The Power of a
Praying®
Woman
BIBLE

GENERAL EDITOR
Stormie Omartian

HARVEST HOUSE
PUBLISHERS
EUGENE, OREGON 97402

Produced with the assistance of The Livingstone Corporation (www.LivingstoneCorporation.com).

Cover design by Kochel Peterson & Associates, Inc.

THE POWER OF A PRAYING is a registered trademark of The Hawkins Children's LLC. Harvest House Publishers, Inc., is the exclusive licensee of the federally registered trademark THE POWER OF A PRAYING.

THE POWER OF A PRAYING® WOMAN BIBLE
Copyright © content and commentary 2006 by Stormie Omartian
Published by Harvest House Publishers, 990 Owen Loop North, Eugene, Oregon 97402
www.harvesthousepublishers.com

Library of Congress Cataloging-in-Publication Data
Bible. English. New International. 2006.
  The power of a praying woman Bible / [commentary by] Stormie Omartian.
    p. cm.
  Includes index.
  ISBN-13: 978-0-7369-1657-8; ISBN-10: 0-7369-1657-1 (bonded leather)
  ISBN-13: 978-0-7369-1659-2; ISBN-10: 0-7369-1659-8 (hardcover)
  ISBN-13: 978-0-7369-1660-8; ISBN-10: 0-7369-1660-1 (bonded leather)
  1. Christian women—Religious life. 2. Bible--Devotional use. I. Omartian, Stormie. II. Title.
BS195.N37 2006
220.5'20814—dc22

                                    2006002432

06 07 08 09 10 11 12 / DP/ 9 8 7 6 5 4 3 2 1

PREFACE TO THE NEW INTERNATIONAL VERSION

THE NEW INTERNATIONAL VERSION is a completely new translation of the Holy Bible made by over a hundred scholars working directly from the best available Hebrew, Aramaic and Greek texts. It had its beginning in 1965 when, after several years of exploratory study by committees from the Christian Reformed Church and the National Association of Evangelicals, a group of scholars met at Palos Heights, Illinois, and concurred in the need for a new translation of the Bible in contemporary English. This group, though not made up of official church representatives, was transdenominational. Its conclusion was endorsed by a large number of leaders from many denominations who met in Chicago in 1966.

Responsibility for the new version was delegated by the Palos Heights group to a self-governing body of fifteen, the Committee on Bible Translation, composed for the most part of biblical scholars from colleges, universities and seminaries. In 1967 the New York Bible Society (now the International Bible Society) generously undertook the financial sponsorship of the project—a sponsorship that made it possible to enlist the help of many distinguished scholars. The fact that participants from the United States, Great Britain, Canada, Australia and New Zealand worked together gave the project its international scope. That they were from many denominations—including Anglican, Assemblies of God, Baptist, Brethren, Christian Reformed, Church of Christ, Evangelical Free, Lutheran, Mennonite, Methodist, Nazarene, Presbyterian, Wesleyan and other churches—helped to safeguard the translation from sectarian bias.

How it was made helps to give the New International Version its distinctiveness. The translation of each book was assigned to a team of scholars. Next, one of the Intermediate Editorial Committees revised the initial translation, with constant reference to the Hebrew, Aramaic or Greek. Their work then went to one of the General Editorial Committees, which checked it in detail and made another thorough revision. This revision in turn was carefully reviewed by the Committee on Bible Translation, which made further changes and then released the final version for publication. In this way the entire Bible underwent three revisions, during each of which the translation was examined for its faithfulness to the original languages and for its English style.

All this involved many thousands of hours of research and discussion regarding the meaning of the texts and the precise way of putting them into English. It may well be that no other translation has been made by a more thorough process of review and revision from committee to committee than this one.

From the beginning of the project, the Committee on Bible Translation held to certain goals for the New International Version: that it would be an accurate translation and one that would have clarity and literary quality and so prove suitable for public and private reading, teaching, preaching, memorizing and liturgical use. The Committee also sought to preserve some measure of continuity with the long tradition of translating the Scriptures into English.

In working toward these goals, the translators were united in their commitment to the authority and infallibility of the Bible as God's Word in written form. They believe that it contains the divine answer to the deepest needs of humanity, that it sheds unique light on our path in a dark world, and that it sets forth the way to our eternal well-being.

The first concern of the translators has been the accuracy of the translation and its fidelity to the thought of the biblical writers. They have weighed the significance of the lexical and grammatical details of the Hebrew, Aramaic and Greek texts. At the same time, they have striven for more than a word-for-word translation. Because thought patterns and syntax differ from language to language, faithful communication of the meaning of the writers of the Bible demands frequent modifications in sentence structure and constant regard for the contextual meanings of words.

A sensitive feeling for style does not always accompany scholarship. Accordingly the Committee on Bible Translation submitted the developing version to a number of stylistic consultants. Two of them read every book of both Old and New Testaments twice—once before and once after the last major revision—and made invaluable suggestions. Samples of the translation were tested for clarity and ease of reading by various kinds of people—young and old, highly educated and less well educated, ministers and laymen.

Concern for clear and natural English—that the New International Version should be idiomatic but not idiosyncratic, contemporary but not dated—motivated the translators and consultants. At the same time, they tried to reflect the differing styles of the biblical writers. In view of the international use of English, the translators sought to avoid obvious Americanisms on the one hand and obvious Anglicisms on the other. A British edition reflects the comparatively few differences of significant idiom and of spelling.

As for the traditional pronouns "thou," "thee" and "thine" in reference to the Deity, the translators judged that to use these archaisms (along with the old verb forms such as "doest," wouldest" and "hadst") would violate accuracy in translation. Neither Hebrew, Aramaic nor Greek uses special pronouns for the persons of the Godhead. A present-day translation is not enhanced by forms that in the time of the King James Version were used in everyday speech, whether referring to God or man.

For the Old Testament the standard Hebrew text, the Masoretic Text as published in the latest editions of *Biblia Hebraica*, was used throughout. The Dead Sea Scrolls contain material bearing on an earlier stage of the Hebrew text. They were consulted, as were the Samaritan Pentateuch and the ancient scribal traditions relating to textual changes. Sometimes a variant Hebrew reading in the margin of the Masoretic Text was followed instead of the text itself. Such instances, being variants within the Masoretic tradition, are not specified by footnotes. In rare cases, words in the consonantal text were divided differently from the way they appear in the Masoretic Text. Footnotes indicate this. The translators also consulted the more important early versions—the Septuagint; Aquila, Symmachus and Theodotion; the Vulgate; the Syriac Peshitta; the Targums; and for the Psalms the *Juxta Hebraica* of Jerome. Readings from these versions were occasionally followed where the Masoretic Text seemed doubtful and where accepted principles of textual criticism showed that one or more of these textual witnesses appeared to provide the correct reading. Such instances are footnoted. Sometimes vowel letters and vowel signs did not, in the judgment of the translators, represent the correct vowels for the original consonantal text. Accordingly some words were read with a different set of vowels. These instances are usually not indicated by footnotes.

The Greek text used in translating the New Testament was an eclectic one. No other piece of ancient literature has such an abundance of manuscript witnesses as does the New Testament. Where existing manuscripts differ, the translators made their choice of readings according to accepted principles of New Testament textual criticism. Footnotes call attention to places where there was uncertainty about what the original text was. The best current printed texts of the Greek New Testament were used.

There is a sense in which the work of translation is never wholly finished. This applies to all great literature and uniquely so to the Bible. In 1973 the New Testament in the New International Version was published. Since then, suggestions for corrections and revisions have been received from various sources. The Committee on Bible Translation carefully considered the suggestions and adopted a number of them. These were incorporated in the first printing of the entire Bible in 1978. Additional revisions were made by the Committee on Bible Translation in 1983 and appear in printings after that date.

As in other ancient documents, the precise meaning of the biblical texts is sometimes uncertain. This is more often the case with the Hebrew and Aramaic texts than with the Greek text. Although archaeological and linguistic discoveries in this century aid in understanding difficult passages, some uncertainties remain. The more significant of these have been called to the reader's attention in the footnotes.

In regard to the divine name *YHWH*, commonly referred to as the *Tetragrammaton*, the translators adopted the device used in most English versions of rendering that name as "LORD" in capital letters to distinguish it from *Adonai*, another Hebrew word rendered "Lord," for which small letters are used. Wherever the two names stand together in the Old Testament as a compound name of God, they are rendered "Sovereign LORD."

Because for most readers today the phrases "the LORD of hosts" and "God of hosts" have little meaning, this version renders them "the LORD Almighty" and "God Almighty." These renderings convey the sense of the Hebrew, namely, "he who is sovereign over all the 'hosts' (powers) in heaven and on earth, especially over the 'hosts' (armies) of Israel." For readers unacquainted with Hebrew this does not make clear the distinction between *Sabaoth* ("hosts" or "Almighty") and *Shaddai* (which can also be translated "Almighty"), but the latter occurs infrequently and is always footnoted. When *Adonai* and *YHWH Sabaoth* occur together, they are rendered "the Lord, the LORD Almighty."

As for other proper nouns, the familiar spellings of the King James Version are generally retained. Names traditionally spelled with "ch," except where it is final, are usually spelled in this translation with "k" or "c," since the biblical languages do not have the sound that "ch" frequently indicates in English—for example, in *chant*. For well-known names such as Zechariah, however, the traditional spelling has been retained. Variation in the spelling of names in the original languages has usually not been indicated. Where a person or place has two or more different names in the Hebrew, Aramaic or Greek texts, the more familiar one has generally been used, with footnotes where needed.

To achieve clarity the translators sometimes supplied words not in the original texts but required by the context. If there was uncertainty about such material, it is enclosed in brackets. Also for the sake of clarity or style, nouns, including some proper nouns, are sometimes substituted for pronouns, and vice versa. And though the Hebrew writers often shifted back and forth between first, second and third personal pronouns without change of antecedent, this translation often makes them uniform, in accordance with English style and without the use of footnotes.

Poetical passages are printed as poetry, that is, with indentation of lines and with separate stanzas. These are generally designed to reflect the structure of Hebrew poetry. This poetry is normally characterized by parallelism in balanced lines. Most of the poetry in the Bible is in the Old Testament, and scholars differ regarding the scansion of Hebrew lines. The translators determined the stanza divisions for the most part by analysis of the subject matter. The stanzas therefore serve as poetic paragraphs.

As an aid to the reader, italicized sectional headings are inserted in most of the books. They are not to be regarded as part of the NIV text, are not for oral reading, and are not intended to dictate the interpretation of the sections they head.

The footnotes in this version are of several kinds, most of which need no explanation. Those giving alternative translations begin with "Or" and generally introduce the alternative with the last word preceding it in the text, except when it is a single-word alternative; in poetry quoted in a footnote a slant mark indicates a line division. Footnotes introduced by "Or" do not have uniform significance. In some cases two possible translations were considered to have about equal validity. In other cases, though the translators were convinced that the translation in the text was correct, they judged that another interpretation was possible and of sufficient importance to be represented in a footnote.

In the New Testament, footnotes that refer to uncertainty regarding the original text are introduced by "Some manuscripts" or similar expressions. In the Old Testament, evidence for the reading chosen is given first and evidence for the alternative is added after a semicolon (for example: Septuagint; Hebrew *father*). In such notes the term "Hebrew" refers to the Masoretic Text.

It should be noted that minerals, flora and fauna, architectural details, articles of clothing and jewelry, musical instruments and other articles cannot always be identified with precision. Also measures of capacity in the biblical period are particularly uncertain (see the table of weights and measures following the text).

Like all translations of the Bible, made as they are by imperfect man, this one undoubtedly falls short of its goals. Yet we are grateful to God for the extent to which he has enabled us to realize these goals and for the strength he has given us and our colleagues to complete our task. We offer this version of the Bible to him in whose name and for whose glory it has been made. We pray that it will lead many into a better understanding of the Holy Scriptures and a fuller knowledge of Jesus Christ the incarnate Word, of whom the Scriptures so faithfully testify.

The Committee on Bible Translation
June 1978
(Revised August 1983)

Names of the translators and editors may be secured from the International Bible Society, translation sponsors of the New International Version, 1820 Jet Stream Drive, Colorado Springs, CO 80921-3696 U.S.A.

TABLE OF *Contents*

WELCOME TO THE
Power of a Praying Woman Bible

Welcome to *The Power of a Praying Woman Bible*. God's Holy Bible is the most important book in the world—it is life-changing, spirit-saving, and soul-transforming. It will be your constant companion because it is the only true and reliable guide for living in a way that makes life work. It is not only God's Word and His map for your walk through life, but it is also His love letter to you.

You may be wondering how this Bible is different from any other edition. The answer is that nothing of the entire NIV Scripture itself has been altered in any way. However, to emphasize *the power of prayer* as it is demonstrated and explained throughout each book of the Bible, I have added six different features, each with its own colorful design. These features emphasize and explain certain parts of Scripture and show what they teach us about prayer.

Each book of this Bible has a brief **Introduction** to help you understand the context of that particular writing. It includes the author who wrote it, the approximate date it was written, the audience for whom it was intended, a brief overview of the book, and the way it highlights the significance of prayer. Also included are two or three prayer themes found in that book that will help you to pray in your own life and situation.

Throughout most of the books you will find articles called **God's People at Prayer**. Here I have highlighted especially significant praying people and important lessons we can all learn from their prayer lives. I know that these amazing men and women of God will inspire you to greater faith and diligence in your own daily prayers.

You will also find **Going Deeper** articles, which are designed to help you better understand what various Scriptures teach about prayer. They will help you to grow in your understanding of what prayer is, how it works, and how to apply it powerfully and practically in your own life.

Page-long articles called **From Stormie's Heart** deal with the kind of tough questions and situations we all are confronted with in our lives. Such titles as "Loving God Through the Tough Times," "Finding Freedom from Anxiety," "What to Do When You Feel Powerless," and "Surviving Disappointment" will help you understand how you can pray for your own life in these specific areas.

You will also find small sections titled **Praying** followed by a Scripture reference and a prayer. These are specific Scriptures turned into prayers. For example, 2 John 1:6 says, "And this is love: that we walk in obedience to his commands." You could pray that Scripture like this: "Help me, Lord, to show my love for You by always living according to Your commands." I hope these examples of using a Scripture in prayer will inspire you to do that very same thing as often as you read the Bible. Reading God's Word should always inspire you to pray in some way.

Also sprinkled throughout are small boxes that say **Prayer is** . . . These are short definitions or explanations of prayer that I believe will be inspiring reminders of what prayer accomplishes and why you need to pray.

My prayer is that this Bible will help you to read God's Word prayerfully, to pray biblically, and to make frequent communication with your heavenly Father a much-loved daily habit that becomes food and life to your soul.

—*Stormie Omartian*

Praying for My Relationships

Use the following Bible verses and prayer starters to help you pray for yourself and for the important relationships in your life.

Praying for My...

DECISIONS
Read Psalm 37:30-31; Proverbs 2:1-6
  Lord, I pray that You would give me wisdom and knowledge so that I can see Your truth in every situation. Give me discernment for each decision I must make. Specifically, I need to know what to do with regard to . . .

DESIRES
Read Psalm 37:4; Psalm 145:16-19
  Lord, I pray that the desires of my heart will be aligned with Your will for my life. Help me to trust Your perfect timing. I surrender all my dreams to You, specifically the dream I have in my heart to do . . .

EMOTIONS
Read Psalm 30:11-12; Psalm 119:28
  Lord, I ask You to be in control of all my thoughts and feelings. Help me to discern when my feelings are not in line with Your heart and Your Word, especially when I experience negative emotions such as . . .

FAITH
Read Matthew 17:20; Hebrews 11:6
  Lord, increase my faith so that I can move mountains in Your name. Give me strength to stand strong on Your promises and believe Your every word. Help me to pray in power about . . .

FEARS
Read Psalm 34:4; 2 Timothy 1:7
  Lord, I don't want to live in fear. Help me remember to always bring my concerns to You in prayer so that Your peace that passes all understanding will permanently reside in my heart. I draw my strength from You and I refuse to be afraid of . . .

FUTURE
Read Proverbs 4:18; Jeremiah 29:11-13
  Lord, I ask that You would give me total peace about my future. I reach out for Your hand today so that I can walk with You into the plans You have for me, especially regarding . . .

HEALTH
Read Jeremiah 30:17; 3 John 1:2

Lord, I thank You that You are the Healer. I look to You for my healing whenever I am injured or sick. I pray that You would strengthen and heal me today. Specifically I pray for . . .

HEART
Read Psalm 51:10-12; 1 John 3:21-22

Lord, I come humbly before You and ask You to cleanse my heart of every fault and renew a steadfast spirit within me. I pray that my heart would always be right before You, specifically in the area of my greatest struggle, which is . . .

LIFE
Read Proverbs 3:5-6; Galatians 2:20

Lord, I bow before You this day and declare that You are Lord over every area of my life. I surrender myself and my life to You and invite You to rule in every part of my mind, soul, body, and spirit. I offer You my life and pray that You will . . .

MIND
Read Isaiah 26:3-4; Romans 12:2-3

Lord, I want Your thoughts to be my thoughts. I pray that my mind will be filled with Your Word so that all my thoughts and ideas will be glorifying to You. Correct my thinking wherever it is not right. Specifically, I am concerned with the thoughts I have had about . . .

PAST
Read Isaiah 43:18-19; Philippians 3:13-14

Lord, help me to let go of anything I have held onto of my past that has kept me from moving into all You have for me. I release my past to You and everyone associated with it so You can restore what has been lost, especially . . .

PURPOSE
Read Ephesians 1:11-12; 2 Thessalonians 1:11

Lord, I want to live my life with a sense of purpose and understanding of the calling You have given me. I choose to lay down anything that would keep me from moving into all You have for me. I pray that You would help me fulfill my purpose regarding . . .

RELATIONSHIPS
Read Ephesians 2:19-22; 1 Peter 3:8-9

Lord, I lift up every one of my relationships to You and ask You to bless them. I pray for godly friends, role models, and mentors to come into my life. Please send people who will speak the truth in love and help me to be the kind of person who . . .

Praying for My Husband's...

(Single women can use these prayers and my *Power of a Praying Wife* book to pray for their future husbands.)

CHOICES
Read Joshua 24:15; Proverbs 16:16

Lord, I pray for my husband (my future husband) and ask You to give him wisdom for every decision he makes. May he reverence You and Your ways and seek to know Your truth. Help him every day to make godly choices, especially in the areas of . . .

FAITH
Read Matthew 17:20; Romans 1:16-17

Lord, I pray that You will give my husband (my future husband) an added measure of faith today. Enlarge his ability to believe in You, Your Word, Your promises, Your ways, and Your power. Put a longing in his heart to talk with You and hear Your voice about . . .

FEARS
Read Psalm 27:1; Isaiah 41:10

Lord, I pray that You will perfect my husband (my future husband) in Your love so that tormenting fear finds no place in him. I pray in the name of Jesus that fear will not rule over him. Instead, I pray that he will . . .

FINANCES
Read Proverbs 11:25; Luke 12:29-31

Lord, I pray that my husband (my future husband) will find it easy to give to You and to others as You have instructed in Your Word. Give him wisdom to handle money wisely. Help him make good decisions as to how he spends, especially in the areas of . . .

MIND
Read Romans 8:6-7; 1 Corinthians 2:14-16

Lord, I pray for Your protection on my husband's (my future husband's) mind. Shield him from the lies of the enemy. Help him to clearly discern between Your voice and any other, especially when he thinks about . . .

PRIORITIES
Read Matthew 6:33; Philippians 2:4

Lord, I pray for my husband's (my future husband's) priorities to be in perfect order. Be Lord and Ruler over his heart. I pray he will seek You first and submit his life to You, especially in the area of . . .

PURPOSE
Read Psalm 20:4; 2 Thessalonians 1:11

Lord, lift my husband's (my future husband's) eyes above the circumstances of the moment so he can see the purpose for which You created him. Give him patience to wait for Your perfect timing with regard to . . .

SELF-IMAGE
Read 2 Corinthians 3:18; 2 Corinthians 5:17

Lord, help my husband (my future husband) see who You really are so he'll know who he really is. May his true self-image be the image of Christ stamped upon his soul. I pray that he would be able to see himself from Your perspective, especially with regard to . . .

SEXUALITY
Read Proverbs 5:15-19; 1 Corinthians 6:13

Lord, bless my husband's (my future husband's) sexuality and make it a part of his life that is totally submitted to Your will. Help me to be all I need to be in that regard. I pray about an area of great concern, which is . . .

TEMPTATIONS
Read Mark 14:38; 1 Corinthians 10:13

Lord, I pray that You would strengthen my husband (my future husband) to resist any temptation that comes his way. Stamp it out of his mind before it ever reaches his heart or personal experience, especially in the area of . . .

TRIALS
Read James 1:2-4; 1 Peter 1:6-7

Lord, I know You work great things in the midst of trials. I don't pray that my husband (my future husband) would have no trials; rather, I pray that he will get through each battle as the winner. In the current trial he is facing, I pray that You would help him to . . .

WIFE
Read Proverbs 18:22; Ephesians 5:28

Lord, teach me how to pray for my husband (my future husband) and make my prayers a true language of love. Teach me what unconditional love really is and how I can communicate it in a way that he will be able to clearly perceive, especially in the way I . . .

WORK
Read Psalm 90:17; Proverbs 22:29

Lord, I pray that You would establish and bless the work of my husband's (my future husband's) hands. May his labor bring not only favor, success, and prosperity, but great fulfillment as well. At the same time, free him from the pressure to . . .

Praying for My Child's...

DESIRE TO LEARN
Read Proverbs 2:1-6; Proverbs 4:13

Lord, I pray that You would give my child a good mind, a teachable spirit, and an ability to learn. Instill in her (him) a desire to attain knowledge and skill, and may she (he) have joy in the process. For areas that are challenging for her (him), I pray that . . .

ETERNAL FUTURE
Read John 6:40; 1 John 5:20

Lord, may my child call You his (her) Savior, be filled with Your Holy Spirit, acknowledge You in every area of his (her) life, and choose always to follow You and Your ways. Help him (her) to walk closely with You today as he (she) . . .

FAITH
Read Mark 11:24; Hebrews 12:2

Lord, I pray that You would take the faith You have planted in my child and multiply it. May the truth of Your Word be firmly established in her (his) heart so that faith will grow daily and guide her (his) life and decisions. Help her (him) to trust You at all times with . . .

SENSE OF LOVE AND ACCEPTANCE
Read Deuteronomy 7:6; 1 John 4:16

Lord, I pray that my child will feel loved and accepted. Penetrate his (her) heart with Your love and help him (her) to fully understand how far-reaching and complete it is. Help me to model Your love and acceptance to my child today in the way I . . .

OBEDIENCE TO THE TRUTH
Read Proverbs 12:22; John 14:15-17

Lord, I pray that You will fill my child with Your Spirit of truth. Give her (him) a heart that loves truth and follows after it. I pray that she (he) will not be blinded or deceived but will always be able to clearly understand Your truth, especially regarding . . .

FREEDOM FROM FEAR
Read Psalm 46:1-3; Isaiah 12:2-3

Lord, I pray that You will deliver my child from any type of fear—real or imagined—that threatens to overtake him (her). Help him (her) not to deny his (her) fears, but instead to remember to take them to You in prayer. Grant my child a sense of peace and safety today as he (she) . . .

FUTURE SPOUSE
Read Genesis 2:22-24; Mark 10:6-9

Unless Your plan is for my child to remain single, Lord, I pray that You will send a marriage partner for him (her). Send the perfect person at the perfect time, and help him (her) to know who that person is. Thank You for providing a wife (husband) who will be . . .

GIFTS AND TALENTS
Read Romans 11:29; 1 Peter 4:10

Lord, I thank You for the gifts and talents You have placed in my child. Please use these blessings for Your glory. Please show me if there is any special nurturing, training, or opportunities I should provide for her (him) and help me see . . .

HEALTH
Read Isaiah 53:5; Malachi 4:2

Lord, I come to You today and pray for healing and wholeness for my child. I ask that sickness and infirmity will have no place or power in his (her) life. I pray for protection against any disease coming into his (her) body and trust that You will . . .

WILLINGNESS TO HONOR AND OBEY HER (HIS) PARENTS
Read Proverbs 1:8-9; Ephesians 6:3

Lord, I pray that You would turn the heart of my child toward You and enable her (him) to honor and obey my husband and me so that her (his) life will be long and good. The specific area of obedience I am most concerned about is . . .

PROTECTION
Read Psalm 4:8; Isaiah 43:2-3

Lord, I lift my child up to You and ask that You would put a hedge of protection around her (him). Protect her (his) spirit, body, mind, and emotions from any kind of evil or harm. I pray specifically for protection from . . .

PURITY AND HOLINESS
Read Psalm 24:3-5; 1 Peter 1:15-16

Lord, I pray that my child will run from evil, from impurity, and from unholy thoughts, words, and deeds. Help him (her) to be drawn toward whatever is pure and holy and choose to be a part of only those things that are pleasing to You. My greatest concern is . . .

RELATIONSHIPS
Read Romans 15:5-6; 1 Corinthians 1:10

Lord, fill my child's heart with Your love and give her (him) an abundance of compassion and forgiveness that will overflow to each friend and family member in her (his) life. Specifically, I pray for her (his) relationship with . . .

Praying for My Friends'...

ABILITY TO BLESS OTHERS

Read John 14:12-14; Galatians 6:9

  Lord, show my friends what You want them to do today to be a blessing to others around them. Specifically, show them how they can serve their families, friends, church, and the people whom You put in their lives. The friends I am most concerned about today are . . .

DECISIONS

Read Proverbs 16:9; Jeremiah 33:3

  Lord, help my friends to walk uprightly, righteously, and obediently to Your commands. May they never be wise in their own eyes, but may they always fear You. Give them the wisdom, knowledge, understanding, direction, and discernment they need. The friends I am specifically praying for today are . . .

DIFFICULT TIMES

Read Matthew 9:22; 2 Corinthians 4:17-18

  Lord, help my friends to embrace the moments of life that are hard to get their arms around. Enable them to see You in those moments. Help me to be an encouragement to them and to remind them of Your goodness. The friends who most need to be encouraged today are . . .

DREAMS AND DESIRES

Read Psalm 21:2; Ephesians 3:20-21

  Lord, I lift up to You the dreams and desires of my friends. May the desires of their hearts line up with the desires of Your heart. I pray that You would hear their requests and lead them in Your path. The friends who most need this prayer today are . . .

HEALTH

Read Jeremiah 17:14; James 5:14-16

  Lord, I pray for good health for my friends. Help them to understand that in Your presence they will find healing. In Your presence they can reach out and touch You and in turn be touched by You. The friends who most need Your healing touch today are . . .

HEARTS

Read Romans 5:5; Hebrews 10:22

  Lord, I pray for my friends and ask that You would pour out Your Spirit in their hearts. May they have a fresh filling of Your love and grace. Help them to draw near to You and feel Your presence. Specifically, the friends who come most strongly to my mind today are . . .

LOSSES

Read Isaiah 53:4; Matthew 5:4

  Lord, I know You are a good God and Your love for my friends is endless. Help them know that too. When they hurt, help them to cast the whole burden of their grief on You and let You carry it, trusting that You will sustain them. The friends who most need You to carry their burdens today are . . .

PROTECTION
Read Psalm 18:2-3; Psalm 32:7

Lord, I pray that You would surround my friends with Your hand of protection. Keep them safe from any accidents, diseases, or evil influences. Protect them wherever they are and keep them out of harm's way. The friends who are most on my heart today are . . .

RELATIONSHIPS
Read John 15:13; 1 John 4:11

Lord, thank You for my friends. They are women who are trustworthy, kind, loving, and faithful. May they encourage and support all their relationships daily through prayer. May forgiveness and love flow freely in their lives so that . . .

SELF-IMAGE
Read Psalm 139:13-16; 1 Peter 3:3-4

Lord, I pray that my friends will not base their worth on appearance but on Your Word. Where anyone in their past has convinced them that they are less than who You made them to be, replace those lies with Your truth. The friends who most need help with that today are . . .

TIMES OF WAITING
Read Psalm 27:14; Psalm 130:5-6

Lord, help my friends to grow in their understanding of Your ways. Help them not to succumb to impatience or discouragement because their timetable does not coincide with Yours. Help them to wait on You. The friends who need patience to wait are . . .

WALK WITH GOD
Read Psalm 119:2-3; 1 John 2:3-6

Lord, I pray that my friends will know You in every way You can be known. Teach them what they need to learn in order to know You better. Draw them close so that they may dwell in Your presence like never before. The friends who most need to know You in a deeper way are . . .

WORDS
Read Psalm 15:1-5; Philippians 4:8

Lord, fill my friends afresh each day with Your Holy Spirit so that Your love and goodness overflow from their hearts and mouths. Help them to speak only about things that are true, noble, right, pure, lovely, admirable, excellent, and praiseworthy. The friends who most need this prayer today are . . .

Praying for the Nation and World

ELECTED OFFICIALS
Read Romans 13:3; Hebrews 13:17

Lord, I pray that the people elected to office in our country and in other countries of the world will be godly and righteous men and women. Raise up men and women who are believers in You. Give them wisdom and favor with the people so they will be able to . . .

AN END TO CRIME AND TERRORISM
Read Luke 12:2-3; John 14:1-3

Lord, I pray that You would expose the plots of those who plan crimes and acts of terrorism. Reveal to the authorities every detail of terrorists' plots against our country and its citizens here and abroad before they take place and help us to . . .

LOCAL GOVERNMENT
Read Jeremiah 29:5-8; 1 Peter 2:13-14

Lord, I pray for the community in which I live. Bless us with peace and protection. Please pour out Your Spirit on this city and state. Give us godly local leaders. Show me how I can make a difference in this community. I especially pray for . . .

THE MEDIA
Read Psalm 112:1,8; Proverbs 14:7

Lord, I pray for all those who work in the media. Place godly people in positions of influence. Give wisdom to those who report the news so that they will not report things that are untrue or that will endanger the lives of others. Help them to . . .

THE MILITARY
Read 2 Chronicles 32:7-8; Psalm 140:6-7

Lord, I pray that You would help us to develop and maintain a strong and skilled military. Give our military leaders godly wisdom to make the right decisions in defending our country. Specifically, I ask that You would . . .

MISSIONARIES
Read Isaiah 52:7; Matthew 28:18-20

Lord, send Your servants into the whole earth to teach people about Jesus and Your ways. Open the eyes of the people of every nation to the truth of Your Word. The missionaries who are most on my heart are . . .

THE NATIONS OF THE WORLD
Read Psalm 96:3-5; Daniel 2:20-21

Lord, I know that what happens in our country affects other nations. And what happens in other nations of the world affects us too. Pour out Your Spirit in every country and every city and on every government and leader. Establish Your kingdom on earth. The countries I am most concerned about are . . .

THE PRESIDENT
Read Proverbs 21:1; 1Timothy 2:1-4

Lord, I pray that You would turn the president's heart toward You at all times so that in the midst of the many voices he hears each day, he will still be able to hear Your voice far above them. Guide the president in every situation. Specifically I pray with regard to . . .

PROTECTION FOR OUR LAND
Read Psalm 5:11-12; Isaiah 32:18

Lord, I pray that You would protect our country from evil enemies. Defend us from anyone who would try to destroy our nation and its people or overtake our nation from within. I ask that You would protect us from . . .

THE SPIRITUAL LIFE OF OUR NATION
Read Mark 1:15; 2 Timothy 3:13-14

Lord, I pray for an outpouring of Your Spirit upon our nation. Bring revival into every city and town in every part of our country and into every church. Help those of us who know You to pray for our country every day. Specifically I pray for . . .

A STRONG ECONOMY
Read Job 22:21; Psalm 128:1-2

Lord, I pray for our nation's economy. Make it strong and stable. Especially protect people who would be most painfully affected by a slipping economy. Put godly and brilliant people in the positions of making decisions about our nation's economy so that . . .

SUPREME COURT JUSTICES AND ALL OTHER JUDGES
Read 2 Samuel 23:3-4; Proverbs 31:9

Lord, I pray that only righteous judges would be appointed in our nation. May each one be a man or woman of God who loves Your laws. Give every judge the wisdom and integrity to judge in accordance with Your will. Especially help them to . . .

TEACHERS AND EDUCATORS
Read Psalm 34:11; Isaiah 54:13

Lord, I pray you would give all teachers, educators, and anyone in authority in every educational facility the ability to lead and instruct. Raise up godly teachers and leaders. Give those who are in charge of the education system wisdom so that they can . . .

What Did Jesus Say About . . . ?

©2006 by Stormie Omartian

Adultery—*Matthew* 5:27-28

Believing—*John* 3:10-21; 5:36-47

Blessing—*Matthew* 5:3-12; *Luke* 6:20-26; 10:23-24

Blindness—*John* 9:35,37,39,41

Born Again—*John* 3:3,5-8; 20:29

Bread of Life—*John* 6:26-27,29,32-33,35-51,53-58,61-65,67,70

Building on the Rock—*Matthew* 7:21-27; *Luke* 6:46-49

Children—*Matthew* 18:3-9; 19:14; *Mark* 9:37,42; 10:14-15; *Luke* 9:48; 18:16-17

Church—*Matthew* 16:18-19

Communion—*Matthew* 26:26-29; *Mark* 14:22,24-25; *Luke* 22:19-20; *1 Corinthians* 11:24-25

Deliverance—*Matthew* 12:43-45; *Mark* 1:25; 5:8-9; *Luke* 4:35; 8:30; 11:17-26

Divorce—*Matthew* 5:31-32; 19:4-6,8-9,11-12; *Mark* 10:3,5-9,11-12; *Luke* 16:17-18

Eternal Life—*Matthew* 19:28-30; *Mark* 10:29-30; *Luke* 18:29-30; *John* 3:14-16; 4:13-14; 5:24-29; 6:27,40; 10:27-29; 12:24-25; 17:1-3

Evangelism—*Matthew* 4:19; 9:37-38; 10:5-16; *Mark* 1:17; 5:19; 6:10-11; *Luke* 5:4,10; 8:39; *John* 4:32, 34-38

Faith—*Matthew* 8:10-13,26; 9:22,24,28-30; 14:27,29,31; 15:24,26,28; 16:8-11; 17:17,20-21; 21:19,21-22; *Mark* 5:30-31,34,36,39,41; 7:27,29; 9:16,19,21,23,25,29; 10:51-52; 11:14,22-26; *Luke* 4:23-27; 7:9; 8:22,25; 9:41; 12:11-12; 17:6,19; 18:41-42

Faithfulness—*Matthew* 24:45-51; *Luke* 12:42-48; *Revelation* 3:7-13

False Prophets—*Matthew* 7:15-20

Fasting—*Matthew* 6:16-18; 9:15; 17:21; *Mark* 2:19-20; *Luke* 5:34-35

Fear—*Matthew* 14:27; 17:7; 28:10; *Mark* 4:35,39,40; 6:50; *Luke* 5:10; 12:32; *John* 6:20

Following Jesus—*Matthew* 4:19; 8:20,22; 9:10; 10:32-39; 16:24-28; 19:17-19,21,23-24,26,28-30; *Mark* 1:17; 2:14; 8:34-38; 9:39-41; 10:18-19,21,23-25,27,29-31; *Luke* 5:4,10,27; 9:3-5,23-26,50,58-60,62; 10:2-12,41-42; 13:24-30; 14:26-35; 18:19-20,22,24-25,27, 29-30; 19:5,9-10; 22:35-36; *John* 1:38-39,42-43,47-48,50-51; 6:26-27,29,32-33,35-51,53-58,61-65,67-70; 7:37-38; 9:35,37,39,41; 10:1-5,7-18,25-30; 12:23-26,44-50; 13:36

Forgiveness—*Matthew* 5:21-26; 6:14-15; 18:22-35; *Mark* 2:5,8-11; *Luke* 5:20,22-24; 7:40-50; 17:3-4; 23:34

Giving—*Mark* 12:43-44; *Luke* 6:38; 14:12-14; 21:3-4; *Acts* 20:35

God the Father—*John* 5:17,19-30; 8:37-47,49-51,54-56,58; 10:32,34-38; 12:44-50; 14:6-7,9-11

God's Will—*Matthew* 12:48-50

Good Fruit—*Matthew* 7:16-20; 12:33-35; *Luke* 6:43-45

Good Shepherd—*John* 10:1-5,7-18,25-30

Grace—*2 Corinthians* 12:9

Great Commission—*Matthew* 28:18-20; *Mark* 16:15-18

Healing—*Matthew* 8:3-4,7,10; 9:2,4-6; 20:32; *Mark* 1:41,44; 3:3-5; *Luke* 5:13-14; 6:8-10; 7:13-14; 8:45-46,48,50,52,54; 13:12,15-16; 14:3,5; 17:14,17-19; 18:41-42; 22:51; *John* 4:48,50,53; 5:6,8,11-12,14; 9:7,11

Holy Spirit—*Luke* 24:49; *John* 7:37-38; 14:15-20,25-26; 15:26-27; 16:5-15; *Acts* 1:4-5,7-8; 11:16

Humility—*Luke* 14:8-11; 22:25-30

Hypocrisy—*Matthew* 15:3-11,13-14,16-20; 16:6,8-11; *Mark* 7:6-16,18-23; 8:15,17-21; 12:38-40; *Luke* 7:31-35; 12:1-3; 20:46-47

Jerusalem—*Matthew* 23:37-39; *Luke* 13:34-35; 19:42-44

Jesus' Baptism—*Matthew* 3:15

Jesus' Identity—*Matthew* 22:42-45; *Luke* 9:18,20; *Mark* 8:26-27,29; *John* 8:58

Jesus Is Lord—*Luke* 6:3-5; 20:41-44

Jesus' Ministry—*Mark* 1:38; *Luke* 4:18-19,21,43

Jesus' Passion—

Passion Prophecies—*Matthew* 17:22-23; 20:18-19; 26:2,31-32; *Mark* 9:31; 10:33-34; 14:27-28; *Luke* 9:22,44; 18:31-33; 22:37-38; 24:7

Judas' Betrayal—*Matthew* 26:21,23-25; *Mark* 14:18,20-21; *Luke* 22:21-22; *John* 13:10,18-21,26-27

Gethsemane—*Matthew* 26:36,38-42,45-46,50,52-56; *Mark*

14:32,34,36-38,41-42,48-49; *Luke* 22:40,42,46,48,51-53; *John* 18:4-9,11

Trials—*Matthew* 26:64; 27:11; *Mark* 14:62; 15:2; *Luke* 22:67-70; 23:3; *John* 18:20-21,23,34,36-37; 19:11

Peter's Denial—*Matthew* 26:34,75; *Mark* 14:30,72; *Luke* 22:34,61; *John* 13:36,38

Crucifixion—*Matthew* 27:46; *Mark* 15:34; *Luke* 23:28-31,34,43,46; *John* 19:26-28,30

Resurrection—*Matthew* 28:9-10; *Luke* 24:17,19,25-26,36,38-39,41,44,46-49; *John* 20:15-17,19,21-23,26-27,29; 21:5-6,10,12,15-19,22-23

Jesus Prays—*Matthew* 11:25-26; *Luke* 10:21-22; 22:42; *John* 17:1-26

Jesus Prophesies—*Matthew* 5:17-18; 11:21-24; 21:2-3,42-44; 24:2,4-44; 26:10-13,18,31-32; 27:63; *Mark* 11:2-3; 13:2,5-32; 14:13-15; *Luke* 12:49-59; 13:32-35; 17:22-37; 19:30-31,42-44; 21:6,8-33; 22:8-12,31-32; 23:28-31; *John* 2:19; 12:7-8,27-28,30-32,34-36; 13:38; 14:1-4,28-31; 16:1-4,16-22

Jesus Questioned—*Matthew* 21:24-25,27; 22:18-21; *Mark* 11:29-30,33; 12:15-17,24-27,29-31,34-37; *Luke* 20:3-4,8,23-25,34-38; *John* 7:16-19,21-24,28-29,33-34,36; 8:7,10-12,14-19,21-26,28-29

Jesus' Return—*Luke* 18:20-37; *Revelation* 16:15; 22:7,12-13,16,20

Jesus' Temptation—*Matthew* 4:4,7,10; *Luke* 4:4,8,12

Jesus, the Vine—*John* 15:1-8

John the Baptist—*Matthew* 11:4-19; 17:11-12; *Mark* 12:13; *Luke* 7:22-28,31-35; *John* 5:33-35

The Old Testament

Author: Moses

Date: Sometime between 1446–1406 BC

Audience: The ancient Israelites, who were about to enter the promised land

Prayer Themes:

- Give thanks for the beauty and wonder of God's awesome creation (1:1-31).

- Praise God for His absolute faithfulness to His promises (9:8-17).

- Pray that during your difficulties and trials, you will have the grace to remember that God is in control of all things—the vast universe as well as the details of your life (45:4-8).

When it comes to prayer, to whom exactly are we praying? Who is this God who claims to hear and answer our prayers?

To properly understand who God is and what it means to know Him intimately, we need to start at the very beginning. In the book of Genesis we find the epic accounts of creation, humankind's "fall" into sin, the great flood of Noah, and the initial stages of God's remarkable plan to rescue a lost humanity. God chooses a man—Abraham—from whom He will bring forth a nation, out of which will come the Savior of the world.

Just like an impossible-to-put-down novel, Genesis is filled with romance and intrigue, unforgettable characters, and nonstop adventure. The only difference? This isn't make-believe. It's the true story of the universe! It's the true story of the one true God, who does indeed hear and answer our every prayer.

Genesis

The Beginning

1 In the beginning God created the heavens and the earth. ²Now the earth was[a] formless and empty, darkness was over the surface of the deep, and the Spirit of God was hovering over the waters.

³And God said, "Let there be light," and there was light. ⁴God saw that the light was good, and he separated the light from the darkness. ⁵God called the light "day," and the darkness he called "night." And there was evening, and there was morning—the first day.

⁶And God said, "Let there be an expanse between the waters to separate water from water." ⁷So God made the expanse and separated the water under the expanse from the water above it. And it was so. ⁸God called the expanse "sky." And there was evening, and there was morning—the second day.

⁹And God said, "Let the water under the sky be gathered to one place, and let dry ground appear." And it was so. ¹⁰God called the dry ground "land," and the gathered waters he called "seas." And God saw that it was good.

¹¹Then God said, "Let the land produce vegetation: seed-bearing plants and trees on the land that bear fruit with seed in it, according to their various kinds." And it was so. ¹²The land produced vegetation: plants bearing seed according to their kinds and

Praying Genesis 1:1-27

Thank You, Lord, for Your beautiful creation. I worship You as my Creator and thank You for creating me in Your image.

[a] 2 Or possibly *became*

trees bearing fruit with seed in it according to their kinds. And God saw that it was good. ¹³And there was evening, and there was morning—the third day.

¹⁴And God said, "Let there be lights in the expanse of the sky to separate the day from the night, and let them serve as signs to mark seasons and days and years, ¹⁵and let them be lights in the expanse of the sky to give light on the earth." And it was so. ¹⁶God made two great lights—the greater light to govern the day and the lesser light to govern the night. He also made the stars. ¹⁷God set them in the expanse of the sky to give light on the earth, ¹⁸to govern the day and the night, and to separate light from darkness. And God saw that it was good. ¹⁹And there was evening, and there was morning—the fourth day.

²⁰And God said, "Let the water teem with living creatures, and let birds fly above the earth across the expanse of the sky." ²¹So God created the great creatures of the sea and every living and moving thing with which the water teems, according to their kinds, and every winged bird according to its kind. And God saw that it was good. ²²God blessed them and said, "Be fruitful and increase in number and fill the water in the seas, and let the birds increase on the earth." ²³And there was evening, and there was morning—the fifth day.

²⁴And God said, "Let the land produce living creatures according to their kinds: livestock, creatures that move along the ground, and wild animals, each according to its kind." And it was so. ²⁵God made the wild animals according to their kinds, the livestock according to their kinds, and all the creatures that move along the ground according to their kinds. And God saw that it was good.

²⁶Then God said, "Let us make man in our image, in our likeness, and let them rule over the fish of the sea and the birds of the air, over the livestock, over all the earth,ᵃ and over all the creatures that move along the ground."

²⁷So God created man in his own image,
in the image of God he created him;
male and female he created them.

²⁸God blessed them and said to them, "Be fruitful and increase in number; fill the earth and subdue it. Rule over the fish of the sea and the birds of the air and over every living creature that moves on the ground."

²⁹Then God said, "I give you every seed-bearing plant on the face of the whole earth and every tree that has fruit with seed in it. They will be yours for food. ³⁰And to all the beasts of the earth and all the birds of the air and all the creatures that move on the ground—everything that has the breath of life in it—I give every green plant for food." And it was so.

³¹God saw all that he had made, and it was very good. And there was evening, and there was morning—the sixth day.

2 Thus the heavens and the earth were completed in all their vast array.

²By the seventh day God had finished the work he had been doing; so on the seventh day he restedᵇ from all his work. ³And God blessed the seventh day and made it holy, because on it he rested from all the work of creating that he had done.

Adam and Eve

⁴This is the account of the heavens and the earth when they were created.

When the LORD God made the earth and the heavens— ⁵and no shrub of the field had yet appeared on the earthᶜ

ᵃ26 Hebrew; Syriac *all the wild animals*   ᵇ2 Or *ceased*; also in verse 3   ᶜ5 Or *land*; also in verse 6

God's Connection With Us

READ AND CONSIDER: GENESIS 1:26–2:7

"The LORD God formed the man from the dust of the ground and breathed into his nostrils the breath of life, and the man became a living being" (Genesis 2:7).

God created the universe with a word. He spoke stars and planets into existence. He formed the world with simple commands. God started the creation process without any preexisting things. He began with nothing. With the presence of the Holy Spirit and the entrance of His Word, creation happened. He brought order, light, life, and beauty out of chaos and darkness. He said, "Let there be . . ." and it happened.

Then He became personally involved with making humans. Other places in Scripture describe God as a "potter" and human beings as the "clay" (Isaiah 64:8), making us think of our heavenly Father bent over a potter's wheel, forming mud figures into the design He had in mind for us. The finishing touch was to breathe into us His breath of life. God got personal, right from the start.

But He didn't stop there. God's action in giving us breath also gave us the ability to speak. The act of breathing that keeps us alive is the same act that we use to communicate. We breathe out to speak (and some languages in the world even breathe in to speak). We are God's image bearers (1:26-27). We breathe and speak because of His breath given to us. We should be in awe of the privilege we have to use the breath of life to speak to our Creator.

We were made to communicate with our Maker. Even though we may not start out doing it very well, He still wants to hear us speak to Him. Just as we are delighted when our babies make their first tiny sounds, so our heavenly Father is delighted when He hears the sound of one of His children speaking words intended for His ears.

So breathe a prayer to God often. If words don't come to mind right away, start by saying, "Thank You." As you say those two words slowly, begin to add "for . . ." until different ways to end the sentence begin to flow. Once you do this a while, you will realize that you can use your inspiration (breathing in) as time to think of the next words and your expiration (breathing out) to express your gratitude. All the way back to the first breath of the first person, you and I were made for this. Giving us the "breath of life" is God's connection with us, and prayer is our connection with Him.

and no plant of the field had yet sprung up, for the LORD God had not sent rain on the earth[a] and there was no man to work the ground, 6but streams[b] came up from the earth and watered the whole surface of the ground— 7the LORD God formed the man[c] from the dust of the ground and breathed into his nostrils the breath of life, and the man became a living being.

8Now the LORD God had planted a garden in the east, in Eden; and there he put the man he had formed. 9And the LORD God made all kinds of trees grow out of the ground—trees that were pleasing to the eye and good for food. In the middle of the garden were the tree of life and the tree of the knowledge of good and evil.

10A river watering the garden flowed

[a]5 Or *land*; also in verse 6   [b]6 Or *mist*   [c]7 The Hebrew for *man (adam)* sounds like and may be related to the Hebrew for *ground (adamah)*; it is also the name *Adam* (see Gen. 2:20).

from Eden; from there it was separated into four headwaters. 11The name of the first is the Pishon; it winds through the entire land of Havilah, where there is gold. 12(The gold of that land is good; aromatic resin[a] and onyx are also there.) 13The name of the second river is the Gihon; it winds through the entire land of Cush.[b] 14The name of the third river is the Tigris; it runs along the east side of Asshur. And the fourth river is the Euphrates.

15The LORD God took the man and put him in the Garden of Eden to work it and take care of it. 16And the LORD God commanded the man, "You are free to eat from any tree in the garden; 17but you must not eat from the tree of the knowledge of good and evil, for when you eat of it you will surely die."

18The LORD God said, "It is not good for the man to be alone. I will make a helper suitable for him."

19Now the LORD God had formed out of the ground all the beasts of the field and all the birds of the air. He brought them to the man to see what he would name them; and whatever the man called each living creature, that was its name. 20So the man gave names to all the livestock, the birds of the air and all the beasts of the field.

But for Adam[c] no suitable helper was found. 21So the LORD God caused the man to fall into a deep sleep; and while he was sleeping, he took one of the man's ribs[d] and closed up the place with flesh. 22Then the LORD God made a woman from the rib[e] he had taken out of the man, and he brought her to the man. 23The man said,

"This is now bone of my bones
  and flesh of my flesh;
she shall be called 'woman,'[f]
  for she was taken out of man."

24For this reason a man will leave his father and mother and be united to his wife, and they will become one flesh. 25The man and his wife were both naked, and they felt no shame.

The Fall of Man

3 Now the serpent was more crafty than any of the wild animals the LORD God had made. He said to the woman, "Did God really say, 'You must not eat from any tree in the garden'?"

2The woman said to the serpent, "We may eat fruit from the trees in the garden, 3but God did say, 'You must not eat fruit from the tree that is in the middle of the garden, and you must not touch it, or you will die.'"

4"You will not surely die," the serpent said to the woman. 5"For God knows that when you eat of it your eyes will be opened, and you will be like God, knowing good and evil."

Praying Genesis 3:1-13
God, help me to obey You at all times
and never assume that I know
what's best for my life.

6When the woman saw that the fruit of the tree was good for food and pleasing to the eye, and also desirable for gaining wisdom, she took some and ate it. She also gave some to her husband, who was with her, and he ate it. 7Then the eyes of both of them were opened, and they realized they were naked; so they sewed fig leaves together and made coverings for themselves.

8Then the man and his wife heard the sound of the LORD God as he was walking in the garden in the cool of the day, and they hid from the LORD God among the trees of the garden. 9But the LORD God called to the man, "Where are you?"

10He answered, "I heard you in the garden, and I was afraid because I was naked; so I hid."

11And he said, "Who told you that

---

a 12 Or good; pearls   b 13 Possibly southeast Mesopotamia   c 20 Or the man   d 21 Or took part of the man's side   e 22 Or part
f 23 The Hebrew for woman sounds like the Hebrew for man.

A Walk in the Garden

READ AND CONSIDER: GENESIS 3:1-9

"Then the man and his wife heard the sound of the LORD God as he was walking in the garden in the cool of the day, and they hid from the LORD God among the trees of the garden. But the LORD God called to the man, 'Where are you?' " (Genesis 3:8-9).

Certain places just feel like this first garden. Something about the lush vegetation, the time of day, or the sounds of nature all provoke an almost overwhelming longing in us to experience what Adam and Eve enjoyed every day—a walk with God.

The world is still a wonderful setting in which to know God, but something has changed. It changed way back there, in the garden. The first two people gave up the pleasure of God's company for their own interests. They heard the sound of God walking in the garden, looking for them, wanting to enjoy their usual walk. But they had sinned. Guilt overwhelmed them. They were ashamed to see God. They lost the close relationship they had with Him, and we've struggled to recapture that closeness ever since.

God didn't hide from man; it was the other way around. Adam and Eve ducked into the bushes in shame, fear, and rebellion. But God came looking. He knew where they were, but He wanted them to know He was willing to seek their company. He was aware of their disobedience, but kept His appointment with them anyway.

What amazing fellowship they forfeited! What peace they lost! And yet, before we criticize them, remember how easily and how often we repeat their mistake. We make choices that draw us away from God. We experience overwhelming moments of His presence that we wish we could wrap up and keep; yet hours later we turn our backs on Him, trying to shut His gentle whisper out of our lives.

The power in our prayer life flows out of God's presence with us. It's not *our* power; it's *His*. We don't experience or witness that power if we insist on our agenda and our schedules. We have to plan and hold sacred the places and times when we meet God. If we don't deliberately build our lives around these "garden walks" with the Lord, the world will rapidly and relentlessly fill our hours with other commitments. As He did with Adam and Eve, God will come looking for us. But how much better would it be if He found us waiting expectantly? I don't want Him to have to call out, "Where are you?" to me. What about you?

you were naked? Have you eaten from the tree that I commanded you not to eat from?"

¹²The man said, "The woman you put here with me—she gave me some fruit from the tree, and I ate it."

¹³Then the LORD God said to the woman, "What is this you have done?"

The woman said, "The serpent deceived me, and I ate."

¹⁴So the LORD God said to the serpent, "Because you have done this,

"Cursed are you above all the livestock
    and all the wild animals!
You will crawl on your belly
    and you will eat dust
    all the days of your life.
¹⁵And I will put enmity
    between you and the woman,
    and between your offspring[a] and hers;
he will crush[b] your head,
    and you will strike his heel."

¹⁶To the woman he said,

---

[a] 15 Or *seed*   [b] 15 Or *strike*

"I will greatly increase your pains in
    childbearing;
  with pain you will give birth to
    children.
Your desire will be for your husband,
  and he will rule over you."

17To Adam he said, "Because you listened to your wife and ate from the tree
about which I commanded you, 'You
must not eat of it,'

"Cursed is the ground because of you;
  through painful toil you will eat of it
  all the days of your life.
18It will produce thorns and thistles for
  you,
  and you will eat the plants of the
  field.
19By the sweat of your brow
  you will eat your food
until you return to the ground,
  since from it you were taken;
for dust you are
  and to dust you will return."

20Adam[a] named his wife Eve,[b] because
she would become the mother of all
the living.

21The LORD God made garments of
skin for Adam and his wife and clothed
them. 22And the LORD God said, "The
man has now become like one of us,
knowing good and evil. He must not be
allowed to reach out his hand and take
also from the tree of life and eat, and live
forever." 23So the LORD God banished
him from the Garden of Eden to work
the ground from which he had been
taken. 24After he drove the man out, he
placed on the east side[c] of the Garden of
Eden cherubim and a flaming sword flashing back and forth to guard the way to
the tree of life.

Cain and Abel

4 Adam[a] lay with his wife Eve, and she
became pregnant and gave birth to
Cain.[d] She said, "With the help of the
LORD I have brought forth[e] a man." 2Later
she gave birth to his brother Abel.

Now Abel kept flocks, and Cain
worked the soil. 3In the course of time
Cain brought some of the fruits of the
soil as an offering to the LORD. 4But Abel
brought fat portions from some of the
firstborn of his flock. The LORD looked
with favor on Abel and his offering, 5but
on Cain and his offering he did not look
with favor. So Cain was very angry, and
his face was downcast.

6Then the LORD said to Cain, "Why
are you angry? Why is your face downcast? 7If you do what is right, will you
not be accepted? But if you do not do
what is right, sin is crouching at your
door; it desires to have you, but you must
master it."

8Now Cain said to his brother Abel,
"Let's go out to the field."[f] And while
they were in the field, Cain attacked his
brother Abel and killed him.

9Then the LORD said to Cain, "Where
is your brother Abel?"

Praying Genesis 4:1-16

*Heavenly Father, show me how to
worship You the way You want me
to so that I will always have a
close relationship with You.*

"I don't know," he replied. "Am I my
brother's keeper?"

10The LORD said, "What have you
done? Listen! Your brother's blood cries
out to me from the ground. 11Now you
are under a curse and driven from the
ground, which opened its mouth to receive your brother's blood from your
hand. 12When you work the ground, it
will no longer yield its crops for you.
You will be a restless wanderer on
the earth."

13Cain said to the LORD, "My punishment is more than I can bear. 14Today

---

a 20,1 Or *The man*   b 20 *Eve* probably means *living.*   c 24 Or *placed in front*   d 1 *Cain* sounds like the Hebrew for *brought forth*
or *acquired.*   e 1 Or *have acquired*   f 8 Samaritan Pentateuch, Septuagint, Vulgate and Syriac; Masoretic Text does not have
"*Let's go out to the field.*"

you are driving me from the land, and I will be hidden from your presence; I will be a restless wanderer on the earth, and whoever finds me will kill me."

¹⁵But the LORD said to him, "Not soᵃ; if anyone kills Cain, he will suffer vengeance seven times over." Then the LORD put a mark on Cain so that no one who found him would kill him. ¹⁶So Cain went out from the LORD's presence and lived in the land of Nod,ᵇ east of Eden.

¹⁷Cain lay with his wife, and she became pregnant and gave birth to Enoch. Cain was then building a city, and he named it after his son Enoch. ¹⁸To Enoch was born Irad, and Irad was the father of Mehujael, and Mehujael was the father of Methushael, and Methushael was the father of Lamech.

¹⁹Lamech married two women, one named Adah and the other Zillah. ²⁰Adah gave birth to Jabal; he was the father of those who live in tents and raise livestock. ²¹His brother's name was Jubal; he was the father of all who play the harp and flute. ²²Zillah also had a son, Tubal-Cain, who forged all kinds of tools out ofᶜ bronze and iron. Tubal-Cain's sister was Naamah.

²³Lamech said to his wives,

"Adah and Zillah, listen to me;
    wives of Lamech, hear my words.
I have killedᵈ a man for wounding
        me,
    a young man for injuring me.
²⁴If Cain is avenged seven times,
    then Lamech seventy-seven times."

²⁵Adam lay with his wife again, and she gave birth to a son and named him Seth,ᵉ saying, "God has granted me another child in place of Abel, since Cain killed him." ²⁶Seth also had a son, and he named him Enosh.

At that time men began to call onᶠ the name of the LORD.

From Adam to Noah

5 This is the written account of Adam's line.

When God created man, he made him in the likeness of God. ²He created them male and female and blessed them. And when they were created, he called them "man.ᵍ"

³When Adam had lived 130 years, he had a son in his own likeness, in his own image; and he named him Seth. ⁴After Seth was born, Adam lived 800 years and had other sons and daughters. ⁵Altogether, Adam lived 930 years, and then he died.

⁶When Seth had lived 105 years, he became the fatherʰ of Enosh. ⁷And after he became the father of Enosh, Seth lived 807 years and had other sons and daughters. ⁸Altogether, Seth lived 912 years, and then he died.

⁹When Enosh had lived 90 years, he became the father of Kenan. ¹⁰And after he became the father of Kenan, Enosh lived 815 years and had other sons and daughters. ¹¹Altogether, Enosh lived 905 years, and then he died.

¹²When Kenan had lived 70 years, he became the father of Mahalalel. ¹³And after he became the father of Mahalalel, Kenan lived 840 years and had other sons and daughters. ¹⁴Altogether, Kenan lived 910 years, and then he died.

¹⁵When Mahalalel had lived 65 years, he became the father of Jared. ¹⁶And after he became the father of Jared, Mahalalel lived 830 years and had other sons and daughters. ¹⁷Altogether, Mahalalel lived 895 years, and then he died.

¹⁸When Jared had lived 162 years, he became the father of Enoch. ¹⁹And after he became the father of Enoch, Jared lived 800 years and had other sons and daughters. ²⁰Altogether, Jared lived 962 years, and then he died.

²¹When Enoch had lived 65 years, he became the father of Methuselah.

ᵃ 15 Septuagint, Vulgate and Syriac; Hebrew *Very well*   ᵇ 16 *Nod* means *wandering* (see verses 12 and 14).   ᶜ 22 Or *who instructed all who work in*   ᵈ 23 Or *I will kill*   ᵉ 25 *Seth* probably means *granted*.   ᶠ 26 Or *to proclaim*   ᵍ 2 Hebrew *adam*   ʰ 6 *Father* may mean *ancestor*; also in verses 7-26.

Powerful Listening

READ AND CONSIDER: GENESIS 6:9-22

"Noah was a righteous man, blameless among the people of his time, and he walked with God" *(Genesis 6:9).*

Noah listened well. When God spoke to him, he paid attention. Genesis tells us that Noah "walked with God." What a beautiful way to say that Noah lived each day with an awareness of God's presence. Beyond that, however, Noah also obeyed. What God told him to do, he did.

Noah obeyed even though God directed him to do something outlandish: "Make yourself an ark" (6:14). And Noah did. What a monstrosity he constructed on dry land, miles from the nearest body of water! How many insults, jokes, and sarcastic questions he must have endured. Yet he kept on task, obeying God's instructions. Hebrews 11:7 lists Noah among the heroes of faith. The picture that develops out of the phrase "walked with God" reveals a person who depended on God's faithfulness across the decades, through times of doubt, against the corruption that surrounded him.

With the exception of his family, Noah stood alone for God in his culture. The memory of God in the world had shrunk to a single man and his household. Many centuries later, Jesus described the people in Noah's day: "For in the days before the flood, people were eating and drinking, marrying and giving in marriage, up to the day Noah entered the ark; and they knew nothing about what would happen until the flood came and took them all away. That is how it will be at the coming of the Son of Man" (Matthew 24:38-39). In Noah's day, as in ours, the noises of busyness can drown out the voice of God. (Little did they know that a different kind of drowning would soon overtake them.) Jesus warned about any time when people are oblivious to the danger of going about life without stopping long enough to listen to God.

Prayer is more than talking to God. While that is vital, too many of us give God our list of requests and then dash off to our next task. What would our lives be like if we took the time not only to talk to God but to listen to Him as well? What if we then determined to obey what He tells us to do—no matter how much our society might scoff at us?

Do you want to walk with God? Then in your prayer time, *listen* carefully for His voice. You may hear Him leading you in a new direction, with a new purpose, and with courage you never knew you had!

22And after he became the father of Methuselah, Enoch walked with God 300 years and had other sons and daughters. 23Altogether, Enoch lived 365 years. 24Enoch walked with God; then he was no more, because God took him away.

25When Methuselah had lived 187 years, he became the father of Lamech. 26And after he became the father of Lamech, Methuselah lived 782 years and had other sons and daughters. 27Altogether, Methuselah lived 969 years, and then he died.

28When Lamech had lived 182 years, he had a son. 29He named him Noah[a] and said, "He will comfort us in the labor and painful toil of our hands caused by the ground the LORD has cursed." 30After Noah was born, Lamech lived 595 years and had other sons and daughters. 31Altogether, Lamech lived 777 years, and then he died.

---

[a] 29 *Noah* sounds like the Hebrew for *comfort.*

32After Noah was 500 years old, he became the father of Shem, Ham and Japheth.

The Flood

6 When men began to increase in number on the earth and daughters were born to them, 2the sons of God saw that the daughters of men were beautiful, and they married any of them they chose. 3Then the LORD said, "My Spirit will not contend with[a] man forever, for he is mortal[b]; his days will be a hundred and twenty years."

4The Nephilim were on the earth in those days—and also afterward—when the sons of God went to the daughters of men and had children by them. They were the heroes of old, men of renown.

5The LORD saw how great man's wickedness on the earth had become, and that every inclination of the thoughts of his heart was only evil all the time. 6The LORD was grieved that he had made man on the earth, and his heart was filled with pain. 7So the LORD said, "I will wipe mankind, whom I have created, from the face of the earth—men and animals, and creatures that move along the ground, and birds of the air—for I am grieved that I have made them." 8But Noah found favor in the eyes of the LORD.

9This is the account of Noah.

Noah was a righteous man, blameless among the people of his time, and he walked with God. 10Noah had three sons: Shem, Ham and Japheth.

11Now the earth was corrupt in God's sight and was full of violence. 12God saw how corrupt the earth had become, for all the people on earth had corrupted their ways. 13So God said to Noah, "I am going to put an end to all people, for the earth is filled with violence because of them. I am surely going to destroy both them and the earth. 14So make yourself an ark of cypress[c] wood; make rooms in it and coat it with pitch inside and out. 15This is how you are to build it: The ark is to be 450 feet long, 75 feet wide and 45 feet high.[d] 16Make a roof for it and finish[e] the ark to within 18 inches[f] of the top. Put a door in the side of the ark and make lower, middle and upper decks. 17I am going to bring floodwaters on the earth to destroy all life under the heavens, every creature that has the breath of life in it. Everything on earth will perish. 18But I will establish my covenant with you, and you will enter the ark—you and your sons and your wife and your sons' wives with you. 19You are to bring into the ark two of all living creatures, male and female, to keep them alive with you. 20Two of every kind of bird, of every kind of animal and of every kind of creature that moves along the ground will come to you to be kept alive. 21You are to take every kind of food that is to be eaten and store it away as food for you and for them."

22Noah did everything just as God commanded him.

Praying Genesis 6:13-22

Dear God, enable me to hear Your voice guiding me so that I can do great things for You.

7 The LORD then said to Noah, "Go into the ark, you and your whole family, because I have found you righteous in this generation. 2Take with you seven[g] of every kind of clean animal, a male and its mate, and two of every kind of unclean animal, a male and its mate, 3and also seven of every kind of bird, male and female, to keep their various kinds alive throughout the earth. 4Seven days from now I will send rain on the earth for forty days and forty nights, and I will wipe from the face of the earth every living creature I have made."

---

[a] 3 Or *My spirit will not remain in*   [b] 3 Or *corrupt*   [c] 14 The meaning of the Hebrew for this word is uncertain.   [d] 15 Hebrew *300 cubits long, 50 cubits wide and 30 cubits high* (about 140 meters long, 23 meters wide and 13.5 meters high)   [e] 16 Or *Make an opening for light by finishing*   [f] 16 Hebrew *a cubit* (about 0.5 meter)   [g] 2 Or *seven pairs*; also in verse 3

The Rewards of Obedience

When your electric bill arrives, you might be able to come up with at least four reasons for not paying it:

1. "I don't have what it takes."
2. "I don't want to."
3. "I didn't know I had to."
4. "I forgot."

Which one of these reasons do you think the electric company will accept as a legitimate excuse for not paying?

You guessed it! None of the above.

Which one of these same four reasons does *God* accept as a good excuse for not living in obedience to His ways?

Right again! None of the above.

It doesn't matter if we feel as though we just don't have it in us to accomplish what He wants, or we openly rebel, or we don't know the right thing to do, or we forget to do the right thing. The consequence is still the same—*darkness*.

When we don't live the way He asks us to, we sacrifice much of the light we could enjoy. We don't experience the degree of His protection, guidance, and answers to prayer that we otherwise would. We forfeit certain blessings when we are not willing to do the things that must precede them.

When we obey God, we are protected. Noah was called to build the ark because God said, "I have found you righteous" (Genesis 7:1). Noah's righteousness ultimately saved him and his family from destruction. We can end up in the most wonderful places in our lives, places we wouldn't have thought to go on our own, simply because God sees that we have a heart to live His way. When we love Him enough to obey what He asks, we come under the covering of His protection.

When we obey God, we can be led by Him.

There are ways that are right and ways that are not, and we cannot confuse the two. If we obey God, He will give us the light of His revelation and get us where we need to go.

When we obey God, we see answers to our prayers. If you find you are not enjoying answers to your prayers, ask God to show you if you have neglected to be obedient to His ways in some area of your life. The Bible says we "receive from him anything we ask, because we obey his commands and do what pleases him" (1 John 3:22). There is a direct correlation between obedience and answered prayer.

God is not trying to be a dictator; He simply wants to show us how life works best. He is saying to us, "If you will do this, I will do that." In whatever area He is asking us to obey, we can be sure He is trying to teach us something that will be for our benefit.

Ask Him to show you if there are certain steps of obedience He wants you to take. He'll tell you. You can depend on it. When you come to a place where you trust Him so thoroughly that you will obey whatever He says, you'll find that obedience won't be a gut-wrenching misery; it will be a privilege. You'll obey because you love God. And because the rewards are great. You'll obey out of the desire to have nothing come between you and God. You'll obey because you'll pay any price to not have your light shut off.

For the next "From Stormie's Heart" article, go to page 60.

⁵And Noah did all that the LORD commanded him.

⁶Noah was six hundred years old when the floodwaters came on the earth. ⁷And Noah and his sons and his wife and his sons' wives entered the ark to escape the waters of the flood. ⁸Pairs of clean and unclean animals, of birds and of all creatures that move along the ground, ⁹male and female, came to Noah and entered the ark, as God had commanded Noah. ¹⁰And after the seven days the floodwaters came on the earth.

¹¹In the six hundredth year of Noah's life, on the seventeenth day of the second month—on that day all the springs of the great deep burst forth, and the floodgates of the heavens were opened. ¹²And rain fell on the earth forty days and forty nights.

¹³On that very day Noah and his sons, Shem, Ham and Japheth, together with his wife and the wives of his three sons, entered the ark. ¹⁴They had with them every wild animal according to its kind, all livestock according to their kinds, every creature that moves along the ground according to its kind and every bird according to its kind, everything with wings. ¹⁵Pairs of all creatures that have the breath of life in them came to Noah and entered the ark. ¹⁶The animals going in were male and female of every living thing, as God had commanded Noah. Then the LORD shut him in.

¹⁷For forty days the flood kept coming on the earth, and as the waters increased they lifted the ark high above the earth. ¹⁸The waters rose and increased greatly on the earth, and the ark floated on the surface of the water. ¹⁹They rose greatly on the earth, and all the high mountains under the entire heavens were covered. ²⁰The waters rose and covered the mountains to a depth of more than twenty feet.ᵃ,ᵇ ²¹Every living thing that moved on the earth perished—birds, livestock, wild animals, all the creatures that swarm over the earth, and all mankind. ²²Everything on dry land that had the breath of life in its nostrils died. ²³Every living thing on the face of the earth was wiped out; men and animals and the creatures that move along the ground and the birds of the air were wiped from the earth. Only Noah was left, and those with him in the ark.

²⁴The waters flooded the earth for a hundred and fifty days.

8 But God remembered Noah and all the wild animals and the livestock that were with him in the ark, and he sent a wind over the earth, and the waters receded. ²Now the springs of the deep and the floodgates of the heavens had been closed, and the rain had stopped falling from the sky. ³The water receded steadily from the earth. At the end of the hundred and fifty days the water had gone down, ⁴and on the seventeenth day of the seventh month the ark came to rest on the mountains of Ararat. ⁵The waters continued to recede until the tenth month, and on the first day of the tenth month the tops of the mountains became visible.

Praying Genesis 8:1-22
Thank You for never forgetting me, Lord.

⁶After forty days Noah opened the window he had made in the ark ⁷and sent out a raven, and it kept flying back and forth until the water had dried up from the earth. ⁸Then he sent out a dove to see if the water had receded from the surface of the ground. ⁹But the dove could find no place to set its feet because there was water over all the surface of the earth; so it returned to Noah in the ark. He reached out his hand and took the dove and brought it back to himself in the ark. ¹⁰He waited seven more days and again sent out the dove from the ark. ¹¹When the dove returned to him in the evening, there in its beak was a freshly plucked olive leaf! Then Noah knew that the water

ᵃ 20 Hebrew *fifteen cubits* (about 6.9 meters)   ᵇ 20 Or *rose more than twenty feet, and the mountains were covered* had receded from the earth. 12He waited seven more days and sent the dove out again, but this time it did not return to him.

13By the first day of the first month of Noah's six hundred and first year, the water had dried up from the earth. Noah then removed the covering from the ark and saw that the surface of the ground was dry. 14By the twenty-seventh day of the second month the earth was completely dry.

15Then God said to Noah, 16"Come out of the ark, you and your wife and your sons and their wives. 17Bring out every kind of living creature that is with you—the birds, the animals, and all the creatures that move along the ground—so they can multiply on the earth and be fruitful and increase in number upon it."

18So Noah came out, together with his sons and his wife and his sons' wives. 19All the animals and all the creatures that move along the ground and all the birds—everything that moves on the earth—came out of the ark, one kind after another.

20Then Noah built an altar to the LORD and, taking some of all the clean animals and clean birds, he sacrificed burnt offerings on it. 21The LORD smelled the pleasing aroma and said in his heart: "Never again will I curse the ground because of man, even though[a] every inclination of his heart is evil from childhood. And never again will I destroy all living creatures, as I have done.

22"As long as the earth endures,
  seedtime and harvest,
  cold and heat,
  summer and winter,
  day and night
  will never cease."

God's Covenant With Noah

9 Then God blessed Noah and his sons, saying to them, "Be fruitful and increase in number and fill the earth. 2The fear and dread of you will fall upon all the beasts of the earth and all the birds of the air, upon every creature that moves along the ground, and upon all the fish of the sea; they are given into your hands. 3Everything that lives and moves will be food for you. Just as I gave you the green plants, I now give you everything.

4"But you must not eat meat that has its lifeblood still in it. 5And for your lifeblood I will surely demand an accounting. I will demand an accounting from every animal. And from each man, too, I will demand an accounting for the life of his fellow man.

6"Whoever sheds the blood of man,
  by man shall his blood be shed;
for in the image of God
  has God made man.

7As for you, be fruitful and increase in number; multiply on the earth and increase upon it."

8Then God said to Noah and to his sons with him: 9"I now establish my covenant with you and with your descendants after you 10and with every living creature that was with you—the birds, the livestock and all the wild animals, all those that came out of the ark with you—every living creature on earth. 11I establish my covenant with you: Never again will all life be cut off by the waters of a flood; never again will there be a flood to destroy the earth."

Praying Genesis 9:11
Thank You, God, for always keeping Your promises to me.

12And God said, "This is the sign of the covenant I am making between me and you and every living creature with you, a covenant for all generations to come: 13I have set my rainbow in the clouds, and it will be the sign of the covenant between me and the earth. 14Whenever I bring clouds over the earth and the

---

[a] 21 Or *man, for*

The Power of God's Promise

READ AND CONSIDER: GENESIS 9:8-17

"Whenever the rainbow appears in the clouds, I will see it and remember the everlasting covenant between God and all living creatures of every kind on the earth" (Genesis 9:16).

When the clouds part after a thundershower revealing a stunning arc of colors, how many times have you stopped to look—and even called to others to join you? "Look at the rainbow!" Never ceasing to be objects of wonder, rainbows are those amazing creations that disappear as quickly as they appear, yet bring joy to our hearts when they surprise us by parting the gray with their luminescence.

That arc of color ties us right back to our ancestor Noah, to the moment after the flood when God made a promise, a covenant, that He would never again destroy the earth with a flood. Many scholars believe that the people of Noah's day had never even seen rain—that instead, the earth had been watered from springs deep in the ground. The flood occurred when "the springs of the great deep burst forth, and the floodgates of the heavens were opened" (7:11). Rain fell from heaven—and would continue to fall for the rest of the ages. But Noah did not need to fear the next time rain clouds gathered because God had made a promise. The rain would subside and the rainbow would appear. That visual sign would be a constant reminder that God always keeps His promises.

What does that have to do with prayer? Everything! When we pray, we reassert our faith that God keeps His promises. What we say out loud, or silently in our hearts, proclaims the truth of God's promises that we have read or heard in His Word. Have you ever noticed that if you are feeling badly and you keep saying negative thoughts out loud, you tend to feel them even stronger? The same is true in believing God's promises. When we speak the truth about God and about what He has promised us, while refusing to believe the lies of the enemy, it causes us to believe God stronger than before. That is not to say we should deny we have real problems or struggles, but the way we interpret them may be different. Satan wants us to believe that God has abandoned us and reneged on His promises, but God wants us to know that His promises are always true in spite of what we can see from our limited human perspective. By asserting our belief in His promises in prayer, we put ourselves in a position to see a lot more from God's perspective and a lot less from the enemy's.

So the next time you stand in wonder at the appearance of a rainbow in the clouds, breathe a prayer of thanks to God that He will always keep His promises.

---

rainbow appears in the clouds, [15]I will remember my covenant between me and you and all living creatures of every kind. Never again will the waters become a flood to destroy all life. [16]Whenever the rainbow appears in the clouds, I will see it and remember the everlasting covenant between God and all living creatures of every kind on the earth."

[17]So God said to Noah, "This is the sign of the covenant I have established between me and all life on the earth."

The Sons of Noah

[18]The sons of Noah who came out of the ark were Shem, Ham and Japheth. (Ham was the father of Canaan.) [19]These were the three sons of Noah, and from them came the people who were scattered over the earth.

20Noah, a man of the soil, proceeded[a] to plant a vineyard. 21When he drank some of its wine, he became drunk and lay uncovered inside his tent. 22Ham, the father of Canaan, saw his father's nakedness and told his two brothers outside. 23But Shem and Japheth took a garment and laid it across their shoulders; then they walked in backward and covered their father's nakedness. Their faces were turned the other way so that they would not see their father's nakedness.

24When Noah awoke from his wine and found out what his youngest son had done to him, 25he said,

> "Cursed be Canaan!
>   The lowest of slaves
>   will he be to his brothers."

26He also said,

> "Blessed be the LORD, the God of
>   Shem!
>   May Canaan be the slave of Shem.[b]
> 27May God extend the territory of
>   Japheth[c];
>   may Japheth live in the tents of
>   Shem,
>   and may Canaan be his[d] slave."

28After the flood Noah lived 350 years. 29Altogether, Noah lived 950 years, and then he died.

The Table of Nations

10 This is the account of Shem, Ham and Japheth, Noah's sons, who themselves had sons after the flood.

The Japhethites

2The sons[e] of Japheth:
  Gomer, Magog, Madai, Javan, Tubal, Meshech and Tiras.
3The sons of Gomer:
  Ashkenaz, Riphath and Togarmah.

4The sons of Javan:
  Elishah, Tarshish, the Kittim and the Rodanim.[f] 5(From these the maritime peoples spread out into their territories by their clans within their nations, each with its own language.)

The Hamites

6The sons of Ham:
  Cush, Mizraim,[g] Put and Canaan.
7The sons of Cush:
  Seba, Havilah, Sabtah, Raamah and Sabteca.
The sons of Raamah:
  Sheba and Dedan.

8Cush was the father[h] of Nimrod, who grew to be a mighty warrior on the earth. 9He was a mighty hunter before the LORD; that is why it is said, "Like Nimrod, a mighty hunter before the LORD." 10The first centers of his kingdom were Babylon, Erech, Akkad and Calneh, in[i] Shinar.[j] 11From that land he went to Assyria, where he built Nineveh, Rehoboth Ir,[k] Calah 12and Resen, which is between Nineveh and Calah; that is the great city.

13Mizraim was the father of
  the Ludites, Anamites, Lehabites, Naphtuhites, 14Pathrusites, Casluhites (from whom the Philistines came) and Caphtorites.
15Canaan was the father of
  Sidon his firstborn,[l] and of the Hittites, 16Jebusites, Amorites, Girgashites, 17Hivites, Arkites, Sinites, 18Arvadites, Zemarites and Hamathites.

Later the Canaanite clans scattered 19and the borders of Canaan reached from Sidon toward Gerar as far as Gaza, and then toward Sodom, Gomorrah, Admah and Zeboiim, as far as Lasha.

---

a 20 Or soil, was the first   b 26 Or be his slave   c 27 Japheth sounds like the Hebrew for extend.   d 27 Or their   e 2 Sons may mean descendants or successors or nations; also in verses 3, 4, 6, 7, 20-23, 29 and 31.   f 4 Some manuscripts of the Masoretic Text and Samaritan Pentateuch (see also Septuagint and 1 Chron. 1:7); most manuscripts of the Masoretic Text Dodanim   g 6 That is, Egypt; also in verse 13   h 8 Father may mean ancestor or predecessor or founder; also in verses 13, 15, 24 and 26.   i 10 Or Erech and Akkad—all of them in   j 10 That is, Babylonia   k 11 Or Nineveh with its city squares   l 15 Or of the Sidonians, the foremost

[20] These are the sons of Ham by their clans and languages, in their territories and nations.

The Semites

[21] Sons were also born to Shem, whose older brother was[a] Japheth; Shem was the ancestor of all the sons of Eber.

[22] The sons of Shem:

Elam, Asshur, Arphaxad, Lud and Aram.

[23] The sons of Aram:

Uz, Hul, Gether and Meshech.[b]

[24] Arphaxad was the father of[c] Shelah, and Shelah the father of Eber.

[25] Two sons were born to Eber:

One was named Peleg,[d] because in his time the earth was divided; his brother was named Joktan.

[26] Joktan was the father of

Almodad, Sheleph, Hazarmaveth, Jerah, [27] Hadoram, Uzal, Diklah, [28] Obal, Abimael, Sheba, [29] Ophir, Havilah and Jobab. All these were sons of Joktan.

[30] The region where they lived stretched from Mesha toward Sephar, in the eastern hill country.

[31] These are the sons of Shem by their clans and languages, in their territories and nations.

[32] These are the clans of Noah's sons, according to their lines of descent, within their nations. From these the nations spread out over the earth after the flood.

The Tower of Babel

11 Now the whole world had one language and a common speech. [2] As men moved eastward,[e] they found a plain in Shinar[f] and settled there.

[3] They said to each other, "Come, let's make bricks and bake them thoroughly." They used brick instead of stone, and tar for mortar. [4] Then they said, "Come, let us build ourselves a city, with a tower that reaches to the heavens, so that we may make a name for ourselves and not be scattered over the face of the whole earth."

[5] But the LORD came down to see the city and the tower that the men were building. [6] The LORD said, "If as one people speaking the same language they have begun to do this, then nothing they plan to do will be impossible for them. [7] Come, let us go down and confuse their language so they will not understand each other."

[8] So the LORD scattered them from there over all the earth, and they stopped building the city. [9] That is why it was called Babel[g]—because there the LORD confused the language of the whole world. From there the LORD scattered them over the face of the whole earth.

Praying Genesis 11:4-9
Lord, show me how to use the gifts and abilities You have given me to bring glory to Your name and not to myself.

From Shem to Abram

[10] This is the account of Shem.

Two years after the flood, when Shem was 100 years old, he became the father[h] of Arphaxad. [11] And after he became the father of Arphaxad, Shem lived 500 years and had other sons and daughters.

[12] When Arphaxad had lived 35 years, he became the father of Shelah. [13] And after he became the father of Shelah, Arphaxad lived 403 years and had other sons and daughters.[i]

[14] When Shelah had lived 30 years, he became the father of Eber. [15] And after he

---

[a] 21 Or *Shem, the older brother of*   [b] 23 See Septuagint and 1 Chron. 1:17; Hebrew *Mash*   [c] 24 Hebrew; Septuagint *father of Cainan, and Cainan was the father of*   [d] 25 *Peleg* means *division.*   [e] 2 Or *from the east;* or *in the east*   [f] 2 That is, Babylonia   [g] 9 That is, Babylon; *Babel* sounds like the Hebrew for *confused.*   [h] 10 *Father* may mean *ancestor;* also in verses 11-25.   [i] 12,13 Hebrew; Septuagint (see also Luke 3:35, 36 and note at Gen. 10:24) *35 years, he became the father of Cainan.* [13] *And after he became the father of Cainan, Arphaxad lived 430 years and had other sons and daughters, and then he died. When Cainan had lived 130 years, he became the father of Shelah. And after he became the father of Shelah, Cainan lived 330 years and had other sons and daughters*

became the father of Eber, Shelah lived 403 years and had other sons and daughters.

16When Eber had lived 34 years, he became the father of Peleg. 17And after he became the father of Peleg, Eber lived 430 years and had other sons and daughters.

18When Peleg had lived 30 years, he became the father of Reu. 19And after he became the father of Reu, Peleg lived 209 years and had other sons and daughters.

20When Reu had lived 32 years, he became the father of Serug. 21And after he became the father of Serug, Reu lived 207 years and had other sons and daughters.

22When Serug had lived 30 years, he became the father of Nahor. 23And after he became the father of Nahor, Serug lived 200 years and had other sons and daughters.

24When Nahor had lived 29 years, he became the father of Terah. 25And after he became the father of Terah, Nahor lived 119 years and had other sons and daughters.

26After Terah had lived 70 years, he became the father of Abram, Nahor and Haran.

27This is the account of Terah.

Terah became the father of Abram, Nahor and Haran. And Haran became the father of Lot. 28While his father Terah was still alive, Haran died in Ur of the Chaldeans, in the land of his birth. 29Abram and Nahor both married. The name of Abram's wife was Sarai, and the name of Nahor's wife was Milcah; she was the daughter of Haran, the father of both Milcah and Iscah. 30Now Sarai was barren; she had no children.

31Terah took his son Abram, his grandson Lot son of Haran, and his daughter-in-law Sarai, the wife of his son Abram, and together they set out from Ur of the Chaldeans to go to Canaan. But when they came to Haran, they settled there. 32Terah lived 205 years, and he died in Haran.

The Call of Abram

12 The LORD had said to Abram, "Leave your country, your people and your father's household and go to the land I will show you.

2 "I will make you into a great nation
   and I will bless you;
I will make your name great,
   and you will be a blessing.
3 I will bless those who bless you,
   and whoever curses you I will curse;
and all peoples on earth
   will be blessed through you."

4So Abram left, as the LORD had told him; and Lot went with him. Abram was seventy-five years old when he set out from Haran. 5He took his wife Sarai, his nephew Lot, all the possessions they had accumulated and the people they had acquired in Haran, and they set out for the land of Canaan, and they arrived there.

6Abram traveled through the land as far as the site of the great tree of Moreh at Shechem. At that time the Canaanites were in the land. 7The LORD appeared to Abram and said, "To your offspringa I will give this land." So he built an altar there to the LORD, who had appeared to him.

Praying Genesis 12:1-8
Holy Father, may I be like Abraham
and always follow You wherever
You want me to go.

8From there he went on toward the hills east of Bethel and pitched his tent, with Bethel on the west and Ai on the east. There he built an altar to the LORD and called on the name of the LORD. 9Then Abram set out and continued toward the Negev.

a 7 Or seed

Abram in Egypt

[10]Now there was a famine in the land, and Abram went down to Egypt to live there for a while because the famine was severe. [11]As he was about to enter Egypt, he said to his wife Sarai, "I know what a beautiful woman you are. [12]When the Egyptians see you, they will say, 'This is his wife.' Then they will kill me but will let you live. [13]Say you are my sister, so that I will be treated well for your sake and my life will be spared because of you."

[14]When Abram came to Egypt, the Egyptians saw that she was a very beautiful woman. [15]And when Pharaoh's officials saw her, they praised her to Pharaoh, and she was taken into his palace. [16]He treated Abram well for her sake, and Abram acquired sheep and cattle, male and female donkeys, menservants and maidservants, and camels.

> Prayer is . . .
>
> *praise, which is*
> *the ultimate love language.*

[17]But the LORD inflicted serious diseases on Pharaoh and his household because of Abram's wife Sarai. [18]So Pharaoh summoned Abram. "What have you done to me?" he said. "Why didn't you tell me she was your wife? [19]Why did you say, 'She is my sister,' so that I took her to be my wife? Now then, here is your wife. Take her and go!" [20]Then Pharaoh gave orders about Abram to his men, and they sent him on his way, with his wife and everything he had.

Abram and Lot Separate

13 So Abram went up from Egypt to the Negev, with his wife and everything he had, and Lot went with him. [2]Abram had become very wealthy in livestock and in silver and gold.

[3]From the Negev he went from place to place until he came to Bethel, to the place between Bethel and Ai where his tent had been earlier [4]and where he had first built an altar. There Abram called on the name of the LORD.

[5]Now Lot, who was moving about with Abram, also had flocks and herds and tents. [6]But the land could not support them while they stayed together, for their possessions were so great that they were not able to stay together. [7]And quarreling arose between Abram's herdsmen and the herdsmen of Lot. The Canaanites and Perizzites were also living in the land at that time.

[8]So Abram said to Lot, "Let's not have any quarreling between you and me, or between your herdsmen and mine, for we are brothers. [9]Is not the whole land before you? Let's part company. If you go to the left, I'll go to the right; if you go to the right, I'll go to the left."

[10]Lot looked up and saw that the whole plain of the Jordan was well watered, like the garden of the LORD, like the land of Egypt, toward Zoar. (This was before the LORD destroyed Sodom and Gomorrah.) [11]So Lot chose for himself the whole plain of the Jordan and set out toward the east. The two men parted company: [12]Abram lived in the land of Canaan, while Lot lived among the cities of the plain and pitched his tents near Sodom. [13]Now the men of Sodom were wicked and were sinning greatly against the LORD.

> *Praying Genesis 13:10-13*
>
> *Lord, guide me so that I never end up living outside Your best for me by choosing what I think is best instead of asking You.*

[14]The LORD said to Abram after Lot had parted from him, "Lift up your eyes from where you are and look north and south, east and west. [15]All the land that you see I will give to you and your offspring[a] forever. [16]I will make your offspring like

---

[a] *15 Or* seed; *also in verse 16*

the dust of the earth, so that if anyone could count the dust, then your offspring could be counted. 17Go, walk through the length and breadth of the land, for I am giving it to you."

18So Abram moved his tents and went to live near the great trees of Mamre at Hebron, where he built an altar to the LORD.

Abram Rescues Lot

14 At this time Amraphel king of Shinar,a Arioch king of Ellasar, Kedorlaomer king of Elam and Tidal king of Goiim 2went to war against Bera king of Sodom, Birsha king of Gomorrah, Shinab king of Admah, Shemeber king of Zeboiim, and the king of Bela (that is, Zoar). 3All these latter kings joined forces in the Valley of Siddim (the Salt Seab). 4For twelve years they had been subject to Kedorlaomer, but in the thirteenth year they rebelled.

5In the fourteenth year, Kedorlaomer and the kings allied with him went out and defeated the Rephaites in Ashteroth Karnaim, the Zuzites in Ham, the Emites in Shaveh Kiriathaim 6and the Horites in the hill country of Seir, as far as El Paran near the desert. 7Then they turned back and went to En Mishpat (that is, Kadesh), and they conquered the whole territory of the Amalekites, as well as the Amorites who were living in Hazazon Tamar.

8Then the king of Sodom, the king of Gomorrah, the king of Admah, the king of Zeboiim and the king of Bela (that is, Zoar) marched out and drew up their battle lines in the Valley of Siddim 9against Kedorlaomer king of Elam, Tidal king of Goiim, Amraphel king of Shinar and Arioch king of Ellasar—four kings against five. 10Now the Valley of Siddim was full of tar pits, and when the kings of Sodom and Gomorrah fled, some of the men fell into them and the rest fled to the hills. 11The four kings seized all the goods of Sodom and Gomorrah and all their food; then they went away. 12They also carried off Abram's nephew Lot and his possessions, since he was living in Sodom.

13One who had escaped came and reported this to Abram the Hebrew. Now Abram was living near the great trees of Mamre the Amorite, a brotherc of Eshcol and Aner, all of whom were allied with Abram. 14When Abram heard that his relative had been taken captive, he called out the 318 trained men born in his household and went in pursuit as far as Dan. 15During the night Abram divided his men to attack them and he routed them, pursuing them as far as Hobah, north of Damascus. 16He recovered all the goods and brought back his relative Lot and his possessions, together with the women and the other people.

17After Abram returned from defeating Kedorlaomer and the kings allied with him, the king of Sodom came out to meet him in the Valley of Shaveh (that is, the King's Valley).

18Then Melchizedek king of Salemd brought out bread and wine. He was priest of God Most High, 19and he blessed Abram, saying,

"Blessed be Abram by God Most High,
    Creatore of heaven and earth.
20And blessed bef God Most High,
    who delivered your enemies into
        your hand."

Then Abram gave him a tenth of everything.

21The king of Sodom said to Abram, "Give me the people and keep the goods for yourself."

22But Abram said to the king of Sodom, "I have raised my hand to the LORD, God Most High, Creator of heaven and earth, and have taken an oath 23that I will accept nothing belonging to you, not even a thread or the thong of a sandal, so that you will never be able to say, 'I made Abram rich.' 24I will accept nothing but what my men have eaten and the share

---

a 1 That is, Babylonia; also in verse 9   b 3 That is, the Dead Sea   c 13 Or a relative; or an ally   d 18 That is, Jerusalem
e 19 Or Possessor; also in verse 22   f 20 Or And praise be to

When We Have to Wait

READ AND CONSIDER: GENESIS 15:1-6

"After this, the word of the LORD came to Abram in a vision: 'Do not be afraid, Abram. I am your shield, your very great reward.' But Abram said, 'O Sovereign LORD, what can you give me since I remain childless and the one who will inherit my estate is Eliezer of Damascus?' " (Genesis 15:1-2).

Can't you just hear the exasperation in Abram's voice? "God, I appreciate that You're my shield and reward. That's great and all. Don't think I don't appreciate it, but . . . what I *really* want is for You to fulfill Your promise of descendants. Let's get on with that promise about becoming a 'great nation.' I want a SON!"

Abram had been waiting a long time. God had promised many descendants to Abram back when he was a mere 75 years old (12:4). He would be 100 years old when Isaac was finally born (21:5). That means Abram and Sarai waited 25 years for God to fulfill His promise.

We don't know how long Abram had already been waiting at this point in the story, but the Bible tells us he was 86 when Ishmael was born (16:16), so we can guess that this exchange between God and Abram occurred sometime in the first decade after God had made the promise.

How long do you patiently wait for answers to your prayers? Does a week seem too long to wait? What about a month? Waiting for a year seems to be beyond our ability. To see that Abram waited for a quarter of a century for an answer should give us hope to wait for our own prayers to be answered.

Abram could have given up. He could have decided that he didn't want to wait on God anymore. (He *did* eventually make a mess of things when he tried to fulfill God's promise on his own by having a child with Hagar.) At this point in the story, however, he chose to believe. If only he had continued to hang on to that belief.

What answer from God are you waiting for? Is it the answer to a prayer for the return of a rebellious child? Is it the answer to a prayer for the salvation of a family member? Is it the answer to a prayer for restoration in your marriage? For a job? For healing? For provision? Whatever it is, keep on praying and waiting. Release it into God's hands and let Him do it in His way and His time. His answer will be worth the wait.

that belongs to the men who went with me—to Aner, Eshcol and Mamre. Let them have their share."

God's Covenant With Abram

15 After this, the word of the LORD came to Abram in a vision:

"Do not be afraid, Abram.
 I am your shield,[a]
 your very great reward.[b]"

²But Abram said, "O Sovereign LORD, what can you give me since I remain childless and the one who will inherit[c] my estate is Eliezer of Damascus?" ³And Abram said, "You have given me no children; so a servant in my household will be my heir."

⁴Then the word of the LORD came to him: "This man will not be your heir, but a son coming from your own body will be your heir." ⁵He took him outside and said, "Look up at the heavens and count the stars—if indeed you can count them."

---

[a] 1 Or *sovereign*   [b] 1 Or *shield; / your reward will be very great*   [c] 2 The meaning of the Hebrew for this phrase is uncertain.

Then he said to him, "So shall your offspring be."

⁶Abram believed the LORD, and he credited it to him as righteousness.

⁷He also said to him, "I am the LORD, who brought you out of Ur of the Chaldeans to give you this land to take possession of it."

⁸But Abram said, "O Sovereign LORD, how can I know that I will gain possession of it?"

⁹So the LORD said to him, "Bring me a heifer, a goat and a ram, each three years old, along with a dove and a young pigeon."

¹⁰Abram brought all these to him, cut them in two and arranged the halves opposite each other; the birds, however, he did not cut in half. ¹¹Then birds of prey came down on the carcasses, but Abram drove them away.

¹²As the sun was setting, Abram fell into a deep sleep, and a thick and dreadful darkness came over him. ¹³Then the LORD said to him, "Know for certain that your descendants will be strangers in a country not their own, and they will be enslaved and mistreated four hundred years. ¹⁴But I will punish the nation they serve as slaves, and afterward they will come out with great possessions. ¹⁵You, however, will go to your fathers in peace and be buried at a good old age. ¹⁶In the fourth generation your descendants will come back here, for the sin of the Amorites has not yet reached its full measure."

¹⁷When the sun had set and darkness had fallen, a smoking firepot with a blazing torch appeared and passed between the pieces. ¹⁸On that day the LORD made a covenant with Abram and said, "To your descendants I give this land, from the river[a] of Egypt to the great river, the Euphrates— ¹⁹the land of the Kenites, Kenizzites, Kadmonites, ²⁰Hittites, Perizzites, Rephaites, ²¹Amorites, Canaanites, Girgashites and Jebusites."

Hagar and Ishmael

16 Now Sarai, Abram's wife, had borne him no children. But she had an Egyptian maidservant named Hagar; ²so she said to Abram, "The LORD has kept me from having children. Go, sleep with my maidservant; perhaps I can build a family through her."

Abram agreed to what Sarai said. ³So after Abram had been living in Canaan ten years, Sarai his wife took her Egyptian maidservant Hagar and gave her to her husband to be his wife. ⁴He slept with Hagar, and she conceived.

When she knew she was pregnant, she began to despise her mistress. ⁵Then Sarai said to Abram, "You are responsible for the wrong I am suffering. I put my servant in your arms, and now that she knows she is pregnant, she despises me. May the LORD judge between you and me."

Praying Genesis 16:1-5

Help me, Lord, to trust in Your promises and not try to make things happen my own way.

⁶"Your servant is in your hands," Abram said. "Do with her whatever you think best." Then Sarai mistreated Hagar; so she fled from her.

⁷The angel of the LORD found Hagar near a spring in the desert; it was the spring that is beside the road to Shur. ⁸And he said, "Hagar, servant of Sarai, where have you come from, and where are you going?"

"I'm running away from my mistress Sarai," she answered.

⁹Then the angel of the LORD told her, "Go back to your mistress and submit to her." ¹⁰The angel added, "I will so increase your descendants that they will be too numerous to count."

¹¹The angel of the LORD also said to her:

"You are now with child
    and you will have a son.
You shall name him Ishmael,[a]
    for the LORD has heard of your
      misery.
[12] He will be a wild donkey of a man;
    his hand will be against everyone
    and everyone's hand against him,
and he will live in hostility
    toward[b] all his brothers."

[13] She gave this name to the LORD who spoke to her: "You are the God who sees me," for she said, "I have now seen[c] the One who sees me." [14] That is why the well was called Beer Lahai Roi[d]; it is still there, between Kadesh and Bered.

[15] So Hagar bore Abram a son, and Abram gave the name Ishmael to the son she had borne. [16] Abram was eighty-six years old when Hagar bore him Ishmael.

The Covenant of Circumcision

17 When Abram was ninety-nine years old, the LORD appeared to him and said, "I am God Almighty[e]; walk before me and be blameless. [2] I will confirm my covenant between me and you and will greatly increase your numbers."

[3] Abram fell facedown, and God said to him, [4] "As for me, this is my covenant with you: You will be the father of many nations. [5] No longer will you be called Abram[f]; your name will be Abraham,[g] for I have made you a father of many nations. [6] I will make you very fruitful; I will make nations of you, and kings will come from you. [7] I will establish my covenant as an everlasting covenant between me and you and your descendants after you for the generations to come, to be your God and the God of your descendants after you. [8] The whole land of Canaan, where you are now an alien, I will give as an everlasting possession to you and your descendants after you; and I will be their God."

[9] Then God said to Abraham, "As for you, you must keep my covenant, you and your descendants after you for the generations to come. [10] This is my covenant with you and your descendants after you, the covenant you are to keep: Every male among you shall be circumcised. [11] You are to undergo circumcision, and it will be the sign of the covenant between me and you. [12] For the generations to come every male among you who is eight days old must be circumcised, including those born in your household or bought with money from a foreigner—those who are not your offspring. [13] Whether born in your household or bought with your money, they must be circumcised. My covenant in your flesh is to be an everlasting covenant. [14] Any uncircumcised male, who has not been circumcised in the flesh, will be cut off from his people; he has broken my covenant."

[15] God also said to Abraham, "As for Sarai your wife, you are no longer to call her Sarai; her name will be Sarah. [16] I will bless her and will surely give you a son by her. I will bless her so that she will be the mother of nations; kings of peoples will come from her."

[17] Abraham fell facedown; he laughed and said to himself, "Will a son be born to a man a hundred years old? Will Sarah bear a child at the age of ninety?" [18] And Abraham said to God, "If only Ishmael might live under your blessing!"

[19] Then God said, "Yes, but your wife Sarah will bear you a son, and you will call him Isaac.[h] I will establish my covenant with him as an everlasting covenant for his descendants after him. [20] And as for Ishmael, I have heard you: I will surely bless him; I will make him fruitful and will greatly increase his numbers. He will be the father of twelve rulers, and I will make him into a great nation. [21] But my covenant I will establish with Isaac, whom Sarah will bear to you by this time next year." [22] When he had finished speaking with Abraham, God went up from him.

---

[a] 11 Ishmael means God hears. [b] 12 Or live to the east / of [c] 13 Or seen the back of [d] 14 Beer Lahai Roi means well of the Living One who sees me. [e] 1 Hebrew El-Shaddai [f] 5 Abram means exalted father. [g] 5 Abraham means father of many. [h] 19 Isaac means he laughs.

23On that very day Abraham took his son Ishmael and all those born in his household or bought with his money, every male in his household, and circumcised them, as God told him. 24Abraham was ninety-nine years old when he was circumcised, 25and his son Ishmael was thirteen; 26Abraham and his son Ishmael were both circumcised on that same day. 27And every male in Abraham's household, including those born in his household or bought from a foreigner, was circumcised with him.

The Three Visitors

18 The LORD appeared to Abraham near the great trees of Mamre while he was sitting at the entrance to his tent in the heat of the day. 2Abraham looked up and saw three men standing nearby. When he saw them, he hurried from the entrance of his tent to meet them and bowed low to the ground.

3He said, "If I have found favor in your eyes, my lord,ᵃ do not pass your servant by. 4Let a little water be brought, and then you may all wash your feet and rest under this tree. 5Let me get you something to eat, so you can be refreshed and then go on your way—now that you have come to your servant."

"Very well," they answered, "do as you say."

6So Abraham hurried into the tent to Sarah. "Quick," he said, "get three seahsᵇ of fine flour and knead it and bake some bread."

7Then he ran to the herd and selected a choice, tender calf and gave it to a servant, who hurried to prepare it. 8He then brought some curds and milk and the calf that had been prepared, and set these before them. While they ate, he stood near them under a tree.

9"Where is your wife Sarah?" they asked him.

"There, in the tent," he said.

10Then the LORDᶜ said, "I will surely return to you about this time next year, and Sarah your wife will have a son."

Now Sarah was listening at the entrance to the tent, which was behind him. 11Abraham and Sarah were already old and well advanced in years, and Sarah was past the age of childbearing. 12So Sarah laughed to herself as she thought, "After I am worn out and my masterᵈ is old, will I now have this pleasure?"

13Then the LORD said to Abraham, "Why did Sarah laugh and say, 'Will I really have a child, now that I am old?' 14Is anything too hard for the LORD? I will return to you at the appointed time next year and Sarah will have a son."

15Sarah was afraid, so she lied and said, "I did not laugh."

But he said, "Yes, you did laugh."

Praying Genesis 18:9-15
Dear God, strengthen my faith so I will always believe that nothing is too hard for You.

Abraham Pleads for Sodom

16When the men got up to leave, they looked down toward Sodom, and Abraham walked along with them to see them on their way. 17Then the LORD said, "Shall I hide from Abraham what I am about to do? 18Abraham will surely become a great and powerful nation, and all nations on earth will be blessed through him. 19For I have chosen him, so that he will direct his children and his household after him to keep the way of the LORD by doing what is right and just, so that the LORD will bring about for Abraham what he has promised him."

20Then the LORD said, "The outcry against Sodom and Gomorrah is so great and their sin so grievous 21that I will go down and see if what they have done is as bad as the outcry that has reached me. If not, I will know."

22The men turned away and went toward Sodom, but Abraham remained standing

---

ᵃ 3 Or O Lord   ᵇ 6 That is, probably about 20 quarts (about 22 liters)   ᶜ 10 Hebrew Then he   ᵈ 12 Or husband before the LORD.ᵃ ²³Then Abraham approached him and said: "Will you sweep away the righteous with the wicked? ²⁴What if there are fifty righteous people in the city? Will you really sweep it away and not spareᵇ the place for the sake of the fifty righteous people in it? ²⁵Far be it from you to do such a thing—to kill the righteous with the wicked, treating the righteous and the wicked alike. Far be it from you! Will not the Judgeᶜ of all the earth do right?"

²⁶The LORD said, "If I find fifty righteous people in the city of Sodom, I will spare the whole place for their sake."

²⁹Once again he spoke to him, "What if only forty are found there?"

He said, "For the sake of forty, I will not do it."

³⁰Then he said, "May the Lord not be angry, but let me speak. What if only thirty can be found there?"

He answered, "I will not do it if I find thirty there."

³¹Abraham said, "Now that I have been so bold as to speak to the Lord, what if only twenty can be found there?"

He said, "For the sake of twenty, I will not destroy it."

³²Then he said, "May the Lord not be

God's people at prayer
INTERCEDING IN HOPE OF SEEING GREAT CHANGE

GENESIS 18:20-33 Abraham knew about the wickedness in Sodom and kept his distance from its evil influence. However, he wasn't eager to see the good folks go down with the bad. He hoped there might be enough decent people in town that God would decide to spare them. Then perhaps, he was only trying to look out for his nephew, Lot, who lived there. In classic bartering fashion, Abraham worked his way down from 50 "righteous people" to ten, gaining God's agreement each time. In the process, Abraham learned a lot about God's patience and compassion.

Given the state of sin in the world, every day that passes represents another occasion when God mercifully withholds judgment. Perhaps you know people in your family, neighborhood, or workplace who appear to be hopeless and unreachable. No matter how unredeemable they may seem, keep asking God to save them. Your prayers can affect the direction of their lives. And who knows what great things you'll learn about God in the process?

²⁷Then Abraham spoke up again: "Now that I have been so bold as to speak to the Lord, though I am nothing but dust and ashes, ²⁸what if the number of the righteous is five less than fifty? Will you destroy the whole city because of five people?"

"If I find forty-five there," he said, "I will not destroy it."

Praying Genesis 18:20-33

Lord, give me the words to pray boldly for the lives of others and not give up or stop interceding too soon.

angry, but let me speak just once more. What if only ten can be found there?"

He answered, "For the sake of ten, I will not destroy it."

³³When the LORD had finished speaking with Abraham, he left, and Abraham returned home.

Sodom and Gomorrah Destroyed

19 The two angels arrived at Sodom in the evening, and Lot was sitting in the gateway of the city. When he saw them, he got up to meet them and bowed down with his face to the ground. ²"My

lords," he said, "please turn aside to your servant's house. You can wash your feet and spend the night and then go on your way early in the morning."

"No," they answered, "we will spend the night in the square."

³But he insisted so strongly that they did go with him and entered his house. He prepared a meal for them, baking bread without yeast, and they ate. ⁴Before they had gone to bed, all the men from every part of the city of Sodom—both young and old—surrounded the house. ⁵They called to Lot, "Where are the men who came to you tonight? Bring them out to us so that we can have sex with them."

⁶Lot went outside to meet them and shut the door behind him ⁷and said, "No, my friends. Don't do this wicked thing. ⁸Look, I have two daughters who have never slept with a man. Let me bring them out to you, and you can do what you like with them. But don't do anything to these men, for they have come under the protection of my roof."

⁹"Get out of our way," they replied. And they said, "This fellow came here as an alien, and now he wants to play the judge! We'll treat you worse than them." They kept bringing pressure on Lot and moved forward to break down the door.

¹⁰But the men inside reached out and pulled Lot back into the house and shut the door. ¹¹Then they struck the men who were at the door of the house, young and old, with blindness so that they could not find the door.

¹²The two men said to Lot, "Do you have anyone else here—sons-in-law, sons or daughters, or anyone else in the city who belongs to you? Get them out of here, ¹³because we are going to destroy this place. The outcry to the LORD against its people is so great that he has sent us to destroy it."

¹⁴So Lot went out and spoke to his sons-in-law, who were pledged to marry[a]

his daughters. He said, "Hurry and get out of this place, because the LORD is about to destroy the city!" But his sons-in-law thought he was joking.

¹⁵With the coming of dawn, the angels urged Lot, saying, "Hurry! Take your wife and your two daughters who are here, or you will be swept away when the city is punished."

¹⁶When he hesitated, the men grasped his hand and the hands of his wife and of his two daughters and led them safely out of the city, for the LORD was merciful to them. ¹⁷As soon as they had brought them out, one of them said, "Flee for your lives! Don't look back, and don't stop anywhere in the plain! Flee to the mountains or you will be swept away!"

¹⁸But Lot said to them, "No, my lords,[b] please! ¹⁹Your[c] servant has found favor in your[c] eyes, and you[c] have shown great kindness to me in sparing my life. But I can't flee to the mountains; this disaster will overtake me, and I'll die. ²⁰Look, here is a town near enough to run to, and it is small. Let me flee to it—it is very small, isn't it? Then my life will be spared."

²¹He said to him, "Very well, I will grant this request too; I will not overthrow the town you speak of. ²²But flee there quickly, because I cannot do anything until you reach it." (That is why the town was called Zoar.[d])

Praying Genesis 19:22-29

Dear Lord, walk with me to where You are leading me; help me not keep looking back to the past so that I become paralyzed by it.

²³By the time Lot reached Zoar, the sun had risen over the land. ²⁴Then the LORD rained down burning sulfur on Sodom and Gomorrah—from the LORD out of the heavens. ²⁵Thus he overthrew those cities and the entire plain, including all those living in the cities—and also the vegetation in the land. ²⁶But Lot's

---

a *14* Or *were married to* b *18* Or *No, Lord*; or *No, my lord* c *19* The Hebrew is singular. d *22 Zoar* means *small.*

wife looked back, and she became a pillar of salt.

27 Early the next morning Abraham got up and returned to the place where he had stood before the LORD. 28 He looked down toward Sodom and Gomorrah, toward all the land of the plain, and he saw dense smoke rising from the land, like smoke from a furnace.

29 So when God destroyed the cities of the plain, he remembered Abraham, and he brought Lot out of the catastrophe that overthrew the cities where Lot had lived.

Lot and His Daughters

30 Lot and his two daughters left Zoar and settled in the mountains, for he was afraid to stay in Zoar. He and his two daughters lived in a cave. 31 One day the older daughter said to the younger, "Our father is old, and there is no man around here to lie with us, as is the custom all over the earth. 32 Let's get our father to drink wine and then lie with him and preserve our family line through our father."

33 That night they got their father to drink wine, and the older daughter went in and lay with him. He was not aware of it when she lay down or when she got up.

34 The next day the older daughter said to the younger, "Last night I lay with my father. Let's get him to drink wine again tonight, and you go in and lie with him so we can preserve our family line through our father." 35 So they got their father to drink wine that night also, and the younger daughter went and lay with him. Again he was not aware of it when she lay down or when she got up.

36 So both of Lot's daughters became pregnant by their father. 37 The older daughter had a son, and she named him Moab[a]; he is the father of the Moabites of today. 38 The younger daughter also had a son, and she named him Ben-Ammi[b]; he is the father of the Ammonites of today.

Abraham and Abimelech

20 Now Abraham moved on from there into the region of the Negev and lived between Kadesh and Shur. For a while he stayed in Gerar, 2 and there Abraham said of his wife Sarah, "She is my sister." Then Abimelech king of Gerar sent for Sarah and took her.

3 But God came to Abimelech in a dream one night and said to him, "You are as good as dead because of the woman you have taken; she is a married woman."

4 Now Abimelech had not gone near her, so he said, "Lord, will you destroy an innocent nation? 5 Did he not say to me, 'She is my sister,' and didn't she also say, 'He is my brother'? I have done this with a clear conscience and clean hands."

6 Then God said to him in the dream, "Yes, I know you did this with a clear conscience, and so I have kept you from sinning against me. That is why I did not let you touch her. 7 Now return the man's wife, for he is a prophet, and he will pray for you and you will live. But if you do not return her, you may be sure that you and all yours will die."

8 Early the next morning Abimelech summoned all his officials, and when he told them all that had happened, they were very much afraid. 9 Then Abimelech called Abraham in and said, "What have you done to us? How have I wronged you that you have brought such great guilt upon me and my kingdom? You have done things to me that should not be done." 10 And Abimelech asked Abraham, "What was your reason for doing this?"

11 Abraham replied, "I said to myself, 'There is surely no fear of God in this place, and they will kill me because of my wife.' 12 Besides, she really is my sister, the daughter of my father though not of my mother; and she became my wife. 13 And when God had me wander from my father's household, I said to her, 'This

---

a 37 Moab sounds like the Hebrew for from father.   b 38 Ben-Ammi means son of my people.

is how you can show your love to me: Everywhere we go, say of me, "He is my brother." '"

14Then Abimelech brought sheep and cattle and male and female slaves and gave them to Abraham, and he returned Sarah his wife to him. 15And Abimelech said, "My land is before you; live wherever you like."

16To Sarah he said, "I am giving your brother a thousand shekelsᵃ of silver. This is to cover the offense against you before all who are with you; you are completely vindicated."

17Then Abraham prayed to God, and God healed Abimelech, his wife and his slave girls so they could have children again, 18for the LORD had closed up every womb in Abimelech's household because of Abraham's wife Sarah.

The Birth of Isaac

21 Now the LORD was gracious to Sarah as he had said, and the LORD did for Sarah what he had promised. 2Sarah became pregnant and bore a son to Abraham in his old age, at the very time God had promised him. 3Abraham gave the name Isaacᵇ to the son Sarah bore him. 4When his son Isaac was eight days old, Abraham circumcised him, as God commanded him. 5Abraham was a hundred years old when his son Isaac was born to him.

6Sarah said, "God has brought me laughter, and everyone who hears about this will laugh with me." 7And she added, "Who would have said to Abraham that Sarah would nurse children? Yet I have borne him a son in his old age."

Hagar and Ishmael Sent Away

8The child grew and was weaned, and on the day Isaac was weaned Abraham held a great feast. 9But Sarah saw that the son whom Hagar the Egyptian had borne to Abraham was mocking, 10and she said to Abraham, "Get rid of that slave woman and her son, for that slave woman's son will never share in the inheritance with my son Isaac."

11The matter distressed Abraham greatly because it concerned his son. 12But God said to him, "Do not be so distressed about the boy and your maidservant. Listen to whatever Sarah tells you, because it is through Isaac that your offspringᶜ will be reckoned. 13I will make the son of the maidservant into a nation also, because he is your offspring."

14Early the next morning Abraham took some food and a skin of water and gave them to Hagar. He set them on her shoulders and then sent her off with the boy. She went on her way and wandered in the desert of Beersheba.

15When the water in the skin was gone, she put the boy under one of the bushes. 16Then she went off and sat down nearby, about a bowshot away, for she thought, "I cannot watch the boy die." And as she sat there nearby, sheᵈ began to sob.

Praying Genesis 21:14-19
My precious Lord, I thank You that when I cry out to You in the dry and thirsty times of my life, You will open my eyes to Your provision of living water for me.

17God heard the boy crying, and the angel of God called to Hagar from heaven and said to her, "What is the matter, Hagar? Do not be afraid; God has heard the boy crying as he lies there. 18Lift the boy up and take him by the hand, for I will make him into a great nation."

19Then God opened her eyes and she saw a well of water. So she went and filled the skin with water and gave the boy a drink.

20God was with the boy as he grew up. He lived in the desert and became an archer. 21While he was living in the Desert of Paran, his mother got a wife for him from Egypt.

ᵃ *16* That is, about 25 pounds (about 11.5 kilograms)   ᵇ *3 Isaac* means *he laughs.*   ᶜ *12* Or *seed*   ᵈ *16* Hebrew; Septuagint *the child*

The Treaty at Beersheba

22At that time Abimelech and Phicol the commander of his forces said to Abraham, "God is with you in everything you do. 23Now swear to me here before God that you will not deal falsely with me or my children or my descendants. Show to me and the country where you are living as an alien the same kindness I have shown to you."

24Abraham said, "I swear it."

25Then Abraham complained to Abimelech about a well of water that Abimelech's servants had seized. 26But Abimelech said, "I don't know who has done this. You did not tell me, and I heard about it only today."

27So Abraham brought sheep and cattle and gave them to Abimelech, and the two men made a treaty. 28Abraham set apart seven ewe lambs from the flock, 29and Abimelech asked Abraham, "What is the meaning of these seven ewe lambs you have set apart by themselves?"

30He replied, "Accept these seven lambs from my hand as a witness that I dug this well."

31So that place was called Beersheba,a because the two men swore an oath there.

32After the treaty had been made at Beersheba, Abimelech and Phicol the commander of his forces returned to the land of the Philistines. 33Abraham planted a tamarisk tree in Beersheba, and there he called upon the name of the LORD, the Eternal God. 34And Abraham stayed in the land of the Philistines for a long time.

Abraham Tested

22 Some time later God tested Abraham. He said to him, "Abraham!"

"Here I am," he replied.

2Then God said, "Take your son, your only son, Isaac, whom you love, and go to the region of Moriah. Sacrifice him there as a burnt offering on one of the mountains I will tell you about."

3Early the next morning Abraham got up and saddled his donkey. He took with him two of his servants and his son Isaac. When he had cut enough wood for the burnt offering, he set out for the place God had told him about. 4On the third day Abraham looked up and saw the place in the distance. 5He said to his servants, "Stay here with the donkey while I and the boy go over there. We will worship and then we will come back to you."

6Abraham took the wood for the burnt offering and placed it on his son Isaac, and he himself carried the fire and the knife. As the two of them went on together, 7Isaac spoke up and said to his father Abraham, "Father?"

"Yes, my son?" Abraham replied.

"The fire and wood are here," Isaac said, "but where is the lamb for the burnt offering?"

8Abraham answered, "God himself will provide the lamb for the burnt offering, my son." And the two of them went on together.

9When they reached the place God had told him about, Abraham built an altar there and arranged the wood on it. He bound his son Isaac and laid him on the altar, on top of the wood. 10Then he reached out his hand and took the knife to slay his son. 11But the angel of the LORD called out to him from heaven, "Abraham! Abraham!"

"Here I am," he replied.

Praying Genesis 22:2, 9-12
Heavenly Father, help me to lay down all that I love so that I can better serve all that You love.

12"Do not lay a hand on the boy," he said. "Do not do anything to him. Now I know that you fear God, because you have not withheld from me your son, your only son."

13Abraham looked up and there in a thicket he saw a ramb caught by its horns.

---

a 31 Beersheba can mean *well of seven* or *well of the oath*. b 13 Many manuscripts of the Masoretic Text, Samaritan Pentateuch, Septuagint and Syriac; most manuscripts of the Masoretic Text *a ram behind him*

Making Sacrifices

GOING *deeper*

READ AND CONSIDER: GENESIS 22:1-19

"Some time later God tested Abraham. He said to him, 'Abraham!' 'Here I am,' he replied. Then God said, 'Take your son, your only son, Isaac, whom you love, and go to the region of Moriah. Sacrifice him there as a burnt offering on one of the mountains I will tell you about.' Early the next morning Abraham got up and saddled his donkey . . ." (Genesis 22:1-3).

Sometimes God asks the strangest things. Noah had to build an ark miles away from any body of water and put in stalls that would somehow be filled with animals. (Surely he wondered how he was going to round up the lions and keep them away from the zebras!)

But nothing quite matches the task given to Abraham. Not only did God ask him to kill his son, God was taking away from Abraham that answer to the promise he had waited 25 years to receive. Isaac was Abraham's heir, the child promised to Abraham and Sarah, the child born in their old age. For Isaac to die would also kill the dream.

Or would it?

It seems that Abraham didn't waste time worrying about it. He got up early the next morning, saddled his donkey, roused the sleepy boy and two servants, cut some wood (he would need kindling to start the fire), and set out for the three-day journey. What went through his mind during those three long days? I imagine that Abraham talked to God *a lot*. And such was Abraham's relationship with God that he trusted God. He didn't understand; he knew that obeying God would hurt him to the core, but he kept right on walking. He kept right on obeying. When he got to the place, he built an altar, bound his son, laid him on the altar, and raised the knife.

Could any of us trust God that much?

Our hearts wince at the thought of sacrificing a human being. But we would be wise to consider how this story gives an astounding picture of what God Himself would one day do for us. As Isaac carried the wood for the burnt offering, so Jesus carried His own cross to Golgotha. As Abraham placed Isaac on the altar, so God placed His Son on the cross. As Abraham raised his knife in order to kill his son in obedience to God, so God allowed Jesus to be put to death so that sin could be punished and forgiveness could be given. Abraham knew that God would provide the lamb for the offering (22:8). Many centuries later, He did. John the Baptist pointed this out to his followers: "Look, the Lamb of God, who takes away the sin of the world!" (John 1:29).

How much do you trust God—*really*? Enough to die for Him? Enough to let a dream in your life die? How about enough to live for Him?

He went over and took the ram and sacrificed it as a burnt offering instead of his son. ¹⁴So Abraham called that place The LORD Will Provide. And to this day it is said, "On the mountain of the LORD it will be provided."

¹⁵The angel of the LORD called to Abraham from heaven a second time ¹⁶and said, "I swear by myself, declares the LORD, that because you have done this and have not withheld your son, your only son, ¹⁷I will surely bless you and make your descendants as numerous as the stars in the sky and as the sand on the seashore. Your descendants will take possession of the cities of their enemies, ¹⁸and through your offspring[a] all nations on earth will be blessed, because you have obeyed me."

19Then Abraham returned to his servants, and they set off together for Beersheba. And Abraham stayed in Beersheba.

Nahor's Sons

20Some time later Abraham was told, "Milcah is also a mother; she has borne sons to your brother Nahor: 21Uz the firstborn, Buz his brother, Kemuel (the father of Aram), 22Kesed, Hazo, Pildash, Jidlaph and Bethuel." 23Bethuel became the father of Rebekah. Milcah bore these eight sons to Abraham's brother Nahor. 24His concubine, whose name was Reumah, also had sons: Tebah, Gaham, Tahash and Maacah.

The Death of Sarah

23 Sarah lived to be a hundred and twenty-seven years old. 2She died at Kiriath Arba (that is, Hebron) in the land of Canaan, and Abraham went to mourn for Sarah and to weep over her.

3Then Abraham rose from beside his dead wife and spoke to the Hittites.a He said, 4"I am an alien and a stranger among you. Sell me some property for a burial site here so I can bury my dead."

5The Hittites replied to Abraham, 6"Sir, listen to us. You are a mighty prince among us. Bury your dead in the choicest of our tombs. None of us will refuse you his tomb for burying your dead."

7Then Abraham rose and bowed down before the people of the land, the Hittites. 8He said to them, "If you are willing to let me bury my dead, then listen to me and intercede with Ephron son of Zohar on my behalf 9so he will sell me the cave of Machpelah, which belongs to him and is at the end of his field. Ask him to sell it to me for the full price as a burial site among you."

10Ephron the Hittite was sitting among his people and he replied to Abraham in the hearing of all the Hittites who had come to the gate of his city. 11"No, my lord," he said. "Listen to me; I giveb you the field, and I giveb you the cave that is in it. I giveb it to you in the presence of my people. Bury your dead."

12Again Abraham bowed down before the people of the land 13and he said to Ephron in their hearing, "Listen to me, if you will. I will pay the price of the field. Accept it from me so I can bury my dead there."

14Ephron answered Abraham, 15"Listen to me, my lord; the land is worth four hundred shekelsc of silver, but what is that between me and you? Bury your dead."

16Abraham agreed to Ephron's terms and weighed out for him the price he had named in the hearing of the Hittites: four hundred shekels of silver, according to the weight current among the merchants.

17So Ephron's field in Machpelah near Mamre—both the field and the cave in it, and all the trees within the borders of the field—was deeded 18to Abraham as his property in the presence of all the Hittites who had come to the gate of the city. 19Afterward Abraham buried his wife Sarah in the cave in the field of Machpelah near Mamre (which is at Hebron) in the land of Canaan. 20So the field and the cave in it were deeded to Abraham by the Hittites as a burial site.

Isaac and Rebekah

24 Abraham was now old and well advanced in years, and the LORD had blessed him in every way. 2He said to the chiefd servant in his household, the one in charge of all that he had, "Put your hand under my thigh. 3I want you to swear by the LORD, the God of heaven and the God of earth, that you will not get a wife for my son from the daughters of the Canaanites, among whom I am living, 4but will go to my country and my own relatives and get a wife for my son Isaac."

5The servant asked him, "What if the woman is unwilling to come back with

---

a 3 Or the sons of Heth; also in verses 5, 7, 10, 16, 18 and 20   b 11 Or sell   c 15 That is, about 10 pounds (about 4.5 kilograms)   d 2 Or oldest

A Prayer for Success

READ AND CONSIDER: GENESIS 24:1-27

"Then he prayed, 'O LORD, God of my master Abraham, give me success today, and show kindness to my master Abraham' " (Genesis 24:12).

When you face a big job or an important responsibility, you want to succeed. The best way to see success is to go directly to God, who wants the very best for your life, and ask for His guidance. That's what Eliezer did.

Abraham had asked his servant to find the right bride for his son Isaac. This was most likely Eliezer, Abraham's trusted servant for many years. Eliezer realized the great weight of the responsibility he carried, so he submitted the matter directly to God rather than depend solely on his own wisdom or on pure luck. He asked God for a sign, and God granted his request almost instantly. Before Eliezer had even finished praying, Rebekah arrived and offered to give him water for both himself and his camels. What a remarkable answer to prayer!

But let's go a little deeper. Who was Eliezer? If we go back to where he is named in Genesis 15:2-3, we discover that not only was he Abraham's trusted servant, but at that point, he stood to inherit all of Abraham's wealth if Abraham had no son. So not only did he lose out when Isaac was born, but Eliezer also had to find a suitable bride for Isaac. A lesser man might have been bitter about all he had lost. A lesser man might have defined "success" as doing whatever it might take to get back into that place of honor in order to gain the inheritance. A lesser man might not have cared what kind of bride he brought back to Isaac. Not Eliezer. He was determined to do the job well, so he prayed for success in the task.

God cares about your responsibilities. He wants to see you do well, to succeed. So don't be afraid to ask for success. Always keep in mind, however, that He may define success very differently than you do. Like Eliezer, walk so close to God that you're able to put aside what you might want for yourself in order to succeed at what God wants for you.

---

me to this land? Shall I then take your son back to the country you came from?"

⁶"Make sure that you do not take my son back there," Abraham said. ⁷"The LORD, the God of heaven, who brought me out of my father's household and my native land and who spoke to me and promised me on oath, saying, 'To your offspring[a] I will give this land'—he will send his angel before you so that you can get a wife for my son from there. ⁸If the woman is unwilling to come back with you, then you will be released from this oath of mine. Only do not take my son back there." ⁹So the servant put his hand under the thigh of his master Abraham

and swore an oath to him concerning this matter.

¹⁰Then the servant took ten of his master's camels and left, taking with him all kinds of good things from his master. He set out for Aram Naharaim[b] and made his way to the town of Nahor. ¹¹He had the camels kneel down near the well outside the town; it was toward evening, the time the women go out to draw water.

¹²Then he prayed, "O LORD, God of my master Abraham, give me success today, and show kindness to my master Abraham. ¹³See, I am standing beside this spring, and the daughters of the towns-people are coming out to draw water.

---

a *7 Or seed*   b *10 That is, Northwest Mesopotamia*

[14]May it be that when I say to a girl, 'Please let down your jar that I may have a drink,' and she says, 'Drink, and I'll water your camels too'—let her be the one you have chosen for your servant Isaac. By this I will know that you have shown kindness to my master."

[15]Before he had finished praying, Rebekah came out with her jar on her shoulder. She was the daughter of Bethuel son of Milcah, who was the wife of Abraham's brother Nahor. [16]The girl was very beautiful, a virgin; no man had ever lain with her. She went down to the spring, filled her jar and came up again.

[17]The servant hurried to meet her and said, "Please give me a little water from your jar."

[18]"Drink, my lord," she said, and quickly lowered the jar to her hands and gave him a drink.

[19]After she had given him a drink, she said, "I'll draw water for your camels too, until they have finished drinking." [20]So she quickly emptied her jar into the trough, ran back to the well to draw more water, and drew enough for all his camels. [21]Without saying a word, the man watched her closely to learn whether or not the LORD had made his journey successful.

[22]When the camels had finished drinking, the man took out a gold nose ring weighing a beka[a] and two gold bracelets weighing ten shekels.[b] [23]Then he asked, "Whose daughter are you? Please tell me, is there room in your father's house for us to spend the night?"

[24]She answered him, "I am the daughter of Bethuel, the son that Milcah bore to Nahor." [25]And she added, "We have plenty of straw and fodder, as well as room for you to spend the night."

[26]Then the man bowed down and worshiped the LORD, [27]saying, "Praise be to the LORD, the God of my master Abraham, who has not abandoned his kindness and faithfulness to my master. As for me, the LORD has led me on the journey to the house of my master's relatives."

[28]The girl ran and told her mother's household about these things. [29]Now Rebekah had a brother named Laban, and he hurried out to the man at the spring. [30]As soon as he had seen the nose ring, and the bracelets on his sister's arms, and had heard Rebekah tell what the man said to her, he went out to the man and found him standing by the camels near the spring. [31]"Come, you who are blessed by the LORD," he said. "Why are you standing out here? I have prepared the house and a place for the camels."

[32]So the man went to the house, and the camels were unloaded. Straw and fodder were brought for the camels, and water for him and his men to wash their feet. [33]Then food was set before him, but he said, "I will not eat until I have told you what I have to say."

"Then tell us," ⌊Laban⌋ said.

[34]So he said, "I am Abraham's servant. [35]The LORD has blessed my master abundantly, and he has become wealthy. He has given him sheep and cattle, silver and gold, menservants and maidservants, and camels and donkeys. [36]My master's wife Sarah has borne him a son in her[c] old age, and he has given him everything he owns. [37]And my master made me swear an oath, and said, 'You must not get a wife for my son from the daughters of the Canaanites, in whose land I live, [38]but go to my father's family and to my own clan, and get a wife for my son.'

[39]"Then I asked my master, 'What if the woman will not come back with me?'

[40]"He replied, 'The LORD, before whom I have walked, will send his angel with you and make your journey a success, so that you can get a wife for my son from my own clan and from my father's family. [41]Then, when you go to my clan, you will be released from my oath even if they refuse to give her to you—you will be released from my oath.'

---

[a] *22* That is, about 1/5 ounce (about 5.5 grams)   [b] *22* That is, about 4 ounces (about 110 grams)   [c] *36* Or *his*

[42]"When I came to the spring today, I said, 'O LORD, God of my master Abraham, if you will, please grant success to the journey on which I have come. [43]See, I am standing beside this spring; if a maiden comes out to draw water and I say to her, "Please let me drink a little water from your jar," [44]and if she says to me, "Drink, and I'll draw water for your camels too," let her be the one the LORD has chosen for my master's son.'

[45]"Before I finished praying in my heart, Rebekah came out, with her jar on her shoulder. She went down to the spring and drew water, and I said to her, 'Please give me a drink.'

[46]"She quickly lowered her jar from her shoulder and said, 'Drink, and I'll water your camels too.' So I drank, and she watered the camels also.

[47]"I asked her, 'Whose daughter are you?'

"She said, 'The daughter of Bethuel son of Nahor, whom Milcah bore to him.'

"Then I put the ring in her nose and the bracelets on her arms, [48]and I bowed down and worshiped the LORD. I praised the LORD, the God of my master Abraham, who had led me on the right road to get the granddaughter of my master's brother for his son. [49]Now if you will show kindness and faithfulness to my master, tell me; and if not, tell me, so I may know which way to turn."

[50]Laban and Bethuel answered, "This is from the LORD; we can say nothing to you one way or the other. [51]Here is Rebekah; take her and go, and let her become the wife of your master's son, as the LORD has directed."

[52]When Abraham's servant heard what they said, he bowed down to the ground before the LORD. [53]Then the servant brought out gold and silver jewelry and articles of clothing and gave them to Rebekah; he also gave costly gifts to her brother and to her mother. [54]Then he and the men who were with him ate and drank and spent the night there.

When they got up the next morning, he said, "Send me on my way to my master."

[55]But her brother and her mother replied, "Let the girl remain with us ten days or so; then you[a] may go."

[56]But he said to them, "Do not detain me, now that the LORD has granted success to my journey. Send me on my way so I may go to my master."

[57]Then they said, "Let's call the girl and ask her about it." [58]So they called Rebekah and asked her, "Will you go with this man?"

"I will go," she said.

[59]So they sent their sister Rebekah on her way, along with her nurse and Abraham's servant and his men. [60]And they blessed Rebekah and said to her,

"Our sister, may you increase
  to thousands upon thousands;
may your offspring possess
  the gates of their enemies."

[61]Then Rebekah and her maids got ready and mounted their camels and went back with the man. So the servant took Rebekah and left.

[62]Now Isaac had come from Beer Lahai Roi, for he was living in the Negev. [63]He went out to the field one evening to meditate,[b] and as he looked up, he saw camels approaching. [64]Rebekah also looked up and saw Isaac. She got down from her camel [65]and asked the servant, "Who is that man in the field coming to meet us?"

"He is my master," the servant answered. So she took her veil and covered herself.

[66]Then the servant told Isaac all he had done. [67]Isaac brought her into the tent of his mother Sarah, and he married Rebekah. So she became his wife, and he loved her; and Isaac was comforted after his mother's death.

---

[a] 55 Or she   [b] 63 The meaning of the Hebrew for this word is uncertain.

The Death of Abraham

25 Abraham took[a] another wife, whose name was Keturah. ²She bore him Zimran, Jokshan, Medan, Midian, Ishbak and Shuah. ³Jokshan was the father of Sheba and Dedan; the descendants of Dedan were the Asshurites, the Letushites and the Leummites. ⁴The sons of Midian were Ephah, Epher, Hanoch, Abida and Eldaah. All these were descendants of Keturah.

⁵Abraham left everything he owned to Isaac. ⁶But while he was still living, he gave gifts to the sons of his concubines and sent them away from his son Isaac to the land of the east.

⁷Altogether, Abraham lived a hundred and seventy-five years. ⁸Then Abraham breathed his last and died at a good old age, an old man and full of years; and he was gathered to his people. ⁹His sons Isaac and Ishmael buried him in the cave of Machpelah near Mamre, in the field of Ephron son of Zohar the Hittite, ¹⁰the field Abraham had bought from the Hittites.[b] There Abraham was buried with his wife Sarah. ¹¹After Abraham's death, God blessed his son Isaac, who then lived near Beer Lahai Roi.

Ishmael's Sons

¹²This is the account of Abraham's son Ishmael, whom Sarah's maidservant, Hagar the Egyptian, bore to Abraham.

¹³These are the names of the sons of Ishmael, listed in the order of their birth: Nebaioth the firstborn of Ishmael, Kedar, Adbeel, Mibsam, ¹⁴Mishma, Dumah, Massa, ¹⁵Hadad, Tema, Jetur, Naphish and Kedemah. ¹⁶These were the sons of Ishmael, and these are the names of the twelve tribal rulers according to their settlements and camps. ¹⁷Altogether, Ishmael lived a hundred and thirty-seven years. He breathed his last and died, and he was gathered to his people. ¹⁸His descendants settled in the area from Havilah to Shur, near the border of Egypt, as you go toward Asshur. And they lived in hostility toward[c] all their brothers.

Jacob and Esau

¹⁹This is the account of Abraham's son Isaac.

Abraham became the father of Isaac, ²⁰and Isaac was forty years old when he married Rebekah daughter of Bethuel the Aramean from Paddan Aram[d] and sister of Laban the Aramean.

[a] 1 Or had taken [b] 10 Or the sons of Heth [c] 18 Or lived to the east of [d] 20 That is, Northwest Mesopotamia

God's people at prayer
ISAAC LONGED FOR A CHILD

GENESIS 25:19-26 Many people who know the pain of infertility today are deeply acquainted with Isaac and Rebekah's grief. Twenty years after getting married, Isaac and Rebekah were still childless. So Isaac talked to God about it. Surely Isaac knew the struggles his own parents, Abraham and Sarah, had endured for many years before his birth. The Bible says, "The LORD answered his prayer, and his wife Rebekah became pregnant." Many infertile couples long to see God answer their own prayers like that. But not all prayers will be answered in the exact way we pray them. That doesn't mean that God hasn't answered however.

His "no" in one direction may be a "yes" in another direction. He may be calling you to be a family to an adopted child. Or He may give you peace about not having a child because of other things He has called you to do. Whatever it is, keep praying and seeking God's will for you and your spouse. Then be willing to trust God's will, God's way, and God's time.

21Isaac prayed to the LORD on behalf of his wife, because she was barren. The LORD answered his prayer, and his wife Rebekah became pregnant. 22The babies jostled each other within her, and she said, "Why is this happening to me?" So she went to inquire of the LORD.

23The LORD said to her,

"Two nations are in your womb,
    and two peoples from within you
        will be separated;
one people will be stronger than the
        other,
    and the older will serve the
        younger."

24When the time came for her to give birth, there were twin boys in her womb. 25The first to come out was red, and his whole body was like a hairy garment; so they named him Esau.ᵃ 26After this, his brother came out, with his hand grasping Esau's heel; so he was named Jacob.ᵇ Isaac was sixty years old when Rebekah gave birth to them.

27The boys grew up, and Esau became a skillful hunter, a man of the open country, while Jacob was a quiet man, staying among the tents. 28Isaac, who had a taste for wild game, loved Esau, but Rebekah loved Jacob.

Praying Genesis 25:29-34

Lord, give me self-control so that I never succumb to the lust of the flesh and end up losing the great spiritual inheritance you have for me.

29Once when Jacob was cooking some stew, Esau came in from the open country, famished. 30He said to Jacob, "Quick, let me have some of that red stew! I'm famished!" (That is why he was also called Edom.ᶜ)

31Jacob replied, "First sell me your birthright."

32"Look, I am about to die," Esau said.

"What good is the birthright to me?"

33But Jacob said, "Swear to me first." So he swore an oath to him, selling his birthright to Jacob.

34Then Jacob gave Esau some bread and some lentil stew. He ate and drank, and then got up and left.

So Esau despised his birthright.

Isaac and Abimelech

26 Now there was a famine in the land—besides the earlier famine of Abraham's time—and Isaac went to Abimelech king of the Philistines in Gerar. 2The LORD appeared to Isaac and said, "Do not go down to Egypt; live in the land where I tell you to live. 3Stay in this land for a while, and I will be with you and will bless you. For to you and your descendants I will give all these lands and will confirm the oath I swore to your father Abraham. 4I will make your descendants as numerous as the stars in the sky and will give them all these lands, and through your offspringᵈ all nations on earth will be blessed, 5because Abraham obeyed me and kept my requirements, my commands, my decrees and my laws." 6So Isaac stayed in Gerar.

7When the men of that place asked him about his wife, he said, "She is my sister," because he was afraid to say, "She is my wife." He thought, "The men of this place might kill me on account of Rebekah, because she is beautiful."

8When Isaac had been there a long time, Abimelech king of the Philistines looked down from a window and saw Isaac caressing his wife Rebekah. 9So Abimelech summoned Isaac and said, "She is really your wife! Why did you say, 'She is my sister'?"

Isaac answered him, "Because I thought I might lose my life on account of her."

10Then Abimelech said, "What is this you have done to us? One of the men might well have slept with your wife, and you would have brought guilt upon us."

ᵃ 25 Esau may mean *hairy*; he was also called Edom, which means *red*. ᵇ 26 Jacob means *he grasps the heel* (figuratively, *he deceives*). ᶜ 30 Edom means *red*. ᵈ 4 Or *seed*

GOING
deeper
Call on the Name of the Lord

READ AND CONSIDER: GENESIS 26:17-25

"Isaac built an altar there and called on the name of the LORD. There he pitched his tent, and there his servants dug a well" (Genesis 26:25).

Isaac was having a difficult time. It seems that everywhere he turned he got into trouble. Abimelech got after him for lying; the Philistines stopped up his wells in order to force him to move away; and even after he moved and dug a new well, someone argued with him about *that* one. He couldn't win.

With each situation, however, he avoided conflict and worked for peace for everyone involved. Finally, when it seemed that everything was peaceful, the Lord appeared, describing Himself as the God of Isaac's father, Abraham. "Do not be afraid, for I am with you; I will bless you and will increase the number of your descendants for the sake of my servant Abraham" (26:24).

This surely must have caused Isaac to flash back to the many times when his dear father had talked about the Lord. What had Abraham taught him? What did Isaac feel about this God who had stopped his father's knife and sent a ram instead as a sacrifice? Did he have memories of being untied and taken back home—and how joyful his dad had looked on that return trip? This God was not to be taken lightly. This God introduced Himself to Isaac, giving him a wonderful promise of future blessing. Isaac acknowledged that promise and "called on the name of the LORD."

What does it mean to call on the name of the Lord? It means to acknowledge who He is and the power of His very existence to do more than we can ask or think. It means to place our trust in Him and praise Him for all He does. When you call on the Lord's name, you give Him the praise that He deserves by recognizing Him in all of His holiness, authority, and glory. In doing so, you open yourself to the power and blessing He wants to bring into your life.

Praise God every day for all the ways that He is sufficient for every need you have, and, like Isaac, declare your faithfulness to Him by calling on His name in prayer.

---

[11]So Abimelech gave orders to all the people: "Anyone who molests this man or his wife shall surely be put to death."

[12]Isaac planted crops in that land and the same year reaped a hundredfold, because the LORD blessed him. [13]The man became rich, and his wealth continued to grow until he became very wealthy. [14]He had so many flocks and herds and servants that the Philistines envied him. [15]So all the wells that his father's servants had dug in the time of his father Abraham, the Philistines stopped up, filling them with earth.

[16]Then Abimelech said to Isaac, "Move away from us; you have become too powerful for us."

[17]So Isaac moved away from there and encamped in the Valley of Gerar and settled there. [18]Isaac reopened the wells that had been dug in the time of his father Abraham, which the Philistines had stopped up after Abraham died, and he gave them the same names his father had given them.

[19]Isaac's servants dug in the valley and discovered a well of fresh water there. [20]But the herdsmen of Gerar quarreled with Isaac's herdsmen and said, "The water is ours!" So he named the well Esek,[a]

---

[a] *20 Esek means dispute.*

because they disputed with him. 21Then they dug another well, but they quarreled over that one also; so he named it Sitnah.ª 22He moved on from there and dug another well, and no one quarreled over it. He named it Rehoboth,ᵇ saying, "Now the LORD has given us room and we will flourish in the land."

23From there he went up to Beersheba. 24That night the LORD appeared to him and said, "I am the God of your father Abraham. Do not be afraid, for I am with you; I will bless you and will increase the number of your descendants for the sake of my servant Abraham."

25Isaac built an altar there and called on the name of the LORD. There he pitched his tent, and there his servants dug a well.

26Meanwhile, Abimelech had come to him from Gerar, with Ahuzzath his personal adviser and Phicol the commander of his forces. 27Isaac asked them, "Why have you come to me, since you were hostile to me and sent me away?"

28They answered, "We saw clearly that the LORD was with you; so we said, 'There ought to be a sworn agreement between us'—between us and you. Let us make a treaty with you 29that you will do us no harm, just as we did not molest you but always treated you well and sent you away in peace. And now you are blessed by the LORD."

30Isaac then made a feast for them, and they ate and drank. 31Early the next morning the men swore an oath to each other. Then Isaac sent them on their way, and they left him in peace.

32That day Isaac's servants came and told him about the well they had dug. They said, "We've found water!" 33He called it Shibah,ᶜ and to this day the name of the town has been Beersheba.ᵈ

34When Esau was forty years old, he married Judith daughter of Beeri the Hittite, and also Basemath daughter of Elon the Hittite. 35They were a source of grief to Isaac and Rebekah.

Jacob Gets Isaac's Blessing

27 When Isaac was old and his eyes were so weak that he could no longer see, he called for Esau his older son and said to him, "My son."

"Here I am," he answered.

2Isaac said, "I am now an old man and don't know the day of my death. 3Now then, get your weapons—your quiver and bow—and go out to the open country to hunt some wild game for me. 4Prepare me the kind of tasty food I like and bring it to me to eat, so that I may give you my blessing before I die."

5Now Rebekah was listening as Isaac spoke to his son Esau. When Esau left for the open country to hunt game and bring it back, 6Rebekah said to her son Jacob, "Look, I overheard your father say to your brother Esau, 7'Bring me some game and prepare me some tasty food to eat, so that I may give you my blessing in the presence of the LORD before I die.' 8Now, my son, listen carefully and do what I tell you: 9Go out to the flock and bring me two choice young goats, so I can prepare some tasty food for your father, just the way he likes it. 10Then take it to your father to eat, so that he may give you his blessing before he dies."

11Jacob said to Rebekah his mother, "But my brother Esau is a hairy man, and I'm a man with smooth skin. 12What if my father touches me? I would appear to be tricking him and would bring down a curse on myself rather than a blessing."

13His mother said to him, "My son, let the curse fall on me. Just do what I say; go and get them for me."

14So he went and got them and brought them to his mother, and she prepared some tasty food, just the way his father liked it. 15Then Rebekah took the best clothes of Esau her older son, which she

---

ª 21 Sitnah means opposition.   ᵇ 22 Rehoboth means room.   ᶜ 33 Shibah can mean oath or seven.   ᵈ 33 Beersheba can mean well of the oath or well of seven.

had in the house, and put them on her younger son Jacob. ¹⁶She also covered his hands and the smooth part of his neck with the goatskins. ¹⁷Then she handed to her son Jacob the tasty food and the bread she had made.

¹⁸He went to his father and said, "My father."

"Yes, my son," he answered. "Who is it?"

¹⁹Jacob said to his father, "I am Esau your firstborn. I have done as you told me. Please sit up and eat some of my game so that you may give me your blessing."

²⁰Isaac asked his son, "How did you find it so quickly, my son?"

"The LORD your God gave me success," he replied.

²¹Then Isaac said to Jacob, "Come near so I can touch you, my son, to know whether you really are my son Esau or not."

²²Jacob went close to his father Isaac, who touched him and said, "The voice is the voice of Jacob, but the hands are the hands of Esau." ²³He did not recognize him, for his hands were hairy like those of his brother Esau; so he blessed him. ²⁴"Are you really my son Esau?" he asked.

"I am," he replied.

²⁵Then he said, "My son, bring me some of your game to eat, so that I may give you my blessing."

Jacob brought it to him and he ate; and he brought some wine and he drank. ²⁶Then his father Isaac said to him, "Come here, my son, and kiss me."

²⁷So he went to him and kissed him. When Isaac caught the smell of his clothes, he blessed him and said,

"Ah, the smell of my son
    is like the smell of a field
    that the LORD has blessed.
²⁸May God give you of heaven's dew
    and of earth's richness—
    an abundance of grain and new
        wine.

²⁹May nations serve you
    and peoples bow down to you.
Be lord over your brothers,
    and may the sons of your mother
        bow down to you.
May those who curse you be cursed
    and those who bless you be blessed."

³⁰After Isaac finished blessing him and Jacob had scarcely left his father's presence, his brother Esau came in from hunting. ³¹He too prepared some tasty food and brought it to his father. Then he said to him, "My father, sit up and eat some of my game, so that you may give me your blessing."

³²His father Isaac asked him, "Who are you?"

"I am your son," he answered, "your firstborn, Esau."

³³Isaac trembled violently and said, "Who was it, then, that hunted game and brought it to me? I ate it just before you came and I blessed him—and indeed he will be blessed!"

³⁴When Esau heard his father's words, he burst out with a loud and bitter cry and said to his father, "Bless me—me too, my father!"

³⁵But he said, "Your brother came deceitfully and took your blessing."

³⁶Esau said, "Isn't he rightly named Jacob[a]? He has deceived me these two times: He took my birthright, and now he's taken my blessing!" Then he asked, "Haven't you reserved any blessing for me?"

³⁷Isaac answered Esau, "I have made him lord over you and have made all his relatives his servants, and I have sustained him with grain and new wine. So what can I possibly do for you, my son?"

³⁸Esau said to his father, "Do you have only one blessing, my father? Bless me too, my father!" Then Esau wept aloud.

³⁹His father Isaac answered him,

"Your dwelling will be
    away from the earth's richness,

---

a 36 *Jacob* means *he grasps the heel* (figuratively, *he deceives*).

away from the dew of heaven
above.
40 You will live by the sword
and you will serve your brother.
But when you grow restless,
you will throw his yoke
from off your neck."

Jacob Flees to Laban

41 Esau held a grudge against Jacob because of the blessing his father had given him. He said to himself, "The days of mourning for my father are near; then I will kill my brother Jacob."

42 When Rebekah was told what her older son Esau had said, she sent for her younger son Jacob and said to him, "Your brother Esau is consoling himself with the thought of killing you. 43 Now then, my son, do what I say: Flee at once to my brother Laban in Haran. 44 Stay with him for a while until your brother's fury subsides. 45 When your brother is no longer angry with you and forgets what you did to him, I'll send word for you to come back from there. Why should I lose both of you in one day?"

46 Then Rebekah said to Isaac, "I'm disgusted with living because of these Hittite women. If Jacob takes a wife from among the women of this land, from Hittite women like these, my life will not be worth living."

28 So Isaac called for Jacob and blessed[a] him and commanded him: "Do not marry a Canaanite woman. 2 Go at once to Paddan Aram,[b] to the house of your mother's father Bethuel. Take a wife for yourself there, from among the daughters of Laban, your mother's brother. 3 May God Almighty[c] bless you and make you fruitful and increase your numbers until you become a community of peoples. 4 May he give you and your descendants the blessing given to Abraham, so that you may take possession of the land where you now live as an alien, the land God gave to Abraham." 5 Then Isaac

sent Jacob on his way, and he went to Paddan Aram, to Laban son of Bethuel the Aramean, the brother of Rebekah, who was the mother of Jacob and Esau.

6 Now Esau learned that Isaac had blessed Jacob and had sent him to Paddan Aram to take a wife from there, and that when he blessed him he commanded him, "Do not marry a Canaanite woman," 7 and that Jacob had obeyed his father and mother and had gone to Paddan Aram. 8 Esau then realized how displeasing the Canaanite women were to his father Isaac; 9 so he went to Ishmael and married Mahalath, the sister of Nebaioth and daughter of Ishmael son of Abraham, in addition to the wives he already had.

Jacob's Dream at Bethel

10 Jacob left Beersheba and set out for Haran. 11 When he reached a certain place, he stopped for the night because the sun had set. Taking one of the stones there, he put it under his head and lay down to sleep. 12 He had a dream in which he saw a stairway[d] resting on the earth, with its top reaching to heaven, and the angels of God were ascending and descending on it. 13 There above it[e] stood the LORD, and he said: "I am the LORD, the God of your father Abraham and the God of Isaac. I will give you and your descendants the land on which you are lying. 14 Your descendants will be like the dust of the earth, and you will spread out to the west and to the east, to the north and to the south. All peoples on earth will be blessed through you and your offspring. 15 I am with you and will watch over you wherever you go, and I

Praying Genesis 28:10-15

Just as Jacob heard Your voice when he was in the middle of obeying You, Father, I pray that I too will always obey You and hear Your voice speaking to my heart.

---

[a] *1* Or *greeted*   [b] *2* That is, Northwest Mesopotamia; also in verses 5, 6 and 7   [c] *3* Hebrew *El-Shaddai*   [d] *12* Or *ladder*
[e] *13* Or *There beside him*

will bring you back to this land. I will not leave you until I have done what I have promised you."

16When Jacob awoke from his sleep, he thought, "Surely the LORD is in this place, and I was not aware of it." 17He was afraid and said, "How awesome is this place! This is none other than the house of God; this is the gate of heaven."

18Early the next morning Jacob took the stone he had placed under his head and set it up as a pillar and poured oil on top of it. 19He called that place Bethel,a though the city used to be called Luz.

20Then Jacob made a vow, saying, "If God will be with me and will watch over me on this journey I am taking and will give me food to eat and clothes to wear 21so that I return safely to my father's house, then the LORDb will be my God 22andc this stone that I have set up as a pillar will be God's house, and of all that you give me I will give you a tenth."

Jacob Arrives in Paddan Aram

29 Then Jacob continued on his journey and came to the land of the eastern peoples. 2There he saw a well in the field, with three flocks of sheep lying near it because the flocks were watered from that well. The stone over the mouth of the well was large. 3When all the flocks were gathered there, the shepherds would roll the stone away from the well's mouth and water the sheep. Then they would return the stone to its place over the mouth of the well.

4Jacob asked the shepherds, "My brothers, where are you from?"

"We're from Haran," they replied.

5He said to them, "Do you know Laban, Nahor's grandson?"

"Yes, we know him," they answered.

6Then Jacob asked them, "Is he well?"

"Yes, he is," they said, "and here comes his daughter Rachel with the sheep."

7"Look," he said, "the sun is still high; it is not time for the flocks to be gath-

ered. Water the sheep and take them back to pasture."

8"We can't," they replied, "until all the flocks are gathered and the stone has been rolled away from the mouth of the well. Then we will water the sheep."

9While he was still talking with them, Rachel came with her father's sheep, for she was a shepherdess. 10When Jacob saw Rachel daughter of Laban, his mother's brother, and Laban's sheep, he went over and rolled the stone away from the mouth of the well and watered his uncle's sheep. 11Then Jacob kissed Rachel and began to weep aloud. 12He had told Rachel that he was a relative of her father and a son of Rebekah. So she ran and told her father.

13As soon as Laban heard the news about Jacob, his sister's son, he hurried to meet him. He embraced him and kissed him and brought him to his home, and there Jacob told him all these things. 14Then Laban said to him, "You are my own flesh and blood."

Jacob Marries Leah and Rachel

After Jacob had stayed with him for a whole month, 15Laban said to him, "Just because you are a relative of mine, should you work for me for nothing? Tell me what your wages should be."

16Now Laban had two daughters; the name of the older was Leah, and the name of the younger was Rachel. 17Leah had weakd eyes, but Rachel was lovely in form, and beautiful. 18Jacob was in love with Rachel and said, "I'll work for you seven years in return for your younger daughter Rachel."

19Laban said, "It's better that I give her to you than to some other man. Stay here with me." 20So Jacob served seven years to get Rachel, but they seemed like only a few days to him because of his love for her.

21Then Jacob said to Laban, "Give me my wife. My time is completed, and I want to lie with her."

---

a 19 Bethel means house of God.   b 20,21 Or Since God ... father's house, the LORD   c 21,22 Or house, and the LORD will be my God, 22then   d 17 Or delicate

²²So Laban brought together all the people of the place and gave a feast. ²³But when evening came, he took his daughter Leah and gave her to Jacob, and Jacob lay with her. ²⁴And Laban gave his servant girl Zilpah to his daughter as her maidservant.

²⁵When morning came, there was Leah! So Jacob said to Laban, "What is this you have done to me? I served you for Rachel, didn't I? Why have you deceived me?"

²⁶Laban replied, "It is not our custom here to give the younger daughter in marriage before the older one. ²⁷Finish this daughter's bridal week; then we will give you the younger one also, in return for another seven years of work."

²⁸And Jacob did so. He finished the week with Leah, and then Laban gave him his daughter Rachel to be his wife. ²⁹Laban gave his servant girl Bilhah to his daughter Rachel as her maidservant. ³⁰Jacob lay with Rachel also, and he loved Rachel more than Leah. And he worked for Laban another seven years.

Jacob's Children

³¹When the LORD saw that Leah was not loved, he opened her womb, but Rachel was barren. ³²Leah became pregnant and gave birth to a son. She named him Reuben,ᵃ for she said, "It is because the LORD has seen my misery. Surely my husband will love me now."

³³She conceived again, and when she gave birth to a son she said, "Because the LORD heard that I am not loved, he gave me this one too." So she named him Simeon.ᵇ

³⁴Again she conceived, and when she gave birth to a son she said, "Now at last my husband will become attached to me, because I have borne him three sons." So he was named Levi.ᶜ

³⁵She conceived again, and when she gave birth to a son she said, "This time I will praise the LORD." So she named him Judah.ᵈ Then she stopped having children.

30 When Rachel saw that she was not bearing Jacob any children, she became jealous of her sister. So she said to Jacob, "Give me children, or I'll die!"

²Jacob became angry with her and said, "Am I in the place of God, who has kept you from having children?"

³Then she said, "Here is Bilhah, my maidservant. Sleep with her so that she can bear children for me and that through her I too can build a family."

⁴So she gave him her servant Bilhah as a wife. Jacob slept with her, ⁵and she became pregnant and bore him a son. ⁶Then Rachel said, "God has vindicated me; he has listened to my plea and given me a son." Because of this she named him Dan.ᵉ

⁷Rachel's servant Bilhah conceived again and bore Jacob a second son. ⁸Then Rachel said, "I have had a great struggle with my sister, and I have won." So she named him Naphtali.ᶠ

⁹When Leah saw that she had stopped having children, she took her maidservant Zilpah and gave her to Jacob as a wife. ¹⁰Leah's servant Zilpah bore Jacob a son. ¹¹Then Leah said, "What good fortune!"ᵍ So she named him Gad.ʰ

¹²Leah's servant Zilpah bore Jacob a second son. ¹³Then Leah said, "How happy I am! The women will call me happy." So she named him Asher.ⁱ

¹⁴During wheat harvest, Reuben went out into the fields and found some mandrake plants, which he brought to his mother Leah. Rachel said to Leah, "Please give me some of your son's mandrakes."

¹⁵But she said to her, "Wasn't it enough that you took away my husband? Will you take my son's mandrakes too?"

"Very well," Rachel said, "he can

ᵃ *32 Reuben sounds like the Hebrew for he has seen my misery; the name means see, a son.*   ᵇ *33 Simeon probably means one who hears.*   ᶜ *34 Levi sounds like and may be derived from the Hebrew for attached.*   ᵈ *35 Judah sounds like and may be derived from the Hebrew for praise.*   ᵉ *6 Dan here means he has vindicated.*   ᶠ *8 Naphtali means my struggle.*   ᵍ *11 Or "A troop is coming!"*   ʰ *11 Gad can mean good fortune or a troop.*   ⁱ *13 Asher means happy.*

sleep with you tonight in return for your son's mandrakes."

¹⁶So when Jacob came in from the fields that evening, Leah went out to meet him. "You must sleep with me," she said. "I have hired you with my son's mandrakes." So he slept with her that night.

¹⁷God listened to Leah, and she became pregnant and bore Jacob a fifth son. ¹⁸Then Leah said, "God has rewarded me for giving my maidservant to my husband." So she named him Issachar.ᵃ

¹⁹Leah conceived again and bore Jacob a sixth son. ²⁰Then Leah said, "God has presented me with a precious gift. This time my husband will treat me with honor, because I have borne him six sons." So she named him Zebulun.ᵇ

²¹Some time later she gave birth to a daughter and named her Dinah.

²²Then God remembered Rachel; he listened to her and opened her womb. ²³She became pregnant and gave birth to a son and said, "God has taken away my disgrace." ²⁴She named him Joseph,ᶜ and said, "May the LORD add to me another son."

Jacob's Flocks Increase

²⁵After Rachel gave birth to Joseph, Jacob said to Laban, "Send me on my way so I can go back to my own homeland. ²⁶Give me my wives and children, for whom I have served you, and I will be on my way. You know how much work I've done for you."

²⁷But Laban said to him, "If I have found favor in your eyes, please stay. I have learned by divination thatᵈ the LORD has blessed me because of you." ²⁸He added, "Name your wages, and I will pay them."

²⁹Jacob said to him, "You know how I have worked for you and how your livestock has fared under my care. ³⁰The little you had before I came has increased greatly, and the LORD has blessed you

wherever I have been. But now, when may I do something for my own household?"

³¹"What shall I give you?" he asked.

"Don't give me anything," Jacob replied. "But if you will do this one thing for me, I will go on tending your flocks and watching over them: ³²Let me go through all your flocks today and remove from them every speckled or spotted sheep, every dark-colored lamb and every spotted or speckled goat. They will be my wages. ³³And my honesty will testify for me in the future, whenever you check on the wages you have paid me. Any goat in my possession that is not speckled or spotted, or any lamb that is not dark-colored, will be considered stolen."

³⁴"Agreed," said Laban. "Let it be as you have said." ³⁵That same day he removed all the male goats that were streaked or spotted, and all the speckled or spotted female goats (all that had white on them) and all the dark-colored lambs, and he placed them in the care of his sons. ³⁶Then he put a three-day journey between himself and Jacob, while Jacob continued to tend the rest of Laban's flocks.

³⁷Jacob, however, took fresh-cut branches from poplar, almond and plane trees and made white stripes on them by peeling the bark and exposing the white inner wood of the branches. ³⁸Then he placed the peeled branches in all the watering troughs, so that they would be directly in front of the flocks when they came to drink. When the flocks were in heat and came to drink, ³⁹they mated in front of the branches. And they bore young that were streaked or speckled or spotted. ⁴⁰Jacob set apart the young of the flock by themselves, but made the rest face the streaked and dark-colored animals that belonged to Laban. Thus he made separate flocks for himself and did not put them with Laban's animals.

ᵃ 18 Issachar sounds like the Hebrew for reward.   ᵇ 20 Zebulun probably means honor.   ᶜ 24 Joseph means may he add.
ᵈ 27 Or possibly have become rich and

41Whenever the stronger females were in heat, Jacob would place the branches in the troughs in front of the animals so they would mate near the branches, 42but if the animals were weak, he would not place them there. So the weak animals went to Laban and the strong ones to Jacob. 43In this way the man grew exceedingly prosperous and came to own large flocks, and maidservants and menservants, and camels and donkeys.

Jacob Flees From Laban

31 Jacob heard that Laban's sons were saying, "Jacob has taken everything our father owned and has gained all this wealth from what belonged to our father." 2And Jacob noticed that Laban's attitude toward him was not what it had been.

3Then the LORD said to Jacob, "Go back to the land of your fathers and to your relatives, and I will be with you."

4So Jacob sent word to Rachel and Leah to come out to the fields where his flocks were. 5He said to them, "I see that your father's attitude toward me is not what it was before, but the God of my father has been with me. 6You know that I've worked for your father with all my strength, 7yet your father has cheated me by changing my wages ten times. However, God has not allowed him to harm me. 8If he said, 'The speckled ones will be your wages,' then all the flocks gave birth to speckled young; and if he said, 'The streaked ones will be your wages,' then all the flocks bore streaked young. 9So God has taken away your father's livestock and has given them to me.

10"In breeding season I once had a dream in which I looked up and saw that the male goats mating with the flock were streaked, speckled or spotted. 11The angel of God said to me in the dream, 'Jacob.' I answered, 'Here I am.' 12And he said, 'Look up and see that all the male goats mating with the flock are streaked, speckled or spotted, for I have seen all that Laban has been doing to you. 13I am the God of Bethel, where you anointed a pillar and where you made a vow to me. Now leave this land at once and go back to your native land.'"

14Then Rachel and Leah replied, "Do we still have any share in the inheritance of our father's estate? 15Does he not regard us as foreigners? Not only has he sold us, but he has used up what was paid for us. 16Surely all the wealth that God took away from our father belongs to us and our children. So do whatever God has told you."

17Then Jacob put his children and his wives on camels, 18and he drove all his livestock ahead of him, along with all the goods he had accumulated in Paddan Aram,ᵃ to go to his father Isaac in the land of Canaan.

19When Laban had gone to shear his sheep, Rachel stole her father's household gods. 20Moreover, Jacob deceived Laban the Aramean by not telling him he was running away. 21So he fled with all he had, and crossing the River,ᵇ he headed for the hill country of Gilead.

Laban Pursues Jacob

22On the third day Laban was told that Jacob had fled. 23Taking his relatives with him, he pursued Jacob for seven days and caught up with him in the hill country of Gilead. 24Then God came to Laban the Aramean in a dream at night and said to him, "Be careful not to say anything to Jacob, either good or bad."

25Jacob had pitched his tent in the hill country of Gilead when Laban overtook him, and Laban and his relatives camped there too. 26Then Laban said to Jacob, "What have you done? You've deceived me, and you've carried off my daughters like captives in war. 27Why did you run off secretly and deceive me? Why didn't you tell me, so I could send you away with joy and singing to the music of tambourines and harps? 28You didn't

---

ᵃ 18 That is, Northwest Mesopotamia   ᵇ 21 That is, the Euphrates even let me kiss my grandchildren and my daughters good-by. You have done a foolish thing. ²⁹I have the power to harm you; but last night the God of your father said to me, 'Be careful not to say anything to Jacob, either good or bad.' ³⁰Now you have gone off because you longed to return to your father's house. But why did you steal my gods?"

³¹Jacob answered Laban, "I was afraid, because I thought you would take your daughters away from me by force. ³²But if you find anyone who has your gods, he shall not live. In the presence of our relatives, see for yourself whether there is anything of yours here with me; and if so, take it." Now Jacob did not know that Rachel had stolen the gods.

³³So Laban went into Jacob's tent and into Leah's tent and into the tent of the two maidservants, but he found nothing. After he came out of Leah's tent, he entered Rachel's tent. ³⁴Now Rachel had taken the household gods and put them inside her camel's saddle and was sitting on them. Laban searched through everything in the tent but found nothing.

³⁵Rachel said to her father, "Don't be angry, my lord, that I cannot stand up in your presence; I'm having my period." So he searched but could not find the household gods.

³⁶Jacob was angry and took Laban to task. "What is my crime?" he asked Laban. "What sin have I committed that you hunt me down? ³⁷Now that you have searched through all my goods, what have you found that belongs to your household? Put it here in front of your relatives and mine, and let them judge between the two of us.

³⁸"I have been with you for twenty years now. Your sheep and goats have not miscarried, nor have I eaten rams from your flocks. ³⁹I did not bring you animals torn by wild beasts; I bore the loss myself. And you demanded payment from me for whatever was stolen by day or night. ⁴⁰This was my situation: The heat consumed me in the daytime and the cold at night, and sleep fled from my eyes. ⁴¹It was like this for the twenty years I was in your household. I worked for you fourteen years for your two daughters and six years for your flocks, and you changed my wages ten times. ⁴²If the God of my father, the God of Abraham and the Fear of Isaac, had not been with me, you would surely have sent me away empty-handed. But God has seen my hardship and the toil of my hands, and last night he rebuked you."

⁴³Laban answered Jacob, "The women are my daughters, the children are my children, and the flocks are my flocks. All you see is mine. Yet what can I do today about these daughters of mine, or about the children they have borne? ⁴⁴Come now, let's make a covenant, you and I, and let it serve as a witness between us."

⁴⁵So Jacob took a stone and set it up as a pillar. ⁴⁶He said to his relatives, "Gather some stones." So they took stones and piled them in a heap, and they ate there by the heap. ⁴⁷Laban called it Jegar Sahadutha,ᵃ and Jacob called it Galeed.ᵇ

⁴⁸Laban said, "This heap is a witness between you and me today." That is why it was called Galeed. ⁴⁹It was also called Mizpah,ᶜ because he said, "May the LORD keep watch between you and me when we are away from each other. ⁵⁰If you mistreat my daughters or if you take any wives besides my daughters, even though no one is with us, remember that God is a witness between you and me."

⁵¹Laban also said to Jacob, "Here is this heap, and here is this pillar I have set up between you and me. ⁵²This heap is a witness, and this pillar is a witness, that I will not go past this heap to your side to harm you and that you will not go past this heap and pillar to my side to harm me. ⁵³May the God of Abraham and the God

---

ᵃ 47 The Aramaic *Jegar Sahadutha* means *witness heap.*   ᵇ 47 The Hebrew *Galeed* means *witness heap.*   ᶜ 49 *Mizpah* means *watchtower.*

of Nahor, the God of their father, judge between us."

So Jacob took an oath in the name of the Fear of his father Isaac. [54]He offered a sacrifice there in the hill country and invited his relatives to a meal. After they had eaten, they spent the night there.

[55]Early the next morning Laban kissed his grandchildren and his daughters and blessed them. Then he left and returned home.

Jacob Prepares to Meet Esau

32 Jacob also went on his way, and the angels of God met him. [2]When Jacob saw them, he said, "This is the camp of God!" So he named that place Mahanaim.[a]

[3]Jacob sent messengers ahead of him to his brother Esau in the land of Seir, the country of Edom. [4]He instructed them: "This is what you are to say to my master Esau: 'Your servant Jacob says, I have been staying with Laban and have remained there till now. [5]I have cattle and donkeys, sheep and goats, menservants and maidservants. Now I am sending this message to my lord, that I may find favor in your eyes.'"

[6]When the messengers returned to Jacob, they said, "We went to your brother Esau, and now he is coming to meet you, and four hundred men are with him."

[7]In great fear and distress Jacob divided the people who were with him into two groups,[b] and the flocks and herds and camels as well. [8]He thought, "If Esau comes and attacks one group,[c] the group[c] that is left may escape."

Praying Genesis 32:9-12

Almighty God, I pray for deliverance from the people and situations I fear might overtake and harm me.

[9]Then Jacob prayed, "O God of my father Abraham, God of my father Isaac, O LORD, who said to me, 'Go back to your country and your relatives, and I will make you prosper,' [10]I am unworthy of all the kindness and faithfulness you have shown your servant. I had only my staff when I crossed this Jordan, but now I have become two groups. [11]Save me, I pray, from the hand of my brother Esau, for I am afraid he will come and attack me, and also the mothers with their chil-

---

[a] 2 Mahanaim means two camps. [b] 7 Or camps; also in verse 10 [c] 8 Or camp

God's people at prayer
JACOB PRAYED THE PROMISES

GENESIS 32:1-12 Jacob was afraid as he approached his homeland, because he got word his brother, Esau, was coming to meet him with a large force. But it wasn't simply Esau's approach that frightened Jacob, it was fear from his past. His last encounter with his older brother involved his own cruel deception that ended up giving him his father Isaac's dying blessing, which rightfully belonged to Esau. And Esau had been filled with anger and resentment. Jacob wrestled between God's promise of protection and his own concerns about Esau's possible desire for revenge.

The old Jacob might have run. On this night, however, he recited God's promises. He held God to His word in prayer, telling God, "Remember what You told me!"

Do you have a good collection of God's promises memorized that you can use in prayer when you wonder about the direction your life is taking? If not, start doing that today. You will find that prayer based on God's promises has an amazing power to energize, comfort, and settle the issue of the next step you are to take.

Struggling in Prayer

READ AND CONSIDER: GENESIS 32:1-32

"Jacob was left alone, and a man wrestled with him till daybreak. When the man saw that he could not overpower him, he touched the socket of Jacob's hip so that his hip was wrenched as he wrestled with the man. Then the man said, 'Let me go, for it is daybreak.' But Jacob replied, 'I will not let you go unless you bless me'" (Genesis 32:24-26).

Does prayer ever seem like a struggle to you? Often our prayer times may seem more like wrestling matches than conversations, but this passage lets us know that amazing transformations can come out of the struggles we experience in prayer.

Up until this particular encounter with God, Jacob's life had been characterized by his attempts to get ahead on his own, his deceitful plots to obtain blessings, and his manipulations to make his life work out the way he wanted it to. He had not given God control and had not trusted the Lord to carry out His plans.

However, when the stranger came along and wrestled with him, Jacob was at a point in his life when he was alone and genuinely fearful about what was going to happen to him and to his family. He was about to meet his brother again, who had every right to hate him. Jacob had no idea what his brother's plans might be. During the struggle with the stranger (who turned out to be God, 32:30), Jacob told the stranger his name—the equivalent of a confession, because his name literally meant "supplanter" or "usurper." This confession led to transformation. Jacob received the blessing from his opponent—a new name and a new future. He had been changed by the confrontation. He also received an injury that resulted in a lifetime limp—an ever-present reminder of what had happened.

If you want to experience life-changing prayer, be honest with God about who you are and confess it. For example, say, "Lord, I have been fearful," or "Lord, I have been a doubter." Then say, "Lord, help me to rise above who I am now to who You have called me to be." Despite Jacob's past, God's plans prevailed in his life, but not without a struggle. Don't be afraid to struggle in prayer, knowing that God will use any measures necessary in order to carry out His plans for your life. Like Jacob, hang on and don't give up until you get the blessing that will change you forever.

dren. ¹²But you have said, 'I will surely make you prosper and will make your descendants like the sand of the sea, which cannot be counted.'"

¹³He spent the night there, and from what he had with him he selected a gift for his brother Esau: ¹⁴two hundred female goats and twenty male goats, two hundred ewes and twenty rams, ¹⁵thirty female camels with their young, forty cows and ten bulls, and twenty female donkeys and ten male donkeys. ¹⁶He put them in the care of his servants, each herd by itself, and said to his servants,

"Go ahead of me, and keep some space between the herds."

¹⁷He instructed the one in the lead: "When my brother Esau meets you and asks, 'To whom do you belong, and where are you going, and who owns all these animals in front of you?' ¹⁸then you are to say, 'They belong to your servant Jacob. They are a gift sent to my lord Esau, and he is coming behind us.'"

¹⁹He also instructed the second, the third and all the others who followed the herds: "You are to say the same thing to Esau when you meet him. ²⁰And be sure

to say, 'Your servant Jacob is coming behind us.'" For he thought, "I will pacify him with these gifts I am sending on ahead; later, when I see him, perhaps he will receive me." ²¹So Jacob's gifts went on ahead of him, but he himself spent the night in the camp.

Jacob Wrestles With God

²²That night Jacob got up and took his two wives, his two maidservants and his eleven sons and crossed the ford of the Jabbok. ²³After he had sent them across the stream, he sent over all his possessions. ²⁴So Jacob was left alone, and a man wrestled with him till daybreak. ²⁵When the man saw that he could not overpower him, he touched the socket of Jacob's hip so that his hip was wrenched as he wrestled with the man. ²⁶Then the man said, "Let me go, for it is daybreak."

But Jacob replied, "I will not let you go unless you bless me."

²⁷The man asked him, "What is your name?"

"Jacob," he answered.

²⁸Then the man said, "Your name will no longer be Jacob, but Israel,ᵃ because you have struggled with God and with men and have overcome."

²⁹Jacob said, "Please tell me your name."

But he replied, "Why do you ask my name?" Then he blessed him there.

³⁰So Jacob called the place Peniel,ᵇ saying, "It is because I saw God face to face, and yet my life was spared."

Praying Genesis 32:24-30

God, I know when You get hold of our lives, we are never the same. Help me to continually surrender myself to You so that I can receive all that You have for me.

³¹The sun rose above him as he passed Peniel,ᶜ and he was limping because of his hip. ³²Therefore to this day the Israelites do not eat the tendon attached to the socket of the hip, because the socket of Jacob's hip was touched near the tendon.

Jacob Meets Esau

33 Jacob looked up and there was Esau, coming with his four hundred men; so he divided the children among Leah, Rachel and the two maidservants. ²He put the maidservants and their children in front, Leah and her children next, and Rachel and Joseph in the rear. ³He himself went on ahead and bowed down to the ground seven times as he approached his brother.

⁴But Esau ran to meet Jacob and embraced him; he threw his arms around his neck and kissed him. And they wept. ⁵Then Esau looked up and saw the women and children. "Who are these with you?" he asked.

Jacob answered, "They are the children God has graciously given your servant."

⁶Then the maidservants and their children approached and bowed down. ⁷Next, Leah and her children came and bowed down. Last of all came Joseph and Rachel, and they too bowed down.

⁸Esau asked, "What do you mean by all these droves I met?"

"To find favor in your eyes, my lord," he said.

⁹But Esau said, "I already have plenty, my brother. Keep what you have for yourself."

¹⁰"No, please!" said Jacob. "If I have found favor in your eyes, accept this gift from me. For to see your face is like seeing the face of God, now that you have received me favorably. ¹¹Please accept the present that was brought to you, for God has been gracious to me and I have all I need." And because Jacob insisted, Esau accepted it.

¹²Then Esau said, "Let us be on our way; I'll accompany you."

¹³But Jacob said to him, "My lord knows that the children are tender and that I must care for the ewes and cows that are nursing their young. If they are

---

ᵃ 28 Israel means *he struggles with God.*   ᵇ 30 Peniel means *face of God.*   ᶜ 31 Hebrew Penuel, a variant of Peniel driven hard just one day, all the animals will die. ¹⁴So let my lord go on ahead of his servant, while I move along slowly at the pace of the droves before me and that of the children, until I come to my lord in Seir."

¹⁵Esau said, "Then let me leave some of my men with you."

"But why do that?" Jacob asked. "Just let me find favor in the eyes of my lord."

¹⁶So that day Esau started on his way back to Seir. ¹⁷Jacob, however, went to Succoth, where he built a place for himself and made shelters for his livestock. That is why the place is called Succoth.ᵃ

¹⁸After Jacob came from Paddan Aram,ᵇ he arrived safely at theᶜ city of Shechem in Canaan and camped within sight of the city. ¹⁹For a hundred pieces of silver,ᵈ he bought from the sons of Hamor, the father of Shechem, the plot of ground where he pitched his tent. ²⁰There he set up an altar and called it El Elohe Israel.ᵉ

Dinah and the Shechemites

34 Now Dinah, the daughter Leah had borne to Jacob, went out to visit the women of the land. ²When Shechem son of Hamor the Hivite, the ruler of that area, saw her, he took her and violated her. ³His heart was drawn to Dinah daughter of Jacob, and he loved the girl and spoke tenderly to her. ⁴And Shechem said to his father Hamor, "Get me this girl as my wife."

⁵When Jacob heard that his daughter Dinah had been defiled, his sons were in the fields with his livestock; so he kept quiet about it until they came home.

⁶Then Shechem's father Hamor went out to talk with Jacob. ⁷Now Jacob's sons had come in from the fields as soon as they heard what had happened. They were filled with grief and fury, because Shechem had done a disgraceful thing inᶠ

Israel by lying with Jacob's daughter—a thing that should not be done.

⁸But Hamor said to them, "My son Shechem has his heart set on your daughter. Please give her to him as his wife. ⁹Intermarry with us; give us your daughters and take our daughters for yourselves. ¹⁰You can settle among us; the land is open to you. Live in it, tradeᵍ in it, and acquire property in it."

¹¹Then Shechem said to Dinah's father and brothers, "Let me find favor in your eyes, and I will give you whatever you ask. ¹²Make the price for the bride and the gift I am to bring as great as you like, and I'll pay whatever you ask me. Only give me the girl as my wife."

¹³Because their sister Dinah had been defiled, Jacob's sons replied deceitfully as they spoke to Shechem and his father Hamor. ¹⁴They said to them, "We can't do such a thing; we can't give our sister to a man who is not circumcised. That would be a disgrace to us. ¹⁵We will give our consent to you on one condition only: that you become like us by circumcising all your males. ¹⁶Then we will give you our daughters and take your daughters for ourselves. We'll settle among you and become one people with you. ¹⁷But if you will not agree to be circumcised, we'll take our sisterʰ and go."

¹⁸Their proposal seemed good to Hamor and his son Shechem. ¹⁹The young man, who was the most honored of all his father's household, lost no time in doing what they said, because he was delighted with Jacob's daughter. ²⁰So Hamor and his son Shechem went to the gate of their city to speak to their fellow townsmen. ²¹"These men are friendly toward us," they said. "Let them live in our land and trade in it; the land has plenty of room for them. We can marry their daughters and they can marry ours. ²²But the men will consent to live with us as one people only on the condition that

ᵃ 17 Succoth means shelters.   ᵇ 18 That is, Northwest Mesopotamia   ᶜ 18 Or arrived at Shalem, a   ᵈ 19 Hebrew hundred kesitahs; a kesitah was a unit of money of unknown weight and value.   ᵉ 20 El Elohe Israel can mean God, the God of Israel or mighty is the God of Israel.   ᶠ 7 Or against   ᵍ 10 Or move about freely; also in verse 21   ʰ 17 Hebrew daughter our males be circumcised, as they themselves are. 23 Won't their livestock, their property and all their other animals become ours? So let us give our consent to them, and they will settle among us."

24 All the men who went out of the city gate agreed with Hamor and his son Shechem, and every male in the city was circumcised.

25 Three days later, while all of them were still in pain, two of Jacob's sons, Simeon and Levi, Dinah's brothers, took their swords and attacked the unsuspecting city, killing every male. 26 They put Hamor and his son Shechem to the sword and took Dinah from Shechem's house and left. 27 The sons of Jacob came upon the dead bodies and looted the city where[a] their sister had been defiled. 28 They seized their flocks and herds and donkeys and everything else of theirs in the city and out in the fields. 29 They carried off all their wealth and all their women and children, taking as plunder everything in the houses.

Praying Genesis 34:1-7,25-27
Creator and Lord, help me to never violate who I was created to be and forfeit the future You have for me by giving place to the desires of my flesh.

30 Then Jacob said to Simeon and Levi, "You have brought trouble on me by making me a stench to the Canaanites and Perizzites, the people living in this land. We are few in number, and if they join forces against me and attack me, I and my household will be destroyed."

31 But they replied, "Should he have treated our sister like a prostitute?"

Jacob Returns to Bethel

35 Then God said to Jacob, "Go up to Bethel and settle there, and build an altar there to God, who appeared to you when you were fleeing from your brother Esau."

2 So Jacob said to his household and to all who were with him, "Get rid of the foreign gods you have with you, and purify yourselves and change your clothes. 3 Then come, let us go up to Bethel, where I will build an altar to God, who answered me in the day of my distress and who has been with me wherever I have gone." 4 So they gave Jacob all the foreign gods they had and the rings in their ears, and Jacob buried them under the oak at Shechem. 5 Then they set out, and the terror of God fell upon the towns all around them so that no one pursued them.

6 Jacob and all the people with him came to Luz (that is, Bethel) in the land of Canaan. 7 There he built an altar, and he called the place El Bethel,[b] because it was there that God revealed himself to him when he was fleeing from his brother.

8 Now Deborah, Rebekah's nurse, died and was buried under the oak below Bethel. So it was named Allon Bacuth.[c]

9 After Jacob returned from Paddan Aram,[d] God appeared to him again and blessed him. 10 God said to him, "Your name is Jacob,[e] but you will no longer be called Jacob; your name will be Israel.[f]" So he named him Israel.

11 And God said to him, "I am God Almighty[g]; be fruitful and increase in number. A nation and a community of nations will come from you, and kings will come from your body. 12 The land I gave to Abraham and Isaac I also give to you, and I will give this land to your descendants after you." 13 Then God went up from him at the place where he had talked with him.

14 Jacob set up a stone pillar at the place where God had talked with him, and he poured out a drink offering on it; he also poured oil on it. 15 Jacob called the place where God had talked with him Bethel.[h]

---

[a] 27 Or because [b] 7 El Bethel means God of Bethel. [c] 8 Allon Bacuth means oak of weeping. [d] 9 That is, Northwest Mesopotamia; also in verse 26 [e] 10 Jacob means he grasps the heel (figuratively, he deceives). [f] 10 Israel means he struggles with God. [g] 11 Hebrew El-Shaddai [h] 15 Bethel means house of God.

GOING
deeper

The Power of Praise

READ AND CONSIDER: GENESIS 35:1-15

"Then come, let us go up to Bethel, where I will build an altar to God, who answered me in the day of my distress and who has been with me wherever I have gone" (Genesis 35:3).

How often do you take the time to remember what God has done for you and thank Him for it? Too often we are so busy that we accept the blessings God gives us as we rush through our hectic days without even stopping to notice them. Deadlines, meetings, and family commitments all crowd out the time we have to praise God. So often we only stop to talk to Him when we need something or when circumstances bring us face-to-face with our own inadequacy.

In this passage, however, Jacob was deliberately taking the time to slow down, stop, and build an altar to the Lord—not to ask for something—but to remember what God had done for him. And this kind of praise has power in it. When we praise God, He renews our strength and reminds us of the truth about who He is and what He wants to do in our lives. When we remember how He has been faithful in the past, it gives us confidence that we can put our trust in Him for our future. When you look back and see His hand guiding your life up to this point, it gives you faith to believe that even though the future is unclear, you can trust that He will not leave you.

It is so important to take time to reflect upon what God has done in your life and how He has been faithful to you. Then you will not fear the future, but anticipate it with the knowledge that God will be with you wherever you go.

The Deaths of Rachel and Isaac

[16]Then they moved on from Bethel. While they were still some distance from Ephrath, Rachel began to give birth and had great difficulty. [17]And as she was having great difficulty in childbirth, the midwife said to her, "Don't be afraid, for you have another son." [18]As she breathed her last—for she was dying—she named her son Ben-Oni.[a] But his father named him Benjamin.[b]

[19]So Rachel died and was buried on the way to Ephrath (that is, Bethlehem). [20]Over her tomb Jacob set up a pillar, and to this day that pillar marks Rachel's tomb.

[21]Israel moved on again and pitched his tent beyond Migdal Eder. [22]While Israel was living in that region, Reuben went in and slept with his father's concubine Bilhah, and Israel heard of it.

Jacob had twelve sons:

[23]The sons of Leah:
Reuben the firstborn of Jacob, Simeon, Levi, Judah, Issachar and Zebulun.

[24]The sons of Rachel:
Joseph and Benjamin.

[25]The sons of Rachel's maidservant Bilhah:
Dan and Naphtali.

[26]The sons of Leah's maidservant Zilpah:
Gad and Asher.

These were the sons of Jacob, who were born to him in Paddan Aram.

[27]Jacob came home to his father Isaac in Mamre, near Kiriath Arba (that is, Hebron), where Abraham and Isaac had stayed. [28]Isaac lived a hundred and eighty years. [29]Then he breathed his last and died and was gathered to his people, old

---

[a] *18 Ben-Oni means* son of my trouble.   [b] *18 Benjamin means* son of my right hand.

and full of years. And his sons Esau and Jacob buried him.

Esau's Descendants

36 This is the account of Esau (that is, Edom).

²Esau took his wives from the women of Canaan: Adah daughter of Elon the Hittite, and Oholibamah daughter of Anah and granddaughter of Zibeon the Hivite— ³also Basemath daughter of Ishmael and sister of Nebaioth.

⁴Adah bore Eliphaz to Esau, Basemath bore Reuel, ⁵and Oholibamah bore Jeush, Jalam and Korah. These were the sons of Esau, who were born to him in Canaan.

⁶Esau took his wives and sons and daughters and all the members of his household, as well as his livestock and all his other animals and all the goods he had acquired in Canaan, and moved to a land some distance from his brother Jacob. ⁷Their possessions were too great for them to remain together; the land where they were staying could not support them both because of their livestock. ⁸So Esau (that is, Edom) settled in the hill country of Seir.

⁹This is the account of Esau the father of the Edomites in the hill country of Seir.

¹⁰These are the names of Esau's sons:
Eliphaz, the son of Esau's wife Adah, and Reuel, the son of Esau's wife Basemath.

¹¹The sons of Eliphaz:
Teman, Omar, Zepho, Gatam and Kenaz.

¹²Esau's son Eliphaz also had a concubine named Timna, who bore him Amalek. These were grandsons of Esau's wife Adah.

¹³The sons of Reuel:
Nahath, Zerah, Shammah and Mizzah. These were grandsons of Esau's wife Basemath.

¹⁴The sons of Esau's wife Oholibamah daughter of Anah and granddaughter of Zibeon, whom she bore to Esau:
Jeush, Jalam and Korah.

¹⁵These were the chiefs among Esau's descendants:
The sons of Eliphaz the firstborn of Esau:
Chiefs Teman, Omar, Zepho, Kenaz, ¹⁶Korah,ᵃ Gatam and Amalek. These were the chiefs descended from Eliphaz in Edom; they were grandsons of Adah.

¹⁷The sons of Esau's son Reuel:
Chiefs Nahath, Zerah, Shammah and Mizzah. These were the chiefs descended from Reuel in Edom; they were grandsons of Esau's wife Basemath.

¹⁸The sons of Esau's wife Oholibamah:
Chiefs Jeush, Jalam and Korah. These were the chiefs descended from Esau's wife Oholibamah daughter of Anah.

¹⁹These were the sons of Esau (that is, Edom), and these were their chiefs.

²⁰These were the sons of Seir the Horite, who were living in the region:
Lotan, Shobal, Zibeon, Anah, ²¹Dishon, Ezer and Dishan. These sons of Seir in Edom were Horite chiefs.

²²The sons of Lotan:
Hori and Homam.ᵇ Timna was Lotan's sister.

²³The sons of Shobal:
Alvan, Manahath, Ebal, Shepho and Onam.

²⁴The sons of Zibeon:
Aiah and Anah. This is the Anah

ᵃ *16* Masoretic Text; Samaritan Pentateuch (see also Gen. 36:11 and 1 Chron. 1:36) does not have *Korah*.   ᵇ *22* Hebrew *Hemam*, a variant of *Homam* (see 1 Chron. 1:39) who discovered the hot springs[a] in the desert while he was grazing the donkeys of his father Zibeon.

25 The children of Anah:

Dishon and Oholibamah daughter of Anah.

26 The sons of Dishon[b]:

Hemdan, Eshban, Ithran and Keran.

27 The sons of Ezer:

Bilhan, Zaavan and Akan.

28 The sons of Dishan:

Uz and Aran.

29 These were the Horite chiefs:

Lotan, Shobal, Zibeon, Anah, 30 Dishon, Ezer and Dishan. These were the Horite chiefs, according to their divisions, in the land of Seir.

The Rulers of Edom

31 These were the kings who reigned in Edom before any Israelite king reigned[c]:

32 Bela son of Beor became king of Edom. His city was named Dinhabah.

33 When Bela died, Jobab son of Zerah from Bozrah succeeded him as king.

34 When Jobab died, Husham from the land of the Temanites succeeded him as king.

35 When Husham died, Hadad son of Bedad, who defeated Midian in the country of Moab, succeeded him as king. His city was named Avith.

36 When Hadad died, Samlah from Masrekah succeeded him as king.

37 When Samlah died, Shaul from Rehoboth on the river[d] succeeded him as king.

38 When Shaul died, Baal-Hanan son of Acbor succeeded him as king.

39 When Baal-Hanan son of Acbor died, Hadad[e] succeeded him as king. His city was named Pau, and his wife's name was Mehetabel

daughter of Matred, the daughter of Me-Zahab.

40 These were the chiefs descended from Esau, by name, according to their clans and regions:

Timna, Alvah, Jetheth, 41 Oholibamah, Elah, Pinon, 42 Kenaz, Teman, Mibzar, 43 Magdiel and Iram. These were the chiefs of Edom, according to their settlements in the land they occupied.

This was Esau the father of the Edomites.

Joseph's Dreams

37 Jacob lived in the land where his father had stayed, the land of Canaan.

2 This is the account of Jacob.

Joseph, a young man of seventeen, was tending the flocks with his brothers, the sons of Bilhah and the sons of Zilpah, his father's wives, and he brought their father a bad report about them.

3 Now Israel loved Joseph more than any of his other sons, because he had been born to him in his old age; and he made a richly ornamented[f] robe for him. 4 When his brothers saw that their father loved him more than any of them, they hated him and could not speak a kind word to him.

5 Joseph had a dream, and when he told it to his brothers, they hated him all the more. 6 He said to them, "Listen to this dream I had: 7 We were binding sheaves of grain out in the field when suddenly my sheaf rose and stood upright, while your sheaves gathered around mine and bowed down to it."

8 His brothers said to him, "Do you intend to reign over us? Will you actually rule us?" And they hated him all the more because of his dream and what he had said.

---

[a] 24 Vulgate; Syriac discovered water; the meaning of the Hebrew for this word is uncertain.   [b] 26 Hebrew Dishan, a variant of Dishon   [c] 31 Or before an Israelite king reigned over them   [d] 37 Possibly the Euphrates   [e] 39 Many manuscripts of the Masoretic Text, Samaritan Pentateuch and Syriac (see also 1 Chron. 1:50); most manuscripts of the Masoretic Text Hadar   [f] 3 The meaning of the Hebrew for richly ornamented is uncertain; also in verses 23 and 32.

9Then he had another dream, and he told it to his brothers. "Listen," he said, "I had another dream, and this time the sun and moon and eleven stars were bowing down to me."

10When he told his father as well as his brothers, his father rebuked him and said, "What is this dream you had? Will your mother and I and your brothers actually come and bow down to the ground before you?" 11His brothers were jealous of him, but his father kept the matter in mind.

Joseph Sold by His Brothers

12Now his brothers had gone to graze their father's flocks near Shechem, 13and Israel said to Joseph, "As you know, your brothers are grazing the flocks near Shechem. Come, I am going to send you to them."

"Very well," he replied.

14So he said to him, "Go and see if all is well with your brothers and with the flocks, and bring word back to me." Then he sent him off from the Valley of Hebron.

When Joseph arrived at Shechem, 15a man found him wandering around in the fields and asked him, "What are you looking for?"

16He replied, "I'm looking for my brothers. Can you tell me where they are grazing their flocks?"

17"They have moved on from here," the man answered. "I heard them say, 'Let's go to Dothan.'"

So Joseph went after his brothers and found them near Dothan. 18But they saw him in the distance, and before he reached them, they plotted to kill him.

19"Here comes that dreamer!" they said to each other. 20"Come now, let's kill him and throw him into one of these cisterns and say that a ferocious animal devoured him. Then we'll see what comes of his dreams."

21When Reuben heard this, he tried to rescue him from their hands. "Let's not take his life," he said. 22"Don't shed any blood. Throw him into this cistern here in the desert, but don't lay a hand on him." Reuben said this to rescue him from them and take him back to his father.

23So when Joseph came to his brothers, they stripped him of his robe—the richly ornamented robe he was wearing— 24and they took him and threw him into the cistern. Now the cistern was empty; there was no water in it.

Praying Genesis 37:23-35

God, remind me that even when life seems unfair and things don't turn out like I expect, You have a plan for my life, and it is good.

25As they sat down to eat their meal, they looked up and saw a caravan of Ishmaelites coming from Gilead. Their camels were loaded with spices, balm and myrrh, and they were on their way to take them down to Egypt.

26Judah said to his brothers, "What will we gain if we kill our brother and cover up his blood? 27Come, let's sell him to the Ishmaelites and not lay our hands on him; after all, he is our brother, our own flesh and blood." His brothers agreed.

28So when the Midianite merchants came by, his brothers pulled Joseph up out of the cistern and sold him for twenty shekels[a] of silver to the Ishmaelites, who took him to Egypt.

29When Reuben returned to the cistern and saw that Joseph was not there, he tore his clothes. 30He went back to his brothers and said, "The boy isn't there! Where can I turn now?"

31Then they got Joseph's robe, slaughtered a goat and dipped the robe in the blood. 32They took the ornamented robe back to their father and said, "We found this. Examine it to see whether it is your son's robe."

33He recognized it and said, "It is my

---

a 28 That is, about 8 ounces (about 0.2 kilogram)

son's robe! Some ferocious animal has devoured him. Joseph has surely been torn to pieces."

³⁴Then Jacob tore his clothes, put on sackcloth and mourned for his son many days. ³⁵All his sons and daughters came to comfort him, but he refused to be comforted. "No," he said, "in mourning will I go down to the grave[a] to my son." So his father wept for him.

³⁶Meanwhile, the Midianites[b] sold Joseph in Egypt to Potiphar, one of Pharaoh's officials, the captain of the guard.

Judah and Tamar

38 At that time, Judah left his brothers and went down to stay with a man of Adullam named Hirah. ²There Judah met the daughter of a Canaanite man named Shua. He married her and lay with her; ³she became pregnant and gave birth to a son, who was named Er. ⁴She conceived again and gave birth to a son and named him Onan. ⁵She gave birth to still another son and named him Shelah. It was at Kezib that she gave birth to him.

⁶Judah got a wife for Er, his firstborn, and her name was Tamar. ⁷But Er, Judah's firstborn, was wicked in the LORD's sight; so the LORD put him to death. ⁸Then Judah said to Onan, "Lie with your brother's wife and fulfill your duty to her as a brother-in-law to produce offspring for your brother." ⁹But Onan knew that the offspring would not be his; so whenever he lay with his brother's wife, he spilled his semen on the ground to keep from producing offspring for his brother. ¹⁰What he did was wicked in the LORD's sight; so he put him to death also.

¹¹Judah then said to his daughter-in-law Tamar, "Live as a widow in your father's house until my son Shelah grows up." For he thought, "He may die too, just like his brothers." So Tamar went to live in her father's house.

¹²After a long time Judah's wife, the daughter of Shua, died. When Judah had recovered from his grief, he went up to Timnah, to the men who were shearing his sheep, and his friend Hirah the Adullamite went with him.

¹³When Tamar was told, "Your father-in-law is on his way to Timnah to shear his sheep," ¹⁴she took off her widow's clothes, covered herself with a veil to disguise herself, and then sat down at the entrance to Enaim, which is on the road to Timnah. For she saw that, though Shelah had now grown up, she had not been given to him as his wife.

¹⁵When Judah saw her, he thought she was a prostitute, for she had covered her face. ¹⁶Not realizing that she was his daughter-in-law, he went over to her by the roadside and said, "Come now, let me sleep with you."

"And what will you give me to sleep with you?" she asked.

¹⁷"I'll send you a young goat from my flock," he said.

"Will you give me something as a pledge until you send it?" she asked.

¹⁸He said, "What pledge should I give you?"

"Your seal and its cord, and the staff in your hand," she answered. So he gave them to her and slept with her, and she became pregnant by him. ¹⁹After she left, she took off her veil and put on her widow's clothes again.

²⁰Meanwhile Judah sent the young goat by his friend the Adullamite in order to get his pledge back from the woman, but he did not find her. ²¹He asked the men who lived there, "Where is the shrine prostitute who was beside the road at Enaim?"

"There hasn't been any shrine prostitute here," they said.

²²So he went back to Judah and said, "I didn't find her. Besides, the men who lived there said, 'There hasn't been any shrine prostitute here.'"

a 35 Hebrew Sheol   b 36 Samaritan Pentateuch, Septuagint, Vulgate and Syriac (see also verse 28); Masoretic Text Medanites

²³Then Judah said, "Let her keep what she has, or we will become a laughingstock. After all, I did send her this young goat, but you didn't find her."

²⁴About three months later Judah was told, "Your daughter-in-law Tamar is guilty of prostitution, and as a result she is now pregnant."

Judah said, "Bring her out and have her burned to death!"

²⁵As she was being brought out, she sent a message to her father-in-law. "I am pregnant by the man who owns these," she said. And she added, "See if you recognize whose seal and cord and staff these are."

²⁶Judah recognized them and said, "She is more righteous than I, since I wouldn't give her to my son Shelah." And he did not sleep with her again.

²⁷When the time came for her to give birth, there were twin boys in her womb. ²⁸As she was giving birth, one of them put out his hand; so the midwife took a scarlet thread and tied it on his wrist and said, "This one came out first." ²⁹But when he drew back his hand, his brother came out, and she said, "So this is how you have broken out!" And he was named Perez.ᵃ ³⁰Then his brother, who had the scarlet thread on his wrist, came out and he was given the name Zerah.ᵇ

Joseph and Potiphar's Wife

39 Now Joseph had been taken down to Egypt. Potiphar, an Egyptian who was one of Pharaoh's officials, the captain of the guard, bought him from the Ishmaelites who had taken him there.

²The LORD was with Joseph and he prospered, and he lived in the house of his Egyptian master. ³When his master saw that the LORD was with him and that the LORD gave him success in everything he did, ⁴Joseph found favor in his eyes and became his attendant. Potiphar put him in charge of his household, and he entrusted to his care everything he owned. ⁵From the time he put him in charge of his household and of all that he owned, the LORD blessed the household of the Egyptian because of Joseph. The blessing of the LORD was on everything Potiphar had, both in the house and in the field. ⁶So he left in Joseph's care everything he had; with Joseph in charge, he did not concern himself with anything except the food he ate.

Now Joseph was well-built and handsome, ⁷and after a while his master's wife took notice of Joseph and said, "Come to bed with me!"

⁸But he refused. "With me in charge," he told her, "my master does not concern himself with anything in the house; everything he owns he has entrusted to my care. ⁹No one is greater in this house than I am. My master has withheld nothing from me except you, because you are his wife. How then could I do such a wicked thing and sin against God?" ¹⁰And though she spoke to Joseph day after day, he refused to go to bed with her or even be with her.

¹¹One day he went into the house to attend to his duties, and none of the household servants was inside. ¹²She caught him by his cloak and said, "Come to bed with me!" But he left his cloak in her hand and ran out of the house.

¹³When she saw that he had left his cloak in her hand and had run out of the house, ¹⁴she called her household servants. "Look," she said to them, "this Hebrew has been brought to us to make sport of us! He came in here to sleep with me, but I screamed. ¹⁵When he heard me scream for help, he left his cloak beside me and ran out of the house."

¹⁶She kept his cloak beside her until his master came home. ¹⁷Then she told him this story: "That Hebrew slave you brought us came to me to make sport of me. ¹⁸But as soon as I screamed for help, he left his cloak beside me and ran out of the house."

¹⁹When his master heard the story his

ᵃ 29 Perez means breaking out.   ᵇ 30 Zerah can mean scarlet or brightness.

God's people at prayer
JOSEPH'S HERE AND NOW PRAYER

GENESIS 39:1-23 We don't know the details of Joseph's prayer life, but we know he walked with God because this passage twice says, "The LORD was with" him (39:2,21). We may look back at situations that have worked out in life and declare, "God was 'there' for me in the past." But the fact is that God is always current, always in the here and now, and always there for us—no matter what we are going through. We need to grow into such a close relationship with Him that we always say, "I'm so glad that God is 'here' for me, right now." Our relationship with God grows closer every time we pray.

The circumstances in Joseph's life were terrible. He lived through devastating setbacks. God's presence didn't keep Joseph out of trouble, but it carried him through it. If you think of prayer as the ticket out of difficulties, you will be disappointed. But if you think of prayer as the conversation you carry on with God through the good times and the bad, His presence will enable you to experience unexpected blessings despite whatever circumstances may come. Just as God has been there in the past, He is also with you right now.

wife told him, saying, "This is how your slave treated me," he burned with anger. ²⁰Joseph's master took him and put him in prison, the place where the king's prisoners were confined.

But while Joseph was there in the prison, ²¹the LORD was with him; he showed him kindness and granted him favor in the eyes of the prison warden. ²²So the warden put Joseph in charge of all those held in the prison, and he was made responsible for all that was done there. ²³The warden paid no attention to anything under Joseph's care, because the LORD was with Joseph and gave him success in whatever he did.

Praying Genesis 39:20-23

Heavenly Father, I thank You for the favor You show to those who love, obey, and serve You. Thank You for being with me and making the things I do prosper.

The Cupbearer and the Baker

40 Some time later, the cupbearer and the baker of the king of Egypt offended their master, the king of Egypt. ²Pharaoh was angry with his two officials, the chief cupbearer and the chief baker, ³and put them in custody in the house of the captain of the guard, in the same prison where Joseph was confined. ⁴The captain of the guard assigned them to Joseph, and he attended them.

After they had been in custody for some time, ⁵each of the two men—the cupbearer and the baker of the king of Egypt, who were being held in prison—had a dream the same night, and each dream had a meaning of its own.

⁶When Joseph came to them the next morning, he saw that they were dejected. ⁷So he asked Pharaoh's officials who were in custody with him in his master's house, "Why are your faces so sad today?"

⁸"We both had dreams," they answered, "but there is no one to interpret them."

Then Joseph said to them, "Do not interpretations belong to God? Tell me your dreams."

⁹So the chief cupbearer told Joseph his dream. He said to him, "In my dream I saw a vine in front of me, ¹⁰and on the vine were three branches. As soon as it budded, it blossomed, and its clusters ripened into grapes. ¹¹Pharaoh's cup was in my hand, and I took the grapes, squeezed them into Pharaoh's cup and put the cup in his hand."

¹²"This is what it means," Joseph said to him. "The three branches are three days. ¹³Within three days Pharaoh will

lift up your head and restore you to your position, and you will put Pharaoh's cup in his hand, just as you used to do when you were his cupbearer. ¹⁴But when all goes well with you, remember me and show me kindness; mention me to Pharaoh and get me out of this prison. ¹⁵For I was forcibly carried off from the land of the Hebrews, and even here I have done nothing to deserve being put in a dungeon."

¹⁶When the chief baker saw that Joseph had given a favorable interpretation, he said to Joseph, "I too had a dream: On my head were three baskets of bread.ᵃ ¹⁷In the top basket were all kinds of baked goods for Pharaoh, but the birds were eating them out of the basket on my head."

¹⁸"This is what it means," Joseph said. "The three baskets are three days. ¹⁹Within three days Pharaoh will lift off your head and hang you on a tree.ᵇ And the birds will eat away your flesh."

²⁰Now the third day was Pharaoh's birthday, and he gave a feast for all his officials. He lifted up the heads of the chief cupbearer and the chief baker in the presence of his officials: ²¹He restored the chief cupbearer to his position, so that he once again put the cup into Pharaoh's hand, ²²but he hangedᶜ the chief baker, just as Joseph had said to them in his interpretation.

²³The chief cupbearer, however, did not remember Joseph; he forgot him.

Pharaoh's Dreams

41 When two full years had passed, Pharaoh had a dream: He was standing by the Nile, ²when out of the river there came up seven cows, sleek and fat, and they grazed among the reeds. ³After them, seven other cows, ugly and gaunt, came up out of the Nile and stood beside those on the riverbank. ⁴And the cows that were ugly and gaunt ate up the seven sleek, fat cows. Then Pharaoh woke up.

⁵He fell asleep again and had a second dream: Seven heads of grain, healthy and good, were growing on a single stalk. ⁶After them, seven other heads of grain sprouted—thin and scorched by the east wind. ⁷The thin heads of grain swallowed up the seven healthy, full heads. Then Pharaoh woke up; it had been a dream.

⁸In the morning his mind was troubled, so he sent for all the magicians and wise men of Egypt. Pharaoh told them his dreams, but no one could interpret them for him.

⁹Then the chief cupbearer said to Pharaoh, "Today I am reminded of my shortcomings. ¹⁰Pharaoh was once angry with his servants, and he imprisoned me and the chief baker in the house of the captain of the guard. ¹¹Each of us had a dream the same night, and each dream had a meaning of its own. ¹²Now a young Hebrew was there with us, a servant of the captain of the guard. We told him our dreams, and he interpreted them for us, giving each man the interpretation of his dream. ¹³And things turned out exactly as he interpreted them to us: I was restored to my position, and the other man was hanged.ᶜ"

¹⁴So Pharaoh sent for Joseph, and he was quickly brought from the dungeon. When he had shaved and changed his clothes, he came before Pharaoh.

¹⁵Pharaoh said to Joseph, "I had a dream, and no one can interpret it. But I have heard it said of you that when you hear a dream you can interpret it."

¹⁶"I cannot do it," Joseph replied to Pharaoh, "but God will give Pharaoh the answer he desires."

¹⁷Then Pharaoh said to Joseph, "In my dream I was standing on the bank of the Nile, ¹⁸when out of the river there came up seven cows, fat and sleek, and they grazed among the reeds. ¹⁹After them, seven other cows came up—scrawny and very ugly and lean. I had never seen such ugly cows in all the land of Egypt. ²⁰The lean, ugly cows ate up the seven fat cows that came up first. ²¹But even after they

ate them, no one could tell that they had done so; they looked just as ugly as before. Then I woke up.

22"In my dreams I also saw seven heads of grain, full and good, growing on a single stalk. 23After them, seven other heads sprouted—withered and thin and scorched by the east wind. 24The thin heads of grain swallowed up the seven good heads. I told this to the magicians, but none could explain it to me."

25Then Joseph said to Pharaoh, "The dreams of Pharaoh are one and the same. God has revealed to Pharaoh what he is about to do. 26The seven good cows are seven years, and the seven good heads of grain are seven years; it is one and the same dream. 27The seven lean, ugly cows that came up afterward are seven years, and so are the seven worthless heads of grain scorched by the east wind: They are seven years of famine.

28"It is just as I said to Pharaoh: God has shown Pharaoh what he is about to do. 29Seven years of great abundance are coming throughout the land of Egypt, 30but seven years of famine will follow them. Then all the abundance in Egypt will be forgotten, and the famine will ravage the land. 31The abundance in the land will not be remembered, because the famine that follows it will be so severe. 32The reason the dream was given to Pharaoh in two forms is that the matter has been firmly decided by God, and God will do it soon.

33"And now let Pharaoh look for a discerning and wise man and put him in charge of the land of Egypt. 34Let Pharaoh appoint commissioners over the land to take a fifth of the harvest of Egypt during the seven years of abundance. 35They should collect all the food of these good years that are coming and store up the grain under the authority of Pharaoh, to be kept in the cities for food. 36This food should be held in reserve for the coun-

try, to be used during the seven years of famine that will come upon Egypt, so that the country may not be ruined by the famine."

37The plan seemed good to Pharaoh and to all his officials. 38So Pharaoh asked them, "Can we find anyone like this man, one in whom is the spirit of God[a]?"

39Then Pharaoh said to Joseph, "Since God has made all this known to you, there is no one so discerning and wise as you. 40You shall be in charge of my palace, and all my people are to submit to your orders. Only with respect to the throne will I be greater than you."

Praying Genesis 41:38-43
Lord, fill me so that I am the type of person in whom people will recognize Your Spirit.

Joseph in Charge of Egypt

41So Pharaoh said to Joseph, "I hereby put you in charge of the whole land of Egypt." 42Then Pharaoh took his signet ring from his finger and put it on Joseph's finger. He dressed him in robes of fine linen and put a gold chain around his neck. 43He had him ride in a chariot as his second-in-command,[b] and men shouted before him, "Make way[c]!" Thus he put him in charge of the whole land of Egypt.

44Then Pharaoh said to Joseph, "I am Pharaoh, but without your word no one will lift hand or foot in all Egypt." 45Pharaoh gave Joseph the name Zaphenath-Paneah and gave him Asenath daughter of Potiphera, priest of On,[d] to be his wife. And Joseph went throughout the land of Egypt.

46Joseph was thirty years old when he entered the service of Pharaoh king of Egypt. And Joseph went out from Pharaoh's presence and traveled throughout Egypt. 47During the seven years of abundance the land produced plentifully. [48]Joseph collected all the food produced in those seven years of abundance in Egypt and stored it in the cities. In each city he put the food grown in the fields surrounding it. [49]Joseph stored up huge quantities of grain, like the sand of the sea; it was so much that he stopped keeping records because it was beyond measure.

[50]Before the years of famine came, two sons were born to Joseph by Asenath daughter of Potiphera, priest of On. [51]Joseph named his firstborn Manasseh[a] and said, "It is because God has made me forget all my trouble and all my father's household." [52]The second son he named Ephraim[b] and said, "It is because God has made me fruitful in the land of my suffering."

[53]The seven years of abundance in Egypt came to an end, [54]and the seven years of famine began, just as Joseph had said. There was famine in all the other lands, but in the whole land of Egypt there was food. [55]When all Egypt began to feel the famine, the people cried to Pharaoh for food. Then Pharaoh told all the Egyptians, "Go to Joseph and do what he tells you."

[56]When the famine had spread over the whole country, Joseph opened the storehouses and sold grain to the Egyptians, for the famine was severe throughout Egypt. [57]And all the countries came to Egypt to buy grain from Joseph, because the famine was severe in all the world.

Joseph's Brothers Go to Egypt

42 When Jacob learned that there was grain in Egypt, he said to his sons, "Why do you just keep looking at each other?" [2]He continued, "I have heard that there is grain in Egypt. Go down there and buy some for us, so that we may live and not die."

[3]Then ten of Joseph's brothers went down to buy grain from Egypt. [4]But Jacob did not send Benjamin, Joseph's brother, with the others, because he was afraid that harm might come to him. [5]So Israel's sons were among those who went to buy grain, for the famine was in the land of Canaan also.

[6]Now Joseph was the governor of the land, the one who sold grain to all its people. So when Joseph's brothers arrived, they bowed down to him with their faces to the ground. [7]As soon as Joseph saw his brothers, he recognized them, but he pretended to be a stranger and spoke harshly to them. "Where do you come from?" he asked.

"From the land of Canaan," they replied, "to buy food."

[8]Although Joseph recognized his brothers, they did not recognize him. [9]Then he remembered his dreams about them and said to them, "You are spies! You have come to see where our land is unprotected."

[10]"No, my lord," they answered. "Your servants have come to buy food. [11]We are all the sons of one man. Your servants are honest men, not spies."

[12]"No!" he said to them. "You have come to see where our land is unprotected."

[13]But they replied, "Your servants were twelve brothers, the sons of one man, who lives in the land of Canaan. The youngest is now with our father, and one is no more."

[14]Joseph said to them, "It is just as I told you: You are spies! [15]And this is how you will be tested: As surely as Pharaoh lives, you will not leave this place unless your youngest brother comes here. [16]Send one of your number to get your brother; the rest of you will be kept in prison, so that your words may be tested to see if you are telling the truth. If you are not, then as surely as Pharaoh lives, you are spies!" [17]And he put them all in custody for three days.

[18]On the third day, Joseph said to them,

---

[a] 51 Manasseh sounds like and may be derived from the Hebrew for forget.   [b] 52 Ephraim sounds like the Hebrew for twice fruitful.

"Do this and you will live, for I fear God: [19]If you are honest men, let one of your brothers stay here in prison, while the rest of you go and take grain back for your starving households. [20]But you must bring your youngest brother to me, so that your words may be verified and that you may not die." This they proceeded to do.

[21]They said to one another, "Surely we are being punished because of our brother. We saw how distressed he was when he pleaded with us for his life, but we would not listen; that's why this distress has come upon us."

[22]Reuben replied, "Didn't I tell you not to sin against the boy? But you wouldn't listen! Now we must give an accounting for his blood." [23]They did not realize that Joseph could understand them, since he was using an interpreter.

[24]He turned away from them and began to weep, but then turned back and spoke to them again. He had Simeon taken from them and bound before their eyes.

[25]Joseph gave orders to fill their bags with grain, to put each man's silver back in his sack, and to give them provisions for their journey. After this was done for them, [26]they loaded their grain on their donkeys and left.

[27]At the place where they stopped for the night one of them opened his sack to get feed for his donkey, and he saw his silver in the mouth of his sack. [28]"My silver has been returned," he said to his brothers. "Here it is in my sack."

Their hearts sank and they turned to each other trembling and said, "What is this that God has done to us?"

[29]When they came to their father Jacob in the land of Canaan, they told him all that had happened to them. They said, [30]"The man who is lord over the land spoke harshly to us and treated us as though we were spying on the land. [31]But we said to him, 'We are honest men; we are not spies. [32]We were twelve brothers, sons of one father. One is no more, and the youngest is now with our father in Canaan.'

[33]"Then the man who is lord over the land said to us, 'This is how I will know whether you are honest men: Leave one of your brothers here with me, and take food for your starving households and go. [34]But bring your youngest brother to me so I will know that you are not spies but honest men. Then I will give your brother back to you, and you can trade[a] in the land.' "

[35]As they were emptying their sacks, there in each man's sack was his pouch of silver! When they and their father saw the money pouches, they were frightened. [36]Their father Jacob said to them, "You have deprived me of my children. Joseph is no more and Simeon is no more, and now you want to take Benjamin. Everything is against me!"

[37]Then Reuben said to his father, "You may put both of my sons to death if I do not bring him back to you. Entrust him to my care, and I will bring him back."

[38]But Jacob said, "My son will not go down there with you; his brother is dead and he is the only one left. If harm comes to him on the journey you are taking, you will bring my gray head down to the grave[b] in sorrow."

The Second Journey to Egypt

43 Now the famine was still severe in the land. [2]So when they had eaten all the grain they had brought from Egypt, their father said to them, "Go back and buy us a little more food."

[3]But Judah said to him, "The man warned us solemnly, 'You will not see my face again unless your brother is with you.' [4]If you will send our brother along with us, we will go down and buy food for you. [5]But if you will not send him, we will not go down, because the man said to us, 'You will not see my face again unless your brother is with you.' "

---

[a] 34 Or *move about freely*   [b] 38 Hebrew *Sheol*

Living a Surrendered Life

Why do some people never seem to grow in the Lord? Why is it they go from one calamity to the next, never able to get beyond survival mode? Why do they seldom, if ever, experience the joy of the Lord? Spiritual breakthrough? A deeper relationship with Him? The release to step out in the area of their gifting? Why can't they move forward into the purposes and destiny God has for them?

The answer, I believe, lies in the word "surrender." They have not fully surrendered everything to God. They have not truly made Jesus Lord over their lives.

Surrendering everything means being willing to say, "Lord, whatever You want me to do I'll do it. I say yes to anything You ask of me, even it means dying to myself and my desires. I will give up the things of the flesh that I want in order to have more of You in my life. I will go to church when I feel like staying home. I will fast when I feel like eating. I will pray when I would rather go to bed. I will read Your Word when I would rather watch TV. I will give when I would rather spend my money on myself. I will enter into praise and worship as my first reaction instead of my last resort. I will do whatever You say so that I can please You and move into all You have for me." This attitude of surrender means putting God first and submitting to His rulership. And it makes all the difference in our lives.

Jesus is Lord whether we declare it or not. That's because "God exalted him to the highest place and gave him the name that is above every name, that at the name of Jesus every knee should bow, in heaven and on earth and under the earth, and every tongue confess that Jesus Christ is Lord, to the glory of God the Father" (Philippians 2:9-11). But He is not only Lord over the universe; He is Lord over our individual lives as well. Whether we acknowledge that or not will determine the success and quality of our life.

Do you remember watching old western movies where the good guy (in the white shirt) catches the bad guy (in the black shirt) and points his gun at him and says, "Stick 'em up!" (It just doesn't sound as menacing to say, "Stick *them* up.")

The bad guy drops everything, raises his hands, and says, "I give up."

Well, this is the kind of surrender God wants. Only you are not the bad guy and God is not pointing a gun at you. He is pointing His finger. But not in an accusatory or embarrassing way. He is pointing to you in a loving way, just as He would if He had picked you for His team. He is saying, "You! I want you! Surrender to Me so I can give you all that I have for you."

If we would drop everything and say, "I give up, Lord. I surrender. Take everything. I will do whatever You say," our lives would be better in every way.

A surrendered life, a life ruled entirely by God, is one that can be used powerfully for His kingdom purposes. God doesn't want just part of you. He wants it all. Pray that you will give God what He wants.

For the next "From Stormie's Heart" article, go to page 78.

⁶Israel asked, "Why did you bring this trouble on me by telling the man you had another brother?"

⁷They replied, "The man questioned us closely about ourselves and our family. 'Is your father still living?' he asked us. 'Do you have another brother?' We simply answered his questions. How were we to know he would say, 'Bring your brother down here'?"

⁸Then Judah said to Israel his father, "Send the boy along with me and we will go at once, so that we and you and our children may live and not die. ⁹I myself will guarantee his safety; you can hold me personally responsible for him. If I do not bring him back to you and set him here before you, I will bear the blame before you all my life. ¹⁰As it is, if we had not delayed, we could have gone and returned twice."

¹¹Then their father Israel said to them, "If it must be, then do this: Put some of the best products of the land in your bags and take them down to the man as a gift—a little balm and a little honey, some spices and myrrh, some pistachio nuts and almonds. ¹²Take double the amount of silver with you, for you must return the silver that was put back into the mouths of your sacks. Perhaps it was a mistake. ¹³Take your brother also and go back to the man at once. ¹⁴And may God Almighty[a] grant you mercy before the man so that he will let your other brother and Benjamin come back with you. As for me, if I am bereaved, I am bereaved."

¹⁵So the men took the gifts and double the amount of silver, and Benjamin also. They hurried down to Egypt and presented themselves to Joseph. ¹⁶When Joseph saw Benjamin with them, he said to the steward of his house, "Take these men to my house, slaughter an animal and prepare dinner; they are to eat with me at noon."

¹⁷The man did as Joseph told him and took the men to Joseph's house. ¹⁸Now the men were frightened when they were taken to his house. They thought, "We were brought here because of the silver that was put back into our sacks the first time. He wants to attack us and overpower us and seize us as slaves and take our donkeys."

¹⁹So they went up to Joseph's steward and spoke to him at the entrance to the house. ²⁰"Please, sir," they said, "we came down here the first time to buy food. ²¹But at the place where we stopped for the night we opened our sacks and each of us found his silver—the exact weight—in the mouth of his sack. So we have brought it back with us. ²²We have also brought additional silver with us to buy food. We don't know who put our silver in our sacks."

²³"It's all right," he said. "Don't be afraid. Your God, the God of your father, has given you treasure in your sacks; I received your silver." Then he brought Simeon out to them.

²⁴The steward took the men into Joseph's house, gave them water to wash their feet and provided fodder for their donkeys. ²⁵They prepared their gifts for Joseph's arrival at noon, because they had heard that they were to eat there.

²⁶When Joseph came home, they presented to him the gifts they had brought into the house, and they bowed down before him to the ground. ²⁷He asked them how they were, and then he said, "How is your aged father you told me about? Is he still living?"

²⁸They replied, "Your servant our father is still alive and well." And they bowed low to pay him honor.

²⁹As he looked about and saw his brother Benjamin, his own mother's son, he asked, "Is this your youngest brother, the one you told me about?" And he said, "God be gracious to you, my son."

³⁰Deeply moved at the sight of his brother, Joseph hurried out and looked for a place

---

a 14 Hebrew El-Shaddai

to weep. He went into his private room and wept there.

31After he had washed his face, he came out and, controlling himself, said, "Serve the food."

32They served him by himself, the brothers by themselves, and the Egyptians who ate with him by themselves, because Egyptians could not eat with Hebrews, for that is detestable to Egyptians. 33The men had been seated before him in the order of their ages, from the firstborn to the youngest; and they looked at each other in astonishment. 34When portions were served to them from Joseph's table, Benjamin's portion was five times as much as anyone else's. So they feasted and drank freely with him.

A Silver Cup in a Sack

44 Now Joseph gave these instructions to the steward of his house: "Fill the men's sacks with as much food as they can carry, and put each man's silver in the mouth of his sack. 2Then put my cup, the silver one, in the mouth of the youngest one's sack, along with the silver for his grain." And he did as Joseph said.

3As morning dawned, the men were sent on their way with their donkeys. 4They had not gone far from the city when Joseph said to his steward, "Go after those men at once, and when you catch up with them, say to them, 'Why have you repaid good with evil? 5Isn't this the cup my master drinks from and also uses for divination? This is a wicked thing you have done.'"

6When he caught up with them, he repeated these words to them. 7But they said to him, "Why does my lord say such things? Far be it from your servants to do anything like that! 8We even brought back to you from the land of Canaan the silver we found inside the mouths of our sacks. So why would we steal silver or gold from your master's house? 9If any of your servants is found to have it, he will die; and the rest of us will become my lord's slaves."

10"Very well, then," he said, "let it be as you say. Whoever is found to have it will become my slave; the rest of you will be free from blame."

11Each of them quickly lowered his sack to the ground and opened it. 12Then the steward proceeded to search, beginning with the oldest and ending with the youngest. And the cup was found in Benjamin's sack. 13At this, they tore their clothes. Then they all loaded their donkeys and returned to the city.

14Joseph was still in the house when Judah and his brothers came in, and they threw themselves to the ground before him. 15Joseph said to them, "What is this you have done? Don't you know that a man like me can find things out by divination?"

16"What can we say to my lord?" Judah replied. "What can we say? How can we prove our innocence? God has uncovered your servants' guilt. We are now my lord's slaves—we ourselves and the one who was found to have the cup."

17But Joseph said, "Far be it from me to do such a thing! Only the man who was found to have the cup will become my slave. The rest of you, go back to your father in peace."

18Then Judah went up to him and said: "Please, my lord, let your servant speak a word to my lord. Do not be angry with your servant, though you are equal to Pharaoh himself. 19My lord asked his servants, 'Do you have a father or a brother?' 20And we answered, 'We have an aged father, and there is a young son born to him in his old age. His brother is dead, and he is the only one of his mother's sons left, and his father loves him.'

21"Then you said to your servants, 'Bring him down to me so I can see him for myself.' 22And we said to my lord, 'The boy cannot leave his father; if he leaves him, his father will die.' 23But you told your servants, 'Unless your youngest brother comes down with you, you will not see my face again.' 24When we went back to your servant my father, we told him what my lord had said.

²⁵"Then our father said, 'Go back and buy a little more food.' ²⁶But we said, 'We cannot go down. Only if our youngest brother is with us will we go. We cannot see the man's face unless our youngest brother is with us.'

²⁷"Your servant my father said to us, 'You know that my wife bore me two sons. ²⁸One of them went away from me, and I said, "He has surely been torn to pieces." And I have not seen him since. ²⁹If you take this one from me too and harm comes to him, you will bring my gray head down to the grave[a] in misery.'

³⁰"So now, if the boy is not with us when I go back to your servant my father and if my father, whose life is closely bound up with the boy's life, ³¹sees that the boy isn't there, he will die. Your servants will bring the gray head of our father down to the grave in sorrow. ³²Your servant guaranteed the boy's safety to my father. I said, 'If I do not bring him back to you, I will bear the blame before you, my father, all my life!'

³³"Now then, please let your servant remain here as my lord's slave in place of the boy, and let the boy return with his brothers. ³⁴How can I go back to my father if the boy is not with me? No! Do not let me see the misery that would come upon my father."

Joseph Makes Himself Known

45 Then Joseph could no longer control himself before all his attendants, and he cried out, "Have everyone leave my presence!" So there was no one with Joseph when he made himself known to his brothers. ²And he wept so loudly that the Egyptians heard him, and Pharaoh's household heard about it.

³Joseph said to his brothers, "I am Joseph! Is my father still living?" But his brothers were not able to answer him, because they were terrified at his presence.

⁴Then Joseph said to his brothers, "Come close to me." When they had done so, he said, "I am your brother Joseph, the one you sold into Egypt! ⁵And now, do not be distressed and do not be angry with yourselves for selling me here, because it was to save lives that God sent me ahead of you. ⁶For two years now there has been famine in the land, and for the next five years there will not be plowing and reaping. ⁷But God sent me ahead of you to preserve for you a remnant on earth and to save your lives by a great deliverance.[b]

Praying Genesis 45:4-8
God, make me a forgiving person just as Joseph was. Help me not to keep an account of wrongs against me but rather to see the bigger picture through Your eyes.

⁸"So then, it was not you who sent me here, but God. He made me father to Pharaoh, lord of his entire household and ruler of all Egypt. ⁹Now hurry back to my father and say to him, 'This is what your son Joseph says: God has made me lord of all Egypt. Come down to me; don't delay. ¹⁰You shall live in the region of Goshen and be near me—you, your children and grandchildren, your flocks and herds, and all you have. ¹¹I will provide for you there, because five years of famine are still to come. Otherwise you and your household and all who belong to you will become destitute.'

¹²"You can see for yourselves, and so can my brother Benjamin, that it is really I who am speaking to you. ¹³Tell my father about all the honor accorded me in Egypt and about everything you have seen. And bring my father down here quickly."

¹⁴Then he threw his arms around his brother Benjamin and wept, and Benjamin embraced him, weeping. ¹⁵And he kissed all his brothers and wept over them. Afterward his brothers talked with him.

¹⁶When the news reached Pharaoh's

palace that Joseph's brothers had come, Pharaoh and all his officials were pleased. [17]Pharaoh said to Joseph, "Tell your brothers, 'Do this: Load your animals and return to the land of Canaan, [18]and bring your father and your families back to me. I will give you the best of the land of Egypt and you can enjoy the fat of the land.'

[19]"You are also directed to tell them, 'Do this: Take some carts from Egypt for your children and your wives, and get your father and come. [20]Never mind about your belongings, because the best of all Egypt will be yours.'"

[21]So the sons of Israel did this. Joseph gave them carts, as Pharaoh had commanded, and he also gave them provisions for their journey. [22]To each of them he gave new clothing, but to Benjamin he gave three hundred shekels[a] of silver and five sets of clothes. [23]And this is what he sent to his father: ten donkeys loaded with the best things of Egypt, and ten female donkeys loaded with grain and bread and other provisions for his journey. [24]Then he sent his brothers away, and as they were leaving he said to them, "Don't quarrel on the way!"

Prayer is . . .

baring your soul to the One
who loved you before you even
knew of Him, and letting
Him speak to your heart.

[25]So they went up out of Egypt and came to their father Jacob in the land of Canaan. [26]They told him, "Joseph is still alive! In fact, he is ruler of all Egypt." Jacob was stunned; he did not believe them. [27]But when they told him everything Joseph had said to them, and when he saw the carts Joseph had sent to carry him

back, the spirit of their father Jacob revived. [28]And Israel said, "I'm convinced! My son Joseph is still alive. I will go and see him before I die."

Jacob Goes to Egypt

46 So Israel set out with all that was his, and when he reached Beersheba, he offered sacrifices to the God of his father Isaac.

[2]And God spoke to Israel in a vision at night and said, "Jacob! Jacob!"

"Here I am," he replied.

[3]"I am God, the God of your father," he said. "Do not be afraid to go down to Egypt, for I will make you into a great nation there. [4]I will go down to Egypt with you, and I will surely bring you back again. And Joseph's own hand will close your eyes."

[5]Then Jacob left Beersheba, and Israel's sons took their father Jacob and their children and their wives in the carts that Pharaoh had sent to transport him. [6]They also took with them their livestock and the possessions they had acquired in Canaan, and Jacob and all his offspring went to Egypt. [7]He took with him to Egypt his sons and grandsons and his daughters and granddaughters—all his offspring.

[8]These are the names of the sons of Israel (Jacob and his descendants) who went to Egypt:

Reuben the firstborn of Jacob.
[9]The sons of Reuben:
   Hanoch, Pallu, Hezron and Carmi.
[10]The sons of Simeon:
   Jemuel, Jamin, Ohad, Jakin, Zohar and Shaul the son of a Canaanite woman.
[11]The sons of Levi:
   Gershon, Kohath and Merari.
[12]The sons of Judah:
   Er, Onan, Shelah, Perez and Zerah (but Er and Onan had died in the land of Canaan).
   The sons of Perez:
   Hezron and Hamul.

---

[a] 22 That is, about 7 1/2 pounds (about 3.5 kilograms)

¹³The sons of Issachar:

Tola, Puah,^a Jashub^b and Shimron.

¹⁴The sons of Zebulun:

Sered, Elon and Jahleel.

¹⁵These were the sons Leah bore to Jacob in Paddan Aram,^c besides his daughter Dinah. These sons and daughters of his were thirty-three in all.

¹⁶The sons of Gad:

Zephon,^d Haggi, Shuni, Ezbon, Eri, Arodi and Areli.

¹⁷The sons of Asher:

Imnah, Ishvah, Ishvi and Beriah.

Their sister was Serah.

The sons of Beriah:

Heber and Malkiel.

¹⁸These were the children born to Jacob by Zilpah, whom Laban had given to his daughter Leah—sixteen in all.

¹⁹The sons of Jacob's wife Rachel:

Joseph and Benjamin. ²⁰In Egypt, Manasseh and Ephraim were born to Joseph by Asenath daughter of Potiphera, priest of On.^e

²¹The sons of Benjamin:

Bela, Beker, Ashbel, Gera, Naaman, Ehi, Rosh, Muppim, Huppim and Ard.

²²These were the sons of Rachel who were born to Jacob—fourteen in all.

²³The son of Dan:

Hushim.

²⁴The sons of Naphtali:

Jahziel, Guni, Jezer and Shillem.

²⁵These were the sons born to Jacob by Bilhah, whom Laban had given to his daughter Rachel—seven in all.

²⁶All those who went to Egypt with Jacob—those who were his direct descendants, not counting his sons' wives—numbered sixty-six persons. ²⁷With the two sons^f who had been born to Joseph in Egypt, the members of Jacob's family, which went to Egypt, were seventy^g in all.

²⁸Now Jacob sent Judah ahead of him to Joseph to get directions to Goshen. When they arrived in the region of Goshen, ²⁹Joseph had his chariot made ready and went to Goshen to meet his father Israel. As soon as Joseph appeared before him, he threw his arms around his father^h and wept for a long time.

³⁰Israel said to Joseph, "Now I am ready to die, since I have seen for myself that you are still alive."

³¹Then Joseph said to his brothers and to his father's household, "I will go up and speak to Pharaoh and will say to him, 'My brothers and my father's household, who were living in the land of Canaan, have come to me. ³²The men are shepherds; they tend livestock, and they have brought along their flocks and herds and everything they own.' ³³When Pharaoh calls you in and asks, 'What is your occupation?' ³⁴you should answer, 'Your servants have tended livestock from our boyhood on, just as our fathers did.' Then you will be allowed to settle in the region of Goshen, for all shepherds are detestable to the Egyptians."

47 Joseph went and told Pharaoh, "My father and brothers, with their flocks and herds and everything they own, have come from the land of Canaan and are now in Goshen." ²He chose five of his brothers and presented them before Pharaoh.

³Pharaoh asked the brothers, "What is your occupation?"

"Your servants are shepherds," they replied to Pharaoh, "just as our fathers were." ⁴They also said to him, "We have come to live here awhile, because the famine is severe in Canaan and your servants' flocks have no pasture. So now, please let your servants settle in Goshen."

⁵Pharaoh said to Joseph, "Your father and your brothers have come to you,

^a 13 Samaritan Pentateuch and Syriac (see also 1 Chron. 7:1); Masoretic Text *Puvah*   ^b 13 Samaritan Pentateuch and some Septuagint manuscripts (see also Num. 26:24 and 1 Chron. 7:1); Masoretic Text *Iob*   ^c 15 That is, Northwest Mesopotamia   ^d 16 Samaritan Pentateuch and Septuagint (see also Num. 26:15); Masoretic Text *Ziphion*   ^e 20 That is, Heliopolis   ^f 27 Hebrew; Septuagint *the nine children*   ^g 27 Hebrew (see also Exodus 1:5 and footnote); Septuagint (see also Acts 7:14) *seventy-five*   ^h 29 Hebrew *around him*

6and the land of Egypt is before you; settle your father and your brothers in the best part of the land. Let them live in Goshen. And if you know of any among them with special ability, put them in charge of my own livestock."

7Then Joseph brought his father Jacob in and presented him before Pharaoh. After Jacob blessed[a] Pharaoh, 8Pharaoh asked him, "How old are you?"

9And Jacob said to Pharaoh, "The years of my pilgrimage are a hundred and thirty. My years have been few and difficult, and they do not equal the years of the pilgrimage of my fathers." 10Then Jacob blessed[b] Pharaoh and went out from his presence.

11So Joseph settled his father and his brothers in Egypt and gave them property in the best part of the land, the district of Rameses, as Pharaoh directed. 12Joseph also provided his father and his brothers and all his father's household with food, according to the number of their children.

Joseph and the Famine

13There was no food, however, in the whole region because the famine was severe; both Egypt and Canaan wasted away because of the famine. 14Joseph collected all the money that was to be found in Egypt and Canaan in payment for the grain they were buying, and he brought it to Pharaoh's palace. 15When the money of the people of Egypt and Canaan was gone, all Egypt came to Joseph and said, "Give us food. Why should we die before your eyes? Our money is used up."

16"Then bring your livestock," said Joseph. "I will sell you food in exchange for your livestock, since your money is gone." 17So they brought their livestock to Joseph, and he gave them food in exchange for their horses, their sheep and goats, their cattle and donkeys. And he brought them through that year with food in exchange for all their livestock.

18When that year was over, they came to him the following year and said, "We cannot hide from our lord the fact that since our money is gone and our livestock belongs to you, there is nothing left for our lord except our bodies and our land. 19Why should we perish before your eyes—we and our land as well? Buy us and our land in exchange for food, and we with our land will be in bondage to Pharaoh. Give us seed so that we may live and not die, and that the land may not become desolate."

20So Joseph bought all the land in Egypt for Pharaoh. The Egyptians, one and all, sold their fields, because the famine was too severe for them. The land became Pharaoh's, 21and Joseph reduced the people to servitude,[c] from one end of Egypt to the other. 22However, he did not buy the land of the priests, because they received a regular allotment from Pharaoh and had food enough from the allotment Pharaoh gave them. That is why they did not sell their land.

23Joseph said to the people, "Now that I have bought you and your land today for Pharaoh, here is seed for you so you can plant the ground. 24But when the crop comes in, give a fifth of it to Pharaoh. The other four-fifths you may keep as seed for the fields and as food for yourselves and your households and your children."

25"You have saved our lives," they said. "May we find favor in the eyes of our lord; we will be in bondage to Pharaoh."

26So Joseph established it as a law concerning land in Egypt—still in force today—that a fifth of the produce belongs to Pharaoh. It was only the land of the priests that did not become Pharaoh's.

27Now the Israelites settled in Egypt in the region of Goshen. They acquired property there and were fruitful and increased greatly in number.

---

a 7 Or greeted   b 10 Or said farewell to   c 21 Samaritan Pentateuch and Septuagint (see also Vulgate); Masoretic Text and he moved the people into the cities

²⁸Jacob lived in Egypt seventeen years, and the years of his life were a hundred and forty-seven. ²⁹When the time drew near for Israel to die, he called for his son Joseph and said to him, "If I have found favor in your eyes, put your hand under my thigh and promise that you will show me kindness and faithfulness. Do not bury me in Egypt, ³⁰but when I rest with my fathers, carry me out of Egypt and bury me where they are buried."

"I will do as you say," he said.

³¹"Swear to me," he said. Then Joseph swore to him, and Israel worshiped as he leaned on the top of his staff.ᵃ

Manasseh and Ephraim

48 Some time later Joseph was told, "Your father is ill." So he took his two sons Manasseh and Ephraim along with him. ²When Jacob was told, "Your son Joseph has come to you," Israel rallied his strength and sat up on the bed.

³Jacob said to Joseph, "God Almightyᵇ appeared to me at Luz in the land of Canaan, and there he blessed me ⁴and said to me, 'I am going to make you fruitful and will increase your numbers. I will make you a community of peoples, and I will give this land as an everlasting possession to your descendants after you.'

⁵"Now then, your two sons born to you in Egypt before I came to you here will be reckoned as mine; Ephraim and Manasseh will be mine, just as Reuben and Simeon are mine. ⁶Any children born to you after them will be yours; in the territory they inherit they will be reckoned under the names of their brothers. ⁷As I was returning from Paddan,ᶜ to my sorrow Rachel died in the land of Canaan while we were still on the way, a little distance from Ephrath. So I buried her there beside the road to Ephrath" (that is, Bethlehem).

⁸When Israel saw the sons of Joseph, he asked, "Who are these?"

⁹"They are the sons God has given me here," Joseph said to his father.

Then Israel said, "Bring them to me so I may bless them."

¹⁰Now Israel's eyes were failing because of old age, and he could hardly see. So Joseph brought his sons close to him, and his father kissed them and embraced them.

¹¹Israel said to Joseph, "I never expected to see your face again, and now God has allowed me to see your children too."

¹²Then Joseph removed them from Israel's knees and bowed down with his face to the ground. ¹³And Joseph took both of them, Ephraim on his right toward Israel's left hand and Manasseh on his left toward Israel's right hand, and brought them close to him. ¹⁴But Israel reached out his right hand and put it on Ephraim's head, though he was the younger, and crossing his arms, he put his left hand on Manasseh's head, even though Manasseh was the firstborn.

¹⁵Then he blessed Joseph and said,

"May the God before whom my
        fathers
    Abraham and Isaac walked,
the God who has been my shepherd
    all my life to this day,
¹⁶the Angel who has delivered me from
        all harm
    —may he bless these boys.
May they be called by my name
    and the names of my fathers
        Abraham and Isaac,
and may they increase greatly
    upon the earth."

¹⁷When Joseph saw his father placing his right hand on Ephraim's head he was displeased; so he took hold of his father's hand to move it from Ephraim's head to Manasseh's head. ¹⁸Joseph said to him, "No, my father, this one is the firstborn; put your right hand on his head."

¹⁹But his father refused and said, "I know, my son, I know. He too will become a people, and he too will become great. Nevertheless, his younger brother

---

ᵃ31 Or Israel bowed down at the head of his bed   ᵇ3 Hebrew El-Shaddai   ᶜ7 That is, Northwest Mesopotamia

GOING deeper

Praying for Your Children

READ AND CONSIDER: GENESIS 48:1-22

"Then he blessed Joseph and said, 'May the God before whom my fathers Abraham and Isaac walked, the God who has been my shepherd all my life to this day, the Angel who has delivered me from all harm—may he bless these boys. May they be called by my name and the names of my fathers Abraham and Isaac, and may they increase greatly upon the earth' "(Genesis 48:15-16).

If you are a parent (or a grandparent), God has given you the authority to pray for your children. You know your children better than anyone else. You know their hopes, their fears, their secret worries, their insecurities, their dreams, their gifts, and their abilities. You love them more than life itself. No one has a heart for their well-being and their future more than you do.

God has not only entrusted you to care for your children's physical, emotional, and spiritual needs, but He has given you a way to bless them as well. Through prayer. The most important thing you can do as a parent is bring your children daily before the Lord and pray for His protection, guidance, wisdom, and love to be infused into every part of their lives. And even though you can't always be with your children every moment, God can. And you can trust that He will be with them in power when you pray.

Each time you intercede for your children, pray that God will bless their lives and give them wisdom and discernment in the choices they face. Pray that He will protect them from the traps the enemy sets for them and that they will follow God and reject evil. Pray that they will love learning and discover the gifts and abilities that God has given them. And pray that their lives will bring glory to God and hope and healing to those around them.

Prayer is the most important gift you can give to your children. They will thrive under the care and power of a praying parent.

---

will be greater than he, and his descendants will become a group of nations." 20He blessed them that day and said,

"In your[a] name will Israel pronounce
　　this blessing:
'May God make you like Ephraim
　　and Manasseh.'"

So he put Ephraim ahead of Manasseh.

21Then Israel said to Joseph, "I am about to die, but God will be with you[b] and take you[b] back to the land of your[b] fathers. 22And to you, as one who is over your brothers, I give the ridge of land[c] I took from the Amorites with my sword and my bow."

Jacob Blesses His Sons

49 Then Jacob called for his sons and said: "Gather around so I can tell you what will happen to you in days to come.

2 "Assemble and listen, sons of Jacob;
　　listen to your father Israel.

3 "Reuben, you are my firstborn,
　　my might, the first sign of my
　　　　strength,
　　excelling in honor, excelling in
　　　　power.
4 Turbulent as the waters, you
　　will no longer excel,

---

a 20 The Hebrew is singular.　b 21 The Hebrew is plural.　c 22 Or And to you I give one portion more than to your brothers—the portion

for you went up onto your father's
   bed,
   onto my couch and defiled it.

5 "Simeon and Levi are brothers—
   their swords[a] are weapons of
      violence.
6 Let me not enter their council,
   let me not join their assembly,
for they have killed men in their
      anger
   and hamstrung oxen as they pleased.
7 Cursed be their anger, so fierce,
   and their fury, so cruel!
I will scatter them in Jacob
   and disperse them in Israel.

8 "Judah,[b] your brothers will praise you;
   your hand will be on the neck of
      your enemies;
   your father's sons will bow down to
      you.
9 You are a lion's cub, O Judah;
   you return from the prey, my son.
Like a lion he crouches and lies down,
   like a lioness—who dares to rouse
      him?
10 The scepter will not depart
      from Judah,
   nor the ruler's staff from between
      his feet,
until he comes to whom it belongs[c]
   and the obedience of the nations is
      his.
11 He will tether his donkey to a vine,
   his colt to the choicest branch;
he will wash his garments in wine,
   his robes in the blood of grapes.
12 His eyes will be darker than wine,
   his teeth whiter than milk.[d]

13 "Zebulun will live by the seashore
   and become a haven for ships;
   his border will extend toward Sidon.

14 "Issachar is a rawboned[e] donkey
   lying down between two saddlebags.[f]

15 When he sees how good is his
      resting place
   and how pleasant is his land,
he will bend his shoulder to the
      burden
   and submit to forced labor.

16 "Dan[g] will provide justice for his
      people
   as one of the tribes of Israel.
17 Dan will be a serpent by the roadside,
   a viper along the path,
that bites the horse's heels
   so that its rider tumbles backward.

18 "I look for your deliverance,
   O LORD.

19 "Gad[h] will be attacked by a
      band of raiders,
   but he will attack them at their heels.

20 "Asher's food will be rich;
   he will provide delicacies fit for a
      king.

21 "Naphtali is a doe set free
   that bears beautiful fawns.[i]

22 "Joseph is a fruitful vine,
   a fruitful vine near a spring,
   whose branches climb over a wall.[j]
23 With bitterness archers attacked
      him;
   they shot at him with hostility.
24 But his bow remained steady,
   his strong arms stayed[k] limber,
because of the hand of the Mighty
      One of Jacob,
   because of the Shepherd, the Rock
      of Israel,
25 because of your father's God, who
      helps you,
   because of the Almighty,[l] who blesses
      you
with blessings of the heavens above,
   blessings of the deep that lies below,
   blessings of the breast and womb.

---

a 5 The meaning of the Hebrew for this word is uncertain.   b 8 Judah sounds like and may be derived from the Hebrew for praise.   c 10 Or until Shiloh comes; or until he comes to whom tribute belongs   d 12 Or will be dull from wine, / his teeth white from milk   e 14 Or strong   f 14 Or campfires   g 16 Dan here means he provides justice.   h 19 Gad can mean attack and band of raiders.   i 21 Or free; / he utters beautiful words   j 22 Or Joseph is a wild colt, / a wild colt near a spring, / a wild donkey on a terraced hill   k 23,24 Or archers will attack... will shoot... will remain... will stay   l 25 Hebrew Shaddai

26 Your father's blessings are
      greater
  than the blessings of the ancient
      mountains,
  than[a] the bounty of the age-old hills.
  Let all these rest on the head of Joseph,
    on the brow of the prince among[b]
      his brothers.

27 "Benjamin is a ravenous wolf;
  in the morning he devours the prey,
  in the evening he divides the
      plunder."

28 All these are the twelve tribes of Israel, and this is what their father said to them when he blessed them, giving each the blessing appropriate to him.

The Death of Jacob

29 Then he gave them these instructions: "I am about to be gathered to my people. Bury me with my fathers in the cave in the field of Ephron the Hittite, 30 the cave in the field of Machpelah, near Mamre in Canaan, which Abraham bought as a burial place from Ephron the Hittite, along with the field. 31 There Abraham and his wife Sarah were buried, there Isaac and his wife Rebekah were buried, and there I buried Leah. 32 The field and the cave in it were bought from the Hittites.[c]"

33 When Jacob had finished giving instructions to his sons, he drew his feet up into the bed, breathed his last and was gathered to his people.

50 Joseph threw himself upon his father and wept over him and kissed him. 2 Then Joseph directed the physicians in his service to embalm his father Israel. So the physicians embalmed him, 3 taking a full forty days, for that was the time required for embalming. And the Egyptians mourned for him seventy days.

4 When the days of mourning had passed, Joseph said to Pharaoh's court, "If I have found favor in your eyes, speak to Pharaoh for me. Tell him, 5 'My father made me swear an oath and said, "I am about to die; bury me in the tomb I dug for myself in the land of Canaan." Now let me go up and bury my father; then I will return.'"

6 Pharaoh said, "Go up and bury your father, as he made you swear to do."

7 So Joseph went up to bury his father. All Pharaoh's officials accompanied him—the dignitaries of his court and all the dignitaries of Egypt— 8 besides all the members of Joseph's household and his brothers and those belonging to his father's household. Only their children and their flocks and herds were left in Goshen. 9 Chariots and horsemen[d] also went up with him. It was a very large company.

10 When they reached the threshing floor of Atad, near the Jordan, they lamented loudly and bitterly; and there Joseph observed a seven-day period of mourning for his father. 11 When the Canaanites who lived there saw the mourning at the threshing floor of Atad, they said, "The Egyptians are holding a solemn ceremony of mourning." That is why that place near the Jordan is called Abel Mizraim.[e]

12 So Jacob's sons did as he had commanded them: 13 They carried him to the land of Canaan and buried him in the cave in the field of Machpelah, near Mamre, which Abraham had bought as a burial place from Ephron the Hittite, along with the field. 14 After burying his father, Joseph returned to Egypt, together with his brothers and all the others who had gone with him to bury his father.

Joseph Reassures His Brothers

15 When Joseph's brothers saw that their father was dead, they said, "What if Joseph holds a grudge against us and pays us back for all the wrongs we did to him?" 16 So they sent word to Joseph, saying, "Your father left these instructions before he died: 17 'This is what you are to say to Joseph: I ask you to forgive your

---

a 26 Or of my progenitors, / as great as   b 26 Or the one separated from   c 32 Or the sons of Heth   d 9 Or charioteers
e 11 Abel Mizraim means mourning of the Egyptians.

brothers the sins and the wrongs they committed in treating you so badly.' Now please forgive the sins of the servants of the God of your father.'" When their message came to him, Joseph wept.

[18] His brothers then came and threw themselves down before him. "We are your slaves," they said.

[19] But Joseph said to them, "Don't be afraid. Am I in the place of God? [20] You intended to harm me, but God intended it for good to accomplish what is now being done, the saving of many lives. [21] So then, don't be afraid. I will provide for you and your children." And he reassured them and spoke kindly to them.

The Death of Joseph

[22] Joseph stayed in Egypt, along with all his father's family. He lived a hundred and ten years [23] and saw the third generation of Ephraim's children. Also the children of Makir son of Manasseh were placed at birth on Joseph's knees.[a]

[24] Then Joseph said to his brothers, "I am about to die. But God will surely come to your aid and take you up out of this land to the land he promised on oath to Abraham, Isaac and Jacob." [25] And Joseph made the sons of Israel swear an oath and said, "God will surely come to your aid, and then you must carry my bones up from this place."

[26] So Joseph died at the age of a hundred and ten. And after they embalmed him, he was placed in a coffin in Egypt.

Praying Genesis 50:15-21

Lord, I thank You that You take the evil that we experience and use it for good. Help me to see Your good in every situation.

---

[a] *23* That is, were counted as his

Author: Moses

Date: Sometime between 1446 and 1406 BC

Audience: The ancient Israelites, who were about to enter the promised land

Trapped. Enslaved. Imprisoned.

Do you ever feel like that... like you needed a divine Deliverer?

Exodus tells of God's miraculous rescue of the ancient Israelites from Egyptian bondage. Then the book reveals how God expected His newly liberated people to live and pray and worship.

Would you like to be free? Unshackled from wrong thoughts and bad habits? Loosed to pursue God with new abandon? Read about the infinite power of God in Exodus. Ask Him to work afresh in your life. When He does, you'll be able to cry out with all those who have tasted God's great deliverance: "In your unfailing love you will lead the people you have redeemed. In your strength you will guide them to your holy dwelling" (15:13).

Prayer Themes:

• *Praise God for His great salvation (14:13-31).*

• *Thank God for His willingness to reveal Himself and His will to a fickle and flawed people (chapters 19–20).*

• *Ask God for more intimate knowledge of Himself—that He would reveal His glory to you and that you would reflect His glory to the world (33:12-23).*

Exodus

The Israelites Oppressed

1 These are the names of the sons of Israel who went to Egypt with Jacob, each with his family: ²Reuben, Simeon, Levi and Judah; ³Issachar, Zebulun and Benjamin; ⁴Dan and Naphtali; Gad and Asher. ⁵The descendants of Jacob numbered seventy[a] in all; Joseph was already in Egypt.

⁶Now Joseph and all his brothers and all that generation died, ⁷but the Israelites were fruitful and multiplied greatly and became exceedingly numerous, so that the land was filled with them.

⁸Then a new king, who did not know about Joseph, came to power in Egypt. ⁹"Look," he said to his people, "the Israelites have become much too numerous for us. ¹⁰Come, we must deal shrewdly with them or they will become even more numerous and, if war breaks out, will join our enemies, fight against us and leave the country."

¹¹So they put slave masters over them to oppress them with forced labor, and they built Pithom and Rameses as store cities for Pharaoh. ¹²But the more they were oppressed, the more they multiplied and spread; so the Egyptians came to dread the Israelites ¹³and worked them ruthlessly. ¹⁴They made their lives bitter with hard labor in brick and mortar and with all kinds of work in the fields; in all their hard labor the Egyptians used them ruthlessly.

¹⁵The king of Egypt said to the Hebrew midwives, whose names were Shiphrah and Puah, ¹⁶"When you help the Hebrew women in childbirth and observe them on the delivery stool, if it is a boy, kill him;

---

a *5* Masoretic Text (also Gen. 46:27); Dead Sea Scrolls and Septuagint (see also Acts 7:14 and note at Gen. 46:27) *seventy-five* but if it is a girl, let her live." 17The midwives, however, feared God and did not do what the king of Egypt had told them to do; they let the boys live. 18Then the king of Egypt summoned the midwives and asked them, "Why have you done this? Why have you let the boys live?"

19The midwives answered Pharaoh, "Hebrew women are not like Egyptian women; they are vigorous and give birth before the midwives arrive."

20So God was kind to the midwives and the people increased and became even more numerous. 21And because the midwives feared God, he gave them families of their own.

22Then Pharaoh gave this order to all his people: "Every boy that is born[a] you must throw into the Nile, but let every girl live."

The Birth of Moses

2 Now a man of the house of Levi married a Levite woman, 2and she became pregnant and gave birth to a son. When she saw that he was a fine child, she hid him for three months. 3But when she could hide him no longer, she got a papyrus basket for him and coated it with tar and pitch. Then she placed the child in it and put it among the reeds along the bank of the Nile. 4His sister stood at a distance to see what would happen to him.

5Then Pharaoh's daughter went down to the Nile to bathe, and her attendants were walking along the river bank. She saw the basket among the reeds and sent her slave girl to get it. 6She opened it and saw the baby. He was crying, and she felt sorry for him. "This is one of the Hebrew babies," she said.

7Then his sister asked Pharaoh's daughter, "Shall I go and get one of the Hebrew women to nurse the baby for you?"

8"Yes, go," she answered. And the girl went and got the baby's mother. 9Pharaoh's daughter said to her, "Take this baby and nurse him for me, and I will pay you."

So the woman took the baby and nursed him. 10When the child grew older, she took him to Pharaoh's daughter and he became her son. She named him Moses,[b] saying, "I drew him out of the water."

Moses Flees to Midian

11One day, after Moses had grown up, he went out to where his own people were and watched them at their hard labor. He saw an Egyptian beating a Hebrew, one of his own people. 12Glancing this way and that and seeing no one, he killed the Egyptian and hid him in the sand. 13The next day he went out and saw two Hebrews fighting. He asked the one in the wrong, "Why are you hitting your fellow Hebrew?"

14The man said, "Who made you ruler and judge over us? Are you thinking of killing me as you killed the Egyptian?" Then Moses was afraid and thought, "What I did must have become known."

15When Pharaoh heard of this, he tried to kill Moses, but Moses fled from Pharaoh and went to live in Midian, where he sat down by a well. 16Now a priest of Midian had seven daughters, and they came to draw water and fill the troughs to water their father's flock. 17Some shepherds came along and drove them away, but Moses got up and came to their rescue and watered their flock.

18When the girls returned to Reuel their father, he asked them, "Why have you returned so early today?"

19They answered, "An Egyptian rescued us from the shepherds. He even drew water for us and watered the flock."

20"And where is he?" he asked his daughters. "Why did you leave him? Invite him to have something to eat."

21Moses agreed to stay with the man, who gave his daughter Zipporah to Moses in marriage. 22Zipporah gave birth to a son, and Moses named him Gershom,[c] saying, "I have become an alien in a foreign land."

a 22 Masoretic Text; Samaritan Pentateuch, Septuagint and Targums born to the Hebrews   b 10 Moses sounds like the Hebrew for draw out.   c 22 Gershom sounds like the Hebrew for an alien there.

Crying Out to God

GOING deeper

READ AND CONSIDER: EXODUS 1:1-14; 2:23-25

"During that long period, the king of Egypt died. The Israelites groaned in their slavery and cried out, and their cry for help because of their slavery went up to God" (Exodus 2:23).

Have you ever felt like the Israelites in this passage? Perhaps you too have endured a long season of repeatedly crying out for deliverance. You might even now be in a difficult situation that seems to offer no apparent means of escape. Perhaps you are hurting, or someone you love is suffering, and you wonder if God can hear your pleas for His help.

When the Israelites cried out, God not only heard them, He answered them far beyond just helping them find relief. He totally liberated them. But it happened God's way—the way that would serve to teach both the Egyptians and the Israelites exactly who He was. God raised up a leader in Moses—two leaders, actually, because He also sent his brother, Aaron. Their first attempt to free the people appeared to fail because the Egyptians ended up giving Israel even more work than they had before. Even when Moses and Aaron performed miracles, Pharaoh hardened his heart. The situation looked more hopeless than ever. But in the midst of situations that are dark and hopeless, God does His greatest work. Even though the children of Israel were in bondage for nearly 400 years, "God heard their groaning and he remembered his covenant. . . God looked on the Israelites and was concerned about them." He will do the same for you. When you cry out to God, your prayers will reach His heart. Just remember that being set free from the past or from a difficult situation may happen quickly or it can be a step-by-step process, depending on what God is wanting to teach you. You can't make it happen on your timetable, so be patient and continue to pray for as long as it takes. Don't ever stop believing that the Lord is a God of miracles.

²³During that long period, the king of Egypt died. The Israelites groaned in their slavery and cried out, and their cry for help because of their slavery went up to God. ²⁴God heard their groaning and he remembered his covenant with Abraham, with Isaac and with Jacob. ²⁵So God looked on the Israelites and was concerned about them.

Praying Exodus 2:24

Thank You, Lord, for hearing my cry for deliverance and rescuing me.

Moses and the Burning Bush

3 Now Moses was tending the flock of Jethro his father-in-law, the priest of Midian, and he led the flock to the far side of the desert and came to Horeb, the mountain of God. ²There the angel of the LORD appeared to him in flames of fire from within a bush. Moses saw that though the bush was on fire it did not burn up. ³So Moses thought, "I will go over and see this strange sight—why the bush does not burn up."

⁴When the LORD saw that he had gone over to look, God called to him from within the bush, "Moses! Moses!"

And Moses said, "Here I am."

⁵"Do not come any closer," God said. "Take off your sandals, for the place where you are standing is holy ground."

Praying Exodus 3:4

Lord, help me to walk so closely with You that I can always hear Your voice speaking to my heart.

⁶Then he said, "I am the God of your father, the God of Abraham, the God of Isaac and the God of Jacob." At this, Moses hid his face, because he was afraid to look at God.

⁷The LORD said, "I have indeed seen the misery of my people in Egypt. I have heard them crying out because of their slave drivers, and I am concerned about their suffering. ⁸So I have come down to rescue them from the hand of the Egyptians and to bring them up out of that land into a good and spacious land, a land flowing with milk and honey—the home of the Canaanites, Hittites, Amorites, Perizzites, Hivites and Jebusites. ⁹And now the cry of the Israelites has reached me, and I have seen the way the Egyptians are oppressing them. ¹⁰So now, go. I am sending you to Pharaoh to bring my people the Israelites out of Egypt."

¹³Moses said to God, "Suppose I go to the Israelites and say to them, 'The God of your fathers has sent me to you,' and they ask me, 'What is his name?' Then what shall I tell them?"

¹⁴God said to Moses, "I AM WHO I AM.ᵇ This is what you are to say to the Israelites: 'I AM has sent me to you.'"

¹⁵God also said to Moses, "Say to the Israelites, 'The LORD,ᶜ the God of your fathers—the God of Abraham, the God of Isaac and the God of Jacob—has sent me to you.' This is my name forever, the name by which I am to be remembered from generation to generation.

¹⁶"Go, assemble the elders of Israel and say to them, 'The LORD, the God of your fathers—the God of Abraham, Isaac and Jacob—appeared to me and said: I have watched over you and have seen what has been done to you in Egypt. ¹⁷And I have

God's people at prayer
MOSES' HESITANT PRAYER

EXODUS 3:11-12 Can you think of a much tougher assignment? God told Moses (who had been herding sheep for 40 years) to go to Pharaoh, the most powerful ruler in the world, and insist on the release of the Egyptian labor force. No wonder Moses responded with this astonished question: "Who am I, that I should go?" Even though he had been raised as a prince of Egypt, Moses had been humbled by his decades in the desert, and he clearly recognized his inadequacy for the monumental task set before him.

The task, however, was *not* too much for the One who assigned it. God's reply to Moses was, "I will be with you." That was all Moses needed. The exact details of how this miracle would be accomplished weren't revealed to Moses at that time. He was to walk by faith, resting in the assurance that God's presence was truly all he required. The same is true for you. The question to ask is not "Who am I?" but "Who is with me?" If God is with you, you have all you need.

¹¹But Moses said to God, "Who am I, that I should go to Pharaoh and bring the Israelites out of Egypt?"

¹²And God said, "I will be with you. And this will be the sign to you that it is I who have sent you: When you have brought the people out of Egypt, youᵃ will worship God on this mountain."

promised to bring you up out of your misery in Egypt into the land of the Canaanites, Hittites, Amorites, Perizzites, Hivites and Jebusites—a land flowing with milk and honey.'

¹⁸"The elders of Israel will listen to you. Then you and the elders are to go to the king of Egypt and say to him, 'The LORD,

ᵃ 12 The Hebrew is plural.   ᵇ 14 Or *I WILL BE WHAT I WILL BE*   ᶜ 15 The Hebrew for LORD sounds like and may be derived from the Hebrew for *I AM* in verse 14.

the God of the Hebrews, has met with us. Let us take a three-day journey into the desert to offer sacrifices to the LORD our God.' ¹⁹But I know that the king of Egypt will not let you go unless a mighty hand compels him. ²⁰So I will stretch out my hand and strike the Egyptians with all the wonders that I will perform among them. After that, he will let you go.

²¹"And I will make the Egyptians favorably disposed toward this people, so that when you leave you will not go empty-handed. ²²Every woman is to ask her neighbor and any woman living in her house for articles of silver and gold and for clothing, which you will put on your sons and daughters. And so you will plunder the Egyptians."

Signs for Moses

4 Moses answered, "What if they do not believe me or listen to me and say, 'The LORD did not appear to you'?"

²Then the LORD said to him, "What is that in your hand?"

"A staff," he replied.

³The LORD said, "Throw it on the ground."

Moses threw it on the ground and it became a snake, and he ran from it. ⁴Then the LORD said to him, "Reach out your hand and take it by the tail." So Moses reached out and took hold of the snake and it turned back into a staff in his hand. ⁵"This," said the LORD, "is so that they may believe that the LORD, the God of their fathers—the God of Abraham, the God of Isaac and the God of Jacob—has appeared to you."

⁶Then the LORD said, "Put your hand inside your cloak." So Moses put his hand into his cloak, and when he took it out, it was leprous,ᵃ like snow.

⁷"Now put it back into your cloak," he said. So Moses put his hand back into his cloak, and when he took it out, it was restored, like the rest of his flesh.

⁸Then the LORD said, "If they do not believe you or pay attention to the first

miraculous sign, they may believe the second. ⁹But if they do not believe these two signs or listen to you, take some water from the Nile and pour it on the dry ground. The water you take from the river will become blood on the ground."

¹⁰Moses said to the LORD, "O Lord, I have never been eloquent, neither in the past nor since you have spoken to your servant. I am slow of speech and tongue."

¹¹The LORD said to him, "Who gave man his mouth? Who makes him deaf or mute? Who gives him sight or makes him blind? Is it not I, the LORD? ¹²Now go; I will help you speak and will teach you what to say."

Praying Exodus 4:10-17
Dear God, help me to trust You completely whenever I am hesitant to move out into what You have called me to do.

¹³But Moses said, "O Lord, please send someone else to do it."

¹⁴Then the LORD's anger burned against Moses and he said, "What about your brother, Aaron the Levite? I know he can speak well. He is already on his way to meet you, and his heart will be glad when he sees you. ¹⁵You shall speak to him and put words in his mouth; I will help both of you speak and will teach you what to do. ¹⁶He will speak to the people for you, and it will be as if he were your mouth and as if you were God to him. ¹⁷But take this staff in your hand so you can perform miraculous signs with it."

Moses Returns to Egypt

¹⁸Then Moses went back to Jethro his father-in-law and said to him, "Let me go back to my own people in Egypt to see if any of them are still alive."

Jethro said, "Go, and I wish you well."

¹⁹Now the LORD had said to Moses in Midian, "Go back to Egypt, for all the men who wanted to kill you are dead." ²⁰So Moses took his wife and sons, put them on a donkey and started back to

ᵃ 6 The Hebrew word was used for various diseases affecting the skin—not necessarily leprosy.

Egypt. And he took the staff of God in his hand.

²¹The Lord said to Moses, "When you return to Egypt, see that you perform before Pharaoh all the wonders I have given you the power to do. But I will harden his heart so that he will not let the people go. ²²Then say to Pharaoh, 'This is what the Lord says: Israel is my firstborn son, ²³and I told you, "Let my son go, so he may worship me." But you refused to let him go; so I will kill your firstborn son.'"

²⁴At a lodging place on the way, the Lord met ⌞Moses⌟ᵃ and was about to kill him. ²⁵But Zipporah took a flint knife, cut off her son's foreskin and touched ⌞Moses'⌟ feet with it.ᵇ "Surely you are a bridegroom of blood to me," she said. ²⁶So the Lord let him alone. (At that time she said "bridegroom of blood," referring to circumcision.)

²⁷The Lord said to Aaron, "Go into the desert to meet Moses." So he met Moses at the mountain of God and kissed him. ²⁸Then Moses told Aaron everything the Lord had sent him to say, and also about all the miraculous signs he had commanded him to perform.

²⁹Moses and Aaron brought together all the elders of the Israelites, ³⁰and Aaron told them everything the Lord had said to Moses. He also performed the signs before the people, ³¹and they believed. And when they heard that the Lord was concerned about them and had seen their misery, they bowed down and worshiped.

Bricks Without Straw

5 Afterward Moses and Aaron went to Pharaoh and said, "This is what the Lord, the God of Israel, says: 'Let my people go, so that they may hold a festival to me in the desert.'"

²Pharaoh said, "Who is the Lord, that I should obey him and let Israel go? I do not know the Lord and I will not let Israel go."

³Then they said, "The God of the Hebrews has met with us. Now let us take a three-day journey into the desert to offer sacrifices to the Lord our God, or he may strike us with plagues or with the sword."

⁴But the king of Egypt said, "Moses and Aaron, why are you taking the people away from their labor? Get back to your work!" ⁵Then Pharaoh said, "Look, the people of the land are now numerous, and you are stopping them from working."

⁶That same day Pharaoh gave this order to the slave drivers and foremen in charge of the people: ⁷"You are no longer to supply the people with straw for making bricks; let them go and gather their own straw. ⁸But require them to make the same number of bricks as before; don't reduce the quota. They are lazy; that is why they are crying out, 'Let us go and sacrifice to our God.' ⁹Make the work harder for the men so that they keep working and pay no attention to lies."

¹⁰Then the slave drivers and the foremen went out and said to the people, "This is what Pharaoh says: 'I will not give you any more straw. ¹¹Go and get your own straw wherever you can find it, but your work will not be reduced at all.'" ¹²So the people scattered all over Egypt to gather stubble to use for straw. ¹³The slave drivers kept pressing them, saying, "Complete the work required of you for each day, just as when you had straw." ¹⁴The Israelite foremen appointed by Pharaoh's slave drivers were beaten and were asked, "Why didn't you meet your quota of bricks yesterday or today, as before?"

¹⁵Then the Israelite foremen went and appealed to Pharaoh: "Why have you treated your servants this way? ¹⁶Your servants are given no straw, yet we are told, 'Make bricks!' Your servants are being beaten, but the fault is with your own people."

ᵃ 24 Or ⌞Moses' son⌟; Hebrew him   ᵇ 25 Or and drew near ⌞Moses'⌟ feet

Expecting a Call

God has a great purpose for each one of us. There is a call from God on your life and mine. The question is, Will we listen to find out what it is?

We can be in the dark about the call of God on our lives for two reasons: either we have *not* heard God's call and we're living as though we *have,* or we *have* heard God's call and we're living as though we have *not.*

I've seen many people who were too busy, too tired, too preoccupied, or too in pursuit of riches and fame to hear God calling them. Others were afraid they might be called to insignificance and so they didn't want to know about it. I've known others still who clearly heard the call of God and ran away from it. The direct line from heaven was ringing and they turned up the volume on their lives so they wouldn't have to hear God and answer. I've also known people with such a low opinion of themselves that they didn't believe God had them destined for anything great. So when the call came, they thought it must be for somebody else and didn't respond.

The only reason it may appear that some people are "more called" by God than others is that they were expecting the call and answered it.

In the early days of telephones, people had party lines. Several households were on the same phone line and anyone in any of those households could pick up the phone and listen in on your conversation. This meant that by afternoon there might be many different opinions and interpretations of the conversation you had that morning.

Receiving God's call does not happen that way. God's line to you is not a party line. You won't hear conflicting opinions. His call is entirely personal and private, and He will speak to you about it.

The Bible says that "God's gifts and his call are irrevocable" (Romans 11:29). When God issues a call, He doesn't take it back. He only waits for us to move into it. Therefore, as long as we are seeking Him, we can never be such a lost cause that His call on our lives is no longer applicable.

All of us share certain calls on our lives. For example, we are all called to partake of God's divine nature (2 Peter 1:3-4), we are called to His eternal glory (1 Peter 5:10), and we are called to bless others (1 Peter 3:9). But we are individually called according to His own purpose. In other words, He has a specific calling for each one of us.

In order to hear God's call, you must be expecting a call. In other words, you need faith that He *will* speak to you, that you *can* hear Him, and that it *will* be good news. Say, "I have set the LORD always before me" (Psalm 16:8), and expect to hear His voice. When an encounter with the living God is your greatest desire, you can be sure you will have it.

For the next "From Stormie's Heart" article, go to page 98.

¹⁷Pharaoh said, "Lazy, that's what you are—lazy! That is why you keep saying, 'Let us go and sacrifice to the LORD.' ¹⁸Now get to work. You will not be given any straw, yet you must produce your full quota of bricks."

¹⁹The Israelite foremen realized they were in trouble when they were told, "You are not to reduce the number of bricks required of you for each day." ²⁰When they left Pharaoh, they found Moses and Aaron waiting to meet them, ²¹and they said, "May the LORD look upon you and judge you! You have made us a stench to Pharaoh and his officials and have put a sword in their hand to kill us."

God Promises Deliverance

²²Moses returned to the LORD and said, "O Lord, why have you brought trouble upon this people? Is this why you sent me? ²³Ever since I went to Pharaoh to speak in your name, he has brought trouble upon this people, and you have not rescued your people at all."

6 Then the LORD said to Moses, "Now you will see what I will do to Pharaoh: Because of my mighty hand he will let them go; because of my mighty hand he will drive them out of his country."

²God also said to Moses, "I am the LORD. ³I appeared to Abraham, to Isaac and to Jacob as God Almighty,ᵃ but by my name the LORDᵇ I did not make myself known to them.ᶜ ⁴I also established my covenant with them to give them the land of Canaan, where they lived as aliens. ⁵Moreover, I have heard the groaning of the Israelites, whom the Egyptians are enslaving, and I have remembered my covenant.

⁶"Therefore, say to the Israelites: 'I am the LORD, and I will bring you out from under the yoke of the Egyptians. I will free you from being slaves to them, and I will redeem you with an outstretched arm and with mighty acts of judgment.

⁷I will take you as my own people, and I will be your God. Then you will know that I am the LORD your God, who brought you out from under the yoke of the Egyptians. ⁸And I will bring you to the land I swore with uplifted hand to give to Abraham, to Isaac and to Jacob. I will give it to you as a possession. I am the LORD.' "

⁹Moses reported this to the Israelites, but they did not listen to him because of their discouragement and cruel bondage.

¹⁰Then the LORD said to Moses, ¹¹"Go, tell Pharaoh king of Egypt to let the Israelites go out of his country."

¹²But Moses said to the LORD, "If the Israelites will not listen to me, why would Pharaoh listen to me, since I speak with faltering lipsᵈ?"

Family Record of Moses and Aaron

¹³Now the LORD spoke to Moses and Aaron about the Israelites and Pharaoh king of Egypt, and he commanded them to bring the Israelites out of Egypt.

¹⁴These were the heads of their familiesᵉ:

The sons of Reuben the firstborn son of Israel were Hanoch and Pallu, Hezron and Carmi. These were the clans of Reuben.

¹⁵The sons of Simeon were Jemuel, Jamin, Ohad, Jakin, Zohar and Shaul the son of a Canaanite woman. These were the clans of Simeon.

¹⁶These were the names of the sons of Levi according to their records: Gershon, Kohath and Merari. Levi lived 137 years.

¹⁷The sons of Gershon, by clans, were Libni and Shimei.

¹⁸The sons of Kohath were Amram, Izhar, Hebron and Uzziel. Kohath lived 133 years.

¹⁹The sons of Merari were Mahli and Mushi.

ᵃ 3 Hebrew El-Shaddai   ᵇ 3 See note at Exodus 3:15.   ᶜ 3 Or Almighty, and by my name the LORD did I not let myself be known to them?   ᵈ 12 Hebrew I am uncircumcised of lips; also in verse 30   ᵉ 14 The Hebrew for families here and in verse 25 refers to units larger than clans.

These were the clans of Levi according to their records.

20Amram married his father's sister Jochebed, who bore him Aaron and Moses. Amram lived 137 years.

21The sons of Izhar were Korah, Nepheg and Zicri.

22The sons of Uzziel were Mishael, Elzaphan and Sithri.

23Aaron married Elisheba, daughter of Amminadab and sister of Nahshon, and she bore him Nadab and Abihu, Eleazar and Ithamar.

24The sons of Korah were Assir, Elkanah and Abiasaph. These were the Korahite clans.

25Eleazar son of Aaron married one of the daughters of Putiel, and she bore him Phinehas.

These were the heads of the Levite families, clan by clan.

26It was this same Aaron and Moses to whom the LORD said, "Bring the Israelites out of Egypt by their divisions." 27They were the ones who spoke to Pharaoh king of Egypt about bringing the Israelites out of Egypt. It was the same Moses and Aaron.

Aaron to Speak for Moses

28Now when the LORD spoke to Moses in Egypt, 29he said to him, "I am the LORD. Tell Pharaoh king of Egypt everything I tell you."

30But Moses said to the LORD, "Since I speak with faltering lips, why would Pharaoh listen to me?"

7 Then the LORD said to Moses, "See, I have made you like God to Pharaoh, and your brother Aaron will be your prophet. 2You are to say everything I command you, and your brother Aaron is to tell Pharaoh to let the Israelites go out of his country. 3But I will harden Pharaoh's heart, and though I multiply my miraculous signs and wonders in Egypt, 4he will not listen to you. Then I will lay my hand on Egypt and with mighty acts of judgment I will bring out my divisions, my

people the Israelites. 5And the Egyptians will know that I am the LORD when I stretch out my hand against Egypt and bring the Israelites out of it."

6Moses and Aaron did just as the LORD commanded them. 7Moses was eighty years old and Aaron eighty-three when they spoke to Pharaoh.

Aaron's Staff Becomes a Snake

8The LORD said to Moses and Aaron, 9"When Pharaoh says to you, 'Perform a miracle,' then say to Aaron, 'Take your staff and throw it down before Pharaoh,' and it will become a snake."

10So Moses and Aaron went to Pharaoh and did just as the LORD commanded. Aaron threw his staff down in front of Pharaoh and his officials, and it became a snake. 11Pharaoh then summoned wise men and sorcerers, and the Egyptian magicians also did the same things by their secret arts: 12Each one threw down his staff and it became a snake. But Aaron's staff swallowed up their staffs. 13Yet Pharaoh's heart became hard and he would not listen to them, just as the LORD had said.

Praying Exodus 7:16
Heavenly Father, help me to not be afraid to boldly deliver Your message to whoever needs to hear it.

The Plague of Blood

14Then the LORD said to Moses, "Pharaoh's heart is unyielding; he refuses to let the people go. 15Go to Pharaoh in the morning as he goes out to the water. Wait on the bank of the Nile to meet him, and take in your hand the staff that was changed into a snake. 16Then say to him, 'The LORD, the God of the Hebrews, has sent me to say to you: Let my people go, so that they may worship me in the desert. But until now you have not listened. 17This is what the LORD says: By this you will know that I am the LORD: With the staff that is in my hand I will strike the water of the Nile, and it will be changed into blood. 18The fish in the Nile will die, and the river will stink; the Egyptians will not be able to drink its water.'"

19 The LORD said to Moses, "Tell Aaron, 'Take your staff and stretch out your hand over the waters of Egypt—over the streams and canals, over the ponds and all the reservoirs'—and they will turn to blood. Blood will be everywhere in Egypt, even in the wooden buckets and stone jars."

20 Moses and Aaron did just as the LORD had commanded. He raised his staff in the presence of Pharaoh and his officials and struck the water of the Nile, and all the water was changed into blood. 21 The fish in the Nile died, and the river smelled so bad that the Egyptians could not drink its water. Blood was everywhere in Egypt.

22 But the Egyptian magicians did the same things by their secret arts, and Pharaoh's heart became hard; he would not listen to Moses and Aaron, just as the LORD had said. 23 Instead, he turned and went into his palace, and did not take even this to heart. 24 And all the Egyptians dug along the Nile to get drinking water, because they could not drink the water of the river.

The Plague of Frogs

25 Seven days passed after the LORD struck the Nile. 1 Then the LORD said to Moses, "Go to Pharaoh and say to him, 'This is what the LORD says: Let my people go, so that they may worship me. 2 If you refuse to let them go, I will plague your whole country with frogs. 3 The Nile will teem with frogs. They will come up into your palace and your bedroom and onto your bed, into the houses of your officials and on your people, and into your ovens and kneading troughs. 4 The frogs will go up on you and your people and all your officials.'"

5 Then the LORD said to Moses, "Tell Aaron, 'Stretch out your hand with your staff over the streams and canals and ponds, and make frogs come up on the land of Egypt.'"

6 So Aaron stretched out his hand over the waters of Egypt, and the frogs came up and covered the land. 7 But the magicians did the same things by their secret arts; they also made frogs come up on the land of Egypt.

8 Pharaoh summoned Moses and Aaron and said, "Pray to the LORD to take the frogs away from me and my people, and I will let your people go to offer sacrifices to the LORD."

9 Moses said to Pharaoh, "I leave to you the honor of setting the time for me to pray for you and your officials and your people that you and your houses may be rid of the frogs, except for those that remain in the Nile."

10 "Tomorrow," Pharaoh said.

Moses replied, "It will be as you say, so that you may know there is no one like the LORD our God. 11 The frogs will leave you and your houses, your officials and your people; they will remain only in the Nile."

12 After Moses and Aaron left Pharaoh, Moses cried out to the LORD about the frogs he had brought on Pharaoh. 13 And the LORD did what Moses asked. The frogs died in the houses, in the courtyards and in the fields. 14 They were piled into heaps, and the land reeked of them. 15 But when Pharaoh saw that there was relief, he hardened his heart and would not listen to Moses and Aaron, just as the LORD had said.

The Plague of Gnats

16 Then the LORD said to Moses, "Tell Aaron, 'Stretch out your staff and strike the dust of the ground,' and throughout the land of Egypt the dust will become gnats." 17 They did this, and when Aaron stretched out his hand with the staff and struck the dust of the ground, gnats came upon men and animals. All the dust throughout the land of Egypt became gnats. 18 But when the magicians tried to produce gnats by their secret arts, they could not. And the gnats were on men and animals.

19 The magicians said to Pharaoh, "This

Praying on Behalf of Others

GOING deeper

READ AND CONSIDER: EXODUS 8:8-11,28-29; 9:27-30; 10:16-19

"Pharaoh quickly summoned Moses and Aaron and said, 'I have sinned against the LORD your God and against you. Now forgive my sin once more and pray to the LORD your God to take this deadly plague away from me'" (Exodus 10:16-17).

Have you ever tried to share your faith with an unbelieving friend, co-worker, or employer, only to have that person demonstrate disinterest or even downright hostility? Those around you may reject your concern for them and ignore their own need for a Savior. However, if a crisis comes, those same people will allow you to pray for them. They may even seek you out—asking for your prayers, knowing you have a "hotline" to heaven.

This becomes extremely difficult when we are called to pray for those who have hurt us. In the Sermon on the Mount, Jesus instructed His followers to disregard the conventional wisdom of the time regarding enemies and practice love through intercession instead. "You have heard that it was said, 'Love your neighbor and hate your enemy.' But I tell you: Love your enemies and pray for those who persecute you, that you may be sons of your Father in heaven'" (Matthew 5:43-45).

Pharaoh put all his faith in the ability of his wise men, sorcerers, and magicians to use their secret arts to perform miracles. But when the plagues were clearly "the finger of God," Pharaoh turned to Moses for help, the one man he knew could truly intercede.

The unbelievers in your world should be able to tell by your life that you are a praying person and that they can depend on you to intercede for them with the only One who can truly make a difference.

is the finger of God." But Pharaoh's heart was hard and he would not listen, just as the LORD had said.

The Plague of Flies

20Then the LORD said to Moses, "Get up early in the morning and confront Pharaoh as he goes to the water and say to him, 'This is what the LORD says: Let my people go, so that they may worship me. 21If you do not let my people go, I will send swarms of flies on you and your officials, on your people and into your houses. The houses of the Egyptians will be full of flies, and even the ground where they are.

22"'But on that day I will deal differently with the land of Goshen, where my people live; no swarms of flies will

be there, so that you will know that I, the LORD, am in this land. 23I will make a distinction[a] between my people and your people. This miraculous sign will occur tomorrow.'"

24And the LORD did this. Dense swarms of flies poured into Pharaoh's palace and into the houses of his officials, and throughout Egypt the land was ruined by the flies.

25Then Pharaoh summoned Moses and Aaron and said, "Go, sacrifice to your God here in the land."

26But Moses said, "That would not be right. The sacrifices we offer the LORD our God would be detestable to the Egyptians. And if we offer sacrifices that are detestable in their eyes, will they not stone us? 27We must take a three-day journey

---

a 23 Septuagint and Vulgate; Hebrew *will put a deliverance* into the desert to offer sacrifices to the LORD our God, as he commands us."

²⁸Pharaoh said, "I will let you go to offer sacrifices to the LORD your God in the desert, but you must not go very far. Now pray for me."

²⁹Moses answered, "As soon as I leave you, I will pray to the LORD, and tomorrow the flies will leave Pharaoh and his officials and his people. Only be sure that Pharaoh does not act deceitfully again by not letting the people go to offer sacrifices to the LORD."

³⁰Then Moses left Pharaoh and prayed to the LORD, ³¹and the LORD did what Moses asked: The flies left Pharaoh and his officials and his people; not a fly remained. ³²But this time also Pharaoh hardened his heart and would not let the people go.

The Plague on Livestock

9 Then the LORD said to Moses, "Go to Pharaoh and say to him, 'This is what the LORD, the God of the Hebrews, says: "Let my people go, so that they may worship me." ²If you refuse to let them go and continue to hold them back, ³the hand of the LORD will bring a terrible plague on your livestock in the field—on your horses and donkeys and camels and on your cattle and sheep and goats. ⁴But the LORD will make a distinction between the livestock of Israel and that of Egypt, so that no animal belonging to the Israelites will die.'"

⁵The LORD set a time and said, "Tomorrow the LORD will do this in the land." ⁶And the next day the LORD did it: All the livestock of the Egyptians died, but not one animal belonging to the Israelites died. ⁷Pharaoh sent men to investigate and found that not even one of the animals of the Israelites had died. Yet his heart was unyielding and he would not let the people go.

The Plague of Boils

⁸Then the LORD said to Moses and Aaron, "Take handfuls of soot from a fur-

nace and have Moses toss it into the air in the presence of Pharaoh. ⁹It will become fine dust over the whole land of Egypt, and festering boils will break out on men and animals throughout the land."

¹⁰So they took soot from a furnace and stood before Pharaoh. Moses tossed it into the air, and festering boils broke out on men and animals. ¹¹The magicians could not stand before Moses because of the boils that were on them and on all the Egyptians. ¹²But the LORD hardened Pharaoh's heart and he would not listen to Moses and Aaron, just as the LORD had said to Moses.

> *Praying Exodus 9:12*
> *Lord, help me to never become hard-hearted toward You and Your ways.*

The Plague of Hail

¹³Then the LORD said to Moses, "Get up early in the morning, confront Pharaoh and say to him, 'This is what the LORD, the God of the Hebrews, says: Let my people go, so that they may worship me, ¹⁴or this time I will send the full force of my plagues against you and against your officials and your people, so you may know that there is no one like me in all the earth. ¹⁵For by now I could have stretched out my hand and struck you and your people with a plague that would have wiped you off the earth. ¹⁶But I have raised you upª for this very purpose, that I might show you my power and that my name might be proclaimed in all the earth. ¹⁷You still set yourself against my people and will not let them go. ¹⁸Therefore, at this time tomorrow I will send the worst hailstorm that has ever fallen on Egypt, from the day it was founded till now. ¹⁹Give an order now to bring your livestock and everything you have in the field to a place of shelter, because the hail will fall on every man and animal that has not been brought in and is still out in the field, and they will die.'"

ª 16 Or have spared you

20Those officials of Pharaoh who feared the word of the LORD hurried to bring their slaves and their livestock inside. 21But those who ignored the word of the LORD left their slaves and livestock in the field.

22Then the LORD said to Moses, "Stretch out your hand toward the sky so that hail will fall all over Egypt—on men and animals and on everything growing in the fields of Egypt." 23When Moses stretched out his staff toward the sky, the LORD sent thunder and hail, and lightning flashed down to the ground. So the LORD rained hail on the land of Egypt; 24hail fell and lightning flashed back and forth. It was the worst storm in all the land of Egypt since it had become a nation. 25Throughout Egypt hail struck everything in the fields—both men and animals; it beat down everything growing in the fields and stripped every tree. 26The only place it did not hail was the land of Goshen, where the Israelites were.

27Then Pharaoh summoned Moses and Aaron. "This time I have sinned," he said to them. "The LORD is in the right, and I and my people are in the wrong. 28Pray to the LORD, for we have had enough thunder and hail. I will let you go; you don't have to stay any longer."

29Moses replied, "When I have gone out of the city, I will spread out my hands in prayer to the LORD. The thunder will stop and there will be no more hail, so you may know that the earth is the LORD's. 30But I know that you and your officials still do not fear the LORD God."

31(The flax and barley were destroyed, since the barley had headed and the flax was in bloom. 32The wheat and spelt, however, were not destroyed, because they ripen later.)

33Then Moses left Pharaoh and went out of the city. He spread out his hands toward the LORD; the thunder and hail stopped, and the rain no longer poured down on the land. 34When Pharaoh saw that the rain and hail and thunder had stopped, he sinned again: He and his officials hardened their hearts. 35So Pharaoh's heart was hard and he would not let the Israelites go, just as the LORD had said through Moses.

The Plague of Locusts

10 Then the LORD said to Moses, "Go to Pharaoh, for I have hardened his heart and the hearts of his officials so that I may perform these miraculous signs of mine among them 2that you may tell your children and grandchildren how I dealt harshly with the Egyptians and how I performed my signs among them, and that you may know that I am the LORD."

3So Moses and Aaron went to Pharaoh and said to him, "This is what the LORD, the God of the Hebrews, says: 'How long will you refuse to humble yourself before me? Let my people go, so that they may worship me. 4If you refuse to let them go, I will bring locusts into your country tomorrow. 5They will cover the face of the ground so that it cannot be seen. They will devour what little you have left after the hail, including every tree that is growing in your fields. 6They will fill your houses and those of all your officials and all the Egyptians—something neither your fathers nor your forefathers have ever seen from the day they settled in this land till now.'" Then Moses turned and left Pharaoh.

7Pharaoh's officials said to him, "How long will this man be a snare to us? Let the people go, so that they may worship the LORD their God. Do you not yet realize that Egypt is ruined?"

8Then Moses and Aaron were brought back to Pharaoh. "Go, worship the LORD your God," he said. "But just who will be going?"

9Moses answered, "We will go with our young and old, with our sons and daughters, and with our flocks and herds, because we are to celebrate a festival to the LORD."

10Pharaoh said, "The LORD be with you—if I let you go, along with your

GOING *deeper*

Praying Against a Hard Heart

READ AND CONSIDER: EXODUS 8:15,30-32; 9:7,12,35; 10:1,20,27

"Then the LORD said to Moses, 'Go to Pharaoh, for I have hardened his heart and the hearts of his officials so that I may perform these miraculous signs of mine among them'" (Exodus 10:1).

Why would God intentionally harden the heart of a man whose permission Moses needed to lead the Israelites out of bondage in Egypt?

Romans 1:21-24 provides a clue when it describes people who neither glorified God nor gave thanks to Him. It tells us that their thinking became futile and their foolish hearts darkened so that "God gave them over in the sinful desires of their hearts." In some cases God takes our willful predisposition to rebel and lets us have our way permanently. The book of Exodus makes it obvious that Pharaoh wasn't a tenderhearted man, whose heart God then hardened; rather, he was a proud and arrogant ruler. In Egypt, Pharaoh's name was Ra, meaning "sun god," and he behaved as if he were a deity whose every wish was to be obeyed, including the enslavement of an entire nation of people forced into labor. The true God chose to debunk Pharaoh's imputed power and demonstrate His own; therefore, He used Pharaoh's own stubbornness to teach him a painful lesson—one that came at great cost.

This passage contains a cautionary word for us as well. Perhaps in our pride we think we can control or manipulate others around us. God loves us but He hates pride (Proverbs 8:13). If necessary, He might give us over to our own sinful desires in order to teach us, sometimes through painful consequences, that we need to be softhearted and always stay open to His leading in our lives.

women and children! Clearly you are bent on evil.[a] 11No! Have only the men go; and worship the LORD, since that's what you have been asking for." Then Moses and Aaron were driven out of Pharaoh's presence.

12And the LORD said to Moses, "Stretch out your hand over Egypt so that locusts will swarm over the land and devour everything growing in the fields, everything left by the hail."

13So Moses stretched out his staff over Egypt, and the LORD made an east wind blow across the land all that day and all that night. By morning the wind had brought the locusts; 14they invaded all Egypt and settled down in every area of the country in great numbers. Never before had there been such a plague of lo-

custs, nor will there ever be again. 15They covered all the ground until it was black. They devoured all that was left after the hail—everything growing in the fields and the fruit on the trees. Nothing green remained on tree or plant in all the land of Egypt.

16Pharaoh quickly summoned Moses and Aaron and said, "I have sinned against the LORD your God and against you. 17Now forgive my sin once more and pray to the LORD your God to take this deadly plague away from me."

18Moses then left Pharaoh and prayed to the LORD. 19And the LORD changed the wind to a very strong west wind, which caught up the locusts and carried them into the Red Sea.[b] Not a locust was left anywhere in Egypt. 20But the LORD

---

[a] 10 Or *Be careful, trouble is in store for you!*   [b] 19 Hebrew *Yam Suph;* that is, Sea of Reeds

hardened Pharaoh's heart, and he would not let the Israelites go.

The Plague of Darkness

²¹Then the LORD said to Moses, "Stretch out your hand toward the sky so that darkness will spread over Egypt—darkness that can be felt." ²²So Moses stretched out his hand toward the sky, and total darkness covered all Egypt for three days. ²³No one could see anyone else or leave his place for three days. Yet all the Israelites had light in the places where they lived.

²⁴Then Pharaoh summoned Moses and said, "Go, worship the LORD. Even your women and children may go with you; only leave your flocks and herds behind."

²⁵But Moses said, "You must allow us to have sacrifices and burnt offerings to present to the LORD our God. ²⁶Our livestock too must go with us; not a hoof is to be left behind. We have to use some of them in worshiping the LORD our God, and until we get there we will not know what we are to use to worship the LORD."

²⁷But the LORD hardened Pharaoh's heart, and he was not willing to let them go. ²⁸Pharaoh said to Moses, "Get out of my sight! Make sure you do not appear before me again! The day you see my face you will die."

²⁹"Just as you say," Moses replied, "I will never appear before you again."

The Plague on the Firstborn

11 Now the LORD had said to Moses, "I will bring one more plague on Pharaoh and on Egypt. After that, he will let you go from here, and when he does, he will drive you out completely. ²Tell the people that men and women alike are to ask their neighbors for articles of silver and gold." ³(The LORD made the Egyptians favorably disposed toward the people, and Moses himself was highly regarded in Egypt by Pharaoh's officials and by the people.)

⁴So Moses said, "This is what the LORD says: 'About midnight I will go throughout Egypt. ⁵Every firstborn son in Egypt will die, from the firstborn son of Pharaoh, who sits on the throne, to the firstborn son of the slave girl, who is at her hand mill, and all the firstborn of the cattle as well. ⁶There will be loud wailing throughout Egypt—worse than there has ever been or ever will be again. ⁷But among the Israelites not a dog will bark at any man or animal.' Then you will know that the LORD makes a distinction between Egypt and Israel. ⁸All these officials of yours will come to me, bowing down before me and saying, 'Go, you and all the people who follow you!' After that I will leave." Then Moses, hot with anger, left Pharaoh.

⁹The LORD had said to Moses, "Pharaoh will refuse to listen to you—so that my wonders may be multiplied in Egypt." ¹⁰Moses and Aaron performed all these wonders before Pharaoh, but the LORD hardened Pharaoh's heart, and he would not let the Israelites go out of his country.

The Passover

12 The LORD said to Moses and Aaron in Egypt, ²"This month is to be for you the first month, the first month of your year. ³Tell the whole community of Israel that on the tenth day of this month each man is to take a lambᵃ for his family, one for each household. ⁴If any household is too small for a whole lamb, they must share one with their nearest neighbor, having taken into account the number of people there are. You are to determine the amount of lamb needed in accordance with what each person will eat. ⁵The animals you choose must be year-old males without defect, and you may take them from the sheep or the goats. ⁶Take care of them until the fourteenth day of the month, when all the people of the community of Israel must slaughter them at twilight. ⁷Then they

ᵃ 3 The Hebrew word can mean *lamb* or *kid*; also in verse 4.

are to take some of the blood and put it on the sides and tops of the doorframes of the houses where they eat the lambs. [8] That same night they are to eat the meat roasted over the fire, along with bitter herbs, and bread made without yeast. [9] Do not eat the meat raw or cooked in water, but roast it over the fire—head, legs and inner parts. [10] Do not leave any of it till morning; if some is left till morning, you must burn it. [11] This is how you are to eat it: with your cloak tucked into your belt, your sandals on your feet and your staff in your hand. Eat it in haste; it is the LORD's Passover.

[12] "On that same night I will pass through Egypt and strike down every firstborn—both men and animals—and I will bring judgment on all the gods of Egypt. I am the LORD. [13] The blood will be a sign for you on the houses where you are; and when I see the blood, I will pass over you. No destructive plague will touch you when I strike Egypt.

[14] "This is a day you are to commemorate; for the generations to come you shall celebrate it as a festival to the LORD—a lasting ordinance. [15] For seven days you are to eat bread made without yeast. On the first day remove the yeast from your houses, for whoever eats anything with yeast in it from the first day through the seventh must be cut off from Israel. [16] On the first day hold a sacred assembly, and another one on the seventh day. Do no work at all on these days, except to prepare food for everyone to eat—that is all you may do.

[17] "Celebrate the Feast of Unleavened Bread, because it was on this very day that I brought your divisions out of Egypt. Celebrate this day as a lasting ordinance for the generations to come. [18] In the first month you are to eat bread made without yeast, from the evening of the fourteenth day until the evening of the twenty-first day. [19] For seven days no yeast is to be found in your houses. And whoever eats anything with yeast in it must be cut off from the community of Israel, whether he is an alien or native-born. [20] Eat nothing made with yeast. Wherever you live, you must eat unleavened bread."

[21] Then Moses summoned all the elders of Israel and said to them, "Go at once and select the animals for your families and slaughter the Passover lamb. [22] Take a bunch of hyssop, dip it into the blood in the basin and put some of the blood on the top and on both sides of the doorframe. Not one of you shall go out the door of his house until morning. [23] When the LORD goes through the land to strike down the Egyptians, he will see the blood on the top and sides of the doorframe and will pass over that doorway, and he will not permit the destroyer to enter your houses and strike you down.

Praying Exodus 12:23
Heavenly Father, I thank You for protecting me from the destroyer.

[24] "Obey these instructions as a lasting ordinance for you and your descendants. [25] When you enter the land that the LORD will give you as he promised, observe this ceremony. [26] And when your children ask you, 'What does this ceremony mean to you?' [27] then tell them, 'It is the Passover sacrifice to the LORD, who passed over the houses of the Israelites in Egypt and spared our homes when he struck down the Egyptians.'" Then the people bowed down and worshiped. [28] The Israelites did just what the LORD commanded Moses and Aaron.

[29] At midnight the LORD struck down all the firstborn in Egypt, from the firstborn of Pharaoh, who sat on the throne, to the firstborn of the prisoner, who was in the dungeon, and the firstborn of all the livestock as well. [30] Pharaoh and all his officials and all the Egyptians got up during the night, and there was loud wailing in Egypt, for there was not a house without someone dead.

The Exodus

31During the night Pharaoh summoned Moses and Aaron and said, "Up! Leave my people, you and the Israelites! Go, worship the LORD as you have requested. 32Take your flocks and herds, as you have said, and go. And also bless me."

33The Egyptians urged the people to hurry and leave the country. "For otherwise," they said, "we will all die!" 34So the people took their dough before the yeast was added, and carried it on their shoulders in kneading troughs wrapped in clothing. 35The Israelites did as Moses instructed and asked the Egyptians for articles of silver and gold and for clothing. 36The LORD had made the Egyptians favorably disposed toward the people, and they gave them what they asked for; so they plundered the Egyptians.

37The Israelites journeyed from Rameses to Succoth. There were about six hundred thousand men on foot, besides women and children. 38Many other people went up with them, as well as large droves of livestock, both flocks and herds. 39With the dough they had brought from Egypt, they baked cakes of unleavened bread. The dough was without yeast because they had been driven out of Egypt and did not have time to prepare food for themselves.

40Now the length of time the Israelite people lived in Egypt[a] was 430 years. 41At the end of the 430 years, to the very day, all the LORD's divisions left Egypt. 42Because the LORD kept vigil that night to bring them out of Egypt, on this night all the Israelites are to keep vigil to honor the LORD for the generations to come.

Passover Restrictions

43The LORD said to Moses and Aaron, "These are the regulations for the Passover:

"No foreigner is to eat of it. 44Any slave you have bought may eat of it after you have circumcised him, 45but a temporary resident and a hired worker may not eat of it.

46"It must be eaten inside one house; take none of the meat outside the house. Do not break any of the bones. 47The whole community of Israel must celebrate it.

48"An alien living among you who wants to celebrate the LORD's Passover must have all the males in his household circumcised; then he may take part like one born in the land. No uncircumcised male may eat of it. 49The same law applies to the native-born and to the alien living among you."

50All the Israelites did just what the LORD had commanded Moses and Aaron. 51And on that very day the LORD brought the Israelites out of Egypt by their divisions.

Consecration of the Firstborn

13 The LORD said to Moses, 2"Consecrate to me every firstborn male. The first offspring of every womb among the Israelites belongs to me, whether man or animal."

3Then Moses said to the people, "Commemorate this day, the day you came out of Egypt, out of the land of slavery, because the LORD brought you out of it with a mighty hand. Eat nothing containing yeast. 4Today, in the month of Abib, you are leaving. 5When the LORD brings you into the land of the Canaanites, Hittites, Amorites, Hivites and Jebusites—the land he swore to your forefathers to give you, a land flowing with milk and honey—you are to observe this ceremony in this month: 6For seven days eat bread made without yeast and on the seventh day hold a festival to the LORD. 7Eat unleavened bread during those seven days; nothing with yeast in it is to be seen among you, nor shall any yeast be seen anywhere within your borders. 8On that day tell your son, 'I do this because of what the LORD did for me when

---

a 40 Masoretic Text; Samaritan Pentateuch and Septuagint Egypt and Canaan

I came out of Egypt.' ⁹This observance will be for you like a sign on your hand and a reminder on your forehead that the law of the LORD is to be on your lips. For the LORD brought you out of Egypt with his mighty hand. ¹⁰You must keep this ordinance at the appointed time year after year.

¹¹"After the LORD brings you into the land of the Canaanites and gives it to you, as he promised on oath to you and your forefathers, ¹²you are to give over to the LORD the first offspring of every womb. All the firstborn males of your livestock belong to the LORD. ¹³Redeem with a lamb every firstborn donkey, but if you do not redeem it, break its neck. Redeem every firstborn among your sons.

¹⁴"In days to come, when your son asks you, 'What does this mean?' say to him, 'With a mighty hand the LORD brought us out of Egypt, out of the land of slavery. ¹⁵When Pharaoh stubbornly refused to let us go, the LORD killed every firstborn in Egypt, both man and animal. This is why I sacrifice to the LORD the first male offspring of every womb and redeem each of my firstborn sons.' ¹⁶And it will be like a sign on your hand and a symbol on your forehead that the LORD brought us out of Egypt with his mighty hand."

Crossing the Sea

¹⁷When Pharaoh let the people go, God did not lead them on the road through the Philistine country, though that was shorter. For God said, "If they face war, they might change their minds and return to Egypt." ¹⁸So God led the people around by the desert road toward the Red Sea.ᵃ The Israelites went up out of Egypt armed for battle.

¹⁹Moses took the bones of Joseph with him because Joseph had made the sons of Israel swear an oath. He had said, "God will surely come to your aid, and then you must carry my bones up with you from this place."ᵇ

²⁰After leaving Succoth they camped at Etham on the edge of the desert. ²¹By day the LORD went ahead of them in a pillar of cloud to guide them on their way and by night in a pillar of fire to give them light, so that they could travel by day or night. ²²Neither the pillar of cloud by day nor the pillar of fire by night left its place in front of the people.

14 Then the LORD said to Moses, ²"Tell the Israelites to turn back and encamp near Pi Hahiroth, between Migdol and the sea. They are to encamp by the sea, directly opposite Baal Zephon. ³Pharaoh will think, 'The Israelites are wandering around the land in confusion, hemmed in by the desert.' ⁴And I will harden Pharaoh's heart, and he will pursue them. But I will gain glory for myself through Pharaoh and all his army, and the Egyptians will know that I am the LORD." So the Israelites did this.

⁵When the king of Egypt was told that the people had fled, Pharaoh and his officials changed their minds about them and said, "What have we done? We have let the Israelites go and have lost their services!" ⁶So he had his chariot made ready and took his army with him. ⁷He took six hundred of the best chariots, along with all the other chariots of Egypt, with officers over all of them. ⁸The LORD hardened the heart of Pharaoh king of Egypt, so that he pursued the Israelites, who were marching out boldly. ⁹The Egyptians—all Pharaoh's horses and chariots, horsemenᶜ and troops—pursued the Israelites and overtook them as they camped by the sea near Pi Hahiroth, opposite Baal Zephon.

¹⁰As Pharaoh approached, the Israelites looked up, and there were the Egyptians, marching after them. They were terrified and cried out to the LORD. ¹¹They said to Moses, "Was it because there were no graves in Egypt that you brought us to the desert to die? What have you done to us by bringing us out of Egypt? ¹²Didn't we say to you in Egypt, 'Leave us alone;

ᵃ 18 Hebrew Yam Suph; that is, Sea of Reeds   ᵇ 19 See Gen. 50:25.   ᶜ 9 Or charioteers; also in verses 17, 18, 23, 26 and 28

GOING *deeper*

Stop Praying and Start Moving

READ AND CONSIDER: EXODUS 14

"Then the LORD said to Moses, 'Why are you crying out to me? Tell the Israelites to move on'"
(Exodus 14:15).

Many passages of Scripture speak of the importance of crying out to God in times of distress. In Lamentations we read, "Arise, cry out in the night . . . pour out your heart like water in the presence of the Lord" (Lamentations 2:19). There comes a point, however, when the time for crying out is past and our clear instruction from the Lord is to take action.

That's what God said to Moses. The Israelites didn't need to worry about the details; God would take care of everything. He would help His people by obstructing the sight of the Egyptians with clouds and darkness. He would give the Israelites light. He would cause the wind to dry up the sea bottom. They didn't need more desperate prayer. They needed to get moving!

They may have been tempted to just wait. "This can't be what God wants us to do! It's too dangerous! It's too frightening! How do we know we'll make it? Let's just keep praying about this."

Sometimes prayer is an excuse for inaction.

Famed missionary Amy Carmichael once wrote a simple rhyme to illustrate the importance of following through with action once we have thoroughly prayed over a matter:

> *A centipede was happy till*
>
> *One day, a toad in fun*
>
> *Said, "Pray, which leg goes after which?"*
>
> *Which strained his mind to such a pitch*
>
> *He lay distracted in a ditch,*
>
> *Considering how to run.*

When you hear God telling you to move in a certain direction, take two words of advice: *Do it!*

If you delay, you may well find yourself "distracted in a ditch, considering how to run." When the way is clear, remember the Lord's instruction to the Israelites through Moses—"Move on!"

---

let us serve the Egyptians'? It would have been better for us to serve the Egyptians than to die in the desert!"

13Moses answered the people, "Do not be afraid. Stand firm and you will see the deliverance the LORD will bring you today. The Egyptians you see today you will never see again. 14The LORD will fight for you; you need only to be still."

15Then the LORD said to Moses, "Why are you crying out to me? Tell the Israelites to move on. 16Raise your staff and stretch out your hand over the sea to divide the water so that the Israelites can go through the sea on dry ground. 17I will harden the hearts of the Egyptians so

Praying Exodus 14:13-14

Dear God, help me to not be afraid in the face of my enemies, but rather to trust that You will fight the battles for me.

that they will go in after them. And I will gain glory through Pharaoh and all his army, through his chariots and his horsemen. ¹⁸The Egyptians will know that I am the LORD when I gain glory through Pharaoh, his chariots and his horsemen."

¹⁹Then the angel of God, who had been traveling in front of Israel's army, withdrew and went behind them. The pillar of cloud also moved from in front and stood behind them, ²⁰coming between the armies of Egypt and Israel. Throughout the night the cloud brought darkness to the one side and light to the other side; so neither went near the other all night long.

²¹Then Moses stretched out his hand over the sea, and all that night the LORD drove the sea back with a strong east wind and turned it into dry land. The waters were divided, ²²and the Israelites went through the sea on dry ground, with a wall of water on their right and on their left.

²³The Egyptians pursued them, and all Pharaoh's horses and chariots and horsemen followed them into the sea. ²⁴During the last watch of the night the LORD looked down from the pillar of fire and cloud at the Egyptian army and threw it into confusion. ²⁵He made the wheels of their chariots come off[a] so that they had difficulty driving. And the Egyptians said, "Let's get away from the Israelites! The LORD is fighting for them against Egypt."

²⁶Then the LORD said to Moses, "Stretch out your hand over the sea so that the waters may flow back over the Egyptians and their chariots and horsemen." ²⁷Moses stretched out his hand over the sea, and at daybreak the sea went back to its place. The Egyptians were fleeing toward[b] it, and the LORD swept them into the sea. ²⁸The water flowed back and covered the chariots and horsemen—the entire army of Pharaoh that had followed

the Israelites into the sea. Not one of them survived.

²⁹But the Israelites went through the sea on dry ground, with a wall of water on their right and on their left. ³⁰That day the LORD saved Israel from the hands of the Egyptians, and Israel saw the Egyptians lying dead on the shore. ³¹And when the Israelites saw the great power the LORD displayed against the Egyptians, the people feared the LORD and put their trust in him and in Moses his servant.

The Song of Moses and Miriam

15 Then Moses and the Israelites sang this song to the LORD:

"I will sing to the LORD,
  for he is highly exalted.
The horse and its rider
  he has hurled into the sea.
²The LORD is my strength and my
    song;
  he has become my salvation.
He is my God, and I will praise him,
  my father's God, and I will exalt
    him.
³The LORD is a warrior;
  the LORD is his name.
⁴Pharaoh's chariots and his army
  he has hurled into the sea.
The best of Pharaoh's officers
  are drowned in the Red Sea.[c]
⁵The deep waters have covered them;
  they sank to the depths like a stone.

⁶"Your right hand, O LORD,
  was majestic in power.
Your right hand, O LORD,
  shattered the enemy.
⁷In the greatness of your majesty
  you threw down those who
    opposed you.
You unleashed your burning anger;
  it consumed them like stubble.
⁸By the blast of your nostrils
  the waters piled up.
The surging waters stood firm like a
    wall;

---

[a] 25 Or *He jammed the wheels of their chariots* (see Samaritan Pentateuch, Septuagint and Syriac)   [b] 27 Or *from*   [c] 4 Hebrew *Yam Suph*; that is, Sea of Reeds; also in verse 22

the deep waters congealed in the
heart of the sea.
9 "The enemy boasted,
'I will pursue, I will overtake them.
I will divide the spoils;
I will gorge myself on them.
I will draw my sword
and my hand will destroy them.'
10 But you blew with your breath,
and the sea covered them.
They sank like lead
in the mighty waters.
11 "Who among the gods is like you,
O Lord?
Who is like you—
majestic in holiness,
awesome in glory,
working wonders?
12 You stretched out your right hand
and the earth swallowed them.

13 "In your unfailing love you will lead
the people you have redeemed.
In your strength you will guide
them
to your holy dwelling.
14 The nations will hear and tremble;
anguish will grip the people of
Philistia.
15 The chiefs of Edom will be terrified,
the leaders of Moab will be seized
with trembling,
the people[a] of Canaan will melt away;
16   terror and dread will fall upon
them.
By the power of your arm
they will be as still as a stone—
until your people pass by, O Lord,
until the people you bought[b] pass
by.
17 You will bring them in and plant
them
on the mountain of your
inheritance—
the place, O Lord, you made for
your dwelling,
the sanctuary, O Lord, your hands
established.

18 The Lord will reign
for ever and ever."

19 When Pharaoh's horses, chariots and
horsemen[c] went into the sea, the Lord
brought the waters of the sea back over
them, but the Israelites walked through
the sea on dry ground. 20 Then Miriam
the prophetess, Aaron's sister, took a tambourine in her hand, and all the women
followed her, with tambourines and dancing. 21 Miriam sang to them:

"Sing to the Lord,
for he is highly exalted.
The horse and its rider
he has hurled into the sea."

The Waters of Marah and Elim

22 Then Moses led Israel from the Red
Sea and they went into the Desert of
Shur. For three days they traveled in the
desert without finding water. 23 When
they came to Marah, they could not
drink its water because it was bitter.
(That is why the place is called Marah.[d])
24 So the people grumbled against Moses,
saying, "What are we to drink?"

25 Then Moses cried out to the Lord,
and the Lord showed him a piece of
wood. He threw it into the water, and
the water became sweet.

There the Lord made a decree and a
law for them, and there he tested them.
26 He said, "If you listen carefully to the
voice of the Lord your God and do what
is right in his eyes, if you pay attention to
his commands and keep all his decrees, I
will not bring on you any of the diseases
I brought on the Egyptians, for I am the
Lord, who heals you."

Praying Exodus 15:26
Thank You, Lord, for being my Healer.

27 Then they came to Elim, where there
were twelve springs and seventy palm
trees, and they camped there near the water.

---

a 15 Or rulers   b 16 Or created   c 19 Or charioteers   d 23 Marah means bitter.

Manna and Quail

16 The whole Israelite community set out from Elim and came to the Desert of Sin, which is between Elim and Sinai, on the fifteenth day of the second month after they had come out of Egypt. ²In the desert the whole community grumbled against Moses and Aaron. ³The Israelites said to them, "If only we had died by the LORD's hand in Egypt! There we sat around pots of meat and ate all the food we wanted, but you have brought us out into this desert to starve this entire assembly to death."

⁴Then the LORD said to Moses, "I will rain down bread from heaven for you. The people are to go out each day and gather enough for that day. In this way I will test them and see whether they will follow my instructions. ⁵On the sixth day they are to prepare what they bring in, and that is to be twice as much as they gather on the other days."

⁶So Moses and Aaron said to all the Israelites, "In the evening you will know that it was the LORD who brought you out of Egypt, ⁷and in the morning you will see the glory of the LORD, because he has heard your grumbling against him. Who are we, that you should grumble against us?" ⁸Moses also said, "You will know that it was the LORD when he gives you meat to eat in the evening and all the bread you want in the morning, because he has heard your grumbling against him. Who are we? You are not grumbling against us, but against the LORD."

⁹Then Moses told Aaron, "Say to the entire Israelite community, 'Come before the LORD, for he has heard your grumbling.'"

¹⁰While Aaron was speaking to the whole Israelite community, they looked toward the desert, and there was the glory of the LORD appearing in the cloud.

¹¹The LORD said to Moses, ¹²"I have heard the grumbling of the Israelites. Tell them, 'At twilight you will eat meat, and in the morning you will be filled with bread. Then you will know that I am the LORD your God.'"

¹³That evening quail came and covered the camp, and in the morning there was a layer of dew around the camp. ¹⁴When the dew was gone, thin flakes like frost on the ground appeared on the desert floor. ¹⁵When the Israelites saw it, they said to each other, "What is it?" For they did not know what it was.

Moses said to them, "It is the bread the LORD has given you to eat. ¹⁶This is what the LORD has commanded: 'Each one is to gather as much as he needs. Take an omerᵃ for each person you have in your tent.'"

¹⁷The Israelites did as they were told; some gathered much, some little. ¹⁸And when they measured it by the omer, he who gathered much did not have too much, and he who gathered little did not have too little. Each one gathered as much as he needed.

¹⁹Then Moses said to them, "No one is to keep any of it until morning."

²⁰However, some of them paid no attention to Moses; they kept part of it until morning, but it was full of maggots and began to smell. So Moses was angry with them.

²¹Each morning everyone gathered as much as he needed, and when the sun grew hot, it melted away. ²²On the sixth day, they gathered twice as much—two omersᵇ for each person—and the leaders of the community came and reported this to Moses. ²³He said to them, "This is what the LORD commanded: 'Tomorrow is to be a day of rest, a holy Sabbath to the LORD. So bake what you want to bake and boil what you want to boil. Save whatever is left and keep it until morning.'"

²⁴So they saved it until morning, as Moses commanded, and it did not stink

ᵃ 16 That is, probably about 2 quarts (about 2 liters); also in verses 18, 32, 33 and 36   ᵇ 22 That is, probably about 4 quarts (about 4.5 liters) or get maggots in it. ²⁵"Eat it today," Moses said, "because today is a Sabbath to the LORD. You will not find any of it on the ground today. ²⁶Six days you are to gather it, but on the seventh day, the Sabbath, there will not be any."

²⁷Nevertheless, some of the people went out on the seventh day to gather it, but they found none. ²⁸Then the LORD said to Moses, "How long will you[a] refuse to keep my commands and my instructions? ²⁹Bear in mind that the LORD has given you the Sabbath; that is why on the sixth day he gives you bread for two days. Everyone is to stay where he is on the seventh day; no one is to go out." ³⁰So the people rested on the seventh day.

³¹The people of Israel called the bread manna.[b] It was white like coriander seed and tasted like wafers made with honey. ³²Moses said, "This is what the LORD has commanded: 'Take an omer of manna and keep it for the generations to come, so they can see the bread I gave you to eat in the desert when I brought you out of Egypt.'"

³³So Moses said to Aaron, "Take a jar and put an omer of manna in it. Then place it before the LORD to be kept for the generations to come."

³⁴As the LORD commanded Moses, Aaron put the manna in front of the Testimony, that it might be kept. ³⁵The Israelites ate manna forty years, until they came to a land that was settled; they ate manna until they reached the border of Canaan.

³⁶(An omer is one tenth of an ephah.)

Water From the Rock

17 The whole Israelite community set out from the Desert of Sin, traveling from place to place as the LORD commanded. They camped at Rephidim, but there was no water for the people to drink. ²So they quarreled with Moses and said, "Give us water to drink."

Moses replied, "Why do you quarrel with me? Why do you put the LORD to the test?"

³But the people were thirsty for water there, and they grumbled against Moses. They said, "Why did you bring us up out of Egypt to make us and our children and livestock die of thirst?"

⁴Then Moses cried out to the LORD, "What am I to do with these people? They are almost ready to stone me."

⁵The LORD answered Moses, "Walk on ahead of the people. Take with you some of the elders of Israel and take in your hand the staff with which you struck the Nile, and go. ⁶I will stand there before you by the rock at Horeb. Strike the rock, and water will come out of it for the people to drink." So Moses did this in the sight of the elders of Israel. ⁷And he called the place Massah[c] and Meribah[d] because the Israelites quarreled and because they tested the LORD saying, "Is the LORD among us or not?"

The Amalekites Defeated

⁸The Amalekites came and attacked the Israelites at Rephidim. ⁹Moses said to Joshua, "Choose some of our men and go out to fight the Amalekites. Tomorrow I will stand on top of the hill with the staff of God in my hands."

¹⁰So Joshua fought the Amalekites as Moses had ordered, and Moses, Aaron and Hur went to the top of the hill. ¹¹As long as Moses held up his hands, the Israelites were winning, but whenever he lowered his hands, the Amalekites were winning. ¹²When Moses' hands grew tired, they took a stone and put it under him and he sat on it. Aaron and Hur held his hands up—one on one side, one on the other—so that his hands remained steady till sunset. ¹³So Joshua overcame the Amalekite army with the sword.

¹⁴Then the LORD said to Moses, "Write this on a scroll as something to be remembered and make sure that Joshua hears it, because I will completely blot out the

---

[a] *28* The Hebrew is plural.   [b] *31 Manna* means *What is it?* (see verse 15).   [c] *7 Massah* means *testing.*   [d] *7 Meribah* means *quarreling.*

memory of Amalek from under heaven."
¹⁵Moses built an altar and called it The
LORD is my Banner. ¹⁶He said, "For hands
were lifted up to the throne of the LORD.
Theᵃ LORD will be at war against the Amalekites from generation to generation."

Jethro Visits Moses

18 Now Jethro, the priest of Midian
and father-in-law of Moses, heard
of everything God had done for Moses
and for his people Israel, and how the
LORD had brought Israel out of Egypt.

²After Moses had sent away his wife
Zipporah, his father-in-law Jethro received her ³and her two sons. One son
was named Gershom,ᵇ for Moses said, "I
have become an alien in a foreign land";
⁴and the other was named Eliezer,ᶜ for he
said, "My father's God was my helper; he
saved me from the sword of Pharaoh."

⁵Jethro, Moses' father-in-law, together
with Moses' sons and wife, came to him
in the desert, where he was camped
near the mountain of God. ⁶Jethro had
sent word to him, "I, your father-in-law
Jethro, am coming to you with your wife
and her two sons."

⁷So Moses went out to meet his father-
in-law and bowed down and kissed him.
They greeted each other and then went
into the tent. ⁸Moses told his father-in-
law about everything the LORD had done
to Pharaoh and the Egyptians for Israel's
sake and about all the hardships they had
met along the way and how the LORD
had saved them.

⁹Jethro was delighted to hear about all
the good things the LORD had done for
Israel in rescuing them from the hand
of the Egyptians. ¹⁰He said, "Praise be
to the LORD, who rescued you from the
hand of the Egyptians and of Pharaoh, and
who rescued the people from the hand
of the Egyptians. ¹¹Now I know that
the LORD is greater than all other gods,
for he did this to those who had treated
Israel arrogantly." ¹²Then Jethro, Moses'
father-in-law, brought a burnt offering
and other sacrifices to God, and Aaron
came with all the elders of Israel to eat
bread with Moses' father-in-law in the
presence of God.

¹³The next day Moses took his seat to
serve as judge for the people, and they
stood around him from morning till evening. ¹⁴When his father-in-law saw all
that Moses was doing for the people, he
said, "What is this you are doing for the
people? Why do you alone sit as judge,
while all these people stand around you
from morning till evening?"

¹⁵Moses answered him, "Because the
people come to me to seek God's will.
¹⁶Whenever they have a dispute, it is
brought to me, and I decide between the
parties and inform them of God's decrees
and laws."

¹⁷Moses' father-in-law replied, "What
you are doing is not good. ¹⁸You and
these people who come to you will only
wear yourselves out. The work is too
heavy for you; you cannot handle it alone.
¹⁹Listen now to me and I will give you
some advice, and may God be with you.
You must be the people's representative
before God and bring their disputes to
him. ²⁰Teach them the decrees and laws,
and show them the way to live and the
duties they are to perform. ²¹But select
capable men from all the people—men
who fear God, trustworthy men who
hate dishonest gain—and appoint them
as officials over thousands, hundreds, fifties and tens. ²²Have them serve as judges
for the people at all times, but have them
bring every difficult case to you; the simple cases they can decide themselves. That
will make your load lighter, because they
will share it with you. ²³If you do this and
God so commands, you will be able to
stand the strain, and all these people will
go home satisfied."

²⁴Moses listened to his father-in-law
and did everything he said. ²⁵He chose

ᵃ *16 Or "Because a hand was against the throne of the LORD, the* ᵇ*3 Gershom sounds like the Hebrew for an alien there.*
ᶜ*4 Eliezer means my God is helper.*

Going Directly to God

READ AND CONSIDER: EXODUS 19:3-8

"So Moses went back and summoned the elders of the people and set before them all the words the LORD had commanded him to speak" (Exodus 19:7).

An intermediary is someone who acts as an agent between two different parties: a go-between, a mediator. As this passage reveals, mediation in the form of intercession was clearly a big part of Moses' role as leader of the nation of Israel. God specifically told him what to say to the people of Israel, and in turn, Moses brought their answer back to the Lord.

Throughout history, various religions have taught that people can only approach God through the intervention of a human mediator. This was also true for the Jewish people during the times recorded in the Old Testament. The people could not approach God directly. Prophets such as Elijah and Elisha arose to speak for the Lord. Kings wouldn't go off to war without consulting a prophet, who also functioned as a mediator or intercessor. This veil between God and humanity was symbolized by the thick, heavy curtain that hung in the Most Holy Place in the tabernacle and later in the temple—a barrier between a holy God and sinful human beings that only priests especially anointed for the task could pass through.

With the crucifixion of Jesus Christ, however, all that changed. At the moment of Christ's death, the curtain in the temple was torn in two (Mark 15:38), representing the dramatic reality that there was no longer any obstruction between God and mankind. When you fully grasp this truth, it will change your life. You do not need the presence of a human intermediary to take your prayers and concerns to your heavenly Father. Instead, Hebrews tells us that we can "approach the throne of grace with confidence, so that we may receive mercy and find grace to help us in our time of need" (Hebrews 4:16).

Jesus is your great High Priest—the only mediator you will ever need. "For there is one God and one mediator between God and men, the man Christ Jesus, who gave himself as a ransom for all men" (1 Timothy 2:5-6).

Nothing is wrong with asking others to pray for and with you, but don't hesitate to take the concerns of your heart directly to God. He is waiting!

capable men from all Israel and made them leaders of the people, officials over thousands, hundreds, fifties and tens. ²⁶They served as judges for the people at all times. The difficult cases they brought to Moses, but the simple ones they decided themselves.

²⁷Then Moses sent his father-in-law on his way, and Jethro returned to his own country.

At Mount Sinai

19 In the third month after the Israelites left Egypt—on the very day—they came to the Desert of Sinai.

²After they set out from Rephidim, they entered the Desert of Sinai, and Israel camped there in the desert in front of the mountain.

³Then Moses went up to God, and the LORD called to him from the mountain and said, "This is what you are to say to the house of Jacob and what you are to tell the people of Israel: ⁴'You yourselves have seen what I did to Egypt, and how I carried you on eagles' wings and brought you to myself. ⁵Now if you obey me fully and keep my covenant, then out of all nations you will be my treasured possession. Although the whole earth is mine,

⁶you[a] will be for me a kingdom of priests and a holy nation.' These are the words you are to speak to the Israelites."

⁷So Moses went back and summoned the elders of the people and set before them all the words the LORD had commanded him to speak. ⁸The people all responded together, "We will do everything the LORD has said." So Moses brought their answer back to the LORD.

⁹The LORD said to Moses, "I am going to come to you in a dense cloud, so that the people will hear me speaking with you and will always put their trust in you." Then Moses told the LORD what the people had said.

¹⁰And the LORD said to Moses, "Go to the people and consecrate them today and tomorrow. Have them wash their clothes ¹¹and be ready by the third day, because on that day the LORD will come down on Mount Sinai in the sight of all the people. ¹²Put limits for the people around the mountain and tell them, 'Be careful that you do not go up the mountain or touch the foot of it. Whoever touches the mountain shall surely be put to death. ¹³He shall surely be stoned or shot with arrows; not a hand is to be laid on him. Whether man or animal, he shall not be permitted to live.' Only when the ram's horn sounds a long blast may they go up to the mountain."

¹⁴After Moses had gone down the mountain to the people, he consecrated them, and they washed their clothes. ¹⁵Then he said to the people, "Prepare yourselves for the third day. Abstain from sexual relations."

¹⁶On the morning of the third day there was thunder and lightning, with a thick cloud over the mountain, and a very loud trumpet blast. Everyone in the camp trembled. ¹⁷Then Moses led the people out of the camp to meet with God, and they stood at the foot of the mountain. ¹⁸Mount Sinai was covered with smoke, because the LORD descended on it in fire. The smoke billowed up from it like smoke from a furnace, the whole mountain[b] trembled violently, ¹⁹and the sound of the trumpet grew louder and louder. Then Moses spoke and the voice of God answered him.[c]

²⁰The LORD descended to the top of Mount Sinai and called Moses to the top of the mountain. So Moses went up ²¹and the LORD said to him, "Go down and warn the people so they do not force their way through to see the LORD and many of them perish. ²²Even the priests, who approach the LORD, must consecrate themselves, or the LORD will break out against them."

²³Moses said to the LORD, "The people cannot come up Mount Sinai, because you yourself warned us, 'Put limits around the mountain and set it apart as holy.'"

²⁴The LORD replied, "Go down and bring Aaron up with you. But the priests and the people must not force their way through to come up to the LORD, or he will break out against them."

²⁵So Moses went down to the people and told them.

The Ten Commandments

20 And God spoke all these words:

²"I am the LORD your God, who brought you out of Egypt, out of the land of slavery.

³"You shall have no other gods before[d] me.

⁴"You shall not make for yourself an idol in the form of anything in heaven above or on the earth beneath or in the waters below. ⁵You shall not bow down to them or worship them; for I, the LORD your God, am a jealous God, punishing the children for the sin of the fathers to the third and fourth generation of those who hate me, ⁶but showing love

---

[a] 5,6 Or *possession, for the whole earth is mine.* [b] *You*   [b] 18 Most Hebrew manuscripts; a few Hebrew manuscripts and Septuagint *all the people*   [c] 19 Or *and God answered him with thunder*   [d] 3 Or *besides*

Your Top Priority

We can't live successfully without right priorities in our lives. Yet some of us try to do that every day. Correct priorities are not something we can figure out on our own. We have to be led by the Holy Spirit and have a clear knowledge of God's Word in order to understand what they should be.

Our two most important priorities come directly from the Word of God. Jesus told us about them saying, " 'Love the Lord your God with all your heart and with all your soul and with all your mind.' This is the first and greatest commandment. And the second is like it: 'Love your neighbor as yourself' " (Matthew 22:37-39). If you maintain these two top priorities—love God and love others—they will guide you in setting all the other priorities in your life.

Your relationship with the Lord must always have top priority over everything else. The Lord said, "You shall have no other gods before me" (Exodus 20:3), and He means it. God wants your *undivided* attention. When you seek Him first every day and ask Him to help you put your life in order, He will do that. I know from experience, and I'm sure you do too, that when we don't seek God first, our lives get out of control. As a result, our lives start ruling *us* instead of us being in charge of *them*.

God is a God of order. We can tell that by looking at the universe. None of it is random or accidental. He doesn't want our lives to be either. His will is that "everything should be done in a fitting and orderly way" (1 Corinthians 14:40). And when we pray to Him about it, He will help us do just that. He will show us how to align ourselves under proper authority so that we can come under the covering of His protection. This is crucial to our moving into all God has for us.

The Bible says we should submit to authority figures designated by God in our church, in our family, in our work, and in our government. To be in right order and have our lives work well, we need to be planted in a church home. It gives us a base of operation. We can't get as far as God wants us to go without it.

We also all need a pastor, a strong Christian leader, or a mentor speaking truth into our lives. God will help you discern who that is. This is not a case for having a guru. The spiritual authority in your life is God's *messenger,* not a person to be worshiped instead of God. This is about having someone in your life to speak truth to you in love and cover you in prayer.

Beyond your submission to God and your submission to other designated authorities in your life, you must be in right relationship to other people: "Submit to one another out of reverence for Christ" (Ephesians 5:21). Submission to others takes a heart that loves others as ourselves. That's the key. When you love God first and others second, all the other priorities in your life will fall into place and you will be in right order. When you ask God to show you clearly what your priorities should be, He will.

For the next "From Stormie's Heart" article, go to page 115.

to a thousand ⌊generations⌋ of those who love me and keep my commandments.

7 "You shall not misuse the name of the LORD your God, for the LORD will not hold anyone guiltless who misuses his name.

8 "Remember the Sabbath day by keeping it holy. 9Six days you shall labor and do all your work, 10but the seventh day is a Sabbath to the LORD your God. On it you shall not do any work, neither you, nor your son or daughter, nor your manservant or maidservant, nor your animals, nor the alien within your gates. 11For in six days the LORD made the heavens and the earth, the sea, and all that is in them, but he rested on the seventh day. Therefore the LORD blessed the Sabbath day and made it holy.

12 "Honor your father and your mother, so that you may live long in the land the LORD your God is giving you.

13 "You shall not murder.

Praying Exodus 20:1-17

Father God, write Your commandments on the tablets of my heart so that I will always remember to obey them.

14 "You shall not commit adultery.

15 "You shall not steal.

16 "You shall not give false testimony against your neighbor.

17 "You shall not covet your neighbor's house. You shall not covet your neighbor's wife, or his manservant or maidservant, his ox or donkey, or anything that belongs to your neighbor."

18When the people saw the thunder and lightning and heard the trumpet and saw the mountain in smoke, they trembled with fear. They stayed at a distance 19and said to Moses, "Speak to us yourself and we will listen. But do not have God speak to us or we will die."

20Moses said to the people, "Do not be afraid. God has come to test you, so that the fear of God will be with you to keep you from sinning."

21The people remained at a distance, while Moses approached the thick darkness where God was.

Idols and Altars

22Then the LORD said to Moses, "Tell the Israelites this: 'You have seen for yourselves that I have spoken to you from heaven: 23Do not make any gods to be alongside me; do not make for yourselves gods of silver or gods of gold.

24 " 'Make an altar of earth for me and sacrifice on it your burnt offerings and fellowship offerings,ᵃ your sheep and goats and your cattle. Wherever I cause my name to be honored, I will come to you and bless you. 25If you make an altar of stones for me, do not build it with dressed stones, for you will defile it if you use a tool on it. 26And do not go up to my altar on steps, lest your nakedness be exposed on it.'

21 "These are the laws you are to set before them:

Hebrew Servants

2"If you buy a Hebrew servant, he is to serve you for six years. But in the seventh year, he shall go free, without paying anything. 3If he comes alone, he is to go free alone; but if he has a wife when he comes, she is to go with him. 4If his master gives him a wife and she bears him sons or daughters, the woman and her children shall belong to her master, and only the man shall go free.

5"But if the servant declares, 'I love my master and my wife and children and do not want to go free,' 6then his master

ᵃ 24 Traditionally *peace offerings*

must take him before the judges.[a] He shall take him to the door or the doorpost and pierce his ear with an awl. Then he will be his servant for life.

7"If a man sells his daughter as a servant, she is not to go free as menservants do. 8If she does not please the master who has selected her for himself,[b] he must let her be redeemed. He has no right to sell her to foreigners, because he has broken faith with her. 9If he selects her for his son, he must grant her the rights of a daughter. 10If he marries another woman, he must not deprive the first one of her food, clothing and marital rights. 11If he does not provide her with these three things, she is to go free, without any payment of money.

Personal Injuries

12"Anyone who strikes a man and kills him shall surely be put to death. 13However, if he does not do it intentionally, but God lets it happen, he is to flee to a place I will designate. 14But if a man schemes and kills another man deliberately, take him away from my altar and put him to death.

15"Anyone who attacks[c] his father or his mother must be put to death.

16"Anyone who kidnaps another and either sells him or still has him when he is caught must be put to death.

17"Anyone who curses his father or mother must be put to death.

18"If men quarrel and one hits the other with a stone or with his fist[d] and he does not die but is confined to bed, 19the one who struck the blow will not be held responsible if the other gets up and walks around outside with his staff; however, he must pay the injured man for the loss of his time and see that he is completely healed.

20"If a man beats his male or female slave with a rod and the slave dies as a direct result, he must be punished, 21but he is not to be punished if the slave gets up after a day or two, since the slave is his property.

22"If men who are fighting hit a pregnant woman and she gives birth prematurely[e] but there is no serious injury, the offender must be fined whatever the woman's husband demands and the court allows. 23But if there is serious injury, you are to take life for life, 24eye for eye, tooth for tooth, hand for hand, foot for foot, 25burn for burn, wound for wound, bruise for bruise.

26"If a man hits a manservant or maidservant in the eye and destroys it, he must let the servant go free to compensate for the eye. 27And if he knocks out the tooth of a manservant or maidservant, he must let the servant go free to compensate for the tooth.

28"If a bull gores a man or a woman to death, the bull must be stoned to death, and its meat must not be eaten. But the owner of the bull will not be held responsible. 29If, however, the bull has had the habit of goring and the owner has been warned but has not kept it penned up and it kills a man or woman, the bull must be stoned and the owner also must be put to death. 30However, if payment is demanded of him, he may redeem his life by paying whatever is demanded. 31This law also applies if the bull gores a son or daughter. 32If the bull gores a male or female slave, the owner must pay thirty shekels[f] of silver to the master of the slave, and the bull must be stoned.

33"If a man uncovers a pit or digs one and fails to cover it and an ox or a donkey falls into it, 34the owner of the pit must pay for the loss; he must pay its owner, and the dead animal will be his.

35"If a man's bull injures the bull of another and it dies, they are to sell the live one and divide both the money and the dead animal equally. 36However, if it was known that the bull had the habit of goring, yet the owner did not keep it penned up, the owner must pay, animal for animal, and the dead animal will be his.

---

a 6 Or before God   b 8 Or master so that he does not choose her   c 15 Or kills   d 18 Or with a tool   e 22 Or she has a miscarriage   f 32 That is, about 12 ounces (about 0.3 kilogram)

Protection of Property

22 "If a man steals an ox or a sheep and slaughters it or sells it, he must pay back five head of cattle for the ox and four sheep for the sheep.

²"If a thief is caught breaking in and is struck so that he dies, the defender is not guilty of bloodshed; ³but if it happens[a] after sunrise, he is guilty of bloodshed.

"A thief must certainly make restitution, but if he has nothing, he must be sold to pay for his theft.

⁴"If the stolen animal is found alive in his possession—whether ox or donkey or sheep—he must pay back double.

⁵"If a man grazes his livestock in a field or vineyard and lets them stray and they graze in another man's field, he must make restitution from the best of his own field or vineyard.

⁶"If a fire breaks out and spreads into thornbushes so that it burns shocks of grain or standing grain or the whole field, the one who started the fire must make restitution.

⁷"If a man gives his neighbor silver or goods for safekeeping and they are stolen from the neighbor's house, the thief, if he is caught, must pay back double. ⁸But if the thief is not found, the owner of the house must appear before the judges[b] to determine whether he has laid his hands on the other man's property. ⁹In all cases of illegal possession of an ox, a donkey, a sheep, a garment, or any other lost property about which somebody says, 'This is mine,' both parties are to bring their cases before the judges. The one whom the judges declare[c] guilty must pay back double to his neighbor.

¹⁰"If a man gives a donkey, an ox, a sheep or any other animal to his neighbor for safekeeping and it dies or is injured or is taken away while no one is looking, ¹¹the issue between them will be settled by the taking of an oath before the LORD that the neighbor did not lay hands on the other person's property. The owner is to accept this, and no restitution is required. ¹²But if the animal was stolen from the neighbor, he must make restitution to the owner. ¹³If it was torn to pieces by a wild animal, he shall bring in the remains as evidence and he will not be required to pay for the torn animal.

¹⁴"If a man borrows an animal from his neighbor and it is injured or dies while the owner is not present, he must make restitution. ¹⁵But if the owner is with the animal, the borrower will not have to pay. If the animal was hired, the money paid for the hire covers the loss.

Social Responsibility

¹⁶"If a man seduces a virgin who is not pledged to be married and sleeps with her, he must pay the bride-price, and she shall be his wife. ¹⁷If her father absolutely refuses to give her to him, he must still pay the bride-price for virgins.

¹⁸"Do not allow a sorceress to live.

¹⁹"Anyone who has sexual relations with an animal must be put to death.

²⁰"Whoever sacrifices to any god other than the LORD must be destroyed.[d]

²¹"Do not mistreat an alien or oppress him, for you were aliens in Egypt.

²²"Do not take advantage of a widow or an orphan. ²³If you do and they cry out to me, I will certainly hear their cry. ²⁴My anger will be aroused, and I will kill you with the sword; your wives will become widows and your children fatherless.

²⁵"If you lend money to one of my people among you who is needy, do not be like a moneylender; charge him no interest.[e] ²⁶If you take your neighbor's cloak as a pledge, return it to him by sunset, ²⁷because his cloak is the only covering he has for his body. What else will he sleep in? When he cries out to me, I will hear, for I am compassionate.

²⁸"Do not blaspheme God[f] or curse the ruler of your people.

---

[a] *3* Or *if he strikes him*   [b] *8* Or *before God*; also in verse 9   [c] *9* Or *whom God declares*   [d] *20* The Hebrew term refers to the irrevocable giving over of things or persons to the LORD, often by totally destroying them.   [e] *25* Or *excessive interest*
[f] *28* Or *Do not revile the judges*

²⁹"Do not hold back offerings from your granaries or your vats.^a

"You must give me the firstborn of your sons. ³⁰Do the same with your cattle and your sheep. Let them stay with their mothers for seven days, but give them to me on the eighth day.

³¹"You are to be my holy people. So do not eat the meat of an animal torn by wild beasts; throw it to the dogs.

Laws of Justice and Mercy

23 "Do not spread false reports. Do not help a wicked man by being a malicious witness.

²"Do not follow the crowd in doing wrong. When you give testimony in a lawsuit, do not pervert justice by siding with the crowd, ³and do not show favoritism to a poor man in his lawsuit.

⁴"If you come across your enemy's ox or donkey wandering off, be sure to take it back to him. ⁵If you see the donkey of someone who hates you fallen down under its load, do not leave it there; be sure you help him with it.

⁶"Do not deny justice to your poor people in their lawsuits. ⁷Have nothing to do with a false charge and do not put an innocent or honest person to death, for I will not acquit the guilty.

⁸"Do not accept a bribe, for a bribe blinds those who see and twists the words of the righteous.

⁹"Do not oppress an alien; you yourselves know how it feels to be aliens, because you were aliens in Egypt.

Sabbath Laws

¹⁰"For six years you are to sow your fields and harvest the crops, ¹¹but during the seventh year let the land lie unplowed and unused. Then the poor among your people may get food from it, and the wild animals may eat what they leave. Do the same with your vineyard and your olive grove.

¹²"Six days do your work, but on the seventh day do not work, so that your ox and your donkey may rest and the slave born in your household, and the alien as well, may be refreshed.

¹³"Be careful to do everything I have said to you. Do not invoke the names of other gods; do not let them be heard on your lips.

The Three Annual Festivals

¹⁴"Three times a year you are to celebrate a festival to me.

¹⁵"Celebrate the Feast of Unleavened Bread; for seven days eat bread made without yeast, as I commanded you. Do this at the appointed time in the month of Abib, for in that month you came out of Egypt.

"No one is to appear before me empty-handed.

¹⁶"Celebrate the Feast of Harvest with the firstfruits of the crops you sow in your field.

"Celebrate the Feast of Ingathering at the end of the year, when you gather in your crops from the field.

¹⁷"Three times a year all the men are to appear before the Sovereign LORD.

¹⁸"Do not offer the blood of a sacrifice to me along with anything containing yeast.

"The fat of my festival offerings must not be kept until morning.

¹⁹"Bring the best of the firstfruits of your soil to the house of the LORD your God.

"Do not cook a young goat in its mother's milk.

God's Angel to Prepare the Way

²⁰"See, I am sending an angel ahead of you to guard you along the way and to bring you to the place I have prepared. ²¹Pay attention to him and listen to what he says. Do not rebel against him; he will not forgive your rebellion, since my Name is in him. ²²If you listen carefully to what he says and do all that I say, I will be an enemy to your enemies and will oppose those who oppose you. ²³My angel

---

^a *29* The meaning of the Hebrew for this phrase is uncertain.

The Power of Little by Little

GOING deeper

READ AND CONSIDER: EXODUS 23:20-30

"Little by little I will drive them out before you, until you have increased enough to take possession of the land" (Exodus 23:30).

Have you ever asked God to do something major in your life, and then experienced disappointment when He appeared to be working little by little rather than all at once?

Perhaps you have a lifestyle habit that you know is unhealthy. You've asked God to remove those persistent physical urges, but you grow discouraged when the progress you're making seems insignificant. Or maybe, like the Israelites, you are coming under attack from adversaries who seem intent on your personal or professional destruction. Why doesn't God, who certainly has the power, give us victory instantaneously or wipe out the enemies that cause so much harm?

There are no simple answers, but this passage provides an important clue about the nature of God's activity on our behalf: He is going by His timetable, not ours, and His will for us is determined by what is ultimately best for us. Scripture tells us that "with the Lord a day is like a thousand years, and a thousand years are like a day. The Lord is not slow in keeping his promise, as some understand slowness. He is patient with you" (2 Peter 3:8-9). Our loving heavenly Father is working for our eternal good, but He is accomplishing His purpose in our lives in His own perfect way and in His own time. God knows that these little steps are better for us now. He doesn't want us to be overtaken by the things that could happen if we experience victory too quickly.

Be encouraged when your prayers reveal progress that can be measured even in the tiniest increments. God is at work in your life and in the lives of those around you, and before long, little by little will add up to major change.

will go ahead of you and bring you into the land of the Amorites, Hittites, Perizzites, Canaanites, Hivites and Jebusites, and I will wipe them out. ²⁴Do not bow down before their gods or worship them or follow their practices. You must demolish them and break their sacred stones to pieces. ²⁵Worship the LORD your God, and his blessing will be on your food and water. I will take away sickness from among you, ²⁶and none will miscarry or be barren in your land. I will give you a full life span.

²⁷"I will send my terror ahead of you and throw into confusion every nation you encounter. I will make all your enemies turn their backs and run. ²⁸I will send the hornet ahead of you to drive the Hivites, Canaanites and Hittites out of your way. ²⁹But I will not drive them out in a single year, because the land would become desolate and the wild animals too numerous for you. ³⁰Little by little I will drive them out before you, until you have increased enough to take possession of the land.

Praying Exodus 23:25-30
Lord, thank You for blessing my food and water and protecting me from sickness.

³¹"I will establish your borders from the Red Sea[a] to the Sea of the Philistines,[b] and from the desert to the River.[c] I will hand over to you the people who live in the land and you will drive them

out before you. 32Do not make a covenant with them or with their gods. 33Do not let them live in your land, or they will cause you to sin against me, because the worship of their gods will certainly be a snare to you."

The Covenant Confirmed

24 Then he said to Moses, "Come up to the LORD, you and Aaron, Nadab and Abihu, and seventy of the elders of Israel. You are to worship at a distance, 2but Moses alone is to approach the LORD; the others must not come near. And the people may not come up with him."

3When Moses went and told the people all the LORD's words and laws, they responded with one voice, "Everything the LORD has said we will do." 4Moses then wrote down everything the LORD had said.

He got up early the next morning and built an altar at the foot of the mountain and set up twelve stone pillars representing the twelve tribes of Israel. 5Then he sent young Israelite men, and they offered burnt offerings and sacrificed young bulls as fellowship offerings[a] to the LORD. 6Moses took half of the blood and put it in bowls, and the other half he sprinkled on the altar. 7Then he took the Book of the Covenant and read it to the people. They responded, "We will do everything the LORD has said; we will obey."

8Moses then took the blood, sprinkled it on the people and said, "This is the blood of the covenant that the LORD has made with you in accordance with all these words."

9Moses and Aaron, Nadab and Abihu, and the seventy elders of Israel went up 10and saw the God of Israel. Under his feet was something like a pavement made of sapphire,[b] clear as the sky itself. 11But God did not raise his hand against these leaders of the Israelites; they saw God, and they ate and drank.

12The LORD said to Moses, "Come up to me on the mountain and stay here, and I will give you the tablets of stone, with the law and commands I have written for their instruction."

13Then Moses set out with Joshua his aide, and Moses went up on the mountain of God. 14He said to the elders, "Wait here for us until we come back to you. Aaron and Hur are with you, and anyone involved in a dispute can go to them."

15When Moses went up on the mountain, the cloud covered it, 16and the glory of the LORD settled on Mount Sinai. For six days the cloud covered the mountain, and on the seventh day the LORD called to Moses from within the cloud. 17To the Israelites the glory of the LORD looked like a consuming fire on top of the mountain. 18Then Moses entered the cloud as he went on up the mountain. And he stayed on the mountain forty days and forty nights.

Offerings for the Tabernacle

25 The LORD said to Moses, 2"Tell the Israelites to bring me an offering. You are to receive the offering for me from each man whose heart prompts him to give. 3These are the offerings you are to receive from them: gold, silver and bronze; 4blue, purple and scarlet yarn and fine linen; goat hair; 5ram skins dyed red and hides of sea cows[c]; acacia wood; 6olive oil for the light; spices for the anointing oil and for the fragrant incense; 7and onyx stones and other gems to be mounted on the ephod and breastpiece.

8"Then have them make a sanctuary for me, and I will dwell among them. 9Make this tabernacle and all its furnishings exactly like the pattern I will show you.

The Ark

10"Have them make a chest of acacia wood—two and a half cubits long, a cubit and a half wide, and a cubit and a half high.[d] 11Overlay it with pure gold, both

---

a 5 Traditionally *peace offerings*   b 10 Or *lapis lazuli*   c 5 That is, dugongs   d 10 That is, about 3 3/4 feet (about 1.1 meters) long and 2 1/4 feet (about 0.7 meter) wide and high inside and out, and make a gold molding around it. 12 Cast four gold rings for it and fasten them to its four feet, with two rings on one side and two rings on the other. 13 Then make poles of acacia wood and overlay them with gold. 14 Insert the poles into the rings on the sides of the chest to carry it. 15 The poles are to remain in the rings of this ark; they are not to be removed. 16 Then put in the ark the Testimony, which I will give you.

17 "Make an atonement cover[a] of pure gold—two and a half cubits long and a cubit and a half wide.[b] 18 And make two cherubim out of hammered gold at the ends of the cover. 19 Make one cherub on one end and the second cherub on the other; make the cherubim of one piece with the cover, at the two ends. 20 The cherubim are to have their wings spread upward, overshadowing the cover with them. The cherubim are to face each other, looking toward the cover. 21 Place the cover on top of the ark and put in the ark the Testimony, which I will give you. 22 There, above the cover between the two cherubim that are over the ark of the Testimony, I will meet with you and give you all my commands for the Israelites.

The Table

23 "Make a table of acacia wood—two cubits long, a cubit wide and a cubit and a half high.[c] 24 Overlay it with pure gold and make a gold molding around it. 25 Also make around it a rim a handbreadth[d] wide and put a gold molding on the rim. 26 Make four gold rings for the table and fasten them to the four corners, where the four legs are. 27 The rings are to be close to the rim to hold the poles used in carrying the table. 28 Make the poles of acacia wood, overlay them with gold and carry the table with them. 29 And make its plates and dishes of pure gold, as well as its pitchers and bowls for the pouring out of offerings. 30 Put the bread of the Presence on this table to be before me at all times.

The Lampstand

31 "Make a lampstand of pure gold and hammer it out, base and shaft; its flowerlike cups, buds and blossoms shall be of one piece with it. 32 Six branches are to extend from the sides of the lampstand—three on one side and three on the other. 33 Three cups shaped like almond flowers with buds and blossoms are to be on one branch, three on the next branch, and the same for all six branches extending from the lampstand. 34 And on the lampstand there are to be four cups shaped like almond flowers with buds and blossoms. 35 One bud shall be under the first pair of branches extending from the lampstand, a second bud under the second pair, and a third bud under the third pair—six branches in all. 36 The buds and branches shall all be of one piece with the lampstand, hammered out of pure gold.

37 "Then make its seven lamps and set them up on it so that they light the space in front of it. 38 Its wick trimmers and trays are to be of pure gold. 39 A talent[e] of pure gold is to be used for the lampstand and all these accessories. 40 See that you make them according to the pattern shown you on the mountain.

The Tabernacle

26 "Make the tabernacle with ten curtains of finely twisted linen and blue, purple and scarlet yarn, with cherubim worked into them by a skilled craftsman. 2 All the curtains are to be the same size—twenty-eight cubits long and four cubits wide.[f] 3 Join five of the curtains together, and do the same with the other five. 4 Make loops of blue material along the edge of the end curtain in one set, and do the same with the end

---

a 17 Traditionally a mercy seat   b 17 That is, about 3 3/4 feet (about 1.1 meters) long and 2 1/4 feet (about 0.7 meter) wide
c 23 That is, about 3 feet (about 0.9 meter) long and 1 1/2 feet (about 0.5 meter) wide and 2 1/4 feet (about 0.7 meter) high
d 25 That is, about 3 inches (about 8 centimeters)   e 39 That is, about 75 pounds (about 34 kilograms)   f 2 That is, about
42 feet (about 12.5 meters) long and 6 feet (about 1.8 meters) wide

curtain in the other set. 5Make fifty loops on one curtain and fifty loops on the end curtain of the other set, with the loops opposite each other. 6Then make fifty gold clasps and use them to fasten the curtains together so that the tabernacle is a unit.

7"Make curtains of goat hair for the tent over the tabernacle—eleven altogether. 8All eleven curtains are to be the same size—thirty cubits long and four cubits wide.a 9Join five of the curtains together into one set and the other six into another set. Fold the sixth curtain double at the front of the tent. 10Make fifty loops along the edge of the end curtain in one set and also along the edge of the end curtain in the other set. 11Then make fifty bronze clasps and put them in the loops to fasten the tent together as a unit. 12As for the additional length of the tent curtains, the half curtain that is left over is to hang down at the rear of the tabernacle. 13The tent curtains will be a cubitb longer on both sides; what is left will hang over the sides of the tabernacle so as to cover it. 14Make for the tent a covering of ram skins dyed red, and over that a covering of hides of sea cows.c

15"Make upright frames of acacia wood for the tabernacle. 16Each frame is to be ten cubits long and a cubit and a half wide,d 17with two projections set parallel to each other. Make all the frames of the tabernacle in this way. 18Make twenty frames for the south side of the tabernacle 19and make forty silver bases to go under them—two bases for each frame, one under each projection. 20For the other side, the north side of the tabernacle, make twenty frames 21and forty silver bases—two under each frame. 22Make six frames for the far end, that is, the west end of the tabernacle, 23and make two frames for the corners at the far end. 24At these two corners they must be double from the bottom all the way to the top, and fitted into a single ring; both shall be like that. 25So

there will be eight frames and sixteen silver bases—two under each frame.

26"Also make crossbars of acacia wood: five for the frames on one side of the tabernacle, 27five for those on the other side, and five for the frames on the west, at the far end of the tabernacle. 28The center crossbar is to extend from end to end at the middle of the frames. 29Overlay the frames with gold and make gold rings to hold the crossbars. Also overlay the crossbars with gold.

30"Set up the tabernacle according to the plan shown you on the mountain.

31"Make a curtain of blue, purple and scarlet yarn and finely twisted linen, with cherubim worked into it by a skilled craftsman. 32Hang it with gold hooks on four posts of acacia wood overlaid with gold and standing on four silver bases. 33Hang the curtain from the clasps and place the ark of the Testimony behind the curtain. The curtain will separate the Holy Place from the Most Holy Place. 34Put the atonement cover on the ark of the Testimony in the Most Holy Place. 35Place the table outside the curtain on the north side of the tabernacle and put the lampstand opposite it on the south side.

36"For the entrance to the tent make a curtain of blue, purple and scarlet yarn and finely twisted linen—the work of an embroiderer. 37Make gold hooks for this curtain and five posts of acacia wood overlaid with gold. And cast five bronze bases for them.

The Altar of Burnt Offering

27 "Build an altar of acacia wood, three cubitse high; it is to be square, five cubits long and five cubits wide.f 2Make a horn at each of the four corners, so that the horns and the altar are of one piece, and overlay the altar with bronze. 3Make all its utensils of bronze—its pots to remove the ashes, and its shovels, sprinkling bowls, meat forks and firepans. 4Make

---

a 8 That is, about 45 feet (about 13.5 meters) long and 6 feet (about 1.8 meters) wide   b 13 That is, about 1 1/2 feet (about 0.5 meter)   c 14 That is, dugongs   d 16 That is, about 15 feet (about 4.5 meters) long and 2 1/4 feet (about 0.7 meter) wide   e 1 That is, about 4 1/2 feet (about 1.3 meters)   f 1 That is, about 7 1/2 feet (about 2.3 meters) long and wide a grating for it, a bronze network, and make a bronze ring at each of the four corners of the network. ⁵Put it under the ledge of the altar so that it is halfway up the altar. ⁶Make poles of acacia wood for the altar and overlay them with bronze. ⁷The poles are to be inserted into the rings so they will be on two sides of the altar when it is carried. ⁸Make the altar hollow, out of boards. It is to be made just as you were shown on the mountain.

The Courtyard

⁹"Make a courtyard for the tabernacle. The south side shall be a hundred cubits^a long and is to have curtains of finely twisted linen, ¹⁰with twenty posts and twenty bronze bases and with silver hooks and bands on the posts. ¹¹The north side shall also be a hundred cubits long and is to have curtains, with twenty posts and twenty bronze bases and with silver hooks and bands on the posts.

¹²"The west end of the courtyard shall be fifty cubits^b wide and have curtains, with ten posts and ten bases. ¹³On the east end, toward the sunrise, the courtyard shall also be fifty cubits wide. ¹⁴Curtains fifteen cubits^c long are to be on one side of the entrance, with three posts and three bases, ¹⁵and curtains fifteen cubits long are to be on the other side, with three posts and three bases.

¹⁶"For the entrance to the courtyard, provide a curtain twenty cubits^d long, of blue, purple and scarlet yarn and finely twisted linen—the work of an embroiderer—with four posts and four bases. ¹⁷All the posts around the courtyard are to have silver bands and hooks, and bronze bases. ¹⁸The courtyard shall be a hundred cubits long and fifty cubits wide,^{e} with curtains of finely twisted linen five cubits^f high, and with bronze bases. ¹⁹All the other articles used in the service of the tabernacle, whatever their function, including all the tent pegs for

it and those for the courtyard, are to be of bronze.

Oil for the Lampstand

²⁰"Command the Israelites to bring you clear oil of pressed olives for the light so that the lamps may be kept burning. ²¹In the Tent of Meeting, outside the curtain that is in front of the Testimony, Aaron and his sons are to keep the lamps burning before the LORD from evening till morning. This is to be a lasting ordinance among the Israelites for the generations to come.

The Priestly Garments

28 "Have Aaron your brother brought to you from among the Israelites, along with his sons Nadab and Abihu, Eleazar and Ithamar, so they may serve me as priests. ²Make sacred garments for your brother Aaron, to give him dignity and honor. ³Tell all the skilled men to whom I have given wisdom in such matters that they are to make garments for Aaron, for his consecration, so he may serve me as priest. ⁴These are the garments they are to make: a breastpiece, an ephod, a robe, a woven tunic, a turban and a sash. They are to make these sacred garments for your brother Aaron and his sons, so they may serve me as priests. ⁵Have them use gold, and blue, purple and scarlet yarn, and fine linen.

The Ephod

⁶"Make the ephod of gold, and of blue, purple and scarlet yarn, and of finely twisted linen—the work of a skilled craftsman. ⁷It is to have two shoulder pieces attached to two of its corners, so it can be fastened. ⁸Its skillfully woven waistband is to be like it—of one piece with the ephod and made with gold, and with blue, purple and scarlet yarn, and with finely twisted linen.

⁹"Take two onyx stones and engrave on them the names of the sons of Israel

---

^{a}*9* That is, about 150 feet (about 46 meters); also in verse 11 ^{b}*12* That is, about 75 feet (about 23 meters); also in verse 13
^{c}*14* That is, about 22 1/2 feet (about 6.9 meters); also in verse 15 ^{d}*16* That is, about 30 feet (about 9 meters) ^{e}*18* That is, about 150 feet (about 46 meters) long and 75 feet (about 23 meters) wide ^{f}*18* That is, about 7 1/2 feet (about 2.3 meters)

¹⁰in the order of their birth—six names on one stone and the remaining six on the other. ¹¹Engrave the names of the sons of Israel on the two stones the way a gem cutter engraves a seal. Then mount the stones in gold filigree settings ¹²and fasten them on the shoulder pieces of the ephod as memorial stones for the sons of Israel. Aaron is to bear the names on his shoulders as a memorial before the LORD. ¹³Make gold filigree settings ¹⁴and two braided chains of pure gold, like a rope, and attach the chains to the settings.

The Breastpiece

¹⁵"Fashion a breastpiece for making decisions—the work of a skilled craftsman. Make it like the ephod: of gold, and of blue, purple and scarlet yarn, and of finely twisted linen. ¹⁶It is to be square—a span[a] long and a span wide—and folded double. ¹⁷Then mount four rows of precious stones on it. In the first row there shall be a ruby, a topaz and a beryl; ¹⁸in the second row a turquoise, a sapphire[b] and an emerald; ¹⁹in the third row a jacinth, an agate and an amethyst; ²⁰in the fourth row a chrysolite, an onyx and a jasper.[c] Mount them in gold filigree settings. ²¹There are to be twelve stones, one for each of the names of the sons of Israel, each engraved like a seal with the name of one of the twelve tribes.

²²"For the breastpiece make braided chains of pure gold, like a rope. ²³Make two gold rings for it and fasten them to two corners of the breastpiece. ²⁴Fasten the two gold chains to the rings at the corners of the breastpiece, ²⁵and the other ends of the chains to the two settings, attaching them to the shoulder pieces of the ephod at the front. ²⁶Make two gold rings and attach them to the other two corners of the breastpiece on the inside edge next to the ephod. ²⁷Make two more gold rings and attach them to the bottom of the shoulder pieces on the front of the ephod, close to the seam just above the waistband of the ephod. ²⁸The rings of the breastpiece are to be tied to the rings of the ephod with blue cord, connecting it to the waistband, so that the breastpiece will not swing out from the ephod.

²⁹"Whenever Aaron enters the Holy Place, he will bear the names of the sons of Israel over his heart on the breastpiece of decision as a continuing memorial before the LORD. ³⁰Also put the Urim and the Thummim in the breastpiece, so they may be over Aaron's heart whenever he enters the presence of the LORD. Thus Aaron will always bear the means of making decisions for the Israelites over his heart before the LORD.

Other Priestly Garments

³¹"Make the robe of the ephod entirely of blue cloth, ³²with an opening for the head in its center. There shall be a woven edge like a collar[d] around this opening, so that it will not tear. ³³Make pomegranates of blue, purple and scarlet yarn around the hem of the robe, with gold bells between them. ³⁴The gold bells and the pomegranates are to alternate around the hem of the robe. ³⁵Aaron must wear it when he ministers. The sound of the bells will be heard when he enters the Holy Place before the LORD and when he comes out, so that he will not die.

³⁶"Make a plate of pure gold and engrave on it as on a seal: HOLY TO THE LORD. ³⁷Fasten a blue cord to it to attach it to the turban; it is to be on the front of the turban. ³⁸It will be on Aaron's forehead, and he will bear the guilt involved in the sacred gifts the Israelites consecrate, whatever their gifts may be. It will be on Aaron's forehead continually so that they will be acceptable to the LORD.

³⁹"Weave the tunic of fine linen and make the turban of fine linen. The sash is to be the work of an embroiderer. ⁴⁰Make tunics, sashes and headbands for Aaron's sons, to give them dignity and

---

a 16 That is, about 9 inches (about 22 centimeters)   b 18 Or lapis lazuli   c 20 The precise identification of some of these precious stones is uncertain.   d 32 The meaning of the Hebrew for this word is uncertain.

honor. 41After you put these clothes on your brother Aaron and his sons, anoint and ordain them. Consecrate them so they may serve me as priests.

42"Make linen undergarments as a covering for the body, reaching from the waist to the thigh. 43Aaron and his sons must wear them whenever they enter the Tent of Meeting or approach the altar to minister in the Holy Place, so that they will not incur guilt and die.

"This is to be a lasting ordinance for Aaron and his descendants.

Consecration of the Priests

29 "This is what you are to do to consecrate them, so they may serve me as priests: Take a young bull and two rams without defect. 2And from fine wheat flour, without yeast, make bread, and cakes mixed with oil, and wafers spread with oil. 3Put them in a basket and present them in it—along with the bull and the two rams. 4Then bring Aaron and his sons to the entrance to the Tent of Meeting and wash them with water. 5Take the garments and dress Aaron with the tunic, the robe of the ephod, the ephod itself and the breastpiece. Fasten the ephod on him by its skillfully woven waistband. 6Put the turban on his head and attach the sacred diadem to the turban. 7Take the anointing oil and anoint him by pouring it on his head. 8Bring his sons and dress them in tunics 9and put headbands on them. Then tie sashes on Aaron and his sons.a The priesthood is theirs by a lasting ordinance. In this way you shall ordain Aaron and his sons.

10"Bring the bull to the front of the Tent of Meeting, and Aaron and his sons shall lay their hands on its head. 11Slaughter it in the LORD's presence at the entrance to the Tent of Meeting. 12Take some of the bull's blood and put it on the horns of the altar with your finger, and pour out the rest of it at the base of the altar. 13Then take all the fat around the inner parts, the covering of the liver, and

both kidneys with the fat on them, and burn them on the altar. 14But burn the bull's flesh and its hide and its offal outside the camp. It is a sin offering.

15"Take one of the rams, and Aaron and his sons shall lay their hands on its head. 16Slaughter it and take the blood and sprinkle it against the altar on all sides. 17Cut the ram into pieces and wash the inner parts and the legs, putting them with the head and the other pieces. 18Then burn the entire ram on the altar. It is a burnt offering to the LORD, a pleasing aroma, an offering made to the LORD by fire.

19"Take the other ram, and Aaron and his sons shall lay their hands on its head. 20Slaughter it, take some of its blood and put it on the lobes of the right ears of Aaron and his sons, on the thumbs of their right hands, and on the big toes of their right feet. Then sprinkle blood against the altar on all sides. 21And take some of the blood on the altar and some of the anointing oil and sprinkle it on Aaron and his garments and on his sons and their garments. Then he and his sons and their garments will be consecrated.

22"Take from this ram the fat, the fat tail, the fat around the inner parts, the covering of the liver, both kidneys with the fat on them, and the right thigh. (This is the ram for the ordination.) 23From the basket of bread made without yeast, which is before the LORD, take a loaf, and a cake made with oil, and a wafer. 24Put all these in the hands of Aaron and his sons and wave them before the LORD as a wave offering. 25Then take them from their hands and burn them on the altar along with the burnt offering for a pleasing aroma to the LORD, an offering made to the LORD by fire. 26After you take the breast of the ram for Aaron's ordination, wave it before the LORD as a wave offering, and it will be your share.

27"Consecrate those parts of the ordination ram that belong to Aaron and his sons: the breast that was waved and the

---

thigh that was presented. [28] This is always to be the regular share from the Israelites for Aaron and his sons. It is the contribution the Israelites are to make to the LORD from their fellowship offerings.[a]

[29] "Aaron's sacred garments will belong to his descendants so that they can be anointed and ordained in them. [30] The son who succeeds him as priest and comes to the Tent of Meeting to minister in the Holy Place is to wear them seven days.

[31] "Take the ram for the ordination and cook the meat in a sacred place. [32] At the entrance to the Tent of Meeting, Aaron and his sons are to eat the meat of the ram and the bread that is in the basket. [33] They are to eat these offerings by which atonement was made for their ordination and consecration. But no one else may eat them, because they are sacred. [34] And if any of the meat of the ordination ram or any bread is left over till morning, burn it up. It must not be eaten, because it is sacred.

[35] "Do for Aaron and his sons everything I have commanded you, taking seven days to ordain them. [36] Sacrifice a bull each day as a sin offering to make atonement. Purify the altar by making atonement for it, and anoint it to consecrate it. [37] For seven days make atonement for the altar and consecrate it. Then the altar will be most holy, and whatever touches it will be holy.

[38] "This is what you are to offer on the altar regularly each day: two lambs a year old. [39] Offer one in the morning and the other at twilight. [40] With the first lamb offer a tenth of an ephah[b] of fine flour mixed with a quarter of a hin[c] of oil from pressed olives, and a quarter of a hin of wine as a drink offering. [41] Sacrifice the other lamb at twilight with the same grain offering and its drink offering as in the morning—a pleasing aroma, an offering made to the LORD by fire.

[42] "For the generations to come this burnt offering is to be made regularly at the entrance to the Tent of Meeting before the LORD. There I will meet you and speak to you; [43] there also I will meet with the Israelites, and the place will be consecrated by my glory.

[44] "So I will consecrate the Tent of Meeting and the altar and will consecrate Aaron and his sons to serve me as priests. [45] Then I will dwell among the Israelites and be their God. [46] They will know that I am the LORD their God, who brought them out of Egypt so that I might dwell among them. I am the LORD their God.

The Altar of Incense

30 "Make an altar of acacia wood for burning incense. [2] It is to be square, a cubit long and a cubit wide, and two cubits high[d]—its horns of one piece with it. [3] Overlay the top and all the sides and the horns with pure gold, and make a gold molding around it. [4] Make two gold rings for the altar below the molding—two on opposite sides—to hold the poles used to carry it. [5] Make the poles of acacia wood and overlay them with gold. [6] Put the altar in front of the curtain that is before the ark of the Testimony—before the atonement cover that is over the Testimony—where I will meet with you.

[7] "Aaron must burn fragrant incense on the altar every morning when he tends the lamps. [8] He must burn incense again when he lights the lamps at twilight so incense will burn regularly before the LORD for the generations to come. [9] Do not offer on this altar any other incense or any burnt offering or grain offering, and do not pour a drink offering on it. [10] Once a year Aaron shall make atonement on its horns. This annual atonement must be made with the blood of the atoning sin offering for the generations to come. It is most holy to the LORD."

Atonement Money

[11] Then the LORD said to Moses, [12] "When you take a census of the Israel-

---

[a] 28 Traditionally *peace offerings*   [b] 40 That is, probably about 2 quarts (about 2 liters)   [c] 40 That is, probably about 1 quart (about 1 liter)   [d] 2 That is, about 1 1/2 feet (about 0.5 meter) long and wide and about 3 feet (about 0.9 meter) high

ites to count them, each one must pay the LORD a ransom for his life at the time he is counted. Then no plague will come on them when you number them. 13Each one who crosses over to those already counted is to give a half shekel,ᵃ according to the sanctuary shekel, which weighs twenty gerahs. This half shekel is an offering to the LORD. 14All who cross over, those twenty years old or more, are to give an offering to the LORD. 15The rich are not to give more than a half shekel and the poor are not to give less when you make the offering to the LORD to atone for your lives. 16Receive the atonement money from the Israelites and use it for the service of the Tent of Meeting. It will be a memorial for the Israelites before the LORD, making atonement for your lives."

Basin for Washing

17Then the LORD said to Moses, 18"Make a bronze basin, with its bronze stand, for washing. Place it between the Tent of Meeting and the altar, and put water in it. 19Aaron and his sons are to wash their hands and feet with water from it. 20Whenever they enter the Tent of Meeting, they shall wash with water so that they will not die. Also, when they approach the altar to minister by presenting an offering made to the LORD by fire, 21they shall wash their hands and feet so that they will not die. This is to be a lasting ordinance for Aaron and his descendants for the generations to come."

Anointing Oil

22Then the LORD said to Moses, 23"Take the following fine spices: 500 shekelsᵇ of liquid myrrh, half as much (that is, 250 shekels) of fragrant cinnamon, 250 shekels of fragrant cane, 24500 shekels of cassia—all according to the sanctuary shekel—and a hinᶜ of olive oil. 25Make these into a sacred anointing oil, a fragrant blend, the work of a perfumer.

It will be the sacred anointing oil. 26Then use it to anoint the Tent of Meeting, the ark of the Testimony, 27the table and all its articles, the lampstand and its accessories, the altar of incense, 28the altar of burnt offering and all its utensils, and the basin with its stand. 29You shall consecrate them so they will be most holy, and whatever touches them will be holy.

30"Anoint Aaron and his sons and consecrate them so they may serve me as priests. 31Say to the Israelites, 'This is to be my sacred anointing oil for the generations to come. 32Do not pour it on men's bodies and do not make any oil with the same formula. It is sacred, and you are to consider it sacred. 33Whoever makes perfume like it and whoever puts it on anyone other than a priest must be cut off from his people.'"

Incense

34Then the LORD said to Moses, "Take fragrant spices—gum resin, onycha and galbanum—and pure frankincense, all in equal amounts, 35and make a fragrant blend of incense, the work of a perfumer. It is to be salted and pure and sacred. 36Grind some of it to powder and place it in front of the Testimony in the Tent of Meeting, where I will meet with you. It shall be most holy to you. 37Do not make any incense with this formula for yourselves; consider it holy to the LORD. 38Whoever makes any like it to enjoy its fragrance must be cut off from his people."

Bezalel and Oholiab

31 Then the LORD said to Moses, 2"See, I have chosen Bezalel son of Uri, the son of Hur, of the tribe of Judah, 3and I have filled him with the Spirit of God, with skill, ability and knowledge in all kinds of crafts— 4to make artistic designs for work in gold, silver and bronze, 5to cut and set stones, to work in wood, and to engage in all kinds

---

ᵃ 13 That is, about 1/5 ounce (about 6 grams); also in verse 15   ᵇ 23 That is, about 12 1/2 pounds (about 6 kilograms)
ᶜ 24 That is, probably about 4 quarts (about 4 liters)

of craftsmanship. [6]Moreover, I have appointed Oholiab son of Ahisamach, of the tribe of Dan, to help him. Also I have given skill to all the craftsmen to make everything I have commanded you: [7]the Tent of Meeting, the ark of the Testimony with the atonement cover on it, and all the other furnishings of the tent— [8]the table and its articles, the pure gold lampstand and all its accessories, the altar of incense, [9]the altar of burnt offering and all its utensils, the basin with its stand— [10]and also the woven garments, both the sacred garments for Aaron the priest and the garments for his sons when they serve as priests, [11]and the anointing oil and fragrant incense for the Holy Place. They are to make them just as I commanded you."

The Sabbath

[12]Then the LORD said to Moses, [13]"Say to the Israelites, 'You must observe my Sabbaths. This will be a sign between me and you for the generations to come, so you may know that I am the LORD, who makes you holy.[a]

[14]"'Observe the Sabbath, because it is holy to you. Anyone who desecrates it must be put to death; whoever does any work on that day must be cut off from his people. [15]For six days, work is to be done, but the seventh day is a Sabbath of rest, holy to the LORD. Whoever does any work on the Sabbath day must be put to death. [16]The Israelites are to observe the Sabbath, celebrating it for the generations to come as a lasting covenant. [17]It will be a sign between me and the Israelites forever, for in six days the LORD made the heavens and the earth, and on the seventh day he abstained from work and rested.'"

[18]When the LORD finished speaking to Moses on Mount Sinai, he gave him the two tablets of the Testimony, the tablets of stone inscribed by the finger of God.

The Golden Calf

32 When the people saw that Moses was so long in coming down from the mountain, they gathered around Aaron and said, "Come, make us gods[b] who will go before us. As for this fellow Moses who brought us up out of Egypt, we don't know what has happened to him."

[2]Aaron answered them, "Take off the gold earrings that your wives, your sons and your daughters are wearing, and bring them to me." [3]So all the people took off their earrings and brought them to Aaron. [4]He took what they handed him and made it into an idol cast in the shape of a calf, fashioning it with a tool. Then they said, "These are your gods,[c] O Israel, who brought you up out of Egypt."

[5]When Aaron saw this, he built an altar in front of the calf and announced, "Tomorrow there will be a festival to the LORD." [6]So the next day the people rose early and sacrificed burnt offerings and presented fellowship offerings.[d] Afterward they sat down to eat and drink and got up to indulge in revelry.

[7]Then the LORD said to Moses, "Go down, because your people, whom you brought up out of Egypt, have become corrupt. [8]They have been quick to turn away from what I commanded them and have made themselves an idol cast in the shape of a calf. They have bowed down to it and sacrificed to it and have said, 'These are your gods, O Israel, who brought you up out of Egypt.'

Praying Exodus 32:7-9
God, show me if I have lifted up my heart
to any kind of idol in my life so that I
may cast it down and destroy its hold.

[9]"I have seen these people," the LORD said to Moses, "and they are a stiff-necked people. [10]Now leave me alone so that my anger may burn against them and that I

---

[a] *13 Or who sanctifies you;* or *who sets you apart as holy*   [b] *1 Or a god;* also in verses 23 and 31   [c] *4 Or This is your god;* also in verse 8   [d] *6 Traditionally peace offerings*

The Power of Intercession

READ AND CONSIDER: EXODUS 32:1-14

"Then the LORD relented and did not bring on his people the disaster he had threatened" (Exodus 32:14).

Can prayer change God's mind? God was angry with the people's disobedience, corruption, and rebellion, and He spoke to Moses of His intent to destroy them. Moses, however, sought God's favor and pleaded with the Lord to spare the very people He had miraculously brought out of Egypt. Exodus 32:14 says the Lord "relented," which means He decided not to do as He had planned. Did Moses actually change the mind of God?

Scripture speaks again and again of the power of intercession. The power is not in us as human beings, of course, or in the order or frequency of the words we speak. The power comes solely from God, the One who hears us. "The prayer of a righteous man [or woman] is powerful" (James 5:16).

Intercession is empowered when it is based on the promises of God. You can pray for another person, but if what you're asking is not consistent with or contradicts His promises, your prayers won't be effective. When your prayers for another are in line with His Word, God *will* respond. This is another good reason to read the Bible daily.

Base your prayers on the truth of God's Word. As Moses did, you can pray God's Word back to Him, reminding Him of what He has promised. You can stand before God "in the gap" (Ezekiel 22:30) and intercede for the lives of others, and for your nation. Intercession is a precious privilege. Who knows what a difference your prayers can make?

---

may destroy them. Then I will make you into a great nation."

¹¹But Moses sought the favor of the LORD his God. "O LORD," he said, "why should your anger burn against your people, whom you brought out of Egypt with great power and a mighty hand? ¹²Why should the Egyptians say, 'It was with evil intent that he brought them out, to kill them in the mountains and to wipe them off the face of the earth'? Turn from your fierce anger; relent and do not bring disaster on your people. ¹³Remember your servants Abraham, Isaac and Israel, to whom you swore by your own self: 'I will make your descendants as numerous as the stars in the sky and I will give your descendants all this land I promised them, and it will be their inheritance forever.'" ¹⁴Then the LORD

relented and did not bring on his people the disaster he had threatened.

¹⁵Moses turned and went down the mountain with the two tablets of the Testimony in his hands. They were inscribed on both sides, front and back. ¹⁶The tablets were the work of God; the writing was the writing of God, engraved on the tablets.

¹⁷When Joshua heard the noise of the people shouting, he said to Moses, "There is the sound of war in the camp."

¹⁸Moses replied:

"It is not the sound of victory,
    it is not the sound of defeat;
    it is the sound of singing that I
        hear."

¹⁹When Moses approached the camp and saw the calf and the dancing, his

anger burned and he threw the tablets out of his hands, breaking them to pieces at the foot of the mountain. 20 And he took the calf they had made and burned it in the fire; then he ground it to powder, scattered it on the water and made the Israelites drink it.

21 He said to Aaron, "What did these people do to you, that you led them into such great sin?"

22 "Do not be angry, my lord," Aaron answered. "You know how prone these people are to evil. 23 They said to me, 'Make us gods who will go before us. As for this fellow Moses who brought us up out of Egypt, we don't know what has happened to him.' 24 So I told them, 'Whoever has any gold jewelry, take it off.' Then they gave me the gold, and I threw it into the fire, and out came this calf!"

25 Moses saw that the people were running wild and that Aaron had let them get out of control and so become a laughingstock to their enemies. 26 So he stood at the entrance to the camp and said, "Whoever is for the LORD, come to me." And all the Levites rallied to him.

27 Then he said to them, "This is what the LORD, the God of Israel, says: 'Each man strap a sword to his side. Go back and forth through the camp from one end to the other, each killing his brother and friend and neighbor.' " 28 The Levites did as Moses commanded, and that day about three thousand of the people died. 29 Then Moses said, "You have been set apart to the LORD today, for you were against your own sons and brothers, and he has blessed you this day."

30 The next day Moses said to the people, "You have committed a great sin. But now I will go up to the LORD; perhaps I can make atonement for your sin."

31 So Moses went back to the LORD and said, "Oh, what a great sin these people have committed! They have made themselves gods of gold. 32 But now, please forgive their sin—but if not, then blot me out of the book you have written."

33 The LORD replied to Moses, "Whoever has sinned against me I will blot out of my book. 34 Now go, lead the people to the place I spoke of, and my angel will go before you. However, when the time comes for me to punish, I will punish them for their sin."

35 And the LORD struck the people with a plague because of what they did with the calf Aaron had made.

33 Then the LORD said to Moses, "Leave this place, you and the people you brought up out of Egypt, and go up to the land I promised on oath to Abraham, Isaac and Jacob, saying, 'I will give it to your descendants.' 2 I will send an angel before you and drive out the Canaanites, Amorites, Hittites, Perizzites, Hivites and Jebusites. 3 Go up to the land flowing with milk and honey. But I will not go with you, because you are a stiffnecked people and I might destroy you on the way."

4 When the people heard these distressing words, they began to mourn and no one put on any ornaments. 5 For the LORD had said to Moses, "Tell the Israelites, 'You are a stiff-necked people. If I were to go with you even for a moment, I might destroy you. Now take off your ornaments and I will decide what to do with you.' " 6 So the Israelites stripped off their ornaments at Mount Horeb.

The Tent of Meeting

7 Now Moses used to take a tent and pitch it outside the camp some distance away, calling it the "tent of meeting." Anyone inquiring of the LORD would go to the tent of meeting outside the camp. 8 And whenever Moses went out to the tent, all the people rose and stood at the entrances to their tents, watching Moses until he entered the tent. 9 As Moses went into the tent, the pillar of cloud would come down and stay at the entrance, while the LORD spoke with Moses. 10 Whenever the people saw the pillar of cloud standing at the entrance to the

Seek God's Greatest Gift

God wants to be with you like a friend. Moses was God's friend. "The LORD would speak to Moses face to face, as a man speaks with his friend" (Exodus 33:11). When Moses wanted to know the way he should go, he said to God, "If you are pleased with me, teach me your ways so I may know you and continue to find favor with you" (Exodus 33:13). His desire was to know *God,* not just get someplace. And God promised that His presence would go with him and give him rest (Exodus 33:14).

Don't you love that? Don't you want that more than anything else in your life? That God would always go with you and give you rest? After God made that promise, Moses said one of the greatest lines in the Bible: "If your Presence does not go with us, do not send us up from here" (Exodus 33:15).

Moses didn't want to go anywhere if God's presence wasn't going with him. He hungered for God. Not just for what God could do for him. He hungered for His presence. That is our hunger as well, whether we know it or not. We hunger to know *God* and the fullness of His presence. God knows that we cannot contain all of His presence. We couldn't handle it, and He only gives us what we can handle. When King Solomon built a place for God to rest—the temple—he dedicated it to the Lord and praised Him, and asked for His presence to live in their midst. Then he said, "But will God really dwell on earth? The heavens, even the highest heaven, cannot contain you. How much less this temple I have built!" (1 Kings 8:27).

Solomon knew that nothing on earth could contain God's presence, let alone this magnificent temple, but he also knew it was God's mercy that allowed His people to experience as much of His presence as they could. God has so much more He wants to give us of Himself. He desires closeness with us. Worship is the way we grow close to Him.

David looked for God. He *went after* Him. He *searched Him out until he found Him.* And then he laid his feelings and longings bare. "All my longings lie open before you, O Lord; my sighing is not hidden from you" (Psalm 38:9). He covered up nothing of his soul.

No matter how much we achieve in life, we will always have a hunger for something more. That's because "we wait in hope for the LORD" (Psalm 33:20). That's why the greatest gift God gives us is His presence. Our deepest desires can only be satisfied by Him alone. Our Creator. Our Father. The true love of our life.

If you don't sense His presence in your life, praise and worship Him until you do. That's not trying to manipulate God; it's breaking down your own barriers in order to allow Him access to your heart.

For the next "From Stormie's Heart" article, go to page 131.

tent, they all stood and worshiped, each at the entrance to his tent. ¹¹The LORD would speak to Moses face to face, as a man speaks with his friend. Then Moses would return to the camp, but his young aide Joshua son of Nun did not leave the tent.

¹⁸Then Moses said, "Now show me your glory."

¹⁹And the LORD said, "I will cause all my goodness to pass in front of you, and I will proclaim my name, the LORD, in your presence. I will have mercy on whom I will have mercy, and I will have

---

God's people at prayer
MOSES' BOLD PRAYER TO SEE GOD'S GLORY

EXODUS 33:12-23 As Moses met with God in the Tent of Meeting each day, he shared a unique face-to-face relationship with the Almighty. He begged God to teach him and to lead him. And then he got so carried away with being in God's presence that he boldly asked to see God's glory. Of course, God knew that no one could see the fullness of His face and live. Elsewhere we are told that God's glory is like a "consuming fire" (24:17). Divine fire and frail human flesh don't mix well. But God loved Moses and accommodated his request, answering as much as Moses could safely receive.

Don't be afraid to pray boldly for big things as Moses did, especially when it comes to seeing more fully who God is. Ask, seek, knock, and you will receive. But be ready to accept whatever God sends. Trust God to answer your prayers in a way that is best for you.

Moses and the Glory of the LORD

¹²Moses said to the LORD, "You have been telling me, 'Lead these people,' but you have not let me know whom you will send with me. You have said, 'I know you by name and you have found favor with me.' ¹³If you are pleased with me, teach me your ways so I may know you and continue to find favor with you. Remember that this nation is your people."

¹⁴The LORD replied, "My Presence will go with you, and I will give you rest."

¹⁵Then Moses said to him, "If your Presence does not go with us, do not send us up from here. ¹⁶How will anyone know that you are pleased with me and with your people unless you go with us? What else will distinguish me and your people from all the other people on the face of the earth?"

¹⁷And the LORD said to Moses, "I will do the very thing you have asked, because I am pleased with you and I know you by name."

compassion on whom I will have compassion. ²⁰But," he said, "you cannot see my face, for no one may see me and live."

²¹Then the LORD said, "There is a place near me where you may stand on a rock. ²²When my glory passes by, I will put you in a cleft in the rock and cover you with my hand until I have passed by. ²³Then I will remove my hand and you will see my back; but my face must not be seen."

Praying Exodus 33:13-15
Heavenly Father, I don't want to go anywhere if Your presence does not go with me.

The New Stone Tablets

34 The LORD said to Moses, "Chisel out two stone tablets like the first ones, and I will write on them the words that were on the first tablets, which you broke. ²Be ready in the morning, and then come up on Mount Sinai. Present yourself to me there on top of the mountain. ³No one is to come with you or be seen anywhere on the mountain; not even the flocks and herds may graze in front of the mountain."

⁴So Moses chiseled out two stone tablets like the first ones and went up Mount Sinai early in the morning, as the LORD had commanded him; and he carried the two stone tablets in his hands. ⁵Then the LORD came down in the cloud and stood there with him and proclaimed his name, the LORD. ⁶And he passed in front of Moses, proclaiming, "The LORD, the LORD, the compassionate and gracious God, slow to anger, abounding in love and faithfulness, ⁷maintaining love to thousands, and forgiving wickedness, rebellion and sin. Yet he does not leave the guilty unpunished; he punishes the children and their children for the sin of the fathers to the third and fourth generation."

Praying Exodus 34:6-7
Thank You, Lord, for always being merciful, gracious, patient, and full of goodness and truth.

⁸Moses bowed to the ground at once and worshiped. ⁹"O Lord, if I have found favor in your eyes," he said, "then let the Lord go with us. Although this is a stiff-necked people, forgive our wickedness and our sin, and take us as your inheritance."

¹⁰Then the LORD said: "I am making a covenant with you. Before all your people I will do wonders never before done in any nation in all the world. The people you live among will see how awesome is the work that I, the LORD, will do for you. ¹¹Obey what I command you today. I will drive out before you the Amorites, Canaanites, Hittites, Perizzites, Hivites and Jebusites. ¹²Be careful not to make a treaty with those who live in the land where you are going, or they will be a snare among you. ¹³Break down their altars, smash their sacred stones and cut down their Asherah poles.ᵃ ¹⁴Do not worship any other god, for the LORD, whose name is Jealous, is a jealous God.

¹⁵"Be careful not to make a treaty with those who live in the land; for when they prostitute themselves to their gods and sacrifice to them, they will invite you and you will eat their sacrifices. ¹⁶And when you choose some of their daughters as wives for your sons and those daughters prostitute themselves to their gods, they will lead your sons to do the same.

¹⁷"Do not make cast idols.

¹⁸"Celebrate the Feast of Unleavened Bread. For seven days eat bread made without yeast, as I commanded you. Do this at the appointed time in the month of Abib, for in that month you came out of Egypt.

¹⁹"The first offspring of every womb belongs to me, including all the firstborn males of your livestock, whether from herd or flock. ²⁰Redeem the firstborn donkey with a lamb, but if you do not redeem it, break its neck. Redeem all your firstborn sons.

"No one is to appear before me empty-handed.

²¹"Six days you shall labor, but on the seventh day you shall rest; even during the plowing season and harvest you must rest.

²²"Celebrate the Feast of Weeks with the firstfruits of the wheat harvest, and the Feast of Ingathering at the turn of the year.ᵇ ²³Three times a year all your men are to appear before the Sovereign LORD, the God of Israel. ²⁴I will drive out nations before you and enlarge your territory, and no one will covet your land when you go up three times each year to appear before the LORD your God.

²⁵"Do not offer the blood of a sacrifice to me along with anything containing yeast, and do not let any of the sacrifice from the Passover Feast remain until morning.

²⁶"Bring the best of the firstfruits of your soil to the house of the LORD your God.

ᵃ *13* That is, symbols of the goddess Asherah   ᵇ *22* That is, in the fall

"Do not cook a young goat in its mother's milk."

27Then the LORD said to Moses, "Write down these words, for in accordance with these words I have made a covenant with you and with Israel." 28Moses was there with the LORD forty days and forty nights without eating bread or drinking water. And he wrote on the tablets the words of the covenant—the Ten Commandments.

The Radiant Face of Moses

29When Moses came down from Mount Sinai with the two tablets of the Testimony in his hands, he was not aware that his face was radiant because he had spoken with the LORD. 30When Aaron and all the Israelites saw Moses, his face was radiant, and they were afraid to come near him. 31But Moses called to them; so Aaron and all the leaders of the community came back to him, and he spoke to them. 32Afterward all the Israelites came near him, and he gave them all the commands the LORD had given him on Mount Sinai.

33When Moses finished speaking to them, he put a veil over his face. 34But whenever he entered the LORD's presence to speak with him, he removed the veil until he came out. And when he came out and told the Israelites what he had been commanded, 35they saw that his face was radiant. Then Moses would put the veil back over his face until he went in to speak with the LORD.

Sabbath Regulations

35 Moses assembled the whole Israelite community and said to them, "These are the things the LORD has commanded you to do: 2For six days, work is to be done, but the seventh day shall be your holy day, a Sabbath of rest to the LORD. Whoever does any work on it must be put to death. 3Do not light a fire in any of your dwellings on the Sabbath day."

Materials for the Tabernacle

4Moses said to the whole Israelite community, "This is what the LORD has commanded: 5From what you have, take an offering for the LORD. Everyone who is willing is to bring to the LORD an offering of gold, silver and bronze; 6blue, purple and scarlet yarn and fine linen; goat hair; 7ram skins dyed red and hides of sea cowsª; acacia wood; 8olive oil for the light; spices for the anointing oil and for the fragrant incense; 9and onyx stones and other gems to be mounted on the ephod and breastpiece.

10"All who are skilled among you are to come and make everything the LORD has commanded: 11the tabernacle with its tent and its covering, clasps, frames, crossbars, posts and bases; 12the ark with its poles and the atonement cover and the curtain that shields it; 13the table with its poles and all its articles and the bread of the Presence; 14the lampstand that is for light with its accessories, lamps and oil for the light; 15the altar of incense with its poles, the anointing oil and the fragrant incense; the curtain for the doorway at the entrance to the tabernacle; 16the altar of burnt offering with its bronze grating, its poles and all its utensils; the bronze basin with its stand; 17the curtains of the courtyard with its posts and bases, and the curtain for the entrance to the courtyard; 18the tent pegs for the tabernacle and for the courtyard, and their ropes; 19the woven garments worn for ministering in the sanctuary—both the sacred garments for Aaron the priest and the garments for his sons when they serve as priests."

20Then the whole Israelite community withdrew from Moses' presence, 21and everyone who was willing and whose heart moved him came and brought an offering to the LORD for the work on the Tent of Meeting, for all its service, and for the sacred garments. 22All who were willing, men and women alike, came and brought gold jewelry of all kinds:

ª 7 That is, dugongs; also in verse 23

brooches, earrings, rings and ornaments. They all presented their gold as a wave offering to the LORD. ²³Everyone who had blue, purple or scarlet yarn or fine linen, or goat hair, ram skins dyed red or hides of sea cows brought them. ²⁴Those presenting an offering of silver or bronze brought it as an offering to the LORD, and everyone who had acacia wood for any part of the work brought it. ²⁵Every skilled woman spun with her hands and brought what she had spun—blue, purple or scarlet yarn or fine linen. ²⁶And all the women who were willing and had the skill spun the goat hair. ²⁷The leaders brought onyx stones and other gems to be mounted on the ephod and breastpiece. ²⁸They also brought spices and olive oil for the light and for the anointing oil and for the fragrant incense. ²⁹All the Israelite men and women who were willing brought to the LORD freewill offerings for all the work the LORD through Moses had commanded them to do.

Bezalel and Oholiab

³⁰Then Moses said to the Israelites, "See, the LORD has chosen Bezalel son of Uri, the son of Hur, of the tribe of Judah, ³¹and he has filled him with the Spirit of God, with skill, ability and knowledge in all kinds of crafts— ³²to make artistic designs for work in gold, silver and bronze, ³³to cut and set stones, to work in wood and to engage in all kinds of artistic craftsmanship. ³⁴And he has given both him and Oholiab son of Ahisamach, of the tribe of Dan, the ability to teach others. ³⁵He has filled them with skill to do all kinds of work as craftsmen, designers, embroiderers in blue, purple and scarlet yarn and fine linen, and weavers—all of them master craftsmen and designers. 36 ¹So Bezalel, Oholiab and every skilled person to whom the LORD has given skill and ability to know how to carry out all the work of constructing the sanctuary are to do the work just as the LORD has commanded."

²Then Moses summoned Bezalel and Oholiab and every skilled person to whom the LORD had given ability and who was willing to come and do the work. ³They received from Moses all the offerings the Israelites had brought to carry out the work of constructing the sanctuary. And the people continued to bring freewill offerings morning after morning. ⁴So all the skilled craftsmen who were doing all the work on the sanctuary left their work ⁵and said to Moses, "The people are bringing more than enough for doing the work the LORD commanded to be done."

⁶Then Moses gave an order and they sent this word throughout the camp: "No man or woman is to make anything else as an offering for the sanctuary." And so the people were restrained from bringing more, ⁷because what they already had was more than enough to do all the work.

The Tabernacle

⁸All the skilled men among the workmen made the tabernacle with ten curtains of finely twisted linen and blue, purple and scarlet yarn, with cherubim worked into them by a skilled craftsman. ⁹All the curtains were the same size—twenty-eight cubits long and four cubits wide.ᵃ ¹⁰They joined five of the curtains together and did the same with the other five. ¹¹Then they made loops of blue material along the edge of the end curtain in one set, and the same was done with the end curtain in the other set. ¹²They also made fifty loops on one curtain and fifty loops on the end curtain of the other set, with the loops opposite each other. ¹³Then they made fifty gold clasps and used them to fasten the two sets of curtains together so that the tabernacle was a unit.

¹⁴They made curtains of goat hair for the tent over the tabernacle—eleven altogether. ¹⁵All eleven curtains were the same size—thirty cubits long and four

---

ᵃ 9 That is, about 42 feet (about 12.5 meters) long and 6 feet (about 1.8 meters) wide cubits wide.[a] 16They joined five of the curtains into one set and the other six into another set. 17Then they made fifty loops along the edge of the end curtain in one set and also along the edge of the end curtain in the other set. 18They made fifty bronze clasps to fasten the tent together as a unit. 19Then they made for the tent a covering of ram skins dyed red, and over that a covering of hides of sea cows.[b]

20They made upright frames of acacia wood for the tabernacle. 21Each frame was ten cubits long and a cubit and a half wide,[c] 22with two projections set parallel to each other. They made all the frames of the tabernacle in this way. 23They made twenty frames for the south side of the tabernacle 24and made forty silver bases to go under them—two bases for each frame, one under each projection. 25For the other side, the north side of the tabernacle, they made twenty frames 26and forty silver bases—two under each frame. 27They made six frames for the far end, that is, the west end of the tabernacle, 28and two frames were made for the corners of the tabernacle at the far end. 29At these two corners the frames were double from the bottom all the way to the top and fitted into a single ring; both were made alike. 30So there were eight frames and sixteen silver bases—two under each frame.

31They also made crossbars of acacia wood: five for the frames on one side of the tabernacle, 32five for those on the other side, and five for the frames on the west, at the far end of the tabernacle. 33They made the center crossbar so that it extended from end to end at the middle of the frames. 34They overlaid the frames with gold and made gold rings to hold the crossbars. They also overlaid the crossbars with gold.

35They made the curtain of blue, purple and scarlet yarn and finely twisted linen, with cherubim worked into it by a skilled craftsman. 36They made four posts of acacia wood for it and overlaid them with gold. They made gold hooks for them and cast their four silver bases. 37For the entrance to the tent they made a curtain of blue, purple and scarlet yarn and finely twisted linen—the work of an embroiderer; 38and they made five posts with hooks for them. They overlaid the tops of the posts and their bands with gold and made their five bases of bronze.

The Ark

37 Bezalel made the ark of acacia wood—two and a half cubits long, a cubit and a half wide, and a cubit and a half high.[d] 2He overlaid it with pure gold, both inside and out, and made a gold molding around it. 3He cast four gold rings for it and fastened them to its four feet, with two rings on one side and two rings on the other. 4Then he made poles of acacia wood and overlaid them with gold. 5And he inserted the poles into the rings on the sides of the ark to carry it.

6He made the atonement cover of pure gold—two and a half cubits long and a cubit and a half wide.[e] 7Then he made two cherubim out of hammered gold at the ends of the cover. 8He made one cherub on one end and the second cherub on the other; at the two ends he made them of one piece with the cover. 9The cherubim had their wings spread upward, overshadowing the cover with them. The cherubim faced each other, looking toward the cover.

The Table

10They[f] made the table of acacia wood—two cubits long, a cubit wide, and a cubit and a half high.[g] 11Then they overlaid it with pure gold and made a gold molding around it. 12They also made

---

[a] 15 That is, about 45 feet (about 13.5 meters) long and 6 feet (about 1.8 meters) wide   [b] 19 That is, dugongs   [c] 21 That is, about 15 feet (about 4.5 meters) long and 2 1/4 feet (about 0.7 meter) wide   [d] 1 That is, about 3 3/4 feet (about 1.1 meters) long and 2 1/4 feet (about 0.7 meter) wide and high   [e] 6 That is, about 3 3/4 feet (about 1.1 meters) long and 2 1/4 feet (about 0.7 meter) wide   [f] 10 Or He; also in verses 11-29   [g] 10 That is, about 3 feet (about 0.9 meter) long, 1 1/2 feet (about 0.5 meter) wide, and 2 1/4 feet (about 0.7 meter) high

around it a rim a handbreadth[a] wide and put a gold molding on the rim. [13]They cast four gold rings for the table and fastened them to the four corners, where the four legs were. [14]The rings were put close to the rim to hold the poles used in carrying the table. [15]The poles for carrying the table were made of acacia wood and were overlaid with gold. [16]And they made from pure gold the articles for the table—its plates and dishes and bowls and its pitchers for the pouring out of drink offerings.

The Lampstand

[17]They made the lampstand of pure gold and hammered it out, base and shaft; its flowerlike cups, buds and blossoms were of one piece with it. [18]Six branches extended from the sides of the lampstand—three on one side and three on the other. [19]Three cups shaped like almond flowers with buds and blossoms were on one branch, three on the next branch and the same for all six branches extending from the lampstand. [20]And on the lampstand were four cups shaped like almond flowers with buds and blossoms. [21]One bud was under the first pair of branches extending from the lampstand, a second bud under the second pair, and a third bud under the third pair—six branches in all. [22]The buds and the branches were all of one piece with the lampstand, hammered out of pure gold.

[23]They made its seven lamps, as well as its wick trimmers and trays, of pure gold. [24]They made the lampstand and all its accessories from one talent[b] of pure gold.

The Altar of Incense

[25]They made the altar of incense out of acacia wood. It was square, a cubit long and a cubit wide, and two cubits high[c]—its horns of one piece with it. [26]They overlaid the top and all the sides and the horns with pure gold, and made a gold molding around it. [27]They made two gold rings below the molding—two on opposite sides—to hold the poles used to carry it. [28]They made the poles of acacia wood and overlaid them with gold.

[29]They also made the sacred anointing oil and the pure, fragrant incense—the work of a perfumer.

The Altar of Burnt Offering

38 They[d] built the altar of burnt offering of acacia wood, three cubits[e] high; it was square, five cubits long and five cubits wide.[f] [2]They made a horn at each of the four corners, so that the horns and the altar were of one piece, and they overlaid the altar with bronze. [3]They made all its utensils of bronze—its pots, shovels, sprinkling bowls, meat forks and firepans. [4]They made a grating for the altar, a bronze network, to be under its ledge, halfway up the altar. [5]They cast bronze rings to hold the poles for the four corners of the bronze grating. [6]They made the poles of acacia wood and overlaid them with bronze. [7]They inserted the poles into the rings so they would be on the sides of the altar for carrying it. They made it hollow, out of boards.

Basin for Washing

[8]They made the bronze basin and its bronze stand from the mirrors of the women who served at the entrance to the Tent of Meeting.

The Courtyard

[9]Next they made the courtyard. The south side was a hundred cubits[g] long and had curtains of finely twisted linen, [10]with twenty posts and twenty bronze bases, and with silver hooks and bands on the posts. [11]The north side was also a hundred cubits long and had twenty posts and twenty bronze bases, with silver hooks and bands on the posts.

[12]The west end was fifty cubits[h] wide

---

[a] 12 That is, about 3 inches (about 8 centimeters)   [b] 24 That is, about 75 pounds (about 34 kilograms)   [c] 25 That is, about 1 1/2 feet (about 0.5 meter) long and wide, and about 3 feet (about 0.9 meter) high   [d] 1 Or He; also in verses 2-9   [e] 1 That is, about 4 1/2 feet (about 1.3 meters)   [f] 1 That is, about 7 1/2 feet (about 2.3 meters) long and wide   [g] 9 That is, about 150 feet (about 46 meters)   [h] 12 That is, about 75 feet (about 23 meters)

and had curtains, with ten posts and ten bases, with silver hooks and bands on the posts. ¹³The east end, toward the sunrise, was also fifty cubits wide. ¹⁴Curtains fifteen cubitsᵃ long were on one side of the entrance, with three posts and three bases, ¹⁵and curtains fifteen cubits long were on the other side of the entrance to the courtyard, with three posts and three bases. ¹⁶All the curtains around the courtyard were of finely twisted linen. ¹⁷The bases for the posts were bronze. The hooks and bands on the posts were silver, and their tops were overlaid with silver; so all the posts of the courtyard had silver bands.

¹⁸The curtain for the entrance to the courtyard was of blue, purple and scarlet yarn and finely twisted linen—the work of an embroiderer. It was twenty cubitsᵇ long and, like the curtains of the courtyard, five cubitsᶜ high, ¹⁹with four posts and four bronze bases. Their hooks and bands were silver, and their tops were overlaid with silver. ²⁰All the tent pegs of the tabernacle and of the surrounding courtyard were bronze.

The Materials Used

²¹These are the amounts of the materials used for the tabernacle, the tabernacle of the Testimony, which were recorded at Moses' command by the Levites under the direction of Ithamar son of Aaron, the priest. ²²(Bezalel son of Uri, the son of Hur, of the tribe of Judah, made everything the LORD commanded Moses; ²³with him was Oholiab son of Ahisamach, of the tribe of Dan—a craftsman and designer, and an embroiderer in blue, purple and scarlet yarn and fine linen.) ²⁴The total amount of the gold from the wave offering used for all the work on the sanctuary was 29 talents and 730 shekels,ᵈ according to the sanctuary shekel.

²⁵The silver obtained from those of the community who were counted in the census was 100 talents and 1,775 shekels,ᵉ according to the sanctuary shekel—²⁶one beka per person, that is, half a shekel,ᶠ according to the sanctuary shekel, from everyone who had crossed over to those counted, twenty years old or more, a total of 603,550 men. ²⁷The 100 talentsᵍ of silver were used to cast the bases for the sanctuary and for the curtain—100 bases from the 100 talents, one talent for each base. ²⁸They used the 1,775 shekelsʰ to make the hooks for the posts, to overlay the tops of the posts, and to make their bands.

²⁹The bronze from the wave offering was 70 talents and 2,400 shekels.ⁱ ³⁰They used it to make the bases for the entrance to the Tent of Meeting, the bronze altar with its bronze grating and all its utensils, ³¹the bases for the surrounding courtyard and those for its entrance and all the tent pegs for the tabernacle and those for the surrounding courtyard.

The Priestly Garments

39 From the blue, purple and scarlet yarn they made woven garments for ministering in the sanctuary. They also made sacred garments for Aaron, as the LORD commanded Moses.

The Ephod

²Theyʲ made the ephod of gold, and of blue, purple and scarlet yarn, and of finely twisted linen. ³They hammered out thin sheets of gold and cut strands to be worked into the blue, purple and scarlet yarn and fine linen—the work of a skilled craftsman. ⁴They made shoulder pieces for the ephod, which were attached to two of its corners, so it could be fastened. ⁵Its skillfully woven waistband was like it—of one piece with the ephod and made with gold, and with blue, purple and scarlet yarn, and

---

ᵃ 14 That is, about 22 1/2 feet (about 6.9 meters) ᵇ 18 That is, about 30 feet (about 9 meters) ᶜ 18 That is, about 7 1/2 feet (about 2.3 meters) ᵈ 24 The weight of the gold was a little over one ton (about 1 metric ton). ᵉ 25 The weight of the silver was a little over 3 3/4 tons (about 3.4 metric tons). ᶠ 26 That is, about 1/5 ounce (about 5.5 grams) ᵍ 27 That is, about 3 3/4 tons (about 3.4 metric tons). ʰ 28 That is, about 45 pounds (about 20 kilograms) ⁱ 29 The weight of the bronze was about 2 1/2 tons (about 2.4 metric tons). ʲ 2 Or He; also in verses 7, 8 and 22 with finely twisted linen, as the LORD commanded Moses.

⁶They mounted the onyx stones in gold filigree settings and engraved them like a seal with the names of the sons of Israel. ⁷Then they fastened them on the shoulder pieces of the ephod as memorial stones for the sons of Israel, as the LORD commanded Moses.

The Breastpiece

⁸They fashioned the breastpiece—the work of a skilled craftsman. They made it like the ephod: of gold, and of blue, purple and scarlet yarn, and of finely twisted linen. ⁹It was square—a span[a] long and a span wide—and folded double. ¹⁰Then they mounted four rows of precious stones on it. In the first row there was a ruby, a topaz and a beryl; ¹¹in the second row a turquoise, a sapphire[b] and an emerald; ¹²in the third row a jacinth, an agate and an amethyst; ¹³in the fourth row a chrysolite, an onyx and a jasper.[c] They were mounted in gold filigree settings. ¹⁴There were twelve stones, one for each of the names of the sons of Israel, each engraved like a seal with the name of one of the twelve tribes.

> ## Prayer is . . .
> being silent before God
> and resting in His presence.

¹⁵For the breastpiece they made braided chains of pure gold, like a rope. ¹⁶They made two gold filigree settings and two gold rings, and fastened the rings to two of the corners of the breastpiece. ¹⁷They fastened the two gold chains to the rings at the corners of the breastpiece, ¹⁸and the other ends of the chains to the two settings, attaching them to the shoulder pieces of the ephod at the front. ¹⁹They made two gold rings and attached them to the other two corners of the breastpiece on the inside edge next to the ephod. ²⁰Then they made two more gold rings and attached them to the bottom of the shoulder pieces on the front of the ephod, close to the seam just above the waistband of the ephod. ²¹They tied the rings of the breastpiece to the rings of the ephod with blue cord, connecting it to the waistband so that the breastpiece would not swing out from the ephod—as the LORD commanded Moses.

Other Priestly Garments

²²They made the robe of the ephod entirely of blue cloth—the work of a weaver— ²³with an opening in the center of the robe like the opening of a collar,[d] and a band around this opening, so that it would not tear. ²⁴They made pomegranates of blue, purple and scarlet yarn and finely twisted linen around the hem of the robe. ²⁵And they made bells of pure gold and attached them around the hem between the pomegranates. ²⁶The bells and pomegranates alternated around the hem of the robe to be worn for ministering, as the LORD commanded Moses.

²⁷For Aaron and his sons, they made tunics of fine linen—the work of a weaver— ²⁸and the turban of fine linen, the linen headbands and the undergarments of finely twisted linen. ²⁹The sash was of finely twisted linen and blue, purple and scarlet yarn—the work of an embroiderer—as the LORD commanded Moses.

³⁰They made the plate, the sacred diadem, out of pure gold and engraved on it, like an inscription on a seal: HOLY TO THE LORD. ³¹Then they fastened a blue cord to it to attach it to the turban, as the LORD commanded Moses.

Moses Inspects the Tabernacle

³²So all the work on the tabernacle, the Tent of Meeting, was completed. The

---

a 9 That is, about 9 inches (about 22 centimeters)   b 11 Or lapis lazuli   c 13 The precise identification of some of these precious stones is uncertain.   d 23 The meaning of the Hebrew for this word is uncertain.

Israelites did everything just as the LORD commanded Moses. 33Then they brought the tabernacle to Moses: the tent and all its furnishings, its clasps, frames, crossbars, posts and bases; 34the covering of ram skins dyed red, the covering of hides of sea cows[a] and the shielding curtain; 35the ark of the Testimony with its poles and the atonement cover; 36the table with all its articles and the bread of the Presence; 37the pure gold lampstand with its row of lamps and all its accessories, and the oil for the light; 38the gold altar, the anointing oil, the fragrant incense, and the curtain for the entrance to the tent; 39the bronze altar with its bronze grating, its poles and all its utensils; the basin with its stand; 40the curtains of the courtyard with its posts and bases, and the curtain for the entrance to the courtyard; the ropes and tent pegs for the courtyard; all the furnishings for the tabernacle, the Tent of Meeting; 41and the woven garments worn for ministering in the sanctuary, both the sacred garments for Aaron the priest and the garments for his sons when serving as priests.

42The Israelites had done all the work just as the LORD had commanded Moses. 43Moses inspected the work and saw that they had done it just as the LORD had commanded. So Moses blessed them.

Setting Up the Tabernacle

40 Then the LORD said to Moses: 2"Set up the tabernacle, the Tent of Meeting, on the first day of the first month. 3Place the ark of the Testimony in it and shield the ark with the curtain. 4Bring in the table and set out what belongs on it. Then bring in the lampstand and set up its lamps. 5Place the gold altar of incense in front of the ark of the Testimony and put the curtain at the entrance to the tabernacle.

6"Place the altar of burnt offering in front of the entrance to the tabernacle, the Tent of Meeting; 7place the basin between the Tent of Meeting and the altar and put water in it. 8Set up the courtyard around it and put the curtain at the entrance to the courtyard.

9"Take the anointing oil and anoint the tabernacle and everything in it; consecrate it and all its furnishings, and it will be holy. 10Then anoint the altar of burnt offering and all its utensils; consecrate the altar, and it will be most holy. 11Anoint the basin and its stand and consecrate them.

12"Bring Aaron and his sons to the entrance to the Tent of Meeting and wash them with water. 13Then dress Aaron in the sacred garments, anoint him and consecrate him so he may serve me as priest. 14Bring his sons and dress them in tunics. 15Anoint them just as you anointed their father, so they may serve me as priests. Their anointing will be to a priesthood that will continue for all generations to come." 16Moses did everything just as the LORD commanded him.

17So the tabernacle was set up on the first day of the first month in the second year. 18When Moses set up the tabernacle, he put the bases in place, erected the frames, inserted the crossbars and set up the posts. 19Then he spread the tent over the tabernacle and put the covering over the tent, as the LORD commanded him.

20He took the Testimony and placed it in the ark, attached the poles to the ark and put the atonement cover over it. 21Then he brought the ark into the tabernacle and hung the shielding curtain and shielded the ark of the Testimony, as the LORD commanded him.

22Moses placed the table in the Tent of Meeting on the north side of the tabernacle outside the curtain 23and set out the bread on it before the LORD, as the LORD commanded him.

24He placed the lampstand in the Tent of Meeting opposite the table on the south side of the tabernacle 25and set up the lamps before the LORD, as the LORD commanded him.

---

a 34 That is, dugongs

²⁶Moses placed the gold altar in the Tent of Meeting in front of the curtain ²⁷and burned fragrant incense on it, as the LORD commanded him. ²⁸Then he put up the curtain at the entrance to the tabernacle.

²⁹He set the altar of burnt offering near the entrance to the tabernacle, the Tent of Meeting, and offered on it burnt offerings and grain offerings, as the LORD commanded him.

³⁰He placed the basin between the Tent of Meeting and the altar and put water in it for washing, ³¹and Moses and Aaron and his sons used it to wash their hands and feet. ³²They washed whenever they entered the Tent of Meeting or approached the altar, as the LORD commanded Moses.

³³Then Moses set up the courtyard around the tabernacle and altar and put up the curtain at the entrance to the courtyard. And so Moses finished the work.

The Glory of the LORD

³⁴Then the cloud covered the Tent of Meeting, and the glory of the LORD filled the tabernacle. ³⁵Moses could not enter the Tent of Meeting because the cloud had settled upon it, and the glory of the LORD filled the tabernacle.

³⁶In all the travels of the Israelites, whenever the cloud lifted from above the tabernacle, they would set out; ³⁷but if the cloud did not lift, they did not set out—until the day it lifted. ³⁸So the cloud of the LORD was over the tabernacle by day, and fire was in the cloud by night, in the sight of all the house of Israel during all their travels.

Author: Moses

Date: Sometime between 1446 and 1406 BC

Audience: Primarily the Levites and priests of Israel

Can flawed people really draw near to a holy God . . . and actually speak to Him? How—in spite of all our inconsistencies—can we bring Him glory? These are the questions answered in the book of Leviticus. Sacrifice opens the way of access to God. And pure motives and right living ensure continued intimacy with God. "Be holy because I, the LORD your God, am holy" (19:2).

Leviticus reminds us that true holiness will extend to every corner and moment of our lives. Prayer and worship are not just for church on Sundays or a quick time each morning. Everything about us—our thoughts, our sexual behavior, the way we treat others, how we fill our days—should reflect our love for God, our concern for His glory, and our undying resolve to point others to Him.

Prayer Themes:

• *Praise Jesus for His atoning sacrifice so that you can always enjoy the presence of God (9:5-7).*

• *Ask God to give you a deep reverence for His holy character (10:1-3).*

• *Ask God to reveal attitudes or actions in your life that do not line up with His ways (chapter 19).*

Leviticus

The Burnt Offering

1 The LORD called to Moses and spoke to him from the Tent of Meeting. He said, 2"Speak to the Israelites and say to them: 'When any of you brings an offering to the LORD, bring as your offering an animal from either the herd or the flock.

3 "'If the offering is a burnt offering from the herd, he is to offer a male without defect. He must present it at the entrance to the Tent of Meeting so that it[a] will be acceptable to the LORD. 4He is to lay his hand on the head of the burnt offering, and it will be accepted on his behalf to make atonement for him. 5He is to slaughter the young bull before the LORD, and then Aaron's sons the priests shall bring the blood and sprinkle it against the altar on all sides at the entrance to the Tent of Meeting. 6He is to skin the burnt offering and cut it into

pieces. 7The sons of Aaron the priest are to put fire on the altar and arrange wood on the fire. 8Then Aaron's sons the priests shall arrange the pieces, including the head and the fat, on the burning wood that is on the altar. 9He is to wash the inner parts and the legs with water, and the priest is to burn all of it on the altar. It is a burnt offering, an offering made by fire, an aroma pleasing to the LORD.

10 "'If the offering is a burnt offering from the flock, from either the sheep or the goats, he is to offer a male without defect. 11He is to slaughter it at the north side of the altar before the LORD, and Aaron's sons the priests shall sprinkle its blood against the altar on all sides. 12He is to cut it into pieces, and the priest shall arrange them, including the head and the fat, on the burning wood that is on the altar. 13He is to wash the inner parts and

a 3 Or *he*

The Cost of Forgiveness

READ AND CONSIDER: LEVITICUS 1:1-13

"He is to lay his hand on the head of the burnt offering, and it will be accepted on his behalf to make atonement for him" (Leviticus 1:4).

In the Old Testament system of sacrifices, forgiveness came at a price—a literal, hands-on, obvious price.

Today we understand forgiveness as we look at Christ's sacrifice. He was our once-and-for-all payment for sin. In the Old Testament, under the law of Moses, the people looked ahead to Christ's salvation. With the Old Testament sacrifices and offerings, they actually *pre*-enacted the provision that was to come through Jesus. The sacrifices were symbols—the lives of innocent animals were offered as payment for the sins of the people. But the people didn't simply drop a suitable animal to be sacrificed at the door of the tabernacle. They took part in the death of the animal. Leviticus 1:4 says that the worshiper put his hand on the head of the animal that was to be killed. Once the animal was slaughtered, *then* the priests handled the rest. The animal's death symbolized the penalty for sin and the people's need for forgiveness in order to be in a relationship with God.

When you go before God to confess your sins and accept His forgiveness, is the price Jesus paid real to you? Is it as real as if you put your hand on Jesus' head as He bore the cross to Golgotha? Today, forgiveness can seem so sanitized, like the meat we buy at the market, wrapped and labeled. We can easily forget that a death occurred in order for us to have the provision.

Keep in mind that the price for your forgiveness was paid out of Jesus' sacrifice. The old sacrificial system gives us an effective reminder that the price was life itself.

---

the legs with water, and the priest is to bring all of it and burn it on the altar. It is a burnt offering, an offering made by fire, an aroma pleasing to the LORD.

¹⁴"'If the offering to the LORD is a burnt offering of birds, he is to offer a dove or a young pigeon. ¹⁵The priest shall bring it to the altar, wring off the head and burn it on the altar; its blood shall be drained out on the side of the altar. ¹⁶He is to remove the crop with its contentsª and throw it to the east side of the altar, where the ashes are. ¹⁷He shall tear it open by the wings, not severing it completely, and then the priest shall burn it on the wood that is on the fire on the altar. It is a burnt offering, an offering made by fire, an aroma pleasing to the LORD.

The Grain Offering

2 "'When someone brings a grain offering to the LORD, his offering is to be of fine flour. He is to pour oil on it, put incense on it ²and take it to Aaron's sons the priests. The priest shall take a handful of the fine flour and oil, together with all the incense, and burn this as a memorial portion on the altar, an offering made by fire, an aroma pleasing to the LORD. ³The rest of the grain offering belongs to Aaron and his sons; it is a most holy part of the offerings made to the LORD by fire.

⁴"'If you bring a grain offering baked in an oven, it is to consist of fine flour: cakes made without yeast and mixed with oil, orᵇ wafers made without yeast and spread with oil. ⁵If your grain offering

---

ª *16* Or *crop and the feathers*; the meaning of the Hebrew for this word is uncertain.   ᵇ *4* Or *and* is prepared on a griddle, it is to be made of fine flour mixed with oil, and without yeast. 6Crumble it and pour oil on it; it is a grain offering. 7If your grain offering is cooked in a pan, it is to be made of fine flour and oil. 8Bring the grain offering made of these things to the LORD; present it to the priest, who shall take it to the altar. 9He shall take out the memorial portion from the grain offering and burn it on the altar as an offering made by fire, an aroma pleasing to the LORD. 10The rest of the grain offering belongs to Aaron and his sons; it is a most holy part of the offerings made to the LORD by fire.

11"'Every grain offering you bring to the LORD must be made without yeast, for you are not to burn any yeast or honey in an offering made to the LORD by fire. 12You may bring them to the LORD as an offering of the firstfruits, but they are not to be offered on the altar as a pleasing aroma. 13Season all your grain offerings with salt. Do not leave the salt of the covenant of your God out of your grain offerings; add salt to all your offerings.

14"'If you bring a grain offering of firstfruits to the LORD, offer crushed heads of new grain roasted in the fire. 15Put oil and incense on it; it is a grain offering. 16The priest shall burn the memorial portion of the crushed grain and the oil, together with all the incense, as an offering made to the LORD by fire.

The Fellowship Offering

3 "'If someone's offering is a fellowship offering,[a] and he offers an animal from the herd, whether male or female, he is to present before the LORD an animal without defect. 2He is to lay his hand on the head of his offering and slaughter it at the entrance to the Tent of Meeting. Then Aaron's sons the priests shall sprinkle the blood against the altar on all sides. 3From the fellowship offering he is to bring a sacrifice made to the LORD by fire: all the fat that covers the inner parts

or is connected to them, 4both kidneys with the fat on them near the loins, and the covering of the liver, which he will remove with the kidneys. 5Then Aaron's sons are to burn it on the altar on top of the burnt offering that is on the burning wood, as an offering made by fire, an aroma pleasing to the LORD.

Prayer is . . .

confessing your sins and errors and any disregard for the ways of God.

6"'If he offers an animal from the flock as a fellowship offering to the LORD, he is to offer a male or female without defect. 7If he offers a lamb, he is to present it before the LORD. 8He is to lay his hand on the head of his offering and slaughter it in front of the Tent of Meeting. Then Aaron's sons shall sprinkle its blood against the altar on all sides. 9From the fellowship offering he is to bring a sacrifice made to the LORD by fire: its fat, the entire fat tail cut off close to the backbone, all the fat that covers the inner parts or is connected to them, 10both kidneys with the fat on them near the loins, and the covering of the liver, which he will remove with the kidneys. 11The priest shall burn them on the altar as food, an offering made to the LORD by fire.

12"'If his offering is a goat, he is to present it before the LORD. 13He is to lay his hand on its head and slaughter it in front of the Tent of Meeting. Then Aaron's sons shall sprinkle its blood against the altar on all sides. 14From what he offers he is to make this offering to the LORD by fire: all the fat that covers the inner parts or is connected to them, 15both kidneys with the fat on them near the loins, and the covering of the liver, which he will remove with the kidneys. 16The priest shall burn them on the altar as food, an offer-

a 1 Traditionally *peace offering*; also in verses 3, 6 and 9 ing made by fire, a pleasing aroma. All the fat is the LORD's.

17 " 'This is a lasting ordinance for the generations to come, wherever you live: You must not eat any fat or any blood.' "

The Sin Offering

4 The LORD said to Moses, 2 "Say to the Israelites: 'When anyone sins unintentionally and does what is forbidden in any of the LORD's commands—

3 " 'If the anointed priest sins, bringing guilt on the people, he must bring to the LORD a young bull without defect as a sin offering for the sin he has committed. 4 He is to present the bull at the entrance to the Tent of Meeting before the LORD. He is to lay his hand on its head and slaughter it before the LORD. 5 Then the anointed priest shall take some of the bull's blood and carry it into the Tent of Meeting. 6 He is to dip his finger into the blood and sprinkle some of it seven times before the LORD, in front of the curtain of the sanctuary. 7 The priest shall then put some of the blood on the horns of the altar of fragrant incense that is before the LORD in the Tent of Meeting. The rest of the bull's blood he shall pour out at the base of the altar of burnt offering at the entrance to the Tent of Meeting. 8 He shall remove all the fat from the bull of the sin offering—the fat that covers the inner parts or is connected to them, 9 both kidneys with the fat on them near the loins, and the covering of the liver, which he will remove with the kidneys— 10 just as the fat is removed from the ox[a] sacrificed as a fellowship offering.[b] Then the priest shall burn them on the altar of burnt offering. 11 But the hide of the bull and all its flesh, as well as the head and legs, the inner parts and offal— 12 that is, all the rest of the bull—he must take outside the camp to a place ceremonially clean, where the ashes are thrown, and burn it in a wood fire on the ash heap.

13 " 'If the whole Israelite community sins unintentionally and does what is for- bidden in any of the LORD's commands, even though the community is unaware of the matter, they are guilty. 14 When they become aware of the sin they com- mitted, the assembly must bring a young bull as a sin offering and present it be- fore the Tent of Meeting. 15 The elders of the community are to lay their hands on the bull's head before the LORD, and the bull shall be slaughtered before the LORD. 16 Then the anointed priest is to take some of the bull's blood into the Tent of Meeting. 17 He shall dip his finger into the blood and sprinkle it before the LORD seven times in front of the curtain. 18 He is to put some of the blood on the horns of the altar that is before the LORD in the Tent of Meeting. The rest of the blood he shall pour out at the base of the altar of burnt offering at the entrance to the Tent of Meeting. 19 He shall remove all the fat from it and burn it on the altar, 20 and do with this bull just as he did with the bull for the sin offering. In this way the priest will make atonement for them, and they will be forgiven. 21 Then he shall take the bull outside the camp and burn it as he burned the first bull. This is the sin offering for the community.

22 " 'When a leader sins unintentionally and does what is forbidden in any of the commands of the LORD his God, he is guilty. 23 When he is made aware of the sin he committed, he must bring as his offering a male goat without defect. 24 He is to lay his hand on the goat's head and slaughter it at the place where the burnt offering is slaughtered before the LORD. It is a sin offering. 25 Then the priest shall take some of the blood of the sin offering with his finger and put it on the horns of the altar of burnt offering and pour out the rest of the blood at the base of the altar. 26 He shall burn all the fat on the al- tar as he burned the fat of the fellowship offering. In this way the priest will make atonement for the man's sin, and he will be forgiven.

---

[a] 10 The Hebrew word can include both male and female.   [b] 10 Traditionally *peace offering*; also in verses 26, 31 and 35

27 "'If a member of the community sins unintentionally and does what is forbidden in any of the LORD's commands, he is guilty. 28 When he is made aware of the sin he committed, he must bring as his offering for the sin he committed a female goat without defect. 29 He is to lay his hand on the head of the sin offering and slaughter it at the place of the burnt offering. 30 Then the priest is to take some of the blood with his finger and put it on the horns of the altar of burnt offering and pour out the rest of the blood at the base of the altar. 31 He shall remove all the fat, just as the fat is removed from the fellowship offering, and the priest shall burn it on the altar as an aroma pleasing to the LORD. In this way the priest will make atonement for him, and he will be forgiven.

32 "'If he brings a lamb as his sin offering, he is to bring a female without defect. 33 He is to lay his hand on its head and slaughter it for a sin offering at the place where the burnt offering is slaughtered. 34 Then the priest shall take some of the blood of the sin offering with his finger and put it on the horns of the altar of burnt offering and pour out the rest of the blood at the base of the altar. 35 He shall remove all the fat, just as the fat is removed from the lamb of the fellowship offering, and the priest shall burn it on the altar on top of the offerings made to the LORD by fire. In this way the priest will make atonement for him for the sin he has committed, and he will be forgiven.

5 "'If a person sins because he does not speak up when he hears a public charge to testify regarding something he has seen or learned about, he will be held responsible.

2 "'Or if a person touches anything ceremonially unclean—whether the carcasses of unclean wild animals or of unclean livestock or of unclean creatures that move along the ground—even though he is unaware of it, he has become unclean and is guilty.

3 "'Or if he touches human uncleanness—anything that would make him unclean—even though he is unaware of it, when he learns of it he will be guilty.

4 "'Or if a person thoughtlessly takes an oath to do anything, whether good or evil—in any matter one might carelessly swear about—even though he is unaware of it, in any case when he learns of it he will be guilty.

5 "'When anyone is guilty in any of these ways, he must confess in what way he has sinned 6 and, as a penalty for the sin he has committed, he must bring to the LORD a female lamb or goat from the flock as a sin offering; and the priest shall make atonement for him for his sin.

7 "'If he cannot afford a lamb, he is to bring two doves or two young pigeons to the LORD as a penalty for his sin—one for a sin offering and the other for a burnt offering. 8 He is to bring them to the priest, who shall first offer the one for the sin offering. He is to wring its head from its neck, not severing it completely, 9 and is to sprinkle some of the blood of the sin offering against the side of the altar; the rest of the blood must be drained out at the base of the altar. It is a sin offering. 10 The priest shall then offer the other as a burnt offering in the prescribed way and make atonement for him for the sin he has committed, and he will be forgiven.

11 "'If, however, he cannot afford two doves or two young pigeons, he is to bring as an offering for his sin a tenth of an ephah[a] of fine flour for a sin offering. He must not put oil or incense on it, because it is a sin offering. 12 He is to bring it to the priest, who shall take a handful of it as a memorial portion and burn it on the altar on top of the offerings made to the LORD by fire. It is a sin offering. 13 In this way the priest will make atonement for him for any of these sins he has committed, and he will be forgiven. The rest

---

a 11 That is, probably about 2 quarts (about 2 liters)

How in the World Can I Be Holy?

God calls us to reflect His holiness. "But just as he who called you is holy, so be holy in all you do; for it is written: 'Be holy, because I am holy' " (1 Peter 1:15-16).

God is not saying, "You be holy!" as a parent would say, "You be quiet!" to a child. He is saying, "I am inviting you to share My holiness. Let My holiness live in you. Come apart and be separate from all that is unholy and allow My holiness to grow in you. Let it become a well in your soul from which you draw your own holiness of character."

It's the difference between telling someone, "Come with me!" and making it a stern command, and saying the same words—"Go with me"—and making it a gentle invitation. With God, it is always a gentle invitation. He doesn't *command* something that we can't begin to do. How can we make ourselves holy like God on our own? We can't do it without *Him*.

Jesus is the greatest example on earth of a holy life and character. He was wholly devoted to God and to God's will in His life. What Jesus did by dying on the cross for us and sending us the Holy Spirit was to ensure that we are guaranteed a way to be released from our unholiness and be holy like God. Because of Him, our sin does not keep us from approaching God's throne. If it did, who could ever come before Him? Instead, our sin is the *reason* to come before Him in confession and repentance, and to praise Him for His holiness.

The more we worship God, the more we see His holiness, wholeness, purity, and goodness making us holy, whole, pure, and good. Coming before God in worship reveals sin in our lives we might not have even been able to acknowledge. What better way to wash it out of us than being in His presence?

Becoming holy should be the goal of our lives because it makes us distinctive. This doesn't mean we gain a holier-than-thou attitude and *lord* it over others. It means we aspire to a holy-as-the-Lord lifestyle so we can be a *blessing* to others.

But we don't just get up one day and say, "I'm going to be holy," and suddenly we are. A deep recognition of the holiness of God and a desire to do whatever it takes to become like Him is absolutely necessary. We can't *make* ourselves holy, but we can *seek* to be holy as God is holy.

How do we seek that when holiness seems so elusive? So unattainable? We do it by worshiping God. And specifically praising Him *for* His holiness. That's what the angels in heaven are doing around the throne all the time. Isaiah heard them saying, "Holy, holy, holy is the LORD Almighty; the whole earth is full of his glory" (Isaiah 6:3). When we praise God for His holiness, we have a closer understanding of what it means to be holy. It is as if His holiness rubs off on us by means of the close proximity we have with God. He imparts His holiness to us as we praise Him.

For the next "From Stormie's Heart" article, go to page 191.

of the offering will belong to the priest, as in the case of the grain offering.'"

The Guilt Offering

¹⁴The LORD said to Moses: ¹⁵"When a person commits a violation and sins unintentionally in regard to any of the LORD's holy things, he is to bring to the LORD as a penalty a ram from the flock, one without defect and of the proper value in silver, according to the sanctuary shekel.ᵃ It is a guilt offering. ¹⁶He must make restitution for what he has failed to do in regard to the holy things, add a fifth of the value to that and give it all to the priest, who will make atonement for him with the ram as a guilt offering, and he will be forgiven.

Praying Leviticus 5:17

Lord, reveal to me any way that
I have not obeyed Your laws so that
I may confess it to You as sin.

---

¹⁷"If a person sins and does what is forbidden in any of the LORD's commands, even though he does not know it, he is guilty and will be held responsible. ¹⁸He is to bring to the priest as a guilt offering a ram from the flock, one without defect and of the proper value. In this way the priest will make atonement for him for the wrong he has committed unintentionally, and he will be forgiven. ¹⁹It is a guilt offering; he has been guilty ofᵇ wrongdoing against the LORD."

6 The LORD said to Moses: ²"If anyone sins and is unfaithful to the LORD by deceiving his neighbor about something entrusted to him or left in his care or stolen, or if he cheats him, ³or if he finds lost property and lies about it, or if he swears falsely, or if he commits any such sin that people may do— ⁴when he thus sins and becomes guilty, he must return what he has stolen or taken by extortion, or what was entrusted to him, or the lost property he found, ⁵or whatever it was

he swore falsely about. He must make restitution in full, add a fifth of the value to it and give it all to the owner on the day he presents his guilt offering. ⁶And as a penalty he must bring to the priest, that is, to the LORD, his guilt offering, a ram from the flock, one without defect and of the proper value. ⁷In this way the priest will make atonement for him before the LORD, and he will be forgiven for any of these things he did that made him guilty."

The Burnt Offering

⁸The LORD said to Moses: ⁹"Give Aaron and his sons this command: 'These are the regulations for the burnt offering: The burnt offering is to remain on the altar hearth throughout the night, till morning, and the fire must be kept burning on the altar. ¹⁰The priest shall then put on his linen clothes, with linen undergarments next to his body, and shall remove the ashes of the burnt offering that the fire has consumed on the altar and place them beside the altar. ¹¹Then he is to take off these clothes and put on others, and carry the ashes outside the camp to a place that is ceremonially clean. ¹²The fire on the altar must be kept burning; it must not go out. Every morning the priest is to add firewood and arrange the burnt offering on the fire and burn the fat of the fellowship offeringsᶜ on it. ¹³The fire must be kept burning on the altar continuously; it must not go out.

The Grain Offering

¹⁴"'These are the regulations for the grain offering: Aaron's sons are to bring it before the LORD, in front of the altar. ¹⁵The priest is to take a handful of fine flour and oil, together with all the incense on the grain offering, and burn the memorial portion on the altar as an aroma pleasing to the LORD. ¹⁶Aaron and his sons shall eat the rest of it, but it is to be eaten without yeast in a holy place;

ᵃ *15* That is, about 2/5 ounce (about 11.5 grams)   ᵇ *19* Or *has made full expiation for his*   ᶜ *12* Traditionally *peace offerings* they are to eat it in the courtyard of the Tent of Meeting. [17]It must not be baked with yeast; I have given it as their share of the offerings made to me by fire. Like the sin offering and the guilt offering, it is most holy. [18]Any male descendant of Aaron may eat it. It is his regular share of the offerings made to the LORD by fire for the generations to come. Whatever touches them will become holy.[a]' "

[19]The LORD also said to Moses, [20]"This is the offering Aaron and his sons are to bring to the LORD on the day he[b] is anointed: a tenth of an ephah[c] of fine flour as a regular grain offering, half of it in the morning and half in the evening. [21]Prepare it with oil on a griddle; bring it well-mixed and present the grain offering broken[d] in pieces as an aroma pleasing to the LORD. [22]The son who is to succeed him as anointed priest shall prepare it. It is the LORD's regular share and is to be burned completely. [23]Every grain offering of a priest shall be burned completely; it must not be eaten."

The Sin Offering

[24]The LORD said to Moses, [25]"Say to Aaron and his sons: 'These are the regulations for the sin offering: The sin offering is to be slaughtered before the LORD in the place the burnt offering is slaughtered; it is most holy. [26]The priest who offers it shall eat it; it is to be eaten in a holy place, in the courtyard of the Tent of Meeting. [27]Whatever touches any of the flesh will become holy, and if any of the blood is spattered on a garment, you must wash it in a holy place. [28]The clay pot the meat is cooked in must be broken; but if it is cooked in a bronze pot, the pot is to be scoured and rinsed with water. [29]Any male in a priest's family may eat it; it is most holy. [30]But any sin offering whose blood is brought into the Tent of Meeting to make atonement in the Holy Place must not be eaten; it must be burned.

The Guilt Offering

7 " 'These are the regulations for the guilt offering, which is most holy: [2]The guilt offering is to be slaughtered in the place where the burnt offering is slaughtered, and its blood is to be sprinkled against the altar on all sides. [3]All its fat shall be offered: the fat tail and the fat that covers the inner parts, [4]both kidneys with the fat on them near the loins, and the covering of the liver, which is to be removed with the kidneys. [5]The priest shall burn them on the altar as an offering made to the LORD by fire. It is a guilt offering. [6]Any male in a priest's family may eat it, but it must be eaten in a holy place; it is most holy.

[7]" 'The same law applies to both the sin offering and the guilt offering: They belong to the priest who makes atonement with them. [8]The priest who offers a burnt offering for anyone may keep its hide for himself. [9]Every grain offering baked in an oven or cooked in a pan or on a griddle belongs to the priest who offers it, [10]and every grain offering, whether mixed with oil or dry, belongs equally to all the sons of Aaron.

The Fellowship Offering

[11]" 'These are the regulations for the fellowship offering[e] a person may present to the LORD:

[12]" 'If he offers it as an expression of thankfulness, then along with this thank offering he is to offer cakes of bread made without yeast and mixed with oil, wafers made without yeast and spread with oil, and cakes of fine flour well-kneaded and mixed with oil. [13]Along with his fellowship offering of thanksgiving he is to present an offering with cakes of bread made with yeast. [14]He is to bring one of each kind as an offering, a contribution to the LORD; it belongs to the priest who sprinkles the blood of the fellowship offerings. [15]The meat of his fellowship offering of thanksgiving must be eaten on

---

[a] 18 Or Whoever touches them must be holy; similarly in verse 27   [b] 20 Or each   [c] 20 That is, probably about 2 quarts (about 2 liters)   [d] 21 The meaning of the Hebrew for this word is uncertain.   [e] 11 Traditionally peace offering; also in verses 13-37

the day it is offered; he must leave none of it till morning.

16 " 'If, however, his offering is the result of a vow or is a freewill offering, the sacrifice shall be eaten on the day he offers it, but anything left over may be eaten on the next day. 17 Any meat of the sacrifice left over till the third day must be burned up. 18 If any meat of the fellowship offering is eaten on the third day, it will not be accepted. It will not be credited to the one who offered it, for it is impure; the person who eats any of it will be held responsible.

19 " 'Meat that touches anything ceremonially unclean must not be eaten; it must be burned up. As for other meat, anyone ceremonially clean may eat it. 20 But if anyone who is unclean eats any meat of the fellowship offering belonging to the LORD, that person must be cut off from his people. 21 If anyone touches something unclean—whether human uncleanness or an unclean animal or any unclean, detestable thing—and then eats any of the meat of the fellowship offering belonging to the LORD, that person must be cut off from his people.' "

Eating Fat and Blood Forbidden

22 The LORD said to Moses, 23 "Say to the Israelites: 'Do not eat any of the fat of cattle, sheep or goats. 24 The fat of an animal found dead or torn by wild animals may be used for any other purpose, but you must not eat it. 25 Anyone who eats the fat of an animal from which an offering by fire may be[a] made to the LORD must be cut off from his people. 26 And wherever you live, you must not eat the blood of any bird or animal. 27 If anyone eats blood, that person must be cut off from his people.' "

The Priests' Share

28 The LORD said to Moses, 29 "Say to the Israelites: 'Anyone who brings a fellowship offering to the LORD is to bring part of it as his sacrifice to the LORD.

30 With his own hands he is to bring the offering made to the LORD by fire; he is to bring the fat, together with the breast, and wave the breast before the LORD as a wave offering. 31 The priest shall burn the fat on the altar, but the breast belongs to Aaron and his sons. 32 You are to give the right thigh of your fellowship offerings to the priest as a contribution. 33 The son of Aaron who offers the blood and the fat of the fellowship offering shall have the right thigh as his share. 34 From the fellowship offerings of the Israelites, I have taken the breast that is waved and the thigh that is presented and have given them to Aaron the priest and his sons as their regular share from the Israelites.' "

35 This is the portion of the offerings made to the LORD by fire that were allotted to Aaron and his sons on the day they were presented to serve the LORD as priests. 36 On the day they were anointed, the LORD commanded that the Israelites give this to them as their regular share for the generations to come.

37 These, then, are the regulations for the burnt offering, the grain offering, the sin offering, the guilt offering, the ordination offering and the fellowship offering, 38 which the LORD gave Moses on Mount Sinai on the day he commanded the Israelites to bring their offerings to the LORD, in the Desert of Sinai.

The Ordination of Aaron and His Sons

8 The LORD said to Moses, 2 "Bring Aaron and his sons, their garments, the anointing oil, the bull for the sin offering, the two rams and the basket containing bread made without yeast, 3 and gather the entire assembly at the entrance to the Tent of Meeting." 4 Moses did as the LORD commanded him, and the assembly gathered at the entrance to the Tent of Meeting.

5 Moses said to the assembly, "This is what the LORD has commanded to be

---

a 25 Or fire is

done." 6Then Moses brought Aaron and his sons forward and washed them with water. 7He put the tunic on Aaron, tied the sash around him, clothed him with the robe and put the ephod on him. He also tied the ephod to him by its skillfully woven waistband; so it was fastened on him. 8He placed the breastpiece on him and put the Urim and Thummim in the breastpiece. 9Then he placed the turban on Aaron's head and set the gold plate, the sacred diadem, on the front of it, as the LORD commanded Moses.

10Then Moses took the anointing oil and anointed the tabernacle and everything in it, and so consecrated them. 11He sprinkled some of the oil on the altar seven times, anointing the altar and all its utensils and the basin with its stand, to consecrate them. 12He poured some of the anointing oil on Aaron's head and anointed him to consecrate him. 13Then he brought Aaron's sons forward, put tunics on them, tied sashes around them and put headbands on them, as the LORD commanded Moses.

14He then presented the bull for the sin offering, and Aaron and his sons laid their hands on its head. 15Moses slaughtered the bull and took some of the blood, and with his finger he put it on all the horns of the altar to purify the altar. He poured out the rest of the blood at the base of the altar. So he consecrated it to make atonement for it. 16Moses also took all the fat around the inner parts, the covering of the liver, and both kidneys and their fat, and burned it on the altar. 17But the bull with its hide and its flesh and its offal he burned up outside the camp, as the LORD commanded Moses.

18He then presented the ram for the burnt offering, and Aaron and his sons laid their hands on its head. 19Then Moses slaughtered the ram and sprinkled the blood against the altar on all sides. 20He cut the ram into pieces and burned the head, the pieces and the fat. 21He washed the inner parts and the legs with water and burned the whole ram on the altar as a burnt offering, a pleasing aroma, an offering made to the LORD by fire, as the LORD commanded Moses.

22He then presented the other ram, the ram for the ordination, and Aaron and his sons laid their hands on its head. 23Moses slaughtered the ram and took some of its blood and put it on the lobe of Aaron's right ear, on the thumb of his right hand and on the big toe of his right foot. 24Moses also brought Aaron's sons forward and put some of the blood on the lobes of their right ears, on the thumbs of their right hands and on the big toes of their right feet. Then he sprinkled blood against the altar on all sides. 25He took the fat, the fat tail, all the fat around the inner parts, the covering of the liver, both kidneys and their fat and the right thigh. 26Then from the basket of bread made without yeast, which was before the LORD, he took a cake of bread, and one made with oil, and a wafer; he put these on the fat portions and on the right thigh. 27He put all these in the hands of Aaron and his sons and waved them before the LORD as a wave offering. 28Then Moses took them from their hands and burned them on the altar on top of the burnt offering as an ordination offering, a pleasing aroma, an offering made to the LORD by fire. 29He also took the breast—Moses' share of the ordination ram—and waved it before the LORD as a wave offering, as the LORD commanded Moses.

30Then Moses took some of the anointing oil and some of the blood from the altar and sprinkled them on Aaron and his garments and on his sons and their garments. So he consecrated Aaron and his garments and his sons and their garments.

31Moses then said to Aaron and his sons, "Cook the meat at the entrance to the Tent of Meeting and eat it there with the bread from the basket of ordination offerings, as I commanded, saying,a 'Aaron and

---

a 31 Or I was commanded:

his sons are to eat it.' ³²Then burn up the rest of the meat and the bread. ³³Do not leave the entrance to the Tent of Meeting for seven days, until the days of your ordination are completed, for your ordination will last seven days. ³⁴What has been done today was commanded by the LORD to make atonement for you. ³⁵You must stay at the entrance to the Tent of Meeting day and night for seven days and do what the LORD requires, so you will not die; for that is what I have been commanded." ³⁶So Aaron and his sons did everything the LORD commanded through Moses.

The Priests Begin Their Ministry

9 On the eighth day Moses summoned Aaron and his sons and the elders of Israel. ²He said to Aaron, "Take a bull calf for your sin offering and a ram for your burnt offering, both without defect, and present them before the LORD. ³Then say to the Israelites: 'Take a male goat for a sin offering, a calf and a lamb—both a year old and without defect—for a burnt offering, ⁴and an ox[a] and a ram for a fellowship offering[b] to sacrifice before the LORD, together with a grain offering mixed with oil. For today the LORD will appear to you.'"

⁵They took the things Moses commanded to the front of the Tent of Meeting, and the entire assembly came near and stood before the LORD. ⁶Then Moses said, "This is what the LORD has commanded you to do, so that the glory of the LORD may appear to you."

⁷Moses said to Aaron, "Come to the altar and sacrifice your sin offering and your burnt offering and make atonement for yourself and the people; sacrifice the offering that is for the people and make atonement for them, as the LORD has commanded."

⁸So Aaron came to the altar and slaughtered the calf as a sin offering for himself. ⁹His sons brought the blood to him, and he dipped his finger into the blood and put it on the horns of the altar; the rest of the blood he poured out at the base of the altar. ¹⁰On the altar he burned the fat, the kidneys and the covering of the liver from the sin offering, as the LORD commanded Moses; ¹¹the flesh and the hide he burned up outside the camp.

¹²Then he slaughtered the burnt offering. His sons handed him the blood, and he sprinkled it against the altar on all sides. ¹³They handed him the burnt offering piece by piece, including the head, and he burned them on the altar. ¹⁴He washed the inner parts and the legs and burned them on top of the burnt offering on the altar.

¹⁵Aaron then brought the offering that was for the people. He took the goat for the people's sin offering and slaughtered it and offered it for a sin offering as he did with the first one.

¹⁶He brought the burnt offering and offered it in the prescribed way. ¹⁷He also brought the grain offering, took a handful of it and burned it on the altar in addition to the morning's burnt offering.

¹⁸He slaughtered the ox and the ram as the fellowship offering for the people. His sons handed him the blood, and he sprinkled it against the altar on all sides. ¹⁹But the fat portions of the ox and the ram—the fat tail, the layer of fat, the kidneys and the covering of the liver— ²⁰these they laid on the breasts, and then Aaron burned the fat on the altar. ²¹Aaron waved the breasts and the right thigh before the LORD as a wave offering, as Moses commanded.

²²Then Aaron lifted his hands toward the people and blessed them. And having sacrificed the sin offering, the burnt offering and the fellowship offering, he stepped down.

²³Moses and Aaron then went into the Tent of Meeting. When they came out, they blessed the people; and the glory

---

[a] 4 The Hebrew word can include both male and female; also in verses 18 and 19.   [b] 4 Traditionally peace offering; also in verses 18 and 22

of the LORD appeared to all the people. ²⁴Fire came out from the presence of the LORD and consumed the burnt offering and the fat portions on the altar. And when all the people saw it, they shouted for joy and fell facedown.

The Death of Nadab and Abihu

10 Aaron's sons Nadab and Abihu took their censers, put fire in them and added incense; and they offered unauthorized fire before the LORD, contrary to his command. ²So fire came out from the presence of the LORD and consumed them, and they died before the LORD.

³Moses then said to Aaron, "This is what the LORD spoke of when he said:

"'Among those who approach me
  I will show myself holy;
 in the sight of all the people
  I will be honored.'"

Aaron remained silent.

⁴Moses summoned Mishael and Elzaphan, sons of Aaron's uncle Uzziel, and said to them, "Come here; carry your cousins outside the camp, away from the front of the sanctuary." ⁵So they came and carried them, still in their tunics, outside the camp, as Moses ordered.

GOING *deeper*

Why We Do What We Do

READ AND CONSIDER: LEVITICUS 10:1-7

"Aaron's sons Nadab and Abihu took their censers, put fire in them and added incense; and they offered unauthorized fire before the LORD, contrary to his command. So fire came out from the presence of the LORD and consumed them, and they died before the LORD" (Leviticus 10:1-2).

Things you do over and over can become very routine. For example, if you perform a ritual enough times, even a sacred one, you can easily forget to honor the full significance of it. What's surprising, however, is to find that even when these Old Testament spiritual rituals were relatively new, some worshipers still struggled to keep the significance of their actions fresh in their minds. Nadab and Abihu were prime examples. They took lightly something that should have been holy, and they paid the ultimate price for their mistake.

From the description given to us at the opening of Leviticus 10, we know that Nadab and Abihu had disregarded instructions they'd been given. This disregard was not simply a mistake—it was an act of disrespect toward God, who had given the instructions. Their disregard seems completely out of place when you consider who these brothers were—the sons of Aaron, the nephews of Moses. They had seen miracles, walked across dry land in the middle of the Red Sea, and eaten manna. They were first-generation eyewitnesses. Their father had become the first high priest of the Israelite nation, and they, as his sons, had been welcomed into the priesthood. Exodus 24:9-10 even tells us that Nadab and Abihu were among 74 men who had climbed the mountain with Moses and had actually *seen* God.

Yet, when the time came to honor God with obedience, they just didn't think it was important enough to do what God wanted.

Have you ever become lax in that way? Do you pray as often as God wants you to? Are you spending time daily in His Word? Are those two spiritual disciplines as fresh and alive as they should be. If not, ask God to give you new excitement about spending time with Him. Ask Him to take away any apathy or carelessness on your part. Do whatever it takes to keep yourself from just going through the motions. Reconnect to the passion and meaning of being in God's presence.

6Then Moses said to Aaron and his sons Eleazar and Ithamar, "Do not let your hair become unkempt,[a] and do not tear your clothes, or you will die and the LORD will be angry with the whole community. But your relatives, all the house of Israel, may mourn for those the LORD has destroyed by fire. 7Do not leave the entrance to the Tent of Meeting or you will die, because the LORD's anointing oil is on you." So they did as Moses said.

Praying Leviticus 10:7-10

Dear God, help me to always be able to distinguish what is holy from what is unholy, and what is polluted and perverted from what is clean and sacred, so that I can stay pure before You.

8Then the LORD said to Aaron, 9"You and your sons are not to drink wine or other fermented drink whenever you go into the Tent of Meeting, or you will die. This is a lasting ordinance for the generations to come. 10You must distinguish between the holy and the common, between the unclean and the clean, 11and you must teach the Israelites all the decrees the LORD has given them through Moses."

12Moses said to Aaron and his remaining sons, Eleazar and Ithamar, "Take the grain offering left over from the offerings made to the LORD by fire and eat it prepared without yeast beside the altar, for it is most holy. 13Eat it in a holy place, because it is your share and your sons' share of the offerings made to the LORD by fire; for so I have been commanded. 14But you and your sons and your daughters may eat the breast that was waved and the thigh that was presented. Eat them in a ceremonially clean place; they have been given to you and your children as your share of the Israelites' fellowship offerings.[b] 15The thigh that was presented and the breast that was waved must be brought with the fat portions of the offer-

ings made by fire, to be waved before the LORD as a wave offering. This will be the regular share for you and your children, as the LORD has commanded."

16When Moses inquired about the goat of the sin offering and found that it had been burned up, he was angry with Eleazar and Ithamar, Aaron's remaining sons, and asked, 17"Why didn't you eat the sin offering in the sanctuary area? It is most holy; it was given to you to take away the guilt of the community by making atonement for them before the LORD. 18Since its blood was not taken into the Holy Place, you should have eaten the goat in the sanctuary area, as I commanded."

19Aaron replied to Moses, "Today they sacrificed their sin offering and their burnt offering before the LORD, but such things as this have happened to me. Would the LORD have been pleased if I had eaten the sin offering today?" 20When Moses heard this, he was satisfied.

Clean and Unclean Food

11 The LORD said to Moses and Aaron, 2"Say to the Israelites: 'Of all the animals that live on land, these are the ones you may eat: 3You may eat any animal that has a split hoof completely divided and that chews the cud.

4"There are some that only chew the cud or only have a split hoof, but you must not eat them. The camel, though it chews the cud, does not have a split hoof; it is ceremonially unclean for you. 5The coney,[c] though it chews the cud, does not have a split hoof; it is unclean for you. 6The rabbit, though it chews the cud, does not have a split hoof; it is unclean for you. 7And the pig, though it has a split hoof completely divided, does not chew the cud; it is unclean for you. 8You must not eat their meat or touch their carcasses; they are unclean for you.

9"Of all the creatures living in the water of the seas and the streams, you may eat any that have fins and scales. 10But all creatures in the seas or streams that

---

[a] 6 Or *Do not uncover your heads*   [b] 14 Traditionally *peace offerings*   [c] 5 That is, the hyrax or rock badger

do not have fins and scales—whether among all the swarming things or among all the other living creatures in the water—you are to detest. [11]And since you are to detest them, you must not eat their meat and you must detest their carcasses. [12]Anything living in the water that does not have fins and scales is to be detestable to you.

[13]" 'These are the birds you are to detest and not eat because they are detestable: the eagle, the vulture, the black vulture, [14]the red kite, any kind of black kite, [15]any kind of raven, [16]the horned owl, the screech owl, the gull, any kind of hawk, [17]the little owl, the cormorant, the great owl, [18]the white owl, the desert owl, the osprey, [19]the stork, any kind of heron, the hoopoe and the bat.[a]

[20]" 'All flying insects that walk on all fours are to be detestable to you. [21]There are, however, some winged creatures that walk on all fours that you may eat: those that have jointed legs for hopping on the ground. [22]Of these you may eat any kind of locust, katydid, cricket or grasshopper. [23]But all other winged creatures that have four legs you are to detest.

[24]" 'You will make yourselves unclean by these; whoever touches their carcasses will be unclean till evening. [25]Whoever picks up one of their carcasses must wash his clothes, and he will be unclean till evening.

[26]" 'Every animal that has a split hoof not completely divided or that does not chew the cud is unclean for you; whoever touches the carcass of any of them will be unclean. [27]Of all the animals that walk on all fours, those that walk on their paws are unclean for you; whoever touches their carcasses will be unclean till evening. [28]Anyone who picks up their carcasses must wash his clothes, and he will be unclean till evening. They are unclean for you.

[29]" 'Of the animals that move about on the ground, these are unclean for you: the weasel, the rat, any kind of great lizard, [30]the gecko, the monitor lizard, the wall lizard, the skink and the chameleon. [31]Of all those that move along the ground, these are unclean for you. Whoever touches them when they are dead will be unclean till evening. [32]When one of them dies and falls on something, that article, whatever its use, will be unclean, whether it is made of wood, cloth, hide or sackcloth. Put it in water; it will be unclean till evening, and then it will be clean. [33]If one of them falls into a clay pot, everything in it will be unclean, and you must break the pot. [34]Any food that could be eaten but has water on it from such a pot is unclean, and any liquid that could be drunk from it is unclean. [35]Anything that one of their carcasses falls on becomes unclean; an oven or cooking pot must be broken up. They are unclean, and you are to regard them as unclean. [36]A spring, however, or a cistern for collecting water remains clean, but anyone who touches one of these carcasses is unclean. [37]If a carcass falls on any seeds that are to be planted, they remain clean. [38]But if water has been put on the seed and a carcass falls on it, it is unclean for you.

[39]" 'If an animal that you are allowed to eat dies, anyone who touches the carcass will be unclean till evening. [40]Anyone who eats some of the carcass must wash his clothes, and he will be unclean till evening. Anyone who picks up the carcass must wash his clothes, and he will be unclean till evening.

[41]" 'Every creature that moves about on the ground is detestable; it is not to be eaten. [42]You are not to eat any creature that moves about on the ground, whether it moves on its belly or walks on all fours or on many feet; it is detestable. [43]Do not defile yourselves by any of these creatures. Do not make yourselves unclean by means of them or be made unclean by them. [44]I am the LORD your God; consecrate yourselves and be holy,

---

[a] [19] The precise identification of some of the birds, insects and animals in this chapter is uncertain.

because I am holy. Do not make yourselves unclean by any creature that moves about on the ground. ⁴⁵I am the LORD who brought you up out of Egypt to be your God; therefore be holy, because I am holy.

⁴⁶"'These are the regulations concerning animals, birds, every living thing that moves in the water and every creature that moves about on the ground. ⁴⁷You must distinguish between the unclean and the clean, between living creatures that may be eaten and those that may not be eaten.'"

Purification After Childbirth

12 The LORD said to Moses, ²"Say to the Israelites: 'A woman who becomes pregnant and gives birth to a son will be ceremonially unclean for seven days, just as she is unclean during her monthly period. ³On the eighth day the boy is to be circumcised. ⁴Then the woman must wait thirty-three days to be purified from her bleeding. She must not touch anything sacred or go to the sanctuary until the days of her purification are over. ⁵If she gives birth to a daughter, for two weeks the woman will be unclean, as during her period. Then she must wait sixty-six days to be purified from her bleeding.

⁶"'When the days of her purification for a son or daughter are over, she is to bring to the priest at the entrance to the Tent of Meeting a year-old lamb for a burnt offering and a young pigeon or a dove for a sin offering. ⁷He shall offer them before the LORD to make atonement for her, and then she will be ceremonially clean from her flow of blood.

"'These are the regulations for the woman who gives birth to a boy or a girl. ⁸If she cannot afford a lamb, she is to bring two doves or two young pigeons, one for a burnt offering and the other for a sin offering. In this way the priest will make atonement for her, and she will be clean.'"

Regulations About Infectious Skin Diseases

13 The LORD said to Moses and Aaron, ²"When anyone has a swelling or a rash or a bright spot on his skin that may become an infectious skin disease,ᵃ he must be brought to Aaron the priest or to one of his sonsᵇ who is a priest. ³The priest is to examine the sore on his skin, and if the hair in the sore has turned white and the sore appears to be more than skin deep,ᶜ it is an infectious skin disease. When the priest examines him, he shall pronounce him ceremonially unclean. ⁴If the spot on his skin is white but does not appear to be more than skin deep and the hair in it has not turned white, the priest is to put the infected person in isolation for seven days. ⁵On the seventh day the priest is to examine him, and if he sees that the sore is unchanged and has not spread in the skin, he is to keep him in isolation another seven days. ⁶On the seventh day the priest is to examine him again, and if the sore has faded and has not spread in the skin, the priest shall pronounce him clean; it is only a rash. The man must wash his clothes, and he will be clean. ⁷But if the rash does spread in his skin after he has shown himself to the priest to be pronounced clean, he must appear before the priest again. ⁸The priest is to examine him, and if the rash has spread in the skin, he shall pronounce him unclean; it is an infectious disease.

⁹"When anyone has an infectious skin disease, he must be brought to the priest. ¹⁰The priest is to examine him, and if there is a white swelling in the skin that has turned the hair white and if there is raw flesh in the swelling, ¹¹it is a chronic skin disease and the priest shall pronounce him unclean. He is not to put him in isolation, because he is already unclean.

¹²"If the disease breaks out all over his skin and, so far as the priest can see, it covers all the skin of the infected person

ᵃ 2 Traditionally leprosy; the Hebrew word was used for various diseases affecting the skin—not necessarily leprosy; also elsewhere in this chapter.   ᵇ 2 Or descendants   ᶜ 3 Or be lower than the rest of the skin; also elsewhere in this chapter from head to foot, 13the priest is to examine him, and if the disease has covered his whole body, he shall pronounce that person clean. Since it has all turned white, he is clean. 14But whenever raw flesh appears on him, he will be unclean. 15When the priest sees the raw flesh, he shall pronounce him unclean. The raw flesh is unclean; he has an infectious disease. 16Should the raw flesh change and turn white, he must go to the priest. 17The priest is to examine him, and if the sores have turned white, the priest shall pronounce the infected person clean; then he will be clean.

18"When someone has a boil on his skin and it heals, 19and in the place where the boil was, a white swelling or reddish-white spot appears, he must present himself to the priest. 20The priest is to examine it, and if it appears to be more than skin deep and the hair in it has turned white, the priest shall pronounce him unclean. It is an infectious skin disease that has broken out where the boil was. 21But if, when the priest examines it, there is no white hair in it and it is not more than skin deep and has faded, then the priest is to put him in isolation for seven days. 22If it is spreading in the skin, the priest shall pronounce him unclean; it is infectious. 23But if the spot is unchanged and has not spread, it is only a scar from the boil, and the priest shall pronounce him clean.

24"When someone has a burn on his skin and a reddish-white or white spot appears in the raw flesh of the burn, 25the priest is to examine the spot, and if the hair in it has turned white, and it appears to be more than skin deep, it is an infectious disease that has broken out in the burn. The priest shall pronounce him unclean; it is an infectious skin disease. 26But if the priest examines it and there is no white hair in the spot and if it is not more than skin deep and has faded, then the priest is to put him in isolation for seven days. 27On the seventh day the priest is to examine him, and if it is spreading in the skin, the priest shall pronounce him unclean; it is an infectious skin disease. 28If, however, the spot is unchanged and has not spread in the skin but has faded, it is a swelling from the burn, and the priest shall pronounce him clean; it is only a scar from the burn.

29"If a man or woman has a sore on the head or on the chin, 30the priest is to examine the sore, and if it appears to be more than skin deep and the hair in it is yellow and thin, the priest shall pronounce that person unclean; it is an itch, an infectious disease of the head or chin. 31But if, when the priest examines this kind of sore, it does not seem to be more than skin deep and there is no black hair in it, then the priest is to put the infected person in isolation for seven days. 32On the seventh day the priest is to examine the sore, and if the itch has not spread and there is no yellow hair in it and it does not appear to be more than skin deep, 33he must be shaved except for the diseased area, and the priest is to keep him in isolation another seven days. 34On the seventh day the priest is to examine the itch, and if it has not spread in the skin and appears to be no more than skin deep, the priest shall pronounce him clean. He must wash his clothes, and he will be clean. 35But if the itch does spread in the skin after he is pronounced clean, 36the priest is to examine him, and if the itch has spread in the skin, the priest does not need to look for yellow hair; the person is unclean. 37If, however, in his judgment it is unchanged and black hair has grown in it, the itch is healed. He is clean, and the priest shall pronounce him clean.

38"When a man or woman has white spots on the skin, 39the priest is to examine them, and if the spots are dull white, it is a harmless rash that has broken out on the skin; that person is clean.

40"When a man has lost his hair and is bald, he is clean. 41If he has lost his hair from the front of his scalp and has a bald forehead, he is clean. 42But if he has a reddish-white sore on his bald head or forehead, it is an infectious disease breaking out on his head or forehead. 43The priest is to examine him, and if the swollen sore on his head or forehead is reddish-white like an infectious skin disease, 44the man is diseased and is unclean. The priest shall pronounce him unclean because of the sore on his head.

45"The person with such an infectious disease must wear torn clothes, let his hair be unkempt,[a] cover the lower part of his face and cry out, 'Unclean! Unclean!' 46As long as he has the infection he remains unclean. He must live alone; he must live outside the camp.

Regulations About Mildew

47"If any clothing is contaminated with mildew—any woolen or linen clothing, 48any woven or knitted material of linen or wool, any leather or anything made of leather— 49and if the contamination in the clothing, or leather, or woven or knitted material, or any leather article, is greenish or reddish, it is a spreading mildew and must be shown to the priest. 50The priest is to examine the mildew and isolate the affected article for seven days. 51On the seventh day he is to examine it, and if the mildew has spread in the clothing, or the woven or knitted material, or the leather, whatever its use, it is a destructive mildew; the article is unclean. 52He must burn up the clothing, or the woven or knitted material of wool or linen, or any leather article that has the contamination in it, because the mildew is destructive; the article must be burned up.

53"But if, when the priest examines it, the mildew has not spread in the clothing, or the woven or knitted material, or the leather article, 54he shall order that the contaminated article be washed. Then he is to isolate it for another seven days. 55After the affected article has been washed, the priest is to examine it, and if the mildew has not changed its appearance, even

though it has not spread, it is unclean. Burn it with fire, whether the mildew has affected one side or the other. 56If, when the priest examines it, the mildew has faded after the article has been washed, he is to tear the contaminated part out of the clothing, or the leather, or the woven or knitted material. 57But if it reappears in the clothing, or in the woven or knitted material, or in the leather article, it is spreading, and whatever has the mildew must be burned with fire. 58The clothing, or the woven or knitted material, or any leather article that has been washed and is rid of the mildew, must be washed again, and it will be clean."

59These are the regulations concerning contamination by mildew in woolen or linen clothing, woven or knitted material, or any leather article, for pronouncing them clean or unclean.

Cleansing From Infectious Skin Diseases

14 The LORD said to Moses, 2"These are the regulations for the diseased person at the time of his ceremonial cleansing, when he is brought to the priest: 3The priest is to go outside the camp and examine him. If the person has been healed of his infectious skin disease,[b] 4the priest shall order that two live clean birds and some cedar wood, scarlet yarn and hyssop be brought for the one to be cleansed. 5Then the priest shall order that one of the birds be killed over fresh water in a clay pot. 6He is then to take the live bird and dip it, together with the cedar wood, the scarlet yarn and the hyssop, into the blood of the bird that was killed over the fresh water. 7Seven times he shall sprinkle the one to be cleansed of the infectious disease and pronounce him clean. Then he is to release the live bird in the open fields.

8"The person to be cleansed must wash his clothes, shave off all his hair and bathe with water; then he will be ceremonially clean. After this he may come into the camp, but he must stay outside his tent for seven days. ⁹On the seventh day he must shave off all his hair; he must shave his head, his beard, his eyebrows and the rest of his hair. He must wash his clothes and bathe himself with water, and he will be clean.

¹⁰"On the eighth day he must bring two male lambs and one ewe lamb a year old, each without defect, along with three-tenths of an ephah* of fine flour mixed with oil for a grain offering, and one logᵇ of oil. ¹¹The priest who pronounces him clean shall present both the one to be cleansed and his offerings before the Lord at the entrance to the Tent of Meeting.

¹²"Then the priest is to take one of the male lambs and offer it as a guilt offering, along with the log of oil; he shall wave them before the Lord as a wave offering. ¹³He is to slaughter the lamb in the holy place where the sin offering and the burnt offering are slaughtered. Like the sin offering, the guilt offering belongs to the priest; it is most holy. ¹⁴The priest is to take some of the blood of the guilt offering and put it on the lobe of the right ear of the one to be cleansed, on the thumb of his right hand and on the big toe of his right foot. ¹⁵The priest shall then take some of the log of oil, pour it in the palm of his own left hand, ¹⁶dip his right forefinger into the oil in his palm, and with his finger sprinkle some of it before the Lord seven times. ¹⁷The priest is to put some of the oil remaining in his palm on the lobe of the right ear of the one to be cleansed, on the thumb of his right hand and on the big toe of his right foot, on top of the blood of the guilt offering. ¹⁸The rest of the oil in his palm the priest shall put on the head of the one to be cleansed and make atonement for him before the Lord.

¹⁹"Then the priest is to sacrifice the sin offering and make atonement for the one to be cleansed from his uncleanness. After that, the priest shall slaughter the burnt offering ²⁰and offer it on the altar, together with the grain offering, and make atonement for him, and he will be clean.

²¹"If, however, he is poor and cannot afford these, he must take one male lamb as a guilt offering to be waved to make atonement for him, together with a tenth of an ephahᶜ of fine flour mixed with oil for a grain offering, a log of oil, ²²and two doves or two young pigeons, which he can afford, one for a sin offering and the other for a burnt offering.

²³"On the eighth day he must bring them for his cleansing to the priest at the entrance to the Tent of Meeting, before the Lord. ²⁴The priest is to take the lamb for the guilt offering, together with the log of oil, and wave them before the Lord as a wave offering. ²⁵He shall slaughter the lamb for the guilt offering and take some of its blood and put it on the lobe of the right ear of the one to be cleansed, on the thumb of his right hand and on the big toe of his right foot. ²⁶The priest is to pour some of the oil into the palm of his own left hand, ²⁷and with his right forefinger sprinkle some of the oil from his palm seven times before the Lord. ²⁸Some of the oil in his palm he is to put on the same places he put the blood of the guilt offering—on the lobe of the right ear of the one to be cleansed, on the thumb of his right hand and on the big toe of his right foot. ²⁹The rest of the oil in his palm the priest shall put on the head of the one to be cleansed, to make atonement for him before the Lord. ³⁰Then he shall sacrifice the doves or the young pigeons, which the person can afford, ³¹oneᵈ as a sin offering and the other as a burnt offering, together with the grain offering. In this way the priest will make atonement before the Lord on behalf of the one to be cleansed."

ᵃ 10 That is, probably about 6 quarts (about 6.5 liters)   ᵇ 10 That is, probably about 2/3 pint (about 0.3 liter); also in verses 12, 15, 21 and 24   ᶜ 21 That is, probably about 2 quarts (about 2 liters)   ᵈ 31 Septuagint and Syriac; Hebrew ³¹such as the person can afford, one

32These are the regulations for anyone who has an infectious skin disease and who cannot afford the regular offerings for his cleansing.

Cleansing From Mildew

33The LORD said to Moses and Aaron, 34"When you enter the land of Canaan, which I am giving you as your possession, and I put a spreading mildew in a house in that land, 35the owner of the house must go and tell the priest, 'I have seen something that looks like mildew in my house.' 36The priest is to order the house to be emptied before he goes in to examine the mildew, so that nothing in the house will be pronounced unclean. After this the priest is to go in and inspect the house. 37He is to examine the mildew on the walls, and if it has greenish or reddish depressions that appear to be deeper than the surface of the wall, 38the priest shall go out the doorway of the house and close it up for seven days. 39On the seventh day the priest shall return to inspect the house. If the mildew has spread on the walls, 40he is to order that the contaminated stones be torn out and thrown into an unclean place outside the town. 41He must have all the inside walls of the house scraped and the material that is scraped off dumped into an unclean place outside the town. 42Then they are to take other stones to replace these and take new clay and plaster the house.

43"If the mildew reappears in the house after the stones have been torn out and the house scraped and plastered, 44the priest is to go and examine it and, if the mildew has spread in the house, it is a destructive mildew; the house is unclean. 45It must be torn down—its stones, timbers and all the plaster—and taken out of the town to an unclean place.

46"Anyone who goes into the house while it is closed up will be unclean till evening. 47Anyone who sleeps or eats in the house must wash his clothes.

48"But if the priest comes to examine it and the mildew has not spread after the house has been plastered, he shall pronounce the house clean, because the mildew is gone. 49To purify the house he is to take two birds and some cedar wood, scarlet yarn and hyssop. 50He shall kill one of the birds over fresh water in a clay pot. 51Then he is to take the cedar wood, the hyssop, the scarlet yarn and the live bird, dip them into the blood of the dead bird and the fresh water, and sprinkle the house seven times. 52He shall purify the house with the bird's blood, the fresh water, the live bird, the cedar wood, the hyssop and the scarlet yarn. 53Then he is to release the live bird in the open fields outside the town. In this way he will make atonement for the house, and it will be clean."

54These are the regulations for any infectious skin disease, for an itch, 55for mildew in clothing or in a house, 56and for a swelling, a rash or a bright spot, 57to determine when something is clean or unclean.

These are the regulations for infectious skin diseases and mildew.

Discharges Causing Uncleanness

15 The LORD said to Moses and Aaron, 2"Speak to the Israelites and say to them: 'When any man has a bodily discharge, the discharge is unclean. 3Whether it continues flowing from his body or is blocked, it will make him unclean. This is how his discharge will bring about uncleanness:

4"'Any bed the man with a discharge lies on will be unclean, and anything he sits on will be unclean. 5Anyone who touches his bed must wash his clothes and bathe with water, and he will be unclean till evening. 6Whoever sits on anything that the man with a discharge sat on must wash his clothes and bathe with water, and he will be unclean till evening.

7"'Whoever touches the man who has a discharge must wash his clothes and bathe with water, and he will be unclean till evening.

8 " 'If the man with the discharge spits on someone who is clean, that person must wash his clothes and bathe with water, and he will be unclean till evening.

9 " 'Everything the man sits on when riding will be unclean, 10and whoever touches any of the things that were under him will be unclean till evening; whoever picks up those things must wash his clothes and bathe with water, and he will be unclean till evening.

11 " 'Anyone the man with a discharge touches without rinsing his hands with water must wash his clothes and bathe with water, and he will be unclean till evening.

12 " 'A clay pot that the man touches must be broken, and any wooden article is to be rinsed with water.

13 " 'When a man is cleansed from his discharge, he is to count off seven days for his ceremonial cleansing; he must wash his clothes and bathe himself with fresh water, and he will be clean. 14On the eighth day he must take two doves or two young pigeons and come before the LORD to the entrance to the Tent of Meeting and give them to the priest. 15The priest is to sacrifice them, the one for a sin offering and the other for a burnt offering. In this way he will make atonement before the LORD for the man because of his discharge.

16 " 'When a man has an emission of semen, he must bathe his whole body with water, and he will be unclean till evening. 17Any clothing or leather that has semen on it must be washed with water, and it will be unclean till evening. 18When a man lies with a woman and there is an emission of semen, both must bathe with water, and they will be unclean till evening.

19 " 'When a woman has her regular flow of blood, the impurity of her monthly period will last seven days, and anyone who touches her will be unclean till evening.

20 " 'Anything she lies on during her period will be unclean, and anything she sits on will be unclean. 21Whoever touches her bed must wash his clothes and bathe with water, and he will be unclean till evening. 22Whoever touches anything she sits on must wash his clothes and bathe with water, and he will be unclean till evening. 23Whether it is the bed or anything she was sitting on, when anyone touches it, he will be unclean till evening.

24 " 'If a man lies with her and her monthly flow touches him, he will be unclean for seven days; any bed he lies on will be unclean.

25 " 'When a woman has a discharge of blood for many days at a time other than her monthly period or has a discharge that continues beyond her period, she will be unclean as long as she has the discharge, just as in the days of her period. 26Any bed she lies on while her discharge continues will be unclean, as is her bed during her monthly period, and anything she sits on will be unclean, as during her period. 27Whoever touches them will be unclean; he must wash his clothes and bathe with water, and he will be unclean till evening.

28 " 'When she is cleansed from her discharge, she must count off seven days, and after that she will be ceremonially clean. 29On the eighth day she must take two doves or two young pigeons and bring them to the priest at the entrance to the Tent of Meeting. 30The priest is to sacrifice one for a sin offering and the other for a burnt offering. In this way he will make atonement for her before the LORD for the uncleanness of her discharge.

31 " 'You must keep the Israelites separate from things that make them unclean, so they will not die in their uncleanness for defiling my dwelling place,a which is among them.' "

32These are the regulations for a man with a discharge, for anyone made

---

a 31 Or *my tabernacle*

unclean by an emission of semen, ³³for a woman in her monthly period, for a man or a woman with a discharge, and for a man who lies with a woman who is ceremonially unclean.

The Day of Atonement

16 The LORD spoke to Moses after the death of the two sons of Aaron who died when they approached the LORD. ²The LORD said to Moses: "Tell your brother Aaron not to come whenever he chooses into the Most Holy Place behind the curtain in front of the atonement cover on the ark, or else he will die, because I appear in the cloud over the atonement cover.

³"This is how Aaron is to enter the sanctuary area: with a young bull for a sin offering and a ram for a burnt offering. ⁴He is to put on the sacred linen tunic, with linen undergarments next to his body; he is to tie the linen sash around him and put on the linen turban. These are sacred garments; so he must bathe himself with water before he puts them on. ⁵From the Israelite community he is to take two male goats for a sin offering and a ram for a burnt offering.

⁶"Aaron is to offer the bull for his own sin offering to make atonement for himself and his household. ⁷Then he is to take the two goats and present them before the LORD at the entrance to the Tent of Meeting. ⁸He is to cast lots for the two goats—one lot for the LORD and the other for the scapegoat.[a] ⁹Aaron shall bring the goat whose lot falls to the LORD and sacrifice it for a sin offering. ¹⁰But the goat chosen by lot as the scapegoat shall be presented alive before the LORD to be used for making atonement by sending it into the desert as a scapegoat.

¹¹"Aaron shall bring the bull for his own sin offering to make atonement for himself and his household, and he is to slaughter the bull for his own sin offering. ¹²He is to take a censer full of burning coals from the altar before the LORD

and two handfuls of finely ground fragrant incense and take them behind the curtain. ¹³He is to put the incense on the fire before the LORD, and the smoke of the incense will conceal the atonement cover above the Testimony, so that he will not die. ¹⁴He is to take some of the bull's blood and with his finger sprinkle it on the front of the atonement cover; then he shall sprinkle some of it with his finger seven times before the atonement cover.

¹⁵"He shall then slaughter the goat for the sin offering for the people and take its blood behind the curtain and do with it as he did with the bull's blood: He shall sprinkle it on the atonement cover and in front of it. ¹⁶In this way he will make atonement for the Most Holy Place because of the uncleanness and rebellion of the Israelites, whatever their sins have been. He is to do the same for the Tent of Meeting, which is among them in the midst of their uncleanness. ¹⁷No one is to be in the Tent of Meeting from the time Aaron goes in to make atonement in the Most Holy Place until he comes out, having made atonement for himself, his household and the whole community of Israel.

¹⁸"Then he shall come out to the altar that is before the LORD and make atonement for it. He shall take some of the bull's blood and some of the goat's blood and put it on all the horns of the altar. ¹⁹He shall sprinkle some of the blood on it with his finger seven times to cleanse it and to consecrate it from the uncleanness of the Israelites.

²⁰"When Aaron has finished making atonement for the Most Holy Place, the Tent of Meeting and the altar, he shall bring forward the live goat. ²¹He is to lay both hands on the head of the live goat and confess over it all the wickedness and rebellion of the Israelites—all their sins—and put them on the goat's head. He shall send the goat away into the desert in the care of a man appointed for

---

^a8 That is, the goat of removal; Hebrew *azazel*; also in verses 10 and 26

the task. ²²The goat will carry on itself all their sins to a solitary place; and the man shall release it in the desert.

²³"Then Aaron is to go into the Tent of Meeting and take off the linen garments he put on before he entered the Most Holy Place, and he is to leave them there. ²⁴He shall bathe himself with water in a holy place and put on his regular garments. Then he shall come out and sacrifice the burnt offering for himself and the burnt offering for the people, to make atonement for himself and for the people. ²⁵He shall also burn the fat of the sin offering on the altar.

²⁶"The man who releases the goat as a scapegoat must wash his clothes and bathe himself with water; afterward he may come into the camp. ²⁷The bull and the goat for the sin offerings, whose blood was brought into the Most Holy Place to make atonement, must be taken outside the camp; their hides, flesh and offal are to be burned up. ²⁸The man who burns them must wash his clothes and bathe himself with water; afterward he may come into the camp.

²⁹"This is to be a lasting ordinance for you: On the tenth day of the seventh month you must deny yourselves[a] and not do any work—whether native-born or an alien living among you— ³⁰because on this day atonement will be made for you, to cleanse you. Then, before the LORD, you will be clean from all your sins. ³¹It is a sabbath of rest, and you must deny yourselves; it is a lasting ordinance. ³²The priest who is anointed and

---

[a] 29 Or *must fast*; also in verse 31

GOING *deeper*

Your Day of Atonement

READ AND CONSIDER: LEVITICUS 16:1-34

"On this day atonement will be made for you, to cleanse you. Then, before the LORD, you will be clean from all your sins" (Leviticus 16:30).

The Day of Atonement, Yom Kippur, was perhaps the most important annual holy day for the ancient Jews. It was the day when the high priest entered the innermost chamber of the tabernacle (and later, the temple) to offer a sacrifice for the sins of the whole nation. The purpose of this sacrifice? The reconciliation of God and His people.

The ritual described in Leviticus 16 had several steps. It included the sacrifice of a bull and the dripping of that bull's blood onto the cover of Israel's most sacred relic—the ark of the covenant. It also included the selection of two goats. One was to be sacrificed, symbolizing the necessary payment for sin. The other goat, the scapegoat, was set free, symbolizing the sins of the people being carried into the desert.

Because of Christ's sacrifice for our sins, every day is our day of atonement. Every day we accept that His death paid for our sins. Every day, our sins are carried into a desert that we will never have to enter.

In light of that reality, how do you approach God in prayer? Do you sit before God as someone God values and loves? Or do you hang your head as if you still have to earn the acceptance you've already been given? Do you rush into His presence, or do you hesitate, hoping that what the Bible teaches about His forgiveness is true. If you tend toward the latter, claim today as your day of atonement. Go to God with a heart of gratitude and thank Him that nothing stands between you and Him.

ordained to succeed his father as high priest is to make atonement. He is to put on the sacred linen garments ³³and make atonement for the Most Holy Place, for the Tent of Meeting and the altar, and for the priests and all the people of the community.

³⁴"This is to be a lasting ordinance for you: Atonement is to be made once a year for all the sins of the Israelites."

And it was done, as the LORD commanded Moses.

Eating Blood Forbidden

17 The LORD said to Moses, ²"Speak to Aaron and his sons and to all the Israelites and say to them: 'This is what the LORD has commanded: ³Any Israelite who sacrifices an ox,^a a lamb or a goat in the camp or outside of it ⁴instead of bringing it to the entrance to the Tent of Meeting to present it as an offering to the LORD in front of the tabernacle of the LORD—that man shall be considered guilty of bloodshed; he has shed blood and must be cut off from his people. ⁵This is so the Israelites will bring to the LORD the sacrifices they are now making in the open fields. They must bring them to the priest, that is, to the LORD, at the entrance to the Tent of Meeting and sacrifice them as fellowship offerings.^b ⁶The priest is to sprinkle the blood against the altar of the LORD at the entrance to the Tent of Meeting and burn the fat as an aroma pleasing to the LORD. ⁷They must no longer offer any of their sacrifices to the goat idols^c to whom they prostitute themselves. This is to be a lasting ordinance for them and for the generations to come.'

⁸"Say to them: 'Any Israelite or any alien living among them who offers a burnt offering or sacrifice ⁹and does not bring it to the entrance to the Tent of Meeting to sacrifice it to the LORD—that man must be cut off from his people.

¹⁰"'Any Israelite or any alien living among them who eats any blood—I will set my face against that person who eats blood and will cut him off from his people. ¹¹For the life of a creature is in the blood, and I have given it to you to make atonement for yourselves on the altar; it is the blood that makes atonement for one's life. ¹²Therefore I say to the Israelites, "None of you may eat blood, nor may an alien living among you eat blood."

¹³"'Any Israelite or any alien living among you who hunts any animal or bird that may be eaten must drain out the blood and cover it with earth, ¹⁴because the life of every creature is its blood. That is why I have said to the Israelites, "You must not eat the blood of any creature, because the life of every creature is its blood; anyone who eats it must be cut off."

¹⁵"'Anyone, whether native-born or alien, who eats anything found dead or torn by wild animals must wash his clothes and bathe with water, and he will be ceremonially unclean till evening; then he will be clean. ¹⁶But if he does not wash his clothes and bathe himself, he will be held responsible.'"

Unlawful Sexual Relations

18 The LORD said to Moses, ²"Speak to the Israelites and say to them: 'I am the LORD your God. ³You must not do as they do in Egypt, where you used to live, and you must not do as they do in the land of Canaan, where I am bringing you. Do not follow their practices. ⁴You must obey my laws and be careful to follow my decrees. I am the LORD your God. ⁵Keep my decrees and laws, for the man who obeys them will live by them. I am the LORD.

⁶"'No one is to approach any close relative to have sexual relations. I am the LORD.

⁷"'Do not dishonor your father by having sexual relations with your mother. She is your mother; do not have relations with her.

⁸"'Do not have sexual relations with your father's wife; that would dishonor your father.

---

^a 3 The Hebrew word can include both male and female.   ^b 5 Traditionally *peace offerings*   ^c 7 Or *demons*

9 "'Do not have sexual relations with your sister, either your father's daughter or your mother's daughter, whether she was born in the same home or elsewhere.

10 "'Do not have sexual relations with your son's daughter or your daughter's daughter; that would dishonor you.

11 "'Do not have sexual relations with the daughter of your father's wife, born to your father; she is your sister.

12 "'Do not have sexual relations with your father's sister; she is your father's close relative.

13 "'Do not have sexual relations with your mother's sister, because she is your mother's close relative.

14 "'Do not dishonor your father's brother by approaching his wife to have sexual relations; she is your aunt.

15 "'Do not have sexual relations with your daughter-in-law. She is your son's wife; do not have relations with her.

16 "'Do not have sexual relations with your brother's wife; that would dishonor your brother.

17 "'Do not have sexual relations with both a woman and her daughter. Do not have sexual relations with either her son's daughter or her daughter's daughter; they are her close relatives. That is wickedness.

Praying Leviticus 18:6-25

Lord, open the eyes of people in my city to all sexual perversion and abuse so that it can be exposed and brought to an end.

---

18 "'Do not take your wife's sister as a rival wife and have sexual relations with her while your wife is living.

19 "'Do not approach a woman to have sexual relations during the uncleanness of her monthly period.

20 "'Do not have sexual relations with your neighbor's wife and defile yourself with her.

21 "'Do not give any of your children to be sacrificed[a] to Molech, for you must not profane the name of your God. I am the LORD.

22 "'Do not lie with a man as one lies with a woman; that is detestable.

23 "'Do not have sexual relations with an animal and defile yourself with it. A woman must not present herself to an animal to have sexual relations with it; that is a perversion.

24 "'Do not defile yourselves in any of these ways, because this is how the nations that I am going to drive out before you became defiled. 25 Even the land was defiled; so I punished it for its sin, and the land vomited out its inhabitants. 26 But you must keep my decrees and my laws. The native-born and the aliens living among you must not do any of these detestable things, 27 for all these things were done by the people who lived in the land before you, and the land became defiled. 28 And if you defile the land, it will vomit you out as it vomited out the nations that were before you.

29 "'Everyone who does any of these detestable things—such persons must be cut off from their people. 30 Keep my requirements and do not follow any of the detestable customs that were practiced before you came and do not defile yourselves with them. I am the LORD your God.'"

Various Laws

19 The LORD said to Moses, 2 "Speak to the entire assembly of Israel and say to them: 'Be holy because I, the LORD your God, am holy.

3 "'Each of you must respect his mother and father, and you must observe my Sabbaths. I am the LORD your God.

4 "'Do not turn to idols or make gods of cast metal for yourselves. I am the LORD your God.

5 "'When you sacrifice a fellowship offering[b] to the LORD, sacrifice it in such a way that it will be accepted on your behalf. 6 It shall be eaten on the day you sacrifice it or on the next day; anything left

---

a 21 Or *to be passed through the fire*   b 5 Traditionally *peace offering*

How Can I Be Holy?

READ AND CONSIDER: LEVITICUS 19:1-10

"Speak to the entire assembly of Israel and say to them: 'Be holy because I, the LORD your God, am holy'" (Leviticus 19:2).

What do you think about when you think of holiness? Do you think of someone who is perfect and untouchable? What do you think about your own holiness? Do you ever wonder, *How can I be holy?*

Throughout Israel's history, holiness was a major issue. As the people's holiness went, so went the state of the nation. Their spiritual strength and their political strength seemed to go hand in hand. In the days of the good King Jehoshaphat, Judah actually won a battle because the people marched before the army singing and praising God for the "splendor of his holiness" (2 Chronicles 20:1-27).

When you think about how to be holy as God is holy, consider this good news: God wants to share His holiness with you. He doesn't stand over you, wagging an index finger in your face like a judgmental teacher saying, "You be holy right now!" Instead, He offers His own holiness to you. He asks you to partake of His holiness.

In Psalm 29, David encouraged us to offer praise to God for His strength and glory and holiness. When we do that, amazing things happen. Because we take the time and attention to see the splendor and beauty of God's holiness, we take on that beauty. The more we lift our heads and hearts to God in praise, the more God is reflected in our faces and in our behavior.

Remember how Moses' face was radiant when he came down from being in the presence of God (Exodus 34:29-35)? When you worship God, you are coming in contact with the beauty of His holiness and allowing that to make you beautifully holy and wonderfully whole.

That's why your time in prayer shouldn't always be squeezed in between running from one thing to the next. You need time with God to really engage and bask in His presence, allowing Him to conform you and remold you in His image. Each time you do that, you become more holy, more like Him.

over until the third day must be burned up. 7If any of it is eaten on the third day, it is impure and will not be accepted. 8Whoever eats it will be held responsible because he has desecrated what is holy to the LORD; that person must be cut off from his people.

9"'When you reap the harvest of your land, do not reap to the very edges of your field or gather the gleanings of your harvest. 10Do not go over your vineyard a second time or pick up the grapes that have fallen. Leave them for the poor and the alien. I am the LORD your God.

11"'Do not steal.

"'Do not lie.

"'Do not deceive one another.

12"'Do not swear falsely by my name and so profane the name of your God. I am the LORD.

13"'Do not defraud your neighbor or rob him.

"'Do not hold back the wages of a hired man overnight.

14"'Do not curse the deaf or put a stumbling block in front of the blind, but fear your God. I am the LORD.

15"'Do not pervert justice; do not show

partiality to the poor or favoritism to the great, but judge your neighbor fairly.

16 " 'Do not go about spreading slander among your people.

" 'Do not do anything that endangers your neighbor's life. I am the LORD.

17 " 'Do not hate your brother in your heart. Rebuke your neighbor frankly so you will not share in his guilt.

18 " 'Do not seek revenge or bear a grudge against one of your people, but love your neighbor as yourself. I am the LORD.

19 " 'Keep my decrees.

" 'Do not mate different kinds of animals.

" 'Do not plant your field with two kinds of seed.

" 'Do not wear clothing woven of two kinds of material.

20 " 'If a man sleeps with a woman who is a slave girl promised to another man but who has not been ransomed or given her freedom, there must be due punishment. Yet they are not to be put to death, because she had not been freed. 21 The man, however, must bring a ram to the entrance to the Tent of Meeting for a guilt offering to the LORD. 22 With the ram of the guilt offering the priest is to make atonement for him before the LORD for the sin he has committed, and his sin will be forgiven.

23 " 'When you enter the land and plant any kind of fruit tree, regard its fruit as forbidden.ᵃ For three years you are to consider it forbiddenᵃ; it must not be eaten. 24 In the fourth year all its fruit will be holy, an offering of praise to the LORD. 25 But in the fifth year you may eat its fruit. In this way your harvest will be increased. I am the LORD your God.

26 " 'Do not eat any meat with the blood still in it.

" 'Do not practice divination or sorcery.

27 " 'Do not cut the hair at the sides of your head or clip off the edges of your beard.

28 " 'Do not cut your bodies for the dead or put tattoo marks on yourselves. I am the LORD.

29 " 'Do not degrade your daughter by making her a prostitute, or the land will turn to prostitution and be filled with wickedness.

30 " 'Observe my Sabbaths and have reverence for my sanctuary. I am the LORD.

31 " 'Do not turn to mediums or seek out spiritists, for you will be defiled by them. I am the LORD your God.

32 " 'Rise in the presence of the aged, show respect for the elderly and revere your God. I am the LORD.

33 " 'When an alien lives with you in your land, do not mistreat him. 34 The alien living with you must be treated as one of your native-born. Love him as yourself, for you were aliens in Egypt. I am the LORD your God.

35 " 'Do not use dishonest standards when measuring length, weight or quantity. 36 Use honest scales and honest weights, an honest ephahᵇ and an honest hin.ᶜ I am the LORD your God, who brought you out of Egypt.

37 " 'Keep all my decrees and all my laws and follow them. I am the LORD.' "

Punishments for Sin

20 The LORD said to Moses, 2 "Say to the Israelites: 'Any Israelite or any alien living in Israel who givesᵈ any of his children to Molech must be put to death. The people of the community are to stone him. 3 I will set my face against that man and I will cut him off from his people; for by giving his children to Molech, he has defiled my sanctuary and profaned my holy name. 4 If the people of the community close their eyes when that man gives one of his children to Molech and they fail to put him to death, 5 I will set my face against that man and his family and will cut off from their people

---

ᵃ 23 Hebrew *uncircumcised*   ᵇ 36 An ephah was a dry measure.   ᶜ 36 A hin was a liquid measure.   ᵈ 2 Or *sacrifices*; also in verses 3 and 4 both him and all who follow him in prostituting themselves to Molech.

6 "'I will set my face against the person who turns to mediums and spiritists to prostitute himself by following them, and I will cut him off from his people.

7 "'Consecrate yourselves and be holy, because I am the LORD your God. 8 Keep my decrees and follow them. I am the LORD, who makes you holy.[a]

9 "'If anyone curses his father or mother, he must be put to death. He has cursed his father or his mother, and his blood will be on his own head.

10 "'If a man commits adultery with another man's wife—with the wife of his neighbor—both the adulterer and the adulteress must be put to death.

11 "'If a man sleeps with his father's wife, he has dishonored his father. Both the man and the woman must be put to death; their blood will be on their own heads.

12 "'If a man sleeps with his daughter-in-law, both of them must be put to death. What they have done is a perversion; their blood will be on their own heads.

13 "'If a man lies with a man as one lies with a woman, both of them have done what is detestable. They must be put to death; their blood will be on their own heads.

14 "'If a man marries both a woman and her mother, it is wicked. Both he and they must be burned in the fire, so that no wickedness will be among you.

15 "'If a man has sexual relations with an animal, he must be put to death, and you must kill the animal.

16 "'If a woman approaches an animal to have sexual relations with it, kill both the woman and the animal. They must be put to death; their blood will be on their own heads.

17 "'If a man marries his sister, the daughter of either his father or his mother, and they have sexual relations, it is a disgrace. They must be cut off before the eyes of their people. He has dishonored his sister and will be held responsible.

18 "'If a man lies with a woman during her monthly period and has sexual relations with her, he has exposed the source of her flow, and she has also uncovered it. Both of them must be cut off from their people.

19 "'Do not have sexual relations with the sister of either your mother or your father, for that would dishonor a close relative; both of you would be held responsible.

20 "'If a man sleeps with his aunt, he has dishonored his uncle. They will be held responsible; they will die childless.

21 "'If a man marries his brother's wife, it is an act of impurity; he has dishonored his brother. They will be childless.

22 "'Keep all my decrees and laws and follow them, so that the land where I am bringing you to live may not vomit you out. 23 You must not live according to the customs of the nations I am going to drive out before you. Because they did all these things, I abhorred them. 24 But I said to you, "You will possess their land; I will give it to you as an inheritance, a land flowing with milk and honey." I am the LORD your God, who has set you apart from the nations.

Praying Leviticus 20:26

Lord, enable me to be holy just as You are holy.

25 "'You must therefore make a distinction between clean and unclean animals and between unclean and clean birds. Do not defile yourselves by any animal or bird or anything that moves along the ground—those which I have set apart as unclean for you. 26 You are to be holy to me[b] because I, the LORD, am holy, and I have set you apart from the nations to be my own.

27 "'A man or woman who is a medium or spiritist among you must be put to

---

[a] 8 Or *who sanctifies you; or who sets you apart as holy*   [b] 26 Or *be my holy ones*

death. You are to stone them; their blood will be on their own heads.'"

Rules for Priests

21 The LORD said to Moses, "Speak to the priests, the sons of Aaron, and say to them: 'A priest must not make himself ceremonially unclean for any of his people who die, ²except for a close relative, such as his mother or father, his son or daughter, his brother, ³or an unmarried sister who is dependent on him since she has no husband—for her he may make himself unclean. ⁴He must not make himself unclean for people related to him by marriage,ᵃ and so defile himself.

⁵"'Priests must not shave their heads or shave off the edges of their beards or cut their bodies. ⁶They must be holy to their God and must not profane the name of their God. Because they present the offerings made to the LORD by fire, the food of their God, they are to be holy.

⁷"'They must not marry women defiled by prostitution or divorced from their husbands, because priests are holy to their God. ⁸Regard them as holy, because they offer up the food of your God. Consider them holy, because I the LORD am holy—I who make you holy.ᵇ

⁹"'If a priest's daughter defiles herself by becoming a prostitute, she disgraces her father; she must be burned in the fire.

¹⁰"'The high priest, the one among his brothers who has had the anointing oil poured on his head and who has been ordained to wear the priestly garments, must not let his hair become unkemptᶜ or tear his clothes. ¹¹He must not enter a place where there is a dead body. He must not make himself unclean, even for his father or mother, ¹²nor leave the sanctuary of his God or desecrate it, because he has been dedicated by the anointing oil of his God. I am the LORD.

¹³"'The woman he marries must be a virgin. ¹⁴He must not marry a widow, a divorced woman, or a woman defiled by prostitution, but only a virgin from his own people, ¹⁵so he will not defile his offspring among his people. I am the LORD, who makes him holy.ᵈ'"

¹⁶The LORD said to Moses, ¹⁷"Say to Aaron: 'For the generations to come none of your descendants who has a defect may come near to offer the food of his God. ¹⁸No man who has any defect may come near: no man who is blind or lame, disfigured or deformed; ¹⁹no man with a crippled foot or hand, ²⁰or who is hunchbacked or dwarfed, or who has any eye defect, or who has festering or running sores or damaged testicles. ²¹No descendant of Aaron the priest who has any defect is to come near to present the offerings made to the LORD by fire. He has a defect; he must not come near to offer the food of his God. ²²He may eat the most holy food of his God, as well as the holy food; ²³yet because of his defect, he must not go near the curtain or approach the altar, and so desecrate my sanctuary. I am the LORD, who makes them holy.ᵉ'"

²⁴So Moses told this to Aaron and his sons and to all the Israelites.

22 The LORD said to Moses, ²"Tell Aaron and his sons to treat with respect the sacred offerings the Israelites consecrate to me, so they will not profane my holy name. I am the LORD.

³"Say to them: 'For the generations to come, if any of your descendants is ceremonially unclean and yet comes near the sacred offerings that the Israelites consecrate to the LORD, that person must be cut off from my presence. I am the LORD.

⁴"'If a descendant of Aaron has an infectious skin diseaseᶠ or a bodily discharge, he may not eat the sacred offerings until he is cleansed. He will also be unclean if he touches something defiled by a corpse or by anyone who has an emission of

---

ᵃ4 Or unclean as a leader among his people   ᵇ8 Or who sanctify you; or who set you apart as holy   ᶜ10 Or not uncover his head   ᵈ15 Or who sanctifies him; or who sets him apart as holy   ᵉ23 Or who sanctifies them; or who sets them apart as holy   ᶠ4 Traditionally leprosy; the Hebrew word was used for various diseases affecting the skin—not necessarily leprosy.

semen, 5or if he touches any crawling thing that makes him unclean, or any person who makes him unclean, whatever the uncleanness may be. 6The one who touches any such thing will be unclean till evening. He must not eat any of the sacred offerings unless he has bathed himself with water. 7When the sun goes down, he will be clean, and after that he may eat the sacred offerings, for they are his food. 8He must not eat anything found dead or torn by wild animals, and so become unclean through it. I am the LORD.

9"'The priests are to keep my requirements so that they do not become guilty and die for treating them with contempt. I am the LORD, who makes them holy.a

10"'No one outside a priest's family may eat the sacred offering, nor may the guest of a priest or his hired worker eat it. 11But if a priest buys a slave with money, or if a slave is born in his household, that slave may eat his food. 12If a priest's daughter marries anyone other than a priest, she may not eat any of the sacred contributions. 13But if a priest's daughter becomes a widow or is divorced, yet has no children, and she returns to live in her father's house as in her youth, she may eat of her father's food. No unauthorized person, however, may eat any of it.

14"'If anyone eats a sacred offering by mistake, he must make restitution to the priest for the offering and add a fifth of the value to it. 15The priests must not desecrate the sacred offerings the Israelites present to the LORD 16by allowing them to eat the sacred offerings and so bring upon them guilt requiring payment. I am the LORD, who makes them holy.'"

Unacceptable Sacrifices

17The LORD said to Moses, 18"Speak to Aaron and his sons and to all the Israelites and say to them: 'If any of you—either an Israelite or an alien living in Israel—presents a gift for a burnt offering to the LORD, either to fulfill a vow or as a freewill offering, 19you must present a male without defect from the cattle, sheep or goats in order that it may be accepted on your behalf. 20Do not bring anything with a defect, because it will not be accepted on your behalf. 21When anyone brings from the herd or flock a fellowship offeringb to the LORD to fulfill a special vow or as a freewill offering, it must be without defect or blemish to be acceptable. 22Do not offer to the LORD the blind, the injured or the maimed, or anything with warts or festering or running sores. Do not place any of these on the altar as an offering made to the LORD by fire. 23You may, however, present as a freewill offering an oxc or a sheep that is deformed or stunted, but it will not be accepted in fulfillment of a vow. 24You must not offer to the LORD an animal whose testicles are bruised, crushed, torn or cut. You must not do this in your own land, 25and you must not accept such animals from the hand of a foreigner and offer them as the food of your God. They will not be accepted on your behalf, because they are deformed and have defects.'"

26The LORD said to Moses, 27"When a calf, a lamb or a goat is born, it is to remain with its mother for seven days. From the eighth day on, it will be acceptable as an offering made to the LORD by fire. 28Do not slaughter a cow or a sheep and its young on the same day.

29"When you sacrifice a thank offering to the LORD, sacrifice it in such a way that it will be accepted on your behalf. 30It must be eaten that same day; leave none of it till morning. I am the LORD.

31"Keep my commands and follow them. I am the LORD. 32Do not profane my holy name. I must be acknowledged as holy by the Israelites. I am the LORD, who makesd you holye 33and who brought you out of Egypt to be your God. I am the LORD."

---

a 9 Or who sanctifies them; or who sets them apart as holy; also in verse 16   b 21 Traditionally peace offering   c 23 The Hebrew word can include both male and female.   d 32 Or made   e 32 Or who sanctifies you; or who sets you apart as holy

GOING

The Act of Celebration

deeper

READ AND CONSIDER: LEVITICUS 23:1-36

"Speak to the Israelites and say to them: 'These are my appointed feasts, the appointed feasts of the LORD, which you are to proclaim as sacred assemblies'" (Leviticus 23:2).

In the Old Testament world, festivals marked the changing of the seasons, the bringing of the harvest, the shearing of the sheep, and so on. For the Israelite nation, these feast days were also spiritual markers of the journey the people had taken under God's care.

The most basic feast was the Sabbath, a day set aside every week to rest as God had in creation. Another frequent feast was the monthly new moon festival. This was a celebration of God's faithfulness to His people and to the covenant He had made with their ancestors.

Then there were the annual feasts. These celebrations commemorated significant historical events in which God had shown Himself in a mighty way. The Feast of Trumpets commemorated the giving of the Ten Commandments. The Passover was a reminder of the final plague by which God freed the people from Egypt. The Feast of Tabernacles memorialized the journey of Israelites to their promised land.

Some of our holidays commemorate spiritual events as well: Easter, Christmas, Lent, and others. We use these holidays to join as communities of faith and remember together what God has done in us and among us.

We can each establish our own times of celebration. What has God done specifically in your life that might be cause for celebration? Part of the celebration of Old Testament feasts involved seeing old friends and returning to old places. Are there people with whom you can connect in order to encourage one another spiritually? Is there someone in your life who led you into a relationship with Jesus or who has had a special impact in your walk with God? Ask God to show you how to best celebrate those special events and show your appreciation to those involved. Praying for that person would be a great way to celebrate. Sending a note of thanks would be another. Invite God to help you build these kinds of living monuments that remind you of your journey with Him.

23 The LORD said to Moses, 2"Speak to the Israelites and say to them: 'These are my appointed feasts, the appointed feasts of the LORD, which you are to proclaim as sacred assemblies.

The Sabbath

3"'There are six days when you may work, but the seventh day is a Sabbath of rest, a day of sacred assembly. You are not to do any work; wherever you live, it is a Sabbath to the LORD.

The Passover and Unleavened Bread

4"'These are the LORD's appointed feasts, the sacred assemblies you are to proclaim at their appointed times: 5 The LORD's Passover begins at twilight on the fourteenth day of the first month. 6On the fifteenth day of that month the LORD's Feast of Unleavened Bread begins; for seven days you must eat bread made without yeast. 7On the first day hold a sacred assembly and do no regular work. 8For seven days present an offering made to the LORD by fire. And on the seventh day hold a sacred assembly and do no regular work.'"

Firstfruits

9The LORD said to Moses, 10"Speak to the Israelites and say to them: 'When you enter the land I am going to give you and you reap its harvest, bring to the priest a sheaf of the first grain you harvest. [11]He is to wave the sheaf before the LORD so it will be accepted on your behalf; the priest is to wave it on the day after the Sabbath. [12]On the day you wave the sheaf, you must sacrifice as a burnt offering to the LORD a lamb a year old without defect, [13]together with its grain offering of two-tenths of an ephah[a] of fine flour mixed with oil—an offering made to the LORD by fire, a pleasing aroma—and its drink offering of a quarter of a hin[b] of wine. [14]You must not eat any bread, or roasted or new grain, until the very day you bring this offering to your God. This is to be a lasting ordinance for the generations to come, wherever you live.

Feast of Weeks

[15]" 'From the day after the Sabbath, the day you brought the sheaf of the wave offering, count off seven full weeks. [16]Count off fifty days up to the day after the seventh Sabbath, and then present an offering of new grain to the LORD. [17]From wherever you live, bring two loaves made of two-tenths of an ephah of fine flour, baked with yeast, as a wave offering of firstfruits to the LORD. [18]Present with this bread seven male lambs, each a year old and without defect, one young bull and two rams. They will be a burnt offering to the LORD, together with their grain offerings and drink offerings—an offering made by fire, an aroma pleasing to the LORD. [19]Then sacrifice one male goat for a sin offering and two lambs, each a year old, for a fellowship offering.[c] [20]The priest is to wave the two lambs before the LORD as a wave offering, together with the bread of the firstfruits. They are a sacred offering to the LORD for the priest. [21]On that same day you are to proclaim a sacred assembly and do no regular work. This is to be a lasting ordinance for the generations to come, wherever you live.

[22]" 'When you reap the harvest of your land, do not reap to the very edges of your field or gather the gleanings of your harvest. Leave them for the poor and the alien. I am the LORD your God.' "

Feast of Trumpets

[23]The LORD said to Moses, [24]"Say to the Israelites: 'On the first day of the seventh month you are to have a day of rest, a sacred assembly commemorated with trumpet blasts. [25]Do no regular work, but present an offering made to the LORD by fire.' "

Day of Atonement

[26]The LORD said to Moses, [27]"The tenth day of this seventh month is the Day of Atonement. Hold a sacred assembly and deny yourselves,[d] and present an offering made to the LORD by fire. [28]Do no work on that day, because it is the Day of Atonement, when atonement is made for you before the LORD your God. [29]Anyone who does not deny himself on that day must be cut off from his people. [30]I will destroy from among his people anyone who does any work on that day. [31]You shall do no work at all. This is to be a lasting ordinance for the generations to come, wherever you live. [32]It is a sabbath of rest for you, and you must deny yourselves. From the evening of the ninth day of the month until the following evening you are to observe your sabbath."

Feast of Tabernacles

[33]The LORD said to Moses, [34]"Say to the Israelites: 'On the fifteenth day of the seventh month the LORD's Feast of Tabernacles begins, and it lasts for seven days. [35]The first day is a sacred assembly; do no regular work. [36]For seven days present offerings made to the LORD by fire, and on the eighth day hold a sacred assembly and present an offering made to the LORD by fire. It is the closing assembly; do no regular work.

[37](" 'These are the LORD's appointed

---

[a] *13* That is, probably about 4 quarts (about 4.5 liters); also in verse 17   [b] *13* That is, probably about 1 quart (about 1 liter)
[c] *19* Traditionally *peace offering*   [d] *27* Or *and fast*; also in verses 29 and 32

feasts, which you are to proclaim as sacred assemblies for bringing offerings made to the LORD by fire—the burnt offerings and grain offerings, sacrifices and drink offerings required for each day. [38] These offerings are in addition to those for the LORD's Sabbaths and[a] in addition to your gifts and whatever you have vowed and all the freewill offerings you give to the LORD.)

[39] "So beginning with the fifteenth day of the seventh month, after you have gathered the crops of the land, celebrate the festival to the LORD for seven days; the first day is a day of rest, and the eighth day also is a day of rest. [40] On the first day you are to take choice fruit from the trees, and palm fronds, leafy branches and poplars, and rejoice before the LORD your God for seven days. [41] Celebrate this as a festival to the LORD for seven days each year. This is to be a lasting ordinance for the generations to come; celebrate it in the seventh month. [42] Live in booths for seven days: All native-born Israelites are to live in booths [43] so your descendants will know that I had the Israelites live in booths when I brought them out of Egypt. I am the LORD your God.'"

[44] So Moses announced to the Israelites the appointed feasts of the LORD.

Oil and Bread Set Before the LORD

24 The LORD said to Moses, [2] "Command the Israelites to bring you clear oil of pressed olives for the light so that the lamps may be kept burning continually. [3] Outside the curtain of the Testimony in the Tent of Meeting, Aaron is to tend the lamps before the LORD from evening till morning, continually. This is to be a lasting ordinance for the generations to come. [4] The lamps on the pure gold lampstand before the LORD must be tended continually.

[5] "Take fine flour and bake twelve loaves of bread, using two-tenths of an ephah[b] for each loaf. [6] Set them in two rows, six in each row, on the table of pure gold before the LORD. [7] Along each row put some pure incense as a memorial portion to represent the bread and to be an offering made to the LORD by fire. [8] This bread is to be set out before the LORD regularly, Sabbath after Sabbath, on behalf of the Israelites, as a lasting covenant. [9] It belongs to Aaron and his sons, who are to eat it in a holy place, because it is a most holy part of their regular share of the offerings made to the LORD by fire."

A Blasphemer Stoned

[10] Now the son of an Israelite mother and an Egyptian father went out among the Israelites, and a fight broke out in the camp between him and an Israelite. [11] The son of the Israelite woman blasphemed the Name with a curse; so they brought him to Moses. (His mother's name was Shelomith, the daughter of Dibri the Danite.) [12] They put him in custody until the will of the LORD should be made clear to them.

[13] Then the LORD said to Moses: [14] "Take the blasphemer outside the camp. All those who heard him are to lay their hands on his head, and the entire assembly is to stone him. [15] Say to the Israelites: 'If anyone curses his God, he will be held responsible; [16] anyone who blasphemes the name of the LORD must be put to death. The entire assembly must stone him. Whether an alien or native-born, when he blasphemes the Name, he must be put to death.

[17] "'If anyone takes the life of a human being, he must be put to death. [18] Anyone who takes the life of someone's animal must make restitution—life for life. [19] If anyone injures his neighbor, whatever he has done must be done to him: [20] fracture for fracture, eye for eye, tooth for tooth. As he has injured the other, so he is to be injured. [21] Whoever kills an animal must make restitution, but whoever kills a man must be put to death. [22] You are to have

---

a 38 Or *These feasts are in addition to the LORD's Sabbaths, and these offerings are*   b 5 That is, probably about 4 quarts (about 4.5 liters) the same law for the alien and the native-born. I am the LORD your God.'"

23 Then Moses spoke to the Israelites, and they took the blasphemer outside the camp and stoned him. The Israelites did as the LORD commanded Moses.

The Sabbath Year

25 The LORD said to Moses on Mount Sinai, 2"Speak to the Israelites and say to them: 'When you enter the land I am going to give you, the land itself must observe a sabbath to the LORD. 3For six years sow your fields, and for six years prune your vineyards and gather their crops. 4But in the seventh year the land is to have a sabbath of rest, a sabbath to the LORD. Do not sow your fields or prune your vineyards. 5Do not reap what grows of itself or harvest the grapes of your untended vines. The land is to have a year of rest. 6Whatever the land yields during the sabbath year will be food for you—for yourself, your manservant and maidservant, and the hired worker and temporary resident who live among you, 7as well as for your livestock and the wild animals in your land. Whatever the land produces may be eaten.

The Year of Jubilee

8"'Count off seven sabbaths of years—seven times seven years—so that the seven sabbaths of years amount to a period of forty-nine years. 9Then have the trumpet sounded everywhere on the tenth day of the seventh month; on the Day of Atonement sound the trumpet throughout your land. 10Consecrate the fiftieth year and proclaim liberty throughout the land to all its inhabitants. It shall be a jubilee for you; each one of you is to return to his family property and each to his own clan. 11The fiftieth year shall be a jubilee for you; do not sow and do not reap what grows of itself or harvest the untended vines. 12For it is a jubilee and is to be holy for you; eat only what is taken directly from the fields.

13"'In this Year of Jubilee everyone is to return to his own property.

14"'If you sell land to one of your countrymen or buy any from him, do not take advantage of each other. 15You are to buy from your countryman on the basis of the number of years since the Jubilee. And he is to sell to you on the basis of the number of years left for harvesting crops. 16When the years are many, you are to increase the price, and when the years are few, you are to decrease the price, because what he is really selling you is the number of crops. 17Do not take advantage of each other, but fear your God. I am the LORD your God.

18"'Follow my decrees and be careful to obey my laws, and you will live safely in the land. 19Then the land will yield its fruit, and you will eat your fill and live there in safety. 20You may ask, "What will we eat in the seventh year if we do not plant or harvest our crops?" 21I will send you such a blessing in the sixth year that the land will yield enough for three years. 22While you plant during the eighth year, you will eat from the old crop and will continue to eat from it until the harvest of the ninth year comes in.

23"'The land must not be sold permanently, because the land is mine and you are but aliens and my tenants. 24Throughout the country that you hold as a possession, you must provide for the redemption of the land.

25"'If one of your countrymen becomes poor and sells some of his property, his nearest relative is to come and redeem what his countryman has sold. 26If, however, a man has no one to redeem it for him but he himself prospers and acquires sufficient means to redeem it, 27he is to determine the value for the years since he sold it and refund the balance to the man to whom he sold it; he can then go back to his own property. 28But if he does not acquire the means to repay him, what he sold will remain in the possession of the buyer until the Year of Jubilee. It will be returned in the Jubilee, and he can then go back to his property.

29 "If a man sells a house in a walled city, he retains the right of redemption a full year after its sale. During that time he may redeem it. 30 If it is not redeemed before a full year has passed, the house in the walled city shall belong permanently to the buyer and his descendants. It is not to be returned in the Jubilee. 31 But houses in villages without walls around them are to be considered as open country. They can be redeemed, and they are to be returned in the Jubilee.

32 "The Levites always have the right to redeem their houses in the Levitical towns, which they possess. 33 So the property of the Levites is redeemable—that is, a house sold in any town they hold—and is to be returned in the Jubilee, because the houses in the towns of the Levites are their property among the Israelites. 34 But the pastureland belonging to their towns must not be sold; it is their permanent possession.

35 "If one of your countrymen becomes poor and is unable to support himself among you, help him as you would an alien or a temporary resident, so he can continue to live among you. 36 Do not take interest of any kind[a] from him, but fear your God, so that your countryman may continue to live among you. 37 You must not lend him money at interest or sell him food at a profit. 38 I am the LORD your God, who brought you out of Egypt to give you the land of Canaan and to be your God.

39 "If one of your countrymen becomes poor among you and sells himself to you, do not make him work as a slave. 40 He is to be treated as a hired worker or a temporary resident among you; he is to work for you until the Year of Jubilee. 41 Then he and his children are to be released, and he will go back to his own clan and to the property of his forefathers. 42 Because the Israelites are my servants, whom I brought out of Egypt, they must not be sold as slaves.

43 Do not rule over them ruthlessly, but fear your God.

44 "Your male and female slaves are to come from the nations around you; from them you may buy slaves. 45 You may also buy some of the temporary residents living among you and members of their clans born in your country, and they will become your property. 46 You can will them to your children as inherited property and can make them slaves for life, but you must not rule over your fellow Israelites ruthlessly.

47 "If an alien or a temporary resident among you becomes rich and one of your countrymen becomes poor and sells himself to the alien living among you or to a member of the alien's clan, 48 he retains the right of redemption after he has sold himself. One of his relatives may redeem him: 49 An uncle or a cousin or any blood relative in his clan may redeem him. Or if he prospers, he may redeem himself. 50 He and his buyer are to count the time from the year he sold himself up to the Year of Jubilee. The price for his release is to be based on the rate paid to a hired man for that number of years. 51 If many years remain, he must pay for his redemption a larger share of the price paid for him. 52 If only a few years remain until the Year of Jubilee, he is to compute that and pay for his redemption accordingly. 53 He is to be treated as a man hired from year to year; you must see to it that his owner does not rule over him ruthlessly.

54 "Even if he is not redeemed in any of these ways, he and his children are to be released in the Year of Jubilee, 55 for the Israelites belong to me as servants. They are my servants, whom I brought out of Egypt. I am the LORD your God.

Reward for Obedience

26 "Do not make idols or set up an image or a sacred stone for yourselves, and do not place a carved stone in your land to bow down before it. I am the LORD your God.

---

a 36 Or *take excessive interest*; similarly in verse 37

2 " 'Observe my Sabbaths and have reverence for my sanctuary. I am the LORD.

3 " 'If you follow my decrees and are careful to obey my commands, 4I will send you rain in its season, and the ground will yield its crops and the trees of the field their fruit. 5Your threshing will continue until grape harvest and the grape harvest will continue until planting, and you will eat all the food you want and live in safety in your land.

6 " 'I will grant peace in the land, and you will lie down and no one will make you afraid. I will remove savage beasts from the land, and the sword will not pass through your country. 7You will pursue your enemies, and they will fall by the sword before you. 8Five of you will chase a hundred, and a hundred of you will chase ten thousand, and your enemies will fall by the sword before you.

9 " 'I will look on you with favor and make you fruitful and increase your numbers, and I will keep my covenant with you. 10You will still be eating last year's harvest when you will have to move it out to make room for the new. 11I will put my dwelling place[a] among you, and I will not abhor you. 12I will walk among you and be your God, and you will be my people. 13I am the LORD your God, who brought you out of Egypt so that you would no longer be slaves to the Egyptians; I broke the bars of your yoke and enabled you to walk with heads held high.

Punishment for Disobedience

14 " 'But if you will not listen to me and carry out all these commands, 15and if you reject my decrees and abhor my laws and fail to carry out all my commands and so violate my covenant, 16then I will do this to you: I will bring upon you sudden terror, wasting diseases and fever that will destroy your sight and drain away your life. You will plant seed in vain, because your enemies will eat it. 17I will set my face against you so that you will be defeated by your enemies; those who hate you will rule over you, and you will flee even when no one is pursuing you.

18 " 'If after all this you will not listen to me, I will punish you for your sins seven times over. 19I will break down your stubborn pride and make the sky above you like iron and the ground beneath you like bronze. 20Your strength will be spent in vain, because your soil will not yield its crops, nor will the trees of the land yield their fruit.

21 " 'If you remain hostile toward me and refuse to listen to me, I will multiply your afflictions seven times over, as your sins deserve. 22I will send wild animals against you, and they will rob you of your children, destroy your cattle and make you so few in number that your roads will be deserted.

23 " 'If in spite of these things you do not accept my correction but continue to be hostile toward me, 24I myself will be hostile toward you and will afflict you for your sins seven times over. 25And I will bring the sword upon you to avenge the breaking of the covenant. When you withdraw into your cities, I will send a plague among you, and you will be given into enemy hands. 26When I cut off your supply of bread, ten women will be able to bake your bread in one oven, and they will dole out the bread by weight. You will eat, but you will not be satisfied.

27 " 'If in spite of this you still do not listen to me but continue to be hostile toward me, 28then in my anger I will be hostile toward you, and I myself will punish you for your sins seven times over. 29You will eat the flesh of your sons and the flesh of your daughters. 30I will destroy your high places, cut down your incense altars and pile your dead bodies on the lifeless forms of your idols, and I will abhor you. 31I will turn your cities into ruins and lay waste your sanctuaries, and I will take no delight in the pleasing

---

a 11 Or my tabernacle

aroma of your offerings. 32I will lay waste the land, so that your enemies who live there will be appalled. 33I will scatter you among the nations and will draw out my sword and pursue you. Your land will be laid waste, and your cities will lie in ruins. 34Then the land will enjoy its sabbath years all the time that it lies desolate and you are in the country of your enemies; then the land will rest and enjoy its sabbaths. 35All the time that it lies desolate, the land will have the rest it did not have during the sabbaths you lived in it.

36"'As for those of you who are left, I will make their hearts so fearful in the lands of their enemies that the sound of a windblown leaf will put them to flight. They will run as though fleeing from the sword, and they will fall, even though no one is pursuing them. 37They will stumble over one another as though fleeing from the sword, even though no one is pursuing them. So you will not be able to stand before your enemies. 38You will perish among the nations; the land of your enemies will devour you. 39Those of you who are left will waste away in the lands of their enemies because of their sins; also because of their fathers' sins they will waste away.

Praying Leviticus 26:40-44

Almighty God, I confess my sins to You and ask that You would forgive me and lead me in Your way.

40"'But if they will confess their sins and the sins of their fathers—their treachery against me and their hostility toward me, 41which made me hostile toward them so that I sent them into the land of their enemies—then when their uncircumcised hearts are humbled and they pay for their sin, 42I will remember my covenant with Jacob and my covenant with Isaac and my covenant with Abraham, and I will remember the land. 43For the land will be deserted by them and will enjoy its sabbaths while it lies desolate without them. They will pay for their sins because they rejected my laws and abhorred my decrees. 44Yet in spite of this, when they are in the land of their enemies, I will not reject them or abhor them so as to destroy them completely, breaking my covenant with them. I am the LORD their God. 45But for their sake I will remember the covenant with their ancestors whom I brought out of Egypt in the sight of the nations to be their God. I am the LORD.'"

46These are the decrees, the laws and the regulations that the LORD established on Mount Sinai between himself and the Israelites through Moses.

Redeeming What Is the LORD's

27 The LORD said to Moses, 2"Speak to the Israelites and say to them: 'If anyone makes a special vow to dedicate persons to the LORD by giving equivalent values, 3set the value of a male between the ages of twenty and sixty at fifty shekels[a] of silver, according to the sanctuary shekel[b]; 4and if it is a female, set her value at thirty shekels.[c] 5If it is a person between the ages of five and twenty, set the value of a male at twenty shekels[d] and of a female at ten shekels.[e] 6If it is a person between one month and five years, set the value of a male at five shekels[f] of silver and that of a female at three shekels[g] of silver. 7If it is a person sixty years old or more, set the value of a male at fifteen shekels[h] and of a female at ten shekels. 8If anyone making the vow is too poor to pay the specified amount, he is to present the person to the priest, who will set the value for him according to what the man making the vow can afford.

9"'If what he vowed is an animal that

---

a 3 That is, about 1 1/4 pounds (about 0.6 kilogram); also in verse 16   b 3 That is, about 2/5 ounce (about 11.5 grams); also in verse 25   c 4 That is, about 12 ounces (about 0.3 kilogram)   d 5 That is, about 8 ounces (about 0.2 kilogram)   e 5 That is, about 4 ounces (about 110 grams); also in verse 7   f 6 That is, about 2 ounces (about 55 grams)   g 6 That is, about 1 1/4 ounces (about 35 grams)   h 7 That is, about 6 ounces (about 170 grams) is acceptable as an offering to the LORD, such an animal given to the LORD becomes holy. 10He must not exchange it or substitute a good one for a bad one, or a bad one for a good one; if he should substitute one animal for another, both it and the substitute become holy. 11If what he vowed is a ceremonially unclean animal—one that is not acceptable as an offering to the LORD—the animal must be presented to the priest, 12who will judge its quality as good or bad. Whatever value the priest then sets, that is what it will be. 13If the owner wishes to redeem the animal, he must add a fifth to its value.

14" 'If a man dedicates his house as something holy to the LORD, the priest will judge its quality as good or bad. Whatever value the priest then sets, so it will remain. 15If the man who dedicates his house redeems it, he must add a fifth to its value, and the house will again become his.

16" 'If a man dedicates to the LORD part of his family land, its value is to be set according to the amount of seed required for it—fifty shekels of silver to a homer[a] of barley seed. 17If he dedicates his field during the Year of Jubilee, the value that has been set remains. 18But if he dedicates his field after the Jubilee, the priest will determine the value according to the number of years that remain until the next Year of Jubilee, and its set value will be reduced. 19If the man who dedicates the field wishes to redeem it, he must add a fifth to its value, and the field will again become his. 20If, however, he does not redeem the field, or if he has sold it to someone else, it can never be redeemed. 21When the field is released in the Jubilee, it will become holy, like a field devoted to the LORD; it will become the property of the priests.[b]

22" 'If a man dedicates to the LORD a field he has bought, which is not part of his family land, 23the priest will determine its value up to the Year of Jubilee, and the man must pay its value on that day as something holy to the LORD. 24In the Year of Jubilee the field will revert to the person from whom he bought it, the one whose land it was. 25Every value is to be set according to the sanctuary shekel, twenty gerahs to the shekel.

26" 'No one, however, may dedicate the firstborn of an animal, since the firstborn already belongs to the LORD; whether an ox[c] or a sheep, it is the LORD's. 27If it is one of the unclean animals, he may buy it back at its set value, adding a fifth of the value to it. If he does not redeem it, it is to be sold at its set value.

28" 'But nothing that a man owns and devotes[d] to the LORD—whether man or animal or family land—may be sold or redeemed; everything so devoted is most holy to the LORD.

29" 'No person devoted to destruction[e] may be ransomed; he must be put to death.

30" 'A tithe of everything from the land, whether grain from the soil or fruit from the trees, belongs to the LORD; it is holy to the LORD. 31If a man redeems any of his tithe, he must add a fifth of the value to it. 32The entire tithe of the herd and flock—every tenth animal that passes under the shepherd's rod—will be holy to the LORD. 33He must not pick out the good from the bad or make any substitution. If he does make a substitution, both the animal and its substitute become holy and cannot be redeemed.' "

34These are the commands the LORD gave Moses on Mount Sinai for the Israelites.

---

a 16 That is, probably about 6 bushels (about 220 liters) b 21 Or priest c 26 The Hebrew word can include both male and female. d 28 The Hebrew term refers to the irrevocable giving over of things or persons to the LORD. e 29 The Hebrew term refers to the irrevocable giving over of things or persons to the LORD, often by totally destroying them.

Author: Moses

Date: Sometime between 1446 and
1406 BC

Audience: The people of Israel

Prayer Themes:

- *Thank God for His desire to bring favor and grace and peace to your life (6:24-26).*

- *Ask God to meet your weakness and need with His unlimited power (11:23).*

- *Intercede for fellow believers and bring their needs to God (14:13-20).*

Are you ever tempted to think that you can alter or ignore God's commands and still ask for His favor and blessing?

The book of Numbers is the sobering account of how the ancient Israelites' unbelief and disobedience turned what should have been a two-week triumphant journey into a 40-year ordeal in the desert. We should never think that just because we speak much of God, or even speak often to God, we are exempted from living as He commands.

Yet mixed into this grim study of the consequences of rebellion are numerous reminders that our God is faithful regardless of our failures. The message of Numbers is that "The LORD is slow to anger, abounding in love and forgiving sin and rebellion. Yet he does not leave the guilty unpunished" (14:18).

Numbers

The Census

1 The LORD spoke to Moses in the Tent of Meeting in the Desert of Sinai on the first day of the second month of the second year after the Israelites came out of Egypt. He said: ²"Take a census of the whole Israelite community by their clans and families, listing every man by name, one by one. ³You and Aaron are to number by their divisions all the men in Israel twenty years old or more who are able to serve in the army. ⁴One man from each tribe, each the head of his family, is to help you. ⁵These are the names of the men who are to assist you:

from Reuben, Elizur son of Shedeur;
⁶from Simeon, Shelumiel son of Zurishaddai;
⁷from Judah, Nahshon son of Amminadab;
⁸from Issachar, Nethanel son of Zuar;
⁹from Zebulun, Eliab son of Helon;
¹⁰from the sons of Joseph:
    from Ephraim, Elishama son of Ammihud;
    from Manasseh, Gamaliel son of Pedahzur;
¹¹from Benjamin, Abidan son of Gideoni;
¹²from Dan, Ahiezer son of Ammishaddai;
¹³from Asher, Pagiel son of Ocran;
¹⁴from Gad, Eliasaph son of Deuel;
¹⁵from Naphtali, Ahira son of Enan."

¹⁶These were the men appointed from the community, the leaders of their ancestral tribes. They were the heads of the clans of Israel.

¹⁷Moses and Aaron took these men whose names had been given, ¹⁸and they called the whole community together on

the first day of the second month. The people indicated their ancestry by their clans and families, and the men twenty years old or more were listed by name, one by one, 19as the LORD commanded Moses. And so he counted them in the Desert of Sinai:

20From the descendants of Reuben the firstborn son of Israel:

All the men twenty years old or more who were able to serve in the army were listed by name, one by one, according to the records of their clans and families. 21The number from the tribe of Reuben was 46,500.

22From the descendants of Simeon:

All the men twenty years old or more who were able to serve in the army were counted and listed by name, one by one, according to the records of their clans and families. 23The number from the tribe of Simeon was 59,300.

24From the descendants of Gad:

All the men twenty years old or more who were able to serve in the army were listed by name, according to the records of their clans and families. 25The number from the tribe of Gad was 45,650.

26From the descendants of Judah:

All the men twenty years old or more who were able to serve in the army were listed by name, according to the records of their clans and families. 27The number from the tribe of Judah was 74,600.

28From the descendants of Issachar:

All the men twenty years old or more who were able to serve in the army were listed by name, according to the records of their clans and families. 29The number from the tribe of Issachar was 54,400.

30From the descendants of Zebulun:

All the men twenty years old or more who were able to serve in the army were listed by name, according to the records of their clans and families. 31The number from the tribe of Zebulun was 57,400.

32From the sons of Joseph:

From the descendants of Ephraim:

All the men twenty years old or more who were able to serve in the army were listed by name, according to the records of their clans and families. 33The number from the tribe of Ephraim was 40,500.

34From the descendants of Manasseh:

All the men twenty years old or more who were able to serve in the army were listed by name, according to the records of their clans and families. 35The number from the tribe of Manasseh was 32,200.

36From the descendants of Benjamin:

All the men twenty years old or more who were able to serve in the army were listed by name, according to the records of their clans and families. 37The number from the tribe of Benjamin was 35,400.

38From the descendants of Dan:

All the men twenty years old or more who were able to serve in the army were listed by name, according to the records of their clans and families. 39The number from the tribe of Dan was 62,700.

40From the descendants of Asher:

All the men twenty years old or more who were able to serve in the army were listed by name, according to the records of their clans and families. 41The number from the tribe of Asher was 41,500.

⁴²From the descendants of Naphtali: All the men twenty years old or more who were able to serve in the army were listed by name, according to the records of their clans and families. ⁴³The number from the tribe of Naphtali was 53,400.

⁴⁴These were the men counted by Moses and Aaron and the twelve leaders of Israel, each one representing his family. ⁴⁵All the Israelites twenty years old or more who were able to serve in Israel's army were counted according to their families. ⁴⁶The total number was 603,550.

⁴⁷The families of the tribe of Levi, however, were not counted along with the others. ⁴⁸The LORD had said to Moses: ⁴⁹"You must not count the tribe of Levi or include them in the census of the other Israelites. ⁵⁰Instead, appoint the Levites to be in charge of the tabernacle of the Testimony—over all its furnishings and everything belonging to it. They are to carry the tabernacle and all its furnishings; they are to take care of it and encamp around it. ⁵¹Whenever the tabernacle is to move, the Levites are to take it down, and whenever the tabernacle is to be set up, the Levites shall do it. Anyone else who goes near it shall be put to death. ⁵²The Israelites are to set up their tents by divisions, each man in his own camp under his own standard. ⁵³The Levites, however, are to set up their tents around the tabernacle of the Testimony so that wrath will not fall on the Israelite community. The Levites are to be responsible for the care of the tabernacle of the Testimony." ⁵⁴The Israelites did all this just as the LORD commanded Moses.

The Arrangement of the Tribal Camps

2 The LORD said to Moses and Aaron: ²"The Israelites are to camp around the Tent of Meeting some distance from it, each man under his standard with the banners of his family."

³On the east, toward the sunrise, the divisions of the camp of Judah are to encamp under their standard. The leader of the people of Judah is Nahshon son of Amminadab. ⁴His division numbers 74,600.

⁵The tribe of Issachar will camp next to them. The leader of the people of Issachar is Nethanel son of Zuar. ⁶His division numbers 54,400.

⁷The tribe of Zebulun will be next. The leader of the people of Zebulun is Eliab son of Helon. ⁸His division numbers 57,400.

⁹All the men assigned to the camp of Judah, according to their divisions, number 186,400. They will set out first.

¹⁰On the south will be the divisions of the camp of Reuben under their standard. The leader of the people of Reuben is Elizur son of Shedeur. ¹¹His division numbers 46,500.

¹²The tribe of Simeon will camp next to them. The leader of the people of Simeon is Shelumiel son of Zurishaddai. ¹³His division numbers 59,300.

¹⁴The tribe of Gad will be next. The leader of the people of Gad is Eliasaph son of Deuel.ᵃ ¹⁵His division numbers 45,650.

¹⁶All the men assigned to the camp of Reuben, according to their divisions, number 151,450. They will set out second.

¹⁷Then the Tent of Meeting and the camp of the Levites will set out in the middle of the camps. They will set out in the same order as they encamp, each in his own place under his standard.

---

^a *14* Many manuscripts of the Masoretic Text, Samaritan Pentateuch and Vulgate (see also Num. 1:14); most manuscripts of the Masoretic Text *Reuel*

¹⁸On the west will be the divisions of the camp of Ephraim under their standard. The leader of the people of Ephraim is Elishama son of Ammihud. ¹⁹His division numbers 40,500.

²⁰The tribe of Manasseh will be next to them. The leader of the people of Manasseh is Gamaliel son of Pedahzur. ²¹His division numbers 32,200.

²²The tribe of Benjamin will be next. The leader of the people of Benjamin is Abidan son of Gideoni. ²³His division numbers 35,400.

²⁴All the men assigned to the camp of Ephraim, according to their divisions, number 108,100. They will set out third.

²⁵On the north will be the divisions of the camp of Dan, under their standard. The leader of the people of Dan is Ahiezer son of Ammishaddai. ²⁶His division numbers 62,700.

²⁷The tribe of Asher will camp next to them. The leader of the people of Asher is Pagiel son of Ocran. ²⁸His division numbers 41,500.

²⁹The tribe of Naphtali will be next. The leader of the people of Naphtali is Ahira son of Enan. ³⁰His division numbers 53,400.

³¹All the men assigned to the camp of Dan number 157,600. They will set out last, under their standards.

³²These are the Israelites, counted according to their families. All those in the camps, by their divisions, number 603,550. ³³The Levites, however, were not counted along with the other Israelites, as the LORD commanded Moses.

³⁴So the Israelites did everything the LORD commanded Moses; that is the way they encamped under their standards, and that is the way they set out, each with his clan and family.

The Levites

3 This is the account of the family of Aaron and Moses at the time the LORD talked with Moses on Mount Sinai.

²The names of the sons of Aaron were Nadab the firstborn and Abihu, Eleazar and Ithamar. ³Those were the names of Aaron's sons, the anointed priests, who were ordained to serve as priests. ⁴Nadab and Abihu, however, fell dead before the LORD when they made an offering with unauthorized fire before him in the Desert of Sinai. They had no sons; so only Eleazar and Ithamar served as priests during the lifetime of their father Aaron.

⁵The LORD said to Moses, ⁶"Bring the tribe of Levi and present them to Aaron the priest to assist him. ⁷They are to perform duties for him and for the whole community at the Tent of Meeting by doing the work of the tabernacle. ⁸They are to take care of all the furnishings of the Tent of Meeting, fulfilling the obligations of the Israelites by doing the work of the tabernacle. ⁹Give the Levites to Aaron and his sons; they are the Israelites who are to be given wholly to him.ᵃ ¹⁰Appoint Aaron and his sons to serve as priests; anyone else who approaches the sanctuary must be put to death."

¹¹The LORD also said to Moses, ¹²"I have taken the Levites from among the Israelites in place of the first male offspring of every Israelite woman. The Levites are mine, ¹³for all the firstborn are mine. When I struck down all the firstborn in Egypt, I set apart for myself every firstborn in Israel, whether man or animal. They are to be mine. I am the LORD."

¹⁴The LORD said to Moses in the Desert of Sinai, ¹⁵"Count the Levites by their families and clans. Count every male a month old or more." ¹⁶So Moses counted them, as he was commanded by the word of the LORD.

ᵃ 9 Most manuscripts of the Masoretic Text; some manuscripts of the Masoretic Text, Samaritan Pentateuch and Septuagint (see also Num. 8:16) *to me*

17 These were the names of the sons
of Levi:

Gershon, Kohath and Merari.
18 These were the names of the Gershonite clans:

Libni and Shimei.
19 The Kohathite clans:

Amram, Izhar, Hebron and Uzziel.
20 The Merarite clans:

Mahli and Mushi.

These were the Levite clans, according
to their families.

21 To Gershon belonged the clans of
the Libnites and Shimeites; these were
the Gershonite clans. 22 The number of
all the males a month old or more who
were counted was 7,500. 23 The Gershonite clans were to camp on the west, behind the tabernacle. 24 The leader of the
families of the Gershonites was Eliasaph
son of Lael. 25 At the Tent of Meeting the
Gershonites were responsible for the care
of the tabernacle and tent, its coverings,
the curtain at the entrance to the Tent of
Meeting, 26 the curtains of the courtyard,
the curtain at the entrance to the courtyard surrounding the tabernacle and altar,
and the ropes—and everything related to
their use.

27 To Kohath belonged the clans of the
Amramites, Izharites, Hebronites and Uzzielites; these were the Kohathite clans.
28 The number of all the males a month
old or more was 8,600.ᵃ The Kohathites were responsible for the care of the
sanctuary. 29 The Kohathite clans were to
camp on the south side of the tabernacle. 30 The leader of the families of the Kohathite clans was Elizaphan son of Uzziel.
31 They were responsible for the care of
the ark, the table, the lampstand, the altars, the articles of the sanctuary used in
ministering, the curtain, and everything
related to their use. 32 The chief leader of
the Levites was Eleazar son of Aaron, the
priest. He was appointed over those who
were responsible for the care of the sanctuary.

33 To Merari belonged the clans of the
Mahlites and the Mushites; these were
the Merarite clans. 34 The number of all
the males a month old or more who were
counted was 6,200. 35 The leader of the
families of the Merarite clans was Zuriel
son of Abihail; they were to camp on the
north side of the tabernacle. 36 The Merarites were appointed to take care of the
frames of the tabernacle, its crossbars,
posts, bases, all its equipment, and everything related to their use, 37 as well as the
posts of the surrounding courtyard with
their bases, tent pegs and ropes.

38 Moses and Aaron and his sons were
to camp to the east of the tabernacle, toward the sunrise, in front of the Tent of
Meeting. They were responsible for the
care of the sanctuary on behalf of the Israelites. Anyone else who approached the
sanctuary was to be put to death.

39 The total number of Levites counted
at the LORD's command by Moses and
Aaron according to their clans, including every male a month old or more,
was 22,000.

40 The LORD said to Moses, "Count all
the firstborn Israelite males who are a
month old or more and make a list of
their names. 41 Take the Levites for me in
place of all the firstborn of the Israelites,
and the livestock of the Levites in place
of all the firstborn of the livestock of the
Israelites. I am the LORD."

42 So Moses counted all the firstborn of
the Israelites, as the LORD commanded
him. 43 The total number of firstborn
males a month old or more, listed by
name, was 22,273.

44 The LORD also said to Moses, 45 "Take
the Levites in place of all the firstborn of
Israel, and the livestock of the Levites in

ᵃ 28 Hebrew; some Septuagint manuscripts 8,300

place of their livestock. The Levites are to be mine. I am the LORD. ⁴⁶To redeem the 273 firstborn Israelites who exceed the number of the Levites, ⁴⁷collect five shekels^a for each one, according to the sanctuary shekel, which weighs twenty gerahs. ⁴⁸Give the money for the redemption of the additional Israelites to Aaron and his sons."

⁴⁹So Moses collected the redemption money from those who exceeded the number redeemed by the Levites. ⁵⁰From the firstborn of the Israelites he collected silver weighing 1,365 shekels,^b according to the sanctuary shekel. ⁵¹Moses gave the redemption money to Aaron and his sons, as he was commanded by the word of the LORD.

The Kohathites

4 The LORD said to Moses and Aaron: ²"Take a census of the Kohathite branch of the Levites by their clans and families. ³Count all the men from thirty to fifty years of age who come to serve in the work in the Tent of Meeting.

⁴"This is the work of the Kohathites in the Tent of Meeting: the care of the most holy things. ⁵When the camp is to move, Aaron and his sons are to go in and take down the shielding curtain and cover the ark of the Testimony with it. ⁶Then they are to cover this with hides of sea cows,^c spread a cloth of solid blue over that and put the poles in place.

⁷"Over the table of the Presence they are to spread a blue cloth and put on it the plates, dishes and bowls, and the jars for drink offerings; the bread that is continually there is to remain on it. ⁸Over these they are to spread a scarlet cloth, cover that with hides of sea cows and put its poles in place.

⁹"They are to take a blue cloth and cover the lampstand that is for light, together with its lamps, its wick trimmers and trays, and all its jars for the oil used to supply it. ¹⁰Then they are to wrap it and all its accessories in a covering of hides of sea cows and put it on a carrying frame.

¹¹"Over the gold altar they are to spread a blue cloth and cover that with hides of sea cows and put its poles in place.

¹²"They are to take all the articles used for ministering in the sanctuary, wrap them in a blue cloth, cover that with hides of sea cows and put them on a carrying frame.

¹³"They are to remove the ashes from the bronze altar and spread a purple cloth over it. ¹⁴Then they are to place on it all the utensils used for ministering at the altar, including the firepans, meat forks, shovels and sprinkling bowls. Over it they are to spread a covering of hides of sea cows and put its poles in place.

¹⁵"After Aaron and his sons have finished covering the holy furnishings and all the holy articles, and when the camp is ready to move, the Kohathites are to come to do the carrying. But they must not touch the holy things or they will die. The Kohathites are to carry those things that are in the Tent of Meeting.

¹⁶"Eleazar son of Aaron, the priest, is to have charge of the oil for the light, the fragrant incense, the regular grain offering and the anointing oil. He is to be in charge of the entire tabernacle and everything in it, including its holy furnishings and articles."

¹⁷The LORD said to Moses and Aaron, ¹⁸"See that the Kohathite tribal clans are not cut off from the Levites. ¹⁹So that they may live and not die when they come near the most holy things, do this for them: Aaron and his sons are to go into the sanctuary and assign to each man his work and what he is to carry. ²⁰But the Kohathites must not go in to look at the holy things, even for a moment, or they will die."

The Gershonites

²¹The LORD said to Moses, ²²"Take a census also of the Gershonites by their

---

^a 47 That is, about 2 ounces (about 55 grams)   ^b 50 That is, about 35 pounds (about 15.5 kilograms)   ^c 6 That is, dugongs; also in verses 8, 10, 11, 12, 14 and 25

families and clans. 23Count all the men from thirty to fifty years of age who come to serve in the work at the Tent of Meeting.

24"This is the service of the Gershonite clans as they work and carry burdens: 25They are to carry the curtains of the tabernacle, the Tent of Meeting, its covering and the outer covering of hides of sea cows, the curtains for the entrance to the Tent of Meeting, 26the curtains of the courtyard surrounding the tabernacle and altar, the curtain for the entrance, the ropes and all the equipment used in its service. The Gershonites are to do all that needs to be done with these things. 27All their service, whether carrying or doing other work, is to be done under the direction of Aaron and his sons. You shall assign to them as their responsibility all they are to carry. 28This is the service of the Gershonite clans at the Tent of Meeting. Their duties are to be under the direction of Ithamar son of Aaron, the priest.

The Merarites

29"Count the Merarites by their clans and families. 30Count all the men from thirty to fifty years of age who come to serve in the work at the Tent of Meeting. 31This is their duty as they perform service at the Tent of Meeting: to carry the frames of the tabernacle, its crossbars, posts and bases, 32as well as the posts of the surrounding courtyard with their bases, tent pegs, ropes, all their equipment and everything related to their use. Assign to each man the specific things he is to carry. 33This is the service of the Merarite clans as they work at the Tent of Meeting under the direction of Ithamar son of Aaron, the priest."

The Numbering of the Levite Clans

34Moses, Aaron and the leaders of the community counted the Kohathites by their clans and families. 35All the men from thirty to fifty years of age who came to serve in the work in the Tent of Meeting, 36counted by clans, were 2,750. 37This was the total of all those in the Kohathite clans who served in the Tent of Meeting. Moses and Aaron counted them according to the LORD's command through Moses.

38The Gershonites were counted by their clans and families. 39All the men from thirty to fifty years of age who came to serve in the work at the Tent of Meeting, 40counted by their clans and families, were 2,630. 41This was the total of those in the Gershonite clans who served at the Tent of Meeting. Moses and Aaron counted them according to the LORD's command.

42The Merarites were counted by their clans and families. 43All the men from thirty to fifty years of age who came to serve in the work at the Tent of Meeting, 44counted by their clans, were 3,200. 45This was the total of those in the Merarite clans. Moses and Aaron counted them according to the LORD's command through Moses.

46So Moses, Aaron and the leaders of Israel counted all the Levites by their clans and families. 47All the men from thirty to fifty years of age who came to do the work of serving and carrying the Tent of Meeting 48numbered 8,580. 49At the LORD's command through Moses, each was assigned his work and told what to carry.

Thus they were counted, as the LORD commanded Moses.

The Purity of the Camp

5 The LORD said to Moses, 2"Command the Israelites to send away from the camp anyone who has an infectious skin disease[a] or a discharge of any kind, or who is ceremonially unclean because of a dead body. 3Send away male and female alike; send them outside the camp so they will not defile their camp, where I dwell among them." 4The Israelites did this; they sent them outside

---

[a] 2 Traditionally *leprosy*; the Hebrew word was used for various diseases affecting the skin—not necessarily leprosy.

GOING *deeper*

The Importance of Restitution

READ AND CONSIDER: NUMBERS 5:5-10

"When a man or woman wrongs another in any way and so is unfaithful to the LORD, that person is guilty and must confess the sin he has committed. He must make full restitution for his wrong, add one fifth to it and give it all to the person he has wronged" (Numbers 5:6-7).

Most of us have experienced the pain of being wronged at some point in life. We may have had personal possessions damaged or stolen. Worse yet, we may have lost someone we loved due to the carelessness or callousness of another individual. There is often no adequate compensation for the pain we suffer, but this passage speaks of God's provision of the concept of restitution as part of His law for the people of Israel. "To make restitution" means to provide compensation or remuneration for the losses someone has experienced due to the actions of another. This passage makes it clear that to simply say "I'm sorry; please forgive me" was not sufficient. Instead, God put into place the stipulation that the guilty party not only had to restore what had been taken but also pay an additional interest penalty as well. Confession included restitution.

We need to accept the fact that justice is not always served in our imperfect world. For example, many crimes are committed for which adequate compensation is impossible. It is usually not within our power to demand and receive remuneration for harm done at the hands of another. However, one avenue of justice is open to all: a heavenly Father who sees each wrongful act committed here on earth. In the life to come we will experience perfect justice, and in the words of Isaiah, "Every valley shall be raised up, every mountain and hill made low; the rough ground shall become level, the rugged places a plain" (Isaiah 40:4).

Until that day comes, we need to be sure that we have not intentionally wronged another. Ask the Lord if you need to apologize and make restitution for anything in your past. The joy and freedom that come from having a clean conscience will lead you to a new level of intimacy with God. Don't put it off; take that first step today.

the camp. They did just as the LORD had instructed Moses.

Restitution for Wrongs

⁵The LORD said to Moses, ⁶"Say to the Israelites: 'When a man or woman wrongs another in any way[a] and so is unfaithful to the LORD, that person is guilty ⁷and must confess the sin he has committed. He must make full restitution for his wrong, add one fifth to it and give it all to the person he has wronged. ⁸But if that person has no close relative to whom restitution can be made for the wrong, the restitution belongs to the LORD and must be given to the priest, along with the ram

with which atonement is made for him. ⁹All the sacred contributions the Israelites bring to a priest will belong to him. ¹⁰Each man's sacred gifts are his own, but what he gives to the priest will belong to the priest.'"

The Test for an Unfaithful Wife

¹¹Then the LORD said to Moses, ¹²"Speak to the Israelites and say to them: 'If a man's wife goes astray and is unfaithful to him ¹³by sleeping with another man, and this is hidden from her husband and her impurity is undetected (since there is no witness against her and she has not been caught in the act), ¹⁴and if feel-

---

ᵃ 6 Or *woman commits any wrong common to mankind*

ings of jealousy come over her husband and he suspects his wife and she is impure—or if he is jealous and suspects her even though she is not impure— 15then he is to take his wife to the priest. He must also take an offering of a tenth of an ephah[a] of barley flour on her behalf. He must not pour oil on it or put incense on it, because it is a grain offering for jealousy, a reminder offering to draw attention to guilt.

16"'The priest shall bring her and have her stand before the LORD. 17Then he shall take some holy water in a clay jar and put some dust from the tabernacle floor into the water. 18After the priest has had the woman stand before the LORD, he shall loosen her hair and place in her hands the reminder offering, the grain offering for jealousy, while he himself holds the bitter water that brings a curse. 19Then the priest shall put the woman under oath and say to her, "If no other man has slept with you and you have not gone astray and become impure while married to your husband, may this bitter water that brings a curse not harm you. 20But if you have gone astray while married to your husband and you have defiled yourself by sleeping with a man other than your husband"— 21here the priest is to put the woman under this curse of the oath—"may the LORD cause your people to curse and denounce you when he causes your thigh to waste away and your abdomen to swell.[b] 22May this water that brings a curse enter your body so that your abdomen swells and your thigh wastes away.[c]"

"'Then the woman is to say, "Amen. So be it."

23"'The priest is to write these curses on a scroll and then wash them off into the bitter water. 24He shall have the woman drink the bitter water that brings a curse, and this water will enter her and cause bitter suffering. 25The priest is to

take from her hands the grain offering for jealousy, wave it before the LORD and bring it to the altar. 26The priest is then to take a handful of the grain offering as a memorial offering and burn it on the altar; after that, he is to have the woman drink the water. 27If she has defiled herself and been unfaithful to her husband, then when she is made to drink the water that brings a curse, it will go into her and cause bitter suffering; her abdomen will swell and her thigh waste away,[d] and she will become accursed among her people. 28If, however, the woman has not defiled herself and is free from impurity, she will be cleared of guilt and will be able to have children.

29"'This, then, is the law of jealousy when a woman goes astray and defiles herself while married to her husband, 30or when feelings of jealousy come over a man because he suspects his wife. The priest is to have her stand before the LORD and is to apply this entire law to her. 31The husband will be innocent of any wrongdoing, but the woman will bear the consequences of her sin.'"

The Nazirite

6 The LORD said to Moses, 2"Speak to the Israelites and say to them: 'If a man or woman wants to make a special vow, a vow of separation to the LORD as a Nazirite, 3he must abstain from wine and other fermented drink and must not drink vinegar made from wine or from other fermented drink. He must not drink grape juice or eat grapes or raisins. 4As long as he is a Nazirite, he must not eat anything that comes from the grapevine, not even the seeds or skins.

5"'During the entire period of his vow of separation no razor may be used on his head. He must be holy until the period of his separation to the LORD is over; he must let the hair of his head grow long. 6Throughout the period of his separation

---

a 15 That is, probably about 2 quarts (about 2 liters)   b 21 Or causes you to have a miscarrying womb and barrenness
c 22 Or body and cause you to be barren and have a miscarrying womb   d 27 Or suffering; she will have barrenness and a miscarrying womb

to the LORD he must not go near a dead body. [7] Even if his own father or mother or brother or sister dies, he must not make himself ceremonially unclean on account of them, because the symbol of his separation to God is on his head. [8] Throughout the period of his separation he is consecrated to the LORD.

[9] "If someone dies suddenly in his presence, thus defiling the hair he has dedicated, he must shave his head on the day of his cleansing—the seventh day. [10] Then on the eighth day he must bring two doves or two young pigeons to the priest at the entrance to the Tent of Meeting. [11] The priest is to offer one as a sin offering and the other as a burnt offering to make atonement for him because he sinned by being in the presence of the dead body. That same day he is to consecrate his head. [12] He must dedicate himself to the LORD for the period of his separation and must bring a year-old male lamb as a guilt offering. The previous days do not count, because he became defiled during his separation.

[13] "Now this is the law for the Nazirite when the period of his separation is over. He is to be brought to the entrance to the Tent of Meeting. [14] There he is to present his offerings to the LORD: a year-old male lamb without defect for a burnt offering, a year-old ewe lamb without defect for a sin offering, a ram without defect for a fellowship offering,[a] [15] together with their grain offerings and drink offerings, and a basket of bread made without yeast—cakes made of fine flour mixed with oil, and wafers spread with oil.

[16] "'The priest is to present them before the LORD and make the sin offering and the burnt offering. [17] He is to present the basket of unleavened bread and is to sacrifice the ram as a fellowship offering to the LORD, together with its grain offering and drink offering.

[18] "'Then at the entrance to the Tent of Meeting, the Nazirite must shave off the hair that he dedicated. He is to take the hair and put it in the fire that is under the sacrifice of the fellowship offering.

[19] "'After the Nazirite has shaved off the hair of his dedication, the priest is to place in his hands a boiled shoulder of the ram, and a cake and a wafer from the basket, both made without yeast. [20] The priest shall then wave them before the LORD as a wave offering; they are holy and belong to the priest, together with the breast that was waved and the thigh that was presented. After that, the Nazirite may drink wine.

[21] "'This is the law of the Nazirite who vows his offering to the LORD in accor-

---

[a] 14 Traditionally *peace offering*; also in verses 17 and 18

God's people at prayer
AARON'S PRAYER OF BLESSING

NUMBERS 6:24-26 God gave this poetic prayer directly to Aaron and his descendants to use in their priestly ministry of blessing the people. Its use certainly isn't confined to clergy, however. These beautiful words have been used in countless settings throughout the centuries as a way of asking God to place His favor upon others. It includes a request for protection ("the LORD keep you"), for love and grace ("the LORD make his face shine upon you"), and for freedom from worry ("give you peace").

Rather than only praying, "God bless Mom and Dad, my relatives, and my friends," consider committing this passage to memory and using these words often to ask the Lord to bless those around you. It is a beautiful and powerful prayer as well as the best gift you can give them.

dance with his separation, in addition to whatever else he can afford. He must fulfill the vow he has made, according to the law of the Nazirite.' "

The Priestly Blessing

22The LORD said to Moses, 23"Tell Aaron and his sons, 'This is how you are to bless the Israelites. Say to them:

24" ' "The LORD bless you
 and keep you;
25the LORD make his face shine upon
  you
 and be gracious to you;
26the LORD turn his face toward you
 and give you peace." '

27"So they will put my name on the Israelites, and I will bless them."

Offerings at the Dedication of the Tabernacle

7 When Moses finished setting up the tabernacle, he anointed it and consecrated it and all its furnishings. He also anointed and consecrated the altar and all its utensils. 2Then the leaders of Israel, the heads of families who were the tribal leaders in charge of those who were counted, made offerings. 3They brought as their gifts before the LORD six covered carts and twelve oxen—an ox from each leader and a cart from every two. These they presented before the tabernacle.

4The LORD said to Moses, 5"Accept these from them, that they may be used in the work at the Tent of Meeting. Give them to the Levites as each man's work requires."

6So Moses took the carts and oxen and gave them to the Levites. 7He gave two carts and four oxen to the Gershonites, as their work required, 8and he gave four carts and eight oxen to the Merarites, as their work required. They were all under the direction of Ithamar son of Aaron, the priest. 9But Moses did not give any to the Kohathites, because they were to carry on their shoulders the holy things, for which they were responsible.

10When the altar was anointed, the leaders brought their offerings for its dedication and presented them before the altar. 11For the LORD had said to Moses, "Each day one leader is to bring his offering for the dedication of the altar."

12The one who brought his offering on the first day was Nahshon son of Amminadab of the tribe of Judah.

13His offering was one silver plate weighing a hundred and thirty shekels,a and one silver sprinkling bowl weighing seventy shekels,b both according to the sanctuary shekel, each filled with fine flour mixed with oil as a grain offering; 14one gold dish weighing ten shekels,c filled with incense; 15one young bull, one ram and one male lamb a year old, for a burnt offering; 16one male goat for a sin offering; 17and two oxen, five rams, five male goats and five male lambs a year old, to be sacrificed as a fellowship offering.d This was the offering of Nahshon son of Amminadab.

18On the second day Nethanel son of Zuar, the leader of Issachar, brought his offering.

19The offering he brought was one silver plate weighing a hundred and thirty shekels, and one silver sprinkling bowl weighing seventy shekels, both according to the sanctuary shekel, each filled with fine flour mixed with oil as a grain offering; 20one gold dish weighing ten shekels, filled with incense; 21one young bull, one ram and one male lamb a year old, for a burnt offering; 22one male goat for a sin offering; 23and two oxen, five rams, five male goats and five male lambs a year old, to be sacrificed as a fellowship offering. This was the offering of Nethanel son of Zuar.

a 13 That is, about 3 1/4 pounds (about 1.5 kilograms); also elsewhere in this chapter   b 13 That is, about 1 3/4 pounds (about 0.8 kilogram); also elsewhere in this chapter   c 14 That is, about 4 ounces (about 110 grams); also elsewhere in this chapter   d 17 Traditionally peace offering; also elsewhere in this chapter

²⁴On the third day, Eliab son of Helon, the leader of the people of Zebulun, brought his offering.

²⁵His offering was one silver plate weighing a hundred and thirty shekels, and one silver sprinkling bowl weighing seventy shekels, both according to the sanctuary shekel, each filled with fine flour mixed with oil as a grain offering; ²⁶one gold dish weighing ten shekels, filled with incense; ²⁷one young bull, one ram and one male lamb a year old, for a burnt offering; ²⁸one male goat for a sin offering; ²⁹and two oxen, five rams, five male goats and five male lambs a year old, to be sacrificed as a fellowship offering. This was the offering of Eliab son of Helon.

³⁰On the fourth day Elizur son of Shedeur, the leader of the people of Reuben, brought his offering.

³¹His offering was one silver plate weighing a hundred and thirty shekels, and one silver sprinkling bowl weighing seventy shekels, both according to the sanctuary shekel, each filled with fine flour mixed with oil as a grain offering; ³²one gold dish weighing ten shekels, filled with incense; ³³one young bull, one ram and one male lamb a year old, for a burnt offering; ³⁴one male goat for a sin offering; ³⁵and two oxen, five rams, five male goats and five male lambs a year old, to be sacrificed as a fellowship offering. This was the offering of Elizur son of Shedeur.

³⁶On the fifth day Shelumiel son of Zurishaddai, the leader of the people of Simeon, brought his offering.

³⁷His offering was one silver plate weighing a hundred and thirty shekels, and one silver sprinkling bowl weighing seventy shekels, both according to the sanctuary shekel, each filled with fine flour mixed with oil as a grain offering; ³⁸one gold dish weighing ten shekels, filled with incense; ³⁹one young bull, one ram and one male lamb a year old, for a burnt offering; ⁴⁰one male goat for a sin offering; ⁴¹and two oxen, five rams, five male goats and five male lambs a year old, to be sacrificed as a fellowship offering. This was the offering of Shelumiel son of Zurishaddai.

⁴²On the sixth day Eliasaph son of Deuel, the leader of the people of Gad, brought his offering.

⁴³His offering was one silver plate weighing a hundred and thirty shekels, and one silver sprinkling bowl weighing seventy shekels, both according to the sanctuary shekel, each filled with fine flour mixed with oil as a grain offering; ⁴⁴one gold dish weighing ten shekels, filled with incense; ⁴⁵one young bull, one ram and one male lamb a year old, for a burnt offering; ⁴⁶one male goat for a sin offering; ⁴⁷and two oxen, five rams, five male goats and five male lambs a year old, to be sacrificed as a fellowship offering. This was the offering of Eliasaph son of Deuel.

⁴⁸On the seventh day Elishama son of Ammihud, the leader of the people of Ephraim, brought his offering.

⁴⁹His offering was one silver plate weighing a hundred and thirty shekels, and one silver sprinkling bowl weighing seventy shekels, both according to the sanctuary shekel, each filled with fine flour mixed with oil as a grain offering; ⁵⁰one gold dish weighing ten shekels, filled with incense; ⁵¹one young bull, one ram and one male lamb a year old, for a burnt offering; ⁵²one male goat for a sin offering; ⁵³and two oxen, five rams, five male goats and five male lambs a year old, to be sacrificed as a fellowship offering. This was the offering of Elishama son of Ammihud.

54On the eighth day Gamaliel son of Pedahzur, the leader of the people of Manasseh, brought his offering.

55His offering was one silver plate weighing a hundred and thirty shekels, and one silver sprinkling bowl weighing seventy shekels, both according to the sanctuary shekel, each filled with fine flour mixed with oil as a grain offering; 56one gold dish weighing ten shekels, filled with incense; 57one young bull, one ram and one male lamb a year old, for a burnt offering; 58one male goat for a sin offering; 59and two oxen, five rams, five male goats and five male lambs a year old, to be sacrificed as a fellowship offering. This was the offering of Gamaliel son of Pedahzur.

60On the ninth day Abidan son of Gideoni, the leader of the people of Benjamin, brought his offering.

61His offering was one silver plate weighing a hundred and thirty shekels, and one silver sprinkling bowl weighing seventy shekels, both according to the sanctuary shekel, each filled with fine flour mixed with oil as a grain offering; 62one gold dish weighing ten shekels, filled with incense; 63one young bull, one ram and one male lamb a year old, for a burnt offering; 64one male goat for a sin offering; 65and two oxen, five rams, five male goats and five male lambs a year old, to be sacrificed as a fellowship offering. This was the offering of Abidan son of Gideoni.

66On the tenth day Ahiezer son of Ammishaddai, the leader of the people of Dan, brought his offering.

67His offering was one silver plate weighing a hundred and thirty shekels, and one silver sprinkling bowl weighing seventy shekels, both according to the sanctuary shekel, each filled with fine flour mixed with oil as a grain offering; 68one gold dish weighing ten shekels, filled with incense; 69one young bull, one ram and one male lamb a year old, for a burnt offering; 70one male goat for a sin offering; 71and two oxen, five rams, five male goats and five male lambs a year old, to be sacrificed as a fellowship offering. This was the offering of Ahiezer son of Ammishaddai.

72On the eleventh day Pagiel son of Ocran, the leader of the people of Asher, brought his offering.

73His offering was one silver plate weighing a hundred and thirty shekels, and one silver sprinkling bowl weighing seventy shekels, both according to the sanctuary shekel, each filled with fine flour mixed with oil as a grain offering; 74one gold dish weighing ten shekels, filled with incense; 75one young bull, one ram and one male lamb a year old, for a burnt offering; 76one male goat for a sin offering; 77and two oxen, five rams, five male goats and five male lambs a year old, to be sacrificed as a fellowship offering. This was the offering of Pagiel son of Ocran.

78On the twelfth day Ahira son of Enan, the leader of the people of Naphtali, brought his offering.

79His offering was one silver plate weighing a hundred and thirty shekels, and one silver sprinkling bowl weighing seventy shekels, both according to the sanctuary shekel, each filled with fine flour mixed with oil as a grain offering; 80one gold dish weighing ten shekels, filled with incense; 81one young bull, one ram and one male lamb a year old, for a burnt offering; 82one male goat for a sin offering; 83and two oxen, five rams, five male goats and five male lambs a year old, to be sacrificed as a fellowship offering. This was the offering of Ahira son of Enan.

84 These were the offerings of the Israelite leaders for the dedication of the altar when it was anointed: twelve silver plates, twelve silver sprinkling bowls and twelve gold dishes. 85 Each silver plate weighed a hundred and thirty shekels, and each sprinkling bowl seventy shekels. Altogether, the silver dishes weighed two thousand four hundred shekels,[a] according to the sanctuary shekel. 86 The twelve gold dishes filled with incense weighed ten shekels each, according to the sanctuary shekel. Altogether, the gold dishes weighed a hundred and twenty shekels.[b] 87 The total number of animals for the burnt offering came to twelve young bulls, twelve rams and twelve male lambs a year old, together with their grain offering. Twelve male goats were used for the sin offering. 88 The total number of animals for the sacrifice of the fellowship offering came to twenty-four oxen, sixty rams, sixty male goats and sixty male lambs a year old. These were the offerings for the dedication of the altar after it was anointed.

89 When Moses entered the Tent of Meeting to speak with the LORD, he heard the voice speaking to him from between the two cherubim above the atonement cover on the ark of the Testimony. And he spoke with him.

Setting Up the Lamps

8 The LORD said to Moses, 2 "Speak to Aaron and say to him, 'When you set up the seven lamps, they are to light the area in front of the lampstand.'"

3 Aaron did so; he set up the lamps so that they faced forward on the lampstand, just as the LORD commanded Moses. 4 This is how the lampstand was made: It was made of hammered gold—from its base to its blossoms. The lampstand was made exactly like the pattern the LORD had shown Moses.

The Setting Apart of the Levites

5 The LORD said to Moses: 6 "Take the Levites from among the other Israelites and make them ceremonially clean. 7 To purify them, do this: Sprinkle the water of cleansing on them; then have them shave their whole bodies and wash their clothes, and so purify themselves. 8 Have them take a young bull with its grain offering of fine flour mixed with oil; then you are to take a second young bull for a sin offering. 9 Bring the Levites to the front of the Tent of Meeting and assemble the whole Israelite community. 10 You are to bring the Levites before the LORD, and the Israelites are to lay their hands on them. 11 Aaron is to present the Levites before the LORD as a wave offering from the Israelites, so that they may be ready to do the work of the LORD.

12 "After the Levites lay their hands on the heads of the bulls, use the one for a sin offering to the LORD and the other for a burnt offering, to make atonement for the Levites. 13 Have the Levites stand in front of Aaron and his sons and then present them as a wave offering to the LORD. 14 In this way you are to set the Levites apart from the other Israelites, and the Levites will be mine.

15 "After you have purified the Levites and presented them as a wave offering, they are to come to do their work at the Tent of Meeting. 16 They are the Israelites who are to be given wholly to me. I have taken them as my own in place of the firstborn, the first male offspring from every Israelite woman. 17 Every firstborn male in Israel, whether man or animal, is mine. When I struck down all the firstborn in Egypt, I set them apart for myself. 18 And I have taken the Levites in place of all the firstborn sons in Israel. 19 Of all the Israelites, I have given the Levites as gifts to Aaron and his sons to do the work at the Tent of Meeting on behalf of the Israelites and to make atonement for them so that no plague will strike the Israelites when they go near the sanctuary."

20 Moses, Aaron and the whole Israelite community did with the Levites just

---

[a] 85 That is, about 60 pounds (about 28 kilograms) [b] 86 That is, about 3 pounds (about 1.4 kilograms)

as the LORD commanded Moses. ²¹The Levites purified themselves and washed their clothes. Then Aaron presented them as a wave offering before the LORD and made atonement for them to purify them. ²²After that, the Levites came to do their work at the Tent of Meeting under the supervision of Aaron and his sons. They did with the Levites just as the LORD commanded Moses.

²³The LORD said to Moses, ²⁴"This applies to the Levites: Men twenty-five years old or more shall come to take part in the work at the Tent of Meeting, ²⁵but at the age of fifty, they must retire from their regular service and work no longer. ²⁶They may assist their brothers in performing their duties at the Tent of Meeting, but they themselves must not do the work. This, then, is how you are to assign the responsibilities of the Levites."

The Passover

9 The LORD spoke to Moses in the Desert of Sinai in the first month of the second year after they came out of Egypt. He said, ²"Have the Israelites celebrate the Passover at the appointed time. ³Celebrate it at the appointed time, at twilight on the fourteenth day of this month, in accordance with all its rules and regulations."

⁴So Moses told the Israelites to celebrate the Passover, ⁵and they did so in the Desert of Sinai at twilight on the fourteenth day of the first month. The Israelites did everything just as the LORD commanded Moses.

⁶But some of them could not celebrate the Passover on that day because they were ceremonially unclean on account of a dead body. So they came to Moses and Aaron that same day ⁷and said to Moses, "We have become unclean because of a dead body, but why should we be kept from presenting the LORD's offering with the other Israelites at the appointed time?"

⁸Moses answered them, "Wait until I find out what the LORD commands concerning you."

⁹Then the LORD said to Moses, ¹⁰"Tell the Israelites: 'When any of you or your descendants are unclean because of a dead body or are away on a journey, they may still celebrate the LORD's Passover. ¹¹They are to celebrate it on the fourteenth day of the second month at twilight. They are to eat the lamb, together with unleavened bread and bitter herbs. ¹²They must not leave any of it till morning or break any of its bones. When they celebrate the Passover, they must follow all the regulations. ¹³But if a man who is ceremonially clean and not on a journey fails to celebrate the Passover, that person must be cut off from his people because he did not present the LORD's offering at the appointed time. That man will bear the consequences of his sin.

¹⁴"'An alien living among you who wants to celebrate the LORD's Passover must do so in accordance with its rules and regulations. You must have the same regulations for the alien and the native-born.'"

The Cloud Above the Tabernacle

¹⁵On the day the tabernacle, the Tent of the Testimony, was set up, the cloud covered it. From evening till morning the cloud above the tabernacle looked like fire. ¹⁶That is how it continued to be; the cloud covered it, and at night it looked like fire. ¹⁷Whenever the cloud lifted from above the Tent, the Israelites set out; wherever the cloud settled, the Israelites encamped. ¹⁸At the LORD's command the Israelites set out, and at his command they encamped. As long as the cloud stayed over the tabernacle, they remained in camp. ¹⁹When the cloud remained over the tabernacle a long time, the Israelites obeyed the LORD's order and did not set out. ²⁰Sometimes the cloud was over the tabernacle only a few days; at the LORD's command they would encamp, and then at his command they would set out. ²¹Sometimes the cloud stayed only from evening till morning, and when it lifted in the morning, they set out. Whether

Guidance for the Journey

GOING *deeper*

READ AND CONSIDER: NUMBERS 9:15-23

"Whenever the cloud lifted from above the Tent, the Israelites set out; wherever the cloud settled, the Israelites encamped ... At the LORD's command they encamped, and at the LORD's command they set out. They obeyed the LORD's order, in accordance with his command through Moses" (Numbers 9:17,23).

We all struggle on occasion with the weight of making a big decision. Should we take this job or that one? Say yes or no to our children when it comes to certain activities? Relocate our family to a different location or stay put? Wouldn't it be wonderful if we had a continual manifestation of God's presence to guide us like the cloud He provided for His children in the desert?

Despite this constant visual reminder of guidance, however, the Israelites still struggled with following and obeying. Learning to walk with God is a process. Just when we think we have it all figured out, God leads us into a new place where our old tricks won't work. In fact, we may feel as if we're learning to walk all over again. And in a way we are. We enter unfamiliar territory and are soon reminded that, on our own, we stumble. Yet when we take His hand, we walk with confidence. God wants us to soar far above the limitations of our circumstances and ourselves. He wants to take us to a place we have never been before and can't get to without His help. When God used Moses to lead the Israelites out of Egypt, they had to learn to depend on the Lord for every step of their journey to the promised land. When they did not do that, they got into trouble. It's the same for us today.

If you are at a place in your life where you feel as if you can't take one step without the Lord's help, be glad. He has you where He wants you. If you're wondering, *Have I done something wrong?* the answer is most likely that you've done something right. God has you on this path, regardless of how difficult and impossible it may seem right now, because you are willing to follow Him. He wants to accomplish great things through you that can only come out of a life of faith. He wants your undivided attention because you can't do these things on your own. The path is not a punishment; it's a privilege. It's not a restriction; it's a reward.

by day or by night, whenever the cloud lifted, they set out. ²²Whether the cloud stayed over the tabernacle for two days or a month or a year, the Israelites would remain in camp and not set out; but when it lifted, they would set out. ²³At the LORD's command they encamped, and at the LORD's command they set out. They obeyed the LORD's order, in accordance with his command through Moses.

The Silver Trumpets

10 The LORD said to Moses: ²"Make two trumpets of hammered silver, and use them for calling the community together and for having the camps set out. ³When both are sounded, the whole community is to assemble before you at the entrance to the Tent of Meeting. ⁴If only one is sounded, the leaders—the heads of the clans of Israel—are to assemble before you. ⁵When a trumpet blast is sounded, the tribes camping on the east are to set out. ⁶At the sounding of a second blast, the camps on the south are to set out. The blast will be the signal for setting out. ⁷To gather the assembly, blow the trumpets, but not with the same signal.

⁸"The sons of Aaron, the priests, are to blow the trumpets. This is to be a lasting ordinance for you and the generations

to come. ⁹When you go into battle in your own land against an enemy who is oppressing you, sound a blast on the trumpets. Then you will be remembered by the LORD your God and rescued from your enemies. ¹⁰Also at your times of rejoicing—your appointed feasts and New Moon festivals—you are to sound the trumpets over your burnt offerings and fellowship offerings,ᵃ and they will be a memorial for you before your God. I am the LORD your God."

The Israelites Leave Sinai

¹¹On the twentieth day of the second month of the second year, the cloud lifted from above the tabernacle of the Testimony. ¹²Then the Israelites set out from the Desert of Sinai and traveled from place to place until the cloud came to rest in the Desert of Paran. ¹³They set out, this first time, at the LORD's command through Moses.

¹⁴The divisions of the camp of Judah went first, under their standard. Nahshon son of Amminadab was in command. ¹⁵Nethanel son of Zuar was over the division of the tribe of Issachar, ¹⁶and Eliab son of Helon was over the division of the tribe of Zebulun. ¹⁷Then the tabernacle was taken down, and the Gershonites and Merarites, who carried it, set out.

¹⁸The divisions of the camp of Reuben went next, under their standard. Elizur son of Shedeur was in command. ¹⁹Shelumiel son of Zurishaddai was over the division of the tribe of Simeon, ²⁰and Eliasaph son of Deuel was over the division of the tribe of Gad. ²¹Then the Kohathites set out, carrying the holy things. The tabernacle was to be set up before they arrived.

²²The divisions of the camp of Ephraim went next, under their standard. Elishama son of Ammihud was in command. ²³Gamaliel son of Pedahzur was over the division of the tribe of Manasseh, ²⁴and Abidan son of Gideoni was over the division of the tribe of Benjamin.

²⁵Finally, as the rear guard for all the units, the divisions of the camp of Dan set out, under their standard. Ahiezer son of Ammishaddai was in command. ²⁶Pagiel son of Ocran was over the division of the tribe of Asher, ²⁷and Ahira son of Enan was over the division of the tribe of Naphtali. ²⁸This was the order of march for the Israelite divisions as they set out.

²⁹Now Moses said to Hobab son of Reuel the Midianite, Moses' father-in-law, "We are setting out for the place about which the LORD said, 'I will give it to you.' Come with us and we will treat you well, for the LORD has promised good things to Israel."

³⁰He answered, "No, I will not go; I am going back to my own land and my own people."

³¹But Moses said, "Please do not leave us. You know where we should camp in the desert, and you can be our eyes. ³²If you come with us, we will share with you whatever good things the LORD gives us."

³³So they set out from the mountain of the LORD and traveled for three days. The ark of the covenant of the LORD went before them during those three days to find them a place to rest. ³⁴The cloud of the LORD was over them by day when they set out from the camp.

³⁵Whenever the ark set out, Moses said,

"Rise up, O LORD!
    May your enemies be scattered;
    may your foes flee before you."

³⁶Whenever it came to rest, he said,

"Return, O LORD,
    to the countless thousands of
        Israel."

Fire From the LORD

11 Now the people complained about their hardships in the hearing of the LORD, and when he heard them his anger

---

ᵃ *10 Traditionally peace offerings*

> ### Praying Numbers 11:1
> Lord, I pray that I will not be a
> complaining person and that I will
> have a heart filled with praise
> and thanksgiving at all times.

was aroused. Then fire from the LORD burned among them and consumed some of the outskirts of the camp. ²When the people cried out to Moses, he prayed to the LORD and the fire died down. ³So that place was called Taberah,ᵃ because fire from the LORD had burned among them.

Quail From the LORD

⁴The rabble with them began to crave other food, and again the Israelites started wailing and said, "If only we had meat to eat! ⁵We remember the fish we ate in Egypt at no cost—also the cucumbers, melons, leeks, onions and garlic. ⁶But now we have lost our appetite; we never see anything but this manna!"

⁷The manna was like coriander seed and looked like resin. ⁸The people went around gathering it, and then ground it in a handmill or crushed it in a mortar. They cooked it in a pot or made it into cakes. And it tasted like something made with olive oil. ⁹When the dew settled on the camp at night, the manna also came down.

¹⁰Moses heard the people of every family wailing, each at the entrance to

ᵃ 3 Taberah means burning.

GOING *deeper*

When You're Feeling Overwhelmed

READ AND CONSIDER: NUMBERS 11:10-17

"I will come down and speak with you there, and I will take of the Spirit that is on you and put the Spirit on them. They will help you carry the burden of the people so that you will not have to carry it alone" (Numbers 11:17).

Have you ever been asked to take on a job that you knew was much too big or too difficult for you, possibly one that did not involve any kind of tangible reward? Perhaps it's a volunteer position at a church or in your community, or you may have even found yourself in the position of raising someone else's child.

Overwhelming as the task might seem, it grows even more challenging when those you are serving don't seem to appreciate your efforts. In return for sacrifice, you get selfishness; your efforts at caretaking are met with complaining. At times like these you may be tempted to cry out to the Lord as Moses did, "Why have you brought this trouble on me? This burden is too heavy for me."

The Israelites were wallowing in the darkness of bitterness, casting blame upon God and His chosen leader. Instead of choosing to see God's hand in the moment, they blamed Moses and God for everything that disappointed them. As a result, their suffering was prolonged.

There is one crucial difference between the complaining that the Israelites did in the desert and the complaints Moses expressed: The people groused to one another, but Moses took his concerns to the only One who could do something about them—God.

As a result of Moses' plea for help, God promised to send additional leaders who would help Moses carry the burden of the needs of the people. Never hesitate to take your troubles to God when you are feeling overwhelmed; He has promised that you do not have to carry them alone.

his tent. The LORD became exceedingly angry, and Moses was troubled. [11]He asked the LORD, "Why have you brought this trouble on your servant? What have I done to displease you that you put the burden of all these people on me? [12]Did I conceive all these people? Did I give them birth? Why do you tell me to carry them in my arms, as a nurse carries an infant, to the land you promised on oath to their forefathers? [13]Where can I get meat for all these people? They keep wailing to me, 'Give us meat to eat!' [14]I cannot carry all these people by myself; the burden is too heavy for me. [15]If this is how you are going to treat me, put me to death right now—if I have found favor in your eyes—and do not let me face my own ruin."

[16]The LORD said to Moses: "Bring me seventy of Israel's elders who are known to you as leaders and officials among the people. Have them come to the Tent of Meeting, that they may stand there with you. [17]I will come down and speak with you there, and I will take of the Spirit that is on you and put the Spirit on them. They will help you carry the burden of the people so that you will not have to carry it alone.

[18]"Tell the people: 'Consecrate yourselves in preparation for tomorrow, when you will eat meat. The LORD heard you when you wailed, "If only we had meat to eat! We were better off in Egypt!" Now the LORD will give you meat, and you will eat it. [19]You will not eat it for just one day, or two days, or five, ten or twenty days, [20]but for a whole month—until it comes out of your nostrils and you loathe it—because you have rejected the LORD, who is among you, and have wailed before him, saying, "Why did we ever leave Egypt?"' "

[21]But Moses said, "Here I am among six hundred thousand men on foot, and you say, 'I will give them meat to eat for a whole month!' [22]Would they have enough if flocks and herds were slaughtered for them? Would they have enough if all the fish in the sea were caught for them?"

[23]The LORD answered Moses, "Is the LORD's arm too short? You will now see whether or not what I say will come true for you."

[24]So Moses went out and told the people what the LORD had said. He brought together seventy of their elders and had them stand around the Tent. [25]Then the LORD came down in the cloud and spoke with him, and he took of the Spirit that was on him and put the Spirit on the seventy elders. When the Spirit rested on them, they prophesied, but they did not do so again.[a]

[26]However, two men, whose names were Eldad and Medad, had remained in the camp. They were listed among the elders, but did not go out to the Tent. Yet the Spirit also rested on them, and they prophesied in the camp. [27]A young man ran and told Moses, "Eldad and Medad are prophesying in the camp."

[28]Joshua son of Nun, who had been Moses' aide since youth, spoke up and said, "Moses, my lord, stop them!"

[29]But Moses replied, "Are you jealous for my sake? I wish that all the LORD's people were prophets and that the LORD would put his Spirit on them!" [30]Then Moses and the elders of Israel returned to the camp.

[31]Now a wind went out from the LORD and drove quail in from the sea. It brought them[b] down all around the camp to about three feet[c] above the ground, as far as a day's walk in any direction. [32]All that day and night and all the next day the people went out and gathered quail. No one gathered less than ten homers.[d] Then they spread them out all around the camp. [33]But while the meat was still between their teeth and before it could be consumed, the anger of the LORD

---

[a]25 Or prophesied and continued to do so   [b]31 Or They flew   [c]31 Hebrew two cubits (about 1 meter)   [d]32 That is, probably about 60 bushels (about 2.2 kiloliters)

burned against the people, and he struck them with a severe plague. [34]Therefore the place was named Kibroth Hattaavah,[a] because there they buried the people who had craved other food.

[35]From Kibroth Hattaavah the people traveled to Hazeroth and stayed there.

Miriam and Aaron Oppose Moses

12 Miriam and Aaron began to talk against Moses because of his Cushite wife, for he had married a Cushite. [2]"Has the LORD spoken only through Moses?" they asked. "Hasn't he also spoken through us?" And the LORD heard this.

[3](Now Moses was a very humble man, more humble than anyone else on the face of the earth.)

Praying Numbers 12:1-15

Dear God, keep my mouth from ever speaking anything against Your anointed sons and daughters.

[4]At once the LORD said to Moses, Aaron and Miriam, "Come out to the Tent of Meeting, all three of you." So the three of them came out. [5]Then the LORD came down in a pillar of cloud; he stood at the entrance to the Tent and summoned Aaron and Miriam. When both of them stepped forward, [6]he said, "Listen to my words:

"When a prophet of the LORD is
  among you,
I reveal myself to him in visions,
I speak to him in dreams.
[7]But this is not true of my servant
  Moses;
he is faithful in all my house.
[8]With him I speak face to face,
  clearly and not in riddles;
he sees the form of the LORD.
Why then were you not afraid
  to speak against my servant Moses?"

[9]The anger of the LORD burned against them, and he left them.

[10]When the cloud lifted from above the Tent, there stood Miriam—leprous,[b] like snow. Aaron turned toward her and saw that she had leprosy; [11]and he said to Moses, "Please, my lord, do not hold against us the sin we have so foolishly committed. [12]Do not let her be like a stillborn infant coming from its mother's womb with its flesh half eaten away."

[13]So Moses cried out to the LORD, "O God, please heal her!"

[14]The LORD replied to Moses, "If her father had spit in her face, would she not have been in disgrace for seven days? Confine her outside the camp for seven days; after that she can be brought back." [15]So Miriam was confined outside the camp for seven days, and the people did not move on till she was brought back.

[16]After that, the people left Hazeroth and encamped in the Desert of Paran.

Exploring Canaan

13 The LORD said to Moses, [2]"Send some men to explore the land of Canaan, which I am giving to the Israelites. From each ancestral tribe send one of its leaders."

[3]So at the LORD's command Moses sent them out from the Desert of Paran. All of them were leaders of the Israelites. [4]These are their names:

from the tribe of Reuben, Shammua
  son of Zaccur;
[5]from the tribe of Simeon, Shaphat
  son of Hori;
[6]from the tribe of Judah, Caleb son
  of Jephunneh;
[7]from the tribe of Issachar, Igal son
  of Joseph;
[8]from the tribe of Ephraim, Hoshea
  son of Nun;
[9]from the tribe of Benjamin, Palti son
  of Raphu;
[10]from the tribe of Zebulun, Gaddiel
  son of Sodi;

---

[a] *34 Kibroth Hattaavah* means *graves of craving.* [b] *10* The Hebrew word was used for various diseases affecting the skin—not necessarily leprosy.

Praying for Those Who Have Hurt You

READ AND CONSIDER: NUMBERS 12:13

"So Moses cried out to the Lord, 'O God, please heal her!' " (Numbers 12:13).

The two people God gave to Moses to help him lead the Israelites out of slavery were his own sister and brother, Miriam and Aaron (see Micah 6:4). You'd think they would be Moses' most ardent supporters. Ironically, however, the opening verse of Numbers 12 tells us that these two family members who should have been most loyal to Moses were speaking out against him.

Family divisions wound us deeply. Friends or colleagues may hurt us, but when betrayal arises from within our own family, the pain is profound. But Moses didn't hang on to any hurt he may have felt. Instead he prayed for his sister.

God confronted both Miriam and Aaron at the Tent of Meeting, but it was upon Miriam that the discipline fell. Since Miriam's name appears before Aaron's, we can assume that she was older and that God was holding her responsible for the division she and Aaron were spreading in the camp because of their critical tongues. As a result, she was afflicted with leprosy, a horrible contagious skin disease that would cause her to be separated from the rest of the camp—perhaps for the remainder of her life. Her younger brother Aaron was horrified when he witnessed the result of their disobedience and disloyalty; he asked Moses to forgive them for their foolishness and sin.

Moses did not hesitate but immediately cried out to the Lord on behalf of his sister: "O God, please heal her!" Though Miriam still had to face the consequence of displeasing the Lord, she was restored to the people after a seven-day time-out. God responded to Moses' plea on behalf of the very one who had wronged him.

Do you have a family member who has hurt you? Have you been able to forgive that person? If not, ask God to help you forgive completely. Then pray for that person because prayer has great power to restore broken family relationships. In the process of praying, you'll begin to sense love growing in your heart for the one who hurt you. God will still hold that person accountable for the sins he or she has committed, but forgiving and praying for that person has the power to free you from all pain and bitterness. Try it and discover the wonderful freedom waiting for you when you forgive.

11 from the tribe of Manasseh (a tribe of Joseph), Gaddi son of Susi; 12 from the tribe of Dan, Ammiel son of Gemalli; 13 from the tribe of Asher, Sethur son of Michael; 14 from the tribe of Naphtali, Nahbi son of Vophsi; 15 from the tribe of Gad, Geuel son of Maki.

16 These are the names of the men Moses sent to explore the land. (Moses gave Hoshea son of Nun the name Joshua.) 17 When Moses sent them to explore Canaan, he said, "Go up through the Negev and on into the hill country. 18 See what the land is like and whether the people who live there are strong or weak, few or many. 19 What kind of land do they live in? Is it good or bad? What kind of

towns do they live in? Are they unwalled or fortified? ²⁰How is the soil? Is it fertile or poor? Are there trees on it or not? Do your best to bring back some of the fruit of the land." (It was the season for the first ripe grapes.)

²¹So they went up and explored the land from the Desert of Zin as far as Rehob, toward Lebo^a Hamath. ²²They went up through the Negev and came to Hebron, where Ahiman, Sheshai and Talmai, the descendants of Anak, lived. (Hebron had been built seven years before Zoan in Egypt.) ²³When they reached the Valley of Eshcol,^b they cut off a branch bearing a single cluster of grapes. Two of them carried it on a pole between them, along with some pomegranates and figs. ²⁴That place was called the Valley of Eshcol because of the cluster of grapes the Israelites cut off there. ²⁵At the end of forty days they returned from exploring the land.

Report on the Exploration

²⁶They came back to Moses and Aaron and the whole Israelite community at Kadesh in the Desert of Paran. There they reported to them and to the whole assembly and showed them the fruit of the land. ²⁷They gave Moses this account: "We went into the land to which you sent us, and it does flow with milk and honey! Here is its fruit. ²⁸But the people who live there are powerful, and the cities are fortified and very large. We even saw descendants of Anak there. ²⁹The Amalekites live in the Negev; the Hittites, Jebusites and Amorites live in the hill country; and the Canaanites live near the sea and along the Jordan."

³⁰Then Caleb silenced the people before Moses and said, "We should go up and take possession of the land, for we can certainly do it."

³¹But the men who had gone up with him said, "We can't attack those people; they are stronger than we are." ³²And they spread among the Israelites a bad report about the land they had explored. They said, "The land we explored devours those living in it. All the people we saw there are of great size. ³³We saw the Nephilim there (the descendants of Anak come from the Nephilim). We seemed like grasshoppers in our own eyes, and we looked the same to them."

The People Rebel

14 That night all the people of the community raised their voices and wept aloud. ²All the Israelites grumbled against Moses and Aaron, and the whole assembly said to them, "If only we had died in Egypt! Or in this desert! ³Why is the LORD bringing us to this land only to let us fall by the sword? Our wives and children will be taken as plunder. Wouldn't it be better for us to go back to Egypt?" ⁴And they said to each other, "We should choose a leader and go back to Egypt."

⁵Then Moses and Aaron fell facedown in front of the whole Israelite assembly gathered there. ⁶Joshua son of Nun and Caleb son of Jephunneh, who were among those who had explored the land, tore their clothes ⁷and said to the entire Israelite assembly, "The land we passed through and explored is exceedingly good. ⁸If the LORD is pleased with us, he will lead us into that land, a land flowing with milk and honey, and will give it to us. ⁹Only do not rebel against the LORD. And do not be afraid of the people of the land, because we will swallow them up. Their protection is gone, but the LORD is with us. Do not be afraid of them."

¹⁰But the whole assembly talked about stoning them. Then the glory of the LORD appeared at the Tent of Meeting to all the Israelites. ¹¹The LORD said to Moses, "How long will these people treat me with contempt? How long will they refuse to believe in me, in spite of all the miraculous signs I have performed among them? ¹²I will strike them down with a plague and destroy them, but I will

---

^a 21 Or *toward the entrance to*   ^b 23 *Eshcol* means *cluster*; also in verse 24.

Just Enough Light for the Step You're On

GOING *deeper*

READ AND CONSIDER: NUMBERS 14:19-23

" 'In accordance with your great love, forgive the sin of these people, just as you have pardoned them from the time they left Egypt until now.' The LORD replied, 'I have forgiven them, as you asked.' " (Numbers 14:19-20).

The history of the Israelites in the desert was checkered with times of eager obedience and great joy along with times of stubborn disobedience and great punishment. God had performed many miracles to deliver His people from Egypt, yet they still continued to doubt Him. He then took them into the desert and tested them.

One test involved water: He let them go without it for three days. God knew the people needed water, and He could easily have provided it for them. But they didn't ask. They didn't pray. They complained. And that was part of the test. God wanted them to ask. He wanted them to be dependent on Him for everything. When Moses cried out to God on their behalf, God said that if the people would listen to Him and do what He commanded, He would meet all their needs. So they listened and obeyed. They got their water and were content.

Until the next crisis.

Instead of learning something from the water situation, the Israelites complained again about their lack of food. God was not trying to starve them. He knew they needed food, and He wanted to provide it for them. But He wanted them to come to Him and rely on Him for it. Once more, Moses prayed and God provided. But this time, God provided only what was needed for each day, one day at a time. God desired that they trust Him for each day's provision. He wanted them to learn to walk with just enough light for the step they were on.

Does this sound at all familiar? Can you think of anyone you know who wants to get to the "promised land" but doesn't want to do what's necessary to make the trip? Are you aware of a person who desires to have everything he or she needs but is not willing to give up anything to get it? Have you ever felt that you should have already arrived, without having to trust God for every step to get there?

This passage illustrates that God's capacity for forgiving the sin and foolishness of His people is unlimited. We need only confess, and He is faithful and just to forgive us (1 John 1:9). At the same time, results follow our rebellious behavior. God will forgive us, but sometimes we have to experience the consequences of our sin. In this case, the people would eventually die in the desert, and of those then alive, only Joshua and Caleb would ever see the promised land.

God often provides just enough light for the step we're on, but we have to trust Him and walk in obedience to His leading. Then He will illuminate the next step we are to take.

make you into a nation greater and stronger than they."

13Moses said to the LORD, "Then the Egyptians will hear about it! By your power you brought these people up from among them. 14And they will tell the inhabitants of this land about it. They have already heard that you, O LORD, are with these people and that you, O LORD, have been seen face to face, that your cloud stays over them, and that you go before them in a pillar of cloud by day and a pillar of fire by night. [15]If you put these people to death all at one time, the nations who have heard this report about you will say, [16]'The LORD was not able to bring these people into the land he promised them on oath; so he slaughtered them in the desert.'

[17]"Now may the Lord's strength be displayed, just as you have declared: [18]'The LORD is slow to anger, abounding in love and forgiving sin and rebellion. Yet he does not leave the guilty unpunished; he punishes the children for the sin of the fathers to the third and fourth generation.' [19]In accordance with your great love, forgive the sin of these people, just as you have pardoned them from the time they left Egypt until now."

Praying Numbers 14:19-20

Help me, Lord, to remember to pray often on behalf of others.

[20]The LORD replied, "I have forgiven them, as you asked. [21]Nevertheless, as surely as I live and as surely as the glory of the LORD fills the whole earth, [22]not one of the men who saw my glory and the miraculous signs I performed in Egypt and in the desert but who disobeyed me and tested me ten times— [23]not one of them will ever see the land I promised on oath to their forefathers. No one who has treated me with contempt will ever see it. [24]But because my servant Caleb has a different spirit and follows me wholeheartedly, I will bring him into the land he went to, and his descendants will inherit it. [25]Since the Amalekites and Canaanites are living in the valleys, turn back tomorrow and set out toward the desert along the route to the Red Sea.[a]"

[26]The LORD said to Moses and Aaron: [27]"How long will this wicked community grumble against me? I have heard the complaints of these grumbling Israel-

ites. [28]So tell them, 'As surely as I live, declares the LORD, I will do to you the very things I heard you say: [29]In this desert your bodies will fall—every one of you twenty years old or more who was counted in the census and who has grumbled against me. [30]Not one of you will enter the land I swore with uplifted hand to make your home, except Caleb son of Jephunneh and Joshua son of Nun. [31]As for your children that you said would be taken as plunder, I will bring them in to enjoy the land you have rejected. [32]But you—your bodies will fall in this desert. [33]Your children will be shepherds here for forty years, suffering for your unfaithfulness, until the last of your bodies lies in the desert. [34]For forty years—one year for each of the forty days you explored the land—you will suffer for your sins and know what it is like to have me against you.' [35]I, the LORD, have spoken, and I will surely do these things to this whole wicked community, which has banded together against me. They will meet their end in this desert; here they will die."

[36]So the men Moses had sent to explore the land, who returned and made the whole community grumble against him by spreading a bad report about it— [37]these men responsible for spreading the bad report about the land were struck down and died of a plague before the LORD. [38]Of the men who went to explore the land, only Joshua son of Nun and Caleb son of Jephunneh survived.

[39]When Moses reported this to all the Israelites, they mourned bitterly. [40]Early the next morning they went up toward the high hill country. "We have sinned," they said. "We will go up to the place the LORD promised."

[41]But Moses said, "Why are you disobeying the LORD's command? This will not succeed! [42]Do not go up, because the LORD is not with you. You will be defeated by your enemies, [43]for the Amalekites and Canaanites will face you there.

---

[a] 25 Hebrew *Yam Suph*; that is, Sea of Reeds

Because you have turned away from the LORD, he will not be with you and you will fall by the sword."

⁴⁴Nevertheless, in their presumption they went up toward the high hill country, though neither Moses nor the ark of the LORD's covenant moved from the camp. ⁴⁵Then the Amalekites and Canaanites who lived in that hill country came down and attacked them and beat them down all the way to Hormah.

Supplementary Offerings

15 The LORD said to Moses, ²"Speak to the Israelites and say to them: 'After you enter the land I am giving you as a home ³and you present to the LORD offerings made by fire, from the herd or the flock, as an aroma pleasing to the LORD—whether burnt offerings or sacrifices, for special vows or freewill offerings or festival offerings— ⁴then the one who brings his offering shall present to the LORD a grain offering of a tenth of an ephahª of fine flour mixed with a quarter of a hinᵇ of oil. ⁵With each lamb for the burnt offering or the sacrifice, prepare a quarter of a hin of wine as a drink offering.

⁶"'With a ram prepare a grain offering of two-tenths of an ephahᶜ of fine flour mixed with a third of a hinᵈ of oil, ⁷and a third of a hin of wine as a drink offering. Offer it as an aroma pleasing to the LORD.

⁸"'When you prepare a young bull as a burnt offering or sacrifice, for a special vow or a fellowship offeringᵉ to the LORD, ⁹bring with the bull a grain offering of three-tenths of an ephahᶠ of fine flour mixed with half a hinᵍ of oil. ¹⁰Also bring half a hin of wine as a drink offering. It will be an offering made by fire, an aroma pleasing to the LORD. ¹¹Each bull or ram, each lamb or young goat, is to be prepared in this manner. ¹²Do this for each one, for as many as you prepare.

¹³"'Everyone who is native-born must do these things in this way when he brings an offering made by fire as an aroma pleasing to the LORD. ¹⁴For the generations to come, whenever an alien or anyone else living among you presents an offering made by fire as an aroma pleasing to the LORD, he must do exactly as you do. ¹⁵The community is to have the same rules for you and for the alien living among you; this is a lasting ordinance for the generations to come. You and the alien shall be the same before the LORD: ¹⁶The same laws and regulations will apply both to you and to the alien living among you.'"

¹⁷The LORD said to Moses, ¹⁸"Speak to the Israelites and say to them: 'When you enter the land to which I am taking you ¹⁹and you eat the food of the land, present a portion as an offering to the LORD. ²⁰Present a cake from the first of your ground meal and present it as an offering from the threshing floor. ²¹Throughout the generations to come you are to give this offering to the LORD from the first of your ground meal.

Offerings for Unintentional Sins

²²"'Now if you unintentionally fail to keep any of these commands the LORD gave Moses— ²³any of the LORD's commands to you through him, from the day the LORD gave them and continuing through the generations to come— ²⁴and if this is done unintentionally without the community being aware of it, then the whole community is to offer a young bull for a burnt offering as an aroma pleasing to the LORD, along with its prescribed grain offering and drink offering, and a male goat for a sin offering. ²⁵The priest is to make atonement for the whole Israelite community, and they will be forgiven, for it was not intentional and they have brought to the LORD for their wrong an

---

ª4 That is, probably about 2 quarts (about 2 liters)   ᵇ4 That is, probably about 1 quart (about 1 liter); also in verse 5
ᶜ6 That is, probably about 4 quarts (about 4.5 liters)   ᵈ6 That is, probably about 1 1/4 quarts (about 1.2 liters); also in verse 7
ᵉ8 Traditionally *peace offering*   ᶠ9 That is, probably about 6 quarts (about 6.5 liters)   ᵍ9 That is, probably about 2 quarts (about 2 liters); also in verse 10

offering made by fire and a sin offering. 26The whole Israelite community and the aliens living among them will be forgiven, because all the people were involved in the unintentional wrong.

27"'But if just one person sins unintentionally, he must bring a year-old female goat for a sin offering. 28The priest is to make atonement before the LORD for the one who erred by sinning unintentionally, and when atonement has been made for him, he will be forgiven. 29One and the same law applies to everyone who sins unintentionally, whether he is a native-born Israelite or an alien.

30"'But anyone who sins defiantly, whether native-born or alien, blasphemes the LORD, and that person must be cut off from his people. 31Because he has despised the LORD's word and broken his commands, that person must surely be cut off; his guilt remains on him.'"

The Sabbath-Breaker Put to Death

32While the Israelites were in the desert, a man was found gathering wood on the Sabbath day. 33Those who found him gathering wood brought him to Moses and Aaron and the whole assembly, 34and they kept him in custody, because it was not clear what should be done to him. 35Then the LORD said to Moses, "The man must die. The whole assembly must stone him outside the camp." 36So the assembly took him outside the camp and stoned him to death, as the LORD commanded Moses.

Tassels on Garments

37The LORD said to Moses, 38"Speak to the Israelites and say to them: 'Throughout the generations to come you are to make tassels on the corners of your garments, with a blue cord on each tassel. 39You will have these tassels to look at and so you will remember all the commands of the LORD, that you may obey them and not prostitute yourselves by going after the lusts of your own hearts and eyes. 40Then you will remember to obey all my commands and will be consecrated to your God. 41I am the LORD your God, who brought you out of Egypt to be your God. I am the LORD your God.'"

Korah, Dathan and Abiram

16 Korah son of Izhar, the son of Kohath, the son of Levi, and certain Reubenites—Dathan and Abiram, sons of Eliab, and On son of Peleth—became insolent[a] 2and rose up against Moses. With them were 250 Israelite men, well-known community leaders who had been appointed members of the council. 3They came as a group to oppose Moses and Aaron and said to them, "You have gone too far! The whole community is holy, every one of them, and the LORD is with them. Why then do you set yourselves above the LORD's assembly?"

4When Moses heard this, he fell facedown. 5Then he said to Korah and all his followers: "In the morning the LORD will show who belongs to him and who is holy, and he will have that person come near him. The man he chooses he will cause to come near him. 6You, Korah, and all your followers are to do this: Take censers 7and tomorrow put fire and incense in them before the LORD. The man the LORD chooses will be the one who is holy. You Levites have gone too far!"

8Moses also said to Korah, "Now listen, you Levites! 9Isn't it enough for you that the God of Israel has separated you from the rest of the Israelite community and brought you near himself to do the work at the LORD's tabernacle and to stand before the community and minister to them? 10He has brought you and all your fellow Levites near himself, but now you are trying to get the priesthood too. 11It is against the LORD that you and all your followers have banded together. Who is Aaron that you should grumble against him?"

12Then Moses summoned Dathan and Abiram, the sons of Eliab. But they said,

---

a 1 Or Peleth—took ⌞men⌟

"We will not come! 13Isn't it enough that you have brought us up out of a land flowing with milk and honey to kill us in the desert? And now you also want to lord it over us? 14Moreover, you haven't brought us into a land flowing with milk and honey or given us an inheritance of fields and vineyards. Will you gouge out the eyes ofᵃ these men? No, we will not come!"

15Then Moses became very angry and said to the LORD, "Do not accept their offering. I have not taken so much as a donkey from them, nor have I wronged any of them."

16Moses said to Korah, "You and all your followers are to appear before the LORD tomorrow—you and they and Aaron. 17Each man is to take his censer and put incense in it—250 censers in all—and present it before the LORD. You and Aaron are to present your censers also." 18So each man took his censer, put fire and incense in it, and stood with Moses and Aaron at the entrance to the Tent of Meeting. 19When Korah had gathered all his followers in opposition to them at the entrance to the Tent of Meeting, the glory of the LORD appeared to the entire assembly. 20The LORD said to Moses and Aaron, 21"Separate yourselves from this assembly so I can put an end to them at once."

22But Moses and Aaron fell facedown and cried out, "O God, God of the spirits of all mankind, will you be angry with the entire assembly when only one man sins?"

23Then the LORD said to Moses, 24"Say to the assembly, 'Move away from the tents of Korah, Dathan and Abiram.'"

25Moses got up and went to Dathan and Abiram, and the elders of Israel followed him. 26He warned the assembly, "Move back from the tents of these wicked men! Do not touch anything belonging to them, or you will be swept away because of all their sins." 27So they moved away from the tents of Korah, Dathan and Abiram. Dathan and Abiram had come out and were standing with their wives, children and little ones at the entrances to their tents.

28Then Moses said, "This is how you will know that the LORD has sent me to do all these things and that it was not my idea: 29If these men die a natural death and experience only what usually happens to men, then the LORD has not sent me. 30But if the LORD brings about something totally new, and the earth opens its mouth and swallows them, with everything that belongs to them, and they go down alive into the grave,ᵇ then you will know that these men have treated the LORD with contempt."

31As soon as he finished saying all this, the ground under them split apart 32and the earth opened its mouth and swallowed them, with their households and all Korah's men and all their possessions. 33They went down alive into the grave, with everything they owned; the earth closed over them, and they perished and were gone from the community. 34At their cries, all the Israelites around them fled, shouting, "The earth is going to swallow us too!"

35And fire came out from the LORD and consumed the 250 men who were offering the incense.

36The LORD said to Moses, 37"Tell Eleazar son of Aaron, the priest, to take the censers out of the smoldering remains and scatter the coals some distance away, for the censers are holy— 38the censers of the men who sinned at the cost of their lives. Hammer the censers into sheets to overlay the altar, for they were presented before the LORD and have become holy. Let them be a sign to the Israelites."

39So Eleazar the priest collected the bronze censers brought by those who had been burned up, and he had them hammered out to overlay the altar, 40as the LORD directed him through Moses.

ᵃ 14 Or you make slaves of; or you deceive   ᵇ 30 Hebrew Sheol; also in verse 33

This was to remind the Israelites that no one except a descendant of Aaron should come to burn incense before the LORD, or he would become like Korah and his followers.

⁴¹The next day the whole Israelite community grumbled against Moses and Aaron. "You have killed the LORD's people," they said.

⁴²But when the assembly gathered in opposition to Moses and Aaron and turned toward the Tent of Meeting, suddenly the cloud covered it and the glory of the LORD appeared. ⁴³Then Moses and Aaron went to the front of the Tent of Meeting, ⁴⁴and the LORD said to Moses, ⁴⁵"Get away from this assembly so I can put an end to them at once." And they fell facedown.

⁴⁶Then Moses said to Aaron, "Take your censer and put incense in it, along with fire from the altar, and hurry to the assembly to make atonement for them. Wrath has come out from the LORD; the plague has started." ⁴⁷So Aaron did as Moses said, and ran into the midst of the assembly. The plague had already started among the people, but Aaron offered the incense and made atonement for them. ⁴⁸He stood between the living and the dead, and the plague stopped. ⁴⁹But 14,700 people died from the plague, in addition to those who had died because of Korah. ⁵⁰Then Aaron returned to Moses at the entrance to the Tent of Meeting, for the plague had stopped.

The Budding of Aaron's Staff

17 The LORD said to Moses, ²"Speak to the Israelites and get twelve staffs from them, one from the leader of each of their ancestral tribes. Write the name of each man on his staff. ³On the staff of Levi write Aaron's name, for there must be one staff for the head of each ancestral tribe. ⁴Place them in the Tent of Meeting in front of the Testimony, where I meet with you. ⁵The staff belonging to the man I choose will sprout, and I will rid myself of this constant grumbling against you by the Israelites."

⁶So Moses spoke to the Israelites, and their leaders gave him twelve staffs, one for the leader of each of their ancestral tribes, and Aaron's staff was among them. ⁷Moses placed the staffs before the LORD in the Tent of the Testimony.

⁸The next day Moses entered the Tent of the Testimony and saw that Aaron's staff, which represented the house of Levi, had not only sprouted but had budded, blossomed and produced almonds. ⁹Then Moses brought out all the staffs from the LORD's presence to all the Israelites. They looked at them, and each man took his own staff.

¹⁰The LORD said to Moses, "Put back Aaron's staff in front of the Testimony, to be kept as a sign to the rebellious. This will put an end to their grumbling against me, so that they will not die." ¹¹Moses did just as the LORD commanded him.

¹²The Israelites said to Moses, "We will die! We are lost, we are all lost! ¹³Anyone who even comes near the tabernacle of the LORD will die. Are we all going to die?"

Duties of Priests and Levites

18 The LORD said to Aaron, "You, your sons and your father's family are to bear the responsibility for offenses against the sanctuary, and you and your sons alone are to bear the responsibility for offenses against the priesthood. ²Bring your fellow Levites from your ancestral tribe to join you and assist you when you and your sons minister before the Tent of the Testimony. ³They are to be responsible to you and are to perform all the duties of the Tent, but they must not go near the furnishings of the sanctuary or the altar, or both they and you will die. ⁴They are to join you and be responsible for the care of the Tent of Meeting—all the work at the Tent—and no one else may come near where you are.

⁵"You are to be responsible for the care of the sanctuary and the altar, so that wrath will not fall on the Israelites again. ⁶I myself have selected your fellow

Surrendering Your Dreams

Most of us have experienced a time when our lives appear to be standing still. No matter how hard we work, it seems like every door is closed and no new ones are opening. Often that's because we have an image in our mind of what we *want* to be happening, and when we see that it isn't, we think *nothing* is happening. We can end up in a stagnant wilderness of frustration and confusion about it if we have made idols out of our dreams.

God wants us to dream. He puts dreams in our heart for His purposes. But in our dreaming, He doesn't want us to exclude *Him*. God's Word says we will perish if we don't have a vision, but the vision we have must be in alignment with His will for our life. In other words, the vision must ultimately be *His*. If we don't get our vision from *Him,* then we don't have a vision that will ever be realized.

God wants us to surrender our dreams because we can't be led by Him if we are chasing after a dream of our own making. And He wants us to surrender *all* of them. That way He can tell us which of them are from Him and in line with *His* will, and which of them are ours and born out of *our* will. If they are only our dreams and visions and not His, we will experience a lifetime of unfulfillment and strife trying to make them happen. Even if the dream in your heart *is* from God, you still won't see it fulfilled until you give it to Him. The dream has to be realized *His* way.

When God wants to make changes in our lives and we're willing to let Him, He starts by cutting away all that is unnecessary. In this process, He strips from us everything that could hinder our future growth in order to prepare us to bring forth good fruit. Our life may look barren during that time, but God is actually freeing us from anything that does not bring forth life.

God puts dreams in our hearts to give us vision and inspiration and to guide us to the right path. That's why we have to make sure the dreams we have are not from our own flesh. The only way to be sure of that is to lay all of our dreams at His feet and let them die. And *we* must also die to *them*. The ones that are not from Him will be buried forever. The ones that *are* from Him will be given new life.

God doesn't want any part of you to be unsurrendered, not even the dreams He has put in your heart. If you give Him *all* of your dreams, then you will see which ones are born of His Spirit. Pursuing the ones that aren't will only lead to misery, frustration, and unfulfillment. Dying to your dreams is difficult, but if you reach up and take your heavenly Father's hand, He will shine His light on the situation and walk you through the process step-by-step.

For the next "From Stormie's Heart" article, go to page 248.

Levites from among the Israelites as a gift to you, dedicated to the LORD to do the work at the Tent of Meeting. 7But only you and your sons may serve as priests in connection with everything at the altar and inside the curtain. I am giving you the service of the priesthood as a gift. Anyone else who comes near the sanctuary must be put to death."

Offerings for Priests and Levites

8Then the LORD said to Aaron, "I myself have put you in charge of the offerings presented to me; all the holy offerings the Israelites give me I give to you and your sons as your portion and regular share. 9You are to have the part of the most holy offerings that is kept from the fire. From all the gifts they bring me as most holy offerings, whether grain or sin or guilt offerings, that part belongs to you and your sons. 10Eat it as something most holy; every male shall eat it. You must regard it as holy.

11"This also is yours: whatever is set aside from the gifts of all the wave offerings of the Israelites. I give this to you and your sons and daughters as your regular share. Everyone in your household who is ceremonially clean may eat it.

12"I give you all the finest olive oil and all the finest new wine and grain they give the LORD as the firstfruits of their harvest. 13All the land's firstfruits that they bring to the LORD will be yours. Everyone in your household who is ceremonially clean may eat it.

14"Everything in Israel that is devoteda to the LORD is yours. 15The first offspring of every womb, both man and animal, that is offered to the LORD is yours. But you must redeem every firstborn son and every firstborn male of unclean animals. 16When they are a month old, you must redeem them at the redemption price set at five shekelsb of silver, according to the sanctuary shekel, which weighs twenty gerahs.

17"But you must not redeem the firstborn of an ox, a sheep or a goat; they are holy. Sprinkle their blood on the altar and burn their fat as an offering made by fire, an aroma pleasing to the LORD. 18Their meat is to be yours, just as the breast of the wave offering and the right thigh are yours. 19Whatever is set aside from the holy offerings the Israelites present to the LORD I give to you and your sons and daughters as your regular share. It is an everlasting covenant of salt before the LORD for both you and your offspring."

20The LORD said to Aaron, "You will have no inheritance in their land, nor will you have any share among them; I am your share and your inheritance among the Israelites.

21"I give to the Levites all the tithes in Israel as their inheritance in return for the work they do while serving at the Tent of Meeting. 22From now on the Israelites must not go near the Tent of Meeting, or they will bear the consequences of their sin and will die. 23It is the Levites who are to do the work at the Tent of Meeting and bear the responsibility for offenses against it. This is a lasting ordinance for the generations to come. They will receive no inheritance among the Israelites. 24Instead, I give to the Levites as their inheritance the tithes that the Israelites present as an offering to the LORD. That is why I said concerning them: 'They will have no inheritance among the Israelites.'"

25The LORD said to Moses, 26"Speak to the Levites and say to them: 'When you receive from the Israelites the tithe I give you as your inheritance, you must present a tenth of that tithe as the LORD's offering. 27Your offering will be reckoned to you as grain from the threshing floor or juice from the winepress. 28In this way you also will present an offering to the LORD from all the tithes you receive from the Israelites. From these tithes you must

---

a 14 The Hebrew term refers to the irrevocable giving over of things or persons to the LORD.   b 16 That is, about 2 ounces (about 55 grams) give the LORD's portion to Aaron the priest. ²⁹You must present as the LORD's portion the best and holiest part of everything given to you.'

³⁰"Say to the Levites: 'When you present the best part, it will be reckoned to you as the product of the threshing floor or the winepress. ³¹You and your households may eat the rest of it anywhere, for it is your wages for your work at the Tent of Meeting. ³²By presenting the best part of it you will not be guilty in this matter; then you will not defile the holy offerings of the Israelites, and you will not die.'"

The Water of Cleansing

19 The LORD said to Moses and Aaron: ²"This is a requirement of the law that the LORD has commanded: Tell the Israelites to bring you a red heifer without defect or blemish and that has never been under a yoke. ³Give it to Eleazar the priest; it is to be taken outside the camp and slaughtered in his presence. ⁴Then Eleazar the priest is to take some of its blood on his finger and sprinkle it seven times toward the front of the Tent of Meeting. ⁵While he watches, the heifer is to be burned—its hide, flesh, blood and offal. ⁶The priest is to take some cedar wood, hyssop and scarlet wool and throw them onto the burning heifer. ⁷After that, the priest must wash his clothes and bathe himself with water. He may then come into the camp, but he will be ceremonially unclean till evening. ⁸The man who burns it must also wash his clothes and bathe with water, and he too will be unclean till evening.

⁹"A man who is clean shall gather up the ashes of the heifer and put them in a ceremonially clean place outside the camp. They shall be kept by the Israelite community for use in the water of cleansing; it is for purification from sin. ¹⁰The man who gathers up the ashes of the heifer must also wash his clothes, and he too will be unclean till evening. This will be a lasting ordinance both for the Israelites and for the aliens living among them.

¹¹"Whoever touches the dead body of anyone will be unclean for seven days. ¹²He must purify himself with the water on the third day and on the seventh day; then he will be clean. But if he does not purify himself on the third and seventh days, he will not be clean. ¹³Whoever touches the dead body of anyone and fails to purify himself defiles the LORD's tabernacle. That person must be cut off from Israel. Because the water of cleansing has not been sprinkled on him, he is unclean; his uncleanness remains on him.

¹⁴"This is the law that applies when a person dies in a tent: Anyone who enters the tent and anyone who is in it will be unclean for seven days, ¹⁵and every open container without a lid fastened on it will be unclean.

¹⁶"Anyone out in the open who touches someone who has been killed with a sword or someone who has died a natural death, or anyone who touches a human bone or a grave, will be unclean for seven days.

¹⁷"For the unclean person, put some ashes from the burned purification offering into a jar and pour fresh water over them. ¹⁸Then a man who is ceremonially clean is to take some hyssop, dip it in the water and sprinkle the tent and all the furnishings and the people who were there. He must also sprinkle anyone who has touched a human bone or a grave or someone who has been killed or someone who has died a natural death. ¹⁹The man who is clean is to sprinkle the unclean person on the third and seventh days, and on the seventh day he is to purify him. The person being cleansed must wash his clothes and bathe with water, and that evening he will be clean. ²⁰But if a person who is unclean does not purify himself, he must be cut off from the community, because he has defiled the sanctuary of the LORD. The water of cleansing has not been sprinkled on him, and he is unclean. ²¹This is a lasting ordinance for them.

"The man who sprinkles the water of cleansing must also wash his clothes, and anyone who touches the water of cleansing will be unclean till evening. 22Anything that an unclean person touches becomes unclean, and anyone who touches it becomes unclean till evening."

Water From the Rock

20 In the first month the whole Israelite community arrived at the Desert of Zin, and they stayed at Kadesh. There Miriam died and was buried.

2Now there was no water for the community, and the people gathered in opposition to Moses and Aaron. 3They quarreled with Moses and said, "If only we had died when our brothers fell dead before the LORD! 4Why did you bring the LORD's community into this desert, that we and our livestock should die here? 5Why did you bring us up out of Egypt to this terrible place? It has no grain or figs, grapevines or pomegranates. And there is no water to drink!"

6Moses and Aaron went from the assembly to the entrance to the Tent of Meeting and fell facedown, and the glory of the LORD appeared to them. 7The LORD said to Moses, 8"Take the staff, and you and your brother Aaron gather the assembly together. Speak to that rock before their eyes and it will pour out its water. You will bring water out of the rock for the community so they and their livestock can drink."

9So Moses took the staff from the LORD's presence, just as he commanded him. 10He and Aaron gathered the assembly together in front of the rock and Moses said to them, "Listen, you rebels, must we bring you water out of this rock?" 11Then Moses raised his arm and struck the rock twice with his staff. Water gushed out, and the community and their livestock drank.

12But the LORD said to Moses and Aaron, "Because you did not trust in me enough to honor me as holy in the sight of the Israelites, you will not bring this community into the land I give them."

13These were the waters of Meribah,ᵃ where the Israelites quarreled with the LORD and where he showed himself holy among them.

Edom Denies Israel Passage

14Moses sent messengers from Kadesh to the king of Edom, saying:

"This is what your brother Israel says: You know about all the hardships that have come upon us. 15Our forefathers went down into Egypt, and we lived there many years. The Egyptians mistreated us and our fathers, 16but when we cried out to the LORD, he heard our cry and sent an angel and brought us out of Egypt.

"Now we are here at Kadesh, a town on the edge of your territory. 17Please let us pass through your country. We will not go through any field or vineyard, or drink water from any well. We will travel along the king's highway and not turn to the right or to the left until we have passed through your territory."

18But Edom answered:

"You may not pass through here; if you try, we will march out and attack you with the sword."

19The Israelites replied:

"We will go along the main road, and if we or our livestock drink any of your water, we will pay for it. We only want to pass through on foot—nothing else."

20Again they answered:

"You may not pass through."

Then Edom came out against them with a large and powerful army. 21Since Edom refused to let them go through their territory, Israel turned away from them.

ᵃ 13 Meribah means quarreling.

The Death of Aaron

22The whole Israelite community set out from Kadesh and came to Mount Hor. 23At Mount Hor, near the border of Edom, the LORD said to Moses and Aaron, 24"Aaron will be gathered to his people. He will not enter the land I give the Israelites, because both of you rebelled against my command at the waters of Meribah. 25Get Aaron and his son Eleazar and take them up Mount Hor. 26Remove Aaron's garments and put them on his son Eleazar, for Aaron will be gathered to his people; he will die there."

27Moses did as the LORD commanded: They went up Mount Hor in the sight of the whole community. 28Moses removed Aaron's garments and put them on his son Eleazar. And Aaron died there on top of the mountain. Then Moses and Eleazar came down from the mountain, 29and when the whole community learned that Aaron had died, the entire house of Israel mourned for him thirty days.

Arad Destroyed

21 When the Canaanite king of Arad, who lived in the Negev, heard that Israel was coming along the road to Atharim, he attacked the Israelites and captured some of them. 2Then Israel made this vow to the LORD: "If you will deliver these people into our hands, we will totally destroy[a] their cities." 3The LORD listened to Israel's plea and gave the Canaanites over to them. They completely destroyed them and their towns; so the place was named Hormah.[b]

The Bronze Snake

4They traveled from Mount Hor along the route to the Red Sea,[c] to go around Edom. But the people grew impatient on the way; 5they spoke against God and against Moses, and said, "Why have you brought us up out of Egypt to die in the desert? There is no bread! There is no water! And we detest this miserable food!"

6Then the LORD sent venomous snakes among them; they bit the people and many Israelites died. 7The people came to Moses and said, "We sinned when we spoke against the LORD and against you. Pray that the LORD will take the snakes away from us." So Moses prayed for the people.

8The LORD said to Moses, "Make a snake and put it up on a pole; anyone who is bitten can look at it and live." 9So Moses made a bronze snake and put it up on a pole. Then when anyone was bitten by a snake and looked at the bronze snake, he lived.

The Journey to Moab

10The Israelites moved on and camped at Oboth. 11Then they set out from Oboth and camped in Iye Abarim, in the desert that faces Moab toward the sunrise. 12From there they moved on and camped in the Zered Valley. 13They set out from there and camped alongside the Arnon, which is in the desert extending into Amorite territory. The Arnon is the border of Moab, between Moab and the Amorites. 14That is why the Book of the Wars of the LORD says:

"... Waheb in Suphah[d] and the ravines,
    the Arnon 15and[e] the slopes of the
        ravines
that lead to the site of Ar
    and lie along the border of Moab."

16From there they continued on to Beer, the well where the LORD said to Moses, "Gather the people together and I will give them water."

17Then Israel sang this song:

"Spring up, O well!
    Sing about it,
18about the well that the princes dug,
    that the nobles of the people sank—
        the nobles with scepters and staffs."

Then they went from the desert to Mattanah, 19from Mattanah to Nahaliel, from

The Power of Faith

READ AND CONSIDER: NUMBERS 21:1-9

"The people came to Moses and said, 'We sinned when we spoke against the Lord and against you. Pray that the Lord will take the snakes away from us.' So Moses prayed for the people. The Lord said to Moses, 'Make a snake and put it up on a pole; anyone who is bitten can look at it and live'" (Numbers 21:7-8).

When you read this passage, do you find yourself becoming frustrated with the stubborn ingratitude of the Israelites? In response to their plea, God had granted them victory over their enemies, the Canaanites. We don't know for certain how long the travels mentioned here lasted, but we do know that "the people grew impatient on the way; they spoke against God and against Moses" and were discontent with the food God provided for them.

Once again we're reminded of the vital importance of the confession of sin. Once again we witness the privilege of intercession, as Moses represented the Israelites' contrition before God. But this passage also bears witness to one of the most compelling principles in Scripture: The power of prayer is most clearly seen in the presence of faith.

Why would God give Moses such a seemingly strange command—to fashion an imitation snake out of bronze metal and put it up on a pole? What's more, God added this promise: Anyone who was bitten by a real snake could simply *look* at the bronze snake and live.

Of course, the artificial snake had no power, but Moses' obedience to the unusual instruction is recorded as well as the result that any person who followed God's command was saved. It was that simple, yet apparently some did not look at the snake. In their stubbornness and rebellion, many refused to believe that something so simple could save them.

It's still that way today. Jesus died on the cross to save us from the venom that infects us and leads to death—which is sin. Yet millions of people are wandering in the desert of their own sin because they refuse to lift their eyes to the cross. They refuse to believe that something so simple could save them.

The bronze snake on the pole is a type or picture of Jesus. Jesus even refers to this imagery in His conversation with Nicodemus recorded in John 3: "Just as Moses lifted up the snake in the desert, so the Son of Man must be lifted up, that everyone who believes in him may have eternal life" (John 3:14-15). In both instances, it takes a willingness to look up and believe.

Christ is our mediator, and He loves us so much that He paid the penalty for our sin with His death. That means that those of us who look to Jesus as our Savior will live eternally with Him.

Nahaliel to Bamoth, 20and from Bamoth to the valley in Moab where the top of Pisgah overlooks the wasteland.

Defeat of Sihon and Og

21Israel sent messengers to say to Sihon king of the Amorites:

22"Let us pass through your country. We will not turn aside into any field or vineyard, or drink water from any well. We will travel along the king's highway until we have passed through your territory."

23But Sihon would not let Israel pass through his territory. He mustered his entire army and marched out into the desert against Israel. When he reached Jahaz, he fought with Israel. 24Israel, however, put him to the sword and took over his land from the Arnon to the Jabbok, but only as far as the Ammonites, because their border was fortified. ²⁵Israel captured all the cities of the Amorites and occupied them, including Heshbon and all its surrounding settlements. ²⁶Heshbon was the city of Sihon king of the Amorites, who had fought against the former king of Moab and had taken from him all his land as far as the Arnon.

²⁷That is why the poets say:

"Come to Heshbon and let it be rebuilt;
    let Sihon's city be restored.

²⁸"Fire went out from Heshbon,
    a blaze from the city of Sihon.
It consumed Ar of Moab,
    the citizens of Arnon's heights.
²⁹Woe to you, O Moab!
    You are destroyed, O people of
        Chemosh!
He has given up his sons as fugitives
    and his daughters as captives
to Sihon king of the Amorites.

³⁰"But we have overthrown them;
    Heshbon is destroyed all the way to
        Dibon.
We have demolished them as far as
        Nophah,
    which extends to Medeba."

³¹So Israel settled in the land of the Amorites.

³²After Moses had sent spies to Jazer, the Israelites captured its surrounding settlements and drove out the Amorites who were there. ³³Then they turned and went up along the road toward Bashan, and Og king of Bashan and his whole army marched out to meet them in battle at Edrei.

³⁴The LORD said to Moses, "Do not be afraid of him, for I have handed him over to you, with his whole army and his land. Do to him what you did to Sihon king of the Amorites, who reigned in Heshbon."

³⁵So they struck him down, together with his sons and his whole army, leaving them no survivors. And they took possession of his land.

Balak Summons Balaam

22 Then the Israelites traveled to the plains of Moab and camped along the Jordan across from Jericho.ᵃ

²Now Balak son of Zippor saw all that Israel had done to the Amorites, ³and Moab was terrified because there were so many people. Indeed, Moab was filled with dread because of the Israelites.

⁴The Moabites said to the elders of Midian, "This horde is going to lick up everything around us, as an ox licks up the grass of the field."

So Balak son of Zippor, who was king of Moab at that time, ⁵sent messengers to summon Balaam son of Beor, who was at Pethor, near the River,ᵇ in his native land. Balak said:

"A people has come out of Egypt; they cover the face of the land and have settled next to me. ⁶Now come and put a curse on these people, because they are too powerful for me. Perhaps then I will be able to defeat them and drive them out of the country. For I know that those you bless are blessed, and those you curse are cursed."

⁷The elders of Moab and Midian left, taking with them the fee for divination. When they came to Balaam, they told him what Balak had said.

⁸"Spend the night here," Balaam said to them, "and I will bring you back the answer the LORD gives me." So the Moabite princes stayed with him.

⁹God came to Balaam and asked, "Who are these men with you?"

¹⁰Balaam said to God, "Balak son of Zippor, king of Moab, sent me this message: ¹¹'A people that has come out of Egypt covers the face of the land. Now come and put a curse on them for me.

ᵃ 1 Hebrew Jordan of Jericho; possibly an ancient name for the Jordan River   ᵇ 5 That is, the Euphrates

Perhaps then I will be able to fight them and drive them away.'"

¹²But God said to Balaam, "Do not go with them. You must not put a curse on those people, because they are blessed."

¹³The next morning Balaam got up and said to Balak's princes, "Go back to your own country, for the LORD has refused to let me go with you."

¹⁴So the Moabite princes returned to Balak and said, "Balaam refused to come with us."

¹⁵Then Balak sent other princes, more numerous and more distinguished than the first. ¹⁶They came to Balaam and said:

"This is what Balak son of Zippor says: Do not let anything keep you from coming to me, ¹⁷because I will reward you handsomely and do whatever you say. Come and put a curse on these people for me."

¹⁸But Balaam answered them, "Even if Balak gave me his palace filled with silver and gold, I could not do anything great or small to go beyond the command of the LORD my God. ¹⁹Now stay here tonight as the others did, and I will find out what else the LORD will tell me."

²⁰That night God came to Balaam and said, "Since these men have come to summon you, go with them, but do only what I tell you."

Balaam's Donkey

²¹Balaam got up in the morning, saddled his donkey and went with the princes of Moab. ²²But God was very angry when he went, and the angel of the LORD stood in the road to oppose him. Balaam was riding on his donkey, and his two servants were with him. ²³When the donkey saw the angel of the LORD standing in the road with a drawn sword in his hand, she turned off the road into a field. Balaam beat her to get her back on the road.

²⁴Then the angel of the LORD stood in a narrow path between two vineyards, with walls on both sides. ²⁵When the donkey saw the angel of the LORD, she pressed close to the wall, crushing Balaam's foot against it. So he beat her again.

²⁶Then the angel of the LORD moved on ahead and stood in a narrow place where there was no room to turn, either to the right or to the left. ²⁷When the donkey saw the angel of the LORD, she lay down under Balaam, and he was angry and beat her with his staff. ²⁸Then the LORD opened the donkey's mouth, and she said to Balaam, "What have I done to you to make you beat me these three times?"

²⁹Balaam answered the donkey, "You have made a fool of me! If I had a sword in my hand, I would kill you right now."

³⁰The donkey said to Balaam, "Am I not your own donkey, which you have always ridden, to this day? Have I been in the habit of doing this to you?"

"No," he said.

³¹Then the LORD opened Balaam's eyes, and he saw the angel of the LORD standing in the road with his sword drawn. So he bowed low and fell facedown.

Praying Numbers 22:31-34
*Heavenly Father, open my eyes
to always see the truth about
myself and my situation.*

³²The angel of the LORD asked him, "Why have you beaten your donkey these three times? I have come here to oppose you because your path is a reckless one before me.ᵃ ³³The donkey saw me and turned away from me these three times. If she had not turned away, I would certainly have killed you by now, but I would have spared her."

³⁴Balaam said to the angel of the LORD, "I have sinned. I did not realize you were standing in the road to oppose me. Now if you are displeased, I will go back."

³⁵The angel of the LORD said to Ba-

ᵃ *32* The meaning of the Hebrew for this clause is uncertain.

laam, "Go with the men, but speak only what I tell you." So Balaam went with the princes of Balak.

³⁶When Balak heard that Balaam was coming, he went out to meet him at the Moabite town on the Arnon border, at the edge of his territory. ³⁷Balak said to Balaam, "Did I not send you an urgent summons? Why didn't you come to me? Am I really not able to reward you?"

³⁸"Well, I have come to you now," Balaam replied. "But can I say just anything? I must speak only what God puts in my mouth."

³⁹Then Balaam went with Balak to Kiriath Huzoth. ⁴⁰Balak sacrificed cattle and sheep, and gave some to Balaam and the princes who were with him. ⁴¹The next morning Balak took Balaam up to Bamoth Baal, and from there he saw part of the people.

Balaam's First Oracle

23 Balaam said, "Build me seven altars here, and prepare seven bulls and seven rams for me." ²Balak did as Balaam said, and the two of them offered a bull and a ram on each altar.

³Then Balaam said to Balak, "Stay here beside your offering while I go aside. Perhaps the LORD will come to meet with me. Whatever he reveals to me I will tell you." Then he went off to a barren height.

⁴God met with him, and Balaam said, "I have prepared seven altars, and on each altar I have offered a bull and a ram."

⁵The LORD put a message in Balaam's mouth and said, "Go back to Balak and give him this message."

⁶So he went back to him and found him standing beside his offering, with all the princes of Moab. ⁷Then Balaam uttered his oracle:

"Balak brought me from Aram,
  the king of Moab from the eastern
    mountains.
'Come,' he said, 'curse Jacob for me;
  come, denounce Israel.'

⁸How can I curse
  those whom God has not cursed?
How can I denounce
  those whom the LORD has not
    denounced?
⁹From the rocky peaks I see them,
  from the heights I view them.
I see a people who live apart
  and do not consider themselves one
    of the nations.
¹⁰Who can count the dust of Jacob
  or number the fourth part of Israel?
Let me die the death of the righteous,
  and may my end be like theirs!"

¹¹Balak said to Balaam, "What have you done to me? I brought you to curse my enemies, but you have done nothing but bless them!"

¹²He answered, "Must I not speak what the LORD puts in my mouth?"

Balaam's Second Oracle

¹³Then Balak said to him, "Come with me to another place where you can see them; you will see only a part but not all of them. And from there, curse them for me." ¹⁴So he took him to the field of Zophim on the top of Pisgah, and there he built seven altars and offered a bull and a ram on each altar.

¹⁵Balaam said to Balak, "Stay here beside your offering while I meet with him over there."

¹⁶The LORD met with Balaam and put a message in his mouth and said, "Go back to Balak and give him this message."

¹⁷So he went to him and found him standing beside his offering, with the princes of Moab. Balak asked him, "What did the LORD say?"

¹⁸Then he uttered his oracle:

"Arise, Balak, and listen;
  hear me, son of Zippor.
¹⁹God is not a man, that he should lie,
  nor a son of man, that he should
    change his mind.
Does he speak and then not act?
  Does he promise and not fulfill?
²⁰I have received a command to bless;

he has blessed, and I cannot
    change it.

21 "No misfortune is seen in Jacob,
    no misery observed in Israel.[a]
The LORD their God is with them;
    the shout of the King is among
    them.
22 God brought them out of Egypt;
    they have the strength of a wild ox.
23 There is no sorcery against Jacob,
    no divination against Israel.
It will now be said of Jacob
    and of Israel, 'See what God has
    done!'
24 The people rise like a lioness;
    they rouse themselves like a lion
that does not rest till he devours his
    prey
    and drinks the blood of his victims."

25 Then Balak said to Balaam, "Neither curse them at all nor bless them at all!"

26 Balaam answered, "Did I not tell you I must do whatever the LORD says?"

Balaam's Third Oracle

27 Then Balak said to Balaam, "Come, let me take you to another place. Perhaps it will please God to let you curse them for me from there." 28 And Balak took Balaam to the top of Peor, overlooking the wasteland.

29 Balaam said, "Build me seven altars here, and prepare seven bulls and seven rams for me." 30 Balak did as Balaam had said, and offered a bull and a ram on each altar.

24 Now when Balaam saw that it pleased the LORD to bless Israel, he did not resort to sorcery as at other times, but turned his face toward the desert. 2 When Balaam looked out and saw Israel encamped tribe by tribe, the Spirit of God came upon him 3 and he uttered his oracle:

"The oracle of Balaam son of Beor,
    the oracle of one whose eye sees
    clearly,

4 the oracle of one who hears the words
    of God,
who sees a vision from the
    Almighty,[b]
who falls prostrate, and whose eyes
    are opened:

5 "How beautiful are your tents,
    O Jacob,
    your dwelling places, O Israel!

6 "Like valleys they spread out,
    like gardens beside a river,
like aloes planted by the LORD,
    like cedars beside the waters.
7 Water will flow from their buckets;
    their seed will have abundant water.

"Their king will be greater than
    Agag;
    their kingdom will be exalted.

8 "God brought them out of Egypt;
    they have the strength of a wild ox.
They devour hostile nations
    and break their bones in pieces;
    with their arrows they pierce them.
9 Like a lion they crouch and lie down,
    like a lioness—who dares to rouse
    them?

"May those who bless you be blessed
    and those who curse you be
    cursed!"

10 Then Balak's anger burned against Balaam. He struck his hands together and said to him, "I summoned you to curse my enemies, but you have blessed them these three times. 11 Now leave at once and go home! I said I would reward you handsomely, but the LORD has kept you from being rewarded."

12 Balaam answered Balak, "Did I not tell the messengers you sent me, 13 'Even if Balak gave me his palace filled with silver and gold, I could not do anything of my own accord, good or bad, to go beyond the command of the LORD—and I must say only what the LORD says'? 14 Now I am going back to my people, but come,

---

a 21 Or He has not looked on Jacob's offenses / or on the wrongs found in Israel.   b 4 Hebrew Shaddai; also in verse 16 let me warn you of what this people will do to your people in days to come."

Balaam's Fourth Oracle

15Then he uttered his oracle:

"The oracle of Balaam son of Beor,
    the oracle of one whose eye sees clearly,
16the oracle of one who hears the words of God,
    who has knowledge from the Most High,
who sees a vision from the Almighty,
    who falls prostrate, and whose eyes are opened:

17"I see him, but not now;
    I behold him, but not near.
A star will come out of Jacob;
    a scepter will rise out of Israel.
He will crush the foreheads of Moab,
    the skulls[a] of[b] all the sons of Sheth.[c]
18Edom will be conquered;
    Seir, his enemy, will be conquered,
    but Israel will grow strong.
19A ruler will come out of Jacob
    and destroy the survivors of the city."

Balaam's Final Oracles

20Then Balaam saw Amalek and uttered his oracle:

"Amalek was first among the nations,
    but he will come to ruin at last."

21Then he saw the Kenites and uttered his oracle:

"Your dwelling place is secure,
    your nest is set in a rock;
22yet you Kenites will be destroyed
    when Asshur takes you captive."

23Then he uttered his oracle:

"Ah, who can live when God does this?[d]
24   Ships will come from the shores of Kittim;

they will subdue Asshur and Eber,
    but they too will come to ruin."

25Then Balaam got up and returned home and Balak went his own way.

Moab Seduces Israel

25 While Israel was staying in Shittim, the men began to indulge in sexual immorality with Moabite women, 2who invited them to the sacrifices to their gods. The people ate and bowed down before these gods. 3So Israel joined in worshiping the Baal of Peor. And the LORD's anger burned against them.

4The LORD said to Moses, "Take all the leaders of these people, kill them and expose them in broad daylight before the LORD, so that the LORD's fierce anger may turn away from Israel."

5So Moses said to Israel's judges, "Each of you must put to death those of your

Prayer is . . .

*letting your heart be softened
in the presence of God.*

men who have joined in worshiping the Baal of Peor."

6Then an Israelite man brought to his family a Midianite woman right before the eyes of Moses and the whole assembly of Israel while they were weeping at the entrance to the Tent of Meeting. 7When Phinehas son of Eleazar, the son of Aaron, the priest, saw this, he left the assembly, took a spear in his hand 8and followed the Israelite into the tent. He drove the spear through both of them—through the Israelite and into the woman's body. Then the plague against the Israelites was stopped; 9but those who died in the plague numbered 24,000.

10The LORD said to Moses, 11"Phinehas

---

a 17 Samaritan Pentateuch (see also Jer. 48:45); the meaning of the word in the Masoretic Text is uncertain.   b 17 Or possibly Moab, / batter   c 17 Or all the noisy boasters   d 23 Masoretic Text; with a different word division of the Hebrew A people will gather from the north.

son of Eleazar, the son of Aaron, the priest, has turned my anger away from the Israelites; for he was as zealous as I am for my honor among them, so that in my zeal I did not put an end to them. [12]Therefore tell him I am making my covenant of peace with him. [13]He and his descendants will have a covenant of a lasting priesthood, because he was zealous for the honor of his God and made atonement for the Israelites."

[14]The name of the Israelite who was killed with the Midianite woman was Zimri son of Salu, the leader of a Simeonite family. [15]And the name of the Midianite woman who was put to death was Cozbi daughter of Zur, a tribal chief of a Midianite family.

[16]The LORD said to Moses, [17]"Treat the Midianites as enemies and kill them, [18]because they treated you as enemies when they deceived you in the affair of Peor and their sister Cozbi, the daughter of a Midianite leader, the woman who was killed when the plague came as a result of Peor."

The Second Census

26 After the plague the LORD said to Moses and Eleazar son of Aaron, the priest, [2]"Take a census of the whole Israelite community by families—all those twenty years old or more who are able to serve in the army of Israel." [3]So on the plains of Moab by the Jordan across from Jericho,[a] Moses and Eleazar the priest spoke with them and said, [4]"Take a census of the men twenty years old or more, as the LORD commanded Moses."

These were the Israelites who came out of Egypt:

[5]The descendants of Reuben, the firstborn son of Israel, were:

through Hanoch, the Hanochite clan;
through Pallu, the Palluite clan;
[6]through Hezron, the Hezronite clan;
through Carmi, the Carmite clan.

[7]These were the clans of Reuben; those numbered were 43,730.

[8]The son of Pallu was Eliab, [9]and the sons of Eliab were Nemuel, Dathan and Abiram. The same Dathan and Abiram were the community officials who rebelled against Moses and Aaron and were among Korah's followers when they rebelled against the LORD. [10]The earth opened its mouth and swallowed them along with Korah, whose followers died when the fire devoured the 250 men. And they served as a warning sign. [11]The line of Korah, however, did not die out.

[12]The descendants of Simeon by their clans were:

through Nemuel, the Nemuelite clan;
through Jamin, the Jaminite clan;
through Jakin, the Jakinite clan;
[13]through Zerah, the Zerahite clan;
through Shaul, the Shaulite clan.
[14]These were the clans of Simeon; there were 22,200 men.

[15]The descendants of Gad by their clans were:

through Zephon, the Zephonite clan;
through Haggi, the Haggite clan;
through Shuni, the Shunite clan;
[16]through Ozni, the Oznite clan;
through Eri, the Erite clan;
[17]through Arodi,[b] the Arodite clan;
through Areli, the Arelite clan.
[18]These were the clans of Gad; those numbered were 40,500.

[19]Er and Onan were sons of Judah, but they died in Canaan. [20]The descendants of Judah by their clans were:

through Shelah, the Shelanite clan;
through Perez, the Perezite clan;
through Zerah, the Zerahite clan.
[21]The descendants of Perez were:
through Hezron, the Hezronite clan;

---

[a] 3 Hebrew *Jordan of Jericho*; possibly an ancient name for the Jordan River; also in verse 63   [b] 17 Samaritan Pentateuch and Syriac (see also Gen. 46:16); Masoretic Text *Arod*

through Hamul, the Hamulite clan.

22 These were the clans of Judah; those numbered were 76,500.

23 The descendants of Issachar by their clans were:

through Tola, the Tolaite clan;
through Puah, the Puite[a] clan;
24 through Jashub, the Jashubite clan;
through Shimron, the Shimronite clan.

25 These were the clans of Issachar; those numbered were 64,300.

26 The descendants of Zebulun by their clans were:

through Sered, the Seredite clan;
through Elon, the Elonite clan;
through Jahleel, the Jahleelite clan.

27 These were the clans of Zebulun; those numbered were 60,500.

28 The descendants of Joseph by their clans through Manasseh and Ephraim were:

29 The descendants of Manasseh:

through Makir, the Makirite clan (Makir was the father of Gilead);
through Gilead, the Gileadite clan.

30 These were the descendants of Gilead:

through Iezer, the Iezerite clan;
through Helek, the Helekite clan;
31 through Asriel, the Asrielite clan;
through Shechem, the Shechemite clan;
32 through Shemida, the Shemidaite clan;
through Hepher, the Hepherite clan.

33 (Zelophehad son of Hepher had no sons; he had only daughters, whose names were Mahlah, Noah, Hoglah, Milcah and Tirzah.)

34 These were the clans of Manasseh; those numbered were 52,700.

35 These were the descendants of Ephraim by their clans:

through Shuthelah, the Shuthelahite clan;
through Beker, the Bekerite clan;
through Tahan, the Tahanite clan.

36 These were the descendants of Shuthelah:

through Eran, the Eranite clan.

37 These were the clans of Ephraim; those numbered were 32,500.

These were the descendants of Joseph by their clans.

38 The descendants of Benjamin by their clans were:

through Bela, the Belaite clan;
through Ashbel, the Ashbelite clan;
through Ahiram, the Ahiramite clan;
39 through Shupham,[b] the Shuphamite clan;
through Hupham, the Huphamite clan.

40 The descendants of Bela through Ard and Naaman were:

through Ard,[c] the Ardite clan;
through Naaman, the Naamite clan.

41 These were the clans of Benjamin; those numbered were 45,600.

42 These were the descendants of Dan by their clans:

through Shuham, the Shuhamite clan.

These were the clans of Dan: 43 All of them were Shuhamite clans; and those numbered were 64,400.

44 The descendants of Asher by their clans were:

through Imnah, the Imnite clan;
through Ishvi, the Ishvite clan;
through Beriah, the Beriite clan;
45 and through the descendants of Beriah:

through Heber, the Heberite clan;

---

a 23 Samaritan Pentateuch, Septuagint, Vulgate and Syriac (see also 1 Chron. 7:1); Masoretic Text *through Puvah, the Punite*   b 39 A few manuscripts of the Masoretic Text, Samaritan Pentateuch, Vulgate and Syriac (see also Septuagint); most manuscripts of the Masoretic Text *Shephupham*   c 40 Samaritan Pentateuch and Vulgate (see also Septuagint); Masoretic Text does not have *through Ard*.

through Malkiel, the Malkielite clan.

46 (Asher had a daughter named Serah.)

47 These were the clans of Asher; those numbered were 53,400.

48 The descendants of Naphtali by their clans were:

through Jahzeel, the Jahzeelite clan;
through Guni, the Gunite clan;
49 through Jezer, the Jezerite clan;
through Shillem, the Shillemite clan.

50 These were the clans of Naphtali; those numbered were 45,400.

51 The total number of the men of Israel was 601,730.

52 The LORD said to Moses, 53 "The land is to be allotted to them as an inheritance based on the number of names. 54 To a larger group give a larger inheritance, and to a smaller group a smaller one; each is to receive its inheritance according to the number of those listed. 55 Be sure that the land is distributed by lot. What each group inherits will be according to the names for its ancestral tribe. 56 Each inheritance is to be distributed by lot among the larger and smaller groups."

57 These were the Levites who were counted by their clans:

through Gershon, the Gershonite clan;
through Kohath, the Kohathite clan;
through Merari, the Merarite clan.

58 These also were Levite clans:

the Libnite clan,
the Hebronite clan,
the Mahlite clan,
the Mushite clan,
the Korahite clan.

(Kohath was the forefather of Amram; 59 the name of Amram's wife was Jochebed, a descendant of Levi, who was born to the Levites[a] in Egypt.

To Amram she bore Aaron, Moses and their sister Miriam. 60 Aaron was the father of Nadab and Abihu, Eleazar and Ithamar. 61 But Nadab and Abihu died when they made an offering before the LORD with unauthorized fire.)

62 All the male Levites a month old or more numbered 23,000. They were not counted along with the other Israelites because they received no inheritance among them.

63 These are the ones counted by Moses and Eleazar the priest when they counted the Israelites on the plains of Moab by the Jordan across from Jericho. 64 Not one of them was among those counted by Moses and Aaron the priest when they counted the Israelites in the Desert of Sinai. 65 For the LORD had told those Israelites they would surely die in the desert, and not one of them was left except Caleb son of Jephunneh and Joshua son of Nun.

Zelophehad's Daughters

27 The daughters of Zelophehad son of Hepher, the son of Gilead, the son of Makir, the son of Manasseh, belonged to the clans of Manasseh son of Joseph. The names of the daughters were Mahlah, Noah, Hoglah, Milcah and Tirzah. They approached 2 the entrance to the Tent of Meeting and stood before Moses, Eleazar the priest, the leaders and the whole assembly, and said, 3 "Our father died in the desert. He was not among Korah's followers, who banded together against the LORD, but he died for his own sin and left no sons. 4 Why should our father's name disappear from his clan because he had no son? Give us property among our father's relatives."

5 So Moses brought their case before the LORD 6 and the LORD said to him, 7 "What Zelophehad's daughters are saying is right. You must certainly give them property as an inheritance among their

---

a 59 Or Jochebed, a daughter of Levi, who was born to Levi

father's relatives and turn their father's inheritance over to them.

8"Say to the Israelites, 'If a man dies and leaves no son, turn his inheritance over to his daughter. 9If he has no daughter, give his inheritance to his brothers. 10If he has no brothers, give his inheritance to his father's brothers. 11If his father had no brothers, give his inheritance to the nearest relative in his clan, that he may possess it. This is to be a legal requirement for the Israelites, as the LORD commanded Moses.'"

in, so the LORD's people will not be like sheep without a shepherd."

18So the LORD said to Moses, "Take Joshua son of Nun, a man in whom is the spirit,[a] and lay your hand on him. 19Have him stand before Eleazar the priest and the entire assembly and commission him in their presence. 20Give him some of your authority so the whole Israelite community will obey him. 21He is to stand before Eleazar the priest, who will obtain decisions for him by inquiring of the Urim before the LORD. At his com-

---

God's people at prayer
MOSES PRAYS FOR GOD'S PROVISION

NUMBERS 27:15-17 As Moses neared the end of his life, the Lord gave him a glimpse of the land that He had promised to the Israelites. But Moses would not lead the people into the promised land because of his disobedience. Rather than sulking about this loss or begging God to change a seemingly unfair situation, Moses' thoughts turned to the beloved and often-maddening children of Israel. What would happen to them? He knew how vulnerable they were, like sheep without a shepherd at times. So he prayed. First he acknowledged God's power and sovereignty ("the God . . . of all mankind"). Then he asked God to send the right person to shepherd His people.

When things are not going your way, take a tip from a godly Old Testament leader. Look to God and His awesome power and, through your prayers, seek to bless, encourage, provide for, and serve others who need it.

Joshua to Succeed Moses

12Then the LORD said to Moses, "Go up this mountain in the Abarim range and see the land I have given the Israelites. 13After you have seen it, you too will be gathered to your people, as your brother Aaron was, 14for when the community rebelled at the waters in the Desert of Zin, both of you disobeyed my command to honor me as holy before their eyes." (These were the waters of Meribah Kadesh, in the Desert of Zin.)

15Moses said to the LORD, 16"May the LORD, the God of the spirits of all mankind, appoint a man over this community 17to go out and come in before them, one who will lead them out and bring them

mand he and the entire community of the Israelites will go out, and at his command they will come in."

22Moses did as the LORD commanded him. He took Joshua and had him stand before Eleazar the priest and the whole assembly. 23Then he laid his hands on him and commissioned him, as the LORD instructed through Moses.

Daily Offerings

28 The LORD said to Moses, 2"Give this command to the Israelites and say to them: 'See that you present to me at the appointed time the food for my offerings made by fire, as an aroma pleasing to me.' 3Say to them: 'This is the offering

---

a 18 Or Spirit

made by fire that you are to present to the LORD: two lambs a year old without defect, as a regular burnt offering each day. [4]Prepare one lamb in the morning and the other at twilight, [5]together with a grain offering of a tenth of an ephah[a] of fine flour mixed with a quarter of a hin[b] of oil from pressed olives. [6]This is the regular burnt offering instituted at Mount Sinai as a pleasing aroma, an offering made to the LORD by fire. [7]The accompanying drink offering is to be a quarter of a hin of fermented drink with each lamb. Pour out the drink offering to the LORD at the sanctuary. [8]Prepare the second lamb at twilight, along with the same kind of grain offering and drink offering that you prepare in the morning. This is an offering made by fire, an aroma pleasing to the LORD.

Sabbath Offerings

[9]"'On the Sabbath day, make an offering of two lambs a year old without defect, together with its drink offering and a grain offering of two-tenths of an ephah[c] of fine flour mixed with oil. [10]This is the burnt offering for every Sabbath, in addition to the regular burnt offering and its drink offering.

Monthly Offerings

[11]"'On the first of every month, present to the LORD a burnt offering of two young bulls, one ram and seven male lambs a year old, all without defect. [12]With each bull there is to be a grain offering of three-tenths of an ephah[d] of fine flour mixed with oil; with the ram, a grain offering of two-tenths of an ephah of fine flour mixed with oil; [13]and with each lamb, a grain offering of a tenth of an ephah of fine flour mixed with oil. This is for a burnt offering, a pleasing aroma, an offering made to the LORD by fire. [14]With each bull there is to be a drink offering of half a hin[e] of wine; with the

ram, a third of a hin[f]; and with each lamb, a quarter of a hin. This is the monthly burnt offering to be made at each new moon during the year. [15]Besides the regular burnt offering with its drink offering, one male goat is to be presented to the LORD as a sin offering.

The Passover

[16]"'On the fourteenth day of the first month the LORD's Passover is to be held. [17]On the fifteenth day of this month there is to be a festival; for seven days eat bread made without yeast. [18]On the first day hold a sacred assembly and do no regular work. [19]Present to the LORD an offering made by fire, a burnt offering of two young bulls, one ram and seven male lambs a year old, all without defect. [20]With each bull prepare a grain offering of three-tenths of an ephah of fine flour mixed with oil; with the ram, two-tenths; [21]and with each of the seven lambs, one-tenth. [22]Include one male goat as a sin offering to make atonement for you. [23]Prepare these in addition to the regular morning burnt offering. [24]In this way prepare the food for the offering made by fire every day for seven days as an aroma pleasing to the LORD; it is to be prepared in addition to the regular burnt offering and its drink offering. [25]On the seventh day hold a sacred assembly and do no regular work.

Feast of Weeks

[26]"'On the day of firstfruits, when you present to the LORD an offering of new grain during the Feast of Weeks, hold a sacred assembly and do no regular work. [27]Present a burnt offering of two young bulls, one ram and seven male lambs a year old as an aroma pleasing to the LORD. [28]With each bull there is to be a grain offering of three-tenths of an ephah of fine flour mixed with oil; with the ram, two-tenths; [29]and with each of

---

[a] 5 That is, probably about 2 quarts (about 2 liters); also in verses 13, 21 and 29   [b] 5 That is, probably about 1 quart (about 1 liter); also in verses 7 and 14   [c] 9 That is, probably about 4 quarts (about 4.5 liters); also in verses 12, 20 and 28   [d] 12 That is, probably about 6 quarts (about 6.5 liters); also in verses 20 and 28   [e] 14 That is, probably about 2 quarts (about 2 liters)   [f] 14 That is, probably about 1 1/4 quarts (about 1.2 liters)

the seven lambs, one-tenth. ³⁰Include one male goat to make atonement for you. ³¹Prepare these together with their drink offerings, in addition to the regular burnt offering and its grain offering. Be sure the animals are without defect.

Feast of Trumpets

29 " 'On the first day of the seventh month hold a sacred assembly and do no regular work. It is a day for you to sound the trumpets. ²As an aroma pleasing to the LORD, prepare a burnt offering of one young bull, one ram and seven male lambs a year old, all without defect. ³With the bull prepare a grain offering of three-tenths of an ephah[a] of fine flour mixed with oil; with the ram, two-tenths[b]; ⁴and with each of the seven lambs, one-tenth.[c] ⁵Include one male goat as a sin offering to make atonement for you. ⁶These are in addition to the monthly and daily burnt offerings with their grain offerings and drink offerings as specified. They are offerings made to the LORD by fire—a pleasing aroma.

Day of Atonement

⁷" 'On the tenth day of this seventh month hold a sacred assembly. You must deny yourselves[d] and do no work. ⁸Present as an aroma pleasing to the LORD a burnt offering of one young bull, one ram and seven male lambs a year old, all without defect. ⁹With the bull prepare a grain offering of three-tenths of an ephah of fine flour mixed with oil; with the ram, two-tenths; ¹⁰and with each of the seven lambs, one-tenth. ¹¹Include one male goat as a sin offering, in addition to the sin offering for atonement and the regular burnt offering with its grain offering, and their drink offerings.

Feast of Tabernacles

¹²" 'On the fifteenth day of the seventh month, hold a sacred assembly and do no regular work. Celebrate a festival to the LORD for seven days. ¹³Present an offering made by fire as an aroma pleasing to the LORD, a burnt offering of thirteen young bulls, two rams and fourteen male lambs a year old, all without defect. ¹⁴With each of the thirteen bulls prepare a grain offering of three-tenths of an ephah of fine flour mixed with oil; with each of the two rams, two-tenths; ¹⁵and with each of the fourteen lambs, one-tenth. ¹⁶Include one male goat as a sin offering, in addition to the regular burnt offering with its grain offering and drink offering.

¹⁷" 'On the second day prepare twelve young bulls, two rams and fourteen male lambs a year old, all without defect. ¹⁸With the bulls, rams and lambs, prepare their grain offerings and drink offerings according to the number specified. ¹⁹Include one male goat as a sin offering, in addition to the regular burnt offering with its grain offering, and their drink offerings.

²⁰" 'On the third day prepare eleven bulls, two rams and fourteen male lambs a year old, all without defect. ²¹With the bulls, rams and lambs, prepare their grain offerings and drink offerings according to the number specified. ²²Include one male goat as a sin offering, in addition to the regular burnt offering with its grain offering and drink offering.

²³" 'On the fourth day prepare ten bulls, two rams and fourteen male lambs a year old, all without defect. ²⁴With the bulls, rams and lambs, prepare their grain offerings and drink offerings according to the number specified. ²⁵Include one male goat as a sin offering, in addition to the regular burnt offering with its grain offering and drink offering.

²⁶" 'On the fifth day prepare nine bulls, two rams and fourteen male lambs a year old, all without defect. ²⁷With the bulls, rams and lambs, prepare their grain offerings and drink offerings according to the number specified. ²⁸Include one male

---

a 3 That is, probably about 6 quarts (about 6.5 liters); also in verses 9 and 14   b 3 That is, probably about 4 quarts (about 4.5 liters); also in verses 9 and 14   c 4 That is, probably about 2 quarts (about 2 liters); also in verses 10 and 15
d 7 Or must fast

goat as a sin offering, in addition to the regular burnt offering with its grain offering and drink offering.

[29] "'On the sixth day prepare eight bulls, two rams and fourteen male lambs a year old, all without defect. [30] With the bulls, rams and lambs, prepare their grain offerings and drink offerings according to the number specified. [31] Include one male goat as a sin offering, in addition to the regular burnt offering with its grain offering and drink offering.

[32] "'On the seventh day prepare seven bulls, two rams and fourteen male lambs a year old, all without defect. [33] With the bulls, rams and lambs, prepare their grain offerings and drink offerings according to the number specified. [34] Include one male goat as a sin offering, in addition to the regular burnt offering with its grain offering and drink offering.

[35] "'On the eighth day hold an assembly and do no regular work. [36] Present an offering made by fire as an aroma pleasing to the LORD, a burnt offering of one bull, one ram and seven male lambs a year old, all without defect. [37] With the bull, the ram and the lambs, prepare their grain offerings and drink offerings according to the number specified. [38] Include one male goat as a sin offering, in addition to the regular burnt offering with its grain offering and drink offering.

[39] "'In addition to what you vow and your freewill offerings, prepare these for the LORD at your appointed feasts: your burnt offerings, grain offerings, drink offerings and fellowship offerings.[a]'"

[40] Moses told the Israelites all that the LORD commanded him.

Vows

30 Moses said to the heads of the tribes of Israel: "This is what the LORD commands: [2] When a man makes a vow to the LORD or takes an oath to obligate himself by a pledge, he must not break his word but must do everything he said.

[3] "When a young woman still living in her father's house makes a vow to the LORD or obligates herself by a pledge [4] and her father hears about her vow or pledge but says nothing to her, then all her vows and every pledge by which she obligated herself will stand. [5] But if her father forbids her when he hears about it, none of her vows or the pledges by which she obligated herself will stand; the LORD will release her because her father has forbidden her.

[6] "If she marries after she makes a vow or after her lips utter a rash promise by which she obligates herself [7] and her husband hears about it but says nothing to her, then her vows or the pledges by which she obligated herself will stand. [8] But if her husband forbids her when he hears about it, he nullifies the vow that obligates her or the rash promise by which she obligates herself, and the LORD will release her.

[9] "Any vow or obligation taken by a widow or divorced woman will be binding on her.

[10] "If a woman living with her husband makes a vow or obligates herself by a pledge under oath [11] and her husband hears about it but says nothing to her and does not forbid her, then all her vows or the pledges by which she obligated herself will stand. [12] But if her husband nullifies them when he hears about them, then none of the vows or pledges that came from her lips will stand. Her husband has nullified them, and the LORD will release her. [13] Her husband may confirm or nullify any vow she makes or any sworn pledge to deny herself. [14] But if her husband says nothing to her about it from day to day, then he confirms all her vows or the pledges binding on her. He confirms them by saying nothing to her when he hears about them. [15] If, however, he nullifies them some time after he hears about them, then he is responsible for her guilt."

---

a 39 Traditionally *peace offerings*

Be Careful What You Promise

READ AND CONSIDER: NUMBERS 30:1-2

"This is what the LORD commands: When a man makes a vow to the LORD or takes an oath to obligate himself by a pledge, he must not break his word but must do everything he said" (Numbers 30:1-2).

"A man's word is his bond," the saying goes. This applies to women too! A "bond" in this case refers to a guarantee or pledge—a verbal agreement that has been made between two parties. Though no written contract has been signed, there is still an understanding that a promise has been made, and there is an obligation to follow through on that promise.

This was especially true in ancient times, when written contracts usually did not exist. Once a vow or oath was made, the trust implicit in that promise was not to be broken. In this passage, Moses was reminding the people that their promises to God and others had to be kept. God commanded it, and integrity demanded it.

Unfortunately we live in an age where words are often carelessly spoken, and promises are too casually made. There are times when we may be tempted to go back on our word or get out of our commitments. But God's Word says that if we make a vow or enter into an agreement, we must not break our word. Broken words are betrayed promises.

Always be careful what you promise. It's best to pray first before you commit to anything. Knowing God's leading will keep you from making a commitment you can't keep and help you to keep one once you have made it.

---

[16] These are the regulations the LORD gave Moses concerning relationships between a man and his wife, and between a father and his young daughter still living in his house.

Vengeance on the Midianites

31 The LORD said to Moses, [2] "Take vengeance on the Midianites for the Israelites. After that, you will be gathered to your people."

[3] So Moses said to the people, "Arm some of your men to go to war against the Midianites and to carry out the LORD's vengeance on them. [4] Send into battle a thousand men from each of the tribes of Israel." [5] So twelve thousand men armed for battle, a thousand from each tribe, were supplied from the clans of Israel. [6] Moses sent them into battle, a thousand from each tribe, along with Phinehas son of Eleazar, the priest, who took with him articles from the sanctuary and the trumpets for signaling.

[7] They fought against Midian, as the LORD commanded Moses, and killed every man. [8] Among their victims were Evi, Rekem, Zur, Hur and Reba—the five kings of Midian. They also killed Balaam son of Beor with the sword. [9] The Israelites captured the Midianite women and children and took all the Midianite herds, flocks and goods as plunder. [10] They burned all the towns where the Midianites had settled, as well as all their camps. [11] They took all the plunder and spoils, including the people and animals, [12] and brought the captives, spoils and plunder to Moses and Eleazar the priest and the Israelite assembly at their camp on the plains of Moab, by the Jordan across from Jericho.[a]

---

[a] *12* Hebrew *Jordan of Jericho*; possibly an ancient name for the Jordan River

¹³Moses, Eleazar the priest and all the leaders of the community went to meet them outside the camp. ¹⁴Moses was angry with the officers of the army—the commanders of thousands and commanders of hundreds—who returned from the battle.

¹⁵"Have you allowed all the women to live?" he asked them. ¹⁶"They were the ones who followed Balaam's advice and were the means of turning the Israelites away from the LORD in what happened at Peor, so that a plague struck the LORD's people. ¹⁷Now kill all the boys. And kill every woman who has slept with a man, ¹⁸but save for yourselves every girl who has never slept with a man.

¹⁹"All of you who have killed anyone or touched anyone who was killed must stay outside the camp seven days. On the third and seventh days you must purify yourselves and your captives. ²⁰Purify every garment as well as everything made of leather, goat hair or wood."

²¹Then Eleazar the priest said to the soldiers who had gone into battle, "This is the requirement of the law that the LORD gave Moses: ²²Gold, silver, bronze, iron, tin, lead ²³and anything else that can withstand fire must be put through the fire, and then it will be clean. But it must also be purified with the water of cleansing. And whatever cannot withstand fire must be put through that water. ²⁴On the seventh day wash your clothes and you will be clean. Then you may come into the camp."

Dividing the Spoils

²⁵The LORD said to Moses, ²⁶"You and Eleazar the priest and the family heads of the community are to count all the people and animals that were captured. ²⁷Divide the spoils between the soldiers who took part in the battle and the rest of the community. ²⁸From the soldiers who fought in the battle, set apart as tribute for the LORD one out of every five hundred, whether persons, cattle, donkeys, sheep or goats. ²⁹Take this tribute from their half share and give it to Eleazar the priest as the LORD's part. ³⁰From the Israelites' half, select one out of every fifty, whether persons, cattle, donkeys, sheep, goats or other animals. Give them to the Levites, who are responsible for the care of the LORD's tabernacle." ³¹So Moses and Eleazar the priest did as the LORD commanded Moses.

³²The plunder remaining from the spoils that the soldiers took was 675,000 sheep, ³³72,000 cattle, ³⁴61,000 donkeys ³⁵and 32,000 women who had never slept with a man.

³⁶The half share of those who fought in the battle was:

337,500 sheep, ³⁷of which the tribute for the LORD was 675;

³⁸36,000 cattle, of which the tribute for the LORD was 72;

³⁹30,500 donkeys, of which the tribute for the LORD was 61;

⁴⁰16,000 people, of which the tribute for the LORD was 32.

⁴¹Moses gave the tribute to Eleazar the priest as the LORD's part, as the LORD commanded Moses.

⁴²The half belonging to the Israelites, which Moses set apart from that of the fighting men— ⁴³the community's half—was 337,500 sheep, ⁴⁴36,000 cattle, ⁴⁵30,500 donkeys ⁴⁶and 16,000 people. ⁴⁷From the Israelites' half, Moses selected one out of every fifty persons and animals, as the LORD commanded him, and gave them to the Levites, who were responsible for the care of the LORD's tabernacle.

⁴⁸Then the officers who were over the units of the army—the commanders of thousands and commanders of hundreds—went to Moses ⁴⁹and said to him, "Your servants have counted the soldiers under our command, and not one is missing. ⁵⁰So we have brought as an offering to the LORD the gold articles each of us acquired—armlets, bracelets, signet rings, earrings and necklaces—to make atonement for ourselves before the LORD."

⁵¹Moses and Eleazar the priest accepted from them the gold—all the crafted articles. ⁵²All the gold from the commanders of thousands and commanders of hundreds that Moses and Eleazar presented as a gift to the LORD weighed 16,750 shekels.ᵃ ⁵³Each soldier had taken plunder for himself. ⁵⁴Moses and Eleazar the priest accepted the gold from the commanders of thousands and commanders of hundreds and brought it into the Tent of Meeting as a memorial for the Israelites before the LORD.

The Transjordan Tribes

32 The Reubenites and Gadites, who had very large herds and flocks, saw that the lands of Jazer and Gilead were suitable for livestock. ²So they came to Moses and Eleazar the priest and to the leaders of the community, and said, ³"Ataroth, Dibon, Jazer, Nimrah, Heshbon, Elealeh, Sebam, Nebo and Beon— ⁴the land the LORD subdued before the people of Israel—are suitable for livestock, and your servants have livestock. ⁵If we have found favor in your eyes," they said, "let this land be given to your servants as our possession. Do not make us cross the Jordan."

⁶Moses said to the Gadites and Reubenites, "Shall your countrymen go to war while you sit here? ⁷Why do you discourage the Israelites from going over into the land the LORD has given them? ⁸This is what your fathers did when I sent them from Kadesh Barnea to look over the land. ⁹After they went up to the Valley of Eshcol and viewed the land, they discouraged the Israelites from entering the land the LORD had given them. ¹⁰The LORD's anger was aroused that day and he swore this oath: ¹¹'Because they have not followed me wholeheartedly, not one of the men twenty years old or more who came up out of Egypt will see the land I promised on oath to Abraham, Isaac and Jacob— ¹²not one except Caleb son of Jephunneh the Kenizzite and Joshua son of Nun, for they followed the LORD wholeheartedly.' ¹³The LORD's anger burned against Israel and he made them wander in the desert forty years, until the whole generation of those who had done evil in his sight was gone.

¹⁴"And here you are, a brood of sinners, standing in the place of your fathers and making the LORD even more angry with Israel. ¹⁵If you turn away from following him, he will again leave all this people in the desert, and you will be the cause of their destruction."

¹⁶Then they came up to him and said, "We would like to build pens here for our livestock and cities for our women and children. ¹⁷But we are ready to arm ourselves and go ahead of the Israelites until we have brought them to their place. Meanwhile our women and children will live in fortified cities, for protection from the inhabitants of the land. ¹⁸We will not return to our homes until every Israelite has received his inheritance. ¹⁹We will not receive any inheritance with them on the other side of the Jordan, because our inheritance has come to us on the east side of the Jordan."

²⁰Then Moses said to them, "If you will do this—if you will arm yourselves before the LORD for battle, ²¹and if all of you will go armed over the Jordan before the LORD until he has driven his enemies out before him— ²²then when the land is subdued before the LORD, you may return and be free from your obligation to the LORD and to Israel. And this land will be your possession before the LORD.

²³"But if you fail to do this, you will be sinning against the LORD; and you may be sure that your sin will find you out. ²⁴Build cities for your women and children, and pens for your flocks, but do what you have promised."

²⁵The Gadites and Reubenites said to Moses, "We your servants will do as our lord commands. ²⁶Our children and wives, our flocks and herds will remain

ᵃ 52 That is, about 420 pounds (about 190 kilograms)

here in the cities of Gilead. 27But your servants, every man armed for battle, will cross over to fight before the LORD, just as our lord says."

28Then Moses gave orders about them to Eleazar the priest and Joshua son of Nun and to the family heads of the Israelite tribes. 29He said to them, "If the Gadites and Reubenites, every man armed for battle, cross over the Jordan with you before the LORD, then when the land is subdued before you, give them the land of Gilead as their possession. 30But if they do not cross over with you armed, they must accept their possession with you in Canaan."

31The Gadites and Reubenites answered, "Your servants will do what the LORD has said. 32We will cross over before the LORD into Canaan armed, but the property we inherit will be on this side of the Jordan."

33Then Moses gave to the Gadites, the Reubenites and the half-tribe of Manasseh son of Joseph the kingdom of Sihon king of the Amorites and the kingdom of Og king of Bashan—the whole land with its cities and the territory around them.

34The Gadites built up Dibon, Ataroth, Aroer, 35Atroth Shophan, Jazer, Jogbehah, 36Beth Nimrah and Beth Haran as fortified cities, and built pens for their flocks. 37And the Reubenites rebuilt Heshbon, Elealeh and Kiriathaim, 38as well as Nebo and Baal Meon (these names were changed) and Sibmah. They gave names to the cities they rebuilt.

39The descendants of Makir son of Manasseh went to Gilead, captured it and drove out the Amorites who were there. 40So Moses gave Gilead to the Makirites, the descendants of Manasseh, and they settled there. 41Jair, a descendant of Manasseh, captured their settlements and called them Havvoth Jair.a 42And Nobah captured Kenath and its surrounding settlements and called it Nobah after himself.

Stages in Israel's Journey

33 Here are the stages in the journey of the Israelites when they came out of Egypt by divisions under the leadership of Moses and Aaron. 2At the LORD's command Moses recorded the stages in their journey. This is their journey by stages:

3The Israelites set out from Rameses on the fifteenth day of the first month, the day after the Passover. They marched out boldly in full view of all the Egyptians, 4who were burying all their firstborn, whom the LORD had struck down among them; for the LORD had brought judgment on their gods.

5The Israelites left Rameses and camped at Succoth.

6They left Succoth and camped at Etham, on the edge of the desert.

7They left Etham, turned back to Pi Hahiroth, to the east of Baal Zephon, and camped near Migdol.

8They left Pi Hahirothb and passed through the sea into the desert, and when they had traveled for three days in the Desert of Etham, they camped at Marah.

9They left Marah and went to Elim, where there were twelve springs and seventy palm trees, and they camped there.

10They left Elim and camped by the Red Sea.c

11They left the Red Sea and camped in the Desert of Sin.

12They left the Desert of Sin and camped at Dophkah.

13They left Dophkah and camped at Alush.

14They left Alush and camped at Rephidim, where there was no water for the people to drink.

15They left Rephidim and camped in the Desert of Sinai.

---

a 41 Or them the settlements of Jair   b 8 Many manuscripts of the Masoretic Text, Samaritan Pentateuch and Vulgate; most manuscripts of the Masoretic Text left from before Hahiroth   c 10 Hebrew Yam Suph; that is, Sea of Reeds; also in verse 11

¹⁶They left the Desert of Sinai and camped at Kibroth Hattaavah.

¹⁷They left Kibroth Hattaavah and camped at Hazeroth.

¹⁸They left Hazeroth and camped at Rithmah.

¹⁹They left Rithmah and camped at Rimmon Perez.

²⁰They left Rimmon Perez and camped at Libnah.

²¹They left Libnah and camped at Rissah.

²²They left Rissah and camped at Kehelathah.

²³They left Kehelathah and camped at Mount Shepher.

²⁴They left Mount Shepher and camped at Haradah.

²⁵They left Haradah and camped at Makheloth.

²⁶They left Makheloth and camped at Tahath.

²⁷They left Tahath and camped at Terah.

²⁸They left Terah and camped at Mithcah.

²⁹They left Mithcah and camped at Hashmonah.

³⁰They left Hashmonah and camped at Moseroth.

³¹They left Moseroth and camped at Bene Jaakan.

³²They left Bene Jaakan and camped at Hor Haggidgad.

³³They left Hor Haggidgad and camped at Jotbathah.

³⁴They left Jotbathah and camped at Abronah.

³⁵They left Abronah and camped at Ezion Geber.

³⁶They left Ezion Geber and camped at Kadesh, in the Desert of Zin.

³⁷They left Kadesh and camped at Mount Hor, on the border of Edom.

³⁸At the LORD's command Aaron the priest went up Mount Hor, where he died on the first day of the fifth month of the fortieth year after the Israelites came out of Egypt. ³⁹Aaron was a hundred and twenty-three years old when he died on Mount Hor.

⁴⁰The Canaanite king of Arad, who lived in the Negev of Canaan, heard that the Israelites were coming.

⁴¹They left Mount Hor and camped at Zalmonah.

⁴²They left Zalmonah and camped at Punon.

⁴³They left Punon and camped at Oboth.

⁴⁴They left Oboth and camped at Iye Abarim, on the border of Moab.

⁴⁵They left Iyim[a] and camped at Dibon Gad.

⁴⁶They left Dibon Gad and camped at Almon Diblathaim.

⁴⁷They left Almon Diblathaim and camped in the mountains of Abarim, near Nebo.

⁴⁸They left the mountains of Abarim and camped on the plains of Moab by the Jordan across from Jericho.[b] ⁴⁹There on the plains of Moab they camped along the Jordan from Beth Jeshimoth to Abel Shittim.

⁵⁰On the plains of Moab by the Jordan across from Jericho the LORD said to Moses, ⁵¹"Speak to the Israelites and say to them: 'When you cross the Jordan into Canaan, ⁵²drive out all the inhabitants of the land before you. Destroy all their carved images and their cast idols, and demolish all their high places. ⁵³Take possession of the land and settle in it, for I have given you the land to possess. ⁵⁴Distribute the land by lot, according to your clans. To a larger group give a larger inheritance, and to a smaller group a smaller one. Whatever falls to them by lot will be theirs. Distribute it according to your ancestral tribes.

⁵⁵"'But if you do not drive out the inhabitants of the land, those you allow to

---

ª 45 That is, Iye Abarim   ᵇ 48 Hebrew *Jordan of Jericho*; possibly an ancient name for the Jordan River; also in verse 50 remain will become barbs in your eyes and thorns in your sides. They will give you trouble in the land where you will live. ⁵⁶And then I will do to you what I plan to do to them.'"

Boundaries of Canaan

34 The LORD said to Moses, ²"Command the Israelites and say to them: 'When you enter Canaan, the land that will be allotted to you as an inheritance will have these boundaries:

³"'Your southern side will include some of the Desert of Zin along the border of Edom. On the east, your southern boundary will start from the end of the Salt Sea,ª ⁴cross south of Scorpionᵇ Pass, continue on to Zin and go south of Kadesh Barnea. Then it will go to Hazar Addar and over to Azmon, ⁵where it will turn, join the Wadi of Egypt and end at the Sea.ᶜ

⁶"'Your western boundary will be the coast of the Great Sea. This will be your boundary on the west.

⁷"'For your northern boundary, run a line from the Great Sea to Mount Hor ⁸and from Mount Hor to Leboᵈ Hamath. Then the boundary will go to Zedad, ⁹continue to Ziphron and end at Hazar Enan. This will be your boundary on the north.

¹⁰"'For your eastern boundary, run a line from Hazar Enan to Shepham. ¹¹The boundary will go down from Shepham to Riblah on the east side of Ain and continue along the slopes east of the Sea of Kinnereth.ᵉ ¹²Then the boundary will go down along the Jordan and end at the Salt Sea.

"'This will be your land, with its boundaries on every side.'"

¹³Moses commanded the Israelites: "Assign this land by lot as an inheritance. The LORD has ordered that it be given to the nine and a half tribes, ¹⁴because the families of the tribe of Reuben, the tribe of Gad and the half-tribe of Manasseh have received their inheritance. ¹⁵These two and a half tribes have received their inheritance on the east side of the Jordan of Jericho,ᶠ toward the sunrise."

¹⁶The LORD said to Moses, ¹⁷"These are the names of the men who are to assign the land for you as an inheritance: Eleazar the priest and Joshua son of Nun. ¹⁸And appoint one leader from each tribe to help assign the land. ¹⁹These are their names:

Caleb son of Jephunneh,
　　from the tribe of Judah;
²⁰Shemuel son of Ammihud,
　　from the tribe of Simeon;
²¹Elidad son of Kislon,
　　from the tribe of Benjamin;
²²Bukki son of Jogli,
　　the leader from the tribe of Dan;
²³Hanniel son of Ephod,
　　the leader from the tribe of Manasseh son of Joseph;
²⁴Kemuel son of Shiphtan,
　　the leader from the tribe of Ephraim son of Joseph;
²⁵Elizaphan son of Parnach,
　　the leader from the tribe of Zebulun;
²⁶Paltiel son of Azzan,
　　the leader from the tribe of Issachar;
²⁷Ahihud son of Shelomi,
　　the leader from the tribe of Asher;
²⁸Pedahel son of Ammihud,
　　the leader from the tribe of Naphtali."

²⁹These are the men the LORD commanded to assign the inheritance to the Israelites in the land of Canaan.

ª *3* That is, the Dead Sea; also in verse 12　ᵇ *4* Hebrew *Akrabbim*　ᶜ *5* That is, the Mediterranean; also in verses 6 and 7　ᵈ *8* Or *to the entrance to*　ᵉ *11* That is, Galilee　ᶠ *15 Jordan of Jericho* was possibly an ancient name for the Jordan River.

Towns for the Levites

35 On the plains of Moab by the Jordan across from Jericho,[a] the LORD said to Moses, 2"Command the Israelites to give the Levites towns to live in from the inheritance the Israelites will possess. And give them pasturelands around the towns. 3Then they will have towns to live in and pasturelands for their cattle, flocks and all their other livestock.

4"The pasturelands around the towns that you give the Levites will extend out fifteen hundred feet[b] from the town wall. 5Outside the town, measure three thousand feet[c] on the east side, three thousand on the south side, three thousand on the west and three thousand on the north, with the town in the center. They will have this area as pastureland for the towns.

Cities of Refuge

6"Six of the towns you give the Levites will be cities of refuge, to which a person who has killed someone may flee. In addition, give them forty-two other towns. 7In all you must give the Levites forty-eight towns, together with their pasturelands. 8The towns you give the Levites from the land the Israelites possess are to be given in proportion to the inheritance of each tribe: Take many towns from a tribe that has many, but few from one that has few."

9Then the LORD said to Moses: 10"Speak to the Israelites and say to them: 'When you cross the Jordan into Canaan, 11select some towns to be your cities of refuge, to which a person who has killed someone accidentally may flee. 12They will be places of refuge from the avenger, so that a person accused of murder may not die before he stands trial before the assembly. 13These six towns you give will be your cities of refuge. 14Give three on this side of the Jordan and three in Canaan as cities of refuge. 15These six towns will be a place of refuge for Israelites, aliens and any other people living among them, so that anyone who has killed another accidentally can flee there.

16"'If a man strikes someone with an iron object so that he dies, he is a murderer; the murderer shall be put to death. 17Or if anyone has a stone in his hand that could kill, and he strikes someone so that he dies, he is a murderer; the murderer shall be put to death. 18Or if anyone has a wooden object in his hand that could kill, and he hits someone so that he dies, he is a murderer; the murderer shall be put to death. 19The avenger of blood shall put the murderer to death; when he meets him, he shall put him to death. 20If anyone with malice aforethought shoves another or throws something at him intentionally so that he dies 21or if in hostility he hits him with his fist so that he dies, that person shall be put to death; he is a murderer. The avenger of blood shall put the murderer to death when he meets him.

22"'But if without hostility someone suddenly shoves another or throws something at him unintentionally 23or, without seeing him, drops a stone on him that could kill him, and he dies, then since he was not his enemy and he did not intend to harm him, 24the assembly must judge between him and the avenger of blood according to these regulations. 25The assembly must protect the one accused of murder from the avenger of blood and send him back to the city of refuge to which he fled. He must stay there until the death of the high priest, who was anointed with the holy oil.

26"'But if the accused ever goes outside the limits of the city of refuge to which he has fled 27and the avenger of blood finds him outside the city, the avenger of blood may kill the accused without being guilty of murder. 28The accused must stay in his city of refuge until the death of the high priest; only after the death

---

a 1 Hebrew *Jordan of Jericho*; possibly an ancient name for the Jordan River   b 4 Hebrew *a thousand cubits* (about 450 meters)
c 5 Hebrew *two thousand cubits* (about 900 meters)

of the high priest may he return to his own property.

29 "'These are to be legal requirements for you throughout the generations to come, wherever you live.

30 "'Anyone who kills a person is to be put to death as a murderer only on the testimony of witnesses. But no one is to be put to death on the testimony of only one witness.

31 "'Do not accept a ransom for the life of a murderer, who deserves to die. He must surely be put to death.

32 "'Do not accept a ransom for anyone who has fled to a city of refuge and so allow him to go back and live on his own land before the death of the high priest.

33 "'Do not pollute the land where you are. Bloodshed pollutes the land, and atonement cannot be made for the land on which blood has been shed, except by the blood of the one who shed it. 34Do not defile the land where you live and where I dwell, for I, the LORD, dwell among the Israelites.'"

Inheritance of Zelophehad's Daughters

36 The family heads of the clan of Gilead son of Makir, the son of Manasseh, who were from the clans of the descendants of Joseph, came and spoke before Moses and the leaders, the heads of the Israelite families. 2They said, "When the LORD commanded my lord to give the land as an inheritance to the Israelites by lot, he ordered you to give the inheritance of our brother Zelophehad to his daughters. 3Now suppose they marry men from other Israelite tribes; then their inheritance will be taken from our ancestral inheritance and added to that of the tribe they marry into. And so part of the inheritance allotted to us will be taken away. 4When the Year of Jubilee for the Israelites comes, their inheritance will be added to that of the tribe into which they marry, and their property will be taken from the tribal inheritance of our forefathers."

5Then at the LORD's command Moses gave this order to the Israelites: "What the tribe of the descendants of Joseph is saying is right. 6This is what the LORD commands for Zelophehad's daughters: They may marry anyone they please as long as they marry within the tribal clan of their father. 7No inheritance in Israel is to pass from tribe to tribe, for every Israelite shall keep the tribal land inherited from his forefathers. 8Every daughter who inherits land in any Israelite tribe must marry someone in her father's tribal clan, so that every Israelite will possess the inheritance of his fathers. 9No inheritance may pass from tribe to tribe, for each Israelite tribe is to keep the land it inherits."

10So Zelophehad's daughters did as the LORD commanded Moses. 11Zelophehad's daughters—Mahlah, Tirzah, Hoglah, Milcah and Noah—married their cousins on their father's side. 12They married within the clans of the descendants of Manasseh son of Joseph, and their inheritance remained in their father's clan and tribe.

13These are the commands and regulations the LORD gave through Moses to the Israelites on the plains of Moab by the Jordan across from Jericho.[a]

---

a 13 Hebrew *Jordan of Jericho*; possibly an ancient name for the Jordan River

Author: Moses (with the final section about Moses' death probably written by Joshua, his successor)

Date: About 1406 BC (shortly before Moses' death)

Audience: The younger generation of Israelites, which was preparing to enter the promised land

Prayer Themes:

- Ask God to deepen, broaden, and strengthen your love and devotion for Him (6:5).

- Ask God to do whatever He needs to do to humble you— so that you might depend on Him always (8:1-3).

- Ask God to help you understand that your daily choices have eternal consequences (chapter 28).

Here is the secret of not only a great prayer life, but a great life altogether: "It is the LORD your God you must follow, and him you must revere. Keep his commands and obey him; serve him and hold fast to him" (13:4).

Poised on the plains of Moab, the children of Israel are ready at long last to cross the Jordan River and move into the promised land. But before the members of this new generation begin their quest, they first need to be reminded of ultimate realities. In his final act of leadership, Moses gathers the 12 tribes and preaches a series of heartfelt sermons. He reviews God's Law and urges the youthful Israelites—and us—to love God wholly and pursue Him fiercely. Our thoughts, our prayers, our entire lives must revolve around Him.

Deuteronomy

The Command to Leave Horeb

1 These are the words Moses spoke to all Israel in the desert east of the Jordan—that is, in the Arabah—opposite Suph, between Paran and Tophel, Laban, Hazeroth and Dizahab. ²(It takes eleven days to go from Horeb to Kadesh Barnea by the Mount Seir road.)

³In the fortieth year, on the first day of the eleventh month, Moses proclaimed to the Israelites all that the LORD had commanded him concerning them. ⁴This was after he had defeated Sihon king of the Amorites, who reigned in Heshbon, and at Edrei had defeated Og king of Bashan, who reigned in Ashtaroth.

⁵East of the Jordan in the territory of Moab, Moses began to expound this law, saying:

⁶The LORD our God said to us at Horeb, "You have stayed long enough at this mountain. ⁷Break camp and advance into the hill country of the Amorites; go to all the neighboring peoples in the Arabah, in the mountains, in the western foothills, in the Negev and along the coast, to the land of the Canaanites and to Lebanon, as far as the great river, the Euphrates. ⁸See, I have given you this land. Go in and take possession of the land that the LORD swore he would give to your fathers—to Abraham, Isaac and Jacob—and to their descendants after them."

The Appointment of Leaders

⁹At that time I said to you, "You are too heavy a burden for me to carry alone. ¹⁰The LORD your God has increased your numbers so that today you are as many as the stars in the sky. ¹¹May the LORD, the God of your fathers, increase you a thousand times and bless you as he has promised! ¹²But how can I bear your problems and your burdens and your disputes all by myself? ¹³Choose some wise,

GOING

deeper

Do Not Be Afraid

READ AND CONSIDER: DEUTERONOMY 1:19-30

"See, the LORD your God has given you the land. Go up and take possession of it as the LORD, the God of your fathers, told you. Do not be afraid; do not be discouraged" (Deuteronomy 1:21).

Many of the people listening to these words had spent 40 long years in the desert. Their parents had stood at this very spot decades earlier, but they had let their fears overwhelm them. In punishment for that blatant lack of faith, God gave that generation a death sentence: "Not one of the men who saw my glory and the miraculous signs I performed in Egypt and in the desert but who disobeyed me and tested me ten times—not one of them will ever see the land I promised on oath to their forefathers" (Numbers 14:22-23). The nation wandered until all the rebellious people died.

That rebellious generation's children now stood poised in the same spot. And what was Moses' message to them? He recounted what had gone before. He told the story of their parents' rebellion and lack of faith. They needed to hear and understand. Would they be prone to the same fear and rebellion, or would they be different? Would they enter and possess the land in full confidence of God's promises? God said to them what He had said to their parents, "Do not be afraid; do not be discouraged."

Walking into a closer relationship with God can be like entering your own personal promised land. You know it's a good place, but it's still filled with unknowns. Following Jesus doesn't mean life is going to be easy. You'll still have giants to battle, territory to claim, and work to do. But God says regarding your journey with Him, "Do not be afraid; do not be discouraged." And the reason is because "the LORD your God, who is going before you, will fight for you."

You see, He already knows the unknowns. He knows about the giants. He has the battle plan. All you need to do is continually look to Him in prayer and follow His lead.

---

understanding and respected men from each of your tribes, and I will set them over you."

[14]You answered me, "What you propose to do is good."

[15]So I took the leading men of your tribes, wise and respected men, and appointed them to have authority over you—as commanders of thousands, of hundreds, of fifties and of tens and as tribal officials. [16]And I charged your judges at that time: Hear the disputes between your brothers and judge fairly, whether the case is between brother Israelites or between one of them and an alien. [17]Do not show partiality in judging; hear both small and great alike. Do not be afraid of any man, for judgment belongs to God.

Bring me any case too hard for you, and I will hear it. [18]And at that time I told you everything you were to do.

Spies Sent Out

[19]Then, as the LORD our God commanded us, we set out from Horeb and went toward the hill country of the Amorites through all that vast and dreadful desert that you have seen, and so we reached Kadesh Barnea. [20]Then I said to you, "You have reached the hill country of the Amorites, which the LORD our God is giving us. [21]See, the LORD your God has given you the land. Go up and take possession of it as the LORD, the God of your fathers, told you. Do not be afraid; do not be discouraged."

²²Then all of you came to me and said, "Let us send men ahead to spy out the land for us and bring back a report about the route we are to take and the towns we will come to."

²³The idea seemed good to me; so I selected twelve of you, one man from each tribe. ²⁴They left and went up into the hill country, and came to the Valley of Eshcol and explored it. ²⁵Taking with them some of the fruit of the land, they brought it down to us and reported, "It is a good land that the LORD our God is giving us."

Rebellion Against the LORD

²⁶But you were unwilling to go up; you rebelled against the command of the LORD your God. ²⁷You grumbled in your tents and said, "The LORD hates us; so he brought us out of Egypt to deliver us into the hands of the Amorites to destroy us. ²⁸Where can we go? Our brothers have made us lose heart. They say, 'The people are stronger and taller than we are; the cities are large, with walls up to the sky. We even saw the Anakites there.'"

²⁹Then I said to you, "Do not be terrified; do not be afraid of them. ³⁰The LORD your God, who is going before you, will fight for you, as he did for you in Egypt, before your very eyes, ³¹and in the desert. There you saw how the LORD your God carried you, as a father carries his son, all the way you went until you reached this place."

³²In spite of this, you did not trust in the LORD your God, ³³who went ahead of you on your journey, in fire by night and in a cloud by day, to search out places for you to camp and to show you the way you should go.

³⁴When the LORD heard what you said, he was angry and solemnly swore: ³⁵"Not a man of this evil generation shall see the good land I swore to give your forefathers, ³⁶except Caleb son of Jephunneh. He will see it, and I will give him and his descendants the land he set his feet on, because he followed the LORD wholeheartedly."

³⁷Because of you the LORD became angry with me also and said, "You shall not enter it, either. ³⁸But your assistant, Joshua son of Nun, will enter it. Encourage him, because he will lead Israel to inherit it. ³⁹And the little ones that you said would be taken captive, your children who do not yet know good from bad—they will enter the land. I will give it to them and they will take possession of it. ⁴⁰But as for you, turn around and set out toward the desert along the route to the Red Sea.ᵃ"

⁴¹Then you replied, "We have sinned against the LORD. We will go up and fight, as the LORD our God commanded us." So every one of you put on his weapons, thinking it easy to go up into the hill country.

⁴²But the LORD said to me, "Tell them, 'Do not go up and fight, because I will not be with you. You will be defeated by your enemies.'"

Praying Deuteronomy 1:43-45
Help me to always listen to You,
Lord, and not rebelliously assume that
I know the right thing to do.

⁴³So I told you, but you would not listen. You rebelled against the LORD's command and in your arrogance you marched up into the hill country. ⁴⁴The Amorites who lived in those hills came out against you; they chased you like a swarm of bees and beat you down from Seir all the way to Hormah. ⁴⁵You came back and wept before the LORD, but he paid no attention to your weeping and turned a deaf ear to you. ⁴⁶And so you stayed in Kadesh many days—all the time you spent there.

Wanderings in the Desert

2 Then we turned back and set out toward the desert along the route to the Red Sea,ᵃ as the LORD had directed me.

ᵃ 40,1 Hebrew *Yam Suph*; that is, Sea of Reeds

For a long time we made our way around the hill country of Seir.

2 Then the LORD said to me, 3 "You have made your way around this hill country long enough; now turn north. 4 Give the people these orders: 'You are about to pass through the territory of your brothers the descendants of Esau, who live in Seir. They will be afraid of you, but be very careful. 5 Do not provoke them to war, for I will not give you any of their land, not even enough to put your foot on. I have given Esau the hill country of Seir as his own. 6 You are to pay them in silver for the food you eat and the water you drink.' "

7 The LORD your God has blessed you in all the work of your hands. He has watched over your journey through this vast desert. These forty years the LORD your God has been with you, and you have not lacked anything.

8 So we went on past our brothers the descendants of Esau, who live in Seir. We turned from the Arabah road, which comes up from Elath and Ezion Geber, and traveled along the desert road of Moab.

9 Then the LORD said to me, "Do not harass the Moabites or provoke them to war, for I will not give you any part of their land. I have given Ar to the descendants of Lot as a possession."

10 (The Emites used to live there—a people strong and numerous, and as tall as the Anakites. 11 Like the Anakites, they too were considered Rephaites, but the Moabites called them Emites. 12 Horites used to live in Seir, but the descendants of Esau drove them out. They destroyed the Horites from before them and settled in their place, just as Israel did in the land the LORD gave them as their possession.)

13 And the LORD said, "Now get up and cross the Zered Valley." So we crossed the valley.

14 Thirty-eight years passed from the time we left Kadesh Barnea until we crossed the Zered Valley. By then, that entire generation of fighting men had perished from the camp, as the LORD had sworn to them. 15 The LORD's hand was against them until he had completely eliminated them from the camp.

16 Now when the last of these fighting men among the people had died, 17 the LORD said to me, 18 "Today you are to pass by the region of Moab at Ar. 19 When you come to the Ammonites, do not harass them or provoke them to war, for I will not give you possession of any land belonging to the Ammonites. I have given it as a possession to the descendants of Lot."

20 (That too was considered a land of the Rephaites, who used to live there; but the Ammonites called them Zamzummites. 21 They were a people strong and numerous, and as tall as the Anakites. The LORD destroyed them from before the Ammonites, who drove them out and settled in their place. 22 The LORD had done the same for the descendants of Esau, who lived in Seir, when he destroyed the Horites from before them. They drove them out and have lived in their place to this day. 23 And as for the Avvites who lived in villages as far as Gaza, the Caphtorites coming out from Caphtor[a] destroyed them and settled in their place.)

Defeat of Sihon King of Heshbon

24 "Set out now and cross the Arnon Gorge. See, I have given into your hand Sihon the Amorite, king of Heshbon, and his country. Begin to take possession of it and engage him in battle. 25 This very day I will begin to put the terror and fear of you on all the nations under heaven. They will hear reports of you and will tremble and be in anguish because of you."

26 From the desert of Kedemoth I sent messengers to Sihon king of Heshbon offering peace and saying, 27 "Let us pass through your country. We will stay on the main road; we will not turn aside to the right or to the left. 28 Sell us food to

---

a 23 That is, Crete

eat and water to drink for their price in silver. Only let us pass through on foot— [29]as the descendants of Esau, who live in Seir, and the Moabites, who live in Ar, did for us—until we cross the Jordan into the land the LORD our God is giving us." [30]But Sihon king of Heshbon refused to let us pass through. For the LORD your God had made his spirit stubborn and his heart obstinate in order to give him into your hands, as he has now done.

[31]The LORD said to me, "See, I have begun to deliver Sihon and his country over to you. Now begin to conquer and possess his land."

[32]When Sihon and all his army came out to meet us in battle at Jahaz, [33]the LORD our God delivered him over to us and we struck him down, together with his sons and his whole army. [34]At that time we took all his towns and completely destroyed[a] them—men, women and children. We left no survivors. [35]But the livestock and the plunder from the towns we had captured we carried off for ourselves. [36]From Aroer on the rim of the Arnon Gorge, and from the town in the gorge, even as far as Gilead, not one town was too strong for us. The LORD our God gave us all of them. [37]But in accordance with the command of the LORD our God, you did not encroach on any of the land of the Ammonites, neither the land along the course of the Jabbok nor that around the towns in the hills.

Defeat of Og King of Bashan

3 Next we turned and went up along the road toward Bashan, and Og king of Bashan with his whole army marched out to meet us in battle at Edrei. [2]The LORD said to me, "Do not be afraid of him, for I have handed him over to you with his whole army and his land. Do to him what you did to Sihon king of the Amorites, who reigned in Heshbon."

[3]So the LORD our God also gave into our hands Og king of Bashan and all his army. We struck them down, leaving no survivors. [4]At that time we took all his cities. There was not one of the sixty cities that we did not take from them—the whole region of Argob, Og's kingdom in Bashan. [5]All these cities were fortified with high walls and with gates and bars, and there were also a great many unwalled villages. [6]We completely destroyed[a] them, as we had done with Sihon king of Heshbon, destroying[a] every city—men, women and children. [7]But all the livestock and the plunder from their cities we carried off for ourselves.

[8]So at that time we took from these two kings of the Amorites the territory east of the Jordan, from the Arnon Gorge as far as Mount Hermon. [9](Hermon is called Sirion by the Sidonians; the Amorites call it Senir.) [10]We took all the towns on the plateau, and all Gilead, and all Bashan as far as Salecah and Edrei, towns of Og's kingdom in Bashan. [11](Only Og king of Bashan was left of the remnant of the Rephaites. His bed[b] was made of iron and was more than thirteen feet long and six feet wide.[c] It is still in Rabbah of the Ammonites.)

Division of the Land

[12]Of the land that we took over at that time, I gave the Reubenites and the Gadites the territory north of Aroer by the Arnon Gorge, including half the hill country of Gilead, together with its towns. [13]The rest of Gilead and also all of Bashan, the kingdom of Og, I gave to the half-tribe of Manasseh. (The whole region of Argob in Bashan used to be known as a land of the Rephaites. [14]Jair, a descendant of Manasseh, took the whole region of Argob as far as the border of the Geshurites and the Maacathites; it was named after him, so that to this day Bashan is called Havvoth Jair.[d]) [15]And I gave Gilead to Makir. [16]But to the Reubenites and the Gadites I

---

[a] *34,6* The Hebrew term refers to the irrevocable giving over of things or persons to the LORD, often by totally destroying them.
[b] *11* Or *sarcophagus*   [c] *11* Hebrew *nine cubits long and four cubits wide* (about 4 meters long and 1.8 meters wide)
[d] *14* Or *called the settlements of Jair*

gave the territory extending from Gilead down to the Arnon Gorge (the middle of the gorge being the border) and out to the Jabbok River, which is the border of the Ammonites. [17]Its western border was the Jordan in the Arabah, from Kinnereth to the Sea of the Arabah (the Salt Sea[a]), below the slopes of Pisgah.

these two kings. The LORD will do the same to all the kingdoms over there where you are going. [22]Do not be afraid of them; the LORD your God himself will fight for you."

[23]At that time I pleaded with the LORD: [24]"O Sovereign LORD, you have begun to show to your servant your greatness and

---

God's people at prayer
MOSES PRAYED HIS HEART'S DESIRE

DEUTERONOMY 3:23-25 The sentence had already been pronounced. Moses, leader of the people of Israel, would not be able to enter the promised land. This sentence boiled down to one mistake, but the outcome was unchangeable. If you had been in Moses' sandals, what kind of prayer would you have prayed?

Even though Moses was facing the consequences of his own actions, he laid his heart's desire once more before the Lord: "Let me go over and see the good land." Moses had been able to avert God's judgment in various intercessions in the past, but not this time. God's answer was final.

Moses never did get to enter the land, but he was able to see it from the top of a mountain. Even when we pray for something, we may not get exactly what we want, exactly the way we want it. But don't let that stop you from praying to God about your heart's desire. And after you pray, thank God for accomplishing His perfect will in your life. Tell Him you trust that His answer is best.

---

[18]I commanded you at that time: "The LORD your God has given you this land to take possession of it. But all your able-bodied men, armed for battle, must cross over ahead of your brother Israelites. [19]However, your wives, your children and your livestock (I know you have much livestock) may stay in the towns I have given you, [20]until the LORD gives rest to your brothers as he has to you, and they too have taken over the land that the LORD your God is giving them, across the Jordan. After that, each of you may go back to the possession I have given you."

Moses Forbidden to Cross the Jordan

[21]At that time I commanded Joshua: "You have seen with your own eyes all that the LORD your God has done to

your strong hand. For what god is there in heaven or on earth who can do the deeds and mighty works you do? [25]Let me go over and see the good land beyond the Jordan—that fine hill country and Lebanon."

[26]But because of you the LORD was angry with me and would not listen to me. "That is enough," the LORD said. "Do not speak to me anymore about this matter. [27]Go up to the top of Pisgah and look west and north and south and east. Look at the land with your own eyes, since you are not going to cross this Jordan. [28]But commission Joshua, and encourage and strengthen him, for he will lead this people across and will cause them to inherit the land that you will see." [29]So we stayed in the valley near Beth Peor.

---

[a] 17 That is, the Dead Sea

Obedience Commanded

4 Hear now, O Israel, the decrees and laws I am about to teach you. Follow them so that you may live and may go in and take possession of the land that the LORD, the God of your fathers, is giving you. ²Do not add to what I command you and do not subtract from it, but keep the commands of the LORD your God that I give you.

³You saw with your own eyes what the LORD did at Baal Peor. The LORD your God destroyed from among you everyone who followed the Baal of Peor, ⁴but all of you who held fast to the LORD your God are still alive today.

⁵See, I have taught you decrees and laws as the LORD my God commanded me, so that you may follow them in the land you are entering to take possession of it. ⁶Observe them carefully, for this will show your wisdom and understanding to the nations, who will hear about all these decrees and say, "Surely this great nation is a wise and understanding people." ⁷What other nation is so great as to have their gods near them the way the LORD our God is near us whenever we pray to him? ⁸And what other nation is so great as to have such righteous decrees and laws as this body of laws I am setting before you today?

⁹Only be careful, and watch yourselves closely so that you do not forget the things your eyes have seen or let them slip from your heart as long as you live. Teach them to your children and to their children after them. ¹⁰Remember the day you stood before the LORD your God at Horeb, when he said to me,

GOING *deeper*

God Is Near When We Pray

READ AND CONSIDER: DEUTERONOMY 4:1-14

"What other nation is so great as to have their gods near them the way the LORD our God is near us whenever we pray to him?" (Deuteronomy 4:7).

It is comforting to know that whenever we pray to our God, He is present with us. The truths that Moses was teaching to the Israelites still hold true for believers today. Our God is alive, He is close, He is responsive. The Lord is here to listen and to bring wisdom, insight, and transformation into hopeless situations. He is here to protect and guide His people on the paths He desires them to walk.

Moses reassured the Israelites about their privileged status as the people of God. He reminded them that they were not like the people of foreign lands whose gods could not respond to them. Their God would remain with them at all times and would hear their prayers whenever they called on Him.

What does this mean for us? Does it mean that God isn't close to us unless we are praying? No. He is always with us, just as His presence traveled constantly with the Israelites to guide them. However, when we pray, we are drawn into a deeper awareness of His presence and a clearer understanding of His nature. Prayer reminds us of who we are in relationship to Him. Prayer puts us in a place where we can hear from Him and be changed by Him. No amount of prayer to a lifeless idol could ever accomplish that. We pray to a living and responsive God who loves us and wants to be an active part of our lives. When we don't pray, we miss out on the benefits of a close walk with Him. Draw near to Him in prayer right now and sense His presence in and around you.

"Assemble the people before me to hear my words so that they may learn to revere me as long as they live in the land and may teach them to their children." ¹¹You came near and stood at the foot of the mountain while it blazed with fire to the very heavens, with black clouds and deep darkness. ¹²Then the LORD spoke to you out of the fire. You heard the sound of words but saw no form; there was only a voice. ¹³He declared to you his covenant, the Ten Commandments, which he commanded you to follow and then wrote them on two stone tablets. ¹⁴And the LORD directed me at that time to teach you the decrees and laws you are to follow in the land that you are crossing the Jordan to possess.

Idolatry Forbidden

¹⁵You saw no form of any kind the day the LORD spoke to you at Horeb out of the fire. Therefore watch yourselves very carefully, ¹⁶so that you do not become corrupt and make for yourselves an idol, an image of any shape, whether formed like a man or a woman, ¹⁷or like any animal on earth or any bird that flies in the air, ¹⁸or like any creature that moves along the ground or any fish in the waters below. ¹⁹And when you look up to the sky and see the sun, the moon and the stars—all the heavenly array—do not be enticed into bowing down to them and worshiping things the LORD your God has apportioned to all the nations under heaven. ²⁰But as for you, the LORD took you and brought you out of the iron-smelting furnace, out of Egypt, to be the people of his inheritance, as you now are.

²¹The LORD was angry with me because of you, and he solemnly swore that I would not cross the Jordan and enter the good land the LORD your God is giving you as your inheritance. ²²I will die in this land; I will not cross the Jordan; but you are about to cross over and take possession of that good land. ²³Be careful not to forget the covenant of the LORD your God that he made with you; do not make for yourselves an idol in the form of anything the LORD your God has forbidden. ²⁴For the LORD your God is a consuming fire, a jealous God.

²⁵After you have had children and grandchildren and have lived in the land a long time—if you then become corrupt and make any kind of idol, doing evil in the eyes of the LORD your God and provoking him to anger, ²⁶I call heaven and earth as witnesses against you this day that you will quickly perish from the land that you are crossing the Jordan to possess. You will not live there long but will certainly be destroyed. ²⁷The LORD will scatter you among the peoples, and only a few of you will survive among the nations to which the LORD will drive you. ²⁸There you will worship man-made gods of wood and stone, which cannot see or hear or eat or smell. ²⁹But if from there you seek the LORD your God, you will find him if you look for him with all your heart and with all your soul. ³⁰When you are in distress and all these things have happened to you, then in later days you will return to the LORD your God and obey him. ³¹For the LORD your God is a merciful God; he will not abandon or destroy you or forget the covenant with your forefathers, which he confirmed to them by oath.

The LORD Is God

³²Ask now about the former days, long before your time, from the day God created man on the earth; ask from one end of the heavens to the other. Has anything so great as this ever happened, or has anything like it ever been heard of? ³³Has any other people heard the voice of God[a] speaking out of fire, as you have, and lived? ³⁴Has any god ever tried to take for himself one nation out of another nation, by testings, by miraculous signs and wonders, by war, by a mighty hand and an outstretched arm, or by great and awesome deeds, like all the things the LORD

ᵃ 33 Or of a god

your God did for you in Egypt before your very eyes?

35 You were shown these things so that you might know that the LORD is God; besides him there is no other. 36 From heaven he made you hear his voice to discipline you. On earth he showed you his great fire, and you heard his words from out of the fire. 37 Because he loved your forefathers and chose their descendants after them, he brought you out of Egypt by his Presence and his great strength, 38 to drive out before you nations greater and stronger than you and to bring you into their land to give it to you for your inheritance, as it is today.

Praying Deuteronomy 4:37-40

Thank You, God, that You will bring me out of hard places with Your presence and Your power.

39 Acknowledge and take to heart this day that the LORD is God in heaven above and on the earth below. There is no other. 40 Keep his decrees and commands, which I am giving you today, so that it may go well with you and your children after you and that you may live long in the land the LORD your God gives you for all time.

Cities of Refuge

41 Then Moses set aside three cities east of the Jordan, 42 to which anyone who had killed a person could flee if he had unintentionally killed his neighbor without malice aforethought. He could flee into one of these cities and save his life. 43 The cities were these: Bezer in the desert plateau, for the Reubenites; Ramoth in Gilead, for the Gadites; and Golan in Bashan, for the Manassites.

Introduction to the Law

44 This is the law Moses set before the Israelites. 45 These are the stipulations, decrees and laws Moses gave them when they came out of Egypt 46 and were in the valley near Beth Peor east of the Jordan,

in the land of Sihon king of the Amorites, who reigned in Heshbon and was defeated by Moses and the Israelites as they came out of Egypt. 47 They took possession of his land and the land of Og king of Bashan, the two Amorite kings east of the Jordan. 48 This land extended from Aroer on the rim of the Arnon Gorge to Mount Siyon[a] (that is, Hermon), 49 and included all the Arabah east of the Jordan, as far as the Sea of the Arabah,[b] below the slopes of Pisgah.

The Ten Commandments

5 Moses summoned all Israel and said:
Hear, O Israel, the decrees and laws I declare in your hearing today. Learn them and be sure to follow them. 2 The LORD our God made a covenant with us at Horeb. 3 It was not with our fathers that the LORD made this covenant, but with us, with all of us who are alive here today. 4 The LORD spoke to you face to face out of the fire on the mountain. 5 (At that time I stood between the LORD and you to declare to you the word of the LORD, because you were afraid of the fire and did not go up the mountain.) And he said:

6 "I am the LORD your God, who brought you out of Egypt, out of the land of slavery.

7 "You shall have no other gods before[c] me.

8 "You shall not make for yourself an idol in the form of anything in heaven above or on the earth beneath or in the waters below. 9 You shall not bow down to them or worship them; for I, the LORD your God, am a jealous God, punishing the children for the sin of the fathers to the third and fourth generation of those who hate me, 10 but showing love to a thousand ⌊generations⌋ of those who love me and keep my commandments.

---

a 48 Hebrew; Syriac (see also Deut. 3:9) *Sirion*   b 49 That is, the Dead Sea   c 7 Or *besides*

11 "You shall not misuse the name of the LORD your God, for the LORD will not hold anyone guiltless who misuses his name.
12 "Observe the Sabbath day by keeping it holy, as the LORD your God has commanded you. 13 Six days you shall labor and do all your work, 14 but the seventh day is a Sabbath to the LORD your God. On it you shall not do any work, neither you, nor your son or daughter, nor your manservant or maidservant, nor your ox, your donkey or any of your animals, nor the alien within your gates, so that your manservant and maidservant may rest, as you do. 15 Remember that you were slaves in Egypt and that the LORD your God brought you out of there with a mighty hand and an outstretched arm. Therefore the LORD your God has commanded you to observe the Sabbath day.
16 "Honor your father and your mother, as the LORD your God has commanded you, so that you may live long and that it may go well with you in the land the LORD your God is giving you.
17 "You shall not murder.
18 "You shall not commit adultery.
19 "You shall not steal.
20 "You shall not give false testimony against your neighbor.
21 "You shall not covet your neighbor's wife. You shall not set your desire on your neighbor's house or land, his manservant or maidservant, his ox or donkey, or anything that belongs to your neighbor."

22 These are the commandments the LORD proclaimed in a loud voice to your whole assembly there on the mountain from out of the fire, the cloud and the deep darkness; and he added nothing more. Then he wrote them on two stone tablets and gave them to me.

23 When you heard the voice out of the darkness, while the mountain was ablaze with fire, all the leading men of your tribes and your elders came to me. 24 And you said, "The LORD our God has shown us his glory and his majesty, and we have heard his voice from the fire. Today we have seen that a man can live even if God speaks with him. 25 But now, why should we die? This great fire will consume us, and we will die if we hear the voice of the LORD our God any longer. 26 For what mortal man has ever heard the voice of the living God speaking out of fire, as we have, and survived? 27 Go near and listen to all that the LORD our God says. Then tell us whatever the LORD our God tells you. We will listen and obey."

Prayer is . . .
fulfilling your main purpose on earth, which is to love, serve, and worship God.

28 The LORD heard you when you spoke to me and the LORD said to me, "I have heard what this people said to you. Everything they said was good. 29 Oh, that their hearts would be inclined to fear me and keep all my commands always, so that it might go well with them and their children forever!
30 "Go, tell them to return to their tents. 31 But you stay here with me so that I may give you all the commands, decrees and laws you are to teach them to follow in the land I am giving them to possess."
32 So be careful to do what the LORD your God has commanded you; do not turn aside to the right or to the left.

[33]Walk in all the way that the LORD your God has commanded you, so that you may live and prosper and prolong your days in the land that you will possess.

Love the LORD Your God

6 These are the commands, decrees and laws the LORD your God directed me to teach you to observe in the land that you are crossing the Jordan to possess, [2]so that you, your children and their children after them may fear the LORD your God as long as you live by keeping all his decrees and commands that I give you, and so that you may enjoy long life. [3]Hear, O Israel, and be careful to obey so that it may go well with you and that you may increase greatly in a land flowing with milk and honey, just as the LORD, the God of your fathers, promised you.

[4]Hear, O Israel: The LORD our God, the LORD is one.[a] [5]Love the LORD your God with all your heart and with all your soul and with all your strength. [6]These commandments that I give you today are to be upon your hearts. [7]Impress them on your children. Talk about them when you sit at home and when you walk along the road, when you lie down and when you get up. [8]Tie them as symbols on your hands and bind them on your foreheads. [9]Write them on the doorframes of your houses and on your gates.

[10]When the LORD your God brings you into the land he swore to your fathers, to Abraham, Isaac and Jacob, to give you—a land with large, flourishing cities you did not build, [11]houses filled with all kinds of good things you did not provide, wells you did not dig, and vineyards and olive groves you did not plant—then when you eat and are satisfied, [12]be careful that you do not forget the LORD, who brought you out of Egypt, out of the land of slavery.

[13]Fear the LORD your God, serve him only and take your oaths in his name.

[14]Do not follow other gods, the gods of the peoples around you; [15]for the LORD your God, who is among you, is a jealous God and his anger will burn against you, and he will destroy you from the face of the land. [16]Do not test the LORD your God as you did at Massah. [17]Be sure to keep the commands of the LORD your God and the stipulations and decrees he has given you. [18]Do what is right and good in the LORD's sight, so that it may go well with you and you may go in and take over the good land that the LORD promised on oath to your forefathers, [19]thrusting out all your enemies before you, as the LORD said.

[20]In the future, when your son asks you, "What is the meaning of the stipulations, decrees and laws the LORD our God has commanded you?" [21]tell him: "We were slaves of Pharaoh in Egypt, but the LORD brought us out of Egypt with a mighty hand. [22]Before our eyes the LORD sent miraculous signs and wonders—great and terrible—upon Egypt and Pharaoh and his whole household. [23]But he brought us out from there to bring us in and give us the land that he promised on oath to our forefathers. [24]The LORD commanded us to obey all these decrees and to fear the LORD our God, so that we might always prosper and be kept alive, as is the case today. [25]And if we are careful to obey all this law before the LORD our God, as he has commanded us, that will be our righteousness."

Driving Out the Nations

7 When the LORD your God brings you into the land you are entering to possess and drives out before you many nations—the Hittites, Girgashites, Amorites, Canaanites, Perizzites, Hivites and Jebusites, seven nations larger and stronger than you— [2]and when the LORD your God has delivered them over to you and you have defeated them, then you must destroy them totally.[b] Make

---

[a]4 Or *The LORD our God is one LORD*; or *The LORD is our God, the LORD is one*; or *The LORD is our God, the LORD alone*   [b]2 The Hebrew term refers to the irrevocable giving over of things or persons to the LORD, often by totally destroying them; also in verse 26.

no treaty with them, and show them no mercy. ³Do not intermarry with them. Do not give your daughters to their sons or take their daughters for your sons, ⁴for they will turn your sons away from following me to serve other gods, and the LORD's anger will burn against you and will quickly destroy you. ⁵This is what you are to do to them: Break down their altars, smash their sacred stones, cut down their Asherah poles^a and burn their idols in the fire. ⁶For you are a people holy to the LORD your God. The LORD your God has chosen you out of all the peoples on the face of the earth to be his people, his treasured possession.

⁷The LORD did not set his affection on you and choose you because you were more numerous than other peoples, for you were the fewest of all peoples. ⁸But it was because the LORD loved you and kept the oath he swore to your forefathers that he brought you out with a mighty hand and redeemed you from the land of slavery, from the power of Pharaoh king of Egypt. ⁹Know therefore that the LORD your God is God; he is the faithful God, keeping his covenant of love to a thousand generations of those who love him and keep his commands. ¹⁰But

those who hate him he will repay to
    their face by destruction;
he will not be slow to repay to their
    face those who hate him.

¹¹Therefore, take care to follow the commands, decrees and laws I give you today.

¹²If you pay attention to these laws and are careful to follow them, then the LORD your God will keep his covenant of love with you, as he swore to your forefathers. ¹³He will love you and bless you and increase your numbers. He will bless the fruit of your womb, the crops of your land—your grain, new wine and oil—the calves of your herds and the lambs of your flocks in the land that he swore to your forefathers to give you. ¹⁴You will be blessed more than any other people; none of your men or women will be childless, nor any of your livestock without young. ¹⁵The LORD will keep you free from every disease. He will not inflict on you the horrible diseases you knew in Egypt, but he will inflict them on all who hate you. ¹⁶You must destroy all the peoples the LORD your God gives over to you. Do not look on them with pity and do not serve their gods, for that will be a snare to you.

Praying Deuteronomy 7:15

Thank You, holy Father, for taking all sickness and disease away from me.

¹⁷You may say to yourselves, "These nations are stronger than we are. How can we drive them out?" ¹⁸But do not be afraid of them; remember well what the LORD your God did to Pharaoh and to all Egypt. ¹⁹You saw with your own eyes the great trials, the miraculous signs and wonders, the mighty hand and outstretched arm, with which the LORD your God brought you out. The LORD your God will do the same to all the peoples you now fear. ²⁰Moreover, the LORD your God will send the hornet among them until even the survivors who hide from you have perished. ²¹Do not be terrified by them, for the LORD your God, who is among you, is a great and awesome God. ²²The LORD your God will drive out those nations before you, little by little. You will not be allowed to eliminate them all at once, or the wild animals will multiply around you. ²³But the LORD your God will deliver them over to you, throwing them into great confusion until they are destroyed. ²⁴He will give their kings into your hand, and you will wipe out their names from under heaven. No one will be able to stand up against you; you will destroy them. ²⁵The images of

---

^a 5 That is, symbols of the goddess Asherah; here and elsewhere in Deuteronomy their gods you are to burn in the fire. Do not covet the silver and gold on them, and do not take it for yourselves, or you will be ensnared by it, for it is detestable to the LORD your God. 26Do not bring a detestable thing into your house or you, like it, will be set apart for destruction. Utterly abhor and detest it, for it is set apart for destruction.

Praying Deuteronomy 7:26

Lord, show me if I have brought anything into my home that is detestable in Your sight.

Do Not Forget the LORD

8 Be careful to follow every command I am giving you today, so that you may live and increase and may enter and possess the land that the LORD promised on oath to your forefathers. 2Remember how the LORD your God led you all the way in the desert these forty years, to humble you and to test you in order to know what was in your heart, whether or not you would keep his commands. 3He humbled you, causing you to hunger and then feeding you with manna, which neither you nor your fathers had known, to teach you that man does not live on bread alone but on every word that comes from the mouth of the LORD. 4Your clothes did not wear out and your feet did not swell during these forty years. 5Know then in your heart that as a man disciplines his son, so the LORD your God disciplines you.

6Observe the commands of the LORD your God, walking in his ways and revering him. 7For the LORD your God is bringing you into a good land—a land with streams and pools of water, with springs flowing in the valleys and hills; 8a land with wheat and barley, vines and fig trees, pomegranates, olive oil and honey; 9a land where bread will not be scarce and you will lack nothing; a land where the rocks are iron and you can dig copper out of the hills.

10When you have eaten and are satisfied, praise the LORD your God for the good land he has given you. 11Be careful that you do not forget the LORD your God, failing to observe his commands, his laws and his decrees that I am giving you this day. 12Otherwise, when you eat and are satisfied, when you build fine houses and settle down, 13and when your herds and flocks grow large and your silver and gold increase and all you have is multiplied, 14then your heart will become proud and you will forget the LORD your God, who brought you out of Egypt, out of the land of slavery. 15He led you through the vast and dreadful desert, that thirsty and waterless land, with its venomous snakes and scorpions. He brought you water out of hard rock. 16He gave you manna to eat in the desert, something your fathers had never known, to humble and to test you so that in the end it might go well with you. 17You may say to yourself, "My power and the strength of my hands have produced this wealth for me." 18But remember the LORD your God, for it is he who gives you the ability to produce wealth, and so confirms his covenant, which he swore to your forefathers, as it is today.

19If you ever forget the LORD your God and follow other gods and worship and bow down to them, I testify against you today that you will surely be destroyed. 20Like the nations the LORD destroyed before you, so you will be destroyed for not obeying the LORD your God.

Not Because of Israel's Righteousness

9 Hear, O Israel. You are now about to cross the Jordan to go in and dispossess nations greater and stronger than you, with large cities that have walls up to the sky. 2The people are strong and tall—Anakites! You know about them and have heard it said: "Who can stand up against the Anakites?" 3But be assured today that the LORD your God is the one who goes across ahead of you like a devouring fire. He will destroy them; he

will subdue them before you. And you will drive them out and annihilate them quickly, as the LORD has promised you.

⁴After the LORD your God has driven them out before you, do not say to yourself, "The LORD has brought me here to take possession of this land because of my righteousness." No, it is on account of the wickedness of these nations that the LORD is going to drive them out before you. ⁵It is not because of your righteousness or your integrity that you are going in to take possession of their land; but on account of the wickedness of these nations, the LORD your God will drive them out before you, to accomplish what he swore to your fathers, to Abraham, Isaac and Jacob. ⁶Understand, then, that it is not because of your righteousness that the LORD your God is giving you this good land to possess, for you are a stiff-necked people.

The Golden Calf

⁷Remember this and never forget how you provoked the LORD your God to anger in the desert. From the day you left Egypt until you arrived here, you have been rebellious against the LORD. ⁸At Horeb you aroused the LORD's wrath so that he was angry enough to destroy you. ⁹When I went up on the mountain to receive the tablets of stone, the tablets of the covenant that the LORD had made with you, I stayed on the mountain forty days and forty nights; I ate no bread and drank no water. ¹⁰The LORD gave me two stone tablets inscribed by the finger of God. On them were all the commandments the LORD proclaimed to you on the mountain out of the fire, on the day of the assembly.

¹¹At the end of the forty days and forty nights, the LORD gave me the two stone tablets, the tablets of the covenant. ¹²Then the LORD told me, "Go down from here at once, because your people whom you brought out of Egypt have become corrupt. They have turned away quickly from what I commanded them and have made a cast idol for themselves."

¹³And the LORD said to me, "I have seen this people, and they are a stiff-necked people indeed! ¹⁴Let me alone, so that I may destroy them and blot out their name from under heaven. And I will make you into a nation stronger and more numerous than they."

¹⁵So I turned and went down from the mountain while it was ablaze with fire. And the two tablets of the covenant were in my hands.ᵃ ¹⁶When I looked, I saw that you had sinned against the LORD your God; you had made for yourselves an idol cast in the shape of a calf. You had turned aside quickly from the way that the LORD had commanded you. ¹⁷So I took the two tablets and threw them out of my hands, breaking them to pieces before your eyes.

¹⁸Then once again I fell prostrate before the LORD for forty days and forty nights; I ate no bread and drank no water, because of all the sin you had committed, doing what was evil in the LORD's sight and so provoking him to anger. ¹⁹I feared the anger and wrath of the LORD, for he was angry enough with you to destroy you. But again the LORD listened to me. ²⁰And the LORD was angry enough with Aaron to destroy him, but at that time I prayed for Aaron too. ²¹Also I took that sinful thing of yours, the calf you had made, and burned it in the fire. Then I crushed it and ground it to powder as fine as dust and threw the dust into a stream that flowed down the mountain.

²²You also made the LORD angry at Taberah, at Massah and at Kibroth Hattaavah.

²³And when the LORD sent you out from Kadesh Barnea, he said, "Go up and take possession of the land I have given you." But you rebelled against the command of the LORD your God. You did not trust him or obey him. ²⁴You have been

---

ᵃ 15 Or *And I had the two tablets of the covenant with me, one in each hand*

GOING *deeper*

Prayers of Intercession

READ AND CONSIDER: DEUTERONOMY 9:7-29

"I feared the anger and wrath of the LORD, for he was angry enough with you to destroy you. But again the LORD listened to me. And the LORD was angry enough with Aaron to destroy him, but at that time I prayed for Aaron too" (Deuteronomy 9:19-20).

When we step in on behalf of others in prayer, amazing things can happen. This is proven over and over again throughout Scripture, and the example in these verses is one of the most powerful in the Bible. In this passage, Moses recounts to the new generation of Israelites the story recorded in Exodus 32.

Picture the scene: Moses was away, meeting with the Lord to receive instruction and guidance for the Israelites from their true and faithful God. During Moses' long absence on the mountain, however, the Israelites grew restless and impatient. They decided that they needed an idol—a golden calf—to worship. And Aaron went along with the plan. God's wrath was stirred toward the people, and in spite of his own anger toward them, Moses intervened on their behalf to prevent God from destroying them. And since Aaron had succumbed to the people's demands and fashioned the idol, he was ultimately responsible. Yet Moses interceded for his brother as well.

Our intercessions for others may be far less dramatic than this example, but the extreme nature of this situation shows how powerful our prayers can be. We may be praying for another's healing, encouragement, guidance, salvation, protection, or strengthening. The Lord's response to Moses reveals that He listens to us and that our prayers matter to Him. We can make a powerful impact on the lives of those around us through our intercessions for them. Take the time to pray diligently for those whom the Spirit puts on your heart. Then watch what God does in their lives.

rebellious against the LORD ever since I have known you.

²⁵I lay prostrate before the LORD those forty days and forty nights because the LORD had said he would destroy you. ²⁶I prayed to the LORD and said, "O Sovereign LORD, do not destroy your people, your own inheritance that you redeemed by your great power and brought out of Egypt with a mighty hand. ²⁷Remember your servants Abraham, Isaac and Jacob. Overlook the stubbornness of this people, their wickedness and their sin. ²⁸Otherwise, the country from which you brought us will say, 'Because the LORD was not able to take them into the land he had promised them, and because he

hated them, he brought them out to put them to death in the desert.' ²⁹But they are your people, your inheritance that you brought out by your great power and your outstretched arm."

Tablets Like the First Ones

10 At that time the LORD said to me, "Chisel out two stone tablets like the first ones and come up to me on the mountain. Also make a wooden chest.ᵃ ²I will write on the tablets the words that were on the first tablets, which you broke. Then you are to put them in the chest."

³So I made the ark out of acacia wood and chiseled out two stone tablets like the first ones, and I went up on the mountain with the two tablets in my hands. ⁴The

ᵃ *1* That is, an ark

LORD wrote on these tablets what he had written before, the Ten Commandments he had proclaimed to you on the mountain, out of the fire, on the day of the assembly. And the LORD gave them to me. ⁵Then I came back down the mountain and put the tablets in the ark I had made, as the LORD commanded me, and they are there now.

⁶(The Israelites traveled from the wells of the Jaakanites to Moserah. There Aaron died and was buried, and Eleazar his son succeeded him as priest. ⁷From there they traveled to Gudgodah and on to Jotbathah, a land with streams of water. ⁸At that time the LORD set apart the tribe of Levi to carry the ark of the covenant of the LORD, to stand before the LORD to minister and to pronounce blessings in his name, as they still do today. ⁹That is why the Levites have no share or inheritance among their brothers; the LORD is their inheritance, as the LORD your God told them.)

¹⁰Now I had stayed on the mountain forty days and nights, as I did the first time, and the LORD listened to me at this time also. It was not his will to destroy you. ¹¹"Go," the LORD said to me, "and lead the people on their way, so that they may enter and possess the land that I swore to their fathers to give them."

Fear the LORD

¹²And now, O Israel, what does the LORD your God ask of you but to fear the LORD your God, to walk in all his ways, to love him, to serve the LORD your God with all your heart and with all your soul, ¹³and to observe the LORD's commands and decrees that I am giving you today for your own good?

¹⁴To the LORD your God belong the heavens, even the highest heavens, the earth and everything in it. ¹⁵Yet the LORD set his affection on your forefathers and loved them, and he chose you, their descendants, above all the nations, as it is today. ¹⁶Circumcise your hearts, there-

fore, and do not be stiff-necked any longer. ¹⁷For the LORD your God is God of gods and Lord of lords, the great God, mighty and awesome, who shows no partiality and accepts no bribes. ¹⁸He defends the cause of the fatherless and the widow, and loves the alien, giving him food and clothing. ¹⁹And you are to love those who are aliens, for you yourselves were aliens in Egypt. ²⁰Fear the LORD your God and serve him. Hold fast to him and take your oaths in his name. ²¹He is your praise; he is your God, who performed for you those great and awesome wonders you saw with your own eyes. ²²Your forefathers who went down into Egypt were seventy in all, and now the LORD your God has made you as numerous as the stars in the sky.

Love and Obey the LORD

11 Love the LORD your God and keep his requirements, his decrees, his laws and his commands always. ²Remember today that your children were not the ones who saw and experienced the discipline of the LORD your God: his majesty, his mighty hand, his outstretched arm; ³the signs he performed and the things he did in the heart of Egypt, both to Pharaoh king of Egypt and to his whole country; ⁴what he did to the Egyptian army, to its horses and chariots, how he overwhelmed them with the waters of the Red Sea[a] as they were pursuing you, and how the LORD brought lasting ruin on them. ⁵It was not your children who saw what he did for you in the desert until you arrived at this place, ⁶and what he did to Dathan and Abiram, sons of Eliab the Reubenite, when the earth opened its mouth right in the middle of all Israel and swallowed them up with their households, their tents and every living thing that belonged to them. ⁷But it was your own eyes that saw all these great things the LORD has done.

⁸Observe therefore all the commands I am giving you today, so that you may

---

ᵃ 4 Hebrew *Yam Suph*; that is, Sea of Reeds

have the strength to go in and take over the land that you are crossing the Jordan to possess, ⁹and so that you may live long in the land that the LORD swore to your forefathers to give to them and their descendants, a land flowing with milk and honey. ¹⁰The land you are entering to take over is not like the land of Egypt, from which you have come, where you planted your seed and irrigated it by foot as in a vegetable garden. ¹¹But the land you are crossing the Jordan to take possession of is a land of mountains and valleys that drinks rain from heaven. ¹²It is a land the LORD your God cares for; the eyes of the LORD your God are continually on it from the beginning of the year to its end.

Praying Deuteronomy 11:8-14

Lord, help me not to be weakened by sin, but to do all You ask me to do so I can possess all that You have for me.

¹³So if you faithfully obey the commands I am giving you today—to love the LORD your God and to serve him with all your heart and with all your soul— ¹⁴then I will send rain on your land in its season, both autumn and spring rains, so that you may gather in your grain, new wine and oil. ¹⁵I will provide grass in the fields for your cattle, and you will eat and be satisfied.

¹⁶Be careful, or you will be enticed to turn away and worship other gods and bow down to them. ¹⁷Then the LORD's anger will burn against you, and he will shut the heavens so that it will not rain and the ground will yield no produce, and you will soon perish from the good land the LORD is giving you. ¹⁸Fix these words of mine in your hearts and minds; tie them as symbols on your hands and bind them on your foreheads. ¹⁹Teach them to your children, talking about them when you sit at home and when

you walk along the road, when you lie down and when you get up. ²⁰Write them on the doorframes of your houses and on your gates, ²¹so that your days and the days of your children may be many in the land that the LORD swore to give your forefathers, as many as the days that the heavens are above the earth.

²²If you carefully observe all these commands I am giving you to follow—to love the LORD your God, to walk in all his ways and to hold fast to him— ²³then the LORD will drive out all these nations before you, and you will dispossess nations larger and stronger than you. ²⁴Every place where you set your foot will be yours: Your territory will extend from the desert to Lebanon, and from the Euphrates River to the western sea.^a ²⁵No man will be able to stand against you. The LORD your God, as he promised you, will put the terror and fear of you on the whole land, wherever you go.

²⁶See, I am setting before you today a blessing and a curse— ²⁷the blessing if you obey the commands of the LORD your God that I am giving you today; ²⁸the curse if you disobey the commands of the LORD your God and turn from the way that I command you today by following other gods, which you have not known. ²⁹When the LORD your God has brought you into the land you are entering to possess, you are to proclaim on Mount Gerizim the blessings, and on Mount Ebal the curses. ³⁰As you know, these mountains are across the Jordan, west of the road,^b toward the setting sun, near the great trees of Moreh, in the territory of those Canaanites living in the Arabah in the vicinity of Gilgal. ³¹You are about to cross the Jordan to enter and take possession of the land the LORD your God is giving you. When you have taken it over and are living there, ³²be sure that you obey all the decrees and laws I am setting before you today.

---

^a *24* That is, the Mediterranean   ^b *30* Or *Jordan, westward*

The One Place of Worship

12 These are the decrees and laws you must be careful to follow in the land that the LORD, the God of your fathers, has given you to possess—as long as you live in the land. 2Destroy completely all the places on the high mountains and on the hills and under every spreading tree where the nations you are dispossessing worship their gods. 3Break down their altars, smash their sacred stones and burn their Asherah poles in the fire; cut down the idols of their gods and wipe out their names from those places.

4You must not worship the LORD your God in their way. 5But you are to seek the place the LORD your God will choose from among all your tribes to put his Name there for his dwelling. To that place you must go; 6there bring your burnt offerings and sacrifices, your tithes and special gifts, what you have vowed to give and your freewill offerings, and the firstborn of your herds and flocks. 7There, in the presence of the LORD your God, you and your families shall eat and shall rejoice in everything you have put your hand to, because the LORD your God has blessed you.

8You are not to do as we do here today, everyone as he sees fit, 9since you have not yet reached the resting place and the inheritance the LORD your God is giving you. 10But you will cross the Jordan and settle in the land the LORD your God is giving you as an inheritance, and he will give you rest from all your enemies around you so that you will live in safety. 11Then to the place the LORD your God will choose as a dwelling for his Name—there you are to bring everything I command you: your burnt offerings and sacrifices, your tithes and special gifts, and all the choice possessions you have vowed to the LORD. 12And there rejoice before the LORD your God, you, your sons and daughters, your menservants and maidservants, and the Levites from your towns, who have no allotment

or inheritance of their own. 13Be careful not to sacrifice your burnt offerings anywhere you please. 14Offer them only at the place the LORD will choose in one of your tribes, and there observe everything I command you.

15Nevertheless, you may slaughter your animals in any of your towns and eat as much of the meat as you want, as if it were gazelle or deer, according to the blessing the LORD your God gives you. Both the ceremonially unclean and the clean may eat it. 16But you must not eat the blood; pour it out on the ground like water. 17You must not eat in your own towns the tithe of your grain and new wine and oil, or the firstborn of your herds and flocks, or whatever you have vowed to give, or your freewill offerings or special gifts. 18Instead, you are to eat them in the presence of the LORD your God at the place the LORD your God will choose—you, your sons and daughters, your menservants and maidservants, and the Levites from your towns—and you are to rejoice before the LORD your God in everything you put your hand to. 19Be careful not to neglect the Levites as long as you live in your land.

20When the LORD your God has enlarged your territory as he promised you, and you crave meat and say, "I would like some meat," then you may eat as much of it as you want. 21If the place where the LORD your God chooses to put his Name is too far away from you, you may slaughter animals from the herds and flocks the LORD has given you, as I have commanded you, and in your own towns you may eat as much of them as you want. 22Eat them as you would gazelle or deer. Both the ceremonially unclean and the clean may eat. 23But be sure you do not eat the blood, because the blood is the life, and you must not eat the life with the meat. 24You must not eat the blood; pour it out on the ground like water. 25Do not eat it, so that it may go well with you and your children after you, because you will be doing what is right in the eyes of the LORD.

26But take your consecrated things and whatever you have vowed to give, and go to the place the LORD will choose. 27Present your burnt offerings on the altar of the LORD your God, both the meat and the blood. The blood of your sacrifices must be poured beside the altar of the LORD your God, but you may eat the meat. 28Be careful to obey all these regulations I am giving you, so that it may always go well with you and your children after you, because you will be doing what is good and right in the eyes of the LORD your God.

29The LORD your God will cut off before you the nations you are about to invade and dispossess. But when you have driven them out and settled in their land, 30and after they have been destroyed before you, be careful not to be ensnared by inquiring about their gods, saying, "How do these nations serve their gods? We will do the same." 31You must not worship the LORD your God in their way, because in worshiping their gods, they do all kinds of detestable things the LORD hates. They even burn their sons and daughters in the fire as sacrifices to their gods.

32See that you do all I command you; do not add to it or take away from it.

Worshiping Other Gods

13 If a prophet, or one who foretells by dreams, appears among you and announces to you a miraculous sign or wonder, 2and if the sign or wonder of which he has spoken takes place, and he says, "Let us follow other gods" (gods you have not known) "and let us worship them," 3you must not listen to the words of that prophet or dreamer. The LORD your God is testing you to find out whether you love him with all your heart and with all your soul. 4It is the LORD your God you must follow, and him you must revere. Keep his commands and obey him; serve him and hold fast

to him. 5That prophet or dreamer must be put to death, because he preached rebellion against the LORD your God, who brought you out of Egypt and redeemed you from the land of slavery; he has tried to turn you from the way the LORD your God commanded you to follow. You must purge the evil from among you.

6If your very own brother, or your son or daughter, or the wife you love, or your closest friend secretly entices you, saying, "Let us go and worship other gods" (gods that neither you nor your fathers have known, 7gods of the peoples around you, whether near or far, from one end of the land to the other), 8do not yield to him or listen to him. Show him no pity. Do not spare him or shield him. 9You must certainly put him to death. Your hand must be the first in putting him to death, and then the hands of all the people. 10Stone him to death, because he tried to turn you away from the LORD your God, who brought you out of Egypt, out of the land of slavery. 11Then all Israel will hear and be afraid, and no one among you will do such an evil thing again.

12If you hear it said about one of the towns the LORD your God is giving you to live in 13that wicked men have arisen among you and have led the people of their town astray, saying, "Let us go and worship other gods" (gods you have not known), 14then you must inquire, probe and investigate it thoroughly. And if it is true and it has been proved that this detestable thing has been done among you, 15you must certainly put to the sword all who live in that town. Destroy it completely,a both its people and its livestock. 16Gather all the plunder of the town into the middle of the public square and completely burn the town and all its plunder as a whole burnt offering to the LORD your God. It is to remain a ruin forever, never to be rebuilt. 17None of those condemned thingsa shall be found in your hands, so that the LORD will turn

---

a 15,17 The Hebrew term refers to the irrevocable giving over of things or persons to the LORD, often by totally destroying them.

from his fierce anger; he will show you mercy, have compassion on you, and increase your numbers, as he promised on oath to your forefathers, 18because you obey the LORD your God, keeping all his commands that I am giving you today and doing what is right in his eyes.

Clean and Unclean Food

14 You are the children of the LORD your God. Do not cut yourselves or shave the front of your heads for the dead, 2for you are a people holy to the LORD your God. Out of all the peoples on the face of the earth, the LORD has chosen you to be his treasured possession.

3Do not eat any detestable thing. 4These are the animals you may eat: the ox, the sheep, the goat, 5the deer, the gazelle, the roe deer, the wild goat, the ibex, the antelope and the mountain sheep.a 6You may eat any animal that has a split hoof divided in two and that chews the cud. 7However, of those that chew the cud or that have a split hoof completely divided you may not eat the camel, the rabbit or the coney.b Although they chew the cud, they do not have a split hoof; they are ceremonially unclean for you. 8The pig is also unclean; although it has a split hoof, it does not chew the cud. You are not to eat their meat or touch their carcasses.

9Of all the creatures living in the water, you may eat any that has fins and scales. 10But anything that does not have fins and scales you may not eat; for you it is unclean.

11You may eat any clean bird. 12But these you may not eat: the eagle, the vulture, the black vulture, 13the red kite, the black kite, any kind of falcon, 14any kind of raven, 15the horned owl, the screech owl, the gull, any kind of hawk, 16the little owl, the great owl, the white owl, 17the desert owl, the osprey, the cormorant, 18the stork, any kind of heron, the hoopoe and the bat.

19All flying insects that swarm are unclean to you; do not eat them. 20But any winged creature that is clean you may eat.

21Do not eat anything you find already dead. You may give it to an alien living in any of your towns, and he may eat it, or you may sell it to a foreigner. But you are a people holy to the LORD your God.

Do not cook a young goat in its mother's milk.

Tithes

22Be sure to set aside a tenth of all that your fields produce each year. 23Eat the tithe of your grain, new wine and oil, and the firstborn of your herds and flocks in the presence of the LORD your God at the place he will choose as a dwelling for his Name, so that you may learn to revere the LORD your God always. 24But if that place is too distant and you have been blessed by the LORD your God and cannot carry your tithe (because the place where the LORD will choose to put his Name is so far away), 25then exchange your tithe for silver, and take the silver with you and go to the place the LORD your God will choose. 26Use the silver to buy whatever you like: cattle, sheep, wine or other fermented drink, or anything you wish. Then you and your household shall eat there in the presence of the LORD your God and rejoice. 27And do not neglect the Levites living in your towns, for they have no allotment or inheritance of their own.

28At the end of every three years, bring all the tithes of that year's produce and store it in your towns, 29so that the Levites (who have no allotment or inheritance of their own) and the aliens, the fatherless and the widows who live in your towns may come and eat and be satisfied, and so that the LORD your God may bless you in all the work of your hands.

The Year for Canceling Debts

15 At the end of every seven years you must cancel debts. 2This is how it is to be done: Every creditor shall cancel

---

a 5 The precise identification of some of the birds and animals in this chapter is uncertain.   b 7 That is, the hyrax or rock badger the loan he has made to his fellow Israelite. He shall not require payment from his fellow Israelite or brother, because the LORD's time for canceling debts has been proclaimed. ³You may require payment from a foreigner, but you must cancel any debt your brother owes you. ⁴However, there should be no poor among you, for in the land the LORD your God is giving you to possess as your inheritance, he will richly bless you, ⁵if only you fully obey the LORD your God and are careful to follow all these commands I am giving you today. ⁶For the LORD your God will bless you as he has promised, and you will lend to many nations but will borrow from none. You will rule over many nations but none will rule over you.

Praying Deuteronomy 15:10
Dear God, show me when, what, and to whom I need to give.

⁷If there is a poor man among your brothers in any of the towns of the land that the LORD your God is giving you, do not be hardhearted or tightfisted toward your poor brother. ⁸Rather be openhanded and freely lend him whatever he needs. ⁹Be careful not to harbor this wicked thought: "The seventh year, the year for canceling debts, is near," so that you do not show ill will toward your needy brother and give him nothing. He may then appeal to the LORD against you, and you will be found guilty of sin. ¹⁰Give generously to him and do so without a grudging heart; then because of this the LORD your God will bless you in all your work and in everything you put your hand to. ¹¹There will always be poor people in the land. Therefore I command you to be openhanded toward your brothers and toward the poor and needy in your land.

Freeing Servants

¹²If a fellow Hebrew, a man or a woman, sells himself to you and serves you six years, in the seventh year you must let him go free. ¹³And when you release him, do not send him away emptyhanded. ¹⁴Supply him liberally from your flock, your threshing floor and your winepress. Give to him as the LORD your God has blessed you. ¹⁵Remember that you were slaves in Egypt and the LORD your God redeemed you. That is why I give you this command today.

¹⁶But if your servant says to you, "I do not want to leave you," because he loves you and your family and is well off with you, ¹⁷then take an awl and push it through his ear lobe into the door, and he will become your servant for life. Do the same for your maidservant.

¹⁸Do not consider it a hardship to set your servant free, because his service to you these six years has been worth twice as much as that of a hired hand. And the LORD your God will bless you in everything you do.

The Firstborn Animals

¹⁹Set apart for the LORD your God every firstborn male of your herds and flocks. Do not put the firstborn of your oxen to work, and do not shear the firstborn of your sheep. ²⁰Each year you and your family are to eat them in the presence of the LORD your God at the place he will choose. ²¹If an animal has a defect, is lame or blind, or has any serious flaw, you must not sacrifice it to the LORD your God. ²²You are to eat it in your own towns. Both the ceremonially unclean and the clean may eat it, as if it were gazelle or deer. ²³But you must not eat the blood; pour it out on the ground like water.

Passover

16 Observe the month of Abib and celebrate the Passover of the LORD your God, because in the month of Abib he brought you out of Egypt by night. ²Sacrifice as the Passover to the LORD your God an animal from your flock or herd at the place the LORD will choose

as a dwelling for his Name. ³Do not eat it with bread made with yeast, but for seven days eat unleavened bread, the bread of affliction, because you left Egypt in haste—so that all the days of your life you may remember the time of your departure from Egypt. ⁴Let no yeast be found in your possession in all your land for seven days. Do not let any of the meat you sacrifice on the evening of the first day remain until morning.

⁵You must not sacrifice the Passover in any town the LORD your God gives you ⁶except in the place he will choose as a dwelling for his Name. There you must sacrifice the Passover in the evening, when the sun goes down, on the anniversary[a] of your departure from Egypt. ⁷Roast it and eat it at the place the LORD your God will choose. Then in the morning return to your tents. ⁸For six days eat unleavened bread and on the seventh day hold an assembly to the LORD your God and do no work.

Feast of Weeks

⁹Count off seven weeks from the time you begin to put the sickle to the standing grain. ¹⁰Then celebrate the Feast of Weeks to the LORD your God by giving a freewill offering in proportion to the blessings the LORD your God has given you. ¹¹And rejoice before the LORD your God at the place he will choose as a dwelling for his Name—you, your sons and daughters, your menservants and maidservants, the Levites in your towns, and the aliens, the fatherless and the widows living among you. ¹²Remember that you were slaves in Egypt, and follow carefully these decrees.

Feast of Tabernacles

¹³Celebrate the Feast of Tabernacles for seven days after you have gathered the produce of your threshing floor and your winepress. ¹⁴Be joyful at your Feast—you, your sons and daughters, your menservants and maidservants, and the Levites,

the aliens, the fatherless and the widows who live in your towns. ¹⁵For seven days celebrate the Feast to the LORD your God at the place the LORD will choose. For the LORD your God will bless you in all your harvest and in all the work of your hands, and your joy will be complete.

¹⁶Three times a year all your men must appear before the LORD your God at the place he will choose: at the Feast of Unleavened Bread, the Feast of Weeks and the Feast of Tabernacles. No man should appear before the LORD empty-handed: ¹⁷Each of you must bring a gift in proportion to the way the LORD your God has blessed you.

Judges

¹⁸Appoint judges and officials for each of your tribes in every town the LORD your God is giving you, and they shall judge the people fairly. ¹⁹Do not pervert justice or show partiality. Do not accept a bribe, for a bribe blinds the eyes of the wise and twists the words of the righteous. ²⁰Follow justice and justice alone, so that you may live and possess the land the LORD your God is giving you.

Worshiping Other Gods

²¹Do not set up any wooden Asherah pole[b] beside the altar you build to the LORD your God, ²²and do not erect a sacred stone, for these the LORD your God hates.

17 Do not sacrifice to the LORD your God an ox or a sheep that has any defect or flaw in it, for that would be detestable to him.

²If a man or woman living among you in one of the towns the LORD gives you is found doing evil in the eyes of the LORD your God in violation of his covenant, ³and contrary to my command has worshiped other gods, bowing down to them or to the sun or the moon or the stars of the sky, ⁴and this has been brought to your attention, then you must investigate it thoroughly. If it is true and it has been

---

a 6 Or down, at the time of day   b 21 Or Do not plant any tree dedicated to Asherah proved that this detestable thing has been done in Israel, [5]take the man or woman who has done this evil deed to your city gate and stone that person to death. [6]On the testimony of two or three witnesses a man shall be put to death, but no one shall be put to death on the testimony of only one witness. [7]The hands of the witnesses must be the first in putting him to death, and then the hands of all the people. You must purge the evil from among you.

Law Courts

[8]If cases come before your courts that are too difficult for you to judge—whether bloodshed, lawsuits or assaults—take them to the place the LORD your God will choose. [9]Go to the priests, who are Levites, and to the judge who is in office at that time. Inquire of them and they will give you the verdict. [10]You must act according to the decisions they give you at the place the LORD will choose. Be careful to do everything they direct you to do. [11]Act according to the law they teach you and the decisions they give you. Do not turn aside from what they tell you, to the right or to the left. [12]The man who shows contempt for the judge or for the priest who stands ministering there to the LORD your God must be put to death. You must purge the evil from Israel. [13]All the people will hear and be afraid, and will not be contemptuous again.

The King

[14]When you enter the land the LORD your God is giving you and have taken possession of it and settled in it, and you say, "Let us set a king over us like all the nations around us," [15]be sure to appoint over you the king the LORD your God chooses. He must be from among your own brothers. Do not place a foreigner over you, one who is not a brother Israelite. [16]The king, moreover, must not acquire great numbers of horses for himself or make the people return to Egypt to get more of them, for the LORD has told you, "You are not to go back that way again." [17]He must not take many wives, or his heart will be led astray. He must not accumulate large amounts of silver and gold.

[18]When he takes the throne of his kingdom, he is to write for himself on a scroll a copy of this law, taken from that of the priests, who are Levites. [19]It is to be with him, and he is to read it all the days of his life so that he may learn to revere the LORD his God and follow carefully all the words of this law and these decrees [20]and not consider himself better than his brothers and turn from the law to the right or to the left. Then he and his descendants will reign a long time over his kingdom in Israel.

Offerings for Priests and Levites

18 The priests, who are Levites—indeed the whole tribe of Levi—are to have no allotment or inheritance with Israel. They shall live on the offerings made to the LORD by fire, for that is their inheritance. [2]They shall have no inheritance among their brothers; the LORD is their inheritance, as he promised them.

[3]This is the share due the priests from the people who sacrifice a bull or a sheep: the shoulder, the jowls and the inner parts. [4]You are to give them the firstfruits of your grain, new wine and oil, and the first wool from the shearing of your sheep, [5]for the LORD your God has chosen them and their descendants out of all your tribes to stand and minister in the LORD's name always.

[6]If a Levite moves from one of your towns anywhere in Israel where he is living, and comes in all earnestness to the place the LORD will choose, [7]he may minister in the name of the LORD his God like all his fellow Levites who serve there in the presence of the LORD. [8]He is to share equally in their benefits, even though he has received money from the sale of family possessions.

Detestable Practices

⁹When you enter the land the LORD your God is giving you, do not learn to imitate the detestable ways of the nations there. ¹⁰Let no one be found among you who sacrifices his son or daughter in ª the fire, who practices divination or sorcery, interprets omens, engages in witchcraft, ¹¹or casts spells, or who is a medium or spiritist or who consults the dead. ¹²Anyone who does these things is detestable to the LORD, and because of these detestable practices the LORD your God will drive out those nations before you. ¹³You must be blameless before the LORD your God.

The Prophet

¹⁴The nations you will dispossess listen to those who practice sorcery or divination. But as for you, the LORD your God has not permitted you to do so. ¹⁵The LORD your God will raise up for you a prophet like me from among your own brothers. You must listen to him. ¹⁶For this is what you asked of the LORD your God at Horeb on the day of the assembly when you said, "Let us not hear the voice of the LORD our God nor see this great fire anymore, or we will die."

¹⁷The LORD said to me: "What they say is good. ¹⁸I will raise up for them a prophet like you from among their brothers; I will put my words in his mouth, and he will tell them everything I command him. ¹⁹If anyone does not listen to my words that the prophet speaks in my name, I myself will call him to account. ²⁰But a prophet who presumes to speak in my name anything I have not commanded him to say, or a prophet who speaks in the name of other gods, must be put to death."

²¹You may say to yourselves, "How can we know when a message has not been spoken by the LORD?" ²²If what a prophet proclaims in the name of the LORD does not take place or come true, that is a message the LORD has not spoken. That prophet has spoken presumptuously. Do not be afraid of him.

Cities of Refuge

19 When the LORD your God has destroyed the nations whose land he is giving you, and when you have driven them out and settled in their towns and houses, ²then set aside for yourselves three cities centrally located in the land the LORD your God is giving you to possess. ³Build roads to them and divide into three parts the land the LORD your God is giving you as an inheritance, so that anyone who kills a man may flee there.

⁴This is the rule concerning the man who kills another and flees there to save his life—one who kills his neighbor unintentionally, without malice aforethought. ⁵For instance, a man may go into the forest with his neighbor to cut wood, and as he swings his ax to fell a tree, the head may fly off and hit his neighbor and kill him. That man may flee to one of these cities and save his life. ⁶Otherwise, the avenger of blood might pursue him in a rage, overtake him if the distance is too great, and kill him even though he is not deserving of death, since he did it to his neighbor without malice aforethought. ⁷This is why I command you to set aside for yourselves three cities.

⁸If the LORD your God enlarges your territory, as he promised on oath to your forefathers, and gives you the whole land he promised them, ⁹because you carefully follow all these laws I command you today—to love the LORD your God and to walk always in his ways—then you are to set aside three more cities. ¹⁰Do this so that innocent blood will not be shed in your land, which the LORD your God is giving you as your inheritance, and so that you will not be guilty of bloodshed.

¹¹But if a man hates his neighbor and lies in wait for him, assaults and kills him, and then flees to one of these cities, ¹²the elders of his town shall send for him, bring him back from the city, and hand him over to the avenger of blood to die. ¹³Show him no pity. You must purge from

ª *10 Or who makes his son or daughter pass through*

Israel the guilt of shedding innocent blood, so that it may go well with you.

14Do not move your neighbor's boundary stone set up by your predecessors in the inheritance you receive in the land the LORD your God is giving you to possess.

Witnesses

15One witness is not enough to convict a man accused of any crime or offense he may have committed. A matter must be established by the testimony of two or three witnesses.

16If a malicious witness takes the stand to accuse a man of a crime, 17the two men involved in the dispute must stand in the presence of the LORD before the priests and the judges who are in office at the time. 18The judges must make a thorough investigation, and if the witness proves to be a liar, giving false testimony against his brother, 19then do to him as he intended to do to his brother. You must purge the evil from among you. 20The rest of the people will hear of this and be afraid, and never again will such an evil thing be done among you. 21Show no pity: life for life, eye for eye, tooth for tooth, hand for hand, foot for foot.

Going to War

20 When you go to war against your enemies and see horses and chariots and an army greater than yours, do not be afraid of them, because the LORD your God, who brought you up out of Egypt, will be with you. 2When you are about to go into battle, the priest shall come forward and address the army. 3He shall say: "Hear, O Israel, today you are going into battle against your enemies. Do not be

---

Praying Deuteronomy 20:1-4

Thank You, Almighty God, that I don't have to be afraid when I face opposition from the enemy because You go with me to fight the battle.

GOING *deeper*

God Is With You

READ AND CONSIDER: DEUTERONOMY 20

"When you go to war against your enemies and see horses and chariots and an army greater than yours, do not be afraid of them, because the LORD your God, who brought you up out of Egypt, will be with you" (Deuteronomy 20:1).

Prayer is one of your strongest weapons against fear. Imagine how the Israelites must have felt every time they faced nation after nation as they made their way toward the promised land. God required that they rely on His strength, not on their numbers or weapons or skills or any other human power they had. He seemed to delight in making sure that they were weaker than the nations they faced so that His power could be revealed in their victories. And when the Israelites believed Him and followed His instructions, God's power was always revealed.

What "wars" are you facing right now? What impossible circumstances are making you draw back in fear? Take them to the Lord in prayer. Think of all the times in your life when God has been faithful to you. It will reinforce your confidence that God will take you through the next "battle" just as He has seen you through past difficulties. When the Israelites thought back on their dramatic rescue from Egypt and remembered God's faithfulness to them, they renewed their strength to face the challenges ahead. Pray that God will open your eyes to all the ways He has upheld you in the past. Ask Him to give you fresh faith to fearlessly face the next battle.

fainthearted or afraid; do not be terrified or give way to panic before them. 4For the LORD your God is the one who goes with you to fight for you against your enemies to give you victory."

5The officers shall say to the army: "Has anyone built a new house and not dedicated it? Let him go home, or he may die in battle and someone else may dedicate it. 6Has anyone planted a vineyard and not begun to enjoy it? Let him go home, or he may die in battle and someone else enjoy it. 7Has anyone become pledged to a woman and not married her? Let him go home, or he may die in battle and someone else marry her." 8Then the officers shall add, "Is any man afraid or fainthearted? Let him go home so that his brothers will not become disheartened too." 9When the officers have finished speaking to the army, they shall appoint commanders over it.

10When you march up to attack a city, make its people an offer of peace. 11If they accept and open their gates, all the people in it shall be subject to forced labor and shall work for you. 12If they refuse to make peace and they engage you in battle, lay siege to that city. 13When the LORD your God delivers it into your hand, put to the sword all the men in it. 14As for the women, the children, the livestock and everything else in the city, you may take these as plunder for yourselves. And you may use the plunder the LORD your God gives you from your enemies. 15This is how you are to treat all the cities that are at a distance from you and do not belong to the nations nearby.

16However, in the cities of the nations the LORD your God is giving you as an inheritance, do not leave alive anything that breathes. 17Completely destroya them—the Hittites, Amorites, Canaanites, Perizzites, Hivites and Jebusites—as the LORD your God has commanded you. 18Otherwise, they will teach you to follow all the detestable things they do in worshiping their gods, and you will sin against the LORD your God.

19When you lay siege to a city for a long time, fighting against it to capture it, do not destroy its trees by putting an ax to them, because you can eat their fruit. Do not cut them down. Are the trees of the field people, that you should besiege them?b 20However, you may cut down trees that you know are not fruit trees and use them to build siege works until the city at war with you falls.

Atonement for an Unsolved Murder

21 If a man is found slain, lying in a field in the land the LORD your God is giving you to possess, and it is not known who killed him, 2your elders and judges shall go out and measure the distance from the body to the neighboring towns. 3Then the elders of the town nearest the body shall take a heifer that has never been worked and has never worn a yoke 4and lead her down to a valley that has not been plowed or planted and where there is a flowing stream. There in the valley they are to break the heifer's neck. 5The priests, the sons of Levi, shall step forward, for the LORD your God has chosen them to minister and to pronounce blessings in the name of the LORD and to decide all cases of dispute and assault. 6Then all the elders of the town nearest the body shall wash their hands over the heifer whose neck was broken in the valley, 7and they shall declare: "Our hands did not shed this blood, nor did our eyes see it done. 8Accept this atonement for your people Israel, whom you have redeemed, O LORD, and do not hold your people guilty of the blood of an innocent man." And the bloodshed will be atoned for. 9So you will purge from yourselves the guilt of shedding innocent blood, since you have done what is right in the eyes of the LORD.

---

a 17 The Hebrew term refers to the irrevocable giving over of things or persons to the LORD, often by totally destroying them.
b 19 Or down to use in the siege, for the fruit trees are for the benefit of man.

Marrying a Captive Woman

¹⁰When you go to war against your enemies and the LORD your God delivers them into your hands and you take captives, ¹¹if you notice among the captives a beautiful woman and are attracted to her, you may take her as your wife. ¹²Bring her into your home and have her shave her head, trim her nails ¹³and put aside the clothes she was wearing when captured. After she has lived in your house and mourned her father and mother for a full month, then you may go to her and be her husband and she shall be your wife. ¹⁴If you are not pleased with her, let her go wherever she wishes. You must not sell her or treat her as a slave, since you have dishonored her.

The Right of the Firstborn

¹⁵If a man has two wives, and he loves one but not the other, and both bear him sons but the firstborn is the son of the wife he does not love, ¹⁶when he wills his property to his sons, he must not give the rights of the firstborn to the son of the wife he loves in preference to his actual firstborn, the son of the wife he does not love. ¹⁷He must acknowledge the son of his unloved wife as the firstborn by giving him a double share of all he has. That son is the first sign of his father's strength. The right of the firstborn belongs to him.

A Rebellious Son

¹⁸If a man has a stubborn and rebellious son who does not obey his father and mother and will not listen to them when they discipline him, ¹⁹his father and mother shall take hold of him and bring him to the elders at the gate of his town. ²⁰They shall say to the elders, "This son of ours is stubborn and rebellious. He will not obey us. He is a profligate and a drunkard." ²¹Then all the men of his town shall stone him to death. You must purge the evil from among you. All Israel will hear of it and be afraid.

Various Laws

²²If a man guilty of a capital offense is put to death and his body is hung on a tree, ²³you must not leave his body on the tree overnight. Be sure to bury him that same day, because anyone who is hung on a tree is under God's curse. You must not desecrate the land the LORD your God is giving you as an inheritance.

22 If you see your brother's ox or sheep straying, do not ignore it but be sure to take it back to him. ²If the brother does not live near you or if you do not know who he is, take it home with you and keep it until he comes looking for it. Then give it back to him. ³Do the same if you find your brother's donkey or his cloak or anything he loses. Do not ignore it.

⁴If you see your brother's donkey or his ox fallen on the road, do not ignore it. Help him get it to its feet.

⁵A woman must not wear men's clothing, nor a man wear women's clothing, for the LORD your God detests anyone who does this.

⁶If you come across a bird's nest beside the road, either in a tree or on the ground, and the mother is sitting on the young or on the eggs, do not take the mother with the young. ⁷You may take the young, but be sure to let the mother go, so that it may go well with you and you may have a long life.

⁸When you build a new house, make a parapet around your roof so that you may not bring the guilt of bloodshed on your house if someone falls from the roof.

⁹Do not plant two kinds of seed in your vineyard; if you do, not only the crops you plant but also the fruit of the vineyard will be defiled.^a

¹⁰Do not plow with an ox and a donkey yoked together.

¹¹Do not wear clothes of wool and linen woven together.

¹²Make tassels on the four corners of the cloak you wear.

---

^a 9 Or be forfeited to the sanctuary

Marriage Violations

¹³If a man takes a wife and, after lying with her, dislikes her ¹⁴and slanders her and gives her a bad name, saying, "I married this woman, but when I approached her, I did not find proof of her virginity," ¹⁵then the girl's father and mother shall bring proof that she was a virgin to the town elders at the gate. ¹⁶The girl's father will say to the elders, "I gave my daughter in marriage to this man, but he dislikes her. ¹⁷Now he has slandered her and said, 'I did not find your daughter to be a virgin.' But here is the proof of my daughter's virginity." Then her parents shall display the cloth before the elders of the town, ¹⁸and the elders shall take the man and punish him. ¹⁹They shall fine him a hundred shekels of silver[a] and give them to the girl's father, because this man has given an Israelite virgin a bad name. She shall continue to be his wife; he must not divorce her as long as he lives.

²⁰If, however, the charge is true and no proof of the girl's virginity can be found, ²¹she shall be brought to the door of her father's house and there the men of her town shall stone her to death. She has done a disgraceful thing in Israel by being promiscuous while still in her father's house. You must purge the evil from among you.

²²If a man is found sleeping with another man's wife, both the man who slept with her and the woman must die. You must purge the evil from Israel.

²³If a man happens to meet in a town a virgin pledged to be married and he sleeps with her, ²⁴you shall take both of them to the gate of that town and stone them to death—the girl because she was in a town and did not scream for help, and the man because he violated another man's wife. You must purge the evil from among you.

²⁵But if out in the country a man happens to meet a girl pledged to be married and rapes her, only the man who has done this shall die. ²⁶Do nothing to the girl; she has committed no sin deserving death. This case is like that of someone who attacks and murders his neighbor, ²⁷for the man found the girl out in the country, and though the betrothed girl screamed, there was no one to rescue her.

²⁸If a man happens to meet a virgin who is not pledged to be married and rapes her and they are discovered, ²⁹he shall pay the girl's father fifty shekels of silver.[b] He must marry the girl, for he has violated her. He can never divorce her as long as he lives.

³⁰A man is not to marry his father's wife; he must not dishonor his father's bed.

Exclusion From the Assembly

23 No one who has been emasculated by crushing or cutting may enter the assembly of the LORD.

²No one born of a forbidden marriage[c] nor any of his descendants may enter the assembly of the LORD, even down to the tenth generation.

³No Ammonite or Moabite or any of his descendants may enter the assembly of the LORD, even down to the tenth generation. ⁴For they did not come to meet you with bread and water on your way when you came out of Egypt, and they hired Balaam son of Beor from Pethor in Aram Naharaim[d] to pronounce a curse on you. ⁵However, the LORD your God would not listen to Balaam but turned the curse into a blessing for you, because the LORD your God loves you. ⁶Do not seek a treaty of friendship with them as long as you live.

⁷Do not abhor an Edomite, for he is your brother. Do not abhor an Egyptian, because you lived as an alien in his country. ⁸The third generation of children born to them may enter the assembly of the LORD.

Uncleanness in the Camp

⁹When you are encamped against your enemies, keep away from everything im-

---

[a] 19 That is, about 2 1/2 pounds (about 1 kilogram) [b] 29 That is, about 1 1/4 pounds (about 0.6 kilogram) [c] 2 Or one of illegitimate birth [d] 4 That is, Northwest Mesopotamia

pure. [10]If one of your men is unclean because of a nocturnal emission, he is to go outside the camp and stay there. [11]But as evening approaches he is to wash himself, and at sunset he may return to the camp.

[12]Designate a place outside the camp where you can go to relieve yourself. [13]As part of your equipment have something to dig with, and when you relieve yourself, dig a hole and cover up your excrement. [14]For the LORD your God moves about in your camp to protect you and to deliver your enemies to you. Your camp must be holy, so that he will not see among you anything indecent and turn away from you.

Miscellaneous Laws

[15]If a slave has taken refuge with you, do not hand him over to his master. [16]Let him live among you wherever he likes and in whatever town he chooses. Do not oppress him.

[17]No Israelite man or woman is to become a shrine prostitute. [18]You must not bring the earnings of a female prostitute or of a male prostitute[a] into the house of the LORD your God to pay any vow, because the LORD your God detests them both.

[19]Do not charge your brother interest, whether on money or food or anything else that may earn interest. [20]You may charge a foreigner interest, but not a brother Israelite, so that the LORD your God may bless you in everything you put your hand to in the land you are entering to possess.

[21]If you make a vow to the LORD your God, do not be slow to pay it, for the LORD your God will certainly demand it of you and you will be guilty of sin. [22]But if you refrain from making a vow, you will not be guilty. [23]Whatever your lips utter you must be sure to do, because you made your vow freely to the LORD your God with your own mouth.

[24]If you enter your neighbor's vineyard, you may eat all the grapes you want, but do not put any in your basket. [25]If you enter your neighbor's grainfield, you may pick kernels with your hands, but you must not put a sickle to his standing grain.

24 If a man marries a woman who becomes displeasing to him because he finds something indecent about her, and he writes her a certificate of divorce, gives it to her and sends her from his house, [2]and if after she leaves his house she becomes the wife of another man, [3]and her second husband dislikes her and writes her a certificate of divorce, gives it to her and sends her from his house, or if he dies, [4]then her first husband, who divorced her, is not allowed to marry her again after she has been defiled. That would be detestable in the eyes of the LORD. Do not bring sin upon the land the LORD your God is giving you as an inheritance.

[5]If a man has recently married, he must not be sent to war or have any other duty laid on him. For one year he is to be free to stay at home and bring happiness to the wife he has married.

[6]Do not take a pair of millstones—not even the upper one—as security for a debt, because that would be taking a man's livelihood as security.

[7]If a man is caught kidnapping one of his brother Israelites and treats him as a slave or sells him, the kidnapper must die. You must purge the evil from among you.

[8]In cases of leprous[b] diseases be very careful to do exactly as the priests, who are Levites, instruct you. You must follow carefully what I have commanded them. [9]Remember what the LORD your God did to Miriam along the way after you came out of Egypt.

[10]When you make a loan of any kind to your neighbor, do not go into his house to get what he is offering as a pledge. [11]Stay outside and let the man to whom you are making the loan bring the pledge

---

[a] 18 Hebrew *of a dog*   [b] 8 The Hebrew word was used for various diseases affecting the skin—not necessarily leprosy.

out to you. ¹²If the man is poor, do not go to sleep with his pledge in your possession. ¹³Return his cloak to him by sunset so that he may sleep in it. Then he will thank you, and it will be regarded as a righteous act in the sight of the LORD your God.

¹⁴Do not take advantage of a hired man who is poor and needy, whether he is a brother Israelite or an alien living in one of your towns. ¹⁵Pay him his wages each day before sunset, because he is poor and is counting on it. Otherwise he may cry to the LORD against you, and you will be guilty of sin.

¹⁶Fathers shall not be put to death for their children, nor children put to death for their fathers; each is to die for his own sin.

¹⁷Do not deprive the alien or the fatherless of justice, or take the cloak of the widow as a pledge. ¹⁸Remember that you were slaves in Egypt and the LORD your God redeemed you from there. That is why I command you to do this.

¹⁹When you are harvesting in your field and you overlook a sheaf, do not go back to get it. Leave it for the alien, the fatherless and the widow, so that the LORD your God may bless you in all the work of your hands. ²⁰When you beat the olives from your trees, do not go over the branches a second time. Leave what remains for the alien, the fatherless and the widow. ²¹When you harvest the grapes in your vineyard, do not go over the vines again. Leave what remains for the alien, the fatherless and the widow. ²²Remember that you were slaves in Egypt. That is why I command you to do this.

25 When men have a dispute, they are to take it to court and the judges will decide the case, acquitting the innocent and condemning the guilty. ²If the guilty man deserves to be beaten, the judge shall make him lie down and have him flogged in his presence with the number of lashes his crime deserves, ³but he must not give him more than forty lashes. If he is flogged more than that, your brother will be degraded in your eyes.

⁴Do not muzzle an ox while it is treading out the grain.

⁵If brothers are living together and one of them dies without a son, his widow must not marry outside the family. Her husband's brother shall take her and marry her and fulfill the duty of a brother-in-law to her. ⁶The first son she bears shall carry on the name of the dead brother so that his name will not be blotted out from Israel.

⁷However, if a man does not want to marry his brother's wife, she shall go to the elders at the town gate and say, "My husband's brother refuses to carry on his brother's name in Israel. He will not fulfill the duty of a brother-in-law to me." ⁸Then the elders of his town shall summon him and talk to him. If he persists in saying, "I do not want to marry her," ⁹his brother's widow shall go up to him in the presence of the elders, take off one of his sandals, spit in his face and say, "This is what is done to the man who will not build up his brother's family line." ¹⁰That man's line shall be known in Israel as The Family of the Unsandaled.

¹¹If two men are fighting and the wife of one of them comes to rescue her husband from his assailant, and she reaches out and seizes him by his private parts, ¹²you shall cut off her hand. Show her no pity.

¹³Do not have two differing weights in your bag—one heavy, one light. ¹⁴Do not have two differing measures in your house—one large, one small. ¹⁵You must have accurate and honest weights and measures, so that you may live long in the land the LORD your God is giving you. ¹⁶For the LORD your God detests anyone who does these things, anyone who deals dishonestly.

¹⁷Remember what the Amalekites did to you along the way when you came out of Egypt. ¹⁸When you were weary

and worn out, they met you on your journey and cut off all who were lagging behind; they had no fear of God. 19When the LORD your God gives you rest from all the enemies around you in the land he is giving you to possess as an inheritance, you shall blot out the memory of Amalek from under heaven. Do not forget!

Firstfruits and Tithes

26 When you have entered the land the LORD your God is giving you as an inheritance and have taken possession of it and settled in it, 2take some of the firstfruits of all that you produce from the soil of the land the LORD your God is giving you and put them in a basket. Then go to the place the LORD your God will choose as a dwelling for his Name 3and say to the priest in office at the time, "I declare today to the LORD your God that I have come to the land the LORD swore to our forefathers to give us." 4The priest shall take the basket from your hands and set it down in front of the altar of the LORD your God. 5Then you shall declare before the LORD your God: "My father was a wandering Aramean, and he went down into Egypt with a few people and lived there and became a great nation, powerful and numerous. 6But the Egyptians mistreated us and made us suffer, putting us to hard labor. 7Then we cried out to the LORD, the God of our fathers, and the LORD heard our voice and saw our misery, toil and oppression. 8So the LORD brought us out of Egypt with a mighty hand and an outstretched arm, with great terror and with miraculous signs and wonders. 9He brought us to this place and gave us this land, a land flowing with milk and honey; 10and now I bring the firstfruits of the soil that you, O LORD, have given me." Place the basket before the LORD your God and bow down before him. 11And you and the Levites and the aliens among you shall rejoice in all the good things the LORD your God has given to you and your household.

12When you have finished setting aside a tenth of all your produce in the third year, the year of the tithe, you shall give it to the Levite, the alien, the fatherless and the widow, so that they may eat in your towns and be satisfied. 13Then say to the LORD your God: "I have removed from my house the sacred portion and have given it to the Levite, the alien, the fatherless and the widow, according to all you commanded. I have not turned aside from your commands nor have I forgotten any of them. 14I have not eaten any of the sacred portion while I was in mourning, nor have I removed any of it while I was unclean, nor have I offered any of it to the dead. I have obeyed the LORD my God; I have done everything you commanded me. 15Look down from heaven, your holy dwelling place, and bless your people Israel and the land you have given us as you promised on oath to our forefathers, a land flowing with milk and honey."

Follow the LORD's Commands

16The LORD your God commands you this day to follow these decrees and laws; carefully observe them with all your heart and with all your soul. 17You have declared this day that the LORD is your God and that you will walk in his ways, that you will keep his decrees, commands and laws, and that you will obey him. 18And the LORD has declared this day that you are his people, his treasured possession as he promised, and that you are to keep all his commands. 19He has declared that he will set you in praise, fame and honor high above all the nations he has made and that you will be a people holy to the LORD your God, as he promised.

The Altar on Mount Ebal

27 Moses and the elders of Israel commanded the people: "Keep all these commands that I give you today. 2When you have crossed the Jordan into the land the LORD your God is giving

Having a Heart to Obey God

The way we learn what God expects of us is by reading His Word. But that is just the beginning. We can study all we want in this holy manual of life and learn everything we are supposed to do, but at some point we still have to act on it. The proof of our sincerity is in the *doing*, not just in the knowing. It's one thing to make a list of dos and don'ts, but it's quite another to have a heart for God's ways and a soul that longs to live them out. It's one thing to read about life; it's another to live it. Obedience is something you *do*; having a heart to obey is something you *pray* about.

When I started learning to pray about every aspect of my life, I asked God to help me be disciplined enough to be daily in His Word, to pray faithfully, and to take the steps of obedience I needed to take. I asked Him to deliver me from depression and anything else that kept me from all He had for me. I was surprised at how quickly God answered those prayers. I have become disciplined, organized, and obedient beyond what I believe are my natural capabilities. I am still learning new levels of obedience, however, even after 35 years of walking with God. My body is getting older, but as a result of obeying God in new ways, my spirit is being renewed with each passing year. And with each new step of obedience I take, I experience new blessings and new freedoms I have not known before and never thought possible.

Don't fall into the trap of thinking that once you are saved you don't have to put forth any effort. That's like getting married and never taking a shower again. You might be able to get away with it for a while, but it's risky business, and your quality of life will definitely suffer. Learning obedience is a lifelong process. There are always new dimensions of obedience to conquer. Even if you have walked with the Lord for 40 years, you still need to ask God to show you any area in which you are not being obedient. We get into trouble when we think we know what to do and we stop asking God if we're doing it. "We must pay more careful attention, therefore, to what we have heard, so that we do not drift away" (Hebrews 2:1).

We can never become prideful about how perfectly we are obeying God because He is continually stretching us and asking us to move into new levels of growth. Nor can we go to the other extreme, saying, "This is just the kind of person I am—undisciplined and unteachable." We have no excuse for not doing what we need to do when God says He will *enable* us to do it if we will just call upon Him for help. All we have to say is, "Lord, help me to be disciplined enough to obey You the way You want me to so I can become the person You created me to be." That is a prayer He loves to answer.

For the next "From Stormie's Heart" article, go to page 266.

you, set up some large stones and coat them with plaster. ³Write on them all the words of this law when you have crossed over to enter the land the LORD your God is giving you, a land flowing with milk and honey, just as the LORD, the God of your fathers, promised you. ⁴And when you have crossed the Jordan, set up these stones on Mount Ebal, as I command you today, and coat them with plaster. ⁵Build there an altar to the LORD your God, an altar of stones. Do not use any iron tool upon them. ⁶Build the altar of the LORD your God with fieldstones and offer burnt offerings on it to the LORD your God. ⁷Sacrifice fellowship offerings[a] there, eating them and rejoicing in the presence of the LORD your God. ⁸And you shall write very clearly all the words of this law on these stones you have set up."

Curses From Mount Ebal

⁹Then Moses and the priests, who are Levites, said to all Israel, "Be silent, O Israel, and listen! You have now become the people of the LORD your God. ¹⁰Obey the LORD your God and follow his commands and decrees that I give you today."

¹¹On the same day Moses commanded the people:

¹²When you have crossed the Jordan, these tribes shall stand on Mount Gerizim to bless the people: Simeon, Levi, Judah, Issachar, Joseph and Benjamin. ¹³And these tribes shall stand on Mount Ebal to pronounce curses: Reuben, Gad, Asher, Zebulun, Dan and Naphtali.

¹⁴The Levites shall recite to all the people of Israel in a loud voice:

¹⁵"Cursed is the man who carves an image or casts an idol—a thing detestable to the LORD, the work of the craftsman's hands—and sets it up in secret."

Then all the people shall say, "Amen!"

¹⁶"Cursed is the man who dishonors his father or his mother."

Then all the people shall say, "Amen!"

¹⁷"Cursed is the man who moves his neighbor's boundary stone."

Then all the people shall say, "Amen!"

¹⁸"Cursed is the man who leads the blind astray on the road."

Then all the people shall say, "Amen!"

¹⁹"Cursed is the man who withholds justice from the alien, the fatherless or the widow."

Then all the people shall say, "Amen!"

²⁰"Cursed is the man who sleeps with his father's wife, for he dishonors his father's bed."

Then all the people shall say, "Amen!"

²¹"Cursed is the man who has sexual relations with any animal."

Then all the people shall say, "Amen!"

²²"Cursed is the man who sleeps with his sister, the daughter of his father or the daughter of his mother."

Then all the people shall say, "Amen!"

²³"Cursed is the man who sleeps with his mother-in-law."

Then all the people shall say, "Amen!"

²⁴"Cursed is the man who kills his neighbor secretly."

Then all the people shall say, "Amen!"

²⁵"Cursed is the man who accepts a bribe to kill an innocent person."

Then all the people shall say, "Amen!"

²⁶"Cursed is the man who does not uphold the words of this law by carrying them out."

Then all the people shall say, "Amen!"

ª 7 Traditionally *peace offerings*

Blessings for Obedience

28 If you fully obey the LORD your God and carefully follow all his commands I give you today, the LORD your God will set you high above all the nations on earth. 2All these blessings will come upon you and accompany you if you obey the LORD your God:

3You will be blessed in the city and blessed in the country.

4The fruit of your womb will be blessed, and the crops of your land and the young of your livestock— the calves of your herds and the lambs of your flocks.

5Your basket and your kneading trough will be blessed.

6You will be blessed when you come in and blessed when you go out.

Praying Deuteronomy 28:1-10

Father, I thank You for all Your many blessings of provision and safety to me.

7The LORD will grant that the enemies who rise up against you will be defeated before you. They will come at you from one direction but flee from you in seven.

8The LORD will send a blessing on your barns and on everything you put your hand to. The LORD your God will bless you in the land he is giving you.

9The LORD will establish you as his holy people, as he promised you on oath, if you keep the commands of the LORD your God and walk in his ways. 10Then all the peoples on earth will see that you are called by the name of the LORD, and they will fear you. 11The LORD will grant you abundant prosperity—in the fruit of your womb, the young of your livestock and the crops of your ground—in the land he swore to your forefathers to give you.

12The LORD will open the heavens, the storehouse of his bounty, to send rain on your land in season and to bless all the work of your hands. You will lend to many nations but will borrow from none. 13The LORD will make you the head, not the tail. If you pay attention to the commands of the LORD your God that I give you this day and carefully follow them, you will always be at the top, never at the bottom. 14Do not turn aside from any of the commands I give you today, to the right or to the left, following other gods and serving them.

Curses for Disobedience

15However, if you do not obey the LORD your God and do not carefully follow all his commands and decrees I am giving you today, all these curses will come upon you and overtake you:

16You will be cursed in the city and cursed in the country.

17Your basket and your kneading trough will be cursed.

18The fruit of your womb will be cursed, and the crops of your land, and the calves of your herds and the lambs of your flocks.

19You will be cursed when you come in and cursed when you go out.

20The LORD will send on you curses, confusion and rebuke in everything you put your hand to, until you are destroyed and come to sudden ruin because of the evil you have done in forsaking him.a 21The LORD will plague you with diseases until he has destroyed you from the land you are entering to possess. 22The LORD will strike you with wasting disease, with fever and inflammation, with scorching heat and drought, with blight and mildew, which will plague you until you perish. 23The sky over your head will be bronze, the ground beneath you iron. 24The LORD will turn the rain of your country into dust and powder; it will come down from the skies until you are destroyed.

25The LORD will cause you to be defeated before your enemies. You will come at them from one direction but flee

a 20 Hebrew me

from them in seven, and you will become a thing of horror to all the kingdoms on earth. 26Your carcasses will be food for all the birds of the air and the beasts of the earth, and there will be no one to frighten them away. 27The LORD will afflict you with the boils of Egypt and with tumors, festering sores and the itch, from which you cannot be cured. 28The LORD will afflict you with madness, blindness and confusion of mind. 29At midday you will grope about like a blind man in the dark. You will be unsuccessful in everything you do; day after day you will be oppressed and robbed, with no one to rescue you.

30You will be pledged to be married to a woman, but another will take her and ravish her. You will build a house, but you will not live in it. You will plant a vineyard, but you will not even begin to enjoy its fruit. 31Your ox will be slaughtered before your eyes, but you will eat none of it. Your donkey will be forcibly taken from you and will not be returned. Your sheep will be given to your enemies, and no one will rescue them. 32Your sons and daughters will be given to another nation, and you will wear out your eyes watching for them day after day, powerless to lift a hand. 33A people that you do not know will eat what your land and labor produce, and you will have nothing but cruel oppression all your days. 34The sights you see will drive you mad. 35The LORD will afflict your knees and legs with painful boils that cannot be cured, spreading from the soles of your feet to the top of your head.

36The LORD will drive you and the king you set over you to a nation unknown to you or your fathers. There you will worship other gods, gods of wood and stone. 37You will become a thing of horror and an object of scorn and ridicule to all the nations where the LORD will drive you.

38You will sow much seed in the field but you will harvest little, because locusts will devour it. 39You will plant vineyards and cultivate them but you will not drink the wine or gather the grapes, because worms will eat them. 40You will have olive trees throughout your country but you will not use the oil, because the olives will drop off. 41You will have sons and daughters but you will not keep them, because they will go into captivity. 42Swarms of locusts will take over all your trees and the crops of your land.

43The alien who lives among you will rise above you higher and higher, but you will sink lower and lower. 44He will lend to you, but you will not lend to him. He will be the head, but you will be the tail.

45All these curses will come upon you. They will pursue you and overtake you until you are destroyed, because you did not obey the LORD your God and observe the commands and decrees he gave you. 46They will be a sign and a wonder to you and your descendants forever. 47Because you did not serve the LORD your God joyfully and gladly in the time of prosperity, 48therefore in hunger and thirst, in nakedness and dire poverty, you will serve the enemies the LORD sends against you. He will put an iron yoke on your neck until he has destroyed you.

49The LORD will bring a nation against you from far away, from the ends of the earth, like an eagle swooping down, a nation whose language you will not understand, 50a fierce-looking nation without respect for the old or pity for the young. 51They will devour the young of your livestock and the crops of your land until you are destroyed. They will leave you no grain, new wine or oil, nor any calves of your herds or lambs of your flocks until you are ruined. 52They will lay siege to all the cities throughout your land until the high fortified walls in which you trust fall down. They will besiege all the cities throughout the land the LORD your God is giving you.

53Because of the suffering that your enemy will inflict on you during the siege, you will eat the fruit of the womb, the flesh of the sons and daughters the LORD your God has given you. ⁵⁴Even the most gentle and sensitive man among you will have no compassion on his own brother or the wife he loves or his surviving children, ⁵⁵and he will not give to one of them any of the flesh of his children that he is eating. It will be all he has left because of the suffering your enemy will inflict on you during the siege of all your cities. ⁵⁶The most gentle and sensitive woman among you—so sensitive and gentle that she would not venture to touch the ground with the sole of her foot—will begrudge the husband she loves and her own son or daughter ⁵⁷the afterbirth from her womb and the children she bears. For she intends to eat them secretly during the siege and in the distress that your enemy will inflict on you in your cities.

⁵⁸If you do not carefully follow all the words of this law, which are written in this book, and do not revere this glorious and awesome name—the LORD your God—⁵⁹the LORD will send fearful plagues on you and your descendants, harsh and prolonged disasters, and severe and lingering illnesses. ⁶⁰He will bring upon you all the diseases of Egypt that you dreaded, and they will cling to you. ⁶¹The LORD will also bring on you every kind of sickness and disaster not recorded in this Book of the Law, until you are destroyed. ⁶²You who were as numerous as the stars in the sky will be left but few in number, because you did not obey the LORD your God. ⁶³Just as it pleased the LORD to make you prosper and increase in number, so it will please him to ruin and destroy you. You will be uprooted from the land you are entering to possess.

⁶⁴Then the LORD will scatter you among all nations, from one end of the earth to the other. There you will worship other gods—gods of wood and stone, which neither you nor your fathers have known. ⁶⁵Among those nations you will find no repose, no resting place for the sole of your foot. There the LORD will give you an anxious mind, eyes weary with longing, and a despairing heart. ⁶⁶You will live in constant suspense, filled with dread both night and day, never sure of your life. ⁶⁷In the morning you will say, "If only it were evening!" and in the evening, "If only it were morning!"—because of the terror that will fill your hearts and the sights that your eyes will see. ⁶⁸The LORD will send you back in ships to Egypt on a journey I said you should never make again. There you will offer yourselves for sale to your enemies as male and female slaves, but no one will buy you.

Renewal of the Covenant

29 These are the terms of the covenant the LORD commanded Moses to make with the Israelites in Moab, in addition to the covenant he had made with them at Horeb.

²Moses summoned all the Israelites and said to them:

Your eyes have seen all that the LORD did in Egypt to Pharaoh, to all his officials and to all his land. ³With your own eyes you saw those great trials, those miraculous signs and great wonders. ⁴But to this day the LORD has not given you a mind that understands or eyes that see or ears that hear. ⁵During the forty years that I led you through the desert, your clothes did not wear out, nor did the sandals on your feet. ⁶You ate no bread and drank no wine or other fermented drink. I did this so that you might know that I am the LORD your God.

⁷When you reached this place, Sihon king of Heshbon and Og king of Bashan came out to fight against us, but we defeated them. ⁸We took their land and gave it as an inheritance to the Reubenites, the Gadites and the half-tribe of Manasseh.

⁹Carefully follow the terms of this covenant, so that you may prosper in everything you do. ¹⁰All of you are standing

today in the presence of the LORD your God—your leaders and chief men, your elders and officials, and all the other men of Israel, ¹¹together with your children and your wives, and the aliens living in your camps who chop your wood and carry your water. ¹²You are standing here in order to enter into a covenant with the LORD your God, a covenant the LORD is making with you this day and sealing with an oath, ¹³to confirm you this day as his people, that he may be your God as he promised you and as he swore to your fathers, Abraham, Isaac and Jacob. ¹⁴I am making this covenant, with its oath, not only with you ¹⁵who are standing here with us today in the presence of the LORD our God but also with those who are not here today.

¹⁶You yourselves know how we lived in Egypt and how we passed through the countries on the way here. ¹⁷You saw among them their detestable images and idols of wood and stone, of silver and gold. ¹⁸Make sure there is no man or woman, clan or tribe among you today whose heart turns away from the LORD our God to go and worship the gods of those nations; make sure there is no root among you that produces such bitter poison.

¹⁹When such a person hears the words of this oath, he invokes a blessing on himself and therefore thinks, "I will be safe, even though I persist in going my own way." This will bring disaster on the watered land as well as the dry.ᵃ ²⁰The LORD will never be willing to forgive him; his wrath and zeal will burn against that man. All the curses written in this book will fall upon him, and the LORD will blot out his name from under heaven. ²¹The LORD will single him out from all the tribes of Israel for disaster, according to all the curses of the covenant written in this Book of the Law.

²²Your children who follow you in later generations and foreigners who come from distant lands will see the calamities that have fallen on the land and the diseases with which the LORD has afflicted it. ²³The whole land will be a burning waste of salt and sulfur—nothing planted, nothing sprouting, no vegetation growing on it. It will be like the destruction of Sodom and Gomorrah, Admah and Zeboiim, which the LORD overthrew in fierce anger. ²⁴All the nations will ask: "Why has the LORD done this to this land? Why this fierce, burning anger?"

²⁵And the answer will be: "It is because this people abandoned the covenant of the LORD, the God of their fathers, the covenant he made with them when he brought them out of Egypt. ²⁶They went off and worshiped other gods and bowed down to them, gods they did not know, gods he had not given them. ²⁷Therefore the LORD's anger burned against this land, so that he brought on it all the curses written in this book. ²⁸In furious anger and in great wrath the LORD uprooted them from their land and thrust them into another land, as it is now."

²⁹The secret things belong to the LORD our God, but the things revealed belong to us and to our children forever, that we may follow all the words of this law.

Prosperity After Turning to the LORD

30 When all these blessings and curses I have set before you come upon you and you take them to heart wherever the LORD your God disperses you among the nations, ²and when you and your children return to the LORD your God and obey him with all your heart and with all your soul according to everything I command you today, ³then the LORD your God will restore your fortunesᵇ and have compassion on you and gather you again from all the nations where he scattered you. ⁴Even if you have been banished to the most distant land under the heavens, from there the LORD your God will gather you and bring you back. ⁵He will bring you to the land that belonged to your fathers, and you will take possession of it. He will make you more prosperous and numerous than your fathers. [6]The LORD your God will circumcise your hearts and the hearts of your descendants, so that you may love him with all your heart and with all your soul, and live. [7]The LORD your God will put all these curses on your enemies who hate and persecute you. [8]You will again obey the LORD and follow all his commands I am giving you today. [9]Then the LORD your God will make you most prosperous in all the work of your hands and in the fruit of your womb, the young of your livestock and the crops of your land. The LORD will again delight in you and make you prosperous, just as he delighted in your fathers, [10]if you obey the LORD your God and keep his commands and decrees that are written in this Book of the Law and turn to the LORD your God with all your heart and with all your soul.

The Offer of Life or Death

[11]Now what I am commanding you today is not too difficult for you or beyond your reach. [12]It is not up in heaven, so that you have to ask, "Who will ascend into heaven to get it and proclaim it to us so we may obey it?" [13]Nor is it beyond the sea, so that you have to ask, "Who will cross the sea to get it and proclaim it to us so we may obey it?" [14]No, the word is very near you; it is in your mouth and in your heart so you may obey it.

[15]See, I set before you today life and prosperity, death and destruction. [16]For I command you today to love the LORD your God, to walk in his ways, and to keep his commands, decrees and laws; then you will live and increase, and the LORD your God will bless you in the land you are entering to possess.

[17]But if your heart turns away and you are not obedient, and if you are drawn away to bow down to other gods and worship them, [18]I declare to you this day that you will certainly be destroyed. You will not live long in the land you are crossing the Jordan to enter and possess.

[19]This day I call heaven and earth as witnesses against you that I have set before you life and death, blessings and curses. Now choose life, so that you and your children may live [20]and that you may love the LORD your God, listen to his voice, and hold fast to him. For the LORD is your life, and he will give you many years in the land he swore to give to your fathers, Abraham, Isaac and Jacob.

Joshua to Succeed Moses

31 Then Moses went out and spoke these words to all Israel: [2]"I am now a hundred and twenty years old and I am no longer able to lead you. The LORD has said to me, 'You shall not cross the Jordan.' [3]The LORD your God himself will cross over ahead of you. He will destroy these nations before you, and you will take possession of their land. Joshua also will cross over ahead of you, as the LORD said. [4]And the LORD will do to them what he did to Sihon and Og, the kings of the Amorites, whom he destroyed along with their land. [5]The LORD will deliver them to you, and you must do to them all that I have commanded you. [6]Be strong and courageous. Do not be afraid or terrified because of them, for the LORD your God goes with you; he will never leave you nor forsake you."

Praying Deuteronomy 31:6
Thank You, God, that You will
not leave or forsake me.

[7]Then Moses summoned Joshua and said to him in the presence of all Israel, "Be strong and courageous, for you must go with this people into the land that the LORD swore to their forefathers to give them, and you must divide it among them as their inheritance. [8]The LORD himself goes before you and will be with you; he will never leave you nor forsake you. Do not be afraid; do not be discouraged."

The Reading of the Law

9So Moses wrote down this law and gave it to the priests, the sons of Levi, who carried the ark of the covenant of the LORD, and to all the elders of Israel. 10Then Moses commanded them: "At the end of every seven years, in the year for canceling debts, during the Feast of Tabernacles, 11when all Israel comes to appear before the LORD your God at the place he will choose, you shall read this law before them in their hearing. 12Assemble the people—men, women and children, and the aliens living in your towns—so they can listen and learn to fear the LORD your God and follow carefully all the words of this law. 13Their children, who do not know this law, must hear it and learn to fear the LORD your God as long as you live in the land you are crossing the Jordan to possess."

Israel's Rebellion Predicted

14The LORD said to Moses, "Now the day of your death is near. Call Joshua and present yourselves at the Tent of Meeting, where I will commission him." So Moses and Joshua came and presented themselves at the Tent of Meeting.

15Then the LORD appeared at the Tent in a pillar of cloud, and the cloud stood over the entrance to the Tent. 16And the LORD said to Moses: "You are going to rest with your fathers, and these people will soon prostitute themselves to the foreign gods of the land they are entering. They will forsake me and break the covenant I made with them. 17On that day I will become angry with them and forsake them; I will hide my face from them, and they will be destroyed. Many disasters and difficulties will come upon them, and on that day they will ask, 'Have not these disasters come upon us because our God is not with us?' 18And I will certainly hide my face on that day because of all their wickedness in turning to other gods.

19"Now write down for yourselves this song and teach it to the Israelites and have them sing it, so that it may be a witness for me against them. 20When I have brought them into the land flowing with milk and honey, the land I promised on oath to their forefathers, and when they eat their fill and thrive, they will turn to other gods and worship them, rejecting me and breaking my covenant. 21And when many disasters and difficulties come upon them, this song will testify against them, because it will not be forgotten by their descendants. I know what they are disposed to do, even before I bring them into the land I promised them on oath." 22So Moses wrote down this song that day and taught it to the Israelites.

23The LORD gave this command to Joshua son of Nun: "Be strong and courageous, for you will bring the Israelites into the land I promised them on oath, and I myself will be with you."

24After Moses finished writing in a book the words of this law from beginning to end, 25he gave this command to the Levites who carried the ark of the covenant of the LORD: 26"Take this Book of the Law and place it beside the ark of the covenant of the LORD your God. There it will remain as a witness against you. 27For I know how rebellious and stiff-necked you are. If you have been rebellious against the LORD while I am still alive and with you, how much more will you rebel after I die! 28Assemble before me all the elders of your tribes and all your officials, so that I can speak these words in their hearing and call heaven and earth to testify against them. 29For I know that after my death you are sure to become utterly corrupt and to turn from the way I have commanded you. In days to come, disaster will fall upon you because you will do evil in the sight of the LORD and provoke him to anger by what your hands have made."

The Song of Moses

30And Moses recited the words of this song from beginning to end in the hearing of the whole assembly of Israel:

32

Listen, O heavens, and I will
speak;
  hear, O earth, the words of my
    mouth.
[2] Let my teaching fall like rain
  and my words descend like dew,
like showers on new grass,
  like abundant rain on tender plants.

[3] I will proclaim the name of the LORD.
  Oh, praise the greatness of our
    God!
[4] He is the Rock, his works are perfect,
  and all his ways are just.
A faithful God who does no wrong,
  upright and just is he.

[5] They have acted corruptly toward
    him;
  to their shame they are no longer
    his children,

but a warped and crooked
  generation.[a]
[6] Is this the way you repay the LORD,
  O foolish and unwise people?
Is he not your Father, your Creator,[b]
  who made you and formed you?

[7] Remember the days of old;
  consider the generations long past.
Ask your father and he will tell you,
  your elders, and they will explain
    to you.
[8] When the Most High gave the
    nations their inheritance,
  when he divided all mankind,
he set up boundaries for the peoples
  according to the number of the
    sons of Israel.[c]
[9] For the LORD's portion is his people,
  Jacob his allotted inheritance.

---

[a] 5 Or Corrupt are they and not his children, / a generation warped and twisted to their shame   [b] 6 Or Father, who bought you
[c] 8 Masoretic Text; Dead Sea Scrolls (see also Septuagint) sons of God

GOING *deeper*

Praise God for His Greatness

READ AND CONSIDER: DEUTERONOMY 32:1-43

"I will proclaim the name of the LORD. Oh, praise the greatness of our God! He is the Rock, his works are perfect, and all his ways are just. A faithful God who does no wrong, upright and just is he" (Deuteronomy 32:3-4).

Nothing we do is more powerful or life changing than praising God. It is one of the means by which God transforms us. Every time we praise and worship Him, His presence changes our hearts and allows the Holy Spirit to soften and mold us into whatever He wants us to be.

Because our flesh does not naturally praise and worship God, we have to *will* ourselves to do it. And because it's not the first thing we think to do, we have to decide to do it regardless of our circumstances. We have to say, "I *will* praise the Lord." Of course, the more we get to know God, the easier praise becomes. When we get to the point where we can't keep from praising Him, then we are at the place we are supposed to be.

Pause many times a day to praise God for the many blessings He's given you. Praise Him that He is your Rock, that His works are perfect, that His ways are just. Praise Him that He is a faithful and good God. Praise Him for how much He loves you and for all the ways He shows it.

Do you want a transformed life? Do you want to be more like Jesus? Do you want to be molded into all that God wants you to be? Then praise Him often. When you think of all He has done for you, praise and worship will come easily.

¹⁰In a desert land he found him,
in a barren and howling waste.
He shielded him and cared for him;
he guarded him as the apple of his
eye,
¹¹like an eagle that stirs up its nest
and hovers over its young,
that spreads its wings to catch them
and carries them on its pinions.
¹²The LORD alone led him;
no foreign god was with him.

¹³He made him ride on the heights of
the land
and fed him with the fruit of the
fields.
He nourished him with honey from
the rock,
and with oil from the flinty crag,
¹⁴with curds and milk from herd and
flock
and with fattened lambs and goats,
with choice rams of Bashan
and the finest kernels of wheat.
You drank the foaming blood of the
grape.

¹⁵Jeshurunª grew fat and kicked;
filled with food, he became heavy
and sleek.
He abandoned the God who made
him
and rejected the Rock his Savior.
¹⁶They made him jealous with their
foreign gods
and angered him with their
detestable idols.
¹⁷They sacrificed to demons, which are
not God—
gods they had not known,
gods that recently appeared,
gods your fathers did not fear.
¹⁸You deserted the Rock, who fathered
you;
you forgot the God who gave you
birth.

¹⁹The LORD saw this and rejected them
because he was angered by his sons
and daughters.

²⁰"I will hide my face from them," he
said,
"and see what their end will be;
for they are a perverse generation,
children who are unfaithful.
²¹They made me jealous by what is no
god
and angered me with their
worthless idols.
I will make them envious by those
who are not a people;
I will make them angry by a nation
that has no understanding.
²²For a fire has been kindled by my
wrath,
one that burns to the realm of
deathᵇ below.
It will devour the earth and its
harvests
and set afire the foundations of the
mountains.

²³"I will heap calamities upon them
and spend my arrows against
them.
²⁴I will send wasting famine against
them,
consuming pestilence and deadly
plague;
I will send against them the fangs of
wild beasts,
the venom of vipers that glide in
the dust.
²⁵In the street the sword will make
them childless;
in their homes terror will reign.
Young men and young women will
perish,
infants and gray-haired men.
²⁶I said I would scatter them
and blot out their memory from
mankind,
²⁷but I dreaded the taunt of the enemy,
lest the adversary misunderstand
and say, 'Our hand has triumphed;
the LORD has not done all this.'"
²⁸They are a nation without sense,
there is no discernment in them.

ª 15 Jeshurun means the upright one, that is, Israel.   ᵇ 22 Hebrew to Sheol

²⁹If only they were wise and would
    understand this
  and discern what their end will be!
³⁰How could one man chase a
    thousand,
  or two put ten thousand to flight,
unless their Rock had sold them,
  unless the LORD had given them
    up?
³¹For their rock is not like our Rock,
  as even our enemies concede.
³²Their vine comes from the vine of
    Sodom
  and from the fields of Gomorrah.
  Their grapes are filled with poison,
  and their clusters with bitterness.
³³Their wine is the venom of serpents,
  the deadly poison of cobras.

³⁴"Have I not kept this in reserve
  and sealed it in my vaults?
³⁵It is mine to avenge; I will repay.
  In due time their foot will slip;
  their day of disaster is near
  and their doom rushes upon them."

³⁶The LORD will judge his people
  and have compassion on his
    servants
when he sees their strength is gone
  and no one is left, slave or free.
³⁷He will say: "Now where are their
    gods,
  the rock they took refuge in,
³⁸the gods who ate the fat of their
    sacrifices
  and drank the wine of their drink
    offerings?
  Let them rise up to help you!
  Let them give you shelter!

³⁹"See now that I myself am He!
  There is no god besides me.
I put to death and I bring to life,
  I have wounded and I will heal,
  and no one can deliver out of my
    hand.
⁴⁰I lift my hand to heaven and declare:
  As surely as I live forever,

⁴¹when I sharpen my flashing sword
  and my hand grasps it in judgment,
I will take vengeance on my
    adversaries
  and repay those who hate me.
⁴²I will make my arrows drunk with
    blood,
  while my sword devours flesh:
  the blood of the slain and the
    captives,
  the heads of the enemy leaders."

⁴³Rejoice, O nations, with his people,ᵃ,ᵇ
  for he will avenge the blood of his
    servants;
he will take vengeance on his
    enemies
  and make atonement for his land
    and people.

⁴⁴Moses came with Joshuaᶜ son of Nun and spoke all the words of this song in the hearing of the people. ⁴⁵When Moses finished reciting all these words to all Israel, ⁴⁶he said to them, "Take to heart all the words I have solemnly declared to you this day, so that you may command your children to obey carefully all the words of this law. ⁴⁷They are not just idle words for you—they are your life. By them you will live long in the land you are crossing the Jordan to possess."

Moses to Die on Mount Nebo

⁴⁸On that same day the LORD told Moses, ⁴⁹"Go up into the Abarim Range to Mount Nebo in Moab, across from Jericho, and view Canaan, the land I am giving the Israelites as their own possession. ⁵⁰There on the mountain that you have climbed you will die and be gathered to your people, just as your brother Aaron died on Mount Hor and was gathered to his people. ⁵¹This is because both of you broke faith with me in the presence of the Israelites at the waters of Meribah Kadesh in the Desert of Zin and because you did not uphold my holiness among the Israelites. ⁵²Therefore, you will see

---

ᵃ43 Or *Make his people rejoice, O nations*   ᵇ43 Masoretic Text; Dead Sea Scrolls (see also Septuagint) *people, / and let all the angels worship him /*   ᶜ44 Hebrew *Hoshea*, a variant of *Joshua* the land only from a distance; you will not enter the land I am giving to the people of Israel."

Moses Blesses the Tribes

33 This is the blessing that Moses the man of God pronounced on the Israelites before his death. ²He said:

"The LORD came from Sinai
  and dawned over them from Seir;
he shone forth from Mount Paran.
He came with ᵃ myriads of holy ones
  from the south, from his mountain
    slopes.ᵇ
³Surely it is you who love the people;
  all the holy ones are in your hand.
At your feet they all bow down,
  and from you receive instruction,
⁴the law that Moses gave us,
  the possession of the assembly of
    Jacob.
⁵He was king over Jeshurunᶜ
  when the leaders of the people
    assembled,
  along with the tribes of Israel.

⁶"Let Reuben live and not die,
  norᵈ his men be few."

⁷And this he said about Judah:

"Hear, O LORD, the cry of Judah;
  bring him to his people.
With his own hands he defends his
    cause.
  Oh, be his help against his foes!"

⁸About Levi he said:

"Your Thummim and Urim belong
  to the man you favored.
You tested him at Massah;
  you contended with him at the
    waters of Meribah.
⁹He said of his father and mother,
  'I have no regard for them.'
He did not recognize his brothers
  or acknowledge his own children,
but he watched over your word
  and guarded your covenant.

¹⁰He teaches your precepts to Jacob
  and your law to Israel.
He offers incense before you
  and whole burnt offerings on your
    altar.
¹¹Bless all his skills, O LORD,
  and be pleased with the work of his
    hands.
Smite the loins of those who rise up
    against him;
  strike his foes till they rise no
    more."

¹²About Benjamin he said:

"Let the beloved of the LORD rest
    secure in him,
  for he shields him all day long,
and the one the LORD loves rests
    between his shoulders."

¹³About Joseph he said:

"May the LORD bless his land
  with the precious dew from heaven
    above
  and with the deep waters that lie
    below;
¹⁴with the best the sun brings forth
  and the finest the moon can yield;
¹⁵with the choicest gifts of the ancient
    mountains
  and the fruitfulness of the
    everlasting hills;
¹⁶with the best gifts of the earth and its
    fullness
  and the favor of him who dwelt in
    the burning bush.
Let all these rest on the head of
    Joseph,
  on the brow of the prince amongᵉ
    his brothers.
¹⁷In majesty he is like a firstborn bull;
  his horns are the horns of a wild
    ox.
With them he will gore the nations,
  even those at the ends of the earth.
Such are the ten thousands of
    Ephraim;

ᵃ2 Or *from*   ᵇ2 The meaning of the Hebrew for this phrase is uncertain.   ᶜ5 *Jeshurun* means *the upright one*, that is, Israel; also in verse 26.   ᵈ6 Or *but let*   ᵉ16 Or *of the one separated from* such are the thousands of Manasseh."

18About Zebulun he said:

"Rejoice, Zebulun, in your going
    out,
and you, Issachar, in your tents.
19They will summon peoples to the
    mountain
    and there offer sacrifices of
    righteousness;
they will feast on the abundance of
    the seas,
    on the treasures hidden in the
    sand."

20About Gad he said:

"Blessed is he who enlarges Gad's
    domain!
Gad lives there like a lion,
    tearing at arm or head.
21He chose the best land for himself;
    the leader's portion was kept for
    him.

When the heads of the people
    assembled,
he carried out the LORD's righteous
    will,
    and his judgments concerning
    Israel."

22About Dan he said:

"Dan is a lion's cub,
    springing out of Bashan."

23About Naphtali he said:

"Naphtali is abounding with the favor
    of the LORD
    and is full of his blessing;
    he will inherit southward to the
    lake."

24About Asher he said:

"Most blessed of sons is Asher;
    let him be favored by his brothers,
    and let him bathe his feet in oil.
25The bolts of your gates will be iron
    and bronze,

God Is Your Refuge

GOING *deeper*

READ AND CONSIDER: DEUTERONOMY 33

"There is no one like the God of Jeshurun, who rides on the heavens to help you and on the clouds in his majesty. The eternal God is your refuge, and underneath are the everlasting arms... Blessed are you, O Israel! Who is like you, a people saved by the LORD? He is your shield and helper and your glorious sword" (Deuteronomy 33:26-27,29).

What an amazing picture! God rides on the heavens to help you. He is your refuge. His arms are holding you up, no matter how heavy your load, how difficult your circumstances, or how strong your fears. God not only fights for you but also provides you with a safe refuge. He actually fights *in your place* while you rest in the safety He gives. He shields you, saves you, and gains victory for you.

As you pray, ask God to show you how this passage applies to your life right now. Think of the specific challenges you face. Picture yourself in His loving protection as He fights your battles for you. Don't try to face your challenges alone. God doesn't want that. Whenever you try to go out on your own strength, He is grieved because you are not allowing Him to do for you all that He longs to do. He is grieved because you make yourself more vulnerable to Satan's attack. Every time you ask God for help, He will rush to your side, and the enemy will be forced to flee from you.

and your strength will equal your
days.

26 "There is no one like the God of
Jeshurun,
who rides on the heavens to help
you
and on the clouds in his majesty.
27 The eternal God is your refuge,
and underneath are the everlasting
arms.
He will drive out your enemy before
you,
saying, 'Destroy him!'
28 So Israel will live in safety alone;
Jacob's spring is secure
in a land of grain and new wine,
where the heavens drop dew.
29 Blessed are you, O Israel!
Who is like you,
a people saved by the LORD?
He is your shield and helper
and your glorious sword.
Your enemies will cower before you,
and you will trample down their
high places.ᵃ"

The Death of Moses

34 Then Moses climbed Mount Nebo
from the plains of Moab to the top
of Pisgah, across from Jericho. There the
LORD showed him the whole land—
from Gilead to Dan, 2 all of Naphtali, the
territory of Ephraim and Manasseh, all
the land of Judah as far as the western

sea,ᵇ ³the Negev and the whole region
from the Valley of Jericho, the City of
Palms, as far as Zoar. ⁴Then the LORD said
to him, "This is the land I promised on
oath to Abraham, Isaac and Jacob when I
said, 'I will give it to your descendants.' I
have let you see it with your eyes, but you
will not cross over into it."

⁵And Moses the servant of the LORD
died there in Moab, as the LORD had said.
⁶He buried himᶜ in Moab, in the valley
opposite Beth Peor, but to this day no
one knows where his grave is. ⁷Moses was
a hundred and twenty years old when he
died, yet his eyes were not weak nor his
strength gone. ⁸The Israelites grieved for
Moses in the plains of Moab thirty days,
until the time of weeping and mourning
was over.

⁹Now Joshua son of Nun was filled
with the spiritᵈ of wisdom because Moses had laid his hands on him. So the Israelites listened to him and did what the
LORD had commanded Moses.

¹⁰Since then, no prophet has risen in
Israel like Moses, whom the LORD knew
face to face, ¹¹who did all those miraculous signs and wonders the LORD sent
him to do in Egypt—to Pharaoh and
to all his officials and to his whole land.
¹²For no one has ever shown the mighty
power or performed the awesome deeds
that Moses did in the sight of all Israel.

ᵃ 29 Or will tread upon their bodies   ᵇ 2 That is, the Mediterranean   ᶜ 6 Or He was buried   ᵈ 9 Or Spirit

Author: Unknown, possibly Samuel

Date: Written after the conquest of Canaan, which took place between 1406 and 1375 BC

Audience: Future generations of God's people—to give them a record of God's mighty acts in history and to encourage them to remain faithful to Him.

When facing difficult struggles or terrifying enemies, nothing is more wonderful than God's peace. The book of Joshua reminds us that true supernatural peace is the reward of those who remember God's presence, rely on His power, and rest in the promises of His Word.

Joshua faced a daunting task—replacing the legendary Moses and leading the inexperienced Israelites into Canaan. He found confidence and strength by drawing near to God. He found victory by calling upon and trusting fully in the Lord.

Whenever "impossible" obstacles stand in your path, ultimate success can be yours if you will call upon the Lord and fully trust His Word (1:8).

Prayer Themes:

- Thank God for His presence with you at all times (1:5; see also Hebrews 13:5).

- Ask God to show you some practical ways you can commemorate His powerful involvement in your life (chapter 4).

- Praise God for His faithfulness to always keep His word and make good on His promises (14:6-15).

Joshua

The LORD Commands Joshua

1 After the death of Moses the servant of the LORD, the LORD said to Joshua son of Nun, Moses' aide: 2"Moses my servant is dead. Now then, you and all these people, get ready to cross the Jordan River into the land I am about to give to them—to the Israelites. 3I will give you every place where you set your foot, as I promised Moses. 4Your territory will extend from the desert to Lebanon, and from the great river, the Euphrates—all the Hittite country—to the Great Sea^a on the west. 5No one will be able to stand up against you all the days of your life. As I was with Moses, so I will be with you; I will never leave you nor forsake you.

6"Be strong and courageous, because you will lead these people to inherit the land I swore to their forefathers to give them. 7Be strong and very courageous. Be careful to obey all the law my servant Moses gave you; do not turn from it to the right or to the left, that you may be successful wherever you go. 8Do not let this Book of the Law depart from your mouth; meditate on it day and night, so that you may be careful to do everything written in it. Then you will be prosperous and successful. 9Have I not commanded you? Be strong and courageous. Do not be terrified; do not be discouraged, for the LORD your God will be with you wherever you go."

Praying Joshua 1:9
Heavenly Father, enable me to be strong and not afraid, knowing that You are with me wherever I go.

10So Joshua ordered the officers of the people: 11"Go through the camp and

---

^a 4 That is, the Mediterranean

Looking for God's Will

READ AND CONSIDER: JOSHUA 1:6-9

"Do not let this Book of the Law depart from your mouth; meditate on it day and night, so that you may be careful to do everything written in it. Then you will be prosperous and successful" (Joshua 1:8).

Who doesn't want to know God's will for their life? And God wants to reveal it. So why does God's will often seem to be such a mystery to us? In order to know what God wants, you need to be aware of four important aspects of His will:

First, God's will is most often found through reading the Bible and letting it sink into your heart. Joshua was commanded to know the Book of the Law backward and forward, to meditate and reflect on it. Then God promised to prosper him. The Bible declares clearly that God will direct and lead us. Psalm 37:23 says, "If the LORD delights in a man's way, he makes his steps firm." And in Psalm 32:8, God promises, "I will instruct you and teach you in the way you should go; I will counsel you and watch over you." He speaks to us through His Word, the Scriptures.

Second, God's will is ongoing in our lives. From the time we are infants until the day we die, God has a will for us—as children, young people, adults, and senior citizens. Isaiah 58:11 says, "The LORD will guide you always; he will satisfy your needs in a sun-scorched land and will strengthen your frame. You will be like a well-watered garden, like a spring whose waters never fail."

Third, God's will is specific. The prophet Isaiah heard the Lord promising His children, "Whether you turn to the right or to the left, your ears will hear a voice behind you, saying, 'This is the way; walk in it'" (Isaiah 30:21).

Fourth, God's will is profitable. The Lord told Joshua, who was to lead the Israelites into the promised land, "Do not let this Book of the Law depart from your mouth . . . be careful to do everything written in it. *Then you will be prosperous and successful*" (Joshua 1:8, emphasis added).

Looking for God's will may be simpler than you ever imagined. It doesn't matter what your situation is at the moment. As you read the Word and prayerfully ask for guidance, then all you have to do is take the next step that the Lord is showing you. As you take one step at a time, you will begin to see a solid way of following after God. As long as you are walking with Him continually in prayer and living His way according to His Word, you are not likely to get off the path of His will. And if by chance you do, He will get you right back on. That's because when you're always listening for God's voice, you will sense in your heart when you violate His directions. Each small step of obedience will turn into a life of obedience lived in the will of God.

---

tell the people, 'Get your supplies ready. Three days from now you will cross the Jordan here to go in and take possession of the land the LORD your God is giving you for your own.'"

¹²But to the Reubenites, the Gadites and the half-tribe of Manasseh, Joshua said, ¹³"Remember the command that Moses the servant of the LORD gave you: 'The LORD your God is giving you rest and has granted you this land.' ¹⁴Your wives, your children and your livestock may stay in the land that Moses gave you east of the Jordan, but all your fighting men, fully armed, must cross over ahead of your brothers. You are to help your brothers ¹⁵until the LORD gives them rest, as he has done for you, and until they

too have taken possession of the land that the LORD your God is giving them. After that, you may go back and occupy your own land, which Moses the servant of the LORD gave you east of the Jordan toward the sunrise."

16 Then they answered Joshua, "Whatever you have commanded us we will do, and wherever you send us we will go. 17 Just as we fully obeyed Moses, so we will obey you. Only may the LORD your God be with you as he was with Moses. 18 Whoever rebels against your word and does not obey your words, whatever you may command them, will be put to death. Only be strong and courageous!"

Rahab and the Spies

2 Then Joshua son of Nun secretly sent two spies from Shittim. "Go, look over the land," he said, "especially Jericho." So they went and entered the house of a prostitute[a] named Rahab and stayed there.

2 The king of Jericho was told, "Look! Some of the Israelites have come here tonight to spy out the land." 3 So the king of Jericho sent this message to Rahab: "Bring out the men who came to you and entered your house, because they have come to spy out the whole land."

4 But the woman had taken the two men and hidden them. She said, "Yes, the men came to me, but I did not know where they had come from. 5 At dusk, when it was time to close the city gate, the men left. I don't know which way they went. Go after them quickly. You may catch up with them." 6 (But she had taken them up to the roof and hidden them under the stalks of flax she had laid out on the roof.) 7 So the men set out in pursuit of the spies on the road that leads to the fords of the Jordan, and as soon as the pursuers had gone out, the gate was shut.

8 Before the spies lay down for the night, she went up on the roof 9 and said

to them, "I know that the LORD has given this land to you and that a great fear of you has fallen on us, so that all who live in this country are melting in fear because of you. 10 We have heard how the LORD dried up the water of the Red Sea[b] for you when you came out of Egypt, and what you did to Sihon and Og, the two kings of the Amorites east of the Jordan, whom you completely destroyed.[c] 11 When we heard of it, our hearts melted and everyone's courage failed because of you, for the LORD your God is God in heaven above and on the earth below. 12 Now then, please swear to me by the LORD that you will show kindness to my family, because I have shown kindness to you. Give me a sure sign 13 that you will spare the lives of my father and mother, my brothers and sisters, and all who belong to them, and that you will save us from death."

14 "Our lives for your lives!" the men assured her. "If you don't tell what we are doing, we will treat you kindly and faithfully when the LORD gives us the land."

15 So she let them down by a rope through the window, for the house she lived in was part of the city wall. 16 Now she had said to them, "Go to the hills so the pursuers will not find you. Hide yourselves there three days until they return, and then go on your way."

17 The men said to her, "This oath you made us swear will not be binding on us 18 unless, when we enter the land, you have tied this scarlet cord in the window through which you let us down, and unless you have brought your father and mother, your brothers and all your family into your house. 19 If anyone goes outside your house into the street, his blood will be on his own head; we will not be responsible. As for anyone who is in the house with you, his blood will be on our head if a hand is laid on him. 20 But if you tell

---

a *1* Or possibly *an innkeeper*   b *10* Hebrew *Yam Suph*; that is, Sea of Reeds   c *10* The Hebrew term refers to the irrevocable giving over of things or persons to the LORD, often by totally destroying them.

what we are doing, we will be released from the oath you made us swear."

²¹"Agreed," she replied. "Let it be as you say." So she sent them away and they departed. And she tied the scarlet cord in the window.

²²When they left, they went into the hills and stayed there three days, until the pursuers had searched all along the road and returned without finding them. ²³Then the two men started back. They went down out of the hills, forded the river and came to Joshua son of Nun and told him everything that had happened to them. ²⁴They said to Joshua, "The LORD has surely given the whole land into our hands; all the people are melting in fear because of us."

Crossing the Jordan

3 Early in the morning Joshua and all the Israelites set out from Shittim and went to the Jordan, where they camped before crossing over. ²After three days the officers went throughout the camp, ³giving orders to the people: "When you see the ark of the covenant of the LORD your God, and the priests, who are Levites, carrying it, you are to move out from your positions and follow it. ⁴Then you will know which way to go, since you have never been this way before. But keep a distance of about a thousand yards³ between you and the ark; do not go near it."

⁵Joshua told the people, "Consecrate yourselves, for tomorrow the LORD will do amazing things among you."

⁶Joshua said to the priests, "Take up the ark of the covenant and pass on ahead of the people." So they took it up and went ahead of them.

⁷And the LORD said to Joshua, "Today I will begin to exalt you in the eyes of all Israel, so they may know that I am with you as I was with Moses. ⁸Tell the priests who carry the ark of the covenant: 'When you reach the edge of the Jordan's waters, go and stand in the river.'"

⁹Joshua said to the Israelites, "Come here and listen to the words of the LORD your God. ¹⁰This is how you will know that the living God is among you and that he will certainly drive out before you the Canaanites, Hittites, Hivites, Perizzites, Girgashites, Amorites and Jebusites. ¹¹See, the ark of the covenant of the Lord of all the earth will go into the Jordan ahead of you. ¹²Now then, choose twelve men from the tribes of Israel, one from each tribe. ¹³And as soon as the priests who carry the ark of the LORD—the Lord of all the earth—set foot in the Jordan, its waters flowing downstream will be cut off and stand up in a heap."

¹⁴So when the people broke camp to cross the Jordan, the priests carrying the ark of the covenant went ahead of them. ¹⁵Now the Jordan is at flood stage all during harvest. Yet as soon as the priests who carried the ark reached the Jordan and their feet touched the water's edge, ¹⁶the water from upstream stopped flowing. It piled up in a heap a great distance away, at a town called Adam in the vicinity of Zarethan, while the water flowing down to the Sea of the Arabah (the Salt Sea³) was completely cut off. So the people crossed over opposite Jericho. ¹⁷The priests who carried the ark of the covenant of the LORD stood firm on dry ground in the middle of the Jordan, while all Israel passed by until the whole nation had completed the crossing on dry ground.

4 When the whole nation had finished crossing the Jordan, the LORD said to Joshua, ²"Choose twelve men from among the people, one from each tribe, ³and tell them to take up twelve stones from the middle of the Jordan from right where the priests stood and to carry them over with you and put them down at the place where you stay tonight."

⁴So Joshua called together the twelve men he had appointed from the Israelites, one from each tribe, ⁵and said to them, "Go over before the ark of the LORD your God into the middle of the Jordan.

---

³ 4 Hebrew *about two thousand cubits* (about 900 meters)   ᵇ 16 That is, the Dead Sea

Learning to Walk With God

When children first learn to walk, they don't get very far without falling. They fare much better if they reach up and take someone else's hand. That helping hand can guide them away from danger and get them safely where they need to go. Soon children will start walking alone—even though they will probably end up falling down and getting hurt or wandering off to someplace that could mean trouble. And parents *allow* those things to happen because they want their children to eventually learn to walk *without* any assistance. Of course, parents step in and protect their children when they see danger, but their goal is always to prepare their children for the day when they will no longer need any help. And they are thrilled when they see their children experience that joy of freedom for the first time.

Learning to walk with our heavenly Father is somewhat different. He wants us to reach up and take His hand, but He doesn't want us to *ever* let go. In fact, His desire is that we become *more* and *more* dependent upon Him for every step. That's because He wants to take us to places we've never been. To heights we can't even imagine. In order to do that, we have to go through the low valleys, treacherous mountains, rough terrain, and narrow paths of life—places where we could easily get lost or off the track.

And there is definitely no way we can just head off on our own and expect to arrive safely in the place He has planned for us. And, quite opposite of the way we teach our children, we will *never* know the joy of *true* freedom until we understand we cannot take a single step without His help.

But it's up to us to take the first step. If we don't, we will never learn to walk with Him. We can be so afraid of taking a wrong step that we fail to take any step at all. God didn't part the waters of the Jordan River for the Israelites until they first put their feet in the water (Joshua 3:15-16). That's because God always requires the first step to be ours. In order to take that first step, we must look into the face of God, reach up to take His hand, and say, "Lead me in the path You have for me, Lord. From this day on I want to walk with You. I take this step of faith and I trust You to meet me here. Align my heart with Yours."

Once you've taken that first step, God will show you other steps to take. He will teach you how to walk in the light of His truth, revelation, and love. You'll discover ways to avoid the things that separate you from Him and all He has for you.

If the path you've been on is crooked, He will make it straight. If you are headed in the wrong direction, He will turn you around. If you have come to a standstill, He will get you moving. If you are going around in circles, He will correct your course and cause you to arrive at your destination. The simple act of giving your life to Him will immediately put you on the correct path and aim you in the right direction.

As you take one step at a time, holding God's hand and letting Him lead, He will get you where you need to go.

For the next "From Stormie's Heart" article, go to page 312.

Each of you is to take up a stone on his shoulder, according to the number of the tribes of the Israelites, 6to serve as a sign among you. In the future, when your children ask you, 'What do these stones mean?' 7tell them that the flow of the Jordan was cut off before the ark of the covenant of the LORD. When it crossed the Jordan, the waters of the Jordan were cut off. These stones are to be a memorial to the people of Israel forever."

8So the Israelites did as Joshua commanded them. They took twelve stones from the middle of the Jordan, according to the number of the tribes of the Israelites, as the LORD had told Joshua; and they carried them over with them to their camp, where they put them down. 9Joshua set up the twelve stones that had been[a] in the middle of the Jordan at the spot where the priests who carried the ark of the covenant had stood. And they are there to this day.

10Now the priests who carried the ark remained standing in the middle of the Jordan until everything the LORD had commanded Joshua was done by the people, just as Moses had directed Joshua. The people hurried over, 11and as soon as all of them had crossed, the ark of the LORD and the priests came to the other side while the people watched. 12The men of Reuben, Gad and the half-tribe of Manasseh crossed over, armed, in front of the Israelites, as Moses had directed them. 13About forty thousand armed for battle crossed over before the LORD to the plains of Jericho for war.

14That day the LORD exalted Joshua in the sight of all Israel; and they revered him all the days of his life, just as they had revered Moses.

15Then the LORD said to Joshua, 16"Command the priests carrying the ark of the Testimony to come up out of the Jordan."

17So Joshua commanded the priests, "Come up out of the Jordan."

18And the priests came up out of the river carrying the ark of the covenant of the LORD. No sooner had they set their feet on the dry ground than the waters of the Jordan returned to their place and ran at flood stage as before.

19On the tenth day of the first month the people went up from the Jordan and camped at Gilgal on the eastern border of Jericho. 20And Joshua set up at Gilgal the twelve stones they had taken out of the Jordan. 21He said to the Israelites, "In the future when your descendants ask their fathers, 'What do these stones mean?' 22tell them, 'Israel crossed the Jordan on dry ground.' 23For the LORD your God dried up the Jordan before you until you had crossed over. The LORD your God did to the Jordan just what he had done to the Red Sea[b] when he dried it up before us until we had crossed over. 24He did this so that all the peoples of the earth might know that the hand of the LORD is powerful and so that you might always fear the LORD your God."

Circumcision at Gilgal

5 Now when all the Amorite kings west of the Jordan and all the Canaanite kings along the coast heard how the LORD had dried up the Jordan before the Israelites until we had crossed over, their hearts melted and they no longer had the courage to face the Israelites.

2At that time the LORD said to Joshua, "Make flint knives and circumcise the Israelites again." 3So Joshua made flint knives and circumcised the Israelites at Gibeath Haaraloth.[c]

4Now this is why he did so: All those who came out of Egypt—all the men of military age—died in the desert on the way after leaving Egypt. 5All the people that came out had been circumcised, but all the people born in the desert during the journey from Egypt had not. 6The Israelites had moved about in the desert forty years until all the men who were

---

[a] 9 Or *Joshua also set up twelve stones* [b] 23 Hebrew *Yam Suph;* that is, Sea of Reeds [c] 3 *Gibeath Haaraloth* means *hill of foreskins.*

of military age when they left Egypt had died, since they had not obeyed the LORD. For the LORD had sworn to them that they would not see the land that he had solemnly promised their fathers to give us, a land flowing with milk and honey. 7So he raised up their sons in their place, and these were the ones Joshua circumcised. They were still uncircumcised because they had not been circumcised on the way. 8And after the whole nation had been circumcised, they remained where they were in camp until they were healed.

Praying Joshua 5:6-9

Lord, if I have to spend time in the wilderness until Egypt is out of my system, I pray You will help me learn my lessons well so I won't have to keep coming back to the same territory.

9Then the LORD said to Joshua, "Today I have rolled away the reproach of Egypt from you." So the place has been called Gilgal[a] to this day.

10On the evening of the fourteenth day of the month, while camped at Gilgal on the plains of Jericho, the Israelites celebrated the Passover. 11The day after the Passover, that very day, they ate some of the produce of the land: unleavened bread and roasted grain. 12The manna stopped the day after[b] they ate this food from the land; there was no longer any manna for the Israelites, but that year they ate of the produce of Canaan.

The Fall of Jericho

13Now when Joshua was near Jericho, he looked up and saw a man standing in front of him with a drawn sword in his hand. Joshua went up to him and asked, "Are you for us or for our enemies?"

14"Neither," he replied, "but as commander of the army of the LORD I have now come." Then Joshua fell facedown to the ground in reverence, and asked

him, "What message does my Lord[c] have for his servant?"

15The commander of the LORD's army replied, "Take off your sandals, for the place where you are standing is holy." And Joshua did so.

6 Now Jericho was tightly shut up because of the Israelites. No one went out and no one came in.

2Then the LORD said to Joshua, "See, I have delivered Jericho into your hands, along with its king and its fighting men. 3March around the city once with all the armed men. Do this for six days. 4Have seven priests carry trumpets of rams' horns in front of the ark. On the seventh day, march around the city seven times, with the priests blowing the trumpets. 5When you hear them sound a long blast on the trumpets, have all the people give a loud shout; then the wall of the city will collapse and the people will go up, every man straight in."

6So Joshua son of Nun called the priests and said to them, "Take up the ark of the covenant of the LORD and have seven priests carry trumpets in front of it." 7And he ordered the people, "Advance! March around the city, with the armed guard going ahead of the ark of the LORD."

8When Joshua had spoken to the people, the seven priests carrying the seven trumpets before the LORD went forward, blowing their trumpets, and the ark of the LORD's covenant followed them. 9The armed guard marched ahead of the priests who blew the trumpets, and the rear guard followed the ark. All this time the trumpets were sounding. 10But Joshua had commanded the people, "Do not give a war cry, do not raise your voices, do not say a word until the day I tell you to shout. Then shout!" 11So he had the ark of the LORD carried around the city, circling it once. Then the people returned to camp and spent the night there.

12Joshua got up early the next morning and the priests took up the ark of the

---

a 9 *Gilgal* sounds like the Hebrew for *roll.*   b 12 Or *the day*   c 14 Or *lord*

Looking for a Breakthrough?

GOING *deeper*

READ AND CONSIDER: JOSHUA 6:1-20

"When the trumpets sounded, the people shouted, and at the sound of the trumpet, when the people gave a loud shout, the wall collapsed; so every man charged straight in, and they took the city" (Joshua 6:20).

Have you ever needed a breakthrough in your life? Or some kind of deliverance? Perhaps you or your situation needed to be transformed, but you were facing a wall as high as the one surrounding Jericho. As far as you could see, there seemed to be no way through it.

The good thing about knowing that you need much more than your own strength in order to break down the walls in your life is that it forces you to rely on the power of God to set you free. And His deliverance and freedom are always far beyond what we can imagine. God wants you to depend on Him and His power whenever you face obstacles in your life. So each time you find that you can't seem to move beyond something you are facing, determine to go deeper into God's Word. Commit to even more fervent prayer. Decide to give God heartfelt worship regardless of what is happening.

Those three steps of obedience are powerful and will destroy whatever is standing in the way of your moving into all God has for you.

The Israelites walked around the city of Jericho 13 times in one week. So don't just stand looking at the walls that are obstructing you. Start encircling them with shouts of praise today and every day for as long as it takes.

LORD. ¹³The seven priests carrying the seven trumpets went forward, marching before the ark of the LORD and blowing the trumpets. The armed men went ahead of them and the rear guard followed the ark of the LORD, while the trumpets kept sounding. ¹⁴So on the second day they marched around the city once and returned to the camp. They did this for six days.

¹⁵On the seventh day, they got up at daybreak and marched around the city seven times in the same manner, except that on that day they circled the city seven times. ¹⁶The seventh time around, when the priests sounded the trumpet blast, Joshua commanded the people, "Shout! For the LORD has given you the city! ¹⁷The city and all that is in it are to be devoted[a] to the LORD. Only Rahab the prostitute[b] and all who are with her in her house shall be spared, because she hid the spies we sent. ¹⁸But keep away from the devoted things, so that you will not bring about your own destruction by taking any of them. Otherwise you will make the camp of Israel liable to destruction and bring trouble on it. ¹⁹All the silver and gold and the articles of bronze and iron are sacred to the LORD and must go into his treasury."

²⁰When the trumpets sounded, the people shouted, and at the sound of the trumpet, when the people gave a loud shout, the wall collapsed; so every man charged straight in, and they took the city. ²¹They devoted the city to the LORD and destroyed with the sword every living thing in it—men and women, young and old, cattle, sheep and donkeys.

---

[a] *17* The Hebrew term refers to the irrevocable giving over of things or persons to the LORD, often by totally destroying them; also in verses 18 and 21.   [b] *17* Or possibly *innkeeper*; also in verses 22 and 25

22Joshua said to the two men who had spied out the land, "Go into the prostitute's house and bring her out and all who belong to her, in accordance with your oath to her." 23So the young men who had done the spying went in and brought out Rahab, her father and mother and brothers and all who belonged to her. They brought out her entire family and put them in a place outside the camp of Israel.

24Then they burned the whole city and everything in it, but they put the silver and gold and the articles of bronze and iron into the treasury of the LORD's house. 25But Joshua spared Rahab the prostitute, with her family and all who belonged to her, because she hid the men Joshua had sent as spies to Jericho—and she lives among the Israelites to this day.

26At that time Joshua pronounced this solemn oath: "Cursed before the LORD is the man who undertakes to rebuild this city, Jericho:

"At the cost of his firstborn son
     will he lay its foundations;
at the cost of his youngest
     will he set up its gates."

27So the LORD was with Joshua, and his fame spread throughout the land.

Achan's Sin

7 But the Israelites acted unfaithfully in regard to the devoted things[a]; Achan son of Carmi, the son of Zimri,[b] the son of Zerah, of the tribe of Judah, took some of them. So the LORD's anger burned against Israel.

2Now Joshua sent men from Jericho to Ai, which is near Beth Aven to the east of Bethel, and told them, "Go up and spy out the region." So the men went up and spied out Ai.

3When they returned to Joshua, they said, "Not all the people will have to go up against Ai. Send two or three thousand men to take it and do not weary all the people, for only a few men are there." 4So about three thousand men went up; but they were routed by the men of Ai, 5who killed about thirty-six of them. They chased the Israelites from the city gate as far as the stone quarries[c] and struck them down on the slopes. At this the hearts of the people melted and became like water.

6Then Joshua tore his clothes and fell facedown to the ground before the ark of the LORD, remaining there till evening. The elders of Israel did the same, and sprinkled dust on their heads. 7And Joshua said, "Ah, Sovereign LORD, why did you ever bring this people across the Jordan to deliver us into the hands of the Amorites to destroy us? If only we had been content to stay on the other side of the Jordan! 8O Lord, what can I say, now that Israel has been routed by its enemies? 9The Canaanites and the other people of the country will hear about this and they will surround us and wipe out our name from the earth. What then will you do for your own great name?"

10The LORD said to Joshua, "Stand up! What are you doing down on your face? 11Israel has sinned; they have violated my covenant, which I commanded them to keep. They have taken some of the devoted things; they have stolen, they have lied, they have put them with their own possessions. 12That is why the Israelites cannot stand against their enemies; they turn their backs and run because they have been made liable to destruction. I will not be with you anymore unless you destroy whatever among you is devoted to destruction.

13"Go, consecrate the people. Tell them, 'Consecrate yourselves in preparation for tomorrow; for this is what the LORD, the God of Israel, says: That which is devoted is among you, O Israel. You

---

a 1 The Hebrew term refers to the irrevocable giving over of things or persons to the LORD, often by totally destroying them; also in verses 11, 12, 13 and 15.   b 1 See Septuagint and 1 Chron. 2:6; Hebrew Zabdi; also in verses 17 and 18.   c 5 Or as far as Shebarim

Roadblocks to Prayer

GOING *deeper*

READ AND CONSIDER: JOSHUA 7:1-13

"The LORD said to Joshua, 'Stand up! What are you doing down on your face? Israel has sinned; they have violated my covenant, which I commanded them to keep' " (Joshua 7:10-11).

At least Joshua had come to the right place. In despair over the nation's recent defeat by the little city of Ai, Joshua and the nation's elders performed the proper rituals of repentance and remained there till evening. But the Lord was not impressed with their weeping and wailing. "Stand up!" God commanded. The problem was sin, and once the sinner was found out and the sin removed from the camp, the problem would be solved. God didn't need Joshua on his face at that moment; He needed Joshua to rout out the sin so the nation could move forward.

When you pray, you've come to the right place. But that's just the beginning. As part of your conversation with God, you will "hear" His words speaking to your heart. He will reveal sins to confess, actions to take, changes to make. As you read His Word, He'll make you aware of what He wants you to do. While it's good to keep reading, keep praying, and keep seeking—we still have to take action, especially where sin is concerned. When God reveals sin to you, "stand up," confess it, and take immediate steps to make any necessary changes. After all, you've got more battles ahead, and you need to be ready.

cannot stand against your enemies until you remove it.

14 " 'In the morning, present yourselves tribe by tribe. The tribe that the LORD takes shall come forward clan by clan; the clan that the LORD takes shall come forward family by family; and the family that the LORD takes shall come forward man by man. 15 He who is caught with the devoted things shall be destroyed by fire, along with all that belongs to him. He has violated the covenant of the LORD and has done a disgraceful thing in Israel!' "

16 Early the next morning Joshua had Israel come forward by tribes, and Judah was taken. 17 The clans of Judah came forward, and he took the Zerahites. He had the clan of the Zerahites come forward by families, and Zimri was taken. 18 Joshua had his family come forward man by man, and Achan son of Carmi, the son of Zimri, the son of Zerah, of the tribe of Judah, was taken.

19 Then Joshua said to Achan, "My son, give glory to the LORD,[a] the God of Israel, and give him the praise.[b] Tell me what you have done; do not hide it from me."

20 Achan replied, "It is true! I have sinned against the LORD, the God of Israel. This is what I have done: 21 When I saw in the plunder a beautiful robe from Babylonia,[c] two hundred shekels[d] of silver and a wedge of gold weighing fifty shekels,[e] I coveted them and took them. They are hidden in the ground inside my tent, with the silver underneath."

22 So Joshua sent messengers, and they ran to the tent, and there it was, hidden in his tent, with the silver underneath. 23 They took the things from the tent, brought them to Joshua and all the Israelites and spread them out before the LORD.

24 Then Joshua, together with all Israel, took Achan son of Zerah, the silver, the robe, the gold wedge, his sons and daughters, his cattle, donkeys and sheep, his tent

---

[a] 19 A solemn charge to tell the truth   [b] 19 Or *and confess to him*   [c] 21 Hebrew *Shinar*   [d] 21 That is, about 5 pounds (about 2.3 kilograms)   [e] 21 That is, about 1 1/4 pounds (about 0.6 kilogram)

and all that he had, to the Valley of Achor. ²⁵Joshua said, "Why have you brought this trouble on us? The LORD will bring trouble on you today."

Then all Israel stoned him, and after they had stoned the rest, they burned them. ²⁶Over Achan they heaped up a large pile of rocks, which remains to this day. Then the LORD turned from his fierce anger. Therefore that place has been called the Valley of Achor[a] ever since.

Ai Destroyed

8 Then the LORD said to Joshua, "Do not be afraid; do not be discouraged. Take the whole army with you, and go up and attack Ai. For I have delivered into your hands the king of Ai, his people, his city and his land. ²You shall do to Ai and its king as you did to Jericho and its king, except that you may carry off their plunder and livestock for yourselves. Set an ambush behind the city."

³So Joshua and the whole army moved out to attack Ai. He chose thirty thousand of his best fighting men and sent them out at night ⁴with these orders: "Listen carefully. You are to set an ambush behind the city. Don't go very far from it. All of you be on the alert. ⁵I and all those with me will advance on the city, and when the men come out against us, as they did before, we will flee from them. ⁶They will pursue us until we have lured them away from the city, for they will say, 'They are running away from us as they did before.' So when we flee from them, ⁷you are to rise up from ambush and take the city. The LORD your God will give it into your hand. ⁸When you have taken the city, set it on fire. Do what the LORD has commanded. See to it; you have my orders."

⁹Then Joshua sent them off, and they went to the place of ambush and lay in wait between Bethel and Ai, to the west of Ai—but Joshua spent that night with the people.

¹⁰Early the next morning Joshua mustered his men, and he and the leaders of Israel marched before them to Ai. ¹¹The entire force that was with him marched up and approached the city and arrived in front of it. They set up camp north of Ai, with the valley between them and the city. ¹²Joshua had taken about five thousand men and set them in ambush between Bethel and Ai, to the west of the city. ¹³They had the soldiers take up their positions—all those in the camp to the north of the city and the ambush to the west of it. That night Joshua went into the valley.

¹⁴When the king of Ai saw this, he and all the men of the city hurried out early in the morning to meet Israel in battle at a certain place overlooking the Arabah. But he did not know that an ambush had been set against him behind the city. ¹⁵Joshua and all Israel let themselves be driven back before them, and they fled toward the desert. ¹⁶All the men of Ai were called to pursue them, and they pursued Joshua and were lured away from the city. ¹⁷Not a man remained in Ai or Bethel who did not go after Israel. They left the city open and went in pursuit of Israel.

¹⁸Then the LORD said to Joshua, "Hold out toward Ai the javelin that is in your hand, for into your hand I will deliver the city." So Joshua held out his javelin toward Ai. ¹⁹As soon as he did this, the men in the ambush rose quickly from their position and rushed forward. They entered the city and captured it and quickly set it on fire.

²⁰The men of Ai looked back and saw the smoke of the city rising against the sky, but they had no chance to escape in any direction, for the Israelites who had been fleeing toward the desert had turned back against their pursuers. ²¹For when Joshua and all Israel saw that the ambush had taken the city and that smoke was going up from the city, they turned around and attacked the men of Ai. ²²The men of the ambush also came

---

a 26 Achor means trouble.

out of the city against them, so that they were caught in the middle, with Israelites on both sides. Israel cut them down, leaving them neither survivors nor fugitives. ²³But they took the king of Ai alive and brought him to Joshua.

²⁴When Israel had finished killing all the men of Ai in the fields and in the desert where they had chased them, and when every one of them had been put to the sword, all the Israelites returned to Ai and killed those who were in it. ²⁵Twelve thousand men and women fell that day— all the people of Ai. ²⁶For Joshua did not draw back the hand that held out his javelin until he had destroyed*a* all who lived in Ai. ²⁷But Israel did carry off for themselves the livestock and plunder of this city, as the LORD had instructed Joshua.

²⁸So Joshua burned Ai and made it a permanent heap of ruins, a desolate place to this day. ²⁹He hung the king of Ai on a tree and left him there until evening. At sunset, Joshua ordered them to take his body from the tree and throw it down at the entrance of the city gate. And they raised a large pile of rocks over it, which remains to this day.

The Covenant Renewed at Mount Ebal

³⁰Then Joshua built on Mount Ebal an altar to the LORD, the God of Israel, ³¹as Moses the servant of the LORD had commanded the Israelites. He built it according to what is written in the Book of the Law of Moses—an altar of uncut stones, on which no iron tool had been used. On it they offered to the LORD burnt offerings and sacrificed fellowship offerings.*b* ³²There, in the presence of the Israelites, Joshua copied on stones the law of Moses, which he had written. ³³All Israel, aliens and citizens alike, with their elders, officials and judges, were standing on both sides of the ark of the covenant of the LORD, facing those who carried

it—the priests, who were Levites. Half of the people stood in front of Mount Gerizim and half of them in front of Mount Ebal, as Moses the servant of the LORD had formerly commanded when he gave instructions to bless the people of Israel.

³⁴Afterward, Joshua read all the words of the law—the blessings and the curses— just as it is written in the Book of the Law. ³⁵There was not a word of all that Moses had commanded that Joshua did not read to the whole assembly of Israel, including the women and children, and the aliens who lived among them.

The Gibeonite Deception

9 Now when all the kings west of the Jordan heard about these things— those in the hill country, in the western foothills, and along the entire coast of the Great Sea*c* as far as Lebanon (the kings of the Hittites, Amorites, Canaanites, Perizzites, Hivites and Jebusites)— ²they came together to make war against Joshua and Israel.

³However, when the people of Gibeon heard what Joshua had done to Jericho and Ai, ⁴they resorted to a ruse: They went as a delegation whose donkeys were loaded*d* with worn-out sacks and old wineskins, cracked and mended. ⁵The men put worn and patched sandals on their feet and wore old clothes. All the bread of their food supply was dry and moldy. ⁶Then they went to Joshua in the camp at Gilgal and said to him and the men of Israel, "We have come from a distant country; make a treaty with us."

⁷The men of Israel said to the Hivites, "But perhaps you live near us. How then can we make a treaty with you?"

⁸"We are your servants," they said to Joshua.

But Joshua asked, "Who are you and where do you come from?"

⁹They answered: "Your servants have come from a very distant country because

a 26 The Hebrew term refers to the irrevocable giving over of things or persons to the LORD, often by totally destroying them. *b 31* Traditionally *peace offerings* *c 1* That is, the Mediterranean *d 4* Most Hebrew manuscripts; some Hebrew manuscripts, Vulgate and Syriac (see also Septuagint) *They prepared provisions and loaded their donkeys* of the fame of the LORD your God. For we have heard reports of him: all that he did in Egypt, [10]and all that he did to the two kings of the Amorites east of the Jordan—Sihon king of Heshbon, and Og king of Bashan, who reigned in Ashtaroth. [11]And our elders and all those living in our country said to us, 'Take provisions for your journey; go and meet them and say to them, "We are your servants; make a treaty with us."' [12]This bread of ours was warm when we packed it at home on the day we left to come to you. But now see how dry and moldy it is. [13]And these wineskins that we filled were new, but see how cracked they are. And our clothes and sandals are worn out by the very long journey."

[14]The men of Israel sampled their provisions but did not inquire of the LORD.

[15]Then Joshua made a treaty of peace with them to let them live, and the leaders of the assembly ratified it by oath.

Praying Joshua 9:14
God, help me not to do just what I think is right without asking You what You want me to do.

[16]Three days after they made the treaty with the Gibeonites, the Israelites heard that they were neighbors, living near them. [17]So the Israelites set out and on the third day came to their cities: Gibeon, Kephirah, Beeroth and Kiriath Jearim. [18]But the Israelites did not attack them, because the leaders of the assembly had sworn an oath to them by the LORD, the God of Israel.

GOING *deeper*

Inquire of the Lord

READ AND CONSIDER: JOSHUA 9

"The men of Israel sampled their provisions but did not inquire of the LORD" (Joshua 9:14).

This sentence is so brief that it can be easily missed, but it is the key to the entire story: The men of Israel "did not inquire of the LORD."

Joshua should have known better—they were in a war. The Israelites were in the middle of a divine takeover of an entire region. They would need God's guidance every step of the way. But this time the travelers had come a long way. Their food was moldy, their wineskins were old and cracked, and their clothes and sandals were worn out. It didn't occur to Israel's leaders that they were being set up. The Israelites were fooled because they didn't ask for God's guidance in deciding what to do.

Does this sound familiar? Do you ever get yourself into trouble because you fail to ask for God's wisdom and direction? Could you have made a better decision if you had "inquired of the Lord" right there in that office, in the classroom, at the doctor's office, or on that date? The passage implies that if the Israelites *had* asked for God's direction, they would have figured out what was really going on.

God wants to be part of your decisions, big and small. No issue is too insignificant to bring to God. He can see the big picture; you can't. He sees the future; you don't. He wants you to ask Him for guidance in all your daily decisions because He cares about everything that concerns you. He is your heavenly Father, and He wants to be involved in every aspect of your life. He wants to help you avoid the pitfalls that come when you don't consult Him before taking action. Pray every day that His Spirit will guide you in each decision you make.

The whole assembly grumbled against the leaders, 19but all the leaders answered, "We have given them our oath by the LORD, the God of Israel, and we cannot touch them now. 20This is what we will do to them: We will let them live, so that wrath will not fall on us for breaking the oath we swore to them." 21They continued, "Let them live, but let them be woodcutters and water carriers for the entire community." So the leaders' promise to them was kept.

26So Joshua saved them from the Israelites, and they did not kill them. 27That day he made the Gibeonites woodcutters and water carriers for the community and for the altar of the LORD at the place the LORD would choose. And that is what they are to this day.

The Sun Stands Still

10 Now Adoni-Zedek king of Jerusalem heard that Joshua had taken Ai and totally destroyed[a] it, doing to Ai and

God's people at prayer
JOSHUA'S BIG PRAYER

JOSHUA 10:1-15 No one could accuse Joshua of lacking boldness in prayer. He ordered the sun and moon to stand still. And they did! The sundial stopped at noon and didn't start again until the following noon. God added an extra day.

God's people were fighting a battle in His name, and darkness would have prevented the army of Israel from wrapping up the victory. The God who created the sun and the moon, light and darkness, could easily suspend the natural process for His purposes.

The lesson we can draw from this is that we should pray big. Too often we ask too small because we don't believe God can or will do that much. We lose our boldness by dwelling on all the reasons why He might *not* answer our prayers. But Joshua shows us how to reach for the sun. He prayed outlandishly! Joshua wasn't proving he was in command; he was letting God display His awesome power!

Say, "Lord, teach me not to limit You with small prayers! Give me the faith to pray big."

22Then Joshua summoned the Gibeonites and said, "Why did you deceive us by saying, 'We live a long way from you,' while actually you live near us? 23You are now under a curse: You will never cease to serve as woodcutters and water carriers for the house of my God."

24They answered Joshua, "Your servants were clearly told how the LORD your God had commanded his servant Moses to give you the whole land and to wipe out all its inhabitants from before you. So we feared for our lives because of you, and that is why we did this. 25We are now in your hands. Do to us whatever seems good and right to you."

its king as he had done to Jericho and its king, and that the people of Gibeon had made a treaty of peace with Israel and were living near them. 2He and his people were very much alarmed at this, because Gibeon was an important city, like one of the royal cities; it was larger than Ai, and all its men were good fighters. 3So Adoni-Zedek king of Jerusalem appealed to Hoham king of Hebron, Piram king of Jarmuth, Japhia king of Lachish and Debir king of Eglon. 4"Come up and help me attack Gibeon," he said, "because it has made peace with Joshua and the Israelites."

5Then the five kings of the Amorites—

[a] 1 The Hebrew term refers to the irrevocable giving over of things or persons to the LORD, often by totally destroying them; also in verses 28, 35, 37, 39 and 40.

the kings of Jerusalem, Hebron, Jarmuth, Lachish and Eglon—joined forces. They moved up with all their troops and took up positions against Gibeon and attacked it.

⁶The Gibeonites then sent word to Joshua in the camp at Gilgal: "Do not abandon your servants. Come up to us quickly and save us! Help us, because all the Amorite kings from the hill country have joined forces against us."

⁷So Joshua marched up from Gilgal with his entire army, including all the best fighting men. ⁸The LORD said to Joshua, "Do not be afraid of them; I have given them into your hand. Not one of them will be able to withstand you."

⁹After an all-night march from Gilgal, Joshua took them by surprise. ¹⁰The LORD threw them into confusion before Israel, who defeated them in a great victory at Gibeon. Israel pursued them along the road going up to Beth Horon and cut them down all the way to Azekah and Makkedah. ¹¹As they fled before Israel on the road down from Beth Horon to Azekah, the LORD hurled large hailstones down on them from the sky, and more of them died from the hailstones than were killed by the swords of the Israelites.

¹²On the day the LORD gave the Amorites over to Israel, Joshua said to the LORD in the presence of Israel:

"O sun, stand still over Gibeon,
    O moon, over the Valley of
        Aijalon."
¹³So the sun stood still,
    and the moon stopped,
    till the nation avenged itself on[a] its
        enemies,

as it is written in the Book of Jashar.

The sun stopped in the middle of the sky and delayed going down about a full day. ¹⁴There has never been a day like it before or since, a day when the LORD listened to a man. Surely the LORD was fighting for Israel!

¹⁵Then Joshua returned with all Israel to the camp at Gilgal.

Five Amorite Kings Killed

¹⁶Now the five kings had fled and hidden in the cave at Makkedah. ¹⁷When Joshua was told that the five kings had been found hiding in the cave at Makkedah, ¹⁸he said, "Roll large rocks up to the mouth of the cave, and post some men there to guard it. ¹⁹But don't stop! Pursue your enemies, attack them from the rear and don't let them reach their cities, for the LORD your God has given them into your hand."

²⁰So Joshua and the Israelites destroyed them completely—almost to a man—but the few who were left reached their fortified cities. ²¹The whole army then returned safely to Joshua in the camp at Makkedah, and no one uttered a word against the Israelites.

²²Joshua said, "Open the mouth of the cave and bring those five kings out to me." ²³So they brought the five kings out of the cave—the kings of Jerusalem, Hebron, Jarmuth, Lachish and Eglon. ²⁴When they had brought these kings to Joshua, he summoned all the men of Israel and said to the army commanders who had come with him, "Come here and put your feet on the necks of these kings." So they came forward and placed their feet on their necks.

²⁵Joshua said to them, "Do not be afraid; do not be discouraged. Be strong and courageous. This is what the LORD will do to all the enemies you are going to fight." ²⁶Then Joshua struck and killed the kings and hung them on five trees, and they were left hanging on the trees until evening.

²⁷At sunset Joshua gave the order and they took them down from the trees and threw them into the cave where they had been hiding. At the mouth of the cave they placed large rocks, which are there to this day.

²⁸That day Joshua took Makkedah. He

---

a 13 Or *nation triumphed over*

put the city and its king to the sword and totally destroyed everyone in it. He left no survivors. And he did to the king of Makkedah as he had done to the king of Jericho.

Southern Cities Conquered

29Then Joshua and all Israel with him moved on from Makkedah to Libnah and attacked it. 30The LORD also gave that city and its king into Israel's hand. The city and everyone in it Joshua put to the sword. He left no survivors there. And he did to its king as he had done to the king of Jericho.

31Then Joshua and all Israel with him moved on from Libnah to Lachish; he took up positions against it and attacked it. 32The LORD handed Lachish over to Israel, and Joshua took it on the second day. The city and everyone in it he put to the sword, just as he had done to Libnah. 33Meanwhile, Horam king of Gezer had come up to help Lachish, but Joshua defeated him and his army—until no survivors were left.

34Then Joshua and all Israel with him moved on from Lachish to Eglon; they took up positions against it and attacked it. 35They captured it that same day and put it to the sword and totally destroyed everyone in it, just as they had done to Lachish.

36Then Joshua and all Israel with him went up from Eglon to Hebron and attacked it. 37They took the city and put it to the sword, together with its king, its villages and everyone in it. They left no survivors. Just as at Eglon, they totally destroyed it and everyone in it.

38Then Joshua and all Israel with him turned around and attacked Debir. 39They took the city, its king and its villages, and put them to the sword. Everyone in it they totally destroyed. They left no survivors. They did to Debir and its king as they had done to Libnah and its king and to Hebron.

40So Joshua subdued the whole region, including the hill country, the Negev, the western foothills and the mountain slopes, together with all their kings. He left no survivors. He totally destroyed all who breathed, just as the LORD, the God of Israel, had commanded. 41Joshua subdued them from Kadesh Barnea to Gaza and from the whole region of Goshen to Gibeon. 42All these kings and their lands Joshua conquered in one campaign, because the LORD, the God of Israel, fought for Israel.

43Then Joshua returned with all Israel to the camp at Gilgal.

Northern Kings Defeated

11 When Jabin king of Hazor heard of this, he sent word to Jobab king of Madon, to the kings of Shimron and Acshaph, 2and to the northern kings who were in the mountains, in the Arabah south of Kinnereth, in the western foothills and in Naphoth Dorᵃ on the west; 3to the Canaanites in the east and west; to the Amorites, Hittites, Perizzites and Jebusites in the hill country; and to the Hivites below Hermon in the region of Mizpah. 4They came out with all their troops and a large number of horses and chariots—a huge army, as numerous as the sand on the seashore. 5All these kings joined forces and made camp together at the Waters of Merom, to fight against Israel.

6The LORD said to Joshua, "Do not be afraid of them, because by this time tomorrow I will hand all of them over to Israel, slain. You are to hamstring their horses and burn their chariots."

7So Joshua and his whole army came against them suddenly at the Waters of Merom and attacked them, 8and the LORD gave them into the hand of Israel. They defeated them and pursued them all the way to Greater Sidon, to Misrephoth Maim, and to the Valley of Mizpah on the east, until no survivors were left. 9Joshua did to them as the LORD had directed: He hamstrung their horses and burned their chariots.

ᵃ2 Or *in the heights of Dor*

10At that time Joshua turned back and captured Hazor and put its king to the sword. (Hazor had been the head of all these kingdoms.) 11Everyone in it they put to the sword. They totally destroyed[a] them, not sparing anything that breathed, and he burned up Hazor itself.

12Joshua took all these royal cities and their kings and put them to the sword. He totally destroyed them, as Moses the servant of the LORD had commanded. 13Yet Israel did not burn any of the cities built on their mounds—except Hazor, which Joshua burned. 14The Israelites carried off for themselves all the plunder and livestock of these cities, but all the people they put to the sword until they completely destroyed them, not sparing anyone that breathed. 15As the LORD commanded his servant Moses, so Moses commanded Joshua, and Joshua did it; he left nothing undone of all that the LORD commanded Moses.

16So Joshua took this entire land: the hill country, all the Negev, the whole region of Goshen, the western foothills, the Arabah and the mountains of Israel with their foothills, 17from Mount Halak, which rises toward Seir, to Baal Gad in the Valley of Lebanon below Mount Hermon. He captured all their kings and struck them down, putting them to death. 18Joshua waged war against all these kings for a long time. 19Except for the Hivites living in Gibeon, not one city made a treaty of peace with the Israelites, who took them all in battle. 20For it was the LORD himself who hardened their hearts to wage war against Israel, so that he might destroy them totally, exterminating them without mercy, as the LORD had commanded Moses.

21At that time Joshua went and destroyed the Anakites from the hill country: from Hebron, Debir and Anab, from all the hill country of Judah, and from all the hill country of Israel. Joshua totally destroyed them and their towns. 22No Anakites were left in Israelite territory; only in Gaza, Gath and Ashdod did any survive. 23So Joshua took the entire land, just as the LORD had directed Moses, and he gave it as an inheritance to Israel according to their tribal divisions.

Then the land had rest from war.

List of Defeated Kings

12 These are the kings of the land whom the Israelites had defeated and whose territory they took over east of the Jordan, from the Arnon Gorge to Mount Hermon, including all the eastern side of the Arabah:

2Sihon king of the Amorites,
who reigned in Heshbon. He ruled from Aroer on the rim of the Arnon Gorge—from the middle of the gorge—to the Jabbok River, which is the border of the Ammonites. This included half of Gilead. 3He also ruled over the eastern Arabah from the Sea of Kinnereth[b] to the Sea of the Arabah (the Salt Sea[c]), to Beth Jeshimoth, and then southward below the slopes of Pisgah.

4And the territory of Og king of Bashan,
one of the last of the Rephaites, who reigned in Ashtaroth and Edrei. 5He ruled over Mount Hermon, Salecah, all of Bashan to the border of the people of Geshur and Maacah, and half of Gilead to the border of Sihon king of Heshbon.

6Moses, the servant of the LORD, and the Israelites conquered them. And Moses the servant of the LORD gave their land to the Reubenites, the Gadites and the half-tribe of Manasseh to be their possession.

7These are the kings of the land that Joshua and the Israelites conquered on the west side of the Jordan, from Baal Gad in the Valley of Lebanon to Mount

---

a 11 The Hebrew term refers to the irrevocable giving over of things or persons to the LORD, often by totally destroying them; also in verses 12, 20 and 21.   b 3 That is, Galilee   c 3 That is, the Dead Sea

Halak, which rises toward Seir (their lands Joshua gave as an inheritance to the tribes of Israel according to their tribal divisions— [8]the hill country, the western foothills, the Arabah, the mountain slopes, the desert and the Negev—the lands of the Hittites, Amorites, Canaanites, Perizzites, Hivites and Jebusites):

[9]	the king of Jericho	one
	the king of Ai (near Bethel)	one
[10]	the king of Jerusalem	one
	the king of Hebron	one
[11]	the king of Jarmuth	one
	the king of Lachish	one
[12]	the king of Eglon	one
	the king of Gezer	one
[13]	the king of Debir	one
	the king of Geder	one
[14]	the king of Hormah	one
	the king of Arad	one
[15]	the king of Libnah	one
	the king of Adullam	one
[16]	the king of Makkedah	one
	the king of Bethel	one
[17]	the king of Tappuah	one
	the king of Hepher	one
[18]	the king of Aphek	one
	the king of Lasharon	one
[19]	the king of Madon	one
	the king of Hazor	one
[20]	the king of Shimron Meron	one
	the king of Acshaph	one
[21]	the king of Taanach	one
	the king of Megiddo	one
[22]	the king of Kedesh	one
	the king of Jokneam in Carmel	one
[23]	the king of Dor (in Naphoth Dor[a])	one
	the king of Goyim in Gilgal	one
[24]	the king of Tirzah	one

thirty-one kings in all.

Land Still to Be Taken

13 When Joshua was old and well advanced in years, the LORD said to him, "You are very old, and there are still very large areas of land to be taken over.

[2]"This is the land that remains: all the regions of the Philistines and Geshurites: [3]from the Shihor River on the east of Egypt to the territory of Ekron on the north, all of it counted as Canaanite (the territory of the five Philistine rulers in Gaza, Ashdod, Ashkelon, Gath and Ekron—that of the Avvites); [4]from the south, all the land of the Canaanites, from Arah of the Sidonians as far as Aphek, the region of the Amorites, [5]the area of the Gebalites[b]; and all Lebanon to the east, from Baal Gad below Mount Hermon to Lebo[c] Hamath.

[6]"As for all the inhabitants of the mountain regions from Lebanon to Misrephoth Maim, that is, all the Sidonians, I myself will drive them out before the Israelites. Be sure to allocate this land to Israel for an inheritance, as I have instructed you, [7]and divide it as an inheritance among the nine tribes and half of the tribe of Manasseh."

Division of the Land East of the Jordan

[8]The other half of Manasseh,[d] the Reubenites and the Gadites had received the inheritance that Moses had given them east of the Jordan, as he, the servant of the LORD, had assigned it to them.

[9]It extended from Aroer on the rim of the Arnon Gorge, and from the town in the middle of the gorge, and included the whole plateau of Medeba as far as Dibon, [10]and all the towns of Sihon king of the Amorites, who ruled in Heshbon, out to the border of the Ammonites. [11]It also included Gilead, the territory of the people of Geshur and Maacah, all of Mount Hermon and all Bashan as far as Salecah— [12]that is, the whole

---

[a] 23 Or *in the heights of Dor* [b] 5 That is, the area of Byblos [c] 5 Or *to the entrance to* [d] 8 Hebrew *With it* (that is, with the other half of Manasseh)

kingdom of Og in Bashan, who had reigned in Ashtaroth and Edrei and had survived as one of the last of the Rephaites. Moses had defeated them and taken over their land. 13But the Israelites did not drive out the people of Geshur and Maacah, so they continue to live among the Israelites to this day.

14But to the tribe of Levi he gave no inheritance, since the offerings made by fire to the LORD, the God of Israel, are their inheritance, as he promised them.

15This is what Moses had given to the tribe of Reuben, clan by clan:

16The territory from Aroer on the rim of the Arnon Gorge, and from the town in the middle of the gorge, and the whole plateau past Medeba 17to Heshbon and all its towns on the plateau, including Dibon, Bamoth Baal, Beth Baal Meon, 18Jahaz, Kedemoth, Mephaath, 19Kiriathaim, Sibmah, Zereth Shahar on the hill in the valley, 20Beth Peor, the slopes of Pisgah, and Beth Jeshimoth— 21all the towns on the plateau and the entire realm of Sihon king of the Amorites, who ruled at Heshbon. Moses had defeated him and the Midianite chiefs, Evi, Rekem, Zur, Hur and Reba—princes allied with Sihon—who lived in that country. 22In addition to those slain in battle, the Israelites had put to the sword Balaam son of Beor, who practiced divination. 23The boundary of the Reubenites was the bank of the Jordan. These towns and their villages were the inheritance of the Reubenites, clan by clan.

24This is what Moses had given to the tribe of Gad, clan by clan:

25The territory of Jazer, all the towns of Gilead and half the Ammonite country as far as Aroer, near Rab-

bah; 26and from Heshbon to Ramath Mizpah and Betonim, and from Mahanaim to the territory of Debir; 27and in the valley, Beth Haram, Beth Nimrah, Succoth and Zaphon with the rest of the realm of Sihon king of Heshbon (the east side of the Jordan, the territory up to the end of the Sea of Kinnereth[a]). 28These towns and their villages were the inheritance of the Gadites, clan by clan.

29This is what Moses had given to the half-tribe of Manasseh, that is, to half the family of the descendants of Manasseh, clan by clan:

30The territory extending from Mahanaim and including all of Bashan, the entire realm of Og king of Bashan—all the settlements of Jair in Bashan, sixty towns, 31half of Gilead, and Ashtaroth and Edrei (the royal cities of Og in Bashan). This was for the descendants of Makir son of Manasseh—for half of the sons of Makir, clan by clan.

32This is the inheritance Moses had given when he was in the plains of Moab across the Jordan east of Jericho. 33But to the tribe of Levi, Moses had given no inheritance; the LORD, the God of Israel, is their inheritance, as he promised them.

Division of the Land West of the Jordan

14 Now these are the areas the Israelites received as an inheritance in the land of Canaan, which Eleazar the priest, Joshua son of Nun and the heads of the tribal clans of Israel allotted to them. 2Their inheritances were assigned by lot to the nine-and-a-half tribes, as the LORD had commanded through Moses. 3Moses had granted the two-and-a-half tribes their inheritance east of the Jordan but had not granted the Levites an inheritance among the rest, 4for the sons of Joseph had become two

---

a 27 That is, Galilee

tribes—Manasseh and Ephraim. The Levites received no share of the land but only towns to live in, with pasturelands for their flocks and herds. ⁵So the Israelites divided the land, just as the LORD had commanded Moses.

Hebron Given to Caleb

⁶Now the men of Judah approached Joshua at Gilgal, and Caleb son of Jephunneh the Kenizzite said to him, "You know what the LORD said to Moses the man of God at Kadesh Barnea about you and me. ⁷I was forty years old when Moses the servant of the LORD sent me from Kadesh Barnea to explore the land. And I brought him back a report according to my convictions, ⁸but my brothers who went up with me made the hearts of the people melt with fear. I, however, followed the LORD my God wholeheartedly. ⁹So on that day Moses swore to me, 'The land on which your feet have walked will be your inheritance and that of your children forever, because you have followed the LORD my God wholeheartedly.'ᵃ

Prayer is . . .

*committing everything you do
to God so He will bless it.*

¹⁰"Now then, just as the LORD promised, he has kept me alive for forty-five years since the time he said this to Moses, while Israel moved about in the desert. So here I am today, eighty-five years old! ¹¹I am still as strong today as the day Moses sent me out; I'm just as vigorous to go out to battle now as I was then. ¹²Now give me this hill country that the LORD promised me that day. You yourself heard then that the Anakites were there and their cities were large and fortified, but, the LORD helping me, I will drive them out just as he said."

¹³Then Joshua blessed Caleb son of Jephunneh and gave him Hebron as his inheritance. ¹⁴So Hebron has belonged to Caleb son of Jephunneh the Kenizzite ever since, because he followed the LORD, the God of Israel, wholeheartedly. ¹⁵(Hebron used to be called Kiriath Arba after Arba, who was the greatest man among the Anakites.)

Then the land had rest from war.

Allotment for Judah

15 The allotment for the tribe of Judah, clan by clan, extended down to the territory of Edom, to the Desert of Zin in the extreme south.

²Their southern boundary started from the bay at the southern end of the Salt Sea,ᵇ ³crossed south of Scorpionᶜ Pass, continued on to Zin and went over to the south of Kadesh Barnea. Then it ran past Hezron up to Addar and curved around to Karka. ⁴It then passed along to Azmon and joined the Wadi of Egypt, ending at the sea. This is theirᵈ southern boundary.

⁵The eastern boundary is the Salt Sea as far as the mouth of the Jordan.

The northern boundary started from the bay of the sea at the mouth of the Jordan, ⁶went up to Beth Hoglah and continued north of Beth Arabah to the Stone of Bohan son of Reuben. ⁷The boundary then went up to Debir from the Valley of Achor and turned north to Gilgal, which faces the Pass of Adummim south of the gorge. It continued along to the waters of En Shemesh and came out at En Rogel. ⁸Then it ran up the Valley of Ben Hinnom along the southern slope of the Jebusite city (that is, Jerusalem). From there it climbed to the top of the hill west of the Hinnom Valley at the northern end of the Valley of Rephaim. ⁹From the hilltop the boundary

---

ᵃ 9 Deut. 1:36   ᵇ 2 That is, the Dead Sea; also in verse 5   ᶜ 3 Hebrew *Akrabbim*   ᵈ 4 Hebrew *your* headed toward the spring of the waters of Nephtoah, came out at the towns of Mount Ephron and went down toward Baalah (that is, Kiriath Jearim). ¹⁰Then it curved westward from Baalah to Mount Seir, ran along the northern slope of Mount Jearim (that is, Kesalon), continued down to Beth Shemesh and crossed to Timnah. ¹¹It went to the northern slope of Ekron, turned toward Shikkeron, passed along to Mount Baalah and reached Jabneel. The boundary ended at the sea.

¹²The western boundary is the coastline of the Great Sea.[a] These are the boundaries around the people of Judah by their clans.

¹³In accordance with the LORD's command to him, Joshua gave to Caleb son of Jephunneh a portion in Judah—Kiriath Arba, that is, Hebron. (Arba was the forefather of Anak.) ¹⁴From Hebron Caleb drove out the three Anakites—Sheshai, Ahiman and Talmai—descendants of Anak. ¹⁵From there he marched against the people living in Debir (formerly called Kiriath Sepher). ¹⁶And Caleb said, "I will give my daughter Acsah in marriage to the man who attacks and captures Kiriath Sepher." ¹⁷Othniel son of Kenaz, Caleb's brother, took it; so Caleb gave his daughter Acsah to him in marriage.

¹⁸One day when she came to Othniel, she urged him[b] to ask her father for a field. When she got off her donkey, Caleb asked her, "What can I do for you?"

¹⁹She replied, "Do me a special favor. Since you have given me land in the Negev, give me also springs of water." So Caleb gave her the upper and lower springs.

²⁰This is the inheritance of the tribe of Judah, clan by clan:

²¹The southernmost towns of the tribe of Judah in the Negev toward the boundary of Edom were:

Kabzeel, Eder, Jagur, ²²Kinah, Dimonah, Adadah, ²³Kedesh, Hazor, Ithnan, ²⁴Ziph, Telem, Bealoth, ²⁵Hazor Hadattah, Kerioth Hezron (that is, Hazor), ²⁶Amam, Shema, Moladah, ²⁷Hazar Gaddah, Heshmon, Beth Pelet, ²⁸Hazar Shual, Beersheba, Biziothiah, ²⁹Baalah, Iim, Ezem, ³⁰Eltolad, Kesil, Hormah, ³¹Ziklag, Madmannah, Sansannah, ³²Lebaoth, Shilhim, Ain and Rimmon—a total of twenty-nine towns and their villages.

³³In the western foothills:

Eshtaol, Zorah, Ashnah, ³⁴Zanoah, En Gannim, Tappuah, Enam, ³⁵Jarmuth, Adullam, Socoh, Azekah, ³⁶Shaaraim, Adithaim and Gederah (or Gederothaim)[c]—fourteen towns and their villages.

³⁷Zenan, Hadashah, Migdal Gad, ³⁸Dilean, Mizpah, Joktheel, ³⁹Lachish, Bozkath, Eglon, ⁴⁰Cabbon, Lahmas, Kitlish, ⁴¹Gederoth, Beth Dagon, Naamah and Makkedah—sixteen towns and their villages.

⁴²Libnah, Ether, Ashan, ⁴³Iphtah, Ashnah, Nezib, ⁴⁴Keilah, Aczib and Mareshah—nine towns and their villages.

⁴⁵Ekron, with its surrounding settlements and villages; ⁴⁶west of Ekron, all that were in the vicinity of Ashdod, together with their villages; ⁴⁷Ashdod, its surrounding settlements and villages; and Gaza, its settlements and villages, as far as the Wadi of Egypt and the coastline of the Great Sea.

⁴⁸In the hill country:

Shamir, Jattir, Socoh, ⁴⁹Dannah, Kiriath Sannah (that is, Debir), ⁵⁰Anab, Eshtemoh, Anim, ⁵¹Goshen, Holon and Giloh—eleven towns and their villages.

⁵²Arab, Dumah, Eshan, ⁵³Janim, Beth Tappuah, Aphekah, ⁵⁴Humtah,

---

^a*12* That is, the Mediterranean; also in verse 47   ^b*18* Hebrew and some Septuagint manuscripts; other Septuagint manuscripts (see also note at Judges 1:14) *Othniel, he urged her*   ^c*36* Or *Gederah and Gederothaim*

Kiriath Arba (that is, Hebron) and Zior—nine towns and their villages.

⁵⁵Maon, Carmel, Ziph, Juttah, ⁵⁶Jezreel, Jokdeam, Zanoah, ⁵⁷Kain, Gibeah and Timnah—ten towns and their villages.

⁵⁸Halhul, Beth Zur, Gedor, ⁵⁹Maarath, Beth Anoth and Eltekon—six towns and their villages.

⁶⁰Kiriath Baal (that is, Kiriath Jearim) and Rabbah—two towns and their villages.

⁶¹In the desert:

Beth Arabah, Middin, Secacah, ⁶²Nibshan, the City of Salt and En Gedi—six towns and their villages.

⁶³Judah could not dislodge the Jebusites, who were living in Jerusalem; to this day the Jebusites live there with the people of Judah.

Allotment for Ephraim and Manasseh

16 The allotment for Joseph began at the Jordan of Jericho,ᵃ east of the waters of Jericho, and went up from there through the desert into the hill country of Bethel. ²It went on from Bethel (that is, Luz),ᵇ crossed over to the territory of the Arkites in Ataroth, ³descended westward to the territory of the Japhletites as far as the region of Lower Beth Horon and on to Gezer, ending at the sea.

⁴So Manasseh and Ephraim, the descendants of Joseph, received their inheritance.

⁵This was the territory of Ephraim, clan by clan:

The boundary of their inheritance went from Ataroth Addar in the east to Upper Beth Horon ⁶and continued to the sea. From Micmethath on the north it curved eastward to Taanath Shiloh, passing by it to Janoah on the east. ⁷Then it went down from Janoah to Ataroth and Naarah, touched Jericho and came out at the Jordan. ⁸From Tappuah the border went west to the Kanah Ravine and ended at the sea. This was the inheritance of the tribe of the Ephraimites, clan by clan. ⁹It also included all the towns and their villages that were set aside for the Ephraimites within the inheritance of the Manassites.

¹⁰They did not dislodge the Canaanites living in Gezer; to this day the Canaanites live among the people of Ephraim but are required to do forced labor.

17 This was the allotment for the tribe of Manasseh as Joseph's firstborn, that is, for Makir, Manasseh's firstborn. Makir was the ancestor of the Gileadites, who had received Gilead and Bashan because the Makirites were great soldiers. ²So this allotment was for the rest of the people of Manasseh—the clans of Abiezer, Helek, Asriel, Shechem, Hepher and Shemida. These are the other male descendants of Manasseh son of Joseph by their clans.

³Now Zelophehad son of Hepher, the son of Gilead, the son of Makir, the son of Manasseh, had no sons but only daughters, whose names were Mahlah, Noah, Hoglah, Milcah and Tirzah. ⁴They went to Eleazar the priest, Joshua son of Nun, and the leaders and said, "The LORD commanded Moses to give us an inheritance among our brothers." So Joshua gave them an inheritance along with the brothers of their father, according to the LORD's command. ⁵Manasseh's share consisted of ten tracts of land besides Gilead and Bashan east of the Jordan, ⁶because the daughters of the tribe of Manasseh received an inheritance among the sons. The land of Gilead belonged to the rest of the descendants of Manasseh.

⁷The territory of Manasseh extended from Asher to Micmethath east of Shechem. The boundary ran southward from there to include the people living at En Tappuah. ⁸(Manasseh had the land of Tappuah, but

---

ᵃ 1 *Jordan of Jericho* was possibly an ancient name for the Jordan River.   ᵇ 2 Septuagint; Hebrew *Bethel to Luz*

Tappuah itself, on the boundary of Manasseh, belonged to the Ephraimites.) 9Then the boundary continued south to the Kanah Ravine. There were towns belonging to Ephraim lying among the towns of Manasseh, but the boundary of Manasseh was the northern side of the ravine and ended at the sea. 10On the south the land belonged to Ephraim, on the north to Manasseh. The territory of Manasseh reached the sea and bordered Asher on the north and Issachar on the east.

11Within Issachar and Asher, Manasseh also had Beth Shan, Ibleam and the people of Dor, Endor, Taanach and Megiddo, together with their surrounding settlements (the third in the list is Naphoth[a]).

12Yet the Manassites were not able to occupy these towns, for the Canaanites were determined to live in that region. 13However, when the Israelites grew stronger, they subjected the Canaanites to forced labor but did not drive them out completely.

14The people of Joseph said to Joshua, "Why have you given us only one allotment and one portion for an inheritance? We are a numerous people and the LORD has blessed us abundantly."

15"If you are so numerous," Joshua answered, "and if the hill country of Ephraim is too small for you, go up into the forest and clear land for yourselves there in the land of the Perizzites and Rephaites."

16The people of Joseph replied, "The hill country is not enough for us, and all the Canaanites who live in the plain have iron chariots, both those in Beth Shan and its settlements and those in the Valley of Jezreel."

17But Joshua said to the house of Joseph—to Ephraim and Manasseh— "You are numerous and very powerful. You will have not only one allotment 18but the forested hill country as well. Clear it, and its farthest limits will be yours; though the Canaanites have iron chariots and though they are strong, you can drive them out."

Division of the Rest of the Land

18 The whole assembly of the Israelites gathered at Shiloh and set up the Tent of Meeting there. The country was brought under their control, 2but there were still seven Israelite tribes who had not yet received their inheritance.

3So Joshua said to the Israelites: "How long will you wait before you begin to take possession of the land that the LORD, the God of your fathers, has given you? 4Appoint three men from each tribe. I will send them out to make a survey of the land and to write a description of it, according to the inheritance of each. Then they will return to me. 5You are to divide the land into seven parts. Judah is to remain in its territory on the south and the house of Joseph in its territory on the north. 6After you have written descriptions of the seven parts of the land, bring them here to me and I will cast lots for you in the presence of the LORD our God. 7The Levites, however, do not get a portion among you, because the priestly service of the LORD is their inheritance. And Gad, Reuben and the half-tribe of Manasseh have already received their inheritance on the east side of the Jordan. Moses the servant of the LORD gave it to them."

8As the men started on their way to map out the land, Joshua instructed them, "Go and make a survey of the land and write a description of it. Then return to me, and I will cast lots for you here at Shiloh in the presence of the LORD." 9So the men left and went through the land. They wrote its description on a scroll, town by town, in seven parts, and returned to Joshua in the camp at Shiloh. 10Joshua then cast lots for them in Shiloh in the presence of the LORD, and there

---

a 11 That is, Naphoth Dor

he distributed the land to the Israelites according to their tribal divisions.

Allotment for Benjamin

[11] The lot came up for the tribe of Benjamin, clan by clan. Their allotted territory lay between the tribes of Judah and Joseph:

[12] On the north side their boundary began at the Jordan, passed the northern slope of Jericho and headed west into the hill country, coming out at the desert of Beth Aven. [13] From there it crossed to the south slope of Luz (that is, Bethel) and went down to Ataroth Addar on the hill south of Lower Beth Horon.

[14] From the hill facing Beth Horon on the south the boundary turned south along the western side and came out at Kiriath Baal (that is, Kiriath Jearim), a town of the people of Judah. This was the western side.

[15] The southern side began at the outskirts of Kiriath Jearim on the west, and the boundary came out at the spring of the waters of Nephtoah. [16] The boundary went down to the foot of the hill facing the Valley of Ben Hinnom, north of the Valley of Rephaim. It continued down the Hinnom Valley along the southern slope of the Jebusite city and so to En Rogel. [17] It then curved north, went to En Shemesh, continued to Geliloth, which faces the Pass of Adummim, and ran down to the Stone of Bohan son of Reuben. [18] It continued to the northern slope of Beth Arabah[a] and on down into the Arabah. [19] It then went to the northern slope of Beth Hoglah and came out at the northern bay of the Salt Sea,[b] at the mouth of the Jordan in the south. This was the southern boundary.

[20] The Jordan formed the boundary on the eastern side.

These were the boundaries that marked out the inheritance of the clans of Benjamin on all sides.

[21] The tribe of Benjamin, clan by clan, had the following cities:

Jericho, Beth Hoglah, Emek Keziz, [22] Beth Arabah, Zemaraim, Bethel, [23] Avvim, Parah, Ophrah, [24] Kephar Ammoni, Ophni and Geba—twelve towns and their villages.

[25] Gibeon, Ramah, Beeroth, [26] Mizpah, Kephirah, Mozah, [27] Rekem, Irpeel, Taralah, [28] Zelah, Haeleph, the Jebusite city (that is, Jerusalem), Gibeah and Kiriath—fourteen towns and their villages.

This was the inheritance of Benjamin for its clans.

Allotment for Simeon

19 The second lot came out for the tribe of Simeon, clan by clan. Their inheritance lay within the territory of Judah. [2] It included:

Beersheba (or Sheba),[c] Moladah, [3] Hazar Shual, Balah, Ezem, [4] Eltolad, Bethul, Hormah, [5] Ziklag, Beth Marcaboth, Hazar Susah, [6] Beth Lebaoth and Sharuhen—thirteen towns and their villages;

[7] Ain, Rimmon, Ether and Ashan—four towns and their villages— [8] and all the villages around these towns as far as Baalath Beer (Ramah in the Negev).

This was the inheritance of the tribe of the Simeonites, clan by clan. [9] The inheritance of the Simeonites was taken from the share of Judah, because Judah's portion was more than they needed. So the Simeonites received their inheritance within the territory of Judah.

Allotment for Zebulun

[10] The third lot came up for Zebulun, clan by clan:

The boundary of their inheritance went as far as Sarid. [11] Going west it

a 18 Septuagint; Hebrew slope facing the Arabah   b 19 That is, the Dead Sea   c 2 Or Beersheba, Sheba; 1 Chron. 4:28 does not have Sheba.

ran to Maralah, touched Dabbesheth, and extended to the ravine near Jokneam. [12]It turned east from Sarid toward the sunrise to the territory of Kisloth Tabor and went on to Daberath and up to Japhia. [13]Then it continued eastward to Gath Hepher and Eth Kazin; it came out at Rimmon and turned toward Neah. [14]There the boundary went around on the north to Hannathon and ended at the Valley of Iphtah El. [15]Included were Kattath, Nahalal, Shimron, Idalah and Bethlehem. There were twelve towns and their villages.
[16]These towns and their villages were the inheritance of Zebulun, clan by clan.

Allotment for Issachar

[17]The fourth lot came out for Issachar, clan by clan. [18]Their territory included:

Jezreel, Kesulloth, Shunem, [19]Hapharaim, Shion, Anaharath, [20]Rabbith, Kishion, Ebez, [21]Remeth, En Gannim, En Haddah and Beth Pazzez. [22]The boundary touched Tabor, Shahazumah and Beth Shemesh, and ended at the Jordan. There were sixteen towns and their villages.

[23]These towns and their villages were the inheritance of the tribe of Issachar, clan by clan.

Allotment for Asher

[24]The fifth lot came out for the tribe of Asher, clan by clan. [25]Their territory included:

Helkath, Hali, Beten, Acshaph, [26]Allammelech, Amad and Mishal. On the west the boundary touched Carmel and Shihor Libnath. [27]It then turned east toward Beth Dagon, touched Zebulun and the Valley of Iphtah El, and went north to Beth Emek and Neiel, passing Cabul on the left. [28]It went to Abdon,[a] Rehob, Hammon and Kanah, as far as Greater Sidon. [29]The boundary then turned back toward Ramah and went to the fortified city of Tyre, turned toward Hosah and came out at the sea in the region of Aczib, [30]Ummah, Aphek and Rehob. There were twenty-two towns and their villages.

[31]These towns and their villages were the inheritance of the tribe of Asher, clan by clan.

Allotment for Naphtali

[32]The sixth lot came out for Naphtali, clan by clan:

[33]Their boundary went from Heleph and the large tree in Zaanannim, passing Adami Nekeb and Jabneel to Lakkum and ending at the Jordan. [34]The boundary ran west through Aznoth Tabor and came out at Hukkok. It touched Zebulun on the south, Asher on the west and the Jordan[b] on the east. [35]The fortified cities were Ziddim, Zer, Hammath, Rakkath, Kinnereth, [36]Adamah, Ramah, Hazor, [37]Kedesh, Edrei, En Hazor, [38]Iron, Migdal El, Horem, Beth Anath and Beth Shemesh. There were nineteen towns and their villages.

[39]These towns and their villages were the inheritance of the tribe of Naphtali, clan by clan.

Allotment for Dan

[40]The seventh lot came out for the tribe of Dan, clan by clan. [41]The territory of their inheritance included:

Zorah, Eshtaol, Ir Shemesh, [42]Shaalabbin, Aijalon, Ithlah, [43]Elon, Timnah, Ekron, [44]Eltekeh, Gibbethon, Baalath, [45]Jehud, Bene Berak, Gath Rimmon, [46]Me Jarkon and Rakkon, with the area facing Joppa.

[47](But the Danites had difficulty taking possession of their territory, so they went up and attacked Leshem, took it, put it to the sword and occupied it. They settled in Leshem and named it Dan after their forefather.)

---

[a] 28 Some Hebrew manuscripts (see also Joshua 21:30); most Hebrew manuscripts *Ebron*   [b] 34 Septuagint; Hebrew *west, and Judah, the Jordan,*

48These towns and their villages were the inheritance of the tribe of Dan, clan by clan.

Allotment for Joshua

49When they had finished dividing the land into its allotted portions, the Israelites gave Joshua son of Nun an inheritance among them, 50as the LORD had commanded. They gave him the town he asked for—Timnath Serah[a] in the hill country of Ephraim. And he built up the town and settled there.

51These are the territories that Eleazar the priest, Joshua son of Nun and the heads of the tribal clans of Israel assigned by lot at Shiloh in the presence of the LORD at the entrance to the Tent of Meeting. And so they finished dividing the land.

Cities of Refuge

20 Then the LORD said to Joshua: 2"Tell the Israelites to designate the cities of refuge, as I instructed you through Moses, 3so that anyone who kills a person accidentally and unintentionally may flee there and find protection from the avenger of blood.

4"When he flees to one of these cities, he is to stand in the entrance of the city gate and state his case before the elders of that city. Then they are to admit him into their city and give him a place to live with them. 5If the avenger of blood pursues him, they must not surrender the one accused, because he killed his neighbor unintentionally and without malice aforethought. 6He is to stay in that city until he has stood trial before the assembly and until the death of the high priest who is serving at that time. Then he may go back to his own home in the town from which he fled."

7So they set apart Kedesh in Galilee in the hill country of Naphtali, Shechem in the hill country of Ephraim, and Kiriath Arba (that is, Hebron) in the hill country of Judah. 8On the east side of the Jordan

of Jericho[b] they designated Bezer in the desert on the plateau in the tribe of Reuben, Ramoth in Gilead in the tribe of Gad, and Golan in Bashan in the tribe of Manasseh. 9Any of the Israelites or any alien living among them who killed someone accidentally could flee to these designated cities and not be killed by the avenger of blood prior to standing trial before the assembly.

Towns for the Levites

21 Now the family heads of the Levites approached Eleazar the priest, Joshua son of Nun, and the heads of the other tribal families of Israel 2at Shiloh in Canaan and said to them, "The LORD commanded through Moses that you give us towns to live in, with pasturelands for our livestock." 3So, as the LORD had commanded, the Israelites gave the Levites the following towns and pasturelands out of their own inheritance:

4The first lot came out for the Kohathites, clan by clan. The Levites who were descendants of Aaron the priest were allotted thirteen towns from the tribes of Judah, Simeon and Benjamin. 5The rest of Kohath's descendants were allotted ten towns from the clans of the tribes of Ephraim, Dan and half of Manasseh.

6The descendants of Gershon were allotted thirteen towns from the clans of the tribes of Issachar, Asher, Naphtali and the half-tribe of Manasseh in Bashan.

7The descendants of Merari, clan by clan, received twelve towns from the tribes of Reuben, Gad and Zebulun.

8So the Israelites allotted to the Levites these towns and their pasturelands, as the LORD had commanded through Moses.

9From the tribes of Judah and Simeon they allotted the following towns by name 10(these towns were assigned to the descendants of Aaron who were from the Kohathite clans of the Levites, because the first lot fell to them):

11They gave them Kiriath Arba (that

---

a 50 Also known as *Timnath Heres* (see Judges 2:9)   b 8 *Jordan of Jericho* was possibly an ancient name for the Jordan River.

is, Hebron), with its surrounding pastureland, in the hill country of Judah. (Arba was the forefather of Anak.) [12]But the fields and villages around the city they had given to Caleb son of Jephunneh as his possession.

[13]So to the descendants of Aaron the priest they gave Hebron (a city of refuge for one accused of murder), Libnah, [14]Jattir, Eshtemoa, [15]Holon, Debir, [16]Ain, Juttah and Beth Shemesh, together with their pasturelands—nine towns from these two tribes.

[17]And from the tribe of Benjamin they gave them Gibeon, Geba, [18]Anathoth and Almon, together with their pasturelands—four towns.

[19]All the towns for the priests, the descendants of Aaron, were thirteen, together with their pasturelands.

[20]The rest of the Kohathite clans of the Levites were allotted towns from the tribe of Ephraim:

[21]In the hill country of Ephraim they were given Shechem (a city of refuge for one accused of murder) and Gezer, [22]Kibzaim and Beth Horon, together with their pasturelands—four towns.

[23]Also from the tribe of Dan they received Eltekeh, Gibbethon, [24]Aijalon and Gath Rimmon, together with their pasturelands—four towns.

[25]From half the tribe of Manasseh they received Taanach and Gath Rimmon, together with their pasturelands—two towns.

[26]All these ten towns and their pasturelands were given to the rest of the Kohathite clans.

[27]The Levite clans of the Gershonites were given:
from the half-tribe of Manasseh, Golan in Bashan (a city of refuge for one accused of murder) and Be Eshtarah, together with their pasturelands—two towns;

[28]from the tribe of Issachar, Kishion, Daberath, [29]Jarmuth and En Gannim, together with their pasturelands—four towns;

[30]from the tribe of Asher, Mishal, Abdon, [31]Helkath and Rehob, together with their pasturelands—four towns;

[32]from the tribe of Naphtali, Kedesh in Galilee (a city of refuge for one accused of murder), Hammoth Dor and Kartan, together with their pasturelands—three towns.

[33]All the towns of the Gershonite clans were thirteen, together with their pasturelands.

[34]The Merarite clans (the rest of the Levites) were given:
from the tribe of Zebulun, Jokneam, Kartah, [35]Dimnah and Nahalal, together with their pasturelands—four towns;

[36]from the tribe of Reuben, Bezer, Jahaz, [37]Kedemoth and Mephaath, together with their pasturelands—four towns;

[38]from the tribe of Gad, Ramoth in Gilead (a city of refuge for one accused of murder), Mahanaim, [39]Heshbon and Jazer, together with their pasturelands—four towns in all.

[40]All the towns allotted to the Merarite clans, who were the rest of the Levites, were twelve.

[41]The towns of the Levites in the territory held by the Israelites were forty-eight in all, together with their pasturelands. [42]Each of these towns had pasturelands surrounding it; this was true for all these towns.

[43]So the LORD gave Israel all the land he had sworn to give their forefathers, and they took possession of it and settled there. [44]The LORD gave them rest on every side, just as he had sworn to their forefathers. Not one of their enemies withstood them; the LORD handed all

their enemies over to them. 45Not one of all the LORD's good promises to the house of Israel failed; every one was fulfilled.

Eastern Tribes Return Home

22 Then Joshua summoned the Reubenites, the Gadites and the half-tribe of Manasseh 2and said to them, "You have done all that Moses the servant of the LORD commanded, and you have obeyed me in everything I commanded. 3For a long time now—to this very day—you have not deserted your brothers but have carried out the mission the LORD your God gave you. 4Now that the LORD your God has given your brothers rest as he promised, return to your homes in the land that Moses the servant of the LORD gave you on the other side of the Jordan. 5But be very careful to keep the commandment and the law that Moses the servant of the LORD gave you: to love the LORD your God, to walk in all his ways, to obey his commands, to hold fast to him and to serve him with all your heart and all your soul."

6Then Joshua blessed them and sent them away, and they went to their homes. 7(To the half-tribe of Manasseh Moses had given land in Bashan, and to the other half of the tribe Joshua gave land on the west side of the Jordan with their brothers.) When Joshua sent them home, he blessed them, 8saying, "Return to your homes with your great wealth—with large herds of livestock, with silver, gold, bronze and iron, and a great quantity of clothing—and divide with your brothers the plunder from your enemies."

9So the Reubenites, the Gadites and the half-tribe of Manasseh left the Israelites at Shiloh in Canaan to return to Gilead, their own land, which they had acquired in accordance with the command of the LORD through Moses.

10When they came to Geliloth near the Jordan in the land of Canaan, the Reubenites, the Gadites and the half-tribe of Manasseh built an imposing altar there by the Jordan. 11And when the Israelites heard that they had built the altar on the border of Canaan at Geliloth near the Jordan on the Israelite side, 12the whole assembly of Israel gathered at Shiloh to go to war against them.

13So the Israelites sent Phinehas son of Eleazar, the priest, to the land of Gilead—to Reuben, Gad and the half-tribe of Manasseh. 14With him they sent ten of the chief men, one for each of the tribes of Israel, each the head of a family division among the Israelite clans.

15When they went to Gilead—to Reuben, Gad and the half-tribe of Manasseh—they said to them: 16"The whole assembly of the LORD says: 'How could you break faith with the God of Israel like this? How could you turn away from the LORD and build yourselves an altar in rebellion against him now? 17Was not the sin of Peor enough for us? Up to this very day we have not cleansed ourselves from that sin, even though a plague fell on the community of the LORD! 18And are you now turning away from the LORD?

"'If you rebel against the LORD today, tomorrow he will be angry with the whole community of Israel. 19If the land you possess is defiled, come over to the LORD's land, where the LORD's tabernacle stands, and share the land with us. But do not rebel against the LORD or against us by building an altar for yourselves, other than the altar of the LORD our God. 20When Achan son of Zerah acted unfaithfully regarding the devoted things,a did not wrath come upon the whole community of Israel? He was not the only one who died for his sin.'"

21Then Reuben, Gad and the half-tribe of Manasseh replied to the heads of the clans of Israel: 22"The Mighty One, God, the LORD! The Mighty One, God, the LORD! He knows! And let Israel know! If this has been in rebellion or disobedience

---

a 20 The Hebrew term refers to the irrevocable giving over of things or persons to the LORD, often by totally destroying them.

to the LORD, do not spare us this day. 23 If we have built our own altar to turn away from the LORD and to offer burnt offerings and grain offerings, or to sacrifice fellowship offerings[a] on it, may the LORD himself call us to account.

24 "No! We did it for fear that some day your descendants might say to ours, 'What do you have to do with the LORD, the God of Israel? 25 The LORD has made the Jordan a boundary between us and you—you Reubenites and Gadites! You have no share in the LORD.' So your descendants might cause ours to stop fearing the LORD.

26 "That is why we said, 'Let us get ready and build an altar—but not for burnt offerings or sacrifices.' 27 On the contrary, it is to be a witness between us and you and the generations that follow, that we will worship the LORD at his sanctuary with our burnt offerings, sacrifices and fellowship offerings. Then in the future your descendants will not be able to say to ours, 'You have no share in the LORD.'

28 "And we said, 'If they ever say this to us, or to our descendants, we will answer: Look at the replica of the LORD's altar, which our fathers built, not for burnt offerings and sacrifices, but as a witness between us and you.'

29 "Far be it from us to rebel against the LORD and turn away from him today by building an altar for burnt offerings, grain offerings and sacrifices, other than the altar of the LORD our God that stands before his tabernacle."

30 When Phinehas the priest and the leaders of the community—the heads of the clans of the Israelites—heard what Reuben, Gad and Manasseh had to say, they were pleased. 31 And Phinehas son of Eleazar, the priest, said to Reuben, Gad and Manasseh, "Today we know that the LORD is with us, because you have not acted unfaithfully toward the LORD in this matter. Now you have rescued the Israelites from the LORD's hand."

32 Then Phinehas son of Eleazar, the priest, and the leaders returned to Canaan from their meeting with the Reubenites and Gadites in Gilead and reported to the Israelites. 33 They were glad to hear the report and praised God. And they talked no more about going to war against them to devastate the country where the Reubenites and the Gadites lived.

34 And the Reubenites and the Gadites gave the altar this name: A Witness Between Us that the LORD is God.

Joshua's Farewell to the Leaders

23 After a long time had passed and the LORD had given Israel rest from all their enemies around them, Joshua, by then old and well advanced in years, 2 summoned all Israel—their elders, leaders, judges and officials—and said to them: "I am old and well advanced in years. 3 You yourselves have seen everything the LORD your God has done to all these nations for your sake; it was the LORD your God who fought for you. 4 Remember how I have allotted as an inheritance for your tribes all the land of the nations that remain—the nations I conquered—between the Jordan and the Great Sea[b] in the west. 5 The LORD your God himself will drive them out of your way. He will push them out before you, and you will take possession of their land, as the LORD your God promised you.

6 "Be very strong; be careful to obey all that is written in the Book of the Law of Moses, without turning aside to the right or to the left. 7 Do not associate with these nations that remain among you; do not invoke the names of their gods or swear by them. You must not serve them or bow down to them. 8 But you are to hold fast to the LORD your God, as you have until now.

9 "The LORD has driven out before you great and powerful nations; to this day no one has been able to withstand you. 10 One of you routs a thousand, because the LORD your God fights for you, just as

---

a 23 Traditionally *peace offerings*; also in verse 27   b 4 That is, the Mediterranean he promised. ¹¹So be very careful to love the LORD your God.

¹²"But if you turn away and ally yourselves with the survivors of these nations that remain among you and if you intermarry with them and associate with them, ¹³then you may be sure that the LORD your God will no longer drive out these nations before you. Instead, they will become snares and traps for you, whips on your backs and thorns in your eyes, until you perish from this good land, which the LORD your God has given you.

¹⁴"Now I am about to go the way of all the earth. You know with all your heart and soul that not one of all the good promises the LORD your God gave you has failed. Every promise has been fulfilled; not one has failed. ¹⁵But just as every good promise of the LORD your God has come true, so the LORD will bring on you all the evil he has threatened, until he has destroyed you from this good land he has given you. ¹⁶If you violate the covenant of the LORD your God, which he commanded you, and go and serve other gods and bow down to them, the LORD's anger will burn against you, and you will quickly perish from the good land he has given you."

The Covenant Renewed at Shechem

24 Then Joshua assembled all the tribes of Israel at Shechem. He summoned the elders, leaders, judges and officials of Israel, and they presented themselves before God.

²Joshua said to all the people, "This is what the LORD, the God of Israel, says: 'Long ago your forefathers, including Terah the father of Abraham and Nahor, lived beyond the River[a] and worshiped other gods. ³But I took your father Abraham from the land beyond the River and led him throughout Canaan and gave him many descendants. I gave him Isaac, ⁴and to Isaac I gave Jacob and Esau. I assigned the hill country of Seir to Esau, but Jacob and his sons went down to Egypt.

⁵"'Then I sent Moses and Aaron, and I afflicted the Egyptians by what I did there, and I brought you out. ⁶When I brought your fathers out of Egypt, you came to the sea, and the Egyptians pursued them with chariots and horsemen[b] as far as the Red Sea.[c] ⁷But they cried to the LORD for help, and he put darkness between you and the Egyptians; he brought the sea over them and covered them. You saw with your own eyes what I did to the Egyptians. Then you lived in the desert for a long time.

⁸"'I brought you to the land of the Amorites who lived east of the Jordan. They fought against you, but I gave them into your hands. I destroyed them from before you, and you took possession of their land. ⁹When Balak son of Zippor, the king of Moab, prepared to fight against Israel, he sent for Balaam son of Beor to put a curse on you. ¹⁰But I would not listen to Balaam, so he blessed you again and again, and I delivered you out of his hand.

Praying Joshua 24:14-16
Father God, I love You with all my heart, and I choose to serve You this day.

¹¹"'Then you crossed the Jordan and came to Jericho. The citizens of Jericho fought against you, as did also the Amorites, Perizzites, Canaanites, Hittites, Girgashites, Hivites and Jebusites, but I gave them into your hands. ¹²I sent the hornet ahead of you, which drove them out before you—also the two Amorite kings. You did not do it with your own sword and bow. ¹³So I gave you a land on which you did not toil and cities you did not build; and you live in them and eat from vineyards and olive groves that you did not plant.'

¹⁴"Now fear the LORD and serve him with all faithfulness. Throw away the gods your forefathers worshiped beyond the River and in Egypt, and serve the LORD.

---

[a] 2 That is, the Euphrates; also in verses 3, 14 and 15   [b] 6 Or *charioteers*   [c] 6 Hebrew *Yam Suph*; that is, Sea of Reeds

15But if serving the LORD seems undesirable to you, then choose for yourselves this day whom you will serve, whether the gods your forefathers served beyond the River, or the gods of the Amorites, in whose land you are living. But as for me and my household, we will serve the LORD."

16Then the people answered, "Far be it from us to forsake the LORD to serve other gods! 17It was the LORD our God himself who brought us and our fathers up out of Egypt, from that land of slavery, and performed those great signs before our eyes. He protected us on our entire journey and among all the nations through which we traveled. 18And the LORD drove out before us all the nations, including the Amorites, who lived in the land. We too will serve the LORD, because he is our God."

19Joshua said to the people, "You are not able to serve the LORD. He is a holy God; he is a jealous God. He will not forgive your rebellion and your sins. 20If you forsake the LORD and serve foreign gods, he will turn and bring disaster on you and make an end of you, after he has been good to you."

21But the people said to Joshua, "No! We will serve the LORD."

22Then Joshua said, "You are witnesses against yourselves that you have chosen to serve the LORD."

"Yes, we are witnesses," they replied.

23"Now then," said Joshua, "throw away the foreign gods that are among you and yield your hearts to the LORD, the God of Israel."

24And the people said to Joshua, "We will serve the LORD our God and obey him."

25On that day Joshua made a covenant for the people, and there at Shechem he drew up for them decrees and laws. 26And Joshua recorded these things in the Book of the Law of God. Then he took a large stone and set it up there under the oak near the holy place of the LORD.

27"See!" he said to all the people. "This stone will be a witness against us. It has heard all the words the LORD has said to us. It will be a witness against you if you are untrue to your God."

Buried in the Promised Land

28Then Joshua sent the people away, each to his own inheritance.

29After these things, Joshua son of Nun, the servant of the LORD, died at the age of a hundred and ten. 30And they buried him in the land of his inheritance, at Timnath Serah[a] in the hill country of Ephraim, north of Mount Gaash.

31Israel served the LORD throughout the lifetime of Joshua and of the elders who outlived him and who had experienced everything the LORD had done for Israel.

32And Joseph's bones, which the Israelites had brought up from Egypt, were buried at Shechem in the tract of land that Jacob bought for a hundred pieces of silver[b] from the sons of Hamor, the father of Shechem. This became the inheritance of Joseph's descendants.

33And Eleazar son of Aaron died and was buried at Gibeah, which had been allotted to his son Phinehas in the hill country of Ephraim.

a 30 Also known as Timnath Heres (see Judges 2:9)   b 32 Hebrew hundred kesitahs; a kesitah was a unit of money of unknown weight and value.

Author: Possibly Samuel

Date: Between 1043 and 1004 BC

Audience: Future generations of God's people who might be tempted to turn away from God

Prayer Themes:

- *Thank God for the gracious way He disciplines you, His child, and pursues you when you stray (2:11-16).*

- *Praise God for the way He rescues you from sin, helping you turn away from false gods and come humbly back to Him (10:15-16).*

- *Ask God for the wisdom and strength to keep from making foolish choices that put you in tempting situations (chapters 14–16).*

Do most of your conversations with God end up being long confessions of the same old sins? Are they repetitive pleas for God to rescue you from your self-made problems? The book of Judges teaches us how to break this rebellion-retribution-repentance cycle.

Be forewarned. Judges is a shocking book. This dark time in Israel's history revealed wholesale lawlessness that pervaded the land: "In those days Israel had no king; everyone did as he saw fit" (21:25). Yet the most astonishing thing is not how time and again the Israelites "refused to give up their evil practices and stubborn ways" (2:19). No, the most stunning revelation from Judges is the way God unfailingly responded with mercy and forgiveness when His people finally confessed their sins and turned from their wicked ways.

Judges

Israel Fights the Remaining Canaanites

After the death of Joshua, the Israelites asked the LORD, "Who will be the first to go up and fight for us against the Canaanites?"

²The LORD answered, "Judah is to go; I have given the land into their hands."

³Then the men of Judah said to the Simeonites their brothers, "Come up with us into the territory allotted to us, to fight against the Canaanites. We in turn will go with you into yours." So the Simeonites went with them.

⁴When Judah attacked, the LORD gave the Canaanites and Perizzites into their hands and they struck down ten thousand men at Bezek. ⁵It was there that they found Adoni-Bezek and fought against him, putting to rout the Canaanites and Perizzites. ⁶Adoni-Bezek fled, but they chased him and caught him, and cut off his thumbs and big toes.

⁷Then Adoni-Bezek said, "Seventy kings with their thumbs and big toes cut off have picked up scraps under my table. Now God has paid me back for what I did to them." They brought him to Jerusalem, and he died there.

⁸The men of Judah attacked Jerusalem also and took it. They put the city to the sword and set it on fire.

⁹After that, the men of Judah went down to fight against the Canaanites living in the hill country, the Negev and the western foothills. ¹⁰They advanced against the Canaanites living in Hebron (formerly called Kiriath Arba) and defeated Sheshai, Ahiman and Talmai.

¹¹From there they advanced against the people living in Debir (formerly called Kiriath Sepher). ¹²And Caleb said, "I will give my daughter Acsah in marriage to

the man who attacks and captures Kiriath Sepher." [13]Othniel son of Kenaz, Caleb's younger brother, took it; so Caleb gave his daughter Acsah to him in marriage.

[14]One day when she came to Othniel, she urged him[a] to ask her father for a field. When she got off her donkey, Caleb asked her, "What can I do for you?"

[15]She replied, "Do me a special favor. Since you have given me land in the Negev, give me also springs of water." Then Caleb gave her the upper and lower springs.

Prayer is . . .

recognizing that you are totally dependent upon God.

[16]The descendants of Moses' father-in-law, the Kenite, went up from the City of Palms[b] with the men of Judah to live among the people of the Desert of Judah in the Negev near Arad.

[17]Then the men of Judah went with the Simeonites their brothers and attacked the Canaanites living in Zephath, and they totally destroyed[c] the city. Therefore it was called Hormah.[d] [18]The men of Judah also took[e] Gaza, Ashkelon and Ekron—each city with its territory.

[19]The LORD was with the men of Judah. They took possession of the hill country, but they were unable to drive the people from the plains, because they had iron chariots. [20]As Moses had promised, Hebron was given to Caleb, who drove from it the three sons of Anak. [21]The Benjamites, however, failed to dislodge the Jebusites, who were living in Jerusalem; to this day the Jebusites live there with the Benjamites.

[22]Now the house of Joseph attacked Bethel, and the LORD was with them. [23]When they sent men to spy out Bethel (formerly called Luz), [24]the spies saw a man coming out of the city and they said to him, "Show us how to get into the city and we will see that you are treated well." [25]So he showed them, and they put the city to the sword but spared the man and his whole family. [26]He then went to the land of the Hittites, where he built a city and called it Luz, which is its name to this day.

[27]But Manasseh did not drive out the people of Beth Shan or Taanach or Dor or Ibleam or Megiddo and their surrounding settlements, for the Canaanites were determined to live in that land. [28]When Israel became strong, they pressed the Canaanites into forced labor but never drove them out completely. [29]Nor did Ephraim drive out the Canaanites living in Gezer, but the Canaanites continued to live there among them. [30]Neither did Zebulun drive out the Canaanites living in Kitron or Nahalol, who remained among them; but they did subject them to forced labor. [31]Nor did Asher drive out those living in Acco or Sidon or Ahlab or Aczib or Helbah or Aphek or Rehob, [32]and because of this the people of Asher lived among the Canaanite inhabitants of the land. [33]Neither did Naphtali drive out those living in Beth Shemesh or Beth Anath; but the Naphtalites too lived among the Canaanite inhabitants of the land, and those living in Beth Shemesh and Beth Anath became forced laborers for them. [34]The Amorites confined the Danites to the hill country, not allowing them to come down into the plain. [35]And the Amorites were determined also to hold out in Mount Heres, Aijalon and Shaalbim, but when the power of the house of Joseph increased, they too were pressed into forced labor. [36]The boundary of the Amorites was from Scorpion[f] Pass to Sela and beyond.

---

[a] 14 Hebrew; Septuagint and Vulgate *Othniel, he urged her* [b] 16 That is, Jericho [c] 17 The Hebrew term refers to the irrevocable giving over of things or persons to the LORD, often by totally destroying them. [d] 17 Hormah means *destruction*. [e] 18 Hebrew; Septuagint *Judah did not take* [f] 36 Hebrew *Akrabbim*

The Angel of the LORD at Bokim

2 The angel of the LORD went up from Gilgal to Bokim and said, "I brought you up out of Egypt and led you into the land that I swore to give to your forefathers. I said, 'I will never break my covenant with you, ²and you shall not make a covenant with the people of this land, but you shall break down their altars.' Yet you have disobeyed me. Why have you done this? ³Now therefore I tell you that I will not drive them out before you; they will be ⌐thorns¬ in your sides and their gods will be a snare to you."

⁴When the angel of the LORD had spoken these things to all the Israelites, the people wept aloud, ⁵and they called that place Bokim.ᵃ There they offered sacrifices to the LORD.

Disobedience and Defeat

⁶After Joshua had dismissed the Israelites, they went to take possession of the land, each to his own inheritance. ⁷The people served the LORD throughout the lifetime of Joshua and of the elders who outlived him and who had seen all the great things the LORD had done for Israel.

⁸Joshua son of Nun, the servant of the LORD, died at the age of a hundred and ten. ⁹And they buried him in the land of his inheritance, at Timnath Heresᵇ in the hill country of Ephraim, north of Mount Gaash.

¹⁰After that whole generation had been gathered to their fathers, another generation grew up, who knew neither the LORD nor what he had done for Israel. ¹¹Then the Israelites did evil in the eyes of the LORD and served the Baals. ¹²They forsook the LORD, the God of their fathers, who had brought them out of Egypt. They followed and worshiped various gods of the peoples around them. They provoked the LORD to anger

---

ᵃ 5 *Bokim* means *weepers.*   ᵇ 9 Also known as *Timnath Serah* (see Joshua 19:50 and 24:30)

GOING *deeper*

Get Personal With God

READ AND CONSIDER: JUDGES 2:6-23

"Therefore the LORD was very angry with Israel and said, 'Because this nation has violated the covenant that I laid down for their forefathers and has not listened to me, I will no longer drive out before them any of the nations Joshua left when he died' " (Judges 2:20-21).

After years of struggle to get to the promised land, the nation of Israel fell away from the Lord who had led them there. Why? Because they did not maintain their own personal connection to Him. Relying on the faith of their fathers wasn't enough to sustain them, and they turned to other gods.

The same principle holds true for us. We cannot rely on other people's faith, or even our own past experiences with God, to sustain our current relationship with Him. We must maintain a living, dynamic, active relationship with Him through our prayer life and Scripture reading in order to know Him at an intimate level.

Prayer is about so much more than just making requests or getting advice. It is our avenue to knowing and being known by the God of the universe. Although He already knows us completely, we don't have any way of experiencing that reality if we do not connect with Him in a personal way.

God created you, and He desires to be part of your life. He doesn't want you to fall into temptations and dangers as the Israelites did. Make sure that you maintain a consistent prayer life and guard against riding on past experiences with Him. Doing so can get you into dangerous territory.

13because they forsook him and served Baal and the Ashtoreths. 14In his anger against Israel the LORD handed them over to raiders who plundered them. He sold them to their enemies all around, whom they were no longer able to resist. 15Whenever Israel went out to fight, the hand of the LORD was against them to defeat them, just as he had sworn to them. They were in great distress.

16Then the LORD raised up judges,[a] who saved them out of the hands of these raiders. 17Yet they would not listen to their judges but prostituted themselves to other gods and worshiped them. Unlike their fathers, they quickly turned from the way in which their fathers had walked, the way of obedience to the LORD's commands. 18Whenever the LORD raised up a judge for them, he was with the judge and saved them out of the hands of their enemies as long as the judge lived; for the LORD had compassion on them as they groaned under those who oppressed and afflicted them. 19But when the judge died, the people returned to ways even more corrupt than those of their fathers, following other gods and serving and worshiping them. They refused to give up their evil practices and stubborn ways.

20Therefore the LORD was very angry with Israel and said, "Because this nation has violated the covenant that I laid down for their forefathers and has not listened to me, 21I will no longer drive out before them any of the nations Joshua left when he died. 22I will use them to test Israel and see whether they will keep the way of the LORD and walk in it as their forefathers did." 23The LORD had allowed those nations to remain; he did not drive them out at once by giving them into the hands of Joshua.

3 These are the nations the LORD left to test all those Israelites who had not experienced any of the wars in Canaan 2(he did this only to teach warfare to the descendants of the Israelites who had not had previous battle experience): 3the five rulers of the Philistines, all the Canaanites, the Sidonians, and the Hivites living in the Lebanon mountains from Mount Baal Hermon to Lebo[b] Hamath. 4They were left to test the Israelites to see whether they would obey the LORD's commands, which he had given their forefathers through Moses.

5The Israelites lived among the Canaanites, Hittites, Amorites, Perizzites, Hivites and Jebusites. 6They took their daughters in marriage and gave their own daughters to their sons, and served their gods.

Othniel

7The Israelites did evil in the eyes of the LORD; they forgot the LORD their God and served the Baals and the Asherahs. 8The anger of the LORD burned against Israel so that he sold them into the hands of Cushan-Rishathaim king of Aram Naharaim,[c] to whom the Israelites were subject for eight years. 9But when they cried out to the LORD, he raised up for them a deliverer, Othniel son of Kenaz, Caleb's younger brother, who saved them. 10The Spirit of the LORD came upon him, so that he became Israel's judge[d] and went to war. The LORD gave Cushan-Rishathaim king of Aram into the hands of Othniel, who overpowered him. 11So the land had peace for forty years, until Othniel son of Kenaz died.

Ehud

12Once again the Israelites did evil in the eyes of the LORD, and because they did this evil the LORD gave Eglon king of Moab power over Israel. 13Getting the Ammonites and Amalekites to join him, Eglon came and attacked Israel, and they took possession of the City of Palms.[e] 14The Israelites were subject to Eglon king of Moab for eighteen years.

15Again the Israelites cried out to the LORD, and he gave them a deliverer—

---

a 16 Or leaders; similarly in verses 17-19   b 3 Or to the entrance to   c 8 That is, Northwest Mesopotamia   d 10 Or leader
e 13 That is, Jericho

God Delivers

GOING *deeper*

READ AND CONSIDER: JUDGES 3:7-30

"But when they cried out to the LORD, he raised up for them a deliverer, Othniel son of Kenaz, Caleb's younger brother, who saved them . . . Again the Israelites cried out to the LORD, and he gave them a deliverer—Ehud, a left-handed man, the son of Gera the Benjamite" (Judges 3:9,15).

The Israelite's sinful ways put them into a place of bondage to foreign nations and foreign gods. But every time they cried out to the Lord, He was faithful to rescue them.

We all need deliverance at one time or another. That's because regardless of how spiritual we may be, we're still made of flesh. And no matter how good we may think we are, we have an enemy who is trying to erect strongholds of evil in our lives. Jesus taught us to pray, "Deliver us from the evil one" (Matthew 6:13). He would not have instructed us in that manner if we didn't need to be delivered. But so often we don't pray that way. So often we live our lives as if we don't realize Jesus paid an enormous price so we could be free. God wants to free us from everything that binds, holds, or separates us from Him. He wants to *continue* to set us free every day of our lives.

Do you feel enslaved to finances, illness, addictions, unhealthy relationships, immorality, or resentments? Do you struggle to be close to God or to believe that He hears your prayers and will answer them? Do you fear that you never have victory over the areas you struggle with, and so you are more discouraged than joyful? God wants to set you free. He wants you to remember that He is the Deliverer. He says, "Call upon me in the day of trouble; I will deliver you, and you will honor me" (Psalm 50:15).

Deliverance is found by praying for it yourself (Psalm 72:12), by having someone else who is a strong believer pray with you for it (Psalm 34:17), by reading the truth of God's Word with great understanding and clarity (John 8:32), and by spending time in the Lord's presence. The most effective and powerful way to spend time in the Lord's presence is in praise and worship. Every time you worship God, something happens to break the power of evil. That's because God inhabits your praises, and this means you are in His presence.

Remember that deliverance is an ongoing process. God wants you whole and will see that process through to the end. Don't give up. "He who began a good work in you will carry it on to completion until the day of Christ Jesus" (Philippians 1:6).

Ehud, a left-handed man, the son of Gera the Benjamite. The Israelites sent him with tribute to Eglon king of Moab. [16]Now Ehud had made a double-edged sword about a foot and a half[a] long, which he strapped to his right thigh under his clothing. [17]He presented the tribute to Eglon king of Moab, who was a very fat man. [18]After Ehud had presented the tribute, he sent on their way the men who had carried it. [19]At the idols[b] near Gilgal he himself turned back and said, "I have a secret message for you, O king."

The king said, "Quiet!" And all his attendants left him.

[20]Ehud then approached him while he was sitting alone in the upper room of his summer palace[c] and said, "I have a

---

[a] *16* Hebrew *a cubit* (about 0.5 meter)   [b] *19* Or *the stone quarries*; also in verse 26   [c] *20* The meaning of the Hebrew for this phrase is uncertain.

message from God for you." As the king rose from his seat, ²¹Ehud reached with his left hand, drew the sword from his right thigh and plunged it into the king's belly. ²²Even the handle sank in after the blade, which came out his back. Ehud did not pull the sword out, and the fat closed in over it. ²³Then Ehud went out to the porchª; he shut the doors of the upper room behind him and locked them.

²⁴After he had gone, the servants came and found the doors of the upper room locked. They said, "He must be relieving himself in the inner room of the house." ²⁵They waited to the point of embarrassment, but when he did not open the doors of the room, they took a key and unlocked them. There they saw their lord fallen to the floor, dead.

²⁶While they waited, Ehud got away. He passed by the idols and escaped to Seirah. ²⁷When he arrived there, he blew a trumpet in the hill country of Ephraim, and the Israelites went down with him from the hills, with him leading them.

²⁸"Follow me," he ordered, "for the LORD has given Moab, your enemy, into your hands." So they followed him down and, taking possession of the fords of the Jordan that led to Moab, they allowed no one to cross over. ²⁹At that time they struck down about ten thousand Moabites, all vigorous and strong; not a man escaped. ³⁰That day Moab was made subject to Israel, and the land had peace for eighty years.

Shamgar

³¹After Ehud came Shamgar son of Anath, who struck down six hundred Philistines with an oxgoad. He too saved Israel.

Deborah

4 After Ehud died, the Israelites once again did evil in the eyes of the LORD. ²So the LORD sold them into the hands of Jabin, a king of Canaan, who reigned in Hazor. The commander of his army was Sisera, who lived in Harosheth Haggoyim. ³Because he had nine hundred iron chariots and had cruelly oppressed the Israelites for twenty years, they cried to the LORD for help.

⁴Deborah, a prophetess, the wife of Lappidoth, was leadingᵇ Israel at that time. ⁵She held court under the Palm of Deborah between Ramah and Bethel in the hill country of Ephraim, and the Israelites came to her to have their disputes decided. ⁶She sent for Barak son of Abinoam from Kedesh in Naphtali and said to him, "The LORD, the God of Israel, commands you: 'Go, take with you ten thousand men of Naphtali and Zebulun and lead the way to Mount Tabor. ⁷I will lure Sisera, the commander of Jabin's army, with his chariots and his troops to the Kishon River and give him into your hands.'"

⁸Barak said to her, "If you go with me, I will go; but if you don't go with me, I won't go."

⁹"Very well," Deborah said, "I will go with you. But because of the way you are going about this,ᶜ the honor will not be yours, for the LORD will hand Sisera over to a woman." So Deborah went with Barak to Kedesh, ¹⁰where he summoned Zebulun and Naphtali. Ten thousand men followed him, and Deborah also went with him.

¹¹Now Heber the Kenite had left the other Kenites, the descendants of Hobab, Moses' brother-in-law,ᵈ and pitched his tent by the great tree in Zaanannim near Kedesh.

¹²When they told Sisera that Barak son of Abinoam had gone up to Mount Tabor, ¹³Sisera gathered together his nine hundred iron chariots and all the men with him, from Harosheth Haggoyim to the Kishon River.

¹⁴Then Deborah said to Barak, "Go! This is the day the LORD has given Sis-

era into your hands. Has not the LORD gone ahead of you?" So Barak went down Mount Tabor, followed by ten thousand men. ¹⁵At Barak's advance, the LORD routed Sisera and all his chariots and army by the sword, and Sisera abandoned his chariot and fled on foot. ¹⁶But Barak pursued the chariots and army as far as Harosheth Haggoyim. All the troops of Sisera fell by the sword; not a man was left.

¹⁷Sisera, however, fled on foot to the tent of Jael, the wife of Heber the Kenite, because there were friendly relations between Jabin king of Hazor and the clan of Heber the Kenite.

¹⁸Jael went out to meet Sisera and said to him, "Come, my lord, come right in. Don't be afraid." So he entered her tent, and she put a covering over him.

²²Barak came by in pursuit of Sisera, and Jael went out to meet him. "Come," she said, "I will show you the man you're looking for." So he went in with her, and there lay Sisera with the tent peg through his temple—dead.

²³On that day God subdued Jabin, the Canaanite king, before the Israelites. ²⁴And the hand of the Israelites grew stronger and stronger against Jabin, the Canaanite king, until they destroyed him.

The Song of Deborah

5 On that day Deborah and Barak son of Abinoam sang this song:

²"When the princes in Israel take the lead,
    when the people willingly offer themselves—
praise the LORD!

God's people at prayer
DEBORAH'S SONG OF PRAISE

JUDGES 5:1-31 What great moments of victory have you faced? Did you ever achieve success over challenging obstacles? Or stand tall when you could have folded in the face of fear or struggle? Whatever your victories, praise God for them.

Of course, victory isn't always the outcome. So God wants us to praise Him in times of defeat as much as we do in times of success. Deborah must have known that all too well because she spent her days mediating trouble for other people. Each day was a reminder that life is not always a winning proposition. But God is Lord in the wins as well as the losses. So when you come out on top, give Him praise like Deborah did. But when you don't, praise Him just as much. Win or lose, God is always worthy of our worship.

---

¹⁹"I'm thirsty," he said. "Please give me some water." She opened a skin of milk, gave him a drink, and covered him up.

²⁰"Stand in the doorway of the tent," he told her. "If someone comes by and asks you, 'Is anyone here?' say 'No.'"

²¹But Jael, Heber's wife, picked up a tent peg and a hammer and went quietly to him while he lay fast asleep, exhausted. She drove the peg through his temple into the ground, and he died.

³"Hear this, you kings! Listen, you rulers!
    I will sing to[a] the LORD, I will sing;
    I will make music to[b] the LORD, the God of Israel.

⁴"O LORD, when you went out from Seir,
    when you marched from the land of Edom,
the earth shook, the heavens poured,

---

[a] 3 Or *of*   [b] 3 Or *I with song I will praise*

the clouds poured down water.
⁵ The mountains quaked before the
  LORD, the One of Sinai,
  before the LORD, the God of Israel.

⁶ "In the days of Shamgar son of
    Anath,
  in the days of Jael, the roads were
    abandoned;
  travelers took to winding paths.
⁷ Village lifeᵃ in Israel ceased,
  ceased until I,ᵇ Deborah, arose,
  arose a mother in Israel.
⁸ When they chose new gods,
  war came to the city gates,
and not a shield or spear was seen
  among forty thousand in Israel.
⁹ My heart is with Israel's princes,
  with the willing volunteers among
    the people.
  Praise the LORD!

¹⁰ "You who ride on white donkeys,
  sitting on your saddle blankets,
  and you who walk along the road,
consider ¹¹the voice of the singersᶜ at
    the watering places.
  They recite the righteous acts of
    the LORD,
  the righteous acts of his warriorsᵈ
    in Israel.

"Then the people of the LORD
  went down to the city gates.
¹²'Wake up, wake up, Deborah!
  Wake up, wake up, break out in
    song!
  Arise, O Barak!
  Take captive your captives, O son
    of Abinoam.'

¹³ "Then the men who were left
  came down to the nobles;
the people of the LORD
  came to me with the mighty.
¹⁴ Some came from Ephraim, whose
    roots were in Amalek;
  Benjamin was with the people who
    followed you.

From Makir captains came down,
  from Zebulun those who bear a
    commander's staff.
¹⁵ The princes of Issachar were with
    Deborah;
  yes, Issachar was with Barak,
  rushing after him into the valley.
In the districts of Reuben
  there was much searching of heart.
¹⁶ Why did you stay among the
    campfiresᵉ
  to hear the whistling for the flocks?
In the districts of Reuben
  there was much searching of heart.
¹⁷ Gilead stayed beyond the Jordan.
  And Dan, why did he linger by the
    ships?
Asher remained on the coast
  and stayed in his coves.
¹⁸ The people of Zebulun risked their
    very lives;
  so did Naphtali on the heights of
    the field.

¹⁹ "Kings came, they fought;
  the kings of Canaan fought
at Taanach by the waters of Megiddo,
  but they carried off no silver, no
    plunder.
²⁰ From the heavens the stars fought,
  from their courses they fought
    against Sisera.
²¹ The river Kishon swept them away,
  the age-old river, the river Kishon.
  March on, my soul; be strong!
²² Then thundered the horses' hoofs—
  galloping, galloping go his mighty
    steeds.
²³ 'Curse Meroz,' said the angel of the
    LORD.
  'Curse its people bitterly,
  because they did not come to help the
    LORD,
  to help the LORD against the
    mighty.'

²⁴ "Most blessed of women be Jael,
  the wife of Heber the Kenite,

ᵃ 7 Or *Warriors* ᵇ 7 Or *you* ᶜ 11 Or *archers*; the meaning of the Hebrew for this word is uncertain. ᵈ 11 Or *villagers*
ᵉ 16 Or *saddlebags*

most blessed of tent-dwelling
   women.
²⁵He asked for water, and she gave him
   milk;
  in a bowl fit for nobles she brought
   him curdled milk.
²⁶Her hand reached for the tent peg,
  her right hand for the workman's
   hammer.
She struck Sisera, she crushed his
   head,
  she shattered and pierced his temple.
²⁷At her feet he sank,
  he fell; there he lay.
At her feet he sank, he fell;
  where he sank, there he fell—dead.

²⁸"Through the window peered Sisera's
   mother;
  behind the lattice she cried out,
'Why is his chariot so long in
   coming?
  Why is the clatter of his chariots
   delayed?'
²⁹The wisest of her ladies answer her;
  indeed, she keeps saying to herself,
³⁰'Are they not finding and dividing the
   spoils:
  a girl or two for each man,
  colorful garments as plunder for
   Sisera,
  colorful garments embroidered,
  highly embroidered garments for
   my neck—
all this as plunder?'

³¹"So may all your enemies perish,
   O Lᴏʀᴅ!
  But may they who love you be like
   the sun
  when it rises in its strength."

Then the land had peace forty years.

Gideon

6 Again the Israelites did evil in the eyes
of the Lᴏʀᴅ, and for seven years he
gave them into the hands of the Midianites. ²Because the power of Midian was so
oppressive, the Israelites prepared shelters
for themselves in mountain clefts, caves
and strongholds. ³Whenever the Israelites
planted their crops, the Midianites, Amalekites and other eastern peoples invaded
the country. ⁴They camped on the land
and ruined the crops all the way to Gaza
and did not spare a living thing for Israel,
neither sheep nor cattle nor donkeys.
⁵They came up with their livestock and
their tents like swarms of locusts. It was
impossible to count the men and their
camels; they invaded the land to ravage
it. ⁶Midian so impoverished the Israelites
that they cried out to the Lᴏʀᴅ for help.

⁷When the Israelites cried to the
Lᴏʀᴅ because of Midian, ⁸he sent them
a prophet, who said, "This is what the
Lᴏʀᴅ, the God of Israel, says: I brought
you up out of Egypt, out of the land of
slavery. ⁹I snatched you from the power
of Egypt and from the hand of all your
oppressors. I drove them from before you
and gave you their land. ¹⁰I said to you,
'I am the Lᴏʀᴅ your God; do not worship the gods of the Amorites, in whose
land you live.' But you have not listened
to me."

¹¹The angel of the Lᴏʀᴅ came and sat
down under the oak in Ophrah that belonged to Joash the Abiezrite, where his
son Gideon was threshing wheat in a
winepress to keep it from the Midianites.
¹²When the angel of the Lᴏʀᴅ appeared
to Gideon, he said, "The Lᴏʀᴅ is with
you, mighty warrior."

¹³"But sir," Gideon replied, "if the
Lᴏʀᴅ is with us, why has all this happened to us? Where are all his wonders
that our fathers told us about when they
said, 'Did not the Lᴏʀᴅ bring us up out
of Egypt?' But now the Lᴏʀᴅ has abandoned us and put us into the hand of
Midian."

¹⁴The Lᴏʀᴅ turned to him and said,
"Go in the strength you have and save
Israel out of Midian's hand. Am I not
sending you?"

¹⁵"But Lord,ᵃ" Gideon asked, "how

can I save Israel? My clan is the weakest in Manasseh, and I am the least in my family."

¹⁶The LORD answered, "I will be with you, and you will strike down all the Midianites together."

Praying Judges 6:15-16

Lord, help me to remember that even though I feel weak, Your presence with me makes me strong.

¹⁷Gideon replied, "If now I have found favor in your eyes, give me a sign that it is really you talking to me. ¹⁸Please do not go away until I come back and bring my offering and set it before you."

And the LORD said, "I will wait until you return."

¹⁹Gideon went in, prepared a young goat, and from an ephahᵃ of flour he made bread without yeast. Putting the meat in a basket and its broth in a pot, he brought them out and offered them to him under the oak.

²⁰The angel of God said to him, "Take the meat and the unleavened bread, place them on this rock, and pour out the broth." And Gideon did so. ²¹With the tip of the staff that was in his hand, the angel of the LORD touched the meat and the unleavened bread. Fire flared from the rock, consuming the meat and the bread. And the angel of the LORD disappeared. ²²When Gideon realized that it was the angel of the LORD, he exclaimed, "Ah, Sovereign LORD! I have seen the angel of the LORD face to face!"

²³But the LORD said to him, "Peace! Do not be afraid. You are not going to die."

²⁴So Gideon built an altar to the LORD there and called it The LORD is Peace. To this day it stands in Ophrah of the Abiezrites.

²⁵That same night the LORD said to him, "Take the second bull from your fa-

ther's herd, the one seven years old.ᵇ Tear down your father's altar to Baal and cut down the Asherah poleᶜ beside it. ²⁶Then build a proper kind ofᵈ altar to the LORD your God on the top of this height. Using the wood of the Asherah pole that you cut down, offer the secondᵉ bull as a burnt offering."

²⁷So Gideon took ten of his servants and did as the LORD told him. But because he was afraid of his family and the men of the town, he did it at night rather than in the daytime.

²⁸In the morning when the men of the town got up, there was Baal's altar, demolished, with the Asherah pole beside it cut down and the second bull sacrificed on the newly built altar!

²⁹They asked each other, "Who did this?"

When they carefully investigated, they were told, "Gideon son of Joash did it."

³⁰The men of the town demanded of Joash, "Bring out your son. He must die, because he has broken down Baal's altar and cut down the Asherah pole beside it."

³¹But Joash replied to the hostile crowd around him, "Are you going to plead Baal's cause? Are you trying to save him? Whoever fights for him shall be put to death by morning! If Baal really is a god, he can defend himself when someone breaks down his altar." ³²So that day they called Gideon "Jerub-Baal,"ᶠ saying, "Let Baal contend with him," because he broke down Baal's altar.

³³Now all the Midianites, Amalekites and other eastern peoples joined forces and crossed over the Jordan and camped in the Valley of Jezreel. ³⁴Then the Spirit of the LORD came upon Gideon, and he blew a trumpet, summoning the Abiezrites to follow him. ³⁵He sent messengers throughout Manasseh, calling them to arms, and also into Asher, Zebulun and Naphtali, so that they too went up to meet them.

ᵃ 19 That is, probably about 3/5 bushel (about 22 liters)   ᵇ 25 Or *Take a full-grown, mature bull from your father's herd*
ᶜ 25 That is, a symbol of the goddess Asherah; here and elsewhere in Judges   ᵈ 26 Or *build with layers of stone an*
ᵉ 26 Or *full-grown*; also in verse 28   ᶠ 32 Jerub-Baal means *let Baal contend*.

³⁶Gideon said to God, "If you will save Israel by my hand as you have promised— ³⁷look, I will place a wool fleece on the threshing floor. If there is dew only on the fleece and all the ground is dry, then I will know that you will save Israel by my hand, as you said." ³⁸And that is what happened. Gideon rose early the next day; he squeezed the fleece and wrung out the dew—a bowlful of water.

and leave Mount Gilead.'" So twenty-two thousand men left, while ten thousand remained.

⁴But the LORD said to Gideon, "There are still too many men. Take them down to the water, and I will sift them for you there. If I say, 'This one shall go with you,' he shall go; but if I say, 'This one shall not go with you,' he shall not go."

⁵So Gideon took the men down to the

God's people at prayer
GIDEON'S FLEECE TEST

JUDGES 6:33-40 Before we decide whether to use Gideon's prayer as a personal example to follow, let's think about the situation. Gideon asked God for signs of victory—first a wet fleece and then a dry one. He prayed that way even though he knew he was all but provoking God's anger. God answered Gideon's request but then required that Gideon's army be reduced in size. Gideon tested God, and then God tested Gideon. The fleece told Gideon that God would bring victory, but Gideon had to surrender every shred of expectation that he and his soldiers would create the victory.

Testing God always turns into a bigger test for us. Whether He does what we ask, the question comes back to whether we will trust Him. This is why God always retains the final say on how He will answer. Rather than asking God for signs to prove Himself, tell Him you trust Him to do what is best.

---

³⁹Then Gideon said to God, "Do not be angry with me. Let me make just one more request. Allow me one more test with the fleece. This time make the fleece dry and the ground covered with dew." ⁴⁰That night God did so. Only the fleece was dry; all the ground was covered with dew.

Gideon Defeats the Midianites

7 Early in the morning, Jerub-Baal (that is, Gideon) and all his men camped at the spring of Harod. The camp of Midian was north of them in the valley near the hill of Moreh. ²The LORD said to Gideon, "You have too many men for me to deliver Midian into their hands. In order that Israel may not boast against me that her own strength has saved her, ³announce now to the people, 'Anyone who trembles with fear may turn back

water. There the LORD told him, "Separate those who lap the water with their tongues like a dog from those who kneel down to drink." ⁶Three hundred men lapped with their hands to their mouths. All the rest got down on their knees to drink.

⁷The LORD said to Gideon, "With the three hundred men that lapped I will save you and give the Midianites into your hands. Let all the other men go, each to his own place." ⁸So Gideon sent the rest of the Israelites to their tents but kept the three hundred, who took over the provisions and trumpets of the others.

Now the camp of Midian lay below him in the valley. ⁹During that night the LORD said to Gideon, "Get up, go down against the camp, because I am going to give it into your hands. ¹⁰If you are afraid to attack, go down to the camp with your servant Purah 11and listen to what they are saying. Afterward, you will be encouraged to attack the camp." So he and Purah his servant went down to the outposts of the camp. 12The Midianites, the Amalekites and all the other eastern peoples had settled in the valley, thick as locusts. Their camels could no more be counted than the sand on the seashore.

13Gideon arrived just as a man was telling a friend his dream. "I had a dream," he was saying. "A round loaf of barley bread came tumbling into the Midianite camp. It struck the tent with such force that the tent overturned and collapsed."

14His friend responded, "This can be nothing other than the sword of Gideon son of Joash, the Israelite. God has given the Midianites and the whole camp into his hands."

15When Gideon heard the dream and its interpretation, he worshiped God. He returned to the camp of Israel and called out, "Get up! The LORD has given the Midianite camp into your hands." 16Dividing the three hundred men into three companies, he placed trumpets and empty jars in the hands of all of them, with torches inside.

17"Watch me," he told them. "Follow my lead. When I get to the edge of the camp, do exactly as I do. 18When I and all who are with me blow our trumpets, then from all around the camp blow yours and shout, 'For the LORD and for Gideon.'"

19Gideon and the hundred men with him reached the edge of the camp at the beginning of the middle watch, just after they had changed the guard. They blew their trumpets and broke the jars that were in their hands. 20The three companies blew the trumpets and smashed the jars. Grasping the torches in their left hands and holding in their right hands the trumpets they were to blow, they shouted, "A sword for the LORD and for Gideon!" 21While each man held his position around the camp, all the Midianites ran, crying out as they fled.

22When the three hundred trumpets sounded, the LORD caused the men throughout the camp to turn on each other with their swords. The army fled to Beth Shittah toward Zererah as far as the border of Abel Meholah near Tabbath. 23Israelites from Naphtali, Asher and all Manasseh were called out, and they pursued the Midianites. 24Gideon sent messengers throughout the hill country of Ephraim, saying, "Come down against the Midianites and seize the waters of the Jordan ahead of them as far as Beth Barah."

So all the men of Ephraim were called out and they took the waters of the Jordan as far as Beth Barah. 25They also captured two of the Midianite leaders, Oreb and Zeeb. They killed Oreb at the rock of Oreb, and Zeeb at the winepress of Zeeb. They pursued the Midianites and brought the heads of Oreb and Zeeb to Gideon, who was by the Jordan.

Zebah and Zalmunna

8 Now the Ephraimites asked Gideon, "Why have you treated us like this? Why didn't you call us when you went to fight Midian?" And they criticized him sharply.

2But he answered them, "What have I accomplished compared to you? Aren't the gleanings of Ephraim's grapes better than the full grape harvest of Abiezer? 3God gave Oreb and Zeeb, the Midianite leaders, into your hands. What was I able to do compared to you?" At this, their resentment against him subsided.

4Gideon and his three hundred men, exhausted yet keeping up the pursuit, came to the Jordan and crossed it. 5He said to the men of Succoth, "Give my troops some bread; they are worn out, and I am still pursuing Zebah and Zalmunna, the kings of Midian."

6But the officials of Succoth said, "Do you already have the hands of Zebah and Zalmunna in your possession? Why should we give bread to your troops?"

7Then Gideon replied, "Just for that,

when the LORD has given Zebah and Zalmunna into my hand, I will tear your flesh with desert thorns and briers."

8From there he went up to Peniel[a] and made the same request of them, but they answered as the men of Succoth had. 9So he said to the men of Peniel, "When I return in triumph, I will tear down this tower."

10Now Zebah and Zalmunna were in Karkor with a force of about fifteen thousand men, all that were left of the armies of the eastern peoples; a hundred and twenty thousand swordsmen had fallen. 11Gideon went up by the route of the nomads east of Nobah and Jogbehah and fell upon the unsuspecting army. 12Zebah and Zalmunna, the two kings of Midian, fled, but he pursued them and captured them, routing their entire army.

13Gideon son of Joash then returned from the battle by the Pass of Heres. 14He caught a young man of Succoth and questioned him, and the young man wrote down for him the names of the seventy-seven officials of Succoth, the elders of the town. 15Then Gideon came and said to the men of Succoth, "Here are Zebah and Zalmunna, about whom you taunted me by saying, 'Do you already have the hands of Zebah and Zalmunna in your possession? Why should we give bread to your exhausted men?'" 16He took the elders of the town and taught the men of Succoth a lesson by punishing them with desert thorns and briers. 17He also pulled down the tower of Peniel and killed the men of the town.

18Then he asked Zebah and Zalmunna, "What kind of men did you kill at Tabor?"

"Men like you," they answered, "each one with the bearing of a prince."

19Gideon replied, "Those were my brothers, the sons of my own mother. As surely as the LORD lives, if you had spared their lives, I would not kill you." 20Turning to Jether, his oldest son, he said,

"Kill them!" But Jether did not draw his sword, because he was only a boy and was afraid.

21Zebah and Zalmunna said, "Come, do it yourself. 'As is the man, so is his strength.'" So Gideon stepped forward and killed them, and took the ornaments off their camels' necks.

Gideon's Ephod

22The Israelites said to Gideon, "Rule over us—you, your son and your grandson—because you have saved us out of the hand of Midian."

23But Gideon told them, "I will not rule over you, nor will my son rule over you. The LORD will rule over you." 24And he said, "I do have one request, that each of you give me an earring from your share of the plunder." (It was the custom of the Ishmaelites to wear gold earrings.)

25They answered, "We'll be glad to give them." So they spread out a garment, and each man threw a ring from his plunder onto it. 26The weight of the gold rings he asked for came to seventeen hundred shekels,[b] not counting the ornaments, the pendants and the purple garments worn by the kings of Midian or the chains that were on their camels' necks. 27Gideon made the gold into an ephod, which he placed in Ophrah, his town. All Israel prostituted themselves by worshiping it there, and it became a snare to Gideon and his family.

Gideon's Death

28Thus Midian was subdued before the Israelites and did not raise its head again. During Gideon's lifetime, the land enjoyed peace forty years.

29Jerub-Baal son of Joash went back home to live. 30He had seventy sons of his own, for he had many wives. 31His concubine, who lived in Shechem, also bore him a son, whom he named Abimelech. 32Gideon son of Joash died at a good old age and was buried in the tomb of his father Joash in Ophrah of the Abiezrites.

---

a 8 Hebrew Penuel, a variant of Peniel; also in verses 9 and 17   b 26 That is, about 43 pounds (about 19.5 kilograms)

33No sooner had Gideon died than the Israelites again prostituted themselves to the Baals. They set up Baal-Berith as their god and 34did not remember the LORD their God, who had rescued them from the hands of all their enemies on every side. 35They also failed to show kindness to the family of Jerub-Baal (that is, Gideon) for all the good things he had done for them.

Abimelech

Abimelech son of Jerub-Baal went to his mother's brothers in Shechem and said to them and to all his mother's clan, 2"Ask all the citizens of Shechem, 'Which is better for you: to have all seventy of Jerub-Baal's sons rule over you, or just one man?' Remember, I am your flesh and blood."

3When the brothers repeated all this to the citizens of Shechem, they were inclined to follow Abimelech, for they said, "He is our brother." 4They gave him seventy shekels[a] of silver from the temple of Baal-Berith, and Abimelech used it to hire reckless adventurers, who became his followers. 5He went to his father's home in Ophrah and on one stone murdered his seventy brothers, the sons of Jerub-Baal. But Jotham, the youngest son of Jerub-Baal, escaped by hiding. 6Then all the citizens of Shechem and Beth Millo gathered beside the great tree at the pillar in Shechem to crown Abimelech king.

7When Jotham was told about this, he climbed up on the top of Mount Gerizim and shouted to them, "Listen to me, citizens of Shechem, so that God may listen to you. 8One day the trees went out to anoint a king for themselves. They said to the olive tree, 'Be our king.'

9"But the olive tree answered, 'Should I give up my oil, by which both gods and men are honored, to hold sway over the trees?'

10"Next, the trees said to the fig tree, 'Come and be our king.'

11"But the fig tree replied, 'Should I give up my fruit, so good and sweet, to hold sway over the trees?'

12"Then the trees said to the vine, 'Come and be our king.'

13"But the vine answered, 'Should I give up my wine, which cheers both gods and men, to hold sway over the trees?'

14"Finally all the trees said to the thornbush, 'Come and be our king.'

15"The thornbush said to the trees, 'If you really want to anoint me king over you, come and take refuge in my shade; but if not, then let fire come out of the thornbush and consume the cedars of Lebanon!'

16"Now if you have acted honorably and in good faith when you made Abimelech king, and if you have been fair to Jerub-Baal and his family, and if you have treated him as he deserves— 17and to think that my father fought for you, risked his life to rescue you from the hand of Midian 18(but today you have revolted against my father's family, murdered his seventy sons on a single stone, and made Abimelech, the son of his slave girl, king over the citizens of Shechem because he is your brother)— 19if then you have acted honorably and in good faith toward Jerub-Baal and his family today, may Abimelech be your joy, and may you be his, too! 20But if you have not, let fire come out from Abimelech and consume you, citizens of Shechem and Beth Millo, and let fire come out from you, citizens of Shechem and Beth Millo, and consume Abimelech!"

21Then Jotham fled, escaping to Beer, and he lived there because he was afraid of his brother Abimelech.

22After Abimelech had governed Israel three years, 23God sent an evil spirit between Abimelech and the citizens of Shechem, who acted treacherously against Abimelech. 24God did this in order that the crime against Jerub-Baal's seventy sons, the shedding of their blood, might be avenged on their brother Abimelech

---

a 4 That is, about 1 3/4 pounds (about 0.8 kilogram)

and on the citizens of Shechem, who had helped him murder his brothers. ²⁵In opposition to him these citizens of Shechem set men on the hilltops to ambush and rob everyone who passed by, and this was reported to Abimelech.

²⁶Now Gaal son of Ebed moved with his brothers into Shechem, and its citizens put their confidence in him. ²⁷After they had gone out into the fields and gathered the grapes and trodden them, they held a festival in the temple of their god. While they were eating and drinking, they cursed Abimelech. ²⁸Then Gaal son of Ebed said, "Who is Abimelech, and who is Shechem, that we should be subject to him? Isn't he Jerub-Baal's son, and isn't Zebul his deputy? Serve the men of Hamor, Shechem's father! Why should we serve Abimelech? ²⁹If only this people were under my command! Then I would get rid of him. I would say to Abimelech, 'Call out your whole army!' "^a

³⁰When Zebul the governor of the city heard what Gaal son of Ebed said, he was very angry. ³¹Under cover he sent messengers to Abimelech, saying, "Gaal son of Ebed and his brothers have come to Shechem and are stirring up the city against you. ³²Now then, during the night you and your men should come and lie in wait in the fields. ³³In the morning at sunrise, advance against the city. When Gaal and his men come out against you, do whatever your hand finds to do."

³⁴So Abimelech and all his troops set out by night and took up concealed positions near Shechem in four companies. ³⁵Now Gaal son of Ebed had gone out and was standing at the entrance to the city gate just as Abimelech and his soldiers came out from their hiding place.

³⁶When Gaal saw them, he said to Zebul, "Look, people are coming down from the tops of the mountains!"

Zebul replied, "You mistake the shadows of the mountains for men."

³⁷But Gaal spoke up again: "Look, people are coming down from the center of the land, and a company is coming from the direction of the soothsayers' tree."

³⁸Then Zebul said to him, "Where is your big talk now, you who said, 'Who is Abimelech that we should be subject to him?' Aren't these the men you ridiculed? Go out and fight them!"

³⁹So Gaal led out^b the citizens of Shechem and fought Abimelech. ⁴⁰Abimelech chased him, and many fell wounded in the flight—all the way to the entrance to the gate. ⁴¹Abimelech stayed in Arumah, and Zebul drove Gaal and his brothers out of Shechem.

⁴²The next day the people of Shechem went out to the fields, and this was reported to Abimelech. ⁴³So he took his men, divided them into three companies and set an ambush in the fields. When he saw the people coming out of the city, he rose to attack them. ⁴⁴Abimelech and the companies with him rushed forward to a position at the entrance to the city gate. Then two companies rushed upon those in the fields and struck them down. ⁴⁵All that day Abimelech pressed his attack against the city until he had captured it and killed its people. Then he destroyed the city and scattered salt over it.

⁴⁶On hearing this, the citizens in the tower of Shechem went into the stronghold of the temple of El-Berith. ⁴⁷When Abimelech heard that they had assembled there, ⁴⁸he and all his men went up Mount Zalmon. He took an ax and cut off some branches, which he lifted to his shoulders. He ordered the men with him, "Quick! Do what you have seen me do!" ⁴⁹So all the men cut branches and followed Abimelech. They piled them against the stronghold and set it on fire over the people inside. So all the people in the tower of Shechem, about a thousand men and women, also died.

⁵⁰Next Abimelech went to Thebez and besieged it and captured it. ⁵¹Inside the city, however, was a strong tower, to which

---

^a *29* Septuagint; Hebrew *him." Then he said to Abimelech, "Call out your whole army!"*   ^b *39* Or *Gaal went out in the sight of*

all the men and women—all the people of the city—fled. They locked themselves in and climbed up on the tower roof. ⁵²Abimelech went to the tower and stormed it. But as he approached the entrance to the tower to set it on fire, ⁵³a woman dropped an upper millstone on his head and cracked his skull.

⁵⁴Hurriedly he called to his armorbearer, "Draw your sword and kill me, so that they can't say, 'A woman killed him.' " So his servant ran him through, and he died. ⁵⁵When the Israelites saw that Abimelech was dead, they went home.

⁵⁶Thus God repaid the wickedness that Abimelech had done to his father by murdering his seventy brothers. ⁵⁷God also made the men of Shechem pay for all their wickedness. The curse of Jotham son of Jerub-Baal came on them.

Tola

10 After the time of Abimelech a man of Issachar, Tola son of Puah, the son of Dodo, rose to save Israel. He lived in Shamir, in the hill country of Ephraim. ²He led[a] Israel twenty-three years; then he died, and was buried in Shamir.

Jair

³He was followed by Jair of Gilead, who led Israel twenty-two years. ⁴He had thirty sons, who rode thirty donkeys. They controlled thirty towns in Gilead, which to this day are called Havvoth Jair.[b] ⁵When Jair died, he was buried in Kamon.

Jephthah

⁶Again the Israelites did evil in the eyes of the LORD. They served the Baals and the Ashtoreths, and the gods of Aram, the gods of Sidon, the gods of Moab, the gods of the Ammonites and the gods of the Philistines. And because the Israelites forsook the LORD and no longer served him, ⁷he became angry with them. He sold them into the hands of the Philistines and the Ammonites, ⁸who that year

shattered and crushed them. For eighteen years they oppressed all the Israelites on the east side of the Jordan in Gilead, the land of the Amorites. ⁹The Ammonites also crossed the Jordan to fight against Judah, Benjamin and the house of Ephraim; and Israel was in great distress. ¹⁰Then the Israelites cried out to the LORD, "We have sinned against you, forsaking our God and serving the Baals."

¹¹The LORD replied, "When the Egyptians, the Amorites, the Ammonites, the Philistines, ¹²the Sidonians, the Amalekites and the Maonites[c] oppressed you and you cried to me for help, did I not save you from their hands? ¹³But you have forsaken me and served other gods, so I will no longer save you. ¹⁴Go and cry out to the gods you have chosen. Let them save you when you are in trouble!"

¹⁵But the Israelites said to the LORD, "We have sinned. Do with us whatever you think best, but please rescue us now." ¹⁶Then they got rid of the foreign gods among them and served the LORD. And he could bear Israel's misery no longer.

¹⁷When the Ammonites were called to arms and camped in Gilead, the Israelites assembled and camped at Mizpah. ¹⁸The leaders of the people of Gilead said to each other, "Whoever will launch the attack against the Ammonites will be the head of all those living in Gilead."

11 Jephthah the Gileadite was a mighty warrior. His father was Gilead; his mother was a prostitute. ²Gilead's wife also bore him sons, and when they were grown up, they drove Jephthah away. "You are not going to get any inheritance in our family," they said, "because you are the son of another woman." ³So Jephthah fled from his brothers and settled in the land of Tob, where a group of adventurers gathered around him and followed him.

⁴Some time later, when the Ammonites made war on Israel, ⁵the elders of

---

[a] 2 Traditionally judged; also in verse 3 [b] 4 Or called the settlements of Jair [c] 12 Hebrew; some Septuagint manuscripts Midianites

GOING *deeper*

Confession and Repentance

READ AND CONSIDER: JUDGES 10:6-18

"But the Israelites said to the LORD, 'We have sinned. Do with us whatever you think best, but please rescue us now.' Then they got rid of the foreign gods among them and served the LORD. And he could bear Israel's misery no longer" (Judges 10:15-16).

Sin separates us from God. It is a simple truth. This passage demonstrates the process we all need to go through in order to remove that barrier and come into right relationship with Him again. The first part of the process involves confession—telling God what you have done wrong. The second part involves repentance—turning away from the wrongdoing. The Israelites confessed that they had worshiped foreign gods; then they got rid of their idols and served the Lord.

When we don't confess our sins, we end up trying to hide from God. Just like Adam and Eve in the garden, we feel we can't face Him. But the problem with attempting to hide from God is that it's impossible. The Bible says that everything we do will be made known—even the things we say and think in secret.

Nothing is heavier and more destructive than sin. We don't realize how heavy it is until we feel its crushing weight in our relationships; we don't see how destructive it is until we hit the wall it has put up between God and us. And, as the Israelites experienced, nothing is more freeing and marvelous than God's compassion and grace. When you confess your sin, you're not informing God of something He doesn't already know. God wants to know that *you* know you've sinned and that you are ready to turn away from it.

Gilead went to get Jephthah from the land of Tob. 6"Come," they said, "be our commander, so we can fight the Ammonites."

7Jephthah said to them, "Didn't you hate me and drive me from my father's house? Why do you come to me now, when you're in trouble?"

8The elders of Gilead said to him, "Nevertheless, we are turning to you now; come with us to fight the Ammonites, and you will be our head over all who live in Gilead."

9Jephthah answered, "Suppose you take me back to fight the Ammonites and the LORD gives them to me—will I really be your head?"

10The elders of Gilead replied, "The LORD is our witness; we will certainly do as you say." 11So Jephthah went with the elders of Gilead, and the people made him head and commander over them. And he repeated all his words before the LORD in Mizpah.

12Then Jephthah sent messengers to the Ammonite king with the question: "What do you have against us that you have attacked our country?"

13The king of the Ammonites answered Jephthah's messengers, "When Israel came up out of Egypt, they took away my land from the Arnon to the Jabbok, all the way to the Jordan. Now give it back peaceably."

14Jephthah sent back messengers to the Ammonite king, 15saying:

"This is what Jephthah says: Israel did not take the land of Moab or the land of the Ammonites. 16But when they came up out of Egypt, Israel went through the desert to the Red Sea[a] and on to Kadesh. 17Then

---

a *16* Hebrew *Yam Suph*; that is, Sea of Reeds

Israel sent messengers to the king of Edom, saying, 'Give us permission to go through your country,' but the king of Edom would not listen. They sent also to the king of Moab, and he refused. So Israel stayed at Kadesh.

18"Next they traveled through the desert, skirted the lands of Edom and Moab, passed along the eastern side of the country of Moab, and camped on the other side of the Arnon. They did not enter the territory of Moab, for the Arnon was its border.

19"Then Israel sent messengers to Sihon king of the Amorites, who ruled in Heshbon, and said to him, 'Let us pass through your country to our own place.' 20Sihon, however, did not trust Israel[a] to pass through his territory. He mustered all his men and encamped at Jahaz and fought with Israel.

21"Then the LORD, the God of Israel, gave Sihon and all his men into Israel's hands, and they defeated them. Israel took over all the land of the Amorites who lived in that country, 22capturing all of it from the Arnon to the Jabbok and from the desert to the Jordan.

23"Now since the LORD, the God of Israel, has driven the Amorites out before his people Israel, what right have you to take it over? 24Will you not take what your god Chemosh gives you? Likewise, whatever the LORD our God has given us, we will possess. 25Are you better than Balak son of Zippor, king of Moab? Did he ever quarrel with Israel or fight with them? 26For three hundred years Israel occupied Heshbon, Aroer, the surrounding settlements and all the towns along the Arnon. Why didn't you retake them during that time? 27I have not wronged you, but you are doing me wrong by waging war against me. Let the LORD, the Judge,[b] decide the dispute this day between the Israelites and the Ammonites."

28The king of Ammon, however, paid no attention to the message Jephthah sent him.

29Then the Spirit of the LORD came upon Jephthah. He crossed Gilead and Manasseh, passed through Mizpah of Gilead, and from there he advanced against the Ammonites. 30And Jephthah made a vow to the LORD: "If you give the Ammonites into my hands, 31whatever comes out of the door of my house to meet me when I return in triumph from the Ammonites will be the LORD's, and I will sacrifice it as a burnt offering."

32Then Jephthah went over to fight the Ammonites, and the LORD gave them into his hands. 33He devastated twenty towns from Aroer to the vicinity of Minnith, as far as Abel Keramim. Thus Israel subdued Ammon.

34When Jephthah returned to his home in Mizpah, who should come out to meet him but his daughter, dancing to the sound of tambourines! She was an only child. Except for her he had neither son nor daughter. 35When he saw her, he tore his clothes and cried, "Oh! My daughter! You have made me miserable and wretched, because I have made a vow to the LORD that I cannot break."

36"My father," she replied, "you have given your word to the LORD. Do to me just as you promised, now that the LORD has avenged you of your enemies, the Ammonites. 37But grant me this one request," she said. "Give me two months to roam the hills and weep with my friends, because I will never marry."

38"You may go," he said. And he let her go for two months. She and the girls went into the hills and wept because she would never marry. 39After the two months, she returned to her father and he did to her as he had vowed. And she was a virgin.

From this comes the Israelite custom

---

a 20 Or *however, would not make an agreement for Israel*   b 27 Or *Ruler*

40that each year the young women of Israel go out for four days to commemorate the daughter of Jephthah the Gileadite.

Jephthah and Ephraim

12 The men of Ephraim called out their forces, crossed over to Zaphon and said to Jephthah, "Why did you go to fight the Ammonites without calling us to go with you? We're going to burn down your house over your head."

2Jephthah answered, "I and my people were engaged in a great struggle with the Ammonites, and although I called, you didn't save me out of their hands. 3When I saw that you wouldn't help, I took my life in my hands and crossed over to fight the Ammonites, and the LORD gave me the victory over them. Now why have you come up today to fight me?"

4Jephthah then called together the men of Gilead and fought against Ephraim. The Gileadites struck them down because the Ephraimites had said, "You Gileadites are renegades from Ephraim and Manasseh." 5The Gileadites captured the fords of the Jordan leading to Ephraim, and whenever a survivor of Ephraim said, "Let me cross over," the men of Gilead asked him, "Are you an Ephraimite?" If he replied, "No," 6they said, "All right, say 'Shibboleth.'" If he said, "Sibboleth," because he could not pronounce the word correctly, they seized him and killed him at the fords of the Jordan. Forty-two thousand Ephraimites were killed at that time.

7Jephthah led[a] Israel six years. Then Jephthah the Gileadite died, and was buried in a town in Gilead.

Ibzan, Elon and Abdon

8After him, Ibzan of Bethlehem led Israel. 9He had thirty sons and thirty daughters. He gave his daughters away in marriage to those outside his clan, and for his sons he brought in thirty young women as wives from outside his clan. Ibzan led Israel seven years. 10Then Ibzan

died, and was buried in Bethlehem.

11After him, Elon the Zebulunite led Israel ten years. 12Then Elon died, and was buried in Aijalon in the land of Zebulun.

13After him, Abdon son of Hillel, from Pirathon, led Israel. 14He had forty sons and thirty grandsons, who rode on seventy donkeys. He led Israel eight years. 15Then Abdon son of Hillel died, and was buried at Pirathon in Ephraim, in the hill country of the Amalekites.

The Birth of Samson

13 Again the Israelites did evil in the eyes of the LORD, so the LORD delivered them into the hands of the Philistines for forty years.

2A certain man of Zorah, named Manoah, from the clan of the Danites, had a wife who was sterile and remained childless. 3The angel of the LORD appeared to her and said, "You are sterile and childless, but you are going to conceive and have a son. 4Now see to it that you drink no wine or other fermented drink and that you do not eat anything unclean, 5because you will conceive and give birth to a son. No razor may be used on his head, because the boy is to be a Nazirite, set apart to God from birth, and he will begin the deliverance of Israel from the hands of the Philistines."

6Then the woman went to her husband and told him, "A man of God came to me. He looked like an angel of God, very awesome. I didn't ask him where he came from, and he didn't tell me his name. 7But he said to me, 'You will conceive and give birth to a son. Now then, drink no wine or other fermented drink and do not eat anything unclean, because the boy will be a Nazirite of God from birth until the day of his death.'"

8Then Manoah prayed to the LORD: "O Lord, I beg you, let the man of God you sent to us come again to teach us how to bring up the boy who is to be born."

9God heard Manoah, and the angel of

---

a 7 Traditionally judged; also in verses 8-14

Maintaining a Clean Heart

Don't think just because you are not a serial killer or have never robbed a bank that you don't have any sin to confess. Don't think because you have walked with the Lord for a number of years and go to church every Sunday morning and Wednesday night and to all prayer meetings in between, that you have nothing for which you need to repent. Sin doesn't have to be glaring and obvious in order for it to be sin. For example, have you ever doubted that God can do what He promises in His Word? Doubt is a sin.

Have you ever said anything about a person to someone else that isn't exactly flattering? Gossip is a sin. Have you ever avoided someone because you thought they might ask something of you that you didn't want to give? Selfishness is a sin. Have you ever had an unloving attitude toward another person? Whatever does not come from love is a sin.

Sin is hard to avoid. That's why confession is crucial. When we don't confess our sins, faults, or errors, they separate us from God. And we don't get our prayers answered. "Your iniquities have separated you from your God; your sins have hidden his face from you, so that he will not hear" (Isaiah 59:2).

It's one thing to recognize when you have done something that has violated God's laws; it's another to be saddened by it to such a degree that you are determined to never do it again. That's repentance. Repentance means to change your mind. To turn and walk the other way. Repenting of something doesn't necessarily mean we will never commit that sin again. It means we don't *intend* to ever commit it again. If you find that you have to confess the same sin again after you have only recently confessed and repented of it, then do so. Confess and repent as many times as necessary to see yourself win the battle over this problem. Don't entertain thoughts such as, *Surely God won't forgive me again for the same thing I just confessed to Him last week.* He forgives *every time* you confess sin before Him and fully repent of it.

"Blessed is he whose transgressions are forgiven, whose sins are covered" (Psalm 32:1). When you turn to the Lord and repent and say, "Create in me a pure heart, O God, and renew a steadfast spirit within me" (Psalm 51:10), then you can turn things around in your life. Ask God every day to show you where your heart is not clean and right before Him. Don't let anything separate you from all He has for you.

For the next "From Stormie's Heart" article, go to page 328.

God came again to the woman while she was out in the field; but her husband Manoah was not with her. [10]The woman hurried to tell her husband, "He's here! The man who appeared to me the other day!"

[11]Manoah got up and followed his wife. When he came to the man, he said, "Are you the one who talked to my wife?"

"I am," he said.

[12]So Manoah asked him, "When your words are fulfilled, what is to be the rule for the boy's life and work?"

[13]The angel of the LORD answered, "Your wife must do all that I have told her. [14]She must not eat anything that comes from the grapevine, nor drink any wine or other fermented drink nor eat anything unclean. She must do everything I have commanded her."

[15]Manoah said to the angel of the LORD, "We would like you to stay until we prepare a young goat for you."

[16]The angel of the LORD replied, "Even though you detain me, I will not eat any of your food. But if you prepare a burnt offering, offer it to the LORD." (Manoah did not realize that it was the angel of the LORD.)

[17]Then Manoah inquired of the angel of the LORD, "What is your name, so that we may honor you when your word comes true?"

[18]He replied, "Why do you ask my name? It is beyond understanding.[a]"
[19]Then Manoah took a young goat, together with the grain offering, and sacrificed it on a rock to the LORD. And the LORD did an amazing thing while Manoah and his wife watched: [20]As the flame blazed up from the altar toward heaven, the angel of the LORD ascended in the flame. Seeing this, Manoah and his wife fell with their faces to the ground. [21]When the angel of the LORD did not show himself again to Manoah and his wife, Manoah realized that it was the angel of the LORD.

[22]"We are doomed to die!" he said to his wife. "We have seen God!"

[23]But his wife answered, "If the LORD had meant to kill us, he would not have accepted a burnt offering and grain offering from our hands, nor shown us all these things or now told us this."

[24]The woman gave birth to a boy and named him Samson. He grew and the LORD blessed him, [25]and the Spirit of the LORD began to stir him while he was in Mahaneh Dan, between Zorah and Eshtaol.

Samson's Marriage

14 Samson went down to Timnah and saw there a young Philistine woman. [2]When he returned, he said to his father and mother, "I have seen a Philistine woman in Timnah; now get her for me as my wife."

[3]His father and mother replied, "Isn't there an acceptable woman among your relatives or among all our people? Must you go to the uncircumcised Philistines to get a wife?"

But Samson said to his father, "Get her for me. She's the right one for me." [4](His parents did not know that this was from the LORD, who was seeking an occasion to confront the Philistines; for at that time they were ruling over Israel.) [5]Samson went down to Timnah together with his father and mother. As they approached the vineyards of Timnah, suddenly a young lion came roaring toward him. [6]The Spirit of the LORD came upon him in power so that he tore the lion apart with his bare hands as he might have torn a young goat. But he told neither his father nor his mother what he had done. [7]Then he went down and talked with the woman, and he liked her.

[8]Some time later, when he went back to marry her, he turned aside to look at the lion's carcass. In it was a swarm of bees and some honey, [9]which he scooped out with his hands and ate as he went along. When he rejoined his parents, he

---

[a] 18 Or is wonderful

gave them some, and they too ate it. But he did not tell them that he had taken the honey from the lion's carcass.

¹⁰Now his father went down to see the woman. And Samson made a feast there, as was customary for bridegrooms. ¹¹When he appeared, he was given thirty companions.

¹²"Let me tell you a riddle," Samson said to them. "If you can give me the answer within the seven days of the feast, I will give you thirty linen garments and thirty sets of clothes. ¹³If you can't tell me the answer, you must give me thirty linen garments and thirty sets of clothes."

"Tell us your riddle," they said. "Let's hear it."

¹⁴He replied,

"Out of the eater, something to eat;
    out of the strong, something sweet."

For three days they could not give the answer.

¹⁵On the fourth[a] day, they said to Samson's wife, "Coax your husband into explaining the riddle for us, or we will burn you and your father's household to death. Did you invite us here to rob us?"

¹⁶Then Samson's wife threw herself on him, sobbing, "You hate me! You don't really love me. You've given my people a riddle, but you haven't told me the answer."

"I haven't even explained it to my father or mother," he replied, "so why should I explain it to you?" ¹⁷She cried the whole seven days of the feast. So on the seventh day he finally told her, because she continued to press him. She in turn explained the riddle to her people.

¹⁸Before sunset on the seventh day the men of the town said to him,

"What is sweeter than honey?
    What is stronger than a lion?"

Samson said to them,

"If you had not plowed with my
    heifer,

you would not have solved my
    riddle."

¹⁹Then the Spirit of the LORD came upon him in power. He went down to Ashkelon, struck down thirty of their men, stripped them of their belongings and gave their clothes to those who had explained the riddle. Burning with anger, he went up to his father's house. ²⁰And Samson's wife was given to the friend who had attended him at his wedding.

Samson's Vengeance on the Philistines

15 Later on, at the time of wheat harvest, Samson took a young goat and went to visit his wife. He said, "I'm going to my wife's room." But her father would not let him go in.

²"I was so sure you thoroughly hated her," he said, "that I gave her to your friend. Isn't her younger sister more attractive? Take her instead."

³Samson said to them, "This time I have a right to get even with the Philistines; I will really harm them." ⁴So he went out and caught three hundred foxes and tied them tail to tail in pairs. He then fastened a torch to every pair of tails, ⁵lit the torches and let the foxes loose in the standing grain of the Philistines. He burned up the shocks and standing grain, together with the vineyards and olive groves.

⁶When the Philistines asked, "Who did this?" they were told, "Samson, the Timnite's son-in-law, because his wife was given to his friend."

So the Philistines went up and burned her and her father to death. ⁷Samson said to them, "Since you've acted like this, I won't stop until I get my revenge on you." ⁸He attacked them viciously and slaughtered many of them. Then he went down and stayed in a cave in the rock of Etam.

⁹The Philistines went up and camped in Judah, spreading out near Lehi. ¹⁰The men of Judah asked, "Why have you come to fight us?"

"We have come to take Samson pris-

---

[a] *15* Some Septuagint manuscripts and Syriac; Hebrew *seventh*

oner," they answered, "to do to him as he did to us."

[11] Then three thousand men from Judah went down to the cave in the rock of Etam and said to Samson, "Don't you realize that the Philistines are rulers over us? What have you done to us?"

He answered, "I merely did to them what they did to me."

[12] They said to him, "We've come to tie you up and hand you over to the Philistines."

Samson said, "Swear to me that you won't kill me yourselves."

[13] "Agreed," they answered. "We will only tie you up and hand you over to them. We will not kill you." So they bound him with two new ropes and led him up from the rock. [14] As he approached Lehi, the Philistines came toward him shouting. The Spirit of the LORD came upon him in power. The ropes on his arms became like charred flax, and the bindings dropped from his hands. [15] Finding a fresh jawbone of a donkey, he grabbed it and struck down a thousand men.

[16] Then Samson said,

"With a donkey's jawbone
  I have made donkeys of them.[a]
With a donkey's jawbone
  I have killed a thousand men."

[17] When he finished speaking, he threw away the jawbone; and the place was called Ramath Lehi.[b]

[18] Because he was very thirsty, he cried out to the LORD, "You have given your servant this great victory. Must I now die of thirst and fall into the hands of the uncircumcised?" [19] Then God opened up the hollow place in Lehi, and water came out of it. When Samson drank, his strength returned and he revived. So the spring was called En Hakkore,[c] and it is still there in Lehi.

[20] Samson led[d] Israel for twenty years in the days of the Philistines.

Samson and Delilah

16 One day Samson went to Gaza, where he saw a prostitute. He went in to spend the night with her. [2] The people of Gaza were told, "Samson is here!" So they surrounded the place and lay in wait for him all night at the city gate. They made no move during the night, saying, "At dawn we'll kill him."

[3] But Samson lay there only until the middle of the night. Then he got up and took hold of the doors of the city gate, together with the two posts, and tore them loose, bar and all. He lifted them to his shoulders and carried them to the top of the hill that faces Hebron.

[4] Some time later, he fell in love with a woman in the Valley of Sorek whose name was Delilah. [5] The rulers of the Philistines went to her and said, "See if you can lure him into showing you the secret of his great strength and how we can overpower him so we may tie him up and subdue him. Each one of us will give you eleven hundred shekels[e] of silver."

[6] So Delilah said to Samson, "Tell me the secret of your great strength and how you can be tied up and subdued."

[7] Samson answered her, "If anyone ties me with seven fresh thongs[f] that have not been dried, I'll become as weak as any other man."

[8] Then the rulers of the Philistines brought her seven fresh thongs that had not been dried, and she tied him with them. [9] With men hidden in the room, she called to him, "Samson, the Philistines are upon you!" But he snapped the thongs as easily as a piece of string snaps when it comes close to a flame. So the secret of his strength was not discovered.

[10] Then Delilah said to Samson, "You have made a fool of me; you lied to me. Come now, tell me how you can be tied."

[11] He said, "If anyone ties me securely with new ropes that have never been used, I'll become as weak as any other man."

---

[a] 16 Or made a heap or two; the Hebrew for donkey sounds like the Hebrew for heap.   [b] 17 Ramath Lehi means jawbone hill.
[c] 19 En Hakkore means caller's spring.   [d] 20 Traditionally judged   [e] 5 That is, about 28 pounds (about 13 kilograms)
[f] 7 Or bowstrings; also in verses 8 and 9

12So Delilah took new ropes and tied him with them. Then, with men hidden in the room, she called to him, "Samson, the Philistines are upon you!" But he snapped the ropes off his arms as if they were threads.

13Delilah then said to Samson, "Until now, you have been making a fool of me and lying to me. Tell me how you can be tied."

He replied, "If you weave the seven braids of my head into the fabric on the loom and tighten it with the pin, I'll become as weak as any other man." So while he was sleeping, Delilah took the seven braids of his head, wove them into the fabric 14anda tightened it with the pin.

Again she called to him, "Samson, the Philistines are upon you!" He awoke from his sleep and pulled up the pin and the loom, with the fabric.

15Then she said to him, "How can you say, 'I love you,' when you won't confide in me? This is the third time you have made a fool of me and haven't told me the secret of your great strength." 16With such nagging she prodded him day after day until he was tired to death.

17So he told her everything. "No razor has ever been used on my head," he said, "because I have been a Nazirite set apart to God since birth. If my head were shaved, my strength would leave me, and I would become as weak as any other man."

18When Delilah saw that he had told her everything, she sent word to the rulers of the Philistines, "Come back once more; he has told me everything." So the rulers of the Philistines returned with the silver in their hands. 19Having put him to sleep on her lap, she called a man to shave off the seven braids of his hair, and so began to subdue him.b And his strength left him.

20Then she called, "Samson, the Philistines are upon you!"

He awoke from his sleep and thought, "I'll go out as before and shake myself free." But he did not know that the LORD had left him.

21Then the Philistines seized him, gouged out his eyes and took him down to Gaza. Binding him with bronze shackles, they set him to grinding in the prison. 22But the hair on his head began to grow again after it had been shaved.

The Death of Samson

23Now the rulers of the Philistines assembled to offer a great sacrifice to Dagon their god and to celebrate, saying, "Our god has delivered Samson, our enemy, into our hands."

24When the people saw him, they praised their god, saying,

"Our god has delivered our enemy
  into our hands,
the one who laid waste our land
  and multiplied our slain."

25While they were in high spirits, they shouted, "Bring out Samson to entertain us." So they called Samson out of the prison, and he performed for them.

Praying Judges 16:20
Heavenly Father, help me to obey You and to resist temptation so that I may always have the fullness of Your presence.

When they stood him among the pillars, 26Samson said to the servant who held his hand, "Put me where I can feel the pillars that support the temple, so that I may lean against them." 27Now the temple was crowded with men and women; all the rulers of the Philistines were there, and on the roof were about three thousand men and women watching Samson perform. 28Then Samson prayed to the LORD, "O Sovereign LORD, remember me. O God, please strengthen me just once more, and let me with one blow get revenge on the Philistines for my two

---

a 13,14 Some Septuagint manuscripts; Hebrew "I can, if you weave the seven braids of my head into the fabric on the loom," 14So she   b 19 Hebrew; some Septuagint manuscripts and he began to weaken eyes." 29Then Samson reached toward the two central pillars on which the temple stood. Bracing himself against them, his right hand on the one and his left hand on the other, 30Samson said, "Let me die with the Philistines!" Then he pushed with all his might, and down came the temple on the rulers and all the people in it. Thus he killed many more when he died than while he lived.

31Then his brothers and his father's whole family went down to get him. They brought him back and buried him between Zorah and Eshtaol in the tomb of Manoah his father. He had led[a] Israel twenty years.

4So he returned the silver to his mother, and she took two hundred shekels[c] of silver and gave them to a silversmith, who made them into the image and the idol. And they were put in Micah's house.

5Now this man Micah had a shrine, and he made an ephod and some idols and installed one of his sons as his priest. 6In those days Israel had no king; everyone did as he saw fit.

7A young Levite from Bethlehem in Judah, who had been living within the clan of Judah, 8left that town in search of some other place to stay. On his way[d] he came to Micah's house in the hill country of Ephraim.

God's people at prayer
SAMSON'S FINAL PRAYER

JUDGES 16:25-31 Samson's powerful final prayer carries a tragic overtone. Samson knew how to pray, but he hadn't done it very much. He apparently realized the source of his strength, but he had failed to ask God about the purpose of his strength and how he should use it. He governed his life too often by God's gift of physical power instead of God's gift of prayer power. Like most of us, Samson had a problem with too much self-reliance. His inconsistent praying led to a scattered life with few accomplishments and a tragic end.

If you're not relying on God in prayer, you are relying on yourself or others. Don't wait until you're at the end of your strength before you turn to God. Don't waste your life relying on yourself when you could be relying on the God who created you for a purpose. Seek God about how to use the gifts He has given you. Make prayer a habit instead of an afterthought. Learn from Samson.

Micah's Idols

17 Now a man named Micah from the hill country of Ephraim 2said to his mother, "The eleven hundred shekels[b] of silver that were taken from you and about which I heard you utter a curse—I have that silver with me; I took it."

Then his mother said, "The LORD bless you, my son!"

3When he returned the eleven hundred shekels of silver to his mother, she said, "I solemnly consecrate my silver to the LORD for my son to make a carved image and a cast idol. I will give it back to you."

9Micah asked him, "Where are you from?"

"I'm a Levite from Bethlehem in Judah," he said, "and I'm looking for a place to stay."

10Then Micah said to him, "Live with me and be my father and priest, and I'll give you ten shekels[e] of silver a year, your clothes and your food." 11So the Levite agreed to live with him, and the young man was to him like one of his sons. 12Then Micah installed the Levite, and the young man became his priest and lived in his house. 13And Micah said,

---

a 31 Traditionally judged   b 2 That is, about 28 pounds (about 13 kilograms)   c 4 That is, about 5 pounds (about 2.3 kilograms)
d 8 Or To carry on his profession   e 10 That is, about 4 ounces (about 110 grams)

"Now I know that the LORD will be good to me, since this Levite has become my priest."

Danites Settle in Laish

18 In those days Israel had no king. And in those days the tribe of the Danites was seeking a place of their own where they might settle, because they had not yet come into an inheritance among the tribes of Israel. 2So the Danites sent five warriors from Zorah and Eshtaol to spy out the land and explore it. These men represented all their clans. They told them, "Go, explore the land."

The men entered the hill country of Ephraim and came to the house of Micah, where they spent the night. 3When they were near Micah's house, they recognized the voice of the young Levite; so they turned in there and asked him, "Who brought you here? What are you doing in this place? Why are you here?"

4He told them what Micah had done for him, and said, "He has hired me and I am his priest."

5Then they said to him, "Please inquire of God to learn whether our journey will be successful."

6The priest answered them, "Go in peace. Your journey has the LORD's approval."

7So the five men left and came to Laish, where they saw that the people were living in safety, like the Sidonians, unsuspecting and secure. And since their land lacked nothing, they were prosperous.ᵃ Also, they lived a long way from the Sidonians and had no relationship with anyone else.ᵇ

8When they returned to Zorah and Eshtaol, their brothers asked them, "How did you find things?"

9They answered, "Come on, let's attack them! We have seen that the land is very good. Aren't you going to do something? Don't hesitate to go there and take it over. 10When you get there, you will find

---

ᵃ 7 The meaning of the Hebrew for this clause is uncertain.   ᵇ 7 Hebrew; some Septuagint manuscripts *with the Arameans*

GOING *deeper*

Know the Source

READ AND CONSIDER: JUDGES 18

"He told them what Micah had done for him and said, 'He has hired me and I am his priest.' Then they said to him, 'Please inquire of God to learn whether our journey will be successful.' The priest answered them, 'Go in peace. Your journey has the LORD's approval'" (Judges 18:4-6).

Looking to other people for counsel can be a very wise thing to do—that is, when we seek wisdom from the right sources. In this case, however, the five warriors from the tribe of Dan looked to a priest who inquired of "god" by using idols and other images, not the true God of Israel. Later in the story, this priest proved to be fickle and disloyal as he abandoned his former master in a time of distress for a better offer. Not exactly a trustworthy source of information!

When you are seeking God's guidance, you might want to ask everyone you know for their opinions—thinking that the more counselors the better. But instead of rushing to get a quick word, stop and pray first. Ask God to give you real discernment. Test the source before you follow any advice. Ask only those who can offer true wisdom from the Lord.

The men from Dan had the right idea—they inquired about God's will. But they stopped inquiring when they heard the priest's word. Take everything you hear and make sure that it is consistent with God's Word. That is the most trustworthy source and one you can always count on.

an unsuspecting people and a spacious land that God has put into your hands, a land that lacks nothing whatever."

¹¹Then six hundred men from the clan of the Danites, armed for battle, set out from Zorah and Eshtaol. ¹²On their way they set up camp near Kiriath Jearim in Judah. This is why the place west of Kiriath Jearim is called Mahaneh Dan[a] to this day. ¹³From there they went on to the hill country of Ephraim and came to Micah's house.

¹⁴Then the five men who had spied out the land of Laish said to their brothers, "Do you know that one of these houses has an ephod, other household gods, a carved image and a cast idol? Now you know what to do." ¹⁵So they turned in there and went to the house of the young Levite at Micah's place and greeted him. ¹⁶The six hundred Danites, armed for battle, stood at the entrance to the gate. ¹⁷The five men who had spied out the land went inside and took the carved image, the ephod, the other household gods and the cast idol while the priest and the six hundred armed men stood at the entrance to the gate.

¹⁸When these men went into Micah's house and took the carved image, the ephod, the other household gods and the cast idol, the priest said to them, "What are you doing?"

¹⁹They answered him, "Be quiet! Don't say a word. Come with us, and be our father and priest. Isn't it better that you serve a tribe and clan in Israel as priest rather than just one man's household?" ²⁰Then the priest was glad. He took the ephod, the other household gods and the carved image and went along with the people. ²¹Putting their little children, their livestock and their possessions in front of them, they turned away and left.

²²When they had gone some distance from Micah's house, the men who lived near Micah were called together and overtook the Danites. ²³As they shouted after them, the Danites turned and said to Micah, "What's the matter with you that you called out your men to fight?"

²⁴He replied, "You took the gods I made, and my priest, and went away. What else do I have? How can you ask, 'What's the matter with you?'"

²⁵The Danites answered, "Don't argue with us, or some hot-tempered men will attack you, and you and your family will lose your lives." ²⁶So the Danites went their way, and Micah, seeing that they were too strong for him, turned around and went back home.

²⁷Then they took what Micah had made, and his priest, and went on to Laish, against a peaceful and unsuspecting people. They attacked them with the sword and burned down their city. ²⁸There was no one to rescue them because they lived a long way from Sidon and had no relationship with anyone else. The city was in a valley near Beth Rehob.

The Danites rebuilt the city and settled there. ²⁹They named it Dan after their forefather Dan, who was born to Israel—though the city used to be called Laish. ³⁰There the Danites set up for themselves the idols, and Jonathan son of Gershom, the son of Moses,[b] and his sons were priests for the tribe of Dan until the time of the captivity of the land. ³¹They continued to use the idols Micah had made, all the time the house of God was in Shiloh.

A Levite and His Concubine

19 In those days Israel had no king.

Now a Levite who lived in a remote area in the hill country of Ephraim took a concubine from Bethlehem in Judah. ²But she was unfaithful to him. She left him and went back to her father's house in Bethlehem, Judah. After she had been there four months, ³her husband went to her to persuade her to return. He had with him his servant and two

---

[a] 12 Mahaneh Dan means Dan's camp.   [b] 30 An ancient Hebrew scribal tradition, some Septuagint manuscripts and Vulgate; Masoretic Text Manasseh

donkeys. She took him into her father's house, and when her father saw him, he gladly welcomed him. ⁴His father-in-law, the girl's father, prevailed upon him to stay; so he remained with him three days, eating and drinking, and sleeping there.

⁵On the fourth day they got up early and he prepared to leave, but the girl's father said to his son-in-law, "Refresh yourself with something to eat; then you can go." ⁶So the two of them sat down to eat and drink together. Afterward the girl's father said, "Please stay tonight and enjoy yourself." ⁷And when the man got up to go, his father-in-law persuaded him, so he stayed there that night. ⁸On the morning of the fifth day, when he rose to go, the girl's father said, "Refresh yourself. Wait till afternoon!" So the two of them ate together.

⁹Then when the man, with his concubine and his servant, got up to leave, his father-in-law, the girl's father, said, "Now look, it's almost evening. Spend the night here; the day is nearly over. Stay and enjoy yourself. Early tomorrow morning you can get up and be on your way home." ¹⁰But, unwilling to stay another night, the man left and went toward Jebus (that is, Jerusalem), with his two saddled donkeys and his concubine.

¹¹When they were near Jebus and the day was almost gone, the servant said to his master, "Come, let's stop at this city of the Jebusites and spend the night."

¹²His master replied, "No. We won't go into an alien city, whose people are not Israelites. We will go on to Gibeah." ¹³He added, "Come, let's try to reach Gibeah or Ramah and spend the night in one of those places." ¹⁴So they went on, and the sun set as they neared Gibeah in Benjamin. ¹⁵There they stopped to spend the night. They went and sat in the city square, but no one took them into his home for the night.

¹⁶That evening an old man from the hill country of Ephraim, who was living in Gibeah (the men of the place were Benjamites), came in from his work in the fields. ¹⁷When he looked and saw the traveler in the city square, the old man asked, "Where are you going? Where did you come from?"

¹⁸He answered, "We are on our way from Bethlehem in Judah to a remote area in the hill country of Ephraim where I live. I have been to Bethlehem in Judah and now I am going to the house of the LORD. No one has taken me into his house. ¹⁹We have both straw and fodder for our donkeys and bread and wine for ourselves your servants—me, your maidservant, and the young man with us. We don't need anything."

²⁰"You are welcome at my house," the old man said. "Let me supply whatever you need. Only don't spend the night in the square." ²¹So he took him into his house and fed his donkeys. After they had washed their feet, they had something to eat and drink.

²²While they were enjoying themselves, some of the wicked men of the city surrounded the house. Pounding on the door, they shouted to the old man who owned the house, "Bring out the man who came to your house so we can have sex with him."

²³The owner of the house went outside and said to them, "No, my friends, don't be so vile. Since this man is my guest, don't do this disgraceful thing. ²⁴Look, here is my virgin daughter, and his concubine. I will bring them out to you now, and you can use them and do to them whatever you wish. But to this man, don't do such a disgraceful thing."

²⁵But the men would not listen to him. So the man took his concubine and sent her outside to them, and they raped her and abused her throughout the night, and at dawn they let her go. ²⁶At daybreak the woman went back to the house where her master was staying, fell down at the door and lay there until daylight.

²⁷When her master got up in the morning and opened the door of the house

and stepped out to continue on his way, there lay his concubine, fallen in the doorway of the house, with her hands on the threshold. 28He said to her, "Get up; let's go." But there was no answer. Then the man put her on his donkey and set out for home.

29When he reached home, he took a knife and cut up his concubine, limb by limb, into twelve parts and sent them into all the areas of Israel. 30Everyone who saw it said, "Such a thing has never been seen or done, not since the day the Israelites came up out of Egypt. Think about it! Consider it! Tell us what to do!"

Israelites Fight the Benjamites

20 Then all the Israelites from Dan to Beersheba and from the land of Gilead came out as one man and assembled before the LORD in Mizpah. 2The leaders of all the people of the tribes of Israel took their places in the assembly of the people of God, four hundred thousand soldiers armed with swords. 3(The Benjamites heard that the Israelites had gone up to Mizpah.) Then the Israelites said, "Tell us how this awful thing happened."

4So the Levite, the husband of the murdered woman, said, "I and my concubine came to Gibeah in Benjamin to spend the night. 5During the night the men of Gibeah came after me and surrounded the house, intending to kill me. They raped my concubine, and she died. 6I took my concubine, cut her into pieces and sent one piece to each region of Israel's inheritance, because they committed this lewd and disgraceful act in Israel. 7Now, all you Israelites, speak up and give your verdict."

8All the people rose as one man, saying, "None of us will go home. No, not one of us will return to his house. 9But now this is what we'll do to Gibeah: We'll go up against it as the lot directs. 10We'll take ten men out of every hundred from all the tribes of Israel, and a hundred from a

thousand, and a thousand from ten thousand, to get provisions for the army. Then, when the army arrives at Gibeah[a] in Benjamin, it can give them what they deserve for all this vileness done in Israel." 11So all the men of Israel got together and united as one man against the city.

12The tribes of Israel sent men throughout the tribe of Benjamin, saying, "What about this awful crime that was committed among you? 13Now surrender those wicked men of Gibeah so that we may put them to death and purge the evil from Israel."

But the Benjamites would not listen to their fellow Israelites. 14From their towns they came together at Gibeah to fight against the Israelites. 15At once the Benjamites mobilized twenty-six thousand swordsmen from their towns, in addition to seven hundred chosen men from those living in Gibeah. 16Among all these soldiers there were seven hundred chosen men who were left-handed, each of whom could sling a stone at a hair and not miss.

17Israel, apart from Benjamin, mustered four hundred thousand swordsmen, all of them fighting men.

18The Israelites went up to Bethel[b] and inquired of God. They said, "Who of us shall go first to fight against the Benjamites?"

The LORD replied, "Judah shall go first."

19The next morning the Israelites got up and pitched camp near Gibeah. 20The men of Israel went out to fight the Benjamites and took up battle positions against them at Gibeah. 21The Benjamites came out of Gibeah and cut down twenty-two thousand Israelites on the battlefield that day. 22But the men of Israel encouraged one another and again took up their positions where they had stationed themselves the first day. 23The Israelites went up and wept before the LORD until evening, and they inquired of the LORD.

---

a 10 One Hebrew manuscript; most Hebrew manuscripts Geba, a variant of Gibeah   b 18 Or to the house of God; also in verse 26

They said, "Shall we go up again to battle against the Benjamites, our brothers?"

The LORD answered, "Go up against them."

²⁴Then the Israelites drew near to Benjamin the second day. ²⁵This time, when the Benjamites came out from Gibeah to oppose them, they cut down another eighteen thousand Israelites, all of them armed with swords.

²⁶Then the Israelites, all the people, went up to Bethel, and there they sat weeping before the LORD. They fasted that day until evening and presented burnt offerings and fellowship offerings^a to the LORD. ²⁷And the Israelites inquired of the LORD. (In those days the ark of the covenant of God was there, ²⁸with Phinehas son of Eleazar, the son of Aaron, ministering before it.) They asked, "Shall we go up again to battle with Benjamin our brother, or not?"

Praying Judges 20:18-28
God, I pray that You will help me not to give up when I face obstacles, but to keep praying until I have victory.

The LORD responded, "Go, for tomorrow I will give them into your hands."

²⁹Then Israel set an ambush around Gibeah. ³⁰They went up against the Benjamites on the third day and took up positions against Gibeah as they had done before. ³¹The Benjamites came out to meet them and were drawn away from the city. They began to inflict casualties on the Israelites as before, so that about thirty men fell in the open field and on the roads—the one leading to Bethel and the other to Gibeah.

³²While the Benjamites were saying, "We are defeating them as before," the Israelites were saying, "Let's retreat and draw them away from the city to the roads."

³³All the men of Israel moved from their places and took up positions at Baal Tamar, and the Israelite ambush charged out of its place on the west^b of Gibeah.^c ³⁴Then ten thousand of Israel's finest men made a frontal attack on Gibeah. The fighting was so heavy that the Benjamites did not realize how near disaster was. ³⁵The LORD defeated Benjamin before Israel, and on that day the Israelites struck down 25,100 Benjamites, all armed with swords. ³⁶Then the Benjamites saw that they were beaten.

Now the men of Israel had given way before Benjamin, because they relied on the ambush they had set near Gibeah. ³⁷The men who had been in ambush made a sudden dash into Gibeah, spread out and put the whole city to the sword. ³⁸The men of Israel had arranged with the ambush that they should send up a great cloud of smoke from the city, ³⁹and then the men of Israel would turn in the battle.

The Benjamites had begun to inflict casualties on the men of Israel (about thirty), and they said, "We are defeating them as in the first battle." ⁴⁰But when the column of smoke began to rise from the city, the Benjamites turned and saw the smoke of the whole city going up into the sky. ⁴¹Then the men of Israel turned on them, and the men of Benjamin were terrified, because they realized that disaster had come upon them. ⁴²So they fled before the Israelites in the direction of the desert, but they could not escape the battle. And the men of Israel who came out of the towns cut them down there. ⁴³They surrounded the Benjamites, chased them and easily^d overran them in the vicinity of Gibeah on the east. ⁴⁴Eighteen thousand Benjamites fell, all of them valiant fighters. ⁴⁵As they turned and fled toward the desert to the rock of Rimmon, the Israelites cut down five thousand men along the roads. They kept pressing after the Benjamites as far as Gidom and struck down two thousand more. [46]On that day twenty-five thousand Benjamite swordsmen fell, all of them valiant fighters. [47]But six hundred men turned and fled into the desert to the rock of Rimmon, where they stayed four months. [48]The men of Israel went back to Benjamin and put all the towns to the sword, including the animals and everything else they found. All the towns they came across they set on fire.

Wives for the Benjamites

21 The men of Israel had taken an oath at Mizpah: "Not one of us will give his daughter in marriage to a Benjamite."

[2]The people went to Bethel,[a] where they sat before God until evening, raising their voices and weeping bitterly. [3]"O LORD, the God of Israel," they cried, "why has this happened to Israel? Why should one tribe be missing from Israel today?"

[4]Early the next day the people built an altar and presented burnt offerings and fellowship offerings.[b]

[5]Then the Israelites asked, "Who from all the tribes of Israel has failed to assemble before the LORD?" For they had taken a solemn oath that anyone who failed to assemble before the LORD at Mizpah should certainly be put to death.

[6]Now the Israelites grieved for their brothers, the Benjamites. "Today one tribe is cut off from Israel," they said. [7]"How can we provide wives for those who are left, since we have taken an oath by the LORD not to give them any of our daughters in marriage?" [8]Then they asked, "Which one of the tribes of Israel failed to assemble before the LORD at Mizpah?" They discovered that no one from Jabesh Gilead had come to the camp for the assembly. [9]For when they counted the people, they found that none of the people of Jabesh Gilead were there.

[10]So the assembly sent twelve thousand fighting men with instructions to go to Jabesh Gilead and put to the sword those living there, including the women and children. [11]"This is what you are to do," they said. "Kill every male and every woman who is not a virgin." [12]They found among the people living in Jabesh Gilead four hundred young women who had never slept with a man, and they took them to the camp at Shiloh in Canaan.

[13]Then the whole assembly sent an offer of peace to the Benjamites at the rock of Rimmon. [14]So the Benjamites returned at that time and were given the women of Jabesh Gilead who had been spared. But there were not enough for all of them.

[15]The people grieved for Benjamin, because the LORD had made a gap in the tribes of Israel. [16]And the elders of the assembly said, "With the women of Benjamin destroyed, how shall we provide wives for the men who are left? [17]The Benjamite survivors must have heirs," they said, "so that a tribe of Israel will not be wiped out. [18]We can't give them our daughters as wives, since we Israelites have taken this oath: 'Cursed be anyone who gives a wife to a Benjamite.' [19]But look, there is the annual festival of the LORD in Shiloh, to the north of Bethel, and east of the road that goes from Bethel to Shechem, and to the south of Lebonah."

[20]So they instructed the Benjamites, saying, "Go and hide in the vineyards [21]and watch. When the girls of Shiloh come out to join in the dancing, then rush from the vineyards and each of you seize a wife from the girls of Shiloh and go to the land of Benjamin. [22]When their fathers or brothers complain to us, we will say to them, 'Do us a kindness by helping them, because we did not get wives for them during the war, and you are innocent, since you did not give your daughters to them.'"

[23]So that is what the Benjamites did.

---

[a] 2 Or *to the house of God*   [b] 4 Traditionally *peace offerings*

While the girls were dancing, each man caught one and carried her off to be his wife. Then they returned to their inheritance and rebuilt the towns and settled in them.

24At that time the Israelites left that place and went home to their tribes and clans, each to his own inheritance.

25In those days Israel had no king; everyone did as he saw fit.

Author: Unknown

Date: During Israel's monarchy

Audience: The Hebrew people, showing them a model of faithfulness and the blessing that comes from devotion to God and His ways

Prayer Themes:

- *Ask God to make you like Ruth—faithful and devoted in an era that is typically marked by unfaithfulness (1:16).*

- *Ask God to help you learn what it means to take refuge in Him (2:12).*

- *Thank God that He is able to use your obedience today to make a difference in future generations (4:13-17).*

Is your current situation tough . . . or even terrible? Take hope. The Ruler of the universe is more than able to rescue and redeem the lives of those who keep seeking Him and doing what's right.

This is the heartwarming message of the book of Ruth, the real-life story that reads like a fairy tale or romance novel. Ruth's story begins tragically amid famine and funerals. It ends happily in unexpected marital and maternal bliss. The blessing Boaz speaks to Ruth, "May you be richly rewarded by the LORD, the God of Israel, under whose wings you have come to take refuge" (2:12), does at last come true.

What a wonderful reminder that our God controls history, orchestrating events, guiding the lives of His faithful followers, and bringing about His perfect purposes. And best of all, He is only a prayer away!

Ruth

Naomi and Ruth

1 In the days when the judges ruled,[a] there was a famine in the land, and a man from Bethlehem in Judah, together with his wife and two sons, went to live for a while in the country of Moab. 2 The man's name was Elimelech, his wife's name Naomi, and the names of his two sons were Mahlon and Kilion. They were Ephrathites from Bethlehem, Judah. And they went to Moab and lived there.

3 Now Elimelech, Naomi's husband, died, and she was left with her two sons. 4 They married Moabite women, one named Orpah and the other Ruth. After they had lived there about ten years, 5 both Mahlon and Kilion also died, and Naomi was left without her two sons and her husband.

6 When she heard in Moab that the LORD had come to the aid of his people by providing food for them, Naomi and her daughters-in-law prepared to return home from there. 7 With her two daughters-in-law she left the place where she had been living and set out on the road that would take them back to the land of Judah.

8 Then Naomi said to her two daughters-in-law, "Go back, each of you, to your mother's home. May the LORD show kindness to you, as you have shown to your dead and to me. 9 May the LORD grant that each of you will find rest in the home of another husband."

Then she kissed them and they wept aloud 10 and said to her, "We will go back with you to your people."

11 But Naomi said, "Return home, my daughters. Why would you come with me? Am I going to have any more sons, who could become your husbands?

---

[a] 1 Traditionally *judged*

¹²Return home, my daughters; I am too old to have another husband. Even if I thought there was still hope for me— even if I had a husband tonight and then gave birth to sons— ¹³would you wait until they grew up? Would you remain unmarried for them? No, my daughters. It is more bitter for me than for you, because the LORD's hand has gone out against me!"

¹⁴At this they wept again. Then Orpah kissed her mother-in-law good-by, but Ruth clung to her.

¹⁵"Look," said Naomi, "your sister-in-law is going back to her people and her gods. Go back with her."

¹⁶But Ruth replied, "Don't urge me to leave you or to turn back from you. Where you go I will go, and where you stay I will stay. Your people will be my people and your God my God. ¹⁷Where you die I will die, and there I will be buried. May the LORD deal with me, be it ever so severely, if anything but death separates you and me." ¹⁸When Naomi realized that Ruth was determined to go with her, she stopped urging her.

¹⁹So the two women went on until they came to Bethlehem. When they arrived in Bethlehem, the whole town was stirred because of them, and the women exclaimed, "Can this be Naomi?"

²⁰"Don't call me Naomi,ᵃ" she told them. "Call me Mara,ᵇ because the Almightyᶜ has made my life very bitter. ²¹I went away full, but the LORD has brought me back empty. Why call me Naomi? The LORD has afflictedᵈ me; the Almighty has brought misfortune upon me."

²²So Naomi returned from Moab accompanied by Ruth the Moabitess, her daughter-in-law, arriving in Bethlehem as the barley harvest was beginning.

Ruth Meets Boaz

2 Now Naomi had a relative on her husband's side, from the clan of Elimelech, a man of standing, whose name was Boaz.

²And Ruth the Moabitess said to Naomi, "Let me go to the fields and pick up the leftover grain behind anyone in whose eyes I find favor."

Naomi said to her, "Go ahead, my daughter." ³So she went out and began to glean in the fields behind the harvesters. As it turned out, she found herself working in a field belonging to Boaz, who was from the clan of Elimelech.

⁴Just then Boaz arrived from Bethlehem and greeted the harvesters, "The LORD be with you!"

"The LORD bless you!" they called back.

⁵Boaz asked the foreman of his harvesters, "Whose young woman is that?"

⁶The foreman replied, "She is the Moabitess who came back from Moab with Naomi. ⁷She said, 'Please let me glean and gather among the sheaves behind the harvesters.' She went into the field and has worked steadily from morning till now, except for a short rest in the shelter."

⁸So Boaz said to Ruth, "My daughter, listen to me. Don't go and glean in another field and don't go away from here. Stay here with my servant girls. ⁹Watch the field where the men are harvesting, and follow along after the girls. I have told the men not to touch you. And whenever you are thirsty, go and get a drink from the water jars the men have filled."

¹⁰At this, she bowed down with her face to the ground. She exclaimed, "Why have I found such favor in your eyes that you notice me—a foreigner?"

¹¹Boaz replied, "I've been told all about what you have done for your mother-in-law since the death of your husband— how you left your father and mother and your homeland and came to live with a people you did not know before. ¹²May the LORD repay you for what you have done. May you be richly rewarded by the LORD, the God of Israel, under whose wings you have come to take refuge."

ᵃ *20 Naomi* means *pleasant*; also in verse 21.   ᵇ *20 Mara* means *bitter*.   ᶜ *20* Hebrew *Shaddai*; also in verse 21   ᵈ *21* Or *has testified against*

[13]"May I continue to find favor in your eyes, my lord," she said. "You have given me comfort and have spoken kindly to your servant—though I do not have the standing of one of your servant girls."

[14]At mealtime Boaz said to her, "Come over here. Have some bread and dip it in the wine vinegar."

When she sat down with the harvesters, he offered her some roasted grain. She ate all she wanted and had some left over. [15]As she got up to glean, Boaz gave orders to his men, "Even if she gathers among the sheaves, don't embarrass her. [16]Rather, pull out some stalks for her from the bundles and leave them for her to pick up, and don't rebuke her."

[17]So Ruth gleaned in the field until evening. Then she threshed the barley she had gathered, and it amounted to about an ephah.[a] [18]She carried it back to town, and her mother-in-law saw how much she had gathered. Ruth also brought out and gave her what she had left over after she had eaten enough.

[19]Her mother-in-law asked her, "Where did you glean today? Where did you work? Blessed be the man who took notice of you!"

Then Ruth told her mother-in-law about the one at whose place she had been working. "The name of the man I worked with today is Boaz," she said.

[20]"The LORD bless him!" Naomi said to her daughter-in-law. "He has not stopped showing his kindness to the living and the dead." She added, "That man is our close relative; he is one of our kinsman-redeemers."

[21]Then Ruth the Moabitess said, "He even said to me, 'Stay with my workers until they finish harvesting all my grain.'"

[22]Naomi said to Ruth her daughter-in-law, "It will be good for you, my daughter, to go with his girls, because in someone else's field you might be harmed."

[23]So Ruth stayed close to the servant girls of Boaz to glean until the barley and wheat harvests were finished. And she lived with her mother-in-law.

Ruth and Boaz at the Threshing Floor

3 One day Naomi her mother-in-law said to her, "My daughter, should I not try to find a home[b] for you, where you will be well provided for? [2]Is not Boaz, with whose servant girls you have been, a kinsman of ours? Tonight he will be winnowing barley on the threshing floor. [3]Wash and perfume yourself, and put on your best clothes. Then go down to the threshing floor, but don't let him know you are there until he has finished eating and drinking. [4]When he lies down, note the place where he is lying. Then go and uncover his feet and lie down. He will tell you what to do."

[5]"I will do whatever you say," Ruth answered. [6]So she went down to the threshing floor and did everything her mother-in-law told her to do.

[7]When Boaz had finished eating and drinking and was in good spirits, he went over to lie down at the far end of the grain pile. Ruth approached quietly, uncovered his feet and lay down. [8]In the middle of the night something startled the man, and he turned and discovered a woman lying at his feet.

[9]"Who are you?" he asked.

"I am your servant Ruth," she said. "Spread the corner of your garment over me, since you are a kinsman-redeemer."

[10]"The LORD bless you, my daughter," he replied. "This kindness is greater than that which you showed earlier: You have not run after the younger men, whether rich or poor. [11]And now, my daughter, don't be afraid. I will do for you all you ask. All my fellow townsmen know that you are a woman of noble character. [12]Although it is true that I am near of kin, there is a kinsman-redeemer nearer than I. [13]Stay here for the night, and in the morning if he wants to redeem, good; let him redeem. But if he is not willing, as

---

[a] 17 That is, probably about 3/5 bushel (about 22 liters)   [b] 1 Hebrew find rest (see Ruth 1:9)

Trusting God with Your Future

God has so much for us. We have no idea.

We look for crumbs under the table; He has prepared a feast for us in the royal banquet hall. We wonder if He remembers who we are; He has been calling our name. We wait for Him to notice our plight; He waits for us to take His hand. We see ourselves in the dark because we've done something wrong; He sees us in the light because we've done something right. We don't recognize the answers to our own prayers; He moves powerfully at our request. We have trouble trusting Him fully with our future; He has a future for us better than the one we dream of for ourselves. "No eye has seen, no ear has heard, no mind has conceived what God has prepared for those who love him" (1 Corinthians 2:9).

We worry so about our future because we can never be completely certain about it. A single event can change our lives. For the better, we hope. For the worse, we fear. When we ask Him about it, He sometimes reveals specifics. But most of the time He doesn't give us anything more than the assurance that our future is secure in His hands. He shows us that we *have* a future, and this simple knowledge must be enough for us.

You have a great future ahead, and it will be reached as you move out of your past and walk step-by-step with God as He reveals Himself to you in the present.

Just as you should not live in the past, resist the urge to live in the future also. Put your future in God's hands, trusting that He will never withhold anything good from you, and then stop worrying about it. This doesn't mean a trumpet will sound announcing that you are spiritually immature if you find yourself concerned about the future. God is not asking you to be perfect. He is asking you to allow *Him* to be perfect in you. God is not asking you to have your whole future figured out. He is asking you to trust that *He* has your future planned. Thinking too much about the future can keep you from fully living the life God has given you now.

This doesn't mean you can't have goals, but some people have goals that are so strong they sacrifice everything to achieve them, even their family and God. Instead of allowing the goal to come *from* God, the goal itself *becomes* god.

Simply follow Him every day on that narrow pathway and you will be free. Free to trust Him for every step. Free to be all He made you to be. Free to do what He called you to do. Free to enjoy all He has for you. You'll walk in a depth of love, peace, fulfillment, and joy you never thought possible.

You don't have to have your life all figured out; you only have to take one step at a time walking with God. And every time you put your hand in God's hand, you'll know you've got a solid hold on your future.

For the next "From Stormie's Heart" article, go to page 355.

surely as the LORD lives I will do it. Lie here until morning."

¹⁴So she lay at his feet until morning, but got up before anyone could be recognized; and he said, "Don't let it be known that a woman came to the threshing floor."

¹⁵He also said, "Bring me the shawl you are wearing and hold it out." When she did so, he poured into it six measures of barley and put it on her. Then he[a] went back to town.

¹⁶When Ruth came to her mother-in-law, Naomi asked, "How did it go, my daughter?"

Then she told her everything Boaz had done for her ¹⁷and added, "He gave me these six measures of barley, saying, 'Don't go back to your mother-in-law empty-handed.'"

¹⁸Then Naomi said, "Wait, my daughter, until you find out what happens. For the man will not rest until the matter is settled today."

Boaz Marries Ruth

Meanwhile Boaz went up to the town gate and sat there. When the kinsman-redeemer he had mentioned came along, Boaz said, "Come over here, my friend, and sit down." So he went over and sat down.

²Boaz took ten of the elders of the town and said, "Sit here," and they did so. ³Then he said to the kinsman-redeemer, "Naomi, who has come back from Moab, is selling the piece of land that belonged to our brother Elimelech. ⁴I thought I should bring the matter to your attention and suggest that you buy it in the presence of these seated here and in the presence of the elders of my people. If you will redeem it, do so. But if you[b] will not, tell me, so I will know. For no one has the right to do it except you, and I am next in line."

"I will redeem it," he said.

⁵Then Boaz said, "On the day you buy the land from Naomi and from Ruth the Moabitess, you acquire[c] the dead man's widow, in order to maintain the name of the dead with his property."

⁶At this, the kinsman-redeemer said, "Then I cannot redeem it because I might endanger my own estate. You redeem it yourself. I cannot do it."

⁷(Now in earlier times in Israel, for the redemption and transfer of property to become final, one party took off his sandal and gave it to the other. This was the method of legalizing transactions in Israel.)

⁸So the kinsman-redeemer said to Boaz, "Buy it yourself." And he removed his sandal.

⁹Then Boaz announced to the elders and all the people, "Today you are witnesses that I have bought from Naomi all the property of Elimelech, Kilion and Mahlon. ¹⁰I have also acquired Ruth the Moabitess, Mahlon's widow, as my wife, in order to maintain the name of the dead with his property, so that his name will not disappear from among his family or from the town records. Today you are witnesses!"

¹¹Then the elders and all those at the gate said, "We are witnesses. May the LORD make the woman who is coming into your home like Rachel and Leah, who together built up the house of Israel. May you have standing in Ephrathah and be famous in Bethlehem. ¹²Through the offspring the LORD gives you by this young woman, may your family be like that of Perez, whom Tamar bore to Judah."

The Genealogy of David

¹³So Boaz took Ruth and she became his wife. Then he went to her, and the LORD enabled her to conceive, and she gave birth to a son. ¹⁴The women said to Naomi: "Praise be to the LORD, who this day has not left you without a kinsman-redeemer. May he become famous

a 15 Most Hebrew manuscripts; many Hebrew manuscripts, Vulgate and Syriac *she*   b 4 Many Hebrew manuscripts, Septuagint, Vulgate and Syriac; most Hebrew manuscripts *he*   c 5 Hebrew; Vulgate and Syriac *Naomi, you acquire Ruth the Moabitess,* throughout Israel! [15]He will renew your life and sustain you in your old age. For your daughter-in-law, who loves you and who is better to you than seven sons, has given him birth."

Praying Ruth 4:13-17

Thank You, Lord, that You will redeem all my difficult situations and use them for Your purposes and glory.

[16]Then Naomi took the child, laid him in her lap and cared for him. [17]The women living there said, "Naomi has a son." And they named him Obed. He was the father of Jesse, the father of David.

[18]This, then, is the family line of Perez:

Perez was the father of Hezron,
[19]Hezron the father of Ram,
   Ram the father of Amminadab,
[20]Amminadab the father of Nahshon,
   Nahshon the father of Salmon,[a]
[21]Salmon the father of Boaz,
   Boaz the father of Obed,
[22]Obed the father of Jesse,
   and Jesse the father of David.

---

[a] 20 A few Hebrew manuscripts, some Septuagint manuscripts and Vulgate (see also verse 21 and Septuagint of 1 Chron. 2:11); most Hebrew manuscripts *Salma*

Author: Unknown

Date: Sometime after 930 BC

Audience: Future generations of Israelites—to exhort them to maintain supreme devotion to God even while being ruled by earthly kings

Prayer Themes:

- Ask God for the grace to hear His voice and the wisdom and courage to do as He leads (3:1-10).

- Ask God to give you a heavenly perspective that sees beyond the surface appearance of people and things (16:7).

- Ask the Lord to send into your life God-loving friends who will prayerfully look out for you and encourage you through discouraging times (23:16).

The way we pray speaks volumes about us. Some people try to use God for selfish reasons, while others selflessly seek to be used *by* God for His purposes.

First Samuel highlights these two ways of praying and living. On the one hand, we meet characters like Hannah, Samuel, and David, who pursued God and His glory. Their top priority was to look for Him, listen to Him, and live for Him. They proclaimed Him King over their lives.

On the other hand, these pages are also filled with people like Hophni, Phinehas, and Saul, who pushed God to the sidelines of life. If they thought of God or spoke to Him at all, they were only trying to manipulate Him into accomplishing their own selfish agendas.

As you read the book of 1 Samuel, ask yourself, *What do my prayer and worship habits say about me?*

1 Samuel

The Birth of Samuel

1 There was a certain man from Ramathaim, a Zuphite[a] from the hill country of Ephraim, whose name was Elkanah son of Jeroham, the son of Elihu, the son of Tohu, the son of Zuph, an Ephraimite. ²He had two wives; one was called Hannah and the other Peninnah. Peninnah had children, but Hannah had none.

³Year after year this man went up from his town to worship and sacrifice to the Lord Almighty at Shiloh, where Hophni and Phinehas, the two sons of Eli, were priests of the Lord. ⁴Whenever the day came for Elkanah to sacrifice, he would give portions of the meat to his wife Peninnah and to all her sons and daughters. ⁵But to Hannah he gave a double portion because he loved her, and the Lord had closed her womb. ⁶And because the Lord had closed her womb, her rival kept provoking her in order to irritate her. ⁷This went on year after year. Whenever Hannah went up to the house of the Lord, her rival provoked her till she wept and would not eat. ⁸Elkanah her husband would say to her, "Hannah, why are you weeping? Why don't you eat? Why are you downhearted? Don't I mean more to you than ten sons?"

⁹Once when they had finished eating and drinking in Shiloh, Hannah stood up. Now Eli the priest was sitting on a chair by the doorpost of the Lord's temple.[b] ¹⁰In bitterness of soul Hannah wept much and prayed to the Lord. ¹¹And she made a vow, saying, "O Lord Almighty, if you will only look upon your servant's misery and remember me, and not forget your servant but give her a son, then I will give him to the Lord for all the days

---

a 1 Or *from Ramathaim Zuphim*   b 9 That is, tabernacle

of his life, and no razor will ever be used on his head."

[12]As she kept on praying to the LORD, Eli observed her mouth. [13]Hannah was praying in her heart, and her lips were moving but her voice was not heard. Eli thought she was drunk [14]and said to her, "How long will you keep on getting drunk? Get rid of your wine."

kanah lay with Hannah his wife, and the LORD remembered her. [20]So in the course of time Hannah conceived and gave birth to a son. She named him Samuel,[a] saying, "Because I asked the LORD for him."

Hannah Dedicates Samuel

[21]When the man Elkanah went up with all his family to offer the annual sacrifice

---

God's people at prayer
HANNAH'S PRAYERS AND PROMISES

1 SAMUEL 1:11; 2:1-11 Hannah faced a deep heartache familiar to many women. She was childless. For women in Old Testament days, barrenness was a shame and disgrace. Her problem was worsened because Peninnah, the other wife in the house, made her life miserable. Peninnah bore several children but resented the fact that their husband, Elkanah, still favored Hannah. So Hannah felt trapped between her husband's affection, her rival's hatred, and her own barrenness.

Hannah turned to God. She prayed long and fervently for a child. She made a promise to God, and when God granted her a child, she kept that promise!

Of course, you cannot sway God with promises about what you will do if He answers your prayer, but if you commit something to God, you must follow through and do what you say you will. Anything else is trying to manipulate God. Hannah followed through, even though it must have been very difficult to give up the one for whom she had prayed so long and fervently.

---

[15]"Not so, my lord," Hannah replied, "I am a woman who is deeply troubled. I have not been drinking wine or beer; I was pouring out my soul to the LORD. [16]Do not take your servant for a wicked woman; I have been praying here out of my great anguish and grief."

[17]Eli answered, "Go in peace, and may the God of Israel grant you what you have asked of him."

[18]She said, "May your servant find favor in your eyes." Then she went her way and ate something, and her face was no longer downcast.

[19]Early the next morning they arose and worshiped before the LORD and then went back to their home at Ramah. El-

to the LORD and to fulfill his vow, [22]Hannah did not go. She said to her husband, "After the boy is weaned, I will take him and present him before the LORD, and he will live there always."

[23]"Do what seems best to you," Elkanah her husband told her. "Stay here until you have weaned him; only may the LORD make good his[b] word." So the woman stayed at home and nursed her son until she had weaned him.

[24]After he was weaned, she took the boy with her, young as he was, along with a three-year-old bull,[c] an ephah[d] of flour and a skin of wine, and brought him to the house of the LORD at Shiloh. [25]When they had slaughtered the bull,

---

[a] 20 Samuel sounds like the Hebrew for heard of God.　[b] 23 Masoretic Text; Dead Sea Scrolls, Septuagint and Syriac your
[c] 24 Dead Sea Scrolls, Septuagint and Syriac; Masoretic Text with three bulls　[d] 24 That is, probably about 3/5 bushel (about 22 liters)

they brought the boy to Eli, 26and she said to him, "As surely as you live, my lord, I am the woman who stood here beside you praying to the LORD. 27I prayed for this child, and the LORD has granted me what I asked of him. 28So now I give him to the LORD. For his whole life he will be given over to the LORD." And he worshiped the LORD there.

Hannah's Prayer

2 Then Hannah prayed and said:

"My heart rejoices in the LORD;
  in the LORD my horn[a] is lifted high.
My mouth boasts over my enemies,
  for I delight in your deliverance.

2 "There is no one holy[b] like the LORD;
  there is no one besides you;
  there is no Rock like our God.

3 "Do not keep talking so proudly
  or let your mouth speak such arrogance,
for the LORD is a God who knows,
  and by him deeds are weighed.

4 "The bows of the warriors are broken,
  but those who stumbled are armed with strength.
5 Those who were full hire themselves out for food,
  but those who were hungry hunger no more.
She who was barren has borne seven children,
  but she who has had many sons pines away.

6 "The LORD brings death and makes alive;
  he brings down to the grave[c] and raises up.
7 The LORD sends poverty and wealth;
  he humbles and he exalts.
8 He raises the poor from the dust
  and lifts the needy from the ash heap;

he seats them with princes
  and has them inherit a throne of honor.

"For the foundations of the earth are the LORD's;
  upon them he has set the world.
9 He will guard the feet of his saints,
  but the wicked will be silenced in darkness.

"It is not by strength that one prevails;
10   those who oppose the LORD will be shattered.
He will thunder against them from heaven;
  the LORD will judge the ends of the earth.

"He will give strength to his king
  and exalt the horn of his anointed."

11Then Elkanah went home to Ramah, but the boy ministered before the LORD under Eli the priest.

Eli's Wicked Sons

12Eli's sons were wicked men; they had no regard for the LORD. 13Now it was the practice of the priests with the people that whenever anyone offered a sacrifice and while the meat was being boiled, the servant of the priest would come with a three-pronged fork in his hand. 14He would plunge it into the pan or kettle or caldron or pot, and the priest would take for himself whatever the fork brought up. This is how they treated all the Israelites who came to Shiloh. 15But even before the fat was burned, the servant of the priest would come and say to the man who was sacrificing, "Give the priest some meat to roast; he won't accept boiled meat from you, but only raw."

16If the man said to him, "Let the fat be burned up first, and then take whatever you want," the servant would then answer, "No, hand it over now; if you don't, I'll take it by force."

17This sin of the young men was very

---

a 1 Horn here symbolizes strength; also in verse 10.   b 2 Or no Holy One   c 6 Hebrew Sheol great in the LORD's sight, for they[a] were treating the LORD's offering with contempt.

18But Samuel was ministering before the LORD—a boy wearing a linen ephod. 19Each year his mother made him a little robe and took it to him when she went up with her husband to offer the annual sacrifice. 20Eli would bless Elkanah and his wife, saying, "May the LORD give you children by this woman to take the place of the one she prayed for and gave to the LORD." Then they would go home. 21And the LORD was gracious to Hannah; she conceived and gave birth to three sons and two daughters. Meanwhile, the boy Samuel grew up in the presence of the LORD.

22Now Eli, who was very old, heard about everything his sons were doing to all Israel and how they slept with the women who served at the entrance to the Tent of Meeting. 23So he said to them, "Why do you do such things? I hear from all the people about these wicked deeds of yours. 24No, my sons; it is not a good report that I hear spreading among the LORD's people. 25If a man sins against another man, God[b] may mediate for him; but if a man sins against the LORD, who will intercede for him?" His sons, however, did not listen to their father's rebuke, for it was the LORD's will to put them to death.

26And the boy Samuel continued to grow in stature and in favor with the LORD and with men.

Prophecy Against the House of Eli

27Now a man of God came to Eli and said to him, "This is what the LORD says: 'Did I not clearly reveal myself to your father's house when they were in Egypt under Pharaoh? 28I chose your father out of all the tribes of Israel to be my priest, to go up to my altar, to burn incense, and to wear an ephod in my presence. I also gave your father's house all the offerings made with fire by the Israelites. 29Why

do you[c] scorn my sacrifice and offering that I prescribed for my dwelling? Why do you honor your sons more than me by fattening yourselves on the choice parts of every offering made by my people Israel?'

30"Therefore the LORD, the God of Israel, declares: 'I promised that your house and your father's house would minister before me forever.' But now the LORD declares: 'Far be it from me! Those who honor me I will honor, but those who despise me will be disdained. 31The time is coming when I will cut short your strength and the strength of your father's house, so that there will not be an old man in your family line 32and you will see distress in my dwelling. Although good will be done to Israel, in your family line there will never be an old man. 33Every one of you that I do not cut off from my altar will be spared only to blind your eyes with tears and to grieve your heart, and all your descendants will die in the prime of life.

34"'And what happens to your two sons, Hophni and Phinehas, will be a sign to you—they will both die on the same day. 35I will raise up for myself a faithful priest, who will do according to what is in my heart and mind. I will firmly establish his house, and he will minister before my anointed one always. 36Then everyone left in your family line will come and bow down before him for a piece of silver and a crust of bread and plead, "Appoint me to some priestly office so I can have food to eat." '"

The LORD Calls Samuel

3 The boy Samuel ministered before the LORD under Eli. In those days the word of the LORD was rare; there were not many visions.

2One night Eli, whose eyes were becoming so weak that he could barely see, was lying down in his usual place. 3The lamp of God had not yet gone out, and Samuel was lying down in the temple[d]

a 17 Or men   b 25 Or the judges   c 29 The Hebrew is plural.   d 3 That is, tabernacle of the LORD, where the ark of God was. [4]Then the LORD called Samuel.

Samuel answered, "Here I am." [5]And he ran to Eli and said, "Here I am; you called me."

But Eli said, "I did not call; go back and lie down." So he went and lay down.

[6]Again the LORD called, "Samuel!" And Samuel got up and went to Eli and said, "Here I am; you called me."

"My son," Eli said, "I did not call; go back and lie down."

[7]Now Samuel did not yet know the LORD: The word of the LORD had not yet been revealed to him.

[11]And the LORD said to Samuel: "See, I am about to do something in Israel that will make the ears of everyone who hears of it tingle. [12]At that time I will carry out against Eli everything I spoke against his family—from beginning to end. [13]For I told him that I would judge his family forever because of the sin he knew about; his sons made themselves contemptible,[a] and he failed to restrain them. [14]Therefore, I swore to the house of Eli, 'The guilt of Eli's house will never be atoned for by sacrifice or offering.'"

[15]Samuel lay down until morning and then opened the doors of the house of

---

God's people at prayer
SAMUEL'S ANSWER OF AVAILABILITY

1 SAMUEL 3:1-21 Being available to God is powerful. It releases God's will in our lives. As Christians, our first desire must be to serve the Lord. When God calls, our response should be like young Samuel's: "Speak, LORD, for your servant is listening." In other words, "God, You are always Number One to me. You are more important than anything else. I will do anything you ask of me."

Availability is simply praying, "Speak to me, Lord, and I will do what You ask." That's what Samuel did, and he influenced a nation. He bridged a gap politically. He anointed and advised kings.

How available are you? Have you told God you are open to His voice and will do what He says regardless of where that leads you? If not, do it now. Be available to whatever He might speak to your heart. Surrender all your plans to Him and be open to anything He instructs you to do.

---

[8]The LORD called Samuel a third time, and Samuel got up and went to Eli and said, "Here I am; you called me."

Then Eli realized that the LORD was calling the boy. [9]So Eli told Samuel, "Go and lie down, and if he calls you, say, 'Speak, LORD, for your servant is listening.'" So Samuel went and lay down in his place.

[10]The LORD came and stood there, calling as at the other times, "Samuel! Samuel!"

Then Samuel said, "Speak, for your servant is listening."

the LORD. He was afraid to tell Eli the vision, [16]but Eli called him and said, "Samuel, my son."

Samuel answered, "Here I am."

[17]"What was it he said to you?" Eli asked. "Do not hide it from me. May God deal with you, be it ever so severely, if you hide from me anything he told you." [18]So Samuel told him everything, hiding nothing from him. Then Eli said, "He is the LORD; let him do what is good in his eyes."

[19]The LORD was with Samuel as he grew up, and he let none of his words fall

---

[a] *13* Masoretic Text; an ancient Hebrew scribal tradition and Septuagint *sons blasphemed God*

to the ground. [20]And all Israel from Dan to Beersheba recognized that Samuel was attested as a prophet of the LORD. [21]The LORD continued to appear at Shiloh, and there he revealed himself to Samuel through his word.

4 And Samuel's word came to all Israel.

The Philistines Capture the Ark

Now the Israelites went out to fight against the Philistines. The Israelites camped at Ebenezer, and the Philistines at Aphek. [2]The Philistines deployed their forces to meet Israel, and as the battle spread, Israel was defeated by the Philistines, who killed about four thousand of them on the battlefield. [3]When the soldiers returned to camp, the elders of Israel asked, "Why did the LORD bring defeat upon us today before the Philistines? Let us bring the ark of the LORD's covenant from Shiloh, so that it[a] may go with us and save us from the hand of our enemies."

[4]So the people sent men to Shiloh, and they brought back the ark of the covenant of the LORD Almighty, who is enthroned between the cherubim. And Eli's two sons, Hophni and Phinehas, were there with the ark of the covenant of God.

[5]When the ark of the LORD's covenant came into the camp, all Israel raised such a great shout that the ground shook. [6]Hearing the uproar, the Philistines asked, "What's all this shouting in the Hebrew camp?"

When they learned that the ark of the LORD had come into the camp, [7]the Philistines were afraid. "A god has come into the camp," they said. "We're in trouble! Nothing like this has happened before. [8]Woe to us! Who will deliver us from the hand of these mighty gods? They are the gods who struck the Egyptians with all kinds of plagues in the desert. [9]Be strong, Philistines! Be men, or you will be subject to the Hebrews, as they have been to you. Be men, and fight!"

[10]So the Philistines fought, and the Israelites were defeated and every man fled to his tent. The slaughter was very great; Israel lost thirty thousand foot soldiers. [11]The ark of God was captured, and Eli's two sons, Hophni and Phinehas, died.

Death of Eli

[12]That same day a Benjamite ran from the battle line and went to Shiloh, his clothes torn and dust on his head. [13]When he arrived, there was Eli sitting on his chair by the side of the road, watching, because his heart feared for the ark of God. When the man entered the town and told what had happened, the whole town sent up a cry.

[14]Eli heard the outcry and asked, "What is the meaning of this uproar?"

The man hurried over to Eli, [15]who was ninety-eight years old and whose eyes were set so that he could not see. [16]He told Eli, "I have just come from the battle line; I fled from it this very day."

Eli asked, "What happened, my son?"

[17]The man who brought the news replied, "Israel fled before the Philistines, and the army has suffered heavy losses. Also your two sons, Hophni and Phinehas, are dead, and the ark of God has been captured."

[18]When he mentioned the ark of God, Eli fell backward off his chair by the side of the gate. His neck was broken and he died, for he was an old man and heavy. He had led[b] Israel forty years.

[19]His daughter-in-law, the wife of Phinehas, was pregnant and near the time of delivery. When she heard the news that the ark of God had been captured and that her father-in-law and her husband were dead, she went into labor and gave birth, but was overcome by her labor pains. [20]As she was dying, the women attending her said, "Don't despair; you have given birth to a son." But she did not respond or pay any attention.

[21]She named the boy Ichabod,[c] saying, "The glory has departed from Israel"—

---

[a] 3 Or he   [b] 18 Traditionally judged   [c] 21 Ichabod means no glory.

because of the capture of the ark of God and the deaths of her father-in-law and her husband. ²²She said, "The glory has departed from Israel, for the ark of God has been captured."

The Ark in Ashdod and Ekron

5 After the Philistines had captured the ark of God, they took it from Ebenezer to Ashdod. ²Then they carried the ark into Dagon's temple and set it beside Dagon. ³When the people of Ashdod rose early the next day, there was Dagon, fallen on his face on the ground before the ark of the LORD! They took Dagon and put him back in his place. ⁴But the following morning when they rose, there was Dagon, fallen on his face on the ground before the ark of the LORD! His head and hands had been broken off and were lying on the threshold; only his body remained. ⁵That is why to this day neither the priests of Dagon nor any others who enter Dagon's temple at Ashdod step on the threshold.

⁶The LORD's hand was heavy upon the people of Ashdod and its vicinity; he brought devastation upon them and afflicted them with tumors.ᵃ ⁷When the men of Ashdod saw what was happening, they said, "The ark of the god of Israel must not stay here with us, because his hand is heavy upon us and upon Dagon our god." ⁸So they called together all the rulers of the Philistines and asked them, "What shall we do with the ark of the god of Israel?"

They answered, "Have the ark of the god of Israel moved to Gath." So they moved the ark of the God of Israel.

⁹But after they had moved it, the LORD's hand was against that city, throwing it into a great panic. He afflicted the people of the city, both young and old, with an outbreak of tumors.ᵇ ¹⁰So they sent the ark of God to Ekron.

As the ark of God was entering Ekron, the people of Ekron cried out, "They have brought the ark of the god of Israel around to us to kill us and our people." ¹¹So they called together all the rulers of the Philistines and said, "Send the ark of the god of Israel away; let it go back to its own place, or itᶜ will kill us and our people." For death had filled the city with panic; God's hand was very heavy upon it. ¹²Those who did not die were afflicted with tumors, and the outcry of the city went up to heaven.

The Ark Returned to Israel

6 When the ark of the LORD had been in Philistine territory seven months, ²the Philistines called for the priests and the diviners and said, "What shall we do with the ark of the LORD? Tell us how we should send it back to its place."

³They answered, "If you return the ark of the god of Israel, do not send it away empty, but by all means send a guilt offering to him. Then you will be healed, and you will know why his hand has not been lifted from you."

⁴The Philistines asked, "What guilt offering should we send to him?"

They replied, "Five gold tumors and five gold rats, according to the number of the Philistine rulers, because the same plague has struck both you and your rulers. ⁵Make models of the tumors and of the rats that are destroying the country, and pay honor to Israel's god. Perhaps he will lift his hand from you and your gods and your land. ⁶Why do you harden your hearts as the Egyptians and Pharaoh did? When heᵈ treated them harshly, did they not send the Israelites out so they could go on their way?

⁷"Now then, get a new cart ready, with two cows that have calved and have never been yoked. Hitch the cows to the cart, but take their calves away and pen them up. ⁸Take the ark of the LORD and put it on the cart, and in a chest beside it put the gold objects you are sending back to him as a guilt offering. Send it on its way, ⁹but

keep watching it. If it goes up to its own territory, toward Beth Shemesh, then the LORD has brought this great disaster on us. But if it does not, then we will know that it was not his hand that struck us and that it happened to us by chance."

¹⁰So they did this. They took two such cows and hitched them to the cart and penned up their calves. ¹¹They placed the ark of the LORD on the cart and along with it the chest containing the gold rats and the models of the tumors. ¹²Then the cows went straight up toward Beth Shemesh, keeping on the road and lowing all the way; they did not turn to the right or to the left. The rulers of the Philistines followed them as far as the border of Beth Shemesh.

¹³Now the people of Beth Shemesh were harvesting their wheat in the valley, and when they looked up and saw the ark, they rejoiced at the sight. ¹⁴The cart came to the field of Joshua of Beth Shemesh, and there it stopped beside a large rock. The people chopped up the wood of the cart and sacrificed the cows as a burnt offering to the LORD. ¹⁵The Levites took down the ark of the LORD, together with the chest containing the gold objects, and placed them on the large rock. On that day the people of Beth Shemesh offered burnt offerings and made sacrifices to the LORD. ¹⁶The five rulers of the Philistines saw all this and then returned that same day to Ekron.

¹⁷These are the gold tumors the Philistines sent as a guilt offering to the LORD—one each for Ashdod, Gaza, Ashkelon, Gath and Ekron. ¹⁸And the number of the gold rats was according to the number of Philistine towns belonging to the five rulers—the fortified towns with their country villages. The large rock, on which[a] they set the ark of the LORD, is a witness to this day in the field of Joshua of Beth Shemesh.

¹⁹But God struck down some of the men of Beth Shemesh, putting seventy[b] of them to death because they had looked into the ark of the LORD. The people mourned because of the heavy blow the LORD had dealt them, ²⁰and the men of Beth Shemesh asked, "Who can stand in the presence of the LORD, this holy God? To whom will the ark go up from here?"

²¹Then they sent messengers to the people of Kiriath Jearim, saying, "The Philistines have returned the ark of the LORD. Come down and take it up to your place." ⁷ ¹So the men of Kiriath Jearim came and took up the ark of the LORD. They took it to Abinadab's house on the hill and consecrated Eleazar his son to guard the ark of the LORD.

Samuel Subdues the Philistines at Mizpah

²It was a long time, twenty years in all, that the ark remained at Kiriath Jearim, and all the people of Israel mourned and sought after the LORD. ³And Samuel said to the whole house of Israel, "If you are returning to the LORD with all your hearts, then rid yourselves of the foreign gods and the Ashtoreths and commit yourselves to the LORD and serve him only, and he will deliver you out of the hand of the Philistines." ⁴So the Israelites put away their Baals and Ashtoreths, and served the LORD only.

> *Praying 1 Samuel 7:3*
> *Lord, help me to reject anything that is an idol in my life and return entirely to You with all of my heart.*

⁵Then Samuel said, "Assemble all Israel at Mizpah and I will intercede with the LORD for you." ⁶When they had assembled at Mizpah, they drew water and poured it out before the LORD. On that day they fasted and there they confessed, "We have sinned against the LORD." And Samuel was leader[c] of Israel at Mizpah. ⁷When the Philistines heard that Israel

---

had assembled at Mizpah, the rulers of the Philistines came up to attack them. And when the Israelites heard of it, they were afraid because of the Philistines. [8]They said to Samuel, "Do not stop crying out to the LORD our God for us, that he may rescue us from the hand of the Philistines." [9]Then Samuel took a suckling lamb and offered it up as a whole burnt offering to the LORD. He cried out to the LORD on Israel's behalf, and the LORD answered him.

[10]While Samuel was sacrificing the burnt offering, the Philistines drew near to engage Israel in battle. But that day the LORD thundered with loud thunder against the Philistines and threw them into such a panic that they were routed before the Israelites. [11]The men of Israel rushed out of Mizpah and pursued the Philistines, slaughtering them along the way to a point below Beth Car.

[12]Then Samuel took a stone and set it up between Mizpah and Shen. He named it Ebenezer,[a] saying, "Thus far has the LORD helped us." [13]So the Philistines were subdued and did not invade Israelite territory again.

Throughout Samuel's lifetime, the hand of the LORD was against the Philistines. [14]The towns from Ekron to Gath that the Philistines had captured from Israel were restored to her, and Israel delivered the neighboring territory from the power of the Philistines. And there was peace between Israel and the Amorites.

[15]Samuel continued as judge over Israel all the days of his life. [16]From year to year he went on a circuit from Bethel to Gilgal to Mizpah, judging Israel in all those places. [17]But he always went back to Ramah, where his home was, and there he also judged Israel. And he built an altar there to the LORD.

Israel Asks for a King

8 When Samuel grew old, he appointed his sons as judges for Israel. [2]The name of his firstborn was Joel and the name of his second was Abijah, and they served at Beersheba. [3]But his sons did not walk in his ways. They turned aside after dishonest gain and accepted bribes and perverted justice.

[4]So all the elders of Israel gathered together and came to Samuel at Ramah. [5]They said to him, "You are old, and your sons do not walk in your ways; now appoint a king to lead[b] us, such as all the other nations have."

[6]But when they said, "Give us a king to lead us," this displeased Samuel; so he prayed to the LORD. [7]And the LORD told him: "Listen to all that the people are saying to you; it is not you they have rejected, but they have rejected me as their king. [8]As they have done from the day I brought them up out of Egypt until this day, forsaking me and serving other gods, so they are doing to you. [9]Now listen to them; but warn them solemnly and let them know what the king who will reign over them will do."

[10]Samuel told all the words of the LORD to the people who were asking him for a king. [11]He said, "This is what the king who will reign over you will do: He will take your sons and make them serve with his chariots and horses, and they will run in front of his chariots. [12]Some he will assign to be commanders of thousands and commanders of fifties, and others to plow his ground and reap his harvest, and still others to make weapons of war and equipment for his chariots. [13]He will take your daughters to be perfumers and cooks and bakers. [14]He will take the best of your fields and vineyards and olive groves and give them to his attendants. [15]He will take a tenth of your grain and of your vintage and give it to his officials and attendants. [16]Your menservants and maidservants and the best of your cattle[c] and donkeys he will take for his own use. [17]He will take a tenth of your flocks, and you yourselves will become his slaves. [18]When that day comes, you will cry out for relief from

---

[a] 12 Ebenezer means stone of help.   [b] 5 Traditionally judge; also in verses 6 and 20   [c] 16 Septuagint; Hebrew young men

Be Careful What You Ask For

READ AND CONSIDER: 1 SAMUEL 8

"So all the elders of Israel gathered together and came to Samuel at Ramah. They said to him, 'You are old, and your sons do not walk in your ways; now appoint a king to lead us, such as all the other nations have'" (1 Samuel 8:4-5).

You can probably recall times in your life when you have prayed for something that, looking back, could have led to disaster. Although we think we know what is best for our lives and our futures, often we pray for the very things that would lead to our own destruction. God knows this; He sees the big picture. He wants us to bring our prayers into alignment with His will. In the case of the Israelites, no amount of instruction—even from the Lord Himself through Samuel—could convince them that they were praying amiss. So the Lord finally gave them the king they begged for, though He knew he would eventually be a burden to them.

Today you have the Holy Spirit to guide you, even in your praying. So always ask the Lord to help you pray according to His will for your life. Also seek wisdom from the Bible so you can pray in alignment with His will. Just as Jesus did in the garden of Gethsemane, pray "not my will, but yours be done" (Luke 22:42). This allows God to work in your heart so you can accept His will, even if it is not what you thought you wanted.

the king you have chosen, and the LORD will not answer you in that day."

19But the people refused to listen to Samuel. "No!" they said. "We want a king over us. 20Then we will be like all the other nations, with a king to lead us and to go out before us and fight our battles."

21When Samuel heard all that the people said, he repeated it before the LORD. 22The LORD answered, "Listen to them and give them a king."

Then Samuel said to the men of Israel, "Everyone go back to his town."

Samuel Anoints Saul

9 There was a Benjamite, a man of standing, whose name was Kish son of Abiel, the son of Zeror, the son of Becorath, the son of Aphiah of Benjamin. 2He had a son named Saul, an impressive young man without equal among the Israelites—a head taller than any of the others.

3Now the donkeys belonging to Saul's father Kish were lost, and Kish said to his son Saul, "Take one of the servants with you and go and look for the donkeys." 4So he passed through the hill country of Ephraim and through the area around Shalisha, but they did not find them. They went on into the district of Shaalim, but the donkeys were not there. Then he passed through the territory of Benjamin, but they did not find them.

5When they reached the district of Zuph, Saul said to the servant who was with him, "Come, let's go back, or my father will stop thinking about the donkeys and start worrying about us."

6But the servant replied, "Look, in this town there is a man of God; he is highly respected, and everything he says comes true. Let's go there now. Perhaps he will tell us what way to take."

7Saul said to his servant, "If we go, what can we give the man? The food in our sacks is gone. We have no gift to take to the man of God. What do we have?"

8The servant answered him again. "Look," he said, "I have a quarter of a shekel[a] of silver. I will give it to the man of God so that he will tell us what way to take." [9](Formerly in Israel, if a man went to inquire of God, he would say, "Come, let us go to the seer," because the prophet of today used to be called a seer.)

[10]"Good," Saul said to his servant. "Come, let's go." So they set out for the town where the man of God was.

[11]As they were going up the hill to the town, they met some girls coming out to draw water, and they asked them, "Is the seer here?"

[12]"He is," they answered. "He's ahead of you. Hurry now; he has just come to our town today, for the people have a sacrifice at the high place. [13]As soon as you enter the town, you will find him before he goes up to the high place to eat. The people will not begin eating until he comes, because he must bless the sacrifice; afterward, those who are invited will eat. Go up now; you should find him about this time."

[14]They went up to the town, and as they were entering it, there was Samuel, coming toward them on his way up to the high place.

[15]Now the day before Saul came, the LORD had revealed this to Samuel: [16]"About this time tomorrow I will send you a man from the land of Benjamin. Anoint him leader over my people Israel; he will deliver my people from the hand of the Philistines. I have looked upon my people, for their cry has reached me."

[17]When Samuel caught sight of Saul, the LORD said to him, "This is the man I spoke to you about; he will govern my people."

[18]Saul approached Samuel in the gateway and asked, "Would you please tell me where the seer's house is?"

[19]"I am the seer," Samuel replied. "Go up ahead of me to the high place, for today you are to eat with me, and in the morning I will let you go and will tell

you all that is in your heart. [20]As for the donkeys you lost three days ago, do not worry about them; they have been found. And to whom is all the desire of Israel turned, if not to you and all your father's family?"

[21]Saul answered, "But am I not a Benjamite, from the smallest tribe of Israel, and is not my clan the least of all the clans of the tribe of Benjamin? Why do you say such a thing to me?"

[22]Then Samuel brought Saul and his servant into the hall and seated them at the head of those who were invited—about thirty in number. [23]Samuel said to the cook, "Bring the piece of meat I gave you, the one I told you to lay aside."

[24]So the cook took up the leg with what was on it and set it in front of Saul. Samuel said, "Here is what has been kept for you. Eat, because it was set aside for you for this occasion, from the time I said, 'I have invited guests.'" And Saul dined with Samuel that day.

[25]After they came down from the high place to the town, Samuel talked with Saul on the roof of his house. [26]They rose about daybreak and Samuel called to Saul on the roof, "Get ready, and I will send you on your way." When Saul got ready, he and Samuel went outside together. [27]As they were going down to the edge of the town, Samuel said to Saul, "Tell the servant to go on ahead of us"—and the servant did so—"but you stay here awhile, so that I may give you a message from God."

10 Then Samuel took a flask of oil and poured it on Saul's head and kissed him, saying, "Has not the LORD anointed you leader over his inheritance?[b] [2]When you leave me today, you will meet two men near Rachel's tomb, at Zelzah on the border of Benjamin. They will say to you, 'The donkeys you set out to look for have been found. And now your father has stopped thinking about them and is

[a] 8 That is, about 1/10 ounce (about 3 grams)   [b] 1 Hebrew; Septuagint and Vulgate over his people Israel? You will reign over the LORD's people and save them from the power of their enemies round about. And this will be a sign to you that the LORD has anointed you leader over his inheritance:

worried about you. He is asking, "What shall I do about my son?"'

³"Then you will go on from there until you reach the great tree of Tabor. Three men going up to God at Bethel will meet you there. One will be carrying three young goats, another three loaves of bread, and another a skin of wine. ⁴They will greet you and offer you two loaves of bread, which you will accept from them.

⁵"After that you will go to Gibeah of God, where there is a Philistine outpost. As you approach the town, you will meet a procession of prophets coming down from the high place with lyres, tambourines, flutes and harps being played before them, and they will be prophesying. ⁶The Spirit of the LORD will come upon you in power, and you will prophesy with them; and you will be changed into a different person. ⁷Once these signs are fulfilled, do whatever your hand finds to do, for God is with you.

⁸"Go down ahead of me to Gilgal. I will surely come down to you to sacrifice burnt offerings and fellowship offerings,ᵃ but you must wait seven days until I come to you and tell you what you are to do."

Saul Made King

⁹As Saul turned to leave Samuel, God changed Saul's heart, and all these signs were fulfilled that day. ¹⁰When they arrived at Gibeah, a procession of prophets met him; the Spirit of God came upon him in power, and he joined in their prophesying. ¹¹When all those who had formerly known him saw him prophesying with the prophets, they asked each other, "What is this that has happened to the son of Kish? Is Saul also among the prophets?"

¹²A man who lived there answered, "And who is their father?" So it became a saying: "Is Saul also among the prophets?" ¹³After Saul stopped prophesying, he went to the high place.

¹⁴Now Saul's uncle asked him and his servant, "Where have you been?"

"Looking for the donkeys," he said. "But when we saw they were not to be found, we went to Samuel."

¹⁵Saul's uncle said, "Tell me what Samuel said to you."

¹⁶Saul replied, "He assured us that the donkeys had been found." But he did not tell his uncle what Samuel had said about the kingship.

¹⁷Samuel summoned the people of Israel to the LORD at Mizpah ¹⁸and said to them, "This is what the LORD, the God of Israel, says: 'I brought Israel up out of Egypt, and I delivered you from the power of Egypt and all the kingdoms that oppressed you.' ¹⁹But you have now rejected your God, who saves you out of all your calamities and distresses. And you have said, 'No, set a king over us.' So now present yourselves before the LORD by your tribes and clans."

²⁰When Samuel brought all the tribes of Israel near, the tribe of Benjamin was chosen. ²¹Then he brought forward the tribe of Benjamin, clan by clan, and Matri's clan was chosen. Finally Saul son of Kish was chosen. But when they looked for him, he was not to be found. ²²So they inquired further of the LORD, "Has the man come here yet?"

And the LORD said, "Yes, he has hidden himself among the baggage."

²³They ran and brought him out, and as he stood among the people he was a head taller than any of the others. ²⁴Samuel said to all the people, "Do you see the man the LORD has chosen? There is no one like him among all the people."

Then the people shouted, "Long live the king!"

²⁵Samuel explained to the people the regulations of the kingship. He wrote them down on a scroll and deposited it before the LORD. Then Samuel dismissed the people, each to his own home.

²⁶Saul also went to his home in Gibeah, accompanied by valiant men whose hearts God had touched. ²⁷But some trou-

---

ᵃ 8 Traditionally *peace offerings*

blemakers said, "How can this fellow save us?" They despised him and brought him no gifts. But Saul kept silent.

Saul Rescues the City of Jabesh

11 Nahash the Ammonite went up and besieged Jabesh Gilead. And all the men of Jabesh said to him, "Make a treaty with us, and we will be subject to you."

2But Nahash the Ammonite replied, "I will make a treaty with you only on the condition that I gouge out the right eye of every one of you and so bring disgrace on all Israel."

3The elders of Jabesh said to him, "Give us seven days so we can send messengers throughout Israel; if no one comes to rescue us, we will surrender to you."

4When the messengers came to Gibeah of Saul and reported these terms to the people, they all wept aloud. 5Just then Saul was returning from the fields, behind his oxen, and he asked, "What is wrong with the people? Why are they weeping?" Then they repeated to him what the men of Jabesh had said.

6When Saul heard their words, the Spirit of God came upon him in power, and he burned with anger. 7He took a pair of oxen, cut them into pieces, and sent the pieces by messengers throughout Israel, proclaiming, "This is what will be done to the oxen of anyone who does not follow Saul and Samuel." Then the terror of the LORD fell on the people, and they turned out as one man. 8When Saul mustered them at Bezek, the men of Israel numbered three hundred thousand and the men of Judah thirty thousand.

9They told the messengers who had come, "Say to the men of Jabesh Gilead, 'By the time the sun is hot tomorrow, you will be delivered.'" When the messengers went and reported this to the men of Jabesh, they were elated. 10They said to the Ammonites, "Tomorrow we will surrender to you, and you can do to us whatever seems good to you."

11The next day Saul separated his men into three divisions; during the last watch of the night they broke into the camp of the Ammonites and slaughtered them until the heat of the day. Those who survived were scattered, so that no two of them were left together.

Saul Confirmed as King

12The people then said to Samuel, "Who was it that asked, 'Shall Saul reign over us?' Bring these men to us and we will put them to death."

13But Saul said, "No one shall be put to death today, for this day the LORD has rescued Israel."

14Then Samuel said to the people, "Come, let us go to Gilgal and there reaffirm the kingship." 15So all the people went to Gilgal and confirmed Saul as king in the presence of the LORD. There they sacrificed fellowship offerings[a] before the LORD, and Saul and all the Israelites held a great celebration.

Samuel's Farewell Speech

12 Samuel said to all Israel, "I have listened to everything you said to me and have set a king over you. 2Now you have a king as your leader. As for me, I am old and gray, and my sons are here with you. I have been your leader from my youth until this day. 3Here I stand. Testify against me in the presence of the LORD and his anointed. Whose ox have I taken? Whose donkey have I taken? Whom have I cheated? Whom have I oppressed? From whose hand have I accepted a bribe to make me shut my eyes? If I have done any of these, I will make it right."

4"You have not cheated or oppressed us," they replied. "You have not taken anything from anyone's hand."

5Samuel said to them, "The LORD is witness against you, and also his anointed is witness this day, that you have not found anything in my hand."

"He is witness," they said.

6Then Samuel said to the people, "It is the LORD who appointed Moses and

---

a 15 Traditionally *peace offerings*

Aaron and brought your forefathers up out of Egypt. [7]Now then, stand here, because I am going to confront you with evidence before the LORD as to all the righteous acts performed by the LORD for you and your fathers.

[8]"After Jacob entered Egypt, they cried to the LORD for help, and the LORD sent Moses and Aaron, who brought your forefathers out of Egypt and settled them in this place.

[9]"But they forgot the LORD their God; so he sold them into the hand of Sisera, the commander of the army of Hazor, and into the hands of the Philistines and the king of Moab, who fought against them. [10]They cried out to the LORD and said, 'We have sinned; we have forsaken the LORD and served the Baals and the Ashtoreths. But now deliver us from the hands of our enemies, and we will serve you.' [11]Then the LORD sent Jerub-Baal,[a] Barak,[b] Jephthah and Samuel,[c] and he delivered you from the hands of your enemies on every side, so that you lived securely.

[12]"But when you saw that Nahash king of the Ammonites was moving against you, you said to me, 'No, we want a king to rule over us'—even though the LORD your God was your king. [13]Now here is the king you have chosen, the one you asked for; see, the LORD has set a king over you. [14]If you fear the LORD and serve and obey him and do not rebel against his commands, and if both you and the king who reigns over you follow the LORD your God—good! [15]But if you do not obey the LORD, and if you rebel against his commands, his hand will be against you, as it was against your fathers.

[16]"Now then, stand still and see this great thing the LORD is about to do before your eyes! [17]Is it not wheat harvest now? I will call upon the LORD to send thunder and rain. And you will realize what an evil thing you did in the eyes of the LORD when you asked for a king."

[18]Then Samuel called upon the LORD, and that same day the LORD sent thunder and rain. So all the people stood in awe of the LORD and of Samuel.

[19]The people all said to Samuel, "Pray to the LORD your God for your servants so that we will not die, for we have added to all our other sins the evil of asking for a king."

Praying 1 Samuel 12:20

Dear God, I thank You that even when I make wrong choices, You will still bless me if I turn to You and follow Your ways.

[20]"Do not be afraid," Samuel replied. "You have done all this evil; yet do not turn away from the LORD, but serve the LORD with all your heart. [21]Do not turn away after useless idols. They can do you no good, nor can they rescue you, because they are useless. [22]For the sake of his great name the LORD will not reject his people, because the LORD was pleased to make you his own. [23]As for me, far be it from me that I should sin against the LORD by failing to pray for you. And I will teach you the way that is good and right. [24]But be sure to fear the LORD and serve him faithfully with all your heart; consider what great things he has done for you. [25]Yet if you persist in doing evil, both you and your king will be swept away."

Samuel Rebukes Saul

13 Saul was ⌊thirty⌋[d] years old when he became king, and he reigned over Israel ⌊forty-⌋[e] two years.

[2]Saul[f] chose three thousand men from Israel; two thousand were with him at Micmash and in the hill country of Bethel, and a thousand were with Jonathan at Gibeah in Benjamin. The rest of the men he sent back to their homes.

[3]Jonathan attacked the Philistine outpost at Geba, and the Philistines heard about it. Then Saul had the trumpet

---

[a] *11* Also called *Gideon*   [b] *11* Some Septuagint manuscripts and Syriac; Hebrew *Bedan*   [c] *11* Hebrew; some Septuagint manuscripts and Syriac *Samson*   [d] *1* A few late manuscripts of the Septuagint; Hebrew does not have *thirty*.   [e] *1* See the round number in Acts 13:21; Hebrew does not have *forty-*.   [f] *1,2* Or *and when he had reigned over Israel two years,* [2]*he*

Give the Gift of Prayer

GOING deeper

READ AND CONSIDER: 1 SAMUEL 12

"As for me, far be it from me that I should sin against the LORD by failing to pray for you. And I will teach you the way that is good and right" (1 Samuel 12:23).

You might not think of a failure to pray for others as a sin against God, but Samuel clearly considered it so. God calls us to support one another, love one another, and pray for one another. When we don't do these acts, we are not living in the unity and fellowship that He desires us to have, and we cannot experience all the blessings that He wants to give us. Samuel knew this and proclaimed that he would be faithful in prayer for the Israelites—in spite of all of the evil they had done in God's eyes.

Prayer is the greatest gift we can give to anyone. Of course, if someone needs food, clothes, and a place to live, those needs must be met too. But in giving that way, we also should not neglect to pray for that person as well. Material things are temporary, but our prayers for another person can affect him or her for a lifetime.

We can never move into all God has for us until we first move into intercessory prayer. This is one part of our calling that all Christians have in common because we are *all* called to intercede for others. God wants us to love others enough to lay down our lives for them in prayer.

blown throughout the land and said, "Let the Hebrews hear!" ⁴So all Israel heard the news: "Saul has attacked the Philistine outpost, and now Israel has become a stench to the Philistines." And the people were summoned to join Saul at Gilgal.

⁵The Philistines assembled to fight Israel, with three thousandᵃ chariots, six thousand charioteers, and soldiers as numerous as the sand on the seashore. They went up and camped at Micmash, east of Beth Aven. ⁶When the men of Israel saw that their situation was critical and that their army was hard pressed, they hid in caves and thickets, among the rocks, and in pits and cisterns. ⁷Some Hebrews even crossed the Jordan to the land of Gad and Gilead.

Saul remained at Gilgal, and all the troops with him were quaking with fear. ⁸He waited seven days, the time set by Samuel; but Samuel did not come to Gilgal, and Saul's men began to scatter. ⁹So

he said, "Bring me the burnt offering and the fellowship offerings.ᵇ" And Saul offered up the burnt offering. ¹⁰Just as he finished making the offering, Samuel arrived, and Saul went out to greet him.

¹¹"What have you done?" asked Samuel.

Saul replied, "When I saw that the men were scattering, and that you did not come at the set time, and that the Philistines were assembling at Micmash, ¹²I thought, 'Now the Philistines will come down against me at Gilgal, and I have not sought the LORD's favor.' So I felt compelled to offer the burnt offering."

¹³"You acted foolishly," Samuel said. "You have not kept the command the LORD your God gave you; if you had, he would have established your kingdom over Israel for all time. ¹⁴But now your kingdom will not endure; the LORD has sought out a man after his own heart and appointed him leader of his people, because you have not kept the LORD's command."

ᵃ*5 Some Septuagint manuscripts and Syriac; Hebrew* thirty thousand   ᵇ*9 Traditionally* peace offerings

[15]Then Samuel left Gilgal[a] and went up to Gibeah in Benjamin, and Saul counted the men who were with him. They numbered about six hundred.

Israel Without Weapons

[16]Saul and his son Jonathan and the men with them were staying in Gibeah[b] in Benjamin, while the Philistines camped at Micmash. [17]Raiding parties went out from the Philistine camp in three detachments. One turned toward Ophrah in the vicinity of Shual, [18]another toward Beth Horon, and the third toward the borderland overlooking the Valley of Zeboim facing the desert.

[19]Not a blacksmith could be found in the whole land of Israel, because the Philistines had said, "Otherwise the Hebrews will make swords or spears!" [20]So all Israel went down to the Philistines to have their plowshares, mattocks, axes and sickles[c] sharpened. [21]The price was two thirds of a shekel[d] for sharpening plowshares and mattocks, and a third of a shekel[e] for sharpening forks and axes and for repointing goads.

[22]So on the day of the battle not a soldier with Saul and Jonathan had a sword or spear in his hand; only Saul and his son Jonathan had them.

Jonathan Attacks the Philistines

[23]Now a detachment of Philistines had gone out to the pass at Micmash. [14:1]One day Jonathan son of Saul said to the young man bearing his armor, "Come, let's go over to the Philistine outpost on the other side." But he did not tell his father.

[2]Saul was staying on the outskirts of Gibeah under a pomegranate tree in Migron. With him were about six hundred men, [3]among whom was Ahijah, who was wearing an ephod. He was a son of Ichabod's brother Ahitub son of Phinehas, the son of Eli, the Lord's priest in Shiloh.

No one was aware that Jonathan had left.

[4]On each side of the pass that Jonathan intended to cross to reach the Philistine outpost was a cliff; one was called Bozez, and the other Seneh. [5]One cliff stood to the north toward Micmash, the other to the south toward Geba.

[6]Jonathan said to his young armor-bearer, "Come, let's go over to the outpost of those uncircumcised fellows. Perhaps the Lord will act in our behalf. Nothing can hinder the Lord from saving, whether by many or by few."

[7]"Do all that you have in mind," his armor-bearer said. "Go ahead; I am with you heart and soul."

[8]Jonathan said, "Come, then; we will cross over toward the men and let them see us. [9]If they say to us, 'Wait there until we come to you,' we will stay where we are and not go up to them. [10]But if they say, 'Come up to us,' we will climb up, because that will be our sign that the Lord has given them into our hands."

[11]So both of them showed themselves to the Philistine outpost. "Look!" said the Philistines. "The Hebrews are crawling out of the holes they were hiding in." [12]The men of the outpost shouted to Jonathan and his armor-bearer, "Come up to us and we'll teach you a lesson."

So Jonathan said to his armor-bearer, "Climb up after me; the Lord has given them into the hand of Israel."

[13]Jonathan climbed up, using his hands and feet, with his armor-bearer right behind him. The Philistines fell before Jonathan, and his armor-bearer followed and killed behind him. [14]In that first attack Jonathan and his armor-bearer killed some twenty men in an area of about half an acre.[f]

Israel Routs the Philistines

[15]Then panic struck the whole army—those in the camp and field, and those in the outposts and raiding parties—and the

---

[a] 15 Hebrew; Septuagint *Gilgal and went his way; the rest of the people went after Saul to meet the army, and they went out of Gilgal*   [b] 16 Two Hebrew manuscripts; most Hebrew manuscripts *Geba*, a variant of *Gibeah*   [c] 20 Septuagint; Hebrew *plowshares*   [d] 21 Hebrew *pim*; that is, about 1/4 ounce (about 8 grams)   [e] 21 That is, about 1/8 ounce (about 4 grams)   [f] 14 Hebrew *half a yoke*; a "yoke" was the land plowed by a yoke of oxen in one day.

ground shook. It was a panic sent by God.[a] [16]Saul's lookouts at Gibeah in Benjamin saw the army melting away in all directions. [17]Then Saul said to the men who were with him, "Muster the forces and see who has left us." When they did, it was Jonathan and his armor-bearer who were not there.

[18]Saul said to Ahijah, "Bring the ark of God." (At that time it was with the Israelites.)[b] [19]While Saul was talking to the priest, the tumult in the Philistine camp increased more and more. So Saul said to the priest, "Withdraw your hand."

[20]Then Saul and all his men assembled and went to the battle. They found the Philistines in total confusion, striking each other with their swords. [21]Those Hebrews who had previously been with the Philistines and had gone up with them to their camp went over to the Israelites who were with Saul and Jonathan. [22]When all the Israelites who had hidden in the hill country of Ephraim heard that the Philistines were on the run, they joined the battle in hot pursuit. [23]So the LORD rescued Israel that day, and the battle moved on beyond Beth Aven.

Jonathan Eats Honey

[24]Now the men of Israel were in distress that day, because Saul had bound the

---

[a] 15 Or a terrible panic   [b] 18 Hebrew; Septuagint "Bring the ephod." (At that time he wore the ephod before the Israelites.)

GOING deeper

God Sees Our Heart Toward Him

READ AND CONSIDER: 1 SAMUEL 14:24-45

"Then Saul built an altar to the LORD; it was the first time he had done this" (1 Samuel 14:35).

What is your relationship with God *really* like?

That question needs to be answered because some people *appear* to have it all together spiritually. They serve in the church and do all the right things, but they don't have a true personal and life-giving relationship with Jesus.

Take Saul, for example. Handsome and strong. King of Israel. Chosen by God. Yet the Bible records here that Saul made an oath to not eat until he avenged his enemies. This may have looked God-honoring, but it was unwise and impulsive and left his army stranded without sustenance. Later, he built an altar to God, but this was the first time Saul had done this—the first time the king of God's people had done the most basic act of honoring God!

The next chapter takes us even deeper, for it tells how Saul imploded as a leader, becoming completely unable to follow God's explicit instructions. In the end, Samuel tells Saul: "Does the LORD delight in burnt offerings and sacrifices as much as in obeying the voice of the LORD? To obey is better than sacrifice, and to heed is better than the fat of rams" (1 Samuel 15:22).

We don't want to be the kind of people who love God with our words only. We don't want to obey Him just because we have to or because our church says we have to. We want to have hearts so full of love for God that we can't contain it. We want to obey God because we can't bear the thought of disappointing Him. We don't want to be the kind of people who pray only when things are rough. We want to eagerly anticipate time with God each day because we love Him and enjoy His presence. God knows the difference.

Always remember that God's love for you is far beyond what you can even imagine. Ask Him to fill your heart with that kind of love for Him in return.

people under an oath, saying, "Cursed be any man who eats food before evening comes, before I have avenged myself on my enemies!" So none of the troops tasted food.

²⁵The entire army[a] entered the woods, and there was honey on the ground. ²⁶When they went into the woods, they saw the honey oozing out, yet no one put his hand to his mouth, because they feared the oath. ²⁷But Jonathan had not heard that his father had bound the people with the oath, so he reached out the end of the staff that was in his hand and dipped it into the honeycomb. He raised his hand to his mouth, and his eyes brightened.[b] ²⁸Then one of the soldiers told him, "Your father bound the army under a strict oath, saying, 'Cursed be any man who eats food today!' That is why the men are faint."

²⁹Jonathan said, "My father has made trouble for the country. See how my eyes brightened[c] when I tasted a little of this honey. ³⁰How much better it would have been if the men had eaten today some of the plunder they took from their enemies. Would not the slaughter of the Philistines have been even greater?"

³¹That day, after the Israelites had struck down the Philistines from Micmash to Aijalon, they were exhausted. ³²They pounced on the plunder and, taking sheep, cattle and calves, they butchered them on the ground and ate them, together with the blood. ³³Then someone said to Saul, "Look, the men are sinning against the LORD by eating meat that has blood in it."

"You have broken faith," he said. "Roll a large stone over here at once." ³⁴Then he said, "Go out among the men and tell them, 'Each of you bring me your cattle and sheep, and slaughter them here and eat them. Do not sin against the LORD by eating meat with blood still in it.'"

So everyone brought his ox that night and slaughtered it there. ³⁵Then Saul built an altar to the LORD; it was the first time he had done this.

³⁶Saul said, "Let us go down after the Philistines by night and plunder them till dawn, and let us not leave one of them alive."

"Do whatever seems best to you," they replied.

But the priest said, "Let us inquire of God here."

³⁷So Saul asked God, "Shall I go down after the Philistines? Will you give them into Israel's hand?" But God did not answer him that day.

³⁸Saul therefore said, "Come here, all you who are leaders of the army, and let us find out what sin has been committed today. ³⁹As surely as the LORD who rescues Israel lives, even if it lies with my son Jonathan, he must die." But not one of the men said a word.

⁴⁰Saul then said to all the Israelites, "You stand over there; I and Jonathan my son will stand over here."

"Do what seems best to you," the men replied.

⁴¹Then Saul prayed to the LORD, the God of Israel, "Give me the right answer."[d] And Jonathan and Saul were taken by lot, and the men were cleared. ⁴²Saul said, "Cast the lot between me and Jonathan my son." And Jonathan was taken.

⁴³Then Saul said to Jonathan, "Tell me what you have done."

So Jonathan told him, "I merely tasted a little honey with the end of my staff. And now must I die?"

⁴⁴Saul said, "May God deal with me, be it ever so severely, if you do not die, Jonathan."

⁴⁵But the men said to Saul, "Should Jonathan die—he who has brought about this great deliverance in Israel? Never! As surely as the LORD lives, not a hair of his head will fall to the ground, for he did this today with God's help." So the men rescued Jonathan, and he was not put to death.

---

a 25 Or Now all the people of the land   b 27 Or his strength was renewed   c 29 Or my strength was renewed   d 41 Hebrew; Septuagint "Why have you not answered your servant today? If the fault is in me or my son Jonathan, respond with Urim, but if the men of Israel are at fault, respond with Thummim."

⁴⁶Then Saul stopped pursuing the Philistines, and they withdrew to their own land.

⁴⁷After Saul had assumed rule over Israel, he fought against their enemies on every side: Moab, the Ammonites, Edom, the kingsᵃ of Zobah, and the Philistines. Wherever he turned, he inflicted punishment on them.ᵇ ⁴⁸He fought valiantly and defeated the Amalekites, delivering Israel from the hands of those who had plundered them.

Saul's Family

⁴⁹Saul's sons were Jonathan, Ishvi and Malki-Shua. The name of his older daughter was Merab, and that of the younger was Michal. ⁵⁰His wife's name was Ahinoam daughter of Ahimaaz. The name of the commander of Saul's army was Abner son of Ner, and Ner was Saul's uncle. ⁵¹Saul's father Kish and Abner's father Ner were sons of Abiel.

⁵²All the days of Saul there was bitter war with the Philistines, and whenever Saul saw a mighty or brave man, he took him into his service.

The Lord Rejects Saul as King

15 Samuel said to Saul, "I am the one the Lord sent to anoint you king over his people Israel; so listen now to the message from the Lord. ²This is what the Lord Almighty says: 'I will punish the Amalekites for what they did to Israel when they waylaid them as they came up from Egypt. ³Now go, attack the Amalekites and totally destroyᶜ everything that belongs to them. Do not spare them; put to death men and women, children and infants, cattle and sheep, camels and donkeys.'"

⁴So Saul summoned the men and mustered them at Telaim—two hundred thousand foot soldiers and ten thousand men from Judah. ⁵Saul went to the city of Amalek and set an ambush in the ravine. ⁶Then he said to the Kenites, "Go

away, leave the Amalekites so that I do not destroy you along with them; for you showed kindness to all the Israelites when they came up out of Egypt." So the Kenites moved away from the Amalekites.

⁷Then Saul attacked the Amalekites all the way from Havilah to Shur, to the east of Egypt. ⁸He took Agag king of the Amalekites alive, and all his people he totally destroyed with the sword. ⁹But Saul and the army spared Agag and the best of the sheep and cattle, the fat calvesᵈ and lambs—everything that was good. These they were unwilling to destroy completely, but everything that was despised and weak they totally destroyed.

¹⁰Then the word of the Lord came to Samuel: ¹¹"I am grieved that I have made Saul king, because he has turned away from me and has not carried out my instructions." Samuel was troubled, and he cried out to the Lord all that night.

¹²Early in the morning Samuel got up and went to meet Saul, but he was told, "Saul has gone to Carmel. There he has set up a monument in his own honor and has turned and gone on down to Gilgal."

¹³When Samuel reached him, Saul said, "The Lord bless you! I have carried out the Lord's instructions."

¹⁴But Samuel said, "What then is this bleating of sheep in my ears? What is this lowing of cattle that I hear?"

¹⁵Saul answered, "The soldiers brought them from the Amalekites; they spared the best of the sheep and cattle to sacrifice to the Lord your God, but we totally destroyed the rest."

¹⁶"Stop!" Samuel said to Saul. "Let me tell you what the Lord said to me last night."

"Tell me," Saul replied.

¹⁷Samuel said, "Although you were once small in your own eyes, did you not become the head of the tribes of

ᵃ47 Masoretic Text; Dead Sea Scrolls and Septuagint king   ᵇ47 Hebrew; Septuagint he was victorious   ᶜ3 The Hebrew term refers to the irrevocable giving over of things or persons to the Lord, often by totally destroying them; also in verses 8, 9, 15, 18, 20 and 21.   ᵈ9 Or the grown bulls; the meaning of the Hebrew for this phrase is uncertain.

Israel? The Lord anointed you king over Israel. [18]And he sent you on a mission, saying, 'Go and completely destroy those wicked people, the Amalekites; make war on them until you have wiped them out.' [19]Why did you not obey the Lord? Why did you pounce on the plunder and do evil in the eyes of the Lord?"

[20]"But I did obey the Lord," Saul said. "I went on the mission the Lord assigned me. I completely destroyed the Amalekites and brought back Agag their king. [21]The soldiers took sheep and cattle from the plunder, the best of what was devoted to God, in order to sacrifice them to the Lord your God at Gilgal."

> *Praying 1 Samuel 15:22-23*
> *Help me to always obey You, Lord, and*
> *let no rebelliousness be found in me.*

[22]But Samuel replied:

"Does the Lord delight in burnt offerings and sacrifices
    as much as in obeying the voice of the Lord?
To obey is better than sacrifice,
    and to heed is better than the fat of rams.
[23]For rebellion is like the sin of divination,
    and arrogance like the evil of idolatry.
Because you have rejected the word of the Lord,
    he has rejected you as king."

[24]Then Saul said to Samuel, "I have sinned. I violated the Lord's command and your instructions. I was afraid of the people and so I gave in to them. [25]Now I beg you, forgive my sin and come back with me, so that I may worship the Lord."

[26]But Samuel said to him, "I will not go back with you. You have rejected the word of the Lord, and the Lord has rejected you as king over Israel!"

[27]As Samuel turned to leave, Saul caught hold of the hem of his robe, and it tore. [28]Samuel said to him, "The Lord has torn the kingdom of Israel from you today and has given it to one of your neighbors—to one better than you. [29]He who is the Glory of Israel does not lie or change his mind; for he is not a man, that he should change his mind."

[30]Saul replied, "I have sinned. But please honor me before the elders of my people and before Israel; come back with me, so that I may worship the Lord your God." [31]So Samuel went back with Saul, and Saul worshiped the Lord.

[32]Then Samuel said, "Bring me Agag king of the Amalekites."

Agag came to him confidently,[a] thinking, "Surely the bitterness of death is past."

[33]But Samuel said,

"As your sword has made women childless,
    so will your mother be childless among women."

And Samuel put Agag to death before the Lord at Gilgal.

[34]Then Samuel left for Ramah, but Saul went up to his home in Gibeah of Saul. [35]Until the day Samuel died, he did not go to see Saul again, though Samuel mourned for him. And the Lord was grieved that he had made Saul king over Israel.

Samuel Anoints David

16 The Lord said to Samuel, "How long will you mourn for Saul, since I have rejected him as king over Israel? Fill your horn with oil and be on your way; I am sending you to Jesse of Bethlehem. I have chosen one of his sons to be king."

[2]But Samuel said, "How can I go? Saul will hear about it and kill me."

The Lord said, "Take a heifer with you and say, 'I have come to sacrifice to the Lord.' [3]Invite Jesse to the sacrifice,

---

[a] 32 Or *him trembling, yet*

and I will show you what to do. You are to anoint for me the one I indicate."

⁴Samuel did what the LORD said. When he arrived at Bethlehem, the elders of the town trembled when they met him. They asked, "Do you come in peace?"

⁵Samuel replied, "Yes, in peace; I have come to sacrifice to the LORD. Consecrate yourselves and come to the sacrifice with me." Then he consecrated Jesse and his sons and invited them to the sacrifice.

⁶When they arrived, Samuel saw Eliab and thought, "Surely the LORD's anointed stands here before the LORD."

⁷But the LORD said to Samuel, "Do not consider his appearance or his height, for I have rejected him. The LORD does not look at the things man looks at. Man looks at the outward appearance, but the LORD looks at the heart."

⁸Then Jesse called Abinadab and had him pass in front of Samuel. But Samuel said, "The LORD has not chosen this one either." ⁹Jesse then had Shammah pass by, but Samuel said, "Nor has the LORD chosen this one." ¹⁰Jesse had seven of his sons pass before Samuel, but Samuel said to him, "The LORD has not chosen these." ¹¹So he asked Jesse, "Are these all the sons you have?"

"There is still the youngest," Jesse answered, "but he is tending the sheep."

Samuel said, "Send for him; we will not sit down^a until he arrives."

¹²So he sent and had him brought in.

---

^a *11* Some Septuagint manuscripts; Hebrew *not gather around*

GOING *deeper*

God Looks on Your Heart

READ AND CONSIDER: 1 SAMUEL 16:1-13

"But the LORD said to Samuel, 'Do not consider his appearance or his height, for I have rejected him. The LORD does not look at the things man looks at. Man looks at the outward appearance, but the LORD looks at the heart'" (1 Samuel 16:7).

Isn't it comforting to know that God does not judge us in the same way that other people often judge us? Or even in the harsh way in which we sometimes judge ourselves? God is concerned with what is in our hearts. That means He cares about our thoughts, passions, attitudes, and whether we trust in Him and love His ways. He does not place value on our outward looks, social status, financial standing, or any other external measure that the world considers so important.

God's selection of David—someone known as a man after God's own heart—demonstrates God's emphasis on internal rather than external characteristics. David's status in his family was so low that he wasn't even called in to meet with Samuel. He was merely the youngest son, out in the fields tending the sheep. However, David was God's choice to be the king of Israel, to perform great deeds, and to be part of the family line that would produce the Savior whom God would provide for Israel. Clearly, God did not see David in the same way that even his own family saw him.

What is God seeing in your heart today? Take a heart inventory right now. First, pray that God would reveal and then remove anything in your heart that doesn't belong there—resentments, anger, sinful thoughts. Second, pray for big things, knowing that if God can use a young shepherd boy, He can use anyone in a big way! Make your heart available to God's power and see what amazing things He will do through you.

He was ruddy, with a fine appearance and handsome features.

Then the LORD said, "Rise and anoint him; he is the one."

¹³So Samuel took the horn of oil and anointed him in the presence of his brothers, and from that day on the Spirit of the LORD came upon David in power. Samuel then went to Ramah.

David in Saul's Service

¹⁴Now the Spirit of the LORD had departed from Saul, and an evil[a] spirit from the LORD tormented him.

¹⁵Saul's attendants said to him, "See, an evil spirit from God is tormenting you. ¹⁶Let our lord command his servants here to search for someone who can play the harp. He will play when the evil spirit from God comes upon you, and you will feel better."

¹⁷So Saul said to his attendants, "Find someone who plays well and bring him to me."

¹⁸One of the servants answered, "I have seen a son of Jesse of Bethlehem who knows how to play the harp. He is a brave man and a warrior. He speaks well and is a fine-looking man. And the LORD is with him."

¹⁹Then Saul sent messengers to Jesse and said, "Send me your son David, who is with the sheep." ²⁰So Jesse took a donkey loaded with bread, a skin of wine and a young goat and sent them with his son David to Saul.

²¹David came to Saul and entered his service. Saul liked him very much, and David became one of his armor-bearers. ²²Then Saul sent word to Jesse, saying, "Allow David to remain in my service, for I am pleased with him."

²³Whenever the spirit from God came upon Saul, David would take his harp and play. Then relief would come to Saul; he would feel better, and the evil spirit would leave him.

David and Goliath

17 Now the Philistines gathered their forces for war and assembled at Socoh in Judah. They pitched camp at Ephes Dammim, between Socoh and Azekah. ²Saul and the Israelites assembled and camped in the Valley of Elah and drew up their battle line to meet the Philistines. ³The Philistines occupied one hill and the Israelites another, with the valley between them.

⁴A champion named Goliath, who was from Gath, came out of the Philistine camp. He was over nine feet[b] tall. ⁵He had a bronze helmet on his head and wore a coat of scale armor of bronze weighing five thousand shekels[c]; ⁶on his legs he wore bronze greaves, and a bronze javelin was slung on his back. ⁷His spear shaft was like a weaver's rod, and its iron point weighed six hundred shekels.[d] His shield bearer went ahead of him.

⁸Goliath stood and shouted to the ranks of Israel, "Why do you come out and line up for battle? Am I not a Philistine, and are you not the servants of Saul? Choose a man and have him come down to me. ⁹If he is able to fight and kill me, we will become your subjects; but if I overcome him and kill him, you will become our subjects and serve us." ¹⁰Then the Philistine said, "This day I defy the ranks of Israel! Give me a man and let us fight each other." ¹¹On hearing the Philistine's words, Saul and all the Israelites were dismayed and terrified.

¹²Now David was the son of an Ephrathite named Jesse, who was from Bethlehem in Judah. Jesse had eight sons, and in Saul's time he was old and well advanced in years. ¹³Jesse's three oldest sons had followed Saul to the war: The firstborn was Eliab; the second, Abinadab; and the third, Shammah. ¹⁴David was the youngest. The three oldest followed Saul, ¹⁵but David went back and forth from Saul to tend his father's sheep at Bethlehem.

---

a 14 Or *injurious*; also in verses 15, 16 and 23   b 4 Hebrew *was six cubits and a span* (about 3 meters)   c 5 That is, about 125 pounds (about 57 kilograms)   d 7 That is, about 15 pounds (about 7 kilograms)

¹⁶For forty days the Philistine came forward every morning and evening and took his stand.

¹⁷Now Jesse said to his son David, "Take this ephah[a] of roasted grain and these ten loaves of bread for your brothers and hurry to their camp. ¹⁸Take along these ten cheeses to the commander of their unit.[b] See how your brothers are and bring back some assurance[c] from them. ¹⁹They are with Saul and all the men of Israel in the Valley of Elah, fighting against the Philistines."

²⁰Early in the morning David left the flock with a shepherd, loaded up and set out, as Jesse had directed. He reached the camp as the army was going out to its battle positions, shouting the war cry. ²¹Israel and the Philistines were drawing up their lines facing each other. ²²David left his things with the keeper of supplies, ran to the battle lines and greeted his brothers. ²³As he was talking with them, Goliath, the Philistine champion from Gath, stepped out from his lines and shouted his usual defiance, and David heard it. ²⁴When the Israelites saw the man, they all ran from him in great fear.

²⁵Now the Israelites had been saying, "Do you see how this man keeps coming out? He comes out to defy Israel. The king will give great wealth to the man who kills him. He will also give him his daughter in marriage and will exempt his father's family from taxes in Israel."

²⁶David asked the men standing near him, "What will be done for the man who kills this Philistine and removes this disgrace from Israel? Who is this uncircumcised Philistine that he should defy the armies of the living God?"

²⁷They repeated to him what they had been saying and told him, "This is what will be done for the man who kills him."

²⁸When Eliab, David's oldest brother, heard him speaking with the men, he burned with anger at him and asked, "Why have you come down here? And with whom did you leave those few sheep in the desert? I know how conceited you are and how wicked your heart is; you came down only to watch the battle."

²⁹"Now what have I done?" said David. "Can't I even speak?" ³⁰He then turned away to someone else and brought up the same matter, and the men answered him as before. ³¹What David said was overheard and reported to Saul, and Saul sent for him.

³²David said to Saul, "Let no one lose heart on account of this Philistine; your servant will go and fight him."

³³Saul replied, "You are not able to go out against this Philistine and fight him; you are only a boy, and he has been a fighting man from his youth."

³⁴But David said to Saul, "Your servant has been keeping his father's sheep. When a lion or a bear came and carried off a sheep from the flock, ³⁵I went after it, struck it and rescued the sheep from its mouth. When it turned on me, I seized it by its hair, struck it and killed it. ³⁶Your servant has killed both the lion and the bear; this uncircumcised Philistine will be like one of them, because he has defied the armies of the living God. ³⁷The LORD who delivered me from the paw of the lion and the paw of the bear will deliver me from the hand of this Philistine."

Saul said to David, "Go, and the LORD be with you."

³⁸Then Saul dressed David in his own tunic. He put a coat of armor on him and a bronze helmet on his head. ³⁹David fastened on his sword over the tunic and tried walking around, because he was not used to them.

"I cannot go in these," he said to Saul, "because I am not used to them." So he took them off. ⁴⁰Then he took his staff in his hand, chose five smooth stones from the stream, put them in the pouch of his shepherd's bag and, with his sling in his hand, approached the Philistine.

⁴¹Meanwhile, the Philistine, with his

---

[a] 17 That is, probably about 3/5 bushel (about 22 liters)   [b] 18 Hebrew *thousand*   [c] 18 Or *some token; or some pledge of spoils*

shield bearer in front of him, kept coming closer to David. 42He looked David over and saw that he was only a boy, ruddy and handsome, and he despised him. 43He said to David, "Am I a dog, that you come at me with sticks?" And the Philistine cursed David by his gods. 44"Come here," he said, "and I'll give your flesh to the birds of the air and the beasts of the field!"

45David said to the Philistine, "You come against me with sword and spear and javelin, but I come against you in the name of the LORD Almighty, the God of the armies of Israel, whom you have defied. 46This day the LORD will hand you over to me, and I'll strike you down and cut off your head. Today I will give the carcasses of the Philistine army to the birds of the air and the beasts of the earth, and the whole world will know that there is a God in Israel. 47All those gathered here will know that it is not by sword or spear that the LORD saves; for the battle is the LORD's, and he will give all of you into our hands."

48As the Philistine moved closer to attack him, David ran quickly toward the battle line to meet him. 49Reaching into his bag and taking out a stone, he slung it and struck the Philistine on the forehead. The stone sank into his forehead, and he fell facedown on the ground.

50So David triumphed over the Philistine with a sling and a stone; without a sword in his hand he struck down the Philistine and killed him.

51David ran and stood over him. He took hold of the Philistine's sword and drew it from the scabbard. After he killed him, he cut off his head with the sword.

When the Philistines saw that their hero was dead, they turned and ran. 52Then the men of Israel and Judah surged forward with a shout and pursued the Philistines to the entrance of Gath[a] and to the gates of Ekron. Their dead were strewn along the Shaaraim road to Gath and Ekron. 53When the Israelites returned from chasing the Philistines, they plundered their camp. 54David took the Philistine's head and brought it to Jerusalem, and he put the Philistine's weapons in his own tent.

55As Saul watched David going out to meet the Philistine, he said to Abner, commander of the army, "Abner, whose son is that young man?"

Abner replied, "As surely as you live, O king, I don't know."

56The king said, "Find out whose son this young man is."

57As soon as David returned from killing the Philistine, Abner took him and brought him before Saul, with David still holding the Philistine's head.

58"Whose son are you, young man?" Saul asked him.

David said, "I am the son of your servant Jesse of Bethlehem."

Saul's Jealousy of David

18 After David had finished talking with Saul, Jonathan became one in spirit with David, and he loved him as himself. 2From that day Saul kept David with him and did not let him return to his father's house. 3And Jonathan made a covenant with David because he loved him as himself. 4Jonathan took off the robe he was wearing and gave it to David, along with his tunic, and even his sword, his bow and his belt.

5Whatever Saul sent him to do, David did it so successfully[b] that Saul gave him a high rank in the army. This pleased all the people, and Saul's officers as well.

6When the men were returning home after David had killed the Philistine, the women came out from all the towns of Israel to meet King Saul with singing and dancing, with joyful songs and with tambourines and lutes. 7As they danced, they sang:

"Saul has slain his thousands,
and David his tens of thousands."

---

a 52 Some Septuagint manuscripts; Hebrew a valley   b 5 Or wisely

When Life Is Overwhelming

At some point in each of our lives, we may find our world being violently shaken. Such traumatic experiences as a devastating illness, a debilitating accident, desertion by a spouse, the death of a loved one, criminal violence, financial ruin, or a natural disaster can occur with disarming suddenness. How can we be prepared to stand strong in the midst of overwhelming circumstances that come without warning?

Circumstances don't have to be catastrophic to be overwhelming. Some people view public speaking as a terrifying experience. They would rather endure an earthquake. For others, confronting a difficult person, having to make a dreaded phone call, or facing the daily challenge of an eating disorder or an addiction are earthshaking challenges. Many people are overwhelmed by raising children, handling the responsibilities of life, or dealing with a strong-willed teenager.

Sometimes the pileup of many little things— each one alone being relatively harmless— becomes more than we can handle. Such things as stress in the workplace, pressure at school, uncomfortable social situations, or anything else that involves expectations we feel we can't live up to, can fill us with unbearable anxiety. No matter what the specifics, the key to overcoming these kinds of overwhelming circumstances is to walk step-by-step with God through them. When we set our anchor in the Lord, we will not be carried away by the storms that threaten to overtake us.

Godly people throughout the Bible, and anyone since who has not lost touch with reality, have all gone through times of being overwhelmed and fearful. Yet being afraid doesn't mean that God is not with you, or that you are out of God's will, or that you are a spiritual weakling. If fear comes upon you without any apparent reason, ask God to show you what it means and where it is coming from. It may be a signal from the Lord to pray.

Any sign of fear should always be a call to prayer. The moment you feel it, draw *immediately* close to God. Get a sense of His presence and leading and allow His love to fully penetrate your situation. Perfect love casts out all fear, but thank God it's not *our* love that has to be perfect. Only *His* love is. The deeper we press into the Lord, the more of His perfect love we experience and the less fear we will have.

When your whole life is shaken, when the circumstances you face are so overwhelming that you feel like an ant in the face of Mount Everest, look to God and see *His* awesome power. Stand before the mountain and say, "Lord, where I am right now I declare to be holy ground. I invite You to reign in this situation, for You are greater than anything I am facing." Sense that His presence is with you to give you peace. There in the darkness of your earthshaking circumstances, reach up to God and know that His mighty hand can reach forth to yours faster than the speed of light.

For the next "From Stormie's Heart" article, go to page 391.

⁸Saul was very angry; this refrain galled him. "They have credited David with tens of thousands," he thought, "but me with only thousands. What more can he get but the kingdom?" ⁹And from that time on Saul kept a jealous eye on David.

¹⁰The next day an evilᵃ spirit from God came forcefully upon Saul. He was prophesying in his house, while David was playing the harp, as he usually did. Saul had a spear in his hand ¹¹and he hurled it, saying to himself, "I'll pin David to the wall." But David eluded him twice.

¹²Saul was afraid of David, because the LORD was with David but had left Saul. ¹³So he sent David away from him and gave him command over a thousand men, and David led the troops in their campaigns. ¹⁴In everything he did he had great success,ᵇ because the LORD was with him. ¹⁵When Saul saw how successfulᶜ he was, he was afraid of him. ¹⁶But all Israel and Judah loved David, because he led them in their campaigns.

¹⁷Saul said to David, "Here is my older daughter Merab. I will give her to you in marriage; only serve me bravely and fight the battles of the LORD." For Saul said to himself, "I will not raise a hand against him. Let the Philistines do that!"

¹⁸But David said to Saul, "Who am I, and what is my family or my father's clan in Israel, that I should become the king's son-in-law?" ¹⁹Soᵈ when the time came for Merab, Saul's daughter, to be given to David, she was given in marriage to Adriel of Meholah.

²⁰Now Saul's daughter Michal was in love with David, and when they told Saul about it, he was pleased. ²¹"I will give her to him," he thought, "so that she may be a snare to him and so that the hand of the Philistines may be against him." So Saul said to David, "Now you have a second opportunity to become my son-in-law."

²²Then Saul ordered his attendants: "Speak to David privately and say, 'Look, the king is pleased with you, and his attendants all like you; now become his son-in-law.'"

²³They repeated these words to David. But David said, "Do you think it is a small matter to become the king's son-in-law? I'm only a poor man and little known."

²⁴When Saul's servants told him what David had said, ²⁵Saul replied, "Say to David, 'The king wants no other price for the bride than a hundred Philistine foreskins, to take revenge on his enemies.'" Saul's plan was to have David fall by the hands of the Philistines.

²⁶When the attendants told David these things, he was pleased to become the king's son-in-law. So before the allotted time elapsed, ²⁷David and his men went out and killed two hundred Philistines. He brought their foreskins and presented the full number to the king so that he might become the king's son-in-law. Then Saul gave him his daughter Michal in marriage.

²⁸When Saul realized that the LORD was with David and that his daughter Michal loved David, ²⁹Saul became still more afraid of him, and he remained his enemy the rest of his days.

³⁰The Philistine commanders continued to go out to battle, and as often as they did, David met with more successᵉ than the rest of Saul's officers, and his name became well known.

Saul Tries to Kill David

19 Saul told his son Jonathan and all the attendants to kill David. But Jonathan was very fond of David ²and warned him, "My father Saul is looking for a chance to kill you. Be on your guard tomorrow morning; go into hiding and stay there. ³I will go out and stand with my father in the field where you are. I'll speak to him about you and will tell you what I find out."

⁴Jonathan spoke well of David to Saul his father and said to him, "Let not the king do wrong to his servant David; he

has not wronged you, and what he has done has benefited you greatly. ⁵He took his life in his hands when he killed the Philistine. The LORD won a great victory for all Israel, and you saw it and were glad. Why then would you do wrong to an innocent man like David by killing him for no reason?"

⁶Saul listened to Jonathan and took this oath: "As surely as the LORD lives, David will not be put to death."

⁷So Jonathan called David and told him the whole conversation. He brought him to Saul, and David was with Saul as before.

⁸Once more war broke out, and David went out and fought the Philistines. He struck them with such force that they fled before him.

⁹But an evil^a spirit from the LORD came upon Saul as he was sitting in his house with his spear in his hand. While David was playing the harp, ¹⁰Saul tried to pin him to the wall with his spear, but David eluded him as Saul drove the spear into the wall. That night David made good his escape.

¹¹Saul sent men to David's house to watch it and to kill him in the morning. But Michal, David's wife, warned him, "If you don't run for your life tonight, tomorrow you'll be killed." ¹²So Michal let David down through a window, and he fled and escaped. ¹³Then Michal took an idol^b and laid it on the bed, covering it with a garment and putting some goats' hair at the head.

¹⁴When Saul sent the men to capture David, Michal said, "He is ill."

¹⁵Then Saul sent the men back to see David and told them, "Bring him up to me in his bed so that I may kill him." ¹⁶But when the men entered, there was the idol in the bed, and at the head was some goats' hair.

¹⁷Saul said to Michal, "Why did you deceive me like this and send my enemy away so that he escaped?"

Michal told him, "He said to me, 'Let me get away. Why should I kill you?'"

¹⁸When David had fled and made his escape, he went to Samuel at Ramah and told him all that Saul had done to him. Then he and Samuel went to Naioth and stayed there. ¹⁹Word came to Saul: "David is in Naioth at Ramah"; ²⁰so he sent men to capture him. But when they saw a group of prophets prophesying, with Samuel standing there as their leader, the Spirit of God came upon Saul's men and they also prophesied. ²¹Saul was told about it, and he sent more men, and they prophesied too. Saul sent men a third time, and they also prophesied. ²²Finally, he himself left for Ramah and went to the great cistern at Secu. And he asked, "Where are Samuel and David?"

"Over in Naioth at Ramah," they said.

²³So Saul went to Naioth at Ramah. But the Spirit of God came even upon him, and he walked along prophesying until he came to Naioth. ²⁴He stripped off his robes and also prophesied in Samuel's presence. He lay that way all that day and night. This is why people say, "Is Saul also among the prophets?"

David and Jonathan

20 Then David fled from Naioth at Ramah and went to Jonathan and asked, "What have I done? What is my crime? How have I wronged your father, that he is trying to take my life?"

²"Never!" Jonathan replied. "You are not going to die! Look, my father doesn't do anything, great or small, without confiding in me. Why would he hide this from me? It's not so!"

³But David took an oath and said, "Your father knows very well that I have found favor in your eyes, and he has said to himself, 'Jonathan must not know this or he will be grieved.' Yet as surely as the LORD lives and as you live, there is only a step between me and death."

⁴Jonathan said to David, "Whatever you want me to do, I'll do for you."

---

^a 9 Or *injurious*   ^b 13 Hebrew *teraphim*; also in verse 16

⁵So David said, "Look, tomorrow is the New Moon festival, and I am supposed to dine with the king; but let me go and hide in the field until the evening of the day after tomorrow. ⁶If your father misses me at all, tell him, 'David earnestly asked my permission to hurry to Bethlehem, his hometown, because an annual sacrifice is being made there for his whole clan.' ⁷If he says, 'Very well,' then your servant is safe. But if he loses his temper, you can be sure that he is determined to harm me. ⁸As for you, show kindness to your servant, for you have brought him into a covenant with you before the LORD. If I am guilty, then kill me yourself! Why hand me over to your father?"

Prayer is . . .

asking God to touch the lives of other people and the situations that affect them.

⁹"Never!" Jonathan said. "If I had the least inkling that my father was determined to harm you, wouldn't I tell you?"

¹⁰David asked, "Who will tell me if your father answers you harshly?"

¹¹"Come," Jonathan said, "let's go out into the field." So they went there together.

¹²Then Jonathan said to David: "By the LORD, the God of Israel, I will surely sound out my father by this time the day after tomorrow! If he is favorably disposed toward you, will I not send you word and let you know? ¹³But if my father is inclined to harm you, may the LORD deal with me, be it ever so severely, if I do not let you know and send you away safely. May the LORD be with you as he has been with my father. ¹⁴But show me unfailing kindness like that of the LORD as

long as I live, so that I may not be killed, ¹⁵and do not ever cut off your kindness from my family—not even when the LORD has cut off every one of David's enemies from the face of the earth."

¹⁶So Jonathan made a covenant with the house of David, saying, "May the LORD call David's enemies to account." ¹⁷And Jonathan had David reaffirm his oath out of love for him, because he loved him as he loved himself.

¹⁸Then Jonathan said to David: "Tomorrow is the New Moon festival. You will be missed, because your seat will be empty. ¹⁹The day after tomorrow, toward evening, go to the place where you hid when this trouble began, and wait by the stone Ezel. ²⁰I will shoot three arrows to the side of it, as though I were shooting at a target. ²¹Then I will send a boy and say, 'Go, find the arrows.' If I say to him, 'Look, the arrows are on this side of you; bring them here,' then come, because, as surely as the LORD lives, you are safe; there is no danger. ²²But if I say to the boy, 'Look, the arrows are beyond you,' then you must go, because the LORD has sent you away. ²³And about the matter you and I discussed—remember, the LORD is witness between you and me forever."

²⁴So David hid in the field, and when the New Moon festival came, the king sat down to eat. ²⁵He sat in his customary place by the wall, opposite Jonathan,ᵃ and Abner sat next to Saul, but David's place was empty. ²⁶Saul said nothing that day, for he thought, "Something must have happened to David to make him ceremonially unclean—surely he is unclean." ²⁷But the next day, the second day of the month, David's place was empty again. Then Saul said to his son Jonathan, "Why hasn't the son of Jesse come to the meal, either yesterday or today?"

²⁸Jonathan answered, "David earnestly asked me for permission to go to Bethlehem. ²⁹He said, 'Let me go, because our family is observing a sacrifice in the

---

ᵃ 25 Septuagint; Hebrew *wall. Jonathan arose*

town and my brother has ordered me to be there. If I have found favor in your eyes, let me get away to see my brothers.' That is why he has not come to the king's table."

30Saul's anger flared up at Jonathan and he said to him, "You son of a perverse and rebellious woman! Don't I know that you have sided with the son of Jesse to your own shame and to the shame of the mother who bore you? 31As long as the son of Jesse lives on this earth, neither you nor your kingdom will be established. Now send and bring him to me, for he must die!"

32"Why should he be put to death? What has he done?" Jonathan asked his father. 33But Saul hurled his spear at him to kill him. Then Jonathan knew that his father intended to kill David.

34Jonathan got up from the table in fierce anger; on that second day of the month he did not eat, because he was grieved at his father's shameful treatment of David.

35In the morning Jonathan went out to the field for his meeting with David. He had a small boy with him, 36and he said to the boy, "Run and find the arrows I shoot." As the boy ran, he shot an arrow beyond him. 37When the boy came to the place where Jonathan's arrow had fallen, Jonathan called out after him, "Isn't the arrow beyond you?" 38Then he shouted, "Hurry! Go quickly! Don't stop!" The boy picked up the arrow and returned to his master. 39(The boy knew nothing of all this; only Jonathan and David knew.) 40Then Jonathan gave his weapons to the boy and said, "Go, carry them back to town."

41After the boy had gone, David got up from the south side ⌊of the stone⌋ and bowed down before Jonathan three times, with his face to the ground. Then they kissed each other and wept together— but David wept the most.

42Jonathan said to David, "Go in peace, for we have sworn friendship with each other in the name of the LORD, saying, 'The LORD is witness between you and me, and between your descendants and my descendants forever.'" Then David left, and Jonathan went back to the town.

David at Nob

21 David went to Nob, to Ahimelech the priest. Ahimelech trembled when he met him, and asked, "Why are you alone? Why is no one with you?"

2David answered Ahimelech the priest, "The king charged me with a certain matter and said to me, 'No one is to know anything about your mission and your instructions.' As for my men, I have told them to meet me at a certain place. 3Now then, what do you have on hand? Give me five loaves of bread, or whatever you can find."

4But the priest answered David, "I don't have any ordinary bread on hand; however, there is some consecrated bread here—provided the men have kept themselves from women."

5David replied, "Indeed women have been kept from us, as usual whenever[a] I set out. The men's things[b] are holy even on missions that are not holy. How much more so today!" 6So the priest gave him the consecrated bread, since there was no bread there except the bread of the Presence that had been removed from before the LORD and replaced by hot bread on the day it was taken away.

7Now one of Saul's servants was there that day, detained before the LORD; he was Doeg the Edomite, Saul's head shepherd.

8David asked Ahimelech, "Don't you have a spear or a sword here? I haven't brought my sword or any other weapon, because the king's business was urgent."

9The priest replied, "The sword of Goliath the Philistine, whom you killed in the Valley of Elah, is here; it is wrapped in a cloth behind the ephod. If you want it, take it; there is no sword here but that one."

---

a 5 Or from us in the past few days since   b 5 Or bodies

David said, "There is none like it; give it to me."

David at Gath

[10] That day David fled from Saul and went to Achish king of Gath. [11] But the servants of Achish said to him, "Isn't this David, the king of the land? Isn't he the one they sing about in their dances:

"'Saul has slain his thousands,
and David his tens of thousands'?"

[12] David took these words to heart and was very much afraid of Achish king of Gath. [13] So he pretended to be insane in their presence; and while he was in their hands he acted like a madman, making marks on the doors of the gate and letting saliva run down his beard.

[14] Achish said to his servants, "Look at the man! He is insane! Why bring him to me? [15] Am I so short of madmen that you have to bring this fellow here to carry on like this in front of me? Must this man come into my house?"

David at Adullam and Mizpah

22 David left Gath and escaped to the cave of Adullam. When his brothers and his father's household heard about it, they went down to him there. [2] All those who were in distress or in debt or discontented gathered around him, and he became their leader. About four hundred men were with him.

[3] From there David went to Mizpah in Moab and said to the king of Moab, "Would you let my father and mother come and stay with you until I learn what God will do for me?" [4] So he left them with the king of Moab, and they stayed with him as long as David was in the stronghold.

[5] But the prophet Gad said to David, "Do not stay in the stronghold. Go into the land of Judah." So David left and went to the forest of Hereth.

Saul Kills the Priests of Nob

[6] Now Saul heard that David and his men had been discovered. And Saul, spear in hand, was seated under the tamarisk tree on the hill at Gibeah, with all his officials standing around him. [7] Saul said to them, "Listen, men of Benjamin! Will the son of Jesse give all of you fields and vineyards? Will he make all of you commanders of thousands and commanders of hundreds? [8] Is that why you have all conspired against me? No one tells me when my son makes a covenant with the son of Jesse. None of you is concerned about me or tells me that my son has incited my servant to lie in wait for me, as he does today."

[9] But Doeg the Edomite, who was standing with Saul's officials, said, "I saw the son of Jesse come to Ahimelech son of Ahitub at Nob. [10] Ahimelech inquired of the LORD for him; he also gave him provisions and the sword of Goliath the Philistine."

[11] Then the king sent for the priest Ahimelech son of Ahitub and his father's whole family, who were the priests at Nob, and they all came to the king. [12] Saul said, "Listen now, son of Ahitub."

"Yes, my lord," he answered.

[13] Saul said to him, "Why have you conspired against me, you and the son of Jesse, giving him bread and a sword and inquiring of God for him, so that he has rebelled against me and lies in wait for me, as he does today?"

[14] Ahimelech answered the king, "Who of all your servants is as loyal as David, the king's son-in-law, captain of your bodyguard and highly respected in your household? [15] Was that day the first time I inquired of God for him? Of course not! Let not the king accuse your servant or any of his father's family, for your servant knows nothing at all about this whole affair."

[16] But the king said, "You will surely die, Ahimelech, you and your father's whole family."

[17] Then the king ordered the guards at his side: "Turn and kill the priests of the LORD, because they too have sided with

David. They knew he was fleeing, yet they did not tell me."

But the king's officials were not willing to raise a hand to strike the priests of the LORD.

18The king then ordered Doeg, "You turn and strike down the priests." So Doeg the Edomite turned and struck them down. That day he killed eighty-five men who wore the linen ephod. 19He also put to the sword Nob, the town of the priests, with its men and women, its children and infants, and its cattle, donkeys and sheep.

20But Abiathar, a son of Ahimelech son of Ahitub, escaped and fled to join David. 21He told David that Saul had killed the priests of the LORD. 22Then David said to Abiathar: "That day, when Doeg the Edomite was there, I knew he would be sure to tell Saul. I am responsible for the death of your father's whole family. 23Stay with me; don't be afraid; the man who is seeking your life is seeking mine also. You will be safe with me."

David Saves Keilah

23 When David was told, "Look, the Philistines are fighting against Keilah and are looting the threshing floors," 2he inquired of the LORD, saying, "Shall I go and attack these Philistines?"

The LORD answered him, "Go, attack the Philistines and save Keilah."

3But David's men said to him, "Here in Judah we are afraid. How much more, then, if we go to Keilah against the Philistine forces!"

4Once again David inquired of the LORD, and the LORD answered him, "Go down to Keilah, for I am going to give the Philistines into your hand." 5So David and his men went to Keilah, fought the Philistines and carried off their livestock. He inflicted heavy losses on the Philistines and saved the people of Keilah. 6(Now Abiathar son of Ahimelech had brought the ephod down with him when he fled to David at Keilah.)

Saul Pursues David

7Saul was told that David had gone to Keilah, and he said, "God has handed him over to me, for David has imprisoned himself by entering a town with gates and bars." 8And Saul called up all his forces for battle, to go down to Keilah to besiege David and his men.

9When David learned that Saul was plotting against him, he said to Abiathar the priest, "Bring the ephod." 10David said, "O LORD, God of Israel, your servant has heard definitely that Saul plans to come to Keilah and destroy the town on account of me. 11Will the citizens of Keilah surrender me to him? Will Saul come down, as your servant has heard? O LORD, God of Israel, tell your servant."

And the LORD said, "He will."

12Again David asked, "Will the citizens of Keilah surrender me and my men to Saul?"

And the LORD said, "They will."

13So David and his men, about six hundred in number, left Keilah and kept moving from place to place. When Saul was told that David had escaped from Keilah, he did not go there.

Praying 1 Samuel 23:4

Father God, help me to always remember to ask You about where I should go and what I should do, and not assume I know the answer.

14David stayed in the desert strongholds and in the hills of the Desert of Ziph. Day after day Saul searched for him, but God did not give David into his hands.

15While David was at Horesh in the Desert of Ziph, he learned that Saul had come out to take his life. 16And Saul's son Jonathan went to David at Horesh and helped him find strength in God. 17"Don't be afraid," he said. "My father Saul will not lay a hand on you. You will be king over Israel, and I will be second to you. Even my father Saul knows this." 18The two of them made a covenant before the LORD. Then Jonathan went home, but David remained at Horesh.

¹⁹The Ziphites went up to Saul at Gibeah and said, "Is not David hiding among us in the strongholds at Horesh, on the hill of Hakilah, south of Jeshimon? ²⁰Now, O king, come down whenever it pleases you to do so, and we will be responsible for handing him over to the king."

²¹Saul replied, "The LORD bless you for your concern for me. ²²Go and make further preparation. Find out where David usually goes and who has seen him there. They tell me he is very crafty. ²³Find out about all the hiding places he uses and come back to me with definite information.ᵃ Then I will go with you; if he is in the area, I will track him down among all the clans of Judah."

²⁴So they set out and went to Ziph ahead of Saul. Now David and his men were in the Desert of Maon, in the Arabah south of Jeshimon. ²⁵Saul and his men began the search, and when David was told about it, he went down to the rock and stayed in the Desert of Maon. When Saul heard this, he went into the Desert of Maon in pursuit of David.

²⁶Saul was going along one side of the mountain, and David and his men were on the other side, hurrying to get away from Saul. As Saul and his forces were closing in on David and his men to capture them, ²⁷a messenger came to Saul, saying, "Come quickly! The Philistines are raiding the land." ²⁸Then Saul broke off his pursuit of David and went to meet the Philistines. That is why they call this place Sela Hammahlekoth.ᵇ ²⁹And David went up from there and lived in the strongholds of En Gedi.

David Spares Saul's Life

24 After Saul returned from pursuing the Philistines, he was told, "David is in the Desert of En Gedi." ²So Saul took three thousand chosen men from all Israel and set out to look for David and his men near the Crags of the Wild Goats.

³He came to the sheep pens along the way; a cave was there, and Saul went in to relieve himself. David and his men were far back in the cave. ⁴The men said, "This is the day the LORD spoke of when he saidᶜ to you, 'I will give your enemy into your hands for you to deal with as you wish.'" Then David crept up unnoticed and cut off a corner of Saul's robe.

⁵Afterward, David was conscience-stricken for having cut off a corner of his robe. ⁶He said to his men, "The LORD forbid that I should do such a thing to my master, the LORD's anointed, or lift my hand against him; for he is the anointed of the LORD." ⁷With these words David rebuked his men and did not allow them to attack Saul. And Saul left the cave and went his way.

⁸Then David went out of the cave and called out to Saul, "My lord the king!" When Saul looked behind him, David bowed down and prostrated himself with his face to the ground. ⁹He said to Saul, "Why do you listen when men say, 'David is bent on harming you'? ¹⁰This day you have seen with your own eyes how the LORD delivered you into my hands in the cave. Some urged me to kill you, but I spared you; I said, 'I will not lift my hand against my master, because he is the LORD's anointed.' ¹¹See, my father, look at this piece of your robe in my hand! I cut off the corner of your robe but did not kill you. Now understand and recognize that I am not guilty of wrongdoing or rebellion. I have not wronged you, but you are hunting me down to take my life. ¹²May the LORD judge between you and me. And may the LORD avenge the wrongs you have done to me, but my hand will not touch you. ¹³As the old saying goes, 'From evildoers come evil deeds,' so my hand will not touch you.

¹⁴"Against whom has the king of Israel

come out? Whom are you pursuing? A dead dog? A flea? [15]May the LORD be our judge and decide between us. May he consider my cause and uphold it; may he vindicate me by delivering me from your hand."

[16]When David finished saying this, Saul asked, "Is that your voice, David my son?" And he wept aloud. [17]"You are more righteous than I," he said. "You have treated me well, but I have treated you badly. [18]You have just now told me of the good you did to me; the LORD delivered me into your hands, but you did not kill me. [19]When a man finds his enemy, does he let him get away unharmed? May the LORD reward you well for the way you treated me today. [20]I know that you will surely be king and that the kingdom of Israel will be established in your hands. [21]Now swear to me by the LORD that you will not cut off my descendants or wipe out my name from my father's family."

[22]So David gave his oath to Saul. Then Saul returned home, but David and his men went up to the stronghold.

David, Nabal and Abigail

25 Now Samuel died, and all Israel assembled and mourned for him; and they buried him at his home in Ramah.

Then David moved down into the Desert of Maon.[a] [2]A certain man in Maon, who had property there at Carmel, was very wealthy. He had a thousand goats and three thousand sheep, which he was shearing in Carmel. [3]His name was Nabal and his wife's name was Abigail. She was an intelligent and beautiful woman, but her husband, a Calebite, was surly and mean in his dealings.

[4]While David was in the desert, he heard that Nabal was shearing sheep. [5]So he sent ten young men and said to them, "Go up to Nabal at Carmel and greet him in my name. [6]Say to him: 'Long life to you! Good health to you and your household! And good health to all that is yours!

[7]"'Now I hear that it is sheep-shearing time. When your shepherds were with us, we did not mistreat them, and the whole time they were at Carmel nothing of theirs was missing. [8]Ask your own servants and they will tell you. Therefore be favorable toward my young men, since we come at a festive time. Please give your servants and your son David whatever you can find for them.'"

[9]When David's men arrived, they gave Nabal this message in David's name. Then they waited.

[10]Nabal answered David's servants, "Who is this David? Who is this son of Jesse? Many servants are breaking away from their masters these days. [11]Why should I take my bread and water, and the meat I have slaughtered for my shearers, and give it to men coming from who knows where?"

[12]David's men turned around and went back. When they arrived, they reported every word. [13]David said to his men, "Put on your swords!" So they put on their swords, and David put on his. About four hundred men went up with David, while two hundred stayed with the supplies.

[14]One of the servants told Nabal's wife Abigail: "David sent messengers from the desert to give our master his greetings, but he hurled insults at them. [15]Yet these men were very good to us. They did not mistreat us, and the whole time we were out in the fields near them nothing was missing. [16]Night and day they were a wall around us all the time we were herding our sheep near them. [17]Now think it over and see what you can do, because disaster is hanging over our master and his whole household. He is such a wicked man that no one can talk to him."

[18]Abigail lost no time. She took two hundred loaves of bread, two skins of wine, five dressed sheep, five seahs[b] of roasted grain, a hundred cakes of raisins

---

a 1 Some Septuagint manuscripts; Hebrew *Paran*   b 18 That is, probably about a bushel (about 37 liters) and two hundred cakes of pressed figs, and loaded them on donkeys. [19] Then she told her servants, "Go on ahead; I'll follow you." But she did not tell her husband Nabal.

[20] As she came riding her donkey into a mountain ravine, there were David and his men descending toward her, and she met them. [21] David had just said, "It's been useless—all my watching over this fellow's property in the desert so that nothing of his was missing. He has paid me back evil for good. [22] May God deal with David,[a] be it ever so severely, if by morning I leave alive one male of all who belong to him!"

[23] When Abigail saw David, she quickly got off her donkey and bowed down before David with her face to the ground. [24] She fell at his feet and said: "My lord, let the blame be on me alone. Please let your servant speak to you; hear what your servant has to say. [25] May my lord pay no attention to that wicked man Nabal. He is just like his name—his name is Fool, and folly goes with him. But as for me, your servant, I did not see the men my master sent.

[26] "Now since the LORD has kept you, my master, from bloodshed and from avenging yourself with your own hands, as surely as the LORD lives and as you live, may your enemies and all who intend to harm my master be like Nabal. [27] And let this gift, which your servant has brought to my master, be given to the men who follow you. [28] Please forgive your servant's offense, for the LORD will certainly make a lasting dynasty for my master, because he fights the LORD's battles. Let no wrongdoing be found in you as long as you live. [29] Even though someone is pursuing you to take your life, the life of my master will be bound securely in the bundle of the living by the LORD your God. But the lives of your enemies he will hurl away as from the pocket of a sling. [30] When the LORD has done for my master every good

thing he promised concerning him and has appointed him leader over Israel, [31] my master will not have on his conscience the staggering burden of needless bloodshed or of having avenged himself. And when the LORD has brought my master success, remember your servant."

[32] David said to Abigail, "Praise be to the LORD, the God of Israel, who has sent you today to meet me. [33] May you be blessed for your good judgment and for keeping me from bloodshed this day and from avenging myself with my own hands. [34] Otherwise, as surely as the LORD, the God of Israel, lives, who has kept me from harming you, if you had not come quickly to meet me, not one male belonging to Nabal would have been left alive by daybreak."

[35] Then David accepted from her hand what she had brought him and said, "Go home in peace. I have heard your words and granted your request."

[36] When Abigail went to Nabal, he was in the house holding a banquet like that of a king. He was in high spirits and very drunk. So she told him nothing until daybreak. [37] Then in the morning, when Nabal was sober, his wife told him all these things, and his heart failed him and he became like a stone. [38] About ten days later, the LORD struck Nabal and he died.

[39] When David heard that Nabal was dead, he said, "Praise be to the LORD, who has upheld my cause against Nabal for treating me with contempt. He has kept his servant from doing wrong and has brought Nabal's wrongdoing down on his own head."

Then David sent word to Abigail, asking her to become his wife. [40] His servants went to Carmel and said to Abigail, "David has sent us to you to take you to become his wife."

[41] She bowed down with her face to the ground and said, "Here is your maidservant, ready to serve you and wash the feet of my master's servants." [42] Abigail quickly

---

[a] 22 Some Septuagint manuscripts; Hebrew *with David's enemies*

got on a donkey and, attended by her five maids, went with David's messengers and became his wife. ⁴³David had also married Ahinoam of Jezreel, and they both were his wives. ⁴⁴But Saul had given his daughter Michal, David's wife, to Paltiel[a] son of Laish, who was from Gallim.

David Again Spares Saul's Life

26 The Ziphites went to Saul at Gibeah and said, "Is not David hiding on the hill of Hakilah, which faces Jeshimon?"

²So Saul went down to the Desert of Ziph, with his three thousand chosen men of Israel, to search there for David. ³Saul made his camp beside the road on the hill of Hakilah facing Jeshimon, but David stayed in the desert. When he saw that Saul had followed him there, ⁴he sent out scouts and learned that Saul had definitely arrived.[b]

⁵Then David set out and went to the place where Saul had camped. He saw where Saul and Abner son of Ner, the commander of the army, had lain down. Saul was lying inside the camp, with the army encamped around him.

⁶David then asked Ahimelech the Hittite and Abishai son of Zeruiah, Joab's brother, "Who will go down into the camp with me to Saul?"

"I'll go with you," said Abishai.

⁷So David and Abishai went to the army by night, and there was Saul, lying asleep inside the camp with his spear stuck in the ground near his head. Abner and the soldiers were lying around him.

⁸Abishai said to David, "Today God has delivered your enemy into your hands. Now let me pin him to the ground with one thrust of my spear; I won't strike him twice."

⁹But David said to Abishai, "Don't destroy him! Who can lay a hand on the LORD's anointed and be guiltless? ¹⁰As surely as the LORD lives," he said, "the LORD himself will strike him; either his time will come and he will die, or he

will go into battle and perish. ¹¹But the LORD forbid that I should lay a hand on the LORD's anointed. Now get the spear and water jug that are near his head, and let's go."

¹²So David took the spear and water jug near Saul's head, and they left. No one saw or knew about it, nor did anyone wake up. They were all sleeping, because the LORD had put them into a deep sleep.

¹³Then David crossed over to the other side and stood on top of the hill some distance away; there was a wide space between them. ¹⁴He called out to the army and to Abner son of Ner, "Aren't you going to answer me, Abner?"

Abner replied, "Who are you who calls to the king?"

¹⁵David said, "You're a man, aren't you? And who is like you in Israel? Why didn't you guard your lord the king? Someone came to destroy your lord the king. ¹⁶What you have done is not good. As surely as the LORD lives, you and your men deserve to die, because you did not guard your master, the LORD's anointed. Look around you. Where are the king's spear and water jug that were near his head?"

¹⁷Saul recognized David's voice and said, "Is that your voice, David my son?"

David replied, "Yes it is, my lord the king." ¹⁸And he added, "Why is my lord pursuing his servant? What have I done, and what wrong am I guilty of? ¹⁹Now let my lord the king listen to his servant's words. If the LORD has incited you against me, then may he accept an offering. If, however, men have done it, may they be cursed before the LORD! They have now driven me from my share in the LORD's inheritance and have said, 'Go, serve other gods.' ²⁰Now do not let my blood fall to the ground far from the presence of the LORD. The king of Israel has come out to look for a flea—as one hunts a partridge in the mountains."

ª 44 Hebrew *Palti*, a variant of *Paltiel*   ᵇ 4 Or *had come to Nacon*

21Then Saul said, "I have sinned. Come back, David my son. Because you considered my life precious today, I will not try to harm you again. Surely I have acted like a fool and have erred greatly."

22"Here is the king's spear," David answered. "Let one of your young men come over and get it. 23The LORD rewards every man for his righteousness and faithfulness. The LORD delivered you into my hands today, but I would not lay a hand on the LORD's anointed. 24As surely as I valued your life today, so may the LORD value my life and deliver me from all trouble."

25Then Saul said to David, "May you be blessed, my son David; you will do great things and surely triumph."

So David went on his way, and Saul returned home.

David Among the Philistines

27 But David thought to himself, "One of these days I will be destroyed by the hand of Saul. The best thing I can do is to escape to the land of the Philistines. Then Saul will give up searching for me anywhere in Israel, and I will slip out of his hand."

2So David and the six hundred men with him left and went over to Achish son of Maoch king of Gath. 3David and his men settled in Gath with Achish. Each man had his family with him, and David had his two wives: Ahinoam of Jezreel and Abigail of Carmel, the widow of Nabal. 4When Saul was told that David had fled to Gath, he no longer searched for him.

5Then David said to Achish, "If I have found favor in your eyes, let a place be assigned to me in one of the country towns, that I may live there. Why should your servant live in the royal city with you?"

6So on that day Achish gave him Ziklag, and it has belonged to the kings of Judah ever since. 7David lived in Philistine territory a year and four months.

8Now David and his men went up and raided the Geshurites, the Girzites and the Amalekites. (From ancient times these peoples had lived in the land extending to Shur and Egypt.) 9Whenever David attacked an area, he did not leave a man or woman alive, but took sheep and cattle, donkeys and camels, and clothes. Then he returned to Achish.

10When Achish asked, "Where did you go raiding today?" David would say, "Against the Negev of Judah" or "Against the Negev of Jerahmeel" or "Against the Negev of the Kenites." 11He did not leave a man or woman alive to be brought to Gath, for he thought, "They might inform on us and say, 'This is what David did.'" And such was his practice as long as he lived in Philistine territory. 12Achish trusted David and said to himself, "He has become so odious to his people, the Israelites, that he will be my servant forever."

Saul and the Witch of Endor

28 In those days the Philistines gathered their forces to fight against Israel. Achish said to David, "You must understand that you and your men will accompany me in the army."

2David said, "Then you will see for yourself what your servant can do."

Achish replied, "Very well, I will make you my bodyguard for life."

3Now Samuel was dead, and all Israel had mourned for him and buried him in his own town of Ramah. Saul had expelled the mediums and spiritists from the land.

4The Philistines assembled and came and set up camp at Shunem, while Saul gathered all the Israelites and set up camp at Gilboa. 5When Saul saw the Philistine army, he was afraid; terror filled his heart. 6He inquired of the LORD, but the LORD did not answer him by dreams or Urim or prophets. 7Saul then said to his attendants, "Find me a woman who is a medium, so I may go and inquire of her."

"There is one in Endor," they said.

8So Saul disguised himself, putting on other clothes, and at night he and two

When God Doesn't Answer

GOING *deeper*

READ AND CONSIDER: 1 SAMUEL 28

"He inquired of the LORD, but the LORD did not answer him by dreams or Urim or prophets" (1 Samuel 28:6).

Sometimes God does not answer our prayers immediately. He may be telling us to wait; He may have another purpose in not giving a direct answer. Whatever the reason, it is always a good idea to "inquire of the Lord," and it is always a bad idea to take matters into our own hands. This is what King Saul did. So desperate was he for some kind of response that he just couldn't wait, so he went to a medium to get an answer.

When God does not answer your prayers, step back and wait. He is giving you an opportunity to trust Him in the midst of the uncertainty and ambiguity you may be feeling. The fact that Saul immediately consulted a medium—something he knew was directly forbidden by God and that he himself had outlawed—showed the shallowness of his trust in the Lord and his lack of commitment to God's ways.

What answer to prayer are you waiting for today? Have you become discouraged about it? Are you tempted to think that God is not listening to your prayers or that He doesn't care about your request? Are you thinking that maybe you need to step in and deal with the problem on your own since you haven't seen any response from God?

If so, ask God to help you to trust Him even when it is hard to do so. Ask Him to help you release the situation into His hands so He can handle it *His way* and in *His time*. Tell Him you are thankful that He knows what to do better than you do.

---

men went to the woman. "Consult a spirit for me," he said, "and bring up for me the one I name."

⁹But the woman said to him, "Surely you know what Saul has done. He has cut off the mediums and spiritists from the land. Why have you set a trap for my life to bring about my death?"

¹⁰Saul swore to her by the LORD, "As surely as the LORD lives, you will not be punished for this."

¹¹Then the woman asked, "Whom shall I bring up for you?"

"Bring up Samuel," he said.

¹²When the woman saw Samuel, she cried out at the top of her voice and said to Saul, "Why have you deceived me? You are Saul!"

¹³The king said to her, "Don't be afraid. What do you see?"

The woman said, "I see a spirit[a] coming up out of the ground."

¹⁴"What does he look like?" he asked.

"An old man wearing a robe is coming up," she said.

Then Saul knew it was Samuel, and he bowed down and prostrated himself with his face to the ground.

¹⁵Samuel said to Saul, "Why have you disturbed me by bringing me up?"

"I am in great distress," Saul said. "The Philistines are fighting against me, and God has turned away from me. He no longer answers me, either by prophets or by dreams. So I have called on you to tell me what to do."

¹⁶Samuel said, "Why do you consult me, now that the LORD has turned away from you and become your enemy? ¹⁷The LORD has done what he predicted

---

ᵃ 13 Or *see spirits*; or *see gods*

through me. The LORD has torn the kingdom out of your hands and given it to one of your neighbors—to David. ¹⁸Because you did not obey the LORD or carry out his fierce wrath against the Amalekites, the LORD has done this to you today. ¹⁹The LORD will hand over both Israel and you to the Philistines, and tomorrow you and your sons will be with me. The LORD will also hand over the army of Israel to the Philistines."

²⁰Immediately Saul fell full length on the ground, filled with fear because of Samuel's words. His strength was gone, for he had eaten nothing all that day and night.

²¹When the woman came to Saul and saw that he was greatly shaken, she said, "Look, your maidservant has obeyed you. I took my life in my hands and did what you told me to do. ²²Now please listen to your servant and let me give you some food so you may eat and have the strength to go on your way."

²³He refused and said, "I will not eat."

But his men joined the woman in urging him, and he listened to them. He got up from the ground and sat on the couch.

²⁴The woman had a fattened calf at the house, which she butchered at once. She took some flour, kneaded it and baked bread without yeast. ²⁵Then she set it before Saul and his men, and they ate. That same night they got up and left.

Achish Sends David Back to Ziklag

29 The Philistines gathered all their forces at Aphek, and Israel camped by the spring in Jezreel. ²As the Philistine rulers marched with their units of hundreds and thousands, David and his men were marching at the rear with Achish. ³The commanders of the Philistines asked, "What about these Hebrews?"

Achish replied, "Is this not David, who was an officer of Saul king of Israel? He has already been with me for over a year, and from the day he left Saul until now, I have found no fault in him."

⁴But the Philistine commanders were angry with him and said, "Send the man back, that he may return to the place you assigned him. He must not go with us into battle, or he will turn against us during the fighting. How better could he regain his master's favor than by taking the heads of our own men? ⁵Isn't this the David they sang about in their dances:

"'Saul has slain his thousands,
and David his tens of thousands'?"

⁶So Achish called David and said to him, "As surely as the LORD lives, you have been reliable, and I would be pleased to have you serve with me in the army. From the day you came to me until now, I have found no fault in you, but the rulers don't approve of you. ⁷Turn back and go in peace; do nothing to displease the Philistine rulers."

⁸"But what have I done?" asked David. "What have you found against your servant from the day I came to you until now? Why can't I go and fight against the enemies of my lord the king?"

⁹Achish answered, "I know that you have been as pleasing in my eyes as an angel of God; nevertheless, the Philistine commanders have said, 'He must not go up with us into battle.' ¹⁰Now get up early, along with your master's servants who have come with you, and leave in the morning as soon as it is light."

¹¹So David and his men got up early in the morning to go back to the land of the Philistines, and the Philistines went up to Jezreel.

David Destroys the Amalekites

30 David and his men reached Ziklag on the third day. Now the Amalekites had raided the Negev and Ziklag. They had attacked Ziklag and burned it, ²and had taken captive the women and all who were in it, both young and old. They killed none of them, but carried them off as they went on their way.

³When David and his men came to Ziklag, they found it destroyed by fire

and their wives and sons and daughters taken captive. ⁴So David and his men wept aloud until they had no strength left to weep. ⁵David's two wives had been captured—Ahinoam of Jezreel and Abigail, the widow of Nabal of Carmel. ⁶David was greatly distressed because the men were talking of stoning him; each one was bitter in spirit because of his sons and daughters. But David found strength in the LORD his God.

⁷Then David said to Abiathar the priest, the son of Ahimelech, "Bring me the ephod." Abiathar brought it to him, ⁸and David inquired of the LORD, "Shall I pursue this raiding party? Will I overtake them?"

"Pursue them," he answered. "You will certainly overtake them and succeed in the rescue."

⁹David and the six hundred men with him came to the Besor Ravine, where some stayed behind, ¹⁰for two hundred men were too exhausted to cross the ravine. But David and four hundred men continued the pursuit.

¹¹They found an Egyptian in a field and brought him to David. They gave him water to drink and food to eat— ¹²part of a cake of pressed figs and two cakes of raisins. He ate and was revived, for he had not eaten any food or drunk any water for three days and three nights.

¹³David asked him, "To whom do you belong, and where do you come from?"

He said, "I am an Egyptian, the slave of an Amalekite. My master abandoned me when I became ill three days ago. ¹⁴We raided the Negev of the Kerethites and the territory belonging to Judah and the Negev of Caleb. And we burned Ziklag."

¹⁵David asked him, "Can you lead me down to this raiding party?"

He answered, "Swear to me before God that you will not kill me or hand me over to my master, and I will take you down to them."

¹⁶He led David down, and there they were, scattered over the countryside, eating, drinking and reveling because of the great amount of plunder they had taken from the land of the Philistines and from Judah. ¹⁷David fought them from dusk until the evening of the next day, and none of them got away, except four hundred young men who rode off on camels and fled. ¹⁸David recovered everything the Amalekites had taken, including his two wives. ¹⁹Nothing was missing: young or old, boy or girl, plunder or anything else they had taken. David brought everything back. ²⁰He took all the flocks and herds, and his men drove them ahead of the other livestock, saying, "This is David's plunder."

²¹Then David came to the two hundred men who had been too exhausted to follow him and who were left behind at the Besor Ravine. They came out to meet David and the people with him. As David and his men approached, he greeted them. ²²But all the evil men and troublemakers among David's followers said, "Because they did not go out with us, we will not share with them the plunder we recovered. However, each man may take his wife and children and go."

²³David replied, "No, my brothers, you must not do that with what the LORD has given us. He has protected us and handed over to us the forces that came against us. ²⁴Who will listen to what you say? The share of the man who stayed with the supplies is to be the same as that of him who went down to the battle. All will share alike." ²⁵David made this a statute and ordinance for Israel from that day to this.

²⁶When David arrived in Ziklag, he sent some of the plunder to the elders of Judah, who were his friends, saying, "Here is a present for you from the plunder of the LORD's enemies."

²⁷He sent it to those who were in Bethel, Ramoth Negev and Jattir; ²⁸to those in Aroer, Siphmoth, Eshtemoa ²⁹and Racal; to those in the towns of the Jerahmeelites and the Kenites; ³⁰to those

in Hormah, Bor Ashan, Athach ³¹and Hebron; and to those in all the other places where David and his men had roamed.

Saul Takes His Life

31 Now the Philistines fought against Israel; the Israelites fled before them, and many fell slain on Mount Gilboa. ²The Philistines pressed hard after Saul and his sons, and they killed his sons Jonathan, Abinadab and Malki-Shua. ³The fighting grew fierce around Saul, and when the archers overtook him, they wounded him critically.

⁴Saul said to his armor-bearer, "Draw your sword and run me through, or these uncircumcised fellows will come and run me through and abuse me."

But his armor-bearer was terrified and would not do it; so Saul took his own sword and fell on it. ⁵When the armor-bearer saw that Saul was dead, he too fell on his sword and died with him. ⁶So Saul and his three sons and his armor-bearer and all his men died together that same day.

⁷When the Israelites along the valley and those across the Jordan saw that the Israelite army had fled and that Saul and his sons had died, they abandoned their towns and fled. And the Philistines came and occupied them.

⁸The next day, when the Philistines came to strip the dead, they found Saul and his three sons fallen on Mount Gilboa. ⁹They cut off his head and stripped off his armor, and they sent messengers throughout the land of the Philistines to proclaim the news in the temple of their idols and among their people. ¹⁰They put his armor in the temple of the Ashtoreths and fastened his body to the wall of Beth Shan.

¹¹When the people of Jabesh Gilead heard of what the Philistines had done to Saul, ¹²all their valiant men journeyed through the night to Beth Shan. They took down the bodies of Saul and his sons from the wall of Beth Shan and went to Jabesh, where they burned them. ¹³Then they took their bones and buried them under a tamarisk tree at Jabesh, and they fasted seven days.

Author: Unknown

Date: Sometime after 930 BC

Audience: Future generations of Israelites—to exhort them to maintain supreme devotion to God even while being ruled by earthly kings

Prayer Themes:

- Ask God for an increasing ability to discern His will for your life (5:17-19).

- Pray that you will develop the character qualities of mercy and kindness so that you will be a blessing to others (chapter 9).

- Tell God that you want to be someone who responds humbly and rightly when confronted with or convicted of wrongdoing (12:1-23).

At the core of an effective prayer life is the issue of our hearts.

- **What does it mean to love God with all my heart?**

- **How can those racked with guilt or filled with shame and regret have clean hearts before a holy God?**

- **What is a man or woman after God's own heart really like?**

Second Samuel tells the remarkable story of how King David rose to power, experienced the terrible disgrace of sin, and yet found God's amazing grace once more. Pay careful attention as you read and study the life of this great prayer warrior, David. You'll never find a better teacher for such matters of the heart than the one who cried, "Search me, O God, and know my heart" (Psalm 139:23).

2 Samuel

David Hears of Saul's Death

1 After the death of Saul, David returned from defeating the Amalekites and stayed in Ziklag two days. ²On the third day a man arrived from Saul's camp, with his clothes torn and with dust on his head. When he came to David, he fell to the ground to pay him honor.

³"Where have you come from?" David asked him.

He answered, "I have escaped from the Israelite camp."

⁴"What happened?" David asked. "Tell me."

He said, "The men fled from the battle. Many of them fell and died. And Saul and his son Jonathan are dead."

⁵Then David said to the young man who brought him the report, "How do you know that Saul and his son Jonathan are dead?"

⁶"I happened to be on Mount Gil-boa," the young man said, "and there was Saul, leaning on his spear, with the chariots and riders almost upon him. ⁷When he turned around and saw me, he called out to me, and I said, 'What can I do?'

⁸"He asked me, 'Who are you?'

"'An Amalekite,' I answered.

⁹"Then he said to me, 'Stand over me and kill me! I am in the throes of death, but I'm still alive.'

¹⁰"So I stood over him and killed him, because I knew that after he had fallen he could not survive. And I took the crown that was on his head and the band on his arm and have brought them here to my lord."

¹¹Then David and all the men with him took hold of their clothes and tore them. ¹²They mourned and wept and fasted till evening for Saul and his son Jonathan, and for the army of the LORD

and the house of Israel, because they had fallen by the sword.

¹³David said to the young man who brought him the report, "Where are you from?"

"I am the son of an alien, an Amalekite," he answered.

¹⁴David asked him, "Why were you not afraid to lift your hand to destroy the LORD's anointed?"

¹⁵Then David called one of his men and said, "Go, strike him down!" So he struck him down, and he died. ¹⁶For David had said to him, "Your blood be on your own head. Your own mouth testified against you when you said, 'I killed the LORD's anointed.'"

David's Lament for Saul and Jonathan

¹⁷David took up this lament concerning Saul and his son Jonathan, ¹⁸and ordered that the men of Judah be taught this lament of the bow (it is written in the Book of Jashar):

¹⁹"Your glory, O Israel, lies slain on
     your heights.
   How the mighty have fallen!

²⁰"Tell it not in Gath,
     proclaim it not in the streets of
       Ashkelon,
   lest the daughters of the Philistines
       be glad,
   lest the daughters of the
       uncircumcised rejoice.

²¹"O mountains of Gilboa,
     may you have neither dew nor rain,
     nor fields that yield offerings ₍of
       grain₎.
   For there the shield of the mighty was
       defiled,
     the shield of Saul—no longer
       rubbed with oil.

²²From the blood of the slain,
     from the flesh of the mighty,
   the bow of Jonathan did not turn
       back,
     the sword of Saul did not return
       unsatisfied.

²³"Saul and Jonathan—
     in life they were loved and
       gracious,
   and in death they were not parted.
   They were swifter than eagles,
     they were stronger than lions.

²⁴"O daughters of Israel,
     weep for Saul,
   who clothed you in scarlet and finery,
     who adorned your garments with
       ornaments of gold.

²⁵"How the mighty have fallen in
       battle!
     Jonathan lies slain on your heights.
²⁶I grieve for you, Jonathan my brother;
     you were very dear to me.
   Your love for me was wonderful,
     more wonderful than that of
       women.

²⁷"How the mighty have fallen!
     The weapons of war have
       perished!"

David Anointed King Over Judah

2 In the course of time, David inquired of the LORD. "Shall I go up to one of the towns of Judah?" he asked.

The LORD said, "Go up."

David asked, "Where shall I go?"

"To Hebron," the LORD answered.

²So David went up there with his two wives, Ahinoam of Jezreel and Abigail, the widow of Nabal of Carmel. ³David also took the men who were with him, each with his family, and they settled in Hebron and its towns. ⁴Then the men of Judah came to Hebron and there they anointed David king over the house of Judah.

When David was told that it was the men of Jabesh Gilead who had buried Saul, ⁵he sent messengers to the men of Jabesh Gilead to say to them, "The LORD bless you for showing this kindness to Saul your master by burying him. ⁶May the LORD now show you kindness and faithfulness, and I too will show you the same favor because you have done this.

[7]Now then, be strong and brave, for Saul your master is dead, and the house of Judah has anointed me king over them."

War Between the Houses of David and Saul

[8]Meanwhile, Abner son of Ner, the commander of Saul's army, had taken Ish-Bosheth son of Saul and brought him over to Mahanaim. [9]He made him king over Gilead, Ashuri[a] and Jezreel, and also over Ephraim, Benjamin and all Israel.

Prayer is . . .

being committed to seeing God move in a situation.

[10]Ish-Bosheth son of Saul was forty years old when he became king over Israel, and he reigned two years. The house of Judah, however, followed David. [11]The length of time David was king in Hebron over the house of Judah was seven years and six months.

[12]Abner son of Ner, together with the men of Ish-Bosheth son of Saul, left Mahanaim and went to Gibeon. [13]Joab son of Zeruiah and David's men went out and met them at the pool of Gibeon. One group sat down on one side of the pool and one group on the other side.

[14]Then Abner said to Joab, "Let's have some of the young men get up and fight hand to hand in front of us."

"All right, let them do it," Joab said.

[15]So they stood up and were counted off—twelve men for Benjamin and Ish-Bosheth son of Saul, and twelve for David. [16]Then each man grabbed his opponent by the head and thrust his dagger into his opponent's side, and they fell down together. So that place in Gibeon was called Helkath Hazzurim.[b]

[17]The battle that day was very fierce, and Abner and the men of Israel were defeated by David's men.

[18]The three sons of Zeruiah were there: Joab, Abishai and Asahel. Now Asahel was as fleet-footed as a wild gazelle. [19]He chased Abner, turning neither to the right nor to the left as he pursued him. [20]Abner looked behind him and asked, "Is that you, Asahel?"

"It is," he answered.

[21]Then Abner said to him, "Turn aside to the right or to the left; take on one of the young men and strip him of his weapons." But Asahel would not stop chasing him.

[22]Again Abner warned Asahel, "Stop chasing me! Why should I strike you down? How could I look your brother Joab in the face?"

[23]But Asahel refused to give up the pursuit; so Abner thrust the butt of his spear into Asahel's stomach, and the spear came out through his back. He fell there and died on the spot. And every man stopped when he came to the place where Asahel had fallen and died.

[24]But Joab and Abishai pursued Abner, and as the sun was setting, they came to the hill of Ammah, near Giah on the way to the wasteland of Gibeon. [25]Then the men of Benjamin rallied behind Abner. They formed themselves into a group and took their stand on top of a hill.

[26]Abner called out to Joab, "Must the sword devour forever? Don't you realize that this will end in bitterness? How long before you order your men to stop pursuing their brothers?"

[27]Joab answered, "As surely as God lives, if you had not spoken, the men would have continued the pursuit of their brothers until morning.[c]"

[28]So Joab blew the trumpet, and all the men came to a halt; they no longer pursued Israel, nor did they fight anymore.

[29]All that night Abner and his men

---

[a] 9 Or *Asher*   [b] 16 *Helkath Hazzurim* means *field of daggers* or *field of hostilities.*   [c] 27 Or *spoken this morning, the men would not have taken up the pursuit of their brothers;* or *spoken, the men would have given up the pursuit of their brothers by morning*

marched through the Arabah. They crossed the Jordan, continued through the whole Bithron[a] and came to Mahanaim.

30Then Joab returned from pursuing Abner and assembled all his men. Besides Asahel, nineteen of David's men were found missing. 31But David's men had killed three hundred and sixty Benjamites who were with Abner. 32They took Asahel and buried him in his father's tomb at Bethlehem. Then Joab and his men marched all night and arrived at Hebron by daybreak.

3 The war between the house of Saul and the house of David lasted a long time. David grew stronger and stronger, while the house of Saul grew weaker and weaker.

2Sons were born to David in Hebron:

His firstborn was Amnon the son of Ahinoam of Jezreel;

3his second, Kileab the son of Abigail the widow of Nabal of Carmel;

the third, Absalom the son of Maacah daughter of Talmai king of Geshur;

4the fourth, Adonijah the son of Haggith;

the fifth, Shephatiah the son of Abital;

5and the sixth, Ithream the son of David's wife Eglah.

These were born to David in Hebron.

Abner Goes Over to David

6During the war between the house of Saul and the house of David, Abner had been strengthening his own position in the house of Saul. 7Now Saul had had a concubine named Rizpah daughter of Aiah. And Ish-Bosheth said to Abner, "Why did you sleep with my father's concubine?"

8Abner was very angry because of what Ish-Bosheth said and he answered, "Am I a dog's head—on Judah's side? This very day I am loyal to the house of your father Saul and to his family and friends. I haven't handed you over to David. Yet now you accuse me of an offense involving this woman! 9May God deal with Abner, be it ever so severely, if I do not do for David what the LORD promised him on oath 10and transfer the kingdom from the house of Saul and establish David's throne over Israel and Judah from Dan to Beersheba." 11Ish-Bosheth did not dare to say another word to Abner, because he was afraid of him.

12Then Abner sent messengers on his behalf to say to David, "Whose land is it? Make an agreement with me, and I will help you bring all Israel over to you."

13"Good," said David. "I will make an agreement with you. But I demand one thing of you: Do not come into my presence unless you bring Michal daughter of Saul when you come to see me." 14Then David sent messengers to Ish-Bosheth son of Saul, demanding, "Give me my wife Michal, whom I betrothed to myself for the price of a hundred Philistine foreskins."

15So Ish-Bosheth gave orders and had her taken away from her husband Paltiel son of Laish. 16Her husband, however, went with her, weeping behind her all the way to Bahurim. Then Abner said to him, "Go back home!" So he went back.

17Abner conferred with the elders of Israel and said, "For some time you have wanted to make David your king. 18Now do it! For the LORD promised David, 'By my servant David I will rescue my people Israel from the hand of the Philistines and from the hand of all their enemies.'"

19Abner also spoke to the Benjamites in person. Then he went to Hebron to tell David everything that Israel and the whole house of Benjamin wanted to do. 20When Abner, who had twenty men with him, came to David at Hebron, David prepared a feast for him and his men. 21Then Abner said to David, "Let me go at once and assemble all Israel for my lord the king, so that they may make a compact with you, and that you may rule over all that your heart desires." So David sent Abner away, and he went in peace.

Joab Murders Abner

22Just then David's men and Joab returned from a raid and brought with them a great deal of plunder. But Abner was no longer with David in Hebron, because David had sent him away, and he had gone in peace. 23When Joab and all the soldiers with him arrived, he was told that Abner son of Ner had come to the king and that the king had sent him away and that he had gone in peace.

24So Joab went to the king and said, "What have you done? Look, Abner came to you. Why did you let him go? Now he is gone! 25You know Abner son of Ner; he came to deceive you and observe your movements and find out everything you are doing."

26Joab then left David and sent messengers after Abner, and they brought him back from the well of Sirah. But David did not know it. 27Now when Abner returned to Hebron, Joab took him aside into the gateway, as though to speak with him privately. And there, to avenge the blood of his brother Asahel, Joab stabbed him in the stomach, and he died.

28Later, when David heard about this, he said, "I and my kingdom are forever innocent before the LORD concerning the blood of Abner son of Ner. 29May his blood fall upon the head of Joab and upon all his father's house! May Joab's house never be without someone who has a running sore or leprosy[a] or who leans on a crutch or who falls by the sword or who lacks food."

30(Joab and his brother Abishai murdered Abner because he had killed their brother Asahel in the battle at Gibeon.)

31Then David said to Joab and all the people with him, "Tear your clothes and put on sackcloth and walk in mourning in front of Abner." King David himself walked behind the bier. 32They buried Abner in Hebron, and the king wept aloud at Abner's tomb. All the people wept also.

33The king sang this lament for Abner:

"Should Abner have died as the
    lawless die?
34   Your hands were not bound,
    your feet were not fettered.
You fell as one falls before wicked men."

And all the people wept over him again.

35Then they all came and urged David to eat something while it was still day; but David took an oath, saying, "May God deal with me, be it ever so severely, if I taste bread or anything else before the sun sets!"

36All the people took note and were pleased; indeed, everything the king did pleased them. 37So on that day all the people and all Israel knew that the king had no part in the murder of Abner son of Ner.

38Then the king said to his men, "Do you not realize that a prince and a great man has fallen in Israel this day? 39And today, though I am the anointed king, I am weak, and these sons of Zeruiah are too strong for me. May the LORD repay the evildoer according to his evil deeds!"

Ish-Bosheth Murdered

4 When Ish-Bosheth son of Saul heard that Abner had died in Hebron, he lost courage, and all Israel became alarmed. 2Now Saul's son had two men who were leaders of raiding bands. One was named Baanah and the other Recab; they were sons of Rimmon the Beerothite from the tribe of Benjamin—Beeroth is considered part of Benjamin, 3because the people of Beeroth fled to Gittaim and have lived there as aliens to this day.

4(Jonathan son of Saul had a son who was lame in both feet. He was five years old when the news about Saul and

---

a 29 The Hebrew word was used for various diseases affecting the skin—not necessarily leprosy.

Jonathan came from Jezreel. His nurse picked him up and fled, but as she hurried to leave, he fell and became crippled. His name was Mephibosheth.)

⁵Now Recab and Baanah, the sons of Rimmon the Beerothite, set out for the house of Ish-Bosheth, and they arrived there in the heat of the day while he was taking his noonday rest. ⁶They went into the inner part of the house as if to get some wheat, and they stabbed him in the stomach. Then Recab and his brother Baanah slipped away.

⁷They had gone into the house while he was lying on the bed in his bedroom. After they stabbed and killed him, they cut off his head. Taking it with them, they traveled all night by way of the Arabah. ⁸They brought the head of Ish-Bosheth to David at Hebron and said to the king, "Here is the head of Ish-Bosheth son of Saul, your enemy, who tried to take your life. This day the LORD has avenged my lord the king against Saul and his offspring."

⁹David answered Recab and his brother Baanah, the sons of Rimmon the Beerothite, "As surely as the LORD lives, who has delivered me out of all trouble, ¹⁰when a man told me, 'Saul is dead,' and thought he was bringing good news, I seized him and put him to death in Ziklag. That was the reward I gave him for his news! ¹¹How much more—when wicked men have killed an innocent man in his own house and on his own bed—should I not now demand his blood from your hand and rid the earth of you!"

¹²So David gave an order to his men, and they killed them. They cut off their hands and feet and hung the bodies by the pool in Hebron. But they took the head of Ish-Bosheth and buried it in Abner's tomb at Hebron.

David Becomes King Over Israel

5 All the tribes of Israel came to David at Hebron and said, "We are your own flesh and blood. ²In the past, while Saul was king over us, you were the one who led Israel on their military campaigns. And the LORD said to you, 'You will shepherd my people Israel, and you will become their ruler.'"

³When all the elders of Israel had come to King David at Hebron, the king made a compact with them at Hebron before the LORD, and they anointed David king over Israel.

⁴David was thirty years old when he became king, and he reigned forty years. ⁵In Hebron he reigned over Judah seven years and six months, and in Jerusalem he reigned over all Israel and Judah thirty-three years.

David Conquers Jerusalem

⁶The king and his men marched to Jerusalem to attack the Jebusites, who lived there. The Jebusites said to David, "You will not get in here; even the blind and the lame can ward you off." They thought, "David cannot get in here." ⁷Nevertheless, David captured the fortress of Zion, the City of David.

⁸On that day, David said, "Anyone who conquers the Jebusites will have to use the water shaft[a] to reach those 'lame and blind' who are David's enemies.[b]" That is why they say, "The 'blind and lame' will not enter the palace."

⁹David then took up residence in the fortress and called it the City of David. He built up the area around it, from the supporting terraces[c] inward. ¹⁰And he became more and more powerful, because the LORD God Almighty was with him.

¹¹Now Hiram king of Tyre sent messengers to David, along with cedar logs and carpenters and stonemasons, and they built a palace for David. ¹²And David knew that the LORD had established him as king over Israel and had exalted his kingdom for the sake of his people Israel.

¹³After he left Hebron, David took more concubines and wives in Jerusalem, and more sons and daughters were born

---

ᵃ 8 Or *use scaling hooks*   ᵇ 8 Or *are hated by David*   ᶜ 9 Or *the Millo* to him. [14]These are the names of the children born to him there: Shammua, Shobab, Nathan, Solomon, [15]Ibhar, Elishua, Nepheg, Japhia, [16]Elishama, Eliada and Eliphelet.

David Defeats the Philistines

[17]When the Philistines heard that David had been anointed king over Israel, they went up in full force to search for him, but David heard about it and went down to the stronghold. [18]Now the Philistines had come and spread out in the Valley of Rephaim; [19]so David inquired of the LORD, "Shall I go and attack the Philistines? Will you hand them over to me?"

The LORD answered him, "Go, for I will surely hand the Philistines over to you."

[20]So David went to Baal Perazim, and there he defeated them. He said, "As waters break out, the LORD has broken out against my enemies before me." So that place was called Baal Perazim.[a] [21]The Philistines abandoned their idols there, and David and his men carried them off.

[22]Once more the Philistines came up and spread out in the Valley of Rephaim; [23]so David inquired of the LORD, and he answered, "Do not go straight up, but circle around behind them and attack them in front of the balsam trees. [24]As soon as you hear the sound of marching in the tops of the balsam trees, move quickly, because that will mean the LORD has gone out in front of you to strike the Philistine army." [25]So David did as the LORD commanded him, and he struck down the Philistines all the way from Gibeon[b] to Gezer.

The Ark Brought to Jerusalem

6 David again brought together out of Israel chosen men, thirty thousand in all. [2]He and all his men set out from Baalah of Judah[c] to bring up from there the ark of God, which is called by the Name,[d] the name of the LORD Almighty, who is enthroned between the cherubim

---

[a] 20 Baal Perazim means the lord who breaks out.   [b] 25 Septuagint (see also 1 Chron. 14:16); Hebrew Geba   [c] 2 That is, Kiriath Jearim; Hebrew Baale Judah, a variant of Baalah of Judah   [d] 2 Hebrew; Septuagint and Vulgate do not have the Name.

GOING deeper
When God Gives Specific Instructions

READ AND CONSIDER: 2 SAMUEL 5:17-25

"So David inquired of the LORD, 'Shall I go and attack the Philistines? Will you hand them over to me?' The LORD answered him, 'Go, for I will surely hand the Philistines over to you'" (2 Samuel 5:19).

God isn't always this direct, but He does occasionally give us very specific instructions in answer to our prayers. If we ask for guidance and depend on Him, He promises to lead us in the direction that we should go (Proverbs 3:5-6). That is what He did for David in this passage, directing him when and how to attack and assuring him of the outcome. So often we do not think to ask God for this kind of specific direction because we don't expect that He will answer us. But He wants to guide our lives—even in the small details—and the more we get in the habit of asking, the more we will learn how to listen for His voice and discern what He is telling us to do.

Don't be afraid to pray for guidance in specific areas of your life, and don't get discouraged if you don't hear answers right away. It may take some time to learn how to hear God's voice leading you. But you will learn, and you will enjoy greater intimacy in your relationship with God. He longs to have this closeness with you, so take Him up on it and start asking questions!

that are on the ark. ³They set the ark of God on a new cart and brought it from the house of Abinadab, which was on the hill. Uzzah and Ahio, sons of Abinadab, were guiding the new cart ⁴with the ark of God on it,ᵃ and Ahio was walking in front of it. ⁵David and the whole house of Israel were celebrating with all their might before the LORD, with songsᵇ and with harps, lyres, tambourines, sistrums and cymbals.

⁶When they came to the threshing floor of Nacon, Uzzah reached out and took hold of the ark of God, because the oxen stumbled. ⁷The LORD's anger burned against Uzzah because of his irreverent act; therefore God struck him down and he died there beside the ark of God.

⁸Then David was angry because the LORD's wrath had broken out against Uzzah, and to this day that place is called Perez Uzzah.ᶜ

⁹David was afraid of the LORD that day and said, "How can the ark of the LORD ever come to me?" ¹⁰He was not willing to take the ark of the LORD to be with him in the City of David. Instead, he took it aside to the house of Obed-Edom the Gittite. ¹¹The ark of the LORD remained in the house of Obed-Edom the Gittite for three months, and the LORD blessed him and his entire household.

¹²Now King David was told, "The LORD has blessed the household of Obed-Edom and everything he has, because of the ark of God." So David went down and brought up the ark of God from the house of Obed-Edom to the City of David with rejoicing. ¹³When those who were carrying the ark of the LORD had taken six steps, he sacrificed a bull and a fattened calf. ¹⁴David, wearing a linen ephod, danced before the LORD with all his might, ¹⁵while he and the entire house of Israel brought up the ark of the LORD with shouts and the sound of trumpets.

¹⁶As the ark of the LORD was entering the City of David, Michal daughter of Saul watched from a window. And when she saw King David leaping and dancing before the LORD, she despised him in her heart.

¹⁷They brought the ark of the LORD and set it in its place inside the tent that David had pitched for it, and David sacrificed burnt offerings and fellowship offeringsᵈ before the LORD. ¹⁸After he had finished sacrificing the burnt offerings and fellowship offerings, he blessed the people in the name of the LORD Almighty. ¹⁹Then he gave a loaf of bread, a cake of dates and a cake of raisins to each person in the whole crowd of Israelites, both men and women. And all the people went to their homes.

²⁰When David returned home to bless his household, Michal daughter of Saul came out to meet him and said, "How the king of Israel has distinguished himself today, disrobing in the sight of the slave girls of his servants as any vulgar fellow would!"

²¹David said to Michal, "It was before the LORD, who chose me rather than your father or anyone from his house when he appointed me ruler over the LORD's people Israel—I will celebrate before the LORD. ²²I will become even more undignified than this, and I will be humiliated in my own eyes. But by these slave girls you spoke of, I will be held in honor."

Praying 2 Samuel 6:13-15
Lord, help me to remember to do as David did and stop often to worship You.

²³And Michal daughter of Saul had no children to the day of her death.

ᵃ *3,4 Dead Sea Scrolls and some Septuagint manuscripts; Masoretic Text* cart ⁴and they brought it with the ark of God from the house of Abinadab, which was on the hill ᵇ *5 See Dead Sea Scrolls, Septuagint and 1 Chronicles 13:8; Masoretic Text* celebrating before the LORD with all kinds of instruments made of pine. ᶜ *8 Perez Uzzah means* outbreak against Uzzah.
ᵈ *17 Traditionally* peace offerings; *also in verse 18*

God's Promise to David

7 After the king was settled in his palace and the LORD had given him rest from all his enemies around him, ²he said to Nathan the prophet, "Here I am, living in a palace of cedar, while the ark of God remains in a tent."

³Nathan replied to the king, "Whatever you have in mind, go ahead and do it, for the LORD is with you."

⁴That night the word of the LORD came to Nathan, saying:

⁵"Go and tell my servant David, 'This is what the LORD says: Are you the one to build me a house to dwell in? ⁶I have not dwelt in a house from the day I brought the Israelites up out of Egypt to this day. I have been moving from place to place with a tent as my dwelling. ⁷Wherever I have moved with all the Israelites, did I ever say to any of their rulers whom I commanded to shepherd my people Israel, "Why have you not built me a house of cedar?"'

⁸"Now then, tell my servant David, 'This is what the LORD Almighty says: I took you from the pasture and from following the flock to be ruler over my people Israel. ⁹I have been

---

GOING *deeper*

When God Says No

READ AND CONSIDER: 2 SAMUEL 7

"Go and tell my servant David, 'This is what the LORD says: Are you the one to build me a house to dwell in? . . . When your days are over and you rest with your fathers, I will raise up your offspring to succeed you, who will come from your own body, and I will establish his kingdom. He is the one who will build a house for my Name, and I will establish the throne of his kingdom forever' " (2 Samuel 7:5,12-13).

Sometimes, God says no.

None of us like to hear no for an answer. We don't want to be told no when we ask for help, or no when we ask someone for something, or no when we want to buy something new. We want to hear yes, yes, yes!

David fully expected a yes from God—and so did Nathan the prophet. After all, David wanted to honor God greatly by building a majestic place of worship. What could be wrong with that? In fact, Nathan was so certain of God's yes that he told David to go ahead and follow his heart. It seemed to him like a good plan with good motivation.

Then God stepped in. "That night the word of the LORD came to Nathan." And Nathan realized he had to tell King David that even though the plan seemed good, it wasn't *God's* plan.

When God says no, it doesn't mean He doesn't care for us. In fact, quite the opposite. It means He has a greater purpose, and He knows the outcome. What you asked for might be dangerous, or unwise, or second-best. Or what you asked for may be wrong—perhaps your motivation or attitude was wrong. God wisely says no. So when you hear a no from God, trust His wisdom. It may even be signaling a *yes* in another direction! David received a disappointing no from God, but he also saw a future yes. David's son, Solomon, would build the temple with more glorious resources at his disposal than anyone ever before him.

When God says no to some of your prayer requests, thank Him for His wisdom and revelation, and tell Him you look forward to the good that He will send your way instead.

with you wherever you have gone, and I have cut off all your enemies from before you. Now I will make your name great, like the names of the greatest men of the earth. 10And I will provide a place for my people Israel and will plant them so that they can have a home of their own and no longer be disturbed. Wicked people will not oppress them anymore, as they did at the beginning 11and have done ever since the time I appointed leaders[a] over my people Israel. I will also give you rest from all your enemies.

" 'The LORD declares to you that the LORD himself will establish a house for you: 12When your days are over and you rest with your fathers, I will raise up your offspring to succeed you, who will come from your own body, and I will establish his kingdom. 13He is the one who will build a house for my Name, and I will establish the throne of his kingdom forever. 14I will be his father, and he will be my son. When he does wrong, I will punish him with the rod of men, with floggings inflicted by men. 15But my love will never be taken away from him, as I took it away from Saul, whom I removed from before you. 16Your house and your kingdom will endure forever before me[b]; your throne will be established forever.' "

17Nathan reported to David all the words of this entire revelation.

David's Prayer

18Then King David went in and sat before the LORD, and he said:

"Who am I, O Sovereign LORD, and what is my family, that you have brought me this far? 19And as if this were not enough in your sight, O Sovereign LORD, you have also spoken about the future of the house of your servant. Is this your usual way of dealing with man, O Sovereign LORD?

20"What more can David say to you? For you know your servant, O Sovereign LORD. 21For the sake of your word and according to your will, you have done this great thing and made it known to your servant.

22"How great you are, O Sovereign LORD! There is no one like you, and there is no God but you, as we have heard with our own ears. 23And who is like your people Israel—the one nation on earth that God went out to redeem as a people for himself, and to make a name for himself, and to perform great and awesome wonders by driving out nations and their gods from before your people, whom you redeemed from Egypt?[c] 24You have established your people Israel as your very own forever, and you, O LORD, have become their God.

25"And now, LORD God, keep forever the promise you have made concerning your servant and his house. Do as you promised, 26so that your name will be great forever. Then men will say, 'The LORD Almighty is God over Israel!' And the house of your servant David will be established before you.

27"O LORD Almighty, God of Israel, you have revealed this to your servant, saying, 'I will build a house for you.' So your servant has found courage to offer you this prayer. 28O Sovereign LORD, you are God! Your words are trustworthy, and you have promised these good things to your servant. 29Now be pleased to bless the house of your servant, that it may continue forever in your sight; for you, O Sovereign LORD, have spoken, and with your blessing the house of your servant will be blessed forever."

David's Victories

8 In the course of time, David defeated the Philistines and subdued them, and he took Metheg Ammah from the control of the Philistines.

2David also defeated the Moabites. He made them lie down on the ground and measured them off with a length of cord. Every two lengths of them were put to death, and the third length was allowed to live. So the Moabites became subject to David and brought tribute.

3Moreover, David fought Hadadezer son of Rehob, king of Zobah, when he went to restore his control along the Euphrates River. 4David captured a thousand of his chariots, seven thousand charioteers[a] and twenty thousand foot soldiers. He hamstrung all but a hundred of the chariot horses.

5When the Arameans of Damascus came to help Hadadezer king of Zobah, David struck down twenty-two thousand of them. 6He put garrisons in the Aramean kingdom of Damascus, and the Arameans became subject to him and brought tribute. The LORD gave David victory wherever he went.

7David took the gold shields that belonged to the officers of Hadadezer and brought them to Jerusalem. 8From Tebah[b] and Berothai, towns that belonged to Hadadezer, King David took a great quantity of bronze.

9When Tou[c] king of Hamath heard that David had defeated the entire army of Hadadezer, 10he sent his son Joram[d] to King David to greet him and congratulate him on his victory in battle over Hadadezer, who had been at war with Tou. Joram brought with him articles of silver and gold and bronze.

11King David dedicated these articles to the LORD, as he had done with the silver and gold from all the nations he had subdued: 12Edom[e] and Moab, the Ammonites and the Philistines, and Amalek. He also dedicated the plunder taken from Hadadezer son of Rehob, king of Zobah.

13And David became famous after he returned from striking down eighteen thousand Edomites[f] in the Valley of Salt.

14He put garrisons throughout Edom, and all the Edomites became subject to David. The LORD gave David victory wherever he went.

David's Officials

15David reigned over all Israel, doing what was just and right for all his people. 16Joab son of Zeruiah was over the army; Jehoshaphat son of Ahilud was recorder; 17Zadok son of Ahitub and Ahimelech son of Abiathar were priests; Seraiah was secretary; 18Benaiah son of Jehoiada was over the Kerethites and Pelethites; and David's sons were royal advisers.[g]

David and Mephibosheth

9 David asked, "Is there anyone still left of the house of Saul to whom I can show kindness for Jonathan's sake?"

2Now there was a servant of Saul's household named Ziba. They called him to appear before David, and the king said to him, "Are you Ziba?"

"Your servant," he replied.

3The king asked, "Is there no one still left of the house of Saul to whom I can show God's kindness?"

Ziba answered the king, "There is still a son of Jonathan; he is crippled in both feet."

4"Where is he?" the king asked.

Ziba answered, "He is at the house of Makir son of Ammiel in Lo Debar."

5So King David had him brought from

---

a 4 Septuagint (see also Dead Sea Scrolls and 1 Chron. 18:4); Masoretic Text captured seventeen hundred of his charioteers
b 8 See some Septuagint manuscripts (see also 1 Chron. 18:8); Hebrew Betah.   c 9 Hebrew Toi, a variant of Tou; also in verse 10
d 10 A variant of Hadoram   e 12 Some Hebrew manuscripts, Septuagint and Syriac (see also 1 Chron. 18:11); most Hebrew manuscripts Aram   f 13 A few Hebrew manuscripts, Septuagint and Syriac (see also 1 Chron. 18:12); most Hebrew manuscripts Aram (that is, Arameans)   g 18 Or were priests

Lo Debar, from the house of Makir son of Ammiel.

⁶When Mephibosheth son of Jonathan, the son of Saul, came to David, he bowed down to pay him honor.

David said, "Mephibosheth!"

"Your servant," he replied.

⁷"Don't be afraid," David said to him, "for I will surely show you kindness for the sake of your father Jonathan. I will restore to you all the land that belonged to your grandfather Saul, and you will always eat at my table."

⁸Mephibosheth bowed down and said, "What is your servant, that you should notice a dead dog like me?"

⁹Then the king summoned Ziba, Saul's servant, and said to him, "I have given your master's grandson everything that belonged to Saul and his family. ¹⁰You and your sons and your servants are to farm the land for him and bring in the crops, so that your master's grandson may be provided for. And Mephibosheth, grandson of your master, will always eat at my table." (Now Ziba had fifteen sons and twenty servants.)

¹¹Then Ziba said to the king, "Your servant will do whatever my lord the king commands his servant to do." So Mephibosheth ate at David's[a] table like one of the king's sons.

¹²Mephibosheth had a young son named Mica, and all the members of Ziba's household were servants of Mephibosheth. ¹³And Mephibosheth lived in Jerusalem, because he always ate at the king's table, and he was crippled in both feet.

David Defeats the Ammonites

10 In the course of time, the king of the Ammonites died, and his son Hanun succeeded him as king. ²David thought, "I will show kindness to Hanun son of Nahash, just as his father showed kindness to me." So David sent a delegation to express his sympathy to Hanun concerning his father.

When David's men came to the land of the Ammonites, ³the Ammonite nobles said to Hanun their lord, "Do you think David is honoring your father by sending men to you to express sympathy? Hasn't David sent them to you to explore the city and spy it out and overthrow it?" ⁴So Hanun seized David's men, shaved off half of each man's beard, cut off their garments in the middle at the buttocks, and sent them away.

⁵When David was told about this, he sent messengers to meet the men, for they were greatly humiliated. The king said, "Stay at Jericho till your beards have grown, and then come back."

⁶When the Ammonites realized that they had become a stench in David's nostrils, they hired twenty thousand Aramean foot soldiers from Beth Rehob and Zobah, as well as the king of Maacah with a thousand men, and also twelve thousand men from Tob.

⁷On hearing this, David sent Joab out with the entire army of fighting men. ⁸The Ammonites came out and drew up in battle formation at the entrance to their city gate, while the Arameans of Zobah and Rehob and the men of Tob and Maacah were by themselves in the open country.

⁹Joab saw that there were battle lines in front of him and behind him; so he selected some of the best troops in Israel and deployed them against the Arameans. ¹⁰He put the rest of the men under the command of Abishai his brother and deployed them against the Ammonites. ¹¹Joab said, "If the Arameans are too strong for me, then you are to come to my rescue; but if the Ammonites are too strong for you, then I will come to rescue you. ¹²Be strong and let us fight bravely for our people and the cities of our God. The LORD will do what is good in his sight."

¹³Then Joab and the troops with him advanced to fight the Arameans, and they

fled before him. ¹⁴When the Ammonites saw that the Arameans were fleeing, they fled before Abishai and went inside the city. So Joab returned from fighting the Ammonites and came to Jerusalem.

¹⁵After the Arameans saw that they had been routed by Israel, they regrouped. ¹⁶Hadadezer had Arameans brought from beyond the River ͣ; they went to Helam, with Shobach the commander of Hadadezer's army leading them.

¹⁷When David was told of this, he gathered all Israel, crossed the Jordan and went to Helam. The Arameans formed their battle lines to meet David and fought against him. ¹⁸But they fled before Israel, and David killed seven hundred of their charioteers and forty thousand of their foot soldiers. ͤ He also struck down Shobach the commander of their army, and he died there. ¹⁹When all the kings who were vassals of Hadadezer saw that they had been defeated by Israel, they made peace with the Israelites and became subject to them.

So the Arameans were afraid to help the Ammonites anymore.

David and Bathsheba

11 In the spring, at the time when kings go off to war, David sent Joab out with the king's men and the whole Israelite army. They destroyed the Ammonites and besieged Rabbah. But David remained in Jerusalem.

Praying 2 Samuel 11:1-5
God, help me to reject temptations to sin when they first cross my mind.

²One evening David got up from his bed and walked around on the roof of the palace. From the roof he saw a woman bathing. The woman was very beautiful, ³and David sent someone to find out about her. The man said, "Isn't this Bathsheba, the daughter of Eliam and the wife of Uriah the Hittite?" ⁴Then David

sent messengers to get her. She came to him, and he slept with her. (She had purified herself from her uncleanness.) Then ͨ she went back home. ⁵The woman conceived and sent word to David, saying, "I am pregnant."

⁶So David sent this word to Joab: "Send me Uriah the Hittite." And Joab sent him to David. ⁷When Uriah came to him, David asked him how Joab was, how the soldiers were and how the war was going. ⁸Then David said to Uriah, "Go down to your house and wash your feet." So Uriah left the palace, and a gift from the king was sent after him. ⁹But Uriah slept at the entrance to the palace with all his master's servants and did not go down to his house.

¹⁰When David was told, "Uriah did not go home," he asked him, "Haven't you just come from a distance? Why didn't you go home?"

¹¹Uriah said to David, "The ark and Israel and Judah are staying in tents, and my master Joab and my lord's men are camped in the open fields. How could I go to my house to eat and drink and lie with my wife? As surely as you live, I will not do such a thing!"

¹²Then David said to him, "Stay here one more day, and tomorrow I will send you back." So Uriah remained in Jerusalem that day and the next. ¹³At David's invitation, he ate and drank with him, and David made him drunk. But in the evening Uriah went out to sleep on his mat among his master's servants; he did not go home.

¹⁴In the morning David wrote a letter to Joab and sent it with Uriah. ¹⁵In it he wrote, "Put Uriah in the front line where the fighting is fiercest. Then withdraw from him so he will be struck down and die."

¹⁶So while Joab had the city under siege, he put Uriah at a place where he knew the strongest defenders were.

ͣ *16* That is, the Euphrates   ͤ *18* Some Septuagint manuscripts (see also 1 Chron. 19:18); Hebrew *horsemen*   ͨ *4* Or *with her. When she purified herself from her uncleanness,*

The Quicksand of Temptation

GOING *deeper*

READ AND CONSIDER: 2 SAMUEL 11

"One evening David got up from his bed and walked around on the roof of the palace. From the roof he saw a woman bathing. The woman was very beautiful, and David sent someone to find out about her" (2 Samuel 11:2-3).

King David was a good man. A man after God's own heart. But one night he wasn't where he was supposed to be, and he wasn't doing what he was supposed to be doing. He was supposed to be fighting with his army. Instead, he was up on his roof watching the *married* lady next door take a bath. Then he sent for her to come to his palace . . . and the story goes downhill from there.

You're probably familiar with it. The beautiful woman, Bathsheba, ended up pregnant, and her husband ended up conveniently dead on the front line of David's battle, being sent there specifically for that purpose by David. The king married Bathsheba, but they lost their baby. And, amazingly, had it not been for a confrontation with the prophet Nathan, David may have come out of the situation thinking he had pulled one over on God just because he had covered his tracks. But that's not how it works.

What could have saved David from the temptation to involve himself with another man's wife? Instead of feasting his eyes on that naked woman, he should have turned his eyes away, admitted his temptation to God *immediately*, and gone right into the privacy of his own room. There he could have done what he had done in the midst of so many other battles or personal struggles—fallen on his face before God in prayer, praise, and worship. If he had stayed there before the Lord until the grip of temptation had released him, these tragedies would have never happened.

But he didn't. David "sent someone to find out about her." He stuck his toe into the quicksand of temptation, and before he knew it, he was in over his head.

All of us face temptation at one time or another. It may not be the same kind that David faced, but anything that draws us away from God and entices us to do what is against God's laws is temptation. Whenever that happens to you, immediately get before God and confess it. Ask Him to set you free from it and help you do the right thing. Then worship God until you feel the temptation broken over you.

The ability to withstand temptation begins the moment you look to your Savior and Deliverer for help.

---

[17] When the men of the city came out and fought against Joab, some of the men in David's army fell; moreover, Uriah the Hittite died.

[18] Joab sent David a full account of the battle. [19] He instructed the messenger: "When you have finished giving the king this account of the battle, [20] the king's anger may flare up, and he may ask you, 'Why did you get so close to the city to fight? Didn't you know they would shoot arrows from the wall? [21] Who killed Abimelech son of Jerub-Besheth[a]? Didn't a woman throw an upper millstone on him from the wall, so that he died in Thebez? Why did you get so close to the wall?' If he asks you this, then say to him, 'Also, your servant Uriah the Hittite is dead.'"

[22] The messenger set out, and when he arrived he told David everything Joab

---

[a] *21* Also known as *Jerub-Baal* (that is, Gideon)

had sent him to say. 23The messenger said to David, "The men overpowered us and came out against us in the open, but we drove them back to the entrance to the city gate. 24Then the archers shot arrows at your servants from the wall, and some of the king's men died. Moreover, your servant Uriah the Hittite is dead."

25David told the messenger, "Say this to Joab: 'Don't let this upset you; the sword devours one as well as another. Press the attack against the city and destroy it.' Say this to encourage Joab."

26When Uriah's wife heard that her husband was dead, she mourned for him. 27After the time of mourning was over, David had her brought to his house, and she became his wife and bore him a son. But the thing David had done displeased the LORD.

Nathan Rebukes David

12 The LORD sent Nathan to David. When he came to him, he said, "There were two men in a certain town, one rich and the other poor. 2The rich man had a very large number of sheep and cattle, 3but the poor man had nothing except one little ewe lamb he had bought. He raised it, and it grew up with him and his children. It shared his food, drank from his cup and even slept in his arms. It was like a daughter to him.

4"Now a traveler came to the rich man, but the rich man refrained from taking one of his own sheep or cattle to prepare a meal for the traveler who had come to him. Instead, he took the ewe lamb that belonged to the poor man and prepared it for the one who had come to him."

5David burned with anger against the man and said to Nathan, "As surely as the LORD lives, the man who did this deserves to die! 6He must pay for that lamb four times over, because he did such a thing and had no pity."

7Then Nathan said to David, "You are the man! This is what the LORD, the God of Israel, says: 'I anointed you king over Israel, and I delivered you from the hand of Saul. 8I gave your master's house to you, and your master's wives into your arms. I gave you the house of Israel and Judah. And if all this had been too little, I would have given you even more. 9Why did you despise the word of the LORD by doing what is evil in his eyes? You struck down Uriah the Hittite with the sword and took his wife to be your own. You killed him with the sword of the Ammonites. 10Now, therefore, the sword will never depart from your house, because you despised me and took the wife of Uriah the Hittite to be your own.'

11"This is what the LORD says: 'Out of your own household I am going to bring calamity upon you. Before your very eyes I will take your wives and give them to one who is close to you, and he will lie with your wives in broad daylight. 12You did it in secret, but I will do this thing in broad daylight before all Israel.'"

13Then David said to Nathan, "I have sinned against the LORD."

Nathan replied, "The LORD has taken away your sin. You are not going to die. 14But because by doing this you have made the enemies of the LORD show utter contempt,a the son born to you will die."

15After Nathan had gone home, the LORD struck the child that Uriah's wife had borne to David, and he became ill. 16David pleaded with God for the child. He fasted and went into his house and spent the nights lying on the ground. 17The elders of his household stood beside him to get him up from the ground, but he refused, and he would not eat any food with them.

18On the seventh day the child died. David's servants were afraid to tell him that the child was dead, for they thought, "While the child was still living, we spoke to David but he would not listen to us. How can we tell him the child is dead? He may do something desperate."

---

a 14 Masoretic Text; an ancient Hebrew scribal tradition *this you have shown utter contempt for the LORD*

¹⁹David noticed that his servants were whispering among themselves and he realized the child was dead. "Is the child dead?" he asked.

"Yes," they replied, "he is dead."

²⁰Then David got up from the ground. After he had washed, put on lotions and changed his clothes, he went into the house of the LORD and worshiped. Then he went to his own house, and at his request they served him food, and he ate.

²¹His servants asked him, "Why are you acting this way? While the child was alive, you fasted and wept, but now that the child is dead, you get up and eat!"

²²He answered, "While the child was still alive, I fasted and wept. I thought, 'Who knows? The LORD may be gracious to me and let the child live.' ²³But now that he is dead, why should I fast? Can I bring him back again? I will go to him, but he will not return to me."

²⁴Then David comforted his wife Bathsheba, and he went to her and lay with her. She gave birth to a son, and they named him Solomon. The LORD loved him; ²⁵and because the LORD loved him, he sent word through Nathan the prophet to name him Jedidiah.ᵃ

²⁶Meanwhile Joab fought against Rabbah of the Ammonites and captured the royal citadel. ²⁷Joab then sent messengers to David, saying, "I have fought against Rabbah and taken its water supply. ²⁸Now muster the rest of the troops and besiege the city and capture it. Otherwise I will take the city, and it will be named after me."

²⁹So David mustered the entire army and went to Rabbah, and attacked and captured it. ³⁰He took the crown from the head of their kingᵇ—its weight was a talentᶜ of gold, and it was set with precious stones—and it was placed on David's head. He took a great quantity of plunder from the city ³¹and brought out the people who were there, consigning them to labor with saws and with iron picks and axes, and he made them work at brickmaking.ᵈ He did this to all the Ammonite towns. Then David and his entire army returned to Jerusalem.

Amnon and Tamar

13 In the course of time, Amnon son of David fell in love with Tamar, the beautiful sister of Absalom son of David.

²Amnon became frustrated to the point of illness on account of his sister Tamar, for she was a virgin, and it seemed impossible for him to do anything to her.

³Now Amnon had a friend named Jonadab son of Shimeah, David's brother. Jonadab was a very shrewd man. ⁴He asked Amnon, "Why do you, the king's son, look so haggard morning after morning? Won't you tell me?"

Amnon said to him, "I'm in love with Tamar, my brother Absalom's sister."

⁵"Go to bed and pretend to be ill," Jonadab said. "When your father comes to see you, say to him, 'I would like my sister Tamar to come and give me something to eat. Let her prepare the food in my sight so I may watch her and then eat it from her hand.'"

⁶So Amnon lay down and pretended to be ill. When the king came to see him, Amnon said to him, "I would like my sister Tamar to come and make some special bread in my sight, so I may eat from her hand."

⁷David sent word to Tamar at the palace: "Go to the house of your brother Amnon and prepare some food for him." ⁸So Tamar went to the house of her brother Amnon, who was lying down. She took some dough, kneaded it, made the bread in his sight and baked it. ⁹Then she took the pan and served him the bread, but he refused to eat.

"Send everyone out of here," Amnon said. So everyone left him. ¹⁰Then Amnon said to Tamar, "Bring the food here into my bedroom so I may eat from your

---

ᵃ *25 Jedidiah* means *loved by the LORD.* ᵇ *30* Or *of Milcom* (that is, Molech) ᶜ *30* That is, about 75 pounds (about 34 kilograms)
ᵈ *31* The meaning of the Hebrew for this clause is uncertain.

hand." And Tamar took the bread she had prepared and brought it to her brother Amnon in his bedroom. [11]But when she took it to him to eat, he grabbed her and said, "Come to bed with me, my sister."

[12]"Don't, my brother!" she said to him. "Don't force me. Such a thing should not be done in Israel! Don't do this wicked thing. [13]What about me? Where could I get rid of my disgrace? And what about you? You would be like one of the wicked fools in Israel. Please speak to the king; he will not keep me from being married to you." [14]But he refused to listen to her, and since he was stronger than she, he raped her.

Praying 2 Samuel 13:12-16

Heavenly Father, please protect me from any kind of violent assault, and keep me safe from those who intend to do evil.

[15]Then Amnon hated her with intense hatred. In fact, he hated her more than he had loved her. Amnon said to her, "Get up and get out!"

[16]"No!" she said to him. "Sending me away would be a greater wrong than what you have already done to me."

But he refused to listen to her. [17]He called his personal servant and said, "Get this woman out of here and bolt the door after her." [18]So his servant put her out and bolted the door after her. She was wearing a richly ornamented[a] robe, for this was the kind of garment the virgin daughters of the king wore. [19]Tamar put ashes on her head and tore the ornamented[b] robe she was wearing. She put her hand on her head and went away, weeping aloud as she went.

[20]Her brother Absalom said to her, "Has that Amnon, your brother, been with you? Be quiet now, my sister; he is your brother. Don't take this thing to heart." And Tamar lived in her brother Absalom's house, a desolate woman.

[21]When King David heard all this, he was furious. [22]Absalom never said a word to Amnon, either good or bad; he hated Amnon because he had disgraced his sister Tamar.

Absalom Kills Amnon

[23]Two years later, when Absalom's sheepshearers were at Baal Hazor near the border of Ephraim, he invited all the king's sons to come there. [24]Absalom went to the king and said, "Your servant has had shearers come. Will the king and his officials please join me?"

[25]"No, my son," the king replied. "All of us should not go; we would only be a burden to you." Although Absalom urged him, he still refused to go, but gave him his blessing.

[26]Then Absalom said, "If not, please let my brother Amnon come with us."

The king asked him, "Why should he go with you?" [27]But Absalom urged him, so he sent with him Amnon and the rest of the king's sons.

[28]Absalom ordered his men, "Listen! When Amnon is in high spirits from drinking wine and I say to you, 'Strike Amnon down,' then kill him. Don't be afraid. Have not I given you this order? Be strong and brave." [29]So Absalom's men did to Amnon what Absalom had ordered. Then all the king's sons got up, mounted their mules and fled.

[30]While they were on their way, the report came to David: "Absalom has struck down all the king's sons; not one of them is left." [31]The king stood up, tore his clothes and lay down on the ground; and all his servants stood by with their clothes torn.

[32]But Jonadab son of Shimeah, David's brother, said, "My lord should not think that they killed all the princes; only Amnon is dead. This has been Absalom's expressed intention ever since the day Amnon raped his sister Tamar. [33]My lord the king should not be concerned about the report that all the king's sons are dead. Only Amnon is dead."

---

[a] *18* The meaning of the Hebrew for this phrase is uncertain.   [b] *19* The meaning of the Hebrew for this word is uncertain.

³⁴Meanwhile, Absalom had fled.

Now the man standing watch looked up and saw many people on the road west of him, coming down the side of the hill. The watchman went and told the king, "I see men in the direction of Horonaim, on the side of the hill."ᵃ

³⁵Jonadab said to the king, "See, the king's sons are here; it has happened just as your servant said."

³⁶As he finished speaking, the king's sons came in, wailing loudly. The king, too, and all his servants wept very bitterly.

³⁷Absalom fled and went to Talmai son of Ammihud, the king of Geshur. But King David mourned for his son every day.

³⁸After Absalom fled and went to Geshur, he stayed there three years. ³⁹And the spirit of the kingᵇ longed to go to Absalom, for he was consoled concerning Amnon's death.

Absalom Returns to Jerusalem

14 Joab son of Zeruiah knew that the king's heart longed for Absalom. ²So Joab sent someone to Tekoa and had a wise woman brought from there. He said to her, "Pretend you are in mourning. Dress in mourning clothes, and don't use any cosmetic lotions. Act like a woman who has spent many days grieving for the dead. ³Then go to the king and speak these words to him." And Joab put the words in her mouth.

⁴When the woman from Tekoa wentᶜ to the king, she fell with her face to the ground to pay him honor, and she said, "Help me, O king!"

⁵The king asked her, "What is troubling you?"

She said, "I am indeed a widow; my husband is dead. ⁶I your servant had two sons. They got into a fight with each other in the field, and no one was there to separate them. One struck the other

and killed him. ⁷Now the whole clan has risen up against your servant; they say, 'Hand over the one who struck his brother down, so that we may put him to death for the life of his brother whom he killed; then we will get rid of the heir as well.' They would put out the only burning coal I have left, leaving my husband neither name nor descendant on the face of the earth."

⁸The king said to the woman, "Go home, and I will issue an order in your behalf."

⁹But the woman from Tekoa said to him, "My lord the king, let the blame rest on me and on my father's family, and let the king and his throne be without guilt."

¹⁰The king replied, "If anyone says anything to you, bring him to me, and he will not bother you again."

¹¹She said, "Then let the king invoke the LORD his God to prevent the avenger of blood from adding to the destruction, so that my son will not be destroyed."

"As surely as the LORD lives," he said, "not one hair of your son's head will fall to the ground."

¹²Then the woman said, "Let your servant speak a word to my lord the king."

"Speak," he replied.

¹³The woman said, "Why then have you devised a thing like this against the people of God? When the king says this, does he not convict himself, for the king has not brought back his banished son? ¹⁴Like water spilled on the ground, which cannot be recovered, so we must die. But God does not take away life; instead, he devises ways so that a banished person may not remain estranged from him.

¹⁵"And now I have come to say this to my lord the king because the people have made me afraid. Your servant thought, 'I will speak to the king; perhaps he will do what his servant asks. ¹⁶Perhaps the king will agree to deliver his servant from the

---

ᵃ 34 Septuagint; Hebrew does not have this sentence.   ᵇ 39 Dead Sea Scrolls and some Septuagint manuscripts; Masoretic Text But the spirit of David the king   ᶜ 4 Many Hebrew manuscripts, Septuagint, Vulgate and Syriac; most Hebrew manuscripts spoke hand of the man who is trying to cut off both me and my son from the inheritance God gave us.'

17 "And now your servant says, 'May the word of my lord the king bring me rest, for my lord the king is like an angel of God in discerning good and evil. May the LORD your God be with you.'"

18 Then the king said to the woman, "Do not keep from me the answer to what I am going to ask you."

"Let my lord the king speak," the woman said.

19 The king asked, "Isn't the hand of Joab with you in all this?"

The woman answered, "As surely as you live, my lord the king, no one can turn to the right or to the left from anything my lord the king says. Yes, it was your servant Joab who instructed me to do this and who put all these words into the mouth of your servant. 20 Your servant Joab did this to change the present situation. My lord has wisdom like that of an angel of God—he knows everything that happens in the land."

21 The king said to Joab, "Very well, I will do it. Go, bring back the young man Absalom."

22 Joab fell with his face to the ground to pay him honor, and he blessed the king. Joab said, "Today your servant knows that he has found favor in your eyes, my lord the king, because the king has granted his servant's request."

23 Then Joab went to Geshur and brought Absalom back to Jerusalem. 24 But the king said, "He must go to his own house; he must not see my face." So Absalom went to his own house and did not see the face of the king.

25 In all Israel there was not a man so highly praised for his handsome appearance as Absalom. From the top of his head to the sole of his foot there was no blemish in him. 26 Whenever he cut the hair of his head—he used to cut his hair from time to time when it became too

heavy for him—he would weigh it, and its weight was two hundred shekels[a] by the royal standard.

27 Three sons and a daughter were born to Absalom. The daughter's name was Tamar, and she became a beautiful woman.

28 Absalom lived two years in Jerusalem without seeing the king's face. 29 Then Absalom sent for Joab in order to send him to the king, but Joab refused to come to him. So he sent a second time, but he refused to come. 30 Then he said to his servants, "Look, Joab's field is next to mine, and he has barley there. Go and set it on fire." So Absalom's servants set the field on fire.

31 Then Joab did go to Absalom's house and he said to him, "Why have your servants set my field on fire?"

32 Absalom said to Joab, "Look, I sent word to you and said, 'Come here so I can send you to the king to ask, "Why have I come from Geshur? It would be better for me if I were still there!"' Now then, I want to see the king's face, and if I am guilty of anything, let him put me to death."

33 So Joab went to the king and told him this. Then the king summoned Absalom, and he came in and bowed down with his face to the ground before the king. And the king kissed Absalom.

Absalom's Conspiracy

15 In the course of time, Absalom provided himself with a chariot and horses and with fifty men to run ahead of him. 2 He would get up early and stand by the side of the road leading to the city gate. Whenever anyone came with a complaint to be placed before the king for a decision, Absalom would call out to him, "What town are you from?" He would answer, "Your servant is from one of the tribes of Israel." 3 Then Absalom would say to him, "Look, your claims are valid and proper, but there is no representative of the king to hear you." 4 And Absalom would add, "If only I were appointed

a 26 That is, about 5 pounds (about 2.3 kilograms)

judge in the land! Then everyone who has a complaint or case could come to me and I would see that he gets justice."

5Also, whenever anyone approached him to bow down before him, Absalom would reach out his hand, take hold of him and kiss him. 6Absalom behaved in this way toward all the Israelites who came to the king asking for justice, and so he stole the hearts of the men of Israel.

7At the end of four[a] years, Absalom said to the king, "Let me go to Hebron and fulfill a vow I made to the LORD. 8While your servant was living at Geshur in Aram, I made this vow: 'If the LORD takes me back to Jerusalem, I will worship the LORD in Hebron.[b]'"

9The king said to him, "Go in peace." So he went to Hebron.

10Then Absalom sent secret messengers throughout the tribes of Israel to say, "As soon as you hear the sound of the trumpets, then say, 'Absalom is king in Hebron.'" 11Two hundred men from Jerusalem had accompanied Absalom. They had been invited as guests and went quite innocently, knowing nothing about the matter. 12While Absalom was offering sacrifices, he also sent for Ahithophel the Gilonite, David's counselor, to come from Giloh, his hometown. And so the conspiracy gained strength, and Absalom's following kept on increasing.

David Flees

13A messenger came and told David, "The hearts of the men of Israel are with Absalom."

14Then David said to all his officials who were with him in Jerusalem, "Come! We must flee, or none of us will escape from Absalom. We must leave immediately, or he will move quickly to overtake us and bring ruin upon us and put the city to the sword."

15The king's officials answered him, "Your servants are ready to do whatever our lord the king chooses."

16The king set out, with his entire household following him; but he left ten concubines to take care of the palace. 17So the king set out, with all the people following him, and they halted at a place some distance away. 18All his men marched past him, along with all the Kerethites and Pelethites; and all the six hundred Gittites who had accompanied him from Gath marched before the king.

19The king said to Ittai the Gittite, "Why should you come along with us? Go back and stay with King Absalom. You are a foreigner, an exile from your homeland. 20You came only yesterday. And today shall I make you wander about with us, when I do not know where I am going? Go back, and take your countrymen. May kindness and faithfulness be with you."

21But Ittai replied to the king, "As surely as the LORD lives, and as my lord the king lives, wherever my lord the king may be, whether it means life or death, there will your servant be."

22David said to Ittai, "Go ahead, march on." So Ittai the Gittite marched on with all his men and the families that were with him.

23The whole countryside wept aloud as all the people passed by. The king also crossed the Kidron Valley, and all the people moved on toward the desert.

24Zadok was there, too, and all the Levites who were with him were carrying the ark of the covenant of God. They set down the ark of God, and Abiathar offered sacrifices[c] until all the people had finished leaving the city.

25Then the king said to Zadok, "Take the ark of God back into the city. If I find favor in the LORD's eyes, he will bring me back and let me see it and his dwelling place again. 26But if he says, 'I am not pleased with you,' then I am ready; let him do to me whatever seems good to him."

---

a 7 Some Septuagint manuscripts, Syriac and Josephus; Hebrew *forty*   b 8 Some Septuagint manuscripts; Hebrew does not have *in Hebron.*   c 24 Or *Abiathar went up*

Navigating the Waters of Relationships

Relationships can be difficult to navigate because of one major variable—*the other person!* Due to that great unknown, we may be going along doing the best we know how and all of a sudden find ourselves in the middle of a relationship crisis. Our darkest hours can come because of the troubled times we have with people.

Any kind of relationship can bring pain. Strife with a mother or father, a brother or sister, a husband or wife, a son or daughter, a relative, friend, pastor, boss, neighbor, boyfriend, girlfriend, or co-worker can cause us to experience a knot in our stomach, a lump in our throat, and a loss of sleep. That's because whether we want to acknowledge it or not, relationships are very important to each of us. We can't live without them. Nor were we ever intended to. God never planned for us to live entirely separate from other people. Much of what God wants to work in us will come about as we grow in our relationships with the people God puts in our lives.

Every relationship requires a sacrifice. Every sacrifice has a reward. If we knew the rewards, we wouldn't hesitate to make the sacrifices. Part of the sacrifice we must pay in a relationship is laying down our pride and our needs. We need to be loved, cared for, valued, and respected, but we never get those needs met when we demand them. We get them met when we give them up. Humbling ourselves and putting the other person's needs before our own can resurrect a relationship that has suffered mortal wounds.

Staying on the right path in *any* relationship means getting rid of excess personal baggage. Unforgiveness and jealousy are examples of such baggage. These negative attitudes will drive a wedge into any relationship. And they are always evident to other people, even if they don't recognize exactly what it is they are observing. The dark moments of relationships can be kept to a minimum if we humble ourselves before God and ask Him to walk us step-by-step through every layer of unforgiveness and jealousy. It's a sacrifice that always brings a great reward.

The best way to protect all of your relationships is to make sure your primary relationship is with the Lord. Then commit each of your relationships to God and ask Him to be Lord over all of them. Cover them in prayer and seek God's hand of reconciliation where that is needed. Even though we can do a great deal to offer our love and forgiveness to other people, only God can soften their hearts enough for them to receive it. Ask Him to do that too.

In ironing out the wrinkles in relationships, I find it's best to remember two things—release people and cling to God. Gaining that perspective can help you rise above the failings of flesh and elevate you to the realm of the miraculous. The stronger your relationship is with the Lord, the better your other relationships will be. The dark moments of any relationship can strengthen your walk with the Lord as you draw closer to Him. So make *Him* the focus of your attention, and trust Him to shine a special light at the crossroads of where your path intersects with the path of another person.

For the next "From Stormie's Heart" article, go to page 460.

²⁷The king also said to Zadok the priest, "Aren't you a seer? Go back to the city in peace, with your son Ahimaaz and Jonathan son of Abiathar. You and Abiathar take your two sons with you. ²⁸I will wait at the fords in the desert until word comes from you to inform me." ²⁹So Zadok and Abiathar took the ark of God back to Jerusalem and stayed there.

³⁰But David continued up the Mount of Olives, weeping as he went; his head was covered and he was barefoot. All the people with him covered their heads too and were weeping as they went up. ³¹Now David had been told, "Ahithophel is among the conspirators with Absalom." So David prayed, "O LORD, turn Ahithophel's counsel into foolishness."

³²When David arrived at the summit, where people used to worship God, Hushai the Arkite was there to meet him, his robe torn and dust on his head. ³³David said to him, "If you go with me, you will be a burden to me. ³⁴But if you return to the city and say to Absalom, 'I will be your servant, O king; I was your father's servant in the past, but now I will be your servant,' then you can help me by frustrating Ahithophel's advice. ³⁵Won't the priests Zadok and Abiathar be there with you? Tell them anything you hear in the king's palace. ³⁶Their two sons, Ahimaaz son of Zadok and Jonathan son of Abiathar, are there with them. Send them to me with anything you hear."

³⁷So David's friend Hushai arrived at Jerusalem as Absalom was entering the city.

David and Ziba

16 When David had gone a short distance beyond the summit, there was Ziba, the steward of Mephibosheth, waiting to meet him. He had a string of donkeys saddled and loaded with two hundred loaves of bread, a hundred cakes of raisins, a hundred cakes of figs and a skin of wine.

²The king asked Ziba, "Why have you brought these?"

Ziba answered, "The donkeys are for the king's household to ride on, the bread and fruit are for the men to eat, and the wine is to refresh those who become exhausted in the desert."

³The king then asked, "Where is your master's grandson?"

Ziba said to him, "He is staying in Jerusalem, because he thinks, 'Today the house of Israel will give me back my grandfather's kingdom.'"

⁴Then the king said to Ziba, "All that belonged to Mephibosheth is now yours."

"I humbly bow," Ziba said. "May I find favor in your eyes, my lord the king."

Shimei Curses David

⁵As King David approached Bahurim, a man from the same clan as Saul's family came out from there. His name was Shimei son of Gera, and he cursed as he came out. ⁶He pelted David and all the king's officials with stones, though all the troops and the special guard were on David's right and left. ⁷As he cursed, Shimei said, "Get out, get out, you man of blood, you scoundrel! ⁸The LORD has repaid you for all the blood you shed in the household of Saul, in whose place you have reigned. The LORD has handed the kingdom over to your son Absalom. You have come to ruin because you are a man of blood!"

⁹Then Abishai son of Zeruiah said to the king, "Why should this dead dog curse my lord the king? Let me go over and cut off his head."

¹⁰But the king said, "What do you and I have in common, you sons of Zeruiah? If he is cursing because the LORD said to him, 'Curse David,' who can ask, 'Why do you do this?'"

¹¹David then said to Abishai and all his officials, "My son, who is of my own flesh, is trying to take my life. How much more, then, this Benjamite! Leave him alone; let him curse, for the LORD has told him to. ¹²It may be that the LORD will see my distress and repay me with good for the cursing I am receiving today."

¹³So David and his men continued along the road while Shimei was going along the hillside opposite him, cursing as he went and throwing stones at him and showering him with dirt. ¹⁴The king and all the people with him arrived at their destination exhausted. And there he refreshed himself.

The Advice of Ahithophel and Hushai

¹⁵Meanwhile, Absalom and all the men of Israel came to Jerusalem, and Ahithophel was with him. ¹⁶Then Hushai the Arkite, David's friend, went to Absalom and said to him, "Long live the king! Long live the king!"

¹⁷Absalom asked Hushai, "Is this the love you show your friend? Why didn't you go with your friend?"

¹⁸Hushai said to Absalom, "No, the one chosen by the LORD, by these people, and by all the men of Israel—his I will be, and I will remain with him. ¹⁹Furthermore, whom should I serve? Should I not serve the son? Just as I served your father, so I will serve you."

²⁰Absalom said to Ahithophel, "Give us your advice. What should we do?"

²¹Ahithophel answered, "Lie with your father's concubines whom he left to take care of the palace. Then all Israel will hear that you have made yourself a stench in your father's nostrils, and the hands of everyone with you will be strengthened." ²²So they pitched a tent for Absalom on the roof, and he lay with his father's concubines in the sight of all Israel.

²³Now in those days the advice Ahithophel gave was like that of one who inquires of God. That was how both David and Absalom regarded all of Ahithophel's advice.

17 Ahithophel said to Absalom, "I would[a] choose twelve thousand men and set out tonight in pursuit of David. ²I would[b] attack him while he is weary and weak. I would[b] strike him with terror, and then all the people with him

will flee. I would[b] strike down only the king ³and bring all the people back to you. The death of the man you seek will mean the return of all; all the people will be unharmed." ⁴This plan seemed good to Absalom and to all the elders of Israel.

⁵But Absalom said, "Summon also Hushai the Arkite, so we can hear what he has to say." ⁶When Hushai came to him, Absalom said, "Ahithophel has given this advice. Should we do what he says? If not, give us your opinion."

⁷Hushai replied to Absalom, "The advice Ahithophel has given is not good this time. ⁸You know your father and his men; they are fighters, and as fierce as a wild bear robbed of her cubs. Besides, your father is an experienced fighter; he will not spend the night with the troops. ⁹Even now, he is hidden in a cave or some other place. If he should attack your troops first,[c] whoever hears about it will say, 'There has been a slaughter among the troops who follow Absalom.' ¹⁰Then even the bravest soldier, whose heart is like the heart of a lion, will melt with fear, for all Israel knows that your father is a fighter and that those with him are brave.

¹¹"So I advise you: Let all Israel, from Dan to Beersheba—as numerous as the sand on the seashore—be gathered to you, with you yourself leading them into battle. ¹²Then we will attack him wherever he may be found, and we will fall on him as dew settles on the ground. Neither he nor any of his men will be left alive. ¹³If he withdraws into a city, then all Israel will bring ropes to that city, and we will drag it down to the valley until not even a piece of it can be found."

¹⁴Absalom and all the men of Israel said, "The advice of Hushai the Arkite is better than that of Ahithophel." For the LORD had determined to frustrate the good advice of Ahithophel in order to bring disaster on Absalom.

¹⁵Hushai told Zadok and Abiathar, the

ᵃ 1 Or Let me   ᵇ 2 Or will   ᶜ 9 Or When some of the men fall at the first attack priests, "Ahithophel has advised Absalom and the elders of Israel to do such and such, but I have advised them to do so and so. 16Now send a message immediately and tell David, 'Do not spend the night at the fords in the desert; cross over without fail, or the king and all the people with him will be swallowed up.'"

17Jonathan and Ahimaaz were staying at En Rogel. A servant girl was to go and inform them, and they were to go and tell King David, for they could not risk being seen entering the city. 18But a young man saw them and told Absalom. So the two of them left quickly and went to the house of a man in Bahurim. He had a well in his courtyard, and they climbed down into it. 19His wife took a covering and spread it out over the opening of the well and scattered grain over it. No one knew anything about it.

20When Absalom's men came to the woman at the house, they asked, "Where are Ahimaaz and Jonathan?"

The woman answered them, "They crossed over the brook."ᵃ The men searched but found no one, so they returned to Jerusalem.

21After the men had gone, the two climbed out of the well and went to inform King David. They said to him, "Set out and cross the river at once; Ahithophel has advised such and such against you." 22So David and all the people with him set out and crossed the Jordan. By daybreak, no one was left who had not crossed the Jordan.

23When Ahithophel saw that his advice had not been followed, he saddled his donkey and set out for his house in his hometown. He put his house in order and then hanged himself. So he died and was buried in his father's tomb.

24David went to Mahanaim, and Absalom crossed the Jordan with all the men of Israel. 25Absalom had appointed Amasa over the army in place of Joab. Amasa was the son of a man named Jether,ᵇ an Israeliteᶜ who had married Abigail,ᵈ the daughter of Nahash and sister of Zeruiah the mother of Joab. 26The Israelites and Absalom camped in the land of Gilead.

27When David came to Mahanaim, Shobi son of Nahash from Rabbah of the Ammonites, and Makir son of Ammiel from Lo Debar, and Barzillai the Gileadite from Rogelim 28brought bedding and bowls and articles of pottery. They also brought wheat and barley, flour and roasted grain, beans and lentils,ᵉ 29honey and curds, sheep, and cheese from cows' milk for David and his people to eat. For they said, "The people have become hungry and tired and thirsty in the desert."

Absalom's Death

18 David mustered the men who were with him and appointed over them commanders of thousands and commanders of hundreds. 2David sent the troops out—a third under the command of Joab, a third under Joab's brother Abishai son of Zeruiah, and a third under Ittai the Gittite. The king told the troops, "I myself will surely march out with you."

3But the men said, "You must not go out; if we are forced to flee, they won't care about us. Even if half of us die, they won't care; but you are worth ten thousand of us.ᶠ It would be better now for you to give us support from the city."

4The king answered, "I will do whatever seems best to you."

So the king stood beside the gate while all the men marched out in units of hundreds and of thousands. 5The king commanded Joab, Abishai and Ittai, "Be gentle with the young man Absalom for my sake." And all the troops heard the king giving orders concerning Absalom to each of the commanders.

⁶The army marched into the field to fight Israel, and the battle took place in the forest of Ephraim. ⁷There the army of Israel was defeated by David's men, and the casualties that day were great— twenty thousand men. ⁸The battle spread out over the whole countryside, and the forest claimed more lives that day than the sword.

⁹Now Absalom happened to meet David's men. He was riding his mule, and as the mule went under the thick branches of a large oak, Absalom's head got caught in the tree. He was left hanging in midair, while the mule he was riding kept on going.

¹⁰When one of the men saw this, he told Joab, "I just saw Absalom hanging in an oak tree."

¹¹Joab said to the man who had told him this, "What! You saw him? Why didn't you strike him to the ground right there? Then I would have had to give you ten shekelsᵃ of silver and a warrior's belt."

¹²But the man replied, "Even if a thousand shekelsᵇ were weighed out into my hands, I would not lift my hand against the king's son. In our hearing the king commanded you and Abishai and Ittai, 'Protect the young man Absalom for my sake.ᶜ' ¹³And if I had put my life in jeopardyᵈ—and nothing is hidden from the king—you would have kept your distance from me."

¹⁴Joab said, "I'm not going to wait like this for you." So he took three javelins in his hand and plunged them into Absalom's heart while Absalom was still alive in the oak tree. ¹⁵And ten of Joab's armor-bearers surrounded Absalom, struck him and killed him.

¹⁶Then Joab sounded the trumpet, and the troops stopped pursuing Israel, for Joab halted them. ¹⁷They took Absalom, threw him into a big pit in the forest and piled up a large heap of rocks over

him. Meanwhile, all the Israelites fled to their homes.

¹⁸During his lifetime Absalom had taken a pillar and erected it in the King's Valley as a monument to himself, for he thought, "I have no son to carry on the memory of my name." He named the pillar after himself, and it is called Absalom's Monument to this day.

David Mourns

¹⁹Now Ahimaaz son of Zadok said, "Let me run and take the news to the king that the LORD has delivered him from the hand of his enemies."

²⁰"You are not the one to take the news today," Joab told him. "You may take the news another time, but you must not do so today, because the king's son is dead."

²¹Then Joab said to a Cushite, "Go, tell the king what you have seen." The Cushite bowed down before Joab and ran off.

²²Ahimaaz son of Zadok again said to Joab, "Come what may, please let me run behind the Cushite."

But Joab replied, "My son, why do you want to go? You don't have any news that will bring you a reward."

²³He said, "Come what may, I want to run."

So Joab said, "Run!" Then Ahimaaz ran by way of the plainᵉ and outran the Cushite.

²⁴While David was sitting between the inner and outer gates, the watchman went up to the roof of the gateway by the wall. As he looked out, he saw a man running alone. ²⁵The watchman called out to the king and reported it.

The king said, "If he is alone, he must have good news." And the man came closer and closer.

²⁶Then the watchman saw another man running, and he called down to the gatekeeper, "Look, another man running alone!"

ᵃ 11 That is, about 4 ounces (about 115 grams)   ᵇ 12 That is, about 25 pounds (about 11 kilograms)   ᶜ 12 A few Hebrew manuscripts, Septuagint, Vulgate and Syriac; most Hebrew manuscripts may be translated *Absalom, whoever you may be.*   ᵈ 13 Or *Otherwise, if I had acted treacherously toward him*   ᵉ 23 That is, the plain of the Jordan

The king said, "He must be bringing good news, too."

27 The watchman said, "It seems to me that the first one runs like Ahimaaz son of Zadok."

"He's a good man," the king said. "He comes with good news."

28 Then Ahimaaz called out to the king, "All is well!" He bowed down before the king with his face to the ground and said, "Praise be to the LORD your God! He has delivered up the men who lifted their hands against my lord the king."

29 The king asked, "Is the young man Absalom safe?"

Ahimaaz answered, "I saw great confusion just as Joab was about to send the king's servant and me, your servant, but I don't know what it was."

30 The king said, "Stand aside and wait here." So he stepped aside and stood there.

31 Then the Cushite arrived and said, "My lord the king, hear the good news! The LORD has delivered you today from all who rose up against you."

32 The king asked the Cushite, "Is the young man Absalom safe?"

The Cushite replied, "May the enemies of my lord the king and all who rise up to harm you be like that young man."

33 The king was shaken. He went up to the room over the gateway and wept. As he went, he said: "O my son Absalom! My son, my son Absalom! If only I had died instead of you—O Absalom, my son, my son!"

19 Joab was told, "The king is weeping and mourning for Absalom." 2 And for the whole army the victory that day was turned into mourning, because on that day the troops heard it said, "The king is grieving for his son." 3 The men stole into the city that day as men steal in who are ashamed when they flee from battle. 4 The king covered his face and cried aloud, "O my son Absalom! O Absalom, my son, my son!"

5 Then Joab went into the house to the king and said, "Today you have humiliated all your men, who have just saved your life and the lives of your sons and daughters and the lives of your wives and concubines. 6 You love those who hate you and hate those who love you. You have made it clear today that the commanders and their men mean nothing to you. I see that you would be pleased if Absalom were alive today and all of us were dead. 7 Now go out and encourage your men. I swear by the LORD that if you don't go out, not a man will be left with you by nightfall. This will be worse for you than all the calamities that have come upon you from your youth till now."

8 So the king got up and took his seat in the gateway. When the men were told, "The king is sitting in the gateway," they all came before him.

David Returns to Jerusalem

Meanwhile, the Israelites had fled to their homes. 9 Throughout the tribes of Israel, the people were all arguing with each other, saying, "The king delivered us from the hand of our enemies; he is the one who rescued us from the hand of the Philistines. But now he has fled the country because of Absalom; 10 and Absalom, whom we anointed to rule over us, has died in battle. So why do you say nothing about bringing the king back?"

11 King David sent this message to Zadok and Abiathar, the priests: "Ask the elders of Judah, 'Why should you be the last to bring the king back to his palace, since what is being said throughout Israel has reached the king at his quarters? 12 You are my brothers, my own flesh and blood. So why should you be the last to bring back the king?' 13 And say to Amasa, 'Are you not my own flesh and blood? May God deal with me, be it ever so severely, if from now on you are not the commander of my army in place of Joab.' "

14 He won over the hearts of all the men of Judah as though they were one man. They sent word to the king, "Return, you and all your men." 15 Then the

king returned and went as far as the Jordan.

Now the men of Judah had come to Gilgal to go out and meet the king and bring him across the Jordan. [16]Shimei son of Gera, the Benjamite from Bahurim, hurried down with the men of Judah to meet King David. [17]With him were a thousand Benjamites, along with Ziba, the steward of Saul's household, and his fifteen sons and twenty servants. They rushed to the Jordan, where the king was. [18]They crossed at the ford to take the king's household over and to do whatever he wished.

When Shimei son of Gera crossed the Jordan, he fell prostrate before the king [19]and said to him, "May my lord not hold me guilty. Do not remember how your servant did wrong on the day my lord the king left Jerusalem. May the king put it out of his mind. [20]For I your servant know that I have sinned, but today I have come here as the first of the whole house of Joseph to come down and meet my lord the king."

[21]Then Abishai son of Zeruiah said, "Shouldn't Shimei be put to death for this? He cursed the LORD's anointed."

[22]David replied, "What do you and I have in common, you sons of Zeruiah? This day you have become my adversaries! Should anyone be put to death in Israel today? Do I not know that today I am king over Israel?" [23]So the king said to Shimei, "You shall not die." And the king promised him on oath.

[24]Mephibosheth, Saul's grandson, also went down to meet the king. He had not taken care of his feet or trimmed his mustache or washed his clothes from the day the king left until the day he returned safely. [25]When he came from Jerusalem to meet the king, the king asked him, "Why didn't you go with me, Mephibosheth?"

[26]He said, "My lord the king, since I your servant am lame, I said, 'I will have my donkey saddled and will ride on it, so I can go with the king.' But Ziba my servant betrayed me. [27]And he has slandered your servant to my lord the king. My lord the king is like an angel of God; so do whatever pleases you. [28]All my grandfather's descendants deserved nothing but death from my lord the king, but you gave your servant a place among those who eat at your table. So what right do I have to make any more appeals to the king?"

[29]The king said to him, "Why say more? I order you and Ziba to divide the fields."

[30]Mephibosheth said to the king, "Let him take everything, now that my lord the king has arrived home safely."

[31]Barzillai the Gileadite also came down from Rogelim to cross the Jordan with the king and to send him on his way from there. [32]Now Barzillai was a very old man, eighty years of age. He had provided for the king during his stay in Mahanaim, for he was a very wealthy man. [33]The king said to Barzillai, "Cross over with me and stay with me in Jerusalem, and I will provide for you."

[34]But Barzillai answered the king, "How many more years will I live, that I should go up to Jerusalem with the king? [35]I am now eighty years old. Can I tell the difference between what is good and what is not? Can your servant taste what he eats and drinks? Can I still hear the voices of men and women singers? Why should your servant be an added burden to my lord the king? [36]Your servant will cross over the Jordan with the king for a short distance, but why should the king reward me in this way? [37]Let your servant return, that I may die in my own town near the tomb of my father and mother. But here is your servant Kimham. Let him cross over with my lord the king. Do for him whatever pleases you."

[38]The king said, "Kimham shall cross over with me, and I will do for him whatever pleases you. And anything you desire from me I will do for you."

[39]So all the people crossed the Jordan,

and then the king crossed over. The king kissed Barzillai and gave him his blessing, and Barzillai returned to his home.

⁴⁰When the king crossed over to Gilgal, Kimham crossed with him. All the troops of Judah and half the troops of Israel had taken the king over.

⁴¹Soon all the men of Israel were coming to the king and saying to him, "Why did our brothers, the men of Judah, steal the king away and bring him and his household across the Jordan, together with all his men?"

⁴²All the men of Judah answered the men of Israel, "We did this because the king is closely related to us. Why are you angry about it? Have we eaten any of the king's provisions? Have we taken anything for ourselves?"

⁴³Then the men of Israel answered the men of Judah, "We have ten shares in the king; and besides, we have a greater claim on David than you have. So why do you treat us with contempt? Were we not the first to speak of bringing back our king?"

But the men of Judah responded even more harshly than the men of Israel.

Sheba Rebels Against David

20 Now a troublemaker named Sheba son of Bicri, a Benjamite, happened to be there. He sounded the trumpet and shouted,

"We have no share in David,
  no part in Jesse's son!
Every man to his tent, O Israel!"

²So all the men of Israel deserted David to follow Sheba son of Bicri. But the men of Judah stayed by their king all the way from the Jordan to Jerusalem.

³When David returned to his palace in Jerusalem, he took the ten concubines he had left to take care of the palace and put them in a house under guard. He provided for them, but did not lie with them. They were kept in confinement till the day of their death, living as widows.

⁴Then the king said to Amasa, "Summon the men of Judah to come to me within three days, and be here yourself." ⁵But when Amasa went to summon Judah, he took longer than the time the king had set for him.

⁶David said to Abishai, "Now Sheba son of Bicri will do us more harm than Absalom did. Take your master's men and pursue him, or he will find fortified cities and escape from us." ⁷So Joab's men and the Kerethites and Pelethites and all the mighty warriors went out under the command of Abishai. They marched out from Jerusalem to pursue Sheba son of Bicri.

⁸While they were at the great rock in Gibeon, Amasa came to meet them. Joab was wearing his military tunic, and strapped over it at his waist was a belt with a dagger in its sheath. As he stepped forward, it dropped out of its sheath.

⁹Joab said to Amasa, "How are you, my brother?" Then Joab took Amasa by the beard with his right hand to kiss him. ¹⁰Amasa was not on his guard against the dagger in Joab's hand, and Joab plunged it into his belly, and his intestines spilled out on the ground. Without being stabbed again, Amasa died. Then Joab and his brother Abishai pursued Sheba son of Bicri.

¹¹One of Joab's men stood beside Amasa and said, "Whoever favors Joab, and whoever is for David, let him follow Joab!" ¹²Amasa lay wallowing in his blood in the middle of the road, and the man saw that all the troops came to a halt there. When he realized that everyone who came up to Amasa stopped, he dragged him from the road into a field and threw a garment over him. ¹³After Amasa had been removed from the road, all the men went on with Joab to pursue Sheba son of Bicri.

¹⁴Sheba passed through all the tribes of Israel to Abel Beth Maacahᵃ and through the entire region of the Berites, who gathered together and followed him. ¹⁵All the

---

ᵃ 14 Or Abel, even Beth Maacah; also in verse 15

troops with Joab came and besieged Sheba in Abel Beth Maacah. They built a siege ramp up to the city, and it stood against the outer fortifications. While they were battering the wall to bring it down, [16]a wise woman called from the city, "Listen! Listen! Tell Joab to come here so I can speak to him." [17]He went toward her, and she asked, "Are you Joab?"

"I am," he answered.

She said, "Listen to what your servant has to say."

"I'm listening," he said.

[18]She continued, "Long ago they used to say, 'Get your answer at Abel,' and that settled it. [19]We are the peaceful and faithful in Israel. You are trying to destroy a city that is a mother in Israel. Why do you want to swallow up the Lord's inheritance?"

[20]"Far be it from me!" Joab replied, "Far be it from me to swallow up or destroy! [21]That is not the case. A man named Sheba son of Bicri, from the hill country of Ephraim, has lifted up his hand against the king, against David. Hand over this one man, and I'll withdraw from the city."

The woman said to Joab, "His head will be thrown to you from the wall."

[22]Then the woman went to all the people with her wise advice, and they cut off the head of Sheba son of Bicri and threw it to Joab. So he sounded the trumpet, and his men dispersed from the city, each returning to his home. And Joab went back to the king in Jerusalem.

[23]Joab was over Israel's entire army; Benaiah son of Jehoiada was over the Kerethites and Pelethites; [24]Adoniram[a] was in charge of forced labor; Jehoshaphat son of Ahilud was recorder; [25]Sheva was secretary; Zadok and Abiathar were priests; [26]and Ira the Jairite was David's priest.

The Gibeonites Avenged

21 During the reign of David, there was a famine for three successive years; so David sought the face of the Lord. The Lord said, "It is on account of Saul and his blood-stained house; it is because he put the Gibeonites to death."

[2]The king summoned the Gibeonites and spoke to them. (Now the Gibeonites were not a part of Israel but were survivors of the Amorites; the Israelites had sworn to ⌊spare⌋ them, but Saul in his zeal for Israel and Judah had tried to annihilate them.) [3]David asked the Gibeonites, "What shall I do for you? How shall I make amends so that you will bless the Lord's inheritance?"

[4]The Gibeonites answered him, "We have no right to demand silver or gold from Saul or his family, nor do we have the right to put anyone in Israel to death."

"What do you want me to do for you?" David asked.

[5]They answered the king, "As for the man who destroyed us and plotted against us so that we have been decimated and have no place anywhere in Israel, [6]let seven of his male descendants be given to us to be killed and exposed before the Lord at Gibeah of Saul—the Lord's chosen one."

So the king said, "I will give them to you."

[7]The king spared Mephibosheth son of Jonathan, the son of Saul, because of the oath before the Lord between David and Jonathan son of Saul. [8]But the king took Armoni and Mephibosheth, the two sons of Aiah's daughter Rizpah, whom she had borne to Saul, together with the five sons of Saul's daughter Merab,[b] whom she had borne to Adriel son of Barzillai the Meholathite. [9]He handed them over to the Gibeonites, who killed and exposed them on a hill before the Lord. All seven of them fell together; they were put to death during the first days of the harvest, just as the barley harvest was beginning.

[10]Rizpah daughter of Aiah took sackcloth

---

a 24 Some Septuagint manuscripts (see also 1 Kings 4:6 and 5:14); Hebrew Adoram   b 8 Two Hebrew manuscripts, some Septuagint manuscripts and Syriac (see also 1 Samuel 18:19); most Hebrew and Septuagint manuscripts Michal and spread it out for herself on a rock. From the beginning of the harvest till the rain poured down from the heavens on the bodies, she did not let the birds of the air touch them by day or the wild animals by night. ¹¹When David was told what Aiah's daughter Rizpah, Saul's concubine, had done, ¹²he went and took the bones of Saul and his son Jonathan from the citizens of Jabesh Gilead. (They had taken them secretly from the public square at Beth Shan, where the Philistines had hung them after they struck Saul down on Gilboa.) ¹³David brought the bones of Saul and his son Jonathan from there, and the bones of those who had been killed and exposed were gathered up.

¹⁴They buried the bones of Saul and his son Jonathan in the tomb of Saul's father Kish, at Zela in Benjamin, and did everything the king commanded. After that, God answered prayer in behalf of the land.

Wars Against the Philistines

¹⁵Once again there was a battle between the Philistines and Israel. David went down with his men to fight against the Philistines, and he became exhausted. ¹⁶And Ishbi-Benob, one of the descendants of Rapha, whose bronze spearhead weighed three hundred shekels[a] and who was armed with a new ⌊sword⌋, said he would kill David. ¹⁷But Abishai son of Zeruiah came to David's rescue; he struck the Philistine down and killed him. Then David's men swore to him, saying, "Never again will you go out with us to battle, so that the lamp of Israel will not be extinguished."

¹⁸In the course of time, there was another battle with the Philistines, at Gob. At that time Sibbecai the Hushathite killed Saph, one of the descendants of Rapha.

¹⁹In another battle with the Philistines

at Gob, Elhanan son of Jaare-Oregim[b] the Bethlehemite killed Goliath[c] the Gittite, who had a spear with a shaft like a weaver's rod.

²⁰In still another battle, which took place at Gath, there was a huge man with six fingers on each hand and six toes on each foot—twenty-four in all. He also was descended from Rapha. ²¹When he taunted Israel, Jonathan son of Shimeah, David's brother, killed him.

²²These four were descendants of Rapha in Gath, and they fell at the hands of David and his men.

David's Song of Praise

22 David sang to the LORD the words of this song when the LORD delivered him from the hand of all his enemies and from the hand of Saul. ²He said:

"The LORD is my rock, my fortress
    and my deliverer;
³ my God is my rock, in whom I take
        refuge,
    my shield and the horn[d] of my
        salvation.
He is my stronghold, my refuge and
        my savior—
    from violent men you save me.
⁴I call to the LORD, who is worthy of
        praise,
    and I am saved from my enemies.

⁵"The waves of death swirled about
        me;
    the torrents of destruction
        overwhelmed me.
⁶The cords of the grave[e] coiled around
        me;
    the snares of death confronted me.
⁷In my distress I called to the LORD;
    I called out to my God.
From his temple he heard my voice;
    my cry came to his ears.

⁸"The earth trembled and quaked,
    the foundations of the heavens[f]
        shook;

---

a 16 That is, about 7 1/2 pounds (about 3.5 kilograms)   b 19 Or son of Jair the weaver   c 19 Hebrew and Septuagint;
1 Chron. 20:5 son of Jair killed Lahmi the brother of Goliath   d 3 Horn here symbolizes strength.   e 6 Hebrew Sheol
f 8 Hebrew; Vulgate and Syriac (see also Psalm 18:7) mountains

they trembled because he was angry.
⁹Smoke rose from his nostrils;
  consuming fire came from his
    mouth,
  burning coals blazed out of it.
¹⁰He parted the heavens and came
    down;
  dark clouds were under his feet.
¹¹He mounted the cherubim and flew;
  he soared[a] on the wings of the wind.
¹²He made darkness his canopy around
    him—
  the dark[b] rain clouds of the sky.

he drew me out of deep
    waters.
¹⁸He rescued me from my powerful
    enemy,
  from my foes, who were too strong
    for me.
¹⁹They confronted me in the day of my
    disaster,
  but the LORD was my support.
²⁰He brought me out into a spacious
    place;
  he rescued me because he delighted
    in me.

God's people at prayer
DAVID PRAISES HIS DELIVERER

2 SAMUEL 22:1-51 It had been a long, weary battle for David. But for the moment, all who intended to cause him harm had been put down. In that moment of calm, when he could have done a lot of other things, David praised God for bringing him through. He had more wars to fight, more enemies to defeat. That was the reality of an ancient king's existence. But when the time came to lay down his sword, David recounted the goodness and the power of the Lord to save, protect, and deliver him. He gave all the glory to God.

What are you struggling with in your life? Are you facing a battle? Is the enemy moving in on you? If so, stop and thank God for all of His deliverance in your life. Sing your own song of praise to Him, thanking Him that He will continue to deliver you. Tell Him that He is worthy of all praise and that you will worship Him in times of battle as well as times of peace.

---

¹³Out of the brightness of his presence
  bolts of lightning blazed forth.
¹⁴The LORD thundered from heaven;
  the voice of the Most High
    resounded.
¹⁵He shot arrows and scattered ₍the
    enemies₎,
  bolts of lightning and routed
    them.
¹⁶The valleys of the sea were exposed
  and the foundations of the earth
    laid bare
at the rebuke of the LORD,
  at the blast of breath from his nostrils.
¹⁷"He reached down from on high and
    took hold of me;

²¹"The LORD has dealt with me
    according to my righteousness;
according to the cleanness of my
    hands he has rewarded me.
²²For I have kept the ways of the
    LORD;
  I have not done evil by turning
    from my God.
²³All his laws are before me;
  I have not turned away from his
    decrees.
²⁴I have been blameless before him
  and have kept myself from sin.
²⁵The LORD has rewarded me
    according to my righteousness,
  according to my cleanness[c] in his
    sight.

---

a *11* Many Hebrew manuscripts (see also Psalm 18:10); most Hebrew manuscripts *appeared*   b *12* Septuagint and Vulgate (see also Psalm 18:11); Hebrew *massed*   c *25* Hebrew; Septuagint and Vulgate (see also Psalm 18:24) *to the cleanness of my hands*

26"To the faithful you show yourself
    faithful,
  to the blameless you show yourself
    blameless,
27to the pure you show yourself pure,
  but to the crooked you show
    yourself shrewd.
28You save the humble,
  but your eyes are on the haughty to
    bring them low.
29You are my lamp, O LORD;
  the LORD turns my darkness into
    light.
30With your help I can advance against
    a troop[a];
  with my God I can scale a wall.

31"As for God, his way is perfect;
  the word of the LORD is flawless.
He is a shield
  for all who take refuge in him.
32For who is God besides the LORD?
  And who is the Rock except our
    God?

Praying 2 Samuel 22:38-41

*Lord, give me persistence and
perseverance in prayer until I see my
enemies defeated and destroyed.*

33It is God who arms me with strength[b]
  and makes my way perfect.
34He makes my feet like the feet of a
    deer;
  he enables me to stand on the
    heights.
35He trains my hands for battle;
  my arms can bend a bow of bronze.
36You give me your shield of victory;
  you stoop down to make me
    great.
37You broaden the path beneath me,
  so that my ankles do not turn.

38"I pursued my enemies and crushed
    them;
  I did not turn back till they were
    destroyed.

39I crushed them completely, and they
    could not rise;
  they fell beneath my feet.
40You armed me with strength for
    battle;
  you made my adversaries bow at
    my feet.
41You made my enemies turn their
    backs in flight,
  and I destroyed my foes.
42They cried for help, but there was no
    one to save them—
  to the LORD, but he did not answer.
43I beat them as fine as the dust of the
    earth;
  I pounded and trampled them like
    mud in the streets.

44"You have delivered me from the
    attacks of my people;
  you have preserved me as the head
    of nations.
People I did not know are subject to
    me,
45 and foreigners come cringing to me;
  as soon as they hear me, they obey
    me.
46They all lose heart;
  they come trembling[c] from their
    strongholds.

47"The LORD lives! Praise be to my
    Rock!
  Exalted be God, the Rock, my
    Savior!
48He is the God who avenges me,
  who puts the nations under me,
49 who sets me free from my enemies.
You exalted me above my foes;
  from violent men you rescued me.
50Therefore I will praise you, O LORD,
    among the nations;
  I will sing praises to your name.
51He gives his king great victories;
  he shows unfailing kindness to his
    anointed,
  to David and his descendants
    forever."

---

a 30 Or can run through a barricade   b 33 Dead Sea Scrolls, some Septuagint manuscripts, Vulgate and Syriac (see also Psalm 18:32); Masoretic Text who is my strong refuge   c 46 Some Septuagint manuscripts and Vulgate (see also Psalm 18:45); Masoretic Text they arm themselves.

The Last Words of David

23 These are the last words of David:

"The oracle of David son of Jesse,
    the oracle of the man exalted by the
        Most High,
the man anointed by the God of
        Jacob,
    Israel's singer of songs[a]:

[2] "The Spirit of the LORD spoke
        through me;
    his word was on my tongue.
[3] The God of Israel spoke,
    the Rock of Israel said to me:
'When one rules over men in
        righteousness,
    when he rules in the fear of God,
[4] he is like the light of morning at
        sunrise
    on a cloudless morning,
like the brightness after rain
    that brings the grass from the
        earth.'

[5] "Is not my house right with God?
    Has he not made with me an
        everlasting covenant,
    arranged and secured in every
        part?
Will he not bring to fruition my
        salvation
    and grant me my every desire?
[6] But evil men are all to be cast aside
        like thorns,
    which are not gathered with the
        hand.
[7] Whoever touches thorns
    uses a tool of iron or the shaft of a
        spear;
    they are burned up where they lie."

David's Mighty Men

[8] These are the names of David's mighty
men:

Josheb-Basshebeth,[b] a Tahkemonite,[c] was
chief of the Three; he raised his spear
against eight hundred men, whom he
killed[d] in one encounter.

[9] Next to him was Eleazar son of Dodai
the Ahohite. As one of the three mighty
men, he was with David when they
taunted the Philistines gathered ⌊at Pas
Dammim⌋[e] for battle. Then the men of
Israel retreated, [10] but he stood his ground
and struck down the Philistines till his
hand grew tired and froze to the sword.
The LORD brought about a great victory
that day. The troops returned to Eleazar,
but only to strip the dead.

[11] Next to him was Shammah son of
Agee the Hararite. When the Philistines
banded together at a place where there
was a field full of lentils, Israel's troops
fled from them. [12] But Shammah took
his stand in the middle of the field. He
defended it and struck the Philistines
down, and the LORD brought about a
great victory.

[13] During harvest time, three of the
thirty chief men came down to David
at the cave of Adullam, while a band of
Philistines was encamped in the Valley
of Rephaim. [14] At that time David was
in the stronghold, and the Philistine garrison was at Bethlehem. [15] David longed
for water and said, "Oh, that someone
would get me a drink of water from the
well near the gate of Bethlehem!" [16] So
the three mighty men broke through the
Philistine lines, drew water from the well
near the gate of Bethlehem and carried
it back to David. But he refused to drink
it; instead, he poured it out before the
LORD. [17] "Far be it from me, O LORD, to
do this!" he said. "Is it not the blood of
men who went at the risk of their lives?"
And David would not drink it.

Such were the exploits of the three
mighty men.

[18] Abishai the brother of Joab son of
Zeruiah was chief of the Three.[f] He

---

[a] 1 Or Israel's beloved singer   [b] 8 Hebrew; some Septuagint manuscripts suggest Ish-Bosheth, that is, Esh-Baal (see also
1 Chron. 11:11 Jashobeam).   [c] 8 Probably a variant of Hacmonite (see 1 Chron. 11:11)   [d] 8 Some Septuagint manuscripts (see
also 1 Chron. 11:11); Hebrew and other Septuagint manuscripts Three; it was Adino the Eznite who killed eight hundred men
[e] 9 See 1 Chron. 11:13; Hebrew gathered there.   [f] 18 Most Hebrew manuscripts (see also 1 Chron. 11:20); two Hebrew
manuscripts and Syriac Thirty

raised his spear against three hundred men, whom he killed, and so he became as famous as the Three. ¹⁹Was he not held in greater honor than the Three? He became their commander, even though he was not included among them.

²⁰Benaiah son of Jehoiada was a valiant fighter from Kabzeel, who performed great exploits. He struck down two of Moab's best men. He also went down into a pit on a snowy day and killed a lion. ²¹And he struck down a huge Egyptian. Although the Egyptian had a spear in his hand, Benaiah went against him with a club. He snatched the spear from the Egyptian's hand and killed him with his own spear. ²²Such were the exploits of Benaiah son of Jehoiada; he too was as famous as the three mighty men. ²³He was held in greater honor than any of the Thirty, but he was not included among the Three. And David put him in charge of his bodyguard.

²⁴Among the Thirty were:
  Asahel the brother of Joab,
  Elhanan son of Dodo from Bethlehem,
²⁵Shammah the Harodite,
  Elika the Harodite,
²⁶Helez the Paltite,
  Ira son of Ikkesh from Tekoa,
²⁷Abiezer from Anathoth,
  Mebunnaiᵃ the Hushathite,
²⁸Zalmon the Ahohite,
  Maharai the Netophathite,
²⁹Heledᵇ son of Baanah the Netophathite,
  Ithai son of Ribai from Gibeah in Benjamin,
³⁰Benaiah the Pirathonite,
  Hiddaiᶜ from the ravines of Gaash,
³¹Abi-Albon the Arbathite,
  Azmaveth the Barhumite,
³²Eliahba the Shaalbonite,
  the sons of Jashen,

Jonathan ³³son ofᵈ Shammah the Hararite,
  Ahiam son of Shararᵉ the Hararite,
³⁴Eliphelet son of Ahasbai the Maacathite,
  Eliam son of Ahithophel the Gilonite,
³⁵Hezro the Carmelite,
  Paarai the Arbite,
³⁶Igal son of Nathan from Zobah,
  the son of Hagri,ᶠ
³⁷Zelek the Ammonite,
  Naharai the Beerothite, the armor-bearer of Joab son of Zeruiah,
³⁸Ira the Ithrite,
  Gareb the Ithrite
³⁹and Uriah the Hittite.
There were thirty-seven in all.

David Counts the Fighting Men

24 Again the anger of the LORD burned against Israel, and he incited David against them, saying, "Go and take a census of Israel and Judah."

²So the king said to Joab and the army commandersᵍ with him, "Go throughout the tribes of Israel from Dan to Beersheba and enroll the fighting men, so that I may know how many there are."

³But Joab replied to the king, "May the LORD your God multiply the troops a hundred times over, and may the eyes of my lord the king see it. But why does my lord the king want to do such a thing?"

⁴The king's word, however, overruled Joab and the army commanders; so they left the presence of the king to enroll the fighting men of Israel.

⁵After crossing the Jordan, they camped near Aroer, south of the town in the gorge, and then went through Gad and on to Jazer. ⁶They went to Gilead and the region of Tahtim Hodshi, and on to Dan Jaan and around toward Sidon. ⁷Then they went toward the fortress of Tyre and

The Importance of Confession

GOING *deeper*

READ AND CONSIDER: 2 SAMUEL 24

"David was conscience-stricken after he had counted the fighting men, and he said to the Lord, 'I have sinned greatly in what I have done. Now, O Lord, I beg you, take away the guilt of your servant. I have done a very foolish thing'" (2 Samuel 24:10).

No one had to say anything—David just *knew* it. The number came back and his conscience immediately pricked him. He realized that he had wanted to count his fighting men because it would make him feel proud, make him feel powerful and in control. But when his arrogance and illusion were revealed, David confessed his sin to God.

When we do something we know is wrong, our conscience usually lets us know. We feel ashamed, tortured, and terrible. But we must be careful that Satan doesn't make us feel so condemned about our sin that we are too ashamed to come before God. The enemy wants us to struggle with guilt to the point that we can't even pray. But the Lord has given us a way out of that kind of condemnation. It's called confession.

Confessing is more than just apologizing. Anyone can do that. We all know people who are good apologizers. The reason they are so good at it is that they get so much practice. They have to say "I'm sorry" over and over again because they never change their ways. In fact, they sometimes say "I'm sorry" without ever actually admitting to any fault. Those are the professional apologizers, and their confessions don't mean anything. But *true* confession means admitting in full detail what you have done, and then fully *repenting* of it. Repentance means being so deeply sorry for what you have done that you will do whatever it takes to keep it from happening again. Confession means *recognizing* we have done wrong and *admitting* our sin. Repentance means being *sorry* about our sin to the point of grief, and so we *turn* and *walk away* from that sin.

Confession and repentance do not negate consequences, however. David went to the right place and did the right thing, but he still had to pay the price. Sometimes our sin sets in motion consequences that we must handle with the Lord's help.

Any time you feel convicted about something and you need to confess it before God, don't hesitate. The sooner you do it, the better you will feel. Also, ask God to show you any sin in your life that *needs* to be confessed. (Too often we don't even see it.) You will be amazed at how quickly God answers that prayer.

---

all the towns of the Hivites and Canaanites. Finally, they went on to Beersheba in the Negev of Judah.

⁸After they had gone through the entire land, they came back to Jerusalem at the end of nine months and twenty days. ⁹Joab reported the number of the fighting men to the king: In Israel there were eight hundred thousand able-bodied men who could handle a sword, and in Judah five hundred thousand.

¹⁰David was conscience-stricken after he had counted the fighting men, and he said to the Lord, "I have sinned greatly in what I have done. Now, O Lord, I beg you, take away the guilt of your servant. I have done a very foolish thing."

¹¹Before David got up the next morning, the word of the Lord had come to Gad the prophet, David's seer: ¹²"Go and tell David, 'This is what the Lord says: I am giving you three options. Choose one of them for me to carry out against you.'"

13So Gad went to David and said to him, "Shall there come upon you three[a] years of famine in your land? Or three months of fleeing from your enemies while they pursue you? Or three days of plague in your land? Now then, think it over and decide how I should answer the one who sent me."

14David said to Gad, "I am in deep distress. Let us fall into the hands of the LORD, for his mercy is great; but do not let me fall into the hands of men."

15So the LORD sent a plague on Israel from that morning until the end of the time designated, and seventy thousand of the people from Dan to Beersheba died. 16When the angel stretched out his hand to destroy Jerusalem, the LORD was grieved because of the calamity and said to the angel who was afflicting the people, "Enough! Withdraw your hand." The angel of the LORD was then at the threshing floor of Araunah the Jebusite.

17When David saw the angel who was striking down the people, he said to the LORD, "I am the one who has sinned and done wrong. These are but sheep. What have they done? Let your hand fall upon me and my family."

David Builds an Altar

18On that day Gad went to David and said to him, "Go up and build an altar to the LORD on the threshing floor of Araunah the Jebusite." 19So David went up, as the LORD had commanded through Gad. 20When Araunah looked and saw the king and his men coming toward him, he went out and bowed down before the king with his face to the ground.

21Araunah said, "Why has my lord the king come to his servant?"

"To buy your threshing floor," David answered, "so I can build an altar to the LORD, that the plague on the people may be stopped."

22Araunah said to David, "Let my lord the king take whatever pleases him and offer it up. Here are oxen for the burnt offering, and here are threshing sledges and ox yokes for the wood. 23O king, Araunah gives all this to the king." Araunah also said to him, "May the LORD your God accept you."

24But the king replied to Araunah, "No, I insist on paying you for it. I will not sacrifice to the LORD my God burnt offerings that cost me nothing."

So David bought the threshing floor and the oxen and paid fifty shekels[b] of silver for them. 25David built an altar to the LORD there and sacrificed burnt offerings and fellowship offerings.[c] Then the LORD answered prayer in behalf of the land, and the plague on Israel was stopped.

---

a 13 Septuagint (see also 1 Chron. 21:12); Hebrew *seven*   b 24 That is, about 1 1/4 pounds (about 0.6 kilogram)
c 25 Traditionally *peace offerings*

Author: Unknown, possibly Jeremiah

Date: Most likely during the time of the exile (between 560 and 538 BC)

Audience: The people of God living during and after the exile—to teach them Israel's history and, more importantly, the spiritual lessons from Israel's past

Prayer Themes:

- *Humbly ask God for heavenly wisdom, so that you always live in a way that honors Him (3:6-14).*

- *Ask God to reveal to you any possessions, desires, and/or relationships in your life that are becoming more important to you than your devotion to Him (11:1-8).*

- *Thank God that when you are quiet before Him, His still, small voice will speak gently to your heart (19:9-12).*

Serving God takes effort. It takes prayer, obedience, and self-sacrifice. Too few kings in Israel's history were willing to do any of those things.

Perhaps the idea that prayer is work explains why so few persist in prayer long term. It requires too much effort. Self-indulgence feels better. And that sad fact may explain why so many begin well in their spiritual walk but do not end well.

Consider, for example, King Solomon. First Kings demonstrates that no one had a more glorious, more blessed beginning ... and few have squandered so much advantage. The king's passion for God cooled, and his pursuit of God and prayers to God waned. As a result, he had a divided heart and left behind a divided kingdom.

What a warning to us to seek the Lord daily. To continue to look to Him for guidance. To pray ongoingly. "May he turn our hearts to him, to walk in all his ways" (8:58).

1 Kings

Adonijah Sets Himself Up as King

1 When King David was old and well advanced in years, he could not keep warm even when they put covers over him. ²So his servants said to him, "Let us look for a young virgin to attend the king and take care of him. She can lie beside him so that our lord the king may keep warm."

³Then they searched throughout Israel for a beautiful girl and found Abishag, a Shunammite, and brought her to the king. ⁴The girl was very beautiful; she took care of the king and waited on him, but the king had no intimate relations with her.

⁵Now Adonijah, whose mother was Haggith, put himself forward and said, "I will be king." So he got chariots and horses[a] ready, with fifty men to run ahead of him. ⁶(His father had never interfered with him by asking, "Why do you behave as you do?" He was also very handsome and was born next after Absalom.)

⁷Adonijah conferred with Joab son of Zeruiah and with Abiathar the priest, and they gave him their support. ⁸But Zadok the priest, Benaiah son of Jehoiada, Nathan the prophet, Shimei and Rei[b] and David's special guard did not join Adonijah.

⁹Adonijah then sacrificed sheep, cattle and fattened calves at the Stone of Zoheleth near En Rogel. He invited all his brothers, the king's sons, and all the men of Judah who were royal officials, ¹⁰but he did not invite Nathan the prophet or Benaiah or the special guard or his brother Solomon.

¹¹Then Nathan asked Bathsheba, Solomon's mother, "Have you not heard that Adonijah, the son of Haggith, has

---

a 5 Or *charioteers*   b 8 Or *and his friends*

become king without our lord David's knowing it? ¹²Now then, let me advise you how you can save your own life and the life of your son Solomon. ¹³Go in to King David and say to him, 'My lord the king, did you not swear to me your servant: "Surely Solomon your son shall be king after me, and he will sit on my throne"? Why then has Adonijah become king?' ¹⁴While you are still there talking to the king, I will come in and confirm what you have said."

¹⁵So Bathsheba went to see the aged king in his room, where Abishag the Shunammite was attending him. ¹⁶Bathsheba bowed low and knelt before the king.

"What is it you want?" the king asked.

¹⁷She said to him, "My lord, you yourself swore to me your servant by the LORD your God: 'Solomon your son shall be king after me, and he will sit on my throne.' ¹⁸But now Adonijah has become king, and you, my lord the king, do not know about it. ¹⁹He has sacrificed great numbers of cattle, fattened calves, and sheep, and has invited all the king's sons, Abiathar the priest and Joab the commander of the army, but he has not invited Solomon your servant. ²⁰My lord the king, the eyes of all Israel are on you, to learn from you who will sit on the throne of my lord the king after him. ²¹Otherwise, as soon as my lord the king is laid to rest with his fathers, I and my son Solomon will be treated as criminals."

²²While she was still speaking with the king, Nathan the prophet arrived. ²³And they told the king, "Nathan the prophet is here." So he went before the king and bowed with his face to the ground.

²⁴Nathan said, "Have you, my lord the king, declared that Adonijah shall be king after you, and that he will sit on your throne? ²⁵Today he has gone down and sacrificed great numbers of cattle, fattened calves, and sheep. He has invited all the king's sons, the commanders of the army and Abiathar the priest. Right now

they are eating and drinking with him and saying, 'Long live King Adonijah!' ²⁶But me your servant, and Zadok the priest, and Benaiah son of Jehoiada, and your servant Solomon he did not invite. ²⁷Is this something my lord the king has done without letting his servants know who should sit on the throne of my lord the king after him?"

David Makes Solomon King

²⁸Then King David said, "Call in Bathsheba." So she came into the king's presence and stood before him.

²⁹The king then took an oath: "As surely as the LORD lives, who has delivered me out of every trouble, ³⁰I will surely carry out today what I swore to you by the LORD, the God of Israel: Solomon your son shall be king after me, and he will sit on my throne in my place."

³¹Then Bathsheba bowed low with her face to the ground and, kneeling before the king, said, "May my lord King David live forever!"

³²King David said, "Call in Zadok the priest, Nathan the prophet and Benaiah son of Jehoiada." When they came before the king, ³³he said to them: "Take your lord's servants with you and set Solomon my son on my own mule and take him down to Gihon. ³⁴There have Zadok the priest and Nathan the prophet anoint him king over Israel. Blow the trumpet and shout, 'Long live King Solomon!' ³⁵Then you are to go up with him, and he is to come and sit on my throne and reign in my place. I have appointed him ruler over Israel and Judah."

³⁶Benaiah son of Jehoiada answered the king, "Amen! May the LORD, the God of my lord the king, so declare it. ³⁷As the LORD was with my lord the king, so may he be with Solomon to make his throne even greater than the throne of my lord King David!"

³⁸So Zadok the priest, Nathan the prophet, Benaiah son of Jehoiada, the Kerethites and the Pelethites went down and put Solomon on King David's mule

and escorted him to Gihon. ³⁹Zadok the priest took the horn of oil from the sacred tent and anointed Solomon. Then they sounded the trumpet and all the people shouted, "Long live King Solomon!" ⁴⁰And all the people went up after him, playing flutes and rejoicing greatly, so that the ground shook with the sound.

⁴¹Adonijah and all the guests who were with him heard it as they were finishing their feast. On hearing the sound of the trumpet, Joab asked, "What's the meaning of all the noise in the city?"

⁴²Even as he was speaking, Jonathan son of Abiathar the priest arrived. Adonijah said, "Come in. A worthy man like you must be bringing good news."

⁴³"Not at all!" Jonathan answered. "Our lord King David has made Solomon king. ⁴⁴The king has sent with him Zadok the priest, Nathan the prophet, Benaiah son of Jehoiada, the Kerethites and the Pelethites, and they have put him on the king's mule, ⁴⁵and Zadok the priest and Nathan the prophet have anointed him king at Gihon. From there they have gone up cheering, and the city resounds with it. That's the noise you hear. ⁴⁶Moreover, Solomon has taken his seat on the royal throne. ⁴⁷Also, the royal officials have come to congratulate our lord King David, saying, 'May your God make Solomon's name more famous than yours and his throne greater than yours!' And the king bowed in worship on his bed ⁴⁸and said, 'Praise be to the LORD, the God of Israel, who has allowed my eyes to see a successor on my throne today.'"

⁴⁹At this, all Adonijah's guests rose in alarm and dispersed. ⁵⁰But Adonijah, in fear of Solomon, went and took hold of the horns of the altar. ⁵¹Then Solomon was told, "Adonijah is afraid of King Solomon and is clinging to the horns of the altar. He says, 'Let King Solomon swear to me today that he will not put his servant to death with the sword.'"

⁵²Solomon replied, "If he shows himself to be a worthy man, not a hair of his head will fall to the ground; but if evil is found in him, he will die." ⁵³Then King Solomon sent men, and they brought him down from the altar. And Adonijah came and bowed down to King Solomon, and Solomon said, "Go to your home."

David's Charge to Solomon

2 When the time drew near for David to die, he gave a charge to Solomon his son.

²"I am about to go the way of all the earth," he said. "So be strong, show yourself a man, ³and observe what the LORD your God requires: Walk in his ways, and keep his decrees and commands, his laws and requirements, as written in the Law of Moses, so that you may prosper in all you do and wherever you go, ⁴and that the LORD may keep his promise to me: 'If your descendants watch how they live, and if they walk faithfully before me with all their heart and soul, you will never fail to have a man on the throne of Israel.'

> *Praying 1 Kings 2:3*
> *Lord, help me to walk in Your ways and keep Your commands so that I may prosper in all I do.*

⁵"Now you yourself know what Joab son of Zeruiah did to me—what he did to the two commanders of Israel's armies, Abner son of Ner and Amasa son of Jether. He killed them, shedding their blood in peacetime as if in battle, and with that blood stained the belt around his waist and the sandals on his feet. ⁶Deal with him according to your wisdom, but do not let his gray head go down to the graveᵃ in peace.

⁷"But show kindness to the sons of Barzillai of Gilead and let them be among those who eat at your table. They stood by me when I fled from your brother Absalom.

⁸"And remember, you have with you Shimei son of Gera, the Benjamite from

---

ᵃ 6 Hebrew *Sheol*; also in verse 9

Bahurim, who called down bitter curses on me the day I went to Mahanaim. When he came down to meet me at the Jordan, I swore to him by the LORD: 'I will not put you to death by the sword.' 9But now, do not consider him innocent. You are a man of wisdom; you will know what to do to him. Bring his gray head down to the grave in blood."

10Then David rested with his fathers and was buried in the City of David. 11He had reigned forty years over Israel—seven years in Hebron and thirty-three in Jerusalem. 12So Solomon sat on the throne of his father David, and his rule was firmly established.

Solomon's Throne Established

13Now Adonijah, the son of Haggith, went to Bathsheba, Solomon's mother. Bathsheba asked him, "Do you come peacefully?"

He answered, "Yes, peacefully." 14Then he added, "I have something to say to you."

"You may say it," she replied.

15"As you know," he said, "the kingdom was mine. All Israel looked to me as their king. But things changed, and the kingdom has gone to my brother; for it has come to him from the LORD. 16Now I have one request to make of you. Do not refuse me."

"You may make it," she said.

17So he continued, "Please ask King Solomon—he will not refuse you—to give me Abishag the Shunammite as my wife."

18"Very well," Bathsheba replied, "I will speak to the king for you."

19When Bathsheba went to King Solomon to speak to him for Adonijah, the king stood up to meet her, bowed down to her and sat down on his throne. He had a throne brought for the king's mother, and she sat down at his right hand.

20"I have one small request to make of you," she said. "Do not refuse me."

The king replied, "Make it, my mother; I will not refuse you."

21So she said, "Let Abishag the Shunammite be given in marriage to your brother Adonijah."

22King Solomon answered his mother, "Why do you request Abishag the Shunammite for Adonijah? You might as well request the kingdom for him—after all, he is my older brother—yes, for him and for Abiathar the priest and Joab son of Zeruiah!"

23Then King Solomon swore by the LORD: "May God deal with me, be it ever so severely, if Adonijah does not pay with his life for this request! 24And now, as surely as the LORD lives—he who has established me securely on the throne of my father David and has founded a dynasty for me as he promised—Adonijah shall be put to death today!" 25So King Solomon gave orders to Benaiah son of Jehoiada, and he struck down Adonijah and he died.

26To Abiathar the priest the king said, "Go back to your fields in Anathoth. You deserve to die, but I will not put you to death now, because you carried the ark of the Sovereign LORD before my father David and shared all my father's hardships." 27So Solomon removed Abiathar from the priesthood of the LORD, fulfilling the word the LORD had spoken at Shiloh about the house of Eli.

28When the news reached Joab, who had conspired with Adonijah though not with Absalom, he fled to the tent of the LORD and took hold of the horns of the altar. 29King Solomon was told that Joab had fled to the tent of the LORD and was beside the altar. Then Solomon ordered Benaiah son of Jehoiada, "Go, strike him down!"

30So Benaiah entered the tent of the LORD and said to Joab, "The king says, 'Come out!'"

But he answered, "No, I will die here."

Benaiah reported to the king, "This is how Joab answered me."

31Then the king commanded Benaiah, "Do as he says. Strike him down and bury him, and so clear me and my father's house of the guilt of the innocent blood that Joab shed. ³²The LORD will repay him for the blood he shed, because without the knowledge of my father David he attacked two men and killed them with the sword. Both of them—Abner son of Ner, commander of Israel's army, and Amasa son of Jether, commander of Judah's army—were better men and more upright than he. ³³May the guilt of their blood rest on the head of Joab and his descendants forever. But on David and his descendants, his house and his throne, may there be the LORD's peace forever."

³⁴So Benaiah son of Jehoiada went up and struck down Joab and killed him, and he was buried on his own land[a] in the desert. ³⁵The king put Benaiah son of Jehoiada over the army in Joab's position and replaced Abiathar with Zadok the priest.

³⁶Then the king sent for Shimei and said to him, "Build yourself a house in Jerusalem and live there, but do not go anywhere else. ³⁷The day you leave and cross the Kidron Valley, you can be sure you will die; your blood will be on your own head."

³⁸Shimei answered the king, "What you say is good. Your servant will do as my lord the king has said." And Shimei stayed in Jerusalem for a long time.

³⁹But three years later, two of Shimei's slaves ran off to Achish son of Maacah, king of Gath, and Shimei was told, "Your slaves are in Gath." ⁴⁰At this, he saddled his donkey and went to Achish at Gath in search of his slaves. So Shimei went away and brought the slaves back from Gath.

⁴¹When Solomon was told that Shimei had gone from Jerusalem to Gath and had returned, ⁴²the king summoned Shimei and said to him, "Did I not make you swear by the LORD and warn you, 'On the day you leave to go anywhere else, you can be sure you will die'? At that time you said to me, 'What you say

is good. I will obey.' ⁴³Why then did you not keep your oath to the LORD and obey the command I gave you?"

⁴⁴The king also said to Shimei, "You know in your heart all the wrong you did to my father David. Now the LORD will repay you for your wrongdoing. ⁴⁵But King Solomon will be blessed, and David's throne will remain secure before the LORD forever."

⁴⁶Then the king gave the order to Benaiah son of Jehoiada, and he went out and struck Shimei down and killed him.

The kingdom was now firmly established in Solomon's hands.

Solomon Asks for Wisdom

3 Solomon made an alliance with Pharaoh king of Egypt and married his daughter. He brought her to the City of David until he finished building his palace and the temple of the LORD, and the wall around Jerusalem. ²The people, however, were still sacrificing at the high places, because a temple had not yet been built for the Name of the LORD. ³Solomon showed his love for the LORD by walking according to the statutes of his father David, except that he offered sacrifices and burned incense on the high places.

⁴The king went to Gibeon to offer sacrifices, for that was the most important high place, and Solomon offered a thousand burnt offerings on that altar. ⁵At Gibeon the LORD appeared to Solomon during the night in a dream, and God said, "Ask for whatever you want me to give you."

⁶Solomon answered, "You have shown great kindness to your servant, my father David, because he was faithful to you and righteous and upright in heart. You have continued this great kindness to him and have given him a son to sit on his throne this very day.

⁷"Now, O LORD my God, you have made your servant king in place of my father David. But I am only a little child and do not know how to carry out my

---

[a] 34 Or buried in his tomb

duties. 8Your servant is here among the people you have chosen, a great people, too numerous to count or number. 9So give your servant a discerning heart to govern your people and to distinguish between right and wrong. For who is able to govern this great people of yours?"

Praying 1 Kings 3:9

Holy Father, I ask that You would always give me the ability to discern between good and evil.

10The Lord was pleased that Solomon had asked for this. 11So God said to him, "Since you have asked for this and not

mon awoke—and he realized it had been a dream.

He returned to Jerusalem, stood before the ark of the Lord's covenant and sacrificed burnt offerings and fellowship offerings.ᵃ Then he gave a feast for all his court.

A Wise Ruling

16Now two prostitutes came to the king and stood before him. 17One of them said, "My lord, this woman and I live in the same house. I had a baby while she was there with me. 18The third day after my child was born, this woman also had a baby. We were alone; there was no one in the house but the two of us.

God's people at prayer
SOLOMON PRAYS FOR WISDOM

1 KINGS 3:4-15 It's hard not to think of Solomon's prayer for wisdom without considering his later mistakes and sins. We see his great wisdom on the throne but so little in his personal life. It's tempting to point a finger at him and say, "If I had the wisdom God poured into you, I certainly wouldn't make the mistakes you made." But the Bible provides more wisdom than Solomon ever dreamed of knowing, yet how often do we ask God to help us glean all the wisdom we can from it?

And how often do we pray for wisdom the way that Solomon prayed? Yet James urges us, "If any of you lacks wisdom, he should ask God, who gives generously to all without finding fault, and it will be given to him" (James 1:5). We are to ask and God will answer. Perhaps our greatest exercise of wisdom comes as we pray that God will help us apply the wisdom He has already given us.

for long life or wealth for yourself, nor have asked for the death of your enemies but for discernment in administering justice, 12I will do what you have asked. I will give you a wise and discerning heart, so that there will never have been anyone like you, nor will there ever be. 13Moreover, I will give you what you have not asked for—both riches and honor—so that in your lifetime you will have no equal among kings. 14And if you walk in my ways and obey my statutes and commands as David your father did, I will give you a long life." 15Then Solo-

19"During the night this woman's son died because she lay on him. 20So she got up in the middle of the night and took my son from my side while I your servant was asleep. She put him by her breast and put her dead son by my breast. 21The next morning, I got up to nurse my son—and he was dead! But when I looked at him closely in the morning light, I saw that it wasn't the son I had borne."

22The other woman said, "No! The living one is my son; the dead one is yours."

But the first one insisted, "No! The

ᵃ 15 Traditionally *peace offerings*

dead one is yours; the living one is mine." And so they argued before the king.

23 The king said, "This one says, 'My son is alive and your son is dead,' while that one says, 'No! Your son is dead and mine is alive.'"

24 Then the king said, "Bring me a sword." So they brought a sword for the king. 25 He then gave an order: "Cut the living child in two and give half to one and half to the other."

26 The woman whose son was alive was filled with compassion for her son and said to the king, "Please, my lord, give her the living baby! Don't kill him!"

But the other said, "Neither I nor you shall have him. Cut him in two!"

27 Then the king gave his ruling: "Give the living baby to the first woman. Do not kill him; she is his mother."

28 When all Israel heard the verdict the king had given, they held the king in awe, because they saw that he had wisdom from God to administer justice.

Solomon's Officials and Governors

4 So King Solomon ruled over all Israel. 2 And these were his chief officials:

Azariah son of Zadok—the priest;

3 Elihoreph and Ahijah, sons of Shisha—secretaries;

Jehoshaphat son of Ahilud—recorder;

4 Benaiah son of Jehoiada—commander in chief;

Zadok and Abiathar—priests;

5 Azariah son of Nathan—in charge of the district officers;

Zabud son of Nathan—a priest and personal adviser to the king;

6 Ahishar—in charge of the palace;

Adoniram son of Abda—in charge of forced labor.

7 Solomon also had twelve district governors over all Israel, who supplied provisions for the king and the royal household. Each one had to provide supplies for one month in the year. 8 These are their names:

Ben-Hur—in the hill country of Ephraim;

9 Ben-Deker—in Makaz, Shaalbim, Beth Shemesh and Elon Bethhanan;

10 Ben-Hesed—in Arubboth (Socoh and all the land of Hepher were his);

11 Ben-Abinadab—in Naphoth Dor[a] (he was married to Taphath daughter of Solomon);

12 Baana son of Ahilud—in Taanach and Megiddo, and in all of Beth Shan next to Zarethan below Jezreel, from Beth Shan to Abel Meholah across to Jokmeam;

13 Ben-Geber—in Ramoth Gilead (the settlements of Jair son of Manasseh in Gilead were his, as well as the district of Argob in Bashan and its sixty large walled cities with bronze gate bars);

14 Ahinadab son of Iddo—in Mahanaim;

15 Ahimaaz—in Naphtali (he had married Basemath daughter of Solomon);

16 Baana son of Hushai—in Asher and in Aloth;

17 Jehoshaphat son of Paruah—in Issachar;

18 Shimei son of Ela—in Benjamin;

19 Geber son of Uri—in Gilead (the country of Sihon king of the Amorites and the country of Og king of Bashan). He was the only governor over the district.

Solomon's Daily Provisions

20 The people of Judah and Israel were as numerous as the sand on the seashore; they ate, they drank and they were happy. 21 And Solomon ruled over all the kingdoms from the River[b] to the land of the Philistines, as far as the border of Egypt. These countries brought tribute and were Solomon's subjects all his life.

22 Solomon's daily provisions were thirty

---

a 11 Or in the heights of Dor   b 21 That is, the Euphrates; also in verse 24 cors^a of fine flour and sixty cors^b of meal, ²³ten head of stall-fed cattle, twenty of pasture-fed cattle and a hundred sheep and goats, as well as deer, gazelles, roebucks and choice fowl. ²⁴For he ruled over all the kingdoms west of the River, from Tiphsah to Gaza, and had peace on all sides. ²⁵During Solomon's lifetime Judah and Israel, from Dan to Beersheba, lived in safety, each man under his own vine and fig tree.

²⁶Solomon had four^c thousand stalls for chariot horses, and twelve thousand horses.^d

²⁷The district officers, each in his month, supplied provisions for King Solomon and all who came to the king's table. They saw to it that nothing was lacking. ²⁸They also brought to the proper place their quotas of barley and straw for the chariot horses and the other horses.

Solomon's Wisdom

²⁹God gave Solomon wisdom and very great insight, and a breadth of understanding as measureless as the sand on the seashore. ³⁰Solomon's wisdom was greater than the wisdom of all the men of the East, and greater than all the wisdom of Egypt. ³¹He was wiser than any other man, including Ethan the Ezrahite—wiser than Heman, Calcol and Darda, the sons of Mahol. And his fame spread to all the surrounding nations. ³²He spoke three thousand proverbs and his songs numbered a thousand and five. ³³He described plant life, from the cedar of Lebanon to the hyssop that grows out of walls. He also taught about animals and birds, reptiles and fish. ³⁴Men of all nations came to listen to Solomon's wisdom, sent by all the kings of the world, who had heard of his wisdom.

Preparations for Building the Temple

5 When Hiram king of Tyre heard that Solomon had been anointed king to succeed his father David, he sent his envoys to Solomon, because he had always been on friendly terms with David. ²Solomon sent back this message to Hiram:

³"You know that because of the wars waged against my father David from all sides, he could not build a temple for the Name of the LORD his God until the LORD put his enemies under his feet. ⁴But now the LORD my God has given me rest on every side, and there is no adversary or disaster. ⁵I intend, therefore, to build a temple for the Name of the LORD my God, as the LORD told my father David, when he said, 'Your son whom I will put on the throne in your place will build the temple for my Name.'

⁶"So give orders that cedars of Lebanon be cut for me. My men will work with yours, and I will pay you for your men whatever wages you set. You know that we have no one so skilled in felling timber as the Sidonians."

⁷When Hiram heard Solomon's message, he was greatly pleased and said, "Praise be to the LORD today, for he has given David a wise son to rule over this great nation."

⁸So Hiram sent word to Solomon:

"I have received the message you sent me and will do all you want in providing the cedar and pine logs. ⁹My men will haul them down from Lebanon to the sea, and I will float them in rafts by sea to the place you specify. There I will separate them and you can take them away. And you are to grant my wish by providing food for my royal household."

¹⁰In this way Hiram kept Solomon supplied with all the cedar and pine logs he wanted, ¹¹and Solomon gave Hiram twenty thousand cors^e of wheat as food

^a22 That is, probably about 185 bushels (about 6.6 kiloliters) ^b22 That is, probably about 375 bushels (about 13.2 kiloliters) ^c26 Some Septuagint manuscripts (see also 2 Chron. 9:25); Hebrew *forty* ^d26 Or *charioteers* ^e11 That is, probably about 125,000 bushels (about 4,400 kiloliters)

for his household, in addition to twenty thousand baths[a,b] of pressed olive oil. Solomon continued to do this for Hiram year after year. [12]The LORD gave Solomon wisdom, just as he had promised him. There were peaceful relations between Hiram and Solomon, and the two of them made a treaty.

[13]King Solomon conscripted laborers from all Israel—thirty thousand men. [14]He sent them off to Lebanon in shifts of ten thousand a month, so that they spent one month in Lebanon and two months at home. Adoniram was in charge of the forced labor. [15]Solomon had seventy thousand carriers and eighty thousand stonecutters in the hills, [16]as well as thirty-three hundred[c] foremen who supervised the project and directed the workmen. [17]At the king's command they removed from the quarry large blocks of quality stone to provide a foundation of dressed stone for the temple. [18]The craftsmen of Solomon and Hiram and the men of Gebal[d] cut and prepared the timber and stone for the building of the temple.

Solomon Builds the Temple

6 In the four hundred and eightieth[e] year after the Israelites had come out of Egypt, in the fourth year of Solomon's reign over Israel, in the month of Ziv, the second month, he began to build the temple of the LORD.

[2]The temple that King Solomon built for the LORD was sixty cubits long, twenty wide and thirty high.[f] [3]The portico at the front of the main hall of the temple extended the width of the temple, that is twenty cubits,[g] and projected ten cubits[h] from the front of the temple. [4]He made narrow clerestory windows in the temple. [5]Against the walls of the main hall and inner sanctuary he built a structure around the building, in which there were side rooms. [6]The lowest floor was five cubits[i] wide, the middle floor six cubits[j] and the third floor seven.[k] He made offset ledges around the outside of the temple so that nothing would be inserted into the temple walls.

[7]In building the temple, only blocks dressed at the quarry were used, and no hammer, chisel or any other iron tool was heard at the temple site while it was being built.

[8]The entrance to the lowest[l] floor was on the south side of the temple; a stairway led up to the middle level and from there to the third. [9]So he built the temple and completed it, roofing it with beams and cedar planks. [10]And he built the side rooms all along the temple. The height of each was five cubits, and they were attached to the temple by beams of cedar.

[11]The word of the LORD came to Solomon: [12]"As for this temple you are building, if you follow my decrees, carry out my regulations and keep all my commands and obey them, I will fulfill through you the promise I gave to David your father. [13]And I will live among the Israelites and will not abandon my people Israel."

[14]So Solomon built the temple and completed it. [15]He lined its interior walls with cedar boards, paneling them from the floor of the temple to the ceiling, and covered the floor of the temple with planks of pine. [16]He partitioned off twenty cubits[g] at the rear of the temple with cedar boards from floor to ceiling to form within the temple an inner sanctuary, the Most Holy Place. [17]The main hall in front of this room was forty cubits[m] long. [18]The inside of the temple was cedar, carved with gourds and open flowers. Everything was cedar; no stone was to be seen.

---

[a] 11 Septuagint (see also 2 Chron. 2:10); Hebrew twenty cors   [b] 11 That is, about 115,000 gallons (about 440 kiloliters)
[c] 16 Hebrew; some Septuagint manuscripts (see also 2 Chron. 2:2, 18) thirty-six hundred   [d] 18 That is, Byblos   [e] 1 Hebrew; Septuagint four hundred and fortieth   [f] 2 That is, about 90 feet (about 27 meters) long and 30 feet (about 9 meters) wide and 45 feet (about 13.5 meters) high   [g] 3,16 That is, about 30 feet (about 9 meters)   [h] 3 That is, about 15 feet (about 4.5 meters)   [i] 6 That is, about 7 1/2 feet (about 2.3 meters); also in verses 10 and 24   [j] 6 That is, about 9 feet (about 2.7 meters)   [k] 6 That is, about 10 1/2 feet (about 3.1 meters)   [l] 8 Septuagint; Hebrew middle   [m] 17 That is, about 60 feet (about 18 meters)

¹⁹He prepared the inner sanctuary within the temple to set the ark of the covenant of the LORD there. ²⁰The inner sanctuary was twenty cubits long, twenty wide and twenty high.^a He overlaid the inside with pure gold, and he also overlaid the altar of cedar. ²¹Solomon covered the inside of the temple with pure gold, and he extended gold chains across the front of the inner sanctuary, which was overlaid with gold. ²²So he overlaid the whole interior with gold. He also overlaid with gold the altar that belonged to the inner sanctuary.

²³In the inner sanctuary he made a pair of cherubim of olive wood, each ten cubits^b high. ²⁴One wing of the first cherub was five cubits long, and the other wing five cubits—ten cubits from wing tip to wing tip. ²⁵The second cherub also measured ten cubits, for the two cherubim were identical in size and shape. ²⁶The height of each cherub was ten cubits. ²⁷He placed the cherubim inside the innermost room of the temple, with their wings spread out. The wing of one cherub touched one wall, while the wing of the other touched the other wall, and their wings touched each other in the middle of the room. ²⁸He overlaid the cherubim with gold.

²⁹On the walls all around the temple, in both the inner and outer rooms, he carved cherubim, palm trees and open flowers. ³⁰He also covered the floors of both the inner and outer rooms of the temple with gold.

³¹For the entrance of the inner sanctuary he made doors of olive wood with five-sided jambs. ³²And on the two olive wood doors he carved cherubim, palm trees and open flowers, and overlaid the cherubim and palm trees with beaten gold. ³³In the same way he made four-sided jambs of olive wood for the entrance to the main hall. ³⁴He also made two pine doors, each having two leaves that turned in sockets. ³⁵He carved cherubim, palm trees and open flowers on them and overlaid them with gold hammered evenly over the carvings.

³⁶And he built the inner courtyard of three courses of dressed stone and one course of trimmed cedar beams.

³⁷The foundation of the temple of the LORD was laid in the fourth year, in the month of Ziv. ³⁸In the eleventh year in the month of Bul, the eighth month, the temple was finished in all its details according to its specifications. He had spent seven years building it.

Solomon Builds His Palace

It took Solomon thirteen years, however, to complete the construction of his palace. ²He built the Palace of the Forest of Lebanon a hundred cubits long, fifty wide and thirty high,^c with four rows of cedar columns supporting trimmed cedar beams. ³It was roofed with cedar above the beams that rested on the columns—forty-five beams, fifteen to a row. ⁴Its windows were placed high in sets of three, facing each other. ⁵All the doorways had rectangular frames; they were in the front part in sets of three, facing each other.^d

⁶He made a colonnade fifty cubits long and thirty wide.^e In front of it was a portico, and in front of that were pillars and an overhanging roof.

⁷He built the throne hall, the Hall of Justice, where he was to judge, and he covered it with cedar from floor to ceiling.^f ⁸And the palace in which he was to live, set farther back, was similar in design. Solomon also made a palace like this hall for Pharaoh's daughter, whom he had married.

⁹All these structures, from the outside to the great courtyard and from foundation to eaves, were made of blocks of

---

^a20 That is, about 30 feet (about 9 meters) long, wide and high   ^b23 That is, about 15 feet (about 4.5 meters)   ^c2 That is, about 150 feet (about 46 meters) long, 75 feet (about 23 meters) wide and 45 feet (about 13.5 meters) high   ^d5 The meaning of the Hebrew for this verse is uncertain.   ^e6 That is, about 75 feet (about 23 meters) long and 45 feet (about 13.5 meters) wide   ^f7 Vulgate and Syriac; Hebrew floor

high-grade stone cut to size and trimmed with a saw on their inner and outer faces. [10]The foundations were laid with large stones of good quality, some measuring ten cubits[a] and some eight.[b] [11]Above were high-grade stones, cut to size, and cedar beams. [12]The great courtyard was surrounded by a wall of three courses of dressed stone and one course of trimmed cedar beams, as was the inner courtyard of the temple of the LORD with its portico.

The Temple's Furnishings

[13]King Solomon sent to Tyre and brought Huram,[c] [14]whose mother was a widow from the tribe of Naphtali and whose father was a man of Tyre and a craftsman in bronze. Huram was highly skilled and experienced in all kinds of bronze work. He came to King Solomon and did all the work assigned to him.

[15]He cast two bronze pillars, each eighteen cubits high and twelve cubits around,[d] by line. [16]He also made two capitals of cast bronze to set on the tops of the pillars; each capital was five cubits[e] high. [17]A network of interwoven chains festooned the capitals on top of the pillars, seven for each capital. [18]He made pomegranates in two rows[f] encircling each network to decorate the capitals on top of the pillars.[g] He did the same for each capital. [19]The capitals on top of the pillars in the portico were in the shape of lilies, four cubits[h] high. [20]On the capitals of both pillars, above the bowl-shaped part next to the network, were the two hundred pomegranates in rows all around. [21]He erected the pillars at the portico of the temple. The pillar to the south he named Jakin[i] and the one to the north Boaz.[j] [22]The capitals on top

were in the shape of lilies. And so the work on the pillars was completed.

[23]He made the Sea of cast metal, circular in shape, measuring ten cubits[a] from rim to rim and five cubits high. It took a line of thirty cubits[k] to measure around it. [24]Below the rim, gourds encircled it—ten to a cubit. The gourds were cast in two rows in one piece with the Sea.

[25]The Sea stood on twelve bulls, three facing north, three facing west, three facing south and three facing east. The Sea rested on top of them, and their hindquarters were toward the center. [26]It was a handbreadth[l] in thickness, and its rim was like the rim of a cup, like a lily blossom. It held two thousand baths.[m]

[27]He also made ten movable stands of bronze; each was four cubits long, four wide and three high.[n] [28]This is how the stands were made: They had side panels attached to uprights. [29]On the panels between the uprights were lions, bulls and cherubim—and on the uprights as well. Above and below the lions and bulls were wreaths of hammered work. [30]Each stand had four bronze wheels with bronze axles, and each had a basin resting on four supports, cast with wreaths on each side. [31]On the inside of the stand there was an opening that had a circular frame one cubit[o] deep. This opening was round, and with its basework it measured a cubit and a half.[p] Around its opening there was engraving. The panels of the stands were square, not round. [32]The four wheels were under the panels, and the axles of the wheels were attached to the stand. The diameter of each wheel was a cubit and a half. [33]The wheels were made like

---

[a] 10,23 That is, about 15 feet (about 4.5 meters)   [b] 10 That is, about 12 feet (about 3.6 meters)   [c] 13 Hebrew *Hiram,* a variant of *Huram;* also in verses 40 and 45   [d] 15 That is, about 27 feet (about 8.1 meters) high and 18 feet (about 5.4 meters) around   [e] 16 That is, about 7 1/2 feet (about 2.3 meters); also in verse 23   [f] 18 Two Hebrew manuscripts and Septuagint; most Hebrew manuscripts *made the pillars, and there were two rows*   [g] 18 Many Hebrew manuscripts and Syriac; most Hebrew manuscripts *pomegranates*   [h] 19 That is, about 6 feet (about 1.8 meters); also in verse 38   [i] 21 *Jakin* probably means *he establishes.*   [j] 21 *Boaz* probably means *in him is strength.*   [k] 23 That is, about 45 feet (about 13.5 meters)   [l] 26 That is, about 3 inches (about 8 centimeters)   [m] 26 That is, probably about 11,500 gallons (about 44 kiloliters); the Septuagint does not have this sentence.   [n] 27 That is, about 6 feet (about 1.8 meters) long and wide and about 4 1/2 feet (about 1.3 meters) high   [o] 31 That is, about 1 1/2 feet (about 0.5 meter)   [p] 31 That is, about 2 1/4 feet (about 0.7 meter); also in verse 32

chariot wheels; the axles, rims, spokes and hubs were all of cast metal.

³⁴Each stand had four handles, one on each corner, projecting from the stand. ³⁵At the top of the stand there was a circular band half a cubit[a] deep. The supports and panels were attached to the top of the stand. ³⁶He engraved cherubim, lions and palm trees on the surfaces of the supports and on the panels, in every available space, with wreaths all around. ³⁷This is the way he made the ten stands. They were all cast in the same molds and were identical in size and shape.

³⁸He then made ten bronze basins, each holding forty baths[b] and measuring four cubits across, one basin to go on each of the ten stands. ³⁹He placed five of the stands on the south side of the temple and five on the north. He placed the Sea on the south side, at the southeast corner of the temple. ⁴⁰He also made the basins and shovels and sprinkling bowls.

So Huram finished all the work he had undertaken for King Solomon in the temple of the LORD:

⁴¹ the two pillars;

the two bowl-shaped capitals on top of the pillars;

the two sets of network decorating the two bowl-shaped capitals on top of the pillars;

⁴² the four hundred pomegranates for the two sets of network (two rows of pomegranates for each network, decorating the bowl-shaped capitals on top of the pillars);

⁴³ the ten stands with their ten basins;

⁴⁴ the Sea and the twelve bulls under it;

⁴⁵ the pots, shovels and sprinkling bowls.

All these objects that Huram made for King Solomon for the temple of the LORD were of burnished bronze. ⁴⁶The king had them cast in clay molds in the plain of the Jordan between Succoth and Zarethan. ⁴⁷Solomon left all these things unweighed, because there were so many; the weight of the bronze was not determined.

⁴⁸Solomon also made all the furnishings that were in the LORD's temple:

the golden altar;

the golden table on which was the bread of the Presence;

⁴⁹ the lampstands of pure gold (five on the right and five on the left, in front of the inner sanctuary);

the gold floral work and lamps and tongs;

⁵⁰ the pure gold basins, wick trimmers, sprinkling bowls, dishes and censers;

and the gold sockets for the doors of the innermost room, the Most Holy Place, and also for the doors of the main hall of the temple.

⁵¹When all the work King Solomon had done for the temple of the LORD was finished, he brought in the things his father David had dedicated—the silver and gold and the furnishings—and he placed them in the treasuries of the LORD's temple.

The Ark Brought to the Temple

8 Then King Solomon summoned into his presence at Jerusalem the elders of Israel, all the heads of the tribes and the chiefs of the Israelite families, to bring up the ark of the LORD's covenant from Zion, the City of David. ²All the men of Israel came together to King Solomon at the time of the festival in the month of Ethanim, the seventh month.

³When all the elders of Israel had arrived, the priests took up the ark, ⁴and they brought up the ark of the LORD and the Tent of Meeting and all the sacred furnishings in it. The priests and Levites carried them up, ⁵and King Solomon and the entire assembly of Israel that had gathered about him were before the ark, sacrificing so many sheep and cattle that they could not be recorded or counted.

ᵃ 35 That is, about 3/4 foot (about 0.2 meter)   ᵇ 38 That is, about 230 gallons (about 880 liters)

⁶The priests then brought the ark of the LORD's covenant to its place in the inner sanctuary of the temple, the Most Holy Place, and put it beneath the wings of the cherubim. ⁷The cherubim spread their wings over the place of the ark and overshadowed the ark and its carrying poles. ⁸These poles were so long that their ends could be seen from the Holy Place in front of the inner sanctuary, but not from outside the Holy Place; and they are still there today. ⁹There was nothing in the ark except the two stone tablets that Moses had placed in it at Horeb, where the LORD made a covenant with the Israelites after they came out of Egypt.

¹⁰When the priests withdrew from the Holy Place, the cloud filled the temple of the LORD. ¹¹And the priests could not perform their service because of the cloud, for the glory of the LORD filled his temple.

¹²Then Solomon said, "The LORD has said that he would dwell in a dark cloud; ¹³I have indeed built a magnificent temple for you, a place for you to dwell forever."

¹⁴While the whole assembly of Israel was standing there, the king turned around and blessed them. ¹⁵Then he said:

"Praise be to the LORD, the God of Israel, who with his own hand has fulfilled what he promised with his own mouth to my father David. For he said, ¹⁶'Since the day I brought my people Israel out of Egypt, I have not chosen a city in any tribe of Israel to have a temple built for my Name to be there, but I have chosen David to rule my people Israel.'

¹⁷"My father David had it in his heart to build a temple for the Name of the LORD, the God of Israel. ¹⁸But the LORD said to my father David, 'Because it was in your heart to build a temple for my Name, you did well to have this in your heart. ¹⁹Nevertheless, you are not the one to build the temple, but your son, who is your own flesh and blood—he is the one who will build the temple for my Name.'

²⁰"The LORD has kept the promise he made: I have succeeded David my father and now I sit on the throne of Israel, just as the LORD promised, and I have built the temple for the Name of the LORD, the God of Israel. ²¹I have provided a place there for the ark, in which is the covenant of the LORD that he made with our fathers when he brought them out of Egypt."

Solomon's Prayer of Dedication

²²Then Solomon stood before the altar of the LORD in front of the whole assembly of Israel, spread out his hands toward heaven ²³and said:

"O LORD, God of Israel, there is no God like you in heaven above or on earth below—you who keep your covenant of love with your servants who continue wholeheartedly in your way. ²⁴You have kept your promise to your servant David my father; with your mouth you have promised and with your hand you have fulfilled it—as it is today.

²⁵"Now LORD, God of Israel, keep for your servant David my father the promises you made to him when you said, 'You shall never fail to have a man to sit before me on the throne of Israel, if only your sons are careful in all they do to walk before me as you have done.' ²⁶And now, O God of Israel, let your word that you promised your servant David my father come true.

²⁷"But will God really dwell on earth? The heavens, even the highest heaven, cannot contain you. How much less this temple I have built! ²⁸Yet give attention to your servant's prayer and his plea for mercy, O LORD my God. Hear the cry and the prayer that your servant

Humbled in His Presence

READ AND CONSIDER: 1 KINGS 8:22-30,56-61

"But will God really dwell on earth? The heavens, even the highest heaven, cannot contain you. How much less this temple I have built!" (1 Kings 8:27).

The magnificent temple was finally complete. All the furnishings had been installed. The ark of the Lord was in the Most Holy Place. Then, before the ribbon cutting celebration could proceed, God's presence in the form of a dark cloud filled the temple. The huge crowd must have been awestruck.

Solomon raised his arms toward heaven, silencing the assembly, and began his prayer. After a brief acknowledgment of his father, David's, (and his) role within God's plan, Solomon asked a wonderful rhetorical question: "How can this temple hold You?" He knew that despite its glory, the temple could not contain God, since even the highest heaven could not contain Him. It was one of the most magnificent structures any human had ever created to honor God, yet the true glory of the temple did not lie in the skill of the builders but in the *presence of God.*

When you come before God in prayer, one way you know you're in His presence is your sense of humility before Him. You can't be full of yourself and filled with His Spirit at the same time. You will always be humbled whenever you realize that this awesome God—whom the heavens cannot contain—is willing to come and live *inside you* through His Holy Spirit.

is praying in your presence this day. 29May your eyes be open toward this temple night and day, this place of which you said, 'My Name shall be there,' so that you will hear the prayer your servant prays toward this place. 30Hear the supplication of your servant and of your people Israel when they pray toward this place. Hear from heaven, your dwelling place, and when you hear, forgive.

31"When a man wrongs his neighbor and is required to take an oath and he comes and swears the oath before your altar in this temple, 32then hear from heaven and act. Judge between your servants, condemning the guilty and bringing down on his own head what he has done. Declare the innocent not guilty, and so establish his innocence.

33"When your people Israel have been defeated by an enemy be-cause they have sinned against you, and when they turn back to you and confess your name, praying and making supplication to you in this temple, 34then hear from heaven and forgive the sin of your people Israel and bring them back to the land you gave to their fathers.

35"When the heavens are shut up and there is no rain because your people have sinned against you, and when they pray toward this place and confess your name and turn from their sin because you have afflicted them, 36then hear from heaven and forgive the sin of your servants, your people Israel. Teach them the right way to live, and send rain on the land you gave your people for an inheritance.

37"When famine or plague comes to the land, or blight or mildew, lo-custs or grasshoppers, or when an enemy besieges them in any of their cities, whatever disaster or disease may come, 38and when a prayer or plea is made by any of your people Israel—each one aware of the afflictions of his own heart, and spreading out his hands toward this temple— 39then hear from heaven, your dwelling place. Forgive and act; deal with each man according to all he does, since you know his heart (for you alone know the hearts of all men), 40so that they will fear you all the time they live in the land you gave our fathers.

41"As for the foreigner who does not belong to your people Israel but has come from a distant land because of your name— 42for men will hear of your great name and your mighty hand and your outstretched arm—when he comes and prays toward this temple, 43then hear from heaven, your dwelling place, and do whatever the foreigner asks of you, so that all the peoples of the earth may know your name and fear you, as do your own people Israel, and may know that this house I have built bears your Name.

44"When your people go to war against their enemies, wherever you send them, and when they pray to the LORD toward the city you have chosen and the temple I have built for your Name, 45then hear from heaven their prayer and their plea, and uphold their cause.

46"When they sin against you— for there is no one who does not sin—and you become angry with them and give them over to the enemy, who takes them captive to his own land, far away or near; 47and if they have a change of heart in the land where they are held captive, and repent and plead with you in the land of their conquerors and say, 'We have sinned, we have done wrong, we have acted wickedly'; 48and if they turn back to you with all their heart and soul in the land of their enemies who took them captive, and pray to you toward the land you gave their fathers, toward the city you have chosen and the temple I have built for your Name; 49then from heaven, your dwelling place, hear their prayer and their plea, and uphold their cause. 50And forgive your people, who have sinned against you; forgive all the offenses they have committed against you, and cause their conquerors to show them mercy; 51for they are your people and your inheritance, whom you brought out of Egypt, out of that iron-smelting furnace.

52"May your eyes be open to your servant's plea and to the plea of your people Israel, and may you listen to them whenever they cry out to you. 53For you singled them out from all the nations of the world to be your own inheritance, just as you declared through your servant Moses when you, O Sovereign LORD, brought our fathers out of Egypt."

54When Solomon had finished all these prayers and supplications to the LORD, he rose from before the altar of the LORD, where he had been kneeling with his hands spread out toward heaven. 55He stood and blessed the whole assembly of Israel in a loud voice, saying:

56"Praise be to the LORD, who has given rest to his people Israel just as he promised. Not one word has failed of all the good promises he gave through his servant Moses. 57May the LORD our God be with us as he was with our fathers; may he never leave us nor forsake us. 58May he turn our hearts to him, to walk in all his ways and to keep the commands, decrees and regulations he gave our fathers. 59And may these words of mine, which I have prayed before the LORD, be near to the LORD our God day and night, that he may uphold the cause of his servant and the cause of his people Israel according to each day's need, 60so that all the peoples of the earth may know that the LORD is God and that there is no other. 61But your hearts must be fully committed to the LORD our God, to live by his decrees and obey his commands, as at this time."

The Dedication of the Temple

62Then the king and all Israel with him offered sacrifices before the LORD. 63Solomon offered a sacrifice of fellowship offerings[a] to the LORD: twenty-two thousand cattle and a hundred and twenty thousand sheep and goats. So the king and all the Israelites dedicated the temple of the LORD.

64On that same day the king consecrated the middle part of the courtyard in front of the temple of the LORD, and there he offered burnt offerings, grain offerings and the fat of the fellowship offerings, because the bronze altar before the LORD was too small to hold the burnt offerings, the grain offerings and the fat of the fellowship offerings.

65So Solomon observed the festival at that time, and all Israel with him—a vast assembly, people from Lebo[b] Hamath to the Wadi of Egypt. They celebrated it before the LORD our God for seven days and seven days more, fourteen days in all. 66On the following day he sent the people away. They blessed the king and then went home, joyful and glad in heart for all the good things the LORD had done for his servant David and his people Israel.

The LORD Appears to Solomon

9 When Solomon had finished building the temple of the LORD and the royal palace, and had achieved all he had desired to do, 2the LORD appeared to him a second time, as he had appeared to him at Gibeon. 3The LORD said to him:

"I have heard the prayer and plea you have made before me; I have consecrated this temple, which you have built, by putting my Name there forever. My eyes and my heart will always be there.

4"As for you, if you walk before me in integrity of heart and uprightness, as David your father did, and do all I command and observe my decrees and laws, 5I will establish your royal throne over Israel forever, as I promised David your father when I said, 'You shall never fail to have a man on the throne of Israel.'

6"But if you[c] or your sons turn away from me and do not observe the commands and decrees I have given you[c] and go off to serve other gods and worship them, 7then I will cut off Israel from the land I have given them and will reject this temple I have consecrated for my Name. Israel will then become a byword and an object of ridicule among all peoples. 8And though this temple is now imposing, all who pass by will be appalled and will scoff and say, 'Why has the LORD done such a thing to this land and to this temple?' 9People will answer, 'Because they have forsaken the LORD their God, who brought their fathers out of Egypt, and have embraced other gods, worshiping and serving them—that is why the LORD brought all this disaster on them.'"

Solomon's Other Activities

10At the end of twenty years, during which Solomon built these two buildings—the temple of the LORD and the royal palace— 11King Solomon gave twenty towns in Galilee to Hiram king of Tyre, because Hiram had supplied him with all the cedar and pine and gold he

---

a 63 Traditionally peace offerings; also in verse 64   b 65 Or from the entrance to   c 6 The Hebrew is plural.

wanted. [12]But when Hiram went from Tyre to see the towns that Solomon had given him, he was not pleased with them. [13]"What kind of towns are these you have given me, my brother?" he asked. And he called them the Land of Cabul,[a] a name they have to this day. [14]Now Hiram had sent to the king 120 talents[b] of gold.

Prayer is . . .

laying aside all work, interests, responsibilities, diversions, and activities in order to spend time with God.

[15]Here is the account of the forced labor King Solomon conscripted to build the LORD's temple, his own palace, the supporting terraces,[c] the wall of Jerusalem, and Hazor, Megiddo and Gezer. [16](Pharaoh king of Egypt had attacked and captured Gezer. He had set it on fire. He killed its Canaanite inhabitants and then gave it as a wedding gift to his daughter, Solomon's wife. [17]And Solomon rebuilt Gezer.) He built up Lower Beth Horon, [18]Baalath, and Tadmor[d] in the desert, within his land, [19]as well as all his store cities and the towns for his chariots and for his horses[e]—whatever he desired to build in Jerusalem, in Lebanon and throughout all the territory he ruled.

[20]All the people left from the Amorites, Hittites, Perizzites, Hivites and Jebusites (these peoples were not Israelites), [21]that is, their descendants remaining in the land, whom the Israelites could not exterminate[f]—these Solomon conscripted for his slave labor force, as it is to this day. [22]But Solomon did not make slaves of any of the Israelites; they were his fight-ing men, his government officials, his officers, his captains, and the commanders of his chariots and charioteers. [23]They were also the chief officials in charge of Solomon's projects—550 officials supervising the men who did the work.

[24]After Pharaoh's daughter had come up from the City of David to the palace Solomon had built for her, he constructed the supporting terraces.

[25]Three times a year Solomon sacrificed burnt offerings and fellowship offerings[g] on the altar he had built for the LORD, burning incense before the LORD along with them, and so fulfilled the temple obligations.

[26]King Solomon also built ships at Ezion Geber, which is near Elath in Edom, on the shore of the Red Sea.[h] [27]And Hiram sent his men—sailors who knew the sea—to serve in the fleet with Solomon's men. [28]They sailed to Ophir and brought back 420 talents[i] of gold, which they delivered to King Solomon.

The Queen of Sheba Visits Solomon

10 When the queen of Sheba heard about the fame of Solomon and his relation to the name of the LORD, she came to test him with hard questions. [2]Arriving at Jerusalem with a very great caravan—with camels carrying spices, large quantities of gold, and precious stones—she came to Solomon and talked with him about all that she had on her mind. [3]Solomon answered all her questions; nothing was too hard for the king to explain to her. [4]When the queen of Sheba saw all the wisdom of Solomon and the palace he had built, [5]the food on his table, the seating of his officials, the attending servants in their robes, his cupbearers, and the burnt offerings he made at[j] the temple of the LORD, she was overwhelmed.

[6]She said to the king, "The report I

---

[a] *13 Cabul* sounds like the Hebrew for *good-for-nothing*.   [b] *14* That is, about 4 1/2 tons (about 4 metric tons)   [c] *15* Or *the Millo*; also in verse 24   [d] *18* The Hebrew may also be read *Tamar.*   [e] *19* Or *charioteers*   [f] *21* The Hebrew term refers to the irrevocable giving over of things or persons to the LORD, often by totally destroying them.   [g] *25* Traditionally *peace offerings*   [h] *26* Hebrew *Yam Suph*; that is, Sea of Reeds   [i] *28* That is, about 16 tons (about 14.5 metric tons)   [j] *5* Or *the ascent by which he went up to*

heard in my own country about your achievements and your wisdom is true. ⁷But I did not believe these things until I came and saw with my own eyes. Indeed, not even half was told me; in wisdom and wealth you have far exceeded the report I heard. ⁸How happy your men must be! How happy your officials, who continually stand before you and hear your wisdom! ⁹Praise be to the LORD your God, who has delighted in you and placed you on the throne of Israel. Because of the LORD's eternal love for Israel, he has made you king, to maintain justice and righteousness."

¹⁰And she gave the king 120 talentsᵃ of gold, large quantities of spices, and precious stones. Never again were so many spices brought in as those the queen of Sheba gave to King Solomon.

¹¹(Hiram's ships brought gold from Ophir; and from there they brought great cargoes of almugwoodᵇ and precious stones. ¹²The king used the almugwood to make supports for the temple of the LORD and for the royal palace, and to make harps and lyres for the musicians. So much almugwood has never been imported or seen since that day.)

¹³King Solomon gave the queen of Sheba all she desired and asked for, besides what he had given her out of his royal bounty. Then she left and returned with her retinue to her own country.

Solomon's Splendor

¹⁴The weight of the gold that Solomon received yearly was 666 talents,ᶜ ¹⁵not including the revenues from merchants and traders and from all the Arabian kings and the governors of the land.

¹⁶King Solomon made two hundred large shields of hammered gold; six hundred bekasᵈ of gold went into each shield. ¹⁷He also made three hundred small shields of hammered gold, with three mi-

nasᵉ of gold in each shield. The king put them in the Palace of the Forest of Lebanon.

¹⁸Then the king made a great throne inlaid with ivory and overlaid with fine gold. ¹⁹The throne had six steps, and its back had a rounded top. On both sides of the seat were armrests, with a lion standing beside each of them. ²⁰Twelve lions stood on the six steps, one at either end of each step. Nothing like it had ever been made for any other kingdom. ²¹All King Solomon's goblets were gold, and all the household articles in the Palace of the Forest of Lebanon were pure gold. Nothing was made of silver, because silver was considered of little value in Solomon's days. ²²The king had a fleet of trading shipsᶠ at sea along with the ships of Hiram. Once every three years it returned, carrying gold, silver and ivory, and apes and baboons.

²³King Solomon was greater in riches and wisdom than all the other kings of the earth. ²⁴The whole world sought audience with Solomon to hear the wisdom God had put in his heart. ²⁵Year after year, everyone who came brought a gift—articles of silver and gold, robes, weapons and spices, and horses and mules.

²⁶Solomon accumulated chariots and horses; he had fourteen hundred chariots and twelve thousand horses,ᵍ which he kept in the chariot cities and also with him in Jerusalem. ²⁷The king made silver as common in Jerusalem as stones, and cedar as plentiful as sycamore-fig trees in the foothills. ²⁸Solomon's horses were imported from Egyptʰ and from Kueⁱ— the royal merchants purchased them from Kue. ²⁹They imported a chariot from Egypt for six hundred shekelsʲ of silver, and a horse for a hundred and fifty.ᵉ They also exported them to all the kings of the Hittites and of the Arameans.

ᵃ 10 That is, about 4 1/2 tons (about 4 metric tons)   ᵇ 11 Probably a variant of algumwood; also in verse 12   ᶜ 14 That is, about 25 tons (about 23 metric tons)   ᵈ 16 That is, about 7 1/2 pounds (about 3.5 kilograms)   ᵉ 17,29 That is, about 3 3/4 pounds (about 1.7 kilograms)   ᶠ 22 Hebrew of ships of Tarshish   ᵍ 26 Or charioteers   ʰ 28 Or possibly Muzur, a region in Cilicia; also in verse 29   ⁱ 28 Probably Cilicia   ʲ 29 That is, about 15 pounds (about 7 kilograms)

Solomon's Wives

11 King Solomon, however, loved many foreign women besides Pharaoh's daughter—Moabites, Ammonites, Edomites, Sidonians and Hittites. ²They were from nations about which the LORD had told the Israelites, "You must not intermarry with them, because they will surely turn your hearts after their gods." Nevertheless, Solomon held fast to them in love. ³He had seven hundred wives of royal birth and three hundred concubines, and his wives led him astray. ⁴As Solomon grew old, his wives turned his heart after other gods, and his heart was not fully devoted to the LORD his God, as the heart of David his father had been. ⁵He followed Ashtoreth the

---

GOING *deeper*

Putting God Above All Else

READ AND CONSIDER: 1 KINGS 11:1-13

"As Solomon grew old, his wives turned his heart after other gods, and his heart was not fully devoted to the LORD his God, as the heart of David his father had been" (1 Kings 11:4).

With all God had given him, how could someone as wise as Solomon get so far off of the narrow path of obedience and so far away from the Lord's ways? Could it be that his wisdom turned out to be a point of pride? Did he think that *he* was the one responsible for all his wealth and blessings, and not God?

For half of his 40-year reign, Solomon seems to have exercised his wisdom in ways that pleased God. But little mention is made of Solomon's prayer life during these years. He presented sacrifices at the temple three times a year, but there is no record of his conversations with God during those visits. Perhaps the temple visits became merely a formality.

At the 20-year mark, cracks began to form in the structure of Solomon's reign. The first indication of a problem can be seen in the way he treated a friend (Hiram) by giving him a cheap gift (9:10-14). The queen of Sheba arrived and heaped praise on Solomon for his wisdom, though she was careful to give God the credit for Solomon's successes. Despite this foreign leader's enthusiastic words about the God of Israel, there's no hint in the passage that Solomon agreed with her or encouraged her interest in the God who had blessed his kingdom.

Solomon's reputation led to great riches. He accumulated things: ships, horses, gold, chariots, palaces, and women—lots of women. He filled his life with treasures, and that's where his heart ended up. "King Solomon was greater in riches and wisdom than all the other kings of the earth" (10:23). God had promised this. After Solomon had asked for wisdom to rule the nation, God had responded, "I will give you what you have not asked for—both riches and honor—so that in your lifetime you will have no equal among kings" (3:13). With all that wisdom, the riches should not have gone to his head. But they did.

Jesus said, "Where your treasure is, there your heart will be also" (Matthew 6:21). Once Solomon's heart was focused on his material wealth, it was easy for his foreign wives to turn his heart away from the God who had so richly blessed him.

Any one of us can be tempted to put the things of this world above our relationship with God. That's why we have to regularly ask Him to show us if any of our possessions or desires are getting in the way of our walk with Him. We must ask the Lord not only for wisdom regarding that, but also for strength to resist anything that tempts our heart to turn away from Him.

goddess of the Sidonians, and Molech[a] the detestable god of the Ammonites. [6]So Solomon did evil in the eyes of the LORD; he did not follow the LORD completely, as David his father had done.

[7]On a hill east of Jerusalem, Solomon built a high place for Chemosh the detestable god of Moab, and for Molech the detestable god of the Ammonites. [8]He did the same for all his foreign wives, who burned incense and offered sacrifices to their gods.

[9]The LORD became angry with Solomon because his heart had turned away from the LORD, the God of Israel, who had appeared to him twice. [10]Although he had forbidden Solomon to follow other gods, Solomon did not keep the LORD's command. [11]So the LORD said to Solomon, "Since this is your attitude and you have not kept my covenant and my decrees, which I commanded you, I will most certainly tear the kingdom away from you and give it to one of your subordinates. [12]Nevertheless, for the sake of David your father, I will not do it during your lifetime. I will tear it out of the hand of your son. [13]Yet I will not tear the whole kingdom from him, but will give him one tribe for the sake of David my servant and for the sake of Jerusalem, which I have chosen."

Solomon's Adversaries

[14]Then the LORD raised up against Solomon an adversary, Hadad the Edomite, from the royal line of Edom. [15]Earlier when David was fighting with Edom, Joab the commander of the army, who had gone up to bury the dead, had struck down all the men in Edom. [16]Joab and all the Israelites stayed there for six months, until they had destroyed all the men in Edom. [17]But Hadad, still only a boy, fled to Egypt with some Edomite officials who had served his father. [18]They set out from Midian and went to Paran. Then taking men from Paran with them, they went to Egypt, to Pharaoh king of Egypt, who gave Hadad a house and land and provided him with food.

[19]Pharaoh was so pleased with Hadad that he gave him a sister of his own wife, Queen Tahpenes, in marriage. [20]The sister of Tahpenes bore him a son named Genubath, whom Tahpenes brought up in the royal palace. There Genubath lived with Pharaoh's own children.

[21]While he was in Egypt, Hadad heard that David rested with his fathers and that Joab the commander of the army was also dead. Then Hadad said to Pharaoh, "Let me go, that I may return to my own country."

[22]"What have you lacked here that you want to go back to your own country?" Pharaoh asked.

"Nothing," Hadad replied, "but do let me go!"

[23]And God raised up against Solomon another adversary, Rezon son of Eliada, who had fled from his master, Hadadezer king of Zobah. [24]He gathered men around him and became the leader of a band of rebels when David destroyed the forces[b] of Zobah; the rebels went to Damascus, where they settled and took control. [25]Rezon was Israel's adversary as long as Solomon lived, adding to the trouble caused by Hadad. So Rezon ruled in Aram and was hostile toward Israel.

Jeroboam Rebels Against Solomon

[26]Also, Jeroboam son of Nebat rebelled against the king. He was one of Solomon's officials, an Ephraimite from Zeredah, and his mother was a widow named Zeruah.

[27]Here is the account of how he rebelled against the king: Solomon had built the supporting terraces[c] and had filled in the gap in the wall of the city of David his father. [28]Now Jeroboam was a man of standing, and when Solomon saw how well the young man did his work, he put him in charge of the whole labor force of the house of Joseph.

[29]About that time Jeroboam was going

---

a 5 Hebrew Milcom; also in verse 33   b 24 Hebrew destroyed them   c 27 Or the Millo out of Jerusalem, and Ahijah the prophet of Shiloh met him on the way, wearing a new cloak. The two of them were alone out in the country, 30and Ahijah took hold of the new cloak he was wearing and tore it into twelve pieces. 31Then he said to Jeroboam, "Take ten pieces for yourself, for this is what the LORD, the God of Israel, says: 'See, I am going to tear the kingdom out of Solomon's hand and give you ten tribes. 32But for the sake of my servant David and the city of Jerusalem, which I have chosen out of all the tribes of Israel, he will have one tribe. 33I will do this because they have[a] forsaken me and worshiped Ashtoreth the goddess of the Sidonians, Chemosh the god of the Moabites, and Molech the god of the Ammonites, and have not walked in my ways, nor done what is right in my eyes, nor kept my statutes and laws as David, Solomon's father, did.

34"'But I will not take the whole kingdom out of Solomon's hand; I have made him ruler all the days of his life for the sake of David my servant, whom I chose and who observed my commands and statutes. 35I will take the kingdom from his son's hands and give you ten tribes. 36I will give one tribe to his son so that David my servant may always have a lamp before me in Jerusalem, the city where I chose to put my Name. 37However, as for you, I will take you, and you will rule over all that your heart desires; you will be king over Israel. 38If you do whatever I command you and walk in my ways and do what is right in my eyes by keeping my statutes and commands, as David my servant did, I will be with you. I will build you a dynasty as enduring as the one I built for David and will give Israel to you. 39I will humble David's descendants because of this, but not forever.'"

40Solomon tried to kill Jeroboam, but Jeroboam fled to Egypt, to Shishak the king, and stayed there until Solomon's death.

Solomon's Death

41As for the other events of Solomon's reign—all he did and the wisdom he displayed—are they not written in the book of the annals of Solomon? 42Solomon reigned in Jerusalem over all Israel forty years. 43Then he rested with his fathers and was buried in the city of David his father. And Rehoboam his son succeeded him as king.

Israel Rebels Against Rehoboam

12 Rehoboam went to Shechem, for all the Israelites had gone there to make him king. 2When Jeroboam son of Nebat heard this (he was still in Egypt, where he had fled from King Solomon), he returned from[b] Egypt. 3So they sent for Jeroboam, and he and the whole assembly of Israel went to Rehoboam and said to him: 4"Your father put a heavy yoke on us, but now lighten the harsh labor and the heavy yoke he put on us, and we will serve you."

5Rehoboam answered, "Go away for three days and then come back to me." So the people went away.

6Then King Rehoboam consulted the elders who had served his father Solomon during his lifetime. "How would you advise me to answer these people?" he asked.

7They replied, "If today you will be a servant to these people and serve them and give them a favorable answer, they will always be your servants."

8But Rehoboam rejected the advice the elders gave him and consulted the young men who had grown up with him and were serving him. 9He asked them, "What is your advice? How should we answer these people who say to me, 'Lighten the yoke your father put on us'?"

10The young men who had grown up with him replied, "Tell these people who have said to you, 'Your father put a heavy yoke on us, but make our yoke lighter'— tell them, 'My little finger is thicker than my father's waist. 11My father laid on you

---

a 33 Hebrew; Septuagint, Vulgate and Syriac *because he has*   b 2 Or *he remained in* a heavy yoke; I will make it even heavier. My father scourged you with whips; I will scourge you with scorpions.'"

12Three days later Jeroboam and all the people returned to Rehoboam, as the king had said, "Come back to me in three days." 13The king answered the people harshly. Rejecting the advice given him by the elders, 14he followed the advice of the young men and said, "My father made your yoke heavy; I will make it even heavier. My father scourged you with whips; I will scourge you with scorpions." 15So the king did not listen to the people, for this turn of events was from the LORD, to fulfill the word the LORD had spoken to Jeroboam son of Nebat through Ahijah the Shilonite.

16When all Israel saw that the king refused to listen to them, they answered the king:

"What share do we have in David,
    what part in Jesse's son?
To your tents, O Israel!
    Look after your own house,
        O David!"

So the Israelites went home. 17But as for the Israelites who were living in the towns of Judah, Rehoboam still ruled over them.

18King Rehoboam sent out Adoniram,a who was in charge of forced labor, but all Israel stoned him to death. King Rehoboam, however, managed to get into his chariot and escape to Jerusalem. 19So Israel has been in rebellion against the house of David to this day.

20When all the Israelites heard that Jeroboam had returned, they sent and called him to the assembly and made him king over all Israel. Only the tribe of Judah remained loyal to the house of David.

21When Rehoboam arrived in Jerusalem, he mustered the whole house of Judah and the tribe of Benjamin—a hundred and eighty thousand fighting men—to make war against the house of Israel and to regain the kingdom for Rehoboam son of Solomon.

22But this word of God came to Shemaiah the man of God: 23"Say to Rehoboam son of Solomon king of Judah, to the whole house of Judah and Benjamin, and to the rest of the people, 24'This is what the LORD says: Do not go up to fight against your brothers, the Israelites. Go home, every one of you, for this is my doing.'" So they obeyed the word of the LORD and went home again, as the LORD had ordered.

Golden Calves at Bethel and Dan

25Then Jeroboam fortified Shechem in the hill country of Ephraim and lived there. From there he went out and built up Peniel.b

26Jeroboam thought to himself, "The kingdom will now likely revert to the house of David. 27If these people go up to offer sacrifices at the temple of the LORD in Jerusalem, they will again give their allegiance to their lord, Rehoboam king of Judah. They will kill me and return to King Rehoboam."

28After seeking advice, the king made two golden calves. He said to the people, "It is too much for you to go up to Jerusalem. Here are your gods, O Israel, who brought you up out of Egypt." 29One he set up in Bethel, and the other in Dan. 30And this thing became a sin; the people went even as far as Dan to worship the one there.

31Jeroboam built shrines on high places and appointed priests from all sorts of people, even though they were not Levites. 32He instituted a festival on the fifteenth day of the eighth month, like the festival held in Judah, and offered sacrifices on the altar. This he did in Bethel, sacrificing to the calves he had made. And at Bethel he also installed priests at the high places he had made. 33On the fifteenth day of

a 18 Some Septuagint manuscripts and Syriac (see also 1 Kings 4:6 and 5:14); Hebrew *Adoram* b 25 Hebrew *Penuel,* a variant of *Peniel* the eighth month, a month of his own choosing, he offered sacrifices on the altar he had built at Bethel. So he instituted the festival for the Israelites and went up to the altar to make offerings.

The Man of God From Judah

13 By the word of the LORD a man of God came from Judah to Bethel, as Jeroboam was standing by the altar to make an offering. ²He cried out against the altar by the word of the LORD: "O altar, altar! This is what the LORD says: 'A son named Josiah will be born to the house of David. On you he will sacrifice the priests of the high places who now make offerings here, and human bones will be burned on you.'" ³That same day the man of God gave a sign: "This is the sign the LORD has declared: The altar will be split apart and the ashes on it will be poured out."

GOING *deeper*

Praying for Someone Who Doesn't Deserve It

READ AND CONSIDER: 1 KINGS 13:1-10

"Then the king said to the man of God, 'Intercede with the LORD your God and pray for me that my hand may be restored.' So the man of God interceded with the LORD, and the king's hand was restored and became as it was before" (1 Kings 13:6).

Have you ever felt God calling you to pray for someone who you thought didn't deserve it? Do you know of people who ignore or even mock God, but when disaster strikes they want God to make it better? Have you ever struggled with the temptation to say, "Why should I pray for you when you show such disrespect for God?" The prophet Ahijah had good reason to feel that way when God sent him to confront the king. But he prayed anyway.

Jeroboam led a rebellion against Solomon's son Rehoboam and became the king of the northern ten tribes of Israel. Ahijah the prophet had foretold Jeroboam's success (11:29-40). Because Jeroboam didn't control Jerusalem, he feared that people's loyalty would be undermined if they continued to travel to the temple there to worship. So he instituted his own religion, complete with golden calves and altars (12:25-33). When God's messenger, Ahijah, showed up with a prophecy against the pagan altar, the king was offended. But when he pointed toward Ahijah to have him arrested, the king's hand instantly shriveled up.

Immediately, Jeroboam asked Ahijah to "intercede with the LORD your God." Even though he needed help, Jeroboam couldn't bring himself to acknowledge God as the God he should worship; instead, this was the *prophet's* God, not his. The fact that God healed him can only be seen as God's grace extended toward a rebel. But Jeroboam missed that point because he continued to promote his own religion. But Jeroboam's persistent rejection of God led to the destruction of his entire family.

And he was willing to pray for Jeroboam immediately, in spite of the fact that Jeroboam had threatened his life. This kind of praying isn't easy. But we are commanded to do it. Ahijah was under orders to announce judgment on the false religion Jeroboam was leading, but given a chance to pray for the wayward king, he didn't hesitate. Jesus said, "Love your enemies and pray for those who persecute you" (Matthew 5:44). We must remember that God is willing to listen to prayers for *us* when we don't deserve it. And we must not hesitate to pray for *others* even when we think *they* don't deserve it.

4When King Jeroboam heard what the man of God cried out against the altar at Bethel, he stretched out his hand from the altar and said, "Seize him!" But the hand he stretched out toward the man shriveled up, so that he could not pull it back. 5Also, the altar was split apart and its ashes poured out according to the sign given by the man of God by the word of the LORD.

6Then the king said to the man of God, "Intercede with the LORD your God and pray for me that my hand may be restored." So the man of God interceded with the LORD, and the king's hand was restored and became as it was before.

7The king said to the man of God, "Come home with me and have something to eat, and I will give you a gift."

8But the man of God answered the king, "Even if you were to give me half your possessions, I would not go with you, nor would I eat bread or drink water here. 9For I was commanded by the word of the LORD: 'You must not eat bread or drink water or return by the way you came.'" 10So he took another road and did not return by the way he had come to Bethel.

Praying 1 Kings 13:6-10

Lord, help me to be strong and obey You regardless of how much I may be enticed to do otherwise.

11Now there was a certain old prophet living in Bethel, whose sons came and told him all that the man of God had done there that day. They also told their father what he had said to the king. 12Their father asked them, "Which way did he go?" And his sons showed him which road the man of God from Judah had taken. 13So he said to his sons, "Saddle the donkey for me." And when they had saddled the donkey for him, he mounted it 14and rode after the man of God. He found him sitting under an oak tree and asked, "Are you the man of God who came from Judah?"

"I am," he replied.

15So the prophet said to him, "Come home with me and eat."

16The man of God said, "I cannot turn back and go with you, nor can I eat bread or drink water with you in this place. 17I have been told by the word of the LORD: 'You must not eat bread or drink water there or return by the way you came.'"

18The old prophet answered, "I too am a prophet, as you are. And an angel said to me by the word of the LORD: 'Bring him back with you to your house so that he may eat bread and drink water.'" (But he was lying to him.) 19So the man of God returned with him and ate and drank in his house.

20While they were sitting at the table, the word of the LORD came to the old prophet who had brought him back. 21He cried out to the man of God who had come from Judah, "This is what the LORD says: 'You have defied the word of the LORD and have not kept the command the LORD your God gave you. 22You came back and ate bread and drank water in the place where he told you not to eat or drink. Therefore your body will not be buried in the tomb of your fathers.'"

23When the man of God had finished eating and drinking, the prophet who had brought him back saddled his donkey for him. 24As he went on his way, a lion met him on the road and killed him, and his body was thrown down on the road, with both the donkey and the lion standing beside it. 25Some people who passed by saw the body thrown down there, with the lion standing beside the body, and they went and reported it in the city where the old prophet lived.

26When the prophet who had brought him back from his journey heard of it, he said, "It is the man of God who defied the word of the LORD. The LORD has given him over to the lion, which has mauled him and killed him, as the word of the LORD had warned him."

²⁷The prophet said to his sons, "Saddle the donkey for me," and they did so. ²⁸Then he went out and found the body thrown down on the road, with the donkey and the lion standing beside it. The lion had neither eaten the body nor mauled the donkey. ²⁹So the prophet picked up the body of the man of God, laid it on the donkey, and brought it back to his own city to mourn for him and bury him. ³⁰Then he laid the body in his own tomb, and they mourned over him and said, "Oh, my brother!"

³¹After burying him, he said to his sons, "When I die, bury me in the grave where the man of God is buried; lay my bones beside his bones. ³²For the message he declared by the word of the LORD against the altar in Bethel and against all the shrines on the high places in the towns of Samaria will certainly come true."

³³Even after this, Jeroboam did not change his evil ways, but once more appointed priests for the high places from all sorts of people. Anyone who wanted to become a priest he consecrated for the high places. ³⁴This was the sin of the house of Jeroboam that led to its downfall and to its destruction from the face of the earth.

Ahijah's Prophecy Against Jeroboam

14 At that time Abijah son of Jeroboam became ill, ²and Jeroboam said to his wife, "Go, disguise yourself, so you won't be recognized as the wife of Jeroboam. Then go to Shiloh. Ahijah the prophet is there—the one who told me I would be king over this people. ³Take ten loaves of bread with you, some cakes and a jar of honey, and go to him. He will tell you what will happen to the boy." ⁴So Jeroboam's wife did what he said and went to Ahijah's house in Shiloh.

Now Ahijah could not see; his sight was gone because of his age. ⁵But the LORD had told Ahijah, "Jeroboam's wife is coming to ask you about her son, for he is ill, and you are to give her such and

such an answer. When she arrives, she will pretend to be someone else."

⁶So when Ahijah heard the sound of her footsteps at the door, he said, "Come in, wife of Jeroboam. Why this pretense? I have been sent to you with bad news. ⁷Go, tell Jeroboam that this is what the LORD, the God of Israel, says: 'I raised you up from among the people and made you a leader over my people Israel. ⁸I tore the kingdom away from the house of David and gave it to you, but you have not been like my servant David, who kept my commands and followed me with all his heart, doing only what was right in my eyes. ⁹You have done more evil than all who lived before you. You have made for yourself other gods, idols made of metal; you have provoked me to anger and thrust me behind your back.

¹⁰"'Because of this, I am going to bring disaster on the house of Jeroboam. I will cut off from Jeroboam every last male in Israel—slave or free. I will burn up the house of Jeroboam as one burns dung, until it is all gone. ¹¹Dogs will eat those belonging to Jeroboam who die in the city, and the birds of the air will feed on those who die in the country. The LORD has spoken!'

¹²"As for you, go back home. When you set foot in your city, the boy will die. ¹³All Israel will mourn for him and bury him. He is the only one belonging to Jeroboam who will be buried, because he is the only one in the house of Jeroboam in whom the LORD, the God of Israel, has found anything good.

¹⁴"The LORD will raise up for himself a king over Israel who will cut off the family of Jeroboam. This is the day! What? Yes, even now.ᵃ ¹⁵And the LORD will strike Israel, so that it will be like a reed swaying in the water. He will uproot Israel from this good land that he gave to their forefathers and scatter them beyond the River,ᵇ because they provoked the LORD to anger by making

---

ᵃ *14* The meaning of the Hebrew for this sentence is uncertain. ᵇ *15* That is, the Euphrates

Asherah poles.[a] 16And he will give Israel up because of the sins Jeroboam has committed and has caused Israel to commit."

17Then Jeroboam's wife got up and left and went to Tirzah. As soon as she stepped over the threshold of the house, the boy died. 18They buried him, and all Israel mourned for him, as the LORD had said through his servant the prophet Ahijah.

19The other events of Jeroboam's reign, his wars and how he ruled, are written in the book of the annals of the kings of Israel. 20He reigned for twenty-two years and then rested with his fathers. And Nadab his son succeeded him as king.

Rehoboam King of Judah

21Rehoboam son of Solomon was king in Judah. He was forty-one years old when he became king, and he reigned seventeen years in Jerusalem, the city the LORD had chosen out of all the tribes of Israel in which to put his Name. His mother's name was Naamah; she was an Ammonite.

22Judah did evil in the eyes of the LORD. By the sins they committed they stirred up his jealous anger more than their fathers had done. 23They also set up for themselves high places, sacred stones and Asherah poles on every high hill and under every spreading tree. 24There were even male shrine prostitutes in the land; the people engaged in all the detestable practices of the nations the LORD had driven out before the Israelites.

25In the fifth year of King Rehoboam, Shishak king of Egypt attacked Jerusalem. 26He carried off the treasures of the temple of the LORD and the treasures of the royal palace. He took everything, including all the gold shields Solomon had made. 27So King Rehoboam made bronze shields to replace them and assigned these to the commanders of the guard on duty at the entrance to the royal palace. 28Whenever the king went to the LORD's temple, the guards bore the shields, and afterward they returned them to the guardroom.

29As for the other events of Rehoboam's reign, and all he did, are they not written in the book of the annals of the kings of Judah? 30There was continual warfare between Rehoboam and Jeroboam. 31And Rehoboam rested with his fathers and was buried with them in the City of David. His mother's name was Naamah; she was an Ammonite. And Abijah[b] his son succeeded him as king.

Abijah King of Judah

15 In the eighteenth year of the reign of Jeroboam son of Nebat, Abijah[c] became king of Judah, 2and he reigned in Jerusalem three years. His mother's name was Maacah daughter of Abishalom.[d]

3He committed all the sins his father had done before him; his heart was not fully devoted to the LORD his God, as the heart of David his forefather had been. 4Nevertheless, for David's sake the LORD his God gave him a lamp in Jerusalem by raising up a son to succeed him and by making Jerusalem strong. 5For David had done what was right in the eyes of the LORD and had not failed to keep any of the LORD's commands all the days of his life—except in the case of Uriah the Hittite.

6There was war between Rehoboam[e] and Jeroboam throughout ⌊Abijah's⌋ lifetime. 7As for the other events of Abijah's reign, and all he did, are they not written in the book of the annals of the kings of Judah? There was war between Abijah and Jeroboam. 8And Abijah rested with his fathers and was buried in the City of David. And Asa his son succeeded him as king.

Asa King of Judah

9In the twentieth year of Jeroboam king of Israel, Asa became king of Judah,

---

a 15 That is, symbols of the goddess Asherah; here and elsewhere in 1 Kings   b 31 Some Hebrew manuscripts and Septuagint (see also 2 Chron. 12:16); most Hebrew manuscripts Abijam   c 1 Some Hebrew manuscripts and Septuagint (see also 2 Chron. 12:16); most Hebrew manuscripts Abijam; also in verses 7 and 8   d 2 A variant of Absalom; also in verse 10   e 6 Most Hebrew manuscripts; some Hebrew manuscripts and Syriac Abijam (that is, Abijah)

10and he reigned in Jerusalem forty-one years. His grandmother's name was Maacah daughter of Abishalom.

11Asa did what was right in the eyes of the LORD, as his father David had done. 12He expelled the male shrine prostitutes from the land and got rid of all the idols his fathers had made. 13He even deposed his grandmother Maacah from her position as queen mother, because she had made a repulsive Asherah pole. Asa cut the pole down and burned it in the Kidron Valley. 14Although he did not remove the high places, Asa's heart was fully committed to the LORD all his life. 15He brought into the temple of the LORD the silver and gold and the articles that he and his father had dedicated.

> *Praying 1 Kings 15:11-12*
> *Give me the ability to recognize any idols in my life, Lord, and help me to remove them.*

16There was war between Asa and Baasha king of Israel throughout their reigns. 17Baasha king of Israel went up against Judah and fortified Ramah to prevent anyone from leaving or entering the territory of Asa king of Judah.

18Asa then took all the silver and gold that was left in the treasuries of the LORD's temple and of his own palace. He entrusted it to his officials and sent them to Ben-Hadad son of Tabrimmon, the son of Hezion, the king of Aram, who was ruling in Damascus. 19"Let there be a treaty between me and you," he said, "as there was between my father and your father. See, I am sending you a gift of silver and gold. Now break your treaty with Baasha king of Israel so he will withdraw from me."

20Ben-Hadad agreed with King Asa and sent the commanders of his forces against the towns of Israel. He conquered Ijon, Dan, Abel Beth Maacah and all Kinnereth in addition to Naphtali. 21When Baasha heard this, he stopped building Ramah and withdrew to Tirzah. 22Then King Asa issued an order to all Judah—no one was exempt—and they carried away from Ramah the stones and timber Baasha had been using there. With them King Asa built up Geba in Benjamin, and also Mizpah.

23As for all the other events of Asa's reign, all his achievements, all he did and the cities he built, are they not written in the book of the annals of the kings of Judah? In his old age, however, his feet became diseased. 24Then Asa rested with his fathers and was buried with them in the city of his father David. And Jehoshaphat his son succeeded him as king.

Nadab King of Israel

25Nadab son of Jeroboam became king of Israel in the second year of Asa king of Judah, and he reigned over Israel two years. 26He did evil in the eyes of the LORD, walking in the ways of his father and in his sin, which he had caused Israel to commit.

27Baasha son of Ahijah of the house of Issachar plotted against him, and he struck him down at Gibbethon, a Philistine town, while Nadab and all Israel were besieging it. 28Baasha killed Nadab in the third year of Asa king of Judah and succeeded him as king.

29As soon as he began to reign, he killed Jeroboam's whole family. He did not leave Jeroboam anyone that breathed, but destroyed them all, according to the word of the LORD given through his servant Ahijah the Shilonite— 30because of the sins Jeroboam had committed and had caused Israel to commit, and because he provoked the LORD, the God of Israel, to anger.

31As for the other events of Nadab's reign, and all he did, are they not written in the book of the annals of the kings of Israel? 32There was war between Asa and Baasha king of Israel throughout their reigns.

Baasha King of Israel

33In the third year of Asa king of Judah, Baasha son of Ahijah became king of all

Israel in Tirzah, and he reigned twenty-four years. ³⁴He did evil in the eyes of the LORD, walking in the ways of Jeroboam and in his sin, which he had caused Israel to commit.

16 Then the word of the LORD came to Jehu son of Hanani against Baasha: ²"I lifted you up from the dust and made you leader of my people Israel, but you walked in the ways of Jeroboam and caused my people Israel to sin and to provoke me to anger by their sins. ³So I am about to consume Baasha and his house, and I will make your house like that of Jeroboam son of Nebat. ⁴Dogs will eat those belonging to Baasha who die in the city, and the birds of the air will feed on those who die in the country."

⁵As for the other events of Baasha's reign, what he did and his achievements, are they not written in the book of the annals of the kings of Israel? ⁶Baasha rested with his fathers and was buried in Tirzah. And Elah his son succeeded him as king.

⁷Moreover, the word of the LORD came through the prophet Jehu son of Hanani to Baasha and his house, because of all the evil he had done in the eyes of the LORD, provoking him to anger by the things he did, and becoming like the house of Jeroboam—and also because he destroyed it.

Elah King of Israel

⁸In the twenty-sixth year of Asa king of Judah, Elah son of Baasha became king of Israel, and he reigned in Tirzah two years.

⁹Zimri, one of his officials, who had command of half his chariots, plotted against him. Elah was in Tirzah at the time, getting drunk in the home of Arza, the man in charge of the palace at Tirzah. ¹⁰Zimri came in, struck him down and killed him in the twenty-seventh year of Asa king of Judah. Then he succeeded him as king.

¹¹As soon as he began to reign and was seated on the throne, he killed off Baasha's whole family. He did not spare a single male, whether relative or friend. ¹²So Zimri destroyed the whole family of Baasha, in accordance with the word of the LORD spoken against Baasha through the prophet Jehu— ¹³because of all the sins Baasha and his son Elah had committed and had caused Israel to commit, so that they provoked the LORD, the God of Israel, to anger by their worthless idols.

¹⁴As for the other events of Elah's reign, and all he did, are they not written in the book of the annals of the kings of Israel?

Zimri King of Israel

¹⁵In the twenty-seventh year of Asa king of Judah, Zimri reigned in Tirzah seven days. The army was encamped near Gibbethon, a Philistine town. ¹⁶When the Israelites in the camp heard that Zimri had plotted against the king and murdered him, they proclaimed Omri, the commander of the army, king over Israel that very day there in the camp. ¹⁷Then Omri and all the Israelites with him withdrew from Gibbethon and laid siege to Tirzah. ¹⁸When Zimri saw that the city was taken, he went into the citadel of the royal palace and set the palace on fire around him. So he died, ¹⁹because of the sins he had committed, doing evil in the eyes of the LORD and walking in the ways of Jeroboam and in the sin he had committed and had caused Israel to commit.

²⁰As for the other events of Zimri's reign, and the rebellion he carried out, are they not written in the book of the annals of the kings of Israel?

Omri King of Israel

²¹Then the people of Israel were split into two factions; half supported Tibni son of Ginath for king, and the other half supported Omri. ²²But Omri's followers proved stronger than those of Tibni son of Ginath. So Tibni died and Omri became king.

²³In the thirty-first year of Asa king of Judah, Omri became king of Israel, and

he reigned twelve years, six of them in Tirzah. ²⁴He bought the hill of Samaria from Shemer for two talents^a of silver and built a city on the hill, calling it Samaria, after Shemer, the name of the former owner of the hill.

²⁵But Omri did evil in the eyes of the LORD and sinned more than all those before him. ²⁶He walked in all the ways of Jeroboam son of Nebat and in his sin, which he had caused Israel to commit, so that they provoked the LORD, the God of Israel, to anger by their worthless idols.

²⁷As for the other events of Omri's reign, what he did and the things he achieved, are they not written in the book of the annals of the kings of Israel? ²⁸Omri rested with his fathers and was buried in Samaria. And Ahab his son succeeded him as king.

Ahab Becomes King of Israel

²⁹In the thirty-eighth year of Asa king of Judah, Ahab son of Omri became king of Israel, and he reigned in Samaria over Israel twenty-two years. ³⁰Ahab son of Omri did more evil in the eyes of the LORD than any of those before him. ³¹He not only considered it trivial to commit the sins of Jeroboam son of Nebat, but he also married Jezebel daughter of Ethbaal king of the Sidonians, and began to serve Baal and worship him. ³²He set up an altar for Baal in the temple of Baal that he built in Samaria. ³³Ahab also made an Asherah pole and did more to provoke the LORD, the God of Israel, to anger than did all the kings of Israel before him.

³⁴In Ahab's time, Hiel of Bethel rebuilt Jericho. He laid its foundations at the cost of his firstborn son Abiram, and he set up its gates at the cost of his youngest son Segub, in accordance with the word of the LORD spoken by Joshua son of Nun.

Elijah Fed by Ravens

17 Now Elijah the Tishbite, from Tishbe^b in Gilead, said to Ahab, "As the LORD, the God of Israel, lives, whom I serve, there will be neither dew nor rain in the next few years except at my word."

²Then the word of the LORD came to Elijah: ³"Leave here, turn eastward and hide in the Kerith Ravine, east of the Jordan. ⁴You will drink from the brook, and I have ordered the ravens to feed you there."

⁵So he did what the LORD had told him. He went to the Kerith Ravine, east of the Jordan, and stayed there. ⁶The ravens brought him bread and meat in the morning and bread and meat in the evening, and he drank from the brook.

The Widow at Zarephath

⁷Some time later the brook dried up because there had been no rain in the land. ⁸Then the word of the LORD came to him: ⁹"Go at once to Zarephath of Sidon and stay there. I have commanded a widow in that place to supply you with food." ¹⁰So he went to Zarephath. When he came to the town gate, a widow was there gathering sticks. He called to her and asked, "Would you bring me a little water in a jar so I may have a drink?" ¹¹As she was going to get it, he called, "And bring me, please, a piece of bread."

¹²"As surely as the LORD your God lives," she replied, "I don't have any bread—only a handful of flour in a jar and a little oil in a jug. I am gathering a few sticks to take home and make a meal for myself and my son, that we may eat it—and die."

¹³Elijah said to her, "Don't be afraid. Go home and do as you have said. But first make a small cake of bread for me from what you have and bring it to me, and then make something for yourself and your son. ¹⁴For this is what the LORD, the God of Israel, says: 'The jar of flour will not be used up and the jug of oil will not run dry until the day the LORD gives rain on the land.'"

¹⁵She went away and did as Elijah had

ᵃ 24 That is, about 150 pounds (about 70 kilograms)   ᵇ 1 Or Tishbite, of the settlers

Learning to Pray Boldly

READ AND CONSIDER: 1 KINGS 17:1-24

"Now Elijah the Tishbite, from Tishbe in Gilead, said to Ahab, 'As the LORD, the God of Israel, lives, whom I serve, there will be neither dew nor rain in the next few years except at my word'" 1 Kings 17:1).

When Elijah prayed, things happened. Clouds dried up or gushed rain, ravens served as food waiters, oil and flour multiplied, fire fell from heaven, and a dead boy came back to life. Some of these miracles were examples of divine timing, and each one of them was an example of divine power. All of them remind us that nothing is impossible when God decides to act.

When people and churches make prayer a priority, they always see answers to their prayers. Those who pray boldly may have the thrill of seeing miracles. When people are unified in the spirit of praise and they pray in unity, God does amazing things.

Some people may question that God would really change the weather because people prayed. But He did it in the Bible. "Elijah was a man just like us. He prayed earnestly that it would not rain, and it did not rain on the land for three and a half years. Again he prayed, and the heavens gave rain, and the earth produced its crops" (James 5:17-18). If Elijah was like us, then why can't we pray like he prayed?

We don't have to understand everything about how prayer works; we just have to believe that it does. Most of us know little about car engines, but that doesn't keep us from driving. We just have to turn the key. Few of us understand electricity, but we still expect our appliances to work when we plug them in. Prayer is the key that gets things going. Prayer is the way we plug in to the power of God. We are instructed to "pray continually" (1 Thessalonians 5:17). And God has promised to hear and answer. Elijah saw some unique answers to prayer, but his ability to pray was not unique. When you pray, big things can happen too. That's because God hears and will answer according to His will.

---

told her. So there was food every day for Elijah and for the woman and her family. ¹⁶For the jar of flour was not used up and the jug of oil did not run dry, in keeping with the word of the LORD spoken by Elijah.

¹⁷Some time later the son of the woman who owned the house became ill. He grew worse and worse, and finally stopped breathing. ¹⁸She said to Elijah, "What do you have against me, man of God? Did you come to remind me of my sin and kill my son?"

¹⁹"Give me your son," Elijah replied. He took him from her arms, carried him to the upper room where he was staying, and laid him on his bed. ²⁰Then he cried out to the LORD, "O LORD my God, have you brought tragedy also upon this widow I am staying with, by causing her son to die?" ²¹Then he stretched himself out on the boy three times and cried to the LORD, "O LORD my God, let this boy's life return to him!"

²²The LORD heard Elijah's cry, and the boy's life returned to him, and he lived. ²³Elijah picked up the child and carried him down from the room into the house. He gave him to his mother and said, "Look, your son is alive!"

²⁴Then the woman said to Elijah, "Now I know that you are a man of God and that the word of the LORD from your mouth is the truth."

Elijah and Obadiah

18 After a long time, in the third year, the word of the LORD came to Elijah: "Go and present yourself to Ahab, and I will send rain on the land." ²So Elijah went to present himself to Ahab.

Now the famine was severe in Samaria, ³and Ahab had summoned Obadiah, who was in charge of his palace. (Obadiah was a devout believer in the LORD. ⁴While Jezebel was killing off the LORD's prophets, Obadiah had taken a hundred prophets and hidden them in two caves, fifty in each, and had supplied them with food and water.) ⁵Ahab had said to Obadiah, "Go through the land to all the springs and valleys. Maybe we can find some grass to keep the horses and mules alive so we will not have to kill any of our animals." ⁶So they divided the land they were to cover, Ahab going in one direction and Obadiah in another.

⁷As Obadiah was walking along, Elijah met him. Obadiah recognized him, bowed down to the ground, and said, "Is it really you, my lord Elijah?"

⁸"Yes," he replied. "Go tell your master, 'Elijah is here.'"

⁹"What have I done wrong," asked Obadiah, "that you are handing your servant over to Ahab to be put to death? ¹⁰As surely as the LORD your God lives, there is not a nation or kingdom where my master has not sent someone to look for you. And whenever a nation or kingdom claimed you were not there, he made them swear they could not find you. ¹¹But now you tell me to go to my master and say, 'Elijah is here.' ¹²I don't know where the Spirit of the LORD may carry you when I leave you. If I go and tell Ahab and he doesn't find you, he will kill me. Yet I your servant have worshiped the LORD since my youth. ¹³Haven't you heard, my lord, what I did while Jezebel was killing the prophets of the LORD? I hid a hundred of the LORD's prophets in two caves, fifty in each, and supplied them with food and water. ¹⁴And now

you tell me to go to my master and say, 'Elijah is here.' He will kill me!"

¹⁵Elijah said, "As the LORD Almighty lives, whom I serve, I will surely present myself to Ahab today."

Elijah on Mount Carmel

¹⁶So Obadiah went to meet Ahab and told him, and Ahab went to meet Elijah. ¹⁷When he saw Elijah, he said to him, "Is that you, you troubler of Israel?"

¹⁸"I have not made trouble for Israel," Elijah replied. "But you and your father's family have. You have abandoned the LORD's commands and have followed the Baals. ¹⁹Now summon the people from all over Israel to meet me on Mount Carmel. And bring the four hundred and fifty prophets of Baal and the four hundred prophets of Asherah, who eat at Jezebel's table."

²⁰So Ahab sent word throughout all Israel and assembled the prophets on Mount Carmel. ²¹Elijah went before the people and said, "How long will you waver between two opinions? If the LORD is God, follow him; but if Baal is God, follow him."

But the people said nothing.

²²Then Elijah said to them, "I am the only one of the LORD's prophets left, but Baal has four hundred and fifty prophets. ²³Get two bulls for us. Let them choose one for themselves, and let them cut it into pieces and put it on the wood but not set fire to it. I will prepare the other bull and put it on the wood but not set fire to it. ²⁴Then you call on the name of your god, and I will call on the name of the LORD. The god who answers by fire—he is God."

Then all the people said, "What you say is good."

²⁵Elijah said to the prophets of Baal, "Choose one of the bulls and prepare it first, since there are so many of you. Call on the name of your god, but do not light the fire." ²⁶So they took the bull given them and prepared it.

Then they called on the name of Baal

GOING *deeper*

Expectant Prayer

READ AND CONSIDER: 1 KINGS 18:16-39

" 'Answer me, O Lord, answer me, so these people will know that you, O Lord, are God, and that you are turning their hearts back again.' Then the fire of the Lord fell and burned up the sacrifice, the wood, the stones and the soil, and also licked up the water in the trench" (1 Kings 18:37-38).

If there is anything like instant replay in heaven, countless believers will want to watch the moment when Elijah gave the signal and God's fire fell and consumed the soggy sacrifice. Elijah had made it impossible to set the sacrifice on fire outside of a miracle from God. And a miracle is what he expected God to do. This is in great contrast to the hours of agonized pleading by the prophets of Baal, urging their mute and impotent god to send a little spark and light the fire under *their* sacrifice.

Years earlier, Moses had warned the people that "God is a consuming fire, a jealous God" (Deuteronomy 4:24). So the way God answered Elijah's prayer was perfectly in character. God doesn't reveal all of His glory because He knows we couldn't handle it. That's why when God makes His presence known, even through messengers, His first words often are "Don't be afraid." But when it came to a showdown with Baal worshipers, God allowed His actions to announce, "Be afraid! God and His consuming fire are here!"

When you pray, do you expect God to do something because you know what He *is able* to do? Or do you half expect to be disappointed because you doubt that God could do something so great for you? If you answered yes to the last question, ask God to give you a heart filled with faith and expectancy of the great things He will do in response to your prayers.

from morning till noon. "O Baal, answer us!" they shouted. But there was no response; no one answered. And they danced around the altar they had made.

27 At noon Elijah began to taunt them. "Shout louder!" he said. "Surely he is a god! Perhaps he is deep in thought, or busy, or traveling. Maybe he is sleeping and must be awakened." 28 So they shouted louder and slashed themselves with swords and spears, as was their custom, until their blood flowed. 29 Midday passed, and they continued their frantic prophesying until the time for the evening sacrifice. But there was no response, no one answered, no one paid attention.

30 Then Elijah said to all the people, "Come here to me." They came to him, and he repaired the altar of the Lord,

which was in ruins. 31 Elijah took twelve stones, one for each of the tribes descended from Jacob, to whom the word of the Lord had come, saying, "Your name shall be Israel." 32 With the stones he built an altar in the name of the Lord, and he dug a trench around it large enough to hold two seahs[a] of seed. 33 He arranged the wood, cut the bull into pieces and laid it on the wood. Then he said to them, "Fill four large jars with water and pour it on the offering and on the wood."

34 "Do it again," he said, and they did it again.

"Do it a third time," he ordered, and they did it the third time. 35 The water ran down around the altar and even filled the trench.

36 At the time of sacrifice, the prophet

a *32* That is, probably about 13 quarts (about 15 liters)

Elijah stepped forward and prayed: "O LORD, God of Abraham, Isaac and Israel, let it be known today that you are God in Israel and that I am your servant and have done all these things at your command. 37 Answer me, O LORD, answer me, so these people will know that you, O LORD, are God, and that you are turning their hearts back again."

38 Then the fire of the LORD fell and burned up the sacrifice, the wood, the stones and the soil, and also licked up the water in the trench.

39 When all the people saw this, they fell prostrate and cried, "The LORD—he is God! The LORD—he is God!"

40 Then Elijah commanded them, "Seize the prophets of Baal. Don't let anyone get away!" They seized them, and Elijah had them brought down to the Kishon Valley and slaughtered there.

41 And Elijah said to Ahab, "Go, eat and drink, for there is the sound of a heavy rain." 42 So Ahab went off to eat and drink, but Elijah climbed to the top of Carmel, bent down to the ground and put his face between his knees.

43 "Go and look toward the sea," he told his servant. And he went up and looked.

"There is nothing there," he said.

Seven times Elijah said, "Go back."

44 The seventh time the servant reported, "A cloud as small as a man's hand is rising from the sea."

So Elijah said, "Go and tell Ahab, 'Hitch up your chariot and go down before the rain stops you.'"

45 Meanwhile, the sky grew black with clouds, the wind rose, a heavy rain came on and Ahab rode off to Jezreel. 46 The power of the LORD came upon Elijah and, tucking his cloak into his belt, he ran ahead of Ahab all the way to Jezreel.

Elijah Flees to Horeb

19 Now Ahab told Jezebel everything Elijah had done and how he had killed all the prophets with the sword. 2 So Jezebel sent a messenger to Elijah to say, "May the gods deal with me, be it ever so severely, if by this time tomorrow I do not make your life like that of one of them."

3 Elijah was afraid[a] and ran for his life. When he came to Beersheba in Judah, he left his servant there, 4 while he himself went a day's journey into the desert. He came to a broom tree, sat down under it and prayed that he might die. "I have had enough, LORD," he said. "Take my life; I am no better than my ancestors." 5 Then he lay down under the tree and fell asleep.

> *Praying 1 Kings 19:1-5*
> *God, help me to not be discouraged when I do what is right and am persecuted for it.*

All at once an angel touched him and said, "Get up and eat." 6 He looked around, and there by his head was a cake of bread baked over hot coals, and a jar of water. He ate and drank and then lay down again.

7 The angel of the LORD came back a second time and touched him and said, "Get up and eat, for the journey is too much for you." 8 So he got up and ate and drank. Strengthened by that food, he traveled forty days and forty nights until he reached Horeb, the mountain of God. 9 There he went into a cave and spent the night.

The LORD Appears to Elijah

And the word of the LORD came to him: "What are you doing here, Elijah?"

10 He replied, "I have been very zealous for the LORD God Almighty. The Israelites have rejected your covenant, broken down your altars, and put your prophets to death with the sword. I am the only one left, and now they are trying to kill me too."

11 The LORD said, "Go out and stand on the mountain in the presence of the LORD, for the LORD is about to pass by."

---

a 3 Or *Elijah saw*

Then a great and powerful wind tore the mountains apart and shattered the rocks before the LORD, but the LORD was not in the wind. After the wind there was an earthquake, but the LORD was not in the earthquake. 12After the earthquake came a fire, but the LORD was not in the fire. And after the fire came a gentle whisper. 13When Elijah heard it, he pulled his cloak over his face and went out and stood at the mouth of the cave.

Then a voice said to him, "What are you doing here, Elijah?"

14He replied, "I have been very zealous for the LORD God Almighty. The Israelites have rejected your covenant, broken down your altars, and put your prophets to death with the sword. I am the only one left, and now they are trying to kill me too."

15The LORD said to him, "Go back the way you came, and go to the Desert of Damascus. When you get there, anoint Hazael king over Aram. 16Also, anoint Jehu son of Nimshi king over Israel, and anoint Elisha son of Shaphat from Abel Meholah to succeed you as prophet. 17Jehu will put to death any who escape the sword of Hazael, and Elisha will put to death any who escape the sword of Jehu. 18Yet I reserve seven thousand in Israel—all whose knees have not bowed down to Baal and all whose mouths have not kissed him."

The Call of Elisha

19So Elijah went from there and found Elisha son of Shaphat. He was plowing with twelve yoke of oxen, and he himself was driving the twelfth pair. Elijah went up to him and threw his cloak around him. 20Elisha then left his oxen and ran after Elijah. "Let me kiss my father and mother good-by," he said, "and then I will come with you."

"Go back," Elijah replied. "What have I done to you?"

21So Elisha left him and went back. He took his yoke of oxen and slaughtered them. He burned the plowing equipment to cook the meat and gave it to the people, and they ate. Then he set out to follow Elijah and became his attendant.

Ben-Hadad Attacks Samaria

20 Now Ben-Hadad king of Aram mustered his entire army. Accompanied by thirty-two kings with their horses and chariots, he went up and besieged Samaria and attacked it. 2He sent messengers into the city to Ahab king of Israel, saying, "This is what Ben-Hadad says: 3'Your silver and gold are mine, and the best of your wives and children are mine.'"

4The king of Israel answered, "Just as you say, my lord the king. I and all I have are yours."

5The messengers came again and said,

"This is what Ben-Hadad says: 'I sent to demand your silver and gold, your wives and your children. 6But about this time tomorrow I am going to send my officials to search your palace and the houses of your officials. They will seize everything you value and carry it away.'"

7The king of Israel summoned all the elders of the land and said to them, "See how this man is looking for trouble! When he sent for my wives and my children, my silver and my gold, I did not refuse him."

8The elders and the people all answered, "Don't listen to him or agree to his demands."

9So he replied to Ben-Hadad's messengers, "Tell my lord the king, 'Your servant will do all you demanded the first time, but this demand I cannot meet.'" They left and took the answer back to Ben-Hadad.

10Then Ben-Hadad sent another message to Ahab: "May the gods deal with me, be it ever so severely, if enough dust remains in Samaria to give each of my men a handful."

11The king of Israel answered, "Tell him: 'One who puts on his armor should not boast like one who takes it off.'"

12Ben-Hadad heard this message while he and the kings were drinking in their tents,ᵃ and he ordered his men: "Prepare to attack." So they prepared to attack the city.

Ahab Defeats Ben-Hadad

13Meanwhile a prophet came to Ahab king of Israel and announced, "This is what the LORD says: 'Do you see this vast army? I will give it into your hand today, and then you will know that I am the LORD.'"

14"But who will do this?" asked Ahab.

The prophet replied, "This is what the LORD says: 'The young officers of the provincial commanders will do it.'"

"And who will start the battle?" he asked.

The prophet answered, "You will."

15So Ahab summoned the young officers of the provincial commanders, 232 men. Then he assembled the rest of the Israelites, 7,000 in all. 16They set out at noon while Ben-Hadad and the 32 kings allied with him were in their tents getting drunk. 17The young officers of the provincial commanders went out first.

Now Ben-Hadad had dispatched scouts, who reported, "Men are advancing from Samaria."

18He said, "If they have come out for peace, take them alive; if they have come out for war, take them alive."

19The young officers of the provincial commanders marched out of the city with the army behind them 20and each one struck down his opponent. At that, the Arameans fled, with the Israelites in pursuit. But Ben-Hadad king of Aram escaped on horseback with some of his horsemen. 21The king of Israel advanced and overpowered the horses and chariots and inflicted heavy losses on the Arameans.

22Afterward, the prophet came to the king of Israel and said, "Strengthen your position and see what must be done, because next spring the king of Aram will attack you again."

23Meanwhile, the officials of the king of Aram advised him, "Their gods are gods of the hills. That is why they were too strong for us. But if we fight them on the plains, surely we will be stronger than they. 24Do this: Remove all the kings from their commands and replace them with other officers. 25You must also raise an army like the one you lost—horse for horse and chariot for chariot—so we can fight Israel on the plains. Then surely we will be stronger than they." He agreed with them and acted accordingly.

26The next spring Ben-Hadad mustered the Arameans and went up to Aphek to fight against Israel. 27When the Israelites were also mustered and given provisions, they marched out to meet them. The Israelites camped opposite them like two small flocks of goats, while the Arameans covered the countryside.

28 The man of God came up and told the king of Israel, "This is what the LORD says: 'Because the Arameans think the LORD is a god of the hills and not a god of the valleys, I will deliver this vast army into your hands, and you will know that I am the LORD.'"

29 For seven days they camped opposite each other, and on the seventh day the battle was joined. The Israelites inflicted a hundred thousand casualties on the Aramean foot soldiers in one day. 30 The rest of them escaped to the city of Aphek, where the wall collapsed on twenty-seven thousand of them. And Ben-Hadad fled to the city and hid in an inner room.

31 His officials said to him, "Look, we have heard that the kings of the house of Israel are merciful. Let us go to the king of Israel with sackcloth around our waists and ropes around our heads. Perhaps he will spare your life."

32 Wearing sackcloth around their waists and ropes around their heads, they went to the king of Israel and said, "Your servant Ben-Hadad says: 'Please let me live.'"

The king answered, "Is he still alive? He is my brother."

33 The men took this as a good sign and were quick to pick up his word. "Yes, your brother Ben-Hadad!" they said.

"Go and get him," the king said. When Ben-Hadad came out, Ahab had him come up into his chariot.

34 "I will return the cities my father took from your father," Ben-Hadad offered. "You may set up your own market areas in Damascus, as my father did in Samaria."

⌊Ahab said,⌋ "On the basis of a treaty I will set you free." So he made a treaty with him, and let him go.

A Prophet Condemns Ahab

35 By the word of the LORD one of the sons of the prophets said to his companion, "Strike me with your weapon," but the man refused.

36 So the prophet said, "Because you have not obeyed the LORD, as soon as you leave me a lion will kill you." And after the man went away, a lion found him and killed him.

37 The prophet found another man and said, "Strike me, please." So the man struck him and wounded him. 38 Then the prophet went and stood by the road waiting for the king. He disguised himself with his headband down over his eyes. 39 As the king passed by, the prophet called out to him, "Your servant went into the thick of the battle, and someone came to me with a captive and said, 'Guard this man. If he is missing, it will be your life for his life, or you must pay a talent[a] of silver.' 40 While your servant was busy here and there, the man disappeared."

"That is your sentence," the king of Israel said. "You have pronounced it yourself."

41 Then the prophet quickly removed the headband from his eyes, and the king of Israel recognized him as one of the prophets. 42 He said to the king, "This is what the LORD says: 'You have set free a man I had determined should die.[b] Therefore it is your life for his life, your people for his people.'" 43 Sullen and angry, the king of Israel went to his palace in Samaria.

Naboth's Vineyard

21 Some time later there was an incident involving a vineyard belonging to Naboth the Jezreelite. The vineyard was in Jezreel, close to the palace of Ahab king of Samaria. 2 Ahab said to Naboth, "Let me have your vineyard to use for a vegetable garden, since it is close to my palace. In exchange I will give you a better vineyard or, if you prefer, I will pay you whatever it is worth."

---

a 39 That is, about 75 pounds (about 34 kilograms)   b 42 The Hebrew term refers to the irrevocable giving over of things or persons to the LORD, often by totally destroying them.

3But Naboth replied, "The LORD forbid that I should give you the inheritance of my fathers."

4So Ahab went home, sullen and angry because Naboth the Jezreelite had said, "I will not give you the inheritance of my fathers." He lay on his bed sulking and refused to eat.

5His wife Jezebel came in and asked him, "Why are you so sullen? Why won't you eat?"

6He answered her, "Because I said to Naboth the Jezreelite, 'Sell me your vineyard; or if you prefer, I will give you another vineyard in its place.' But he said, 'I will not give you my vineyard.'"

7Jezebel his wife said, "Is this how you act as king over Israel? Get up and eat! Cheer up. I'll get you the vineyard of Naboth the Jezreelite."

8So she wrote letters in Ahab's name, placed his seal on them, and sent them to the elders and nobles who lived in Naboth's city with him. 9In those letters she wrote:

"Proclaim a day of fasting and seat Naboth in a prominent place among the people. 10But seat two scoundrels opposite him and have them testify that he has cursed both God and the king. Then take him out and stone him to death."

11So the elders and nobles who lived in Naboth's city did as Jezebel directed in the letters she had written to them. 12They proclaimed a fast and seated Naboth in a prominent place among the people. 13Then two scoundrels came and sat opposite him and brought charges against Naboth before the people, saying, "Naboth has cursed both God and the king." So they took him outside the city and stoned him to death. 14Then they sent word to Jezebel: "Naboth has been stoned and is dead."

15As soon as Jezebel heard that Naboth had been stoned to death, she said to Ahab, "Get up and take possession of the vineyard of Naboth the Jezreelite that he refused to sell you. He is no longer alive, but dead." 16When Ahab heard that Naboth was dead, he got up and went down to take possession of Naboth's vineyard.

17Then the word of the LORD came to Elijah the Tishbite: 18"Go down to meet Ahab king of Israel, who rules in Samaria. He is now in Naboth's vineyard, where he has gone to take possession of it. 19Say to him, 'This is what the LORD says: Have you not murdered a man and seized his property?' Then say to him, 'This is what the LORD says: In the place where dogs licked up Naboth's blood, dogs will lick up your blood—yes, yours!'"

20Ahab said to Elijah, "So you have found me, my enemy!"

"I have found you," he answered, "because you have sold yourself to do evil in the eyes of the LORD. 21'I am going to bring disaster on you. I will consume your descendants and cut off from Ahab every last male in Israel—slave or free. 22I will make your house like that of Jeroboam son of Nebat and that of Baasha son of Ahijah, because you have provoked me to anger and have caused Israel to sin.'

23"And also concerning Jezebel the LORD says: 'Dogs will devour Jezebel by the wall of[a] Jezreel.'

24"Dogs will eat those belonging to Ahab who die in the city, and the birds of the air will feed on those who die in the country."

25(There was never a man like Ahab, who sold himself to do evil in the eyes of the LORD, urged on by Jezebel his wife. 26He behaved in the vilest manner by going after idols, like the Amorites the LORD drove out before Israel.)

27When Ahab heard these words, he tore his clothes, put on sackcloth and fasted. He lay in sackcloth and went around meekly.

28Then the word of the LORD came to Elijah the Tishbite: 29"Have you noticed how Ahab has humbled himself before me? Because he has humbled himself, I will not bring this disaster in his day, but I will bring it on his house in the days of his son."

Micaiah Prophesies Against Ahab

22 For three years there was no war between Aram and Israel. ²But in the third year Jehoshaphat king of Judah went down to see the king of Israel. ³The king of Israel had said to his officials, "Don't you know that Ramoth Gilead belongs to us and yet we are doing nothing to retake it from the king of Aram?"

⁴So he asked Jehoshaphat, "Will you go with me to fight against Ramoth Gilead?"

Jehoshaphat replied to the king of Israel, "I am as you are, my people as your people, my horses as your horses." ⁵But Jehoshaphat also said to the king of Israel, "First seek the counsel of the Lord."

⁶So the king of Israel brought together the prophets—about four hundred men—and asked them, "Shall I go to war against Ramoth Gilead, or shall I refrain?"

"Go," they answered, "for the Lord will give it into the king's hand."

⁷But Jehoshaphat asked, "Is there not a prophet of the Lord here whom we can inquire of?"

⁸The king of Israel answered Jehoshaphat, "There is still one man through whom we can inquire of the Lord, but I hate him because he never prophesies anything good about me, but always bad. He is Micaiah son of Imlah."

"The king should not say that," Jehoshaphat replied.

⁹So the king of Israel called one of his officials and said, "Bring Micaiah son of Imlah at once."

¹⁰Dressed in their royal robes, the king of Israel and Jehoshaphat king of Judah were sitting on their thrones at the threshing floor by the entrance of the gate of Samaria, with all the prophets prophesying before them. ¹¹Now Zedekiah son of Kenaanah had made iron horns and

he declared, "This is what the Lord says: 'With these you will gore the Arameans until they are destroyed.'"

¹²All the other prophets were prophesying the same thing. "Attack Ramoth Gilead and be victorious," they said, "for the Lord will give it into the king's hand."

¹³The messenger who had gone to summon Micaiah said to him, "Look, as one man the other prophets are predicting success for the king. Let your word agree with theirs, and speak favorably."

¹⁴But Micaiah said, "As surely as the Lord lives, I can tell him only what the Lord tells me."

¹⁵When he arrived, the king asked him, "Micaiah, shall we go to war against Ramoth Gilead, or shall I refrain?"

"Attack and be victorious," he answered, "for the Lord will give it into the king's hand."

¹⁶The king said to him, "How many times must I make you swear to tell me nothing but the truth in the name of the Lord?"

¹⁷Then Micaiah answered, "I saw all Israel scattered on the hills like sheep without a shepherd, and the Lord said, 'These people have no master. Let each one go home in peace.'"

¹⁸The king of Israel said to Jehoshaphat, "Didn't I tell you that he never prophesies anything good about me, but only bad?"

¹⁹Micaiah continued, "Therefore hear the word of the Lord: I saw the Lord sitting on his throne with all the host of heaven standing around him on his right and on his left. ²⁰And the Lord said, 'Who will entice Ahab into attacking Ramoth Gilead and going to his death there?'

"One suggested this, and another that. ²¹Finally, a spirit came forward, stood before the Lord and said, 'I will entice him.'

²²"'By what means?' the Lord asked.

"'I will go out and be a lying spirit in the mouths of all his prophets,' he said.

"'You will succeed in enticing him,' said the Lord. 'Go and do it.'

23"So now the LORD has put a lying spirit in the mouths of all these prophets of yours. The LORD has decreed disaster for you."

24Then Zedekiah son of Kenaanah went up and slapped Micaiah in the face. "Which way did the spirit from[a] the LORD go when he went from me to speak to you?" he asked.

25Micaiah replied, "You will find out on the day you go to hide in an inner room."

26The king of Israel then ordered, "Take Micaiah and send him back to Amon the ruler of the city and to Joash the king's son 27and say, 'This is what the king says: Put this fellow in prison and give him nothing but bread and water until I return safely.'"

28Micaiah declared, "If you ever return safely, the LORD has not spoken through me." Then he added, "Mark my words, all you people!"

Ahab Killed at Ramoth Gilead

29So the king of Israel and Jehoshaphat king of Judah went up to Ramoth Gilead. 30The king of Israel said to Jehoshaphat, "I will enter the battle in disguise, but you wear your royal robes." So the king of Israel disguised himself and went into battle.

31Now the king of Aram had ordered his thirty-two chariot commanders, "Do not fight with anyone, small or great, except the king of Israel." 32When the chariot commanders saw Jehoshaphat, they thought, "Surely this is the king of Israel." So they turned to attack him, but when Jehoshaphat cried out, 33the chariot commanders saw that he was not the king of Israel and stopped pursuing him.

34But someone drew his bow at random and hit the king of Israel between the sections of his armor. The king told his chariot driver, "Wheel around and get me out of the fighting. I've been wounded." 35All day long the battle raged, and the king was propped up in his chariot facing the Arameans. The blood from his wound ran onto the floor of the chariot, and that evening he died. 36As the sun was setting, a cry spread through the army: "Every man to his town; everyone to his land!"

37So the king died and was brought to Samaria, and they buried him there. 38They washed the chariot at a pool in Samaria (where the prostitutes bathed),[b] and the dogs licked up his blood, as the word of the LORD had declared.

39As for the other events of Ahab's reign, including all he did, the palace he built and inlaid with ivory, and the cities he fortified, are they not written in the book of the annals of the kings of Israel? 40Ahab rested with his fathers. And Ahaziah his son succeeded him as king.

Jehoshaphat King of Judah

41Jehoshaphat son of Asa became king of Judah in the fourth year of Ahab king of Israel. 42Jehoshaphat was thirty-five years old when he became king, and he reigned in Jerusalem twenty-five years. His mother's name was Azubah daughter of Shilhi. 43In everything he walked in the ways of his father Asa and did not stray from them; he did what was right in the eyes of the LORD. The high places, however, were not removed, and the people continued to offer sacrifices and burn incense there. 44Jehoshaphat was also at peace with the king of Israel.

45As for the other events of Jehoshaphat's reign, the things he achieved and his military exploits, are they not written in the book of the annals of the kings of Judah? 46He rid the land of the rest of the male shrine prostitutes who remained there even after the reign of his father Asa. 47There was then no king in Edom; a deputy ruled.

48Now Jehoshaphat built a fleet of trading ships[c] to go to Ophir for gold, but they never set sail—they were wrecked at Ezion Geber. 49At that time Ahaziah son of Ahab said to Jehoshaphat, "Let my

---

a 24 Or Spirit of   b 38 Or Samaria and cleaned the weapons   c 48 Hebrew of ships of Tarshish men sail with your men," but Jehoshaphat refused.

50 Then Jehoshaphat rested with his fathers and was buried with them in the city of David his father. And Jehoram his son succeeded him.

Ahaziah King of Israel

51 Ahaziah son of Ahab became king of Israel in Samaria in the seventeenth year of Jehoshaphat king of Judah, and he reigned over Israel two years. 52 He did evil in the eyes of the LORD, because he walked in the ways of his father and mother and in the ways of Jeroboam son of Nebat, who caused Israel to sin. 53 He served and worshiped Baal and provoked the LORD, the God of Israel, to anger, just as his father had done.

Author: Unknown, possibly Jeremiah

Date: Most likely during the time of the exile (between 560 and 538 BC)

Audience: Future generations—to record Israel's history so that readers might learn practical spiritual lessons from Israel's example, both good and bad

Prayer Themes:

- Ask God to give you a selfless heart that is always willing to share good news with others—especially the good news of forgiveness and new life in Christ (7:3-9).

- Tell God you want to be like Hezekiah—full of faith and a desire to obey—in an era marked by doubt and disobedience (18:5-6).

- Thank God for all your leaders (spiritual, military, civic, political, etc.) who have hearts like Josiah—a desire to walk with God and live as His servants (22:2).

There's been a concerted effort in recent years by Christians to pray faithfully and fervently for world leaders (1 Timothy 2:2). How important is this prayer focus? Do such prayers really make a difference?

Absolutely! When we pray *for* those in positions of power, we are praying *to* the One with *all* power. Our God is the "King of kings" (1 Timothy 6:15). All presidents and princes are subject to Him (Psalm 2:1-12; 72:11). The Bible assures us that God has a direct hand in the affairs of world governments. He is the One who "sets up kings and deposes them" (Daniel 2:21).

Second Kings demonstrates how critical it is for a people to have rulers who love God—as well as the severe consequences when a nation's political leaders are not godly.

2 Kings

The LORD's Judgment on Ahaziah

1 After Ahab's death, Moab rebelled against Israel. ²Now Ahaziah had fallen through the lattice of his upper room in Samaria and injured himself. So he sent messengers, saying to them, "Go and consult Baal-Zebub, the god of Ekron, to see if I will recover from this injury."

³But the angel of the LORD said to Elijah the Tishbite, "Go up and meet the messengers of the king of Samaria and ask them, 'Is it because there is no God in Israel that you are going off to consult Baal-Zebub, the god of Ekron?' ⁴Therefore this is what the LORD says: 'You will not leave the bed you are lying on. You will certainly die!'" So Elijah went.

⁵When the messengers returned to the king, he asked them, "Why have you come back?"

⁶"A man came to meet us," they replied. "And he said to us, 'Go back to the king who sent you and tell him, "This is what the LORD says: Is it because there is no God in Israel that you are sending men to consult Baal-Zebub, the god of Ekron? Therefore you will not leave the bed you are lying on. You will certainly die!"'"

⁷The king asked them, "What kind of man was it who came to meet you and told you this?"

⁸They replied, "He was a man with a garment of hair and with a leather belt around his waist."

The king said, "That was Elijah the Tishbite."

⁹Then he sent to Elijah a captain with his company of fifty men. The captain went up to Elijah, who was sitting on the top of a hill, and said to him, "Man of God, the king says, 'Come down!'"

¹⁰Elijah answered the captain, "If I am a man of God, may fire come down from heaven and consume you and your fifty

men!"Then fire fell from heaven and consumed the captain and his men.

11At this the king sent to Elijah another captain with his fifty men. The captain said to him, "Man of God, this is what the king says, 'Come down at once!'"

12"If I am a man of God," Elijah replied, "may fire come down from heaven and consume you and your fifty men!" Then the fire of God fell from heaven and consumed him and his fifty men.

13So the king sent a third captain with his fifty men. This third captain went up and fell on his knees before Elijah. "Man of God," he begged, "please have respect for my life and the lives of these fifty men, your servants! 14See, fire has fallen from heaven and consumed the first two captains and all their men. But now have respect for my life!"

Prayer is...
welcoming God's presence.

15The angel of the LORD said to Elijah, "Go down with him; do not be afraid of him." So Elijah got up and went down with him to the king.

16He told the king, "This is what the LORD says: Is it because there is no God in Israel for you to consult that you have sent messengers to consult Baal-Zebub, the god of Ekron? Because you have done this, you will never leave the bed you are lying on. You will certainly die!" 17So he died, according to the word of the LORD that Elijah had spoken.

Because Ahaziah had no son, Joram[a] succeeded him as king in the second year of Jehoram son of Jehoshaphat king of Judah. 18As for all the other events of Ahaziah's reign, and what he did, are they not written in the book of the annals of the kings of Israel?

Elijah Taken Up to Heaven

2 When the LORD was about to take Elijah up to heaven in a whirlwind, Elijah and Elisha were on their way from Gilgal. 2Elijah said to Elisha, "Stay here; the LORD has sent me to Bethel."

But Elisha said, "As surely as the LORD lives and as you live, I will not leave you." So they went down to Bethel.

3The company of the prophets at Bethel came out to Elisha and asked, "Do you know that the LORD is going to take your master from you today?"

"Yes, I know," Elisha replied, "but do not speak of it."

4Then Elijah said to him, "Stay here, Elisha; the LORD has sent me to Jericho."

And he replied, "As surely as the LORD lives and as you live, I will not leave you." So they went to Jericho.

5The company of the prophets at Jericho went up to Elisha and asked him, "Do you know that the LORD is going to take your master from you today?"

"Yes, I know," he replied, "but do not speak of it."

6Then Elijah said to him, "Stay here; the LORD has sent me to the Jordan."

And he replied, "As surely as the LORD lives and as you live, I will not leave you." So the two of them walked on.

7Fifty men of the company of the prophets went and stood at a distance, facing the place where Elijah and Elisha had stopped at the Jordan. 8Elijah took his cloak, rolled it up and struck the water with it. The water divided to the right and to the left, and the two of them crossed over on dry ground.

9When they had crossed, Elijah said to Elisha, "Tell me, what can I do for you before I am taken from you?"

"Let me inherit a double portion of your spirit," Elisha replied.

10"You have asked a difficult thing," Elijah said, "yet if you see me when I am taken from you, it will be yours—otherwise not."

---

a *17* Hebrew *Jehoram,* a variant of *Joram*

[11] As they were walking along and talking together, suddenly a chariot of fire and horses of fire appeared and separated the two of them, and Elijah went up to heaven in a whirlwind. [12] Elisha saw this and cried out, "My father! My father! The chariots and horsemen of Israel!" And Elisha saw him no more. Then he took hold of his own clothes and tore them apart.

[13] He picked up the cloak that had fallen from Elijah and went back and stood on the bank of the Jordan. [14] Then he took the cloak that had fallen from him and struck the water with it. "Where now is the LORD, the God of Elijah?" he asked. When he struck the water, it divided to the right and to the left, and he crossed over.

[15] The company of the prophets from Jericho, who were watching, said, "The spirit of Elijah is resting on Elisha." And they went to meet him and bowed to the ground before him. [16] "Look," they said, "we your servants have fifty able men. Let them go and look for your master. Perhaps the Spirit of the LORD has picked him up and set him down on some mountain or in some valley."

"No," Elisha replied, "do not send them."

[17] But they persisted until he was too ashamed to refuse. So he said, "Send them." And they sent fifty men, who searched for three days but did not find him. [18] When they returned to Elisha, who was staying in Jericho, he said to them, "Didn't I tell you not to go?"

Healing of the Water

[19] The men of the city said to Elisha, "Look, our lord, this town is well situated, as you can see, but the water is bad and the land is unproductive."

[20] "Bring me a new bowl," he said, "and put salt in it." So they brought it to him.

[21] Then he went out to the spring and threw the salt into it, saying, "This is what the LORD says: 'I have healed this water. Never again will it cause death or make the land unproductive.'" [22] And the water has remained wholesome to this day, according to the word Elisha had spoken.

Elisha Is Jeered

[23] From there Elisha went up to Bethel. As he was walking along the road, some youths came out of the town and jeered at him. "Go on up, you baldhead!" they said. "Go on up, you baldhead!" [24] He turned around, looked at them and called down a curse on them in the name of the LORD. Then two bears came out of the woods and mauled forty-two of the youths. [25] And he went on to Mount Carmel and from there returned to Samaria.

Moab Revolts

Joram[a] son of Ahab became king of Israel in Samaria in the eighteenth year of Jehoshaphat king of Judah, and he reigned twelve years. [2] He did evil in the eyes of the LORD, but not as his father and mother had done. He got rid of the sacred stone of Baal that his father had made. [3] Nevertheless he clung to the sins of Jeroboam son of Nebat, which he had caused Israel to commit; he did not turn away from them.

[4] Now Mesha king of Moab raised sheep, and he had to supply the king of Israel with a hundred thousand lambs and with the wool of a hundred thousand rams. [5] But after Ahab died, the king of Moab rebelled against the king of Israel. [6] So at that time King Joram set out from Samaria and mobilized all Israel. [7] He also sent this message to Jehoshaphat king of Judah: "The king of Moab has rebelled against me. Will you go with me to fight against Moab?"

"I will go with you," he replied. "I am as you are, my people as your people, my horses as your horses."

[8] "By what route shall we attack?" he asked.

"Through the Desert of Edom," he answered.

---

[a] 1 Hebrew *Jehoram*, a variant of *Joram*; also in verse 6

9So the king of Israel set out with the king of Judah and the king of Edom. After a roundabout march of seven days, the army had no more water for themselves or for the animals with them.

10"What!" exclaimed the king of Israel. "Has the LORD called us three kings together only to hand us over to Moab?"

11But Jehoshaphat asked, "Is there no prophet of the LORD here, that we may inquire of the LORD through him?"

An officer of the king of Israel answered, "Elisha son of Shaphat is here. He used to pour water on the hands of Elijah.ª"

12Jehoshaphat said, "The word of the LORD is with him." So the king of Israel and Jehoshaphat and the king of Edom went down to him.

13Elisha said to the king of Israel, "What do we have to do with each other? Go to the prophets of your father and the prophets of your mother."

"No," the king of Israel answered, "because it was the LORD who called us three kings together to hand us over to Moab."

14Elisha said, "As surely as the LORD Almighty lives, whom I serve, if I did not have respect for the presence of Jehoshaphat king of Judah, I would not look at you or even notice you. 15But now bring me a harpist."

While the harpist was playing, the hand of the LORD came upon Elisha 16and he said, "This is what the LORD says: Make this valley full of ditches. 17For this is what the LORD says: You will see neither wind nor rain, yet this valley will be filled with water, and you, your cattle and your other animals will drink. 18This is an easy thing in the eyes of the LORD; he will also hand Moab over to you. 19You will overthrow every fortified city and every major town. You will cut down every good tree, stop up all the springs, and ruin every good field with stones."

20The next morning, about the time for offering the sacrifice, there it was—water flowing from the direction of Edom! And the land was filled with water.

21Now all the Moabites had heard that the kings had come to fight against them; so every man, young and old, who could bear arms was called up and stationed on the border. 22When they got up early in the morning, the sun was shining on the water. To the Moabites across the way, the water looked red—like blood. 23"That's blood!" they said. "Those kings must have fought and slaughtered each other. Now to the plunder, Moab!"

24But when the Moabites came to the camp of Israel, the Israelites rose up and fought them until they fled. And the Israelites invaded the land and slaughtered the Moabites. 25They destroyed the towns, and each man threw a stone on every good field until it was covered. They stopped up all the springs and cut down every good tree. Only Kir Hareseth was left with its stones in place, but men armed with slings surrounded it and attacked it as well.

26When the king of Moab saw that the battle had gone against him, he took with him seven hundred swordsmen to break through to the king of Edom, but they failed. 27Then he took his firstborn son, who was to succeed him as king, and offered him as a sacrifice on the city wall. The fury against Israel was great; they withdrew and returned to their own land.

The Widow's Oil

4 The wife of a man from the company of the prophets cried out to Elisha, "Your servant my husband is dead, and you know that he revered the LORD. But now his creditor is coming to take my two boys as his slaves."

Praying 2 Kings 4:1-6
Lord, enlarge my heart to
contain all You have for me.

ª *11* That is, he was Elijah's personal servant.

God Will Pour Out as Much as You Can Receive

READ AND CONSIDER: 2 KINGS 4:1-7

"Elisha said, 'Go around and ask all your neighbors for empty jars. Don't ask for just a few. Then go inside and shut the door behind you and your sons. Pour oil into all the jars, and as each is filled, put it to one side' " (2 Kings 4:3-4).

The widow came to Elisha for help because her sons were about to be sold into slavery to cover her debts. When he asked her what she had in her house, she said all she had was one jar of oil. He instructed her to borrow empty jars, *but not just a few.*

The widow didn't know what God would do with these empty jars; she only knew He asked her to gather *many.* This woman's faith would be measured by how many jars she collected.

God took what the widow had in her one jar and multiplied it to fill all the containers she had borrowed and brought into her house. She was then able to sell the oil and pay her debts.

God will take what you have and multiply it to meet your needs as well. But how well are you able to contain all God has for you? Do you have faith enough to embrace the big things God wants to do in your life? If not, ask Him to give you big faith, and then determine to shut the door on doubt.

---

²Elisha replied to her, "How can I help you? Tell me, what do you have in your house?"

"Your servant has nothing there at all," she said, "except a little oil."

³Elisha said, "Go around and ask all your neighbors for empty jars. Don't ask for just a few. ⁴Then go inside and shut the door behind you and your sons. Pour oil into all the jars, and as each is filled, put it to one side."

⁵She left him and afterward shut the door behind her and her sons. They brought the jars to her and she kept pouring. ⁶When all the jars were full, she said to her son, "Bring me another one."

But he replied, "There is not a jar left." Then the oil stopped flowing.

⁷She went and told the man of God, and he said, "Go, sell the oil and pay your debts. You and your sons can live on what is left."

The Shunammite's Son Restored to Life

⁸One day Elisha went to Shunem. And a well-to-do woman was there, who urged him to stay for a meal. So whenever he came by, he stopped there to eat. ⁹She said to her husband, "I know that this man who often comes our way is a holy man of God. ¹⁰Let's make a small room on the roof and put in it a bed and a table, a chair and a lamp for him. Then he can stay there whenever he comes to us."

¹¹One day when Elisha came, he went up to his room and lay down there. ¹²He said to his servant Gehazi, "Call the Shunammite." So he called her, and she stood before him. ¹³Elisha said to him, "Tell her, 'You have gone to all this trouble for us. Now what can be done for you? Can we speak on your behalf to the king or the commander of the army?' "

She replied, "I have a home among my own people."

14"What can be done for her?" Elisha asked.

Gehazi said, "Well, she has no son and her husband is old."

15Then Elisha said, "Call her." So he called her, and she stood in the doorway. 16"About this time next year," Elisha said, "you will hold a son in your arms."

"No, my lord," she objected. "Don't mislead your servant, O man of God!"

17But the woman became pregnant, and the next year about that same time she gave birth to a son, just as Elisha had told her.

18The child grew, and one day he went out to his father, who was with the reapers. 19"My head! My head!" he said to his father.

His father told a servant, "Carry him to his mother." 20After the servant had lifted him up and carried him to his mother, the boy sat on her lap until noon, and then he died. 21She went up and laid him on the bed of the man of God, then shut the door and went out.

22She called her husband and said, "Please send me one of the servants and a donkey so I can go to the man of God quickly and return."

23"Why go to him today?" he asked. "It's not the New Moon or the Sabbath."

"It's all right," she said.

24She saddled the donkey and said to her servant, "Lead on; don't slow down for me unless I tell you." 25So she set out and came to the man of God at Mount Carmel.

When he saw her in the distance, the man of God said to his servant Gehazi, "Look! There's the Shunammite! 26Run to meet her and ask her, 'Are you all right? Is your husband all right? Is your child all right?'"

"Everything is all right," she said.

27When she reached the man of God at the mountain, she took hold of his feet. Gehazi came over to push her away, but the man of God said, "Leave her alone!

She is in bitter distress, but the LORD has hidden it from me and has not told me why."

28"Did I ask you for a son, my lord?" she said. "Didn't I tell you, 'Don't raise my hopes'?"

29Elisha said to Gehazi, "Tuck your cloak into your belt, take my staff in your hand and run. If you meet anyone, do not greet him, and if anyone greets you, do not answer. Lay my staff on the boy's face."

30But the child's mother said, "As surely as the LORD lives and as you live, I will not leave you." So he got up and followed her.

31Gehazi went on ahead and laid the staff on the boy's face, but there was no sound or response. So Gehazi went back to meet Elisha and told him, "The boy has not awakened."

32When Elisha reached the house, there was the boy lying dead on his couch. 33He went in, shut the door on the two of them and prayed to the LORD. 34Then he got on the bed and lay upon the boy, mouth to mouth, eyes to eyes, hands to hands. As he stretched himself out upon him, the boy's body grew warm. 35Elisha turned away and walked back and forth in the room and then got on the bed and stretched out upon him once more. The boy sneezed seven times and opened his eyes.

36Elisha summoned Gehazi and said, "Call the Shunammite." And he did. When she came, he said, "Take your son." 37She came in, fell at his feet and bowed to the ground. Then she took her son and went out.

Death in the Pot

38Elisha returned to Gilgal and there was a famine in that region. While the company of the prophets was meeting with him, he said to his servant, "Put on the large pot and cook some stew for these men."

39One of them went out into the fields to gather herbs and found a wild vine. He gathered some of its gourds and filled the fold of his cloak. When he returned, he cut them up into the pot of stew, though no one knew what they were. [40]The stew was poured out for the men, but as they began to eat it, they cried out, "O man of God, there is death in the pot!" And they could not eat it.

[41]Elisha said, "Get some flour." He put it into the pot and said, "Serve it to the people to eat." And there was nothing harmful in the pot.

Feeding of a Hundred

[42]A man came from Baal Shalishah, bringing the man of God twenty loaves of barley bread baked from the first ripe grain, along with some heads of new grain. "Give it to the people to eat," Elisha said.

[43]"How can I set this before a hundred men?" his servant asked.

But Elisha answered, "Give it to the people to eat. For this is what the LORD says: 'They will eat and have some left over.'" [44]Then he set it before them, and they ate and had some left over, according to the word of the LORD.

Naaman Healed of Leprosy

5 Now Naaman was commander of the army of the king of Aram. He was a great man in the sight of his master and highly regarded, because through him the LORD had given victory to Aram. He was a valiant soldier, but he had leprosy.[a]

[2]Now bands from Aram had gone out and had taken captive a young girl from Israel, and she served Naaman's wife. [3]She said to her mistress, "If only my master would see the prophet who is in Samaria! He would cure him of his leprosy."

[4]Naaman went to his master and told him what the girl from Israel had said. [5]"By all means, go," the king of Aram replied. "I will send a letter to the king of Israel." So Naaman left, taking with him ten talents[b] of silver, six thousand shekels[c]

of gold and ten sets of clothing. [6]The letter that he took to the king of Israel read: "With this letter I am sending my servant Naaman to you so that you may cure him of his leprosy."

[7]As soon as the king of Israel read the letter, he tore his robes and said, "Am I God? Can I kill and bring back to life? Why does this fellow send someone to me to be cured of his leprosy? See how he is trying to pick a quarrel with me!"

[8]When Elisha the man of God heard that the king of Israel had torn his robes, he sent him this message: "Why have you torn your robes? Have the man come to me and he will know that there is a prophet in Israel." [9]So Naaman went with his horses and chariots and stopped at the door of Elisha's house. [10]Elisha sent a messenger to say to him, "Go, wash yourself seven times in the Jordan, and your flesh will be restored and you will be cleansed."

[11]But Naaman went away angry and said, "I thought that he would surely come out to me and stand and call on the name of the LORD his God, wave his hand over the spot and cure me of my leprosy. [12]Are not Abana and Pharpar, the rivers of Damascus, better than any of the waters of Israel? Couldn't I wash in them and be cleansed?" So he turned and went off in a rage.

[13]Naaman's servants went to him and said, "My father, if the prophet had told you to do some great thing, would you not have done it? How much more, then, when he tells you, 'Wash and be cleansed'!" [14]So he went down and dipped himself in the Jordan seven times, as the man of God had told him, and his flesh was restored and became clean like that of a young boy.

[15]Then Naaman and all his attendants went back to the man of God. He stood before him and said, "Now I know that there is no God in all the world except

---

[a] 1 The Hebrew word was used for various diseases affecting the skin—not necessarily leprosy; also in verses 3, 6, 7, 11 and 27.   [b] 5 That is, about 750 pounds (about 340 kilograms)   [c] 5 That is, about 150 pounds (about 70 kilograms)

in Israel. Please accept now a gift from your servant."

16 The prophet answered, "As surely as the LORD lives, whom I serve, I will not accept a thing." And even though Naaman urged him, he refused.

17 "If you will not," said Naaman, "please let me, your servant, be given as much earth as a pair of mules can carry, for your servant will never again make burnt offerings and sacrifices to any other god but the LORD. 18 But may the LORD forgive your servant for this one thing: When my master enters the temple of Rimmon to bow down and he is leaning on my arm and I bow there also—when I bow down in the temple of Rimmon, may the LORD forgive your servant for this."

19 "Go in peace," Elisha said.

After Naaman had traveled some distance, 20 Gehazi, the servant of Elisha the man of God, said to himself, "My master was too easy on Naaman, this Aramean, by not accepting from him what he brought. As surely as the LORD lives, I will run after him and get something from him."

21 So Gehazi hurried after Naaman. When Naaman saw him running toward him, he got down from the chariot to meet him. "Is everything all right?" he asked.

22 "Everything is all right," Gehazi answered. "My master sent me to say, 'Two young men from the company of the prophets have just come to me from the hill country of Ephraim. Please give them a talent[a] of silver and two sets of clothing.'"

23 "By all means, take two talents," said Naaman. He urged Gehazi to accept them, and then tied up the two talents of silver in two bags, with two sets of clothing. He gave them to two of his servants, and they carried them ahead of Gehazi. 24 When Gehazi came to the hill, he took the things from the servants and put them away in the house. He sent the men away and they left. 25 Then he went in and stood before his master Elisha.

"Where have you been, Gehazi?" Elisha asked.

"Your servant didn't go anywhere," Gehazi answered.

26 But Elisha said to him, "Was not my spirit with you when the man got down from his chariot to meet you? Is this the time to take money, or to accept clothes, olive groves, vineyards, flocks, herds, or menservants and maidservants? 27 Naaman's leprosy will cling to you and to your descendants forever." Then Gehazi went from Elisha's presence and he was leprous, as white as snow.

An Axhead Floats

6 The company of the prophets said to Elisha, "Look, the place where we meet with you is too small for us. 2 Let us go to the Jordan, where each of us can get a pole; and let us build a place there for us to live."

And he said, "Go."

3 Then one of them said, "Won't you please come with your servants?"

"I will," Elisha replied. 4 And he went with them.

They went to the Jordan and began to cut down trees. 5 As one of them was cutting down a tree, the iron axhead fell into the water. "Oh, my lord," he cried out, "it was borrowed!"

6 The man of God asked, "Where did it fall?" When he showed him the place, Elisha cut a stick and threw it there, and made the iron float. 7 "Lift it out," he said. Then the man reached out his hand and took it.

Elisha Traps Blinded Arameans

8 Now the king of Aram was at war with Israel. After conferring with his officers, he said, "I will set up my camp in such and such a place."

9 The man of God sent word to the king of Israel: "Beware of passing that place, because the Arameans are going down

---

[a] 22 That is, about 75 pounds (about 34 kilograms)

there." [10]So the king of Israel checked on the place indicated by the man of God. Time and again Elisha warned the king, so that he was on his guard in such places.

[11]This enraged the king of Aram. He summoned his officers and demanded of them, "Will you not tell me which of us is on the side of the king of Israel?"

[12]"None of us, my lord the king," said one of his officers, "but Elisha, the prophet who is in Israel, tells the king of Israel the very words you speak in your bedroom."

[13]"Go, find out where he is," the king ordered, "so I can send men and capture him." The report came back: "He is in Dothan." [14]Then he sent horses and chariots and a strong force there. They went by night and surrounded the city.

[15]When the servant of the man of God got up and went out early the next morning, an army with horses and chariots had surrounded the city. "Oh, my lord, what shall we do?" the servant asked.

[16]"Don't be afraid," the prophet answered. "Those who are with us are more than those who are with them."

Praying 2 Kings 6:16-17

Lord, open my eyes to see the truth in all situations.

[17]And Elisha prayed, "O LORD, open his eyes so he may see." Then the LORD opened the servant's eyes, and he looked and saw the hills full of horses and chariots of fire all around Elisha.

[18]As the enemy came down toward him, Elisha prayed to the LORD, "Strike these people with blindness." So he struck them with blindness, as Elisha had asked.

[19]Elisha told them, "This is not the road

Open My Eyes, Lord

GOING *deeper*

READ AND CONSIDER: 2 KINGS 6:8-23

"And Elisha prayed, 'O LORD, open his eyes so he may see.' Then the LORD opened the servant's eyes, and he looked and saw the hills full of horses and chariots of fire all around Elisha. As the enemy came down toward him, Elisha prayed to the LORD, 'Strike these people with blindness.' So he struck them with blindness, as Elisha had asked" (2 Kings 6:17-18).

Elisha and his servant were surrounded by an enemy army, but Elisha knew something his servant didn't, so he prayed that God would open his servant's eyes—*really* open them. When God did just that, the servant saw an even greater army of God surrounding the whole scene.

Elisha's prayer is one we can all pray too. "Open my eyes, Lord. Help me to see the *real* picture, the big picture, the supernatural picture. Help me to see what You are doing. Lift the curtain off of my spiritual eyes so that I can see Your hand at work behind the scenes of the battles I face in life."

But there is another prayer in this story. After Elisha prayed that his servant would see the truth of God's supernatural protection, he then prayed that his enemies would be struck blind so they couldn't see what was around them. This would cause them to follow a different path. Both of Elisha's prayers were answered. There are times when we also need to pray Elisha's second prayer. We need to ask God to blind and confuse our enemy.

Ask God to give you the ability to see with spiritual eyes so you can better understand things from *His* perspective.

and this is not the city. Follow me, and I will lead you to the man you are looking for." And he led them to Samaria.

20 After they entered the city, Elisha said, "LORD, open the eyes of these men so they can see." Then the LORD opened their eyes and they looked, and there they were, inside Samaria.

21 When the king of Israel saw them, he asked Elisha, "Shall I kill them, my father? Shall I kill them?"

22 "Do not kill them," he answered. "Would you kill men you have captured with your own sword or bow? Set food and water before them so that they may eat and drink and then go back to their master." 23 So he prepared a great feast for them, and after they had finished eating and drinking, he sent them away, and they returned to their master. So the bands from Aram stopped raiding Israel's territory.

Famine in Besieged Samaria

24 Some time later, Ben-Hadad king of Aram mobilized his entire army and marched up and laid siege to Samaria. 25 There was a great famine in the city; the siege lasted so long that a donkey's head sold for eighty shekels[a] of silver, and a quarter of a cab[b] of seed pods[c] for five shekels.[d]

26 As the king of Israel was passing by on the wall, a woman cried to him, "Help me, my lord the king!"

27 The king replied, "If the LORD does not help you, where can I get help for you? From the threshing floor? From the winepress?" 28 Then he asked her, "What's the matter?"

She answered, "This woman said to me, 'Give up your son so we may eat him today, and tomorrow we'll eat my son.' 29 So we cooked my son and ate him. The next day I said to her, 'Give up your son so we may eat him,' but she had hidden him."

30 When the king heard the woman's words, he tore his robes. As he went along the wall, the people looked, and there, underneath, he had sackcloth on his body. 31 He said, "May God deal with me, be it ever so severely, if the head of Elisha son of Shaphat remains on his shoulders today!"

32 Now Elisha was sitting in his house, and the elders were sitting with him. The king sent a messenger ahead, but before he arrived, Elisha said to the elders, "Don't you see how this murderer is sending someone to cut off my head? Look, when the messenger comes, shut the door and hold it shut against him. Is not the sound of his master's footsteps behind him?" 33 While he was still talking to them, the messenger came down to him. And the king said, "This disaster is from the LORD. Why should I wait for the LORD any longer?"

7 Elisha said, "Hear the word of the LORD. This is what the LORD says: About this time tomorrow, a seah[e] of flour will sell for a shekel[f] and two seahs[g] of barley for a shekel at the gate of Samaria."

2 The officer on whose arm the king was leaning said to the man of God, "Look, even if the LORD should open the floodgates of the heavens, could this happen?"

"You will see it with your own eyes," answered Elisha, "but you will not eat any of it!"

The Siege Lifted

3 Now there were four men with leprosy[h] at the entrance of the city gate. They said to each other, "Why stay here until we die? 4 If we say, 'We'll go into the city'—the famine is there, and we will die. And if we stay here, we will die. So let's go over to the camp of the Arameans

---

a 25 That is, about 2 pounds (about 1 kilogram)   b 25 That is, probably about 1/2 pint (about 0.3 liter)   c 25 Or of doves' dung
d 25 That is, about 2 ounces (about 55 grams)   e 1 That is, probably about 7 quarts (about 7.3 liters); also in verses 16 and 18   f 1 That is, about 2/5 ounce (about 11 grams); also in verses 16 and 18   g 1 That is, probably about 13 quarts (about 15 liters); also in verses 16 and 18   h 3 The Hebrew word is used for various diseases affecting the skin—not necessarily leprosy; also in verse 8.

and surrender. If they spare us, we live; if they kill us, then we die."

⁵At dusk they got up and went to the camp of the Arameans. When they reached the edge of the camp, not a man was there, ⁶for the Lord had caused the Arameans to hear the sound of chariots and horses and a great army, so that they said to one another, "Look, the king of Israel has hired the Hittite and Egyptian kings to attack us!" ⁷So they got up and fled in the dusk and abandoned their tents and their horses and donkeys. They left the camp as it was and ran for their lives.

⁸The men who had leprosy reached the edge of the camp and entered one of the tents. They ate and drank, and carried away silver, gold and clothes, and went off and hid them. They returned and entered another tent and took some things from it and hid them also.

⁹Then they said to each other, "We're not doing right. This is a day of good news and we are keeping it to ourselves. If we wait until daylight, punishment will overtake us. Let's go at once and report this to the royal palace."

¹⁰So they went and called out to the city gatekeepers and told them, "We went into the Aramean camp and not a man was there—not a sound of anyone—only tethered horses and donkeys, and the tents left just as they were." ¹¹The gatekeepers shouted the news, and it was reported within the palace.

¹²The king got up in the night and said to his officers, "I will tell you what the Arameans have done to us. They know we are starving; so they have left the camp to hide in the countryside, thinking, 'They will surely come out, and then we will take them alive and get into the city.'"

¹³One of his officers answered, "Have some men take five of the horses that are left in the city. Their plight will be like that of all the Israelites left here—yes, they will only be like all these Israelites who are doomed. So let us send them to find out what happened."

¹⁴So they selected two chariots with their horses, and the king sent them after the Aramean army. He commanded the drivers, "Go and find out what has happened." ¹⁵They followed them as far as the Jordan, and they found the whole road strewn with the clothing and equipment the Arameans had thrown away in their headlong flight. So the messengers returned and reported to the king. ¹⁶Then the people went out and plundered the camp of the Arameans. So a seah of flour sold for a shekel, and two seahs of barley sold for a shekel, as the Lord had said.

¹⁷Now the king had put the officer on whose arm he leaned in charge of the gate, and the people trampled him in the gateway, and he died, just as the man of God had foretold when the king came down to his house. ¹⁸It happened as the man of God had said to the king: "About this time tomorrow, a seah of flour will sell for a shekel and two seahs of barley for a shekel at the gate of Samaria."

¹⁹The officer had said to the man of God, "Look, even if the Lord should open the floodgates of the heavens, could this happen?" The man of God had replied, "You will see it with your own eyes, but you will not eat any of it!" ²⁰And that is exactly what happened to him, for the people trampled him in the gateway, and he died.

The Shunammite's Land Restored

8 Now Elisha had said to the woman whose son he had restored to life, "Go away with your family and stay for a while wherever you can, because the Lord has decreed a famine in the land that will last seven years." ²The woman proceeded to do as the man of God said. She and her family went away and stayed in the land of the Philistines seven years.

³At the end of the seven years she came back from the land of the Philistines and went to the king to beg for her house and land. ⁴The king was talking to Gehazi, the servant of the man of God, and had said, "Tell me about all the great things Elisha

has done." 5Just as Gehazi was telling the king how Elisha had restored the dead to life, the woman whose son Elisha had brought back to life came to beg the king for her house and land.

Gehazi said, "This is the woman, my lord the king, and this is her son whom Elisha restored to life." 6The king asked the woman about it, and she told him.

Then he assigned an official to her case and said to him, "Give back everything that belonged to her, including all the income from her land from the day she left the country until now."

Hazael Murders Ben-Hadad

7Elisha went to Damascus, and Ben-Hadad king of Aram was ill. When the king was told, "The man of God has come all the way up here," 8he said to Hazael, "Take a gift with you and go to meet the man of God. Consult the LORD through him; ask him, 'Will I recover from this illness?'"

9Hazael went to meet Elisha, taking with him as a gift forty camel-loads of all the finest wares of Damascus. He went in and stood before him, and said, "Your son Ben-Hadad king of Aram has sent me to ask, 'Will I recover from this illness?'"

10Elisha answered, "Go and say to him, 'You will certainly recover'; buta the LORD has revealed to me that he will in fact die." 11He stared at him with a fixed gaze until Hazael felt ashamed. Then the man of God began to weep.

12"Why is my lord weeping?" asked Hazael.

"Because I know the harm you will do to the Israelites," he answered. "You will set fire to their fortified places, kill their young men with the sword, dash their little children to the ground, and rip open their pregnant women."

13Hazael said, "How could your servant, a mere dog, accomplish such a feat?"

"The LORD has shown me that you will become king of Aram," answered Elisha.

14Then Hazael left Elisha and returned to his master. When Ben-Hadad asked, "What did Elisha say to you?" Hazael replied, "He told me that you would certainly recover." 15But the next day he took a thick cloth, soaked it in water and spread it over the king's face, so that he died. Then Hazael succeeded him as king.

Jehoram King of Judah

16In the fifth year of Joram son of Ahab king of Israel, when Jehoshaphat was king of Judah, Jehoram son of Jehoshaphat began his reign as king of Judah. 17He was thirty-two years old when he became king, and he reigned in Jerusalem eight years. 18He walked in the ways of the kings of Israel, as the house of Ahab had done, for he married a daughter of Ahab. He did evil in the eyes of the LORD. 19Nevertheless, for the sake of his servant David, the LORD was not willing to destroy Judah. He had promised to maintain a lamp for David and his descendants forever.

20In the time of Jehoram, Edom rebelled against Judah and set up its own king. 21So Jehoramb went to Zair with all his chariots. The Edomites surrounded him and his chariot commanders, but he rose up and broke through by night; his army, however, fled back home. 22To this day Edom has been in rebellion against Judah. Libnah revolted at the same time.

23As for the other events of Jehoram's reign, and all he did, are they not written in the book of the annals of the kings of Judah? 24Jehoram rested with his fathers and was buried with them in the City of David. And Ahaziah his son succeeded him as king.

Ahaziah King of Judah

25In the twelfth year of Joram son of Ahab king of Israel, Ahaziah son of Jehoram king of Judah began to reign. 26Ahaziah was twenty-two years old when he became king, and he reigned in Jerusalem one year. His mother's name was Athaliah, a granddaughter of Omri king of Israel. 27He walked in the ways of the house of Ahab and did evil in the eyes of the LORD, as the house of Ahab had done, for he was related by marriage to Ahab's family.

28Ahaziah went with Joram son of Ahab to war against Hazael king of Aram at Ramoth Gilead. The Arameans wounded Joram; 29so King Joram returned to Jezreel to recover from the wounds the Arameans had inflicted on him at Ramoth[a] in his battle with Hazael king of Aram.

Then Ahaziah son of Jehoram king of Judah went down to Jezreel to see Joram son of Ahab, because he had been wounded.

Jehu Anointed King of Israel

9 The prophet Elisha summoned a man from the company of the prophets and said to him, "Tuck your cloak into your belt, take this flask of oil with you and go to Ramoth Gilead. 2When you get there, look for Jehu son of Jehoshaphat, the son of Nimshi. Go to him, get him away from his companions and take him into an inner room. 3Then take the flask and pour the oil on his head and declare, 'This is what the LORD says: I anoint you king over Israel.' Then open the door and run; don't delay!"

4So the young man, the prophet, went to Ramoth Gilead. 5When he arrived, he found the army officers sitting together. "I have a message for you, commander," he said.

"For which of us?" asked Jehu.

"For you, commander," he replied.

6Jehu got up and went into the house. Then the prophet poured the oil on Jehu's head and declared, "This is what the LORD, the God of Israel, says: 'I anoint you king over the LORD's people Israel. 7You are to destroy the house of Ahab your master, and I will avenge the blood of my servants the prophets and the blood of all the LORD's servants shed by Jezebel.

8The whole house of Ahab will perish. I will cut off from Ahab every last male in Israel—slave or free. 9I will make the house of Ahab like the house of Jeroboam son of Nebat and like the house of Baasha son of Ahijah. 10As for Jezebel, dogs will devour her on the plot of ground at Jezreel, and no one will bury her.' " Then he opened the door and ran.

11When Jehu went out to his fellow officers, one of them asked him, "Is everything all right? Why did this madman come to you?"

"You know the man and the sort of things he says," Jehu replied.

12"That's not true!" they said. "Tell us."

Jehu said, "Here is what he told me: 'This is what the LORD says: I anoint you king over Israel.' "

13They hurried and took their cloaks and spread them under him on the bare steps. Then they blew the trumpet and shouted, "Jehu is king!"

Jehu Kills Joram and Ahaziah

14So Jehu son of Jehoshaphat, the son of Nimshi, conspired against Joram. (Now Joram and all Israel had been defending Ramoth Gilead against Hazael king of Aram, 15but King Joram[b] had returned to Jezreel to recover from the wounds the Arameans had inflicted on him in the battle with Hazael king of Aram.) Jehu said, "If this is the way you feel, don't let anyone slip out of the city to go and tell the news in Jezreel." 16Then he got into his chariot and rode to Jezreel, because Joram was resting there and Ahaziah king of Judah had gone down to see him.

17When the lookout standing on the tower in Jezreel saw Jehu's troops approaching, he called out, "I see some troops coming."

"Get a horseman," Joram ordered. "Send him to meet them and ask, 'Do you come in peace?' "

18The horseman rode off to meet Jehu and said, "This is what the king says: 'Do you come in peace?' "

---

a 29 Hebrew Ramah, a variant of Ramoth   b 15 Hebrew Jehoram, a variant of Joram; also in verses 17 and 21-24

You Have a Great Purpose

Each one of us has a purpose in the Lord, but many of us don't realize that. And when we don't have an accurate understanding of our identity, we either strive to be like someone else or something we're not. We compare ourselves to others and feel as though we always fall short. When we don't become who *we* think we're *supposed* to be, it makes us critical of ourselves and our lives. It causes us to be insecure, oversensitive, judgmental, frustrated, and unfulfilled. We become self-absorbed, constantly having to think about ourselves and what we *should* be. It forces us to try too hard to make life happen the way we think it is supposed to. In the extreme, it makes us tell lies about ourselves and become dishonest about who we really are. When you are around people who don't have any idea of what they are called to do, you sense their unrest, unfulfillment, anxiety, and lack of peace.

God doesn't want that for you. He wants you to have a clear vision for your life. He wants to reveal to you what your gifts and talents are and show you how to best develop them and use them for His glory.

We all need to have a sense of why we are here. We all need to know we were created for a purpose. We will never find fulfillment and happiness until we are doing the thing for which we were created. But God won't move us into the big things He has called us to unless we have been proven faithful in the small things He has given us. So if you are doing what you deem to be small things right now, rejoice! God's getting you ready for big things ahead.

Don't think that if you haven't moved into the purposes God has for you by now that it's too late. It is *never* too late. I did everything late. I didn't come to the Lord until I was 28. I got married late, had children late, and didn't even start writing professionally until I was over 40. The full fruit of my ministry didn't appear until I was into my fifties. So don't give up. No matter what age you are, God has a purpose for you. He has something for you to do *now*.

Keep in mind that God "has saved us and called us to a holy life—not because of anything we have done but because of his own purpose and grace. This grace was given us in Christ Jesus before the beginning of time" (2 Timothy 1:9). "We have different gifts, according to the grace given us" (Romans 12:6). For "each man has his own gift from God; one has this gift, another has that" (1 Corinthians 7:7). So then, "each one should retain the place in life that the Lord assigned to him and to which God has called him" (1 Corinthians 7:17). I pray that God will "give you the Spirit of wisdom and revelation, so that you may know him better" (Ephesians 1:17). "May he give you the desire of your heart and make all your plans succeed" (Psalm 20:4).

Don't ever forget that God has an important purpose for your life and that it is good. Pray often, asking Him to enable you to move into it.

For the next "From Stormie's Heart" article, go to page 553.

"What do you have to do with peace?" Jehu replied. "Fall in behind me."

The lookout reported, "The messenger has reached them, but he isn't coming back."

¹⁹So the king sent out a second horseman. When he came to them he said, "This is what the king says: 'Do you come in peace?'"

Jehu replied, "What do you have to do with peace? Fall in behind me."

²⁰The lookout reported, "He has reached them, but he isn't coming back either. The driving is like that of Jehu son of Nimshi—he drives like a madman."

²¹"Hitch up my chariot," Joram ordered. And when it was hitched up, Joram king of Israel and Ahaziah king of Judah rode out, each in his own chariot, to meet Jehu. They met him at the plot of ground that had belonged to Naboth the Jezreelite. ²²When Joram saw Jehu he asked, "Have you come in peace, Jehu?"

"How can there be peace," Jehu replied, "as long as all the idolatry and witchcraft of your mother Jezebel abound?"

²³Joram turned about and fled, calling out to Ahaziah, "Treachery, Ahaziah!"

²⁴Then Jehu drew his bow and shot Joram between the shoulders. The arrow pierced his heart and he slumped down in his chariot. ²⁵Jehu said to Bidkar, his chariot officer, "Pick him up and throw him on the field that belonged to Naboth the Jezreelite. Remember how you and I were riding together in chariots behind Ahab his father when the LORD made this prophecy about him: ²⁶'Yesterday I saw the blood of Naboth and the blood of his sons, declares the LORD, and I will surely make you pay for it on this plot of ground, declares the LORD.'ᵃ Now then, pick him up and throw him on that plot, in accordance with the word of the LORD."

²⁷When Ahaziah king of Judah saw what had happened, he fled up the road

to Beth Haggan.ᵇ Jehu chased him, shouting, "Kill him too!" They wounded him in his chariot on the way up to Gur near Ibleam, but he escaped to Megiddo and died there. ²⁸His servants took him by chariot to Jerusalem and buried him with his fathers in his tomb in the City of David. ²⁹(In the eleventh year of Joram son of Ahab, Ahaziah had become king of Judah.)

Jezebel Killed

³⁰Then Jehu went to Jezreel. When Jezebel heard about it, she painted her eyes, arranged her hair and looked out of a window. ³¹As Jehu entered the gate, she asked, "Have you come in peace, Zimri, you murderer of your master?"ᶜ

³²He looked up at the window and called out, "Who is on my side? Who?" Two or three eunuchs looked down at him. ³³"Throw her down!" Jehu said. So they threw her down, and some of her blood spattered the wall and the horses as they trampled her underfoot.

³⁴Jehu went in and ate and drank. "Take care of that cursed woman," he said, "and bury her, for she was a king's daughter." ³⁵But when they went out to bury her, they found nothing except her skull, her feet and her hands. ³⁶They went back and told Jehu, who said, "This is the word of the LORD that he spoke through his servant Elijah the Tishbite: On the plot of ground at Jezreel dogs will devour Jezebel's flesh.ᵈ ³⁷Jezebel's body will be like refuse on the ground in the plot at Jezreel, so that no one will be able to say, 'This is Jezebel.'"

Ahab's Family Killed

10 Now there were in Samaria seventy sons of the house of Ahab. So Jehu wrote letters and sent them to Samaria: to the officials of Jezreel,ᵉ to the elders and to the guardians of Ahab's children. He said, ²"As soon as this letter reaches you, since your master's sons are with you

and you have chariots and horses, a fortified city and weapons, ³choose the best
and most worthy of your master's sons
and set him on his father's throne. Then
fight for your master's house."

⁴But they were terrified and said, "If
two kings could not resist him, how
can we?"

⁵So the palace administrator, the city
governor, the elders and the guardians
sent this message to Jehu: "We are your
servants and we will do anything you say.
We will not appoint anyone as king; you
do whatever you think best."

⁶Then Jehu wrote them a second letter,
saying, "If you are on my side and will
obey me, take the heads of your master's
sons and come to me in Jezreel by this
time tomorrow."

Now the royal princes, seventy of
them, were with the leading men of the
city, who were rearing them. ⁷When the
letter arrived, these men took the princes
and slaughtered all seventy of them. They
put their heads in baskets and sent them
to Jehu in Jezreel. ⁸When the messenger
arrived, he told Jehu, "They have brought
the heads of the princes."

Then Jehu ordered, "Put them in two
piles at the entrance of the city gate until morning."

⁹The next morning Jehu went out. He
stood before all the people and said, "You
are innocent. It was I who conspired
against my master and killed him, but
who killed all these? ¹⁰Know then, that
not a word the LORD has spoken against
the house of Ahab will fail. The LORD
has done what he promised through his
servant Elijah." ¹¹So Jehu killed everyone
in Jezreel who remained of the house of
Ahab, as well as all his chief men, his close
friends and his priests, leaving him no survivor.

¹²Jehu then set out and went toward
Samaria. At Beth Eked of the Shepherds,
¹³he met some relatives of Ahaziah king
of Judah and asked, "Who are you?"

They said, "We are relatives of Aha-

ziah, and we have come down to greet
the families of the king and of the queen
mother."

¹⁴"Take them alive!" he ordered. So
they took them alive and slaughtered
them by the well of Beth Eked—forty-
two men. He left no survivor.

¹⁵After he left there, he came upon Jehonadab son of Recab, who was on his
way to meet him. Jehu greeted him and
said, "Are you in accord with me, as I am
with you?"

"I am," Jehonadab answered.

"If so," said Jehu, "give me your hand."
So he did, and Jehu helped him up into
the chariot. ¹⁶Jehu said, "Come with me
and see my zeal for the LORD." Then he
had him ride along in his chariot.

¹⁷When Jehu came to Samaria, he
killed all who were left there of Ahab's
family; he destroyed them, according to
the word of the LORD spoken to Elijah.

Ministers of Baal Killed

¹⁸Then Jehu brought all the people
together and said to them, "Ahab served
Baal a little; Jehu will serve him much.
¹⁹Now summon all the prophets of Baal,
all his ministers and all his priests. See that
no one is missing, because I am going to
hold a great sacrifice for Baal. Anyone
who fails to come will no longer live."
But Jehu was acting deceptively in order
to destroy the ministers of Baal.

²⁰Jehu said, "Call an assembly in honor
of Baal." So they proclaimed it. ²¹Then he
sent word throughout Israel, and all the
ministers of Baal came; not one stayed
away. They crowded into the temple of
Baal until it was full from one end to the
other. ²²And Jehu said to the keeper of
the wardrobe, "Bring robes for all the
ministers of Baal." So he brought out
robes for them.

²³Then Jehu and Jehonadab son of
Recab went into the temple of Baal.
Jehu said to the ministers of Baal, "Look
around and see that no servants of the
LORD are here with you—only minis-
ters of Baal." ²⁴So they went in to make

sacrifices and burnt offerings. Now Jehu had posted eighty men outside with this warning: "If one of you lets any of the men I am placing in your hands escape, it will be your life for his life."

25As soon as Jehu had finished making the burnt offering, he ordered the guards and officers: "Go in and kill them; let no one escape." So they cut them down with the sword. The guards and officers threw the bodies out and then entered the inner shrine of the temple of Baal. 26They brought the sacred stone out of the temple of Baal and burned it. 27They demolished the sacred stone of Baal and tore down the temple of Baal, and people have used it for a latrine to this day.

28So Jehu destroyed Baal worship in Israel. 29However, he did not turn away from the sins of Jeroboam son of Nebat, which he had caused Israel to commit—the worship of the golden calves at Bethel and Dan.

30The LORD said to Jehu, "Because you have done well in accomplishing what is right in my eyes and have done to the house of Ahab all I had in mind to do, your descendants will sit on the throne of Israel to the fourth generation." 31Yet Jehu was not careful to keep the law of the LORD, the God of Israel, with all his heart. He did not turn away from the sins of Jeroboam, which he had caused Israel to commit.

32In those days the LORD began to reduce the size of Israel. Hazael overpowered the Israelites throughout their territory 33east of the Jordan in all the land of Gilead (the region of Gad, Reuben and Manasseh), from Aroer by the Arnon Gorge through Gilead to Bashan.

34As for the other events of Jehu's reign, all he did, and all his achievements, are they not written in the book of the annals of the kings of Israel?

35Jehu rested with his fathers and was buried in Samaria. And Jehoahaz his son succeeded him as king. 36The time that Jehu reigned over Israel in Samaria was twenty-eight years.

Athaliah and Joash

11 When Athaliah the mother of Ahaziah saw that her son was dead, she proceeded to destroy the whole royal family. 2But Jehosheba, the daughter of King Jehoram[a] and sister of Ahaziah, took Joash son of Ahaziah and stole him away from among the royal princes, who were about to be murdered. She put him and his nurse in a bedroom to hide him from Athaliah; so he was not killed. 3He remained hidden with his nurse at the temple of the LORD for six years while Athaliah ruled the land.

4In the seventh year Jehoiada sent for the commanders of units of a hundred, the Carites and the guards and had them brought to him at the temple of the LORD. He made a covenant with them and put them under oath at the temple of the LORD. Then he showed them the king's son. 5He commanded them, saying, "This is what you are to do: You who are in the three companies that are going on duty on the Sabbath—a third of you guarding the royal palace, 6a third at the Sur Gate, and a third at the gate behind the guard, who take turns guarding the temple— 7and you who are in the other two companies that normally go off Sabbath duty are all to guard the temple for the king. 8Station yourselves around the king, each man with his weapon in his hand. Anyone who approaches your ranks[b] must be put to death. Stay close to the king wherever he goes."

9The commanders of units of a hundred did just as Jehoiada the priest ordered. Each one took his men—those who were going on duty on the Sabbath and those who were going off duty—and came to Jehoiada the priest. 10Then he gave the commanders the spears and shields that had belonged to King David and that were in the temple of the LORD. 11The guards, each with his weapon in his hand, stationed themselves around the king—near the altar and the temple, from the south side to the north side of the temple.

12Jehoiada brought out the king's son and put the crown on him; he presented him with a copy of the covenant and proclaimed him king. They anointed him, and the people clapped their hands and shouted, "Long live the king!"

13When Athaliah heard the noise made by the guards and the people, she went to the people at the temple of the LORD. 14She looked and there was the king, standing by the pillar, as the custom was. The officers and the trumpeters were beside the king, and all the people of the land were rejoicing and blowing trumpets. Then Athaliah tore her robes and called out, "Treason! Treason!"

15Jehoiada the priest ordered the commanders of units of a hundred, who were in charge of the troops: "Bring her out between the ranks[a] and put to the sword anyone who follows her." For the priest had said, "She must not be put to death in the temple of the LORD." 16So they seized her as she reached the place where the horses enter the palace grounds, and there she was put to death.

17Jehoiada then made a covenant between the LORD and the king and people that they would be the LORD's people. He also made a covenant between the king and the people. 18All the people of the land went to the temple of Baal and tore it down. They smashed the altars and idols to pieces and killed Mattan the priest of Baal in front of the altars.

Then Jehoiada the priest posted guards at the temple of the LORD. 19He took with him the commanders of hundreds, the Carites, the guards and all the people of the land, and together they brought the king down from the temple of the LORD and went into the palace, entering by way of the gate of the guards. The king then took his place on the royal throne, 20and all the people of the land rejoiced. And the city was quiet, because Athaliah had been slain with the sword at the palace.

21Joash[b] was seven years old when he began to reign.

Joash Repairs the Temple

12 In the seventh year of Jehu, Joash[c] became king, and he reigned in Jerusalem forty years. His mother's name was Zibiah; she was from Beersheba. 2Joash did what was right in the eyes of the LORD all the years Jehoiada the priest instructed him. 3The high places, however, were not removed; the people continued to offer sacrifices and burn incense there.

4Joash said to the priests, "Collect all the money that is brought as sacred offerings to the temple of the LORD—the money collected in the census, the money received from personal vows and the money brought voluntarily to the temple. 5Let every priest receive the money from one of the treasurers, and let it be used to repair whatever damage is found in the temple."

6But by the twenty-third year of King Joash the priests still had not repaired the temple. 7Therefore King Joash summoned Jehoiada the priest and the other priests and asked them, "Why aren't you repairing the damage done to the temple? Take no more money from your treasurers, but hand it over for repairing the temple." 8The priests agreed that they would not collect any more money from the people and that they would not repair the temple themselves.

9Jehoiada the priest took a chest and bored a hole in its lid. He placed it beside the altar, on the right side as one enters the temple of the LORD. The priests who guarded the entrance put into the chest all the money that was brought to the temple of the LORD. 10Whenever

a 15 Or out from the precincts   b 21 Hebrew Jehoash, a variant of Joash   c 1 Hebrew Jehoash, a variant of Joash; also in verses 2, 4, 6, 7 and 18 they saw that there was a large amount of money in the chest, the royal secretary and the high priest came, counted the money that had been brought into the temple of the LORD and put it into bags. [11]When the amount had been determined, they gave the money to the men appointed to supervise the work on the temple. With it they paid those who worked on the temple of the LORD—the carpenters and builders, [12]the masons and stonecutters. They purchased timber and dressed stone for the repair of the temple of the LORD, and met all the other expenses of restoring the temple.

[13]The money brought into the temple was not spent for making silver basins, wick trimmers, sprinkling bowls, trumpets or any other articles of gold or silver for the temple of the LORD; [14]it was paid to the workmen, who used it to repair the temple. [15]They did not require an accounting from those to whom they gave the money to pay the workers, because they acted with complete honesty. [16]The money from the guilt offerings and sin offerings was not brought into the temple of the LORD; it belonged to the priests.

[17]About this time Hazael king of Aram went up and attacked Gath and captured it. Then he turned to attack Jerusalem. [18]But Joash king of Judah took all the sacred objects dedicated by his fathers—Jehoshaphat, Jehoram and Ahaziah, the kings of Judah—and the gifts he himself had dedicated and all the gold found in the treasuries of the temple of the LORD and of the royal palace, and he sent them to Hazael king of Aram, who then withdrew from Jerusalem.

[19]As for the other events of the reign of Joash, and all he did, are they not written in the book of the annals of the kings of Judah? [20]His officials conspired against him and assassinated him at Beth Millo, on the road down to Silla. [21]The officials who murdered him were Jozabad son of Shimeath and Jehozabad son of Shomer. He died and was buried with his fathers in the City of David. And Amaziah his son succeeded him as king.

Jehoahaz King of Israel

13 In the twenty-third year of Joash son of Ahaziah king of Judah, Jehoahaz son of Jehu became king of Israel in Samaria, and he reigned seventeen years. [2]He did evil in the eyes of the LORD by following the sins of Jeroboam son of Nebat, which he had caused Israel to commit, and he did not turn away from them. [3]So the LORD's anger burned against Israel, and for a long time he kept them under the power of Hazael king of Aram and Ben-Hadad his son.

[4]Then Jehoahaz sought the LORD's favor, and the LORD listened to him, for he saw how severely the king of Aram was oppressing Israel. [5]The LORD provided a deliverer for Israel, and they escaped from the power of Aram. So the Israelites lived in their own homes as they had before. [6]But they did not turn away from the sins of the house of Jeroboam, which he had caused Israel to commit; they continued in them. Also, the Asherah pole[a] remained standing in Samaria.

[7]Nothing had been left of the army of Jehoahaz except fifty horsemen, ten chariots and ten thousand foot soldiers, for the king of Aram had destroyed the rest and made them like the dust at threshing time.

[8]As for the other events of the reign of Jehoahaz, all he did and his achievements, are they not written in the book of the annals of the kings of Israel? [9]Jehoahaz rested with his fathers and was buried in Samaria. And Jehoash[b] his son succeeded him as king.

Jehoash King of Israel

[10]In the thirty-seventh year of Joash king of Judah, Jehoash son of Jehoahaz became king of Israel in Samaria, and he

---

[a] 6 That is, a symbol of the goddess Asherah; here and elsewhere in 2 Kings   [b] 9 Hebrew Joash, a variant of Jehoash; also in verses 12-14 and 25

GOING *deeper*

Undeserved Answers to Prayer

READ AND CONSIDER: 2 KINGS 13:1-9

"Then Jehoahaz sought the LORD's favor, and the LORD listened to him, for he saw how severely the king of Aram was oppressing Israel. The LORD provided a deliverer for Israel, and they escaped from the power of Aram. So the Israelites lived in their own homes as they had before" (2 Kings 13:4-5).

Jehoahaz was not known for his wisdom and virtue. He was such an evil king that God sent the oppressive team of King Hazael and Prince Ben-Hadad of Aram as Jehoahaz's judgment. It seemed he was finally getting what he deserved.

But then Jehoahaz did an unexpected thing. When the oppression became too great, he did what any of us would do when our backs are against the wall and our best efforts are not enough—he prayed. An evil man was desperate and turned to God. He asked for God's help, and God gave it. That's what God does. He answers the prayers of people *who don't deserve it.*

How easy it is to believe that our answered prayers have something to do with our being good enough. Or we think that if God *hasn't* answered our prayer yet, it must be because we *aren't* good enough. Or worse, we don't pray because we think we can't impress God enough with our goodness to make Him want to answer. We forget that our best goodness still would not *deserve* God's favor.

Jehoahaz's prayer has a lot to teach us. He called out to God, knowing full well that he had given God no good reason to answer. He received God's favor, not because of who he was, but because of who God is—a gracious and compassionate God who listens to honest, humble prayers. Don't forget that God always listens whenever you pray.

reigned sixteen years. [11]He did evil in the eyes of the LORD and did not turn away from any of the sins of Jeroboam son of Nebat, which he had caused Israel to commit; he continued in them.

[12]As for the other events of the reign of Jehoash, all he did and his achievements, including his war against Amaziah king of Judah, are they not written in the book of the annals of the kings of Israel? [13]Jehoash rested with his fathers, and Jeroboam succeeded him on the throne. Jehoash was buried in Samaria with the kings of Israel.

[14]Now Elisha was suffering from the illness from which he died. Jehoash king of Israel went down to see him and wept over him. "My father! My father!" he cried. "The chariots and horsemen of Israel!"

[15]Elisha said, "Get a bow and some arrows," and he did so. [16]"Take the bow in your hands," he said to the king of Israel. When he had taken it, Elisha put his hands on the king's hands.

[17]"Open the east window," he said, and he opened it. "Shoot!" Elisha said, and he shot. "The LORD's arrow of victory, the arrow of victory over Aram!" Elisha declared. "You will completely destroy the Arameans at Aphek."

[18]Then he said, "Take the arrows," and the king took them. Elisha told him, "Strike the ground." He struck it three times and stopped. [19]The man of God was angry with him and said, "You should have struck the ground five or six times; then you would have defeated Aram and completely destroyed it. But now you will defeat it only three times."

²⁰Elisha died and was buried.

Now Moabite raiders used to enter the country every spring. ²¹Once while some Israelites were burying a man, suddenly they saw a band of raiders; so they threw the man's body into Elisha's tomb. When the body touched Elisha's bones, the man came to life and stood up on his feet.

²²Hazael king of Aram oppressed Israel throughout the reign of Jehoahaz. ²³But the LORD was gracious to them and had compassion and showed concern for them because of his covenant with Abraham, Isaac and Jacob. To this day he has been unwilling to destroy them or banish them from his presence.

²⁴Hazael king of Aram died, and Ben-Hadad his son succeeded him as king. ²⁵Then Jehoash son of Jehoahaz recaptured from Ben-Hadad son of Hazael the towns he had taken in battle from his father Jehoahaz. Three times Jehoash defeated him, and so he recovered the Israelite towns.

Amaziah King of Judah

14 In the second year of Jehoash[a] son of Jehoahaz king of Israel, Amaziah son of Joash king of Judah began to reign. ²He was twenty-five years old when he became king, and he reigned in Jerusalem twenty-nine years. His mother's name was Jehoaddin; she was from Jerusalem. ³He did what was right in the eyes of the LORD, but not as his father David had done. In everything he followed the example of his father Joash. ⁴The high places, however, were not removed; the people continued to offer sacrifices and burn incense there.

⁵After the kingdom was firmly in his grasp, he executed the officials who had murdered his father the king. ⁶Yet he did not put the sons of the assassins to death, in accordance with what is written in the Book of the Law of Moses where the LORD commanded: "Fathers shall not be put to death for their children, nor children put to death for their fathers; each is to die for his own sins."[b]

⁷He was the one who defeated ten thousand Edomites in the Valley of Salt and captured Sela in battle, calling it Joktheel, the name it has to this day.

⁸Then Amaziah sent messengers to Jehoash son of Jehoahaz, the son of Jehu, king of Israel, with the challenge: "Come, meet me face to face."

⁹But Jehoash king of Israel replied to Amaziah king of Judah: "A thistle in Lebanon sent a message to a cedar in Lebanon, 'Give your daughter to my son in marriage.' Then a wild beast in Lebanon came along and trampled the thistle underfoot. ¹⁰You have indeed defeated Edom and now you are arrogant. Glory in your victory, but stay at home! Why ask for trouble and cause your own downfall and that of Judah also?"

¹¹Amaziah, however, would not listen, so Jehoash king of Israel attacked. He and Amaziah king of Judah faced each other at Beth Shemesh in Judah. ¹²Judah was routed by Israel, and every man fled to his home. ¹³Jehoash king of Israel captured Amaziah king of Judah, the son of Joash, the son of Ahaziah, at Beth Shemesh. Then Jehoash went to Jerusalem and broke down the wall of Jerusalem from the Ephraim Gate to the Corner Gate—a section about six hundred feet long.[c] ¹⁴He took all the gold and silver and all the articles found in the temple of the LORD and in the treasuries of the royal palace. He also took hostages and returned to Samaria.

¹⁵As for the other events of the reign of Jehoash, what he did and his achievements, including his war against Amaziah king of Judah, are they not written in the book of the annals of the kings of Israel? ¹⁶Jehoash rested with his fathers and was buried in Samaria with the kings of Israel. And Jeroboam his son succeeded him as king.

¹⁷Amaziah son of Joash king of Judah

ᵃ *1* Hebrew *Joash,* a variant of *Jehoash*; also in verses 13, 23 and 27   ᵇ *6* Deut. 24:16   ᶜ *13* Hebrew *four hundred cubits* (about 180 meters) lived for fifteen years after the death of Jehoash son of Jehoahaz king of Israel. [18]As for the other events of Amaziah's reign, are they not written in the book of the annals of the kings of Judah?

[19]They conspired against him in Jerusalem, and he fled to Lachish, but they sent men after him to Lachish and killed him there. [20]He was brought back by horse and was buried in Jerusalem with his fathers, in the City of David.

[21]Then all the people of Judah took Azariah,[a] who was sixteen years old, and made him king in place of his father Amaziah. [22]He was the one who rebuilt Elath and restored it to Judah after Amaziah rested with his fathers.

Jeroboam II King of Israel

[23]In the fifteenth year of Amaziah son of Joash king of Judah, Jeroboam son of Jehoash king of Israel became king in Samaria, and he reigned forty-one years. [24]He did evil in the eyes of the LORD and did not turn away from any of the sins of Jeroboam son of Nebat, which he had caused Israel to commit. [25]He was the one who restored the boundaries of Israel from Lebo[b] Hamath to the Sea of the Arabah,[c] in accordance with the word of the LORD, the God of Israel, spoken through his servant Jonah son of Amittai, the prophet from Gath Hepher.

[26]The LORD had seen how bitterly everyone in Israel, whether slave or free, was suffering; there was no one to help them. [27]And since the LORD had not said he would blot out the name of Israel from under heaven, he saved them by the hand of Jeroboam son of Jehoash.

[28]As for the other events of Jeroboam's reign, all he did, and his military achievements, including how he recovered for Israel both Damascus and Hamath, which had belonged to Yaudi,[d] are they not written in the book of the annals of the kings of Israel? [29]Jeroboam rested with his fa-

thers, the kings of Israel. And Zechariah his son succeeded him as king.

Azariah King of Judah

15 In the twenty-seventh year of Jeroboam king of Israel, Azariah son of Amaziah king of Judah began to reign. [2]He was sixteen years old when he became king, and he reigned in Jerusalem fifty-two years. His mother's name was Jecoliah; she was from Jerusalem. [3]He did what was right in the eyes of the LORD, just as his father Amaziah had done. [4]The high places, however, were not removed; the people continued to offer sacrifices and burn incense there.

[5]The LORD afflicted the king with leprosy[e] until the day he died, and he lived in a separate house.[f] Jotham the king's son had charge of the palace and governed the people of the land.

[6]As for the other events of Azariah's reign, and all he did, are they not written in the book of the annals of the kings of Judah? [7]Azariah rested with his fathers and was buried near them in the City of David. And Jotham his son succeeded him as king.

Zechariah King of Israel

[8]In the thirty-eighth year of Azariah king of Judah, Zechariah son of Jeroboam became king of Israel in Samaria, and he reigned six months. [9]He did evil in the eyes of the LORD, as his fathers had done. He did not turn away from the sins of Jeroboam son of Nebat, which he had caused Israel to commit.

[10]Shallum son of Jabesh conspired against Zechariah. He attacked him in front of the people,[g] assassinated him and succeeded him as king. [11]The other events of Zechariah's reign are written in the book of the annals of the kings of Israel. [12]So the word of the LORD spoken to Jehu was fulfilled: "Your descendants will sit on the throne of Israel to the fourth generation."[h]

---

[a] 21 Also called *Uzziah* [b] 25 Or *from the entrance to* [c] 25 That is, the Dead Sea [d] 28 Or *Judah* [e] 5 The Hebrew word was used for various diseases affecting the skin—not necessarily leprosy. [f] 5 Or *in a house where he was relieved of responsibility* [g] 10 Hebrew; some Septuagint manuscripts *in Ibleam* [h] 12 2 Kings 10:30

Shallum King of Israel

[13]Shallum son of Jabesh became king in the thirty-ninth year of Uzziah king of Judah, and he reigned in Samaria one month. [14]Then Menahem son of Gadi went from Tirzah up to Samaria. He attacked Shallum son of Jabesh in Samaria, assassinated him and succeeded him as king.

[15]The other events of Shallum's reign, and the conspiracy he led, are written in the book of the annals of the kings of Israel.

[16]At that time Menahem, starting out from Tirzah, attacked Tiphsah and everyone in the city and its vicinity, because they refused to open their gates. He sacked Tiphsah and ripped open all the pregnant women.

Menahem King of Israel

[17]In the thirty-ninth year of Azariah king of Judah, Menahem son of Gadi became king of Israel, and he reigned in Samaria ten years. [18]He did evil in the eyes of the LORD. During his entire reign he did not turn away from the sins of Jeroboam son of Nebat, which he had caused Israel to commit.

[19]Then Pul[a] king of Assyria invaded the land, and Menahem gave him a thousand talents[b] of silver to gain his support and strengthen his own hold on the kingdom. [20]Menahem exacted this money from Israel. Every wealthy man had to contribute fifty shekels[c] of silver to be given to the king of Assyria. So the king of Assyria withdrew and stayed in the land no longer.

[21]As for the other events of Menahem's reign, and all he did, are they not written in the book of the annals of the kings of Israel? [22]Menahem rested with his fathers. And Pekahiah his son succeeded him as king.

Pekahiah King of Israel

[23]In the fiftieth year of Azariah king of Judah, Pekahiah son of Menahem became king of Israel in Samaria, and he reigned two years. [24]Pekahiah did evil in the eyes of the LORD. He did not turn away from the sins of Jeroboam son of Nebat, which he had caused Israel to commit. [25]One of his chief officers, Pekah son of Remaliah, conspired against him. Taking fifty men of Gilead with him, he assassinated Pekahiah, along with Argob and Arieh, in the citadel of the royal palace at Samaria. So Pekah killed Pekahiah and succeeded him as king.

[26]The other events of Pekahiah's reign, and all he did, are written in the book of the annals of the kings of Israel.

Pekah King of Israel

[27]In the fifty-second year of Azariah king of Judah, Pekah son of Remaliah became king of Israel in Samaria, and he reigned twenty years. [28]He did evil in the eyes of the LORD. He did not turn away from the sins of Jeroboam son of Nebat, which he had caused Israel to commit.

[29]In the time of Pekah king of Israel, Tiglath-Pileser king of Assyria came and took Ijon, Abel Beth Maacah, Janoah, Kedesh and Hazor. He took Gilead and Galilee, including all the land of Naphtali, and deported the people to Assyria. [30]Then Hoshea son of Elah conspired against Pekah son of Remaliah. He attacked and assassinated him, and then succeeded him as king in the twentieth year of Jotham son of Uzziah.

[31]As for the other events of Pekah's reign, and all he did, are they not written in the book of the annals of the kings of Israel?

Jotham King of Judah

[32]In the second year of Pekah son of Remaliah king of Israel, Jotham son of Uzziah king of Judah began to reign. [33]He was twenty-five years old when he became king, and he reigned in Jerusalem sixteen years. His mother's name was Jerusha daughter of Zadok. [34]He did what

---

a 19 Also called *Tiglath-Pileser*   *b 19* That is, about 37 tons (about 34 metric tons)   *c 20* That is, about 1 1/4 pounds (about 0.6 kilogram) was right in the eyes of the LORD, just as his father Uzziah had done. 35The high places, however, were not removed; the people continued to offer sacrifices and burn incense there. Jotham rebuilt the Upper Gate of the temple of the LORD.

36As for the other events of Jotham's reign, and what he did, are they not written in the book of the annals of the kings of Judah? 37(In those days the LORD began to send Rezin king of Aram and Pekah son of Remaliah against Judah.) 38Jotham rested with his fathers and was buried with them in the City of David, the city of his father. And Ahaz his son succeeded him as king.

Ahaz King of Judah

16 In the seventeenth year of Pekah son of Remaliah, Ahaz son of Jotham king of Judah began to reign. 2Ahaz was twenty years old when he became king, and he reigned in Jerusalem sixteen years. Unlike David his father, he did not do what was right in the eyes of the LORD his God. 3He walked in the ways of the kings of Israel and even sacrificed his son in[a] the fire, following the detestable ways of the nations the LORD had driven out before the Israelites. 4He offered sacrifices and burned incense at the high places, on the hilltops and under every spreading tree.

5Then Rezin king of Aram and Pekah son of Remaliah king of Israel marched up to fight against Jerusalem and besieged Ahaz, but they could not overpower him. 6At that time, Rezin king of Aram recovered Elath for Aram by driving out the men of Judah. Edomites then moved into Elath and have lived there to this day.

7Ahaz sent messengers to say to Tiglath-Pileser king of Assyria, "I am your servant and vassal. Come up and save me out of the hand of the king of Aram and of the king of Israel, who are attacking me." 8And Ahaz took the silver and gold found in the temple of the LORD and in the treasuries of the royal palace and sent it as a gift to the king of Assyria. 9The king of Assyria complied by attacking Damascus and capturing it. He deported its inhabitants to Kir and put Rezin to death.

10Then King Ahaz went to Damascus to meet Tiglath-Pileser king of Assyria. He saw an altar in Damascus and sent to Uriah the priest a sketch of the altar, with detailed plans for its construction. 11So Uriah the priest built an altar in accordance with all the plans that King Ahaz had sent from Damascus and finished it before King Ahaz returned. 12When the king came back from Damascus and saw the altar, he approached it and presented offerings[b] on it. 13He offered up his burnt offering and grain offering, poured out his drink offering, and sprinkled the blood of his fellowship offerings[c] on the altar. 14The bronze altar that stood before the LORD he brought from the front of the temple—from between the new altar and the temple of the LORD—and put it on the north side of the new altar.

15King Ahaz then gave these orders to Uriah the priest: "On the large new altar, offer the morning burnt offering and the evening grain offering, the king's burnt offering and his grain offering, and the burnt offering of all the people of the land, and their grain offering and their drink offering. Sprinkle on the altar all the blood of the burnt offerings and sacrifices. But I will use the bronze altar for seeking guidance." 16And Uriah the priest did just as King Ahaz had ordered.

17King Ahaz took away the side panels and removed the basins from the movable stands. He removed the Sea from the bronze bulls that supported it and set it on a stone base. 18He took away the Sabbath canopy[d] that had been built at the temple and removed the royal entryway outside the temple of the LORD, in deference to the king of Assyria.

19As for the other events of the reign of

---

[a] 3 Or even made his son pass through (see Septuagint)   [b] 12 Or and went up   [c] 13 Traditionally peace offerings   [d] 18 Or the dais of his throne

Ahaz, and what he did, are they not written in the book of the annals of the kings of Judah? [20]Ahaz rested with his fathers and was buried with them in the City of David. And Hezekiah his son succeeded him as king.

Hoshea Last King of Israel

[17] In the twelfth year of Ahaz king of Judah, Hoshea son of Elah became king of Israel in Samaria, and he reigned nine years. [2]He did evil in the eyes of the LORD, but not like the kings of Israel who preceded him.

[3]Shalmaneser king of Assyria came up to attack Hoshea, who had been Shalmaneser's vassal and had paid him tribute. [4]But the king of Assyria discovered that Hoshea was a traitor, for he had sent envoys to So[a] king of Egypt, and he no longer paid tribute to the king of Assyria, as he had done year by year. Therefore Shalmaneser seized him and put him in prison. [5]The king of Assyria invaded the entire land, marched against Samaria and laid siege to it for three years. [6]In the ninth year of Hoshea, the king of Assyria captured Samaria and deported the Israelites to Assyria. He settled them in Halah, in Gozan on the Habor River and in the towns of the Medes.

Israel Exiled Because of Sin

[7]All this took place because the Israelites had sinned against the LORD their God, who had brought them up out of Egypt from under the power of Pharaoh king of Egypt. They worshiped other gods [8]and followed the practices of the nations the LORD had driven out before them, as well as the practices that the kings of Israel had introduced. [9]The Israelites secretly did things against the LORD their God that were not right. From watchtower to fortified city they built themselves high places in all their towns. [10]They set up sacred stones and Asherah poles on every high hill and under every spreading tree. [11]At every high place they burned incense, as the nations whom the LORD had driven out before them had done. They did wicked things that provoked the LORD to anger. [12]They worshiped idols, though the LORD had said, "You shall not do this."[b] [13]The LORD warned Israel and Judah through all his prophets and seers: "Turn from your evil ways. Observe my commands and decrees, in accordance with the entire Law that I commanded your fathers to obey and that I delivered to you through my servants the prophets."

[14]But they would not listen and were as stiff-necked as their fathers, who did not trust in the LORD their God. [15]They rejected his decrees and the covenant he had made with their fathers and the warnings he had given them. They followed worthless idols and themselves became worthless. They imitated the nations around them although the LORD had ordered them, "Do not do as they do," and they did the things the LORD had forbidden them to do.

[16]They forsook all the commands of the LORD their God and made for themselves two idols cast in the shape of calves, and an Asherah pole. They bowed down to all the starry hosts, and they worshiped Baal. [17]They sacrificed their sons and daughters in[c] the fire. They practiced divination and sorcery and sold themselves to do evil in the eyes of the LORD, provoking him to anger.

[18]So the LORD was very angry with Israel and removed them from his presence. Only the tribe of Judah was left, [19]and even Judah did not keep the commands of the LORD their God. They followed the practices Israel had introduced. [20]Therefore the LORD rejected all the people of Israel; he afflicted them and gave them into the hands of plunderers, until he thrust them from his presence.

[21]When he tore Israel away from the

---

[a] 4 Or to Sais, to the; So is possibly an abbreviation for Osorkon.   [b] 12 Exodus 20:4,5   [c] 17 Or They made their sons and daughters pass through

GOING *deeper*

An Undivided Heart

READ AND CONSIDER: 2 KINGS 17:24-33

"They worshiped the LORD, but they also appointed all sorts of their own people to officiate for them as priests in the shrines at the high places. They worshiped the LORD, but they also served their own gods in accordance with the customs of the nations from which they had been brought" (2 Kings 17:32-33).

If Samaria was anything, it was a house divided. Starting with King Jeroboam, this northern kingdom had allowed the worship of foreign gods—forgetting their spiritual roots. A succession of evil kings spiraled the nation deeper and deeper into sin, until God finally allowed it to be taken into exile by the Assyrians. The people of the northern kingdom were taken captive; then the king of Assyria brought other people from foreign lands and resettled them in Samaria. After some concerns about "what the god of that country requires" (17:26), the king sent a few exiled priests back to teach the resettled foreigners about the god of that land. The result was that people tried to combine the worship of Jehovah God with that of all the various false gods—including those whose worship practices were in direct violation of God's laws. That was a combination that was sure to bring serious consequences. When it comes to serving God, our loyalty to Him cannot be divided.

Centuries later, Jesus talked about a house divided. He had been accused of casting out demons by the power of Satan (a ludicrous accusation made by jealous people). Jesus pointed out to these accusers that He wouldn't be working against Satan by the power of Satan. A house divided is a house that will fall (see Matthew 12:24-29). And that's what happened to Samaria, not that the nation immediately disappeared, but that it never regained spiritual or political power.

Samaria is a good lesson for us. In the rush of our lives, it's easy to be divided—in our time, our energies, our focus. Without realizing it, we can be a lot like the Samaritans, serving God along with our other allegiances.

That's why prayer is so important. It unites your heart with God's. And it connects you to *who* matters more than anything else in your life. Prayer keeps your heart undivided.

house of David, they made Jeroboam son of Nebat their king. Jeroboam enticed Israel away from following the LORD and caused them to commit a great sin. ²²The Israelites persisted in all the sins of Jeroboam and did not turn away from them ²³until the LORD removed them from his presence, as he had warned through all his servants the prophets. So the people of Israel were taken from their homeland into exile in Assyria, and they are still there.

Samaria Resettled

²⁴The king of Assyria brought people from Babylon, Cuthah, Avva, Hamath and Sepharvaim and settled them in the towns of Samaria to replace the Israelites. They took over Samaria and lived in its towns. ²⁵When they first lived there, they did not worship the LORD; so he sent lions among them and they killed some of the people. ²⁶It was reported to the king of Assyria: "The people you deported and resettled in the towns of Samaria do not know what the god of that country requires. He has sent lions among them, which are killing them off, because the people do not know what he requires."

²⁷Then the king of Assyria gave this

order: "Have one of the priests you took captive from Samaria go back to live there and teach the people what the god of the land requires." ²⁸So one of the priests who had been exiled from Samaria came to live in Bethel and taught them how to worship the LORD.

²⁹Nevertheless, each national group made its own gods in the several towns where they settled, and set them up in the shrines the people of Samaria had made at the high places. ³⁰The men from Babylon made Succoth Benoth, the men from Cuthah made Nergal, and the men from Hamath made Ashima; ³¹the Avvites made Nibhaz and Tartak, and the Sepharvites burned their children in the fire as sacrifices to Adrammelech and Anammelech, the gods of Sepharvaim. ³²They worshiped the LORD, but they also appointed all sorts of their own people to officiate for them as priests in the shrines at the high places. ³³They worshiped the LORD, but they also served their own gods in accordance with the customs of the nations from which they had been brought.

Praying 2 Kings 17:39
Thank You, Lord, that because I fear You, You will deliver me from the hands of my enemies.

³⁴To this day they persist in their former practices. They neither worship the LORD nor adhere to the decrees and ordinances, the laws and commands that the LORD gave the descendants of Jacob, whom he named Israel. ³⁵When the LORD made a covenant with the Israelites, he commanded them: "Do not worship any other gods or bow down to them, serve them or sacrifice to them. ³⁶But the LORD, who brought you up out of Egypt with mighty power and outstretched arm, is the one you must worship. To him you shall bow down and to him offer sacrifices. ³⁷You must always be careful to

keep the decrees and ordinances, the laws and commands he wrote for you. Do not worship other gods. ³⁸Do not forget the covenant I have made with you, and do not worship other gods. ³⁹Rather, worship the LORD your God; it is he who will deliver you from the hand of all your enemies."

⁴⁰They would not listen, however, but persisted in their former practices. ⁴¹Even while these people were worshiping the LORD, they were serving their idols. To this day their children and grandchildren continue to do as their fathers did.

Hezekiah King of Judah

18 In the third year of Hoshea son of Elah king of Israel, Hezekiah son of Ahaz king of Judah began to reign. ²He was twenty-five years old when he became king, and he reigned in Jerusalem twenty-nine years. His mother's name was Abijah[a] daughter of Zechariah. ³He did what was right in the eyes of the LORD, just as his father David had done. ⁴He removed the high places, smashed the sacred stones and cut down the Asherah poles. He broke into pieces the bronze snake Moses had made, for up to that time the Israelites had been burning incense to it. (It was called[b] Nehushtan.[c])

⁵Hezekiah trusted in the LORD, the God of Israel. There was no one like him among all the kings of Judah, either before him or after him. ⁶He held fast to the LORD and did not cease to follow him; he kept the commands the LORD had given Moses. ⁷And the LORD was with him; he was successful in whatever he undertook. He rebelled against the king of Assyria and did not serve him. ⁸From watchtower to fortified city, he defeated the Philistines, as far as Gaza and its territory.

⁹In King Hezekiah's fourth year, which was the seventh year of Hoshea son of Elah king of Israel, Shalmaneser king of Assyria marched against Samaria and laid siege to it. ¹⁰At the end of three years the

---

ᵃ *2* Hebrew *Abi,* a variant of *Abijah*   ᵇ*4* Or *He called it*   ᶜ*4* Nehushtan sounds like the Hebrew for *bronze* and *snake* and *unclean thing.*

Assyrians took it. So Samaria was captured in Hezekiah's sixth year, which was the ninth year of Hoshea king of Israel. ¹¹The king of Assyria deported Israel to Assyria and settled them in Halah, in Gozan on the Habor River and in towns of the Medes. ¹²This happened because they had not obeyed the LORD their God, but had violated his covenant—all that Moses the servant of the LORD commanded. They neither listened to the commands nor carried them out.

¹³In the fourteenth year of King Hezekiah's reign, Sennacherib king of Assyria attacked all the fortified cities of Judah and captured them. ¹⁴So Hezekiah king of Judah sent this message to the king of Assyria at Lachish: "I have done wrong. Withdraw from me, and I will pay whatever you demand of me." The king of Assyria exacted from Hezekiah king of Judah three hundred talentsª of silver and thirty talentsᵇ of gold. ¹⁵So Hezekiah gave him all the silver that was found in the temple of the LORD and in the treasuries of the royal palace.

¹⁶At this time Hezekiah king of Judah stripped off the gold with which he had covered the doors and doorposts of the temple of the LORD, and gave it to the king of Assyria.

Sennacherib Threatens Jerusalem

¹⁷The king of Assyria sent his supreme commander, his chief officer and his field commander with a large army, from Lachish to King Hezekiah at Jerusalem. They came up to Jerusalem and stopped at the aqueduct of the Upper Pool, on the road to the Washerman's Field. ¹⁸They called for the king; and Eliakim son of Hilkiah the palace administrator, Shebna the secretary, and Joah son of Asaph the recorder went out to them.

¹⁹The field commander said to them, "Tell Hezekiah:

"'This is what the great king, the king of Assyria, says: On what are you basing this confidence of yours? ²⁰You say you have strategy and military strength—but you speak only empty words. On whom are you depending, that you rebel against me? ²¹Look now, you are depending on Egypt, that splintered reed of a staff, which pierces a man's hand and wounds him if he leans on it! Such is Pharaoh king of Egypt to all who depend on him. ²²And if you say to me, "We are depending on the LORD our God"—isn't he the one whose high places and altars Hezekiah removed, saying to Judah and Jerusalem, "You must worship before this altar in Jerusalem"?

²³"'Come now, make a bargain with my master, the king of Assyria: I will give you two thousand horses—if you can put riders on them! ²⁴How can you repulse one officer of the least of my master's officials, even though you are depending on Egypt for chariots and horsemenᶜ? ²⁵Furthermore, have I come to attack and destroy this place without word from the LORD? The LORD himself told me to march against this country and destroy it.'"

²⁶Then Eliakim son of Hilkiah, and Shebna and Joah said to the field commander, "Please speak to your servants in Aramaic, since we understand it. Don't speak to us in Hebrew in the hearing of the people on the wall."

²⁷But the commander replied, "Was it only to your master and you that my master sent me to say these things, and not to the men sitting on the wall—who, like you, will have to eat their own filth and drink their own urine?"

²⁸Then the commander stood and called out in Hebrew: "Hear the word of the great king, the king of Assyria! ²⁹This is what the king says: Do not let Hezekiah deceive you. He cannot deliver you from my hand. ³⁰Do not let Hezekiah persuade

---

ª 14 That is, about 11 tons (about 10 metric tons)   ᵇ 14 That is, about 1 ton (about 1 metric ton)   ᶜ 24 Or charioteers you to trust in the LORD when he says, 'The LORD will surely deliver us; this city will not be given into the hand of the king of Assyria.'

³¹"Do not listen to Hezekiah. This is what the king of Assyria says: Make peace with me and come out to me. Then every one of you will eat from his own vine and fig tree and drink water from his own cistern, ³²until I come and take you to a land like your own, a land of grain and new wine, a land of bread and vineyards, a land of olive trees and honey. Choose life and not death!

"Do not listen to Hezekiah, for he is misleading you when he says, 'The LORD will deliver us.' ³³Has the god of any nation ever delivered his land from the hand of the king of Assyria? ³⁴Where are the gods of Hamath and Arpad? Where are the gods of Sepharvaim, Hena and Ivvah? Have they rescued Samaria from my hand? ³⁵Who of all the gods of these countries has been able to save his land from me? How then can the LORD deliver Jerusalem from my hand?"

³⁶But the people remained silent and said nothing in reply, because the king had commanded, "Do not answer him."

³⁷Then Eliakim son of Hilkiah the palace administrator, Shebna the secretary and Joah son of Asaph the recorder went to Hezekiah, with their clothes torn, and told him what the field commander had said.

Jerusalem's Deliverance Foretold

19 When King Hezekiah heard this, he tore his clothes and put on sackcloth and went into the temple of the LORD. ²He sent Eliakim the palace administrator, Shebna the secretary and the leading priests, all wearing sackcloth, to the prophet Isaiah son of Amoz. ³They told him, "This is what Hezekiah says: This day is a day of distress and rebuke and disgrace, as when children come to the point of birth and there is no strength to deliver them. ⁴It may be that the LORD

your God will hear all the words of the field commander, whom his master, the king of Assyria, has sent to ridicule the living God, and that he will rebuke him for the words the LORD your God has heard. Therefore pray for the remnant that still survives."

⁵When King Hezekiah's officials came to Isaiah, ⁶Isaiah said to them, "Tell your master, 'This is what the LORD says: Do not be afraid of what you have heard—those words with which the underlings of the king of Assyria have blasphemed me. ⁷Listen! I am going to put such a spirit in him that when he hears a certain report, he will return to his own country, and there I will have him cut down with the sword.'"

⁸When the field commander heard that the king of Assyria had left Lachish, he withdrew and found the king fighting against Libnah.

⁹Now Sennacherib received a report that Tirhakah, the Cushite[a] king of Egypt, was marching out to fight against him. So he again sent messengers to Hezekiah with this word: ¹⁰"Say to Hezekiah king of Judah: Do not let the god you depend on deceive you when he says, 'Jerusalem will not be handed over to the king of Assyria.' ¹¹Surely you have heard what the kings of Assyria have done to all the countries, destroying them completely. And will you be delivered? ¹²Did the gods of the nations that were destroyed by my forefathers deliver them: the gods of Gozan, Haran, Rezeph and the people of Eden who were in Tel Assar? ¹³Where is the king of Hamath, the king of Arpad, the king of the city of Sepharvaim, or of Hena or Ivvah?"

Hezekiah's Prayer

¹⁴Hezekiah received the letter from the messengers and read it. Then he went up to the temple of the LORD and spread it out before the LORD. ¹⁵And Hezekiah prayed to the LORD: "O LORD, God of Israel, enthroned between the cherubim,

you alone are God over all the kingdoms of the earth. You have made heaven and earth. 16Give ear, O LORD, and hear; open your eyes, O LORD, and see; listen to the words Sennacherib has sent to insult the living God.

17"It is true, O LORD, that the Assyrian kings have laid waste these nations and their lands. 18They have thrown their gods into the fire and destroyed them, for they were not gods but only wood and stone, fashioned by men's hands. 19Now, O LORD our God, deliver us from his hand, so that all kingdoms on earth may know that you alone, O LORD, are God."

Against the Holy One of Israel!
23By your messengers
    you have heaped insults on the
        Lord.
And you have said,
    "With my many chariots
I have ascended the heights of the
        mountains,
    the utmost heights of Lebanon.
I have cut down its tallest cedars,
    the choicest of its pines.
I have reached its remotest parts,
    the finest of its forests.
24I have dug wells in foreign lands
    and drunk the water there.

God's people at prayer
HEZEKIAH'S PRAYER FOR GOD'S INTERVENTION

2 KINGS 19:14-19 When King Hezekiah ruled in Jerusalem, the Assyrians were the scourge of Judah and all the nations around them. The arrogant Assyrian king, Sennacherib, taunted the people of Judah with a message: Their God would be powerless against him, just as all the other conquered nations' gods had been!

It looked hopeless for the little nation of Judah. So Hezekiah did the most powerful thing he could do—he prayed. He took the message that had arrived from Sennacherib, went to the temple, and spread the letter out in front of the Lord. Then he prayed for God to deliver His people.

What devastating "letter" has arrived in your life? An unexpected bill? A final notice? A rejection? A difficult message from family or friends? Divorce papers? A doctor's report? Spread them out before God and ask Him what you should do next. Then listen for God to tell you.

Isaiah Prophesies Sennacherib's Fall

20Then Isaiah son of Amoz sent a message to Hezekiah: "This is what the LORD, the God of Israel, says: I have heard your prayer concerning Sennacherib king of Assyria. 21This is the word that the LORD has spoken against him:

" 'The Virgin Daughter of Zion
        despises you and mocks you.
The Daughter of Jerusalem
        tosses her head as you flee.
22Who is it you have insulted and
        blasphemed?
    Against whom have you raised your
        voice
    and lifted your eyes in pride?

With the soles of my feet
    I have dried up all the streams of
        Egypt."

25" 'Have you not heard?
    Long ago I ordained it.
In days of old I planned it;
    now I have brought it to pass,
that you have turned fortified cities
    into piles of stone.
26Their people, drained of power,
    are dismayed and put to
        shame.
They are like plants in the field,
    like tender green shoots,
like grass sprouting on the roof,
    scorched before it grows up.

27 " 'But I know where you stay
and when you come and go
and how you rage against me.
28 Because you rage against me
and your insolence has reached my
ears,
I will put my hook in your nose
and my bit in your mouth,
and I will make you return
by the way you came.'

29 "This will be the sign for you,
O Hezekiah:

"This year you will eat what grows
by itself,
and the second year what springs
from that.
But in the third year sow and reap,
plant vineyards and eat their fruit.
30 Once more a remnant of the house of
Judah
will take root below and bear fruit
above.
31 For out of Jerusalem will come a
remnant,
and out of Mount Zion a band of
survivors.

The zeal of the LORD Almighty will accomplish this.

32 "Therefore this is what the LORD says
concerning the king of Assyria:

"He will not enter this city
or shoot an arrow here.
He will not come before it with
shield
or build a siege ramp against it.
33 By the way that he came he will
return;
he will not enter this city,
declares the LORD.
34 I will defend this city and save it,
for my sake and for the sake of
David my servant."

35 That night the angel of the LORD
went out and put to death a hundred and
eighty-five thousand men in the Assyrian camp. When the people got up the
next morning—there were all the dead
bodies! 36 So Sennacherib king of Assyria
broke camp and withdrew. He returned
to Nineveh and stayed there.

37 One day, while he was worshiping in
the temple of his god Nisroch, his sons
Adrammelech and Sharezer cut him
down with the sword, and they escaped
to the land of Ararat. And Esarhaddon
his son succeeded him as king.

Hezekiah's Illness

20 In those days Hezekiah became ill
and was at the point of death. The
prophet Isaiah son of Amoz went to him
and said, "This is what the LORD says: Put
your house in order, because you are going to die; you will not recover."

2 Hezekiah turned his face to the wall
and prayed to the LORD, 3 "Remember,
O LORD, how I have walked before you
faithfully and with wholehearted devotion and have done what is good in your
eyes." And Hezekiah wept bitterly.

Praying 2 Kings 20:1-5
*How grateful I am, Lord, that
You hear my prayers when I am
in a life-and-death situation.*

4 Before Isaiah had left the middle court,
the word of the LORD came to him: 5 "Go
back and tell Hezekiah, the leader of my
people, 'This is what the LORD, the God
of your father David, says: I have heard
your prayer and seen your tears; I will
heal you. On the third day from now you
will go up to the temple of the LORD.
6 I will add fifteen years to your life. And
I will deliver you and this city from the
hand of the king of Assyria. I will defend
this city for my sake and for the sake of
my servant David.'"

7 Then Isaiah said, "Prepare a poultice
of figs." They did so and applied it to the
boil, and he recovered.

8 Hezekiah had asked Isaiah, "What will
be the sign that the LORD will heal me
and that I will go up to the temple of the
LORD on the third day from now?"

GOING *deeper*

Remember Me, Lord

READ AND CONSIDER: 2 KINGS 20:1-11

"Hezekiah turned his face to the wall and prayed to the LORD, 'Remember, O LORD, how I have walked before you faithfully and with wholehearted devotion and have done what is good in your eyes.' And Hezekiah wept bitterly" (2 Kings 20:2-3).

The prophet Isaiah had informed Hezekiah that he was going to die. Perhaps you've faced a similar situation, whether from a potentially terminal illness, a near fatal accident, or an iffy report from a medical test. Whenever you face your own mortality, what do you do? Hezekiah prayed.

His prayer was a plea not to be forgotten by God. "Remember how I've served you, Lord. Remember the good things I have done."

When we find ourselves in desperate circumstances—especially in a life and death situation—we want to say, "Remember me, Lord. I love You and want to serve You longer." We know God doesn't owe us that. But we also know He is a God of mercy and grace. And we are asking for His grace to be extended to us now.

One of the things Hezekiah's prayer did was to clearly identify God as the source of his healing and deliverance. By turning to God with his whole heart, he was coming to the only One who could change his fate. God heard his prayer and the cry of his heart and not only healed him but gave him 15 more years to live and serve.

When you are in a difficult situation, cry out to God as the source of your healing and deliverance. Thank Him that He is a God of mercy and grace.

---

⁹Isaiah answered, "This is the LORD's sign to you that the LORD will do what he has promised: Shall the shadow go forward ten steps, or shall it go back ten steps?"

¹⁰"It is a simple matter for the shadow to go forward ten steps," said Hezekiah. "Rather, have it go back ten steps."

¹¹Then the prophet Isaiah called upon the LORD, and the LORD made the shadow go back the ten steps it had gone down on the stairway of Ahaz.

Envoys From Babylon

¹²At that time Merodach-Baladan son of Baladan king of Babylon sent Hezekiah letters and a gift, because he had heard of Hezekiah's illness. ¹³Hezekiah received the messengers and showed them all that was in his storehouses—the silver, the gold, the spices and the fine oil—his ar-

mory and everything found among his treasures. There was nothing in his palace or in all his kingdom that Hezekiah did not show them.

¹⁴Then Isaiah the prophet went to King Hezekiah and asked, "What did those men say, and where did they come from?"

"From a distant land," Hezekiah replied. "They came from Babylon."

¹⁵The prophet asked, "What did they see in your palace?"

"They saw everything in my palace," Hezekiah said. "There is nothing among my treasures that I did not show them."

¹⁶Then Isaiah said to Hezekiah, "Hear the word of the LORD: ¹⁷The time will surely come when everything in your palace, and all that your fathers have stored up until this day, will be carried off to

Babylon. Nothing will be left, says the LORD. [18]And some of your descendants, your own flesh and blood, that will be born to you, will be taken away, and they will become eunuchs in the palace of the king of Babylon."

[19]"The word of the LORD you have spoken is good," Hezekiah replied. For he thought, "Will there not be peace and security in my lifetime?"

[20]As for the other events of Hezekiah's reign, all his achievements and how he made the pool and the tunnel by which he brought water into the city, are they not written in the book of the annals of the kings of Judah? [21]Hezekiah rested with his fathers. And Manasseh his son succeeded him as king.

Manasseh King of Judah

21 Manasseh was twelve years old when he became king, and he reigned in Jerusalem fifty-five years. His mother's name was Hephzibah. [2]He did evil in the eyes of the LORD, following the detestable practices of the nations the LORD had driven out before the Israelites. [3]He rebuilt the high places his father Hezekiah had destroyed; he also erected altars to Baal and made an Asherah pole, as Ahab king of Israel had done. He bowed down to all the starry hosts and worshiped them. [4]He built altars in the temple of the LORD, of which the LORD had said, "In Jerusalem I will put my Name." [5]In both courts of the temple of the LORD, he built altars to all the starry hosts. [6]He sacrificed his own son in[a] the fire, practiced sorcery and divination, and consulted mediums and spiritists. He did much evil in the eyes of the LORD, provoking him to anger.

[7]He took the carved Asherah pole he had made and put it in the temple, of which the LORD had said to David and to his son Solomon, "In this temple and in Jerusalem, which I have chosen out of all the tribes of Israel, I will put my Name forever. [8]I will not again make the feet

of the Israelites wander from the land I gave their forefathers, if only they will be careful to do everything I commanded them and will keep the whole Law that my servant Moses gave them." [9]But the people did not listen. Manasseh led them astray, so that they did more evil than the nations the LORD had destroyed before the Israelites.

[10]The LORD said through his servants the prophets: [11]"Manasseh king of Judah has committed these detestable sins. He has done more evil than the Amorites who preceded him and has led Judah into sin with his idols. [12]Therefore this is what the LORD, the God of Israel, says: I am going to bring such disaster on Jerusalem and Judah that the ears of everyone who hears of it will tingle. [13]I will stretch out over Jerusalem the measuring line used against Samaria and the plumb line used against the house of Ahab. I will wipe out Jerusalem as one wipes a dish, wiping it and turning it upside down. [14]I will forsake the remnant of my inheritance and hand them over to their enemies. They will be looted and plundered by all their foes, [15]because they have done evil in my eyes and have provoked me to anger from the day their forefathers came out of Egypt until this day."

[16]Moreover, Manasseh also shed so much innocent blood that he filled Jerusalem from end to end—besides the sin that he had caused Judah to commit, so that they did evil in the eyes of the LORD.

[17]As for the other events of Manasseh's reign, and all he did, including the sin he committed, are they not written in the book of the annals of the kings of Judah? [18]Manasseh rested with his fathers and was buried in his palace garden, the garden of Uzza. And Amon his son succeeded him as king.

Amon King of Judah

[19]Amon was twenty-two years old when he became king, and he reigned in Jerusalem two years. His mother's name

---

[a]6 Or *He made his own son pass through*

was Meshullemeth daughter of Haruz; she was from Jotbah. 20He did evil in the eyes of the LORD, as his father Manasseh had done. 21He walked in all the ways of his father; he worshiped the idols his father had worshiped, and bowed down to them. 22He forsook the LORD, the God of his fathers, and did not walk in the way of the LORD.

23Amon's officials conspired against him and assassinated the king in his palace. 24Then the people of the land killed all who had plotted against King Amon, and they made Josiah his son king in his place.

25As for the other events of Amon's reign, and what he did, are they not written in the book of the annals of the kings of Judah? 26He was buried in his grave in the garden of Uzza. And Josiah his son succeeded him as king.

The Book of the Law Found

22 Josiah was eight years old when he became king, and he reigned in Jerusalem thirty-one years. His mother's name was Jedidah daughter of Adaiah; she was from Bozkath. 2He did what was right in the eyes of the LORD and walked in all the ways of his father David, not turning aside to the right or to the left.

3In the eighteenth year of his reign, King Josiah sent the secretary, Shaphan son of Azaliah, the son of Meshullam, to the temple of the LORD. He said: 4"Go up to Hilkiah the high priest and have him get ready the money that has been brought into the temple of the LORD, which the doorkeepers have collected from the people. 5Have them entrust it to the men appointed to supervise the work on the temple. And have these men pay the workers who repair the temple of the LORD— 6the carpenters, the builders and the masons. Also have them purchase timber and dressed stone to repair the temple. 7But they need not account for the money entrusted to them, because they are acting faithfully."

8Hilkiah the high priest said to Shaphan the secretary, "I have found the Book of the Law in the temple of the LORD." He gave it to Shaphan, who read it. 9Then Shaphan the secretary went to the king and reported to him: "Your officials have paid out the money that was in the temple of the LORD and have entrusted it to the workers and supervisors at the temple." 10Then Shaphan the secretary informed the king, "Hilkiah the priest has given me a book." And Shaphan read from it in the presence of the king.

11When the king heard the words of the Book of the Law, he tore his robes. 12He gave these orders to Hilkiah the priest, Ahikam son of Shaphan, Acbor son of Micaiah, Shaphan the secretary and Asaiah the king's attendant: 13"Go and inquire of the LORD for me and for the people and for all Judah about what is written in this book that has been found. Great is the LORD's anger that burns against us because our fathers have not obeyed the words of this book; they have not acted in accordance with all that is written there concerning us."

14Hilkiah the priest, Ahikam, Acbor, Shaphan and Asaiah went to speak to the prophetess Huldah, who was the wife of Shallum son of Tikvah, the son of Harhas, keeper of the wardrobe. She lived in Jerusalem, in the Second District.

15She said to them, "This is what the LORD, the God of Israel, says: Tell the man who sent you to me, 16This is what the LORD says: I am going to bring disaster on this place and its people, according to everything written in the book the king of Judah has read. 17Because they have forsaken me and burned incense to other gods and provoked me to anger by all the idols their hands have made,ᵃ my anger will burn against this place and will not be quenched.' 18Tell the king of Judah, who sent you to inquire of the LORD, 'This is what the LORD, the God of Israel, says concerning the words you

---

ᵃ 17 Or by everything they have done

heard: [19]Because your heart was responsive and you humbled yourself before the LORD when you heard what I have spoken against this place and its people, that they would become accursed and laid waste, and because you tore your robes and wept in my presence, I have heard you, declares the LORD. [20]Therefore I will gather you to your fathers, and you will be buried in peace. Your eyes will not see all the disaster I am going to bring on this place.'"

So they took her answer back to the king.

Josiah Renews the Covenant

23 Then the king called together all the elders of Judah and Jerusalem. [2]He went up to the temple of the LORD with the men of Judah, the people of Jerusalem, the priests and the prophets—all the people from the least to the greatest. He read in their hearing all the words of the Book of the Covenant, which had been found in the temple of the LORD. [3]The king stood by the pillar and renewed the covenant in the presence of the LORD—to follow the LORD and keep his commands, regulations and decrees with all his heart and all his soul, thus confirming the words of the covenant written in this book. Then all the people pledged themselves to the covenant.

> **Praying 2 Kings 23:3**
> *I long to follow You with all my heart, Lord, and to obey You to the very best of my ability.*

[4]The king ordered Hilkiah the high priest, the priests next in rank and the doorkeepers to remove from the temple of the LORD all the articles made for Baal and Asherah and all the starry hosts. He burned them outside Jerusalem in the fields of the Kidron Valley and took the ashes to Bethel. [5]He did away with the pagan priests appointed by the kings of Judah to burn incense on the high places of the towns of Judah and on those around Jerusalem—those who burned incense to Baal, to the sun and moon, to the constellations and to all the starry hosts. [6]He took the Asherah pole from the temple of the LORD to the Kidron Valley outside Jerusalem and burned it there. He ground it to powder and scattered the dust over the graves of the common people. [7]He also tore down the quarters of the male shrine prostitutes, which were in the temple of the LORD and where women did weaving for Asherah.

[8]Josiah brought all the priests from the towns of Judah and desecrated the high places, from Geba to Beersheba, where the priests had burned incense. He broke down the shrines[a] at the gates—at the entrance to the Gate of Joshua, the city governor, which is on the left of the city gate. [9]Although the priests of the high places did not serve at the altar of the LORD in Jerusalem, they ate unleavened bread with their fellow priests.

[10]He desecrated Topheth, which was in the Valley of Ben Hinnom, so no one could use it to sacrifice his son or daughter in[b] the fire to Molech. [11]He removed from the entrance to the temple of the LORD the horses that the kings of Judah had dedicated to the sun. They were in the court near the room of an official named Nathan-Melech. Josiah then burned the chariots dedicated to the sun.

[12]He pulled down the altars the kings of Judah had erected on the roof near the upper room of Ahaz, and the altars Manasseh had built in the two courts of the temple of the LORD. He removed them from there, smashed them to pieces and threw the rubble into the Kidron Valley. [13]The king also desecrated the high places that were east of Jerusalem on the south of the Hill of Corruption—the ones Solomon king of Israel had built for Ashtoreth the vile goddess of the Sidonians, for Chemosh the vile god of Moab, and for Molech[c] the detestable god of the people

---

[a] 8 Or high places   [b] 10 Or to make his son or daughter pass through   [c] 13 Hebrew Milcom

of Ammon. ¹⁴Josiah smashed the sacred stones and cut down the Asherah poles and covered the sites with human bones.

¹⁵Even the altar at Bethel, the high place made by Jeroboam son of Nebat, who had caused Israel to sin—even that altar and high place he demolished. He burned the high place and ground it to powder, and burned the Asherah pole also. ¹⁶Then Josiah looked around, and when he saw the tombs that were there on the hillside, he had the bones removed from them and burned on the altar to defile it, in accordance with the word of the LORD proclaimed by the man of God who foretold these things.

¹⁷The king asked, "What is that tombstone I see?"

The men of the city said, "It marks the tomb of the man of God who came from Judah and pronounced against the altar of Bethel the very things you have done to it."

¹⁸"Leave it alone," he said. "Don't let anyone disturb his bones." So they spared his bones and those of the prophet who had come from Samaria.

¹⁹Just as he had done at Bethel, Josiah removed and defiled all the shrines at the high places that the kings of Israel had built in the towns of Samaria that had provoked the LORD to anger. ²⁰Josiah slaughtered all the priests of those high places on the altars and burned human bones on them. Then he went back to Jerusalem.

²¹The king gave this order to all the people: "Celebrate the Passover to the LORD your God, as it is written in this Book of the Covenant." ²²Not since the days of the judges who led Israel, nor throughout the days of the kings of Israel and the kings of Judah, had any such Passover been observed. ²³But in the eighteenth year of King Josiah, this Passover was celebrated to the LORD in Jerusalem.

²⁴Furthermore, Josiah got rid of the mediums and spiritists, the household gods, the idols and all the other detestable things seen in Judah and Jerusalem. This he did to fulfill the requirements of the law written in the book that Hilkiah the priest had discovered in the temple of the LORD. ²⁵Neither before nor after Josiah was there a king like him who turned to the LORD as he did—with all his heart and with all his soul and with all his strength, in accordance with all the Law of Moses.

²⁶Nevertheless, the LORD did not turn away from the heat of his fierce anger, which burned against Judah because of all that Manasseh had done to provoke him to anger. ²⁷So the LORD said, "I will remove Judah also from my presence as I removed Israel, and I will reject Jerusalem, the city I chose, and this temple, about which I said, 'There shall my Name be.'ᵃ"

²⁸As for the other events of Josiah's reign, and all he did, are they not written in the book of the annals of the kings of Judah?

²⁹While Josiah was king, Pharaoh Neco king of Egypt went up to the Euphrates River to help the king of Assyria. King Josiah marched out to meet him in battle, but Neco faced him and killed him at Megiddo. ³⁰Josiah's servants brought his body in a chariot from Megiddo to Jerusalem and buried him in his own tomb. And the people of the land took Jehoahaz son of Josiah and anointed him and made him king in place of his father.

Jehoahaz King of Judah

³¹Jehoahaz was twenty-three years old when he became king, and he reigned in Jerusalem three months. His mother's name was Hamutal daughter of Jeremiah; she was from Libnah. ³²He did evil in the eyes of the LORD, just as his fathers had done. ³³Pharaoh Neco put him in chains at Riblah in the land of Hamathᵇ so that he might not reign in Jerusalem, and he imposed on Judah a levy of a hundred

ᵃ27 1 Kings 8:29   ᵇ33 Hebrew; Septuagint (see also 2 Chron. 36:3) Neco at Riblah in Hamath removed him

talents[a] of silver and a talent[b] of gold.
34Pharaoh Neco made Eliakim son of
Josiah king in place of his father Josiah
and changed Eliakim's name to Jehoiakim. But he took Jehoahaz and carried
him off to Egypt, and there he died. 35Je-
hoiakim paid Pharaoh Neco the silver
and gold he demanded. In order to do so,
he taxed the land and exacted the silver
and gold from the people of the land according to their assessments.

Jehoiakim King of Judah

36Jehoiakim was twenty-five years old
when he became king, and he reigned in
Jerusalem eleven years. His mother's name
was Zebidah daughter of Pedaiah; she was
from Rumah. 37And he did evil in the eyes
of the LORD, just as his fathers had done.

24 During Jehoiakim's reign, Nebuchadnezzar king of Babylon invaded the land, and Jehoiakim became his
vassal for three years. But then he changed
his mind and rebelled against Nebuchadnezzar. 2The LORD sent Babylonian,[c]
Aramean, Moabite and Ammonite raiders against him. He sent them to destroy
Judah, in accordance with the word of
the LORD proclaimed by his servants the
prophets. 3Surely these things happened
to Judah according to the LORD's command, in order to remove them from his
presence because of the sins of Manasseh
and all he had done, 4including the shedding of innocent blood. For he had filled
Jerusalem with innocent blood, and the
LORD was not willing to forgive.

5As for the other events of Jehoiakim's
reign, and all he did, are they not written
in the book of the annals of the kings of
Judah? 6Jehoiakim rested with his fathers.
And Jehoiachin his son succeeded him
as king.

7The king of Egypt did not march out
from his own country again, because
the king of Babylon had taken all his
territory, from the Wadi of Egypt to the
Euphrates River.

Jehoiachin King of Judah

8Jehoiachin was eighteen years old
when he became king, and he reigned
in Jerusalem three months. His mother's
name was Nehushta daughter of Elnathan; she was from Jerusalem. 9He did
evil in the eyes of the LORD, just as his
father had done.

10At that time the officers of Nebuchadnezzar king of Babylon advanced on
Jerusalem and laid siege to it, 11and Nebuchadnezzar himself came up to the city
while his officers were besieging it. 12Je-
hoiachin king of Judah, his mother, his
attendants, his nobles and his officials all
surrendered to him.

In the eighth year of the reign of the
king of Babylon, he took Jehoiachin
prisoner. 13As the LORD had declared,
Nebuchadnezzar removed all the treasures from the temple of the LORD and
from the royal palace, and took away all
the gold articles that Solomon king of
Israel had made for the temple of the
LORD. 14He carried into exile all Jerusalem: all the officers and fighting men, and
all the craftsmen and artisans—a total of
ten thousand. Only the poorest people of
the land were left.

15Nebuchadnezzar took Jehoiachin
captive to Babylon. He also took from
Jerusalem to Babylon the king's mother,
his wives, his officials and the leading
men of the land. 16The king of Babylon
also deported to Babylon the entire force
of seven thousand fighting men, strong
and fit for war, and a thousand craftsmen
and artisans. 17He made Mattaniah, Jehoiachin's uncle, king in his place and
changed his name to Zedekiah.

Zedekiah King of Judah

18Zedekiah was twenty-one years old
when he became king, and he reigned
in Jerusalem eleven years. His mother's
name was Hamutal daughter of Jeremiah;
she was from Libnah. 19He did evil in
the eyes of the LORD, just as Jehoiakim
had done. 20It was because of the LORD's

---

[a] 33 That is, about 3 3/4 tons (about 3.4 metric tons)   [b] 33 That is, about 75 pounds (about 34 kilograms)   [c] 2 Or Chaldean

anger that all this happened to Jerusalem and Judah, and in the end he thrust them from his presence.

The Fall of Jerusalem

Now Zedekiah rebelled against the king of Babylon.

25 So in the ninth year of Zedekiah's reign, on the tenth day of the tenth month, Nebuchadnezzar king of Babylon marched against Jerusalem with his whole army. He encamped outside the city and built siege works all around it. 2The city was kept under siege until the eleventh year of King Zedekiah. 3By the ninth day of the fourth[a] month the famine in the city had become so severe that there was no food for the people to eat. 4Then the city wall was broken through, and the whole army fled at night through the gate between the two walls near the king's garden, though the Babylonians[b] were surrounding the city. They fled toward the Arabah,[c] 5but the Babylonian[d] army pursued the king and overtook him in the plains of Jericho. All his soldiers were separated from him and scattered, 6and he was captured. He was taken to the king of Babylon at Riblah, where sentence was pronounced on him. 7They killed the sons of Zedekiah before his eyes. Then they put out his eyes, bound him with bronze shackles and took him to Babylon.

8On the seventh day of the fifth month, in the nineteenth year of Nebuchadnezzar king of Babylon, Nebuzaradan commander of the imperial guard, an official of the king of Babylon, came to Jerusalem. 9He set fire to the temple of the LORD, the royal palace and all the houses of Jerusalem. Every important building he burned down. 10The whole Babylonian army, under the commander of the imperial guard, broke down the walls around Jerusalem. 11Nebuzaradan the commander of the guard carried into exile the people who remained in the city, along with the rest of the populace and those who had gone over to the king of Babylon. 12But the commander left behind some of the poorest people of the land to work the vineyards and fields.

13The Babylonians broke up the bronze pillars, the movable stands and the bronze Sea that were at the temple of the LORD and they carried the bronze to Babylon. 14They also took away the pots, shovels, wick trimmers, dishes and all the bronze articles used in the temple service. 15The commander of the imperial guard took away the censers and sprinkling bowls—all that were made of pure gold or silver.

16The bronze from the two pillars, the Sea and the movable stands, which Solomon had made for the temple of the LORD, was more than could be weighed. 17Each pillar was twenty-seven feet[e] high. The bronze capital on top of one pillar was four and a half feet[f] high and was decorated with a network and pomegranates of bronze all around. The other pillar, with its network, was similar.

18The commander of the guard took as prisoners Seraiah the chief priest, Zephaniah the priest next in rank and the three doorkeepers. 19Of those still in the city, he took the officer in charge of the fighting men and five royal advisers. He also took the secretary who was chief officer in charge of conscripting the people of the land and sixty of his men who were found in the city. 20Nebuzaradan the commander took them all and brought them to the king of Babylon at Riblah. 21There at Riblah, in the land of Hamath, the king had them executed.

So Judah went into captivity, away from her land.

22Nebuchadnezzar king of Babylon appointed Gedaliah son of Ahikam, the son of Shaphan, to be over the people he had left behind in Judah. 23When all the army officers and their men heard that the king of Babylon had appointed

a 3 See Jer. 52:6. b 4 Or Chaldeans; also in verses 13, 25 and 26 c 4 Or the Jordan Valley d 5 Or Chaldean; also in verses 10 and 24 e 17 Hebrew eighteen cubits (about 8.1 meters) f 17 Hebrew three cubits (about 1.3 meters)

Gedaliah as governor, they came to Gedaliah at Mizpah—Ishmael son of Nethaniah, Johanan son of Kareah, Seraiah son of Tanhumeth the Netophathite, Jaazaniah the son of the Maacathite, and their men. ²⁴Gedaliah took an oath to reassure them and their men. "Do not be afraid of the Babylonian officials," he said. "Settle down in the land and serve the king of Babylon, and it will go well with you."

²⁵In the seventh month, however, Ishmael son of Nethaniah, the son of Elishama, who was of royal blood, came with ten men and assassinated Gedaliah and also the men of Judah and the Babylonians who were with him at Mizpah. ²⁶At

this, all the people from the least to the greatest, together with the army officers, fled to Egypt for fear of the Babylonians.

Jehoiachin Released

²⁷In the thirty-seventh year of the exile of Jehoiachin king of Judah, in the year Evil-Merodach[a] became king of Babylon, he released Jehoiachin from prison on the twenty-seventh day of the twelfth month. ²⁸He spoke kindly to him and gave him a seat of honor higher than those of the other kings who were with him in Babylon. ²⁹So Jehoiachin put aside his prison clothes and for the rest of his life ate regularly at the king's table. ³⁰Day by day the king gave Jehoiachin a regular allowance as long as he lived.

---

[a] 27 Also called Amel-Marduk

Author: Unknown, possibly Ezra

Date: About 400 BC

Audience: The remnant of Jews living after the exile, who needed a reminder of God's promises to bring about a Messiah through King David's descendants

What do you think when you read this famous New Testament verse on prayer: "Pray continually" (1 Thessalonians 5:17)? Perhaps, like so many, you've pondered that command and wondered, *Continually? Without ceasing? How in the world do I do that? What does that look like in a busy life?*

King David, the dominant character in 1 Chronicles, is the best example of a person who prayed often. His "God-ward" perspective is clearly seen. He instinctively and regularly turned to God as he governed the people and led Israel's armies. Though he had several enormous failures in his life, David somehow managed, for the most part, to keep his own heart (and the nation's attention) focused on God.

Prayer Themes:

- *Thank God that He knows each individual by name, and He knows you by name (1:1–9:44).*

- *Tell the Lord that you want to develop an ever-increasing reverence for Him—a holy fear and a sense of awe and wonder in worship (13:7-10).*

- *Thank God for His many blessings in your life, for His works on your behalf (16:7-36).*

1 Chronicles

Historical Records From Adam to Abraham

To Noah's Sons

1 Adam, Seth, Enosh, [2]Kenan, Mahalalel, Jared, [3]Enoch, Methuselah, Lamech, Noah.

[4]The sons of Noah:[a]
Shem, Ham and Japheth.

The Japhethites

[5]The sons[b] of Japheth:
Gomer, Magog, Madai, Javan, Tubal, Meshech and Tiras.
[6]The sons of Gomer:
Ashkenaz, Riphath[c] and Togarmah.
[7]The sons of Javan:
Elishah, Tarshish, the Kittim and the Rodanim.

The Hamites

[8]The sons of Ham:
Cush, Mizraim,[d] Put and Canaan.
[9]The sons of Cush:
Seba, Havilah, Sabta, Raamah and Sabteca.
The sons of Raamah:
Sheba and Dedan.
[10]Cush was the father[e] of
Nimrod, who grew to be a mighty warrior on earth.
[11]Mizraim was the father of
the Ludites, Anamites, Lehabites, Naphtuhites, [12]Pathrusites, Casluhites (from whom the Philistines came) and Caphtorites.
[13]Canaan was the father of
Sidon his firstborn,[f] and of the Hittites, [14]Jebusites, Amorites, Gir-

---

[a] 4 Septuagint; Hebrew does not have this line.   [b] 5 Sons may mean descendants or successors or nations; also in verses 6-10, 17 and 20.   [c] 6 Many Hebrew manuscripts and Vulgate (see also Septuagint and Gen. 10:3); most Hebrew manuscripts Diphath   [d] 8 That is, Egypt; also in verse 11   [e] 10 Father may mean ancestor or predecessor or founder; also in verses 11, 13, 18 and 20.   [f] 13 Or of the Sidonians, the foremost

gashites, 15Hivites, Arkites, Sinites, 16Arvadites, Zemarites and Ha-mathites.

The Semites
17 The sons of Shem:
Elam, Asshur, Arphaxad, Lud and Aram.
The sons of Aram:ᵃ
Uz, Hul, Gether and Meshech.
18 Arphaxad was the father of Shelah, and Shelah the father of Eber.
19 Two sons were born to Eber:
One was named Peleg,ᵇ because in his time the earth was divided; his brother was named Joktan.
20 Joktan was the father of
Almodad, Sheleph, Hazarmaveth, Jerah, 21Hadoram, Uzal, Diklah, 22Obal,ᶜ Abimael, Sheba, 23Ophir, Havilah and Jobab. All these were sons of Joktan.

24 Shem, Arphaxad,ᵈ Shelah,
25 Eber, Peleg, Reu,
26 Serug, Nahor, Terah
27 and Abram (that is, Abraham).

The Family of Abraham
28 The sons of Abraham:
Isaac and Ishmael.

Descendants of Hagar
29 These were their descendants:
Nebaioth the firstborn of Ishmael, Kedar, Adbeel, Mibsam, 30Mishma, Dumah, Massa, Hadad, Tema, 31Jetur, Naphish and Kedemah. These were the sons of Ishmael.

Descendants of Keturah
32 The sons born to Keturah, Abra-ham's concubine:
Zimran, Jokshan, Medan, Midian, Ishbak and Shuah.

The sons of Jokshan:
Sheba and Dedan.
33 The sons of Midian:
Ephah, Epher, Hanoch, Abida and Eldaah.
All these were descendants of Ketu-rah.

Descendants of Sarah
34 Abraham was the father of Isaac.
The sons of Isaac:
Esau and Israel.

Esau's Sons
35 The sons of Esau:
Eliphaz, Reuel, Jeush, Jalam and Korah.
36 The sons of Eliphaz:
Teman, Omar, Zepho,ᵉ Gatam and Kenaz;
by Timna: Amalek.ᶠ
37 The sons of Reuel:
Nahath, Zerah, Shammah and Mizzah.

The People of Seir in Edom
38 The sons of Seir:
Lotan, Shobal, Zibeon, Anah, Di-shon, Ezer and Dishan.
39 The sons of Lotan:
Hori and Homam. Timna was Lo-tan's sister.
40 The sons of Shobal:
Alvan,ᵍ Manahath, Ebal, Shepho and Onam.
The sons of Zibeon:
Aiah and Anah.
41 The son of Anah:
Dishon.
The sons of Dishon:
Hemdan,ʰ Eshban, Ithran and Ke-ran.
42 The sons of Ezer:
Bilhan, Zaavan and Akan.ⁱ

ᵃ 17 One Hebrew manuscript and some Septuagint manuscripts (see also Gen. 10:23); most Hebrew manuscripts do not have this line.   ᵇ 19 Peleg means division.   ᶜ 22 Some Hebrew manuscripts and Syriac (see also Gen. 10:28); most Hebrew manuscripts Ebal   ᵈ 24 Hebrew; some Septuagint manuscripts Arphaxad, Cainan (see also note at Gen. 11:10)   ᵉ 36 Many Hebrew manuscripts, some Septuagint manuscripts and Syriac (see also Gen. 36:11); most Hebrew manuscripts Zephi   ᶠ 36 Some Septuagint manuscripts (see also Gen. 36:12); Hebrew Gatam, Kenaz, Timna and Amalek   ᵍ 40 Many Hebrew manuscripts and some Septuagint manuscripts (see also Gen. 36:23); most Hebrew manuscripts Alian   ʰ 41 Many Hebrew manuscripts and some Septuagint manuscripts (see also Gen. 36:26); most Hebrew manuscripts Hamran   ⁱ 42 Many Hebrew and Septuagint manuscripts (see also Gen. 36:27); most Hebrew manuscripts Zaavan, Jaakan

The sons of Dishan[a]:
Uz and Aran.

The Rulers of Edom

43 These were the kings who reigned in Edom before any Israelite king reigned[b]:
Bela son of Beor, whose city was named Dinhabah.

44 When Bela died, Jobab son of Zerah from Bozrah succeeded him as king.

45 When Jobab died, Husham from the land of the Temanites succeeded him as king.

46 When Husham died, Hadad son of Bedad, who defeated Midian in the country of Moab, succeeded him as king. His city was named Avith.

47 When Hadad died, Samlah from Masrekah succeeded him as king.

48 When Samlah died, Shaul from Rehoboth on the river[c] succeeded him as king.

49 When Shaul died, Baal-Hanan son of Acbor succeeded him as king.

50 When Baal-Hanan died, Hadad succeeded him as king. His city was named Pau,[d] and his wife's name was Mehetabel daughter of Matred, the daughter of Me-Zahab. 51 Hadad also died.

The chiefs of Edom were:
Timna, Alvah, Jetheth, 52 Oholibamah, Elah, Pinon, 53 Kenaz, Teman, Mibzar, 54 Magdiel and Iram. These were the chiefs of Edom.

Israel's Sons

2 These were the sons of Israel:
Reuben, Simeon, Levi, Judah, Issachar, Zebulun, 2 Dan, Joseph, Benjamin, Naphtali, Gad and Asher.

Judah

To Hezron's Sons

3 The sons of Judah:
Er, Onan and Shelah. These three were born to him by a Canaanite woman, the daughter of Shua. Er, Judah's firstborn, was wicked in the LORD's sight; so the LORD put him to death. 4 Tamar, Judah's daughter-in-law, bore him Perez and Zerah. Judah had five sons in all.

5 The sons of Perez:
Hezron and Hamul.

6 The sons of Zerah:
Zimri, Ethan, Heman, Calcol and Darda[e]—five in all.

7 The son of Carmi:
Achar,[f] who brought trouble on Israel by violating the ban on taking devoted things.[g]

8 The son of Ethan:
Azariah.

9 The sons born to Hezron were:
Jerahmeel, Ram and Caleb.[h]

From Ram Son of Hezron

10 Ram was the father of Amminadab, and Amminadab the father of Nahshon, the leader of the people of Judah. 11 Nahshon was the father of Salmon,[i] Salmon the father of Boaz, 12 Boaz the father of Obed and Obed the father of Jesse.

13 Jesse was the father of Eliab his firstborn; the second son was Abinadab, the third Shimea, 14 the fourth Nethanel, the fifth Raddai, 15 the sixth Ozem and the seventh David. 16 Their sisters were Zeruiah and Abigail. Zeruiah's three sons were Abishai, Joab and Asahel. 17 Abigail was the mother

a 42 Hebrew Dishon, a variant of Dishan   b 43 Or before an Israelite king reigned over them   c 48 Possibly the Euphrates   d 50 Many Hebrew manuscripts, some Septuagint manuscripts, Vulgate and Syriac (see also Gen. 36:39); most Hebrew manuscripts Pai   e 6 Many Hebrew manuscripts, some Septuagint manuscripts and Syriac (see also 1 Kings 4:31); most Hebrew manuscripts Dara   f 7 Achar means trouble; Achar is called Achan in Joshua.   g 7 The Hebrew term refers to the irrevocable giving over of things or persons to the LORD, often by totally destroying them.   h 9 Hebrew Kelubai, a variant of Caleb   i 11 Septuagint (see also Ruth 4:21); Hebrew Salma of Amasa, whose father was Jether the Ishmaelite.

Caleb Son of Hezron

¹⁸ Caleb son of Hezron had children by his wife Azubah (and by Jerioth). These were her sons: Jesher, Shobab and Ardon. ¹⁹ When Azubah died, Caleb married Ephrath, who bore him Hur. ²⁰ Hur was the father of Uri, and Uri the father of Bezalel.

²¹ Later, Hezron lay with the daughter of Makir the father of Gilead (he had married her when he was sixty years old), and she bore him Segub. ²² Segub was the father of Jair, who controlled twenty-three towns in Gilead. ²³ (But Geshur and Aram captured Havvoth Jair,ᵃ as well as Kenath with its surrounding settlements—sixty towns.) All these were descendants of Makir the father of Gilead.

²⁴ After Hezron died in Caleb Ephrathah, Abijah the wife of Hezron bore him Ashhur the fatherᵇ of Tekoa.

Jerahmeel Son of Hezron

²⁵ The sons of Jerahmeel the firstborn of Hezron:
Ram his firstborn, Bunah, Oren, Ozem andᶜ Ahijah. ²⁶ Jerahmeel had another wife, whose name was Atarah; she was the mother of Onam.

²⁷ The sons of Ram the firstborn of Jerahmeel:
Maaz, Jamin and Eker.

²⁸ The sons of Onam:
Shammai and Jada.

The sons of Shammai:
Nadab and Abishur.

²⁹ Abishur's wife was named Abihail, who bore him Ahban and Molid.

³⁰ The sons of Nadab:
Seled and Appaim. Seled died without children.

³¹ The son of Appaim:
Ishi, who was the father of Sheshan.

Sheshan was the father of Ahlai.

³² The sons of Jada, Shammai's brother:
Jether and Jonathan. Jether died without children.

³³ The sons of Jonathan:
Peleth and Zaza.

These were the descendants of Jerahmeel.

³⁴ Sheshan had no sons—only daughters.

He had an Egyptian servant named Jarha. ³⁵ Sheshan gave his daughter in marriage to his servant Jarha, and she bore him Attai.

³⁶ Attai was the father of Nathan,
Nathan the father of Zabad,
³⁷ Zabad the father of Ephlal,
Ephlal the father of Obed,
³⁸ Obed the father of Jehu,
Jehu the father of Azariah,
³⁹ Azariah the father of Helez,
Helez the father of Eleasah,
⁴⁰ Eleasah the father of Sismai,
Sismai the father of Shallum,
⁴¹ Shallum the father of Jekamiah,
and Jekamiah the father of Elishama.

The Clans of Caleb

⁴² The sons of Caleb the brother of Jerahmeel:
Mesha his firstborn, who was the father of Ziph, and his son Mareshah,ᵈ who was the father of Hebron.

⁴³ The sons of Hebron:
Korah, Tappuah, Rekem and Shema. ⁴⁴ Shema was the father of Raham, and Raham the father of Jorkeam. Rekem was the father of Shammai. ⁴⁵ The son of Shammai was Maon, and Maon was the father of Beth Zur.

⁴⁶ Caleb's concubine Ephah was the

ᵃ 23 Or captured the settlements of Jair   ᵇ 24 Father may mean civic leader or military leader; also in verses 42, 45, 49-52 and possibly elsewhere.   ᶜ 25 Or Oren and Ozem, by   ᵈ 42 The meaning of the Hebrew for this phrase is uncertain.

mother of Haran, Moza and Gazez. Haran was the father of Gazez.

47 The sons of Jahdai:

Regem, Jotham, Geshan, Pelet, Ephah and Shaaph.

48 Caleb's concubine Maacah was the mother of Sheber and Tirhanah. 49 She also gave birth to Shaaph the father of Madmannah and to Sheva the father of Macbenah and Gibea. Caleb's daughter was Acsah. 50 These were the descendants of Caleb.

The sons of Hur the firstborn of Ephrathah:

Shobal the father of Kiriath Jearim, 51 Salma the father of Bethlehem, and Hareph the father of Beth Gader.

52 The descendants of Shobal the father of Kiriath Jearim were:

Haroeh, half the Manahathites, 53 and the clans of Kiriath Jearim: the Ithrites, Puthites, Shumathites and Mishraites. From these descended the Zorathites and Eshtaolites.

54 The descendants of Salma:

Bethlehem, the Netophathites, Atroth Beth Joab, half the Manahathites, the Zorites, 55 and the clans of scribes[a] who lived at Jabez: the Tirathites, Shimeathites and Sucathites. These are the Kenites who came from Hammath, the father of the house of Recab.[b]

The Sons of David

3 These were the sons of David born to him in Hebron:

The firstborn was Amnon the son of Ahinoam of Jezreel;

the second, Daniel the son of Abigail of Carmel;

2 the third, Absalom the son of Maacah daughter of Talmai king of Geshur;

the fourth, Adonijah the son of Haggith;

3 the fifth, Shephatiah the son of Abital;

and the sixth, Ithream, by his wife Eglah.

4 These six were born to David in Hebron, where he reigned seven years and six months.

David reigned in Jerusalem thirty-three years, 5 and these were the children born to him there:

Shammua,[c] Shobab, Nathan and Solomon. These four were by Bathsheba[d] daughter of Ammiel. 6 There were also Ibhar, Elishua,[e] Eliphelet, 7 Nogah, Nepheg, Japhia, 8 Elishama, Eliada and Eliphelet—nine in all. 9 All these were the sons of David, besides his sons by his concubines. And Tamar was their sister.

The Kings of Judah

10 Solomon's son was Rehoboam,

Abijah his son,

Asa his son,

Jehoshaphat his son,

11 Jehoram[f] his son,

Ahaziah his son,

Joash his son,

12 Amaziah his son,

Azariah his son,

Jotham his son,

13 Ahaz his son,

Hezekiah his son,

Manasseh his son,

14 Amon his son,

Josiah his son.

15 The sons of Josiah:

Johanan the firstborn,

Jehoiakim the second son,

Zedekiah the third,

Shallum the fourth.

---

16 The successors of Jehoiakim:
Jehoiachin[a] his son,
and Zedekiah.

The Royal Line After the Exile

17 The descendants of Jehoiachin the captive:
Shealtiel his son, 18 Malkiram, Pedaiah, Shenazzar, Jekamiah, Hoshama and Nedabiah.

19 The sons of Pedaiah:
Zerubbabel and Shimei.
The sons of Zerubbabel:
Meshullam and Hananiah.
Shelomith was their sister.

20 There were also five others:
Hashubah, Ohel, Berekiah, Hasadiah and Jushab-Hesed.

21 The descendants of Hananiah:
Pelatiah and Jeshaiah, and the sons of Rephaiah, of Arnan, of Obadiah and of Shecaniah.

22 The descendants of Shecaniah:
Shemaiah and his sons:
Hattush, Igal, Bariah, Neariah and Shaphat—six in all.

23 The sons of Neariah:
Elioenai, Hizkiah and Azrikam—three in all.

24 The sons of Elioenai:
Hodaviah, Eliashib, Pelaiah, Akkub, Johanan, Delaiah and Anani—seven in all.

Other Clans of Judah

4 The descendants of Judah:
Perez, Hezron, Carmi, Hur and Shobal.

2 Reaiah son of Shobal was the father of Jahath, and Jahath the father of Ahumai and Lahad. These were the clans of the Zorathites.

3 These were the sons[b] of Etam:
Jezreel, Ishma and Idbash. Their sister was named Hazzelelponi.
4 Penuel was the father of Gedor, and Ezer the father of Hushah.

These were the descendants of Hur, the firstborn of Ephrathah and father[c] of Bethlehem.

5 Ashhur the father of Tekoa had two wives, Helah and Naarah.

6 Naarah bore him Ahuzzam, Hepher, Temeni and Haahashtari. These were the descendants of Naarah.

7 The sons of Helah:
Zereth, Zohar, Ethnan, 8 and Koz, who was the father of Anub and Hazzobebah and of the clans of Aharhel son of Harum.

Praying 1 Chronicles 4:10

God, bless me and enlarge my sphere of influence; be with me and deliver me from evil.

9 Jabez was more honorable than his brothers. His mother had named him Jabez,[d] saying, "I gave birth to him in pain." 10 Jabez cried out to the God of Israel, "Oh, that you would bless me and enlarge my territory! Let your hand be with me, and keep me from harm so that I will be free from pain." And God granted his request.

11 Kelub, Shuhah's brother, was the father of Mehir, who was the father of Eshton. 12 Eshton was the father of Beth Rapha, Paseah and Tehinnah the father of Ir Nahash.[e] These were the men of Recah.

13 The sons of Kenaz:
Othniel and Seraiah.
The sons of Othniel:
Hathath and Meonothai.[f] 14 Meonothai was the father of Ophrah.
Seraiah was the father of Joab, the father of Ge Harashim.[g] It was called this because its people were craftsmen.

15 The sons of Caleb son of Jephunneh:

---

[a] *16 Hebrew* Jeconiah, *a variant of* Jehoiachin; *also in verse 17*   [b] *3 Some Septuagint manuscripts (see also Vulgate); Hebrew* father   [c] *4* Father *may mean* civic leader *or* military leader; *also in verses 12, 14, 17, 18 and possibly elsewhere.*   [d] *9* Jabez *sounds like the Hebrew for* pain.   [e] *12 Or* of the city of Nahash   [f] *13 Some Septuagint manuscripts and Vulgate; Hebrew does not have* and Meonothai.   [g] *14* Ge Harashim *means* valley of craftsmen.

Be Bold to Ask

READ AND CONSIDER: 1 CHRONICLES 4:9-10

"Jabez cried out to the God of Israel, 'Oh, that you would bless me and enlarge my territory! Let your hand be with me, and keep me from harm so that I will be free from pain.' And God granted his request" (1 Chronicles 4:10).

Apart from these two verses, Jabez doesn't show up anywhere else in Scripture. Yet his brief mention here left a lasting impression. He prayed boldly, and then "God granted his request."

Jabez, whose name sounded like the Hebrew word for "pain," made four requests: for God's blessing ("bless me"), for God's provision ("enlarge my territory"), for God's presence ("let your hand be with me"), and for God's protection ("keep me from harm"). All of these things are what God wants for us. It is God's pleasure to bless us and provide for us, to be with us and protect us. But He wants us to pray and ask. And so often we don't. Too often we think we don't deserve His blessings or that it is being selfish to ask. Sometimes we pursue things in our own strength and fail to recognize God's goodness in wanting to be our provider. Often we don't want to seem as if we are asking for too much, as if God is limited in what He has to give.

If you have ever had thoughts like that, consider the words of Jesus when He said, "Your Father has been pleased to give you the kingdom" (Luke 12:32). That sounds like He wants to give us more than we realize.

Have you ever prayed boldly like Jabez did? If not, start by thanking God for all He has already given you and then ask for the desires of your heart. Ask Him to bless you so you can serve His purposes and bless others.

Don't worry that in asking boldly you will ask for too much. God is not going to give you something that is not good for you or before you are ready to receive it. He will always answer your prayers according to His will and in His perfect timing.

Iru, Elah and Naam.
The son of Elah:
Kenaz.
16 The sons of Jehallelel:
Ziph, Ziphah, Tiria and Asarel.
17 The sons of Ezrah:
Jether, Mered, Epher and Jalon. One of Mered's wives gave birth to Miriam, Shammai and Ishbah the father of Eshtemoa. 18 (His Judean wife gave birth to Jered the father of Gedor, Heber the father of Soco, and Jekuthiel the father of Zanoah.) These were the children of Pharaoh's daughter Bithiah, whom Mered had married.
19 The sons of Hodiah's wife, the sister of Naham:

the father of Keilah the Garmite, and Eshtemoa the Maacathite.
20 The sons of Shimon:
Amnon, Rinnah, Ben-Hanan and Tilon.
The descendants of Ishi:
Zoheth and Ben-Zoheth.
21 The sons of Shelah son of Judah:
Er the father of Lecah, Laadah the father of Mareshah and the clans of the linen workers at Beth Ashbea, 22 Jokim, the men of Cozeba, and Joash and Saraph, who ruled in Moab and Jashubi Lehem. (These records are from ancient times.) 23 They were the potters who lived at Netaim and Gederah; they stayed there and worked for the king.

Simeon

24 The descendants of Simeon:

Nemuel, Jamin, Jarib, Zerah and Shaul;

25 Shallum was Shaul's son, Mibsam his son and Mishma his son.

26 The descendants of Mishma:

Hammuel his son, Zaccur his son and Shimei his son.

27 Shimei had sixteen sons and six daughters, but his brothers did not have many children; so their entire clan did not become as numerous as the people of Judah. 28 They lived in Beersheba, Moladah, Hazar Shual, 29 Bilhah, Ezem, Tolad, 30 Bethuel, Hormah, Ziklag, 31 Beth Marcaboth, Hazar Susim, Beth Biri and Shaaraim. These were their towns until the reign of David. 32 Their surrounding villages were Etam, Ain, Rimmon, Token and Ashan—five towns— 33 and all the villages around these towns as far as Baalath.a These were their settlements. And they kept a genealogical record.

34 Meshobab, Jamlech, Joshah son of Amaziah, 35 Joel, Jehu son of Joshibiah, the son of Seraiah, the son of Asiel, 36 also Elioenai, Jaakobah, Jeshohaiah, Asaiah, Adiel, Jesimiel, Benaiah, 37 and Ziza son of Shiphi, the son of Allon, the son of Jedaiah, the son of Shimri, the son of Shemaiah.

38 The men listed above by name were leaders of their clans. Their families increased greatly, 39 and they went to the outskirts of Gedor to the east of the valley in search of pasture for their flocks. 40 They found rich, good pasture, and the land was spacious, peaceful and quiet. Some Hamites had lived there formerly.

41 The men whose names were listed came in the days of Hezekiah king of Judah. They attacked the Hamites in their dwellings and also the Meunites who were there and completely destroyedb them, as is evident to this day. Then they settled in their place, because there was pasture for their flocks. 42 And five hundred of these Simeonites, led by Pelatiah, Neariah, Rephaiah and Uzziel, the sons of Ishi, invaded the hill country of Seir. 43 They killed the remaining Amalekites who had escaped, and they have lived there to this day.

Reuben

5 The sons of Reuben the firstborn of Israel (he was the firstborn, but when he defiled his father's marriage bed, his rights as firstborn were given to the sons of Joseph son of Israel; so he could not be listed in the genealogical record in accordance with his birthright, 2 and though Judah was the strongest of his brothers and a ruler came from him, the rights of the firstborn belonged to Joseph)— 3 the sons of Reuben the firstborn of Israel:

Hanoch, Pallu, Hezron and Carmi.

4 The descendants of Joel:

Shemaiah his son, Gog his son, Shimei his son, 5 Micah his son, Reaiah his son, Baal his son,

6 and Beerah his son, whom Tiglath-Pileserc king of Assyria took into exile. Beerah was a leader of the Reubenites.

7 Their relatives by clans, listed according to their genealogical records: Jeiel the chief, Zechariah, 8 and Bela son of Azaz, the son of Shema, the son of Joel. They settled in the area from Aroer to Nebo and Baal Meon. 9 To the east they occupied the land up to the edge of the desert that extends to the Euphrates River, because their livestock had increased in Gilead.

10 During Saul's reign they waged war against the Hagrites, who were defeated at their hands; they occupied the dwellings of the Hagrites throughout the entire region east of Gilead.

a 33 Some Septuagint manuscripts (see also Joshua 19:8); Hebrew Baal   b 41 The Hebrew term refers to the irrevocable giving over of things or persons to the Lord, often by totally destroying them.   c 6 Hebrew Tilgath-Pilneser, a variant of Tiglath-Pileser; also in verse 26

Gad

11 The Gadites lived next to them in Bashan, as far as Salecah:

12 Joel was the chief, Shapham the second, then Janai and Shaphat, in Bashan.

13 Their relatives, by families, were:
Michael, Meshullam, Sheba, Jorai, Jacan, Zia and Eber—seven in all.

14 These were the sons of Abihail son of Huri, the son of Jaroah, the son of Gilead, the son of Michael, the son of Jeshishai, the son of Jahdo, the son of Buz.

15 Ahi son of Abdiel, the son of Guni, was head of their family.

16 The Gadites lived in Gilead, in Bashan and its outlying villages, and on all the pasturelands of Sharon as far as they extended.

17 All these were entered in the genealogical records during the reigns of Jotham king of Judah and Jeroboam king of Israel.

18 The Reubenites, the Gadites and the half-tribe of Manasseh had 44,760 men ready for military service—able-bodied men who could handle shield and sword, who could use a bow, and who were trained for battle. 19 They waged war against the Hagrites, Jetur, Naphish and Nodab. 20 They were helped in fighting them, and God handed the Hagrites and all their allies over to them, because they cried out to him during the battle. He answered their prayers, because they trusted in him. 21 They seized the livestock of the Hagrites—fifty thousand camels, two hundred fifty thousand sheep and two thousand donkeys. They also took one hundred thousand people captive, 22 and many others fell slain, because the battle was God's. And they occupied the land until the exile.

The Half-Tribe of Manasseh

23 The people of the half-tribe of Manasseh were numerous; they settled in the land from Bashan to Baal Hermon, that is, to Senir (Mount Hermon).

24 These were the heads of their families: Epher, Ishi, Eliel, Azriel, Jeremiah, Hodaviah and Jahdiel. They were brave warriors, famous men, and heads of their families. 25 But they were unfaithful to the God of their fathers and prostituted themselves to the gods of the peoples of the land, whom God had destroyed before them. 26 So the God of Israel stirred up the spirit of Pul king of Assyria (that is, Tiglath-Pileser king of Assyria), who took the Reubenites, the Gadites and the half-tribe of Manasseh into exile. He took them to Halah, Habor, Hara and the river of Gozan, where they are to this day.

Levi

6 The sons of Levi:
Gershon, Kohath and Merari.

2 The sons of Kohath:
Amram, Izhar, Hebron and Uzziel.

3 The children of Amram:
Aaron, Moses and Miriam.

The sons of Aaron:
Nadab, Abihu, Eleazar and Ithamar.

4 Eleazar was the father of Phinehas,
Phinehas the father of Abishua,

5 Abishua the father of Bukki,
Bukki the father of Uzzi,

6 Uzzi the father of Zerahiah,
Zerahiah the father of Meraioth,

7 Meraioth the father of Amariah,
Amariah the father of Ahitub,

8 Ahitub the father of Zadok,
Zadok the father of Ahimaaz,

9 Ahimaaz the father of Azariah,
Azariah the father of Johanan,

10 Johanan the father of Azariah (it was he who served as priest in the temple Solomon built in Jerusalem),

11 Azariah the father of Amariah,
Amariah the father of Ahitub,

12 Ahitub the father of Zadok,
Zadok the father of Shallum,

13 Shallum the father of Hilkiah,
Hilkiah the father of Azariah,

¹⁴ Azariah the father of Seraiah,
and Seraiah the father of Jehoza-
dak.

¹⁵ Jehozadak was deported when the
LORD sent Judah and Jerusalem into
exile by the hand of Nebuchadnezzar.

¹⁶ The sons of Levi:
Gershon,ᵃ Kohath and Merari.
¹⁷ These are the names of the sons of
Gershon:
Libni and Shimei.
¹⁸ The sons of Kohath:
Amram, Izhar, Hebron and Uzziel.
¹⁹ The sons of Merari:
Mahli and Mushi.
These are the clans of the Levites
listed according to their fathers:
²⁰ Of Gershon:
Libni his son, Jehath his son,
Zimmah his son, ²¹Joah his son,
Iddo his son, Zerah his son
and Jeatherai his son.
²² The descendants of Kohath:
Amminadab his son, Korah his
son,
Assir his son, ²³Elkanah his son,
Ebiasaph his son, Assir his son,
²⁴ Tahath his son, Uriel his son,
Uzziah his son and Shaul his
son.
²⁵ The descendants of Elkanah:
Amasai, Ahimoth,
²⁶ Elkanah his son,ᵇ Zophai his son,
Nahath his son, ²⁷Eliab his son,
Jeroham his son, Elkanah his son
and Samuel his son.ᶜ
²⁸ The sons of Samuel:
Joelᵈ the firstborn
and Abijah the second son.
²⁹ The descendants of Merari:
Mahli, Libni his son,
Shimei his son, Uzzah his son,
³⁰ Shimea his son, Haggiah his son
and Asaiah his son.

The Temple Musicians

³¹ These are the men David put in
charge of the music in the house of the
LORD after the ark came to rest there.
³² They ministered with music before the
tabernacle, the Tent of Meeting, until Solomon built the temple of the LORD in
Jerusalem. They performed their duties
according to the regulations laid down
for them.
³³ Here are the men who served,
together with their sons:
From the Kohathites:
Heman, the musician,
the son of Joel, the son of Samuel,
³⁴ the son of Elkanah, the son of Jero-
ham,
the son of Eliel, the son of Toah,
³⁵ the son of Zuph, the son of Elka-
nah,
the son of Mahath, the son of
Amasai,
³⁶ the son of Elkanah, the son of Joel,
the son of Azariah, the son of
Zephaniah,
³⁷ the son of Tahath, the son of Assir,
the son of Ebiasaph, the son of Ko-
rah,
³⁸ the son of Izhar, the son of Ko-
hath,
the son of Levi, the son of Israel;
³⁹ and Heman's associate Asaph, who
served at his right hand:
Asaph son of Berekiah, the son of
Shimea,
⁴⁰ the son of Michael, the son of Baa-
seiah,ᵉ
the son of Malkijah, ⁴¹the son of
Ethni,
the son of Zerah, the son of Adaiah,
⁴² the son of Ethan, the son of Zim-
mah,
the son of Shimei, ⁴³the son of Jahath,

ᵃ *16* Hebrew *Gershom*, a variant of *Gershon*; also in verses 17, 20, 43, 62 and 71   ᵇ *26* Some Hebrew manuscripts, Septuagint
and Syriac; most Hebrew manuscripts *Ahimoth ²⁶and Elkanah. The sons of Elkanah:*   ᶜ*27* Some Septuagint manuscripts (see
also 1 Samuel 1:19,20 and 1 Chron. 6:33,34); Hebrew does not have *and Samuel his son.*   ᵈ*28* Some Septuagint manuscripts
and Syriac (see also 1 Samuel 8:2 and 1 Chron. 6:33); Hebrew does not have *Joel.*   ᵉ*40* Most Hebrew manuscripts; some
Hebrew manuscripts, one Septuagint manuscript and Syriac *Maaseiah*

the son of Gershon, the son of
Levi;
44 and from their associates, the Merarites, at his left hand:
Ethan son of Kishi, the son of
Abdi,
the son of Malluch, 45 the son of
Hashabiah,
the son of Amaziah, the son of
Hilkiah,
46 the son of Amzi, the son of Bani,
the son of Shemer, 47 the son of
Mahli,
the son of Mushi, the son of
Merari,
the son of Levi.

48 Their fellow Levites were assigned
to all the other duties of the tabernacle,
the house of God. 49 But Aaron and his descendants were the ones who presented
offerings on the altar of burnt offering
and on the altar of incense in connection
with all that was done in the Most Holy
Place, making atonement for Israel, in accordance with all that Moses the servant
of God had commanded.

50 These were the descendants of
Aaron:
Eleazar his son, Phinehas his son,
Abishua his son, 51 Bukki his son,
Uzzi his son, Zerahiah his son,
52 Meraioth his son, Amariah his
son,
Ahitub his son, 53 Zadok his son
and Ahimaaz his son.

54 These were the locations of their
settlements allotted as their territory
(they were assigned to the descendants
of Aaron who were from the Kohathite
clan, because the first lot was for them):
55 They were given Hebron in
Judah with its surrounding pasturelands. 56 But the fields and villages
around the city were given to Caleb
son of Jephunneh.

57 So the descendants of Aaron
were given Hebron (a city of refuge),
and Libnah,[a] Jattir, Eshtemoa, 58 Hi-
len, Debir, 59 Ashan, Juttah[b] and Beth
Shemesh, together with their pasturelands. 60 And from the tribe of
Benjamin they were given Gibeon,[c]
Geba, Alemeth and Anathoth, together with their pasturelands.
   These towns, which were distributed among the Kohathite clans,
were thirteen in all.
61 The rest of Kohath's descendants
were allotted ten towns from the clans of
half the tribe of Manasseh.
62 The descendants of Gershon, clan by
clan, were allotted thirteen towns from
the tribes of Issachar, Asher and Naphtali,
and from the part of the tribe of Manasseh that is in Bashan.
63 The descendants of Merari, clan by
clan, were allotted twelve towns from the
tribes of Reuben, Gad and Zebulun.
64 So the Israelites gave the Levites
these towns and their pasturelands.
65 From the tribes of Judah, Simeon and
Benjamin they allotted the previously
named towns.
66 Some of the Kohathite clans were
given as their territory towns from the
tribe of Ephraim.
67 In the hill country of Ephraim
they were given Shechem (a city of
refuge), and Gezer,[d] 68 Jokmeam, Beth
Horon, 69 Aijalon and Gath Rimmon,
together with their pasturelands.
70 And from half the tribe of Manasseh the Israelites gave Aner and
Bileam, together with their pasturelands, to the rest of the Kohathite clans.

71 The Gershonites received the following:
From the clan of the half-tribe of
Manasseh
they received Golan in Bashan

---

a 57 See Joshua 21:13; Hebrew *given the cities of refuge: Hebron, Libnah.* b 59 Syriac (see also Septuagint and Joshua 21:16);
Hebrew does not have *Juttah.* c 60 See Joshua 21:17; Hebrew does not have *Gibeon.* d 67 See Joshua 21:21; Hebrew *given
the cities of refuge: Shechem, Gezer.*

and also Ashtaroth, together with their pasturelands;

72 from the tribe of Issachar they received Kedesh, Daberath, 73 Ramoth and Anem, together with their pasturelands;

74 from the tribe of Asher they received Mashal, Abdon, 75 Hukok and Rehob, together with their pasturelands;

76 and from the tribe of Naphtali they received Kedesh in Galilee, Hammon and Kiriathaim, together with their pasturelands.

77 The Merarites (the rest of the Levites) received the following:

From the tribe of Zebulun they received Jokneam, Kartah,ª Rimmono and Tabor, together with their pasturelands;

78 from the tribe of Reuben across the Jordan east of Jericho they received Bezer in the desert, Jahzah, 79 Kedemoth and Mephaath, together with their pasturelands;

80 and from the tribe of Gad they received Ramoth in Gilead, Mahanaim, 81 Heshbon and Jazer, together with their pasturelands.

Issachar

7 The sons of Issachar:
Tola, Puah, Jashub and Shimron—four in all.

2 The sons of Tola:
Uzzi, Rephaiah, Jeriel, Jahmai, Ibsam and Samuel—heads of their families. During the reign of David, the descendants of Tola listed as fighting men in their genealogy numbered 22,600.

3 The son of Uzzi:
Izrahiah.

The sons of Izrahiah:
Michael, Obadiah, Joel and Isshiah. All five of them were chiefs. 4 According to their family genealogy,

they had 36,000 men ready for battle, for they had many wives and children.

5 The relatives who were fighting men belonging to all the clans of Issachar, as listed in their genealogy, were 87,000 in all.

Benjamin

6 Three sons of Benjamin:
Bela, Beker and Jediael.

7 The sons of Bela:
Ezbon, Uzzi, Uzziel, Jerimoth and Iri, heads of families—five in all. Their genealogical record listed 22,034 fighting men.

8 The sons of Beker:
Zemirah, Joash, Eliezer, Elioenai, Omri, Jeremoth, Abijah, Anathoth and Alemeth. All these were the sons of Beker. 9 Their genealogical record listed the heads of families and 20,200 fighting men.

10 The son of Jediael:
Bilhan.

The sons of Bilhan:
Jeush, Benjamin, Ehud, Kenaanah, Zethan, Tarshish and Ahishahar. 11 All these sons of Jediael were heads of families. There were 17,200 fighting men ready to go out to war. 12 The Shuppites and Huppites were the descendants of Ir, and the Hushites the descendants of Aher.

Naphtali

13 The sons of Naphtali:
Jahziel, Guni, Jezer and Shillemᵇ—the descendants of Bilhah.

Manasseh

14 The descendants of Manasseh:
Asriel was his descendant through his Aramean concubine. She gave birth to Makir the father of Gilead. 15 Makir took a wife from among the Huppites and Shuppites. His sister's name was Maacah.

---

a 77 See Septuagint and Joshua 21:34; Hebrew does not have *Jokneam, Kartah*. b 13 Some Hebrew and Septuagint manuscripts (see also Gen. 46:24 and Num. 26:49); most Hebrew manuscripts *Shallum*

Another descendant was named Zelophehad, who had only daughters.

¹⁶Makir's wife Maacah gave birth to a son and named him Peresh. His brother was named Sheresh, and his sons were Ulam and Rakem. ¹⁷The son of Ulam:

Bedan.

These were the sons of Gilead son of Makir, the son of Manasseh. ¹⁸His sister Hammoleketh gave birth to Ishhod, Abiezer and Mahlah. ¹⁹The sons of Shemida were:

Ahian, Shechem, Likhi and Aniam.

Ephraim

²⁰The descendants of Ephraim:

Shuthelah, Bered his son,
Tahath his son, Eleadah his son,
Tahath his son, ²¹Zabad his son
and Shuthelah his son.

Ezer and Elead were killed by the native-born men of Gath, when they went down to seize their livestock. ²²Their father Ephraim mourned for them many days, and his relatives came to comfort him. ²³Then he lay with his wife again, and she became pregnant and gave birth to a son. He named him Beriah,ᵃ because there had been misfortune in his family. ²⁴His daughter was Sheerah, who built Lower and Upper Beth Horon as well as Uzzen Sheerah.

²⁵Rephah was his son, Resheph his son,ᵇ
Telah his son, Tahan his son,
²⁶Ladan his son, Ammihud his son,
Elishama his son, ²⁷Nun his son
and Joshua his son.

²⁸Their lands and settlements included Bethel and its surrounding villages, Naaran to the east, Gezer and its villages to the west, and Shechem and its villages all the way to Ayyah and its villages. ²⁹Along the borders of Manasseh were Beth Shan, Taanach, Megiddo and Dor, together with their villages. The descendants of Joseph son of Israel lived in these towns.

Asher

³⁰The sons of Asher:

Imnah, Ishvah, Ishvi and Beriah. Their sister was Serah.

³¹The sons of Beriah:

Heber and Malkiel, who was the father of Birzaith.

³²Heber was the father of Japhlet, Shomer and Hotham and of their sister Shua.

³³The sons of Japhlet:

Pasach, Bimhal and Ashvath. These were Japhlet's sons.

³⁴The sons of Shomer:

Ahi, Rohgah,ᶜ Hubbah and Aram.

³⁵The sons of his brother Helem:

Zophah, Imna, Shelesh and Amal.

³⁶The sons of Zophah:

Suah, Harnepher, Shual, Beri, Imrah, ³⁷Bezer, Hod, Shamma, Shilshah, Ithranᵈ and Beera.

³⁸The sons of Jether:

Jephunneh, Pispah and Ara.

³⁹The sons of Ulla:

Arah, Hanniel and Rizia.

⁴⁰All these were descendants of Asher—heads of families, choice men, brave warriors and outstanding leaders. The number of men ready for battle, as listed in their genealogy, was 26,000.

The Genealogy of Saul the Benjamite

8 Benjamin was the father of Bela his firstborn,

Ashbel the second son, Aharah the third,
²Nohah the fourth and Rapha the fifth.

³The sons of Bela were:

Addar, Gera, Abihud,ᵉ ⁴Abishua, Naaman, Ahoah, ⁵Gera, Shephuphan and Huram.

⁶These were the descendants of Ehud, who were heads of families

---

ᵃ 23 Beriah sounds like the Hebrew for misfortune.   ᵇ 25 Some Septuagint manuscripts; Hebrew does not have his son.
ᶜ 34 Or of his brother Shomer: Rohgah   ᵈ 37 Possibly a variant of Jether   ᵉ 3 Or Gera the father of Ehud

of those living in Geba and were deported to Manahath:

⁷Naaman, Ahijah, and Gera, who deported them and who was the father of Uzza and Ahihud.

⁸Sons were born to Shaharaim in Moab after he had divorced his wives Hushim and Baara. ⁹By his wife Hodesh he had Jobab, Zibia, Mesha, Malcam, ¹⁰Jeuz, Sakia and Mirmah. These were his sons, heads of families. ¹¹By Hushim he had Abitub and Elpaal.

¹²The sons of Elpaal:

Eber, Misham, Shemed (who built Ono and Lod with its surrounding villages), ¹³and Beriah and Shema, who were heads of families of those living in Aijalon and who drove out the inhabitants of Gath.

¹⁴Ahio, Shashak, Jeremoth, ¹⁵Zebadiah, Arad, Eder, ¹⁶Michael, Ishpah and Joha were the sons of Beriah.

¹⁷Zebadiah, Meshullam, Hizki, Heber, ¹⁸Ishmerai, Izliah and Jobab were the sons of Elpaal.

¹⁹Jakim, Zicri, Zabdi, ²⁰Elienai, Zillethai, Eliel, ²¹Adaiah, Beraiah and Shimrath were the sons of Shimei.

²²Ishpan, Eber, Eliel, ²³Abdon, Zicri, Hanan, ²⁴Hananiah, Elam, Anthothijah, ²⁵Iphdeiah and Penuel were the sons of Shashak.

²⁶Shamsherai, Shehariah, Athaliah, ²⁷Jaareshiah, Elijah and Zicri were the sons of Jeroham.

²⁸All these were heads of families, chiefs as listed in their genealogy, and they lived in Jerusalem.

²⁹Jeielᵃ the fatherᵇ of Gibeon lived in Gibeon.

His wife's name was Maacah, ³⁰and his firstborn son was Abdon, followed by Zur, Kish, Baal, Ner,ᶜ Nadab, ³¹Gedor, Ahio, Zeker ³²and Mikloth, who was the father of Shimeah. They too lived near their relatives in Jerusalem.

³³Ner was the father of Kish, Kish the father of Saul, and Saul the father of Jonathan, Malki-Shua, Abinadab and Esh-Baal.ᵈ

³⁴The son of Jonathan:

Merib-Baal,ᵉ who was the father of Micah.

³⁵The sons of Micah:

Pithon, Melech, Tarea and Ahaz.

³⁶Ahaz was the father of Jehoaddah, Jehoaddah was the father of Alemeth, Azmaveth and Zimri, and Zimri was the father of Moza. ³⁷Moza was the father of Binea; Raphah was his son, Eleasah his son and Azel his son.

³⁸Azel had six sons, and these were their names:

Azrikam, Bokeru, Ishmael, Sheariah, Obadiah and Hanan. All these were the sons of Azel.

³⁹The sons of his brother Eshek:

Ulam his firstborn, Jeush the second son and Eliphelet the third. ⁴⁰The sons of Ulam were brave warriors who could handle the bow. They had many sons and grandsons—150 in all.

All these were the descendants of Benjamin.

9 All Israel was listed in the genealogies recorded in the book of the kings of Israel.

The People in Jerusalem

The people of Judah were taken captive to Babylon because of their unfaithfulness. ²Now the first to resettle on their own property in their own towns were some Israelites, priests, Levites and temple servants.

³Those from Judah, from Benjamin, and from Ephraim and Manasseh who lived in Jerusalem were:

⁴Uthai son of Ammihud, the son of

Omri, the son of Imri, the son of Bani, a descendant of Perez son of Judah.

5 Of the Shilonites:

Asaiah the firstborn and his sons.

6 Of the Zerahites:

Jeuel.

The people from Judah numbered 690.

7 Of the Benjamites:

Sallu son of Meshullam, the son of Hodaviah, the son of Hassenuah;

8 Ibneiah son of Jeroham; Elah son of Uzzi, the son of Micri; and Meshullam son of Shephatiah, the son of Reuel, the son of Ibnijah.

9 The people from Benjamin, as listed in their genealogy, numbered 956. All these men were heads of their families.

10 Of the priests:

Jedaiah; Jehoiarib; Jakin;

11 Azariah son of Hilkiah, the son of Meshullam, the son of Zadok, the son of Meraioth, the son of Ahitub, the official in charge of the house of God;

12 Adaiah son of Jeroham, the son of Pashhur, the son of Malkijah; and Maasai son of Adiel, the son of Jahzerah, the son of Meshullam, the son of Meshillemith, the son of Immer.

13 The priests, who were heads of families, numbered 1,760. They were able men, responsible for ministering in the house of God.

14 Of the Levites:

Shemaiah son of Hasshub, the son of Azrikam, the son of Hashabiah, a Merarite; 15 Bakbakkar, Heresh, Galal and Mattaniah son of Mica, the son of Zicri, the son of Asaph; 16 Obadiah son of Shemaiah, the son of Galal, the son of Jeduthun; and Berekiah son of Asa, the son of Elkanah, who lived in the villages of the Netophathites.

17 The gatekeepers:

Shallum, Akkub, Talmon, Ahiman and their brothers, Shallum their chief 18 being stationed at the King's Gate on the east, up to the present time. These were the gatekeepers belonging to the camp of the Levites. 19 Shallum son of Kore, the son of Ebiasaph, the son of Korah, and his fellow gatekeepers from his family (the Korahites) were responsible for guarding the thresholds of the Tent[a] just as their fathers had been responsible for guarding the entrance to the dwelling of the LORD. 20 In earlier times Phinehas son of Eleazar was in charge of the gatekeepers, and the LORD was with him. 21 Zechariah son of Meshelemiah was the gatekeeper at the entrance to the Tent of Meeting.

22 Altogether, those chosen to be gatekeepers at the thresholds numbered 212. They were registered by genealogy in their villages. The gatekeepers had been assigned to their positions of trust by David and Samuel the seer. 23 They and their descendants were in charge of guarding the gates of the house of the LORD—the house called the Tent. 24 The gatekeepers were on the four sides: east, west, north and south. 25 Their brothers in their villages had to come from time to time and share their duties for seven-day periods. 26 But the four principal gatekeepers, who were Levites, were entrusted with the responsibility for the rooms and treasuries in the house of God. 27 They would spend the night stationed around the house of God, because they had to guard it; and they had charge of the key for opening it each morning.

28 Some of them were in charge of the articles used in the temple service; they counted them when they were brought in and when they were taken out. 29 Others were assigned to take care of the fur-

---

a 19 That is, the temple; also in verses 21 and 23

nishings and all the other articles of the sanctuary, as well as the flour and wine, and the oil, incense and spices. ³⁰But some of the priests took care of mixing the spices. ³¹A Levite named Mattithiah, the firstborn son of Shallum the Korahite, was entrusted with the responsibility for baking the offering bread. ³²Some of their Kohathite brothers were in charge of preparing for every Sabbath the bread set out on the table.

³³Those who were musicians, heads of Levite families, stayed in the rooms of the temple and were exempt from other duties because they were responsible for the work day and night.

³⁴All these were heads of Levite families, chiefs as listed in their genealogy, and they lived in Jerusalem.

The Genealogy of Saul

³⁵Jeiel the father[a] of Gibeon lived in Gibeon.

His wife's name was Maacah, ³⁶and his firstborn son was Abdon, followed by Zur, Kish, Baal, Ner, Nadab, ³⁷Gedor, Ahio, Zechariah and Mikloth. ³⁸Mikloth was the father of Shimeam. They too lived near their relatives in Jerusalem.

³⁹Ner was the father of Kish, Kish the father of Saul, and Saul the father of Jonathan, Malki-Shua, Abinadab and Esh-Baal.[b]

⁴⁰The son of Jonathan:
Merib-Baal,[c] who was the father of Micah.

⁴¹The sons of Micah:
Pithon, Melech, Tahrea and Ahaz.[d]

⁴²Ahaz was the father of Jadah, Jadah[e] was the father of Alemeth, Azmaveth and Zimri, and Zimri was the father of Moza. ⁴³Moza was the father of Binea; Rephaiah was his son, Eleasah his son and Azel his son.

⁴⁴Azel had six sons, and these were their names:

Azrikam, Bokeru, Ishmael, Sheariah, Obadiah and Hanan. These were the sons of Azel.

Saul Takes His Life

10 Now the Philistines fought against Israel; the Israelites fled before them, and many fell slain on Mount Gilboa. ²The Philistines pressed hard after Saul and his sons, and they killed his sons Jonathan, Abinadab and Malki-Shua. ³The fighting grew fierce around Saul, and when the archers overtook him, they wounded him.

⁴Saul said to his armor-bearer, "Draw your sword and run me through, or these uncircumcised fellows will come and abuse me."

But his armor-bearer was terrified and would not do it; so Saul took his own sword and fell on it. ⁵When the armor-bearer saw that Saul was dead, he too fell on his sword and died. ⁶So Saul and his three sons died, and all his house died together.

⁷When all the Israelites in the valley saw that the army had fled and that Saul and his sons had died, they abandoned their towns and fled. And the Philistines came and occupied them.

⁸The next day, when the Philistines came to strip the dead, they found Saul and his sons fallen on Mount Gilboa. ⁹They stripped him and took his head and his armor, and sent messengers throughout the land of the Philistines to proclaim the news among their idols and their people. ¹⁰They put his armor in the temple of their gods and hung up his head in the temple of Dagon.

¹¹When all the inhabitants of Jabesh Gilead heard of everything the Philistines had done to Saul, ¹²all their valiant men went and took the bodies of Saul and his sons and brought them to Jabesh. Then they buried their bones under the great tree in Jabesh, and they fasted seven days.

---

[a] *35 Father* may mean *civic leader* or *military leader.* [b] *39* Also known as *Ish-Bosheth* [c] *40* Also known as *Mephibosheth*
[d] *41* Vulgate and Syriac (see also Septuagint and 1 Chron. 8:35); Hebrew does not have *and Ahaz.* [e] *42* Some Hebrew manuscripts and Septuagint (see also 1 Chron. 8:36); most Hebrew manuscripts *Jarah, Jarah*

¹³Saul died because he was unfaithful to the Lord; he did not keep the word of the Lord and even consulted a medium for guidance, ¹⁴and did not inquire of the Lord. So the Lord put him to death and turned the kingdom over to David son of Jesse.

Praying 1 Chronicles 10:13-14

God, help me to always seek You and not any ungodly source.

David Becomes King Over Israel

11 All Israel came together to David at Hebron and said, "We are your own flesh and blood. ²In the past, even while Saul was king, you were the one who led Israel on their military campaigns. And the Lord your God said to you, 'You will shepherd my people Israel, and you will become their ruler.'"

³When all the elders of Israel had come to King David at Hebron, he made a compact with them at Hebron before the Lord, and they anointed David king over Israel, as the Lord had promised through Samuel.

David Conquers Jerusalem

⁴David and all the Israelites marched to Jerusalem (that is, Jebus). The Jebusites who lived there ⁵said to David, "You will not get in here." Nevertheless, David captured the fortress of Zion, the City of David.

⁶David had said, "Whoever leads the attack on the Jebusites will become commander-in-chief." Joab son of Zeruiah went up first, and so he received the command.

⁷David then took up residence in the fortress, and so it was called the City of David. ⁸He built up the city around it, from the supporting terraces[a] to the surrounding wall, while Joab restored the rest of the city. ⁹And David became more and more powerful, because the Lord Almighty was with him.

David's Mighty Men

¹⁰These were the chiefs of David's mighty men—they, together with all Israel, gave his kingship strong support to extend it over the whole land, as the Lord had promised— ¹¹this is the list of David's mighty men:

Jashobeam,[b] a Hacmonite, was chief of the officers[c]; he raised his spear against three hundred men, whom he killed in one encounter.

¹²Next to him was Eleazar son of Dodai the Ahohite, one of the three mighty men. ¹³He was with David at Pas Dammim when the Philistines gathered there for battle. At a place where there was a field full of barley, the troops fled from the Philistines. ¹⁴But they took their stand in the middle of the field. They defended it and struck the Philistines down, and the Lord brought about a great victory.

¹⁵Three of the thirty chiefs came down to David to the rock at the cave of Adullam, while a band of Philistines was encamped in the Valley of Rephaim. ¹⁶At that time David was in the stronghold, and the Philistine garrison was at Bethlehem. ¹⁷David longed for water and said, "Oh, that someone would get me a drink of water from the well near the gate of Bethlehem!" ¹⁸So the Three broke through the Philistine lines, drew water from the well near the gate of Bethlehem and carried it back to David. But he refused to drink it; instead, he poured it out before the Lord. ¹⁹"God forbid that I should do this!" he said. "Should I drink the blood of these men who went at the risk of their lives?" Because they risked their lives to bring it back, David would not drink it.

Such were the exploits of the three mighty men.

²⁰Abishai the brother of Joab was chief of the Three. He raised his spear against three hundred men, whom he killed, and so he became as famous as the Three. ²¹He

---

[a] 8 Or *the Millo* [b] 11 Possibly a variant of *Jashob-Baal* [c] 11 Or *Thirty*; some Septuagint manuscripts *Three* (see also 2 Samuel 23:8)

was doubly honored above the Three and became their commander, even though he was not included among them.

[22] Benaiah son of Jehoiada was a valiant fighter from Kabzeel, who performed great exploits. He struck down two of Moab's best men. He also went down into a pit on a snowy day and killed a lion. [23] And he struck down an Egyptian who was seven and a half feet[a] tall. Although the Egyptian had a spear like a weaver's rod in his hand, Benaiah went against him with a club. He snatched the spear from the Egyptian's hand and killed him with his own spear. [24] Such were the exploits of Benaiah son of Jehoiada; he too was as famous as the three mighty men. [25] He was held in greater honor than any of the Thirty, but he was not included among the Three. And David put him in charge of his bodyguard.

[26] The mighty men were:

Asahel the brother of Joab,
Elhanan son of Dodo from Bethlehem,
[27] Shammoth the Harorite,
Helez the Pelonite,
[28] Ira son of Ikkesh from Tekoa,
Abiezer from Anathoth,
[29] Sibbecai the Hushathite,
Ilai the Ahohite,
[30] Maharai the Netophathite,
Heled son of Baanah the Netophathite,
[31] Ithai son of Ribai from Gibeah in Benjamin,
Benaiah the Pirathonite,
[32] Hurai from the ravines of Gaash,
Abiel the Arbathite,
[33] Azmaveth the Baharumite,
Eliahba the Shaalbonite,
[34] the sons of Hashem the Gizonite,
Jonathan son of Shagee the Hararite,
[35] Ahiam son of Sacar the Hararite,
Eliphal son of Ur,
[36] Hepher the Mekerathite,
Ahijah the Pelonite,
[37] Hezro the Carmelite,
Naarai son of Ezbai,
[38] Joel the brother of Nathan,
Mibhar son of Hagri,
[39] Zelek the Ammonite,
Naharai the Berothite, the armor-bearer of Joab son of Zeruiah,
[40] Ira the Ithrite,
Gareb the Ithrite,
[41] Uriah the Hittite,
Zabad son of Ahlai,
[42] Adina son of Shiza the Reubenite, who was chief of the Reubenites, and the thirty with him,
[43] Hanan son of Maacah,
Joshaphat the Mithnite,
[44] Uzzia the Ashterathite,
Shama and Jeiel the sons of Hotham the Aroerite,
[45] Jediael son of Shimri,
his brother Joha the Tizite,
[46] Eliel the Mahavite,
Jeribai and Joshaviah the sons of Elnaam,
Ithmah the Moabite,
[47] Eliel, Obed and Jaasiel the Mezobaite.

Warriors Join David

12 These were the men who came to David at Ziklag, while he was banished from the presence of Saul son of Kish (they were among the warriors who helped him in battle; [2] they were armed with bows and were able to shoot arrows or to sling stones right-handed or left-handed; they were kinsmen of Saul from the tribe of Benjamin):

[3] Ahiezer their chief and Joash the sons of Shemaah the Gibeathite; Jeziel and Pelet the sons of Azmaveth; Beracah, Jehu the Anathothite, [4] and Ishmaiah the Gibeonite, a mighty man among the Thirty, who was a leader of the Thirty; Jeremiah, Jahaziel, Johanan, Jozabad the Gederathite, [5] Eluzai, Jerimoth, Bealiah, Shemariah and Shephatiah

---

[a] 23 Hebrew *five cubits* (about 2.3 meters)

the Haruphite; ⁶Elkanah, Isshiah, Azarel, Joezer and Jashobeam the Korahites; ⁷and Joelah and Zebadiah the sons of Jeroham from Gedor.

⁸Some Gadites defected to David at his stronghold in the desert. They were brave warriors, ready for battle and able to handle the shield and spear. Their faces were the faces of lions, and they were as swift as gazelles in the mountains.
⁹Ezer was the chief,
   Obadiah the second in command,
      Eliab the third,
¹⁰Mishmannah the fourth, Jeremiah the fifth,
¹¹Attai the sixth, Eliel the seventh,
¹²Johanan the eighth, Elzabad the ninth,
¹³Jeremiah the tenth and Macbannai the eleventh.

¹⁴These Gadites were army commanders; the least was a match for a hundred, and the greatest for a thousand. ¹⁵It was they who crossed the Jordan in the first month when it was overflowing all its banks, and they put to flight everyone living in the valleys, to the east and to the west.

¹⁶Other Benjamites and some men from Judah also came to David in his stronghold. ¹⁷David went out to meet them and said to them, "If you have come to me in peace, to help me, I am ready to have you unite with me. But if you have come to betray me to my enemies when my hands are free from violence, may the God of our fathers see it and judge you."

¹⁸Then the Spirit came upon Amasai, chief of the Thirty, and he said:

"We are yours, O David!
   We are with you, O son of Jesse!
Success, success to you,
   and success to those who help you,
      for your God will help you."

So David received them and made them leaders of his raiding bands.

¹⁹Some of the men of Manasseh defected to David when he went with the Philistines to fight against Saul. (He and his men did not help the Philistines because, after consultation, their rulers sent him away. They said, "It will cost us our heads if he deserts to his master Saul.") ²⁰When David went to Ziklag, these were the men of Manasseh who defected to him: Adnah, Jozabad, Jediael, Michael, Jozabad, Elihu and Zillethai, leaders of units of a thousand in Manasseh. ²¹They helped David against raiding bands, for all of them were brave warriors, and they were commanders in his army. ²²Day after day men came to help David, until he had a great army, like the army of God.ᵃ

> # Prayer is . . .
> *asking God to protect you from all attacks of the enemy.*

Others Join David at Hebron

²³These are the numbers of the men armed for battle who came to David at Hebron to turn Saul's kingdom over to him, as the LORD had said:
²⁴men of Judah, carrying shield and spear—6,800 armed for battle;
²⁵men of Simeon, warriors ready for battle—7,100;
²⁶men of Levi—4,600, ²⁷including Jehoiada, leader of the family of Aaron, with 3,700 men, ²⁸and Zadok, a brave young warrior, with 22 officers from his family;
²⁹men of Benjamin, Saul's kinsmen—3,000, most of whom had remained loyal to Saul's house until then;
³⁰men of Ephraim, brave warriors, famous in their own clans—20,800;
³¹men of half the tribe of Manasseh,

ᵃ 22 Or *a great and mighty army*

designated by name to come and make David king—18,000;

³²men of Issachar, who understood the times and knew what Israel should do—200 chiefs, with all their relatives under their command;

³³men of Zebulun, experienced soldiers prepared for battle with every type of weapon, to help David with undivided loyalty—50,000;

³⁴men of Naphtali—1,000 officers, together with 37,000 men carrying shields and spears;

³⁵men of Dan, ready for battle—28,600;

³⁶men of Asher, experienced soldiers prepared for battle—40,000;

³⁷and from east of the Jordan, men of Reuben, Gad and the half-tribe of Manasseh, armed with every type of weapon—120,000.

³⁸All these were fighting men who volunteered to serve in the ranks. They came to Hebron fully determined to make David king over all Israel. All the rest of the Israelites were also of one mind to make David king. ³⁹The men spent three days there with David, eating and drinking, for their families had supplied provisions for them. ⁴⁰Also, their neighbors from as far away as Issachar, Zebulun and Naphtali came bringing food on donkeys, camels, mules and oxen. There were plentiful supplies of flour, fig cakes, raisin cakes, wine, oil, cattle and sheep, for there was joy in Israel.

Bringing Back the Ark

13 David conferred with each of his officers, the commanders of thousands and commanders of hundreds. ²He then said to the whole assembly of Israel, "If it seems good to you and if it is the will of the LORD our God, let us send word far and wide to the rest of our brothers throughout the territories of Israel, and also to the priests and Levites who are with them in their towns and pasturelands, to come and join us.

³Let us bring the ark of our God back to us, for we did not inquire ofᵃ itᵇ during the reign of Saul." ⁴The whole assembly agreed to do this, because it seemed right to all the people.

⁵So David assembled all the Israelites, from the Shihor River in Egypt to Leboᶜ Hamath, to bring the ark of God from Kiriath Jearim. ⁶David and all the Israelites with him went to Baalah of Judah (Kiriath Jearim) to bring up from there the ark of God the LORD, who is enthroned between the cherubim—the ark that is called by the Name.

⁷They moved the ark of God from Abinadab's house on a new cart, with Uzzah and Ahio guiding it. ⁸David and all the Israelites were celebrating with all their might before God, with songs and with harps, lyres, tambourines, cymbals and trumpets.

⁹When they came to the threshing floor of Kidon, Uzzah reached out his hand to steady the ark, because the oxen stumbled. ¹⁰The LORD's anger burned against Uzzah, and he struck him down because he had put his hand on the ark. So he died there before God.

¹¹Then David was angry because the LORD's wrath had broken out against Uzzah, and to this day that place is called Perez Uzzah.ᵈ

¹²David was afraid of God that day and asked, "How can I ever bring the ark of God to me?" ¹³He did not take the ark to be with him in the City of David. Instead, he took it aside to the house of Obed-Edom the Gittite. ¹⁴The ark of God remained with the family of Obed-Edom in his house for three months, and the LORD blessed his household and everything he had.

David's House and Family

14 Now Hiram king of Tyre sent messengers to David, along with cedar logs, stonemasons and carpenters to build a palace for him. ²And David knew that the LORD had established him as king

---

ᵃ3 Or we neglected   ᵇ3 Or him   ᶜ5 Or to the entrance to   ᵈ11 Perez Uzzah means outbreak against Uzzah.

Pray Before You Act

READ AND CONSIDER: 1 CHRONICLES 14:8-17

"Now the Philistines had come and raided the Valley of Rephaim; so David inquired of God: 'Shall I go and attack the Philistines? Will you hand them over to me?' The LORD answered him, 'Go, I will hand them over to you' " (1 Chronicles 14:9-10).

David was finally made king of all Israel. Suddenly, he faced his first challenge as the ruler of the land. The Philistines decided to test his strength by invading territory under his control. The new king could have taken this threat as a personal challenge to prove his fitness to rule. Instead, he turned to God for wisdom in responding to the attack. He didn't do anything before asking God for direction. He prayed before proceeding.

Twice God instructed David to attack. His permission was specific. So was His promise of victory. Israel would defeat the Philistines because God would "hand them over." Interestingly, both armies took their "gods" into battle. The true God of Israel won; the gods of the Philistines were left lying on the battlefield like dry wood ready for burning. "The Philistines had abandoned their gods there, and David gave orders to burn them in the fire" (14:12).

Then the Philistines returned for round two. It's not clear exactly why. Perhaps they needed to rescue their gods or try out some new ones, or perhaps they thought David's first victory was just beginner's luck. David prayed again and received new marching orders. The Philistines were defeated again.

David's actions in this passage reveal several significant lessons about prayer. First, no matter how sudden or major a threat, we need to pray *before* we respond. Second, God brings the victory. Third, just because we have prayed and seen an "enemy" defeated doesn't mean we won't face that same threat again. Fourth, prayer allows us to receive direction from God that may include a different kind of action than we have taken previously.

Although we can't always see the problems we avoided because we prayed, all too often we see the bad things that happen when we act and don't pray. Ask God to help you always pray before you take any action or make any decision.

over Israel and that his kingdom had been highly exalted for the sake of his people Israel.

³In Jerusalem David took more wives and became the father of more sons and daughters. ⁴These are the names of the children born to him there: Shammua, Shobab, Nathan, Solomon, ⁵Ibhar, Elishua, Elpelet, ⁶Nogah, Nepheg, Japhia, ⁷Elishama, Beeliada[a] and Eliphelet.

David Defeats the Philistines

⁸When the Philistines heard that David had been anointed king over all Israel, they went up in full force to search for him, but David heard about it and went out to meet them. ⁹Now the Philistines had come and raided the Valley of Rephaim; ¹⁰so David inquired of God: "Shall I go and attack the Philistines? Will you hand them over to me?"

The LORD answered him, "Go, I will hand them over to you."

¹¹So David and his men went up to Baal Perazim, and there he defeated them. He said, "As waters break out, God has broken out against my enemies by my hand." So that place was called Baal

---

[a] 7 A variant of *Eliada*

Perazim.[a] [12]The Philistines had abandoned their gods there, and David gave orders to burn them in the fire.

[13]Once more the Philistines raided the valley; [14]so David inquired of God again, and God answered him, "Do not go straight up, but circle around them and attack them in front of the balsam trees. [15]As soon as you hear the sound of marching in the tops of the balsam trees, move out to battle, because that will mean God has gone out in front of you to strike the Philistine army." [16]So David did as God commanded him, and they struck down the Philistine army, all the way from Gibeon to Gezer.

Praying 1 Chronicles 14:14-15
Thank You, Lord, that when I am confronted by the enemy, You will go before me into battle.

[17]So David's fame spread throughout every land, and the LORD made all the nations fear him.

The Ark Brought to Jerusalem

15 After David had constructed buildings for himself in the City of David, he prepared a place for the ark of God and pitched a tent for it. [2]Then David said, "No one but the Levites may carry the ark of God, because the LORD chose them to carry the ark of the LORD and to minister before him forever."

[3]David assembled all Israel in Jerusalem to bring up the ark of the LORD to the place he had prepared for it. [4]He called together the descendants of Aaron and the Levites:

[5]From the descendants of Kohath,
Uriel the leader and 120 relatives;
[6]from the descendants of Merari,
Asaiah the leader and 220 relatives;
[7]from the descendants of Gershon,[b]
Joel the leader and 130 relatives;

[8]from the descendants of Elizaphan,
Shemaiah the leader and 200 relatives;
[9]from the descendants of Hebron,
Eliel the leader and 80 relatives;
[10]from the descendants of Uzziel,
Amminadab the leader and 112 relatives.

[11]Then David summoned Zadok and Abiathar the priests, and Uriel, Asaiah, Joel, Shemaiah, Eliel and Amminadab the Levites. [12]He said to them, "You are the heads of the Levitical families; you and your fellow Levites are to consecrate yourselves and bring up the ark of the LORD, the God of Israel, to the place I have prepared for it. [13]It was because you, the Levites, did not bring it up the first time that the LORD our God broke out in anger against us. We did not inquire of him about how to do it in the prescribed way." [14]So the priests and Levites consecrated themselves in order to bring up the ark of the LORD, the God of Israel. [15]And the Levites carried the ark of God with the poles on their shoulders, as Moses had commanded in accordance with the word of the LORD.

[16]David told the leaders of the Levites to appoint their brothers as singers to sing joyful songs, accompanied by musical instruments: lyres, harps and cymbals.

[17]So the Levites appointed Heman son of Joel; from his brothers, Asaph son of Berekiah; and from their brothers the Merarites, Ethan son of Kushaiah; [18]and with them their brothers next in rank: Zechariah,[c] Jaaziel, Shemiramoth, Jehiel, Unni, Eliab, Benaiah, Maaseiah, Mattithiah, Eliphelehu, Mikneiah, Obed-Edom and Jeiel,[d] the gatekeepers. [19]The musicians Heman, Asaph and Ethan were to sound the bronze cymbals; [20]Zechariah, Aziel, Shemiramoth, Jehiel, Unni, Eliab, Maaseiah and Benaiah were to play the lyres according to *alamoth*,[e] [21]and Mattithiah, Eliphelehu, Mikneiah,

---

[a] *11 Baal Perazim means the lord who breaks out.*   [b] *7 Hebrew Gershom, a variant of Gershon*   [c] *18 Three Hebrew manuscripts and most Septuagint manuscripts (see also verse 20 and 1 Chron. 16:5); most Hebrew manuscripts Zechariah son and or Zechariah, Ben and*   [d] *18 Hebrew; Septuagint (see also verse 21) Jeiel and Azaziah*   [e] *20 Probably a musical term*

Obed-Edom, Jeiel and Azaziah were to play the harps, directing according to *sheminith*.[a] 22Kenaniah the head Levite was in charge of the singing; that was his responsibility because he was skillful at it.

23Berekiah and Elkanah were to be doorkeepers for the ark. 24Shebaniah, Joshaphat, Nethanel, Amasai, Zechariah, Benaiah and Eliezer the priests were to blow trumpets before the ark of God. Obed-Edom and Jehiah were also to be doorkeepers for the ark.

25So David and the elders of Israel and the commanders of units of a thousand went to bring up the ark of the covenant of the LORD from the house of Obed-Edom, with rejoicing. 26Because God had helped the Levites who were carrying the ark of the covenant of the LORD, seven bulls and seven rams were sacrificed. 27Now David was clothed in a robe of fine linen, as were all the Levites who were carrying the ark, and as were the singers, and Kenaniah, who was in charge of the singing of the choirs. David also wore a linen ephod. 28So all Israel brought up the ark of the covenant of the LORD with shouts, with the sounding of rams' horns and trumpets, and of cymbals, and the playing of lyres and harps.

29As the ark of the covenant of the LORD was entering the City of David, Michal daughter of Saul watched from a window. And when she saw King David dancing and celebrating, she despised him in her heart.

16 They brought the ark of God and set it inside the tent that David had pitched for it, and they presented burnt offerings and fellowship offerings[b] before God. 2After David had finished sacrificing the burnt offerings and fellowship offerings, he blessed the people in the name of the LORD. 3Then he gave a loaf of bread, a cake of dates and a cake of raisins to each Israelite man and woman.

4He appointed some of the Levites to minister before the ark of the LORD, to make petition, to give thanks, and to praise the LORD, the God of Israel: 5Asaph was the chief, Zechariah second, then Jeiel, Shemiramoth, Jehiel, Mattithiah, Eliab, Benaiah, Obed-Edom and Jeiel. They were to play the lyres and harps, Asaph was to sound the cymbals, 6and Benaiah and Jahaziel the priests were to blow the trumpets regularly before the ark of the covenant of God.

David's Psalm of Thanks

7That day David first committed to Asaph and his associates this psalm of thanks to the LORD:

8Give thanks to the LORD, call on his
    name;
  make known among the nations
    what he has done.
9Sing to him, sing praise to him;
  tell of all his wonderful acts.

Praying 1 Chronicles 16:8-12
I give thanks to You, Lord, for filling my heart with joy every time I seek You.

10Glory in his holy name;
  let the hearts of those who seek the
    LORD rejoice.
11Look to the LORD and his strength;
  seek his face always.
12Remember the wonders he has done,
  his miracles, and the judgments he
    pronounced,
13O descendants of Israel his servant,
  O sons of Jacob, his chosen ones.

14He is the LORD our God;
  his judgments are in all the earth.
15He remembers[c] his covenant forever,
  the word he commanded, for a
    thousand generations,
16the covenant he made with Abraham,
  the oath he swore to Isaac.
17He confirmed it to Jacob as a decree,
  to Israel as an everlasting covenant:

---

a 21 Probably a musical term   b 1 Traditionally *peace offerings*; also in verse 2   c 15 Some Septuagint manuscripts (see also Psalm 105:8); Hebrew *Remember*

¹⁸"To you I will give the land of
  Canaan
  as the portion you will inherit."

¹⁹When they were but few in number,
  few indeed, and strangers in it,
²⁰they^a wandered from nation to nation,
  from one kingdom to another.
²¹He allowed no man to oppress them;
  for their sake he rebuked kings:
²²"Do not touch my anointed ones;
  do my prophets no harm."

²³Sing to the LORD, all the earth;
  proclaim his salvation day after day.
²⁴Declare his glory among the nations,
  his marvelous deeds among all
    peoples.
²⁵For great is the LORD and most
    worthy of praise;
  he is to be feared above all gods.
²⁶For all the gods of the nations are
    idols,
  but the LORD made the heavens.
²⁷Splendor and majesty are before him;
  strength and joy in his dwelling
    place.
²⁸Ascribe to the LORD, O families of
    nations,
  ascribe to the LORD glory and
    strength,
²⁹ ascribe to the LORD the glory due
    his name.
  Bring an offering and come before
    him;
  worship the LORD in the splendor
    of his^b holiness.
³⁰Tremble before him, all the earth!
  The world is firmly established; it
    cannot be moved.
³¹Let the heavens rejoice, let the earth
    be glad;
  let them say among the nations,
    "The LORD reigns!"
³²Let the sea resound, and all that is in
    it;
  let the fields be jubilant, and
    everything in them!

³³Then the trees of the forest will sing,
  they will sing for joy before the
    LORD,
  for he comes to judge the earth.

³⁴Give thanks to the LORD, for he is
    good;
  his love endures forever.
³⁵Cry out, "Save us, O God our Savior;
  gather us and deliver us from the
    nations,
  that we may give thanks to your holy
    name,
  that we may glory in your praise."
³⁶Praise be to the LORD, the God of
    Israel,
  from everlasting to everlasting.

Then all the people said "Amen" and
"Praise the LORD."

³⁷David left Asaph and his associates
before the ark of the covenant of the
LORD to minister there regularly, according
to each day's requirements. ³⁸He also
left Obed-Edom and his sixty-eight associates
to minister with them. Obed-
Edom son of Jeduthun, and also Hosah,
were gatekeepers.

³⁹David left Zadok the priest and his
fellow priests before the tabernacle of the
LORD at the high place in Gibeon ⁴⁰to
present burnt offerings to the LORD on
the altar of burnt offering regularly, morning
and evening, in accordance with everything
written in the Law of the LORD,
which he had given Israel. ⁴¹With them
were Heman and Jeduthun and the rest
of those chosen and designated by name
to give thanks to the LORD, "for his love
endures forever." ⁴²Heman and Jeduthun
were responsible for the sounding of the
trumpets and cymbals and for the playing
of the other instruments for sacred song.
The sons of Jeduthun were stationed at
the gate.

⁴³Then all the people left, each for his
own home, and David returned home to
bless his family.

---

^a 18-20 One Hebrew manuscript, Septuagint and Vulgate (see also Psalm 105:12); most Hebrew manuscripts inherit, / ¹⁹though you are but few in number, / few indeed, and strangers in it." / ²⁰They   ^b 29 Or LORD with the splendor of

God's Promise to David

17 After David was settled in his palace, he said to Nathan the prophet, "Here I am, living in a palace of cedar, while the ark of the covenant of the LORD is under a tent."

2 Nathan replied to David, "Whatever you have in mind, do it, for God is with you."

3 That night the word of God came to Nathan, saying:

4 "Go and tell my servant David, 'This is what the LORD says: You are not the one to build me a house to dwell in. 5 I have not dwelt in a house from the day I brought Israel up out of Egypt to this day. I have moved from one tent site to another, from one dwelling place to another. 6 Wherever I have moved with all the Israelites, did I ever say to any of their leaders[a] whom I commanded to shepherd my people, "Why have you not built me a house of cedar?"'

7 "Now then, tell my servant David, 'This is what the LORD Almighty says: I took you from the pasture and from following the flock, to be ruler over my people Israel. 8 I have been with you wherever you have gone, and I have cut off all your enemies from before you. Now I will make your name like the names of the greatest men of the earth. 9 And I will provide a place for my people Israel and will plant them so that they can have a home of their own and no longer be disturbed. Wicked people will not oppress them anymore, as they did at the beginning 10 and have done ever since the time I appointed leaders over my people Israel. I will also subdue all your enemies.

"'I declare to you that the LORD will build a house for you: 11 When your days are over and you go to be with your fathers, I will raise up your offspring to succeed you, one of your own sons, and I will establish his kingdom. 12 He is the one who will build a house for me, and I will establish his throne forever. 13 I will be his father, and he will be my son. I will never take my love away from him, as I took it away from your predecessor. 14 I will set him over my house and my kingdom forever; his throne will be established forever.'"

15 Nathan reported to David all the words of this entire revelation.

David's Prayer

16 Then King David went in and sat before the LORD, and he said:

"Who am I, O LORD God, and what is my family, that you have brought me this far? 17 And as if this were not enough in your sight, O God, you have spoken about the future of the house of your servant. You have looked on me as though I were the most exalted of men, O LORD God.

18 "What more can David say to you for honoring your servant? For you know your servant, 19 O LORD. For the sake of your servant and according to your will, you have done this great thing and made known all these great promises.

20 "There is no one like you, O LORD, and there is no God but you, as we have heard with our own ears. 21 And who is like your people Israel—the one nation on earth whose God went out to redeem a people for himself, and to make a name for yourself, and to perform great and awesome wonders by driving out nations from before your people, whom you redeemed from Egypt? 22 You made your people Israel your very own forever, and you, O LORD, have become their God.

23 "And now, LORD, let the prom-

---

[a] 6 Traditionally *judges*; also in verse 10

God Does More Than You Can Imagine

READ AND CONSIDER: 1 CHRONICLES 17:1-27

"And now, LORD, let the promise you have made concerning your servant and his house be established forever. Do as you promised, so that it will be established and that your name will be great forever. Then men will say, 'The LORD Almighty, the God over Israel, is Israel's God!' And the house of your servant David will be established before you" (1 Chronicles 17:23-24).

More than anything David desired to build a magnificent temple to honor the Lord. He had big plans and all kinds of resources ready. Even Nathan the prophet thought a temple was a great idea. Then God spoke. Through a revelation to Nathan, God revealed that David would not be the one to achieve that goal. The message Nathan shared began with God's "no" but ended with amazing promises to David. One of David's offspring (Solomon) would indeed build the temple, and David's throne would be established forever.

Rather than complaining about being denied the temple project, David responded with deep humility, gratitude, and praise. God was giving more than he ever dreamed—a temple and an everlasting kingdom! David acknowledged that this great blessing had to do with God's character and grace, not David's own worthiness (17:16-19). He praised God saying, "There is no one like you, O LORD" (17:20). He described the parallel between God's gracious choice of his family and God's faithfulness to Israel, both examples of God's amazing willingness to work out His plans through frail and flawed people. Then David made a request: "Let the promise you have made . . . be established forever" (17:23). In today's language, David was praying, "Lord, these are the amazing promises You have made about my family. I know that because You have said it, it will be done!"

Whenever you sense that God is saying no to your prayer, don't focus on your disappointment over not having *your* will done. If you do that, you may miss the joy of something much better that can come about if *God's* will is done. God's will is always richer and better than anything you can imagine.

ise you have made concerning your servant and his house be established forever. Do as you promised, ²⁴so that it will be established and that your name will be great forever. Then men will say, 'The LORD Almighty, the God over Israel, is Israel's God!' And the house of your servant David will be established before you.

²⁵"You, my God, have revealed to your servant that you will build a house for him. So your servant has found courage to pray to you. ²⁶O LORD, you are God! You have promised these good things to your

servant. ²⁷Now you have been pleased to bless the house of your servant, that it may continue forever in your sight; for you, O LORD, have blessed it, and it will be blessed forever."

David's Victories

18 In the course of time, David defeated the Philistines and subdued them, and he took Gath and its surrounding villages from the control of the Philistines.

²David also defeated the Moabites, and they became subject to him and brought tribute.

³Moreover, David fought Hadadezer king of Zobah, as far as Hamath, when he went to establish his control along the Euphrates River. ⁴David captured a thousand of his chariots, seven thousand charioteers and twenty thousand foot soldiers. He hamstrung all but a hundred of the chariot horses.

⁵When the Arameans of Damascus came to help Hadadezer king of Zobah, David struck down twenty-two thousand of them. ⁶He put garrisons in the Aramean kingdom of Damascus, and the Arameans became subject to him and brought tribute. The LORD gave David victory everywhere he went.

⁷David took the gold shields carried by the officers of Hadadezer and brought them to Jerusalem. ⁸From Tebah[a] and Cun, towns that belonged to Hadadezer, David took a great quantity of bronze, which Solomon used to make the bronze Sea, the pillars and various bronze articles.

⁹When Tou king of Hamath heard that David had defeated the entire army of Hadadezer king of Zobah, ¹⁰he sent his son Hadoram to King David to greet him and congratulate him on his victory in battle over Hadadezer, who had been at war with Tou. Hadoram brought all kinds of articles of gold and silver and bronze.

¹¹King David dedicated these articles to the LORD, as he had done with the silver and gold he had taken from all these nations: Edom and Moab, the Ammonites and the Philistines, and Amalek.

¹²Abishai son of Zeruiah struck down eighteen thousand Edomites in the Valley of Salt. ¹³He put garrisons in Edom, and all the Edomites became subject to David. The LORD gave David victory everywhere he went.

David's Officials

¹⁴David reigned over all Israel, doing what was just and right for all his people. ¹⁵Joab son of Zeruiah was over the army; Jehoshaphat son of Ahilud was recorder; ¹⁶Zadok son of Ahitub and Ahimelech[b] son of Abiathar were priests; Shavsha was secretary; ¹⁷Benaiah son of Jehoiada was over the Kerethites and Pelethites; and David's sons were chief officials at the king's side.

The Battle Against the Ammonites

19 In the course of time, Nahash king of the Ammonites died, and his son succeeded him as king. ²David thought, "I will show kindness to Hanun son of Nahash, because his father showed kindness to me." So David sent a delegation to express his sympathy to Hanun concerning his father.

When David's men came to Hanun in the land of the Ammonites to express sympathy to him, ³the Ammonite nobles said to Hanun, "Do you think David is honoring your father by sending men to you to express sympathy? Haven't his men come to you to explore and spy out the country and overthrow it?" ⁴So Hanun seized David's men, shaved them, cut off their garments in the middle at the buttocks, and sent them away.

⁵When someone came and told David about the men, he sent messengers to meet them, for they were greatly humiliated. The king said, "Stay at Jericho till your beards have grown, and then come back."

⁶When the Ammonites realized that they had become a stench in David's nostrils, Hanun and the Ammonites sent a thousand talents[c] of silver to hire chariots and charioteers from Aram Naharaim,[d] Aram Maacah and Zobah. ⁷They hired thirty-two thousand chariots and charioteers, as well as the king of Maacah with his troops, who came and camped near Medeba, while the Ammonites were mustered from their towns and moved out for battle.

⁸On hearing this, David sent Joab out with the entire army of fighting men.

ᵃ 8 Hebrew Tibhath, a variant of Tebah   ᵇ 16 Some Hebrew manuscripts, Vulgate and Syriac (see also 2 Samuel 8:17); most Hebrew manuscripts Abimelech   ᶜ 6 That is, about 37 tons (about 34 metric tons)   ᵈ 6 That is, Northwest Mesopotamia

9The Ammonites came out and drew up in battle formation at the entrance to their city, while the kings who had come were by themselves in the open country. 10Joab saw that there were battle lines in front of him and behind him; so he selected some of the best troops in Israel and deployed them against the Arameans. 11He put the rest of the men under the command of Abishai his brother, and they were deployed against the Ammonites. 12Joab said, "If the Arameans are too strong for me, then you are to rescue me; but if the Ammonites are too strong for you, then I will rescue you. 13Be strong and let us fight bravely for our people and the cities of our God. The LORD will do what is good in his sight."

14Then Joab and the troops with him advanced to fight the Arameans, and they fled before him. 15When the Ammonites saw that the Arameans were fleeing, they too fled before his brother Abishai and went inside the city. So Joab went back to Jerusalem.

16After the Arameans saw that they had been routed by Israel, they sent messengers and had Arameans brought from beyond the River,a with Shophach the commander of Hadadezer's army leading them.

17When David was told of this, he gathered all Israel and crossed the Jordan; he advanced against them and formed his battle lines opposite them. David formed his lines to meet the Arameans in battle, and they fought against him. 18But they fled before Israel, and David killed seven thousand of their charioteers and forty thousand of their foot soldiers. He also killed Shophach the commander of their army.

19When the vassals of Hadadezer saw that they had been defeated by Israel, they made peace with David and became subject to him.

So the Arameans were not willing to help the Ammonites anymore.

The Capture of Rabbah

20 In the spring, at the time when kings go off to war, Joab led out the armed forces. He laid waste the land of the Ammonites and went to Rabbah and besieged it, but David remained in Jerusalem. Joab attacked Rabbah and left it in ruins. 2David took the crown from the head of their kingb—its weight was found to be a talentc of gold, and it was set with precious stones—and it was placed on David's head. He took a great quantity of plunder from the city 3and brought out the people who were there, consigning them to labor with saws and with iron picks and axes. David did this to all the Ammonite towns. Then David and his entire army returned to Jerusalem.

War With the Philistines

4In the course of time, war broke out with the Philistines, at Gezer. At that time Sibbecai the Hushathite killed Sippai, one of the descendants of the Rephaites, and the Philistines were subjugated.

5In another battle with the Philistines, Elhanan son of Jair killed Lahmi the brother of Goliath the Gittite, who had a spear with a shaft like a weaver's rod.

6In still another battle, which took place at Gath, there was a huge man with six fingers on each hand and six toes on each foot—twenty-four in all. He also was descended from Rapha. 7When he taunted Israel, Jonathan son of Shimea, David's brother, killed him.

8These were descendants of Rapha in Gath, and they fell at the hands of David and his men.

David Numbers the Fighting Men

21 Satan rose up against Israel and incited David to take a census of Israel. 2So David said to Joab and the commanders of the troops, "Go and count the Israelites from Beersheba to Dan. Then report back to me so that I may know how many there are."

3But Joab replied, "May the LORD

---

a 16 That is, the Euphrates   b 2 Or of Milcom, that is, Molech   c 2 That is, about 75 pounds (about 34 kilograms) multiply his troops a hundred times over. My lord the king, are they not all my lord's subjects? Why does my lord want to do this? Why should he bring guilt on Israel?"

⁴The king's word, however, overruled Joab; so Joab left and went throughout Israel and then came back to Jerusalem. ⁵Joab reported the number of the fighting men to David: In all Israel there were one million one hundred thousand men who could handle a sword, including four hundred and seventy thousand in Judah.

⁶But Joab did not include Levi and Benjamin in the numbering, because the king's command was repulsive to him. ⁷This command was also evil in the sight of God; so he punished Israel.

⁸Then David said to God, "I have sinned greatly by doing this. Now, I beg you, take away the guilt of your servant. I have done a very foolish thing."

⁹The LORD said to Gad, David's seer, ¹⁰"Go and tell David, 'This is what the LORD says: I am giving you three options. Choose one of them for me to carry out against you.'"

GOING deeper

Repenting Before God in Prayer

READ AND CONSIDER: 1 CHRONICLES 21:1-19

"David said to God, 'Was it not I who ordered the fighting men to be counted? I am the one who has sinned and done wrong. These are but sheep. What have they done? O LORD my God, let your hand fall upon me and my family, but do not let this plague remain on your people'" (1 Chronicles 21:17).

King David had many highs of faith and obedience and some real lows of sin and disobedience. How can someone with such capacity for harmony with God be guilty of such sinful actions? This episode begins with a reminder that David was a prime target of Satan. Humiliating and defeating people whom God has called seems to be a specialty of the enemy of our souls.

Satan tempted ("incited") David, and David took the bait (21:1-2). Taking a census of fighting men appealed to the king's sense of authority and power. It was a matter of sinful pride. Satan knew just where David was weakest.

By the time Joab returned with the numbers, the king realized he had sinned. To his great credit, David owned up to his sin. He took responsibility and confessed it all to God in prayer. God used this occasion to teach David an indelible lesson about responsibility: When we sin, the consequences are real and often hurt others. When a king sins, all the people suffer. God gave David a choice of consequences, each affecting both king and people. David chose to submit to God's direct punishment rather than suffer under "the hands of men" (21:13). But the effects of his choice overwhelmed David: Seventy thousand men died from the plague. The king gained a deeper, humbler, more painful perspective on the seriousness of sin and the holiness of God. He begged God to punish him personally and spare the rest of the people. God called off the plague, and David offered sacrifices. Our last glimpse of David in this episode shows a king chastened and respectful before God, careful not to take Him for granted.

We all need to confess our sins in prayer to God. Especially the sin of pride, which we are each tempted to have. But if we include repentance and confession as part of our prayers and then ask God to help us not commit those sins again, it enables us to stay on target with God. Even though there may be hard consequences for sin we've committed, when we come before God with humble hearts, we can be forgiven and good can come out of it.

¹¹So Gad went to David and said to him, "This is what the LORD says: 'Take your choice: ¹²three years of famine, three months of being swept away[a] before your enemies, with their swords overtaking you, or three days of the sword of the LORD—days of plague in the land, with the angel of the LORD ravaging every part of Israel.' Now then, decide how I should answer the one who sent me."

¹³David said to Gad, "I am in deep distress. Let me fall into the hands of the LORD, for his mercy is very great; but do not let me fall into the hands of men."

¹⁴So the LORD sent a plague on Israel, and seventy thousand men of Israel fell dead. ¹⁵And God sent an angel to destroy Jerusalem. But as the angel was doing so, the LORD saw it and was grieved because of the calamity and said to the angel who was destroying the people, "Enough! Withdraw your hand." The angel of the LORD was then standing at the threshing floor of Araunah[b] the Jebusite.

¹⁶David looked up and saw the angel of the LORD standing between heaven and earth, with a drawn sword in his hand extended over Jerusalem. Then David and the elders, clothed in sackcloth, fell facedown.

¹⁷David said to God, "Was it not I who ordered the fighting men to be counted? I am the one who has sinned and done wrong. These are but sheep. What have they done? O LORD my God, let your hand fall upon me and my family, but do not let this plague remain on your people."

¹⁸Then the angel of the LORD ordered Gad to tell David to go up and build an altar to the LORD on the threshing floor of Araunah the Jebusite. ¹⁹So David went up in obedience to the word that Gad had spoken in the name of the LORD.

²⁰While Araunah was threshing wheat, he turned and saw the angel; his four sons who were with him hid themselves.

²¹Then David approached, and when Araunah looked and saw him, he left the threshing floor and bowed down before David with his face to the ground.

²²David said to him, "Let me have the site of your threshing floor so I can build an altar to the LORD, that the plague on the people may be stopped. Sell it to me at the full price."

²³Araunah said to David, "Take it! Let my lord the king do whatever pleases him. Look, I will give the oxen for the burnt offerings, the threshing sledges for the wood, and the wheat for the grain offering. I will give all this."

Praying 1 Chronicles 21:24
Lord, I don't want to offer anything to You that costs me nothing.

²⁴But King David replied to Araunah, "No, I insist on paying the full price. I will not take for the LORD what is yours, or sacrifice a burnt offering that costs me nothing."

²⁵So David paid Araunah six hundred shekels[c] of gold for the site. ²⁶David built an altar to the LORD there and sacrificed burnt offerings and fellowship offerings.[d] He called on the LORD, and the LORD answered him with fire from heaven on the altar of burnt offering.

²⁷Then the LORD spoke to the angel, and he put his sword back into its sheath. ²⁸At that time, when David saw that the LORD had answered him on the threshing floor of Araunah the Jebusite, he offered sacrifices there. ²⁹The tabernacle of the LORD, which Moses had made in the desert, and the altar of burnt offering were at that time on the high place at Gibeon. ³⁰But David could not go before it to inquire of God, because he was afraid of the sword of the angel of the LORD.

22 Then David said, "The house of the LORD God is to be here, and also the altar of burnt offering for Israel."

---

[a] 12 Hebrew; Septuagint and Vulgate (see also 2 Samuel 24:13) of fleeing [b] 15 Hebrew Ornan, a variant of Araunah; also in verses 18-28 [c] 25 That is, about 15 pounds (about 7 kilograms) [d] 26 Traditionally peace offerings

Preparations for the Temple

²So David gave orders to assemble the aliens living in Israel, and from among them he appointed stonecutters to prepare dressed stone for building the house of God. ³He provided a large amount of iron to make nails for the doors of the gateways and for the fittings, and more bronze than could be weighed. ⁴He also provided more cedar logs than could be counted, for the Sidonians and Tyrians had brought large numbers of them to David.

⁵David said, "My son Solomon is young and inexperienced, and the house to be built for the LORD should be of great magnificence and fame and splendor in the sight of all the nations. Therefore I will make preparations for it." So David made extensive preparations before his death.

⁶Then he called for his son Solomon and charged him to build a house for the LORD, the God of Israel. ⁷David said to Solomon: "My son, I had it in my heart to build a house for the Name of the LORD my God. ⁸But this word of the LORD came to me: 'You have shed much blood and have fought many wars. You are not to build a house for my Name, because you have shed much blood on the earth in my sight. ⁹But you will have a son who will be a man of peace and rest, and I will give him rest from all his enemies on every side. His name will be Solomon,ᵃ and I will grant Israel peace and quiet during his reign. ¹⁰He is the one who will build a house for my Name. He will be my son, and I will be his father. And I will establish the throne of his kingdom over Israel forever.'

¹¹"Now, my son, the LORD be with you, and may you have success and build the house of the LORD your God, as he said you would. ¹²May the LORD give you discretion and understanding when he puts you in command over Israel, so that you may keep the law of the LORD your God.

¹³Then you will have success if you are careful to observe the decrees and laws that the LORD gave Moses for Israel. Be strong and courageous. Do not be afraid or discouraged.

¹⁴"I have taken great pains to provide for the temple of the LORD a hundred thousand talentsᵇ of gold, a million talentsᶜ of silver, quantities of bronze and iron too great to be weighed, and wood and stone. And you may add to them. ¹⁵You have many workmen: stonecutters, masons and carpenters, as well as men skilled in every kind of work ¹⁶in gold and silver, bronze and iron—craftsmen beyond number. Now begin the work, and the LORD be with you."

¹⁷Then David ordered all the leaders of Israel to help his son Solomon. ¹⁸He said to them, "Is not the LORD your God with you? And has he not granted you rest on every side? For he has handed the inhabitants of the land over to me, and the land is subject to the LORD and to his people. ¹⁹Now devote your heart and soul to seeking the LORD your God. Begin to build the sanctuary of the LORD God, so that you may bring the ark of the covenant of the LORD and the sacred articles belonging to God into the temple that will be built for the Name of the LORD."

The Levites

23 When David was old and full of years, he made his son Solomon king over Israel.

²He also gathered together all the leaders of Israel, as well as the priests and Levites. ³The Levites thirty years old or more were counted, and the total number of men was thirty-eight thousand. ⁴David said, "Of these, twenty-four thousand are to supervise the work of the temple of the LORD and six thousand are to be officials and judges. ⁵Four thousand are to be gatekeepers and four thousand are to praise the LORD with the musical instruments I have provided for that purpose."

ᵃ 9 Solomon sounds like and may be derived from the Hebrew for peace.   ᵇ 14 That is, about 3,750 tons (about 3,450 metric tons)   ᶜ 14 That is, about 37,500 tons (about 34,500 metric tons)

⁶David divided the Levites into groups corresponding to the sons of Levi: Gershon, Kohath and Merari.

Gershonites

⁷Belonging to the Gershonites:
Ladan and Shimei.
⁸The sons of Ladan:
Jehiel the first, Zetham and Joel—three in all.
⁹The sons of Shimei:
Shelomoth, Haziel and Haran—three in all.
These were the heads of the families of Ladan.
¹⁰And the sons of Shimei:
Jahath, Ziza,ᵃ Jeush and Beriah.
These were the sons of Shimei—four in all.
¹¹Jahath was the first and Ziza the second, but Jeush and Beriah did not have many sons; so they were counted as one family with one assignment.

Kohathites

¹²The sons of Kohath:
Amram, Izhar, Hebron and Uzziel—four in all.
¹³The sons of Amram:
Aaron and Moses.
Aaron was set apart, he and his descendants forever, to consecrate the most holy things, to offer sacrifices before the LORD, to minister before him and to pronounce blessings in his name forever.
¹⁴The sons of Moses the man of God were counted as part of the tribe of Levi.
¹⁵The sons of Moses:
Gershom and Eliezer.
¹⁶The descendants of Gershom:
Shubael was the first.
¹⁷The descendants of Eliezer:
Rehabiah was the first.
Eliezer had no other sons, but the sons of Rehabiah were very numerous.

¹⁸The sons of Izhar:
Shelomith was the first.
¹⁹The sons of Hebron:
Jeriah the first, Amariah the second, Jahaziel the third and Jekameam the fourth.
²⁰The sons of Uzziel:
Micah the first and Isshiah the second.

Merarites

²¹The sons of Merari:
Mahli and Mushi.
The sons of Mahli:
Eleazar and Kish.
²²Eleazar died without having sons: he had only daughters. Their cousins, the sons of Kish, married them.
²³The sons of Mushi:
Mahli, Eder and Jerimoth—three in all.

²⁴These were the descendants of Levi by their families—the heads of families as they were registered under their names and counted individually, that is, the workers twenty years old or more who served in the temple of the LORD. ²⁵For David had said, "Since the LORD, the God of Israel, has granted rest to his people and has come to dwell in Jerusalem forever, ²⁶the Levites no longer need to carry the tabernacle or any of the articles used in its service." ²⁷According to the last instructions of David, the Levites were counted from those twenty years old or more.

²⁸The duty of the Levites was to help Aaron's descendants in the service of the temple of the LORD: to be in charge of the courtyards, the side rooms, the purification of all sacred things and the performance of other duties at the house of God. ²⁹They were in charge of the bread set out on the table, the flour for the grain offerings, the unleavened wafers, the baking and the mixing, and all measurements of quantity and size. ³⁰They were also to

---

ᵃ 10 One Hebrew manuscript, Septuagint and Vulgate (see also verse 11); most Hebrew manuscripts Zina stand every morning to thank and praise the LORD. They were to do the same in the evening ³¹and whenever burnt offerings were presented to the LORD on Sabbaths and at New Moon festivals and at appointed feasts. They were to serve before the LORD regularly in the proper number and in the way prescribed for them.

³²And so the Levites carried out their responsibilities for the Tent of Meeting, for the Holy Place and, under their brothers the descendants of Aaron, for the service of the temple of the LORD.

The Divisions of Priests

24 These were the divisions of the sons of Aaron:

The sons of Aaron were Nadab, Abihu, Eleazar and Ithamar. ²But Nadab and Abihu died before their father did, and they had no sons; so Eleazar and Ithamar served as the priests. ³With the help of Zadok a descendant of Eleazar and Ahimelech a descendant of Ithamar, David separated them into divisions for their appointed order of ministering. ⁴A larger number of leaders were found among Eleazar's descendants than among Ithamar's, and they were divided accordingly: sixteen heads of families from Eleazar's descendants and eight heads of families from Ithamar's descendants. ⁵They divided them impartially by drawing lots, for there were officials of the sanctuary and officials of God among the descendants of both Eleazar and Ithamar.

⁶The scribe Shemaiah son of Nethanel, a Levite, recorded their names in the presence of the king and of the officials: Zadok the priest, Ahimelech son of Abiathar and the heads of families of the priests and of the Levites—one family being taken from Eleazar and then one from Ithamar.

⁷The first lot fell to Jehoiarib, the second to Jedaiah,

⁸the third to Harim, the fourth to Seorim, ⁹the fifth to Malkijah, the sixth to Mijamin, ¹⁰the seventh to Hakkoz, the eighth to Abijah, ¹¹the ninth to Jeshua, the tenth to Shecaniah, ¹²the eleventh to Eliashib, the twelfth to Jakim, ¹³the thirteenth to Huppah, the fourteenth to Jeshebeab, ¹⁴the fifteenth to Bilgah, the sixteenth to Immer, ¹⁵the seventeenth to Hezir, the eighteenth to Happizzez, ¹⁶the nineteenth to Pethahiah, the twentieth to Jehezkel, ¹⁷the twenty-first to Jakin, the twenty-second to Gamul, ¹⁸the twenty-third to Delaiah and the twenty-fourth to Maaziah.

¹⁹This was their appointed order of ministering when they entered the temple of the LORD, according to the regulations prescribed for them by their forefather Aaron, as the LORD, the God of Israel, had commanded him.

The Rest of the Levites

²⁰As for the rest of the descendants of Levi:

from the sons of Amram: Shubael; from the sons of Shubael: Jehdeiah.

²¹As for Rehabiah, from his sons: Isshiah was the first.

²²From the Izharites: Shelomoth; from the sons of Shelomoth: Jahath.

²³The sons of Hebron: Jeriah the first,ᵃ Amariah the second, Jahaziel the third and Jekameam the fourth.

²⁴The son of Uzziel: Micah; from the sons of Micah: Shamir.

²⁵The brother of Micah: Isshiah;

ᵃ 23 Two Hebrew manuscripts and some Septuagint manuscripts (see also 1 Chron. 23:19); most Hebrew manuscripts The sons of Jeriah:

from the sons of Isshiah: Zechariah.
²⁶ The sons of Merari: Mahli and Mushi.
The son of Jaaziah: Beno.
²⁷ The sons of Merari:
from Jaaziah: Beno, Shoham, Zaccur and Ibri.
²⁸ From Mahli: Eleazar, who had no
sons.
²⁹ From Kish: the son of Kish:
Jerahmeel.
³⁰ And the sons of Mushi: Mahli, Eder
and Jerimoth.

These were the Levites, according to
their families. ³¹ They also cast lots, just as
their brothers the descendants of Aaron
did, in the presence of King David and
of Zadok, Ahimelech, and the heads of
families of the priests and of the Levites.
The families of the oldest brother were
treated the same as those of the youngest.

The Singers

25 David, together with the commanders of the army, set apart some
of the sons of Asaph, Heman and Jeduthun for the ministry of prophesying, accompanied by harps, lyres and cymbals.
Here is the list of the men who performed this service:

² From the sons of Asaph:
Zaccur, Joseph, Nethaniah and Asare-
lah. The sons of Asaph were under
the supervision of Asaph, who prophesied under the king's supervision.
³ As for Jeduthun, from his sons:
Gedaliah, Zeri, Jeshaiah, Shimei,ᵃ
Hashabiah and Mattithiah, six in all,
under the supervision of their father
Jeduthun, who prophesied, using
the harp in thanking and praising
the LORD.
⁴ As for Heman, from his sons:
Bukkiah, Mattaniah, Uzziel, Shubael

and Jerimoth; Hananiah, Hanani, Eli-
athah, Giddalti and Romamti-Ezer;
Joshbekashah, Mallothi, Hothir and
Mahazioth. ⁵ All these were sons of
Heman the king's seer. They were
given him through the promises of
God to exalt him.ᵇ God gave Heman
fourteen sons and three daughters.

⁶ All these men were under the supervision of their fathers for the music of
the temple of the LORD, with cymbals,
lyres and harps, for the ministry at the
house of God. Asaph, Jeduthun and Heman were under the supervision of the
king. ⁷ Along with their relatives—all of
them trained and skilled in music for the
LORD—they numbered 288. ⁸ Young and
old alike, teacher as well as student, cast
lots for their duties.

⁹ The first lot, which was for
Asaph, fell to Joseph,
his sons and relatives,ᶜ   12ᵈ
the second to Gedaliah,
he and his relatives and sons,   12
¹⁰ the third to Zaccur,
his sons and relatives,   12
¹¹ the fourth to Izri,ᵉ
his sons and relatives,   12
¹² the fifth to Nethaniah,
his sons and relatives,   12
¹³ the sixth to Bukkiah,
his sons and relatives,   12
¹⁴ the seventh to Jesarelah,ᶠ
his sons and relatives,   12
¹⁵ the eighth to Jeshaiah,
his sons and relatives,   12
¹⁶ the ninth to Mattaniah,
his sons and relatives,   12
¹⁷ the tenth to Shimei,
his sons and relatives,   12
¹⁸ the eleventh to Azarel,ᵍ
his sons and relatives,   12
¹⁹ the twelfth to Hashabiah,
his sons and relatives,   12
²⁰ the thirteenth to Shubael,
his sons and relatives,   12

²¹ the fourteenth to Mattithiah,
his sons and relatives,   12
²² the fifteenth to Jerimoth,
his sons and relatives,   12
²³ the sixteenth to Hananiah,
his sons and relatives,   12
²⁴ the seventeenth to Joshbekashah,
his sons and relatives,   12
²⁵ the eighteenth to Hanani,
his sons and relatives,   12
²⁶ the nineteenth to Mallothi,
his sons and relatives,   12
²⁷ the twentieth to Eliathah,
his sons and relatives,   12
²⁸ the twenty-first to Hothir,
his sons and relatives,   12
²⁹ the twenty-second to Giddalti,
his sons and relatives,   12
³⁰ the twenty-third to Mahazioth,
his sons and relatives,   12
³¹ the twenty-fourth to Romamti-
Ezer,
his sons and relatives,   12

The Gatekeepers

26 The divisions of the gatekeepers:

From the Korahites: Meshelemiah son
of Kore, one of the sons of Asaph.
² Meshelemiah had sons:
Zechariah the firstborn,
Jediael the second,
Zebadiah the third,
Jathniel the fourth,
³ Elam the fifth,
Jehohanan the sixth
and Eliehoenai the seventh.
⁴ Obed-Edom also had sons:
Shemaiah the firstborn,
Jehozabad the second,
Joah the third,
Sacar the fourth,
Nethanel the fifth,
⁵ Ammiel the sixth,
Issachar the seventh
and Peullethai the eighth.
(For God had blessed Obed-
Edom.)

⁶ His son Shemaiah also had sons,
who were leaders in their father's
family because they were very capable men. ⁷ The sons of Shemaiah: Othni, Rephael, Obed and
Elzabad; his relatives Elihu and
Semakiah were also able men.
⁸ All these were descendants of
Obed-Edom; they and their sons
and their relatives were capable
men with the strength to do the
work—descendants of Obed-
Edom, 62 in all.
⁹ Meshelemiah had sons and relatives,
who were able men—18 in all.

¹⁰ Hosah the Merarite had sons: Shimri
the first (although he was not the
firstborn, his father had appointed
him the first), ¹¹ Hilkiah the second,
Tabaliah the third and Zechariah
the fourth. The sons and relatives
of Hosah were 13 in all.

¹² These divisions of the gatekeepers,
through their chief men, had duties for
ministering in the temple of the LORD,
just as their relatives had. ¹³ Lots were cast
for each gate, according to their families,
young and old alike.

¹⁴ The lot for the East Gate fell to
Shelemiah.ᵃ Then lots were cast for his
son Zechariah, a wise counselor, and the
lot for the North Gate fell to him. ¹⁵ The
lot for the South Gate fell to Obed-
Edom, and the lot for the storehouse fell
to his sons. ¹⁶ The lots for the West Gate
and the Shalleketh Gate on the upper
road fell to Shuppim and Hosah.

Guard was alongside of guard: ¹⁷ There
were six Levites a day on the east, four
a day on the north, four a day on the
south and two at a time at the storehouse. ¹⁸ As for the court to the west,
there were four at the road and two at
the court itself.

¹⁹ These were the divisions of the gatekeepers who were descendants of Korah
and Merari.

ᵃ 14 A variant of *Meshelemiah*

The Treasurers and Other Officials

20Their fellow Levites were[a] in charge of the treasuries of the house of God and the treasuries for the dedicated things.

21The descendants of Ladan, who were Gershonites through Ladan and who were heads of families belonging to Ladan the Gershonite, were Jehieli, 22the sons of Jehieli, Zetham and his brother Joel. They were in charge of the treasuries of the temple of the LORD.

23From the Amramites, the Izharites, the Hebronites and the Uzzielites:

24Shubael, a descendant of Gershom son of Moses, was the officer in charge of the treasuries. 25His relatives through Eliezer: Rehabiah his son, Jeshaiah his son, Joram his son, Zicri his son and Shelomith his son. 26Shelomith and his relatives were in charge of all the treasuries for the things dedicated by King David, by the heads of families who were the commanders of thousands and commanders of hundreds, and by the other army commanders. 27Some of the plunder taken in battle they dedicated for the repair of the temple of the LORD. 28And everything dedicated by Samuel the seer and by Saul son of Kish, Abner son of Ner and Joab son of Zeruiah, and all the other dedicated things were in the care of Shelomith and his relatives.

29From the Izharites: Kenaniah and his sons were assigned duties away from the temple, as officials and judges over Israel.

30From the Hebronites: Hashabiah and his relatives—seventeen hundred able men—were responsible in Israel west of the Jordan for all the work of the LORD and for the king's service. 31As for the Hebronites, Jeriah was their chief according to the genealogical records of their families. In the fortieth year of David's reign a search was made in the records, and capable men among the Hebronites were found at Jazer in Gilead. 32Jeriah had twenty-seven hundred relatives, who were able men and heads of families, and King David put them in charge of the Reubenites, the Gadites and the half-tribe of Manasseh for every matter pertaining to God and for the affairs of the king.

Army Divisions

27 This is the list of the Israelites—heads of families, commanders of thousands and commanders of hundreds, and their officers, who served the king in all that concerned the army divisions that were on duty month by month throughout the year. Each division consisted of 24,000 men.

2In charge of the first division, for the first month, was Jashobeam son of Zabdiel. There were 24,000 men in his division. 3He was a descendant of Perez and chief of all the army officers for the first month.

4In charge of the division for the second month was Dodai the Ahohite; Mikloth was the leader of his division. There were 24,000 men in his division.

5The third army commander, for the third month, was Benaiah son of Jehoiada the priest. He was chief and there were 24,000 men in his division. 6This was the Benaiah who was a mighty man among the Thirty and was over the Thirty. His son Ammizabad was in charge of his division.

7The fourth, for the fourth month, was Asahel the brother of Joab; his son Zebadiah was his successor. There were 24,000 men in his division.

8The fifth, for the fifth month, was the commander Shamhuth the Izrahite. There were 24,000 men in his division.

9 The sixth, for the sixth month, was Ira the son of Ikkesh the Tekoite. There were 24,000 men in his division.

10 The seventh, for the seventh month, was Helez the Pelonite, an Ephraimite. There were 24,000 men in his division.

11 The eighth, for the eighth month, was Sibbecai the Hushathite, a Zerahite. There were 24,000 men in his division.

12 The ninth, for the ninth month, was Abiezer the Anathothite, a Benjamite. There were 24,000 men in his division.

13 The tenth, for the tenth month, was Maharai the Netophathite, a Zerahite. There were 24,000 men in his division.

14 The eleventh, for the eleventh month, was Benaiah the Pirathonite, an Ephraimite. There were 24,000 men in his division.

15 The twelfth, for the twelfth month, was Heldai the Netophathite, from the family of Othniel. There were 24,000 men in his division.

Officers of the Tribes

16 The officers over the tribes of Israel:

over the Reubenites: Eliezer son of Zicri;

over the Simeonites: Shephatiah son of Maacah;

17 over Levi: Hashabiah son of Kemuel;

over Aaron: Zadok;

18 over Judah: Elihu, a brother of David;

over Issachar: Omri son of Michael;

19 over Zebulun: Ishmaiah son of Obadiah;

over Naphtali: Jerimoth son of Azriel;

20 over the Ephraimites: Hoshea son of Azaziah;

over half the tribe of Manasseh: Joel son of Pedaiah;

21 over the half-tribe of Manasseh in Gilead: Iddo son of Zechariah;

over Benjamin: Jaasiel son of Abner;

22 over Dan: Azarel son of Jeroham.

These were the officers over the tribes of Israel.

23 David did not take the number of the men twenty years old or less, because the LORD had promised to make Israel as numerous as the stars in the sky. 24 Joab son of Zeruiah began to count the men but did not finish. Wrath came on Israel on account of this numbering, and the number was not entered in the book[a] of the annals of King David.

The King's Overseers

25 Azmaveth son of Adiel was in charge of the royal storehouses.

Jonathan son of Uzziah was in charge of the storehouses in the outlying districts, in the towns, the villages and the watchtowers.

26 Ezri son of Kelub was in charge of the field workers who farmed the land.

27 Shimei the Ramathite was in charge of the vineyards.

Zabdi the Shiphmite was in charge of the produce of the vineyards for the wine vats.

28 Baal-Hanan the Gederite was in charge of the olive and sycamore-fig trees in the western foothills.

Joash was in charge of the supplies of olive oil.

29 Shitrai the Sharonite was in charge of the herds grazing in Sharon.

Shaphat son of Adlai was in charge of the herds in the valleys.

30 Obil the Ishmaelite was in charge of the camels.

Jehdeiah the Meronothite was in charge of the donkeys.

31 Jaziz the Hagrite was in charge of the flocks.

All these were the officials in charge of King David's property.

a 24 Septuagint; Hebrew number

³²Jonathan, David's uncle, was a counselor, a man of insight and a scribe. Jehiel son of Hacmoni took care of the king's sons.

³³Ahithophel was the king's counselor. Hushai the Arkite was the king's friend. ³⁴Ahithophel was succeeded by Jehoiada son of Benaiah and by Abiathar.

Joab was the commander of the royal army.

David's Plans for the Temple

28 David summoned all the officials of Israel to assemble at Jerusalem: the officers over the tribes, the commanders of the divisions in the service of the king, the commanders of thousands and commanders of hundreds, and the officials in charge of all the property and livestock belonging to the king and his sons, together with the palace officials, the mighty men and all the brave warriors.

²King David rose to his feet and said: "Listen to me, my brothers and my people. I had it in my heart to build a house as a place of rest for the ark of the covenant of the LORD, for the footstool of our God, and I made plans to build it. ³But God said to me, 'You are not to build a house for my Name, because you are a warrior and have shed blood.'

⁴"Yet the LORD, the God of Israel, chose me from my whole family to be king over Israel forever. He chose Judah as leader, and from the house of Judah he chose my family, and from my father's sons he was pleased to make me king over all Israel. ⁵Of all my sons—and the LORD has given me many—he has chosen my son Solomon to sit on the throne of the kingdom of the LORD over Israel. ⁶He said to me: 'Solomon your son is the one who will build my house and my courts, for I have chosen him to be my son, and I will be his father. ⁷I will establish his kingdom forever if he is unswerving in carrying out my commands and laws, as is being done at this time.'

⁸"So now I charge you in the sight of all Israel and of the assembly of the LORD, and in the hearing of our God: Be careful to follow all the commands of the LORD your God, that you may possess this good land and pass it on as an inheritance to your descendants forever.

⁹"And you, my son Solomon, acknowledge the God of your father, and serve him with wholehearted devotion and with a willing mind, for the LORD searches every heart and understands every motive behind the thoughts. If you seek him, he will be found by you; but if you forsake him, he will reject you forever. ¹⁰Consider now, for the LORD has chosen you to build a temple as a sanctuary. Be strong and do the work."

¹¹Then David gave his son Solomon the plans for the portico of the temple, its buildings, its storerooms, its upper parts, its inner rooms and the place of atonement. ¹²He gave him the plans of all that the Spirit had put in his mind for the courts of the temple of the LORD and all the surrounding rooms, for the treasuries of the temple of God and for the treasuries for the dedicated things. ¹³He gave him instructions for the divisions of the priests and Levites, and for all the work of serving in the temple of the LORD, as well as for all the articles to be used in its service. ¹⁴He designated the weight of gold for all the gold articles to be used in various kinds of service, and the weight of silver for all the silver articles to be used in various kinds of service: ¹⁵the weight of gold for the gold lampstands and their lamps, with the weight for each lampstand and its lamps; and the weight of silver for each silver lampstand and its lamps, according to the use of each lampstand; ¹⁶the weight of gold for each table for consecrated bread; the weight of silver for the silver tables; ¹⁷the weight of pure gold for the forks, sprinkling bowls and pitchers; the weight of gold for each gold dish; the weight of silver for each silver dish; ¹⁸and the weight of the refined gold for the altar of incense. He also gave him the plan for the chariot, that is, the

cherubim of gold that spread their wings and shelter the ark of the covenant of the LORD.

[19]"All this," David said, "I have in writing from the hand of the LORD upon me, and he gave me understanding in all the details of the plan."

[20]David also said to Solomon his son, "Be strong and courageous, and do the work. Do not be afraid or discouraged, for the LORD God, my God, is with you. He will not fail you or forsake you until all the work for the service of the temple of the LORD is finished. [21]The divisions of the priests and Levites are ready for all the work on the temple of God, and every willing man skilled in any craft will help you in all the work. The officials and all the people will obey your every command."

Gifts for Building the Temple

29 Then King David said to the whole assembly: "My son Solomon, the one whom God has chosen, is young and inexperienced. The task is great, because this palatial structure is not for man but for the LORD God. [2]With all my resources I have provided for the temple of my God—gold for the gold work, silver for the silver, bronze for the bronze, iron for the iron and wood for the wood, as well as onyx for the settings, turquoise,[a] stones of various colors, and all kinds of fine stone and marble—all of these in large quantities. [3]Besides, in my devotion to the temple of my God I now give my personal treasures of gold and silver for the temple of my God, over and above everything I have provided for this holy temple: [4]three thousand talents[b] of gold (gold of Ophir) and seven thousand talents[c] of refined silver, for the overlaying of the walls of the buildings, [5]for the gold work and the silver work, and for all the work to be done by the craftsmen. Now,

who is willing to consecrate himself today to the LORD?"

[6]Then the leaders of families, the officers of the tribes of Israel, the commanders of thousands and commanders of hundreds, and the officials in charge of the king's work gave willingly. [7]They gave toward the work on the temple of God five thousand talents[d] and ten thousand darics[e] of gold, ten thousand talents[f] of silver, eighteen thousand talents[g] of bronze and a hundred thousand talents[h] of iron. [8]Any who had precious stones gave them to the treasury of the temple of the LORD in the custody of Jehiel the Gershonite. [9]The people rejoiced at the willing response of their leaders, for they had given freely and wholeheartedly to the LORD. David the king also rejoiced greatly.

David's Prayer

[10]David praised the LORD in the presence of the whole assembly, saying,

"Praise be to you, O LORD,
    God of our father Israel,
    from everlasting to everlasting.
[11]Yours, O LORD, is the greatness and
        the power
    and the glory and the majesty and
        the splendor,
    for everything in heaven and earth
        is yours.
Yours, O LORD, is the kingdom;
    you are exalted as head over all.
[12]Wealth and honor come from you;
    you are the ruler of all things.
In your hands are strength and power
    to exalt and give strength to all.
[13]Now, our God, we give you thanks,
    and praise your glorious name.

[14]"But who am I, and who are my people, that we should be able to give as generously as this? Everything comes from you, and we have given you only

---

[a]2 The meaning of the Hebrew for this word is uncertain.   [b]4 That is, about 110 tons (about 100 metric tons)   [c]4 That is, about 260 tons (about 240 metric tons)   [d]7 That is, about 190 tons (about 170 metric tons)   [e]7 That is, about 185 pounds (about 84 kilograms)   [f]7 That is, about 375 tons (about 345 metric tons)   [g]7 That is, about 675 tons (about 610 metric tons)   [h]7 That is, about 3,750 tons (about 3,450 metric tons)

The Power of Praise-Filled Giving

READ AND CONSIDER: 1 CHRONICLES 29:1-20

"Wealth and honor come from you; you are the ruler of all things. In your hands are strength and power to exalt and give strength to all. Now, our God, we give you thanks, and praise your glorious name" (1 Chronicles 29:12-13).

David's life was winding down, and he wanted to pave the way for his son's reign and for the construction of the great temple. He arranged for vast sums of raw materials to be stockpiled for the project. As one of his last official gestures as king, David announced he would add his own personal gift from out of his treasures as the king. He challenged others to give in the same spirit, out of honor to God. "Now," he said, "who is willing to consecrate himself today to the LORD?" (29:5). Other leaders stepped up and gave. The resulting offering provided much of the funding for the construction of the temple.

The people were amazed at their own generosity. King David was deeply touched by their giving and lifted up one of the greatest prayers of praise in the Bible. It wasn't a long prayer, but every word exalted God and recognized Him as the ultimate supplier of all things. What more appropriate way to acknowledge God as the head over all and the owner of everything than by contributing generously to the building of a grand temple that would honor Him? What better way to show trust in God's future faithfulness than to give from the abundance of His present faithfulness?

After King David gave his personal treasure and praised God, he acknowledged the profound effect he had felt as the people gave their offerings. And he fervently prayed that this spirit of generosity and trust would always be a hallmark of God's people. David concluded by urging the people to "Praise the LORD your God" (29:20). They gave to God from their earthly treasures as well as giving praise to Him from their whole hearts.

Powerful prayer includes lavish praise to God for His generosity. It also includes giving to God out of a praise-filled heart. To do otherwise reveals that we revere our possessions more than our God, who has given us all that we have.

what comes from your hand. [15]We are aliens and strangers in your sight, as were all our forefathers. Our days on earth are like a shadow, without hope. [16]O LORD our God, as for all this abundance that we have provided for building you a temple for your Holy Name, it comes from your hand, and all of it belongs to you. [17]I know, my God, that you test the heart and are pleased with integrity. All these things have I given willingly and with honest intent. And now I have seen with joy how willingly your people who are here have given to you. [18]O LORD, God of our fathers Abraham, Isaac and Israel, keep this desire in the hearts of your people forever, and keep their hearts loyal to you. [19]And give my son Solomon the wholehearted devotion to keep your commands, requirements and decrees and to do everything to build the palatial structure for which I have provided."

[20]Then David said to the whole assembly, "Praise the LORD your God." So they all praised the LORD, the God of their fathers; they bowed low and fell prostrate before the LORD and the king.

Solomon Acknowledged as King

[21]The next day they made sacrifices to the LORD and presented burnt offerings

to him: a thousand bulls, a thousand rams and a thousand male lambs, together with their drink offerings, and other sacrifices in abundance for all Israel. 22 They ate and drank with great joy in the presence of the LORD that day.

Then they acknowledged Solomon son of David as king a second time, anointing him before the LORD to be ruler and Zadok to be priest. 23 So Solomon sat on the throne of the LORD as king in place of his father David. He prospered and all Israel obeyed him. 24 All the officers and mighty men, as well as all of King David's sons, pledged their submission to King Solomon.

25 The LORD highly exalted Solomon in the sight of all Israel and bestowed on him royal splendor such as no king over Israel ever had before.

The Death of David

26 David son of Jesse was king over all Israel. 27 He ruled over Israel forty years—seven in Hebron and thirty-three in Jerusalem. 28 He died at a good old age, having enjoyed long life, wealth and honor. His son Solomon succeeded him as king.

29 As for the events of King David's reign, from beginning to end, they are written in the records of Samuel the seer, the records of Nathan the prophet and the records of Gad the seer, 30 together with the details of his reign and power, and the circumstances that surrounded him and Israel and the kingdoms of all the other lands.

Author: Unknown, possibly Ezra

Date: About 400 BC

Audience: The remnant of Jews living after the exile, who needed a reminder of God's promises to bring about a Messiah through King David's descendants

Prayer Themes:

- Bring your "impossible" situations to God and trust in His infinite power (14:11).

- Ask God to give you a heart that hungers for Him and seeks Him . . . ask for the wisdom and grace to stay close to Him (15:2).

- Thank God that He is able to soften and change even the hardest heart (33:13).

Why should we be diligent to pursue God every day?

Our impact on others is directly proportional to our intimacy with God.

Second Chronicles warns us of the consequences of not seeking God. And it inspires us to follow hard after Him:

"If my people, who are called by my name, will humble themselves and pray and seek my face and turn from their wicked ways, then will I hear from heaven and will forgive their sin and will heal their land" (7:14).

Watch the parade of kings go by in 2 Chronicles. Observe their reigns. Whenever a ruler led in a godly manner, the people followed and prospered. Whenever a king turned away from God, the nation disintegrated spiritually.

The same is true for us. Following God brings blessing. Not following God brings destruction. This is reason alone to pray often throughout each day and to seek a close walk with God.

2 Chronicles

Solomon Asks for Wisdom

1 Solomon son of David established himself firmly over his kingdom, for the LORD his God was with him and made him exceedingly great.

²Then Solomon spoke to all Israel—to the commanders of thousands and commanders of hundreds, to the judges and to all the leaders in Israel, the heads of families— ³and Solomon and the whole assembly went to the high place at Gibeon, for God's Tent of Meeting was there, which Moses the LORD's servant had made in the desert. ⁴Now David had brought up the ark of God from Kiriath Jearim to the place he had prepared for it, because he had pitched a tent for it in Jerusalem. ⁵But the bronze altar that Bezalel son of Uri, the son of Hur, had made was in Gibeon in front of the tabernacle of the LORD; so Solomon and the assembly inquired of him there. ⁶Solomon went up to the bronze altar before the LORD in the Tent of Meeting and offered a thousand burnt offerings on it.

⁷That night God appeared to Solomon and said to him, "Ask for whatever you want me to give you."

⁸Solomon answered God, "You have shown great kindness to David my father and have made me king in his place. ⁹Now, LORD God, let your promise to my father David be confirmed, for you have made me king over a people who are as numerous as the dust of the earth. ¹⁰Give me wisdom and knowledge, that I may lead this people, for who is able to govern this great people of yours?"

¹¹God said to Solomon, "Since this is your heart's desire and you have not asked for wealth, riches or honor, nor for the death of your enemies, and since you have not asked for a long life but for wisdom and knowledge to govern my

people over whom I have made you king, [12]therefore wisdom and knowledge will be given you. And I will also give you wealth, riches and honor, such as no king who was before you ever had and none after you will have."

[13]Then Solomon went to Jerusalem from the high place at Gibeon, from before the Tent of Meeting. And he reigned over Israel.

[14]Solomon accumulated chariots and horses; he had fourteen hundred chariots and twelve thousand horses,[a] which he kept in the chariot cities and also with him in Jerusalem. [15]The king made silver and gold as common in Jerusalem as stones, and cedar as plentiful as sycamore-fig trees in the foothills. [16]Solomon's horses were imported from Egypt[b] and from Kue[c]—the royal merchants purchased them from Kue. [17]They imported a chariot from Egypt for six hundred shekels[d] of silver, and a horse for a hundred and fifty.[e] They also exported them to all the kings of the Hittites and of the Arameans.

Preparations for Building the Temple

2 Solomon gave orders to build a temple for the Name of the LORD and a royal palace for himself. [2]He conscripted seventy thousand men as carriers and eighty thousand as stonecutters in the hills and thirty-six hundred as foremen over them.

Praying 2 Chronicles 2:1

Help me to do something great for You, Lord.

[3]Solomon sent this message to Hiram[f] king of Tyre:

"Send me cedar logs as you did for my father David when you sent him cedar to build a palace to live in. [4]Now I am about to build a temple for the Name of the LORD my God and to dedicate it to him for burning fragrant incense before him, for setting out the consecrated bread regularly, and for making burnt offerings every morning and evening and on Sabbaths and New Moons and at the appointed feasts of the LORD our God. This is a lasting ordinance for Israel.

[5]"The temple I am going to build will be great, because our God is greater than all other gods. [6]But who is able to build a temple for him, since the heavens, even the highest heavens, cannot contain him? Who then am I to build a temple for him, except as a place to burn sacrifices before him?

[7]"Send me, therefore, a man skilled to work in gold and silver, bronze and iron, and in purple, crimson and blue yarn, and experienced in the art of engraving, to work in Judah and Jerusalem with my skilled craftsmen, whom my father David provided.

[8]"Send me also cedar, pine and algum[g] logs from Lebanon, for I know that your men are skilled in cutting timber there. My men will work with yours [9]to provide me with plenty of lumber, because the temple I build must be large and magnificent. [10]I will give your servants, the woodsmen who cut the timber, twenty thousand cors[h] of ground wheat, twenty thousand cors of barley, twenty thousand baths[i] of wine and twenty thousand baths of olive oil."

[11]Hiram king of Tyre replied by letter to Solomon:

"Because the LORD loves his people, he has made you their king."

---

[a] *14* Or *charioteers*   [b] *16* Or possibly *Muzur*, a region in Cilicia; also in verse 17   [c] *16* Probably Cilicia   [d] *17* That is, about 15 pounds (about 7 kilograms)   [e] *17* That is, about 3 3/4 pounds (about 1.7 kilograms)   [f] *3* Hebrew *Huram*, a variant of *Hiram*; also in verses 11 and 12   [g] *8* Probably a variant of *almug*; possibly juniper   [h] *10* That is, probably about 125,000 bushels (about 4,400 kiloliters)   [i] *10* That is, probably about 115,000 gallons (about 440 kiloliters)

¹²And Hiram added:

"Praise be to the LORD, the God of Israel, who made heaven and earth! He has given King David a wise son, endowed with intelligence and discernment, who will build a temple for the LORD and a palace for himself.

¹³"I am sending you Huram-Abi, a man of great skill, ¹⁴whose mother was from Dan and whose father was from Tyre. He is trained to work in gold and silver, bronze and iron, stone and wood, and with purple and blue and crimson yarn and fine linen. He is experienced in all kinds of engraving and can execute any design given to him. He will work with your craftsmen and with those of my lord, David your father.

¹⁵"Now let my lord send his servants the wheat and barley and the olive oil and wine he promised, ¹⁶and we will cut all the logs from Lebanon that you need and will float them in rafts by sea down to Joppa. You can then take them up to Jerusalem."

¹⁷Solomon took a census of all the aliens who were in Israel, after the census his father David had taken; and they were found to be 153,600. ¹⁸He assigned 70,000 of them to be carriers and 80,000 to be stonecutters in the hills, with 3,600 foremen over them to keep the people working.

Solomon Builds the Temple

3 Then Solomon began to build the temple of the LORD in Jerusalem on Mount Moriah, where the LORD had appeared to his father David. It was on the threshing floor of Araunah[a] the Jebusite, the place provided by David. ²He began building on the second day of the second month in the fourth year of his reign.

³The foundation Solomon laid for building the temple of God was sixty cubits long and twenty cubits wide[b] (using the cubit of the old standard). ⁴The portico at the front of the temple was twenty cubits[c] long across the width of the building and twenty cubits[d] high.

He overlaid the inside with pure gold. ⁵He paneled the main hall with pine and covered it with fine gold and decorated it with palm tree and chain designs. ⁶He adorned the temple with precious stones. And the gold he used was gold of Parvaim. ⁷He overlaid the ceiling beams, doorframes, walls and doors of the temple with gold, and he carved cherubim on the walls.

⁸He built the Most Holy Place, its length corresponding to the width of the temple—twenty cubits long and twenty cubits wide. He overlaid the inside with six hundred talents[e] of fine gold. ⁹The gold nails weighed fifty shekels.[f] He also overlaid the upper parts with gold.

¹⁰In the Most Holy Place he made a pair of sculptured cherubim and overlaid them with gold. ¹¹The total wingspan of the cherubim was twenty cubits. One wing of the first cherub was five cubits[g] long and touched the temple wall, while its other wing, also five cubits long, touched the wing of the other cherub. ¹²Similarly one wing of the second cherub was five cubits long and touched the other temple wall, and its other wing, also five cubits long, touched the wing of the first cherub. ¹³The wings of these cherubim extended twenty cubits. They stood on their feet, facing the main hall.[h]

¹⁴He made the curtain of blue, purple and crimson yarn and fine linen, with cherubim worked into it.

¹⁵In the front of the temple he made two pillars, which ⌊together⌋ were thirty-five cubits[i] long, each with a capital on

---

ᵃ 1 Hebrew Ornan, a variant of Araunah   ᵇ 3 That is, about 90 feet (about 27 meters) long and 30 feet (about 9 meters) wide
ᶜ 4 That is, about 30 feet (about 9 meters); also in verses 8, 11 and 13   ᵈ 4 Some Septuagint and Syriac manuscripts; Hebrew
and a hundred and twenty   ᵉ 8 That is, about 23 tons (about 21 metric tons)   ᶠ 9 That is, about 1 1/4 pounds (about
0.6 kilogram)   ᵍ 11 That is, about 7 1/2 feet (about 2.3 meters); also in verse 15   ʰ 13 Or facing inward   ⁱ 15 That is, about
52 feet (about 16 meters)

top measuring five cubits. [16]He made interwoven chains[a] and put them on top of the pillars. He also made a hundred pomegranates and attached them to the chains. [17]He erected the pillars in the front of the temple, one to the south and one to the north. The one to the south he named Jakin[b] and the one to the north Boaz.[c]

The Temple's Furnishings

4 He made a bronze altar twenty cubits long, twenty cubits wide and ten cubits high.[d] [2]He made the Sea of cast metal, circular in shape, measuring ten cubits from rim to rim and five cubits[e] high. It took a line of thirty cubits[f] to measure around it. [3]Below the rim, figures of bulls encircled it—ten to a cubit.[g] The bulls were cast in two rows in one piece with the Sea.

[4]The Sea stood on twelve bulls, three facing north, three facing west, three facing south and three facing east. The Sea rested on top of them, and their hindquarters were toward the center. [5]It was a handbreadth[h] in thickness, and its rim was like the rim of a cup, like a lily blossom. It held three thousand baths.[i]

[6]He then made ten basins for washing and placed five on the south side and five on the north. In them the things to be used for the burnt offerings were rinsed, but the Sea was to be used by the priests for washing.

[7]He made ten gold lampstands according to the specifications for them and placed them in the temple, five on the south side and five on the north.

[8]He made ten tables and placed them in the temple, five on the south side and five on the north. He also made a hundred gold sprinkling bowls.

[9]He made the courtyard of the priests, and the large court and the doors for the court, and overlaid the doors with bronze. [10]He placed the Sea on the south side, at the southeast corner.

[11]He also made the pots and shovels and sprinkling bowls.

So Huram finished the work he had undertaken for King Solomon in the temple of God:

[12]the two pillars;

the two bowl-shaped capitals on top of the pillars;

the two sets of network decorating the two bowl-shaped capitals on top of the pillars;

[13]the four hundred pomegranates for the two sets of network (two rows of pomegranates for each network, decorating the bowl-shaped capitals on top of the pillars);

[14]the stands with their basins;

[15]the Sea and the twelve bulls under it;

[16]the pots, shovels, meat forks and all related articles.

All the objects that Huram-Abi made for King Solomon for the temple of the LORD were of polished bronze. [17]The king had them cast in clay molds in the plain of the Jordan between Succoth and Zarethan.[j] [18]All these things that Solomon made amounted to so much that the weight of the bronze was not determined.

[19]Solomon also made all the furnishings that were in God's temple:

the golden altar;

the tables on which was the bread of the Presence;

[20]the lampstands of pure gold with their lamps, to burn in front of the inner sanctuary as prescribed;

[21]the gold floral work and lamps and tongs (they were solid gold);

[22]the pure gold wick trimmers, sprinkling bowls, dishes and censers; and the gold doors of the temple: the inner doors to the Most

---

[a] 16 Or possibly *made chains in the inner sanctuary*; the meaning of the Hebrew for this phrase is uncertain.   [b] 17 Jakin probably means *he establishes.*   [c] 17 Boaz probably means *in him is strength.*   [d] 1 That is, about 30 feet (about 9 meters) long and wide, and about 15 feet (about 4.5 meters) high   [e] 2 That is, about 7 1/2 feet (about 2.3 meters)   [f] 2 That is, about 45 feet (about 13.5 meters)   [g] 3 That is, about 1 1/2 feet (about 0.5 meter)   [h] 5 That is, about 3 inches (about 8 centimeters)   [i] 5 That is, about 17,500 gallons (about 66 kiloliters)   [j] 17 Hebrew *Zeredatha*, a variant of *Zarethan*

Holy Place and the doors of the main hall.

5 When all the work Solomon had done for the temple of the LORD was finished, he brought in the things his father David had dedicated—the silver and gold and all the furnishings—and he placed them in the treasuries of God's temple.

The Ark Brought to the Temple

2 Then Solomon summoned to Jerusalem the elders of Israel, all the heads of the tribes and the chiefs of the Israelite families, to bring up the ark of the LORD's covenant from Zion, the City of David. 3 And all the men of Israel came together to the king at the time of the festival in the seventh month.

4 When all the elders of Israel had arrived, the Levites took up the ark, 5 and they brought up the ark and the Tent of Meeting and all the sacred furnishings in it. The priests, who were Levites, carried them up; 6 and King Solomon and the entire assembly of Israel that had gathered about him were before the ark, sacrificing so many sheep and cattle that they could not be recorded or counted.

7 The priests then brought the ark of the LORD's covenant to its place in the inner sanctuary of the temple, the Most Holy Place, and put it beneath the wings of the cherubim. 8 The cherubim spread their wings over the place of the ark and covered the ark and its carrying poles. 9 These poles were so long that their ends, extending from the ark, could be seen from in front of the inner sanctuary, but not from outside the Holy Place; and they are still there today. 10 There was nothing in the ark except the two tablets that Moses had placed in it at Horeb, where the LORD made a covenant with the Israelites after they came out of Egypt.

11 The priests then withdrew from the Holy Place. All the priests who were there had consecrated themselves, regardless of their divisions. 12 All the Levites who were

musicians—Asaph, Heman, Jeduthun and their sons and relatives—stood on the east side of the altar, dressed in fine linen and playing cymbals, harps and lyres. They were accompanied by 120 priests sounding trumpets. 13 The trumpeters and singers joined in unison, as with one voice, to give praise and thanks to the LORD. Accompanied by trumpets, cymbals and other instruments, they raised their voices in praise to the LORD and sang:

"He is good;
his love endures forever."

Then the temple of the LORD was filled with a cloud, 14 and the priests could not perform their service because of the cloud, for the glory of the LORD filled the temple of God.

6 Then Solomon said, "The LORD has said that he would dwell in a dark cloud; 2 I have built a magnificent temple for you, a place for you to dwell forever."

3 While the whole assembly of Israel was standing there, the king turned around and blessed them. 4 Then he said:

"Praise be to the LORD, the God of Israel, who with his hands has fulfilled what he promised with his mouth to my father David. For he said, 5 'Since the day I brought my people out of Egypt, I have not chosen a city in any tribe of Israel to have a temple built for my Name to be there, nor have I chosen anyone to be the leader over my people Israel. 6 But now I have chosen Jerusalem for my Name to be there, and I have chosen David to rule my people Israel.'

7 "My father David had it in his heart to build a temple for the Name of the LORD, the God of Israel. 8 But the LORD said to my father David, 'Because it was in your heart to build a temple for my Name, you did well to have this in your heart. 9 Nevertheless, you are not the one to

GOING *deeper*

Inviting God's Presence and Forgiveness

READ AND CONSIDER: 2 CHRONICLES 6:12-42

"Now, my God, may your eyes be open and your ears attentive to the prayers offered in this place. Now arise, O LORD God, and come to your resting place, you and the ark of your might. May your priests, O LORD God, be clothed with salvation, may your saints rejoice in your goodness" (2 Chronicles 6:40-41).

Solomon's workers had completed the temple construction. David, Solomon's father and predecessor, had gathered the materials, but Solomon was charged with completing the actual structure. Such attention to detail was given to this process that it took seven years to complete the majestic temple. The walls and furniture were covered with gold. The king of Tyre himself shipped the lumber in from Lebanon.

Yet even with all its finery, it wasn't the temple building that prompted Solomon's thoughtful prayer here. It was God's glorious presence filling that temple. Finally there was a place for God to dwell more permanently among His people. Since the nation's whole identity was based on its relationship with God and His blessing, this was a very significant moment.

In light of that, it's interesting to really listen to Solomon's prayer. Rather than a formal prayer laced with high and holy phrases, it is a very down-to-earth prayer filled with the tough stuff of real life. Solomon covered the gamut of life situations that these people were going to face as they worshiped for—what he hopes will be—many centuries at this temple.

After describing all the possible tragedies that could happen, Solomon's prayer was, in essence, "Be with us." No matter how the people might stray, he wanted God to hear their prayers of repentance and forgive them. He wanted God's presence.

We should pray the same way—inviting God's presence to dwell in us and to forgive us whenever we stray from His ways.

build the temple, but your son, who is your own flesh and blood—he is the one who will build the temple for my Name.'

¹⁰"The LORD has kept the promise he made. I have succeeded David my father and now I sit on the throne of Israel, just as the LORD promised, and I have built the temple for the Name of the LORD, the God of Israel. ¹¹There I have placed the ark, in which is the covenant of the LORD that he made with the people of Israel."

Solomon's Prayer of Dedication

¹²Then Solomon stood before the altar of the LORD in front of the whole assembly of Israel and spread out his hands. ¹³Now he had made a bronze platform, five cubits[a] long, five cubits wide and three cubits[b] high, and had placed it in the center of the outer court. He stood on the platform and then knelt down before the whole assembly of Israel and spread out his hands toward heaven. ¹⁴He said:

"O LORD, God of Israel, there is no God like you in heaven or on earth —you who keep your covenant of

---

a *13* That is, about 7 1/2 feet (about 2.3 meters)   b *13* That is, about 4 1/2 feet (about 1.3 meters) love with your servants who continue wholeheartedly in your way. 15 You have kept your promise to your servant David my father; with your mouth you have promised and with your hand you have fulfilled it—as it is today.

16 "Now LORD, God of Israel, keep for your servant David my father the promises you made to him when you said, 'You shall never fail to have a man to sit before me on the throne of Israel, if only your sons are careful in all they do to walk before me according to my law, as you have done.' 17 And now, O LORD, God of Israel, let your word that you promised your servant David come true.

18 "But will God really dwell on earth with men? The heavens, even the highest heavens, cannot contain you. How much less this temple I have built! 19 Yet give attention to your servant's prayer and his plea for mercy, O LORD my God. Hear the cry and the prayer that your servant is praying in your presence. 20 May your eyes be open toward this temple day and night, this place of which you said you would put your Name there. May you hear the prayer your servant prays toward this place. 21 Hear the supplications of your servant and of your people Israel when they pray toward this place. Hear from heaven, your dwelling place; and when you hear, forgive.

22 "When a man wrongs his neighbor and is required to take an oath and he comes and swears the oath before your altar in this temple, 23 then hear from heaven and act. Judge between your servants, repaying the guilty by bringing down on his own head what he has done. Declare the innocent not guilty and so establish his innocence.

24 "When your people Israel have been defeated by an enemy because they have sinned against you and when they turn back and confess your name, praying and making supplication before you in this temple, 25 then hear from heaven and forgive the sin of your people Israel and bring them back to the land you gave to them and their fathers.

26 "When the heavens are shut up and there is no rain because your people have sinned against you, and when they pray toward this place and confess your name and turn from their sin because you have afflicted them, 27 then hear from heaven and forgive the sin of your servants, your people Israel. Teach them the right way to live, and send rain on the land you gave your people for an inheritance.

28 "When famine or plague comes to the land, or blight or mildew, locusts or grasshoppers, or when enemies besiege them in any of their cities, whatever disaster or disease may come, 29 and when a prayer or plea is made by any of your people Israel—each one aware of his afflictions and pains, and spreading out his hands toward this temple— 30 then hear from heaven, your dwelling place. Forgive, and deal with each man according to all he does, since you know his heart (for you alone know the hearts of men), 31 so that they will fear you and walk in your ways all the time they live in the land you gave our fathers.

32 "As for the foreigner who does not belong to your people Israel but has come from a distant land because of your great name and your mighty hand and your outstretched arm—when he comes and prays toward this temple, 33 then hear from heaven, your dwelling place, and do whatever the foreigner asks of you, so that all the peoples of the earth may know your name and fear you,

as do your own people Israel, and may know that this house I have built bears your Name.

34"When your people go to war against their enemies, wherever you send them, and when they pray to you toward this city you have chosen and the temple I have built for your Name, 35then hear from heaven their prayer and their plea, and uphold their cause.

36"When they sin against you—for there is no one who does not sin—and you become angry with them and give them over to the enemy, who takes them captive to a land far away or near; 37and if they have a change of heart in the land where they are held captive, and repent and plead with you in the land of their captivity and say, 'We have sinned, we have done wrong and acted wickedly'; 38and if they turn back to you with all their heart and soul in the land of their captivity where they were taken, and pray toward the land you gave their fathers, toward the city you have chosen and toward the temple I have built for your Name; 39then from heaven, your dwelling place, hear their prayer and their pleas, and uphold their cause. And forgive your people, who have sinned against you.

40"Now, my God, may your eyes be open and your ears attentive to the prayers offered in this place.

41"Now arise, O Lord God, and
  come to your resting place,
  you and the ark of your might.
May your priests, O Lord God,
  be clothed with salvation,
  may your saints rejoice in your
    goodness.
42O Lord God, do not reject your
    anointed one.
  Remember the great love
    promised to David your
    servant."

The Dedication of the Temple

7 When Solomon finished praying, fire came down from heaven and consumed the burnt offering and the sacrifices, and the glory of the Lord filled the temple. 2The priests could not enter the temple of the Lord because the glory of the Lord filled it. 3When all the Israelites saw the fire coming down and the glory of the Lord above the temple, they knelt on the pavement with their faces to the ground, and they worshiped and gave thanks to the Lord, saying,

"He is good;
  his love endures forever."

4Then the king and all the people offered sacrifices before the Lord. 5And King Solomon offered a sacrifice of twenty-two thousand head of cattle and a hundred and twenty thousand sheep and goats. So the king and all the people dedicated the temple of God. 6The priests took their positions, as did the Levites with the Lord's musical instruments, which King David had made for praising the Lord and which were used when he gave thanks, saying, "His love endures forever." Opposite the Levites, the priests blew their trumpets, and all the Israelites were standing.

7Solomon consecrated the middle part of the courtyard in front of the temple of the Lord, and there he offered burnt offerings and the fat of the fellowship offerings,[a] because the bronze altar he had made could not hold the burnt offerings, the grain offerings and the fat portions.

8So Solomon observed the festival at that time for seven days, and all Israel with him—a vast assembly, people from Lebo[b] Hamath to the Wadi of Egypt. 9On the eighth day they held an assembly, for they had celebrated the dedication of the altar for seven days and the festival for seven days more. 10On the twenty-third day of the seventh month he sent the people to their homes, joyful and glad in

---

a 7 Traditionally *peace offerings*   b 8 Or *from the entrance to*

Why We Must Pray for Our Nation

READ AND CONSIDER: 2 CHRONICLES 7:11-22

"If my people, who are called by my name, will humble themselves and pray and seek my face and turn from their wicked ways, then will I hear from heaven and will forgive their sin and will heal their land" (2 Chronicles 7:14).

King Solomon dedicated the temple and saw God's awesome presence there. The people feasted for days and days. The king prayed a prayer that seemed to cover all possible contingencies, asking God for guidance, deliverance, and forgiveness. Once the festivities were over, God answered. Coming to Solomon in the night, God laid it out, plain and simple. *If* the people would follow God's ways, *then* He would hear their prayers and heal their land.

Looking back through Israel's history, it is obvious that every time the people did not follow God's plan, they didn't receive what God had planned for them. When they worshiped other gods and did whatever they wanted, when they married into other tribes and made deals with wicked nations, they lost political strength and were ultimately defeated and taken away as exiles.

We can ask ourselves, how could they have missed it? God couldn't have been clearer in His instructions. And yet, we too often miss what God is saying. God is still saying that if we follow His ways our lives will be better, yet often we don't follow and then wonder why things go the way they do.

God is still saying, "Pray for your nation." Whether we like our leaders or greatly disagree with them, God calls us to humble ourselves and pray for them.

Our land needs healing. God's promise is that if we turn from our wicked ways, He will forgive and heal. That won't happen without prayer.

heart for the good things the LORD had done for David and Solomon and for his people Israel.

The LORD Appears to Solomon

[11]When Solomon had finished the temple of the LORD and the royal palace, and had succeeded in carrying out all he had in mind to do in the temple of the LORD and in his own palace, [12]the LORD appeared to him at night and said:

"I have heard your prayer and have chosen this place for myself as a temple for sacrifices.

[13]"When I shut up the heavens so that there is no rain, or command locusts to devour the land or send a plague among my people, [14]if my people, who are called by my name, will humble themselves and pray and seek my face and turn from their wicked ways, then will I hear from heaven and will forgive their sin and will heal their land. [15]Now my eyes will be open and my ears attentive to the prayers offered in this place.

Praying 2 Chronicles 7:14

Lord, I humble myself before You and pray that You would forgive the sins of my people and heal our land.

[16]I have chosen and consecrated this temple so that my Name may be there forever. My eyes and my heart will always be there.

[17]"As for you, if you walk before

me as David your father did, and do all I command, and observe my decrees and laws, 18I will establish your royal throne, as I covenanted with David your father when I said, 'You shall never fail to have a man to rule over Israel.'

19"But if you[a] turn away and forsake the decrees and commands I have given you[a] and go off to serve other gods and worship them, 20then I will uproot Israel from my land, which I have given them, and will reject this temple I have consecrated for my Name. I will make it a byword and an object of ridicule among all peoples. 21And though this temple is now so imposing, all who pass by will be appalled and say, 'Why has the LORD done such a thing to this land and to this temple?' 22People will answer, 'Because they have forsaken the LORD, the God of their fathers, who brought them out of Egypt, and have embraced other gods, worshiping and serving them—that is why he brought all this disaster on them.'"

Solomon's Other Activities

8 At the end of twenty years, during which Solomon built the temple of the LORD and his own palace, 2Solomon rebuilt the villages that Hiram[b] had given him, and settled Israelites in them. 3Solomon then went to Hamath Zobah and captured it. 4He also built up Tadmor in the desert and all the store cities he had built in Hamath. 5He rebuilt Upper Beth Horon and Lower Beth Horon as fortified cities, with walls and with gates and bars, 6as well as Baalath and all his store cities, and all the cities for his chariots and for his horses[c]—whatever he desired to build in Jerusalem, in Lebanon and throughout all the territory he ruled.

7All the people left from the Hittites, Amorites, Perizzites, Hivites and Jebusites (these peoples were not Israelites), 8that is, their descendants remaining in the land, whom the Israelites had not destroyed—these Solomon conscripted for his slave labor force, as it is to this day. 9But Solomon did not make slaves of the Israelites for his work; they were his fighting men, commanders of his captains, and commanders of his chariots and charioteers. 10They were also King Solomon's chief officials—two hundred and fifty officials supervising the men.

11Solomon brought Pharaoh's daughter up from the City of David to the palace he had built for her, for he said, "My wife must not live in the palace of David king of Israel, because the places the ark of the LORD has entered are holy."

12On the altar of the LORD that he had built in front of the portico, Solomon sacrificed burnt offerings to the LORD, 13according to the daily requirement for offerings commanded by Moses for Sabbaths, New Moons and the three annual feasts—the Feast of Unleavened Bread, the Feast of Weeks and the Feast of Tabernacles. 14In keeping with the ordinance of his father David, he appointed the divisions of the priests for their duties, and the Levites to lead the praise and to assist the priests according to each day's requirement. He also appointed the gatekeepers by divisions for the various gates, because this was what David the man of God had ordered. 15They did not deviate from the king's commands to the priests or to the Levites in any matter, including that of the treasuries.

16All Solomon's work was carried out, from the day the foundation of the temple of the LORD was laid until its completion. So the temple of the LORD was finished.

17Then Solomon went to Ezion Geber and Elath on the coast of Edom. 18And Hiram sent him ships commanded by his own officers, men who knew the sea. These, with Solomon's men, sailed to Ophir and brought back four hundred

---

a 19 The Hebrew is plural.   b 2 Hebrew Huram, a variant of Hiram; also in verse 18   c 6 Or charioteers and fifty talents[a] of gold, which they delivered to King Solomon.

The Queen of Sheba Visits Solomon

9 When the queen of Sheba heard of Solomon's fame, she came to Jerusalem to test him with hard questions. Arriving with a very great caravan—with camels carrying spices, large quantities of gold, and precious stones—she came to Solomon and talked with him about all she had on her mind. [2]Solomon answered all her questions; nothing was too hard for him to explain to her. [3]When the queen of Sheba saw the wisdom of Solomon, as well as the palace he had built, [4]the food on his table, the seating of his officials, the attending servants in their robes, the cupbearers in their robes and the burnt offerings he made at[b] the temple of the LORD, she was overwhelmed.

[5]She said to the king, "The report I heard in my own country about your achievements and your wisdom is true. [6]But I did not believe what they said until I came and saw with my own eyes. Indeed, not even half the greatness of your wisdom was told me; you have far exceeded the report I heard. [7]How happy your men must be! How happy your officials, who continually stand before you and hear your wisdom! [8]Praise be to the LORD your God, who has delighted in you and placed you on his throne as king to rule for the LORD your God. Because of the love of your God for Israel and his desire to uphold them forever, he has made you king over them, to maintain justice and righteousness."

[9]Then she gave the king 120 talents[c] of gold, large quantities of spices, and precious stones. There had never been such spices as those the queen of Sheba gave to King Solomon.

[10](The men of Hiram and the men of Solomon brought gold from Ophir; they also brought algumwood[d] and precious stones. [11]The king used the algumwood to make steps for the temple of the LORD and for the royal palace, and to make harps and lyres for the musicians. Nothing like them had ever been seen in Judah.)

[12]King Solomon gave the queen of Sheba all she desired and asked for; he gave her more than she had brought to him. Then she left and returned with her retinue to her own country.

Solomon's Splendor

[13]The weight of the gold that Solomon received yearly was 666 talents,[e] [14]not including the revenues brought in by merchants and traders. Also all the kings of Arabia and the governors of the land brought gold and silver to Solomon.

[15]King Solomon made two hundred large shields of hammered gold; six hundred bekas[f] of hammered gold went into each shield. [16]He also made three hundred small shields of hammered gold, with three hundred bekas[g] of gold in each shield. The king put them in the Palace of the Forest of Lebanon.

[17]Then the king made a great throne inlaid with ivory and overlaid with pure gold. [18]The throne had six steps, and a footstool of gold was attached to it. On both sides of the seat were armrests, with a lion standing beside each of them. [19]Twelve lions stood on the six steps, one at either end of each step. Nothing like it had ever been made for any other kingdom. [20]All King Solomon's goblets were gold, and all the household articles in the Palace of the Forest of Lebanon were pure gold. Nothing was made of silver, because silver was considered of little value in Solomon's day. [21]The king had a fleet of trading ships[h] manned by Hiram's[i] men. Once every three years it returned, carrying gold, silver and ivory, and apes and baboons.

---

[a] 18 That is, about 17 tons (about 16 metric tons)   [b] 4 Or the ascent by which he went up to   [c] 9 That is, about 4 1/2 tons (about 4 metric tons)   [d] 10 Probably a variant of almugwood   [e] 13 That is, about 25 tons (about 23 metric tons)   [f] 15 That is, about 7 1/2 pounds (about 3.5 kilograms)   [g] 16 That is, about 3 3/4 pounds (about 1.7 kilograms)   [h] 21 Hebrew of ships that could go to Tarshish   [i] 21 Hebrew Huram, a variant of Hiram

²²King Solomon was greater in riches and wisdom than all the other kings of the earth. ²³All the kings of the earth sought audience with Solomon to hear the wisdom God had put in his heart. ²⁴Year after year, everyone who came brought a gift—articles of silver and gold, and robes, weapons and spices, and horses and mules.

²⁵Solomon had four thousand stalls for horses and chariots, and twelve thousand horses,ᵃ which he kept in the chariot cities and also with him in Jerusalem. ²⁶He ruled over all the kings from the Riverᵇ to the land of the Philistines, as far as the border of Egypt. ²⁷The king made silver as common in Jerusalem as stones, and cedar as plentiful as sycamore-fig trees in the foothills. ²⁸Solomon's horses were imported from Egyptᶜ and from all other countries.

Solomon's Death

²⁹As for the other events of Solomon's reign, from beginning to end, are they not written in the records of Nathan the prophet, in the prophecy of Ahijah the Shilonite and in the visions of Iddo the seer concerning Jeroboam son of Nebat? ³⁰Solomon reigned in Jerusalem over all Israel forty years. ³¹Then he rested with his fathers and was buried in the city of David his father. And Rehoboam his son succeeded him as king.

Israel Rebels Against Rehoboam

10 Rehoboam went to Shechem, for all the Israelites had gone there to make him king. ²When Jeroboam son of Nebat heard this (he was in Egypt, where he had fled from King Solomon), he returned from Egypt. ³So they sent for Jeroboam, and he and all Israel went to Rehoboam and said to him: ⁴"Your father put a heavy yoke on us, but now lighten the harsh labor and the heavy yoke he put on us, and we will serve you."

⁵Rehoboam answered, "Come back to me in three days." So the people went away.

⁶Then King Rehoboam consulted the elders who had served his father Solomon during his lifetime. "How would you advise me to answer these people?" he asked.

⁷They replied, "If you will be kind to these people and please them and give them a favorable answer, they will always be your servants."

⁸But Rehoboam rejected the advice the elders gave him and consulted the young men who had grown up with him and were serving him. ⁹He asked them, "What is your advice? How should we answer these people who say to me, 'Lighten the yoke your father put on us'?"

Prayer is . . .

how you see God's purpose for your life realized.

¹⁰The young men who had grown up with him replied, "Tell the people who have said to you, 'Your father put a heavy yoke on us, but make our yoke lighter'—tell them, 'My little finger is thicker than my father's waist. ¹¹My father laid on you a heavy yoke; I will make it even heavier. My father scourged you with whips; I will scourge you with scorpions.'"

¹²Three days later Jeroboam and all the people returned to Rehoboam, as the king had said, "Come back to me in three days." ¹³The king answered them harshly. Rejecting the advice of the elders, ¹⁴he followed the advice of the young men and said, "My father made your yoke heavy; I will make it even heavier. My father scourged you with whips; I will scourge you with scorpions." ¹⁵So the king did not listen to the people, for this turn of events was from God, to fulfill the word the LORD had spoken to Jeroboam son of Nebat through Ahijah the Shilonite.

¹⁶When all Israel saw that the king re-

ᵃ 25 Or *charioteers*   ᵇ 26 That is, the Euphrates   ᶜ 28 Or possibly *Muzur,* a region in Cilicia fused to listen to them, they answered the king:

"What share do we have in David,
    what part in Jesse's son?
To your tents, O Israel!
    Look after your own house,
        O David!"

So all the Israelites went home. [17]But as for the Israelites who were living in the towns of Judah, Rehoboam still ruled over them.

[18]King Rehoboam sent out Adoniram,[a] who was in charge of forced labor, but the Israelites stoned him to death. King Rehoboam, however, managed to get into his chariot and escape to Jerusalem. [19]So Israel has been in rebellion against the house of David to this day.

[11] When Rehoboam arrived in Jerusalem, he mustered the house of Judah and Benjamin—a hundred and eighty thousand fighting men—to make war against Israel and to regain the kingdom for Rehoboam.

[2]But this word of the LORD came to Shemaiah the man of God: [3]"Say to Rehoboam son of Solomon king of Judah and to all the Israelites in Judah and Benjamin, [4]'This is what the LORD says: Do not go up to fight against your brothers. Go home, every one of you, for this is my doing.'" So they obeyed the words of the LORD and turned back from marching against Jeroboam.

Rehoboam Fortifies Judah

[5]Rehoboam lived in Jerusalem and built up towns for defense in Judah: [6]Bethlehem, Etam, Tekoa, [7]Beth Zur, Soco, Adullam, [8]Gath, Mareshah, Ziph, [9]Adoraim, Lachish, Azekah, [10]Zorah, Aijalon and Hebron. These were fortified cities in Judah and Benjamin. [11]He strengthened their defenses and put commanders in them, with supplies of food, olive oil and wine. [12]He put shields and spears in all the cities, and made them very strong. So Judah and Benjamin were his.

[13]The priests and Levites from all their districts throughout Israel sided with him. [14]The Levites even abandoned their pasturelands and property, and came to Judah and Jerusalem because Jeroboam and his sons had rejected them as priests of the LORD. [15]And he appointed his own priests for the high places and for the goat and calf idols he had made. [16]Those from every tribe of Israel who set their hearts on seeking the LORD, the God of Israel, followed the Levites to Jerusalem to offer sacrifices to the LORD, the God of their fathers. [17]They strengthened the kingdom of Judah and supported Rehoboam son of Solomon three years, walking in the ways of David and Solomon during this time.

Rehoboam's Family

[18]Rehoboam married Mahalath, who was the daughter of David's son Jerimoth and of Abihail, the daughter of Jesse's son Eliab. [19]She bore him sons: Jeush, Shemariah and Zaham. [20]Then he married Maacah daughter of Absalom, who bore him Abijah, Attai, Ziza and Shelomith. [21]Rehoboam loved Maacah daughter of Absalom more than any of his other wives and concubines. In all, he had eighteen wives and sixty concubines, twenty-eight sons and sixty daughters.

[22]Rehoboam appointed Abijah son of Maacah to be the chief prince among his brothers, in order to make him king. [23]He acted wisely, dispersing some of his sons throughout the districts of Judah and Benjamin, and to all the fortified cities. He gave them abundant provisions and took many wives for them.

Shishak Attacks Jerusalem

[12] After Rehoboam's position as king was established and he had become strong, he and all Israel[b] with him abandoned the law of the LORD. [2]Because they had been unfaithful to the LORD, Shishak king of Egypt attacked Jerusalem in the fifth year of King Rehoboam.

---

[a] 18 Hebrew *Hadoram*, a variant of *Adoniram*   [b] 1 That is, Judah, as frequently in 2 Chronicles

³With twelve hundred chariots and sixty thousand horsemen and the innumerable troops of Libyans, Sukkites and Cushites[a] that came with him from Egypt, ⁴he captured the fortified cities of Judah and came as far as Jerusalem.

⁵Then the prophet Shemaiah came to Rehoboam and to the leaders of Judah who had assembled in Jerusalem for fear of Shishak, and he said to them, "This is what the LORD says, 'You have abandoned me; therefore, I now abandon you to Shishak.'"

⁶The leaders of Israel and the king humbled themselves and said, "The LORD is just."

⁷When the LORD saw that they humbled themselves, this word of the LORD came to Shemaiah: "Since they have humbled themselves, I will not destroy them but will soon give them deliverance. My wrath will not be poured out on Jerusalem through Shishak. ⁸They will, however, become subject to him, so that they may learn the difference between serving me and serving the kings of other lands."

⁹When Shishak king of Egypt attacked Jerusalem, he carried off the treasures of the temple of the LORD and the treasures of the royal palace. He took everything, including the gold shields Solomon had made. ¹⁰So King Rehoboam made bronze shields to replace them and assigned these to the commanders of the guard on duty at the entrance to the royal palace. ¹¹Whenever the king went to the LORD's temple, the guards went with him, bearing the shields, and afterward they returned them to the guardroom.

¹²Because Rehoboam humbled himself, the LORD's anger turned from him, and he was not totally destroyed. Indeed, there was some good in Judah.

¹³King Rehoboam established himself firmly in Jerusalem and continued as king. He was forty-one years old when he became king, and he reigned seventeen years in Jerusalem, the city the LORD had chosen out of all the tribes of Israel in which to put his Name. His mother's name was Naamah; she was an Ammonite. ¹⁴He did evil because he had not set his heart on seeking the LORD.

¹⁵As for the events of Rehoboam's reign, from beginning to end, are they not written in the records of Shemaiah the prophet and of Iddo the seer that deal with genealogies? There was continual warfare between Rehoboam and Jeroboam. ¹⁶Rehoboam rested with his fathers and was buried in the City of David. And Abijah his son succeeded him as king.

Abijah King of Judah

13 In the eighteenth year of the reign of Jeroboam, Abijah became king of Judah, ²and he reigned in Jerusalem three years. His mother's name was Maacah,[b] a daughter[c] of Uriel of Gibeah.

There was war between Abijah and Jeroboam. ³Abijah went into battle with a force of four hundred thousand able fighting men, and Jeroboam drew up a battle line against him with eight hundred thousand able troops.

⁴Abijah stood on Mount Zemaraim, in the hill country of Ephraim, and said, "Jeroboam and all Israel, listen to me! ⁵Don't you know that the LORD, the God of Israel, has given the kingship of Israel to David and his descendants forever by a covenant of salt? ⁶Yet Jeroboam son of Nebat, an official of Solomon son of David, rebelled against his master. ⁷Some worthless scoundrels gathered around him and opposed Rehoboam son of Solomon when he was young and indecisive and not strong enough to resist them.

⁸"And now you plan to resist the kingdom of the LORD, which is in the hands of David's descendants. You are indeed a vast army and have with you the golden calves that Jeroboam made to be your gods. ⁹But didn't you drive out the priests

a 3 That is, people from the upper Nile region   b 2 Most Septuagint manuscripts and Syriac (see also 2 Chron. 11:20 and 1 Kings 15:2); Hebrew Micaiah   c 2 Or granddaughter of the LORD, the sons of Aaron, and the Levites, and make priests of your own as the peoples of other lands do? Whoever comes to consecrate himself with a young bull and seven rams may become a priest of what are not gods.

10 "As for us, the LORD is our God, and we have not forsaken him. The priests who serve the LORD are sons of Aaron, and the Levites assist them. 11 Every morning and evening they present burnt offerings and fragrant incense to the LORD. They set out the bread on the ceremonially clean table and light the lamps on the gold lampstand every evening. We are observing the requirements of the LORD our God. But you have forsaken him. 12 God is with us; he is our leader. His priests with their trumpets will sound the battle cry against you. Men of Israel, do not fight against the LORD, the God of your fathers, for you will not succeed."

13 Now Jeroboam had sent troops around to the rear, so that while he was in front of Judah the ambush was behind them. 14 Judah turned and saw that they were being attacked at both front and rear. Then they cried out to the LORD. The priests blew their trumpets 15 and the men of Judah raised the battle cry. At the sound of their battle cry, God routed Jeroboam and all Israel before Abijah and Judah. 16 The Israelites fled before Judah, and God delivered them into their hands. 17 Abijah and his men inflicted heavy losses on them, so that there were five hundred thousand casualties among Israel's able men. 18 The men of Israel were subdued on that occasion, and the men of Judah were victorious because they relied on the LORD, the God of their fathers.

19 Abijah pursued Jeroboam and took from him the towns of Bethel, Jeshanah and Ephron, with their surrounding villages. 20 Jeroboam did not regain power during the time of Abijah. And the LORD struck him down and he died.

21 But Abijah grew in strength. He married fourteen wives and had twenty-two sons and sixteen daughters.

22 The other events of Abijah's reign, what he did and what he said, are written in the annotations of the prophet Iddo.

14 And Abijah rested with his fathers and was buried in the City of David. Asa his son succeeded him as king, and in his days the country was at peace for ten years.

Asa King of Judah

2 Asa did what was good and right in the eyes of the LORD his God. 3 He removed the foreign altars and the high places, smashed the sacred stones and cut down the Asherah poles.ᵃ 4 He commanded Judah to seek the LORD, the God of their fathers, and to obey his laws and commands. 5 He removed the high places and incense altars in every town in Judah, and the kingdom was at peace under him. 6 He built up the fortified cities of Judah, since the land was at peace. No one was at war with him during those years, for the LORD gave him rest.

7 "Let us build up these towns," he said to Judah, "and put walls around them, with towers, gates and bars. The land is still ours, because we have sought the LORD our God; we sought him and he has given us rest on every side." So they built and prospered.

8 Asa had an army of three hundred thousand men from Judah, equipped with large shields and with spears, and two hundred and eighty thousand from Benjamin, armed with small shields and with bows. All these were brave fighting men.

9 Zerah the Cushite marched out against them with a vast armyᵇ and three hundred chariots, and came as far as Mareshah. 10 Asa went out to meet him, and they took up battle positions in the Valley of Zephathah near Mareshah.

11 Then Asa called to the LORD his God

God's people at prayer
ASA REVEALS A PART-TIME FAITH

2 CHRONICLES 14:11 Asa was known as one of the good kings of Judah. His reign was set apart by a time in his rule when he faced national crises by trusting in God. He was also among the kings who destroyed pagan shrines in an attempt to purify the worship of the people.

If you look more closely at Asa's career, however, you'll find that his "good king" status was only part of the story. Faced with an opportunity to build a strong military alliance, Asa gave away the temple treasures and abandoned his trust in God (chapter 16). Asa ended his life as a sick, old man so disconnected from his faith that he didn't even ask for God's help or healing.

Many of us do the same thing. A crisis comes and we pray. But when things are going well, often we don't pray as fervently or frequently. But we must, because prayer keeps us connected to God.

and said, "LORD, there is no one like you to help the powerless against the mighty. Help us, O LORD our God, for we rely on you, and in your name we have come against this vast army. O LORD, you are our God; do not let man prevail against you."

¹²The LORD struck down the Cushites before Asa and Judah. The Cushites fled, ¹³and Asa and his army pursued them as far as Gerar. Such a great number of Cushites fell that they could not recover; they were crushed before the LORD and his forces. The men of Judah carried off a large amount of plunder. ¹⁴They destroyed all the villages around Gerar, for the terror of the LORD had fallen upon them. They plundered all these villages, since there was much booty there. ¹⁵They also attacked the camps of the herdsmen and carried off droves of sheep and goats and camels. Then they returned to Jerusalem.

Asa's Reform

15 The Spirit of God came upon Azariah son of Oded. ²He went out to meet Asa and said to him, "Listen to me, Asa and all Judah and Benjamin. The LORD is with you when you are with him. If you seek him, he will be found by you, but if you forsake him, he will forsake you. ³For a long time Israel was without the true God, without a priest to teach and without the law. ⁴But in their distress they turned to the LORD, the God of Israel, and sought him, and he was found by them. ⁵In those days it was not safe to travel about, for all the inhabitants of the lands were in great turmoil. ⁶One nation was being crushed by another and one city by another, because God was troubling them with every kind of distress. ⁷But as for you, be strong and do not give up, for your work will be rewarded."

Praying 2 Chronicles 15:7
Reward the work of my hands with success, Lord.

⁸When Asa heard these words and the prophecy of Azariah son of[a] Oded the prophet, he took courage. He removed the detestable idols from the whole land of Judah and Benjamin and from the towns he had captured in the hills of Ephraim. He repaired the altar of the LORD that was in front of the portico of the LORD's temple.

⁹Then he assembled all Judah and Benjamin and the people from Ephraim, Manasseh and Simeon who had settled among them, for large numbers had come over to him from Israel when they saw that the LORD his God was with him.

¹⁰They assembled at Jerusalem in the

---

[a] *8* Vulgate and Syriac (see also Septuagint and verse 1); Hebrew does not have *Azariah son of*.

GOING *deeper* 1

Praying in the Good Times

READ AND CONSIDER: 2 CHRONICLES 15:1-19

"Although he did not remove the high places from Israel, Asa's heart was fully committed ⌊to the LORD⌋ all his life" (2 Chronicles 15:17).

When we live a lifestyle of praise and worship, we keep our heart fresh and open to the working of the Holy Spirit in us. Spending time in prayerful worship keeps us in the right attitude to hear from God and be guided by Him. It positions Him as first priority in our lives and helps us stay dependent upon Him, whether things in our lives are going well or not.

When the Spirit of God came upon the prophet Azariah, he told King Asa, "The LORD is with you when you are with him. If you seek him, he will be found by you, but if you forsake him, he will forsake you" (15:2). It can't get any clearer than that. If God is with *us* as long as we're with *Him*, that should increase our motivation to be with *Him*.

So what does it mean to be "with God"? We understand it pretty clearly in the bad times. We come to God desperate for help. What about when things are going well? The best advice when you are in a season of peace and rest is to use that time to build and fortify yourself in the Lord. Study His Word. Communicate with Him in prayer. Spend time in His presence in worship and praise. Get closer. Stay *with* Him. Use that time to fall in love with Jesus all over again.

King Asa didn't always do everything right, but in the end he was described as a king who had a heart fully committed to the Lord. Even when you don't act perfectly, you can show God that your heart is perfectly in love with Him by the praise you give Him every day.

third month of the fifteenth year of Asa's reign. ¹¹At that time they sacrificed to the LORD seven hundred head of cattle and seven thousand sheep and goats from the plunder they had brought back. ¹²They entered into a covenant to seek the LORD, the God of their fathers, with all their heart and soul. ¹³All who would not seek the LORD, the God of Israel, were to be put to death, whether small or great, man or woman. ¹⁴They took an oath to the LORD with loud acclamation, with shouting and with trumpets and horns. ¹⁵All Judah rejoiced about the oath because they had sworn it wholeheartedly. They sought God eagerly, and he was found by them. So the LORD gave them rest on every side.

¹⁶King Asa also deposed his grandmother Maacah from her position as queen mother, because she had made a repulsive Asherah pole. Asa cut the pole

down, broke it up and burned it in the Kidron Valley. ¹⁷Although he did not remove the high places from Israel, Asa's heart was fully committed ⌊to the LORD⌋ all his life. ¹⁸He brought into the temple of God the silver and gold and the articles that he and his father had dedicated.

¹⁹There was no more war until the thirty-fifth year of Asa's reign.

Asa's Last Years

16 In the thirty-sixth year of Asa's reign Baasha king of Israel went up against Judah and fortified Ramah to prevent anyone from leaving or entering the territory of Asa king of Judah.

²Asa then took the silver and gold out of the treasuries of the LORD's temple and of his own palace and sent it to Ben-Hadad king of Aram, who was ruling in Damascus. ³"Let there be a treaty between me and you," he said, "as there

was between my father and your father. See, I am sending you silver and gold. Now break your treaty with Baasha king of Israel so he will withdraw from me."

⁴Ben-Hadad agreed with King Asa and sent the commanders of his forces against the towns of Israel. They conquered Ijon, Dan, Abel Maim[a] and all the store cities of Naphtali. ⁵When Baasha heard this, he stopped building Ramah and abandoned his work. ⁶Then King Asa brought all the men of Judah, and they carried away from Ramah the stones and timber Baasha had been using. With them he built up Geba and Mizpah.

⁷At that time Hanani the seer came to Asa king of Judah and said to him: "Because you relied on the king of Aram and not on the LORD your God, the army of the king of Aram has escaped from your hand. ⁸Were not the Cushites[b] and Libyans a mighty army with great numbers of chariots and horsemen[c]? Yet when you relied on the LORD, he delivered them into your hand. ⁹For the eyes of the LORD range throughout the earth to strengthen those whose hearts are fully committed to him. You have done a foolish thing, and from now on you will be at war."

¹⁰Asa was angry with the seer because of this; he was so enraged that he put him in prison. At the same time Asa brutally oppressed some of the people.

¹¹The events of Asa's reign, from beginning to end, are written in the book of the kings of Judah and Israel. ¹²In the thirty-ninth year of his reign Asa was afflicted with a disease in his feet. Though his disease was severe, even in his illness he did not seek help from the LORD, but only from the physicians. ¹³Then in the forty-first year of his reign Asa died and rested with his fathers. ¹⁴They buried him in the tomb that he had cut out for himself in the City of David. They laid him on a bier covered with spices and various blended perfumes, and they made a huge fire in his honor.

Jehoshaphat King of Judah

17 Jehoshaphat his son succeeded him as king and strengthened himself against Israel. ²He stationed troops in all the fortified cities of Judah and put garrisons in Judah and in the towns of Ephraim that his father Asa had captured.

³The LORD was with Jehoshaphat because in his early years he walked in the ways his father David had followed. He did not consult the Baals ⁴but sought the God of his father and followed his commands rather than the practices of Israel. ⁵The LORD established the kingdom under his control; and all Judah brought gifts to Jehoshaphat, so that he had great wealth and honor. ⁶His heart was devoted to the ways of the LORD; furthermore, he removed the high places and the Asherah poles from Judah.

⁷In the third year of his reign he sent his officials Ben-Hail, Obadiah, Zechariah, Nethanel and Micaiah to teach in the towns of Judah. ⁸With them were certain Levites—Shemaiah, Nethaniah, Zebadiah, Asahel, Shemiramoth, Jehonathan, Adonijah, Tobijah and Tob-Adonijah—and the priests Elishama and Jehoram. ⁹They taught throughout Judah, taking with them the Book of the Law of the LORD; they went around to all the towns of Judah and taught the people.

¹⁰The fear of the LORD fell on all the kingdoms of the lands surrounding Judah, so that they did not make war with Jehoshaphat. ¹¹Some Philistines brought Jehoshaphat gifts and silver as tribute, and the Arabs brought him flocks: seven thousand seven hundred rams and seven thousand seven hundred goats.

¹²Jehoshaphat became more and more powerful; he built forts and store cities in Judah ¹³and had large supplies in the towns of Judah. He also kept experienced fighting men in Jerusalem. ¹⁴Their enrollment by families was as follows:

From Judah, commanders of units of 1,000:

Adnah the commander, with 300,000 fighting men;

15 next, Jehohanan the commander, with 280,000;

16 next, Amasiah son of Zicri, who volunteered himself for the service of the LORD, with 200,000.

17 From Benjamin:

Eliada, a valiant soldier, with 200,000 men armed with bows and shields;

18 next, Jehozabad, with 180,000 men armed for battle.

19 These were the men who served the king, besides those he stationed in the fortified cities throughout Judah.

Micaiah Prophesies Against Ahab

18 Now Jehoshaphat had great wealth and honor, and he allied himself with Ahab by marriage. 2 Some years later he went down to visit Ahab in Samaria. Ahab slaughtered many sheep and cattle for him and the people with him and urged him to attack Ramoth Gilead. 3 Ahab king of Israel asked Jehoshaphat king of Judah, "Will you go with me against Ramoth Gilead?"

Praying 2 Chronicles 18:13

Help me to speak only Your truth, Lord.

Jehoshaphat replied, "I am as you are, and my people as your people; we will join you in the war." 4 But Jehoshaphat also said to the king of Israel, "First seek the counsel of the LORD."

5 So the king of Israel brought together the prophets—four hundred men—and asked them, "Shall we go to war against Ramoth Gilead, or shall I refrain?"

"Go," they answered, "for God will give it into the king's hand."

6 But Jehoshaphat asked, "Is there not a prophet of the LORD here whom we can inquire of?"

7 The king of Israel answered Jehoshaphat, "There is still one man through whom we can inquire of the LORD, but I hate him because he never prophesies anything good about me, but always bad. He is Micaiah son of Imlah."

"The king should not say that," Jehoshaphat replied.

8 So the king of Israel called one of his officials and said, "Bring Micaiah son of Imlah at once."

9 Dressed in their royal robes, the king of Israel and Jehoshaphat king of Judah were sitting on their thrones at the threshing floor by the entrance to the gate of Samaria, with all the prophets prophesying before them. 10 Now Zedekiah son of Kenaanah had made iron horns, and he declared, "This is what the LORD says: 'With these you will gore the Arameans until they are destroyed.'"

11 All the other prophets were prophesying the same thing. "Attack Ramoth Gilead and be victorious," they said, "for the LORD will give it into the king's hand."

12 The messenger who had gone to summon Micaiah said to him, "Look, as one man the other prophets are predicting success for the king. Let your word agree with theirs, and speak favorably."

13 But Micaiah said, "As surely as the LORD lives, I can tell him only what my God says."

14 When he arrived, the king asked him, "Micaiah, shall we go to war against Ramoth Gilead, or shall I refrain?"

"Attack and be victorious," he answered, "for they will be given into your hand."

15 The king said to him, "How many times must I make you swear to tell me nothing but the truth in the name of the LORD?"

16 Then Micaiah answered, "I saw all Israel scattered on the hills like sheep without a shepherd, and the LORD said, 'These people have no master. Let each one go home in peace.'"

17 The king of Israel said to Jehoshaphat, "Didn't I tell you that he never prophesies anything good about me, but only bad?"

¹⁸Micaiah continued, "Therefore hear the word of the LORD: I saw the LORD sitting on his throne with all the host of heaven standing on his right and on his left. ¹⁹And the LORD said, 'Who will entice Ahab king of Israel into attacking Ramoth Gilead and going to his death there?'

"One suggested this, and another that. ²⁰Finally, a spirit came forward, stood before the LORD and said, 'I will entice him.'

"'By what means?' the LORD asked.

²¹"'I will go and be a lying spirit in the mouths of all his prophets,' he said.

"'You will succeed in enticing him,' said the LORD. 'Go and do it.'

²²"So now the LORD has put a lying spirit in the mouths of these prophets of yours. The LORD has decreed disaster for you."

²³Then Zedekiah son of Kenaanah went up and slapped Micaiah in the face. "Which way did the spirit from[a] the LORD go when he went from me to speak to you?" he asked.

ᵃ 23 Or Spirit of

GOING *deeper*

Deliverance May Be Only a Prayer Away

READ AND CONSIDER: 2 CHRONICLES 18:28-34

"When the chariot commanders saw Jehoshaphat, they thought, 'This is the king of Israel.' So they turned to attack him, but Jehoshaphat cried out, and the LORD helped him. God drew them away from him" (2 Chronicles 18:31).

The kingdom of Israel had divided into two kingdoms, Israel and Judah. While these kingdoms were often at odds, they did join together to fight Aram. Judah's king, Jehoshaphat, was known for being a righteous king, but this was not a trait that could be used to describe Israel's wicked King Ahab. Even though the prophet Micaiah had foreseen doom for Israel and the death of Ahab, the two nations had a common enemy in Aram, so it seemed to make political sense to go into battle together.

As a precaution against the prophecy of his own death, King Ahab shrewdly suggested that he remain in disguise as a soldier, while Jehoshaphat enter the battle in a king's full regalia. Even those of us who've never entered a battlefield would know that the enemy army is going to want to take out the leader. If the king is leading his army, he is the primary target. But Jehoshaphat agreed. And sure enough, when the enemy attacked, they went after the only king they saw. But Jehosphaphat prayed, and God protected him. And in keeping with the prophecy, a stray arrow found the chink in Ahab's armor even though he was disguised as a mere soldier.

Jehoshaphat made several errors that day, not the least of which was building an alliance with a competing and wicked king. He asked for a prophet of God but didn't really listen when he came. He let his faith slip in the face of political expediency, pride, or even fear. But one choice Jehoshaphat made was impeccable. Even in the heat of battle, he cried out to God.

Prayer is not something that only happens in the quietness of a moment. Acknowledging God's presence and power—talking to God—should be part of every aspect of life, the battles as well as the peace times. Always cry out to God in your desperate moments, remembering that deliverance is often only a prayer away.

[24]Micaiah replied, "You will find out on the day you go to hide in an inner room."

[25]The king of Israel then ordered, "Take Micaiah and send him back to Amon the ruler of the city and to Joash the king's son, [26]and say, 'This is what the king says: Put this fellow in prison and give him nothing but bread and water until I return safely.'"

[27]Micaiah declared, "If you ever return safely, the LORD has not spoken through me." Then he added, "Mark my words, all you people!"

Ahab Killed at Ramoth Gilead

[28]So the king of Israel and Jehoshaphat king of Judah went up to Ramoth Gilead. [29]The king of Israel said to Jehoshaphat, "I will enter the battle in disguise, but you wear your royal robes." So the king of Israel disguised himself and went into battle.

[30]Now the king of Aram had ordered his chariot commanders, "Do not fight with anyone, small or great, except the king of Israel." [31]When the chariot commanders saw Jehoshaphat, they thought, "This is the king of Israel." So they turned to attack him, but Jehoshaphat cried out, and the LORD helped him. God drew them away from him, [32]for when the chariot commanders saw that he was not the king of Israel, they stopped pursuing him.

[33]But someone drew his bow at random and hit the king of Israel between the sections of his armor. The king told the chariot driver, "Wheel around and get me out of the fighting. I've been wounded." [34]All day long the battle raged, and the king of Israel propped himself up in his chariot facing the Arameans until evening. Then at sunset he died.

19 When Jehoshaphat king of Judah returned safely to his palace in Jerusalem, [2]Jehu the seer, the son of Hanani, went out to meet him and said to the king, "Should you help the wicked and love[a] those who hate the LORD? Because of this, the wrath of the LORD is upon

you. [3]There is, however, some good in you, for you have rid the land of the Asherah poles and have set your heart on seeking God."

Jehoshaphat Appoints Judges

[4]Jehoshaphat lived in Jerusalem, and he went out again among the people from Beersheba to the hill country of Ephraim and turned them back to the LORD, the God of their fathers. [5]He appointed judges in the land, in each of the fortified cities of Judah. [6]He told them, "Consider carefully what you do, because you are not judging for man but for the LORD, who is with you whenever you give a verdict. [7]Now let the fear of the LORD be upon you. Judge carefully, for with the LORD our God there is no injustice or partiality or bribery."

[8]In Jerusalem also, Jehoshaphat appointed some of the Levites, priests and heads of Israelite families to administer the law of the LORD and to settle disputes. And they lived in Jerusalem. [9]He gave them these orders: "You must serve faithfully and wholeheartedly in the fear of the LORD. [10]In every case that comes before you from your fellow countrymen who live in the cities—whether bloodshed or other concerns of the law, commands, decrees or ordinances—you are to warn them not to sin against the LORD; otherwise his wrath will come on you and your brothers. Do this, and you will not sin.

[11]"Amariah the chief priest will be over you in any matter concerning the LORD, and Zebadiah son of Ishmael, the leader of the tribe of Judah, will be over you in any matter concerning the king, and the Levites will serve as officials before you. Act with courage, and may the LORD be with those who do well."

Jehoshaphat Defeats Moab and Ammon

20 After this, the Moabites and Ammonites with some of the Meunites[b] came to make war on Jehoshaphat.

---

[a] 2 Or *and make alliances with*   [b] 1 Some Septuagint manuscripts; Hebrew *Ammonites*

God's people at prayer
JEHOSHAPHAT REPLACES FEAR WITH FAITH

2 CHRONICLES 20:1-13 King Jehoshaphat offers one of the best biblical examples of the power of praising God when we're faced with an enemy. As an enormous multitude of enemy soldiers gathered against him, Jehoshaphat called his people to fast in order to connect with God more fully.

And then, Jehoshaphat prayed. He affirmed God's omnipotence. He spoke of his people's reliance on God. He cried out about the specific need. He said to God, "We have no power ... We do not know what to do." But—and this is key—he added, "Our eyes are upon you."

When you are faced with an enemy or a battle that threatens you, stop everything and declare your dependence on God. Express your need. Tell God you don't know what to do. Turn your eyes upon Him. Then wait for Him to answer.

²Some men came and told Jehoshaphat, "A vast army is coming against you from Edom,ᵃ from the other side of the Sea.ᵇ It is already in Hazazon Tamar" (that is, En Gedi). ³Alarmed, Jehoshaphat resolved to inquire of the LORD, and he proclaimed a fast for all Judah. ⁴The people of Judah came together to seek help from the LORD; indeed, they came from every town in Judah to seek him.

⁵Then Jehoshaphat stood up in the assembly of Judah and Jerusalem at the temple of the LORD in the front of the new courtyard ⁶and said:

"O LORD, God of our fathers, are you not the God who is in heaven? You rule over all the kingdoms of the nations. Power and might are in your hand, and no one can withstand you. ⁷O our God, did you not drive out the inhabitants of this land before your people Israel and give it forever to the descendants of Abraham your friend? ⁸They have lived in it and have built in it a sanctuary for your Name, saying, ⁹'If calamity comes upon us, whether the sword of judgment, or plague or famine, we will stand in your presence before this temple that bears your Name and will cry out to you in our distress, and you will hear us and save us.'

¹⁰"But now here are men from Ammon, Moab and Mount Seir, whose territory you would not allow Israel to invade when they came from Egypt; so they turned away from them and did not destroy them. ¹¹See how they are repaying us by coming to drive us out of the possession you gave us as an inheritance. ¹²O our God, will you not judge them? For we have no power to face this vast army that is attacking us. We do not know what to do, but our eyes are upon you."

¹³All the men of Judah, with their wives and children and little ones, stood there before the LORD.

¹⁴Then the Spirit of the LORD came upon Jahaziel son of Zechariah, the son of Benaiah, the son of Jeiel, the son of Mattaniah, a Levite and descendant of Asaph, as he stood in the assembly.

Praying 2 Chronicles 20:15
Thank You that the battles I face are Yours, Lord.

¹⁵He said: "Listen, King Jehoshaphat and all who live in Judah and Jerusalem! This is what the LORD says to you: 'Do not be afraid or discouraged because of this vast army. For the battle is not yours,

---

ᵃ *2* One Hebrew manuscript; most Hebrew manuscripts, Septuagint and Vulgate *Aram*   ᵇ *2* That is, the Dead Sea but God's. [16]Tomorrow march down against them. They will be climbing up by the Pass of Ziz, and you will find them at the end of the gorge in the Desert of Jeruel. [17]You will not have to fight this battle. Take up your positions; stand firm and see the deliverance the LORD will give you, O Judah and Jerusalem. Do not be afraid; do not be discouraged. Go out to face them tomorrow, and the LORD will be with you.'"

[18]Jehoshaphat bowed with his face to the ground, and all the people of Judah and Jerusalem fell down in worship before the LORD. [19]Then some Levites from the Kohathites and Korahites stood up and praised the LORD, the God of Israel, with a very loud voice.

[20]Early in the morning they left for the Desert of Tekoa. As they set out, Jehoshaphat stood and said, "Listen to me, Judah and people of Jerusalem! Have faith in the LORD your God and you will be upheld; have faith in his prophets and you will be successful." [21]After consulting the people, Jehoshaphat appointed men to sing to the LORD and to praise him for the splendor of his[a] holiness as they went out at the head of the army, saying:

"Give thanks to the LORD,
    for his love endures forever."

[22]As they began to sing and praise, the LORD set ambushes against the men of Ammon and Moab and Mount Seir who were invading Judah, and they were defeated. [23]The men of Ammon and Moab rose up against the men from Mount Seir to destroy and annihilate them. After they finished slaughtering the men from Seir, they helped to destroy one another.

[24]When the men of Judah came to the place that overlooks the desert and looked toward the vast army, they saw only dead bodies lying on the ground; no one had escaped. [25]So Jehoshaphat and his men went to carry off their plunder, and they found among them a great amount of equipment and clothing[b] and also articles of value—more than they could take away. There was so much plunder that it took three days to collect it. [26]On the fourth day they assembled in the Valley of Beracah, where they praised the LORD. This is why it is called the Valley of Beracah[c] to this day.

[27]Then, led by Jehoshaphat, all the men of Judah and Jerusalem returned joyfully to Jerusalem, for the LORD had given them cause to rejoice over their enemies. [28]They entered Jerusalem and went to the temple of the LORD with harps and lutes and trumpets.

[29]The fear of God came upon all the kingdoms of the countries when they heard how the LORD had fought against the enemies of Israel. [30]And the kingdom of Jehoshaphat was at peace, for his God had given him rest on every side.

The End of Jehoshaphat's Reign

[31]So Jehoshaphat reigned over Judah. He was thirty-five years old when he became king of Judah, and he reigned in Jerusalem twenty-five years. His mother's name was Azubah daughter of Shilhi. [32]He walked in the ways of his father Asa and did not stray from them; he did what was right in the eyes of the LORD. [33]The high places, however, were not removed, and the people still had not set their hearts on the God of their fathers.

[34]The other events of Jehoshaphat's reign, from beginning to end, are written in the annals of Jehu son of Hanani, which are recorded in the book of the kings of Israel.

[35]Later, Jehoshaphat king of Judah made an alliance with Ahaziah king of Israel, who was guilty of wickedness. [36]He agreed with him to construct a fleet of trading ships.[d] After these were built at Ezion Geber, [37]Eliezer son of Dodavahu of Mareshah prophesied against Jehoshaphat, saying, "Because you have made

---

[a] 21 Or him with the splendor of   [b] 25 Some Hebrew manuscripts and Vulgate; most Hebrew manuscripts corpses
[c] 26 Beracah means praise.   [d] 36 Hebrew of ships that could go to Tarshish

an alliance with Ahaziah, the Lord will destroy what you have made." The ships were wrecked and were not able to set sail to trade.[a]

21 Then Jehoshaphat rested with his fathers and was buried with them in the City of David. And Jehoram his son succeeded him as king. [2]Jehoram's brothers, the sons of Jehoshaphat, were Azariah, Jehiel, Zechariah, Azariahu, Michael and Shephatiah. All these were sons of Jehoshaphat king of Israel.[b] [3]Their father had given them many gifts of silver and gold and articles of value, as well as fortified cities in Judah, but he had given the kingdom to Jehoram because he was his firstborn son.

Jehoram King of Judah

[4]When Jehoram established himself firmly over his father's kingdom, he put all his brothers to the sword along with some of the princes of Israel. [5]Jehoram was thirty-two years old when he became king, and he reigned in Jerusalem eight years. [6]He walked in the ways of the kings of Israel, as the house of Ahab had done, for he married a daughter of Ahab. He did evil in the eyes of the Lord. [7]Nevertheless, because of the covenant the Lord had made with David, the Lord was not willing to destroy the house of David. He had promised to maintain a lamp for him and his descendants forever.

[8]In the time of Jehoram, Edom rebelled against Judah and set up its own king. [9]So Jehoram went there with his officers and all his chariots. The Edomites surrounded him and his chariot commanders, but he rose up and broke through by night. [10]To this day Edom has been in rebellion against Judah.

Libnah revolted at the same time, because Jehoram had forsaken the Lord, the God of his fathers. [11]He had also built high places on the hills of Judah and had caused the people of Jerusalem to prostitute themselves and had led Judah astray.

[12]Jehoram received a letter from Elijah the prophet, which said:

"This is what the Lord, the God of your father David, says: 'You have not walked in the ways of your father Jehoshaphat or of Asa king of Judah. [13]But you have walked in the ways of the kings of Israel, and you have led Judah and the people of Jerusalem to prostitute themselves, just as the house of Ahab did. You have also murdered your own brothers, members of your father's house, men who were better than you. [14]So now the Lord is about to strike your people, your sons, your wives and everything that is yours, with a heavy blow. [15]You yourself will be very ill with a lingering disease of the bowels, until the disease causes your bowels to come out.'"

[16]The Lord aroused against Jehoram the hostility of the Philistines and of the Arabs who lived near the Cushites. [17]They attacked Judah, invaded it and carried off all the goods found in the king's palace, together with his sons and wives. Not a son was left to him except Ahaziah,[c] the youngest.

[18]After all this, the Lord afflicted Jehoram with an incurable disease of the bowels. [19]In the course of time, at the end of the second year, his bowels came out because of the disease, and he died in great pain. His people made no fire in his honor, as they had for his fathers.

[20]Jehoram was thirty-two years old when he became king, and he reigned in Jerusalem eight years. He passed away, to no one's regret, and was buried in the City of David, but not in the tombs of the kings.

Ahaziah King of Judah

22 The people of Jerusalem made Ahaziah, Jehoram's youngest son, king in his place, since the raiders, who came with the Arabs into the camp, had

---

[a] 37 Hebrew sail for Tarshish   [b] 2 That is, Judah, as frequently in 2 Chronicles   [c] 17 Hebrew Jehoahaz, a variant of Ahaziah

killed all the older sons. So Ahaziah son of Jehoram king of Judah began to reign.

²Ahaziah was twenty-twoᵃ years old when he became king, and he reigned in Jerusalem one year. His mother's name was Athaliah, a granddaughter of Omri.

³He too walked in the ways of the house of Ahab, for his mother encouraged him in doing wrong. ⁴He did evil in the eyes of the LORD, as the house of Ahab had done, for after his father's death they became his advisers, to his undoing. ⁵He also followed their counsel when he went with Joramᵇ son of Ahab king of Israel to war against Hazael king of Aram at Ramoth Gilead. The Arameans wounded Joram; ⁶so he returned to Jezreel to recover from the wounds they had inflicted on him at Ramothᶜ in his battle with Hazael king of Aram.

Then Ahaziahᵈ son of Jehoram king of Judah went down to Jezreel to see Joram son of Ahab because he had been wounded.

⁷Through Ahaziah's visit to Joram, God brought about Ahaziah's downfall. When Ahaziah arrived, he went out with Joram to meet Jehu son of Nimshi, whom the LORD had anointed to destroy the house of Ahab. ⁸While Jehu was executing judgment on the house of Ahab, he found the princes of Judah and the sons of Ahaziah's relatives, who had been attending Ahaziah, and he killed them. ⁹He then went in search of Ahaziah, and his men captured him while he was hiding in Samaria. He was brought to Jehu and put to death. They buried him, for they said, "He was a son of Jehoshaphat, who sought the LORD with all his heart." So there was no one in the house of Ahaziah powerful enough to retain the kingdom.

Athaliah and Joash

¹⁰When Athaliah the mother of Ahaziah saw that her son was dead, she proceeded to destroy the whole royal family of the house of Judah. ¹¹But Jehosheba,ᵉ the daughter of King Jehoram, took Joash son of Ahaziah and stole him away from among the royal princes who were about to be murdered and put him and his nurse in a bedroom. Because Jehosheba,ᵉ the daughter of King Jehoram and wife of the priest Jehoiada, was Ahaziah's sister, she hid the child from Athaliah so she could not kill him. ¹²He remained hidden with them at the temple of God for six years while Athaliah ruled the land.

23 In the seventh year Jehoiada showed his strength. He made a covenant with the commanders of units of a hundred: Azariah son of Jeroham, Ishmael son of Jehohanan, Azariah son of Obed, Maaseiah son of Adaiah, and Elishaphat son of Zicri. ²They went throughout Judah and gathered the Levites and the heads of Israelite families from all the towns. When they came to Jerusalem, ³the whole assembly made a covenant with the king at the temple of God.

Jehoiada said to them, "The king's son shall reign, as the LORD promised concerning the descendants of David. ⁴Now this is what you are to do: A third of you priests and Levites who are going on duty on the Sabbath are to keep watch at the doors, ⁵a third of you at the royal palace and a third at the Foundation Gate, and all the other men are to be in the courtyards of the temple of the LORD. ⁶No one is to enter the temple of the LORD except the priests and Levites on duty; they may enter because they are consecrated, but all the other men are to guard what the LORD has assigned to them.ᶠ ⁷The Levites are to station themselves around the king, each man with his weapons in his hand. Anyone who enters the temple must be put to death. Stay close to the king wherever he goes."

⁸The Levites and all the men of Judah

ᵃ *2* Some Septuagint manuscripts and Syriac (see also 2 Kings 8:26); Hebrew *forty-two*   ᵇ *5* Hebrew *Jehoram*, a variant of *Joram*; also in verses 6 and 7   ᶜ *6* Hebrew *Ramah*, a variant of *Ramoth*   ᵈ *6* Some Hebrew manuscripts, Septuagint, Vulgate and Syriac (see also 2 Kings 8:29); most Hebrew manuscripts *Azariah*   ᵉ *11* Hebrew *Jehoshabeath*, a variant of *Jehosheba*   ᶠ *6* Or *to observe the LORD's command ₍not to enter₎*

did just as Jehoiada the priest ordered. Each one took his men—those who were going on duty on the Sabbath and those who were going off duty—for Jehoiada the priest had not released any of the divisions. 9Then he gave the commanders of units of a hundred the spears and the large and small shields that had belonged to King David and that were in the temple of God. 10He stationed all the men, each with his weapon in his hand, around the king—near the altar and the temple, from the south side to the north side of the temple.

11Jehoiada and his sons brought out the king's son and put the crown on him; they presented him with a copy of the covenant and proclaimed him king. They anointed him and shouted, "Long live the king!"

12When Athaliah heard the noise of the people running and cheering the king, she went to them at the temple of the LORD. 13She looked, and there was the king, standing by his pillar at the entrance. The officers and the trumpeters were beside the king, and all the people of the land were rejoicing and blowing trumpets, and singers with musical instruments were leading the praises. Then Athaliah tore her robes and shouted, "Treason! Treason!"

14Jehoiada the priest sent out the commanders of units of a hundred, who were in charge of the troops, and said to them: "Bring her out between the ranksa and put to the sword anyone who follows her." For the priest had said, "Do not put her to death at the temple of the LORD." 15So they seized her as she reached the entrance of the Horse Gate on the palace grounds, and there they put her to death.

16Jehoiada then made a covenant that he and the people and the kingb would be the LORD's people. 17All the people went to the temple of Baal and tore it down. They smashed the altars and idols and killed Mattan the priest of Baal in front of the altars.

18Then Jehoiada placed the oversight of the temple of the LORD in the hands of the priests, who were Levites, to whom David had made assignments in the temple, to present the burnt offerings of the LORD as written in the Law of Moses, with rejoicing and singing, as David had ordered. 19He also stationed doorkeepers at the gates of the LORD's temple so that no one who was in any way unclean might enter.

20He took with him the commanders of hundreds, the nobles, the rulers of the people and all the people of the land and brought the king down from the temple of the LORD. They went into the palace through the Upper Gate and seated the king on the royal throne, 21and all the people of the land rejoiced. And the city was quiet, because Athaliah had been slain with the sword.

Joash Repairs the Temple

24 Joash was seven years old when he became king, and he reigned in Jerusalem forty years. His mother's name was Zibiah; she was from Beersheba. 2Joash did what was right in the eyes of the LORD all the years of Jehoiada the priest. 3Jehoiada chose two wives for him, and he had sons and daughters.

4Some time later Joash decided to restore the temple of the LORD. 5He called together the priests and Levites and said to them, "Go to the towns of Judah and collect the money due annually from all Israel, to repair the temple of your God. Do it now." But the Levites did not act at once.

6Therefore the king summoned Jehoiada the chief priest and said to him, "Why haven't you required the Levites to bring in from Judah and Jerusalem the tax imposed by Moses the servant of the LORD and by the assembly of Israel for the Tent of the Testimony?"

7Now the sons of that wicked woman

---

a 14 Or out from the precincts   b 16 Or covenant between ⸤the LORD⸥ and the people and the king that they (see 2 Kings 11:17)

Stepping Into Something Great

Many people know their calling but can't see how it will ever be realized in the details of their lives. That's because they are trying to accomplish it in their own strength. But God doesn't say, "Here's what I want you to do with your life, now go do it." He first gives you a vision and then says, "Walk step-by-step with Me, and *I'll* do it through you." Also, the whole of our call does not suddenly drop in our laps. We grow into it a step at a time, and it is realized gradually.

If you feel called to something better than what you are doing at this time, let me assure you that it is probably because you are. If you have never sought God about His plans and purposes for your life, do that now. If you have already done that, then there must be a purpose for what you are doing at this moment that you cannot see. Or perhaps you have not surrendered your dreams to the Lord. In any case, know that He will not leave you where you are forever.

Don't be afraid of the perfecting process that prepares you to move into God's call on your life. It will establish, strengthen, and settle you (1 Peter 5:10). Just stand strong through the fire and you will be purified, molded, humbled, and made ready for what He has for you to do. If you walk step-by-step with God, you'll come out of that time with a sense of His presence and power that will make it all worthwhile. It will set you on the path to greatness.

Let me clarify the meaning of greatness. Too often when people think of greatness, it stirs up images in their minds of having great talent, great riches, great fame, great influence, great power, or great accomplishments. They mistakenly believe that greatness comes about because of something they are or something they have. But greatness is not about *us*; it's about *His*

greatness *in* us. God's idea of greatness is having a heart, soul, and spirit so full of His greatness that it manifests through us.

In the Bible, the word "great" is nearly always used to describe who God is: "For great is the LORD and most worthy of praise" (1 Chronicles 16:25). Or what God has done: "The LORD has done great things for us, and we are filled with joy" (Psalm 126:3).

A great person is one who obeys God: "Anyone who breaks one of the least of these commandments and teaches others to do the same will be called least in the kingdom of heaven, but whoever practices and teaches these commands will be called great in the kingdom of heaven" (Matthew 5:19). A great person is one who is a servant: "Not so with you. Instead, whoever wants to become great among you must be your servant" (Matthew 20:26).

When we acknowledge God's greatness through our worship of Him, we invite His greatness to dwell *in* us. When we obey God and serve Him and others, we open the door for Him to do great things *through* us. This is the kind of greatness God has called us to in our lives.

For the next "From Stormie's Heart" article, go to page 611.

Athaliah had broken into the temple of God and had used even its sacred objects for the Baals.

8At the king's command, a chest was made and placed outside, at the gate of the temple of the LORD. 9A proclamation was then issued in Judah and Jerusalem that they should bring to the LORD the tax that Moses the servant of God had required of Israel in the desert. 10All the officials and all the people brought their contributions gladly, dropping them into the chest until it was full. 11Whenever the chest was brought in by the Levites to the king's officials and they saw that there was a large amount of money, the royal secretary and the officer of the chief priest would come and empty the chest and carry it back to its place. They did this regularly and collected a great amount of money. 12The king and Jehoiada gave it to the men who carried out the work required for the temple of the LORD. They hired masons and carpenters to restore the LORD's temple, and also workers in iron and bronze to repair the temple.

13The men in charge of the work were diligent, and the repairs progressed under them. They rebuilt the temple of God according to its original design and reinforced it. 14When they had finished, they brought the rest of the money to the king and Jehoiada, and with it were made articles for the LORD's temple: articles for the service and for the burnt offerings, and also dishes and other objects of gold and silver. As long as Jehoiada lived, burnt offerings were presented continually in the temple of the LORD.

15Now Jehoiada was old and full of years, and he died at the age of a hundred and thirty. 16He was buried with the kings in the City of David, because of the good he had done in Israel for God and his temple.

The Wickedness of Joash

17After the death of Jehoiada, the officials of Judah came and paid homage to the king, and he listened to them. 18They abandoned the temple of the LORD, the God of their fathers, and worshiped Asherah poles and idols. Because of their guilt, God's anger came upon Judah and Jerusalem. 19Although the LORD sent prophets to the people to bring them back to him, and though they testified against them, they would not listen.

20Then the Spirit of God came upon Zechariah son of Jehoiada the priest. He stood before the people and said, "This is what God says: 'Why do you disobey the LORD's commands? You will not prosper. Because you have forsaken the LORD, he has forsaken you.'"

21But they plotted against him, and by order of the king they stoned him to death in the courtyard of the LORD's temple. 22King Joash did not remember the kindness Zechariah's father Jehoiada had shown him but killed his son, who said as he lay dying, "May the LORD see this and call you to account."

23At the turn of the year,a the army of Aram marched against Joash; it invaded Judah and Jerusalem and killed all the leaders of the people. They sent all the plunder to their king in Damascus. 24Although the Aramean army had come with only a few men, the LORD delivered into their hands a much larger army. Because Judah had forsaken the LORD, the God of their fathers, judgment was executed on Joash. 25When the Arameans withdrew, they left Joash severely wounded. His officials conspired against him for murdering the son of Jehoiada the priest, and they killed him in his bed. So he died and was buried in the City of David, but not in the tombs of the kings.

26Those who conspired against him were Zabad,b son of Shimeath an Ammonite woman, and Jehozabad, son of Shimrithc a Moabite woman. 27The account of his sons, the many prophecies about him, and the record of the restoration of the temple of God are written in the annotations on the book of the kings. And Amaziah his son succeeded him as king.

Amaziah King of Judah

25 Amaziah was twenty-five years old when he became king, and he reigned in Jerusalem twenty-nine years. His mother's name was Jehoaddin[a]; she was from Jerusalem. 2He did what was right in the eyes of the LORD, but not wholeheartedly. 3After the kingdom was firmly in his control, he executed the officials who had murdered his father the king. 4Yet he did not put their sons to death, but acted in accordance with what is written in the Law, in the Book of Moses, where the LORD commanded: "Fathers shall not be put to death for their children, nor children put to death for their fathers; each is to die for his own sins."[b]

5Amaziah called the people of Judah together and assigned them according to their families to commanders of thousands and commanders of hundreds for all Judah and Benjamin. He then mustered those twenty years old or more and found that there were three hundred thousand men ready for military service, able to handle the spear and shield. 6He also hired a hundred thousand fighting men from Israel for a hundred talents[c] of silver.

7But a man of God came to him and said, "O king, these troops from Israel must not march with you, for the LORD is not with Israel—not with any of the people of Ephraim. 8Even if you go and fight courageously in battle, God will overthrow you before the enemy, for God has the power to help or to overthrow."

9Amaziah asked the man of God, "But what about the hundred talents I paid for these Israelite troops?"

The man of God replied, "The LORD can give you much more than that."

10So Amaziah dismissed the troops who had come to him from Ephraim and sent them home. They were furious with Judah and left for home in a great rage.

11Amaziah then marshaled his strength and led his army to the Valley of Salt, where he killed ten thousand men of Seir. 12The army of Judah also captured ten thousand men alive, took them to the top of a cliff and threw them down so that all were dashed to pieces.

13Meanwhile the troops that Amaziah had sent back and had not allowed to take part in the war raided Judean towns from Samaria to Beth Horon. They killed three thousand people and carried off great quantities of plunder.

14When Amaziah returned from slaughtering the Edomites, he brought back the gods of the people of Seir. He set them up as his own gods, bowed down to them and burned sacrifices to them. 15The anger of the LORD burned against Amaziah, and he sent a prophet to him, who said, "Why do you consult this people's gods, which could not save their own people from your hand?"

16While he was still speaking, the king said to him, "Have we appointed you an adviser to the king? Stop! Why be struck down?"

So the prophet stopped but said, "I know that God has determined to destroy you, because you have done this and have not listened to my counsel."

17After Amaziah king of Judah consulted his advisers, he sent this challenge to Jehoash[d] son of Jehoahaz, the son of Jehu, king of Israel: "Come, meet me face to face."

18But Jehoash king of Israel replied to Amaziah king of Judah: "A thistle in Lebanon sent a message to a cedar in Lebanon, 'Give your daughter to my son in marriage.' Then a wild beast in Lebanon came along and trampled the thistle underfoot. 19You say to yourself that you have defeated Edom, and now you are arrogant and proud. But stay at home! Why

---

a 1 Hebrew *Jehoaddan,* a variant of *Jehoaddin*   b 4 Deut. 24:16   c 6 That is, about 3 3/4 tons (about 3.4 metric tons); also in verse 9   d 17 Hebrew *Joash,* a variant of *Jehoash*; also in verses 18, 21, 23 and 25 ask for trouble and cause your own downfall and that of Judah also?"

20 Amaziah, however, would not listen, for God so worked that he might hand them over to Jehoash, because they sought the gods of Edom. 21 So Jehoash king of Israel attacked. He and Amaziah king of Judah faced each other at Beth Shemesh in Judah. 22 Judah was routed by Israel, and every man fled to his home. 23 Jehoash king of Israel captured Amaziah king of Judah, the son of Joash, the son of Ahaziah,[a] at Beth Shemesh. Then Jehoash brought him to Jerusalem and broke down the wall of Jerusalem from the Ephraim Gate to the Corner Gate—a section about six hundred feet[b] long. 24 He took all the gold and silver and all the articles found in the temple of God that had been in the care of Obed-Edom, together with the palace treasures and the hostages, and returned to Samaria.

25 Amaziah son of Joash king of Judah lived for fifteen years after the death of Jehoash son of Jehoahaz king of Israel. 26 As for the other events of Amaziah's reign, from beginning to end, are they not written in the book of the kings of Judah and Israel? 27 From the time that Amaziah turned away from following the LORD, they conspired against him in Jerusalem and he fled to Lachish, but they sent men after him to Lachish and killed him there. 28 He was brought back by horse and was buried with his fathers in the City of Judah.

Uzziah King of Judah

26 Then all the people of Judah took Uzziah,[c] who was sixteen years old, and made him king in place of his father Amaziah. 2 He was the one who rebuilt Elath and restored it to Judah after Amaziah rested with his fathers.

3 Uzziah was sixteen years old when he became king, and he reigned in Jerusalem fifty-two years. His mother's name was Jecoliah; she was from Jerusalem.

4 He did what was right in the eyes of the LORD, just as his father Amaziah had done. 5 He sought God during the days of Zechariah, who instructed him in the fear[d] of God. As long as he sought the LORD, God gave him success.

6 He went to war against the Philistines and broke down the walls of Gath, Jabneh and Ashdod. He then rebuilt towns near Ashdod and elsewhere among the Philistines. 7 God helped him against the Philistines and against the Arabs who lived in Gur Baal and against the Meunites. 8 The Ammonites brought tribute to Uzziah, and his fame spread as far as the border of Egypt, because he had become very powerful.

9 Uzziah built towers in Jerusalem at the Corner Gate, at the Valley Gate and at the angle of the wall, and he fortified them. 10 He also built towers in the desert and dug many cisterns, because he had much livestock in the foothills and in the plain. He had people working his fields and vineyards in the hills and in the fertile lands, for he loved the soil.

11 Uzziah had a well-trained army, ready to go out by divisions according to their numbers as mustered by Jeiel the secretary and Maaseiah the officer under the direction of Hananiah, one of the royal officials. 12 The total number of family leaders over the fighting men was 2,600. 13 Under their command was an army of 307,500 men trained for war, a powerful force to support the king against his enemies. 14 Uzziah provided shields, spears, helmets, coats of armor, bows and slingstones for the entire army. 15 In Jerusalem he made machines designed by skillful men for use on the towers and on the corner defenses to shoot arrows and hurl large stones. His fame spread far and wide, for he was greatly helped until he became powerful.

16 But after Uzziah became powerful, his pride led to his downfall. He was unfaith-

---

a 23 Hebrew *Jehoahaz*, a variant of *Ahaziah*   b 23 Hebrew *four hundred cubits* (about 180 meters)   c 1 Also called *Azariah*
d 5 Many Hebrew manuscripts, Septuagint and Syriac; other Hebrew manuscripts *vision*

ful to the LORD his God, and entered the temple of the LORD to burn incense on the altar of incense. [17]Azariah the priest with eighty other courageous priests of the LORD followed him in. [18]They confronted him and said, "It is not right for you, Uzziah, to burn incense to the LORD. That is for the priests, the descendants of Aaron, who have been consecrated to burn incense. Leave the sanctuary, for you have been unfaithful; and you will not be honored by the LORD God."

[19]Uzziah, who had a censer in his hand ready to burn incense, became angry. While he was raging at the priests in their presence before the incense altar in the LORD's temple, leprosy[a] broke out on his forehead. [20]When Azariah the chief priest and all the other priests looked at him, they saw that he had leprosy on his forehead, so they hurried him out. Indeed, he himself was eager to leave, because the LORD had afflicted him.

[21]King Uzziah had leprosy until the day he died. He lived in a separate house[b]—leprous, and excluded from the temple of the LORD. Jotham his son had charge of the palace and governed the people of the land.

[22]The other events of Uzziah's reign, from beginning to end, are recorded by the prophet Isaiah son of Amoz. [23]Uzziah rested with his fathers and was buried near them in a field for burial that belonged to the kings, for people said, "He had leprosy." And Jotham his son succeeded him as king.

Jotham King of Judah

27 Jotham was twenty-five years old when he became king, and he reigned in Jerusalem sixteen years. His mother's name was Jerusha daughter of Zadok. [2]He did what was right in the eyes of the LORD, just as his father Uzziah had done, but unlike him he did not enter the temple of the LORD. The

people, however, continued their corrupt practices. [3]Jotham rebuilt the Upper Gate of the temple of the LORD and did extensive work on the wall at the hill of Ophel. [4]He built towns in the Judean hills and forts and towers in the wooded areas.

[5]Jotham made war on the king of the Ammonites and conquered them. That year the Ammonites paid him a hundred talents[c] of silver, ten thousand cors[d] of wheat and ten thousand cors of barley. The Ammonites brought him the same amount also in the second and third years.

[6]Jotham grew powerful because he walked steadfastly before the LORD his God.

[7]The other events in Jotham's reign, including all his wars and the other things he did, are written in the book of the kings of Israel and Judah. [8]He was twenty-five years old when he became king, and he reigned in Jerusalem sixteen years. [9]Jotham rested with his fathers and was buried in the City of David. And Ahaz his son succeeded him as king.

Ahaz King of Judah

28 Ahaz was twenty years old when he became king, and he reigned in Jerusalem sixteen years. Unlike David his father, he did not do what was right in the eyes of the LORD. [2]He walked in the ways of the kings of Israel and also made cast idols for worshiping the Baals. [3]He burned sacrifices in the Valley of Ben Hinnom and sacrificed his sons in the fire, following the detestable ways of the nations the LORD had driven out before the Israelites. [4]He offered sacrifices and burned incense at the high places, on the hilltops and under every spreading tree.

[5]Therefore the LORD his God handed him over to the king of Aram. The Arameans defeated him and took many of his people as prisoners and brought them to Damascus.

---

[a] *19* The Hebrew word was used for various diseases affecting the skin—not necessarily leprosy; also in verses 20, 21 and 23.   [b] *21* Or *in a house where he was relieved of responsibilities*   [c] *5* That is, about 3 3/4 tons (about 3.4 metric tons)   [d] *5* That is, probably about 62,000 bushels (about 2,200 kiloliters)

He was also given into the hands of the king of Israel, who inflicted heavy casualties on him. [6]In one day Pekah son of Remaliah killed a hundred and twenty thousand soldiers in Judah—because Judah had forsaken the LORD, the God of their fathers. [7]Zicri, an Ephraimite warrior, killed Maaseiah the king's son, Azrikam the officer in charge of the palace, and Elkanah, second to the king. [8]The Israelites took captive from their kinsmen two hundred thousand wives, sons and daughters. They also took a great deal of plunder, which they carried back to Samaria.

[9]But a prophet of the LORD named Oded was there, and he went out to meet the army when it returned to Samaria. He said to them, "Because the LORD, the God of your fathers, was angry with Judah, he gave them into your hand. But you have slaughtered them in a rage that reaches to heaven. [10]And now you intend to make the men and women of Judah and Jerusalem your slaves. But aren't you also guilty of sins against the LORD your God? [11]Now listen to me! Send back your fellow countrymen you have taken as prisoners, for the LORD's fierce anger rests on you."

[12]Then some of the leaders in Ephraim —Azariah son of Jehohanan, Berekiah son of Meshillemoth, Jehizkiah son of Shallum, and Amasa son of Hadlai— confronted those who were arriving from the war. [13]"You must not bring those prisoners here," they said, "or we will be guilty before the LORD. Do you intend to add to our sin and guilt? For our guilt is already great, and his fierce anger rests on Israel."

[14]So the soldiers gave up the prisoners and plunder in the presence of the officials and all the assembly. [15]The men designated by name took the prisoners, and from the plunder they clothed all who were naked. They provided them with clothes and sandals, food and drink, and healing balm. All those who were weak they put on donkeys. So they took them back to their fellow countrymen at Jericho, the City of Palms, and returned to Samaria.

[16]At that time King Ahaz sent to the king[a] of Assyria for help. [17]The Edomites had again come and attacked Judah and carried away prisoners, [18]while the Philistines had raided towns in the foothills and in the Negev of Judah. They captured and occupied Beth Shemesh, Aijalon and Gederoth, as well as Soco, Timnah and Gimzo, with their surrounding villages. [19]The LORD had humbled Judah because of Ahaz king of Israel,[b] for he had promoted wickedness in Judah and had been most unfaithful to the LORD. [20]Tiglath-Pileser[c] king of Assyria came to him, but he gave him trouble instead of help. [21]Ahaz took some of the things from the temple of the LORD and from the royal palace and from the princes and presented them to the king of Assyria, but that did not help him.

[22]In his time of trouble King Ahaz became even more unfaithful to the LORD. [23]He offered sacrifices to the gods of Damascus, who had defeated him; for he thought, "Since the gods of the kings of Aram have helped them, I will sacrifice to them so they will help me." But they were his downfall and the downfall of all Israel.

[24]Ahaz gathered together the furnishings from the temple of God and took them away.[d] He shut the doors of the LORD's temple and set up altars at every street corner in Jerusalem. [25]In every town in Judah he built high places to burn sacrifices to other gods and provoked the LORD, the God of his fathers, to anger.

[26]The other events of his reign and all his ways, from beginning to end, are written in the book of the kings of Judah

---

and Israel. [27]Ahaz rested with his fathers and was buried in the city of Jerusalem, but he was not placed in the tombs of the kings of Israel. And Hezekiah his son succeeded him as king.

Hezekiah Purifies the Temple

29 Hezekiah was twenty-five years old when he became king, and he reigned in Jerusalem twenty-nine years. His mother's name was Abijah daughter of Zechariah. [2]He did what was right in the eyes of the LORD, just as his father David had done.

[3]In the first month of the first year of his reign, he opened the doors of the temple of the LORD and repaired them. [4]He brought in the priests and the Levites, assembled them in the square on the east side [5]and said: "Listen to me, Levites! Consecrate yourselves now and consecrate the temple of the LORD, the God of your fathers. Remove all defilement from the sanctuary. [6]Our fathers were unfaithful; they did evil in the eyes of the LORD our God and forsook him. They turned their faces away from the LORD's dwelling place and turned their backs on him. [7]They also shut the doors of the portico and put out the lamps. They did not burn incense or present any burnt offerings at the sanctuary to the God of Israel. [8]Therefore, the anger of the LORD has fallen on Judah and Jerusalem; he has made them an object of dread and horror and scorn, as you can see with your own eyes. [9]This is why our fathers have fallen by the sword and why our sons and daughters and our wives are in captivity. [10]Now I intend to make a covenant with the LORD, the God of Israel, so that his fierce anger will turn away from us. [11]My sons, do not be negligent now, for the LORD has chosen you to stand before him and serve him, to minister before him and to burn incense."

[12]Then these Levites set to work:

from the Kohathites,
Mahath son of Amasai and Joel son of Azariah;

from the Merarites,
Kish son of Abdi and Azariah son of Jehallelel;
from the Gershonites,
Joah son of Zimmah and Eden son of Joah;
[13]from the descendants of Elizaphan, Shimri and Jeiel;
from the descendants of Asaph, Zechariah and Mattaniah;
[14]from the descendants of Heman, Jehiel and Shimei;
from the descendants of Jeduthun, Shemaiah and Uzziel.

[15]When they had assembled their brothers and consecrated themselves, they went in to purify the temple of the LORD, as the king had ordered, following the word of the LORD. [16]The priests went into the sanctuary of the LORD to purify it. They brought out to the courtyard of the LORD's temple everything unclean that they found in the temple of the LORD. The Levites took it and carried it out to the Kidron Valley. [17]They began the consecration on the first day of the first month, and by the eighth day of the month they reached the portico of the LORD. For eight more days they consecrated the temple of the LORD itself, finishing on the sixteenth day of the first month.

[18]Then they went in to King Hezekiah and reported: "We have purified the entire temple of the LORD, the altar of burnt offering with all its utensils, and the table for setting out the consecrated bread, with all its articles. [19]We have prepared and consecrated all the articles that King Ahaz removed in his unfaithfulness while he was king. They are now in front of the LORD's altar."

[20]Early the next morning King Hezekiah gathered the city officials together and went up to the temple of the LORD. [21]They brought seven bulls, seven rams, seven male lambs and seven male goats as a sin offering for the kingdom, for the sanctuary and for Judah. The king commanded the priests, the descendants

of Aaron, to offer these on the altar of the LORD. ²²So they slaughtered the bulls, and the priests took the blood and sprinkled it on the altar; next they slaughtered the rams and sprinkled their blood on the altar; then they slaughtered the lambs and sprinkled their blood on the altar. ²³The goats for the sin offering were brought before the king and the assembly, and they laid their hands on them. ²⁴The priests then slaughtered the goats and presented their blood on the altar for a sin offering to atone for all Israel, because the king had ordered the burnt offering and the sin offering for all Israel.

²⁵He stationed the Levites in the temple of the LORD with cymbals, harps and lyres in the way prescribed by David and Gad the king's seer and Nathan the prophet; this was commanded by the LORD through his prophets. ²⁶So the Levites stood ready with David's instruments, and the priests with their trumpets.

²⁷Hezekiah gave the order to sacrifice the burnt offering on the altar. As the offering began, singing to the LORD began also, accompanied by trumpets and the instruments of David king of Israel. ²⁸The whole assembly bowed in worship, while the singers sang and the trumpeters played. All this continued until the sacrifice of the burnt offering was completed.

²⁹When the offerings were finished, the king and everyone present with him knelt down and worshiped. ³⁰King Hezekiah and his officials ordered the Levites to praise the LORD with the words of David and of Asaph the seer. So they sang praises with gladness and bowed their heads and worshiped.

³¹Then Hezekiah said, "You have now dedicated yourselves to the LORD. Come and bring sacrifices and thank offerings to the temple of the LORD." So the assembly brought sacrifices and thank offerings, and all whose hearts were willing brought burnt offerings.

³²The number of burnt offerings the assembly brought was seventy bulls, a hundred rams and two hundred male lambs—all of them for burnt offerings to the LORD. ³³The animals consecrated as sacrifices amounted to six hundred bulls and three thousand sheep and goats. ³⁴The priests, however, were too few to skin all the burnt offerings; so their kinsmen the Levites helped them until the task was finished and until other priests had been consecrated, for the Levites had been more conscientious in consecrating themselves than the priests had been. ³⁵There were burnt offerings in abundance, together with the fat of the fellowship offerings^a and the drink offerings that accompanied the burnt offerings.

So the service of the temple of the LORD was reestablished. ³⁶Hezekiah and all the people rejoiced at what God had brought about for his people, because it was done so quickly.

Hezekiah Celebrates the Passover

30 Hezekiah sent word to all Israel and Judah and also wrote letters to Ephraim and Manasseh, inviting them to come to the temple of the LORD in Jerusalem and celebrate the Passover to the LORD, the God of Israel. ²The king and his officials and the whole assembly in Jerusalem decided to celebrate the Passover in the second month. ³They had not been able to celebrate it at the regular time because not enough priests had consecrated themselves and the people had not assembled in Jerusalem. ⁴The plan seemed right both to the king and to the whole assembly. ⁵They decided to send a proclamation throughout Israel, from Beersheba to Dan, calling the people to come to Jerusalem and celebrate the Passover to the LORD, the God of Israel. It had not been celebrated in large numbers according to what was written.

⁶At the king's command, couriers went throughout Israel and Judah with letters from the king and from his officials, which read:

---

^a ³⁵ Traditionally *peace offerings*

"People of Israel, return to the Lord, the God of Abraham, Isaac and Israel, that he may return to you who are left, who have escaped from the hand of the kings of Assyria. 7Do not be like your fathers and brothers, who were unfaithful to the Lord, the God of their fathers, so that he made them an object of horror, as you see. 8Do not be stiff-necked, as your fathers were; submit to the Lord. Come to the sanctuary, which he has consecrated forever. Serve the Lord your God, so that his fierce anger will turn away from you. 9If you return to the Lord, then your brothers and your children will be shown compassion by their captors and will come back to this land, for the Lord your God is gracious and compassionate. He will not turn his face from you if you return to him."

10The couriers went from town to town in Ephraim and Manasseh, as far as Zebulun, but the people scorned and ridiculed them. 11Nevertheless, some men of Asher, Manasseh and Zebulun humbled themselves and went to Jerusalem. 12Also in Judah the hand of God was on the people to give them unity of mind to carry out what the king and his officials had ordered, following the word of the Lord.

13A very large crowd of people assembled

GOING *deeper*

Even When We Don't Do Everything Right

READ AND CONSIDER: 2 CHRONICLES 30:1-20

"Although most of the many people who came from Ephraim, Manasseh, Issachar and Zebulun had not purified themselves, yet they ate the Passover, contrary to what was written. But Hezekiah prayed for them, saying, 'May the Lord, who is good, pardon everyone who sets his heart on seeking God—the Lord, the God of his fathers—even if he is not clean according to the rules of the sanctuary.' And the Lord heard Hezekiah and healed the people" (2 Chronicles 30:18-20).

Hezekiah had a heart like Jesus. Over and over again, Jesus broke the religious rules of His day. He understood that God's heart was bigger than any set of rules, even the ones meant to govern worship and holiness. Hezekiah's prayer revealed the same thing in him.

The people had come from far and wide to feast and worship. But some were not prepared. They were ceremonially unclean. Hezekiah realized, however, that what was happening—the reinstitution of the Passover, the most important national and spiritual ritual—was much larger than any rule regarding that ritual. If Hezekiah hadn't realized that, the festival would have caused division rather than unity. The work of God would have moved backward rather than forward. The whole point of the feast would have been missed—the point being that God saves His people based on His mercy, love, and the blood of a lamb.

Hezekiah's prayer showed how much he believed that God would be gracious and merciful to overlook imperfection and help His children worship Him. He healed them even though they had not done everything right.

Don't hesitate to come to God. Don't be afraid to ask God to help you honor and worship Him, even when you don't do everything perfectly. He will enable you to do that.

in Jerusalem to celebrate the Feast of Unleavened Bread in the second month. [14]They removed the altars in Jerusalem and cleared away the incense altars and threw them into the Kidron Valley.

[15]They slaughtered the Passover lamb on the fourteenth day of the second month. The priests and the Levites were ashamed and consecrated themselves and brought burnt offerings to the temple of the LORD. [16]Then they took up their regular positions as prescribed in the Law of Moses the man of God. The priests sprinkled the blood handed to them by the Levites. [17]Since many in the crowd had not consecrated themselves, the Levites had to kill the Passover lambs for all those who were not ceremonially clean and could not consecrate ⌊their lambs⌋ to the LORD. [18]Although most of the many people who came from Ephraim, Manasseh, Issachar and Zebulun had not purified themselves, yet they ate the Passover, contrary to what was written. But Hezekiah prayed for them, saying, "May the LORD, who is good, pardon everyone [19]who sets his heart on seeking God—the LORD, the God of his fathers—even if he is not clean according to the rules of the sanctuary." [20]And the LORD heard Hezekiah and healed the people.

[21]The Israelites who were present in Jerusalem celebrated the Feast of Unleavened Bread for seven days with great rejoicing, while the Levites and priests sang to the LORD every day, accompanied by the LORD's instruments of praise.[a]

[22]Hezekiah spoke encouragingly to all the Levites, who showed good understanding of the service of the LORD. For the seven days they ate their assigned portion and offered fellowship offerings[b] and praised the LORD, the God of their fathers.

[23]The whole assembly then agreed to celebrate the festival seven more days; so for another seven days they celebrated joyfully. [24]Hezekiah king of Judah provided a thousand bulls and seven thousand sheep and goats for the assembly, and the officials provided them with a thousand bulls and ten thousand sheep and goats. A great number of priests consecrated themselves. [25]The entire assembly of Judah rejoiced, along with the priests and Levites and all who had assembled from Israel, including the aliens who had come from Israel and those who lived in Judah. [26]There was great joy in Jerusalem, for since the days of Solomon son of David king of Israel there had been nothing like this in Jerusalem. [27]The priests and the Levites stood to bless the people, and God heard them, for their prayer reached heaven, his holy dwelling place.

31 When all this had ended, the Israelites who were there went out to the towns of Judah, smashed the sacred stones and cut down the Asherah poles. They destroyed the high places and the altars throughout Judah and Benjamin and in Ephraim and Manasseh. After they had destroyed all of them, the Israelites returned to their own towns and to their own property.

Contributions for Worship

[2]Hezekiah assigned the priests and Levites to divisions—each of them according to their duties as priests or Levites—to offer burnt offerings and fellowship offerings,[b] to minister, to give thanks and to sing praises at the gates of the LORD's dwelling. [3]The king contributed from his own possessions for the morning and evening burnt offerings and for the burnt offerings on the Sabbaths, New Moons and appointed feasts as written in the Law of the LORD. [4]He ordered the people living in Jerusalem to give the portion due the priests and Levites so they could devote themselves to the Law of the LORD. [5]As soon as the order went out, the Israelites generously gave the firstfruits of their grain, new wine, oil and honey and all that the fields produced. They brought a

---

[a] 21 Or priests praised the LORD every day with resounding instruments belonging to the LORD   [b] 22,2 Traditionally peace offerings

great amount, a tithe of everything. 6The men of Israel and Judah who lived in the towns of Judah also brought a tithe of their herds and flocks and a tithe of the holy things dedicated to the LORD their God, and they piled them in heaps. 7They began doing this in the third month and finished in the seventh month. 8When Hezekiah and his officials came and saw the heaps, they praised the LORD and blessed his people Israel.

9Hezekiah asked the priests and Levites about the heaps; 10and Azariah the chief priest, from the family of Zadok, answered, "Since the people began to bring their contributions to the temple of the LORD, we have had enough to eat and plenty to spare, because the LORD has blessed his people, and this great amount is left over."

11Hezekiah gave orders to prepare storerooms in the temple of the LORD, and this was done. 12Then they faithfully brought in the contributions, tithes and dedicated gifts. Conaniah, a Levite, was in charge of these things, and his brother Shimei was next in rank. 13Jehiel, Azaziah, Nahath, Asahel, Jerimoth, Jozabad, Eliel, Ismakiah, Mahath and Benaiah were supervisors under Conaniah and Shimei his brother, by appointment of King Hezekiah and Azariah the official in charge of the temple of God.

14Kore son of Imnah the Levite, keeper of the East Gate, was in charge of the freewill offerings given to God, distributing the contributions made to the LORD and also the consecrated gifts. 15Eden, Miniamin, Jeshua, Shemaiah, Amariah and Shecaniah assisted him faithfully in the towns of the priests, distributing to their fellow priests according to their divisions, old and young alike.

16In addition, they distributed to the males three years old or more whose names were in the genealogical records—all who would enter the temple of the LORD to perform the daily duties

of their various tasks, according to their responsibilities and their divisions. 17And they distributed to the priests enrolled by their families in the genealogical records and likewise to the Levites twenty years old or more, according to their responsibilities and their divisions. 18They included all the little ones, the wives, and the sons and daughters of the whole community listed in these genealogical records. For they were faithful in consecrating themselves.

19As for the priests, the descendants of Aaron, who lived on the farm lands around their towns or in any other towns, men were designated by name to distribute portions to every male among them and to all who were recorded in the genealogies of the Levites.

20This is what Hezekiah did throughout Judah, doing what was good and right and faithful before the LORD his God. 21In everything that he undertook in the service of God's temple and in obedience to the law and the commands, he sought his God and worked wholeheartedly. And so he prospered.

Sennacherib Threatens Jerusalem

32 After all that Hezekiah had so faithfully done, Sennacherib king of Assyria came and invaded Judah. He laid siege to the fortified cities, thinking to conquer them for himself. 2When Hezekiah saw that Sennacherib had come and that he intended to make war on Jerusalem, 3he consulted with his officials and military staff about blocking off the water from the springs outside the city, and they helped him. 4A large force of men assembled, and they blocked all the springs and the stream that flowed through the land. "Why should the kings[a] of Assyria come and find plenty of water?" they said. 5Then he worked hard repairing all the broken sections of the wall and building towers on it. He built another wall outside that one and reinforced the supporting terraces[b] of the

---

a 4 Hebrew; Septuagint and Syriac *king*   b 5 Or *the Millo*

GOING *deeper*

God Is on Your Side

READ AND CONSIDER: 2 CHRONICLES 32:1-23

" 'Be strong and courageous. Do not be afraid or discouraged because of the king of Assyria and the vast army with him, for there is a greater power with us than with him. With him is only the arm of flesh, but with us is the LORD our God to help us and to fight our battles.' And the people gained confidence from what Hezekiah the king of Judah said" (2 Chronicles 32:7-8).

King Hezekiah knew the king of Assyria was going to attack Jerusalem. It was only a matter of time. So he gathered his advisors and worked hard to build up his defenses and prepare the city. Then he gathered the people and reminded them that no matter the size of the army against them, God was bigger. "And the people gained confidence." By acknowledging and remembering who God was, they all found strength.

It's not wrong to be afraid of what you see *could* happen. That's realism. What *is* wrong is to not seek God's help immediately and humble yourself in worship before Him. Among other things, our praise reminds the enemy of who God is and how well we know Him. Always keep in mind that the enemy does not want you to worship God. So every time you attempt to build an altar to God in your life, the enemy will try to stop you.

Have you faced any frightening opposition in your life lately? Have you felt the enemy of your soul waging a full attack against you? Are you sometimes overwhelmed at how little strength and power you feel in the midst of it all? Don't worry; pray, and remember, "The one who is in you is greater than the one who is in the world" (1 John 4:4).

When King Hezekiah faced a strong enemy, he told his people the truth—God is greater. Keep in mind that when you acknowledge and praise God in the midst of enemy opposition, there is far more power with you than there is with the enemy.

City of David. He also made large numbers of weapons and shields.

⁶He appointed military officers over the people and assembled them before him in the square at the city gate and encouraged them with these words: ⁷"Be strong and courageous. Do not be afraid or discouraged because of the king of Assyria and the vast army with him, for there is a greater power with us than with him. ⁸With him is only the arm of flesh, but with us is the LORD our God to help us and to fight our battles." And the people gained confidence from what Hezekiah the king of Judah said.

⁹Later, when Sennacherib king of Assyria and all his forces were laying siege to Lachish, he sent his officers to Jerusalem with this message for Hezekiah king of Judah and for all the people of Judah who were there:

¹⁰"This is what Sennacherib king of Assyria says: On what are you basing your confidence, that you remain in Jerusalem under siege? ¹¹When Hezekiah says, 'The LORD our God will save us from the hand of the king of Assyria,' he is misleading you, to let you die of hunger and thirst. ¹²Did not Hezekiah himself remove this god's high places and altars, saying to Judah and Jerusalem, 'You must worship before one altar and burn sacrifices on it'?

¹³"Do you not know what I and my fathers have done to all the peoples of the other lands? Were the gods

of those nations ever able to deliver their land from my hand? [14]Who of all the gods of these nations that my fathers destroyed has been able to save his people from me? How then can your god deliver you from my hand? [15]Now do not let Hezekiah deceive you and mislead you like this. Do not believe him, for no god of any nation or kingdom has been able to deliver his people from my hand or the hand of my fathers. How much less will your god deliver you from my hand!"

[16]Sennacherib's officers spoke further against the LORD God and against his servant Hezekiah. [17]The king also wrote letters insulting the LORD, the God of Israel, and saying this against him: "Just as the gods of the peoples of the other lands did not rescue their people from my hand, so the god of Hezekiah will not rescue his people from my hand." [18]Then they called out in Hebrew to the people of Jerusalem who were on the wall, to terrify them and make them afraid in order to capture the city. [19]They spoke about the God of Jerusalem as they did about the gods of the other peoples of the world— the work of men's hands.

[20]King Hezekiah and the prophet Isaiah son of Amoz cried out in prayer to heaven about this. [21]And the LORD sent an angel, who annihilated all the fighting men and the leaders and officers in the camp of the Assyrian king. So he withdrew to his own land in disgrace. And when he went into the temple of his god, some of his sons cut him down with the sword.

[22]So the LORD saved Hezekiah and the people of Jerusalem from the hand of Sennacherib king of Assyria and from the hand of all others. He took care of them[a] on every side. [23]Many brought offerings to Jerusalem for the LORD and valuable gifts for Hezekiah king of Judah. From then on he was highly regarded by all the nations.

Hezekiah's Pride, Success and Death

[24]In those days Hezekiah became ill and was at the point of death. He prayed to the LORD, who answered him and gave him a miraculous sign. [25]But Hezekiah's heart was proud and he did not respond to the kindness shown him; therefore the LORD's wrath was on him and on Judah and Jerusalem. [26]Then Hezekiah repented of the pride of his heart, as did the people of Jerusalem; therefore the LORD's wrath did not come upon them during the days of Hezekiah.

[27]Hezekiah had very great riches and honor, and he made treasuries for his silver and gold and for his precious stones, spices, shields and all kinds of valuables. [28]He also made buildings to store the harvest of grain, new wine and oil; and he made stalls for various kinds of cattle, and pens for the flocks. [29]He built villages and acquired great numbers of flocks and herds, for God had given him very great riches.

[30]It was Hezekiah who blocked the upper outlet of the Gihon spring and channeled the water down to the west side of the City of David. He succeeded in everything he undertook. [31]But when envoys were sent by the rulers of Babylon to ask him about the miraculous sign that had occurred in the land, God left him to test him and to know everything that was in his heart.

[32]The other events of Hezekiah's reign and his acts of devotion are written in the vision of the prophet Isaiah son of Amoz in the book of the kings of Judah and Israel. [33]Hezekiah rested with his fathers and was buried on the hill where the tombs of David's descendants are. All Judah and the people of Jerusalem honored him when he died. And Manasseh his son succeeded him as king.

Manasseh King of Judah

33 Manasseh was twelve years old when he became king, and he reigned in Jerusalem fifty-five years. [2]He

---

[a] 22 Hebrew; Septuagint and Vulgate *He gave them rest*

God's people at prayer
MANASSEH MAKES A TURNAROUND?

2 CHRONICLES 33:1-20 Manasseh's reign was the longest of the Judean kings, and one of the most evil. He had worshiped pagan gods and even sacrificed his children to them. Eventually, punishment came. "In his distress he sought the favor of the LORD his God and humbled himself greatly" (33:12).

While we might be tempted to say "too little too late," God willingly listened to the distraught king's plea and forgave him. Manasseh then made an attempt to undo many of the evil things he had done.

Manasseh's past was firmly established, yet when it came to a moment of confrontation, he reached out to God and was restored. Too many times we let our past—blemished or unblemished—dictate how we will approach God. But God is Lord of this moment, and He can make it new when you reach out to Him. He did it for Manasseh. He can do it for you.

did evil in the eyes of the LORD, following the detestable practices of the nations the LORD had driven out before the Israelites. ³He rebuilt the high places his father Hezekiah had demolished; he also erected altars to the Baals and made Asherah poles. He bowed down to all the starry hosts and worshiped them. ⁴He built altars in the temple of the LORD, of which the LORD had said, "My Name will remain in Jerusalem forever." ⁵In both courts of the temple of the LORD, he built altars to all the starry hosts. ⁶He sacrificed his sons in ᵃ the fire in the Valley of Ben Hinnom, practiced sorcery, divination and witchcraft, and consulted mediums and spiritists. He did much evil in the eyes of the LORD, provoking him to anger.

⁷He took the carved image he had made and put it in God's temple, of which God had said to David and to his son Solomon, "In this temple and in Jerusalem, which I have chosen out of all the tribes of Israel, I will put my Name forever. ⁸I will not again make the feet of the Israelites leave the land I assigned to your forefathers, if only they will be careful to do everything I commanded them concerning all the laws, decrees and ordinances given through Moses." ⁹But

Manasseh led Judah and the people of Jerusalem astray, so that they did more evil than the nations the LORD had destroyed before the Israelites.

¹⁰The LORD spoke to Manasseh and his people, but they paid no attention. ¹¹So the LORD brought against them the army commanders of the king of Assyria, who took Manasseh prisoner, put a hook in his nose, bound him with bronze shackles and took him to Babylon. ¹²In his distress he sought the favor of the LORD his God and humbled himself greatly before the God of his fathers. ¹³And when he prayed to him, the LORD was moved by his entreaty and listened to his plea; so he brought him back to Jerusalem and to his kingdom. Then Manasseh knew that the LORD is God.

Praying
2 Chronicles 33:10-13
I am grateful, Lord, that You will hear the prayer of even the worst sinner who repents.

¹⁴Afterward he rebuilt the outer wall of the City of David, west of the Gihon spring in the valley, as far as the entrance of the Fish Gate and encircling the hill of Ophel; he also made it much higher. He

---

ᵃ 6 Or *He made his sons pass through*

stationed military commanders in all the fortified cities in Judah.

[15]He got rid of the foreign gods and removed the image from the temple of the LORD, as well as all the altars he had built on the temple hill and in Jerusalem; and he threw them out of the city. [16]Then he restored the altar of the LORD and sacrificed fellowship offerings[a] and thank offerings on it, and told Judah to serve the LORD, the God of Israel. [17]The people, however, continued to sacrifice at the high places, but only to the LORD their God.

[18]The other events of Manasseh's reign, including his prayer to his God and the words the seers spoke to him in the name of the LORD, the God of Israel, are written in the annals of the kings of Israel.[b] [19]His prayer and how God was moved by his entreaty, as well as all his sins and unfaithfulness, and the sites where he built high places and set up Asherah poles and idols before he humbled himself—all are written in the records of the seers.[c] [20]Manasseh rested with his fathers and was buried in his palace. And Amon his son succeeded him as king.

Amon King of Judah

[21]Amon was twenty-two years old when he became king, and he reigned in Jerusalem two years. [22]He did evil in the eyes of the LORD, as his father Manasseh had done. Amon worshiped and offered sacrifices to all the idols Manasseh had made. [23]But unlike his father Manasseh, he did not humble himself before the LORD; Amon increased his guilt.

[24]Amon's officials conspired against him and assassinated him in his palace. [25]Then the people of the land killed all who had plotted against King Amon, and they made Josiah his son king in his place.

Josiah's Reforms

34 Josiah was eight years old when he became king, and he reigned in Jerusalem thirty-one years. [2]He did what was right in the eyes of the LORD and walked in the ways of his father David, not turning aside to the right or to the left.

[3]In the eighth year of his reign, while he was still young, he began to seek the God of his father David. In his twelfth year he began to purge Judah and Jerusalem of high places, Asherah poles, carved idols and cast images. [4]Under his direction the altars of the Baals were torn down; he cut to pieces the incense altars that were above them, and smashed the Asherah poles, the idols and the images. These he broke to pieces and scattered over the graves of those who had sacrificed to them. [5]He burned the bones of the priests on their altars, and so he purged Judah and Jerusalem. [6]In the towns of Manasseh, Ephraim and Simeon, as far as Naphtali, and in the ruins around them, [7]he tore down the altars and the Asherah poles and crushed the idols to powder and cut to pieces all the incense altars throughout Israel. Then he went back to Jerusalem.

[8]In the eighteenth year of Josiah's reign, to purify the land and the temple, he sent Shaphan son of Azaliah and Maaseiah the ruler of the city, with Joah son of Joahaz, the recorder, to repair the temple of the LORD his God.

[9]They went to Hilkiah the high priest and gave him the money that had been brought into the temple of God, which the Levites who were the doorkeepers had collected from the people of Manasseh, Ephraim and the entire remnant of Israel and from all the people of Judah and Benjamin and the inhabitants of Jerusalem. [10]Then they entrusted it to the men appointed to supervise the work on the LORD's temple. These men paid the workers who repaired and restored the temple. [11]They also gave money to the carpenters and builders to purchase dressed stone, and timber for joists and beams for the buildings that the kings of Judah had allowed to fall into ruin.

---

[a] 16 Traditionally *peace offerings*   [b] 18 That is, Judah, as frequently in 2 Chronicles   [c] 19 One Hebrew manuscript and Septuagint; most Hebrew manuscripts *of Hozai*

12The men did the work faithfully. Over them to direct them were Jahath and Obadiah, Levites descended from Merari, and Zechariah and Meshullam, descended from Kohath. The Levites—all who were skilled in playing musical instruments— 13had charge of the laborers and supervised all the workers from job to job. Some of the Levites were secretaries, scribes and doorkeepers.

The Book of the Law Found

14While they were bringing out the money that had been taken into the temple of the LORD, Hilkiah the priest found the Book of the Law of the LORD that had been given through Moses. 15Hilkiah said to Shaphan the secretary, "I have found the Book of the Law in the temple of the LORD." He gave it to Shaphan.

16Then Shaphan took the book to the king and reported to him: "Your officials are doing everything that has been committed to them. 17They have paid out the money that was in the temple of the LORD and have entrusted it to the supervisors and workers." 18Then Shaphan the secretary informed the king, "Hilkiah the priest has given me a book." And Shaphan read from it in the presence of the king.

19When the king heard the words of the Law, he tore his robes. 20He gave these orders to Hilkiah, Ahikam son of Shaphan, Abdon son of Micah,a Shaphan the secretary and Asaiah the king's attendant: 21"Go and inquire of the LORD for me and for the remnant in Israel and Judah about what is written in this book that has been found. Great is the LORD's anger that is poured out on us because our fathers have not kept the word of the LORD; they have not acted in accordance with all that is written in this book."

22Hilkiah and those the king had sent with himb went to speak to the prophetess Huldah, who was the wife of Shallum son of Tokhath,c the son of Hasrah,d

keeper of the wardrobe. She lived in Jerusalem, in the Second District.

23She said to them, "This is what the LORD, the God of Israel, says: Tell the man who sent you to me, 24'This is what the LORD says: I am going to bring disaster on this place and its people—all the curses written in the book that has been read in the presence of the king of Judah. 25Because they have forsaken me and burned incense to other gods and provoked me to anger by all that their hands have made,e my anger will be poured out on this place and will not be quenched.' 26Tell the king of Judah, who sent you to inquire of the LORD, 'This is what the LORD, the God of Israel, says concerning the words you heard: 27Because your heart was responsive and you humbled yourself before God when you heard what he spoke against this place and its people, and because you humbled yourself before me and tore your robes and wept in my presence, I have heard you, declares the LORD. 28Now I will gather you to your fathers, and you will be buried in peace. Your eyes will not see all the disaster I am going to bring on this place and on those who live here.'"

So they took her answer back to the king.

29Then the king called together all the elders of Judah and Jerusalem. 30He went up to the temple of the LORD with the men of Judah, the people of Jerusalem, the priests and the Levites—all the people from the least to the greatest. He read in their hearing all the words of the Book of the Covenant, which had been found in the temple of the LORD. 31The king stood by his pillar and renewed the covenant in the presence of the LORD—to follow the LORD and keep his commands, regulations and decrees with all his heart and all his soul, and to obey the words of the covenant written in this book.

32Then he had everyone in Jerusalem

a 20 Also called *Acbor son of Micaiah*   b 22 One Hebrew manuscript, Vulgate and Syriac; most Hebrew manuscripts do not have *had sent with him*.   c 22 Also called *Tikvah*   d 22 Also called *Harhas*   e 25 Or *by everything they have done* and Benjamin pledge themselves to it; the people of Jerusalem did this in accordance with the covenant of God, the God of their fathers.

33Josiah removed all the detestable idols from all the territory belonging to the Israelites, and he had all who were present in Israel serve the LORD their God. As long as he lived, they did not fail to follow the LORD, the God of their fathers.

Josiah Celebrates the Passover

35 Josiah celebrated the Passover to the LORD in Jerusalem, and the Passover lamb was slaughtered on the fourteenth day of the first month. 2He appointed the priests to their duties and encouraged them in the service of the LORD's temple. 3He said to the Levites, who instructed all Israel and who had been consecrated to the LORD: "Put the sacred ark in the temple that Solomon son of David king of Israel built. It is not to be carried about on your shoulders. Now serve the LORD your God and his people Israel. 4Prepare yourselves by families in your divisions, according to the directions written by David king of Israel and by his son Solomon.

5"Stand in the holy place with a group of Levites for each subdivision of the families of your fellow countrymen, the lay people.6Slaughter the Passover lambs, consecrate yourselves and prepare ⌊the lambs⌋ for your fellow countrymen, doing what the LORD commanded through Moses."

7Josiah provided for all the lay people who were there a total of thirty thousand sheep and goats for the Passover offerings, and also three thousand cattle—all from the king's own possessions.

8His officials also contributed voluntarily to the people and the priests and Levites. Hilkiah, Zechariah and Jehiel, the administrators of God's temple, gave the priests twenty-six hundred Passover offerings and three hundred cattle. 9Also Conaniah along with Shemaiah and Nethanel, his brothers, and Hashabiah, Jeiel and Jozabad, the leaders of the Le-

vites, provided five thousand Passover offerings and five hundred head of cattle for the Levites.

10The service was arranged and the priests stood in their places with the Levites in their divisions as the king had ordered. 11The Passover lambs were slaughtered, and the priests sprinkled the blood handed to them, while the Levites skinned the animals. 12They set aside the burnt offerings to give them to the subdivisions of the families of the people to offer to the LORD, as is written in the Book of Moses. They did the same with the cattle. 13They roasted the Passover animals over the fire as prescribed, and boiled the holy offerings in pots, caldrons and pans and served them quickly to all the people. 14After this, they made preparations for themselves and for the priests, because the priests, the descendants of Aaron, were sacrificing the burnt offerings and the fat portions until nightfall. So the Levites made preparations for themselves and for the Aaronic priests.

15The musicians, the descendants of Asaph, were in the places prescribed by David, Asaph, Heman and Jeduthun the king's seer. The gatekeepers at each gate did not need to leave their posts, because their fellow Levites made the preparations for them.

16So at that time the entire service of the LORD was carried out for the celebration of the Passover and the offering of burnt offerings on the altar of the LORD, as King Josiah had ordered. 17The Israelites who were present celebrated the Passover at that time and observed the Feast of Unleavened Bread for seven days. 18The Passover had not been observed like this in Israel since the days of the prophet Samuel; and none of the kings of Israel had ever celebrated such a Passover as did Josiah, with the priests, the Levites and all Judah and Israel who were there with the people of Jerusalem. 19This Passover was celebrated in the eighteenth year of Josiah's reign.

The Death of Josiah

20After all this, when Josiah had set the temple in order, Neco king of Egypt went up to fight at Carchemish on the Euphrates, and Josiah marched out to meet him in battle. 21But Neco sent messengers to him, saying, "What quarrel is there between you and me, O king of Judah? It is not you I am attacking at this time, but the house with which I am at war. God has told me to hurry; so stop opposing God, who is with me, or he will destroy you."

22Josiah, however, would not turn away from him, but disguised himself to engage him in battle. He would not listen to what Neco had said at God's command but went to fight him on the plain of Megiddo.

23Archers shot King Josiah, and he told his officers, "Take me away; I am badly wounded." 24So they took him out of his chariot, put him in the other chariot he had and brought him to Jerusalem, where he died. He was buried in the tombs of his fathers, and all Judah and Jerusalem mourned for him.

25Jeremiah composed laments for Josiah, and to this day all the men and women singers commemorate Josiah in the laments. These became a tradition in Israel and are written in the Laments.

26The other events of Josiah's reign and his acts of devotion, according to what is written in the Law of the LORD— 27all the events, from beginning to end, are written in the book of the kings of Israel 36 and Judah. 1And the people of the land took Jehoahaz son of Josiah and made him king in Jerusalem in place of his father.

Jehoahaz King of Judah

2Jehoahaz[a] was twenty-three years old when he became king, and he reigned in Jerusalem three months. 3The king of Egypt dethroned him in Jerusalem and imposed on Judah a levy of a hundred talents[b] of silver and a talent[c] of gold. 4The king of Egypt made Eliakim, a brother of Jehoahaz, king over Judah and Jerusalem and changed Eliakim's name to Jehoiakim. But Neco took Eliakim's brother Jehoahaz and carried him off to Egypt.

Jehoiakim King of Judah

5Jehoiakim was twenty-five years old when he became king, and he reigned in Jerusalem eleven years. He did evil in the eyes of the LORD his God. 6Nebuchadnezzar king of Babylon attacked him and bound him with bronze shackles to take him to Babylon. 7Nebuchadnezzar also took to Babylon articles from the temple of the LORD and put them in his temple[d] there.

8The other events of Jehoiakim's reign, the detestable things he did and all that was found against him, are written in the book of the kings of Israel and Judah. And Jehoiachin his son succeeded him as king.

Jehoiachin King of Judah

9Jehoiachin was eighteen[e] years old when he became king, and he reigned in Jerusalem three months and ten days. He did evil in the eyes of the LORD. 10In the spring, King Nebuchadnezzar sent for him and brought him to Babylon, together with articles of value from the temple of the LORD, and he made Jehoiachin's uncle,[f] Zedekiah, king over Judah and Jerusalem.

Zedekiah King of Judah

11Zedekiah was twenty-one years old when he became king, and he reigned in Jerusalem eleven years. 12He did evil in the eyes of the LORD his God and did not humble himself before Jeremiah the prophet, who spoke the word of the LORD. 13He also rebelled against King Nebuchadnezzar, who had made him take an oath in God's name. He became stiff-necked and hardened his heart and

a 2 Hebrew Joahaz, a variant of Jehoahaz; also in verse 4   b 3 That is, about 3 3/4 tons (about 3.4 metric tons)   c 3 That is, about 75 pounds (about 34 kilograms)   d 7 Or palace   e 9 One Hebrew manuscript, some Septuagint manuscripts and Syriac (see also 2 Kings 24:8); most Hebrew manuscripts eight   f 10 Hebrew brother, that is, relative (see 2 Kings 24:17) would not turn to the LORD, the God of Israel. [14]Furthermore, all the leaders of the priests and the people became more and more unfaithful, following all the detestable practices of the nations and defiling the temple of the LORD, which he had consecrated in Jerusalem.

The Fall of Jerusalem

[15]The LORD, the God of their fathers, sent word to them through his messengers again and again, because he had pity on his people and on his dwelling place. [16]But they mocked God's messengers, despised his words and scoffed at his prophets until the wrath of the LORD was aroused against his people and there was no remedy. [17]He brought up against them the king of the Babylonians,[a] who killed their young men with the sword in the sanctuary, and spared neither young man nor young woman, old man or aged. God handed all of them over to Nebuchadnezzar. [18]He carried to Babylon all the articles from the temple of God, both large and small, and the treasures of the LORD's temple and the treasures of the king and his officials. [19]They set fire to God's temple and broke down the wall of Jerusalem; they burned all the palaces and destroyed everything of value there.

[20]He carried into exile to Babylon the remnant, who escaped from the sword, and they became servants to him and his sons until the kingdom of Persia came to power. [21]The land enjoyed its sabbath rests; all the time of its desolation it rested, until the seventy years were completed in fulfillment of the word of the LORD spoken by Jeremiah.

[22]In the first year of Cyrus king of Persia, in order to fulfill the word of the LORD spoken by Jeremiah, the LORD moved the heart of Cyrus king of Persia to make a proclamation throughout his realm and to put it in writing:

[23]"This is what Cyrus king of Persia says:

"'The LORD, the God of heaven, has given me all the kingdoms of the earth and he has appointed me to build a temple for him at Jerusalem in Judah. Anyone of his people among you—may the LORD his God be with him, and let him go up.'"

---

[a] 17 Or *Chaldeans*

Author: Probably Ezra

Date: 440 BC

Audience: The post-exile Jews—to remind them of God's past faithfulness and to prompt them to love and worship and serve Him in the land, according to His covenant promises

Alfred Lord Tennyson once observed, "More things are wrought by prayer than this world dreams of." John Wesley went a step further: "God does nothing but by prayer."

Can this really be true? Has God actually decreed our prayers to be the keys that unlock heaven's greatest miracles? The answer is yes! When we pray—humbly, persistently, and in faith—lives get turned around. Marriages are saved. "Dead" churches experience resurrection. Entire nations undergo revival.

The book of Ezra tells such a story of God's mighty work. After 70 years of exile—seven decades of waiting and watching, praying and persevering—the Jews were allowed to return to the land of Israel and begin rebuilding their beloved temple.

Here is a remarkable account of faith and worship as well as a reminder of the necessity of obedience. Here is a prompt for those who consider themselves "the servants of the God of heaven and earth" (5:11) to lift up bold prayers and petitions.

Prayer Themes:

- *Praise our sovereign God that He works in and through the decisions of world leaders—no one is able to thwart His plans and purposes (1:2).*

- *Ask God to make you more and more generous . . . always willing to give back to His work (2:64–3:7).*

- *Thank God that He is able to watch over and protect His servants (8:21-32).*

Ezra

Cyrus Helps the Exiles to Return

1 In the first year of Cyrus king of Persia, in order to fulfill the word of the LORD spoken by Jeremiah, the LORD moved the heart of Cyrus king of Persia to make a proclamation throughout his realm and to put it in writing:

2 "This is what Cyrus king of Persia says:

"'The LORD, the God of heaven, has given me all the kingdoms of the earth and he has appointed me to build a temple for him at Jerusalem in Judah. 3 Anyone of his people among you—may his God be with him, and let him go up to Jerusalem in Judah and build the temple of the LORD, the God of Israel, the God who is in Jerusalem. 4 And the people of any place where survivors may now be living are to provide him with silver and gold, with goods and livestock, and with freewill offerings for the temple of God in Jerusalem.'"

5 Then the family heads of Judah and Benjamin, and the priests and Levites—everyone whose heart God had moved—prepared to go up and build the house of the LORD in Jerusalem. 6 All their neighbors assisted them with articles of silver and gold, with goods and livestock, and with valuable gifts, in addition to all the freewill offerings. 7 Moreover, King Cyrus brought out the articles belonging to the temple of the LORD, which Nebuchadnezzar had carried away from Jerusalem and had placed in the temple of his god. 8 Cyrus king of Persia had them brought by Mithredath the treasurer, who counted

a 7 Or *gods*

them out to Sheshbazzar the prince of Judah.

9This was the inventory:

gold dishes	30
silver dishes	1,000
silver pans[a]	29
10gold bowls	30
matching silver bowls	410
other articles	1,000

11In all, there were 5,400 articles of gold and of silver. Sheshbazzar brought all these along when the exiles came up from Babylon to Jerusalem.

The List of the Exiles Who Returned

2 Now these are the people of the province who came up from the captivity of the exiles, whom Nebuchadnezzar king of Babylon had taken captive to Babylon (they returned to Jerusalem and Judah, each to his own town, 2in company with Zerubbabel, Jeshua, Nehemiah, Seraiah, Reelaiah, Mordecai, Bilshan, Mispar, Bigvai, Rehum and Baanah):

The list of the men of the people of Israel:

3the descendants of Parosh	2,172
4of Shephatiah	372
5of Arah	775
6of Pahath-Moab (through the line of Jeshua and Joab)	2,812
7of Elam	1,254
8of Zattu	945
9of Zaccai	760
10of Bani	642
11of Bebai	623
12of Azgad	1,222
13of Adonikam	666
14of Bigvai	2,056
15of Adin	454
16of Ater (through Hezekiah)	98
17of Bezai	323
18of Jorah	112
19of Hashum	223
20of Gibbar	95

21the men of Bethlehem	123
22of Netophah	56
23of Anathoth	128
24of Azmaveth	42
25of Kiriath Jearim,[b] Kephirah and Beeroth	743
26of Ramah and Geba	621
27of Micmash	122
28of Bethel and Ai	223
29of Nebo	52
30of Magbish	156
31of the other Elam	1,254
32of Harim	320
33of Lod, Hadid and Ono	725
34of Jericho	345
35of Senaah	3,630

36The priests:

the descendants of Jedaiah (through the family of Jeshua)	973
37of Immer	1,052
38of Pashhur	1,247
39of Harim	1,017

40The Levites:

the descendants of Jeshua and Kadmiel (through the line of Hodaviah)	74

41The singers:

the descendants of Asaph	128

42The gatekeepers of the temple:

the descendants of Shallum, Ater, Talmon, Akkub, Hatita and Shobai	139

43The temple servants:

the descendants of
Ziha, Hasupha, Tabbaoth,
44Keros, Siaha, Padon,
45Lebanah, Hagabah, Akkub,
46Hagab, Shalmai, Hanan,
47Giddel, Gahar, Reaiah,
48Rezin, Nekoda, Gazzam,
49Uzza, Paseah, Besai,
50Asnah, Meunim, Nephusim,

---

a 9 The meaning of the Hebrew for this word is uncertain.   b 25 See Septuagint (see also Neh. 7:29); Hebrew Kiriath Arim.

51 Bakbuk, Hakupha, Harhur,
52 Bazluth, Mehida, Harsha,
53 Barkos, Sisera, Temah,
54 Neziah and Hatipha

55 The descendants of the servants of Solomon:

the descendants of
  Sotai, Hassophereth, Peruda,
56 Jaala, Darkon, Giddel,
57 Shephatiah, Hattil,
  Pokereth-Hazzebaim and Ami

58 The temple servants and the
  descendants of the servants
  of Solomon   392

59 The following came up from the towns of Tel Melah, Tel Harsha, Kerub, Addon and Immer, but they could not show that their families were descended from Israel:

60 The descendants of
  Delaiah, Tobiah and
  Nekoda   652

61 And from among the priests:

The descendants of
  Hobaiah, Hakkoz and Barzillai
  (a man who had married
  a daughter of Barzillai the
  Gileadite and was called by
  that name).
62 These searched for their family records, but they could not find them and so were excluded from the priesthood as unclean. 63 The governor ordered them not to eat any of the most sacred food until there was a priest ministering with the Urim and Thummim.

64 The whole company numbered 42,360, 65 besides their 7,337 menservants and maidservants; and they also had 200 men and women singers. 66 They had 736 horses, 245 mules, 67 435 camels and 6,720 donkeys.

68 When they arrived at the house of the LORD in Jerusalem, some of the heads of the families gave freewill offerings toward the rebuilding of the house of God on its site. 69 According to their ability they gave to the treasury for this work 61,000 drachmas[a] of gold, 5,000 minas[b] of silver and 100 priestly garments.

70 The priests, the Levites, the singers, the gatekeepers and the temple servants settled in their own towns, along with some of the other people, and the rest of the Israelites settled in their towns.

Rebuilding the Altar

3 When the seventh month came and the Israelites had settled in their towns, the people assembled as one man in Jerusalem. 2 Then Jeshua son of Jozadak and his fellow priests and Zerubbabel son of Shealtiel and his associates began to build the altar of the God of Israel to sacrifice burnt offerings on it, in accordance with what is written in the Law of Moses the man of God. 3 Despite their fear of the peoples around them, they built the altar on its foundation and sacrificed burnt offerings on it to the LORD, both the morning and evening sacrifices. 4 Then in accordance with what is written, they celebrated the Feast of Tabernacles with the required number of burnt offerings prescribed for each day. 5 After that, they presented the regular burnt offerings, the New Moon sacrifices and the sacrifices for all the appointed sacred feasts of the LORD, as well as those brought as freewill offerings to the LORD. 6 On the first day of the seventh month they began to offer burnt offerings to the LORD, though the foundation of the LORD's temple had not yet been laid.

Rebuilding the Temple

7 Then they gave money to the masons and carpenters, and gave food and drink and oil to the people of Sidon and Tyre, so that they would bring cedar logs by sea from Lebanon to Joppa, as authorized by Cyrus king of Persia.

---

a 69 That is, about 1,100 pounds (about 500 kilograms)   b 69 That is, about 3 tons (about 2.9 metric tons)

GOING deeper

The Antidote for Fear

READ AND CONSIDER: EZRA 3:7-13

"With praise and thanksgiving they sang to the Lord: 'He is good; his love to Israel endures forever.' And all the people gave a great shout of praise to the Lord, because the foundation of the house of the Lord was laid" (Ezra 3:11).

The people of Judah had been exiled. Jerusalem and its temple were in ruins. Outsiders had taken over the land—people who did not understand or revere the customs of the Jewish nation. So when the first Jews returned from their exile, they were fearful and a bit intimidated by the people around them. But they knew they must rebuild, and so they began. It was a slow and arduous process, but finally the foundation of the temple was laid.

And then the people pulled out all the stops, praising God, singing songs, shouting, and playing trumpets and cymbals. They were so *loud* that all the foreign neighbors heard them.

When you're struggling, or doubting, or fearful, or feel as if your foundation has crumbled, don't ever underestimate the power of praise! Don't just think about it. Do it. Pull out all the stops. Make praise your *first* response to fearful situations in your life. God wants us to praise Him at all times, but especially when we are afraid or discouraged. When we do, not only will He take away our fear, but He will also give us joy (Psalm 34:1-5).

Fear will tell you things that are not God's truth for your life. Fear denies that God's presence is powerful and fully active in your life. It cancels all hope and faith in God's desire to work in your behalf. But the truth is that faith, prayer, praise, and the Word of God will conquer your every fear.

---

[8]In the second month of the second year after their arrival at the house of God in Jerusalem, Zerubbabel son of Shealtiel, Jeshua son of Jozadak and the rest of their brothers (the priests and the Levites and all who had returned from the captivity to Jerusalem) began the work, appointing Levites twenty years of age and older to supervise the building of the house of the Lord. [9]Jeshua and his sons and brothers and Kadmiel and his sons (descendants of Hodaviah[a]) and the sons of Henadad and their sons and brothers—all Levites—joined together in supervising those working on the house of God.

[10]When the builders laid the foundation of the temple of the Lord, the priests in their vestments and with trumpets, and the Levites (the sons of Asaph) with cymbals, took their places to praise the Lord, as prescribed by David king of Israel. [11]With praise and thanksgiving they sang to the Lord:

"He is good;
    his love to Israel endures forever."

Praying Ezra 3:11
*Lord, I thank You for the solid foundation
You have laid in my life.*

And all the people gave a great shout of praise to the Lord, because the foundation of the house of the Lord was laid. [12]But many of the older priests and Levites and family heads, who had seen the former temple, wept aloud when they saw the foundation of this temple being laid, while many others shouted for joy. [13]No one could distinguish the sound of

---

[a] 9 Hebrew *Yehudah*, probably a variant of *Hodaviah*

the shouts of joy from the sound of weeping, because the people made so much noise. And the sound was heard far away.

Opposition to the Rebuilding

4 When the enemies of Judah and Benjamin heard that the exiles were building a temple for the LORD, the God of Israel, ²they came to Zerubbabel and to the heads of the families and said, "Let us help you build because, like you, we seek your God and have been sacrificing to him since the time of Esarhaddon king of Assyria, who brought us here."

³But Zerubbabel, Jeshua and the rest of the heads of the families of Israel answered, "You have no part with us in building a temple to our God. We alone will build it for the LORD, the God of Israel, as King Cyrus, the king of Persia, commanded us."

⁴Then the peoples around them set out to discourage the people of Judah and make them afraid to go on building.ᵃ ⁵They hired counselors to work against them and frustrate their plans during the entire reign of Cyrus king of Persia and down to the reign of Darius king of Persia.

Later Opposition Under Xerxes and Artaxerxes

⁶At the beginning of the reign of Xerxes,ᵇ they lodged an accusation against the people of Judah and Jerusalem.

⁷And in the days of Artaxerxes king of Persia, Bishlam, Mithredath, Tabeel and the rest of his associates wrote a letter to Artaxerxes. The letter was written in Aramaic script and in the Aramaic language.ᶜ,ᵈ

⁸Rehum the commanding officer and Shimshai the secretary wrote a letter against Jerusalem to Artaxerxes the king as follows:

⁹Rehum the commanding officer and Shimshai the secretary, together with the rest of their associates—the judges and officials over the men from Tripolis, Persia,ᵉ Erech and Babylon, the Elamites of Susa, ¹⁰and the other people whom the great and honorable Ashurbanipalᶠ deported and settled in the city of Samaria and elsewhere in Trans-Euphrates.

Prayer is . . .
an act of faith, believing that God will hear and answer.

¹¹(This is a copy of the letter they sent him.)

To King Artaxerxes,

From your servants, the men of Trans-Euphrates:

¹²The king should know that the Jews who came up to us from you have gone to Jerusalem and are rebuilding that rebellious and wicked city. They are restoring the walls and repairing the foundations.

¹³Furthermore, the king should know that if this city is built and its walls are restored, no more taxes, tribute or duty will be paid, and the royal revenues will suffer. ¹⁴Now since we are under obligation to the palace and it is not proper for us to see the king dishonored, we are sending this message to inform the king, ¹⁵so that a search may be made in the archives of your predecessors. In these records you will find that this city is a rebellious city, troublesome to kings and provinces, a place of rebellion from ancient times. That is why this city was destroyed. ¹⁶We inform the king that if this city is built and its walls are restored, you will be left with nothing in Trans-Euphrates.

¹⁷The king sent this reply:

To Rehum the commanding officer, Shimshai the secretary and the rest of their associates living in Samaria and elsewhere in Trans-Euphrates:

Greetings.

¹⁸The letter you sent us has been read and translated in my presence. ¹⁹I issued an order and a search was made, and it was found that this city has a long history of revolt against kings and has been a place of rebellion and sedition. ²⁰Jerusalem has had powerful kings ruling over the whole of Trans-Euphrates, and taxes, tribute and duty were paid to them. ²¹Now issue an order to these men to stop work, so that this city will not be rebuilt until I so order. ²²Be careful not to neglect this matter. Why let this threat grow, to the detriment of the royal interests?

²³As soon as the copy of the letter of King Artaxerxes was read to Rehum and Shimshai the secretary and their associates, they went immediately to the Jews in Jerusalem and compelled them by force to stop.

²⁴Thus the work on the house of God in Jerusalem came to a standstill until the second year of the reign of Darius king of Persia.

Tattenai's Letter to Darius

5 Now Haggai the prophet and Zechariah the prophet, a descendant of Iddo, prophesied to the Jews in Judah and Jerusalem in the name of the God of Israel, who was over them. ²Then Zerubbabel son of Shealtiel and Jeshua son of Jozadak set to work to rebuild the house of God in Jerusalem. And the prophets of God were with them, helping them.

³At that time Tattenai, governor of Trans-Euphrates, and Shethar-Bozenai and their associates went to them and asked, "Who authorized you to rebuild this temple and restore this structure?" ⁴They also asked, "What are the names of the men constructing this building?"ᵃ ⁵But the eye of their God was watching over the elders of the Jews, and they were not stopped until a report could go to Darius and his written reply be received.

⁶This is a copy of the letter that Tattenai, governor of Trans-Euphrates, and Shethar-Bozenai and their associates, the officials of Trans-Euphrates, sent to King Darius. ⁷The report they sent him read as follows:

To King Darius:

Cordial greetings.

⁸The king should know that we went to the district of Judah, to the temple of the great God. The people are building it with large stones and placing the timbers in the walls. The work is being carried on with diligence and is making rapid progress under their direction.

⁹We questioned the elders and asked them, "Who authorized you to rebuild this temple and restore this structure?" ¹⁰We also asked them their names, so that we could write down the names of their leaders for your information.

¹¹This is the answer they gave us:

"We are the servants of the God of heaven and earth, and we are rebuilding the temple that was built many years ago, one that a great king of Israel built and finished. ¹²But because our fathers angered the God of heaven, he handed them over to Nebuchadnezzar the Chaldean, king of Babylon, who destroyed this temple and deported the people to Babylon.

¹³"However, in the first year of Cyrus king of Babylon, King Cyrus issued a decree to rebuild this house

---

ᵃ 4 See Septuagint; Aramaic ⁴We told them the names of the men constructing this building.

of God. [14]He even removed from the temple[a] of Babylon the gold and silver articles of the house of God, which Nebuchadnezzar had taken from the temple in Jerusalem and brought to the temple[a] in Babylon.

"Then King Cyrus gave them to a man named Sheshbazzar, whom he had appointed governor, [15]and he told him, 'Take these articles and go and deposit them in the temple in Jerusalem. And rebuild the house of God on its site.' [16]So this Sheshbazzar came and laid the foundations of the house of God in Jerusalem. From that day to the present it has been under construction but is not yet finished."

[17]Now if it pleases the king, let a search be made in the royal archives of Babylon to see if King Cyrus did in fact issue a decree to rebuild this house of God in Jerusalem. Then let the king send us his decision in this matter.

The Decree of Darius

6 King Darius then issued an order, and they searched in the archives stored in the treasury at Babylon. [2]A scroll was found in the citadel of Ecbatana in the province of Media, and this was written on it:

Memorandum:

[3]In the first year of King Cyrus, the king issued a decree concerning the temple of God in Jerusalem:

Let the temple be rebuilt as a place to present sacrifices, and let its foundations be laid. It is to be ninety feet[b] high and ninety feet wide, [4]with three courses of large stones and one of timbers. The costs are to be paid by the royal treasury. [5]Also, the gold and silver articles of the house of God, which Nebuchadnezzar took from the temple in Jerusalem and brought

to Babylon, are to be returned to their places in the temple in Jerusalem; they are to be deposited in the house of God.

[6]Now then, Tattenai, governor of Trans-Euphrates, and Shethar-Bozenai and you, their fellow officials of that province, stay away from there. [7]Do not interfere with the work on this temple of God. Let the governor of the Jews and the Jewish elders rebuild this house of God on its site.

[8]Moreover, I hereby decree what you are to do for these elders of the Jews in the construction of this house of God:

The expenses of these men are to be fully paid out of the royal treasury, from the revenues of Trans-Euphrates, so that the work will not stop. [9]Whatever is needed—young bulls, rams, male lambs for burnt offerings to the God of heaven, and wheat, salt, wine and oil, as requested by the priests in Jerusalem—must be given them daily without fail, [10]so that they may offer sacrifices pleasing to the God of heaven and pray for the well-being of the king and his sons.

[11]Furthermore, I decree that if anyone changes this edict, a beam is to be pulled from his house and he is to be lifted up and impaled on it. And for this crime his house is to be made a pile of rubble. [12]May God, who has caused his Name to dwell there, overthrow any king or people who lifts a hand to change this decree or to destroy this temple in Jerusalem.

I Darius have decreed it. Let it be carried out with diligence.

Completion and Dedication of the Temple

[13]Then, because of the decree King Darius had sent, Tattenai, governor of Trans-Euphrates, and Shethar-Bozenai and their associates carried it out with

---

diligence. ¹⁴So the elders of the Jews continued to build and prosper under the preaching of Haggai the prophet and Zechariah, a descendant of Iddo. They finished building the temple according to the command of the God of Israel and the decrees of Cyrus, Darius and Artaxerxes, kings of Persia. ¹⁵The temple was completed on the third day of the month Adar, in the sixth year of the reign of King Darius.

¹⁶Then the people of Israel—the priests, the Levites and the rest of the exiles—celebrated the dedication of the house of God with joy. ¹⁷For the dedication of this house of God they offered a hundred bulls, two hundred rams, four hundred male lambs and, as a sin offering for all Israel, twelve male goats, one for each of the tribes of Israel. ¹⁸And they installed the priests in their divisions and the Levites in their groups for the service of God at Jerusalem, according to what is written in the Book of Moses.

The Passover

¹⁹On the fourteenth day of the first month, the exiles celebrated the Passover. ²⁰The priests and Levites had purified themselves and were all ceremonially clean. The Levites slaughtered the Passover lamb for all the exiles, for their brothers the priests and for themselves. ²¹So the Israelites who had returned from the exile ate it, together with all who had separated themselves from the unclean practices of their Gentile neighbors in order to seek the LORD, the God of Israel. ²²For seven days they celebrated with joy the Feast of Unleavened Bread, because the LORD had filled them with joy by changing the attitude of the king of Assyria, so that he assisted them in the work on the house of God, the God of Israel.

Ezra Comes to Jerusalem

7 After these things, during the reign of Artaxerxes king of Persia, Ezra son of Seraiah, the son of Azariah, the son

of Hilkiah, ²the son of Shallum, the son of Zadok, the son of Ahitub, ³the son of Amariah, the son of Azariah, the son of Meraioth, ⁴the son of Zerahiah, the son of Uzzi, the son of Bukki, ⁵the son of Abishua, the son of Phinehas, the son of Eleazar, the son of Aaron the chief priest— ⁶this Ezra came up from Babylon. He was a teacher well versed in the Law of Moses, which the LORD, the God of Israel, had given. The king had granted him everything he asked, for the hand of the LORD his God was on him. ⁷Some of the Israelites, including priests, Levites, singers, gatekeepers and temple servants, also came up to Jerusalem in the seventh year of King Artaxerxes.

⁸Ezra arrived in Jerusalem in the fifth month of the seventh year of the king. ⁹He had begun his journey from Babylon on the first day of the first month, and he arrived in Jerusalem on the first day of the fifth month, for the gracious hand of his God was on him. ¹⁰For Ezra had devoted himself to the study and observance of the Law of the LORD, and to teaching its decrees and laws in Israel.

King Artaxerxes' Letter to Ezra

¹¹This is a copy of the letter King Artaxerxes had given to Ezra the priest and teacher, a man learned in matters concerning the commands and decrees of the LORD for Israel:

¹²ᵃArtaxerxes, king of kings,

To Ezra the priest, a teacher of the Law of the God of heaven:

Greetings.

¹³Now I decree that any of the Israelites in my kingdom, including priests and Levites, who wish to go to Jerusalem with you, may go. ¹⁴You are sent by the king and his seven advisers to inquire about Judah and Jerusalem with regard to the Law of your God, which is in your hand. ¹⁵Moreover, you are to take with you

---

ᵃ *12* The text of Ezra 7:12-26 is in Aramaic.

the silver and gold that the king and his advisers have freely given to the God of Israel, whose dwelling is in Jerusalem, [16]together with all the silver and gold you may obtain from the province of Babylon, as well as the freewill offerings of the people and priests for the temple of their God in Jerusalem. [17]With this money be sure to buy bulls, rams and male lambs, together with their grain offerings and drink offerings, and sacrifice them on the altar of the temple of your God in Jerusalem.

[18]You and your brother Jews may then do whatever seems best with the rest of the silver and gold, in accordance with the will of your God. [19]Deliver to the God of Jerusalem all the articles entrusted to you for worship in the temple of your God. [20]And anything else needed for the temple of your God that you may have occasion to supply, you may provide from the royal treasury.

[21]Now I, King Artaxerxes, order all the treasurers of Trans-Euphrates to provide with diligence whatever Ezra the priest, a teacher of the Law of the God of heaven, may ask of you— [22]up to a hundred talents[a] of silver, a hundred cors[b] of wheat, a hundred baths[c] of wine, a hundred baths[c] of olive oil, and salt without limit. [23]Whatever the God of heaven has prescribed, let it be done with diligence for the temple of the God of heaven. Why should there be wrath against the realm of the king and of his sons? [24]You are also to know that you have no authority to impose taxes, tribute or duty on any of the priests, Levites, singers, gatekeepers, temple servants or other workers at this house of God.

[25]And you, Ezra, in accordance with the wisdom of your God, which you possess, appoint magistrates and judges to administer justice to all the people of Trans-Euphrates—all who know the laws of your God. And you are to teach any who do not know them. [26]Whoever does not obey the law of your God and the law of the king must surely be punished by death, banishment, confiscation of property, or imprisonment.

[27]Praise be to the LORD, the God of our fathers, who has put it into the king's heart to bring honor to the house of the LORD in Jerusalem in this way [28]and who has extended his good favor to me before the king and his advisers and all the king's powerful officials. Because the hand of the LORD my God was on me, I took courage and gathered leading men from Israel to go up with me.

List of the Family Heads Returning With Ezra

8 These are the family heads and those registered with them who came up with me from Babylon during the reign of King Artaxerxes:

[2]of the descendants of Phinehas, Gershom;

of the descendants of Ithamar, Daniel;

of the descendants of David, Hattush [3]of the descendants of Shecaniah;

of the descendants of Parosh, Zechariah, and with him were registered 150 men;

[4]of the descendants of Pahath-Moab, Eliehoenai son of Zerahiah, and with him 200 men;

[5]of the descendants of Zattu,[d] Shecaniah son of Jahaziel, and with him 300 men;

[6]of the descendants of Adin, Ebed son of Jonathan, and with him 50 men;

---

[a] 22 That is, about 3 3/4 tons (about 3.4 metric tons) [b] 22 That is, probably about 600 bushels (about 22 kiloliters) [c] 22 That is, probably about 600 gallons (about 2.2 kiloliters) [d] 5 Some Septuagint manuscripts (also 1 Esdras 8:32); Hebrew does not have Zattu.

7 of the descendants of Elam, Jeshaiah son of Athaliah, and with him 70 men;

8 of the descendants of Shephatiah, Zebadiah son of Michael, and with him 80 men;

9 of the descendants of Joab, Obadiah son of Jehiel, and with him 218 men;

10 of the descendants of Bani,ª Shelomith son of Josiphiah, and with him 160 men;

11 of the descendants of Bebai, Zechariah son of Bebai, and with him 28 men;

12 of the descendants of Azgad, Johanan son of Hakkatan, and with him 110 men;

13 of the descendants of Adonikam, the last ones, whose names were

ª *10* Some Septuagint manuscripts (also 1 Esdras 8:36); Hebrew does not have *Bani*.

GOING *deeper*

The Power of Fasting With Prayer

READ AND CONSIDER: EZRA 8:21-32

"So we fasted and petitioned our God about this, and he answered our prayer" (Ezra 8:23).

Ezra the priest, and those traveling with him, needed protection for what would be a long and difficult journey. They could have asked the king for horses and soldiers, but they didn't. They could have hired guards, but they didn't. In fact, Ezra says he was ashamed to do that. After all, they had told the king how powerful their God was. Surely He could protect them on their way.

So they fasted and prayed.

Prayer is always a strong weapon against the enemy. Fasting makes it even more so. When the Lord puts on your heart that a particular request needs to be accompanied by fasting, you would be wise to listen. Fasting takes prayer to a whole new level, keeping evil at bay and breaking down strongholds. Fasting is a way of saying, "I deny myself what I want most and put God first in my life." The enemy hates that because he knows it's a sure way of resisting and defeating him. Fasting cripples the power of evil spiritual forces in the realm of darkness so they cannot sustain their grip on your life, your mind, and your circumstances.

Fasting and prayer bring your body into submission by informing it that it is not in charge. Fasting says, "I'm a spiritual being before I'm a physical being. I'm physical, so I need to eat, but I'm spiritual too. I'm going to assert the supremacy of my spiritual allegiance beyond and before my allegiance to my body and its desire for food."

Ezra was facing a difficult but very important trip, so he fasted and prayed. Whenever you are facing a difficult circumstance or decision, you can be sure that when you fast and pray about it, much is being accomplished in the spiritual realm. In fact, far more is accomplished in the realm of the spirit during a fast than is ever manifested immediately in the physical realm.

The kind of fast God wants is that of an obedient heart willing to say, "Yes, God, I'll go without food for a period if that means a child may be healed, a friend in bondage may be set free, a lost family member may be found, someone in darkness may be moved into light, or that I might live in greater wisdom, peace, and power. Yes, God, a fast is a small price to pay for all that."

Be open to hear what the Lord says to you about fasting, for He *is* saying something. If you are able to fast, He wants you to do so because you trust Him, love Him, and acknowledge His power.

Eliphelet, Jeuel and Shemaiah, and with them 60 men;

[14] of the descendants of Bigvai, Uthai and Zaccur, and with them 70 men.

The Return to Jerusalem

[15] I assembled them at the canal that flows toward Ahava, and we camped there three days. When I checked among the people and the priests, I found no Levites there. [16] So I summoned Eliezer, Ariel, Shemaiah, Elnathan, Jarib, Elnathan, Nathan, Zechariah and Meshullam, who were leaders, and Joiarib and Elnathan, who were men of learning, [17] and I sent them to Iddo, the leader in Casiphia. I told them what to say to Iddo and his kinsmen, the temple servants in Casiphia, so that they might bring attendants to us for the house of our God. [18] Because the gracious hand of our God was on us, they brought us Sherebiah, a capable man, from the descendants of Mahli son of Levi, the son of Israel, and Sherebiah's sons and brothers, 18 men; [19] and Hashabiah, together with Jeshaiah from the descendants of Merari, and his brothers and nephews, 20 men. [20] They also brought 220 of the temple servants—a body that David and the officials had established to assist the Levites. All were registered by name.

[21] There, by the Ahava Canal, I proclaimed a fast, so that we might humble ourselves before our God and ask him for a safe journey for us and our children, with all our possessions. [22] I was ashamed to ask the king for soldiers and horsemen to protect us from enemies on the road, because we had told the king, "The gracious hand of our God is on everyone who looks to him, but his great anger is against all who forsake him." [23] So we fasted and petitioned our God about this, and he answered our prayer.

[24] Then I set apart twelve of the leading priests, together with Sherebiah, Hashabiah and ten of their brothers, [25] and I weighed out to them the offering of silver and gold and the articles that the king, his advisers, his officials and all Israel present there had donated for the house of our God. [26] I weighed out to them 650 talents[a] of silver, silver articles weighing 100 talents,[b] 100 talents[b] of gold, [27] 20 bowls of gold valued at 1,000 darics,[c] and two fine articles of polished bronze, as precious as gold.

[28] I said to them, "You as well as these articles are consecrated to the LORD. The silver and gold are a freewill offering to the LORD, the God of your fathers. [29] Guard them carefully until you weigh them out in the chambers of the house of the LORD in Jerusalem before the leading priests and the Levites and the family heads of Israel." [30] Then the priests and Levites received the silver and gold and sacred articles that had been weighed out to be taken to the house of our God in Jerusalem.

Praying Ezra 8:31

Thank You, Lord, that Your hand is upon me and You will deliver me from the hand of the enemy.

[31] On the twelfth day of the first month we set out from the Ahava Canal to go to Jerusalem. The hand of our God was on us, and he protected us from enemies and bandits along the way. [32] So we arrived in Jerusalem, where we rested three days.

[33] On the fourth day, in the house of our God, we weighed out the silver and gold and the sacred articles into the hands of Meremoth son of Uriah, the priest. Eleazar son of Phinehas was with him, and so were the Levites Jozabad son of Jeshua and Noadiah son of Binnui. [34] Everything was accounted for by number and weight, and the entire weight was recorded at that time.

[35] Then the exiles who had returned

---

[a] *26* That is, about 25 tons (about 22 metric tons)   [b] *26* That is, about 3 3/4 tons (about 3.4 metric tons)   [c] *27* That is, about 19 pounds (about 8.5 kilograms)

from captivity sacrificed burnt offerings to the God of Israel: twelve bulls for all Israel, ninety-six rams, seventy-seven male lambs and, as a sin offering, twelve male goats. All this was a burnt offering to the LORD. 36 They also delivered the king's orders to the royal satraps and to the governors of Trans-Euphrates, who then gave assistance to the people and to the house of God.

Ezra's Prayer About Intermarriage

9 After these things had been done, the leaders came to me and said, "The people of Israel, including the priests and the Levites, have not kept themselves separate from the neighboring peoples with their detestable practices, like those of the Canaanites, Hittites, Perizzites, Jebusites, Ammonites, Moabites, Egyptians and Amorites. 2 They have taken some of their daughters as wives for themselves and their sons, and have mingled the holy race with the peoples around them. And the leaders and officials have led the way in this unfaithfulness."

3 When I heard this, I tore my tunic and cloak, pulled hair from my head and beard and sat down appalled. 4 Then everyone who trembled at the words of the God of Israel gathered around me because of this unfaithfulness of the exiles. And I sat there appalled until the evening sacrifice.

5 Then, at the evening sacrifice, I rose from my self-abasement, with my tunic and cloak torn, and fell on my knees with my hands spread out to the LORD my God 6 and prayed:

"O my God, I am too ashamed and disgraced to lift up my face to you, my God, because our sins are higher than our heads and our guilt has reached to the heavens. 7 From the days of our forefathers until now, our guilt has been great. Because of our sins, we and our kings and our priests have been subjected to the sword and captivity, to pillage and humiliation at the hand of foreign kings, as it is today.

8 "But now, for a brief moment, the LORD our God has been gracious in leaving us a remnant and giving us a firm place in his sanctuary, and so our God gives light to our eyes and a little relief in our bondage. 9 Though we are slaves, our God has not deserted us in our bondage. He has shown us kindness in the sight of the kings of Persia: He has granted us new life to rebuild the house of our God and repair its ruins, and he

---

God's people at prayer
EZRA CONFESSES THE SINS OF HIS PEOPLE

EZRA 9:5-15 Ezra lived at a time when Judah was rebuilding itself as a nation. His prayer was the prayer of a man who had awakened in the uncomfortable situation his people had been making for generations. The consequences of their years of disregarding God's laws had piled up on them until it seemed there was no way home again to the presence of the Lord.

But there was.

Ezra's prayer hearkened back to God's original mandate that His people not intermarry in order to keep their worship pure. Yet, here they were generations later, with hardly an ethnic identity. Can you imagine trying to untangle that web? Marriages would have to be dissolved. Families separated. People disenfranchised. What a mess.

Yet, a mess is what it sometimes takes for us to return to God's presence. When we find ourselves in a situation that is beyond our ability to rectify and we know it is a situation of our own making, we must humble ourselves before God and confess it. And He will restore us.

has given us a wall of protection in Judah and Jerusalem.

10"But now, O our God, what can we say after this? For we have disregarded the commands 11you gave through your servants the prophets when you said:'The land you are entering to possess is a land polluted by the corruption of its peoples. By their detestable practices they have filled it with their impurity from one end to the other. 12Therefore, do not give your daughters in marriage to their sons or take their daughters for your sons. Do not seek a treaty of friendship with them at any time, that you may be strong and eat the good things of the land and leave it to your children as an everlasting inheritance.'

13"What has happened to us is a result of our evil deeds and our great guilt, and yet, our God, you have punished us less than our sins have deserved and have given us a remnant like this. 14Shall we again break your commands and intermarry with the peoples who commit such detestable practices? Would you not be angry enough with us to destroy us, leaving us no remnant or survivor? 15O LORD, God of Israel, you are righteous! We are left this day as a remnant. Here we are before you in our guilt, though because of it not one of us can stand in your presence."

The People's Confession of Sin

10 While Ezra was praying and confessing, weeping and throwing himself down before the house of God, a large crowd of Israelites—men, women and children—gathered around him. They too wept bitterly. 2Then Shecaniah son of Jehiel, one of the descendants of Elam, said to Ezra, "We have been unfaithful to our God by marrying foreign women from the peoples around us. But in spite of this, there is still hope for Israel. 3Now let us make a covenant before our God to send away all these women and their children, in accordance with the counsel of my lord and of those who fear the commands of our God. Let it be done according to the Law. 4Rise up; this matter is in your hands. We will support you, so take courage and do it."

5So Ezra rose up and put the leading priests and Levites and all Israel under oath to do what had been suggested. And they took the oath. 6Then Ezra withdrew from before the house of God and went to the room of Jehohanan son of Eliashib. While he was there, he ate no food and drank no water, because he continued to mourn over the unfaithfulness of the exiles.

7A proclamation was then issued throughout Judah and Jerusalem for all the exiles to assemble in Jerusalem. 8Anyone who failed to appear within three days would forfeit all his property, in accordance with the decision of the officials and elders, and would himself be expelled from the assembly of the exiles.

9Within the three days, all the men of Judah and Benjamin had gathered in Jerusalem. And on the twentieth day of the ninth month, all the people were sitting in the square before the house of God, greatly distressed by the occasion and because of the rain. 10Then Ezra the priest stood up and said to them, "You have been unfaithful; you have married foreign women, adding to Israel's guilt. 11Now make confession to the LORD, the God of your fathers, and do his will. Separate yourselves from the peoples around you and from your foreign wives."

12The whole assembly responded with a loud voice: "You are right! We must do as you say. 13But there are many people here and it is the rainy season; so we cannot stand outside. Besides, this matter cannot be taken care of in a day or two, because we have sinned greatly in this thing. 14Let our officials act for the whole assembly. Then let everyone in our towns who has married a foreign woman come at a set time, along with the elders and judges of each town, until the fierce anger of our God in this matter is turned away from us." ¹⁵Only Jonathan son of Asahel and Jahzeiah son of Tikvah, supported by Meshullam and Shabbethai the Levite, opposed this.

¹⁶So the exiles did as was proposed. Ezra the priest selected men who were family heads, one from each family division, and all of them designated by name. On the first day of the tenth month they sat down to investigate the cases, ¹⁷and by the first day of the first month they finished dealing with all the men who had married foreign women.

Those Guilty of Intermarriage

¹⁸Among the descendants of the priests, the following had married foreign women:

From the descendants of Jeshua son of Jozadak, and his brothers: Maaseiah, Eliezer, Jarib and Gedaliah. ¹⁹(They all gave their hands in pledge to put away their wives, and for their guilt they each presented a ram from the flock as a guilt offering.)

²⁰From the descendants of Immer:
Hanani and Zebadiah.

²¹From the descendants of Harim:
Maaseiah, Elijah, Shemaiah, Jehiel and Uzziah.

²²From the descendants of Pashhur:
Elioenai, Maaseiah, Ishmael, Nethanel, Jozabad and Elasah.

²³Among the Levites:

Jozabad, Shimei, Kelaiah (that is, Kelita), Pethahiah, Judah and Eliezer.

²⁴From the singers:
Eliashib.
From the gatekeepers:
Shallum, Telem and Uri.

²⁵And among the other Israelites:

From the descendants of Parosh:
Ramiah, Izziah, Malkijah, Mijamin, Eleazar, Malkijah and Benaiah.

²⁶From the descendants of Elam:
Mattaniah, Zechariah, Jehiel, Abdi, Jeremoth and Elijah.

²⁷From the descendants of Zattu:
Elioenai, Eliashib, Mattaniah, Jeremoth, Zabad and Aziza.

²⁸From the descendants of Bebai:
Jehohanan, Hananiah, Zabbai and Athlai.

²⁹From the descendants of Bani:
Meshullam, Malluch, Adaiah, Jashub, Sheal and Jeremoth.

³⁰From the descendants of Pahath-Moab:
Adna, Kelal, Benaiah, Maaseiah, Mattaniah, Bezalel, Binnui and Manasseh.

³¹From the descendants of Harim:
Eliezer, Ishijah, Malkijah, Shemaiah, Shimeon, ³²Benjamin, Malluch and Shemariah.

³³From the descendants of Hashum:
Mattenai, Mattattah, Zabad, Eliphelet, Jeremai, Manasseh and Shimei.

³⁴From the descendants of Bani:
Maadai, Amram, Uel, ³⁵Benaiah, Bedeiah, Keluhi, ³⁶Vaniah, Meremoth, Eliashib, ³⁷Mattaniah, Mattenai and Jaasu.

³⁸From the descendants of Binnui:ᵃ
Shimei, ³⁹Shelemiah, Nathan, Adaiah, ⁴⁰Macnadebai, Shashai, Sharai, ⁴¹Azarel, Shelemiah, Shemariah, ⁴²Shallum, Amariah and Joseph.

⁴³From the descendants of Nebo:
Jeiel, Mattithiah, Zabad, Zebina, Jaddai, Joel and Benaiah.

⁴⁴All these had married foreign women, and some of them had children by these wives.ᵇ

ᵃ 37,38 See Septuagint (also 1 Esdras 9:34); Hebrew *Jaasu* ³⁸*and Bani and Binnui,*   ᵇ 44 Or *and they sent them away with their children*

Author: Probably the same unknown author of 1 and 2 Chronicles, so possibly Ezra

Date: 430 BC

Audience: Future generations of Hebrews—to remind them of God's past faithfulness and to encourage future trust and obedience

What are you trying to build or rebuild? A godly character? A career? A marriage? A home? A ministry? Whatever it is, remember this much-needed reminder from Nehemiah: *Great, enduring "building projects" are always (and only!) accomplished with much prayer.*

Read this amazing account of the rebuilding of the walls of Jerusalem. This massive undertaking was accomplished in less than two months despite fierce opposition and an unskilled labor force! How? Nehemiah and his colleagues not only *worked* tirelessly, but they *prayed* fervently and constantly!

Prayer Themes:

• *Ask God to impress upon you the need for a life of integrity . . . so that, like Nehemiah, you'll have a platform upon which to build great things for Him (2:2-8).*

• *Ask God for the wisdom and courage to ignore the destructive critics in your life (6:1-9).*

• *Ask God to enable you to be someone who always hears and obeys His Word with deep reverence and joy (8:9-18).*

Nehemiah

Nehemiah's Prayer

1 The words of Nehemiah son of Hacaliah:

In the month of Kislev in the twentieth year, while I was in the citadel of Susa, ²Hanani, one of my brothers, came from Judah with some other men, and I questioned them about the Jewish remnant that survived the exile, and also about Jerusalem.

³They said to me, "Those who survived the exile and are back in the province are in great trouble and disgrace. The wall of Jerusalem is broken down, and its gates have been burned with fire."

⁴When I heard these things, I sat down and wept. For some days I mourned and fasted and prayed before the God of heaven. ⁵Then I said:

"O LORD, God of heaven, the great and awesome God, who keeps his covenant of love with those who love him and obey his commands, ⁶let your ear be attentive and your eyes open to hear the prayer your servant is praying before you day and night for your servants, the people of Israel. I confess the sins we Israelites, including myself and my father's house, have committed against you. ⁷We have acted very wickedly toward you. We have not obeyed the commands, decrees and laws you gave your servant Moses.

⁸"Remember the instruction you gave your servant Moses, saying, 'If you are unfaithful, I will scatter you among the nations, ⁹but if you return to me and obey my commands, then even if your exiled people are at the farthest horizon, I will gather them from there and bring them to the place I have chosen as a dwelling for my Name.'

[10] "They are your servants and your people, whom you redeemed by your great strength and your mighty hand. [11] O Lord, let your ear be attentive to the prayer of this your servant and to the prayer of your servants who delight in revering your name. Give your servant success today by granting him favor in the presence of this man."

I was cupbearer to the king.

[5] and I answered the king, "If it pleases the king and if your servant has found favor in his sight, let him send me to the city in Judah where my fathers are buried so that I can rebuild it."

[6] Then the king, with the queen sitting beside him, asked me, "How long will your journey take, and when will you get back?" It pleased the king to send me; so I set a time.

[7] I also said to him, "If it pleases the king, may I have letters to the governors

God's people at prayer
NEHEMIAH'S INTIMATE DEPENDENCE ON GOD

NEHEMIAH 1:5-11 In the middle of a busy life and stressful events, Nehemiah lets us feel the pulse of his prayer habit. On nine occasions Nehemiah recorded his words to God. He prayed often, and he prayed short prayers. Four times Nehemiah simply said little more than, "Remember me for this, O my God" (5:19, 13:14,22,31).

Though he was clearly a decisive leader, Nehemiah practiced intimate dependence on God. Feeling the intense spotlight of King Artaxerxes's question, Nehemiah made the earthly king wait while he spoke to the King of the universe. Nehemiah's confessions were transparent; his requests were urgent and direct. He spoke without fear that God would misunderstand him. Nehemiah's example shows us we can talk to God about anything.

What conversations and interactions with God would you like to have today? Open up your heart and your voice and tell Him everything that's on your mind right now.

Artaxerxes Sends Nehemiah to Jerusalem

2 In the month of Nisan in the twentieth year of King Artaxerxes, when wine was brought for him, I took the wine and gave it to the king. I had not been sad in his presence before; [2] so the king asked me, "Why does your face look so sad when you are not ill? This can be nothing but sadness of heart."

I was very much afraid, [3] but I said to the king, "May the king live forever! Why should my face not look sad when the city where my fathers are buried lies in ruins, and its gates have been destroyed by fire?"

[4] The king said to me, "What is it you want?"

Then I prayed to the God of heaven, of Trans-Euphrates, so that they will provide me safe-conduct until I arrive in Judah? [8] And may I have a letter to Asaph, keeper of the king's forest, so he will give me timber to make beams for the gates of the citadel by the temple and for the city wall and for the residence I will occupy?" And because the gracious hand of my God was upon me, the king granted my requests. [9] So I went to the governors of Trans-Euphrates and gave them the king's letters. The king had also sent army officers and cavalry with me.

[10] When Sanballat the Horonite and Tobiah the Ammonite official heard about this, they were very much disturbed that someone had come to promote the welfare of the Israelites.

Nehemiah Inspects Jerusalem's Walls

¹¹I went to Jerusalem, and after staying there three days ¹²I set out during the night with a few men. I had not told anyone what my God had put in my heart to do for Jerusalem. There were no mounts with me except the one I was riding on.

¹³By night I went out through the Valley Gate toward the Jackalᵃ Well and the Dung Gate, examining the walls of Jerusalem, which had been broken down, and its gates, which had been destroyed by fire. ¹⁴Then I moved on toward the Fountain Gate and the King's Pool, but there was not enough room for my mount to get through; ¹⁵so I went up the valley by night, examining the wall. Finally, I turned back and reentered through the Valley Gate. ¹⁶The officials did not know where I had gone or what I was doing, because as yet I had said nothing to the Jews or the priests or nobles or officials or any others who would be doing the work.

¹⁷Then I said to them, "You see the trouble we are in: Jerusalem lies in ruins, and its gates have been burned with fire. Come, let us rebuild the wall of Jerusalem, and we will no longer be in disgrace." ¹⁸I also told them about the gracious hand of my God upon me and what the king had said to me.

They replied, "Let us start rebuilding." So they began this good work.

¹⁹But when Sanballat the Horonite, Tobiah the Ammonite official and Geshem the Arab heard about it, they mocked and ridiculed us. "What is this you are doing?" they asked. "Are you rebelling against the king?"

²⁰I answered them by saying, "The God of heaven will give us success. We his servants will start rebuilding, but as for you, you have no share in Jerusalem or any claim or historic right to it."

Builders of the Wall

3 Eliashib the high priest and his fellow priests went to work and rebuilt the Sheep Gate. They dedicated it and set its doors in place, building as far as the Tower of the Hundred, which they dedicated, and as far as the Tower of Hananel. ²The men of Jericho built the adjoining section, and Zaccur son of Imri built next to them.

³The Fish Gate was rebuilt by the sons of Hassenaah. They laid its beams and put its doors and bolts and bars in place. ⁴Meremoth son of Uriah, the son of Hakkoz, repaired the next section. Next to him Meshullam son of Berekiah, the son of Meshezabel, made repairs, and next to him Zadok son of Baana also made repairs. ⁵The next section was repaired by the men of Tekoa, but their nobles would not put their shoulders to the work under their supervisors.ᵇ

⁶The Jeshanahᶜ Gate was repaired by Joiada son of Paseah and Meshullam son of Besodeiah. They laid its beams and put its doors and bolts and bars in place. ⁷Next to them, repairs were made by men from Gibeon and Mizpah—Melatiah of Gibeon and Jadon of Meronoth—places under the authority of the governor of Trans-Euphrates. ⁸Uzziel son of Harhaiah, one of the goldsmiths, repaired the next section; and Hananiah, one of the perfume-makers, made repairs next to that. They restoredᵈ Jerusalem as far as the Broad Wall. ⁹Rephaiah son of Hur, ruler of a half-district of Jerusalem, repaired the next section. ¹⁰Adjoining this, Jedaiah son of Harumaph made repairs opposite his house, and Hattush son of Hashabneiah made repairs next to him. ¹¹Malkijah son of Harim and Hasshub son of Pahath-Moab repaired another section and the Tower of the Ovens. ¹²Shallum son of Hallohesh, ruler of a half-district of Jerusalem, repaired the next section with the help of his daughters.

¹³The Valley Gate was repaired by Hanun and the residents of Zanoah. They rebuilt it and put its doors and bolts and bars in place. They also repaired five

---

ᵃ 13 Or Serpent or Fig   ᵇ 5 Or their Lord or the governor   ᶜ 6 Or Old   ᵈ 8 Or They left out part of hundred yards[a] of the wall as far as the Dung Gate.

[14]The Dung Gate was repaired by Malkijah son of Recab, ruler of the district of Beth Hakkerem. He rebuilt it and put its doors and bolts and bars in place.

[15]The Fountain Gate was repaired by Shallun son of Col-Hozeh, ruler of the district of Mizpah. He rebuilt it, roofing it over and putting its doors and bolts and bars in place. He also repaired the wall of the Pool of Siloam,[b] by the King's Garden, as far as the steps going down from the City of David. [16]Beyond him, Nehemiah son of Azbuk, ruler of a half-district of Beth Zur, made repairs up to a point opposite the tombs[c] of David, as far as the artificial pool and the House of the Heroes.

[17]Next to him, the repairs were made by the Levites under Rehum son of Bani. Beside him, Hashabiah, ruler of half the district of Keilah, carried out repairs for his district. [18]Next to him, the repairs were made by their countrymen under Binnui[d] son of Henadad, ruler of the other half-district of Keilah. [19]Next to him, Ezer son of Jeshua, ruler of Mizpah, repaired another section, from a point facing the ascent to the armory as far as the angle. [20]Next to him, Baruch son of Zabbai zealously repaired another section, from the angle to the entrance of the house of Eliashib the high priest. [21]Next to him, Meremoth son of Uriah, the son of Hakkoz, repaired another section, from the entrance of Eliashib's house to the end of it.

[22]The repairs next to him were made by the priests from the surrounding region. [23]Beyond them, Benjamin and Hasshub made repairs in front of their house; and next to them, Azariah son of Maaseiah, the son of Ananiah, made repairs beside his house. [24]Next to him, Binnui son of Henadad repaired another section, from Azariah's house to the angle and the corner, [25]and Palal son of Uzai worked opposite the angle and the tower projecting from the upper palace near the court of the guard. Next to him, Pedaiah son of Parosh [26]and the temple servants living on the hill of Ophel made repairs up to a point opposite the Water Gate toward the east and the projecting tower. [27]Next to them, the men of Tekoa repaired another section, from the great projecting tower to the wall of Ophel.

[28]Above the Horse Gate, the priests made repairs, each in front of his own house. [29]Next to them, Zadok son of Immer made repairs opposite his house. Next to him, Shemaiah son of Shecaniah, the guard at the East Gate, made repairs. [30]Next to him, Hananiah son of Shelemiah, and Hanun, the sixth son of Zalaph, repaired another section. Next to them, Meshullam son of Berekiah made repairs opposite his living quarters. [31]Next to him, Malkijah, one of the goldsmiths, made repairs as far as the house of the temple servants and the merchants, opposite the Inspection Gate, and as far as the room above the corner; [32]and between the room above the corner and the Sheep Gate the goldsmiths and merchants made repairs.

Opposition to the Rebuilding

4 When Sanballat heard that we were rebuilding the wall, he became angry and was greatly incensed. He ridiculed the Jews, [2]and in the presence of his associates and the army of Samaria, he said, "What are those feeble Jews doing? Will they restore their wall? Will they offer sacrifices? Will they finish in a day? Can they bring the stones back to life from those heaps of rubble—burned as they are?"

[3]Tobiah the Ammonite, who was at his side, said, "What they are building—if even a fox climbed up on it, he would break down their wall of stones!"

---

[a] 13 Hebrew a thousand cubits (about 450 meters)   [b] 15 Hebrew Shelah, a variant of Shiloah, that is, Siloam   [c] 16 Hebrew; Septuagint, some Vulgate manuscripts and Syriac tomb   [d] 18 Two Hebrew manuscripts and Syriac (see also Septuagint and verse 24); most Hebrew manuscripts Bavvai

Be Watchful in Prayer

GOING deeper

READ AND CONSIDER: NEHEMIAH 4:1-9

"But we prayed to our God and posted a guard day and night to meet this threat" (Nehemiah 4:9).

Working for good in this world will always meet opposition. The enemies of Jerusalem wanted the city to remain in ruins. They were angry when Nehemiah organized the people to rebuild the walls. First they ridiculed, then they threatened, then they planned to attack. The pressure to stop the work grew. Nehemiah prayed against the ridicule and the threats. He trusted God, and he "posted a guard day and night."

There are examples in Scripture when God instructed people to pray and stand back to see Him work (for example, in 2 Kings 19:35, where God wiped out an army laying siege to Jerusalem). But these occasions are rare. Prayer and faith are vital, but so is doing our part.

So how do we know when we should just pray, or when we should pray *and* do something else? The answer is to keep praying, and God will show you. Nehemiah was a man of constant prayer. His ongoing conversations with God gave him insight into what he was to do. At times, God said, "I'll take care of it." At times, God said, "I'll take care of it, but have the people post a guard. They'll all feel better about that." In any case, you can know what to do when you become sensitive to God's guidance as Nehemiah was. Nehemiah and the people never had to fight, but they had to be ready to do so. Their prayers renewed their trust in God; their actions showed that they were willing to have God work things out any way He decided. Whether they had to fight or not, they were not going to stop building the wall, for they were under God's orders. That was a greater motivator for Nehemiah and his people than anything the enemies could throw at them.

We have to be watchful in prayer and always available to do what God has instructed us to do. As we stay in close communication with Him, He will show us what action to take.

⁴Hear us, O our God, for we are despised. Turn their insults back on their own heads. Give them over as plunder in a land of captivity. ⁵Do not cover up their guilt or blot out their sins from your sight, for they have thrown insults in the face of ᵃ the builders.

⁶So we rebuilt the wall till all of it reached half its height, for the people worked with all their heart.

⁷But when Sanballat, Tobiah, the Arabs, the Ammonites and the men of Ashdod heard that the repairs to Jerusalem's walls had gone ahead and that the gaps were being closed, they were very angry. ⁸They all plotted together to come and fight against Jerusalem and stir up trouble against it. ⁹But we prayed to our God and posted a guard day and night to meet this threat.

¹⁰Meanwhile, the people in Judah said, "The strength of the laborers is giving out, and there is so much rubble that we cannot rebuild the wall."

Praying Nehemiah 4:7-11

Lord, help me to be watchful in prayer so the enemy cannot come in and undermine the work You have given me to do.

¹¹Also our enemies said, "Before they know it or see us, we will be right there

ᵃ 5 Or *have provoked you to anger before*

among them and will kill them and put an end to the work."

¹²Then the Jews who lived near them came and told us ten times over, "Wherever you turn, they will attack us."

¹³Therefore I stationed some of the people behind the lowest points of the wall at the exposed places, posting them by families, with their swords, spears and bows. ¹⁴After I looked things over, I stood up and said to the nobles, the officials and the rest of the people, "Don't be afraid of them. Remember the Lord, who is great and awesome, and fight for your brothers, your sons and your daughters, your wives and your homes."

¹⁵When our enemies heard that we were aware of their plot and that God had frustrated it, we all returned to the wall, each to his own work.

¹⁶From that day on, half of my men did the work, while the other half were equipped with spears, shields, bows and armor. The officers posted themselves behind all the people of Judah ¹⁷who were building the wall. Those who carried materials did their work with one hand and held a weapon in the other, ¹⁸and each of the builders wore his sword at his side as he worked. But the man who sounded the trumpet stayed with me.

¹⁹Then I said to the nobles, the officials and the rest of the people, "The work is extensive and spread out, and we are widely separated from each other along the wall. ²⁰Wherever you hear the sound of the trumpet, join us there. Our God will fight for us!"

²¹So we continued the work with half the men holding spears, from the first light of dawn till the stars came out. ²²At that time I also said to the people, "Have every man and his helper stay inside Jerusalem at night, so they can serve us as guards by night and workmen by day." ²³Neither I nor my brothers nor my men nor the guards with me took off our clothes; each had his weapon, even when he went for water.[a]

Nehemiah Helps the Poor

5 Now the men and their wives raised a great outcry against their Jewish brothers. ²Some were saying, "We and our sons and daughters are numerous; in order for us to eat and stay alive, we must get grain."

³Others were saying, "We are mortgaging our fields, our vineyards and our homes to get grain during the famine."

⁴Still others were saying, "We have had to borrow money to pay the king's tax on our fields and vineyards. ⁵Although we are of the same flesh and blood as our countrymen and though our sons are as good as theirs, yet we have to subject our sons and daughters to slavery. Some of our daughters have already been enslaved, but we are powerless, because our fields and our vineyards belong to others."

⁶When I heard their outcry and these charges, I was very angry. ⁷I pondered them in my mind and then accused the nobles and officials. I told them, "You are exacting usury from your own countrymen!" So I called together a large meeting to deal with them ⁸and said: "As far as possible, we have bought back our Jewish brothers who were sold to the Gentiles. Now you are selling your brothers, only for them to be sold back to us!" They kept quiet, because they could find nothing to say.

⁹So I continued, "What you are doing is not right. Shouldn't you walk in the fear of our God to avoid the reproach of our Gentile enemies? ¹⁰I and my brothers and my men are also lending the people money and grain. But let the exacting of usury stop! ¹¹Give back to them immediately their fields, vineyards, olive groves and houses, and also the usury you are charging them—the hundredth part of the money, grain, new wine and oil."

¹²"We will give it back," they said. "And

we will not demand anything more from them. We will do as you say."

Then I summoned the priests and made the nobles and officials take an oath to do what they had promised. [13]I also shook out the folds of my robe and said, "In this way may God shake out of his house and possessions every man who does not keep this promise. So may such a man be shaken out and emptied!"

At this the whole assembly said, "Amen," and praised the LORD. And the people did as they had promised.

[14]Moreover, from the twentieth year of King Artaxerxes, when I was appointed to be their governor in the land of Judah, until his thirty-second year—twelve years—neither I nor my brothers ate the food allotted to the governor. [15]But the earlier governors—those preceding me—placed a heavy burden on the people and took forty shekels[a] of silver from them in addition to food and wine. Their assistants also lorded it over the people. But out of reverence for God I did not act like that. [16]Instead, I devoted myself to the work on this wall. All my men were assembled there for the work; we[b] did not acquire any land.

[17]Furthermore, a hundred and fifty Jews and officials ate at my table, as well as those who came to us from the surrounding nations. [18]Each day one ox, six choice sheep and some poultry were prepared for me, and every ten days an abundant supply of wine of all kinds. In spite of all this, I never demanded the food allotted to the governor, because the demands were heavy on these people.

[19]Remember me with favor, O my God, for all I have done for these people.

Further Opposition to the Rebuilding

6 When word came to Sanballat, Tobiah, Geshem the Arab and the rest of our enemies that I had rebuilt the wall and not a gap was left in it—though up to that time I had not set the doors in the gates— [2]Sanballat and Geshem sent me this message: "Come, let us meet together in one of the villages[c] on the plain of Ono."

But they were scheming to harm me; [3]so I sent messengers to them with this reply: "I am carrying on a great project and cannot go down. Why should the work stop while I leave it and go down to you?" [4]Four times they sent me the same message, and each time I gave them the same answer.

[5]Then, the fifth time, Sanballat sent his aide to me with the same message, and in his hand was an unsealed letter [6]in which was written:

"It is reported among the nations—and Geshem[d] says it is true—that you and the Jews are plotting to revolt, and therefore you are building the wall. Moreover, according to these reports you are about to become their king [7]and have even appointed prophets to make this proclamation about you in Jerusalem: 'There is a king in Judah!' Now this report will get back to the king; so come, let us confer together."

[8]I sent him this reply: "Nothing like what you are saying is happening; you are just making it up out of your head."

Praying Nehemiah 6:9-11
Enable me to not succumb to fear, which I know is part of Satan's plan for my destruction.

---

[9]They were all trying to frighten us, thinking, "Their hands will get too weak for the work, and it will not be completed."

⌊But I prayed,⌋ "Now strengthen my hands."

[10]One day I went to the house of Shemaiah son of Delaiah, the son of Mehetabel, who was shut in at his home.

---

[a] 15 That is, about 1 pound (about 0.5 kilogram)   [b] 16 Most Hebrew manuscripts; some Hebrew manuscripts, Septuagint, Vulgate and Syriac /   [c] 2 Or in Kephirim   [d] 6 Hebrew Gashmu, a variant of Geshem

He said, "Let us meet in the house of God, inside the temple, and let us close the temple doors, because men are coming to kill you—by night they are coming to kill you."

11But I said, "Should a man like me run away? Or should one like me go into the temple to save his life? I will not go!" 12I realized that God had not sent him, but that he had prophesied against me because Tobiah and Sanballat had hired him. 13He had been hired to intimidate me so that I would commit a sin by doing this, and then they would give me a bad name to discredit me.

14Remember Tobiah and Sanballat, O my God, because of what they have done; remember also the prophetess Noadiah and the rest of the prophets who have been trying to intimidate me.

The Completion of the Wall

15So the wall was completed on the twenty-fifth of Elul, in fifty-two days. 16When all our enemies heard about this, all the surrounding nations were afraid and lost their self-confidence, because they realized that this work had been done with the help of our God.

17Also, in those days the nobles of Judah were sending many letters to Tobiah, and replies from Tobiah kept coming to them. 18For many in Judah were under oath to him, since he was son-in-law to Shecaniah son of Arah, and his son Jehohanan had married the daughter of Meshullam son of Berekiah. 19Moreover, they kept reporting to me his good deeds and then telling him what I said. And Tobiah sent letters to intimidate me.

7 After the wall had been rebuilt and I had set the doors in place, the gatekeepers and the singers and the Levites were appointed. 2I put in charge of Jerusalem my brother Hanani, along with[a] Hananiah the commander of the citadel, because he was a man of integrity and feared God more than most men do. 3I

said to them, "The gates of Jerusalem are not to be opened until the sun is hot. While the gatekeepers are still on duty, have them shut the doors and bar them. Also appoint residents of Jerusalem as guards, some at their posts and some near their own houses."

The List of the Exiles Who Returned

4Now the city was large and spacious, but there were few people in it, and the houses had not yet been rebuilt. 5So my God put it into my heart to assemble the nobles, the officials and the common people for registration by families. I found the genealogical record of those who had been the first to return. This is what I found written there:

6These are the people of the province who came up from the captivity of the exiles whom Nebuchadnezzar king of Babylon had taken captive (they returned to Jerusalem and Judah, each to his own town, 7in company with Zerubbabel, Jeshua, Nehemiah, Azariah, Raamiah, Nahamani, Mordecai, Bilshan, Mispereth, Bigvai, Nehum and Baanah):

The list of the men of Israel:

8the descendants of Parosh	2,172
9of Shephatiah	372
10of Arah	652
11of Pahath-Moab (through the line of Jeshua and Joab)	2,818
12of Elam	1,254
13of Zattu	845
14of Zaccai	760
15of Binnui	648
16of Bebai	628
17of Azgad	2,322
18of Adonikam	667
19of Bigvai	2,067
20of Adin	655
21of Ater (through Hezekiah)	98
22of Hashum	328
23of Bezai	324

---

a 2 Or Hanani, that is,

24 of Hariph	112
25 of Gibeon	95
26 the men of Bethlehem and Netophah	188
27 of Anathoth	128
28 of Beth Azmaveth	42
29 of Kiriath Jearim, Kephirah and Beeroth	743
30 of Ramah and Geba	621
31 of Micmash	122
32 of Bethel and Ai	123
33 of the other Nebo	52
34 of the other Elam	1,254
35 of Harim	320
36 of Jericho	345
37 of Lod, Hadid and Ono	721
38 of Senaah	3,930

39 The priests:

the descendants of Jedaiah (through the family of Jeshua)	973
40 of Immer	1,052
41 of Pashhur	1,247
42 of Harim	1,017

43 The Levites:

the descendants of Jeshua (through Kadmiel through the line of Hodaviah)	74

44 The singers:

the descendants of Asaph	148

45 The gatekeepers:

the descendants of Shallum, Ater, Talmon, Akkub, Hatita and Shobai	138

46 The temple servants:

the descendants of
Ziha, Hasupha, Tabbaoth,
47 Keros, Sia, Padon,
48 Lebana, Hagaba, Shalmai,
49 Hanan, Giddel, Gahar,
50 Reaiah, Rezin, Nekoda,
51 Gazzam, Uzza, Paseah,
52 Besai, Meunim, Nephusim,
53 Bakbuk, Hakupha, Harhur,
54 Bazluth, Mehida, Harsha,
55 Barkos, Sisera, Temah,
56 Neziah and Hatipha

57 The descendants of the servants of Solomon:

the descendants of
Sotai, Sophereth, Perida,
58 Jaala, Darkon, Giddel,
59 Shephatiah, Hattil,
Pokereth-Hazzebaim and Amon

60 The temple servants and the descendants of the servants of Solomon	392

61 The following came up from the towns of Tel Melah, Tel Harsha, Kerub, Addon and Immer, but they could not show that their families were descended from Israel:

62 the descendants of Delaiah, Tobiah and Nekoda	642

63 And from among the priests:

the descendants of
Hobaiah, Hakkoz and Barzillai
(a man who had married
a daughter of Barzillai the
Gileadite and was called by
that name).

64 These searched for their family records, but they could not find them and so were excluded from the priesthood as unclean. 65 The governor, therefore, ordered them not to eat any of the most sacred food until there should be a priest ministering with the Urim and Thummim.

66 The whole company numbered 42,360, 67 besides their 7,337 menservants and maidservants; and they also had 245 men and women singers. 68 There were 736 horses, 245 mules,[a] 69 435 camels and 6,720 donkeys.

70 Some of the heads of the families contributed to the work. The

---

a 68 Some Hebrew manuscripts (see also Ezra 2:66); most Hebrew manuscripts do not have this verse.

governor gave to the treasury 1,000 drachmas[a] of gold, 50 bowls and 530 garments for priests. [71]Some of the heads of the families gave to the treasury for the work 20,000 drachmas[b] of gold and 2,200 minas[c] of silver. [72]The total given by the rest of the people was 20,000 drachmas of gold, 2,000 minas[d] of silver and 67 garments for priests.

[73]The priests, the Levites, the gate-keepers, the singers and the temple servants, along with certain of the people and the rest of the Israelites, settled in their own towns.

Ezra Reads the Law

When the seventh month came and the Israelites had settled in their towns, 8 [1]all the people assembled as one man in the square before the Water Gate. They told Ezra the scribe to bring out the Book of the Law of Moses, which the LORD had commanded for Israel.

[2]So on the first day of the seventh month Ezra the priest brought the Law before the assembly, which was made up of men and women and all who were able to understand. [3]He read it aloud from day-break till noon as he faced the square be-fore the Water Gate in the presence of the men, women and others who could understand. And all the people listened attentively to the Book of the Law.

[4]Ezra the scribe stood on a high wooden platform built for the occasion. Beside him on his right stood Mattithiah, Shema, Anaiah, Uriah, Hilkiah and Ma-aseiah; and on his left were Pedaiah, Mishael, Malkijah, Hashum, Hashbadda-nah, Zechariah and Meshullam.

[5]Ezra opened the book. All the people could see him because he was standing above them; and as he opened it, the peo-ple all stood up. [6]Ezra praised the LORD, the great God; and all the people lifted their hands and responded, "Amen! Amen!"

Then they bowed down and worshiped the LORD with their faces to the ground.

[7]The Levites—Jeshua, Bani, Sherebiah, Jamin, Akkub, Shabbethai, Hodiah, Ma-aseiah, Kelita, Azariah, Jozabad, Hanan and Pelaiah—instructed the people in the Law while the people were standing there. [8]They read from the Book of the Law of God, making it clear[e] and giving the meaning so that the people could un-derstand what was being read.

[9]Then Nehemiah the governor, Ezra the priest and scribe, and the Levites who were instructing the people said to them all, "This day is sacred to the LORD your God. Do not mourn or weep." For all the people had been weeping as they listened to the words of the Law.

[10]Nehemiah said, "Go and enjoy choice food and sweet drinks, and send some to those who have nothing prepared. This day is sacred to our Lord. Do not grieve, for the joy of the LORD is your strength."

[11]The Levites calmed all the people, say-ing, "Be still, for this is a sacred day. Do not grieve."

[12]Then all the people went away to eat and drink, to send portions of food and to celebrate with great joy, because they now understood the words that had been made known to them.

[13]On the second day of the month, the heads of all the families, along with the priests and the Levites, gathered around Ezra the scribe to give attention to the words of the Law. [14]They found writ-ten in the Law, which the LORD had commanded through Moses, that the Israelites were to live in booths during the feast of the seventh month [15]and that they should proclaim this word and spread it throughout their towns and in Jerusalem: "Go out into the hill country and bring back branches from olive and wild olive trees, and from myrtles, palms and shade trees, to make booths"—as it is written.[f]

---

[a] 70 That is, about 19 pounds (about 8.5 kilograms)   [b] 71 That is, about 375 pounds (about 170 kilograms); also in verse 72   [c] 71 That is, about 1 1/3 tons (about 1.2 metric tons)   [d] 72 That is, about 1 1/4 tons (about 1.1 metric tons)   [e] 8 Or God, translating it   [f] 15 See Lev. 23:37-40.

¹⁶So the people went out and brought back branches and built themselves booths on their own roofs, in their courtyards, in the courts of the house of God and in the square by the Water Gate and the one by the Gate of Ephraim. ¹⁷The whole company that had returned from exile built booths and lived in them. From the days of Joshua son of Nun until that day, the Israelites had not celebrated it like this. And their joy was very great.

¹⁸Day after day, from the first day to the last, Ezra read from the Book of the Law of God. They celebrated the feast for seven days, and on the eighth day, in accordance with the regulation, there was an assembly.

The Israelites Confess Their Sins

9 On the twenty-fourth day of the same month, the Israelites gathered together, fasting and wearing sackcloth and having dust on their heads. ²Those of Israelite descent had separated themselves from all foreigners. They stood in their places and confessed their sins and the wickedness of their fathers. ³They stood where they were and read from the Book of the Law of the LORD their God for a quarter of the day, and spent another quarter in confession and in worshiping the LORD their God. ⁴Standing on the stairs were the Levites—Jeshua, Bani, Kadmiel, Shebaniah, Bunni, Sherebiah, Bani and Kenani—who called with loud voices to the LORD their God. ⁵And the Levites—Jeshua, Kadmiel, Bani, Hashabneiah, Sherebiah, Hodiah, Shebaniah and Pethahiah—said: "Stand up and praise the LORD your God, who is from everlasting to everlasting.ᵃ"

"Blessed be your glorious name, and may it be exalted above all blessing and praise. ⁶You alone are the LORD. You made the heavens, even the highest heavens, and all their starry host, the earth and all that is on it, the seas and all that is in them.

You give life to everything, and the multitudes of heaven worship you.

⁷"You are the LORD God, who chose Abram and brought him out of Ur of the Chaldeans and named him Abraham. ⁸You found his heart faithful to you, and you made a covenant with him to give to his descendants the land of the Canaanites, Hittites, Amorites, Perizzites, Jebusites and Girgashites. You have kept your promise because you are righteous.

⁹"You saw the suffering of our forefathers in Egypt; you heard their cry at the Red Sea.ᵇ ¹⁰You sent miraculous signs and wonders against Pharaoh, against all his officials and all the people of his land, for you knew how arrogantly the Egyptians treated them. You made a name for yourself, which remains to this day. ¹¹You divided the sea before them, so that they passed through it on dry ground, but you hurled their pursuers into the depths, like a stone into mighty waters. ¹²By day you led them with a pillar of cloud, and by night with a pillar of fire to give them light on the way they were to take.

¹³"You came down on Mount Sinai; you spoke to them from heaven. You gave them regulations and laws that are just and right, and decrees and commands that are good. ¹⁴You made known to them your holy Sabbath and gave them commands, decrees and laws through your servant Moses. ¹⁵In their hunger you gave them bread from heaven and in their thirst you brought them water from the rock; you told them to go in and take possession of the land you had sworn with uplifted hand to give them.

¹⁶"But they, our forefathers, became arrogant and stiff-necked, and

---

ᵃ 5 Or God for ever and ever   ᵇ 9 Hebrew Yam Suph; that is, Sea of Reeds

Thank God for His Mercy to You

READ AND CONSIDER: NEHEMIAH 9:1-37

"But in your great mercy you did not put an end to them or abandon them, for you are a gracious and merciful God" (Nehemiah 9:31).

Nehemiah and the people of Israel had just accomplished an impossible mission. They had rebuilt the massive walls of Jerusalem in record time. Against all odds and opposition they had succeeded. Now it was time for another kind of rebuilding—accepting and applying God's written instructions for His people. Nehemiah chapter 8 describes a national Bible study of sorts, as Ezra reintroduced God's law to the people. Chapter 9 records the effects of God's Word settling into the hearts and minds of God's people. They arrived at a clear understanding of how far they had drifted from God's ways, and so they gathered for a great service of national repentance and worship.

In God's presence, the people reviewed their history, highlighting the repeated sins of the nation as well as God's repeated mercy and faithfulness. This review wasn't to inform God, but to demonstrate to themselves that they understood how things had come to be. They were standing as a small remnant of a great nation that had been humbled under God's just judgment. In God's mercy they had returned to their land. Their very existence was an amazing tribute to God's faithfulness. Despite everything His people had done to violate the covenants He had made with them in the past, God had kept His word. They knew God was faithful, so they dared to start over.

Their prayer of confession offers us a good example. We need to review our spiritual history in prayer from time to time. Particularly when we have followed the Lord for a long time, we need to trace the journey we have traveled with Him. Perhaps we hesitate to do this because we realize our history with God is like the Israelites' was—full of our failures as well as God's faithfulness. God certainly takes no pleasure in our review of sins unless it leads us to repentance and a clearer understanding of all He has done to guard and guide us along the way. Thank God for all the times He has shown His mercy and grace to you.

did not obey your commands. 17 They refused to listen and failed to remember the miracles you performed among them. They became stiff-necked and in their rebellion appointed a leader in order to return to their slavery. But you are a forgiving God, gracious and compassionate, slow to anger and abounding in love. Therefore you did not desert them, 18 even when they cast for themselves an image of a calf and said, 'This is your god, who brought you up out of Egypt,' or when they committed awful blasphemies.

19 "Because of your great compassion you did not abandon them in the desert. By day the pillar of cloud did not cease to guide them on their path, nor the pillar of fire by night to shine on the way they were to take. 20 You gave your good Spirit to instruct them. You did not withhold your manna from their mouths, and you gave them water for their thirst. 21 For forty years you sustained them in the desert; they lacked nothing, their clothes did not wear out nor did their feet become swollen.

22 "You gave them kingdoms and nations, allotting to them even the remotest frontiers. They took over

the country of Sihon[a] king of Heshbon and the country of Og king of Bashan. 23 You made their sons as numerous as the stars in the sky, and you brought them into the land that you told their fathers to enter and possess. 24 Their sons went in and took possession of the land. You subdued before them the Canaanites, who lived in the land; you handed the Canaanites over to them, along with their kings and the peoples of the land, to deal with them as they pleased. 25 They captured fortified cities and fertile land; they took possession of houses filled with all kinds of good things, wells already dug, vineyards, olive groves and fruit trees in abundance. They ate to the full and were well-nourished; they reveled in your great goodness.

26 "But they were disobedient and rebelled against you; they put your law behind their backs. They killed your prophets, who had admonished them in order to turn them back to you; they committed awful blasphemies. 27 So you handed them over to their enemies, who oppressed them. But when they were oppressed they cried out to you. From heaven you heard them, and in your great compassion you gave them deliverers, who rescued them from the hand of their enemies.

28 "But as soon as they were at rest, they again did what was evil in your sight. Then you abandoned them to the hand of their enemies so that they ruled over them. And when they cried out to you again, you heard from heaven, and in your compassion you delivered them time after time.

29 "You warned them to return to your law, but they became arrogant and disobeyed your commands. They sinned against your ordinances, by which a man will live if he obeys them. Stubbornly they turned their backs on you, became stiff-necked and refused to listen. 30 For many years you were patient with them. By your Spirit you admonished them through your prophets. Yet they paid no attention, so you handed them over to the neighboring peoples. 31 But in your great mercy you did not put an end to them or abandon them, for you are a gracious and merciful God.

32 "Now therefore, O our God, the great, mighty and awesome God, who keeps his covenant of love, do not let all this hardship seem trifling in your eyes—the hardship that has come upon us, upon our kings and leaders, upon our priests and prophets, upon our fathers and all your people, from the days of the kings of Assyria until today. 33 In all that has happened to us, you have been just; you have acted faithfully, while we did wrong. 34 Our kings, our leaders, our priests and our fathers did not follow your law; they did not pay attention to your commands or the warnings you gave them. 35 Even while they were in their kingdom, enjoying your great goodness to them in the spacious and fertile land you gave them, they did not serve you or turn from their evil ways.

36 "But see, we are slaves today, slaves in the land you gave our forefathers so they could eat its fruit and the other good things it produces. 37 Because of our sins, its abundant harvest goes to the kings you have placed over us. They rule over our bodies and our cattle as they please. We are in great distress.

The Agreement of the People

38 "In view of all this, we are making a binding agreement, putting it in writing, and our leaders, our Levites and our priests are affixing their seals to it."

---

a 22 One Hebrew manuscript and Septuagint; most Hebrew manuscripts Sihon, that is, the country of the

10 Those who sealed it were:

Nehemiah the governor, the son of Hacaliah.

Zedekiah, ²Seraiah, Azariah, Jeremiah,
³Pashhur, Amariah, Malkijah,
⁴Hattush, Shebaniah, Malluch,
⁵Harim, Meremoth, Obadiah,
⁶Daniel, Ginnethon, Baruch,
⁷Meshullam, Abijah, Mijamin,
⁸Maaziah, Bilgai and Shemaiah.
These were the priests.

⁹The Levites:

Jeshua son of Azaniah, Binnui of the sons of Henadad, Kadmiel,
¹⁰and their associates: Shebaniah, Hodiah, Kelita, Pelaiah, Hanan,
¹¹Mica, Rehob, Hashabiah,
¹²Zaccur, Sherebiah, Shebaniah,
¹³Hodiah, Bani and Beninu.

¹⁴The leaders of the people:

Parosh, Pahath-Moab, Elam, Zattu, Bani,
¹⁵Bunni, Azgad, Bebai,
¹⁶Adonijah, Bigvai, Adin,
¹⁷Ater, Hezekiah, Azzur,
¹⁸Hodiah, Hashum, Bezai,
¹⁹Hariph, Anathoth, Nebai,
²⁰Magpiash, Meshullam, Hezir,
²¹Meshezabel, Zadok, Jaddua,
²²Pelatiah, Hanan, Anaiah,
²³Hoshea, Hananiah, Hasshub,
²⁴Hallohesh, Pilha, Shobek,
²⁵Rehum, Hashabnah, Maaseiah,
²⁶Ahiah, Hanan, Anan,
²⁷Malluch, Harim and Baanah.

²⁸"The rest of the people—priests, Levites, gatekeepers, singers, temple servants and all who separated themselves from the neighboring peoples for the sake of the Law of God, together with their wives and all their sons and daughters who are able to understand— ²⁹all these now join their brothers the nobles, and bind themselves with a curse and an oath to follow the Law of God given through Moses the servant of God and to obey carefully all the commands, regulations and decrees of the LORD our Lord.

³⁰"We promise not to give our daughters in marriage to the peoples around us or take their daughters for our sons.

³¹"When the neighboring peoples bring merchandise or grain to sell on the Sabbath, we will not buy from them on the Sabbath or on any holy day. Every seventh year we will forgo working the land and will cancel all debts.

³²"We assume the responsibility for carrying out the commands to give a third of a shekel[a] each year for the service of the house of our God: ³³for the bread set out on the table; for the regular grain offerings and burnt offerings; for the offerings on the Sabbaths, New Moon festivals and appointed feasts; for the holy offerings; for sin offerings to make atonement for Israel; and for all the duties of the house of our God.

³⁴"We—the priests, the Levites and the people—have cast lots to determine when each of our families is to bring to the house of our God at set times each year a contribution of wood to burn on the altar of the LORD our God, as it is written in the Law.

³⁵"We also assume responsibility for bringing to the house of the LORD each year the firstfruits of our crops and of every fruit tree.

³⁶"As it is also written in the Law, we will bring the firstborn of our sons and of our cattle, of our herds and of our flocks to the house of our God, to the priests ministering there.

---

a *32* That is, about 1/8 ounce (about 4 grams)

37"Moreover, we will bring to the storerooms of the house of our God, to the priests, the first of our ground meal, of our ⌊grain⌋ offerings, of the fruit of all our trees and of our new wine and oil. And we will bring a tithe of our crops to the Levites, for it is the Levites who collect the tithes in all the towns where we work. 38A priest descended from Aaron is to accompany the Levites when they receive the tithes, and the Levites are to bring a tenth of the tithes up to the house of our God, to the storerooms of the treasury. 39The people of Israel, including the Levites, are to bring their contributions of grain, new wine and oil to the storerooms where the articles for the sanctuary are kept and where the ministering priests, the gatekeepers and the singers stay.

"We will not neglect the house of our God."

The New Residents of Jerusalem

11 Now the leaders of the people settled in Jerusalem, and the rest of the people cast lots to bring one out of every ten to live in Jerusalem, the holy city, while the remaining nine were to stay in their own towns. 2The people commended all the men who volunteered to live in Jerusalem.

3These are the provincial leaders who settled in Jerusalem (now some Israelites, priests, Levites, temple servants and descendants of Solomon's servants lived in the towns of Judah, each on his own property in the various towns, 4while other people from both Judah and Benjamin lived in Jerusalem):

From the descendants of Judah:

Athaiah son of Uzziah, the son of Zechariah, the son of Amariah, the son of Shephatiah, the son of Mahalalel, a descendant of Perez; 5and Maaseiah son of Baruch, the son of Col-Hozeh, the son of Hazaiah, the son of Adaiah, the son of Joiarib, the son of Zechariah, a descendant of Shelah. 6The descendants of Perez who lived in Jerusalem totaled 468 able men.

7From the descendants of Benjamin:

Sallu son of Meshullam, the son of Joed, the son of Pedaiah, the son of Kolaiah, the son of Maaseiah, the son of Ithiel, the son of Jeshaiah, 8and his followers, Gabbai and Sallai—928 men. 9Joel son of Zicri was their chief officer, and Judah son of Hassenuah was over the Second District of the city.

10From the priests:

Jedaiah; the son of Joiarib; Jakin; 11Seraiah son of Hilkiah, the son of Meshullam, the son of Zadok, the son of Meraioth, the son of Ahitub, supervisor in the house of God, 12and their associates, who carried on work for the temple—822 men; Adaiah son of Jeroham, the son of Pelaliah, the son of Amzi, the son of Zechariah, the son of Pashhur, the son of Malkijah, 13and his associates, who were heads of families—242 men; Amashsai son of Azarel, the son of Ahzai, the son of Meshillemoth, the son of Immer, 14and his[a] associates, who were able men—128. Their chief officer was Zabdiel son of Haggedolim.

15From the Levites:

Shemaiah son of Hasshub, the son of Azrikam, the son of Hashabiah, the son of Bunni; 16Shabbethai and Jozabad, two of the heads of the Levites, who had charge of the outside work of the house of God; 17Mattaniah son of Mica, the son of Zabdi, the son of Asaph, the director who led in thanksgiving and prayer; Bakbukiah, second among his associates; and

---

a 14 Most Septuagint manuscripts; Hebrew their

Abda son of Shammua, the son of Galal, the son of Jeduthun. 18 The Levites in the holy city totaled 284.

19 The gatekeepers:

Akkub, Talmon and their associates, who kept watch at the gates—172 men.

20 The rest of the Israelites, with the priests and Levites, were in all the towns of Judah, each on his ancestral property. 21 The temple servants lived on the hill of Ophel, and Ziha and Gishpa were in charge of them.

22 The chief officer of the Levites in Jerusalem was Uzzi son of Bani, the son of Hashabiah, the son of Mattaniah, the son of Mica. Uzzi was one of Asaph's descendants, who were the singers responsible for the service of the house of God. 23 The singers were under the king's orders, which regulated their daily activity. 24 Pethahiah son of Meshezabel, one of the descendants of Zerah son of Judah, was the king's agent in all affairs relating to the people.

25 As for the villages with their fields, some of the people of Judah lived in Kiriath Arba and its surrounding settlements, in Dibon and its settlements, in Jekabzeel and its villages, 26 in Jeshua, in Moladah, in Beth Pelet, 27 in Hazar Shual, in Beersheba and its settlements, 28 in Ziklag, in Meconah and its settlements, 29 in En Rimmon, in Zorah, in Jarmuth, 30 Zanoah, Adullam and their villages, in Lachish and its fields, and in Azekah and its settlements. So they were living all the way from Beersheba to the Valley of Hinnom.

31 The descendants of the Benjamites from Geba lived in Micmash, Aija, Bethel and its settlements, 32 in Anathoth, Nob and Ananiah, 33 in Hazor, Ramah and Gittaim, 34 in Hadid, Zeboim and Neballat, 35 in Lod and Ono, and in the Valley of the Craftsmen.

36 Some of the divisions of the Levites of Judah settled in Benjamin.

Priests and Levites

12 These were the priests and Levites who returned with Zerubbabel son of Shealtiel and with Jeshua:

Seraiah, Jeremiah, Ezra,
2 Amariah, Malluch, Hattush,
3 Shecaniah, Rehum, Meremoth,
4 Iddo, Ginnethon,ª Abijah,
5 Mijamin,ᵇ Moadiah, Bilgah,
6 Shemaiah, Joiarib, Jedaiah,
7 Sallu, Amok, Hilkiah and Jedaiah.

These were the leaders of the priests and their associates in the days of Jeshua.

8 The Levites were Jeshua, Binnui, Kadmiel, Sherebiah, Judah, and also Mattaniah, who, together with his associates, was in charge of the songs of thanksgiving. 9 Bakbukiah and Unni, their associates, stood opposite them in the services.

10 Jeshua was the father of Joiakim, Joiakim the father of Eliashib, Eliashib the father of Joiada, 11 Joiada the father of Jonathan, and Jonathan the father of Jaddua.

12 In the days of Joiakim, these were the heads of the priestly families:

of Seraiah's family, Meraiah;
of Jeremiah's, Hananiah;
13 of Ezra's, Meshullam;
of Amariah's, Jehohanan;
14 of Malluch's, Jonathan;
of Shecaniah's,ᶜ Joseph;
15 of Harim's, Adna;
of Meremoth's,ᵈ Helkai;
16 of Iddo's, Zechariah;
of Ginnethon's, Meshullam;
17 of Abijah's, Zicri;
of Miniamin's and of Moadiah's, Piltai;
18 of Bilgah's, Shammua;
of Shemaiah's, Jehonathan;
19 of Joiarib's, Mattenai;
of Jedaiah's, Uzzi;
20 of Sallu's, Kallai;

of Amok's, Eber; 21of Hilkiah's, Hashabiah; of Jedaiah's, Nethanel.

22The family heads of the Levites in the days of Eliashib, Joiada, Johanan and Jaddua, as well as those of the priests, were recorded in the reign of Darius the Persian. 23The family heads among the descendants of Levi up to the time of Johanan son of Eliashib were recorded in the book of the annals. 24And the leaders of the Levites were Hashabiah, Sherebiah, Jeshua son of Kadmiel, and their associates, who stood opposite them to give praise and thanksgiving, one section responding to the other, as prescribed by David the man of God.

> *Prayer is ...*
> giving all your concerns to God
> so He can carry the weight of them.

25Mattaniah, Bakbukiah, Obadiah, Meshullam, Talmon and Akkub were gatekeepers who guarded the storerooms at the gates. 26They served in the days of Joiakim son of Jeshua, the son of Jozadak, and in the days of Nehemiah the governor and of Ezra the priest and scribe.

Dedication of the Wall of Jerusalem

27At the dedication of the wall of Jerusalem, the Levites were sought out from where they lived and were brought to Jerusalem to celebrate joyfully the dedication with songs of thanksgiving and with the music of cymbals, harps and lyres. 28The singers also were brought together from the region around Jerusalem—from the villages of the Netophathites, 29from Beth Gilgal, and from the area of Geba and Azmaveth, for the singers had built villages for themselves around Jerusalem. 30When the priests and Levites had purified themselves ceremonially, they purified the people, the gates and the wall.

31I had the leaders of Judah go up on top[a] of the wall. I also assigned two large choirs to give thanks. One was to proceed on top[b] of the wall to the right, toward the Dung Gate. 32Hoshaiah and half the leaders of Judah followed them, 33along with Azariah, Ezra, Meshullam, 34Judah, Benjamin, Shemaiah, Jeremiah, 35as well as some priests with trumpets, and also Zechariah son of Jonathan, the son of Shemaiah, the son of Mattaniah, the son of Micaiah, the son of Zaccur, the son of Asaph, 36and his associates—Shemaiah, Azarel, Milalai, Gilalai, Maai, Nethanel, Judah and Hanani—with musical instruments ⌊prescribed by⌋ David the man of God. Ezra the scribe led the procession. 37At the Fountain Gate they continued directly up the steps of the City of David on the ascent to the wall and passed above the house of David to the Water Gate on the east.

38The second choir proceeded in the opposite direction. I followed them on top[c] of the wall, together with half the people—past the Tower of the Ovens to the Broad Wall, 39over the Gate of Ephraim, the Jeshanah[d] Gate, the Fish Gate, the Tower of Hananel and the Tower of the Hundred, as far as the Sheep Gate. At the Gate of the Guard they stopped.

40The two choirs that gave thanks then took their places in the house of God; so did I, together with half the officials, 41as well as the priests—Eliakim, Maaseiah, Miniamin, Micaiah, Elioenai, Zechariah and Hananiah with their trumpets— 42and also Maaseiah, Shemaiah, Eleazar, Uzzi, Jehohanan, Malkijah, Elam and Ezer. The choirs sang under the direction of Jezrahiah. 43And on that day they offered great sacrifices, rejoicing because God had given them great joy. The women and children also rejoiced. The sound of rejoicing in Jerusalem could be heard far away.

---

a 31 Or go alongside   b 31 Or proceed alongside   c 38 Or them alongside   d 39 Or Old

44At that time men were appointed to be in charge of the storerooms for the contributions, firstfruits and tithes. From the fields around the towns they were to bring into the storerooms the portions required by the Law for the priests and the Levites, for Judah was pleased with the ministering priests and Levites. 45They performed the service of their God and the service of purification, as did also the singers and gatekeepers, according to the commands of David and his son Solomon. 46For long ago, in the days of David and Asaph, there had been directors for the singers and for the songs of praise and thanksgiving to God. 47So in the days of Zerubbabel and of Nehemiah, all Israel contributed the daily portions for the singers and gatekeepers. They also set aside the portion for the other Levites, and the Levites set aside the portion for the descendants of Aaron.

Nehemiah's Final Reforms

13 On that day the Book of Moses was read aloud in the hearing of the people and there it was found written that no Ammonite or Moabite should ever be admitted into the assembly of God, 2because they had not met the Israelites with food and water but had hired Balaam to call a curse down on them. (Our God, however, turned the curse into a blessing.) 3When the people heard this law, they excluded from Israel all who were of foreign descent.

4Before this, Eliashib the priest had been put in charge of the storerooms of the house of our God. He was closely associated with Tobiah, 5and he had provided him with a large room formerly used to store the grain offerings and incense and temple articles, and also the tithes of grain, new wine and oil prescribed for the Levites, singers and gatekeepers, as well as the contributions for the priests.

6But while all this was going on, I was not in Jerusalem, for in the thirty-second year of Artaxerxes king of Babylon I had returned to the king. Some time later I asked his permission 7and came back to Jerusalem. Here I learned about the evil thing Eliashib had done in providing Tobiah a room in the courts of the house of God. 8I was greatly displeased and threw all Tobiah's household goods out of the room. 9I gave orders to purify the rooms, and then I put back into them the equipment of the house of God, with the grain offerings and the incense.

10I also learned that the portions assigned to the Levites had not been given to them, and that all the Levites and singers responsible for the service had gone back to their own fields. 11So I rebuked the officials and asked them, "Why is the house of God neglected?" Then I called them together and stationed them at their posts.

12All Judah brought the tithes of grain, new wine and oil into the storerooms. 13I put Shelemiah the priest, Zadok the scribe, and a Levite named Pedaiah in charge of the storerooms and made Hanan son of Zaccur, the son of Mattaniah, their assistant, because these men were considered trustworthy. They were made responsible for distributing the supplies to their brothers.

14Remember me for this, O my God, and do not blot out what I have so faithfully done for the house of my God and its services.

15In those days I saw men in Judah treading winepresses on the Sabbath and bringing in grain and loading it on donkeys, together with wine, grapes, figs and all other kinds of loads. And they were bringing all this into Jerusalem on the Sabbath. Therefore I warned them against selling food on that day. 16Men from Tyre who lived in Jerusalem were bringing in fish and all kinds of merchandise and selling them in Jerusalem on the Sabbath to the people of Judah. 17I rebuked the nobles of Judah and said to them, "What is this wicked thing you are doing—

desecrating the Sabbath day? ¹⁸Didn't your forefathers do the same things, so that our God brought all this calamity upon us and upon this city? Now you are stirring up more wrath against Israel by desecrating the Sabbath."

¹⁹When evening shadows fell on the gates of Jerusalem before the Sabbath, I ordered the doors to be shut and not opened until the Sabbath was over. I stationed some of my own men at the gates so that no load could be brought in on the Sabbath day. ²⁰Once or twice the merchants and sellers of all kinds of goods spent the night outside Jerusalem. ²¹But I warned them and said, "Why do you spend the night by the wall? If you do this again, I will lay hands on you." From that time on they no longer came on the Sabbath. ²²Then I commanded the Levites to purify themselves and go and guard the gates in order to keep the Sabbath day holy.

Remember me for this also, O my God, and show mercy to me according to your great love.

²³Moreover, in those days I saw men of Judah who had married women from Ashdod, Ammon and Moab. ²⁴Half of their children spoke the language of Ashdod or the language of one of the other peoples, and did not know how to speak the language of Judah. ²⁵I rebuked them and called curses down on them. I beat some of the men and pulled out their hair. I made them take an oath in God's name and said: "You are not to give your daughters in marriage to their sons, nor are you to take their daughters in marriage for your sons or for yourselves. ²⁶Was it not because of marriages like these that Solomon king of Israel sinned? Among the many nations there was no king like him. He was loved by his God, and God made him king over all Israel, but even he was led into sin by foreign women. ²⁷Must we hear now that you too are doing all this terrible wickedness and are being unfaithful to our God by marrying foreign women?"

²⁸One of the sons of Joiada son of Eliashib the high priest was son-in-law to Sanballat the Horonite. And I drove him away from me.

²⁹Remember them, O my God, because they defiled the priestly office and the covenant of the priesthood and of the Levites.

³⁰So I purified the priests and the Levites of everything foreign, and assigned them duties, each to his own task. ³¹I also made provision for contributions of wood at designated times, and for the firstfruits.

Remember me with favor, O my God.

Author: Unknown

Date: 460 BC

Audience: Later generations of the Jewish people—to record the events surrounding their ancestors' deliverance in Persia, which led to the establishment of the annual Feast of Purim

Prayer Themes:

- *Thank God for the encouraging truth that He has made you just as you are so that you can better serve His purposes in the world (2:7-9).*

- *Ask God for the courage and faith to do what is right, no matter what the consequences may be (4:12-16).*

- *Trust God to honor your past faithfulness and to exalt you in His perfect time (6:1-12).*

It is common for Christians to fall into the subtle trap of supposing that prayer works by formula. "Assume the preferred posture, address God by the right name, use the proper words and phrases, and presto—your prayers will be answered."

The book of Esther shatters such myths.

In this surprising account of a beautiful queen who was used by God to save the Jewish people from genocide in Persia, we find not a single overt reference to prayer! Not only that, but the book doesn't even mention the name of God!

And yet, given the plight of the Jews, it's safe to assume that their times of fasting (4:3,16; 9:31) were filled with desperate prayer to the Lord of heaven. And given the way the story ends, it is obvious that God was both aware and at work during their whole ordeal.

Prayer doesn't have to be formal or flowery—or even public or audible—to be effective. It has to be heartfelt.

Esther

Queen Vashti Deposed

1 This is what happened during the time of Xerxes,[a] the Xerxes who ruled over 127 provinces stretching from India to Cush[b]: ²At that time King Xerxes reigned from his royal throne in the citadel of Susa, ³and in the third year of his reign he gave a banquet for all his nobles and officials. The military leaders of Persia and Media, the princes, and the nobles of the provinces were present.

⁴For a full 180 days he displayed the vast wealth of his kingdom and the splendor and glory of his majesty. ⁵When these days were over, the king gave a banquet, lasting seven days, in the enclosed garden of the king's palace, for all the people from the least to the greatest, who were in the citadel of Susa. ⁶The garden had hangings of white and blue linen, fastened with cords of white linen and purple material to silver rings on marble pillars. There were couches of gold and silver on a mosaic pavement of porphyry, marble, mother-of-pearl and other costly stones. ⁷Wine was served in goblets of gold, each one different from the other, and the royal wine was abundant, in keeping with the king's liberality. ⁸By the king's command each guest was allowed to drink in his own way, for the king instructed all the wine stewards to serve each man what he wished.

⁹Queen Vashti also gave a banquet for the women in the royal palace of King Xerxes.

¹⁰On the seventh day, when King Xerxes was in high spirits from wine, he

---

a 1 Hebrew *Ahasuerus*, a variant of Xerxes' Persian name; here and throughout Esther   b 1 That is, the upper Nile region commanded the seven eunuchs who served him—Mehuman, Biztha, Harbona, Bigtha, Abagtha, Zethar and Carcas— 11to bring before him Queen Vashti, wearing her royal crown, in order to display her beauty to the people and nobles, for she was lovely to look at. 12But when the attendants delivered the king's command, Queen Vashti refused to come. Then the king became furious and burned with anger.

13Since it was customary for the king to consult experts in matters of law and justice, he spoke with the wise men who understood the times 14and were closest to the king—Carshena, Shethar, Admatha, Tarshish, Meres, Marsena and Memucan, the seven nobles of Persia and Media who had special access to the king and were highest in the kingdom.

15"According to law, what must be done to Queen Vashti?" he asked. "She has not obeyed the command of King Xerxes that the eunuchs have taken to her."

16Then Memucan replied in the presence of the king and the nobles, "Queen Vashti has done wrong, not only against the king but also against all the nobles and the peoples of all the provinces of King Xerxes. 17For the queen's conduct will become known to all the women, and so they will despise their husbands and say, 'King Xerxes commanded Queen Vashti to be brought before him, but she would not come.' 18This very day the Persian and Median women of the nobility who have heard about the queen's conduct will respond to all the king's nobles in the same way. There will be no end of disrespect and discord.

19"Therefore, if it pleases the king, let him issue a royal decree and let it be written in the laws of Persia and Media, which cannot be repealed, that Vashti is never again to enter the presence of King Xerxes. Also let the king give her royal position to someone else who is better than she. 20Then when the king's edict is proclaimed throughout all his vast realm, all the women will respect their husbands, from the least to the greatest."

21The king and his nobles were pleased with this advice, so the king did as Memucan proposed. 22He sent dispatches to all parts of the kingdom, to each province in its own script and to each people in its own language, proclaiming in each people's tongue that every man should be ruler over his own household.

Esther Made Queen

2 Later when the anger of King Xerxes had subsided, he remembered Vashti and what she had done and what he had decreed about her. 2Then the king's personal attendants proposed, "Let a search be made for beautiful young virgins for the king. 3Let the king appoint commissioners in every province of his realm to bring all these beautiful girls into the harem at the citadel of Susa. Let them be placed under the care of Hegai, the king's eunuch, who is in charge of the women; and let beauty treatments be given to them. 4Then let the girl who pleases the king be queen instead of Vashti." This advice appealed to the king, and he followed it.

5Now there was in the citadel of Susa a Jew of the tribe of Benjamin, named Mordecai son of Jair, the son of Shimei, the son of Kish, 6who had been carried into exile from Jerusalem by Nebuchadnezzar king of Babylon, among those taken captive with Jehoiachin[a] king of Judah. 7Mordecai had a cousin named Hadassah, whom he had brought up because she had neither father nor mother. This girl, who was also known as Esther, was lovely in form and features, and Mordecai had taken her as his own daughter when her father and mother died.

8When the king's order and edict had been proclaimed, many girls were brought to the citadel of Susa and put under the care of Hegai. Esther also was taken to the king's palace and entrusted

---

a 6 Hebrew *Jeconiah*, a variant of *Jehoiachin*

to Hegai, who had charge of the harem. ⁹The girl pleased him and won his favor. Immediately he provided her with her beauty treatments and special food. He assigned to her seven maids selected from the king's palace and moved her and her maids into the best place in the harem.

¹⁰Esther had not revealed her nationality and family background, because Mordecai had forbidden her to do so. ¹¹Every day he walked back and forth near the courtyard of the harem to find out how Esther was and what was happening to her.

¹²Before a girl's turn came to go in to King Xerxes, she had to complete twelve months of beauty treatments prescribed for the women, six months with oil of myrrh and six with perfumes and cosmetics. ¹³And this is how she would go to the king: Anything she wanted was given her to take with her from the harem to the king's palace. ¹⁴In the evening she would go there and in the morning return to another part of the harem to the care of Shaashgaz, the king's eunuch who was in charge of the concubines. She would not return to the king unless he was pleased with her and summoned her by name.

¹⁵When the turn came for Esther (the girl Mordecai had adopted, the daughter of his uncle Abihail) to go to the king, she asked for nothing other than what Hegai, the king's eunuch who was in charge of the harem, suggested. And Esther won the favor of everyone who saw her. ¹⁶She was taken to King Xerxes in the royal residence in the tenth month, the month of Tebeth, in the seventh year of his reign.

¹⁷Now the king was attracted to Esther more than to any of the other women, and she won his favor and approval more than any of the other virgins. So he set a royal crown on her head and made her queen instead of Vashti. ¹⁸And the king gave a great banquet, Esther's banquet, for all his nobles and officials. He proclaimed a holiday throughout the provinces and distributed gifts with royal liberality.

Mordecai Uncovers a Conspiracy

¹⁹When the virgins were assembled a second time, Mordecai was sitting at the king's gate. ²⁰But Esther had kept secret her family background and nationality just as Mordecai had told her to do, for she continued to follow Mordecai's instructions as she had done when he was bringing her up.

²¹During the time Mordecai was sitting at the king's gate, Bigthana[a] and Teresh, two of the king's officers who guarded the doorway, became angry and conspired to assassinate King Xerxes. ²²But Mordecai found out about the plot and told Queen Esther, who in turn reported it to the king, giving credit to Mordecai. ²³And when the report was investigated and found to be true, the two officials were hanged on a gallows.[b] All this was recorded in the book of the annals in the presence of the king.

Haman's Plot to Destroy the Jews

3 After these events, King Xerxes honored Haman son of Hammedatha, the Agagite, elevating him and giving him a seat of honor higher than that of all the other nobles. ²All the royal officials at the king's gate knelt down and paid honor to Haman, for the king had commanded this concerning him. But Mordecai would not kneel down or pay him honor.

³Then the royal officials at the king's gate asked Mordecai, "Why do you disobey the king's command?" ⁴Day after day they spoke to him but he refused to comply. Therefore they told Haman about it to see whether Mordecai's behavior would be tolerated, for he had told them he was a Jew.

⁵When Haman saw that Mordecai would not kneel down or pay him honor, he was enraged. ⁶Yet having learned who Mordecai's people were, he scorned the idea of killing only Mordecai. Instead

---

ᵃ 21 Hebrew *Bigthan*, a variant of *Bigthana*   ᵇ 23 Or *were hung* (or *impaled*) *on poles*; similarly elsewhere in Esther

Haman looked for a way to destroy all Mordecai's people, the Jews, throughout the whole kingdom of Xerxes.

7In the twelfth year of King Xerxes, in the first month, the month of Nisan, they cast the *pur* (that is, the lot) in the presence of Haman to select a day and month. And the lot fell on[a] the twelfth month, the month of Adar.

8Then Haman said to King Xerxes, "There is a certain people dispersed and scattered among the peoples in all the provinces of your kingdom whose customs are different from those of all other people and who do not obey the king's laws; it is not in the king's best interest to tolerate them. 9If it pleases the king, let a decree be issued to destroy them, and I will put ten thousand talents[b] of silver into the royal treasury for the men who carry out this business."

10So the king took his signet ring from his finger and gave it to Haman son of Hammedatha, the Agagite, the enemy of the Jews. 11"Keep the money," the king said to Haman, "and do with the people as you please."

12Then on the thirteenth day of the first month the royal secretaries were summoned. They wrote out in the script of each province and in the language of each people all Haman's orders to the king's satraps, the governors of the various provinces and the nobles of the various peoples. These were written in the name of King Xerxes himself and sealed with his own ring. 13Dispatches were sent by couriers to all the king's provinces with the order to destroy, kill and annihilate all the Jews—young and old, women and little children—on a single day, the thirteenth day of the twelfth month, the month of Adar, and to plunder their goods. 14A copy of the text of the edict was to be issued as law in every province and made known to the people of every nationality so they would be ready for that day.

15Spurred on by the king's command, the couriers went out, and the edict was issued in the citadel of Susa. The king and Haman sat down to drink, but the city of Susa was bewildered.

Mordecai Persuades Esther to Help

4 When Mordecai learned of all that had been done, he tore his clothes, put on sackcloth and ashes, and went out into the city, wailing loudly and bitterly. 2But he went only as far as the king's gate, because no one clothed in sackcloth was allowed to enter it. 3In every province to which the edict and order of the king came, there was great mourning among the Jews, with fasting, weeping and wailing. Many lay in sackcloth and ashes.

4When Esther's maids and eunuchs came and told her about Mordecai, she was in great distress. She sent clothes for him to put on instead of his sackcloth, but he would not accept them. 5Then Esther summoned Hathach, one of the king's eunuchs assigned to attend her, and ordered him to find out what was troubling Mordecai and why.

6So Hathach went out to Mordecai in the open square of the city in front of the king's gate. 7Mordecai told him everything that had happened to him, including the exact amount of money Haman had promised to pay into the royal treasury for the destruction of the Jews. 8He also gave him a copy of the text of the edict for their annihilation, which had been published in Susa, to show to Esther and explain it to her, and he told him to urge her to go into the king's presence to beg for mercy and plead with him for her people.

9Hathach went back and reported to Esther what Mordecai had said. 10Then she instructed him to say to Mordecai, 11"All the king's officials and the people of the royal provinces know that for any man or woman who approaches the king in the inner court without being summoned the king has but one law: that he be put to death. The only exception to

GOING *deeper*

The Power of One

READ AND CONSIDER: ESTHER 4:1-17

"Go, gather together all the Jews who are in Susa, and fast for me. Do not eat or drink for three days, night or day. I and my maids will fast as you do. When this is done, I will go to the king, even though it is against the law. And if I perish, I perish" (Esther 4:16).

Have you ever thought, "I'm just one person. My prayers can't make a difference"?

Many of us think that from time to time. But it's not true.

Esther was the chosen wife of Xerxes, the powerful king of the Persian Empire. This king had made an example of his previous wife by banishing her for her disobedience to him. Now Esther was faced with an even more severe punishment if she dared approach the king on his throne without being summoned. She was literally risking her life. Yet her cousin, Mordecai, asked her to do just that. Her people, the Jews, were in great danger, and Esther was queen of the empire. "Who knows," her cousin had said, "but that you have come to royal position for such a time as this?"

Esther was just one person, but she was the one person in the right place at the right time—put there by God Himself to intercede for her people. So she called the people together and asked them to fast and pray for three days. She may have been the queen, but she still needed great courage, great faith, and God's guidance through the circumstances. More than her own life was at stake; the lives of millions of her countrymen were in jeopardy as well. But she courageously did what she had to do and saved her nation.

As believers, we each have to stand up for what is right, even if the result of our actions may bring ridicule or something worse. It's easy to talk the talk when we're with our Christian friends, but those times when we are surrounded by scoffing unbelievers can be very challenging. Maybe you are the only Christian at work or at a family gathering—what do you do when confronted about your faith? Are you willing to risk banishment by your peers by standing up for what is right?

It would be easier to sit back and quietly wait for the moment to pass—that moment when you could have spoken up for the truth. It's far more challenging to take a risk and stand up for what's right. Esther fasted and prayed and followed God's leading. You can do the same. And you never know when it will result in the very thing for which you were created. You never know when your intercession and actions may save lives.

this is for the king to extend the gold scepter to him and spare his life. But thirty days have passed since I was called to go to the king."

¹²When Esther's words were reported to Mordecai, ¹³he sent back this answer: "Do not think that because you are in the king's house you alone of all the Jews will escape. ¹⁴For if you remain silent at this time, relief and deliverance for the Jews will arise from another place, but

you and your father's family will perish. And who knows but that you have come to royal position for such a time as this?"

¹⁵Then Esther sent this reply to Mor-

Praying Esther 4:13-17
Prepare me, Lord, for such a time when I can be Your instrument of salvation and deliverance for others.

God's people at prayer
ESTHER'S DILEMMAS AND DECISIONS

ESTHER 4:15-17 Queen Esther had a dilemma. There was a lot at stake, and she knew it. She didn't run in to her husband, the king, and scream, "Your hoodlum friends are going to ruin our lives!" Rather, she prayed first and then ministered to him in love while God prepared his heart.

Esther risked her life for the sake of what was right. Her courage and calm demeanor in the face of death is a model in character for every Christian to follow. There were no split-second decisions, no rash behaviors. Her actions were threefold: prayer, fasting, and gathering the support of others. God gave her the words to say and a plan to set in motion. Then she went to the royal courtroom, knowing that whatever happened, she was in God's hands.

In a tough situation when you don't know what to do, start by fasting and praying, and then get others to join you, at least in prayer. Take courage and be calm. The answers will come.

decai: ¹⁶"Go, gather together all the Jews who are in Susa, and fast for me. Do not eat or drink for three days, night or day. I and my maids will fast as you do. When this is done, I will go to the king, even though it is against the law. And if I perish, I perish."

¹⁷So Mordecai went away and carried out all of Esther's instructions.

Esther's Request to the King

5 On the third day Esther put on her royal robes and stood in the inner court of the palace, in front of the king's hall. The king was sitting on his royal throne in the hall, facing the entrance. ²When he saw Queen Esther standing in the court, he was pleased with her and held out to her the gold scepter that was in his hand. So Esther approached and touched the tip of the scepter.

³Then the king asked, "What is it, Queen Esther? What is your request? Even up to half the kingdom, it will be given you."

⁴"If it pleases the king," replied Esther, "let the king, together with Haman, come today to a banquet I have prepared for him."

⁵"Bring Haman at once," the king said, "so that we may do what Esther asks."

So the king and Haman went to the banquet Esther had prepared. ⁶As they were drinking wine, the king again asked

Esther, "Now what is your petition? It will be given you. And what is your request? Even up to half the kingdom, it will be granted."

⁷Esther replied, "My petition and my request is this: ⁸If the king regards me with favor and if it pleases the king to grant my petition and fulfill my request, let the king and Haman come tomorrow to the banquet I will prepare for them. Then I will answer the king's question."

Haman's Rage Against Mordecai

⁹Haman went out that day happy and in high spirits. But when he saw Mordecai at the king's gate and observed that he neither rose nor showed fear in his presence, he was filled with rage against Mordecai. ¹⁰Nevertheless, Haman restrained himself and went home.

Calling together his friends and Zeresh, his wife, ¹¹Haman boasted to them about his vast wealth, his many sons, and all the ways the king had honored him and how he had elevated him above the other nobles and officials. ¹²"And that's not all," Haman added. "I'm the only person Queen Esther invited to accompany the king to the banquet she gave. And she has invited me along with the king tomorrow. ¹³But all this gives me no satisfaction as long as I see that Jew Mordecai sitting at the king's gate."

¹⁴His wife Zeresh and all his friends said

How a Wise Woman Speaks

When *a wise woman speaks, she gives a reason for the hope that is within her.* The most important words we can speak are ones that explain our faith to anyone who asks or who will listen. We must be able to give a reason for the hope we have within us (1 Peter 3:15). We have to pray that God will help us become bold enough to clearly explain our faith in God. We have to ask God to help us tell others why we call Jesus our Messiah, why we can't live without the Holy Spirit, and why we choose to live God's way. And we must be able to do this in a manner that is loving and humble. Otherwise, we will alienate those whom God wants to draw to Himself. If the love of God and the testimony of His goodness are not in our heart, then they will not come out of our mouth. And what we say will not draw people to the Lord. It may, in fact, do the exact opposite.

When a wise woman speaks, she knows that timing is important. When things need to be said that are difficult for the hearer to receive, timing is everything. Certain words cannot be uttered with any success if the person listening is not open and ready to hear them. It's important to discern that, and the only way to know for certain when to speak and what to say is to pray about it in advance. The Bible says that we are not to be too hasty to speak (Proverbs 29:20). A wise woman knows she shouldn't share every single thought that comes into her head. "A fool gives full vent to his anger, but a wise man keeps himself under control" (Proverbs 29:11). You may have good things to say, but people aren't always ready to hear them. Only God knows for sure when someone is ready. Ask Him to show you.

When a wise woman speaks, she tells the truth. When we don't speak the truth, we hurt others as well as ourselves. "Therefore each of you must put off falsehood and speak truthfully to his neighbor, for we are all members of one body" (Ephesians 4:25). But we can't run around speaking the truth without wisdom, sensitivity, and a sense of the Lord's timing. People don't want to hear every bit of truth about themselves every moment. It's too much for them. Sometimes it's better to say nothing and pray for God to show you when a person is ready to hear the truth.

When a wise woman speaks, she doesn't talk too much. We have to be careful that we don't spend more time talking than is necessary. "As a dream comes when there are many cares, so the speech of a fool when there are many words" (Ecclesiastes 5:3). I always told my prayer group that we shouldn't spend more time talking about our requests than we do praying for them. And we can't just spill words out of our mouth without giving thought to what we are saying. We will give account of every idle word in the day of judgment (Matthew 12:36). This is a very scary thought. We must ask God to make us wise in the amount of talking we do.

When a wise woman speaks, her words are gracious. We can't speak words that are mean, insensitive, harsh, coarse, rude, deceitful, offensive, or arrogant without reaping the consequences. With our words we will either build lives or we will tear them down. "The things that come out of the mouth come from the heart, and these make a man 'unclean' " (Matthew 15:18). "Words from a wise man's mouth are gracious, but a fool is consumed by his own lips" (Ecclesiastes 10:12). Ask God to create in you a clean heart so filled with His Spirit, His love, and His truth that it will overflow love, truth, and healing in your speech. Ask Him to help you find words that speak life to those around you.

For the next "From Stormie's Heart" article, go to page 635.

to him, "Have a gallows built, seventy-five feet[a] high, and ask the king in the morning to have Mordecai hanged on it. Then go with the king to the dinner and be happy." This suggestion delighted Haman, and he had the gallows built.

Mordecai Honored

6 That night the king could not sleep; so he ordered the book of the chronicles, the record of his reign, to be brought in and read to him. [2]It was found recorded there that Mordecai had exposed Bigthana and Teresh, two of the king's officers who guarded the doorway, who had conspired to assassinate King Xerxes.

[3]"What honor and recognition has Mordecai received for this?" the king asked.

"Nothing has been done for him," his attendants answered.

[4]The king said, "Who is in the court?" Now Haman had just entered the outer court of the palace to speak to the king about hanging Mordecai on the gallows he had erected for him.

[5]His attendants answered, "Haman is standing in the court."

"Bring him in," the king ordered.

[6]When Haman entered, the king asked him, "What should be done for the man the king delights to honor?"

Now Haman thought to himself, "Who is there that the king would rather honor than me?" [7]So he answered the king, "For the man the king delights to honor, [8]have them bring a royal robe the king has worn and a horse the king has ridden, one with a royal crest placed on its head. [9]Then let the robe and horse be entrusted to one of the king's most noble princes. Let them robe the man the king delights to honor, and lead him on the horse through the city streets, proclaiming before him, 'This is what is done for the man the king delights to honor!'"

[10]"Go at once," the king commanded Haman. "Get the robe and the horse and do just as you have suggested for Mordecai the Jew, who sits at the king's gate. Do not neglect anything you have recommended."

[11]So Haman got the robe and the horse. He robed Mordecai, and led him on horseback through the city streets, proclaiming before him, "This is what is done for the man the king delights to honor!"

[12]Afterward Mordecai returned to the king's gate. But Haman rushed home, with his head covered in grief, [13]and told Zeresh his wife and all his friends everything that had happened to him.

His advisers and his wife Zeresh said to him, "Since Mordecai, before whom your downfall has started, is of Jewish origin, you cannot stand against him—you will surely come to ruin!" [14]While they were still talking with him, the king's eunuchs arrived and hurried Haman away to the banquet Esther had prepared.

Haman Hanged

7 So the king and Haman went to dine with Queen Esther, [2]and as they were drinking wine on that second day, the king again asked, "Queen Esther, what is your petition? It will be given you. What is your request? Even up to half the kingdom, it will be granted."

[3]Then Queen Esther answered, "If I have found favor with you, O king, and if it pleases your majesty, grant me my life—this is my petition. And spare my people—this is my request. [4]For I and my people have been sold for destruction and slaughter and annihilation. If we had merely been sold as male and female slaves, I would have kept quiet, because no such distress would justify disturbing the king.[b]"

[5]King Xerxes asked Queen Esther, "Who is he? Where is the man who has dared to do such a thing?"

[6]Esther said, "The adversary and enemy is this vile Haman."

---

[a] 14 Hebrew fifty cubits (about 23 meters)   [b] 4 Or quiet, but the compensation our adversary offers cannot be compared with the loss the king would suffer

Then Haman was terrified before the king and queen. [7]The king got up in a rage, left his wine and went out into the palace garden. But Haman, realizing that the king had already decided his fate, stayed behind to beg Queen Esther for his life.

[8]Just as the king returned from the palace garden to the banquet hall, Haman was falling on the couch where Esther was reclining.

The king exclaimed, "Will he even molest the queen while she is with me in the house?"

As soon as the word left the king's mouth, they covered Haman's face. [9]Then Harbona, one of the eunuchs attending the king, said, "A gallows seventy-five feet[a] high stands by Haman's house. He had it made for Mordecai, who spoke up to help the king."

The king said, "Hang him on it!" [10]So they hanged Haman on the gallows he had prepared for Mordecai. Then the king's fury subsided.

The King's Edict in Behalf of the Jews

8 That same day King Xerxes gave Queen Esther the estate of Haman, the enemy of the Jews. And Mordecai came into the presence of the king, for Esther had told how he was related to her. [2]The king took off his signet ring, which he had reclaimed from Haman, and presented it to Mordecai. And Esther appointed him over Haman's estate.

[3]Esther again pleaded with the king, falling at his feet and weeping. She begged him to put an end to the evil plan of Haman the Agagite, which he had devised against the Jews. [4]Then the king extended the gold scepter to Esther and she arose and stood before him.

[5]"If it pleases the king," she said, "and if he regards me with favor and thinks it the right thing to do, and if he is pleased with me, let an order be written overruling the dispatches that Haman son of Hammedatha, the Agagite, devised and wrote to destroy the Jews in all the king's provinces. [6]For how can I bear to see disaster fall on my people? How can I bear to see the destruction of my family?"

[7]King Xerxes replied to Queen Esther and to Mordecai the Jew, "Because Haman attacked the Jews, I have given his estate to Esther, and they have hanged him on the gallows. [8]Now write another decree in the king's name in behalf of the Jews as seems best to you, and seal it with the king's signet ring—for no document written in the king's name and sealed with his ring can be revoked."

[9]At once the royal secretaries were summoned—on the twenty-third day of the third month, the month of Sivan. They wrote out all Mordecai's orders to the Jews, and to the satraps, governors and nobles of the 127 provinces stretching from India to Cush.[b] These orders were written in the script of each province and the language of each people and also to the Jews in their own script and language. [10]Mordecai wrote in the name of King Xerxes, sealed the dispatches with the king's signet ring, and sent them by mounted couriers, who rode fast horses especially bred for the king.

[11]The king's edict granted the Jews in every city the right to assemble and protect themselves; to destroy, kill and annihilate any armed force of any nationality or province that might attack them and their women and children; and to plunder the property of their enemies. [12]The day appointed for the Jews to do this in all the provinces of King Xerxes was the thirteenth day of the twelfth month, the month of Adar. [13]A copy of the text of the edict was to be issued as law in every province and made known to the people of every nationality so that the Jews would be ready on that day to avenge themselves on their enemies.

[14]The couriers, riding the royal horses, raced out, spurred on by the king's

---

[a]9 Hebrew *fifty cubits* (about 23 meters)   [b]9 That is, the upper Nile region

command. And the edict was also issued in the citadel of Susa.

15Mordecai left the king's presence wearing royal garments of blue and white, a large crown of gold and a purple robe of fine linen. And the city of Susa held a joyous celebration. 16For the Jews it was a time of happiness and joy, gladness and honor. 17In every province and in every city, wherever the edict of the king went, there was joy and gladness among the Jews, with feasting and celebrating. And many people of other nationalities became Jews because fear of the Jews had seized them.

Triumph of the Jews

9 On the thirteenth day of the twelfth month, the month of Adar, the edict commanded by the king was to be carried out. On this day the enemies of the Jews had hoped to overpower them, but now the tables were turned and the Jews got the upper hand over those who hated them. 2The Jews assembled in their cities in all the provinces of King Xerxes to attack those seeking their destruction. No one could stand against them, because the people of all the other nationalities were afraid of them. 3And all the nobles of the provinces, the satraps, the governors and the king's administrators helped the Jews, because fear of Mordecai had seized them. 4Mordecai was prominent in the palace; his reputation spread throughout the provinces, and he became more and more powerful.

5The Jews struck down all their enemies with the sword, killing and destroying them, and they did what they pleased to those who hated them. 6In the citadel of Susa, the Jews killed and destroyed five hundred men. 7They also killed Parshandatha, Dalphon, Aspatha, 8Poratha, Adalia, Aridatha, 9Parmashta, Arisai, Aridai and Vaizatha, 10the ten sons of Haman son of Hammedatha, the enemy of the Jews. But they did not lay their hands on the plunder.

11The number of those slain in the cita-

del of Susa was reported to the king that same day. 12The king said to Queen Esther, "The Jews have killed and destroyed five hundred men and the ten sons of Haman in the citadel of Susa. What have they done in the rest of the king's provinces? Now what is your petition? It will be given you. What is your request? It will also be granted."

13"If it pleases the king," Esther answered, "give the Jews in Susa permission to carry out this day's edict tomorrow also, and let Haman's ten sons be hanged on gallows."

14So the king commanded that this be done. An edict was issued in Susa, and they hanged the ten sons of Haman. 15The Jews in Susa came together on the fourteenth day of the month of Adar, and they put to death in Susa three hundred men, but they did not lay their hands on the plunder.

16Meanwhile, the remainder of the Jews who were in the king's provinces also assembled to protect themselves and get relief from their enemies. They killed seventy-five thousand of them but did not lay their hands on the plunder. 17This happened on the thirteenth day of the month of Adar, and on the fourteenth they rested and made it a day of feasting and joy.

Purim Celebrated

18The Jews in Susa, however, had assembled on the thirteenth and fourteenth, and then on the fifteenth they rested and made it a day of feasting and joy.

19That is why rural Jews—those living in villages—observe the fourteenth of the month of Adar as a day of joy and feasting, a day for giving presents to each other.

20Mordecai recorded these events, and he sent letters to all the Jews throughout the provinces of King Xerxes, near and far, 21to have them celebrate annually the fourteenth and fifteenth days of the month of Adar 22as the time when the Jews got relief from their enemies, and as the month when their sorrow was turned into joy and their mourning into a day of celebration. He wrote them to observe the days as days of feasting and joy and giving presents of food to one another and gifts to the poor.

23So the Jews agreed to continue the celebration they had begun, doing what Mordecai had written to them. 24For Haman son of Hammedatha, the Agagite, the enemy of all the Jews, had plotted against the Jews to destroy them and had cast the *pur* (that is, the lot) for their ruin and destruction. 25But when the plot came to the king's attention,[a] he issued written orders that the evil scheme Haman had devised against the Jews should come back onto his own head, and that he and his sons should be hanged on the gallows. 26(Therefore these days were called Purim, from the word *pur*.) Because of everything written in this letter and because of what they had seen and what had happened to them, 27the Jews took it upon themselves to establish the custom that they and their descendants and all who join them should without fail observe these two days every year, in the way prescribed and at the time appointed. 28These days should be remembered and observed in every generation by every family, and in every province and in every city. And these days of Purim should never cease to be celebrated by the Jews, nor should the memory of them die out among their descendants.

29So Queen Esther, daughter of Abihail, along with Mordecai the Jew, wrote with full authority to confirm this second letter concerning Purim. 30And Mordecai sent letters to all the Jews in the 127 provinces of the kingdom of Xerxes—words of goodwill and assurance— 31to establish these days of Purim at their designated times, as Mordecai the Jew and Queen Esther had decreed for them, and as they had established for themselves and their descendants in regard to their times of fasting and lamentation. 32Esther's decree confirmed these regulations about Purim, and it was written down in the records.

The Greatness of Mordecai

10 King Xerxes imposed tribute throughout the empire, to its distant shores. 2And all his acts of power and might, together with a full account of the greatness of Mordecai to which the king had raised him, are they not written in the book of the annals of the kings of Media and Persia? 3Mordecai the Jew was second in rank to King Xerxes, preeminent among the Jews, and held in high esteem by his many fellow Jews, because he worked for the good of his people and spoke up for the welfare of all the Jews.

---

[a] 25 Or *when Esther came before the king*

Author: An unknown Israelite (possibly Moses, Solomon, or Elihu)

Date: Unknown (though the events described occurred approximately 2000–1000 BC)

Audience: To remind the people of God that despite human suffering, God is both just and good

We so often view prayer as a means of obtaining needed things:

Healing from a debilitating illness

Relief from emotional torment

Financial help or rescue

Strength to face arduous tasks

Wisdom during life's confusing times

While these kinds of prayers are not wrong (and, in fact, are invited by our loving heavenly Father), they can gradually cause us to lose sight of a larger and deeper truth: Prayer is not so much about getting things *from* God as it is being *with* God.

This is the message of Job. God is the point. He is the One our hearts hunger for. More than gifts, more than blessings, we need the One who gives and blesses.

More than theological answers to all our "why?" questions, we need a steady faith in the "who" who holds the universe and our lives in His hand.

Prayer Themes:

- Pray for an alert, discerning, and bold heart and mind so that you can be aware of the schemes of the accuser and be able to stand firm against his attacks (1:6-12).

- Ask God for the kind of openhanded trust that enjoys His blessings but does not grab them, demand them, or complain when they are withdrawn (1:20-22).

- Ask God for fresh glimpses of His awesome power and holiness so that you might live with a humble reverence for Him (42:1-6).

Job

Prologue

1 In the land of Uz there lived a man whose name was Job. This man was blameless and upright; he feared God and shunned evil. ²He had seven sons and three daughters, ³and he owned seven thousand sheep, three thousand camels, five hundred yoke of oxen and five hundred donkeys, and had a large number of servants. He was the greatest man among all the people of the East.

⁴His sons used to take turns holding feasts in their homes, and they would invite their three sisters to eat and drink with them. ⁵When a period of feasting had run its course, Job would send and have them purified. Early in the morning he would sacrifice a burnt offering for each of them, thinking, "Perhaps my children have sinned and cursed God in their hearts." This was Job's regular custom.

Praying Job 1:6-12

Help me to remember when I go through tough times that Satan is my enemy, and You, Lord, are always on my side.

Job's First Test

⁶One day the angels[a] came to present themselves before the LORD, and Satan[b] also came with them. ⁷The LORD said to Satan, "Where have you come from?"

Satan answered the LORD, "From roam-

---

[a] 6 Hebrew *the sons of God*   [b] 6 *Satan* means *accuser*.

Praising God in Good Times and Bad

GOING deeper

READ AND CONSIDER: JOB 1:1-22

"At this, Job got up and tore his robe and shaved his head. Then he fell to the ground in worship and said: 'Naked I came from my mother's womb, and naked I will depart. The LORD gave and the LORD has taken away; may the name of the LORD be praised' " (Job 1:20-21).

If God is in control, then why is this happening to me? This may be your first reaction when calamity strikes. Everyone has times of suffering, some to a greater extent than others. It is unavoidable, inescapable, and often undeserved.

Job, the man who did nothing to deserve his fate, lost everything, including all of his children and his health. Life can't get worse than that. Through it all, however, and even in his greatest hour of grief, he never cursed God. He could have blamed God, but he didn't. He trusted Him instead. His reaction to the tremendous loss was to humble himself and worship God.

Job endured that terrible time without wavering in his worship of God, and his life was eventually restored. Job lost seven sons and three daughters, and in the end God gave him seven new sons and three new daughters. "The LORD blessed the latter part of Job's life more than the first" (42:12). You may be thinking, "Yes, that's nice, but Job still lost the first seven sons and three daughters. You can't just replace a child the way you can replace a house or a herd of sheep."

It's true that Job suffered greatly. But because of his attitude, God brought good out of it. Job did not blame the Lord and say, "Why did You let this happen, God?" Instead, he said that life contains good and bad situations, and we should accept each with the same amount of reverence for God. The Bible says to "consider blessed those who have persevered. You have heard of Job's perseverance and have seen what the Lord finally brought about. The Lord is full of compassion and mercy" (James 5:11). No matter what difficult time we go through, there will be a time when life is good again.

What a powerful illustration of what we should do in response to tragedy in our own lives. God gives us what we have, and He takes it away as He sees fit. We are to praise Him for all of it. We won't always know the reason for our suffering, but we can know that God allows things to happen to us for His purpose. This doesn't make our suffering any easier, but it does give us hope for the future.

Don't give up in the midst of great loss, disappointment, or failure, or you will miss the greatest miracle in your life. If instead you praise God through it, you will see the birth of something new and good.

---

ing through the earth and going back and forth in it."

⁸Then the LORD said to Satan, "Have you considered my servant Job? There is no one on earth like him; he is blameless and upright, a man who fears God and shuns evil."

⁹"Does Job fear God for nothing?" Sa- tan replied. ¹⁰"Have you not put a hedge around him and his household and everything he has? You have blessed the work of his hands, so that his flocks and herds are spread throughout the land. ¹¹But stretch out your hand and strike everything he has, and he will surely curse you to your face."

12The LORD said to Satan, "Very well, then, everything he has is in your hands, but on the man himself do not lay a finger."

Then Satan went out from the presence of the LORD.

13One day when Job's sons and daughters were feasting and drinking wine at the oldest brother's house, 14a messenger came to Job and said, "The oxen were plowing and the donkeys were grazing nearby, 15and the Sabeans attacked and carried them off. They put the servants to the sword, and I am the only one who has escaped to tell you!"

16While he was still speaking, another messenger came and said, "The fire of God fell from the sky and burned up the sheep and the servants, and I am the only one who has escaped to tell you!"

17While he was still speaking, another messenger came and said, "The Chaldeans formed three raiding parties and swept down on your camels and carried them off. They put the servants to the sword, and I am the only one who has escaped to tell you!"

18While he was still speaking, yet another messenger came and said, "Your sons and daughters were feasting and drinking wine at the oldest brother's house, 19when suddenly a mighty wind swept in from the desert and struck the four corners of the house. It collapsed on them and they are dead, and I am the only one who has escaped to tell you!"

20At this, Job got up and tore his robe and shaved his head. Then he fell to the ground in worship 21and said:

"Naked I came from my mother's
    womb,
  and naked I will depart.a
The LORD gave and the LORD has
    taken away;
  may the name of the LORD be
    praised."

22In all this, Job did not sin by charging God with wrongdoing.

Job's Second Test

2 On another day the angelsb came to present themselves before the LORD, and Satan also came with them to present himself before him. 2And the LORD said to Satan, "Where have you come from?"

Satan answered the LORD, "From roaming through the earth and going back and forth in it."

3Then the LORD said to Satan, "Have you considered my servant Job? There is no one on earth like him; he is blameless and upright, a man who fears God and shuns evil. And he still maintains his integrity, though you incited me against him to ruin him without any reason."

4"Skin for skin!" Satan replied. "A man will give all he has for his own life. 5But stretch out your hand and strike his flesh and bones, and he will surely curse you to your face."

6The LORD said to Satan, "Very well, then, he is in your hands; but you must spare his life."

7So Satan went out from the presence of the LORD and afflicted Job with painful sores from the soles of his feet to the top of his head. 8Then Job took a piece of broken pottery and scraped himself with it as he sat among the ashes.

9His wife said to him, "Are you still holding on to your integrity? Curse God and die!"

10He replied, "You are talking like a foolishc woman. Shall we accept good from God, and not trouble?"

In all this, Job did not sin in what he said.

Job's Three Friends

11When Job's three friends, Eliphaz the Temanite, Bildad the Shuhite and Zophar the Naamathite, heard about all the troubles that had come upon him, they set out from their homes and met together by agreement to go and sympathize with him and comfort him. 12When they saw him from a distance, they could hardly recognize him; they began to weep aloud,

---

a 21 Or will return there   b 1 Hebrew the sons of God   c 10 The Hebrew word rendered foolish denotes moral deficiency.

Facing Your Fears

GOING *deeper*

READ AND CONSIDER: JOB 3:1-26

"What I feared has come upon me; what I dreaded has happened to me. I have no peace, no quietness; I have no rest, but only turmoil" (Job 3:25-26).

Job was considered by God to be a righteous man, yet Job had fear. He feared something happening to his children. He feared failing health. He feared losing everything. When each one of these fears came true, he said, "I have no rest, but only turmoil." Overwhelmed with grief, Job wished he had never been born. He had lived according to God's laws, had worshiped God rather than his possessions, and still he was afflicted. Who can criticize Job for his reaction? How many of us have lost everything—including our children, health, and possessions? How would we respond to such a horrible situation?

When the thing we fear most comes upon us, the only way to react is to praise God in the midst of it. That doesn't mean we have to act as though nothing bad has happened. Besides, healthy grief is important. But we must still recognize the things about God that are always true no matter what is happening and how afraid we are.

Whatever your deepest fears are right now, bring every one of them to God. Thank Him that He is greater than any of them. Thank Him that in His presence all fear is gone. "Blessed is the man who fears the LORD, who finds great delight in his commands ... He will have no fear of bad news; his heart is steadfast, trusting in the LORD (Psalm 112:1,7).

God's love can take away your fear. His love gives the power to stand against the enemy of your soul when he wants fear to overwhelm you. And even if your worst fears do come upon you, God's love assures you that He will walk with you every step of the way toward restoration.

and they tore their robes and sprinkled dust on their heads. ¹³Then they sat on the ground with him for seven days and seven nights. No one said a word to him, because they saw how great his suffering was.

Job Speaks

3 After this, Job opened his mouth and cursed the day of his birth. ²He said:

³ "May the day of my birth perish,
    and the night it was said, 'A boy is
        born!'
⁴ That day—may it turn to darkness;
    may God above not care about it;
    may no light shine upon it.
⁵ May darkness and deep shadowᵃ claim
        it once more;
    may a cloud settle over it;

may blackness overwhelm its light.
⁶ That night—may thick darkness seize
        it;
    may it not be included among the
        days of the year
    nor be entered in any of the
        months.
⁷ May that night be barren;
    may no shout of joy be heard in it.
⁸ May those who curse daysᵇ curse that
        day,
    those who are ready to rouse
        Leviathan.
⁹ May its morning stars become dark;
    may it wait for daylight in vain
    and not see the first rays of dawn,
¹⁰ for it did not shut the doors of the
        womb on me
    to hide trouble from my eyes.

ᵃ 5 Or *and the shadow of death*   ᵇ 8 Or *the sea*

11"Why did I not perish at birth,
    and die as I came from the womb?
12Why were there knees to receive me
    and breasts that I might be nursed?
13For now I would be lying down in
        peace;
    I would be asleep and at rest
14with kings and counselors of the earth,
    who built for themselves places
        now lying in ruins,
15with rulers who had gold,
    who filled their houses with silver.
16Or why was I not hidden in the
        ground like a stillborn child,
    like an infant who never saw the
        light of day?
17There the wicked cease from turmoil,
    and there the weary are at rest.
18Captives also enjoy their ease;
    they no longer hear the slave
        driver's shout.
19The small and the great are there,
    and the slave is freed from his
        master.

20"Why is light given to those in misery,
    and life to the bitter of soul,
21to those who long for death that does
        not come,
    who search for it more than for
        hidden treasure,
22who are filled with gladness
    and rejoice when they reach the
        grave?
23Why is life given to a man
    whose way is hidden,
    whom God has hedged in?
24For sighing comes to me instead of
        food;
    my groans pour out like water.
25What I feared has come upon me;
    what I dreaded has happened to me.
26I have no peace, no quietness;
    I have no rest, but only turmoil."

Eliphaz

4 Then Eliphaz the Temanite replied:

2"If someone ventures a word with
        you, will you be impatient?
But who can keep from speaking?
3Think how you have instructed
        many,
    how you have strengthened feeble
        hands.
4Your words have supported those
        who stumbled;
    you have strengthened faltering
        knees.
5But now trouble comes to you, and
        you are discouraged;
    it strikes you, and you are
        dismayed.
6Should not your piety be your
        confidence
    and your blameless ways your hope?

7"Consider now: Who, being
        innocent, has ever perished?
    Where were the upright ever
        destroyed?
8As I have observed, those who plow
        evil
    and those who sow trouble reap it.
9At the breath of God they are
        destroyed;
    at the blast of his anger they perish.
10The lions may roar and growl,
    yet the teeth of the great lions are
        broken.
11The lion perishes for lack of prey,
    and the cubs of the lioness are
        scattered.

12"A word was secretly brought to me,
    my ears caught a whisper of it.
13Amid disquieting dreams in the
        night,
    when deep sleep falls on men,
14fear and trembling seized me
    and made all my bones shake.
15A spirit glided past my face,
    and the hair on my body stood on
        end.
16It stopped,
    but I could not tell what it was.
A form stood before my eyes,
    and I heard a hushed voice:
17'Can a mortal be more righteous than
        God?

Can a man be more pure than his
   Maker?
18If God places no trust in his servants,
   if he charges his angels with error,
19how much more those who live in
      houses of clay,
   whose foundations are in the dust,
   who are crushed more readily than
      a moth!
20Between dawn and dusk they are
      broken to pieces;
   unnoticed, they perish forever.
21Are not the cords of their tent pulled
      up,
   so that they die without wisdom?'ᵃ

5 "Call if you will, but who will
   answer you?
   To which of the holy ones will you
      turn?
2Resentment kills a fool,
   and envy slays the simple.
3I myself have seen a fool taking root,
   but suddenly his house was cursed.
4His children are far from safety,
   crushed in court without a
      defender.
5The hungry consume his harvest,
   taking it even from among thorns,
   and the thirsty pant after his wealth.
6For hardship does not spring from the
      soil,
   nor does trouble sprout from the
      ground.
7Yet man is born to trouble
   as surely as sparks fly upward.

8"But if it were I, I would appeal to
      God;
   I would lay my cause before him.
9He performs wonders that cannot be
      fathomed,
   miracles that cannot be counted.
10He bestows rain on the earth;
   he sends water upon the
      countryside.
11The lowly he sets on high,
   and those who mourn are lifted to
      safety.

12He thwarts the plans of the crafty,
   so that their hands achieve no
      success.
13He catches the wise in their
      craftiness,
   and the schemes of the wily are
      swept away.
14Darkness comes upon them in the
      daytime;
   at noon they grope as in the night.
15He saves the needy from the sword in
      their mouth;
   he saves them from the clutches of
      the powerful.
16So the poor have hope,
   and injustice shuts its mouth.

17"Blessed is the man whom God
      corrects;
   so do not despise the discipline of
      the Almighty.ᵇ
18For he wounds, but he also binds up;
   he injures, but his hands also heal.
19From six calamities he will rescue
      you;
   in seven no harm will befall you.
20In famine he will ransom you from
      death,
   and in battle from the stroke of the
      sword.
21You will be protected from the lash
      of the tongue,
   and need not fear when destruction
      comes.
22You will laugh at destruction and
      famine,
   and need not fear the beasts of the
      earth.
23For you will have a covenant with the
      stones of the field,
   and the wild animals will be at
      peace with you.
24You will know that your tent is
      secure;
   you will take stock of your
      property and find nothing
      missing.
25You will know that your children
      will be many,

ᵃ21 Some interpreters end the quotation after verse 17.   ᵇ17 Hebrew *Shaddai*; here and throughout Job

and your descendants like the grass
    of the earth.
26 You will come to the grave in full
    vigor,
  like sheaves gathered in season.

27 "We have examined this, and it is
    true.
  So hear it and apply it to yourself."

Job

6 Then Job replied:

2 "If only my anguish could be weighed
  and all my misery be placed on the
    scales!
3 It would surely outweigh the sand of
    the seas—
  no wonder my words have been
    impetuous.
4 The arrows of the Almighty are in
    me,
  my spirit drinks in their poison;
  God's terrors are marshaled against
    me.
5 Does a wild donkey bray when it has
    grass,
  or an ox bellow when it has fodder?
6 Is tasteless food eaten without salt,
  or is there flavor in the white of an
    egg^a?
7 I refuse to touch it;
  such food makes me ill.

8 "Oh, that I might have my request,
  that God would grant what I hope
    for,
9 that God would be willing to crush
    me,
  to let loose his hand and cut me off!
10 Then I would still have this
    consolation—
  my joy in unrelenting pain—
  that I had not denied the words of
    the Holy One.

11 "What strength do I have, that I
    should still hope?
  What prospects, that I should be
    patient?
12 Do I have the strength of stone?
  Is my flesh bronze?
13 Do I have any power to help myself,
  now that success has been driven
    from me?

14 "A despairing man should have the
    devotion of his friends,
  even though he forsakes the fear of
    the Almighty.
15 But my brothers are as undependable
    as intermittent streams,
  as the streams that overflow
16 when darkened by thawing ice
  and swollen with melting snow,
17 but that cease to flow in the dry
    season,
  and in the heat vanish from their
    channels.
18 Caravans turn aside from their routes;
  they go up into the wasteland and
    perish.
19 The caravans of Tema look for water,
  the traveling merchants of Sheba
    look in hope.
20 They are distressed, because they had
    been confident;
  they arrive there, only to be
    disappointed.
21 Now you too have proved to be of no
    help;
  you see something dreadful and are
    afraid.
22 Have I ever said, 'Give something on
    my behalf,
  pay a ransom for me from your
    wealth,
23 deliver me from the hand of the
    enemy,
  ransom me from the clutches of the
    ruthless'?

24 "Teach me, and I will be quiet;
  show me where I have been wrong.
25 How painful are honest words!
  But what do your arguments prove?
26 Do you mean to correct what I say,
  and treat the words of a despairing
    man as wind?

---

^a 6 The meaning of the Hebrew for this phrase is uncertain.

27 You would even cast lots for the
fatherless
and barter away your friend.

28 "But now be so kind as to look at me.
Would I lie to your face?
29 Relent, do not be unjust;
reconsider, for my integrity is at
stake.[a]
30 Is there any wickedness on my lips?
Can my mouth not discern malice?

7 "Does not man have hard service on
earth?
Are not his days like those of a
hired man?
2 Like a slave longing for the evening
shadows,

or a hired man waiting eagerly for
his wages,
3 so I have been allotted months of
futility,
and nights of misery have been
assigned to me.
4 When I lie down I think, 'How long
before I get up?'
The night drags on, and I toss till
dawn.
5 My body is clothed with worms and
scabs,
my skin is broken and festering.

6 "My days are swifter than a weaver's
shuttle,
and they come to an end without
hope.

a 29 Or my righteousness still stands

GOING deeper

Knowing God Is With You

READ AND CONSIDER: JOB 7:1-21

"What is man that you make so much of him, that you give him so much attention?" (Job 7:17).

Job was at the end of his rope. He was suffering greatly, with no understanding of why. His question came out of his frustration. In essence, he was saying, "We're worthless, God, so stop paying attention to us humans! Maybe then we'd be left in peace. Maybe then we wouldn't be tested and examined and constantly found wanting."

Job knew he wasn't a hypocrite. He knew he'd lived a life pleasing to God. In his pain he lashed out at God. But his friends concluded that he must have committed some horrible sin in order to deserve such unbearable punishment. Surely they understood that all people suffer—yet the extent of Job's suffering seemed to need an explanation.

When we are careful to obey God's rules and directions for our lives and repent when we sin, we may feel as if we should be exempt from suffering. After all, why would God allow faithful people to endure such hardships? But God uses difficulties, pain, suffering, and trials to make us stronger, wiser, and more able to comfort others.

God is the Lord, the Savior of our souls, the Lover of our hearts. He isn't sitting up in heaven watching us in our misery. He is with us every step of the way, working His perfect will in our lives.

God says, "As the heavens are higher than the earth, so are my ways higher than your ways and my thoughts than your thoughts" (Isaiah 55:9). You may not understand your suffering, just as you cannot understand the depth of God's love for you. But keep open the lines of communication between you and Him. If you feel angry because of your situation, tell Him. He understands. As you praise Him for who He is, He will heal your heart and bring good out of the situation.

⁷Remember, O God, that my life is
  but a breath;
  my eyes will never see happiness
  again.
⁸The eye that now sees me will see me
  no longer;
  you will look for me, but I will be
  no more.
⁹As a cloud vanishes and is gone,
  so he who goes down to the graveᵃ
  does not return.
¹⁰He will never come to his house
  again;
  his place will know him no more.

¹¹"Therefore I will not keep silent;
  I will speak out in the anguish of
  my spirit,
  I will complain in the bitterness of
  my soul.
¹²Am I the sea, or the monster of the
  deep,
  that you put me under guard?
¹³When I think my bed will comfort
  me
  and my couch will ease my
  complaint,
¹⁴even then you frighten me with
  dreams
  and terrify me with visions,
¹⁵so that I prefer strangling and death,
  rather than this body of mine.
¹⁶I despise my life; I would not live
  forever.
  Let me alone; my days have no
  meaning.

¹⁷"What is man that you make so much
  of him,
  that you give him so much
  attention,
¹⁸that you examine him every morning
  and test him every moment?
¹⁹Will you never look away from me,
  or let me alone even for an instant?
²⁰If I have sinned, what have I done to
  you,
  O watcher of men?

Why have you made me your target?
  Have I become a burden to you?ᵇ
²¹Why do you not pardon my offenses
  and forgive my sins?
For I will soon lie down in the dust;
  you will search for me, but I will be
  no more."

Bildad

8 Then Bildad the Shuhite replied:

²"How long will you say such
  things?
  Your words are a blustering wind.
³Does God pervert justice?
  Does the Almighty pervert what is
  right?
⁴When your children sinned against
  him,
  he gave them over to the penalty of
  their sin.
⁵But if you will look to God
  and plead with the Almighty,
⁶if you are pure and upright,
  even now he will rouse himself on
  your behalf
  and restore you to your rightful
  place.
⁷Your beginnings will seem humble,
  so prosperous will your future be.

⁸"Ask the former generations
  and find out what their fathers
  learned,
⁹for we were born only yesterday and
  know nothing,
  and our days on earth are but a
  shadow.
¹⁰Will they not instruct you and tell
  you?
  Will they not bring forth words
  from their understanding?
¹¹Can papyrus grow tall where there is
  no marsh?
  Can reeds thrive without water?
¹²While still growing and uncut,
  they wither more quickly than
  grass.

ᵃ 9 Hebrew Sheol   ᵇ 20 A few manuscripts of the Masoretic Text, an ancient Hebrew scribal tradition and Septuagint; most manuscripts of the Masoretic Text I have become a burden to myself.

¹³Such is the destiny of all who forget God;
so perishes the hope of the godless.
¹⁴What he trusts in is fragile^a;
what he relies on is a spider's web.
¹⁵He leans on his web, but it gives way;
he clings to it, but it does not hold.
¹⁶He is like a well-watered plant in the sunshine,
spreading its shoots over the garden;
¹⁷it entwines its roots around a pile of rocks
and looks for a place among the stones.
¹⁸But when it is torn from its spot,
that place disowns it and says, 'I never saw you.'
¹⁹Surely its life withers away,
and^b from the soil other plants grow.

²⁰"Surely God does not reject a blameless man
or strengthen the hands of evildoers.
²¹He will yet fill your mouth with laughter
and your lips with shouts of joy.
²²Your enemies will be clothed in shame,
and the tents of the wicked will be no more."

Job

9 Then Job replied:

²"Indeed, I know that this is true.
But how can a mortal be righteous before God?
³Though one wished to dispute with him,
he could not answer him one time out of a thousand.
⁴His wisdom is profound, his power is vast.
Who has resisted him and come out unscathed?

⁵He moves mountains without their knowing it
and overturns them in his anger.
⁶He shakes the earth from its place
and makes its pillars tremble.
⁷He speaks to the sun and it does not shine;
he seals off the light of the stars.
⁸He alone stretches out the heavens
and treads on the waves of the sea.
⁹He is the Maker of the Bear and Orion,
the Pleiades and the constellations of the south.
¹⁰He performs wonders that cannot be fathomed,
miracles that cannot be counted.
¹¹When he passes me, I cannot see him;
when he goes by, I cannot perceive him.
¹²If he snatches away, who can stop him?
Who can say to him, 'What are you doing?'
¹³God does not restrain his anger;
even the cohorts of Rahab cowered at his feet.

¹⁴"How then can I dispute with him?
How can I find words to argue with him?
¹⁵Though I were innocent, I could not answer him;
I could only plead with my Judge for mercy.
¹⁶Even if I summoned him and he responded,
I do not believe he would give me a hearing.
¹⁷He would crush me with a storm
and multiply my wounds for no reason.
¹⁸He would not let me regain my breath
but would overwhelm me with misery.
¹⁹If it is a matter of strength, he is mighty!

---

^a 14 The meaning of the Hebrew for this word is uncertain.   ^b 19 Or *Surely all the joy it has / is that*

And if it is a matter of justice, who
  will summon him[a]?

²⁰Even if I were innocent, my mouth
  would condemn me;
  if I were blameless, it would
  pronounce me guilty.

²¹"Although I am blameless,
  I have no concern for myself;
  I despise my own life.

²²It is all the same; that is why I say,
  'He destroys both the blameless and
  the wicked.'

²³When a scourge brings sudden death,
  he mocks the despair of the
  innocent.

²⁴When a land falls into the hands of
  the wicked,
  he blindfolds its judges.
  If it is not he, then who is it?

²⁵"My days are swifter than a runner;
  they fly away without a glimpse of
  joy.

²⁶They skim past like boats of papyrus,
  like eagles swooping down on their
  prey.

²⁷If I say, 'I will forget my complaint,
  I will change my expression, and
  smile,'

²⁸I still dread all my sufferings,
  for I know you will not hold me
  innocent.

²⁹Since I am already found guilty,
  why should I struggle in vain?

³⁰Even if I washed myself with soap[b]
  and my hands with washing soda,

³¹you would plunge me into a slime pit
  so that even my clothes would
  detest me.

³²"He is not a man like me that I might
  answer him,
  that we might confront each other
  in court.

³³If only there were someone to
  arbitrate between us,
  to lay his hand upon us both,

³⁴someone to remove God's rod from
  me,

so that his terror would frighten me
  no more.

³⁵Then I would speak up without fear
  of him,
  but as it now stands with me, I
  cannot.

10 "I loathe my very life;
  therefore I will give free rein to
  my complaint
  and speak out in the bitterness of
  my soul.

²I will say to God: Do not condemn
  me,
  but tell me what charges you have
  against me.

³Does it please you to oppress me,
  to spurn the work of your hands,
  while you smile on the schemes of
  the wicked?

⁴Do you have eyes of flesh?
  Do you see as a mortal sees?

⁵Are your days like those of a mortal
  or your years like those of a man,

⁶that you must search out my faults
  and probe after my sin—

⁷though you know that I am not
  guilty
  and that no one can rescue me from
  your hand?

⁸"Your hands shaped me and made
  me.
  Will you now turn and destroy me?

⁹Remember that you molded me like
  clay.
  Will you now turn me to dust
  again?

¹⁰Did you not pour me out like milk
  and curdle me like cheese,

¹¹clothe me with skin and flesh
  and knit me together with bones
  and sinews?

¹²You gave me life and showed me
  kindness,
  and in your providence watched
  over my spirit.

¹³"But this is what you concealed in
  your heart,

---

[a] 19 See Septuagint; Hebrew *me*. [b] 30 Or *snow*

and I know that this was in your mind:

¹⁴If I sinned, you would be watching me
and would not let my offense go unpunished.

¹⁵If I am guilty—woe to me!
Even if I am innocent, I cannot lift my head,
for I am full of shame
and drowned in° my affliction.

¹⁶If I hold my head high, you stalk me like a lion
and again display your awesome power against me.

¹⁷You bring new witnesses against me
and increase your anger toward me;
your forces come against me wave upon wave.

¹⁸"Why then did you bring me out of the womb?
I wish I had died before any eye saw me.

¹⁹If only I had never come into being,
or had been carried straight from the womb to the grave!

²⁰Are not my few days almost over?
Turn away from me so I can have a moment's joy

²¹before I go to the place of no return,
to the land of gloom and deep shadow,ᵇ

²²to the land of deepest night,
of deep shadow and disorder,
where even the light is like darkness."

Zophar

11 Then Zophar the Naamathite replied:

²"Are all these words to go unanswered?
Is this talker to be vindicated?

³Will your idle talk reduce men to silence?
Will no one rebuke you when you mock?

⁴You say to God, 'My beliefs are flawless
and I am pure in your sight.'

⁵Oh, how I wish that God would speak,
that he would open his lips against you

⁶and disclose to you the secrets of wisdom,
for true wisdom has two sides.
Know this: God has even forgotten some of your sin.

⁷"Can you fathom the mysteries of God?
Can you probe the limits of the Almighty?

⁸They are higher than the heavens— what can you do?
They are deeper than the depths of the graveᶜ—what can you know?

⁹Their measure is longer than the earth
and wider than the sea.

¹⁰"If he comes along and confines you in prison
and convenes a court, who can oppose him?

¹¹Surely he recognizes deceitful men;
and when he sees evil, does he not take note?

¹²But a witless man can no more become wise
than a wild donkey's colt can be born a man.ᵈ

¹³"Yet if you devote your heart to him
and stretch out your hands to him,

¹⁴if you put away the sin that is in your hand
and allow no evil to dwell in your tent,

¹⁵then you will lift up your face without shame;
you will stand firm and without fear.

¹⁶You will surely forget your trouble,

ᵃ 15 Or and aware of   ᵇ 21 Or and the shadow of death; also in verse 22   ᶜ 8 Hebrew than Sheol   ᵈ 12 Or wild donkey can be born tame

recalling it only as waters gone by.
17Life will be brighter than noonday,
and darkness will become like
morning.
18You will be secure, because there is
hope;
you will look about you and take
your rest in safety.
19You will lie down, with no one to
make you afraid,
and many will court your favor.
20But the eyes of the wicked will fail,
and escape will elude them;
their hope will become a dying
gasp."

Job

12 Then Job replied:

2"Doubtless you are the people,
and wisdom will die with you!
3But I have a mind as well as you;
I am not inferior to you.
Who does not know all these
things?

4"I have become a laughingstock to
my friends,
though I called upon God and he
answered—
a mere laughingstock, though
righteous and blameless!
5Men at ease have contempt for
misfortune
as the fate of those whose feet are
slipping.
6The tents of marauders are
undisturbed,
and those who provoke God are
secure—
those who carry their god in their
hands.ᵃ

7"But ask the animals, and they will
teach you,
or the birds of the air, and they will
tell you;
8or speak to the earth, and it will teach
you,
or let the fish of the sea inform you.

9Which of all these does not know
that the hand of the LORD has done
this?
10In his hand is the life of every
creature
and the breath of all mankind.
11Does not the ear test words
as the tongue tastes food?
12Is not wisdom found among the aged?
Does not long life bring
understanding?

13"To God belong wisdom and power;
counsel and understanding are his.
14What he tears down cannot be
rebuilt;
the man he imprisons cannot be
released.
15If he holds back the waters, there is
drought;
if he lets them loose, they devastate
the land.
16To him belong strength and victory;
both deceived and deceiver are his.
17He leads counselors away stripped
and makes fools of judges.
18He takes off the shackles put on by
kings
and ties a loincloth ᵇ around their
waist.
19He leads priests away stripped
and overthrows men long
established.
20He silences the lips of trusted advisers
and takes away the discernment of
elders.
21He pours contempt on nobles
and disarms the mighty.
22He reveals the deep things of darkness
and brings deep shadows into the
light.
23He makes nations great, and destroys
them;
he enlarges nations, and disperses
them.
24He deprives the leaders of the earth of
their reason;
he sends them wandering through a
trackless waste.

ᵃ 6 Or secure / in what God's hand brings them   ᵇ 18 Or shackles of kings / and ties a belt

²⁵They grope in darkness with no light;
    he makes them stagger like
        drunkards.

¹³ "My eyes have seen all this,
    my ears have heard and
        understood it.
²What you know, I also know;
    I am not inferior to you.
³But I desire to speak to the Almighty
    and to argue my case with God.
⁴You, however, smear me with lies;
    you are worthless physicians, all of
        you!
⁵If only you would be altogether
        silent!
    For you, that would be wisdom.
⁶Hear now my argument;
    listen to the plea of my lips.
⁷Will you speak wickedly on God's
        behalf?
    Will you speak deceitfully for
        him?
⁸Will you show him partiality?
    Will you argue the case for God?
⁹Would it turn out well if he
        examined you?
    Could you deceive him as you
        might deceive men?
¹⁰He would surely rebuke you
    if you secretly showed partiality.
¹¹Would not his splendor terrify you?
    Would not the dread of him fall on
        you?
¹²Your maxims are proverbs of ashes;
    your defenses are defenses of clay.

¹³"Keep silent and let me speak;
    then let come to me what may.
¹⁴Why do I put myself in jeopardy
    and take my life in my hands?

Praying Job 13:15
Lord, may I trust You in the
hard times with the same faith
as when things are going well.

¹⁵Though he slay me, yet will I hope in
        him;

^a 15 Or *He will surely slay me; I have no hope — / yet I will*

    I will surely^a defend my ways to his
        face.
¹⁶Indeed, this will turn out for my
        deliverance,
    for no godless man would dare
        come before him!
¹⁷Listen carefully to my words;
    let your ears take in what I say.
¹⁸Now that I have prepared my case,
    I know I will be vindicated.
¹⁹Can anyone bring charges against
        me?
    If so, I will be silent and die.

²⁰"Only grant me these two things,
        O God,
    and then I will not hide from you:
²¹Withdraw your hand far from me,
    and stop frightening me with your
        terrors.
²²Then summon me and I will answer,
    or let me speak, and you reply.
²³How many wrongs and sins have I
        committed?
    Show me my offense and my sin.
²⁴Why do you hide your face
    and consider me your enemy?
²⁵Will you torment a windblown leaf?
    Will you chase after dry chaff?
²⁶For you write down bitter things
        against me
    and make me inherit the sins of my
        youth.
²⁷You fasten my feet in shackles;
    you keep close watch on all my
        paths
    by putting marks on the soles of my
        feet.

²⁸"So man wastes away like something
        rotten,
    like a garment eaten by moths.

¹⁴ "Man born of woman
    is of few days and full of trouble.
²He springs up like a flower and
        withers away;
    like a fleeting shadow, he does not
        endure.
³Do you fix your eye on such a one?

Will you bring him[a] before you for
  judgment?
4 Who can bring what is pure from the
  impure?
  No one!
5 Man's days are determined;
  you have decreed the number of his
    months
  and have set limits he cannot
    exceed.
6 So look away from him and let him
    alone,
  till he has put in his time like a
    hired man.

7 "At least there is hope for a tree:
  If it is cut down, it will sprout
    again,
  and its new shoots will not fail.
8 Its roots may grow old in the
    ground
  and its stump die in the soil,
9 yet at the scent of water it will bud
  and put forth shoots like a plant.
10 But man dies and is laid low;
  he breathes his last and is no more.
11 As water disappears from the sea
  or a riverbed becomes parched and
    dry,
12 so man lies down and does not rise;
  till the heavens are no more, men
    will not awake
  or be roused from their sleep.

13 "If only you would hide me in the
    grave[b]
  and conceal me till your anger has
    passed!
  If only you would set me a time
  and then remember me!
14 If a man dies, will he live again?
  All the days of my hard service
  I will wait for my renewal[c] to
    come.
15 You will call and I will answer you;
  you will long for the creature your
    hands have made.
16 Surely then you will count my steps
  but not keep track of my sin.

17 My offenses will be sealed up in a
    bag;
  you will cover over my sin.

18 "But as a mountain erodes and
    crumbles
  and as a rock is moved from its
    place,
19 as water wears away stones
  and torrents wash away the soil,
  so you destroy man's hope.
20 You overpower him once for all, and
    he is gone;
  you change his countenance and
    send him away.
21 If his sons are honored, he does not
    know it;
  if they are brought low, he does not
    see it.
22 He feels but the pain of his own body
  and mourns only for himself."

Eliphaz

15 Then Eliphaz the Temanite replied:

2 "Would a wise man answer with
    empty notions
  or fill his belly with the hot east
    wind?
3 Would he argue with useless words,
  with speeches that have no value?
4 But you even undermine piety
  and hinder devotion to God.
5 Your sin prompts your mouth;
  you adopt the tongue of the crafty.
6 Your own mouth condemns you, not
    mine;
  your own lips testify against you.

7 "Are you the first man ever born?
  Were you brought forth before the
    hills?
8 Do you listen in on God's council?
  Do you limit wisdom to yourself?
9 What do you know that we do not
    know?
  What insights do you have that we
    do not have?
10 The gray-haired and the aged are on
    our side,

---

a 3 Septuagint, Vulgate and Syriac; Hebrew me   b 13 Hebrew Sheol   c 14 Or release

men even older than your father.
[11]Are God's consolations not enough
for you,
words spoken gently to you?
[12]Why has your heart carried you away,
and why do your eyes flash,
[13]so that you vent your rage against
God
and pour out such words from your
mouth?

[14]"What is man, that he could be pure,
or one born of woman, that he
could be righteous?

Prayer is . . .

*the way you find comfort
from life's pain.*

---

[15]If God places no trust in his holy ones,
if even the heavens are not pure in
his eyes,
[16]how much less man, who is vile and
corrupt,
who drinks up evil like water!

[17]"Listen to me and I will explain to
you;
let me tell you what I have seen,
[18]what wise men have declared,
hiding nothing received from their
fathers
[19](to whom alone the land was given
when no alien passed among them):
[20]All his days the wicked man suffers
torment,
the ruthless through all the years
stored up for him.
[21]Terrifying sounds fill his ears;
when all seems well, marauders
attack him.
[22]He despairs of escaping the darkness;
he is marked for the sword.
[23]He wanders about—food for
vultures[a];

he knows the day of darkness is at
hand.
[24]Distress and anguish fill him with
terror;
they overwhelm him, like a king
poised to attack,
[25]because he shakes his fist at God
and vaunts himself against the
Almighty,
[26]defiantly charging against him
with a thick, strong shield.

[27]"Though his face is covered with fat
and his waist bulges with flesh,
[28]he will inhabit ruined towns
and houses where no one lives,
houses crumbling to rubble.
[29]He will no longer be rich and his
wealth will not endure,
nor will his possessions spread over
the land.
[30]He will not escape the darkness;
a flame will wither his shoots,
and the breath of God's mouth will
carry him away.
[31]Let him not deceive himself by
trusting what is worthless,
for he will get nothing in return.
[32]Before his time he will be paid in full,
and his branches will not flourish.
[33]He will be like a vine stripped of its
unripe grapes,
like an olive tree shedding its
blossoms.
[34]For the company of the godless will
be barren,
and fire will consume the tents of
those who love bribes.
[35]They conceive trouble and give birth
to evil;
their womb fashions deceit."

Job

16 Then Job replied:

[2]"I have heard many things like these;
miserable comforters are you all!
[3]Will your long-winded speeches
never end?

---

[a] 23 Or *about, looking for food*

What ails you that you keep on
    arguing?
⁴I also could speak like you,
    if you were in my place;
I could make fine speeches against
    you
    and shake my head at you.
⁵But my mouth would encourage you;
    comfort from my lips would bring
        you relief.

⁶"Yet if I speak, my pain is not
    relieved;
    and if I refrain, it does not go
        away.
⁷Surely, O God, you have worn me
    out;
    you have devastated my entire
        household.
⁸You have bound me—and it has
    become a witness;
    my gauntness rises up and testifies
        against me.
⁹God assails me and tears me in his
    anger
    and gnashes his teeth at me;
    my opponent fastens on me his
        piercing eyes.
¹⁰Men open their mouths to jeer at me;
    they strike my cheek in scorn
    and unite together against me.
¹¹God has turned me over to evil men
    and thrown me into the clutches of
        the wicked.
¹²All was well with me, but he
    shattered me;
    he seized me by the neck and
        crushed me.
    He has made me his target;
¹³   his archers surround me.
    Without pity, he pierces my kidneys
    and spills my gall on the ground.
¹⁴Again and again he bursts upon me;
    he rushes at me like a warrior.

¹⁵"I have sewed sackcloth over my skin
    and buried my brow in the dust.
¹⁶My face is red with weeping,
    deep shadows ring my eyes;

¹⁷yet my hands have been free of
    violence
    and my prayer is pure.

¹⁸"O earth, do not cover my blood;
    may my cry never be laid to rest!
¹⁹Even now my witness is in heaven;
    my advocate is on high.
²⁰My intercessor is my friendᵃ
    as my eyes pour out tears to God;
²¹on behalf of a man he pleads with God
    as a man pleads for his friend.

²²"Only a few years will pass
    before I go on the journey of no
        return.

17 ¹My spirit is broken,
    my days are cut short,
    the grave awaits me.
²Surely mockers surround me;
    my eyes must dwell on their
        hostility.

³"Give me, O God, the pledge you
    demand.
    Who else will put up security for
        me?
⁴You have closed their minds to
    understanding;
    therefore you will not let them
        triumph.
⁵If a man denounces his friends for
    reward,
    the eyes of his children will fail.

⁶"God has made me a byword to
    everyone,
    a man in whose face people spit.
⁷My eyes have grown dim with grief;
    my whole frame is but a shadow.
⁸Upright men are appalled at this;
    the innocent are aroused against the
        ungodly.
⁹Nevertheless, the righteous will hold
    to their ways,
    and those with clean hands will
        grow stronger.
¹⁰"But come on, all of you, try again!
    I will not find a wise man among
        you.

ᵃ20 Or My friends treat me with scorn

11My days have passed, my plans are
      shattered,
   and so are the desires of my heart.
12These men turn night into day;
   in the face of darkness they say,
      'Light is near.'
13If the only home I hope for is the
      grave,[a]
   if I spread out my bed in darkness,
14if I say to corruption, 'You are my
      father,'
   and to the worm, 'My mother' or
      'My sister,'
15where then is my hope?
   Who can see any hope for me?
16Will it go down to the gates of
      death[a]?
   Will we descend together into the
      dust?"

Bildad

18 Then Bildad the Shuhite replied:

2"When will you end these speeches?
   Be sensible, and then we can talk.
3Why are we regarded as cattle
   and considered stupid in your
      sight?
4You who tear yourself to pieces in
      your anger,
   is the earth to be abandoned for
      your sake?
   Or must the rocks be moved from
      their place?

5"The lamp of the wicked is snuffed
      out;
   the flame of his fire stops burning.
6The light in his tent becomes dark;
   the lamp beside him goes out.
7The vigor of his step is weakened;
   his own schemes throw him down.
8His feet thrust him into a net
   and he wanders into its mesh.
9A trap seizes him by the heel;
   a snare holds him fast.
10A noose is hidden for him on the
      ground;
   a trap lies in his path.

11Terrors startle him on every side
   and dog his every step.
12Calamity is hungry for him;
   disaster is ready for him when he
      falls.
13It eats away parts of his skin;
   death's firstborn devours his limbs.
14He is torn from the security of his
      tent
   and marched off to the king of
      terrors.
15Fire resides[b] in his tent;
   burning sulfur is scattered over his
      dwelling.
16His roots dry up below
   and his branches wither above.
17The memory of him perishes from
      the earth;
   he has no name in the land.
18He is driven from light into darkness
   and is banished from the world.
19He has no offspring or descendants
      among his people,
   no survivor where once he lived.
20Men of the west are appalled at his
      fate;
   men of the east are seized with
      horror.
21Surely such is the dwelling of an evil
      man;
   such is the place of one who knows
      not God."

Job

19 Then Job replied:

2"How long will you torment me
   and crush me with words?
3Ten times now you have reproached
      me;
   shamelessly you attack me.
4If it is true that I have gone astray,
   my error remains my concern
      alone.
5If indeed you would exalt yourselves
      above me
   and use my humiliation against me,
6then know that God has wronged me
   and drawn his net around me.

---

a 13,16 Hebrew *Sheol*   b 15 Or *Nothing he had remains*

⁷"Though I cry, 'I've been wronged!'
  I get no response;
though I call for help, there is no
  justice.
⁸He has blocked my way so I cannot
  pass;
he has shrouded my paths in
  darkness.
⁹He has stripped me of my honor
  and removed the crown from my
  head.
¹⁰He tears me down on every side till I
  am gone;
he uproots my hope like a tree.
¹¹His anger burns against me;
  he counts me among his enemies.
¹²His troops advance in force;
  they build a siege ramp against me
  and encamp around my tent.

¹³"He has alienated my brothers from
  me;
my acquaintances are completely
  estranged from me.
¹⁴My kinsmen have gone away;
  my friends have forgotten me.
¹⁵My guests and my maidservants count
  me a stranger;
they look upon me as an alien.
¹⁶I summon my servant, but he does
  not answer,
though I beg him with my own
  mouth.
¹⁷My breath is offensive to my wife;
  I am loathsome to my own
  brothers.
¹⁸Even the little boys scorn me;
  when I appear, they ridicule me.
¹⁹All my intimate friends detest me;
  those I love have turned against me.
²⁰I am nothing but skin and bones;
  I have escaped with only the skin of
  my teeth.ᵃ

²¹"Have pity on me, my friends, have
  pity,
for the hand of God has struck me.
²²Why do you pursue me as God does?
Will you never get enough of my
  flesh?

²³"Oh, that my words were recorded,
  that they were written on a scroll,
²⁴that they were inscribed with an iron
  tool onᵇ lead,
or engraved in rock forever!
²⁵I know that my Redeemerᶜ lives,
  and that in the end he will stand
  upon the earth.ᵈ
²⁶And after my skin has been destroyed,
  yetᵉ inᶠ my flesh I will see God;
²⁷I myself will see him
  with my own eyes—I, and not
  another.
How my heart yearns within me!

²⁸"If you say, 'How we will hound
  him,
since the root of the trouble lies in
  him,ᵍ'
²⁹you should fear the sword yourselves;
  for wrath will bring punishment by
  the sword,
and then you will know that there
  is judgment.ʰ'"

Zophar

20 Then Zophar the Naamathite re-
    plied:

²"My troubled thoughts prompt me to
  answer
because I am greatly disturbed.
³I hear a rebuke that dishonors me,
  and my understanding inspires me
  to reply.

⁴"Surely you know how it has been
  from of old,
ever since manⁱ was placed on the
  earth,
⁵that the mirth of the wicked is brief,
  the joy of the godless lasts but a
  moment.
⁶Though his pride reaches to the
  heavens
and his head touches the clouds,

ᵃ20 Or only my gums   ᵇ24 Or and   ᶜ25 Or defender   ᵈ25 Or upon my grave   ᵉ26 Or And after I awake, / though this
body_ has been destroyed, / then   ᶠ26 Or / apart from   ᵍ28 Many Hebrew manuscripts, Septuagint and Vulgate; most
Hebrew manuscripts me   ʰ29 Or / that you may come to know the Almighty   ⁱ4 Or Adam

Passing the Test

Do you remember how each time you took a test in school you had to study hard so you'd know the material and be able to pass the test? The purpose of the test was for the teacher to determine how much you knew and, consequently, what grade you would receive. The more you knew, the better your grade.

God's tests are not like school tests. First of all, He already knows how much we know. The test is not for Him. It's for us. God's test helps us clearly see what we're made of. It teaches us about ourselves and about God. The test itself is part of our learning process.

The results of the test God gives us, depending on our attitude in the midst of the testing, will determine whether we are refined like gold by the process or become cold and hard like steel. It won't necessarily be how much we know that counts, but what we do with the knowledge we've got. It's *how* we take the test.

In the test that God gives us, we receive no grade. We will either pass, or we'll have to keep taking it until we get it right. We have two choices with regard to God's tests. We can resist God, have a bad attitude, and try to run from it. Or we can embrace *Him* in it and welcome His perfecting hand in our lives. Our reaction will determine the outcome.

The most miserable times in my life as a believer have been during what I see now were periods of testing. And they came just before the most significant breakthrough of God's light. The good news is that the more challenging the test, the more monumental the reward waiting for us on the other side of it—*if* we react to it in the right way.

We are often put to our most difficult test just before the greatest work of God in our lives is about to be accomplished.

The Bible's story of Job is important because the magnitude of Job's suffering in his time of testing is unimaginable. It is the worst case scenario. He lost everything, including his children and his health. Although he suffered such agony, he never doubted or turned against God. His reward for faithfulness was that "the LORD blessed the latter part of Job's life more than the first" (Job 42:12).

I know that most of us feel we would just as soon not be quite so blessed in our latter days and forget the whole trial and testing thing. But we aren't given that choice. God decides the time, place, and manner of testing. No matter what the test entails, God wants us to have unflinching faith in the midst of it, just like Job had.

Don't fear the times of testing God allows you to go through. It doesn't have to be miserable. Think of it as a refining that will reveal anything amiss in your life and show you where changes need to be made. The only way God can lead you to where you've never been, and can't get to without Him, is to call you to a new place in your life that requires more purity of heart, more faith, and more obedience than you've ever known. Ask Him to help you pass any test necessary in order to receive all He has for you.

For the next "From Stormie's Heart" article, go to page 722.

⁷he will perish forever, like his own
dung;
those who have seen him will say,
'Where is he?'
⁸Like a dream he flies away, no more
to be found,
banished like a vision of the night.
⁹The eye that saw him will not see
him again;
his place will look on him no more.
¹⁰His children must make amends to
the poor;
his own hands must give back his
wealth.
¹¹The youthful vigor that fills his bones
will lie with him in the dust.

¹²"Though evil is sweet in his mouth
and he hides it under his tongue,
¹³though he cannot bear to let it go
and keeps it in his mouth,
¹⁴yet his food will turn sour in his
stomach;
it will become the venom of
serpents within him.
¹⁵He will spit out the riches he
swallowed;
God will make his stomach vomit
them up.
¹⁶He will suck the poison of serpents;
the fangs of an adder will kill him.
¹⁷He will not enjoy the streams,
the rivers flowing with honey and
cream.
¹⁸What he toiled for he must give back
uneaten;
he will not enjoy the profit from
his trading.
¹⁹For he has oppressed the poor and left
them destitute;
he has seized houses he did not
build.

²⁰"Surely he will have no respite from
his craving;
he cannot save himself by his
treasure.
²¹Nothing is left for him to devour;
his prosperity will not endure.

²²In the midst of his plenty, distress will
overtake him;
the full force of misery will come
upon him.
²³When he has filled his belly,
God will vent his burning anger
against him
and rain down his blows upon him.
²⁴Though he flees from an iron
weapon,
a bronze-tipped arrow pierces him.
²⁵He pulls it out of his back,
the gleaming point out of his liver.
Terrors will come over him;
²⁶   total darkness lies in wait for his
treasures.
A fire unfanned will consume him
and devour what is left in his tent.
²⁷The heavens will expose his guilt;
the earth will rise up against him.
²⁸A flood will carry off his house,
rushing watersᵃ on the day of God's
wrath.
²⁹Such is the fate God allots the
wicked,
the heritage appointed for them by
God."

Job

21

Then Job replied:
²"Listen carefully to my words;
let this be the consolation you give
me.
³Bear with me while I speak,
and after I have spoken, mock on.

⁴"Is my complaint directed to man?
Why should I not be impatient?
⁵Look at me and be astonished;
clap your hand over your mouth.
⁶When I think about this, I am
terrified;
trembling seizes my body.
⁷Why do the wicked live on,
growing old and increasing in
power?
⁸They see their children established
around them,

ᵃ 28 Or *The possessions in his house will be carried off, / washed away* their offspring before their eyes.

⁹Their homes are safe and free from
  fear;
  the rod of God is not upon them.
¹⁰Their bulls never fail to breed;
  their cows calve and do not
    miscarry.
¹¹They send forth their children as a
    flock;
  their little ones dance about.
¹²They sing to the music of tambourine
    and harp;
  they make merry to the sound of
    the flute.
¹³They spend their years in prosperity
  and go down to the graveᵃ in peace.ᵇ
¹⁴Yet they say to God, 'Leave us alone!
  We have no desire to know your
    ways.
¹⁵Who is the Almighty, that we should
    serve him?
  What would we gain by praying to
    him?'
¹⁶But their prosperity is not in their
    own hands,
  so I stand aloof from the counsel of
    the wicked.

¹⁷"Yet how often is the lamp of the
    wicked snuffed out?
  How often does calamity come
    upon them,
  the fate God allots in his anger?
¹⁸How often are they like straw before
    the wind,
  like chaff swept away by a gale?
¹⁹It is said, 'God stores up a man's
    punishment for his sons.'
  Let him repay the man himself, so
    that he will know it!
²⁰Let his own eyes see his destruction;
  let him drink of the wrath of the
    Almighty.ᶜ
²¹For what does he care about the
    family he leaves behind
  when his allotted months come to
    an end?

²²"Can anyone teach knowledge to
    God,
  since he judges even the highest?
²³One man dies in full vigor,
  completely secure and at ease,
²⁴his bodyᵈ well nourished,
  his bones rich with marrow.
²⁵Another man dies in bitterness of soul,
  never having enjoyed anything
    good.
²⁶Side by side they lie in the dust,
  and worms cover them both.

²⁷"I know full well what you are
    thinking,
  the schemes by which you would
    wrong me.
²⁸You say, 'Where now is the great
    man's house,
  the tents where wicked men lived?'
²⁹Have you never questioned those who
    travel?
  Have you paid no regard to their
    accounts—
³⁰that the evil man is spared from the
    day of calamity,
  that he is delivered fromᵉ the day of
    wrath?
³¹Who denounces his conduct to his
    face?
  Who repays him for what he has
    done?
³²He is carried to the grave,
  and watch is kept over his tomb.
³³The soil in the valley is sweet to him;
  all men follow after him,
  and a countless throng goesᶠ before
    him.

³⁴"So how can you console me with
    your nonsense?
  Nothing is left of your answers but
    falsehood!"

Eliphaz

22 Then Eliphaz the Temanite replied:

²"Can a man be of benefit to God?

ᵃ 13 Hebrew *Sheol*   ᵇ 13 Or *in an instant*   ᶜ 17-20 *Verses* 17 and 18 may be taken as exclamations and 19 and 20 as declarations.   ᵈ 24 The meaning of the Hebrew for this word is uncertain.   ᵉ 30 Or *man is reserved for the day of calamity, / that he is brought forth to*   ᶠ 33 Or */ as a countless throng went*

Can even a wise man benefit him?
3 What pleasure would it give the
    Almighty if you were
    righteous?
  What would he gain if your ways
    were blameless?

4 "Is it for your piety that he rebukes
    you
  and brings charges against you?
5 Is not your wickedness great?
  Are not your sins endless?
6 You demanded security from your
    brothers for no reason;
  you stripped men of their clothing,
    leaving them naked.
7 You gave no water to the weary
  and you withheld food from the
    hungry,
8 though you were a powerful man,
    owning land—
  an honored man, living on it.
9 And you sent widows away empty-
    handed
  and broke the strength of the
    fatherless.
10 That is why snares are all around you,
  why sudden peril terrifies you,
11 why it is so dark you cannot see,
  and why a flood of water covers
    you.

12 "Is not God in the heights of heaven?
  And see how lofty are the highest
    stars!
13 Yet you say, 'What does God know?
  Does he judge through such
    darkness?
14 Thick clouds veil him, so he does not
    see us
  as he goes about in the vaulted
    heavens.'
15 Will you keep to the old path
  that evil men have trod?
16 They were carried off before their
    time,
  their foundations washed away by
    a flood.
17 They said to God, 'Leave us alone!

What can the Almighty do to us?'
18 Yet it was he who filled their houses
    with good things,
  so I stand aloof from the counsel of
    the wicked.

19 "The righteous see their ruin and
    rejoice;
  the innocent mock them, saying,
20 'Surely our foes are destroyed,
  and fire devours their wealth.'

21 "Submit to God and be at peace with
    him;
  in this way prosperity will come to
    you.
22 Accept instruction from his mouth
  and lay up his words in your heart.
23 If you return to the Almighty, you
    will be restored:
  If you remove wickedness far from
    your tent
24 and assign your nuggets to the dust,
  your gold of Ophir to the rocks in
    the ravines,
25 then the Almighty will be your gold,
  the choicest silver for you.
26 Surely then you will find delight in
    the Almighty
  and will lift up your face to God.
27 You will pray to him, and he will
    hear you,
  and you will fulfill your vows.
28 What you decide on will be done,
  and light will shine on your ways.
29 When men are brought low and you
    say, 'Lift them up!'
  then he will save the downcast.
30 He will deliver even one who is not
    innocent,
  who will be delivered through the
    cleanness of your hands."

Job

23 Then Job replied:

2 "Even today my complaint is bitter;
  his hand[a] is heavy in spite of[b] my
    groaning.
3 If only I knew where to find him;

---

[a] 2 Septuagint and Syriac; Hebrew / the hand on me [b] 2 Or heavy on me in

if only I could go to his dwelling!
⁴I would state my case before him
  and fill my mouth with arguments.
⁵I would find out what he would
    answer me,
  and consider what he would say.
⁶Would he oppose me with great
    power?
  No, he would not press charges
    against me.
⁷There an upright man could present
    his case before him,
  and I would be delivered forever
    from my judge.

⁸"But if I go to the east, he is not
    there;
  if I go to the west, I do not find
    him.
⁹When he is at work in the north, I do
    not see him;
  when he turns to the south, I catch
    no glimpse of him.
¹⁰But he knows the way that I take;
  when he has tested me, I will come
    forth as gold.
¹¹My feet have closely followed his
    steps;
  I have kept to his way without
    turning aside.
¹²I have not departed from the
    commands of his lips;
  I have treasured the words of his
    mouth more than my daily
    bread.

¹³"But he stands alone, and who can
    oppose him?
  He does whatever he pleases.
¹⁴He carries out his decree against me,
  and many such plans he still has in
    store.
¹⁵That is why I am terrified before him;
  when I think of all this, I fear him.
¹⁶God has made my heart faint;
  the Almighty has terrified me.
¹⁷Yet I am not silenced by the darkness,
  by the thick darkness that covers
    my face.

24 "Why does the Almighty not set
    times for judgment?
  Why must those who know him
    look in vain for such days?
²Men move boundary stones;
  they pasture flocks they have stolen.
³They drive away the orphan's
    donkey
  and take the widow's ox in pledge.
⁴They thrust the needy from the path
  and force all the poor of the land
    into hiding.
⁵Like wild donkeys in the desert,
  the poor go about their labor of
    foraging food;
  the wasteland provides food for
    their children.
⁶They gather fodder in the fields
  and glean in the vineyards of the
    wicked.
⁷Lacking clothes, they spend the night
    naked;
  they have nothing to cover
    themselves in the cold.
⁸They are drenched by mountain rains
  and hug the rocks for lack of
    shelter.
⁹The fatherless child is snatched from
    the breast;
  the infant of the poor is seized for
    a debt.
¹⁰Lacking clothes, they go about naked;
  they carry the sheaves, but still go
    hungry.
¹¹They crush olives among the
    terracesᵃ;
  they tread the winepresses, yet
    suffer thirst.
¹²The groans of the dying rise from the
    city,
  and the souls of the wounded cry
    out for help.
  But God charges no one with
    wrongdoing.

¹³"There are those who rebel against
    the light,
  who do not know its ways
    or stay in its paths.

ᵃ *11* Or *olives between the millstones*; the meaning of the Hebrew for this word is uncertain.

14 When daylight is gone, the murderer
  rises up
  and kills the poor and needy;
  in the night he steals forth like a
  thief.
15 The eye of the adulterer watches for
  dusk;
  he thinks, 'No eye will see me,'
  and he keeps his face concealed.
16 In the dark, men break into houses,
  but by day they shut themselves in;
  they want nothing to do with the
  light.
17 For all of them, deep darkness is their
  morning[a];
  they make friends with the terrors
  of darkness.[b]

18 "Yet they are foam on the surface of
  the water;
  their portion of the land is
  cursed,
  so that no one goes to the
  vineyards.
19 As heat and drought snatch away the
  melted snow,
  so the grave[c] snatches away those
  who have sinned.
20 The womb forgets them,
  the worm feasts on them;
  evil men are no longer remembered
  but are broken like a tree.
21 They prey on the barren and childless
  woman,
  and to the widow show no
  kindness.
22 But God drags away the mighty by
  his power;
  though they become established,
  they have no assurance of life.
23 He may let them rest in a feeling of
  security,
  but his eyes are on their ways.
24 For a little while they are exalted, and
  then they are gone;
  they are brought low and gathered
  up like all others;
  they are cut off like heads of grain.

25 "If this is not so, who can prove me
  false
  and reduce my words to nothing?"

Bildad

25 Then Bildad the Shuhite replied:

2 "Dominion and awe belong to God;
  he establishes order in the heights
  of heaven.
3 Can his forces be numbered?
  Upon whom does his light not rise?
4 How then can a man be righteous
  before God?
  How can one born of woman be
  pure?
5 If even the moon is not bright
  and the stars are not pure in his
  eyes,
6 how much less man, who is but a
  maggot—
  a son of man, who is only a
  worm!"

Job

26 Then Job replied:

2 "How you have helped the
  powerless!
  How you have saved the arm that
  is feeble!
3 What advice you have offered to one
  without wisdom!
  And what great insight you have
  displayed!
4 Who has helped you utter these
  words?
  And whose spirit spoke from your
  mouth?

5 "The dead are in deep anguish,
  those beneath the waters and all
  that live in them.
6 Death[c] is naked before God;
  Destruction[d] lies uncovered.
7 He spreads out the northern ⌊skies⌋
  over empty space;
  he suspends the earth over
  nothing.

---

[a] 17 Or them, their morning is like the shadow of death   [b] 17 Or of the shadow of death   [c] 19,6 Hebrew Sheol   [d] 6 Hebrew Abaddon

Finding Peace in the Midst of Suffering

READ AND CONSIDER: JOB 26:1-14

"And these are but the outer fringe of his works; how faint the whisper we hear of him! Who then can understand the thunder of his power?" (Job 26:14).

God's power and ways are immeasurable, far beyond our comprehension. We will never fully understand them this side of heaven. We don't understand His ways that allow us to suffer. And we don't understand His power to redeem and restore us. That's why we must praise God no matter what is happening in our lives. We should praise Him even in the midst of suffering because it strengthens us and refines our faith in Him. Trials, hardships, and pain all serve to strengthen not only the individual, but also a society or nation. How much more should we praise God when we know for certain that God loves us, has a purpose, and is working out His plan through our every experience.

Our suffering can be compared to the refining process of silver. The heat is turned up and as the impurities rise to the surface, they are skimmed away by the refiner. Because God is sovereign, nothing that happens to us surprises Him. And as difficult as it is to accept sometimes, God even allows us, His children, to suffer.

It is in those times of suffering that we may feel as if we're on a roller coaster, vacillating up and down as we wonder why God would allow us to endure such pain. Yet if we draw close to Him, we will have a sense of peace, knowing He is in control of the situation. In spite of all that Job went through, he never doubted God's unlimited power. Job said that God's power terrified him (23:15-16). He said, when referring to God's ability to calm a raging storm, "These are but the outer fringe of his works" (26:14).

So even in the midst of turmoil and grief, praise God for the path He has chosen for you and for His refining power and love. When the heat is on, allow the Refiner to purify your soul.

---

⁸He wraps up the waters in his clouds,
    yet the clouds do not burst under
      their weight.
⁹He covers the face of the full moon,
    spreading his clouds over it.
¹⁰He marks out the horizon on the face
      of the waters
    for a boundary between light and
      darkness.
¹¹The pillars of the heavens quake,
    aghast at his rebuke.
¹²By his power he churned up the sea;
    by his wisdom he cut Rahab to
      pieces.
¹³By his breath the skies became fair;

his hand pierced the gliding
      serpent.
¹⁴And these are but the outer fringe of
      his works;
  how faint the whisper we hear of
      him!
  Who then can understand the
      thunder of his power?"

27 And Job continued his discourse:

²"As surely as God lives, who has
      denied me justice,
    the Almighty, who has made me
      taste bitterness of soul,

3 as long as I have life within me,
  the breath of God in my nostrils,
4 my lips will not speak wickedness,
  and my tongue will utter no deceit.
5 I will never admit you are in the
    right;
  till I die, I will not deny my
    integrity.
6 I will maintain my righteousness and
    never let go of it;
  my conscience will not reproach
    me as long as I live.

7 "May my enemies be like the wicked,
  my adversaries like the unjust!
8 For what hope has the godless when
    he is cut off,
  when God takes away his life?
9 Does God listen to his cry
  when distress comes upon him?
10 Will he find delight in the Almighty?
  Will he call upon God at all times?

11 "I will teach you about the power of
    God;
  the ways of the Almighty I will not
    conceal.
12 You have all seen this yourselves.
  Why then this meaningless talk?

13 "Here is the fate God allots to the
    wicked,
  the heritage a ruthless man receives
    from the Almighty:
14 However many his children, their fate
    is the sword;
  his offspring will never have
    enough to eat.
15 The plague will bury those who
    survive him,
  and their widows will not weep for
    them.
16 Though he heaps up silver like dust
  and clothes like piles of clay,
17 what he lays up the righteous will
    wear,
  and the innocent will divide his
    silver.
18 The house he builds is like a moth's
    cocoon,

like a hut made by a watchman.
19 He lies down wealthy, but will do so
    no more;
  when he opens his eyes, all is gone.
20 Terrors overtake him like a flood;
  a tempest snatches him away in the
    night.
21 The east wind carries him off, and he
    is gone;
  it sweeps him out of his place.
22 It hurls itself against him without
    mercy
  as he flees headlong from its power.
23 It claps its hands in derision
  and hisses him out of his place.

28 "There is a mine for silver
  and a place where gold is refined.
2 Iron is taken from the earth,
  and copper is smelted from ore.
3 Man puts an end to the darkness;
  he searches the farthest recesses
  for ore in the blackest darkness.
4 Far from where people dwell he cuts
    a shaft,
  in places forgotten by the foot of
    man;
  far from men he dangles and sways.
5 The earth, from which food comes,
  is transformed below as by fire;
6 sapphires[a] come from its rocks,
  and its dust contains nuggets of
    gold.
7 No bird of prey knows that hidden
    path,
  no falcon's eye has seen it.
8 Proud beasts do not set foot on it,
  and no lion prowls there.
9 Man's hand assaults the flinty rock
  and lays bare the roots of the
    mountains.
10 He tunnels through the rock;
  his eyes see all its treasures.
11 He searches[b] the sources of the rivers
  and brings hidden things to light.

12 "But where can wisdom be found?
  Where does understanding dwell?
13 Man does not comprehend its worth;

---

a 6 Or lapis lazuli; also in verse 16   b 11 Septuagint, Aquila and Vulgate; Hebrew He dams up

it cannot be found in the land of
  the living.
14 The deep says, 'It is not in me';
  the sea says, 'It is not with me.'
15 It cannot be bought with the finest
    gold,
  nor can its price be weighed in
    silver.
16 It cannot be bought with the gold of
    Ophir,
  with precious onyx or sapphires.
17 Neither gold nor crystal can compare
    with it,
  nor can it be had for jewels of gold.
18 Coral and jasper are not worthy of
    mention;
  the price of wisdom is beyond
    rubies.
19 The topaz of Cush cannot compare
    with it;
  it cannot be bought with pure gold.

20 "Where then does wisdom come
    from?
  Where does understanding dwell?
21 It is hidden from the eyes of every
    living thing,
  concealed even from the birds of
    the air.
22 Destruction[a] and Death say,
  'Only a rumor of it has reached our
    ears.'
23 God understands the way to it
  and he alone knows where it dwells,
24 for he views the ends of the earth
  and sees everything under the
    heavens.
25 When he established the force of the
    wind
  and measured out the waters,
26 when he made a decree for the rain
  and a path for the thunderstorm,
27 then he looked at wisdom and
    appraised it;
  he confirmed it and tested it.
28 And he said to man,
  'The fear of the Lord—that is
    wisdom,
  and to shun evil is understanding.'"

29 Job continued his discourse:

2 "How I long for the months gone by,
  for the days when God watched
    over me,
3 when his lamp shone upon my head
  and by his light I walked through
    darkness!
4 Oh, for the days when I was in my
    prime,
  when God's intimate friendship
    blessed my house,
5 when the Almighty was still with me
  and my children were around me,
6 when my path was drenched with
    cream
  and the rock poured out for me
    streams of olive oil.

7 "When I went to the gate of the city
  and took my seat in the public
    square,
8 the young men saw me and stepped
    aside
  and the old men rose to their feet;
9 the chief men refrained from speaking
  and covered their mouths with
    their hands;
10 the voices of the nobles were hushed,
  and their tongues stuck to the roof
    of their mouths.
11 Whoever heard me spoke well of me,
  and those who saw me commended
    me,
12 because I rescued the poor who cried
    for help,
  and the fatherless who had none to
    assist him.
13 The man who was dying blessed me;
  I made the widow's heart sing.
14 I put on righteousness as my clothing;
  justice was my robe and my turban.
15 I was eyes to the blind
  and feet to the lame.
16 I was a father to the needy;
  I took up the case of the stranger.
17 I broke the fangs of the wicked
  and snatched the victims from their
    teeth.

---

a 22 Hebrew *Abaddon*

¹⁸"I thought, 'I will die in my own
house,
my days as numerous as the grains
of sand.
¹⁹My roots will reach to the water,
and the dew will lie all night on
my branches.
²⁰My glory will remain fresh in me,
the bow ever new in my hand.'

²¹"Men listened to me expectantly,
waiting in silence for my counsel.
²²After I had spoken, they spoke no
more;
my words fell gently on their ears.
²³They waited for me as for showers
and drank in my words as the
spring rain.
²⁴When I smiled at them, they scarcely
believed it;
the light of my face was precious to
them.^a
²⁵I chose the way for them and sat as
their chief;
I dwelt as a king among his troops;
I was like one who comforts
mourners.

30 "But now they mock me,
men younger than I,
whose fathers I would have disdained
to put with my sheep dogs.
²Of what use was the strength of their
hands to me,
since their vigor had gone from
them?
³Haggard from want and hunger,
they roamed^b the parched land
in desolate wastelands at night.
⁴In the brush they gathered salt
herbs,
and their food^c was the root of the
broom tree.
⁵They were banished from their fellow
men,
shouted at as if they were thieves.
⁶They were forced to live in the dry
stream beds,

among the rocks and in holes in the
ground.
⁷They brayed among the bushes
and huddled in the undergrowth.
⁸A base and nameless brood,
they were driven out of the land.

⁹"And now their sons mock me in
song;
I have become a byword among
them.
¹⁰They detest me and keep their
distance;
they do not hesitate to spit in my
face.
¹¹Now that God has unstrung my bow
and afflicted me,
they throw off restraint in my
presence.
¹²On my right the tribe^d attacks;
they lay snares for my feet,
they build their siege ramps against
me.
¹³They break up my road;
they succeed in destroying me—
without anyone's helping them.^e
¹⁴They advance as through a gaping
breach;
amid the ruins they come rolling in.
¹⁵Terrors overwhelm me;
my dignity is driven away as by the
wind,
my safety vanishes like a cloud.

¹⁶"And now my life ebbs away;
days of suffering grip me.
¹⁷Night pierces my bones;
my gnawing pains never rest.
¹⁸In his great power ⌊God⌋ becomes like
clothing to me^f;
he binds me like the neck of my
garment.
¹⁹He throws me into the mud,
and I am reduced to dust and ashes.

²⁰"I cry out to you, O God, but you do
not answer;
I stand up, but you merely look at
me.

---

^a24 The meaning of the Hebrew for this clause is uncertain.   ^b3 Or *gnawed*   ^c4 Or *fuel*   ^d12 The meaning of the Hebrew for
this word is uncertain.   ^e13 Or *me.* / *'No one can help him,'* ⌊*they say*⌋.   ^f18 Hebrew; Septuagint ⌊*God grasps my clothing*⌋

21You turn on me ruthlessly;
    with the might of your hand you
        attack me.
22You snatch me up and drive me
        before the wind;
    you toss me about in the storm.
23I know you will bring me down to
        death,
    to the place appointed for all the
        living.

24"Surely no one lays a hand on a
        broken man
    when he cries for help in his distress.
25Have I not wept for those in trouble?
    Has not my soul grieved for the
        poor?
26Yet when I hoped for good, evil
        came;
    when I looked for light, then came
        darkness.
27The churning inside me never stops;
    days of suffering confront me.
28I go about blackened, but not by the
        sun;
    I stand up in the assembly and cry
        for help.
29I have become a brother of jackals,
    a companion of owls.
30My skin grows black and peels;
    my body burns with fever.
31My harp is tuned to mourning,
    and my flute to the sound of
        wailing.

31 "I made a covenant with my eyes
    not to look lustfully at a girl.
2For what is man's lot from God
        above,
    his heritage from the Almighty on
        high?
3Is it not ruin for the wicked,
    disaster for those who do wrong?
4Does he not see my ways
    and count my every step?

Praying Job 31:4
Thank You, Lord, that You know me,
and You see everything I do.

5"If I have walked in falsehood
    or my foot has hurried after
        deceit—
6let God weigh me in honest scales
    and he will know that I am
        blameless—
7if my steps have turned from the
        path,
    if my heart has been led by my
        eyes,
    or if my hands have been defiled,
8then may others eat what I have
        sown,
    and may my crops be uprooted.

9"If my heart has been enticed by a
        woman,
    or if I have lurked at my neighbor's
        door,
10then may my wife grind another
        man's grain,
    and may other men sleep with her.
11For that would have been shameful,
    a sin to be judged.
12It is a fire that burns to Destruction[a];
    it would have uprooted my harvest.

13"If I have denied justice to my
        menservants and maidservants
    when they had a grievance against
        me,
14what will I do when God confronts
        me?
    What will I answer when called to
        account?
15Did not he who made me in the
        womb make them?
    Did not the same one form us both
        within our mothers?

16"If I have denied the desires of the
        poor
    or let the eyes of the widow grow
        weary,
17if I have kept my bread to myself,
    not sharing it with the fatherless—
18but from my youth I reared him as
        would a father,
    and from my birth I guided the
        widow—

---

a 12 Hebrew *Abaddon*

19if I have seen anyone perishing for
     lack of clothing,
   or a needy man without a garment,
20and his heart did not bless me
   for warming him with the fleece
     from my sheep,
21if I have raised my hand against the
     fatherless,
   knowing that I had influence in
     court,
22then let my arm fall from the
     shoulder,
   let it be broken off at the joint.
23For I dreaded destruction from God,
   and for fear of his splendor I could
     not do such things.

24"If I have put my trust in gold
   or said to pure gold, 'You are my
     security,'
25if I have rejoiced over my great
     wealth,
   the fortune my hands had gained,
26if I have regarded the sun in its
     radiance
   or the moon moving in splendor,
27so that my heart was secretly enticed
   and my hand offered them a kiss of
     homage,
28then these also would be sins to be
     judged,
   for I would have been unfaithful to
     God on high.

29"If I have rejoiced at my enemy's
     misfortune
   or gloated over the trouble that
     came to him—
30I have not allowed my mouth to sin
   by invoking a curse against his
     life—
31if the men of my household have
     never said,
   'Who has not had his fill of Job's
     meat?'—
32but no stranger had to spend the night
     in the street,
   for my door was always open to the
     traveler—

33if I have concealed my sin as men do,ª
   by hiding my guilt in my heart
34because I so feared the crowd
   and so dreaded the contempt of the
     clans
   that I kept silent and would not go
     outside—

35("Oh, that I had someone to hear me!
   I sign now my defense—let the
     Almighty answer me;
   let my accuser put his indictment in
     writing.
36Surely I would wear it on my shoulder,
   I would put it on like a crown.
37I would give him an account of my
     every step;
   like a prince I would approach
     him.)—

38"if my land cries out against me
   and all its furrows are wet with
     tears,
39if I have devoured its yield without
     payment
   or broken the spirit of its tenants,
40then let briers come up instead of
     wheat
   and weeds instead of barley."

The words of Job are ended.

Elihu

32 So these three men stopped answering Job, because he was righteous in his own eyes. 2But Elihu son of
Barakel the Buzite, of the family of Ram,
became very angry with Job for justifying
himself rather than God. 3He was also angry with the three friends, because they
had found no way to refute Job, and yet
had condemned him.ᵇ 4Now Elihu had
waited before speaking to Job because
they were older than he. 5But when he
saw that the three men had nothing more
to say, his anger was aroused.

6So Elihu son of Barakel the Buzite
said:

"I am young in years,
   and you are old;

ª 33 Or as Adam did   ᵇ 3 Masoretic Text; an ancient Hebrew scribal tradition Job, and so had condemned God

that is why I was fearful,
not daring to tell you what I know.
⁷I thought, 'Age should speak;
advanced years should teach
wisdom.'
⁸But it is the spiritᵃ in a man,
the breath of the Almighty, that
gives him understanding.
⁹It is not only the oldᵇ who are wise,
not only the aged who understand
what is right.

¹⁰"Therefore I say: Listen to me;
I too will tell you what I know.
¹¹I waited while you spoke,
I listened to your reasoning;
while you were searching for words,
¹² I gave you my full attention.
But not one of you has proved Job
wrong;
none of you has answered his
arguments.
¹³Do not say, 'We have found wisdom;
let God refute him, not man.'
¹⁴But Job has not marshaled his words
against me,
and I will not answer him with
your arguments.

¹⁵"They are dismayed and have no
more to say;
words have failed them.
¹⁶Must I wait, now that they are silent,
now that they stand there with no
reply?
¹⁷I too will have my say;
I too will tell what I know.
¹⁸For I am full of words,
and the spirit within me compels me;
¹⁹inside I am like bottled-up wine,
like new wineskins ready to burst.
²⁰I must speak and find relief;
I must open my lips and reply.
²¹I will show partiality to no one,
nor will I flatter any man;
²²for if I were skilled in flattery,
my Maker would soon take me
away.

33 "But now, Job, listen to my
words;
pay attention to everything I say.
²I am about to open my mouth;
my words are on the tip of my
tongue.
³My words come from an upright
heart;
my lips sincerely speak what I
know.
⁴The Spirit of God has made me;
the breath of the Almighty gives
me life.
⁵Answer me then, if you can;
prepare yourself and confront me.
⁶I am just like you before God;
I too have been taken from clay.
⁷No fear of me should alarm you,
nor should my hand be heavy upon
you.

⁸"But you have said in my hearing—
I heard the very words—
⁹'I am pure and without sin;
I am clean and free from guilt.
¹⁰Yet God has found fault with me;
he considers me his enemy.
¹¹He fastens my feet in shackles;
he keeps close watch on all my
paths.'

¹²"But I tell you, in this you are not
right,
for God is greater than man.
¹³Why do you complain to him
that he answers none of man's
wordsᶜ?
¹⁴For God does speak—now one way,
now another—
though man may not perceive it.
¹⁵In a dream, in a vision of the night,
when deep sleep falls on men
as they slumber in their beds,
¹⁶he may speak in their ears
and terrify them with warnings,
¹⁷to turn man from wrongdoing
and keep him from pride,
¹⁸to preserve his soul from the pit,ᵈ

ᵃ8 Or Spirit; also in verse 18   ᵇ9 Or many; or great   ᶜ13 Or that he does not answer for any of his actions   ᵈ18 Or preserve him from the grave

his life from perishing by the
sword.[a]

¹⁹Or a man may be chastened on a bed
of pain
with constant distress in his bones,

²⁰so that his very being finds food
repulsive
and his soul loathes the choicest
meal.

²¹His flesh wastes away to nothing,
and his bones, once hidden, now
stick out.

²²His soul draws near to the pit,[b]
and his life to the messengers of
death.[c]

²³"Yet if there is an angel on his side
as a mediator, one out of a
thousand,
to tell a man what is right for him,

²⁴to be gracious to him and say,
'Spare him from going down to the
pit[d];
I have found a ransom for him'—

²⁵then his flesh is renewed like a child's;
it is restored as in the days of his
youth.

²⁶He prays to God and finds favor with
him,
he sees God's face and shouts for
joy;
he is restored by God to his
righteous state.

²⁷Then he comes to men and says,
'I sinned, and perverted what was
right,
but I did not get what I deserved.

²⁸He redeemed my soul from going
down to the pit,[e]
and I will live to enjoy the light.'

²⁹"God does all these things to a man—
twice, even three times—

³⁰to turn back his soul from the pit,[f]
that the light of life may shine on
him.

³¹"Pay attention, Job, and listen to me;
be silent, and I will speak.

³²If you have anything to say, answer
me;
speak up, for I want you to be
cleared.

³³But if not, then listen to me;
be silent, and I will teach you
wisdom."

34 Then Elihu said:

²"Hear my words, you wise men;
listen to me, you men of learning.

³For the ear tests words
as the tongue tastes food.

⁴Let us discern for ourselves what is
right;
let us learn together what is good.

⁵"Job says, 'I am innocent,
but God denies me justice.

⁶Although I am right,
I am considered a liar;
although I am guiltless,
his arrow inflicts an incurable
wound.'

⁷What man is like Job,
who drinks scorn like water?

⁸He keeps company with evildoers;
he associates with wicked men.

⁹For he says, 'It profits a man
nothing
when he tries to please God.'

¹⁰"So listen to me, you men of
understanding.
Far be it from God to do evil,
from the Almighty to do wrong.

¹¹He repays a man for what he has
done;
he brings upon him what his
conduct deserves.

¹²It is unthinkable that God would do
wrong,
that the Almighty would pervert
justice.

¹³Who appointed him over the earth?
Who put him in charge of the
whole world?

¹⁴If it were his intention

---

[a] 18 Or from crossing the River   [b] 22 Or He draws near to the grave   [c] 22 Or to the dead   [d] 24 Or grave   [e] 28 Or redeemed me
from going down to the grave   [f] 30 Or turn him back from the grave

and he withdrew his spirit[a] and breath,

15 all mankind would perish together
and man would return to the dust.

16 "If you have understanding, hear this;
listen to what I say.

17 Can he who hates justice govern?
Will you condemn the just and mighty One?

18 Is he not the One who says to kings, 'You are worthless,'
and to nobles, 'You are wicked,'

19 who shows no partiality to princes
and does not favor the rich over the poor,
for they are all the work of his hands?

20 They die in an instant, in the middle of the night;
the people are shaken and they pass away;
the mighty are removed without human hand.

21 "His eyes are on the ways of men;
he sees their every step.

22 There is no dark place, no deep shadow,
where evildoers can hide.

23 God has no need to examine men further,
that they should come before him for judgment.

24 Without inquiry he shatters the mighty
and sets up others in their place.

25 Because he takes note of their deeds,
he overthrows them in the night and they are crushed.

26 He punishes them for their wickedness
where everyone can see them,

27 because they turned from following him
and had no regard for any of his ways.

28 They caused the cry of the poor to come before him,

so that he heard the cry of the needy.

29 But if he remains silent, who can condemn him?
If he hides his face, who can see him?
Yet he is over man and nation alike,

30 to keep a godless man from ruling,
from laying snares for the people.

31 "Suppose a man says to God, 'I am guilty but will offend no more.

32 Teach me what I cannot see;
if I have done wrong, I will not do so again.'

33 Should God then reward you on your terms,
when you refuse to repent?
You must decide, not I;
so tell me what you know.

34 "Men of understanding declare,
wise men who hear me say to me,

35 'Job speaks without knowledge;
his words lack insight.'

36 Oh, that Job might be tested to the utmost
for answering like a wicked man!

37 To his sin he adds rebellion;
scornfully he claps his hands among us
and multiplies his words against God."

35 Then Elihu said:

2 "Do you think this is just?
You say, 'I will be cleared by God.'[b]

3 Yet you ask him, 'What profit is it to me,[c]
and what do I gain by not sinning?'

4 "I would like to reply to you
and to your friends with you.

5 Look up at the heavens and see;
gaze at the clouds so high above you.

6 If you sin, how does that affect him?
If your sins are many, what does that do to him?

---

a 14 Or *Spirit*   b 2 Or *My righteousness is more than God's*   c 3 Or *you*

GOING *deeper*

Finding a Song in the Night

READ AND CONSIDER: JOB 35:1-16

"But no one says, 'Where is God my Maker, who gives songs in the night?" (Job 35:10).

Of all Job's friends, only Elihu had a glimmer of wisdom. In fact, God rebukes the other three men for their inaccurate explanations of Job's pain (42:7-9). Elihu wasn't completely in tune with the sovereignty of God, but he understood that something good would come from Job's pain. He observed that people often cry out to God for deliverance, but rarely cry out for God Himself (35:10).

King David experienced suffering, and God gave him a song:

> I waited patiently for the LORD; he turned to me and heard my cry.
> He lifted me out of the slimy pit, out of the mud and mire;
> he set my feet on a rock and gave me a firm place to stand.
> He put a new song in my mouth, a hymn of praise to our God.
> Many will see and fear and put their trust in the LORD (Psalm 40:1-3).

In your darkest time, when you seek God, He will give you a song in the night. It will be a song of worship and praise, and your heart will sing once more. It doesn't matter how terrible or difficult your situation is. Every time you praise God, He will move into the situation to redeem and transform it in some way. Praise God for how He will work through your pain, for the lives He will touch through your witness. You may never know how far-reaching your testimony will be, but rest assured that God will use you to glorify Him and to draw others closer to Jesus.

7 If you are righteous, what do you
   give to him,
   or what does he receive from your
   hand?
8 Your wickedness affects only a man
   like yourself,
   and your righteousness only the
   sons of men.
9 "Men cry out under a load of
   oppression;
   they plead for relief from the arm of
   the powerful.
10 But no one says, 'Where is God my
   Maker,
   who gives songs in the
   night,
11 who teaches more to us than to[a] the
   beasts of the earth

and makes us wiser than[b] the birds
   of the air?'
12 He does not answer when men cry
   out
   because of the arrogance of the
   wicked.
13 Indeed, God does not listen to their
   empty plea;
   the Almighty pays no attention
   to it.
14 How much less, then, will he listen
   when you say that you do not see
   him,
   that your case is before him
   and you must wait for him,
15 and further, that his anger never
   punishes
   and he does not take the least
   notice of wickedness.[c]

---

[a] 11 Or *teaches us by* [b] 11 Or *us wise by* [c] 15 Symmachus, Theodotion and Vulgate; the meaning of the Hebrew for this word is uncertain.

¹⁶So Job opens his mouth with empty
  talk;
    without knowledge he multiplies
      words."

36 Elihu continued:

²"Bear with me a little longer and I
  will show you
    that there is more to be said in
      God's behalf.
³I get my knowledge from afar;
  I will ascribe justice to my Maker.
⁴Be assured that my words are not
  false;
    one perfect in knowledge is with
      you.

⁵"God is mighty, but does not despise
  men;
    he is mighty, and firm in his
      purpose.
⁶He does not keep the wicked alive
  but gives the afflicted their rights.
⁷He does not take his eyes off the
  righteous;
    he enthrones them with kings
    and exalts them forever.
⁸But if men are bound in chains,
  held fast by cords of affliction,
⁹he tells them what they have done—
  that they have sinned arrogantly.
¹⁰He makes them listen to correction
  and commands them to repent of
    their evil.
¹¹If they obey and serve him,
  they will spend the rest of their
    days in prosperity
  and their years in contentment.
¹²But if they do not listen,
  they will perish by the sword[a]
  and die without knowledge.

¹³"The godless in heart harbor
  resentment;
    even when he fetters them, they do
      not cry for help.
¹⁴They die in their youth,
  among male prostitutes of the
    shrines.

¹⁵But those who suffer he delivers in
  their suffering;
    he speaks to them in their affliction.
¹⁶"He is wooing you from the jaws of
  distress
    to a spacious place free from
      restriction,
    to the comfort of your table laden
      with choice food.
¹⁷But now you are laden with the
  judgment due the wicked;
    judgment and justice have taken
      hold of you.
¹⁸Be careful that no one entices you by
  riches;
    do not let a large bribe turn you
      aside.
¹⁹Would your wealth
  or even all your mighty efforts
    sustain you so you would not be in
      distress?
²⁰Do not long for the night,
  to drag people away from their
    homes.[b]
²¹Beware of turning to evil,
  which you seem to prefer to
    affliction.

²²"God is exalted in his power.
  Who is a teacher like him?
²³Who has prescribed his ways for him,
  or said to him, 'You have done
    wrong'?
²⁴Remember to extol his work,
  which men have praised in song.
²⁵All mankind has seen it;
  men gaze on it from afar.
²⁶How great is God—beyond our
  understanding!
    The number of his years is past
      finding out.

²⁷"He draws up the drops of water,
  which distill as rain to the streams[c];
²⁸the clouds pour down their moisture
  and abundant showers fall on
    mankind.
²⁹Who can understand how he spreads
  out the clouds,

---

[a] 12 Or will cross the River [b] 20 The meaning of the Hebrew for verses 18-20 is uncertain. [c] 27 Or distill from the mist as rain

how he thunders from his pavilion?
30See how he scatters his lightning
    about him,
bathing the depths of the sea.
31This is the way he governs[a] the
    nations
and provides food in abundance.
32He fills his hands with lightning
and commands it to strike its mark.
33His thunder announces the coming
    storm;
even the cattle make known its
    approach.[b]

37 "At this my heart pounds
    and leaps from its place.
2Listen! Listen to the roar of his voice,
to the rumbling that comes from
    his mouth.
3He unleashes his lightning beneath
    the whole heaven
and sends it to the ends of the
    earth.
4After that comes the sound of his
    roar;
he thunders with his majestic voice.
When his voice resounds,
    he holds nothing back.
5God's voice thunders in marvelous
    ways;
he does great things beyond our
    understanding.
6He says to the snow, 'Fall on the
    earth,'
and to the rain shower, 'Be a
    mighty downpour.'
7So that all men he has made may
    know his work,
he stops every man from his labor.[c]
8The animals take cover;
they remain in their dens.
9The tempest comes out from its
    chamber,
the cold from the driving winds.
10The breath of God produces ice,
and the broad waters become
    frozen.
11He loads the clouds with moisture;

he scatters his lightning through
    them.
12At his direction they swirl around
over the face of the whole earth
to do whatever he commands
    them.
13He brings the clouds to punish men,
or to water his earth[d] and show his
    love.

14"Listen to this, Job;
stop and consider God's wonders.
15Do you know how God controls the
    clouds
and makes his lightning flash?
16Do you know how the clouds hang
    poised,
those wonders of him who is
    perfect in knowledge?
17You who swelter in your clothes
when the land lies hushed under
    the south wind,
18can you join him in spreading out the
    skies,
hard as a mirror of cast bronze?

19"Tell us what we should say to him;
we cannot draw up our case
because of our darkness.
20Should he be told that I want to
    speak?
Would any man ask to be
    swallowed up?
21Now no one can look at the sun,
bright as it is in the skies
after the wind has swept them
    clean.
22Out of the north he comes in golden
    splendor;
God comes in awesome majesty.
23The Almighty is beyond our reach
and exalted in power;
in his justice and great
    righteousness, he does not
    oppress.
24Therefore, men revere him,
for does he not have regard for all
    the wise in heart?[e]"

---

a 31 Or nourishes   b 33 Or announces his coming—/ the One zealous against evil   c 7 Or / he fills all men with fear by his power   d 13 Or to favor them   e 24 Or for he does not have regard for any who think they are wise.

The LORD Speaks

38 Then the LORD answered Job out of the storm. He said:

2 "Who is this that darkens my counsel
    with words without knowledge?
3 Brace yourself like a man;
    I will question you,
    and you shall answer me.

4 "Where were you when I laid the
        earth's foundation?
    Tell me, if you understand.
5 Who marked off its dimensions?
        Surely you know!
    Who stretched a measuring line
        across it?
6 On what were its footings set,
    or who laid its cornerstone—
7 while the morning stars sang together
    and all the angels[a] shouted for joy?

8 "Who shut up the sea behind doors
    when it burst forth from the womb,
9 when I made the clouds its garment
    and wrapped it in thick darkness,
10 when I fixed limits for it
    and set its doors and bars in place,
11 when I said, 'This far you may come
        and no farther;
    here is where your proud waves
        halt'?

12 "Have you ever given orders to the
        morning,
    or shown the dawn its place,
13 that it might take the earth by the
        edges
    and shake the wicked out of it?
14 The earth takes shape like clay under
        a seal;
    its features stand out like those of a
        garment.
15 The wicked are denied their light,
    and their upraised arm is broken.

16 "Have you journeyed to the springs
        of the sea
    or walked in the recesses of the
        deep?

17 Have the gates of death been shown
        to you?
    Have you seen the gates of the
        shadow of death[b]?
18 Have you comprehended the vast
        expanses of the earth?
    Tell me, if you know all this.

19 "What is the way to the abode of
        light?
    And where does darkness reside?
20 Can you take them to their places?
    Do you know the paths to their
        dwellings?
21 Surely you know, for you were
        already born!
    You have lived so many years!

22 "Have you entered the storehouses of
        the snow
    or seen the storehouses of the hail,
23 which I reserve for times of trouble,
    for days of war and battle?
24 What is the way to the place where
        the lightning is dispersed,
    or the place where the east winds
        are scattered over the earth?
25 Who cuts a channel for the torrents of
        rain,
    and a path for the thunderstorm,
26 to water a land where no man lives,
    a desert with no one in it,
27 to satisfy a desolate wasteland
    and make it sprout with grass?
28 Does the rain have a father?
    Who fathers the drops of dew?
29 From whose womb comes the ice?
    Who gives birth to the frost from
        the heavens
30 when the waters become hard as
        stone,
    when the surface of the deep is
        frozen?

31 "Can you bind the beautiful[c]
        Pleiades?
    Can you loose the cords of Orion?
32 Can you bring forth the constellations
        in their seasons[d]

---

a 7 Hebrew the sons of God   b 17 Or gates of deep shadows   c 31 Or the twinkling; or the chains of the   d 32 Or the morning
star in its season

or lead out the Bear[a] with its cubs?

³³Do you know the laws of the
heavens?
Can you set up ⌊God's[b]⌋ dominion
over the earth?

³⁴"Can you raise your voice to the
clouds
and cover yourself with a flood of
water?
³⁵Do you send the lightning bolts on
their way?
Do they report to you, 'Here we
are'?
³⁶Who endowed the heart[c] with
wisdom
or gave understanding to the
mind[c]?
³⁷Who has the wisdom to count the
clouds?
Who can tip over the water jars of
the heavens
³⁸when the dust becomes hard
and the clods of earth stick
together?

³⁹"Do you hunt the prey for the lioness
and satisfy the hunger of the lions
⁴⁰when they crouch in their dens
or lie in wait in a thicket?
⁴¹Who provides food for the raven
when its young cry out to God
and wander about for lack of food?

39 "Do you know when the
mountain goats give birth?
Do you watch when the doe bears
her fawn?
²Do you count the months till they
bear?
Do you know the time they give
birth?
³They crouch down and bring forth
their young;
their labor pains are ended.
⁴Their young thrive and grow strong
in the wilds;
they leave and do not return.

⁵"Who let the wild donkey go free?

Who untied his ropes?
⁶I gave him the wasteland as his home,
the salt flats as his habitat.
⁷He laughs at the commotion in the
town;
he does not hear a driver's shout.
⁸He ranges the hills for his pasture
and searches for any green thing.

⁹"Will the wild ox consent to serve
you?
Will he stay by your manger at
night?
¹⁰Can you hold him to the furrow with
a harness?
Will he till the valleys behind you?
¹¹Will you rely on him for his great
strength?
Will you leave your heavy work to
him?
¹²Can you trust him to bring in your
grain
and gather it to your threshing
floor?

¹³"The wings of the ostrich flap
joyfully,
but they cannot compare with the
pinions and feathers of the
stork.
¹⁴She lays her eggs on the ground
and lets them warm in the sand,
¹⁵unmindful that a foot may crush
them,
that some wild animal may trample
them.
¹⁶She treats her young harshly, as if
they were not hers;
she cares not that her labor was in
vain,
¹⁷for God did not endow her with
wisdom
or give her a share of good sense.
¹⁸Yet when she spreads her feathers to
run,
she laughs at horse and rider.

¹⁹"Do you give the horse his strength
or clothe his neck with a flowing
mane?

---

[a] 32 Or out Leo   [b] 33 Or his; or their   [c] 36 The meaning of the Hebrew for this word is uncertain.

20Do you make him leap like a locust,
striking terror with his proud
snorting?
21He paws fiercely, rejoicing in his
strength,
and charges into the fray.
22He laughs at fear, afraid of nothing;
he does not shy away from the
sword.
23The quiver rattles against his side,
along with the flashing spear and
lance.
24In frenzied excitement he eats up the
ground;
he cannot stand still when the
trumpet sounds.
25At the blast of the trumpet he snorts,
'Aha!'

a rocky crag is his stronghold.
29From there he seeks out his food;
his eyes detect it from afar.
30His young ones feast on blood,
and where the slain are, there is
he."

40 The LORD said to Job:

2"Will the one who contends with the
Almighty correct him?
Let him who accuses God answer
him!"

3Then Job answered the LORD:

4"I am unworthy—how can I reply to
you?
I put my hand over my mouth.

God's people at prayer
JOB ASKS WHY

JOB 40:1-5 When we are in the midst of great pain, whether it is physical or emotional, our natural response is to cry out to God and ask along with Job, "Why me? What have I done to deserve this?"

We've all had times in which we've asked God why we have a certain affliction. We're troubled by the times when there is no apparent reason for the pain we must endure. It is in those times when we must rely upon God's strength and accept that we may never understand the "why." In His great wisdom, God will do what is best for us, no matter what. But that doesn't mean we should sit back and do nothing. We have the ability to speak to God and make our requests known to Him. And we should ask for healing, deliverance, or provision when we need it.

It's okay to ask God for a reason. But in the end it's best to accept God's will for you whether you know the reason or not, trusting that He will see you through any and all difficulties.

He catches the scent of battle from
afar,
the shout of commanders and the
battle cry.
26"Does the hawk take flight by your
wisdom
and spread his wings toward the
south?
27Does the eagle soar at your command
and build his nest on high?
28He dwells on a cliff and stays there at
night;

5I spoke once, but I have no answer—
twice, but I will say no more."

6Then the LORD spoke to Job out of
the storm:

7"Brace yourself like a man;
I will question you,
and you shall answer me.

8"Would you discredit my justice?
Would you condemn me to justify
yourself?
9Do you have an arm like God's,

and can your voice thunder like
his?
¹⁰ Then adorn yourself with glory and
splendor,
and clothe yourself in honor and
majesty.
¹¹ Unleash the fury of your wrath,
look at every proud man and bring
him low,

Praying Job 40:8-14
*Lord, forgive me if I have ever
questioned Your ways or judgments.*

¹² look at every proud man and humble
him,
crush the wicked where they stand.
¹³ Bury them all in the dust together;
shroud their faces in the grave.
¹⁴ Then I myself will admit to you
that your own right hand can save
you.

¹⁵ "Look at the behemoth,ᵃ
which I made along with you
and which feeds on grass like an ox.
¹⁶ What strength he has in his loins,
what power in the muscles of his
belly!
¹⁷ His tailᵇ sways like a cedar;
the sinews of his thighs are close-
knit.
¹⁸ His bones are tubes of bronze,
his limbs like rods of iron.
¹⁹ He ranks first among the works of
God,
yet his Maker can approach him
with his sword.
²⁰ The hills bring him their produce,
and all the wild animals play
nearby.
²¹ Under the lotus plants he lies,
hidden among the reeds in the
marsh.
²² The lotuses conceal him in their
shadow;
the poplars by the stream surround
him.

²³ When the river rages, he is not
alarmed;
he is secure, though the Jordan
should surge against his mouth.
²⁴ Can anyone capture him by the eyes,ᶜ
or trap him and pierce his nose?

41 "Can you pull in the leviathanᵈ
with a fishhook
or tie down his tongue with a rope?
² Can you put a cord through his nose
or pierce his jaw with a hook?
³ Will he keep begging you for mercy?
Will he speak to you with gentle
words?
⁴ Will he make an agreement with you
for you to take him as your slave
for life?
⁵ Can you make a pet of him like a bird
or put him on a leash for your girls?
⁶ Will traders barter for him?
Will they divide him up among the
merchants?
⁷ Can you fill his hide with harpoons
or his head with fishing spears?
⁸ If you lay a hand on him,
you will remember the struggle and
never do it again!
⁹ Any hope of subduing him is false;
the mere sight of him is
overpowering.
¹⁰ No one is fierce enough to rouse
him.
Who then is able to stand against
me?
¹¹ Who has a claim against me that I
must pay?
Everything under heaven belongs
to me.

¹² "I will not fail to speak of his limbs,
his strength and his graceful form.
¹³ Who can strip off his outer coat?
Who would approach him with a
bridle?
¹⁴ Who dares open the doors of his
mouth,
ringed about with his fearsome
teeth?

ᵃ *15* Possibly the hippopotamus or the elephant   ᵇ *17* Possibly trunk   ᶜ *24* Or *by a water hole*   ᵈ *1* Possibly the crocodile

¹⁵His back has[a] rows of shields
   tightly sealed together;
¹⁶each is so close to the next
   that no air can pass between.
¹⁷They are joined fast to one another;
   they cling together and cannot be
      parted.
¹⁸His snorting throws out flashes of
      light;
   his eyes are like the rays of dawn.
¹⁹Firebrands stream from his mouth;
   sparks of fire shoot out.
²⁰Smoke pours from his nostrils
   as from a boiling pot over a fire of
      reeds.
²¹His breath sets coals ablaze,
   and flames dart from his mouth.
²²Strength resides in his neck;
   dismay goes before him.
²³The folds of his flesh are tightly
      joined;
   they are firm and immovable.
²⁴His chest is hard as rock,
   hard as a lower millstone.
²⁵When he rises up, the mighty are
      terrified;
   they retreat before his thrashing.
²⁶The sword that reaches him has no
      effect,
   nor does the spear or the dart or the
      javelin.
²⁷Iron he treats like straw
   and bronze like rotten wood.
²⁸Arrows do not make him flee;
   slingstones are like chaff to him.
²⁹A club seems to him but a piece of
      straw;
   he laughs at the rattling of the
      lance.
³⁰His undersides are jagged potsherds,
   leaving a trail in the mud like a
      threshing sledge.
³¹He makes the depths churn like a
      boiling caldron
   and stirs up the sea like a pot of
      ointment.
³²Behind him he leaves a glistening
      wake;

one would think the deep had
   white hair.
³³Nothing on earth is his equal—
   a creature without fear.
³⁴He looks down on all that are
      haughty;
   he is king over all that are proud."

Job

42 Then Job replied to the LORD:

²"I know that you can do all things;
   no plan of yours can be thwarted.
³⌊You asked,⌋ 'Who is this that
      obscures my counsel without
      knowledge?'
   Surely I spoke of things I did not
      understand,
   things too wonderful for me to
      know.

⁴⌊"You said,⌋ 'Listen now, and I will
      speak;
   I will question you,
      and you shall answer me.'
⁵My ears had heard of you
   but now my eyes have seen you.
⁶Therefore I despise myself
   and repent in dust and ashes."

Epilogue

⁷After the LORD had said these things
to Job, he said to Eliphaz the Temanite,
"I am angry with you and your two
friends, because you have not spoken of
me what is right, as my servant Job has.
⁸So now take seven bulls and seven rams
and go to my servant Job and sacrifice a
burnt offering for yourselves. My servant
Job will pray for you, and I will accept his
prayer and not deal with you according
to your folly. You have not spoken of me
what is right, as my servant Job has." ⁹So
Eliphaz the Temanite, Bildad the Shuhite
and Zophar the Naamathite did what the
LORD told them; and the LORD accepted
Job's prayer.

¹⁰After Job had prayed for his friends,
the LORD made him prosperous again

ᵃ 15 Or *His pride is his*

> *Praying Job 42:10*
> Father God, help me to forgive
> others when they are thoughtless
> and lack compassion.

and gave him twice as much as he had before. ¹¹All his brothers and sisters and everyone who had known him before came and ate with him in his house. They comforted and consoled him over all the trouble the LORD had brought upon him, and each one gave him a piece of silver[a] and a gold ring.

¹²The LORD blessed the latter part of Job's life more than the first. He had fourteen thousand sheep, six thousand camels, a thousand yoke of oxen and a thousand donkeys. ¹³And he also had seven sons and three daughters. ¹⁴The first daughter he named Jemimah, the second Keziah and the third Keren-Happuch. ¹⁵Nowhere in all the land were there found women as beautiful as Job's daughters, and their father granted them an inheritance along with their brothers.

¹⁶After this, Job lived a hundred and forty years; he saw his children and their children to the fourth generation. ¹⁷And so he died, old and full of years.

---

[a] *11* Hebrew *him a kesitah*; a kesitah was a unit of money of unknown weight and value.

Author: David, Asaph, the sons of Korah, Solomon, Heman, Ethan, Moses, and other unknown authors

Date: Written over a period of centuries and compiled following Israel's exile, about the third century BC

Audience: Worshipers of Yahweh who would gather to pray at the temple in Jerusalem or in synagogues throughout the land of Israel

Prayer Themes:

- *Tell the Lord you want to have the integrity and character of a true worshiper so that you can always be close to Him (15:1-5).*

- *Tell God you are hungry and thirsty for more of Him, and only He can satisfy your soul (63:1-4).*

- *Call on God to give you a deep and unshakeable love for His Word so that you can stand strong and live pure in this generation (119:33-40).*

Psalms is the ultimate textbook on prayer and praise.

Here, in Israel's ancient hymnal, we find every kind of prayer imaginable: exuberant praises and terrified cries for help, spontaneous songs of thanksgiving and carefully constructed statements of divine truth, national laments and individual confessions, lengthy expressions of trust and concise pleas for justice.

No matter what the state of your soul—sorrow, doubt, joy, anger, gratitude, guilt, or wonder—Psalms will teach you how to express your heart honestly. Authentically. Thoroughly.

If you spend time reading and understanding these prayers and then take them and make them your own, you will find a more-satisfying prayer life. Much more than that, you will find God Himself. Then you will be able to exult with the psalmist: "Taste and see that the LORD is good; blessed is the man [or woman!] who takes refuge in him" (34:8).

Psalms

BOOK I

Psalms 1—41

Psalm 1

¹Blessed is the man
who does not walk in the counsel
of the wicked
or stand in the way of sinners
or sit in the seat of mockers.
²But his delight is in the law of the
LORD,
and on his law he meditates day and
night.
³He is like a tree planted by streams of
water,
which yields its fruit in season
and whose leaf does not wither.
Whatever he does prospers.

⁴Not so the wicked!
They are like chaff
that the wind blows away.
⁵Therefore the wicked will not stand
in the judgment,
nor sinners in the assembly of the
righteous.

⁶For the LORD watches over the way of
the righteous,
but the way of the wicked will
perish.

Psalm 2

¹Why do the nations conspire[a]
and the peoples plot in vain?
²The kings of the earth take their
stand

---

[a] *1 Hebrew; Septuagint* rage

and the rulers gather together
against the LORD
and against his Anointed One.[a]
3 "Let us break their chains," they say,
"and throw off their fetters."

4 The One enthroned in heaven laughs;
the Lord scoffs at them.
5 Then he rebukes them in his anger
and terrifies them in his wrath,
saying,
6 "I have installed my King[b]
on Zion, my holy hill."

7 I will proclaim the decree of the
LORD:

He said to me, "You are my Son[c];
today I have become your
Father.[d]
8 Ask of me,
and I will make the nations your
inheritance,
the ends of the earth your
possession.
9 You will rule them with an iron
scepter[e];
you will dash them to pieces like
pottery."

10 Therefore, you kings, be wise;
be warned, you rulers of the earth.
11 Serve the LORD with fear
and rejoice with trembling.
12 Kiss the Son, lest he be angry
and you be destroyed in your
way,
for his wrath can flare up in a
moment.
Blessed are all who take refuge in
him.

Psalm 3

A psalm of David. When he fled
from his son Absalom.

1 O LORD, how many are my foes!
How many rise up against me!

2 Many are saying of me,
"God will not deliver him."   Selah[f]

3 But you are a shield around me,
O LORD;
you bestow glory on me and lift[g] up
my head.
4 To the LORD I cry aloud,
and he answers me from his holy
hill.   Selah

5 I lie down and sleep;
I wake again, because the LORD
sustains me.
6 I will not fear the tens of thousands
drawn up against me on every side.

7 Arise, O LORD!
Deliver me, O my God!
Strike all my enemies on the jaw;
break the teeth of the wicked.

8 From the LORD comes deliverance.
May your blessing be on your
people.   Selah

Psalm 4

For the director of music. With stringed
instruments. A psalm of David.

1 Answer me when I call to you,
O my righteous God.
Give me relief from my distress;
be merciful to me and hear my
prayer.

2 How long, O men, will you turn my
glory into shame[h]?
How long will you love delusions
and seek false gods[i]?   Selah
3 Know that the LORD has set apart the
godly for himself;
the LORD will hear when I call to
him.

4 In your anger do not sin;
when you are on your beds,
search your hearts and be silent.
Selah

---

[a] 2 Or anointed one   [b] 6 Or king   [c] 7 Or son; also in verse 12   [d] 7 Or have begotten you   [e] 9 Or will break them with a rod of iron   [f] 2 A word of uncertain meaning, occurring frequently in the Psalms; possibly a musical term   [g] 3 Or LORD, / my Glorious One, who lifts   [h] 2 Or you dishonor my Glorious One   [i] 2 Or seek lies

Praying Psalm 4:4

*Father, keep me from the sin of anger
and help me to trust You more.*

---

⁵Offer right sacrifices
  and trust in the LORD.

⁶Many are asking, "Who can show us
    any good?"
  Let the light of your face shine
    upon us, O LORD.

⁷You have filled my heart with greater
    joy
  than when their grain and new
    wine abound.

⁸I will lie down and sleep in
    peace,
  for you alone, O LORD,
  make me dwell in safety.

Psalm 5

For the director of music. For flutes.
A psalm of David.

¹Give ear to my words, O LORD,
  consider my sighing.

²Listen to my cry for help,
  my King and my God,
  for to you I pray.

³In the morning, O LORD, you hear
    my voice;
  in the morning I lay my requests
    before you
  and wait in expectation.

⁴You are not a God who takes pleasure
    in evil;
  with you the wicked cannot dwell.

⁵The arrogant cannot stand in your
    presence;
  you hate all who do wrong.

GOING *deeper*

God Hears When You Call

READ AND CONSIDER: PSALM 4:1-8

"Know that the LORD has set apart the godly for himself; the LORD will hear when I call to him" (Psalm 4:3).

Psalms is one of the most encouraging books in all of Scripture. There is no emotion we can experience, whether elation or depression, guilt or gladness, that we won't find first expressed in Psalms. This book is the ancient hymnal of the Israelites, and the 150 psalms contained in its pages are a combination of prayer, poetry, and praise. When you don't know what to say to God, pray the psalms back to Him!

Whenever you feel *desperate* to know that God is close and that He is hearing your prayers and will answer you, read this verse again. Remember that God hears the prayers of the godly. The Hebrew word for *godly* is often translated "saints." God sees you as a saint, and He has set you apart for Himself. If you've accepted Christ as your Savior, you are a saint, a child of God, set apart for His glory (Romans 8:16-17). Yet even though we know this is how God sees us, there are times when we don't feel close to God—times when He feels far away and our prayers seem to go no further than the ceiling.

Your prayers may appear to go unanswered for many reasons. God may simply be giving you the answer that you are to wait. It could be that some sin in your life is clouding your communication with Him. Isaiah wrote, "Your iniquities have separated you from your God; your sins have hidden his face from you, so that he will not hear" (Isaiah 59:2). Make sure that nothing in your life is acting as a barrier between you and God.

Be encouraged! As God's child, you have His ear. Stay close, and He promises to hear when you call.

6 You destroy those who tell lies;
  bloodthirsty and deceitful men
    the LORD abhors.

7 But I, by your great mercy,
  will come into your house;
  in reverence will I bow down
    toward your holy temple.
8 Lead me, O LORD, in your
    righteousness
  because of my enemies—
    make straight your way before me.

9 Not a word from their mouth can be
    trusted;
  their heart is filled with
    destruction.
  Their throat is an open grave;
    with their tongue they speak deceit.
10 Declare them guilty, O God!
  Let their intrigues be their
    downfall.
  Banish them for their many sins,
    for they have rebelled against you.

11 But let all who take refuge in you be
    glad;
  let them ever sing for joy.
  Spread your protection over them,
    that those who love your name may
    rejoice in you.
12 For surely, O LORD, you bless the
    righteous;
  you surround them with your favor
    as with a shield.

Psalm 6

*For the director of music. With stringed
instruments. According to sheminith.[a]
A psalm of David.*

1 O LORD, do not rebuke me in your
    anger
  or discipline me in your wrath.
2 Be merciful to me, LORD, for I am
    faint;
  O LORD, heal me, for my bones are
    in agony.
3 My soul is in anguish.
  How long, O LORD, how long?

4 Turn, O Lord, and deliver me;
  save me because of your unfailing
    love.
5 No one remembers you when he is
    dead.
  Who praises you from the grave[b]?

6 I am worn out from groaning;
  all night long I flood my bed with
    weeping
  and drench my couch with tears.
7 My eyes grow weak with sorrow;
  they fail because of all my foes.

8 Away from me, all you who do evil,
  for the LORD has heard my
    weeping.
9 The LORD has heard my cry for
    mercy;
  the LORD accepts my prayer.

Praying Psalm 6:8-9
*Thank You for always hearing
my prayer, Lord.*

10 All my enemies will be ashamed and
    dismayed;
  they will turn back in sudden
    disgrace.

Psalm 7

*A shiggaion[c] of David, which he sang to
the LORD concerning Cush, a Benjamite.*

1 O LORD my God, I take refuge in
    you;
  save and deliver me from all who
    pursue me,
2 or they will tear me like a lion
  and rip me to pieces with no one to
    rescue me.

3 O LORD my God, if I have done
    this
  and there is guilt on my hands—
4 if I have done evil to him who is at
    peace with me
  or without cause have robbed my
    foe—

---

a Title: Probably a musical term   b 5 Hebrew *Sheol*   c Title: Probably a literary or musical term

5then let my enemy pursue and
    overtake me;
  let him trample my life to the
    ground
  and make me sleep in the dust.
                                    Selah

6Arise, O LORD, in your anger;
  rise up against the rage of my
    enemies.
  Awake, my God; decree justice.
7Let the assembled peoples gather
    around you.
  Rule over them from on high;
8   let the LORD judge the peoples.
  Judge me, O LORD, according to my
    righteousness,
  according to my integrity, O Most
    High.
9O righteous God,
  who searches minds and hearts,
  bring to an end the violence of the
    wicked
  and make the righteous secure.

10My shielda is God Most High,
  who saves the upright in heart.
11God is a righteous judge,
  a God who expresses his wrath
    every day.
12If he does not relent,
  heb will sharpen his sword;
  he will bend and string his bow.
13He has prepared his deadly
    weapons;
  he makes ready his flaming
    arrows.

14He who is pregnant with evil
  and conceives trouble gives birth to
    disillusionment.
15He who digs a hole and scoops it out
  falls into the pit he has made.
16The trouble he causes recoils on
    himself;
  his violence comes down on his
    own head.

17I will give thanks to the LORD
  because of his righteousness

and will sing praise to the name of
  the LORD Most High.

Psalm 8

For the director of music. According
to *gittith*.c A psalm of David.

1O LORD, our Lord,
  how majestic is your name in all
    the earth!

You have set your glory
  above the heavens.
2From the lips of children and
    infants
  you have ordained praised
because of your enemies,
  to silence the foe and the avenger.

Praying Psalm 8:1

*Lord, You are excellent and
worthy of all praise.*

3When I consider your heavens,
  the work of your fingers,
  the moon and the stars,
  which you have set in place,
4what is man that you are mindful of
    him,
  the son of man that you care for
    him?
5You made him a little lower than the
    heavenly beingse
  and crowned him with glory and
    honor.

6You made him ruler over the works
    of your hands;
  you put everything under his
    feet:
7all flocks and herds,
  and the beasts of the field,
8the birds of the air,
  and the fish of the sea,
  all that swim the paths of the seas.

9O LORD, our Lord,
  how majestic is your name in all
    the earth!

---

a 10 Or *sovereign* b 12 Or *If a man does not repent, / God* c Title: Probably a musical term d 2 Or *strength* e 5 Or *than God*

GOING deeper

Praise Is Your Greatest Weapon

READ AND CONSIDER: PSALM 9:1-20

"I will praise you, O LORD, with all my heart; I will tell of all your wonders . . . For he who avenges blood remembers; he does not ignore the cry of the afflicted" (Psalm 9:1,12).

Have you noticed how many psalms either begin or end with praise? Praise is *not* denial. The Bible never tells us to bury our pain. Instead, we are to pour it out like water from a pitcher: "I pour out my complaint before him; before him I tell my trouble" (142:2). However, once we've expressed our distressing emotions to God, He gives us a powerful weapon with which we can fight our battles—the weapon of praise.

God wants us to *destroy* evil, not just try to outrun it. He doesn't want us to only try to defend ourselves and stay alive; He wants us to push the enemy back. He wants us to say as David did, "I pursued my enemies and crushed them; I did not turn back till they were destroyed. I crushed them completely, and they could not rise; they fell beneath my feet. You armed me with strength for battle; you made my adversaries bow at my feet" (2 Samuel 22:38-40).

Praise is one of our greatest weapons of warfare. "The weapons we fight with are not the weapons of the world. On the contrary, they have divine power to demolish strongholds" (2 Corinthians 10:4). When we praise God, our enemies have to turn back from attacking because they cannot stand in His presence. Every time you praise Jesus for His victory on the cross, it reminds the devil of his greatest defeat. And he hates that.

You don't have to praise God *for* your troubles, but you can praise Him in the *midst* of them. And rest secure that He "remembers; he does not ignore the cry of the afflicted" (9:12).

Psalm 9[a]

For the director of music. To the tune of "The Death of the Son." A psalm of David.

1 I will praise you, O LORD, with all
    my heart;
  I will tell of all your wonders.
2 I will be glad and rejoice in you;
  I will sing praise to your name,
    O Most High.

3 My enemies turn back;
  they stumble and perish before you.
4 For you have upheld my right and my
    cause;
  you have sat on your throne,
    judging righteously.
5 You have rebuked the nations and
    destroyed the wicked;

  you have blotted out their name for
    ever and ever.
6 Endless ruin has overtaken the enemy,
  you have uprooted their cities;
  even the memory of them has
    perished.

7 The LORD reigns forever;
  he has established his throne for
    judgment.
8 He will judge the world in
    righteousness;
  he will govern the peoples with
    justice.
9 The LORD is a refuge for the
    oppressed,
  a stronghold in times of trouble.
10 Those who know your name will
    trust in you,

---

[a] Psalms 9 and 10 may have been originally a single acrostic poem, the stanzas of which begin with the successive letters of the Hebrew alphabet. In the Septuagint they constitute one psalm.

for you, LORD, have never forsaken
those who seek you.

[11] Sing praises to the LORD, enthroned
in Zion;
proclaim among the nations what
he has done.
[12] For he who avenges blood
remembers;
he does not ignore the cry of the
afflicted.

[13] O LORD, see how my enemies
persecute me!
Have mercy and lift me up from
the gates of death,
[14] that I may declare your praises
in the gates of the Daughter of
Zion
and there rejoice in your salvation.
[15] The nations have fallen into the pit
they have dug;
their feet are caught in the net they
have hidden.
[16] The LORD is known by his justice;
the wicked are ensnared by the
work of their hands.

Higgaion.[a] *Selah*

[17] The wicked return to the grave,[b]
all the nations that forget God.
[18] But the needy will not always be
forgotten,
nor the hope of the afflicted ever
perish.

[19] Arise, O LORD, let not man triumph;
let the nations be judged in your
presence.
[20] Strike them with terror, O LORD;
let the nations know they are but
men.   *Selah*

Psalm 10[c]

[1] Why, O LORD, do you stand far off?
Why do you hide yourself in times
of trouble?

[2] In his arrogance the wicked man
hunts down the weak,

who are caught in the schemes he
devises.
[3] He boasts of the cravings of his heart;
he blesses the greedy and reviles the
LORD.
[4] In his pride the wicked does not seek
him;
in all his thoughts there is no room
for God.
[5] His ways are always prosperous;
he is haughty and your laws are far
from him;
he sneers at all his enemies.
[6] He says to himself, "Nothing will
shake me;
I'll always be happy and never have
trouble."
[7] His mouth is full of curses and lies
and threats;
trouble and evil are under his
tongue.
[8] He lies in wait near the villages;
from ambush he murders the
innocent,
watching in secret for his victims.
[9] He lies in wait like a lion in cover;
he lies in wait to catch the helpless;
he catches the helpless and drags
them off in his net.
[10] His victims are crushed, they
collapse;
they fall under his strength.
[11] He says to himself, "God has
forgotten;
he covers his face and never sees."

[12] Arise, LORD! Lift up your hand,
O God.
Do not forget the helpless.
[13] Why does the wicked man revile
God?
Why does he say to himself,
"He won't call me to account"?
[14] But you, O God, do see trouble and
grief;
you consider it to take it in hand.
The victim commits himself to you;

---

[a] *16* Or *Meditation*; possibly a musical notation [b] *17* Hebrew *Sheol* [c] Psalms 9 and 10 may have been originally a single acrostic poem, the stanzas of which begin with the successive letters of the Hebrew alphabet. In the Septuagint they constitute one psalm.

you are the helper of the fatherless.
15Break the arm of the wicked and evil
man;
call him to account for his wickedness
that would not be found out.

16The LORD is King for ever and ever;
the nations will perish from his
land.
17You hear, O LORD, the desire of the
afflicted;
you encourage them, and you listen
to their cry,
18defending the fatherless and the
oppressed,
in order that man, who is of the
earth, may terrify no more.

Psalm 11

For the director of music. Of David.

1In the LORD I take refuge.
How then can you say to me:
"Flee like a bird to your mountain.
2For look, the wicked bend their
bows;
they set their arrows against the
strings
to shoot from the shadows
at the upright in heart.
3When the foundations are being
destroyed,
what can the righteous doa?"

4The LORD is in his holy temple;
the LORD is on his heavenly throne.
He observes the sons of men;
his eyes examine them.
5The LORD examines the righteous,
but the wickedb and those who love
violence
his soul hates.
6On the wicked he will rain
fiery coals and burning sulfur;
a scorching wind will be their lot.

7For the LORD is righteous,
he loves justice;
upright men will see his face.

Psalm 12

For the director of music. According
to sheminith.c A psalm of David.

1Help, LORD, for the godly are no
more;
the faithful have vanished from
among men.
2Everyone lies to his neighbor;
their flattering lips speak with
deception.

3May the LORD cut off all flattering
lips
and every boastful tongue
4that says, "We will triumph with our
tongues;
we own our lipsd—who is our
master?"

5"Because of the oppression of the
weak
and the groaning of the needy,
I will now arise," says the LORD.
"I will protect them from those
who malign them."
6And the words of the LORD are
flawless,
like silver refined in a furnace of
clay,
purified seven times.

Praying Psalm 12:5
Thank You, Lord, for keeping me safe.

7O LORD, you will keep us safe
and protect us from such people
forever.
8The wicked freely strut about
when what is vile is honored
among men.

Psalm 13

For the director of music. A psalm of David.

1How long, O LORD? Will you forget
me forever?
How long will you hide your face
from me?

---

a3 Or what is the Righteous One doing   b5 Or The LORD, the Righteous One, examines the wicked, /   cTitle: Probably a
musical term   d4 Or / our lips are our plowshares

Look to God as Your Protector

GOING *deeper*

READ AND CONSIDER: PSALM 12:1-8

"'Because of the oppression of the weak and the groaning of the needy, I will now arise,' says the LORD. *'I will protect them from those who malign them'" (Psalm 12:5).*

I know what it's like to have lived in the "bad part of town," where people are murdered, mugged, raped, and robbed. Where it wasn't safe to go out of the house. Fearing for my safety became a way of life there. In fact, many times I wondered if I would ever make it out of that place alive. No one stays in the bad part of town if they can possibly afford to live anywhere else.

After I came to know the Lord, I found the greatest comfort in being able to trust God as my Protector. God promises to rise up and protect the oppressed and needy from their oppressors. God did that for me. I intensely *yearned* for safety for years. He not only protected me in the dangerous place where I lived, but He led me to a place of safety.

We should never take for granted the protection of the Lord in our lives. We should not enter a plane, train, or automobile without praising Him as our Protector. We should not enter a day without *asking* Him for His protection and then thanking Him for it in advance. How many times have we been protected and spared from harm or disaster that we are not even aware of?

Remember, God also promises protection from those who malign you or who try to destroy your reputation without just cause. "It is mine to avenge; I will repay. In due time their foot will slip; their day of disaster is near and their doom rushes upon them" (Deuteronomy 32:35). He hears your prayerful groanings. He knows your needs. When you are slandered or your life is threatened, rest assured that God promises divine protection. Your life is safe in His hands.

²How long must I wrestle with my
    thoughts
  and every day have sorrow in my
    heart?
  How long will my enemy triumph
    over me?

³Look on me and answer, O LORD my
    God.
  Give light to my eyes, or I will
    sleep in death;
⁴my enemy will say, "I have overcome
    him,"
  and my foes will rejoice when I
    fall.

⁵But I trust in your unfailing love;
  my heart rejoices in your salvation.
⁶I will sing to the LORD,
  for he has been good to me.

Psalm 14

For the director of music. Of David.

¹The fool[a] says in his heart,
  "There is no God."
They are corrupt, their deeds are vile;
  there is no one who does good.

²The LORD looks down from heaven
    on the sons of men
to see if there are any who
    understand,
  any who seek God.
³All have turned aside,
  they have together become corrupt;
there is no one who does good,
  not even one.

⁴Will evildoers never learn—
  those who devour my people as
    men eat bread

---

[a] *1* The Hebrew words rendered *fool* in Psalms denote one who is morally deficient.

and who do not call on the LORD?
5 There they are, overwhelmed with
    dread,
  for God is present in the company
    of the righteous.
6 You evildoers frustrate the plans of
    the poor,
  but the LORD is their refuge.

7 Oh, that salvation for Israel would
    come out of Zion!
  When the LORD restores the
    fortunes of his people,
  let Jacob rejoice and Israel be glad!

Psalm 15

A psalm of David.

1 LORD, who may dwell in your
    sanctuary?
  Who may live on your holy hill?

2 He whose walk is blameless
    and who does what is righteous,
  who speaks the truth from his heart
3   and has no slander on his tongue,
  who does his neighbor no wrong
    and casts no slur on his fellowman,
4 who despises a vile man
    but honors those who fear the
    LORD,
  who keeps his oath
    even when it hurts,
5 who lends his money without usury
    and does not accept a bribe against
    the innocent.

He who does these things
  will never be shaken.

Psalm 16

A miktam[a] of David.

1 Keep me safe, O God,
  for in you I take refuge.

2 I said to the LORD, "You are my Lord;
  apart from you I have no good
    thing."
3 As for the saints who are in the land,

they are the glorious ones in whom
  is all my delight.[b]
4 The sorrows of those will increase
  who run after other gods.
  I will not pour out their libations of
    blood
  or take up their names on my lips.

5 LORD, you have assigned me my
    portion and my cup;
  you have made my lot secure.
6 The boundary lines have fallen for me
    in pleasant places;
  surely I have a delightful
    inheritance.

7 I will praise the LORD, who counsels
    me;
  even at night my heart instructs
    me.
8 I have set the LORD always before me.
  Because he is at my right hand,
  I will not be shaken.

9 Therefore my heart is glad and my
    tongue rejoices;
  my body also will rest secure,
10 because you will not abandon me to
    the grave,[c]
  nor will you let your Holy One[d] see
    decay.
11 You have made[e] known to me the
    path of life;
  you will fill me with joy in your
    presence,
  with eternal pleasures at your right
    hand.

Psalm 17

A prayer of David.

1 Hear, O LORD, my righteous plea;
  listen to my cry.
  Give ear to my prayer—
  it does not rise from deceitful lips.
2 May my vindication come from you;
  may your eyes see what is right.

3 Though you probe my heart and
    examine me at night,

---

though you test me, you will find
nothing;
I have resolved that my mouth will
not sin.
⁴As for the deeds of men—
by the word of your lips
I have kept myself
from the ways of the violent.
⁵My steps have held to your paths;
my feet have not slipped.

⁶I call on you, O God, for you will
answer me;
give ear to me and hear my prayer.
⁷Show the wonder of your great love,
you who save by your right hand
those who take refuge in you from
their foes.

⁸Keep me as the apple of your eye;
hide me in the shadow of your
wings
⁹from the wicked who assail me,
from my mortal enemies who
surround me.

¹⁰They close up their callous hearts,
and their mouths speak with
arrogance.
¹¹They have tracked me down, they
now surround me,
with eyes alert, to throw me to the
ground.
¹²They are like a lion hungry for prey,
like a great lion crouching in
cover.

¹³Rise up, O LORD, confront them,
bring them down;
rescue me from the wicked by your
sword.
¹⁴O LORD, by your hand save me from
such men,
from men of this world whose
reward is in this life.

You still the hunger of those you
cherish;
their sons have plenty,
and they store up wealth for their
children.

¹⁵And I—in righteousness I will see
your face;
when I awake, I will be satisfied
with seeing your likeness.

Psalm 18

For the director of music. Of David
the servant of the LORD. He sang to
the LORD the words of this song
when the LORD delivered him from
the hand of all his enemies and
from the hand of Saul. He said:

¹I love you, O LORD, my strength.

²The LORD is my rock, my fortress and
my deliverer;
my God is my rock, in whom I
take refuge.
He is my shield and the horn[a] of my
salvation, my stronghold.
³I call to the LORD, who is worthy of
praise,
and I am saved from my enemies.

⁴The cords of death entangled me;
the torrents of destruction
overwhelmed me.
⁵The cords of the grave[b] coiled around
me;
the snares of death confronted me.
⁶In my distress I called to the LORD;
I cried to my God for help.
From his temple he heard my voice;
my cry came before him, into his
ears.

⁷The earth trembled and quaked,
and the foundations of the
mountains shook;
they trembled because he was
angry.
⁸Smoke rose from his nostrils;
consuming fire came from his
mouth,
burning coals blazed out of it.
⁹He parted the heavens and came
down;
dark clouds were under his feet.
¹⁰He mounted the cherubim and flew;
he soared on the wings of the wind.

---

[a] 2 *Horn* here symbolizes strength.   [b] 5 Hebrew *Sheol*

11 He made darkness his covering, his
canopy around him—
the dark rain clouds of the sky.
12 Out of the brightness of his presence
clouds advanced,
with hailstones and bolts of
lightning.
13 The LORD thundered from heaven;
the voice of the Most High
resounded.[a]
14 He shot his arrows and scattered ⌊the
enemies⌋,
great bolts of lightning and routed
them.
15 The valleys of the sea were exposed
and the foundations of the earth
laid bare
at your rebuke, O LORD,
at the blast of breath from your
nostrils.

16 He reached down from on high and
took hold of me;
he drew me out of deep waters.
17 He rescued me from my powerful
enemy,
from my foes, who were too strong
for me.
18 They confronted me in the day of my
disaster,
but the LORD was my support.
19 He brought me out into a spacious
place;
he rescued me because he delighted
in me.

20 The LORD has dealt with me
according to my righteousness;
according to the cleanness of my
hands he has rewarded me.
21 For I have kept the ways of the LORD;
I have not done evil by turning
from my God.
22 All his laws are before me;
I have not turned away from his
decrees.
23 I have been blameless before him
and have kept myself from sin.

24 The LORD has rewarded me
according to my righteousness,
according to the cleanness of my
hands in his sight.

25 To the faithful you show yourself
faithful,
to the blameless you show yourself
blameless,
26 to the pure you show yourself pure,
but to the crooked you show
yourself shrewd.
27 You save the humble
but bring low those whose eyes are
haughty.
28 You, O LORD, keep my lamp
burning;
my God turns my darkness into
light.
29 With your help I can advance against
a troop[b];
with my God I can scale a wall.

30 As for God, his way is perfect;
the word of the LORD is flawless.
He is a shield
for all who take refuge in him.
31 For who is God besides the LORD?
And who is the Rock except our
God?
32 It is God who arms me with strength
and makes my way perfect.
33 He makes my feet like the feet of a
deer;
he enables me to stand on the
heights.
34 He trains my hands for battle;
my arms can bend a bow of bronze.
35 You give me your shield of victory,
and your right hand sustains me;
you stoop down to make me great.
36 You broaden the path beneath me,
so that my ankles do not turn.

37 I pursued my enemies and overtook
them;
I did not turn back till they were
destroyed.

---

a 13 Some Hebrew manuscripts and Septuagint (see also 2 Samuel 22:14); most Hebrew manuscripts resounded, / amid
hailstones and bolts of lightning   b 29 Or can run through a barricade

Persevering Prayer

GOING *deeper*

READ AND CONSIDER: PSALM 18:28-42

"You armed me with strength for battle; you made my adversaries bow at my feet" (Psalm 18:39).

Perseverance has been described as the ability to see a problem or a situation through to its resolution despite the difficulties encountered on the way. It's not hard to persevere when everything's going your way, but when the road to resolution becomes a virtual obstacle course, we need the strength to persevere through the pressure.

God's Word tells us over and over again that perseverance, while it may not be fun, is actually good for us, "because we know that suffering produces perseverance; perseverance, character; and character, hope" (Romans 5:3-4). In fact, we are actually *commanded* to stay with the course God puts us on. "Run with perseverance the race marked out for us" (Hebrews 12:1).

Ask the Lord to help you do as David did and be aggressive against the enemy, who would try to wear you down with discouragement. Ask Him to help you stand strong against this enemy until he is completely destroyed. David didn't stop until the job was done, and neither should we. We should pray through until we see the answer.

Ask God to give you the strength you need in order to persevere in prayer. With His power flowing through you, you can not only withstand whatever pressures are coming your way, you can eliminate them. Remember, you don't run this obstacle course alone. God is with you and will arm you with strength for the battle. Because of that you will have the victory.

38 I crushed them so that they could not rise;
    they fell beneath my feet.
39 You armed me with strength for battle;
    you made my adversaries bow at my feet.
40 You made my enemies turn their backs in flight,
    and I destroyed my foes.
41 They cried for help, but there was no one to save them—
    to the LORD, but he did not answer.
42 I beat them as fine as dust borne on the wind;
    I poured them out like mud in the streets.
43 You have delivered me from the attacks of the people;
    you have made me the head of nations;
    people I did not know are subject to me.
44 As soon as they hear me, they obey me;
    foreigners cringe before me.
45 They all lose heart;
    they come trembling from their strongholds.
46 The LORD lives! Praise be to my Rock!
    Exalted be God my Savior!
47 He is the God who avenges me,
    who subdues nations under me,
48   who saves me from my enemies.
You exalted me above my foes;
    from violent men you rescued me.
49 Therefore I will praise you among the nations, O LORD;

I will sing praises to your name.
50 He gives his king great victories;
  he shows unfailing kindness to his
    anointed,
  to David and his descendants
    forever.

Psalm 19

For the director of music. A psalm of David.

1 The heavens declare the glory of
    God;
  the skies proclaim the work of his
    hands.
2 Day after day they pour forth speech;
  night after night they display
    knowledge.
3 There is no speech or language
  where their voice is not heard.[a]
4 Their voice[b] goes out into all the
    earth,
  their words to the ends of the
    world.

In the heavens he has pitched a tent
    for the sun,
5   which is like a bridegroom coming
    forth from his pavilion,
  like a champion rejoicing to run his
    course.
6 It rises at one end of the heavens
  and makes its circuit to the other;
  nothing is hidden from its heat.

7 The law of the LORD is perfect,
  reviving the soul.
The statutes of the LORD are
    trustworthy,
  making wise the simple.
8 The precepts of the LORD are right,
  giving joy to the heart.
The commands of the LORD are
    radiant,
  giving light to the eyes.
9 The fear of the LORD is pure,
  enduring forever.
The ordinances of the LORD are sure
  and altogether righteous.
10 They are more precious than gold,
  than much pure gold;

they are sweeter than honey,
  than honey from the comb.
11 By them is your servant warned;
  in keeping them there is great
    reward.

12 Who can discern his errors?
  Forgive my hidden faults.
13 Keep your servant also from willful
    sins;
  may they not rule over me.
Then will I be blameless,
  innocent of great transgression.

14 May the words of my mouth and the
    meditation of my heart
  be pleasing in your sight,
  O LORD, my Rock and my
    Redeemer.

Psalm 20

For the director of music. A psalm of David.

1 May the LORD answer you when you
    are in distress;
  may the name of the God of Jacob
    protect you.
2 May he send you help from the
    sanctuary
  and grant you support from Zion.
3 May he remember all your sacrifices
  and accept your burnt offerings.
                                    Selah
4 May he give you the desire of your
    heart
  and make all your plans succeed.
5 We will shout for joy when you are
    victorious
  and will lift up our banners in the
    name of our God.
May the LORD grant all your requests.

6 Now I know that the LORD saves his
    anointed;
  he answers him from his holy
    heaven
  with the saving power of his right
    hand.
7 Some trust in chariots and some in
    horses,

---

a 3 Or They have no speech, there are no words; / no sound is heard from them   b 4 Septuagint, Jerome and Syriac; Hebrew line

but we trust in the name of the
    LORD our God.
8 They are brought to their knees and
    fall,
    but we rise up and stand firm.

9 O LORD, save the king!
    Answer[a] us when we call!

Psalm 21

For the director of music. A psalm of David.

1 O LORD, the king rejoices in your
    strength.
    How great is his joy in the victories
        you give!
2 You have granted him the desire of
        his heart
    and have not withheld the request
        of his lips.   *Selah*
3 You welcomed him with rich
        blessings
    and placed a crown of pure gold on
        his head.
4 He asked you for life, and you gave it
        to him—
    length of days, for ever and ever.
5 Through the victories you gave, his
        glory is great;
    you have bestowed on him splendor
        and majesty.
6 Surely you have granted him eternal
        blessings
    and made him glad with the joy of
        your presence.
7 For the king trusts in the LORD;
    through the unfailing love of the
        Most High
    he will not be shaken.

8 Your hand will lay hold on all your
        enemies;
    your right hand will seize your
        foes.
9 At the time of your appearing
    you will make them like a fiery
        furnace.
In his wrath the LORD will swallow
        them up,
    and his fire will consume them.

10 You will destroy their descendants
        from the earth,
    their posterity from mankind.
11 Though they plot evil against you
    and devise wicked schemes, they
        cannot succeed;
12 for you will make them turn their
        backs
    when you aim at them with drawn
        bow.

13 Be exalted, O LORD, in your strength;
    we will sing and praise your might.

Psalm 22

For the director of music. To ⌞the tune of⌟
    "The Doe of the Morning."
    A psalm of David.

1 My God, my God, why have you
        forsaken me?
    Why are you so far from saving me,
    so far from the words of my
        groaning?
2 O my God, I cry out by day, but you
        do not answer,
    by night, and am not silent.

3 Yet you are enthroned as the Holy
        One;
    you are the praise of Israel.[b]
4 In you our fathers put their trust;
    they trusted and you delivered
        them.
5 They cried to you and were saved;
    in you they trusted and were not
        disappointed.

Praying Psalm 22:3

Lord, how grateful I am that You
live in the praises of Your people.

6 But I am a worm and not a man,
    scorned by men and despised by the
        people.
7 All who see me mock me;
    they hurl insults, shaking their
        heads:
8 "He trusts in the LORD;

---

[a] 9 Or save! / O King, answer   [b] 3 Or Yet you are holy, / enthroned on the praises of Israel

let the LORD rescue him.
Let him deliver him,
   since he delights in him."

9 Yet you brought me out of the womb;
   you made me trust in you
   even at my mother's breast.
10 From birth I was cast upon you;
   from my mother's womb you have
      been my God.
11 Do not be far from me,
   for trouble is near
   and there is no one to help.

12 Many bulls surround me;
   strong bulls of Bashan encircle me.
13 Roaring lions tearing their prey
   open their mouths wide against me.
14 I am poured out like water,
   and all my bones are out of joint.
My heart has turned to wax;
   it has melted away within me.
15 My strength is dried up like a
      potsherd,
   and my tongue sticks to the roof of
      my mouth;
   you lay me^a in the dust of death.
16 Dogs have surrounded me;
   a band of evil men has encircled
      me,
   they have pierced^b my hands and
      my feet.
17 I can count all my bones;
   people stare and gloat over me.
18 They divide my garments among
      them
   and cast lots for my clothing.

19 But you, O LORD, be not far off;
   O my Strength, come quickly to
      help me.
20 Deliver my life from the sword,
   my precious life from the power of
      the dogs.
21 Rescue me from the mouth of the
      lions;
   save^c me from the horns of the wild
      oxen.

22 I will declare your name to my
      brothers;
   in the congregation I will praise
      you.
23 You who fear the LORD, praise him!
   All you descendants of Jacob, honor
      him!
   Revere him, all you descendants of
      Israel!
24 For he has not despised or disdained
   the suffering of the afflicted one;
he has not hidden his face from him
   but has listened to his cry for help.

25 From you comes the theme of my
      praise in the great assembly;
   before those who fear you^d will I
      fulfill my vows.
26 The poor will eat and be satisfied;
   they who seek the LORD will praise
      him—
   may your hearts live forever!
27 All the ends of the earth
   will remember and turn to the
      LORD,
and all the families of the nations
   will bow down before him,
28 for dominion belongs to the LORD
   and he rules over the nations.

29 All the rich of the earth will feast and
      worship;
   all who go down to the dust will
      kneel before him—
   those who cannot keep themselves
      alive.
30 Posterity will serve him;
   future generations will be told
      about the Lord.
31 They will proclaim his righteousness
   to a people yet unborn—
   for he has done it.

Psalm 23

A psalm of David.

1 The LORD is my shepherd, I shall not
   be in want.

---

^a15 Or /I am laid   ^b16 Some Hebrew manuscripts, Septuagint and Syriac; most Hebrew manuscripts /like the lion,
^c21 Or /you have heard   ^d25 Hebrew him

2 He makes me lie down in green
   pastures,
he leads me beside quiet waters,
3 he restores my soul.
He guides me in paths of
   righteousness
   for his name's sake.
4 Even though I walk
   through the valley of the shadow of
      death,[a]
I will fear no evil,
   for you are with me;
your rod and your staff,
   they comfort me.

Praying Psalm 23:3

*I pray that You, Father, would
restore my soul and lead me on the
path You have for my life.*

5 You prepare a table before me
   in the presence of my enemies.
You anoint my head with oil;
   my cup overflows.
6 Surely goodness and love will
   follow me
all the days of my life,
and I will dwell in the house of the
   LORD
   forever.

Psalm 24

Of David. A psalm.

1 The earth is the LORD's, and
   everything in it,
   the world, and all who live in it;
2 for he founded it upon the seas
   and established it upon the waters.

3 Who may ascend the hill of the
   LORD?
   Who may stand in his holy place?
4 He who has clean hands and a pure
      heart,
   who does not lift up his soul to an
      idol

or swear by what is false.[b]
5 He will receive blessing from the
   LORD
   and vindication from God his
      Savior.
6 Such is the generation of those who
   seek him,
   who seek your face, O God of
      Jacob.[c]   *Selah*

7 Lift up your heads, O you gates;
   be lifted up, you ancient doors,
   that the King of glory may come
      in.
8 Who is this King of glory?
   The LORD strong and mighty,
   the LORD mighty in battle.
9 Lift up your heads, O you gates;
   lift them up, you ancient doors,
   that the King of glory may come
      in.
10 Who is he, this King of glory?
   The LORD Almighty—
   he is the King of glory.   *Selah*

Psalm 25[d]

Of David.

1 To you, O LORD, I lift up my soul;
2 in you I trust, O my God.
Do not let me be put to shame,
   nor let my enemies triumph over
      me.
3 No one whose hope is in you
   will ever be put to shame,
but they will be put to shame
   who are treacherous without
      excuse.

4 Show me your ways, O LORD,
   teach me your paths;
5 guide me in your truth and teach me,
   for you are God my Savior,
   and my hope is in you all day long.
6 Remember, O LORD, your great
   mercy and love,
   for they are from of old.
7 Remember not the sins of my youth

and my rebellious ways;
according to your love remember me,
  for you are good, O LORD.

8 Good and upright is the LORD;
  therefore he instructs sinners in his
    ways.
9 He guides the humble in what is right
  and teaches them his way.
10 All the ways of the LORD are loving
    and faithful
  for those who keep the demands of
    his covenant.
11 For the sake of your name, O LORD,
  forgive my iniquity, though it is
    great.
12 Who, then, is the man that fears the
    LORD?
  He will instruct him in the way
    chosen for him.
13 He will spend his days in prosperity,
  and his descendants will inherit the
    land.
14 The LORD confides in those who fear
    him;
  he makes his covenant known to
    them.
15 My eyes are ever on the LORD,
  for only he will release my feet
    from the snare.

16 Turn to me and be gracious to me,
  for I am lonely and afflicted.
17 The troubles of my heart have
    multiplied;
  free me from my anguish.
18 Look upon my affliction and my
    distress
  and take away all my sins.
19 See how my enemies have increased
  and how fiercely they hate me!
20 Guard my life and rescue me;
  let me not be put to shame,
  for I take refuge in you.
21 May integrity and uprightness protect
    me,
  because my hope is in you.

22 Redeem Israel, O God,
  from all their troubles!

Psalm 26

Of David.

1 Vindicate me, O LORD,
  for I have led a blameless life;
I have trusted in the LORD
  without wavering.
2 Test me, O LORD, and try me,
  examine my heart and my mind;
3 for your love is ever before me,
  and I walk continually in your
    truth.
4 I do not sit with deceitful men,
  nor do I consort with hypocrites;
5 I abhor the assembly of evildoers
  and refuse to sit with the wicked.
6 I wash my hands in innocence,
  and go about your altar, O LORD,
7 proclaiming aloud your praise
  and telling of all your wonderful
    deeds.
8 I love the house where you live,
    O LORD,
  the place where your glory dwells.

9 Do not take away my soul along with
    sinners,
  my life with bloodthirsty men,
10 in whose hands are wicked schemes,
  whose right hands are full of bribes.
11 But I lead a blameless life;
  redeem me and be merciful to me.

12 My feet stand on level ground;
  in the great assembly I will praise
    the LORD.

Psalm 27

Of David.

1 The LORD is my light and my
    salvation—
  whom shall I fear?
The LORD is the stronghold of my
    life—
  of whom shall I be afraid?
2 When evil men advance against me
  to devour my flesh,[a]
  when my enemies and my foes attack
    me,

---

a 2 Or to slander me

GOING deeper

Your Heavenly Father Waits to Hear From You

READ AND CONSIDER: PSALM 27:1-13

"Though my father and mother forsake me, the LORD will receive me" (Psalm 27:10).

When Jesus' disciples asked Him to teach them to pray, He gave them a model beginning with the words "Our Father" (Matthew 6:9-13). Some of us have no problem thinking of God as a Father. We had good dads, or at least adequate ones, and the imagery of God in relationship to us as our Father is a positive one.

For others of us, however, thinking of God as a Father is troublesome, if not downright painful. Perhaps you're in that category. Your earthly father may have abandoned you or neglected you or even abused you. How do you wrap your mind around the concept of a heavenly Father when you have conflicted feelings about the earthly father who failed you in that category?

God says that in order to have a long, fruitful life and move into all He has for you, you must honor your father and mother (Exodus 20:12). It's a command! You may have had parents who were around and provided food and a place to live—and for that you certainly need to be grateful— but maybe they never put anything of themselves into your life. Maybe you could never expect Dad or Mom to support, encourage, or teach you anything. But you still need to honor them, if for no other reason than that they gave you life. Without them, you wouldn't be here.

But you can't fully honor your father and mother if you haven't forgiven them. No parent is perfect. No parent always does everything right. Ask God to show you if there is anything you need to forgive. Even if your parents are no longer living, forgiving them will clear the way for you to fully see God as your heavenly Father and to feel His love for you. He will heal and restore whatever you suffered or lost in your relationship with them.

Praise God that He is the perfect Father—loving, kind, accessible, helpful, encouraging, guiding, and comforting. Regardless of what your earthly father was like, your heavenly Father will be everything you need. Look to Him every day.

---

they will stumble and fall.
3 Though an army besiege me,
  my heart will not fear;
though war break out against me,
  even then will I be confident.

4 One thing I ask of the LORD,
  this is what I seek:
that I may dwell in the house of the
    LORD
  all the days of my life,
to gaze upon the beauty of the
    LORD
  and to seek him in his temple.
5 For in the day of trouble

he will keep me safe in his
    dwelling;
he will hide me in the shelter of his
    tabernacle
  and set me high upon a rock.
6 Then my head will be exalted
  above the enemies who surround
    me;
at his tabernacle will I sacrifice with
    shouts of joy;
  I will sing and make music to the
    LORD.

7 Hear my voice when I call, O LORD;
  be merciful to me and answer me.

8 My heart says of you, "Seek his[a]
    face!"
    Your face, LORD, I will seek.
9 Do not hide your face from me,
    do not turn your servant away in
        anger;
    you have been my helper.
  Do not reject me or forsake me,
    O God my Savior.
10 Though my father and mother forsake
        me,
    the LORD will receive me.
11 Teach me your way, O LORD;
    lead me in a straight path
    because of my oppressors.
12 Do not turn me over to the desire of
        my foes,
    for false witnesses rise up against
        me,
    breathing out violence.

13 I am still confident of this:
    I will see the goodness of the
        LORD
    in the land of the living.
14 Wait for the LORD;
    be strong and take heart
    and wait for the LORD.

Psalm 28

Of David.

1 To you I call, O LORD my Rock;
    do not turn a deaf ear to me.
  For if you remain silent,
    I will be like those who have gone
        down to the pit.
2 Hear my cry for mercy
    as I call to you for help,
  as I lift up my hands
    toward your Most Holy Place.

3 Do not drag me away with the
        wicked,
    with those who do evil,
  who speak cordially with their
        neighbors
    but harbor malice in their hearts.
4 Repay them for their deeds

and for their evil work;
repay them for what their hands have
    done
and bring back upon them what
    they deserve.
5 Since they show no regard for the
    works of the LORD
and what his hands have done,
he will tear them down
and never build them up again.

6 Praise be to the LORD,
    for he has heard my cry for mercy.
7 The LORD is my strength and my
        shield;
    my heart trusts in him, and I am
        helped.
  My heart leaps for joy
    and I will give thanks to him in
        song.

8 The LORD is the strength of his
        people,
    a fortress of salvation for his
        anointed one.
9 Save your people and bless your
        inheritance;
    be their shepherd and carry them
        forever.

Psalm 29

A psalm of David.

1 Ascribe to the LORD, O mighty ones,
    ascribe to the LORD glory and
        strength.
2 Ascribe to the LORD the glory due his
        name;
    worship the LORD in the splendor
        of his[b] holiness.

3 The voice of the LORD is over the
        waters;
    the God of glory thunders,
    the LORD thunders over the mighty
        waters.
4 The voice of the LORD is powerful;
    the voice of the LORD is majestic.
5 The voice of the LORD breaks the
        cedars;

---

a 8 Or To you, O my heart, he has said, "Seek my   b 2 Or LORD with the splendor of

the LORD breaks in pieces the
cedars of Lebanon.
⁶He makes Lebanon skip like a calf,
Sirionᵃ like a young wild ox.
⁷The voice of the LORD strikes
with flashes of lightning.
⁸The voice of the LORD shakes the
desert;
the LORD shakes the Desert of
Kadesh.
⁹The voice of the LORD twists the oaksᵇ
and strips the forests bare.
And in his temple all cry, "Glory!"

¹⁰The LORD sitsᶜ enthroned over the
flood;
the LORD is enthroned as King
forever.
¹¹The LORD gives strength to his
people;
the LORD blesses his people with
peace.

Psalm 30

A psalm. A song. For the dedication
of the temple.ᵈ Of David.

¹I will exalt you, O LORD,
for you lifted me out of the depths
and did not let my enemies gloat
over me.
²O LORD my God, I called to you for
help
and you healed me.
³O LORD, you brought me up from
the graveᵉ;
you spared me from going down
into the pit.

⁴Sing to the LORD, you saints of his;
praise his holy name.
⁵For his anger lasts only a moment,
but his favor lasts a lifetime;
weeping may remain for a night,
but rejoicing comes in the
morning.

⁶When I felt secure, I said,
"I will never be shaken."

⁷O LORD, when you favored me,
you made my mountainᶠ stand firm;
but when you hid your face,
I was dismayed.

⁸To you, O LORD, I called;
to the Lord I cried for mercy:
⁹"What gain is there in my
destruction,ᵍ
in my going down into the pit?
Will the dust praise you?
Will it proclaim your faithfulness?
¹⁰Hear, O LORD, and be merciful to
me;
O LORD, be my help."

¹¹You turned my wailing into dancing;
you removed my sackcloth and
clothed me with joy,
¹²that my heart may sing to you and
not be silent.
O LORD my God, I will give you
thanks forever.

Psalm 31

For the director of music.
A psalm of David.

¹In you, O LORD, I have taken refuge;
let me never be put to shame;
deliver me in your righteousness.
²Turn your ear to me,
come quickly to my rescue;
be my rock of refuge,
a strong fortress to save me.
³Since you are my rock and my
fortress,
for the sake of your name lead and
guide me.
⁴Free me from the trap that is set for
me,
for you are my refuge.
⁵Into your hands I commit my spirit;
redeem me, O LORD, the God of
truth.

⁶I hate those who cling to worthless
idols;
I trust in the LORD.

ᵃ6 That is, Mount Hermon   ᵇ9 Or LORD makes the deer give birth   ᶜ10 Or sat   ᵈTitle: Or palace   ᵉ3 Hebrew Sheol   ᶠ7 Or hill
country   ᵍ9 Or there if I am silenced

7 I will be glad and rejoice in your love,
  for you saw my affliction
  and knew the anguish of my soul.
8 You have not handed me over to the
    enemy
  but have set my feet in a spacious
    place.

9 Be merciful to me, O LORD, for I am
    in distress;
  my eyes grow weak with sorrow,
  my soul and my body with grief.
10 My life is consumed by anguish
  and my years by groaning;
  my strength fails because of my
    affliction,ª
  and my bones grow weak.
11 Because of all my enemies,
  I am the utter contempt of my
    neighbors;
  I am a dread to my friends—
    those who see me on the street flee
      from me.
12 I am forgotten by them as though I
    were dead;
    I have become like broken pottery.
13 For I hear the slander of many;
    there is terror on every side;
  they conspire against me
    and plot to take my life.

14 But I trust in you, O LORD;
  I say, "You are my God."
15 My times are in your hands;
  deliver me from my enemies
    and from those who pursue me.
16 Let your face shine on your servant;
  save me in your unfailing love.
17 Let me not be put to shame, O LORD,
    for I have cried out to you;
  but let the wicked be put to shame
    and lie silent in the grave.ᵇ
18 Let their lying lips be silenced,
    for with pride and contempt
  they speak arrogantly against the
    righteous.

19 How great is your goodness,
  which you have stored up for those
    who fear you,
which you bestow in the sight of men
  on those who take refuge in you.
20 In the shelter of your presence you
    hide them
  from the intrigues of men;
in your dwelling you keep them safe
  from accusing tongues.

21 Praise be to the LORD,
  for he showed his wonderful love
    to me
  when I was in a besieged city.
22 In my alarm I said,
  "I am cut off from your sight!"
Yet you heard my cry for mercy
  when I called to you for help.

23 Love the LORD, all his saints!
  The LORD preserves the faithful,
  but the proud he pays back in full.
24 Be strong and take heart,
  all you who hope in the LORD.

Psalm 32

Of David. A *maskil.*ᶜ

1 Blessed is he
  whose transgressions are forgiven,
  whose sins are covered.
2 Blessed is the man
  whose sin the LORD does not count
    against him
  and in whose spirit is no deceit.

3 When I kept silent,
  my bones wasted away
  through my groaning all day long.
4 For day and night
  your hand was heavy upon me;
my strength was sapped
  as in the heat of summer.   *Selah*
5 Then I acknowledged my sin to you
  and did not cover up my iniquity.
I said, "I will confess
  my transgressions to the LORD"—

Praying Psalm 32:1-5

*Lord, show me any sin in my life that
needs to be confessed before You so
that my heart can be clean.*

ª *10* Or *guilt* ᵇ *17* Hebrew *Sheol* ᶜTitle: Probably a literary or musical term

The Blessing of Confessing

READ AND CONSIDER: PSALM 32:1-11

"Then I acknowledged my sin to you and did not cover up my iniquity. I said, 'I will confess my transgressions to the LORD'—and you forgave the guilt of my sin" (Psalm 32:5).

Sin always brings separation. When we behave badly toward our family members or use our tongues carelessly so that others are wounded, our sinful actions lead to barriers being built between ourselves and other people.

Sin separates us from God as well. When we break any of the commandments that He lovingly set forth for our own protection, we put up a wall between ourselves and the One who made us. It's a wall of our own construction. But God's Word provides a solution to this barrier. It's called confession.

Confession has been defined as "agreeing with God about our sin." The most common Old Testament words for sin are "transgressions" and "iniquity," and Psalm 32 contains frequent references to these actions that serve to separate us from God.

When we don't confess our sins, we end up trying to hide ourselves from God. Just like Adam and Eve in the garden, we feel we can't face Him. But the problem with attempting to hide from God is that it's impossible. The Bible says that everything we do will be made known—even the things we said and thought in secret. "Nothing in all creation is hidden from God's sight. Everything is uncovered and laid bare before the eyes of him to whom we must give account" (Hebrews 4:13).

What a frightening thought! If each of us will have to give an account, the quicker we get it straight with God—the better. In fact, the sooner we deal with the sins we *can* see, the sooner God can reveal to us the ones we *can't*. And only God knows how much of that is residing in each of us. Sin always has consequences. King David described it best when he wrote of his own unconfessed sin: "When I kept silent, my bones wasted away through my groaning all day long. For day and night your hand was heavy upon me; my strength was sapped as in the heat of summer" (32:3-4).

Confession has a "consequence" too—a good consequence! A free and happy heart! When we confess our sins to God, we are blessed. To be blessed means to enjoy the favor of God. There is no greater blessing than knowing that your sins have been forgiven by God.

and you forgave
   the guilt of my sin.   *Selah*

⁶Therefore let everyone who is godly
      pray to you
   while you may be found;
surely when the mighty waters rise,
   they will not reach him.
⁷You are my hiding place;
   you will protect me from trouble
   and surround me with songs of
      deliverance.   *Selah*

⁸I will instruct you and teach you in
      the way you should go;
   I will counsel you and watch over
      you.
⁹Do not be like the horse or the mule,
   which have no understanding
but must be controlled by bit and
      bridle
   or they will not come to you.
¹⁰Many are the woes of the wicked,
   but the LORD's unfailing love

surrounds the man who trusts in
him.

11 Rejoice in the LORD and be glad, you
righteous;
sing, all you who are upright in
heart!

Psalm 33

1 Sing joyfully to the LORD, you
righteous;
it is fitting for the upright to praise
him.
2 Praise the LORD with the harp;
make music to him on the
ten-stringed lyre.
3 Sing to him a new song;
play skillfully, and shout for joy.

4 For the word of the LORD is right and
true;
he is faithful in all he does.
5 The LORD loves righteousness and
justice;
the earth is full of his unfailing
love.

6 By the word of the LORD were the
heavens made,
their starry host by the breath of his
mouth.
7 He gathers the waters of the sea into
jars[a];
he puts the deep into storehouses.
8 Let all the earth fear the LORD;
let all the people of the world
revere him.
9 For he spoke, and it came to be;
he commanded, and it stood
firm.
10 The LORD foils the plans of the
nations;
he thwarts the purposes of the
peoples.
11 But the plans of the LORD stand firm
forever,
the purposes of his heart through
all generations.

12 Blessed is the nation whose God is the
LORD,
the people he chose for his
inheritance.
13 From heaven the LORD looks down
and sees all mankind;
14 from his dwelling place he watches
all who live on earth—
15 he who forms the hearts of all,
who considers everything they do.
16 No king is saved by the size of his
army;
no warrior escapes by his great
strength.
17 A horse is a vain hope for deliverance;
despite all its great strength it
cannot save.
18 But the eyes of the LORD are on those
who fear him,
on those whose hope is in his
unfailing love,
19 to deliver them from death
and keep them alive in famine.

20 We wait in hope for the LORD;
he is our help and our shield.
21 In him our hearts rejoice,
for we trust in his holy name.
22 May your unfailing love rest upon us,
O LORD,
even as we put our hope in you.

Psalm 34[b]

Of David. When he pretended to be insane
before Abimelech, who drove
him away, and he left.

1 I will extol the LORD at all times;
his praise will always be on my lips.
2 My soul will boast in the LORD;
let the afflicted hear and rejoice.
3 Glorify the LORD with me;
let us exalt his name together.

4 I sought the LORD, and he answered me;
he delivered me from all my fears.
5 Those who look to him are radiant;
their faces are never covered with
shame.

---

[a] 7 Or sea as into a heap   [b] This psalm is an acrostic poem, the verses of which begin with the successive letters of the
Hebrew alphabet.

> *Praying Psalm 34:4*
> *Thank You, heavenly Father,*
> *for setting me free from all fear.*

6 This poor man called, and the LORD
  heard him;
  he saved him out of all his
  troubles.
7 The angel of the LORD encamps
  around those who fear him,
  and he delivers them.

8 Taste and see that the LORD is good;
  blessed is the man who takes refuge
  in him.
9 Fear the LORD, you his saints,
  for those who fear him lack
  nothing.
10 The lions may grow weak and
  hungry,
  but those who seek the LORD lack
  no good thing.

11 Come, my children, listen to me;
  I will teach you the fear of the
  LORD.
12 Whoever of you loves life
  and desires to see many good days,
13 keep your tongue from evil
  and your lips from speaking lies.
14 Turn from evil and do good;
  seek peace and pursue it.

15 The eyes of the LORD are on the
  righteous
  and his ears are attentive to their
  cry;
16 the face of the LORD is against those
  who do evil,
  to cut off the memory of them
  from the earth.

17 The righteous cry out, and the LORD
  hears them;
  he delivers them from all their
  troubles.
18 The LORD is close to the
  brokenhearted
  and saves those who are crushed in
  spirit.

19 A righteous man may have many
  troubles,
  but the LORD delivers him from
  them all;
20 he protects all his bones,
  not one of them will be broken.

21 Evil will slay the wicked;
  the foes of the righteous will be
  condemned.
22 The LORD redeems his servants;
  no one will be condemned who
  takes refuge in him.

Psalm 35

Of David.

1 Contend, O LORD, with those who
  contend with me;
  fight against those who fight
  against me.
2 Take up shield and buckler;
  arise and come to my aid.
3 Brandish spear and javelin[a]
  against those who pursue me.
Say to my soul,
  "I am your salvation."

4 May those who seek my life
  be disgraced and put to shame;
  may those who plot my ruin
  be turned back in dismay.
5 May they be like chaff before the
  wind,
  with the angel of the LORD driving
  them away;
6 may their path be dark and slippery,
  with the angel of the LORD
  pursuing them.
7 Since they hid their net for me
  without cause
  and without cause dug a pit for me,
8 may ruin overtake them by surprise—
  may the net they hid entangle
  them,
  may they fall into the pit, to their
  ruin.
9 Then my soul will rejoice in the
  LORD
  and delight in his salvation.

a 3 Or *and block the way*

10 My whole being will exclaim,
    "Who is like you, O LORD?
You rescue the poor from those too
      strong for them,
    the poor and needy from those who
      rob them."

11 Ruthless witnesses come forward;
    they question me on things I know
      nothing about.
12 They repay me evil for good
    and leave my soul forlorn.
13 Yet when they were ill, I put on
      sackcloth
    and humbled myself with fasting.
  When my prayers returned to me
      unanswered,
14   I went about mourning
    as though for my friend or brother.
  I bowed my head in grief
    as though weeping for my mother.
15 But when I stumbled, they gathered
      in glee;
    attackers gathered against me when
      I was unaware.
  They slandered me without
      ceasing.
16 Like the ungodly they maliciously
      mocked[a];
    they gnashed their teeth at me.
17 O Lord, how long will you look on?
    Rescue my life from their ravages,
    my precious life from these lions.
18 I will give you thanks in the great
      assembly;
    among throngs of people I will
      praise you.

19 Let not those gloat over me
    who are my enemies without cause;
  let not those who hate me without
      reason
    maliciously wink the eye.
20 They do not speak peaceably,
    but devise false accusations
    against those who live quietly in
      the land.
21 They gape at me and say, "Aha! Aha!
    With our own eyes we have seen it."

22 O LORD, you have seen this; be not
      silent.
    Do not be far from me, O Lord.
23 Awake, and rise to my defense!
    Contend for me, my God and Lord.
24 Vindicate me in your righteousness,
      O LORD my God;
    do not let them gloat over me.
25 Do not let them think, "Aha, just
      what we wanted!"
    or say, "We have swallowed him
      up."

26 May all who gloat over my distress
    be put to shame and confusion;
  may all who exalt themselves over me
    be clothed with shame and
      disgrace.
27 May those who delight in my
      vindication
    shout for joy and gladness;
  may they always say, "The LORD be
      exalted,
    who delights in the well-being of
      his servant."
28 My tongue will speak of your
      righteousness
    and of your praises all day long.

Psalm 36

For the director of music.
Of David the servant of the LORD.

1 An oracle is within my heart
    concerning the sinfulness of the
      wicked:[b]
  There is no fear of God
    before his eyes.
2 For in his own eyes he flatters
      himself
    too much to detect or hate his sin.
3 The words of his mouth are wicked
      and deceitful;
    he has ceased to be wise and to do
      good.
4 Even on his bed he plots evil;
    he commits himself to a sinful
      course
    and does not reject what is wrong.

---

a 16 Septuagint; Hebrew may mean *ungodly circle of mockers.*   b 1 Or heart: / Sin proceeds from the wicked.

5 Your love, O LORD, reaches to the
heavens,
your faithfulness to the skies.
6 Your righteousness is like the mighty
mountains,
your justice like the great deep.
O LORD, you preserve both man and
beast.
7 How priceless is your unfailing
love!
Both high and low among men
find[a] refuge in the shadow of your
wings.
8 They feast on the abundance of your
house;
you give them drink from your
river of delights.
9 For with you is the fountain of life;
in your light we see light.

10 Continue your love to those who
know you,
your righteousness to the upright
in heart.
11 May the foot of the proud not come
against me,
nor the hand of the wicked drive
me away.
12 See how the evildoers lie fallen—
thrown down, not able to rise!

Psalm 37[b]

Of David.

1 Do not fret because of evil men
or be envious of those who do
wrong;
2 for like the grass they will soon
wither,
like green plants they will soon die
away.

3 Trust in the LORD and do good;
dwell in the land and enjoy safe
pasture.
4 Delight yourself in the LORD
and he will give you the desires of
your heart.

5 Commit your way to the LORD;
trust in him and he will do this:
6 He will make your righteousness
shine like the dawn,
the justice of your cause like the
noonday sun.

7 Be still before the LORD and wait
patiently for him;
do not fret when men succeed in
their ways,
when they carry out their wicked
schemes.

8 Refrain from anger and turn from
wrath;
do not fret—it leads only to evil.
9 For evil men will be cut off,
but those who hope in the LORD
will inherit the land.

10 A little while, and the wicked will be
no more;
though you look for them, they
will not be found.
11 But the meek will inherit the land
and enjoy great peace.

12 The wicked plot against the
righteous
and gnash their teeth at them;
13 but the Lord laughs at the wicked,
for he knows their day is coming.

14 The wicked draw the sword
and bend the bow
to bring down the poor and needy,
to slay those whose ways are
upright.
15 But their swords will pierce their own
hearts,
and their bows will be broken.

16 Better the little that the righteous
have
than the wealth of many wicked;
17 for the power of the wicked will be
broken,
but the LORD upholds the
righteous.

---

a 7 Or love, O God! / Men find; or love! / Both heavenly beings and men / find   b This psalm is an acrostic poem, the stanzas of
which begin with the successive letters of the Hebrew alphabet.

18The days of the blameless are known
  to the LORD,
  and their inheritance will endure
    forever.
19In times of disaster they will not
    wither;
  in days of famine they will enjoy
    plenty.

20But the wicked will perish:
  The LORD's enemies will be like
    the beauty of the fields,
  they will vanish—vanish like
    smoke.

21The wicked borrow and do not
    repay,
  but the righteous give generously;
22those the LORD blesses will inherit
    the land,
  but those he curses will be cut off.

23If the LORD delights in a man's way,
  he makes his steps firm;
24though he stumble, he will not fall,
  for the LORD upholds him with his
    hand.

25I was young and now I am old,
  yet I have never seen the righteous
    forsaken
  or their children begging bread.
26They are always generous and lend
    freely;
  their children will be blessed.

27Turn from evil and do good;
  then you will dwell in the land
    forever.
28For the LORD loves the just
  and will not forsake his faithful
    ones.

  They will be protected forever,
    but the offspring of the wicked will
      be cut off;
29the righteous will inherit the land
  and dwell in it forever.

30The mouth of the righteous man
    utters wisdom,
  and his tongue speaks what is just.

31The law of his God is in his heart;
  his feet do not slip.

32The wicked lie in wait for the
    righteous,
  seeking their very lives;
33but the LORD will not leave them in
    their power
  or let them be condemned when
    brought to trial.

34Wait for the LORD
  and keep his way.
  He will exalt you to inherit the land;
    when the wicked are cut off, you
      will see it.

35I have seen a wicked and ruthless man
  flourishing like a green tree in its
    native soil,
36but he soon passed away and was no
    more;
  though I looked for him, he could
    not be found.

37Consider the blameless, observe the
    upright;
  there is a futureª for the man of
    peace.
38But all sinners will be destroyed;
  the futureᵇ of the wicked will be
    cut off.

39The salvation of the righteous comes
    from the LORD;
  he is their stronghold in time of
    trouble.
40The LORD helps them and delivers
    them;
  he delivers them from the wicked
    and saves them,
  because they take refuge in him.

Psalm 38

A psalm of David. A petition.

1O LORD, do not rebuke me in your
    anger
  or discipline me in your wrath.
2For your arrows have pierced me,

ª 37 Or there will be posterity   ᵇ 38 Or posterity

and your hand has come down
upon me.
3Because of your wrath there is no
health in my body;
my bones have no soundness
because of my sin.
4My guilt has overwhelmed me
like a burden too heavy to bear.

5My wounds fester and are loathsome
because of my sinful folly.
6I am bowed down and brought very
low;
all day long I go about mourning.
7My back is filled with searing pain;
there is no health in my body.
8I am feeble and utterly crushed;
I groan in anguish of heart.

9All my longings lie open before you,
O Lord;
my sighing is not hidden from you.
10My heart pounds, my strength fails
me;
even the light has gone from my
eyes.
11My friends and companions avoid me
because of my wounds;
my neighbors stay far away.
12Those who seek my life set their
traps,
those who would harm me talk of
my ruin;
all day long they plot deception.

13I am like a deaf man, who cannot
hear,
like a mute, who cannot open his
mouth;
14I have become like a man who does
not hear,
whose mouth can offer no reply.
15I wait for you, O Lord;
you will answer, O Lord my God.
16For I said, "Do not let them gloat
or exalt themselves over me when
my foot slips."

17For I am about to fall,
and my pain is ever with me.
18I confess my iniquity;

I am troubled by my sin.
19Many are those who are my vigorous
enemies;
those who hate me without reason
are numerous.
20Those who repay my good with evil
slander me when I pursue what is
good.

Prayer is . . .

pouring out your heart
and soul before God.

21O Lord, do not forsake me;
be not far from me, O my God.
22Come quickly to help me,
O Lord my Savior.

Psalm 39

For the director of music. For Jeduthun.
A psalm of David.

1I said, "I will watch my ways
and keep my tongue from sin;
I will put a muzzle on my mouth
as long as the wicked are in my
presence."
2But when I was silent and still,
not even saying anything good,
my anguish increased.
3My heart grew hot within me,
and as I meditated, the fire burned;
then I spoke with my tongue:

4"Show me, O Lord, my life's end
and the number of my days;
let me know how fleeting is my life.
5You have made my days a mere
handbreadth;
the span of my years is as nothing
before you.
Each man's life is but a breath.
Selah
6Man is a mere phantom as he goes to
and fro:

He bustles about, but only in vain;
he heaps up wealth, not knowing
who will get it.

7 "But now, Lord, what do I look for?
My hope is in you.
8 Save me from all my transgressions;
do not make me the scorn of fools.
9 I was silent; I would not open my
mouth,
for you are the one who has done
this.
10 Remove your scourge from me;
I am overcome by the blow of your
hand.
11 You rebuke and discipline men for
their sin;
you consume their wealth like a
moth—
each man is but a breath.   *Selah*

12 "Hear my prayer, O LORD,
listen to my cry for help;
be not deaf to my weeping.
For I dwell with you as an alien,
a stranger, as all my fathers were.
13 Look away from me, that I may
rejoice again
before I depart and am no more."

Psalm 40

For the director of music.
Of David. A psalm.

1 I waited patiently for the LORD;
he turned to me and heard my cry.
2 He lifted me out of the slimy pit,
out of the mud and mire;
he set my feet on a rock
and gave me a firm place to stand.
3 He put a new song in my mouth,
a hymn of praise to our God.
Many will see and fear
and put their trust in the LORD.

4 Blessed is the man
who makes the LORD his trust,
who does not look to the proud,

to those who turn aside to false
gods.[a]
5 Many, O LORD my God,
are the wonders you have done.
The things you planned for us
no one can recount to you;
were I to speak and tell of them,
they would be too many to declare.

6 Sacrifice and offering you did not
desire,
but my ears you have pierced[b,c];
burnt offerings and sin offerings
you did not require.
7 Then I said, "Here I am, I have
come—
it is written about me in the scroll.[d]
8 I desire to do your will, O my God;
your law is within my heart."

9 I proclaim righteousness in the great
assembly;
I do not seal my lips,
as you know, O LORD.
10 I do not hide your righteousness in
my heart;
I speak of your faithfulness and
salvation.
I do not conceal your love and your
truth
from the great assembly.

11 Do not withhold your mercy from
me, O LORD;
may your love and your truth
always protect me.
12 For troubles without number
surround me;
my sins have overtaken me, and I
cannot see.
They are more than the hairs of my
head,
and my heart fails within me.

13 Be pleased, O LORD, to save me;
O LORD, come quickly to help me.
14 May all who seek to take my life
be put to shame and confusion;
may all who desire my ruin

---

a 4 Or *to falsehood*   b 6 Hebrew; Septuagint *but a body you have prepared for me* (see also Symmachus and Theodotion)
c 6 Or *opened*   d 7 Or *come / with the scroll written for me*

be turned back in disgrace.
15May those who say to me, "Aha!
Aha!"
be appalled at their own shame.
16But may all who seek you
rejoice and be glad in you;
may those who love your salvation
always say,
"The LORD be exalted!"

17Yet I am poor and needy;
may the Lord think of me.
You are my help and my deliverer;
O my God, do not delay.

Psalm 41

For the director of music.
A psalm of David.

1Blessed is he who has regard for the
weak;
the LORD delivers him in times of
trouble.
2The LORD will protect him and
preserve his life;
he will bless him in the land
and not surrender him to the desire
of his foes.
3The LORD will sustain him on his
sickbed
and restore him from his bed of
illness.

4I said, "O LORD, have mercy on me;
heal me, for I have sinned against
you."
5My enemies say of me in malice,
"When will he die and his name
perish?"
6Whenever one comes to see me,
he speaks falsely, while his heart
gathers slander;
then he goes out and spreads it
abroad.

7All my enemies whisper together
against me;
they imagine the worst for me,
saying,
8"A vile disease has beset him;

he will never get up from the place
where he lies."
9Even my close friend, whom I
trusted,
he who shared my bread,
has lifted up his heel against me.

10But you, O LORD, have mercy on me;
raise me up, that I may repay them.
11I know that you are pleased with me,
for my enemy does not triumph
over me.
12In my integrity you uphold me
and set me in your presence forever.

13Praise be to the LORD, the God of
Israel,
from everlasting to everlasting.
Amen and Amen.

BOOK II
Psalms 42—72

Psalm 42[a]

For the director of music.
A *maskil*[b] of the Sons of Korah.

1As the deer pants for streams of water,
so my soul pants for you, O God.
2My soul thirsts for God, for the living
God.
When can I go and meet with God?
3My tears have been my food
day and night,
while men say to me all day long,
"Where is your God?"
4These things I remember
as I pour out my soul:
how I used to go with the multitude,
leading the procession to the house
of God,
with shouts of joy and thanksgiving
among the festive throng.

5Why are you downcast, O my soul?
Why so disturbed within me?
Put your hope in God,

---

[a]In many Hebrew manuscripts Psalms 42 and 43 constitute one psalm.   [b]Title: Probably a literary or musical term

for I will yet praise him,
my Savior and [6]my God.

My[a] soul is downcast within me;
  therefore I will remember you
from the land of the Jordan,
  the heights of Hermon—from
    Mount Mizar.
[7]Deep calls to deep
  in the roar of your waterfalls;
all your waves and breakers
  have swept over me.

Praying Psalm 42:5

Lord, I refuse to be discouraged,
for I know my hope is in You.

---

[8]By day the LORD directs his love,
  at night his song is with me—
  a prayer to the God of my life.

[9]I say to God my Rock,
  "Why have you forgotten me?
Why must I go about mourning,
  oppressed by the enemy?"
[10]My bones suffer mortal agony
  as my foes taunt me,
saying to me all day long,
  "Where is your God?"

[11]Why are you downcast, O my soul?
  Why so disturbed within me?
Put your hope in God,
  for I will yet praise him,
  my Savior and my God.

Psalm 43[b]

[1]Vindicate me, O God,
  and plead my cause against an
    ungodly nation;
  rescue me from deceitful and
    wicked men.
[2]You are God my stronghold.
  Why have you rejected me?
Why must I go about mourning,
  oppressed by the enemy?
[3]Send forth your light and your truth,
  let them guide me;

let them bring me to your holy
    mountain,
  to the place where you dwell.
[4]Then will I go to the altar of God,
  to God, my joy and my delight.
I will praise you with the harp,
  O God, my God.

[5]Why are you downcast, O my soul?
  Why so disturbed within me?
Put your hope in God,
  for I will yet praise him,
  my Savior and my God.

Psalm 44

For the director of music. Of the Sons
of Korah. A *maskil*.[c]

[1]We have heard with our ears,
    O God;
  our fathers have told us
what you did in their days,
  in days long ago.
[2]With your hand you drove out the
    nations
  and planted our fathers;
you crushed the peoples
  and made our fathers flourish.
[3]It was not by their sword that they
    won the land,
  nor did their arm bring them
    victory;
  it was your right hand, your arm,
    and the light of your face, for you
    loved them.

[4]You are my King and my God,
  who decrees[d] victories for Jacob.
[5]Through you we push back our
    enemies;
  through your name we trample our
    foes.
[6]I do not trust in my bow,
  my sword does not bring me
    victory;
[7]but you give us victory over our
    enemies,
  you put our adversaries to shame.

---

a 5,6 A few Hebrew manuscripts, Septuagint and Syriac; most Hebrew manuscripts *praise him for his saving help.* / [6]*O my God,*
my   b In many Hebrew manuscripts Psalms 42 and 43 constitute one psalm.   c Title: Probably a literary or musical term
d 4 Septuagint, Aquila and Syriac; Hebrew *King, O God; / command*

⁸In God we make our boast all day
    long,
    and we will praise your name
        forever.   *Selah*

⁹But now you have rejected and
    humbled us;
    you no longer go out with our
        armies.
¹⁰You made us retreat before the
    enemy,
    and our adversaries have plundered
        us.
¹¹You gave us up to be devoured like
    sheep
    and have scattered us among the
        nations.
¹²You sold your people for a pittance,
    gaining nothing from their sale.

¹³You have made us a reproach to our
    neighbors,
    the scorn and derision of those
        around us.
¹⁴You have made us a byword among
    the nations;
    the peoples shake their heads at us.
¹⁵My disgrace is before me all day long,
    and my face is covered with shame
¹⁶at the taunts of those who reproach
    and revile me,
    because of the enemy, who is bent
        on revenge.

¹⁷All this happened to us,
    though we had not forgotten you
    or been false to your covenant.
¹⁸Our hearts had not turned back;
    our feet had not strayed from your
        path.
¹⁹But you crushed us and made us a
    haunt for jackals
    and covered us over with deep
        darkness.

²⁰If we had forgotten the name of our
    God
    or spread out our hands to a foreign
        god,
²¹would not God have discovered it,

since he knows the secrets of the
    heart?
²²Yet for your sake we face death all
    day long;
    we are considered as sheep to be
        slaughtered.

²³Awake, O Lord! Why do you sleep?
    Rouse yourself! Do not reject us
        forever.
²⁴Why do you hide your face
    and forget our misery and
        oppression?

²⁵We are brought down to the dust;
    our bodies cling to the ground.
²⁶Rise up and help us;
    redeem us because of your
        unfailing love.

Psalm 45

For the director of music. To the tune
of "Lilies." Of the Sons of Korah.
A *maskil.*[a] A wedding song.

¹My heart is stirred by a noble theme
    as I recite my verses for the king;
    my tongue is the pen of a skillful
        writer.

²You are the most excellent of men
    and your lips have been anointed
        with grace,
    since God has blessed you forever.
³Gird your sword upon your side,
    O mighty one;
    clothe yourself with splendor and
        majesty.
⁴In your majesty ride forth victoriously
    in behalf of truth, humility and
        righteousness;
    let your right hand display awesome
        deeds.
⁵Let your sharp arrows pierce the
    hearts of the king's enemies;
    let the nations fall beneath your
        feet.
⁶Your throne, O God, will last for
    ever and ever;
    a scepter of justice will be the
        scepter of your kingdom.

---

[a] Title: Probably a literary or musical term

7 You love righteousness and hate
    wickedness;
  therefore God, your God, has set
      you above your companions
  by anointing you with the oil of joy.
8 All your robes are fragrant with
      myrrh and aloes and cassia;
  from palaces adorned with ivory
    the music of the strings makes you
      glad.
9 Daughters of kings are among your
      honored women;
  at your right hand is the royal bride
    in gold of Ophir.

10 Listen, O daughter, consider and give
      ear:
  Forget your people and your
      father's house.
11 The king is enthralled by your
      beauty;
  honor him, for he is your lord.
12 The Daughter of Tyre will come with
    a gift,[a]
  men of wealth will seek your favor.

13 All glorious is the princess within
    ⌊her chamber⌋;
  her gown is interwoven with gold.
14 In embroidered garments she is led to
      the king;
  her virgin companions follow her
    and are brought to you.
15 They are led in with joy and gladness;
    they enter the palace of the king.

16 Your sons will take the place of your
      fathers;
  you will make them princes
      throughout the land.
17 I will perpetuate your memory
      through all generations;
  therefore the nations will praise
    you for ever and ever.

Psalm 46

*For the director of music. Of the Sons of Korah.
According to* alamoth.[b] *A song.*

1 God is our refuge and strength,

    an ever-present help in trouble.
2 Therefore we will not fear, though
      the earth give way
  and the mountains fall into the
      heart of the sea,
3 though its waters roar and foam
  and the mountains quake with their
      surging.   *Selah*

4 There is a river whose streams make
      glad the city of God,
  the holy place where the Most
      High dwells.
5 God is within her, she will not fall;
    God will help her at break of day.
6 Nations are in uproar, kingdoms fall;
    he lifts his voice, the earth melts.

7 The LORD Almighty is with us;
    the God of Jacob is our fortress.
                                  Selah

8 Come and see the works of the LORD,
    the desolations he has brought on
      the earth.
9 He makes wars cease to the ends of
      the earth;
  he breaks the bow and shatters the
      spear,
  he burns the shields[c] with fire.
10 "Be still, and know that I am God;
    I will be exalted among the
      nations,
    I will be exalted in the earth."

11 The LORD Almighty is with us;
    the God of Jacob is our fortress.
                                  Selah

Psalm 47

*For the director of music. Of the Sons
of Korah. A psalm.*

1 Clap your hands, all you nations;
    shout to God with cries of joy.
2 How awesome is the LORD Most
      High,
  the great King over all the earth!
3 He subdued nations under us,
    peoples under our feet.
4 He chose our inheritance for us,

---

a 12 Or *A Tyrian robe is among the gifts*   b Title: Probably a musical term   c 9 Or *chariots* the pride of Jacob, whom he loved.

Selah

⁵God has ascended amid shouts of joy,
  the LORD amid the sounding of
    trumpets.
⁶Sing praises to God, sing praises;
  sing praises to our King, sing
    praises.
⁷For God is the King of all the earth;
  sing to him a psalm[a] of praise.
⁸God reigns over the nations;
  God is seated on his holy throne.
⁹The nobles of the nations assemble
  as the people of the God of
    Abraham,
  for the kings[b] of the earth belong to
    God;
  he is greatly exalted.

Psalm 48

A song. A psalm of the Sons of Korah.

¹Great is the LORD, and most worthy
    of praise,
  in the city of our God, his holy
    mountain.
²It is beautiful in its loftiness,
  the joy of the whole earth.
Like the utmost heights of Zaphon[c] is
    Mount Zion,
  the[d] city of the Great King.
³God is in her citadels;
  he has shown himself to be her
    fortress.

⁴When the kings joined forces,
  when they advanced together,
⁵they saw ⌊her⌋ and were astounded;
  they fled in terror.
⁶Trembling seized them there,
  pain like that of a woman in labor.
⁷You destroyed them like ships of
    Tarshish
  shattered by an east wind.
⁸As we have heard,
  so have we seen
in the city of the LORD Almighty,

in the city of our God:
  God makes her secure forever.

Selah

⁹Within your temple, O God,
  we meditate on your unfailing
    love.
¹⁰Like your name, O God,
  your praise reaches to the ends of
    the earth;
  your right hand is filled with
    righteousness.
¹¹Mount Zion rejoices,
  the villages of Judah are glad
  because of your judgments.

¹²Walk about Zion, go around her,
  count her towers,
¹³consider well her ramparts,
  view her citadels,
  that you may tell of them to the
    next generation.
¹⁴For this God is our God for ever and
    ever;
  he will be our guide even to the
    end.

Psalm 49

*For the director of music. Of the Sons
of Korah. A psalm.*

¹Hear this, all you peoples;
  listen, all who live in this world,
²both low and high,
  rich and poor alike:
³My mouth will speak words of
    wisdom;
  the utterance from my heart will
    give understanding.
⁴I will turn my ear to a proverb;
  with the harp I will expound my
    riddle:

⁵Why should I fear when evil days
    come,
  when wicked deceivers surround
    me—
⁶those who trust in their wealth
  and boast of their great riches?

---

a 7 Or *a maskil* (probably a literary or musical term)   b 9 Or *shields*   c 2 *Zaphon* can refer to a sacred mountain or the
direction north.   d 2 Or *earth, / Mount Zion, on the northern side / of the*

7 No man can redeem the life of
    another
    or give to God a ransom for him—
8 the ransom for a life is costly,
    no payment is ever enough—
9 that he should live on forever
    and not see decay.

10 For all can see that wise men die;
    the foolish and the senseless alike
      perish
    and leave their wealth to others.
11 Their tombs will remain their houses[a]
    forever,
    their dwellings for endless
      generations,
    though they had[b] named lands after
      themselves.

12 But man, despite his riches, does not
    endure;
    he is[c] like the beasts that perish.

13 This is the fate of those who trust in
    themselves,
    and of their followers, who approve
      their sayings.   *Selah*
14 Like sheep they are destined for the
    grave,[d]
    and death will feed on them.
The upright will rule over them in
    the morning;
    their forms will decay in the grave,[d]
    far from their princely mansions.
15 But God will redeem my life[e] from
    the grave;
    he will surely take me to himself.
        Selah

16 Do not be overawed when a man
    grows rich,
    when the splendor of his house
      increases;
17 for he will take nothing with him
    when he dies,
    his splendor will not descend with
      him.
18 Though while he lived he counted
    himself blessed—

and men praise you when you
    prosper—
19 he will join the generation of his
    fathers,
    who will never see the light ⌊of
      life⌋.

20 A man who has riches without
    understanding
    is like the beasts that perish.

Psalm 50
A psalm of Asaph.

1 The Mighty One, God, the LORD,
    speaks and summons the earth
    from the rising of the sun to the
      place where it sets.
2 From Zion, perfect in beauty,
    God shines forth.
3 Our God comes and will not be
    silent;
    a fire devours before him,
    and around him a tempest rages.
4 He summons the heavens above,
    and the earth, that he may judge his
      people:
5 "Gather to me my consecrated ones,
    who made a covenant with me by
      sacrifice."
6 And the heavens proclaim his
    righteousness,
    for God himself is judge.   *Selah*

7 "Hear, O my people, and I will
    speak,
    O Israel, and I will testify against
      you:
    I am God, your God.
8 I do not rebuke you for your
    sacrifices
    or your burnt offerings, which are
      ever before me.
9 I have no need of a bull from your
    stall
    or of goats from your pens,
10 for every animal of the forest is mine,
    and the cattle on a thousand hills.

---

[a] *11* Septuagint and Syriac; Hebrew *In their thoughts their houses will remain*   [b] *11* Or */ for they have*   [c] *12* Hebrew; Septuagint
and Syriac read verse 12 the same as verse 20.   [d] *14* Hebrew *Sheol*; also in verse 15   [e] *15* Or *soul*

11I know every bird in the mountains,
  and the creatures of the field are
    mine.
12If I were hungry I would not tell you,
  for the world is mine, and all that
    is in it.
13Do I eat the flesh of bulls
  or drink the blood of goats?
14Sacrifice thank offerings to God,
  fulfill your vows to the Most
    High,
15and call upon me in the day of
    trouble;
  I will deliver you, and you will
    honor me."

16But to the wicked, God says:

"What right have you to recite my
    laws
  or take my covenant on your lips?
17You hate my instruction
  and cast my words behind you.
18When you see a thief, you join with
    him;
  you throw in your lot with
    adulterers.
19You use your mouth for evil
  and harness your tongue to deceit.
20You speak continually against your
    brother
  and slander your own mother's
    son.
21These things you have done and I
    kept silent;
  you thought I was altogether[a] like
    you.
  But I will rebuke you
  and accuse you to your face.

22"Consider this, you who forget
    God,
  or I will tear you to pieces, with
    none to rescue:
23He who sacrifices thank offerings
    honors me,
  and he prepares the way
  so that I may show him[b] the
    salvation of God."

Psalm 51

For the director of music. A psalm of David.
When the prophet Nathan came to him after
David had committed adultery with Bathsheba.

1Have mercy on me, O God,
  according to your unfailing love;
according to your great compassion
  blot out my transgressions.
2Wash away all my iniquity
  and cleanse me from my sin.

3For I know my transgressions,
  and my sin is always before me.
4Against you, you only, have I sinned
  and done what is evil in your sight,
so that you are proved right when you
    speak
  and justified when you judge.
5Surely I was sinful at birth,
  sinful from the time my mother
    conceived me.
6Surely you desire truth in the inner
    parts[c];
  you teach[d] me wisdom in the
    inmost place.

7Cleanse me with hyssop, and I will be
    clean;
  wash me, and I will be whiter than
    snow.
8Let me hear joy and gladness;
  let the bones you have crushed
    rejoice.
9Hide your face from my sins
  and blot out all my iniquity.

10Create in me a pure heart, O God,
  and renew a steadfast spirit within
    me.
11Do not cast me from your presence
  or take your Holy Spirit from me.
12Restore to me the joy of your
    salvation
  and grant me a willing spirit, to
    sustain me.

13Then I will teach transgressors your
    ways,
  and sinners will turn back to you.

---

a 21 Or thought the 'I AM' was   b 23 Or and to him who considers his way / I will show   c 6 The meaning of the Hebrew for this phrase is uncertain.   d 6 Or you desired…; / you taught

Pray to Resist Temptation

GOING deeper

READ AND CONSIDER: PSALM 51:1-19

"Create in me a pure heart, O God, and renew a steadfast spirit within me. Do not cast me from your presence or take your Holy Spirit from me. Restore to me the joy of your salvation and grant me a willing spirit, to sustain me" (Psalm 51:10-12).

David wrote the words of this psalm after the prophet Nathan confronted him following David's adultery with Bathsheba. To his credit, David recognized his own sin, and this psalm is both a passionate plea for purity and a prayer in which David is crying out to God to be restored into the joy of right relationship. However, David could have spared himself much grief and sorrow (as well as for Bathsheba and her husband) if he had taken his feelings for Bathsheba to God in the first place.

God wants us to live in stark contrast to the world. The world is absorbed totally in the flesh. Sexual temptation of one sort or another is everywhere. The attitude toward casual sex and immorality in our society has gone far beyond what most people imagined it ever could. Those who have any sense of their own purpose and who God created them to be know that they cannot compromise in this area. The price is way too high. The consequences are far too great.

God says we are to "abstain from sinful desires, which war against your soul" (1 Peter 2:11). The things we lust after, whether they be sex, material goods, prestige, money, or power, create havoc in our souls. They cause peace to elude us. It's not that God doesn't want us to ever have any of these things; it's that we are to submit to His way and His timing and let *Him* bless us as He wills.

There is a way to resist all temptation of the flesh—especially sexual temptation—and that is to worship God. But it must be our *first* reaction, and not after the fact.

King David *should* have done this. Instead, when Bathsheba discovered she was pregnant, David tried to cover up the adultery by arranging to have her husband killed in battle.

This all began as one sinful thought. No one ends up in adultery without thinking about it first. It's at the *first thought* that prayer should arise. David was later confronted by the prophet Nathan about what he had done, and to his credit David confessed everything and was deeply repentant. Even so, there were stiff consequences for his actions, not the least of which was the death of David and Bathsheba's baby boy. And from that time on murder, death, and treachery became a part of his family and his reign.

Everyone makes mistakes. Don't let guilt over them separate you from God or make you feel distant from Him. That is the enemy's plan to keep you from all God has for you. The way to have victory over temptation is to go immediately before the Lord when temptation first crosses your mind. Don't wait the way David did. Don't entertain it for even a moment. Go to God right away and confess it. Then praise Him as the God who is more powerful than anything that tempts you.

14 Save me from bloodguilt,
    O God,
  the God who saves me,
  and my tongue will sing of your
    righteousness.

15 O Lord, open my lips,
  and my mouth will declare your
    praise.
16 You do not delight in sacrifice, or I
    would bring it;

you do not take pleasure in burnt
offerings.
17 The sacrifices of God are[a] a broken
spirit;
a broken and contrite heart,
O God, you will not despise.

18 In your good pleasure make Zion
prosper;
build up the walls of Jerusalem.
19 Then there will be righteous
sacrifices,
whole burnt offerings to delight
you;
then bulls will be offered on your
altar.

Psalm 52

For the director of music. A *maskil*[b] of David.
When Doeg the Edomite had gone to Saul
and told him: "David has gone
to the house of Ahimelech."

1 Why do you boast of evil, you
mighty man?
Why do you boast all day long,
you who are a disgrace in the eyes
of God?
2 Your tongue plots destruction;
it is like a sharpened razor,
you who practice deceit.
3 You love evil rather than good,
falsehood rather than speaking the
truth.   *Selah*
4 You love every harmful word,
O you deceitful tongue!

5 Surely God will bring you down to
everlasting ruin:
He will snatch you up and tear you
from your tent;
he will uproot you from the land of
the living.   *Selah*
6 The righteous will see and fear;
they will laugh at him, saying,
7 "Here now is the man
who did not make God his
stronghold
but trusted in his great wealth

and grew strong by destroying
others!"

8 But I am like an olive tree
flourishing in the house of God;
I trust in God's unfailing love
for ever and ever.
9 I will praise you forever for what you
have done;
in your name I will hope, for your
name is good.
I will praise you in the presence of
your saints.

Psalm 53

For the director of music. According
to *mahalath*.[c] A *maskil*[b] of David.

1 The fool says in his heart,
"There is no God."
They are corrupt, and their ways are
vile;
there is no one who does good.

2 God looks down from heaven
on the sons of men
to see if there are any who
understand,
any who seek God.
3 Everyone has turned away,
they have together become corrupt;
there is no one who does good,
not even one.

4 Will the evildoers never learn—
those who devour my people as
men eat bread
and who do not call on God?
5 There they were, overwhelmed with
dread,
where there was nothing to dread.
God scattered the bones of those who
attacked you;
you put them to shame, for God
despised them.

6 Oh, that salvation for Israel would
come out of Zion!
When God restores the fortunes of
his people,
let Jacob rejoice and Israel be glad!

---

[a] 17 Or *My sacrifice, O God, is*   [b] Title: Probably a literary or musical term   [c] Title: Probably a musical term

Psalm 54

For the director of music. With stringed instruments. A *maskil*[a] of David. When the Ziphites had gone to Saul and said, "Is not David hiding among us?"

1 Save me, O God, by your name;
   vindicate me by your might.
2 Hear my prayer, O God;
   listen to the words of my mouth.

3 Strangers are attacking me;
   ruthless men seek my life—
   men without regard for God.   *Selah*

4 Surely God is my help;
   the Lord is the one who sustains me.

5 Let evil recoil on those who slander me;
   in your faithfulness destroy them.

6 I will sacrifice a freewill offering to you;
   I will praise your name, O LORD,
   for it is good.
7 For he has delivered me from all my troubles,
   and my eyes have looked in triumph on my foes.

Psalm 55

For the director of music. With stringed instruments. A *maskil*[a] of David.

1 Listen to my prayer, O God,
   do not ignore my plea;
2   hear me and answer me.
   My thoughts trouble me and I am distraught
3   at the voice of the enemy,
   at the stares of the wicked;
   for they bring down suffering upon me
   and revile me in their anger.

4 My heart is in anguish within me;
   the terrors of death assail me.
5 Fear and trembling have beset me;
   horror has overwhelmed me.

6 I said, "Oh, that I had the wings of a dove!
   I would fly away and be at rest—
7 I would flee far away
   and stay in the desert;   *Selah*
8 I would hurry to my place of shelter,
   far from the tempest and storm."

9 Confuse the wicked, O Lord,
   confound their speech,
   for I see violence and strife in the city.
10 Day and night they prowl about on its walls;
   malice and abuse are within it.
11 Destructive forces are at work in the city;
   threats and lies never leave its streets.

12 If an enemy were insulting me,
   I could endure it;
   if a foe were raising himself against me,
   I could hide from him.
13 But it is you, a man like myself,
   my companion, my close friend,
14 with whom I once enjoyed sweet fellowship
   as we walked with the throng at the house of God.

15 Let death take my enemies by surprise;
   let them go down alive to the grave,[b]
   for evil finds lodging among them.

16 But I call to God,
   and the LORD saves me.
17 Evening, morning and noon
   I cry out in distress,
   and he hears my voice.
18 He ransoms me unharmed
   from the battle waged against me,
   even though many oppose me.
19 God, who is enthroned forever,
   will hear them and afflict them—
   Selah

---

a Title: Probably a literary or musical term   b 15 Hebrew *Sheol*

men who never change their ways
and have no fear of God.

20 My companion attacks his friends;
he violates his covenant.
21 His speech is smooth as butter,
yet war is in his heart;
his words are more soothing than oil,
yet they are drawn swords.

22 Cast your cares on the LORD
and he will sustain you;
he will never let the righteous fall.
23 But you, O God, will bring down the
wicked
into the pit of corruption;
bloodthirsty and deceitful men
will not live out half their days.

But as for me, I trust in you.

Psalm 56

For the director of music. To the tune of
"A Dove on Distant Oaks." Of David.
A *miktam*.[a] When the Philistines
had seized him in Gath.

1 Be merciful to me, O God, for men
hotly pursue me;
all day long they press their attack.
2 My slanderers pursue me all day long;
many are attacking me in their
pride.

3 When I am afraid,
I will trust in you.
4 In God, whose word I praise,
in God I trust; I will not be afraid.
What can mortal man do to me?

5 All day long they twist my words;
they are always plotting to harm
me.
6 They conspire, they lurk,
they watch my steps,
eager to take my life.

7 On no account let them escape;
in your anger, O God, bring down
the nations.
8 Record my lament;

list my tears on your scroll[b]—
are they not in your record?

9 Then my enemies will turn back
when I call for help.
By this I will know that God is for
me.
10 In God, whose word I praise,
in the LORD, whose word I praise—
11 in God I trust; I will not be afraid.
What can man do to me?

> *Praying Psalm 56:8-9*
> *Thank You, Lord, for seeing my tears*
> *and knowing my situation.*

12 I am under vows to you, O God;
I will present my thank offerings
to you.
13 For you have delivered me[c] from
death
and my feet from stumbling,
that I may walk before God
in the light of life.[d]

Psalm 57

For the director of music. To the tune
of "Do Not Destroy." Of David.
A *miktam*.[a] When he had fled
from Saul into the cave.

1 Have mercy on me, O God, have
mercy on me,
for in you my soul takes refuge.
I will take refuge in the shadow of
your wings
until the disaster has passed.

2 I cry out to God Most High,
to God, who fulfills his purpose
for me.
3 He sends from heaven and saves me,
rebuking those who hotly pursue
me;   *Selah*
God sends his love and his
faithfulness.
4 I am in the midst of lions;
I lie among ravenous beasts—

---

[a]Title: Probably a literary or musical term   [b]8 Or / put my tears in your wineskin   [c]13 Or my soul   [d]13 Or the land of the living

men whose teeth are spears and
arrows,
whose tongues are sharp swords.

5 Be exalted, O God, above the
heavens;
let your glory be over all the earth.

6 They spread a net for my feet—
I was bowed down in distress.
They dug a pit in my path—
but they have fallen into it
themselves.   *Selah*

7 My heart is steadfast, O God,
my heart is steadfast;
I will sing and make music.
8 Awake, my soul!
Awake, harp and lyre!
I will awaken the dawn.

9 I will praise you, O Lord, among the
nations;
I will sing of you among the
peoples.
10 For great is your love, reaching to the
heavens;
your faithfulness reaches to the skies.

11 Be exalted, O God, above the
heavens;
let your glory be over all the earth.

Psalm 58

For the director of music. ⌊To the tune of⌋
"Do Not Destroy." Of David. A *miktam.*[a]

1 Do you rulers indeed speak justly?
Do you judge uprightly among
men?
2 No, in your heart you devise
injustice,
and your hands mete out violence
on the earth.
3 Even from birth the wicked go astray;
from the womb they are wayward
and speak lies.
4 Their venom is like the venom of a
snake,
like that of a cobra that has stopped
its ears,

5 that will not heed the tune of the
charmer,
however skillful the enchanter may
be.

6 Break the teeth in their mouths,
O God;
tear out, O LORD, the fangs of the
lions!
7 Let them vanish like water that flows
away;
when they draw the bow, let their
arrows be blunted.
8 Like a slug melting away as it moves
along,
like a stillborn child, may they not
see the sun.

9 Before your pots can feel ⌊the heat of⌋
the thorns—
whether they be green or dry—the
wicked will be swept away.[b]
10 The righteous will be glad when they
are avenged,
when they bathe their feet in the
blood of the wicked.
11 Then men will say,
"Surely the righteous still are
rewarded;
surely there is a God who judges
the earth."

Psalm 59

For the director of music. ⌊To the tune of⌋
"Do Not Destroy." Of David. A *miktam.*[a]
When Saul had sent men to watch
David's house in order to kill him.[b]

1 Deliver me from my enemies,
O God;
protect me from those who rise up
against me.
2 Deliver me from evildoers
and save me from bloodthirsty men.

3 See how they lie in wait for me!
Fierce men conspire against me
for no offense or sin of mine,
O LORD.
4 I have done no wrong, yet they are
ready to attack me.

---

a Title: Probably a literary or musical term b 9 The meaning of the Hebrew for this verse is uncertain.

Arise to help me; look on my plight!

⁵O Lᴏʀᴅ God Almighty, the God of Israel,
rouse yourself to punish all the nations;
show no mercy to wicked traitors.
Selah

⁶They return at evening,
snarling like dogs,
and prowl about the city.
⁷See what they spew from their mouths—
they spew out swords from their lips,
and they say, "Who can hear us?"
⁸But you, O Lᴏʀᴅ, laugh at them;
you scoff at all those nations.

⁹O my Strength, I watch for you;
you, O God, are my fortress, ¹⁰my loving God.

God will go before me
and will let me gloat over those who slander me.
¹¹But do not kill them, O Lord our shield,ᵃ
or my people will forget.
In your might make them wander about,
and bring them down.
¹²For the sins of their mouths,
for the words of their lips,
let them be caught in their pride.
For the curses and lies they utter,
¹³   consume them in wrath,
consume them till they are no more.
Then it will be known to the ends of the earth
that God rules over Jacob.   *Selah*

¹⁴They return at evening,
snarling like dogs,
and prowl about the city.
¹⁵They wander about for food
and howl if not satisfied.

¹⁶But I will sing of your strength,
in the morning I will sing of your love;
for you are my fortress,
my refuge in times of trouble.

¹⁷O my Strength, I sing praise to you;
you, O God, are my fortress, my loving God.

Psalm 60

For the director of music. To the tune of "The Lily of the Covenant." A miktamᵇ of David. For teaching. When he fought Aram Naharaimᶜ and Aram Zobah,ᵈ and when Joab returned and struck down twelve thousand Edomites in the Valley of Salt.

¹You have rejected us, O God, and burst forth upon us;
you have been angry—now restore us!
²You have shaken the land and torn it open;
mend its fractures, for it is quaking.
³You have shown your people desperate times;
you have given us wine that makes us stagger.
⁴But for those who fear you, you have raised a banner
to be unfurled against the bow.
Selah

⁵Save us and help us with your right hand,
that those you love may be delivered.
⁶God has spoken from his sanctuary:
"In triumph I will parcel out Shechem
and measure off the Valley of Succoth.
⁷Gilead is mine, and Manasseh is mine;
Ephraim is my helmet,
Judah my scepter.
⁸Moab is my washbasin,
upon Edom I toss my sandal;
over Philistia I shout in triumph."

⁹Who will bring me to the fortified
        city?
    Who will lead me to Edom?
¹⁰Is it not you, O God, you who have
        rejected us
    and no longer go out with our
        armies?
¹¹Give us aid against the enemy,
    for the help of man is worthless.
¹²With God we will gain the victory,
    and he will trample down our
        enemies.

Psalm 61

For the director of music. With stringed
instruments. Of David.

¹Hear my cry, O God;
    listen to my prayer.

²From the ends of the earth I call to
        you,
    I call as my heart grows faint;
    lead me to the rock that is higher
        than I.
³For you have been my refuge,
    a strong tower against the foe.

⁴I long to dwell in your tent forever
    and take refuge in the shelter of
        your wings.   *Selah*
⁵For you have heard my vows, O God;
    you have given me the heritage of
        those who fear your name.

⁶Increase the days of the king's life,
    his years for many generations.
⁷May he be enthroned in God's
        presence forever;
    appoint your love and faithfulness
        to protect him.

⁸Then will I ever sing praise to your
        name
    and fulfill my vows day after day.

Psalm 62

For the director of music. For Jeduthun.
A psalm of David.

¹My soul finds rest in God alone;

my salvation comes from him.
²He alone is my rock and my salvation;
    he is my fortress, I will never be
        shaken.

³How long will you assault a man?
    Would all of you throw him
        down—
    this leaning wall, this tottering
        fence?
⁴They fully intend to topple him
    from his lofty place;
    they take delight in lies.
With their mouths they bless,
    but in their hearts they curse. *Selah*

⁵Find rest, O my soul, in God alone;
    my hope comes from him.
⁶He alone is my rock and my salvation;
    he is my fortress, I will not be
        shaken.
⁷My salvation and my honor depend
        on God[a];
    he is my mighty rock, my refuge.
⁸Trust in him at all times, O people;
    pour out your hearts to him,
    for God is our refuge.   *Selah*

⁹Lowborn men are but a breath,
    the highborn are but a lie;
if weighed on a balance, they are
        nothing;
    together they are only a breath.
¹⁰Do not trust in extortion
    or take pride in stolen goods;
though your riches increase,
    do not set your heart on them.

¹¹One thing God has spoken,
    two things have I heard:
that you, O God, are strong,
¹²   and that you, O Lord, are loving.
Surely you will reward each person
    according to what he has done.

Psalm 63

A psalm of David. When he was
in the Desert of Judah.

¹O God, you are my God,
    earnestly I seek you;

---

a 7 Or / God Most High is my salvation and my honor

Thirsting After God

GOING *deeper*

"O God, you are my God, earnestly I seek you; my soul thirsts for you, my body longs for you, in a dry and weary land where there is no water" (Psalm 63:1).

If you were lost in the desert without anything to eat or drink, you would seek food and water anywhere you could find it, even if it wasn't good for you. You wouldn't care how many impurities it had in it or how bad it tasted because you want to survive. But God has so much more for you than just survival.

What do *you* hunger and thirst for right now? Is it more of the Lord?

When King David hungered and thirsted for the Lord, he said, "As the deer pants for streams of water, so my soul pants for you, O God. My soul thirsts for God, for the living God. When can I go and meet with God?" (42:1-2). He wanted the Lord more than anything else. God's presence was food and water to him.

Have you ever been that thirsty for God? Sometimes we don't experience that deep thirst until we know what it's like to wander in the desert of our own desires. We grab for what the world has to offer only to discover that it leaves us empty.

Jesus once said, "If anyone is thirsty, let him come to me and drink. Whoever believes in me, as the Scripture has said, streams of living water will flow from within him" (John 7:37-38). Jesus was quoting from an invitation given in the Old Testament book of Isaiah, in which the prophet recorded these words: "Come, all you who are thirsty, come to the waters" (Isaiah 55:1). When we quench our spiritual thirst in the Lord, His Spirit will flow *through* us, and streams of living water will flow *from* us.

Drink deeply of all that God has for you in His Word, in His presence, and in prayer and praise, and you will never be thirsty again!

my soul thirsts for you,
　my body longs for you,
in a dry and weary land
　where there is no water.

2 I have seen you in the sanctuary
　and beheld your power and your
　　glory.
3 Because your love is better than life,
　my lips will glorify you.
4 I will praise you as long as I live,
　and in your name I will lift up my
　　hands.
5 My soul will be satisfied as with the
　　richest of foods;
　with singing lips my mouth will
　　praise you.

6 On my bed I remember you;
　I think of you through the watches
　　of the night.
7 Because you are my help,
　I sing in the shadow of your wings.
8 My soul clings to you;
　your right hand upholds me.
9 They who seek my life will be
　　destroyed;
　they will go down to the depths of
　　the earth.
10 They will be given over to the sword
　　and become food for jackals.

11 But the king will rejoice in God;
　all who swear by God's name will
　　praise him,

while the mouths of liars will be
silenced.

Psalm 64

For the director of music. A psalm of David.

[1]Hear me, O God, as I voice my
complaint;
protect my life from the threat of
the enemy.
[2]Hide me from the conspiracy of the
wicked,
from that noisy crowd of evildoers.

[3]They sharpen their tongues like
swords
and aim their words like deadly
arrows.
[4]They shoot from ambush at the
innocent man;
they shoot at him suddenly,
without fear.

[5]They encourage each other in evil
plans,
they talk about hiding their snares;
they say, "Who will see them[a]?"
[6]They plot injustice and say,
"We have devised a perfect plan!"
Surely the mind and heart of man
are cunning.

[7]But God will shoot them with
arrows;
suddenly they will be struck down.
[8]He will turn their own tongues
against them
and bring them to ruin;
all who see them will shake their
heads in scorn.

[9]All mankind will fear;
they will proclaim the works of
God
and ponder what he has done.
[10]Let the righteous rejoice in the LORD
and take refuge in him;
let all the upright in heart praise
him!

Psalm 65

For the director of music. A psalm
of David. A song.

[1]Praise awaits[b] you, O God, in Zion;
to you our vows will be fulfilled.
[2]O you who hear prayer,
to you all men will come.
[3]When we were overwhelmed by sins,
you forgave[c] our transgressions.
[4]Blessed are those you choose
and bring near to live in your
courts!
We are filled with the good things of
your house,
of your holy temple.

[5]You answer us with awesome deeds
of righteousness,
O God our Savior,
the hope of all the ends of the earth
and of the farthest seas,
[6]who formed the mountains by your
power,
having armed yourself with
strength,
[7]who stilled the roaring of the seas,
the roaring of their waves,
and the turmoil of the nations.
[8]Those living far away fear your
wonders;
where morning dawns and evening
fades
you call forth songs of joy.

[9]You care for the land and water it;
you enrich it abundantly.
The streams of God are filled with
water
to provide the people with grain,
for so you have ordained it.[d]
[10]You drench its furrows
and level its ridges;
you soften it with showers
and bless its crops.
[11]You crown the year with your
bounty,
and your carts overflow with
abundance.

---

[a]5 Or us   [b]1 Or befits; the meaning of the Hebrew for this word is uncertain.   [c]3 Or made atonement for   [d]9 Or for that is
how you prepare the land

Praying From a Right Heart

GOING *deeper*

READ AND CONSIDER: PSALM 66:1-20

"If I had cherished sin in my heart, the Lord would not have listened; but God has surely listened and heard my voice in prayer. Praise be to God, who has not rejected my prayer or withheld his love from me!" (Psalm 66:18-20).

The good thing about prayer—or the problem with prayer, depending on our perspective—is that we have to go to God to do it. This means we can't get away with anything. It means that any negative thoughts, bad attitudes, hardness of heart, or selfish motives are going to be revealed by the Lord. Fervent and honest prayer causes the depths of our hearts to be exposed. That can be uncomfortable. Even downright miserable. The verses above make it crystal clear that if we have any unforgiveness, bitterness, selfishness, pride, anger, irritation, or resentment in our hearts, our prayers will not be answered. Our hearts have to be right when we pray.

In the same way, God wants us to be right with others before we take our concerns or even our acts of service—our "gifts"—to Him. In what is called The Sermon on the Mount, Jesus explicitly instructed His followers on the importance of setting things right: "Therefore, if you are offering your gift at the altar and there remember that your brother has something against you, leave your gift there in front of the altar. First go and be reconciled to your brother; then come and offer your gift" (Matthew 5:23-24).

All of us jeopardize our own prayers when we don't pray them from a right heart. What is in our hearts when we pray has more effect on whether our prayers are answered than the actual prayer itself. That's why, when we come before God to pray, He asks us to first confess anything in our hearts that shouldn't be there. He does that so nothing will separate us from Him.

If you ever feel as if your prayers are not being heard, examine your heart and ask God to clearly reveal anything that you might need to confess before Him. Then that joy David felt will be your joy as well.

---

12 The grasslands of the desert overflow;
   the hills are clothed with gladness.
13 The meadows are covered with flocks
   and the valleys are mantled with
        grain;
   they shout for joy and sing.

Psalm 66

For the director of music. A song. A psalm.

1 Shout with joy to God, all the earth!
2   Sing the glory of his name;
   make his praise glorious!
3 Say to God, "How awesome are your
        deeds!
   So great is your power
   that your enemies cringe before you.
4 All the earth bows down to you;

they sing praise to you,
   they sing praise to your name."
                                    Selah

5 Come and see what God has done,
   how awesome his works in man's
        behalf!
6 He turned the sea into dry land,
   they passed through the waters on
        foot—
   come, let us rejoice in him.
7 He rules forever by his power,
   his eyes watch the nations—
   let not the rebellious rise up against
        him.   *Selah*

8 Praise our God, O peoples,
   let the sound of his praise be heard;

⁹he has preserved our lives
and kept our feet from slipping.
¹⁰For you, O God, tested us;
you refined us like silver.
¹¹You brought us into prison
and laid burdens on our backs.
¹²You let men ride over our heads;
we went through fire and water,
but you brought us to a place of
abundance.

¹³I will come to your temple with
burnt offerings
and fulfill my vows to you—
¹⁴vows my lips promised and my mouth
spoke
when I was in trouble.
¹⁵I will sacrifice fat animals to you
and an offering of rams;
I will offer bulls and goats.   *Selah*

¹⁶Come and listen, all you who fear
God;
let me tell you what he has done
for me.
¹⁷I cried out to him with my mouth;
his praise was on my tongue.
¹⁸If I had cherished sin in my heart,
the Lord would not have
listened;
¹⁹but God has surely listened
and heard my voice in prayer.
²⁰Praise be to God,
who has not rejected my prayer
or withheld his love from me!

Psalm 67

*For the director of music. With stringed
instruments. A psalm. A song.*

¹May God be gracious to us and
bless us
and make his face shine upon us,
Selah
²that your ways may be known on
earth,
your salvation among all nations.

³May the peoples praise you, O God;
may all the peoples praise you.

⁴May the nations be glad and sing for
joy,
for you rule the peoples justly
and guide the nations of the earth.
Selah
⁵May the peoples praise you, O God;
may all the peoples praise you.

⁶Then the land will yield its harvest,
and God, our God, will bless us.
⁷God will bless us,
and all the ends of the earth will
fear him.

Psalm 68

*For the director of music. Of David.
A psalm. A song.*

¹May God arise, may his enemies be
scattered;
may his foes flee before him.
²As smoke is blown away by the wind,
may you blow them away;
as wax melts before the fire,
may the wicked perish before God.
³But may the righteous be glad
and rejoice before God;
may they be happy and joyful.

⁴Sing to God, sing praise to his name,
extol him who rides on the
cloudsᵃ—
his name is the LORD—
and rejoice before him.
⁵A father to the fatherless, a defender
of widows,
is God in his holy dwelling.
⁶God sets the lonely in families,ᵇ
he leads forth the prisoners with
singing;
but the rebellious live in a sun-
scorched land.

⁷When you went out before your
people, O God,
when you marched through the
wasteland,   *Selah*
⁸the earth shook,
the heavens poured down rain,
before God, the One of Sinai,

ᵃ4 Or / *prepare the way for him who rides through the deserts*   ᵇ6 Or *the desolate in a homeland*

before God, the God of Israel.
⁹You gave abundant showers, O God;
    you refreshed your weary
        inheritance.
¹⁰Your people settled in it,
    and from your bounty, O God, you
        provided for the poor.

¹¹The Lord announced the word,
    and great was the company of those
        who proclaimed it:
¹²"Kings and armies flee in haste;
    in the camps men divide the
        plunder.
¹³Even while you sleep among the
        campfires,ᵃ
    the wings of ⌞my⌟ dove are sheathed
        with silver,
    its feathers with shining gold."
¹⁴When the Almightyᵇ scattered the
        kings in the land,
    it was like snow fallen on Zalmon.

¹⁵The mountains of Bashan are majestic
        mountains;
    rugged are the mountains of
        Bashan.
¹⁶Why gaze in envy, O rugged
        mountains,
    at the mountain where God
        chooses to reign,
    where the LORD himself will dwell
        forever?
¹⁷The chariots of God are tens of
        thousands
    and thousands of thousands;
    the Lord ⌞has come⌟ from Sinai into
        his sanctuary.
¹⁸When you ascended on high,
    you led captives in your train;
    you received gifts from men,
    even fromᶜ the rebellious—
    that you,ᵈ O LORD God, might
        dwell there.

¹⁹Praise be to the Lord, to God our
        Savior,
    who daily bears our burdens. *Selah*
²⁰Our God is a God who saves;

from the Sovereign LORD comes
    escape from death.
²¹Surely God will crush the heads of his
        enemies,
    the hairy crowns of those who go
        on in their sins.
²²The Lord says, "I will bring them
        from Bashan;
    I will bring them from the depths
        of the sea,
²³that you may plunge your feet in the
        blood of your foes,
    while the tongues of your dogs
        have their share."

²⁴Your procession has come into view,
        O God,
    the procession of my God and King
        into the sanctuary.
²⁵In front are the singers, after them the
        musicians;
    with them are the maidens playing
        tambourines.
²⁶Praise God in the great congregation;
    praise the LORD in the assembly of
        Israel.
²⁷There is the little tribe of Benjamin,
        leading them,
    there the great throng of Judah's
        princes,
    and there the princes of Zebulun
        and of Naphtali.

²⁸Summon your power, O Godᵉ;
    show us your strength, O God, as
        you have done before.
²⁹Because of your temple at Jerusalem
    kings will bring you gifts.
³⁰Rebuke the beast among the reeds,
    the herd of bulls among the calves
        of the nations.
    Humbled, may it bring bars of silver.
    Scatter the nations who delight in
        war.
³¹Envoys will come from Egypt;
    Cushᶠ will submit herself to God.
³²Sing to God, O kingdoms of the
        earth,

ᵃ *13* Or *saddlebags*   ᵇ *14* Hebrew *Shaddai*   ᶜ *18* Or *gifts for men, / even*   ᵈ *18* Or *they*   ᵉ *28* Many Hebrew manuscripts, Septuagint and Syriac; most Hebrew manuscripts *Your God has summoned power for you*   ᶠ *31* That is, the upper Nile region

sing praise to the Lord,   *Selah*
33to him who rides the ancient skies
    above,
  who thunders with mighty voice.
34Proclaim the power of God,
    whose majesty is over Israel,
    whose power is in the skies.
35You are awesome, O God, in your
    sanctuary;
  the God of Israel gives power and
    strength to his people.

Praise be to God!

Psalm 69

For the director of music. To the tune
of "Lilies." Of David.

1Save me, O God,
  for the waters have come up to my
    neck.
2I sink in the miry depths,
  where there is no foothold.
I have come into the deep waters;
  the floods engulf me.
3I am worn out calling for help;
  my throat is parched.
My eyes fail,
  looking for my God.
4Those who hate me without reason
  outnumber the hairs of my head;
many are my enemies without cause,
  those who seek to destroy me.
I am forced to restore
  what I did not steal.

5You know my folly, O God;
  my guilt is not hidden from you.

6May those who hope in you
  not be disgraced because of me,
  O Lord, the LORD Almighty;
may those who seek you
  not be put to shame because of me,
  O God of Israel.
7For I endure scorn for your sake,
  and shame covers my face.
8I am a stranger to my brothers,
  an alien to my own mother's sons;
9for zeal for your house consumes me,

and the insults of those who insult
  you fall on me.
10When I weep and fast,
  I must endure scorn;
11when I put on sackcloth,
  people make sport of me.
12Those who sit at the gate mock me,
  and I am the song of the drunkards.

13But I pray to you, O LORD,
  in the time of your favor;
in your great love, O God,
  answer me with your sure salvation.
14Rescue me from the mire,
  do not let me sink;
deliver me from those who hate me,
  from the deep waters.
15Do not let the floodwaters engulf me
  or the depths swallow me up
  or the pit close its mouth over me.
16Answer me, O LORD, out of the
    goodness of your love;
  in your great mercy turn to me.
17Do not hide your face from your
    servant;
  answer me quickly, for I am in
    trouble.
18Come near and rescue me;
  redeem me because of my foes.

19You know how I am scorned,
    disgraced and shamed;
  all my enemies are before you.
20Scorn has broken my heart
  and has left me helpless;
I looked for sympathy, but there was
    none,
  for comforters, but I found none.
21They put gall in my food
  and gave me vinegar for my thirst.

22May the table set before them become
    a snare;
  may it become retribution and[a] a
    trap.
23May their eyes be darkened so they
    cannot see,
  and their backs be bent forever.
24Pour out your wrath on them;
  let your fierce anger overtake them.

---

[a] 22 Or *snare / and their fellowship become*

²⁵May their place be deserted;
    let there be no one to dwell in their
        tents.
²⁶For they persecute those you wound
    and talk about the pain of those you
        hurt.
²⁷Charge them with crime upon crime;
    do not let them share in your
        salvation.
²⁸May they be blotted out of the book
        of life
    and not be listed with the
        righteous.

²⁹I am in pain and distress;
    may your salvation, O God, protect
        me.

³⁰I will praise God's name in song
    and glorify him with thanksgiving.
³¹This will please the LORD more than
        an ox,
    more than a bull with its horns and
        hoofs.
³²The poor will see and be glad—
    you who seek God, may your
        hearts live!
³³The LORD hears the needy
    and does not despise his captive
        people.

³⁴Let heaven and earth praise him,
    the seas and all that move in them,
³⁵for God will save Zion
    and rebuild the cities of Judah.
    Then people will settle there and
        possess it;
³⁶   the children of his servants will
        inherit it,
    and those who love his name will
        dwell there.

Psalm 70

For the director of music. Of David.
A petition.

¹Hasten, O God, to save me;
    O LORD, come quickly to help me.
²May those who seek my life
    be put to shame and confusion;
may all who desire my ruin

be turned back in disgrace.
³May those who say to me, "Aha!
        Aha!"
    turn back because of their shame.
⁴But may all who seek you
    rejoice and be glad in you;
may those who love your salvation
    always say,
    "Let God be exalted!"

⁵Yet I am poor and needy;
    come quickly to me, O God.
You are my help and my deliverer;
    O LORD, do not delay.

Psalm 71

¹In you, O LORD, I have taken refuge;
    let me never be put to shame.
²Rescue me and deliver me in your
        righteousness;
    turn your ear to me and save me.
³Be my rock of refuge,
    to which I can always go;
give the command to save me,
    for you are my rock and my
        fortress.
⁴Deliver me, O my God, from the
        hand of the wicked,
    from the grasp of evil and cruel
        men.

⁵For you have been my hope,
    O Sovereign LORD,
    my confidence since my youth.
⁶From birth I have relied on you;
    you brought me forth from my
        mother's womb.
    I will ever praise you.
⁷I have become like a portent to many,
    but you are my strong refuge.
⁸My mouth is filled with your praise,
    declaring your splendor all day
        long.

⁹Do not cast me away when I am old;
    do not forsake me when my
        strength is gone.
¹⁰For my enemies speak against me;
    those who wait to kill me conspire
        together.
¹¹They say, "God has forsaken him;

pursue him and seize him,
for no one will rescue him."
12 Be not far from me, O God;
come quickly, O my God, to help
me.
13 May my accusers perish in shame;
may those who want to harm me
be covered with scorn and disgrace.

14 But as for me, I will always have
hope;
I will praise you more and more.
15 My mouth will tell of your
righteousness,
of your salvation all day long,
though I know not its measure.
16 I will come and proclaim your
mighty acts, O Sovereign
LORD;
I will proclaim your righteousness,
yours alone.
17 Since my youth, O God, you have
taught me,
and to this day I declare your
marvelous deeds.
18 Even when I am old and gray,
do not forsake me, O God,
till I declare your power to the next
generation,
your might to all who are to come.

19 Your righteousness reaches to the
skies, O God,
you who have done great things.
Who, O God, is like you?
20 Though you have made me see
troubles, many and bitter,
you will restore my life again;
from the depths of the earth
you will again bring me up.
21 You will increase my honor
and comfort me once again.

22 I will praise you with the harp
for your faithfulness, O my God;
I will sing praise to you with the lyre,
O Holy One of Israel.
23 My lips will shout for joy
when I sing praise to you—

I, whom you have redeemed.
24 My tongue will tell of your righteous
acts
all day long,
for those who wanted to harm me
have been put to shame and
confusion.

Psalm 72

Of Solomon.

1 Endow the king with your justice,
O God,
the royal son with your
righteousness.
2 He will[a] judge your people in
righteousness,
your afflicted ones with justice.
3 The mountains will bring prosperity
to the people,
the hills the fruit of righteousness.
4 He will defend the afflicted among
the people
and save the children of the needy;
he will crush the oppressor.

5 He will endure[b] as long as the sun,
as long as the moon, through all
generations.
6 He will be like rain falling on a
mown field,
like showers watering the earth.
7 In his days the righteous will flourish;
prosperity will abound till the
moon is no more.

8 He will rule from sea to sea
and from the River[c] to the ends of
the earth.[d]
9 The desert tribes will bow before him
and his enemies will lick the dust.
10 The kings of Tarshish and of distant
shores
will bring tribute to him;
the kings of Sheba and Seba
will present him gifts.
11 All kings will bow down to him
and all nations will serve him.

---

[a] 2 Or May he; similarly in verses 3-11 and 17   [b] 5 Septuagint; Hebrew You will be feared   [c] 8 That is, the Euphrates
[d] 8 Or the end of the land

¹²For he will deliver the needy who cry
out,
the afflicted who have no one to
help.
¹³He will take pity on the weak and the
needy
and save the needy from death.
¹⁴He will rescue them from oppression
and violence,
for precious is their blood in his
sight.

Prayer is . . .

conversation with God, the closest
Friend you will ever have.

¹⁵Long may he live!
May gold from Sheba be given him.
May people ever pray for him
and bless him all day long.
¹⁶Let grain abound throughout the
land;
on the tops of the hills may it sway.
Let its fruit flourish like Lebanon;
let it thrive like the grass of the
field.
¹⁷May his name endure forever;
may it continue as long as the sun.

All nations will be blessed through
him,
and they will call him blessed.

¹⁸Praise be to the LORD God, the God
of Israel,
who alone does marvelous deeds.
¹⁹Praise be to his glorious name
forever;
may the whole earth be filled with
his glory.
Amen and Amen.

²⁰This concludes the prayers of David
son of Jesse.

BOOK III
Psalms 73—89

Psalm 73
A psalm of Asaph.

¹Surely God is good to Israel,
to those who are pure in heart.

²But as for me, my feet had almost
slipped;
I had nearly lost my foothold.
³For I envied the arrogant
when I saw the prosperity of the
wicked.

⁴They have no struggles;
their bodies are healthy and strong.ᵃ
⁵They are free from the burdens
common to man;
they are not plagued by human ills.
⁶Therefore pride is their necklace;
they clothe themselves with
violence.
⁷From their callous hearts comes
iniquityᵇ;
the evil conceits of their minds
know no limits.
⁸They scoff, and speak with malice;
in their arrogance they threaten
oppression.
⁹Their mouths lay claim to heaven,
and their tongues take possession of
the earth.
¹⁰Therefore their people turn to them
and drink up waters in
abundance.ᶜ
¹¹They say, "How can God know?
Does the Most High have
knowledge?"

¹²This is what the wicked are like—
always carefree, they increase in
wealth.

¹³Surely in vain have I kept my heart
pure;
in vain have I washed my hands in
innocence.
¹⁴All day long I have been plagued;

ᵃ*4* With a different word division of the Hebrew; Masoretic Text *struggles at their death; / their bodies are healthy*   ᵇ*7* Syriac
(see also Septuagint); Hebrew *Their eyes bulge with fat*   ᶜ*10* The meaning of the Hebrew for this verse is uncertain.

I have been punished every
morning.

15If I had said, "I will speak thus,"
I would have betrayed your children.
16When I tried to understand all this,
it was oppressive to me
17till I entered the sanctuary of God;
then I understood their final destiny.

18Surely you place them on slippery
ground;
you cast them down to ruin.
19How suddenly are they destroyed,
completely swept away by terrors!
20As a dream when one awakes,
so when you arise, O Lord,
you will despise them as fantasies.

21When my heart was grieved
and my spirit embittered,
22I was senseless and ignorant;
I was a brute beast before you.

23Yet I am always with you;
you hold me by my right hand.
24You guide me with your counsel,
and afterward you will take me
into glory.
25Whom have I in heaven but you?
And earth has nothing I desire
besides you.
26My flesh and my heart may fail,
but God is the strength of my heart
and my portion forever.

27Those who are far from you will
perish;
you destroy all who are unfaithful
to you.
28But as for me, it is good to be near
God.
I have made the Sovereign LORD
my refuge;
I will tell of all your deeds.

Psalm 74
A *maskil*a of Asaph.

1Why have you rejected us forever,
O God?

Why does your anger smolder
against the sheep of your
pasture?
2Remember the people you purchased
of old,
the tribe of your inheritance,
whom you redeemed—
Mount Zion, where you dwelt.
3Turn your steps toward these
everlasting ruins,
all this destruction the enemy has
brought on the sanctuary.

4Your foes roared in the place where
you met with us;
they set up their standards as signs.
5They behaved like men wielding axes
to cut through a thicket of trees.
6They smashed all the carved paneling
with their axes and hatchets.
7They burned your sanctuary to the
ground;
they defiled the dwelling place of
your Name.
8They said in their hearts, "We will
crush them completely!"
They burned every place where
God was worshiped in the
land.
9We are given no miraculous signs;
no prophets are left,
and none of us knows how long
this will be.

10How long will the enemy mock you,
O God?
Will the foe revile your name
forever?
11Why do you hold back your hand,
your right hand?
Take it from the folds of your
garment and destroy them!

12But you, O God, are my king from of
old;
you bring salvation upon the earth.
13It was you who split open the sea by
your power;
you broke the heads of the monster
in the waters.

---

aTitle: Probably a literary or musical term

¹⁴It was you who crushed the heads of
Leviathan
and gave him as food to the
creatures of the desert.
¹⁵It was you who opened up springs
and streams;
you dried up the ever flowing
rivers.
¹⁶The day is yours, and yours also the
night;
you established the sun and moon.
¹⁷It was you who set all the boundaries
of the earth;
you made both summer and winter.

¹⁸Remember how the enemy has
mocked you, O LORD,
how foolish people have reviled
your name.
¹⁹Do not hand over the life of your
dove to wild beasts;
do not forget the lives of your
afflicted people forever.
²⁰Have regard for your covenant,
because haunts of violence fill the
dark places of the land.
²¹Do not let the oppressed retreat in
disgrace;
may the poor and needy praise your
name.
²²Rise up, O God, and defend your
cause;
remember how fools mock you all
day long.
²³Do not ignore the clamor of your
adversaries,
the uproar of your enemies, which
rises continually.

Psalm 75

For the director of music. To the tune of, "Do
Not Destroy." A psalm of Asaph. A song.

¹We give thanks to you, O God,
we give thanks, for your Name is
near;
men tell of your wonderful deeds.

²You say, "I choose the appointed
time;

it is I who judge uprightly.
³When the earth and all its people
quake,
it is I who hold its pillars firm. *Selah*
⁴To the arrogant I say, 'Boast no
more,'
and to the wicked, 'Do not lift up
your horns.
⁵Do not lift your horns against heaven;
do not speak with outstretched
neck.'"

⁶No one from the east or the west
or from the desert can exalt a man.
⁷But it is God who judges:
He brings one down, he exalts
another.
⁸In the hand of the LORD is a cup
full of foaming wine mixed with
spices;
he pours it out, and all the wicked of
the earth
drink it down to its very dregs.

⁹As for me, I will declare this forever;
I will sing praise to the God of
Jacob.
¹⁰I will cut off the horns of all the
wicked,
but the horns of the righteous will
be lifted up.

Psalm 76

For the director of music. With stringed
instruments. A psalm of Asaph. A song.

¹In Judah God is known;
his name is great in Israel.
²His tent is in Salem,
his dwelling place in Zion.
³There he broke the flashing arrows,
the shields and the swords, the
weapons of war.   *Selah*

⁴You are resplendent with light,
more majestic than mountains rich
with game.
⁵Valiant men lie plundered,
they sleep their last sleep;
not one of the warriors
can lift his hands.

⁶At your rebuke, O God of Jacob,
  both horse and chariot lie still.
⁷You alone are to be feared.
  Who can stand before you when
    you are angry?
⁸From heaven you pronounced
    judgment,
  and the land feared and was quiet—
⁹when you, O God, rose up to judge,
  to save all the afflicted of the land.
                                    Selah

¹⁰Surely your wrath against men brings
    you praise,
  and the survivors of your wrath are
    restrained.ᵃ

¹¹Make vows to the LORD your God
    and fulfill them;
  let all the neighboring lands
    bring gifts to the One to be feared.
¹²He breaks the spirit of rulers;
  he is feared by the kings of the
    earth.

Psalm 77

For the director of music. For Jeduthun.
Of Asaph. A psalm.

¹I cried out to God for help;
  I cried out to God to hear me.
²When I was in distress, I sought the
    Lord;
  at night I stretched out untiring
    hands
  and my soul refused to be
    comforted.

³I remembered you, O God, and I
    groaned;
  I mused, and my spirit grew faint.
                                    Selah
⁴You kept my eyes from closing;
  I was too troubled to speak.
⁵I thought about the former days,
  the years of long ago;
⁶I remembered my songs in the night.
  My heart mused and my spirit
    inquired:

⁷"Will the Lord reject forever?
  Will he never show his favor again?
⁸Has his unfailing love vanished
    forever?
  Has his promise failed for all time?
⁹Has God forgotten to be merciful?
  Has he in anger withheld his
    compassion?"   *Selah*

¹⁰Then I thought, "To this I will
    appeal:
  the years of the right hand of the
    Most High."
¹¹I will remember the deeds of the
    LORD;
  yes, I will remember your miracles
    of long ago.
¹²I will meditate on all your works
  and consider all your mighty deeds.

¹³Your ways, O God, are holy.
  What god is so great as our God?
¹⁴You are the God who performs
    miracles;
  you display your power among the
    peoples.
¹⁵With your mighty arm you redeemed
    your people,
  the descendants of Jacob and
    Joseph.   *Selah*

¹⁶The waters saw you, O God,
  the waters saw you and writhed;
  the very depths were convulsed.
¹⁷The clouds poured down water,
  the skies resounded with thunder;
  your arrows flashed back and forth.
¹⁸Your thunder was heard in the
    whirlwind,
  your lightning lit up the world;
  the earth trembled and quaked.
¹⁹Your path led through the sea,
  your way through the mighty
    waters,
  though your footprints were not
    seen.

²⁰You led your people like a flock
  by the hand of Moses and Aaron.

ᵃ 10 Or *Surely the wrath of men brings you praise, / and with the remainder of wrath you arm yourself*

Psalm 78

A *maskil*[a] of Asaph.

¹O my people, hear my teaching;
  listen to the words of my mouth.
²I will open my mouth in parables,
  I will utter hidden things, things
    from of old—
³what we have heard and known,
  what our fathers have told us.
⁴We will not hide them from their
    children;
  we will tell the next generation
the praiseworthy deeds of the LORD,
  his power, and the wonders he has
    done.
⁵He decreed statutes for Jacob
  and established the law in Israel,
which he commanded our
    forefathers
  to teach their children,
⁶so the next generation would know
    them,
  even the children yet to be born,
  and they in turn would tell their
    children.
⁷Then they would put their trust in
    God
  and would not forget his deeds
  but would keep his commands.
⁸They would not be like their
    forefathers—
  a stubborn and rebellious
    generation,
whose hearts were not loyal to God,
  whose spirits were not faithful to
    him.

⁹The men of Ephraim, though armed
    with bows,
  turned back on the day of battle;
¹⁰they did not keep God's covenant
  and refused to live by his law.
¹¹They forgot what he had done,
  the wonders he had shown them.
¹²He did miracles in the sight of their
    fathers
  in the land of Egypt, in the region
    of Zoan.
¹³He divided the sea and led them
    through;
  he made the water stand firm like
    a wall.
¹⁴He guided them with the cloud by
    day
  and with light from the fire all
    night.
¹⁵He split the rocks in the desert
  and gave them water as abundant as
    the seas;
¹⁶he brought streams out of a rocky
    crag
  and made water flow down like
    rivers.

¹⁷But they continued to sin against him,
  rebelling in the desert against the
    Most High.
¹⁸They willfully put God to the test
  by demanding the food they
    craved.
¹⁹They spoke against God, saying,
  "Can God spread a table in the
    desert?
²⁰When he struck the rock, water
    gushed out,
  and streams flowed abundantly.
But can he also give us food?
  Can he supply meat for his
    people?"
²¹When the LORD heard them, he was
    very angry;
  his fire broke out against Jacob,
  and his wrath rose against Israel,
²²for they did not believe in God
  or trust in his deliverance.
²³Yet he gave a command to the skies
    above
  and opened the doors of the
    heavens;
²⁴he rained down manna for the people
    to eat,
  he gave them the grain of heaven.
²⁵Men ate the bread of angels;
  he sent them all the food they
    could eat.
²⁶He let loose the east wind from the
    heavens

---

[a]Title: Probably a literary or musical term

and led forth the south wind by his
    power.
27He rained meat down on them like
    dust,
    flying birds like sand on the
      seashore.
28He made them come down inside
    their camp,
    all around their tents.
29They ate till they had more than
    enough,
    for he had given them what they
      craved.
30But before they turned from the food
    they craved,
    even while it was still in their
      mouths,
31God's anger rose against them;
    he put to death the sturdiest among
      them,
    cutting down the young men of
      Israel.
32In spite of all this, they kept on
    sinning;
    in spite of his wonders, they did not
      believe.
33So he ended their days in futility
    and their years in terror.
34Whenever God slew them, they
    would seek him;
    they eagerly turned to him again.
35They remembered that God was their
    Rock,
    that God Most High was their
      Redeemer.
36But then they would flatter him with
    their mouths,
    lying to him with their tongues;
37their hearts were not loyal to him,
    they were not faithful to his
      covenant.
38Yet he was merciful;
    he forgave their iniquities
    and did not destroy them.
    Time after time he restrained his
      anger
    and did not stir up his full wrath.
39He remembered that they were but
    flesh,

a passing breeze that does not
    return.
40How often they rebelled against him
    in the desert
    and grieved him in the wasteland!
41Again and again they put God to the
    test;
    they vexed the Holy One of Israel.
42They did not remember his power—
    the day he redeemed them from the
      oppressor,
43the day he displayed his miraculous
    signs in Egypt,
    his wonders in the region of Zoan.
44He turned their rivers to blood;
    they could not drink from their
      streams.
45He sent swarms of flies that devoured
    them,
    and frogs that devastated them.
46He gave their crops to the
    grasshopper,
    their produce to the locust.
47He destroyed their vines with hail
    and their sycamore-figs with sleet.
48He gave over their cattle to the hail,
    their livestock to bolts of
      lightning.
49He unleashed against them his hot
    anger,
    his wrath, indignation and
      hostility—
    a band of destroying angels.
50He prepared a path for his anger;
    he did not spare them from death
    but gave them over to the plague.
51He struck down all the firstborn of
    Egypt,
    the firstfruits of manhood in the
      tents of Ham.
52But he brought his people out like a
    flock;
    he led them like sheep through the
      desert.
53He guided them safely, so they were
    unafraid;
    but the sea engulfed their enemies.
54Thus he brought them to the border
    of his holy land,

to the hill country his right hand
  had taken.
⁵⁵He drove out nations before them
  and allotted their lands to them as
    an inheritance;
  he settled the tribes of Israel in their
    homes.

⁵⁶But they put God to the test
  and rebelled against the Most High;
  they did not keep his statutes.
⁵⁷Like their fathers they were disloyal
    and faithless,
  as unreliable as a faulty bow.
⁵⁸They angered him with their high
    places;
  they aroused his jealousy with their
    idols.
⁵⁹When God heard them, he was very
    angry;
  he rejected Israel completely.
⁶⁰He abandoned the tabernacle of
    Shiloh,
  the tent he had set up among men.
⁶¹He sent ⌊the ark of⌋ his might into
    captivity,
  his splendor into the hands of the
    enemy.
⁶²He gave his people over to the
    sword;
  he was very angry with his
    inheritance.
⁶³Fire consumed their young men,
  and their maidens had no wedding
    songs;
⁶⁴their priests were put to the sword,
  and their widows could not weep.

⁶⁵Then the Lord awoke as from sleep,
  as a man wakes from the stupor of
    wine.
⁶⁶He beat back his enemies;
  he put them to everlasting shame.
⁶⁷Then he rejected the tents of Joseph,
  he did not choose the tribe of
    Ephraim;
⁶⁸but he chose the tribe of Judah,
  Mount Zion, which he loved.
⁶⁹He built his sanctuary like the
    heights,

like the earth that he established
    forever.
⁷⁰He chose David his servant
  and took him from the sheep pens;
⁷¹from tending the sheep he brought
    him
  to be the shepherd of his people
    Jacob,
  of Israel his inheritance.
⁷²And David shepherded them with
    integrity of heart;
  with skillful hands he led them.

Psalm 79

A psalm of Asaph.

¹O God, the nations have invaded
    your inheritance;
  they have defiled your holy temple,
  they have reduced Jerusalem to
    rubble.
²They have given the dead bodies of
    your servants
  as food to the birds of the air,
  the flesh of your saints to the beasts
    of the earth.
³They have poured out blood like
    water
  all around Jerusalem,
  and there is no one to bury the dead.
⁴We are objects of reproach to our
    neighbors,
  of scorn and derision to those
    around us.

⁵How long, O Lord? Will you be
    angry forever?
  How long will your jealousy burn
    like fire?
⁶Pour out your wrath on the nations
    that do not acknowledge you,
  on the kingdoms
    that do not call on your name;
⁷for they have devoured Jacob
  and destroyed his homeland.
⁸Do not hold against us the sins of the
    fathers;
  may your mercy come quickly to
    meet us,
  for we are in desperate need.

⁹Help us, O God our Savior,
  for the glory of your name;
deliver us and forgive our sins
  for your name's sake.
¹⁰Why should the nations say,
  "Where is their God?"
Before our eyes, make known among
    the nations
  that you avenge the outpoured
    blood of your servants.
¹¹May the groans of the prisoners come
    before you;
  by the strength of your arm
  preserve those condemned to die.

¹²Pay back into the laps of our
    neighbors seven times
  the reproach they have hurled at
    you, O Lord.
¹³Then we your people, the sheep of
    your pasture,
  will praise you forever;
from generation to generation
  we will recount your praise.

Prayer is . . .

communicating your thoughts,
feelings, and longings to God.

Psalm 80

For the director of music. To the tune of
"The Lilies of the Covenant."
Of Asaph. A psalm.

¹Hear us, O Shepherd of Israel,
  you who lead Joseph like a flock;
you who sit enthroned between the
    cherubim, shine forth
² before Ephraim, Benjamin and
    Manasseh.
  Awaken your might;
  come and save us.

³Restore us, O God;
  make your face shine upon us,
  that we may be saved.

⁴O LORD God Almighty,
  how long will your anger smolder
  against the prayers of your people?
⁵You have fed them with the bread of
    tears;
  you have made them drink tears by
    the bowlful.
⁶You have made us a source of
    contention to our neighbors,
  and our enemies mock us.

⁷Restore us, O God Almighty;
  make your face shine upon us,
  that we may be saved.

⁸You brought a vine out of Egypt;
  you drove out the nations and
    planted it.
⁹You cleared the ground for it,
  and it took root and filled the land.
¹⁰The mountains were covered with its
    shade,
  the mighty cedars with its branches.
¹¹It sent out its boughs to the Sea,[a]
  its shoots as far as the River.[b]

¹²Why have you broken down its walls
  so that all who pass by pick its
    grapes?
¹³Boars from the forest ravage it
  and the creatures of the field feed
    on it.
¹⁴Return to us, O God Almighty!
  Look down from heaven and see!
  Watch over this vine,
¹⁵ the root your right hand has
    planted,
  the son[c] you have raised up for
    yourself.

¹⁶Your vine is cut down, it is burned
    with fire;
  at your rebuke your people perish.
¹⁷Let your hand rest on the man at your
    right hand,
  the son of man you have raised up
    for yourself.
¹⁸Then we will not turn away from you;
  revive us, and we will call on your
    name.

a 11 Probably the Mediterranean   b 11 That is, the Euphrates   c 15 Or branch

¹⁹Restore us, O Lord God Almighty;
make your face shine upon us,
that we may be saved.

Psalm 81

For the director of music. According
to *gittith*.^a Of Asaph.

¹Sing for joy to God our strength;
shout aloud to the God of Jacob!
²Begin the music, strike the
tambourine,
play the melodious harp and lyre.

³Sound the ram's horn at the New
Moon,
and when the moon is full, on the
day of our Feast;
⁴this is a decree for Israel,
an ordinance of the God of Jacob.
⁵He established it as a statute for
Joseph
when he went out against Egypt,
where we heard a language we did
not understand.^b

⁶He says, "I removed the burden from
their shoulders;
their hands were set free from the
basket.
⁷In your distress you called and I
rescued you,
I answered you out of a
thundercloud;
I tested you at the waters of
Meribah.   *Selah*

⁸"Hear, O my people, and I will warn
you—
if you would but listen to me,
O Israel!
⁹You shall have no foreign god among
you;
you shall not bow down to an alien
god.
¹⁰I am the Lord your God,
who brought you up out of
Egypt.
Open wide your mouth and I will
fill it.

¹¹"But my people would not listen to
me;
Israel would not submit to me.
¹²So I gave them over to their stubborn
hearts
to follow their own devices.

¹³"If my people would but listen to me,
if Israel would follow my ways,
¹⁴how quickly would I subdue their
enemies
and turn my hand against their
foes!
¹⁵Those who hate the Lord would
cringe before him,
and their punishment would last
forever.
¹⁶But you would be fed with the finest
of wheat;
with honey from the rock I would
satisfy you."

Psalm 82

A psalm of Asaph.

¹God presides in the great assembly;
he gives judgment among the
"gods":

²"How long will you^c defend the
unjust
and show partiality to the wicked?
        Selah
³Defend the cause of the weak and
fatherless;
maintain the rights of the poor and
oppressed.
⁴Rescue the weak and needy;
deliver them from the hand of the
wicked.

⁵"They know nothing, they
understand nothing.
They walk about in darkness;
all the foundations of the earth are
shaken.

⁶"I said, 'You are "gods";
you are all sons of the Most High.'
⁷But you will die like mere men;
you will fall like every other ruler."

---

^aTitle: Probably a musical term   ^b5 Or / and we heard a voice we had not known   ^c2 The Hebrew is plural.

8 Rise up, O God, judge the earth,
  for all the nations are your
    inheritance.

Psalm 83

A song. A psalm of Asaph.

1 O God, do not keep silent;
  be not quiet, O God, be not still.
2 See how your enemies are astir,
  how your foes rear their heads.
3 With cunning they conspire against
    your people;
  they plot against those you cherish.
4 "Come," they say, "let us destroy
      them as a nation,
    that the name of Israel be
      remembered no more."

5 With one mind they plot together;
  they form an alliance against you—
6 the tents of Edom and the Ishmaelites,
  of Moab and the Hagrites,
7 Gebal,[a] Ammon and Amalek,
  Philistia, with the people of Tyre.
8 Even Assyria has joined them
  to lend strength to the descendants
    of Lot.   *Selah*

9 Do to them as you did to Midian,
    as you did to Sisera and Jabin at the
      river Kishon,
10 who perished at Endor
  and became like refuse on the
    ground.
11 Make their nobles like Oreb and
    Zeeb,
  all their princes like Zebah and
    Zalmunna,
12 who said, "Let us take possession
  of the pasturelands of God."

13 Make them like tumbleweed, O my
    God,
  like chaff before the wind.
14 As fire consumes the forest
  or a flame sets the mountains
    ablaze,
15 so pursue them with your tempest
  and terrify them with your storm.

16 Cover their faces with shame
  so that men will seek your name,
    O LORD.

17 May they ever be ashamed and
    dismayed;
  may they perish in disgrace.
18 Let them know that you, whose name
  is the LORD—
  that you alone are the Most High
    over all the earth.

Psalm 84

For the director of music. According to *gittith.*[b] Of the Sons of Korah. A psalm.

1 How lovely is your dwelling place,
  O LORD Almighty!
2 My soul yearns, even faints,
  for the courts of the LORD;
  my heart and my flesh cry out
  for the living God.

3 Even the sparrow has found a home,
  and the swallow a nest for herself,
  where she may have her young—
  a place near your altar,
  O LORD Almighty, my King and
    my God.
4 Blessed are those who dwell in your
    house;
  they are ever praising you.   *Selah*

5 Blessed are those whose strength is in
    you,
  who have set their hearts on
    pilgrimage.
6 As they pass through the Valley of
    Baca,
  they make it a place of springs;
  the autumn rains also cover it with
    pools.[c]
7 They go from strength to strength,
  till each appears before God in Zion.

8 Hear my prayer, O LORD God
    Almighty;
  listen to me, O God of Jacob.   *Selah*
9 Look upon our shield,[d] O God;
  look with favor on your anointed
    one.

---

[a] 7 That is, Byblos   [b] Title: Probably a musical term   [c] 6 Or *blessings*   [d] 9 Or *sovereign*

[10]Better is one day in your courts
  than a thousand elsewhere;
I would rather be a doorkeeper in the
    house of my God
  than dwell in the tents of the wicked.
[11]For the Lord God is a sun and shield;
  the Lord bestows favor and honor;
no good thing does he withhold
  from those whose walk is blameless.

[12]O Lord Almighty,
  blessed is the man who trusts in you.

Psalm 85

For the director of music. Of the Sons
of Korah. A psalm.

[1]You showed favor to your land,
    O Lord;
  you restored the fortunes of Jacob.
[2]You forgave the iniquity of your
    people
  and covered all their sins.   *Selah*
[3]You set aside all your wrath
  and turned from your fierce anger.

[4]Restore us again, O God our Savior,
  and put away your displeasure
    toward us.
[5]Will you be angry with us forever?
  Will you prolong your anger
    through all generations?
[6]Will you not revive us again,
  that your people may rejoice in
    you?
[7]Show us your unfailing love,
    O Lord,
  and grant us your salvation.

[8]I will listen to what God the Lord
    will say;
  he promises peace to his people, his
    saints—
  but let them not return to folly.
[9]Surely his salvation is near those who
    fear him,
  that his glory may dwell in our
    land.

[10]Love and faithfulness meet together;
  righteousness and peace kiss each
    other.

[11]Faithfulness springs forth from the
    earth,
  and righteousness looks down from
    heaven.
[12]The Lord will indeed give what is
    good,
  and our land will yield its harvest.
[13]Righteousness goes before him
  and prepares the way for his steps.

Psalm 86

A prayer of David.

[1]Hear, O Lord, and answer me,
  for I am poor and needy.
[2]Guard my life, for I am devoted to
    you.
  You are my God; save your servant
  who trusts in you.
[3]Have mercy on me, O Lord,
  for I call to you all day long.
[4]Bring joy to your servant,
  for to you, O Lord,
  I lift up my soul.

[5]You are forgiving and good, O Lord,
  abounding in love to all who call
    to you.
[6]Hear my prayer, O Lord;
  listen to my cry for mercy.
[7]In the day of my trouble I will call to
    you,
  for you will answer me.

[8]Among the gods there is none like
    you, O Lord;
  no deeds can compare with yours.
[9]All the nations you have made
  will come and worship before you,
    O Lord;
  they will bring glory to your name.
[10]For you are great and do marvelous
    deeds;
  you alone are God.

[11]Teach me your way, O Lord,
  and I will walk in your truth;
give me an undivided heart,
  that I may fear your name.
[12]I will praise you, O Lord my God,
  with all my heart;

Remembering God's Goodness in Bad Times

What are some of the most beautiful things you have ever seen? A field of vibrantly colored flowers? A waterfall? A loved one's smile? A crystal clear lake? A painting? A baby's face? A sparkling jewel? An act of love toward someone? Take everything that has ever touched you deeply with its beauty, put them all together, and you have only a fraction of the beauty of the Lord. It's hard to imagine.

David said, "One thing I ask of the LORD, this is what I seek: that I may dwell in the house of the LORD all the days of my life, to gaze upon the beauty of the LORD and to seek him in his temple" (Psalm 27:4). Above all else, David wanted to look on the splendor, radiance, holiness, goodness, and glory of God, and be close to Him forever. Isn't that what *we* want too?

Everything God *is,* is not only beautiful, it is also good.

When you think of the *goodness* of the Lord, what do you think of? Perfection? Purity? Grandness? Holiness? Love? Grace? Mercy? Our minds can't comprehend it. We know God is good, but we forget *how* good. When something happens to us that hurts, we often fail to remember what a good God He is. We start having doubts and wonder, *If God is good, why did He let this happen?* We forget that God is good even when things are bad.

David said, "You are my Lord; apart from you I have no good thing" (Psalm 16:2). The Bible says to "taste and see that the LORD is good; blessed is the man who takes refuge in him" (Psalm 34:8).

In tough times we may doubt that God is really good because, just like His beauty, His goodness is greater than we can imagine.

Our minds cannot even comprehend the breadth and the depth of it.

That's why, when we go through bad times, we have to *remind* ourselves of God's goodness. Otherwise, we too easily forget. One of the ways we keep ourselves reminded of God's goodness is to read His Word. It helps us remember that no matter what happens, He is a God of mercy and grace. "You are forgiving and good, O Lord, abounding in love to all who call to you" (Psalm 86:5).

His mercy means He has compassion on us. His grace means He gives us what we don't deserve. His mercy and grace are signs of His goodness. His goodness is a sign of His amazing love. And we should love that about Him.

Another way we can learn to completely trust that God is good is to praise Him for His goodness, no matter what is happening in our lives. Every time we do, it opens up the channels through which that particular aspect of His nature is poured into our hearts. You will be amazed when you pray this way how God will open your eyes to see things you haven't seen before. The Lord has done or is doing so many good things we don't even think to give Him credit for. We either don't see them, or we take them for granted. The more you praise God for His goodness, the more you will see it manifested in your life.

Because of Jesus, we can experience God's goodness whenever we come to Him and worship Him. Our praise of Him opens our eyes to His goodness in our lives.

And that's a beautiful thing!

For the next "From Stormie's Heart" article, go to page 735.

I will glorify your name forever.
[13] For great is your love toward me;
   you have delivered me from the
      depths of the grave.[a]

[14] The arrogant are attacking me,
      O God;
   a band of ruthless men seeks my
      life—
   men without regard for you.
[15] But you, O Lord, are a compassionate
      and gracious God,
   slow to anger, abounding in love
      and faithfulness.
[16] Turn to me and have mercy on me;
   grant your strength to your servant
   and save the son of your
      maidservant.[b]
[17] Give me a sign of your goodness,
   that my enemies may see it and be
      put to shame,
   for you, O Lord, have helped me
      and comforted me.

Psalm 87

Of the Sons of Korah. A psalm. A song.

[1] He has set his foundation on the holy
      mountain;
[2] the Lord loves the gates of Zion
   more than all the dwellings of
      Jacob.
[3] Glorious things are said of you,
   O city of God: *Selah*
[4] "I will record Rahab[c] and Babylon
   among those who acknowledge
      me—
Philistia too, and Tyre, along with
   Cush[d]—
   and will say, 'This[e] one was born in
      Zion.'"

[5] Indeed, of Zion it will be said,
   "This one and that one were born
      in her,
   and the Most High himself will
      establish her."

[6] The Lord will write in the register of
      the peoples:
   "This one was born in Zion." *Selah*
[7] As they make music they will sing,
   "All my fountains are in you."

Psalm 88

A song. A psalm of the Sons of Korah. For the director of music. According to *mahalath leannoth*.[f] A *maskil*[g] of Heman the Ezrahite.

[1] O Lord, the God who saves me,
   day and night I cry out before you.
[2] May my prayer come before you;
   turn your ear to my cry.

[3] For my soul is full of trouble
   and my life draws near the grave.[h]
[4] I am counted among those who go
      down to the pit;
   I am like a man without strength.
[5] I am set apart with the dead,
   like the slain who lie in the grave,
   whom you remember no more,
   who are cut off from your care.

[6] You have put me in the lowest pit,
   in the darkest depths.
[7] Your wrath lies heavily upon me;
   you have overwhelmed me with all
      your waves.   *Selah*
[8] You have taken from me my closest
      friends
   and have made me repulsive to
      them.
   I am confined and cannot escape;
[9] my eyes are dim with grief.

   I call to you, O Lord, every day;
   I spread out my hands to you.
[10] Do you show your wonders to the
      dead?
   Do those who are dead rise up and
      praise you?   *Selah*
[11] Is your love declared in the grave,
   your faithfulness in Destruction[i]?
[12] Are your wonders known in the place
      of darkness,

---

[a] *13* Hebrew *Sheol*   [b] *16* Or *save your faithful son*   [c] *4* A poetic name for Egypt   [d] *4* That is, the upper Nile region   [e] *4* Or "O Rahab and Babylon, / Philistia, Tyre and Cush, / I will record concerning those who acknowledge me: / 'This   [f] Title: Possibly a tune, "The Suffering of Affliction"   [g] Title: Probably a literary or musical term   [h] *3* Hebrew *Sheol*   [i] *11* Hebrew *Abaddon*

or your righteous deeds in the land
    of oblivion?

13But I cry to you for help, O Lord;
    in the morning my prayer comes
       before you.
14Why, O Lord, do you reject me
    and hide your face from me?
15From my youth I have been afflicted
    and close to death;
    I have suffered your terrors and am
       in despair.
16Your wrath has swept over me;
    your terrors have destroyed me.
17All day long they surround me like a
    flood;
    they have completely engulfed me.
18You have taken my companions and
    loved ones from me;
    the darkness is my closest friend.

Psalm 89

A *maskil*[a] of Ethan the Ezrahite.

1I will sing of the Lord's great love
    forever;
    with my mouth I will make your
       faithfulness known through all
       generations.
2I will declare that your love stands
    firm forever,
    that you established your
       faithfulness in heaven itself.

3You said, "I have made a covenant
    with my chosen one,
    I have sworn to David my servant,
4'I will establish your line forever
    and make your throne firm through
       all generations.'"   *Selah*

5The heavens praise your wonders,
    O Lord,
    your faithfulness too, in the
       assembly of the holy ones.
6For who in the skies above can
    compare with the Lord?
    Who is like the Lord among the
       heavenly beings?

7In the council of the holy ones God is
    greatly feared;
    he is more awesome than all who
       surround him.
8O Lord God Almighty, who is like
    you?
    You are mighty, O Lord, and your
       faithfulness surrounds you.

9You rule over the surging sea;
    when its waves mount up, you still
       them.
10You crushed Rahab like one of the
    slain;
    with your strong arm you scattered
       your enemies.
11The heavens are yours, and yours also
    the earth;
    you founded the world and all that
       is in it.
12You created the north and the south;
    Tabor and Hermon sing for joy at
       your name.
13Your arm is endued with power;
    your hand is strong, your right
       hand exalted.

14Righteousness and justice are the
    foundation of your throne;
    love and faithfulness go before you.
15Blessed are those who have learned to
    acclaim you,
    who walk in the light of your
       presence, O Lord.
16They rejoice in your name all day
    long;
    they exult in your righteousness.
17For you are their glory and strength,
    and by your favor you exalt our
       horn.[b]
18Indeed, our shield[c] belongs to the
    Lord,
    our king to the Holy One of Israel.

19Once you spoke in a vision,
    to your faithful people you said:
"I have bestowed strength on a
    warrior;
    I have exalted a young man from
       among the people.

---

aTitle: Probably a literary or musical term   b17 *Horn* here symbolizes strong one.   c18 Or *sovereign*

20I have found David my servant;
　　with my sacred oil I have anointed
　　　him.
21My hand will sustain him;
　　surely my arm will strengthen him.
22No enemy will subject him to tribute;
　　no wicked man will oppress him.
23I will crush his foes before him
　　and strike down his adversaries.
24My faithful love will be with him,
　　and through my name his horn[a]
　　　will be exalted.
25I will set his hand over the sea,
　　his right hand over the rivers.
26He will call out to me, 'You are my
　　　Father,
　　my God, the Rock my Savior.'
27I will also appoint him my firstborn,
　　the most exalted of the kings of the
　　　earth.
28I will maintain my love to him
　　　forever,
　　and my covenant with him will
　　　never fail.
29I will establish his line forever,
　　his throne as long as the heavens
　　　endure.

30"If his sons forsake my law
　　and do not follow my statutes,
31if they violate my decrees
　　and fail to keep my commands,
32I will punish their sin with the rod,
　　their iniquity with flogging;
33but I will not take my love from him,
　　nor will I ever betray my
　　　faithfulness.
34I will not violate my covenant
　　or alter what my lips have uttered.
35Once for all, I have sworn by my
　　　holiness—
　　and I will not lie to David—
36that his line will continue forever
　　and his throne endure before me
　　　like the sun;
37it will be established forever like the
　　　moon,
　　the faithful witness in the sky."
　　　　　　　　　　　　　　　Selah

38But you have rejected, you have
　　　spurned,
　　you have been very angry with
　　　your anointed one.
39You have renounced the covenant
　　　with your servant
　　and have defiled his crown in the
　　　dust.
40You have broken through all his walls
　　and reduced his strongholds to
　　　ruins.
41All who pass by have plundered him;
　　he has become the scorn of his
　　　neighbors.
42You have exalted the right hand of his
　　　foes;
　　you have made all his enemies
　　　rejoice.
43You have turned back the edge of his
　　　sword
　　and have not supported him in
　　　battle.
44You have put an end to his splendor
　　and cast his throne to the ground.
45You have cut short the days of his
　　　youth;
　　you have covered him with a
　　mantle of shame.　　　　Selah

46How long, O LORD? Will you hide
　　　yourself forever?
　　How long will your wrath burn
　　　like fire?
47Remember how fleeting is my life.
　　For what futility you have created
　　　all men!
48What man can live and not see death,
　　or save himself from the power of
　　　the grave[b]?　　　　　　Selah
49O Lord, where is your former great
　　　love,
　　which in your faithfulness you
　　　swore to David?
50Remember, Lord, how your servant
　　　has[c] been mocked,
　　how I bear in my heart the taunts
　　　of all the nations,
51the taunts with which your enemies
　　　have mocked, O LORD,

---

a 24 Horn here symbolizes strength.　　b 48 Hebrew Sheol　　c 50 Or your servants have

with which they have mocked
 every step of your anointed
  one.

52Praise be to the LORD forever!
 Amen and Amen.

BOOK IV
Psalms 90—106

Psalm 90

A prayer of Moses the man of God.

1Lord, you have been our dwelling
  place
 throughout all generations.
2Before the mountains were born
 or you brought forth the earth and
  the world,
 from everlasting to everlasting you
  are God.

3You turn men back to dust,
 saying, "Return to dust, O sons of
  men."

4For a thousand years in your sight
 are like a day that has just gone
  by,
 or like a watch in the night.
5You sweep men away in the sleep of
  death;
 they are like the new grass of the
  morning—
6though in the morning it springs up
  new,
 by evening it is dry and
  withered.

7We are consumed by your anger
 and terrified by your indignation.
8You have set our iniquities before
  you,
 our secret sins in the light of your
  presence.
9All our days pass away under your
  wrath;
 we finish our years with a moan.
10The length of our days is seventy
  years—
 or eighty, if we have the strength;

GOING *deeper*

Commit Your Work to God

READ AND CONSIDER: PSALM 90:1-17

"May the favor of the Lord our God rest upon us; establish the work of our hands for us—yes, establish the work of our hands" (Psalm 90:17).

What's on your "To Do" list for today? Do you have a job to get to, a home to clean, someone to care for? Do you feel sometimes as if you're constantly busy, continually on the move, and yet at the end of the day you wonder if you have accomplished all that you should have? How about your work? Do you regularly ask God to bless it?

The psalmist recognized that people "are like the new grass of the morning—though in the morning it springs up new, by evening it is dry and withered" (90:5-6). Our days, quite literally, are numbered. "The length of our days is seventy years—or eighty, if we have the strength" (90:10). This reminder of our own mortality reinforces the need to commit every task we undertake to God and to ask for His blessing upon it.

We can start by making it a habit to turn our day over to the Lord when we first wake up. Then ask for His help in all that we have to do and thank Him that He will enable us to do it. "The one who calls you is faithful and he will do it" (1 Thessalonians 5:24).

When you thank God and give Him charge over every endeavor you undertake, right down to the smallest detail of your day, He will establish the work of your hands.

yet their span[a] is but trouble and
sorrow,
for they quickly pass, and we fly
away.

11 Who knows the power of your anger?
For your wrath is as great as the
fear that is due you.
12 Teach us to number our days aright,
that we may gain a heart of
wisdom.

13 Relent, O LORD! How long will it
be?
Have compassion on your servants.
14 Satisfy us in the morning with your
unfailing love,
that we may sing for joy and be
glad all our days.
15 Make us glad for as many days as you
have afflicted us,
for as many years as we have seen
trouble.
16 May your deeds be shown to your
servants,
your splendor to their children.

17 May the favor[b] of the Lord our God
rest upon us;
establish the work of our hands for
us—
yes, establish the work of our hands.

Psalm 91

1 He who dwells in the shelter of the
Most High
will rest in the shadow of the
Almighty.[c]
2 I will say[d] of the LORD, "He is my
refuge and my fortress,
my God, in whom I trust."

3 Surely he will save you from the
fowler's snare
and from the deadly pestilence.
4 He will cover you with his feathers,
and under his wings you will find
refuge;
his faithfulness will be your shield
and rampart.

5 You will not fear the terror of night,
nor the arrow that flies by day,
6 nor the pestilence that stalks in the
darkness,
nor the plague that destroys at
midday.
7 A thousand may fall at your side,
ten thousand at your right hand,
but it will not come near you.
8 You will only observe with your eyes
and see the punishment of the
wicked.

9 If you make the Most High your
dwelling—
even the LORD, who is my refuge—
10 then no harm will befall you,
no disaster will come near your
tent.
11 For he will command his angels
concerning you
to guard you in all your ways;
12 they will lift you up in their hands,
so that you will not strike your foot
against a stone.
13 You will tread upon the lion and the
cobra;
you will trample the great lion and
the serpent.

14 "Because he loves me," says the
LORD, "I will rescue him;
I will protect him, for he
acknowledges my name.
15 He will call upon me, and I will
answer him;
I will be with him in trouble,
I will deliver him and honor him.
16 With long life will I satisfy him
and show him my salvation."

Psalm 92

A psalm. A song. For the Sabbath day.

1 It is good to praise the LORD
and make music to your name,
O Most High,
2 to proclaim your love in the
morning
and your faithfulness at night,

---

[a] 10 Or *yet the best of them*   [b] 17 Or *beauty*   [c] 1 Hebrew *Shaddai*   [d] 2 Or *He says*

³to the music of the ten-stringed lyre
   and the melody of the harp.

⁴For you make me glad by your deeds,
      O Lord;
   I sing for joy at the works of your
      hands.
⁵How great are your works, O Lord,
   how profound your thoughts!
⁶The senseless man does not know,
   fools do not understand,
⁷that though the wicked spring up like
      grass
   and all evildoers flourish,
   they will be forever destroyed.

⁸But you, O Lord, are exalted forever.

⁹For surely your enemies, O Lord,
   surely your enemies will perish;
   all evildoers will be scattered.
¹⁰You have exalted my horn[a] like that
      of a wild ox;
   fine oils have been poured upon
      me.
¹¹My eyes have seen the defeat of my
      adversaries;
   my ears have heard the rout of my
      wicked foes.

¹²The righteous will flourish like a
      palm tree,
   they will grow like a cedar of
      Lebanon;
¹³planted in the house of the Lord,
   they will flourish in the courts of
      our God.
¹⁴They will still bear fruit in old age,
   they will stay fresh and green,
¹⁵proclaiming, "The Lord is upright;
   he is my Rock, and there is no
      wickedness in him."

Psalm 93

¹The Lord reigns, he is robed in
      majesty;
   the Lord is robed in majesty
   and is armed with strength.
   The world is firmly established;
   it cannot be moved.

²Your throne was established long ago;
   you are from all eternity.

³The seas have lifted up, O Lord,
   the seas have lifted up their voice;
   the seas have lifted up their
      pounding waves.
⁴Mightier than the thunder of the
      great waters,
   mightier than the breakers of the
      sea—
   the Lord on high is mighty.

⁵Your statutes stand firm;
   holiness adorns your house
   for endless days, O Lord.

Psalm 94

¹O Lord, the God who avenges,
   O God who avenges, shine forth.
²Rise up, O Judge of the earth;
   pay back to the proud what they
      deserve.
³How long will the wicked, O Lord,
   how long will the wicked be
      jubilant?

⁴They pour out arrogant words;
   all the evildoers are full of boasting.
⁵They crush your people, O Lord;
   they oppress your inheritance.
⁶They slay the widow and the alien;
   they murder the fatherless.
⁷They say, "The Lord does not see;
   the God of Jacob pays no heed."

⁸Take heed, you senseless ones among
      the people;
   you fools, when will you become
      wise?
⁹Does he who implanted the ear not
      hear?
   Does he who formed the eye not
      see?
¹⁰Does he who disciplines nations not
      punish?
   Does he who teaches man lack
      knowledge?
¹¹The Lord knows the thoughts of man;
   he knows that they are futile.

---

[a] 10 Horn here symbolizes strength.

12Blessed is the man you discipline,
     O Lord,
   the man you teach from your law;
13you grant him relief from days of
     trouble,
   till a pit is dug for the wicked.
14For the Lord will not reject his
     people;
   he will never forsake his
     inheritance.
15Judgment will again be founded on
     righteousness,
   and all the upright in heart will
     follow it.

16Who will rise up for me against the
     wicked?
   Who will take a stand for me
     against evildoers?
17Unless the Lord had given me help,
   I would soon have dwelt in the
     silence of death.
18When I said, "My foot is slipping,"
   your love, O Lord, supported me.
19When anxiety was great within me,
   your consolation brought joy to my
     soul.

20Can a corrupt throne be allied with
     you—
   one that brings on misery by its
     decrees?
21They band together against the
     righteous
   and condemn the innocent to
     death.
22But the Lord has become my fortress,
   and my God the rock in whom I
     take refuge.
23He will repay them for their sins
   and destroy them for their
     wickedness;
   the Lord our God will destroy
     them.

Psalm 95

1Come, let us sing for joy to the Lord;
   let us shout aloud to the Rock of
     our salvation.

2Let us come before him with
     thanksgiving
   and extol him with music and song.
3For the Lord is the great God,
   the great King above all gods.
4In his hand are the depths of the
     earth,
   and the mountain peaks belong to
     him.
5The sea is his, for he made it,
   and his hands formed the dry land.

6Come, let us bow down in worship,
   let us kneel before the Lord our
     Maker;
7for he is our God
   and we are the people of his
     pasture,
   the flock under his care.

Today, if you hear his voice,
8   do not harden your hearts as you
       did at Meribah,a
   as you did that day at Massahb in
     the desert,
9where your fathers tested and tried
     me,
   though they had seen what I did.
10For forty years I was angry with that
     generation;
   I said, "They are a people whose
     hearts go astray,
   and they have not known my
     ways."
11So I declared on oath in my anger,
   "They shall never enter my rest."

Psalm 96

1Sing to the Lord a new song;
   sing to the Lord, all the earth.
2Sing to the Lord, praise his name;
   proclaim his salvation day after day.
3Declare his glory among the nations,
   his marvelous deeds among all
     peoples.

4For great is the Lord and most
     worthy of praise;
   he is to be feared above all gods.

---

a 8 Meribah means quarreling.   b 8 Massah means testing.

5 For all the gods of the nations are
    idols,
  but the LORD made the heavens.
6 Splendor and majesty are before him;
    strength and glory are in his
    sanctuary.

7 Ascribe to the LORD, O families of
    nations,
  ascribe to the LORD glory and
    strength.
8 Ascribe to the LORD the glory due his
    name;
  bring an offering and come into his
    courts.
9 Worship the LORD in the splendor of
    his[a] holiness;
  tremble before him, all the earth.

10 Say among the nations, "The LORD
    reigns."
  The world is firmly established, it
    cannot be moved;
  he will judge the peoples with
    equity.
11 Let the heavens rejoice, let the earth
    be glad;
  let the sea resound, and all that is
    in it;
12   let the fields be jubilant, and
    everything in them.
  Then all the trees of the forest will
    sing for joy;
13   they will sing before the LORD, for
    he comes,
  he comes to judge the earth.
  He will judge the world in
    righteousness
  and the peoples in his truth.

Psalm 97

1 The LORD reigns, let the earth be
    glad;
  let the distant shores rejoice.

2 Clouds and thick darkness surround
    him;
  righteousness and justice are the
    foundation of his throne.
3 Fire goes before him

and consumes his foes on every
    side.
4 His lightning lights up the world;
  the earth sees and trembles.
5 The mountains melt like wax before
    the LORD,
  before the Lord of all the earth.
6 The heavens proclaim his
    righteousness,
  and all the peoples see his glory.

7 All who worship images are put to
    shame,
  those who boast in idols—
  worship him, all you gods!

8 Zion hears and rejoices
  and the villages of Judah are glad
  because of your judgments,
    O LORD.
9 For you, O LORD, are the Most High
    over all the earth;
  you are exalted far above all gods.

10 Let those who love the LORD hate
    evil,
  for he guards the lives of his faithful
    ones
  and delivers them from the hand of
    the wicked.
11 Light is shed upon the righteous
  and joy on the upright in heart.
12 Rejoice in the LORD, you who are
    righteous,
  and praise his holy name.

Psalm 98

A psalm.

1 Sing to the LORD a new song,
  for he has done marvelous things;
  his right hand and his holy arm
  have worked salvation for him.
2 The LORD has made his salvation
    known
  and revealed his righteousness to
    the nations.
3 He has remembered his love
  and his faithfulness to the house of
    Israel;

---

a 9 Or LORD with the splendor of

all the ends of the earth have seen
  the salvation of our God.

4 Shout for joy to the LORD, all the
    earth,
  burst into jubilant song with music;
5 make music to the LORD with the
    harp,
  with the harp and the sound of
    singing,
6 with trumpets and the blast of the
    ram's horn—
  shout for joy before the LORD, the
    King.

7 Let the sea resound, and everything
    in it,
  the world, and all who live in it.
8 Let the rivers clap their hands,
  let the mountains sing together for
    joy;
9 let them sing before the LORD,
  for he comes to judge the earth.
He will judge the world in
    righteousness
  and the peoples with equity.

Psalm 99

1 The LORD reigns,
  let the nations tremble;
he sits enthroned between the
    cherubim,
  let the earth shake.
2 Great is the LORD in Zion;
  he is exalted over all the nations.
3 Let them praise your great and
    awesome name—
  he is holy.

4 The King is mighty, he loves
    justice—
  you have established equity;
in Jacob you have done
  what is just and right.
5 Exalt the LORD our God
  and worship at his footstool;
  he is holy.

6 Moses and Aaron were among his
    priests,

Samuel was among those who
    called on his name;
they called on the LORD
  and he answered them.
7 He spoke to them from the pillar of
    cloud;
  they kept his statutes and the
    decrees he gave them.

8 O LORD our God,
  you answered them;
you were to Israel[a] a forgiving God,
  though you punished their
    misdeeds.[b]
9 Exalt the LORD our God
  and worship at his holy mountain,
  for the LORD our God is holy.

Psalm 100

A psalm. For giving thanks.

1 Shout for joy to the LORD, all the
    earth.
2   Worship the LORD with gladness;
  come before him with joyful songs.
3 Know that the LORD is God.
  It is he who made us, and we are
    his[c];
  we are his people, the sheep of his
    pasture.

4 Enter his gates with thanksgiving
  and his courts with praise;
  give thanks to him and praise his
    name.
5 For the LORD is good and his love
    endures forever;
  his faithfulness continues through
    all generations.

Psalm 101

Of David. A psalm.

1 I will sing of your love and justice;
  to you, O LORD, I will sing praise.
2 I will be careful to lead a blameless
    life—
  when will you come to me?

I will walk in my house
  with blameless heart.

---

a 8 Hebrew *them* b 8 Or / *an avenger of the wrongs done to them* c 3 Or *and not we ourselves*

GOING *deeper*

Experiencing the Power of Praise

READ AND CONSIDER: PSALM 100:1-5

"Enter his gates with thanksgiving and his courts with praise" (Psalm 100:4).

Praising God is not just about singing praise songs in church once a week. Praise should be a part of every moment of your life. Praise should be what you do in the car while on the way to work, to school, or to the store. It's what you should have in your heart when you're in the mall, the airport, or the doctor's office. It's what you do when the kitchen sink stops up, the car has a flat tire, you become sick, or you've lost your keys for the fortieth time. It's what you speak fervently when you are in the emergency room, at a loved one's burial, or in the middle of a tornado. Praise should be an ongoing attitude of the heart—an attitude that doesn't change, no matter what else in your life does.

This is not about some kind of positive thinking. This is not a plunge into denial that says, "This isn't really happening" or "I'm going to pretend that I'm not actually feeling this way." Instead, it means, "Don't let yourself sink to the level of the problem; make yourself rise to the level of the solution."

One of the secrets of experiencing the power of praise is to make a decision that you will worship God no matter what your circumstances. When you get to the place where praise comes automatically, no matter what is going on, you will come to know God more intimately. And when you do, you won't be able to *stop* yourself from praising Him.

It's easy to praise God when great things happen or when you see answers to your prayers, but what about when everything is going wrong? What is your first reaction to difficult or bad things that happen? If you blame others, yourself, or God, this only compounds the problem, leading to more distress, misery, and difficulty. Instead, if you refuse to react to your problems in the flesh and move immediately into the realm of the spirit by praising God, you will find that everything turns out differently. When you make your first reaction to what happens in your life a reaffirming praise to God for who He is, you invite His presence to inhabit the situation and His power to come and change things. This is the hidden power of praising God.

God wants you to exalt Him and not your problems. This doesn't mean trying to convince yourself that your problems don't exist. It means you are saying, "Although I have these problems, I know that You, Lord, are greater than they are. You are my heavenly Father. You are a good God. In You is everything I need for my life, and I choose to exalt You above all."

When you become convinced of the power of praise in every situation and understand all that is accomplished when you truly praise God, your life will be changed forever.

3 I will set before my eyes
  no vile thing.

The deeds of faithless men I hate;
  they will not cling to me.
4 Men of perverse heart shall be far
    from me;
  I will have nothing to do with
    evil.

5 Whoever slanders his neighbor in
    secret,
  him will I put to silence;
whoever has haughty eyes and a
    proud heart,
  him will I not endure.

6 My eyes will be on the faithful in the
    land,

that they may dwell with me;
he whose walk is blameless
    will minister to me.

⁷No one who practices deceit
    will dwell in my house;
no one who speaks falsely
    will stand in my presence.

⁸Every morning I will put to silence
    all the wicked in the land;
I will cut off every evildoer
    from the city of the LORD.

Praying Psalm 101:3
*Lord, keep my eyes from ever
looking at anything evil.*

Psalm 102

A prayer of an afflicted man. When he is faint
and pours out his lament before the LORD.

¹Hear my prayer, O LORD;
    let my cry for help come to you.
²Do not hide your face from me
    when I am in distress.
Turn your ear to me;
    when I call, answer me quickly.

³For my days vanish like smoke;
    my bones burn like glowing
        embers.
⁴My heart is blighted and withered
        like grass;
    I forget to eat my food.
⁵Because of my loud groaning
    I am reduced to skin and bones.
⁶I am like a desert owl,
    like an owl among the ruins.
⁷I lie awake; I have become
    like a bird alone on a roof.
⁸All day long my enemies taunt me;
    those who rail against me use my
        name as a curse.
⁹For I eat ashes as my food
    and mingle my drink with tears
¹⁰because of your great wrath,
    for you have taken me up and
        thrown me aside.

¹¹My days are like the evening shadow;
    I wither away like grass.

¹²But you, O LORD, sit enthroned
        forever;
    your renown endures through all
        generations.
¹³You will arise and have compassion
        on Zion,
    for it is time to show favor to her;
    the appointed time has come.
¹⁴For her stones are dear to your
        servants;
    her very dust moves them to pity.
¹⁵The nations will fear the name of the
        LORD,
    all the kings of the earth will revere
        your glory.
¹⁶For the LORD will rebuild Zion
    and appear in his glory.
¹⁷He will respond to the prayer of the
        destitute;
    he will not despise their plea.

¹⁸Let this be written for a future
        generation,
    that a people not yet created may
        praise the LORD:
¹⁹"The LORD looked down from his
        sanctuary on high,
    from heaven he viewed the earth,
²⁰to hear the groans of the prisoners
    and release those condemned to
        death."
²¹So the name of the LORD will be
        declared in Zion
    and his praise in Jerusalem
²²when the peoples and the kingdoms
    assemble to worship the LORD.

²³In the course of my life[a] he broke my
        strength;
    he cut short my days.
²⁴So I said:
"Do not take me away, O my God,
    in the midst of my days;
    your years go on through all
        generations.
²⁵In the beginning you laid the
    foundations of the earth,

[a] 23 Or *By his power*

Praise Is the Prayer That Changes Everything

READ AND CONSIDER: PSALM 102:1-28

"Hear my prayer, O LORD; let my cry for help come to you. Do not hide your face from me when I am in distress. Turn your ear to me; when I call, answer me quickly" (Psalm 102:1-2).

Once when I was enduring tremendous physical suffering, I randomly opened my Bible for comfort. Instead of turning to where the ribbon marked my place of ongoing reading, I found myself at Psalm 102. What I read there was written thousands of years ago, yet it could have been written for me right then in terms of what I was experiencing. The writer was honest before God about the way he was feeling and all that he was suffering, and he cried out to God to hear his prayer and give him a future. After reading the psalm, I did the same thing. Like the writer, I recognized that God will exist forever and will never change, and I have an eternal future with Him. No matter how bad it is here, I have the hope that whether God chooses to heal me or not, I have a life forever with Him that is free of pain, and I praise Him for that.

I have found that no matter how bad I feel, when I praise God I always feel better. I have found great healing in worship services where many people are worshiping God together. I have also found healing when worshiping God by myself. Things happen when we worship Him because praising God is the prayer that changes everything.

If you need to see a change in your life, your health, your circumstances, your financial situation, your attitude, your spouse, your children, or your church, then praise God! Thank Him for all that He can and will do—and invite Him to do it in His way and in His time. The Lord "will respond to the prayers of the destitute; he will not despise their plea" (102:17). And His answers will be far better than anything you could have thought up for yourself!

and the heavens are the work of
 your hands.
26 They will perish, but you remain;
 they will all wear out like a
 garment.
Like clothing you will change them
 and they will be discarded.
27 But you remain the same,
 and your years will never end.
28 The children of your servants will
 live in your presence;
 their descendants will be
 established before you."

Psalm 103

Of David.

1 Praise the LORD, O my soul;

all my inmost being, praise his holy
 name.
2 Praise the LORD, O my soul,
 and forget not all his benefits—
3 who forgives all your sins
 and heals all your diseases,
4 who redeems your life from the pit
 and crowns you with love and
 compassion,
5 who satisfies your desires with good
 things
 so that your youth is renewed like
 the eagle's.

6 The LORD works righteousness
 and justice for all the oppressed.
7 He made known his ways to Moses,
 his deeds to the people of Israel:

The Most Important Thing You Can Do

Nothing we do is more powerful

or more life-changing than praising God. It is one of the means by which God transforms us. Every time we praise and worship Him, His presence comes to dwell in us and changes our hearts and allows the Holy Spirit to soften and mold them into whatever He wants them to be.

Because praise and worship is not something our flesh naturally *wants* to do, we have to *will* ourselves to do it. And because it's not the first thing we think of to do, we have to decide to do it no matter what our circumstances. We have to say, "I *will* praise the Lord." Of course, the more we get to know God, the easier praise becomes. When we get to the point where we can't keep from praising Him, then we are at the place we are supposed to be. If you ever find yourself unmotivated in this regard, try reading the following 20 reasons to worship God from Psalm 103. It works for me every time.

Twenty Good Reasons to Worship God

1. He forgives my sins.
2. He heals all my diseases.
3. He redeems my life from the pit.
4. He crowns me with love and compassion.
5. He satisfies my desires with good things.
6. He works righteousness and justice for all the oppressed.
7. He makes His ways known.
8. He is compassionate.
9. He is gracious.
10. He is slow to anger.
11. He will not accuse us.
12. He will not harbor His anger forever.
13. He does not treat us as our sins deserve.
14. He shows great love to those who fear Him.
15. He removes our transgressions from us.
16. He has compassion for us.
17. He remembers we are dust.
18. His love is everlasting.
19. He blesses our children and grandchildren who obey Him.
20. He rules over all, and His throne is established.

Praising and worshiping God with other believers is one of the most powerful and significant things we can do in our lives. Corporate worship causes bondages to be broken, and it makes the way for wonderful changes in us that might never happen otherwise. A powerful dynamic occurs in the spirit realm when we worship God together. It can't happen any other way.

No matter what your church background is or has been, ask God to make you into the true worshiper He wants you to be. Give your whole self to it. As long as you have breath you can "be joyful always; pray continually; give thanks in all circumstances, for this is God's will for you in Christ Jesus" (1 Thessalonians 5:16-18). Remember that the songs of worship you sing over and over in your heart during the day will fill your soul in the night. And you will have peaceful rest.

For the next "From Stormie's Heart" article, go to page 749.

8The LORD is compassionate and
gracious,
slow to anger, abounding in love.
9He will not always accuse,
nor will he harbor his anger
forever;
10he does not treat us as our sins
deserve
or repay us according to our
iniquities.
11For as high as the heavens are above
the earth,
so great is his love for those who
fear him;
12as far as the east is from the west,
so far has he removed our
transgressions from us.
13As a father has compassion on his
children,
so the LORD has compassion on
those who fear him;
14for he knows how we are formed,
he remembers that we are dust.
15As for man, his days are like grass,
he flourishes like a flower of the
field;
16the wind blows over it and it is gone,
and its place remembers it no
more.
17But from everlasting to everlasting
the LORD's love is with those who
fear him,
and his righteousness with their
children's children—
18with those who keep his covenant
and remember to obey his
precepts.

19The LORD has established his throne
in heaven,
and his kingdom rules over all.

20Praise the LORD, you his angels,
you mighty ones who do his
bidding,
who obey his word.
21Praise the LORD, all his heavenly
hosts,
you his servants who do his will.

22Praise the LORD, all his works
everywhere in his dominion.

Praise the LORD, O my soul.

Psalm 104

1Praise the LORD, O my soul.

O LORD my God, you are very great;
you are clothed with splendor and
majesty.
2He wraps himself in light as with a
garment;
he stretches out the heavens like a
tent
3   and lays the beams of his upper
chambers on their waters.
He makes the clouds his chariot
and rides on the wings of the wind.
4He makes winds his messengers,[a]
flames of fire his servants.

5He set the earth on its foundations;
it can never be moved.
6You covered it with the deep as with
a garment;
the waters stood above the
mountains.
7But at your rebuke the waters fled,
at the sound of your thunder they
took to flight;
8they flowed over the mountains,
they went down into the valleys,
to the place you assigned for them.
9You set a boundary they cannot cross;
never again will they cover the
earth.

10He makes springs pour water into the
ravines;
it flows between the mountains.
11They give water to all the beasts of
the field;
the wild donkeys quench their
thirst.
12The birds of the air nest by the
waters;
they sing among the branches.
13He waters the mountains from his
upper chambers;

---

a 4 Or angels

the earth is satisfied by the fruit of
his work.

¹⁴He makes grass grow for the cattle,
and plants for man to cultivate—
bringing forth food from the earth:
¹⁵wine that gladdens the heart of man,
oil to make his face shine,
and bread that sustains his heart.
¹⁶The trees of the LORD are well
watered,
the cedars of Lebanon that he
planted.
¹⁷There the birds make their nests;
the stork has its home in the pine
trees.
¹⁸The high mountains belong to the
wild goats;
the crags are a refuge for the
coneys.ᵃ

¹⁹The moon marks off the seasons,
and the sun knows when to go
down.
²⁰You bring darkness, it becomes night,
and all the beasts of the forest
prowl.
²¹The lions roar for their prey
and seek their food from God.
²²The sun rises, and they steal away;
they return and lie down in their
dens.
²³Then man goes out to his work,
to his labor until evening.

²⁴How many are your works, O LORD!
In wisdom you made them all;
the earth is full of your creatures.
²⁵There is the sea, vast and spacious,
teeming with creatures beyond
number—
living things both large and small.
²⁶There the ships go to and fro,
and the leviathan, which you
formed to frolic there.

²⁷These all look to you
to give them their food at the
proper time.
²⁸When you give it to them,

they gather it up;
when you open your hand,
they are satisfied with good things.
²⁹When you hide your face,
they are terrified;
when you take away their breath,
they die and return to the dust.
³⁰When you send your Spirit,
they are created,
and you renew the face of the
earth.

³¹May the glory of the LORD endure
forever;
may the LORD rejoice in his
works—
³²he who looks at the earth, and it
trembles,
who touches the mountains, and
they smoke.

³³I will sing to the LORD all my life;
I will sing praise to my God as long
as I live.
³⁴May my meditation be pleasing to
him,
as I rejoice in the LORD.
³⁵But may sinners vanish from the earth
and the wicked be no more.

Praise the LORD, O my soul.

Praise the LORD.ᵇ

Psalm 105

¹Give thanks to the LORD, call on his
name;
make known among the nations
what he has done.
²Sing to him, sing praise to him;
tell of all his wonderful acts.
³Glory in his holy name;
let the hearts of those who seek the
LORD rejoice.
⁴Look to the LORD and his strength;
seek his face always.

⁵Remember the wonders he has done,
his miracles, and the judgments he
pronounced,

ᵃ 18 That is, the hyrax or rock badger   ᵇ 35 Hebrew Hallelu Yah; in the Septuagint this line stands at the beginning of
Psalm 105.

6 O descendants of Abraham his
 servant,
 O sons of Jacob, his chosen ones.
7 He is the LORD our God;
 his judgments are in all the earth.

8 He remembers his covenant forever,
 the word he commanded, for a
 thousand generations,
9 the covenant he made with Abraham,
 the oath he swore to Isaac.
10 He confirmed it to Jacob as a decree,
 to Israel as an everlasting covenant:
11 "To you I will give the land of
 Canaan
 as the portion you will inherit."

12 When they were but few in number,
 few indeed, and strangers in it,
13 they wandered from nation to nation,
 from one kingdom to another.
14 He allowed no one to oppress them;
 for their sake he rebuked kings:
15 "Do not touch my anointed ones;
 do my prophets no harm."

16 He called down famine on the land
 and destroyed all their supplies of
 food;
17 and he sent a man before them—
 Joseph, sold as a slave.
18 They bruised his feet with shackles,
 his neck was put in irons,
19 till what he foretold came to pass,
 till the word of the LORD proved
 him true.
20 The king sent and released him,
 the ruler of peoples set him free.
21 He made him master of his
 household,
 ruler over all he possessed,
22 to instruct his princes as he pleased
 and teach his elders wisdom.

23 Then Israel entered Egypt;
 Jacob lived as an alien in the land
 of Ham.
24 The LORD made his people very
 fruitful;
 he made them too numerous for
 their foes,

25 whose hearts he turned to hate his
 people,
 to conspire against his servants.
26 He sent Moses his servant,
 and Aaron, whom he had chosen.
27 They performed his miraculous signs
 among them,
 his wonders in the land of Ham.
28 He sent darkness and made the land
 dark—
 for had they not rebelled against his
 words?
29 He turned their waters into blood,
 causing their fish to die.
30 Their land teemed with frogs,
 which went up into the bedrooms
 of their rulers.
31 He spoke, and there came swarms of
 flies,
 and gnats throughout their
 country.
32 He turned their rain into hail,
 with lightning throughout their
 land;
33 he struck down their vines and fig
 trees
 and shattered the trees of their
 country.
34 He spoke, and the locusts came,
 grasshoppers without number;
35 they ate up every green thing in their
 land,
 ate up the produce of their soil.
36 Then he struck down all the firstborn
 in their land,
 the firstfruits of all their manhood.

37 He brought out Israel, laden with
 silver and gold,
 and from among their tribes no one
 faltered.
38 Egypt was glad when they left,
 because dread of Israel had fallen
 on them.
39 He spread out a cloud as a covering,
 and a fire to give light at night.
40 They asked, and he brought them
 quail
 and satisfied them with the bread of
 heaven.

⁴¹He opened the rock, and water
gushed out;
like a river it flowed in the desert.

⁴²For he remembered his holy promise
given to his servant Abraham.
⁴³He brought out his people with
rejoicing,
his chosen ones with shouts of joy;
⁴⁴he gave them the lands of the nations,
and they fell heir to what others
had toiled for—
⁴⁵that they might keep his precepts
and observe his laws.

Praise the Lord.ᵃ

Psalm 106

¹Praise the Lord.ᵇ

Give thanks to the Lord, for he is
good;
his love endures forever.
²Who can proclaim the mighty acts of
the Lord
or fully declare his praise?
³Blessed are they who maintain justice,
who constantly do what is right.
⁴Remember me, O Lord, when you
show favor to your people,
come to my aid when you save them,
⁵that I may enjoy the prosperity of
your chosen ones,
that I may share in the joy of your
nation
and join your inheritance in giving
praise.

⁶We have sinned, even as our fathers
did;
we have done wrong and acted
wickedly.
⁷When our fathers were in Egypt,
they gave no thought to your
miracles;
they did not remember your many
kindnesses,
and they rebelled by the sea, the
Red Sea.ᶜ

⁸Yet he saved them for his name's sake,
to make his mighty power known.
⁹He rebuked the Red Sea, and it dried
up;
he led them through the depths as
through a desert.
¹⁰He saved them from the hand of the
foe;
from the hand of the enemy he
redeemed them.
¹¹The waters covered their adversaries;
not one of them survived.
¹²Then they believed his promises
and sang his praise.

¹³But they soon forgot what he had
done
and did not wait for his counsel.
¹⁴In the desert they gave in to their
craving;
in the wasteland they put God to
the test.
¹⁵So he gave them what they asked for,
but sent a wasting disease upon
them.

¹⁶In the camp they grew envious of
Moses
and of Aaron, who was consecrated
to the Lord.
¹⁷The earth opened up and swallowed
Dathan;
it buried the company of Abiram.
¹⁸Fire blazed among their followers;
a flame consumed the wicked.

¹⁹At Horeb they made a calf
and worshiped an idol cast from
metal.
²⁰They exchanged their Glory
for an image of a bull, which eats
grass.
²¹They forgot the God who saved
them,
who had done great things in
Egypt,
²²miracles in the land of Ham
and awesome deeds by the Red Sea.
²³So he said he would destroy them—

ᵃ 45 Hebrew *Hallelu Yah*   ᵇ 1 Hebrew *Hallelu Yah*; also in verse 48   ᶜ 7 Hebrew *Yam Suph*; that is, Sea of Reeds; also in verses 9 and 22

had not Moses, his chosen one,
stood in the breach before him
  to keep his wrath from destroying
    them.

24 Then they despised the pleasant land;
  they did not believe his promise.
25 They grumbled in their tents
  and did not obey the LORD.
26 So he swore to them with uplifted
    hand
  that he would make them fall in
    the desert,
27 make their descendants fall among
    the nations
  and scatter them throughout the
    lands.

28 They yoked themselves to the Baal of
    Peor
  and ate sacrifices offered to lifeless
    gods;
29 they provoked the LORD to anger by
    their wicked deeds,
  and a plague broke out among
    them.
30 But Phinehas stood up and
    intervened,
  and the plague was checked.
31 This was credited to him as
    righteousness
  for endless generations to come.

32 By the waters of Meribah they
    angered the LORD,
  and trouble came to Moses because
    of them;
33 for they rebelled against the Spirit of
    God,
  and rash words came from Moses'
    lips.[a]

34 They did not destroy the peoples
  as the LORD had commanded them,
35 but they mingled with the nations
  and adopted their customs.
36 They worshiped their idols,
  which became a snare to them.
37 They sacrificed their sons
  and their daughters to demons.

38 They shed innocent blood,
  the blood of their sons and
    daughters,
whom they sacrificed to the idols of
    Canaan,
  and the land was desecrated by
    their blood.
39 They defiled themselves by what they
    did;
  by their deeds they prostituted
    themselves.

40 Therefore the LORD was angry with
    his people
  and abhorred his inheritance.
41 He handed them over to the nations,
  and their foes ruled over them.
42 Their enemies oppressed them
  and subjected them to their power.
43 Many times he delivered them,
  but they were bent on rebellion
  and they wasted away in their sin.

44 But he took note of their distress
  when he heard their cry;
45 for their sake he remembered his
    covenant
  and out of his great love he
    relented.
46 He caused them to be pitied
  by all who held them captive.

47 Save us, O LORD our God,
  and gather us from the nations,
that we may give thanks to your holy
    name
  and glory in your praise.

48 Praise be to the LORD, the God of
    Israel,
  from everlasting to everlasting.
Let all the people say, "Amen!"

Praise the LORD.

BOOK V
Psalms 107—150

Psalm 107
1 Give thanks to the LORD, for he is
    good;

---

a 33 Or *against his spirit, / and rash words came from his lips*

his love endures forever.
²Let the redeemed of the LORD say
this—
those he redeemed from the hand
of the foe,
³those he gathered from the lands,
from east and west, from north and
south.ᵃ

⁴Some wandered in desert wastelands,
finding no way to a city where they
could settle.
⁵They were hungry and thirsty,
and their lives ebbed away.
⁶Then they cried out to the LORD in
their trouble,
and he delivered them from their
distress.
⁷He led them by a straight way
to a city where they could settle.
⁸Let them give thanks to the LORD for
his unfailing love
and his wonderful deeds for men,
⁹for he satisfies the thirsty
and fills the hungry with good
things.

¹⁰Some sat in darkness and the deepest
gloom,
prisoners suffering in iron chains,
¹¹for they had rebelled against the
words of God
and despised the counsel of the
Most High.
¹²So he subjected them to bitter labor;
they stumbled, and there was no
one to help.
¹³Then they cried to the LORD in their
trouble,
and he saved them from their
distress.
¹⁴He brought them out of darkness and
the deepest gloom
and broke away their chains.

Praying Psalm 107:10-13

*Thank You, Lord, for delivering me out of
darkness and saving me from my distress.*

¹⁵Let them give thanks to the LORD for
his unfailing love
and his wonderful deeds for men,
¹⁶for he breaks down gates of bronze
and cuts through bars of iron.

¹⁷Some became fools through their
rebellious ways
and suffered affliction because of
their iniquities.
¹⁸They loathed all food
and drew near the gates of death.
¹⁹Then they cried to the LORD in their
trouble,
and he saved them from their
distress.
²⁰He sent forth his word and healed
them;
he rescued them from the grave.
²¹Let them give thanks to the LORD for
his unfailing love
and his wonderful deeds for men.
²²Let them sacrifice thank offerings
and tell of his works with songs of
joy.

²³Others went out on the sea in ships;
they were merchants on the mighty
waters.
²⁴They saw the works of the LORD,
his wonderful deeds in the deep.
²⁵For he spoke and stirred up a tempest
that lifted high the waves.
²⁶They mounted up to the heavens and
went down to the depths;
in their peril their courage melted
away.
²⁷They reeled and staggered like
drunken men;
they were at their wits' end.
²⁸Then they cried out to the LORD in
their trouble,
and he brought them out of their
distress.
²⁹He stilled the storm to a whisper;
the waves of the sea were hushed.
³⁰They were glad when it grew calm,
and he guided them to their desired
haven.

ᵃ *3 Hebrew north and the sea*

31Let them give thanks to the LORD for
his unfailing love
and his wonderful deeds for men.
32Let them exalt him in the assembly of
the people
and praise him in the council of the
elders.

33He turned rivers into a desert,
flowing springs into thirsty ground,
34and fruitful land into a salt waste,
because of the wickedness of those
who lived there.
35He turned the desert into pools of
water
and the parched ground into
flowing springs;
36there he brought the hungry to live,
and they founded a city where they
could settle.
37They sowed fields and planted vineyards
that yielded a fruitful harvest;
38he blessed them, and their numbers
greatly increased,
and he did not let their herds
diminish.

39Then their numbers decreased, and
they were humbled
by oppression, calamity and sorrow;
40he who pours contempt on nobles
made them wander in a trackless
waste.
41But he lifted the needy out of their
affliction
and increased their families like
flocks.
42The upright see and rejoice,
but all the wicked shut their mouths.

43Whoever is wise, let him heed these
things
and consider the great love of the
LORD.

Psalm 108

A song. A psalm of David.

1My heart is steadfast, O God;
I will sing and make music with all
my soul.

2Awake, harp and lyre!
I will awaken the dawn.
3I will praise you, O LORD, among the
nations;
I will sing of you among the
peoples.
4For great is your love, higher than the
heavens;
your faithfulness reaches to the
skies.
5Be exalted, O God, above the
heavens,
and let your glory be over all the
earth.

6Save us and help us with your right
hand,
that those you love may be
delivered.
7God has spoken from his sanctuary:
"In triumph I will parcel out
Shechem
and measure off the Valley of
Succoth.
8Gilead is mine, Manasseh is mine;
Ephraim is my helmet,
Judah my scepter.
9Moab is my washbasin,
upon Edom I toss my sandal;
over Philistia I shout in triumph."

10Who will bring me to the fortified
city?
Who will lead me to Edom?
11Is it not you, O God, you who have
rejected us
and no longer go out with our
armies?
12Give us aid against the enemy,
for the help of man is worthless.
13With God we will gain the victory,
and he will trample down our
enemies.

Psalm 109

For the director of music.
Of David. A psalm.

1O God, whom I praise,
do not remain silent,
2for wicked and deceitful men

have opened their mouths against
　　me;
they have spoken against me with
　　lying tongues.
³With words of hatred they surround
　　me;
they attack me without cause.
⁴In return for my friendship they
　　accuse me,
but I am a man of prayer.
⁵They repay me evil for good,
　　and hatred for my friendship.

⁶Appointᵃ an evil manᵇ to oppose him;
　　let an accuserᶜ stand at his right
　　hand.
⁷When he is tried, let him be found
　　guilty,
and may his prayers condemn him.
⁸May his days be few;
　　may another take his place of
　　leadership.
⁹May his children be fatherless
　　and his wife a widow.
¹⁰May his children be wandering
　　beggars;
may they be drivenᵈ from their
　　ruined homes.
¹¹May a creditor seize all he has;
　　may strangers plunder the fruits of
　　his labor.
¹²May no one extend kindness to him
　　or take pity on his fatherless
　　children.
¹³May his descendants be cut off,
　　their names blotted out from the
　　next generation.
¹⁴May the iniquity of his fathers be
　　remembered before the LORD;
may the sin of his mother never be
　　blotted out.
¹⁵May their sins always remain before
　　the LORD,
that he may cut off the memory of
　　them from the earth.

¹⁶For he never thought of doing a
　　kindness,
but hounded to death the poor
　　and the needy and the
　　brokenhearted.
¹⁷He loved to pronounce a curse—
　　may itᵉ come on him;
he found no pleasure in blessing—
　　may it beᶠ far from him.
¹⁸He wore cursing as his garment;
　　it entered into his body like water,
　　into his bones like oil.
¹⁹May it be like a cloak wrapped about
　　him,
like a belt tied forever around him.
²⁰May this be the LORD's payment to
　　my accusers,
to those who speak evil of me.

²¹But you, O Sovereign LORD,
　　deal well with me for your name's
　　sake;
out of the goodness of your love,
　　deliver me.
²²For I am poor and needy,
　　and my heart is wounded within
　　me.
²³I fade away like an evening shadow;
　　I am shaken off like a locust.
²⁴My knees give way from fasting;
　　my body is thin and gaunt.
²⁵I am an object of scorn to my
　　accusers;
when they see me, they shake their
　　heads.

²⁶Help me, O LORD my God;
　　save me in accordance with your
　　love.
²⁷Let them know that it is your hand,
　　that you, O LORD, have done it.
²⁸They may curse, but you will bless;
　　when they attack they will be put
　　to shame,
but your servant will rejoice.
²⁹My accusers will be clothed with
　　disgrace
and wrapped in shame as in a cloak.

³⁰With my mouth I will greatly extol
　　the LORD;

ᵃ 6 Or ⌊They say:⌋ "Appoint (with quotation marks at the end of verse 19)　　ᵇ 6 Or the Evil One　　ᶜ 6 Or let Satan
ᵈ 10 Septuagint; Hebrew sought　　ᵉ 17 Or curse, / and it has　　ᶠ 17 Or blessing, / and it is

in the great throng I will praise
him.
³¹For he stands at the right hand of the
needy one,
to save his life from those who
condemn him.

Psalm 110

Of David. A psalm.

¹The LORD says to my Lord:
"Sit at my right hand
until I make your enemies
a footstool for your feet."

²The LORD will extend your mighty
scepter from Zion;
you will rule in the midst of your
enemies.
³Your troops will be willing
on your day of battle.
Arrayed in holy majesty,
from the womb of the dawn
you will receive the dew of your
youth.ᵃ

⁴The LORD has sworn
and will not change his mind:
"You are a priest forever,
in the order of Melchizedek."

⁵The Lord is at your right hand;
he will crush kings on the day of
his wrath.
⁶He will judge the nations, heaping up
the dead
and crushing the rulers of the
whole earth.
⁷He will drink from a brook beside
the wayᵇ;
therefore he will lift up his head.

Psalm 111ᶜ

¹Praise the LORD.ᵈ

I will extol the LORD with all my
heart
in the council of the upright and in
the assembly.

²Great are the works of the LORD;
they are pondered by all who
delight in them.
³Glorious and majestic are his deeds,
and his righteousness endures
forever.
⁴He has caused his wonders to be
remembered;
the LORD is gracious and
compassionate.
⁵He provides food for those who fear
him;
he remembers his covenant forever.
⁶He has shown his people the power of
his works,
giving them the lands of other
nations.
⁷The works of his hands are faithful
and just;
all his precepts are trustworthy.
⁸They are steadfast for ever and ever,
done in faithfulness and
uprightness.
⁹He provided redemption for his
people;
he ordained his covenant
forever—
holy and awesome is his name.
¹⁰The fear of the LORD is the beginning
of wisdom;
all who follow his precepts have
good understanding.
To him belongs eternal praise.

Psalm 112ᶜ

¹Praise the LORD.ᵈ

Blessed is the man who fears the
LORD,
who finds great delight in his
commands.

²His children will be mighty in the
land;
the generation of the upright will
be blessed.
³Wealth and riches are in his house,

ᵃ 3 Or / your young men will come to you like the dew   ᵇ 7 Or / The One who grants succession will set him in authority
ᶜThis psalm is an acrostic poem, the lines of which begin with the successive letters of the Hebrew alphabet.   ᵈ 1 Hebrew
Hallelu Yah

and his righteousness endures
  forever.
[4] Even in darkness light dawns for the
  upright,
  for the gracious and compassionate
  and righteous man.[a]
[5] Good will come to him who is
  generous and lends freely,
  who conducts his affairs with
  justice.
[6] Surely he will never be shaken;
  a righteous man will be
  remembered forever.
[7] He will have no fear of bad news;
  his heart is steadfast, trusting in the
  LORD.
[8] His heart is secure, he will have no
  fear;
  in the end he will look in triumph
  on his foes.
[9] He has scattered abroad his gifts to
  the poor,
  his righteousness endures forever;
  his horn[b] will be lifted high in
  honor.

Praying Psalm 112:6-8

*Father, I thank You that I don't
have to be afraid of bad news.*

[10] The wicked man will see and be
  vexed,
  he will gnash his teeth and waste
  away;
  the longings of the wicked will
  come to nothing.

Psalm 113

[1] Praise the LORD.[c]

Praise, O servants of the LORD,
  praise the name of the LORD.
[2] Let the name of the LORD be praised,
  both now and forevermore.
[3] From the rising of the sun to the
  place where it sets,
  the name of the LORD is to be
  praised.

[4] The LORD is exalted over all the
  nations,
  his glory above the heavens.
[5] Who is like the LORD our God,
  the One who sits enthroned on
  high,
[6] who stoops down to look
  on the heavens and the earth?
[7] He raises the poor from the dust
  and lifts the needy from the ash
  heap;
[8] he seats them with princes,
  with the princes of their people.
[9] He settles the barren woman in her
  home
  as a happy mother of children.

Praise the LORD.

Psalm 114

[1] When Israel came out of Egypt,
  the house of Jacob from a people of
  foreign tongue,
[2] Judah became God's sanctuary,
  Israel his dominion.

[3] The sea looked and fled,
  the Jordan turned back;
[4] the mountains skipped like rams,
  the hills like lambs.

[5] Why was it, O sea, that you fled,
  O Jordan, that you turned back,
[6] you mountains, that you skipped like
  rams,
  you hills, like lambs?

[7] Tremble, O earth, at the presence of
  the Lord,
  at the presence of the God of Jacob,
[8] who turned the rock into a pool,
  the hard rock into springs of water.

Psalm 115

[1] Not to us, O LORD, not to us
  but to your name be the glory,
  because of your love and
  faithfulness.

---

[a] *4* Or / *for ⌊the* LORD⌋ *is gracious and compassionate and righteous*   [b] *9 Horn* here symbolizes dignity.   [c] *1* Hebrew *Hallelu Yah;*
also in verse 9

2 Why do the nations say,
  "Where is their God?"
3 Our God is in heaven;
  he does whatever pleases him.
4 But their idols are silver and gold,
  made by the hands of men.
5 They have mouths, but cannot speak,
  eyes, but they cannot see;
6 they have ears, but cannot hear,
  noses, but they cannot smell;
7 they have hands, but cannot feel,
  feet, but they cannot walk;
  nor can they utter a sound with
    their throats.
8 Those who make them will be like
    them,
  and so will all who trust in them.

9 O house of Israel, trust in the
    LORD—
  he is their help and shield.
10 O house of Aaron, trust in the
    LORD—
  he is their help and shield.
11 You who fear him, trust in the
    LORD—
  he is their help and shield.

12 The LORD remembers us and will
    bless us:
  He will bless the house of Israel,
  he will bless the house of Aaron,
13 he will bless those who fear the
    LORD—
  small and great alike.

14 May the LORD make you increase,
  both you and your children.
15 May you be blessed by the LORD,
  the Maker of heaven and earth.

16 The highest heavens belong to the
    LORD,
  but the earth he has given to man.
17 It is not the dead who praise the
    LORD,
  those who go down to silence;
18 it is we who extol the LORD,
  both now and forevermore.

Praise the LORD.[a]

Psalm 116

1 I love the LORD, for he heard my
    voice;
  he heard my cry for mercy.
2 Because he turned his ear to me,
  I will call on him as long as I live.

3 The cords of death entangled me,
  the anguish of the grave[b] came
    upon me;
  I was overcome by trouble and
    sorrow.
4 Then I called on the name of the LORD:
  "O LORD, save me!"

5 The LORD is gracious and righteous;
  our God is full of compassion.
6 The LORD protects the simplehearted;
  when I was in great need, he saved
    me.

7 Be at rest once more, O my soul,
  for the LORD has been good to you.

8 For you, O LORD, have delivered my
    soul from death,
  my eyes from tears,
  my feet from stumbling,
9 that I may walk before the LORD
  in the land of the living.
10 I believed; therefore[c] I said,
  "I am greatly afflicted."
11 And in my dismay I said,
  "All men are liars."

12 How can I repay the LORD
  for all his goodness to me?
13 I will lift up the cup of salvation
  and call on the name of the LORD.
14 I will fulfill my vows to the LORD
  in the presence of all his people.

15 Precious in the sight of the LORD
  is the death of his saints.
16 O LORD, truly I am your servant;
  I am your servant, the son of your
    maidservant[d];
  you have freed me from my chains.

17 I will sacrifice a thank offering to you
  and call on the name of the LORD.
18 I will fulfill my vows to the LORD

---

a 18 Hebrew Hallelu Yah   b 3 Hebrew Sheol   c 10 Or believed even when   d 16 Or servant, your faithful son

God Hears You When You Pray

GOING deeper

READ AND CONSIDER: PSALM 116:1-19

"I love the LORD, for he heard my voice; he heard my cry for mercy. Because he turned his ear to me, I will call on him as long as I live" (Psalm 116:1-2).

Do you have someone in your life who listens to you—I mean truly *listens?* Maybe it's a sister or a close friend, or even a coworker who is empathetic. If so, you are blessed. We've all experienced times when it seems as if everyone we know is either too busy or too distracted by their own problems to sit and listen to the cries of our heart. There are few times as lonely as when we are hurting and have no one to tell.

As a child of God, however, you always have someone who will listen to you: God Himself!

Over and over again we find these declarations in the psalms: "God has surely listened and heard my voice in prayer" (66:19). "I waited patiently for the LORD; he turned to me and heard my cry" (40:1). Waiting is never easy, but when the answer to one of your prayers comes, you know without a doubt that God has heard your cries.

God is never so far away that He cannot hear us. Scripture tells us that He turns His ear to us, and it is never a deaf ear. He loves us. He is ever present in our lives. And He hears us when we call to Him.

Never doubt that you have Someone in your life who is always willing to listen. And He alone has the power to change the situation you are facing. Take comfort in the reality that you are loved by God, and He has your best interests at heart. "Be at rest once more, O my soul, for the LORD has been good to you" (116:7).

in the presence of all his people,
¹⁹in the courts of the house of the
    LORD—
in your midst, O Jerusalem.

Praise the LORD.ᵃ

Psalm 117

¹Praise the LORD, all you nations;
    extol him, all you peoples.
²For great is his love toward us,
    and the faithfulness of the LORD
        endures forever.

Praise the LORD.ᵃ

Psalm 118

¹Give thanks to the LORD, for he is
        good;
    his love endures forever.

²Let Israel say:
    "His love endures forever."
³Let the house of Aaron say:
    "His love endures forever."
⁴Let those who fear the LORD say:
    "His love endures forever."

⁵In my anguish I cried to the LORD,
    and he answered by setting me
        free.
⁶The LORD is with me; I will not be
        afraid.
    What can man do to me?
⁷The LORD is with me; he is my
        helper.
    I will look in triumph on my
        enemies.

⁸It is better to take refuge in the LORD
    than to trust in man.

ᵃ *19,2* Hebrew *Hallelu Yah*

9It is better to take refuge in the LORD
    than to trust in princes.

10All the nations surrounded me,
    but in the name of the LORD I cut
        them off.
11They surrounded me on every side,
    but in the name of the LORD I cut
        them off.
12They swarmed around me like bees,
    but they died out as quickly as
        burning thorns;
    in the name of the LORD I cut them
        off.
13I was pushed back and about to fall,
    but the LORD helped me.
14The LORD is my strength and my
        song;
    he has become my salvation.

15Shouts of joy and victory
    resound in the tents of the
        righteous:
    "The LORD's right hand has done
        mighty things!
16   The LORD's right hand is lifted high;
    the LORD's right hand has done
        mighty things!"

17I will not die but live,
    and will proclaim what the LORD
        has done.
18The LORD has chastened me severely,
    but he has not given me over to
        death.

19Open for me the gates of
        righteousness;
    I will enter and give thanks to the
        LORD.
20This is the gate of the LORD
    through which the righteous may
        enter.
21I will give you thanks, for you
        answered me;
    you have become my salvation.

22The stone the builders rejected
    has become the capstone;
23the LORD has done this,
    and it is marvelous in our eyes.
24This is the day the LORD has made;
    let us rejoice and be glad in it.

25O LORD, save us;
    O LORD, grant us success.
26Blessed is he who comes in the name
        of the LORD.
    From the house of the LORD we
        bless you.[a]
27The LORD is God,
    and he has made his light shine
        upon us.
    With boughs in hand, join in the
        festal procession
    up[b] to the horns of the altar.

28You are my God, and I will give you
        thanks;
    you are my God, and I will exalt
        you.

29Give thanks to the LORD, for he is
        good;
    his love endures forever.

Psalm 119[c]

א Aleph

1Blessed are they whose ways are
        blameless,
    who walk according to the law of
        the LORD.
2Blessed are they who keep his statutes
    and seek him with all their heart.
3They do nothing wrong;
    they walk in his ways.
4You have laid down precepts
    that are to be fully obeyed.
5Oh, that my ways were steadfast
    in obeying your decrees!
6Then I would not be put to shame
    when I consider all your
        commands.
7I will praise you with an upright
        heart
    as I learn your righteous laws.

---

a 26 The Hebrew is plural.   b 27 Or Bind the festal sacrifice with ropes / and take it   cThis psalm is an acrostic poem; the verses of each stanza begin with the same letter of the Hebrew alphabet.

Ten Good Reasons to Read God's Word

If you have trouble being in God's Word every day, here are just a few of the many reasons to read the Bible that should inspire you:

1. *To know where you are going.* You can't foresee the future or *exactly* where you are heading, but God's Word will guide you. "Direct my footsteps according to your word; let no sin rule over me" (Psalm 119:133).

2. *To have wisdom.* Knowledge of God's Word is where wisdom begins to grow in you. "The law of the LORD is perfect, reviving the soul. The statutes of the LORD are trustworthy, making wise the simple" (Psalm 19:7).

3. *To find success.* When you live according to the teachings of the Bible, life works. "Do not let this Book of the Law depart from your mouth; meditate on it day and night, so that you may be careful to do everything written in it. Then you will be prosperous and successful" (Joshua 1:8).

4. *To live in purity.* You must live a life of holiness and purity in order to enjoy more of the Lord's presence, but you can't be made pure without being cleansed through God's Word. "How can a young man keep his way pure? By living according to your word" (Psalm 119:9).

5. *To obey God.* If you don't understand what God's laws are, how can you obey them? "Teach me, O LORD, to follow your decrees; then I will keep them to the end. Give me understanding, and I will keep your law and obey it with all my heart. Direct me in the path of your commands, for there I find delight" (Psalm 119:33-35).

6. *To have joy.* You cannot be free of anxiety and unrest without the Word of God in your heart. "The precepts of the LORD are right, giving joy to the heart. The commands of the LORD are radiant, giving light to the eyes" (Psalm 19:8).

7. *To grow in faith.* You can't grow in faith without reading and hearing the Word of God. "Consequently, faith comes from hearing the message, and the message is heard through the word of Christ" (Romans 10:17).

8. *To find deliverance.* You won't know what you need to be free of unless you study God's Word to find out. "If you hold to my teaching, you are really my disciples. Then you will know the truth, and the truth will set you free" (John 8:31-32).

9. *To have peace.* God will give you a peace that the world can't give, but you must find it first in His Word. "Great peace have they who love your law, and nothing can make them stumble" (Psalm 119:165).

10. *To distinguish good from evil.* Everything has become so relative today, how can you know for sure what is right and wrong without God's Word? "I have hidden your word in my heart that I might not sin against you" (Psalm 119:11).

For the next "From Stormie's Heart" article, go to page 808.

8I will obey your decrees;
  do not utterly forsake me.

ב   Beth

9How can a young man keep his way
    pure?
  By living according to your word.
10I seek you with all my heart;
  do not let me stray from your
    commands.
11I have hidden your word in my heart
  that I might not sin against you.
12Praise be to you, O LORD;
  teach me your decrees.
13With my lips I recount
  all the laws that come from your
    mouth.
14I rejoice in following your statutes
  as one rejoices in great riches.
15I meditate on your precepts
  and consider your ways.
16I delight in your decrees;
  I will not neglect your word.

ג   Gimel

17Do good to your servant, and I will
    live;
  I will obey your word.
18Open my eyes that I may see
  wonderful things in your law.
19I am a stranger on earth;
  do not hide your commands from
    me.
20My soul is consumed with longing
  for your laws at all times.
21You rebuke the arrogant, who are
    cursed
  and who stray from your
    commands.
22Remove from me scorn and
    contempt,
  for I keep your statutes.
23Though rulers sit together and slander
    me,
  your servant will meditate on your
    decrees.
24Your statutes are my delight;
  they are my counselors.

ד   Daleth

25I am laid low in the dust;
  preserve my life according to your
    word.
26I recounted my ways and you
    answered me;
  teach me your decrees.
27Let me understand the teaching of
    your precepts;
  then I will meditate on your
    wonders.
28My soul is weary with sorrow;
  strengthen me according to your
    word.
29Keep me from deceitful ways;
  be gracious to me through your
    law.
30I have chosen the way of truth;
  I have set my heart on your laws.
31I hold fast to your statutes, O LORD;
  do not let me be put to shame.
32I run in the path of your commands,
  for you have set my heart free.

ה   He

33Teach me, O LORD, to follow your
    decrees;
  then I will keep them to the end.
34Give me understanding, and I will
    keep your law
  and obey it with all my heart.
35Direct me in the path of your
    commands,
  for there I find delight.
36Turn my heart toward your statutes
  and not toward selfish gain.
37Turn my eyes away from worthless
    things;
  preserve my life according to your
    word.a
38Fulfill your promise to your servant,
  so that you may be feared.
39Take away the disgrace I dread,
  for your laws are good.
40How I long for your precepts!
  Preserve my life in your
    righteousness.

---

a 37 Two manuscripts of the Masoretic Text and Dead Sea Scrolls; most manuscripts of the Masoretic Text life in your way

ו Waw

⁴¹May your unfailing love come to me,
O LORD,
    your salvation according to your
    promise;
⁴²then I will answer the one who taunts
me,
    for I trust in your word.
⁴³Do not snatch the word of truth from
my mouth,
    for I have put my hope in your
    laws.
⁴⁴I will always obey your law,
    for ever and ever.
⁴⁵I will walk about in freedom,
    for I have sought out your precepts.
⁴⁶I will speak of your statutes before
kings
    and will not be put to shame,
⁴⁷for I delight in your commands
    because I love them.
⁴⁸I lift up my hands toᵃ your
       commands, which I love,
    and I meditate on your decrees.

ז Zayin

⁴⁹Remember your word to your
       servant,
    for you have given me hope.
⁵⁰My comfort in my suffering is this:
    Your promise preserves my life.
⁵¹The arrogant mock me without
       restraint,
    but I do not turn from your law.
⁵²I remember your ancient laws,
    O LORD,
    and I find comfort in them.
⁵³Indignation grips me because of the
       wicked,
    who have forsaken your law.
⁵⁴Your decrees are the theme of my
       song
    wherever I lodge.
⁵⁵In the night I remember your name,
    O LORD,
    and I will keep your law.
⁵⁶This has been my practice:
    I obey your precepts.

ח Heth

⁵⁷You are my portion, O LORD;
    I have promised to obey your
    words.
⁵⁸I have sought your face with all my
heart;
    be gracious to me according to
    your promise.
⁵⁹I have considered my ways
    and have turned my steps to your
    statutes.
⁶⁰I will hasten and not delay
    to obey your commands.
⁶¹Though the wicked bind me with
ropes,
    I will not forget your law.
⁶²At midnight I rise to give you thanks
    for your righteous laws.
⁶³I am a friend to all who fear you,
    to all who follow your precepts.
⁶⁴The earth is filled with your love,
    O LORD;
    teach me your decrees.

ט Teth

⁶⁵Do good to your servant
    according to your word, O LORD.
⁶⁶Teach me knowledge and good
       judgment,
    for I believe in your commands.
⁶⁷Before I was afflicted I went astray,
    but now I obey your word.
⁶⁸You are good, and what you do is
good;
    teach me your decrees.
⁶⁹Though the arrogant have smeared
       me with lies,
    I keep your precepts with all my
    heart.
⁷⁰Their hearts are callous and
       unfeeling,
    but I delight in your law.
⁷¹It was good for me to be afflicted
    so that I might learn your decrees.
⁷²The law from your mouth is more
       precious to me
    than thousands of pieces of silver
    and gold.

ᵃ *48 Or for*

י Yodh

73 Your hands made me and formed me;
  give me understanding to learn
    your commands.
74 May those who fear you rejoice when
    they see me,
  for I have put my hope in your
    word.
75 I know, O LORD, that your laws are
    righteous,
  and in faithfulness you have
    afflicted me.
76 May your unfailing love be my
    comfort,
  according to your promise to your
    servant.
77 Let your compassion come to me that
    I may live,
  for your law is my delight.
78 May the arrogant be put to shame for
    wronging me without cause;
  but I will meditate on your
    precepts.
79 May those who fear you turn to me,
  those who understand your statutes.
80 May my heart be blameless toward
    your decrees,
  that I may not be put to shame.

כ Kaph

81 My soul faints with longing for your
    salvation,
  but I have put my hope in your
    word.
82 My eyes fail, looking for your
    promise;
  I say, "When will you comfort
    me?"
83 Though I am like a wineskin in the
    smoke,
  I do not forget your decrees.
84 How long must your servant wait?
  When will you punish my
    persecutors?
85 The arrogant dig pitfalls for me,
  contrary to your law.
86 All your commands are trustworthy;
  help me, for men persecute me
    without cause.

87 They almost wiped me from the
    earth,
  but I have not forsaken your
    precepts.
88 Preserve my life according to your
    love,
  and I will obey the statutes of your
    mouth.

ל Lamedh

89 Your word, O LORD, is eternal;
  it stands firm in the heavens.
90 Your faithfulness continues through
    all generations;
  you established the earth, and it
    endures.
91 Your laws endure to this day,
  for all things serve you.
92 If your law had not been my delight,
  I would have perished in my
    affliction.
93 I will never forget your precepts,
  for by them you have preserved my
    life.
94 Save me, for I am yours;
  I have sought out your precepts.
95 The wicked are waiting to destroy
    me,
  but I will ponder your statutes.
96 To all perfection I see a limit;
  but your commands are boundless.

מ Mem

97 Oh, how I love your law!
  I meditate on it all day long.
98 Your commands make me wiser than
    my enemies,
  for they are ever with me.
99 I have more insight than all
    my teachers,
  for I meditate on your statutes.
100 I have more understanding than
    the elders,
  for I obey your precepts.
101 I have kept my feet from every
    evil path
  so that I might obey your word.
102 I have not departed from your laws,
  for you yourself have taught me.

103 How sweet are your words to
     my taste,
     sweeter than honey to my mouth!
104 I gain understanding from
     your precepts;
     therefore I hate every wrong path.

ב Nun

105 Your word is a lamp to my feet
     and a light for my path.
106 I have taken an oath and
     confirmed it,
     that I will follow your righteous
     laws.
107 I have suffered much;
     preserve my life, O LORD,
     according to your word.
108 Accept, O LORD, the willing praise
     of my mouth,
     and teach me your laws.
109 Though I constantly take my life in
     my hands,
     I will not forget your law.
110 The wicked have set a snare for me,
     but I have not strayed from your
     precepts.
111 Your statutes are my heritage forever;
     they are the joy of my heart.
112 My heart is set on keeping
     your decrees
     to the very end.

ס Samekh

113 I hate double-minded men,
     but I love your law.
114 You are my refuge and my shield;
     I have put my hope in your word.
115 Away from me, you evildoers,
     that I may keep the commands of
     my God!
116 Sustain me according to your
     promise, and I will live;
     do not let my hopes be dashed.
117 Uphold me, and I will be delivered;
     I will always have regard for your
     decrees.
118 You reject all who stray from
     your decrees,
     for their deceitfulness is in vain.

119 All the wicked of the earth you
     discard like dross;
     therefore I love your statutes.
120 My flesh trembles in fear of you;
     I stand in awe of your laws.

ע Ayin

121 I have done what is righteous
     and just;
     do not leave me to my oppressors.
122 Ensure your servant's well-being;
     let not the arrogant oppress me.
123 My eyes fail, looking for
     your salvation,
     looking for your righteous promise.
124 Deal with your servant according to
     your love
     and teach me your decrees.
125 I am your servant; give
     me discernment
     that I may understand your
     statutes.
126 It is time for you to act, O LORD;
     your law is being broken.
127 Because I love your commands
     more than gold, more than pure
     gold,
128 and because I consider all your
     precepts right,
     I hate every wrong path.

פ Pe

129 Your statutes are wonderful;
     therefore I obey them.
130 The unfolding of your words
     gives light;
     it gives understanding to the
     simple.
131 I open my mouth and pant,
     longing for your commands.
132 Turn to me and have mercy on me,
     as you always do to those who love
     your name.
133 Direct my footsteps according to
     your word;
     let no sin rule over me.
134 Redeem me from the oppression
     of men,
     that I may obey your precepts.

135 Make your face shine upon
        your servant
    and teach me your decrees.
136 Streams of tears flow from my eyes,
    for your law is not obeyed.

צ Tsadhe

137 Righteous are you, O LORD,
    and your laws are right.
138 The statutes you have laid down
        are righteous;
    they are fully trustworthy.
139 My zeal wears me out,
    for my enemies ignore your words.
140 Your promises have been
        thoroughly tested,
    and your servant loves them.
141 Though I am lowly and despised,
    I do not forget your precepts.
142 Your righteousness is everlasting
    and your law is true.
143 Trouble and distress have come
        upon me,
    but your commands are my
        delight.
144 Your statutes are forever right;
    give me understanding that I may
        live.

ק Qoph

145 I call with all my heart; answer me,
        O LORD,
    and I will obey your decrees.
146 I call out to you; save me
    and I will keep your statutes.
147 I rise before dawn and cry for help;
    I have put my hope in your word.
148 My eyes stay open through the
        watches of the night,
    that I may meditate on your
        promises.
149 Hear my voice in accordance with
        your love;
    preserve my life, O LORD,
        according to your laws.
150 Those who devise wicked schemes
        are near,
    but they are far from your law.
151 Yet you are near, O LORD,

    and all your commands are true.
152 Long ago I learned from
        your statutes
    that you established them to last
        forever.

ר Resh

153 Look upon my suffering and
        deliver me,
    for I have not forgotten your law.
154 Defend my cause and redeem me;
    preserve my life according to your
        promise.
155 Salvation is far from the wicked,
    for they do not seek out your
        decrees.
156 Your compassion is great, O LORD;
    preserve my life according to your
        laws.
157 Many are the foes who persecute me,
    but I have not turned from your
        statutes.
158 I look on the faithless with
        loathing,
    for they do not obey your word.
159 See how I love your precepts;
    preserve my life, O LORD,
        according to your love.
160 All your words are true;
    all your righteous laws are eternal.

ש Sin and Shin

161 Rulers persecute me without cause,
    but my heart trembles at your
        word.
162 I rejoice in your promise
    like one who finds great spoil.
163 I hate and abhor falsehood
    but I love your law.
164 Seven times a day I praise you
    for your righteous laws.
165 Great peace have they who love
        your law,
    and nothing can make them
        stumble.
166 I wait for your salvation, O LORD,
    and I follow your commands.
167 I obey your statutes,
    for I love them greatly.

168 I obey your precepts and
your statutes,
for all my ways are known to you.

ת Taw

169 May my cry come before you,
O LORD;
give me understanding according
to your word.
170 May my supplication come
before you;
deliver me according to your
promise.
171 May my lips overflow with praise,
for you teach me your decrees.
172 May my tongue sing of your word,
for all your commands are
righteous.
173 May your hand be ready to help
me,
for I have chosen your precepts.
174 I long for your salvation, O LORD,
and your law is my delight.
175 Let me live that I may praise you,
and may your laws sustain me.
176 I have strayed like a lost sheep.
Seek your servant,
for I have not forgotten your
commands.

Psalm 120

A song of ascents.

1 I call on the LORD in my distress,
and he answers me.
2 Save me, O LORD, from lying lips
and from deceitful tongues.

3 What will he do to you,
and what more besides, O deceitful
tongue?
4 He will punish you with a warrior's
sharp arrows,
with burning coals of the broom
tree.

5 Woe to me that I dwell in Meshech,
that I live among the tents of
Kedar!
6 Too long have I lived
among those who hate peace.

7 I am a man of peace;
but when I speak, they are for war.

Psalm 121

A song of ascents.

1 I lift up my eyes to the hills—
where does my help come from?
2 My help comes from the LORD,
the Maker of heaven and earth.

3 He will not let your foot slip—
he who watches over you will not
slumber;
4 indeed, he who watches over Israel
will neither slumber nor sleep.

5 The LORD watches over you—
the LORD is your shade at your
right hand;
6 the sun will not harm you by day,
nor the moon by night.

7 The LORD will keep you from all
harm—
he will watch over your life;
8 the LORD will watch over your
coming and going
both now and forevermore.

Psalm 122

A song of ascents. Of David.

1 I rejoiced with those who said to me,
"Let us go to the house of the
LORD."
2 Our feet are standing
in your gates, O Jerusalem.

3 Jerusalem is built like a city
that is closely compacted together.
4 That is where the tribes go up,
the tribes of the LORD,
to praise the name of the LORD
according to the statute given to
Israel.
5 There the thrones for judgment stand,
the thrones of the house of David.

6 Pray for the peace of Jerusalem:
"May those who love you be
secure.
7 May there be peace within your walls

and security within your citadels."
8 For the sake of my brothers and
friends,
   I will say, "Peace be within you."
9 For the sake of the house of the LORD
our God,
   I will seek your prosperity.

Psalm 123

A song of ascents.

1 I lift up my eyes to you,
   to you whose throne is in heaven.
2 As the eyes of slaves look to the hand
of their master,
   as the eyes of a maid look to the
   hand of her mistress,
so our eyes look to the LORD our
God,
   till he shows us his mercy.

3 Have mercy on us, O LORD, have
   mercy on us,
   for we have endured much
   contempt.
4 We have endured much ridicule from
the proud,
   much contempt from the arrogant.

Psalm 124

A song of ascents. Of David.

1 If the LORD had not been on our
side—
   let Israel say—
2 if the LORD had not been on our side
when men attacked us,
3 when their anger flared against us,
   they would have swallowed us
   alive;
4 the flood would have engulfed us,
   the torrent would have swept over
   us,
5 the raging waters
   would have swept us away.

6 Praise be to the LORD,
   who has not let us be torn by their
   teeth.
7 We have escaped like a bird

out of the fowler's snare;
   the snare has been broken,
   and we have escaped.
8 Our help is in the name of the LORD,
   the Maker of heaven and earth.

Psalm 125

A song of ascents.

1 Those who trust in the LORD are like
Mount Zion,
   which cannot be shaken but
   endures forever.
2 As the mountains surround Jerusalem,
   so the LORD surrounds his people
   both now and forevermore.

3 The scepter of the wicked will not
remain
   over the land allotted to the
   righteous,
for then the righteous might use
   their hands to do evil.

4 Do good, O LORD, to those who are
good,
   to those who are upright in heart.
5 But those who turn to crooked ways
   the LORD will banish with the
   evildoers.

Peace be upon Israel.

Psalm 126

A song of ascents.

1 When the LORD brought back the
captives to[a] Zion,
   we were like men who dreamed.[b]
2 Our mouths were filled with
laughter,
   our tongues with songs of joy.
Then it was said among the nations,
   "The LORD has done great things
   for them."
3 The LORD has done great things for
us,
   and we are filled with joy.

4 Restore our fortunes,[c] O LORD,
   like streams in the Negev.

---

a 1 Or LORD restored the fortunes of   b 1 Or men restored to health   c 4 Or Bring back our captives

5 Those who sow in tears
will reap with songs of joy.
6 He who goes out weeping,
carrying seed to sow,
will return with songs of joy,
carrying sheaves with him.

Psalm 127

A song of ascents. Of Solomon.

1 Unless the LORD builds the house,
its builders labor in vain.
Unless the LORD watches over the
city,
the watchmen stand guard in vain.
2 In vain you rise early
and stay up late,
toiling for food to eat—
for he grants sleep to[a] those he
loves.

3 Sons are a heritage from the LORD,
children a reward from him.
4 Like arrows in the hands of a warrior
are sons born in one's youth.
5 Blessed is the man
whose quiver is full of them.
They will not be put to shame
when they contend with their
enemies in the gate.

Psalm 128

A song of ascents.

1 Blessed are all who fear the LORD,
who walk in his ways.
2 You will eat the fruit of your labor;
blessings and prosperity will be
yours.
3 Your wife will be like a fruitful vine
within your house;
your sons will be like olive shoots
around your table.
4 Thus is the man blessed
who fears the LORD.

5 May the LORD bless you from Zion
all the days of your life;
may you see the prosperity of
Jerusalem,

6   and may you live to see your
children's children.

Peace be upon Israel.

Psalm 129

A song of ascents.

1 They have greatly oppressed me from
my youth—
let Israel say—
2 they have greatly oppressed me from
my youth,
but they have not gained the
victory over me.
3 Plowmen have plowed my back
and made their furrows long.
4 But the LORD is righteous;
he has cut me free from the cords
of the wicked.

5 May all who hate Zion
be turned back in shame.
6 May they be like grass on the roof,
which withers before it can grow;
7 with it the reaper cannot fill his
hands,
nor the one who gathers fill his
arms.
8 May those who pass by not say,
"The blessing of the LORD be upon
you;
we bless you in the name of the
LORD."

Psalm 130

A song of ascents.

1 Out of the depths I cry to you,
O LORD;
2   O Lord, hear my voice.
Let your ears be attentive
to my cry for mercy.

3 If you, O LORD, kept a record of sins,
O Lord, who could stand?
4 But with you there is forgiveness;
therefore you are feared.

5 I wait for the LORD, my soul waits,
and in his word I put my hope.

---

a 2 Or eat— / for while they sleep he provides for

⁶My soul waits for the Lord
more than watchmen wait for the
morning,
more than watchmen wait for the
morning.

Praying Psalm 130:5-6

*Help me to wait patiently on You,
Lord, for Your perfect timing
and answer to my prayers.*

⁷O Israel, put your hope in the Lord,
for with the Lord is unfailing love
and with him is full redemption.
⁸He himself will redeem Israel
from all their sins.

Psalm 131

A song of ascents. Of David.

¹My heart is not proud, O Lord,
my eyes are not haughty;
I do not concern myself with great
matters
or things too wonderful for me.
²But I have stilled and quieted my soul;
like a weaned child with its mother,
like a weaned child is my soul
within me.

³O Israel, put your hope in the Lord
both now and forevermore.

Psalm 132

A song of ascents.

¹O Lord, remember David
and all the hardships he endured.

²He swore an oath to the Lord
and made a vow to the Mighty
One of Jacob:
³"I will not enter my house
or go to my bed—
⁴I will allow no sleep to my eyes,
no slumber to my eyelids,
⁵till I find a place for the Lord,
a dwelling for the Mighty One of
Jacob."

⁶We heard it in Ephrathah,
we came upon it in the fields of
Jaarᵃ:ᵇ
⁷"Let us go to his dwelling place;
let us worship at his footstool—
⁸arise, O Lord, and come to your
resting place,
you and the ark of your might.
⁹May your priests be clothed with
righteousness;
may your saints sing for joy."

¹⁰For the sake of David your servant,
do not reject your anointed one.

¹¹The Lord swore an oath to David,
a sure oath that he will not revoke:
"One of your own descendants
I will place on your throne—
¹²if your sons keep my covenant
and the statutes I teach them,
then their sons will sit
on your throne for ever and ever."

¹³For the Lord has chosen Zion,
he has desired it for his dwelling:
¹⁴"This is my resting place for ever and
ever;
here I will sit enthroned, for I have
desired it—
¹⁵I will bless her with abundant
provisions;
her poor will I satisfy with food.
¹⁶I will clothe her priests with
salvation,
and her saints will ever sing for joy.

¹⁷"Here I will make a hornᶜ grow for
David
and set up a lamp for my anointed
one.
¹⁸I will clothe his enemies with shame,
but the crown on his head will be
resplendent."

Psalm 133

A song of ascents. Of David.

¹How good and pleasant it is
when brothers live together in unity!

ᵃ 6 That is, Kiriath Jearim   ᵇ 6 Or *heard of it in Ephrathah, / we found it in the fields of Jaar.* (And no quotes around verses 7-9)
ᶜ 17 Horn here symbolizes strong one, that is, king.

2 It is like precious oil poured on the
head,
   running down on the beard,
running down on Aaron's beard,
   down upon the collar of his robes.
3 It is as if the dew of Hermon
were falling on Mount Zion.
For there the LORD bestows his
blessing,
   even life forevermore.

Psalm 134

A song of ascents.

1 Praise the LORD, all you servants of
the LORD
who minister by night in the house
of the LORD.
2 Lift up your hands in the sanctuary
and praise the LORD.

3 May the LORD, the Maker of heaven
and earth,
bless you from Zion.

Prayer is . . .

*praise, which is taking the
focus off of yourself and placing
it entirely upon God.*

Psalm 135

1 Praise the LORD.[a]

Praise the name of the LORD;
   praise him, you servants of the
LORD,
2 you who minister in the house of the
LORD,
   in the courts of the house of our
God.

3 Praise the LORD, for the LORD is
good;
   sing praise to his name, for that is
pleasant.

4 For the LORD has chosen Jacob to be
his own,
   Israel to be his treasured possession.
5 I know that the LORD is great,
   that our Lord is greater than all
gods.
6 The LORD does whatever pleases him,
   in the heavens and on the earth,
   in the seas and all their depths.
7 He makes clouds rise from the ends of
the earth;
   he sends lightning with the rain
   and brings out the wind from his
storehouses.

8 He struck down the firstborn of
Egypt,
   the firstborn of men and animals.
9 He sent his signs and wonders into
your midst, O Egypt,
   against Pharaoh and all his servants.
10 He struck down many nations
   and killed mighty kings—
11 Sihon king of the Amorites,
   Og king of Bashan
   and all the kings of Canaan—
12 and he gave their land as an
inheritance,
   an inheritance to his people Israel.

13 Your name, O LORD, endures forever,
   your renown, O LORD, through all
generations.
14 For the LORD will vindicate his
people
   and have compassion on his servants.

15 The idols of the nations are silver and
gold,
   made by the hands of men.
16 They have mouths, but cannot speak,
   eyes, but they cannot see;
17 they have ears, but cannot hear,
   nor is there breath in their mouths.
18 Those who make them will be like
them,
   and so will all who trust in them.

19 O house of Israel, praise the LORD;
   O house of Aaron, praise the LORD;

---

a 1 Hebrew *Hallelu Yah*; also in verses 3 and 21

20O house of Levi, praise the LORD;
  you who fear him, praise the LORD.
21Praise be to the LORD from Zion,
  to him who dwells in Jerusalem.

Praise the LORD.

Psalm 136

1Give thanks to the LORD, for he is
  good.
      His love endures forever.
2Give thanks to the God of gods.
      His love endures forever.
3Give thanks to the Lord of lords:
      His love endures forever.

4to him who alone does great wonders,
      His love endures forever.
5who by his understanding made the
  heavens,
      His love endures forever.
6who spread out the earth upon the
  waters,
      His love endures forever.
7who made the great lights—
      His love endures forever.
8the sun to govern the day,
      His love endures forever.
9the moon and stars to govern the night;
      His love endures forever.

10to him who struck down the firstborn
  of Egypt
      His love endures forever.
11and brought Israel out from among
  them
      His love endures forever.
12with a mighty hand and outstretched
  arm;
      His love endures forever.
13to him who divided the Red Sea[a]
  asunder
      His love endures forever.
14and brought Israel through the midst
  of it,
      His love endures forever.
15but swept Pharaoh and his army into
  the Red Sea;
      His love endures forever.

16to him who led his people through
  the desert,
      His love endures forever.
17who struck down great kings,
      His love endures forever.
18and killed mighty kings—
      His love endures forever.
19Sihon king of the Amorites
      His love endures forever.
20and Og king of Bashan—
      His love endures forever.
21and gave their land as an inheritance,
      His love endures forever.
22an inheritance to his servant Israel;
      His love endures forever.

23to the One who remembered us in
  our low estate
      His love endures forever.
24and freed us from our enemies,
      His love endures forever.
25and who gives food to every creature.
      His love endures forever.

26Give thanks to the God of heaven.
      His love endures forever.

Psalm 137

1By the rivers of Babylon we sat and
  wept
  when we remembered Zion.
2There on the poplars
  we hung our harps,
3for there our captors asked us for
  songs,
  our tormentors demanded songs of
    joy;
  they said, "Sing us one of the songs
    of Zion!"

4How can we sing the songs of the
  LORD
  while in a foreign land?
5If I forget you, O Jerusalem,
  may my right hand forget ⌊its skill⌋
6May my tongue cling to the roof of
  my mouth
  if I do not remember you,
  if I do not consider Jerusalem
  my highest joy.

---

a *13* Hebrew *Yam Suph*; that is, Sea of Reeds; also in verse 15

⁷Remember, O LORD, what the
Edomites did
on the day Jerusalem fell.
"Tear it down," they cried,
"tear it down to its foundations!"

⁸O Daughter of Babylon, doomed to
destruction,
happy is he who repays you
for what you have done to us—
⁹he who seizes your infants
and dashes them against the rocks.

Psalm 138

Of David.

¹I will praise you, O LORD, with all
my heart;
before the "gods" I will sing your
praise.
²I will bow down toward your holy
temple
and will praise your name
for your love and your faithfulness,
for you have exalted above all things
your name and your word.
³When I called, you answered me;
you made me bold and stouthearted.

⁴May all the kings of the earth praise
you, O LORD,
when they hear the words of your
mouth.
⁵May they sing of the ways of the
LORD,
for the glory of the LORD is great.

⁶Though the LORD is on high, he
looks upon the lowly,
but the proud he knows from afar.
⁷Though I walk in the midst of
trouble,
you preserve my life;
you stretch out your hand against the
anger of my foes,
with your right hand you save me.
⁸The LORD will fulfill ⌊his purpose⌋
for me;
your love, O LORD, endures
forever—

do not abandon the works of your
hands.

Psalm 139

For the director of music.
Of David. A psalm.

¹O LORD, you have searched me
and you know me.
²You know when I sit and when I rise;
you perceive my thoughts from
afar.
³You discern my going out and my
lying down;
you are familiar with all my ways.
⁴Before a word is on my tongue
you know it completely, O LORD.

⁵You hem me in—behind and before;
you have laid your hand upon me.
⁶Such knowledge is too wonderful for
me,
too lofty for me to attain.

⁷Where can I go from your Spirit?
Where can I flee from your
presence?
⁸If I go up to the heavens, you are
there;
if I make my bed in the depths,ᵃ
you are there.
⁹If I rise on the wings of the dawn,
if I settle on the far side of the sea,
¹⁰even there your hand will guide me,
your right hand will hold me fast.

¹¹If I say, "Surely the darkness will
hide me
and the light become night around
me,"
¹²even the darkness will not be dark to
you;
the night will shine like the day,
for darkness is as light to you.

¹³For you created my inmost being;
you knit me together in my
mother's womb.
¹⁴I praise you because I am fearfully
and wonderfully made;
your works are wonderful,

ᵃ 8 Hebrew *Sheol*

Thank God That He Knows and Loves You

GOING *deeper*

READ AND CONSIDER: PSALM 139:1-24

"O LORD, you have searched me and you know me. You know when I sit and when I rise; you perceive my thoughts from afar. You discern my going out and my lying down; you are familiar with all my ways" (Psalm 139:1-3).

God knows everything about you. He knows your thoughts even before you think them. "Before a word is on my tongue you know it completely, O LORD" (139:4). He knows your actions from the time you rise in the morning until the moment you go to bed at night. Even when sleep reduces you to unconsciousness, He is watching over you still.

God is everywhere around you. There is nowhere you can go that God is not there too. He is with you in the mountaintop experiences of life, and He is with you in the valleys of despair. He is omnipresent. Corrie ten Boom suffered in a Nazi prison camp during World War II yet was able to write, "There is no pit so deep that God is not deeper still."

God did a miracle in creating you! You may struggle with the way you feel or how you look, and you may not feel much like a "miracle" at all, but you are. You may feel more like a mistake, but you are not. God formed you and loved you even when you were in your mother's womb. You bear His image (Genesis 1:27).

Your life is no accident, and the purpose of your life was ordained even before you were born. Your heavenly Father knows everything about you, is present everywhere around you, and performed a miracle when He made you. Praise God every day that He knows you and loves you!

I know that full well.
15 My frame was not hidden from you
  when I was made in the secret
   place.
When I was woven together in the
   depths of the earth,
16 your eyes saw my unformed body.
All the days ordained for me
  were written in your book
  before one of them came to be.

17 How precious to[a] me are your
   thoughts, O God!
How vast is the sum of them!
18 Were I to count them,
  they would outnumber the grains
   of sand.
When I awake,
  I am still with you.

19 If only you would slay the wicked,
   O God!
Away from me, you bloodthirsty
   men!
20 They speak of you with evil intent;
  your adversaries misuse your name.
21 Do I not hate those who hate you,
   O LORD,
  and abhor those who rise up against
   you?
22 I have nothing but hatred for them;
  I count them my enemies.

23 Search me, O God, and know my
   heart;
  test me and know my anxious
   thoughts.
24 See if there is any offensive way in me,
  and lead me in the way everlasting.

a 17 Or *concerning*

Psalm 140

For the director of music.
A psalm of David.

¹Rescue me, O LORD, from evil men;
   protect me from men of violence,
²who devise evil plans in their hearts
   and stir up war every day.
³They make their tongues as sharp as a
      serpent's;
   the poison of vipers is on their lips.
                                    Selah

⁴Keep me, O LORD, from the hands of
      the wicked;
   protect me from men of violence
   who plan to trip my feet.
⁵Proud men have hidden a snare for
      me;
   they have spread out the cords of
      their net
   and have set traps for me along my
      path.   *Selah*

⁶O LORD, I say to you, "You are my
      God."
   Hear, O LORD, my cry for mercy.
⁷O Sovereign LORD, my strong
      deliverer,
   who shields my head in the day of
      battle—
⁸do not grant the wicked their desires,
      O LORD;
   do not let their plans succeed,
   or they will become proud.   *Selah*

⁹Let the heads of those who
      surround me
   be covered with the trouble their
      lips have caused.
¹⁰Let burning coals fall upon them;
   may they be thrown into the fire,
   into miry pits, never to rise.
¹¹Let slanderers not be established in
      the land;
   may disaster hunt down men of
      violence.

¹²I know that the LORD secures justice
      for the poor
   and upholds the cause of the needy.

¹³Surely the righteous will praise your
      name
   and the upright will live before
      you.

Psalm 141

A psalm of David.

¹O LORD, I call to you; come quickly
      to me.
   Hear my voice when I call to you.
²May my prayer be set before you like
      incense;
   may the lifting up of my hands be
      like the evening sacrifice.

³Set a guard over my mouth, O LORD;
   keep watch over the door of my
      lips.
⁴Let not my heart be drawn to what is
      evil,
   to take part in wicked deeds
with men who are evildoers;
   let me not eat of their delicacies.

Praying Psalm 141:3
Put a guard over my lips, Lord, so that I
will never say anything wrong or hurtful.

⁵Let a righteous manᵃ strike me—it is
      a kindness;
   let him rebuke me—it is oil on my
      head.
   My head will not refuse it.

Yet my prayer is ever against the
      deeds of evildoers;
⁶ their rulers will be thrown down
      from the cliffs,
   and the wicked will learn that my
      words were well spoken.
⁷⌞They will say,⌟ "As one plows and
      breaks up the earth,
   so our bones have been scattered at
      the mouth of the grave.ᵇ"

⁸But my eyes are fixed on you,
      O Sovereign LORD;
   in you I take refuge—do not give
      me over to death.

ᵃ 5 Or *Let the Righteous One*   ᵇ 7 Hebrew *Sheol*

⁹Keep me from the snares they have
  laid for me,
  from the traps set by evildoers.
¹⁰Let the wicked fall into their own
  nets,
  while I pass by in safety.

Psalm 142

A *maskil*ᵃ of David. When he was
in the cave. A prayer.

¹I cry aloud to the LORD;
  I lift up my voice to the LORD for
  mercy.
²I pour out my complaint before him;
  before him I tell my trouble.

³When my spirit grows faint within
  me,
  it is you who know my way.
In the path where I walk
  men have hidden a snare for me.
⁴Look to my right and see;
  no one is concerned for me.
I have no refuge;
  no one cares for my life.

⁵I cry to you, O LORD;
  I say, "You are my refuge,
  my portion in the land of the
  living."
⁶Listen to my cry,
  for I am in desperate need;
rescue me from those who pursue me,
  for they are too strong for me.
⁷Set me free from my prison,
  that I may praise your name.

Then the righteous will gather
  about me
  because of your goodness to me.

Psalm 143

A psalm of David.

¹O LORD, hear my prayer,
  listen to my cry for mercy;
in your faithfulness and righteousness
  come to my relief.
²Do not bring your servant into
  judgment,

for no one living is righteous before
  you.

³The enemy pursues me,
  he crushes me to the ground;
he makes me dwell in darkness
  like those long dead.
⁴So my spirit grows faint within me;
  my heart within me is dismayed.
⁵I remember the days of long ago;
  I meditate on all your works
  and consider what your hands have
  done.
⁶I spread out my hands to you;
  my soul thirsts for you like a
  parched land.   *Selah*

⁷Answer me quickly, O LORD;
  my spirit fails.
Do not hide your face from me
  or I will be like those who go
  down to the pit.
⁸Let the morning bring me word of
  your unfailing love,
  for I have put my trust in you.
Show me the way I should go,
  for to you I lift up my soul.
⁹Rescue me from my enemies,
  O LORD,
  for I hide myself in you.
¹⁰Teach me to do your will,
  for you are my God;
may your good Spirit
  lead me on level ground.

¹¹For your name's sake, O LORD,
  preserve my life;
in your righteousness, bring me out
  of trouble.
¹²In your unfailing love, silence my
  enemies;
  destroy all my foes,
  for I am your servant.

Psalm 144

Of David.

¹Praise be to the LORD my Rock,
  who trains my hands for war,
  my fingers for battle.

ᵃTitle: Probably a literary or musical term

2He is my loving God and my fortress,
  my stronghold and my deliverer,
my shield, in whom I take refuge,
  who subdues peoples[a] under me.

3O Lord, what is man that you care
    for him,
  the son of man that you think of
    him?
4Man is like a breath;
  his days are like a fleeting shadow.

5Part your heavens, O Lord, and
    come down;
  touch the mountains, so that they
    smoke.
6Send forth lightning and scatter ˻the
    enemies ˼;
  shoot your arrows and rout them.
7Reach down your hand from on
    high;
  deliver me and rescue me
from the mighty waters,
  from the hands of foreigners
8whose mouths are full of lies,
  whose right hands are deceitful.

9I will sing a new song to you, O God;
  on the ten-stringed lyre I will make
    music to you,
10to the One who gives victory to
    kings,
  who delivers his servant David
    from the deadly sword.

11Deliver me and rescue me
  from the hands of foreigners
whose mouths are full of lies,
  whose right hands are deceitful.

12Then our sons in their youth
  will be like well-nurtured plants,
and our daughters will be like pillars
  carved to adorn a palace.
13Our barns will be filled
  with every kind of provision.
Our sheep will increase by thousands,
  by tens of thousands in our fields;

14 our oxen will draw heavy loads.[b]
There will be no breaching of walls,
  no going into captivity,
  no cry of distress in our streets.

15Blessed are the people of whom this is
    true;
  blessed are the people whose God is
    the Lord.

Psalm 145[c]

A psalm of praise. Of David.

1I will exalt you, my God the King;
  I will praise your name for ever and
    ever.
2Every day I will praise you
  and extol your name for ever and
    ever.

3Great is the Lord and most worthy of
    praise;
  his greatness no one can fathom.
4One generation will commend your
    works to another;
  they will tell of your mighty acts.
5They will speak of the glorious
    splendor of your majesty,
  and I will meditate on your
    wonderful works.[d]
6They will tell of the power of your
    awesome works,
  and I will proclaim your great
    deeds.
7They will celebrate your abundant
    goodness
  and joyfully sing of your
    righteousness.

8The Lord is gracious and
    compassionate,
  slow to anger and rich in love.
9The Lord is good to all;
  he has compassion on all he has
    made.
10All you have made will praise you,
    O Lord;
  your saints will extol you.

---

a 2 Many manuscripts of the Masoretic Text, Dead Sea Scrolls, Aquila, Jerome and Syriac; most manuscripts of the Masoretic Text *subdues my people*   b 14 Or *our chieftains will be firmly established*   c This psalm is an acrostic poem, the verses of which (including verse 13b) begin with the successive letters of the Hebrew alphabet.   d 5 Dead Sea Scrolls and Syriac (see also Septuagint); Masoretic Text *On the glorious splendor of your majesty / and on your wonderful works I will meditate*

The Lord Is Near When We Pray

GOING

deeper

READ AND CONSIDER: PSALM 145:1-21

"The Lord is near to all who call on him, to all who call on him in truth" (Psalm 145:18).

Do you experience times when God seems far away? Most of us do. The psalmist speaks for us when he cries out, "Why, O Lord, do you stand far off? Why do you hide yourself in times of trouble?" (10:1). When He was hanging on the cross, Jesus cried out, "My God, my God, why have you forsaken me?" (Matthew 27:46).

Our feelings may tell us that God is distant, but Scripture tells us otherwise. When we call on Him in prayer, God is near to us whether we *feel* it or not. At the same time, we might pray for something we need and fail to see an answer after weeks, months, or even years of passionate intercession. Why does God so often cause us to wait for what we are so sure we need right away?

We may be denied certain things for a time because God wants us to fervently pray and intercede for them. He wants to do something great in response to our prayers, something that can only be birthed in prayer. There may be things that won't happen in your life unless you are praying long and fervently about them.

If you start becoming discouraged and feel as if your life won't ever be any different than it is at this moment, know that the truth is quite the opposite. It's at these very times, when you feel as though you're not getting anywhere or you're missing the future God has for you, that God is actually *preparing* you for your future. And when the time is right, He has been known to do a very quick work. Draw close to God in prayer, trusting that He is near. Thank Him that He hears your prayers and will answer in His perfect way.

11 They will tell of the glory of your
kingdom
and speak of your might,
12 so that all men may know of your
mighty acts
and the glorious splendor of your
kingdom.
13 Your kingdom is an everlasting
kingdom,
and your dominion endures
through all generations.

The Lord is faithful to all his
promises
and loving toward all he has made.[a]
14 The Lord upholds all those who fall
and lifts up all who are bowed
down.

15 The eyes of all look to you,
and you give them their food at the
proper time.
16 You open your hand
and satisfy the desires of every
living thing.
17 The Lord is righteous in all his ways
and loving toward all he has made.
18 The Lord is near to all who call on
him,
to all who call on him in truth.
19 He fulfills the desires of those who
fear him;
he hears their cry and saves them.
20 The Lord watches over all who love
him,
but all the wicked he will destroy.

---

a *13* One manuscript of the Masoretic Text, Dead Sea Scrolls and Syriac (see also Septuagint); most manuscripts of the Masoretic Text do not have the last two lines of verse 13.

²¹My mouth will speak in praise of the
LORD.
Let every creature praise his holy
name
for ever and ever.

Psalm 146

¹Praise the LORD.ᵃ

Praise the LORD, O my soul.
² I will praise the LORD all my life;
I will sing praise to my God as long
as I live.

³Do not put your trust in princes,
in mortal men, who cannot save.
⁴When their spirit departs, they return
to the ground;
on that very day their plans come
to nothing.

⁵Blessed is he whose help is the God of
Jacob,
whose hope is in the LORD his God,
⁶the Maker of heaven and earth,
the sea, and everything in them—
the LORD, who remains faithful
forever.
⁷He upholds the cause of the oppressed
and gives food to the hungry.
The LORD sets prisoners free,
⁸ the LORD gives sight to the blind,
the LORD lifts up those who are
bowed down,
the LORD loves the righteous.
⁹The LORD watches over the alien
and sustains the fatherless and the
widow,
but he frustrates the ways of the
wicked.

¹⁰The LORD reigns forever,
your God, O Zion, for all generations.

Praise the LORD.

Psalm 147

¹Praise the LORD.ᵇ

How good it is to sing praises to our
God,
how pleasant and fitting to praise
him!

²The LORD builds up Jerusalem;
he gathers the exiles of Israel.
³He heals the brokenhearted
and binds up their wounds.
⁴He determines the number of the
stars
and calls them each by name.
⁵Great is our Lord and mighty in
power;
his understanding has no limit.
⁶The LORD sustains the humble
but casts the wicked to the ground.

⁷Sing to the LORD with thanksgiving;
make music to our God on the
harp.
⁸He covers the sky with clouds;
he supplies the earth with rain
and makes grass grow on the hills.
⁹He provides food for the cattle
and for the young ravens when they
call.

¹⁰His pleasure is not in the strength of
the horse,
nor his delight in the legs of a man;
¹¹the LORD delights in those who fear
him,
who put their hope in his unfailing
love.

¹²Extol the LORD, O Jerusalem;
praise your God, O Zion,
¹³for he strengthens the bars of your
gates
and blesses your people within you.
¹⁴He grants peace to your borders
and satisfies you with the finest of
wheat.

¹⁵He sends his command to the earth;
his word runs swiftly.
¹⁶He spreads the snow like wool
and scatters the frost like ashes.
¹⁷He hurls down his hail like pebbles.
Who can withstand his icy blast?
¹⁸He sends his word and melts them;

ᵃ 1 Hebrew *Hallelu Yah*; also in verse 10   ᵇ 1 Hebrew *Hallelu Yah*; also in verse 20

he stirs up his breezes, and the
   waters flow.

19 He has revealed his word to Jacob,
   his laws and decrees to Israel.
20 He has done this for no other nation;
   they do not know his laws.

Praise the LORD.

Psalm 148

1 Praise the LORD.[a]

Praise the LORD from the heavens,
   praise him in the heights above.
2 Praise him, all his angels,
   praise him, all his heavenly hosts.
3 Praise him, sun and moon,
   praise him, all you shining stars.
4 Praise him, you highest heavens
   and you waters above the skies.
5 Let them praise the name of the LORD,
   for he commanded and they were
      created.
6 He set them in place for ever and
      ever;
   he gave a decree that will never
      pass away.

7 Praise the LORD from the earth,
   you great sea creatures and all
      ocean depths,
8 lightning and hail, snow and clouds,
   stormy winds that do his bidding,
9 you mountains and all hills,
   fruit trees and all cedars,
10 wild animals and all cattle,
   small creatures and flying birds,
11 kings of the earth and all nations,
   you princes and all rulers on earth,
12 young men and maidens,
   old men and children.

13 Let them praise the name of the
      LORD,
   for his name alone is exalted;
   his splendor is above the earth and
      the heavens.
14 He has raised up for his people a
      horn,[b]

the praise of all his saints,
   of Israel, the people close to his
      heart.

Praise the LORD.

Psalm 149

1 Praise the LORD.[c]

Sing to the LORD a new song,
   his praise in the assembly of the
      saints.
2 Let Israel rejoice in their Maker;
   let the people of Zion be glad in
      their King.
3 Let them praise his name with
      dancing
   and make music to him with
      tambourine and harp.
4 For the LORD takes delight in his
      people;
   he crowns the humble with
      salvation.
5 Let the saints rejoice in this honor
   and sing for joy on their beds.
6 May the praise of God be in their
      mouths
   and a double-edged sword in their
      hands,
7 to inflict vengeance on the nations
   and punishment on the peoples,
8 to bind their kings with fetters,
   their nobles with shackles of
      iron,
9 to carry out the sentence written
      against them.
   This is the glory of all his saints.

Praise the LORD.

Psalm 150

1 Praise the LORD.[d]

Praise God in his sanctuary;
   praise him in his mighty heavens.
2 Praise him for his acts of power;
   praise him for his surpassing
      greatness.

---

a 1 Hebrew Hallelu Yah; also in verse 14   b 14 Horn here symbolizes strong one, that is, king.   c 1 Hebrew Hallelu Yah; also in verse 9   d 1 Hebrew Hallelu Yah; also in verse 6

³Praise him with the sounding of the
trumpet,
   praise him with the harp and lyre,
⁴praise him with tambourine and
dancing,
   praise him with the strings and
flute,

⁵praise him with the clash of cymbals,
   praise him with resounding
cymbals.

⁶Let everything that has breath praise
the LORD.

Praise the LORD.

Author: Mostly Solomon—with contributions by Agur, King Lemuel, and others

Date: Compiled about the tenth century BC

Audience: Everyone—young and old alike—who desires a happy and prosperous life

"The LORD is far from the wicked but he hears the prayer of the righteous" (15:29).

God doesn't respond favorably to the prayers of people who aren't right with Him. He hears the prayers of those who live His way. A study and search through the rest of the book of Proverbs will reveal practical insight into exactly what it means to live a righteous life.

No other book offers so much wide-ranging teaching on how to live in a way that honors God. So read it, and heed its profoundly simple instruction. Then get ready for your prayer life to explode!

"The LORD detests the sacrifice of the wicked, but the prayer of the upright pleases him" (15:8).

Prayer Themes:

- *Tell God you want to learn more and more what it means to trust Him with all your heart and to acknowledge Him in all your ways (3:5-6).*

- *Thank God that He gives wisdom and understanding to those who seek them (4:5-9).*

- *Ask God to teach you what it means to "fear" Him so that you'll be wise and have understanding (9:10).*

Proverbs

Prologue: Purpose and Theme

1 The proverbs of Solomon son of David, king of Israel:

2 for attaining wisdom and discipline;
for understanding words of insight;

3 for acquiring a disciplined and prudent life,
doing what is right and just and fair;

4 for giving prudence to the simple,
knowledge and discretion to the young—

5 let the wise listen and add to their learning,
and let the discerning get guidance—

6 for understanding proverbs and parables,
the sayings and riddles of the wise.

7 The fear of the LORD is the beginning of knowledge,
but fools[a] despise wisdom and discipline.

Exhortations to Embrace Wisdom

Warning Against Enticement

8 Listen, my son, to your father's instruction
and do not forsake your mother's teaching.

9 They will be a garland to grace your head
and a chain to adorn your neck.

10 My son, if sinners entice you,
do not give in to them.

11 If they say, "Come along with us;
let's lie in wait for someone's blood,
let's waylay some harmless soul;

---

a *7* The Hebrew words rendered *fool* in Proverbs, and often elsewhere in the Old Testament, denote one who is morally deficient.

¹²let's swallow them alive, like the
    grave,ᵃ
  and whole, like those who go down
    to the pit;
¹³we will get all sorts of valuable things
  and fill our houses with plunder;
¹⁴throw in your lot with us,
  and we will share a common
    purse"—
¹⁵my son, do not go along with them,
  do not set foot on their paths;
¹⁶for their feet rush into sin,
  they are swift to shed blood.
¹⁷How useless to spread a net
  in full view of all the birds!
¹⁸These men lie in wait for their own
    blood;
  they waylay only themselves!
¹⁹Such is the end of all who go after
    ill-gotten gain;
  it takes away the lives of those who
    get it.

Warning Against Rejecting Wisdom

²⁰Wisdom calls aloud in the street,
  she raises her voice in the public
    squares;
²¹at the head of the noisy streetsᵇ she
    cries out,
  in the gateways of the city she
    makes her speech:

²²"How long will you simple onesᶜ love
    your simple ways?
  How long will mockers delight in
    mockery
  and fools hate knowledge?
²³If you had responded to my rebuke,
  I would have poured out my heart
    to you
  and made my thoughts known to
    you.
²⁴But since you rejected me when I
    called
  and no one gave heed when I
    stretched out my hand,
²⁵since you ignored all my advice
  and would not accept my rebuke,

²⁶I in turn will laugh at your disaster;
  I will mock when calamity
    overtakes you—
²⁷when calamity overtakes you like a
    storm,
  when disaster sweeps over you like
    a whirlwind,
  when distress and trouble
    overwhelm you.

²⁸"Then they will call to me but I will
    not answer;
  they will look for me but will not
    find me.
²⁹Since they hated knowledge
  and did not choose to fear the
    LORD,
³⁰since they would not accept my
    advice
  and spurned my rebuke,
³¹they will eat the fruit of their ways
  and be filled with the fruit of their
    schemes.
³²For the waywardness of the simple
    will kill them,
  and the complacency of fools will
    destroy them;
³³but whoever listens to me will live in
    safety
  and be at ease, without fear of
    harm."

Moral Benefits of Wisdom

2 My son, if you accept my words
  and store up my commands within
    you,
²turning your ear to wisdom
  and applying your heart to
    understanding,
³and if you call out for insight
  and cry aloud for understanding,
⁴and if you look for it as for silver
  and search for it as for hidden
    treasure,
⁵then you will understand the fear of
    the LORD
  and find the knowledge of God.
⁶For the LORD gives wisdom,

ᵃ 12 Hebrew Sheol   ᵇ 21 Hebrew; Septuagint / on the tops of the walls   ᶜ 22 The Hebrew word rendered *simple* in Proverbs
generally denotes one without moral direction and inclined to evil.

and from his mouth come
knowledge and understanding.
7 He holds victory in store for the
upright,
he is a shield to those whose walk is
blameless,
8 for he guards the course of the just
and protects the way of his faithful
ones.

9 Then you will understand what is
right and just
and fair—every good path.
10 For wisdom will enter your heart,
and knowledge will be pleasant to
your soul.
11 Discretion will protect you,
and understanding will guard you.

12 Wisdom will save you from the ways
of wicked men,
from men whose words are
perverse,
13 who leave the straight paths
to walk in dark ways,
14 who delight in doing wrong
and rejoice in the perverseness of
evil,
15 whose paths are crooked
and who are devious in their ways.

16 It will save you also from the
adulteress,
from the wayward wife with her
seductive words,
17 who has left the partner of her youth
and ignored the covenant she made
before God.[a]
18 For her house leads down to death
and her paths to the spirits of the
dead.
19 None who go to her return
or attain the paths of life.

20 Thus you will walk in the ways of
good men
and keep to the paths of the
righteous.
21 For the upright will live in the land,
and the blameless will remain in it;
22 but the wicked will be cut off from
the land,
and the unfaithful will be torn
from it.

Further Benefits of Wisdom

3 My son, do not forget my teaching,
but keep my commands in your
heart,
2 for they will prolong your life many
years
and bring you prosperity.

3 Let love and faithfulness never leave
you;
bind them around your neck,
write them on the tablet of your
heart.
4 Then you will win favor and a good
name
in the sight of God and man.

5 Trust in the LORD with all your heart
and lean not on your own
understanding;
6 in all your ways acknowledge him,
and he will make your paths
straight.[b]

7 Do not be wise in your own eyes;
fear the LORD and shun evil.
8 This will bring health to your body
and nourishment to your bones.

9 Honor the LORD with your wealth,
with the firstfruits of all your crops;
10 then your barns will be filled to
overflowing,
and your vats will brim over with
new wine.

11 My son, do not despise the LORD's
discipline
and do not resent his rebuke,
12 because the LORD disciplines those he
loves,
as a father[c] the son he delights in.

13 Blessed is the man who finds wisdom,
the man who gains understanding,
14 for she is more profitable than silver
and yields better returns than gold.

---

a 17 Or covenant of her God   b 6 Or will direct your paths   c 12 Hebrew; Septuagint / and he punishes

Acknowledge God in Every Area of Your Life

GOING deeper

READ AND CONSIDER: PROVERBS 3:1-18

"Trust in the LORD with all your heart and lean not on your own understanding; in all your ways acknowledge him, and he will make your paths straight" (Proverbs 3:5-6).

We have to trust that God's ways are always right and not try to figure things out on our own or make up our own rules. And we have to acknowledge God in every area of our lives.

We have to acknowledge Him first of all as Jesus our Savior, as our heavenly Father, and as the Holy Spirit our Comforter. Then we have to acknowledge Him as the One who meets all of our needs and is Lord over every area of our lives. That means we acknowledge Him as Lord over our relationships, our work, our activities, our finances, our homes, our bodies, and our marriages.

Is there any place in your life that you have not turned completely over to God? If so, say, "Lord, I invite You to be Lord over this area of my life." If you are not sure, ask God to show you. He will. And when you see some area where you have not fully acknowledged God as Lord, pray, "Lord, I acknowledge You in this area of my life, and I ask You to reign there. I want to recognize You in everything I do so that I can honor and serve You. Thank You that You will direct my steps and make my paths straight."

15 She is more precious than rubies;
  nothing you desire can compare
    with her.
16 Long life is in her right hand;
  in her left hand are riches and
    honor.
17 Her ways are pleasant ways,
  and all her paths are peace.
18 She is a tree of life to those who
    embrace her;
  those who lay hold of her will be
    blessed.

Praying Proverbs 3:13-18

Lord, give me wisdom so that I may bless others and live in joy and happiness.

19 By wisdom the LORD laid the earth's
    foundations,
  by understanding he set the heavens
    in place;
20 by his knowledge the deeps were
    divided,
  and the clouds let drop the dew.

21 My son, preserve sound judgment and
    discernment,
  do not let them out of your sight;
22 they will be life for you,
  an ornament to grace your neck.
23 Then you will go on your way in
    safety,
  and your foot will not stumble;
24 when you lie down, you will not be
    afraid;
  when you lie down, your sleep will
    be sweet.
25 Have no fear of sudden disaster
  or of the ruin that overtakes the
    wicked,
26 for the LORD will be your
    confidence
  and will keep your foot from being
    snared.
27 Do not withhold good from those
  who deserve it,
  when it is in your power to act.
28 Do not say to your neighbor,

"Come back later; I'll give it
  tomorrow"—
when you now have it with you.

29Do not plot harm against your
  neighbor,
who lives trustfully near you.
30Do not accuse a man for no reason—
when he has done you no harm.

31Do not envy a violent man
or choose any of his ways,
32for the LORD detests a perverse man
but takes the upright into his
  confidence.

33The LORD's curse is on the house of
  the wicked,
but he blesses the home of the
  righteous.
34He mocks proud mockers
but gives grace to the humble.
35The wise inherit honor,
but fools he holds up to shame.

Wisdom Is Supreme

4 Listen, my sons, to a father's
  instruction;
pay attention and gain
  understanding.
2I give you sound learning,
so do not forsake my teaching.
3When I was a boy in my father's
  house,
still tender, and an only child of my
  mother,
4he taught me and said,
"Lay hold of my words with all
  your heart;
keep my commands and you will
  live.
5Get wisdom, get understanding;
do not forget my words or swerve
  from them.
6Do not forsake wisdom, and she will
  protect you;
love her, and she will watch over
  you.
7Wisdom is supreme; therefore get
  wisdom.

Though it cost all you have,[a] get
  understanding.
8Esteem her, and she will exalt you;
embrace her, and she will honor
  you.
9She will set a garland of grace on
  your head
and present you with a crown of
  splendor."

10Listen, my son, accept what I say,
and the years of your life will be
  many.
11I guide you in the way of wisdom
and lead you along straight paths.
12When you walk, your steps will not
  be hampered;
when you run, you will not
  stumble.
13Hold on to instruction, do not let it
  go;
guard it well, for it is your life.
14Do not set foot on the path of the
  wicked
or walk in the way of evil men.
15Avoid it, do not travel on it;
turn from it and go on your way.
16For they cannot sleep till they do
  evil;
they are robbed of slumber till they
  make someone fall.
17They eat the bread of wickedness
and drink the wine of violence.

18The path of the righteous is like the
  first gleam of dawn,
shining ever brighter till the full
  light of day.
19But the way of the wicked is like
  deep darkness;
they do not know what makes
  them stumble.

20My son, pay attention to what I say;
listen closely to my words.
21Do not let them out of your sight,
keep them within your heart;
22for they are life to those who find
  them
and health to a man's whole body.

a 7 Or Whatever else you get

23Above all else, guard your heart,
  for it is the wellspring of life.
24Put away perversity from your
    mouth;
  keep corrupt talk far from your lips.
25Let your eyes look straight ahead,
  fix your gaze directly before you.
26Make level[a] paths for your feet
  and take only ways that are firm.
27Do not swerve to the right or the left;
  keep your foot from evil.

Warning Against Adultery

5 My son, pay attention to my
    wisdom,
  listen well to my words of insight,
2that you may maintain discretion
  and your lips may preserve
    knowledge.
3For the lips of an adulteress drip
    honey,
  and her speech is smoother than oil;
4but in the end she is bitter as gall,
  sharp as a double-edged sword.
5Her feet go down to death;
  her steps lead straight to the grave.[b]
6She gives no thought to the way of
    life;
  her paths are crooked, but she
    knows it not.

7Now then, my sons, listen to me;
  do not turn aside from what I say.
8Keep to a path far from her,
  do not go near the door of her
    house,
9lest you give your best strength to
    others
  and your years to one who is cruel,
10lest strangers feast on your wealth
  and your toil enrich another man's
    house.
11At the end of your life you will
    groan,
  when your flesh and body are spent.
12You will say, "How I hated
    discipline!
  How my heart spurned correction!
13I would not obey my teachers

or listen to my instructors.
14I have come to the brink of utter ruin
  in the midst of the whole
    assembly."

15Drink water from your own cistern,
  running water from your own well.
16Should your springs overflow in the
    streets,
  your streams of water in the public
    squares?
17Let them be yours alone,
  never to be shared with strangers.
18May your fountain be blessed,
  and may you rejoice in the wife of
    your youth.
19A loving doe, a graceful deer—
  may her breasts satisfy you always,
  may you ever be captivated by her
    love.
20Why be captivated, my son, by an
    adulteress?
  Why embrace the bosom of another
    man's wife?

21For a man's ways are in full view of
    the LORD,
  and he examines all his paths.
22The evil deeds of a wicked man
    ensnare him;
  the cords of his sin hold him fast.
23He will die for lack of discipline,
  led astray by his own great folly.

Warnings Against Folly

6 My son, if you have put up security
    for your neighbor,
  if you have struck hands in pledge
    for another,
2if you have been trapped by what you
    said,
  ensnared by the words of your
    mouth,
3then do this, my son, to free yourself,
  since you have fallen into your
    neighbor's hands:
Go and humble yourself;
  press your plea with your neighbor!
4Allow no sleep to your eyes,
  no slumber to your eyelids.

---

[a] 26 Or Consider the [b] 5 Hebrew Sheol

5 Free yourself, like a gazelle from the
    hand of the hunter,
  like a bird from the snare of the
    fowler.

6 Go to the ant, you sluggard;
  consider its ways and be wise!
7 It has no commander,
  no overseer or ruler,
8 yet it stores its provisions in summer
  and gathers its food at harvest.

9 How long will you lie there, you
    sluggard?
  When will you get up from your
    sleep?
10 A little sleep, a little slumber,
  a little folding of the hands to
    rest—
11 and poverty will come on you like a
    bandit
  and scarcity like an armed man.[a]

12 A scoundrel and villain,
  who goes about with a corrupt
    mouth,
13   who winks with his eye,
  signals with his feet
  and motions with his fingers,
14   who plots evil with deceit in his
    heart—
  he always stirs up dissension.
15 Therefore disaster will overtake him
  in an instant;
  he will suddenly be destroyed—
    without remedy.

16 There are six things the LORD hates,
  seven that are detestable to him:
17   haughty eyes,
  a lying tongue,
  hands that shed innocent blood,
18   a heart that devises wicked
    schemes,
  feet that are quick to rush into
    evil,
19   a false witness who pours out
    lies
  and a man who stirs up dissension
    among brothers.

Warning Against Adultery

20 My son, keep your father's commands
  and do not forsake your mother's
    teaching.
21 Bind them upon your heart forever;
  fasten them around your neck.
22 When you walk, they will guide you;
  when you sleep, they will watch
    over you;
  when you awake, they will speak
    to you.
23 For these commands are a lamp,
  this teaching is a light,
  and the corrections of discipline
  are the way to life,
24 keeping you from the immoral
    woman,
  from the smooth tongue of the
    wayward wife.
25 Do not lust in your heart after her
    beauty
  or let her captivate you with her
    eyes,
26 for the prostitute reduces you to a loaf
    of bread,
  and the adulteress preys upon your
    very life.
27 Can a man scoop fire into his lap
  without his clothes being burned?
28 Can a man walk on hot coals
  without his feet being scorched?
29 So is he who sleeps with another
    man's wife;
  no one who touches her will go
    unpunished.

30 Men do not despise a thief if he steals
  to satisfy his hunger when he is
    starving.
31 Yet if he is caught, he must pay
    sevenfold,
  though it costs him all the wealth
    of his house.
32 But a man who commits adultery
    lacks judgment;
  whoever does so destroys himself.
33 Blows and disgrace are his lot,
  and his shame will never be wiped
    away;

---

a 11 Or like a vagrant / and scarcity like a beggar

³⁴for jealousy arouses a husband's fury,
and he will show no mercy when
he takes revenge.
³⁵He will not accept any compensation;
he will refuse the bribe, however
great it is.

Warning Against the Adulteress

7 My son, keep my words
and store up my commands within
you.
²Keep my commands and you will
live;
guard my teachings as the apple of
your eye.
³Bind them on your fingers;
write them on the tablet of your
heart.
⁴Say to wisdom, "You are my sister,"
and call understanding your
kinsman;
⁵they will keep you from the
adulteress,
from the wayward wife with her
seductive words.

⁶At the window of my house
I looked out through the lattice.
⁷I saw among the simple,
I noticed among the young men,
a youth who lacked judgment.
⁸He was going down the street near
her corner,
walking along in the direction of
her house
⁹at twilight, as the day was fading,
as the dark of night set in.

¹⁰Then out came a woman to meet
him,
dressed like a prostitute and with
crafty intent.
¹¹(She is loud and defiant,
her feet never stay at home;
¹²now in the street, now in the squares,
at every corner she lurks.)
¹³She took hold of him and kissed
him
and with a brazen face she said:

¹⁴"I have fellowship offerings[a] at home;
today I fulfilled my vows.
¹⁵So I came out to meet you;
I looked for you and have found
you!
¹⁶I have covered my bed
with colored linens from Egypt.
¹⁷I have perfumed my bed
with myrrh, aloes and cinnamon.
¹⁸Come, let's drink deep of love till
morning;
let's enjoy ourselves with love!
¹⁹My husband is not at home;
he has gone on a long journey.
²⁰He took his purse filled with money
and will not be home till full
moon."

²¹With persuasive words she led him
astray;
she seduced him with her smooth
talk.
²²All at once he followed her
like an ox going to the slaughter,
like a deer[b] stepping into a noose[c]
²³   till an arrow pierces his liver,
like a bird darting into a snare,
little knowing it will cost him his
life.

²⁴Now then, my sons, listen to me;
pay attention to what I say.
²⁵Do not let your heart turn to her
ways
or stray into her paths.
²⁶Many are the victims she has brought
down;
her slain are a mighty throng.
²⁷Her house is a highway to the grave,[d]
leading down to the chambers of
death.

Wisdom's Call

8 Does not wisdom call out?
Does not understanding raise her
voice?
²On the heights along the way,
where the paths meet, she takes her
stand;

ᵃ 14 Traditionally *peace offerings*   ᵇ 22 Syriac (see also Septuagint); Hebrew *fool*   ᶜ 22 The meaning of the Hebrew for this line
is uncertain.   ᵈ 27 Hebrew *Sheol*

3beside the gates leading into the city,
 at the entrances, she cries aloud:
4"To you, O men, I call out;
 I raise my voice to all mankind.
5You who are simple, gain prudence;
 you who are foolish, gain
  understanding.
6Listen, for I have worthy things to
  say;
 I open my lips to speak what is
  right.
7My mouth speaks what is true,
 for my lips detest wickedness.
8All the words of my mouth are just;
 none of them is crooked or
  perverse.
9To the discerning all of them are
  right;
 they are faultless to those who have
  knowledge.
10Choose my instruction instead of
  silver,
 knowledge rather than choice gold,
11for wisdom is more precious than
  rubies,
 and nothing you desire can
  compare with her.

12"I, wisdom, dwell together with
  prudence;
 I possess knowledge and discretion.
13To fear the LORD is to hate evil;
 I hate pride and arrogance,
 evil behavior and perverse speech.
14Counsel and sound judgment are
  mine;
 I have understanding and power.
15By me kings reign
 and rulers make laws that are just;
16by me princes govern,
 and all nobles who rule on earth.a
17I love those who love me,
 and those who seek me find me.
18With me are riches and honor,
 enduring wealth and prosperity.
19My fruit is better than fine gold;
 what I yield surpasses choice silver.

20I walk in the way of righteousness,
 along the paths of justice,
21bestowing wealth on those who
  love me
 and making their treasuries full.

22"The LORD brought me forth as the
  first of his works,b,c
 before his deeds of old;
23I was appointedd from eternity,
 from the beginning, before the
  world began.
24When there were no oceans, I was
  given birth,
 when there were no springs
  abounding with water;
25before the mountains were settled in
  place,
 before the hills, I was given birth,
26before he made the earth or its fields
 or any of the dust of the world.
27I was there when he set the heavens
  in place,
 when he marked out the horizon
  on the face of the deep,
28when he established the clouds above
 and fixed securely the fountains of
  the deep,
29when he gave the sea its boundary
 so the waters would not overstep
  his command,
 and when he marked out the
  foundations of the earth.
30   Then I was the craftsman at his
  side.
 I was filled with delight day after day,
  rejoicing always in his presence,
31rejoicing in his whole world
 and delighting in mankind.

32"Now then, my sons, listen to me;
 blessed are those who keep my ways.
33Listen to my instruction and be wise;
 do not ignore it.
34Blessed is the man who listens to me,
 watching daily at my doors,
 waiting at my doorway.
35For whoever finds me finds life

---

a 16 Many Hebrew manuscripts and Septuagint; most Hebrew manuscripts and nobles—all righteous rulers   b 22 Or way;
or dominion   c 22 Or The LORD possessed me at the beginning of his work; or The LORD brought me forth at the beginning of
his work   d 23 Or fashioned

The Benefits of Waiting on God

GOING *deeper*

READ AND CONSIDER: PROVERBS 8:22-36

"Blessed is the man who listens to me, watching daily at my doors, waiting at my doorway" (Proverbs 8:34).

When you are sitting at a stoplight, standing in a long checkout line at the supermarket, or flipping idly through an old magazine in a physician's waiting room, do you ever think, "What a blessing it is to wait"?

If you're like most people, you probably hate to wait. We are busy people; we usually have more to do in any given day than we can possibly accomplish. And yet over and over again, Scripture speaks of the need for us to wait—and *commands* us to do so. "Be still before the LORD and wait patiently for him" (Psalm 37:7). The key is waiting for *Him*.

The Bible teaches that waiting for *Him* is actually a blessing in our lives.

This verse tells us that we are blessed when we listen to God and watch and wait daily at His doors. But how does God use times of waiting to bless us?

When God permits life's circumstances to delay us from our intended goal, we can be sure He has good reason. It might be to build our faith because the New Testament teaches that "faith is being sure of what we hope for and certain of what we do not see" (Hebrews 11:1). When we are forced to wait, our faith must become stronger.

Or God might use times of waiting to build our character as we wait for the character of Christ to be formed in us. "And we, who with unveiled faces all reflect the Lord's glory, are being transformed into his likeness with ever-increasing glory, which comes from the Lord, who is the Spirit" (2 Corinthians 3:18).

Or God may be wanting us to wait so that we can learn to be patient. As we wait with hopeful anticipation for Him to work in our situation, He has promised that we will be "strengthened with all power according to his glorious might so that you may have great endurance and patience, and joyfully giving thanks to the Father" (Colossians 1:11-12).

God loves us, so our times of waiting on Him must be ultimately beneficial to our emotional and spiritual growth. The next time you are tempted to become restless during a time of waiting on God, use that time instead to praise God for all the benefits and blessings that He has in store for you. And don't forget to thank Him that His timing is perfect.

and receives favor from the LORD.
36 But whoever fails to find me harms himself;
all who hate me love death."

Invitations of Wisdom and of Folly

9 Wisdom has built her house;
she has hewn out its seven pillars.
2 She has prepared her meat and mixed her wine;
she has also set her table.
3 She has sent out her maids, and she calls
from the highest point of the city.
4 "Let all who are simple come in here!"
she says to those who lack judgment.
5 "Come, eat my food
and drink the wine I have mixed.

6 Leave your simple ways and you will
live;
walk in the way of understanding.

7 "Whoever corrects a mocker invites
insult;
whoever rebukes a wicked man
incurs abuse.
8 Do not rebuke a mocker or he will
hate you;
rebuke a wise man and he will love
you.
9 Instruct a wise man and he will be
wiser still;
teach a righteous man and he will
add to his learning.

10 "The fear of the Lord is the
beginning of wisdom,
and knowledge of the Holy One is
understanding.
11 For through me your days will be many,
and years will be added to your life.
12 If you are wise, your wisdom will
reward you;
if you are a mocker, you alone will
suffer."

13 The woman Folly is loud;
she is undisciplined and without
knowledge.
14 She sits at the door of her house,
on a seat at the highest point of the
city,
15 calling out to those who pass by,
who go straight on their way.
16 "Let all who are simple come in here!"
she says to those who lack judgment.
17 "Stolen water is sweet;
food eaten in secret is delicious!"
18 But little do they know that the dead
are there,
that her guests are in the depths of
the grave.ª

Proverbs of Solomon

10 The proverbs of Solomon:

A wise son brings joy to his father,
but a foolish son grief to his
mother.
2 Ill-gotten treasures are of no value,
but righteousness delivers from
death.
3 The Lord does not let the righteous
go hungry
but he thwarts the craving of the
wicked.
4 Lazy hands make a man poor,
but diligent hands bring wealth.
5 He who gathers crops in summer is a
wise son,
but he who sleeps during harvest is
a disgraceful son.
6 Blessings crown the head of the
righteous,
but violence overwhelms the
mouth of the wicked.b
7 The memory of the righteous will be
a blessing,
but the name of the wicked will
rot.
8 The wise in heart accept commands,
but a chattering fool comes to
ruin.
9 The man of integrity walks securely,
but he who takes crooked paths
will be found out.
10 He who winks maliciously causes
grief,
and a chattering fool comes to ruin.
11 The mouth of the righteous is a
fountain of life,
but violence overwhelms the
mouth of the wicked.
12 Hatred stirs up dissension,
but love covers over all wrongs.
13 Wisdom is found on the lips of the
discerning,
but a rod is for the back of him
who lacks judgment.

ª 18 Hebrew Sheol b 6 Or but the mouth of the wicked conceals violence; also in verse 11

¹⁴Wise men store up knowledge,
but the mouth of a fool invites ruin.

¹⁵The wealth of the rich is their
fortified city,
but poverty is the ruin of the poor.

¹⁶The wages of the righteous bring
them life,
but the income of the wicked
brings them punishment.

¹⁷He who heeds discipline shows the
way to life,
but whoever ignores correction
leads others astray.

¹⁸He who conceals his hatred has lying
lips,
and whoever spreads slander is a
fool.

¹⁹When words are many, sin is not
absent,
but he who holds his tongue is wise.

²⁰The tongue of the righteous is choice
silver,
but the heart of the wicked is of
little value.

²¹The lips of the righteous nourish
many,
but fools die for lack of judgment.

Praying Proverbs 10:22

*Bless me, Lord, for I know that no sorrow
comes without Your blessing,*

²²The blessing of the LORD brings
wealth,
and he adds no trouble to it.

²³A fool finds pleasure in evil conduct,
but a man of understanding delights
in wisdom.

²⁴What the wicked dreads will overtake
him;
what the righteous desire will be
granted.

²⁵When the storm has swept by, the
wicked are gone,
but the righteous stand firm
forever.

²⁶As vinegar to the teeth and smoke to
the eyes,
so is a sluggard to those who send
him.

²⁷The fear of the LORD adds length to
life,
but the years of the wicked are cut
short.

²⁸The prospect of the righteous is
joy,
but the hopes of the wicked come
to nothing.

²⁹The way of the LORD is a refuge for
the righteous,
but it is the ruin of those who do
evil.

³⁰The righteous will never be
uprooted,
but the wicked will not remain in
the land.

³¹The mouth of the righteous brings
forth wisdom,
but a perverse tongue will be cut
out.

³²The lips of the righteous know what
is fitting,
but the mouth of the wicked only
what is perverse.

11 The LORD abhors dishonest scales,
but accurate weights are his
delight.

²When pride comes, then comes
disgrace,
but with humility comes wisdom.

³The integrity of the upright guides
them,
but the unfaithful are destroyed by
their duplicity.

⁴Wealth is worthless in the day of
wrath,
but righteousness delivers from
death.

5 The righteousness of the blameless
     makes a straight way for them,
   but the wicked are brought down
     by their own wickedness.

6 The righteousness of the upright
     delivers them,
   but the unfaithful are trapped by
     evil desires.

7 When a wicked man dies, his hope
     perishes;
   all he expected from his power
     comes to nothing.

8 The righteous man is rescued from
     trouble,
   and it comes on the wicked instead.

9 With his mouth the godless destroys
     his neighbor,
   but through knowledge the
     righteous escape.

10 When the righteous prosper, the city
     rejoices;
   when the wicked perish, there are
     shouts of joy.

11 Through the blessing of the upright a
     city is exalted,
   but by the mouth of the wicked it is
     destroyed.

12 A man who lacks judgment derides
     his neighbor,
   but a man of understanding holds
     his tongue.

13 A gossip betrays a confidence,
   but a trustworthy man keeps a
     secret.

14 For lack of guidance a nation falls,
   but many advisers make victory
     sure.

15 He who puts up security for another
     will surely suffer,
   but whoever refuses to strike hands
     in pledge is safe.

16 A kindhearted woman gains
     respect,
   but ruthless men gain only wealth.

17 A kind man benefits himself,
   but a cruel man brings trouble on
     himself.

18 The wicked man earns deceptive
     wages,
   but he who sows righteousness
     reaps a sure reward.

19 The truly righteous man attains
     life,
   but he who pursues evil goes to his
     death.

20 The LORD detests men of perverse
     heart
   but he delights in those whose ways
     are blameless.

21 Be sure of this: The wicked will not
     go unpunished,
   but those who are righteous will
     go free.

22 Like a gold ring in a pig's snout
   is a beautiful woman who shows no
     discretion.

23 The desire of the righteous ends only
     in good,
   but the hope of the wicked only in
     wrath.

24 One man gives freely, yet gains even
     more;
   another withholds unduly, but
     comes to poverty.

25 A generous man will prosper;
   he who refreshes others will
     himself be refreshed.

26 People curse the man who hoards
     grain,
   but blessing crowns him who is
     willing to sell.

27 He who seeks good finds goodwill,
   but evil comes to him who searches
     for it.

28 Whoever trusts in his riches will
     fall,
   but the righteous will thrive like a
     green leaf.

²⁹He who brings trouble on his family
will inherit only wind,
and the fool will be servant to the
wise.

³⁰The fruit of the righteous is a tree of
life,
and he who wins souls is wise.

³¹If the righteous receive their due on
earth,
how much more the ungodly and
the sinner!

12 Whoever loves discipline loves
knowledge,
but he who hates correction is
stupid.

²A good man obtains favor from the
LORD,
but the LORD condemns a crafty
man.

³A man cannot be established through
wickedness,
but the righteous cannot be
uprooted.

⁴A wife of noble character is her
husband's crown,
but a disgraceful wife is like decay
in his bones.

⁵The plans of the righteous are just,
but the advice of the wicked is
deceitful.

⁶The words of the wicked lie in wait
for blood,
but the speech of the upright
rescues them.

⁷Wicked men are overthrown and are
no more,
but the house of the righteous
stands firm.

⁸A man is praised according to his
wisdom,
but men with warped minds are
despised.

⁹Better to be a nobody and yet have a
servant

than pretend to be somebody and
have no food.

¹⁰A righteous man cares for the needs
of his animal,
but the kindest acts of the wicked
are cruel.

¹¹He who works his land will have
abundant food,
but he who chases fantasies lacks
judgment.

¹²The wicked desire the plunder of evil
men,
but the root of the righteous
flourishes.

¹³An evil man is trapped by his sinful
talk,
but a righteous man escapes
trouble.

¹⁴From the fruit of his lips a man is
filled with good things
as surely as the work of his hands
rewards him.

¹⁵The way of a fool seems right to him,
but a wise man listens to advice.

¹⁶A fool shows his annoyance at once,
but a prudent man overlooks an
insult.

¹⁷A truthful witness gives honest
testimony,
but a false witness tells lies.

¹⁸Reckless words pierce like a sword,
but the tongue of the wise brings
healing.

¹⁹Truthful lips endure forever,
but a lying tongue lasts only a
moment.

²⁰There is deceit in the hearts of those
who plot evil,
but joy for those who promote
peace.

²¹No harm befalls the righteous,
but the wicked have their fill of
trouble.

²²The LORD detests lying lips,
but he delights in men who are
truthful.

²³A prudent man keeps his knowledge
to himself,
but the heart of fools blurts out
folly.

²⁴Diligent hands will rule,
but laziness ends in slave labor.

²⁵An anxious heart weighs a man
down,
but a kind word cheers him up.

²⁶A righteous man is cautious in
friendship,ᵃ
but the way of the wicked leads
them astray.

²⁷The lazy man does not roastᵇ his game,
but the diligent man prizes his
possessions.

²⁸In the way of righteousness there is
life;
along that path is immortality.

13 A wise son heeds his father's
instruction,
but a mocker does not listen to
rebuke.

²From the fruit of his lips a man enjoys
good things,
but the unfaithful have a craving
for violence.

³He who guards his lips guards his life,
but he who speaks rashly will come
to ruin.

⁴The sluggard craves and gets nothing,
but the desires of the diligent are
fully satisfied.

⁵The righteous hate what is false,
but the wicked bring shame and
disgrace.

⁶Righteousness guards the man of
integrity,

but wickedness overthrows the
sinner.

⁷One man pretends to be rich, yet has
nothing;
another pretends to be poor, yet has
great wealth.

⁸A man's riches may ransom his life,
but a poor man hears no threat.

⁹The light of the righteous shines
brightly,
but the lamp of the wicked is
snuffed out.

¹⁰Pride only breeds quarrels,
but wisdom is found in those who
take advice.

¹¹Dishonest money dwindles away,
but he who gathers money little by
little makes it grow.

¹²Hope deferred makes the heart sick,
but a longing fulfilled is a tree of
life.

¹³He who scorns instruction will pay
for it,
but he who respects a command is
rewarded.

¹⁴The teaching of the wise is a fountain
of life,
turning a man from the snares of
death.

¹⁵Good understanding wins favor,
but the way of the unfaithful is
hard.ᶜ

¹⁶Every prudent man acts out of
knowledge,
but a fool exposes his folly.

¹⁷A wicked messenger falls into
trouble,
but a trustworthy envoy brings
healing.

¹⁸He who ignores discipline comes to
poverty and shame,

ᵃ 26 Or man is a guide to his neighbor   ᵇ 27 The meaning of the Hebrew for this word is uncertain.   ᶜ 15 Or unfaithful does
not endure

but whoever heeds correction is honored.

19 A longing fulfilled is sweet to the soul,
  but fools detest turning from evil.

20 He who walks with the wise grows wise,
  but a companion of fools suffers harm.

21 Misfortune pursues the sinner,
  but prosperity is the reward of the righteous.

22 A good man leaves an inheritance for his children's children,
  but a sinner's wealth is stored up for the righteous.

23 A poor man's field may produce abundant food,
  but injustice sweeps it away.

24 He who spares the rod hates his son,
  but he who loves him is careful to discipline him.

25 The righteous eat to their hearts' content,
  but the stomach of the wicked goes hungry.

14 The wise woman builds her house,
  but with her own hands the foolish one tears hers down.

2 He whose walk is upright fears the LORD,
  but he whose ways are devious despises him.

3 A fool's talk brings a rod to his back,
  but the lips of the wise protect them.

4 Where there are no oxen, the manger is empty,
  but from the strength of an ox comes an abundant harvest.

5 A truthful witness does not deceive,
  but a false witness pours out lies.

6 The mocker seeks wisdom and finds none,
  but knowledge comes easily to the discerning.

7 Stay away from a foolish man,
  for you will not find knowledge on his lips.

8 The wisdom of the prudent is to give thought to their ways,
  but the folly of fools is deception.

9 Fools mock at making amends for sin,
  but goodwill is found among the upright.

10 Each heart knows its own bitterness,
  and no one else can share its joy.

11 The house of the wicked will be destroyed,
  but the tent of the upright will flourish.

12 There is a way that seems right to a man,
  but in the end it leads to death.

13 Even in laughter the heart may ache,
  and joy may end in grief.

14 The faithless will be fully repaid for their ways,
  and the good man rewarded for his.

15 A simple man believes anything,
  but a prudent man gives thought to his steps.

16 A wise man fears the LORD and shuns evil,
  but a fool is hotheaded and reckless.

17 A quick-tempered man does foolish things,
  and a crafty man is hated.

18 The simple inherit folly,
  but the prudent are crowned with knowledge.

19 Evil men will bow down in the presence of the good,
  and the wicked at the gates of the righteous.

20 The poor are shunned even by their
   neighbors,
   but the rich have many friends.

21 He who despises his neighbor sins,
   but blessed is he who is kind to the
   needy.

22 Do not those who plot evil go astray?
   But those who plan what is good
   find[a] love and faithfulness.

23 All hard work brings a profit,
   but mere talk leads only to poverty.

24 The wealth of the wise is their crown,
   but the folly of fools yields folly.

25 A truthful witness saves lives,
   but a false witness is deceitful.

26 He who fears the LORD has a secure
   fortress,
   and for his children it will be a
   refuge.

27 The fear of the LORD is a fountain of
   life,
   turning a man from the snares of
   death.

28 A large population is a king's glory,
   but without subjects a prince is
   ruined.

29 A patient man has great
   understanding,
   but a quick-tempered man displays
   folly.

30 A heart at peace gives life to the body,
   but envy rots the bones.

31 He who oppresses the poor shows
   contempt for their Maker,
   but whoever is kind to the needy
   honors God.

32 When calamity comes, the wicked
   are brought down,
   but even in death the righteous
   have a refuge.

33 Wisdom reposes in the heart of the
   discerning
   and even among fools she lets
   herself be known.[b]

34 Righteousness exalts a nation,
   but sin is a disgrace to any people.

35 A king delights in a wise servant,
   but a shameful servant incurs his
   wrath.

15 A gentle answer turns away
   wrath,
   but a harsh word stirs up anger.

2 The tongue of the wise commends
   knowledge,
   but the mouth of the fool gushes
   folly.

3 The eyes of the LORD are everywhere,
   keeping watch on the wicked and
   the good.

4 The tongue that brings healing is a
   tree of life,
   but a deceitful tongue crushes the
   spirit.

5 A fool spurns his father's discipline,
   but whoever heeds correction
   shows prudence.

6 The house of the righteous contains
   great treasure,
   but the income of the wicked
   brings them trouble.

7 The lips of the wise spread
   knowledge;
   not so the hearts of fools.

8 The LORD detests the sacrifice of the
   wicked,
   but the prayer of the upright pleases
   him.

9 The LORD detests the way of the
   wicked
   but he loves those who pursue
   righteousness.

10 Stern discipline awaits him who
   leaves the path;
   he who hates correction will die.

---

a 22 Or show   b 33 Hebrew; Septuagint and Syriac / but in the heart of fools she is not known

11 Death and Destruction[a] lie open
    before the LORD—
  how much more the hearts of men!

12 A mocker resents correction;
    he will not consult the wise.

13 A happy heart makes the face
    cheerful,
  but heartache crushes the spirit.

14 The discerning heart seeks
    knowledge,
  but the mouth of a fool feeds on
    folly.

15 All the days of the oppressed are
    wretched,
  but the cheerful heart has a
    continual feast.

16 Better a little with the fear of the
    LORD
  than great wealth with turmoil.

17 Better a meal of vegetables where
    there is love
  than a fattened calf with hatred.

18 A hot-tempered man stirs up
    dissension,
  but a patient man calms a quarrel.

19 The way of the sluggard is blocked
    with thorns,
  but the path of the upright is a
    highway.

20 A wise son brings joy to his father,
  but a foolish man despises his
    mother.

a 11 Hebrew *Sheol and Abaddon*

GOING *deeper*

God Hears the Prayers of the Righteous

READ AND CONSIDER: PROVERBS 15:8-9,26,29

"The LORD detests the sacrifice of the wicked, but the prayer of the upright pleases him" *(Proverbs 15:8).*

Certain principles in Scripture are repeated over and over again. Consider this chapter of Proverbs. Again and again we are reminded that "the LORD detests the way of the wicked but he loves those who pursue righteousness . . . The Lord detests the thoughts of the wicked, but those of the pure are pleasing to him" (15:9,26). Why the continual repetition of the importance of righteousness?

First, we need to remember what righteousness is *not:* It is not simply doing "good works." Scripture does not teach that we will obtain righteousness through our own efforts. Rather, we *become* righteous through our relationship with Jesus Christ. This is spelled out for us in the New Testament: "But now a righteousness from God, apart from law, has been made known . . . This righteousness from God comes through faith in Jesus Christ to all who believe" (Romans 3:21-22).

Any righteousness imparted to us, then, is due to our faith in Christ. Yet once we receive Christ as our Savior, God expects us to live as redeemed people—individuals who are characterized by spirits of humility, repentance, and submission to God's will in our lives. "What does the LORD require of you? To act justly and to love mercy and to walk humbly with your God" (Micah 6:8). Living according to His commandments and all the teaching found in His Word is righteous living. And we are promised that God will hear our prayers when we live His way.

21 Folly delights a man who lacks
     judgment,
    but a man of understanding keeps a
     straight course.

22 Plans fail for lack of counsel,
    but with many advisers they
     succeed.

23 A man finds joy in giving an apt
     reply—
    and how good is a timely word!

24 The path of life leads upward for the
     wise
    to keep him from going down to
     the grave.ᵃ

25 The LORD tears down the proud
     man's house
    but he keeps the widow's
     boundaries intact.

26 The LORD detests the thoughts of the
     wicked,
    but those of the pure are pleasing
     to him.

27 A greedy man brings trouble to his
     family,
    but he who hates bribes will live.

28 The heart of the righteous weighs its
     answers,
    but the mouth of the wicked gushes
     evil.

29 The LORD is far from the wicked
    but he hears the prayer of the
     righteous.

30 A cheerful look brings joy to the
     heart,
    and good news gives health to the
     bones.

31 He who listens to a life-giving
     rebuke
    will be at home among the wise.

32 He who ignores discipline despises
     himself,
    but whoever heeds correction gains
     understanding.

33 The fear of the LORD teaches a man
     wisdom,ᵇ
    and humility comes before honor.

16 To man belong the plans of the
     heart,
    but from the LORD comes the reply
     of the tongue.

2 All a man's ways seem innocent to
     him,
    but motives are weighed by the
     LORD.

3 Commit to the LORD whatever you
     do,
    and your plans will succeed.

4 The LORD works out everything for
     his own ends—
    even the wicked for a day of
     disaster.

5 The LORD detests all the proud of
     heart.
    Be sure of this: They will not go
     unpunished.

6 Through love and faithfulness sin is
     atoned for;
    through the fear of the LORD a man
     avoids evil.

7 When a man's ways are pleasing to
     the LORD,
    he makes even his enemies live at
     peace with him.

8 Better a little with righteousness
    than much gain with injustice.

9 In his heart a man plans his course,
    but the LORD determines his
     steps.

10 The lips of a king speak as an oracle,
    and his mouth should not betray
     justice.

11 Honest scales and balances are from
     the LORD;
    all the weights in the bag are of his
     making.

ᵃ 24 Hebrew Sheol   ᵇ 33 Or Wisdom teaches the fear of the LORD

¹²Kings detest wrongdoing,
for a throne is established through
righteousness.

¹³Kings take pleasure in honest lips;
they value a man who speaks the
truth.

¹⁴A king's wrath is a messenger of death,
but a wise man will appease it.

¹⁵When a king's face brightens, it
means life;
his favor is like a rain cloud in
spring.

¹⁶How much better to get wisdom than
gold,
to choose understanding rather
than silver!

¹⁷The highway of the upright avoids
evil;
he who guards his way guards his
life.

¹⁸Pride goes before destruction,
a haughty spirit before a fall.

¹⁹Better to be lowly in spirit and among
the oppressed
than to share plunder with the
proud.

²⁰Whoever gives heed to instruction
prospers,
and blessed is he who trusts in the
LORD.

²¹The wise in heart are called
discerning,
and pleasant words promote
instruction.ᵃ

²²Understanding is a fountain of life to
those who have it,
but folly brings punishment to fools.

²³A wise man's heart guides his mouth,
and his lips promote instruction.ᵇ

²⁴Pleasant words are a honeycomb,
sweet to the soul and healing to the
bones.

²⁵There is a way that seems right to a
man,
but in the end it leads to death.

²⁶The laborer's appetite works for him;
his hunger drives him on.

²⁷A scoundrel plots evil,
and his speech is like a scorching
fire.

²⁸A perverse man stirs up dissension,
and a gossip separates close
friends.

²⁹A violent man entices his neighbor
and leads him down a path that is
not good.

³⁰He who winks with his eye is
plotting perversity;
he who purses his lips is bent on
evil.

³¹Gray hair is a crown of splendor;
it is attained by a righteous life.

³²Better a patient man than a warrior,
a man who controls his temper
than one who takes a city.

³³The lot is cast into the lap,
but its every decision is from the
LORD.

17 Better a dry crust with peace and
quiet
than a house full of feasting,ᶜ with
strife.

²A wise servant will rule over a
disgraceful son,
and will share the inheritance as
one of the brothers.

³The crucible for silver and the
furnace for gold,
but the LORD tests the heart.

⁴A wicked man listens to evil lips;
a liar pays attention to a malicious
tongue.

⁵He who mocks the poor shows
contempt for their Maker;

ᵃ 21 Or *words make a man persuasive*   ᵇ 23 Or *mouth / and makes his lips persuasive*   ᶜ 1 Hebrew *sacrifices*

whoever gloats over disaster will
not go unpunished.

6 Children's children are a crown to the
aged,
and parents are the pride of their
children.

7 Arrogant[a] lips are unsuited to a fool—
how much worse lying lips to a
ruler!

8 A bribe is a charm to the one who
gives it;
wherever he turns, he succeeds.

9 He who covers over an offense
promotes love,
but whoever repeats the matter
separates close friends.

10 A rebuke impresses a man of
discernment
more than a hundred lashes a fool.

11 An evil man is bent only on rebellion;
a merciless official will be sent
against him.

12 Better to meet a bear robbed of her
cubs
than a fool in his folly.

13 If a man pays back evil for good,
evil will never leave his house.

14 Starting a quarrel is like breaching a
dam;
so drop the matter before a dispute
breaks out.

15 Acquitting the guilty and
condemning the innocent—
the LORD detests them both.

16 Of what use is money in the hand of a
fool,
since he has no desire to get
wisdom?

17 A friend loves at all times,
and a brother is born for adversity.

18 A man lacking in judgment strikes
hands in pledge

and puts up security for his
neighbor.

19 He who loves a quarrel loves sin;
he who builds a high gate invites
destruction.

20 A man of perverse heart does not
prosper;
he whose tongue is deceitful falls
into trouble.

21 To have a fool for a son brings grief;
there is no joy for the father of a
fool.

22 A cheerful heart is good medicine,
but a crushed spirit dries up the
bones.

23 A wicked man accepts a bribe in
secret
to pervert the course of justice.

24 A discerning man keeps wisdom in
view,
but a fool's eyes wander to the ends
of the earth.

25 A foolish son brings grief to his father
and bitterness to the one who bore
him.

26 It is not good to punish an innocent
man,
or to flog officials for their
integrity.

27 A man of knowledge uses words with
restraint,
and a man of understanding is
even-tempered.

28 Even a fool is thought wise if he keeps
silent,
and discerning if he holds his
tongue.

18 An unfriendly man pursues
selfish ends;
he defies all sound judgment.

2 A fool finds no pleasure in
understanding

---

a 7 Or *Eloquent*

but delights in airing his own
   opinions.

3 When wickedness comes, so does
   contempt,
   and with shame comes disgrace.

4 The words of a man's mouth are deep
   waters,
   but the fountain of wisdom is a
   bubbling brook.

5 It is not good to be partial to the
   wicked
   or to deprive the innocent of
   justice.

6 A fool's lips bring him strife,
   and his mouth invites a beating.

7 A fool's mouth is his undoing,
   and his lips are a snare to his soul.

8 The words of a gossip are like choice
   morsels;
   they go down to a man's inmost
   parts.

9 One who is slack in his work
   is brother to one who destroys.

10 The name of the LORD is a strong
   tower;
   the righteous run to it and are safe.

11 The wealth of the rich is their
   fortified city;
   they imagine it an unscalable wall.

12 Before his downfall a man's heart is
   proud,
   but humility comes before honor.

13 He who answers before listening—
   that is his folly and his shame.

14 A man's spirit sustains him in sickness,
   but a crushed spirit who can bear?

15 The heart of the discerning acquires
   knowledge;
   the ears of the wise seek it out.

16 A gift opens the way for the giver
   and ushers him into the presence of
   the great.

17 The first to present his case seems
   right,
   till another comes forward and
   questions him.

18 Casting the lot settles disputes
   and keeps strong opponents apart.

19 An offended brother is more
   unyielding than a fortified
   city,
   and disputes are like the barred
   gates of a citadel.

20 From the fruit of his mouth a man's
   stomach is filled;
   with the harvest from his lips he is
   satisfied.

21 The tongue has the power of life and
   death,
   and those who love it will eat its
   fruit.

Praying Proverbs 18:21

*God, give me words that
speak life to people.*

22 He who finds a wife finds what is
   good
   and receives favor from the LORD.

23 A poor man pleads for mercy,
   but a rich man answers harshly.

24 A man of many companions may
   come to ruin,
   but there is a friend who sticks
   closer than a brother.

19 Better a poor man whose walk is
   blameless
   than a fool whose lips are perverse.

2 It is not good to have zeal without
   knowledge,
   nor to be hasty and miss the way.

3 A man's own folly ruins his life,
   yet his heart rages against the
   LORD.

4 Wealth brings many friends,
   but a poor man's friend deserts him.

5A false witness will not go
    unpunished,
  and he who pours out lies will not
    go free.

6Many curry favor with a ruler,
  and everyone is the friend of a man
    who gives gifts.

7A poor man is shunned by all his
    relatives—
  how much more do his friends
    avoid him!
Though he pursues them with
    pleading,
  they are nowhere to be found.ᵃ

8He who gets wisdom loves his own
    soul;
  he who cherishes understanding
    prospers.

9A false witness will not go
    unpunished,
  and he who pours out lies will
    perish.

10It is not fitting for a fool to live in
    luxury—
  how much worse for a slave to rule
    over princes!

11A man's wisdom gives him patience;
  it is to his glory to overlook an
    offense.

12A king's rage is like the roar of a lion,
  but his favor is like dew on the
    grass.

13A foolish son is his father's ruin,
  and a quarrelsome wife is like a
    constant dripping.

14Houses and wealth are inherited from
    parents,
  but a prudent wife is from the
    LORD.

15Laziness brings on deep sleep,
  and the shiftless man goes hungry.

16He who obeys instructions guards his
    life,

but he who is contemptuous of his
    ways will die.

17He who is kind to the poor lends to
    the LORD,
  and he will reward him for what he
    has done.

18Discipline your son, for in that there
    is hope;
  do not be a willing party to his
    death.

19A hot-tempered man must pay the
    penalty;
  if you rescue him, you will have to
    do it again.

Prayer is . . .
walking daily with God.

20Listen to advice and accept
    instruction,
  and in the end you will be wise.

21Many are the plans in a man's heart,
  but it is the LORD's purpose that
    prevails.

22What a man desires is unfailing loveᵇ;
  better to be poor than a liar.

23The fear of the LORD leads to life:
  Then one rests content, untouched
    by trouble.

24The sluggard buries his hand in the
    dish;
  he will not even bring it back to his
    mouth!

25Flog a mocker, and the simple will
    learn prudence;
  rebuke a discerning man, and he
    will gain knowledge.

26He who robs his father and drives out
    his mother

ᵃ 7 The meaning of the Hebrew for this sentence is uncertain. ᵇ 22 Or *A man's greed is his shame*

is a son who brings shame and
disgrace.

²⁷Stop listening to instruction, my son,
and you will stray from the words
of knowledge.

²⁸A corrupt witness mocks at justice,
and the mouth of the wicked gulps
down evil.

²⁹Penalties are prepared for mockers,
and beatings for the backs of
fools.

20 Wine is a mocker and beer a
brawler;
whoever is led astray by them is not
wise.

²A king's wrath is like the roar of a
lion;
he who angers him forfeits his life.

³It is to a man's honor to avoid strife,
but every fool is quick to quarrel.

⁴A sluggard does not plow in season;
so at harvest time he looks but finds
nothing.

⁵The purposes of a man's heart are
deep waters,
but a man of understanding draws
them out.

⁶Many a man claims to have unfailing
love,
but a faithful man who can find?

⁷The righteous man leads a blameless
life;
blessed are his children after him.

⁸When a king sits on his throne to
judge,
he winnows out all evil with his
eyes.

⁹Who can say, "I have kept my heart
pure;
I am clean and without sin"?

¹⁰Differing weights and differing
measures—
the LORD detests them both.

¹¹Even a child is known by his actions,
by whether his conduct is pure and
right.

¹²Ears that hear and eyes that see—
the LORD has made them both.

¹³Do not love sleep or you will grow
poor;
stay awake and you will have food
to spare.

¹⁴"It's no good, it's no good!" says the
buyer;
then off he goes and boasts about
his purchase.

¹⁵Gold there is, and rubies in abundance,
but lips that speak knowledge are a
rare jewel.

¹⁶Take the garment of one who puts up
security for a stranger;
hold it in pledge if he does it for a
wayward woman.

¹⁷Food gained by fraud tastes sweet to a
man,
but he ends up with a mouth full of
gravel.

¹⁸Make plans by seeking advice;
if you wage war, obtain guidance.

¹⁹A gossip betrays a confidence;
so avoid a man who talks too much.

²⁰If a man curses his father or mother,
his lamp will be snuffed out in
pitch darkness.

²¹An inheritance quickly gained at the
beginning
will not be blessed at the end.

²²Do not say, "I'll pay you back for this
wrong!"
Wait for the LORD, and he will
deliver you.

²³The LORD detests differing weights,
and dishonest scales do not please
him.

²⁴A man's steps are directed by the
LORD.

How then can anyone understand
 his own way?

25 It is a trap for a man to dedicate
 something rashly
 and only later to consider his vows.

26 A wise king winnows out the wicked;
 he drives the threshing wheel over
 them.

27 The lamp of the LORD searches the
 spirit of a man[a];
 it searches out his inmost being.

28 Love and faithfulness keep a king
 safe;
 through love his throne is made
 secure.

29 The glory of young men is their
 strength,
 gray hair the splendor of the old.

30 Blows and wounds cleanse away evil,
 and beatings purge the inmost
 being.

21 The king's heart is in the hand of
 the LORD;
 he directs it like a watercourse
 wherever he pleases.

2 All a man's ways seem right to him,
 but the LORD weighs the heart.

3 To do what is right and just
 is more acceptable to the LORD
 than sacrifice.

4 Haughty eyes and a proud heart,
 the lamp of the wicked, are sin!

5 The plans of the diligent lead to
 profit
 as surely as haste leads to poverty.

6 A fortune made by a lying tongue
 is a fleeting vapor and a deadly
 snare.[b]

7 The violence of the wicked will drag
 them away,
 for they refuse to do what is right.

8 The way of the guilty is devious,
 but the conduct of the innocent is
 upright.

9 Better to live on a corner of the
 roof
 than share a house with a
 quarrelsome wife.

10 The wicked man craves evil;
 his neighbor gets no mercy from
 him.

11 When a mocker is punished, the
 simple gain wisdom;
 when a wise man is instructed, he
 gets knowledge.

12 The Righteous One[c] takes note of the
 house of the wicked
 and brings the wicked to ruin.

13 If a man shuts his ears to the cry of
 the poor,
 he too will cry out and not be
 answered.

14 A gift given in secret soothes
 anger,
 and a bribe concealed in the cloak
 pacifies great wrath.

15 When justice is done, it brings joy to
 the righteous
 but terror to evildoers.

16 A man who strays from the path of
 understanding
 comes to rest in the company of the
 dead.

17 He who loves pleasure will become
 poor;
 whoever loves wine and oil will
 never be rich.

18 The wicked become a ransom for the
 righteous,
 and the unfaithful for the upright.

19 Better to live in a desert
 than with a quarrelsome and ill-
 tempered wife.

---

a 27 Or *The spirit of man is the LORD's lamp*   b 6 Some Hebrew manuscripts, Septuagint and Vulgate; most Hebrew manuscripts
vapor for those who seek death   c 12 Or *The righteous man*

²⁰In the house of the wise are stores of
    choice food and oil,
  but a foolish man devours all he
    has.

²¹He who pursues righteousness and
    love
  finds life, prosperity[a] and honor.

²²A wise man attacks the city of the
    mighty
  and pulls down the stronghold in
    which they trust.

²³He who guards his mouth and his
    tongue
  keeps himself from calamity.

²⁴The proud and arrogant man—
    "Mocker" is his name;
  he behaves with overweening pride.

²⁵The sluggard's craving will be the
    death of him,
  because his hands refuse to work.
²⁶All day long he craves for more,
  but the righteous give without
    sparing.

²⁷The sacrifice of the wicked is
    detestable—
  how much more so when brought
    with evil intent!

²⁸A false witness will perish,
  and whoever listens to him will be
    destroyed forever.[b]

²⁹A wicked man puts up a bold front,
  but an upright man gives thought
    to his ways.

³⁰There is no wisdom, no insight, no
    plan
  that can succeed against the LORD.

³¹The horse is made ready for the day
    of battle,
  but victory rests with the LORD.

22 A good name is more desirable
    than great riches;
  to be esteemed is better than silver
    or gold.

²Rich and poor have this in common:
  The LORD is the Maker of them all.

³A prudent man sees danger and takes
    refuge,
  but the simple keep going and
    suffer for it.

⁴Humility and the fear of the LORD
  bring wealth and honor and life.

⁵In the paths of the wicked lie thorns
    and snares,
  but he who guards his soul stays far
    from them.

⁶Train[c] a child in the way he should go,
  and when he is old he will not turn
    from it.

⁷The rich rule over the poor,
  and the borrower is servant to the
    lender.

⁸He who sows wickedness reaps
    trouble,
  and the rod of his fury will be
    destroyed.

⁹A generous man will himself be blessed,
  for he shares his food with the poor.

¹⁰Drive out the mocker, and out goes
    strife;
  quarrels and insults are ended.

¹¹He who loves a pure heart and whose
    speech is gracious
  will have the king for his friend.

¹²The eyes of the LORD keep watch
    over knowledge,
  but he frustrates the words of the
    unfaithful.

¹³The sluggard says, "There is a lion
    outside!"
  or, "I will be murdered in the
    streets!"

¹⁴The mouth of an adulteress is a deep
    pit;
  he who is under the LORD's wrath
    will fall into it.

---

a 21 Or righteousness   b 28 Or / but the words of an obedient man will live on   c 6 Or Start

15Folly is bound up in the heart of a child,
  but the rod of discipline will drive
    it far from him.
16He who oppresses the poor to
    increase his wealth
  and he who gives gifts to the rich—
    both come to poverty.

Sayings of the Wise

17Pay attention and listen to the sayings
    of the wise;
  apply your heart to what I teach,
18for it is pleasing when you keep them
    in your heart
  and have all of them ready on your
    lips.
19So that your trust may be in the LORD,
  I teach you today, even you.
20Have I not written thirtyᵃ sayings for
    you,
  sayings of counsel and knowledge,
21teaching you true and reliable words,
  so that you can give sound answers
    to him who sent you?

22Do not exploit the poor because they
    are poor
  and do not crush the needy in court,
23for the LORD will take up their case
  and will plunder those who plunder
    them.

24Do not make friends with a hot-
    tempered man,
  do not associate with one easily
    angered,
25or you may learn his ways
  and get yourself ensnared.

26Do not be a man who strikes hands in
    pledge
  or puts up security for debts;
27if you lack the means to pay,
  your very bed will be snatched
    from under you.

28Do not move an ancient boundary
    stone
  set up by your forefathers.

29Do you see a man skilled in his work?
  He will serve before kings;
  he will not serve before obscure
    men.

23 When you sit to dine with a
    ruler,
  note well whatᵇ is before you,
2and put a knife to your throat
  if you are given to gluttony.
3Do not crave his delicacies,
  for that food is deceptive.

4Do not wear yourself out to get rich;
  have the wisdom to show restraint.
5Cast but a glance at riches, and they
    are gone,
  for they will surely sprout wings
  and fly off to the sky like an eagle.

6Do not eat the food of a stingy man,
  do not crave his delicacies;
7for he is the kind of man
  who is always thinking about the
    cost.ᶜ
  "Eat and drink," he says to you,
    but his heart is not with you.
8You will vomit up the little you have
    eaten
  and will have wasted your
    compliments.

9Do not speak to a fool,
  for he will scorn the wisdom of
    your words.

10Do not move an ancient boundary
    stone
  or encroach on the fields of the
    fatherless,
11for their Defender is strong;
  he will take up their case against
    you.

12Apply your heart to instruction
  and your ears to words of knowledge.

13Do not withhold discipline from a
    child;
  if you punish him with the rod, he
    will not die.

ᵃ 20 Or not formerly written; or not written excellent ᵇ 1 Or who ᶜ 7 Or for as he thinks within himself, / so he is; or for as he
puts on a feast, / so he is

GOING deeper

Ten Good Reasons to Ask God for Wisdom

READ AND CONSIDER: PROVERBS 23:12,19,23

"Buy the truth and do not sell it; get wisdom, discipline and understanding" (Proverbs 23:23).

If you were given a choice between wealth and wisdom, which would you choose?

The Bible never promises that financial gain will bring us increased happiness, but Scripture consistently teaches that we *should* ask for wisdom. Think of wisdom as the ability to exercise good judgment and discern correctly at all times. Wouldn't it be wonderful to have that ability? All we have to do is ask God for it! "Wisdom is supreme; therefore get wisdom. Though it cost all you have, get understanding" (4:7).

Here are ten good reasons to ask God for wisdom:

1. *To have longevity, blessings, and honor.* "Long life is in her right hand; in her left hand are riches and honor" (3:16).

2. *To live a good, peaceful life.* "Her ways are pleasant ways, and all her paths are peace" (3:17).

3. *To enjoy vitality and happiness.* "She is a tree of life to those who embrace her; those who lay hold of her will be blessed" (3:18).

4. *To be protected.* "Then you will go on your way in safety, and your foot will not stumble" (3:23).

5. *To experience refreshing rest.* "When you lie down, you will not be afraid; when you lie down, your sleep will be sweet" (3:24).

6. *To gain confidence.* "The LORD will be your confidence and will keep your foot from being snared" (3:26).

7. *To live in security.* "Do not forsake wisdom, and she will protect you; love her, and she will watch over you . . . When you walk, your steps will not be hampered; when you run, you will not stumble" (4:6,12).

8. *To be promoted.* "Esteem her, and she will exalt you; embrace her, and she will honor you" (4:8).

9. *To be saved from evil.* "For wisdom will enter your heart, and knowledge will be pleasant to your soul. Discretion will protect you, and understanding will guard you. Wisdom will save you from the ways of wicked men, from men whose words are perverse" (2:10-12).

10. *To be guided in the way you should go.* "Let the wise listen and add to their learning, and let the discerning get guidance" (1:5).

Ask God today to give you wisdom in all things.

---

¹⁴Punish him with the rod
　　and save his soul from death.[a]

¹⁵My son, if your heart is wise,
　　then my heart will be glad;
¹⁶my inmost being will rejoice
　　when your lips speak what is
　　right.

¹⁷Do not let your heart envy sinners,
　　but always be zealous for the fear of
　　the LORD.

---

[a] *14* Hebrew *Sheol*

¹⁸There is surely a future hope for you,
and your hope will not be cut off.

¹⁹Listen, my son, and be wise,
and keep your heart on the right
path.
²⁰Do not join those who drink too
much wine
or gorge themselves on meat,
²¹for drunkards and gluttons become
poor,
and drowsiness clothes them in
rags.

²²Listen to your father, who gave you
life,
and do not despise your mother
when she is old.
²³Buy the truth and do not sell it;
get wisdom, discipline and
understanding.
²⁴The father of a righteous man has
great joy;
he who has a wise son delights in
him.
²⁵May your father and mother be glad;
may she who gave you birth
rejoice!

²⁶My son, give me your heart
and let your eyes keep to my ways,
²⁷for a prostitute is a deep pit
and a wayward wife is a narrow
well.
²⁸Like a bandit she lies in wait,
and multiplies the unfaithful among
men.

²⁹Who has woe? Who has sorrow?
Who has strife? Who has
complaints?
Who has needless bruises? Who has
bloodshot eyes?
³⁰Those who linger over wine,
who go to sample bowls of mixed
wine.
³¹Do not gaze at wine when it is red,
when it sparkles in the cup,
when it goes down smoothly!
³²In the end it bites like a snake
and poisons like a viper.

³³Your eyes will see strange sights
and your mind imagine confusing
things.
³⁴You will be like one sleeping on the
high seas,
lying on top of the rigging.
³⁵"They hit me," you will say, "but I'm
not hurt!
They beat me, but I don't feel it!
When will I wake up
so I can find another drink?"

24 Do not envy wicked men,
do not desire their company;
²for their hearts plot violence,
and their lips talk about making
trouble.

³By wisdom a house is built,
and through understanding it is
established;
⁴through knowledge its rooms are
filled
with rare and beautiful treasures.

⁵A wise man has great power,
and a man of knowledge increases
strength;
⁶for waging war you need guidance,
and for victory many advisers.

⁷Wisdom is too high for a fool;
in the assembly at the gate he has
nothing to say.

⁸He who plots evil
will be known as a schemer.
⁹The schemes of folly are sin,
and men detest a mocker.

¹⁰If you falter in times of trouble,
how small is your strength!

¹¹Rescue those being led away to
death;
hold back those staggering toward
slaughter.
¹²If you say, "But we knew nothing
about this,"
does not he who weighs the heart
perceive it?
Does not he who guards your life
know it?

Will he not repay each person
   according to what he has done?

13Eat honey, my son, for it is good;
   honey from the comb is sweet to
      your taste.
14Know also that wisdom is sweet to
      your soul;
   if you find it, there is a future hope
      for you,
   and your hope will not be cut off.

15Do not lie in wait like an outlaw
      against a righteous man's
      house,
   do not raid his dwelling place;
16for though a righteous man falls seven
      times, he rises again,
   but the wicked are brought down
      by calamity.

17Do not gloat when your enemy falls;
   when he stumbles, do not let your
      heart rejoice,
18or the LORD will see and disapprove
   and turn his wrath away from him.

19Do not fret because of evil men
   or be envious of the wicked,
20for the evil man has no future hope,
   and the lamp of the wicked will be
      snuffed out.

21Fear the LORD and the king, my son,
   and do not join with the rebellious,
22for those two will send sudden
      destruction upon them,
   and who knows what calamities
      they can bring?

Further Sayings of the Wise
23These also are sayings of the wise:

To show partiality in judging is not
      good:
24Whoever says to the guilty, "You are
      innocent"—
   peoples will curse him and nations
      denounce him.
25But it will go well with those who
   convict the guilty,

and rich blessing will come upon
      them.

26An honest answer
   is like a kiss on the lips.

27Finish your outdoor work
   and get your fields ready;
   after that, build your house.

28Do not testify against your neighbor
      without cause,
   or use your lips to deceive.
29Do not say, "I'll do to him as he has
      done to me;
   I'll pay that man back for what he
      did."

30I went past the field of the sluggard,
   past the vineyard of the man who
      lacks judgment;
31thorns had come up everywhere,
   the ground was covered with
      weeds,
   and the stone wall was in ruins.
32I applied my heart to what I observed
   and learned a lesson from what I
      saw:
33A little sleep, a little slumber,
   a little folding of the hands to rest—
34and poverty will come on you like a
      bandit
   and scarcity like an armed man.[a]

More Proverbs of Solomon
25 These are more proverbs of Solomon, copied by the men of
Hezekiah king of Judah:

2It is the glory of God to conceal a
      matter;
   to search out a matter is the glory
      of kings.

3As the heavens are high and the earth
      is deep,
   so the hearts of kings are
      unsearchable.

4Remove the dross from the silver,
   and out comes material for[b] the
      silversmith;

---

[a] 34 Or like a vagrant / and scarcity like a beggar   [b] 4 Or comes a vessel from

⁵ remove the wicked from the king's
  presence,
    and his throne will be established
      through righteousness.

⁶ Do not exalt yourself in the king's
  presence,
    and do not claim a place among
      great men;
⁷ it is better for him to say to you,
  "Come up here,"
    than for him to humiliate you
      before a nobleman.

What you have seen with your eyes
⁸   do not bring[a] hastily to court,
  for what will you do in the end
    if your neighbor puts you to shame?

⁹ If you argue your case with a
  neighbor,
    do not betray another man's
      confidence,
¹⁰ or he who hears it may shame you
  and you will never lose your bad
    reputation.

¹¹ A word aptly spoken
  is like apples of gold in settings of
    silver.

¹² Like an earring of gold or an
  ornament of fine gold
    is a wise man's rebuke to a listening
      ear.

¹³ Like the coolness of snow at harvest
  time
    is a trustworthy messenger to those
      who send him;
  he refreshes the spirit of his masters.

¹⁴ Like clouds and wind without rain
  is a man who boasts of gifts he does
    not give.

¹⁵ Through patience a ruler can be
  persuaded,
    and a gentle tongue can break a
      bone.

¹⁶ If you find honey, eat just enough—
  too much of it, and you will vomit.

¹⁷ Seldom set foot in your neighbor's
  house—
    too much of you, and he will hate
      you.

¹⁸ Like a club or a sword or a sharp arrow
  is the man who gives false
    testimony against his neighbor.

¹⁹ Like a bad tooth or a lame foot
  is reliance on the unfaithful in
    times of trouble.

²⁰ Like one who takes away a garment
  on a cold day,
    or like vinegar poured on soda,
  is one who sings songs to a heavy
    heart.

²¹ If your enemy is hungry, give him
  food to eat;
    if he is thirsty, give him water to
      drink.
²² In doing this, you will heap burning
  coals on his head,
    and the LORD will reward you.

²³ As a north wind brings rain,
  so a sly tongue brings angry looks.

²⁴ Better to live on a corner of the roof
  than share a house with a
    quarrelsome wife.

²⁵ Like cold water to a weary soul
  is good news from a distant land.

²⁶ Like a muddied spring or a polluted
  well
    is a righteous man who gives way
      to the wicked.

²⁷ It is not good to eat too much honey,
  nor is it honorable to seek one's
    own honor.

Praying Proverbs 25:28
  *Lord, help me to rule over
    my mind and emotions.*

²⁸ Like a city whose walls are broken
  down
    is a man who lacks self-control.

---

[a] 7,8 Or *nobleman* / *on whom you had set your eyes.* / [8] Do not go

26 Like snow in summer or rain in
harvest,
  honor is not fitting for a fool.

² Like a fluttering sparrow or a darting
swallow,
  an undeserved curse does not come
  to rest.

³ A whip for the horse, a halter for the
donkey,
  and a rod for the backs of fools!

⁴ Do not answer a fool according to his
folly,
  or you will be like him yourself.

⁵ Answer a fool according to his folly,
  or he will be wise in his own eyes.

⁶ Like cutting off one's feet or drinking
violence
  is the sending of a message by the
  hand of a fool.

⁷ Like a lame man's legs that hang
limp
  is a proverb in the mouth of a fool.

⁸ Like tying a stone in a sling
  is the giving of honor to a fool.

⁹ Like a thornbush in a drunkard's
hand
  is a proverb in the mouth of a fool.

¹⁰ Like an archer who wounds at
random
  is he who hires a fool or any
  passer-by.

¹¹ As a dog returns to its vomit,
  so a fool repeats his folly.

¹² Do you see a man wise in his own
eyes?
  There is more hope for a fool than
  for him.

¹³ The sluggard says, "There is a lion in
the road,
  a fierce lion roaming the streets!"

¹⁴ As a door turns on its hinges,
  so a sluggard turns on his bed.

¹⁵ The sluggard buries his hand in the
dish;
  he is too lazy to bring it back to his
  mouth.

¹⁶ The sluggard is wiser in his own eyes
  than seven men who answer
  discreetly.

¹⁷ Like one who seizes a dog by the ears
  is a passer-by who meddles in a
  quarrel not his own.

¹⁸ Like a madman shooting
  firebrands or deadly arrows
¹⁹ is a man who deceives his neighbor
  and says, "I was only joking!"

²⁰ Without wood a fire goes out;
  without gossip a quarrel dies down.

²¹ As charcoal to embers and as wood to
fire,
  so is a quarrelsome man for
  kindling strife.

²² The words of a gossip are like choice
morsels;
  they go down to a man's inmost
  parts.

²³ Like a coating of glazeᵃ over
earthenware
  are fervent lips with an evil heart.

²⁴ A malicious man disguises himself
  with his lips,
  but in his heart he harbors deceit.
²⁵ Though his speech is charming, do
  not believe him,
  for seven abominations fill his
  heart.
²⁶ His malice may be concealed by
  deception,
  but his wickedness will be exposed
  in the assembly.

²⁷ If a man digs a pit, he will fall into it;
  if a man rolls a stone, it will roll
  back on him.

²⁸ A lying tongue hates those it hurts,
  and a flattering mouth works ruin.

ᵃ 23 With a different word division of the Hebrew; Masoretic Text *of silver dross*

27 Do not boast about tomorrow,
for you do not know what a day
may bring forth.

2 Let another praise you, and not your
own mouth;
someone else, and not your own
lips.

3 Stone is heavy and sand a burden,
but provocation by a fool is heavier
than both.

4 Anger is cruel and fury
overwhelming,
but who can stand before jealousy?

5 Better is open rebuke
than hidden love.

6 Wounds from a friend can be trusted,
but an enemy multiplies kisses.

7 He who is full loathes honey,
but to the hungry even what is
bitter tastes sweet.

8 Like a bird that strays from its nest
is a man who strays from his
home.

9 Perfume and incense bring joy to the
heart,
and the pleasantness of one's
friend springs from his earnest
counsel.

10 Do not forsake your friend and the
friend of your father,
and do not go to your brother's
house when disaster strikes
you—
better a neighbor nearby than a
brother far away.

11 Be wise, my son, and bring joy to my
heart;
then I can answer anyone who
treats me with contempt.

12 The prudent see danger and take
refuge,
but the simple keep going and
suffer for it.

13 Take the garment of one who puts up
security for a stranger;
hold it in pledge if he does it for a
wayward woman.

14 If a man loudly blesses his neighbor
early in the morning,
it will be taken as a curse.

15 A quarrelsome wife is like
a constant dripping on a rainy day;

16 restraining her is like restraining the
wind
or grasping oil with the hand.

17 As iron sharpens iron,
so one man sharpens another.

18 He who tends a fig tree will eat its
fruit,
and he who looks after his master
will be honored.

19 As water reflects a face,
so a man's heart reflects the man.

20 Death and Destruction[a] are never
satisfied,
and neither are the eyes of man.

21 The crucible for silver and the
furnace for gold,
but man is tested by the praise he
receives.

22 Though you grind a fool in a mortar,
grinding him like grain with a
pestle,
you will not remove his folly from
him.

23 Be sure you know the condition of
your flocks,
give careful attention to your herds;

24 for riches do not endure forever,
and a crown is not secure for all
generations.

25 When the hay is removed and new
growth appears
and the grass from the hills is
gathered in,

26 the lambs will provide you with
clothing,

---

a 20 Hebrew *Sheol and Abaddon*

and the goats with the price of a field.
27 You will have plenty of goats' milk
   to feed you and your family
   and to nourish your servant girls.

28 The wicked man flees though no
   one pursues,
   but the righteous are as bold as a
   lion.

2 When a country is rebellious, it has
   many rulers,
   but a man of understanding and
   knowledge maintains order.

3 A ruler[a] who oppresses the poor
   is like a driving rain that leaves no
   crops.

4 Those who forsake the law praise the
   wicked,
   but those who keep the law resist
   them.

5 Evil men do not understand justice,
   but those who seek the Lord
   understand it fully.

6 Better a poor man whose walk is
   blameless
   than a rich man whose ways are
   perverse.

7 He who keeps the law is a discerning
   son,
   but a companion of gluttons
   disgraces his father.

8 He who increases his wealth by
   exorbitant interest
   amasses it for another, who will be
   kind to the poor.

9 If anyone turns a deaf ear to the law,
   even his prayers are detestable.

10 He who leads the upright along an
   evil path
   will fall into his own trap,
   but the blameless will receive a
   good inheritance.

11 A rich man may be wise in his own
   eyes,

but a poor man who has
   discernment sees through him.

12 When the righteous triumph, there is
   great elation;
   but when the wicked rise to power,
   men go into hiding.

13 He who conceals his sins does not
   prosper,
   but whoever confesses and
   renounces them finds mercy.

14 Blessed is the man who always fears
   the Lord,
   but he who hardens his heart falls
   into trouble.

15 Like a roaring lion or a charging bear
   is a wicked man ruling over a
   helpless people.

16 A tyrannical ruler lacks judgment,
   but he who hates ill-gotten gain
   will enjoy a long life.

17 A man tormented by the guilt of
   murder
   will be a fugitive till death;
   let no one support him.

18 He whose walk is blameless is kept safe,
   but he whose ways are perverse will
   suddenly fall.

19 He who works his land will have
   abundant food,
   but the one who chases fantasies
   will have his fill of poverty.

20 A faithful man will be richly blessed,
   but one eager to get rich will not
   go unpunished.

21 To show partiality is not good—
   yet a man will do wrong for a piece
   of bread.

22 A stingy man is eager to get rich
   and is unaware that poverty awaits
   him.

23 He who rebukes a man will in the
   end gain more favor

---

a 3 Or A poor man

GOING *deeper*

When Our Prayers Displease God

READ AND CONSIDER: PROVERBS 28:9

"If anyone turns a deaf ear to the law, even his prayers are detestable" (Proverbs 28:9).
Can it be that there is a time when our prayers actually *displease* God?

Scripture tells us that a consequence of disobedience is that our prayers will not be heard. In fact, the word "detestable" means something that is revolting, abominable, or loathsome. None of us wants God to see our prayers that way!

In order to grow in the Lord, it's important to keep asking God to show us what He wants us to do. If we don't ask, we won't know. Even when we think we are doing everything right, it's always good to pray, "Lord, show me any place in my life where I am not obeying You. I want to live by Your rules."

One of the consequences for disobedience is not getting your prayers answered. You cannot receive all God has for you if you are not living in obedience. Jesus said, "If you want to enter life, obey the commandments" (Matthew 19:17). He knew that nothing would give people more peace and confidence than knowing they are doing what God wants them to do. God's Word promises that by being obedient to His ways you will find mercy (Psalm 28:6), peace (Psalm 37:37), and blessing (Proverbs 29:18). *Not* living in obedience brings harsh consequences (15:10), unanswered prayers (28:9), and the inability to enter into the great things God has for us (1 Corinthians 6:9).

Walking in obedience has to do not only with keeping God's commandments but also with heeding God's *specific* instructions. For example, if God has instructed you to rest and you don't do it, that's disobedience. If He has told you to stop doing a certain type of work and you keep doing it, that's disobedience. If He has told you to move to another place and you don't move, that's disobedience too. Or God may ask you to take a different job, stop a certain activity, join a certain church, or change the way you've always done something. Whatever He asks you to do, remember He does this for your greatest good.

God's ways are always better than ours, and obedience to His Word clears the path for our prayers to be heard.

than he who has a flattering
tongue.

24 He who robs his father or mother
and says, "It's not wrong"—
he is partner to him who
destroys.

25 A greedy man stirs up dissension,
but he who trusts in the LORD will
prosper.

26 He who trusts in himself is a fool,
but he who walks in wisdom is
kept safe.

27 He who gives to the poor will lack
nothing,
but he who closes his eyes to them
receives many curses.

28 When the wicked rise to power,
people go into hiding;
but when the wicked perish, the
righteous thrive.

29 A man who remains stiff-necked
after many rebukes
will suddenly be destroyed—
without remedy.

²When the righteous thrive, the
people rejoice;
when the wicked rule, the people
groan.

³A man who loves wisdom brings joy
to his father,
but a companion of prostitutes
squanders his wealth.

⁴By justice a king gives a country
stability,
but one who is greedy for bribes
tears it down.

⁵Whoever flatters his neighbor
is spreading a net for his feet.

⁶An evil man is snared by his own sin,
but a righteous one can sing and be
glad.

⁷The righteous care about justice for
the poor,
but the wicked have no such
concern.

⁸Mockers stir up a city,
but wise men turn away anger.

⁹If a wise man goes to court with a
fool,
the fool rages and scoffs, and there
is no peace.

¹⁰Bloodthirsty men hate a man of
integrity
and seek to kill the upright.

¹¹A fool gives full vent to his anger,
but a wise man keeps himself under
control.

¹²If a ruler listens to lies,
all his officials become wicked.

¹³The poor man and the oppressor have
this in common:
The LORD gives sight to the eyes of
both.

¹⁴If a king judges the poor with
fairness,
his throne will always be secure.

¹⁵The rod of correction imparts
wisdom,
but a child left to himself disgraces
his mother.

¹⁶When the wicked thrive, so does sin,
but the righteous will see their
downfall.

¹⁷Discipline your son, and he will give
you peace;
he will bring delight to your soul.

¹⁸Where there is no revelation, the
people cast off restraint;
but blessed is he who keeps the law.

¹⁹A servant cannot be corrected by
mere words;
though he understands, he will not
respond.

²⁰Do you see a man who speaks in
haste?
There is more hope for a fool than
for him.

²¹If a man pampers his servant from
youth,
he will bring grief^a in the end.

²²An angry man stirs up dissension,
and a hot-tempered one commits
many sins.

²³A man's pride brings him low,
but a man of lowly spirit gains
honor.

²⁴The accomplice of a thief is his own
enemy;
he is put under oath and dare not
testify.

²⁵Fear of man will prove to be a snare,
but whoever trusts in the LORD is
kept safe.

²⁶Many seek an audience with a ruler,
but it is from the LORD that man
gets justice.

²⁷The righteous detest the dishonest;
the wicked detest the upright.

---

^{a} 21 The meaning of the Hebrew for this word is uncertain.

Sayings of Agur

30 The sayings of Agur son of Jakeh—an oracle[a]:

This man declared to Ithiel,
to Ithiel and to Ucal:[b]

2 "I am the most ignorant of men;
I do not have a man's understanding.
3 I have not learned wisdom,
nor have I knowledge of the Holy
One.
4 Who has gone up to heaven and
come down?
Who has gathered up the wind in
the hollow of his hands?
Who has wrapped up the waters in
his cloak?
Who has established all the ends of
the earth?
What is his name, and the name of
his son?
Tell me if you know!

5 "Every word of God is flawless;
he is a shield to those who take
refuge in him.
6 Do not add to his words,
or he will rebuke you and prove
you a liar.

7 "Two things I ask of you, O Lord;
do not refuse me before I die:
8 Keep falsehood and lies far from me;
give me neither poverty nor riches,
but give me only my daily bread.
9 Otherwise, I may have too much and
disown you
and say, 'Who is the Lord?'
Or I may become poor and steal,
and so dishonor the name of my
God.

10 "Do not slander a servant to his
master,
or he will curse you, and you will
pay for it.

11 "There are those who curse their
fathers
and do not bless their mothers;
12 those who are pure in their own eyes
and yet are not cleansed of their
filth;
13 those whose eyes are ever so
haughty,
whose glances are so disdainful;
14 those whose teeth are swords
and whose jaws are set with knives
to devour the poor from the earth,
the needy from among mankind.

15 "The leech has two daughters.
'Give! Give!' they cry.

"There are three things that are never
satisfied,
four that never say, 'Enough!':
16 the grave,[c] the barren womb,
land, which is never satisfied with
water,
and fire, which never says,
'Enough!'

17 "The eye that mocks a father,
that scorns obedience to a mother,
will be pecked out by the ravens of
the valley,
will be eaten by the vultures.

18 "There are three things that are too
amazing for me,
four that I do not understand:
19 the way of an eagle in the sky,
the way of a snake on a rock,
the way of a ship on the high seas,
and the way of a man with a
maiden.

20 "This is the way of an adulteress:
She eats and wipes her mouth
and says, 'I've done nothing
wrong.'

21 "Under three things the earth
trembles,
under four it cannot bear up:
22 a servant who becomes king,
a fool who is full of food,
23 an unloved woman who is married,

---

[a] 1 Or Jakeh of Massa [b] 1 Masoretic Text; with a different word division of the Hebrew declared, "I am weary, O God; / I am weary, O God, and faint. [c] 16 Hebrew Sheol

and a maidservant who displaces
    her mistress.

24 "Four things on earth are small,
    yet they are extremely wise:
25 Ants are creatures of little strength,
    yet they store up their food in the
      summer;
26 coneys[a] are creatures of little power,
    yet they make their home in the
      crags;
27 locusts have no king,
    yet they advance together in ranks;
28 a lizard can be caught with the hand,
    yet it is found in kings' palaces.

29 "There are three things that are
    stately in their stride,
    four that move with stately bearing:
30 a lion, mighty among beasts,
    who retreats before nothing;
31 a strutting rooster, a he-goat,
    and a king with his army around
      him.[b]

32 "If you have played the fool and
    exalted yourself,
    or if you have planned evil,
    clap your hand over your mouth!
33 For as churning the milk produces
    butter,
    and as twisting the nose produces
      blood,
    so stirring up anger produces
      strife."

Sayings of King Lemuel

31 The sayings of King Lemuel—an
oracle[c] his mother taught him:

2 "O my son, O son of my womb,
    O son of my vows,[d]
3 do not spend your strength on
    women,
    your vigor on those who ruin
      kings.

4 "It is not for kings, O Lemuel—
    not for kings to drink wine,
    not for rulers to crave beer,
5 lest they drink and forget what the
    law decrees,
    and deprive all the oppressed of
      their rights.
6 Give beer to those who are
    perishing,
    wine to those who are in anguish;
7 let them drink and forget their
    poverty
    and remember their misery no
      more.

8 "Speak up for those who cannot
    speak for themselves,
    for the rights of all who are
      destitute.
9 Speak up and judge fairly;
    defend the rights of the poor and
      needy."

Epilogue: The Wife of Noble Character

10e A wife of noble character who
    can find?
    She is worth far more than rubies.
11 Her husband has full confidence in
    her
    and lacks nothing of value.
12 She brings him good, not harm,
    all the days of her life.
13 She selects wool and flax
    and works with eager hands.
14 She is like the merchant ships,
    bringing her food from afar.
15 She gets up while it is still dark;
    she provides food for her family
    and portions for her servant girls.
16 She considers a field and buys it;
    out of her earnings she plants a
      vineyard.
17 She sets about her work vigorously;
    her arms are strong for her tasks.
18 She sees that her trading is profitable,
    and her lamp does not go out at
      night.
19 In her hand she holds the distaff

---

a *26* That is, the hyrax or rock badger   b *31* Or *king secure against revolt*   c *1* Or *of Lemuel king of Massa, which*   d *2* Or /
the answer to my prayers   e *10* Verses 10-31 are an acrostic, each verse beginning with a successive letter of the Hebrew
alphabet.

Ask God to Bless the Work You Do

It doesn't matter if you are a stay-at-home mom, a full-time student, a CEO of a giant corporation, a single woman who is self-supporting, a married woman running a home, a skilled career woman, a disabled person, a babysitter, a house sitter, a single working mom, or a volunteer at the rescue mission downtown—you have work to do. It doesn't matter if your work is recognized by the whole world or only God sees it. It doesn't matter if you are getting paid big bucks or receiving no financial compensation whatsoever. Your work is valuable. And you want it to be blessed by God.

Whatever work we do, we want to do it well and be successful. When our work is good, it gives us fulfillment. When we accomplish something worthwhile that makes life better for other people, our families, or ourselves, it gives us satisfaction. But when the work of our hands is not blessed, we are weighed down with frustration and unfulfillment.

The ideal woman described in the Bible is a hard worker (Proverbs 31). She buys and sells property (a real estate agent?). She plants a vineyard (a landscaper?). She makes clothing (a designer?). And she sells it (manager of a clothing store?). She is a woman of strength, energy, and vision who works hard into the night and knows that what she has to offer is good. God wants us to experience that kind of success and satisfaction. But it doesn't happen without prayer.

Prayer helps us to find the balance between being greedy for "gain," which depletes our life (Proverbs 1:19), and having "lazy hands," which makes us poor (Proverbs 10:4).

Prayer helps us to not wear ourselves out

trying to be rich (Proverbs 23:4) and yet still be diligent in our work, which may ultimately bring us monetary rewards (Proverbs 10:4). Prayer helps us find the balance between laziness and obsession, between gaining the whole world and losing our own soul (Matthew 16:26).

The Bible says that "the worker deserves his wages" (1 Timothy 5:18). This means you deserve to be paid or rewarded for your work. Sometimes the reward is in the actual doing of the work itself. You don't get paid for maintaining a home, serving soup at the rescue mission, or teaching a child to tie his shoes, but your reward for seeing the result of your labor is priceless. "The wages of the righteous bring them life" (Proverbs 10:16).

If you have a paying job, don't hesitate to pray that you will be compensated fairly and generously. Pray for your employer to be blessed in his business so he in turn can afford to pay all employees well. Pray that your work is recognized and appreciated by others. Pray to receive promotions and advancement in line with God's will. Say, "Lord, I would like to have that promotion and that raise if it's Your will for my life." As you pray that way and commit your work to the Lord, He will bless it.

No matter what your paycheck reflects, your work is important to God, it's important to others, and it's important to you. You can't afford not to pray about it. Commit your work to the Lord and ask Him to bless it.

For the next "From Stormie's Heart" article, go to page 824.

and grasps the spindle with her
    fingers.
20 She opens her arms to the poor
    and extends her hands to the
       needy.
21 When it snows, she has no fear for her
    household;
    for all of them are clothed in
       scarlet.
22 She makes coverings for her bed;
    she is clothed in fine linen and
       purple.
23 Her husband is respected at the city
    gate,
    where he takes his seat among the
       elders of the land.
24 She makes linen garments and sells
    them,
    and supplies the merchants with
       sashes.
25 She is clothed with strength and
    dignity;
    she can laugh at the days to come.
26 She speaks with wisdom,

and faithful instruction is on her
    tongue.
27 She watches over the affairs of her
    household
    and does not eat the bread of
       idleness.
28 Her children arise and call her
    blessed;
    her husband also, and he praises her:
29 "Many women do noble things,
    but you surpass them all."

Praying Proverbs 31:30

*Lord, help me to be a woman who fears
You and finds favor in Your eyes.*

30 Charm is deceptive, and beauty is
    fleeting;
    but a woman who fears the LORD is
       to be praised.
31 Give her the reward she has earned,
    and let her works bring her praise at
       the city gate.

Author: King Solomon

Date: Approximately 935 BC

Audience: To all those searching for the meaning of life

According to some surveys, about nine out of every ten people say they pray. (Interestingly, even some self-proclaimed atheists admit to praying! One can only wonder to whom or what they are praying.) Yet despite this almost universal effort to connect with God, huge numbers remain frustrated. Thirsty. Searching. Empty.

The problem is, many people don't really know God or how to relate to Him in prayer. Their prayers are more desperate praying rather than an ongoing communication with their heavenly Father.

How can a person avoid this kind of desperate existence? After pondering this question, King Solomon said, "Here is the conclusion of the matter: Fear God and keep his commandments, for this is the whole ⌊duty⌋ of man" (12:13).

Ultimate meaning and satisfaction in life are found only in relating rightly to God. That means getting to know Him through His Word and constantly communicating with Him in prayer.

Ecclesiastes will convince you that there is nothing more important in life than your relationship with God.

Prayer Themes:

- *Thank the Lord that you are an eternal creature made by Him and for Him, and earthly pleasures will never be able to satisfy your soul (3:11).*

- *Ask God to give you His perspective on wealth (5:10-20).*

- *Tell God you want to live bravely and boldly, with a strong faith that rejects a fearful or overly cautious approach to life (11:1-6).*

Ecclesiastes

Everything Is Meaningless

1 The words of the Teacher,[a] son of David, king in Jerusalem:

2 "Meaningless! Meaningless!"
　　says the Teacher.
　"Utterly meaningless!
　　Everything is meaningless."

3 What does man gain from all his labor
　　at which he toils under the sun?
4 Generations come and generations go,
　　but the earth remains forever.
5 The sun rises and the sun sets,
　　and hurries back to where it rises.
6 The wind blows to the south
　　and turns to the north;
　round and round it goes,
　　ever returning on its course.
7 All streams flow into the sea,
　　yet the sea is never full.
To the place the streams come from,
　　there they return again.
8 All things are wearisome,
　　more than one can say.
The eye never has enough of seeing,
　　nor the ear its fill of hearing.
9 What has been will be again,
　　what has been done will be done
　　again;
　there is nothing new under the sun.
10 Is there anything of which one can
　　say,
　"Look! This is something new"?
It was here already, long ago;
　　it was here before our time.
11 There is no remembrance of men of
　　old,
　　and even those who are yet to come
will not be remembered
　　by those who follow.

---

[a] *1* Or *leader of the assembly*; also in verses 2 and 12

Wisdom Is Meaningless

12I, the Teacher, was king over Israel in Jerusalem. 13I devoted myself to study and to explore by wisdom all that is done under heaven. What a heavy burden God has laid on men! 14I have seen all the things that are done under the sun; all of them are meaningless, a chasing after the wind.

15What is twisted cannot be
    straightened;
  what is lacking cannot be counted.

16I thought to myself, "Look, I have grown and increased in wisdom more than anyone who has ruled over Jerusalem before me; I have experienced much of wisdom and knowledge." 17Then I applied myself to the understanding of wisdom, and also of madness and folly, but I learned that this, too, is a chasing after the wind.

18For with much wisdom comes much
    sorrow;
  the more knowledge, the more
    grief.

Pleasures Are Meaningless

2 I thought in my heart, "Come now, I will test you with pleasure to find out what is good." But that also proved to be meaningless. 2"Laughter," I said, "is foolish. And what does pleasure accomplish?" 3I tried cheering myself with wine, and embracing folly—my mind still guiding me with wisdom. I wanted to see what was worthwhile for men to do under heaven during the few days of their lives.

4I undertook great projects: I built houses for myself and planted vineyards. 5I made gardens and parks and planted all kinds of fruit trees in them. 6I made reservoirs to water groves of flourishing trees. 7I bought male and female slaves and had other slaves who were born in my house. I also owned more herds and flocks than anyone in Jerusalem before me. 8I amassed silver and gold for myself,

and the treasure of kings and provinces. I acquired men and women singers, and a harem[a] as well—the delights of the heart of man. 9I became greater by far than anyone in Jerusalem before me. In all this my wisdom stayed with me.

10I denied myself nothing my eyes
    desired;
  I refused my heart no pleasure.
  My heart took delight in all my work,
    and this was the reward for all my
    labor.
11Yet when I surveyed all that my
    hands had done
  and what I had toiled to achieve,
everything was meaningless, a
    chasing after the wind;
  nothing was gained under the sun.

Wisdom and Folly Are Meaningless

12Then I turned my thoughts to
    consider wisdom,
  and also madness and folly.
  What more can the king's
    successor do
  than what has already been done?
13I saw that wisdom is better than folly,
  just as light is better than darkness.
14The wise man has eyes in his head,
  while the fool walks in the
    darkness;
  but I came to realize
  that the same fate overtakes them
    both.

15Then I thought in my heart,

"The fate of the fool will overtake
    me also.
  What then do I gain by being
    wise?"
I said in my heart,
  "This too is meaningless."
16For the wise man, like the fool, will
    not be long remembered;
  in days to come both will be
    forgotten.
Like the fool, the wise man too must
    die!

---

a 8 The meaning of the Hebrew for this phrase is uncertain.

Toil Is Meaningless

17So I hated life, because the work that is done under the sun was grievous to me. All of it is meaningless, a chasing after the wind. 18I hated all the things I had toiled for under the sun, because I must leave them to the one who comes after me. 19And who knows whether he will be a wise man or a fool? Yet he will have control over all the work into which I have poured my effort and skill under the sun. This too is meaningless. 20So my heart began to despair over all my toilsome labor under the sun. 21For a man may do his work with wisdom, knowledge and skill, and then he must leave all he owns to someone who has not worked for it. This too is meaningless and a great misfortune. 22What does a man get for all the toil and anxious striving with which he labors under the sun? 23All his days his work is pain and grief; even at night his mind does not rest. This too is meaningless.

24A man can do nothing better than to eat and drink and find satisfaction in his work. This too, I see, is from the hand of God, 25for without him, who can eat or find enjoyment? 26To the man who pleases him, God gives wisdom, knowledge and happiness, but to the sinner he gives the task of gathering and storing up wealth to hand it over to the one who pleases God. This too is meaningless, a chasing after the wind.

A Time for Everything

3 There is a time for everything,
   and a season for every activity
      under heaven:

2 a time to be born and a time to die,
   a time to plant and a time to uproot,
3 a time to kill and a time to heal,
   a time to tear down and a time to
      build,
4 a time to weep and a time to laugh,
   a time to mourn and a time to dance,
5 a time to scatter stones and a time
      to gather them,
   a time to embrace and a time to
      refrain,
6 a time to search and a time to give
      up,
   a time to keep and a time to throw
      away,
7 a time to tear and a time to mend,
   a time to be silent and a time to
      speak,
8 a time to love and a time to hate,
   a time for war and a time for peace.

9What does the worker gain from his toil? 10I have seen the burden God has laid on men. 11He has made everything beautiful in its time. He has also set eternity in the hearts of men; yet they cannot fathom what God has done from beginning to end. 12I know that there is nothing better for men than to be happy and do good while they live. 13That everyone may eat and drink, and find satisfaction in all his toil—this is the gift of God. 14I know that everything God does will endure forever; nothing can be added to it and nothing taken from it. God does it so that men will revere him.

15Whatever is has already been,
   and what will be has been before;
   and God will call the past to
      account.[a]

16And I saw something else under the sun:

In the place of judgment—wickedness
      was there,
   in the place of justice—wickedness
      was there.

17I thought in my heart,

"God will bring to judgment
   both the righteous and the wicked,
for there will be a time for every
      activity,
   a time for every deed."

18I also thought, "As for men, God tests them so that they may see that they are like the animals. 19Man's fate is like

---

a 15 Or God calls back the past

Timing Is Everything

READ AND CONSIDER: ECCLESIASTES 3:1-11

"He has made everything beautiful in its time. He has also set eternity in the hearts of men; yet they cannot fathom what God has done from beginning to end" (Ecclesiastes 3:11).

When it comes to prayer, most of us think about timing—that is, we think about what the timing of God's answers should be. *When the answer doesn't come immediately,* we anxiously wonder why. But Ecclesiastes tells us, "There is a time for everything, and a season for every activity under heaven." God's timing is not the same as ours. His ways are not our ways. We live our lives with a sense of earthly time. God sees things from an eternal perspective. Living in our time-bound world and waiting for God's timing is often hard, especially when we ask for things we want or need now.

We have to remember that even though we pray and have faith, the final outcome and timing are in *God's* hands. He says there is "a time to heal" (3:3). So if you pray for healing and nothing happens, don't beat yourself up or be mad at God. God sometimes uses physical ailments to get our attention so He can speak to us. He wants us to fervently turn to Him. So keep praying and don't give up hope.

The same is true when praying that God will save someone's life. We don't have the final say over anyone's hour of death. The Bible says there is "a time to die" (3:2), but we are not the ones who decide that. God does. And we must accept His decision. We can pray, but *He* determines the outcome. We have to allow Him to do that without resenting or getting angry at Him.

God's timing is perfect. And it is liberating when we surrender to it. There is great freedom in simply laying our concerns and desires before Him and then trusting Him for the outcome. What joy there is in looking for God's goodness to us in the midst of our times of waiting. While you may not be able to understand exactly what God is doing, you can trust that He is doing something. He has your best interests at heart. And He will make everything in your life beautiful in *His* perfect time.

---

that of the animals; the same fate awaits them both: As one dies, so dies the other. All have the same breath[a]; man has no advantage over the animal. Everything is meaningless. ²⁰All go to the same place; all come from dust, and to dust all return. ²¹Who knows if the spirit of man rises upward and if the spirit of the animal[b] goes down into the earth?"

²²So I saw that there is nothing better for a man than to enjoy his work, because that is his lot. For who can bring him to see what will happen after him?

Oppression, Toil, Friendlessness

4 Again I looked and saw all the oppression that was taking place under the sun:

I saw the tears of the oppressed—
and they have no comforter;
power was on the side of their
oppressors—
and they have no comforter.
² And I declared that the dead,
who had already died,
are happier than the living,
who are still alive.
³ But better than both
is he who has not yet been,
who has not seen the evil
that is done under the sun.

⁴ And I saw that all labor and all achievement spring from man's envy of his neighbor. This too is meaningless, a chasing after the wind.

---

[a] 19 Or *spirit*   [b] 21 Or *Who knows the spirit of man, which rises upward, or the spirit of the animal, which*

⁵The fool folds his hands
and ruins himself.
⁶Better one handful with
tranquillity
than two handfuls with toil
and chasing after the wind.

⁷Again I saw something meaningless
under the sun:

⁸There was a man all alone;
he had neither son nor brother.
There was no end to his toil,
yet his eyes were not content with
his wealth.
"For whom am I toiling," he asked,
"and why am I depriving myself of
enjoyment?"
This too is meaningless—
a miserable business!

⁹Two are better than one,
because they have a good return for
their work:
¹⁰If one falls down,
his friend can help him up.
But pity the man who falls
and has no one to help him up!
¹¹Also, if two lie down together, they
will keep warm.
But how can one keep warm
alone?
¹²Though one may be overpowered,
two can defend themselves.
A cord of three strands is not quickly
broken.

Advancement Is Meaningless

¹³Better a poor but wise youth than
an old but foolish king who no longer knows how to take warning. ¹⁴The
youth may have come from prison to the
kingship, or he may have been born in
poverty within his kingdom. ¹⁵I saw that
all who lived and walked under the sun
followed the youth, the king's successor.
¹⁶There was no end to all the people who
were before them. But those who came
later were not pleased with the successor.
This too is meaningless, a chasing after
the wind.

Stand in Awe of God

5 Guard your steps when you go to
the house of God. Go near to listen
rather than to offer the sacrifice of fools,
who do not know that they do wrong.

²Do not be quick with your mouth,
do not be hasty in your heart
to utter anything before God.
God is in heaven
and you are on earth,
so let your words be few.
³As a dream comes when there are
many cares,
so the speech of a fool when there
are many words.

⁴When you make a vow to God, do not
delay in fulfilling it. He has no pleasure in
fools; fulfill your vow. ⁵It is better not to
vow than to make a vow and not fulfill
it. ⁶Do not let your mouth lead you into
sin. And do not protest to the ⌊temple⌋
messenger, "My vow was a mistake." Why
should God be angry at what you say and
destroy the work of your hands? ⁷Much
dreaming and many words are meaningless. Therefore stand in awe of God.

Riches Are Meaningless

⁸If you see the poor oppressed in a district, and justice and rights denied, do
not be surprised at such things; for one
official is eyed by a higher one, and over
them both are others higher still. ⁹The
increase from the land is taken by all; the
king himself profits from the fields.

¹⁰Whoever loves money never has
money enough;
whoever loves wealth is never
satisfied with his income.
This too is meaningless.

¹¹As goods increase,
so do those who consume them.
And what benefit are they to the
owner
except to feast his eyes on them?

¹²The sleep of a laborer is sweet,
whether he eats little or much,

but the abundance of a rich man
   permits him no sleep.

13I have seen a grievous evil under the
sun:

wealth hoarded to the harm of its
   owner,
14 or wealth lost through some
    misfortune,
so that when he has a son
   there is nothing left for him.
15Naked a man comes from his
    mother's womb,
   and as he comes, so he departs.
He takes nothing from his labor
   that he can carry in his hand.

16This too is a grievous evil:

As a man comes, so he departs,
   and what does he gain,
    since he toils for the wind?
17All his days he eats in darkness,
   with great frustration, affliction and
    anger.

18Then I realized that it is good and
proper for a man to eat and drink, and
to find satisfaction in his toilsome labor
under the sun during the few days of life
God has given him—for this is his lot.
19Moreover, when God gives any man
wealth and possessions, and enables him
to enjoy them, to accept his lot and be
happy in his work—this is a gift of God.
20He seldom reflects on the days of his
life, because God keeps him occupied
with gladness of heart.

6 I have seen another evil under the
sun, and it weighs heavily on men:
2God gives a man wealth, possessions and
honor, so that he lacks nothing his heart
desires, but God does not enable him to
enjoy them, and a stranger enjoys them instead. This is meaningless, a grievous evil.
3A man may have a hundred children
and live many years; yet no matter how
long he lives, if he cannot enjoy his
prosperity and does not receive proper
burial, I say that a stillborn child is better
off than he. 4It comes without meaning,

it departs in darkness, and in darkness its
name is shrouded. 5Though it never saw
the sun or knew anything, it has more
rest than does that man— 6even if he
lives a thousand years twice over but fails
to enjoy his prosperity. Do not all go to
the same place?

7All man's efforts are for his mouth,
   yet his appetite is never satisfied.
8What advantage has a wise man
   over a fool?
What does a poor man gain
   by knowing how to conduct
    himself before others?
9Better what the eye sees
   than the roving of the appetite.
This too is meaningless,
   a chasing after the wind.

10Whatever exists has already been
    named,
   and what man is has been known;
no man can contend
   with one who is stronger than he.
11The more the words,
   the less the meaning,
   and how does that profit anyone?

12For who knows what is good for a
man in life, during the few and meaningless days he passes through like a shadow?
Who can tell him what will happen under the sun after he is gone?

Wisdom

7 A good name is better than fine
   perfume,
   and the day of death better than the
    day of birth.
2It is better to go to a house of
    mourning
   than to go to a house of feasting,
for death is the destiny of every man;
   the living should take this to
    heart.
3Sorrow is better than laughter,
   because a sad face is good for the
    heart.
4The heart of the wise is in the house
   of mourning,

but the heart of fools is in the house
of pleasure.
⁵It is better to heed a wise man's
rebuke
than to listen to the song of fools.
⁶Like the crackling of thorns under the
pot,
so is the laughter of fools.
This too is meaningless.

⁷Extortion turns a wise man into a
fool,
and a bribe corrupts the heart.

⁸The end of a matter is better than its
beginning,
and patience is better than pride.
⁹Do not be quickly provoked in your
spirit,
for anger resides in the lap of fools.

¹⁰Do not say, "Why were the old days
better than these?"
For it is not wise to ask such
questions.

¹¹Wisdom, like an inheritance, is a
good thing
and benefits those who see the sun.
¹²Wisdom is a shelter
as money is a shelter,
but the advantage of knowledge is
this:
that wisdom preserves the life of its
possessor.

¹³Consider what God has done:

Who can straighten
what he has made crooked?
¹⁴When times are good, be happy;
but when times are bad, consider:
God has made the one
as well as the other.
Therefore, a man cannot discover
anything about his future.

¹⁵In this meaningless life of mine I have
seen both of these:

a righteous man perishing in his
righteousness,
and a wicked man living long in his
wickedness.
¹⁶Do not be overrighteous,
neither be overwise—
why destroy yourself?
¹⁷Do not be overwicked,
and do not be a fool—
why die before your time?
¹⁸It is good to grasp the one
and not let go of the other.
The man who fears God will avoid
all ⌊extremes⌋.ᵃ

¹⁹Wisdom makes one wise man more
powerful
than ten rulers in a city.

²⁰There is not a righteous man on
earth
who does what is right and never
sins.

²¹Do not pay attention to every word
people say,
or you may hear your servant
cursing you—
²²for you know in your heart
that many times you yourself have
cursed others.

²³All this I tested by wisdom and I
said,

"I am determined to be wise"—
but this was beyond me.
²⁴Whatever wisdom may be,
it is far off and most profound—
who can discover it?
²⁵So I turned my mind to
understand,
to investigate and to search out
wisdom and the scheme of
things
and to understand the stupidity of
wickedness
and the madness of folly.

²⁶I find more bitter than death
the woman who is a snare,
whose heart is a trap
and whose hands are chains.

ᵃ 18 Or will follow them both

The man who pleases God will escape
her,
but the sinner she will ensnare.

[27]"Look," says the Teacher,[a] "this is
what I have discovered:

"Adding one thing to another to
discover the scheme of things—
[28] while I was still searching
but not finding—
I found one ⌊upright⌋ man among a
thousand,
but not one ⌊upright⌋ woman
among them all.
[29]This only have I found:
God made mankind upright,
but men have gone in search of
many schemes."

8 Who is like the wise man?
Who knows the explanation of
things?
Wisdom brightens a man's face
and changes its hard appearance.

Obey the King

[2]Obey the king's command, I say, because you took an oath before God. [3]Do
not be in a hurry to leave the king's presence. Do not stand up for a bad cause, for
he will do whatever he pleases. [4]Since a
king's word is supreme, who can say to
him, "What are you doing?"

[5]Whoever obeys his command will
come to no harm,
and the wise heart will know the
proper time and procedure.
[6]For there is a proper time and
procedure for every matter,
though a man's misery weighs
heavily upon him.

[7]Since no man knows the future,
who can tell him what is to come?
[8]No man has power over the wind to
contain it[b];
so no one has power over the day of
his death.

As no one is discharged in time of war,
so wickedness will not release those
who practice it.

[9]All this I saw, as I applied my mind
to everything done under the sun. There
is a time when a man lords it over others to his own[c] hurt. [10]Then too, I saw
the wicked buried—those who used to
come and go from the holy place and receive praise[d] in the city where they did
this. This too is meaningless.

[11]When the sentence for a crime is not
quickly carried out, the hearts of the people are filled with schemes to do wrong.
[12]Although a wicked man commits a hundred crimes and still lives a long time, I
know that it will go better with God-
fearing men, who are reverent before
God. [13]Yet because the wicked do not
fear God, it will not go well with them,
and their days will not lengthen like a
shadow.

[14]There is something else meaningless
that occurs on earth: righteous men who
get what the wicked deserve, and wicked
men who get what the righteous deserve.
This too, I say, is meaningless. [15]So I commend the enjoyment of life, because
nothing is better for a man under the sun
than to eat and drink and be glad. Then
joy will accompany him in his work all
the days of the life God has given him
under the sun.

[16]When I applied my mind to know
wisdom and to observe man's labor on
earth—his eyes not seeing sleep day or
night— [17]then I saw all that God has
done. No one can comprehend what
goes on under the sun. Despite all his efforts to search it out, man cannot discover
its meaning. Even if a wise man claims he
knows, he cannot really comprehend it.

A Common Destiny for All

9 So I reflected on all this and concluded that the righteous and the
wise and what they do are in God's

---

[a] 27 Or *leader of the assembly*   [b] 8 Or *over his spirit to retain it*   [c] 9 Or *to their*   [d] 10 Some Hebrew manuscripts and
Septuagint (Aquila); most Hebrew manuscripts *and are forgotten*

hands, but no man knows whether love or hate awaits him. [2]All share a common destiny—the righteous and the wicked, the good and the bad,[a] the clean and the unclean, those who offer sacrifices and those who do not.

As it is with the good man,
    so with the sinner;
as it is with those who take oaths,
    so with those who are afraid to take
        them.

[3]This is the evil in everything that happens under the sun: The same destiny overtakes all. The hearts of men, moreover, are full of evil and there is madness in their hearts while they live, and afterward they join the dead. [4]Anyone who is among the living has hope[b]—even a live dog is better off than a dead lion!

[5]For the living know that they will die,
    but the dead know nothing;
they have no further reward,
    and even the memory of them is
        forgotten.
[6]Their love, their hate
    and their jealousy have long since
        vanished;
never again will they have a part
    in anything that happens under the
        sun.

[7]Go, eat your food with gladness, and drink your wine with a joyful heart, for it is now that God favors what you do. [8]Always be clothed in white, and always anoint your head with oil. [9]Enjoy life with your wife, whom you love, all the days of this meaningless life that God has given you under the sun—all your meaningless days. For this is your lot in life and in your toilsome labor under the sun. [10]Whatever your hand finds to do, do it with all your might, for in the grave,[c] where you are going, there is neither working nor planning nor knowledge nor wisdom.

[11]I have seen something else under the sun:

The race is not to the swift
    or the battle to the strong,
nor does food come to the wise
    or wealth to the brilliant
    or favor to the learned;
but time and chance happen to them
    all.

[12]Moreover, no man knows when his hour will come:

As fish are caught in a cruel net,
    or birds are taken in a snare,
so men are trapped by evil times
    that fall unexpectedly upon them.

Wisdom Better Than Folly

[13]I also saw under the sun this example of wisdom that greatly impressed me: [14]There was once a small city with only a few people in it. And a powerful king came against it, surrounded it and built huge siegeworks against it. [15]Now there lived in that city a man poor but wise, and he saved the city by his wisdom. But nobody remembered that poor man. [16]So I said, "Wisdom is better than strength." But the poor man's wisdom is despised, and his words are no longer heeded.

[17]The quiet words of the wise are more
        to be heeded
    than the shouts of a ruler of fools.
[18]Wisdom is better than weapons of war,
    but one sinner destroys much good.

10 As dead flies give perfume a bad
        smell,
    so a little folly outweighs wisdom
        and honor.
[2]The heart of the wise inclines to the
        right,
    but the heart of the fool to the left.
[3]Even as he walks along the road,
    the fool lacks sense
    and shows everyone how stupid
        he is.

---

[a]2 Septuagint (Aquila), Vulgate and Syriac; Hebrew does not have *and the bad.*   [b]4 Or *What then is to be chosen? With all who live, there is hope*   [c]10 Hebrew *Sheol*

⁴If a ruler's anger rises against you,
do not leave your post;
calmness can lay great errors to rest.

⁵There is an evil I have seen under the
sun,
the sort of error that arises from a
ruler:
⁶Fools are put in many high positions,
while the rich occupy the low ones.
⁷I have seen slaves on horseback,
while princes go on foot like slaves.

⁸Whoever digs a pit may fall into it;
whoever breaks through a wall may
be bitten by a snake.
⁹Whoever quarries stones may be
injured by them;
whoever splits logs may be
endangered by them.

Prayer is . . .

*acknowledging God in
every area of your life.*

¹⁰If the ax is dull
and its edge unsharpened,
more strength is needed
but skill will bring success.

¹¹If a snake bites before it is charmed,
there is no profit for the charmer.

¹²Words from a wise man's mouth are
gracious,
but a fool is consumed by his own
lips.
¹³At the beginning his words are folly;
at the end they are wicked
madness—
¹⁴   and the fool multiplies words.

No one knows what is coming—
who can tell him what will happen
after him?

¹⁵A fool's work wearies him;
he does not know the way to town.

¹⁶Woe to you, O land whose king was
a servant[a]
and whose princes feast in the
morning.
¹⁷Blessed are you, O land whose king is
of noble birth
and whose princes eat at a proper
time—
for strength and not for
drunkenness.

¹⁸If a man is lazy, the rafters sag;
if his hands are idle, the house
leaks.

¹⁹A feast is made for laughter,
and wine makes life merry,
but money is the answer for
everything.

²⁰Do not revile the king even in your
thoughts,
or curse the rich in your bedroom,
because a bird of the air may carry
your words,
and a bird on the wing may report
what you say.

Bread Upon the Waters

11 Cast your bread upon the waters,
for after many days you will find
it again.
²Give portions to seven, yes to eight,
for you do not know what disaster
may come upon the land.

³If clouds are full of water,
they pour rain upon the earth.
Whether a tree falls to the south or to
the north,
in the place where it falls, there
will it lie.
⁴Whoever watches the wind will not
plant;
whoever looks at the clouds will
not reap.

⁵As you do not know the path of the
wind,
or how the body is formed[b] in a
mother's womb,

---

a 16 Or *king is a child*   b 5 Or *know how life* (or *the spirit*) / *enters the body being formed*

so you cannot understand the work
of God,
the Maker of all things.

6 Sow your seed in the morning,
and at evening let not your hands
be idle,
for you do not know which will
succeed,
whether this or that,
or whether both will do equally
well.

Remember Your Creator
While Young

7 Light is sweet,
and it pleases the eyes to see the
sun.
8 However many years a man may
live,
let him enjoy them all.
But let him remember the days of
darkness,
for they will be many.
Everything to come is meaningless.

9 Be happy, young man, while you are
young,
and let your heart give you joy in
the days of your youth.
Follow the ways of your heart
and whatever your eyes see,
but know that for all these things
God will bring you to judgment.
10 So then, banish anxiety from your
heart
and cast off the troubles of your
body,
for youth and vigor are
meaningless.

12 Remember your Creator
in the days of your youth,
before the days of trouble come
and the years approach when you
will say,
"I find no pleasure in them"—
2 before the sun and the light
and the moon and the stars grow
dark,

and the clouds return after the
rain;
3 when the keepers of the house
tremble,
and the strong men stoop,
when the grinders cease because they
are few,
and those looking through the
windows grow dim;
4 when the doors to the street are
closed
and the sound of grinding fades;
when men rise up at the sound of
birds,
but all their songs grow faint;
5 when men are afraid of heights
and of dangers in the streets;
when the almond tree blossoms
and the grasshopper drags himself
along
and desire no longer is stirred.
Then man goes to his eternal home
and mourners go about the
streets.

6 Remember him—before the silver
cord is severed,
or the golden bowl is broken;
before the pitcher is shattered at the
spring,
or the wheel broken at the well,
7 and the dust returns to the ground it
came from,
and the spirit returns to God who
gave it.

8 "Meaningless! Meaningless!" says the
Teacher.[a]
"Everything is meaningless!"

The Conclusion of the Matter

9 Not only was the Teacher wise, but
also he imparted knowledge to the people. He pondered and searched out and
set in order many proverbs. 10 The Teacher
searched to find just the right words, and
what he wrote was upright and true.

11 The words of the wise are like goads,
their collected sayings like firmly embed-
ded nails—given by one Shepherd. 12 Be

---

[a] 8 Or the leader of the assembly; also in verses 9 and 10

warned, my son, of anything in addition to them.

Of making many books there is no end, and much study wearies the body.

13 Now all has been heard;
here is the conclusion of the matter:
Fear God and keep his
commandments,
for this is the whole ⸤duty⸥ of man.

14 For God will bring every deed into
judgment,
including every hidden thing,
whether it is good or evil.

Praying Ecclesiastes 12:13-14

Lord, help me to remember that nothing is more important in this life than knowing, serving, obeying, and reverencing You.

Author: King Solomon

Date: During the tenth century BC

Audience: The people of God who need a positive example of pure marital love, as well as a reminder of God's passion for His beloved people

Heart-to-heart communication is an essential ingredient of good relationships.

Whether you're talking about a friendship, a marriage, or a relationship with God, intimacy requires deep and heartfelt words of love, affection, truthfulness, and tenderness. That kind of open expression of appreciation and devotion draws hearts together.

On the face of it, the Song of Songs is about love in marriage. With its sensual imagery and dialogue, this unabashedly passionate book shows us what pure and committed love is like. At a deeper spiritual level, however, many scholars believe this ancient love song was also meant to point to the kind of intimate relationship God longs to have with His people.

If your prayer life has lost its excitement, if your relationship with God has become mechanical and passionless, read the Song of Songs with the desire to learn how to pour out your love to the Lord and receive love from the great Lover of your soul.

Prayer Themes:

- *Thank God for the wonders of His deep and unfailing love for you (1:1-4).*

- *As you speak words of love to God, wait quietly before Him and hear Him speak words of love and affection to your heart (4:1; 6:4).*

- *Ask God to purify and strengthen your love for Him, so you can love Him as passionately as He loves you (8:6-7).*

Song of Songs

1 Solomon's Song of Songs.

Beloved[a]

² Let him kiss me with the kisses of his
    mouth—
  for your love is more delightful
    than wine.
³ Pleasing is the fragrance of your
    perfumes;
  your name is like perfume poured
    out.
  No wonder the maidens love you!
⁴ Take me away with you—let us hurry!
  Let the king bring me into his
    chambers.

Friends

  We rejoice and delight in you[b];
    we will praise your love more than
    wine.

Beloved

  How right they are to adore you!

⁵ Dark am I, yet lovely,
    O daughters of Jerusalem,
  dark like the tents of Kedar,
    like the tent curtains of Solomon.[c]
⁶ Do not stare at me because I am
    dark,
  because I am darkened by the sun.
  My mother's sons were angry
    with me
  and made me take care of the
    vineyards;
  my own vineyard I have
    neglected.
⁷ Tell me, you whom I love, where you
    graze your flock
  and where you rest your sheep at
    midday.

ᵃPrimarily on the basis of the gender of the Hebrew pronouns used, male and female speakers are indicated in the margins by the captions *Lover* and *Beloved* respectively. The words of others are marked *Friends*. In some instances the divisions and their captions are debatable. ᵇ*4* The Hebrew is masculine singular. ᶜ*5* Or *Salma*

Why should I be like a veiled
        woman
    beside the flocks of your friends?

Friends
8 If you do not know, most beautiful of
        women,
    follow the tracks of the sheep
and graze your young goats
    by the tents of the shepherds.

Lover
9 I liken you, my darling, to a mare
        harnessed to one of the chariots of
        Pharaoh.
10 Your cheeks are beautiful with
        earrings,
    your neck with strings of jewels.
11 We will make you earrings of gold,
        studded with silver.

Beloved
12 While the king was at his table,
    my perfume spread its fragrance.
13 My lover is to me a sachet of
        myrrh
    resting between my breasts.
14 My lover is to me a cluster of henna
        blossoms
    from the vineyards of En Gedi.

Lover
15 How beautiful you are, my darling!
    Oh, how beautiful!
    Your eyes are doves.

Beloved
16 How handsome you are, my lover!
    Oh, how charming!
    And our bed is verdant.

Lover
17 The beams of our house are cedars;
    our rafters are firs.

Beloved [a]
2 I am a rose [b] of Sharon,
    a lily of the valleys.

Lover
2 Like a lily among thorns
    is my darling among the maidens.

Beloved
3 Like an apple tree among the trees of
        the forest
    is my lover among the young men.
I delight to sit in his shade,
    and his fruit is sweet to my taste.
4 He has taken me to the banquet hall,
    and his banner over me is love.
5 Strengthen me with raisins,
    refresh me with apples,
    for I am faint with love.
6 His left arm is under my head,
    and his right arm embraces me.
7 Daughters of Jerusalem, I charge you
    by the gazelles and by the does of
        the field:
Do not arouse or awaken love
    until it so desires.

8 Listen! My lover!
    Look! Here he comes,
leaping across the mountains,
    bounding over the hills.
9 My lover is like a gazelle or a young
        stag.
    Look! There he stands behind our
        wall,
gazing through the windows,
    peering through the lattice.
10 My lover spoke and said to me,
    "Arise, my darling,
    my beautiful one, and come with
        me.
11 See! The winter is past;
    the rains are over and gone.
12 Flowers appear on the earth;
    the season of singing has come,
the cooing of doves
    is heard in our land.
13 The fig tree forms its early fruit;
    the blossoming vines spread their
        fragrance.
Arise, come, my darling;
    my beautiful one, come with me."

Lover
14 My dove in the clefts of the rock,
    in the hiding places on the
        mountainside,

---

a Or Lover   b 1 Possibly a member of the crocus family

Loving the One Who Loves You Most

The love issue is a big one. There is no one who doesn't want or need love, especially if it was completely missing during some period of their development as a child. But we don't have to live without it, because God loves us completely and continually. There is nothing you can do that would make Him love you any more or any less than He does right now. And God's love is the same for everyone.

When you think of the worst person on earth, whom do you think of? An evil dictator? A serial killer? A child molester? A wife abuser? Well, God loves each one of them. He hates their sins, just the way He hates yours and mine, but He loves the person. Though it's hard to imagine, it's true.

When a child does things his parents don't like, they still love him. It's the same with your heavenly Father. His love is always there for you no matter what you have done. *People's* love for us may change, depending on what we do or don't do to please them. But *God's* does not. He loves you with an eternal, undying, everlasting, unconditional love. The love we feel from some people often depends on how valuable we are to them at the moment.

God says we are valuable to Him at all times. The times when I most sense God's love for me is when I worship in a group of people gathered together for that purpose. An extremely powerful dynamic happens when people worship together. I'm not talking about just getting together to sing nice songs *about* God. I'm talking about worshiping God for who He is with all we have in us. There is nothing more healing, restoring, or life changing.

Once you sense God's love through those times of corporate praise and worship, you won't want to ever live without it.

God doesn't want us to praise Him just with our mouths; He wants us to praise Him with our whole hearts. He doesn't want us to praise Him just because someone said to; He wants us to praise Him because we love Him. "These people come near to me with their mouth and honor me with their lips, but their hearts are far from me. Their worship of me is made up only of rules taught by men" (Isaiah 29:13). When you understand how much God loves you, you can't help but praise Him for it.

One of the wonderful things that happens when we worship the God of love is that He fills us with His love and then we become a conduit of His love to others. His love *for* us causes love to grow *in* us for other people, some of whom we might not even think to love. "Whoever does not love does not know God, because God is love" (1 John 4:8).

One thing about falling in love with someone who loves you back is that no matter how much you see each other, it is never enough. You always want more. Once you feel God's love *for* you, *in* you, and *around* you, you will want to be in His presence all the time. Jesus said, "Love the Lord your God with all your heart and with all your soul and with all your mind" (Matthew 22:37). *That's a lot of love.*

That's with everything we have in us.

With our whole being.

Unconditional. Complete.

For the next "From Stormie's Heart" article, go to page 886.

show me your face,
  let me hear your voice;
for your voice is sweet,
  and your face is lovely.
¹⁵Catch for us the foxes,
  the little foxes
that ruin the vineyards,
  our vineyards that are in bloom.

Beloved
¹⁶My lover is mine and I am his;
  he browses among the lilies.
¹⁷Until the day breaks
  and the shadows flee,
turn, my lover,
  and be like a gazelle
or like a young stag
  on the rugged hills.^a

3 All night long on my bed
  I looked for the one my heart loves;
  I looked for him but did not find
    him.
²I will get up now and go about the
    city,
  through its streets and squares;
I will search for the one my heart
    loves.
  So I looked for him but did not
    find him.
³The watchmen found me
  as they made their rounds in the
    city.
  "Have you seen the one my heart
    loves?"
⁴Scarcely had I passed them
  when I found the one my heart
    loves.
I held him and would not let
    him go
till I had brought him to my
    mother's house,
  to the room of the one who
    conceived me.
⁵Daughters of Jerusalem, I charge you
  by the gazelles and by the does of
    the field:
Do not arouse or awaken love
  until it so desires.

⁶Who is this coming up from the
    desert
  like a column of smoke,
perfumed with myrrh and incense
  made from all the spices of the
    merchant?
⁷Look! It is Solomon's carriage,
  escorted by sixty warriors,
  the noblest of Israel,
⁸all of them wearing the sword,
  all experienced in battle,
each with his sword at his side,
  prepared for the terrors of the
    night.
⁹King Solomon made for himself the
    carriage;
  he made it of wood from Lebanon.
¹⁰Its posts he made of silver,
  its base of gold.
Its seat was upholstered with purple,
  its interior lovingly inlaid
  by^b the daughters of Jerusalem.
¹¹Come out, you daughters of Zion,
  and look at King Solomon wearing
    the crown,
  the crown with which his mother
    crowned him
on the day of his wedding,
  the day his heart rejoiced.

Lover
4 How beautiful you are, my darling!
  Oh, how beautiful!
  Your eyes behind your veil are
    doves.
Your hair is like a flock of goats
  descending from Mount Gilead.
²Your teeth are like a flock of sheep
    just shorn,
  coming up from the washing.
Each has its twin;
  not one of them is alone.
³Your lips are like a scarlet ribbon;
  your mouth is lovely.
Your temples behind your veil
  are like the halves of a
    pomegranate.
⁴Your neck is like the tower of David,
  built with elegance^c;

---

^a 17 Or the hills of Bether   ^b 10 Or its inlaid interior a gift of love / from   ^c 4 The meaning of the Hebrew for this word is uncertain.

A Stream of Refreshing

GOING deeper

READ AND CONSIDER: SONG OF SONGS 4

"You are a garden fountain, a well of flowing water streaming down from Lebanon" (Song of Songs 4:15).

Wouldn't it be wonderful to be thought of as a well of living water, flowing like a refreshing stream? Especially by the people around us and those closest to us in our lives. Wouldn't it be great to be loved, adored, and appreciated in the way that adoration is described in chapter 4? But that is the way God thinks about His people. He loves us with a beautiful and unfailing love.

We all want to have a committed, deep, pure, unconditional, sacrificing, heart-uniting relationship in our lives with someone who will not leave or forsake us for someone better. We all want to be thought of as spotless and flawless. We all want to be remembered as pleasing and beautiful. And that is the way God already thinks of us. He sees us through His Son, Jesus, who is all those things. And because we have received Jesus into our lives, His beauty, purity, and perfection is what God sees in us. And the more we spend time with the Lord and surrender our lives completely to His will, the more others will see *Him* in us.

The Holy Spirit flowing in us is what enables us to be a stream of refreshing for other people. All we have to do is open up to His flow in our lives by inviting His presence to fill us afresh each day. When we do, He will pour out on us His river of living water and His everlasting flow of love. That, along with the beauty of His presence in us, will be more than enough to attract others with a refreshing that will wash over their souls.

on it hang a thousand shields,
  all of them shields of warriors.
5 Your two breasts are like two fawns,
  like twin fawns of a gazelle
  that browse among the lilies.
6 Until the day breaks
  and the shadows flee,
 I will go to the mountain of myrrh
  and to the hill of incense.
7 All beautiful you are, my darling;
  there is no flaw in you.

8 Come with me from Lebanon, my
  bride,
  come with me from Lebanon.
 Descend from the crest of Amana,
  from the top of Senir, the summit
   of Hermon,
 from the lions' dens
  and the mountain haunts of the
   leopards.
9 You have stolen my heart, my sister,
  my bride;

you have stolen my heart
 with one glance of your eyes,
 with one jewel of your necklace.
10 How delightful is your love, my
  sister, my bride!
 How much more pleasing is your
  love than wine,
 and the fragrance of your perfume
  than any spice!
11 Your lips drop sweetness as the
  honeycomb, my bride;
 milk and honey are under your
  tongue.
 The fragrance of your garments is
  like that of Lebanon.
12 You are a garden locked up, my sister,
  my bride;
 you are a spring enclosed, a sealed
  fountain.
13 Your plants are an orchard of
  pomegranates
  with choice fruits,

with henna and nard,
14 nard and saffron,
   calamus and cinnamon,
   with every kind of incense tree,
   with myrrh and aloes
   and all the finest spices.
15 You are[a] a garden fountain,
   a well of flowing water
   streaming down from Lebanon.

Beloved
16 Awake, north wind,
   and come, south wind!
 Blow on my garden,
   that its fragrance may spread
     abroad.
 Let my lover come into his garden
   and taste its choice fruits.

Lover
5 I have come into my garden, my
   sister, my bride;
 I have gathered my myrrh with my
   spice.
 I have eaten my honeycomb and my
   honey;
 I have drunk my wine and my
   milk.

Friends
 Eat, O friends, and drink;
   drink your fill, O lovers.

Beloved
2 I slept but my heart was awake.
   Listen! My lover is knocking:
 "Open to me, my sister, my darling,
   my dove, my flawless one.
 My head is drenched with dew,
   my hair with the dampness of the
     night."
3 I have taken off my robe—
   must I put it on again?
 I have washed my feet—
   must I soil them again?
4 My lover thrust his hand through the
   latch-opening;
   my heart began to pound for him.
5 I arose to open for my lover,
   and my hands dripped with myrrh,

my fingers with flowing myrrh,
   on the handles of the lock.
6 I opened for my lover,
   but my lover had left; he was gone.
   My heart sank at his departure.[b]
 I looked for him but did not find him.
   I called him but he did not answer.
7 The watchmen found me
   as they made their rounds in the
     city.
 They beat me, they bruised me;
   they took away my cloak,
   those watchmen of the walls!
8 O daughters of Jerusalem, I charge
     you—
   if you find my lover,
 what will you tell him?
   Tell him I am faint with love.

Friends
9 How is your beloved better than
     others,
   most beautiful of women?
 How is your beloved better than
     others,
   that you charge us so?

Beloved
10 My lover is radiant and ruddy,
   outstanding among ten thousand.
11 His head is purest gold;
   his hair is wavy
   and black as a raven.
12 His eyes are like doves
   by the water streams,
 washed in milk,
   mounted like jewels.
13 His cheeks are like beds of spice
   yielding perfume.
 His lips are like lilies
   dripping with myrrh.
14 His arms are rods of gold
   set with chrysolite.
 His body is like polished ivory
   decorated with sapphires.[c]
15 His legs are pillars of marble
   set on bases of pure gold.
 His appearance is like Lebanon,
   choice as its cedars.

a 15 Or I am (spoken by the Beloved)   b 6 Or heart had gone out to him when he spoke   c 14 Or lapis lazuli

16His mouth is sweetness itself;
   he is altogether lovely.
This is my lover, this my friend,
   O daughters of Jerusalem.

Friends

6 Where has your lover gone,
   most beautiful of women?
Which way did your lover turn,
   that we may look for him with
     you?

Beloved

2My lover has gone down to his
     garden,
   to the beds of spices,
to browse in the gardens
   and to gather lilies.
3I am my lover's and my lover is
     mine;
   he browses among the lilies.

Lover

4You are beautiful, my darling, as
     Tirzah,
   lovely as Jerusalem,
   majestic as troops with banners.
5Turn your eyes from me;
   they overwhelm me.
Your hair is like a flock of goats
   descending from Gilead.
6Your teeth are like a flock of sheep
   coming up from the washing.
Each has its twin,
   not one of them is alone.
7Your temples behind your veil
   are like the halves of a
     pomegranate.
8Sixty queens there may be,
   and eighty concubines,
   and virgins beyond number;
9but my dove, my perfect one, is
     unique,
   the only daughter of her mother,
   the favorite of the one who bore
     her.
The maidens saw her and called her
     blessed;
   the queens and concubines praised
     her.

Friends

10Who is this that appears like the dawn,
   fair as the moon, bright as the sun,
   majestic as the stars in procession?

Lover

11I went down to the grove of nut trees
   to look at the new growth in the
     valley,
to see if the vines had budded
   or the pomegranates were in
     bloom.
12Before I realized it,
   my desire set me among the royal
     chariots of my people.[a]

Friends

13Come back, come back,
   O Shulammite;
   come back, come back, that we
     may gaze on you!

Lover

Why would you gaze on the
     Shulammite
   as on the dance of Mahanaim?

7 How beautiful your sandaled feet,
   O prince's daughter!
Your graceful legs are like jewels,
   the work of a craftsman's hands.
2Your navel is a rounded goblet
   that never lacks blended wine.
Your waist is a mound of wheat
   encircled by lilies.
3Your breasts are like two fawns,
   twins of a gazelle.
4Your neck is like an ivory tower.
Your eyes are the pools of Heshbon
   by the gate of Bath Rabbim.
Your nose is like the tower of
     Lebanon
   looking toward Damascus.
5Your head crowns you like Mount
     Carmel.
   Your hair is like royal tapestry;
   the king is held captive by its
     tresses.
6How beautiful you are and how
     pleasing,

---

a 12 Or *among the chariots of Amminadab;* or *among the chariots of the people of the prince*

O love, with your delights!
⁷Your stature is like that of the palm,
  and your breasts like clusters of
    fruit.
⁸I said, "I will climb the palm tree;
  I will take hold of its fruit."
May your breasts be like the clusters
    of the vine,
  the fragrance of your breath like
    apples,
⁹ and your mouth like the best wine.

Beloved
  May the wine go straight to my lover,
    flowing gently over lips and teeth.ᵃ
¹⁰I belong to my lover,
  and his desire is for me.
¹¹Come, my lover, let us go to the
    countryside,
  let us spend the night in the
    villages.ᵇ
¹²Let us go early to the vineyards
  to see if the vines have budded,
  if their blossoms have opened,
    and if the pomegranates are in
      bloom—
  there I will give you my love.
¹³The mandrakes send out their
    fragrance,
  and at our door is every delicacy,
  both new and old,
    that I have stored up for you, my
      lover.

8 If only you were to me like a
    brother,
  who was nursed at my mother's
    breasts!
Then, if I found you outside,
  I would kiss you,
  and no one would despise me.
²I would lead you
  and bring you to my mother's
    house—
  she who has taught me.
I would give you spiced wine to
    drink,
  the nectar of my pomegranates.

³His left arm is under my head
  and his right arm embraces me.
⁴Daughters of Jerusalem, I charge you:
  Do not arouse or awaken love
  until it so desires.

Friends
⁵Who is this coming up from the desert
  leaning on her lover?

Beloved
  Under the apple tree I roused you;
    there your mother conceived you,
      there she who was in labor gave
        you birth.
⁶Place me like a seal over your heart,
  like a seal on your arm;
  for love is as strong as death,
    its jealousyᶜ unyielding as the
      grave.ᵈ
  It burns like blazing fire,
    like a mighty flame.ᵉ

Praying Song of Songs 8:6
*Teach me, Lord, to love others
the way that You love me.*

⁷Many waters cannot quench love;
  rivers cannot wash it away.
If one were to give
  all the wealth of his house for love,
  itᶠ would be utterly scorned.

Friends
⁸We have a young sister,
  and her breasts are not yet grown.
What shall we do for our sister
  for the day she is spoken for?
⁹If she is a wall,
  we will build towers of silver on her.
If she is a door,
  we will enclose her with panels of
    cedar.

Beloved
¹⁰I am a wall,
  and my breasts are like towers.
Thus I have become in his eyes
  like one bringing contentment.

ᵃ 9 Septuagint, Aquila, Vulgate and Syriac; Hebrew *lips of sleepers*   ᵇ 11 Or *henna bushes*   ᶜ 6 Or *ardor*   ᵈ 6 Hebrew *Sheol*
ᵉ 6 Or / *like the very flame of the* LORD   ᶠ 7 Or *he*

11Solomon had a vineyard in Baal
    Hamon;
  he let out his vineyard to tenants.
  Each was to bring for its fruit
  a thousand shekels[a] of silver.
12But my own vineyard is mine to give;
  the thousand shekels are for you,
    O Solomon,
  and two hundred[b] are for those
  who tend its fruit.

Lover

13You who dwell in the gardens
  with friends in attendance,
  let me hear your voice!

Beloved

14Come away, my lover,
  and be like a gazelle
  or like a young stag
  on the spice-laden mountains.

---

[a] *11* That is, about 25 pounds (about 11.5 kilograms); also in verse 12   [b] *12* That is, about 5 pounds (about 2.3 kilograms)

Author: Isaiah

Date: Between 701 and 681 BC

Audience: The southern kingdom of Judah—to warn of coming judgment for sin, to encourage with reminders of God's unending love for His people

Prayer Themes:

- Tell God that you desire a close relationship with Him, that you want to love and trust Him above all else (5:11-17).

- Thank God for the promise that you do not have to fear death or eternal judgment; instead, you can forever walk with Him and rejoice in His great salvation (25:8-9).

- Thank God for His greatness and power that allow you to "run and not grow weary . . . walk and not be faint" (40:12-31).

The very idea of prayer is amazing. Through prayer we have access to God. Even though we are sin-tainted creatures, we can come before the throne of the King of heaven and earth and make requests, knowing that He hears us. But too often we don't stay in communication with God long enough to hear what He wants to speak to our hearts. When we don't listen to God or don't heed God's messengers, there is a price to pay for it. That is what Isaiah was trying to tell the people of Judah.

Isaiah prophesied coming judgment on Judah if they didn't repent of their ways. He wanted them to hear what God was saying to them. But in his warnings, there was always a message of hope: If they would listen to God and repent, He would hear and forgive.

Prayer needs to become *more* than a list of requests we bring before God, although He does want us to ask for things. It needs to be, above all, a relationship with Him. In a close relationship, both parties get to talk. And both need to listen. Too often, with God, we do all the talking and we don't take time to listen.

God is always willing to hear us and forgive us when we have repentant hearts. So let's never forget to heed the divine invitation to "seek the Lord while he may be found; call on him while he is near" (55:6). And let's remember to ask Him what He desires to speak to our hearts.

Isaiah

1 The vision concerning Judah and Jerusalem that Isaiah son of Amoz saw during the reigns of Uzziah, Jotham, Ahaz and Hezekiah, kings of Judah.

A Rebellious Nation

2 Hear, O heavens! Listen, O earth!
    For the Lord has spoken:
"I reared children and brought them
        up,
    but they have rebelled against
        me.
3 The ox knows his master,
    the donkey his owner's manger,

but Israel does not know,
    my people do not understand."

4 Ah, sinful nation,
    a people loaded with guilt,
a brood of evildoers,
    children given to corruption!
They have forsaken the Lord;
    they have spurned the Holy One of
        Israel
    and turned their backs on him.

5 Why should you be beaten anymore?
    Why do you persist in rebellion?
Your whole head is injured,

your whole heart afflicted.
6 From the sole of your foot to the top
of your head
there is no soundness—
only wounds and welts
and open sores,
not cleansed or bandaged
or soothed with oil.

7 Your country is desolate,
your cities burned with fire;
your fields are being stripped by
foreigners
right before you,
laid waste as when overthrown by
strangers.
8 The Daughter of Zion is left
like a shelter in a vineyard,
like a hut in a field of melons,
like a city under siege.
9 Unless the LORD Almighty
had left us some survivors,
we would have become like Sodom,
we would have been like
Gomorrah.

10 Hear the word of the LORD,
you rulers of Sodom;
listen to the law of our God,
you people of Gomorrah!
11 "The multitude of your sacrifices—
what are they to me?" says the
LORD.
"I have more than enough of burnt
offerings,
of rams and the fat of fattened
animals;
I have no pleasure
in the blood of bulls and lambs and
goats.
12 When you come to appear before me,
who has asked this of you,
this trampling of my courts?
13 Stop bringing meaningless
offerings!
Your incense is detestable to me.
New Moons, Sabbaths and
convocations—
I cannot bear your evil assemblies.

14 Your New Moon festivals and your
appointed feasts
my soul hates.
They have become a burden to me;
I am weary of bearing them.
15 When you spread out your hands in
prayer,
I will hide my eyes from you;
even if you offer many prayers,
I will not listen.
Your hands are full of blood;
16   wash and make yourselves clean.
Take your evil deeds
out of my sight!
Stop doing wrong,
17   learn to do right!
Seek justice,
encourage the oppressed.ª
Defend the cause of the fatherless,
plead the case of the widow.

Praying Isaiah 1:16-17
*Lord, help me to cleanse myself
from all evil so that I can be an
instrument in Your hands to help
those who can't help themselves.*

18 "Come now, let us reason together,"
says the LORD.
"Though your sins are like scarlet,
they shall be as white as snow;
though they are red as crimson,
they shall be like wool.
19 If you are willing and obedient,
you will eat the best from the land;
20 but if you resist and rebel,
you will be devoured by the sword."
For the mouth of the LORD
has spoken.

21 See how the faithful city
has become a harlot!
She once was full of justice;
righteousness used to dwell in her—
but now murderers!
22 Your silver has become dross,
your choice wine is diluted with
water.
23 Your rulers are rebels,

ª 17 Or / rebuke the oppressor

companions of thieves;
  they all love bribes
  and chase after gifts.
They do not defend the cause of the
    fatherless;
  the widow's case does not come
    before them.
²⁴Therefore the Lord, the LORD
    Almighty,
  the Mighty One of Israel, declares:
"Ah, I will get relief from my foes
  and avenge myself on my enemies.
²⁵I will turn my hand against you;
  I will thoroughly purge away your
    dross
  and remove all your impurities.
²⁶I will restore your judges as in days of
    old,
  your counselors as at the beginning.
Afterward you will be called
  the City of Righteousness,
  the Faithful City."

²⁷Zion will be redeemed with justice,
  her penitent ones with
    righteousness.
²⁸But rebels and sinners will both be
    broken,
  and those who forsake the LORD
    will perish.

²⁹"You will be ashamed because of the
    sacred oaks
  in which you have delighted;
you will be disgraced because of the
    gardens
  that you have chosen.
³⁰You will be like an oak with fading
    leaves,
  like a garden without water.
³¹The mighty man will become tinder
  and his work a spark;
  both will burn together,
  with no one to quench the fire."

The Mountain of the LORD

2 This is what Isaiah son of Amoz saw
  concerning Judah and Jerusalem:

²In the last days

the mountain of the LORD's temple
  will be established
  as chief among the mountains;
it will be raised above the hills,
  and all nations will stream to it.

³Many peoples will come and say,

"Come, let us go up to the mountain
    of the LORD,
  to the house of the God of Jacob.
He will teach us his ways,
  so that we may walk in his paths."
The law will go out from Zion,
  the word of the LORD from
    Jerusalem.
⁴He will judge between the nations
  and will settle disputes for many
    peoples.
They will beat their swords into
    plowshares
  and their spears into pruning
    hooks.
Nation will not take up sword against
    nation,
  nor will they train for war
    anymore.

⁵Come, O house of Jacob,
  let us walk in the light of the LORD.

The Day of the LORD

⁶You have abandoned your people,
  the house of Jacob.
They are full of superstitions from the
    East;
  they practice divination like the
    Philistines
  and clasp hands with pagans.
⁷Their land is full of silver and gold;
  there is no end to their treasures.
Their land is full of horses;
  there is no end to their chariots.
⁸Their land is full of idols;
  they bow down to the work of
    their hands,
  to what their fingers have made.
⁹So man will be brought low
  and mankind humbled—
  do not forgive them.ᵃ

ᵃ 9 Or *not raise them up*

10 Go into the rocks,
  hide in the ground
from dread of the LORD
  and the splendor of his majesty!
11 The eyes of the arrogant man will be
    humbled
  and the pride of men brought low;
the LORD alone will be exalted in that
    day.

12 The LORD Almighty has a day in
    store
  for all the proud and lofty,
  for all that is exalted
  (and they will be humbled),
13 for all the cedars of Lebanon, tall and
    lofty,
  and all the oaks of Bashan,
14 for all the towering mountains
  and all the high hills,
15 for every lofty tower
  and every fortified wall,
16 for every trading ship[a]
  and every stately vessel.
17 The arrogance of man will be
    brought low
  and the pride of men humbled;
the LORD alone will be exalted in that
    day,
18   and the idols will totally disappear.

19 Men will flee to caves in the rocks
  and to holes in the ground
from dread of the LORD
  and the splendor of his majesty,
  when he rises to shake the earth.
20 In that day men will throw away
  to the rodents and bats
their idols of silver and idols of
    gold,
  which they made to worship.
21 They will flee to caverns in the rocks
  and to the overhanging crags
from dread of the LORD
  and the splendor of his majesty,
  when he rises to shake the earth.

22 Stop trusting in man,
  who has but a breath in his nostrils.
Of what account is he?

Judgment on Jerusalem and Judah

3 See now, the Lord,
  the LORD Almighty,
is about to take from Jerusalem and
    Judah
  both supply and support:
all supplies of food and all supplies of
    water,
2   the hero and warrior,
  the judge and prophet,
  the soothsayer and elder,
3 the captain of fifty and man of rank,
  the counselor, skilled craftsman and
    clever enchanter.

4 I will make boys their officials;
  mere children will govern them.
5 People will oppress each other—
  man against man, neighbor against
    neighbor.
The young will rise up against the
    old,
  the base against the honorable.

6 A man will seize one of his brothers
  at his father's home, and say,
"You have a cloak, you be our leader;
  take charge of this heap of ruins!"
7 But in that day he will cry out,
  "I have no remedy.
I have no food or clothing in my
    house;
  do not make me the leader of the
    people."

8 Jerusalem staggers,
  Judah is falling;
their words and deeds are against the
    LORD,
  defying his glorious presence.
9 The look on their faces testifies
    against them;
  they parade their sin like Sodom;
  they do not hide it.
Woe to them!
  They have brought disaster upon
    themselves.

10 Tell the righteous it will be well with
    them,

---

a 16 Hebrew *every ship of Tarshish*

for they will enjoy the fruit of their
  deeds.
11 Woe to the wicked! Disaster is upon
  them!
They will be paid back for what their
  hands have done.

12 Youths oppress my people,
  women rule over them.
O my people, your guides lead you
  astray;
  they turn you from the path.

13 The LORD takes his place in court;
  he rises to judge the people.
14 The LORD enters into judgment
  against the elders and leaders of his
  people:
"It is you who have ruined my
  vineyard;
  the plunder from the poor is in
  your houses.
15 What do you mean by crushing my
  people
  and grinding the faces of the
  poor?"
          declares the Lord,
          the LORD Almighty.

16 The LORD says,
"The women of Zion are haughty,
  walking along with outstretched
  necks,
  flirting with their eyes,
tripping along with mincing steps,
  with ornaments jingling on their
  ankles.
17 Therefore the Lord will bring sores
  on the heads of the women of
  Zion;
  the LORD will make their scalps
  bald."

18 In that day the Lord will snatch away
their finery: the bangles and headbands
and crescent necklaces, 19 the earrings and
bracelets and veils, 20 the headdresses and
ankle chains and sashes, the perfume bot-
tles and charms, 21 the signet rings and
nose rings, 22 the fine robes and the capes

and cloaks, the purses 23 and mirrors, and
the linen garments and tiaras and shawls.

24 Instead of fragrance there will be a
  stench;
  instead of a sash, a rope;
instead of well-dressed hair, baldness;
  instead of fine clothing, sackcloth;
  instead of beauty, branding.
25 Your men will fall by the sword,
  your warriors in battle.
26 The gates of Zion will lament and
  mourn;
  destitute, she will sit on the
  ground.
4 1 In that day seven women
  will take hold of one man
and say, "We will eat our own food
  and provide our own clothes;
  only let us be called by your name.
  Take away our disgrace!"

The Branch of the LORD

2 In that day the Branch of the LORD
will be beautiful and glorious, and the
fruit of the land will be the pride and
glory of the survivors in Israel. 3 Those
who are left in Zion, who remain in Jerusalem, will be called holy, all who are
recorded among the living in Jerusalem.
4 The Lord will wash away the filth of
the women of Zion; he will cleanse the
bloodstains from Jerusalem by a spirit[a] of
judgment and a spirit[a] of fire. 5 Then the
LORD will create over all of Mount Zion
and over those who assemble there a
cloud of smoke by day and a glow of flaming fire by night; over all the glory will be
a canopy. 6 It will be a shelter and shade
from the heat of the day, and a refuge and
hiding place from the storm and rain.

The Song of the Vineyard

5 I will sing for the one I love
  a song about his vineyard:
My loved one had a vineyard
  on a fertile hillside.
2 He dug it up and cleared it of stones
  and planted it with the choicest
  vines.

He built a watchtower in it
   and cut out a winepress as well.
Then he looked for a crop of good
     grapes,
   but it yielded only bad fruit.

3 "Now you dwellers in Jerusalem and
     men of Judah,
   judge between me and my
     vineyard.
4 What more could have been done for
     my vineyard
   than I have done for it?
When I looked for good grapes,
   why did it yield only bad?
5 Now I will tell you
   what I am going to do to my
     vineyard:
I will take away its hedge,
   and it will be destroyed;
I will break down its wall,
   and it will be trampled.
6 I will make it a wasteland,
   neither pruned nor cultivated,
   and briers and thorns will grow
     there.
I will command the clouds
   not to rain on it."

7 The vineyard of the LORD Almighty
   is the house of Israel,
and the men of Judah
   are the garden of his delight.
And he looked for justice, but saw
     bloodshed;
   for righteousness, but heard cries of
     distress.

Woes and Judgments

8 Woe to you who add house to house
   and join field to field
till no space is left
   and you live alone in the land.

9 The LORD Almighty has declared in
my hearing:

   "Surely the great houses will become
     desolate,

   the fine mansions left without
     occupants.
10 A ten-acre[a] vineyard will produce
   only a bath[b] of wine,
   a homer[c] of seed only an ephah[d] of
     grain."

11 Woe to those who rise early in the
     morning
   to run after their drinks,
who stay up late at night
   till they are inflamed with wine.
12 They have harps and lyres at their
     banquets,
   tambourines and flutes and wine,
but they have no regard for the deeds
     of the LORD,
   no respect for the work of his
     hands.
13 Therefore my people will go into
     exile
   for lack of understanding;
their men of rank will die of hunger
   and their masses will be parched
     with thirst.
14 Therefore the grave[e] enlarges its
     appetite
   and opens its mouth without limit;
into it will descend their nobles and
     masses
   with all their brawlers and revelers.
15 So man will be brought low
   and mankind humbled,
   the eyes of the arrogant humbled.
16 But the LORD Almighty will be
     exalted by his justice,
   and the holy God will show himself
     holy by his righteousness.
17 Then sheep will graze as in their own
     pasture;
   lambs will feed[f] among the ruins of
     the rich.

18 Woe to those who draw sin along
     with cords of deceit,
   and wickedness as with cart ropes,
19 to those who say, "Let God hurry,
   let him hasten his work

---

a 10 Hebrew *ten-yoke*, that is, the land plowed by 10 yoke of oxen in one day   b 10 That is, probably about 6 gallons (about
22 liters)   c 10 That is, probably about 6 bushels (about 220 liters)   d 10 That is, probably about 3/5 bushel (about 22 liters)
e 14 Hebrew *Sheol*   f 17 Septuagint; Hebrew / strangers will eat

so we may see it.
Let it approach,
let the plan of the Holy One of
Israel come,
so we may know it."

20 Woe to those who call evil good
and good evil,
who put darkness for light
and light for darkness,
who put bitter for sweet
and sweet for bitter.

21 Woe to those who are wise in their
own eyes
and clever in their own sight.

Praying Isaiah 5:20-21

*Dear God, may I never fall into
the confusion of the world and become
so wise in my own eyes that I can
see evil and call it good.*

22 Woe to those who are heroes at
drinking wine
and champions at mixing
drinks,
23 who acquit the guilty for a bribe,
but deny justice to the innocent.
24 Therefore, as tongues of fire lick up
straw
and as dry grass sinks down in the
flames,
so their roots will decay
and their flowers blow away like
dust;
for they have rejected the law of the
LORD Almighty
and spurned the word of the Holy
One of Israel.
25 Therefore the LORD's anger burns
against his people;
his hand is raised and he strikes
them down.
The mountains shake,
and the dead bodies are like refuse
in the streets.
Yet for all this, his anger is not turned
away,
his hand is still upraised.

26 He lifts up a banner for the distant
nations,
he whistles for those at the ends of
the earth.
Here they come,
swiftly and speedily!
27 Not one of them grows tired or
stumbles,
not one slumbers or sleeps;
not a belt is loosened at the waist,
not a sandal thong is broken.
28 Their arrows are sharp,
all their bows are strung;
their horses' hoofs seem like flint,
their chariot wheels like a
whirlwind.
29 Their roar is like that of the lion,
they roar like young lions;
they growl as they seize their prey
and carry it off with no one to
rescue.
30 In that day they will roar over it
like the roaring of the sea.
And if one looks at the land,
he will see darkness and
distress;
even the light will be darkened by
the clouds.

Isaiah's Commission

6 In the year that King Uzziah died,
I saw the Lord seated on a throne,
high and exalted, and the train of his
robe filled the temple. 2 Above him were
seraphs, each with six wings: With two
wings they covered their faces, with
two they covered their feet, and with two
they were flying. 3 And they were calling
to one another:

"Holy, holy, holy is the LORD
Almighty;
the whole earth is full of his
glory."

4 At the sound of their voices the doorposts and thresholds shook and the temple was filled with smoke.
5 "Woe to me!" I cried. "I am ruined!
For I am a man of unclean lips, and I live
among a people of unclean lips, and my

Standing Before Our Holy God

GOING deeper

READ AND CONSIDER: ISAIAH 6:1-8

"'Woe to me!' I cried. 'I am ruined! For I am a man of unclean lips, and I live among a people of unclean lips, and my eyes have seen the King, the LORD Almighty'" (Isaiah 6:5).

When Isaiah, one of God's greatest prophets, had a vision of God with the angels worshiping Him around His throne, he realized his own unworthiness and sin. He said, "I am ruined!" When he confessed his sin, God touched him and purified him. God's holiness made him aware of his own lack of it. It also made him whole.

Sin chips away pieces of our soul. With enough sin, we become a pile of broken pieces. But God's holiness is what purifies us and helps us to separate ourselves from all that is *unholy*. There is a correlation between God's holiness and our wholeness. That's why when we are in His presence, we become more whole. *God's holiness makes us whole.* Whenever the great men of faith in the Bible, such as Job, Abraham, and Moses, had a close encounter with God, they saw their own failings. That's what happens to us too.

You may be thinking, *Why do I need to become more aware of my own failings? I am already well aware of them. Thinking about them is just going to make me feel worse about myself than I already do.*

But understanding God's holiness doesn't make you feel bad about yourself in a way that leads to depression. It makes you feel drawn toward His holiness in a way that leads to restoration. It convicts you rather than condemns you. It's actually liberating.

The Bible tells us to "approach the throne of grace with confidence, so that we may receive mercy and find grace to help us in our time of need" (Hebrews 4:16). We certainly should be humble as we bring our unworthiness to His throne. Yet we can be confident because we know we are called and loved. We can come to God anytime, knowing that He wants us there and that He will cleanse our hearts and make us more like Him.

Ask the Lord to help you comprehend His holiness. Then acknowledge your own lack of it and pray that who He is will rub off on you.

---

eyes have seen the King, the LORD Almighty."

⁶Then one of the seraphs flew to me with a live coal in his hand, which he had taken with tongs from the altar. ⁷With it he touched my mouth and said, "See, this has touched your lips; your guilt is taken away and your sin atoned for."

⁸Then I heard the voice of the Lord saying, "Whom shall I send? And who will go for us?"

And I said, "Here am I. Send me!"

⁹He said, "Go and tell this people:

"'Be ever hearing, but never understanding;
be ever seeing, but never perceiving.'
¹⁰Make the heart of this people calloused;
make their ears dull
and close their eyes.ᵃ
Otherwise they might see with their eyes,
hear with their ears,
understand with their hearts,
and turn and be healed."

ᵃ 9,10 Hebrew; Septuagint *'You will be ever hearing, but never understanding; / you will be ever seeing, but never perceiving.' /* ¹⁰*This people's heart has become calloused; / they hardly hear with their ears, / and they have closed their eyes*

[11] Then I said, "For how long, O Lord?"
And he answered:

"Until the cities lie ruined
    and without inhabitant,
until the houses are left deserted
    and the fields ruined and ravaged,
[12] until the LORD has sent everyone far
        away
    and the land is utterly forsaken.
[13] And though a tenth remains in the
        land,
    it will again be laid waste.
But as the terebinth and oak
    leave stumps when they are cut
        down,
    so the holy seed will be the stump
        in the land."

The Sign of Immanuel

7 When Ahaz son of Jotham, the son of
Uzziah, was king of Judah, King Rezin
of Aram and Pekah son of Remaliah king
of Israel marched up to fight against Jerusalem, but they could not overpower it.

[2] Now the house of David was told,
"Aram has allied itself with[a] Ephraim";
so the hearts of Ahaz and his people
were shaken, as the trees of the forest are
shaken by the wind.

[3] Then the LORD said to Isaiah, "Go out,
you and your son Shear-Jashub,[b] to meet
Ahaz at the end of the aqueduct of the
Upper Pool, on the road to the Washerman's Field. [4] Say to him, 'Be careful, keep
calm and don't be afraid. Do not lose
heart because of these two smoldering
stubs of firewood—because of the fierce
anger of Rezin and Aram and of the son
of Remaliah. [5] Aram, Ephraim and Remaliah's son have plotted your ruin, saying,
[6] "Let us invade Judah; let us tear it apart
and divide it among ourselves, and make
the son of Tabeel king over it." [7] Yet this
is what the Sovereign LORD says:

"'It will not take place,
    it will not happen,
[8] for the head of Aram is Damascus,

and the head of Damascus is only
        Rezin.
Within sixty-five years
    Ephraim will be too shattered to be
        a people.
[9] The head of Ephraim is Samaria,
    and the head of Samaria is only
        Remaliah's son.
If you do not stand firm in your faith,
    you will not stand at all.'"

[10] Again the LORD spoke to Ahaz,
[11] "Ask the LORD your God for a sign,
whether in the deepest depths or in the
highest heights."

[12] But Ahaz said, "I will not ask; I will
not put the LORD to the test."

[13] Then Isaiah said, "Hear now, you
house of David! Is it not enough to try
the patience of men? Will you try the patience of my God also? [14] Therefore the
Lord himself will give you[c] a sign: The virgin will be with child and will give birth
to a son, and[d] will call him Immanuel.[e]
[15] He will eat curds and honey when he
knows enough to reject the wrong and
choose the right. [16] But before the boy
knows enough to reject the wrong and
choose the right, the land of the two
kings you dread will be laid waste. [17] The
LORD will bring on you and on your
people and on the house of your father
a time unlike any since Ephraim broke
away from Judah—he will bring the king
of Assyria."

[18] In that day the LORD will whistle for
flies from the distant streams of Egypt and
for bees from the land of Assyria. [19] They
will all come and settle in the steep ravines and in the crevices in the rocks, on
all the thornbushes and at all the water
holes. [20] In that day the Lord will use a
razor hired from beyond the River[f]—the
king of Assyria—to shave your head and
the hair of your legs, and to take off your
beards also. [21] In that day, a man will keep
alive a young cow and two goats. [22] And
because of the abundance of the milk

---

[a] 2 Or has set up camp in   [b] 3 Shear-Jashub means a remnant will return.   [c] 14 The Hebrew is plural.   [d] 14 Masoretic Text;
Dead Sea Scrolls and he or and they   [e] 14 Immanuel means God with us.   [f] 20 That is, the Euphrates

they give, he will have curds to eat. All who remain in the land will eat curds and honey. [23]In that day, in every place where there were a thousand vines worth a thousand silver shekels,[a] there will be only briers and thorns. [24]Men will go there with bow and arrow, for the land will be covered with briers and thorns. [25]As for all the hills once cultivated by the hoe, you will no longer go there for fear of the briers and thorns; they will become places where cattle are turned loose and where sheep run.

Assyria, the LORD's Instrument

8 The LORD said to me, "Take a large scroll and write on it with an ordinary pen: Maher-Shalal-Hash-Baz.[b] [2]And I will call in Uriah the priest and Zechariah son of Jeberekiah as reliable witnesses for me."

[3]Then I went to the prophetess, and she conceived and gave birth to a son. And the LORD said to me, "Name him Maher-Shalal-Hash-Baz. [4]Before the boy knows how to say 'My father' or 'My mother,' the wealth of Damascus and the plunder of Samaria will be carried off by the king of Assyria."

[5]The LORD spoke to me again:

[6]"Because this people has rejected
    the gently flowing waters of
        Shiloah
  and rejoices over Rezin
    and the son of Remaliah,
[7]therefore the Lord is about to bring
        against them
    the mighty floodwaters of the
        River[c]—
    the king of Assyria with all his
        pomp.
  It will overflow all its channels,
    run over all its banks
[8]and sweep on into Judah, swirling
        over it,
    passing through it and reaching up
        to the neck.

Its outspread wings will cover the
        breadth of your land,
    O Immanuel[d]!"

[9]Raise the war cry,[e] you nations, and
        be shattered!
    Listen, all you distant lands.
  Prepare for battle, and be shattered!
    Prepare for battle, and be
        shattered!
[10]Devise your strategy, but it will be
        thwarted;
    propose your plan, but it will not
        stand,
  for God is with us.[f]

Fear God

[11]The LORD spoke to me with his strong hand upon me, warning me not to follow the way of this people. He said:

[12]"Do not call conspiracy
    everything that these people call
        conspiracy[g];
  do not fear what they fear,
    and do not dread it.
[13]The LORD Almighty is the one you
        are to regard as holy,
    he is the one you are to fear,
    he is the one you are to dread,
[14]and he will be a sanctuary;
    but for both houses of Israel he will
        be
  a stone that causes men to stumble
    and a rock that makes them fall.
  And for the people of Jerusalem he
        will be
    a trap and a snare.
[15]Many of them will stumble;
    they will fall and be broken,
    they will be snared and captured."

[16]Bind up the testimony
    and seal up the law among my
        disciples.
[17]I will wait for the LORD,
    who is hiding his face from the
        house of Jacob.
  I will put my trust in him.

---

[a] 23 That is, about 25 pounds (about 11.5 kilograms)   [b] 1 Maher-Shalal-Hash-Baz means quick to the plunder, swift to the spoil; also in verse 3.   [c] 7 That is, the Euphrates   [d] 8 Immanuel means God with us.   [e] 9 Or Do your worst   [f] 10 Hebrew Immanuel   [g] 12 Or Do not call for a treaty / every time these people call for a treaty

[18]Here am I, and the children the LORD has given me. We are signs and symbols in Israel from the LORD Almighty, who dwells on Mount Zion.

[19]When men tell you to consult mediums and spiritists, who whisper and mutter, should not a people inquire of their God? Why consult the dead on behalf of the living? [20]To the law and to the testimony! If they do not speak according to this word, they have no light of dawn. [21]Distressed and hungry, they will roam through the land; when they are famished, they will become enraged and, looking upward, will curse their king and their God. [22]Then they will look toward the earth and see only distress and darkness and fearful gloom, and they will be thrust into utter darkness.

To Us a Child Is Born

9 Nevertheless, there will be no more gloom for those who were in distress. In the past he humbled the land of Zebulun and the land of Naphtali, but in the future he will honor Galilee of the Gentiles, by the way of the sea, along the Jordan—

[2] The people walking in darkness
    have seen a great light;
on those living in the land of the
        shadow of death[a]
    a light has dawned.
[3] You have enlarged the nation
    and increased their joy;
they rejoice before you
    as people rejoice at the harvest,
as men rejoice
    when dividing the plunder.
[4] For as in the day of Midian's defeat,
    you have shattered

the yoke that burdens them,
    the bar across their shoulders,
    the rod of their oppressor.
[5] Every warrior's boot used in battle
    and every garment rolled in
        blood
will be destined for burning,
    will be fuel for the fire.
[6] For to us a child is born,
    to us a son is given,
    and the government will be on his
        shoulders.
And he will be called
    Wonderful Counselor,[b] Mighty
        God,
    Everlasting Father, Prince of Peace.
[7] Of the increase of his government
        and peace
    there will be no end.
He will reign on David's throne
    and over his kingdom,
establishing and upholding it
    with justice and righteousness
    from that time on and forever.
The zeal of the LORD Almighty
    will accomplish this.

The LORD's Anger Against Israel

[8] The Lord has sent a message against
        Jacob;
    it will fall on Israel.
[9] All the people will know it—
    Ephraim and the inhabitants of
        Samaria—
who say with pride
    and arrogance of heart,
[10] "The bricks have fallen down,
    but we will rebuild with dressed
        stone;
the fig trees have been felled,
    but we will replace them with
        cedars."
[11] But the LORD has strengthened
    Rezin's foes against them
    and has spurred their enemies on.
[12] Arameans from the east and
    Philistines from the west
have devoured Israel with open
    mouth.

---

[a] 2 Or *land of darkness*   [b] 6 Or *Wonderful, Counselor*

Yet for all this, his anger is not turned
    away,
    his hand is still upraised.

¹³But the people have not returned to
        him who struck them,
    nor have they sought the LORD
        Almighty.
¹⁴So the LORD will cut off from Israel
        both head and tail,
    both palm branch and reed in a
        single day;
¹⁵the elders and prominent men are the
        head,
    the prophets who teach lies are the
        tail.
¹⁶Those who guide this people mislead
        them,
    and those who are guided are led
        astray.
¹⁷Therefore the Lord will take no
        pleasure in the young men,
    nor will he pity the fatherless and
        widows,
for everyone is ungodly and
        wicked,
    every mouth speaks vileness.

Yet for all this, his anger is not turned
    away,
    his hand is still upraised.

¹⁸Surely wickedness burns like a fire;
    it consumes briers and thorns,
it sets the forest thickets ablaze,
    so that it rolls upward in a column
        of smoke.
¹⁹By the wrath of the LORD Almighty
    the land will be scorched
and the people will be fuel for the
        fire;
    no one will spare his brother.
²⁰On the right they will devour,
    but still be hungry;
on the left they will eat,
    but not be satisfied.
Each will feed on the flesh of his own
        offspringª:
²¹   Manasseh will feed on Ephraim,
        and Ephraim on Manasseh;

together they will turn against
    Judah.

Yet for all this, his anger is not turned
    away,
    his hand is still upraised.

10 Woe to those who make unjust
        laws,
    to those who issue oppressive
        decrees,
²to deprive the poor of their rights
    and withhold justice from the
        oppressed of my people,
making widows their prey
    and robbing the fatherless.
³What will you do on the day of
        reckoning,
    when disaster comes from afar?
To whom will you run for help?
    Where will you leave your riches?
⁴Nothing will remain but to cringe
        among the captives
    or fall among the slain.

Yet for all this, his anger is not turned
    away,
    his hand is still upraised.

God's Judgment on Assyria
⁵"Woe to the Assyrian, the rod of my
        anger,
    in whose hand is the club of my
        wrath!
⁶I send him against a godless nation,
    I dispatch him against a people who
        anger me,
to seize loot and snatch plunder,
    and to trample them down like
        mud in the streets.
⁷But this is not what he intends,
    this is not what he has in mind;
his purpose is to destroy,
    to put an end to many nations.
⁸'Are not my commanders all kings?'
        he says.
⁹   'Has not Calno fared like
            Carchemish?
Is not Hamath like Arpad,
    and Samaria like Damascus?

ª 20 Or arm

¹⁰As my hand seized the kingdoms of the idols,
  kingdoms whose images excelled those of Jerusalem and Samaria—
¹¹shall I not deal with Jerusalem and her images
  as I dealt with Samaria and her idols?' "

¹²When the Lord has finished all his work against Mount Zion and Jerusalem, he will say, "I will punish the king of Assyria for the willful pride of his heart and the haughty look in his eyes. ¹³For he says:

" 'By the strength of my hand I have done this,
  and by my wisdom, because I have understanding.
I removed the boundaries of nations,
  I plundered their treasures;
  like a mighty one I subdued[a] their kings.
¹⁴As one reaches into a nest,
  so my hand reached for the wealth of the nations;
as men gather abandoned eggs,
  so I gathered all the countries;
not one flapped a wing,
  or opened its mouth to chirp.' "

¹⁵Does the ax raise itself above him who swings it,
  or the saw boast against him who uses it?
As if a rod were to wield him who lifts it up,
  or a club brandish him who is not wood!
¹⁶Therefore, the Lord, the LORD Almighty,
  will send a wasting disease upon his sturdy warriors;
under his pomp a fire will be kindled
  like a blazing flame.
¹⁷The Light of Israel will become a fire,
  their Holy One a flame;

in a single day it will burn and consume
  his thorns and his briers.
¹⁸The splendor of his forests and fertile fields
  it will completely destroy,
  as when a sick man wastes away.
¹⁹And the remaining trees of his forests will be so few
  that a child could write them down.

The Remnant of Israel

²⁰In that day the remnant of Israel,
  the survivors of the house of Jacob,
will no longer rely on him
  who struck them down
but will truly rely on the LORD,
  the Holy One of Israel.
²¹A remnant will return,[b] a remnant of Jacob
  will return to the Mighty God.
²²Though your people, O Israel, be like the sand by the sea,
  only a remnant will return.
Destruction has been decreed,
  overwhelming and righteous.
²³The Lord, the LORD Almighty, will carry out
  the destruction decreed upon the whole land.

²⁴Therefore, this is what the Lord, the LORD Almighty, says:

"O my people who live in Zion,
  do not be afraid of the Assyrians,
who beat you with a rod
  and lift up a club against you, as Egypt did.
²⁵Very soon my anger against you will end
  and my wrath will be directed to their destruction."
²⁶The LORD Almighty will lash them with a whip,
  as when he struck down Midian at the rock of Oreb;
and he will raise his staff over the waters,

---

a 13 Or */ I subdued the mighty,*   *b 21* Hebrew *shear-jashub;* also in verse 22

as he did in Egypt.
27In that day their burden will be lifted
from your shoulders,
their yoke from your neck;
the yoke will be broken
because you have grown so fat.[a]

28They enter Aiath;
they pass through Migron;
they store supplies at Micmash.
29They go over the pass, and say,
"We will camp overnight at Geba."
Ramah trembles;
Gibeah of Saul flees.
30Cry out, O Daughter of Gallim!
Listen, O Laishah!
Poor Anathoth!
31Madmenah is in flight;
the people of Gebim take cover.
32This day they will halt at Nob;
they will shake their fist
at the mount of the Daughter of Zion,
at the hill of Jerusalem.

33See, the Lord, the LORD Almighty,
will lop off the boughs with great
power.
The lofty trees will be felled,
the tall ones will be brought low.
34He will cut down the forest thickets
with an ax;
Lebanon will fall before the Mighty
One.

The Branch From Jesse

11 A shoot will come up from the
stump of Jesse;
from his roots a Branch will bear
fruit.
2The Spirit of the LORD will rest on
him—
the Spirit of wisdom and of
understanding,
the Spirit of counsel and of
power,
the Spirit of knowledge and of the
fear of the LORD—
3and he will delight in the fear of the
LORD.

He will not judge by what he sees
with his eyes,
or decide by what he hears with his
ears;
4but with righteousness he will judge
the needy,
with justice he will give decisions
for the poor of the earth.
He will strike the earth with the rod
of his mouth;
with the breath of his lips he will
slay the wicked.
5Righteousness will be his belt
and faithfulness the sash around his
waist.

6The wolf will live with the lamb,
the leopard will lie down with the
goat,
the calf and the lion and the yearling[b]
together;
and a little child will lead them.
7The cow will feed with the bear,
their young will lie down together,
and the lion will eat straw like the
ox.
8The infant will play near the hole of
the cobra,
and the young child put his hand
into the viper's nest.
9They will neither harm nor destroy
on all my holy mountain,
for the earth will be full of the
knowledge of the LORD
as the waters cover the sea.

10In that day the Root of Jesse will
stand as a banner for the peoples; the
nations will rally to him, and his place
of rest will be glorious. 11In that day the
Lord will reach out his hand a second
time to reclaim the remnant that is left
of his people from Assyria, from Lower
Egypt, from Upper Egypt,[c] from Cush,[d]
from Elam, from Babylonia,[e] from Hamath and from the islands of the sea.

12He will raise a banner for the nations
and gather the exiles of Israel;

---

[a] 27 Hebrew; Septuagint broken / from your shoulders   [b] 6 Hebrew; Septuagint lion will feed   [c] 11 Hebrew from Pathros
[d] 11 That is, the upper Nile region   [e] 11 Hebrew Shinar

he will assemble the scattered people
   of Judah
from the four quarters of the earth.
[13] Ephraim's jealousy will vanish,
   and Judah's enemies[a] will be cut
      off;
Ephraim will not be jealous of Judah,
   nor Judah hostile toward Ephraim.

[14] They will swoop down on the slopes
   of Philistia to the west;
together they will plunder the
   people to the east.
They will lay hands on Edom and
   Moab,
and the Ammonites will be subject
   to them.

_____
a 13 Or hostility

GOING deeper

I Will Praise You

READ AND CONSIDER: ISAIAH 12

"I will praise you, O LORD. Although you were angry with me, your anger has turned away and you have comforted me. Surely God is my salvation; I will trust and not be afraid. The LORD, the LORD is my strength and my song; he has become my salvation" (Isaiah 12:1-2).

The Lord gets angry about sin. We must not fool ourselves by thinking that God overlooks our sin just because He loves us, or that we can somehow get away with sin because we're one of God's kids. Sin is ugly. Sin caused the death of His beloved Son. Sin will not be tolerated by our holy God.

But sin is a part of our nature. Paul wrote, "I know that nothing good lives in me, that is, in my sinful nature. For I have the desire to do what is good, but I cannot carry it out. For what I do is not the good I want to do; no, the evil I do not want to do—this I keep on doing" (Romans 7:18-19). Although we are saved from sin, we continue to struggle with it. We've been set free from sin, but our sin nature still rears its ugly head. Satan constantly tries to wear us down and tempt us to sin so we can be rendered ineffective for God's kingdom.

While sin is a reality, and God's anger at sin is a reality, so is our good standing with God. The battle is real, but He has armed us for the battle (Ephesians 6:10-17). We have the ultimate weapons, which are God's Word and our praise.

The Bible says, "The angel of the LORD encamps around those who fear him, and he delivers them" (Psalm 34:7). Whenever the enemy tries to drag you into sin, use your sword, which is the Word of God, and drown the enemy out with praise. Thank God that He is the Deliverer and you are being delivered even as you praise Him.

If you ever seem to be sliding back into the very sin you've already been set free of, don't even waste time getting discouraged. Often what seems like the same old sin coming back again may be another layer surfacing that needs to come off. You're not going backward—you are going deeper. Those deep layers of bondage can hurt far worse than the earlier ones. But the deeper you go, the stronger you get, the more mature you become, the readier you are to move into all God has for you.

If you fall (and everybody does at times), remember that you have the weapon of repentance. Go to God immediately. Confess your sin and clear the air. Show Him your repentant heart. His anger will turn away, and He will comfort you (Isaiah 12:1).

Then praise God for all the glorious things He has done and is doing in your life.

¹⁵The LORD will dry up
    the gulf of the Egyptian sea;
with a scorching wind he will sweep
    his hand
    over the Euphrates River.ᵃ
He will break it up into seven streams
    so that men can cross over in
    sandals.
¹⁶There will be a highway for the
    remnant of his people
    that is left from Assyria,
as there was for Israel
    when they came up from Egypt.

Songs of Praise

12 In that day you will say:

"I will praise you, O LORD.
    Although you were angry with me,
your anger has turned away
    and you have comforted me.
²Surely God is my salvation;
    I will trust and not be afraid.
The LORD, the LORD, is my strength
    and my song;
    he has become my salvation."
³With joy you will draw water
    from the wells of salvation.

⁴In that day you will say:

"Give thanks to the LORD, call on his
    name;
    make known among the nations
    what he has done,
    and proclaim that his name is
    exalted.
⁵Sing to the LORD, for he has done
    glorious things;
    let this be known to all the world.
⁶Shout aloud and sing for joy, people
    of Zion,
    for great is the Holy One of Israel
    among you."

A Prophecy Against Babylon

13 An oracle concerning Babylon that
Isaiah son of Amoz saw:

²Raise a banner on a bare hilltop,
    shout to them;

beckon to them
    to enter the gates of the nobles.
³I have commanded my holy ones;
    I have summoned my warriors to
    carry out my wrath—
    those who rejoice in my triumph.

⁴Listen, a noise on the mountains,
    like that of a great multitude!
Listen, an uproar among the
    kingdoms,
    like nations massing together!
The LORD Almighty is mustering
    an army for war.
⁵They come from faraway lands,
    from the ends of the heavens—
the LORD and the weapons of his
    wrath—
    to destroy the whole country.

⁶Wail, for the day of the LORD is near;
    it will come like destruction from
    the Almighty.ᵇ
⁷Because of this, all hands will go
    limp,
    every man's heart will melt.
⁸Terror will seize them,
    pain and anguish will grip them;
    they will writhe like a woman in
    labor.
They will look aghast at each other,
    their faces aflame.

⁹See, the day of the LORD is coming
    —a cruel day, with wrath and
    fierce anger—
to make the land desolate
    and destroy the sinners within it.
¹⁰The stars of heaven and their
    constellations
    will not show their light.
The rising sun will be darkened
    and the moon will not give its
    light.
¹¹I will punish the world for its evil,
    the wicked for their sins.
I will put an end to the arrogance of
    the haughty
    and will humble the pride of the
    ruthless.

ᵃ 15 Hebrew *the River*   ᵇ 6 Hebrew *Shaddai*

¹²I will make man scarcer than pure
gold,
more rare than the gold of Ophir.
¹³Therefore I will make the heavens
tremble;
and the earth will shake from its
place
at the wrath of the LORD Almighty,
in the day of his burning anger.

¹⁴Like a hunted gazelle,
like sheep without a shepherd,
each will return to his own people,
each will flee to his native land.
¹⁵Whoever is captured will be thrust
through;
all who are caught will fall by the
sword.
¹⁶Their infants will be dashed to pieces
before their eyes;
their houses will be looted and
their wives ravished.

¹⁷See, I will stir up against them the
Medes,
who do not care for silver
and have no delight in gold.
¹⁸Their bows will strike down the
young men;
they will have no mercy on infants
nor will they look with compassion
on children.
¹⁹Babylon, the jewel of kingdoms,
the glory of the Babylonians'ᵃ pride,
will be overthrown by God
like Sodom and Gomorrah.
²⁰She will never be inhabited
or lived in through all generations;
no Arab will pitch his tent there,
no shepherd will rest his flocks
there.
²¹But desert creatures will lie there,
jackals will fill her houses;
there the owls will dwell,
and there the wild goats will leap
about.
²²Hyenas will howl in her strongholds,
jackals in her luxurious palaces.

Her time is at hand,
and her days will not be prolonged.

14 The LORD will have compassion
on Jacob;
once again he will choose Israel
and will settle them in their own
land.
Aliens will join them
and unite with the house of Jacob.
²Nations will take them
and bring them to their own
place.
And the house of Israel will possess
the nations
as menservants and maidservants in
the LORD's land.
They will make captives of their
captors
and rule over their oppressors.

³On the day the LORD gives you relief
from suffering and turmoil and cruel bondage, ⁴you will take up this taunt against the
king of Babylon:

How the oppressor has come to an
end!
How his furyᵇ has ended!
⁵The LORD has broken the rod of the
wicked,
the scepter of the rulers,
⁶which in anger struck down peoples
with unceasing blows,
and in fury subdued nations
with relentless aggression.
⁷All the lands are at rest and at peace;
they break into singing.
⁸Even the pine trees and the cedars of
Lebanon
exult over you and say,
"Now that you have been laid low,
no woodsman comes to cut us
down."

⁹The graveᶜ below is all astir
to meet you at your coming;
it rouses the spirits of the departed to
greet you—

ᵃ 19 Or Chaldeans'   ᵇ 4 Dead Sea Scrolls, Septuagint and Syriac; the meaning of the word in the Masoretic Text is uncertain.
ᶜ 9 Hebrew Sheol; also in verses 11 and 15

all those who were leaders in the
world;
it makes them rise from their
thrones—
all those who were kings over the
nations.
10 They will all respond,
they will say to you,
"You also have become weak, as we
are;
you have become like us."
11 All your pomp has been brought
down to the grave,
along with the noise of your harps;
maggots are spread out beneath you
and worms cover you.

12 How you have fallen from heaven,
O morning star, son of the dawn!
You have been cast down to the
earth,
you who once laid low the nations!
13 You said in your heart,
"I will ascend to heaven;
I will raise my throne
above the stars of God;
I will sit enthroned on the mount of
assembly,
on the utmost heights of the sacred
mountain.ᵃ
14 I will ascend above the tops of the
clouds;
I will make myself like the Most
High."
15 But you are brought down to the
grave,
to the depths of the pit.

16 Those who see you stare at you,
they ponder your fate:
"Is this the man who shook the earth
and made kingdoms tremble,
17 the man who made the world a
desert,
who overthrew its cities
and would not let his captives go
home?"
18 All the kings of the nations lie in
state,

each in his own tomb.
19 But you are cast out of your tomb
like a rejected branch;
you are covered with the slain,
with those pierced by the sword,
those who descend to the stones of
the pit.
Like a corpse trampled underfoot,
20   you will not join them in burial,
for you have destroyed your land
and killed your people.

The offspring of the wicked
will never be mentioned again.
21 Prepare a place to slaughter his sons
for the sins of their forefathers;
they are not to rise to inherit the land
and cover the earth with their cities.

22 "I will rise up against them,"
declares the LORD Almighty.
"I will cut off from Babylon her name
and survivors,
her offspring and descendants,"
declares the LORD.
23 "I will turn her into a place for owls
and into swampland;
I will sweep her with the broom of
destruction,"
declares the LORD Almighty.

A Prophecy Against Assyria
24 The LORD Almighty has sworn,

"Surely, as I have planned, so it will
be,
and as I have purposed, so it will
stand.
25 I will crush the Assyrian in my land;
on my mountains I will trample
him down.
His yoke will be taken from my
people,
and his burden removed from their
shoulders."

26 This is the plan determined for the
whole world;
this is the hand stretched out over
all nations.

ᵃ *13* Or *the north*; Hebrew *Zaphon*

27For the LORD Almighty has
        purposed, and who can thwart
        him?
    His hand is stretched out, and who
        can turn it back?

A Prophecy Against the Philistines

28This oracle came in the year King
Ahaz died:

29Do not rejoice, all you Philistines,
    that the rod that struck you is
        broken;
    from the root of that snake will spring
        up a viper,
    its fruit will be a darting, venomous
        serpent.
30The poorest of the poor will find
        pasture,
    and the needy will lie down in
        safety.
    But your root I will destroy by
        famine;
    it will slay your survivors.

31Wail, O gate! Howl, O city!
    Melt away, all you Philistines!
    A cloud of smoke comes from the
        north,
    and there is not a straggler in its
        ranks.
32What answer shall be given
    to the envoys of that nation?
    "The LORD has established Zion,
    and in her his afflicted people will
        find refuge."

A Prophecy Against Moab

15 An oracle concerning Moab:

    Ar in Moab is ruined,
        destroyed in a night!
    Kir in Moab is ruined,
        destroyed in a night!
2Dibon goes up to its temple,
    to its high places to weep;
    Moab wails over Nebo and Medeba.
    Every head is shaved
    and every beard cut off.
3In the streets they wear sackcloth;
    on the roofs and in the public
        squares
    they all wail,
    prostrate with weeping.
4Heshbon and Elealeh cry out,
    their voices are heard all the way to
        Jahaz.
    Therefore the armed men of Moab
        cry out,
    and their hearts are faint.

5My heart cries out over Moab;
    her fugitives flee as far as Zoar,
    as far as Eglath Shelishiyah.
    They go up the way to Luhith,
    weeping as they go;
    on the road to Horonaim
    they lament their destruction.
6The waters of Nimrim are dried up
    and the grass is withered;
    the vegetation is gone
    and nothing green is left.
7So the wealth they have acquired and
        stored up
    they carry away over the Ravine of
        the Poplars.
8Their outcry echoes along the border
        of Moab;
    their wailing reaches as far as
        Eglaim,
    their lamentation as far as Beer
        Elim.
9Dimon's[a] waters are full of blood,
    but I will bring still more upon
        Dimon[a]—
    a lion upon the fugitives of Moab
    and upon those who remain in the
        land.

16 Send lambs as tribute
    to the ruler of the land,
    from Sela, across the desert,
    to the mount of the Daughter of
        Zion.
2Like fluttering birds
    pushed from the nest,
    so are the women of Moab
    at the fords of the Arnon.

---

a 9 Masoretic Text; Dead Sea Scrolls, some Septuagint manuscripts and Vulgate Dibon

³"Give us counsel,
   render a decision.
Make your shadow like night—
   at high noon.
Hide the fugitives,
   do not betray the refugees.
⁴Let the Moabite fugitives stay with
      you;
   be their shelter from the destroyer."

The oppressor will come to an end,
   and destruction will cease;
   the aggressor will vanish from the
      land.
⁵In love a throne will be established;
   in faithfulness a man will sit
      on it—
   one from the houseª of David—
one who in judging seeks justice
   and speeds the cause of
      righteousness.

⁶We have heard of Moab's pride—
   her overweening pride and conceit,
her pride and her insolence—
   but her boasts are empty.
⁷Therefore the Moabites wail,
   they wail together for Moab.
Lament and grieve
   for the menᵇ of Kir Hareseth.
⁸The fields of Heshbon wither,
   the vines of Sibmah also.
The rulers of the nations
   have trampled down the choicest
      vines,
which once reached Jazer
   and spread toward the desert.
Their shoots spread out
   and went as far as the sea.
⁹So I weep, as Jazer weeps,
   for the vines of Sibmah.
O Heshbon, O Elealeh,
   I drench you with tears!
The shouts of joy over your ripened
      fruit
   and over your harvests have been
      stilled.
¹⁰Joy and gladness are taken away from
      the orchards;

no one sings or shouts in the
      vineyards;
no one treads out wine at the presses,
   for I have put an end to the
      shouting.
¹¹My heart laments for Moab like a
      harp,
   my inmost being for Kir Hareseth.
¹²When Moab appears at her high
      place,
   she only wears herself out;
when she goes to her shrine to pray,
   it is to no avail.

¹³This is the word the LORD has already
spoken concerning Moab. ¹⁴But now the
LORD says: "Within three years, as a servant bound by contract would count
them, Moab's splendor and all her many
people will be despised, and her survivors
will be very few and feeble."

An Oracle Against Damascus

17 An oracle concerning Damascus:

"See, Damascus will no longer be a
      city
   but will become a heap of ruins.
²The cities of Aroer will be deserted
   and left to flocks, which will lie
      down,
   with no one to make them afraid.
³The fortified city will disappear from
      Ephraim,
   and royal power from Damascus;
the remnant of Aram will be
   like the glory of the Israelites,"
         declares the LORD Almighty.

⁴"In that day the glory of Jacob will
      fade;
   the fat of his body will waste away.
⁵It will be as when a reaper gathers the
      standing grain
   and harvests the grain with his
      arm—
as when a man gleans heads of grain
   in the Valley of Rephaim.
⁶Yet some gleanings will remain,
   as when an olive tree is beaten,

ª 5 Hebrew *tent*   ᵇ 7 Or "*raisin cakes,*" a wordplay

leaving two or three olives on the
topmost branches,
four or five on the fruitful boughs,"
declares the LORD,
the God of Israel.

[7] In that day men will look to their
Maker
and turn their eyes to the Holy
One of Israel.
[8] They will not look to the altars,
the work of their hands,
and they will have no regard for the
Asherah poles[a]
and the incense altars their fingers
have made.

[9] In that day their strong cities, which
they left because of the Israelites, will be
like places abandoned to thickets and undergrowth. And all will be desolation.

[10] You have forgotten God your Savior;
you have not remembered the
Rock, your fortress.
Therefore, though you set out the
finest plants
and plant imported vines,

Praying Isaiah 17:10

*Lord, I pray that I will always be
mindful of Your presence and power in
my life so that I can avoid the sorrow
that is inevitable in not doing so.*

[11] though on the day you set them out,
you make them grow,
and on the morning when you plant
them, you bring them to bud,
yet the harvest will be as nothing
in the day of disease and incurable
pain.

[12] Oh, the raging of many nations—
they rage like the raging sea!
Oh, the uproar of the peoples—
they roar like the roaring of great
waters!
[13] Although the peoples roar like the
roar of surging waters,

when he rebukes them they flee far
away,
driven before the wind like chaff on
the hills,
like tumbleweed before a gale.
[14] In the evening, sudden terror!
Before the morning, they are gone!
This is the portion of those who loot
us,
the lot of those who plunder us.

Prayer is . . .

*seeking God and believing
you will find Him.*

A Prophecy Against Cush

18 Woe to the land of whirring
wings[b]
along the rivers of Cush,[c]
[2] which sends envoys by sea
in papyrus boats over the water.

Go, swift messengers,
to a people tall and smooth-skinned,
to a people feared far and wide,
an aggressive nation of strange
speech,
whose land is divided by rivers.

[3] All you people of the world,
you who live on the earth,
when a banner is raised on the
mountains,
you will see it,
and when a trumpet sounds,
you will hear it.
[4] This is what the LORD says to me:
"I will remain quiet and will look
on from my dwelling place,
like shimmering heat in the
sunshine,
like a cloud of dew in the heat of
harvest."
[5] For, before the harvest, when the
blossom is gone

---

[a] *8* That is, symbols of the goddess Asherah   [b] *1* Or *of locusts*   [c] *1* That is, the upper Nile region

and the flower becomes a ripening
grape,
he will cut off the shoots with
pruning knives,
and cut down and take away the
spreading branches.
6 They will all be left to the mountain
birds of prey
and to the wild animals;
the birds will feed on them all
summer,
the wild animals all winter.

7 At that time gifts will be brought to
the LORD Almighty

from a people tall and smooth-
skinned,
from a people feared far and wide,
an aggressive nation of strange
speech,
whose land is divided by rivers—

the gifts will be brought to Mount Zion,
the place of the Name of the LORD Almighty.

A Prophecy About Egypt

19 An oracle concerning Egypt:

See, the LORD rides on a swift cloud
and is coming to Egypt.
The idols of Egypt tremble before
him,
and the hearts of the Egyptians
melt within them.

2 "I will stir up Egyptian against
Egyptian—
brother will fight against brother,
neighbor against neighbor,
city against city,
kingdom against kingdom.
3 The Egyptians will lose heart,
and I will bring their plans to
nothing;
they will consult the idols and the
spirits of the dead,
the mediums and the spiritists.
4 I will hand the Egyptians over
to the power of a cruel master,

and a fierce king will rule over
them,"
declares the Lord, the LORD
Almighty.

5 The waters of the river will dry up,
and the riverbed will be parched
and dry.
6 The canals will stink;
the streams of Egypt will dwindle
and dry up.
The reeds and rushes will wither,
7 also the plants along the Nile,
at the mouth of the river.
Every sown field along the Nile
will become parched, will blow
away and be no more.
8 The fishermen will groan and lament,
all who cast hooks into the Nile;
those who throw nets on the water
will pine away.
9 Those who work with combed flax
will despair,
the weavers of fine linen will lose
hope.
10 The workers in cloth will be dejected,
and all the wage earners will be
sick at heart.

11 The officials of Zoan are nothing but
fools;
the wise counselors of Pharaoh give
senseless advice.
How can you say to Pharaoh,
"I am one of the wise men,
a disciple of the ancient kings"?

12 Where are your wise men now?
Let them show you and make
known
what the LORD Almighty
has planned against Egypt.
13 The officials of Zoan have become
fools,
the leaders of Memphis[a] are
deceived;
the cornerstones of her peoples
have led Egypt astray.
14 The LORD has poured into them
a spirit of dizziness;

---

a 13 Hebrew Noph

they make Egypt stagger in all that
  she does,
    as a drunkard staggers around in his
      vomit.
¹⁵There is nothing Egypt can do—
  head or tail, palm branch or reed.

¹⁶In that day the Egyptians will be like
women. They will shudder with fear at
the uplifted hand that the LORD Almighty
raises against them. ¹⁷And the land of Judah will bring terror to the Egyptians; everyone to whom Judah is mentioned will
be terrified, because of what the LORD
Almighty is planning against them.

¹⁸In that day five cities in Egypt will
speak the language of Canaan and swear
allegiance to the LORD Almighty. One of
them will be called the City of Destruc-
tion.ᵃ

¹⁹In that day there will be an altar to
the LORD in the heart of Egypt, and a
monument to the LORD at its border. ²⁰It
will be a sign and witness to the LORD Almighty in the land of Egypt. When they
cry out to the LORD because of their oppressors, he will send them a savior and
defender, and he will rescue them. ²¹So
the LORD will make himself known to
the Egyptians, and in that day they will acknowledge the LORD. They will worship
with sacrifices and grain offerings; they
will make vows to the LORD and keep
them. ²²The LORD will strike Egypt with
a plague; he will strike them and heal
them. They will turn to the LORD, and
he will respond to their pleas and heal
them.

²³In that day there will be a highway
from Egypt to Assyria. The Assyrians will
go to Egypt and the Egyptians to Assyria.
The Egyptians and Assyrians will worship together. ²⁴In that day Israel will be
the third, along with Egypt and Assyria,
a blessing on the earth. ²⁵The LORD Almighty will bless them, saying, "Blessed
be Egypt my people, Assyria my handi-
work, and Israel my inheritance."

A Prophecy Against Egypt and Cush

20 In the year that the supreme
commander, sent by Sargon king
of Assyria, came to Ashdod and attacked
and captured it— ²at that time the LORD
spoke through Isaiah son of Amoz. He
said to him, "Take off the sackcloth
from your body and the sandals from
your feet." And he did so, going around
stripped and barefoot.

³Then the LORD said, "Just as my servant Isaiah has gone stripped and barefoot for three years, as a sign and portent
against Egypt and Cush,ᵇ ⁴so the king of
Assyria will lead away stripped and barefoot the Egyptian captives and Cushite
exiles, young and old, with buttocks
bared—to Egypt's shame. ⁵Those who
trusted in Cush and boasted in Egypt
will be afraid and put to shame. ⁶In that
day the people who live on this coast will
say, 'See what has happened to those we
relied on, those we fled to for help and deliverance from the king of Assyria! How
then can we escape?' "

A Prophecy Against Babylon

21 An oracle concerning the Desert
by the Sea:

Like whirlwinds sweeping through
  the southland,
    an invader comes from the desert,
    from a land of terror.

²A dire vision has been shown to me:
  The traitor betrays, the looter takes
    loot.
Elam, attack! Media, lay siege!
  I will bring to an end all the
    groaning she caused.

³At this my body is racked with pain,
  pangs seize me, like those of a
    woman in labor;
I am staggered by what I hear,
  I am bewildered by what I see.
⁴My heart falters,
  fear makes me tremble;

ᵃ 18 Most manuscripts of the Masoretic Text; some manuscripts of the Masoretic Text, Dead Sea Scrolls and Vulgate *City of the
Sun* (that is, Heliopolis)   ᵇ 3 That is, the upper Nile region; also in verse 5

the twilight I longed for
   has become a horror to me.

5 They set the tables,
   they spread the rugs,
   they eat, they drink!
Get up, you officers,
   oil the shields!

6 This is what the Lord says to me:

"Go, post a lookout
   and have him report what he sees.
7 When he sees chariots
   with teams of horses,
riders on donkeys
   or riders on camels,
let him be alert,
   fully alert."

8 And the lookout[a] shouted,

"Day after day, my lord, I stand on
   the watchtower;
   every night I stay at my post.
9 Look, here comes a man in a
   chariot
   with a team of horses.
And he gives back the answer:
   'Babylon has fallen, has fallen!
All the images of its gods
   lie shattered on the ground!'"

10 O my people, crushed on the
   threshing floor,
   I tell you what I have heard
from the Lord Almighty,
   from the God of Israel.

A Prophecy Against Edom

11 An oracle concerning Dumah[b]:

Someone calls to me from Seir,
   "Watchman, what is left of the
     night?
   Watchman, what is left of the
     night?"
12 The watchman replies,
   "Morning is coming, but also the
     night.
If you would ask, then ask;
   and come back yet again."

A Prophecy Against Arabia

13 An oracle concerning Arabia:

You caravans of Dedanites,
   who camp in the thickets of Arabia,
14   bring water for the thirsty;
you who live in Tema,
   bring food for the fugitives.
15 They flee from the sword,
   from the drawn sword,
from the bent bow
   and from the heat of battle.

16 This is what the Lord says to me: "Within one year, as a servant bound by contract would count it, all the pomp of Kedar will come to an end. 17 The survivors of the bowmen, the warriors of Kedar, will be few." The Lord, the God of Israel, has spoken.

A Prophecy About Jerusalem

22 An oracle concerning the Valley of Vision:

What troubles you now,
   that you have all gone up on the
     roofs,
2 O town full of commotion,
   O city of tumult and revelry?
Your slain were not killed by the
     sword,
   nor did they die in battle.
3 All your leaders have fled together;
   they have been captured without
     using the bow.
All you who were caught were taken
     prisoner together,
   having fled while the enemy was
     still far away.
4 Therefore I said, "Turn away from
     me;
   let me weep bitterly.
Do not try to console me
   over the destruction of my people."

5 The Lord, the Lord Almighty, has a
     day
   of tumult and trampling and terror
   in the Valley of Vision,
a day of battering down walls

---

[a] 8 Dead Sea Scrolls and Syriac; Masoretic Text *A lion*   [b] 11 Dumah means *silence* or *stillness*, a wordplay on *Edom*.

and of crying out to the mountains.
⁶Elam takes up the quiver,
  with her charioteers and horses;
  Kir uncovers the shield.
⁷Your choicest valleys are full of
  chariots,
  and horsemen are posted at the city
  gates;
⁸ the defenses of Judah are stripped
  away.

And you looked in that day
  to the weapons in the Palace of the
  Forest;
⁹you saw that the City of David
  had many breaches in its defenses;
you stored up water
  in the Lower Pool.
¹⁰You counted the buildings in
  Jerusalem
  and tore down houses to strengthen
  the wall.
¹¹You built a reservoir between the two
  walls
  for the water of the Old Pool,
but you did not look to the One who
  made it,
  or have regard for the One who
  planned it long ago.

¹²The Lord, the LORD Almighty,
  called you on that day
to weep and to wail,
  to tear out your hair and put on
  sackcloth.
¹³But see, there is joy and revelry,
  slaughtering of cattle and killing of
  sheep,
  eating of meat and drinking of
  wine!
"Let us eat and drink," you say,
  "for tomorrow we die!"

¹⁴The LORD Almighty has revealed this
in my hearing: "Till your dying day this
sin will not be atoned for," says the Lord,
the LORD Almighty.

¹⁵This is what the Lord, the LORD Almighty, says:

"Go, say to this steward,
  to Shebna, who is in charge of the
  palace:
¹⁶What are you doing here and who
  gave you permission
to cut out a grave for yourself here,
hewing your grave on the height
  and chiseling your resting place in
  the rock?

¹⁷"Beware, the LORD is about to take
  firm hold of you
  and hurl you away, O you mighty
  man.
¹⁸He will roll you up tightly like a ball
  and throw you into a large country.
There you will die
  and there your splendid chariots
  will remain—
  you disgrace to your master's house!
¹⁹I will depose you from your office,
  and you will be ousted from your
  position.

²⁰"In that day I will summon my servant, Eliakim son of Hilkiah. ²¹I will clothe him with your robe and fasten your sash around him and hand your authority over to him. He will be a father to those who live in Jerusalem and to the house of Judah. ²²I will place on his shoulder the key to the house of David; what he opens no one can shut, and what he shuts no one can open. ²³I will drive him like a peg into a firm place; he will be a seatᵃ of honor for the house of his father. ²⁴All the glory of his family will hang on him: its offspring and offshoots—all its lesser vessels, from the bowls to all the jars.

²⁵"In that day," declares the LORD Almighty, "the peg driven into the firm place will give way; it will be sheared off and will fall, and the load hanging on it will be cut down." The LORD has spoken.

A Prophecy About Tyre

23 An oracle concerning Tyre:

Wail, O ships of Tarshish!

For Tyre is destroyed
and left without house or harbor.
From the land of Cyprus[a]
word has come to them.

2 Be silent, you people of the island,
and you merchants of Sidon,
whom the seafarers have
enriched.
3 On the great waters
came the grain of the Shihor;
the harvest of the Nile[b] was the
revenue of Tyre,
and she became the marketplace of
the nations.

4 Be ashamed, O Sidon, and you,
O fortress of the sea,
for the sea has spoken:
"I have neither been in labor nor
given birth;
I have neither reared sons nor
brought up daughters."
5 When word comes to Egypt,
they will be in anguish at the
report from Tyre.

6 Cross over to Tarshish;
wail, you people of the island.
7 Is this your city of revelry,
the old, old city,
whose feet have taken her
to settle in far-off lands?
8 Who planned this against Tyre,
the bestower of crowns,
whose merchants are princes,
whose traders are renowned in the
earth?
9 The LORD Almighty planned it,
to bring low the pride of all glory
and to humble all who are
renowned on the earth.

10 Till[c] your land as along the Nile,
O Daughter of Tarshish,
for you no longer have a harbor.
11 The LORD has stretched out his hand
over the sea
and made its kingdoms tremble.

He has given an order concerning
Phoenicia[d]
that her fortresses be destroyed.
12 He said, "No more of your reveling,
O Virgin Daughter of Sidon, now
crushed!

"Up, cross over to Cyprus[a];
even there you will find no rest."
13 Look at the land of the Babylonians,[e]
this people that is now of no
account!
The Assyrians have made it
a place for desert creatures;
they raised up their siege towers,
they stripped its fortresses bare
and turned it into a ruin.

14 Wail, you ships of Tarshish;
your fortress is destroyed!

15 At that time Tyre will be forgotten for seventy years, the span of a king's life. But at the end of these seventy years, it will happen to Tyre as in the song of the prostitute:

16 "Take up a harp, walk through the
city,
O prostitute forgotten;
play the harp well, sing many a song,
so that you will be remembered."

17 At the end of seventy years, the LORD will deal with Tyre. She will return to her hire as a prostitute and will ply her trade with all the kingdoms on the face of the earth. 18 Yet her profit and her earnings will be set apart for the LORD; they will not be stored up or hoarded. Her profits will go to those who live before the LORD, for abundant food and fine clothes.

The LORD's Devastation of the Earth

24 See, the LORD is going to lay
waste the earth
and devastate it;
he will ruin its face
and scatter its inhabitants—
2 it will be the same

---

[a] 1,12 Hebrew Kittim   [b] 2,3 Masoretic Text; one Dead Sea Scroll Sidon, / who cross over the sea; / your envoys 3 are on the great waters. / The grain of the Shihor, / the harvest of the Nile,   [c] 10 Dead Sea Scrolls and some Septuagint manuscripts; Masoretic Text Go through   [d] 11 Hebrew Canaan   [e] 13 Or Chaldeans

for priest as for people,
for master as for servant,
for mistress as for maid,
for seller as for buyer,
for borrower as for lender,
for debtor as for creditor.
³The earth will be completely laid
    waste
and totally plundered.
      The LORD has spoken this word.

⁴The earth dries up and withers,
    the world languishes and withers,
    the exalted of the earth languish.
⁵The earth is defiled by its people;
    they have disobeyed the laws,
violated the statutes
and broken the everlasting
    covenant.
⁶Therefore a curse consumes the earth;
    its people must bear their guilt.
Therefore earth's inhabitants are
    burned up,
and very few are left.
⁷The new wine dries up and the vine
    withers;
all the merrymakers groan.
⁸The gaiety of the tambourines is
    stilled,
the noise of the revelers has
    stopped,
the joyful harp is silent.
⁹No longer do they drink wine with a
    song;
the beer is bitter to its drinkers.
¹⁰The ruined city lies desolate;
    the entrance to every house is
    barred.
¹¹In the streets they cry out for wine;
    all joy turns to gloom,
all gaiety is banished from the
    earth.
¹²The city is left in ruins,
    its gate is battered to pieces.
¹³So will it be on the earth
    and among the nations,
as when an olive tree is beaten,
    or as when gleanings are left after
    the grape harvest.

¹⁴They raise their voices, they shout for
    joy;
from the west they acclaim the
    LORD's majesty.
¹⁵Therefore in the east give glory to the
    LORD;
exalt the name of the LORD, the
    God of Israel,
in the islands of the sea.
¹⁶From the ends of the earth we hear
    singing:
    "Glory to the Righteous One."

But I said, "I waste away, I waste
    away!
    Woe to me!
The treacherous betray!
    With treachery the treacherous
    betray!"
¹⁷Terror and pit and snare await you,
    O people of the earth.
¹⁸Whoever flees at the sound of terror
    will fall into a pit;
whoever climbs out of the pit
    will be caught in a snare.

The floodgates of the heavens are
    opened,
    the foundations of the earth shake.
¹⁹The earth is broken up,
    the earth is split asunder,
    the earth is thoroughly shaken.
²⁰The earth reels like a drunkard,
    it sways like a hut in the wind;
so heavy upon it is the guilt of its
    rebellion
that it falls—never to rise again.

²¹In that day the LORD will punish
    the powers in the heavens above
    and the kings on the earth below.
²²They will be herded together
    like prisoners bound in a dungeon;
they will be shut up in prison
    and be punished[a] after many days.
²³The moon will be abashed, the sun
    ashamed;
for the LORD Almighty will reign
on Mount Zion and in Jerusalem,
and before its elders, gloriously.

---

[a] 22 Or released

Praise to the Lord

25 O Lord, you are my God;
    I will exalt you and praise your
      name,
for in perfect faithfulness
    you have done marvelous things,
    things planned long ago.
2 You have made the city a heap of
      rubble,
    the fortified town a ruin,
  the foreigners' stronghold a city no
      more;
    it will never be rebuilt.
3 Therefore strong peoples will honor
      you;

a banquet of aged wine—
    the best of meats and the finest of
      wines.
7 On this mountain he will destroy
    the shroud that enfolds all
      peoples,
  the sheet that covers all nations;
8 he will swallow up death forever.
  The Sovereign Lord will wipe away
      the tears
    from all faces;
  he will remove the disgrace of his
      people
    from all the earth.
                The Lord has spoken.

God's people at prayer
ISAIAH PRAYS WITH BALANCE

ISAIAH 25:1-5; 26:7-9 Sometimes we don't have a balanced view of God. We can get so focused on His love and forgiveness that we forget about His anger at sin and the seriousness of His judgment. On the other hand, we can be so worried about His displeasure and high standards that we don't remember His loving mercy toward us.

Isaiah praised God for the way in which He would stand against wickedness, as well as the way in which He would save His people. Isaiah had a balanced view of God—the one and only Judge of mankind and his one and only Savior.

Do you stand in awe of God's power and judgment, yet fall at His feet in thankfulness for His mercy? Both are right responses of those who love Him.

---

  cities of ruthless nations will revere
      you.
4 You have been a refuge for the poor,
    a refuge for the needy in his
      distress,
  a shelter from the storm
    and a shade from the heat.
  For the breath of the ruthless
    is like a storm driving against a wall
5   and like the heat of the desert.
  You silence the uproar of foreigners;
    as heat is reduced by the shadow of
      a cloud,
    so the song of the ruthless is stilled.

6 On this mountain the Lord
      Almighty will prepare
    a feast of rich food for all peoples,

9 In that day they will say,

  "Surely this is our God;
    we trusted in him, and he saved us.
  This is the Lord, we trusted in him;
    let us rejoice and be glad in his
      salvation."

10 The hand of the Lord will rest on
      this mountain;
    but Moab will be trampled under
      him
    as straw is trampled down in the
      manure.
11 They will spread out their hands in it,
    as a swimmer spreads out his hands
      to swim.
  God will bring down their pride

despite the cleverness[a] of their hands.
12He will bring down your high
        fortified walls
    and lay them low;
he will bring them down to the
        ground,
    to the very dust.

A Song of Praise

26 In that day this song will be sung
    in the land of Judah:

We have a strong city;
    God makes salvation
    its walls and ramparts.

---

[a] *11* The meaning of the Hebrew for this word is uncertain.

GOING *deeper*

Having Peace About Your Future

READ AND CONSIDER: ISAIAH 26:1-9

"You will keep in perfect peace him whose mind is steadfast, because he trusts in you" (Isaiah 26:3).

We all would like to experience "perfect peace," but as we look around at our world, at our lives, at our futures, it's hard to imagine that the peace we experience can ever be perfect. Although God promises us a future full of hope and blessing, it doesn't just happen automatically. There are some things *we* have to do. One of them is to pray (Jeremiah 29:11-13). Another is to obey God.

Every time you pray and obey, you are investing in your future. Although you live in a world where everything in your life can change in an instant, and you can't be certain what tomorrow will bring, God is unchanging. Although you may not know the specific details about what is ahead, you can trust that God knows. And He will get you safely where you need to go. In fact, the way to get to the future God has for you is to walk closely with Him today.

Walking with God doesn't mean there won't be obstacles. Satan will see to it that there are. While God has a plan for your future that is good, the devil has one too, and it's not good. But the devil's plan for your life cannot succeed as long as you are walking with God, living in obedience to His ways, worshiping only Him, standing strong in His Word, and praying without ceasing.

Your future is in *God's* hands. The only thing that is important is what *He* says about it. He doesn't want you to be concerned about your future anyway. He wants you to be concerned with *Him*, because *He* is your future. Remember that you are God's child, and He loves you. As you *walk* with Him, you will become more like Him every day (1 John 3:1-3). As you *look* to Him, you will be "transformed into his likeness with ever-increasing glory, which comes from the Lord, who is Spirit" (2 Corinthians 3:18). As you *live* with Him, He will take you from strength to strength.

God is looking for people who will be committed to living His way and stepping into the purposes He has for their lives. You are one of those people. I pray that you will be equipped and ready when God says, "Now is the time," and the doors of opportunity open. Just keep doing what's right, and when you least expect it, you will get a call from God giving you your assignment.

Perfect peace can be a reality. Remember, God "is able to do immeasurably more than all we ask or imagine, according to his power that is at work within us" (Ephesians 3:20). He has more for you than you can imagine. And now may "the God of hope fill you with all joy and peace as you trust in him, so that you may overflow with hope by the power of the Holy Spirit" (Romans 15:13). Stay focused on God. As Isaiah wrote, God will keep you in "perfect peace" because you trust in Him.

2 Open the gates
  that the righteous nation may enter,
  the nation that keeps faith.
3 You will keep in perfect peace
  him whose mind is steadfast,
  because he trusts in you.
4 Trust in the LORD forever,
  for the LORD, the LORD, is the
    Rock eternal.
5 He humbles those who dwell on high,
  he lays the lofty city low;
 he levels it to the ground
  and casts it down to the dust.
6 Feet trample it down—
  the feet of the oppressed,
  the footsteps of the poor.

7 The path of the righteous is level;
  O upright One, you make the way
    of the righteous smooth.
8 Yes, LORD, walking in the way of
    your laws,[a]
  we wait for you;
 your name and renown
  are the desire of our hearts.
9 My soul yearns for you in the night;
  in the morning my spirit longs for
    you.
 When your judgments come upon the
    earth,
  the people of the world learn
    righteousness.
10 Though grace is shown to the
    wicked,
  they do not learn righteousness;
 even in a land of uprightness they go
    on doing evil
  and regard not the majesty of the
    LORD.
11 O LORD, your hand is lifted high,
  but they do not see it.
 Let them see your zeal for your
    people and be put to shame;
 let the fire reserved for your
    enemies consume them.
12 LORD, you establish peace for us;
  all that we have accomplished you
    have done for us.

13 O LORD, our God, other lords besides
    you have ruled over us,
  but your name alone do we honor.
14 They are now dead, they live no
    more;
  those departed spirits do not rise.
 You punished them and brought
    them to ruin;
  you wiped out all memory of them.
15 You have enlarged the nation,
    O LORD;
  you have enlarged the nation.
 You have gained glory for yourself;
  you have extended all the borders
    of the land.

16 LORD, they came to you in their
    distress;
  when you disciplined them,
  they could barely whisper a prayer.[b]
17 As a woman with child and about to
    give birth
  writhes and cries out in her pain,
  so were we in your presence,
    O LORD.
18 We were with child, we writhed in
    pain,
  but we gave birth to wind.
 We have not brought salvation to the
    earth;
  we have not given birth to people
    of the world.

19 But your dead will live;
  their bodies will rise.
 You who dwell in the dust,
  wake up and shout for joy.
 Your dew is like the dew of the
    morning;
  the earth will give birth to her
    dead.

20 Go, my people, enter your rooms
  and shut the doors behind you;
 hide yourselves for a little while
  until his wrath has passed by.
21 See, the LORD is coming out of his
    dwelling
  to punish the people of the earth
    for their sins.

---

a 8 Or judgments b 16 The meaning of the Hebrew for this clause is uncertain.

The earth will disclose the blood shed
  upon her;
  she will conceal her slain no longer.

Deliverance of Israel

27 In that day,

the LORD will punish with his sword,
  his fierce, great and powerful
    sword,
Leviathan the gliding serpent,
  Leviathan the coiling serpent;
he will slay the monster of the sea.

²In that day—

"Sing about a fruitful vineyard:
³ I, the LORD, watch over it;
  I water it continually.
I guard it day and night
  so that no one may harm it.
⁴ I am not angry.
If only there were briers and thorns
    confronting me!
  I would march against them in
    battle;
  I would set them all on fire.
⁵Or else let them come to me for
    refuge;
  let them make peace with me,
  yes, let them make peace with me."

⁶In days to come Jacob will take root,
  Israel will bud and blossom
  and fill all the world with fruit.

⁷Has ⌊the LORD⌋ struck her
  as he struck down those who struck
    her?
  Has she been killed
  as those were killed who killed her?
⁸By warfareᵃ and exile you contend
    with her—
  with his fierce blast he drives her
    out,
  as on a day the east wind blows.
⁹By this, then, will Jacob's guilt be
    atoned for,
  and this will be the full fruitage of
    the removal of his sin:

When he makes all the altar stones
  to be like chalk stones crushed to
    pieces,
no Asherah polesᵇ or incense altars
  will be left standing.
¹⁰The fortified city stands desolate,
  an abandoned settlement, forsaken
    like the desert;
  there the calves graze,
    there they lie down;
  they strip its branches bare.
¹¹When its twigs are dry, they are
    broken off
  and women come and make fires
    with them.
For this is a people without
    understanding;
  so their Maker has no compassion
    on them,
  and their Creator shows them no
    favor.

¹²In that day the LORD will thresh
from the flowing Euphratesᶜ to the Wadi
of Egypt, and you, O Israelites, will be
gathered up one by one. ¹³And in that
day a great trumpet will sound. Those
who were perishing in Assyria and those
who were exiled in Egypt will come and
worship the LORD on the holy mountain
in Jerusalem.

Woe to Ephraim

28 Woe to that wreath, the pride of
  Ephraim's drunkards,
  to the fading flower, his glorious
    beauty,
set on the head of a fertile valley—
  to that city, the pride of those laid
    low by wine!
²See, the Lord has one who is
    powerful and strong.
  Like a hailstorm and a destructive
    wind,
like a driving rain and a flooding
    downpour,
  he will throw it forcefully to the
    ground.

ᵃ8 See Septuagint; the meaning of the Hebrew for this word is uncertain.   ᵇ9 That is, symbols of the goddess Asherah
ᶜ12 Hebrew River

3 That wreath, the pride of Ephraim's
      drunkards,
   will be trampled underfoot.
4 That fading flower, his glorious
      beauty,
   set on the head of a fertile valley,
 will be like a fig ripe before harvest—
   as soon as someone sees it and takes
      it in his hand,
   he swallows it.

5 In that day the LORD Almighty
   will be a glorious crown,
 a beautiful wreath
   for the remnant of his people.
6 He will be a spirit of justice
   to him who sits in judgment,
 a source of strength
   to those who turn back the battle at
      the gate.

7 And these also stagger from wine
   and reel from beer:
 Priests and prophets stagger from beer
   and are befuddled with wine;
 they reel from beer,
   they stagger when seeing visions,
   they stumble when rendering
      decisions.
8 All the tables are covered with vomit
   and there is not a spot without filth.

9 "Who is it he is trying to teach?
   To whom is he explaining his
      message?
 To children weaned from their milk,
   to those just taken from the breast?
10 For it is:
   Do and do, do and do,
   rule on rule, rule on rule[a];
   a little here, a little there."

11 Very well then, with foreign lips and
      strange tongues
   God will speak to this people,
12 to whom he said,
   "This is the resting place, let the
      weary rest";
 and, "This is the place of repose"—

Praying Isaiah 28:12
*Thank You, Lord, that when
I am weary I can always find rest
and refreshment in You.*

but they would not listen.
13 So then, the word of the LORD to
      them will become:
   Do and do, do and do,
   rule on rule, rule on rule;
   a little here, a little there—
 so that they will go and fall backward,
   be injured and snared and captured.

14 Therefore hear the word of the LORD,
      you scoffers
   who rule this people in Jerusalem.
15 You boast, "We have entered into a
      covenant with death,
   with the grave[b] we have made an
      agreement.
 When an overwhelming scourge
      sweeps by,
   it cannot touch us,
 for we have made a lie our refuge
   and falsehood[c] our hiding place."

16 So this is what the Sovereign LORD
says:

 "See, I lay a stone in Zion,
   a tested stone,
 a precious cornerstone for a sure
      foundation;
   the one who trusts will never be
      dismayed.
17 I will make justice the measuring line
   and righteousness the plumb line;
 hail will sweep away your refuge, the
      lie,
   and water will overflow your
      hiding place.
18 Your covenant with death will be
      annulled;
   your agreement with the grave will
      not stand.
 When the overwhelming scourge
      sweeps by,

---

a 10 Hebrew / sav lasav sav lasav / kav lakav kav lakav (possibly meaningless sounds; perhaps a mimicking of the prophet's words); also in verse 13   b 15 Hebrew Sheol; also in verse 18   c 15 Or false gods

you will be beaten down by it.
19 As often as it comes it will carry you
   away;
   morning after morning, by day and
   by night,
   it will sweep through."

The understanding of this message
   will bring sheer terror.
20 The bed is too short to stretch out on,
   the blanket too narrow to wrap
   around you.
21 The LORD will rise up as he did at
   Mount Perazim,
   he will rouse himself as in the
   Valley of Gibeon—
to do his work, his strange work,
   and perform his task, his alien task.
22 Now stop your mocking,
   or your chains will become
   heavier;
the Lord, the LORD Almighty, has
   told me
of the destruction decreed against
   the whole land.

23 Listen and hear my voice;
   pay attention and hear what I say.
24 When a farmer plows for planting,
      does he plow continually?
   Does he keep on breaking up and
      harrowing the soil?
25 When he has leveled the surface,
   does he not sow caraway and scatter
      cummin?
Does he not plant wheat in its place,[a]
   barley in its plot,[a]
   and spelt in its field?
26 His God instructs him
   and teaches him the right way.

27 Caraway is not threshed with a
      sledge,
   nor is a cartwheel rolled over
      cummin;
caraway is beaten out with a rod,
   and cummin with a stick.
28 Grain must be ground to make bread;
   so one does not go on threshing it
      forever.

Though he drives the wheels of his
   threshing cart over it,
   his horses do not grind it.
29 All this also comes from the LORD
   Almighty,
   wonderful in counsel and
   magnificent in wisdom.

Woe to David's City

29 Woe to you, Ariel, Ariel,
   the city where David settled!
Add year to year
   and let your cycle of festivals go on.
2 Yet I will besiege Ariel;
   she will mourn and lament,
   she will be to me like an altar
   hearth.[b]
3 I will encamp against you all
   around;
   I will encircle you with towers
   and set up my siege works against
   you.
4 Brought low, you will speak from the
   ground;
   your speech will mumble out of the
   dust.
Your voice will come ghostlike from
   the earth;
   out of the dust your speech will
   whisper.

5 But your many enemies will become
   like fine dust,
   the ruthless hordes like blown
   chaff.
Suddenly, in an instant,
6   the LORD Almighty will come
with thunder and earthquake and
   great noise,
   with windstorm and tempest and
   flames of a devouring fire.
7 Then the hordes of all the nations
   that fight against Ariel,
   that attack her and her fortress and
   besiege her,
will be as it is with a dream,
   with a vision in the night—
8 as when a hungry man dreams that he
   is eating,

---

a 25 The meaning of the Hebrew for this word is uncertain.   b 2 The Hebrew for *altar hearth* sounds like the Hebrew for *Ariel*.

but he awakens, and his hunger
remains;
as when a thirsty man dreams that he
is drinking,
but he awakens faint, with his thirst
unquenched.
So will it be with the hordes of all the
nations
that fight against Mount Zion.

9 Be stunned and amazed,
blind yourselves and be sightless;
be drunk, but not from wine,
stagger, but not from beer.
10 The LORD has brought over you a
deep sleep:
He has sealed your eyes (the
prophets);
he has covered your heads (the
seers).

11 For you this whole vision is nothing
but words sealed in a scroll. And if you
give the scroll to someone who can read,
and say to him, "Read this, please," he
will answer, "I can't; it is sealed." 12 Or if
you give the scroll to someone who cannot read, and say, "Read this, please," he
will answer, "I don't know how to read."

13 The Lord says:

"These people come near to me with
their mouth
and honor me with their lips,
but their hearts are far from me.
Their worship of me
is made up only of rules taught by
men.[a]
14 Therefore once more I will astound
these people
with wonder upon wonder;
the wisdom of the wise will perish,
the intelligence of the intelligent
will vanish."
15 Woe to those who go to great depths
to hide their plans from the LORD,
who do their work in darkness and
think,
"Who sees us? Who will know?"

16 You turn things upside down,
as if the potter were thought to be
like the clay!
Shall what is formed say to him who
formed it,
"He did not make me"?
Can the pot say of the potter,
"He knows nothing"?

17 In a very short time, will not
Lebanon be turned into a
fertile field
and the fertile field seem like a
forest?
18 In that day the deaf will hear the
words of the scroll,
and out of gloom and darkness
the eyes of the blind will see.
19 Once more the humble will rejoice in
the LORD;
the needy will rejoice in the Holy
One of Israel.
20 The ruthless will vanish,
the mockers will disappear,
and all who have an eye for evil
will be cut down—
21 those who with a word make a man
out to be guilty,
who ensnare the defender in court
and with false testimony deprive
the innocent of justice.

22 Therefore this is what the LORD, who
redeemed Abraham, says to the house
of Jacob:

"No longer will Jacob be ashamed;
no longer will their faces grow pale.
23 When they see among them their
children,
the work of my hands,
they will keep my name holy;
they will acknowledge the holiness
of the Holy One of Jacob,
and will stand in awe of the God of
Israel.
24 Those who are wayward in spirit will
gain understanding;
those who complain will accept
instruction."

---

a 13 Hebrew; Septuagint They worship me in vain; / their teachings are but rules taught by men

Woe to the Obstinate Nation

30 "Woe to the obstinate children,"
declares the LORD,
"to those who carry out plans that are
not mine,
forming an alliance, but not by my
Spirit,
heaping sin upon sin;
² who go down to Egypt
without consulting me;
who look for help to Pharaoh's
protection,
to Egypt's shade for refuge.
³ But Pharaoh's protection will be to
your shame,
Egypt's shade will bring you
disgrace.
⁴ Though they have officials in Zoan
and their envoys have arrived in
Hanes,
⁵ everyone will be put to shame
because of a people useless to them,
who bring neither help nor advantage,
but only shame and disgrace."

⁶ An oracle concerning the animals of
the Negev:

Through a land of hardship and
distress,
of lions and lionesses,
of adders and darting snakes,
the envoys carry their riches on
donkeys' backs,
their treasures on the humps of
camels,
to that unprofitable nation,
⁷   to Egypt, whose help is utterly
useless.
Therefore I call her
Rahab the Do-Nothing.

⁸ Go now, write it on a tablet for them,
inscribe it on a scroll,
that for the days to come
it may be an everlasting witness.
⁹ These are rebellious people, deceitful
children,
children unwilling to listen to the
LORD's instruction.
¹⁰ They say to the seers,

"See no more visions!"
and to the prophets,
"Give us no more visions of what
is right!
Tell us pleasant things,
prophesy illusions.
¹¹ Leave this way,
get off this path,
and stop confronting us
with the Holy One of Israel!"

¹² Therefore, this is what the Holy One
of Israel says:

"Because you have rejected this
message,
relied on oppression
and depended on deceit,
¹³ this sin will become for you
like a high wall, cracked and
bulging,
that collapses suddenly, in an
instant.
¹⁴ It will break in pieces like pottery,
shattered so mercilessly
that among its pieces not a fragment
will be found
for taking coals from a hearth
or scooping water out of a cistern."

¹⁵ This is what the Sovereign LORD, the
Holy One of Israel, says:

"In repentance and rest is your
salvation,
in quietness and trust is your
strength,
but you would have none of it.
¹⁶ You said, 'No, we will flee on horses.'
Therefore you will flee!
You said, 'We will ride off on swift
horses.'
Therefore your pursuers will be
swift!
¹⁷ A thousand will flee
at the threat of one;
at the threat of five
you will all flee away,
till you are left
like a flagstaff on a mountaintop,
like a banner on a hill."

Knowing Which Way to Go

GOING deeper

READ AND CONSIDER: ISAIAH 30:19-26

"Whether you turn to the right or to the left, your ears will hear a voice behind you, saying, 'This is the way; walk in it' " (Isaiah 30:21).

We pray about a lot of things—things we need, things we want, safety for our families, traveling mercies, strength in times of grief. Very often, we pray for guidance. We need to know God's will about a big decision, how to solve a problem, how to deal with people, how to face adversity. We want to know God's will because it is a place of safety. When we live outside of God's will, we forfeit His protection.

We all want to be in the center of God's will. That's why we shouldn't pursue a career, move to another place, or make any major life change without knowing that it is the will of God. The way we find out is to regularly ask God to show us what His will is and then ask Him to lead us in it. When you ask Him to speak to your heart, He will do that. He will give you peace about a certain thing and *lack* of peace about others. What joy to have peace that as we confidently set foot in a certain direction, God is leading us on that particular path. We can be confident that whatever happens along the way, we don't have to worry because we are right where God wants us to be.

But all too often we don't hear that voice behind us. We hear the voices clamoring around us instead; we hear our own internal concerns and issues; we're in a hurry, and so we just forge ahead on the path and hope that everything will work out in the end.

When Isaiah gave this promise of God's guidance, it was in the midst of a description of people turning their hearts back to God. He had just prophesied to them about God's compassion in waiting for them to get their priorities in line. When they established right priorities, when their hearts were drawn in the right direction, God's voice would guide them.

As you seek guidance, listen for God's voice. It will be there. Take a few quiet moments to wait on Him and give Him time to respond.

18 Yet the LORD longs to be gracious to you;
    he rises to show you compassion.
For the LORD is a God of justice.
    Blessed are all who wait for him!

19 O people of Zion, who live in Jerusalem, you will weep no more. How gracious he will be when you cry for help! As soon as he hears, he will answer you. 20 Although the Lord gives you the bread of adversity and the water of affliction, your teachers will be hidden no more; with your own eyes you will see them. 21 Whether you turn to the right or to the left, your ears will hear a voice behind you, saying, "This is the way; walk in it." 22 Then you will defile your idols overlaid with silver and your images covered with gold; you will throw them away like a menstrual cloth and say to them, "Away with you!"

23 He will also send you rain for the seed you sow in the ground, and the food that comes from the land will be rich and plentiful. In that day your cattle will graze in broad meadows. 24 The oxen and donkeys that work the soil will eat fodder and mash, spread out with fork and shovel. 25 In the day of great slaughter, when the towers fall, streams of water will flow on

every high mountain and every lofty hill. ²⁶The moon will shine like the sun, and the sunlight will be seven times brighter, like the light of seven full days, when the LORD binds up the bruises of his people and heals the wounds he inflicted.

²⁷See, the Name of the LORD comes
    from afar,
  with burning anger and dense
    clouds of smoke;
his lips are full of wrath,
  and his tongue is a consuming fire.
²⁸His breath is like a rushing torrent,
  rising up to the neck.
He shakes the nations in the sieve of
    destruction;
  he places in the jaws of the peoples
  a bit that leads them astray.
²⁹And you will sing
    as on the night you celebrate a holy
      festival;
  your hearts will rejoice
    as when people go up with flutes
  to the mountain of the LORD,
    to the Rock of Israel.
³⁰The LORD will cause men to hear his
    majestic voice
    and will make them see his arm
      coming down
  with raging anger and consuming fire,
    with cloudburst, thunderstorm and
      hail.
³¹The voice of the LORD will shatter
    Assyria;
    with his scepter he will strike them
      down.
³²Every stroke the LORD lays on them
    with his punishing rod
  will be to the music of tambourines
    and harps,
    as he fights them in battle with the
      blows of his arm.
³³Topheth has long been prepared;
  it has been made ready for the king.
Its fire pit has been made deep and
    wide,
  with an abundance of fire and
    wood;
the breath of the LORD,

like a stream of burning sulfur,
  sets it ablaze.

Woe to Those Who Rely on Egypt

31 Woe to those who go down to
      Egypt for help,
  who rely on horses,
  who trust in the multitude of their
    chariots
    and in the great strength of their
      horsemen,
  but do not look to the Holy One of
    Israel,
    or seek help from the LORD.
²Yet he too is wise and can bring
    disaster;
    he does not take back his words.
He will rise up against the house of
    the wicked,
    against those who help evildoers.
³But the Egyptians are men and not
    God;
    their horses are flesh and not spirit.
When the LORD stretches out his
    hand,
  he who helps will stumble,
  he who is helped will fall;
  both will perish together.

⁴This is what the LORD says to me:

"As a lion growls,
  a great lion over his prey—
and though a whole band of
    shepherds
  is called together against him,
he is not frightened by their shouts
  or disturbed by their clamor—
so the LORD Almighty will come
    down
    to do battle on Mount Zion and on
      its heights.
⁵Like birds hovering overhead,
  the LORD Almighty will shield
    Jerusalem;
he will shield it and deliver it,
  he will 'pass over' it and will rescue
    it."

⁶Return to him you have so greatly revolted against, O Israelites. ⁷For in

that day every one of you will reject the
idols of silver and gold your sinful hands
have made.

8 "Assyria will fall by a sword that is
not of man;
a sword, not of mortals, will devour
them.
They will flee before the sword
and their young men will be put to
forced labor.
9 Their stronghold will fall because of
terror;
at sight of the battle standard their
commanders will panic,"
declares the LORD,
whose fire is in Zion,
whose furnace is in Jerusalem.

The Kingdom of Righteousness

32 See, a king will reign in
righteousness
and rulers will rule with justice.
2 Each man will be like a shelter from
the wind
and a refuge from the storm,
like streams of water in the desert
and the shadow of a great rock in a
thirsty land.

3 Then the eyes of those who see will
no longer be closed,
and the ears of those who hear will
listen.
4 The mind of the rash will know and
understand,
and the stammering tongue will be
fluent and clear.
5 No longer will the fool be called
noble
nor the scoundrel be highly
respected.
6 For the fool speaks folly,
his mind is busy with evil:
He practices ungodliness
and spreads error concerning the
LORD;
the hungry he leaves empty
and from the thirsty he withholds
water.
7 The scoundrel's methods are wicked,

he makes up evil schemes
to destroy the poor with lies,
even when the plea of the needy is
just.
8 But the noble man makes noble plans,
and by noble deeds he stands.

The Women of Jerusalem

9 You women who are so complacent,
rise up and listen to me;
you daughters who feel secure,
hear what I have to say!
10 In little more than a year
you who feel secure will tremble;
the grape harvest will fail,
and the harvest of fruit will not
come.
11 Tremble, you complacent women;
shudder, you daughters who feel
secure!
Strip off your clothes,
put sackcloth around your waists.
12 Beat your breasts for the pleasant
fields,
for the fruitful vines
13 and for the land of my people,
a land overgrown with thorns and
briers—
yes, mourn for all houses of merriment
and for this city of revelry.
14 The fortress will be abandoned,
the noisy city deserted;
citadel and watchtower will become a
wasteland forever,
the delight of donkeys, a pasture for
flocks,
15 till the Spirit is poured upon us from
on high,
and the desert becomes a fertile
field,
and the fertile field seems like a
forest.
16 Justice will dwell in the desert
and righteousness live in the fertile
field.
17 The fruit of righteousness will be
peace;
the effect of righteousness will
be quietness and confidence
forever.

18My people will live in peaceful
    dwelling places,
  in secure homes,
  in undisturbed places of rest.

Praying Isaiah 32:17-18
Help me, God, to live a righteous life
so that I may always dwell in a peaceful,
quiet, secure, and restful place.

19Though hail flattens the forest
    and the city is leveled completely,
20how blessed you will be,
    sowing your seed by every stream,
    and letting your cattle and donkeys
      range free.

Distress and Help

33 Woe to you, O destroyer,
    you who have not been
      destroyed!
  Woe to you, O traitor,
    you who have not been betrayed!
  When you stop destroying,
    you will be destroyed;
  when you stop betraying,
    you will be betrayed.

2O LORD, be gracious to us;
    we long for you.
  Be our strength every morning,
    our salvation in time of distress.
3At the thunder of your voice, the
    peoples flee;
  when you rise up, the nations
    scatter.
4Your plunder, O nations, is harvested
    as by young locusts;
  like a swarm of locusts men pounce
    on it.

5The LORD is exalted, for he dwells on
    high;
  he will fill Zion with justice and
    righteousness.
6He will be the sure foundation for
    your times,
  a rich store of salvation and wisdom
    and knowledge;

the fear of the LORD is the key to
    this treasure.a
7Look, their brave men cry aloud in
    the streets;
  the envoys of peace weep bitterly.
8The highways are deserted,
    no travelers are on the roads.
  The treaty is broken,
    its witnessesb are despised,
    no one is respected.
9The land mournsc and wastes away,
    Lebanon is ashamed and withers;
  Sharon is like the Arabah,
    and Bashan and Carmel drop their
      leaves.

10"Now will I arise," says the LORD.
    "Now will I be exalted;
    now will I be lifted up.
11You conceive chaff,
    you give birth to straw;
  your breath is a fire that consumes
    you.
12The peoples will be burned as if to
    lime;
  like cut thornbushes they will be
    set ablaze."

13You who are far away, hear what I
    have done;
  you who are near, acknowledge my
    power!
14The sinners in Zion are terrified;
    trembling grips the godless:
  "Who of us can dwell with the
    consuming fire?
  Who of us can dwell with
    everlasting burning?"
15He who walks righteously
    and speaks what is right,
  who rejects gain from extortion
    and keeps his hand from accepting
      bribes,
  who stops his ears against plots of
    murder
    and shuts his eyes against
      contemplating evil—
16this is the man who will dwell on the
    heights,

---

a 6 Or *is a treasure from him*   b 8 Dead Sea Scrolls; Masoretic Text / *the cities*   c 9 Or *dries up*

whose refuge will be the mountain
fortress.
His bread will be supplied,
and water will not fail him.

[17] Your eyes will see the king in his
beauty
and view a land that stretches
afar.
[18] In your thoughts you will ponder the
former terror:
"Where is that chief officer?
Where is the one who took the
revenue?
Where is the officer in charge of
the towers?"
[19] You will see those arrogant people no
more,
those people of an obscure speech,
with their strange,
incomprehensible tongue.

[20] Look upon Zion, the city of our
festivals;
your eyes will see Jerusalem,
a peaceful abode, a tent that will
not be moved;
its stakes will never be pulled up,
nor any of its ropes broken.
[21] There the LORD will be our Mighty
One.
It will be like a place of broad rivers
and streams.
No galley with oars will ride them,
no mighty ship will sail them.
[22] For the LORD is our judge,
the LORD is our lawgiver,
the LORD is our king;
it is he who will save us.

[23] Your rigging hangs loose:
The mast is not held secure,
the sail is not spread.
Then an abundance of spoils will be
divided
and even the lame will carry off
plunder.
[24] No one living in Zion will say, "I am
ill";

and the sins of those who dwell
there will be forgiven.

Judgment Against the Nations

34 Come near, you nations, and
listen;
pay attention, you peoples!
Let the earth hear, and all that is in it,
the world, and all that comes out
of it!
[2] The LORD is angry with all nations;
his wrath is upon all their armies.
He will totally destroy[a] them,
he will give them over to slaughter.
[3] Their slain will be thrown out,
their dead bodies will send up a
stench;
the mountains will be soaked with
their blood.
[4] All the stars of the heavens will be
dissolved
and the sky rolled up like a scroll;
all the starry host will fall
like withered leaves from the vine,
like shriveled figs from the fig tree.

[5] My sword has drunk its fill in the
heavens;
see, it descends in judgment on
Edom,
the people I have totally destroyed.
[6] The sword of the LORD is bathed in
blood,
it is covered with fat—
the blood of lambs and goats,
fat from the kidneys of rams.
For the LORD has a sacrifice in Bozrah
and a great slaughter in Edom.
[7] And the wild oxen will fall with
them,
the bull calves and the great bulls.
Their land will be drenched with
blood,
and the dust will be soaked with
fat.

[8] For the LORD has a day of vengeance,
a year of retribution, to uphold
Zion's cause.

---

[a] 2 The Hebrew term refers to the irrevocable giving over of things or persons to the LORD, often by totally destroying them; also
in verse 5.

⁹ Edom's streams will be turned into
  pitch,
  her dust into burning sulfur;
  her land will become blazing pitch!
¹⁰ It will not be quenched night and day;
  its smoke will rise forever.
From generation to generation it will
  lie desolate;
  no one will ever pass through it
  again.
¹¹ The desert owlᵃ and screech owlᵃ will
  possess it;
  the great owlᵃ and the raven will
  nest there.
God will stretch out over Edom
  the measuring line of chaos
  and the plumb line of desolation.
¹² Her nobles will have nothing there to
  be called a kingdom,
  all her princes will vanish away.
¹³ Thorns will overrun her citadels,
  nettles and brambles her
  strongholds.
She will become a haunt for jackals,
  a home for owls.
¹⁴ Desert creatures will meet with
  hyenas,
  and wild goats will bleat to each
  other;
  there the night creatures will also
  repose
  and find for themselves places of
  rest.
¹⁵ The owl will nest there and lay eggs,
  she will hatch them, and care for
  her young under the shadow of
  her wings;
  there also the falcons will gather,
  each with its mate.

¹⁶ Look in the scroll of the LORD and
read:
None of these will be missing,
  not one will lack her mate.
For it is his mouth that has given the
  order,
  and his Spirit will gather them
  together.

¹⁷ He allots their portions;
  his hand distributes them by
  measure.
They will possess it forever
  and dwell there from generation to
  generation.

Joy of the Redeemed

35 The desert and the parched land
  will be glad;
  the wilderness will rejoice and
  blossom.
Like the crocus, ² it will burst into
  bloom;
  it will rejoice greatly and shout for
  joy.
The glory of Lebanon will be given
  to it,
  the splendor of Carmel and Sharon;
  they will see the glory of the LORD,
  the splendor of our God.

³ Strengthen the feeble hands,
  steady the knees that give way;
⁴ say to those with fearful hearts,
  "Be strong, do not fear;
  your God will come,
  he will come with vengeance;
  with divine retribution
  he will come to save you."

⁵ Then will the eyes of the blind be
  opened
  and the ears of the deaf unstopped.
⁶ Then will the lame leap like a deer,
  and the mute tongue shout for joy.
Water will gush forth in the
  wilderness
  and streams in the desert.
⁷ The burning sand will become a
  pool,
  the thirsty ground bubbling
  springs.
In the haunts where jackals once lay,
  grass and reeds and papyrus will
  grow.
⁸ And a highway will be there;
  it will be called the Way of
  Holiness.

ᵃ *11* The precise identification of these birds is uncertain.

The unclean will not journey on it;
it will be for those who walk in
that Way;
wicked fools will not go about on
it.[a]
9 No lion will be there,
nor will any ferocious beast get up
on it;
they will not be found there.
But only the redeemed will walk
there,
10 and the ransomed of the LORD will
return.
They will enter Zion with singing;
everlasting joy will crown their
heads.
Gladness and joy will overtake them,
and sorrow and sighing will flee
away.

Praying Isaiah 35:8-10

*I pray that I can always walk in the
way of Your holiness, Lord, so that
I will obtain the joy and gladness
and safety You have for me there.*

Sennacherib Threatens Jerusalem

36 In the fourteenth year of King Hezekiah's reign, Sennacherib king of Assyria attacked all the fortified cities of Judah and captured them. ²Then the king of Assyria sent his field commander with a large army from Lachish to King Hezekiah at Jerusalem. When the commander stopped at the aqueduct of the Upper Pool, on the road to the Washerman's Field, ³Eliakim son of Hilkiah the palace administrator, Shebna the secretary, and Joah son of Asaph the recorder went out to him.

⁴The field commander said to them, "Tell Hezekiah,

" 'This is what the great king, the king of Assyria, says: On what are you basing this confidence of yours? ⁵You say you have strategy and military strength—but you speak only empty words. On whom are you

depending, that you rebel against me? ⁶Look now, you are depending on Egypt, that splintered reed of a staff, which pierces a man's hand and wounds him if he leans on it! Such is Pharaoh king of Egypt to all who depend on him. ⁷And if you say to me, "We are depending on the LORD our God"—isn't he the one whose high places and altars Hezekiah removed, saying to Judah and Jerusalem, "You must worship before this altar"?

⁸" 'Come now, make a bargain with my master, the king of Assyria: I will give you two thousand horses—if you can put riders on them! ⁹How then can you repulse one officer of the least of my master's officials, even though you are depending on Egypt for chariots and horsemen? ¹⁰Furthermore, have I come to attack and destroy this land without the LORD? The LORD himself told me to march against this country and destroy it.' "

¹¹Then Eliakim, Shebna and Joah said to the field commander, "Please speak to your servants in Aramaic, since we understand it. Don't speak to us in Hebrew in the hearing of the people on the wall."

¹²But the commander replied, "Was it only to your master and you that my master sent me to say these things, and not to the men sitting on the wall—who, like you, will have to eat their own filth and drink their own urine?"

¹³Then the commander stood and called out in Hebrew, "Hear the words of the great king, the king of Assyria! ¹⁴This is what the king says: Do not let Hezekiah deceive you. He cannot deliver you! ¹⁵Do not let Hezekiah persuade you to trust in the LORD when he says, 'The LORD will surely deliver us; this city will not be given into the hand of the king of Assyria.'

¹⁶"Do not listen to Hezekiah. This is what the king of Assyria says: Make peace with me and come out to me. Then every

one of you will eat from his own vine and fig tree and drink water from his own cistern, [17]until I come and take you to a land like your own—a land of grain and new wine, a land of bread and vineyards.

[18]"Do not let Hezekiah mislead you when he says, 'The LORD will deliver us.' Has the god of any nation ever delivered his land from the hand of the king of Assyria? [19]Where are the gods of Hamath and Arpad? Where are the gods of Sepharvaim? Have they rescued Samaria from my hand? [20]Who of all the gods of these countries has been able to save his land from me? How then can the LORD deliver Jerusalem from my hand?"

[21]But the people remained silent and said nothing in reply, because the king had commanded, "Do not answer him."

[22]Then Eliakim son of Hilkiah the palace administrator, Shebna the secretary, and Joah son of Asaph the recorder went to Hezekiah, with their clothes torn, and told him what the field commander had said.

Jerusalem's Deliverance Foretold

37 When King Hezekiah heard this, he tore his clothes and put on sackcloth and went into the temple of the LORD. [2]He sent Eliakim the palace administrator, Shebna the secretary, and the leading priests, all wearing sackcloth, to the prophet Isaiah son of Amoz. [3]They told him, "This is what Hezekiah says: This day is a day of distress and rebuke and disgrace, as when children come to the point of birth and there is no strength to deliver them. [4]It may be that the LORD your God will hear the words of the field commander, whom his master, the king of Assyria, has sent to ridicule the living God, and that he will rebuke him for the words the LORD your God has heard. Therefore pray for the remnant that still survives."

[5]When King Hezekiah's officials came to Isaiah, [6]Isaiah said to them, "Tell your master, 'This is what the LORD says: Do not be afraid of what you have heard—those words with which the underlings of the king of Assyria have blasphemed me. [7]Listen! I am going to put a spirit in him so that when he hears a certain report, he will return to his own country, and there I will have him cut down with the sword.'"

[8]When the field commander heard that the king of Assyria had left Lachish, he withdrew and found the king fighting against Libnah.

[9]Now Sennacherib received a report that Tirhakah, the Cushite[a] king ¸of Egypt¸ was marching out to fight against him. When he heard it, he sent messengers to Hezekiah with this word: [10]"Say to Hezekiah king of Judah: Do not let the god you depend on deceive you when he says, 'Jerusalem will not be handed over to the king of Assyria.' [11]Surely you have heard what the kings of Assyria have done to all the countries, destroying them completely. And will you be delivered? [12]Did the gods of the nations that were destroyed by my forefathers deliver them—the gods of Gozan, Haran, Rezeph and the people of Eden who were in Tel Assar? [13]Where is the king of Hamath, the king of Arpad, the king of the city of Sepharvaim, or of Hena or Ivvah?"

Hezekiah's Prayer

[14]Hezekiah received the letter from the messengers and read it. Then he went up to the temple of the LORD and spread it out before the LORD. [15]And Hezekiah prayed to the LORD: [16]"O LORD Almighty, God of Israel, enthroned between the cherubim, you alone are God over all the kingdoms of the earth. You have made heaven and earth. [17]Give ear, O LORD, and hear; open your eyes, O LORD, and see; listen to all the words Sennacherib has sent to insult the living God.

[18]"It is true, O LORD, that the Assyrian kings have laid waste all these peoples and their lands. [19]They have thrown their gods into the fire and destroyed them, for

---

a [9] That is, from the upper Nile region

they were not gods but only wood and stone, fashioned by human hands. ²⁰Now, O LORD our God, deliver us from his hand, so that all kingdoms on earth may know that you alone, O LORD, are God.ª"

Sennacherib's Fall

²¹Then Isaiah son of Amoz sent a message to Hezekiah: "This is what the LORD, the God of Israel, says: Because you have prayed to me concerning Sennacherib king of Assyria, ²²this is the word the LORD has spoken against him:

"The Virgin Daughter of Zion
  despises and mocks you.
The Daughter of Jerusalem
  tosses her head as you flee.
²³Who is it you have insulted and
    blasphemed?
  Against whom have you raised your
    voice
and lifted your eyes in pride?
  Against the Holy One of Israel!
²⁴By your messengers
  you have heaped insults on the
    Lord.
And you have said,
  'With my many chariots
I have ascended the heights of the
    mountains,
  the utmost heights of Lebanon.
I have cut down its tallest cedars,
  the choicest of its pines.
I have reached its remotest heights,
  the finest of its forests.
²⁵I have dug wells in foreign landsᵇ
  and drunk the water there.
With the soles of my feet
  I have dried up all the streams of
    Egypt.'

²⁶"Have you not heard?
  Long ago I ordained it.
In days of old I planned it;
  now I have brought it to pass,
that you have turned fortified cities
  into piles of stone.

²⁷Their people, drained of power,
  are dismayed and put to shame.
They are like plants in the field,
  like tender green shoots,
like grass sprouting on the roof,
  scorchedᶜ before it grows up.

²⁸"But I know where you stay
  and when you come and go
  and how you rage against me.
²⁹Because you rage against me
  and because your insolence has
    reached my ears,
I will put my hook in your nose
  and my bit in your mouth,
and I will make you return
  by the way you came.

³⁰"This will be the sign for you, O Hezekiah:

"This year you will eat what grows
    by itself,
  and the second year what springs
    from that.
But in the third year sow and reap,
  plant vineyards and eat their fruit.
³¹Once more a remnant of the house of
    Judah
  will take root below and bear fruit
    above.
³²For out of Jerusalem will come a
    remnant,
  and out of Mount Zion a band of
    survivors.
The zeal of the LORD Almighty
  will accomplish this.

³³"Therefore this is what the LORD says concerning the king of Assyria:

"He will not enter this city
  or shoot an arrow here.
He will not come before it with shield
  or build a siege ramp against it.
³⁴By the way that he came he will
    return;
  he will not enter this city,"
            declares the LORD.

ª 20 Dead Sea Scrolls (see also 2 Kings 19:19); Masoretic Text alone are the Lord   ᵇ 25 Dead Sea Scrolls (see also 2 Kings 19:24); Masoretic Text does not have in foreign lands.   ᶜ 27 Some manuscripts of the Masoretic Text, Dead Sea Scrolls and some Septuagint manuscripts (see also 2 Kings 19:26); most manuscripts of the Masoretic Text roof / and terraced fields

35"I will defend this city and save it,
for my sake and for the sake of
David my servant!"

36Then the angel of the LORD went out and put to death a hundred and eighty-five thousand men in the Assyrian camp. When the people got up the next morning—there were all the dead bodies! 37So Sennacherib king of Assyria broke camp and withdrew. He returned to Nineveh and stayed there.

38One day, while he was worshiping in the temple of his god Nisroch, his sons Adrammelech and Sharezer cut him down with the sword, and they escaped to the land of Ararat. And Esarhaddon his son succeeded him as king.

Hezekiah's Illness

38 In those days Hezekiah became ill and was at the point of death. The prophet Isaiah son of Amoz went to him and said, "This is what the LORD says: Put your house in order, because you are going to die; you will not recover."

2Hezekiah turned his face to the wall and prayed to the LORD, 3"Remember, O LORD, how I have walked before you faithfully and with wholehearted devotion and have done what is good in your eyes." And Hezekiah wept bitterly.

4Then the word of the LORD came to Isaiah: 5"Go and tell Hezekiah, 'This is what the LORD, the God of your father David, says: I have heard your prayer and seen your tears; I will add fifteen years to your life. 6And I will deliver you and this city from the hand of the king of Assyria. I will defend this city.

7"This is the LORD's sign to you that the LORD will do what he has promised: 8I will make the shadow cast by the sun go back the ten steps it has gone down on the stairway of Ahaz.'" So the sunlight went back the ten steps it had gone down.

9A writing of Hezekiah king of Judah after his illness and recovery:

10I said, "In the prime of my life
must I go through the gates of
death[a]
and be robbed of the rest of my
years?"
11I said, "I will not again see the LORD,
the LORD, in the land of the living;
no longer will I look on mankind,
or be with those who now dwell in
this world.[b]
12Like a shepherd's tent my house
has been pulled down and taken
from me.
Like a weaver I have rolled up my
life,
and he has cut me off from the
loom;
day and night you made an end of
me.
13I waited patiently till dawn,
but like a lion he broke all my
bones;
day and night you made an end of
me.
14I cried like a swift or thrush,
I moaned like a mourning dove.
My eyes grew weak as I looked to the
heavens.
I am troubled; O Lord, come to my
aid!"
15But what can I say?
He has spoken to me, and he
himself has done this.
I will walk humbly all my years
because of this anguish of my
soul.
16Lord, by such things men live;
and my spirit finds life in them
too.
You restored me to health
and let me live.
17Surely it was for my benefit
that I suffered such anguish.
In your love you kept me
from the pit of destruction;
you have put all my sins
behind your back.
18For the grave[a] cannot praise you,

---

a 10,18 Hebrew *Sheol*   b 11 A few Hebrew manuscripts; most Hebrew manuscripts *in the place of cessation*

death cannot sing your praise;
those who go down to the pit
cannot hope for your faithfulness.
¹⁹The living, the living—they praise
you,
as I am doing today;
fathers tell their children
about your faithfulness.

²⁰The LORD will save me,
and we will sing with stringed
instruments
all the days of our lives
in the temple of the LORD.

²¹Isaiah had said, "Prepare a poultice of figs and apply it to the boil, and he will recover."

²²Hezekiah had asked, "What will be the sign that I will go up to the temple of the LORD?"

Envoys From Babylon

39 At that time Merodach-Baladan son of Baladan king of Babylon sent Hezekiah letters and a gift, because he had heard of his illness and recovery. ²Hezekiah received the envoys gladly and showed them what was in his storehouses—the silver, the gold, the spices, the fine oil, his entire armory and everything found among his treasures. There was nothing in his palace or in all his kingdom that Hezekiah did not show them.

³Then Isaiah the prophet went to King Hezekiah and asked, "What did those men say, and where did they come from?"

"From a distant land," Hezekiah replied. "They came to me from Babylon."

⁴The prophet asked, "What did they see in your palace?"

"They saw everything in my palace," Hezekiah said. "There is nothing among my treasures that I did not show them."

⁵Then Isaiah said to Hezekiah, "Hear the word of the LORD Almighty: ⁶The time will surely come when everything in your palace, and all that your fathers have stored up until this day, will be carried off to Babylon. Nothing will be left, says the LORD. ⁷And some of your descendants, your own flesh and blood who will be born to you, will be taken away, and they will become eunuchs in the palace of the king of Babylon."

⁸"The word of the LORD you have spoken is good," Hezekiah replied. For he thought, "There will be peace and security in my lifetime."

Comfort for God's People

40 Comfort, comfort my people,
says your God.
²Speak tenderly to Jerusalem,
and proclaim to her
that her hard service has been
completed,
that her sin has been paid for,
that she has received from the LORD's
hand
double for all her sins.

³A voice of one calling:
"In the desert prepare
the way for the LORD^a;
make straight in the wilderness
a highway for our God.^b
⁴Every valley shall be raised up,
every mountain and hill made low;
the rough ground shall become level,
the rugged places a plain.
⁵And the glory of the LORD will be
revealed,
and all mankind together will see it.
For the mouth of the LORD
has spoken."

⁶A voice says, "Cry out."
And I said, "What shall I cry?"

"All men are like grass,
and all their glory is like the flowers
of the field.
⁷The grass withers and the flowers fall,
because the breath of the LORD
blows on them.
Surely the people are grass.

---

^a 3 Or *A voice of one calling in the desert: / "Prepare the way for the LORD* ^b 3 Hebrew; Septuagint *make straight the paths of our God*

8 The grass withers and the flowers fall,
    but the word of our God stands
        forever."

9 You who bring good tidings to
        Zion,
    go up on a high mountain.
You who bring good tidings to
        Jerusalem,[a]
    lift up your voice with a shout,
lift it up, do not be afraid;
    say to the towns of Judah,
    "Here is your God!"
10 See, the Sovereign LORD comes with
        power,
    and his arm rules for him.
See, his reward is with him,
    and his recompense accompanies
        him.
11 He tends his flock like a shepherd:
    He gathers the lambs in his arms
and carries them close to his heart;
    he gently leads those that have
        young.

12 Who has measured the waters in the
        hollow of his hand,
    or with the breadth of his hand
        marked off the heavens?
Who has held the dust of the earth in
        a basket,
    or weighed the mountains on the
        scales
    and the hills in a balance?
13 Who has understood the mind[b] of the
        LORD,
    or instructed him as his counselor?
14 Whom did the LORD consult to
        enlighten him,
    and who taught him the right
        way?
Who was it that taught him
        knowledge
    or showed him the path of
        understanding?

15 Surely the nations are like a drop in a
        bucket;
    they are regarded as dust on the
        scales;

he weighs the islands as though
    they were fine dust.
16 Lebanon is not sufficient for altar
        fires,
    nor its animals enough for burnt
        offerings.
17 Before him all the nations are as
        nothing;
    they are regarded by him as
        worthless
    and less than nothing.

18 To whom, then, will you compare
        God?
    What image will you compare him
        to?
19 As for an idol, a craftsman casts it,
    and a goldsmith overlays it with
        gold
    and fashions silver chains for it.
20 A man too poor to present such an
        offering
    selects wood that will not rot.
He looks for a skilled craftsman
    to set up an idol that will not
        topple.

21 Do you not know?
    Have you not heard?
Has it not been told you from the
        beginning?
    Have you not understood since the
        earth was founded?
22 He sits enthroned above the circle of
        the earth,
    and its people are like grasshoppers.
He stretches out the heavens like a
        canopy,
    and spreads them out like a tent to
        live in.
23 He brings princes to naught
    and reduces the rulers of this world
        to nothing.
24 No sooner are they planted,
    no sooner are they sown,
    no sooner do they take root in the
        ground,
than he blows on them and they
        wither,

---

[a] 9 Or O Zion, bringer of good tidings, / go up on a high mountain. / O Jerusalem, bringer of good tidings   [b] 13 Or Spirit; or spirit

and a whirlwind sweeps them away
like chaff.

25 "To whom will you compare me?
Or who is my equal?" says the
Holy One.
26 Lift your eyes and look to the
heavens:
Who created all these?
He who brings out the starry host one
by one,
and calls them each by name.
Because of his great power and
mighty strength,
not one of them is missing.

27 Why do you say, O Jacob,
and complain, O Israel,
"My way is hidden from the LORD;
my cause is disregarded by my
God"?
28 Do you not know?
Have you not heard?
The LORD is the everlasting God,
the Creator of the ends of the earth.
He will not grow tired or weary,
and his understanding no one can
fathom.
29 He gives strength to the weary
and increases the power of the
weak.
30 Even youths grow tired and weary,
and young men stumble and fall;

Praying Isaiah 40:31

*Lord, I wait on You to renew my strength
so that I can rise up and run the race
and not become weary or weak.*

31 but those who hope in the LORD
will renew their strength.
They will soar on wings like eagles;
they will run and not grow weary,
they will walk and not be faint.

The Helper of Israel

41 "Be silent before me, you islands!
Let the nations renew their
strength!

Let them come forward and speak;
let us meet together at the place of
judgment.

2 "Who has stirred up one from the
east,
calling him in righteousness to his
service[a]?
He hands nations over to him
and subdues kings before him.
He turns them to dust with his
sword,
to windblown chaff with his bow.
3 He pursues them and moves on
unscathed,
by a path his feet have not traveled
before.
4 Who has done this and carried it
through,
calling forth the generations from
the beginning?
I, the LORD—with the first of them
and with the last—I am he."

5 The islands have seen it and fear;
the ends of the earth tremble.
They approach and come forward;
6   each helps the other
and says to his brother, "Be
strong!"
7 The craftsman encourages the
goldsmith,
and he who smooths with the
hammer
spurs on him who strikes the anvil.
He says of the welding, "It is good."
He nails down the idol so it will
not topple.

8 "But you, O Israel, my servant,
Jacob, whom I have chosen,
you descendants of Abraham my
friend,
9 I took you from the ends of the earth,
from its farthest corners I called
you.
I said, 'You are my servant';
I have chosen you and have not
rejected you.
10 So do not fear, for I am with you;

---

a 2 Or / whom victory meets at every step

do not be dismayed, for I am your
God.
I will strengthen you and help you;
I will uphold you with my
righteous right hand.

11"All who rage against you
will surely be ashamed and
disgraced;
those who oppose you
will be as nothing and perish.
12Though you search for your enemies,
you will not find them.
Those who wage war against you
will be as nothing at all.
13For I am the LORD, your God,
who takes hold of your right hand
and says to you, Do not fear;
I will help you.
14Do not be afraid, O worm Jacob,
O little Israel,
for I myself will help you," declares
the LORD,
your Redeemer, the Holy One of
Israel.
15"See, I will make you into a
threshing sledge,
new and sharp, with many teeth.
You will thresh the mountains and
crush them,
and reduce the hills to chaff.
16You will winnow them, the wind
will pick them up,
and a gale will blow them away.
But you will rejoice in the LORD
and glory in the Holy One of Israel.

17"The poor and needy search for
water,
but there is none;
their tongues are parched with
thirst.
But I the LORD will answer them;
I, the God of Israel, will not forsake
them.
18I will make rivers flow on barren
heights,
and springs within the valleys.
I will turn the desert into pools of
water,

and the parched ground into
springs.
19I will put in the desert
the cedar and the acacia, the myrtle
and the olive.
I will set pines in the wasteland,
the fir and the cypress together,

Prayer is . . .

*receiving a drink of cool,
refreshing living water when your
spirit is dry and thirsty.*

20so that people may see and know,
may consider and understand,
that the hand of the LORD has done
this,
that the Holy One of Israel has
created it.

21"Present your case," says the LORD.
"Set forth your arguments," says
Jacob's King.
22"Bring in ⌊your idols⌋ to tell us
what is going to happen.
Tell us what the former things were,
so that we may consider them
and know their final outcome.
Or declare to us the things to come,
23   tell us what the future holds,
so we may know that you are
gods.
Do something, whether good or bad,
so that we will be dismayed and
filled with fear.
24But you are less than nothing
and your works are utterly
worthless;
he who chooses you is detestable.

25"I have stirred up one from the north,
and he comes—
one from the rising sun who calls
on my name.
He treads on rulers as if they were
mortar,

as if he were a potter treading the
clay.
26Who told of this from the beginning,
so we could know,
or beforehand, so we could say, 'He
was right'?
No one told of this,
no one foretold it,
no one heard any words from you.
27I was the first to tell Zion, 'Look,
here they are!'
I gave to Jerusalem a messenger of
good tidings.
28I look but there is no one—
no one among them to give counsel,
no one to give answer when I ask
them.
29See, they are all false!
Their deeds amount to nothing;
their images are but wind and
confusion.

The Servant of the LORD

42 "Here is my servant, whom I
uphold,
my chosen one in whom I delight;
I will put my Spirit on him
and he will bring justice to the
nations.
2He will not shout or cry out,
or raise his voice in the streets.
3A bruised reed he will not break,
and a smoldering wick he will not
snuff out.
In faithfulness he will bring forth
justice;
4 he will not falter or be discouraged
till he establishes justice on earth.
In his law the islands will put their
hope."

5This is what God the LORD says—
he who created the heavens and
stretched them out,
who spread out the earth and all
that comes out of it,
who gives breath to its people,
and life to those who walk on it:
6"I, the LORD, have called you in
righteousness;

I will take hold of your hand.
I will keep you and will make you
to be a covenant for the people
and a light for the Gentiles,
7to open eyes that are blind,
to free captives from prison
and to release from the dungeon
those who sit in darkness.

8"I am the LORD; that is my name!
I will not give my glory to another
or my praise to idols.
9See, the former things have taken
place,
and new things I declare;
before they spring into being
I announce them to you."

Song of Praise to the LORD

10Sing to the LORD a new song,
his praise from the ends of the
earth,
you who go down to the sea, and all
that is in it,
you islands, and all who live in
them.
11Let the desert and its towns raise their
voices;
let the settlements where Kedar
lives rejoice.
Let the people of Sela sing for joy;
let them shout from the
mountaintops.
12Let them give glory to the LORD
and proclaim his praise in the
islands.
13The LORD will march out like a
mighty man,
like a warrior he will stir up his
zeal;
with a shout he will raise the battle
cry
and will triumph over his enemies.

14"For a long time I have kept silent,
I have been quiet and held myself
back.
But now, like a woman in childbirth,
I cry out, I gasp and pant.
15I will lay waste the mountains and
hills

and dry up all their vegetation;
I will turn rivers into islands
and dry up the pools.
16I will lead the blind by ways they
have not known,
along unfamiliar paths I will guide
them;
I will turn the darkness into light
before them
and make the rough places smooth.
These are the things I will do;
I will not forsake them.
17But those who trust in idols,
who say to images, 'You are our
gods,'
will be turned back in utter shame.

Israel Blind and Deaf

18"Hear, you deaf;
look, you blind, and see!
19Who is blind but my servant,
and deaf like the messenger I send?
Who is blind like the one committed
to me,
blind like the servant of the LORD?
20You have seen many things, but have
paid no attention;
your ears are open, but you hear
nothing."
21It pleased the LORD
for the sake of his righteousness
to make his law great and glorious.
22But this is a people plundered and
looted,
all of them trapped in pits
or hidden away in prisons.
They have become plunder,
with no one to rescue them;
they have been made loot,
with no one to say, "Send them
back."

23Which of you will listen to this
or pay close attention in time to
come?
24Who handed Jacob over to become
loot,
and Israel to the plunderers?
Was it not the LORD,

against whom we have sinned?
For they would not follow his ways;
they did not obey his law.
25So he poured out on them his
burning anger,
the violence of war.
It enveloped them in flames, yet they
did not understand;
it consumed them, but they did not
take it to heart.

Israel's Only Savior

43 But now, this is what the LORD
says—
he who created you, O Jacob,
he who formed you, O Israel:
"Fear not, for I have redeemed you;
I have summoned you by name;
you are mine.
2When you pass through the waters,
I will be with you;
and when you pass through the rivers,
they will not sweep over you.
When you walk through the fire,
you will not be burned;
the flames will not set you ablaze.
3For I am the LORD, your God,
the Holy One of Israel, your Savior;
I give Egypt for your ransom,
Cusha and Seba in your stead.
4Since you are precious and honored
in my sight,
and because I love you,
I will give men in exchange for you,
and people in exchange for your
life.
5Do not be afraid, for I am with you;
I will bring your children from the
east
and gather you from the west.
6I will say to the north, 'Give them up!'
and to the south, 'Do not hold
them back.'
Bring my sons from afar
and my daughters from the ends of
the earth—
7everyone who is called by my name,
whom I created for my glory,
whom I formed and made."

---

a 3 That is, the upper Nile region

⁸Lead out those who have eyes but are
blind,
who have ears but are deaf.
⁹All the nations gather together
and the peoples assemble.
Which of them foretold this
and proclaimed to us the former
things?
Let them bring in their witnesses to
prove they were right,
so that others may hear and say, "It
is true."
¹⁰"You are my witnesses," declares the
Lord,
"and my servant whom I have
chosen,
so that you may know and believe me
and understand that I am he.
Before me no god was formed,
nor will there be one after me.
¹¹I, even I, am the Lord,
and apart from me there is no
savior.
¹²I have revealed and saved and
proclaimed—
I, and not some foreign god among
you.
You are my witnesses," declares the
Lord, "that I am God.
¹³   Yes, and from ancient days I am he.
No one can deliver out of my hand.
When I act, who can reverse it?"

God's Mercy and Israel's Unfaithfulness

¹⁴This is what the Lord says—
your Redeemer, the Holy One of
Israel:
"For your sake I will send to Babylon
and bring down as fugitives all the
Babylonians,ᵃ
in the ships in which they took
pride.
¹⁵I am the Lord, your Holy One,
Israel's Creator, your King."

¹⁶This is what the Lord says—
he who made a way through the
sea,
a path through the mighty waters,
¹⁷who drew out the chariots and horses,
the army and reinforcements
together,
and they lay there, never to rise again,
extinguished, snuffed out like a
wick:
¹⁸"Forget the former things;
do not dwell on the past.
¹⁹See, I am doing a new thing!
Now it springs up; do you not
perceive it?
I am making a way in the desert
and streams in the wasteland.
²⁰The wild animals honor me,
the jackals and the owls,
because I provide water in the desert
and streams in the wasteland,
to give drink to my people, my
chosen,
²¹   the people I formed for myself
that they may proclaim my praise.

²²"Yet you have not called upon me,
O Jacob,
you have not wearied yourselves for
me, O Israel.
²³You have not brought me sheep for
burnt offerings,
nor honored me with your
sacrifices.
I have not burdened you with grain
offerings
nor wearied you with demands for
incense.
²⁴You have not bought any fragrant
calamus for me,
or lavished on me the fat of your
sacrifices.
But you have burdened me with your
sins
and wearied me with your offenses.
²⁵"I, even I, am he who blots out
your transgressions, for my own
sake,
and remembers your sins no more.
²⁶Review the past for me,
let us argue the matter together;

ᵃ *14* Or *Chaldeans*

Praise Is the Purest Form of Prayer

GOING deeper

READ AND CONSIDER: ISAIAH 43:16-21

"I provide water in the desert and streams in the wasteland, to give drink to my people, my chosen, the people I formed for myself that they may proclaim my praise" (Isaiah 43:20-21).

My definition of prayer is simply *communicating with God*. It's a love relationship first and foremost. Prayer is baring your soul to the One who loved you before you even knew of Him and letting Him speak to your heart.

Far too often prayer becomes a complicated issue for people. In fact, there can seem to be so many aspects to it that people can become intimidated. They fear that they can't pray well enough, or right enough, or long enough, or eloquently enough. They are afraid that their prayers won't be heard because they themselves are not good enough or holy enough or knowledgeable enough. In all the books I have written, I have sought to dispel that kind of fear and intimidation and make prayer accessible to everyone.

One of the most important forms of prayer—or *communicating with God*—is worship and praise. Worship is the *purest* form of prayer because it causes our minds and souls to focus entirely on God and away from ourselves. It communicates our love, devotion, reverence, appreciation, and thankfulness to God, exalting Him for who He is, communicating our longing for Him, and drawing close to Him for the sake of being close. When we worship God, we are the closest to Him we will ever be. That's because praise welcomes His presence in our midst.

We were created to praise God. And God wants to make praise and worship of Him a way of life. Not necessarily with a hymn and a harp, but with a song in our heart that breaks forth through our lips as praise to the One who created us, formed us, gave us life. When we walk with Him, stay in fellowship with Him, use the gifts He has given us, serve Him wherever we find ourselves, and live for Him at all times, we can't help but praise Him for who He is and all He has done. When we do that for which we were created, we connect with our purpose. It fills our souls. It sets our path right.

Make praise and worship of God the way you live your life every day, and you'll sleep in peace every night.

---

state the case for your innocence.
²⁷Your first father sinned;
   your spokesmen rebelled against me.
²⁸So I will disgrace the dignitaries of
      your temple,
   and I will consign Jacob to
      destruction[a]
   and Israel to scorn.

Israel the Chosen

44 "But now listen, O Jacob, my
      servant,
   Israel, whom I have chosen.

²This is what the LORD says—
   he who made you, who formed you
      in the womb,
   and who will help you:
Do not be afraid, O Jacob, my servant,
   Jeshurun, whom I have chosen.
³For I will pour water on the thirsty
      land,
   and streams on the dry ground;
I will pour out my Spirit on your
      offspring,
   and my blessing on your
      descendants.

---

[a] *28* The Hebrew term refers to the irrevocable giving over of things or persons to the LORD, often by totally destroying them.

4 They will spring up like grass in a
     meadow,
   like poplar trees by flowing
     streams.
5 One will say, 'I belong to the LORD';
     another will call himself by the
     name of Jacob;
   still another will write on his hand,
     'The LORD's,'
   and will take the name Israel.

Praying Isaiah 44:5

*Help me to always remember
that I belong to You, Lord, so that
I never forget who I am.*

The LORD, Not Idols

6 "This is what the LORD says—
     Israel's King and Redeemer, the
     LORD Almighty:
   I am the first and I am the last;
     apart from me there is no God.
7 Who then is like me? Let him
     proclaim it.
   Let him declare and lay out
     before me
   what has happened since I established
     my ancient people,
   and what is yet to come—
     yes, let him foretell what will
     come.
8 Do not tremble, do not be afraid.
     Did I not proclaim this and foretell
     it long ago?
   You are my witnesses. Is there any
     God besides me?
     No, there is no other Rock; I know
     not one."

9 All who make idols are nothing,
     and the things they treasure are
     worthless.
   Those who would speak up for them
     are blind;
     they are ignorant, to their own
     shame.
10 Who shapes a god and casts an idol,
     which can profit him nothing?
11 He and his kind will be put to shame;
     craftsmen are nothing but men.

Let them all come together and take
     their stand;
   they will be brought down to
     terror and infamy.
12 The blacksmith takes a tool
     and works with it in the coals;
   he shapes an idol with hammers,
     he forges it with the might of his
     arm.
   He gets hungry and loses his strength;
     he drinks no water and grows faint.
13 The carpenter measures with a line
     and makes an outline with a
     marker;
   he roughs it out with chisels
     and marks it with compasses.
   He shapes it in the form of man,
     of man in all his glory,
     that it may dwell in a shrine.
14 He cut down cedars,
     or perhaps took a cypress or oak.
   He let it grow among the trees of the
     forest,
     or planted a pine, and the rain
     made it grow.
15 It is man's fuel for burning;
     some of it he takes and warms
     himself,
   he kindles a fire and bakes bread.
   But he also fashions a god and
     worships it;
     he makes an idol and bows down
     to it.
16 Half of the wood he burns in the fire;
     over it he prepares his meal,
   he roasts his meat and eats his fill.
   He also warms himself and says,
     "Ah! I am warm; I see the fire."
17 From the rest he makes a god, his
     idol;
   he bows down to it and worships.
   He prays to it and says,
     "Save me; you are my god."
18 They know nothing, they understand
     nothing;
   their eyes are plastered over so they
     cannot see,
   and their minds closed so they
     cannot understand.

¹⁹No one stops to think,
no one has the knowledge or
understanding to say,
"Half of it I used for fuel;
I even baked bread over its coals,
I roasted meat and I ate.
Shall I make a detestable thing from
what is left?
Shall I bow down to a block of
wood?"
²⁰He feeds on ashes, a deluded heart
misleads him;
he cannot save himself, or say,
"Is not this thing in my right hand
a lie?"

²¹"Remember these things, O Jacob,
for you are my servant, O Israel.
I have made you, you are my servant;
O Israel, I will not forget you.
²²I have swept away your offenses like a
cloud,
your sins like the morning mist.
Return to me,
for I have redeemed you."

²³Sing for joy, O heavens, for the LORD
has done this;
shout aloud, O earth beneath.
Burst into song, you mountains,
you forests and all your trees,
for the LORD has redeemed Jacob,
he displays his glory in Israel.

Jerusalem to Be Inhabited

²⁴"This is what the LORD says—
your Redeemer, who formed you
in the womb:

I am the LORD,
who has made all things,
who alone stretched out the heavens,
who spread out the earth by myself,

²⁵who foils the signs of false prophets
and makes fools of diviners,
who overthrows the learning of the
wise
and turns it into nonsense,
²⁶who carries out the words of his
servants

and fulfills the predictions of his
messengers,

who says of Jerusalem, 'It shall be
inhabited,'
of the towns of Judah, 'They shall
be built,'
and of their ruins, 'I will restore
them,'
²⁷who says to the watery deep, 'Be dry,
and I will dry up your streams,'
²⁸who says of Cyrus, 'He is my
shepherd
and will accomplish all that I please;
he will say of Jerusalem, "Let it be
rebuilt,"
and of the temple, "Let its
foundations be laid."'

45 "This is what the LORD says to
his anointed,
to Cyrus, whose right hand I take
hold of
to subdue nations before him
and to strip kings of their armor,
to open doors before him
so that gates will not be shut:
²I will go before you
and will level the mountainsᵃ;
I will break down gates of bronze
and cut through bars of iron.
³I will give you the treasures of
darkness,
riches stored in secret places,
so that you may know that I am the
LORD,
the God of Israel, who summons
you by name.
⁴For the sake of Jacob my servant,
of Israel my chosen,
I summon you by name
and bestow on you a title of honor,
though you do not acknowledge
me.
⁵I am the LORD, and there is no other;
apart from me there is no God.
I will strengthen you,
though you have not acknowledged
me,

ᵃ 2 Dead Sea Scrolls and Septuagint; the meaning of the word in the Masoretic Text is uncertain.

The Treasure You Find in Darkness

When I gave birth to my first baby, the doctor told me, "You have a boy." I didn't forget that information and have to keep asking him over and over, "What was my baby?" I did not wake up in the hospital the next morning and say to the nurse, "Tell me again what I had." I didn't call my best friend the following week and wonder, "Do you happen to remember whether I gave birth to a boy or girl?" The minute I heard I had a son, no one had to tell me again. From that moment, I knew. An entire vision for my child's future was in place the second I was told the truth.

This experience is the same for every mother and every father. Or anyone who receives life-changing good news.

God wants you to have that same certainty about Him. He wants you to be so convinced of His presence in your life that even when you can't feel it, sense it, or see it, you know He is there. He wants you to be completely sure that the light of His Spirit *in* you will never be put out. You don't have to keep looking for it. You don't have to doubt it. No circumstance can dim it. It is there for now and all eternity.

One of the ways God makes us certain of His light is by allowing us to test it in the darkness. But this darkness is not to be dreaded. It is the darkness God has created for His purposes. "I form the light and create darkness" (Isaiah 45:7). God sometimes allows things to get very dark in our lives in order to grow us up and teach us about Himself. And some things that we accomplish in darkness cannot happen in any other setting.

Think about what it's like when the power goes out in your home at night. You can barely function in the dark. You walk carefully, one step at a time, reaching out for familiar things to steady and guide you until you can find a flashlight, candle, or generator switch. If someone is holding a source of light, you reach out and take their hand so you can move together. You don't take a step until you're certain that both of you are going in the same direction.

That's exactly how God uses darkness in our lives. We're in the dark until we see *His* light in it. He wants us to reach out for *Him* so we can walk together in the same direction. He desires that we draw close so that we sense His presence at all times.

This is not like the darkness of evil, which you can clearly sense. Or the darkness of our own disobedience, which we know in our hearts. This is a different kind of darkness, and God says there are treasures to be found there. "I will give you the treasures of darkness, riches stored in secret places, so that you may know that I am the LORD, the God of Israel, who summons you by name" (Isaiah 45:3).

The treasure we find in the darkness is Him.

For the next "From Stormie's Heart" article, go to page 940.

⁶so that from the rising of the sun
  to the place of its setting
men may know there is none besides
    me.
  I am the LORD, and there is no
    other.
⁷I form the light and create darkness,
  I bring prosperity and create
    disaster;
  I, the LORD, do all these things.

⁸"You heavens above, rain down
    righteousness;
  let the clouds shower it down.
Let the earth open wide,
  let salvation spring up,
let righteousness grow with it;
  I, the LORD, have created it.

⁹"Woe to him who quarrels with his
    Maker,
  to him who is but a potsherd
      among the potsherds on the
      ground.
Does the clay say to the potter,
  'What are you making?'
Does your work say,
  'He has no hands'?
¹⁰Woe to him who says to his father,
  'What have you begotten?'
or to his mother,
  'What have you brought to birth?'

¹¹"This is what the LORD says—
  the Holy One of Israel, and its
    Maker:
Concerning things to come,
  do you question me about my
    children,
  or give me orders about the work
    of my hands?
¹²It is I who made the earth
  and created mankind upon it.
My own hands stretched out the
    heavens;
  I marshaled their starry hosts.
¹³I will raise up Cyrusᵃ in my
    righteousness:
  I will make all his ways straight.
He will rebuild my city

and set my exiles free,
but not for a price or reward,
  says the LORD Almighty."

¹⁴This is what the LORD says:

"The products of Egypt and the
    merchandise of Cush,ᵇ
  and those tall Sabeans—
they will come over to you
  and will be yours;
they will trudge behind you,
  coming over to you in chains.
They will bow down before you
  and plead with you, saying,
'Surely God is with you, and there is
    no other;
  there is no other god.'"

¹⁵Truly you are a God who hides
    himself,
  O God and Savior of Israel.
¹⁶All the makers of idols will be put to
    shame and disgraced;
  they will go off into disgrace
    together.
¹⁷But Israel will be saved by the LORD
  with an everlasting salvation;
you will never be put to shame or
    disgraced,
  to ages everlasting.

¹⁸For this is what the LORD says—
  he who created the heavens,
    he is God;
he who fashioned and made the earth,
    he founded it;
he did not create it to be empty,
    but formed it to be inhabited—
  he says:
"I am the LORD,
  and there is no other.
¹⁹I have not spoken in secret,
    from somewhere in a land of
      darkness;
I have not said to Jacob's
    descendants,
  'Seek me in vain.'
I, the LORD, speak the truth;
  I declare what is right.

ᵃ 13 Hebrew *him*   ᵇ 14 That is, the upper Nile region

20"Gather together and come;
   assemble, you fugitives from the
      nations.
Ignorant are those who carry about
   idols of wood,
   who pray to gods that cannot save.
21Declare what is to be, present it—
   let them take counsel together.
Who foretold this long ago,
   who declared it from the distant
      past?
Was it not I, the LORD?
   And there is no God apart from
      me,
a righteous God and a Savior;
   there is none but me.

22"Turn to me and be saved,
   all you ends of the earth;
   for I am God, and there is no other.
23By myself I have sworn,
   my mouth has uttered in all
      integrity
a word that will not be revoked:
Before me every knee will bow;
   by me every tongue will swear.
24They will say of me, 'In the LORD
      alone
are righteousness and strength.'"
All who have raged against him
   will come to him and be put to
      shame.
25But in the LORD all the descendants
   of Israel
   will be found righteous and will
      exult.

Gods of Babylon

46 Bel bows down, Nebo stoops
   low;
   their idols are borne by beasts of
      burden.ᵃ
The images that are carried about are
   burdensome,
   a burden for the weary.
2They stoop and bow down together;
   unable to rescue the burden,
   they themselves go off into
      captivity.

3"Listen to me, O house of Jacob,
   all you who remain of the house of
      Israel,
you whom I have upheld since you
      were conceived,
   and have carried since your birth.
4Even to your old age and gray hairs
   I am he, I am he who will sustain
      you.
I have made you and I will carry you;
   I will sustain you and I will rescue
      you.

5"To whom will you compare me or
      count me equal?
To whom will you liken me that
      we may be compared?
6Some pour out gold from their bags
   and weigh out silver on the scales;
they hire a goldsmith to make it into
   a god,
   and they bow down and worship it.
7They lift it to their shoulders and
      carry it;
   they set it up in its place, and there
      it stands.
From that spot it cannot move.
Though one cries out to it, it does not
      answer;
   it cannot save him from his
      troubles.

8"Remember this, fix it in mind,
   take it to heart, you rebels.
9Remember the former things, those
      of long ago;
I am God, and there is no other;
   I am God, and there is none like
      me.
10I make known the end from the
      beginning,
   from ancient times, what is still to
      come.
I say: My purpose will stand,
   and I will do all that I please.
11From the east I summon a bird of
      prey;
   from a far-off land, a man to fulfill
      my purpose.

ᵃ *1 Or are but beasts and cattle*

What I have said, that will I bring
about;
what I have planned, that will I do.
[12]Listen to me, you stubborn-hearted,
you who are far from righteousness.
[13]I am bringing my righteousness near,
it is not far away;
and my salvation will not be
delayed.
I will grant salvation to Zion,
my splendor to Israel.

The Fall of Babylon

47 "Go down, sit in the dust,
Virgin Daughter of Babylon;
sit on the ground without a throne,
Daughter of the Babylonians.[a]
No more will you be called
tender or delicate.
[2]Take millstones and grind flour;
take off your veil.
Lift up your skirts, bare your legs,
and wade through the streams.
[3]Your nakedness will be exposed
and your shame uncovered.
I will take vengeance;
I will spare no one."

[4]Our Redeemer—the LORD Almighty
is his name—
is the Holy One of Israel.

[5]"Sit in silence, go into darkness,
Daughter of the Babylonians;
no more will you be called
queen of kingdoms.
[6]I was angry with my people
and desecrated my inheritance;
I gave them into your hand,
and you showed them no mercy.
Even on the aged
you laid a very heavy yoke.
[7]You said, 'I will continue forever—
the eternal queen!'
But you did not consider these things
or reflect on what might happen.

[8]"Now then, listen, you wanton
creature,
lounging in your security
and saying to yourself,
'I am, and there is none besides
me.
I will never be a widow
or suffer the loss of children.'
[9]Both of these will overtake you
in a moment, on a single day:
loss of children and widowhood.
They will come upon you in full
measure,
in spite of your many sorceries
and all your potent spells.
[10]You have trusted in your wickedness
and have said, 'No one sees me.'
Your wisdom and knowledge mislead
you
when you say to yourself,
'I am, and there is none besides me.'
[11]Disaster will come upon you,
and you will not know how to
conjure it away.
A calamity will fall upon you
that you cannot ward off with a
ransom;
a catastrophe you cannot foresee
will suddenly come upon you.

[12]"Keep on, then, with your magic
spells
and with your many sorceries,
which you have labored at since
childhood.
Perhaps you will succeed,
perhaps you will cause terror.
[13]All the counsel you have received has
only worn you out!
Let your astrologers come forward,
those stargazers who make predictions
month by month,
let them save you from what is
coming upon you.
[14]Surely they are like stubble;
the fire will burn them up.
They cannot even save themselves
from the power of the flame.
Here are no coals to warm anyone;
here is no fire to sit by.
[15]That is all they can do for you—
these you have labored with

---

[a] 1 Or *Chaldeans*; also in verse 5

and trafficked with since
childhood.
Each of them goes on in his error;
there is not one that can save you.

Stubborn Israel

48 "Listen to this, O house of Jacob,
you who are called by the name
of Israel
and come from the line of Judah,
you who take oaths in the name of
the LORD
and invoke the God of Israel—
but not in truth or righteousness—
2 you who call yourselves citizens of
the holy city
and rely on the God of Israel—
the LORD Almighty is his name:
3 I foretold the former things long ago,
my mouth announced them and I
made them known;
then suddenly I acted, and they
came to pass.
4 For I knew how stubborn you were;
the sinews of your neck were iron,
your forehead was bronze.
5 Therefore I told you these things long
ago;
before they happened I announced
them to you
so that you could not say,
'My idols did them;
my wooden image and metal god
ordained them.'
6 You have heard these things; look at
them all.
Will you not admit them?

"From now on I will tell you of new
things,
of hidden things unknown to you.
7 They are created now, and not long
ago;
you have not heard of them before
today.
So you cannot say,
'Yes, I knew of them.'
8 You have neither heard nor
understood;

from of old your ear has not been
open.
Well do I know how treacherous you
are;
you were called a rebel from birth.
9 For my own name's sake I delay my
wrath;
for the sake of my praise I hold it
back from you,
so as not to cut you off.
10 See, I have refined you, though not as
silver;
I have tested you in the furnace of
affliction.
11 For my own sake, for my own sake, I
do this.
How can I let myself be defamed?
I will not yield my glory to another.

Israel Freed

12 "Listen to me, O Jacob,
Israel, whom I have called:
I am he;
I am the first and I am the last.
13 My own hand laid the foundations of
the earth,
and my right hand spread out the
heavens;
when I summon them,
they all stand up together.

14 "Come together, all of you, and
listen:
Which of ⌊the idols⌋ has foretold
these things?
The LORD's chosen ally
will carry out his purpose against
Babylon;
his arm will be against the
Babylonians.ᵃ
15 I, even I, have spoken;
yes, I have called him.
I will bring him,
and he will succeed in his mission.

16 "Come near me and listen to this:

"From the first announcement I have
not spoken in secret;
at the time it happens, I am there."

ᵃ 14 Or Chaldeans; also in verse 20

And now the Sovereign LORD has
　　sent me,
　　with his Spirit.

[17]This is what the LORD says—
　　your Redeemer, the Holy One of
　　　Israel:
"I am the LORD your God,
　　who teaches you what is best for
　　　you,
　　who directs you in the way you
　　　should go.
[18]If only you had paid attention to my
　　commands,
　　your peace would have been like a
　　　river,
　　your righteousness like the waves of
　　　the sea.
[19]Your descendants would have been
　　like the sand,
　　your children like its numberless
　　　grains;
their name would never be cut off
　　nor destroyed from before me."

[20]Leave Babylon,
　　flee from the Babylonians!
Announce this with shouts of joy
　　and proclaim it.
Send it out to the ends of the earth;
　　say, "The LORD has redeemed his
　　　servant Jacob."
[21]They did not thirst when he led them
　　through the deserts;
　　he made water flow for them from
　　　the rock;
he split the rock
　　and water gushed out.

[22]"There is no peace," says the LORD,
　　"for the wicked."

The Servant of the LORD

49 Listen to me, you islands;
　　hear this, you distant nations:
Before I was born the LORD called
　　me;
　　from my birth he has made
　　　mention of my name.
[2]He made my mouth like a sharpened
　　sword,

in the shadow of his hand he hid me;
　　he made me into a polished arrow
　　and concealed me in his quiver.
[3]He said to me, "You are my servant,
　　Israel, in whom I will display my
　　　splendor."
[4]But I said, "I have labored to no
　　purpose;
　　I have spent my strength in vain
　　　and for nothing.
Yet what is due me is in the LORD's
　　hand,
　　and my reward is with my God."

[5]And now the LORD says—
　　he who formed me in the womb to
　　　be his servant
to bring Jacob back to him
　　and gather Israel to himself,
for I am honored in the eyes of the
　　LORD
　　and my God has been my
　　　strength—
[6]he says:
"It is too small a thing for you to be
　　my servant
　　to restore the tribes of Jacob
　　and bring back those of Israel I have
　　　kept.
I will also make you a light for the
　　Gentiles,
　　that you may bring my salvation to
　　　the ends of the earth."

[7]This is what the LORD says—
　　the Redeemer and Holy One of
　　　Israel—
to him who was despised and
　　abhorred by the nation,
　　to the servant of rulers:
"Kings will see you and rise up,
　　princes will see and bow down,
because of the LORD, who is faithful,
　　the Holy One of Israel, who has
　　　chosen you."

Restoration of Israel

[8]This is what the LORD says:

"In the time of my favor I will answer
　　you,

and in the day of salvation I will
  help you;
I will keep you and will make you
  to be a covenant for the people,
to restore the land
  and to reassign its desolate
  inheritances,
9 to say to the captives, 'Come out,'
  and to those in darkness, 'Be free!'

"They will feed beside the roads
  and find pasture on every barren
  hill.
10 They will neither hunger nor thirst,
  nor will the desert heat or the sun
  beat upon them.
He who has compassion on them will
  guide them
  and lead them beside springs of
  water.
11 I will turn all my mountains into
  roads,
  and my highways will be raised
  up.
12 See, they will come from afar—
  some from the north, some from
  the west,
  some from the region of Aswan.ᵃ"

13 Shout for joy, O heavens;
  rejoice, O earth;
  burst into song, O mountains!
For the LORD comforts his people
  and will have compassion on his
  afflicted ones.

14 But Zion said, "The LORD has
  forsaken me,
  the Lord has forgotten me."
15 "Can a mother forget the baby at her
  breast
  and have no compassion on the
  child she has borne?
Though she may forget,
  I will not forget you!
16 See, I have engraved you on the
  palms of my hands;
  your walls are ever before me.
17 Your sons hasten back,

and those who laid you waste
  depart from you.
18 Lift up your eyes and look around;
  all your sons gather and come to
  you.
As surely as I live," declares the LORD,
  "you will wear them all as
  ornaments;
  you will put them on, like a bride.

19 "Though you were ruined and made
  desolate
  and your land laid waste,
now you will be too small for your
  people,
  and those who devoured you will
  be far away.
20 The children born during your
  bereavement
  will yet say in your hearing,
'This place is too small for us;
  give us more space to live in.'
21 Then you will say in your heart,
  'Who bore me these?
I was bereaved and barren;
  I was exiled and rejected.
Who brought these up?
I was left all alone,
  but these—where have they come
  from?'"

22 This is what the Sovereign LORD
says:

"See, I will beckon to the Gentiles,
  I will lift up my banner to the
  peoples;
they will bring your sons in their
  arms
  and carry your daughters on their
  shoulders.
23 Kings will be your foster fathers,
  and their queens your nursing
  mothers.
They will bow down before you with
  their faces to the ground;
  they will lick the dust at your feet.
Then you will know that I am the
  LORD;

ᵃ 12 Dead Sea Scrolls; Masoretic Text Sinim

those who hope in me will not be
disappointed."

24Can plunder be taken from warriors,
or captives rescued from the fierce[a]?

25But this is what the LORD says:

"Yes, captives will be taken from
warriors,
and plunder retrieved from the
fierce;
I will contend with those who
contend with you,
and your children I will save.
26I will make your oppressors eat their
own flesh;
they will be drunk on their own
blood, as with wine.
Then all mankind will know
that I, the LORD, am your Savior,
your Redeemer, the Mighty One
of Jacob."

Israel's Sin and the Servant's Obedience

50 This is what the LORD says:

"Where is your mother's certificate of
divorce
with which I sent her away?
Or to which of my creditors
did I sell you?
Because of your sins you were sold;
because of your transgressions your
mother was sent away.
2When I came, why was there no one?
When I called, why was there no
one to answer?
Was my arm too short to ransom you?
Do I lack the strength to rescue
you?
By a mere rebuke I dry up the sea,
I turn rivers into a desert;
their fish rot for lack of water
and die of thirst.
3I clothe the sky with darkness
and make sackcloth its covering."

4The Sovereign LORD has given me an
instructed tongue,

to know the word that sustains the
weary.
He wakens me morning by morning,
wakens my ear to listen like one
being taught.
5The Sovereign LORD has opened my
ears,
and I have not been rebellious;
I have not drawn back.
6I offered my back to those who beat
me,
my cheeks to those who pulled out
my beard;
I did not hide my face
from mocking and spitting.
7Because the Sovereign LORD helps
me,
I will not be disgraced.
Therefore have I set my face like flint,
and I know I will not be put to
shame.
8He who vindicates me is near.
Who then will bring charges
against me?
Let us face each other!
Who is my accuser?
Let him confront me!
9It is the Sovereign LORD who helps
me.
Who is he that will condemn me?
They will all wear out like a garment;
the moths will eat them up.

10Who among you fears the LORD
and obeys the word of his servant?
Let him who walks in the dark,
who has no light,
trust in the name of the LORD
and rely on his God.
11But now, all you who light fires
and provide yourselves with
flaming torches,
go, walk in the light of your fires
and of the torches you have set
ablaze.
This is what you shall receive from
my hand:
You will lie down in torment.

---

a 24 Dead Sea Scrolls, Vulgate and Syriac (see also Septuagint and verse 25); Masoretic Text *righteous*

Everlasting Salvation for Zion

51 "Listen to me, you who pursue righteousness
and who seek the Lord:
Look to the rock from which you
were cut
and to the quarry from which you
were hewn;
²look to Abraham, your father,
and to Sarah, who gave you birth.
When I called him he was but one,
and I blessed him and made him
many.
³The Lord will surely comfort Zion
and will look with compassion on
all her ruins;
he will make her deserts like Eden,
her wastelands like the garden of
the Lord.
Joy and gladness will be found in her,
thanksgiving and the sound of
singing.

⁴"Listen to me, my people;
hear me, my nation:
The law will go out from me;
my justice will become a light to
the nations.
⁵My righteousness draws near
speedily,
my salvation is on the way,
and my arm will bring justice to
the nations.
The islands will look to me
and wait in hope for my arm.
⁶Lift up your eyes to the heavens,
look at the earth beneath;
the heavens will vanish like smoke,
the earth will wear out like a
garment
and its inhabitants die like flies.
But my salvation will last forever,
my righteousness will never fail.

⁷"Hear me, you who know what is
right,
you people who have my law in
your hearts:
Do not fear the reproach of men
or be terrified by their insults.

⁸For the moth will eat them up like a
garment;
the worm will devour them like
wool.
But my righteousness will last forever,
my salvation through all
generations."

⁹Awake, awake! Clothe yourself with
strength,
O arm of the Lord;
awake, as in days gone by,
as in generations of old.
Was it not you who cut Rahab to
pieces,
who pierced that monster through?
¹⁰Was it not you who dried up the sea,
the waters of the great deep,
who made a road in the depths of the
sea
so that the redeemed might cross
over?
¹¹The ransomed of the Lord will
return.
They will enter Zion with singing;
everlasting joy will crown their
heads.
Gladness and joy will overtake them,
and sorrow and sighing will flee
away.

¹²"I, even I, am he who comforts you.
Who are you that you fear mortal
men,
the sons of men, who are but grass,
¹³that you forget the Lord your Maker,
who stretched out the heavens
and laid the foundations of the
earth,
that you live in constant terror every
day
because of the wrath of the
oppressor,
who is bent on destruction?
For where is the wrath of the
oppressor?
¹⁴ The cowering prisoners will soon
be set free;
they will not die in their dungeon,
nor will they lack bread.

¹⁵For I am the LORD your God,
  who churns up the sea so that its
    waves roar—
  the LORD Almighty is his name.
¹⁶I have put my words in your mouth
  and covered you with the shadow
    of my hand—
  I who set the heavens in place,
  who laid the foundations of the
    earth,
  and who say to Zion, 'You are my
    people.'"

The Cup of the LORD's Wrath
¹⁷Awake, awake!
  Rise up, O Jerusalem,
you who have drunk from the hand
    of the LORD
  the cup of his wrath,
you who have drained to its dregs
  the goblet that makes men stagger.
¹⁸Of all the sons she bore
  there was none to guide her;
of all the sons she reared
  there was none to take her by the
    hand.
¹⁹These double calamities have come
    upon you—
  who can comfort you?—
ruin and destruction, famine and
    sword—
  who canᵃ console you?
²⁰Your sons have fainted;
  they lie at the head of every street,
  like antelope caught in a net.
They are filled with the wrath of the
    LORD
  and the rebuke of your God.

²¹Therefore hear this, you afflicted one,
  made drunk, but not with wine.
²²This is what your Sovereign LORD
    says,
  your God, who defends his people:
"See, I have taken out of your hand
  the cup that made you stagger;
from that cup, the goblet of my
    wrath,

you will never drink again.
²³I will put it into the hands of your
    tormentors,
  who said to you,
  'Fall prostrate that we may walk
    over you.'
And you made your back like the
    ground,
  like a street to be walked over."

52 Awake, awake, O Zion,
  clothe yourself with strength.
Put on your garments of splendor,
  O Jerusalem, the holy city.
The uncircumcised and defiled
  will not enter you again.
²Shake off your dust;
  rise up, sit enthroned, O Jerusalem.
Free yourself from the chains on your
    neck,
  O captive Daughter of Zion.

³For this is what the LORD says:

"You were sold for nothing,
  and without money you will be
    redeemed."

⁴For this is what the Sovereign LORD
says:

"At first my people went down to
    Egypt to live;
  lately, Assyria has oppressed them.

⁵"And now what do I have here?" declares the LORD.

"For my people have been taken away
    for nothing,
  and those who rule them mock,ᵇ"
                    declares the LORD.
"And all day long
  my name is constantly blasphemed.
⁶Therefore my people will know my
    name;
  therefore in that day they will
    know
that it is I who foretold it.
  Yes, it is I."

ᵃ 19 Dead Sea Scrolls, Septuagint, Vulgate and Syriac; Masoretic Text / how can I   ᵇ 5 Dead Sea Scrolls and Vulgate; Masoretic Text wail

7 How beautiful on the mountains
   are the feet of those who bring
      good news,
who proclaim peace,
   who bring good tidings,
   who proclaim salvation,
   who say to Zion,
   "Your God reigns!"
8 Listen! Your watchmen lift up their
      voices;
   together they shout for joy.
When the LORD returns to Zion,
   they will see it with their own eyes.
9 Burst into songs of joy together,
   you ruins of Jerusalem,
for the LORD has comforted his people,
   he has redeemed Jerusalem.
10 The LORD will lay bare his holy arm
   in the sight of all the nations,
and all the ends of the earth will see
   the salvation of our God.

11 Depart, depart, go out from there!
   Touch no unclean thing!
Come out from it and be pure,
   you who carry the vessels of the
      LORD.
12 But you will not leave in haste
   or go in flight;
for the LORD will go before you,
   the God of Israel will be your rear
      guard.

The Suffering and Glory
of the Servant

13 See, my servant will act wisely[a];
   he will be raised and lifted up and
      highly exalted.
14 Just as there were many who were
      appalled at him[b]—
   his appearance was so disfigured
      beyond that of any man
   and his form marred beyond
      human likeness—
15 so will he sprinkle many nations,[c]
   and kings will shut their mouths
      because of him.
For what they were not told, they
   will see,

and what they have not heard, they
   will understand.

53 Who has believed our message
   and to whom has the arm of the
      LORD been revealed?
2 He grew up before him like a tender
      shoot,
   and like a root out of dry ground.
He had no beauty or majesty to
      attract us to him,
   nothing in his appearance that we
      should desire him.
3 He was despised and rejected by men,
   a man of sorrows, and familiar with
      suffering.
Like one from whom men hide their
      faces
   he was despised, and we esteemed
      him not.

4 Surely he took up our infirmities
   and carried our sorrows,
yet we considered him stricken by
      God,
   smitten by him, and afflicted.
5 But he was pierced for our
      transgressions,
   he was crushed for our iniquities;
the punishment that brought us peace
      was upon him,
   and by his wounds we are healed.

Praying Isaiah 53:4-5
*Thank You, Lord, that You have
borne my grief and sorrow, You have
paid the price for my sin, and because
of Your suffering I can be healed.*

6 We all, like sheep, have gone astray,
   each of us has turned to his own
      way;
and the LORD has laid on him
   the iniquity of us all.

7 He was oppressed and afflicted,
   yet he did not open his mouth;
he was led like a lamb to the
      slaughter,

<hr>

a 13 Or will prosper b 14 Hebrew you c 15 Hebrew; Septuagint so will many nations marvel at him

and as a sheep before her shearers
   is silent,
   so he did not open his mouth.
⁸By oppression[a] and judgment he was
   taken away.
   And who can speak of his
     descendants?
   For he was cut off from the land of
     the living;
   for the transgression of my people
     he was stricken.[b]

> *Prayer is . . .*
>
> *choosing to sit at the feet of Jesus.*

⁹He was assigned a grave with the
   wicked,
   and with the rich in his death,
   though he had done no violence,
   nor was any deceit in his mouth.

¹⁰Yet it was the LORD's will to crush
   him and cause him to
   suffer,
   and though the LORD makes[c] his
     life a guilt offering,
   he will see his offspring and prolong
     his days,
   and the will of the LORD will
     prosper in his hand.
¹¹After the suffering of his soul,
   he will see the light ⌊of life⌋[d] and be
     satisfied[e];
   by his knowledge[f] my righteous
     servant will justify many,
   and he will bear their iniquities.
¹²Therefore I will give him a portion
     among the great,[g]
   and he will divide the spoils with
     the strong,[h]
   because he poured out his life unto
     death,

and was numbered with the
   transgressors.
For he bore the sin of many,
   and made intercession for the
     transgressors.

The Future Glory of Zion

54 "Sing, O barren woman,
   you who never bore a child;
burst into song, shout for joy,
   you who were never in labor;
because more are the children of the
     desolate woman
   than of her who has a husband,"
       says the LORD.
²"Enlarge the place of your tent,
   stretch your tent curtains wide,
   do not hold back;
   lengthen your cords,
   strengthen your stakes.
³For you will spread out to the right
     and to the left;
   your descendants will dispossess
     nations
   and settle in their desolate cities.

⁴"Do not be afraid; you will not suffer
   shame.
Do not fear disgrace; you will not
   be humiliated.
You will forget the shame of your
   youth
   and remember no more the
     reproach of your widowhood.
⁵For your Maker is your husband—
   the LORD Almighty is his name—
   the Holy One of Israel is your
     Redeemer;
   he is called the God of all the earth.
⁶The LORD will call you back
   as if you were a wife deserted and
     distressed in spirit—
a wife who married young,
   only to be rejected," says your
     God.
⁷"For a brief moment I abandoned
   you,

---

[a]8 Or *From arrest* [b]8 Or *away. / Yet who of his generation considered / that he was cut off from the land of the living / for the transgression of my people, / to whom the blow was due?* [c]10 Hebrew *though you make* [d]11 Dead Sea Scrolls (see also Septuagint); Masoretic Text does not have *the light ⌊of life⌋.* [e]11 Or (with Masoretic Text) ¹¹*He will see the result of the suffering of his soul / and be satisfied* [f]11 Or *by knowledge of him* [g]12 Or *many* [h]12 Or *numerous*

GOING *deeper*

How to Respond to Unanswered Prayer

READ AND CONSIDER: ISAIAH 54:1-8

"'Sing, O barren woman, you who never bore a child; burst into song, shout for joy, you who were never in labor; because more are the children of the desolate woman than of her who has a husband,' says the LORD" (Isaiah 54:1).

When the prophet Isaiah foretold of Jerusalem's coming restoration, he likened its condition to a barren woman. He told the Israelites to sing in the face of it. This is exactly how we should respond to unanswered prayer or to the barren or unfruitful situations in our own lives. We are to sing praise to the One who can bring to life the places in us and our situations that appear to be dead. The One who can birth something new in us and our circumstances. The One who hears our prayers and answers in His way and His time. Whenever you have a dream in your life that seems to go unfulfilled year after year and there is no way possible to make it happen, determine to worship God in the face of it. When hope that this thing can ever be brought to life completely dies, then praise God for His resurrection power. The Bible tells us that not only can God bring to life things that are dead, but we are actually to prepare for that possibility because of who He is and what He does.

Have you ever experienced times when you are praying fervently from your whole heart and yet it seems that heaven and earth are silent? Do you ever wonder if God has even heard your prayers? If so, you are not alone. We've all felt that at times. But be assured that God hears and will answer. He may fall silent for a time, but His silence does not mean that He has not heard or that He has forgotten your request. What God has promised, He will perform. And when He does, you will be amazed that the answer is far beyond what you could have imagined. Until that time, sing praise to the Lord and see things come to life that you thought never would.

but with deep compassion I will
bring you back.
⁸In a surge of anger
I hid my face from you for a
moment,
but with everlasting kindness
I will have compassion on you,"
says the LORD your Redeemer.

⁹"To me this is like the days of Noah,
when I swore that the waters of
Noah would never again cover
the earth.
So now I have sworn not to be angry
with you,
never to rebuke you again.

¹⁰Though the mountains be shaken
and the hills be removed,
yet my unfailing love for you will not
be shaken
nor my covenant of peace be
removed,"
says the LORD, who has compassion
on you.

¹¹"O afflicted city, lashed by storms and
not comforted,
I will build you with stones of
turquoise,ᵃ
your foundations with sapphires.ᵇ
¹²I will make your battlements of
rubies,

ᵃ *11* The meaning of the Hebrew for this word is uncertain.   ᵇ *11* Or *lapis lazuli*

your gates of sparkling jewels,
and all your walls of precious
stones.
¹³All your sons will be taught by the
Lord,
and great will be your children's
peace.
¹⁴In righteousness you will be
established:
Tyranny will be far from you;
you will have nothing to fear.
Terror will be far removed;
it will not come near you.
¹⁵If anyone does attack you, it will not
be my doing;
whoever attacks you will surrender
to you.

¹⁶"See, it is I who created the blacksmith
who fans the coals into flame
and forges a weapon fit for its work.
And it is I who have created the
destroyer to work havoc;
¹⁷   no weapon forged against you will
prevail,
and you will refute every tongue
that accuses you.
This is the heritage of the servants of
the Lord,
and this is their vindication from
me,"
declares the Lord.

Invitation to the Thirsty

55 "Come, all you who are thirsty,
come to the waters;
and you who have no money,
come, buy and eat!
Come, buy wine and milk
without money and without cost.
²Why spend money on what is not
bread,
and your labor on what does not
satisfy?
Listen, listen to me, and eat what is
good,
and your soul will delight in the
richest of fare.
³Give ear and come to me;
hear me, that your soul may live.

I will make an everlasting covenant
with you,
my faithful love promised to David.
⁴See, I have made him a witness to the
peoples,
a leader and commander of the
peoples.
⁵Surely you will summon nations you
know not,
and nations that do not know you
will hasten to you,
because of the Lord your God,
the Holy One of Israel,
for he has endowed you with
splendor."

⁶Seek the Lord while he may be
found;
call on him while he is near.
⁷Let the wicked forsake his way
and the evil man his thoughts.
Let him turn to the Lord, and he
will have mercy on him,
and to our God, for he will freely
pardon.

⁸"For my thoughts are not your
thoughts,
neither are your ways my ways,"
declares the Lord.
⁹"As the heavens are higher than the
earth,
so are my ways higher than your
ways
and my thoughts than your
thoughts.
¹⁰As the rain and the snow
come down from heaven,
and do not return to it
without watering the earth
and making it bud and flourish,
so that it yields seed for the sower
and bread for the eater,
¹¹so is my word that goes out from my
mouth:
It will not return to me empty,
but will accomplish what I desire
and achieve the purpose for which
I sent it.
¹²You will go out in joy

Praying God's Word

READ AND CONSIDER: ISAIAH 55

"As the rain and the snow come down from heaven, and do not return to it without watering the earth and making it bud and flourish . . . so is my word that goes out from my mouth: It will not return to me empty, but will accomplish what I desire and achieve the purpose for which I sent it" (Isaiah 55:10-11).

Sometimes we get discouraged when we pray fervently about a situation and get no response. We may even wonder if God hears us. But Isaiah 55 promises that God's Word, like the rain and snow, does what it needs to do wherever it goes. It accomplishes what God desires and achieves the purpose for which He sends it.

That means there is a power in praying God's Word. And we need to remember that, especially when we are in the midst of a battle. We can't see it in the quiet of our prayer time, but the words we raise to heaven are weapons of warfare. Because of our prayers, angels fight with demons to bring about God's will.

God's Word is "living and active. Sharper than any double-edged sword, it penetrates even to dividing soul and spirit, joints and marrow; it judges the thoughts and attitudes of the heart" (Hebrews 4:12). Paul placed the Word of God as part of every Christian's armor, saying that we must carry "the sword of the Spirit, which is the word of God" (Ephesians 6:17). In short, God's Word pierces everything it touches. It is *never* ineffectual.

That's why it is so important for you to not only pray, but to also read your Bible daily. Underline it, claim its promises, pray the words back to God. When you don't know what to pray, look up a psalm and read it aloud as your prayer. You can never be at a loss for words when it comes to prayer because God has given you everything you need. When you pray His words, you tap into His power and wield His sword. God promises that great things will happen when you do.

The battle for our lives, and the lives and souls of our children, our husbands, our friends, our families, our neighbors, and our nation is waged on our knees. When we don't pray, it's like sitting on the sidelines watching those we love and care about scrambling through a war zone, getting shot at from every angle. When we *do* pray, however, we're in the battle alongside them, appropriating God's power on their behalf. If we also declare the Word of God in our prayers, then we wield a powerful weapon against which no enemy can prevail.

and be led forth in peace;
the mountains and hills
 will burst into song before you,
and all the trees of the field
 will clap their hands.
13 Instead of the thornbush will grow
 the pine tree,
 and instead of briers the myrtle will
 grow.
This will be for the LORD's renown,
 for an everlasting sign,
 which will not be destroyed."

Salvation for Others

56 This is what the LORD says:

"Maintain justice
 and do what is right,
for my salvation is close at hand
 and my righteousness will soon be
 revealed.
2 Blessed is the man who does this,
 the man who holds it fast,
who keeps the Sabbath without
 desecrating it,

and keeps his hand from doing any
   evil."

³Let no foreigner who has bound
      himself to the LORD say,
   "The LORD will surely exclude me
      from his people."
And let not any eunuch complain,
   "I am only a dry tree."

⁴For this is what the LORD says:

"To the eunuchs who keep my
      Sabbaths,
   who choose what pleases me
   and hold fast to my covenant—
⁵to them I will give within my temple
      and its walls
   a memorial and a name
   better than sons and daughters;
I will give them an everlasting name
   that will not be cut off.
⁶And foreigners who bind themselves
      to the LORD
   to serve him,
to love the name of the LORD,
   and to worship him,
all who keep the Sabbath without
      desecrating it
   and who hold fast to my
      covenant—
⁷these I will bring to my holy
      mountain
   and give them joy in my house of
      prayer.
Their burnt offerings and sacrifices
   will be accepted on my altar;
for my house will be called
   a house of prayer for all nations."
⁸The Sovereign LORD declares—
   he who gathers the exiles of Israel:
"I will gather still others to them
   besides those already gathered."

God's Accusation Against the Wicked

⁹Come, all you beasts of the field,
   come and devour, all you beasts of
      the forest!
¹⁰Israel's watchmen are blind,
   they all lack knowledge;
they are all mute dogs,

they cannot bark;
they lie around and dream,
   they love to sleep.
¹¹They are dogs with mighty appetites;
   they never have enough.
They are shepherds who lack
      understanding;
   they all turn to their own way,
   each seeks his own gain.
¹²"Come," each one cries, "let me get
      wine!
   Let us drink our fill of beer!
And tomorrow will be like today,
   or even far better."

57 The righteous perish,
   and no one ponders it in his
      heart;
devout men are taken away,
   and no one understands
that the righteous are taken away
   to be spared from evil.
²Those who walk uprightly
   enter into peace;
   they find rest as they lie in death.

³"But you—come here, you sons of a
      sorceress,
   you offspring of adulterers and
      prostitutes!
⁴Whom are you mocking?
   At whom do you sneer
   and stick out your tongue?
Are you not a brood of rebels,
   the offspring of liars?
⁵You burn with lust among the oaks
   and under every spreading tree;
you sacrifice your children in the
      ravines
   and under the overhanging crags.
⁶The idols among the smooth stones
   of the ravines are your portion;
they, they are your lot.
Yes, to them you have poured out
      drink offerings
   and offered grain offerings.
In the light of these things, should
   I relent?
⁷You have made your bed on a high
   and lofty hill;

there you went up to offer your
sacrifices.
8 Behind your doors and your doorposts
you have put your pagan symbols.
Forsaking me, you uncovered your
bed,
you climbed into it and opened it
wide;
you made a pact with those whose
beds you love,
and you looked on their nakedness.
9 You went to Molech[a] with olive oil
and increased your perfumes.
You sent your ambassadors[b] far away;
you descended to the grave[c] itself!
10 You were wearied by all your ways,
but you would not say, 'It is
hopeless.'
You found renewal of your strength,
and so you did not faint.

11 "Whom have you so dreaded and
feared
that you have been false to me,
and have neither remembered me
nor pondered this in your hearts?
Is it not because I have long been silent
that you do not fear me?
12 I will expose your righteousness and
your works,
and they will not benefit you.
13 When you cry out for help,
let your collection ⌊of idols⌋ save you!
The wind will carry all of them off,
a mere breath will blow them away.
But the man who makes me his
refuge
will inherit the land
and possess my holy mountain."

Comfort for the Contrite

14 And it will be said:

"Build up, build up, prepare the road!
Remove the obstacles out of the
way of my people."
15 For this is what the high and lofty
One says—
he who lives forever, whose name
is holy:

"I live in a high and holy place,
but also with him who is contrite
and lowly in spirit,
to revive the spirit of the lowly
and to revive the heart of the
contrite.
16 I will not accuse forever,
nor will I always be angry,
for then the spirit of man would grow
faint before me—
the breath of man that I have created.
17 I was enraged by his sinful greed;
I punished him, and hid my face in
anger,
yet he kept on in his willful ways.
18 I have seen his ways, but I will heal
him;
I will guide him and restore
comfort to him,
19 creating praise on the lips of the
mourners in Israel.
Peace, peace, to those far and near,"
says the LORD. "And I will heal
them."
20 But the wicked are like the tossing sea,
which cannot rest,
whose waves cast up mire and mud.
21 "There is no peace," says my God,
"for the wicked."

True Fasting

58 "Shout it aloud, do not hold
back.
Raise your voice like a trumpet.
Declare to my people their rebellion
and to the house of Jacob their sins.
2 For day after day they seek me out;
they seem eager to know my ways,
as if they were a nation that does
what is right
and has not forsaken the commands
of its God.
They ask me for just decisions
and seem eager for God to come
near them.
3 'Why have we fasted,' they say,
'and you have not seen it?
Why have we humbled ourselves,
and you have not noticed?'

---

a 9 Or to the king b 9 Or idols c 9 Hebrew Sheol

"Yet on the day of your fasting, you
do as you please
and exploit all your workers.
⁴ Your fasting ends in quarreling and
strife,

and in striking each other with
wicked fists.
You cannot fast as you do today
and expect your voice to be heard
on high.

GOING deeper

God's Chosen Fast

READ AND CONSIDER: ISAIAH 58:6-14

"Is not this the kind of fasting I have chosen: to loose the chains of injustice and untie the cords of the yoke, to set the oppressed free and break every yoke?" (Isaiah 58:6).

God gives us many wonderful keys for spiritual growth—keys such as speaking and reading His Word, praise, prayer, faith, and also fasting. Don't let your life be locked up because you are not using all of your keys. Fasting is a key to total health in every part of your being.

Fasting is not the easiest of disciplines, but it's not the hardest either. If you have a disease or health problems, check with your physician to see if it is safe for you. If it is, fasting can provide an especially close time with your heavenly Father. If you can begin the discipline of fasting for even one day each month, you will feel fresh, renewed, and cleansed in body, mind, and soul. And you will experience a special fellowship with God as you deny your physical desire for food and turn your focus on God.

Fasting is a spiritual discipline that is a denial of self. When you deny yourself, you position the Lord as *everything* in your life. This breaks the bonds of oppression. It causes things to change. Deliberately denying yourself food for a set period of time in order to give yourself more completely to prayer and closer communication with God has great rewards.

There are many religions in which fasting is a regular spiritual practice. There are also many people who fast who have no religious beliefs related to fasting but want a natural cure or cleansing for the body. We, as believers in Jesus who take seriously the written Word of God, must do our fasting unto the Lord to honor, worship, and glorify Him. It is not just a religious exercise; it is a step of obedience to God for the purpose of ministering unto Him. This is a personal matter between you and God—an offering to Him—and should be approached prayerfully and by the leading of the Holy Spirit.

Fasting goes hand in hand with prayer, so always fast with the intent of praying too. Fasting is not intended to twist God's arm into getting what you want out of Him, nor is it something you do to win His approval, but it is a time of offering your concerns to Him.

If you desire to delve into the discipline of fasting, or if you already do it, take the time to read Isaiah 58 every time you fast. It's rich with purposes, promises, and truth. This passage describes the kind of fasting God desires—the kind of fast He has chosen, what fasting is intended to accomplish, and what the promise is for those who fast. God will speak to you through it. You will be reminded of why you are fasting: "to loose the chains of injustice," "to set the oppressed free," and to "break every yoke." It also serves as a reminder of what you should do: "Share your food with the hungry," "provide the poor wanderer with shelter," and do not "turn away from your own flesh and blood." And He tells you of your rewards: "Your light will break forth like the dawn, and your healing will quickly appear," and "the glory of the LORD will be your rear guard. Then you will call, and the LORD will answer." Ultimately, you are assured that "you will find your joy in the LORD." Now that's worth skipping a meal for and praying instead.

⁵Is this the kind of fast I have chosen,
  only a day for a man to humble
    himself?
  Is it only for bowing one's head like
    a reed
    and for lying on sackcloth and
      ashes?
  Is that what you call a fast,
    a day acceptable to the LORD?

⁶"Is not this the kind of fasting I have
    chosen:
  to loose the chains of injustice
    and untie the cords of the yoke,
  to set the oppressed free
    and break every yoke?
⁷Is it not to share your food with the
    hungry
    and to provide the poor wanderer
      with shelter—
  when you see the naked, to clothe
    him,
    and not to turn away from your
      own flesh and blood?
⁸Then your light will break forth like
    the dawn,
    and your healing will quickly
      appear;
  then your righteousnessᵃ will go
    before you,
    and the glory of the LORD will be
      your rear guard.
⁹Then you will call, and the LORD
    will answer;
  you will cry for help, and he will
    say: Here am I.

  "If you do away with the yoke of
    oppression,
  with the pointing finger and
    malicious talk,
¹⁰and if you spend yourselves in behalf
    of the hungry
    and satisfy the needs of the
      oppressed,
  then your light will rise in the
    darkness,
    and your night will become like
      the noonday.

¹¹The LORD will guide you always;
  he will satisfy your needs in a sun-
    scorched land
    and will strengthen your frame.
  You will be like a well-watered
    garden,
    like a spring whose waters never
      fail.
¹²Your people will rebuild the ancient
    ruins
    and will raise up the age-old
      foundations;
  you will be called Repairer of Broken
    Walls,
    Restorer of Streets with Dwellings.

¹³"If you keep your feet from breaking
    the Sabbath
    and from doing as you please on my
      holy day,
  if you call the Sabbath a delight
    and the LORD's holy day honorable,
  and if you honor it by not going your
    own way
    and not doing as you please or
      speaking idle words,
¹⁴then you will find your joy in the
    LORD,
    and I will cause you to ride on the
      heights of the land
    and to feast on the inheritance of
      your father Jacob."
  The mouth of the LORD has spoken.

Sin, Confession and Redemption

59 Surely the arm of the LORD is
    not too short to save,
  nor his ear too dull to hear.
²But your iniquities have separated
    you from your God;
  your sins have hidden his face from
    you,
    so that he will not hear.
³For your hands are stained with
    blood,
    your fingers with guilt.
  Your lips have spoken lies,
    and your tongue mutters wicked
      things.

ᵃ 8 Or your righteous One

Tearing Down the Wall of Separation

READ AND CONSIDER: ISAIAH 59:1-8

"But your iniquities have separated you from your God; your sins have hidden his face from you, so that he will not hear" (Isaiah 59:2).

Nothing works in our lives when we don't live God's way, not the least of which is that our prayers are not answered. This verse says that our sins separate us from God so that He will not hear us when we pray. Don't let unconfessed sin separate you from God and hinder your prayers.

If you can't think of any sin in your life, ask God to show you whatever you need to see in that regard. All of us get things in our hearts, souls, minds, attitudes, and emotions that shouldn't be there and are not God's best for our lives. Often we have sin in our hearts and lives and don't even realize it until we start paying the consequences for it. Don't let any separation happen between you and God. Talk to Him daily about the condition of your heart. Ask God often to keep you undeceived. And when He reveals any sin, confess it immediately so that you can be cleansed of it.

We all fail at times, so don't let any failure on your part hinder your prayers in any way. If you take care of this issue by yourself with God in the daytime, by confessing and repenting of all sin as soon as you are aware of it, then you won't have to be dealing with the effects of it when you are trying to sleep at night.

⁴No one calls for justice;
  no one pleads his case with
    integrity.
They rely on empty arguments and
    speak lies;
  they conceive trouble and give
    birth to evil.
⁵They hatch the eggs of vipers
  and spin a spider's web.
Whoever eats their eggs will die,
  and when one is broken, an adder is
    hatched.
⁶Their cobwebs are useless for
    clothing;
  they cannot cover themselves with
    what they make.
Their deeds are evil deeds,
  and acts of violence are in their
    hands.
⁷Their feet rush into sin;
  they are swift to shed innocent
    blood.
Their thoughts are evil thoughts;

ruin and destruction mark their
    ways.
⁸The way of peace they do not know;
  there is no justice in their paths.
They have turned them into crooked
    roads;
  no one who walks in them will
    know peace.

⁹So justice is far from us,
  and righteousness does not reach us.
We look for light, but all is darkness;
  for brightness, but we walk in deep
    shadows.
¹⁰Like the blind we grope along the
    wall,
  feeling our way like men without
    eyes.
At midday we stumble as if it were
    twilight;
  among the strong, we are like the
    dead.
¹¹We all growl like bears;
  we moan mournfully like doves.

We look for justice, but find none;
  for deliverance, but it is far away.

12For our offenses are many in your
    sight,
  and our sins testify against us.
Our offenses are ever with us,
  and we acknowledge our iniquities:
13rebellion and treachery against the
    LORD,
  turning our backs on our God,
fomenting oppression and revolt,
  uttering lies our hearts have
    conceived.
14So justice is driven back,
  and righteousness stands at a
    distance;
truth has stumbled in the streets,
  honesty cannot enter.
15Truth is nowhere to be found,
  and whoever shuns evil becomes a
    prey.

The LORD looked and was displeased
  that there was no justice.
16He saw that there was no one,
  he was appalled that there was no
    one to intervene;
so his own arm worked salvation for
    him,
  and his own righteousness sustained
    him.
17He put on righteousness as his
    breastplate,
  and the helmet of salvation on his
    head;
he put on the garments of vengeance
  and wrapped himself in zeal as in a
    cloak.
18According to what they have done,
  so will he repay
wrath to his enemies
  and retribution to his foes;
  he will repay the islands their due.
19From the west, men will fear the
    name of the LORD,
  and from the rising of the sun, they
    will revere his glory.
For he will come like a pent-up flood

that the breath of the LORD drives
  along.[a]
20"The Redeemer will come to Zion,
  to those in Jacob who repent of
    their sins,"
                      declares the LORD.

21"As for me, this is my covenant with
them," says the LORD. "My Spirit, who is
on you, and my words that I have put in
your mouth will not depart from your
mouth, or from the mouths of your children, or from the mouths of their descendants from this time on and forever," says
the LORD.

The Glory of Zion

60 "Arise, shine, for your light has
    come,
  and the glory of the LORD rises
    upon you.
2See, darkness covers the earth
  and thick darkness is over the
    peoples,
but the LORD rises upon you
  and his glory appears over you.
3Nations will come to your light,
  and kings to the brightness of your
    dawn.

4"Lift up your eyes and look about you:
  All assemble and come to you;
your sons come from afar,
  and your daughters are carried on
    the arm.
5Then you will look and be radiant,
  your heart will throb and swell
    with joy;
the wealth on the seas will be brought
    to you,
  to you the riches of the nations will
    come.
6Herds of camels will cover your land,
  young camels of Midian and
    Ephah.
And all from Sheba will come,
  bearing gold and incense
  and proclaiming the praise of the
    LORD.

---

[a] 19 Or When the enemy comes in like a flood, / the Spirit of the LORD will put him to flight

⁷All Kedar's flocks will be gathered to
you,
   the rams of Nebaioth will serve
     you;
they will be accepted as offerings on
   my altar,
   and I will adorn my glorious
     temple.

⁸"Who are these that fly along like
clouds,
   like doves to their nests?
⁹Surely the islands look to me;
   in the lead are the ships of
     Tarshish,ᵃ
bringing your sons from afar,
   with their silver and gold,
to the honor of the LORD your God,
   the Holy One of Israel,
   for he has endowed you with
     splendor.

¹⁰"Foreigners will rebuild your walls,
   and their kings will serve you.
Though in anger I struck you,
   in favor I will show you
     compassion.
¹¹Your gates will always stand open,
   they will never be shut, day or
     night,
so that men may bring you the wealth
   of the nations—
   their kings led in triumphal
     procession.
¹²For the nation or kingdom that will
   not serve you will perish;
   it will be utterly ruined.

¹³"The glory of Lebanon will come to
you,
   the pine, the fir and the cypress
     together,
to adorn the place of my sanctuary;
   and I will glorify the place of my
     feet.
¹⁴The sons of your oppressors will
   come bowing before you;
   all who despise you will bow down
     at your feet

and will call you the City of the
   LORD,
   Zion of the Holy One of Israel.

¹⁵"Although you have been forsaken
   and hated,
   with no one traveling through,
I will make you the everlasting pride
   and the joy of all generations.
¹⁶You will drink the milk of nations
   and be nursed at royal breasts.
Then you will know that I, the LORD,
   am your Savior,
   your Redeemer, the Mighty One
     of Jacob.
¹⁷Instead of bronze I will bring you
   gold,
   and silver in place of iron.
Instead of wood I will bring you
   bronze,
   and iron in place of stones.
I will make peace your governor
   and righteousness your ruler.
¹⁸No longer will violence be heard in
   your land,
   nor ruin or destruction within your
     borders,
but you will call your walls Salvation
   and your gates Praise.
¹⁹The sun will no more be your light
   by day,
   nor will the brightness of the moon
     shine on you,
for the LORD will be your everlasting
   light,
   and your God will be your glory.
²⁰Your sun will never set again,
   and your moon will wane no
     more;
the LORD will be your everlasting
   light,
   and your days of sorrow will end.
²¹Then will all your people be
   righteous
   and they will possess the land
     forever.
They are the shoot I have planted,
   the work of my hands,
   for the display of my splendor.

ᵃ 9 Or the trading ships

22 The least of you will become a
    thousand,
  the smallest a mighty nation.
I am the LORD;
  in its time I will do this swiftly."

The Year of the LORD's Favor

61 The Spirit of the Sovereign LORD
    is on me,
  because the LORD has anointed me
  to preach good news to the poor.
He has sent me to bind up the
    brokenhearted,
  to proclaim freedom for the
    captives
  and release from darkness for the
    prisoners,[a]
2 to proclaim the year of the LORD's
  favor

and the day of vengeance of our
  God,
to comfort all who mourn,
3 and provide for those who grieve in
  Zion—
to bestow on them a crown of beauty
  instead of ashes,
the oil of gladness
  instead of mourning,
and a garment of praise
  instead of a spirit of despair.
They will be called oaks of
  righteousness,
  a planting of the LORD
  for the display of his splendor.

4 They will rebuild the ancient ruins
  and restore the places long
    devastated;

---

a 1 Hebrew; Septuagint *the blind*

GOING *deeper*

Receive Beauty for Ashes

READ AND CONSIDER: ISAIAH 61

"He has sent me . . . to bestow on them a crown of beauty instead of ashes, the oil of gladness instead of mourning, and a garment of praise instead of a spirit of despair" (Isaiah 61:1,3).

The Jews had plenty to grieve about. The nation had struggled for many generations with taking God at His word and following Him faithfully. The prophet Isaiah was a strong voice for God, calling His people to renewed faithfulness. And he didn't leave anyone out. Isaiah confronted the wealthy and even the royalty with their lack of commitment to God's ways. The real problem in Jerusalem was that not *enough* people were grieving. In fact, they were not concerned at all that they were, in essence, snubbing their noses at God.

But for those who willingly turned their faces to God and repented of their sins, Isaiah had some good news. God promised comfort for those who grieved, beauty instead of ashes, oil instead of mourning, praise instead of despair. There was hope for those who understood that the Lord's favor would come upon all who sincerely sought to love and obey Him.

Do you ever grieve over the sins of your life or your own community or nation? If so, bring your grief to God and let Him trade it for gladness. Do you ever look at the ashes of your life or the lives of others and feel that great sense of loss? If so, God wants to give you beauty in exchange.

God knows what to do with despair. So seek Him. Sit with Him. Grieve with Him. Repent before Him. Let Him renew your life. Ask Him for beauty, gladness, and a garment of praise. Then you can say with the ancient prophet, "I delight greatly in the LORD; my soul rejoices in my God. For he has clothed me with garments of salvation and arrayed me in a robe of righteousness" (61:10).

they will renew the ruined cities
  that have been devastated for
  generations.
⁵Aliens will shepherd your flocks;
  foreigners will work your fields and
  vineyards.
⁶And you will be called priests of the
  LORD,
  you will be named ministers of our
  God.
You will feed on the wealth of
  nations,
  and in their riches you will boast.

⁷Instead of their shame
  my people will receive a double
  portion,
  and instead of disgrace
  they will rejoice in their
  inheritance;
and so they will inherit a double
  portion in their land,
  and everlasting joy will be theirs.

⁸"For I, the LORD, love justice;
  I hate robbery and iniquity.
In my faithfulness I will reward them
  and make an everlasting covenant
  with them.
⁹Their descendants will be known
  among the nations
  and their offspring among the
  peoples.
All who see them will acknowledge
  that they are a people the LORD has
  blessed."

¹⁰I delight greatly in the LORD;
  my soul rejoices in my God.
For he has clothed me with garments
  of salvation
  and arrayed me in a robe of
  righteousness,
as a bridegroom adorns his head like
  a priest,
  and as a bride adorns herself with
  her jewels.
¹¹For as the soil makes the sprout
  come up
  and a garden causes seeds to grow,

so the Sovereign LORD will make
  righteousness and praise
  spring up before all nations.

Zion's New Name

62 For Zion's sake I will not keep
  silent,
  for Jerusalem's sake I will not
  remain quiet,
till her righteousness shines out like
  the dawn,
  her salvation like a blazing torch.
²The nations will see your
  righteousness,
  and all kings your glory;
you will be called by a new name
  that the mouth of the LORD will
  bestow.
³You will be a crown of splendor in
  the LORD's hand,
  a royal diadem in the hand of your
  God.
⁴No longer will they call you Deserted,
  or name your land Desolate.
But you will be called Hephzibah,ᵃ
  and your land Beulahᵇ;
for the LORD will take delight in you,
  and your land will be married.
⁵As a young man marries a maiden,
  so will your sonsᶜ marry you;
as a bridegroom rejoices over his
  bride,
  so will your God rejoice over you.

⁶I have posted watchmen on your
  walls, O Jerusalem;
  they will never be silent day or
  night.
You who call on the LORD,
  give yourselves no rest,
⁷and give him no rest till he establishes
  Jerusalem
  and makes her the praise of the
  earth.

⁸The LORD has sworn by his right
  hand
  and by his mighty arm:
"Never again will I give your grain
  as food for your enemies,

ᵃ4 Hephzibah means *my delight is in her.*   ᵇ4 Beulah means *married.*   ᶜ5 Or Builder

Finding Deliverance

GOING deeper

READ AND CONSIDER: ISAIAH 62

"For Zion's sake I will not keep silent, for Jerusalem's sake I will not remain quiet, till her righteousness shines out like the dawn, her salvation like a blazing torch" (Isaiah 62:1).

Isaiah interceded for the deliverance and restoration of his nation with fervency and desperation. Yet he also prayed with the hope of a man who had a vision for the future of his people.

We need to pray with that same combination of desperation and vision. Once we recognize that our only hope for deliverance and restoration in our lives is found in God, it causes us to pray with passion. Yet we are hopeful because we know that nothing is impossible with God. We know that in His hands, anything is possible. In His hands, the situation will be resolved, the question answered, the wound mended, the oppression dissipated.

Isaiah's prayer reminds us of several things. First, it reminds us of the passion we must have in prayer not only for our own lives, but for the lives of others in our family, our city, and our nation. Next, it reminds us that our only hope is in God, even if we fool ourselves into believing for a time that we can take care of things ourselves. Finally, Isaiah's prayer reminds us that no matter how hopeless the situation seems, God is our hope. We are never in a dark situation with no light. He is our light, and we just have to open our eyes and see Him.

All lasting deliverance and restoration come from the Lord, and it is an ongoing process. It is God who has "delivered us from such a deadly peril, and he will deliver us. On him we have set our hope that he will continue to deliver us" (2 Corinthians 1:10). God does a complete work, and He will see it through to the end. So don't give up because it's taking longer than you hoped. Be confident that "he who began a good work in you will carry it on to completion until the day of Christ Jesus" (Philippians 1:6).

No matter how difficult your situation seems, don't give up because God will not rest until your righteousness shines out like the dawn and your salvation like a blazing torch (Isaiah 62:1).

---

and never again will foreigners drink
the new wine
for which you have toiled;
⁹but those who harvest it will eat it
and praise the LORD,
and those who gather the grapes will
drink it
in the courts of my sanctuary."

¹⁰Pass through, pass through the gates!
Prepare the way for the people.
Build up, build up the highway!
Remove the stones.
Raise a banner for the nations.

¹¹The LORD has made proclamation
to the ends of the earth:
"Say to the Daughter of Zion,

'See, your Savior comes!
See, his reward is with him,
and his recompense accompanies
him.'"
¹²They will be called the Holy People,
the Redeemed of the LORD;
and you will be called Sought After,
the City No Longer Deserted.

God's Day of Vengeance and Redemption

63 Who is this coming from Edom,
from Bozrah, with his garments
stained crimson?
Who is this, robed in splendor,
striding forward in the greatness of
his strength?

"It is I, speaking in righteousness,
  mighty to save."

2 Why are your garments red,
  like those of one treading the
    winepress?

3 "I have trodden the winepress alone;
  from the nations no one was with
    me.
I trampled them in my anger
  and trod them down in my wrath;
their blood spattered my garments,
  and I stained all my clothing.
4 For the day of vengeance was in my
    heart,
  and the year of my redemption has
    come.
5 I looked, but there was no one to help,
  I was appalled that no one gave
    support;
so my own arm worked salvation for
    me,
  and my own wrath sustained me.
6 I trampled the nations in my anger;
  in my wrath I made them drunk
and poured their blood on the
    ground."

Praise and Prayer

7 I will tell of the kindnesses of the
    LORD,
  the deeds for which he is to be
    praised,
according to all the LORD has done
    for us—
yes, the many good things he has
    done
  for the house of Israel,
according to his compassion and
    many kindnesses.
8 He said, "Surely they are my people,
  sons who will not be false to me";
and so he became their Savior.
9 In all their distress he too was
    distressed,
  and the angel of his presence saved
    them.
In his love and mercy he redeemed
    them;

he lifted them up and carried them
  all the days of old.
10 Yet they rebelled
  and grieved his Holy Spirit.
So he turned and became their enemy
  and he himself fought against them.

11 Then his people recalled[a] the days of
    old,
  the days of Moses and his people—
where is he who brought them
    through the sea,
  with the shepherd of his flock?
Where is he who set
  his Holy Spirit among them,
12 who sent his glorious arm of power
  to be at Moses' right hand,
who divided the waters before them,
  to gain for himself everlasting
    renown,
13 who led them through the depths?
Like a horse in open country,
  they did not stumble;
14 like cattle that go down to the plain,
  they were given rest by the Spirit of
    the LORD.
This is how you guided your people
  to make for yourself a glorious
    name.

15 Look down from heaven and see
  from your lofty throne, holy and
    glorious.
Where are your zeal and your
    might?
  Your tenderness and compassion are
    withheld from us.
16 But you are our Father,
  though Abraham does not know us
or Israel acknowledge us;
you, O LORD, are our Father,
  our Redeemer from of old is your
    name.
17 Why, O LORD, do you make us
    wander from your ways
  and harden our hearts so we do not
    revere you?
Return for the sake of your servants,
  the tribes that are your inheritance.

---

a 11 Or But may he recall

18 For a little while your people
      possessed your holy place,
  but now our enemies have trampled
      down your sanctuary.
19 We are yours from of old;
  but you have not ruled over them,
  they have not been called by your
      name.^a

64 Oh, that you would rend the
      heavens and come down,
  that the mountains would tremble
      before you!
2 As when fire sets twigs ablaze
  and causes water to boil,
  come down to make your name
      known to your enemies
  and cause the nations to quake
      before you!
3 For when you did awesome things
      that we did not expect,
  you came down, and the mountains
      trembled before you.
4 Since ancient times no one has
      heard,
  no ear has perceived,
  no eye has seen any God besides you,
  who acts on behalf of those who
      wait for him.
5 You come to the help of those who
      gladly do right,
  who remember your ways.
  But when we continued to sin against
      them,
  you were angry.
  How then can we be saved?
6 All of us have become like one who is
      unclean,
  and all our righteous acts are like
      filthy rags;
  we all shrivel up like a leaf,
      and like the wind our sins sweep us
      away.
7 No one calls on your name
    or strives to lay hold of you;
  for you have hidden your face from us
    and made us waste away because of
      our sins.

8 Yet, O LORD, you are our Father.
  We are the clay, you are the
      potter;
  we are all the work of your hand.
9 Do not be angry beyond measure,
      O LORD;
  do not remember our sins forever.
  Oh, look upon us, we pray,
    for we are all your people.
10 Your sacred cities have become a
      desert;
  even Zion is a desert, Jerusalem a
      desolation.
11 Our holy and glorious temple, where
      our fathers praised you,
  has been burned with fire,
  and all that we treasured lies in
      ruins.
12 After all this, O LORD, will you hold
      yourself back?
  Will you keep silent and punish us
      beyond measure?

Judgment and Salvation

65 "I revealed myself to those who
      did not ask for me;
  I was found by those who did not
      seek me.
  To a nation that did not call on my
      name,
  I said, 'Here am I, here am I.'
2 All day long I have held out my hands
    to an obstinate people,
  who walk in ways not good,
      pursuing their own imaginations—
3 a people who continually provoke me
    to my very face,
  offering sacrifices in gardens
    and burning incense on altars of
      brick;
4 who sit among the graves
    and spend their nights keeping
      secret vigil;
  who eat the flesh of pigs,
    and whose pots hold broth of
      unclean meat;
5 who say, 'Keep away; don't come near
      me,
  for I am too sacred for you!'

---

^a 19 Or *We are like those you have never ruled, / like those never called by your name*

Such people are smoke in my nostrils,
a fire that keeps burning all day.

6 "See, it stands written before me:
I will not keep silent but will pay
back in full;
I will pay it back into their laps—
7 both your sins and the sins of your
fathers,"
says the LORD.
"Because they burned sacrifices on
the mountains
and defied me on the hills,
I will measure into their laps
the full payment for their former
deeds."

8 This is what the LORD says:

"As when juice is still found in a
cluster of grapes
and men say, 'Don't destroy it,
there is yet some good in it,'
so will I do in behalf of my servants;
I will not destroy them all.
9 I will bring forth descendants from
Jacob,
and from Judah those who will
possess my mountains;
my chosen people will inherit them,
and there will my servants live.
10 Sharon will become a pasture for
flocks,
and the Valley of Achor a resting
place for herds,
for my people who seek me.

11 "But as for you who forsake the
LORD
and forget my holy mountain,
who spread a table for Fortune
and fill bowls of mixed wine for
Destiny,
12 I will destine you for the sword,
and you will all bend down for the
slaughter;
for I called but you did not answer,
I spoke but you did not listen.
You did evil in my sight
and chose what displeases me."

13 Therefore this is what the Sovereign
LORD says:

"My servants will eat,
but you will go hungry;
my servants will drink,
but you will go thirsty;
my servants will rejoice,
but you will be put to shame.
14 My servants will sing
out of the joy of their hearts,
but you will cry out
from anguish of heart
and wail in brokenness of spirit.
15 You will leave your name
to my chosen ones as a curse;
the Sovereign LORD will put you to
death,
but to his servants he will give
another name.
16 Whoever invokes a blessing in the land
will do so by the God of truth;
he who takes an oath in the land
will swear by the God of truth.
For the past troubles will be forgotten
and hidden from my eyes.

New Heavens and a New Earth
17 "Behold, I will create
new heavens and a new earth.
The former things will not be
remembered,
nor will they come to mind.
18 But be glad and rejoice forever
in what I will create,
for I will create Jerusalem to be a
delight
and its people a joy.
19 I will rejoice over Jerusalem
and take delight in my people;
the sound of weeping and of crying
will be heard in it no more.

20 "Never again will there be in it
an infant who lives but a few days,
or an old man who does not live
out his years;
he who dies at a hundred
will be thought a mere youth;
he who fails to reach[a] a hundred

---
a 20 Or / the sinner who reaches

will be considered accursed.
21 They will build houses and dwell in
them;
they will plant vineyards and eat
their fruit.
22 No longer will they build houses and
others live in them,
or plant and others eat.
For as the days of a tree,
so will be the days of my people;
my chosen ones will long enjoy
the works of their hands.
23 They will not toil in vain
or bear children doomed to
misfortune;
for they will be a people blessed by
the LORD,
they and their descendants with
them.
24 Before they call I will answer;
while they are still speaking I will
hear.

Praying Isaiah 65:24

*Lord, I thank You for hearing
my prayers, and even before I call,
You have set Yourself to answer.*

25 The wolf and the lamb will feed
together,
and the lion will eat straw like the
ox,
but dust will be the serpent's food.
They will neither harm nor destroy
on all my holy mountain,"
says the LORD.

Judgment and Hope

66 This is what the LORD says:

"Heaven is my throne,
and the earth is my footstool.
Where is the house you will build for
me?
Where will my resting place be?
2 Has not my hand made all these
things,
and so they came into being?"
declares the LORD.

"This is the one I esteem:
he who is humble and contrite in
spirit,
and trembles at my word.
3 But whoever sacrifices a bull
is like one who kills a man,
and whoever offers a lamb,
like one who breaks a dog's neck;
whoever makes a grain offering
is like one who presents pig's blood,
and whoever burns memorial incense,
like one who worships an idol.
They have chosen their own ways,
and their souls delight in their
abominations;
4 so I also will choose harsh treatment
for them
and will bring upon them what
they dread.
For when I called, no one answered,
when I spoke, no one listened.
They did evil in my sight
and chose what displeases me."

5 Hear the word of the LORD,
you who tremble at his word:
"Your brothers who hate you,
and exclude you because of my
name, have said,
'Let the LORD be glorified,
that we may see your joy!'
Yet they will be put to shame.
6 Hear that uproar from the city,
hear that noise from the temple!
It is the sound of the LORD
repaying his enemies all they
deserve.

7 "Before she goes into labor,
she gives birth;
before the pains come upon her,
she delivers a son.
8 Who has ever heard of such a thing?
Who has ever seen such things?
Can a country be born in a day
or a nation be brought forth in a
moment?
Yet no sooner is Zion in labor
than she gives birth to her children.
9 Do I bring to the moment of birth

and not give delivery?" says the
LORD.
"Do I close up the womb
    when I bring to delivery?" says
        your God.
[10]"Rejoice with Jerusalem and be glad
        for her,
    all you who love her;
rejoice greatly with her,
    all you who mourn over her.
[11]For you will nurse and be satisfied
        at her comforting breasts;
you will drink deeply
    and delight in her overflowing
        abundance."

[12]For this is what the LORD says:

"I will extend peace to her like a river,
    and the wealth of nations like a
        flooding stream;
you will nurse and be carried on her
        arm
    and dandled on her knees.
[13]As a mother comforts her child,
    so will I comfort you;
    and you will be comforted over
        Jerusalem."

[14]When you see this, your heart will
        rejoice
    and you will flourish like grass;
the hand of the LORD will be made
        known to his servants,
    but his fury will be shown to his
        foes.
[15]See, the LORD is coming with fire,
    and his chariots are like a
        whirlwind;
he will bring down his anger with
        fury,
    and his rebuke with flames of fire.
[16]For with fire and with his sword
    the LORD will execute judgment
        upon all men,

and many will be those slain by the
    LORD.

[17]"Those who consecrate and purify
themselves to go into the gardens, following the one in the midst of[a] those who
eat the flesh of pigs and rats and other
abominable things—they will meet their
end together," declares the LORD.

[18]"And I, because of their actions and
their imaginations, am about to come[b]
and gather all nations and tongues, and
they will come and see my glory.

[19]"I will set a sign among them, and
I will send some of those who survive
to the nations—to Tarshish, to the Libyans[c] and Lydians (famous as archers), to
Tubal and Greece, and to the distant islands that have not heard of my fame or
seen my glory. They will proclaim my
glory among the nations. [20]And they will
bring all your brothers, from all the nations, to my holy mountain in Jerusalem
as an offering to the LORD—on horses, in
chariots and wagons, and on mules and
camels," says the LORD. "They will bring
them, as the Israelites bring their grain
offerings, to the temple of the LORD in
ceremonially clean vessels. [21]And I will select some of them also to be priests and
Levites," says the LORD.

[22]"As the new heavens and the new
earth that I make will endure before
me," declares the LORD, "so will your
name and descendants endure. [23]From
one New Moon to another and from
one Sabbath to another, all mankind will
come and bow down before me," says the
LORD. [24]"And they will go out and look
upon the dead bodies of those who rebelled against me; their worm will not
die, nor will their fire be quenched, and
they will be loathsome to all mankind."

---

[a] *17* Or *gardens behind one of your temples, and*   [b] *18* The meaning of the Hebrew for this clause is uncertain.   [c] *19* Some
Septuagint manuscripts *Put* (Libyans); Hebrew *Pul*

Author: Jeremiah (sometimes dictated to his scribe Baruch)

Date: Between 626 and 586 BC

Audience: God's people, who were facing the consequences of their sin and needed encouragement that God still loved them.

Suppose you sensed God convicting and nudging and prompting you to confront a friend about some wrong behavior. How would you respond? Would you be nervous? Do you think such a divine assignment might motivate you to do some serious praying?

Jeremiah was called by God to confront not just a friend, but an entire nation. And he had to speak hard words, not on one or two uncomfortable occasions, but continually, for four long decades. It was his job description, and Jeremiah's dogged obedience to it, that transformed the so-called "weeping prophet" into a role model of godliness and devotion.

As you read this fascinating book (the longest in the Bible), pay careful attention to Jeremiah's ongoing, lifelong conversation with God. Clearly, he grasped the concept later expressed by Jesus, "Apart from me you can do nothing" (John 15:5).

Prayer Themes:

- Thank God that He has made you and called you for a unique purpose—you have a key role in His eternal plan (1:4-10).

- Tell God honestly what is in your heart, not what "ought" to be in your heart (20:7-8).

- Praise God for His new covenant and the inner spiritual power to live for His glory. Ask Him to help you better understand the spiritual gifts He has given you (31:31-35).

Jeremiah

1 The words of Jeremiah son of Hilkiah, one of the priests at Anathoth in the territory of Benjamin. ²The word of the LORD came to him in the thirteenth year of the reign of Josiah son of Amon king of Judah, ³and through the reign of Jehoiakim son of Josiah king of Judah, down to the fifth month of the eleventh year of Zedekiah son of Josiah king of Judah, when the people of Jerusalem went into exile.

The Call of Jeremiah

⁴The word of the LORD came to me, saying,

⁵"Before I formed you in the womb I knew[a] you,
    before you were born I set you apart;
    I appointed you as a prophet to the nations."

⁶"Ah, Sovereign LORD," I said, "I do not know how to speak; I am only a child."

⁷But the LORD said to me, "Do not say, 'I am only a child.' You must go to everyone I send you to and say whatever I command you. ⁸Do not be afraid of them, for I am with you and will rescue you," declares the LORD.

⁹Then the LORD reached out his hand and touched my mouth and said to me, "Now, I have put my words in your mouth. ¹⁰See, today I appoint you over nations and kingdoms to uproot and tear down, to destroy and overthrow, to build and to plant."

¹¹The word of the LORD came to me: "What do you see, Jeremiah?"

"I see the branch of an almond tree," I replied.

¹²The LORD said to me, "You have seen

ᵃ 5 Or *chose*

GOING *deeper*

Praying Without Excuses

READ AND CONSIDER: JEREMIAH 1:1-10

"But the LORD said to me, 'Do not say, "I am only a child." You must go to everyone I send you to and say whatever I command you . . . Then the LORD reached out his hand and touched my mouth and said to me, 'Now, I have put my words in your mouth'"(Jeremiah 1:7,9).

There was Jeremiah, simply minding his own business, when "the word of the LORD came." And not just any word, but a word of divine appointment. God was giving him a whole new job description: to speak for Him to the nations. Feeling completely inadequate, Jeremiah humbly declined. After all, he couldn't speak well, and besides, he was just a kid. But God completely rejected Jeremiah's excuses.

The Lord immediately dismissed Jeremiah's concern about his youthfulness, but He did respond to Jeremiah's fear about speaking in a very specific way. The prophet described it like this: "The LORD reached out his hand and touched my mouth" (1:9). How wonderful and comforting that touch must have been. Jeremiah knew he did not need to worry any longer.

When we think up excuses for not doing God's will, what we are really saying is that we understand things better than God does. We are also saying that we think it's up to us and our abilities, rather than up to God's power and enablement. Feeling inadequate is good when it drives us to depend on God. But it's not good when that insecurity and fear cause us to say no to what God wants.

When it comes to prayer, we often have excuses for why we can't. We may see someone who needs prayer and yet we don't step out and do it. We may think, "My prayers aren't powerful enough." "God can't use me, I'm not eloquent." "I haven't walked with God long enough."

But we must remember how God told Jeremiah that He had put words in his mouth. The Lord will do that for us when we ask Him to help us pray.

God has given us the most powerful tool in the universe: *prayer.* The power of prayer is unlimited because it's God's power, not ours. If our words release God's power to change people's hearts, bring down spiritual strongholds, or build up nations, then we are participating in the most potent force in the universe.

When you pray, start by saying, "Lord, please touch my mind and mouth and give me Your words to pray." And then pray as the Lord leads. Of course, it's only in heaven that you will be able to see all the miracles that have been brought about by your prayers. But even on earth you will one day say, "I prayed about that situation, and look what God did!"

---

correctly, for I am watching[a] to see that my word is fulfilled."

¹³The word of the LORD came to me again: "What do you see?"

"I see a boiling pot, tilting away from the north," I answered.

¹⁴The LORD said to me, "From the north disaster will be poured out on all who live in the land. ¹⁵I am about to sum-

mon all the peoples of the northern kingdoms," declares the LORD.

"Their kings will come and set up
    their thrones
in the entrance of the gates of
    Jerusalem;
they will come against all her
    surrounding walls

---

^a *12* The Hebrew for *watching* sounds like the Hebrew for *almond tree.*

and against all the towns of Judah.
¹⁶I will pronounce my judgments on
my people
because of their wickedness in
forsaking me,
in burning incense to other gods
and in worshiping what their hands
have made.

¹⁷"Get yourself ready! Stand up and say to them whatever I command you. Do not be terrified by them, or I will terrify you before them. ¹⁸Today I have made you a fortified city, an iron pillar and a bronze wall to stand against the whole land—against the kings of Judah, its officials, its priests and the people of the land. ¹⁹They will fight against you but will not overcome you, for I am with you and will rescue you," declares the LORD.

Israel Forsakes God

2 The word of the LORD came to me: ²"Go and proclaim in the hearing of Jerusalem:

"'I remember the devotion of your
youth,
how as a bride you loved me
and followed me through the desert,
through a land not sown.
³Israel was holy to the LORD,
the firstfruits of his harvest;
all who devoured her were held
guilty,
and disaster overtook them,'"
declares the LORD.

⁴Hear the word of the LORD, O house
of Jacob,
all you clans of the house of Israel.

⁵This is what the LORD says:

"What fault did your fathers find in
me,
that they strayed so far from me?
They followed worthless idols
and became worthless themselves.
⁶They did not ask, 'Where is the LORD,

who brought us up out of Egypt
and led us through the barren
wilderness,
through a land of deserts and rifts,
a land of drought and darkness,ᵃ
a land where no one travels and no
one lives?'
⁷I brought you into a fertile land
to eat its fruit and rich produce.
But you came and defiled my land
and made my inheritance
detestable.
⁸The priests did not ask,
'Where is the LORD?'
Those who deal with the law did not
know me;
the leaders rebelled against me.
The prophets prophesied by Baal,
following worthless idols.

⁹"Therefore I bring charges against
you again,"
declares the LORD.
"And I will bring charges against
your children's children.
¹⁰Cross over to the coasts of Kittimᵇ
and look,
send to Kedarᶜ and observe closely;
see if there has ever been anything
like this:
¹¹Has a nation ever changed its gods?
(Yet they are not gods at all.)
But my people have exchanged theirᵈ
Glory
for worthless idols.
¹²Be appalled at this, O heavens,
and shudder with great horror,"
declares the LORD.
¹³"My people have committed two
sins:
They have forsaken me,
the spring of living water,
and have dug their own cisterns,
broken cisterns that cannot hold
water.
¹⁴Is Israel a servant, a slave by birth?
Why then has he become plunder?
¹⁵Lions have roared;

they have growled at him.
They have laid waste his land;
  his towns are burned and deserted.
¹⁶Also, the men of Memphis^a and
    Tahpanhes
  have shaved the crown of your
    head.^b
¹⁷Have you not brought this on
    yourselves
  by forsaking the LORD your God
  when he led you in the way?
¹⁸Now why go to Egypt
  to drink water from the Shihor^c?
And why go to Assyria
  to drink water from the River^d?
¹⁹Your wickedness will punish you;
  your backsliding will rebuke you.
Consider then and realize
  how evil and bitter it is for you
when you forsake the LORD your God
  and have no awe of me,"
                    declares the Lord,
            the LORD Almighty.

²⁰"Long ago you broke off your yoke
  and tore off your bonds;
  you said, 'I will not serve you!'
Indeed, on every high hill
  and under every spreading tree
  you lay down as a prostitute.
²¹I had planted you like a choice vine
  of sound and reliable stock.
How then did you turn against me
  into a corrupt, wild vine?
²²Although you wash yourself with
    soda
  and use an abundance of soap,
  the stain of your guilt is still before
    me,"
            declares the Sovereign LORD.
²³"How can you say, 'I am not defiled;
  I have not run after the Baals'?
See how you behaved in the valley;
  consider what you have done.
You are a swift she-camel
  running here and there,
²⁴a wild donkey accustomed to the
    desert,
  sniffing the wind in her craving—

in her heat who can restrain her?
Any males that pursue her need not
    tire themselves;
  at mating time they will find her.
²⁵Do not run until your feet are bare
  and your throat is dry.
But you said, 'It's no use!
  I love foreign gods,
  and I must go after them.'

²⁶"As a thief is disgraced when he is
    caught,
  so the house of Israel is disgraced—
they, their kings and their officials,
  their priests and their prophets.
²⁷They say to wood, 'You are my
    father,'
  and to stone, 'You gave me birth.'
They have turned their backs to me
  and not their faces;
yet when they are in trouble, they say,
  'Come and save us!'
²⁸Where then are the gods you made
    for yourselves?
  Let them come if they can save you
  when you are in trouble!
For you have as many gods
  as you have towns, O Judah.

²⁹"Why do you bring charges against
    me?
  You have all rebelled against me,"
                    declares the LORD.
³⁰"In vain I punished your people;
  they did not respond to correction.
Your sword has devoured your
    prophets
  like a ravening lion.

³¹"You of this generation, consider the
word of the LORD:

"Have I been a desert to Israel
  or a land of great darkness?
Why do my people say, 'We are free
    to roam;
  we will come to you no more'?
³²Does a maiden forget her jewelry,
  a bride her wedding ornaments?
Yet my people have forgotten me,

---

^a 16 Hebrew *Noph*   ^b 16 Or *have cracked your skull*   ^c 18 That is, a branch of the Nile   ^d 18 That is, the Euphrates

days without number.
33 How skilled you are at pursuing love!
Even the worst of women can learn
from your ways.
34 On your clothes men find
the lifeblood of the innocent poor,
though you did not catch them
breaking in.
Yet in spite of all this
35 you say, 'I am innocent;
he is not angry with me.'
But I will pass judgment on you
because you say, 'I have not sinned.'
36 Why do you go about so much,
changing your ways?
You will be disappointed by Egypt
as you were by Assyria.
37 You will also leave that place
with your hands on your head,
for the LORD has rejected those you
trust;
you will not be helped by them.

3 "If a man divorces his wife
and she leaves him and marries
another man,
should he return to her again?
Would not the land be completely
defiled?
But you have lived as a prostitute
with many lovers—
would you now return to me?"
declares the LORD.
2 "Look up to the barren heights and
see.
Is there any place where you have
not been ravished?
By the roadside you sat waiting for
lovers,
sat like a nomad[a] in the desert.
You have defiled the land
with your prostitution and
wickedness.
3 Therefore the showers have been
withheld,
and no spring rains have fallen.
Yet you have the brazen look of a
prostitute;

you refuse to blush with shame.
4 Have you not just called to me:
'My Father, my friend from my
youth,
5 will you always be angry?
Will your wrath continue
forever?'
This is how you talk,
but you do all the evil you can."

Prayer is . . .

*asking God to use you
to accomplish His will on earth.*

Unfaithful Israel

6 During the reign of King Josiah, the LORD said to me, "Have you seen what faithless Israel has done? She has gone up on every high hill and under every spreading tree and has committed adultery there. 7 I thought that after she had done all this she would return to me but she did not, and her unfaithful sister Judah saw it. 8 I gave faithless Israel her certificate of divorce and sent her away because of all her adulteries. Yet I saw that her unfaithful sister Judah had no fear; she also went out and committed adultery. 9 Because Israel's immorality mattered so little to her, she defiled the land and committed adultery with stone and wood. 10 In spite of all this, her unfaithful sister Judah did not return to me with all her heart, but only in pretense," declares the LORD.

11 The LORD said to me, "Faithless Israel is more righteous than unfaithful Judah. 12 Go, proclaim this message toward the north:

" 'Return, faithless Israel,' declares the
LORD,
'I will frown on you no longer,
for I am merciful,' declares the LORD,
'I will not be angry forever.
13 Only acknowledge your guilt—

you have rebelled against the LORD
　　your God,
you have scattered your favors to
　　foreign gods
　under every spreading tree,
　and have not obeyed me,'"
　　　　　　　declares the LORD.

¹⁴"Return, faithless people," declares
the LORD, "for I am your husband. I will
choose you—one from a town and two
from a clan—and bring you to Zion.
¹⁵Then I will give you shepherds after
my own heart, who will lead you with
knowledge and understanding. ¹⁶In those
days, when your numbers have increased
greatly in the land," declares the LORD,
"men will no longer say, 'The ark of the
covenant of the LORD.' It will never enter their minds or be remembered; it will
not be missed, nor will another one be
made. ¹⁷At that time they will call Jerusalem The Throne of the LORD, and all
nations will gather in Jerusalem to honor
the name of the LORD. No longer will
they follow the stubbornness of their evil
hearts. ¹⁸In those days the house of Judah
will join the house of Israel, and together
they will come from a northern land to
the land I gave your forefathers as an inheritance.

¹⁹"I myself said,

" 'How gladly would I treat you like
　　sons
　and give you a desirable land,
　the most beautiful inheritance of
　　any nation.'
I thought you would call me 'Father'
　and not turn away from following
　　me.
²⁰But like a woman unfaithful to her
　　husband,
　so you have been unfaithful to me,
　O house of Israel,"
　　　　　　　declares the LORD.

²¹A cry is heard on the barren heights,
　the weeping and pleading of the
　　people of Israel,
because they have perverted their ways

and have forgotten the LORD their
　　God.

²²"Return, faithless people;
　I will cure you of backsliding."

"Yes, we will come to you,
　for you are the LORD our God.
²³Surely the ⌐idolatrous¬ commotion on
　　the hills
　and mountains is a deception;
surely in the LORD our God
　is the salvation of Israel.
²⁴From our youth shameful gods have
　　consumed
　the fruits of our fathers' labor—
their flocks and herds,
　their sons and daughters.
²⁵Let us lie down in our shame,
　and let our disgrace cover us.
We have sinned against the LORD our
　　God,
　both we and our fathers;
from our youth till this day
　we have not obeyed the LORD our
　　God."

4 "If you will return, O Israel,
　return to me,"
　　　　　　　declares the LORD.
"If you put your detestable idols out
　　of my sight
　and no longer go astray,
²and if in a truthful, just and righteous
　　way
　you swear, 'As surely as the LORD
　　lives,'
then the nations will be blessed by him
　and in him they will glory."

³This is what the LORD says to the men
of Judah and to Jerusalem:

"Break up your unplowed ground
　and do not sow among thorns.
⁴Circumcise yourselves to the LORD,
　circumcise your hearts,
　you men of Judah and people of
　　Jerusalem,
or my wrath will break out and burn
　like fire

because of the evil you have
done—
burn with no one to quench it.

Disaster From the North

5 "Announce in Judah and proclaim in
Jerusalem and say:
'Sound the trumpet throughout the
land!'
Cry aloud and say:
'Gather together!
Let us flee to the fortified cities!'
6 Raise the signal to go to Zion!
Flee for safety without delay!
For I am bringing disaster from the
north,
even terrible destruction."

7 A lion has come out of his lair;
a destroyer of nations has set out.
He has left his place
to lay waste your land.
Your towns will lie in ruins
without inhabitant.
8 So put on sackcloth,
lament and wail,
for the fierce anger of the LORD
has not turned away from us.

9 "In that day," declares the LORD,
"the king and the officials will lose
heart,
the priests will be horrified,
and the prophets will be appalled."

10 Then I said, "Ah, Sovereign LORD,
how completely you have deceived this
people and Jerusalem by saying, 'You
will have peace,' when the sword is at
our throats."

11 At that time this people and Jerusalem will be told, "A scorching wind from
the barren heights in the desert blows
toward my people, but not to winnow
or cleanse; 12 a wind too strong for that
comes from me.a Now I pronounce my
judgments against them."

13 Look! He advances like the clouds,
his chariots come like a whirlwind,
his horses are swifter than eagles.

Woe to us! We are ruined!
14 O Jerusalem, wash the evil from your
heart and be saved.
How long will you harbor wicked
thoughts?
15 A voice is announcing from Dan,
proclaiming disaster from the hills
of Ephraim.
16 "Tell this to the nations,
proclaim it to Jerusalem:
'A besieging army is coming from a
distant land,
raising a war cry against the cities
of Judah.
17 They surround her like men guarding
a field,
because she has rebelled against
me,'"
declares the LORD.
18 "Your own conduct and actions
have brought this upon you.
This is your punishment.
How bitter it is!
How it pierces to the heart!"

19 Oh, my anguish, my anguish!
I writhe in pain.
Oh, the agony of my heart!
My heart pounds within me,
I cannot keep silent.
For I have heard the sound of the
trumpet;
I have heard the battle cry.
20 Disaster follows disaster;
the whole land lies in ruins.
In an instant my tents are destroyed,
my shelter in a moment.
21 How long must I see the battle
standard
and hear the sound of the trumpet?

22 "My people are fools;
they do not know me.
They are senseless children;
they have no understanding.
They are skilled in doing evil;
they know not how to do good."

23 I looked at the earth,
and it was formless and empty;

---

a 12 Or comes at my command

and at the heavens,
and their light was gone.
24 I looked at the mountains,
and they were quaking;
all the hills were swaying.
25 I looked, and there were no people;
every bird in the sky had flown
away.
26 I looked, and the fruitful land was a
desert;
all its towns lay in ruins
before the LORD, before his fierce
anger.

27 This is what the LORD says:

"The whole land will be ruined,
though I will not destroy it
completely.
28 Therefore the earth will mourn
and the heavens above grow dark,
because I have spoken and will not
relent,
I have decided and will not turn
back."

29 At the sound of horsemen and
archers
every town takes to flight.
Some go into the thickets;
some climb up among the rocks.
All the towns are deserted;
no one lives in them.

30 What are you doing, O devastated
one?
Why dress yourself in scarlet
and put on jewels of gold?
Why shade your eyes with paint?
You adorn yourself in vain.
Your lovers despise you;
they seek your life.

31 I hear a cry as of a woman in labor,
a groan as of one bearing her first
child—
the cry of the Daughter of Zion
gasping for breath,
stretching out her hands and
saying,
"Alas! I am fainting;
my life is given over to murderers."

Not One Is Upright

5 "Go up and down the streets of
Jerusalem,
look around and consider,
search through her squares.
If you can find but one person
who deals honestly and seeks the
truth,
I will forgive this city.
2 Although they say, 'As surely as the
LORD lives,'
still they are swearing falsely."

3 O LORD, do not your eyes look for
truth?
You struck them, but they felt no
pain;
you crushed them, but they refused
correction.
They made their faces harder than
stone
and refused to repent.
4 I thought, "These are only the poor;
they are foolish,
for they do not know the way of the
LORD,
the requirements of their God.
5 So I will go to the leaders
and speak to them;
surely they know the way of the
LORD,
the requirements of their God."
But with one accord they too had
broken off the yoke
and torn off the bonds.
6 Therefore a lion from the forest will
attack them,
a wolf from the desert will ravage
them,
a leopard will lie in wait near their
towns
to tear to pieces any who venture
out,
for their rebellion is great
and their backslidings many.

7 "Why should I forgive you?
Your children have forsaken me
and sworn by gods that are not
gods.

I supplied all their needs,
  yet they committed adultery
  and thronged to the houses of
    prostitutes.
8 They are well-fed, lusty stallions,
  each neighing for another man's
    wife.
9 Should I not punish them for this?"
    declares the LORD.
  "Should I not avenge myself
    on such a nation as this?

10 "Go through her vineyards and
    ravage them,
  but do not destroy them
    completely.
  Strip off her branches,
    for these people do not belong to
      the LORD.
11 The house of Israel and the house of
    Judah
  have been utterly unfaithful to me,"
    declares the LORD.

12 They have lied about the LORD;
  they said, "He will do nothing!
  No harm will come to us;
  we will never see sword or famine.
13 The prophets are but wind
  and the word is not in them;
  so let what they say be done to
    them."

14 Therefore this is what the LORD God
  Almighty says:

"Because the people have spoken
  these words,
  I will make my words in your
    mouth a fire
  and these people the wood it
    consumes.
15 O house of Israel," declares the LORD,
  "I am bringing a distant nation
    against you—
  an ancient and enduring nation,
  a people whose language you do
    not know,
  whose speech you do not
    understand.
16 Their quivers are like an open grave;

all of them are mighty warriors.
17 They will devour your harvests and
    food,
  devour your sons and daughters;
  they will devour your flocks and
    herds,
  devour your vines and fig trees.
  With the sword they will destroy
    the fortified cities in which you
      trust.

18 "Yet even in those days," declares the
  LORD, "I will not destroy you completely.
19 And when the people ask, 'Why has
  the LORD our God done all this to us?'
  you will tell them, 'As you have forsaken
  me and served foreign gods in your own
  land, so now you will serve foreigners in
  a land not your own.'

20 "Announce this to the house of Jacob
    and proclaim it in Judah:
21 Hear this, you foolish and senseless
    people,
  who have eyes but do not see,
  who have ears but do not hear:
22 Should you not fear me?" declares the
    LORD.
  "Should you not tremble in my
    presence?
  I made the sand a boundary for the
    sea,
  an everlasting barrier it cannot
    cross.
  The waves may roll, but they cannot
    prevail;
  they may roar, but they cannot
    cross it.
23 But these people have stubborn and
    rebellious hearts;
  they have turned aside and gone
    away.
24 They do not say to themselves,
  'Let us fear the LORD our God,
  who gives autumn and spring rains in
    season,
  who assures us of the regular weeks
    of harvest.'
25 Your wrongdoings have kept these
    away;

your sins have deprived you of
good.

26 "Among my people are wicked men
who lie in wait like men who snare
birds
and like those who set traps to
catch men.
27 Like cages full of birds,
their houses are full of deceit;
they have become rich and powerful
28   and have grown fat and sleek.
Their evil deeds have no limit;
they do not plead the case of the
fatherless to win it,
they do not defend the rights of the
poor.
29 Should I not punish them for this?"
declares the LORD.
"Should I not avenge myself
on such a nation as this?

30 "A horrible and shocking thing
has happened in the land:
31 The prophets prophesy lies,
the priests rule by their own
authority,
and my people love it this way.
But what will you do in the end?

Jerusalem Under Siege

6 "Flee for safety, people of
Benjamin!
Flee from Jerusalem!
Sound the trumpet in Tekoa!
Raise the signal over Beth
Hakkerem!
For disaster looms out of the north,
even terrible destruction.
2 I will destroy the Daughter of Zion,
so beautiful and delicate.
3 Shepherds with their flocks will come
against her;
they will pitch their tents around
her,
each tending his own portion."

4 "Prepare for battle against her!
Arise, let us attack at noon!
But, alas, the daylight is fading,

and the shadows of evening grow
long.
5 So arise, let us attack at night
and destroy her fortresses!"

6 This is what the LORD Almighty says:

"Cut down the trees
and build siege ramps against
Jerusalem.
This city must be punished;
it is filled with oppression.
7 As a well pours out its water,
so she pours out her wickedness.
Violence and destruction resound in
her;
her sickness and wounds are ever
before me.
8 Take warning, O Jerusalem,
or I will turn away from you
and make your land desolate
so no one can live in it."

9 This is what the LORD Almighty says:

"Let them glean the remnant of Israel
as thoroughly as a vine;
pass your hand over the branches
again,
like one gathering grapes."

10 To whom can I speak and give
warning?
Who will listen to me?
Their ears are closed[a]
so they cannot hear.
The word of the LORD is offensive to
them;
they find no pleasure in it.
11 But I am full of the wrath of the
LORD,
and I cannot hold it in.

"Pour it out on the children in the
street
and on the young men gathered
together;
both husband and wife will be caught
in it,
and the old, those weighed down
with years.

---

a 10 Hebrew uncircumcised

12 Their houses will be turned over to
  others,
    together with their fields and their
    wives,
  when I stretch out my hand
    against those who live in the land,"
      declares the LORD.
13 "From the least to the greatest,
  all are greedy for gain;
  prophets and priests alike,
  all practice deceit.
14 They dress the wound of my people
  as though it were not serious.
  'Peace, peace,' they say,
    when there is no peace.
15 Are they ashamed of their loathsome
  conduct?
    No, they have no shame at all;
    they do not even know how to
    blush.
  So they will fall among the fallen;
    they will be brought down when I
    punish them,"
      says the LORD.

16 This is what the LORD says:

"Stand at the crossroads and look;
  ask for the ancient paths,
ask where the good way is, and walk
  in it,
  and you will find rest for your
  souls.
But you said, 'We will not walk in
  it.'

Praying Jeremiah 6:16

*Lord, show me the path You
have for me so that I may walk
in it and find rest for my soul.*

17 I appointed watchmen over you and
  said,
    'Listen to the sound of the
    trumpet!'
  But you said, 'We will not listen.'
18 Therefore hear, O nations;
  observe, O witnesses,
  what will happen to them.
19 Hear, O earth:

I am bringing disaster on this people,
  the fruit of their schemes,
because they have not listened to my
  words
  and have rejected my law.
20 What do I care about incense from
  Sheba
  or sweet calamus from a distant
  land?
Your burnt offerings are not
  acceptable;
  your sacrifices do not please me."

21 Therefore this is what the LORD says:

"I will put obstacles before this
  people.
  Fathers and sons alike will stumble
  over them;
  neighbors and friends will perish."

22 This is what the LORD says:

"Look, an army is coming
  from the land of the north;
a great nation is being stirred up
  from the ends of the earth.
23 They are armed with bow and
  spear;
  they are cruel and show no mercy.
They sound like the roaring sea
  as they ride on their horses;
they come like men in battle
  formation
  to attack you, O Daughter of
  Zion."

24 We have heard reports about them,
  and our hands hang limp.
Anguish has gripped us,
  pain like that of a woman in labor.
25 Do not go out to the fields
  or walk on the roads,
for the enemy has a sword,
  and there is terror on every side.
26 O my people, put on sackcloth
  and roll in ashes;
  mourn with bitter wailing
  as for an only son,
for suddenly the destroyer
  will come upon us.

GOING deeper

Praying for Your Nation

READ AND CONSIDER: JEREMIAH 6:16-19

"This is what the LORD says: 'Stand at the crossroads and look; ask for the ancient paths, ask where the good way is, and walk in it, and you will find rest for your souls. But you said, "We will not walk in it."... I am bringing disaster on this people, the fruit of their schemes, because they have not listened to my words'" (Jeremiah 6:16,19).

Notice what God said to the sinful nations: "Stand . . . look . . . ask . . . walk." In other words, "Look for the right way to go and then follow it." And the reward for doing that meets everyone's deepest longing—"and you will find rest for your souls." Unfortunately, the response of far too many nations to God is, "We will not walk in it."

The consequence for any nation that forsakes God and His ways is serious. Even though you and I and millions of other believers have not forsaken God and His ways, many others in our nation have. But God gives us a way to respond to His warnings of judgment by confessing the sins of our nation before Him and asking Him to heal our land: "If my people, who are called by my name, will humble themselves and pray and seek my face and turn from their wicked ways, then will I hear from heaven and will forgive their sin and will heal their land" (2 Chronicles 7:14).

He didn't say that all people in a nation must be perfect in their heart and actions in order to receive His blessings. If that were the case, there would never be a nation that was blessed. We can, however, "stand in the gap" and be the one person willing to pray. Ezekiel described the sad situation when not one person could be found to pray: "I looked for a man among them who would build up the wall and stand before me in the gap on behalf of the land so I would not have to destroy it, but I found none" (Ezekiel 22:30).

God allows those of us who are called by His name to humble ourselves and repent for the sins of our nation so that we can continue to receive the blessings He has for us. We can stand in the gap on behalf of our unrepentant nation. Let's pray that we will be the ones who stand at the crossroads, look for the ancient paths, ask where the good way is, and walk in it. And may many others follow our example.

27 "I have made you a tester of metals
  and my people the ore,
that you may observe
  and test their ways.
28 They are all hardened rebels,
  going about to slander.
They are bronze and iron;
  they all act corruptly.
29 The bellows blow fiercely
  to burn away the lead with fire,
but the refining goes on in vain;
  the wicked are not purged out.
30 They are called rejected silver,
  because the LORD has rejected
    them."

False Religion Worthless

7 This is the word that came to Jeremiah from the LORD: 2 "Stand at the gate of the LORD's house and there proclaim this message:

"'Hear the word of the LORD, all you people of Judah who come through these gates to worship the LORD. 3 This is what the LORD Almighty, the God of Israel, says: Reform your ways and your actions, and I will let you live in this place. 4 Do not trust in deceptive words and say, "This is the temple of the LORD, the temple of the LORD, the temple of the LORD!" 5 If you really change your ways and your actions and deal with each other justly, 6if you do not oppress the alien, the fatherless or the widow and do not shed innocent blood in this place, and if you do not follow other gods to your own harm, 7then I will let you live in this place, in the land I gave your forefathers for ever and ever. 8But look, you are trusting in deceptive words that are worthless.

9 "Will you steal and murder, commit adultery and perjury,[a] burn incense to Baal and follow other gods you have not known, 10and then come and stand before me in this house, which bears my Name, and say, "We are safe"—safe to do all these detestable things? 11Has this house, which bears my Name, become a den of robbers to you? But I have been watching! declares the LORD.

12 "Go now to the place in Shiloh where I first made a dwelling for my Name, and see what I did to it because of the wickedness of my people Israel. 13While you were doing all these things, declares the LORD, I spoke to you again and again, but you did not listen; I called you, but you did not answer. 14Therefore, what I did to Shiloh I will now do to the house that bears my Name, the temple you trust in, the place I gave to you and your fathers. 15I will thrust you from my presence, just as I did all your brothers, the people of Ephraim.'

16 "So do not pray for this people nor offer any plea or petition for them; do not plead with me, for I will not listen to you. 17Do you not see what they are doing in the towns of Judah and in the streets of Jerusalem? 18The children gather wood, the fathers light the fire, and the women knead the dough and make cakes of bread for the Queen of Heaven. They pour out drink offerings to other gods to provoke me to anger. 19But am I the one they are provoking? declares the LORD. Are they not rather harming themselves, to their own shame?

20 "Therefore this is what the Sovereign LORD says: My anger and my wrath will be poured out on this place, on man and beast, on the trees of the field and on the fruit of the ground, and it will burn and not be quenched.

21 "'This is what the LORD Almighty, the God of Israel, says: Go ahead, add your burnt offerings to your other sacrifices and eat the meat yourselves! 22For when I brought your forefathers out of Egypt and spoke to them, I did not just give them commands about burnt offerings and sacrifices, 23but I gave them this command: Obey me, and I will be your God and you will be my people. Walk in all the ways I command you, that it may go well with you. 24But they did not listen or pay attention; instead, they followed the stubborn inclinations of their evil hearts. They went backward and not forward. 25From the time your forefathers left Egypt until now, day after day, again and again I sent you my servants the prophets. 26But they did not listen to me or pay attention. They were stiff-necked and did more evil than their forefathers.'

27 "When you tell them all this, they will not listen to you; when you call to them, they will not answer. 28Therefore say to them, 'This is the nation that has not obeyed the LORD its God or responded to correction. Truth has perished; it has vanished from their lips. 29Cut off your hair and throw it away; take up a lament on the barren heights, for the LORD has rejected and abandoned this generation that is under his wrath.

The Valley of Slaughter

30 "'The people of Judah have done evil in my eyes, declares the LORD. They have set up their detestable idols in the house that bears my Name and have defiled it. 31They have built the high places of Topheth in the Valley of Ben Hinnom to burn their sons and daughters in the fire—something I did not command, nor did it enter my mind. 32So beware, the days are coming, declares the LORD, when

---

a 9 Or and swear by false gods

people will no longer call it Topheth or the Valley of Ben Hinnom, but the Valley of Slaughter, for they will bury the dead in Topheth until there is no more room. [33] Then the carcasses of this people will become food for the birds of the air and the beasts of the earth, and there will be no one to frighten them away. [34] I will bring an end to the sounds of joy and gladness and to the voices of bride and bridegroom in the towns of Judah and the streets of Jerusalem, for the land will become desolate.

8 "'At that time, declares the LORD, the bones of the kings and officials of Judah, the bones of the priests and prophets, and the bones of the people of Jerusalem will be removed from their graves. [2] They will be exposed to the sun and the moon and all the stars of the heavens, which they have loved and served and which they have followed and consulted and worshiped. They will not be gathered up or buried, but will be like refuse lying on the ground. [3] Wherever I banish them, all the survivors of this evil nation will prefer death to life, declares the LORD Almighty.'

Sin and Punishment

[4] "Say to them, 'This is what the LORD says:

"'When men fall down, do they not
    get up?
  When a man turns away, does he
    not return?
[5] Why then have these people turned
    away?
  Why does Jerusalem always turn
    away?
They cling to deceit;
  they refuse to return.
[6] I have listened attentively,
  but they do not say what is right.
No one repents of his wickedness,
  saying, "What have I done?"
Each pursues his own course
  like a horse charging into battle.

[7] Even the stork in the sky
  knows her appointed seasons,
and the dove, the swift and the thrush
  observe the time of their migration.
But my people do not know
  the requirements of the LORD.

[8] "'How can you say, "We are wise,
  for we have the law of the LORD,"
when actually the lying pen of the
    scribes
  has handled it falsely?
[9] The wise will be put to shame;
  they will be dismayed and trapped.
Since they have rejected the word of
    the LORD,
  what kind of wisdom do they have?
[10] Therefore I will give their wives to
    other men
  and their fields to new owners.
From the least to the greatest,
  all are greedy for gain;
prophets and priests alike,
  all practice deceit.
[11] They dress the wound of my people
  as though it were not serious.
"Peace, peace," they say,
  when there is no peace.
[12] Are they ashamed of their loathsome
    conduct?
  No, they have no shame at all;
  they do not even know how to
    blush.
So they will fall among the fallen;
  they will be brought down when
    they are punished,
                    says the LORD.
[13] "'I will take away their harvest,
                    declares the LORD.
  There will be no grapes on the
    vine.
There will be no figs on the tree,
  and their leaves will wither.
What I have given them
  will be taken from them.[a]'"

[14] "Why are we sitting here?
  Gather together!
Let us flee to the fortified cities

---

a 13 The meaning of the Hebrew for this sentence is uncertain.

and perish there!
For the LORD our God has doomed us
　to perish
and given us poisoned water to
　drink,
because we have sinned against
　him.
15 We hoped for peace
　but no good has come,
for a time of healing
　but there was only terror.
16 The snorting of the enemy's horses
　is heard from Dan;
at the neighing of their stallions
　the whole land trembles.
They have come to devour
　the land and everything in it,
　the city and all who live there."

17 "See, I will send venomous snakes
　　among you,
vipers that cannot be charmed,
　and they will bite you,"
　　　　　　　declares the LORD.

18 O my Comforter[a] in sorrow,
　my heart is faint within me.
19 Listen to the cry of my people
　from a land far away:
"Is the LORD not in Zion?
　Is her King no longer there?"

"Why have they provoked me to
　　anger with their images,
with their worthless foreign idols?"

20 "The harvest is past,
　the summer has ended,
　and we are not saved."

21 Since my people are crushed, I am
　　crushed;
I mourn, and horror grips me.
22 Is there no balm in Gilead?
　Is there no physician there?
Why then is there no healing
　for the wound of my people?
9 1 Oh, that my head were a spring of
　　water
and my eyes a fountain of tears!

I would weep day and night
　for the slain of my people.
2 Oh, that I had in the desert
　a lodging place for travelers,
so that I might leave my people
　and go away from them;
for they are all adulterers,
　a crowd of unfaithful people.

3 "They make ready their tongue
　like a bow, to shoot lies;
it is not by truth
　that they triumph[b] in the land.
They go from one sin to another;
　they do not acknowledge me,"
　　　　　　　declares the LORD.
4 "Beware of your friends;
　do not trust your brothers.
For every brother is a deceiver,[c]
　and every friend a slanderer.
5 Friend deceives friend,
　and no one speaks the truth.
They have taught their tongues to lie;
　they weary themselves with sinning.
6 You[d] live in the midst of deception;
　in their deceit they refuse to
　　acknowledge me,"
　　　　　　　declares the LORD.

Praying Jeremiah 9:5-6

*Heavenly Father, please keep me
from committing any kind of deception
or speaking anything but truth.*

7 Therefore this is what the LORD Almighty says:

"See, I will refine and test them,
　for what else can I do
　because of the sin of my people?
8 Their tongue is a deadly arrow;
　it speaks with deceit.
With his mouth each speaks cordially
　to his neighbor,
but in his heart he sets a trap for
　him.
9 Should I not punish them for this?"
　declares the LORD.

---

a 18 The meaning of the Hebrew for this word is uncertain.　　b 3 Or *lies; / they are not valiant for truth*　　c 4 Or *a deceiving Jacob*
d 6 That is, Jeremiah (the Hebrew is singular)

GOING
deeper 1

Boasting in God Alone

READ AND CONSIDER: JEREMIAH 9:13-26

"This is what the LORD says: 'Let not the wise man boast of his wisdom or the strong man boast of his strength or the rich man boast of his riches, but let him who boasts boast about this: that he understands and knows me, that I am the LORD, who exercises kindness, justice and righteousness on earth, for in these I delight' " (Jeremiah 9:23-24).

Everyone wants to accomplish something significant with his life. We all desire to do things well. Who doesn't want to accomplish something worth boasting about, even if we are not the ones doing the boasting? But God says we are to boast about one thing only, and this is that we know *Him.*

Men and women of the world boast about their accomplishments. These verses mention three things people commonly boast about, and those are wisdom, strength, and riches. But even if we have *all* of these characteristics, we can't get prideful about them as though *we* did something great. That's because everything we have comes from God.

The one thing we can brag about is that we have a relationship with the Lord. The only reason we have the potential to do something great is that we are His and His Spirit dwells in us. Because of His greatness *in* us, He will accomplish great things *through* us. Perhaps the greatest things we will do in life are acts that no one will ever know about—such as interceding in prayer or caring for the needy—the impact of which we will not comprehend this side of eternity.

"Should I not avenge myself
  on such a nation as this?"

¹⁰I will weep and wail for the
    mountains
  and take up a lament concerning
    the desert pastures.
They are desolate and untraveled,
  and the lowing of cattle is not
    heard.
The birds of the air have fled
  and the animals are gone.

¹¹"I will make Jerusalem a heap of ruins,
    a haunt of jackals;
and I will lay waste the towns of
    Judah
  so no one can live there."

¹²What man is wise enough to understand this? Who has been instructed by the LORD and can explain it? Why has the land been ruined and laid waste like a desert that no one can cross?

¹³The LORD said, "It is because they have forsaken my law, which I set before them; they have not obeyed me or followed my law. ¹⁴Instead, they have followed the stubbornness of their hearts; they have followed the Baals, as their fathers taught them." ¹⁵Therefore, this is what the LORD Almighty, the God of Israel, says: "See, I will make this people eat bitter food and drink poisoned water. ¹⁶I will scatter them among nations that neither they nor their fathers have known, and I will pursue them with the sword until I have destroyed them."

¹⁷This is what the LORD Almighty says:

"Consider now! Call for the wailing
    women to come;
  send for the most skillful of them.
¹⁸Let them come quickly
  and wail over us
till our eyes overflow with tears

and water streams from our eyelids.
¹⁹The sound of wailing is heard from
Zion:
'How ruined we are!
How great is our shame!
We must leave our land
because our houses are in ruins.'"

²⁰Now, O women, hear the word of the
LORD;
open your ears to the words of his
mouth.
Teach your daughters how to wail;
teach one another a lament.
²¹Death has climbed in through our
windows
and has entered our fortresses;
it has cut off the children from the
streets
and the young men from the public
squares.

²²Say, "This is what the LORD declares:

"'The dead bodies of men will lie
like refuse on the open field,
like cut grain behind the reaper,
with no one to gather them.'"

²³This is what the LORD says:

"Let not the wise man boast of his
wisdom
or the strong man boast of his
strength
or the rich man boast of his riches,
²⁴but let him who boasts boast about
this:
that he understands and knows me,
that I am the LORD, who exercises
kindness,
justice and righteousness on earth,
for in these I delight,"
declares the LORD.

²⁵"The days are coming," declares the
LORD, "when I will punish all who are circumcised only in the flesh— ²⁶Egypt, Judah, Edom, Ammon, Moab and all who
live in the desert in distant places.ᵃ For
all these nations are really uncircumcised,

and even the whole house of Israel is uncircumcised in heart."

God and Idols

10 Hear what the LORD says to you,
O house of Israel. ²This is what the
LORD says:

"Do not learn the ways of the nations
or be terrified by signs in the sky,
though the nations are terrified by
them.
³For the customs of the peoples are
worthless;
they cut a tree out of the forest,
and a craftsman shapes it with his
chisel.
⁴They adorn it with silver and gold;
they fasten it with hammer and
nails
so it will not totter.
⁵Like a scarecrow in a melon patch,
their idols cannot speak;
they must be carried
because they cannot walk.
Do not fear them;
they can do no harm
nor can they do any good."

⁶No one is like you, O LORD;
you are great,
and your name is mighty in power.
⁷Who should not revere you,
O King of the nations?
This is your due.
Among all the wise men of the
nations
and in all their kingdoms,
there is no one like you.
⁸They are all senseless and foolish;
they are taught by worthless
wooden idols.
⁹Hammered silver is brought from
Tarshish
and gold from Uphaz.
What the craftsman and goldsmith
have made
is then dressed in blue and purple—
all made by skilled workers.
¹⁰But the LORD is the true God;

ᵃ 26 Or desert and who clip the hair by their foreheads

he is the living God, the eternal
King.
When he is angry, the earth trembles;
the nations cannot endure his
wrath.

[11] "Tell them this: 'These gods, who did
not make the heavens and the earth, will
perish from the earth and from under
the heavens.'"[a]

[12] But God made the earth by his power;
he founded the world by his
wisdom
and stretched out the heavens by his
understanding.
[13] When he thunders, the waters in the
heavens roar;
he makes clouds rise from the ends
of the earth.
He sends lightning with the rain
and brings out the wind from his
storehouses.

[14] Everyone is senseless and without
knowledge;
every goldsmith is shamed by his
idols.
His images are a fraud;
they have no breath in them.
[15] They are worthless, the objects of
mockery;
when their judgment comes, they
will perish.
[16] He who is the Portion of Jacob is not
like these,
for he is the Maker of all things,
including Israel, the tribe of his
inheritance—
the LORD Almighty is his name.

Coming Destruction

[17] Gather up your belongings to leave
the land,
you who live under siege.
[18] For this is what the LORD says:
"At this time I will hurl out
those who live in this land;
I will bring distress on them
so that they may be captured."

[19] Woe to me because of my injury!
My wound is incurable!
Yet I said to myself,
"This is my sickness, and I must
endure it."
[20] My tent is destroyed;
all its ropes are snapped.
My sons are gone from me and are no
more;
no one is left now to pitch my tent
or to set up my shelter.
[21] The shepherds are senseless
and do not inquire of the LORD;
so they do not prosper
and all their flock is scattered.
[22] Listen! The report is coming—
a great commotion from the land of
the north!
It will make the towns of Judah
desolate,
a haunt of jackals.

Jeremiah's Prayer

[23] I know, O LORD, that a man's life is
not his own;
it is not for man to direct his steps.
[24] Correct me, LORD, but only with
justice—
not in your anger,
lest you reduce me to nothing.
[25] Pour out your wrath on the nations
that do not acknowledge you,
on the peoples who do not call on
your name.
For they have devoured Jacob;
they have devoured him completely
and destroyed his homeland.

The Covenant Is Broken

11 This is the word that came to
Jeremiah from the LORD: [2] "Listen
to the terms of this covenant and tell
them to the people of Judah and to those
who live in Jerusalem. [3] Tell them that this
is what the LORD, the God of Israel, says:
'Cursed is the man who does not obey
the terms of this covenant— [4] the terms
I commanded your forefathers when I
brought them out of Egypt, out of the

---

[a] 11 The text of this verse is in Aramaic.

iron-smelting furnace.' I said, 'Obey me and do everything I command you, and you will be my people, and I will be your God. 5Then I will fulfill the oath I swore to your forefathers, to give them a land flowing with milk and honey'—the land you possess today."

I answered, "Amen, LORD."

6The LORD said to me, "Proclaim all these words in the towns of Judah and in the streets of Jerusalem: 'Listen to the terms of this covenant and follow them. 7From the time I brought your forefathers up from Egypt until today, I warned them again and again, saying, "Obey me." 8But they did not listen or pay attention; instead, they followed the stubbornness of their evil hearts. So I brought on them all the curses of the covenant I had commanded them to follow but that they did not keep.'"

9Then the LORD said to me, "There is a conspiracy among the people of Judah and those who live in Jerusalem. 10They have returned to the sins of their forefathers, who refused to listen to my words. They have followed other gods to serve them. Both the house of Israel and the house of Judah have broken the covenant I made with their forefathers. 11Therefore this is what the LORD says: 'I will bring on them a disaster they cannot escape. Although they cry out to me, I will not listen to them. 12The towns of Judah and the people of Jerusalem will go and cry out to the gods to whom they burn incense, but they will not help them at all when disaster strikes. 13You have as many gods as you have towns, O Judah; and the altars you have set up to burn incense to that shameful god Baal are as many as the streets of Jerusalem.'

14"Do not pray for this people nor offer any plea or petition for them, because I will not listen when they call to me in the time of their distress.

15"What is my beloved doing in my
   temple

as she works out her evil schemes
   with many?
Can consecrated meat avert ⌐your
   punishment⌐?
When you engage in your
   wickedness,
then you rejoice.ᵃ'"

16The LORD called you a thriving olive
   tree
   with fruit beautiful in form.
But with the roar of a mighty storm
   he will set it on fire,
   and its branches will be broken.

17The LORD Almighty, who planted you, has decreed disaster for you, because the house of Israel and the house of Judah have done evil and provoked me to anger by burning incense to Baal.

Plot Against Jeremiah

18Because the LORD revealed their plot to me, I knew it, for at that time he showed me what they were doing. 19I had been like a gentle lamb led to the slaughter; I did not realize that they had plotted against me, saying,

"Let us destroy the tree and its fruit;
   let us cut him off from the land of
   the living,
   that his name be remembered no
   more."
20But, O LORD Almighty, you who
   judge righteously
   and test the heart and mind,
let me see your vengeance upon
   them,
   for to you I have committed my
   cause.

21"Therefore this is what the LORD says about the men of Anathoth who are seeking your life and saying, 'Do not prophesy in the name of the LORD or you will die by our hands'— 22therefore this is what the LORD Almighty says: 'I will punish them. Their young men will die by the sword, their sons and daughters by famine. 23Not even a remnant will

---

ᵃ 15 Or Could consecrated meat avert your punishment? / Then you would rejoice be left to them, because I will bring disaster on the men of Anathoth in the year of their punishment.'"

Jeremiah's Complaint

12 You are always righteous,
O LORD,
when I bring a case before you.
Yet I would speak with you about
your justice:
Why does the way of the wicked
prosper?
Why do all the faithless live at
ease?
2 You have planted them, and they
have taken root;
they grow and bear fruit.
You are always on their lips
but far from their hearts.
3 Yet you know me, O LORD;
you see me and test my thoughts
about you.

Drag them off like sheep to be
butchered!
Set them apart for the day of
slaughter!
4 How long will the land lie parched[a]
and the grass in every field be
withered?
Because those who live in it are
wicked,
the animals and birds have
perished.
Moreover, the people are saying,
"He will not see what happens to
us."

God's Answer

5 "If you have raced with men on foot
and they have worn you out,
how can you compete with horses?
If you stumble in safe country,[b]
how will you manage in the
thickets by[c] the Jordan?

---

[a] 4 Or land mourn   [b] 5 Or If you put your trust in a land of safety   [c] 5 Or the flooding of

---

GOING *deeper*

Being Honest Before God

READ AND CONSIDER: JEREMIAH 12:1-13

"You are always righteous, O LORD, when I bring a case before you. Yet I would speak with you about your justice: Why does the way of the wicked prosper? Why do all the faithless live at ease?" (Jeremiah 12:1).

One remarkable thing about Jeremiah was he never hesitated to tell God what was on his mind. He didn't edit his prayers. He trusted God enough to be completely honest. God listened and responded with mercy. In this particular case, Jeremiah came to God with a compliment and two complaints. He recognized God's faithfulness—"You are always righteous" (12:1). Then Jeremiah began to pour out a list of issues he felt God needed to resolve. Among these were the prosperity and peaceful living of wicked people, which greatly irritated the prophet. Why did God allow such people to succeed?

God's response presents a beautiful picture of His patience. He gently told Jeremiah that he was out of his league in attempting to give God direction. He didn't rebuke Jeremiah; He simply told him that what he observed was a small part of a much larger picture.

God wants us to be honest with Him. He lets us bare our souls and share our hearts. Like a loving parent, He listens and is not angry or impatient. So if you have concerns and questions, bring them before your heavenly Father and lay them all at His feet. Often He will help you to see things from His perspective.

6 Your brothers, your own family—
even they have betrayed you;
they have raised a loud cry against
you.
Do not trust them,
though they speak well of you.

7 "I will forsake my house,
abandon my inheritance;
I will give the one I love
into the hands of her enemies.
8 My inheritance has become to me
like a lion in the forest.
She roars at me;
therefore I hate her.
9 Has not my inheritance become to me
like a speckled bird of prey
that other birds of prey surround
and attack?
Go and gather all the wild beasts;
bring them to devour.
10 Many shepherds will ruin my vineyard
and trample down my field;
they will turn my pleasant field
into a desolate wasteland.
11 It will be made a wasteland,
parched and desolate before me;
the whole land will be laid waste
because there is no one who cares.
12 Over all the barren heights in the
desert
destroyers will swarm,
for the sword of the LORD will devour
from one end of the land to the
other;
no one will be safe.
13 They will sow wheat but reap thorns;
they will wear themselves out but
gain nothing.
So bear the shame of your harvest
because of the LORD's fierce anger."

14 This is what the LORD says: "As for
all my wicked neighbors who seize the
inheritance I gave my people Israel, I
will uproot them from their lands and
I will uproot the house of Judah from
among them. 15 But after I uproot them,
I will again have compassion and will
bring each of them back to his own inheritance and his own country. 16 And if
they learn well the ways of my people
and swear by my name, saying, 'As surely
as the LORD lives'—even as they once
taught my people to swear by Baal—then
they will be established among my people. 17 But if any nation does not listen,
I will completely uproot and destroy it,"
declares the LORD.

A Linen Belt

13 This is what the LORD said to me:
"Go and buy a linen belt and put it
around your waist, but do not let it touch
water." 2 So I bought a belt, as the LORD
directed, and put it around my waist.

3 Then the word of the LORD came to
me a second time: 4 "Take the belt you
bought and are wearing around your
waist, and go now to Perath[a] and hide
it there in a crevice in the rocks." 5 So I
went and hid it at Perath, as the LORD
told me.

6 Many days later the LORD said to me,
"Go now to Perath and get the belt I told
you to hide there." 7 So I went to Perath
and dug up the belt and took it from the
place where I had hidden it, but now it
was ruined and completely useless.

8 Then the word of the LORD came to
me: 9 "This is what the LORD says: 'In the
same way I will ruin the pride of Judah
and the great pride of Jerusalem. 10 These
wicked people, who refuse to listen to
my words, who follow the stubbornness
of their hearts and go after other gods to
serve and worship them, will be like this
belt—completely useless! 11 For as a belt is
bound around a man's waist, so I bound
the whole house of Israel and the whole
house of Judah to me,' declares the LORD,
'to be my people for my renown and
praise and honor. But they have not listened.'

Wineskins

12 "Say to them: 'This is what the LORD,
the God of Israel, says: Every wineskin

---

a 4 Or possibly *the Euphrates*; also in verses 5-7

should be filled with wine.' And if they say to you, 'Don't we know that every wineskin should be filled with wine?' [13]then tell them, 'This is what the LORD says: I am going to fill with drunkenness all who live in this land, including the kings who sit on David's throne, the priests, the prophets and all those living in Jerusalem. [14]I will smash them one against the other, fathers and sons alike, declares the LORD. I will allow no pity or mercy or compassion to keep me from destroying them.' "

Praying Jeremiah 13:15-17

Lord, help me to never give way to pride so that I end up grieving You and walking in the darkness of being full of myself.

Threat of Captivity

[15]Hear and pay attention,
  do not be arrogant,
  for the LORD has spoken.
[16]Give glory to the LORD your God
  before he brings the darkness,
 before your feet stumble
  on the darkening hills.
 You hope for light,
  but he will turn it to thick darkness
  and change it to deep gloom.
[17]But if you do not listen,
  I will weep in secret
  because of your pride;
 my eyes will weep bitterly,
  overflowing with tears,
  because the LORD's flock will be
   taken captive.

[18]Say to the king and to the queen
   mother,
 "Come down from your thrones,
 for your glorious crowns
  will fall from your heads."
[19]The cities in the Negev will be shut
   up,
  and there will be no one to open
   them.
 All Judah will be carried into exile,
  carried completely away.

[20]Lift up your eyes and see
  those who are coming from the
   north.
 Where is the flock that was entrusted
  to you,
  the sheep of which you boasted?
[21]What will you say when ⌊the LORD⌋
   sets over you
  those you cultivated as your special
   allies?
 Will not pain grip you
  like that of a woman in labor?
[22]And if you ask yourself,
  "Why has this happened to me?"—
 it is because of your many sins
  that your skirts have been torn off
  and your body mistreated.
[23]Can the Ethiopian[a] change his skin
  or the leopard its spots?
 Neither can you do good
  who are accustomed to doing evil.

[24]"I will scatter you like chaff
  driven by the desert wind.
[25]This is your lot,
  the portion I have decreed for you,"
   declares the LORD,
 "because you have forgotten me
  and trusted in false gods.
[26]I will pull up your skirts over your
   face
  that your shame may be seen—
[27]your adulteries and lustful neighings,
  your shameless prostitution!
 I have seen your detestable acts
  on the hills and in the fields.
 Woe to you, O Jerusalem!
  How long will you be unclean?"

Drought, Famine, Sword

14 This is the word of the LORD to Jeremiah concerning the drought:

[2]"Judah mourns,
  her cities languish;
 they wail for the land,
  and a cry goes up from Jerusalem.
[3]The nobles send their servants for
   water;
  they go to the cisterns

---

[a] 23 Hebrew *Cushite* (probably a person from the upper Nile region)

but find no water.
They return with their jars unfilled;
    dismayed and despairing,
    they cover their heads.
4 The ground is cracked
    because there is no rain in the land;
the farmers are dismayed
    and cover their heads.
5 Even the doe in the field
    deserts her newborn fawn
    because there is no grass.
6 Wild donkeys stand on the barren
        heights
    and pant like jackals;
their eyesight fails
    for lack of pasture."

7 Although our sins testify against us,
    O LORD, do something for the sake
        of your name.
For our backsliding is great;
    we have sinned against you.
8 O Hope of Israel,
    its Savior in times of distress,
why are you like a stranger in the
        land,
    like a traveler who stays only a
        night?
9 Why are you like a man taken by
        surprise,
    like a warrior powerless to save?
You are among us, O LORD,
    and we bear your name;
    do not forsake us!

10 This is what the LORD says about
this people:

"They greatly love to wander;
    they do not restrain their feet.
So the LORD does not accept them;
    he will now remember their
        wickedness
    and punish them for their sins."

11 Then the LORD said to me, "Do not
pray for the well-being of this people.
12 Although they fast, I will not listen to
their cry; though they offer burnt offerings and grain offerings, I will not accept

them. Instead, I will destroy them with
the sword, famine and plague."

13 But I said, "Ah, Sovereign LORD, the
prophets keep telling them, 'You will
not see the sword or suffer famine. Indeed, I will give you lasting peace in this
place.'"

14 Then the LORD said to me, "The
prophets are prophesying lies in my
name. I have not sent them or appointed
them or spoken to them. They are prophesying to you false visions, divinations,
idolatries[a] and the delusions of their own
minds. 15 Therefore, this is what the LORD
says about the prophets who are prophesying in my name: I did not send them,
yet they are saying, 'No sword or famine
will touch this land.' Those same prophets will perish by sword and famine.
16 And the people they are prophesying to
will be thrown out into the streets of Jerusalem because of the famine and sword.
There will be no one to bury them or
their wives, their sons or their daughters.
I will pour out on them the calamity
they deserve.

17 "Speak this word to them:

"'Let my eyes overflow with tears
    night and day without ceasing;
for my virgin daughter—my people—
    has suffered a grievous wound,
    a crushing blow.
18 If I go into the country,
    I see those slain by the sword;
if I go into the city,
    I see the ravages of famine.
Both prophet and priest
    have gone to a land they know
        not.'"

19 Have you rejected Judah completely?
    Do you despise Zion?
Why have you afflicted us
    so that we cannot be healed?
We hoped for peace
    but no good has come,
for a time of healing
    but there is only terror.

---

a 14 Or visions, worthless divinations

²⁰O Lord, we acknowledge our
        wickedness
    and the guilt of our fathers;
    we have indeed sinned against
        you.
²¹For the sake of your name do not
        despise us;
    do not dishonor your glorious
        throne.
Remember your covenant with us
    and do not break it.
²²Do any of the worthless idols of the
        nations bring rain?
    Do the skies themselves send down
        showers?
No, it is you, O Lord our God.
    Therefore our hope is in you,
    for you are the one who does all
        this.

15 Then the Lord said to me: "Even if Moses and Samuel were to stand before me, my heart would not go out to this people. Send them away from my presence! Let them go! ²And if they ask you, 'Where shall we go?' tell them, 'This is what the Lord says:

" 'Those destined for death, to death;
    those for the sword, to the sword;
    those for starvation, to starvation;
    those for captivity, to captivity.'

³"I will send four kinds of destroyers against them," declares the Lord, "the sword to kill and the dogs to drag away and the birds of the air and the beasts of the earth to devour and destroy. ⁴I will make them abhorrent to all the kingdoms of the earth because of what Manasseh son of Hezekiah king of Judah did in Jerusalem.

⁵"Who will have pity on you,
        O Jerusalem?
    Who will mourn for you?
    Who will stop to ask how you
        are?
⁶You have rejected me," declares the
        Lord.
    "You keep on backsliding.
So I will lay hands on you and
        destroy you;
    I can no longer show compassion.
⁷I will winnow them with a
        winnowing fork
    at the city gates of the land.
I will bring bereavement and
        destruction on my people,
    for they have not changed their
        ways.
⁸I will make their widows more
        numerous
    than the sand of the sea.
At midday I will bring a destroyer
    against the mothers of their young
        men;
suddenly I will bring down on them
    anguish and terror.
⁹The mother of seven will grow faint
    and breathe her last.
Her sun will set while it is still day;
    she will be disgraced and
        humiliated.
I will put the survivors to the sword
    before their enemies,"
                        declares the Lord.

¹⁰Alas, my mother, that you gave me
        birth,
    a man with whom the whole land
        strives and contends!
I have neither lent nor borrowed,
    yet everyone curses me.

¹¹The Lord said,

"Surely I will deliver you for a good
        purpose;
    surely I will make your enemies
        plead with you
    in times of disaster and times of
        distress.

¹²"Can a man break iron—
    iron from the north—or bronze?
¹³Your wealth and your treasures
    I will give as plunder, without
        charge,
because of all your sins
    throughout your country.
¹⁴I will enslave you to your enemies

What Do You Need Redeemed in Your Life?

God is all about redemption and restoration.

We look for perfect things in our lives. Perfect situations. Perfect work. Perfect people. Perfect relationships. Perfect marriages. Perfect timing.

God is all about taking the imperfect and injecting His perfection into it.

So often we are willing to throw things out because we think they are unredeemable. Things like relationships, marriages, situations, hopes, dreams, people, and even our own lives.

God wants to redeem things we never dreamed possible.

God's most important act of redemption was when He redeemed our lost relationship with Him through His Son, Jesus. It was lost a long time before you and I were born, and Jesus paid the price to redeem it. But God redeems our life in many other ways too.

His redemption is one of the most beautiful and touching things about the Lord. It is nothing less than solid evidence of His love for us. When you understand that, it'll change your perspective on things. You'll see possibilities for your life like never before. It will cause you to be expectant and hopeful about what God can do in difficult situations.

God's redemption is all about His love for us.

What do you need God to redeem in your life? He has redeemed you from *hell* (Job 33:28), from *death* (Job 5:20), from *condemnation* (Psalm 34:22), from your enemies (Job 6:23), from your *troubles* (Psalm 25:22), from *sin* (Psalm 130:8). *And He wants you to trust Him to be your Redeemer for all time and in all things.* He asks, "Was my arm too short to ransom you?" (Isaiah 50:2). He says, "I will save you from the hands of the wicked and redeem you from the grasp of the cruel" (Jeremiah 15:21).

Whatever has been lost or stolen from you, God will restore it in some way. He will take all the broken and missing pieces of your life and put them together again. And there will come a point when you no longer feel the pain of loss. "The LORD redeems his servants" (Psalm 34:22). But it has to be done in *His* way and in *His* time. And worshiping and praising God as your Redeemer is a big part of seeing Him accomplish that. He does it most visibly in an environment of praise. He comes into our worship to infuse our situation with Himself and cause it to be transformed.

Because God loves us so much, He wants to totally restore, repair, rebuild, recover, renew, and redeem our souls and our lives. No matter how much damage has occurred, we cannot experience a loss so great that He cannot restore or redeem it in some way. God's redemption doesn't always happen in the way we expect. But isn't that often how the Lord does things? He doesn't do what we *think* He's going to. He always does something *greater*.

For the next "From Stormie's Heart" article, go to page 1004.

in[a] a land you do not know,
for my anger will kindle a fire
   that will burn against you."

15 You understand, O LORD;
   remember me and care for me.
   Avenge me on my persecutors.
You are long-suffering—do not take
   me away;
   think of how I suffer reproach for
   your sake.
16 When your words came, I ate them;
   they were my joy and my heart's
   delight,
for I bear your name,
   O LORD God Almighty.
17 I never sat in the company of revelers,
   never made merry with them;
I sat alone because your hand was
   on me
   and you had filled me with
   indignation.
18 Why is my pain unending
   and my wound grievous and
   incurable?
Will you be to me like a deceptive
   brook,
   like a spring that fails?

19 Therefore this is what the LORD says:

"If you repent, I will restore you
   that you may serve me;
if you utter worthy, not worthless,
   words,
   you will be my spokesman.
Let this people turn to you,
   but you must not turn to them.
20 I will make you a wall to this people,
   a fortified wall of bronze;
they will fight against you
   but will not overcome you,
for I am with you
   to rescue and save you,"
                  declares the LORD.
21 "I will save you from the hands of the
   wicked
   and redeem you from the grasp of
   the cruel."

Day of Disaster

16 Then the word of the LORD came
to me: 2 "You must not marry and
have sons or daughters in this place." 3 For
this is what the LORD says about the sons
and daughters born in this land and about
the women who are their mothers and
the men who are their fathers: 4 "They
will die of deadly diseases. They will not
be mourned or buried but will be like
refuse lying on the ground. They will perish by sword and famine, and their dead
bodies will become food for the birds of
the air and the beasts of the earth."

5 For this is what the LORD says: "Do
not enter a house where there is a funeral
meal; do not go to mourn or show sympathy, because I have withdrawn my
blessing, my love and my pity from this
people," declares the LORD. 6 "Both high
and low will die in this land. They will not
be buried or mourned, and no one will
cut himself or shave his head for them.
7 No one will offer food to comfort those
who mourn for the dead—not even for a
father or a mother—nor will anyone give
them a drink to console them.

8 "And do not enter a house where
there is feasting and sit down to eat and
drink. 9 For this is what the LORD Almighty, the God of Israel, says: Before
your eyes and in your days I will bring an
end to the sounds of joy and gladness and
to the voices of bride and bridegroom in
this place.

10 "When you tell these people all this
and they ask you, 'Why has the LORD
decreed such a great disaster against us?
What wrong have we done? What sin
have we committed against the LORD
our God?' 11 then say to them, 'It is because your fathers forsook me,' declares
the LORD, 'and followed other gods and
served and worshiped them. They forsook
me and did not keep my law. 12 But you
have behaved more wickedly than your
fathers. See how each of you is following

---

[a] 14 Some Hebrew manuscripts, Septuagint and Syriac (see also Jer. 17:4); most Hebrew manuscripts *I will cause your enemies
to bring you / into*

the stubbornness of his evil heart instead of obeying me. 13So I will throw you out of this land into a land neither you nor your fathers have known, and there you will serve other gods day and night, for I will show you no favor.'

Praying Jeremiah 16:11-13

Help me, God, to not just do what I want instead of listening to You and doing what You want.

14"However, the days are coming," declares the LORD, "when men will no longer say, 'As surely as the LORD lives, who brought the Israelites up out of Egypt,' 15but they will say, 'As surely as the LORD lives, who brought the Israelites up out of the land of the north and out of all the countries where he had banished them.' For I will restore them to the land I gave their forefathers.

16"But now I will send for many fishermen," declares the LORD, "and they will catch them. After that I will send for many hunters, and they will hunt them down on every mountain and hill and from the crevices of the rocks. 17My eyes are on all their ways; they are not hidden from me, nor is their sin concealed from my eyes. 18I will repay them double for their wickedness and their sin, because they have defiled my land with the lifeless forms of their vile images and have filled my inheritance with their detestable idols."

19O LORD, my strength and my fortress,
  my refuge in time of distress,
to you the nations will come
  from the ends of the earth and say,
"Our fathers possessed nothing but
    false gods,
  worthless idols that did them no
    good.
20Do men make their own gods?
  Yes, but they are not gods!"

21"Therefore I will teach them—
  this time I will teach them

my power and might.
Then they will know
  that my name is the LORD.

17 "Judah's sin is engraved with an
    iron tool,
  inscribed with a flint point,
on the tablets of their hearts
  and on the horns of their altars.
2Even their children remember
  their altars and Asherah poles[a]
beside the spreading trees
  and on the high hills.
3My mountain in the land
  and your[b] wealth and all your
    treasures
I will give away as plunder,
  together with your high places,
  because of sin throughout your
    country.
4Through your own fault you will lose
  the inheritance I gave you.
I will enslave you to your enemies
  in a land you do not know,
for you have kindled my anger,
  and it will burn forever."

5This is what the LORD says:

"Cursed is the one who trusts in man,
  who depends on flesh for his
    strength
  and whose heart turns away from
    the LORD.
6He will be like a bush in the
    wastelands;
  he will not see prosperity when it
    comes.
He will dwell in the parched places of
    the desert,
  in a salt land where no one lives.

7"But blessed is the man who trusts in
    the LORD,
  whose confidence is in him.
8He will be like a tree planted by the
    water
  that sends out its roots by the stream.
It does not fear when heat comes;
  its leaves are always green.

---

a 2 That is, symbols of the goddess Asherah   b 2,3 Or hills / 3and the mountains of the land. / Your

It has no worries in a year of drought
and never fails to bear fruit."

⁹The heart is deceitful above all things
and beyond cure.
Who can understand it?

¹⁰"I the LORD search the heart
and examine the mind,
to reward a man according to his
conduct,
according to what his deeds
deserve."

¹¹Like a partridge that hatches eggs it
did not lay
is the man who gains riches by
unjust means.

When his life is half gone, they will
desert him,
and in the end he will prove to be
a fool.

¹²A glorious throne, exalted from the
beginning,
is the place of our sanctuary.
¹³O LORD, the hope of Israel,
all who forsake you will be put to
shame.
Those who turn away from you will
be written in the dust
because they have forsaken the LORD,
the spring of living water.

¹⁴Heal me, O LORD, and I will be
healed;

GOING deeper

Praying for Healing

READ AND CONSIDER: JEREMIAH 17:14-18

"Heal me, O LORD, and I will be healed" (Jeremiah 17:14).

Healing and body care are two different things. When you ask God to heal you, this is something *He* does. Taking care of your body is something *you* do. Both are vitally important.

God knows we are a fallen race and can't do everything perfectly. That's why He sent Jesus to be our Healer. But He also calls us to be good stewards over everything He gives us, including our body. He wants us to live in balance and temperance and to take care not to abuse our body in any way. He wants us to glorify Him in the care of our bodies because we are the temple of His Holy Spirit.

Many of us tend to think, "Everything I have is the Lord's—except for my eating habits. Those are mine." Or we think, "My life is the Lord's, but my body belongs to me, and I can do with it whatever feels good." But when we are the Lord's, our body has to be surrendered to Him just like everything else. Caring for our body is not something we can do successfully independent of God.

I've actually heard people say, "I don't worry about taking care of my body because the Lord can just heal me when I get sick." This kind of presumptuous thinking is dangerous and can get us into trouble. Satan's plan for our lives is to do the very thing that will hurt us the most. We help him along by that kind of attitude. We sabotage our lives by not doing what's best for our bodies and our health. Ask God to help you resist what is bad for you and to be disciplined enough to do what's right. God loves and values you. He created you. You are where His Holy Spirit dwells. He wants you to love and value yourself enough to take good care of your body.

However, even after all of our efforts toward taking proper care of ourselves, we can still get sick. And we need Jesus, our Healer, to heal us. Don't hesitate to ask Him for His healing touch upon your body.

save me and I will be saved,
for you are the one I praise.
15They keep saying to me,
"Where is the word of the LORD?
Let it now be fulfilled!"
16I have not run away from being your
shepherd;
you know I have not desired the
day of despair.
What passes my lips is open before
you.
17Do not be a terror to me;
you are my refuge in the day of
disaster.
18Let my persecutors be put to shame,
but keep me from shame;
let them be terrified,
but keep me from terror.
Bring on them the day of disaster;
destroy them with double
destruction.

Keeping the Sabbath Holy

19This is what the LORD said to me:
"Go and stand at the gate of the people,
through which the kings of Judah go in
and out; stand also at all the other gates of
Jerusalem. 20Say to them, 'Hear the word
of the LORD, O kings of Judah and all
people of Judah and everyone living in
Jerusalem who come through these gates.
21This is what the LORD says: Be careful
not to carry a load on the Sabbath day or
bring it through the gates of Jerusalem.
22Do not bring a load out of your houses
or do any work on the Sabbath, but keep
the Sabbath day holy, as I commanded
your forefathers. 23Yet they did not listen
or pay attention; they were stiff-necked
and would not listen or respond to discipline. 24But if you are careful to obey
me, declares the LORD, and bring no load
through the gates of this city on the Sabbath, but keep the Sabbath day holy by not
doing any work on it, 25then kings who
sit on David's throne will come through
the gates of this city with their officials.
They and their officials will come riding
in chariots and on horses, accompanied
by the men of Judah and those living in

Jerusalem, and this city will be inhabited
forever. 26People will come from the
towns of Judah and the villages around Jerusalem, from the territory of Benjamin
and the western foothills, from the hill
country and the Negev, bringing burnt
offerings and sacrifices, grain offerings, incense and thank offerings to the house
of the LORD. 27But if you do not obey
me to keep the Sabbath day holy by not
carrying any load as you come through
the gates of Jerusalem on the Sabbath day,
then I will kindle an unquenchable fire
in the gates of Jerusalem that will consume her fortresses.'"

At the Potter's House

18 This is the word that came to
Jeremiah from the LORD: 2"Go
down to the potter's house, and there I
will give you my message." 3So I went
down to the potter's house, and I saw
him working at the wheel. 4But the pot
he was shaping from the clay was marred
in his hands; so the potter formed it into
another pot, shaping it as seemed best
to him.

5Then the word of the LORD came
to me: 6"O house of Israel, can I not do
with you as this potter does?" declares
the LORD. "Like clay in the hand of the
potter, so are you in my hand, O house of
Israel. 7If at any time I announce that a nation or kingdom is to be uprooted, torn
down and destroyed, 8and if that nation
I warned repents of its evil, then I will
relent and not inflict on it the disaster I
had planned. 9And if at another time I announce that a nation or kingdom is to be
built up and planted, 10and if it does evil
in my sight and does not obey me, then I
will reconsider the good I had intended
to do for it.

11"Now therefore say to the people of
Judah and those living in Jerusalem, 'This
is what the LORD says: Look! I am preparing a disaster for you and devising a plan
against you. So turn from your evil ways,
each one of you, and reform your ways
and your actions.' 12But they will reply,

'It's no use. We will continue with our own plans; each of us will follow the stubbornness of his evil heart.'"

13Therefore this is what the LORD says:

"Inquire among the nations:
  Who has ever heard anything like
    this?
A most horrible thing has been done
  by Virgin Israel.
14Does the snow of Lebanon
  ever vanish from its rocky slopes?
Do its cool waters from distant
    sources
  ever cease to flow?ᵃ
15Yet my people have forgotten me;
  they burn incense to worthless idols,
which made them stumble in their
    ways
  and in the ancient paths.
They made them walk in bypaths
  and on roads not built up.
16Their land will be laid waste,
  an object of lasting scorn;
all who pass by will be appalled
  and will shake their heads.
17Like a wind from the east,
  I will scatter them before their
    enemies;
I will show them my back and not
    my face
  in the day of their disaster."

18They said, "Come, let's make plans against Jeremiah; for the teaching of the law by the priest will not be lost, nor will counsel from the wise, nor the word from the prophets. So come, let's attack him with our tongues and pay no attention to anything he says."

19Listen to me, O LORD;
  hear what my accusers are saying!
20Should good be repaid with evil?
  Yet they have dug a pit for me.
Remember that I stood before you
  and spoke in their behalf
to turn your wrath away from
    them.

21So give their children over to famine;
  hand them over to the power of the
    sword.
Let their wives be made childless and
    widows;
  let their men be put to death,
  their young men slain by the sword
    in battle.
22Let a cry be heard from their houses
  when you suddenly bring invaders
    against them,
for they have dug a pit to capture me
  and have hidden snares for my feet.
23But you know, O LORD,
  all their plots to kill me.
Do not forgive their crimes
  or blot out their sins from your sight.
Let them be overthrown before you;
  deal with them in the time of your
    anger.

19 This is what the LORD says: "Go and buy a clay jar from a potter. Take along some of the elders of the people and of the priests 2and go out to the Valley of Ben Hinnom, near the entrance of the Potsherd Gate. There proclaim the words I tell you, 3and say, 'Hear the word of the LORD, O kings of Judah and people of Jerusalem. This is what the LORD Almighty, the God of Israel, says: Listen! I am going to bring a disaster on this place that will make the ears of everyone who hears of it tingle. 4For they have forsaken me and made this a place of foreign gods; they have burned sacrifices in it to gods that neither they nor their fathers nor the kings of Judah ever knew, and they have filled this place with the blood of the innocent. 5They have built the high places of Baal to burn their sons in the fire as offerings to Baal—something I did not command or mention, nor did it enter my mind. 6So beware, the days are coming, declares the LORD, when people will no longer call this place Topheth or the Valley of Ben Hinnom, but the Valley of Slaughter.

ᵃ 14 The meaning of the Hebrew for this sentence is uncertain.

7 "'In this place I will ruin[a] the plans of Judah and Jerusalem. I will make them fall by the sword before their enemies, at the hands of those who seek their lives, and I will give their carcasses as food to the birds of the air and the beasts of the earth. 8 I will devastate this city and make it an object of scorn; all who pass by will be appalled and will scoff because of all its wounds. 9 I will make them eat the flesh of their sons and daughters, and they will eat one another's flesh during the stress of the siege imposed on them by the enemies who seek their lives.'

10 "Then break the jar while those who go with you are watching, 11 and say to them, 'This is what the LORD Almighty says: I will smash this nation and this city just as this potter's jar is smashed and cannot be repaired. They will bury the dead in Topheth until there is no more room. 12 This is what I will do to this place and to those who live here, declares the LORD. I will make this city like Topheth. 13 The houses in Jerusalem and those of the kings of Judah will be defiled like this place, Topheth—all the houses where they burned incense on the roofs to all the starry hosts and poured out drink offerings to other gods.'"

14 Jeremiah then returned from Topheth, where the LORD had sent him to prophesy, and stood in the court of the LORD's temple and said to all the people, 15 "This is what the LORD Almighty, the God of Israel, says: 'Listen! I am going to bring on this city and the villages around it every disaster I pronounced against them, because they were stiff-necked and would not listen to my words.'"

Jeremiah and Pashhur

20 When the priest Pashhur son of Immer, the chief officer in the temple of the LORD, heard Jeremiah prophesying these things, 2 he had Jeremiah the prophet beaten and put in the stocks at the Upper Gate of Benjamin at the LORD's temple. 3 The next day, when Pashhur released him from the stocks, Jeremiah said to him, "The LORD's name for you is not Pashhur, but Magor-Missabib.[b] 4 For this is what the LORD says: 'I will make you a terror to yourself and to all your friends; with your own eyes you will see them fall by the sword of their enemies. I will hand all Judah over to the king of Babylon, who will carry them away to Babylon or put them to the sword. 5 I will hand over to their enemies all the wealth of this city—all its products, all its valuables and all the treasures of the kings of Judah. They will take it away as plunder and carry it off to Babylon. 6 And you, Pashhur, and all who live in your house will go into exile to Babylon. There you will die and be buried, you and all your friends to whom you have prophesied lies.'"

Jeremiah's Complaint

7 O LORD, you deceived[c] me, and I was deceived[c];
  you overpowered me and prevailed.
I am ridiculed all day long;
  everyone mocks me.
8 Whenever I speak, I cry out
  proclaiming violence and
    destruction.
So the word of the LORD has
    brought me
  insult and reproach all day long.
9 But if I say, "I will not mention him
  or speak any more in his name,"
his word is in my heart like a fire,
  a fire shut up in my bones.
I am weary of holding it in;
  indeed, I cannot.
10 I hear many whispering,
  "Terror on every side!
  Report him! Let's report him!"
All my friends
  are waiting for me to slip, saying,
"Perhaps he will be deceived;
  then we will prevail over him
  and take our revenge on him."

---

a 7 The Hebrew for ruin sounds like the Hebrew for jar (see verses 1 and 10).   b 3 Magor-Missabib means terror on every side.
c 7 Or persuaded

God's people at prayer
JEREMIAH'S PRAYERS OF COMPLAINT

JEREMIAH 20:7-18 Jeremiah had a habit of arguing with himself and complaining to God in the same prayer. This passage is a prayer of complaint to God that includes accusation (20:7), sarcasm (20:8), exasperation (20:9), fear (20:10), praise (20:13), anger (20:14), and grief (20:18). Jeremiah didn't hesitate to tell God what was on his mind . . . even when he had a hard time making up his mind. And God listened.

Have you ever been so absorbed in a complex situation that you don't know where to begin to pray about it? Whenever that happens, don't let that stop you from praying. Your prayers don't have to be eloquent, they just have to be honest and from the heart. God values a truthful heart.

11 But the LORD is with me like a
    mighty warrior;
  so my persecutors will stumble and
      not prevail.
  They will fail and be thoroughly
      disgraced;
    their dishonor will never be
      forgotten.
12 O LORD Almighty, you who examine
      the righteous
  and probe the heart and mind,
  let me see your vengeance upon
      them,
    for to you I have committed my
      cause.

13 Sing to the LORD!
  Give praise to the LORD!
  He rescues the life of the needy
    from the hands of the wicked.

14 Cursed be the day I was born!
  May the day my mother bore me
      not be blessed!
15 Cursed be the man who brought my
      father the news,
  who made him very glad, saying,
    "A child is born to you—a son!"
16 May that man be like the towns
    the LORD overthrew without pity.
  May he hear wailing in the morning,
    a battle cry at noon.
17 For he did not kill me in the womb,

  with my mother as my grave,
    her womb enlarged forever.
18 Why did I ever come out of the
      womb
    to see trouble and sorrow
    and to end my days in shame?

God Rejects Zedekiah's Request

21 The word came to Jeremiah from the LORD when King Zedekiah sent to him Pashhur son of Malkijah and the priest Zephaniah son of Maaseiah. They said: 2 "Inquire now of the LORD for us because Nebuchadnezzar[a] king of Babylon is attacking us. Perhaps the LORD will perform wonders for us as in times past so that he will withdraw from us."

3 But Jeremiah answered them, "Tell Zedekiah, 4 'This is what the LORD, the God of Israel, says: I am about to turn against you the weapons of war that are in your hands, which you are using to fight the king of Babylon and the Babylonians[b] who are outside the wall besieging you. And I will gather them inside this city. 5 I myself will fight against you with an outstretched hand and a mighty arm in anger and fury and great wrath. 6 I will strike down those who live in this city—both men and animals—and they will die of a terrible plague. 7 After that, declares the LORD, I will hand over Zedekiah king of Judah, his officials and

---

a 2 Hebrew *Nebuchadrezzar*, of which *Nebuchadnezzar* is a variant; here and often in Jeremiah and Ezekiel   b 4 Or *Chaldeans*; also in verse 9 the people in this city who survive the plague, sword and famine, to Nebuchadnezzar king of Babylon and to their enemies who seek their lives. He will put them to the sword; he will show them no mercy or pity or compassion.'

8"Furthermore, tell the people, 'This is what the LORD says: See, I am setting before you the way of life and the way of death. 9Whoever stays in this city will die by the sword, famine or plague. But whoever goes out and surrenders to the Babylonians who are besieging you will live; he will escape with his life. 10I have determined to do this city harm and not good, declares the LORD. It will be given into the hands of the king of Babylon, and he will destroy it with fire.'

11"Moreover, say to the royal house of Judah, 'Hear the word of the LORD; 12O house of David, this is what the LORD says:

" 'Administer justice every morning;
    rescue from the hand of his
        oppressor
    the one who has been robbed,
or my wrath will break out and burn
        like fire
    because of the evil you have done—
    burn with no one to quench it.
13I am against you, ⌊Jerusalem,⌋
    you who live above this valley
    on the rocky plateau,
                declares the LORD—
you who say, "Who can come against
        us?
    Who can enter our refuge?"
14I will punish you as your deeds
        deserve,
                declares the LORD.
I will kindle a fire in your forests
    that will consume everything
        around you.' "

Judgment Against Evil Kings

22 This is what the LORD says: "Go down to the palace of the king of Judah and proclaim this message there:

2'Hear the word of the LORD, O king of Judah, you who sit on David's throne—you, your officials and your people who come through these gates. 3This is what the LORD says: Do what is just and right. Rescue from the hand of his oppressor the one who has been robbed. Do no wrong or violence to the alien, the fatherless or the widow, and do not shed innocent blood in this place. 4For if you are careful to carry out these commands, then kings who sit on David's throne will come through the gates of this palace, riding in chariots and on horses, accompanied by their officials and their people. 5But if you do not obey these commands, declares the LORD, I swear by myself that this palace will become a ruin.' "

6For this is what the LORD says about the palace of the king of Judah:

"Though you are like Gilead to me,
    like the summit of Lebanon,
I will surely make you like a desert,
    like towns not inhabited.
7I will send destroyers against you,
    each man with his weapons,
and they will cut up your fine cedar
        beams
    and throw them into the fire.

8"People from many nations will pass by this city and will ask one another, 'Why has the LORD done such a thing to this great city?' 9And the answer will be: 'Because they have forsaken the covenant of the LORD their God and have worshiped and served other gods.' "

10Do not weep for the dead ⌊king⌋ or
        mourn his loss;
rather, weep bitterly for him who
        is exiled,
because he will never return
    nor see his native land again.

11For this is what the LORD says about Shallum[a] son of Josiah, who succeeded his father as king of Judah but has gone from this place: "He will never return.

---

a 11 Also called Jehoahaz

¹²He will die in the place where they have led him captive; he will not see this land again."

¹³"Woe to him who builds his palace
    by unrighteousness,
  his upper rooms by injustice,
making his countrymen work for
    nothing,
  not paying them for their labor.
¹⁴He says, 'I will build myself a great
    palace
  with spacious upper rooms.'
So he makes large windows in it,
  panels it with cedar
  and decorates it in red.

¹⁵"Does it make you a king
  to have more and more cedar?
Did not your father have food and
    drink?
  He did what was right and just,
  so all went well with him.
¹⁶He defended the cause of the poor
    and needy,
  and so all went well.
Is that not what it means to know
    me?"
  declares the LORD.
¹⁷"But your eyes and your heart
  are set only on dishonest gain,
on shedding innocent blood
  and on oppression and extortion."

¹⁸Therefore this is what the LORD says about Jehoiakim son of Josiah king of Judah:

"They will not mourn for him:
  'Alas, my brother! Alas, my sister!'
They will not mourn for him:
  'Alas, my master! Alas, his
    splendor!'
¹⁹He will have the burial of a donkey—
  dragged away and thrown
  outside the gates of Jerusalem."

²⁰"Go up to Lebanon and cry out,
  let your voice be heard in Bashan,
cry out from Abarim,

for all your allies are crushed.
²¹I warned you when you felt secure,
  but you said, 'I will not listen!'
This has been your way from your
    youth;
  you have not obeyed me.

²²The wind will drive all your
    shepherds away,
  and your allies will go into exile.
Then you will be ashamed and
    disgraced
  because of all your wickedness.
²³You who live in 'Lebanon,'ᵃ
  who are nestled in cedar buildings,
how you will groan when pangs
    come upon you,
  pain like that of a woman in labor!

²⁴"As surely as I live," declares the LORD, "even if you, Jehoiachinᵇ son of Jehoiakim king of Judah, were a signet ring on my right hand, I would still pull you off. ²⁵I will hand you over to those who seek your life, those you fear—to Nebuchadnezzar king of Babylon and to the Babylonians.ᶜ ²⁶I will hurl you and the mother who gave you birth into another country, where neither of you was born, and there you both will die. ²⁷You will never come back to the land you long to return to."

²⁸Is this man Jehoiachin a despised,
    broken pot,
  an object no one wants?
Why will he and his children be
    hurled out,
  cast into a land they do not know?
²⁹O land, land, land,
  hear the word of the LORD!
³⁰This is what the LORD says:
  "Record this man as if childless,

ᵃ 23 That is, the palace in Jerusalem (see 1 Kings 7:2)   ᵇ 24 Hebrew *Coniah*, a variant of *Jehoiachin*; also in verse 28
ᶜ 25 Or *Chaldeans*

a man who will not prosper in his
lifetime,
for none of his offspring will prosper,
none will sit on the throne of
David
or rule anymore in Judah.”

The Righteous Branch

23 “Woe to the shepherds who are destroying and scattering the sheep of my pasture!” declares the LORD. 2 Therefore this is what the LORD, the God of Israel, says to the shepherds who tend my people: “Because you have scattered my flock and driven them away and have not bestowed care on them, I will bestow punishment on you for the evil you have done,” declares the LORD. 3 “I myself will gather the remnant of my flock out of all the countries where I have driven them and will bring them back to their pasture, where they will be fruitful and increase in number. 4 I will place shepherds over them who will tend them, and they will no longer be afraid or terrified, nor will any be missing,” declares the LORD.

5 “The days are coming,” declares the
LORD,
“when I will raise up to David[a] a
righteous Branch,
a King who will reign wisely
and do what is just and right in the
land.
6 In his days Judah will be saved
and Israel will live in safety.
This is the name by which he will be
called:
The LORD Our Righteousness.

7 “So then, the days are coming,” declares the LORD, “when people will no longer say, ‘As surely as the LORD lives, who brought the Israelites up out of Egypt,’ 8 but they will say, ‘As surely as the LORD lives, who brought the descendants of Israel up out of the land of the north and out of all the countries where he had banished them.’ Then they will live in their own land.”

Lying Prophets

9 Concerning the prophets:

My heart is broken within me;
all my bones tremble.
I am like a drunken man,
like a man overcome by wine,
because of the LORD
and his holy words.
10 The land is full of adulterers;
because of the curse[b] the land lies
parched[c]
and the pastures in the desert are
withered.
The ⌐prophets⌐ follow an evil course
and use their power unjustly.

11 “Both prophet and priest are godless;
even in my temple I find their
wickedness,”
declares the LORD.
12 “Therefore their path will become
slippery;
they will be banished to darkness
and there they will fall.
I will bring disaster on them
in the year they are punished,”
declares the LORD.

13 “Among the prophets of Samaria
I saw this repulsive thing:
They prophesied by Baal
and led my people Israel astray.
14 And among the prophets of Jerusalem
I have seen something horrible:
They commit adultery and live a lie.
They strengthen the hands of
evildoers,
so that no one turns from his
wickedness.
They are all like Sodom to me;
the people of Jerusalem are like
Gomorrah.”

15 Therefore, this is what the LORD Almighty says concerning the prophets:

“I will make them eat bitter food
and drink poisoned water,
because from the prophets of
Jerusalem

---

a 5 Or up from David's line   b 10 Or because of these things   c 10 Or land mourns

Ask God for Discernment

READ AND CONSIDER: JEREMIAH 23:16-32

"This is what the LORD Almighty says: 'Do not listen to what the prophets are prophesying to you; they fill you with false hopes. They speak visions from their own minds, not from the mouth of the LORD' " (Jeremiah 23:16).

Just as the Israelites centuries ago, we all long to hear directly from God. We want to hear prophetic words of truth. We need words of hope. Sometimes we're so desperate for it that we're willing to listen to just about anyone who says, "God told me . . ." But Jeremiah spoke about the dangers of listening to the wrong voices.

Someone claiming to speak for God must meet a very high standard—perfection! God declared that His prophets would always be correct in their pronouncements. What they said would come true. Any mistake would make their message null and void (Deuteronomy 18:20-22). We make a serious mistake if we describe predictions as truly "prophetic" when they come from someone with a track record of wild guesses and incorrect declarations.

But then, how do we know for sure whether what we are hearing from someone is the truth?

Our first tool of evaluation is God's Word. Those who contradict or twist what God has already declared cannot be trusted. God says not to listen to voices that speak lies, for "they speak visions from their own minds, not from the mouth of the LORD" (Jeremiah 23:16). Any vision for the future that is full of failure and empty of hope is not from God (Jeremiah 29:11). And "positive" visions that discount God's power often express someone's wishful thinking. So always check out what you hear against the teachings of Scripture.

Our second tool of evaluation is the Holy Spirit. When we are born again, the Holy Spirit comes to dwell in us. Jesus called the Holy Spirit our "Counselor" and the "Spirit of truth," promising that He would "guide you into all truth" (John 16:7,13). When in doubt about what someone is saying or teaching, always pray for the Spirit to show you the truth.

Whenever you pray, ask the Holy Spirit to give you discernment and the ability to identify what is from Him and what is not. If people are giving you advice you're not sure about, ask Him to give you revelation regarding that.

Each time you read God's Word, ask Him to speak to you through it. If you have confusion about things people have spoken to you, ask Him to show you whether their words line up with *His* Word. Don't listen to people with visions from their own minds and not from the mouth of God.

---

ungodliness has spread throughout
   the land."

16 This is what the LORD Almighty says:

"Do not listen to what the prophets
   are prophesying to you;
they fill you with false hopes.
They speak visions from their own
      minds,
   not from the mouth of the LORD.

17 They keep saying to those who
      despise me,
   'The LORD says: You will have
      peace.'
And to all who follow the
      stubbornness of their hearts
   they say, 'No harm will come to
      you.'
18 But which of them has stood in the
      council of the LORD

to see or to hear his word?
Who has listened and heard his word?
¹⁹See, the storm of the LORD
    will burst out in wrath,
a whirlwind swirling down
    on the heads of the wicked.
²⁰The anger of the LORD will not turn
    back
    until he fully accomplishes
    the purposes of his heart.
In days to come
    you will understand it clearly.
²¹I did not send these prophets,
    yet they have run with their message;
I did not speak to them,
    yet they have prophesied.
²²But if they had stood in my council,
    they would have proclaimed my
        words to my people
and would have turned them from
        their evil ways
    and from their evil deeds.

²³"Am I only a God nearby,"
                declares the LORD,
    "and not a God far away?
²⁴Can anyone hide in secret places
    so that I cannot see him?"
                declares the LORD.
    "Do not I fill heaven and earth?"
                declares the LORD.

²⁵"I have heard what the prophets say who prophesy lies in my name. They say, 'I had a dream! I had a dream!' ²⁶How long will this continue in the hearts of these lying prophets, who prophesy the delusions of their own minds? ²⁷They think the dreams they tell one another will make my people forget my name, just as their fathers forgot my name through Baal worship. ²⁸Let the prophet who has a dream tell his dream, but let the one who has my word speak it faithfully. For what has straw to do with grain?" declares the LORD. ²⁹"Is not my word like fire," declares the LORD, "and like a hammer that breaks a rock in pieces?

³⁰"Therefore," declares the LORD, "I am against the prophets who steal from one another words supposedly from me. ³¹Yes," declares the LORD, "I am against the prophets who wag their own tongues and yet declare, 'The LORD declares.' ³²Indeed, I am against those who prophesy false dreams," declares the LORD. "They tell them and lead my people astray with their reckless lies, yet I did not send or appoint them. They do not benefit these people in the least," declares the LORD.

False Oracles and False Prophets

³³"When these people, or a prophet or a priest, ask you, 'What is the oracleᵃ of the LORD?' say to them, 'What oracle?ᵇ I will forsake you, declares the LORD.' ³⁴If a prophet or a priest or anyone else claims, 'This is the oracle of the LORD,' I will punish that man and his household. ³⁵This is what each of you keeps on saying to his friend or relative: 'What is the LORD's answer?' or 'What has the LORD spoken?' ³⁶But you must not mention 'the oracle of the LORD' again, because every man's own word becomes his oracle and so you distort the words of the living God, the LORD Almighty, our God. ³⁷This is what you keep saying to a prophet: 'What is the LORD's answer to you?' or 'What has the LORD spoken?' ³⁸Although you claim, 'This is the oracle of the LORD,' this is what the LORD says: You used the words, 'This is the oracle of the LORD,' even though I told you that you must not claim, 'This is the oracle of the LORD.' ³⁹Therefore, I will surely forget you and cast you out of my presence along with the city I gave to you and your fathers. ⁴⁰I will bring upon you everlasting disgrace—everlasting shame that will not be forgotten."

Two Baskets of Figs

24 After Jehoiachinᶜ son of Jehoiakim king of Judah and the officials, the craftsmen and the artisans of Judah

---

ᵃ *33* Or *burden* (see Septuagint and Vulgate)   ᵇ *33* Hebrew; Septuagint and Vulgate *'You are the burden.'* (The Hebrew for *oracle* and *burden* is the same.)   ᶜ *1* Hebrew *Jeconiah,* a variant of *Jehoiachin* were carried into exile from Jerusalem to Babylon by Nebuchadnezzar king of Babylon, the LORD showed me two baskets of figs placed in front of the temple of the LORD. ²One basket had very good figs, like those that ripen early; the other basket had very poor figs, so bad they could not be eaten.

³Then the LORD asked me, "What do you see, Jeremiah?"

"Figs," I answered. "The good ones are very good, but the poor ones are so bad they cannot be eaten."

⁴Then the word of the LORD came to me: ⁵"This is what the LORD, the God of Israel, says: 'Like these good figs, I regard as good the exiles from Judah, whom I sent away from this place to the land of the Babylonians.ᵃ ⁶My eyes will watch over them for their good, and I will bring them back to this land. I will build them up and not tear them down; I will plant them and not uproot them. ⁷I will give them a heart to know me, that I am the LORD. They will be my people, and I will be their God, for they will return to me with all their heart.

Praying Jeremiah 24:7

Dear God, help me to always turn to You with my whole heart and acknowledge that You are my Lord.

⁸" 'But like the poor figs, which are so bad they cannot be eaten,' says the LORD, 'so will I deal with Zedekiah king of Judah, his officials and the survivors from Jerusalem, whether they remain in this land or live in Egypt. ⁹I will make them abhorrent and an offense to all the kingdoms of the earth, a reproach and a byword, an object of ridicule and cursing, wherever I banish them. ¹⁰I will send the sword, famine and plague against them until they are destroyed from the land I gave to them and their fathers.' "

Seventy Years of Captivity

25 The word came to Jeremiah concerning all the people of Judah in the fourth year of Jehoiakim son of Josiah king of Judah, which was the first year of Nebuchadnezzar king of Babylon. ²So Jeremiah the prophet said to all the people of Judah and to all those living in Jerusalem: ³For twenty-three years—from the thirteenth year of Josiah son of Amon king of Judah until this very day—the word of the LORD has come to me and I have spoken to you again and again, but you have not listened.

⁴And though the LORD has sent all his servants the prophets to you again and again, you have not listened or paid any attention. ⁵They said, "Turn now, each of you, from your evil ways and your evil practices, and you can stay in the land the LORD gave to you and your fathers for ever and ever. ⁶Do not follow other gods to serve and worship them; do not provoke me to anger with what your hands have made. Then I will not harm you."

⁷"But you did not listen to me," declares the LORD, "and you have provoked me with what your hands have made, and you have brought harm to yourselves."

⁸Therefore the LORD Almighty says this: "Because you have not listened to my words, ⁹I will summon all the peoples of the north and my servant Nebuchadnezzar king of Babylon," declares the LORD, "and I will bring them against this land and its inhabitants and against all the surrounding nations. I will completely destroyᵇ them and make them an object of horror and scorn, and an everlasting ruin. ¹⁰I will banish from them the sounds of joy and gladness, the voices of bride and bridegroom, the sound of millstones and the light of the lamp. ¹¹This whole country will become a desolate wasteland, and these nations will serve the king of Babylon seventy years.

¹²"But when the seventy years are

ᵃ 5 Or *Chaldeans*   ᵇ 9 The Hebrew term refers to the irrevocable giving over of things or persons to the LORD, often by totally destroying them.

fulfilled, I will punish the king of Babylon and his nation, the land of the Babylonians,[a] for their guilt," declares the LORD, "and will make it desolate forever. [13]I will bring upon that land all the things I have spoken against it, all that are written in this book and prophesied by Jeremiah against all the nations. [14]They themselves will be enslaved by many nations and great kings; I will repay them according to their deeds and the work of their hands."

The Cup of God's Wrath

[15]This is what the LORD, the God of Israel, said to me: "Take from my hand this cup filled with the wine of my wrath and make all the nations to whom I send you drink it. [16]When they drink it, they will stagger and go mad because of the sword I will send among them."

[17]So I took the cup from the LORD's hand and made all the nations to whom he sent me drink it: [18]Jerusalem and the towns of Judah, its kings and officials, to make them a ruin and an object of horror and scorn and cursing, as they are today; [19]Pharaoh king of Egypt, his attendants, his officials and all his people, [20]and all the foreign people there; all the kings of Uz; all the kings of the Philistines (those of Ashkelon, Gaza, Ekron, and the people left at Ashdod); [21]Edom, Moab and Ammon; [22]all the kings of Tyre and Sidon; the kings of the coastlands across the sea; [23]Dedan, Tema, Buz and all who are in distant places[b]; [24]all the kings of Arabia and all the kings of the foreign people who live in the desert; [25]all the kings of Zimri, Elam and Media; [26]and all the kings of the north, near and far, one after the other—all the kingdoms on the face of the earth. And after all of them, the king of Sheshach[c] will drink it too.

[27]"Then tell them, 'This is what the LORD Almighty, the God of Israel, says: Drink, get drunk and vomit, and fall to rise no more because of the sword I will send among you.' [28]But if they re-

fuse to take the cup from your hand and drink, tell them, 'This is what the LORD Almighty says: You must drink it! [29]See, I am beginning to bring disaster on the city that bears my Name, and will you indeed go unpunished? You will not go unpunished, for I am calling down a sword upon all who live on the earth, declares the LORD Almighty.'

[30]"Now prophesy all these words against them and say to them:

"'The LORD will roar from on high;
  he will thunder from his holy
    dwelling
  and roar mightily against his land.
He will shout like those who tread
    the grapes,
  shout against all who live on the
    earth.
[31]The tumult will resound to the ends
    of the earth,
  for the LORD will bring charges
    against the nations;
he will bring judgment on all
    mankind
  and put the wicked to the sword,'"
              declares the LORD.

[32]This is what the LORD Almighty says:

"Look! Disaster is spreading
  from nation to nation;
a mighty storm is rising
  from the ends of the earth."

[33]At that time those slain by the LORD will be everywhere—from one end of the earth to the other. They will not be mourned or gathered up or buried, but will be like refuse lying on the ground.

[34]Weep and wail, you shepherds;
  roll in the dust, you leaders of the
    flock.
For your time to be slaughtered has
    come;
  you will fall and be shattered like
    fine pottery.
[35]The shepherds will have nowhere to
    flee,

---

[a] 12 Or Chaldeans   [b] 23 Or who clip the hair by their foreheads   [c] 26 Sheshach is a cryptogram for Babylon.

the leaders of the flock no place to
   escape.
[36] Hear the cry of the shepherds,
   the wailing of the leaders of the
      flock,
   for the LORD is destroying their
      pasture.
[37] The peaceful meadows will be laid
      waste
   because of the fierce anger of the
      LORD.
[38] Like a lion he will leave his lair,
   and their land will become
      desolate
   because of the sword[a] of the oppressor
   and because of the LORD's fierce
      anger.

Jeremiah Threatened With Death

26 Early in the reign of Jehoiakim son
   of Josiah king of Judah, this word
came from the LORD: [2] "This is what the
LORD says: Stand in the courtyard of the
LORD's house and speak to all the people
of the towns of Judah who come to worship in the house of the LORD. Tell them
everything I command you; do not omit
a word. [3] Perhaps they will listen and each
will turn from his evil way. Then I will
relent and not bring on them the disaster
I was planning because of the evil they
have done. [4] Say to them, 'This is what
the LORD says: If you do not listen to
me and follow my law, which I have set
before you, [5] and if you do not listen to
the words of my servants the prophets,
whom I have sent to you again and again
(though you have not listened), [6] then I
will make this house like Shiloh and this
city an object of cursing among all the
nations of the earth.'"

[7] The priests, the prophets and all the
people heard Jeremiah speak these words
in the house of the LORD. [8] But as soon
as Jeremiah finished telling all the people
everything the LORD had commanded
him to say, the priests, the prophets
and all the people seized him and said,
"You must die! [9] Why do you prophesy

in the LORD's name that this house will
be like Shiloh and this city will be desolate and deserted?" And all the people
crowded around Jeremiah in the house
of the LORD.

[10] When the officials of Judah heard
about these things, they went up from the
royal palace to the house of the LORD and
took their places at the entrance of the
New Gate of the LORD's house. [11] Then
the priests and the prophets said to the
officials and all the people, "This man
should be sentenced to death because he
has prophesied against this city. You have
heard it with your own ears!"

[12] Then Jeremiah said to all the officials
and all the people: "The LORD sent me
to prophesy against this house and this
city all the things you have heard. [13] Now
reform your ways and your actions and
obey the LORD your God. Then the LORD
will relent and not bring the disaster he
has pronounced against you. [14] As for me,
I am in your hands; do with me whatever
you think is good and right. [15] Be assured,
however, that if you put me to death, you
will bring the guilt of innocent blood on
yourselves and on this city and on those
who live in it, for in truth the LORD has
sent me to you to speak all these words
in your hearing."

[16] Then the officials and all the people
said to the priests and the prophets, "This
man should not be sentenced to death!
He has spoken to us in the name of the
LORD our God."

[17] Some of the elders of the land
stepped forward and said to the entire assembly of people, [18] "Micah of Moresheth
prophesied in the days of Hezekiah king
of Judah. He told all the people of Judah,
'This is what the LORD Almighty says:

" 'Zion will be plowed like a field,
   Jerusalem will become a heap of
      rubble,
   the temple hill a mound overgrown
      with thickets.'[b]

---

a 38 Some Hebrew manuscripts and Septuagint (see also Jer. 46:16 and 50:16); most Hebrew manuscripts *anger*   b 18 Micah 3:12

19 "Did Hezekiah king of Judah or anyone else in Judah put him to death? Did not Hezekiah fear the LORD and seek his favor? And did not the LORD relent, so that he did not bring the disaster he pronounced against them? We are about to bring a terrible disaster on ourselves!"

20 (Now Uriah son of Shemaiah from Kiriath Jearim was another man who prophesied in the name of the LORD; he prophesied the same things against this city and this land as Jeremiah did. 21 When King Jehoiakim and all his officers and officials heard his words, the king sought to put him to death. But Uriah heard of it and fled in fear to Egypt. 22 King Jehoiakim, however, sent Elnathan son of Acbor to Egypt, along with some other men. 23 They brought Uriah out of Egypt and took him to King Jehoiakim, who had him struck down with a sword and his body thrown into the burial place of the common people.)

24 Furthermore, Ahikam son of Shaphan supported Jeremiah, and so he was not handed over to the people to be put to death.

Judah to Serve Nebuchadnezzar

27 Early in the reign of Zedekiah[a] son of Josiah king of Judah, this word came to Jeremiah from the LORD: 2 This is what the LORD said to me: "Make a yoke out of straps and crossbars and put it on your neck. 3 Then send word to the kings of Edom, Moab, Ammon, Tyre and Sidon through the envoys who have come to Jerusalem to Zedekiah king of Judah. 4 Give them a message for their masters and say, 'This is what the LORD Almighty, the God of Israel, says: "Tell this to your masters: 5 With my great power and outstretched arm I made the earth and its people and the animals that are on it, and I give it to anyone I please. 6 Now I will hand all your countries over to my servant Nebuchadnezzar king of Babylon; I will make even the wild animals subject to him. 7 All nations will serve him and his son and his grandson until the time for his land comes; then many nations and great kings will subjugate him.

8 " ' "If, however, any nation or kingdom will not serve Nebuchadnezzar king of Babylon or bow its neck under his yoke, I will punish that nation with the sword, famine and plague, declares the LORD, until I destroy it by his hand. 9 So do not listen to your prophets, your diviners, your interpreters of dreams, your mediums or your sorcerers who tell you, 'You will not serve the king of Babylon.' 10 They prophesy lies to you that will only serve to remove you far from your lands; I will banish you and you will perish. 11 But if any nation will bow its neck under the yoke of the king of Babylon and serve him, I will let that nation remain in its own land to till it and to live there, declares the LORD." ' "

12 I gave the same message to Zedekiah king of Judah. I said, "Bow your neck under the yoke of the king of Babylon; serve him and his people, and you will live. 13 Why will you and your people die by the sword, famine and plague with which the LORD has threatened any nation that will not serve the king of Babylon? 14 Do not listen to the words of the prophets who say to you, 'You will not serve the king of Babylon,' for they are prophesying lies to you. 15 'I have not sent them,' declares the LORD. 'They are prophesying lies in my name. Therefore, I will banish you and you will perish, both you and the prophets who prophesy to you.' "

16 Then I said to the priests and all these people, "This is what the LORD says: Do not listen to the prophets who say, 'Very soon now the articles from the LORD's house will be brought back from Babylon.' They are prophesying lies to you. 17 Do not listen to them. Serve the king of Babylon, and you will live. Why should this city become a ruin? 18 If they are

---

a 1 A few Hebrew manuscripts and Syriac (see also Jer. 27:3, 12 and 28:1); most Hebrew manuscripts Jehoiakim (Most Septuagint manuscripts do not have this verse.)

prophets and have the word of the LORD, let them plead with the LORD Almighty that the furnishings remaining in the house of the LORD and in the palace of the king of Judah and in Jerusalem not be taken to Babylon. ¹⁹For this is what the LORD Almighty says about the pillars, the Sea, the movable stands and the other furnishings that are left in this city, ²⁰which Nebuchadnezzar king of Babylon did not take away when he carried Jehoiachinª son of Jehoiakim king of Judah into exile from Jerusalem to Babylon, along with all the nobles of Judah and Jerusalem— ²¹yes, this is what the LORD Almighty, the God of Israel, says about the things that are left in the house of the LORD and in the palace of the king of Judah and in Jerusalem: ²²'They will be taken to Babylon and there they will remain until the day I come for them,' declares the LORD. 'Then I will bring them back and restore them to this place.'"

The False Prophet Hananiah

28 In the fifth month of that same year, the fourth year, early in the reign of Zedekiah king of Judah, the prophet Hananiah son of Azzur, who was from Gibeon, said to me in the house of the LORD in the presence of the priests and all the people: ²"This is what the LORD Almighty, the God of Israel, says: 'I will break the yoke of the king of Babylon. ³Within two years I will bring back to this place all the articles of the LORD's house that Nebuchadnezzar king of Babylon removed from here and took to Babylon. ⁴I will also bring back to this place Jehoiachinª son of Jehoiakim king of Judah and all the other exiles from Judah who went to Babylon,' declares the LORD, 'for I will break the yoke of the king of Babylon.'"

⁵Then the prophet Jeremiah replied to the prophet Hananiah before the priests and all the people who were standing in the house of the LORD. ⁶He said, "Amen! May the LORD do so! May the LORD fulfill the words you have prophesied by bringing the articles of the LORD's house and all the exiles back to this place from Babylon. ⁷Nevertheless, listen to what I have to say in your hearing and in the hearing of all the people: ⁸From early times the prophets who preceded you and me have prophesied war, disaster and plague against many countries and great kingdoms. ⁹But the prophet who prophesies peace will be recognized as one truly sent by the LORD only if his prediction comes true."

¹⁰Then the prophet Hananiah took the yoke off the neck of the prophet Jeremiah and broke it, ¹¹and he said before all the people, "This is what the LORD says: 'In the same way will I break the yoke of Nebuchadnezzar king of Babylon off the neck of all the nations within two years.'" At this, the prophet Jeremiah went on his way.

¹²Shortly after the prophet Hananiah had broken the yoke off the neck of the prophet Jeremiah, the word of the LORD came to Jeremiah: ¹³"Go and tell Hananiah, 'This is what the LORD says: You have broken a wooden yoke, but in its place you will get a yoke of iron. ¹⁴This is what the LORD Almighty, the God of Israel, says: I will put an iron yoke on the necks of all these nations to make them serve Nebuchadnezzar king of Babylon, and they will serve him. I will even give him control over the wild animals.'"

¹⁵Then the prophet Jeremiah said to Hananiah the prophet, "Listen, Hananiah! The LORD has not sent you, yet you have persuaded this nation to trust in lies. ¹⁶Therefore, this is what the LORD says: 'I am about to remove you from the face of the earth. This very year you are going to die, because you have preached rebellion against the LORD.'"

¹⁷In the seventh month of that same year, Hananiah the prophet died.

A Letter to the Exiles

29 This is the text of the letter that the prophet Jeremiah sent from Jerusalem to the surviving elders among the

---

ª 20,4 Hebrew *Jeconiah*, a variant of *Jehoiachin*

exiles and to the priests, the prophets and all the other people Nebuchadnezzar had carried into exile from Jerusalem to Babylon. ²(This was after King Jehoiachinᵃ and the queen mother, the court officials and the leaders of Judah and Jerusalem, the craftsmen and the artisans had gone into exile from Jerusalem.) ³He entrusted the letter to Elasah son of Shaphan and to Gemariah son of Hilkiah, whom

Zedekiah king of Judah sent to King Nebuchadnezzar in Babylon. It said:

⁴This is what the LORD Almighty, the God of Israel, says to all those I carried into exile from Jerusalem to Babylon: ⁵"Build houses and settle down; plant gardens and eat what they produce. ⁶Marry and have sons and daughters; find wives for your

---

ᵃ 2 Hebrew *Jeconiah*, a variant of *Jehoiachin*

GOING *deeper*

God's Plans Still Require Prayer on Our Part

READ AND CONSIDER: JEREMIAH 29:4-14

" 'For I know the plans I have for you,' declares the LORD, 'plans to prosper you and not to harm you, plans to give you hope and a future' " (Jeremiah 29:11).

Jeremiah had some good news and some bad news from God for the people. The bad news was extremely bad. They would spend 70 years in captivity in Babylon (29:10). The good news was that God would bring His people home in the end. He had plans for them—plans to prosper and not harm them, plans to give them hope and a future. But that still meant that an entire generation would come and go before the hopeful promise in Jeremiah 29:11 would come true.

Sometimes God's plans can take a long time to come to pass. (You probably know that already.) And in those long waiting times, we can lose heart or get discouraged. That's why it's important to remember that a future filled with hope and blessing doesn't just happen automatically. There are things we need to do.

The first thing you need to do is to seek God and pray about your future. "Then you will call upon me and come and pray to me, and I will listen to you. You will seek me and find me when you seek me with all your heart" (29:12-13).

The second thing you need to do is to be diligent to obey God. Every step of obedience you take today will take you into the future God has planned for you. "Whether you turn to the right or to the left, your ears will hear a voice behind you, saying, 'This is the way; walk in it' " (Isaiah 30:21). You have to listen for God's voice leading you every step of the way.

The Holy Spirit is God's guarantee to you that He will help you do what you need to do and bring to pass everything He promised. "Having believed, you were marked in him with a seal, the promised Holy Spirit, who is a deposit guaranteeing our inheritance until the redemption of those who are God's possession—to the praise of his glory" (Ephesians 1:13-14).

Every time you seek God and obey Him, every time you pray and listen for His voice, you are investing in your future. God promises that you have a good future and a reason to have hope. Trust Him for both. It may not happen as quickly as you would like, but God promises, and He will deliver.

sons and give your daughters in marriage, so that they too may have sons and daughters. Increase in number there; do not decrease. [7]Also, seek the peace and prosperity of the city to which I have carried you into exile. Pray to the LORD for it, because if it prospers, you too will prosper." [8]Yes, this is what the LORD Almighty, the God of Israel, says: "Do not let the prophets and diviners among you deceive you. Do not listen to the dreams you encourage them to have. [9]They are prophesying lies to you in my name. I have not sent them," declares the LORD.

[10]This is what the LORD says: "When seventy years are completed for Babylon, I will come to you and fulfill my gracious promise to bring you back to this place. [11]For I know the plans I have for you," declares the LORD, "plans to prosper you and not to harm you, plans to give you hope and a future. [12]Then you will call upon me and come and pray to me, and I will listen to you. [13]You will seek me and find me when you seek me with all your heart. [14]I will be found by you," declares the LORD, "and will bring you back from captivity.[a] I will gather you from all the nations and places where I have banished you," declares the LORD, "and will bring you back to the place from which I carried you into exile."

[15]You may say, "The LORD has raised up prophets for us in Babylon," [16]but this is what the LORD says about the king who sits on David's throne and all the people who remain in this city, your countrymen who did not go with you into exile— [17]yes, this is what the LORD Almighty says: "I will send the sword, famine and plague against them and I will make them like poor figs that are so bad they cannot be eaten. [18]I will pursue them with the sword, famine and plague and will make them abhorrent to all the kingdoms of the earth and an object of cursing and horror, of scorn and reproach, among all the nations where I drive them. [19]For they have not listened to my words," declares the LORD, "words that I sent to them again and again by my servants the prophets. And you exiles have not listened either," declares the LORD.

[20]Therefore, hear the word of the LORD, all you exiles whom I have sent away from Jerusalem to Babylon. [21]This is what the LORD Almighty, the God of Israel, says about Ahab son of Kolaiah and Zedekiah son of Maaseiah, who are prophesying lies to you in my name: "I will hand them over to Nebuchadnezzar king of Babylon, and he will put them to death before your very eyes. [22]Because of them, all the exiles from Judah who are in Babylon will use this curse: 'The LORD treat you like Zedekiah and Ahab, whom the king of Babylon burned in the fire.' [23]For they have done outrageous things in Israel; they have committed adultery with their neighbors' wives and in my name have spoken lies, which I did not tell them to do. I know it and am a witness to it," declares the LORD.

Message to Shemaiah

[24]Tell Shemaiah the Nehelamite, [25]"This is what the LORD Almighty, the God of Israel, says: You sent letters in your own name to all the people in Jerusalem, to Zephaniah son of Maaseiah the priest, and to all the other priests. You said to Zephaniah, [26]'The LORD has appointed you priest in place of Jehoiada to be in charge of the house of the LORD; you should put any madman who acts like a prophet into the stocks and neck-irons.

[a] 14 Or will restore your fortunes

27So why have you not reprimanded Jeremiah from Anathoth, who poses as a prophet among you? 28He has sent this message to us in Babylon: It will be a long time. Therefore build houses and settle down; plant gardens and eat what they produce.'"

29Zephaniah the priest, however, read the letter to Jeremiah the prophet. 30Then the word of the LORD came to Jeremiah: 31"Send this message to all the exiles: 'This is what the LORD says about Shemaiah the Nehelamite: Because Shemaiah has prophesied to you, even though I did not send him, and has led you to believe a lie, 32this is what the LORD says: I will surely punish Shemaiah the Nehelamite and his descendants. He will have no one left among this people, nor will he see the good things I will do for my people, declares the LORD, because he has preached rebellion against me.'"

Restoration of Israel

30 This is the word that came to Jeremiah from the LORD: 2"This is what the LORD, the God of Israel, says: 'Write in a book all the words I have spoken to you. 3The days are coming,' declares the LORD, 'when I will bring my people Israel and Judah back from captivity[a] and restore them to the land I gave their forefathers to possess,' says the LORD."

Praying Jeremiah 30:2

Lord, help me to remember all You have taught me in Your Word and have spoken to me in times of prayer and devotions.

4These are the words the LORD spoke concerning Israel and Judah: 5"This is what the LORD says:

" 'Cries of fear are heard—
    terror, not peace.
6Ask and see:
    Can a man bear children?
Then why do I see every strong man
    with his hands on his stomach like
        a woman in labor,
    every face turned deathly pale?
7How awful that day will be!
    None will be like it.
It will be a time of trouble for Jacob,
    but he will be saved out of it.

8" 'In that day,' declares the LORD
        Almighty,
    'I will break the yoke off their
        necks
and will tear off their bonds;
    no longer will foreigners enslave
        them.
9Instead, they will serve the LORD
        their God
    and David their king,
    whom I will raise up for them.

10" 'So do not fear, O Jacob my servant;
    do not be dismayed, O Israel,'
                declares the LORD.
'I will surely save you out of a distant
        place,
    your descendants from the land of
        their exile.
Jacob will again have peace and
        security,
    and no one will make him afraid.
11I am with you and will save you,'
    declares the LORD.
'Though I completely destroy all the
        nations
    among which I scatter you,
    I will not completely destroy you.
I will discipline you but only with
        justice;
    I will not let you go entirely
        unpunished.'

12"This is what the LORD says:

" 'Your wound is incurable,
    your injury beyond healing.
13There is no one to plead your cause,
    no remedy for your sore,
    no healing for you.
14All your allies have forgotten you;
    they care nothing for you.

---

a 3 Or *will restore the fortunes of my people Israel and Judah*

I have struck you as an enemy would
  and punished you as would the
    cruel,
because your guilt is so great
  and your sins so many.
15 Why do you cry out over your wound,
  your pain that has no cure?
Because of your great guilt and many
    sins
  I have done these things to you.

16 "'But all who devour you will be
    devoured;
  all your enemies will go into exile.
Those who plunder you will be
    plundered;
  all who make spoil of you I will
    despoil.
17 But I will restore you to health
  and heal your wounds,'
                declares the LORD,
'because you are called an outcast,
  Zion for whom no one cares.'

18 "This is what the LORD says:

"'I will restore the fortunes of Jacob's
    tents
  and have compassion on his
    dwellings;
the city will be rebuilt on her ruins,
  and the palace will stand in its
    proper place.
19 From them will come songs of
    thanksgiving
  and the sound of rejoicing.
I will add to their numbers,
  and they will not be decreased;
I will bring them honor,
  and they will not be disdained.
20 Their children will be as in days of
    old,
  and their community will be
    established before me;
  I will punish all who oppress them.
21 Their leader will be one of their own;
  their ruler will arise from among
    them.
I will bring him near and he will
  come close to me,

for who is he who will devote
    himself
  to be close to me?'
                declares the LORD.
22 "'So you will be my people,
  and I will be your God.'"

23 See, the storm of the LORD
  will burst out in wrath,
a driving wind swirling down
  on the heads of the wicked.
24 The fierce anger of the LORD will not
    turn back
  until he fully accomplishes
  the purposes of his heart.
In days to come
  you will understand this.

31 "At that time," declares the LORD,
  "I will be the God of all the clans
of Israel, and they will be my people."

2 This is what the LORD says:

"The people who survive the sword
  will find favor in the desert;
  I will come to give rest to Israel."

3 The LORD appeared to us in the past,[a]
saying:

"I have loved you with an everlasting
    love;
  I have drawn you with loving-
    kindness.
4 I will build you up again
  and you will be rebuilt, O Virgin
    Israel.
Again you will take up your
    tambourines
  and go out to dance with the
    joyful.
5 Again you will plant vineyards
  on the hills of Samaria;
the farmers will plant them
  and enjoy their fruit.
6 There will be a day when watchmen
    cry out
  on the hills of Ephraim,
'Come, let us go up to Zion,
  to the LORD our God.'"

---

a 3 Or LORD has appeared to us from afar

⁷This is what the LORD says:

"Sing with joy for Jacob;
  shout for the foremost of the nations.
Make your praises heard, and say,
  'O LORD, save your people,
  the remnant of Israel.'
⁸See, I will bring them from the land
    of the north
  and gather them from the ends of
    the earth.
Among them will be the blind and
    the lame,
  expectant mothers and women in
    labor;
  a great throng will return.
⁹They will come with weeping;
  they will pray as I bring them back.
I will lead them beside streams of
    water
  on a level path where they will not
    stumble,
because I am Israel's father,
  and Ephraim is my firstborn son.

¹⁰"Hear the word of the LORD,
    O nations;
  proclaim it in distant coastlands:
'He who scattered Israel will gather
    them
  and will watch over his flock like a
    shepherd.'
¹¹For the LORD will ransom Jacob
  and redeem them from the hand of
    those stronger than they.
¹²They will come and shout for joy on
    the heights of Zion;
  they will rejoice in the bounty of
    the LORD—
the grain, the new wine and the oil,
  the young of the flocks and herds.
They will be like a well-watered
    garden,
  and they will sorrow no more.
¹³Then maidens will dance and be glad,
  young men and old as well.
I will turn their mourning into
    gladness;
  I will give them comfort and joy
    instead of sorrow.

¹⁴I will satisfy the priests with
    abundance,
  and my people will be filled with
    my bounty,"
          declares the LORD.

¹⁵This is what the LORD says:

"A voice is heard in Ramah,
  mourning and great weeping,
Rachel weeping for her children
  and refusing to be comforted,
  because her children are no more."

¹⁶This is what the LORD says:

"Restrain your voice from weeping
  and your eyes from tears,
for your work will be rewarded,"
          declares the LORD.
"They will return from the land of
    the enemy.

Prayer is . . .

*drawing near to God with your heart,
mind, and spirit, knowing He
will draw near to you.*

¹⁷So there is hope for your future,"
          declares the LORD.
"Your children will return to their
    own land.

¹⁸"I have surely heard Ephraim's
    moaning:
'You disciplined me like an unruly
    calf,
  and I have been disciplined.
Restore me, and I will return,
  because you are the LORD my God.
¹⁹After I strayed,
  I repented;
after I came to understand,
  I beat my breast.
I was ashamed and humiliated
  because I bore the disgrace of my
    youth.'
²⁰Is not Ephraim my dear son,

the child in whom I delight?
Though I often speak against him,
I still remember him.
Therefore my heart yearns for him;
I have great compassion for him,"
                    declares the LORD.

21 "Set up road signs;
put up guideposts.
Take note of the highway,
the road that you take.
Return, O Virgin Israel,
return to your towns.
22 How long will you wander,
O unfaithful daughter?
The LORD will create a new thing on
        earth—
a woman will surround[a] a man."

23 This is what the LORD Almighty, the God of Israel, says: "When I bring them back from captivity,[b] the people in the land of Judah and in its towns will once again use these words: 'The LORD bless you, O righteous dwelling, O sacred mountain.' 24 People will live together in Judah and all its towns—farmers and those who move about with their flocks. 25 I will refresh the weary and satisfy the faint."

26 At this I awoke and looked around. My sleep had been pleasant to me.

27 "The days are coming," declares the LORD, "when I will plant the house of Israel and the house of Judah with the offspring of men and of animals. 28 Just as I watched over them to uproot and tear down, and to overthrow, destroy and bring disaster, so I will watch over them to build and to plant," declares the LORD. 29 "In those days people will no longer say,

'The fathers have eaten sour grapes,
    and the children's teeth are set on
        edge.'

30 Instead, everyone will die for his own sin; whoever eats sour grapes—his own teeth will be set on edge.

31 "The time is coming," declares the
        LORD,
"when I will make a new covenant
with the house of Israel
    and with the house of Judah.
32 It will not be like the covenant
    I made with their forefathers
when I took them by the hand
    to lead them out of Egypt,
because they broke my covenant,
    though I was a husband to[c] them,[d]"
                    declares the LORD.
33 "This is the covenant I will make
        with the house of Israel
after that time," declares the
        LORD.
"I will put my law in their minds
    and write it on their hearts.
I will be their God,
    and they will be my people.
34 No longer will a man teach his
        neighbor,
    or a man his brother, saying, 'Know
        the LORD,'
because they will all know me,
    from the least of them to the
        greatest,"
                    declares the LORD.
"For I will forgive their wickedness
    and will remember their sins no
        more."

35 This is what the LORD says,

he who appoints the sun
    to shine by day,
who decrees the moon and stars
    to shine by night,
who stirs up the sea
    so that its waves roar—
    the LORD Almighty is his name:
36 "Only if these decrees vanish from
        my sight,"
declares the LORD,
"will the descendants of Israel ever
        cease
    to be a nation before me."

37 This is what the LORD says:

---

a 22 Or will go about seeking; or will protect   b 23 Or I restore their fortunes   c 32 Hebrew; Septuagint and Syriac / and I turned away from   d 32 Or was their master

"Only if the heavens above can be
measured
and the foundations of the earth
below be searched out
will I reject all the descendants of
Israel
because of all they have done,"
declares the LORD.

³⁸"The days are coming," declares the LORD, "when this city will be rebuilt for me from the Tower of Hananel to the Corner Gate. ³⁹The measuring line will stretch from there straight to the hill of Gareb and then turn to Goah. ⁴⁰The whole valley where dead bodies and ashes are thrown, and all the terraces out to the Kidron Valley on the east as far as the corner of the Horse Gate, will be holy to the LORD. The city will never again be uprooted or demolished."

Jeremiah Buys a Field

32 This is the word that came to Jeremiah from the LORD in the tenth year of Zedekiah king of Judah, which was the eighteenth year of Nebuchadnezzar. ²The army of the king of Babylon was then besieging Jerusalem, and Jeremiah the prophet was confined in the courtyard of the guard in the royal palace of Judah.

³Now Zedekiah king of Judah had imprisoned him there, saying, "Why do you prophesy as you do? You say, 'This is what the LORD says: I am about to hand this city over to the king of Babylon, and he will capture it. ⁴Zedekiah king of Judah will not escape out of the hands of the Babylonians[a] but will certainly be handed over to the king of Babylon, and will speak with him face to face and see him with his own eyes. ⁵He will take Zedekiah to Babylon, where he will remain until I deal with him, declares the LORD. If you fight against the Babylonians, you will not succeed.'"

⁶Jeremiah said, "The word of the LORD came to me: ⁷Hanamel son of Shallum your uncle is going to come to you and say, 'Buy my field at Anathoth, because as nearest relative it is your right and duty to buy it.'

⁸"Then, just as the LORD had said, my cousin Hanamel came to me in the courtyard of the guard and said, 'Buy my field at Anathoth in the territory of Benjamin. Since it is your right to redeem it and possess it, buy it for yourself.'

"I knew that this was the word of the LORD; ⁹so I bought the field at Anathoth from my cousin Hanamel and weighed out for him seventeen shekels[b] of silver. ¹⁰I signed and sealed the deed, had it witnessed, and weighed out the silver on the scales. ¹¹I took the deed of purchase—the sealed copy containing the terms and conditions, as well as the unsealed copy— ¹²and I gave this deed to Baruch son of Neriah, the son of Mahseiah, in the presence of my cousin Hanamel and of the witnesses who had signed the deed and of all the Jews sitting in the courtyard of the guard.

¹³"In their presence I gave Baruch these instructions: ¹⁴'This is what the LORD Almighty, the God of Israel, says: Take these documents, both the sealed and unsealed copies of the deed of purchase, and put them in a clay jar so they will last a long time. ¹⁵For this is what the LORD Almighty, the God of Israel, says: Houses, fields and vineyards will again be bought in this land.'

¹⁶"After I had given the deed of purchase to Baruch son of Neriah, I prayed to the LORD:

Praying Jeremiah 32:17
I am grateful, Lord, that You are the Creator of heaven and earth, and because of Your power, nothing is too hard for You.

¹⁷"Ah, Sovereign LORD, you have made the heavens and the earth by your great power and outstretched arm. Nothing is too hard for you.

---

[a] *4 Or Chaldeans*; also in verses 5, 24, 25, 28, 29 and 43   [b] *9 That is, about 7 ounces (about 200 grams)*

¹⁸You show love to thousands but bring the punishment for the fathers' sins into the laps of their children after them. O great and powerful God, whose name is the LORD Almighty, ¹⁹great are your purposes and mighty are your deeds. Your eyes are open to all the ways of men; you reward everyone according to his conduct and as his deeds deserve. ²⁰You performed miraculous signs and wonders in Egypt and have continued them to this day, both in Israel and among all mankind, and have gained the renown that is still yours. ²¹You brought your people Israel out of Egypt with signs and wonders, by a mighty hand and an outstretched arm and with great terror. ²²You gave them this land you had sworn to give their forefathers, a land flowing with milk and honey. ²³They came in and took possession of it, but they did not obey you or follow your law; they did not do what you commanded them to do. So you brought all this disaster upon them.

²⁴"See how the siege ramps are built up to take the city. Because of the sword, famine and plague, the city will be handed over to the Babylonians who are attacking it. What you said has happened, as you now see. ²⁵And though the city will be handed over to the Babylonians, you, O Sovereign LORD, say to me, 'Buy the field with silver and have the transaction witnessed.'"

²⁶Then the word of the LORD came to Jeremiah: ²⁷"I am the LORD, the God of all mankind. Is anything too hard for me? ²⁸Therefore, this is what the LORD says: I am about to hand this city over to the Babylonians and to Nebuchadnezzar king of Babylon, who will capture it. ²⁹The Babylonians who are attacking this city will come in and set it on fire; they will burn it down, along with the houses where the people provoked me to anger by burning incense on the roofs to Baal and by pouring out drink offerings to other gods.

³⁰"The people of Israel and Judah have done nothing but evil in my sight from their youth; indeed, the people of Israel have done nothing but provoke me with what their hands have made, declares the LORD. ³¹From the day it was built until now, this city has so aroused my anger and wrath that I must remove it from my sight. ³²The people of Israel and Judah have provoked me by all the evil they have done—they, their kings and officials, their priests and prophets, the men of Judah and the people of Jerusalem. ³³They turned their backs to me and not their faces; though I taught them again and again, they would not listen or respond to discipline. ³⁴They set up their abominable idols in the house that bears my Name and defiled it. ³⁵They built high places for Baal in the Valley of Ben Hinnom to sacrifice their sons and daughters[a] to Molech, though I never commanded, nor did it enter my mind, that they should do such a detestable thing and so make Judah sin.

³⁶"You are saying about this city, 'By the sword, famine and plague it will be handed over to the king of Babylon'; but this is what the LORD, the God of Israel, says: ³⁷I will surely gather them from all the lands where I banish them in my furious anger and great wrath; I will bring them back to this place and let them live in safety. ³⁸They will be my people, and I will be their God. ³⁹I will give them singleness of heart and action, so that they will always fear me for their own good and the good of their children after them. ⁴⁰I will make an everlasting covenant with them: I will never stop doing good to them, and I will inspire them to fear me, so that they will never turn away from me. ⁴¹I will rejoice in doing them good and will assuredly plant them in this land with all my heart and soul.

---

a 35 Or *to make their sons and daughters pass through the fire*

42"This is what the LORD says: As I have brought all this great calamity on this people, so I will give them all the prosperity I have promised them. 43Once more fields will be bought in this land of which you say, 'It is a desolate waste, without men or animals, for it has been handed over to the Babylonians.' 44Fields will be bought for silver, and deeds will be signed, sealed and witnessed in the territory of Benjamin, in the villages around Jerusalem, in the towns of Judah and in the towns of the hill country, of the western foothills and of the Negev, because I will restore their fortunes,[a] declares the LORD."

Promise of Restoration

33 While Jeremiah was still confined in the courtyard of the guard, the word of the LORD came to him a second time: 2"This is what the LORD says, he who made the earth, the LORD who formed it and established it—the LORD is his name: 3'Call to me and I will answer you and tell you great and unsearchable things you do not know.' 4For this is what the LORD, the God of Israel, says about the houses in this city and the royal palaces of Judah that have been torn down to be used against the siege ramps and the sword 5in the fight with the Babylonians[b]: 'They will be filled with the dead bodies of the men I will slay in my anger and wrath. I will hide my face from this city because of all its wickedness.

6"'Nevertheless, I will bring health and healing to it; I will heal my people and will let them enjoy abundant peace and security. 7I will bring Judah and Israel back from captivity[c] and will rebuild them as they were before. 8I will cleanse them from all the sin they have committed against me and will forgive all their sins of rebellion against me. 9Then this city will bring me renown, joy, praise and honor before all nations on earth that hear of all the good things I do for it; and they will be in awe and will tremble at the abundant prosperity and peace I provide for it.'

10"This is what the LORD says: 'You say about this place, "It is a desolate waste, without men or animals." Yet in the towns of Judah and the streets of Jerusalem that are deserted, inhabited by neither men nor animals, there will be heard once more 11the sounds of joy and gladness, the voices of bride and bridegroom, and the voices of those who bring thank offerings to the house of the LORD, saying,

"Give thanks to the LORD Almighty,
    for the LORD is good;
    his love endures forever."

For I will restore the fortunes of the land as they were before,' says the LORD.

12"This is what the LORD Almighty says: 'In this place, desolate and without men or animals—in all its towns there will again be pastures for shepherds to rest their flocks. 13In the towns of the hill country, of the western foothills and of the Negev, in the territory of Benjamin, in the villages around Jerusalem and in the towns of Judah, flocks will again pass under the hand of the one who counts them,' says the LORD.

14"'The days are coming,' declares the LORD, 'when I will fulfill the gracious promise I made to the house of Israel and to the house of Judah.

15"'In those days and at that time
    I will make a righteous Branch
        sprout from David's line;
    he will do what is just and right in
        the land.
16In those days Judah will be saved
    and Jerusalem will live in safety.
    This is the name by which it[d] will be
        called:
    The LORD Our Righteousness.'

17For this is what the LORD says: 'David will never fail to have a man to sit on the throne of the house of Israel, 18nor will the priests, who are Levites, ever fail to have a man to stand before me continually to

---

[a] 44 Or will bring them back from captivity [b] 5 Or Chaldeans [c] 7 Or will restore the fortunes of Judah and Israel [d] 16 Or he

offer burnt offerings, to burn grain offerings and to present sacrifices.'"

[19]The word of the LORD came to Jeremiah: [20]"This is what the LORD says: 'If you can break my covenant with the day and my covenant with the night, so that day and night no longer come at their appointed time, [21]then my covenant with David my servant—and my covenant with the Levites who are priests ministering before me—can be broken and David will no longer have a descendant to reign on his throne. [22]I will make the descendants of David my servant and the Levites who minister before me as countless as the stars of the sky and as measureless as the sand on the seashore.'"

[23]The word of the LORD came to Jeremiah: [24]"Have you not noticed that these people are saying, 'The LORD has rejected the two kingdoms[a] he chose'? So they despise my people and no longer regard them as a nation. [25]This is what the LORD says: 'If I have not established my covenant with day and night and the fixed laws of heaven and earth, [26]then I will reject the descendants of Jacob and David my servant and will not choose one of his sons to rule over the descendants of Abraham, Isaac and Jacob. For I will restore their fortunes[b] and have compassion on them.'"

Warning to Zedekiah

34 While Nebuchadnezzar king of Babylon and all his army and all the kingdoms and peoples in the empire he ruled were fighting against Jerusalem and all its surrounding towns, this word came to Jeremiah from the LORD: [2]"This is what the LORD, the God of Israel, says: Go to Zedekiah king of Judah and tell him, 'This is what the LORD says: I am about to hand this city over to the king of Babylon, and he will burn it down. [3]You will not escape from his grasp but will surely be captured and handed over to him. You will see the king of Babylon with your own eyes, and he will speak with you face to face. And you will go to Babylon.

[4]"'Yet hear the promise of the LORD, O Zedekiah king of Judah. This is what the LORD says concerning you: You will not die by the sword; [5]you will die peacefully. As people made a funeral fire in honor of your fathers, the former kings who preceded you, so they will make a fire in your honor and lament, "Alas, O master!" I myself make this promise, declares the LORD.'"

[6]Then Jeremiah the prophet told all this to Zedekiah king of Judah, in Jerusalem, [7]while the army of the king of Babylon was fighting against Jerusalem and the other cities of Judah that were still holding out—Lachish and Azekah. These were the only fortified cities left in Judah.

Freedom for Slaves

[8]The word came to Jeremiah from the LORD after King Zedekiah had made a covenant with all the people in Jerusalem to proclaim freedom for the slaves. [9]Everyone was to free his Hebrew slaves, both male and female; no one was to hold a fellow Jew in bondage. [10]So all the officials and people who entered into this covenant agreed that they would free their male and female slaves and no longer hold them in bondage. They agreed, and set them free. [11]But afterward they changed their minds and took back the slaves they had freed and enslaved them again.

[12]Then the word of the LORD came to Jeremiah: [13]"This is what the LORD, the God of Israel, says: I made a covenant with your forefathers when I brought them out of Egypt, out of the land of slavery. I said, [14]'Every seventh year each of you must free any fellow Hebrew who has sold himself to you. After he has served you six years, you must let him go free.'[c] Your fathers, however, did not listen to me or pay attention to me. [15]Recently you repented and did what is right in my sight: Each of you proclaimed freedom

---

[a] 24 Or *families* [b] 26 Or *will bring them back from captivity* [c] 14 Deut. 15:12

to his countrymen. You even made a covenant before me in the house that bears my Name. 16But now you have turned around and profaned my name; each of you has taken back the male and female slaves you had set free to go where they wished. You have forced them to become your slaves again.

17"Therefore, this is what the LORD says: You have not obeyed me; you have not proclaimed freedom for your fellow countrymen. So I now proclaim 'freedom' for you, declares the LORD—'freedom' to fall by the sword, plague and famine. I will make you abhorrent to all the kingdoms of the earth. 18The men who have violated my covenant and have not fulfilled the terms of the covenant they made before me, I will treat like the calf they cut in two and then walked between its pieces. 19The leaders of Judah and Jerusalem, the court officials, the priests and all the people of the land who walked between the pieces of the calf, 20I will hand over to their enemies who seek their lives. Their dead bodies will become food for the birds of the air and the beasts of the earth.

21"I will hand Zedekiah king of Judah and his officials over to their enemies who seek their lives, to the army of the king of Babylon, which has withdrawn from you. 22I am going to give the order, declares the LORD, and I will bring them back to this city. They will fight against it, take it and burn it down. And I will lay waste the towns of Judah so no one can live there."

The Recabites

35 This is the word that came to Jeremiah from the LORD during the reign of Jehoiakim son of Josiah king of Judah: 2"Go to the Recabite family and invite them to come to one of the side rooms of the house of the LORD and give them wine to drink."

3So I went to get Jaazaniah son of Jeremiah, the son of Habazziniah, and his brothers and all his sons—the whole family of the Recabites. 4I brought them into the house of the LORD, into the room of the sons of Hanan son of Igdaliah the man of God. It was next to the room of the officials, which was over that of Maaseiah son of Shallum the doorkeeper. 5Then I set bowls full of wine and some cups before the men of the Recabite family and said to them, "Drink some wine."

6But they replied, "We do not drink wine, because our forefather Jonadab son of Recab gave us this command: 'Neither you nor your descendants must ever drink wine. 7Also you must never build houses, sow seed or plant vineyards; you must never have any of these things, but must always live in tents. Then you will live a long time in the land where you are nomads.' 8We have obeyed everything our forefather Jonadab son of Recab commanded us. Neither we nor our wives nor our sons and daughters have ever drunk wine 9or built houses to live in or had vineyards, fields or crops. 10We have lived in tents and have fully obeyed everything our forefather Jonadab commanded us. 11But when Nebuchadnezzar king of Babylon invaded this land, we said, 'Come, we must go to Jerusalem to escape the Babylonian[a] and Aramean armies.' So we have remained in Jerusalem."

12Then the word of the LORD came to Jeremiah, saying: 13"This is what the LORD Almighty, the God of Israel, says: Go and tell the men of Judah and the people of Jerusalem, 'Will you not learn a lesson and obey my words?' declares the LORD. 14'Jonadab son of Recab ordered his sons not to drink wine and this command has been kept. To this day they do not drink wine, because they obey their forefather's command. But I have spoken to you again and again, yet you have not obeyed me. 15Again and again I sent all my servants the prophets to you. They

---

a 11 Or Chaldean

said, "Each of you must turn from your wicked ways and reform your actions; do not follow other gods to serve them. Then you will live in the land I have given to you and your fathers." But you have not paid attention or listened to me. ¹⁶The descendants of Jonadab son of Recab have carried out the command their forefather gave them, but these people have not obeyed me.'

¹⁷"Therefore, this is what the LORD God Almighty, the God of Israel, says:

'Listen! I am going to bring on Judah and on everyone living in Jerusalem every disaster I pronounced against them. I spoke to them, but they did not listen; I called to them, but they did not answer.'"

¹⁸Then Jeremiah said to the family of the Recabites, "This is what the LORD Almighty, the God of Israel, says: 'You have obeyed the command of your forefather Jonadab and have followed all his instructions and have done everything he ordered.' ¹⁹Therefore, this is what the

GOING deeper

Learning to Listen

READ AND CONSIDER: JEREMIAH 35

"Therefore, this is what the LORD God Almighty, the God of Israel, says: 'Listen!' " (Jeremiah 35:17).

This is not a complicated direction God is giving His people. It can't get any simpler than, "Listen!" He said it then, and He's still saying it today. God wants us to listen to Him only. That's why we have to be discerning about what we allow into our minds.

We have a choice about what we will accept into our minds and what we won't. We can choose to "take captive every thought to make it obedient to Christ" (2 Corinthians 10:5), or we can allow the devil to feed us lies and manipulate our lives. Every sin begins as a thought in the mind. "For from within, out of men's hearts, come evil thoughts, sexual immorality, theft, murder, adultery, greed, malice, deceit, lewdness, envy, slander, arrogance and folly" (Mark 7:21-22). If we don't take control of our minds, the devil will.

That's why you must be diligent to monitor what you allow into your mind. What TV shows, magazines, and books do you look at? What music, radio programs, or CDs do you listen to? Do they fill your mind with godly thoughts and feed your spirit so you feel enriched, clear-minded, peaceful, and blessed, or do they deplete you and leave you feeling empty, confused, anxious, and fearful? "God is not a God of disorder but of peace" (1 Corinthians 14:33). When we fill our minds with God's Word and godly books and magazines written by people in whom God's Spirit resides, and we listen to music that praises and glorifies Him, we leave no room for the enemy's propaganda.

Refusing to entertain unrighteousness in your thought life is part of resisting the devil. If you want to determine whether your thoughts are from the enemy or the Lord, ask yourself, "Are these thoughts I would *choose* to have?" If you answer no, then they are probably from your enemy.

Don't live with confusion or mental oppression. You never have to "live as the Gentiles do, in the futility of their thinking. They are darkened in their understanding and separated from the life of God because of the ignorance that is in them due to the hardening of their hearts" (Ephesians 4:17-18). Instead, ask God to give you clarity and knowledge. Ask Him to give you ears to hear His voice. Ask Him to make you a good listener.

LORD Almighty, the God of Israel, says: 'Jonadab son of Recab will never fail to have a man to serve me.'"

Jehoiakim Burns Jeremiah's Scroll

36 In the fourth year of Jehoiakim son of Josiah king of Judah, this word came to Jeremiah from the LORD: ²"Take a scroll and write on it all the words I have spoken to you concerning Israel, Judah and all the other nations from the time I began speaking to you in the reign of Josiah till now. ³Perhaps when the people of Judah hear about every disaster I plan to inflict on them, each of them will turn from his wicked way; then I will forgive their wickedness and their sin."

⁴So Jeremiah called Baruch son of Neriah, and while Jeremiah dictated all the words the LORD had spoken to him, Baruch wrote them on the scroll. ⁵Then Jeremiah told Baruch, "I am restricted; I cannot go to the LORD's temple. ⁶So you go to the house of the LORD on a day of fasting and read to the people from the scroll the words of the LORD that you wrote as I dictated. Read them to all the people of Judah who come in from their towns. ⁷Perhaps they will bring their petition before the LORD, and each will turn from his wicked ways, for the anger and wrath pronounced against this people by the LORD are great."

⁸Baruch son of Neriah did everything Jeremiah the prophet told him to do; at the LORD's temple he read the words of the LORD from the scroll. ⁹In the ninth month of the fifth year of Jehoiakim son of Josiah king of Judah, a time of fasting before the LORD was proclaimed for all the people in Jerusalem and those who had come from the towns of Judah. ¹⁰From the room of Gemariah son of Shaphan the secretary, which was in the upper courtyard at the entrance of the New Gate of the temple, Baruch read to all the people at the LORD's temple the words of Jeremiah from the scroll.

¹¹When Micaiah son of Gemariah, the son of Shaphan, heard all the words of the LORD from the scroll, ¹²he went down to the secretary's room in the royal palace, where all the officials were sitting: Elishama the secretary, Delaiah son of Shemaiah, Elnathan son of Acbor, Gemariah son of Shaphan, Zedekiah son of Hananiah, and all the other officials. ¹³After Micaiah told them everything he had heard Baruch read to the people from the scroll, ¹⁴all the officials sent Jehudi son of Nethaniah, the son of Shelemiah, the son of Cushi, to say to Baruch, "Bring the scroll from which you have read to the people and come." So Baruch son of Neriah went to them with the scroll in his hand. ¹⁵They said to him, "Sit down, please, and read it to us."

So Baruch read it to them. ¹⁶When they heard all these words, they looked at each other in fear and said to Baruch, "We must report all these words to the king." ¹⁷Then they asked Baruch, "Tell us, how did you come to write all this? Did Jeremiah dictate it?"

¹⁸"Yes," Baruch replied, "he dictated all these words to me, and I wrote them in ink on the scroll."

¹⁹Then the officials said to Baruch, "You and Jeremiah, go and hide. Don't let anyone know where you are."

²⁰After they put the scroll in the room of Elishama the secretary, they went to the king in the courtyard and reported everything to him. ²¹The king sent Jehudi to get the scroll, and Jehudi brought it from the room of Elishama the secretary and read it to the king and all the officials standing beside him. ²²It was the ninth month and the king was sitting in the winter apartment, with a fire burning in the firepot in front of him. ²³Whenever Jehudi had read three or four columns of the scroll, the king cut them off with a scribe's knife and threw them into the firepot, until the entire scroll was burned in the fire. ²⁴The king and all his attendants who heard all these words showed no fear, nor did they tear their clothes. ²⁵Even though Elnathan, Delaiah and

Gemariah urged the king not to burn the scroll, he would not listen to them. ²⁶Instead, the king commanded Jerahmeel, a son of the king, Seraiah son of Azriel and Shelemiah son of Abdeel to arrest Baruch the scribe and Jeremiah the prophet. But the LORD had hidden them.

²⁷After the king burned the scroll containing the words that Baruch had written at Jeremiah's dictation, the word of the LORD came to Jeremiah: ²⁸"Take another scroll and write on it all the words that were on the first scroll, which Jehoiakim king of Judah burned up. ²⁹Also tell Jehoiakim king of Judah, 'This is what the LORD says: You burned that scroll and said, "Why did you write on it that the king of Babylon would certainly come and destroy this land and cut off both men and animals from it?" ³⁰Therefore, this is what the LORD says about Jehoiakim king of Judah: He will have no one to sit on the throne of David; his body will be thrown out and exposed to the heat by day and the frost by night. ³¹I will punish him and his children and his attendants for their wickedness; I will bring on them and those living in Jerusalem and the people of Judah every disaster I pronounced against them, because they have not listened.' "

³²So Jeremiah took another scroll and gave it to the scribe Baruch son of Neriah, and as Jeremiah dictated, Baruch wrote on it all the words of the scroll that Jehoiakim king of Judah had burned in the fire. And many similar words were added to them.

Jeremiah in Prison

37 Zedekiah son of Josiah was made king of Judah by Nebuchadnezzar king of Babylon; he reigned in place of Jehoiachin^a son of Jehoiakim. ²Neither he nor his attendants nor the people of the land paid any attention to the words the LORD had spoken through Jeremiah the prophet.

³King Zedekiah, however, sent Jehucal son of Shelemiah with the priest Zephaniah son of Maaseiah to Jeremiah the prophet with this message: "Please pray to the LORD our God for us."

⁴Now Jeremiah was free to come and go among the people, for he had not yet been put in prison. ⁵Pharaoh's army had marched out of Egypt, and when the Babylonians^b who were besieging Jerusalem heard the report about them, they withdrew from Jerusalem.

⁶Then the word of the LORD came to Jeremiah the prophet: ⁷"This is what the LORD, the God of Israel, says: Tell the king of Judah, who sent you to inquire of me, 'Pharaoh's army, which has marched out to support you, will go back to its own land, to Egypt. ⁸Then the Babylonians will return and attack this city; they will capture it and burn it down.'

⁹"This is what the LORD says: Do not deceive yourselves, thinking, 'The Babylonians will surely leave us.' They will not! ¹⁰Even if you were to defeat the entire Babylonian^c army that is attacking you and only wounded men were left in their tents, they would come out and burn this city down."

¹¹After the Babylonian army had withdrawn from Jerusalem because of Pharaoh's army, ¹²Jeremiah started to leave the city to go to the territory of Benjamin to get his share of the property among the people there. ¹³But when he reached the Benjamin Gate, the captain of the guard, whose name was Irijah son of Shelemiah, the son of Hananiah, arrested him and said, "You are deserting to the Babylonians!"

¹⁴"That's not true!" Jeremiah said. "I am not deserting to the Babylonians." But Irijah would not listen to him; instead, he arrested Jeremiah and brought him to the officials. ¹⁵They were angry with Jeremiah and had him beaten and imprisoned in the house of Jonathan the secretary, which they had made into a prison.

---

^a 1 Hebrew *Coniah*, a variant of *Jehoiachin*   ^b 5 Or *Chaldeans*; also in verses 8, 9, 13 and 14   ^c 10 Or *Chaldean*; also in verse 11

16 Jeremiah was put into a vaulted cell in a dungeon, where he remained a long time. 17 Then King Zedekiah sent for him and had him brought to the palace, where he asked him privately, "Is there any word from the LORD?"

"Yes," Jeremiah replied, "you will be handed over to the king of Babylon."

18 Then Jeremiah said to King Zedekiah, "What crime have I committed against you or your officials or this people, that you have put me in prison? 19 Where are your prophets who prophesied to you, 'The king of Babylon will not attack you or this land'? 20 But now, my lord the king, please listen. Let me bring my petition before you: Do not send me back to the house of Jonathan the secretary, or I will die there."

21 King Zedekiah then gave orders for Jeremiah to be placed in the courtyard of the guard and given bread from the street of the bakers each day until all the bread in the city was gone. So Jeremiah remained in the courtyard of the guard.

Jeremiah Thrown Into a Cistern

38 Shephatiah son of Mattan, Gedaliah son of Pashhur, Jehucal[a] son of Shelemiah, and Pashhur son of Malkijah heard what Jeremiah was telling all the people when he said, 2 "This is what the LORD says: 'Whoever stays in this city will die by the sword, famine or plague, but whoever goes over to the Babylonians[b] will live. He will escape with his life; he will live.' 3 And this is what the LORD says: 'This city will certainly be handed over to the army of the king of Babylon, who will capture it.'"

4 Then the officials said to the king, "This man should be put to death. He is discouraging the soldiers who are left in this city, as well as all the people, by the things he is saying to them. This man is not seeking the good of these people but their ruin."

5 "He is in your hands," King Zedekiah answered. "The king can do nothing to oppose you."

6 So they took Jeremiah and put him into the cistern of Malkijah, the king's son, which was in the courtyard of the guard. They lowered Jeremiah by ropes into the cistern; it had no water in it, only mud, and Jeremiah sank down into the mud.

7 But Ebed-Melech, a Cushite,[c] an official[d] in the royal palace, heard that they had put Jeremiah into the cistern. While the king was sitting in the Benjamin Gate, 8 Ebed-Melech went out of the palace and said to him, 9 "My lord the king, these men have acted wickedly in all they have done to Jeremiah the prophet. They have thrown him into a cistern, where he will starve to death when there is no longer any bread in the city."

10 Then the king commanded Ebed-Melech the Cushite, "Take thirty men from here with you and lift Jeremiah the prophet out of the cistern before he dies."

11 So Ebed-Melech took the men with him and went to a room under the treasury in the palace. He took some old rags and worn-out clothes from there and let them down with ropes to Jeremiah in the cistern. 12 Ebed-Melech the Cushite said to Jeremiah, "Put these old rags and worn-out clothes under your arms to pad the ropes." Jeremiah did so, 13 and they pulled him up with the ropes and lifted him out of the cistern. And Jeremiah remained in the courtyard of the guard.

Zedekiah Questions Jeremiah Again

14 Then King Zedekiah sent for Jeremiah the prophet and had him brought to the third entrance to the temple of the LORD. "I am going to ask you something," the king said to Jeremiah. "Do not hide anything from me."

15 Jeremiah said to Zedekiah, "If I give you an answer, will you not kill me? Even if I did give you counsel, you would not listen to me."

---

a 1 Hebrew Jucal, a variant of Jehucal   b 2 Or Chaldeans; also in verses 18, 19 and 23   c 7 Probably from the upper Nile region
d 7 Or a eunuch

Paying Attention to God's Direction
GOING deeper

READ AND CONSIDER: JEREMIAH 37–38

"Zedekiah son of Josiah was made king of Judah by Nebuchadnezzar king of Babylon; he reigned in place of Jehoiachin son of Jehoiakim. Neither he nor his attendants nor the people of the land paid any attention to the words the LORD had spoken through Jeremiah the prophet" (Jeremiah 37:1-2).

This passage in Jeremiah reads like a script for a movie. Danger, courage, betrayal, drama, war, and political intrigue abound. Tensions stay at a fever pitch in a large city under siege. Our hero Jeremiah may not live to see another day. Special forces led by Ebed-Melech the Cushite have to pull off a daring rescue. Outside the walls, the mighty Chaldeans are waiting for the city to collapse. When and how will Jerusalem fall? Will God actually let that happen? When the end comes, who will be left standing? And why isn't anyone listening to the one prophet who is speaking for God? He's the good guy. We can see it so clearly, why can't they?

We can see things in that Old Testament scene because we have perspective and access to other information. But when you're in the middle of a situation, things aren't always so clear. As our life stories unfold, sometimes it's obvious who to listen to and who *not* to listen to; sometimes it's not. Sometimes we pay attention; sometimes we don't. The Director of our life movie is giving just enough information to bring us along on the right path. There may be surprises in the plot along the way—but He is not surprised. It's all part of the story. He gives directions and guidance, telling us where to go and what to do so that the story falls into place as it should. We just have to pay attention.

King Zedekiah kept asking Jeremiah for God's counsel, but then when he received God's directions, he didn't act on them. The king *wanted* to know, but he was unwilling to do anything with that knowledge. How often do we plead for God's direction and, not liking what we hear, decide to go our own way? We hear from God but then, for one reason or another, we don't immediately act on it.

When you are asking God for direction, ask Him to give you ears to hear it and the will and strength to follow it. Say, "God, show me what to do and enable me to do it."

16But King Zedekiah swore this oath secretly to Jeremiah: "As surely as the LORD lives, who has given us breath, I will neither kill you nor hand you over to those who are seeking your life." 17Then Jeremiah said to Zedekiah, "This is what the LORD God Almighty, the God of Israel, says:'If you surrender to the officers of the king of Babylon, your life will be spared and this city will not be burned down; you and your family will live. 18But if you will not surrender to the officers of the king of Babylon, this city will be handed over to the Babylonians and they will burn it down; you yourself will not escape from their hands.'"

19King Zedekiah said to Jeremiah, "I am afraid of the Jews who have gone over to the Babylonians, for the Babylonians may hand me over to them and they will mistreat me."

20"They will not hand you over," Jeremiah replied. "Obey the LORD by doing what I tell you. Then it will go well with you, and your life will be spared. 21But if you refuse to surrender, this is what the LORD has revealed to me: 22All the women left in the palace of the king of Judah will be brought out to the officials of the king of Babylon. Those women will say to you:

> " 'They misled you and overcame
> you—
> those trusted friends of yours.
> Your feet are sunk in the mud;
> your friends have deserted you.'

23 "All your wives and children will be brought out to the Babylonians. You yourself will not escape from their hands but will be captured by the king of Babylon; and this city will[a] be burned down."

24 Then Zedekiah said to Jeremiah, "Do not let anyone know about this conversation, or you may die. 25 If the officials hear that I talked with you, and they come to you and say, 'Tell us what you said to the king and what the king said to you; do not hide it from us or we will kill you,' 26 then tell them, 'I was pleading with the king not to send me back to Jonathan's house to die there.' "

27 All the officials did come to Jeremiah and question him, and he told them everything the king had ordered him to say. So they said no more to him, for no one had heard his conversation with the king.

28 And Jeremiah remained in the courtyard of the guard until the day Jerusalem was captured.

The Fall of Jerusalem

39 This is how Jerusalem was taken: 1 In the ninth year of Zedekiah king of Judah, in the tenth month, Nebuchadnezzar king of Babylon marched against Jerusalem with his whole army and laid siege to it. 2 And on the ninth day of the fourth month of Zedekiah's eleventh year, the city wall was broken through. 3 Then all the officials of the king of Babylon came and took seats in the Middle Gate: Nergal-Sharezer of Samgar, Nebo-Sarsekim[b] a chief officer, Nergal-Sharezer a high official and all the other officials of the king of Babylon.

4 When Zedekiah king of Judah and all the soldiers saw them, they fled; they left the city at night by way of the king's garden, through the gate between the two walls, and headed toward the Arabah.[c]

5 But the Babylonian[d] army pursued them and overtook Zedekiah in the plains of Jericho. They captured him and took him to Nebuchadnezzar king of Babylon at Riblah in the land of Hamath, where he pronounced sentence on him. 6 There at Riblah the king of Babylon slaughtered the sons of Zedekiah before his eyes and also killed all the nobles of Judah. 7 Then he put out Zedekiah's eyes and bound him with bronze shackles to take him to Babylon.

8 The Babylonians[e] set fire to the royal palace and the houses of the people and broke down the walls of Jerusalem. 9 Nebuzaradan commander of the imperial guard carried into exile to Babylon the people who remained in the city, along with those who had gone over to him, and the rest of the people. 10 But Nebuzaradan the commander of the guard left behind in the land of Judah some of the poor people, who owned nothing; and at that time he gave them vineyards and fields.

11 Now Nebuchadnezzar king of Babylon had given these orders about Jeremiah through Nebuzaradan commander of the imperial guard: 12 "Take him and look after him; don't harm him but do for him whatever he asks." 13 So Nebuzaradan the commander of the guard, Nebushazban a chief officer, Nergal-Sharezer a high official and all the other officers of the king of Babylon 14 sent and had Jeremiah taken out of the courtyard of the guard. They turned him over to Gedaliah son of Ahikam, the son of Shaphan, to take him back to his home. So he remained among his own people.

15 While Jeremiah had been confined in the courtyard of the guard, the word of

---

a 23 Or and you will cause this city to   b 3 Or Nergal-Sharezer, Samgar-Nebo, Sarsekim   c 4 Or the Jordan Valley
d 5 Or Chaldean   e 8 Or Chaldeans

the LORD came to him: [16]"Go and tell Ebed-Melech the Cushite, 'This is what the LORD Almighty, the God of Israel, says: I am about to fulfill my words against this city through disaster, not prosperity. At that time they will be fulfilled before your eyes. [17]But I will rescue you on that day, declares the LORD; you will not be handed over to those you fear. [18]I will save you; you will not fall by the sword but will escape with your life, because you trust in me, declares the LORD.'"

Praying Jeremiah 39:17-18
Lord, I thank You for protecting those who trust in You and who listen to You and obey.

Jeremiah Freed

40 The word came to Jeremiah from the LORD after Nebuzaradan commander of the imperial guard had released him at Ramah. He had found Jeremiah bound in chains among all the captives from Jerusalem and Judah who were being carried into exile to Babylon. [2]When the commander of the guard found Jeremiah, he said to him, "The LORD your God decreed this disaster for this place. [3]And now the LORD has brought it about; he has done just as he said he would. All this happened because you people sinned against the LORD and did not obey him. [4]But today I am freeing you from the chains on your wrists. Come with me to Babylon, if you like, and I will look after you; but if you do not want to, then don't come. Look, the whole country lies before you; go wherever you please." [5]However, before Jeremiah turned to go,[a] Nebuzaradan added, "Go back to Gedaliah son of Ahikam, the son of Shaphan, whom the king of Babylon has appointed over the towns of Judah, and live with him among the people, or go anywhere else you please."

Then the commander gave him provisions and a present and let him go.

[6]So Jeremiah went to Gedaliah son of Ahikam at Mizpah and stayed with him among the people who were left behind in the land.

Gedaliah Assassinated

[7]When all the army officers and their men who were still in the open country heard that the king of Babylon had appointed Gedaliah son of Ahikam as governor over the land and had put him in charge of the men, women and children who were the poorest in the land and who had not been carried into exile to Babylon, [8]they came to Gedaliah at Mizpah—Ishmael son of Nethaniah, Johanan and Jonathan the sons of Kareah, Seraiah son of Tanhumeth, the sons of Ephai the Netophathite, and Jaazaniah[b] the son of the Maacathite, and their men. [9]Gedaliah son of Ahikam, the son of Shaphan, took an oath to reassure them and their men. "Do not be afraid to serve the Babylonians,[c]" he said. "Settle down in the land and serve the king of Babylon, and it will go well with you. [10]I myself will stay at Mizpah to represent you before the Babylonians who come to us, but you are to harvest the wine, summer fruit and oil, and put them in your storage jars, and live in the towns you have taken over."

[11]When all the Jews in Moab, Ammon, Edom and all the other countries heard that the king of Babylon had left a remnant in Judah and had appointed Gedaliah son of Ahikam, the son of Shaphan, as governor over them, [12]they all came back to the land of Judah, to Gedaliah at Mizpah, from all the countries where they had been scattered. And they harvested an abundance of wine and summer fruit.

[13]Johanan son of Kareah and all the army officers still in the open country came to Gedaliah at Mizpah [14]and said to him, "Don't you know that Baalis king of the Ammonites has sent Ishmael son of Nethaniah to take your life?" But Gedaliah son of Ahikam did not believe them.

[15]Then Johanan son of Kareah said privately to Gedaliah in Mizpah, "Let me go and kill Ishmael son of Nethaniah, and no one will know it. Why should he take your life and cause all the Jews who are gathered around you to be scattered and the remnant of Judah to perish?"

[16]But Gedaliah son of Ahikam said to Johanan son of Kareah, "Don't do such a thing! What you are saying about Ishmael is not true."

41 In the seventh month Ishmael son of Nethaniah, the son of Elishama, who was of royal blood and had been one of the king's officers, came with ten men to Gedaliah son of Ahikam at Mizpah. While they were eating together there, [2]Ishmael son of Nethaniah and the ten men who were with him got up and struck down Gedaliah son of Ahikam, the son of Shaphan, with the sword, killing the one whom the king of Babylon had appointed as governor over the land. [3]Ishmael also killed all the Jews who were with Gedaliah at Mizpah, as well as the Babylonian[a] soldiers who were there.

[4]The day after Gedaliah's assassination, before anyone knew about it, [5]eighty men who had shaved off their beards, torn their clothes and cut themselves came from Shechem, Shiloh and Samaria, bringing grain offerings and incense with them to the house of the LORD. [6]Ishmael son of Nethaniah went out from Mizpah to meet them, weeping as he went. When he met them, he said, "Come to Gedaliah son of Ahikam." [7]When they went into the city, Ishmael son of Nethaniah and the men who were with him slaughtered them and threw them into a cistern. [8]But ten of them said to Ishmael, "Don't kill us! We have wheat and barley, oil and honey, hidden in a field." So he let them alone and did not kill them with the others. [9]Now the cistern where he threw all the bodies of the men he had killed along with Gedaliah was the one King Asa had made as part of his defense against Baasha

king of Israel. Ishmael son of Nethaniah filled it with the dead.

[10]Ishmael made captives of all the rest of the people who were in Mizpah—the king's daughters along with all the others who were left there, over whom Nebuzaradan commander of the imperial guard had appointed Gedaliah son of Ahikam. Ishmael son of Nethaniah took them captive and set out to cross over to the Ammonites.

[11]When Johanan son of Kareah and all the army officers who were with him heard about all the crimes Ishmael son of Nethaniah had committed, [12]they took all their men and went to fight Ishmael son of Nethaniah. They caught up with him near the great pool in Gibeon. [13]When all the people Ishmael had with him saw Johanan son of Kareah and the army officers who were with him, they were glad. [14]All the people Ishmael had taken captive at Mizpah turned and went over to Johanan son of Kareah. [15]But Ishmael son of Nethaniah and eight of his men escaped from Johanan and fled to the Ammonites.

Flight to Egypt

[16]Then Johanan son of Kareah and all the army officers who were with him led away all the survivors from Mizpah whom he had recovered from Ishmael son of Nethaniah after he had assassinated Gedaliah son of Ahikam: the soldiers, women, children and court officials he had brought from Gibeon. [17]And they went on, stopping at Geruth Kimham near Bethlehem on their way to Egypt [18]to escape the Babylonians.[b] They were afraid of them because Ishmael son of Nethaniah had killed Gedaliah son of Ahikam, whom the king of Babylon had appointed as governor over the land.

42 Then all the army officers, including Johanan son of Kareah and Jezaniah[c] son of Hoshaiah, and all the people from the least to the greatest approached [2]Jeremiah the prophet and said

---

[a] 3 Or Chaldean   [b] 18 Or Chaldeans   [c] 1 Hebrew; Septuagint (see also 43:2) Azariah

GOING *deeper*

Knowing What to Do

READ AND CONSIDER: JEREMIAH 41:16–42:22

"Pray that the LORD your God will tell us where we should go and what we should do" (Jeremiah 42:3).

Jerusalem had fallen. The king, humiliated and abused, had been led off to Babylon. Most of the nobles had been put to death. The working class had been taken away in chains. A remnant of poor people was left behind. Things looked desperate.

The people came to Jeremiah for a word from God. They promised to carry out God's directions. Jeremiah prayed and waited. And when God's word came... the people did exactly the *opposite* of the instructions they received. They demonstrated a spirit of blatant disobedience. They believed their eyes (present circumstances), their hearts (fears), and their false leaders. They rejected God's promise of blessing. Even though they asked for God's guidance, they had already decided what they would do.

We're all like that sometimes. We pray, "Lord, do I really need to do this?" And when He says yes, we act as if we didn't hear anything.

Every time we ask God to show us what to do in a situation, we also need to ask Him to help us do it.

---

to him, "Please hear our petition and pray to the LORD your God for this entire remnant. For as you now see, though we were once many, now only a few are left. ³Pray that the LORD your God will tell us where we should go and what we should do."

⁴"I have heard you," replied Jeremiah the prophet. "I will certainly pray to the LORD your God as you have requested; I will tell you everything the LORD says and will keep nothing back from you."

⁵Then they said to Jeremiah, "May the LORD be a true and faithful witness against us if we do not act in accordance with everything the LORD your God sends you to tell us. ⁶Whether it is favorable or unfavorable, we will obey the LORD our God, to whom we are sending you, so that it will go well with us, for we will obey the LORD our God."

⁷Ten days later the word of the LORD came to Jeremiah. ⁸So he called together Johanan son of Kareah and all the army officers who were with him and all the people from the least to the greatest. ⁹He

said to them, "This is what the LORD, the God of Israel, to whom you sent me to present your petition, says: ¹⁰'If you stay in this land, I will build you up and not tear you down; I will plant you and not uproot you, for I am grieved over the disaster I have inflicted on you. ¹¹Do not be afraid of the king of Babylon, whom you now fear. Do not be afraid of him, declares the LORD, for I am with you and will save you and deliver you from his hands. ¹²I will show you compassion so that he will have compassion on you and restore you to your land.'

¹³"However, if you say, 'We will not stay in this land,' and so disobey the LORD your God, ¹⁴and if you say, 'No, we will go and live in Egypt, where we will not see war or hear the trumpet or be hungry for bread,' ¹⁵then hear the word of the LORD, O remnant of Judah. This is what the LORD Almighty, the God of Israel, says: 'If you are determined to go to Egypt and you do go to settle there, ¹⁶then the sword you fear will overtake you there, and the famine you dread will

follow you into Egypt, and there you will die. ¹⁷Indeed, all who are determined to go to Egypt to settle there will die by the sword, famine and plague; not one of them will survive or escape the disaster I will bring on them.' ¹⁸This is what the LORD Almighty, the God of Israel, says: 'As my anger and wrath have been poured out on those who lived in Jerusalem, so will my wrath be poured out on you when you go to Egypt. You will be an object of cursing and horror, of condemnation and reproach; you will never see this place again.'

¹⁹"O remnant of Judah, the LORD has told you, 'Do not go to Egypt.' Be sure of this: I warn you today ²⁰that you made a fatal mistake[a] when you sent me to the LORD your God and said, 'Pray to the LORD our God for us; tell us everything he says and we will do it.' ²¹I have told you today, but you still have not obeyed the LORD your God in all he sent me to tell you. ²²So now, be sure of this: You will die by the sword, famine and plague in the place where you want to go to settle."

43 When Jeremiah finished telling the people all the words of the LORD their God—everything the LORD had sent him to tell them— ²Azariah son of Hoshaiah and Johanan son of Kareah and all the arrogant men said to Jeremiah, "You are lying! The LORD our God has not sent you to say, 'You must not go to Egypt to settle there.' ³But Baruch son of Neriah is inciting you against us to hand us over to the Babylonians,[b] so they may kill us or carry us into exile to Babylon."

⁴So Johanan son of Kareah and all the army officers and all the people disobeyed the LORD's command to stay in the land of Judah. ⁵Instead, Johanan son of Kareah and all the army officers led away all the remnant of Judah who had come back to live in the land of Judah from all the nations where they had been scattered. ⁶They also led away all the men, women and children and the king's daughters

whom Nebuzaradan commander of the imperial guard had left with Gedaliah son of Ahikam, the son of Shaphan, and Jeremiah the prophet and Baruch son of Neriah. ⁷So they entered Egypt in disobedience to the LORD and went as far as Tahpanhes.

⁸In Tahpanhes the word of the LORD came to Jeremiah: ⁹"While the Jews are watching, take some large stones with you and bury them in clay in the brick pavement at the entrance to Pharaoh's palace in Tahpanhes. ¹⁰Then say to them, 'This is what the LORD Almighty, the God of Israel, says: I will send for my servant Nebuchadnezzar king of Babylon, and I will set his throne over these stones I have buried here; he will spread his royal canopy above them. ¹¹He will come and attack Egypt, bringing death to those destined for death, captivity to those destined for captivity, and the sword to those destined for the sword. ¹²He[c] will set fire to the temples of the gods of Egypt; he will burn their temples and take their gods captive. As a shepherd wraps his garment around him, so will he wrap Egypt around himself and depart from there unscathed. ¹³There in the temple of the sun[d] in Egypt he will demolish the sacred pillars and will burn down the temples of the gods of Egypt.'"

Disaster Because of Idolatry

44 This word came to Jeremiah concerning all the Jews living in Lower Egypt—in Migdol, Tahpanhes and Memphis[e]—and in Upper Egypt[f]: ²"This is what the LORD Almighty, the God of Israel, says: You saw the great disaster I brought on Jerusalem and on all the towns of Judah. Today they lie deserted and in ruins ³because of the evil they have done. They provoked me to anger by burning incense and by worshiping other gods that neither they nor you nor your fathers ever knew. ⁴Again and again I sent my servants the prophets, who said, 'Do not do this detestable thing that I

---

a 20 Or *you erred in your hearts*   b 3 Or *Chaldeans*   c 12 Or *I*   d 13 Or *in Heliopolis*   e 1 Hebrew *Noph*   f 1 Hebrew *in Pathros* hate!' ⁵But they did not listen or pay attention; they did not turn from their wickedness or stop burning incense to other gods. ⁶Therefore, my fierce anger was poured out; it raged against the towns of Judah and the streets of Jerusalem and made them the desolate ruins they are today.

⁷"Now this is what the LORD God Almighty, the God of Israel, says: Why bring such great disaster on yourselves by cutting off from Judah the men and women, the children and infants, and so leave yourselves without a remnant? ⁸Why provoke me to anger with what your hands have made, burning incense to other gods in Egypt, where you have come to live? You will destroy yourselves and make yourselves an object of cursing and reproach among all the nations on earth. ⁹Have you forgotten the wickedness committed by your fathers and by the kings and queens of Judah and the wickedness committed by you and your wives in the land of Judah and the streets of Jerusalem? ¹⁰To this day they have not humbled themselves or shown reverence, nor have they followed my law and the decrees I set before you and your fathers.

¹¹"Therefore, this is what the LORD Almighty, the God of Israel, says: I am determined to bring disaster on you and to destroy all Judah. ¹²I will take away the remnant of Judah who were determined to go to Egypt to settle there. They will all perish in Egypt; they will fall by the sword or die from famine. From the least to the greatest, they will die by sword or famine. They will become an object of cursing and horror, of condemnation and reproach. ¹³I will punish those who live in Egypt with the sword, famine and plague, as I punished Jerusalem. ¹⁴None of the remnant of Judah who have gone to live in Egypt will escape or survive to return to the land of Judah, to which they long to return and live; none will return except a few fugitives."

¹⁵Then all the men who knew that their wives were burning incense to other gods, along with all the women who were present—a large assembly—and all the people living in Lower and Upper Egypt,[a] said to Jeremiah, ¹⁶"We will not listen to the message you have spoken to us in the name of the LORD! ¹⁷We will certainly do everything we said we would: We will burn incense to the Queen of Heaven and will pour out drink offerings to her just as we and our fathers, our kings and our officials did in the towns of Judah and in the streets of Jerusalem. At that time we had plenty of food and were well off and suffered no harm. ¹⁸But ever since we stopped burning incense to the Queen of Heaven and pouring out drink offerings to her, we have had nothing and have been perishing by sword and famine."

¹⁹The women added, "When we burned incense to the Queen of Heaven and poured out drink offerings to her, did not our husbands know that we were making cakes like her image and pouring out drink offerings to her?"

²⁰Then Jeremiah said to all the people, both men and women, who were answering him, ²¹"Did not the LORD remember and think about the incense burned in the towns of Judah and the streets of Jerusalem by you and your fathers, your kings and your officials and the people of the land? ²²When the LORD could no longer endure your wicked actions and the detestable things you did, your land became an object of cursing and a desolate waste without inhabitants, as it is today. ²³Because you have burned incense and have sinned against the LORD and have not obeyed him or followed his law or his decrees or his stipulations, this disaster has come upon you, as you now see."

²⁴Then Jeremiah said to all the people, including the women, "Hear the word of the LORD, all you people of Judah in

---

Egypt. 25This is what the LORD Almighty, the God of Israel, says: You and your wives have shown by your actions what you promised when you said, 'We will certainly carry out the vows we made to burn incense and pour out drink offerings to the Queen of Heaven.'

"Go ahead then, do what you promised! Keep your vows! 26But hear the word of the LORD, all Jews living in Egypt: 'I swear by my great name,' says the LORD, 'that no one from Judah living anywhere in Egypt will ever again invoke my name or swear,"As surely as the Sovereign LORD lives." 27For I am watching over them for harm, not for good; the Jews in Egypt will perish by sword and famine until they are all destroyed. 28Those who escape the sword and return to the land of Judah from Egypt will be very few. Then the whole remnant of Judah who came to live in Egypt will know whose word will stand—mine or theirs.

29"'This will be the sign to you that I will punish you in this place,' declares the LORD, 'so that you will know that my threats of harm against you will surely stand.' 30This is what the LORD says: 'I am going to hand Pharaoh Hophra king of Egypt over to his enemies who seek his life, just as I handed Zedekiah king of Judah over to Nebuchadnezzar king of Babylon, the enemy who was seeking his life.'"

A Message to Baruch

45 This is what Jeremiah the prophet told Baruch son of Neriah in the fourth year of Jehoiakim son of Josiah king of Judah, after Baruch had written on a scroll the words Jeremiah was then dictating: 2"This is what the LORD, the God of Israel, says to you, Baruch: 3You said, 'Woe to me! The LORD has added sorrow to my pain; I am worn out with groaning and find no rest.'"

4The LORD said, "Say this to him: 'This is what the LORD says: I will overthrow what I have built and uproot what I have planted, throughout the land.

5Should you then seek great things for yourself? Seek them not. For I will bring disaster on all people, declares the LORD, but wherever you go I will let you escape with your life.'"

A Message About Egypt

46 This is the word of the LORD that came to Jeremiah the prophet concerning the nations:

2Concerning Egypt:

This is the message against the army of Pharaoh Neco king of Egypt, which was defeated at Carchemish on the Euphrates River by Nebuchadnezzar king of Babylon in the fourth year of Jehoiakim son of Josiah king of Judah:

3"Prepare your shields, both large and
small,
and march out for battle!
4Harness the horses,
mount the steeds!
Take your positions
with helmets on!
Polish your spears,
put on your armor!
5What do I see?
They are terrified,
they are retreating,
their warriors are defeated.
They flee in haste
without looking back,
and there is terror on every side,"
declares the LORD.
6"The swift cannot flee
nor the strong escape.
In the north by the River Euphrates
they stumble and fall.

7"Who is this that rises like the Nile,
like rivers of surging waters?
8Egypt rises like the Nile,
like rivers of surging waters.
She says, 'I will rise and cover the
earth;
I will destroy cities and their
people.'
9Charge, O horses!

God Will Get You Through

GOING deeper

READ AND CONSIDER: JEREMIAH 45

"Should you then seek great things for yourself? Seek them not. For I will bring disaster on all people, declares the LORD, but wherever you go I will let you escape with your life" (Jeremiah 45:5).

Jeremiah's scribe, Baruch, surely suffered as much as Jeremiah. After he recorded everything Jeremiah heard from the Lord, he read the prophecies publicly. Then he had to read them again before a group of leaders, after which he was instructed to go into hiding with Jeremiah. A little later he heard his scroll had been sliced to pieces and burned. To his surprise (and probably terror), Jeremiah gave Baruch another scroll and said, "God has told me to do it over. Let's start." Baruch became discouraged and afraid, but he also prayed. And God answered.

God gave Jeremiah a special message for Baruch. He told Baruch he would preserve his life in all circumstances. God warned him not to seek great things for himself because *everyone* would experience adversity. But God promised to rescue *him*.

The assurance of God's presence must have been a powerful comfort to Baruch. That same assurance is available to us. God has said, "Never will I leave you; never will I forsake you" (Hebrews 13:5). Jesus promised, "I am with you always, to the very end of the age" (Matthew 28:20).

These promises do not mean that nothing bad will ever happen to us. They mean that we can count on God's presence as we face all that life brings our way. Even in the midst of terrible circumstances, God is with us, saving us in ways we may not even be able to comprehend at the time. Jesus said, "I have told you these things, so that in me you may have peace. In this world you will have trouble. But take heart! I have overcome the world" (John 16:33).

It doesn't matter what your circumstances are at this moment, God has a future for you that is filled with good things. Even though you may have to go through tough times, take God's hand and walk with Him. He promises He won't let you fall.

Drive furiously, O charioteers!
March on, O warriors—
    men of Cush[a] and Put who carry
        shields,
    men of Lydia who draw the
        bow.
¹⁰But that day belongs to the Lord, the
        LORD Almighty—
    a day of vengeance, for vengeance
        on his foes.
The sword will devour till it is
        satisfied,

till it has quenched its thirst with
        blood.
For the Lord, the LORD Almighty,
    will offer sacrifice
in the land of the north by the
        River Euphrates.

¹¹"Go up to Gilead and get balm,
    O Virgin Daughter of Egypt.
But you multiply remedies in vain;
    there is no healing for you.
¹²The nations will hear of your shame;

---

a 9 That is, the upper Nile region

your cries will fill the earth.
One warrior will stumble over
    another;
  both will fall down together."

13 This is the message the LORD spoke to Jeremiah the prophet about the coming of Nebuchadnezzar king of Babylon to attack Egypt:

14 "Announce this in Egypt, and
    proclaim it in Migdol;
  proclaim it also in Memphis[a] and
    Tahpanhes:
 'Take your positions and get ready,
  for the sword devours those around
    you.'
15 Why will your warriors be laid low?
  They cannot stand, for the LORD
    will push them down.
16 They will stumble repeatedly;
  they will fall over each other.
 They will say, 'Get up, let us go back
  to our own people and our native
    lands,
  away from the sword of the
    oppressor.'
17 There they will exclaim,
  'Pharaoh king of Egypt is only a
    loud noise;
  he has missed his opportunity.'

18 "As surely as I live," declares the
    King,
  whose name is the LORD Almighty,
 "one will come who is like Tabor
    among the mountains,
  like Carmel by the sea.
19 Pack your belongings for exile,
  you who live in Egypt,
 for Memphis will be laid waste
  and lie in ruins without inhabitant.

20 "Egypt is a beautiful heifer,
  but a gadfly is coming
    against her from the north.
21 The mercenaries in her ranks
  are like fattened calves.
 They too will turn and flee together,
  they will not stand their ground,

for the day of disaster is coming upon
    them,
  the time for them to be punished.
22 Egypt will hiss like a fleeing serpent
  as the enemy advances in force;
 they will come against her with axes,
  like men who cut down trees.
23 They will chop down her forest,"
        declares the LORD,
 "dense though it be.
 They are more numerous than
    locusts,
  they cannot be counted.
24 The Daughter of Egypt will be put to
    shame,
  handed over to the people of the
    north."

25 The LORD Almighty, the God of Israel, says: "I am about to bring punishment on Amon god of Thebes,[b] on Pharaoh, on Egypt and her gods and her kings, and on those who rely on Pharaoh. 26 I will hand them over to those who seek their lives, to Nebuchadnezzar king of Babylon and his officers. Later, however, Egypt will be inhabited as in times past," declares the LORD.

Praying Jeremiah 46:27

I pray that You, Lord, would save me, my children, and my family members from the things that would try to hold us captive.

27 "Do not fear, O Jacob my servant;
  do not be dismayed, O Israel.
 I will surely save you out of a distant
    place,
  your descendants from the land of
    their exile.
 Jacob will again have peace and
    security,
  and no one will make him afraid.
28 Do not fear, O Jacob my servant,
  for I am with you," declares the
    LORD.
 "Though I completely destroy all the
    nations

---

a 14 Hebrew *Noph*; also in verse 19   b 25 Hebrew *No*

among which I scatter you,
   I will not completely destroy you.
I will discipline you but only with
      justice;
   I will not let you go entirely
      unpunished."

A Message About the Philistines

47 This is the word of the LORD that
came to Jeremiah the prophet concerning the Philistines before Pharaoh
attacked Gaza:

²This is what the LORD says:

"See how the waters are rising in the
      north;
   they will become an overflowing
      torrent.
They will overflow the land and
      everything in it,
   the towns and those who live in
      them.
The people will cry out;
   all who dwell in the land will wail
³at the sound of the hoofs of galloping
      steeds,
   at the noise of enemy chariots
   and the rumble of their wheels.
Fathers will not turn to help their
      children;
   their hands will hang limp.
⁴For the day has come
   to destroy all the Philistines
and to cut off all survivors
   who could help Tyre and Sidon.
The LORD is about to destroy the
      Philistines,
   the remnant from the coasts of
      Caphtor.ᵃ
⁵Gaza will shave her head in
      mourning;
   Ashkelon will be silenced.
O remnant on the plain,
   how long will you cut yourselves?

⁶"'Ah, sword of the LORD,' ⌊you cry,⌋
   'how long till you rest?
Return to your scabbard;

cease and be still.'
⁷But how can it rest
   when the LORD has commanded it,
when he has ordered it
   to attack Ashkelon and the coast?"

A Message About Moab

48 Concerning Moab:

This is what the LORD Almighty, the
God of Israel, says:

"Woe to Nebo, for it will be ruined.
   Kiriathaim will be disgraced and
      captured;
   the strongholdᵇ will be disgraced
      and shattered.
²Moab will be praised no more;
   in Heshbonᶜ men will plot her
      downfall:
   'Come, let us put an end to that
      nation.'
You too, O Madmen,ᵈ will be
      silenced;
   the sword will pursue you.
³Listen to the cries from Horonaim,
   cries of great havoc and
      destruction.
⁴Moab will be broken;
   her little ones will cry out.ᵉ
⁵They go up the way to Luhith,
   weeping bitterly as they go;
on the road down to Horonaim
   anguished cries over the destruction
      are heard.
⁶Flee! Run for your lives;
   become like a bushᶠ in the desert.
⁷Since you trust in your deeds and
      riches,
   you too will be taken captive,
and Chemosh will go into exile,
   together with his priests and
      officials.
⁸The destroyer will come against
      every town,
   and not a town will escape.
The valley will be ruined
   and the plateau destroyed,

ᵃ4 That is, Crete   ᵇ1 Or /Misgab   ᶜ2 The Hebrew for Heshbon sounds like the Hebrew for plot.   ᵈ2 The name of the Moabite
town Madmen sounds like the Hebrew for be silenced.   ᵉ4 Hebrew; Septuagint /proclaim it to Zoar   ᶠ6 Or like Aroer

because the LORD has spoken.
9 Put salt on Moab,
   for she will be laid waste[a];
her towns will become desolate,
   with no one to live in them.

10 "A curse on him who is lax in doing
   the LORD's work!
A curse on him who keeps his
   sword from bloodshed!

Praying Jeremiah 48:10

Lord, I pray that I will never do Your work in a deceitful or lax way, but always in a spirit of truth and devotion to serving You.

11 "Moab has been at rest from youth,
   like wine left on its dregs,
not poured from one jar to
   another—
she has not gone into exile.
So she tastes as she did,
   and her aroma is unchanged.
12 But days are coming,"
   declares the LORD,
"when I will send men who pour
   from jars,
   and they will pour her out;
they will empty her jars
   and smash her jugs.
13 Then Moab will be ashamed of
   Chemosh,
   as the house of Israel was ashamed
when they trusted in Bethel.

14 "How can you say, 'We are
   warriors,
   men valiant in battle'?
15 Moab will be destroyed and her
   towns invaded;
her finest young men will go down
   in the slaughter,"
   declares the King, whose name is
   the LORD Almighty.
16 "The fall of Moab is at hand;
   her calamity will come quickly.
17 Mourn for her, all who live around
   her,
   all who know her fame;

say, 'How broken is the mighty
   scepter,
   how broken the glorious staff!'
18 "Come down from your glory
   and sit on the parched ground,
O inhabitants of the Daughter of
   Dibon,
for he who destroys Moab
   will come up against you
   and ruin your fortified cities.
19 Stand by the road and watch,
   you who live in Aroer.
Ask the man fleeing and the woman
   escaping,
   ask them, 'What has happened?'
20 Moab is disgraced, for she is shattered.
   Wail and cry out!
Announce by the Arnon
   that Moab is destroyed.
21 Judgment has come to the plateau—
   to Holon, Jahzah and Mephaath,
22   to Dibon, Nebo and Beth
     Diblathaim,
23   to Kiriathaim, Beth Gamul and
     Beth Meon,
24   to Kerioth and Bozrah—
   to all the towns of Moab, far and
     near.
25 Moab's horn[b] is cut off;
   her arm is broken,"
          declares the LORD.

26 "Make her drunk,
   for she has defied the LORD.
Let Moab wallow in her vomit;
   let her be an object of ridicule.
27 Was not Israel the object of your
   ridicule?
Was she caught among thieves,
that you shake your head in scorn
   whenever you speak of her?
28 Abandon your towns and dwell
   among the rocks,
   you who live in Moab.
Be like a dove that makes its nest
   at the mouth of a cave.
29 "We have heard of Moab's pride—
   her overweening pride and conceit,

---

a 9 Or *Give wings to Moab, / for she will fly away*   b 25 Horn here symbolizes strength.

her pride and arrogance
and the haughtiness of her heart.
³⁰I know her insolence but it is futile,"
declares the LORD,
"and her boasts accomplish
nothing.
³¹Therefore I wail over Moab,
for all Moab I cry out,
I moan for the men of Kir
Hareseth.
³²I weep for you, as Jazer weeps,
O vines of Sibmah.
Your branches spread as far as the sea;
they reached as far as the sea of
Jazer.
The destroyer has fallen
on your ripened fruit and grapes.
³³Joy and gladness are gone
from the orchards and fields of
Moab.
I have stopped the flow of wine from
the presses;
no one treads them with shouts of
joy.
Although there are shouts,
they are not shouts of joy.

³⁴"The sound of their cry rises
from Heshbon to Elealeh and Jahaz,
from Zoar as far as Horonaim and
Eglath Shelishiyah,
for even the waters of Nimrim are
dried up.
³⁵In Moab I will put an end
to those who make offerings on the
high places
and burn incense to their gods,"
declares the LORD.
³⁶"So my heart laments for Moab like a
flute;
it laments like a flute for the men of
Kir Hareseth.
The wealth they acquired is gone.
³⁷Every head is shaved
and every beard cut off;
every hand is slashed
and every waist is covered with
sackcloth.
³⁸On all the roofs in Moab

and in the public squares
there is nothing but mourning,
for I have broken Moab
like a jar that no one wants,"
declares the LORD.
³⁹"How shattered she is! How they
wail!
How Moab turns her back in
shame!
Moab has become an object of
ridicule,
an object of horror to all those
around her."

⁴⁰This is what the LORD says:

"Look! An eagle is swooping down,
spreading its wings over Moab.
⁴¹Kerioth[a] will be captured
and the strongholds taken.
In that day the hearts of Moab's
warriors
will be like the heart of a woman
in labor.
⁴²Moab will be destroyed as a nation
because she defied the LORD.
⁴³Terror and pit and snare await you,
O people of Moab,"
declares the LORD.
⁴⁴"Whoever flees from the terror
will fall into a pit,
whoever climbs out of the pit
will be caught in a snare;
for I will bring upon Moab
the year of her punishment,"
declares the LORD.
⁴⁵"In the shadow of Heshbon
the fugitives stand helpless,
for a fire has gone out from
Heshbon,
a blaze from the midst of Sihon;
it burns the foreheads of Moab,
the skulls of the noisy boasters.
⁴⁶Woe to you, O Moab!
The people of Chemosh are
destroyed;
your sons are taken into exile
and your daughters into captivity.

^a 41 Or *The cities*

47 "Yet I will restore the fortunes of
   Moab
   in days to come,"
                    declares the LORD.

Here ends the judgment on Moab.

A Message About Ammon

49 Concerning the Ammonites:

This is what the LORD says:

"Has Israel no sons?
   Has she no heirs?
Why then has Molech[a] taken
   possession of Gad?
   Why do his people live in its
   towns?
2 But the days are coming,"
   declares the LORD,
"when I will sound the battle cry
   against Rabbah of the Ammonites;
it will become a mound of ruins,
   and its surrounding villages will be
   set on fire.
Then Israel will drive out
   those who drove her out,"
                    says the LORD.
3 "Wail, O Heshbon, for Ai is
   destroyed!
   Cry out, O inhabitants of Rabbah!
Put on sackcloth and mourn;
   rush here and there inside the
   walls,
for Molech will go into exile,
   together with his priests and
   officials.
4 Why do you boast of your valleys,
   boast of your valleys so fruitful?
O unfaithful daughter,
   you trust in your riches and say,
   'Who will attack me?'
5 I will bring terror on you
   from all those around you,"
                    declares the Lord,
                    the LORD Almighty.
"Every one of you will be driven
   away,
   and no one will gather the
   fugitives.

6 "Yet afterward, I will restore the
   fortunes of the Ammonites,"
                    declares the LORD.

A Message About Edom

7 Concerning Edom:

This is what the LORD Almighty says:

"Is there no longer wisdom in
   Teman?
   Has counsel perished from the
   prudent?
   Has their wisdom decayed?
8 Turn and flee, hide in deep caves,
   you who live in Dedan,
for I will bring disaster on Esau
   at the time I punish him.
9 If grape pickers came to you,
   would they not leave a few grapes?
If thieves came during the night,
   would they not steal only as much
   as they wanted?
10 But I will strip Esau bare;
   I will uncover his hiding places,
   so that he cannot conceal himself.
His children, relatives and neighbors
   will perish,
   and he will be no more.
11 Leave your orphans; I will protect
   their lives.
   Your widows too can trust in me."

12 This is what the LORD says: "If those
who do not deserve to drink the cup
must drink it, why should you go unpunished? You will not go unpunished,
but must drink it. 13 I swear by myself,"
declares the LORD, "that Bozrah will become a ruin and an object of horror, of
reproach and of cursing; and all its towns
will be in ruins forever."

14 I have heard a message from the LORD:
   An envoy was sent to the nations
   to say,
"Assemble yourselves to attack it!
   Rise up for battle!"

15 "Now I will make you small among
   the nations,

---

a 1 Or their king; Hebrew malcam; also in verse 3

despised among men.
¹⁶The terror you inspire
and the pride of your heart have
deceived you,
you who live in the clefts of the
rocks,
who occupy the heights of the hill.
Though you build your nest as high
as the eagle's,
from there I will bring you down,"
declares the LORD.
¹⁷"Edom will become an object of
horror;
all who pass by will be appalled and
will scoff
because of all its wounds.
¹⁸As Sodom and Gomorrah were
overthrown,
along with their neighboring
towns,"
says the LORD,
"so no one will live there;
no man will dwell in it.

¹⁹"Like a lion coming up from Jordan's
thickets
to a rich pastureland,
I will chase Edom from its land in an
instant.
Who is the chosen one I will
appoint for this?
Who is like me and who can
challenge me?
And what shepherd can stand
against me?"
²⁰Therefore, hear what the LORD has
planned against Edom,
what he has purposed against those
who live in Teman:
The young of the flock will be
dragged away;
he will completely destroy their
pasture because of them.
²¹At the sound of their fall the earth
will tremble;
their cry will resound to the Red
Sea.ᵃ
²²Look! An eagle will soar and swoop
down,

spreading its wings over Bozrah.
In that day the hearts of Edom's
warriors
will be like the heart of a woman
in labor.

A Message About Damascus
²³Concerning Damascus:

"Hamath and Arpad are dismayed,
for they have heard bad news.
They are disheartened,
troubled likeᵇ the restless sea.
²⁴Damascus has become feeble,
she has turned to flee
and panic has gripped her;
anguish and pain have seized her,
pain like that of a woman in labor.
²⁵Why has the city of renown not been
abandoned,
the town in which I delight?
²⁶Surely, her young men will fall in the
streets;
all her soldiers will be silenced in
that day,"
declares the LORD Almighty.
²⁷"I will set fire to the walls of
Damascus;
it will consume the fortresses of
Ben-Hadad."

A Message About Kedar and Hazor
²⁸Concerning Kedar and the kingdoms
of Hazor, which Nebuchadnezzar king
of Babylon attacked:

This is what the LORD says:

"Arise, and attack Kedar
and destroy the people of the East.
²⁹Their tents and their flocks will be
taken;
their shelters will be carried off
with all their goods and camels.
Men will shout to them,
'Terror on every side!'

³⁰"Flee quickly away!
Stay in deep caves, you who live in
Hazor,"
declares the LORD.

ᵃ 21 Hebrew Yam Suph; that is, Sea of Reeds   ᵇ 23 Hebrew on or by

"Nebuchadnezzar king of Babylon
 has plotted against you;
he has devised a plan against you.

31"Arise and attack a nation at ease,
 which lives in confidence,"
    declares the LORD,
"a nation that has neither gates nor
  bars;
 its people live alone.
32Their camels will become plunder,
 and their large herds will be booty.
I will scatter to the winds those who
  are in distant places[a]
and will bring disaster on them
  from every side,"
    declares the LORD.
33"Hazor will become a haunt of jackals,
 a desolate place forever.
No one will live there;
 no man will dwell in it."

A Message About Elam

34This is the word of the LORD that
came to Jeremiah the prophet concerning Elam, early in the reign of Zedekiah
king of Judah:

35This is what the LORD Almighty
says:

"See, I will break the bow of Elam,
 the mainstay of their might.
36I will bring against Elam the four
  winds
 from the four quarters of the
  heavens;
I will scatter them to the four winds,
 and there will not be a nation
where Elam's exiles do not go.
37I will shatter Elam before their foes,
 before those who seek their lives;
I will bring disaster upon them,
 even my fierce anger,"
    declares the LORD.
"I will pursue them with the sword
 until I have made an end of them.
38I will set my throne in Elam
 and destroy her king and officials,"
    declares the LORD.

39"Yet I will restore the fortunes of
  Elam
in days to come,"
    declares the LORD.

A Message About Babylon

50 This is the word the LORD spoke
through Jeremiah the prophet concerning Babylon and the land of the Babylonians[b]:

2"Announce and proclaim among the
  nations,
 lift up a banner and proclaim it;
keep nothing back, but say,
'Babylon will be captured;
 Bel will be put to shame,
 Marduk filled with terror.
Her images will be put to shame
 and her idols filled with terror.'
3A nation from the north will attack
  her
 and lay waste her land.
No one will live in it;
 both men and animals will flee
  away.

4"In those days, at that time,"
 declares the LORD,
"the people of Israel and the people of
  Judah together
will go in tears to seek the LORD
 their God.
5They will ask the way to Zion
 and turn their faces toward it.
They will come and bind themselves
  to the LORD
in an everlasting covenant
 that will not be forgotten.

6"My people have been lost sheep;
 their shepherds have led them astray
and caused them to roam on the
  mountains.
They wandered over mountain and
  hill
 and forgot their own resting place.
7Whoever found them devoured them;
 their enemies said, 'We are not
  guilty,

---

a 32 Or who clip the hair by their foreheads   b 1 Or Chaldeans; also in verses 8, 25, 35 and 45

for they sinned against the LORD,
  their true pasture,
  the LORD, the hope of their fathers.'

8 "Flee out of Babylon;
  leave the land of the Babylonians,
  and be like the goats that lead the
    flock.
9 For I will stir up and bring against
    Babylon
  an alliance of great nations from
    the land of the north.
  They will take up their positions
    against her,
  and from the north she will be
    captured.
  Their arrows will be like skilled
    warriors
  who do not return empty-handed.
10 So Babylonia[a] will be plundered;
  all who plunder her will have their
    fill,"

            declares the LORD.

11 "Because you rejoice and are glad,
  you who pillage my inheritance,
  because you frolic like a heifer
    threshing grain
  and neigh like stallions,
12 your mother will be greatly ashamed;
  she who gave you birth will be
    disgraced.
  She will be the least of the nations—
  a wilderness, a dry land, a desert.
13 Because of the LORD's anger she will
    not be inhabited
  but will be completely desolate.
  All who pass Babylon will be
    horrified and scoff
  because of all her wounds.

14 "Take up your positions around
    Babylon,
  all you who draw the bow.
  Shoot at her! Spare no arrows,
  for she has sinned against the LORD.
15 Shout against her on every side!
  She surrenders, her towers fall,
  her walls are torn down.

Since this is the vengeance of the
    LORD,
  take vengeance on her;
  do to her as she has done to others.
16 Cut off from Babylon the sower,
  and the reaper with his sickle at
    harvest.
  Because of the sword of the oppressor
  let everyone return to his own
    people,
  let everyone flee to his own land.

17 "Israel is a scattered flock
  that lions have chased away.
  The first to devour him
  was the king of Assyria;
  the last to crush his bones
  was Nebuchadnezzar king of
    Babylon."

18 Therefore this is what the LORD Almighty, the God of Israel, says:

"I will punish the king of Babylon
    and his land
  as I punished the king of Assyria.
19 But I will bring Israel back to his own
    pasture
  and he will graze on Carmel and
    Bashan;
  his appetite will be satisfied
  on the hills of Ephraim and Gilead.
20 In those days, at that time,"
            declares the LORD,
  "search will be made for Israel's guilt,
  but there will be none,
  and for the sins of Judah,
  but none will be found,
  for I will forgive the remnant I
    spare.

21 "Attack the land of Merathaim
  and those who live in Pekod.
  Pursue, kill and completely destroy[b]
    them,"
            declares the LORD.
  "Do everything I have commanded
    you.
22 The noise of battle is in the land,

---

a 10 Or Chaldea   b 21 The Hebrew term refers to the irrevocable giving over of things or persons to the LORD, often by totally
destroying them; also in verse 26.

the noise of great destruction!

²³How broken and shattered
  is the hammer of the whole earth!
How desolate is Babylon
  among the nations!

²⁴I set a trap for you, O Babylon,
  and you were caught before you
    knew it;
you were found and captured
  because you opposed the LORD.

²⁵The LORD has opened his arsenal
  and brought out the weapons of his
    wrath,
for the Sovereign LORD Almighty has
    work to do
  in the land of the Babylonians.

²⁶Come against her from afar.
  Break open her granaries;
  pile her up like heaps of grain.
Completely destroy her
  and leave her no remnant.

²⁷Kill all her young bulls;
  let them go down to the slaughter!
Woe to them! For their day has come,
  the time for them to be punished.

²⁸Listen to the fugitives and refugees
    from Babylon
  declaring in Zion
how the LORD our God has taken
    vengeance,
  vengeance for his temple.

²⁹"Summon archers against Babylon,
  all those who draw the bow.
Encamp all around her;
  let no one escape.
Repay her for her deeds;
  do to her as she has done.
For she has defied the LORD,
  the Holy One of Israel.

³⁰Therefore, her young men will fall in
    the streets;
  all her soldiers will be silenced in
    that day,"
              declares the LORD.

³¹"See, I am against you, O arrogant
    one,"
  declares the Lord, the LORD
    Almighty,

"for your day has come,
  the time for you to be punished.

³²The arrogant one will stumble and
    fall
  and no one will help her up;
I will kindle a fire in her towns
  that will consume all who are
    around her."

³³This is what the LORD Almighty says:

"The people of Israel are oppressed,
  and the people of Judah as well.
All their captors hold them fast,
  refusing to let them go.

³⁴Yet their Redeemer is strong;
  the LORD Almighty is his name.
He will vigorously defend their
    cause
  so that he may bring rest to their
    land,
  but unrest to those who live in
    Babylon.

³⁵"A sword against the Babylonians!"
  declares the LORD—
"against those who live in Babylon
  and against her officials and wise
    men!

³⁶A sword against her false prophets!
  They will become fools.
A sword against her warriors!
  They will be filled with terror.

³⁷A sword against her horses and
    chariots
  and all the foreigners in her ranks!
  They will become women.
A sword against her treasures!
  They will be plundered.

³⁸A drought onª her waters!
  They will dry up.
For it is a land of idols,
  idols that will go mad with terror.

³⁹"So desert creatures and hyenas will
    live there,
  and there the owl will dwell.
It will never again be inhabited
  or lived in from generation to
    generation.

ª 38 Or A sword against

[40]As God overthrew Sodom and
  Gomorrah
along with their neighboring
    towns,"
              declares the LORD,
"so no one will live there;
  no man will dwell in it.

[41]"Look! An army is coming from the
    north;
  a great nation and many kings
  are being stirred up from the ends
    of the earth.
[42]They are armed with bows and
    spears;
  they are cruel and without mercy.
They sound like the roaring sea
  as they ride on their horses;
they come like men in battle
    formation
  to attack you, O Daughter of
    Babylon.
[43]The king of Babylon has heard
    reports about them,
  and his hands hang limp.
Anguish has gripped him,
  pain like that of a woman in labor.
[44]Like a lion coming up from Jordan's
    thickets
  to a rich pastureland,
I will chase Babylon from its land in
  an instant.
  Who is the chosen one I will
    appoint for this?
Who is like me and who can
    challenge me?
  And what shepherd can stand
    against me?"
[45]Therefore, hear what the LORD has
    planned against Babylon,
  what he has purposed against the
    land of the Babylonians:
The young of the flock will be
    dragged away;
  he will completely destroy their
    pasture because of them.
[46]At the sound of Babylon's capture the
  earth will tremble;

its cry will resound among the
  nations.

51 This is what the LORD says:

"See, I will stir up the spirit of a
  destroyer
against Babylon and the people of
    Leb Kamai.[a]
[2]I will send foreigners to Babylon
  to winnow her and to devastate her
    land;
they will oppose her on every side
  in the day of her disaster.
[3]Let not the archer string his bow,
  nor let him put on his armor.
Do not spare her young men;
  completely destroy[b] her army.
[4]They will fall down slain in
    Babylon,[c]
  fatally wounded in her streets.
[5]For Israel and Judah have not been
    forsaken
  by their God, the LORD Almighty,
though their land[d] is full of guilt
  before the Holy One of Israel.

[6]"Flee from Babylon!
  Run for your lives!
  Do not be destroyed because of her
    sins.
It is time for the LORD's vengeance;
  he will pay her what she deserves.
[7]Babylon was a gold cup in the LORD's
    hand;
  she made the whole earth drunk.
The nations drank her wine;
  therefore they have now gone mad.
[8]Babylon will suddenly fall and be
    broken.
  Wail over her!
Get balm for her pain;
  perhaps she can be healed.

[9]"'We would have healed Babylon,
  but she cannot be healed;
let us leave her and each go to his
    own land,

---

[a] 1 Leb Kamai is a cryptogram for Chaldea, that is, Babylonia. [b] 3 The Hebrew term refers to the irrevocable giving over of
things or persons to the LORD, often by totally destroying them. [c] 4 Or Chaldea [d] 5 Or / and the land of the Babylonians,

for her judgment reaches to the
    skies,
it rises as high as the clouds.'

10 "'The LORD has vindicated us;
    come, let us tell in Zion
what the LORD our God has done.'

11 "Sharpen the arrows,
    take up the shields!
The LORD has stirred up the kings of
    the Medes,
    because his purpose is to destroy
    Babylon.
The LORD will take vengeance,
    vengeance for his temple.
12 Lift up a banner against the walls of
    Babylon!
    Reinforce the guard,
station the watchmen,
    prepare an ambush!
The LORD will carry out his purpose,
    his decree against the people of
    Babylon.
13 You who live by many waters
    and are rich in treasures,
your end has come,
    the time for you to be cut off.
14 The LORD Almighty has sworn by
    himself:
I will surely fill you with men, as
    with a swarm of locusts,
    and they will shout in triumph over
    you.

15 "He made the earth by his power;
    he founded the world by his
    wisdom
    and stretched out the heavens by his
    understanding.
16 When he thunders, the waters in the
    heavens roar;
    he makes clouds rise from the ends
    of the earth.
He sends lightning with the rain
    and brings out the wind from his
    storehouses.

17 "Every man is senseless and without
    knowledge;

every goldsmith is shamed by his
    idols.
His images are a fraud;
    they have no breath in them.
18 They are worthless, the objects of
    mockery;
    when their judgment comes, they
    will perish.
19 He who is the Portion of Jacob is not
    like these,
for he is the Maker of all things,
    including the tribe of his
    inheritance—
    the LORD Almighty is his name.

20 "You are my war club,
    my weapon for battle—
with you I shatter nations,
    with you I destroy kingdoms,
21 with you I shatter horse and rider,
    with you I shatter chariot and
    driver,
22 with you I shatter man and woman,
    with you I shatter old man and
    youth,
    with you I shatter young man and
    maiden,
23 with you I shatter shepherd and flock,
    with you I shatter farmer and oxen,
    with you I shatter governors and
    officials.

24 "Before your eyes I will repay Babylon and all who live in Babylonia[a] for all the wrong they have done in Zion," declares the LORD.

25 "I am against you, O destroying
    mountain,
    you who destroy the whole earth,"
             declares the LORD.
"I will stretch out my hand against
    you,
    roll you off the cliffs,
    and make you a burned-out mountain.
26 No rock will be taken from you for a
    cornerstone,
    nor any stone for a foundation,
for you will be desolate forever,"
             declares the LORD.

---

a 24 Or Chaldea; also in verse 35

27 "Lift up a banner in the land!
　Blow the trumpet among the
　　nations!
　Prepare the nations for battle against
　　her;
　summon against her these
　　kingdoms:
　Ararat, Minni and Ashkenaz.
　Appoint a commander against her;
　send up horses like a swarm of
　　locusts.
28 Prepare the nations for battle against
　　her—
　the kings of the Medes,
　their governors and all their officials,
　and all the countries they rule.
29 The land trembles and writhes,
　for the LORD's purposes against
　　Babylon stand—
　to lay waste the land of Babylon
　so that no one will live there.
30 Babylon's warriors have stopped
　　fighting;
　they remain in their strongholds.
　Their strength is exhausted;
　they have become like women.
　Her dwellings are set on fire;
　the bars of her gates are broken.
31 One courier follows another
　and messenger follows messenger
　to announce to the king of Babylon
　that his entire city is captured,
32 the river crossings seized,
　the marshes set on fire,
　and the soldiers terrified."

33 This is what the LORD Almighty, the
God of Israel, says:

"The Daughter of Babylon is like a
　　threshing floor
　at the time it is trampled;
　the time to harvest her will soon
　　come."

34 "Nebuchadnezzar king of Babylon
　　has devoured us,
　he has thrown us into confusion,
　he has made us an empty jar.
　Like a serpent he has swallowed us

and filled his stomach with our
　　delicacies,
　and then has spewed us out.
35 May the violence done to our flesh[a]
　　be upon Babylon,"
　say the inhabitants of Zion.
"May our blood be on those who live
　　in Babylonia,"
　says Jerusalem.

36 Therefore, this is what the LORD says:

"See, I will defend your cause
　and avenge you;
　I will dry up her sea
　and make her springs dry.
37 Babylon will be a heap of ruins,
　a haunt of jackals,
　an object of horror and scorn,
　a place where no one lives.
38 Her people all roar like young lions,
　they growl like lion cubs.
39 But while they are aroused,
　I will set out a feast for them
　and make them drunk,
　so that they shout with laughter—
　then sleep forever and not awake,"
　　　　　　　　　declares the LORD.
40 "I will bring them down
　like lambs to the slaughter,
　like rams and goats.

41 "How Sheshach[b] will be captured,
　the boast of the whole earth
　　seized!
　What a horror Babylon will be
　among the nations!
42 The sea will rise over Babylon;
　its roaring waves will cover her.
43 Her towns will be desolate,
　a dry and desert land,
　a land where no one lives,
　through which no man travels.
44 I will punish Bel in Babylon
　and make him spew out what he
　　has swallowed.
　The nations will no longer stream to
　　him.
　And the wall of Babylon will fall.

---

a 35 Or done to us and to our children　b 41 Sheshach is a cryptogram for Babylon.

45"Come out of her, my people!
Run for your lives!
Run from the fierce anger of the
LORD.
46Do not lose heart or be afraid
when rumors are heard in the
land;
one rumor comes this year, another
the next,
rumors of violence in the land
and of ruler against ruler.
47For the time will surely come
when I will punish the idols of
Babylon;
her whole land will be disgraced
and her slain will all lie fallen
within her.
48Then heaven and earth and all that is
in them
will shout for joy over Babylon,
for out of the north
destroyers will attack her,"
declares the LORD.

49"Babylon must fall because of Israel's
slain,
just as the slain in all the earth
have fallen because of Babylon.
50You who have escaped the sword,
leave and do not linger!
Remember the LORD in a distant
land,
and think on Jerusalem."

51"We are disgraced,
for we have been insulted
and shame covers our faces,
because foreigners have entered
the holy places of the LORD's
house."

52"But days are coming," declares the
LORD,
"when I will punish her idols,
and throughout her land
the wounded will groan.
53Even if Babylon reaches the sky
and fortifies her lofty stronghold,
I will send destroyers against her,"
declares the LORD.

54"The sound of a cry comes from
Babylon,
the sound of great destruction
from the land of the Babylonians.[a]
55The LORD will destroy Babylon;
he will silence her noisy din.
Waves ⌊of enemies⌋ will rage like great
waters;
the roar of their voices will
resound.
56A destroyer will come against
Babylon;
her warriors will be captured,
and their bows will be broken.
For the LORD is a God of retribution;
he will repay in full.
57I will make her officials and wise men
drunk,
her governors, officers and warriors
as well;
they will sleep forever and not
awake,"
declares the King, whose name is
the LORD Almighty.

58This is what the LORD Almighty
says:

"Babylon's thick wall will be leveled
and her high gates set on fire;
the peoples exhaust themselves for
nothing,
the nations' labor is only fuel for
the flames."

59This is the message Jeremiah gave to the staff officer Seraiah son of Neriah, the son of Mahseiah, when he went to Babylon with Zedekiah king of Judah in the fourth year of his reign. 60Jeremiah had written on a scroll about all the disasters that would come upon Babylon—all that had been recorded concerning Babylon. 61He said to Seraiah, "When you get to Babylon, see that you read all these words aloud. 62Then say, 'O LORD, you have said you will destroy this place, so that neither man nor animal will live in it; it will be desolate forever.' 63When you finish reading this scroll, tie a stone to it and throw

---

a 54 Or Chaldeans

it into the Euphrates. 64Then say, 'So will Babylon sink to rise no more because of the disaster I will bring upon her. And her people will fall.' "

The words of Jeremiah end here.

The Fall of Jerusalem

52 Zedekiah was twenty-one years old when he became king, and he reigned in Jerusalem eleven years. His mother's name was Hamutal daughter of Jeremiah; she was from Libnah. 2He did evil in the eyes of the LORD, just as Jehoiakim had done. 3It was because of the LORD's anger that all this happened to Jerusalem and Judah, and in the end he thrust them from his presence.

Now Zedekiah rebelled against the king of Babylon.

4So in the ninth year of Zedekiah's reign, on the tenth day of the tenth month, Nebuchadnezzar king of Babylon marched against Jerusalem with his whole army. They camped outside the city and built siege works all around it. 5The city was kept under siege until the eleventh year of King Zedekiah.

6By the ninth day of the fourth month the famine in the city had become so severe that there was no food for the people to eat. 7Then the city wall was broken through, and the whole army fled. They left the city at night through the gate between the two walls near the king's garden, though the Babylonians[a] were surrounding the city. They fled toward the Arabah,[b] 8but the Babylonian[c] army pursued King Zedekiah and overtook him in the plains of Jericho. All his soldiers were separated from him and scattered, 9and he was captured.

He was taken to the king of Babylon at Riblah in the land of Hamath, where he pronounced sentence on him. 10There at Riblah the king of Babylon slaughtered the sons of Zedekiah before his eyes; he also killed all the officials of Judah. 11Then he put out Zedekiah's eyes, bound him with bronze shackles and took him to Babylon, where he put him in prison till the day of his death.

12On the tenth day of the fifth month, in the nineteenth year of Nebuchadnezzar king of Babylon, Nebuzaradan commander of the imperial guard, who served the king of Babylon, came to Jerusalem. 13He set fire to the temple of the LORD, the royal palace and all the houses of Jerusalem. Every important building he burned down. 14The whole Babylonian army under the commander of the imperial guard broke down all the walls around Jerusalem. 15Nebuzaradan the commander of the guard carried into exile some of the poorest people and those who remained in the city, along with the rest of the craftsmen[d] and those who had gone over to the king of Babylon. 16But Nebuzaradan left behind the rest of the poorest people of the land to work the vineyards and fields.

17The Babylonians broke up the bronze pillars, the movable stands and the bronze Sea that were at the temple of the LORD and they carried all the bronze to Babylon. 18They also took away the pots, shovels, wick trimmers, sprinkling bowls, dishes and all the bronze articles used in the temple service. 19The commander of the imperial guard took away the basins, censers, sprinkling bowls, pots, lampstands, dishes and bowls used for drink offerings—all that were made of pure gold or silver.

20The bronze from the two pillars, the Sea and the twelve bronze bulls under it, and the movable stands, which King Solomon had made for the temple of the LORD, was more than could be weighed. 21Each of the pillars was eighteen cubits high and twelve cubits in circumference[e]; each was four fingers thick, and hollow. 22The bronze capital on top of the one pillar was five cubits[f] high and

---

was decorated with a network and pomegranates of bronze all around. The other pillar, with its pomegranates, was similar. 23There were ninety-six pomegranates on the sides; the total number of pomegranates above the surrounding network was a hundred.

24The commander of the guard took as prisoners Seraiah the chief priest, Zephaniah the priest next in rank and the three doorkeepers. 25Of those still in the city, he took the officer in charge of the fighting men, and seven royal advisers. He also took the secretary who was chief officer in charge of conscripting the people of the land and sixty of his men who were found in the city. 26Nebuzaradan the commander took them all and brought them to the king of Babylon at Riblah. 27There at Riblah, in the land of Hamath, the king had them executed.

So Judah went into captivity, away from her land. 28This is the number of the people Nebuchadnezzar carried into exile:

in the seventh year, 3,023 Jews;
29in Nebuchadnezzar's eighteenth year,
   832 people from Jerusalem;
30in his twenty-third year,
   745 Jews taken into exile by Nebuzaradan the commander of the imperial guard.
   There were 4,600 people in all.

Jehoiachin Released

31In the thirty-seventh year of the exile of Jehoiachin king of Judah, in the year Evil-Merodach[a] became king of Babylon, he released Jehoiachin king of Judah and freed him from prison on the twenty-fifth day of the twelfth month. 32He spoke kindly to him and gave him a seat of honor higher than those of the other kings who were with him in Babylon. 33So Jehoiachin put aside his prison clothes and for the rest of his life ate regularly at the king's table. 34Day by day the king of Babylon gave Jehoiachin a regular allowance as long as he lived, till the day of his death.

---

a 31 Also called Amel-Marduk

Author: Jeremiah

Date: Approximately 575 BC

Audience: Worshipers of God—not only to document the fall of Jerusalem in 586 BC but also to remind them of the consequences of forsaking the Lord

Prayer Themes:

- *Thank God for His faithfulness, love, and goodness to all who trust in Him (3:22-25).*

- *Ask God to give you the courage to examine your own heart and the humility to turn from sin (3:39-41).*

- *Praise the Lord that He reigns forever and that His "throne endures from generation to generation" (5:19).*

Almost every believer cries out to God when trouble first comes. But few have the spiritual character or maturity to cling faithfully to God *all the way through* life's darkest hours.

The short book of Lamentations (actually more like a diary) shows us how to keep praying and trusting when hope is all but gone. These five chapters vividly capture the prophet Jeremiah's anguish as he helplessly watched both the destruction of Judah and the captivity of his wayward countrymen.

And yet in the midst of his grief and confusion, Jeremiah continued to pursue God. His declaration in 3:22-23 is a model prayer for us during our tough times: "Because of the LORD's great love we are not consumed, for his compassions never fail. They are new every morning; great is your faithfulness."

Lamentations

1 [a] How deserted lies the city,
  once so full of people!
How like a widow is she,
  who once was great among the
    nations!
She who was queen among the
    provinces
  has now become a slave.

2 Bitterly she weeps at night,
  tears are upon her cheeks.
Among all her lovers
  there is none to comfort her.
All her friends have betrayed her;
  they have become her enemies.

3 After affliction and harsh labor,
  Judah has gone into exile.
She dwells among the nations;
  she finds no resting place.
All who pursue her have overtaken her
  in the midst of her distress.

4 The roads to Zion mourn,
  for no one comes to her appointed
    feasts.
All her gateways are desolate,
  her priests groan,
her maidens grieve,
  and she is in bitter anguish.

5 Her foes have become her
    masters;
  her enemies are at ease.
The LORD has brought her grief
  because of her many sins.
Her children have gone into exile,
  captive before the foe.

6 All the splendor has departed
  from the Daughter of Zion.
Her princes are like deer
  that find no pasture;
in weakness they have fled
  before the pursuer.

---

[a] This chapter is an acrostic poem, the verses of which begin with the successive letters of the Hebrew alphabet.

⁷In the days of her affliction and
    wandering
  Jerusalem remembers all the
    treasures
    that were hers in days of old.
  When her people fell into enemy
    hands,
    there was no one to help her.
  Her enemies looked at her
    and laughed at her destruction.

⁸Jerusalem has sinned greatly
    and so has become unclean.
  All who honored her despise her,
    for they have seen her nakedness;
  she herself groans
    and turns away.

⁹Her filthiness clung to her skirts;
    she did not consider her future.
  Her fall was astounding;
    there was none to comfort her.
  "Look, O LORD, on my affliction,
    for the enemy has triumphed."

¹⁰The enemy laid hands
    on all her treasures;
  she saw pagan nations
    enter her sanctuary—
  those you had forbidden
    to enter your assembly.

¹¹All her people groan
    as they search for bread;
  they barter their treasures for food
    to keep themselves alive.
  "Look, O LORD, and consider,
    for I am despised."

¹²"Is it nothing to you, all you who pass
    by?
  Look around and see.
  Is any suffering like my suffering
    that was inflicted on me,
  that the LORD brought on me
    in the day of his fierce anger?

¹³"From on high he sent fire,
    sent it down into my bones.
  He spread a net for my feet
    and turned me back.

He made me desolate,
  faint all the day long.

¹⁴"My sins have been bound into a
    yoke[a];
  by his hands they were woven
    together.
  They have come upon my neck
    and the Lord has sapped my
      strength.
  He has handed me over
    to those I cannot withstand.

¹⁵"The Lord has rejected
    all the warriors in my midst;
  he has summoned an army against me
    to[b] crush my young men.
  In his winepress the Lord has
      trampled
    the Virgin Daughter of Judah.

¹⁶"This is why I weep
    and my eyes overflow with tears.
  No one is near to comfort me,
    no one to restore my spirit.
  My children are destitute
    because the enemy has prevailed."

¹⁷Zion stretches out her hands,
    but there is no one to comfort her.
  The LORD has decreed for Jacob
    that his neighbors become his foes;
  Jerusalem has become
    an unclean thing among them.

¹⁸"The LORD is righteous,
    yet I rebelled against his command.
  Listen, all you peoples;
    look upon my suffering.
  My young men and maidens
    have gone into exile.

¹⁹"I called to my allies
    but they betrayed me.
  My priests and my elders
    perished in the city
  while they searched for food
    to keep themselves alive.

²⁰"See, O LORD, how distressed I am!
    I am in torment within,
  and in my heart I am disturbed,

ᵃ *14* Most Hebrew manuscripts; Septuagint *He kept watch over my sins*   ᵇ *15* Or *has set a time for me / when he will*

for I have been most rebellious.
Outside, the sword bereaves;
inside, there is only death.

21 "People have heard my groaning,
but there is no one to comfort me.
All my enemies have heard of my
distress;
they rejoice at what you have
done.
May you bring the day you have
announced
so they may become like me.

22 "Let all their wickedness come before
you;
deal with them
as you have dealt with me
because of all my sins.
My groans are many
and my heart is faint."

2ᵃ How the Lord has covered the
Daughter of Zion
with the cloud of his angerᵇ!
He has hurled down the splendor of
Israel
from heaven to earth;
he has not remembered his footstool
in the day of his anger.

2 Without pity the Lord has
swallowed up
all the dwellings of Jacob;
in his wrath he has torn down
the strongholds of the Daughter of
Judah.
He has brought her kingdom and its
princes
down to the ground in dishonor.

3 In fierce anger he has cut off
every hornᶜ of Israel.
He has withdrawn his right hand
at the approach of the enemy.
He has burned in Jacob like a flaming
fire
that consumes everything around
it.

4 Like an enemy he has strung his bow;
his right hand is ready.
Like a foe he has slain
all who were pleasing to the eye;
he has poured out his wrath like fire
on the tent of the Daughter of
Zion.

5 The Lord is like an enemy;
he has swallowed up Israel.
He has swallowed up all her palaces
and destroyed her strongholds.
He has multiplied mourning and
lamentation
for the Daughter of Judah.

6 He has laid waste his dwelling like a
garden;
he has destroyed his place of
meeting.
The LORD has made Zion forget
her appointed feasts and her
Sabbaths;
in his fierce anger he has spurned
both king and priest.

7 The Lord has rejected his altar
and abandoned his sanctuary.
He has handed over to the enemy
the walls of her palaces;
they have raised a shout in the house
of the LORD
as on the day of an appointed feast.

8 The LORD determined to tear down
the wall around the Daughter of
Zion.
He stretched out a measuring line
and did not withhold his hand from
destroying.
He made ramparts and walls lament;
together they wasted away.

9 Her gates have sunk into the ground;
their bars he has broken and
destroyed.
Her king and her princes are exiled
among the nations,
the law is no more,

ᵃThis chapter is an acrostic poem, the verses of which begin with the successive letters of the Hebrew alphabet.   ᵇ1 Or *How
the Lord in his anger / has treated the Daughter of Zion with contempt*   ᶜ3 Or / *all the strength*; or *every king*; horn here
symbolizes strength.

and her prophets no longer find
  visions from the LORD.

10 The elders of the Daughter of Zion
  sit on the ground in silence;
they have sprinkled dust on their
    heads
  and put on sackcloth.
The young women of Jerusalem
  have bowed their heads to the
    ground.

11 My eyes fail from weeping,
  I am in torment within,
my heart is poured out on the ground
  because my people are destroyed,
because children and infants faint
  in the streets of the city.

12 They say to their mothers,
  "Where is bread and wine?"
as they faint like wounded men
  in the streets of the city,
as their lives ebb away
  in their mothers' arms.

13 What can I say for you?
  With what can I compare you,
  O Daughter of Jerusalem?
To what can I liken you,
  that I may comfort you,
  O Virgin Daughter of Zion?
Your wound is as deep as the sea.
  Who can heal you?

14 The visions of your prophets
  were false and worthless;
they did not expose your sin
  to ward off your captivity.
The oracles they gave you
  were false and misleading.

15 All who pass your way
  clap their hands at you;
they scoff and shake their heads
  at the Daughter of Jerusalem:
"Is this the city that was called
  the perfection of beauty,
  the joy of the whole earth?"

16 All your enemies open their mouths
  wide against you;

they scoff and gnash their teeth
  and say, "We have swallowed her up.
This is the day we have waited for;
  we have lived to see it."

17 The LORD has done what he planned;
  he has fulfilled his word,
  which he decreed long ago.
He has overthrown you without pity,
  he has let the enemy gloat over you,
  he has exalted the horn[a] of your
    foes.

18 The hearts of the people
  cry out to the Lord.
O wall of the Daughter of Zion,
  let your tears flow like a river
  day and night;
give yourself no relief,
  your eyes no rest.

19 Arise, cry out in the night,
  as the watches of the night begin;
pour out your heart like water
  in the presence of the Lord.
Lift up your hands to him
  for the lives of your children,
who faint from hunger
  at the head of every street.

20 "Look, O LORD, and consider:
  Whom have you ever treated like
    this?
Should women eat their offspring,
  the children they have cared for?
Should priest and prophet be killed
  in the sanctuary of the Lord?

21 "Young and old lie together
  in the dust of the streets;
my young men and maidens
  have fallen by the sword.
You have slain them in the day of
    your anger;
  you have slaughtered them without
    pity.

22 "As you summon to a feast day,
  so you summoned against me
  terrors on every side.
In the day of the LORD's anger

a 17 Horn here symbolizes strength.

Finding Hope in the Midst of Sorrow

READ AND CONSIDER: LAMENTATIONS 2

"Arise, cry out in the night, as the watches of the night begin; pour out your heart like water in the presence of the Lord. Lift up your hands to him" (Lamentations 2:19).

When Jeremiah wrote Lamentations, the echo of Jerusalem's crumbling walls were possibly still ringing in his ears. The cries of despair and weeping over those who had died could yet be heard. All that was left for the Israelites was the grim prospect of a bleak future.

Jeremiah, known as the "weeping prophet," responded with a grief-filled lament over the city and over the people. Like much of Jeremiah's prayer life, these verses are filled with raw emotion. They include deep reverence, anger, worship, confidence, despair, questions, and answers. All aspects of grief find expression in this brief book. Here we see how deeply the human heart can break. There's no joyful worship here, only agony.

If you ever feel such sorrow, do as Jeremiah says and "pour out your heart like water in the presence of the Lord." In your toughest hour, God invites you to hold nothing back, not even your raw emotions. In God's loving presence you will find hope.

Jeremiah finds hope in the midst of his affliction, but the promises God made to Jeremiah are for you as well. As you pour out your pain to God, as you are surrounded with bitterness and hardship (3:5), as you call out for help and it feels as if He has shut out your prayers (3:8), as your heart is pierced (3:13), as you are deprived of peace and prosperity (3:17), remember these words of Jeremiah: "Yet this I call to mind and therefore I have hope: Because of the LORD's great love we are not consumed, for his compassions never fail. They are new every morning; great is your faithfulness. I say to myself, 'The LORD is my portion; therefore I will wait for him.' The LORD is good to those whose hope is in him, to the one who seeks him; it is good to wait quietly for the salvation of the LORD" (3:21-26).

There is hope to be found in the midst of your pain. The darkness, the heartbreak, the sorrow, and the grief are not permanent. The Lord's compassion never fails. He is good to those who hope in Him, who seek Him, who wait quietly for Him.

---

no one escaped or survived;
those I cared for and reared,
my enemy has destroyed."

3 [a] I am the man who has seen
affliction
by the rod of his wrath.
² He has driven me away and made me
walk
in darkness rather than light;
³ indeed, he has turned his hand
against me
again and again, all day long.

⁴ He has made my skin and my flesh
grow old
and has broken my bones.
⁵ He has besieged me and
surrounded me
with bitterness and hardship.
⁶ He has made me dwell in darkness
like those long dead.

⁷ He has walled me in so I cannot
escape;
he has weighed me down with
chains.

---

[a] This chapter is an acrostic poem; the verses of each stanza begin with the successive letters of the Hebrew alphabet, and the verses within each stanza begin with the same letter.

8 Even when I call out or cry for help,
  he shuts out my prayer.
9 He has barred my way with blocks of
    stone;
  he has made my paths crooked.

10 Like a bear lying in wait,
   like a lion in hiding,
11 he dragged me from the path and
     mangled me
   and left me without help.
12 He drew his bow
   and made me the target for his
     arrows.

13 He pierced my heart
   with arrows from his quiver.
14 I became the laughingstock of all my
     people;
   they mock me in song all day long.
15 He has filled me with bitter herbs
   and sated me with gall.

16 He has broken my teeth with gravel;
   he has trampled me in the dust.
17 I have been deprived of peace;
   I have forgotten what prosperity is.
18 So I say, "My splendor is gone
   and all that I had hoped from the
     LORD."

19 I remember my affliction and my
     wandering,
   the bitterness and the gall.
20 I well remember them,
   and my soul is downcast within me.
21 Yet this I call to mind
   and therefore I have hope:

Praying
Lamentations 3:22-24

*Thank You, Lord, that Your mercies to
me are new every morning, and Your love,
faithfulness, and compassion increasingly
strengthen my hope in You each day.*

22 Because of the LORD's great love we
     are not consumed,
   for his compassions never fail.
23 They are new every morning;
   great is your faithfulness.

24 I say to myself, "The LORD is my
     portion;
   therefore I will wait for him."

25 The LORD is good to those whose
     hope is in him,
   to the one who seeks him;
26 it is good to wait quietly
   for the salvation of the LORD.
27 It is good for a man to bear the yoke
   while he is young.

28 Let him sit alone in silence,
   for the LORD has laid it on him.
29 Let him bury his face in the dust—
   there may yet be hope.
30 Let him offer his cheek to one who
     would strike him,
   and let him be filled with disgrace.

31 For men are not cast off
   by the Lord forever.
32 Though he brings grief, he will show
     compassion,
   so great is his unfailing love.
33 For he does not willingly bring
     affliction
   or grief to the children of men.

34 To crush underfoot
   all prisoners in the land,
35 to deny a man his rights
   before the Most High,
36 to deprive a man of justice—
   would not the Lord see such
     things?

37 Who can speak and have it happen
   if the Lord has not decreed it?
38 Is it not from the mouth of the Most
     High
   that both calamities and good
     things come?
39 Why should any living man complain
   when punished for his sins?
40 Let us examine our ways and test
     them,
   and let us return to the LORD.
41 Let us lift up our hearts and our
     hands
   to God in heaven, and say:

42"We have sinned and rebelled
and you have not forgiven.

43"You have covered yourself with
anger and pursued us;
you have slain without pity.
44You have covered yourself with a
cloud
so that no prayer can get through.
45You have made us scum and refuse
among the nations.

46"All our enemies have opened their
mouths
wide against us.
47We have suffered terror and
pitfalls,
ruin and destruction."
48Streams of tears flow from my eyes
because my people are destroyed.

49My eyes will flow unceasingly,
without relief,
50until the LORD looks down
from heaven and sees.
51What I see brings grief to my soul
because of all the women of my
city.

52Those who were my enemies without
cause
hunted me like a bird.
53They tried to end my life in a pit
and threw stones at me;
54the waters closed over my head,
and I thought I was about to be cut
off.

55I called on your name, O LORD,
from the depths of the pit.
56You heard my plea: "Do not close
your ears
to my cry for relief."
57You came near when I called you,
and you said, "Do not fear."

58O Lord, you took up my case;
you redeemed my life.
59You have seen, O LORD, the wrong
done to me.
Uphold my cause!

60You have seen the depth of their
vengeance,
all their plots against me.

61O LORD, you have heard their insults,
all their plots against me—
62what my enemies whisper and mutter
against me all day long.
63Look at them! Sitting or standing,
they mock me in their songs.

64Pay them back what they deserve,
O LORD,
for what their hands have done.
65Put a veil over their hearts,
and may your curse be on them!
66Pursue them in anger and destroy
them
from under the heavens of the LORD.

4 a How the gold has lost its luster,
the fine gold become dull!
The sacred gems are scattered
at the head of every street.

2How the precious sons of Zion,
once worth their weight in gold,
are now considered as pots of clay,
the work of a potter's hands!

3Even jackals offer their breasts
to nurse their young,
but my people have become heartless
like ostriches in the desert.

4Because of thirst the infant's tongue
sticks to the roof of its mouth;
the children beg for bread,
but no one gives it to them.

5Those who once ate delicacies
are destitute in the streets.
Those nurtured in purple
now lie on ash heaps.

6The punishment of my people
is greater than that of Sodom,
which was overthrown in a moment
without a hand turned to help her.

7Their princes were brighter than
snow

---

aThis chapter is an acrostic poem, the verses of which begin with the successive letters of the Hebrew alphabet.

Reaching for God's Hand in Times of Loss

Everyone experiences loss. It's a part of life. It's the part we don't like and wish we never had to go through. But we all will.

When our losses are severe, we feel as if a light has gone out inside of us. And nothing can turn it back on except the restoration of that which is no more. It leaves a hole in our heart the size of the Grand Canyon. But even if what was lost can never be brought back, the part of our life that has died as a result *can* be made to live again. When we walk in the light of God's resurrecting power, He can soothe our pain, heal our wounds, and fill the empty places in our heart.

During the dark times of loss, whether it's the death of a loved one, a crippling disease or injury, divorce, a straying child, the end of a relationship, or the loss of home and finances, we grieve because someone or something we love is no longer part of us. Life as we once knew it is forever destroyed. The way we envisioned our future—with that person, with that security, with that capability—is severely shattered. These kinds of losses can bring such pain that we wonder if we will survive them, and if we do, will we ever feel anything other than the pain? Will we hurt forever? Will life ever feel normal again?

If you suffer any kind of loss, don't try to get your arms around *it*. Let God get His arms around *you*. He knows your suffering and will give you the comfort of His presence and the healing balm of His love. If you walk step-by-step with God through each day of your loss, in time this pain that seems to be without end will actually subside and you will know happiness again.

There is no medal given for getting over loss quickly, so don't try to rush the healing process. Submit to every stage of it. Waves of grief come and go and return again when you least expect them. Even when you begin to forget, something will suddenly remind you of what you lost, and you will feel the pain all over again. Don't dread those times. Embrace the Lord *in* them. All moments traveled on this road will bring about another part of the healing. Every tear will cleanse a layer of the wound. Each memory will become a salve to the soul.

When a tragedy happens, it's normal to feel that life has come to a complete standstill. But it's life as you *knew* it that has stopped. Your new life, *without* that which was lost, is going forward. You just can't see it yet. Even though it's hard to imagine the future being any different than it is at that moment, healing and restoration are happening. You won't always feel this way. There *will* be an end. The loss may have been sudden, but the transition to your new life must be traveled one step at a time.

In times of loss, reach up and take your heavenly Father's hand. He wants to comfort you and shoulder your grief. He wants to walk with you and bear your burdens. Seek His steadying arm moment by moment and He will draw you closer to Him. Even if your well of tears seems to never run dry, continue to walk in the light of God's presence, and you *will* make it through the river of grief to the other side. If you can't see ahead, it's okay. God will not only provide enough light for your next step, He will also enable you to take it.

For the next "From Stormie's Heart" article, go to page 1036.

and whiter than milk,
    their bodies more ruddy than rubies,
    their appearance like sapphires.[a]

⁸But now they are blacker than soot;
    they are not recognized in the
        streets.
Their skin has shriveled on their
        bones;
    it has become as dry as a stick.

⁹Those killed by the sword are better
        off
    than those who die of famine;
racked with hunger, they waste away
    for lack of food from the field.

¹⁰With their own hands compassionate
        women
    have cooked their own children,
who became their food
    when my people were destroyed.

¹¹The LORD has given full vent to his
        wrath;
    he has poured out his fierce anger.
He kindled a fire in Zion
    that consumed her foundations.

¹²The kings of the earth did not believe,
    nor did any of the world's people,
that enemies and foes could enter
    the gates of Jerusalem.

¹³But it happened because of the sins of
        her prophets
    and the iniquities of her priests,
who shed within her
    the blood of the righteous.

¹⁴Now they grope through the streets
    like men who are blind.
They are so defiled with blood
    that no one dares to touch their
        garments.

¹⁵"Go away! You are unclean!" men
        cry to them.
    "Away! Away! Don't touch us!"
When they flee and wander about,
    people among the nations say,
    "They can stay here no longer."

¹⁶The LORD himself has scattered them;
    he no longer watches over them.
The priests are shown no honor,
    the elders no favor.

¹⁷Moreover, our eyes failed,
    looking in vain for help;
from our towers we watched
    for a nation that could not save us.

¹⁸Men stalked us at every step,
    so we could not walk in our streets.
Our end was near, our days were
        numbered,
    for our end had come.

¹⁹Our pursuers were swifter
    than eagles in the sky;
they chased us over the mountains
    and lay in wait for us in the desert.

²⁰The LORD's anointed, our very life
        breath,
    was caught in their traps.
We thought that under his shadow
    we would live among the nations.

²¹Rejoice and be glad, O Daughter of
        Edom,
    you who live in the land of Uz.
But to you also the cup will be
        passed;
    you will be drunk and stripped
        naked.

²²O Daughter of Zion, your
        punishment will end;
    he will not prolong your exile.
But, O Daughter of Edom, he will
        punish your sin
    and expose your wickedness.

5 Remember, O LORD, what has
        happened to us;
    look, and see our disgrace.
²Our inheritance has been turned over
        to aliens,
    our homes to foreigners.
³We have become orphans and
        fatherless,
    our mothers like widows.

---

a 7 Or lapis lazuli

⁴We must buy the water we drink;
  our wood can be had only at a
    price.
⁵Those who pursue us are at our
    heels;
  we are weary and find no rest.
⁶We submitted to Egypt and Assyria
    to get enough bread.
⁷Our fathers sinned and are no more,
  and we bear their punishment.
⁸Slaves rule over us,
  and there is none to free us from
    their hands.
⁹We get our bread at the risk of our
    lives
  because of the sword in the desert.
¹⁰Our skin is hot as an oven,
  feverish from hunger.
¹¹Women have been ravished in Zion,
  and virgins in the towns of Judah.
¹²Princes have been hung up by their
    hands;
  elders are shown no respect.
¹³Young men toil at the millstones;
  boys stagger under loads of wood.

¹⁴The elders are gone from the city
    gate;
  the young men have stopped their
    music.
¹⁵Joy is gone from our hearts;
  our dancing has turned to
    mourning.
¹⁶The crown has fallen from our head.
  Woe to us, for we have sinned!
¹⁷Because of this our hearts are faint,
  because of these things our eyes
    grow dim
¹⁸for Mount Zion, which lies desolate,
  with jackals prowling over it.

¹⁹You, O LORD, reign forever;
  your throne endures from
    generation to generation.
²⁰Why do you always forget us?
  Why do you forsake us so long?
²¹Restore us to yourself, O LORD, that
    we may return;
  renew our days as of old
²²unless you have utterly rejected us
  and are angry with us beyond
    measure.

Author: Ezekiel

Date: Between 593 and 571 BC

Audience: God's people, to remind them of His sovereign rule and to call them to live according to His holy purposes

Prayer Themes:

- *Ask God to reveal to you His specific role for you to play in the building of His church and kingdom (2:1-8).*

- *Thank God for the wonderful gift of the Holy Spirit, who enables you to know God and who empowers you to live for Him (36:24-26).*

- *Tell God you want His glory to fill your life—that you want to be a living temple filled with His presence and power (43:1-4).*

God instructed Ezekiel to warn the people of Jerusalem about the coming destruction of the city and their ultimate loss of God's presence. God also gave Ezekiel a prophesy of future restoration. God spoke and Ezekiel listened.

The habit of "listening to God's voice" is often neglected today, but it was the first order of business for God's prophets in the Bible. No one can speak for God unless he or she has heard God speak. Before servants of God like Ezekiel ever set out to deliver God's message, they first had to stop and hear God's voice.

Even though Ezekiel's prophecies and heavenly visions may be hard to understand, do not let their strange content obscure their clear intent—to call people back to God and give them hope.

God wants to use each one of us to draw others to God and give them a message of hope. But only as we speak constantly with Him and listen for His voice speaking to us, can we have life-altering and life-giving words to share with others.

Ezekiel

The Living Creatures and the Glory of the LORD

1 In the[a] thirtieth year, in the fourth month on the fifth day, while I was among the exiles by the Kebar River, the heavens were opened and I saw visions of God.

²On the fifth of the month—it was the fifth year of the exile of King Jehoiachin— ³the word of the LORD came to Ezekiel the priest, the son of Buzi,[b] by the Kebar River in the land of the Babylonians.[c] There the hand of the LORD was upon him.

⁴I looked, and I saw a windstorm coming out of the north—an immense cloud with flashing lightning and surrounded by brilliant light. The center of the fire looked like glowing metal, ⁵and in the fire was what looked like four living creatures. In appearance their form was that of a man, ⁶but each of them had four faces and four wings. ⁷Their legs were straight; their feet were like those of a calf and gleamed like burnished bronze. ⁸Under their wings on their four sides they had the hands of a man. All four of them had faces and wings, ⁹and their wings touched one another. Each one went straight ahead; they did not turn as they moved.

¹⁰Their faces looked like this: Each of the four had the face of a man, and on the right side each had the face of a lion, and on the left the face of an ox; each also had the face of an eagle. ¹¹Such were their faces. Their wings were spread out upward; each had two wings, one touching the wing of another creature on either side, and two wings covering its body. ¹²Each one went straight ahead. Wherever the spirit would go, they would

---

[a] *1* Or ⌞my⌟   [b] *3* Or *Ezekiel son of Buzi the priest*   [c] *3* Or *Chaldeans*

go, without turning as they went. ¹³The appearance of the living creatures was like burning coals of fire or like torches. Fire moved back and forth among the creatures; it was bright, and lightning flashed out of it. ¹⁴The creatures sped back and forth like flashes of lightning.

¹⁵As I looked at the living creatures, I saw a wheel on the ground beside each creature with its four faces. ¹⁶This was the appearance and structure of the wheels: They sparkled like chrysolite, and all four looked alike. Each appeared to be made like a wheel intersecting a wheel. ¹⁷As they moved, they would go in any one of the four directions the creatures faced; the wheels did not turn about[a] as the creatures went. ¹⁸Their rims were high and awesome, and all four rims were full of eyes all around.

¹⁹When the living creatures moved, the wheels beside them moved; and when the living creatures rose from the ground, the wheels also rose. ²⁰Wherever the spirit would go, they would go, and the wheels would rise along with them, because the spirit of the living creatures was in the wheels. ²¹When the creatures moved, they also moved; when the creatures stood still, they also stood still; and when the creatures rose from the ground, the wheels rose along with them, because the spirit of the living creatures was in the wheels.

²²Spread out above the heads of the living creatures was what looked like an expanse, sparkling like ice, and awesome. ²³Under the expanse their wings were stretched out one toward the other, and each had two wings covering its body. ²⁴When the creatures moved, I heard the sound of their wings, like the roar of rushing waters, like the voice of the Almighty,[b] like the tumult of an army. When they stood still, they lowered their wings.

²⁵Then there came a voice from above the expanse over their heads as they stood with lowered wings. ²⁶Above the expanse over their heads was what looked like a throne of sapphire,[c] and high above on the throne was a figure like that of a man. ²⁷I saw that from what appeared to be his waist up he looked like glowing metal, as if full of fire, and that from there down he looked like fire; and brilliant light surrounded him. ²⁸Like the appearance of a rainbow in the clouds on a rainy day, so was the radiance around him.

This was the appearance of the likeness of the glory of the LORD. When I saw it, I fell facedown, and I heard the voice of one speaking.

Ezekiel's Call

2 He said to me, "Son of man, stand up on your feet and I will speak to you." ²As he spoke, the Spirit came into me and raised me to my feet, and I heard him speaking to me.

³He said: "Son of man, I am sending you to the Israelites, to a rebellious nation that has rebelled against me; they and their fathers have been in revolt against me to this very day. ⁴The people to whom I am sending you are obstinate and stubborn. Say to them, 'This is what the Sovereign LORD says.' ⁵And whether they listen or fail to listen—for they are a rebellious house—they will know that a prophet has been among them. ⁶And you, son of man, do not be afraid of them or their words. Do not be afraid, though briers and thorns are all around you and you live among scorpions. Do not be afraid of what they say or terrified by them, though they are a rebellious house. ⁷You must speak my words to them, whether they listen or fail to listen, for they are rebellious. ⁸But you, son of man, listen to what I say to you. Do not rebel like that rebellious house; open your mouth and eat what I give you."

⁹Then I looked, and I saw a hand stretched out to me. In it was a scroll, ¹⁰which he unrolled before me. On both sides of it were written words of lament and mourning and woe.

ᵃ 17 Or aside   ᵇ 24 Hebrew Shaddai   ᶜ 26 Or lapis lazuli

3 And he said to me, "Son of man, eat what is before you, eat this scroll; then go and speak to the house of Israel." ²So I opened my mouth, and he gave me the scroll to eat.

³Then he said to me, "Son of man, eat this scroll I am giving you and fill your stomach with it." So I ate it, and it tasted as sweet as honey in my mouth.

⁴He then said to me: "Son of man, go now to the house of Israel and speak my words to them. ⁵You are not being sent to a people of obscure speech and difficult language, but to the house of Israel— ⁶not to many peoples of obscure speech and difficult language, whose words you cannot understand. Surely if I had sent you to them, they would have listened to you. ⁷But the house of Israel is not willing to listen to you because they are not willing to listen to me, for the whole house of Israel is hardened and obstinate. ⁸But I will make you as unyielding and hardened as they are. ⁹I will make your forehead like the hardest stone, harder than flint. Do not be afraid of them or terrified by them, though they are a rebellious house."

¹⁰And he said to me, "Son of man, listen carefully and take to heart all the words I speak to you. ¹¹Go now to your countrymen in exile and speak to them. Say to them, 'This is what the Sovereign LORD says,' whether they listen or fail to listen."

¹²Then the Spirit lifted me up, and I heard behind me a loud rumbling sound—May the glory of the LORD be praised in his dwelling place!— ¹³the sound of the wings of the living creatures brushing against each other and the sound of the wheels beside them, a loud rumbling sound. ¹⁴The Spirit then lifted me up and took me away, and I went in bitterness and in the anger of my spirit, with the strong hand of the LORD upon me. ¹⁵I came to the exiles who lived at Tel Abib near the Kebar River. And

there, where they were living, I sat among them for seven days—overwhelmed.

Warning to Israel

¹⁶At the end of seven days the word of the LORD came to me: ¹⁷"Son of man, I have made you a watchman for the house of Israel; so hear the word I speak and give them warning from me. ¹⁸When I say to a wicked man, 'You will surely die,' and you do not warn him or speak out to dissuade him from his evil ways in order to save his life, that wicked man will die for[a] his sin, and I will hold you accountable for his blood. ¹⁹But if you do warn the wicked man and he does not turn from his wickedness or from his evil ways, he will die for his sin; but you will have saved yourself.

²⁰"Again, when a righteous man turns from his righteousness and does evil, and I put a stumbling block before him, he will die. Since you did not warn him, he will die for his sin. The righteous things he did will not be remembered, and I will hold you accountable for his blood. ²¹But if you do warn the righteous man not to sin and he does not sin, he will surely live because he took warning, and you will have saved yourself."

Praying Ezekiel 3:21
Lord, help me to always say what I need to say to the person who I see is about to fall into sin or temptation so that I may cause Your blessings to fall upon us both.

²²The hand of the LORD was upon me there, and he said to me, "Get up and go out to the plain, and there I will speak to you." ²³So I got up and went out to the plain. And the glory of the LORD was standing there, like the glory I had seen by the Kebar River, and I fell facedown.

²⁴Then the Spirit came into me and raised me to my feet. He spoke to me and said: "Go, shut yourself inside your house. ²⁵And you, son of man, they will

tie with ropes; you will be bound so that you cannot go out among the people. 26I will make your tongue stick to the roof of your mouth so that you will be silent and unable to rebuke them, though they are a rebellious house. 27But when I speak to you, I will open your mouth and you shall say to them, 'This is what the Sovereign LORD says.' Whoever will listen let him listen, and whoever will refuse let him refuse; for they are a rebellious house.

Siege of Jerusalem Symbolized

4 "Now, son of man, take a clay tablet, put it in front of you and draw the city of Jerusalem on it. 2Then lay siege to it: Erect siege works against it, build a ramp up to it, set up camps against it and put battering rams around it. 3Then take an iron pan, place it as an iron wall between you and the city and turn your face toward it. It will be under siege, and you shall besiege it. This will be a sign to the house of Israel.

4"Then lie on your left side and put the sin of the house of Israel upon yourself.a You are to bear their sin for the number of days you lie on your side. 5I have assigned you the same number of days as the years of their sin. So for 390 days you will bear the sin of the house of Israel.

6"After you have finished this, lie down again, this time on your right side, and bear the sin of the house of Judah. I have assigned you 40 days, a day for each year. 7Turn your face toward the siege of Jerusalem and with bared arm prophesy against her. 8I will tie you up with ropes so that you cannot turn from one side to the other until you have finished the days of your siege.

9"Take wheat and barley, beans and lentils, millet and spelt; put them in a storage jar and use them to make bread for yourself. You are to eat it during the 390 days you lie on your side. 10Weigh out twenty shekelsb of food to eat each day and eat it at set times. 11Also measure out

a sixth of a hinc of water and drink it at set times. 12Eat the food as you would a barley cake; bake it in the sight of the people, using human excrement for fuel." 13The LORD said, "In this way the people of Israel will eat defiled food among the nations where I will drive them."

14Then I said, "Not so, Sovereign LORD! I have never defiled myself. From my youth until now I have never eaten anything found dead or torn by wild animals. No unclean meat has ever entered my mouth."

15"Very well," he said, "I will let you bake your bread over cow manure instead of human excrement."

16He then said to me: "Son of man, I will cut off the supply of food in Jerusalem. The people will eat rationed food in anxiety and drink rationed water in despair, 17for food and water will be scarce. They will be appalled at the sight of each other and will waste away because ofd their sin.

5 "Now, son of man, take a sharp sword and use it as a barber's razor to shave your head and your beard. Then take a set of scales and divide up the hair. 2When the days of your siege come to an end, burn a third of the hair with fire inside the city. Take a third and strike it with the sword all around the city. And scatter a third to the wind. For I will pursue them with drawn sword. 3But take a few strands of hair and tuck them away in the folds of your garment. 4Again, take a few of these and throw them into the fire and burn them up. A fire will spread from there to the whole house of Israel.

5"This is what the Sovereign LORD says: This is Jerusalem, which I have set in the center of the nations, with countries all around her. 6Yet in her wickedness she has rebelled against my laws and decrees more than the nations and countries around her. She has rejected my laws and has not followed my decrees.

7"Therefore this is what the Sovereign

---

a 4 Or your side   b 10 That is, about 8 ounces (about 0.2 kilogram)   c 11 That is, about 2/3 quart (about 0.6 liter)   d 17 Or away in

LORD says: You have been more unruly than the nations around you and have not followed my decrees or kept my laws. You have not even[a] conformed to the standards of the nations around you.

8"Therefore this is what the Sovereign LORD says: I myself am against you, Jerusalem, and I will inflict punishment on you in the sight of the nations. 9Because of all your detestable idols, I will do to you what I have never done before and will never do again. 10Therefore in your midst fathers will eat their children, and children will eat their fathers. I will inflict punishment on you and will scatter all your survivors to the winds. 11Therefore as surely as I live, declares the Sovereign LORD, because you have defiled my sanctuary with all your vile images and detestable practices, I myself will withdraw my favor; I will not look on you with pity or spare you. 12A third of your people will die of the plague or perish by famine inside you; a third will fall by the sword outside your walls; and a third I will scatter to the winds and pursue with drawn sword.

13"Then my anger will cease and my wrath against them will subside, and I will be avenged. And when I have spent my wrath upon them, they will know that I the LORD have spoken in my zeal.

14"I will make you a ruin and a reproach among the nations around you, in the sight of all who pass by. 15You will be a reproach and a taunt, a warning and an object of horror to the nations around you when I inflict punishment on you in anger and in wrath and with stinging rebuke. I the LORD have spoken. 16When I shoot at you with my deadly and destructive arrows of famine, I will shoot to destroy you. I will bring more and more famine upon you and cut off your supply of food. 17I will send famine and wild beasts against you, and they will leave you childless. Plague and bloodshed will sweep through you, and I will bring the sword against you. I the LORD have spoken."

A Prophecy Against the Mountains of Israel

6 The word of the LORD came to me: 2"Son of man, set your face against the mountains of Israel; prophesy against them 3and say: 'O mountains of Israel, hear the word of the Sovereign LORD. This is what the Sovereign LORD says to the mountains and hills, to the ravines and valleys: I am about to bring a sword against you, and I will destroy your high places. 4Your altars will be demolished and your incense altars will be smashed; and I will slay your people in front of your idols. 5I will lay the dead bodies of the Israelites in front of their idols, and I will scatter your bones around your altars. 6Wherever you live, the towns will be laid waste and the high places demolished, so that your altars will be laid waste and devastated, your idols smashed and ruined, your incense altars broken down, and what you have made wiped out. 7Your people will fall slain among you, and you will know that I am the LORD.

8"'But I will spare some, for some of you will escape the sword when you are scattered among the lands and nations. 9Then in the nations where they have been carried captive, those who escape will remember me—how I have been grieved by their adulterous hearts, which have turned away from me, and by their eyes, which have lusted after their idols. They will loathe themselves for the evil they have done and for all their detestable practices. 10And they will know that I am the LORD; I did not threaten in vain to bring this calamity on them.

11"'This is what the Sovereign LORD says: Strike your hands together and stamp your feet and cry out "Alas!" because of all the wicked and detestable practices of the house of Israel, for they will fall by the sword, famine and plague. 12He that is far away will die of the

---

[a] 7 Most Hebrew manuscripts; some Hebrew manuscripts and Syriac You have

plague, and he that is near will fall by the sword, and he that survives and is spared will die of famine. So will I spend my wrath upon them. 13And they will know that I am the LORD, when their people lie slain among their idols around their altars, on every high hill and on all the mountaintops, under every spreading tree and every leafy oak—places where they offered fragrant incense to all their idols. 14And I will stretch out my hand against them and make the land a desolate waste from the desert to Diblah^a—wherever they live. Then they will know that I am the LORD.'"

The End Has Come

7 The word of the LORD came to me: 2"Son of man, this is what the Sovereign LORD says to the land of Israel: The end! The end has come upon the four corners of the land. 3The end is now upon you and I will unleash my anger against you. I will judge you according to your conduct and repay you for all your detestable practices. 4I will not look on you with pity or spare you; I will surely repay you for your conduct and the detestable practices among you. Then you will know that I am the LORD.

5"This is what the Sovereign LORD says: Disaster! An unheard-of^b disaster is coming. 6The end has come! The end has come! It has roused itself against you. It has come! 7Doom has come upon you— you who dwell in the land. The time has come, the day is near; there is panic, not joy, upon the mountains. 8I am about to pour out my wrath on you and spend my anger against you; I will judge you according to your conduct and repay you for all your detestable practices. 9I will not look on you with pity or spare you; I will repay you in accordance with your conduct and the detestable practices among you. Then you will know that it is I the LORD who strikes the blow.

10"The day is here! It has come! Doom

has burst forth, the rod has budded, arrogance has blossomed! 11Violence has grown into^c a rod to punish wickedness; none of the people will be left, none of that crowd—no wealth, nothing of value. 12The time has come, the day has arrived. Let not the buyer rejoice nor the seller grieve, for wrath is upon the whole crowd. 13The seller will not recover the land he has sold as long as both of them live, for the vision concerning the whole crowd will not be reversed. Because of their sins, not one of them will preserve his life. 14Though they blow the trumpet and get everything ready, no one will go into battle, for my wrath is upon the whole crowd.

15"Outside is the sword, inside are plague and famine; those in the country will die by the sword, and those in the city will be devoured by famine and plague. 16All who survive and escape will be in the mountains, moaning like doves of the valleys, each because of his sins. 17Every hand will go limp, and every knee will become as weak as water. 18They will put on sackcloth and be clothed with terror. Their faces will be covered with shame and their heads will be shaved. 19They will throw their silver into the streets, and their gold will be an unclean thing. Their silver and gold will not be able to save them in the day of the LORD's wrath. They will not satisfy their hunger or fill their stomachs with it, for it has made them stumble into sin. 20They were proud of their beautiful jewelry and used it to make their detestable idols and vile images. Therefore I will turn these into an unclean thing for them. 21I will hand it all over as plunder to foreigners and as loot to the wicked of the earth, and they will defile it. 22I will turn my face away from them, and they will desecrate my treasured place; robbers will enter it and desecrate it.

23"Prepare chains, because the land is

---

^a 14 Most Hebrew manuscripts; a few Hebrew manuscripts *Riblah* and Syriac *Disaster after*   ^c 11 Or *The violent one has become*   ^b 5 Most Hebrew manuscripts; some Hebrew manuscripts

full of bloodshed and the city is full of violence. 24 I will bring the most wicked of the nations to take possession of their houses; I will put an end to the pride of the mighty, and their sanctuaries will be desecrated. 25 When terror comes, they will seek peace, but there will be none. 26 Calamity upon calamity will come, and rumor upon rumor. They will try to get a vision from the prophet; the teaching of the law by the priest will be lost, as will the counsel of the elders. 27 The king will mourn, the prince will be clothed with despair, and the hands of the people of the land will tremble. I will deal with them according to their conduct, and by their own standards I will judge them. Then they will know that I am the LORD."

Praying Ezekiel 7:27

Thank You, Lord, that because of Jesus living in me, You do not judge me according to what I deserve.

Idolatry in the Temple

8 In the sixth year, in the sixth month on the fifth day, while I was sitting in my house and the elders of Judah were sitting before me, the hand of the Sovereign LORD came upon me there. 2 I looked, and I saw a figure like that of a man.ª From what appeared to be his waist down he was like fire, and from there up his appearance was as bright as glowing metal. 3 He stretched out what looked like a hand and took me by the hair of my head. The Spirit lifted me up between earth and heaven and in visions of God he took me to Jerusalem, to the entrance to the north gate of the inner court, where the idol that provokes to jealousy stood. 4 And there before me was the glory of the God of Israel, as in the vision I had seen in the plain.

5 Then he said to me, "Son of man, look toward the north." So I looked, and in the entrance north of the gate of the altar I saw this idol of jealousy.

6 And he said to me, "Son of man, do you see what they are doing—the utterly detestable things the house of Israel is doing here, things that will drive me far from my sanctuary? But you will see things that are even more detestable."

7 Then he brought me to the entrance to the court. I looked, and I saw a hole in the wall. 8 He said to me, "Son of man, now dig into the wall." So I dug into the wall and saw a doorway there.

9 And he said to me, "Go in and see the wicked and detestable things they are doing here." 10 So I went in and looked, and I saw portrayed all over the walls all kinds of crawling things and detestable animals and all the idols of the house of Israel. 11 In front of them stood seventy elders of the house of Israel, and Jaazaniah son of Shaphan was standing among them. Each had a censer in his hand, and a fragrant cloud of incense was rising.

12 He said to me, "Son of man, have you seen what the elders of the house of Israel are doing in the darkness, each at the shrine of his own idol? They say, 'The LORD does not see us; the LORD has forsaken the land.'" 13 Again, he said, "You will see them doing things that are even more detestable."

14 Then he brought me to the entrance to the north gate of the house of the LORD, and I saw women sitting there, mourning for Tammuz. 15 He said to me, "Do you see this, son of man? You will see things that are even more detestable than this."

16 He then brought me into the inner court of the house of the LORD, and there at the entrance to the temple, between the portico and the altar, were about twenty-five men. With their backs toward the temple of the LORD and their faces toward the east, they were bowing down to the sun in the east.

17 He said to me, "Have you seen this, son of man? Is it a trivial matter for the house of Judah to do the detestable things

---

ª 2 Or *saw a fiery figure*

they are doing here? Must they also fill the land with violence and continually provoke me to anger? Look at them putting the branch to their nose! [18]Therefore I will deal with them in anger; I will not look on them with pity or spare them. Although they shout in my ears, I will not listen to them."

Idolaters Killed

9 Then I heard him call out in a loud voice, "Bring the guards of the city here, each with a weapon in his hand." [2]And I saw six men coming from the direction of the upper gate, which faces north, each with a deadly weapon in his hand. With them was a man clothed in linen who had a writing kit at his side. They came in and stood beside the bronze altar.

[3]Now the glory of the God of Israel went up from above the cherubim, where it had been, and moved to the threshold of the temple. Then the LORD called to the man clothed in linen who had the writing kit at his side [4]and said to him, "Go throughout the city of Jerusalem and put a mark on the foreheads of those who grieve and lament over all the detestable things that are done in it."

[5]As I listened, he said to the others, "Follow him through the city and kill, without showing pity or compassion. [6]Slaughter old men, young men and maidens, women and children, but do not touch anyone who has the mark. Begin at my sanctuary." So they began with the elders who were in front of the temple.

[7]Then he said to them, "Defile the temple and fill the courts with the slain. Go!" So they went out and began killing throughout the city. [8]While they were killing and I was left alone, I fell facedown, crying out, "Ah, Sovereign LORD! Are you going to destroy the entire remnant of Israel in this outpouring of your wrath on Jerusalem?"

[9]He answered me, "The sin of the house of Israel and Judah is exceedingly great; the land is full of bloodshed and the city is full of injustice. They say, 'The LORD has forsaken the land; the LORD does not see.' [10]So I will not look on them with pity or spare them, but I will bring down on their own heads what they have done."

[11]Then the man in linen with the writing kit at his side brought back word, saying, "I have done as you commanded."

The Glory Departs From the Temple

10 I looked, and I saw the likeness of a throne of sapphire[a] above the expanse that was over the heads of the cherubim. [2]The LORD said to the man clothed in linen, "Go in among the wheels beneath the cherubim. Fill your hands with burning coals from among the cherubim and scatter them over the city." And as I watched, he went in.

[3]Now the cherubim were standing on the south side of the temple when the man went in, and a cloud filled the inner court. [4]Then the glory of the LORD rose from above the cherubim and moved to the threshold of the temple. The cloud filled the temple, and the court was full of the radiance of the glory of the LORD. [5]The sound of the wings of the cherubim could be heard as far away as the outer court, like the voice of God Almighty[b] when he speaks.

[6]When the LORD commanded the man in linen, "Take fire from among the wheels, from among the cherubim," the man went in and stood beside a wheel. [7]Then one of the cherubim reached out his hand to the fire that was among them. He took up some of it and put it into the hands of the man in linen, who took it and went out. [8](Under the wings of the cherubim could be seen what looked like the hands of a man.)

[9]I looked, and I saw beside the cherubim four wheels, one beside each of the cherubim; the wheels sparkled like chrysolite. [10]As for their appearance, the four of them looked alike; each was like

---

[a] 1 Or lapis lazuli   [b] 5 Hebrew El-Shaddai

a wheel intersecting a wheel. 11As they moved, they would go in any one of the four directions the cherubim faced; the wheels did not turn about[a] as the cherubim went. The cherubim went in whatever direction the head faced, without turning as they went. 12Their entire bodies, including their backs, their hands and their wings, were completely full of eyes, as were their four wheels. 13I heard the wheels being called "the whirling wheels." 14Each of the cherubim had four faces: One face was that of a cherub, the second the face of a man, the third the face of a lion, and the fourth the face of an eagle.

15Then the cherubim rose upward. These were the living creatures I had seen by the Kebar River. 16When the cherubim moved, the wheels beside them moved; and when the cherubim spread their wings to rise from the ground, the wheels did not leave their side. 17When the cherubim stood still, they also stood still; and when the cherubim rose, they rose with them, because the spirit of the living creatures was in them.

Praying Ezekiel 10:18

Lord, I thank You for always being with me, for I can think of nothing more horrible than to have Your presence depart from me as it departed from Your temple long ago.

18Then the glory of the LORD departed from over the threshold of the temple and stopped above the cherubim. 19While I watched, the cherubim spread their wings and rose from the ground, and as they went, the wheels went with them. They stopped at the entrance to the east gate of the LORD's house, and the glory of the God of Israel was above them.

20These were the living creatures I had seen beneath the God of Israel by the Kebar River, and I realized that they were cherubim. 21Each had four faces and four

wings, and under their wings was what looked like the hands of a man. 22Their faces had the same appearance as those I had seen by the Kebar River. Each one went straight ahead.

Judgment on Israel's Leaders

11 Then the Spirit lifted me up and brought me to the gate of the house of the LORD that faces east. There at the entrance to the gate were twenty-five men, and I saw among them Jaazaniah son of Azzur and Pelatiah son of Benaiah, leaders of the people. 2The LORD said to me, "Son of man, these are the men who are plotting evil and giving wicked advice in this city. 3They say, 'Will it not soon be time to build houses?[b] This city is a cooking pot, and we are the meat.' 4Therefore prophesy against them; prophesy, son of man."

5Then the Spirit of the LORD came upon me, and he told me to say: "This is what the LORD says: That is what you are saying, O house of Israel, but I know what is going through your mind. 6You have killed many people in this city and filled its streets with the dead.

7"Therefore this is what the Sovereign LORD says: The bodies you have thrown there are the meat and this city is the pot, but I will drive you out of it. 8You fear the sword, and the sword is what I will bring against you, declares the Sovereign LORD. 9I will drive you out of the city and hand you over to foreigners and inflict punishment on you. 10You will fall by the sword, and I will execute judgment on you at the borders of Israel. Then you will know that I am the LORD. 11This city will not be a pot for you, nor will you be the meat in it; I will execute judgment on you at the borders of Israel. 12And you will know that I am the LORD, for you have not followed my decrees or kept my laws but have conformed to the standards of the nations around you."

13Now as I was prophesying, Pelatiah son of Benaiah died. Then I fell facedown

---

a 11 Or *aside*   b 3 Or *This is not the time to build houses.*

God's people at prayer
EZEKIEL PLEADS FOR HIS NATION

EZEKIEL 11:13-16 Israel was a rebel nation. The people thought they were "spiritual," yet they were anything *but* that. Many people gave up on Israel, but not Ezekiel. He cried out for God's mercy on their behalf.

No matter how much we may be tempted to give up on our own country, believing there is nothing we can do about the moral decay around us, we need to remember the fervent pleading of Ezekiel and cry out, "Preserve and protect our nation!"

Everyone must pray that God will pour out His Spirit on their nation. We all should pray for our leaders and decision makers. Let's pray that God will give the nation an undivided heart and a new spirit (11:19).

and cried out in a loud voice, "Ah, Sovereign LORD! Will you completely destroy the remnant of Israel?"

¹⁴The word of the LORD came to me: ¹⁵"Son of man, your brothers—your brothers who are your blood relatives[a] and the whole house of Israel—are those of whom the people of Jerusalem have said, 'They are[b] far away from the LORD; this land was given to us as our possession.'

Promised Return of Israel

¹⁶"Therefore say: 'This is what the Sovereign LORD says: Although I sent them far away among the nations and scattered them among the countries, yet for a little while I have been a sanctuary for them in the countries where they have gone.'

¹⁷"Therefore say: 'This is what the Sovereign LORD says: I will gather you from the nations and bring you back from the countries where you have been scattered, and I will give you back the land of Israel again.'

¹⁸"They will return to it and remove all its vile images and detestable idols. ¹⁹I will give them an undivided heart and put a new spirit in them; I will remove from them their heart of stone and give them a heart of flesh. ²⁰Then they will follow my decrees and be careful to keep

my laws. They will be my people, and I will be their God. ²¹But as for those whose hearts are devoted to their vile images and detestable idols, I will bring down on their own heads what they have done, declares the Sovereign LORD."

²²Then the cherubim, with the wheels beside them, spread their wings, and the glory of the God of Israel was above them. ²³The glory of the LORD went up from within the city and stopped above the mountain east of it. ²⁴The Spirit lifted me up and brought me to the exiles in Babylonia[c] in the vision given by the Spirit of God.

Then the vision I had seen went up from me, ²⁵and I told the exiles everything the LORD had shown me.

The Exile Symbolized

12 The word of the LORD came to me: ²"Son of man, you are living among a rebellious people. They have eyes to see but do not see and ears to hear but do not hear, for they are a rebellious people.

³"Therefore, son of man, pack your belongings for exile and in the daytime, as they watch, set out and go from where you are to another place. Perhaps they will understand, though they are a rebellious house. ⁴During the daytime, while they watch, bring out your belongings

---

a 15 Or *are in exile with you* (see Septuagint and Syriac)   b 15 Or *those to whom the people of Jerusalem have said, 'Stay*
c 24 Or *Chaldea*

Finding a New Heart

READ AND CONSIDER: EZEKIEL 11:16-25

"I will give them an undivided heart and put a new spirit in them; I will remove from them their heart of stone and give them a heart of flesh" (Ezekiel 11:19).

There's an old hymn that contains these poignant words: "Prone to wander, Lord, I feel it; prone to leave the God I love." Many of us experience the temptation to wander spiritually—to drift away from the God we love. Our hearts and emotions can be desperately deceptive, convincing us all too easily that we want what someone else has and not what God has planned for us. "The heart is deceitful above all things and beyond cure. Who can understand it?" (Jeremiah 17:9).

There is One, however, who *does* understand how emotionally fragmented our hearts can become, and He has promised to give us an undivided heart. What does this mean? Simply this: God promises that when we relinquish control of our hearts to Him, He will transform us from the inside out. If you think you can't give up that destructive habit, those inappropriate thoughts, that illicit relationship, then seek God. Cry out for His help. Ask Him to give you an undivided heart. God specializes in spiritual surgery on hearts that are open to Him.

God also promises to remove our hearts of stone. Have you experienced such pain and trauma in your life that you have determined never to allow yourself to be that hurt again? Has your warm heart for the things of the Lord ever become cold and distant? When we invite God's Spirit to truly take up residence within us, He lights a fire in the hearth of our hearts that cannot be put out. Ask God today to ignite a fire within your heart so that it can burn away all hardness. Ask Him to give you a new heart filled with His love.

packed for exile. Then in the evening, while they are watching, go out like those who go into exile. ⁵While they watch, dig through the wall and take your belongings out through it. ⁶Put them on your shoulder as they are watching and carry them out at dusk. Cover your face so that you cannot see the land, for I have made you a sign to the house of Israel."

⁷So I did as I was commanded. During the day I brought out my things packed for exile. Then in the evening I dug through the wall with my hands. I took my belongings out at dusk, carrying them on my shoulders while they watched.

⁸In the morning the word of the LORD came to me: ⁹"Son of man, did not that rebellious house of Israel ask you, 'What are you doing?'

¹⁰"Say to them, 'This is what the Sovereign LORD says: This oracle concerns the prince in Jerusalem and the whole house of Israel who are there.' ¹¹Say to them, 'I am a sign to you.'

"As I have done, so it will be done to them. They will go into exile as captives.

¹²"The prince among them will put his things on his shoulder at dusk and leave, and a hole will be dug in the wall for him to go through. He will cover his face so that he cannot see the land. ¹³I will spread my net for him, and he will be caught in my snare; I will bring him to Babylonia, the land of the Chaldeans, but he will not see it, and there he will die. ¹⁴I will scatter to the winds all those around him—his staff and all his troops—and I will pursue them with drawn sword.

¹⁵"They will know that I am the LORD, when I disperse them among the nations and scatter them through the countries. ¹⁶But I will spare a few of them from the

sword, famine and plague, so that in the nations where they go they may acknowledge all their detestable practices. Then they will know that I am the LORD."

17 The word of the LORD came to me: 18 "Son of man, tremble as you eat your food, and shudder in fear as you drink your water. 19 Say to the people of the land: 'This is what the Sovereign LORD says about those living in Jerusalem and in the land of Israel: They will eat their food in anxiety and drink their water in despair, for their land will be stripped of everything in it because of the violence of all who live there. 20 The inhabited towns will be laid waste and the land will be desolate. Then you will know that I am the LORD.'"

21 The word of the LORD came to me: 22 "Son of man, what is this proverb you have in the land of Israel: 'The days go by and every vision comes to nothing'? 23 Say to them, 'This is what the Sovereign LORD says: I am going to put an end to this proverb, and they will no longer quote it in Israel.' Say to them, 'The days are near when every vision will be fulfilled. 24 For there will be no more false visions or flattering divinations among the people of Israel. 25 But I the LORD will speak what I will, and it shall be fulfilled without delay. For in your days, you rebellious house, I will fulfill whatever I say, declares the Sovereign LORD.'"

26 The word of the LORD came to me: 27 "Son of man, the house of Israel is saying, 'The vision he sees is for many years from now, and he prophesies about the distant future.'

28 "Therefore say to them, 'This is what the Sovereign LORD says: None of my words will be delayed any longer; whatever I say will be fulfilled, declares the Sovereign LORD.'"

False Prophets Condemned

13 The word of the LORD came to me: 2 "Son of man, prophesy against the prophets of Israel who are now prophe-

sying. Say to those who prophesy out of their own imagination: 'Hear the word of the LORD! 3 This is what the Sovereign LORD says: Woe to the foolish[a] prophets who follow their own spirit and have seen nothing! 4 Your prophets, O Israel, are like jackals among ruins. 5 You have not gone up to the breaks in the wall to repair it for the house of Israel so that it will stand firm in the battle on the day of the LORD. 6 Their visions are false and their divinations a lie. They say, "The LORD declares," when the LORD has not sent them; yet they expect their words to be fulfilled. 7 Have you not seen false visions and uttered lying divinations when you say, "The LORD declares," though I have not spoken?

Praying Ezekiel 13:7

Help me, Lord, to never speak a word that is not from You or share a vision that is strictly from my own heart and not from Yours.

8 "'Therefore this is what the Sovereign LORD says: Because of your false words and lying visions, I am against you, declares the Sovereign LORD. 9 My hand will be against the prophets who see false visions and utter lying divinations. They will not belong to the council of my people or be listed in the records of the house of Israel, nor will they enter the land of Israel. Then you will know that I am the Sovereign LORD.

10 "'Because they lead my people astray, saying, "Peace," when there is no peace, and because, when a flimsy wall is built, they cover it with whitewash, 11 therefore tell those who cover it with whitewash that it is going to fall. Rain will come in torrents, and I will send hailstones hurtling down, and violent winds will burst forth. 12 When the wall collapses, will people not ask you, "Where is the whitewash you covered it with?"

13 "'Therefore this is what the Sovereign

---

a 3 Or wicked

LORD says: In my wrath I will unleash a violent wind, and in my anger hailstones and torrents of rain will fall with destructive fury. ¹⁴I will tear down the wall you have covered with whitewash and will level it to the ground so that its foundation will be laid bare. When it^a falls, you will be destroyed in it; and you will know that I am the LORD. ¹⁵So I will spend my wrath against the wall and against those who covered it with whitewash. I will say to you, "The wall is gone and so are those who whitewashed it, ¹⁶those prophets of Israel who prophesied to Jerusalem and saw visions of peace for her when there was no peace, declares the Sovereign LORD."'

¹⁷"Now, son of man, set your face against the daughters of your people who prophesy out of their own imagination. Prophesy against them ¹⁸and say, 'This is what the Sovereign LORD says: Woe to the women who sew magic charms on all their wrists and make veils of various lengths for their heads in order to ensnare people. Will you ensnare the lives of my people but preserve your own? ¹⁹You have profaned me among my people for a few handfuls of barley and scraps of bread. By lying to my people, who listen to lies, you have killed those who should not have died and have spared those who should not live.

²⁰"'Therefore this is what the Sovereign LORD says: I am against your magic charms with which you ensnare people like birds and I will tear them from your arms; I will set free the people that you ensnare like birds. ²¹I will tear off your veils and save my people from your hands, and they will no longer fall prey to your power. Then you will know that I am the LORD. ²²Because you disheartened the righteous with your lies, when I had brought them no grief, and because you encouraged the wicked not to turn from their evil ways and so save their lives, ²³therefore you will no longer see false

visions or practice divination. I will save my people from your hands. And then you will know that I am the LORD.'"

Idolaters Condemned

14 Some of the elders of Israel came to me and sat down in front of me. ²Then the word of the LORD came to me: ³"Son of man, these men have set up idols in their hearts and put wicked stumbling blocks before their faces. Should I let them inquire of me at all? ⁴Therefore speak to them and tell them, 'This is what the Sovereign LORD says: When any Israelite sets up idols in his heart and puts a wicked stumbling block before his face and then goes to a prophet, I the LORD will answer him myself in keeping with his great idolatry. ⁵I will do this to recapture the hearts of the people of Israel, who have all deserted me for their idols.'

⁶"Therefore say to the house of Israel, 'This is what the Sovereign LORD says: Repent! Turn from your idols and renounce all your detestable practices!

Praying Ezekiel 14:6
God, I pray that I will turn away from any idol in my life and not allow myself to look on anything that is an abomination to You.

⁷"'When any Israelite or any alien living in Israel separates himself from me and sets up idols in his heart and puts a wicked stumbling block before his face and then goes to a prophet to inquire of me, I the LORD will answer him myself. ⁸I will set my face against that man and make him an example and a byword. I will cut him off from my people. Then you will know that I am the LORD.

⁹"'And if the prophet is enticed to utter a prophecy, I the LORD have enticed that prophet, and I will stretch out my hand against him and destroy him from among my people Israel. ¹⁰They will bear their guilt—the prophet will be as guilty

as the one who consults him. [11] Then the people of Israel will no longer stray from me, nor will they defile themselves anymore with all their sins. They will be my people, and I will be their God, declares the Sovereign LORD.'"

Judgment Inescapable

[12] The word of the LORD came to me: [13] "Son of man, if a country sins against me by being unfaithful and I stretch out my hand against it to cut off its food supply and send famine upon it and kill its men and their animals, [14] even if these three men—Noah, Daniel[a] and Job— were in it, they could save only themselves by their righteousness, declares the Sovereign LORD.

[15] "Or if I send wild beasts through that country and they leave it childless and it becomes desolate so that no one can pass through it because of the beasts, [16] as surely as I live, declares the Sovereign LORD, even if these three men were in it, they could not save their own sons or daughters. They alone would be saved, but the land would be desolate.

[17] "Or if I bring a sword against that country and say, 'Let the sword pass throughout the land,' and I kill its men and their animals, [18] as surely as I live, declares the Sovereign LORD, even if these three men were in it, they could not save their own sons or daughters. They alone would be saved.

[19] "Or if I send a plague into that land and pour out my wrath upon it through bloodshed, killing its men and their animals, [20] as surely as I live, declares the Sovereign LORD, even if Noah, Daniel and Job were in it, they could save neither son nor daughter. They would save only themselves by their righteousness.

[21] "For this is what the Sovereign LORD says: How much worse will it be when I send against Jerusalem my four dreadful judgments—sword and famine and wild beasts and plague—to kill its men and their animals! [22] Yet there will be some survivors—sons and daughters who will be brought out of it. They will come to you, and when you see their conduct and their actions, you will be consoled regarding the disaster I have brought upon Jerusalem—every disaster I have brought upon it. [23] You will be consoled when you see their conduct and their actions, for you will know that I have done nothing in it without cause, declares the Sovereign LORD."

Jerusalem, A Useless Vine

15 The word of the LORD came to me: [2] "Son of man, how is the wood of a vine better than that of a branch on any of the trees in the forest? [3] Is wood ever taken from it to make anything useful? Do they make pegs from it to hang things on? [4] And after it is thrown on the fire as fuel and the fire burns both ends and chars the middle, is it then useful for anything? [5] If it was not useful for anything when it was whole, how much less can it be made into something useful when the fire has burned it and it is charred?

[6] "Therefore this is what the Sovereign LORD says: As I have given the wood of the vine among the trees of the forest as fuel for the fire, so will I treat the people living in Jerusalem. [7] I will set my face against them. Although they have come out of the fire, the fire will yet consume them. And when I set my face against them, you will know that I am the LORD. [8] I will make the land desolate because they have been unfaithful, declares the Sovereign LORD."

An Allegory of Unfaithful Jerusalem

16 The word of the LORD came to me: [2] "Son of man, confront Jerusalem with her detestable practices [3] and say, 'This is what the Sovereign LORD says to Jerusalem: Your ancestry and birth were in the land of the Canaanites; your father was an Amorite and your mother a Hittite. [4] On the day you were born your cord was not cut, nor were you washed with

---

[a] 14 Or Danel; the Hebrew spelling may suggest a person other than the prophet Daniel; also in verse 20.

water to make you clean, nor were you rubbed with salt or wrapped in cloths. [5]No one looked on you with pity or had compassion enough to do any of these things for you. Rather, you were thrown out into the open field, for on the day you were born you were despised.

[6]"'Then I passed by and saw you kicking about in your blood, and as you lay there in your blood I said to you, "Live!"[a] [7]I made you grow like a plant of the field. You grew up and developed and became the most beautiful of jewels.[b] Your breasts were formed and your hair grew, you who were naked and bare.

[8]"'Later I passed by, and when I looked at you and saw that you were old enough for love, I spread the corner of my garment over you and covered your nakedness. I gave you my solemn oath and entered into a covenant with you, declares the Sovereign LORD, and you became mine.

[9]"'I bathed[c] you with water and washed the blood from you and put ointments on you. [10]I clothed you with an embroidered dress and put leather sandals on you. I dressed you in fine linen and covered you with costly garments. [11]I adorned you with jewelry: I put bracelets on your arms and a necklace around your neck, [12]and I put a ring on your nose, earrings on your ears and a beautiful crown on your head. [13]So you were adorned with gold and silver; your clothes were of fine linen and costly fabric and embroidered cloth. Your food was fine flour, honey and olive oil. You became very beautiful and rose to be a queen. [14]And your fame spread among the nations on account of your beauty, because the splendor I had given you made your beauty perfect, declares the Sovereign LORD.

[15]"'But you trusted in your beauty and used your fame to become a prostitute. You lavished your favors on anyone who passed by and your beauty became

Praying Ezekiel 16:14-15

Dear God, I ask You to keep my heart from ever trusting in the good things You give me instead of trusting in You, the Giver of all that I have.

his.[d] [16]You took some of your garments to make gaudy high places, where you carried on your prostitution. Such things should not happen, nor should they ever occur. [17]You also took the fine jewelry I gave you, the jewelry made of my gold and silver, and you made for yourself male idols and engaged in prostitution with them. [18]And you took your embroidered clothes to put on them, and you offered my oil and incense before them. [19]Also the food I provided for you—the fine flour, olive oil and honey I gave you to eat—you offered as fragrant incense before them. That is what happened, declares the Sovereign LORD.

[20]"'And you took your sons and daughters whom you bore to me and sacrificed them as food to the idols. Was your prostitution not enough? [21]You slaughtered my children and sacrificed them[e] to the idols. [22]In all your detestable practices and your prostitution you did not remember the days of your youth, when you were naked and bare, kicking about in your blood.

[23]"'Woe! Woe to you, declares the Sovereign LORD. In addition to all your other wickedness, [24]you built a mound for yourself and made a lofty shrine in every public square. [25]At the head of every street you built your lofty shrines and degraded your beauty, offering your body with increasing promiscuity to anyone who passed by. [26]You engaged in prostitution with the Egyptians, your lustful neighbors, and provoked me to anger with your increasing promiscuity. [27]So I stretched out my hand against you and reduced your territory; I gave you over to the greed of your enemies, the daughters

---

[a]6 A few Hebrew manuscripts, Septuagint and Syriac; most Hebrew manuscripts *"Live!" And as you lay there in your blood I said to you, "Live!"* [b]7 Or *became mature* [c]9 Or *I had bathed* [d]15 Most Hebrew manuscripts; one Hebrew manuscript (see some Septuagint manuscripts) *by. Such a thing should not happen* [e]21 Or *and made them pass through the fire*

of the Philistines, who were shocked by your lewd conduct. 28 You engaged in prostitution with the Assyrians too, because you were insatiable; and even after that, you still were not satisfied. 29 Then you increased your promiscuity to include Babylonia,[a] a land of merchants, but even with this you were not satisfied.

30 "'How weak-willed you are, declares the Sovereign LORD, when you do all these things, acting like a brazen prostitute! 31 When you built your mounds at the head of every street and made your lofty shrines in every public square, you were unlike a prostitute, because you scorned payment.

32 "'You adulterous wife! You prefer strangers to your own husband! 33 Every prostitute receives a fee, but you give gifts to all your lovers, bribing them to come to you from everywhere for your illicit favors. 34 So in your prostitution you are the opposite of others; no one runs after you for your favors. You are the very opposite, for you give payment and none is given to you.

35 "'Therefore, you prostitute, hear the word of the LORD! 36 This is what the Sovereign LORD says: Because you poured out your wealth[b] and exposed your nakedness in your promiscuity with your lovers, and because of all your detestable idols, and because you gave them your children's blood, 37 therefore I am going to gather all your lovers, with whom you found pleasure, those you loved as well as those you hated. I will gather them against you from all around and will strip you in front of them, and they will see all your nakedness. 38 I will sentence you to the punishment of women who commit adultery and who shed blood; I will bring upon you the blood vengeance of my wrath and jealous anger. 39 Then I will hand you over to your lovers, and they will tear down your mounds and destroy your lofty shrines. They will strip you of your clothes and take your fine jewelry

and leave you naked and bare. 40 They will bring a mob against you, who will stone you and hack you to pieces with their swords. 41 They will burn down your houses and inflict punishment on you in the sight of many women. I will put a stop to your prostitution, and you will no longer pay your lovers. 42 Then my wrath against you will subside and my jealous anger will turn away from you; I will be calm and no longer angry.

43 "'Because you did not remember the days of your youth but enraged me with all these things, I will surely bring down on your head what you have done, declares the Sovereign LORD. Did you not add lewdness to all your other detestable practices?

44 "'Everyone who quotes proverbs will quote this proverb about you: "Like mother, like daughter." 45 You are a true daughter of your mother, who despised her husband and her children; and you are a true sister of your sisters, who despised their husbands and their children. Your mother was a Hittite and your father an Amorite. 46 Your older sister was Samaria, who lived to the north of you with her daughters; and your younger sister, who lived to the south of you with her daughters, was Sodom. 47 You not only walked in their ways and copied their detestable practices, but in all your ways you soon became more depraved than they. 48 As surely as I live, declares the Sovereign LORD, your sister Sodom and her daughters never did what you and your daughters have done.

Praying Ezekiel 16:49

Lord, help me to never get so full of myself and what I have that I fail to share it with the poor and needy.

49 "'Now this was the sin of your sister Sodom: She and her daughters were arrogant, overfed and unconcerned; they did not help the poor and needy. 50 They

---

[a] 29 Or *Chaldea*   [b] 36 Or *lust*

were haughty and did detestable things before me. Therefore I did away with them as you have seen. 51Samaria did not commit half the sins you did. You have done more detestable things than they, and have made your sisters seem righteous by all these things you have done. 52Bear your disgrace, for you have furnished some justification for your sisters. Because your sins were more vile than theirs, they appear more righteous than you. So then, be ashamed and bear your disgrace, for you have made your sisters appear righteous.

53"However, I will restore the fortunes of Sodom and her daughters and of Samaria and her daughters, and your fortunes along with them, 54so that you may bear your disgrace and be ashamed of all you have done in giving them comfort. 55And your sisters, Sodom with her daughters and Samaria with her daughters, will return to what they were before; and you and your daughters will return to what you were before. 56You would not even mention your sister Sodom in the day of your pride, 57before your wickedness was uncovered. Even so, you are now scorned by the daughters of Edom[a] and all her neighbors and the daughters of the Philistines—all those around you who despise you. 58You will bear the consequences of your lewdness and your detestable practices, declares the LORD.

59"'This is what the Sovereign LORD says: I will deal with you as you deserve, because you have despised my oath by breaking the covenant. 60Yet I will remember the covenant I made with you in the days of your youth, and I will establish an everlasting covenant with you. 61Then you will remember your ways and be ashamed when you receive your sisters, both those who are older than you and those who are younger. I will give them to you as daughters, but not on the basis of my covenant with you. 62So I will establish my covenant with you, and you

will know that I am the LORD. 63Then, when I make atonement for you for all you have done, you will remember and be ashamed and never again open your mouth because of your humiliation, declares the Sovereign LORD.'"

Two Eagles and a Vine

17 The word of the LORD came to me: 2"Son of man, set forth an allegory and tell the house of Israel a parable. 3Say to them, 'This is what the Sovereign LORD says: A great eagle with powerful wings, long feathers and full plumage of varied colors came to Lebanon. Taking hold of the top of a cedar, 4he broke off its topmost shoot and carried it away to a land of merchants, where he planted it in a city of traders.

5"'He took some of the seed of your land and put it in fertile soil. He planted it like a willow by abundant water, 6and it sprouted and became a low, spreading vine. Its branches turned toward him, but its roots remained under it. So it became a vine and produced branches and put out leafy boughs.

7"'But there was another great eagle with powerful wings and full plumage. The vine now sent out its roots toward him from the plot where it was planted and stretched out its branches to him for water. 8It had been planted in good soil by abundant water so that it would produce branches, bear fruit and become a splendid vine.'

9"Say to them, 'This is what the Sovereign LORD says: Will it thrive? Will it not be uprooted and stripped of its fruit so that it withers? All its new growth will wither. It will not take a strong arm or many people to pull it up by the roots. 10Even if it is transplanted, will it thrive? Will it not wither completely when the east wind strikes it—wither away in the plot where it grew?'"

11Then the word of the LORD came to me: 12"Say to this rebellious house, 'Do you not know what these things mean?'

---

[a] 57 Many Hebrew manuscripts and Syriac; most Hebrew manuscripts, Septuagint and Vulgate *Aram*

Say to them: 'The king of Babylon went to Jerusalem and carried off her king and her nobles, bringing them back with him to Babylon. 13Then he took a member of the royal family and made a treaty with him, putting him under oath. He also carried away the leading men of the land, 14so that the kingdom would be brought low, unable to rise again, surviving only by keeping his treaty. 15But the king rebelled against him by sending his envoys to Egypt to get horses and a large army. Will he succeed? Will he who does such things escape? Will he break the treaty and yet escape?

16"'As surely as I live, declares the Sovereign LORD, he shall die in Babylon, in the land of the king who put him on the throne, whose oath he despised and whose treaty he broke. 17Pharaoh with his mighty army and great horde will be of no help to him in war, when ramps are built and siege works erected to destroy many lives. 18He despised the oath by breaking the covenant. Because he had given his hand in pledge and yet did all these things, he shall not escape.

19"'Therefore this is what the Sovereign LORD says: As surely as I live, I will bring down on his head my oath that he despised and my covenant that he broke. 20I will spread my net for him, and he will be caught in my snare. I will bring him to Babylon and execute judgment upon him there because he was unfaithful to me. 21All his fleeing troops will fall by the sword, and the survivors will be scattered to the winds. Then you will know that I the LORD have spoken.

22"'This is what the Sovereign LORD says: I myself will take a shoot from the very top of a cedar and plant it; I will break off a tender sprig from its topmost shoots and plant it on a high and lofty mountain. 23On the mountain heights of Israel I will plant it; it will produce branches and bear fruit and become a splendid cedar. Birds of every kind will nest in it; they will find shelter in the shade of its branches. 24All the trees of the field will know that I the LORD bring down the tall tree and make the low tree grow tall. I dry up the green tree and make the dry tree flourish.

"'I the LORD have spoken, and I will do it.'"

The Soul Who Sins Will Die

18 The word of the LORD came to me: 2"What do you people mean by quoting this proverb about the land of Israel:

"'The fathers eat sour grapes,
    and the children's teeth are set on
      edge'?

3"As surely as I live, declares the Sovereign LORD, you will no longer quote this proverb in Israel. 4For every living soul belongs to me, the father as well as the son—both alike belong to me. The soul who sins is the one who will die.

5"Suppose there is a righteous man
    who does what is just and right.
6He does not eat at the mountain
      shrines
    or look to the idols of the house of
      Israel.
He does not defile his neighbor's wife
    or lie with a woman during her
      period.
7He does not oppress anyone,
    but returns what he took in pledge
      for a loan.
He does not commit robbery
    but gives his food to the hungry
    and provides clothing for the
      naked.
8He does not lend at usury
    or take excessive interest.[a]
He withholds his hand from doing
      wrong
    and judges fairly between man and
      man.
9He follows my decrees
    and faithfully keeps my laws.

---

[a] 8 Or take interest; similarly in verses 13 and 17

That man is righteous;
   he will surely live,
         declares the Sovereign LORD.

¹⁰"Suppose he has a violent son, who sheds blood or does any of these other things[a] ¹¹(though the father has done none of them):

"He eats at the mountain shrines.
He defiles his neighbor's wife.
¹²He oppresses the poor and needy.
He commits robbery.
He does not return what he took in
      pledge.
He looks to the idols.
He does detestable things.
¹³He lends at usury and takes excessive
      interest.

Will such a man live? He will not! Because he has done all these detestable things, he will surely be put to death and his blood will be on his own head.

¹⁴"But suppose this son has a son who sees all the sins his father commits, and though he sees them, he does not do such things:

¹⁵"He does not eat at the mountain
      shrines
   or look to the idols of the house of
      Israel.
He does not defile his neighbor's wife.
¹⁶He does not oppress anyone
   or require a pledge for a loan.
He does not commit robbery
   but gives his food to the hungry
   and provides clothing for the
      naked.
¹⁷He withholds his hand from sin[b]
   and takes no usury or excessive
      interest.
He keeps my laws and follows my
      decrees.

He will not die for his father's sin; he will surely live. ¹⁸But his father will die for his own sin, because he practiced extortion, robbed his brother and did what was wrong among his people.

¹⁹"Yet you ask, 'Why does the son not share the guilt of his father?' Since the son has done what is just and right and has been careful to keep all my decrees, he will surely live. ²⁰The soul who sins is the one who will die. The son will not share the guilt of the father, nor will the father share the guilt of the son. The righteousness of the righteous man will be credited to him, and the wickedness of the wicked will be charged against him.

²¹"But if a wicked man turns away from all the sins he has committed and keeps all my decrees and does what is just and right, he will surely live; he will not die. ²²None of the offenses he has committed will be remembered against him. Because of the righteous things he has done, he will live. ²³Do I take any pleasure in the death of the wicked? declares the Sovereign LORD. Rather, am I not pleased when they turn from their ways and live?

²⁴"But if a righteous man turns from his righteousness and commits sin and does the same detestable things the wicked man does, will he live? None of the righteous things he has done will be remembered. Because of the unfaithfulness he is guilty of and because of the sins he has committed, he will die.

²⁵"Yet you say, 'The way of the Lord is not just.' Hear, O house of Israel: Is my way unjust? Is it not your ways that are unjust? ²⁶If a righteous man turns from his righteousness and commits sin, he will die for it; because of the sin he has committed he will die. ²⁷But if a wicked man turns away from the wickedness he has committed and does what is just and right, he will save his life. ²⁸Because he considers all the offenses he has committed and turns away from them, he will surely live; he will not die. ²⁹Yet the house of Israel says, 'The way of the Lord is not just.' Are my ways unjust, O house of Israel? Is it not your ways that are unjust?

---

[a] 10 Or things to a brother   [b] 17 Septuagint (see also verse 8); Hebrew from the poor

30"Therefore, O house of Israel, I will judge you, each one according to his ways, declares the Sovereign LORD. Repent! Turn away from all your offenses; then sin will not be your downfall. 31Rid yourselves of all the offenses you have committed, and get a new heart and a new spirit. Why will you die, O house of Israel? 32For I take no pleasure in the death of anyone, declares the Sovereign LORD. Repent and live!

A Lament for Israel's Princes

19 "Take up a lament concerning the princes of Israel 2and say:

"'What a lioness was your mother
among the lions!
She lay down among the young lions
and reared her cubs.

3She brought up one of her cubs,
and he became a strong lion.
He learned to tear the prey
and he devoured men.
4The nations heard about him,
and he was trapped in their pit.
They led him with hooks
to the land of Egypt.

5"'When she saw her hope unfulfilled,
her expectation gone,
she took another of her cubs
and made him a strong lion.
6He prowled among the lions,
for he was now a strong lion.
He learned to tear the prey
and he devoured men.
7He broke down[a] their strongholds
and devastated their towns.

---

a 7 Targum (see Septuagint); Hebrew *He knew*

GOING *deeper*

The Promise of a Fresh Start

READ AND CONSIDER: EZEKIEL 18

"Rid yourselves of all the offenses you have committed, and get a new heart and a new spirit. Why will you die, O house of Israel?" (Ezekiel 18:31).

How do we get rid of each and every transgression from our lives? How can we divest ourselves of those sins of which we're not even aware? How do we get free of attitudes and actions we don't yet even recognize as being wrong? The answer is to ask God for it.

Scripture teaches that none of us is perfect. "All have sinned and fall short of the glory of God" (Romans 3:23). Because of our fallen nature, we need to ask God to bring to light any hidden sins that have taken root in our hearts so they can be dealt with now rather than later, when the consequences may be far more serious. God will do that, for "He knows the secrets of the heart" (Psalm 44:21). We've all heard stories of the "nice, likeable man" who beats his wife, abuses his children, or goes on a killing spree. You can be sure that he was a man who had hidden sin in his heart. We can be just as sure that any hidden sin in us will eventually display itself in an undesirable way. The time to catch it is now. "Turn away from all your offenses; then sin will not be your downfall" (Ezekiel 18:30). Ask God to bring any hidden sin to light so there won't be a physical or emotional price to pay for it.

Sin leads to death, but repentance leads to life. "For the wages of sin is death, but the gift of God is eternal life" (Romans 6:23). We don't confess our sins in order for God to know about them. He already knows. Confession is a chance for us to clear the slate. Repentance is an opportunity for us to start over. We need to do both! We need a new heart and a new spirit. We need a fresh start—today and every day.

The land and all who were in it
  were terrified by his roaring.
⁸ Then the nations came against him,
  those from regions round about.
They spread their net for him,
  and he was trapped in their pit.
⁹ With hooks they pulled him into a
    cage
  and brought him to the king of
    Babylon.
They put him in prison,
  so his roar was heard no longer
  on the mountains of Israel.

¹⁰ " 'Your mother was like a vine in
    your vineyard[a]
  planted by the water;
it was fruitful and full of branches
  because of abundant water.
¹¹ Its branches were strong,
  fit for a ruler's scepter.
It towered high
  above the thick foliage,
conspicuous for its height
  and for its many branches.
¹² But it was uprooted in fury
  and thrown to the ground.
The east wind made it shrivel,
  it was stripped of its fruit;
its strong branches withered
  and fire consumed them.
¹³ Now it is planted in the desert,
  in a dry and thirsty land.
¹⁴ Fire spread from one of its main[b]
    branches
  and consumed its fruit.
No strong branch is left on it
  fit for a ruler's scepter.'

This is a lament and is to be used as a lament."

Rebellious Israel

20 In the seventh year, in the fifth month on the tenth day, some of the elders of Israel came to inquire of the LORD, and they sat down in front of me.

² Then the word of the LORD came to me: ³ "Son of man, speak to the elders of Israel and say to them, 'This is what the Sovereign LORD says: Have you come to inquire of me? As surely as I live, I will not let you inquire of me, declares the Sovereign LORD.'

⁴ "Will you judge them? Will you judge them, son of man? Then confront them with the detestable practices of their fathers ⁵ and say to them: 'This is what the Sovereign LORD says: On the day I chose Israel, I swore with uplifted hand to the descendants of the house of Jacob and revealed myself to them in Egypt. With uplifted hand I said to them, "I am the LORD your God." ⁶ On that day I swore to them that I would bring them out of Egypt into a land I had searched out for them, a land flowing with milk and honey, the most beautiful of all lands. ⁷ And I said to them, "Each of you, get rid of the vile images you have set your eyes on, and do not defile yourselves with the idols of Egypt. I am the LORD your God."

⁸ " 'But they rebelled against me and would not listen to me; they did not get rid of the vile images they had set their eyes on, nor did they forsake the idols of Egypt. So I said I would pour out my wrath on them and spend my anger against them in Egypt. ⁹ But for the sake of my name I did what would keep it from being profaned in the eyes of the nations they lived among and in whose sight I had revealed myself to the Israelites by bringing them out of Egypt. ¹⁰ Therefore I led them out of Egypt and brought them into the desert. ¹¹ I gave them my decrees and made known to them my laws, for the man who obeys them will live by them. ¹² Also I gave them my Sabbaths as a sign between us, so they would know that I the LORD made them holy.

¹³ " 'Yet the people of Israel rebelled against me in the desert. They did not follow my decrees but rejected my laws—although the man who obeys them will live by them—and they utterly desecrated my Sabbaths. So I said I would pour out my wrath on them and destroy them in

---

[a] 10 Two Hebrew manuscripts; most Hebrew manuscripts *your blood*   [b] 14 Or *from under its*

the desert. 14But for the sake of my name I did what would keep it from being profaned in the eyes of the nations in whose sight I had brought them out. 15Also with uplifted hand I swore to them in the desert that I would not bring them into the land I had given them—a land flowing with milk and honey, most beautiful of all lands— 16because they rejected my laws and did not follow my decrees and desecrated my Sabbaths. For their hearts were devoted to their idols. 17Yet I looked on them with pity and did not destroy them or put an end to them in the desert. 18I said to their children in the desert, "Do not follow the statutes of your fathers or keep their laws or defile yourselves with their idols. 19I am the LORD your God; follow my decrees and be careful to keep my laws. 20Keep my Sabbaths holy, that they may be a sign between us. Then you will know that I am the LORD your God."

21"But the children rebelled against me: They did not follow my decrees, they were not careful to keep my laws—although the man who obeys them will live by them—and they desecrated my Sabbaths. So I said I would pour out my wrath on them and spend my anger against them in the desert. 22But I withheld my hand, and for the sake of my name I did what would keep it from being profaned in the eyes of the nations in whose sight I had brought them out. 23Also with uplifted hand I swore to them in the desert that I would disperse them among the nations and scatter them through the countries, 24because they had not obeyed my laws but had rejected my decrees and desecrated my Sabbaths, and their eyes lusted after their fathers' idols. 25I also gave them over to statutes that were not good and laws they could not live by; 26I let them become defiled through their gifts—the sacrifice of every firstborn[a]—that I might fill them with horror so they would know that I am the LORD.'

27"Therefore, son of man, speak to the people of Israel and say to them, 'This is what the Sovereign LORD says: In this also your fathers blasphemed me by forsaking me: 28When I brought them into the land I had sworn to give them and they saw any high hill or any leafy tree, there they offered their sacrifices, made offerings that provoked me to anger, presented their fragrant incense and poured out their drink offerings. 29Then I said to them: What is this high place you go to?'" (It is called Bamah[b] to this day.)

Judgment and Restoration

30"Therefore say to the house of Israel: 'This is what the Sovereign LORD says: Will you defile yourselves the way your fathers did and lust after their vile images? 31When you offer your gifts—the sacrifice of your sons in[c] the fire—you continue to defile yourselves with all your idols to this day. Am I to let you inquire of me, O house of Israel? As surely as I live, declares the Sovereign LORD, I will not let you inquire of me.

32"'You say, "We want to be like the nations, like the peoples of the world, who serve wood and stone." But what you have in mind will never happen. 33As surely as I live, declares the Sovereign LORD, I will rule over you with a mighty hand and an outstretched arm and with outpoured wrath. 34I will bring you from the nations and gather you from the countries where you have been scattered—with a mighty hand and an outstretched arm and with outpoured wrath. 35I will bring you into the desert of the nations and there, face to face, I will execute judgment upon you. 36As I judged your fathers in the desert of the land of Egypt, so I will judge you, declares the Sovereign LORD. 37I will take note of you as you pass under my rod, and I will bring you into the bond of the covenant. 38I will purge you of those who revolt and rebel

---

a 26 Or —making every firstborn pass through the fire, b 29 Bamah means high place. c 31 Or —making your sons pass through against me. Although I will bring them out of the land where they are living, yet they will not enter the land of Israel. Then you will know that I am the LORD.

³⁹"'As for you, O house of Israel, this is what the Sovereign LORD says: Go and serve your idols, every one of you! But afterward you will surely listen to me and no longer profane my holy name with your gifts and idols. ⁴⁰For on my holy mountain, the high mountain of Israel, declares the Sovereign LORD, there in the land the entire house of Israel will serve me, and there I will accept them. There I will require your offerings and your choice gifts,ᵃ along with all your holy sacrifices. ⁴¹I will accept you as fragrant incense when I bring you out from the nations and gather you from the countries where you have been scattered, and I will show myself holy among you in the sight of the nations. ⁴²Then you will know that I am the LORD, when I bring you into the land of Israel, the land I had sworn with uplifted hand to give to your fathers. ⁴³There you will remember your conduct and all the actions by which you have defiled yourselves, and you will loathe yourselves for all the evil you have done. ⁴⁴You will know that I am the LORD, when I deal with you for my name's sake and not according to your evil ways and your corrupt practices, O house of Israel, declares the Sovereign LORD.'"

ᵃ 40 Or and the gifts of your firstfruits

GOING *deeper*

Getting Free of the Burden of Sin

READ AND CONSIDER: EZEKIEL 20:30-44

"There you will remember your conduct and all the actions by which you have defiled your-selves, and you will loathe yourselves for all the evil you have done" (Ezekiel 20:43).

If you have children of your own or you work with children in any capacity, you know the importance of insisting that they admit when they've done wrong. If a child lies or steals or cheats and is never held accountable for his actions, he will be tempted to see what more he can get away with the next time.

The same principle holds true for us as adults. Just as confession and repentance are two life principles we insist upon for our children, they are equally important for us as children of God. Unconfessed sin puts a wall between us and God. Repentance, which literally means "turning away and deciding not to do it again," is manifested when we say, in effect, "I did this, I'm sorry about it, and I'm not going to do it again." If sin is not confessed and repented of in that way, we can't be free of the bondage that goes along with it.

King David knew all about unconfessed sin when he wrote, "When I kept silent, my bones wasted away through my groaning all day long . . . Then I acknowledged my sin to you and did not cover up my iniquity. I said, 'I will confess my transgressions to the LORD'—and you forgave the guilt of my sin" (Psalm 32:3,5).

What God said to the Israelites who disobeyed Him and didn't repent was that they would remember their evil and hate themselves for it. We all have experienced that sense of shame when we remember some words we've said or actions we've done that we now deeply regret. But even though we may never forget those things, we can still be set free from the bondage and the burden of guilt by confessing and repenting of those sins. This allows God to take away the burden and make us new.

Prophecy Against the South

45The word of the LORD came to me: 46"Son of man, set your face toward the south; preach against the south and prophesy against the forest of the southland. 47Say to the southern forest: 'Hear the word of the LORD. This is what the Sovereign LORD says: I am about to set fire to you, and it will consume all your trees, both green and dry. The blazing flame will not be quenched, and every face from south to north will be scorched by it. 48Everyone will see that I the LORD have kindled it; it will not be quenched.'"

49Then I said, "Ah, Sovereign LORD! They are saying of me, 'Isn't he just telling parables?'"

Babylon, God's Sword of Judgment

21 The word of the LORD came to me: 2"Son of man, set your face against Jerusalem and preach against the sanctuary. Prophesy against the land of Israel 3and say to her: 'This is what the LORD says: I am against you. I will draw my sword from its scabbard and cut off from you both the righteous and the wicked. 4Because I am going to cut off the righteous and the wicked, my sword will be unsheathed against everyone from south to north. 5Then all people will know that I the LORD have drawn my sword from its scabbard; it will not return again.'

6"Therefore groan, son of man! Groan before them with broken heart and bitter grief. 7And when they ask you, 'Why are you groaning?' you shall say, 'Because of the news that is coming. Every heart will melt and every hand go limp; every spirit will become faint and every knee become as weak as water.' It is coming! It will surely take place, declares the Sovereign LORD."

8The word of the LORD came to me: 9"Son of man, prophesy and say, 'This is what the Lord says:

"'A sword, a sword,
    sharpened and polished—
10sharpened for the slaughter,
    polished to flash like lightning!

"'Shall we rejoice in the scepter of my son ⌊Judah⌋? The sword despises every such stick.

11"'The sword is appointed to be
        polished,
    to be grasped with the hand;
it is sharpened and polished,
    made ready for the hand of the
        slayer.
12Cry out and wail, son of man,
    for it is against my people;
    it is against all the princes of Israel.
They are thrown to the sword
    along with my people.
Therefore beat your breast.

13"'Testing will surely come. And what if the scepter ⌊of Judah⌋, which the sword despises, does not continue? declares the Sovereign LORD.'

14"So then, son of man, prophesy
    and strike your hands together.
Let the sword strike twice,
    even three times.
It is a sword for slaughter—
    a sword for great slaughter,
    closing in on them from every side.
15So that hearts may melt
    and the fallen be many,
I have stationed the sword for
        slaughter[a]
    at all their gates.
Oh! It is made to flash like lightning,
    it is grasped for slaughter.
16O sword, slash to the right,
    then to the left,
    wherever your blade is turned.
17I too will strike my hands together,
    and my wrath will subside.
I the LORD have spoken."

18The word of the LORD came to me: 19"Son of man, mark out two roads for the sword of the king of Babylon to take, both starting from the same country. Make a signpost where the road branches

---

a 15 Septuagint; the meaning of the Hebrew for this word is uncertain.

off to the city. ²⁰Mark out one road for the sword to come against Rabbah of the Ammonites and another against Judah and fortified Jerusalem. ²¹For the king of Babylon will stop at the fork in the road, at the junction of the two roads, to seek an omen: He will cast lots with arrows, he will consult his idols, he will examine the liver. ²²Into his right hand will come the lot for Jerusalem, where he is to set up battering rams, to give the command to slaughter, to sound the battle cry, to set battering rams against the gates, to build a ramp and to erect siege works. ²³It will seem like a false omen to those who have sworn allegiance to him, but he will remind them of their guilt and take them captive.

²⁴"Therefore this is what the Sovereign LORD says: 'Because you people have brought to mind your guilt by your open rebellion, revealing your sins in all that you do—because you have done this, you will be taken captive.

²⁵"'O profane and wicked prince of Israel, whose day has come, whose time of punishment has reached its climax, ²⁶this is what the Sovereign LORD says: Take off the turban, remove the crown. It will not be as it was: The lowly will be exalted and the exalted will be brought low. ²⁷A ruin! A ruin! I will make it a ruin! It will not be restored until he comes to whom it rightfully belongs; to him I will give it.'

²⁸"And you, son of man, prophesy and say, 'This is what the Sovereign LORD says about the Ammonites and their insults:

"'A sword, a sword,
    drawn for the slaughter,
polished to consume
    and to flash like lightning!
²⁹Despite false visions concerning you
    and lying divinations about you,
it will be laid on the necks
    of the wicked who are to be slain,
whose day has come,
    whose time of punishment has
        reached its climax.

³⁰Return the sword to its scabbard.
    In the place where you were
        created,
in the land of your ancestry,
    I will judge you.
³¹I will pour out my wrath upon you
    and breathe out my fiery anger
        against you;
I will hand you over to brutal men,
    men skilled in destruction.
³²You will be fuel for the fire,
    your blood will be shed in your
        land,
you will be remembered no more;
    for I the LORD have spoken.'"

Jerusalem's Sins

22 The word of the LORD came to me: ²"Son of man, will you judge her? Will you judge this city of bloodshed? Then confront her with all her detestable practices ³and say: 'This is what the Sovereign LORD says: O city that brings on herself doom by shedding blood in her midst and defiles herself by making idols, ⁴you have become guilty because of the blood you have shed and have become defiled by the idols you have made. You have brought your days to a close, and the end of your years has come. Therefore I will make you an object of scorn to the nations and a laughingstock to all the countries. ⁵Those who are near and those who are far away will mock you, O infamous city, full of turmoil.

⁶"'See how each of the princes of Israel who are in you uses his power to shed blood. ⁷In you they have treated father and mother with contempt; in you they have oppressed the alien and mistreated the fatherless and the widow. ⁸You have despised my holy things and desecrated my Sabbaths. ⁹In you are slanderous men bent on shedding blood; in you are those who eat at the mountain shrines and commit lewd acts. ¹⁰In you are those who dishonor their fathers' bed; in you are those who violate women during their period, when they are ceremonially unclean. ¹¹In you one

man commits a detestable offense with his neighbor's wife, another shamefully defiles his daughter-in-law, and another violates his sister, his own father's daughter. 12In you men accept bribes to shed blood; you take usury and excessive interest[a] and make unjust gain from your neighbors by extortion. And you have forgotten me, declares the Sovereign LORD.

13"'I will surely strike my hands together at the unjust gain you have made and at the blood you have shed in your midst. 14Will your courage endure or your hands be strong in the day I deal with you? I the LORD have spoken, and I will do it. 15I will disperse you among the nations and scatter you through the countries; and I will put an end to your uncleanness. 16When you have been defiled[b] in the eyes of the nations, you will know that I am the LORD.'"

17Then the word of the LORD came to me: 18"Son of man, the house of Israel has become dross to me; all of them are the copper, tin, iron and lead left inside a furnace. They are but the dross of silver. 19Therefore this is what the Sovereign LORD says: 'Because you have all become dross, I will gather you into Jerusalem. 20As men gather silver, copper, iron, lead and tin into a furnace to melt it with a fiery blast, so will I gather you in my anger and my wrath and put you inside the city and melt you. 21I will gather you and

---

a 12 Or usury and interest   b 16 Or When I have allotted you your inheritance

---

GOING deeper

Standing in the Gap for Our Nation

READ AND CONSIDER: EZEKIEL 22:23-31

"I looked for a man among them who would build up the wall and stand before me in the gap on behalf of the land so I would not have to destroy it, but I found none" (Ezekiel 22:30).

It's difficult to read this verse without feeling tremendously sad. The Lord is speaking through the prophet Ezekiel to the people of Israel and explaining why judgment could not be averted on their land. God said He was looking for just one person who would pray and intercede for the nation so it wouldn't be destroyed, but He could not find even one person. What a tragedy.

How can we read this passage and not think of our own country with all its sin and rebellion? Our day of judgment will come as well. As surely as there is a physical law of gravity, there is also a spiritual law of reaping what we sow. There may be a time lapse between what we have sown and what we reap, but the harvest will come.

Bad things don't come from God. They happen because we have sown bad seeds or as a result of the enemy's work. Either way, God gives us the opportunity to avert both of those things by standing in the gap through prayer. In spite of everything that is wrong in our country, we still enjoy the blessings we have because countless people have stood in the gap on behalf of our nation.

When God looked for a person to pray and couldn't find *one*, the land of Israel was taken over by enemies. Do you see how significant a role each of us can play as we learn to pray together for the protection of our nation today? As we pray according to God's Word and invoke God's power as intercessors, we can affect the outcome of events and avert judgment on our land.

Let's stand in the gap together and see what great things God will do.

I will blow on you with my fiery wrath, and you will be melted inside her. [22]As silver is melted in a furnace, so you will be melted inside her, and you will know that I the LORD have poured out my wrath upon you.'"

[23]Again the word of the LORD came to me: [24]"Son of man, say to the land, 'You are a land that has had no rain or showers[a] in the day of wrath.' [25]There is a conspiracy of her princes[b] within her like a roaring lion tearing its prey; they devour people, take treasures and precious things and make many widows within her. [26]Her priests do violence to my law and profane my holy things; they do not distinguish between the holy and the common; they teach that there is no difference between the unclean and the clean; and they shut their eyes to the keeping of my Sabbaths, so that I am profaned among them. [27]Her officials within her are like wolves tearing their prey; they shed blood and kill people to make unjust gain. [28]Her prophets whitewash these deeds for them by false visions and lying divinations. They say, 'This is what the Sovereign LORD says'—when the LORD has not spoken. [29]The people of the land practice extortion and commit robbery; they oppress the poor and needy and mistreat the alien, denying them justice.

[30]"I looked for a man among them who would build up the wall and stand before me in the gap on behalf of the land so I would not have to destroy it, but I found none. [31]So I will pour out my wrath on them and consume them with my fiery anger, bringing down on their own heads all they have done, declares the Sovereign LORD."

Two Adulterous Sisters

23 The word of the LORD came to me: [2]"Son of man, there were two women, daughters of the same mother. [3]They became prostitutes in Egypt, engaging in prostitution from their youth. In that land their breasts were fondled and their virgin bosoms caressed. [4]The older was named Oholah, and her sister was Oholibah. They were mine and gave birth to sons and daughters. Oholah is Samaria, and Oholibah is Jerusalem.

[5]"Oholah engaged in prostitution while she was still mine; and she lusted after her lovers, the Assyrians—warriors [6]clothed in blue, governors and commanders, all of them handsome young men, and mounted horsemen. [7]She gave herself as a prostitute to all the elite of the Assyrians and defiled herself with all the idols of everyone she lusted after. [8]She did not give up the prostitution she began in Egypt, when during her youth men slept with her, caressed her virgin bosom and poured out their lust upon her.

[9]"Therefore I handed her over to her lovers, the Assyrians, for whom she lusted. [10]They stripped her naked, took away her sons and daughters and killed her with the sword. She became a byword among women, and punishment was inflicted on her.

[11]"Her sister Oholibah saw this, yet in her lust and prostitution she was more depraved than her sister. [12]She too lusted after the Assyrians—governors and commanders, warriors in full dress, mounted horsemen, all handsome young men. [13]I saw that she too defiled herself; both of them went the same way.

[14]"But she carried her prostitution still further. She saw men portrayed on a wall, figures of Chaldeans[c] portrayed in red, [15]with belts around their waists and flowing turbans on their heads; all of them looked like Babylonian chariot officers, natives of Chaldea.[d] [16]As soon as she saw them, she lusted after them and sent messengers to them in Chaldea. [17]Then the Babylonians came to her, to the bed of love, and in their lust they defiled her. After she had been defiled by them, she turned away from them in disgust.

---

[a] 24 Septuagint; Hebrew has not been cleansed or rained on   [b] 25 Septuagint; Hebrew prophets   [c] 14 Or Babylonians
[d] 15 Or Babylonia; also in verse 16

18When she carried on her prostitution openly and exposed her nakedness, I turned away from her in disgust, just as I had turned away from her sister. 19Yet she became more and more promiscuous as she recalled the days of her youth, when she was a prostitute in Egypt. 20There she lusted after her lovers, whose genitals were like those of donkeys and whose emission was like that of horses. 21So you longed for the lewdness of your youth, when in Egypt your bosom was caressed and your young breasts fondled.[a]

22"Therefore, Oholibah, this is what the Sovereign LORD says: I will stir up your lovers against you, those you turned away from in disgust, and I will bring them against you from every side— 23the Babylonians and all the Chaldeans, the men of Pekod and Shoa and Koa, and all the Assyrians with them, handsome young men, all of them governors and commanders, chariot officers and men of high rank, all mounted on horses. 24They will come against you with weapons,[b] chariots and wagons and with a throng of people; they will take up positions against you on every side with large and small shields and with helmets. I will turn you over to them for punishment, and they will punish you according to their standards. 25I will direct my jealous anger against you, and they will deal with you in fury. They will cut off your noses and your ears, and those of you who are left will fall by the sword. They will take away your sons and daughters, and those of you who are left will be consumed by fire. 26They will also strip you of your clothes and take your fine jewelry. 27So I will put a stop to the lewdness and prostitution you began in Egypt. You will not look on these things with longing or remember Egypt anymore.

28"For this is what the Sovereign LORD says: I am about to hand you over to those you hate, to those you turned away

from in disgust. 29They will deal with you in hatred and take away everything you have worked for. They will leave you naked and bare, and the shame of your prostitution will be exposed. Your lewdness and promiscuity 30have brought this upon you, because you lusted after the nations and defiled yourself with their idols. 31You have gone the way of your sister; so I will put her cup into your hand.

32"This is what the Sovereign LORD says:

"You will drink your sister's cup,
    a cup large and deep;
it will bring scorn and derision,
    for it holds so much.
33You will be filled with drunkenness
        and sorrow,
    the cup of ruin and desolation,
    the cup of your sister Samaria.
34You will drink it and drain it dry;
    you will dash it to pieces
    and tear your breasts.

I have spoken, declares the Sovereign LORD.

35"Therefore this is what the Sovereign LORD says: Since you have forgotten me and thrust me behind your back, you must bear the consequences of your lewdness and prostitution."

36The LORD said to me: "Son of man, will you judge Oholah and Oholibah? Then confront them with their detestable practices, 37for they have committed adultery and blood is on their hands. They committed adultery with their idols; they even sacrificed their children, whom they bore to me,[c] as food for them. 38They have also done this to me: At that same time they defiled my sanctuary and desecrated my Sabbaths. 39On the very day they sacrificed their children to their idols, they entered my sanctuary and desecrated it. That is what they did in my house.

40"They even sent messengers for men

---

who came from far away, and when they arrived you bathed yourself for them, painted your eyes and put on your jewelry. [41]You sat on an elegant couch, with a table spread before it on which you had placed the incense and oil that belonged to me.

[42]"The noise of a carefree crowd was around her; Sabeans[a] were brought from the desert along with men from the rabble, and they put bracelets on the arms of the woman and her sister and beautiful crowns on their heads. [43]Then I said about the one worn out by adultery, 'Now let them use her as a prostitute, for that is all she is.' [44]And they slept with her. As men sleep with a prostitute, so they slept with those lewd women, Oholah and Oholibah. [45]But righteous men will sentence them to the punishment of women who commit adultery and shed blood, because they are adulterous and blood is on their hands.

[46]"This is what the Sovereign LORD says: Bring a mob against them and give them over to terror and plunder. [47]The mob will stone them and cut them down with their swords; they will kill their sons and daughters and burn down their houses.

[48]"So I will put an end to lewdness in the land, that all women may take warning and not imitate you. [49]You will suffer the penalty for your lewdness and bear the consequences of your sins of idolatry. Then you will know that I am the Sovereign LORD."

The Cooking Pot

24 In the ninth year, in the tenth month on the tenth day, the word of the LORD came to me: [2]"Son of man, record this date, this very date, because the king of Babylon has laid siege to Jerusalem this very day. [3]Tell this rebellious house a parable and say to them: 'This is what the Sovereign LORD says:

"'Put on the cooking pot; put it on
and pour water into it.

[4]Put into it the pieces of meat,
all the choice pieces—the leg and
the shoulder.
Fill it with the best of these bones;
[5]   take the pick of the flock.
Pile wood beneath it for the bones;
bring it to a boil
and cook the bones in it.

[6]"'For this is what the Sovereign LORD says:

"'Woe to the city of bloodshed,
to the pot now encrusted,
whose deposit will not go away!
Empty it piece by piece
without casting lots for them.

[7]"'For the blood she shed is in her
midst:
She poured it on the bare rock;
she did not pour it on the ground,
where the dust would cover it.
[8]To stir up wrath and take revenge
I put her blood on the bare rock,
so that it would not be covered.

[9]"'Therefore this is what the Sovereign LORD says:

"'Woe to the city of bloodshed!
I, too, will pile the wood high.
[10]So heap on the wood
and kindle the fire.
Cook the meat well,
mixing in the spices;
and let the bones be charred.
[11]Then set the empty pot on the
coals
till it becomes hot and its copper
glows
so its impurities may be melted
and its deposit burned away.
[12]It has frustrated all efforts;
its heavy deposit has not been
removed,
not even by fire.

[13]"'Now your impurity is lewdness. Because I tried to cleanse you but you would not be cleansed from your impurity, you

Four Things That Are True About Following God's Will

1. *Following God's will does not mean we will never have trouble.* Trouble is a part of life. Having fulfillment and peace in the midst of trouble is what living in God's will is all about. There is great confidence in knowing that you are walking in the will of God and doing what He wants you to do. When you are sure of that, you can better deal with what life brings you. So don't think that trouble in your life means you are out of God's will. God uses the trouble you have to perfect you. There is a big difference between being out of God's will and being pruned or tested by God. Both are uncomfortable, but one leads to life and one doesn't. In one you will have peace, no matter how uncomfortable it gets. In the other, you won't.

2. *Following God's will is not easy.* The life of Jesus confirms that following God's will is not always fun, enjoyable, pleasant, or easy. Jesus was doing God's will when He went to the cross. He said, "For I have come down from heaven not to do my will but to do the will of him who sent me" (John 6:38). If anyone could have said, "I don't want to follow God's will today," I think it would have been Him. But He did it perfectly. And now He will enable us to do it too.

3. *Following God's will can make you very uncomfortable.* In fact, if you don't ever feel stretched or uncomfortable in your walk with the Lord, then I would question whether you are actually *in* the will of God. It has been my personal experience that stretched and uncomfortable is a way of life when walking in the will of God.

4. *Following God's will doesn't happen automatically.* That's because God gave us a choice as to whether we subject our will to Him or not. We make that decision every day. Will we *seek* His will? Will we *ask* Him for wisdom? Will we *do* what He says? "Do not be foolish, but understand what the Lord's will is" (Ephesians 5:17). Knowing God's will is the way we choose to live each day of our lives.

God doesn't want you to live your life for the lusts of the flesh, "but rather for the will of God" (1 Peter 4:2). He wants to "equip you with everything good for doing his will, and may he work in us what is pleasing to him" (Hebrews 13:21). "For it is God who works in you to will and to act according to his good purpose" (Philippians 2:13). I pray that in everything you do "you may stand firm in all the will of God" (Colossians 4:12). The best place to start seeking God's will for your life is to begin to "give thanks in all circumstances, for this is God's will for you in Christ Jesus" (1 Thessalonians 5:18). Thank Him for keeping you in the center of His will. Then ask Him to guide your every step. It feels so good to be confident you are on the right path and doing what God *wants* that I know you will do whatever it takes to experience it.

For the next "From Stormie's Heart" article, go to page 1077.

will not be clean again until my wrath against you has subsided.

[14] "'I the LORD have spoken. The time has come for me to act. I will not hold back; I will not have pity, nor will I relent. You will be judged according to your conduct and your actions, declares the Sovereign LORD.'"

Ezekiel's Wife Dies

[15] The word of the LORD came to me: [16] "Son of man, with one blow I am about to take away from you the delight of your eyes. Yet do not lament or weep or shed any tears. [17] Groan quietly; do not mourn for the dead. Keep your turban fastened and your sandals on your feet; do not cover the lower part of your face or eat the customary food ⌊of mourners⌋."

[18] So I spoke to the people in the morning, and in the evening my wife died. The next morning I did as I had been commanded.

[19] Then the people asked me, "Won't you tell us what these things have to do with us?"

[20] So I said to them, "The word of the LORD came to me: [21] Say to the house of Israel, 'This is what the Sovereign LORD says: I am about to desecrate my sanctuary—the stronghold in which you take pride, the delight of your eyes, the object of your affection. The sons and daughters you left behind will fall by the sword. [22] And you will do as I have done. You will not cover the lower part of your face or eat the customary food ⌊of mourners⌋. [23] You will keep your turbans on your heads and your sandals on your feet. You will not mourn or weep but will waste away because of[a] your sins and groan among yourselves. [24] Ezekiel will be a sign to you; you will do just as he has done. When this happens, you will know that I am the Sovereign LORD.'

[25] "And you, son of man, on the day I take away their stronghold, their joy and glory, the delight of their eyes, their heart's desire, and their sons and daughters as well— [26] on that day a fugitive will come to tell you the news. [27] At that time your mouth will be opened; you will speak with him and will no longer be silent. So you will be a sign to them, and they will know that I am the LORD."

A Prophecy Against Ammon

25 The word of the LORD came to me: [2] "Son of man, set your face against the Ammonites and prophesy against them. [3] Say to them, 'Hear the word of the Sovereign LORD. This is what the Sovereign LORD says: Because you said "Aha!" over my sanctuary when it was desecrated and over the land of Israel when it was laid waste and over the people of Judah when they went into exile, [4] therefore I am going to give you to the people of the East as a possession. They will set up their camps and pitch their tents among you; they will eat your fruit and drink your milk. [5] I will turn Rabbah into a pasture for camels and Ammon into a resting place for sheep. Then you will know that I am the LORD. [6] For this is what the Sovereign LORD says: Because you have clapped your hands and stamped your feet, rejoicing with all the malice of your heart against the land of Israel, [7] therefore I will stretch out my hand against you and give you as plunder to the nations. I will cut you off from the nations and exterminate you from the countries. I will destroy you, and you will know that I am the LORD.'"

A Prophecy Against Moab

[8] "This is what the Sovereign LORD says: 'Because Moab and Seir said, "Look, the house of Judah has become like all the other nations," [9] therefore I will expose the flank of Moab, beginning at its frontier towns—Beth Jeshimoth, Baal Meon and Kiriathaim—the glory of that land. [10] I will give Moab along with the Ammonites to the people of the East as a possession, so that the Ammonites will not

---

[a] 23 Or *away in*

be remembered among the nations; [11]and I will inflict punishment on Moab. Then they will know that I am the LORD.'"

A Prophecy Against Edom

[12]"This is what the Sovereign LORD says: 'Because Edom took revenge on the house of Judah and became very guilty by doing so, [13]therefore this is what the Sovereign LORD says: I will stretch out my hand against Edom and kill its men and their animals. I will lay it waste, and from Teman to Dedan they will fall by the sword. [14]I will take vengeance on Edom by the hand of my people Israel, and they will deal with Edom in accordance with my anger and my wrath; they will know my vengeance, declares the Sovereign LORD.'"

A Prophecy Against Philistia

[15]"This is what the Sovereign LORD says: 'Because the Philistines acted in vengeance and took revenge with malice in their hearts, and with ancient hostility sought to destroy Judah, [16]therefore this is what the Sovereign LORD says: I am about to stretch out my hand against the Philistines, and I will cut off the Kerethites and destroy those remaining along the coast. [17]I will carry out great vengeance on them and punish them in my wrath. Then they will know that I am the LORD, when I take vengeance on them.'"

A Prophecy Against Tyre

26 In the eleventh year, on the first day of the month, the word of the LORD came to me: [2]"Son of man, because Tyre has said of Jerusalem, 'Aha! The gate to the nations is broken, and its doors have swung open to me; now that she lies in ruins I will prosper,' [3]therefore this is what the Sovereign LORD says: I am against you, O Tyre, and I will bring many nations against you, like the sea casting up its waves. [4]They will destroy the walls of Tyre and pull down her towers; I will scrape away her rubble and make her a bare rock. [5]Out in the sea she will be-

come a place to spread fishnets, for I have spoken, declares the Sovereign LORD. She will become plunder for the nations, [6]and her settlements on the mainland will be ravaged by the sword. Then they will know that I am the LORD.

[7]"For this is what the Sovereign LORD says: From the north I am going to bring against Tyre Nebuchadnezzar[a] king of Babylon, king of kings, with horses and chariots, with horsemen and a great army. [8]He will ravage your settlements on the mainland with the sword; he will set up siege works against you, build a ramp up to your walls and raise his shields against you. [9]He will direct the blows of his battering rams against your walls and demolish your towers with his weapons. [10]His horses will be so many that they will cover you with dust. Your walls will tremble at the noise of the war horses, wagons and chariots when he enters your gates as men enter a city whose walls have been broken through. [11]The hoofs of his horses will trample all your streets; he will kill your people with the sword, and your strong pillars will fall to the ground. [12]They will plunder your wealth and loot your merchandise; they will break down your walls and demolish your fine houses and throw your stones, timber and rubble into the sea. [13]I will put an end to your noisy songs, and the music of your harps will be heard no more. [14]I will make you a bare rock, and you will become a place to spread fishnets. You will never be rebuilt, for I the LORD have spoken, declares the Sovereign LORD.

[15]"This is what the Sovereign LORD says to Tyre: Will not the coastlands tremble at the sound of your fall, when the wounded groan and the slaughter takes place in you? [16]Then all the princes of the coast will step down from their thrones and lay aside their robes and take off their embroidered garments. Clothed with terror, they will sit on the ground, trembling every moment, appalled at you. [17]Then

---

[a] 7 Hebrew *Nebuchadrezzar*, of which *Nebuchadnezzar* is a variant; here and often in Ezekiel and Jeremiah

they will take up a lament concerning you and say to you:

"'How you are destroyed, O city of renown,
  peopled by men of the sea!
You were a power on the seas,
  you and your citizens;
you put your terror
  on all who lived there.
18 Now the coastlands tremble
  on the day of your fall;
the islands in the sea
  are terrified at your collapse.'

19 "This is what the Sovereign LORD says: When I make you a desolate city, like cities no longer inhabited, and when I bring the ocean depths over you and its vast waters cover you, 20 then I will bring you down with those who go down to the pit, to the people of long ago. I will make you dwell in the earth below, as in ancient ruins, with those who go down to the pit, and you will not return or take your place[a] in the land of the living. 21 I will bring you to a horrible end and you will be no more. You will be sought, but you will never again be found, declares the Sovereign LORD."

A Lament for Tyre

27 The word of the LORD came to me: 2 "Son of man, take up a lament concerning Tyre. 3 Say to Tyre, situated at the gateway to the sea, merchant of peoples on many coasts, 'This is what the Sovereign LORD says:

"'You say, O Tyre,
  "I am perfect in beauty."
4 Your domain was on the high seas;
  your builders brought your beauty
    to perfection.
5 They made all your timbers
  of pine trees from Senir[b];
they took a cedar from Lebanon
  to make a mast for you.
6 Of oaks from Bashan

they made your oars;
of cypress wood[c] from the coasts of
  Cyprus[d]
they made your deck, inlaid with
  ivory.
7 Fine embroidered linen from Egypt
  was your sail
and served as your banner;
your awnings were of blue and purple
  from the coasts of Elishah.
8 Men of Sidon and Arvad were your
  oarsmen;
your skilled men, O Tyre, were
  aboard as your seamen.
9 Veteran craftsmen of Gebal[e] were on
  board
  as shipwrights to caulk your seams.
All the ships of the sea and their
  sailors
came alongside to trade for your
  wares.

10 "'Men of Persia, Lydia and Put
  served as soldiers in your army.
They hung their shields and helmets
  on your walls,
  bringing you splendor.
11 Men of Arvad and Helech
  manned your walls on every side;
men of Gammad
  were in your towers.
They hung their shields around your
  walls;
  they brought your beauty to
    perfection.

12 "'Tarshish did business with you because of your great wealth of goods; they exchanged silver, iron, tin and lead for your merchandise.

13 "'Greece, Tubal and Meshech traded with you; they exchanged slaves and articles of bronze for your wares.

14 "'Men of Beth Togarmah exchanged work horses, war horses and mules for your merchandise.

15 "'The men of Rhodes[f] traded with you, and many coastlands were your

---

a 20 Septuagint; Hebrew *return, and I will give glory*   b 5 That is, Hermon   c 6 Targum; the Masoretic Text has a different division of the consonants.   d 6 Hebrew *Kittim*   e 9 That is, Byblos   f 15 Septuagint; Hebrew *Dedan* customers; they paid you with ivory tusks and ebony.

16 "'Aram[a] did business with you because of your many products; they exchanged turquoise, purple fabric, embroidered work, fine linen, coral and rubies for your merchandise.

17 "'Judah and Israel traded with you; they exchanged wheat from Minnith and confections,[b] honey, oil and balm for your wares.

18 "'Damascus, because of your many products and great wealth of goods, did business with you in wine from Helbon and wool from Zahar.

19 "'Danites and Greeks from Uzal bought your merchandise; they exchanged wrought iron, cassia and calamus for your wares.

20 "'Dedan traded in saddle blankets with you.

21 "'Arabia and all the princes of Kedar were your customers; they did business with you in lambs, rams and goats.

22 "'The merchants of Sheba and Raamah traded with you; for your merchandise they exchanged the finest of all kinds of spices and precious stones, and gold.

23 "'Haran, Canneh and Eden and merchants of Sheba, Asshur and Kilmad traded with you. 24 In your marketplace they traded with you beautiful garments, blue fabric, embroidered work and multicolored rugs with cords twisted and tightly knotted.

25 "'The ships of Tarshish serve
    as carriers for your wares.
You are filled with heavy cargo
    in the heart of the sea.
26 Your oarsmen take you
    out to the high seas.
But the east wind will break you to
        pieces
    in the heart of the sea.
27 Your wealth, merchandise and wares,
    your mariners, seamen and
        shipwrights,

your merchants and all your soldiers,
    and everyone else on board
will sink into the heart of the sea
    on the day of your shipwreck.
28 The shorelands will quake
    when your seamen cry out.
29 All who handle the oars
    will abandon their ships;
the mariners and all the seamen
    will stand on the shore.
30 They will raise their voice
    and cry bitterly over you;
they will sprinkle dust on their heads
    and roll in ashes.
31 They will shave their heads because
        of you
    and will put on sackcloth.
They will weep over you with
        anguish of soul
    and with bitter mourning.
32 As they wail and mourn over you,
    they will take up a lament
        concerning you:
"Who was ever silenced like Tyre,
    surrounded by the sea?"
33 When your merchandise went out on
        the seas,
    you satisfied many nations;
with your great wealth and your wares
    you enriched the kings of the earth.
34 Now you are shattered by the sea
    in the depths of the waters;
your wares and all your company
    have gone down with you.
35 All who live in the coastlands
    are appalled at you;
their kings shudder with horror
    and their faces are distorted with fear.
36 The merchants among the nations
        hiss at you;
    you have come to a horrible end
    and will be no more.'"

A Prophecy Against the King of Tyre

28 The word of the LORD came to me: 2 "Son of man, say to the ruler of Tyre, 'This is what the Sovereign LORD says:

---

a 16 Most Hebrew manuscripts; some Hebrew manuscripts and Syriac Edom   b 17 The meaning of the Hebrew for this word is uncertain.

" 'In the pride of your heart
    you say, "I am a god;
I sit on the throne of a god
    in the heart of the seas."
But you are a man and not a god,
    though you think you are as wise
        as a god.
³ Are you wiser than Daniel[a]?
    Is no secret hidden from you?
⁴ By your wisdom and understanding
    you have gained wealth for
        yourself
and amassed gold and silver
    in your treasuries.
⁵ By your great skill in trading
    you have increased your wealth,
and because of your wealth
    your heart has grown proud.

⁶ " 'Therefore this is what the Sovereign Lord says:

" 'Because you think you are wise,
    as wise as a god,
⁷ I am going to bring foreigners against
        you,
    the most ruthless of nations;
they will draw their swords against
        your beauty and wisdom
    and pierce your shining splendor.
⁸ They will bring you down to the pit,
    and you will die a violent death
    in the heart of the seas.
⁹ Will you then say, "I am a god,"
    in the presence of those who kill
        you?
You will be but a man, not a god,
    in the hands of those who slay you.
¹⁰ You will die the death of the
        uncircumcised
    at the hands of foreigners.

I have spoken, declares the Sovereign
Lord.' "

¹¹ The word of the Lord came to me:
¹² "Son of man, take up a lament concerning the king of Tyre and say to him: 'This is what the Sovereign Lord says:

" 'You were the model of perfection,
    full of wisdom and perfect in
        beauty.
¹³ You were in Eden,
    the garden of God;
every precious stone adorned you:
    ruby, topaz and emerald,
    chrysolite, onyx and jasper,
    sapphire,[b] turquoise and beryl.[c]
Your settings and mountings[d] were
        made of gold;
    on the day you were created they
        were prepared.
¹⁴ You were anointed as a guardian
        cherub,
    for so I ordained you.
You were on the holy mount of God;
    you walked among the fiery stones.
¹⁵ You were blameless in your ways
    from the day you were created
    till wickedness was found in you.
¹⁶ Through your widespread trade
    you were filled with violence,
    and you sinned.
So I drove you in disgrace from the
        mount of God,
    and I expelled you, O guardian
        cherub,
    from among the fiery stones.
¹⁷ Your heart became proud
    on account of your beauty,
and you corrupted your wisdom
    because of your splendor.
So I threw you to the earth;
    I made a spectacle of you before
        kings.
¹⁸ By your many sins and dishonest
        trade
    you have desecrated your
        sanctuaries.
So I made a fire come out from you,
    and it consumed you,
and I reduced you to ashes on the
        ground
    in the sight of all who were
        watching.
¹⁹ All the nations who knew you

ᵃ *3* Or *Danel*; the Hebrew spelling may suggest a person other than the prophet Daniel.   ᵇ *13* Or *lapis lazuli*   ᶜ *13* The precise identification of some of these precious stones is uncertain.   ᵈ *13* The meaning of the Hebrew for this phrase is uncertain.

are appalled at you;
you have come to a horrible end
and will be no more.'"

A Prophecy Against Sidon

²⁰The word of the LORD came to me: ²¹"Son of man, set your face against Sidon; prophesy against her ²²and say: 'This is what the Sovereign LORD says:

"'I am against you, O Sidon,
and I will gain glory within you.
They will know that I am the LORD,
when I inflict punishment on her
and show myself holy within her.
²³I will send a plague upon her
and make blood flow in her streets.
The slain will fall within her,
with the sword against her on every
side.
Then they will know that I am the
LORD.

²⁴"'No longer will the people of Israel have malicious neighbors who are painful briers and sharp thorns. Then they will know that I am the Sovereign LORD.

²⁵"'This is what the Sovereign LORD says: When I gather the people of Israel from the nations where they have been scattered, I will show myself holy among them in the sight of the nations. Then they will live in their own land, which I gave to my servant Jacob. ²⁶They will live there in safety and will build houses and plant vineyards; they will live in safety when I inflict punishment on all their neighbors who maligned them. Then they will know that I am the LORD their God.'"

A Prophecy Against Egypt

29 In the tenth year, in the tenth month on the twelfth day, the word of the LORD came to me: ²"Son of man, set your face against Pharaoh king of Egypt and prophesy against him and against all Egypt. ³Speak to him and say: 'This is what the Sovereign LORD says:

"'I am against you, Pharaoh king of
Egypt,

you great monster lying among
your streams.
You say, "The Nile is mine;
I made it for myself."
⁴But I will put hooks in your jaws
and make the fish of your streams
stick to your scales.
I will pull you out from among your
streams,
with all the fish sticking to your
scales.
⁵I will leave you in the desert,
you and all the fish of your streams.
You will fall on the open field
and not be gathered or picked up.
I will give you as food
to the beasts of the earth and the
birds of the air.

> ### Prayer is . . .
>
> *letting your physical self be quiet so
> that your spiritual self can be ignited.*

⁶Then all who live in Egypt will know that I am the LORD.

"'You have been a staff of reed for the house of Israel. ⁷When they grasped you with their hands, you splintered and you tore open their shoulders; when they leaned on you, you broke and their backs were wrenched.^a

⁸"'Therefore this is what the Sovereign LORD says: I will bring a sword against you and kill your men and their animals. ⁹Egypt will become a desolate wasteland. Then they will know that I am the LORD.

"'Because you said, "The Nile is mine; I made it," ¹⁰therefore I am against you and against your streams, and I will make the land of Egypt a ruin and a desolate waste from Migdol to Aswan, as far as the border of Cush.^b ¹¹No foot of man or animal will pass through it; no one will live there for forty years. ¹²I will make the

---

^a 7 Syriac (see also Septuagint and Vulgate); Hebrew *and you caused their backs to stand*   ^b 10 That is, the upper Nile region

land of Egypt desolate among devastated lands, and her cities will lie desolate forty years among ruined cities. And I will disperse the Egyptians among the nations and scatter them through the countries.

13 "'Yet this is what the Sovereign LORD says: At the end of forty years I will gather the Egyptians from the nations where they were scattered. 14 I will bring them back from captivity and return them to Upper Egypt,[a] the land of their ancestry. There they will be a lowly kingdom. 15 It will be the lowliest of kingdoms and will never again exalt itself above the other nations. I will make it so weak that it will never again rule over the nations. 16 Egypt will no longer be a source of confidence for the people of Israel but will be a reminder of their sin in turning to her for help. Then they will know that I am the Sovereign LORD.'"

17 In the twenty-seventh year, in the first month on the first day, the word of the LORD came to me: 18 "Son of man, Nebuchadnezzar king of Babylon drove his army in a hard campaign against Tyre; every head was rubbed bare and every shoulder made raw. Yet he and his army got no reward from the campaign he led against Tyre. 19 Therefore this is what the Sovereign LORD says: I am going to give Egypt to Nebuchadnezzar king of Babylon, and he will carry off its wealth. He will loot and plunder the land as pay for his army. 20 I have given him Egypt as a reward for his efforts because he and his army did it for me, declares the Sovereign LORD.

21 "On that day I will make a horn[b] grow for the house of Israel, and I will open your mouth among them. Then they will know that I am the LORD."

A Lament for Egypt

30 The word of the LORD came to me: 2 "Son of man, prophesy and say: 'This is what the Sovereign LORD says:

"'Wail and say,
  "Alas for that day!"
3 For the day is near,
  the day of the LORD is near—
a day of clouds,
  a time of doom for the nations.
4 A sword will come against Egypt,
  and anguish will come upon
    Cush.[c]
When the slain fall in Egypt,
  her wealth will be carried away
  and her foundations torn down.

5 Cush and Put, Lydia and all Arabia, Libya[d] and the people of the covenant land will fall by the sword along with Egypt.

6 "'This is what the LORD says:

"'The allies of Egypt will fall
  and her proud strength will fail.
From Migdol to Aswan
  they will fall by the sword within
    her,
      declares the Sovereign LORD.
7 "'They will be desolate
  among desolate lands,
and their cities will lie
  among ruined cities.
8 Then they will know that I am the
    LORD,
  when I set fire to Egypt
  and all her helpers are crushed.

9 "'On that day messengers will go out from me in ships to frighten Cush out of her complacency. Anguish will take hold of them on the day of Egypt's doom, for it is sure to come.

10 "'This is what the Sovereign LORD says:

"'I will put an end to the hordes of
    Egypt
  by the hand of Nebuchadnezzar
    king of Babylon.
11 He and his army—the most ruthless
    of nations—
  will be brought in to destroy the
    land.

---

[a] 14 Hebrew to Pathros   [b] 21 Horn here symbolizes strength.   [c] 4 That is, the upper Nile region; also in verses 5 and 9
[d] 5 Hebrew Cub

They will draw their swords against
    Egypt
    and fill the land with the slain.
¹²I will dry up the streams of the Nile
    and sell the land to evil men;
by the hand of foreigners
    I will lay waste the land and
        everything in it.

I the LORD have spoken.

    ¹³"This is what the Sovereign LORD
says:

  "'I will destroy the idols
    and put an end to the images in
        Memphis.ᵃ
No longer will there be a prince in
    Egypt,
    and I will spread fear throughout
        the land.
¹⁴I will lay waste Upper Egypt,ᵇ
    set fire to Zoan
    and inflict punishment on Thebes.ᶜ
¹⁵I will pour out my wrath on Pelusium,ᵈ
    the stronghold of Egypt,
    and cut off the hordes of Thebes.
¹⁶I will set fire to Egypt;
    Pelusium will writhe in agony.
Thebes will be taken by storm;
    Memphis will be in constant distress.
¹⁷The young men of Heliopolisᵉ and
        Bubastisᶠ
    will fall by the sword,
    and the cities themselves will go
        into captivity.
¹⁸Dark will be the day at Tahpanhes
    when I break the yoke of Egypt;
    there her proud strength will come
        to an end.
She will be covered with clouds,
    and her villages will go into
        captivity.
¹⁹So I will inflict punishment on Egypt,
    and they will know that I am the
        LORD.'"

    ²⁰In the eleventh year, in the first month
on the seventh day, the word of the LORD

came to me: ²¹"Son of man, I have broken
the arm of Pharaoh king of Egypt. It has
not been bound up for healing or put in
a splint so as to become strong enough
to hold a sword. ²²Therefore this is what
the Sovereign LORD says: I am against
Pharaoh king of Egypt. I will break both
his arms, the good arm as well as the broken one, and make the sword fall from
his hand. ²³I will disperse the Egyptians
among the nations and scatter them
through the countries. ²⁴I will strengthen
the arms of the king of Babylon and put
my sword in his hand, but I will break
the arms of Pharaoh, and he will groan
before him like a mortally wounded man.
²⁵I will strengthen the arms of the king of
Babylon, but the arms of Pharaoh will fall
limp. Then they will know that I am the
LORD, when I put my sword into the hand
of the king of Babylon and he brandishes
it against Egypt. ²⁶I will disperse the Egyptians among the nations and scatter them
through the countries. Then they will
know that I am the LORD."

A Cedar in Lebanon

31 In the eleventh year, in the third
month on the first day, the word
of the LORD came to me: ²"Son of man,
say to Pharaoh king of Egypt and to his
hordes:

  "'Who can be compared with you in
        majesty?
³Consider Assyria, once a cedar in
    Lebanon,
  with beautiful branches
    overshadowing the forest;
it towered on high,
    its top above the thick foliage.
⁴The waters nourished it,
    deep springs made it grow tall;
  their streams flowed
    all around its base
and sent their channels
    to all the trees of the field.
⁵So it towered higher

ᵃ 13 Hebrew *Noph*; also in verse 16   ᵇ 14 Hebrew *waste Pathros*   ᶜ 14 Hebrew *No*; also in verses 15 and 16   ᵈ 15 Hebrew *Sin*;
also in verse 16   ᵉ 17 Hebrew *Awen* (or *On*)   ᶠ 17 Hebrew *Pi Beseth*

than all the trees of the field;
  its boughs increased
    and its branches grew long,
    spreading because of abundant
      waters.
⁶All the birds of the air
    nested in its boughs,
  all the beasts of the field
    gave birth under its branches;
  all the great nations
    lived in its shade.
⁷It was majestic in beauty,
    with its spreading boughs,
  for its roots went down
    to abundant waters.
⁸The cedars in the garden of God
    could not rival it,
  nor could the pine trees
    equal its boughs,
  nor could the plane trees
    compare with its branches—
  no tree in the garden of God
    could match its beauty.
⁹I made it beautiful
    with abundant branches,
  the envy of all the trees of Eden
    in the garden of God.

¹⁰"'Therefore this is what the Sovereign LORD says: Because it towered on high, lifting its top above the thick foliage, and because it was proud of its height, ¹¹I handed it over to the ruler of the nations, for him to deal with according to its wickedness. I cast it aside, ¹²and the most ruthless of foreign nations cut it down and left it. Its boughs fell on the mountains and in all the valleys; its branches lay broken in all the ravines of the land. All the nations of the earth came out from under its shade and left it. ¹³All the birds of the air settled on the fallen tree, and all the beasts of the field were among its branches. ¹⁴Therefore no other trees by the waters are ever to tower proudly on high, lifting their tops above the thick foliage. No other trees so well-watered are ever to reach such a height; they are all destined for death, for the earth below,

among mortal men, with those who go down to the pit.

¹⁵"'This is what the Sovereign LORD says: On the day it was brought down to the grave[a] I covered the deep springs with mourning for it; I held back its streams, and its abundant waters were restrained. Because of it I clothed Lebanon with gloom, and all the trees of the field withered away. ¹⁶I made the nations tremble at the sound of its fall when I brought it down to the grave with those who go down to the pit. Then all the trees of Eden, the choicest and best of Lebanon, all the trees that were well-watered, were consoled in the earth below. ¹⁷Those who lived in its shade, its allies among the nations, had also gone down to the grave with it, joining those killed by the sword.

¹⁸"'Which of the trees of Eden can be compared with you in splendor and majesty? Yet you, too, will be brought down with the trees of Eden to the earth below; you will lie among the uncircumcised, with those killed by the sword.

"'This is Pharaoh and all his hordes, declares the Sovereign LORD.'"

A Lament for Pharaoh

32 In the twelfth year, in the twelfth month on the first day, the word of the LORD came to me: ²"Son of man, take up a lament concerning Pharaoh king of Egypt and say to him:

"'You are like a lion among the nations;
    you are like a monster in the seas
  thrashing about in your streams,
    churning the water with your feet
    and muddying the streams.

³"'This is what the Sovereign LORD says:

"'With a great throng of people
    I will cast my net over you,
    and they will haul you up in my net.
⁴I will throw you on the land
    and hurl you on the open field.

I will let all the birds of the air settle
    on you
and all the beasts of the earth gorge
    themselves on you.
5 I will spread your flesh on the
    mountains
    and fill the valleys with your remains.
6 I will drench the land with your
    flowing blood
    all the way to the mountains,
and the ravines will be filled with
    your flesh.
7 When I snuff you out, I will cover
    the heavens
    and darken their stars;
I will cover the sun with a cloud,
    and the moon will not give its light.
8 All the shining lights in the heavens
    I will darken over you;
I will bring darkness over your
    land,
      declares the Sovereign LORD.
9 I will trouble the hearts of many
    peoples
    when I bring about your
      destruction among the nations,
among[a] lands you have not known.
10 I will cause many peoples to be
    appalled at you,
and their kings will shudder with
    horror because of you
when I brandish my sword before
    them.
On the day of your downfall
    each of them will tremble
    every moment for his life.

11 "For this is what the Sovereign
LORD says:

" 'The sword of the king of Babylon
    will come against you.
12 I will cause your hordes to fall
    by the swords of mighty men—
    the most ruthless of all nations.
They will shatter the pride of Egypt,
    and all her hordes will be
      overthrown.
13 I will destroy all her cattle

from beside abundant waters
no longer to be stirred by the foot of
    man
    or muddied by the hoofs of cattle.
14 Then I will let her waters settle
    and make her streams flow like oil,
      declares the Sovereign LORD.
15 When I make Egypt desolate
    and strip the land of everything in it,
when I strike down all who live there,
    then they will know that I am the
      LORD.'

16 "This is the lament they will chant for her. The daughters of the nations will chant it; for Egypt and all her hordes they will chant it, declares the Sovereign LORD."

17 In the twelfth year, on the fifteenth day of the month, the word of the LORD came to me: 18 "Son of man, wail for the hordes of Egypt and consign to the earth below both her and the daughters of mighty nations, with those who go down to the pit. 19 Say to them, 'Are you more favored than others? Go down and be laid among the uncircumcised.' 20 They will fall among those killed by the sword. The sword is drawn; let her be dragged off with all her hordes. 21 From within the grave[b] the mighty leaders will say of Egypt and her allies, 'They have come down and they lie with the uncircumcised, with those killed by the sword.'

22 "Assyria is there with her whole army; she is surrounded by the graves of all her slain, all who have fallen by the sword. 23 Their graves are in the depths of the pit and her army lies around her grave. All who had spread terror in the land of the living are slain, fallen by the sword.

24 "Elam is there, with all her hordes around her grave. All of them are slain, fallen by the sword. All who had spread terror in the land of the living went down uncircumcised to the earth below. They bear their shame with those who go down to the pit. 25 A bed is made for

---

her among the slain, with all her hordes around her grave. All of them are uncircumcised, killed by the sword. Because their terror had spread in the land of the living, they bear their shame with those who go down to the pit; they are laid among the slain.

²⁶"Meshech and Tubal are there, with all their hordes around their graves. All of them are uncircumcised, killed by the sword because they spread their terror in the land of the living. ²⁷Do they not lie with the other uncircumcised warriors who have fallen, who went down to the grave with their weapons of war, whose swords were placed under their heads? The punishment for their sins rested on their bones, though the terror of these warriors had stalked through the land of the living.

²⁸"You too, O Pharaoh, will be broken and will lie among the uncircumcised, with those killed by the sword.

²⁹"Edom is there, her kings and all her princes; despite their power, they are laid with those killed by the sword. They lie with the uncircumcised, with those who go down to the pit.

³⁰"All the princes of the north and all the Sidonians are there; they went down with the slain in disgrace despite the terror caused by their power. They lie uncircumcised with those killed by the sword and bear their shame with those who go down to the pit.

³¹"Pharaoh—he and all his army—will see them and he will be consoled for all his hordes that were killed by the sword, declares the Sovereign LORD. ³²Although I had him spread terror in the land of the living, Pharaoh and all his hordes will be laid among the uncircumcised, with those killed by the sword, declares the Sovereign LORD."

Ezekiel a Watchman

33 The word of the LORD came to me: ²"Son of man, speak to your countrymen and say to them: 'When I bring the sword against a land, and the people of the land choose one of their men and make him their watchman, ³and he sees the sword coming against the land and blows the trumpet to warn the people, ⁴then if anyone hears the trumpet but does not take warning and the sword comes and takes his life, his blood will be on his own head. ⁵Since he heard the sound of the trumpet but did not take warning, his blood will be on his own head. If he had taken warning, he would have saved himself. ⁶But if the watchman sees the sword coming and does not blow the trumpet to warn the people and the sword comes and takes the life of one of them, that man will be taken away because of his sin, but I will hold the watchman accountable for his blood.'

⁷"Son of man, I have made you a watchman for the house of Israel; so hear the word I speak and give them warning from me. ⁸When I say to the wicked, 'O wicked man, you will surely die,' and you do not speak out to dissuade him from his ways, that wicked man will die for[a] his sin, and I will hold you accountable for his blood. ⁹But if you do warn the wicked man to turn from his ways and he does not do so, he will die for his sin, but you will have saved yourself.

Praying Ezekiel 33:9

Heavenly Father, I pray for people in my own community who have set themselves to do evil, that they would turn from their wicked ways and serve only You.

¹⁰"Son of man, say to the house of Israel, 'This is what you are saying: "Our offenses and sins weigh us down, and we are wasting away because of[b] them. How then can we live?"' ¹¹Say to them, 'As surely as I live, declares the Sovereign LORD, I take no pleasure in the death of the wicked, but rather that they turn from their ways and live. Turn! Turn from your evil ways! Why will you die, O house of Israel?'

ᵃ *8 Or in; also in verse 9* ᵇ *10 Or away in*

¹²"Therefore, son of man, say to your countrymen, 'The righteousness of the righteous man will not save him when he disobeys, and the wickedness of the wicked man will not cause him to fall when he turns from it. The righteous man, if he sins, will not be allowed to live because of his former righteousness.' ¹³If I tell the righteous man that he will surely live, but then he trusts in his righteousness and does evil, none of the righteous things he has done will be remembered; he will die for the evil he has done. ¹⁴And if I say to the wicked man, 'You will surely die,' but he then turns away from his sin and does what is just and right— ¹⁵if he gives back what he took in pledge for a loan, returns what he has stolen, follows the decrees that give life, and does no evil, he will surely live; he will not die. ¹⁶None of the sins he has committed will be remembered against him. He has done what is just and right; he will surely live.

¹⁷"Yet your countrymen say, 'The way of the Lord is not just.' But it is their way that is not just. ¹⁸If a righteous man turns from his righteousness and does evil, he will die for it. ¹⁹And if a wicked man turns away from his wickedness and does what is just and right, he will live by doing so. ²⁰Yet, O house of Israel, you say, 'The way of the Lord is not just.' But I will judge each of you according to his own ways."

Jerusalem's Fall Explained

²¹In the twelfth year of our exile, in the tenth month on the fifth day, a man who had escaped from Jerusalem came to me and said, "The city has fallen!" ²²Now the evening before the man arrived, the hand of the LORD was upon me, and he opened my mouth before the man came to me in the morning. So my mouth was opened and I was no longer silent.

²³Then the word of the LORD came to me: ²⁴"Son of man, the people living in those ruins in the land of Israel are saying, 'Abraham was only one man, yet he possessed the land. But we are many; surely the land has been given to us as our possession.' ²⁵Therefore say to them, 'This is what the Sovereign LORD says: Since you eat meat with the blood still in it and look to your idols and shed blood, should you then possess the land? ²⁶You rely on your sword, you do detestable things, and each of you defiles his neighbor's wife. Should you then possess the land?'

²⁷"Say this to them: 'This is what the Sovereign LORD says: As surely as I live, those who are left in the ruins will fall by the sword, those out in the country I will give to the wild animals to be devoured, and those in strongholds and caves will die of a plague. ²⁸I will make the land a desolate waste, and her proud strength will come to an end, and the mountains of Israel will become desolate so that no one will cross them. ²⁹Then they will know that I am the LORD, when I have made the land a desolate waste because of all the detestable things they have done.'

³⁰"As for you, son of man, your countrymen are talking together about you by the walls and at the doors of the houses, saying to each other, 'Come and hear the message that has come from the LORD.' ³¹My people come to you, as they usually do, and sit before you to listen to your words, but they do not put them into practice. With their mouths they express devotion, but their hearts are greedy for unjust gain. ³²Indeed, to them you are nothing more than one who sings love songs with a beautiful voice and plays an instrument well, for they hear your words but do not put them into practice.

Praying Ezekiel 33:31
I pray that I will never hear Your Word and not do it, Lord, or speak words of love to You while at the same time pursuing my own gain.

³³"When all this comes true—and it surely will—then they will know that a prophet has been among them."

Shepherds and Sheep

34 The word of the LORD came to me: ²"Son of man, prophesy against the shepherds of Israel; prophesy and say to them:'This is what the Sovereign LORD says: Woe to the shepherds of Israel who only take care of themselves! Should not shepherds take care of the flock? ³You eat the curds, clothe yourselves with the wool and slaughter the choice animals, but you do not take care of the flock. ⁴You have not strengthened the weak or healed the sick or bound up the injured. You have not brought back the strays or searched for the lost. You have ruled them harshly and brutally. ⁵So they were scattered because there was no shepherd, and when they were scattered they became food for all the wild animals. ⁶My sheep wandered over all the mountains and on every high hill. They were scattered over the whole earth, and no one searched or looked for them.

⁷"'Therefore, you shepherds, hear the word of the LORD: ⁸As surely as I live, declares the Sovereign LORD, because my flock lacks a shepherd and so has been plundered and has become food for all the wild animals, and because my shepherds did not search for my flock but cared for themselves rather than for my flock, ⁹therefore, O shepherds, hear the word of the LORD: ¹⁰This is what the Sovereign LORD says: I am against the shepherds and will hold them accountable for my flock. I will remove them from tending the flock so that the shepherds can no longer feed themselves. I will rescue my flock from their mouths, and it will no longer be food for them.

¹¹"'For this is what the Sovereign LORD says: I myself will search for my sheep and look after them. ¹²As a shepherd looks after his scattered flock when he is with them, so will I look after my sheep. I will rescue them from all the places where they were scattered on a day of clouds and darkness. ¹³I will bring them out from the nations and gather them from the countries, and I will bring them into their own land. I will pasture them on the mountains of Israel, in the ravines and in all the settlements in the land. ¹⁴I will tend them in a good pasture, and the mountain heights of Israel will be their grazing land. There they will lie down in good grazing land, and there they will feed in a rich pasture on the mountains of Israel. ¹⁵I myself will tend my sheep and have them lie down, declares the Sovereign LORD. ¹⁶I will search for the lost and bring back the strays. I will bind up the injured and strengthen the weak, but the sleek and the strong I will destroy. I will shepherd the flock with justice.

¹⁷"'As for you, my flock, this is what the Sovereign LORD says: I will judge between one sheep and another, and between rams and goats. ¹⁸Is it not enough for you to feed on the good pasture? Must you also trample the rest of your pasture with your feet? Is it not enough for you to drink clear water? Must you also muddy the rest with your feet? ¹⁹Must my flock feed on what you have trampled and drink what you have muddied with your feet?

²⁰"'Therefore this is what the Sovereign LORD says to them: See, I myself will judge between the fat sheep and the lean sheep. ²¹Because you shove with flank and shoulder, butting all the weak sheep with your horns until you have driven them away, ²²I will save my flock, and they will no longer be plundered. I will judge between one sheep and another. ²³I will place over them one shepherd, my servant David, and he will tend them; he will tend them and be their shepherd. ²⁴I the LORD will be their God, and my servant David will be prince among them. I the LORD have spoken.

²⁵"'I will make a covenant of peace with them and rid the land of wild beasts so that they may live in the desert and sleep in the forests in safety. ²⁶I will bless them and the places surrounding my

hill.[a] I will send down showers in season; there will be showers of blessing. 27The trees of the field will yield their fruit and the ground will yield its crops; the people will be secure in their land. They will know that I am the LORD, when I break the bars of their yoke and rescue them from the hands of those who enslaved them. 28They will no longer be plundered by the nations, nor will wild animals devour them. They will live in safety, and no one will make them afraid. 29I will provide for them a land renowned for its crops, and they will no longer be victims of famine in the land or bear the scorn of the nations. 30Then they will know that I, the LORD their God, am with them and that they, the house of Israel, are my people, declares the Sovereign LORD. 31You my sheep, the sheep of my pasture, are people, and I am your God, declares the Sovereign LORD.' "

A Prophecy Against Edom

35 The word of the LORD came to me: 2"Son of man, set your face against Mount Seir; prophesy against it 3and say: 'This is what the Sovereign LORD says: I am against you, Mount Seir, and I will stretch out my hand against you and make you a desolate waste. 4I will turn your towns into ruins and you will be desolate. Then you will know that I am the LORD.

5" 'Because you harbored an ancient hostility and delivered the Israelites over to the sword at the time of their calamity, the time their punishment reached its climax, 6therefore as surely as I live, declares the Sovereign LORD, I will give you over to bloodshed and it will pursue you. Since you did not hate bloodshed, bloodshed will pursue you. 7I will make Mount Seir a desolate waste and cut off from it all who come and go. 8I will fill your mountains with the slain; those killed by the sword will fall on your hills and in your valleys and in all your ravines. 9I will make you desolate forever; your

towns will not be inhabited. Then you will know that I am the LORD.

10" 'Because you have said, "These two nations and countries will be ours and we will take possession of them," even though I the LORD was there, 11therefore as surely as I live, declares the Sovereign LORD, I will treat you in accordance with the anger and jealousy you showed in your hatred of them and I will make myself known among them when I judge you. 12Then you will know that I the LORD have heard all the contemptible things you have said against the mountains of Israel. You said, "They have been laid waste and have been given over to us to devour." 13You boasted against me and spoke against me without restraint, and I heard it. 14This is what the Sovereign LORD says: While the whole earth rejoices, I will make you desolate. 15Because you rejoiced when the inheritance of the house of Israel became desolate, that is how I will treat you. You will be desolate, O Mount Seir, you and all of Edom. Then they will know that I am the LORD.' "

A Prophecy to the Mountains of Israel

36 "Son of man, prophesy to the mountains of Israel and say, 'O mountains of Israel, hear the word of the LORD. 2This is what the Sovereign LORD says: The enemy said of you, "Aha! The ancient heights have become our possession." ' 3Therefore prophesy and say, 'This is what the Sovereign LORD says: Because they ravaged and hounded you from every side so that you became the possession of the rest of the nations and the object of people's malicious talk and slander, 4therefore, O mountains of Israel, hear the word of the Sovereign LORD: This is what the Sovereign LORD says to the mountains and hills, to the ravines and valleys, to the desolate ruins and the deserted towns that have been plundered and ridiculed by the rest of

---

[a] 26 Or I will make them and the places surrounding my hill a blessing

the nations around you— [5]this is what the Sovereign LORD says: In my burning zeal I have spoken against the rest of the nations, and against all Edom, for with glee and with malice in their hearts they made my land their own possession so that they might plunder its pastureland.' [6]Therefore prophesy concerning the land of Israel and say to the mountains and hills, to the ravines and valleys: 'This is what the Sovereign LORD says: I speak in my jealous wrath because you have suffered the scorn of the nations. [7]Therefore this is what the Sovereign LORD says: I swear with uplifted hand that the nations around you will also suffer scorn.

[8]"'But you, O mountains of Israel, will produce branches and fruit for my people Israel, for they will soon come home. [9]I am concerned for you and will look on you with favor; you will be plowed and sown, [10]and I will multiply the number of people upon you, even the whole house of Israel. The towns will be inhabited and the ruins rebuilt. [11]I will increase the number of men and animals upon you, and they will be fruitful and become numerous. I will settle people on you as in the past and will make you prosper more than before. Then you will know that I am the LORD. [12]I will cause people, my people Israel, to walk upon you. They will possess you, and you will be their inheritance; you will never again deprive them of their children.

[13]"'This is what the Sovereign LORD says: Because people say to you, "You devour men and deprive your nation of its children," [14]therefore you will no longer devour men or make your nation childless, declares the Sovereign LORD. [15]No longer will I make you hear the taunts of the nations, and no longer will you suffer the scorn of the peoples or cause your nation to fall, declares the Sovereign LORD.'"

[16]Again the word of the LORD came to me: [17]"Son of man, when the people of Israel were living in their own land, they defiled it by their conduct and their actions. Their conduct was like a woman's monthly uncleanness in my sight. [18]So I poured out my wrath on them because they had shed blood in the land and because they had defiled it with their idols. [19]I dispersed them among the nations, and they were scattered through the countries; I judged them according to their conduct and their actions. [20]And wherever they went among the nations they profaned my holy name, for it was said of them, 'These are the LORD's people, and yet they had to leave his land.' [21]I had concern for my holy name, which the house of Israel profaned among the nations where they had gone.

[22]"Therefore say to the house of Israel, 'This is what the Sovereign LORD says: It is not for your sake, O house of Israel, that I am going to do these things, but for the sake of my holy name, which you have profaned among the nations where you have gone. [23]I will show the holiness of my great name, which has been profaned among the nations, the name you have profaned among them. Then the nations will know that I am the LORD, declares the Sovereign LORD, when I show myself holy through you before their eyes.

[24]"'For I will take you out of the nations; I will gather you from all the countries and bring you back into your own land. [25]I will sprinkle clean water on you, and you will be clean; I will cleanse you from all your impurities and from all your idols. [26]I will give you a new heart and put a new spirit in you; I will remove from you your heart of stone and give you a heart of flesh. [27]And I will put my Spirit in you and move you to follow my decrees and be careful to keep my laws. [28]You will live in the land I gave your forefathers; you will be my people, and I will be your God. [29]I will save you from all your uncleanness. I will call for the grain and make it plentiful and will not bring famine upon you. [30]I will increase

Moving in the Spirit

GOING deeper

READ AND CONSIDER: EZEKIEL 36:24-32

"And I will put my Spirit in you and move you to follow my decrees and be careful to keep my laws" (Ezekiel 36:27).

We all have to do things we don't want to do. Even in the best of jobs, there are still aspects we don't enjoy. When we do things we don't like simply because we know we need to do them, it builds character in us, makes us disciplined, and forms us into leaders God can trust. Besides, there's always a price to pay when we forsake the things we *need* to do in order to do only the things we *feel* like doing. We must be willing to make sacrifices for the blessings we want.

When we ask God for it, He will give us the discipline we need in order to do all the tasks that are distasteful to us. When God asks us to do something, He also promises to equip us to carry it out. "The one who calls you is faithful and he will do it" (1 Thessalonians 5:24). Look at the men and women in Scripture whom God singled out for extraordinary assignments. Moses was in his senior years, David was only a shepherd boy, and Jesus' mother, Mary, was most likely just a teenager. None of them felt qualified for the work to which God called them, and yet they responded in obedience and faith, and God enabled them to do what they needed to do.

God has promised to put His Spirit within you. Wherever you go and whatever tasks are before you, you have the pledge of His powerful guidance. But you have to be continually tapped into Him. You have to be in constant communication with Him in order to be plugged into His power. You have to be moving in the Spirit in order to do all He has for you to do.

the fruit of the trees and the crops of the field, so that you will no longer suffer disgrace among the nations because of famine. ³¹Then you will remember your evil ways and wicked deeds, and you will loathe yourselves for your sins and detestable practices. ³²I want you to know that I am not doing this for your sake, declares the Sovereign LORD. Be ashamed and disgraced for your conduct, O house of Israel!

³³"'This is what the Sovereign LORD says: On the day I cleanse you from all your sins, I will resettle your towns, and the ruins will be rebuilt. ³⁴The desolate land will be cultivated instead of lying desolate in the sight of all who pass through it. ³⁵They will say, "This land that was laid waste has become like the garden of Eden; the cities that were lying in ruins, desolate and destroyed, are now fortified and inhabited." ³⁶Then the na-

tions around you that remain will know that I the LORD have rebuilt what was destroyed and have replanted what was desolate. I the LORD have spoken, and I will do it.'

³⁷"This is what the Sovereign LORD says: Once again I will yield to the plea of the house of Israel and do this for them: I will make their people as numerous as sheep, ³⁸as numerous as the flocks for offerings at Jerusalem during her appointed feasts. So will the ruined cities be filled with flocks of people. Then they will know that I am the LORD."

The Valley of Dry Bones

37 The hand of the LORD was upon me, and he brought me out by the Spirit of the LORD and set me in the middle of a valley; it was full of bones. ²He led me back and forth among them, and I saw a great many bones on the floor of the valley, bones that were very dry. ³He

asked me, "Son of man, can these bones live?"

I said, "O Sovereign LORD, you alone know."

⁴Then he said to me, "Prophesy to these bones and say to them, 'Dry bones, hear the word of the LORD! ⁵This is what the Sovereign LORD says to these bones: I will make breathª enter you, and you will come to life. ⁶I will attach tendons to you and make flesh come upon you and cover you with skin; I will put breath in you, and you will come to life. Then you will know that I am the LORD.' "

⁷So I prophesied as I was commanded.

And as I was prophesying, there was a noise, a rattling sound, and the bones came together, bone to bone. ⁸I looked, and tendons and flesh appeared on them and skin covered them, but there was no breath in them.

⁹Then he said to me, "Prophesy to the breath; prophesy, son of man, and say to it, 'This is what the Sovereign LORD says: Come from the four winds, O breath, and breathe into these slain, that they may live.' " ¹⁰So I prophesied as he commanded me, and breath entered them; they came to life and stood up on their feet—a vast army.

ª 5 The Hebrew for this word can also mean *wind* or *spirit* (see verses 6-14).

GOING *deeper*

Bringing Dead Things to Life

READ AND CONSIDER: EZEKIEL 37:1-14

"This is what the Sovereign LORD says to these bones: I will make breath enter you, and you will come to life" (Ezekiel 37:5).

One of the most amazing things that God has placed within nature is its ability to recreate itself. Who doesn't rejoice at seeing flowers pop up from the ground, or leaves and blossoms budding on trees after a long winter when everything appeared lifeless and dead?

On the spiritual level as well, God specializes in bringing life where things might have seemed dead. This powerful story in Ezekiel is actually a metaphor—a word picture—of God's ability to restore life in seemingly hopeless situations. With God's hand upon him and led by His Spirit, the prophet Ezekiel sees a vision of an entire valley full of dry bones. God asks Ezekiel whether he thinks these bones can live. The prophet answers wisely: "You alone know," and God proceeds to cover the bones with tendons, flesh, and skin. Then God gives Ezekiel the order to use His holy name to command the breath of life to enter the bones. To Ezekiel's amazement, a great army rises to its feet.

Just as this vision was a symbolic representation of God's intention to restore the nation of Israel after its years of captivity, it has also come to signify His ability to breathe new life into any seemingly hopeless situation. Have you ever used the word "dead" in connection with your life? Has the life gone out of your marriage? Does the church you attend seem lifeless and dull? Is your own heart for God without vibrancy? Does your work feel like it's sucking the life out of you? Just as God commanded Ezekiel to take action in His power, He has given us the power of prayer.

If your marriage lacks love, pray! If your church is without vitality, pray! If your walk with God is dry, pray! If your work is killing you slowly, pray! God is waiting to work through you to bring His life into places and situations you thought were dead. If dry bones can become a vast army, your situation is not beyond hope. You can see dead things brought to life through prayer.

¹¹Then he said to me: "Son of man, these bones are the whole house of Israel. They say, 'Our bones are dried up and our hope is gone; we are cut off.' ¹²Therefore prophesy and say to them: 'This is what the Sovereign LORD says: O my people, I am going to open your graves and bring you up from them; I will bring you back to the land of Israel. ¹³Then you, my people, will know that I am the LORD, when I open your graves and bring you up from them. ¹⁴I will put my Spirit in you and you will live, and I will settle you in your own land. Then you will know that I the LORD have spoken, and I have done it, declares the LORD.' "

One Nation Under One King

¹⁵The word of the LORD came to me: ¹⁶"Son of man, take a stick of wood and write on it, 'Belonging to Judah and the Israelites associated with him.' Then take another stick of wood, and write on it, 'Ephraim's stick, belonging to Joseph and all the house of Israel associated with him.' ¹⁷Join them together into one stick so that they will become one in your hand.

¹⁸"When your countrymen ask you, 'Won't you tell us what you mean by this?' ¹⁹say to them, 'This is what the Sovereign LORD says: I am going to take the stick of Joseph—which is in Ephraim's hand—and of the Israelite tribes associated with him, and join it to Judah's stick, making them a single stick of wood, and they will become one in my hand.' ²⁰Hold before their eyes the sticks you have written on ²¹and say to them, 'This is what the Sovereign LORD says: I will take the Israelites out of the nations where they have gone. I will gather them from all around and bring them back into their own land. ²²I will make them one nation in the land, on the mountains of Israel. There will be one king over all of them and they will never again be two nations or be divided into two kingdoms. ²³They will no longer defile themselves with their idols and vile images or with any of their offenses, for I will save them from all their sinful backsliding,ᵃ and I will cleanse them. They will be my people, and I will be their God.

²⁴'My servant David will be king over them, and they will all have one shepherd. They will follow my laws and be careful to keep my decrees. ²⁵They will live in the land I gave to my servant Jacob, the land where your fathers lived. They and their children and their children's children will live there forever, and David my servant will be their prince forever. ²⁶I will make a covenant of peace with them; it will be an everlasting covenant. I will establish them and increase their numbers, and I will put my sanctuary among them forever. ²⁷My dwelling place will be with them; I will be their God, and they will be my people. ²⁸Then the nations will know that I the LORD make Israel holy, when my sanctuary is among them forever.' "

A Prophecy Against Gog

38 The word of the LORD came to me: ²"Son of man, set your face against Gog, of the land of Magog, the chief prince ofᵇ Meshech and Tubal; prophesy against him ³and say: 'This is what the Sovereign LORD says: I am against you, O Gog, chief prince ofᶜ Meshech and Tubal. ⁴I will turn you around, put hooks in your jaws and bring you out with your whole army—your horses, your horsemen fully armed, and a great horde with large and small shields, all of them brandishing their swords. ⁵Persia, Cushᵈ and Put will be with them, all with shields and helmets, ⁶also Gomer with all its troops, and Beth Togarmah from the far north with all its troops—the many nations with you.

⁷'Get ready; be prepared, you and all the hordes gathered about you, and take command of them. ⁸After many days you will be called to arms. In future years you

---

ᵃ 23 Many Hebrew manuscripts (see also Septuagint); most Hebrew manuscripts *all their dwelling places where they sinned*
ᵇ 2 Or *the prince of Rosh,* ᶜ 3 Or *Gog, prince of Rosh,* ᵈ 5 That is, the upper Nile region

will invade a land that has recovered from war, whose people were gathered from many nations to the mountains of Israel, which had long been desolate. They had been brought out from the nations, and now all of them live in safety. ⁹You and all your troops and the many nations with you will go up, advancing like a storm; you will be like a cloud covering the land.

¹⁰"'This is what the Sovereign LORD says: On that day thoughts will come into your mind and you will devise an evil scheme. ¹¹You will say, "I will invade a land of unwalled villages; I will attack a peaceful and unsuspecting people—all of them living without walls and without gates and bars. ¹²I will plunder and loot and turn my hand against the resettled ruins and the people gathered from the nations, rich in livestock and goods, living at the center of the land." ¹³Sheba and Dedan and the merchants of Tarshish and all her villages[a] will say to you, "Have you come to plunder? Have you gathered your hordes to loot, to carry off silver and gold, to take away livestock and goods and to seize much plunder?"'

¹⁴"Therefore, son of man, prophesy and say to Gog: 'This is what the Sovereign LORD says: In that day, when my people Israel are living in safety, will you not take notice of it? ¹⁵You will come from your place in the far north, you and many nations with you, all of them riding on horses, a great horde, a mighty army. ¹⁶You will advance against my people Israel like a cloud that covers the land. In days to come, O Gog, I will bring you against my land, so that the nations may know me when I show myself holy through you before their eyes.

¹⁷"'This is what the Sovereign LORD says: Are you not the one I spoke of in former days by my servants the prophets of Israel? At that time they prophesied for years that I would bring you against them. ¹⁸This is what will happen in that day: When Gog attacks the land of Israel, my hot anger will be aroused, declares the Sovereign LORD. ¹⁹In my zeal and fiery wrath I declare that at that time there shall be a great earthquake in the land of Israel. ²⁰The fish of the sea, the birds of the air, the beasts of the field, every creature that moves along the ground, and all the people on the face of the earth will tremble at my presence. The mountains will be overturned, the cliffs will crumble and every wall will fall to the ground. ²¹I will summon a sword against Gog on all my mountains, declares the Sovereign LORD. Every man's sword will be against his brother. ²²I will execute judgment upon him with plague and bloodshed; I will pour down torrents of rain, hailstones and burning sulfur on him and on his troops and on the many nations with him. ²³And so I will show my greatness and my holiness, and I will make myself known in the sight of many nations. Then they will know that I am the LORD.'

39 "Son of man, prophesy against Gog and say: 'This is what the Sovereign LORD says: I am against you, O Gog, chief prince of[b] Meshech and Tubal. ²I will turn you around and drag you along. I will bring you from the far north and send you against the mountains of Israel. ³Then I will strike your bow from your left hand and make your arrows drop from your right hand. ⁴On the mountains of Israel you will fall, you and all your troops and the nations with you. I will give you as food to all kinds of carrion birds and to the wild animals. ⁵You will fall in the open field, for I have spoken, declares the Sovereign LORD. ⁶I will send fire on Magog and on those who live in safety in the coastlands, and they will know that I am the LORD.

⁷"'I will make known my holy name among my people Israel. I will no longer let my holy name be profaned, and the nations will know that I the LORD am the Holy One in Israel. ⁸It is coming! It will

---

surely take place, declares the Sovereign LORD. This is the day I have spoken of.

9 " 'Then those who live in the towns of Israel will go out and use the weapons for fuel and burn them up—the small and large shields, the bows and arrows, the war clubs and spears. For seven years they will use them for fuel. 10They will not need to gather wood from the fields or cut it from the forests, because they will use the weapons for fuel. And they will plunder those who plundered them and loot those who looted them, declares the Sovereign LORD.

11 " 'On that day I will give Gog a burial place in Israel, in the valley of those who travel east toward[a] the Sea.[b] It will block the way of travelers, because Gog and all his hordes will be buried there. So it will be called the Valley of Hamon Gog.[c]

12 " 'For seven months the house of Israel will be burying them in order to cleanse the land. 13All the people of the land will bury them, and the day I am glorified will be a memorable day for them, declares the Sovereign LORD.

14 " 'Men will be regularly employed to cleanse the land. Some will go throughout the land and, in addition to them, others will bury those that remain on the ground. At the end of the seven months they will begin their search. 15As they go through the land and one of them sees a human bone, he will set up a marker beside it until the gravediggers have buried it in the Valley of Hamon Gog. 16(Also a town called Hamonah[d] will be there.) And so they will cleanse the land.'

17"Son of man, this is what the Sovereign LORD says: Call out to every kind of bird and all the wild animals: 'Assemble and come together from all around to the sacrifice I am preparing for you, the great sacrifice on the mountains of Israel. There you will eat flesh and drink blood. 18You will eat the flesh of mighty men and drink the blood of the princes of the earth as if they were rams and lambs, goats and bulls—all of them fattened animals from Bashan. 19At the sacrifice I am preparing for you, you will eat fat till you are glutted and drink blood till you are drunk. 20At my table you will eat your fill of horses and riders, mighty men and soldiers of every kind,' declares the Sovereign LORD.

21"I will display my glory among the nations, and all the nations will see the punishment I inflict and the hand I lay upon them. 22From that day forward the house of Israel will know that I am the LORD their God. 23And the nations will know that the people of Israel went into exile for their sin, because they were unfaithful to me. So I hid my face from them and handed them over to their enemies, and they all fell by the sword. 24I dealt with them according to their uncleanness and their offenses, and I hid my face from them.

25"Therefore this is what the Sovereign LORD says: I will now bring Jacob back from captivity[e] and will have compassion on all the people of Israel, and I will be zealous for my holy name. 26They will forget their shame and all the unfaithfulness they showed toward me when they lived in safety in their land with no one to make them afraid. 27When I have brought them back from the nations and have gathered them from the countries of their enemies, I will show myself holy through them in the sight of many nations. 28Then they will know that I am the LORD their God, for though I sent them into exile among the nations, I will gather them to their own land, not leaving any behind. 29I will no longer hide

---

a *11* Or *of*   b *11* That is, the Dead Sea   c *11* *Hamon Gog* means *hordes of Gog.*   d *16* *Hamonah* means *horde.*   e *25* Or *now restore the fortunes of Jacob* my face from them, for I will pour out my Spirit on the house of Israel, declares the Sovereign LORD."

The New Temple Area

40 In the twenty-fifth year of our exile, at the beginning of the year, on the tenth of the month, in the fourteenth year after the fall of the city—on that very day the hand of the LORD was upon me and he took me there. ²In visions of God he took me to the land of Israel and set me on a very high mountain, on whose south side were some buildings that looked like a city. ³He took me there, and I saw a man whose appearance was like bronze; he was standing in the gateway with a linen cord and a measuring rod in his hand. ⁴The man said to me, "Son of man, look with your eyes and hear with your ears and pay attention to everything I am going to show you, for that is why you have been brought here. Tell the house of Israel everything you see."

The East Gate to the Outer Court

⁵I saw a wall completely surrounding the temple area. The length of the measuring rod in the man's hand was six long cubits, each of which was a cubitᵃ and a handbreadth.ᵇ He measured the wall; it was one measuring rod thick and one rod high.

⁶Then he went to the gate facing east. He climbed its steps and measured the threshold of the gate; it was one rod deep.ᶜ ⁷The alcoves for the guards were one rod long and one rod wide, and the projecting walls between the alcoves were five cubits thick. And the threshold of the gate next to the portico facing the temple was one rod deep.

⁸Then he measured the portico of the gateway; ⁹itᵈ was eight cubits deep and its jambs were two cubits thick. The portico of the gateway faced the temple.

¹⁰Inside the east gate were three alcoves on each side; the three had the same measurements, and the faces of the projecting walls on each side had the same measurements. ¹¹Then he measured the width of the entrance to the gateway; it was ten cubits and its length was thirteen cubits. ¹²In front of each alcove was a wall one cubit high, and the alcoves were six cubits square. ¹³Then he measured the gateway from the top of the rear wall of one alcove to the top of the opposite one; the distance was twenty-five cubits from one parapet opening to the opposite one. ¹⁴He measured along the faces of the projecting walls all around the inside of the gateway—sixty cubits. The measurement was up to the porticoᵉ facing the courtyard.ᶠ ¹⁵The distance from the entrance of the gateway to the far end of its portico was fifty cubits. ¹⁶The alcoves and the projecting walls inside the gateway were surmounted by narrow parapet openings all around, as was the portico; the openings all around faced inward. The faces of the projecting walls were decorated with palm trees.

The Outer Court

¹⁷Then he brought me into the outer court. There I saw some rooms and a pavement that had been constructed all around the court; there were thirty rooms along the pavement. ¹⁸It abutted the sides of the gateways and was as wide as they were long; this was the lower pavement. ¹⁹Then he measured the distance from the inside of the lower gateway to the outside of the inner court; it was a hundred cubits on the east side as well as on the north.

The North Gate

²⁰Then he measured the length and width of the gate facing north, leading into the outer court. ²¹Its alcoves—three on each side—its projecting walls and its portico had the same measurements

---

ᵃ5 The common cubit was about 1 1/2 feet (about 0.5 meter). ᵇ5 That is, about 3 inches (about 8 centimeters) ᶜ6 Septuagint; Hebrew *deep, the first threshold, one rod deep* ᵈ8,9 Many Hebrew manuscripts, Septuagint, Vulgate and Syriac; most Hebrew manuscripts *gateway facing the temple; it was one rod deep. ⁹Then he measured the portico of the gateway; it* ᵉ14 Septuagint; Hebrew *projecting wall* ᶠ14 The meaning of the Hebrew for this verse is uncertain.

as those of the first gateway. It was fifty cubits long and twenty-five cubits wide. 22Its openings, its portico and its palm tree decorations had the same measurements as those of the gate facing east. Seven steps led up to it, with its portico opposite them. 23There was a gate to the inner court facing the north gate, just as there was on the east. He measured from one gate to the opposite one; it was a hundred cubits.

The South Gate

24Then he led me to the south side and I saw a gate facing south. He measured its jambs and its portico, and they had the same measurements as the others. 25The gateway and its portico had narrow openings all around, like the openings of the others. It was fifty cubits long and twenty-five cubits wide. 26Seven steps led up to it, with its portico opposite them; it had palm tree decorations on the faces of the projecting walls on each side. 27The inner court also had a gate facing south, and he measured from this gate to the outer gate on the south side; it was a hundred cubits.

Gates to the Inner Court

28Then he brought me into the inner court through the south gate, and he measured the south gate; it had the same measurements as the others. 29Its alcoves, its projecting walls and its portico had the same measurements as the others. The gateway and its portico had openings all around. It was fifty cubits long and twenty-five cubits wide. 30(The porticoes of the gateways around the inner court were twenty-five cubits wide and five cubits deep.) 31Its portico faced the outer court; palm trees decorated its jambs, and eight steps led up to it.

32Then he brought me to the inner court on the east side, and he measured the gateway; it had the same measurements as the others. 33Its alcoves, its pro-

jecting walls and its portico had the same measurements as the others. The gateway and its portico had openings all around. It was fifty cubits long and twenty-five cubits wide. 34Its portico faced the outer court; palm trees decorated the jambs on either side, and eight steps led up to it.

35Then he brought me to the north gate and measured it. It had the same measurements as the others, 36as did its alcoves, its projecting walls and its portico, and it had openings all around. It was fifty cubits long and twenty-five cubits wide. 37Its porticoᵃ faced the outer court; palm trees decorated the jambs on either side, and eight steps led up to it.

The Rooms for Preparing Sacrifices

38A room with a doorway was by the portico in each of the inner gateways, where the burnt offerings were washed. 39In the portico of the gateway were two tables on each side, on which the burnt offerings, sin offerings and guilt offerings were slaughtered. 40By the outside wall of the portico of the gateway, near the steps at the entrance to the north gateway were two tables, and on the other side of the steps were two tables. 41So there were four tables on one side of the gateway and four on the other—eight tables in all—on which the sacrifices were slaughtered. 42There were also four tables of dressed stone for the burnt offerings, each a cubit and a half long, a cubit and a half wide and a cubit high. On them were placed the utensils for slaughtering the burnt offerings and the other sacrifices. 43And double-pronged hooks, each a handbreadth long, were attached to the wall all around. The tables were for the flesh of the offerings.

Rooms for the Priests

44Outside the inner gate, within the inner court, were two rooms, oneᵇ at the side of the north gate and facing south, and another at the side of the southᶜ gate and facing north. 45He said to me, "The

---

ᵃ 37 Septuagint (see also verses 31 and 34); Hebrew *jambs*   ᵇ 44 Septuagint; Hebrew *were rooms for singers, which were*
ᶜ 44 Septuagint; Hebrew *east*

room facing south is for the priests who have charge of the temple, [46] and the room facing north is for the priests who have charge of the altar. These are the sons of Zadok, who are the only Levites who may draw near to the LORD to minister before him."

[47] Then he measured the court: It was square—a hundred cubits long and a hundred cubits wide. And the altar was in front of the temple.

The Temple

[48] He brought me to the portico of the temple and measured the jambs of the portico; they were five cubits wide on either side. The width of the entrance was fourteen cubits and its projecting walls were[a] three cubits wide on either side. [49] The portico was twenty cubits wide, and twelve[b] cubits from front to back. It was reached by a flight of stairs,[c] and there were pillars on each side of the jambs.

41 Then the man brought me to the outer sanctuary and measured the jambs; the width of the jambs was six cubits[d] on each side.[e] [2] The entrance was ten cubits wide, and the projecting walls on each side of it were five cubits wide. He also measured the outer sanctuary; it was forty cubits long and twenty cubits wide.

[3] Then he went into the inner sanctuary and measured the jambs of the entrance; each was two cubits wide. The entrance was six cubits wide, and the projecting walls on each side of it were seven cubits wide. [4] And he measured the length of the inner sanctuary; it was twenty cubits, and its width was twenty cubits across the end of the outer sanctuary. He said to me, "This is the Most Holy Place."

[5] Then he measured the wall of the temple; it was six cubits thick, and each side room around the temple was four cubits wide. [6] The side rooms were on three levels, one above another, thirty on each level. There were ledges all around the wall of the temple to serve as supports for the side rooms, so that the supports were not inserted into the wall of the temple. [7] The side rooms all around the temple were wider at each successive level. The structure surrounding the temple was built in ascending stages, so that the rooms widened as one went upward. A stairway went up from the lowest floor to the top floor through the middle floor.

[8] I saw that the temple had a raised base all around it, forming the foundation of the side rooms. It was the length of the rod, six long cubits. [9] The outer wall of the side rooms was five cubits thick. The open area between the side rooms of the temple [10] and the ˌpriests'ˌ rooms was twenty cubits wide all around the temple. [11] There were entrances to the side rooms from the open area, one on the north and another on the south; and the base adjoining the open area was five cubits wide all around.

[12] The building facing the temple courtyard on the west side was seventy cubits wide. The wall of the building was five cubits thick all around, and its length was ninety cubits.

[13] Then he measured the temple; it was a hundred cubits long, and the temple courtyard and the building with its walls were also a hundred cubits long. [14] The width of the temple courtyard on the east, including the front of the temple, was a hundred cubits.

[15] Then he measured the length of the building facing the courtyard at the rear of the temple, including its galleries on each side; it was a hundred cubits.

The outer sanctuary, the inner sanctuary and the portico facing the court, [16] as well as the thresholds and the narrow windows and galleries around the three of them—everything beyond and including the threshold was covered with wood. The floor, the wall up to the windows,

---

[a] *48* Septuagint; Hebrew *entrance was*   [b] *49* Septuagint; Hebrew *eleven*   [c] *49* Hebrew; Septuagint *Ten steps led up to it*
[d] *1* The common cubit was about 1 1/2 feet (about 0.5 meter).   [e] *1* One Hebrew manuscript and Septuagint; most Hebrew manuscripts *side, the width of the tent*

and the windows were covered. 17In the space above the outside of the entrance to the inner sanctuary and on the walls at regular intervals all around the inner and outer sanctuary 18were carved cherubim and palm trees. Palm trees alternated with cherubim. Each cherub had two faces: 19the face of a man toward the palm tree on one side and the face of a lion toward the palm tree on the other. They were carved all around the whole temple. 20From the floor to the area above the entrance, cherubim and palm trees were carved on the wall of the outer sanctuary.

21The outer sanctuary had a rectangular doorframe, and the one at the front of the Most Holy Place was similar. 22There was a wooden altar three cubits high and two cubits square[a]; its corners, its base[b] and its sides were of wood. The man said to me, "This is the table that is before the LORD." 23Both the outer sanctuary and the Most Holy Place had double doors. 24Each door had two leaves—two hinged leaves for each door. 25And on the doors of the outer sanctuary were carved cherubim and palm trees like those carved on the walls, and there was a wooden overhang on the front of the portico. 26On the sidewalls of the portico were narrow windows with palm trees carved on each side. The side rooms of the temple also had overhangs.

Rooms for the Priests

42 Then the man led me northward into the outer court and brought me to the rooms opposite the temple courtyard and opposite the outer wall on the north side. 2The building whose door faced north was a hundred cubits[c] long and fifty cubits wide. 3Both in the section twenty cubits from the inner court and in the section opposite the pavement of the outer court, gallery faced gallery at the three levels. 4In front of the rooms was an inner passageway ten cubits wide and a hundred cubits[d] long. Their doors

were on the north. 5Now the upper rooms were narrower, for the galleries took more space from them than from the rooms on the lower and middle floors of the building. 6The rooms on the third floor had no pillars, as the courts had; so they were smaller in floor space than those on the lower and middle floors. 7There was an outer wall parallel to the rooms and the outer court; it extended in front of the rooms for fifty cubits. 8While the row of rooms on the side next to the outer court was fifty cubits long, the row on the side nearest the sanctuary was a hundred cubits long. 9The lower rooms had an entrance on the east side as one enters them from the outer court.

10On the south side[e] along the length of the wall of the outer court, adjoining the temple courtyard and opposite the outer wall, were rooms 11with a passageway in front of them. These were like the rooms on the north; they had the same length and width, with similar exits and dimensions. Similar to the doorways on the north 12were the doorways of the rooms on the south. There was a doorway at the beginning of the passageway that was parallel to the corresponding wall extending eastward, by which one enters the rooms.

13Then he said to me, "The north and south rooms facing the temple courtyard are the priests' rooms, where the priests who approach the LORD will eat the most holy offerings. There they will put the most holy offerings—the grain offerings, the sin offerings and the guilt offerings— for the place is holy. 14Once the priests enter the holy precincts, they are not to go into the outer court until they leave behind the garments in which they minister, for these are holy. They are to put on other clothes before they go near the places that are for the people."

15When he had finished measuring what was inside the temple area, he led

---

[a] 22 Septuagint; Hebrew *long*   [b] 22 Septuagint; Hebrew *length*   [c] 2 The common cubit was about 1 1/2 feet (about 0.5 meter).
[d] 4 Septuagint and Syriac; Hebrew *and one cubit*   [e] 10 Septuagint; Hebrew *Eastward*

me out by the east gate and measured the area all around: [16]He measured the east side with the measuring rod; it was five hundred cubits.[a] [17]He measured the north side; it was five hundred cubits[b] by the measuring rod. [18]He measured the south side; it was five hundred cubits by the measuring rod. [19]Then he turned to the west side and measured; it was five hundred cubits by the measuring rod. [20]So he measured the area on all four sides. It had a wall around it, five hundred cubits long and five hundred cubits wide, to separate the holy from the common.

The Glory Returns to the Temple

43 Then the man brought me to the gate facing east, [2]and I saw the glory of the God of Israel coming from the east. His voice was like the roar of rushing waters, and the land was radiant with his glory. [3]The vision I saw was like the vision I had seen when he[c] came to destroy the city and like the visions I had seen by the Kebar River, and I fell facedown. [4]The glory of the LORD entered the temple through the gate facing east. [5]Then the Spirit lifted me up and brought me into the inner court, and the glory of the LORD filled the temple.

[6]While the man was standing beside me, I heard someone speaking to me from inside the temple. [7]He said: "Son of man, this is the place of my throne and the place for the soles of my feet. This is where I will live among the Israelites forever. The house of Israel will never again defile my holy name—neither they nor their kings—by their prostitution[d] and the lifeless idols[e] of their kings at their high places. [8]When they placed their threshold next to my threshold and their doorposts beside my doorposts, with only a wall between me and them, they defiled my holy name by their detestable practices. So I destroyed them in

my anger. [9]Now let them put away from me their prostitution and the lifeless idols of their kings, and I will live among them forever.

> *Praying Ezekiel 43:7*
> *Thank You, Lord, for making me to be a temple in which Your Holy Spirit dwells.*

[10]"Son of man, describe the temple to the people of Israel, that they may be ashamed of their sins. Let them consider the plan, [11]and if they are ashamed of all they have done, make known to them the design of the temple—its arrangement, its exits and entrances—its whole design and all its regulations[f] and laws. Write these down before them so that they may be faithful to its design and follow all its regulations.

[12]"This is the law of the temple: All the surrounding area on top of the mountain will be most holy. Such is the law of the temple.

The Altar

[13]"These are the measurements of the altar in long cubits, that cubit being a cubit[g] and a handbreadth[h]: Its gutter is a cubit deep and a cubit wide, with a rim of one span[i] around the edge. And this is the height of the altar: [14]From the gutter on the ground up to the lower ledge it is two cubits high and a cubit wide, and from the smaller ledge up to the larger ledge it is four cubits high and a cubit wide. [15]The altar hearth is four cubits high, and four horns project upward from the hearth. [16]The altar hearth is square, twelve cubits long and twelve cubits wide. [17]The upper ledge also is square, fourteen cubits long and fourteen cubits wide, with a rim of half a cubit and a gutter of a cubit all around. The steps of the altar face east."

[18]Then he said to me, "Son of man, this is what the Sovereign LORD says:

---

[a] *16* See Septuagint of verse 17; Hebrew *rods*; also in verses 18 and 19.   [b] *17* Septuagint; Hebrew *rods*   [c] *3* Some Hebrew manuscripts and Vulgate; most Hebrew manuscripts *I*   [d] *7* Or *their spiritual adultery*; also in verse 9   [e] *7* Or *the corpses*; also in verse 9   [f] *11* Some Hebrew manuscripts and Septuagint; most Hebrew manuscripts *regulations and its whole design*
[g] *13* The common cubit was about 1 1/2 feet (about 0.5 meter).   [h] *13* That is, about 3 inches (about 8 centimeters)   [i] *13* That is, about 9 inches (about 22 centimeters)

These will be the regulations for sacrificing burnt offerings and sprinkling blood upon the altar when it is built: 19You are to give a young bull as a sin offering to the priests, who are Levites, of the family of Zadok, who come near to minister before me, declares the Sovereign LORD. 20You are to take some of its blood and put it on the four horns of the altar and on the four corners of the upper ledge and all around the rim, and so purify the altar and make atonement for it. 21You are to take the bull for the sin offering and burn it in the designated part of the temple area outside the sanctuary.

22"On the second day you are to offer a male goat without defect for a sin offering, and the altar is to be purified as it was purified with the bull. 23When you have finished purifying it, you are to offer a young bull and a ram from the flock, both without defect. 24You are to offer them before the LORD, and the priests are to sprinkle salt on them and sacrifice them as a burnt offering to the LORD.

25"For seven days you are to provide a male goat daily for a sin offering; you are also to provide a young bull and a ram from the flock, both without defect. 26For seven days they are to make atonement for the altar and cleanse it; thus they will dedicate it. 27At the end of these days, from the eighth day on, the priests are to present your burnt offerings and fellowship offerings[a] on the altar. Then I will accept you, declares the Sovereign LORD."

The Prince, the Levites, the Priests

44 Then the man brought me back to the outer gate of the sanctuary, the one facing east, and it was shut. 2The LORD said to me, "This gate is to remain shut. It must not be opened; no one may enter through it. It is to remain shut because the LORD, the God of Israel, has entered through it. 3The prince himself is the only one who may sit inside the gateway to eat in the presence of the LORD. He is to enter by way of the portico of the gateway and go out the same way."

4Then the man brought me by way of the north gate to the front of the temple. I looked and saw the glory of the LORD filling the temple of the LORD, and I fell facedown.

5The LORD said to me, "Son of man, look carefully, listen closely and give attention to everything I tell you concerning all the regulations regarding the temple of the LORD. Give attention to the entrance of the temple and all the exits of the sanctuary. 6Say to the rebellious house of Israel, 'This is what the Sovereign LORD says: Enough of your detestable practices, O house of Israel! 7In addition to all your other detestable practices, you brought foreigners uncircumcised in heart and flesh into my sanctuary, desecrating my temple while you offered me food, fat and blood, and you broke my covenant. 8Instead of carrying out your duty in regard to my holy things, you put others in charge of my sanctuary. 9This is what the Sovereign LORD says: No foreigner uncircumcised in heart and flesh is to enter my sanctuary, not even the foreigners who live among the Israelites.

10"'The Levites who went far from me when Israel went astray and who wandered from me after their idols must bear the consequences of their sin. 11They may serve in my sanctuary, having charge of the gates of the temple and serving in it; they may slaughter the burnt offerings and sacrifices for the people and stand before the people and serve them. 12But because they served them in the presence of their idols and made the house of Israel fall into sin, therefore I have sworn with

Prayer is . . .

drawing close to God because you delight in Him.

---

a 27 Traditionally *peace offerings*

uplifted hand that they must bear the consequences of their sin, declares the Sovereign LORD. 13They are not to come near to serve me as priests or come near any of my holy things or my most holy offerings; they must bear the shame of their detestable practices. 14Yet I will put them in charge of the duties of the temple and all the work that is to be done in it.

15"'But the priests, who are Levites and descendants of Zadok and who faithfully carried out the duties of my sanctuary when the Israelites went astray from me, are to come near to minister before me; they are to stand before me to offer sacrifices of fat and blood, declares the Sovereign LORD. 16They alone are to enter my sanctuary; they alone are to come near my table to minister before me and perform my service.

17"'When they enter the gates of the inner court, they are to wear linen clothes; they must not wear any woolen garment while ministering at the gates of the inner court or inside the temple. 18They are to wear linen turbans on their heads and linen undergarments around their waists. They must not wear anything that makes them perspire. 19When they go out into the outer court where the people are, they are to take off the clothes they have been ministering in and are to leave them in the sacred rooms, and put on other clothes, so that they do not consecrate the people by means of their garments.

20"'They must not shave their heads or let their hair grow long, but they are to keep the hair of their heads trimmed. 21No priest is to drink wine when he enters the inner court. 22They must not marry widows or divorced women; they may marry only virgins of Israelite descent or widows of priests. 23They are to teach my people the difference between the holy and the common and show them how to distinguish between the unclean and the clean.

24"'In any dispute, the priests are to serve as judges and decide it according to my ordinances. They are to keep my laws and my decrees for all my appointed feasts, and they are to keep my Sabbaths holy.

25"'A priest must not defile himself by going near a dead person; however, if the dead person was his father or mother, son or daughter, brother or unmarried sister, then he may defile himself. 26After he is cleansed, he must wait seven days. 27On the day he goes into the inner court of the sanctuary to minister in the sanctuary, he is to offer a sin offering for himself, declares the Sovereign LORD.

28"'I am to be the only inheritance the priests have. You are to give them no possession in Israel; I will be their possession. 29They will eat the grain offerings, the sin offerings and the guilt offerings; and everything in Israel devoted[a] to the LORD will belong to them. 30The best of all the firstfruits and of all your special gifts will belong to the priests. You are to give them the first portion of your ground meal so that a blessing may rest on your household. 31The priests must not eat anything, bird or animal, found dead or torn by wild animals.

Division of the Land

45 "'When you allot the land as an inheritance, you are to present to the LORD a portion of the land as a sacred district, 25,000 cubits long and 20,000[b] cubits wide; the entire area will be holy. 2Of this, a section 500 cubits square is to be for the sanctuary, with 50 cubits around it for open land. 3In the sacred district, measure off a section 25,000 cubits[c] long and 10,000 cubits[d] wide. In it will be the sanctuary, the Most Holy Place. 4It will be the sacred portion of the land for the priests, who minister in the sanctuary and who draw near to minister before the LORD. It will be a place for their houses as well as a holy place for the sanctuary.

---

a 29 The Hebrew term refers to the irrevocable giving over of things or persons to the LORD.   b 1 Septuagint (see also verses 3 and 5 and 48:9); Hebrew 10,000   c 3 That is, about 7 miles (about 12 kilometers)   d 3 That is, about 3 miles (about 5 kilometers)

⁵An area 25,000 cubits long and 10,000 cubits wide will belong to the Levites, who serve in the temple, as their possession for towns to live in.ᵃ

⁶" 'You are to give the city as its property an area 5,000 cubits wide and 25,000 cubits long, adjoining the sacred portion; it will belong to the whole house of Israel.

⁷" 'The prince will have the land bordering each side of the area formed by the sacred district and the property of the city. It will extend westward from the west side and eastward from the east side, running lengthwise from the western to the eastern border parallel to one of the tribal portions. ⁸This land will be his possession in Israel. And my princes will no longer oppress my people but will allow the house of Israel to possess the land according to their tribes.

⁹" 'This is what the Sovereign LORD says: You have gone far enough, O princes of Israel! Give up your violence and oppression and do what is just and right. Stop dispossessing my people, declares the Sovereign LORD. ¹⁰You are to use accurate scales, an accurate ephahᵇ and an accurate bath.ᶜ ¹¹The ephah and the bath are to be the same size, the bath containing a tenth of a homerᵈ and the ephah a tenth of a homer; the homer is to be the standard measure for both. ¹²The shekelᵉ is to consist of twenty gerahs. Twenty shekels plus twenty-five shekels plus fifteen shekels equal one mina.ᶠ

Offerings and Holy Days

¹³" 'This is the special gift you are to offer: a sixth of an ephah from each homer of wheat and a sixth of an ephah from each homer of barley. ¹⁴The prescribed portion of oil, measured by the bath, is a tenth of a bath from each cor (which consists of ten baths or one homer, for ten baths are equivalent to a homer). ¹⁵Also

one sheep is to be taken from every flock of two hundred from the well-watered pastures of Israel. These will be used for the grain offerings, burnt offerings and fellowship offeringsᵍ to make atonement for the people, declares the Sovereign LORD. ¹⁶All the people of the land will participate in this special gift for the use of the prince in Israel. ¹⁷It will be the duty of the prince to provide the burnt offerings, grain offerings and drink offerings at the festivals, the New Moons and the Sabbaths—at all the appointed feasts of the house of Israel. He will provide the sin offerings, grain offerings, burnt offerings and fellowship offerings to make atonement for the house of Israel.

¹⁸" 'This is what the Sovereign LORD says: In the first month on the first day you are to take a young bull without defect and purify the sanctuary. ¹⁹The priest is to take some of the blood of the sin offering and put it on the doorposts of the temple, on the four corners of the upper ledge of the altar and on the gateposts of the inner court. ²⁰You are to do the same on the seventh day of the month for anyone who sins unintentionally or through ignorance; so you are to make atonement for the temple.

²¹" 'In the first month on the fourteenth day you are to observe the Passover, a feast lasting seven days, during which you shall eat bread made without yeast. ²²On that day the prince is to provide a bull as a sin offering for himself and for all the people of the land. ²³Every day during the seven days of the Feast he is to provide seven bulls and seven rams without defect as a burnt offering to the LORD, and a male goat for a sin offering. ²⁴He is to provide as a grain offering an ephah for each bull and an ephah for each ram, along with a hinʰ of oil for each ephah.

²⁵" 'During the seven days of the Feast, which begins in the seventh month on

---

ᵃ 5 Septuagint; Hebrew *temple; they will have as their possession 20 rooms*   ᵇ 10 An ephah was a dry measure.   ᶜ 10 A bath was a liquid measure.   ᵈ 11 A homer was a dry measure.   ᵉ 12 A shekel weighed about 2/5 ounce (about 11.5 grams).   ᶠ 12 That is, 60 shekels; the common mina was 50 shekels.   ᵍ 15 Traditionally *peace offerings*; also in verse 17   ʰ 24 That is, probably about 4 quarts (about 4 liters) the fifteenth day, he is to make the same provision for sin offerings, burnt offerings, grain offerings and oil.

46 " 'This is what the Sovereign LORD says: The gate of the inner court facing east is to be shut on the six working days, but on the Sabbath day and on the day of the New Moon it is to be opened. [2] The prince is to enter from the outside through the portico of the gateway and stand by the gatepost. The priests are to sacrifice his burnt offering and his fellowship offerings.[a] He is to worship at the threshold of the gateway and then go out, but the gate will not be shut until evening. [3] On the Sabbaths and New Moons the people of the land are to worship in the presence of the LORD at the entrance to that gateway. [4] The burnt offering the prince brings to the LORD on the Sabbath day is to be six male lambs and a ram, all without defect. [5] The grain offering given with the ram is to be an ephah,[b] and the grain offering with the lambs is to be as much as he pleases, along with a hin[c] of oil for each ephah. [6] On the day of the New Moon he is to offer a young bull, six lambs and a ram, all without defect. [7] He is to provide as a grain offering one ephah with the bull, one ephah with the ram, and with the lambs as much as he wants to give, along with a hin of oil with each ephah. [8] When the prince enters, he is to go in through the portico of the gateway, and he is to come out the same way.

Praying Ezekiel 46:3

Heavenly Father, I thank You that because Jesus has broken down every wall of separation, I can worship You any place and any time, and I never have to stand far off from Your presence.

[9] " 'When the people of the land come before the LORD at the appointed feasts, whoever enters by the north gate to worship is to go out the south gate; and whoever enters by the south gate is to go out the north gate. No one is to return through the gate by which he entered, but each is to go out the opposite gate. [10] The prince is to be among them, going in when they go in and going out when they go out.

[11] " 'At the festivals and the appointed feasts, the grain offering is to be an ephah with a bull, an ephah with a ram, and with the lambs as much as one pleases, along with a hin of oil for each ephah. [12] When the prince provides a freewill offering to the LORD—whether a burnt offering or fellowship offerings—the gate facing east is to be opened for him. He shall offer his burnt offering or his fellowship offerings as he does on the Sabbath day. Then he shall go out, and after he has gone out, the gate will be shut.

[13] " 'Every day you are to provide a year-old lamb without defect for a burnt offering to the LORD; morning by morning you shall provide it. [14] You are also to provide with it morning by morning a grain offering, consisting of a sixth of an ephah with a third of a hin of oil to moisten the flour. The presenting of this grain offering to the LORD is a lasting ordinance. [15] So the lamb and the grain offering and the oil shall be provided morning by morning for a regular burnt offering.

[16] " 'This is what the Sovereign LORD says: If the prince makes a gift from his inheritance to one of his sons, it will also belong to his descendants; it is to be their property by inheritance. [17] If, however, he makes a gift from his inheritance to one of his servants, the servant may keep it until the year of freedom; then it will revert to the prince. His inheritance belongs to his sons only; it is theirs. [18] The prince must not take any of the inheritance of the people, driving them off their property. He is to give his sons their inheritance out of his own property, so

---

[a] *2* Traditionally *peace offerings*; also in verse 12   [b] *5* That is, probably about 3/5 bushel (about 22 liters)   [c] *5* That is, probably about 4 quarts (about 4 liters)

that none of my people will be separated from his property.' "

19 Then the man brought me through the entrance at the side of the gate to the sacred rooms facing north, which belonged to the priests, and showed me a place at the western end. 20 He said to me, "This is the place where the priests will cook the guilt offering and the sin offering and bake the grain offering, to avoid bringing them into the outer court and consecrating the people."

21 He then brought me to the outer court and led me around to its four corners, and I saw in each corner another court. 22 In the four corners of the outer court were enclosed[a] courts, forty cubits long and thirty cubits wide; each of the courts in the four corners was the same size. 23 Around the inside of each of the four courts was a ledge of stone, with places for fire built all around under the ledge. 24 He said to me, "These are the kitchens where those who minister at the temple will cook the sacrifices of the people."

The River From the Temple

47 The man brought me back to the entrance of the temple, and I saw water coming out from under the threshold of the temple toward the east (for the temple faced east). The water was coming down from under the south side of the temple, south of the altar. 2 He then brought me out through the north gate and led me around the outside to the outer gate facing east, and the water was flowing from the south side.

3 As the man went eastward with a measuring line in his hand, he measured off a thousand cubits[b] and then led me through water that was ankle-deep. 4 He measured off another thousand cubits and led me through water that was knee-deep. He measured off another thousand and led me through water that was up to the waist. 5 He measured off another

thousand, but now it was a river that I could not cross, because the water had risen and was deep enough to swim in—a river that no one could cross. 6 He asked me, "Son of man, do you see this?"

Then he led me back to the bank of the river. 7 When I arrived there, I saw a great number of trees on each side of the river. 8 He said to me, "This water flows toward the eastern region and goes down into the Arabah,[c] where it enters the Sea.[d] When it empties into the Sea,[d] the water there becomes fresh. 9 Swarms of living creatures will live wherever the river flows. There will be large numbers of fish, because this water flows there and makes the salt water fresh; so where the river flows everything will live. 10 Fishermen will stand along the shore; from En Gedi to En Eglaim there will be places for spreading nets. The fish will be of many kinds—like the fish of the Great Sea.[e] 11 But the swamps and marshes will not become fresh; they will be left for salt. 12 Fruit trees of all kinds will grow on both banks of the river. Their leaves will not wither, nor will their fruit fail. Every month they will bear, because the water from the sanctuary flows to them. Their fruit will serve for food and their leaves for healing."

> *Praying Ezekiel 47:12*
> *Lord, may I continually produce the fruit of Your Spirit because of the edifying and healing stream of living water flowing from You into me.*

The Boundaries of the Land

13 This is what the Sovereign LORD says: "These are the boundaries by which you are to divide the land for an inheritance among the twelve tribes of Israel, with two portions for Joseph. 14 You are to divide it equally among them. Because I swore with uplifted hand to give it to your forefathers, this land will become your inheritance.

---

a 22 The meaning of the Hebrew for this word is uncertain.   b 3 That is, about 1,500 feet (about 450 meters)   c 8 Or the Jordan Valley   d 8 That is, the Dead Sea   e 10 That is, the Mediterranean; also in verses 15, 19 and 20

15"This is to be the boundary of the land:

"On the north side it will run from the Great Sea by the Hethlon road past Lebo[a] Hamath to Zedad, 16Berothah[b] and Sibraim (which lies on the border between Damascus and Hamath), as far as Hazer Hatticon, which is on the border of Hauran. 17The boundary will extend from the sea to Hazar Enan,[c] along the northern border of Damascus, with the border of Hamath to the north. This will be the north boundary.
18"On the east side the boundary will run between Hauran and Damascus, along the Jordan between Gilead and the land of Israel, to the eastern sea and as far as Tamar.[d] This will be the east boundary.
19"On the south side it will run from Tamar as far as the waters of Meribah Kadesh, then along the Wadi ⌊of Egypt⌋ to the Great Sea. This will be the south boundary.
20"On the west side, the Great Sea will be the boundary to a point opposite Lebo[e] Hamath. This will be the west boundary.

21"You are to distribute this land among yourselves according to the tribes of Israel. 22You are to allot it as an inheritance for yourselves and for the aliens who have settled among you and who have children. You are to consider them as native-born Israelites; along with you they are to be allotted an inheritance among the tribes of Israel. 23In whatever tribe the alien settles, there you are to give him his inheritance," declares the Sovereign LORD.

The Division of the Land

48 "These are the tribes, listed by name: At the northern frontier, Dan will have one portion; it will follow the Hethlon road to Lebo[f] Hamath; Hazar Enan and the northern border of Damascus next to Hamath will be part of its border from the east side to the west side.

2"Asher will have one portion; it will border the territory of Dan from east to west.
3"Naphtali will have one portion; it will border the territory of Asher from east to west.
4"Manasseh will have one portion; it will border the territory of Naphtali from east to west.
5"Ephraim will have one portion; it will border the territory of Manasseh from east to west.
6"Reuben will have one portion; it will border the territory of Ephraim from east to west.
7"Judah will have one portion; it will border the territory of Reuben from east to west.
8"Bordering the territory of Judah from east to west will be the portion you are to present as a special gift. It will be 25,000 cubits[g] wide, and its length from east to west will equal one of the tribal portions; the sanctuary will be in the center of it.
9"The special portion you are to offer to the LORD will be 25,000 cubits long and 10,000 cubits[h] wide. 10This will be the sacred portion for the priests. It will be 25,000 cubits long on the north side, 10,000 cubits wide on the west side, 10,000 cubits wide on the east side and 25,000 cubits long on the south side. In the center of it will be the sanctuary of the LORD. 11This will be for the consecrated priests, the Zadokites, who were faithful in serving me and did not go astray as the Levites did when the Israelites went astray. 12It will be a special gift to them from the sacred portion of the land, a most holy portion, bordering the territory of the Levites.

---

a 15 Or *past the entrance to* b 15,16 See Septuagint and Ezekiel 48:1; Hebrew *road to go into Zedad,* 16Hamath, Berothah
c 17 Hebrew *Enon,* a variant of *Enan* d 18 Septuagint and Syriac; Hebrew *Israel. You will measure to the eastern sea*
e 20 Or *opposite the entrance to* f 1 Or *to the entrance to* g 8 That is, about 7 miles (about 12 kilometers) h 9 That is, about 3 miles (about 5 kilometers)

13 "Alongside the territory of the priests, the Levites will have an allotment 25,000 cubits long and 10,000 cubits wide. Its total length will be 25,000 cubits and its width 10,000 cubits. 14 They must not sell or exchange any of it. This is the best of the land and must not pass into other hands, because it is holy to the LORD.

15 "The remaining area, 5,000 cubits wide and 25,000 cubits long, will be for the common use of the city, for houses and for pastureland. The city will be in the center of it 16 and will have these measurements: the north side 4,500 cubits, the south side 4,500 cubits, the east side 4,500 cubits, and the west side 4,500 cubits. 17 The pastureland for the city will be 250 cubits on the north, 250 cubits on the south, 250 cubits on the east, and 250 cubits on the west. 18 What remains of the area, bordering on the sacred portion and running the length of it, will be 10,000 cubits on the east side and 10,000 cubits on the west side. Its produce will supply food for the workers of the city. 19 The workers from the city who farm it will come from all the tribes of Israel. 20 The entire portion will be a square, 25,000 cubits on each side. As a special gift you will set aside the sacred portion, along with the property of the city.

21 "What remains on both sides of the area formed by the sacred portion and the city property will belong to the prince. It will extend eastward from the 25,000 cubits of the sacred portion to the eastern border, and westward from the 25,000 cubits to the western border. Both these areas running the length of the tribal portions will belong to the prince, and the sacred portion with the temple sanctuary will be in the center of them. 22 So the property of the Levites and the property of the city will lie in the center of the area that belongs to the prince. The area belonging to the prince will lie between the border of Judah and the border of Benjamin.

23 "As for the rest of the tribes: Benja-

min will have one portion; it will extend from the east side to the west side.

24 "Simeon will have one portion; it will border the territory of Benjamin from east to west.

25 "Issachar will have one portion; it will border the territory of Simeon from east to west.

26 "Zebulun will have one portion; it will border the territory of Issachar from east to west.

27 "Gad will have one portion; it will border the territory of Zebulun from east to west.

28 "The southern boundary of Gad will run south from Tamar to the waters of Meribah Kadesh, then along the Wadi ⌊of Egypt⌋ to the Great Sea.ᵃ

29 "This is the land you are to allot as an inheritance to the tribes of Israel, and these will be their portions," declares the Sovereign LORD.

The Gates of the City

30 "These will be the exits of the city: Beginning on the north side, which is 4,500 cubits long, 31 the gates of the city will be named after the tribes of Israel. The three gates on the north side will be the gate of Reuben, the gate of Judah and the gate of Levi.

32 "On the east side, which is 4,500 cubits long, will be three gates: the gate of Joseph, the gate of Benjamin and the gate of Dan.

33 "On the south side, which measures 4,500 cubits, will be three gates: the gate of Simeon, the gate of Issachar and the gate of Zebulun.

34 "On the west side, which is 4,500 cubits long, will be three gates: the gate of Gad, the gate of Asher and the gate of Naphtali.

35 "The distance all around will be 18,000 cubits.

"And the name of the city from that time on will be:

THE LORD IS THERE."

ᵃ 28 That is, the Mediterranean

Author: Daniel

Date: 530 BC

Audience: God's people in exile, to remind them of God's absolute, triumphant rule, no matter how bleak or uncertain world events might seem

Prayer Themes:

• Ask God to give you the strength of character to go against the flow of a godless culture (1:8-19).

• Ask the Lord to give you a sturdier faith, one that obeys no matter what the costs (3:16-18).

• Praise God for the comforting truth that He is "sovereign over the kingdoms of men" (5:21).

The clear message behind the fiery furnace and lions' den in the book of Daniel is that God is bigger than anything we face.

Daniel reminds us of the awesome nature and infinite power of the God to whom we pray.

God is absolutely in charge. He controls not only the affairs of people and nations but the entire universe. Everything and everyone everywhere is subject to His perfect rule.

Once we grasp this powerful truth about the greatness of God, prayer ceases to be an uncertain, nervous kind of "spiritual wishing." Because our God sits enthroned above the heavens, the King above all kings, we can both rest and revel in Him when we pray. We have nothing to fear and everything to hope for. We can watch in wonder as His will is done in our lives.

Daniel

Daniel's Training in Babylon

1 In the third year of the reign of Jehoiakim king of Judah, Nebuchadnezzar king of Babylon came to Jerusalem and besieged it. ²And the Lord delivered Jehoiakim king of Judah into his hand, along with some of the articles from the temple of God. These he carried off to the temple of his god in Babylonia[a] and put in the treasure house of his god.

³Then the king ordered Ashpenaz, chief of his court officials, to bring in some of the Israelites from the royal family and the nobility— ⁴young men without any physical defect, handsome, showing aptitude for every kind of learning, well informed, quick to understand, and qualified to serve in the king's palace. He was to teach them the language and literature of the Babylonians.[b] ⁵The king assigned them a daily amount of food and wine

from the king's table. They were to be trained for three years, and after that they were to enter the king's service.

⁶Among these were some from Judah: Daniel, Hananiah, Mishael and Azariah. ⁷The chief official gave them new names: to Daniel, the name Belteshazzar; to Hananiah, Shadrach; to Mishael, Meshach; and to Azariah, Abednego.

Praying Daniel 1:7-8

God, help me to always have a sense of my own destiny and not let the world affect my identity or compromise my purpose in any way.

⁸But Daniel resolved not to defile himself with the royal food and wine, and he asked the chief official for permission not to defile himself this way. ⁹Now God had caused the official to show favor and

---

ᵃ 2 Hebrew *Shinar* ᵇ 4 Or *Chaldeans*

sympathy to Daniel, [10]but the official told Daniel, "I am afraid of my lord the king, who has assigned your[a] food and drink. Why should he see you looking worse than the other young men your age? The king would then have my head because of you."

[11]Daniel then said to the guard whom the chief official had appointed over Daniel, Hananiah, Mishael and Azariah, [12]"Please test your servants for ten days: Give us nothing but vegetables to eat and water to drink. [13]Then compare our appearance with that of the young men who eat the royal food, and treat your servants in accordance with what you see." [14]So he agreed to this and tested them for ten days.

[15]At the end of the ten days they looked healthier and better nourished than any of the young men who ate the royal food. [16]So the guard took away their choice food and the wine they were to drink and gave them vegetables instead.

[17]To these four young men God gave knowledge and understanding of all kinds of literature and learning. And Daniel could understand visions and dreams of all kinds.

[18]At the end of the time set by the king to bring them in, the chief official presented them to Nebuchadnezzar. [19]The king talked with them, and he found none equal to Daniel, Hananiah, Mishael and Azariah; so they entered the king's service. [20]In every matter of wisdom and understanding about which the king questioned them, he found them ten times better than all the magicians and enchanters in his whole kingdom.

[21]And Daniel remained there until the first year of King Cyrus.

Nebuchadnezzar's Dream

2 In the second year of his reign, Nebuchadnezzar had dreams; his mind was troubled and he could not sleep. [2]So the king summoned the magicians, enchant-

ers, sorcerers and astrologers[b] to tell him what he had dreamed. When they came in and stood before the king, [3]he said to them, "I have had a dream that troubles me and I want to know what it means.[c]"

[4]Then the astrologers answered the king in Aramaic,[d] "O king, live forever! Tell your servants the dream, and we will interpret it."

[5]The king replied to the astrologers, "This is what I have firmly decided: If you do not tell me what my dream was and interpret it, I will have you cut into pieces and your houses turned into piles of rubble. [6]But if you tell me the dream and explain it, you will receive from me gifts and rewards and great honor. So tell me the dream and interpret it for me."

[7]Once more they replied, "Let the king tell his servants the dream, and we will interpret it."

[8]Then the king answered, "I am certain that you are trying to gain time, because you realize that this is what I have firmly decided: [9]If you do not tell me the dream, there is just one penalty for you. You have conspired to tell me misleading and wicked things, hoping the situation will change. So then, tell me the dream, and I will know that you can interpret it for me."

[10]The astrologers answered the king, "There is not a man on earth who can do what the king asks! No king, however great and mighty, has ever asked such a thing of any magician or enchanter or astrologer. [11]What the king asks is too difficult. No one can reveal it to the king except the gods, and they do not live among men."

[12]This made the king so angry and furious that he ordered the execution of all the wise men of Babylon. [13]So the decree was issued to put the wise men to death, and men were sent to look for Daniel and his friends to put them to death.

[14]When Arioch, the commander of

---

[a] 10 The Hebrew for *your* and *you* in this verse is plural.   [b] 2 Or *Chaldeans*; also in verses 4, 5 and 10   [c] 3 Or *was*   [d] 4 The text from here through chapter 7 is in Aramaic.

the king's guard, had gone out to put to death the wise men of Babylon, Daniel spoke to him with wisdom and tact. ¹⁵He asked the king's officer, "Why did the king issue such a harsh decree?" Arioch then explained the matter to Daniel. ¹⁶At this, Daniel went in to the king and asked for time, so that he might interpret the dream for him.

¹⁷Then Daniel returned to his house and explained the matter to his friends Hananiah, Mishael and Azariah. ¹⁸He urged them to plead for mercy from the God of heaven concerning this mystery, so that he and his friends might not be executed with the rest of the wise men of Babylon. ¹⁹During the night the mystery was revealed to Daniel in a vision.

Then Daniel praised the God of heaven ²⁰and said:

> "Praise be to the name of God for
>   ever and ever;
>   wisdom and power are his.
> ²¹He changes times and seasons;
>   he sets up kings and deposes them.
> He gives wisdom to the wise
>   and knowledge to the discerning.
> ²²He reveals deep and hidden things;
>   he knows what lies in darkness,
>   and light dwells with him.
> ²³I thank and praise you, O God of my
>   fathers:
>   You have given me wisdom and
>   power,
> you have made known to me what
>   we asked of you,

GOING deeper

Seeing God in the Dark

READ AND CONSIDER: DANIEL 2:17-23

"During the night the mystery was revealed to Daniel in a vision. Then Daniel praised the God of heaven and said: 'Praise be to the name of God for ever and ever; wisdom and power are his' " *(Daniel 2:19-20).*

Why is it that during the daylight hours when we're active and busy, our problems don't seem as serious? But when darkness falls and the lights go out, our fears and worries loom larger. Perhaps it's because we forget that we serve a God who never sleeps and is sovereign over our affairs both day and night. The sovereignty of God is a major theme of the book of Daniel. Throughout this book we see multiple reasons that Daniel and his friends had to praise God for His power and ultimate authority over the situations that literally kept them up at night.

Are you facing situations that cause you to lose sleep at night? If so, you're not alone. For centuries God's people have experienced what are sometimes called "dark nights of the soul." Take comfort in the fact that God uses these times of darkness to teach us invaluable lessons we might never learn in the light. He desires to teach us things about Himself that we will only learn in the dark—when we are holding tightly to Him and He has our undivided attention. During those times, we will be the losers if we resist Him and what He is trying to teach us. He wants to share His secrets with us. "He reveals deep and hidden things; he knows what lies in darkness, and light dwells with him" (2:22).

One of the biggest mistakes we can make is to be angry with God because of things that happen. Or *don't* happen. "Woe to him who quarrels with his Maker" (Isaiah 45:9). Instead, allow God to use these dark times to give you "the treasures of darkness, riches stored in secret places, so that you may know that I am the LORD, the God of Israel, who summons you by name" (Isaiah 45:3).

you have made known to us the dream of the king."

Daniel Interprets the Dream

24Then Daniel went to Arioch, whom the king had appointed to execute the wise men of Babylon, and said to him, "Do not execute the wise men of Babylon. Take me to the king, and I will interpret his dream for him."

25Arioch took Daniel to the king at once and said, "I have found a man among the exiles from Judah who can tell the king what his dream means."

26The king asked Daniel (also called Belteshazzar), "Are you able to tell me what I saw in my dream and interpret it?"

27Daniel replied, "No wise man, enchanter, magician or diviner can explain to the king the mystery he has asked about, 28but there is a God in heaven who reveals mysteries. He has shown King Nebuchadnezzar what will happen in days to come. Your dream and the visions that passed through your mind as you lay on your bed are these:

29"As you were lying there, O king, your mind turned to things to come, and the revealer of mysteries showed you what is going to happen. 30As for me, this mystery has been revealed to me, not because I have greater wisdom than other living men, but so that you, O king, may know the interpretation and that you may understand what went through your mind.

31"You looked, O king, and there before you stood a large statue—an enormous, dazzling statue, awesome in appearance. 32The head of the statue was made of pure gold, its chest and arms of silver, its belly and thighs of bronze, 33its legs of iron, its feet partly of iron and partly of baked clay. 34While you were watching, a rock was cut out, but not by human hands. It struck the statue on its feet of iron and clay and smashed them. 35Then the iron, the clay, the bronze, the silver and the gold were broken to pieces at the same time and became like chaff on a threshing floor in the summer. The wind swept them away without leaving a trace. But the rock that struck the statue became a huge mountain and filled the whole earth.

36"This was the dream, and now we will interpret it to the king. 37You, O king, are the king of kings. The God of heaven has given you dominion and power and might and glory; 38in your hands he has placed mankind and the beasts of the field and the birds of the air. Wherever they live, he has made you ruler over them all. You are that head of gold.

39"After you, another kingdom will rise, inferior to yours. Next, a third kingdom, one of bronze, will rule over the whole earth. 40Finally, there will be a fourth kingdom, strong as iron—for iron breaks and smashes everything—and as iron breaks things to pieces, so it will crush and break all the others. 41Just as you saw that the feet and toes were partly of baked clay and partly of iron, so this will be a divided kingdom; yet it will have some of the strength of iron in it, even as you saw iron mixed with clay. 42As the toes were partly iron and partly clay, so this kingdom will be partly strong and partly brittle. 43And just as you saw the iron mixed with baked clay, so the people will be a mixture and will not remain united, any more than iron mixes with clay.

44"In the time of those kings, the God of heaven will set up a kingdom that will never be destroyed, nor will it be left to another people. It will crush all those kingdoms and bring them to an end, but it will itself endure forever. 45This is the meaning of the vision of the rock cut out of a mountain, but not by human hands—a rock that broke the iron, the bronze, the clay, the silver and the gold to pieces.

"The great God has shown the king what will take place in the future. The dream is true and the interpretation is trustworthy."

46Then King Nebuchadnezzar fell prostrate before Daniel and paid him honor and ordered that an offering and incense be presented to him. 47The king said to Daniel, "Surely your God is the God of gods and the Lord of kings and a revealer of mysteries, for you were able to reveal this mystery."

48Then the king placed Daniel in a high position and lavished many gifts on him. He made him ruler over the entire province of Babylon and placed him in charge of all its wise men. 49Moreover, at Daniel's request the king appointed Shadrach, Meshach and Abednego administrators over the province of Babylon, while Daniel himself remained at the royal court.

The Image of Gold and the Fiery Furnace

3 King Nebuchadnezzar made an image of gold, ninety feet high and nine feet[a] wide, and set it up on the plain of Dura in the province of Babylon. 2He then summoned the satraps, prefects, governors, advisers, treasurers, judges, magistrates and all the other provincial officials to come to the dedication of the image he had set up. 3So the satraps, prefects, governors, advisers, treasurers, judges, magistrates and all the other provincial officials assembled for the dedication of the image that King Nebuchadnezzar had set up, and they stood before it.

4Then the herald loudly proclaimed, "This is what you are commanded to do, O peoples, nations and men of every language: 5As soon as you hear the sound of the horn, flute, zither, lyre, harp, pipes and all kinds of music, you must fall down and worship the image of gold that King Nebuchadnezzar has set up. 6Whoever does not fall down and worship will immediately be thrown into a blazing furnace."

7Therefore, as soon as they heard the sound of the horn, flute, zither, lyre, harp and all kinds of music, all the peoples, nations and men of every language fell down and worshiped the image of gold that King Nebuchadnezzar had set up.

8At this time some astrologers[b] came forward and denounced the Jews. 9They said to King Nebuchadnezzar, "O king, live forever! 10You have issued a decree, O king, that everyone who hears the sound of the horn, flute, zither, lyre, harp, pipes and all kinds of music must fall down and worship the image of gold, 11and that whoever does not fall down and worship will be thrown into a blazing furnace. 12But there are some Jews whom you have set over the affairs of the province of Babylon—Shadrach, Meshach and Abednego—who pay no attention to you, O king. They neither serve your gods nor worship the image of gold you have set up."

13Furious with rage, Nebuchadnezzar summoned Shadrach, Meshach and Abednego. So these men were brought before the king, 14and Nebuchadnezzar said to them, "Is it true, Shadrach, Meshach and Abednego, that you do not serve my gods or worship the image of gold I have set up? 15Now when you hear the sound of the horn, flute, zither, lyre, harp, pipes and all kinds of music, if you are ready to fall down and worship the image I made, very good. But if you do not worship it, you will be thrown immediately into a blazing furnace. Then what god will be able to rescue you from my hand?"

16Shadrach, Meshach and Abednego replied to the king, "O Nebuchadnezzar, we do not need to defend ourselves before you in this matter. 17If we are thrown into the blazing furnace, the God we serve is able to save us from it, and he will rescue us from your hand, O king. 18But even if he does not, we want you to know, O king, that we will not serve your gods or worship the image of gold you have set up."

19Then Nebuchadnezzar was furious with Shadrach, Meshach and Abednego, and his attitude toward them changed. He ordered the furnace heated seven times hotter than usual 20and commanded some

---

a 1 Aramaic *sixty cubits high and six cubits wide* (about 27 meters high and 2.7 meters wide)   b 8 Or *Chaldeans* of the strongest soldiers in his army to tie up Shadrach, Meshach and Abednego and throw them into the blazing furnace. 21So these men, wearing their robes, trousers, turbans and other clothes, were bound and thrown into the blazing furnace. 22The king's command was so urgent and the furnace so hot that the flames of the fire killed the soldiers who took up Shadrach, Meshach and Abednego, 23and these three men, firmly tied, fell into the blazing furnace.

24Then King Nebuchadnezzar leaped to his feet in amazement and asked his advisers, "Weren't there three men that we tied up and threw into the fire?"

They replied, "Certainly, O king."

25He said, "Look! I see four men walking around in the fire, unbound and unharmed, and the fourth looks like a son of the gods."

Praying Daniel 3:25

Thank You, Jesus, that when the heat is on in our lives, You get in the fire with us and are faithful to those who are faithful to You.

26Nebuchadnezzar then approached the opening of the blazing furnace and shouted, "Shadrach, Meshach and Abednego, servants of the Most High God, come out! Come here!"

So Shadrach, Meshach and Abednego came out of the fire, 27and the satraps, prefects, governors and royal advisers crowded around them. They saw that the fire had not harmed their bodies, nor was a hair of their heads singed; their robes were not scorched, and there was no smell of fire on them.

28Then Nebuchadnezzar said, "Praise be to the God of Shadrach, Meshach and Abednego, who has sent his angel and rescued his servants! They trusted in him and defied the king's command and were willing to give up their lives rather than serve or worship any god except their own God. 29Therefore I decree that the people of any nation or language who say anything against the God of Shadrach, Meshach and Abednego be cut into pieces and their houses be turned into piles of rubble, for no other god can save in this way."

30Then the king promoted Shadrach, Meshach and Abednego in the province of Babylon.

Nebuchadnezzar's Dream of a Tree

4 King Nebuchadnezzar,

To the peoples, nations and men of every language, who live in all the world:

May you prosper greatly!

2It is my pleasure to tell you about the miraculous signs and wonders that the Most High God has performed for me.

3How great are his signs,
    how mighty his wonders!
His kingdom is an eternal
        kingdom;
    his dominion endures from
        generation to generation.

4I, Nebuchadnezzar, was at home in my palace, contented and prosperous. 5I had a dream that made me afraid. As I was lying in my bed, the images and visions that passed through my mind terrified me. 6So I commanded that all the wise men of Babylon be brought before me to interpret the dream for me. 7When the magicians, enchanters, astrologersa and diviners came, I told them the dream, but they could not interpret it for me. 8Finally, Daniel came into my presence and I told him the dream. (He is called Belteshazzar, after the name of my god, and the spirit of the holy gods is in him.) 9I said, "Belteshazzar, chief of the magicians, I know that the spirit of

---

a 7 Or *Chaldeans*

the holy gods is in you, and no mystery is too difficult for you. Here is my dream; interpret it for me. 10 These are the visions I saw while lying in my bed: I looked, and there before me stood a tree in the middle of the land. Its height was enormous. 11 The tree grew large and strong and its top touched the sky; it was visible to the ends of the earth. 12 Its leaves were beautiful, its fruit abundant, and on it was food for all. Under it the beasts of the field found shelter, and the birds of the air lived in its branches; from it every creature was fed.

13 "In the visions I saw while lying in my bed, I looked, and there before me was a messenger,[a] a holy one, coming down from heaven. 14 He called in a loud voice: 'Cut down the tree and trim off its branches; strip off its leaves and scatter its fruit. Let the animals flee from under it and the birds from its branches. 15 But let the stump and its roots, bound with iron and bronze, remain in the ground, in the grass of the field.

" 'Let him be drenched with the dew of heaven, and let him live with the animals among the plants of the earth. 16 Let his mind be changed from that of a man and let him be given the mind of an animal, till seven times[b] pass by for him.

17 " 'The decision is announced by messengers, the holy ones declare the verdict, so that the living may know that the Most High is sovereign over the kingdoms of men and gives them to anyone he wishes and sets over them the lowliest of men.'

18 "This is the dream that I, King Nebuchadnezzar, had. Now, Belteshazzar, tell me what it means, for none of the wise men in my kingdom can interpret it for me. But you can, because the spirit of the holy gods is in you."

Daniel Interprets the Dream

19 Then Daniel (also called Belteshazzar) was greatly perplexed for a time, and his thoughts terrified him. So the king said, "Belteshazzar, do not let the dream or its meaning alarm you."

Belteshazzar answered, "My lord, if only the dream applied to your enemies and its meaning to your adversaries! 20 The tree you saw, which grew large and strong, with its top touching the sky, visible to the whole earth, 21 with beautiful leaves and abundant fruit, providing food for all, giving shelter to the beasts of the field, and having nesting places in its branches for the birds of the air— 22 you, O king, are that tree! You have become great and strong; your greatness has grown until it reaches the sky, and your dominion extends to distant parts of the earth.

23 "You, O king, saw a messenger, a holy one, coming down from heaven and saying, 'Cut down the tree and destroy it, but leave the stump, bound with iron and bronze, in the grass of the field, while its roots remain in the ground. Let him be drenched with the dew of heaven; let him live like the wild animals, until seven times pass by for him.'

24 "This is the interpretation, O king, and this is the decree the Most High has issued against my lord the king: 25 You will be driven away from people and will live with the wild animals; you will eat grass like cattle and be drenched with the dew of heaven. Seven times will pass by for you until you acknowledge that the Most High is sovereign over the kingdoms of men and gives them to anyone he wishes. 26 The command to leave the stump of the tree with its roots means that your kingdom will be restored to you when you

---

a 13 Or watchman; also in verses 17 and 23   b 16 Or years; also in verses 23, 25 and 32 acknowledge that Heaven rules. 27Therefore, O king, be pleased to accept my advice: Renounce your sins by doing what is right, and your wickedness by being kind to the oppressed. It may be that then your prosperity will continue."

The Dream Is Fulfilled

28All this happened to King Nebuchadnezzar. 29Twelve months later, as the king was walking on the roof of the royal palace of Babylon, 30he said, "Is not this the great Babylon I have built as the royal residence, by my mighty power and for the glory of my majesty?"

31The words were still on his lips when a voice came from heaven, "This is what is decreed for you, King Nebuchadnezzar: Your royal authority has been taken from you. 32You will be driven away from people and will live with the wild animals; you will eat grass like cattle. Seven times will pass by for you until you acknowledge that the Most High is sovereign over the kingdoms of men and gives them to anyone he wishes."

33Immediately what had been said about Nebuchadnezzar was fulfilled. He was driven away from people and ate grass like cattle. His body was drenched with the dew of heaven until his hair grew like the feathers of an eagle and his nails like the claws of a bird.

34At the end of that time, I, Nebuchadnezzar, raised my eyes toward heaven, and my sanity was restored. Then I praised the Most High; I honored and glorified him who lives forever.

His dominion is an eternal dominion;
  his kingdom endures from
    generation to generation.
35All the peoples of the earth
  are regarded as nothing.

He does as he pleases
  with the powers of heaven
  and the peoples of the earth.
No one can hold back his hand
  or say to him: "What have you
    done?"

36At the same time that my sanity was restored, my honor and splendor were returned to me for the glory of my kingdom. My advisers and nobles sought me out, and I was restored to my throne and became even greater than before. 37Now I, Nebuchadnezzar, praise and exalt and glorify the King of heaven, because everything he does is right and all his ways are just. And those who walk in pride he is able to humble.

The Writing on the Wall

5 King Belshazzar gave a great banquet for a thousand of his nobles and drank wine with them. 2While Belshazzar was drinking his wine, he gave orders to bring in the gold and silver goblets that Nebuchadnezzar his father[a] had taken from the temple in Jerusalem, so that the king and his nobles, his wives and his concubines might drink from them. 3So they brought in the gold goblets that had been taken from the temple of God in Jerusalem, and the king and his nobles, his wives and his concubines drank from them. 4As they drank the wine, they praised the gods of gold and silver, of bronze, iron, wood and stone.

5Suddenly the fingers of a human hand appeared and wrote on the plaster of the wall, near the lampstand in the royal palace. The king watched the hand as it wrote. 6His face turned pale and he was so frightened that his knees knocked together and his legs gave way.

7The king called out for the enchanters, astrologers[b] and diviners to be brought and said to these wise men of Babylon, "Whoever reads this writing and tells me what it means will be clothed in purple

---

[a] 2 Or ancestor, or predecessor; also in verses 11, 13 and 18   [b] 7 Or Chaldeans; also in verse 11

How Can I Make Prayer a Daily Habit?

We need to determine what time each day we can be with God alone or the opportunity will slip through our fingers. I have found that it is best to pray in the morning when I first get up. If I don't do it then, it becomes much harder later, and I find myself struggling to have something more than a pray-and-run time. But it might be better for you at midmorning, lunchtime, sometime in the afternoon, or in the evening after dinner. I've tried having my main prayer time before I go to bed, but I am usually so tired by then that I spend a lot less time and I am not as clear thinking. Also, doing it then doesn't provide the advantage of having the day covered from the beginning. On the other hand, spending time with God at night helps me sleep peacefully. Regardless of when you do it, the point is to *allow* time for daily prayer so it becomes a habit.

Ask God to *help* you carve out the time you need to spend with Him. He will show you things you can eliminate from your schedule, or at least shorten to the point of giving you an extra 20 to 30 minutes. I have found that if I can get on my knees and pray *before* I do much else, then my day is not off and running without me while I am trying to catch up. Just as you would never leave the house in the morning without brushing your teeth, it should also be that you wouldn't think of starting your day without being alone with God. Even if it is only for a few minutes, you have at least started the day on the right track.

It is good to have some paper and a pencil handy when coming before God so that you can write down what He speaks to your heart in your prayer time. He may remind you of something you would otherwise have forgotten. He might bring to mind something you need to do that you would not have thought of. These kinds of things make your life easier and less confusing or haphazard.

Your personal prayer time with God is the foundation for all other kinds of effective prayer. It's not that you *can't* pray with other people until you have prayed alone with God. If that were the case, most of us would not even be saved. Nor would we have experienced the healing, deliverance, or restoration we have due to the prayers of others for us. And we've all had times where the troubles in our lives were so great that we were sustained by the prayers of others. But eventually, in order to move on in the things of God, we have to establish our own personal prayer time with the Lord. Ask God to help you do that. He will.

For the next "From Stormie's Heart" article, go to page 1094.

and have a gold chain placed around his neck, and he will be made the third highest ruler in the kingdom."

8 Then all the king's wise men came in, but they could not read the writing or tell the king what it meant. 9 So King Belshazzar became even more terrified and his face grew more pale. His nobles were baffled.

10 The queen,[a] hearing the voices of the king and his nobles, came into the banquet hall. "O king, live forever!" she said. "Don't be alarmed! Don't look so pale! 11 There is a man in your kingdom who has the spirit of the holy gods in him. In the time of your father he was found to have insight and intelligence and wisdom like that of the gods. King Nebuchadnezzar your father—your father the king, I say—appointed him chief of the magicians, enchanters, astrologers and diviners. 12 This man Daniel, whom the king called Belteshazzar, was found to have a keen mind and knowledge and understanding, and also the ability to interpret dreams, explain riddles and solve difficult problems. Call for Daniel, and he will tell you what the writing means."

13 So Daniel was brought before the king, and the king said to him, "Are you Daniel, one of the exiles my father the king brought from Judah? 14 I have heard that the spirit of the gods is in you and that you have insight, intelligence and outstanding wisdom. 15 The wise men and enchanters were brought before me to read this writing and tell me what it means, but they could not explain it. 16 Now I have heard that you are able to give interpretations and to solve difficult problems. If you can read this writing and tell me what it means, you will be clothed in purple and have a gold chain placed around your neck, and you will be made the third highest ruler in the kingdom."

17 Then Daniel answered the king, "You may keep your gifts for yourself and give your rewards to someone else. Nevertheless, I will read the writing for the king and tell him what it means.

18 "O king, the Most High God gave your father Nebuchadnezzar sovereignty and greatness and glory and splendor. 19 Because of the high position he gave him, all the peoples and nations and men of every language dreaded and feared him. Those the king wanted to put to death, he put to death; those he wanted to spare, he spared; those he wanted to promote, he promoted; and those he wanted to humble, he humbled. 20 But when his heart became arrogant and hardened with pride, he was deposed from his royal throne and stripped of his glory. 21 He was driven away from people and given the mind of an animal; he lived with the wild donkeys and ate grass like cattle; and his body was drenched with the dew of heaven, until he acknowledged that the Most High God is sovereign over the kingdoms of men and sets over them anyone he wishes.

22 "But you his son,[b] O Belshazzar, have not humbled yourself, though you knew all this. 23 Instead, you have set yourself up against the Lord of heaven. You had the goblets from his temple brought to you, and you and your nobles, your wives and your concubines drank wine from them. You praised the gods of silver and gold, of bronze, iron, wood and stone, which cannot see or hear or understand. But you did not honor the God who holds in his hand your life and all your ways. 24 Therefore he sent the hand that wrote the inscription.

25 "This is the inscription that was written:

MENE, MENE, TEKEL, PARSIN[c]

26 "This is what these words mean:

Mene[d]: God has numbered the days of your reign and brought it to an end.

---

a 10 Or queen mother   b 22 Or descendant; or successor   c 25 Aramaic UPARSIN (that is, AND PARSIN)   d 26 Mene can mean numbered or mina (a unit of money).

27 *Tekel*[a]: You have been weighed on the scales and found wanting.

28 *Peres*[b]: Your kingdom is divided and given to the Medes and Persians."

29 Then at Belshazzar's command, Daniel was clothed in purple, a gold chain was placed around his neck, and he was proclaimed the third highest ruler in the kingdom.

30 That very night Belshazzar, king of the Babylonians,[c] was slain, 31 and Darius the Mede took over the kingdom, at the age of sixty-two.

Daniel in the Den of Lions

6 It pleased Darius to appoint 120 satraps to rule throughout the kingdom, 2 with three administrators over them, one of whom was Daniel. The satraps were made accountable to them so that the king might not suffer loss. 3 Now Daniel so distinguished himself among the administrators and the satraps by his exceptional qualities that the king planned to set him over the whole kingdom. 4 At this, the administrators and the satraps tried to find grounds for charges against Daniel in his conduct of government affairs, but they were unable to do so. They could find no corruption in him, because he was trustworthy and neither corrupt nor negligent. 5 Finally these men said, "We will never find any basis for charges against this man Daniel unless it has something to do with the law of his God."

6 So the administrators and the satraps went as a group to the king and said: "O King Darius, live forever! 7 The royal administrators, prefects, satraps, advisers and governors have all agreed that the king should issue an edict and enforce the decree that anyone who prays to any god or man during the next thirty days, except to you, O king, shall be thrown into the lions' den. 8 Now, O king, issue the decree and put it in writing so that it cannot be altered—in accordance with the laws of the Medes and Persians, which cannot be repealed." 9 So King Darius put the decree in writing.

10 Now when Daniel learned that the decree had been published, he went home to his upstairs room where the windows

---

[a] 27 *Tekel* can mean *weighed* or *shekel*.   [b] 28 *Peres* (the singular of *Parsin*) can mean *divided* or *Persia* or *a half mina* or *a half shekel*.   [c] 30 Or *Chaldeans*

God's people at prayer
DANIEL'S DISCIPLINED PRAYER LIFE

DANIEL 6:1-13 Imagine that the civil authorities in your area have enacted a law prohibiting prayer, public or private, upon penalty of death. Knowing that your very life is at stake, you have a choice to make. You can obey the edict, you can "go underground" with your prayer life, or you can continue on praying as you have always done and pay the consequences.

Daniel faced this same choice, and Scripture is very clear on his decision. He continued to pray on his knees three times each day, "just as he had done before." The spiritual disciplines Daniel had established early on stayed with him throughout his life. He refused to be intimidated by the threats of those in power. He refused to worship any other god. Daniel understood then what Jesus later talked about when He instructed people not to fear those who could only harm the body (Matthew 10:28).

Regardless of how pressured you feel by the demands of your life and schedule, no matter what ridicule you might face from those around you, dare to be a Daniel and pray when you need to pray. God is greater than any intimidation or diversion you might face.

opened toward Jerusalem. Three times a day he got down on his knees and prayed, giving thanks to his God, just as he had done before. ¹¹Then these men went as a group and found Daniel praying and asking God for help. ¹²So they went to the king and spoke to him about his royal decree: "Did you not publish a decree that during the next thirty days anyone who prays to any god or man except to you, O king, would be thrown into the lions' den?"

The king answered, "The decree stands—in accordance with the laws of the Medes and Persians, which cannot be repealed."

¹³Then they said to the king, "Daniel, who is one of the exiles from Judah, pays no attention to you, O king, or to the decree you put in writing. He still prays three times a day." ¹⁴When the king heard this, he was greatly distressed; he was determined to rescue Daniel and made every effort until sundown to save him.

¹⁵Then the men went as a group to the king and said to him, "Remember, O king, that according to the law of the Medes and Persians no decree or edict that the king issues can be changed."

¹⁶So the king gave the order, and they brought Daniel and threw him into the lions' den. The king said to Daniel, "May your God, whom you serve continually, rescue you!"

¹⁷A stone was brought and placed over the mouth of the den, and the king sealed it with his own signet ring and with the rings of his nobles, so that Daniel's situation might not be changed. ¹⁸Then the king returned to his palace and spent the night without eating and without any entertainment being brought to him. And he could not sleep.

¹⁹At the first light of dawn, the king got up and hurried to the lions' den. ²⁰When he came near the den, he called to Daniel in an anguished voice, "Daniel, servant of the living God, has your God, whom you

serve continually, been able to rescue you from the lions?"

²¹Daniel answered, "O king, live forever! ²²My God sent his angel, and he shut the mouths of the lions. They have not hurt me, because I was found innocent in his sight. Nor have I ever done any wrong before you, O king."

²³The king was overjoyed and gave orders to lift Daniel out of the den. And when Daniel was lifted from the den, no wound was found on him, because he had trusted in his God.

²⁴At the king's command, the men who had falsely accused Daniel were brought in and thrown into the lions' den, along with their wives and children. And before they reached the floor of the den, the lions overpowered them and crushed all their bones.

²⁵Then King Darius wrote to all the peoples, nations and men of every language throughout the land:

"May you prosper greatly!

²⁶"I issue a decree that in every part of my kingdom people must fear and reverence the God of Daniel.

"For he is the living God
    and he endures forever;
his kingdom will not be destroyed,
    his dominion will never end.
²⁷He rescues and he saves;
    he performs signs and wonders
    in the heavens and on the earth.
He has rescued Daniel
    from the power of the lions."

²⁸So Daniel prospered during the reign of Darius and the reign of Cyrusᵃ the Persian.

Daniel's Dream of Four Beasts

7 In the first year of Belshazzar king of Babylon, Daniel had a dream, and visions passed through his mind as he was lying on his bed. He wrote down the substance of his dream.

ᵃ 28 Or Darius, that is, the reign of Cyrus

²Daniel said: "In my vision at night I looked, and there before me were the four winds of heaven churning up the great sea. ³Four great beasts, each different from the others, came up out of the sea.

⁴"The first was like a lion, and it had the wings of an eagle. I watched until its wings were torn off and it was lifted from the ground so that it stood on two feet like a man, and the heart of a man was given to it.

⁵"And there before me was a second beast, which looked like a bear. It was raised up on one of its sides, and it had three ribs in its mouth between its teeth. It was told, 'Get up and eat your fill of flesh!'

⁶"After that, I looked, and there before me was another beast, one that looked like a leopard. And on its back it had four wings like those of a bird. This beast had four heads, and it was given authority to rule.

⁷"After that, in my vision at night I looked, and there before me was a fourth beast—terrifying and frightening and very powerful. It had large iron teeth; it crushed and devoured its victims and trampled underfoot whatever was left. It was different from all the former beasts, and it had ten horns.

⁸"While I was thinking about the horns, there before me was another horn, a little one, which came up among them; and three of the first horns were uprooted before it. This horn had eyes like the eyes of a man and a mouth that spoke boastfully.

⁹"As I looked,

"thrones were set in place,
    and the Ancient of Days took his
        seat.
His clothing was as white as snow;
    the hair of his head was white like
        wool.
His throne was flaming with fire,
    and its wheels were all ablaze.
¹⁰A river of fire was flowing,

coming out from before him.
Thousands upon thousands attended
    him;
    ten thousand times ten thousand
        stood before him.
The court was seated,
    and the books were opened.

¹¹"Then I continued to watch because of the boastful words the horn was speaking. I kept looking until the beast was slain and its body destroyed and thrown into the blazing fire. ¹²(The other beasts had been stripped of their authority, but were allowed to live for a period of time.)

¹³"In my vision at night I looked, and there before me was one like a son of man, coming with the clouds of heaven. He approached the Ancient of Days and was led into his presence. ¹⁴He was given authority, glory and sovereign power; all peoples, nations and men of every language worshiped him. His dominion is an everlasting dominion that will not pass away, and his kingdom is one that will never be destroyed.

The Interpretation of the Dream

¹⁵"I, Daniel, was troubled in spirit, and the visions that passed through my mind disturbed me. ¹⁶I approached one of those standing there and asked him the true meaning of all this.

"So he told me and gave me the interpretation of these things: ¹⁷'The four great beasts are four kingdoms that will rise from the earth. ¹⁸But the saints of the Most High will receive the kingdom and will possess it forever—yes, for ever and ever.'

¹⁹"Then I wanted to know the true meaning of the fourth beast, which was different from all the others and most terrifying, with its iron teeth and bronze claws—the beast that crushed and devoured its victims and trampled underfoot whatever was left. ²⁰I also wanted to know about the ten horns on its head and about the other horn that came up, before which three of them fell—the

horn that looked more imposing than the others and that had eyes and a mouth that spoke boastfully. 21As I watched, this horn was waging war against the saints and defeating them, 22until the Ancient of Days came and pronounced judgment in favor of the saints of the Most High, and the time came when they possessed the kingdom.

23"He gave me this explanation: 'The fourth beast is a fourth kingdom that will appear on earth. It will be different from all the other kingdoms and will devour the whole earth, trampling it down and crushing it. 24The ten horns are ten kings who will come from this kingdom. After them another king will arise, different from the earlier ones; he will subdue three kings. 25He will speak against the Most High and oppress his saints and try to change the set times and the laws. The saints will be handed over to him for a time, times and half a time.[a]

26"'But the court will sit, and his power will be taken away and completely destroyed forever. 27Then the sovereignty, power and greatness of the kingdoms under the whole heaven will be handed over to the saints, the people of the Most High. His kingdom will be an everlasting kingdom, and all rulers will worship and obey him.'

28"This is the end of the matter. I, Daniel, was deeply troubled by my thoughts, and my face turned pale, but I kept the matter to myself."

Daniel's Vision of a Ram and a Goat

8 In the third year of King Belshazzar's reign, I, Daniel, had a vision, after the one that had already appeared to me. 2In my vision I saw myself in the citadel of Susa in the province of Elam; in the vision I was beside the Ulai Canal. 3I looked up, and there before me was a ram with two horns, standing beside the canal, and the horns were long. One of the horns was longer than the other but grew up later. 4I watched the ram as he charged toward the west and the north and the south. No animal could stand against him, and none could rescue from his power. He did as he pleased and became great.

5As I was thinking about this, suddenly a goat with a prominent horn between his eyes came from the west, crossing the whole earth without touching the ground. 6He came toward the two-horned ram I had seen standing beside the canal and charged at him in great rage. 7I saw him attack the ram furiously, striking the ram and shattering his two horns. The ram was powerless to stand against him; the goat knocked him to the ground and trampled on him, and none could rescue the ram from his power. 8The goat became very great, but at the height of his power his large horn was broken off, and in its place four prominent horns grew up toward the four winds of heaven.

9Out of one of them came another horn, which started small but grew in power to the south and to the east and toward the Beautiful Land. 10It grew until it reached the host of the heavens, and it threw some of the starry host down to the earth and trampled on them. 11It set itself up to be as great as the Prince of the host; it took away the daily sacrifice from him, and the place of his sanctuary was brought low. 12Because of rebellion, the host ⌊of the saints⌋[b] and the daily sacrifice were given over to it. It prospered in everything it did, and truth was thrown to the ground.

13Then I heard a holy one speaking, and another holy one said to him, "How long will it take for the vision to be fulfilled—the vision concerning the daily sacrifice, the rebellion that causes desolation, and the surrender of the sanctuary and of the host that will be trampled underfoot?"

14He said to me, "It will take 2,300 evenings and mornings; then the sanctuary will be reconsecrated."

---

a 25 Or for a year, two years and half a year   b 12 Or rebellion, the armies

The Interpretation of the Vision

15While I, Daniel, was watching the vision and trying to understand it, there before me stood one who looked like a man. 16And I heard a man's voice from the Ulai calling, "Gabriel, tell this man the meaning of the vision."

17As he came near the place where I was standing, I was terrified and fell prostrate. "Son of man," he said to me, "understand that the vision concerns the time of the end."

18While he was speaking to me, I was in a deep sleep, with my face to the ground. Then he touched me and raised me to my feet.

19He said: "I am going to tell you what will happen later in the time of wrath, because the vision concerns the appointed time of the end.ª 20The two-horned ram that you saw represents the kings of Media and Persia. 21The shaggy goat is the king of Greece, and the large horn between his eyes is the first king. 22The four horns that replaced the one that was broken off represent four kingdoms that will emerge from his nation but will not have the same power.

23"In the latter part of their reign, when rebels have become completely wicked, a stern-faced king, a master of intrigue, will arise. 24He will become very strong, but not by his own power. He will cause astounding devastation and will succeed in whatever he does. He will destroy the mighty men and the holy people. 25He will cause deceit to prosper, and he will consider himself superior. When they feel secure, he will destroy many and take his stand against the Prince of princes. Yet he will be destroyed, but not by human power.

26"The vision of the evenings and mornings that has been given you is true, but seal up the vision, for it concerns the distant future."

27I, Daniel, was exhausted and lay ill for several days. Then I got up and went about the king's business. I was appalled by the vision; it was beyond understanding.

Daniel's Prayer

9 In the first year of Darius son of Xerxesᵇ (a Mede by descent), who was made ruler over the Babylonianᶜ kingdom— 2in the first year of his reign, I, Daniel, understood from the Scriptures, according to the word of the LORD given to Jeremiah the prophet, that the desolation of Jerusalem would last seventy years. 3So I turned to the Lord God and pleaded with him in prayer and petition, in fasting, and in sackcloth and ashes.

4I prayed to the LORD my God and confessed:

"O Lord, the great and awesome God, who keeps his covenant of love with all who love him and obey his commands, 5we have sinned and done wrong. We have been wicked and have rebelled; we have turned away from your commands and laws. 6We have not listened to your servants the prophets, who spoke in your name to our kings, our princes and our fathers, and to all the people of the land.

7"Lord, you are righteous, but this day we are covered with shame—the men of Judah and people of Jerusalem and all Israel, both near and far, in all the countries where you have scattered us because of our unfaithfulness to you. 8O LORD, we and our kings, our princes and our fathers are covered with shame because we have sinned against you. 9The Lord our God is merciful and forgiving, even though we have rebelled against him; 10we have not obeyed the LORD our God or kept the laws he gave us through his servants the prophets. 11All Israel has transgressed your law and turned away, refusing to obey you.

ª 19 Or because the end will be at the appointed time   ᵇ 1 Hebrew Ahasuerus   ᶜ 1 Or Chaldean

"Therefore the curses and sworn judgments written in the Law of Moses, the servant of God, have been poured out on us, because we have sinned against you. [12]You have fulfilled the words spoken against us and against our rulers by bringing upon us great disaster. Under the whole heaven nothing has ever been done like what has been done to Jerusalem. [13]Just as it is written in the Law of Moses, all this disaster has come upon us, yet we have not sought the favor of the LORD our God by turning from our sins and giving attention to your truth. [14]The LORD did not hesitate to bring the disaster upon us, for the LORD our God is righteous in everything he does; yet we have not obeyed him.

[15]"Now, O Lord our God, who brought your people out of Egypt with a mighty hand and who made for yourself a name that endures to this day, we have sinned, we have done wrong. [16]O Lord, in keeping with all your righteous acts, turn away your anger and your wrath from Jerusalem, your city, your holy hill. Our sins and the iniquities of our fathers have made Jerusalem and your people an object of scorn to all those around us.

[17]"Now, our God, hear the prayers and petitions of your servant. For your sake, O Lord, look with favor on your desolate sanctuary. [18]Give ear, O God, and hear; open your eyes and see the desolation of the city that bears your Name. We do not make requests of you because we are righteous, but because of your great mercy. [19]O Lord, listen! O Lord, forgive! O Lord, hear and act! For your sake, O my God, do not delay, because your city and your people bear your Name."

GOING *deeper*

Crying Out for God's Mercy

READ AND CONSIDER: DANIEL 9:4-19

"Now, our God, hear the prayers and petitions of your servant . . . We do not make requests of you because we are righteous, but because of your great mercy" (Daniel 9:17-18).

Daniel had many reasons to be deeply alarmed. His own people were in exile, and he was pleading with God for the end of their captivity and their return to Jerusalem. But Daniel wasn't asking God for His help because the people deserved it. He was making his request because he knew God was a merciful God. Daniel cried out, "but because of your great mercy." Daniel was begging God to extend compassion and mercy to the people because of who *the Lord* was, not because of who the people were. His passionate prayer was a petition to a holy and righteous God—a God who grants grace in difficult situations because of His nature. Grace is not something that we can ever earn or deserve. Even our very salvation is a work of God's grace. "For it is by grace you have been saved, through faith—and this not from yourselves, it is the gift of God—not by works, so that no one can boast" (Ephesians 2:8-9).

When we are going through difficult circumstances, we can ask God's help even though we don't deserve it. Just like the tax collector Jesus described in one of His parables, we can say, "God, have mercy on me, a sinner" (Luke 18:13). Then praise Him that His help isn't dependent on what we do or on our "works," but on who *He* is.

The Seventy "Sevens"

20While I was speaking and praying, confessing my sin and the sin of my people Israel and making my request to the LORD my God for his holy hill— 21while I was still in prayer, Gabriel, the man I had seen in the earlier vision, came to me in swift flight about the time of the evening sacrifice. 22He instructed me and said to me, "Daniel, I have now come to give you insight and understanding. 23As soon as you began to pray, an answer was given, which I have come to tell you, for you are highly esteemed. Therefore, consider the message and understand the vision:

24"Seventy 'sevens'a are decreed for your people and your holy city to finishb transgression, to put an end to sin, to atone for wickedness, to bring in everlasting righteousness, to seal up vision and prophecy and to anoint the most holy.c

25"Know and understand this: From the issuing of the decreed to restore and rebuild Jerusalem until the Anointed One,e the ruler, comes, there will be seven 'sevens,' and sixty-two 'sevens.' It will be rebuilt with streets and a trench, but in times of trouble. 26After the sixty-two 'sevens,' the Anointed One will be cut off and will have nothing.f The people of the ruler who will come will destroy the city and the sanctuary. The end will come like a flood: War will continue until the end, and desolations have been decreed. 27He will confirm a covenant with many for one 'seven.'g In the middle of the 'seven'g he will put an end to sacrifice and offering. And on a wing ⸤of the temple⸥ he will set up an abomination that causes desolation, until the end that is decreed is poured out on him.h"i

Daniel's Vision of a Man

10 In the third year of Cyrus king of Persia, a revelation was given to Daniel (who was called Belteshazzar).

Its message was true and it concerned a great war.j The understanding of the message came to him in a vision.

2At that time I, Daniel, mourned for three weeks. 3I ate no choice food; no meat or wine touched my lips; and I used no lotions at all until the three weeks were over.

4On the twenty-fourth day of the first month, as I was standing on the bank of the great river, the Tigris, 5I looked up and there before me was a man dressed in linen, with a belt of the finest gold around his waist. 6His body was like chrysolite, his face like lightning, his eyes like flaming torches, his arms and legs like the gleam of burnished bronze, and his voice like the sound of a multitude.

7I, Daniel, was the only one who saw the vision; the men with me did not see it, but such terror overwhelmed them that they fled and hid themselves. 8So I was left alone, gazing at this great vision; I had no strength left, my face turned deathly pale and I was helpless. 9Then I heard him speaking, and as I listened to him, I fell into a deep sleep, my face to the ground.

10A hand touched me and set me trembling on my hands and knees. 11He said, "Daniel, you who are highly esteemed, consider carefully the words I am about to speak to you, and stand up, for I have now been sent to you." And when he said this to me, I stood up trembling.

12Then he continued, "Do not be afraid, Daniel. Since the first day that you set your mind to gain understanding and to humble yourself before your God, your words were heard, and I have come in response to them. 13But the prince of the Persian kingdom resisted me twenty-one days. Then Michael, one of the chief princes, came to help me, because I was detained there with the king of Persia. 14Now I have come to explain to you

a 24 Or 'weeks'; also in verses 25 and 26   b 24 Or restrain   c 24 Or Most Holy Place; or most holy One   d 25 Or word   e 25 Or an anointed one; also in verse 26   f 26 Or off and will have no one; or off, but not for himself   g 27 Or 'week'   h 27 Or it   i 27 Or And one who causes desolation will come upon the pinnacle of the abominable ⸤temple⸥, until the end that is decreed is poured out on the desolated ⸤city⸥   j 1 Or true and burdensome

Finding Faith to Wait for the Answer

READ AND CONSIDER: DANIEL 10:1-14

"Then he continued, 'Do not be afraid, Daniel. Since the first day that you set your mind to gain understanding and to humble yourself before your God, your words were heard, and I have come in response to them. But the prince of the Persian kingdom resisted me twenty-one days'" (Daniel 10:12-13).

Have you ever waited anxiously for a promised letter or package to arrive, only to have days, weeks, or maybe even months pass by with no sign of it? How do you know for certain that it was placed in the mail in the first place or that it wasn't delivered to the wrong address?

When it comes to prayer, most of us will have times when we wonder whether the answer to our request has been "lost." Did God hear us at all, and is He planning to respond?

The book of Daniel contains one of the most encouraging yet sobering conversations recorded in the Bible when it comes to receiving an answer to prayer. Daniel had been faithfully fasting and praying for weeks without seeing any response. After 21 days, he had a vision of an angelic being who appeared to him and told him the reason for the delay: A spiritual battle was being waged in the heavens. Daniel was told that the messenger had been sent in response to his prayers from the first day, but he had been detained by opposition from "the prince of the Persian kingdom," a reference to an evil supernatural force. When Daniel persisted in prayer, help was sent to the first messenger in the form of the archangel Michael, and the messenger finally reached Daniel with a word from God for the future.

What an encouragement this is for us! God has promised to hear our prayers when we come to Him in faith, but we need to remember that Satan may throw obstacles in the way of our receiving the answers God has sent. What are we to do? Continue to pray! The prayers of a righteous man or woman are powerful and effective (James 5:16). Don't give up when the answer doesn't come right away. God hears and will answer. You have His Word on it!

---

what will happen to your people in the future, for the vision concerns a time yet to come."

15While he was saying this to me, I bowed with my face toward the ground and was speechless. 16Then one who looked like a man[a] touched my lips, and I opened my mouth and began to speak. I said to the one standing before me, "I am overcome with anguish because of the vision, my lord, and I am helpless. 17How can I, your servant, talk with you, my lord? My strength is gone and I can hardly breathe."

18Again the one who looked like a man touched me and gave me strength.

19"Do not be afraid, O man highly esteemed," he said. "Peace! Be strong now; be strong."

When he spoke to me, I was strengthened and said, "Speak, my lord, since you have given me strength."

20So he said, "Do you know why I have come to you? Soon I will return to fight against the prince of Persia, and when I go, the prince of Greece will come; 21but first I will tell you what is written in the Book of Truth. (No one supports me against them except Michael, your prince. 1And in the first year of Darius the Mede, I took my stand to support and protect him.)

---

a *16* Most manuscripts of the Masoretic Text; one manuscript of the Masoretic Text, Dead Sea Scrolls and Septuagint *Then something that looked like a man's hand*

The Kings of the South and the North

2"Now then, I tell you the truth: Three more kings will appear in Persia, and then a fourth, who will be far richer than all the others. When he has gained power by his wealth, he will stir up everyone against the kingdom of Greece. 3Then a mighty king will appear, who will rule with great power and do as he pleases. 4After he has appeared, his empire will be broken up and parceled out toward the four winds of heaven. It will not go to his descendants, nor will it have the power he exercised, because his empire will be uprooted and given to others.

5"The king of the South will become strong, but one of his commanders will become even stronger than he and will rule his own kingdom with great power. 6After some years, they will become allies. The daughter of the king of the South will go to the king of the North to make an alliance, but she will not retain her power, and he and his power[a] will not last. In those days she will be handed over, together with her royal escort and her father[b] and the one who supported her.

7"One from her family line will arise to take her place. He will attack the forces of the king of the North and enter his fortress; he will fight against them and be victorious. 8He will also seize their gods, their metal images and their valuable articles of silver and gold and carry them off to Egypt. For some years he will leave the king of the North alone. 9Then the king of the North will invade the realm of the king of the South but will retreat to his own country. 10His sons will prepare for war and assemble a great army, which will sweep on like an irresistible flood and carry the battle as far as his fortress.

11"Then the king of the South will march out in a rage and fight against the king of the North, who will raise a large army, but it will be defeated. 12When the army is carried off, the king of the South will be filled with pride and will slaughter many thousands, yet he will not remain triumphant. 13For the king of the North will muster another army, larger than the first; and after several years, he will advance with a huge army fully equipped.

14"In those times many will rise against the king of the South. The violent men among your own people will rebel in fulfillment of the vision, but without success. 15Then the king of the North will come and build up siege ramps and will capture a fortified city. The forces of the South will be powerless to resist; even their best troops will not have the strength to stand. 16The invader will do as he pleases; no one will be able to stand against him. He will establish himself in the Beautiful Land and will have the power to destroy it. 17He will determine to come with the might of his entire kingdom and will make an alliance with the king of the South. And he will give him a daughter in marriage in order to overthrow the kingdom, but his plans[c] will not succeed or help him. 18Then he will turn his attention to the coastlands and will take many of them, but a commander will put an end to his insolence and will turn his insolence back upon him. 19After this, he will turn back toward the fortresses of his own country but will stumble and fall, to be seen no more.

20"His successor will send out a tax collector to maintain the royal splendor. In a few years, however, he will be destroyed, yet not in anger or in battle.

21"He will be succeeded by a contemptible person who has not been given the honor of royalty. He will invade the kingdom when its people feel secure, and he will seize it through intrigue. 22Then an overwhelming army will be swept away before him; both it and a prince of the covenant will be destroyed. 23After coming to an agreement with him, he will act deceitfully, and with only a few people he will rise to power. 24When the richest provinces feel secure, he will invade them

---

a 6 Or offspring   b 6 Or child (see Vulgate and Syriac)   c 17 Or but she and will achieve what neither his fathers nor his forefathers did. He will distribute plunder, loot and wealth among his followers. He will plot the overthrow of fortresses—but only for a time.

25 "With a large army he will stir up his strength and courage against the king of the South. The king of the South will wage war with a large and very powerful army, but he will not be able to stand because of the plots devised against him. 26 Those who eat from the king's provisions will try to destroy him; his army will be swept away, and many will fall in battle. 27 The two kings, with their hearts bent on evil, will sit at the same table and lie to each other, but to no avail, because an end will still come at the appointed time. 28 The king of the North will return to his own country with great wealth, but his heart will be set against the holy covenant. He will take action against it and then return to his own country.

29 "At the appointed time he will invade the South again, but this time the outcome will be different from what it was before. 30 Ships of the western coastlandsᵃ will oppose him, and he will lose heart. Then he will turn back and vent his fury against the holy covenant. He will return and show favor to those who forsake the holy covenant.

31 "His armed forces will rise up to desecrate the temple fortress and will abolish the daily sacrifice. Then they will set up the abomination that causes desolation. 32 With flattery he will corrupt those who have violated the covenant, but the people who know their God will firmly resist him.

33 "Those who are wise will instruct many, though for a time they will fall by the sword or be burned or captured or plundered. 34 When they fall, they will receive a little help, and many who are not sincere will join them. 35 Some of the wise will stumble, so that they may be refined, purified and made spotless until the time of the end, for it will still come at the appointed time.

The King Who Exalts Himself

36 "The king will do as he pleases. He will exalt and magnify himself above every god and will say unheard-of things against the God of gods. He will be successful until the time of wrath is completed, for what has been determined must take place. 37 He will show no regard for the gods of his fathers or for the one desired by women, nor will he regard any god, but will exalt himself above them all. 38 Instead of them, he will honor a god of fortresses; a god unknown to his fathers he will honor with gold and silver, with precious stones and costly gifts. 39 He will attack the mightiest fortresses with the help of a foreign god and will greatly honor those who acknowledge him. He will make them rulers over many people and will distribute the land at a price.ᵇ

40 "At the time of the end the king of the South will engage him in battle, and the king of the North will storm out against him with chariots and cavalry and a great fleet of ships. He will invade many countries and sweep through them like a flood. 41 He will also invade the Beautiful Land. Many countries will fall, but Edom, Moab and the leaders of Ammon will be delivered from his hand. 42 He will extend his power over many countries; Egypt will not escape. 43 He will gain control of the treasures of gold and silver and all the riches of Egypt, with the Libyans and Nubians in submission. 44 But reports from the east and the north will alarm him, and he will set out in a great rage to destroy and annihilate many. 45 He will pitch his royal tents between the seas atᶜ the beautiful holy mountain. Yet he will come to his end, and no one will help him.

The End Times

12 "At that time Michael, the great prince who protects your people, will arise. There will be a time of dis-

---

tress such as has not happened from the beginning of nations until then. But at that time your people—everyone whose name is found written in the book—will be delivered. [2]Multitudes who sleep in the dust of the earth will awake: some to everlasting life, others to shame and everlasting contempt. [3]Those who are wise[a] will shine like the brightness of the heavens, and those who lead many to righteousness, like the stars for ever and ever. [4]But you, Daniel, close up and seal the words of the scroll until the time of the end. Many will go here and there to increase knowledge."

[5]Then I, Daniel, looked, and there before me stood two others, one on this bank of the river and one on the opposite bank. [6]One of them said to the man clothed in linen, who was above the waters of the river, "How long will it be before these astonishing things are fulfilled?"

[7]The man clothed in linen, who was above the waters of the river, lifted his right hand and his left hand toward heaven, and I heard him swear by him who lives forever, saying, "It will be for a time, times and half a time.[b] When the power of the holy people has been finally broken, all these things will be completed."

[8]I heard, but I did not understand. So I asked, "My lord, what will the outcome of all this be?"

[9]He replied, "Go your way, Daniel, because the words are closed up and sealed until the time of the end. [10]Many will be purified, made spotless and refined, but the wicked will continue to be wicked. None of the wicked will understand, but those who are wise will understand.

[11]"From the time that the daily sacrifice is abolished and the abomination that causes desolation is set up, there will be 1,290 days. [12]Blessed is the one who waits for and reaches the end of the 1,335 days.

[13]"As for you, go your way till the end. You will rest, and then at the end of the days you will rise to receive your allotted inheritance."

---

[a] 3 Or *who impart wisdom*   [b] 7 Or *a year, two years and half a year*

Author: Hosea

Date: About the middle of the eighth century BC

Audience: The unfaithful tribes of the northern kingdom of Israel—to graphically show them the undying love of God despite their blatant spiritual infidelity

Sometimes we get so caught up in the theology of prayer, so concerned with the "how to" of it, so obsessed with what words to use and in what order, we lose sight of the One to whom we're speaking.

When we get to that place, Hosea jolts us back to reality by revealing God not as an unfeeling "force" who dispenses answers to prayers like some kind of impersonal heavenly vending machine, but as a compassionate Creator. In this heart-wrenching book, through the unlikely marriage of the prophet Hosea and an immoral woman named Gomer, God shows Himself to be a lover who has been betrayed.

What a shock to think that when we stop talking to God and no longer pursue Him, when we turn away from Him in order to go after unimportant things, we don't merely break God's law . . . we break His heart.

Prayer Themes:

• *Praise God for His endless commitment to you—that nothing will stop Him from loving you and pursuing you (2:5-20).*

• *Ask God to deliver you from any superficial religious commitment or devotion that is merely outward and ritualistic (6:1-6).*

• *Ask the Lord to teach you what genuine, heartfelt repentance is and to correct any tendencies you may have to wander away from Him (14:1-9).*

Hosea

1 The word of the LORD that came to Hosea son of Beeri during the reigns of Uzziah, Jotham, Ahaz and Hezekiah, kings of Judah, and during the reign of Jeroboam son of Jehoash[a] king of Israel:

Hosea's Wife and Children

²When the LORD began to speak through Hosea, the LORD said to him, "Go, take to yourself an adulterous wife and children of unfaithfulness, because the land is guilty of the vilest adultery in departing from the LORD." ³So he married Gomer daughter of Diblaim, and she conceived and bore him a son.

⁴Then the LORD said to Hosea, "Call him Jezreel, because I will soon punish the house of Jehu for the massacre at Jezreel, and I will put an end to the kingdom of Israel. ⁵In that day I will break Israel's bow in the Valley of Jezreel."

⁶Gomer conceived again and gave birth to a daughter. Then the LORD said to Hosea, "Call her Lo-Ruhamah,[b] for I will no longer show love to the house of Israel, that I should at all forgive them. ⁷Yet I will show love to the house of Judah; and I will save them—not by bow, sword or battle, or by horses and horsemen, but by the LORD their God."

⁸After she had weaned Lo-Ruhamah, Gomer had another son. ⁹Then the LORD said, "Call him Lo-Ammi,[c] for you are not my people, and I am not your God.

¹⁰"Yet the Israelites will be like the sand on the seashore, which cannot be measured or counted. In the place where it was said to them, 'You are not my people,' they will be called 'sons of the living God.' ¹¹The people of Judah and the people of Israel will be reunited, and they will appoint one leader and will come up out of the land, for great will be the day of Jezreel.

ᵃ 1 Hebrew *Joash*, a variant of *Jehoash*   ᵇ 6 *Lo-Ruhamah* means *not loved*.   ᶜ 9 *Lo-Ammi* means *not my people*.

2 "Say of your brothers, 'My people,'
and of your sisters, 'My loved one.'

Israel Punished and Restored

2 "Rebuke your mother, rebuke her,
for she is not my wife,
and I am not her husband.
Let her remove the adulterous look
from her face
and the unfaithfulness from
between her breasts.
3 Otherwise I will strip her naked
and make her as bare as on the day
she was born;
I will make her like a desert,
turn her into a parched land,
and slay her with thirst.
4 I will not show my love to her
children,
because they are the children of
adultery.
5 Their mother has been unfaithful
and has conceived them in disgrace.
She said, 'I will go after my lovers,
who give me my food and my water,
my wool and my linen, my oil and
my drink.'
6 Therefore I will block her path with
thornbushes;
I will wall her in so that she cannot
find her way.
7 She will chase after her lovers but not
catch them;
she will look for them but not find
them.
Then she will say,
'I will go back to my husband as at
first,
for then I was better off than now.'
8 She has not acknowledged that I was
the one
who gave her the grain, the new
wine and oil,
who lavished on her the silver and
gold—
which they used for Baal.

9 "Therefore I will take away my grain
when it ripens,

and my new wine when it is ready.
I will take back my wool and my
linen,
intended to cover her nakedness.
10 So now I will expose her lewdness
before the eyes of her lovers;
no one will take her out of my
hands.
11 I will stop all her celebrations:
her yearly festivals, her New
Moons,
her Sabbath days—all her appointed
feasts.
12 I will ruin her vines and her fig trees,
which she said were her pay from
her lovers;
I will make them a thicket,
and wild animals will devour them.
13 I will punish her for the days
she burned incense to the Baals;
she decked herself with rings and
jewelry,
and went after her lovers,
but me she forgot,"
declares the LORD.

14 "Therefore I am now going to allure
her;
I will lead her into the desert
and speak tenderly to her.
15 There I will give her back her
vineyards,
and will make the Valley of Achor[a]
a door of hope.
There she will sing[b] as in the days of
her youth,
as in the day she came up out of
Egypt.

16 "In that day," declares the LORD,
"you will call me 'my husband';
you will no longer call me 'my
master.[c]'
17 I will remove the names of the Baals
from her lips;
no longer will their names be
invoked.
18 In that day I will make a covenant for
them

---

a 15 Achor means trouble.   b 15 Or respond   c 16 Hebrew baal

with the beasts of the field and the
   birds of the air
and the creatures that move along
   the ground.
Bow and sword and battle
   I will abolish from the land,
   so that all may lie down in safety.
[19] I will betroth you to me forever;
   I will betroth you in[a] righteousness
      and justice,
   in[b] love and compassion.
[20] I will betroth you in faithfulness,
   and you will acknowledge the
      LORD.

[21] "In that day I will respond,"
   declares the LORD—
   "I will respond to the skies,
      and they will respond to the earth;
[22] and the earth will respond to the
      grain,
   the new wine and oil,
      and they will respond to Jezreel.[c]
[23] I will plant her for myself in the land;
   I will show my love to the one I
      called 'Not my loved one.[d]'
   I will say to those called 'Not my
      people,[e]' 'You are my people';
   and they will say, 'You are my
      God.'"

Hosea's Reconciliation With His Wife

3 The LORD said to me, "Go, show your
   love to your wife again, though she
is loved by another and is an adulteress.
Love her as the LORD loves the Israelites,
though they turn to other gods and love
the sacred raisin cakes."

   [2] So I bought her for fifteen shekels[f] of
silver and about a homer and a lethek[g] of
barley. [3] Then I told her, "You are to live
with[h] me many days; you must not be a
prostitute or be intimate with any man,
and I will live with[h] you."

   [4] For the Israelites will live many days
without king or prince, without sacrifice or sacred stones, without ephod or

idol. [5] Afterward the Israelites will return
and seek the LORD their God and David
their king. They will come trembling
to the LORD and to his blessings in the
last days.

The Charge Against Israel

4 Hear the word of the LORD, you
   Israelites,
   because the LORD has a charge to
      bring
   against you who live in the land:
"There is no faithfulness, no love,
   no acknowledgment of God in the
      land.
[2] There is only cursing,[i] lying and
      murder,
   stealing and adultery;
   they break all bounds,
      and bloodshed follows bloodshed.
[3] Because of this the land mourns,[j]
   and all who live in it waste away;
   the beasts of the field and the birds of
      the air
   and the fish of the sea are dying.

[4] "But let no man bring a charge,
   let no man accuse another,
for your people are like those
   who bring charges against a priest.
[5] You stumble day and night,
   and the prophets stumble with you.
So I will destroy your mother—

> *Praying Hosea 4:6*
> *Lord, give me wisdom and knowledge*
> *so that I will not do things in*
> *ignorance and perish because of it.*

[6]   my people are destroyed from lack
         of knowledge.

"Because you have rejected
      knowledge,
   I also reject you as my priests;
because you have ignored the law of
      your God,
   I also will ignore your children.

---

[a] 19 Or with; also in verse 20 [b] 19 Or with [c] 22 Jezreel means God plants. [d] 23 Hebrew Lo-Ruhamah [e] 23 Hebrew Lo-Ammi
[f] 2 That is, about 6 ounces (about 170 grams) [g] 2 That is, probably about 10 bushels (about 330 liters) [h] 3 Or wait for
[i] 2 That is, to pronounce a curse upon [j] 3 Or dries up

7 The more the priests increased,
  the more they sinned against me;
  they exchanged[a] their[b] Glory for
    something disgraceful.
8 They feed on the sins of my people
  and relish their wickedness.
9 And it will be: Like people, like
    priests.
  I will punish both of them for their
    ways
  and repay them for their deeds.

10 "They will eat but not have enough;
  they will engage in prostitution but
    not increase,
  because they have deserted the LORD
  to give themselves 11 to prostitution,
  to old wine and new,
  which take away the understanding
    12 of my people.
  They consult a wooden idol
  and are answered by a stick of
    wood.
  A spirit of prostitution leads them
    astray;
  they are unfaithful to their God.
13 They sacrifice on the mountaintops
  and burn offerings on the hills,
  under oak, poplar and terebinth,
  where the shade is pleasant.
  Therefore your daughters turn to
    prostitution
  and your daughters-in-law to
    adultery.

14 "I will not punish your daughters
  when they turn to prostitution,
  nor your daughters-in-law
  when they commit adultery,
  because the men themselves consort
    with harlots
  and sacrifice with shrine
    prostitutes—
  a people without understanding
  will come to ruin!

15 "Though you commit adultery,
    O Israel,
  let not Judah become guilty.

"Do not go to Gilgal;
  do not go up to Beth Aven.[c]
  And do not swear, 'As surely as the
    LORD lives!'
16 The Israelites are stubborn,
  like a stubborn heifer.
  How then can the LORD pasture them
  like lambs in a meadow?
17 Ephraim is joined to idols;
  leave him alone!
18 Even when their drinks are gone,
  they continue their prostitution;
  their rulers dearly love shameful
    ways.
19 A whirlwind will sweep them away,
  and their sacrifices will bring them
    shame.

Judgment Against Israel

5 "Hear this, you priests!
  Pay attention, you Israelites!
  Listen, O royal house!
  This judgment is against you:
  You have been a snare at Mizpah,
  a net spread out on Tabor.
2 The rebels are deep in slaughter.
  I will discipline all of them.
3 I know all about Ephraim;
  Israel is not hidden from me.
  Ephraim, you have now turned to
    prostitution;
  Israel is corrupt.

4 "Their deeds do not permit them
  to return to their God.
  A spirit of prostitution is in their
    heart;
  they do not acknowledge the LORD.
5 Israel's arrogance testifies against them;
  the Israelites, even Ephraim,
  stumble in their sin;
  Judah also stumbles with them.
6 When they go with their flocks and
    herds
  to seek the LORD,
  they will not find him;
  he has withdrawn himself from
    them.

---

a 7 Syriac and an ancient Hebrew scribal tradition; Masoretic Text *I will exchange*   b 7 Masoretic Text; an ancient Hebrew scribal tradition *my*   c 15 Beth Aven means *house of wickedness* (a name for Bethel, which means *house of God*).

Four Reasons We Go Through Difficult Times

1. *Sometimes difficult things happen to us so that the glory and power of God can be revealed in and through us.* When Jesus passed by a man who was born blind, His disciples asked Him if the man's blindness was because he had sinned or because his parents had sinned. Jesus replied, "Neither this man nor his parents sinned...but this happened so that the work of God might be displayed in his life" (John 9:3). We may not be able to understand why certain things are happening at the time, and we may never know why we have to go through them until we go to be with the Lord, but when we turn to God in the midst of difficult situations, God's glory will be seen in them and on you.

2. *Sometimes God uses difficult times to purify us.* The Bible says, "Since Christ suffered in his body, arm yourselves also with the same attitude, because he who has suffered in his body is done with sin" (1 Peter 4:1). This means our suffering during difficult times will burn sin and selfishness out of our lives. God allows suffering to happen so that we will learn to live for Him and not for ourselves. So that we will pursue His will and not our own. It's not pleasant at the time, but God's desire is "that we may share in his holiness" (Hebrews 12:10). He wants us to let go of the things we lust after and cling to what is most important in life—Him.

3. *Sometimes our misery is caused by God disciplining us.* "No discipline seems pleasant at the time, but painful. Later on, however, it produces a harvest of righteousness and peace for those who have been trained by it" (Hebrews 12:11). The fruit that this godly disciplining and pruning produces in us is worth the trouble we have to go through to get it, and we have to be careful not to resist it or hate it. "Do not make light of the Lord's discipline, and do not lose heart when he rebukes you, because the Lord disciplines those he loves, and he punishes everyone he accepts as a son" (Hebrews 12:5-6).

4. *Sometimes we are caught in the midst of the enemy's work.* It's the enemy's delight to make you miserable and try to destroy your life. Often the reason for the anguish, sorrow, sadness, grief, or pain you feel is entirely his doing and no fault of your own or anyone else's. Your comfort is in knowing that as you praise God in the midst of it, He will defeat the enemy and bring good out of it that you can't even fathom. He wants you to walk with Him in faith as He leads you through it, and He will teach you to trust Him in the midst of it.

Every time you rise above the pain in your life and find the goodness, clarity, peace, and light of the Lord there, your faith will increase. God will meet you in the midst of your pain and not only perfect you, but increase your compassion for the sufferings of others. As you continue to live in the presence of the Lord, His glory will be revealed in you.

For the next "From Stormie's Heart" article, go to page 1131.

7 They are unfaithful to the LORD;
   they give birth to illegitimate
      children.
Now their New Moon festivals
   will devour them and their fields.

8 "Sound the trumpet in Gibeah,
   the horn in Ramah.
Raise the battle cry in Beth Aven[a];
   lead on, O Benjamin.
9 Ephraim will be laid waste
   on the day of reckoning.
Among the tribes of Israel
   I proclaim what is certain.
10 Judah's leaders are like those
   who move boundary stones.
I will pour out my wrath on them
   like a flood of water.
11 Ephraim is oppressed,
   trampled in judgment,
   intent on pursuing idols.[b]
12 I am like a moth to Ephraim,
   like rot to the people of Judah.

13 "When Ephraim saw his sickness,
   and Judah his sores,
then Ephraim turned to Assyria,
   and sent to the great king for help.
But he is not able to cure you,
   not able to heal your sores.
14 For I will be like a lion to Ephraim,
   like a great lion to Judah.
I will tear them to pieces and go
      away;
   I will carry them off, with no one
      to rescue them.
15 Then I will go back to my place
   until they admit their guilt.
And they will seek my face;
   in their misery they will earnestly
      seek me."

Israel Unrepentant

6 "Come, let us return to the LORD.
   He has torn us to pieces
      but he will heal us;
he has injured us
   but he will bind up our wounds.
2 After two days he will revive us;

on the third day he will restore us,
   that we may live in his presence.
3 Let us acknowledge the LORD;
   let us press on to acknowledge him.
As surely as the sun rises,
   he will appear;
he will come to us like the winter
      rains,
   like the spring rains that water the
      earth."

4 "What can I do with you, Ephraim?
   What can I do with you, Judah?
Your love is like the morning mist,
   like the early dew that disappears.
5 Therefore I cut you in pieces with my
      prophets,
   I killed you with the words of my
      mouth;
   my judgments flashed like lightning
      upon you.
6 For I desire mercy, not sacrifice,
   and acknowledgment of God rather
      than burnt offerings.
7 Like Adam,[c] they have broken the
      covenant—
   they were unfaithful to me there.
8 Gilead is a city of wicked men,
   stained with footprints of blood.
9 As marauders lie in ambush for a
      man,
   so do bands of priests;
they murder on the road to Shechem,
   committing shameful crimes.
10 I have seen a horrible thing
   in the house of Israel.
There Ephraim is given to
      prostitution
   and Israel is defiled.

11 "Also for you, Judah,
   a harvest is appointed.

"Whenever I would restore the
      fortunes of my people,
7 1 whenever I would heal Israel,
   the sins of Ephraim are exposed
   and the crimes of Samaria revealed.
They practice deceit,

---

[a] 8 Beth Aven means *house of wickedness* (a name for Bethel, which means *house of God*).   [b] 11 The meaning of the Hebrew
for this word is uncertain.   [c] 7 Or *As at Adam*; or *Like men*

thieves break into houses,
bandits rob in the streets;
2 but they do not realize
that I remember all their evil
deeds.
Their sins engulf them;
they are always before me.

3 "They delight the king with their
wickedness,
the princes with their lies.
4 They are all adulterers,
burning like an oven
whose fire the baker need not stir
from the kneading of the dough till
it rises.
5 On the day of the festival of our king
the princes become inflamed with
wine,
and he joins hands with the
mockers.
6 Their hearts are like an oven;
they approach him with intrigue.
Their passion smolders all night;
in the morning it blazes like a
flaming fire.
7 All of them are hot as an oven;
they devour their rulers.
All their kings fall,
and none of them calls on me.

8 "Ephraim mixes with the nations;
Ephraim is a flat cake not turned
over.
9 Foreigners sap his strength,
but he does not realize it.
His hair is sprinkled with gray,
but he does not notice.
10 Israel's arrogance testifies against him,
but despite all this
he does not return to the LORD his
God
or search for him.

11 "Ephraim is like a dove,
easily deceived and senseless—
now calling to Egypt,
now turning to Assyria.
12 When they go, I will throw my net
over them;

I will pull them down like birds of
the air.
When I hear them flocking together,
I will catch them.
13 Woe to them,
because they have strayed from me!
Destruction to them,
because they have rebelled against
me!
I long to redeem them
but they speak lies against me.
14 They do not cry out to me from their
hearts
but wail upon their beds.
They gather together[a] for grain and
new wine
but turn away from me.
15 I trained them and strengthened
them,
but they plot evil against me.
16 They do not turn to the Most High;
they are like a faulty bow.
Their leaders will fall by the sword
because of their insolent words.
For this they will be ridiculed
in the land of Egypt.

Israel to Reap the Whirlwind

8 "Put the trumpet to your lips!
An eagle is over the house of the
LORD
because the people have broken my
covenant
and rebelled against my law.
2 Israel cries out to me,
'O our God, we acknowledge you!'
3 But Israel has rejected what is good;
an enemy will pursue him.
4 They set up kings without my
consent;
they choose princes without my
approval.
With their silver and gold
they make idols for themselves
to their own destruction.
5 Throw out your calf-idol, O Samaria!
My anger burns against them.
How long will they be incapable of
purity?

---

a 14 Most Hebrew manuscripts; some Hebrew manuscripts and Septuagint *They slash themselves*

⁶   They are from Israel!
This calf—a craftsman has made it;
    it is not God.
It will be broken in pieces,
    that calf of Samaria.

⁷ "They sow the wind
    and reap the whirlwind.
The stalk has no head;
    it will produce no flour.
Were it to yield grain,
    foreigners would swallow it up.
⁸ Israel is swallowed up;
    now she is among the nations
    like a worthless thing.
⁹ For they have gone up to Assyria
    like a wild donkey wandering alone.
    Ephraim has sold herself to lovers.
¹⁰ Although they have sold themselves
        among the nations,
    I will now gather them together.
They will begin to waste away
    under the oppression of the mighty
        king.

¹¹ "Though Ephraim built many altars
        for sin offerings,
    these have become altars for sinning.
¹² I wrote for them the many things of
        my law,
    but they regarded them as
        something alien.
¹³ They offer sacrifices given to me
    and they eat the meat,
    but the LORD is not pleased with
        them.
Now he will remember their
        wickedness
    and punish their sins:
They will return to Egypt.
¹⁴ Israel has forgotten his Maker
    and built palaces;
Judah has fortified many towns.
But I will send fire upon their cities
    that will consume their fortresses."

Punishment for Israel

9 Do not rejoice, O Israel;
    do not be jubilant like the other
        nations.

For you have been unfaithful to your
        God;
    you love the wages of a prostitute
        at every threshing floor.
² Threshing floors and winepresses will
        not feed the people;
    the new wine will fail them.
³ They will not remain in the LORD's
        land;
    Ephraim will return to Egypt
    and eat unclean[a] food in Assyria.
⁴ They will not pour out wine
        offerings to the LORD,
    nor will their sacrifices please him.
Such sacrifices will be to them like
        the bread of mourners;
    all who eat them will be unclean.
This food will be for themselves;
    it will not come into the temple of
        the LORD.

⁵ What will you do on the day of your
        appointed feasts,
    on the festival days of the LORD?
⁶ Even if they escape from destruction,
    Egypt will gather them,
    and Memphis will bury them.
Their treasures of silver will be taken
        over by briers,
    and thorns will overrun their tents.
⁷ The days of punishment are coming,
    the days of reckoning are at hand.
    Let Israel know this.
Because your sins are so many
    and your hostility so great,
the prophet is considered a fool,
    the inspired man a maniac.
⁸ The prophet, along with my God,
    is the watchman over Ephraim,[b]
yet snares await him on all his paths,
    and hostility in the house of his God.
⁹ They have sunk deep into corruption,
    as in the days of Gibeah.
God will remember their wickedness
    and punish them for their sins.

¹⁰ "When I found Israel,
    it was like finding grapes in the
        desert;

---

[a] 3 That is, ceremonially unclean   [b] 8 Or *The prophet is the watchman over Ephraim, / the people of my God*

when I saw your fathers,
  it was like seeing the early fruit on
    the fig tree.
But when they came to Baal Peor,
  they consecrated themselves to that
    shameful idol
and became as vile as the thing they
    loved.

11 Ephraim's glory will fly away like a
    bird—
  no birth, no pregnancy, no
    conception.
12 Even if they rear children,
  I will bereave them of every one.
Woe to them
  when I turn away from them!
13 I have seen Ephraim, like Tyre,
  planted in a pleasant place.
But Ephraim will bring out
  their children to the slayer."

14 Give them, O LORD—
  what will you give them?
Give them wombs that miscarry
  and breasts that are dry.

15 "Because of all their wickedness in
    Gilgal,
  I hated them there.
Because of their sinful deeds,
  I will drive them out of my house.
I will no longer love them;
  all their leaders are rebellious.
16 Ephraim is blighted,
  their root is withered,
  they yield no fruit.
Even if they bear children,
  I will slay their cherished
    offspring."

17 My God will reject them
  because they have not obeyed him;
  they will be wanderers among the
    nations.

10 Israel was a spreading vine;
  he brought forth fruit for
    himself.
As his fruit increased,

he built more altars;
as his land prospered,
  he adorned his sacred stones.
2 Their heart is deceitful,
  and now they must bear their guilt.
The LORD will demolish their altars
  and destroy their sacred stones.

3 Then they will say, "We have no king
  because we did not revere the
    LORD.
But even if we had a king,
  what could he do for us?"
4 They make many promises,
  take false oaths
  and make agreements;
therefore lawsuits spring up
  like poisonous weeds in a plowed
    field.
5 The people who live in Samaria fear
  for the calf-idol of Beth Aven.ª
Its people will mourn over it,
  and so will its idolatrous priests,
those who had rejoiced over its
    splendor,
  because it is taken from them into
    exile.
6 It will be carried to Assyria
  as tribute for the great king.
Ephraim will be disgraced;
  Israel will be ashamed of its
    wooden idols.ᵇ
7 Samaria and its king will float away
  like a twig on the surface of the
    waters.
8 The high places of wickednessᶜ will
    be destroyed—
  it is the sin of Israel.
Thorns and thistles will grow up
  and cover their altars.
Then they will say to the mountains,
  "Cover us!"
and to the hills, "Fall on us!"

9 "Since the days of Gibeah, you have
    sinned, O Israel,
  and there you have remained.ᵈ
Did not war overtake

the evildoers in Gibeah?
¹⁰When I please, I will punish them;
  nations will be gathered against
    them
  to put them in bonds for their
    double sin.
¹¹Ephraim is a trained heifer
  that loves to thresh;
so I will put a yoke
  on her fair neck.
I will drive Ephraim,
  Judah must plow,
  and Jacob must break up the
    ground.
¹²Sow for yourselves righteousness,
  reap the fruit of unfailing love,
and break up your unplowed ground;
  for it is time to seek the LORD,
until he comes
  and showers righteousness on you.
¹³But you have planted wickedness,
  you have reaped evil,
  you have eaten the fruit of
    deception.
Because you have depended on your
    own strength
  and on your many warriors,
¹⁴the roar of battle will rise against
    your people,
  so that all your fortresses will be
    devastated—
as Shalman devastated Beth Arbel on
    the day of battle,
  when mothers were dashed to the
    ground with their children.
¹⁵Thus will it happen to you, O Bethel,
  because your wickedness is great.
When that day dawns,
  the king of Israel will be completely
    destroyed.

God's Love for Israel

11 "When Israel was a child, I loved
    him,
  and out of Egypt I called my son.
²But the more Iᵃ called Israel,
  the further they went from me.ᵇ
They sacrificed to the Baals
  and they burned incense to images.

³It was I who taught Ephraim to walk,
  taking them by the arms;
but they did not realize
  it was I who healed them.
⁴I led them with cords of human
    kindness,
  with ties of love;
I lifted the yoke from their neck
  and bent down to feed them.

⁵"Will they not return to Egypt
  and will not Assyria rule over them
  because they refuse to repent?
⁶Swords will flash in their cities,
  will destroy the bars of their gates
  and put an end to their plans.
⁷My people are determined to turn
    from me.
  Even if they call to the Most High,
  he will by no means exalt them.

⁸"How can I give you up, Ephraim?
  How can I hand you over, Israel?
How can I treat you like Admah?
  How can I make you like
    Zeboiim?
My heart is changed within me;
  all my compassion is aroused.
⁹I will not carry out my fierce anger,
  nor will I turn and devastate
    Ephraim.
For I am God, and not man—
  the Holy One among you.
  I will not come in wrath.ᶜ
¹⁰They will follow the LORD;
  he will roar like a lion.
When he roars,
  his children will come trembling
    from the west.
¹¹They will come trembling
  like birds from Egypt,
  like doves from Assyria.
I will settle them in their homes,"
  declares the LORD.

Israel's Sin

¹²Ephraim has surrounded me with lies,
  the house of Israel with deceit.
And Judah is unruly against God,
  even against the faithful Holy One.

ᵃ2 Some Septuagint manuscripts; Hebrew *they*   ᵇ2 Septuagint; Hebrew *them*   ᶜ9 Or *come against any city*

12 ¹Ephraim feeds on the wind;
he pursues the east wind all day
and multiplies lies and violence.
He makes a treaty with Assyria
and sends olive oil to Egypt.
²The LORD has a charge to bring
against Judah;
he will punish Jacob[a] according to
his ways
and repay him according to his
deeds.
³In the womb he grasped his brother's
heel;
as a man he struggled with God.
⁴He struggled with the angel and
overcame him;
he wept and begged for his favor.
He found him at Bethel
and talked with him there—
⁵the LORD God Almighty,
the LORD is his name of renown!
⁶But you must return to your God;
maintain love and justice,
and wait for your God always.

⁷The merchant uses dishonest scales;
he loves to defraud.
⁸Ephraim boasts,
"I am very rich; I have become
wealthy.
With all my wealth they will not find
in me
any iniquity or sin."

⁹"I am the LORD your God,
⌐who brought you⌐ out of[b] Egypt;
I will make you live in tents again,
as in the days of your appointed
feasts.
¹⁰I spoke to the prophets,
gave them many visions
and told parables through them."

¹¹Is Gilead wicked?
Its people are worthless!
Do they sacrifice bulls in Gilgal?
Their altars will be like piles of
stones
on a plowed field.

¹²Jacob fled to the country of Aram[c];
Israel served to get a wife,
and to pay for her he tended sheep.
¹³The LORD used a prophet to bring
Israel up from Egypt,
by a prophet he cared for him.
¹⁴But Ephraim has bitterly provoked
him to anger;
his Lord will leave upon him the
guilt of his bloodshed
and will repay him for his
contempt.

The LORD's Anger Against Israel

13 When Ephraim spoke, men
trembled;
he was exalted in Israel.
But he became guilty of Baal
worship and died.
²Now they sin more and more;
they make idols for themselves from
their silver,
cleverly fashioned images,
all of them the work of craftsmen.
It is said of these people,
"They offer human sacrifice
and kiss[d] the calf-idols."
³Therefore they will be like the
morning mist,
like the early dew that disappears,
like chaff swirling from a threshing
floor,
like smoke escaping through a
window.

⁴"But I am the LORD your God,
⌐who brought you⌐ out of[b] Egypt.
You shall acknowledge no God but
me,
no Savior except me.
⁵I cared for you in the desert,
in the land of burning heat.
⁶When I fed them, they were satisfied;
when they were satisfied, they
became proud;
then they forgot me.
⁷So I will come upon them like a lion,
like a leopard I will lurk by the path.

---

[a] 2 Jacob means he grasps the heel (figuratively, he deceives). [b] 9,4 Or God / ever since you were in [c] 12 That is, Northwest Mesopotamia [d] 2 Or "Men who sacrifice / kiss"

⁸Like a bear robbed of her cubs,
    I will attack them and rip them
        open.
Like a lion I will devour them;
    a wild animal will tear them apart.

⁹"You are destroyed, O Israel,
    because you are against me, against
        your helper.
¹⁰Where is your king, that he may save
        you?
    Where are your rulers in all your
        towns,

of whom you said,
    'Give me a king and princes'?
¹¹So in my anger I gave you a king,
    and in my wrath I took him
        away.
¹²The guilt of Ephraim is stored up,
    his sins are kept on record.
¹³Pains as of a woman in childbirth
        come to him,
    but he is a child without wisdom;
when the time arrives,
    he does not come to the opening of
        the womb.

GOING *deeper*

Finding God's Forgiveness and Love

READ AND CONSIDER: HOSEA 14

"Take words with you and return to the LORD. Say to him: 'Forgive all our sins and receive us graciously, that we may offer the fruit of our lips' " (Hosea 14:2).

The book of Hosea is an unusual love story of a husband, an unfaithful wife, and a love that forgives and redeems even when the relationship seems irreparably broken. Put yourself in Hosea's place. God tells you to take an adulterous wife, give your kids odd names that represent divine messages, and pay to get your wife back after she has disgraced herself with other men. Then God instructs you to forgive her and love her more than before.

Your reaction might be, "Are you joking, God? You want me to what?" But Hosea didn't question God. Instead, he did exactly as God said. As a result his life became a beautiful metaphor of God's love for the unfaithful nation of Israel and for each of us individually. It parallels God's love for His "bride" (His people) and the reconciliation that God's true love brings about.

Hosea calls the people of Israel to repentance, to turn back to God. He even gives them the words to say: "Forgive all our sins and receive us graciously . . . for in you the fatherless [we] find compassion" (14:2-3). These simple but amazing words, when prayed with honesty and a contrite heart, are as relevant today as they were 2500 years ago. No matter how faithless we have been, God will be faithful and just to forgive us (1 John 1:9).

Forgiveness begins when we recognize how sinful and needy we are. We can't save ourselves, and no amount of money, fame, or power can save us either. Our only hope is to throw ourselves upon the mercy of our Creator, knowing we don't deserve it. God loves us so much that He paid in blood to redeem us. Jesus Christ, His only Son, gave His life that we might forever have God's compassionate forgiveness.

When you are tired of trying to be good on your own, weary of a life of sin, when your friends and family desert you, when you feel yourself sinking in the quicksand of guilt, lift your voice to God. Ask Him to forgive you for your sins and for trying to do it all on your own. He will wash away your past, start you on a new path, and walk with you. Together, you and He will write your own love story, a story that will last forever.

14 "I will ransom them from the power
    of the grave[a];
  I will redeem them from death.
Where, O death, are your plagues?
  Where, O grave,[a] is your
    destruction?

"I will have no compassion,
15   even though he thrives among his
    brothers.
An east wind from the LORD will
    come,
  blowing in from the desert;
his spring will fail
  and his well dry up.
His storehouse will be plundered
  of all its treasures.
16 The people of Samaria must bear
    their guilt,
  because they have rebelled against
    their God.
They will fall by the sword;
  their little ones will be dashed to
    the ground,
  their pregnant women ripped
    open."

Repentance to Bring Blessing

14 Return, O Israel, to the LORD
    your God.
  Your sins have been your downfall!
2 Take words with you
  and return to the LORD.
Say to him:
  "Forgive all our sins
and receive us graciously,
  that we may offer the fruit of our
    lips.[b]

3 Assyria cannot save us;
  we will not mount war-horses.
We will never again say 'Our gods'
  to what our own hands have made,
  for in you the fatherless find
    compassion."

4 "I will heal their waywardness
  and love them freely,
  for my anger has turned away from
    them.
5 I will be like the dew to Israel;
  he will blossom like a lily.
Like a cedar of Lebanon
  he will send down his roots;
6   his young shoots will grow.
His splendor will be like an olive
    tree,
  his fragrance like a cedar of
    Lebanon.
7 Men will dwell again in his shade.
  He will flourish like the grain.
He will blossom like a vine,
  and his fame will be like the wine
    from Lebanon.
8 O Ephraim, what more have I[c] to do
    with idols?
  I will answer him and care for him.
I am like a green pine tree;
  your fruitfulness comes from me."

9 Who is wise? He will realize these
    things.
  Who is discerning? He will
    understand them.
The ways of the LORD are right;
  the righteous walk in them,
  but the rebellious stumble in them.

---

[a] 14 Hebrew *Sheol*   [b] 2 Or *offer our lips as sacrifices of bulls*   [c] 8 Or *What more has Ephraim*

Author: Joel

Date: About the ninth century BC

Audience: The unfaithful people of God—
to urge them to turn from sin so
that God's judgment might be
averted in favor of blessing and
restoration

Prayer Themes:

- *Praise God that He gives us fasting, prayer, and repentence as ways to cleanse ourselves from sin (1:13-15).*

- *Thank God for His grace and compassion, which He shows to all who turn to Him (2:11-14).*

- *Ask God to turn the hearts of your friends and neighbors toward Him so that they might make a decision to repent and believe in Christ (3:14)*

The need for repentance is the dominant theme underlying the prophetic book of Joel. The prophet tells his people: "Your rebellion is not only sinful, it is senseless. Why would you reject the One who longs to bless you? Come to your senses. Come back to God."

Joel speaks of a coming age when those who acknowledge their wrongdoing and seek forgiveness will find unparalleled favor. Those who do not confess their need for cleansing, and then trust God to forgive, will eventually face the holy but fierce judgment of the Lord.

Confession and repentance are crucial parts of our prayer life. When we confess our sins to God, it's not so He can find out what we've been doing. He already knows! It's so we can take responsibility for what we've done and not let it become a wall of separation between us and God.

If you ever find yourself feeling as if your prayers aren't getting past the ceiling, ask God to show you if you have any unconfessed sin in your life. He will.

Joel

1 The word of the LORD that came to Joel son of Pethuel.

An Invasion of Locusts

2 Hear this, you elders;
  listen, all who live in the land.
Has anything like this ever happened
      in your days
  or in the days of your forefathers?
3 Tell it to your children,
  and let your children tell it to their
      children,
  and their children to the next
      generation.
4 What the locust swarm has left
  the great locusts have eaten;
what the great locusts have left
  the young locusts have eaten;

what the young locusts have left
  other locusts[a] have eaten.

5 Wake up, you drunkards, and
      weep!
  Wail, all you drinkers of wine;
wail because of the new wine,
  for it has been snatched from your
      lips.
6 A nation has invaded my land,
  powerful and without number;
it has the teeth of a lion,
  the fangs of a lioness.
7 It has laid waste my vines
  and ruined my fig trees.
It has stripped off their bark
  and thrown it away,
  leaving their branches white.

---

[a] 4 The precise meaning of the four Hebrew words used here for locusts is uncertain.

8 Mourn like a virgin[a] in sackcloth
  grieving for the husband[b] of her
    youth.
9 Grain offerings and drink
    offerings
  are cut off from the house of the
    LORD.
The priests are in mourning,
  those who minister before the
    LORD.
10 The fields are ruined,
  the ground is dried up[c];
the grain is destroyed,
  the new wine is dried up,
  the oil fails.
11 Despair, you farmers,
  wail, you vine growers;
grieve for the wheat and the barley,
  because the harvest of the field is
    destroyed.
12 The vine is dried up
  and the fig tree is withered;
the pomegranate, the palm and the
    apple tree—
  all the trees of the field—are dried
    up.
Surely the joy of mankind
  is withered away.

A Call to Repentance

13 Put on sackcloth, O priests, and
    mourn;
  wail, you who minister before the
    altar.
Come, spend the night in sackcloth,
  you who minister before my God;
for the grain offerings and drink
    offerings
  are withheld from the house of
    your God.
14 Declare a holy fast;
  call a sacred assembly.
Summon the elders
  and all who live in the land
to the house of the LORD your God,
  and cry out to the LORD.

15 Alas for that day!
  For the day of the LORD is near;
  it will come like destruction from
    the Almighty.[d]

16 Has not the food been cut off
  before our very eyes—
joy and gladness
  from the house of our God?
17 The seeds are shriveled
  beneath the clods.[e]

---

a 8 Or *young woman* b 8 Or *betrothed* c 10 Or *ground mourns* d 15 Hebrew *Shaddai* e 17 The meaning of the Hebrew for this word is uncertain.

God's people at prayer
JOEL'S PRAYER WHEN ALL SEEMED LOST

JOEL 1:19-20 Hurricanes, tornadoes, and tsunamis are powerful and unstoppable forces. The actions of others—from terrorists to drunk drivers—are a part of life over which we have no control. What can we do when life seems out of control or all seems lost?

The first thing to do is not allow our heart to harden against God. If our heart becomes hard, we cannot have a vision from God's perspective. We won't be able to see the whole picture. We will only see the way it is, not the way God wants it to become. We won't see that the forces on this earth—natural, man-made, or satanic—cannot touch His power.

God understands our pain, our confusion, and our feelings of hopelessness.

Because of His great love for each of us, He hears our cries. So remember to call out to God when all seems overwhelming and hopeless saying, "To you, O LORD, I call," just like the prophet Joel. God will hear you and give you the peace, comfort, and protection you seek.

The storehouses are in ruins,
  the granaries have been broken
    down,
  for the grain has dried up.
¹⁸How the cattle moan!
  The herds mill about
because they have no pasture;
  even the flocks of sheep are
    suffering.

¹⁹To you, O Lord, I call,
  for fire has devoured the open
    pastures
  and flames have burned up all the
    trees of the field.
²⁰Even the wild animals pant for you;
  the streams of water have dried up
  and fire has devoured the open
    pastures.

An Army of Locusts

2 Blow the trumpet in Zion;
  sound the alarm on my holy hill.
Let all who live in the land tremble,
  for the day of the Lord is coming.
It is close at hand—
² a day of darkness and gloom,
  a day of clouds and blackness.
Like dawn spreading across the
    mountains
  a large and mighty army comes,
such as never was of old
  nor ever will be in ages to come.

³Before them fire devours,
  behind them a flame blazes.
Before them the land is like the
    garden of Eden,
  behind them, a desert waste—
nothing escapes them.
⁴They have the appearance of horses;
  they gallop along like cavalry.
⁵With a noise like that of chariots
  they leap over the mountaintops,
like a crackling fire consuming
    stubble,
  like a mighty army drawn up for
    battle.

⁶At the sight of them, nations are in
    anguish;

every face turns pale.
⁷They charge like warriors;
  they scale walls like soldiers.
They all march in line,
  not swerving from their course.
⁸They do not jostle each other;
  each marches straight ahead.
They plunge through defenses
  without breaking ranks.
⁹They rush upon the city;
  they run along the wall.
They climb into the houses;
  like thieves they enter through the
    windows.

¹⁰Before them the earth shakes,
  the sky trembles,
the sun and moon are darkened,
  and the stars no longer shine.
¹¹The Lord thunders
  at the head of his army;
his forces are beyond number,
  and mighty are those who obey his
    command.
The day of the Lord is great;
  it is dreadful.
  Who can endure it?

Rend Your Heart

¹²"Even now," declares the Lord,
  "return to me with all your heart,
  with fasting and weeping and
    mourning."

¹³Rend your heart
  and not your garments.
Return to the Lord your God,
  for he is gracious and
    compassionate,
slow to anger and abounding in love,
  and he relents from sending
    calamity.
¹⁴Who knows? He may turn and have
    pity
  and leave behind a blessing—
grain offerings and drink offerings
  for the Lord your God.

¹⁵Blow the trumpet in Zion,
  declare a holy fast,
  call a sacred assembly.

¹⁶Gather the people,
consecrate the assembly;
bring together the elders,
gather the children,
those nursing at the breast.
Let the bridegroom leave his room
and the bride her chamber.
¹⁷Let the priests, who minister before
the LORD,
weep between the temple porch
and the altar.
Let them say, "Spare your people,
O LORD.
Do not make your inheritance an
object of scorn,
a byword among the nations.
Why should they say among the
peoples,
'Where is their God?'"

The LORD's Answer
¹⁸Then the LORD will be jealous for his
land
and take pity on his people.

¹⁹The LORD will reply^a to them:

"I am sending you grain, new wine
and oil,
enough to satisfy you fully;
never again will I make you
an object of scorn to the nations.

²⁰"I will drive the northern army far
from you,
pushing it into a parched and
barren land,
with its front columns going into the
eastern sea^b
and those in the rear into the
western sea.^c
And its stench will go up;
its smell will rise."

Surely he has done great things.^d
²¹ Be not afraid, O land;
be glad and rejoice.
Surely the LORD has done great
things.

²² Be not afraid, O wild animals,
for the open pastures are becoming
green.
The trees are bearing their fruit;
the fig tree and the vine yield their
riches.
²³Be glad, O people of Zion,
rejoice in the LORD your God,
for he has given you
the autumn rains in righteousness.^e
He sends you abundant showers,
both autumn and spring rains, as
before.
²⁴The threshing floors will be filled
with grain;
the vats will overflow with new
wine and oil.

²⁵"I will repay you for the years the
locusts have eaten—
the great locust and the young
locust,
the other locusts and the locust
swarm^f—
my great army that I sent among
you.
²⁶You will have plenty to eat, until you
are full,
and you will praise the name of the
LORD your God,
who has worked wonders for you;
never again will my people be
shamed.
²⁷Then you will know that I am in
Israel,
that I am the LORD your God,
and that there is no other;
never again will my people be
shamed.

The Day of the LORD
²⁸"And afterward,
I will pour out my Spirit on all
people.
Your sons and daughters will
prophesy,
your old men will dream dreams,
your young men will see visions.

It's Never Too Late to Turn to God

READ AND CONSIDER: JOEL 2:12-27

"I will repay you for the years the locusts have eaten—the great locust and the young locust, the other locusts and the locust swarm—my great army that I sent among you" (Joel 2:25).

Up to this point, Joel's prophecy was gloom and doom for those who had turned their backs on God. He warned of a day of judgment coming—a day so dreadful that he asked, "Who can endure it?" Even so, Joel kept reminding the people to repent and seek God's forgiveness.

The people had sinned greatly. They had bowed to other gods and succumbed to the idolatry in the world around them. They had been far from God for a long time.

Joel says it's not too late. God would forgive and bless them if they would return to Him in prayer and repentance.

When we pray, repenting of our sinfulness, our hearts become soft toward God, and we gain a renewed vision. We see there is hope. We have faith that He will restore all that has been devoured, destroyed, and eaten away. Even years of life that have been wasted in godless living can be restored. Trust God to take away all pain, hopelessness, hardness, and unforgiveness. Have faith in His ability to resurrect love and life from the deadest of places. Understand that He wants to restore what has been lost so that you will know He is God and glorify His name.

What is broken in your life? What have the "locusts" eaten? What has been lost, destroyed, or ruined? God says He will restore it when you turn to Him. It's never too late.

29 Even on my servants, both men and women,
I will pour out my Spirit in those days.
30 I will show wonders in the heavens and on the earth,
blood and fire and billows of smoke.
31 The sun will be turned to darkness and the moon to blood
before the coming of the great and dreadful day of the LORD.
32 And everyone who calls on the name of the LORD will be saved;
for on Mount Zion and in Jerusalem there will be deliverance,
as the LORD has said,
among the survivors whom the LORD calls.

The Nations Judged

3 "In those days and at that time, when I restore the fortunes of Judah and Jerusalem,
2 I will gather all nations and bring them down to the Valley of Jehoshaphat.[a]
There I will enter into judgment against them
concerning my inheritance, my people Israel,
for they scattered my people among the nations
and divided up my land.
3 They cast lots for my people and traded boys for prostitutes;
they sold girls for wine that they might drink.

4 "Now what have you against me, O Tyre and Sidon and all you regions of Philistia? Are you repaying me for

---

[a] 2 Jehoshaphat means *the LORD judges*; also in verse 12.

something I have done? If you are paying me back, I will swiftly and speedily return on your own heads what you have done. ⁵For you took my silver and my gold and carried off my finest treasures to your temples. ⁶You sold the people of Judah and Jerusalem to the Greeks, that you might send them far from their homeland.

⁷"See, I am going to rouse them out of the places to which you sold them, and I will return on your own heads what you have done. ⁸I will sell your sons and daughters to the people of Judah, and they will sell them to the Sabeans, a nation far away." The LORD has spoken.

⁹Proclaim this among the nations:
  Prepare for war!
 Rouse the warriors!
  Let all the fighting men draw near
    and attack.
¹⁰Beat your plowshares into swords
  and your pruning hooks into
    spears.
 Let the weakling say,
  "I am strong!"
¹¹Come quickly, all you nations from
    every side,
  and assemble there.

 Bring down your warriors, O LORD!

¹²"Let the nations be roused;
  let them advance into the Valley of
    Jehoshaphat,
 for there I will sit
  to judge all the nations on every
    side.
¹³Swing the sickle,
  for the harvest is ripe.
 Come, trample the grapes,
  for the winepress is full
  and the vats overflow—
 so great is their wickedness!"

¹⁴Multitudes, multitudes
  in the valley of decision!
 For the day of the LORD is near
  in the valley of decision.
¹⁵The sun and moon will be darkened,
  and the stars no longer shine.
¹⁶The LORD will roar from Zion
  and thunder from Jerusalem;
  the earth and the sky will tremble.
 But the LORD will be a refuge for his
    people,
  a stronghold for the people of Israel.

Blessings for God's People

¹⁷"Then you will know that I, the
    LORD your God,
  dwell in Zion, my holy hill.
 Jerusalem will be holy;
  never again will foreigners invade
    her.

¹⁸"In that day the mountains will drip
    new wine,
  and the hills will flow with milk;
  all the ravines of Judah will run
    with water.
 A fountain will flow out of the
    LORD's house
  and will water the valley of
    acacias.ᵃ
¹⁹But Egypt will be desolate,
  Edom a desert waste,
 because of violence done to the
    people of Judah,
  in whose land they shed innocent
    blood.
²⁰Judah will be inhabited forever
  and Jerusalem through all
    generations.
²¹Their bloodguilt, which I have not
    pardoned,
  I will pardon."

 The LORD dwells in Zion!

ᵃ 18 Or Valley of Shittim

Author: Amos

Date: Between 760 and 750 BC

Audience: Primarily the ten tribes of the northern kingdom of Israel—to announce God's imminent judgment due to their rampant unfaithfulness

Prayer Themes:

- Praise God that He is Almighty and nothing is too hard for Him (4:13).

- Ask God to show you practical ways you can pray that will promote justice in a world filled with injustice (5:24).

- Thank God for giving you His Word, your dependable guidebook for life (8:11-12).

Have you ever been deeply burdened to pray for someone or something and then had those prayer efforts turn into agonizing exercises in waiting? Have you ever wondered if and when God would answer your prayers?

If so, you understand what the prophet Amos felt and experienced. Ironically, his name means "burden bearer." A shepherd and farmer by trade, his unexpected divine assignment was to deliver a series of grim warnings to a hard-hearted nation.

For at least a decade he labored without apparent success. His efforts fell on deaf ears. And yet it is clear, God looked down on Amos's tireless obedience and was pleased.

Remember Amos every time God speaks to your heart to pray for an impossible situation. Though you cannot control the results, you can resolve to be faithful to what God has spoken to you and not give up.

Amos

1 The words of Amos, one of the shepherds of Tekoa—what he saw concerning Israel two years before the earthquake, when Uzziah was king of Judah and Jeroboam son of Jehoash[a] was king of Israel.

²He said:

"The LORD roars from Zion
and thunders from Jerusalem;
the pastures of the shepherds dry up,[b]
and the top of Carmel withers."

Judgment on Israel's Neighbors

³This is what the LORD says:

"For three sins of Damascus,
even for four, I will not turn back
⌊my wrath⌋.
Because she threshed Gilead
with sledges having iron teeth,
⁴I will send fire upon the house of
Hazael

that will consume the fortresses of
Ben-Hadad.
⁵I will break down the gate of
Damascus;
I will destroy the king who is in[c]
the Valley of Aven[d]
and the one who holds the scepter in
Beth Eden.
The people of Aram will go into
exile to Kir,"
says the LORD.

⁶This is what the LORD says:

"For three sins of Gaza,
even for four, I will not turn back
⌊my wrath⌋.
Because she took captive whole
communities
and sold them to Edom,
⁷I will send fire upon the walls of Gaza
that will consume her fortresses.

---

a *1* Hebrew *Joash,* a variant of *Jehoash*   b *2* Or *shepherds mourn*   c *5* Or *the inhabitants of*   d *5 Aven* means *wickedness.*

⁸I will destroy the king[a] of Ashdod
and the one who holds the scepter
in Ashkelon.
I will turn my hand against Ekron,
till the last of the Philistines is
dead,"
says the Sovereign LORD.

⁹This is what the LORD says:

"For three sins of Tyre,
even for four, I will not turn back
⌐my wrath⌐.
Because she sold whole communities
of captives to Edom,
disregarding a treaty of
brotherhood,
¹⁰I will send fire upon the walls of Tyre
that will consume her fortresses."

¹¹This is what the LORD says:

"For three sins of Edom,
even for four, I will not turn back
⌐my wrath⌐.
Because he pursued his brother with
a sword,
stifling all compassion,[b]
because his anger raged continually
and his fury flamed unchecked,
¹²I will send fire upon Teman
that will consume the fortresses of
Bozrah."

¹³This is what the LORD says:

"For three sins of Ammon,
even for four, I will not turn back
⌐my wrath⌐.
Because he ripped open the pregnant
women of Gilead
in order to extend his borders,
¹⁴I will set fire to the walls of Rabbah
that will consume her fortresses
amid war cries on the day of battle,
amid violent winds on a stormy
day.
¹⁵Her king[c] will go into exile,
he and his officials together,"
says the LORD.

2 This is what the LORD says:

"For three sins of Moab,
even for four, I will not turn back
⌐my wrath⌐.
Because he burned, as if to lime,
the bones of Edom's king,
²I will send fire upon Moab
that will consume the fortresses of
Kerioth.[d]
Moab will go down in great tumult
amid war cries and the blast of the
trumpet.
³I will destroy her ruler
and kill all her officials with him,"
says the LORD.

⁴This is what the LORD says:

"For three sins of Judah,
even for four, I will not turn back
⌐my wrath⌐.
Because they have rejected the law of
the LORD
and have not kept his decrees,
because they have been led astray by
false gods,[e]
the gods[f] their ancestors followed,
⁵I will send fire upon Judah
that will consume the fortresses of
Jerusalem."

Judgment on Israel

⁶This is what the LORD says:

"For three sins of Israel,
even for four, I will not turn back
⌐my wrath⌐.
They sell the righteous for silver,
and the needy for a pair of sandals.
⁷They trample on the heads of the poor
as upon the dust of the ground
and deny justice to the oppressed.
Father and son use the same girl
and so profane my holy name.
⁸They lie down beside every altar
on garments taken in pledge.
In the house of their god
they drink wine taken as fines.

---

[a] 8 Or inhabitants   [b] 11 Or sword / and destroyed his allies   [c] 15 Or / Molech; Hebrew malcam   [d] 2 Or of her cities
[e] 4 Or by lies   [f] 4 Or lies

9 "I destroyed the Amorite before
   them,
 though he was tall as the cedars
 and strong as the oaks.
 I destroyed his fruit above
 and his roots below.

10 "I brought you up out of Egypt,
   and I led you forty years in the
      desert
   to give you the land of the
      Amorites.
11 I also raised up prophets from among
   your sons
   and Nazirites from among your
      young men.
 Is this not true, people of Israel?"
                  declares the LORD.
12 "But you made the Nazirites drink
   wine
   and commanded the prophets not
   to prophesy.

13 "Now then, I will crush you
   as a cart crushes when loaded with
      grain.
14 The swift will not escape,
   the strong will not muster their
      strength,
   and the warrior will not save his life.
15 The archer will not stand his ground,
   the fleet-footed soldier will not get
      away,
   and the horseman will not save his
      life.
16 Even the bravest warriors
   will flee naked on that day,"
                  declares the LORD.

Witnesses Summoned Against Israel

3 Hear this word the LORD has spoken
   against you, O people of Israel—
against the whole family I brought up
out of Egypt:

2 "You only have I chosen
   of all the families of the earth;
 therefore I will punish you
   for all your sins."

3 Do two walk together
   unless they have agreed to do so?

4 Does a lion roar in the thicket
   when he has no prey?
 Does he growl in his den
   when he has caught nothing?
5 Does a bird fall into a trap on the
      ground
   where no snare has been set?
 Does a trap spring up from the earth
   when there is nothing to catch?
6 When a trumpet sounds in a city,
   do not the people tremble?
 When disaster comes to a city,
   has not the LORD caused it?

7 Surely the Sovereign LORD does
      nothing
   without revealing his plan
   to his servants the prophets.

8 The lion has roared—
   who will not fear?
 The Sovereign LORD has spoken—
   who can but prophesy?

9 Proclaim to the fortresses of Ashdod
   and to the fortresses of Egypt:
 "Assemble yourselves on the
      mountains of Samaria;
   see the great unrest within her
   and the oppression among her
      people."

10 "They do not know how to do
      right," declares the LORD,
 "who hoard plunder and loot in
      their fortresses."

11 Therefore this is what the Sovereign
LORD says:

"An enemy will overrun the land;
   he will pull down your strongholds
   and plunder your fortresses."

12 This is what the LORD says:

"As a shepherd saves from the lion's
      mouth
   only two leg bones or a piece of an
      ear,
 so will the Israelites be saved,
 those who sit in Samaria
   on the edge of their beds

Pray for Godly Friends

READ AND CONSIDER: AMOS 3

"Do two walk together unless they have agreed to do so?" (Amos 3:3).

So much is made of the importance of the right kind of friends in the Bible that we can't treat this part of our lives lightly.

The main quality to look for in a close friend is how much that person loves and fears God. What Amos wrote is a picture of being in agreement on many levels. You will have all different kinds of friends, but your closest friends—those with whom you walk closely—should be the kind of friends who impart something of the goodness of the Lord to you every time you are with them.

Following are signs of a desirable friend:

A desirable friend tells you the truth in love. "Wounds from a friend can be trusted, but an enemy multiplies kisses" (Proverbs 27:6).

A desirable friend gives you sound advice. "Perfume and incense bring joy to the heart, and the pleasantness of one's friend springs from his earnest counsel" (Proverbs 27:9).

A desirable friend refines you. "As iron sharpens iron, so one man sharpens another" (Proverbs 27:17).

A desirable friend helps you grow in wisdom. "He who walks with the wise grows wise, but a companion of fools suffers harm" (Proverbs 13:20).

A desirable friend stays close to you. "A man of many companions may come to ruin, but there is a friend who sticks closer than a brother" (Proverbs 18:24).

A desirable friend loves you and stands by you. "A friend loves at all times, and a brother is born for adversity" (Proverbs 17:17).

A desirable friend helps in time of trouble. "Two are better than one, because they have a good return for their work: If one falls down, his friend can help him up!" (Ecclesiastes 4:9-10).

Following are signs of an undesirable friend:

An undesirable friend is immoral and has no regard for others. "But now I am writing you that you must not associate with anyone who calls himself a brother but is sexually immoral or greedy, an idolater or a slanderer, a drunkard or a swindler. With such a man do not even eat" (1 Corinthians 5:11).

An undesirable friend is changeable and unstable. "Do not join with the rebellious, for those two [the LORD and the King] will send sudden destruction upon them, and who knows what calamities they can bring?" (Proverbs 24:21-22).

An undesirable friend is frequently angry. "Do not make friends with a hot-tempered man, do not associate with one easily angered, or you may learn his ways and get yourself ensnared" (Proverbs 22:24-25).

An undesirable friend gives ungodly counsel. "Blessed is the man who does not walk in the counsel of the wicked or stand in the way of sinners or sit in the seat of mockers" (Psalm 1:1).

An undesirable friend is a lawless unbeliever. "Do not be yoked together with unbelievers. For what do righteousness and wickedness have in common? Or what fellowship can light have with darkness? What harmony is there between Christ and Belial? What does a believer have in common with an unbeliever?" (2 Corinthians 6:14-15).

An undesirable friend is irreverent toward God and His laws. "I am a friend to all who fear you, to all who follow your precepts" (Psalm 119:63).

Ask God to give you good, godly friends who will influence and encourage *you* to grow deeper in Him.

and in Damascus on their
    couches.ª"

¹³"Hear this and testify against the
house of Jacob," declares the Lord, the
LORD God Almighty.

¹⁴"On the day I punish Israel for her
    sins,
  I will destroy the altars of Bethel;
  the horns of the altar will be cut off
    and fall to the ground.
¹⁵I will tear down the winter house
    along with the summer house;
  the houses adorned with ivory will be
    destroyed
  and the mansions will be demolished,"
            declares the LORD.

Israel Has Not Returned to God

4 Hear this word, you cows of Bashan
    on Mount Samaria,
  you women who oppress the poor
    and crush the needy
  and say to your husbands, "Bring us
    some drinks!"
²The Sovereign LORD has sworn by his
    holiness:
  "The time will surely come
  when you will be taken away with
    hooks,
  the last of you with fishhooks.
³You will each go straight out
    through breaks in the wall,
  and you will be cast out toward
    Harmon,ᵇ"
            declares the LORD.
⁴"Go to Bethel and sin;
    go to Gilgal and sin yet more.
  Bring your sacrifices every morning,
    your tithes every three years.ᶜ
⁵Burn leavened bread as a thank
    offering
  and brag about your freewill
    offerings—
  boast about them, you Israelites,
    for this is what you love to do,"
            declares the Sovereign LORD.

⁶"I gave you empty stomachsᵈ in every
    city
  and lack of bread in every town,
  yet you have not returned to me,"
            declares the LORD.

⁷"I also withheld rain from you
    when the harvest was still three
      months away.
  I sent rain on one town,
    but withheld it from another.
  One field had rain;
    another had none and dried up.
⁸People staggered from town to town
    for water
  but did not get enough to drink,
    yet you have not returned to me,"
            declares the LORD.

⁹"Many times I struck your gardens
    and vineyards,
  I struck them with blight and
    mildew.
  Locusts devoured your fig and olive
    trees,
  yet you have not returned to me,"
            declares the LORD.

¹⁰"I sent plagues among you
    as I did to Egypt.
  I killed your young men with the
    sword,
  along with your captured horses.
  I filled your nostrils with the stench
    of your camps,
  yet you have not returned to me,"
            declares the LORD.

¹¹"I overthrew some of you
    as Iᵉ overthrew Sodom and
      Gomorrah.
  You were like a burning stick
    snatched from the fire,
  yet you have not returned to me,"
            declares the LORD.

¹²"Therefore this is what I will do to
    you, Israel,
  and because I will do this to you,

ª 12 The meaning of the Hebrew for this line is uncertain.   ᵇ 3 Masoretic Text; with a different word division of the Hebrew
(see Septuagint) out, O mountain of oppression   ᶜ 4 Or tithes on the third day   ᵈ 6 Hebrew you cleanness of teeth
ᵉ 11 Hebrew God

prepare to meet your God,
O Israel."

13He who forms the mountains,
creates the wind,
and reveals his thoughts to man,
he who turns dawn to darkness,
and treads the high places of the
earth—
the LORD God Almighty is his
name.

A Lament and Call to Repentance

5 Hear this word, O house of Israel, this lament I take up concerning you:

2"Fallen is Virgin Israel,
never to rise again,
deserted in her own land,
with no one to lift her up."

3This is what the Sovereign LORD says:

"The city that marches out a
thousand strong for Israel
will have only a hundred left;
the town that marches out a hundred
strong
will have only ten left."

4This is what the LORD says to the house of Israel:

"Seek me and live;
5   do not seek Bethel,
do not go to Gilgal,
do not journey to Beersheba.
For Gilgal will surely go into exile,
and Bethel will be reduced to
nothing.ᵃ"
6Seek the LORD and live,
or he will sweep through the house
of Joseph like a fire;
it will devour,
and Bethel will have no one to
quench it.

7You who turn justice into bitterness
and cast righteousness to the
ground
8(he who made the Pleiades and
Orion,

who turns blackness into dawn
and darkens day into night,
who calls for the waters of the sea
and pours them out over the face of
the land—
the LORD is his name—
9he flashes destruction on the
stronghold
and brings the fortified city to ruin),
10you hate the one who reproves in
court
and despise him who tells the truth.

11You trample on the poor
and force him to give you grain.
Therefore, though you have built
stone mansions,
you will not live in them;
though you have planted lush
vineyards,
you will not drink their wine.
12For I know how many are your
offenses
and how great your sins.

You oppress the righteous and take
bribes
and you deprive the poor of justice
in the courts.
13Therefore the prudent man keeps
quiet in such times,
for the times are evil.

14Seek good, not evil,
that you may live.
Then the LORD God Almighty will
be with you,
just as you say he is.
15Hate evil, love good;
maintain justice in the courts.
Perhaps the LORD God Almighty will
have mercy
on the remnant of Joseph.

16Therefore this is what the Lord, the LORD God Almighty, says:

"There will be wailing in all the
streets
and cries of anguish in every public
square.

ᵃ 5 Or grief; or wickedness; Hebrew aven, a reference to Beth Aven (a derogatory name for Bethel)

The farmers will be summoned to
weep
and the mourners to wail.
¹⁷There will be wailing in all the
vineyards,
for I will pass through your midst,"
says the LORD.

The Day of the LORD
¹⁸Woe to you who long
for the day of the LORD!
Why do you long for the day of the
LORD?
That day will be darkness, not
light.
¹⁹It will be as though a man fled from a
lion
only to meet a bear,
as though he entered his house
and rested his hand on the wall
only to have a snake bite him.
²⁰Will not the day of the LORD be
darkness, not light—
pitch-dark, without a ray of
brightness?

²¹"I hate, I despise your religious feasts;
I cannot stand your assemblies.
²²Even though you bring me burnt
offerings and grain offerings,
I will not accept them.
Though you bring choice fellowship
offerings,ª
I will have no regard for them.
²³Away with the noise of your songs!
I will not listen to the music of
your harps.
²⁴But let justice roll on like a river,
righteousness like a never-failing
stream!

²⁵"Did you bring me sacrifices and
offerings
forty years in the desert, O house
of Israel?
²⁶You have lifted up the shrine of your
king,
the pedestal of your idols,
the star of your godᵇ—

which you made for yourselves.
²⁷Therefore I will send you into exile
beyond Damascus,"
says the LORD, whose name is God
Almighty.

Woe to the Complacent
6 Woe to you who are complacent in
Zion,
and to you who feel secure on
Mount Samaria,
you notable men of the foremost
nation,
to whom the people of Israel come!
²Go to Calneh and look at it;
go from there to great Hamath,
and then go down to Gath in
Philistia.
Are they better off than your two
kingdoms?
Is their land larger than yours?
³You put off the evil day
and bring near a reign of terror.
⁴You lie on beds inlaid with ivory
and lounge on your couches.
You dine on choice lambs
and fattened calves.
⁵You strum away on your harps like
David
and improvise on musical
instruments.
⁶You drink wine by the bowlful
and use the finest lotions,
but you do not grieve over the ruin
of Joseph.
⁷Therefore you will be among the first
to go into exile;
your feasting and lounging will
end.

The LORD Abhors the Pride of Israel
⁸The Sovereign LORD has sworn by
himself—the LORD God Almighty declares:

"I abhor the pride of Jacob
and detest his fortresses;
I will deliver up the city
and everything in it."

ª 22 Traditionally *peace offerings* ᵇ 26 Or *lifted up Sakkuth your king / and Kaiwan your idols, / your star-gods*; Septuagint
lifted up the shrine of Molech / and the star of your god Rephan, / their idols

⁹If ten men are left in one house, they too will die. ¹⁰And if a relative who is to burn the bodies comes to carry them out of the house and asks anyone still hiding there, "Is anyone with you?" and he says, "No," then he will say, "Hush! We must not mention the name of the Lord."

¹¹For the Lord has given the command,
and he will smash the great house
into pieces
and the small house into bits.

¹²Do horses run on the rocky crags?
Does one plow there with oxen?
But you have turned justice into
poison
and the fruit of righteousness into
bitterness—
¹³you who rejoice in the conquest of Lo
Debar[a]
and say, "Did we not take Karnaim[b]
by our own strength?"

¹⁴For the Lord God Almighty declares,
"I will stir up a nation against you,
O house of Israel,
that will oppress you all the way
from Lebo[c] Hamath to the valley of
the Arabah."

Locusts, Fire and a Plumb Line

7 This is what the Sovereign Lord showed me: He was preparing swarms of locusts after the king's share had been harvested and just as the second crop was coming up. ²When they had stripped the land clean, I cried out, "Sovereign Lord, forgive! How can Jacob survive? He is so small!"

³So the Lord relented.

"This will not happen," the Lord said.

⁴This is what the Sovereign Lord showed me: The Sovereign Lord was calling for judgment by fire; it dried up the great deep and devoured the land. ⁵Then I cried out, "Sovereign Lord, I beg you, stop! How can Jacob survive? He is so small!"

⁶So the Lord relented.

"This will not happen either," the Sovereign Lord said.

⁷This is what he showed me: The Lord was standing by a wall that had been built true to plumb, with a plumb line in his hand. ⁸And the Lord asked me, "What do you see, Amos?"

"A plumb line," I replied.

Then the Lord said, "Look, I am setting a plumb line among my people Israel; I will spare them no longer.

⁹"The high places of Isaac will be
destroyed
and the sanctuaries of Israel will be
ruined;
with my sword I will rise against
the house of Jeroboam."

Amos and Amaziah

¹⁰Then Amaziah the priest of Bethel sent a message to Jeroboam king of Israel: "Amos is raising a conspiracy against you in the very heart of Israel. The land cannot bear all his words. ¹¹For this is what Amos is saying:

"'Jeroboam will die by the sword,
and Israel will surely go into exile,
away from their native land.'"

¹²Then Amaziah said to Amos, "Get out, you seer! Go back to the land of Judah. Earn your bread there and do your prophesying there. ¹³Don't prophesy anymore at Bethel, because this is the king's sanctuary and the temple of the kingdom."

¹⁴Amos answered Amaziah, "I was neither a prophet nor a prophet's son, but I was a shepherd, and I also took care of sycamore-fig trees. ¹⁵But the Lord took me from tending the flock and said to me, 'Go, prophesy to my people Israel.' ¹⁶Now then, hear the word of the Lord. You say,

"'Do not prophesy against Israel,
and stop preaching against the
house of Isaac.'

---

a 13 Lo Debar means nothing.   b 13 Karnaim means horns; horn here symbolizes strength.   c 14 Or from the entrance to

¹⁷"Therefore this is what the LORD says:

"'Your wife will become a prostitute
    in the city,
and your sons and daughters will
    fall by the sword.
Your land will be measured and
    divided up,
and you yourself will die in a
    paganᵃ country.
And Israel will certainly go into
    exile,
    away from their native land.'"

A Basket of Ripe Fruit

8 This is what the Sovereign LORD showed me: a basket of ripe fruit. ²"What do you see, Amos?" he asked.

"A basket of ripe fruit," I answered.

Then the LORD said to me, "The time is ripe for my people Israel; I will spare them no longer.

³"In that day," declares the Sovereign LORD, "the songs in the temple will turn to wailing.ᵇ Many, many bodies—flung everywhere! Silence!"

⁴Hear this, you who trample the needy
    and do away with the poor of the
    land,

⁵saying,

"When will the New Moon be over
    that we may sell grain,
and the Sabbath be ended
    that we may market wheat?"—
skimping the measure,
    boosting the price
    and cheating with dishonest scales,
⁶buying the poor with silver
    and the needy for a pair of sandals,
selling even the sweepings with the
    wheat.

⁷The LORD has sworn by the Pride of Jacob: "I will never forget anything they have done.

⁸"Will not the land tremble for this,
    and all who live in it mourn?

The whole land will rise like the
    Nile;
it will be stirred up and then sink
    like the river of Egypt.

⁹"In that day," declares the Sovereign LORD,

"I will make the sun go down at
    noon
    and darken the earth in broad
    daylight.
¹⁰I will turn your religious feasts into
    mourning
    and all your singing into weeping.
I will make all of you wear sackcloth
    and shave your heads.
I will make that time like mourning
    for an only son
    and the end of it like a bitter day.

Praying Amos 8:11

*Heavenly Father, I pray that my
soul will never experience the famine
of not hearing Your words to my heart
or the drought of not having a fresh
flow of Your Spirit in my life.*

¹¹"The days are coming," declares the
    Sovereign LORD,
    "when I will send a famine through
    the land—
not a famine of food or a thirst for
    water,
    but a famine of hearing the words
    of the LORD.
¹²Men will stagger from sea to sea
    and wander from north to east,
searching for the word of the LORD,
    but they will not find it.

¹³"In that day

"the lovely young women and strong
    young men
    will faint because of thirst.
¹⁴They who swear by the shameᶜ of
    Samaria,
    or say, 'As surely as your god lives,
    O Dan,'

ᵃ *17* Hebrew *an unclean*   ᵇ *3* Or *"the temple singers will wail*   ᶜ *14* Or *by Ashima;* or *by the idol*

or, 'As surely as the god[a] of
Beersheba lives'—
they will fall,
never to rise again."

Israel to Be Destroyed

9 I saw the Lord standing by the altar,
and he said:

"Strike the tops of the pillars
so that the thresholds shake.
Bring them down on the heads of all
the people;
those who are left I will kill with
the sword.
Not one will get away,
none will escape.
[2] Though they dig down to the depths
of the grave,[b]
from there my hand will take them.
Though they climb up to the
heavens,
from there I will bring them down.
[3] Though they hide themselves on the
top of Carmel,
there I will hunt them down and
seize them.
Though they hide from me at the
bottom of the sea,
there I will command the serpent
to bite them.
[4] Though they are driven into exile by
their enemies,
there I will command the sword to
slay them.
I will fix my eyes upon them
for evil and not for good."

[5] The Lord, the LORD Almighty,
he who touches the earth and it
melts,
and all who live in it mourn—
the whole land rises like the Nile,
then sinks like the river of Egypt—
[6] he who builds his lofty palace[c] in the
heavens
and sets its foundation[d] on the
earth,

who calls for the waters of the sea
and pours them out over the face of
the land—
the LORD is his name.

[7] "Are not you Israelites
the same to me as the Cushites[e]?"
declares the LORD.
"Did I not bring Israel up from
Egypt,
the Philistines from Caphtor[f]
and the Arameans from Kir?

[8] "Surely the eyes of the Sovereign
LORD
are on the sinful kingdom.
I will destroy it
from the face of the earth—
yet I will not totally destroy
the house of Jacob,"
declares the LORD.
[9] "For I will give the command,
and I will shake the house of
Israel
among all the nations
as grain is shaken in a sieve,
and not a pebble will reach the
ground.
[10] All the sinners among my people
will die by the sword,
all those who say,
'Disaster will not overtake or meet
us.'

Israel's Restoration

[11] "In that day I will restore
David's fallen tent.
I will repair its broken places,
restore its ruins,
and build it as it used to be,
[12] so that they may possess the remnant
of Edom
and all the nations that bear my
name,[g]"
declares the LORD,
who will do these things.

[13] "The days are coming," declares the
LORD,

---

[a] 14 Or power [b] 2 Hebrew to Sheol [c] 6 The meaning of the Hebrew for this phrase is uncertain. [d] 6 The meaning of the
Hebrew for this word is uncertain. [e] 7 That is, people from the upper Nile region [f] 7 That is, Crete [g] 12 Hebrew; Septuagint
so that the remnant of men / and all the nations that bear my name may seek the Lord

"when the reaper will be overtaken
    by the plowman
and the planter by the one treading
    grapes.
New wine will drip from the mountains
    and flow from all the hills.
14I will bring back my exiled[a] people
    Israel;
they will rebuild the ruined cities
    and live in them.

They will plant vineyards and drink
    their wine;
they will make gardens and eat
    their fruit.
15I will plant Israel in their own
    land,
never again to be uprooted
from the land I have given them,"

        says the LORD your God.

---

a 14 Or *will restore the fortunes of my*

Author: Obadiah

Date: Between 605 and 586 BC

Audience: The nation of Edom, announcing judgment for their callous refusal to help Israel (their blood brothers—Israel descended from Jacob, Edom from Esau) during a military crisis

If we pray while we are harboring unconfessed sin in our lives, we may as well save our breath (Psalm 66:18).

While all sin is offensive to God, certain attitudes and actions seem to elicit especially sharp condemnation. Take for example the list of "things the LORD hates" in Proverbs 6:16-19. Item number one: "Haughty eyes," or pride. It was for prideful behavior that God sent the prophet Obadiah to announce judgment on Edom.

There is always a steep price to pay for pride. Pride is what caused Lucifer to fall from heaven and become the devil (Isaiah 14:12-15). We must ask God to reveal any pride in us and then confess it as sin the moment we recognize it. If we ask God to give us understanding about who He really is, it will help us keep our heart humble before Him.

Prayer Themes:

• Ask God to keep you from succumbing to the sin of pride (1:3).

• Pray for God to bless those who are poor, and to give you His heart of mercy so that you mourn the misfortunes of others enough to help them (1:12).

• Ask the Lord to help you sow good seed so that you will reap good things (1:15).

Obadiah

¹The vision of Obadiah.

This is what the Sovereign LORD says about Edom—

We have heard a message from the
    LORD:
    An envoy was sent to the nations
        to say,
"Rise, and let us go against her for
    battle"—
²"See, I will make you small among
    the nations;
    you will be utterly despised.
³The pride of your heart has deceived
    you,
    you who live in the clefts of the
        rocksᵃ
    and make your home on the
        heights,
    you who say to yourself,

'Who can bring me down to the
    ground?'
⁴Though you soar like the eagle
    and make your nest among the
        stars,
    from there I will bring you down,"
        declares the LORD.
⁵"If thieves came to you,
    if robbers in the night—
Oh, what a disaster awaits you—
    would they not steal only as much
        as they wanted?
If grape pickers came to you,
    would they not leave a few
        grapes?
⁶But how Esau will be ransacked,
    his hidden treasures pillaged!
⁷All your allies will force you to the
    border;
    your friends will deceive and
        overpower you;

ᵃ 3 Or of Sela

those who eat your bread will set a
trap for you,[a]
but you will not detect it.

[8]"In that day," declares the LORD,
"will I not destroy the wise men of
Edom,
men of understanding in the
mountains of Esau?
[9]Your warriors, O Teman, will be
terrified,
and everyone in Esau's mountains
will be cut down in the slaughter.
[10]Because of the violence against your
brother Jacob,
you will be covered with shame;
you will be destroyed forever.

Prayer is . . .

being honest with God.

[11]On the day you stood aloof
while strangers carried off his
wealth
and foreigners entered his gates
and cast lots for Jerusalem,
you were like one of them.
[12]You should not look down on your
brother
in the day of his misfortune,
nor rejoice over the people of Judah
in the day of their destruction,
nor boast so much
in the day of their trouble.
[13]You should not march through the
gates of my people
in the day of their disaster,
nor look down on them in their
calamity
in the day of their disaster,
nor seize their wealth
in the day of their disaster.
[14]You should not wait at the crossroads
to cut down their fugitives,

nor hand over their survivors
in the day of their trouble.

[15]"The day of the LORD is near
for all nations.
As you have done, it will be done to
you;
your deeds will return upon your
own head.
[16]Just as you drank on my holy hill,
so all the nations will drink
continually;
they will drink and drink
and be as if they had never been.
[17]But on Mount Zion will be
deliverance;
it will be holy,
and the house of Jacob
will possess its inheritance.
[18]The house of Jacob will be a fire
and the house of Joseph a flame;
the house of Esau will be stubble,
and they will set it on fire and
consume it.
There will be no survivors
from the house of Esau."
The LORD has spoken.

[19]People from the Negev will occupy
the mountains of Esau,
and people from the foothills will
possess
the land of the Philistines.
They will occupy the fields of
Ephraim and Samaria,
and Benjamin will possess Gilead.
[20]This company of Israelite exiles who
are in Canaan
will possess ⌊the land⌋ as far as
Zarephath;
the exiles from Jerusalem who are in
Sepharad
will possess the towns of the Negev.
[21]Deliverers will go up on[b] Mount
Zion
to govern the mountains of Esau.
And the kingdom will be the
LORD's.

---

a 7 The meaning of the Hebrew for this clause is uncertain.   b 21 Or *from*

Author: Jonah

Date: About 750 BC

Audience: Jonah preached to the Ninevites (the residents of the capital city of Assyria); the written record of his mission was intended to remind Israel of her God-given calling to be a light to all the nations of the world.

Do you ever wrestle with God? Have you argued with Him or tried to do something other than what He was calling you to do?

If so, you'll appreciate the short and fascinating account of Jonah. It's one of the most familiar and best-loved Bible stories. And yet it's about so much more than a reluctant prophet being swallowed by a great fish. The book of Jonah reveals God's heart for the world. It speaks of wrong attitudes and the lengths God will go to get us where we need to be. It's about submitting our lives and accepting our part in His plan.

As you read Jonah, contrast the prophet's pettiness with God's great mercy. Compare his prickly, pouty nature with the deep reverence and instant obedience displayed by everyone else in the book. And pay careful attention to exactly where Jonah was when he prayed his best and most God-honoring prayer (chapter 2).

Prayer Themes:

- *Pray that God will keep you from running away from Him and His will (1:10).*

- *Praise the Lord that He is a God of second chances (3:1).*

- *Ask God to break your heart for the very things that break His heart (4:10-11).*

Jonah

Jonah Flees From the LORD

1 The word of the LORD came to Jonah son of Amittai: ²"Go to the great city of Nineveh and preach against it, because its wickedness has come up before me."

³But Jonah ran away from the LORD and headed for Tarshish. He went down to Joppa, where he found a ship bound for that port. After paying the fare, he went aboard and sailed for Tarshish to flee from the LORD.

⁴Then the LORD sent a great wind on the sea, and such a violent storm arose that the ship threatened to break up. ⁵All the sailors were afraid and each cried out to his own god. And they threw the cargo into the sea to lighten the ship.

But Jonah had gone below deck, where he lay down and fell into a deep sleep. ⁶The captain went to him and said, "How can you sleep? Get up and call on your god! Maybe he will take notice of us, and we will not perish."

⁷Then the sailors said to each other, "Come, let us cast lots to find out who is responsible for this calamity." They cast lots and the lot fell on Jonah.

⁸So they asked him, "Tell us, who is responsible for making all this trouble for us? What do you do? Where do you come from? What is your country? From what people are you?"

⁹He answered, "I am a Hebrew and I worship the LORD, the God of heaven, who made the sea and the land."

¹⁰This terrified them and they asked, "What have you done?" (They knew he was running away from the LORD, because he had already told them so.)

¹¹The sea was getting rougher and rougher. So they asked him, "What should we do to you to make the sea calm down for us?"

¹²"Pick me up and throw me into the sea," he replied, "and it will become calm. I know that it is my fault that this great storm has come upon you."

¹³Instead, the men did their best to row back to land. But they could not, for the sea grew even wilder than before. ¹⁴Then they cried to the LORD, "O LORD, please do not let us die for taking this man's life. Do not hold us accountable for killing an innocent man, for you, O LORD, have done as you pleased." ¹⁵Then they took Jonah and threw him overboard, and the raging sea grew calm. ¹⁶At this the men greatly feared the LORD, and they offered a sacrifice to the LORD and made vows to him.

¹⁷But the LORD provided a great fish to swallow Jonah, and Jonah was inside the fish three days and three nights.

Jonah's Prayer

2 From inside the fish Jonah prayed to the LORD his God. ²He said:

"In my distress I called to the LORD,
and he answered me.
From the depths of the grave[a] I called
for help,
and you listened to my cry.
³You hurled me into the deep,
into the very heart of the seas,
and the currents swirled about me;

all your waves and breakers
swept over me.
⁴I said, 'I have been banished
from your sight;
yet I will look again
toward your holy temple.'
⁵The engulfing waters threatened me,[b]
the deep surrounded me;
seaweed was wrapped around my
head.
⁶To the roots of the mountains I sank
down;
the earth beneath barred me in
forever.
But you brought my life up from the
pit,
O LORD my God.

⁷"When my life was ebbing away,
I remembered you, LORD,
and my prayer rose to you,
to your holy temple.

⁸"Those who cling to worthless idols
forfeit the grace that could be theirs.
⁹But I, with a song of thanksgiving,
will sacrifice to you.
What I have vowed I will make
good.
Salvation comes from the LORD."

¹⁰And the LORD commanded the fish, and it vomited Jonah onto dry land.

---

a 2 Hebrew Sheol   b 5 Or waters were at my throat

God's people at prayer
JONAH'S PRAYER FROM THE DEPTHS

JONAH 2:1-10 Jonah was in no position to bargain with the Lord. He had completely disobeyed God and was running from Him. But his plan was foiled when he was swallowed by a great fish! God gave him three days inside the fish's stomach to think about how he had come to be there. And what did Jonah do? He prayed as "the deep surrounded" him. He sought the Lord as the "currents swirled." He pledged to sing a "song of thanksgiving" and keep his vow. Jonah quickly realized it would have been far better to obey God from the start.

God had mercy on Jonah, and He will be merciful to us when we repent and humble ourselves before Him. No matter how far off the path God has for you that you find yourself, no matter what troubling currents may be swirling around you, no matter how far away from God you feel, He will hear you when you call on Him and will lift you from any pit into which you have fallen.

Jonah Goes to Nineveh

3 Then the word of the LORD came to Jonah a second time: ²"Go to the great city of Nineveh and proclaim to it the message I give you."

Praying Jonah 3:1

Lord, help me to never run from
what You are instructing me to do,
but thank You that if I were to do that,
You are a God of second chances.

---

³Jonah obeyed the word of the LORD and went to Nineveh. Now Nineveh was a very important city—a visit required three days. ⁴On the first day, Jonah started into the city. He proclaimed: "Forty more days and Nineveh will be overturned." ⁵The Ninevites be-lieved God. They declared a fast, and all of them, from the greatest to the least, put on sackcloth.

⁶When the news reached the king of Nineveh, he rose from his throne, took off his royal robes, covered himself with sackcloth and sat down in the dust. ⁷Then he issued a proclamation in Nineveh:

"By the decree of the king and his nobles:

Do not let any man or beast, herd or flock, taste anything; do not let them eat or drink. ⁸But let man and beast be covered with sackcloth. Let everyone call urgently on God. Let them give up their evil ways and their violence. ⁹Who knows? God may yet relent and with compassion

---

Delivering God's Message

GOING deeper

READ AND CONSIDER: JONAH 4

"Should I not be concerned about that great city?" (Jonah 4:11).

God had given Jonah a second chance. "Go to the great city of Nineveh" had been the directive (1:2), and Jonah had gone the other direction. But God caught up with him, sent a fish to provide personal transportation back to shore, and said again to Jonah, "Go to the great city of Nineveh" (3:2). And this time, Jonah went.

What a compassionate God! He could have let His reluctant prophet drown in the ocean, but He didn't. He had a message for Nineveh, and He wanted Jonah to deliver it.

God always offers His grace and compassion to everyone—even those who might seem to be least deserving. Somewhere in Nineveh surely someone was seeking divine intervention, someone believed there had to be more to life, and they were looking to God for help. And God heard their prayer and sent Jonah to bring a message—with powerful results. The people's hearts were ripe to hear from God.

God hears the cries of those who seek Him. When people call out to Him on behalf of a city, He will send someone with a message. When people don't seek God, and when their hearts become hard and filled with evil desires, God will allow destruction to come upon them.

You have received God's compassion and seen His loving touch on your life. All around you are people who need to know God's love and compassion for them, too. Many of them may look carefree, but who knows the deep longings in their hearts and the questions they may be asking. They may be praying, "Lord, send someone to speak the truth and show me the right way to live."

Ask God to show you if perhaps He is sending you or asking you to intercede on someone's behalf.

turn from his fierce anger so that we will not perish."

¹⁰When God saw what they did and how they turned from their evil ways, he had compassion and did not bring upon them the destruction he had threatened.

Jonah's Anger at the LORD's Compassion

4 But Jonah was greatly displeased and became angry. ²He prayed to the LORD, "O LORD, is this not what I said when I was still at home? That is why I was so quick to flee to Tarshish. I knew that you are a gracious and compassionate God, slow to anger and abounding in love, a God who relents from sending calamity. ³Now, O LORD, take away my life, for it is better for me to die than to live."

⁴But the LORD replied, "Have you any right to be angry?"

⁵Jonah went out and sat down at a place east of the city. There he made himself a shelter, sat in its shade and waited to see what would happen to the city. ⁶Then the LORD God provided a vine and made it grow up over Jonah to give shade for his head to ease his discomfort, and Jonah was very happy about the vine. ⁷But at dawn the next day God provided a worm, which chewed the vine so that it withered. ⁸When the sun rose, God provided a scorching east wind, and the sun blazed on Jonah's head so that he grew faint. He wanted to die, and said, "It would be better for me to die than to live."

⁹But God said to Jonah, "Do you have a right to be angry about the vine?"

"I do," he said. "I am angry enough to die."

¹⁰But the LORD said, "You have been concerned about this vine, though you did not tend it or make it grow. It sprang up overnight and died overnight. ¹¹But Nineveh has more than a hundred and twenty thousand people who cannot tell their right hand from their left, and many cattle as well. Should I not be concerned about that great city?"

Author: Micah

Date: Between 750 and 686 BC

Audience: The people of God, warning them of short-term judgment and comforting them with assurances of long-term deliverance and hope

Micah was an obscure prophet in ancient Israel, given the unenviable task of assessing and addressing his own stubborn, sin-soaked culture. His message was to remind them of what God wanted. "What does the LORD require of you? To act justly and to love mercy and to walk humbly with your God" (6:8).

When you hear or read the news every day, does it cause you to shake your head and throw up your hands in despair, or does it prompt you to bow your head and fold your hands in prayer?

We all need to pray more. We must pray that people's hearts will be softened to the things of the Lord so they will "turn in fear to the LORD our God" (7:17). We can pray that they come to a clear understanding that God will have compassion on them and remove their sins and iniquities to the depths of the sea (7:19). Praying for people helps them to better hear God's voice.

Prayer Themes:

- *Ask the Lord to give your nation leaders who will seek to honor Him in all their decisions (3:1-4).*

- *Thank God for the fulfillment of all the messianic prophecies in the Old Testament and for sending Christ to save you, shepherd you, and reign in your life (5:2-5).*

- *Pray for a deeper and stronger faith in God, and a growing confidence that He will hear your prayers and answer them (7:7).*

Micah

1 The word of the LORD that came to Micah of Moresheth during the reigns of Jotham, Ahaz and Hezekiah, kings of Judah—the vision he saw concerning Samaria and Jerusalem.

2 Hear, O peoples, all of you,
   listen, O earth and all who are
      in it,
that the Sovereign LORD may witness
      against you,
   the Lord from his holy temple.

Judgment Against Samaria and Jerusalem

3 Look! The LORD is coming from his
      dwelling place;
   he comes down and treads the high
      places of the earth.
4 The mountains melt beneath him
   and the valleys split apart,
like wax before the fire,
   like water rushing down a slope.

5 All this is because of Jacob's
      transgression,
   because of the sins of the house of
      Israel.
What is Jacob's transgression?
   Is it not Samaria?
What is Judah's high place?
   Is it not Jerusalem?

6 "Therefore I will make Samaria a
      heap of rubble,
   a place for planting vineyards.
I will pour her stones into the valley
   and lay bare her foundations.
7 All her idols will be broken to
      pieces;
   all her temple gifts will be burned
      with fire;
   I will destroy all her images.
Since she gathered her gifts from the
      wages of prostitutes,
   as the wages of prostitutes they will
      again be used."

Weeping and Mourning

8 Because of this I will weep and wail;
    I will go about barefoot and naked.
I will howl like a jackal
    and moan like an owl.
9 For her wound is incurable;
    it has come to Judah.
It[a] has reached the very gate of my
        people,
    even to Jerusalem itself.
10 Tell it not in Gath[b];
    weep not at all.[c]
In Beth Ophrah[d]
    roll in the dust.
11 Pass on in nakedness and shame,
    you who live in Shaphir.[e]
Those who live in Zaanan[f]
    will not come out.
Beth Ezel is in mourning;
    its protection is taken from you.
12 Those who live in Maroth[g] writhe in
        pain,
    waiting for relief,
because disaster has come from the
        LORD,
    even to the gate of Jerusalem.
13 You who live in Lachish,[h]
    harness the team to the chariot.
You were the beginning of sin
    to the Daughter of Zion,
for the transgressions of Israel
    were found in you.
14 Therefore you will give parting gifts
    to Moresheth Gath.
The town of Aczib[i] will prove
        deceptive
    to the kings of Israel.
15 I will bring a conqueror against you
    who live in Mareshah.[j]
He who is the glory of Israel
    will come to Adullam.
16 Shave your heads in mourning
    for the children in whom you
        delight;
make yourselves as bald as the
        vulture,

for they will go from you into
    exile.

Man's Plans and God's

2 Woe to those who plan iniquity,
    to those who plot evil on their
        beds!
At morning's light they carry it out
    because it is in their power to do it.
2 They covet fields and seize them,
    and houses, and take them.
They defraud a man of his home,
    a fellowman of his inheritance.

3 Therefore, the LORD says:

"I am planning disaster against this
        people,
    from which you cannot save
        yourselves.
You will no longer walk proudly,
    for it will be a time of calamity.
4 In that day men will ridicule you;
    they will taunt you with this
        mournful song:
'We are utterly ruined;
    my people's possession is divided
        up.
He takes it from me!
    He assigns our fields to traitors.'"

5 Therefore you will have no one in
    the assembly of the LORD
to divide the land by lot.

False Prophets

6 "Do not prophesy," their prophets say.
    "Do not prophesy about these
        things;
    disgrace will not overtake us."
7 Should it be said, O house of Jacob:
    "Is the Spirit of the LORD angry?
    Does he do such things?"

"Do not my words do good
    to him whose ways are upright?
8 Lately my people have risen up
    like an enemy.
You strip off the rich robe

---

a 9 Or He   b 10 Gath sounds like the Hebrew for tell.   c 10 Hebrew; Septuagint may suggest not in Acco. The Hebrew for
in Acco sounds like the Hebrew for weep.   d 10 Beth Ophrah means house of dust.   e 11 Shaphir means pleasant.
f 11 Zaanan sounds like the Hebrew for come out.   g 12 Maroth sounds like the Hebrew for bitter.   h 13 Lachish sounds like the
Hebrew for team.   i 14 Aczib means deception.   j 15 Mareshah sounds like the Hebrew for conqueror.

from those who pass by without a
care,
like men returning from battle.
⁹You drive the women of my
people
from their pleasant homes.
You take away my blessing
from their children forever.
¹⁰Get up, go away!
For this is not your resting place,
because it is defiled,
it is ruined, beyond all remedy.
¹¹If a liar and deceiver comes and says,
'I will prophesy for you plenty of
wine and beer,'
he would be just the prophet for
this people!

Deliverance Promised

¹²"I will surely gather all of you,
O Jacob;
I will surely bring together the
remnant of Israel.
I will bring them together like sheep
in a pen,
like a flock in its pasture;
the place will throng with people.
¹³One who breaks open the way will
go up before them;
they will break through the gate
and go out.
Their king will pass through before
them,
the LORD at their head."

Leaders and Prophets Rebuked

3 Then I said,

"Listen, you leaders of Jacob,
you rulers of the house of Israel.
Should you not know justice,
² you who hate good and love evil;
who tear the skin from my people
and the flesh from their bones;
³who eat my people's flesh,
strip off their skin
and break their bones in pieces;
who chop them up like meat for the
pan,
like flesh for the pot?"

⁴Then they will cry out to the LORD,
but he will not answer them.
At that time he will hide his face
from them
because of the evil they have done.

Praying Micah 3:4

*Heavenly Father, I pray that I will never
cause distance or separation between You
and me by doing anything that would be
considered evil in Your sight.*

⁵This is what the LORD says:

"As for the prophets
who lead my people astray,
if one feeds them,
they proclaim 'peace';
if he does not,
they prepare to wage war against
him.
⁶Therefore night will come over you,
without visions,
and darkness, without divination.
The sun will set for the prophets,
and the day will go dark for them.
⁷The seers will be ashamed
and the diviners disgraced.
They will all cover their faces
because there is no answer from
God."

⁸But as for me, I am filled with power,
with the Spirit of the LORD,
and with justice and might,
to declare to Jacob his transgression,
to Israel his sin.
⁹Hear this, you leaders of the house of
Jacob,
you rulers of the house of Israel,
who despise justice
and distort all that is right;
¹⁰who build Zion with bloodshed,
and Jerusalem with wickedness.
¹¹Her leaders judge for a bribe,
her priests teach for a price,
and her prophets tell fortunes for
money.
Yet they lean upon the LORD and say,
"Is not the LORD among us?

No disaster will come upon us."
¹²Therefore because of you,
　Zion will be plowed like a field,
Jerusalem will become a heap of
　　rubble,
　the temple hill a mound overgrown
　　with thickets.

The Mountain of the LORD

4 In the last days

the mountain of the LORD's temple
　　will be established
　as chief among the mountains;
it will be raised above the hills,
　and peoples will stream to it.

²Many nations will come and say,

"Come, let us go up to the mountain
　　of the LORD,
　to the house of the God of Jacob.
He will teach us his ways,
　so that we may walk in his paths."
The law will go out from Zion,
　the word of the LORD from
　　Jerusalem.
³He will judge between many peoples
　and will settle disputes for strong
　　nations far and wide.
They will beat their swords into
　　plowshares
　and their spears into pruning
　　hooks.
Nation will not take up sword against
　　nation,
　nor will they train for war
　　anymore.
⁴Every man will sit under his own vine
　and under his own fig tree,
and no one will make them afraid,
　for the LORD Almighty has spoken.
⁵All the nations may walk
　in the name of their gods;
we will walk in the name of the LORD
　our God for ever and ever.

The LORD's Plan

⁶"In that day," declares the LORD,

"I will gather the lame;

I will assemble the exiles
　and those I have brought to grief.
⁷I will make the lame a remnant,
　those driven away a strong nation.
The LORD will rule over them in
　　Mount Zion
from that day and forever.
⁸As for you, O watchtower of the
　　flock,
　O stronghold[a] of the Daughter of
　　Zion,
the former dominion will be restored
　　to you;
　kingship will come to the Daughter
　　of Jerusalem."

⁹Why do you now cry aloud—
　have you no king?
Has your counselor perished,
　that pain seizes you like that of a
　　woman in labor?
¹⁰Writhe in agony, O Daughter of
　　Zion,
　like a woman in labor,
for now you must leave the city
　to camp in the open field.
You will go to Babylon;
　there you will be rescued.
There the LORD will redeem you
　out of the hand of your enemies.

¹¹But now many nations
　are gathered against you.
They say, "Let her be defiled,
　let our eyes gloat over Zion!"
¹²But they do not know
　the thoughts of the LORD;
they do not understand his plan,
　he who gathers them like sheaves to
　　the threshing floor.
¹³"Rise and thresh, O Daughter of
　　Zion,
　for I will give you horns of iron;
I will give you hoofs of bronze
　and you will break to pieces many
　　nations."

You will devote their ill-gotten gains
　to the LORD,

ᵃ8 Or hill

their wealth to the Lord of all the
earth.

A Promised Ruler From Bethlehem

5 Marshal your troops, O city of
troops,[a]
for a siege is laid against us.
They will strike Israel's ruler
on the cheek with a rod.

2 "But you, Bethlehem Ephrathah,
though you are small among the
clans[b] of Judah,
out of you will come for me
one who will be ruler over Israel,
whose origins[c] are from of old,
from ancient times.[d]"

3 Therefore Israel will be abandoned
until the time when she who is in
labor gives birth
and the rest of his brothers return
to join the Israelites.

4 He will stand and shepherd his flock
in the strength of the LORD,
in the majesty of the name of the
LORD his God.
And they will live securely, for then
his greatness
will reach to the ends of the earth.
5 And he will be their peace.

Deliverance and Destruction

When the Assyrian invades our land
and marches through our fortresses,
we will raise against him seven
shepherds,
even eight leaders of men.
6 They will rule[e] the land of Assyria
with the sword,
the land of Nimrod with drawn
sword.[f]
He will deliver us from the Assyrian
when he invades our land
and marches into our borders.

7 The remnant of Jacob will be
in the midst of many peoples
like dew from the LORD,

like showers on the grass,
which do not wait for man
or linger for mankind.
8 The remnant of Jacob will be among
the nations,
in the midst of many peoples,
like a lion among the beasts of the
forest,
like a young lion among flocks of
sheep,
which mauls and mangles as it goes,
and no one can rescue.
9 Your hand will be lifted up in
triumph over your enemies,
and all your foes will be destroyed.

10 "In that day," declares the LORD,

"I will destroy your horses from
among you
and demolish your chariots.
11 I will destroy the cities of your land
and tear down all your strongholds.
12 I will destroy your witchcraft
and you will no longer cast spells.
13 I will destroy your carved images
and your sacred stones from among
you;
you will no longer bow down
to the work of your hands.
14 I will uproot from among you your
Asherah poles[g]
and demolish your cities.
15 I will take vengeance in anger and
wrath
upon the nations that have not
obeyed me."

The LORD's Case Against Israel

6 Listen to what the LORD says:

"Stand up, plead your case before the
mountains;
let the hills hear what you have to
say.
2 Hear, O mountains, the LORD's
accusation;
listen, you everlasting foundations
of the earth.

a 1 Or Strengthen your walls, O walled city   b 2 Or rulers   c 2 Hebrew goings out   d 2 Or from days of eternity   e 6 Or crush
f 6 Or Nimrod in its gates   g 14 That is, symbols of the goddess Asherah

Surviving Disappointment

Disappointment

is inevitable. That's because life doesn't always turn out the way we imagine it will. When it doesn't, how can we survive the disappointment? How can we get through those dark times? What kind of comfort can we hope to have?

Often our greatest times of disappointment come when someone fails us, or we at least *feel* that they have. People can hurt us deeply. Sometimes they know what they are doing, while other times they're only doing the best they know how to do with the tools they have. In either case, the level of fulfillment and happiness we experience in our lives doesn't depend on other people; it depends on God. Of course, we do rely on other people for certain things, and it's painful when they let us down. But the ultimate success or joy of our life should not depend on them. We don't have to prolong suffering over what others do or don't do to us, because ultimately our reward is in God's hands.

It's also seriously disappointing when we believe *we* have failed in some way, perhaps due to our own carelessness or in spite of our best efforts. Or we *think* we have failed when we really haven't at all. And we sit in darkness over it, torturing ourselves. The regret and condemnation pounds us down like a giant sledgehammer to our soul. "If only I hadn't . . ." "If I just would have . . ." "Why didn't I . . ." It's a weight we can't carry and were never meant to.

Even when we have to bear the consequences for the wrong choices we've made, God is still on our side. "Though I have fallen, I will rise. Though I sit in darkness, the LORD will be my light" (Micah 7:8). How wonderful it is to know that even in a darkness of our own creation, God is still there, and so is

His light. I think that's what makes us love Him most. His grace. We realize how little we deserve it and how far short of His glory we fall, yet He loves and accepts us anyway. Even in our greatest depth of failure, God brings good out of it as long as we reach humbly to Him.

God often allows hard things to happen in our lives in order to bless us in some way. If we are willing to allow for that possibility in everything that happens, it saves us from being devastated by people and situations that are ultimately going to be used for God's glory. If we surrender our disappointment to God and say, "Be my light and lead me through this, Lord," His work will be accomplished faster.

When disappointing things happen to you, ask God to help you discern His truth about what you are experiencing. Ask *Him* to reign in the situation instead of your feelings. It's easy to go with anger or hurt, but far more rewarding to find God's blessing in the situation instead. It pleases Him when you have faith enough in the midst of your disappointment to put your hope and expectations in Him.

When you experience disappointment, do not run into the arms of bitterness or unforgiveness. Run to your Father's arms instead so He can hold, comfort, and sustain you. If you will maintain a humble, submitted, faith-filled, expectant heart, you will see God's goodness manifest in the midst of all that's happening to you. He will use this experience to bring you closer to Him, and your greatest treasure will be a deep sense of His presence.

For the next "From Stormie's Heart" article, go to page 1172.

For the LORD has a case against his
people;
he is lodging a charge against Israel.

3 "My people, what have I done to you?
How have I burdened you? Answer
me.
4 I brought you up out of Egypt
and redeemed you from the land of
slavery.
I sent Moses to lead you,
also Aaron and Miriam.
5 My people, remember
what Balak king of Moab counseled
and what Balaam son of Beor
answered.
Remember ⌞your journey⌟ from
Shittim to Gilgal,
that you may know the righteous
acts of the LORD."

6 With what shall I come before the
LORD
and bow down before the exalted
God?
Shall I come before him with burnt
offerings,
with calves a year old?
7 Will the LORD be pleased with
thousands of rams,
with ten thousand rivers of oil?
Shall I offer my firstborn for my
transgression,
the fruit of my body for the sin of
my soul?
8 He has showed you, O man, what is
good.
And what does the LORD require
of you?
To act justly and to love mercy
and to walk humbly with your God.

Israel's Guilt and Punishment

9 Listen! The LORD is calling to the
city—
and to fear your name is wisdom—
"Heed the rod and the One who
appointed it.[a]
10 Am I still to forget, O wicked house,

your ill-gotten treasures
and the short ephah,[b] which is
accursed?
11 Shall I acquit a man with dishonest
scales,
with a bag of false weights?
12 Her rich men are violent;
her people are liars
and their tongues speak deceitfully.
13 Therefore, I have begun to destroy
you,
to ruin you because of your sins.
14 You will eat but not be satisfied;
your stomach will still be empty.[c]
You will store up but save nothing,
because what you save I will give to
the sword.
15 You will plant but not harvest;
you will press olives but not use the
oil on yourselves,
you will crush grapes but not drink
the wine.
16 You have observed the statutes of
Omri
and all the practices of Ahab's
house,
and you have followed their
traditions.
Therefore I will give you over to ruin
and your people to derision;
you will bear the scorn of the
nations.[d]"

Israel's Misery

7 What misery is mine!
I am like one who gathers summer
fruit
at the gleaning of the vineyard;
there is no cluster of grapes to eat,
none of the early figs that I crave.
2 The godly have been swept from the
land;
not one upright man remains.
All men lie in wait to shed blood;
each hunts his brother with a net.
3 Both hands are skilled in doing evil;
the ruler demands gifts,
the judge accepts bribes,

---

[a] 9 The meaning of the Hebrew for this line is uncertain.   [b] 10 An ephah was a dry measure.   [c] 14 The meaning of the Hebrew
for this word is uncertain.   [d] 16 Septuagint; Hebrew *scorn due my people*

the powerful dictate what they
desire—
they all conspire together.
⁴ The best of them is like a brier,
the most upright worse than a
thorn hedge.
The day of your watchmen has come,
the day God visits you.
Now is the time of their confusion.
⁵ Do not trust a neighbor;
put no confidence in a friend.
Even with her who lies in your
embrace

be careful of your words.
⁶ For a son dishonors his
father,
a daughter rises up against her
mother,
a daughter-in-law against her
mother-in-law—
a man's enemies are the members of
his own household.

⁷ But as for me, I watch in hope for the
LORD,
I wait for God my Savior;
my God will hear me.

GOING *deeper*

Rising Up out of the Darkness

READ AND CONSIDER: MICAH 7

"Do not gloat over me, my enemy! Though I have fallen, I will rise. Though I sit in darkness, the LORD will be my light" (Micah 7:8).

No one is perfect. The people of Judah knew this very well—they had failed God miserably. And to make matters worse, their enemies were laughing at them.

Being good can be a daily struggle for many people. Our human nature is instinctively selfish, causing us to strive to satisfy our own desires. Yet God has given us His Word and His Spirit to help us combat our sinful nature. Still, we all fall into sin, some deeper than others. In those times we have a choice to make: wallow in the darkness of self-pity or repent and look to Jesus. "The LORD will be my light," wrote Micah. Sin is a dark path that first draws us in with promises of the gratification of our human desires. But when the light of the Word shines upon it, all the snares, traps, and quagmires are revealed.

Always remember that no matter how much we've failed, God is ready to forgive us when we ask Him to. He doesn't want any of His children to sink without hope of rescue. That's why He gave us His Son, Jesus, to offer us His lifeline. Reaching out in repentance is our decision. Picture a person drowning and crying out for help, when suddenly a strong arm reaches into the water. That the person would obviously reach for the strong hand immediately and be saved. Confession of sin and repentance are a strong hand that reaches to us when we are drowning in our own failures, yet many people choose to reject that means of restoration. Perhaps they don't realize the danger they are in, or maybe they reject the hope offered, thinking they can save themselves. But Jesus is always there ready to pull us up and out of the darkness, no matter how deep or how many times we slip and fall. Whenever you feel yourself sinking into the darkness, say this prayer:

Lord, help me to trust Your light in my life. I look to You to be my treasure in darkness. I know that You are light and in You is no darkness at all. Lord, You see what is in the dark. And when I am in darkness, You will be my light. I know that when I fall, You will lift me up again. I worship You as the Light of my life and thank You that You will enlighten the dark for me. Though I have fallen, I will rise. Though I sit in darkness, You, Lord, will be my light.

Israel Will Rise

8 Do not gloat over me, my enemy!
  Though I have fallen, I will rise.
Though I sit in darkness,
  the LORD will be my light.
9 Because I have sinned against him,
  I will bear the LORD's wrath,
until he pleads my case
  and establishes my right.
He will bring me out into the light;
  I will see his righteousness.
10 Then my enemy will see it
  and will be covered with shame,
she who said to me,
  "Where is the LORD your God?"
My eyes will see her downfall;
  even now she will be trampled
    underfoot
  like mire in the streets.

11 The day for building your walls will
    come,
  the day for extending your
    boundaries.
12 In that day people will come to you
  from Assyria and the cities of
    Egypt,
  even from Egypt to the Euphrates
  and from sea to sea
  and from mountain to mountain.
13 The earth will become desolate
    because of its inhabitants,
  as the result of their deeds.

Prayer and Praise

14 Shepherd your people with your staff,
  the flock of your inheritance,
which lives by itself in a forest,
  in fertile pasturelands.[a]
Let them feed in Bashan and Gilead
  as in days long ago.

15 "As in the days when you came out of
    Egypt,
  I will show them my wonders."

16 Nations will see and be ashamed,
  deprived of all their power.
They will lay their hands on their
    mouths
  and their ears will become deaf.
17 They will lick dust like a snake,
  like creatures that crawl on the
    ground.
They will come trembling out of
    their dens;
  they will turn in fear to the LORD
    our God
  and will be afraid of you.
18 Who is a God like you,
  who pardons sin and forgives the
    transgression
  of the remnant of his inheritance?
You do not stay angry forever
  but delight to show mercy.
19 You will again have compassion on
    us;
  you will tread our sins underfoot
  and hurl all our iniquities into the
    depths of the sea.
20 You will be true to Jacob,
  and show mercy to Abraham,
as you pledged on oath to our fathers
  in days long ago.

---

a 14 Or in the middle of Carmel

Author: Nahum

Date: Between 663 and 612 BC

Audience: The doom that Nahum prophesied on Assyria was intended to bring comfort to the nation of Israel by reminding them that the Lord is a powerful and just Judge.

Prayer Themes:

- *Thank God for the promise that though He is slow to anger, He "will not leave the guilty unpunished" (1:3).*

- *Praise God for His goodness in your life, for the specific ways He has demonstrated care for you (1:7).*

- *Ask God to enable you to be His powerful messenger who brings the good news of salvation and proclaims peace with God (1:15).*

Nahum, whose name means "comfort," was a Jewish prophet who announced the doom of ancient Assyria. Though God had mercifully spared this empire a century earlier—by sending Jonah with a warning to repent—the Assyrians under King Ashurbanipal had quickly reverted to their evil ways. No nation was ever more sadistic or savage.

The comforting message underlying the book of Nahum is that our God reigns and He is the great King over all. He is the supreme Judge of the universe, and every dictator and evil leader *will* answer to him.

Even though God *will* have the last word in human history, we must not neglect our call to pray for the nations. As you watch global events unfold, pray for all oppressed peoples. Pray for an outpouring of God's Spirit upon them, their city, and their nation. Pray that more and more people will hear the good news and come to know Jesus as their Savior.

Nahum

1 An oracle concerning Nineveh. The book of the vision of Nahum the Elkoshite.

The Lord's Anger Against Nineveh

² The Lord is a jealous and avenging God;
   the Lord takes vengeance and is filled with wrath.
The Lord takes vengeance on his foes
   and maintains his wrath against his enemies.
³ The Lord is slow to anger and great in power;
   the Lord will not leave the guilty unpunished.
His way is in the whirlwind and the storm,
   and clouds are the dust of his feet.
⁴ He rebukes the sea and dries it up;
   he makes all the rivers run dry.
Bashan and Carmel wither
   and the blossoms of Lebanon fade.
⁵ The mountains quake before him
   and the hills melt away.
The earth trembles at his presence,
   the world and all who live in it.
⁶ Who can withstand his indignation?
   Who can endure his fierce anger?
His wrath is poured out like fire;
   the rocks are shattered before him.

⁷ The Lord is good,
   a refuge in times of trouble.
He cares for those who trust in him,

Praying Nahum 1:7
Thank You, Lord, that You are a refuge in times of trouble and that You love all who trust in You.

> ## Prayer is . . .
>
> *coming to God in childlike humility,*
> *expecting to receive something good*
> *from your heavenly Father.*

8 but with an overwhelming flood
   he will make an end of ⌊Nineveh⌋;
      he will pursue his foes into darkness.

9 Whatever they plot against the LORD
      he[a] will bring to an end;
   trouble will not come a second time.
10 They will be entangled among thorns
      and drunk from their wine;
   they will be consumed like dry
      stubble.[b]
11 From you, ⌊O Nineveh,⌋ has one
      come forth
   who plots evil against the LORD
      and counsels wickedness.

12 This is what the LORD says:

"Although they have allies and are
      numerous,
   they will be cut off and pass away.
Although I have afflicted you,
   ⌊O Judah,⌋
   I will afflict you no more.
13 Now I will break their yoke from
      your neck
   and tear your shackles away."

14 The LORD has given a command
      concerning you, ⌊Nineveh⌋:
   "You will have no descendants to
      bear your name.
I will destroy the carved images and
      cast idols
   that are in the temple of your gods.
I will prepare your grave,
   for you are vile."

15 Look, there on the mountains,
   the feet of one who brings good
      news,

who proclaims peace!
Celebrate your festivals, O Judah,
   and fulfill your vows.
No more will the wicked invade you;
   they will be completely destroyed.

Nineveh to Fall

2 An attacker advances against you,
      ⌊Nineveh⌋.
   Guard the fortress,
   watch the road,
   brace yourselves,
   marshal all your strength!

2 The LORD will restore the splendor of
      Jacob
   like the splendor of Israel,
though destroyers have laid them
      waste
   and have ruined their vines.

3 The shields of his soldiers are red;
   the warriors are clad in scarlet.
The metal on the chariots flashes
   on the day they are made ready;
   the spears of pine are brandished.[c]
4 The chariots storm through the
      streets,
   rushing back and forth through the
      squares.
They look like flaming torches;
   they dart about like lightning.

5 He summons his picked troops,
   yet they stumble on their way.
They dash to the city wall;
   the protective shield is put in place.
6 The river gates are thrown open
   and the palace collapses.
7 It is decreed[d] that ⌊the city⌋
   be exiled and carried away.
Its slave girls moan like doves
   and beat upon their breasts.
8 Nineveh is like a pool,
   and its water is draining away.
"Stop! Stop!" they cry,
   but no one turns back.
9 Plunder the silver!
   Plunder the gold!

---

[a] 9 Or *What do you foes plot against the LORD? / He*   [b] 10 The meaning of the Hebrew for this verse is uncertain.   [c] 3 Hebrew;
Septuagint and Syriac / *the horsemen rush to and fro*   [d] 7 The meaning of the Hebrew for this word is uncertain.

The supply is endless,
the wealth from all its treasures!
¹⁰She is pillaged, plundered, stripped!
Hearts melt, knees give way,
bodies tremble, every face grows
pale.

¹¹Where now is the lions' den,
the place where they fed their
young,
where the lion and lioness went,
and the cubs, with nothing to fear?
¹²The lion killed enough for his cubs
and strangled the prey for his mate,
filling his lairs with the kill
and his dens with the prey.

¹³"I am against you,"
declares the LORD Almighty.
"I will burn up your chariots in
smoke,
and the sword will devour your
young lions.
I will leave you no prey on the
earth.
The voices of your messengers
will no longer be heard."

Woe to Nineveh

3 Woe to the city of blood,
full of lies,
full of plunder,
never without victims!
²The crack of whips,
the clatter of wheels,
galloping horses
and jolting chariots!
³Charging cavalry,
flashing swords
and glittering spears!
Many casualties,
piles of dead,
bodies without number,
people stumbling over the corpses—
⁴all because of the wanton lust of a
harlot,
alluring, the mistress of sorceries,
who enslaved nations by her
prostitution
and peoples by her witchcraft.

⁵"I am against you," declares the LORD
Almighty.
"I will lift your skirts over your
face.
I will show the nations your
nakedness
and the kingdoms your shame.
⁶I will pelt you with filth,
I will treat you with contempt
and make you a spectacle.
⁷All who see you will flee from you
and say,
'Nineveh is in ruins—who will
mourn for her?'
Where can I find anyone to
comfort you?"

⁸Are you better than Thebes,ᵃ
situated on the Nile,
with water around her?
The river was her defense,
the waters her wall.
⁹Cushᵇ and Egypt were her boundless
strength;
Put and Libya were among her
allies.
¹⁰Yet she was taken captive
and went into exile.
Her infants were dashed to pieces
at the head of every street.
Lots were cast for her nobles,
and all her great men were put in
chains.
¹¹You too will become drunk;
you will go into hiding
and seek refuge from the enemy.

¹²All your fortresses are like fig trees
with their first ripe fruit;
when they are shaken,
the figs fall into the mouth of the
eater.
¹³Look at your troops—
they are all women!
The gates of your land
are wide open to your enemies;
fire has consumed their bars.

¹⁴Draw water for the siege,
strengthen your defenses!

ᵃ 8 Hebrew *No Amon*   ᵇ 9 That is, the upper Nile region

Work the clay,
tread the mortar,
repair the brickwork!
15There the fire will devour you;
the sword will cut you down
and, like grasshoppers, consume
you.
Multiply like grasshoppers,
multiply like locusts!
16You have increased the number of
your merchants
till they are more than the stars of
the sky,
but like locusts they strip the land
and then fly away.
17Your guards are like locusts,
your officials like swarms of
locusts

that settle in the walls on a cold
day—
but when the sun appears they fly
away,
and no one knows where.

18O king of Assyria, your shepherds[a]
slumber;
your nobles lie down to rest.
Your people are scattered on the
mountains
with no one to gather them.
19Nothing can heal your wound;
your injury is fatal.
Everyone who hears the news about
you
claps his hands at your fall,
for who has not felt
your endless cruelty?

---

[a] 18 Or rulers

Author: Habakkuk

Date: About 605 BC

Audience: The nation of Israel, specifically those who were questioning the mysterious ways of God

Prayer Themes:

- Ask God to help you grow in your knowledge of Him so you can learn to live by faith (2:4).

- Thank the Lord that nothing will prevent His glory from filling the earth (2:14).

- Ask God for the perseverance and strength to continue trusting and worshiping Him, even in dark and uncertain times (3:17-19).

Have you ever been overwhelmed by all the negative things you see going on in the world around you? Do you sometimes wonder, *Where is God in the midst of certain devastating events?* We've all questioned God at some point in our lives. We've all seen or experienced some tragedy or perplexing predicament and said, "Lord, why did this happen?"

That is what happened to Habakkuk. After experiencing doubt about all the troubling things that were happening around him, he reverently inquired of the Lord. He focused on God and ended up bowing low in worship, which is the place we all will ultimately come to when we ask God questions that begin with "Why?" We must live by faith in God, who is far greater and more powerful than all the disturbing things we see in the world, and worship Him for who He is.

Habakkuk

1

The oracle that Habakkuk the prophet received.

Habakkuk's Complaint

² How long, O LORD, must I call for help,
  but you do not listen?
Or cry out to you, "Violence!"
  but you do not save?
³ Why do you make me look at injustice?
  Why do you tolerate wrong?
Destruction and violence are before me;
  there is strife, and conflict abounds.
⁴ Therefore the law is paralyzed,
  and justice never prevails.
The wicked hem in the righteous,
  so that justice is perverted.

The LORD's Answer

⁵ "Look at the nations and watch—
  and be utterly amazed.
For I am going to do something in
    your days
  that you would not believe,
  even if you were told.
⁶ I am raising up the Babylonians,^a
  that ruthless and impetuous people,
who sweep across the whole earth
  to seize dwelling places not their
    own.
⁷ They are a feared and dreaded people;
  they are a law to themselves
  and promote their own honor.
⁸ Their horses are swifter than leopards,
  fiercer than wolves at dusk.
Their cavalry gallops headlong;
  their horsemen come from afar.
They fly like a vulture swooping to
    devour;
⁹   they all come bent on violence.
Their hordes^b advance like a desert
    wind

---

^a 6 Or *Chaldeans*   ^b 9 The meaning of the Hebrew for this word is uncertain.

GOING *deeper*

Keep Praying No Matter What

READ AND CONSIDER: HABAKKUK 1:1-11

"How long, O LORD, must I call for help, but you do not listen? Or cry out to you, 'Violence!' but you do not save?" (Habakkuk 1:2).

Isn't it interesting to note that Habakkuk felt the same way about society as Christians feel today? There seems to be no justice upon the wicked.

You might see a situation and wonder, *Where is God in the midst of this? Why do bad things happen to good people? How are the evildoers getting away with cheating, violence, oppression, and perversion?* Habakkuk saw the evil around him, and he cried out to God for answers. He didn't doubt God's omnipotence; rather, he didn't understand why God would allow sin to run rampant in the world. God answered the prophet, telling him exactly what He planned to do.

Today injustice, evil, and sin continue to appear to prosper, but not because God is indifferent. God has a plan. He wants us to partner with Him in this plan by praying. Whenever you feel sad over what you see happening in the world today, pour out your concerns to God in prayer. Pray that you and your fellow believers might be a light in a darkened world, bringing the hope and peace of Jesus to those with whom you interact every day. God will answer those prayers.

Habakkuk knew that he would need to persevere no matter what. We must do the same. "Though the fig tree does not bud and there are no grapes on the vines, though the olive crop fails and the fields produce no food, though there are no sheep in the pen and no cattle in the stalls, yet I will rejoice in the LORD, I will be joyful in God my Savior" (3:17-18). We must learn to say, "No matter how bad it gets, Lord, I will be joyful and not stop praying until Your will is done on earth."

---

and gather prisoners like sand.
¹⁰They deride kings
and scoff at rulers.
They laugh at all fortified cities;
they build earthen ramps and
capture them.
¹¹Then they sweep past like the wind
and go on—
guilty men, whose own strength is
their god."

Habakkuk's Second Complaint

¹²O LORD, are you not from
everlasting?
My God, my Holy One, we will
not die.
O LORD, you have appointed them to
execute judgment;
O Rock, you have ordained them
to punish.
¹³Your eyes are too pure to look on evil;

you cannot tolerate wrong.
Why then do you tolerate the
treacherous?
Why are you silent while the
wicked
swallow up those more righteous
than themselves?
¹⁴You have made men like fish in the
sea,
like sea creatures that have no ruler.
¹⁵The wicked foe pulls all of them up
with hooks,
he catches them in his net,
he gathers them up in his dragnet;
and so he rejoices and is glad.
¹⁶Therefore he sacrifices to his net
and burns incense to his dragnet,
for by his net he lives in luxury
and enjoys the choicest food.
¹⁷Is he to keep on emptying his net,
destroying nations without mercy?

2 I will stand at my watch
  and station myself on the ramparts;
I will look to see what he will say to
    me,
  and what answer I am to give to
    this complaint.[a]

The Lord's Answer

[2] Then the Lord replied:

"Write down the revelation
  and make it plain on tablets
  so that a herald[b] may run with it.
[3] For the revelation awaits an appointed
    time;
  it speaks of the end
    and will not prove false.
Though it linger, wait for it;
  it[c] will certainly come and will not
    delay.

[4] "See, he is puffed up;
  his desires are not upright—
  but the righteous will live by his
    faith[d]—
[5] indeed, wine betrays him;
  he is arrogant and never at rest.
Because he is as greedy as the grave[e]
  and like death is never satisfied,
he gathers to himself all the nations
  and takes captive all the peoples.

[6] "Will not all of them taunt him with
ridicule and scorn, saying,

"'Woe to him who piles up stolen
    goods
  and makes himself wealthy by
    extortion!
  How long must this go on?'
[7] Will not your debtors[f] suddenly arise?
  Will they not wake up and make
    you tremble?
  Then you will become their victim.
[8] Because you have plundered many
    nations,
  the peoples who are left will
    plunder you.
For you have shed man's blood;

you have destroyed lands and cities
  and everyone in them.

[9] "Woe to him who builds his realm by
    unjust gain
  to set his nest on high,
  to escape the clutches of ruin!
[10] You have plotted the ruin of many
    peoples,
  shaming your own house and
    forfeiting your life.
[11] The stones of the wall will cry out,
  and the beams of the woodwork
    will echo it.

[12] "Woe to him who builds a city with
    bloodshed
  and establishes a town by crime!
[13] Has not the Lord Almighty
    determined
  that the people's labor is only fuel
    for the fire,
  that the nations exhaust themselves
    for nothing?
[14] For the earth will be filled with the
    knowledge of the glory of the
    Lord,
  as the waters cover the sea.

[15] "Woe to him who gives drink to his
    neighbors,
  pouring it from the wineskin till
    they are drunk,
  so that he can gaze on their naked
    bodies.
[16] You will be filled with shame instead
    of glory.
  Now it is your turn! Drink and be
    exposed[g]!
The cup from the Lord's right hand
    is coming around to you,
  and disgrace will cover your glory.
[17] The violence you have done to
    Lebanon will overwhelm
    you,
  and your destruction of animals
    will terrify you.
For you have shed man's blood;

---

[a] 1 Or and what to answer when I am rebuked   [b] 2 Or so that whoever reads it   [c] 3 Or Though he linger, wait for him; / he
[d] 4 Or faithfulness   [e] 5 Hebrew Sheol   [f] 7 Or creditors   [g] 16 Masoretic Text; Dead Sea Scrolls, Aquila, Vulgate and Syriac (see
also Septuagint) and stagger

you have destroyed lands and cities
    and everyone in them.

18 "Of what value is an idol, since a man
        has carved it?
    Or an image that teaches lies?
For he who makes it trusts in his own
        creation;
    he makes idols that cannot speak.
19 Woe to him who says to wood,
        'Come to life!'
    Or to lifeless stone, 'Wake up!'
Can it give guidance?
    It is covered with gold and silver;
    there is no breath in it.
20 But the LORD is in his holy temple;
    let all the earth be silent before
        him."

Praying Habakkuk 2:18-20

*Lord, show me anything in my life
that has become an idol to me, and
reveal whatever has captured my heart
more than You, and I will bow before
You in repentance and reverence.*

Habakkuk's Prayer

3 A prayer of Habakkuk the prophet.
    On *shigionoth.*[a]

2 LORD, I have heard of your fame;
    I stand in awe of your deeds,
        O LORD.

Renew them in our day,
    in our time make them known;
    in wrath remember mercy.

3 God came from Teman,
    the Holy One from Mount Paran.
                                Selah[b]
His glory covered the heavens
    and his praise filled the earth.
4 His splendor was like the sunrise;
    rays flashed from his hand,
    where his power was hidden.
5 Plague went before him;
    pestilence followed his steps.
6 He stood, and shook the earth;
    he looked, and made the nations
        tremble.
The ancient mountains crumbled
    and the age-old hills collapsed.
    His ways are eternal.
7 I saw the tents of Cushan in distress,
    the dwellings of Midian in anguish.

8 Were you angry with the rivers,
        O LORD?
    Was your wrath against the
        streams?
Did you rage against the sea
    when you rode with your horses
    and your victorious chariots?
9 You uncovered your bow,
    you called for many arrows.   *Selah*
You split the earth with rivers;

---

a 1 Probably a literary or musical term   b 3 A word of uncertain meaning; possibly a musical term; also in verses 9 and 13

God's people at prayer
HABAKKUK STANDS IN AWE

HABAKKUK 3:1-19 When evil people finally come face-to-face with God, they will tremble in fright as God reveals their punishment. But when we as Christians meet God, our fear will be of a different kind. We will tremble, just as Habakkuk (3:16), but out of reverence, awe, and respect.

When we come before God in prayer, we need to approach Him with the respect He deserves. We must seek His presence above all and not just give Him our list of what we want Him to do. Although He cares about the things that concern us, He cares even more about our relationship with Him. So quiet your heart as Habakkuk did in this passage, and draw close to God in praise and worship. Then, as you make your requests known, don't forget to intercede for others.

¹⁰   the mountains saw you and
        writhed.
    Torrents of water swept by;
        the deep roared
        and lifted its waves on high.

¹¹Sun and moon stood still in the
        heavens
        at the glint of your flying arrows,
        at the lightning of your flashing
        spear.
¹²In wrath you strode through the
        earth
        and in anger you threshed the
        nations.
¹³You came out to deliver your people,
        to save your anointed one.
    You crushed the leader of the land of
        wickedness,
        you stripped him from head to foot.
                                    Selah
¹⁴With his own spear you pierced his
        head
        when his warriors stormed out to
        scatter us,
    gloating as though about to devour
        the wretched who were in hiding.

¹⁵You trampled the sea with your
        horses,
        churning the great waters.

¹⁶I heard and my heart pounded,
        my lips quivered at the sound;
    decay crept into my bones,
        and my legs trembled.
    Yet I will wait patiently for the day of
        calamity
        to come on the nation invading us.
¹⁷Though the fig tree does not bud
        and there are no grapes on the
        vines,
    though the olive crop fails
        and the fields produce no food,
    though there are no sheep in the pen
        and no cattle in the stalls,
¹⁸yet I will rejoice in the LORD,
        I will be joyful in God my Savior.

¹⁹The Sovereign LORD is my strength;
        he makes my feet like the feet of a
        deer,
        he enables me to go on the heights.

For the director of music. On my
    stringed instruments.

Author: Zephaniah

Date: Between 640 and 630 BC

Audience: A message to the backslidden nation of Judah of imminent judgment, but also of future mercy

The better you know God, the greater your worship and the more powerful your prayers will be.

How eager would you be to approach the Lord in prayer if deep down you thought Him to be a moody deity always on the verge of wrath? Would any of us be motivated to spend a lot of time seeking God's help if we thought He was powerless or disinterested?

The Bible is full of revealing passages about God that challenge our misconceptions and give us a more complete picture of God's nature. And few are as intriguing as this one from the prophecy of Zephaniah: "The LORD your God is with you, he is mighty to save. He will take great delight in you, he will quiet you with his love, he will rejoice over you with singing" (3:17).

Who wouldn't want to serve a God like that? Who wouldn't be inspired to know and talk to this God of love, tenderness, and compassion? Although Zephaniah is a book that is full of grim words of judgment, that is only one aspect of God's character, and it is in response to sin. He is, and always will be, a God of love and restoration.

Prayer Themes:

- As you sit quietly before your sovereign Lord, ask Him to give you a clear view of His greatness (1:7).

- Ask God to give you a thirst for more of Him and a hunger for His righteousness (2:3).

- Thank the Lord that He is a God of justice and will restore what has been lost to us (3:19-20).

Zephaniah

1 The word of the LORD that came to Zephaniah son of Cushi, the son of Gedaliah, the son of Amariah, the son of Hezekiah, during the reign of Josiah son of Amon king of Judah:

Warning of Coming Destruction

2 "I will sweep away everything
   from the face of the earth,"
                declares the LORD.
3 "I will sweep away both men and
      animals;
   I will sweep away the birds of the
      air
   and the fish of the sea.
   The wicked will have only heaps of
      rubble[a]
   when I cut off man from the face of
      the earth,"
                declares the LORD.

Against Judah

4 "I will stretch out my hand against
      Judah
   and against all who live in
      Jerusalem.
   I will cut off from this place every
      remnant of Baal,
   the names of the pagan and the
      idolatrous priests—
5 those who bow down on the roofs
   to worship the starry host,
   those who bow down and swear by
      the LORD
   and who also swear by Molech,[b]
6 those who turn back from following
      the LORD
   and neither seek the LORD nor
      inquire of him.
7 Be silent before the Sovereign LORD,
   for the day of the LORD is near.

---

[a] 3 The meaning of the Hebrew for this line is uncertain.   [b] 5 Hebrew *Malcam*, that is, Milcom

The Lord has prepared a sacrifice;
  he has consecrated those he has
    invited.
[8] On the day of the Lord's sacrifice
  I will punish the princes
  and the king's sons
and all those clad
  in foreign clothes.
[9] On that day I will punish
  all who avoid stepping on the
    threshold,[a]
who fill the temple of their gods
  with violence and deceit.

[10] "On that day," declares the Lord,
  "a cry will go up from the Fish
    Gate,
  wailing from the New Quarter,
  and a loud crash from the hills.
[11] Wail, you who live in the market
    district[b];
  all your merchants will be wiped
    out,
  all who trade with[c] silver will be
    ruined.
[12] At that time I will search Jerusalem
    with lamps
  and punish those who are
    complacent,
  who are like wine left on its dregs,
who think, 'The Lord will do
    nothing,
  either good or bad.'
[13] Their wealth will be plundered,
  their houses demolished.
They will build houses
  but not live in them;
they will plant vineyards
  but not drink the wine.

The Great Day of the Lord

[14] "The great day of the Lord is near—
  near and coming quickly.
Listen! The cry on the day of the
    Lord will be bitter,
  the shouting of the warrior there.
[15] That day will be a day of wrath,
  a day of distress and anguish,
a day of trouble and ruin,

a day of darkness and gloom,
  a day of clouds and blackness,
[16] a day of trumpet and battle cry
  against the fortified cities
  and against the corner towers.
[17] I will bring distress on the people
  and they will walk like blind men,
  because they have sinned against
    the Lord.
Their blood will be poured out like
    dust
  and their entrails like filth.
[18] Neither their silver nor their gold
  will be able to save them
  on the day of the Lord's wrath.
In the fire of his jealousy
  the whole world will be consumed,
for he will make a sudden end
  of all who live in the earth."

[2] Gather together, gather together,
  O shameful nation,
[2] before the appointed time arrives
  and that day sweeps on like chaff,
before the fierce anger of the Lord
  comes upon you,
  before the day of the Lord's wrath
    comes upon you.
[3] Seek the Lord, all you humble of the
    land,
  you who do what he commands.
Seek righteousness, seek humility;
  perhaps you will be sheltered
  on the day of the Lord's anger.

Praying Zephaniah 2:3
*Heavenly Father, I humble
myself before You and seek Your face
and Your righteousness this day, and
I ask that I will always have the
courage to do what's right.*

Against Philistia

[4] Gaza will be abandoned
  and Ashkelon left in ruins.
At midday Ashdod will be emptied
  and Ekron uprooted.
[5] Woe to you who live by the sea,

---

[a] 9 See 1 Samuel 5:5. [b] 11 Or the Mortar [c] 11 Or in

O Kerethite people;
the word of the LORD is against you,
O Canaan, land of the Philistines.

"I will destroy you,
and none will be left."

6 The land by the sea, where the
Kerethites[a] dwell,
will be a place for shepherds and
sheep pens.
7 It will belong to the remnant of the
house of Judah;
there they will find pasture.
In the evening they will lie down
in the houses of Ashkelon.
The LORD their God will care for
them;
he will restore their fortunes.[b]

Against Moab and Ammon

8 "I have heard the insults of Moab
and the taunts of the Ammonites,
who insulted my people
and made threats against their
land.
9 Therefore, as surely as I live,"
declares the LORD Almighty, the
God of Israel,
"surely Moab will become like
Sodom,
the Ammonites like Gomorrah—
a place of weeds and salt pits,
a wasteland forever.
The remnant of my people will
plunder them;
the survivors of my nation will
inherit their land."

10 This is what they will get in return
for their pride,
for insulting and mocking the
people of the LORD Almighty.
11 The LORD will be awesome to them
when he destroys all the gods of the
land.
The nations on every shore will
worship him,
every one in its own land.

Against Cush

12 "You too, O Cushites,[c]
will be slain by my sword."

Against Assyria

13 He will stretch out his hand against
the north
and destroy Assyria,
leaving Nineveh utterly desolate
and dry as the desert.
14 Flocks and herds will lie down there,
creatures of every kind.
The desert owl and the screech owl
will roost on her columns.
Their calls will echo through the
windows,
rubble will be in the doorways,
the beams of cedar will be exposed.
15 This is the carefree city
that lived in safety.
She said to herself,
"I am, and there is none besides me."
What a ruin she has become,
a lair for wild beasts!
All who pass by her scoff
and shake their fists.

The Future of Jerusalem

3 Woe to the city of oppressors,
rebellious and defiled!
2 She obeys no one,
she accepts no correction.
She does not trust in the LORD,
she does not draw near to her God.
3 Her officials are roaring lions,
her rulers are evening wolves,
who leave nothing for the morning.
4 Her prophets are arrogant;
they are treacherous men.
Her priests profane the sanctuary
and do violence to the law.
5 The LORD within her is righteous;
he does no wrong.
Morning by morning he dispenses his
justice,
and every new day he does not fail,
yet the unrighteous know no
shame.

---

a 6 The meaning of the Hebrew for this word is uncertain.   b 7 Or *will bring back their captives*   c 12 That is, people from the upper Nile region

6 "I have cut off nations;
　　their strongholds are demolished.
I have left their streets deserted,
　　with no one passing through.
Their cities are destroyed;
　　no one will be left—no one at all.
7 I said to the city,
　　'Surely you will fear me
　　and accept correction!'
Then her dwelling would not be cut
　　off,
　　nor all my punishments come upon
　　　her.
But they were still eager
　　to act corruptly in all they did.
8 Therefore wait for me," declares the
　　LORD,
　　"for the day I will stand up to
　　　testify.[a]

I have decided to assemble the
　　nations,
　　to gather the kingdoms
and to pour out my wrath on them—
　　all my fierce anger.
The whole world will be consumed
　　by the fire of my jealous anger.

9 "Then will I purify the lips of the
　　peoples,
　　that all of them may call on the
　　　name of the LORD
　　and serve him shoulder to shoulder.
10 From beyond the rivers of Cush[b]
　　my worshipers, my scattered people,
　　will bring me offerings.
11 On that day you will not be put to
　　shame
　　for all the wrongs you have done
　　　to me,

---

[a] 8 Septuagint and Syriac; Hebrew *will rise up to plunder*　　[b] 10 That is, the upper Nile region

GOING *deeper*

Thank God for His Love

READ AND CONSIDER: ZEPHANIAH 3:8-20

"The LORD your God is with you, he is mighty to save. He will take great delight in you, he will quiet you with his love, he will rejoice over you with singing" (Zephaniah 3:17).

The Lord is with you. What joy there is in knowing that God is with you! You always have a line of open communication with Him because He is omnipresent. Whether your prayers are long or short, the Lord hears them all. Thank Him that He is a God who is close to you.

The Lord is mighty to save. Rejoice that you have been snatched from the jaws of hell because of God's great love. He has provided salvation through His Son, Jesus Christ, and He accepts your repentance for sin no matter how many times you come to Him with a repentant heart. Thank Him for His salvation and continuing forgiveness.

The Lord takes great delight in you . . . He will rejoice over you with singing. Just as you rejoice in the victories of others, God will rejoice over you with gladness. Like the Father that He is, He is proud of His children. He is glad when you follow His will and live a life that will cause others to want to know Him. Thank Him for His joyful delight in you.

The Lord will quiet you with His love. In times of turmoil, if you turn to the Lord, He will quiet you with His love. There is peace in knowing that whatever circumstances come your way, God will be there to guide you through. In good times and bad, His love will comfort your pain and soothe your weariness. Thank Him for His peace in you.

Rejoice daily in this profound relationship you have with the Almighty God. Thank Him again and again for His presence and love in your life, even when you know you don't deserve it.

because I will remove from this city
those who rejoice in their pride.
Never again will you be haughty
on my holy hill.
12But I will leave within you
the meek and humble,
who trust in the name of the LORD.
13The remnant of Israel will do no
wrong;
they will speak no lies,
nor will deceit be found in their
mouths.
They will eat and lie down
and no one will make them afraid."

14Sing, O Daughter of Zion;
shout aloud, O Israel!
Be glad and rejoice with all your
heart,
O Daughter of Jerusalem!
15The LORD has taken away your
punishment,
he has turned back your enemy.
The LORD, the King of Israel, is with
you;
never again will you fear any harm.
16On that day they will say to
Jerusalem,

"Do not fear, O Zion;
do not let your hands hang limp.
17The LORD your God is with you,
he is mighty to save.
He will take great delight in you,
he will quiet you with his love,
he will rejoice over you with
singing."

18"The sorrows for the appointed feasts
I will remove from you;
they are a burden and a reproach to
you.ª
19At that time I will deal
with all who oppressed you;
I will rescue the lame
and gather those who have been
scattered.
I will give them praise and honor
in every land where they were put
to shame.
20At that time I will gather you;
at that time I will bring you home.
I will give you honor and praise
among all the peoples of the earth
when I restore your fortunesᵇ
before your very eyes,"
says the LORD.

ª18 Or "I will gather you who mourn for the appointed feasts; / your reproach is a burden to you   ᵇ20 Or I bring back your
captives

Author: Haggai

Date: About 520 BC

Audience: The Jews who had returned from Babylonian exile and were beginning the work of rebuilding the temple. Haggai challenged them to finish the task

Prayer Themes:

- Ask God to help you keep a watchful eye on your priorities—that you might always put Him and His work first (1:4-9).

- Ask the Lord to enable you to be His messenger so that you can always speak words of life and hope to those around you (1:13-14).

- Tell God that you give all your possessions to Him knowing that everything you have comes from His hand (2:8).

As you read this brief prophetic book of Haggai, you will notice how many times you see the phrases "declares the LORD" (12 times), "this is what the LORD Almighty says" (five times), "the word of the LORD came" (five times).

God obviously had much to say to His people, and Haggai (like all the rest of the prophets) went to great pains to quote the Lord's messages accurately.

What we need to remember all these centuries later is that God is *still* speaking to His people, and we must continually be listening for His voice. A huge part of prayer is listening *for* His divine voice and then paying close attention to what He is instructing us to do. That's how we will know for certain what work He is calling us to and how it will be accomplished.

Haggai

A Call to Build the House of the LORD

1 In the second year of King Darius, on the first day of the sixth month, the word of the LORD came through the prophet Haggai to Zerubbabel son of Shealtiel, governor of Judah, and to Joshua[a] son of Jehozadak, the high priest:

2 This is what the LORD Almighty says: "These people say, 'The time has not yet come for the LORD's house to be built.'"

3 Then the word of the LORD came through the prophet Haggai: 4 "Is it a time for you yourselves to be living in your paneled houses, while this house remains a ruin?"

5 Now this is what the LORD Almighty says: "Give careful thought to your ways. 6 You have planted much, but have harvested little. You eat, but never have enough. You drink, but never have your fill. You put on clothes, but are not warm. You earn wages, only to put them in a purse with holes in it."

7 This is what the LORD Almighty says: "Give careful thought to your ways. 8 Go up into the mountains and bring down timber and build the house, so that I may take pleasure in it and be honored," says the LORD. 9 "You expected much, but see, it turned out to be little. What you brought home, I blew away. Why?" declares the LORD Almighty. "Because of my house, which remains a ruin, while each of you is busy with his own house. 10 Therefore, because of you the heavens have withheld their dew and the earth its crops. 11 I called for a drought on the fields and the mountains, on the grain, the new wine, the oil and whatever the ground produces, on men and cattle, and on the labor of your hands."

---

a *1* A variant of *Jeshua;* here and elsewhere in Haggai

Don't Neglect Your Walk With God

GOING *deeper*

READ AND CONSIDER: HAGGAI 1:1-11

"'You expected much, but see, it turned out to be little. What you brought home, I blew away. Why?' declares the LORD Almighty. 'Because of my house, which remains a ruin, while each of you is busy with his own house'" (Haggai 1:9).

In Haggai's time, the people had been returned to their land after exile in Babylon. But instead of getting down to work rebuilding their spiritual lives by rebuilding God's temple, they were more concerned with the condition of their own homes, more concerned with how they looked to others than with the time they spent in communion with God.

It is a warning to us to not be concerned with outward appearances and selfish pursuits, but rather to be concerned with the condition of our hearts and the things that touch the heart of God.

Haggai had stern words for his people. He admonished them to get their priorities straight! We too have to always place God first in our lives and remember that any work we attempt for Him without His blessing and guidance will be unproductive. Our material possessions will not satisfy us like He will.

Don't allow anything to keep you from your daily prayer time. Do whatever it takes to be with God. Ask Him to help you not neglect your relationship with Him. What you do in the Spirit— your praise, worship, and prayer—lasts for eternity.

12 Then Zerubbabel son of Shealtiel, Joshua son of Jehozadak, the high priest, and the whole remnant of the people obeyed the voice of the LORD their God and the message of the prophet Haggai, because the LORD their God had sent him. And the people feared the LORD.

13 Then Haggai, the LORD's messenger, gave this message of the LORD to the people: "I am with you," declares the LORD. 14 So the LORD stirred up the spirit of Zerubbabel son of Shealtiel, governor of Judah, and the spirit of Joshua son of Jehozadak, the high priest, and the spirit of the whole remnant of the people. They came and began to work on the house of the LORD Almighty, their God, 15 on the twenty-fourth day of the sixth month in the second year of King Darius.

The Promised Glory of the New House

2 On the twenty-first day of the seventh month, the word of the LORD came through the prophet Haggai:

2 "Speak to Zerubbabel son of Shealtiel, governor of Judah, to Joshua son of Jehozadak, the high priest, and to the remnant of the people. Ask them, 3 'Who of you is left who saw this house in its former glory? How does it look to you now? Does it not seem to you like nothing? 4 But now be strong, O Zerubbabel,' declares the LORD. 'Be strong, O Joshua son of Jehozadak, the high priest. Be strong, all you people of the land,' declares the LORD, 'and work. For I am with you,' declares the LORD Almighty. 5 'This is what I covenanted with you when you came out of Egypt. And my Spirit remains among you. Do not fear.'

6 "This is what the LORD Almighty says: 'In a little while I will once more shake the heavens and the earth, the sea and the dry land. 7 I will shake all nations, and the desired of all nations will come, and I will fill this house with glory,' says the LORD Almighty. 8 'The silver is mine and the gold is mine,' declares the LORD Almighty.

9'The glory of this present house will be greater than the glory of the former house,' says the LORD Almighty. 'And in this place I will grant peace,' declares the LORD Almighty."

Blessings for a Defiled People

10On the twenty-fourth day of the ninth month, in the second year of Darius, the word of the LORD came to the prophet Haggai: 11"This is what the LORD Almighty says: 'Ask the priests what the law says: 12If a person carries consecrated meat in the fold of his garment, and that fold touches some bread or stew, some wine, oil or other food, does it become consecrated?'"

The priests answered, "No."

13Then Haggai said, "If a person defiled by contact with a dead body touches one of these things, does it become defiled?"

"Yes," the priests replied, "it becomes defiled."

14Then Haggai said, "'So it is with this people and this nation in my sight,' declares the LORD. 'Whatever they do and whatever they offer there is defiled.

15"'Now give careful thought to this from this day on[a]—consider how things were before one stone was laid on another in the LORD's temple. 16When anyone came to a heap of twenty measures, there were only ten. When anyone went to a wine vat to draw fifty measures, there were only twenty. 17I struck all the work of your hands with blight, mildew and hail, yet you did not turn to me,' declares the LORD. 18'From this day on, from this twenty-fourth day of the ninth month, give careful thought to the day when the foundation of the LORD's temple was laid. Give careful thought: 19Is there yet any seed left in the barn? Until now, the vine and the fig tree, the pomegranate and the olive tree have not borne fruit.

"'From this day on I will bless you.'"

Zerubbabel the LORD's Signet Ring

20The word of the LORD came to Haggai a second time on the twenty-fourth day of the month: 21"Tell Zerubbabel governor of Judah that I will shake the heavens and the earth. 22I will overturn royal thrones and shatter the power of the foreign kingdoms. I will overthrow chariots and their drivers; horses and their riders will fall, each by the sword of his brother.

23"'On that day,' declares the LORD Almighty, 'I will take you, my servant Zerubbabel son of Shealtiel,' declares the LORD, 'and I will make you like my signet ring, for I have chosen you,' declares the LORD Almighty."

---

a 15 Or to the days past

Author: Zechariah

Date: Between 520 and 480 BC

Audience: The people of Judah—to encourage them to complete the job of rebuilding the temple

Two of the biggest obstacles to a rich prayer life are discouragement and distraction.

Discouragement means to be completely without courage. It is that beaten, dejected sense that all is lost. A disintegrating marriage, a dead-end job, a rebellious child, a chronic illness, or a large debt—such long-term problems tempt us to wonder, *What's the use?* But the truth is, we can find our encouragement in the Lord.

Distraction is another danger. Far too often we find ourselves starting to pray, only to be sidetracked by something clamoring for our attention. But the more we are attracted to the Lord, the less we will be distracted by other things.

If discouragement and distraction are all too common in your life, you'll find help and hope in Zechariah's encouraging exhortation. His message to the ancient Jews is this: Get busy and stay focused... your Messiah is coming!

And the reason we believers shouldn't lose heart or lose sight of the goal is because... our Messiah is coming *back!*

Prayer Themes:

- Praise God for His complete forgiveness, for taking away all your sin and giving you His righteousness (3:1-4).

- Ask God to help you complete whatever He gives you to do and to do it with right motives (7:4-6).

- Thank God for His constant blessings, abundance, and care in your life (10:1).

Zechariah

A Call to Return to the LORD

1 In the eighth month of the second year of Darius, the word of the LORD came to the prophet Zechariah son of Berekiah, the son of Iddo:

2 "The LORD was very angry with your forefathers. 3 Therefore tell the people: This is what the LORD Almighty says: 'Return to me,' declares the LORD Almighty, 'and I will return to you,' says the LORD Almighty. 4 Do not be like your forefathers, to whom the earlier prophets proclaimed: This is what the LORD Almighty says: 'Turn from your evil ways and your evil practices.' But they would not listen or pay attention to me, declares the LORD. 5 Where are your forefathers now? And the prophets, do they live forever? 6 But did not my words and my decrees, which I commanded my servants the prophets, overtake your forefathers?

"Then they repented and said, 'The LORD Almighty has done to us what our ways and practices deserve, just as he determined to do.'"

The Man Among the Myrtle Trees

7 On the twenty-fourth day of the eleventh month, the month of Shebat, in the second year of Darius, the word of the LORD came to the prophet Zechariah son of Berekiah, the son of Iddo.

8 During the night I had a vision—and there before me was a man riding a red horse! He was standing among the myrtle trees in a ravine. Behind him were red, brown and white horses.

9 I asked, "What are these, my lord?"

The angel who was talking with me answered, "I will show you what they are."

[10]Then the man standing among the myrtle trees explained, "They are the ones the LORD has sent to go throughout the earth."

[11]And they reported to the angel of the LORD, who was standing among the myrtle trees, "We have gone throughout the earth and found the whole world at rest and in peace."

[12]Then the angel of the LORD said, "LORD Almighty, how long will you withhold mercy from Jerusalem and from the towns of Judah, which you have been angry with these seventy years?" [13]So the LORD spoke kind and comforting words to the angel who talked with me.

[14]Then the angel who was speaking to me said, "Proclaim this word: This is what the LORD Almighty says: 'I am very jealous for Jerusalem and Zion, [15]but I am very angry with the nations that feel secure. I was only a little angry, but they added to the calamity.'

[16]"Therefore, this is what the LORD says: 'I will return to Jerusalem with mercy, and there my house will be rebuilt. And the measuring line will be stretched out over Jerusalem,' declares the LORD Almighty.

[17]"Proclaim further: This is what the LORD Almighty says: 'My towns will again overflow with prosperity, and the LORD will again comfort Zion and choose Jerusalem.' "

Four Horns and Four Craftsmen

[18]Then I looked up—and there before me were four horns! [19]I asked the angel who was speaking to me, "What are these?"

He answered me, "These are the horns that scattered Judah, Israel and Jerusalem."

[20]Then the LORD showed me four craftsmen. [21]I asked, "What are these coming to do?"

He answered, "These are the horns that scattered Judah so that no one could raise his head, but the craftsmen have come to terrify them and throw down these horns of the nations who lifted up their horns against the land of Judah to scatter its people."

A Man With a Measuring Line

2 Then I looked up—and there before me was a man with a measuring line in his hand! [2]I asked, "Where are you going?"

He answered me, "To measure Jerusalem, to find out how wide and how long it is."

[3]Then the angel who was speaking to me left, and another angel came to meet him [4]and said to him: "Run, tell that young man, 'Jerusalem will be a city without walls because of the great number of men and livestock in it. [5]And I myself will be a wall of fire around it,' declares the LORD, 'and I will be its glory within.'

[6]"Come! Come! Flee from the land of the north," declares the LORD, "for I have scattered you to the four winds of heaven," declares the LORD.

[7]"Come, O Zion! Escape, you who live in the Daughter of Babylon!" [8]For this is what the LORD Almighty says: "After he has honored me and has sent me against the nations that have plundered you—for whoever touches you touches the apple of his eye— [9]I will surely raise my hand against them so that their slaves will plunder them.[a] Then you will know that the LORD Almighty has sent me.

[10]"Shout and be glad, O Daughter of Zion. For I am coming, and I will live among you," declares the LORD. [11]"Many nations will be joined with the LORD in that day and will become my people. I will live among you and you will know that the LORD Almighty has sent me to you. [12]The LORD will inherit Judah as his portion in the holy land and will again choose Jerusalem. [13]Be still before the LORD, all mankind, because he has roused himself from his holy dwelling."

---

[a] 8,9 Or says after... eye: [9]"I... plunder them."

Clean Garments for the High Priest

3 Then he showed me Joshua[a] the high priest standing before the angel of the LORD, and Satan[b] standing at his right side to accuse him. [2] The LORD said to Satan, "The LORD rebuke you, Satan! The LORD, who has chosen Jerusalem, rebuke you! Is not this man a burning stick snatched from the fire?"

[3] Now Joshua was dressed in filthy clothes as he stood before the angel. [4] The angel said to those who were standing before him, "Take off his filthy clothes."

Then he said to Joshua, "See, I have taken away your sin, and I will put rich garments on you."

[5] Then I said, "Put a clean turban on his head." So they put a clean turban on his head and clothed him, while the angel of the LORD stood by.

[6] The angel of the LORD gave this charge to Joshua: [7] "This is what the LORD Almighty says: 'If you will walk in my ways and keep my requirements, then you will govern my house and have charge of my courts, and I will give you a place among these standing here.

[8] "'Listen, O high priest Joshua and your associates seated before you, who are men symbolic of things to come: I am going to bring my servant, the Branch. [9] See, the stone I have set in front of Joshua! There are seven eyes[c] on that one stone, and I will engrave an inscription on it,' says the LORD Almighty, 'and I will remove the sin of this land in a single day.

[10] "'In that day each of you will invite his neighbor to sit under his vine and fig tree,' declares the LORD Almighty."

The Gold Lampstand and the Two Olive Trees

4 Then the angel who talked with me returned and wakened me, as a man is wakened from his sleep. [2] He asked me, "What do you see?"

---

[a] 1 A variant of *Jeshua*; here and elsewhere in Zechariah   [b] 1 *Satan* means *accuser.*   [c] 9 Or *facets*

GOING *deeper*

By His Spirit

READ AND CONSIDER: ZECHARIAH 4

"So he said to me, 'This is the word of the LORD to Zerubbabel: "Not by might nor by power, but by my Spirit," says the LORD Almighty' " (Zechariah 4:6).

Zerubbabel was given a huge responsibility: to rebuild the temple in Jerusalem. While the prophets encouraged him in this task, it was Zerubbabel's sole responsibility to see it through to completion. How inadequate he must have felt!

Every time you feel you are unable to do what God has called you to do, when you feel as though you don't have what it takes to move into the life God has for you, worship is the way to respond. First of all, be grateful that you feel the way you do because that means you are humble and dependent on God. Rejoice if you feel inadequate to the task because that means you are going to have to depend on God to enable you to do it. And He will, because "the one who calls you is faithful and he will do it" (1 Thessalonians 5:24).

You don't have to make your life happen; you just have to worship God and let *Him* make it happen. You don't have to strive to figure out your purpose; you have to strive to know God, for *He* knows your purpose. Your praise will illuminate the path by which God will guide you into your future and the purpose He has for you. You won't accomplish it; He will. Not by might or power, but by His Spirit.

I answered, "I see a solid gold lamp-stand with a bowl at the top and seven lights on it, with seven channels to the lights. ³Also there are two olive trees by it, one on the right of the bowl and the other on its left."

⁴I asked the angel who talked with me, "What are these, my lord?"

⁵He answered, "Do you not know what these are?"

"No, my lord," I replied.

⁶So he said to me, "This is the word of the LORD to Zerubbabel: 'Not by might nor by power, but by my Spirit,' says the LORD Almighty.

⁷"What[a] are you, O mighty mountain? Before Zerubbabel you will become level ground. Then he will bring out the capstone to shouts of 'God bless it! God bless it!'"

⁸Then the word of the LORD came to me: ⁹"The hands of Zerubbabel have laid the foundation of this temple; his hands will also complete it. Then you will know that the LORD Almighty has sent me to you.

¹⁰"Who despises the day of small things? Men will rejoice when they see the plumb line in the hand of Zerubbabel.

"(These seven are the eyes of the LORD, which range throughout the earth.)"

¹¹Then I asked the angel, "What are these two olive trees on the right and the left of the lampstand?"

¹²Again I asked him, "What are these two olive branches beside the two gold pipes that pour out golden oil?"

¹³He replied, "Do you not know what these are?"

"No, my lord," I said.

¹⁴So he said, "These are the two who are anointed to[b] serve the Lord of all the earth."

The Flying Scroll

5 I looked again—and there before me was a flying scroll!

²He asked me, "What do you see?"

I answered, "I see a flying scroll, thirty feet long and fifteen feet wide.[c]"

³And he said to me, "This is the curse that is going out over the whole land; for according to what it says on one side, every thief will be banished, and according to what it says on the other, everyone who swears falsely will be banished. ⁴The LORD Almighty declares, 'I will send it out, and it will enter the house of the thief and the house of him who swears falsely by my name. It will remain in his house and destroy it, both its timbers and its stones.'"

The Woman in a Basket

⁵Then the angel who was speaking to me came forward and said to me, "Look up and see what this is that is appearing."

⁶I asked, "What is it?"

He replied, "It is a measuring basket.[d]" And he added, "This is the iniquity[e] of the people throughout the land."

⁷Then the cover of lead was raised, and there in the basket sat a woman! ⁸He said, "This is wickedness," and he pushed her back into the basket and pushed the lead cover down over its mouth.

⁹Then I looked up—and there before me were two women, with the wind in their wings! They had wings like those of a stork, and they lifted up the basket between heaven and earth.

¹⁰"Where are they taking the basket?" I asked the angel who was speaking to me.

¹¹He replied, "To the country of Babylonia[f] to build a house for it. When it is ready, the basket will be set there in its place."

Four Chariots

6 I looked up again—and there before me were four chariots coming out from between two mountains—mountains of bronze! ²The first chariot had red horses, the second black, ³the third white, and the fourth dappled—all of them powerful. ⁴I asked the angel who

---

[a]7 Or Who [b]14 Or two who bring oil and [c]2 Hebrew twenty cubits long and ten cubits wide (about 9 meters long and 4.5 meters wide) [d]6 Hebrew an ephah; also in verses 7-11 [e]6 Or appearance [f]11 Hebrew Shinar

was speaking to me, "What are these, my lord?"

5 The angel answered me, "These are the four spirits[a] of heaven, going out from standing in the presence of the Lord of the whole world. 6 The one with the black horses is going toward the north country, the one with the white horses toward the west,[b] and the one with the dappled horses toward the south."

7 When the powerful horses went out, they were straining to go throughout the earth. And he said, "Go throughout the earth!" So they went throughout the earth.

8 Then he called to me, "Look, those going toward the north country have given my Spirit[c] rest in the land of the north."

A Crown for Joshua

9 The word of the LORD came to me: 10 "Take ⌊silver and gold⌋ from the exiles Heldai, Tobijah and Jedaiah, who have arrived from Babylon. Go the same day to the house of Josiah son of Zephaniah. 11 Take the silver and gold and make a crown, and set it on the head of the high priest, Joshua son of Jehozadak. 12 Tell him this is what the LORD Almighty says: 'Here is the man whose name is the Branch, and he will branch out from his place and build the temple of the LORD. 13 It is he who will build the temple of the LORD, and he will be clothed with majesty and will sit and rule on his throne. And he will be a priest on his throne. And there will be harmony between the two.' 14 The crown will be given to Heldai,[d] Tobijah, Jedaiah and Hen[e] son of Zephaniah as a memorial in the temple of the LORD. 15 Those who are far away will come and help to build the temple of the LORD, and you will know that the LORD Almighty has sent me to you. This will happen if you diligently obey the LORD your God."

Justice and Mercy, Not Fasting

7 In the fourth year of King Darius, the word of the LORD came to Zechariah on the fourth day of the ninth month,

the month of Kislev. 2 The people of Bethel had sent Sharezer and Regem-Melech, together with their men, to entreat the LORD 3 by asking the priests of the house of the LORD Almighty and the prophets, "Should I mourn and fast in the fifth month, as I have done for so many years?"

4 Then the word of the LORD Almighty came to me: 5 "Ask all the people of the land and the priests, 'When you fasted and mourned in the fifth and seventh months for the past seventy years, was it really for me that you fasted? 6 And when you were eating and drinking, were you not just feasting for yourselves? 7 Are these not the words the LORD proclaimed through the earlier prophets when Jerusalem and its surrounding towns were at rest and prosperous, and the Negev and the western foothills were settled?'"

8 And the word of the LORD came again to Zechariah: 9 "This is what the LORD Almighty says: 'Administer true justice; show mercy and compassion to one another. 10 Do not oppress the widow or the fatherless, the alien or the poor. In your hearts do not think evil of each other.'

11 "But they refused to pay attention; stubbornly they turned their backs and stopped up their ears. 12 They made their hearts as hard as flint and would not listen to the law or to the words that the LORD Almighty had sent by his Spirit through the earlier prophets. So the LORD Almighty was very angry.

13 "'When I called, they did not listen; so when they called, I would not listen,' says the LORD Almighty. 14 'I scattered them with a whirlwind among all the nations, where they were strangers. The land was left so desolate behind them that no one could come or go. This is how they made the pleasant land desolate.'"

The LORD Promises to Bless Jerusalem

8 Again the word of the LORD Almighty came to me. 2 This is what the LORD Almighty says: "I am very jealous

---

a 5 Or winds   b 6 Or horses after them   c 8 Or spirit   d 14 Syriac; Hebrew Helem   e 14 Or and the gracious one, the

Developing a Heart for Worship *GOING deeper*

READ AND CONSIDER: ZECHARIAH 7

"Ask all the people of the land and the priests, 'When you fasted and mourned in the fifth and seventh months for the past seventy years, was it really for me that you fasted?'" (Zechariah 7:5).

Zechariah had a message for his people—and it wasn't a pleasant one. He wanted them to understand that just worshiping, fasting, and keeping all the rituals of the faith was of no value. It meant nothing to God because it meant nothing to the people. They were not doing these acts out of love and devotion for God.

It's not enough that you should read about worship, hear worship songs, or listen to other people worship; you must actually worship God with a heart full of love for Him. It's in your own personal worship times that you will develop an intimate relationship with Him. If you are ever worshiping God by yourself and you don't sense His intimate presence, continue to praise and worship Him until you do. It's not that you have to try hard to get God to be close to you. He has chosen to dwell in your praise. But you do have to give Him time to break down the barriers in your soul and penetrate the walls of your heart so that He can pour Himself into you.

God must always be the complete focus of your worship. But when you worship Him, there will be gifts and blessings that He will pour out on you.

In worship you will sense why you were created. You will hear God speak to your heart because He has softened it and made it less resistant. In worship you will experience God's love. He will change your emotions, attitudes, and patterns of thought. He will pour out His Spirit upon you and make your heart open to receive all He has for you. He will give you clarity of mind so you can better understand His Word. He will refresh, renew, enrich, enlighten, heal, free, and fulfill you. He will breathe life into the dead areas of your existence. He will infuse you with His power and His joy. He will redeem and transform you and your situation. He will fill your empty places, liberate you from bondage, take away your fear and doubt, grow your faith, and give you peace. He will break the chains that imprison you and restore you to wholeness. He will lift you above your circumstances and limitations, and motivate you to help others find life in Him.

for Zion; I am burning with jealousy for her."

³This is what the LORD says: "I will return to Zion and dwell in Jerusalem. Then Jerusalem will be called the City of Truth, and the mountain of the LORD Almighty will be called the Holy Mountain."

⁴This is what the LORD Almighty says: "Once again men and women of ripe old age will sit in the streets of Jerusalem, each with cane in hand because of his age. ⁵The city streets will be filled with boys and girls playing there."

⁶This is what the LORD Almighty says: "It may seem marvelous to the remnant of this people at that time, but will it seem marvelous to me?" declares the LORD Almighty.

⁷This is what the LORD Almighty says: "I will save my people from the countries of the east and the west. ⁸I will bring them back to live in Jerusalem; they will be my people, and I will be faithful and righteous to them as their God."

⁹This is what the LORD Almighty says: "You who now hear these words spoken by the prophets who were there when

the foundation was laid for the house of the LORD Almighty, let your hands be strong so that the temple may be built. ¹⁰Before that time there were no wages for man or beast. No one could go about his business safely because of his enemy, for I had turned every man against his neighbor. ¹¹But now I will not deal with the remnant of this people as I did in the past," declares the LORD Almighty.

¹²"The seed will grow well, the vine will yield its fruit, the ground will produce its crops, and the heavens will drop their dew. I will give all these things as an inheritance to the remnant of this people. ¹³As you have been an object of cursing among the nations, O Judah and Israel, so will I save you, and you will be a blessing. Do not be afraid, but let your hands be strong."

¹⁴This is what the LORD Almighty says: "Just as I had determined to bring disaster upon you and showed no pity when your fathers angered me," says the LORD Almighty, ¹⁵"so now I have determined to do good again to Jerusalem and Judah. Do not be afraid. ¹⁶These are the things you are to do: Speak the truth to each other, and render true and sound judgment in your courts; ¹⁷do not plot evil against your neighbor, and do not love to swear falsely. I hate all this," declares the LORD.

¹⁸Again the word of the LORD Almighty came to me. ¹⁹This is what the LORD Almighty says: "The fasts of the fourth, fifth, seventh and tenth months will become joyful and glad occasions and happy festivals for Judah. Therefore love truth and peace."

²⁰This is what the LORD Almighty says: "Many peoples and the inhabitants of many cities will yet come, ²¹and the inhabitants of one city will go to another and say, 'Let us go at once to entreat the LORD and seek the LORD Almighty. I myself am going.' ²²And many peoples and powerful nations will come to Jerusalem to seek the LORD Almighty and to entreat him."

²³This is what the LORD Almighty says: "In those days ten men from all languages and nations will take firm hold of one Jew by the hem of his robe and say, 'Let us go with you, because we have heard that God is with you.'"

Judgment on Israel's Enemies
AN ORACLE

9 The word of the LORD is against
    the land of Hadrach
  and will rest upon Damascus—
for the eyes of men and all the tribes
    of Israel
  are on the LORD—ᵃ
²and upon Hamath too, which borders
    on it,
  and upon Tyre and Sidon, though
    they are very skillful.
³Tyre has built herself a stronghold;
  she has heaped up silver like dust,
  and gold like the dirt of the streets.
⁴But the Lord will take away her
    possessions
  and destroy her power on the sea,
  and she will be consumed by fire.
⁵Ashkelon will see it and fear;
  Gaza will writhe in agony,
  and Ekron too, for her hope will
    wither.
 Gaza will lose her king
  and Ashkelon will be deserted.
⁶Foreigners will occupy Ashdod,
  and I will cut off the pride of the
    Philistines.
⁷I will take the blood from their
    mouths,
  the forbidden food from between
    their teeth.
 Those who are left will belong to our
    God
  and become leaders in Judah,
  and Ekron will be like the
    Jebusites.
⁸But I will defend my house
  against marauding forces.

ᵃ 1 Or Damascus. / For the eye of the LORD is on all mankind, / as well as on the tribes of Israel,

Never again will an oppressor
    overrun my people,
  for now I am keeping watch.

The Coming of Zion's King
⁹Rejoice greatly, O Daughter of Zion!
  Shout, Daughter of Jerusalem!
See, your kingᵃ comes to you,
  righteous and having salvation,
  gentle and riding on a donkey,
  on a colt, the foal of a donkey.
¹⁰I will take away the chariots from
    Ephraim
  and the war-horses from Jerusalem,
  and the battle bow will be broken.
He will proclaim peace to the
    nations.
  His rule will extend from sea to sea
  and from the Riverᵇ to the ends of
    the earth.ᶜ
¹¹As for you, because of the blood of
    my covenant with you,
  I will free your prisoners from the
    waterless pit.

Praying Zechariah 9:12

*Lord, You are my stronghold, and
I thank You for restoring double to me
of all that has been lost in my life.*

¹²Return to your fortress, O prisoners
    of hope;
  even now I announce that I will
    restore twice as much to you.
¹³I will bend Judah as I bend my bow
  and fill it with Ephraim.
I will rouse your sons, O Zion,
  against your sons, O Greece,
  and make you like a warrior's
    sword.

The Lord Will Appear
¹⁴Then the Lord will appear over
    them;
  his arrow will flash like lightning.
The Sovereign Lord will sound the
    trumpet;
  he will march in the storms of the
    south,

¹⁵ and the Lord Almighty will shield
    them.
They will destroy
  and overcome with slingstones.
They will drink and roar as with
    wine;
  they will be full like a bowl
  used for sprinklingᵈ the corners of
    the altar.
¹⁶The Lord their God will save them
    on that day
  as the flock of his people.
They will sparkle in his land
  like jewels in a crown.
¹⁷How attractive and beautiful they
    will be!
Grain will make the young men
    thrive,
  and new wine the young women.

The Lord Will Care for Judah
10 Ask the Lord for rain in the
    springtime;
  it is the Lord who makes the storm
    clouds.
He gives showers of rain to men,
  and plants of the field to everyone.
²The idols speak deceit,
  diviners see visions that lie;
they tell dreams that are false,
  they give comfort in vain.
Therefore the people wander like
    sheep
  oppressed for lack of a shepherd.

³"My anger burns against the
    shepherds,
  and I will punish the leaders;
for the Lord Almighty will care
  for his flock, the house of Judah,
  and make them like a proud horse
    in battle.
⁴From Judah will come the
    cornerstone,
  from him the tent peg,
  from him the battle bow,
  from him every ruler.
⁵Together theyᵉ will be like mighty
    men

trampling the muddy streets in
battle.
Because the LORD is with them,
they will fight and overthrow the
horsemen.

6 "I will strengthen the house of Judah
and save the house of Joseph.
I will restore them
because I have compassion on
them.
They will be as though
I had not rejected them,
for I am the LORD their God
and I will answer them.
7 The Ephraimites will become like
mighty men,
and their hearts will be glad as with
wine.
Their children will see it and be
joyful;
their hearts will rejoice in the
LORD.
8 I will signal for them
and gather them in.
Surely I will redeem them;
they will be as numerous as
before.
9 Though I scatter them among the
peoples,
yet in distant lands they will
remember me.
They and their children will survive,
and they will return.
10 I will bring them back from Egypt
and gather them from Assyria.
I will bring them to Gilead and
Lebanon,
and there will not be room enough
for them.
11 They will pass through the sea of
trouble;
the surging sea will be subdued
and all the depths of the Nile will
dry up.
Assyria's pride will be brought down
and Egypt's scepter will pass away.
12 I will strengthen them in the LORD
and in his name they will walk,"
declares the LORD.

11 Open your doors, O Lebanon,
so that fire may devour your
cedars!
2 Wail, O pine tree, for the cedar has
fallen;
the stately trees are ruined!
Wail, oaks of Bashan;
the dense forest has been cut down!
3 Listen to the wail of the shepherds;
their rich pastures are destroyed!
Listen to the roar of the lions;
the lush thicket of the Jordan is
ruined!

Two Shepherds

4 This is what the LORD my God says:
"Pasture the flock marked for slaughter.
5 Their buyers slaughter them and go
unpunished. Those who sell them say,
'Praise the LORD, I am rich!' Their own
shepherds do not spare them. 6 For I will
no longer have pity on the people of the
land," declares the LORD. "I will hand
everyone over to his neighbor and his
king. They will oppress the land, and I
will not rescue them from their hands."

7 So I pastured the flock marked for
slaughter, particularly the oppressed of
the flock. Then I took two staffs and
called one Favor and the other Union,
and I pastured the flock. 8 In one month I
got rid of the three shepherds.

The flock detested me, and I grew
weary of them 9 and said, "I will not be
your shepherd. Let the dying die, and the
perishing perish. Let those who are left
eat one another's flesh."

10 Then I took my staff called Favor
and broke it, revoking the covenant I
had made with all the nations. 11 It was revoked on that day, and so the afflicted of
the flock who were watching me knew
it was the word of the LORD.

12 I told them, "If you think it best, give
me my pay; but if not, keep it." So they
paid me thirty pieces of silver.

13 And the LORD said to me, "Throw
it to the potter"—the handsome price
at which they priced me! So I took the
thirty pieces of silver and threw them

into the house of the LORD to the potter. 14Then I broke my second staff called Union, breaking the brotherhood between Judah and Israel.

15Then the LORD said to me, "Take again the equipment of a foolish shepherd. 16For I am going to raise up a shepherd over the land who will not care for the lost, or seek the young, or heal the injured, or feed the healthy, but will eat the meat of the choice sheep, tearing off their hoofs.

17"Woe to the worthless shepherd,
  who deserts the flock!
May the sword strike his arm and his
    right eye!
May his arm be completely withered,
  his right eye totally blinded!"

Jerusalem's Enemies to Be Destroyed
AN ORACLE

12 This is the word of the LORD concerning Israel. The LORD, who stretches out the heavens, who lays the foundation of the earth, and who forms the spirit of man within him, declares: 2"I am going to make Jerusalem a cup that sends all the surrounding peoples reeling. Judah will be besieged as well as Jerusalem. 3On that day, when all the nations of the earth are gathered against her, I will make Jerusalem an immovable rock for all the nations. All who try to move it will injure themselves. 4On that day I will strike every horse with panic and its rider with madness," declares the LORD. "I will keep a watchful eye over the house of Judah, but I will blind all the horses of the nations. 5Then the leaders of Judah will say in their hearts, 'The people of Jerusalem are strong, because the LORD Almighty is their God.'

6"On that day I will make the leaders of Judah like a firepot in a woodpile, like a flaming torch among sheaves. They will consume right and left all the surrounding peoples, but Jerusalem will remain intact in her place.

7"The LORD will save the dwellings of Judah first, so that the honor of the house of David and of Jerusalem's inhabitants may not be greater than that of Judah. 8On that day the LORD will shield those who live in Jerusalem, so that the feeblest among them will be like David, and the house of David will be like God, like the Angel of the LORD going before them. 9On that day I will set out to destroy all the nations that attack Jerusalem.

Mourning for the One They Pierced

10"And I will pour out on the house of David and the inhabitants of Jerusalem a spirit[a] of grace and supplication. They will look on[b] me, the one they have pierced, and they will mourn for him as one mourns for an only child, and grieve bitterly for him as one grieves for a firstborn son. 11On that day the weeping in Jerusalem will be great, like the weeping of Hadad Rimmon in the plain of Megiddo. 12The land will mourn, each clan by itself, with their wives by themselves: the clan of the house of David and their wives, the clan of the house of Nathan and their wives, 13the clan of the house of Levi and their wives, the clan of Shimei and their wives, 14and all the rest of the clans and their wives.

Cleansing From Sin

13 "On that day a fountain will be opened to the house of David and the inhabitants of Jerusalem, to cleanse them from sin and impurity.

2"On that day, I will banish the names of the idols from the land, and they will be remembered no more," declares the LORD Almighty. "I will remove both the prophets and the spirit of impurity from the land. 3And if anyone still prophesies, his father and mother, to whom he was born, will say to him, 'You must die, because you have told lies in the LORD's name.' When he prophesies, his own parents will stab him.

4"On that day every prophet will be

ashamed of his prophetic vision. He will not put on a prophet's garment of hair in order to deceive. [5]He will say, 'I am not a prophet. I am a farmer; the land has been my livelihood since my youth.[a]' [6]If someone asks him, 'What are these wounds on your body[b]?' he will answer, 'The wounds I was given at the house of my friends.'

The Shepherd Struck, the Sheep Scattered

[7]"Awake, O sword, against my
    shepherd,
  against the man who is close to
    me!"
  declares the LORD Almighty.
"Strike the shepherd,
  and the sheep will be scattered,
  and I will turn my hand against the
    little ones.
[8]In the whole land," declares the
  LORD,
  "two-thirds will be struck down
    and perish;
  yet one-third will be left in it.

Praying Zechariah 13:9

Heavenly Father, I thank You that because my hope is in You, You will continue to refine and purify me.

[9]This third I will bring into the fire;
  I will refine them like silver
  and test them like gold.
They will call on my name
  and I will answer them;
I will say, 'They are my people,'
  and they will say, 'The LORD is our
    God.'"

The LORD Comes and Reigns

14 A day of the LORD is coming when your plunder will be divided among you.

[2]I will gather all the nations to Jerusalem to fight against it; the city will be captured, the houses ransacked, and the women raped. Half of the city will go into exile, but the rest of the people will not be taken from the city.

[3]Then the LORD will go out and fight against those nations, as he fights in the day of battle. [4]On that day his feet will stand on the Mount of Olives, east of Jerusalem, and the Mount of Olives will be split in two from east to west, forming a great valley, with half of the mountain moving north and half moving south. [5]You will flee by my mountain valley, for it will extend to Azel. You will flee as you fled from the earthquake[c] in the days of Uzziah king of Judah. Then the LORD my God will come, and all the holy ones with him.

[6]On that day there will be no light, no cold or frost. [7]It will be a unique day, without daytime or nighttime—a day known to the LORD. When evening comes, there will be light.

[8]On that day living water will flow out from Jerusalem, half to the eastern sea[d] and half to the western sea,[e] in summer and in winter.

[9]The LORD will be king over the whole earth. On that day there will be one LORD, and his name the only name.

[10]The whole land, from Geba to Rimmon, south of Jerusalem, will become like the Arabah. But Jerusalem will be raised up and remain in its place, from the Benjamin Gate to the site of the First Gate, to the Corner Gate, and from the Tower of Hananel to the royal winepresses. [11]It will be inhabited; never again will it be destroyed. Jerusalem will be secure.

[12]This is the plague with which the LORD will strike all the nations that fought against Jerusalem: Their flesh will rot while they are still standing on their feet, their eyes will rot in their sockets, and their tongues will rot in their mouths. [13]On that day men will be stricken by the LORD with great panic. Each man will seize the hand of another, and they will

[a]5 Or farmer; a man sold me in my youth [b]6 Or wounds between your hands [c]5 Or [5]My mountain valley will be blocked and will extend to Azel. It will be blocked as it was blocked because of the earthquake [d]8 That is, the Dead Sea [e]8 That is, the Mediterranean

attack each other. [14]Judah too will fight at Jerusalem. The wealth of all the surrounding nations will be collected—great quantities of gold and silver and clothing. [15]A similar plague will strike the horses and mules, the camels and donkeys, and all the animals in those camps.

[16]Then the survivors from all the nations that have attacked Jerusalem will go up year after year to worship the King, the LORD Almighty, and to celebrate the Feast of Tabernacles. [17]If any of the peoples of the earth do not go up to Jerusalem to worship the King, the LORD Almighty, they will have no rain. [18]If the Egyptian people do not go up and take part, they will have no rain. The LORD[a]

will bring on them the plague he inflicts on the nations that do not go up to celebrate the Feast of Tabernacles. [19]This will be the punishment of Egypt and the punishment of all the nations that do not go up to celebrate the Feast of Tabernacles.

[20]On that day HOLY TO THE LORD will be inscribed on the bells of the horses, and the cooking pots in the LORD's house will be like the sacred bowls in front of the altar. [21]Every pot in Jerusalem and Judah will be holy to the LORD Almighty, and all who come to sacrifice will take some of the pots and cook in them. And on that day there will no longer be a Canaanite[b] in the house of the LORD Almighty.

---

[a] 18 Or part, then the LORD   [b] 21 Or merchant

Author: Malachi

Date: About 430 BC

Audience: The doubting, disconsolate people of the Lord

Malachi preached and prophesied to a jaded group of Israelites. They were doing all the required religious rituals, but it was empty routine. Their hearts weren't in it.

We all go through seasons when we are on fire for God, and then other times when we are not as eager and excited. Sometimes our worship can become more like a ritual than a vibrant, life-changing adoration of the God of the universe who loves us and saves us.

For that reason, we must frequently ask God to show us when our love cools, and pray that He will reignite it by the power of His Spirit. Ask Him to reveal any lifeless rituals in your life. Ask Him to show you any part of your walk with Him where your heart is not in it.

Prayer Themes:

- Ask the Lord to show you whenever you are giving Him anything but the best offerings of your time, talents, and treasure (1:6-9).

- Intercede for your married friends—not only that they not divorce, but that they would have marriages that honor God and amaze the watching world (2:16).

- Ask God to give you faith and the desire to become a generous giver (3:8-10).

Malachi

1 An oracle: The word of the LORD to Israel through Malachi.[a]

Jacob Loved, Esau Hated

2 "I have loved you," says the LORD.

"But you ask, 'How have you loved us?'

"Was not Esau Jacob's brother?" the LORD says. "Yet I have loved Jacob, 3but Esau I have hated, and I have turned his mountains into a wasteland and left his inheritance to the desert jackals."

4 Edom may say, "Though we have been crushed, we will rebuild the ruins."

But this is what the LORD Almighty says: "They may build, but I will demolish. They will be called the Wicked Land, a people always under the wrath of the LORD. 5You will see it with your own eyes and say, 'Great is the LORD—even beyond the borders of Israel!'

Blemished Sacrifices

6 "A son honors his father, and a servant his master. If I am a father, where is the honor due me? If I am a master, where is the respect due me?" says the LORD Almighty. "It is you, O priests, who show contempt for my name.

"But you ask, 'How have we shown contempt for your name?'

7 "You place defiled food on my altar.

"But you ask, 'How have we defiled you?'

"By saying that the LORD's table is contemptible. 8When you bring blind animals for sacrifice, is that not wrong? When you sacrifice crippled or diseased animals, is that not wrong? Try offering them to your governor! Would he be pleased with you? Would he accept you?" says the LORD Almighty.

9 "Now implore God to be gracious to

---

[a] *1 Malachi means* my messenger.

us. With such offerings from your hands, will he accept you?"—says the LORD Almighty.

10 "Oh, that one of you would shut the temple doors, so that you would not light useless fires on my altar! I am not pleased with you," says the LORD Almighty, "and I will accept no offering from your hands. 11 My name will be great among the nations, from the rising to the setting of the sun. In every place incense and pure offerings will be brought to my name, because my name will be great among the nations," says the LORD Almighty.

12 "But you profane it by saying of the Lord's table, 'It is defiled,' and of its food, 'It is contemptible.' 13 And you say, 'What a burden!' and you sniff at it contemptuously," says the LORD Almighty.

"When you bring injured, crippled or diseased animals and offer them as sacrifices, should I accept them from your hands?" says the LORD. 14 "Cursed is the cheat who has an acceptable male in his flock and vows to give it, but then sacrifices a blemished animal to the Lord. For I am a great king," says the LORD Almighty, "and my name is to be feared among the nations.

Admonition for the Priests

2 "And now this admonition is for you, O priests. 2 If you do not listen, and if you do not set your heart to honor my name," says the LORD Almighty, "I will send a curse upon you, and I will curse your blessings. Yes, I have already cursed them, because you have not set your heart to honor me.

3 "Because of you I will rebuke[a] your descendants[b]; I will spread on your faces the offal from your festival sacrifices, and you will be carried off with it. 4 And you will know that I have sent you this admonition so that my covenant with Levi may continue," says the LORD Almighty. 5 "My covenant was with him, a covenant of life and peace, and I gave them to him;

this called for reverence and he revered me and stood in awe of my name. 6 True instruction was in his mouth and nothing false was found on his lips. He walked with me in peace and uprightness, and turned many from sin.

7 "For the lips of a priest ought to preserve knowledge, and from his mouth men should seek instruction—because he is the messenger of the LORD Almighty. 8 But you have turned from the way and by your teaching have caused many to stumble; you have violated the covenant with Levi," says the LORD Almighty. 9 "So I have caused you to be despised and humiliated before all the people, because you have not followed my ways but have shown partiality in matters of the law."

Judah Unfaithful

10 Have we not all one Father[c]? Did not one God create us? Why do we profane the covenant of our fathers by breaking faith with one another?

11 Judah has broken faith. A detestable thing has been committed in Israel and in Jerusalem: Judah has desecrated the sanctuary the LORD loves, by marrying the daughter of a foreign god. 12 As for the man who does this, whoever he may be, may the LORD cut him off from the tents of Jacob[d]—even though he brings offerings to the LORD Almighty.

13 Another thing you do: You flood the LORD's altar with tears. You weep and wail because he no longer pays attention to your offerings or accepts them with pleasure from your hands. 14 You ask, "Why?" It is because the LORD is acting as the witness between you and the wife of your youth, because you have broken faith with her, though she is your partner, the wife of your marriage covenant.

15 Has not ⌊the LORD⌋ made them one? In flesh and spirit they are his. And why one? Because he was seeking godly offspring.[a] So guard yourself in your spirit,

---

a 3 Or cut off (see Septuagint)   b 3 Or will blight your grain   c 10 Or father   d 12 Or 12 May the LORD cut off from the tents of Jacob anyone who gives testimony in behalf of the man who does this and do not break faith with the wife of your youth.

16 "I hate divorce," says the LORD God of Israel, "and I hate a man's covering himself[b] with violence as well as with his garment," says the LORD Almighty.

So guard yourself in your spirit, and do not break faith.

The Day of Judgment

17 You have wearied the LORD with your words.

"How have we wearied him?" you ask.

By saying, "All who do evil are good in the eyes of the LORD, and he is pleased with them" or "Where is the God of justice?"

3 "See, I will send my messenger, who will prepare the way before me. Then suddenly the Lord you are seeking will come to his temple; the messenger of the covenant, whom you desire, will come," says the LORD Almighty.

2 But who can endure the day of his

> ## Prayer is . . .
>
> seeking God and His kingdom above all else and trusting that He will supply all your needs.

coming? Who can stand when he appears? For he will be like a refiner's fire or a launderer's soap. 3 He will sit as a refiner and purifier of silver; he will purify the Levites and refine them like gold and silver. Then the LORD will have men who will bring offerings in righteousness, 4 and the offerings of Judah and Jerusalem will be acceptable to the LORD, as in days gone by, as in former years.

5 "So I will come near to you for judgment. I will be quick to testify against sorcerers, adulterers and perjurers, against

those who defraud laborers of their wages, who oppress the widows and the fatherless, and deprive aliens of justice, but do not fear me," says the LORD Almighty.

Robbing God

6 "I the LORD do not change. So you, O descendants of Jacob, are not destroyed. 7 Ever since the time of your forefathers you have turned away from my decrees and have not kept them. Return to me, and I will return to you," says the LORD Almighty.

"But you ask, 'How are we to return?'

> ## Praying Malachi 3:8-11
>
> God, help me to never rob You of the tithes and offerings I owe You, and thank You for opening up the windows of heaven and pouring out Your blessing upon me.

8 "Will a man rob God? Yet you rob me.

"But you ask, 'How do we rob you?'

"In tithes and offerings. 9 You are under a curse—the whole nation of you—because you are robbing me. 10 Bring the whole tithe into the storehouse, that there may be food in my house. Test me in this," says the LORD Almighty, "and see if I will not throw open the floodgates of heaven and pour out so much blessing that you will not have room enough for it. 11 I will prevent pests from devouring your crops, and the vines in your fields will not cast their fruit," says the LORD Almighty. 12 "Then all the nations will call you blessed, for yours will be a delightful land," says the LORD Almighty.

13 "You have said harsh things against me," says the LORD.

"Yet you ask, 'What have we said against you?'

14 "You have said, 'It is futile to serve God. What did we gain by carrying out his requirements and going about like mourners before the LORD Almighty? 15 But now we call the arrogant blessed.

---

a 15 Or 15But the one who is our father, did not do this, not as long as life remained in him. And what was he seeking? An offspring from God   b 16 Or his wife

Certainly the evildoers prosper, and even those who challenge God escape.'"

16Then those who feared the LORD talked with each other, and the LORD listened and heard. A scroll of remembrance was written in his presence concerning those who feared the LORD and honored his name.

17"They will be mine," says the LORD Almighty, "in the day when I make up my treasured possession.ª I will spare them, just as in compassion a man spares his son who serves him. 18And you will again see the distinction between the righteous and the wicked, between those who serve God and those who do not.

The Day of the LORD

4 "Surely the day is coming; it will burn like a furnace. All the arrogant and every evildoer will be stubble, and that day that is coming will set them on fire," says the LORD Almighty. "Not a root or a branch will be left to them. 2But for you who revere my name, the sun of righteousness will rise with healing in its wings. And you will go out and leap like calves released from the stall. 3Then you will trample down the wicked; they will be ashes under the soles of your feet on the day when I do these things," says the LORD Almighty.

4"Remember the law of my servant Moses, the decrees and laws I gave him at Horeb for all Israel.

5"See, I will send you the prophet Elijah before that great and dreadful day of the LORD comes. 6He will turn the hearts of the fathers to their children, and the hearts of the children to their fathers; or else I will come and strike the land with a curse."

ª 17 Or Almighty, "my treasured possession, in the day when I act

The New Testament

Author: Matthew

Date: Between AD 58 and 70

Audience: Greek-speaking Jews, to prove that Jesus is their long-awaited Messiah

Prayer Themes:

- Ask God to develop within you the character of a true disciple of Christ (5:1-10).

- Praise Jesus for being our all-powerful Savior who is able and willing to do miraculous things in the lives of those who believe in Him (8:1–9:38).

- Thank God for His willingness to use you for His kingdom purposes, and for His promised presence in your life as you serve Him (28:18-20).

Imagine a good and powerful king choosing *you* to play a key role in his empire. He taps you to be his emissary, trains you for the task, authorizes you to act on his behalf, helps you to teach others, assures you of his favor and protection, and promises to supply whatever you need to complete the mission. All you have to do is ask.

This is what happens in the Gospel of Matthew. Jesus of Nazareth is shown to be the King of the Jews, the Messiah promised in the ancient Hebrew Scriptures.

Gathering twelve devoted followers, King Jesus lays the groundwork for His kingdom. For three years, He shows and tells His disciples how to think, how to pray, how to trust, how to love—how to live. Then, when the religious leaders of that time become threatened, the King is assassinated. But Jesus doesn't stay dead. He is resurrected out of the grave, and before ascending into heaven, He commissions His subjects and promises to come again and take them with Him to His eternal kingdom.

Matthew

The Genealogy of Jesus

1 A record of the genealogy of Jesus Christ the son of David, the son of Abraham:

2 Abraham was the father of Isaac,
Isaac the father of Jacob,
Jacob the father of Judah and his brothers,
3 Judah the father of Perez and Zerah, whose mother was Tamar,
Perez the father of Hezron,
Hezron the father of Ram,
4 Ram the father of Amminadab,
Amminadab the father of Nahshon,
Nahshon the father of Salmon,
5 Salmon the father of Boaz, whose mother was Rahab,
Boaz the father of Obed, whose mother was Ruth,
Obed the father of Jesse,
6 and Jesse the father of King David.

David was the father of Solomon, whose mother had been Uriah's wife,
7 Solomon the father of Rehoboam,
Rehoboam the father of Abijah,
Abijah the father of Asa,
8 Asa the father of Jehoshaphat,
Jehoshaphat the father of Jehoram,
Jehoram the father of Uzziah,
9 Uzziah the father of Jotham,
Jotham the father of Ahaz,
Ahaz the father of Hezekiah,
10 Hezekiah the father of Manasseh,
Manasseh the father of Amon,
Amon the father of Josiah,

What Is Prayer, Exactly?

Prayer is communicating with God. When we struggle with such things as unrealized dreams, an unfulfilling life, lack of mental clarity, or emotional pain, we have access to the God who can touch every area of our lives to transform them and bring about wholeness. He wants to reach down and touch *us,* but first we have to reach up and touch *Him* in prayer. When we pray, we're saying, "I know You are real, Lord, and I want to spend time with You."

Prayer is praising and worshiping God for who He is. This takes our focus off of ourselves and places it on Him. It positions Him first in our hearts and allows Him full access to our lives. When we pray, we're saying, "Lord, You are wonderful, almighty, all-powerful, the God and Creator of all things. I exalt You above everything, and I worship You for who You are."

Prayer is telling God we love and adore Him. It's coming humbly before God and speaking to Him the way we would to someone we dearly love. Prayer is telling God how grateful we are that He loved us before we were even aware He existed. When we pray, we're saying, "I love You, Lord, and I thank You for loving me."

Prayer is telling God we need Him. We need God for everything. We need Him to save us, forgive us, heal us, deliver us, fill us, restore us, redeem us, free us, guide us, protect us, lift us above our limitations, and move us into the plans and purposes He has for us. We can't get there without Him. When we pray, we're saying, "I can't live without You, Lord. If You don't intervene in my life, nothing good is going to happen."

Prayer is making our requests known to God. It's sharing with Him all that is on our hearts, knowing that He cares about each one of those things. Prayer is acknowledging that, even though what we are praying for may seem impossible to us, with God all things are possible (19:26). When we pray, we're saying, "Lord, I have these needs, and I know You care about them and will hear my requests."

Prayer is serving God His way. God has things for each of us to do, and they start with prayer. The good news is that it's never too late to sow the seeds of prayer and gain a different harvest than the seeds of sin and death we have produced in our world. We can invite God's power to enter specific situations right now. When we pray, we're saying, "Lord, I want to be Your instrument through which You do what You want to do on this planet. Help me to pray according to Your will, so that *Your* will is done on earth."

For the next "From Stormie's Heart" article, go to page 1183.

11and Josiah the father of Jeconiah[a] and his brothers at the time of the exile to Babylon.

12After the exile to Babylon:
Jeconiah was the father of Shealtiel,
Shealtiel the father of Zerubbabel,
13Zerubbabel the father of Abiud,
Abiud the father of Eliakim,
Eliakim the father of Azor,
14Azor the father of Zadok,
Zadok the father of Akim,
Akim the father of Eliud,
15Eliud the father of Eleazar,
Eleazar the father of Matthan,
Matthan the father of Jacob,
16and Jacob the father of Joseph, the husband of Mary, of whom was born Jesus, who is called Christ.

17Thus there were fourteen generations in all from Abraham to David, fourteen from David to the exile to Babylon, and fourteen from the exile to the Christ.[b]

The Birth of Jesus Christ

18This is how the birth of Jesus Christ came about: His mother Mary was pledged to be married to Joseph, but before they came together, she was found to be with child through the Holy Spirit. 19Because Joseph her husband was a righteous man and did not want to expose her to public disgrace, he had in mind to divorce her quietly.

20But after he had considered this, an angel of the Lord appeared to him in a dream and said, "Joseph son of David, do not be afraid to take Mary home as your wife, because what is conceived in her is from the Holy Spirit. 21She will give birth to a son, and you are to give him the name Jesus,[c] because he will save his people from their sins."

22All this took place to fulfill what the Lord had said through the prophet: 23"The virgin will be with child and will give birth to a son, and they will call him Immanuel"[d]—which means, "God with us."

24When Joseph woke up, he did what the angel of the Lord had commanded him and took Mary home as his wife. 25But he had no union with her until she gave birth to a son. And he gave him the name Jesus.

The Visit of the Magi

2 After Jesus was born in Bethlehem in Judea, during the time of King Herod, Magi[e] from the east came to Jerusalem 2and asked, "Where is the one who has been born king of the Jews? We saw his star in the east[f] and have come to worship him."

3When King Herod heard this he was disturbed, and all Jerusalem with him. 4When he had called together all the people's chief priests and teachers of the law, he asked them where the Christ[g] was to be born. 5"In Bethlehem in Judea," they replied, "for this is what the prophet has written:

6"'But you, Bethlehem, in the land of Judah,
are by no means least among the rulers of Judah;
for out of you will come a ruler
who will be the shepherd of my people Israel.'[h]"

7Then Herod called the Magi secretly and found out from them the exact time the star had appeared. 8He sent them to Bethlehem and said, "Go and make a careful search for the child. As soon as you find him, report to me, so that I too may go and worship him."

9After they had heard the king, they went on their way, and the star they had seen in the east[i] went ahead of them until it stopped over the place where the child was. 10When they saw the star, they were

a 11 That is, Jehoiachin; also in verse 12   b 17 Or Messiah. "The Christ" (Greek) and "the Messiah" (Hebrew) both mean "the Anointed One."   c 21 Jesus is the Greek form of Joshua, which means the Lord saves.   d 23 Isaiah 7:14   e 1 Traditionally Wise Men   f 2 Or star when it rose   g 4 Or Messiah   h 6 Micah 5:2   i 9 Or seen when it rose overjoyed. ¹¹On coming to the house, they saw the child with his mother Mary, and they bowed down and worshiped him. Then they opened their treasures and presented him with gifts of gold and of incense and of myrrh. ¹²And having been warned in a dream not to go back to Herod, they returned to their country by another route.

The Escape to Egypt

¹³When they had gone, an angel of the Lord appeared to Joseph in a dream. "Get up," he said, "take the child and his mother and escape to Egypt. Stay there until I tell you, for Herod is going to search for the child to kill him."

¹⁴So he got up, took the child and his mother during the night and left for Egypt, ¹⁵where he stayed until the death of Herod. And so was fulfilled what the Lord had said through the prophet: "Out of Egypt I called my son."[a]

¹⁶When Herod realized that he had been outwitted by the Magi, he was furious, and he gave orders to kill all the boys in Bethlehem and its vicinity who were two years old and under, in accordance with the time he had learned from the Magi. ¹⁷Then what was said through the prophet Jeremiah was fulfilled:

¹⁸"A voice is heard in Ramah,
    weeping and great mourning,
Rachel weeping for her children
    and refusing to be comforted,
because they are no more."[b]

The Return to Nazareth

¹⁹After Herod died, an angel of the Lord appeared in a dream to Joseph in Egypt ²⁰and said, "Get up, take the child and his mother and go to the land of Israel, for those who were trying to take the child's life are dead."

²¹So he got up, took the child and his mother and went to the land of Israel. ²²But when he heard that Archelaus was reigning in Judea in place of his father Herod, he was afraid to go there. Having

been warned in a dream, he withdrew to the district of Galilee, ²³and he went and lived in a town called Nazareth. So was fulfilled what was said through the prophets: "He will be called a Nazarene."

John the Baptist Prepares the Way

3 In those days John the Baptist came, preaching in the Desert of Judea ²and saying, "Repent, for the kingdom of heaven is near." ³This is he who was spoken of through the prophet Isaiah:

"A voice of one calling in the desert,
'Prepare the way for the Lord,
    make straight paths for him.'"[c]

Praying Matthew 3:1-3
Heavenly Father, I repent of all my sins before You, because I know that repentance prepares the way in my heart for You to do Your perfect work in me.

⁴John's clothes were made of camel's hair, and he had a leather belt around his waist. His food was locusts and wild honey. ⁵People went out to him from Jerusalem and all Judea and the whole region of the Jordan. ⁶Confessing their sins, they were baptized by him in the Jordan River.

⁷But when he saw many of the Pharisees and Sadducees coming to where he was baptizing, he said to them: "You brood of vipers! Who warned you to flee from the coming wrath? ⁸Produce fruit in keeping with repentance. ⁹And do not think you can say to yourselves, 'We have Abraham as our father.' I tell you that out of these stones God can raise up children for Abraham. ¹⁰The ax is already at the root of the trees, and every tree that does not produce good fruit will be cut down and thrown into the fire.

¹¹"I baptize you with[d] water for repentance. But after me will come one who is more powerful than I, whose sandals I am not fit to carry. He will baptize you with the Holy Spirit and with fire. ¹²His

---

[a] *15* Hosea 11:1 [b] *18* Jer. 31:15 [c] *3* Isaiah 40:3 [d] *11* Or *in*

winnowing fork is in his hand, and he will clear his threshing floor, gathering his wheat into the barn and burning up the chaff with unquenchable fire."

The Baptism of Jesus

[13] Then Jesus came from Galilee to the Jordan to be baptized by John. [14] But John tried to deter him, saying, "I need to be baptized by you, and do you come to me?"

[15] Jesus replied, "Let it be so now; it is proper for us to do this to fulfill all righteousness." Then John consented.

[16] As soon as Jesus was baptized, he went up out of the water. At that moment heaven was opened, and he saw the Spirit of God descending like a dove and lighting on him. [17] And a voice from heaven said, "This is my Son, whom I love; with him I am well pleased."

The Temptation of Jesus

4 Then Jesus was led by the Spirit into the desert to be tempted by the devil. [2] After fasting forty days and forty nights, he was hungry. [3] The tempter came to him and said, "If you are the Son of God, tell these stones to become bread."

[4] Jesus answered, "It is written: 'Man does not live on bread alone, but on every word that comes from the mouth of God.'[a]"

Praying Matthew 4:4
Lord, help me to feed on Your Word daily so that I will never hunger after things that do not give life.

[5] Then the devil took him to the holy city and had him stand on the highest point of the temple. [6] "If you are the Son of God," he said, "throw yourself down. For it is written:

"'He will command his angels
    concerning you,
and they will lift you up in their
    hands,

so that you will not strike your foot
    against a stone.'[b]"

[7] Jesus answered him, "It is also written: 'Do not put the Lord your God to the test.'[c]"

[8] Again, the devil took him to a very high mountain and showed him all the kingdoms of the world and their splendor. [9] "All this I will give you," he said, "if you will bow down and worship me."

[10] Jesus said to him, "Away from me, Satan! For it is written: 'Worship the Lord your God, and serve him only.'[d]"

[11] Then the devil left him, and angels came and attended him.

Jesus Begins to Preach

[12] When Jesus heard that John had been put in prison, he returned to Galilee. [13] Leaving Nazareth, he went and lived in Capernaum, which was by the lake in the area of Zebulun and Naphtali— [14] to fulfill what was said through the prophet Isaiah:

[15] "Land of Zebulun and land of
    Naphtali,
  the way to the sea, along the
    Jordan,
  Galilee of the Gentiles—
[16] the people living in darkness
  have seen a great light;
on those living in the land of the
    shadow of death
  a light has dawned."[e]

[17] From that time on Jesus began to preach, "Repent, for the kingdom of heaven is near."

The Calling of the First Disciples

[18] As Jesus was walking beside the Sea of Galilee, he saw two brothers, Simon called Peter and his brother Andrew. They were casting a net into the lake, for they were fishermen. [19] "Come, follow me," Jesus said, "and I will make you fishers of men." [20] At once they left their nets and followed him.

[21] Going on from there, he saw two

---

[a]4 Deut. 8:3   [b]6 Psalm 91:11,12   [c]7 Deut. 6:16   [d]10 Deut. 6:13   [e]16 Isaiah 9:1,2

other brothers, James son of Zebedee and his brother John. They were in a boat with their father Zebedee, preparing their nets. Jesus called them, 22and immediately they left the boat and their father and followed him.

Jesus Heals the Sick

23Jesus went throughout Galilee, teaching in their synagogues, preaching the good news of the kingdom, and healing every disease and sickness among the people. 24News about him spread all over Syria, and people brought to him all who were ill with various diseases, those suffering severe pain, the demon-possessed, those having seizures, and the paralyzed, and he healed them. 25Large crowds from Galilee, the Decapolis,ª Jerusalem, Judea and the region across the Jordan followed him.

The Beatitudes

5 Now when he saw the crowds, he went up on a mountainside and sat down. His disciples came to him, 2and he began to teach them, saying:

3 "Blessed are the poor in spirit,
   for theirs is the kingdom of
      heaven.
4 Blessed are those who mourn,
   for they will be comforted.
5 Blessed are the meek,
   for they will inherit the earth.

Prayer is . . .

*the way you satisfy the longing of
your soul to be close to God.*

6 Blessed are those who hunger and
      thirst for righteousness,
   for they will be filled.
7 Blessed are the merciful,
   for they will be shown mercy.
8 Blessed are the pure in heart,

for they will see God.
9 Blessed are the peacemakers,
   for they will be called sons of God.
10 Blessed are those who are persecuted
      because of righteousness,
   for theirs is the kingdom of heaven.

11 "Blessed are you when people insult you, persecute you and falsely say all kinds of evil against you because of me. 12Rejoice and be glad, because great is your reward in heaven, for in the same way they persecuted the prophets who were before you.

Salt and Light

13 "You are the salt of the earth. But if the salt loses its saltiness, how can it be made salty again? It is no longer good for anything, except to be thrown out and trampled by men.

14 "You are the light of the world. A city on a hill cannot be hidden. 15Neither do people light a lamp and put it under a bowl. Instead they put it on its stand, and it gives light to everyone in the house. 16In the same way, let your light shine before men, that they may see your good deeds and praise your Father in heaven.

The Fulfillment of the Law

17 "Do not think that I have come to abolish the Law or the Prophets; I have not come to abolish them but to fulfill them. 18I tell you the truth, until heaven and earth disappear, not the smallest letter, not the least stroke of a pen, will by any means disappear from the Law until everything is accomplished. 19Anyone who breaks one of the least of these commandments and teaches others to do the same will be called least in the kingdom of heaven, but whoever practices and teaches these commands will be called great in the kingdom of heaven. 20For I tell you that unless your righteousness surpasses that of the Pharisees and the teachers of the law, you will certainly not enter the kingdom of heaven.

ª 25 That is, the Ten Cities

Murder

21 "You have heard that it was said to the people long ago, 'Do not murder,[a] and anyone who murders will be subject to judgment.' 22 But I tell you that anyone who is angry with his brother[b] will be subject to judgment. Again, anyone who says to his brother, 'Raca,[c]' is answerable to the Sanhedrin. But anyone who says, 'You fool!' will be in danger of the fire of hell.

23 "Therefore, if you are offering your gift at the altar and there remember that your brother has something against you, 24 leave your gift there in front of the altar. First go and be reconciled to your brother; then come and offer your gift.

25 "Settle matters quickly with your adversary who is taking you to court. Do it while you are still with him on the way, or he may hand you over to the judge, and the judge may hand you over to the officer, and you may be thrown into prison. 26 I tell you the truth, you will not get out until you have paid the last penny.[d]

Adultery

27 "You have heard that it was said, 'Do not commit adultery.'[e] 28 But I tell you that anyone who looks at a woman lustfully has already committed adultery with her in his heart. 29 If your right eye causes you to sin, gouge it out and throw it away. It is better for you to lose one part of your body than for your whole body to be thrown into hell. 30 And if your right hand causes you to sin, cut it off and throw it away. It is better for you to lose one part of your body than for your whole body to go into hell.

Divorce

31 "It has been said, 'Anyone who divorces his wife must give her a certificate of divorce.'[f] 32 But I tell you that anyone who divorces his wife, except for marital unfaithfulness, causes her to become an adulteress, and anyone who marries the divorced woman commits adultery.

Oaths

33 "Again, you have heard that it was said to the people long ago, 'Do not break your oath, but keep the oaths you have made to the Lord.' 34 But I tell you, Do not swear at all: either by heaven, for it is God's throne; 35 or by the earth, for it is his footstool; or by Jerusalem, for it is the city of the Great King. 36 And do not swear by your head, for you cannot make even one hair white or black. 37 Simply let your 'Yes' be 'Yes,' and your 'No,' 'No'; anything beyond this comes from the evil one.

An Eye for an Eye

38 "You have heard that it was said, 'Eye for eye, and tooth for tooth.'[g] 39 But I tell you, Do not resist an evil person. If someone strikes you on the right cheek, turn to him the other also. 40 And if someone wants to sue you and take your tunic, let him have your cloak as well. 41 If someone forces you to go one mile, go with him two miles. 42 Give to the one who asks you, and do not turn away from the one who wants to borrow from you.

Love for Enemies

43 "You have heard that it was said, 'Love your neighbor[h] and hate your enemy.' 44 But I tell you: Love your enemies[i] and pray for those who persecute you, 45 that you may be sons of your Father in heaven. He causes his sun to rise on the evil and the good, and sends rain on the righteous and the unrighteous. 46 If you love those who love you, what reward will you get? Are not even the tax collectors doing that? 47 And if you greet only your brothers, what are you doing more than others? Do not even pagans do that? 48 Be perfect, therefore, as your heavenly Father is perfect.

---

a 21 Exodus 20:13   b 22 Some manuscripts brother without cause   c 22 An Aramaic term of contempt   d 26 Greek kodrantes   e 27 Exodus 20:14   f 31 Deut. 24:1   g 38 Exodus 21:24; Lev. 24:20; Deut. 19:21   h 43 Lev. 19:18   i 44 Some late manuscripts enemies, bless those who curse you, do good to those who hate you

Giving to the Needy

6 "Be careful not to do your 'acts of righteousness' before men, to be seen by them. If you do, you will have no reward from your Father in heaven.

2"So when you give to the needy, do not announce it with trumpets, as the hypocrites do in the synagogues and on the streets, to be honored by men. I tell you the truth, they have received their reward in full. 3But when you give to the needy, do not let your left hand know what your right hand is doing, 4so that your giving may be in secret. Then your Father, who sees what is done in secret, will reward you.

Prayer

5"And when you pray, do not be like the hypocrites, for they love to pray standing in the synagogues and on the street corners to be seen by men. I tell you the truth, they have received their reward in full. 6But when you pray, go into your room, close the door and pray to your Father, who is unseen. Then your Father, who sees what is done in secret, will reward you. 7And when you pray, do not keep on babbling like pagans, for they think they will be heard because of their many words. 8Do not be like them, for your Father knows what you need before you ask him.

9"This, then, is how you should pray:

"'Our Father in heaven,
    hallowed be your name,
10your kingdom come,
    your will be done
        on earth as it is in heaven.
11Give us today our daily bread.
12Forgive us our debts,
    as we also have forgiven our debtors.
13And lead us not into temptation,
    but deliver us from the evil one.ᵃ'

14For if you forgive men when they sin against you, your heavenly Father will also forgive you. 15But if you do not for-give men their sins, your Father will not forgive your sins.

Fasting

16"When you fast, do not look somber as the hypocrites do, for they disfigure their faces to show men they are fasting. I tell you the truth, they have received their reward in full. 17But when you fast, put oil on your head and wash your face, 18so that it will not be obvious to men that you are fasting, but only to your Father, who is unseen; and your Father, who sees what is done in secret, will reward you.

Treasures in Heaven

19"Do not store up for yourselves treasures on earth, where moth and rust destroy, and where thieves break in and steal. 20But store up for yourselves treasures in heaven, where moth and rust do not destroy, and where thieves do not break in and steal. 21For where your treasure is, there your heart will be also.

22"The eye is the lamp of the body. If your eyes are good, your whole body will be full of light. 23But if your eyes are bad, your whole body will be full of darkness. If then the light within you is darkness, how great is that darkness!

24"No one can serve two masters. Either he will hate the one and love the other, or he will be devoted to the one and despise the other. You cannot serve both God and Money.

Do Not Worry

25"Therefore I tell you, do not worry about your life, what you will eat or drink; or about your body, what you will wear. Is not life more important than food, and the body more important than clothes? 26Look at the birds of the air; they do not sow or reap or store away in barns, and yet your heavenly Father feeds them. Are you not much more valuable than they? 27Who of you by worrying can add a single hour to his lifeᵇ?

28"And why do you worry about

ᵃ 13 Or from evil; some late manuscripts one, / for yours is the kingdom and the power and the glory forever. Amen.
ᵇ 27 Or single cubit to his height

Jesus Teaches Us How to Pray

GOING *deeper*

READ AND CONSIDER: MATTHEW 6:9-13

"This, then, is how you should pray: 'Our Father in heaven, hallowed be your name, your kingdom come, your will be done on earth as it is in heaven. Give us today our daily bread. Forgive us our debts, as we also have forgiven our debtors. And lead us not into temptation, but deliver us from the evil one' " (Matthew 6:9-13).

Few people can enter a church without hearing this prayer either spoken or sung. It's known around the world. In Jerusalem there is a building that has over one hundred beautiful ceramic tiles inscribed with the words of this prayer in many languages of the world. Some people call it the "Our Father" or "The Lord's Prayer." Whatever title you use, it's accurate to say that this is probably the best known and most repeated prayer in the Christian world.

It is called the Lord's Prayer because Jesus, our Lord, taught His disciples to pray in this manner. He did not intend for them to mindlessly repeat this prayer over and over. Rather, He was laying out a pattern of prayer for them, and for us today as His disciples, to follow. There is rich meaning in each phrase.

Our Father in heaven, hallowed be your name is a declaration of praise acknowledging that God is holy and to be revered. His name is never to be taken lightly. Not only is He Lord of heaven and earth, but He is also our heavenly Father.

Your kingdom come, your will be done on earth as it is in heaven reminds us that God wants us to pray for His will to rule and reign in our world. As we pray and invite God to manifest His power in the midst of earth's suffering and pain, He will move in response to our prayers. His power and presence will enter our lives and will work out on earth what He has willed in heaven.

Give us today our daily bread declares our dependence upon God as our provider. All that we have now has been provided by His gracious hand. Everything we need in the future will come from Him day by day as we seek Him for it.

Forgive us our debts, as we also have forgiven our debtors is a statement in which we not only ask God for forgiveness, but we are also reminded that we must forgive others. Just as we are indebted to God because He forgave our sins, so we must willingly forgive those who have sinned against us.

Lead us not into temptation, but deliver us from the evil one. Jesus was not saying that God tempts people but that we have an enemy of our souls who would like nothing better than to defeat us. We all go through difficulties and times of temptation from which we need divine deliverance. But Jesus paid an enormous price so we could be free and have power over the evil one.

Some manuscripts include: *For yours is the kingdom and the power and the glory forever. Amen.* All that God is and all that God does lives forever. There has never been and never will be anything greater than God in all the universe. This declaration reminds us of that.

clothes? See how the lilies of the field grow. They do not labor or spin. [29]Yet I tell you that not even Solomon in all his splendor was dressed like one of these. [30]If that is how God clothes the grass of the field, which is here today and tomorrow is thrown into the fire, will he not much more clothe you, O you of little faith?

31So do not worry, saying, 'What shall we eat?' or 'What shall we drink?' or 'What shall we wear?' 32For the pagans run after all these things, and your heavenly Father knows that you need them. 33But seek first his kingdom and his righteousness, and all these things will be given to you as well. 34Therefore do not worry about tomorrow, for tomorrow will worry about itself. Each day has enough trouble of its own.

Judging Others

7 "Do not judge, or you too will be judged. 2For in the same way you judge others, you will be judged, and with the measure you use, it will be measured to you.

3"Why do you look at the speck of sawdust in your brother's eye and pay no attention to the plank in your own eye? 4How can you say to your brother, 'Let me take the speck out of your eye,' when all the time there is a plank in your own eye? 5You hypocrite, first take the plank out of your own eye, and then you will see clearly to remove the speck from your brother's eye.

6"Do not give dogs what is sacred; do not throw your pearls to pigs. If you do, they may trample them under their feet, and then turn and tear you to pieces.

Ask, Seek, Knock

7"Ask and it will be given to you; seek and you will find; knock and the door will be opened to you. 8For everyone who asks receives; he who seeks finds; and to him who knocks, the door will be opened.

9"Which of you, if his son asks for bread, will give him a stone? 10Or if he

---

GOING *deeper*

Ask, Seek, and Knock

READ AND CONSIDER: MATTHEW 7:7-12

"Ask and it will be given to you; seek and you will find; knock and the door will be opened to you. For everyone who asks receives; he who seeks finds; and to him who knocks, the door will be opened" (Matthew 7:7-8).

If Jesus instructs us to ask, seek, and knock, why do we sometimes struggle to pray as much as we should? One reason could be that we doubt God will really hear and answer. Or we fear being disappointed if we ask for too much or for the wrong thing. Or our own self-sufficiency may keep us from total dependency upon God. Or perhaps we feel that if God knows what we need before we ask, why do we need to ask?

Yet Jesus Himself, who knew the heart of Father God better than anyone, teaches us that we must be diligent to tell God our needs and pursue Him by faith. "Without faith it is impossible to please God, because anyone who comes to him must believe that he exists and that he rewards those who earnestly seek him" (Hebrews 11:6).

Often we feel reluctant to bring our needs to God because we think our problems are too big, or too small, or our own fault—therefore, we can't bother God about them. But the good news is that we are God's beloved children, and He is our loving Father. We can feel free to ask Him for the desires of our heart and that they be in alignment with His will. "Seek his kingdom, and these things will be given to you as well" (Luke 12:31).

Jesus' promise is that if we imperfect parents desire to give good gifts to our children, "how much more will your Father in heaven give good gifts to those who ask him!" (Matthew 7:11). So don't hesitate to ask, seek, and knock, knowing that your heavenly Father hears and will answer.

asks for a fish, will give him a snake? 11If you, then, though you are evil, know how to give good gifts to your children, how much more will your Father in heaven give good gifts to those who ask him! 12So in everything, do to others what you would have them do to you, for this sums up the Law and the Prophets.

The Narrow and Wide Gates

13"Enter through the narrow gate. For wide is the gate and broad is the road that leads to destruction, and many enter through it. 14But small is the gate and narrow the road that leads to life, and only a few find it.

A Tree and Its Fruit

15"Watch out for false prophets. They come to you in sheep's clothing, but inwardly they are ferocious wolves. 16By their fruit you will recognize them. Do people pick grapes from thornbushes, or figs from thistles? 17Likewise every good tree bears good fruit, but a bad tree bears bad fruit. 18A good tree cannot bear bad fruit, and a bad tree cannot bear good fruit. 19Every tree that does not bear good fruit is cut down and thrown into the fire. 20Thus, by their fruit you will recognize them.

21"Not everyone who says to me, 'Lord, Lord,' will enter the kingdom of heaven, but only he who does the will of my Father who is in heaven. 22Many will say to me on that day, 'Lord, Lord, did we not prophesy in your name, and in your name drive out demons and perform many miracles?' 23Then I will tell them plainly, 'I never knew you. Away from me, you evildoers!'

The Wise and Foolish Builders

24"Therefore everyone who hears these words of mine and puts them into practice is like a wise man who built his house on the rock. 25The rain came down, the streams rose, and the winds blew and beat against that house; yet it did not fall, because it had its foundation on the rock.

26But everyone who hears these words of mine and does not put them into practice is like a foolish man who built his house on sand. 27The rain came down, the streams rose, and the winds blew and beat against that house, and it fell with a great crash."

28When Jesus had finished saying these things, the crowds were amazed at his teaching, 29because he taught as one who had authority, and not as their teachers of the law.

The Man With Leprosy

8 When he came down from the mountainside, large crowds followed him. 2A man with leprosy[a] came and knelt before him and said, "Lord, if you are willing, you can make me clean."

3Jesus reached out his hand and touched the man. "I am willing," he said. "Be clean!" Immediately he was cured[b] of his leprosy. 4Then Jesus said to him, "See that you don't tell anyone. But go, show yourself to the priest and offer the gift Moses commanded, as a testimony to them."

The Faith of the Centurion

5When Jesus had entered Capernaum, a centurion came to him, asking for help. 6"Lord," he said, "my servant lies at home paralyzed and in terrible suffering."

7Jesus said to him, "I will go and heal him."

8The centurion replied, "Lord, I do not deserve to have you come under my roof. But just say the word, and my servant will be healed. 9For I myself am a man under authority, with soldiers under me. I tell this one, 'Go,' and he goes; and that one, 'Come,' and he comes. I say to my servant, 'Do this,' and he does it."

10When Jesus heard this, he was astonished and said to those following him, "I tell you the truth, I have not found anyone in Israel with such great faith. 11I say to you that many will come from the east and the west, and will take their places at

a 2 The Greek word was used for various diseases affecting the skin—not necessarily leprosy. b 3 Greek made clean the feast with Abraham, Isaac and Jacob in the kingdom of heaven. 12But the subjects of the kingdom will be thrown outside, into the darkness, where there will be weeping and gnashing of teeth."

13Then Jesus said to the centurion, "Go! It will be done just as you believed it would." And his servant was healed at that very hour.

Jesus Heals Many

14When Jesus came into Peter's house, he saw Peter's mother-in-law lying in bed with a fever. 15He touched her hand and the fever left her, and she got up and began to wait on him.

16When evening came, many who were demon-possessed were brought to him, and he drove out the spirits with a word and healed all the sick. 17This was to fulfill what was spoken through the prophet Isaiah:

"He took up our infirmities
    and carried our diseases."[a]

The Cost of Following Jesus

18When Jesus saw the crowd around him, he gave orders to cross to the other side of the lake. 19Then a teacher of the law came to him and said, "Teacher, I will follow you wherever you go."

20Jesus replied, "Foxes have holes and birds of the air have nests, but the Son of Man has no place to lay his head."

21Another disciple said to him, "Lord, first let me go and bury my father."

22But Jesus told him, "Follow me, and let the dead bury their own dead."

Jesus Calms the Storm

23Then he got into the boat and his disciples followed him. 24Without warning, a furious storm came up on the lake, so that the waves swept over the boat. But Jesus was sleeping. 25The disciples went and woke him, saying, "Lord, save us! We're going to drown!"

26He replied, "You of little faith, why are you so afraid?" Then he got up and rebuked the winds and the waves, and it was completely calm.

> ### Praying Matthew 8:26
> *Jesus, help me to have big faith so that I can pray to You, believing that You will calm the storms in my life.*

27The men were amazed and asked, "What kind of man is this? Even the winds and the waves obey him!"

The Healing of Two Demon-possessed Men

28When he arrived at the other side in the region of the Gadarenes,[b] two demon-possessed men coming from the tombs met him. They were so violent that no one could pass that way. 29"What do you want with us, Son of God?" they shouted. "Have you come here to torture us before the appointed time?"

30Some distance from them a large herd of pigs was feeding. 31The demons begged Jesus, "If you drive us out, send us into the herd of pigs."

32He said to them, "Go!" So they came out and went into the pigs, and the whole herd rushed down the steep bank into the lake and died in the water. 33Those tending the pigs ran off, went into the town and reported all this, including what had happened to the demon-possessed men. 34Then the whole town went out to meet Jesus. And when they saw him, they pleaded with him to leave their region.

Jesus Heals a Paralytic

9 Jesus stepped into a boat, crossed over and came to his own town. 2Some men brought to him a paralytic, lying on a mat. When Jesus saw their faith, he said to the paralytic, "Take heart, son; your sins are forgiven."

3At this, some of the teachers of the law said to themselves, "This fellow is blaspheming!"

4Knowing their thoughts, Jesus said, "Why do you entertain evil thoughts in

---

Have Faith That With God All Things Are Possible

Miracles happen because people have faith. Not faith in miracles; faith in God, who performs miracles.

When a woman who had had a flow of blood for 12 years touched the hem of Jesus' garment, Jesus turned around and said, "Take heart, daughter . . . your faith has healed you." The woman was made well from that moment (9:22). Jesus healed blind men after He touched them and said, "According to your faith will it be done to you" (9:29). It is by faith the Israelites passed through the Red Sea as though it were dry land, while the Egyptians drowned trying to do the same thing (Hebrews 11:29).

In order to see miracles in our lives, we have to touch Jesus and have faith in His ability and desire to touch us. Praise and worship enable us to do that. Our worship will influence what emanates from our life— whether it be great faith or great doubt.

What do you do when you hear bad news? If you received a bad report from the doctor after your test results were in, would it cause your heart to sink and fear to rise? Would depression settle over you like a dark blanket of dread? If that ever happens to you for any reason, begin immediately to praise God. Praise Him out loud if you are in a position to do so. Sing praise and worship songs to Him until the grip of sadness or shock is broken. Thank Him that because of who He is, anything is possible. Pray about the specifics. Tell Him your needs, requests, concerns, and fears. Tell Him all the reasons you love Him. Thank Him for His Word and quote His Word in your prayers. As you do all that, you will find your faith increasing. The more it increases, the more you will be able to face your doubts and fears and say, "With God, all things are possible. Blessed be the name of the Lord."

The fact that God responds to our faith is a sign of His love for us. He rewards us for believing in Him. For trusting Him. For loving Him. It is His great love for us that causes us to have faith in Him. You know how it is when you fall in love with someone. Their love for you causes you to trust that person. It's the same with God. The more you realize how much He loves you, the more you will have faith in Him. The more you worship Him, the more you will understand and trust His love for you.

The more you express your love to God in praise, the more you will understand His greatness. Then you will see that nothing is too hard for Him—not even the miracle you need in your life right now.

For the next "From Stormie's Heart" article, go to page 1222.

your hearts? 5Which is easier: to say, 'Your sins are forgiven,' or to say, 'Get up and walk'? 6But so that you may know that the Son of Man has authority on earth to forgive sins…" Then he said to the paralytic, "Get up, take your mat and go home." 7And the man got up and went home. 8When the crowd saw this, they were filled with awe; and they praised God, who had given such authority to men.

The Calling of Matthew

9As Jesus went on from there, he saw a man named Matthew sitting at the tax collector's booth. "Follow me," he told him, and Matthew got up and followed him.

10While Jesus was having dinner at Matthew's house, many tax collectors and "sinners" came and ate with him and his disciples. 11When the Pharisees saw this, they asked his disciples, "Why does your teacher eat with tax collectors and 'sinners'?"

12On hearing this, Jesus said, "It is not the healthy who need a doctor, but the sick. 13But go and learn what this means: 'I desire mercy, not sacrifice.'[a] For I have not come to call the righteous, but sinners."

Jesus Questioned About Fasting

14Then John's disciples came and asked him, "How is it that we and the Pharisees fast, but your disciples do not fast?"

15Jesus answered, "How can the guests of the bridegroom mourn while he is with them? The time will come when the bridegroom will be taken from them; then they will fast.

16"No one sews a patch of unshrunk cloth on an old garment, for the patch will pull away from the garment, making the tear worse. 17Neither do men pour new wine into old wineskins. If they do, the skins will burst, the wine will run out and the wineskins will be ruined. No, they pour new wine into new wineskins, and both are preserved."

A Dead Girl and a Sick Woman

18While he was saying this, a ruler came and knelt before him and said, "My daughter has just died. But come and put your hand on her, and she will live." 19Jesus got up and went with him, and so did his disciples.

20Just then a woman who had been subject to bleeding for twelve years came up behind him and touched the edge of his cloak. 21She said to herself, "If I only touch his cloak, I will be healed."

22Jesus turned and saw her. "Take heart, daughter," he said, "your faith has healed you." And the woman was healed from that moment.

23When Jesus entered the ruler's house and saw the flute players and the noisy crowd, 24he said, "Go away. The girl is not dead but asleep." But they laughed at him. 25After the crowd had been put outside, he went in and took the girl by the hand, and she got up. 26News of this spread through all that region.

Jesus Heals the Blind and Mute

27As Jesus went on from there, two blind men followed him, calling out, "Have mercy on us, Son of David!"

28When he had gone indoors, the blind men came to him, and he asked them, "Do you believe that I am able to do this?"

"Yes, Lord," they replied.

29Then he touched their eyes and said, "According to your faith will it be done to you"; 30and their sight was restored. Jesus warned them sternly, "See that no one knows about this." 31But they went out and spread the news about him all over that region.

32While they were going out, a man who was demon-possessed and could not talk was brought to Jesus. 33And when the demon was driven out, the man who had been mute spoke. The crowd was amazed and said, "Nothing like this has ever been seen in Israel."

34But the Pharisees said, "It is by the

a 13 Hosea 6:6

prince of demons that he drives out demons."

The Workers Are Few

35 Jesus went through all the towns and villages, teaching in their synagogues, preaching the good news of the kingdom and healing every disease and sickness. 36 When he saw the crowds, he had compassion on them, because they were harassed and helpless, like sheep without a shepherd. 37 Then he said to his disciples, "The harvest is plentiful but the workers are few. 38 Ask the Lord of the harvest, therefore, to send out workers into his harvest field."

Jesus Sends Out the Twelve

10 He called his twelve disciples to him and gave them authority to drive out evil[a] spirits and to heal every disease and sickness.

2 These are the names of the twelve apostles: first, Simon (who is called Peter) and his brother Andrew; James son of Zebedee, and his brother John; 3 Philip and Bartholomew; Thomas and Matthew the tax collector; James son of Alphaeus, and Thaddaeus; 4 Simon the Zealot and Judas Iscariot, who betrayed him.

5 These twelve Jesus sent out with the following instructions: "Do not go among the Gentiles or enter any town of the Samaritans. 6 Go rather to the lost sheep of Israel. 7 As you go, preach this message: 'The kingdom of heaven is near.' 8 Heal the sick, raise the dead, cleanse those who have leprosy,[b] drive out demons. Freely you have received, freely give. 9 Do not take along any gold or silver or copper in your belts; 10 take no bag for the journey, or extra tunic, or sandals or a staff; for the worker is worth his keep.

11 "Whatever town or village you enter, search for some worthy person there and stay at his house until you leave. 12 As you enter the home, give it your greeting. 13 If the home is deserving, let your peace rest

on it; if it is not, let your peace return to you. 14 If anyone will not welcome you or listen to your words, shake the dust off your feet when you leave that home or town. 15 I tell you the truth, it will be more bearable for Sodom and Gomorrah on the day of judgment than for that town. 16 I am sending you out like sheep among wolves. Therefore be as shrewd as snakes and as innocent as doves.

17 "Be on your guard against men; they will hand you over to the local councils and flog you in their synagogues. 18 On my account you will be brought before governors and kings as witnesses to them and to the Gentiles. 19 But when they arrest you, do not worry about what to say or how to say it. At that time you will be given what to say, 20 for it will not be you speaking, but the Spirit of your Father speaking through you.

21 "Brother will betray brother to death, and a father his child; children will rebel against their parents and have them put to death. 22 All men will hate you because of me, but he who stands firm to the end will be saved. 23 When you are persecuted in one place, flee to another. I tell you the truth, you will not finish going through the cities of Israel before the Son of Man comes.

24 "A student is not above his teacher, nor a servant above his master. 25 It is enough for the student to be like his teacher, and the servant like his master. If the head of the house has been called Beelzebub,[c] how much more the members of his household!

26 "So do not be afraid of them. There is nothing concealed that will not be disclosed, or hidden that will not be made known. 27 What I tell you in the dark, speak in the daylight; what is whispered in your ear, proclaim from the roofs. 28 Do not be afraid of those who kill the body but cannot kill the soul. Rather, be afraid of the One who can destroy both soul

---

[a] 1 Greek unclean   [b] 8 The Greek word was used for various diseases affecting the skin—not necessarily leprosy.   [c] 25 Greek Beezeboul or Beelzeboul

and body in hell. ²⁹Are not two sparrows sold for a penny[a]? Yet not one of them will fall to the ground apart from the will of your Father. ³⁰And even the very hairs of your head are all numbered. ³¹So don't be afraid; you are worth more than many sparrows.

³²"Whoever acknowledges me before men, I will also acknowledge him before my Father in heaven. ³³But whoever disowns me before men, I will disown him before my Father in heaven.

Praying Matthew 10:32-33
Dear Jesus, give me courage so that I will never deny You in any way, regardless of the circumstances I may face.

³⁴"Do not suppose that I have come to bring peace to the earth. I did not come to bring peace, but a sword. ³⁵For I have come to turn

"'a man against his father,
    a daughter against her mother,
a daughter-in-law against her
        mother-in-law—
³⁶   a man's enemies will be the
        members of his own
        household.'[b]

³⁷"Anyone who loves his father or mother more than me is not worthy of me; anyone who loves his son or daughter more than me is not worthy of me; ³⁸and anyone who does not take his cross and follow me is not worthy of me. ³⁹Whoever finds his life will lose it, and whoever loses his life for my sake will find it.

⁴⁰"He who receives you receives me, and he who receives me receives the one who sent me. ⁴¹Anyone who receives a prophet because he is a prophet will receive a prophet's reward, and anyone who receives a righteous man because he is a righteous man will receive a righteous man's reward. ⁴²And if anyone gives even

a cup of cold water to one of these little ones because he is my disciple, I tell you the truth, he will certainly not lose his reward."

Jesus and John the Baptist

11 After Jesus had finished instructing his twelve disciples, he went on from there to teach and preach in the towns of Galilee.[c]

²When John heard in prison what Christ was doing, he sent his disciples ³to ask him, "Are you the one who was to come, or should we expect someone else?"

⁴Jesus replied, "Go back and report to John what you hear and see: ⁵The blind receive sight, the lame walk, those who have leprosy[d] are cured, the deaf hear, the dead are raised, and the good news is preached to the poor. ⁶Blessed is the man who does not fall away on account of me."

⁷As John's disciples were leaving, Jesus began to speak to the crowd about John: "What did you go out into the desert to see? A reed swayed by the wind? ⁸If not, what did you go out to see? A man dressed in fine clothes? No, those who wear fine clothes are in kings' palaces. ⁹Then what did you go out to see? A prophet? Yes, I tell you, and more than a prophet. ¹⁰This is the one about whom it is written:

"'I will send my messenger ahead of
        you,
    who will prepare your way before
        you.'[e]

¹¹I tell you the truth: Among those born of women there has not risen anyone greater than John the Baptist; yet he who is least in the kingdom of heaven is greater than he. ¹²From the days of John the Baptist until now, the kingdom of heaven has been forcefully advancing, and forceful men lay hold of it. ¹³For all the Prophets and the Law prophesied un-

---

[a] *29* Greek *an assarion*   [b] *36* Micah 7:6   [c] *1* Greek *in their towns*   [d] *5* The Greek word was used for various diseases affecting the skin—not necessarily leprosy.   [e] *10* Mal. 3:1

til John. ¹⁴And if you are willing to accept it, he is the Elijah who was to come. ¹⁵He who has ears, let him hear.

¹⁶"To what can I compare this generation? They are like children sitting in the marketplaces and calling out to others:

¹⁷"'We played the flute for you,
   and you did not dance;
we sang a dirge,
   and you did not mourn.'

¹⁸For John came neither eating nor drinking, and they say, 'He has a demon.' ¹⁹The Son of Man came eating and drinking, and they say, 'Here is a glutton and a drunkard, a friend of tax collectors and "sinners."' But wisdom is proved right by her actions."

Woe on Unrepentant Cities

²⁰Then Jesus began to denounce the cities in which most of his miracles had been performed, because they did not repent. ²¹"Woe to you, Korazin! Woe to you, Bethsaida! If the miracles that were performed in you had been performed in Tyre and Sidon, they would have repented long ago in sackcloth and ashes. ²²But I tell you, it will be more bearable for Tyre and Sidon on the day of judgment than for you. ²³And you, Capernaum, will you be lifted up to the skies? No, you will go down to the depths.ᵃ If the miracles that were performed in you had been performed in Sodom, it would have remained to this day. ²⁴But I tell you that it will be more bearable for Sodom on the day of judgment than for you."

Rest for the Weary

²⁵At that time Jesus said, "I praise you, Father, Lord of heaven and earth, because you have hidden these things from the wise and learned, and revealed them to little children. ²⁶Yes, Father, for this was your good pleasure.

²⁷"All things have been committed to me by my Father. No one knows the Son except the Father, and no one knows the Father except the Son and those to whom the Son chooses to reveal him.

²⁸"Come to me, all you who are weary and burdened, and I will give you rest. ²⁹Take my yoke upon you and learn from me, for I am gentle and humble in heart, and you will find rest for your souls. ³⁰For my yoke is easy and my burden is light."

Lord of the Sabbath

12 At that time Jesus went through the grainfields on the Sabbath. His disciples were hungry and began to pick some heads of grain and eat them. ²When the Pharisees saw this, they said to him, "Look! Your disciples are doing what is unlawful on the Sabbath."

³He answered, "Haven't you read what David did when he and his companions were hungry? ⁴He entered the house of God, and he and his companions ate the consecrated bread—which was not lawful for them to do, but only for the priests. ⁵Or haven't you read in the Law that on the Sabbath the priests in the temple desecrate the day and yet are innocent? ⁶I tell you that oneᵇ greater than the temple is here. ⁷If you had known what these words mean, 'I desire mercy, not sacrifice,'ᶜ you would not have condemned the innocent. ⁸For the Son of Man is Lord of the Sabbath."

⁹Going on from that place, he went into their synagogue, ¹⁰and a man with a shriveled hand was there. Looking for a reason to accuse Jesus, they asked him, "Is it lawful to heal on the Sabbath?"

¹¹He said to them, "If any of you has a sheep and it falls into a pit on the Sabbath, will you not take hold of it and lift it out? ¹²How much more valuable is a man than a sheep! Therefore it is lawful to do good on the Sabbath."

¹³Then he said to the man, "Stretch out your hand." So he stretched it out and it was completely restored, just as sound as the other. ¹⁴But the Pharisees went out and plotted how they might kill Jesus.

ᵃ23 Greek *Hades*   ᵇ6 Or *something*; also in verses 41 and 42   ᶜ7 Hosea 6:6

God's Chosen Servant

15 Aware of this, Jesus withdrew from that place. Many followed him, and he healed all their sick, 16 warning them not to tell who he was. 17 This was to fulfill what was spoken through the prophet Isaiah:

18 "Here is my servant whom I have
      chosen,
   the one I love, in whom I delight;
 I will put my Spirit on him,
      and he will proclaim justice to the
         nations.
19 He will not quarrel or cry out;
   no one will hear his voice in the
      streets.
20 A bruised reed he will not break,
   and a smoldering wick he will not
      snuff out,
 till he leads justice to victory.
21   In his name the nations will put
         their hope."ᵃ

Jesus and Beelzebub

22 Then they brought him a demon-possessed man who was blind and mute, and Jesus healed him, so that he could both talk and see. 23 All the people were astonished and said, "Could this be the Son of David?"

24 But when the Pharisees heard this, they said, "It is only by Beelzebub,ᵇ the prince of demons, that this fellow drives out demons."

25 Jesus knew their thoughts and said to them, "Every kingdom divided against itself will be ruined, and every city or household divided against itself will not stand. 26 If Satan drives out Satan, he is divided against himself. How then can his kingdom stand? 27 And if I drive out demons by Beelzebub, by whom do your people drive them out? So then, they will be your judges. 28 But if I drive out demons by the Spirit of God, then the kingdom of God has come upon you.

29 "Or again, how can anyone enter a strong man's house and carry off his possessions unless he first ties up the strong man? Then he can rob his house.

30 "He who is not with me is against me, and he who does not gather with me scatters. 31 And so I tell you, every sin and blasphemy will be forgiven men, but the blasphemy against the Spirit will not be forgiven. 32 Anyone who speaks a word against the Son of Man will be forgiven, but anyone who speaks against the Holy Spirit will not be forgiven, either in this age or in the age to come.

33 "Make a tree good and its fruit will be good, or make a tree bad and its fruit will be bad, for a tree is recognized by its fruit. 34 You brood of vipers, how can you who are evil say anything good? For out of the overflow of the heart the mouth speaks. 35 The good man brings good things out of the good stored up in him, and the evil man brings evil things out of the evil stored up in him. 36 But I tell you that men will have to give account on the day of judgment for every careless word they have spoken. 37 For by your words you will be acquitted, and by your words you will be condemned."

The Sign of Jonah

38 Then some of the Pharisees and teachers of the law said to him, "Teacher, we want to see a miraculous sign from you."

39 He answered, "A wicked and adulterous generation asks for a miraculous sign! But none will be given it except the sign of the prophet Jonah. 40 For as Jonah was three days and three nights in the belly of a huge fish, so the Son of Man will be three days and three nights in the heart of the earth. 41 The men of Nineveh will stand up at the judgment with this generation and condemn it; for they repented at the preaching of Jonah, and now oneᶜ greater than Jonah is here. 42 The Queen of the South will rise at the judgment with this generation and condemn it; for she came from the ends of the earth to listen to Solomon's wisdom, and now one greater than Solomon is here.

ᵃ 21 Isaiah 42:1-4   ᵇ 24 Greek *Beezeboul* or *Beelzeboul*; also in verse 27   ᶜ 41 Or *something*; also in verse 42

[43]"When an evil[a] spirit comes out of a man, it goes through arid places seeking rest and does not find it. [44]Then it says, 'I will return to the house I left.' When it arrives, it finds the house unoccupied, swept clean and put in order. [45]Then it goes and takes with it seven other spirits more wicked than itself, and they go in and live there. And the final condition of that man is worse than the first. That is how it will be with this wicked generation."

Jesus' Mother and Brothers

[46]While Jesus was still talking to the crowd, his mother and brothers stood outside, wanting to speak to him. [47]Someone told him, "Your mother and brothers are standing outside, wanting to speak to you."[b]

[48]He replied to him, "Who is my mother, and who are my brothers?" [49]Pointing to his disciples, he said, "Here are my mother and my brothers. [50]For whoever does the will of my Father in heaven is my brother and sister and mother."

The Parable of the Sower

13 That same day Jesus went out of the house and sat by the lake. [2]Such large crowds gathered around him that he got into a boat and sat in it, while all the people stood on the shore. [3]Then he told them many things in parables, saying: "A farmer went out to sow his seed. [4]As he was scattering the seed, some fell along the path, and the birds came and ate it up. [5]Some fell on rocky places, where it did not have much soil. It sprang up quickly, because the soil was shallow. [6]But when the sun came up, the plants were scorched, and they withered because they had no root. [7]Other seed fell among thorns, which grew up and choked the plants. [8]Still other seed fell on good soil, where it produced a crop—a hundred, sixty or thirty times what was sown. [9]He who has ears, let him hear."

[10]The disciples came to him and asked, "Why do you speak to the people in parables?"

[11]He replied, "The knowledge of the secrets of the kingdom of heaven has been given to you, but not to them. [12]Whoever has will be given more, and he will have an abundance. Whoever does not have, even what he has will be taken from him. [13]This is why I speak to them in parables:

"Though seeing, they do not see;
    though hearing, they do not hear
        or understand.

[14]In them is fulfilled the prophecy of Isaiah:

"'You will be ever hearing but never
        understanding;
    you will be ever seeing but never
        perceiving.
[15]For this people's heart has become
        calloused;
    they hardly hear with their ears,
        and they have closed their eyes.
Otherwise they might see with their
        eyes,
    hear with their ears,
    understand with their hearts
and turn, and I would heal them.'[c]

[16]But blessed are your eyes because they see, and your ears because they hear. [17]For I tell you the truth, many prophets and righteous men longed to see what you see but did not see it, and to hear what you hear but did not hear it.

[18]"Listen then to what the parable of the sower means: [19]When anyone hears the message about the kingdom and does not understand it, the evil one comes and snatches away what was sown in his heart. This is the seed sown along the path. [20]The one who received the seed that fell on rocky places is the man who hears the word and at once receives it with joy. [21]But since he has no root, he lasts only a short time. When trouble or persecution comes because of the word, he quickly

falls away. ²²The one who received the seed that fell among the thorns is the man who hears the word, but the worries of this life and the deceitfulness of wealth choke it, making it unfruitful. ²³But the one who received the seed that fell on good soil is the man who hears the word and understands it. He produces a crop, yielding a hundred, sixty or thirty times what was sown."

The Parable of the Weeds

²⁴Jesus told them another parable:"The kingdom of heaven is like a man who sowed good seed in his field. ²⁵But while everyone was sleeping, his enemy came and sowed weeds among the wheat, and went away. ²⁶When the wheat sprouted and formed heads, then the weeds also appeared.

²⁷"The owner's servants came to him and said, 'Sir, didn't you sow good seed in your field? Where then did the weeds come from?'

²⁸"'An enemy did this,' he replied.

"The servants asked him, 'Do you want us to go and pull them up?'

²⁹"'No,' he answered, 'because while you are pulling the weeds, you may root up the wheat with them. ³⁰Let both grow together until the harvest. At that time I will tell the harvesters: First collect the weeds and tie them in bundles to be burned; then gather the wheat and bring it into my barn.'"

The Parables of the Mustard Seed and the Yeast

³¹He told them another parable: "The kingdom of heaven is like a mustard seed, which a man took and planted in his field. ³²Though it is the smallest of all your seeds, yet when it grows, it is the largest of garden plants and becomes a tree, so that the birds of the air come and perch in its branches."

³³He told them still another parable: "The kingdom of heaven is like yeast that a woman took and mixed into a large amount[a] of flour until it worked all through the dough."

³⁴Jesus spoke all these things to the crowd in parables; he did not say anything to them without using a parable. ³⁵So was fulfilled what was spoken through the prophet:

"I will open my mouth in parables,
  I will utter things hidden since the creation of the world."[b]

The Parable of the Weeds Explained

³⁶Then he left the crowd and went into the house. His disciples came to him and said, "Explain to us the parable of the weeds in the field."

³⁷He answered, "The one who sowed the good seed is the Son of Man. ³⁸The field is the world, and the good seed stands for the sons of the kingdom. The weeds are the sons of the evil one, ³⁹and the enemy who sows them is the devil. The harvest is the end of the age, and the harvesters are angels.

⁴⁰"As the weeds are pulled up and burned in the fire, so it will be at the end of the age. ⁴¹The Son of Man will send out his angels, and they will weed out of his kingdom everything that causes sin and all who do evil. ⁴²They will throw them into the fiery furnace, where there will be weeping and gnashing of teeth. ⁴³Then the righteous will shine like the sun in the kingdom of their Father. He who has ears, let him hear.

The Parables of the Hidden Treasure and the Pearl

⁴⁴"The kingdom of heaven is like treasure hidden in a field. When a man found it, he hid it again, and then in his joy went and sold all he had and bought that field.

Praying Matthew 13:46
*Father God, show me what I need
to give up in my life so that I can have
more of You; help me to sacrifice all
else for what is most important.*

---

a 33 Greek *three satas* (probably about 1/2 bushel or 22 liters)   b 35 Psalm 78:2

⁴⁵"Again, the kingdom of heaven is like a merchant looking for fine pearls. ⁴⁶When he found one of great value, he went away and sold everything he had and bought it.

The Parable of the Net

⁴⁷"Once again, the kingdom of heaven is like a net that was let down into the lake and caught all kinds of fish. ⁴⁸When it was full, the fishermen pulled it up on the shore. Then they sat down and collected the good fish in baskets, but threw the bad away. ⁴⁹This is how it will be at the end of the age. The angels will come and separate the wicked from the righteous ⁵⁰and throw them into the fiery furnace, where there will be weeping and gnashing of teeth.

⁵¹"Have you understood all these things?" Jesus asked.

"Yes," they replied.

⁵²He said to them, "Therefore every teacher of the law who has been instructed about the kingdom of heaven is like the owner of a house who brings out of his storeroom new treasures as well as old."

A Prophet Without Honor

⁵³When Jesus had finished these parables, he moved on from there. ⁵⁴Coming to his hometown, he began teaching the people in their synagogue, and they were amazed. "Where did this man get this wisdom and these miraculous powers?" they asked. ⁵⁵"Isn't this the carpenter's son? Isn't his mother's name Mary, and aren't his brothers James, Joseph, Simon and Judas? ⁵⁶Aren't all his sisters with us? Where then did this man get all these things?" ⁵⁷And they took offense at him.

But Jesus said to them, "Only in his hometown and in his own house is a prophet without honor."

⁵⁸And he did not do many miracles there because of their lack of faith.

John the Baptist Beheaded

14 At that time Herod the tetrarch heard the reports about Jesus, ²and he said to his attendants, "This is John the Baptist; he has risen from the dead! That is why miraculous powers are at work in him."

³Now Herod had arrested John and bound him and put him in prison because of Herodias, his brother Philip's wife, ⁴for John had been saying to him: "It is not lawful for you to have her." ⁵Herod wanted to kill John, but he was afraid of the people, because they considered him a prophet.

⁶On Herod's birthday the daughter of Herodias danced for them and pleased Herod so much ⁷that he promised with an oath to give her whatever she asked. ⁸Prompted by her mother, she said, "Give me here on a platter the head of John the Baptist." ⁹The king was distressed, but because of his oaths and his dinner guests, he ordered that her request be granted ¹⁰and had John beheaded in the prison. ¹¹His head was brought in on a platter and given to the girl, who carried it to her mother. ¹²John's disciples came and took his body and buried it. Then they went and told Jesus.

Jesus Feeds the Five Thousand

¹³When Jesus heard what had happened, he withdrew by boat privately to a solitary place. Hearing of this, the crowds followed him on foot from the towns. ¹⁴When Jesus landed and saw a large crowd, he had compassion on them and healed their sick.

¹⁵As evening approached, the disciples came to him and said, "This is a remote place, and it's already getting late. Send the crowds away, so they can go to the villages and buy themselves some food."

¹⁶Jesus replied, "They do not need to go away. You give them something to eat."

¹⁷"We have here only five loaves of bread and two fish," they answered.

¹⁸"Bring them here to me," he said. ¹⁹And he directed the people to sit down on the grass. Taking the five loaves and the two fish and looking up to heaven, he gave thanks and broke the loaves. Then he gave them to the disciples, and the

disciples gave them to the people. 20 They all ate and were satisfied, and the disciples picked up twelve basketfuls of broken pieces that were left over. 21 The number of those who ate was about five thousand men, besides women and children.

Jesus Walks on the Water

22 Immediately Jesus made the disciples get into the boat and go on ahead of him to the other side, while he dismissed the crowd. 23 After he had dismissed them, he went up on a mountainside by himself to pray. When evening came, he was there alone, 24 but the boat was already a considerable distance[a] from land, buffeted by the waves because the wind was against it.

25 During the fourth watch of the night Jesus went out to them, walking on the lake. 26 When the disciples saw him walking on the lake, they were ter-

---

[a] 24 Greek *many stadia*

GOING *deeper*

The Value of Time Alone With God

READ AND CONSIDER: MATTHEW 14:22-23

"After he had dismissed them, he went up on a mountainside by himself to pray. When evening came, he was there alone" (Matthew 14:23).

Solitude—time alone—means different things to different people. Some have too little of it and treasure times of quiet with no one else around. Others who live alone may feel they have too much of it. "Alone" to them means "lonely."

There are examples throughout the Gospels of the value Jesus placed on solitude. He was surrounded each day by His disciples who He was teaching and training, and also by crowds of people who were hungry for His touch. Although He was fully God, He was also fully human. In order for Jesus to have the strength to minister continually, He had to make prayer a priority. When painful things happened, Jesus handled them by spending time alone with His Father. "When Jesus heard what had happened [the death of John the Baptist], he withdrew by boat privately to a solitary place" (14:13). Jesus was often alone, but never lonely. He was always spending time with God.

We don't have to ever be lonely either. When we are alone, we can be with God. On the other hand, if Jesus depended on regular times away to communicate with God in solitude, how much more do *we* need to make such times of quiet a priority in our lives!

We often speak of "finding" time to be alone with God, but that valuable time has a way of getting lost in the midst of our overcrowded schedules. We must change our focus from trying to *find* time to *making* time. I heard of one mother who paused each day and threw her apron over her head. When the children saw that, they knew it was Mama's time alone with God! It doesn't matter *how* we do it, we just have to do it.

If you find it hard to make time for solitude, remember that your heavenly Father is wanting and waiting to spend time with you. "The LORD your God is with you, he is mighty to save. He will take great delight in you, he will quiet you with his love, he will rejoice over you with singing" (Zephaniah 3:17). Don't keep God waiting.

Whether you are surrounded by a noisy family or you live entirely isolated, take great joy in making time to be alone with God. "Alone" never has to mean "lonely" when you have the Lord in your life!

rified. "It's a ghost," they said, and cried out in fear.

27But Jesus immediately said to them: "Take courage! It is I. Don't be afraid."

28"Lord, if it's you," Peter replied, "tell me to come to you on the water."

29"Come," he said.

Then Peter got down out of the boat, walked on the water and came toward Jesus. 30But when he saw the wind, he was afraid and, beginning to sink, cried out, "Lord, save me!"

31Immediately Jesus reached out his hand and caught him. "You of little faith," he said, "why did you doubt?"

32And when they climbed into the boat, the wind died down. 33Then those who were in the boat worshiped him, saying, "Truly you are the Son of God."

34When they had crossed over, they landed at Gennesaret. 35And when the men of that place recognized Jesus, they sent word to all the surrounding country. People brought all their sick to him 36and begged him to let the sick just touch the edge of his cloak, and all who touched him were healed.

Clean and Unclean

15 Then some Pharisees and teachers of the law came to Jesus from Jerusalem and asked, 2"Why do your disciples break the tradition of the elders? They don't wash their hands before they eat!"

3Jesus replied, "And why do you break the command of God for the sake of your tradition? 4For God said, 'Honor your father and mother'a and 'Anyone who curses his father or mother must be put to death.'b 5But you say that if a man says to his father or mother, 'Whatever help you might otherwise have received from me is a gift devoted to God,' 6he is not to 'honor his father'c with it. Thus you nullify the word of God for the sake of your tradition. 7You hypocrites! Isaiah was right when he prophesied about you:

8"'These people honor me with their lips,
    but their hearts are far from me.
9They worship me in vain;
    their teachings are but rules taught by men.'d"

10Jesus called the crowd to him and said, "Listen and understand. 11What goes into a man's mouth does not make him 'unclean,' but what comes out of his mouth, that is what makes him 'unclean.'"

12Then the disciples came to him and asked, "Do you know that the Pharisees were offended when they heard this?"

13He replied, "Every plant that my heavenly Father has not planted will be pulled up by the roots. 14Leave them; they are blind guides.e If a blind man leads a blind man, both will fall into a pit."

15Peter said, "Explain the parable to us."

16"Are you still so dull?" Jesus asked them. 17"Don't you see that whatever enters the mouth goes into the stomach and then out of the body? 18But the things that come out of the mouth come from the heart, and these make a man 'unclean.' 19For out of the heart come evil thoughts, murder, adultery, sexual immorality, theft, false testimony, slander. 20These are what make a man 'unclean'; but eating with unwashed hands does not make him 'unclean.'"

The Faith of the Canaanite Woman

21Leaving that place, Jesus withdrew to the region of Tyre and Sidon. 22A Canaanite woman from that vicinity came to him, crying out, "Lord, Son of David, have mercy on me! My daughter is suffering terribly from demon-possession."

23Jesus did not answer a word. So his disciples came to him and urged him, "Send her away, for she keeps crying out after us."

24He answered, "I was sent only to the lost sheep of Israel."

---

a 4 Exodus 20:12; Deut. 5:16   b 4 Exodus 21:17; Lev. 20:9   c 6 Some manuscripts father or his mother   d 9 Isaiah 29:13
e 14 Some manuscripts guides of the blind

25 The woman came and knelt before him. "Lord, help me!" she said.

26 He replied, "It is not right to take the children's bread and toss it to their dogs."

27 "Yes, Lord," she said, "but even the dogs eat the crumbs that fall from their masters' table."

28 Then Jesus answered, "Woman, you have great faith! Your request is granted." And her daughter was healed from that very hour.

Jesus Feeds the Four Thousand

29 Jesus left there and went along the Sea of Galilee. Then he went up on a mountainside and sat down. 30 Great crowds came to him, bringing the lame, the blind, the crippled, the mute and many others, and laid them at his feet; and he healed them. 31 The people were amazed when they saw the mute speaking, the crippled made well, the lame walking and the blind seeing. And they praised the God of Israel.

32 Jesus called his disciples to him and said, "I have compassion for these people; they have already been with me three days and have nothing to eat. I do not want to send them away hungry, or they may collapse on the way."

33 His disciples answered, "Where could we get enough bread in this remote place to feed such a crowd?"

34 "How many loaves do you have?" Jesus asked.

"Seven," they replied, "and a few small fish."

35 He told the crowd to sit down on the ground. 36 Then he took the seven loaves and the fish, and when he had given thanks, he broke them and gave them to the disciples, and they in turn to the people. 37 They all ate and were satisfied. Afterward the disciples picked up seven basketfuls of broken pieces that were left over. 38 The number of those who ate was four thousand, besides women and children. 39 After Jesus had sent the crowd away, he got into the boat and went to the vicinity of Magadan.

The Demand for a Sign

16 The Pharisees and Sadducees came to Jesus and tested him by asking him to show them a sign from heaven.

2 He replied,[a] "When evening comes, you say, 'It will be fair weather, for the sky is red,' 3 and in the morning, 'Today it will be stormy, for the sky is red and overcast.' You know how to interpret the appearance of the sky, but you cannot interpret the signs of the times. 4 A wicked and adulterous generation looks for a miraculous sign, but none will be given it except the sign of Jonah." Jesus then left them and went away.

The Yeast of the Pharisees and Sadducees

5 When they went across the lake, the disciples forgot to take bread. 6 "Be careful," Jesus said to them. "Be on your guard against the yeast of the Pharisees and Sadducees."

7 They discussed this among themselves and said, "It is because we didn't bring any bread."

8 Aware of their discussion, Jesus asked, "You of little faith, why are you talking among yourselves about having no bread? 9 Do you still not understand? Don't you remember the five loaves for the five thousand, and how many basketfuls you gathered? 10 Or the seven loaves for the four thousand, and how many basketfuls you gathered? 11 How is it you don't understand that I was not talking to you about bread? But be on your guard against the yeast of the Pharisees and Sadducees." 12 Then they understood that he was not telling them to guard against the yeast used in bread, but against the teaching of the Pharisees and Sadducees.

Peter's Confession of Christ

13 When Jesus came to the region of Caesarea Philippi, he asked his disciples, "Who do people say the Son of Man is?"

a 2 Some early manuscripts do not have the rest of verse 2 and all of verse 3.

[14]They replied, "Some say John the Baptist; others say Elijah; and still others, Jeremiah or one of the prophets."

[15]"But what about you?" he asked. "Who do you say I am?"

[16]Simon Peter answered, "You are the Christ,[a] the Son of the living God."

[17]Jesus replied, "Blessed are you, Simon son of Jonah, for this was not revealed to you by man, but by my Father in heaven. [18]And I tell you that you are Peter,[b] and on this rock I will build my church, and the gates of Hades[c] will not overcome it.[d] [19]I will give you the keys of the kingdom of heaven; whatever you bind on earth will be[e] bound in heaven, and whatever you loose on earth will be[e] loosed in heaven." [20]Then he warned his disciples not to tell anyone that he was the Christ.

Jesus Predicts His Death

[21]From that time on Jesus began to explain to his disciples that he must go to Jerusalem and suffer many things at the hands of the elders, chief priests and teachers of the law, and that he must be killed and on the third day be raised to life.

[22]Peter took him aside and began to rebuke him. "Never, Lord!" he said. "This shall never happen to you!"

[23]Jesus turned and said to Peter, "Get behind me, Satan! You are a stumbling block to me; you do not have in mind the things of God, but the things of men."

[24]Then Jesus said to his disciples, "If anyone would come after me, he must deny himself and take up his cross and follow me. [25]For whoever wants to save his life[f] will lose it, but whoever loses his life for me will find it. [26]What good will it be for a man if he gains the whole world, yet forfeits his soul? Or what can a man give in exchange for his soul? [27]For the Son of Man is going to come in his Father's glory with his angels, and then he will reward each person according to what he has done. [28]I tell you the truth, some who are standing here will not taste death before they see the Son of Man coming in his kingdom."

The Transfiguration

17 After six days Jesus took with him Peter, James and John the brother of James, and led them up a high mountain by themselves. [2]There he was transfigured before them. His face shone like the sun, and his clothes became as white as the light. [3]Just then there appeared before them Moses and Elijah, talking with Jesus.

[4]Peter said to Jesus, "Lord, it is good for us to be here. If you wish, I will put up three shelters—one for you, one for Moses and one for Elijah."

[5]While he was still speaking, a bright cloud enveloped them, and a voice from the cloud said, "This is my Son, whom I love; with him I am well pleased. Listen to him!"

[6]When the disciples heard this, they fell facedown to the ground, terrified. [7]But Jesus came and touched them. "Get up," he said. "Don't be afraid." [8]When they looked up, they saw no one except Jesus.

[9]As they were coming down the mountain, Jesus instructed them, "Don't tell anyone what you have seen, until the Son of Man has been raised from the dead."

[10]The disciples asked him, "Why then do the teachers of the law say that Elijah must come first?"

[11]Jesus replied, "To be sure, Elijah comes and will restore all things. [12]But I tell you, Elijah has already come, and they did not recognize him, but have done to him everything they wished. In the same way the Son of Man is going to suffer at their hands." [13]Then the disciples understood that he was talking to them about John the Baptist.

The Healing of a Boy With a Demon

[14]When they came to the crowd, a man approached Jesus and knelt before him. [15]"Lord, have mercy on my son," he said.

---

[a] 16 Or Messiah; also in verse 20   [b] 18 Peter means rock.   [c] 18 Or hell   [d] 18 Or not prove stronger than it   [e] 19 Or have been
[f] 25 The Greek word means either life or soul; also in verse 26.

"He has seizures and is suffering greatly. He often falls into the fire or into the water. 16I brought him to your disciples, but they could not heal him."

17"O unbelieving and perverse generation," Jesus replied, "how long shall I stay with you? How long shall I put up with you? Bring the boy here to me." 18Jesus rebuked the demon, and it came out of the boy, and he was healed from that moment.

19Then the disciples came to Jesus in private and asked, "Why couldn't we drive it out?"

20He replied, "Because you have so little faith. I tell you the truth, if you have faith as small as a mustard seed, you can say to this mountain, 'Move from here to there' and it will move. Nothing will be impossible for you.ᵃ"

Praying Matthew 17:20

Lord, give me the kind of faith that can move mountains in my life.

22When they came together in Galilee, he said to them, "The Son of Man is going to be betrayed into the hands of men. 23They will kill him, and on the third day he will be raised to life." And the disciples were filled with grief.

The Temple Tax

24After Jesus and his disciples arrived in Capernaum, the collectors of the two-drachma tax came to Peter and asked, "Doesn't your teacher pay the temple taxᵇ?"

25"Yes, he does," he replied.

When Peter came into the house, Jesus was the first to speak. "What do you think, Simon?" he asked. "From whom do the kings of the earth collect duty and taxes— from their own sons or from others?"

26"From others," Peter answered.

"Then the sons are exempt," Jesus said to him. 27"But so that we may not offend them, go to the lake and throw out your line. Take the first fish you catch; open its mouth and you will find a four-drachma coin. Take it and give it to them for my tax and yours."

The Greatest in the Kingdom of Heaven

18 At that time the disciples came to Jesus and asked, "Who is the greatest in the kingdom of heaven?"

2He called a little child and had him stand among them. 3And he said: "I tell you the truth, unless you change and become like little children, you will never enter the kingdom of heaven. 4Therefore, whoever humbles himself like this child is the greatest in the kingdom of heaven.

5"And whoever welcomes a little child like this in my name welcomes me. 6But if anyone causes one of these little ones who believe in me to sin, it would be better for him to have a large millstone hung around his neck and to be drowned in the depths of the sea.

7"Woe to the world because of the things that cause people to sin! Such things must come, but woe to the man through whom they come! 8If your hand or your foot causes you to sin, cut it off and throw it away. It is better for you to enter life maimed or crippled than to have two hands or two feet and be thrown into eternal fire. 9And if your eye causes you to sin, gouge it out and throw it away. It is better for you to enter life with one eye than to have two eyes and be thrown into the fire of hell.

The Parable of the Lost Sheep

10"See that you do not look down on one of these little ones. For I tell you that their angels in heaven always see the face of my Father in heaven.ᶜ

12"What do you think? If a man owns a hundred sheep, and one of them wanders away, will he not leave the ninety-nine on the hills and go to look for the one that wandered off? 13And if he finds it, I

ᵃ *20 Some manuscripts you. 21But this kind does not go out except by prayer and fasting.*   ᵇ *24 Greek the two drachmas*
ᶜ *10 Some manuscripts heaven. 11The Son of Man came to save what was lost.*

Creating a Symphony of Prayer

GOING deeper

READ AND CONSIDER: MATTHEW 18:18-20

"Again, I tell you that if two of you on earth agree about anything you ask for, it will be done for you by my Father in heaven" (Matthew 18:19).

One of the first things we need to learn about praying with others is the need for unity. Jesus said "If you agree . . . it will be done." That word *agree* is very important. The Greek word for "unity" is *sumphoneo*. It's where we get the word "symphony." In order to have harmony, there are a number of things we need to agree on.

First of all, we need to agree on the basics, which are the very foundation of our faith. Foremost among these is that Jesus is "the way and the truth and the life" and "no one comes to the Father except through" Him (John 14:6). We must also agree that the Bible is inerrant—without fault in its original translation—and inspired by God. We agree that Jesus was born of a virgin and lived a sinless life, that He died for our sins and rose from the dead, and that whoever believes in Him will have everlasting life.

Second, we need to be in agreement about what we are requesting from God. For example, if your marriage is in trouble, you can pray with your spouse or with a trusted friend and agree together that marriage is a covenant ordained by God. Then ask God to be at the center of your marriage and a reflection of Christ's love for His people (Ephesians 5:31-32). Or another example is if you are in need or struggling in an area, you can join one or more people and agree that Satan will not have victory in this situation.

The Bible says that one can put a thousand to flight and two can put ten thousand to flight (Deuteronomy 32:30). If you do the math, you will see how powerful two or more people can be when they join together and agree in prayer about whatever concerns them.

Unity within the body of Christ is extremely important to God, and unity in prayer is a critical part of that. The very night He was betrayed, Jesus prayed for all believers everywhere that we might experience true unity. "May they be brought to complete unity to let the world know that you sent me and have loved them even as you have loved me" (John 17:23).

When we agree together in prayer, our words create a rich symphony of intercession that is carried to the very throne of God. Nothing is more beautiful to the ear of the Lord than the sound of the unified prayers of His people. Let the music begin.

---

tell you the truth, he is happier about that one sheep than about the ninety-nine that did not wander off. [14]In the same way your Father in heaven is not willing that any of these little ones should be lost.

A Brother Who Sins Against You

[15]"If your brother sins against you,[a] go and show him his fault, just between the two of you. If he listens to you, you have won your brother over. [16]But if he will not listen, take one or two others along, so that 'every matter may be established by the testimony of two or three witnesses.'[b] [17]If he refuses to listen to them, tell it to the church; and if he refuses to listen even to the church, treat him as you would a pagan or a tax collector.

[18]"I tell you the truth, whatever you bind on earth will be[c] bound in heaven, and whatever you loose on earth will be[c] loosed in heaven.

---

[a] *15* Some manuscripts do not have *against you.*   [b] *16* Deut. 19:15   [c] *18* Or *have been*

[19]"Again, I tell you that if two of you on earth agree about anything you ask for, it will be done for you by my Father in heaven. [20]For where two or three come together in my name, there am I with them."

The Parable of the Unmerciful Servant

[21]Then Peter came to Jesus and asked, "Lord, how many times shall I forgive my brother when he sins against me? Up to seven times?"

[22]Jesus answered, "I tell you, not seven times, but seventy-seven times.[a]

[23]"Therefore, the kingdom of heaven is like a king who wanted to settle accounts with his servants. [24]As he began the settlement, a man who owed him ten thousand talents[b] was brought to him. [25]Since he was not able to pay, the master ordered that he and his wife and his children and all that he had be sold to repay the debt.

[26]"The servant fell on his knees before him. 'Be patient with me,' he begged, 'and I will pay back everything.' [27]The servant's master took pity on him, canceled the debt and let him go.

[28]"But when that servant went out, he found one of his fellow servants who owed him a hundred denarii.[c] He grabbed him and began to choke him. 'Pay back what you owe me!' he demanded.

[29]"His fellow servant fell to his knees and begged him, 'Be patient with me, and I will pay you back.'

[30]"But he refused. Instead, he went off and had the man thrown into prison until he could pay the debt. [31]When the other servants saw what had happened, they were greatly distressed and went and told their master everything that had happened.

[32]"Then the master called the servant in. 'You wicked servant,' he said, 'I canceled all that debt of yours because you begged me to. [33]Shouldn't you have had mercy on your fellow servant just as I had on you?' [34]In anger his master turned him over to the jailers to be tortured, until he should pay back all he owed.

[35]"This is how my heavenly Father will treat each of you unless you forgive your brother from your heart."

Divorce

19 When Jesus had finished saying these things, he left Galilee and went into the region of Judea to the other side of the Jordan. [2]Large crowds followed him, and he healed them there.

[3]Some Pharisees came to him to test him. They asked, "Is it lawful for a man to divorce his wife for any and every reason?"

[4]"Haven't you read," he replied, "that at the beginning the Creator 'made them male and female,'[d] [5]and said, 'For this reason a man will leave his father and mother and be united to his wife, and the two will become one flesh'[e]? [6]So they are no longer two, but one. Therefore what God has joined together, let man not separate."

[7]"Why then," they asked, "did Moses command that a man give his wife a certificate of divorce and send her away?"

[8]Jesus replied, "Moses permitted you to divorce your wives because your hearts were hard. But it was not this way from the beginning. [9]I tell you that anyone who divorces his wife, except for marital unfaithfulness, and marries another woman commits adultery."

[10]The disciples said to him, "If this is the situation between a husband and wife, it is better not to marry."

[11]Jesus replied, "Not everyone can accept this word, but only those to whom it has been given. [12]For some are eunuchs because they were born that way; others were made that way by men; and others have renounced marriage[f] because of the kingdom of heaven. The one who can accept this should accept it."

---

[a]22 Or seventy times seven   [b]24 That is, millions of dollars   [c]28 That is, a few dollars   [d]4 Gen. 1:27   [e]5 Gen. 2:24
[f]12 Or have made themselves eunuchs

The Little Children and Jesus

¹³Then little children were brought to Jesus for him to place his hands on them and pray for them. But the disciples rebuked those who brought them.

¹⁴Jesus said, "Let the little children come to me, and do not hinder them, for the kingdom of heaven belongs to such as these." ¹⁵When he had placed his hands on them, he went on from there.

The Rich Young Man

¹⁶Now a man came up to Jesus and asked, "Teacher, what good thing must I do to get eternal life?"

¹⁷"Why do you ask me about what is good?" Jesus replied. "There is only One who is good. If you want to enter life, obey the commandments."

¹⁸"Which ones?" the man inquired.

Jesus replied, " 'Do not murder, do not commit adultery, do not steal, do not give false testimony, ¹⁹honor your father and mother,'ᵃ and 'love your neighbor as yourself.'ᵇ"

²⁰"All these I have kept," the young man said. "What do I still lack?"

²¹Jesus answered, "If you want to be perfect, go, sell your possessions and give to the poor, and you will have treasure in heaven. Then come, follow me."

²²When the young man heard this, he went away sad, because he had great wealth.

²³Then Jesus said to his disciples, "I tell you the truth, it is hard for a rich man to enter the kingdom of heaven. ²⁴Again I tell you, it is easier for a camel to go through the eye of a needle than for a rich man to enter the kingdom of God."

²⁵When the disciples heard this, they were greatly astonished and asked, "Who then can be saved?"

²⁶Jesus looked at them and said, "With man this is impossible, but with God all things are possible."

²⁷Peter answered him, "We have left everything to follow you! What then will there be for us?"

Praying Matthew 19:26

Thank You, Lord, that with You all things are possible and I can face the seemingly impossible situations in my life with faith and hope.

²⁸Jesus said to them, "I tell you the truth, at the renewal of all things, when the Son of Man sits on his glorious throne, you who have followed me will also sit on twelve thrones, judging the twelve tribes of Israel. ²⁹And everyone who has left houses or brothers or sisters or father or motherᶜ or children or fields for my sake will receive a hundred times as much and will inherit eternal life. ³⁰But many who are first will be last, and many who are last will be first.

The Parable of the Workers in the Vineyard

20 "For the kingdom of heaven is like a landowner who went out early in the morning to hire men to work in his vineyard. ²He agreed to pay them a denarius for the day and sent them into his vineyard.

³"About the third hour he went out and saw others standing in the marketplace doing nothing. ⁴He told them, 'You also go and work in my vineyard, and I will pay you whatever is right.' ⁵So they went.

"He went out again about the sixth hour and the ninth hour and did the same thing. ⁶About the eleventh hour he went out and found still others standing around. He asked them, 'Why have you been standing here all day long doing nothing?'

⁷" 'Because no one has hired us,' they answered.

"He said to them, 'You also go and work in my vineyard.'

⁸"When evening came, the owner of the vineyard said to his foreman, 'Call the workers and pay them their wages, beginning with the last ones hired and going on to the first.'

ᵃ *19* Exodus 20:12-16; Deut. 5:16-20   ᵇ *19* Lev. 19:18   ᶜ *29* Some manuscripts *mother or wife*

9"The workers who were hired about the eleventh hour came and each received a denarius. 10So when those came who were hired first, they expected to receive more. But each one of them also received a denarius. 11When they received it, they began to grumble against the landowner. 12'These men who were hired last worked only one hour,' they said, 'and you have made them equal to us who have borne the burden of the work and the heat of the day.'

13"But he answered one of them, 'Friend, I am not being unfair to you. Didn't you agree to work for a denarius? 14Take your pay and go. I want to give the man who was hired last the same as I gave you. 15Don't I have the right to do what I want with my own money? Or are you envious because I am generous?'

16"So the last will be first, and the first will be last."

Jesus Again Predicts His Death

17Now as Jesus was going up to Jerusalem, he took the twelve disciples aside and said to them, 18"We are going up to Jerusalem, and the Son of Man will be betrayed to the chief priests and the teachers of the law. They will condemn him to death 19and will turn him over to the Gentiles to be mocked and flogged and crucified. On the third day he will be raised to life!"

A Mother's Request

20Then the mother of Zebedee's sons came to Jesus with her sons and, kneeling down, asked a favor of him.

21"What is it you want?" he asked.

She said, "Grant that one of these two sons of mine may sit at your right and the other at your left in your kingdom."

22"You don't know what you are asking," Jesus said to them. "Can you drink the cup I am going to drink?"

"We can," they answered.

23Jesus said to them, "You will indeed drink from my cup, but to sit at my right or left is not for me to grant. These places belong to those for whom they have been prepared by my Father."

24When the ten heard about this, they were indignant with the two brothers. 25Jesus called them together and said, "You know that the rulers of the Gentiles lord it over them, and their high officials exercise authority over them. 26Not so with you. Instead, whoever wants to become great among you must be your servant, 27and whoever wants to be first must be your slave— 28just as the Son of Man did not come to be served, but to serve, and to give his life as a ransom for many."

Two Blind Men Receive Sight

29As Jesus and his disciples were leaving Jericho, a large crowd followed him. 30Two blind men were sitting by the roadside, and when they heard that Jesus was going by, they shouted, "Lord, Son of David, have mercy on us!"

31The crowd rebuked them and told them to be quiet, but they shouted all the louder, "Lord, Son of David, have mercy on us!"

32Jesus stopped and called them. "What do you want me to do for you?" he asked.

33"Lord," they answered, "we want our sight."

34Jesus had compassion on them and touched their eyes. Immediately they received their sight and followed him.

The Triumphal Entry

21 As they approached Jerusalem and came to Bethphage on the Mount of Olives, Jesus sent two disciples, 2saying to them, "Go to the village ahead of you, and at once you will find a donkey tied there, with her colt by her. Untie them and bring them to me. 3If anyone says anything to you, tell him that the Lord needs them, and he will send them right away."

4This took place to fulfill what was spoken through the prophet:

5"Say to the Daughter of Zion,
    'See, your king comes to you,

gentle and riding on a donkey,
  on a colt, the foal of a donkey.' "[a]

[6]The disciples went and did as Jesus had instructed them. [7]They brought the donkey and the colt, placed their cloaks on them, and Jesus sat on them. [8]A very large crowd spread their cloaks on the road, while others cut branches from the trees and spread them on the road. [9]The crowds that went ahead of him and those that followed shouted,

"Hosanna[b] to the Son of David!"

"Blessed is he who comes in the name
  of the Lord!"[c]

"Hosanna[b] in the highest!"

[10]When Jesus entered Jerusalem, the whole city was stirred and asked, "Who is this?"

[11]The crowds answered, "This is Jesus, the prophet from Nazareth in Galilee."

Jesus at the Temple

[12]Jesus entered the temple area and drove out all who were buying and selling there. He overturned the tables of the money changers and the benches of those selling doves. [13]"It is written," he said to them, " 'My house will be called a house of prayer,'[d] but you are making it a 'den of robbers.'[e]"

[14]The blind and the lame came to him at the temple, and he healed them. [15]But when the chief priests and the teachers of the law saw the wonderful things he did and the children shouting in the temple area, "Hosanna to the Son of David," they were indignant.

[16]"Do you hear what these children are saying?" they asked him.

"Yes," replied Jesus, "have you never read,

" 'From the lips of children and
    infants
  you have ordained praise'[f]?"

[17]And he left them and went out of the city to Bethany, where he spent the night.

The Fig Tree Withers

[18]Early in the morning, as he was on his way back to the city, he was hungry. [19]Seeing a fig tree by the road, he went up to it but found nothing on it except leaves. Then he said to it, "May you never bear fruit again!" Immediately the tree withered.

[20]When the disciples saw this, they were amazed. "How did the fig tree wither so quickly?" they asked.

[21]Jesus replied, "I tell you the truth, if you have faith and do not doubt, not only can you do what was done to the fig tree, but also you can say to this mountain, 'Go, throw yourself into the sea,' and it will be done. [22]If you believe, you will receive whatever you ask for in prayer."

The Authority of Jesus Questioned

[23]Jesus entered the temple courts, and, while he was teaching, the chief priests and the elders of the people came to him. "By what authority are you doing these things?" they asked. "And who gave you this authority?"

[24]Jesus replied, "I will also ask you one question. If you answer me, I will tell you by what authority I am doing these things. [25]John's baptism—where did it come from? Was it from heaven, or from men?"

They discussed it among themselves and said, "If we say, 'From heaven,' he will ask, 'Then why didn't you believe him?' [26]But if we say, 'From men'—we are afraid of the people, for they all hold that John was a prophet."

[27]So they answered Jesus, "We don't know."

Then he said, "Neither will I tell you by what authority I am doing these things.

---

[a] 5 Zech. 9:9   [b] 9 A Hebrew expression meaning "Save!" which became an exclamation of praise; also in verse 15
[c] 9 Psalm 118:26   [d] 13 Isaiah 56:7   [e] 13 Jer. 7:11   [f] 16 Psalm 8:2

GOING *deeper*

Learning to Believe

READ AND CONSIDER: MATTHEW 21:21-22

"If you believe, you will receive whatever you ask for in prayer" (Matthew 21:22).

What a great promise from our Lord! All we have to do is believe. But that's not so easy, is it? It's easier to doubt than it is to have faith to believe for the answers to our prayers. But faith is not about trusting in faith itself, it's about trusting God and what He says in His Word. It's about confidently claiming the promises of God, believing that God means what He says.

Jesus promised His disciples, "You'll receive whatever you ask for in prayer," on one condition: "If you believe." Believe in what? In our own request? Does this mean we can get whatever we ask for, anything at all, no matter how grandiose our desires? The answer is no. Are we to believe in our own great faith? We would be foolish to do that. We are to believe God and trust in His perfect will.

It's important to remember that God's will never contradicts His Word. Yes, we are to pray for whatever we need, but if those needs and desires run contrary to the will of God, He is not going to give them to us. Our loving Father will not go against His own nature or give us that which is detrimental to the best that He has for us. At times, something may seem to us to be perfectly within God's will—and we should pray with all our heart—but we should still remember that only God sees the big picture. In the long run, what we are praying for may not be what's best at all.

Praying is not telling God what to do. Praying is communicating the desires of your heart. It's trusting that *God* knows what to do, and He will answer in His way and in His time. Faith is believing God hears and will do the right thing. When you also pray that God's will be done in your life, you can release your requests into God's hands, believing He has heard you and will do what's best.

Faith has to do with believing that God is who He says He is and will do what He says He will. In order to increase your faith, read God's Word and ask Him to help you learn to believe Him. Ask Him to give you a greater measure of faith and the ability to walk confidently in the faith He has given you.

The Parable of the Two Sons

28 "What do you think? There was a man who had two sons. He went to the first and said, 'Son, go and work today in the vineyard.'

29 " 'I will not,' he answered, but later he changed his mind and went.

30 "Then the father went to the other son and said the same thing. He answered, 'I will, sir,' but he did not go.

31 "Which of the two did what his father wanted?"

"The first," they answered.

Jesus said to them, "I tell you the truth, the tax collectors and the prostitutes are entering the kingdom of God ahead of you. 32 For John came to you to show you the way of righteousness, and you did not believe him, but the tax collectors and the prostitutes did. And even after you saw this, you did not repent and believe him.

The Parable of the Tenants

33 "Listen to another parable: There was a landowner who planted a vineyard. He put a wall around it, dug a winepress in it and built a watchtower. Then he rented

the vineyard to some farmers and went away on a journey. 34When the harvest time approached, he sent his servants to the tenants to collect his fruit.

35"The tenants seized his servants; they beat one, killed another, and stoned a third. 36Then he sent other servants to them, more than the first time, and the tenants treated them the same way. 37Last of all, he sent his son to them. 'They will respect my son,' he said.

38"But when the tenants saw the son, they said to each other, 'This is the heir. Come, let's kill him and take his inheritance.' 39So they took him and threw him out of the vineyard and killed him.

40"Therefore, when the owner of the vineyard comes, what will he do to those tenants?"

41"He will bring those wretches to a wretched end," they replied, "and he will rent the vineyard to other tenants, who will give him his share of the crop at harvest time."

42Jesus said to them, "Have you never read in the Scriptures:

"'The stone the builders rejected
    has become the capstone[a];
  the Lord has done this,
    and it is marvelous in our eyes'[b]?

43"Therefore I tell you that the kingdom of God will be taken away from you and given to a people who will produce its fruit. 44He who falls on this stone will be broken to pieces, but he on whom it falls will be crushed."[c]

45When the chief priests and the Pharisees heard Jesus' parables, they knew he was talking about them. 46They looked for a way to arrest him, but they were afraid of the crowd because the people held that he was a prophet.

The Parable of the Wedding Banquet

22 Jesus spoke to them again in parables, saying: 2"The kingdom of heaven is like a king who prepared a wedding banquet for his son. 3He sent his servants to those who had been invited to the banquet to tell them to come, but they refused to come.

4"Then he sent some more servants and said, 'Tell those who have been invited that I have prepared my dinner: My oxen and fattened cattle have been butchered, and everything is ready. Come to the wedding banquet.'

5"But they paid no attention and went off—one to his field, another to his business. 6The rest seized his servants, mistreated them and killed them. 7The king was enraged. He sent his army and destroyed those murderers and burned their city.

8"Then he said to his servants, 'The wedding banquet is ready, but those I invited did not deserve to come. 9Go to the street corners and invite to the banquet anyone you find.' 10So the servants went out into the streets and gathered all the people they could find, both good and bad, and the wedding hall was filled with guests.

11"But when the king came in to see the guests, he noticed a man there who was not wearing wedding clothes. 12'Friend,' he asked, 'how did you get in here without wedding clothes?' The man was speechless.

13"Then the king told the attendants, 'Tie him hand and foot, and throw him outside, into the darkness, where there will be weeping and gnashing of teeth.'

14"For many are invited, but few are chosen."

Paying Taxes to Caesar

15Then the Pharisees went out and laid plans to trap him in his words. 16They sent their disciples to him along with the Herodians. "Teacher," they said, "we know you are a man of integrity and that you teach the way of God in accordance with the truth. You aren't swayed by men, because you pay no attention to who they are. 17Tell us then, what is your opinion? Is it right to pay taxes to Caesar or not?"

---

a 42 Or cornerstone   b 42 Psalm 118:22,23   c 44 Some manuscripts do not have verse 44.

18But Jesus, knowing their evil intent, said, "You hypocrites, why are you trying to trap me? 19Show me the coin used for paying the tax." They brought him a denarius, 20and he asked them, "Whose portrait is this? And whose inscription?"

21"Caesar's," they replied.

Then he said to them, "Give to Caesar what is Caesar's, and to God what is God's."

22When they heard this, they were amazed. So they left him and went away.

Marriage at the Resurrection

23That same day the Sadducees, who say there is no resurrection, came to him with a question. 24"Teacher," they said, "Moses told us that if a man dies without having children, his brother must marry the widow and have children for him. 25Now there were seven brothers among us. The first one married and died, and since he had no children, he left his wife to his brother. 26The same thing happened to the second and third brother, right on down to the seventh. 27Finally, the woman died. 28Now then, at the resurrection, whose wife will she be of the seven, since all of them were married to her?"

29Jesus replied, "You are in error because you do not know the Scriptures or the power of God. 30At the resurrection people will neither marry nor be given in marriage; they will be like the angels in heaven. 31But about the resurrection of the dead—have you not read what God said to you, 32'I am the God of Abraham, the God of Isaac, and the God of Jacob'a? He is not the God of the dead but of the living."

33When the crowds heard this, they were astonished at his teaching.

The Greatest Commandment

34Hearing that Jesus had silenced the Sadducees, the Pharisees got together. 35One of them, an expert in the law, tested him with this question: 36"Teacher, which is the greatest commandment in the Law?"

37Jesus replied: "'Love the Lord your God with all your heart and with all your soul and with all your mind.'b 38This is the first and greatest commandment. 39And the second is like it: 'Love your neighbor as yourself.'c 40All the Law and the Prophets hang on these two commandments."

Whose Son Is the Christ?

41While the Pharisees were gathered together, Jesus asked them, 42"What do you think about the Christd? Whose son is he?"

"The son of David," they replied.

43He said to them, "How is it then that David, speaking by the Spirit, calls him 'Lord'? For he says,

44"'The Lord said to my Lord:
  "Sit at my right hand
  until I put your enemies
    under your feet."'e

45If then David calls him 'Lord,' how can he be his son?" 46No one could say a word in reply, and from that day on no one dared to ask him any more questions.

Seven Woes

23 Then Jesus said to the crowds and to his disciples: 2"The teachers of the law and the Pharisees sit in Moses' seat. 3So you must obey them and do everything they tell you. But do not do what they do, for they do not practice what they preach. 4They tie up heavy loads and put them on men's shoulders, but they themselves are not willing to lift a finger to move them.

5"Everything they do is done for men to see: They make their phylacteriesf wide and the tassels on their garments long; 6they love the place of honor at banquets and the most important seats in the synagogues; 7they love to be greeted in the marketplaces and to have men call them 'Rabbi.'

---

a 32 Exodus 3:6   b 37 Deut. 6:5   c 39 Lev. 19:18   d 42 Or Messiah   e 44 Psalm 110:1   f 5 That is, boxes containing Scripture verses, worn on forehead and arm

8"But you are not to be called 'Rabbi,' for you have only one Master and you are all brothers. 9And do not call anyone on earth 'father,' for you have one Father, and he is in heaven. 10Nor are you to be called 'teacher,' for you have one Teacher, the Christ.[a] 11The greatest among you will be your servant. 12For whoever exalts himself will be humbled, and whoever humbles himself will be exalted.

Praying Matthew 23:10-11

Father, I pray that You would give me a servant's heart and show me how I can serve You and others better.

13"Woe to you, teachers of the law and Pharisees, you hypocrites! You shut the kingdom of heaven in men's faces. You yourselves do not enter, nor will you let those who are trying to.[b]

15"Woe to you, teachers of the law and Pharisees, you hypocrites! You travel over land and sea to win a single convert, and when he becomes one, you make him twice as much a son of hell as you are.

16"Woe to you, blind guides! You say, 'If anyone swears by the temple, it means nothing; but if anyone swears by the gold of the temple, he is bound by his oath.' 17You blind fools! Which is greater: the gold, or the temple that makes the gold sacred? 18You also say, 'If anyone swears by the altar, it means nothing; but if anyone swears by the gift on it, he is bound by his oath.' 19You blind men! Which is greater: the gift, or the altar that makes the gift sacred? 20Therefore, he who swears by the altar swears by it and by everything on it. 21And he who swears by the temple swears by it and by the one who dwells in it. 22And he who swears by heaven swears by God's throne and by the one who sits on it.

23"Woe to you, teachers of the law and Pharisees, you hypocrites! You give a tenth of your spices—mint, dill and cum-min. But you have neglected the more important matters of the law—justice, mercy and faithfulness. You should have practiced the latter, without neglecting the former. 24You blind guides! You strain out a gnat but swallow a camel.

25"Woe to you, teachers of the law and Pharisees, you hypocrites! You clean the outside of the cup and dish, but inside they are full of greed and self-indulgence. 26Blind Pharisee! First clean the inside of the cup and dish, and then the outside also will be clean.

27"Woe to you, teachers of the law and Pharisees, you hypocrites! You are like whitewashed tombs, which look beautiful on the outside but on the inside are full of dead men's bones and everything unclean. 28In the same way, on the outside you appear to people as righteous but on the inside you are full of hypocrisy and wickedness.

29"Woe to you, teachers of the law and Pharisees, you hypocrites! You build tombs for the prophets and decorate the graves of the righteous. 30And you say, 'If we had lived in the days of our forefathers, we would not have taken part with them in shedding the blood of the prophets.' 31So you testify against yourselves that you are the descendants of those who murdered the prophets. 32Fill up, then, the measure of the sin of your forefathers!

33"You snakes! You brood of vipers! How will you escape being condemned to hell? 34Therefore I am sending you prophets and wise men and teachers. Some of them you will kill and crucify; others you will flog in your synagogues and pursue from town to town. 35And so upon you will come all the righteous blood that has been shed on earth, from the blood of righteous Abel to the blood of Zechariah son of Berekiah, whom you murdered between the temple and the altar. 36I tell you the truth, all this will come upon this generation.

---

a 10 Or *Messiah*   b 13 Some manuscripts *to.* 14*Woe to you, teachers of the law and Pharisees, you hypocrites! You devour widows' houses and for a show make lengthy prayers. Therefore you will be punished more severely.*

37"O Jerusalem, Jerusalem, you who kill the prophets and stone those sent to you, how often I have longed to gather your children together, as a hen gathers her chicks under her wings, but you were not willing. 38Look, your house is left to you desolate. 39For I tell you, you will not see me again until you say, 'Blessed is he who comes in the name of the Lord.'ᵃ"

Signs of the End of the Age

24 Jesus left the temple and was walking away when his disciples came up to him to call his attention to its buildings. 2"Do you see all these things?" he asked. "I tell you the truth, not one stone here will be left on another; every one will be thrown down."

3As Jesus was sitting on the Mount of Olives, the disciples came to him privately. "Tell us," they said, "when will this happen, and what will be the sign of your coming and of the end of the age?"

4Jesus answered: "Watch out that no one deceives you. 5For many will come in my name, claiming, 'I am the Christ,ᵇ' and will deceive many. 6You will hear of wars and rumors of wars, but see to it that you are not alarmed. Such things must happen, but the end is still to come. 7Nation will rise against nation, and kingdom against kingdom. There will be famines and earthquakes in various places. 8All these are the beginning of birth pains.

9"Then you will be handed over to be persecuted and put to death, and you will be hated by all nations because of me. 10At that time many will turn away from the faith and will betray and hate each other, 11and many false prophets will appear and deceive many people. 12Because of the increase of wickedness, the love of most will grow cold, 13but he who stands firm to the end will be saved. 14And this gospel of the kingdom will be preached in the whole world as a testimony to all nations, and then the end will come.

15"So when you see standing in the holy place 'the abomination that causes desolation,'ᶜ spoken of through the prophet Daniel—let the reader understand—16then let those who are in Judea flee to the mountains. 17Let no one on the roof of his house go down to take anything out of the house. 18Let no one in the field go back to get his cloak. 19How dreadful it will be in those days for pregnant women and nursing mothers! 20Pray that your flight will not take place in winter or on the Sabbath. 21For then there will be great distress, unequaled from the beginning of the world until now—and never to be equaled again. 22If those days had not been cut short, no one would survive, but for the sake of the elect those days will be shortened. 23At that time if anyone says to you, 'Look, here is the Christ!' or, 'There he is!' do not believe it. 24For false Christs and false prophets will appear and perform great signs and miracles to deceive even the elect—if that were possible. 25See, I have told you ahead of time.

Prayer is . . .

putting tomorrow's burdens in God's hands today.

26"So if anyone tells you, 'There he is, out in the desert,' do not go out; or, 'Here he is, in the inner rooms,' do not believe it. 27For as lightning that comes from the east is visible even in the west, so will be the coming of the Son of Man. 28Wherever there is a carcass, there the vultures will gather.

29"Immediately after the distress of those days

"'the sun will be darkened,
and the moon will not give its light;
the stars will fall from the sky,
and the heavenly bodies will be shaken.'ᵈ

ᵃ39 Psalm 118:26 ᵇ5 Or *Messiah*; also in verse 23 ᶜ15 Daniel 9:27; 11:31; 12:11 ᵈ29 Isaiah 13:10; 34:4

30"At that time the sign of the Son of Man will appear in the sky, and all the nations of the earth will mourn. They will see the Son of Man coming on the clouds of the sky, with power and great glory. 31And he will send his angels with a loud trumpet call, and they will gather his elect from the four winds, from one end of the heavens to the other.

32"Now learn this lesson from the fig tree: As soon as its twigs get tender and its leaves come out, you know that summer is near. 33Even so, when you see all these things, you know that it[a] is near, right at the door. 34I tell you the truth, this generation[b] will certainly not pass away until all these things have happened. 35Heaven and earth will pass away, but my words will never pass away.

The Day and Hour Unknown

36"No one knows about that day or hour, not even the angels in heaven, nor the Son,[c] but only the Father. 37As it was in the days of Noah, so it will be at the coming of the Son of Man. 38For in the days before the flood, people were eating and drinking, marrying and giving in marriage, up to the day Noah entered the ark; 39and they knew nothing about what would happen until the flood came and took them all away. That is how it will be at the coming of the Son of Man. 40Two men will be in the field; one will be taken and the other left. 41Two women will be grinding with a hand mill; one will be taken and the other left.

42"Therefore keep watch, because you do not know on what day your Lord will come. 43But understand this: If the owner of the house had known at what time of night the thief was coming, he would have kept watch and would not have let his house be broken into. 44So you also must be ready, because the Son of Man will come at an hour when you do not expect him.

45"Who then is the faithful and wise servant, whom the master has put in charge of the servants in his household to give them their food at the proper time? 46It will be good for that servant whose master finds him doing so when he returns. 47I tell you the truth, he will put him in charge of all his possessions. 48But suppose that servant is wicked and says to himself, 'My master is staying away a long time,' 49and he then begins to beat his fellow servants and to eat and drink with drunkards. 50The master of that servant will come on a day when he does not expect him and at an hour he is not aware of. 51He will cut him to pieces and assign him a place with the hypocrites, where there will be weeping and gnashing of teeth.

The Parable of the Ten Virgins

25 "At that time the kingdom of heaven will be like ten virgins who took their lamps and went out to meet the bridegroom. 2Five of them were foolish and five were wise. 3The foolish ones took their lamps but did not take any oil with them. 4The wise, however, took oil in jars along with their lamps. 5The bridegroom was a long time in coming, and they all became drowsy and fell asleep.

6"At midnight the cry rang out: 'Here's the bridegroom! Come out to meet him!'

7"Then all the virgins woke up and trimmed their lamps. 8The foolish ones said to the wise, 'Give us some of your oil; our lamps are going out.'

9"'No,' they replied, 'there may not be enough for both us and you. Instead, go to those who sell oil and buy some for yourselves.'

10"But while they were on their way to buy the oil, the bridegroom arrived. The virgins who were ready went in with him to the wedding banquet. And the door was shut.

11"Later the others also came. 'Sir! Sir!' they said. 'Open the door for us!'

12"But he replied, 'I tell you the truth, I don't know you.'

---

a 33 Or he b 34 Or race c 36 Some manuscripts do not have nor the Son.

13"Therefore keep watch, because you do not know the day or the hour.

The Parable of the Talents

14"Again, it will be like a man going on a journey, who called his servants and entrusted his property to them. 15To one he gave five talents[a] of money, to another two talents, and to another one talent, each according to his ability. Then he went on his journey. 16The man who had received the five talents went at once and put his money to work and gained five more. 17So also, the one with the two talents gained two more. 18But the man who had received the one talent went off, dug a hole in the ground and hid his master's money.

19"After a long time the master of those servants returned and settled accounts with them. 20The man who had received the five talents brought the other five. 'Master,' he said, 'you entrusted me with five talents. See, I have gained five more.'

Praying Matthew 25:21

Father God, enable me to always be faithful over everything You entrust to my care so that I may enter into the fullness of joy found in You.

21"His master replied, 'Well done, good and faithful servant! You have been faithful with a few things; I will put you in charge of many things. Come and share your master's happiness!'

22"The man with the two talents also came. 'Master,' he said, 'you entrusted me with two talents; see, I have gained two more.'

23"His master replied, 'Well done, good and faithful servant! You have been faithful with a few things; I will put you in charge of many things. Come and share your master's happiness!'

24"Then the man who had received the one talent came. 'Master,' he said, 'I knew that you are a hard man, harvesting where you have not sown and gathering where you have not scattered seed. 25So I was afraid and went out and hid your talent in the ground. See, here is what belongs to you.'

26"His master replied, 'You wicked, lazy servant! So you knew that I harvest where I have not sown and gather where I have not scattered seed? 27Well then, you should have put my money on deposit with the bankers, so that when I returned I would have received it back with interest.

28"'Take the talent from him and give it to the one who has the ten talents. 29For everyone who has will be given more, and he will have an abundance. Whoever does not have, even what he has will be taken from him. 30And throw that worthless servant outside, into the darkness, where there will be weeping and gnashing of teeth.'

The Sheep and the Goats

31"When the Son of Man comes in his glory, and all the angels with him, he will sit on his throne in heavenly glory. 32All the nations will be gathered before him, and he will separate the people one from another as a shepherd separates the sheep from the goats. 33He will put the sheep on his right and the goats on his left.

34"Then the King will say to those on his right, 'Come, you who are blessed by my Father; take your inheritance, the kingdom prepared for you since the creation of the world. 35For I was hungry and you gave me something to eat, I was thirsty and you gave me something to drink, I was a stranger and you invited me in, 36I needed clothes and you clothed me, I was sick and you looked after me, I was in prison and you came to visit me.'

37"Then the righteous will answer him, 'Lord, when did we see you hungry and feed you, or thirsty and give you something to drink? 38When did we see you a stranger and invite you in, or needing clothes and clothe you? 39When did

---

a 15 A talent was worth more than a thousand dollars.

we see you sick or in prison and go to visit you?'

⁴⁰"The King will reply, 'I tell you the truth, whatever you did for one of the least of these brothers of mine, you did for me.'

⁴¹"Then he will say to those on his left, 'Depart from me, you who are cursed, into the eternal fire prepared for the devil and his angels. ⁴²For I was hungry and you gave me nothing to eat, I was thirsty and you gave me nothing to drink, ⁴³I was a stranger and you did not invite me in, I needed clothes and you did not clothe me, I was sick and in prison and you did not look after me.'

⁴⁴"They also will answer, 'Lord, when did we see you hungry or thirsty or a stranger or needing clothes or sick or in prison, and did not help you?'

⁴⁵"He will reply, 'I tell you the truth, whatever you did not do for one of the least of these, you did not do for me.'

⁴⁶"Then they will go away to eternal punishment, but the righteous to eternal life."

The Plot Against Jesus

26 When Jesus had finished saying all these things, he said to his disciples, ²"As you know, the Passover is two days away—and the Son of Man will be handed over to be crucified."

³Then the chief priests and the elders of the people assembled in the palace of the high priest, whose name was Caiaphas, ⁴and they plotted to arrest Jesus in some sly way and kill him. ⁵"But not during the Feast," they said, "or there may be a riot among the people."

Jesus Anointed at Bethany

⁶While Jesus was in Bethany in the home of a man known as Simon the Leper, ⁷a woman came to him with an alabaster jar of very expensive perfume, which she poured on his head as he was reclining at the table.

⁸When the disciples saw this, they were indignant. "Why this waste?" they asked.

⁹"This perfume could have been sold at a high price and the money given to the poor."

¹⁰Aware of this, Jesus said to them, "Why are you bothering this woman? She has done a beautiful thing to me. ¹¹The poor you will always have with you, but you will not always have me. ¹²When she poured this perfume on my body, she did it to prepare me for burial. ¹³I tell you the truth, wherever this gospel is preached throughout the world, what she has done will also be told, in memory of her."

Judas Agrees to Betray Jesus

¹⁴Then one of the Twelve—the one called Judas Iscariot—went to the chief priests ¹⁵and asked, "What are you willing to give me if I hand him over to you?" So they counted out for him thirty silver coins. ¹⁶From then on Judas watched for an opportunity to hand him over.

The Lord's Supper

¹⁷On the first day of the Feast of Unleavened Bread, the disciples came to Jesus and asked, "Where do you want us to make preparations for you to eat the Passover?"

¹⁸He replied, "Go into the city to a certain man and tell him, 'The Teacher says: My appointed time is near. I am going to celebrate the Passover with my disciples at your house.'" ¹⁹So the disciples did as Jesus had directed them and prepared the Passover.

²⁰When evening came, Jesus was reclining at the table with the Twelve. ²¹And while they were eating, he said, "I tell you the truth, one of you will betray me."

²²They were very sad and began to say to him one after the other, "Surely not I, Lord?"

²³Jesus replied, "The one who has dipped his hand into the bowl with me will betray me. ²⁴The Son of Man will go just as it is written about him. But woe to that man who betrays the Son of Man! It would be better for him if he had not been born."

25Then Judas, the one who would betray him, said, "Surely not I, Rabbi?"

Jesus answered, "Yes, it is you."[a]

26While they were eating, Jesus took bread, gave thanks and broke it, and gave it to his disciples, saying, "Take and eat; this is my body."

27Then he took the cup, gave thanks and offered it to them, saying, "Drink from it, all of you. 28This is my blood of the[b] covenant, which is poured out for many for the forgiveness of sins. 29I tell you, I will not drink of this fruit of the vine from now on until that day when I drink it anew with you in my Father's kingdom."

30When they had sung a hymn, they went out to the Mount of Olives.

Jesus Predicts Peter's Denial

31Then Jesus told them, "This very night you will all fall away on account of me, for it is written:

"'I will strike the shepherd,
    and the sheep of the flock will be
        scattered.'[c]

32But after I have risen, I will go ahead of you into Galilee."

33Peter replied, "Even if all fall away on account of you, I never will."

34"I tell you the truth," Jesus answered, "this very night, before the rooster crows, you will disown me three times."

35But Peter declared, "Even if I have to die with you, I will never disown you." And all the other disciples said the same.

Gethsemane

36Then Jesus went with his disciples to a place called Gethsemane, and he said to them, "Sit here while I go over there and pray." 37He took Peter and the two sons of Zebedee along with him, and he began to be sorrowful and troubled. 38Then he said to them, "My soul is overwhelmed with sorrow to the point of death. Stay here and keep watch with me."

39Going a little farther, he fell with his face to the ground and prayed, "My Father, if it is possible, may this cup be taken from me. Yet not as I will, but as you will."

40Then he returned to his disciples and found them sleeping. "Could you men not keep watch with me for one hour?" he asked Peter. 41"Watch and pray so that you will not fall into temptation. The spirit is willing, but the body is weak."

42He went away a second time and prayed, "My Father, if it is not possible for this cup to be taken away unless I drink it, may your will be done."

43When he came back, he again found them sleeping, because their eyes were heavy. 44So he left them and went away once more and prayed the third time, saying the same thing.

45Then he returned to the disciples and said to them, "Are you still sleeping and resting? Look, the hour is near, and the Son of Man is betrayed into the hands of sinners. 46Rise, let us go! Here comes my betrayer!"

Jesus Arrested

47While he was still speaking, Judas, one of the Twelve, arrived. With him was a large crowd armed with swords and clubs, sent from the chief priests and the elders of the people. 48Now the betrayer had arranged a signal with them: "The one I kiss is the man; arrest him." 49Going at once to Jesus, Judas said, "Greetings, Rabbi!" and kissed him.

50Jesus replied, "Friend, do what you came for."[d]

Then the men stepped forward, seized Jesus and arrested him. 51With that, one of Jesus' companions reached for his sword, drew it out and struck the servant of the high priest, cutting off his ear.

52"Put your sword back in its place," Jesus said to him, "for all who draw the sword will die by the sword. 53Do you think I cannot call on my Father, and he will at once put at my disposal more than twelve legions of angels? 54But how then would the Scriptures be fulfilled that say it must happen in this way?"

---

[a]25 Or "You yourself have said it"   [b]28 Some manuscripts the new   [c]31 Zech. 13:7   [d]50 Or "Friend, why have you come?"

GOING *deeper*

Wanting God's Will

READ AND CONSIDER: MATTHEW 26:36-46

"Going a little farther, he fell with his face to the ground and prayed, 'My Father, if it is possible, may this cup be taken from me. Yet not as I will, but as you will' " (Matthew 26:39).

It's important to pray for God's will to be done in our lives, but how do we align our own desires and will with what God wants? How do we learn to *want* God's plan for us more than we want our own?

Jesus' passionate prayer in the garden of Gethsemane is the greatest model for us of praying with absolute honesty and total submission. He knew He would be arrested, tortured, and put to death as part of God's plan of redemption for the world. The "cup" that He was about to drink was the cup of divine wrath for the sins of humanity, and He was about to take upon Himself the penalty for that sin. He anticipated the physical pain and suffering as well as the emotional agony of being separated from His Father, and He asked that this cup of suffering be taken away. The intensity of this prayer gives us a glimpse of Jesus' humanity. If it wasn't going to be painful, He would not have agonized to this extent.

You and I face times that aren't easy. We look ahead and sense God saying, "Stay in this difficult marriage," "Love that rebellious child," "Return kindness to that belligerent boss." Just like Jesus did, we can ask God to remove the cup of pain from our lives, to give us an easier way out. But like Jesus, we have to also say: "Yet not as I will, but as You will." The easy way may not be the best way. The easy way is often not the way God has for you.

God wants us to pray about all things, but He wants us to pray according to His will. That's why it's important to ask God to reveal His will to us and help us pray accordingly. When we don't know what God's will is, we should always include in our prayer, "Lord, let Your perfect will be done in this situation."

[55]At that time Jesus said to the crowd, "Am I leading a rebellion, that you have come out with swords and clubs to capture me? Every day I sat in the temple courts teaching, and you did not arrest me. [56]But this has all taken place that the writings of the prophets might be fulfilled." Then all the disciples deserted him and fled.

Before the Sanhedrin

[57]Those who had arrested Jesus took him to Caiaphas, the high priest, where the teachers of the law and the elders had assembled. [58]But Peter followed him at a distance, right up to the courtyard of the high priest. He entered and sat down with the guards to see the outcome.

[59]The chief priests and the whole Sanhedrin were looking for false evidence against Jesus so that they could put him to death. [60]But they did not find any, though many false witnesses came forward.

Finally two came forward [61]and declared, "This fellow said, 'I am able to destroy the temple of God and rebuild it in three days.' "

[62]Then the high priest stood up and said to Jesus, "Are you not going to answer? What is this testimony that these men are bringing against you?" [63]But Jesus remained silent.

The high priest said to him, "I charge you under oath by the living God: Tell us if you are the Christ,[a] the Son of God."

---

[a] *63* Or *Messiah*; also in verse 68

64"Yes, it is as you say," Jesus replied. "But I say to all of you: In the future you will see the Son of Man sitting at the right hand of the Mighty One and coming on the clouds of heaven."

65Then the high priest tore his clothes and said, "He has spoken blasphemy! Why do we need any more witnesses? Look, now you have heard the blasphemy. 66What do you think?"

"He is worthy of death," they answered.

67Then they spit in his face and struck him with their fists. Others slapped him 68and said, "Prophesy to us, Christ. Who hit you?"

Peter Disowns Jesus

69Now Peter was sitting out in the courtyard, and a servant girl came to him. "You also were with Jesus of Galilee," she said.

70But he denied it before them all. "I don't know what you're talking about," he said.

71Then he went out to the gateway, where another girl saw him and said to the people there, "This fellow was with Jesus of Nazareth."

72He denied it again, with an oath: "I don't know the man!"

73After a little while, those standing there went up to Peter and said, "Surely you are one of them, for your accent gives you away."

74Then he began to call down curses on himself and he swore to them, "I don't know the man!"

Immediately a rooster crowed. 75Then Peter remembered the word Jesus had spoken: "Before the rooster crows, you will disown me three times." And he went outside and wept bitterly.

Judas Hangs Himself

27 Early in the morning, all the chief priests and the elders of the people came to the decision to put Jesus to death. 2They bound him, led him away and handed him over to Pilate, the governor.

3When Judas, who had betrayed him, saw that Jesus was condemned, he was seized with remorse and returned the thirty silver coins to the chief priests and the elders. 4"I have sinned," he said, "for I have betrayed innocent blood."

"What is that to us?" they replied. "That's your responsibility."

5So Judas threw the money into the temple and left. Then he went away and hanged himself.

6The chief priests picked up the coins and said, "It is against the law to put this into the treasury, since it is blood money." 7So they decided to use the money to buy the potter's field as a burial place for foreigners. 8That is why it has been called the Field of Blood to this day. 9Then what was spoken by Jeremiah the prophet was fulfilled: "They took the thirty silver coins, the price set on him by the people of Israel, 10and they used them to buy the potter's field, as the Lord commanded me."a

Jesus Before Pilate

11Meanwhile Jesus stood before the governor, and the governor asked him, "Are you the king of the Jews?"

"Yes, it is as you say," Jesus replied.

12When he was accused by the chief priests and the elders, he gave no answer. 13Then Pilate asked him, "Don't you hear the testimony they are bringing against you?" 14But Jesus made no reply, not even to a single charge—to the great amazement of the governor.

15Now it was the governor's custom at the Feast to release a prisoner chosen by the crowd. 16At that time they had a notorious prisoner, called Barabbas. 17So when the crowd had gathered, Pilate asked them, "Which one do you want me to release to you: Barabbas, or Jesus who is called Christ?" 18For he knew it was out of envy that they had handed Jesus over to him.

19While Pilate was sitting on the judge's

---

a 10 See Zech. 11:12,13; Jer. 19:1-13; 32:6-9.

seat, his wife sent him this message: "Don't have anything to do with that innocent man, for I have suffered a great deal today in a dream because of him."

20 But the chief priests and the elders persuaded the crowd to ask for Barabbas and to have Jesus executed.

21 "Which of the two do you want me to release to you?" asked the governor.

"Barabbas," they answered.

22 "What shall I do, then, with Jesus who is called Christ?" Pilate asked.

They all answered, "Crucify him!"

23 "Why? What crime has he committed?" asked Pilate.

But they shouted all the louder, "Crucify him!"

24 When Pilate saw that he was getting nowhere, but that instead an uproar was starting, he took water and washed his hands in front of the crowd. "I am innocent of this man's blood," he said. "It is your responsibility!"

25 All the people answered, "Let his blood be on us and on our children!"

26 Then he released Barabbas to them. But he had Jesus flogged, and handed him over to be crucified.

The Soldiers Mock Jesus

27 Then the governor's soldiers took Jesus into the Praetorium and gathered the whole company of soldiers around him. 28 They stripped him and put a scarlet robe on him, 29 and then twisted together a crown of thorns and set it on his head. They put a staff in his right hand and knelt in front of him and mocked him. "Hail, king of the Jews!" they said. 30 They spit on him, and took the staff and struck him on the head again and again. 31 After they had mocked him, they took off the robe and put his own clothes on him. Then they led him away to crucify him.

The Crucifixion

32 As they were going out, they met a man from Cyrene, named Simon, and

they forced him to carry the cross. 33 They came to a place called Golgotha (which means The Place of the Skull). 34 There they offered Jesus wine to drink, mixed with gall; but after tasting it, he refused to drink it. 35 When they had crucified him, they divided up his clothes by casting lots.[a] 36 And sitting down, they kept watch over him there. 37 Above his head they placed the written charge against him: THIS IS JESUS, THE KING OF THE JEWS. 38 Two robbers were crucified with him, one on his right and one on his left. 39 Those who passed by hurled insults at him, shaking their heads 40 and saying, "You who are going to destroy the temple and build it in three days, save yourself! Come down from the cross, if you are the Son of God!"

41 In the same way the chief priests, the teachers of the law and the elders mocked him. 42 "He saved others," they said, "but he can't save himself! He's the King of Israel! Let him come down now from the cross, and we will believe in him. 43 He trusts in God. Let God rescue him now if he wants him, for he said, 'I am the Son of God.'" 44 In the same way the robbers who were crucified with him also heaped insults on him.

The Death of Jesus

45 From the sixth hour until the ninth hour darkness came over all the land. 46 About the ninth hour Jesus cried out in a loud voice, *"Eloi, Eloi,[b] lama sabachthani?"*—which means, "My God, my God, why have you forsaken me?"[c]

47 When some of those standing there heard this, they said, "He's calling Elijah."

48 Immediately one of them ran and got a sponge. He filled it with wine vinegar, put it on a stick, and offered it to Jesus to drink. 49 The rest said, "Now leave him alone. Let's see if Elijah comes to save him."

50 And when Jesus had cried out again in a loud voice, he gave up his spirit.

51At that moment the curtain of the temple was torn in two from top to bottom. The earth shook and the rocks split. 52The tombs broke open and the bodies of many holy people who had died were raised to life. 53They came out of the tombs, and after Jesus' resurrection they went into the holy city and appeared to many people.

54When the centurion and those with him who were guarding Jesus saw the earthquake and all that had happened, they were terrified, and exclaimed, "Surely he was the Son[a] of God!"

55Many women were there, watching from a distance. They had followed Jesus from Galilee to care for his needs. 56Among them were Mary Magdalene, Mary the mother of James and Joses, and the mother of Zebedee's sons.

The Burial of Jesus

57As evening approached, there came a rich man from Arimathea, named Joseph, who had himself become a disciple of Jesus. 58Going to Pilate, he asked for Jesus' body, and Pilate ordered that it be given to him. 59Joseph took the body, wrapped it in a clean linen cloth, 60and placed it in his own new tomb that he had cut out of the rock. He rolled a big stone in front of the entrance to the tomb and went away. 61Mary Magdalene and the other Mary were sitting there opposite the tomb.

The Guard at the Tomb

62The next day, the one after Preparation Day, the chief priests and the Pharisees went to Pilate. 63"Sir," they said, "we remember that while he was still alive that deceiver said, 'After three days I will rise again.' 64So give the order for the tomb to be made secure until the third day. Otherwise, his disciples may come and steal the body and tell the people that he has been raised from the dead. This last deception will be worse than the first."

65"Take a guard," Pilate answered. "Go, make the tomb as secure as you know how." 66So they went and made the tomb secure by putting a seal on the stone and posting the guard.

The Resurrection

28 After the Sabbath, at dawn on the first day of the week, Mary Magdalene and the other Mary went to look at the tomb.

2There was a violent earthquake, for an angel of the Lord came down from heaven and, going to the tomb, rolled back the stone and sat on it. 3His appearance was like lightning, and his clothes were white as snow. 4The guards were so afraid of him that they shook and became like dead men.

5The angel said to the women, "Do not be afraid, for I know that you are looking for Jesus, who was crucified. 6He is not here; he has risen, just as he said. Come and see the place where he lay. 7Then go quickly and tell his disciples: 'He has risen from the dead and is going ahead of you into Galilee. There you will see him.' Now I have told you."

Praying Matthew 28:5-6
Precious Jesus, thank You that You died and rose again for me so that I may have life forever in You.

8So the women hurried away from the tomb, afraid yet filled with joy, and ran to tell his disciples. 9Suddenly Jesus met them. "Greetings," he said. They came to him, clasped his feet and worshiped him. 10Then Jesus said to them, "Do not be afraid. Go and tell my brothers to go to Galilee; there they will see me."

The Guards' Report

11While the women were on their way, some of the guards went into the city and reported to the chief priests everything that had happened. 12When the chief priests had met with the elders and devised a plan, they gave the soldiers a large sum of money, 13telling them, "You are to say, 'His disciples came during the night and stole him away while we were asleep.' [14]If this report gets to the governor, we will satisfy him and keep you out of trouble." [15]So the soldiers took the money and did as they were instructed. And this story has been widely circulated among the Jews to this very day.

The Great Commission

[16]Then the eleven disciples went to Galilee, to the mountain where Jesus had told them to go. [17]When they saw him, they worshiped him; but some doubted. [18]Then Jesus came to them and said, "All authority in heaven and on earth has been given to me. [19]Therefore go and make disciples of all nations, baptizing them in[a] the name of the Father and of the Son and of the Holy Spirit, [20]and teaching them to obey everything I have commanded you. And surely I am with you always, to the very end of the age."

---

[a] *19* Or *into*; see Acts 8:16; 19:5; Romans 6:3; 1 Cor. 1:13; 10:2 and Gal. 3:27.

Author: John Mark

Date: In the AD 50s or 60s

Audience: Gentiles in general and Roman believers in particular

Mark intended his biography of Christ to be read throughout the Roman Empire by a non-Jewish audience, so he focused on Jesus' actions and miracles, as well as His teachings, in order to prove that He was the Son of God. Even the evil spirits identified Jesus as God's Son.

This Gospel also shows Jesus to be the ultimate Servant and challenges us to be the same by losing our lives for His sake in order to save them (8:34-35). Mark reveals the "secret" behind the Lord's powerful ministry. "Very early in the morning, while it was still dark, Jesus got up, left the house and went off to a solitary place, where he prayed" (1:35).

If anyone would not have had to get up early and pray, it surely would have been Him—Jesus, the Son of God. But He never ceased to rely completely on His Father in heaven. His top priority was always intimacy with the Father.

That must be our goal too.

Prayer Themes:

• *Ask the Lord to help you be continually aware that being with Him must always take priority over doing things for Him (3:14).*

• *Pray for God to give you a deep and unshakable faith so that His work is not limited in your life by any unbelief (6:4-6).*

• *Relinquish your rights to all you own and tell God that everything you have is His. Ask Him to help you remember that you are only a steward of His gracious gifts (10:17-31).*

Mark

John the Baptist Prepares the Way

1 The beginning of the gospel about Jesus Christ, the Son of God.[a]

²It is written in Isaiah the prophet:

"I will send my messenger ahead of you,
    who will prepare your way"[b]—
³"a voice of one calling in the desert,
    'Prepare the way for the Lord,
    make straight paths for him.' "[c]

⁴And so John came, baptizing in the desert region and preaching a baptism of repentance for the forgiveness of sins. ⁵The whole Judean countryside and all the people of Jerusalem went out to him. Confessing their sins, they were baptized by him in the Jordan River. ⁶John wore clothing made of camel's hair, with a leather belt around his waist, and he ate locusts and wild honey. ⁷And this was his message: "After me will come one more powerful than I, the thongs of whose sandals I am not worthy to stoop down and untie. ⁸I baptize you with[d] water, but he will baptize you with the Holy Spirit."

The Baptism and Temptation of Jesus

⁹At that time Jesus came from Nazareth in Galilee and was baptized by John in the Jordan. ¹⁰As Jesus was coming up out of the water, he saw heaven being torn open and the Spirit descending on him like a dove. ¹¹And a voice came from heaven: "You are my Son, whom I love; with you I am well pleased."

¹²At once the Spirit sent him out into the desert, ¹³and he was in the desert forty days, being tempted by Satan. He was with the wild animals, and angels attended him.

---

[a] *1* Some manuscripts do not have *the Son of God.*   [b] *2* Mal. 3:1   [c] *3* Isaiah 40:3   [d] *8* Or *in*

GOING deeper

The Power to Fight Temptation

READ AND CONSIDER: MARK 1:9-13

"He was in the desert forty days, being tempted by Satan. He was with the wild animals, and angels attended him" (Mark 1:13).

How often is the word *temptation* used lightly? We might comment on some food that looks particularly "tempting," or we laughingly say we're "yielding to temptation" when we buy something we want but don't absolutely need.

Most often, however, temptation is not a laughing matter. When we crave, desire, or are enticed by something that is wrong for us, we are experiencing temptation in its most dangerous form. The Bible says we have an enemy, Satan, who would like nothing more than to tempt us to sin and destroy our lives.

Jesus knew what it was to experience temptation. Immediately following His baptism, Jesus was led into the desert by the Holy Spirit where He was tempted by Satan for 40 days. God allowed this time of testing in Jesus' life, but it was Satan who did the tempting (Matthew 4:1-11).

Even though Jesus was God incarnate, He was also fully human. How could any human being withstand a full 40 days of intensive satanic attack? Based on what Scripture relates of the life of Christ and His regular habit of spending time alone with God, we know that Jesus did not enter this grueling time of temptation unprepared. Prayer and His knowledge of the Scriptures girded Him for battle. We should strive to be like Him in our preparation for enemy attacks.

The best time to pray about temptation is *before* you fall into it. After the lure presents itself, resisting temptation becomes much more difficult. The model prayer Jesus taught us to pray as a matter of course is a good place to start. "Lead us not into temptation, but deliver us from the evil one" (Matthew 6:13). We can also prepare to do as Jesus did and rebuke the enemy with God's Word. That means we must read it enough to know what it says. In addition to that, we can call on the Lord. "Because he himself suffered when he was tempted, he is able to help those who are being tempted" (Hebrews 2:18).

None of us is immune to temptation. We might think that as we mature in the Lord, temptation will be less intense. But the truth is, we must continue to watch out for subtle temptations and ask God to give us discernment. Never hesitate to cry out to God when you are tempted. The temptation is not the sin. Whether we sin or not has to do with whether we *entertain* the temptation or turn to God immediately. God is not only able to help us stand strong against temptation, but He can also deliver us out of it.

The Calling of the First Disciples

¹⁴After John was put in prison, Jesus went into Galilee, proclaiming the good news of God. ¹⁵"The time has come," he said. "The kingdom of God is near. Repent and believe the good news!"

¹⁶As Jesus walked beside the Sea of Galilee, he saw Simon and his brother Andrew casting a net into the lake, for they were fishermen. ¹⁷"Come, follow me," Jesus said, "and I will make you fishers of men." ¹⁸At once they left their nets and followed him.

¹⁹When he had gone a little farther, he saw James son of Zebedee and his brother John in a boat, preparing their nets. ²⁰Without delay he called them, and they left their father Zebedee in the

boat with the hired men and followed him.

Jesus Drives Out an Evil Spirit

21 They went to Capernaum, and when the Sabbath came, Jesus went into the synagogue and began to teach. 22 The people were amazed at his teaching, because he taught them as one who had authority, not as the teachers of the law. 23 Just then a man in their synagogue who was possessed by an evil[a] spirit cried out, 24 "What do you want with us, Jesus of Nazareth? Have you come to destroy us? I know who you are—the Holy One of God!"

25 "Be quiet!" said Jesus sternly. "Come out of him!" 26 The evil spirit shook the man violently and came out of him with a shriek.

27 The people were all so amazed that they asked each other, "What is this? A new teaching—and with authority! He even gives orders to evil spirits and they obey him." 28 News about him spread quickly over the whole region of Galilee.

Jesus Heals Many

29 As soon as they left the synagogue, they went with James and John to the home of Simon and Andrew. 30 Simon's mother-in-law was in bed with a fever, and they told Jesus about her. 31 So he went to her, took her hand and helped her up. The fever left her and she began to wait on them.

32 That evening after sunset the people brought to Jesus all the sick and demon-possessed. 33 The whole town gathered at the door, 34 and Jesus healed many who had various diseases. He also drove out many demons, but he would not let the demons speak because they knew who he was.

Jesus Prays in a Solitary Place

35 Very early in the morning, while it was still dark, Jesus got up, left the house and went off to a solitary place, where he prayed. 36 Simon and his companions went to look for him, 37 and when they found him, they exclaimed: "Everyone is looking for you!"

38 Jesus replied, "Let us go somewhere else—to the nearby villages—so I can preach there also. That is why I have come." 39 So he traveled throughout Galilee, preaching in their synagogues and driving out demons.

A Man With Leprosy

40 A man with leprosy[b] came to him and begged him on his knees, "If you are willing, you can make me clean."

---

[a] 23 Greek *unclean*; also in verses 26 and 27 [b] 40 The Greek word was used for various diseases affecting the skin—not necessarily leprosy.

God's people at prayer
JESUS MAKES PRAYER A HABIT

MARK 1:35 A habit is an action or behavior that is regular and repetitive—a long-standing practice. The fact that Jesus had a habit of praying is clear throughout the four Gospels. In order to have time alone with God, He would often rise long before daybreak and go alone into a solitary place to pray. Prayer was the vital connection between Him and His Father, and Jesus made it a priority in His life.

Most of us struggle to find room in our schedules for prayer. But when we don't take time to pray, it's like saying we don't believe prayer is really necessary. Jesus gave us the greatest example of habitual and fervent prayer. If the Son of God—the only perfect man who ever lived—knew that He couldn't function without prayer, how much more do we need to be dependent enough upon God to set aside time for daily prayer in our lives!

[41] Filled with compassion, Jesus reached out his hand and touched the man. "I am willing," he said. "Be clean!" [42] Immediately the leprosy left him and he was cured.

[43] Jesus sent him away at once with a strong warning: [44] "See that you don't tell this to anyone. But go, show yourself to the priest and offer the sacrifices that Moses commanded for your cleansing, as a testimony to them." [45] Instead he went out and began to talk freely, spreading the news. As a result, Jesus could no longer enter a town openly but stayed outside in lonely places. Yet the people still came to him from everywhere.

Jesus Heals a Paralytic

2 A few days later, when Jesus again entered Capernaum, the people heard that he had come home. [2] So many gathered that there was no room left, not even outside the door, and he preached the word to them. [3] Some men came, bringing to him a paralytic, carried by four of them. [4] Since they could not get him to Jesus because of the crowd, they made an opening in the roof above Jesus and, after digging through it, lowered the mat the paralyzed man was lying on. [5] When Jesus saw their faith, he said to the paralytic, "Son, your sins are forgiven."

[6] Now some teachers of the law were sitting there, thinking to themselves, [7] "Why does this fellow talk like that? He's blaspheming! Who can forgive sins but God alone?"

[8] Immediately Jesus knew in his spirit that this was what they were thinking in their hearts, and he said to them, "Why are you thinking these things? [9] Which is easier: to say to the paralytic, 'Your sins are forgiven,' or to say, 'Get up, take your mat and walk'? [10] But that you may know that the Son of Man has authority on earth to forgive sins..." He said to the paralytic, [11] "I tell you, get up, take your mat and go home." [12] He got up, took his mat and walked out in full view of them all. This amazed everyone and they praised God, saying, "We have never seen anything like this!"

The Calling of Levi

[13] Once again Jesus went out beside the lake. A large crowd came to him, and he began to teach them. [14] As he walked along, he saw Levi son of Alphaeus sitting at the tax collector's booth. "Follow me," Jesus told him, and Levi got up and followed him.

[15] While Jesus was having dinner at Levi's house, many tax collectors and "sinners" were eating with him and his disciples, for there were many who followed him. [16] When the teachers of the law who were Pharisees saw him eating with the "sinners" and tax collectors, they asked his disciples: "Why does he eat with tax collectors and 'sinners'?"

[17] On hearing this, Jesus said to them, "It is not the healthy who need a doctor, but the sick. I have not come to call the righteous, but sinners."

Jesus Questioned About Fasting

[18] Now John's disciples and the Pharisees were fasting. Some people came and asked Jesus, "How is it that John's disciples and the disciples of the Pharisees are fasting, but yours are not?"

[19] Jesus answered, "How can the guests of the bridegroom fast while he is with them? They cannot, so long as they have him with them. [20] But the time will come when the bridegroom will be taken from them, and on that day they will fast.

[21] "No one sews a patch of unshrunk cloth on an old garment. If he does, the new piece will pull away from the old, making the tear worse. [22] And no one pours new wine into old wineskins. If he does, the wine will burst the skins, and both the wine and the wineskins will be ruined. No, he pours new wine into new wineskins."

Lord of the Sabbath

[23] One Sabbath Jesus was going through the grainfields, and as his disciples walked along, they began to pick some heads of

grain. 24The Pharisees said to him, "Look, why are they doing what is unlawful on the Sabbath?"

25He answered, "Have you never read what David did when he and his companions were hungry and in need? 26In the days of Abiathar the high priest, he entered the house of God and ate the consecrated bread, which is lawful only for priests to eat. And he also gave some to his companions."

27Then he said to them, "The Sabbath was made for man, not man for the Sabbath. 28So the Son of Man is Lord even of the Sabbath."

3 Another time he went into the synagogue, and a man with a shriveled hand was there. 2Some of them were looking for a reason to accuse Jesus, so they watched him closely to see if he would heal him on the Sabbath. 3Jesus said to the man with the shriveled hand, "Stand up in front of everyone."

4Then Jesus asked them, "Which is lawful on the Sabbath: to do good or to do evil, to save life or to kill?" But they remained silent.

5He looked around at them in anger and, deeply distressed at their stubborn hearts, said to the man, "Stretch out your hand." He stretched it out, and his hand was completely restored. 6Then the Pharisees went out and began to plot with the Herodians how they might kill Jesus.

Crowds Follow Jesus

7Jesus withdrew with his disciples to the lake, and a large crowd from Galilee followed. 8When they heard all he was doing, many people came to him from Judea, Jerusalem, Idumea, and the regions across the Jordan and around Tyre and Sidon. 9Because of the crowd he told his disciples to have a small boat ready for him, to keep the people from crowding him. 10For he had healed many, so that those with diseases were pushing forward to touch him. 11Whenever the evil[a] spir-

its saw him, they fell down before him and cried out, "You are the Son of God." 12But he gave them strict orders not to tell who he was.

The Appointing of the Twelve Apostles

13Jesus went up on a mountainside and called to him those he wanted, and they came to him. 14He appointed twelve—designating them apostles[b]—that they might be with him and that he might send them out to preach 15and to have authority to drive out demons. 16These are the twelve he appointed: Simon (to whom he gave the name Peter); 17James son of Zebedee and his brother John (to them he gave the name Boanerges, which means Sons of Thunder); 18Andrew, Philip, Bartholomew, Matthew, Thomas, James son of Alphaeus, Thaddaeus, Simon the Zealot 19and Judas Iscariot, who betrayed him.

Jesus and Beelzebub

20Then Jesus entered a house, and again a crowd gathered, so that he and his disciples were not even able to eat. 21When his family heard about this, they went to take charge of him, for they said, "He is out of his mind."

22And the teachers of the law who came down from Jerusalem said, "He is possessed by Beelzebub[c]! By the prince of demons he is driving out demons."

23So Jesus called them and spoke to them in parables: "How can Satan drive out Satan? 24If a kingdom is divided against itself, that kingdom cannot stand. 25If a house is divided against itself, that house cannot stand. 26And if Satan opposes himself and is divided, he cannot stand; his end has come. 27In fact, no one can enter a strong man's house and carry off his possessions unless he first ties up the strong man. Then he can rob his house. 28I tell you the truth, all the sins and blasphemies of men will be forgiven them. 29But whoever blasphemes against

---

a 11 Greek unclean; also in verse 30   b 14 Some manuscripts do not have designating them apostles.   c 22 Greek Beezeboul or Beelzeboul the Holy Spirit will never be forgiven; he is guilty of an eternal sin."

30He said this because they were saying, "He has an evil spirit."

Jesus' Mother and Brothers

31Then Jesus' mother and brothers arrived. Standing outside, they sent someone in to call him. 32A crowd was sitting around him, and they told him, "Your mother and brothers are outside looking for you."

33"Who are my mother and my brothers?" he asked.

34Then he looked at those seated in a circle around him and said, "Here are my mother and my brothers! 35Whoever does God's will is my brother and sister and mother."

The Parable of the Sower

4 Again Jesus began to teach by the lake. The crowd that gathered around him was so large that he got into a boat and sat in it out on the lake, while all the people were along the shore at the water's edge. 2He taught them many things by parables, and in his teaching said: 3"Listen! A farmer went out to sow his seed. 4As he was scattering the seed, some fell along the path, and the birds came and ate it up. 5Some fell on rocky places, where it did not have much soil. It sprang up quickly, because the soil was shallow. 6But when the sun came up, the plants were scorched, and they withered because they had no root. 7Other seed fell among thorns, which grew up and choked the plants, so that they did not bear grain. 8Still other seed fell on good soil. It came up, grew and produced a crop, multiplying thirty, sixty, or even a hundred times."

9Then Jesus said, "He who has ears to hear, let him hear."

10When he was alone, the Twelve and the others around him asked him about the parables. 11He told them, "The secret of the kingdom of God has been given

to you. But to those on the outside everything is said in parables 12so that,

> " 'they may be ever seeing but never
>   perceiving,
> and ever hearing but never
>   understanding;
> otherwise they might turn and be
>   forgiven!'ᵃ"

13Then Jesus said to them, "Don't you understand this parable? How then will you understand any parable? 14The farmer sows the word. 15Some people are like seed along the path, where the word is sown. As soon as they hear it, Satan comes and takes away the word that was sown in them. 16Others, like seed sown on rocky places, hear the word and at once receive it with joy. 17But since they have no root, they last only a short time. When trouble or persecution comes because of the word, they quickly fall away. 18Still others, like seed sown among thorns, hear the word; 19but the worries of this life, the deceitfulness of wealth and the desires for other things come in and choke the word, making it unfruitful. 20Others, like seed sown on good soil, hear the word, accept it, and produce a crop—thirty, sixty or even a hundred times what was sown."

A Lamp on a Stand

21He said to them, "Do you bring in a lamp to put it under a bowl or a bed? Instead, don't you put it on its stand? 22For whatever is hidden is meant to be disclosed, and whatever is concealed is meant to be brought out into the open. 23If anyone has ears to hear, let him hear."

24"Consider carefully what you hear," he continued. "With the measure you use, it will be measured to you—and even more. 25Whoever has will be given

Praying Mark 4:24-25
Lord, enable me to understand what I hear
from You and apply it to my life so that
my spiritual understanding will grow.

ᵃ 12 Isaiah 6:9,10

Waiting in the Wings

Has it ever seemed like you are waiting in the wings for the next scene of your life to start? The stage is dark and you're expecting the lights to go up and the curtain to rise. The first act may or may not have gone smoothly, but by now you've been on an extended intermission and you're beginning to wonder if the second act will ever begin.

How many times in our lives have we found ourselves waiting like that? Waiting for things to change. Waiting for something to happen. Waiting for life to get back to normal. Waiting for more time or more money. Waiting for the relationship to get better. Waiting for the right door to open. Waiting for the right person to come along. Waiting for somebody to notice. Waiting, waiting, waiting.

We don't like waiting. We want action. But God says waiting can be good, because that's how we learn patience. We respond that there's nothing wrong with patience, but we want it now!

We can't have patience, however, without the waiting. And God says we need patience because it will ultimately make us complete. That's because patience is one of the attributes of God. When we are patient, we are like Him. When we are being tested, or feel like we are walking in the wilderness, part of what we are learning is to be patient.

I've found that it's best to view these waiting times by thinking of them as times of waiting on the Lord. Try it. You'll see. It's much easier to think about waiting on God than it is to be patient with your circumstances. Waiting on the Lord gives you the sense that something is going on— only you just can't see it. You are waiting in eager anticipation of what God is going to do next. Going through a waiting period doesn't mean there is nothing happening, because when you are waiting on the Lord, He is always moving in your life.

Even though it may not seem like it, as long as you are walking with the Lord you are going from glory to glory and strength to strength (2 Corinthians 3:18; Psalm 84:7). You are always going somewhere in God's plan. And His purpose for you is constantly being realized. But you have to be patient and wait for Him to accomplish it His way and in His time.

If you ever feel like you are just going through the motions in your own life, don't let yourself become frustrated over it. Know that God's mercies to you are new every morning and as a result, God freshly hears your words spoken to Him as well. There is no such thing as the same old prayer. Each prayer you pray, even if it's about the same thing, has new life to it every time you pray it. Every day you have another opportunity to affect your future with the words you speak to God. Even though you may not see results as soon as you would like, much is happening in the spirit realm that you don't see. Each prayer sets something in motion.

If you continue to walk with God and take the steps you know are right, you will get where you need to go. It may seem like it's taking forever, but don't be discouraged. God has been known to do a quick work for which He has been preparing a long time. Let Him sustain you in the interim. Tell yourself that you will "Be still before the Lord and wait patiently for him" (Psalm 37:7).

For the next "From Stormie's Heart" article, go to page 1254.

more; whoever does not have, even what he has will be taken from him."

The Parable of the Growing Seed

26He also said, "This is what the kingdom of God is like. A man scatters seed on the ground. 27Night and day, whether he sleeps or gets up, the seed sprouts and grows, though he does not know how. 28All by itself the soil produces grain—first the stalk, then the head, then the full kernel in the head. 29As soon as the grain is ripe, he puts the sickle to it, because the harvest has come."

The Parable of the Mustard Seed

30Again he said, "What shall we say the kingdom of God is like, or what parable shall we use to describe it? 31It is like a mustard seed, which is the smallest seed you plant in the ground. 32Yet when planted, it grows and becomes the largest of all garden plants, with such big branches that the birds of the air can perch in its shade."

33With many similar parables Jesus spoke the word to them, as much as they could understand. 34He did not say anything to them without using a parable. But when he was alone with his own disciples, he explained everything.

Jesus Calms the Storm

35That day when evening came, he said to his disciples, "Let us go over to the other side." 36Leaving the crowd behind, they took him along, just as he was, in the boat. There were also other boats with him. 37A furious squall came up, and the waves broke over the boat, so that it was nearly swamped. 38Jesus was in the stern, sleeping on a cushion. The disciples woke him and said to him, "Teacher, don't you care if we drown?"

39He got up, rebuked the wind and said to the waves, "Quiet! Be still!" Then the wind died down and it was completely calm.

40He said to his disciples, "Why are you so afraid? Do you still have no faith?"

41They were terrified and asked each other, "Who is this? Even the wind and the waves obey him!"

The Healing of a Demon-possessed Man

5 They went across the lake to the region of the Gerasenes.a 2When Jesus got out of the boat, a man with an evilb spirit came from the tombs to meet him. 3This man lived in the tombs, and no one could bind him any more, not even with a chain. 4For he had often been chained hand and foot, but he tore the chains apart and broke the irons on his feet. No one was strong enough to subdue him. 5Night and day among the tombs and in the hills he would cry out and cut himself with stones.

6When he saw Jesus from a distance, he ran and fell on his knees in front of him. 7He shouted at the top of his voice, "What do you want with me, Jesus, Son of the Most High God? Swear to God that you won't torture me!" 8For Jesus had said to him, "Come out of this man, you evil spirit!"

9Then Jesus asked him, "What is your name?"

"My name is Legion," he replied, "for we are many." 10And he begged Jesus again and again not to send them out of the area.

11A large herd of pigs was feeding on the nearby hillside. 12The demons begged Jesus, "Send us among the pigs; allow us to go into them." 13He gave them permission, and the evil spirits came out and went into the pigs. The herd, about two thousand in number, rushed down the steep bank into the lake and were drowned.

14Those tending the pigs ran off and reported this in the town and countryside, and the people went out to see what had happened. 15When they came to Jesus, they saw the man who had been possessed by the legion of demons, sitting there, dressed and in his right mind; and

---

a 1 Some manuscripts Gadarenes; other manuscripts Gergesenes   b 2 Greek unclean; also in verses 8 and 13 they were afraid. ¹⁶Those who had seen it told the people what had happened to the demon-possessed man—and told about the pigs as well. ¹⁷Then the people began to plead with Jesus to leave their region.

¹⁸As Jesus was getting into the boat, the man who had been demon-possessed begged to go with him. ¹⁹Jesus did not let him, but said, "Go home to your family and tell them how much the Lord has done for you, and how he has had mercy on you." ²⁰So the man went away and began to tell in the Decapolis[a] how much Jesus had done for him. And all the people were amazed.

A Dead Girl and a Sick Woman

²¹When Jesus had again crossed over by boat to the other side of the lake, a large crowd gathered around him while he was by the lake. ²²Then one of the synagogue rulers, named Jairus, came there. Seeing Jesus, he fell at his feet ²³and pleaded earnestly with him, "My little daughter is dying. Please come and put your hands on her so that she will be healed and live." ²⁴So Jesus went with him.

A large crowd followed and pressed around him. ²⁵And a woman was there who had been subject to bleeding for twelve years. ²⁶She had suffered a great deal under the care of many doctors and had spent all she had, yet instead of getting better she grew worse. ²⁷When she heard about Jesus, she came up behind him in the crowd and touched his cloak, ²⁸because she thought, "If I just touch his clothes, I will be healed." ²⁹Immediately her bleeding stopped and she felt in her body that she was freed from her suffering.

³⁰At once Jesus realized that power had gone out from him. He turned around in the crowd and asked, "Who touched my clothes?"

³¹"You see the people crowding against you," his disciples answered, "and yet you can ask, 'Who touched me?'"

³²But Jesus kept looking around to see who had done it. ³³Then the woman, knowing what had happened to her, came and fell at his feet and, trembling with fear, told him the whole truth. ³⁴He said to her, "Daughter, your faith has healed you. Go in peace and be freed from your suffering."

³⁵While Jesus was still speaking, some men came from the house of Jairus, the synagogue ruler. "Your daughter is dead," they said. "Why bother the teacher any more?"

³⁶Ignoring what they said, Jesus told the synagogue ruler, "Don't be afraid; just believe."

Praying Mark 5:35-36
Jesus, help me not be afraid when bad news comes, but rather look to You and have faith that You will work a miracle in my life.

³⁷He did not let anyone follow him except Peter, James and John the brother of James. ³⁸When they came to the home of the synagogue ruler, Jesus saw a commotion, with people crying and wailing loudly. ³⁹He went in and said to them, "Why all this commotion and wailing? The child is not dead but asleep." ⁴⁰But they laughed at him.

After he put them all out, he took the child's father and mother and the disciples who were with him, and went in where the child was. ⁴¹He took her by the hand and said to her, *"Talitha koum!"* (which means, "Little girl, I say to you, get up!"). ⁴²Immediately the girl stood up and walked around (she was twelve years old). At this they were completely astonished. ⁴³He gave strict orders not to let anyone know about this, and told them to give her something to eat.

A Prophet Without Honor

6 Jesus left there and went to his hometown, accompanied by his disciples. ²When the Sabbath came, he began to

---

[a] *20* That is, the Ten Cities

teach in the synagogue, and many who heard him were amazed.

"Where did this man get these things?" they asked. "What's this wisdom that has been given him, that he even does miracles! ³Isn't this the carpenter? Isn't this Mary's son and the brother of James, Joseph,ᵃ Judas and Simon? Aren't his sisters here with us?" And they took offense at him.

⁴Jesus said to them, "Only in his hometown, among his relatives and in his own house is a prophet without honor." ⁵He could not do any miracles there, except lay his hands on a few sick people and heal them. ⁶And he was amazed at their lack of faith.

Jesus Sends Out the Twelve

Then Jesus went around teaching from village to village. ⁷Calling the Twelve to him, he sent them out two by two and gave them authority over evilᵇ spirits.

⁸These were his instructions: "Take nothing for the journey except a staff—no bread, no bag, no money in your belts. ⁹Wear sandals but not an extra tunic. ¹⁰Whenever you enter a house, stay there until you leave that town. ¹¹And if any place will not welcome you or listen to you, shake the dust off your feet when you leave, as a testimony against them."

¹²They went out and preached that people should repent. ¹³They drove out many demons and anointed many sick people with oil and healed them.

John the Baptist Beheaded

¹⁴King Herod heard about this, for Jesus' name had become well known. Some were saying,ᶜ "John the Baptist has been raised from the dead, and that is why miraculous powers are at work in him."

¹⁵Others said, "He is Elijah."

And still others claimed, "He is a prophet, like one of the prophets of long ago."

¹⁶But when Herod heard this, he said, "John, the man I beheaded, has been raised from the dead!"

¹⁷For Herod himself had given orders to have John arrested, and he had him bound and put in prison. He did this because of Herodias, his brother Philip's wife, whom he had married. ¹⁸For John had been saying to Herod, "It is not lawful for you to have your brother's wife." ¹⁹So Herodias nursed a grudge against John and wanted to kill him. But she was not able to, ²⁰because Herod feared John and protected him, knowing him to be a righteous and holy man. When Herod heard John, he was greatly puzzled;ᵈ yet he liked to listen to him.

²¹Finally the opportune time came. On his birthday Herod gave a banquet for his high officials and military commanders and the leading men of Galilee. ²²When the daughter of Herodias came in and danced, she pleased Herod and his dinner guests.

The king said to the girl, "Ask me for anything you want, and I'll give it to you." ²³And he promised her with an oath, "Whatever you ask I will give you, up to half my kingdom."

²⁴She went out and said to her mother, "What shall I ask for?"

"The head of John the Baptist," she answered.

²⁵At once the girl hurried in to the king with the request: "I want you to give me right now the head of John the Baptist on a platter."

²⁶The king was greatly distressed, but because of his oaths and his dinner guests, he did not want to refuse her. ²⁷So he immediately sent an executioner with orders to bring John's head. The man went, beheaded John in the prison, ²⁸and brought back his head on a platter. He presented it to the girl, and she gave it to her mother. ²⁹On hearing of this, John's disciples came and took his body and laid it in a tomb.

ᵃ 3 Greek *Joses*, a variant of *Joseph*   ᵇ 7 Greek *unclean*   ᶜ 14 Some early manuscripts *He was saying*   ᵈ 20 Some early manuscripts *he did many things*

Jesus Feeds the Five Thousand

30The apostles gathered around Jesus and reported to him all they had done and taught. 31Then, because so many people were coming and going that they did not even have a chance to eat, he said to them, "Come with me by yourselves to a quiet place and get some rest."

32So they went away by themselves in a boat to a solitary place. 33But many who saw them leaving recognized them and ran on foot from all the towns and got there ahead of them. 34When Jesus landed and saw a large crowd, he had compassion on them, because they were like sheep without a shepherd. So he began teaching them many things.

35By this time it was late in the day, so his disciples came to him. "This is a remote place," they said, "and it's already very late. 36Send the people away so they can go to the surrounding countryside and villages and buy themselves something to eat."

37But he answered, "You give them something to eat."

They said to him, "That would take eight months of a man's wages[a]! Are we to go and spend that much on bread and give it to them to eat?"

38"How many loaves do you have?" he asked. "Go and see."

When they found out, they said, "Five—and two fish."

39Then Jesus directed them to have all the people sit down in groups on the green grass. 40So they sat down in groups of hundreds and fifties. 41Taking the five loaves and the two fish and looking up to heaven, he gave thanks and broke the loaves. Then he gave them to his disciples to set before the people. He also divided the two fish among them all. 42They all ate and were satisfied, 43and the disciples picked up twelve basketfuls of broken pieces of bread and fish. 44The number of the men who had eaten was five thousand.

Jesus Walks on the Water

45Immediately Jesus made his disciples get into the boat and go on ahead of him to Bethsaida, while he dismissed the crowd. 46After leaving them, he went up on a mountainside to pray.

47When evening came, the boat was in the middle of the lake, and he was alone on land. 48He saw the disciples straining at the oars, because the wind was against them. About the fourth watch of the night he went out to them, walking on the lake. He was about to pass by them, 49but when they saw him walking on the lake, they thought he was a ghost. They cried out, 50because they all saw him and were terrified.

Immediately he spoke to them and said, "Take courage! It is I. Don't be afraid." 51Then he climbed into the boat with them, and the wind died down. They were completely amazed, 52for they had not understood about the loaves; their hearts were hardened.

53When they had crossed over, they landed at Gennesaret and anchored there. 54As soon as they got out of the boat, people recognized Jesus. 55They ran throughout that whole region and carried the sick on mats to wherever they heard he was. 56And wherever he went—into villages, towns or countryside—they placed the sick in the marketplaces. They begged him to let him to let them touch even the edge of his cloak, and all who touched him were healed.

Clean and Unclean

7 The Pharisees and some of the teachers of the law who had come from Jerusalem gathered around Jesus and 2saw some of his disciples eating food with hands that were "unclean," that is, unwashed. 3(The Pharisees and all the Jews do not eat unless they give their hands a ceremonial washing, holding to the tradition of the elders. 4When they come from the marketplace they do not eat unless they wash. And they observe many

---

a 37 Greek take two hundred denarii

other traditions, such as the washing of cups, pitchers and kettles.ᵃ)

⁵So the Pharisees and teachers of the law asked Jesus, "Why don't your disciples live according to the tradition of the elders instead of eating their food with 'unclean' hands?"

⁶He replied, "Isaiah was right when he prophesied about you hypocrites; as it is written:

" 'These people honor me with their lips,
     but their hearts are far from me.
⁷They worship me in vain;
     their teachings are but rules taught by men.'ᵇ

⁸You have let go of the commands of God and are holding on to the traditions of men."

⁹And he said to them: "You have a fine way of setting aside the commands of God in order to observeᶜ your own traditions! ¹⁰For Moses said, 'Honor your father and your mother,'ᵈ and, 'Anyone who curses his father or mother must be put to death.'ᵉ ¹¹But you say that if a man says to his father or mother: 'Whatever help you might otherwise have received from me is Corban' (that is, a gift devoted to God), ¹²then you no longer let him do anything for his father or mother. ¹³Thus you nullify the word of God by your tradition that you have handed down. And you do many things like that."

¹⁴Again Jesus called the crowd to him and said, "Listen to me, everyone, and understand this. ¹⁵Nothing outside a man can make him 'unclean' by going into him. Rather, it is what comes out of a man that makes him 'unclean.'ᶠ"

¹⁷After he had left the crowd and entered the house, his disciples asked him about this parable. ¹⁸"Are you so dull?" he asked. "Don't you see that nothing that enters a man from the outside can make him 'unclean'? ¹⁹For it doesn't go into his

heart but into his stomach, and then out of his body." (In saying this, Jesus declared all foods "clean.")

²⁰He went on: "What comes out of a man is what makes him 'unclean.' ²¹For from within, out of men's hearts, come evil thoughts, sexual immorality, theft, murder, adultery, ²²greed, malice, deceit, lewdness, envy, slander, arrogance and folly. ²³All these evils come from inside and make a man 'unclean.' "

The Faith of a Syrophoenician Woman

²⁴Jesus left that place and went to the vicinity of Tyre.ᵍ He entered a house and did not want anyone to know it; yet he could not keep his presence secret. ²⁵In fact, as soon as she heard about him, a woman whose little daughter was possessed by an evilʰ spirit came and fell at his feet. ²⁶The woman was a Greek, born in Syrian Phoenicia. She begged Jesus to drive the demon out of her daughter.

²⁷"First let the children eat all they want," he told her, "for it is not right to take the children's bread and toss it to their dogs."

²⁸"Yes, Lord," she replied, "but even the dogs under the table eat the children's crumbs."

²⁹Then he told her, "For such a reply, you may go; the demon has left your daughter."

³⁰She went home and found her child lying on the bed, and the demon gone.

The Healing of a Deaf and Mute Man

³¹Then Jesus left the vicinity of Tyre and went through Sidon, down to the Sea of Galilee and into the region of the Decapolis.ⁱ ³²There some people brought to him a man who was deaf and could hardly talk, and they begged him to place his hand on the man.

³³After he took him aside, away from the crowd, Jesus put his fingers into the

---

ᵃ4 Some early manuscripts *pitchers, kettles and dining couches* ᵇ6,7 Isaiah 29:13 ᶜ9 Some manuscripts *set up* ᵈ10 Exodus 20:12; Deut. 5:16 ᵉ10 Exodus 21:17; Lev. 20:9 ᶠ15 Some early manuscripts *'unclean.'* ¹⁶*If anyone has ears to hear, let him hear.* ᵍ24 Many early manuscripts *Tyre and Sidon* ʰ25 Greek *unclean* ⁱ31 That is, the Ten Cities man's ears. Then he spit and touched the man's tongue. ³⁴He looked up to heaven and with a deep sigh said to him, *"Eph-phatha!"* (which means, "Be opened!"). ³⁵At this, the man's ears were opened, his tongue was loosened and he began to speak plainly.

³⁶Jesus commanded them not to tell anyone. But the more he did so, the more they kept talking about it. ³⁷People were overwhelmed with amazement. "He has done everything well," they said. "He even makes the deaf hear and the mute speak."

Jesus Feeds the Four Thousand

8 During those days another large crowd gathered. Since they had nothing to eat, Jesus called his disciples to him and said, ²"I have compassion for these people; they have already been with me three days and have nothing to eat. ³If I send them home hungry, they will collapse on the way, because some of them have come a long distance."

⁴His disciples answered, "But where in this remote place can anyone get enough bread to feed them?"

⁵"How many loaves do you have?" Jesus asked.

"Seven," they replied.

⁶He told the crowd to sit down on the ground. When he had taken the seven loaves and given thanks, he broke them and gave them to his disciples to set before the people, and they did so. ⁷They had a few small fish as well; he gave thanks for them also and told the disciples to distribute them. ⁸The people ate and were satisfied. Afterward the disciples picked up seven basketfuls of broken pieces that were left over. ⁹About four thousand men were present. And having sent them away, ¹⁰he got into the boat with his disciples and went to the region of Dalmanutha.

¹¹The Pharisees came and began to question Jesus. To test him, they asked him for a sign from heaven. ¹²He sighed deeply and said, "Why does this generation ask for a miraculous sign? I tell you

the truth, no sign will be given to it." ¹³Then he left them, got back into the boat and crossed to the other side.

The Yeast of the Pharisees and Herod

¹⁴The disciples had forgotten to bring bread, except for one loaf they had with them in the boat. ¹⁵"Be careful," Jesus warned them. "Watch out for the yeast of the Pharisees and that of Herod."

¹⁶They discussed this with one another and said, "It is because we have no bread."

¹⁷Aware of their discussion, Jesus asked them: "Why are you talking about having no bread? Do you still not see or understand? Are your hearts hardened? ¹⁸Do you have eyes but fail to see, and ears but fail to hear? And don't you remember? ¹⁹When I broke the five loaves for the five thousand, how many basketfuls of pieces did you pick up?"

"Twelve," they replied.

²⁰"And when I broke the seven loaves for the four thousand, how many basketfuls of pieces did you pick up?"

They answered, "Seven."

²¹He said to them, "Do you still not understand?"

The Healing of a Blind Man at Bethsaida

²²They came to Bethsaida, and some people brought a blind man and begged Jesus to touch him. ²³He took the blind man by the hand and led him outside the village. When he had spit on the man's eyes and put his hands on him, Jesus asked, "Do you see anything?"

²⁴He looked up and said, "I see people; they look like trees walking around."

²⁵Once more Jesus put his hands on the man's eyes. Then his eyes were opened, his sight was restored, and he saw everything clearly. ²⁶Jesus sent him home, saying, "Don't go into the village.ᵃ"

Peter's Confession of Christ

²⁷Jesus and his disciples went on to the villages around Caesarea Philippi. On the

---

ᵃ 26 Some manuscripts *Don't go and tell anyone in the village* way he asked them, "Who do people say I am?"

28They replied, "Some say John the Baptist; others say Elijah; and still others, one of the prophets."

29"But what about you?" he asked. "Who do you say I am?"

Peter answered, "You are the Christ.[a]"

30Jesus warned them not to tell anyone about him.

Jesus Predicts His Death

31He then began to teach them that the Son of Man must suffer many things and be rejected by the elders, chief priests and teachers of the law, and that he must be killed and after three days rise again. 32He spoke plainly about this, and Peter took him aside and began to rebuke him.

33But when Jesus turned and looked at his disciples, he rebuked Peter. "Get behind me, Satan!" he said. "You do not have in mind the things of God, but the things of men."

34Then he called the crowd to him along with his disciples and said: "If anyone would come after me, he must deny himself and take up his cross and follow me. 35For whoever wants to save his life[b] will lose it, but whoever loses his life for me and for the gospel will save it. 36What good is it for a man to gain the whole world, yet forfeit his soul? 37Or what can a man give in exchange for his soul? 38If anyone is ashamed of me and my words in this adulterous and sinful generation, the Son of Man will be ashamed of him when he comes in his Father's glory with the holy angels."

9 And he said to them, "I tell you the truth, some who are standing here will not taste death before they see the kingdom of God come with power."

The Transfiguration

2After six days Jesus took Peter, James and John with him and led them up a high mountain, where they were all alone. There he was transfigured before them. 3His clothes became dazzling white, whiter than anyone in the world could bleach them. 4And there appeared before them Elijah and Moses, who were talking with Jesus.

5Peter said to Jesus, "Rabbi, it is good for us to be here. Let us put up three shelters—one for you, one for Moses and one for Elijah." 6(He did not know what to say, they were so frightened.)

7Then a cloud appeared and enveloped them, and a voice came from the cloud: "This is my Son, whom I love. Listen to him!"

8Suddenly, when they looked around, they no longer saw anyone with them except Jesus.

9As they were coming down the mountain, Jesus gave them orders not to tell anyone what they had seen until the Son of Man had risen from the dead. 10They kept the matter to themselves, discussing what "rising from the dead" meant.

11And they asked him, "Why do the teachers of the law say that Elijah must come first?"

12Jesus replied, "To be sure, Elijah does come first, and restores all things. Why then is it written that the Son of Man must suffer much and be rejected? 13But I tell you, Elijah has come, and they have done to him everything they wished, just as it is written about him."

The Healing of a Boy With an Evil Spirit

14When they came to the other disciples, they saw a large crowd around them and the teachers of the law arguing with them. 15As soon as all the people saw Jesus, they were overwhelmed with wonder and ran to greet him.

16"What are you arguing with them about?" he asked.

17A man in the crowd answered, "Teacher, I brought you my son, who is possessed by a spirit that has robbed him

a 29 Or Messiah. "The Christ" (Greek) and "the Messiah" (Hebrew) both mean "the Anointed One."   b 35 The Greek word means either life or soul; also in verse 36.

of speech. 18Whenever it seizes him, it throws him to the ground. He foams at the mouth, gnashes his teeth and becomes rigid. I asked your disciples to drive out the spirit, but they could not."

19"O unbelieving generation," Jesus replied, "how long shall I stay with you? How long shall I put up with you? Bring the boy to me."

20So they brought him. When the spirit saw Jesus, it immediately threw the boy into a convulsion. He fell to the ground and rolled around, foaming at the mouth.

21Jesus asked the boy's father, "How long has he been like this?"

"From childhood," he answered. 22"It has often thrown him into fire or water to kill him. But if you can do anything, take pity on us and help us."

23"'If you can'?" said Jesus. "Everything is possible for him who believes."

24Immediately the boy's father exclaimed, "I do believe; help me overcome my unbelief!"

25When Jesus saw that a crowd was running to the scene, he rebuked the evil[a] spirit. "You deaf and mute spirit," he said, "I command you, come out of him and never enter him again."

26The spirit shrieked, convulsed him violently and came out. The boy looked so much like a corpse that many said, "He's dead." 27But Jesus took him by the hand and lifted him to his feet, and he stood up.

28After Jesus had gone indoors, his disciples asked him privately, "Why couldn't we drive it out?"

29He replied, "This kind can come out only by prayer.[b]"

30They left that place and passed through Galilee. Jesus did not want anyone to know where they were, 31because he was teaching his disciples. He said to them, "The Son of Man is going to be betrayed into the hands of men. They will kill him, and after three days he will rise." 32But they did not understand what he meant and were afraid to ask him about it.

Who Is the Greatest?

33They came to Capernaum. When he was in the house, he asked them, "What were you arguing about on the road?" 34But they kept quiet because on the way they had argued about who was the greatest.

35Sitting down, Jesus called the Twelve and said, "If anyone wants to be first, he must be the very last, and the servant of all."

36He took a little child and had him stand among them. Taking him in his arms, he said to them, 37"Whoever welcomes one of these little children in my name welcomes me; and whoever welcomes me does not welcome me but the one who sent me."

Whoever Is Not Against Us Is for Us

38"Teacher," said John, "we saw a man driving out demons in your name and we told him to stop, because he was not one of us."

39"Do not stop him," Jesus said. "No one who does a miracle in my name can in the next moment say anything bad about me, 40for whoever is not against us is for us. 41I tell you the truth, anyone who gives you a cup of water in my name because you belong to Christ will certainly not lose his reward.

Causing to Sin

42"And if anyone causes one of these little ones who believe in me to sin, it would be better for him to be thrown into the sea with a large millstone tied around his neck. 43If your hand causes you to sin, cut it off. It is better for you to enter life maimed than with two hands to go into hell, where the fire never goes out.[c] 45And if your foot causes you to sin, cut it off. It is better for you to enter life crippled than to have two feet and be thrown into hell.[d] 47And if your eye

---

a 25 Greek unclean   b 29 Some manuscripts prayer and fasting   c 43 Some manuscripts out, 44where / " 'their worm does not die, / and the fire is not quenched.'   d 45 Some manuscripts hell, 46where / " 'their worm does not die, / and the fire is not quenched.'

Finding Freedom From What Keeps You Bound

GOING *deeper*

READ AND CONSIDER: MARK 9:14-32

"He replied, 'This kind can come out only by prayer'" (Mark 9:29).

Jesus' disciples attempted to exorcise a demon from an afflicted boy, but they failed. After Jesus responded to the frantic father's plea for help, the demon left the child and the disciples were left bewildered. Why had Jesus succeeded where their sincere efforts had not?

Jesus said that prayer was the key to releasing this person from bondage to satanic forces. Some manuscripts include fasting along with prayer. Fasting always increases the power of our prayers. The disciples had apparently not prepared themselves well enough by praying and fasting first.

In Matthew 18:18, Christ taught, "Whatever you bind on earth will be bound in heaven, and whatever you loose on earth will be loosed in heaven." God gives us His authority on earth. When we call on that authority, God releases power to us from heaven. Because it's God's power and not ours, we become the vessel through which His power flows. When we pray, we bring that power to bear upon the situation, allowing the power of God to work through our powerlessness. When we pray, we are humbling ourselves before God and saying, "I need Your presence and Your power, Lord. I can't do this without You." When we don't pray, we are in effect saying that we have no need of anything outside of ourselves.

If you are facing a difficult situation within your own life, you have authority in the name of Jesus to stop evil and permit good. You can submit to God in prayer whatever bondage controls you—such as alcoholism, addiction, laziness, depression, infirmity, abusiveness, confusion, anxiety, fear, or failure—and fast and pray to be released from it. God will set you free.

causes you to sin, pluck it out. It is better for you to enter the kingdom of God with one eye than to have two eyes and be thrown into hell, [48]where

"'their worm does not die,
and the fire is not quenched.'[a]

[49]Everyone will be salted with fire.

[50]"Salt is good, but if it loses its saltiness, how can you make it salty again? Have salt in yourselves, and be at peace with each other."

Divorce

10 Jesus then left that place and went into the region of Judea and across the Jordan. Again crowds of people came to him, and as was his custom, he taught them.

[2]Some Pharisees came and tested him by asking, "Is it lawful for a man to divorce his wife?"

[3]"What did Moses command you?" he replied.

[4]They said, "Moses permitted a man to write a certificate of divorce and send her away."

[5]"It was because your hearts were hard that Moses wrote you this law," Jesus replied. [6]"But at the beginning of creation God 'made them male and female.'[b] [7]'For this reason a man will leave his father and mother and be united to his wife,[c] [8]and the two will become one flesh.'[d] So they

[a]48 Isaiah 66:24   [b]6 Gen. 1:27   [c]7 Some early manuscripts do not have *and be united to his wife.*   [d]8 Gen. 2:24

are no longer two, but one. [9] Therefore what God has joined together, let man not separate."

[10] When they were in the house again, the disciples asked Jesus about this. [11] He answered, "Anyone who divorces his wife and marries another woman commits adultery against her. [12] And if she divorces her husband and marries another man, she commits adultery."

The Little Children and Jesus

[13] People were bringing little children to Jesus to have him touch them, but the disciples rebuked them. [14] When Jesus saw this, he was indignant. He said to them, "Let the little children come to me, and do not hinder them, for the kingdom of God belongs to such as these. [15] I tell you the truth, anyone who will not receive the kingdom of God like a little child will never enter it." [16] And he took the children in his arms, put his hands on them and blessed them.

The Rich Young Man

[17] As Jesus started on his way, a man ran up to him and fell on his knees before him. "Good teacher," he asked, "what must I do to inherit eternal life?"

[18] "Why do you call me good?" Jesus answered. "No one is good—except God alone. [19] You know the commandments: 'Do not murder, do not commit adultery, do not steal, do not give false testimony, do not defraud, honor your father and mother.'[a]"

[20] "Teacher," he declared, "all these I have kept since I was a boy."

[21] Jesus looked at him and loved him. "One thing you lack," he said. "Go, sell everything you have and give to the poor, and you will have treasure in heaven. Then come, follow me."

[22] At this the man's face fell. He went away sad, because he had great wealth.

[23] Jesus looked around and said to his disciples, "How hard it is for the rich to enter the kingdom of God!"

[24] The disciples were amazed at his

---

[a] 19 Exodus 20:12-16; Deut. 5:16-20

GOING deeper

Nothing Is Impossible With God

READ AND CONSIDER: MARK 10:17-31

"Jesus looked at them and said, 'With man this is impossible, but not with God; all things are possible with God'" (Mark 10:27).

The most exciting thing about God being all-powerful is that it means *with God, all things are possible.* There is nothing too hard for Him. Gabriel told Mary that "nothing is impossible with God," and look what happened to her (Luke 1:37). Jesus said, "All things are possible with God," and look what He accomplished! There is nothing that God cannot do. God's power is not limited.

If you have ever lived through an earthquake, tornado, or hurricane, you know that the power of it is overwhelming and frightening. Yet God has absolute power over all those things. May I suggest that we don't really *want* to experience the *full* magnitude of God's power?

Suffice it to say that God has far more power than is necessary to meet your needs and lift you above your situation. He has more than enough power to rescue you from your circumstances and help you do things you could not do without Him. If God is so powerful that He can create something from nothing or give life to the dead, then think what He can do in your life. He has the power to do whatever is necessary, and He doesn't want you to doubt it.

words. But Jesus said again, "Children, how hard it is[a] to enter the kingdom of God! 25It is easier for a camel to go through the eye of a needle than for a rich man to enter the kingdom of God."

26The disciples were even more amazed, and said to each other, "Who then can be saved?"

27Jesus looked at them and said, "With man this is impossible, but not with God; all things are possible with God."

28Peter said to him, "We have left everything to follow you!"

29"I tell you the truth," Jesus replied, "no one who has left home or brothers or sisters or mother or father or children or fields for me and the gospel 30will fail to receive a hundred times as much in this present age (homes, brothers, sisters, mothers, children and fields—and with them, persecutions) and in the age to come, eternal life. 31But many who are first will be last, and the last first."

Jesus Again Predicts His Death

32They were on their way up to Jerusalem, with Jesus leading the way, and the disciples were astonished, while those who followed were afraid. Again he took the Twelve aside and told them what was going to happen to him. 33"We are going up to Jerusalem," he said, "and the Son of Man will be betrayed to the chief priests and teachers of the law. They will condemn him to death and will hand him over to the Gentiles, 34who will mock him and spit on him, flog him and kill him. Three days later he will rise."

The Request of James and John

35Then James and John, the sons of Zebedee, came to him. "Teacher," they said, "we want you to do for us whatever we ask."

36"What do you want me to do for you?" he asked.

37They replied, "Let one of us sit at your right and the other at your left in your glory."

38"You don't know what you are asking," Jesus said. "Can you drink the cup I drink or be baptized with the baptism I am baptized with?"

39"We can," they answered.

Jesus said to them, "You will drink the cup I drink and be baptized with the baptism I am baptized with, 40but to sit at my right or left is not for me to grant. These places belong to those for whom they have been prepared."

41When the ten heard about this, they became indignant with James and John. 42Jesus called them together and said, "You know that those who are regarded as rulers of the Gentiles lord it over them, and their high officials exercise authority over them. 43Not so with you. Instead, whoever wants to become great among you must be your servant, 44and whoever wants to be first must be slave of all. 45For even the Son of Man did not come to be served, but to serve, and to give his life as a ransom for many."

Blind Bartimaeus Receives His Sight

46Then they came to Jericho. As Jesus and his disciples, together with a large crowd, were leaving the city, a blind man, Bartimaeus (that is, the Son of Timaeus), was sitting by the roadside begging. 47When he heard that it was Jesus of Nazareth, he began to shout, "Jesus, Son of David, have mercy on me!"

48Many rebuked him and told him to be quiet, but he shouted all the more, "Son of David, have mercy on me!"

49Jesus stopped and said, "Call him."

So they called to the blind man, "Cheer up! On your feet! He's calling you." 50Throwing his cloak aside, he jumped to his feet and came to Jesus.

51"What do you want me to do for you?" Jesus asked him.

The blind man said, "Rabbi, I want to see."

52"Go," said Jesus, "your faith has healed you." Immediately he received his sight and followed Jesus along the road.

---

[a] 24 Some manuscripts *is for those who trust in riches*

The Triumphal Entry

11 As they approached Jerusalem and came to Bethphage and Bethany at the Mount of Olives, Jesus sent two of his disciples, ²saying to them, "Go to the village ahead of you, and just as you enter it, you will find a colt tied there, which no one has ever ridden. Untie it and bring it here. ³If anyone asks you, 'Why are you doing this?' tell him, 'The Lord needs it and will send it back here shortly.'"

⁴They went and found a colt outside in the street, tied at a doorway. As they untied it, ⁵some people standing there asked, "What are you doing, untying that colt?" ⁶They answered as Jesus had told them to, and the people let them go. ⁷When they brought the colt to Jesus and threw their cloaks over it, he sat on it. ⁸Many people spread their cloaks on the road, while others spread branches they had cut in the fields. ⁹Those who went ahead and those who followed shouted,

"Hosanna!ᵃ"

"Blessed is he who comes in the name of the Lord!"ᵇ

¹⁰"Blessed is the coming kingdom of our father David!"

"Hosanna in the highest!"

¹¹Jesus entered Jerusalem and went to the temple. He looked around at everything, but since it was already late, he went out to Bethany with the Twelve.

Jesus Clears the Temple

¹²The next day as they were leaving Bethany, Jesus was hungry. ¹³Seeing in the distance a fig tree in leaf, he went to find out if it had any fruit. When he reached it, he found nothing but leaves, because it was not the season for figs. ¹⁴Then he said to the tree, "May no one ever eat fruit from you again." And his disciples heard him say it.

¹⁵On reaching Jerusalem, Jesus entered the temple area and began driving out those who were buying and selling there. He overturned the tables of the money changers and the benches of those selling doves, ¹⁶and would not allow anyone to carry merchandise through the temple courts. ¹⁷And as he taught them, he said, "Is it not written:

"'My house will be called
a house of prayer for all nations'ᶜ?

But you have made it 'a den of robbers.'ᵈ"

¹⁸The chief priests and the teachers of the law heard this and began looking for a way to kill him, for they feared him, because the whole crowd was amazed at his teaching.

¹⁹When evening came, theyᵉ went out of the city.

The Withered Fig Tree

²⁰In the morning, as they went along, they saw the fig tree withered from the roots. ²¹Peter remembered and said to Jesus, "Rabbi, look! The fig tree you cursed has withered!"

²²"Haveᶠ faith in God," Jesus answered. ²³"I tell you the truth, if anyone says to this mountain, 'Go, throw yourself into the sea,' and does not doubt in his heart but believes that what he says will happen, it will be done for him. ²⁴Therefore I tell you, whatever you ask for in prayer, believe that you have received it, and it will be yours. ²⁵And when you stand praying, if you hold anything against anyone, forgive him, so that your Father in heaven may forgive you your sins.ᵍ"

The Authority of Jesus Questioned

²⁷They arrived again in Jerusalem, and while Jesus was walking in the temple courts, the chief priests, the teachers of the law and the elders came to him.

ᵃ *9* A Hebrew expression meaning "Save!" which became an exclamation of praise; also in verse 10   ᵇ *9* Psalm 118:25,26
ᶜ *17* Isaiah 56:7   ᵈ *17* Jer. 7:11   ᵉ *19* Some early manuscripts *he*   ᶠ *22* Some early manuscripts *If you have*   ᵍ *25* Some manuscripts *sins.* ²⁶*But if you do not forgive, neither will your Father who is in heaven forgive your sins.*

The Power of Forgiveness

READ AND CONSIDER: MARK 11:20-25

"And when you stand praying, if you hold anything against anyone, forgive him, so that your Father in heaven may forgive you your sins" (Mark 11:25).

Of all the commands in Scripture, the instruction to forgive those who have hurt us is one of the most difficult to keep. Our natural human tendency is to hold on to the hurt inflicted upon us, to nurse our wounds and hold grudges. Or, at the very least, we separate ourselves forever from the individual who is the source of our pain so that we cannot be hurt by that person again.

There are times, such as in cases of abuse, when physical separation is necessary. When a crime has been committed, justice and forgiveness go hand in hand. The courts of law must hold a perpetrator accountable, and God will hold that person accountable in the final judgment, but we must still forgive that person. In these verses, Jesus was talking about the spiritual obligation that we have to forgive each other because we have been so graciously forgiven by our heavenly Father. To refuse to forgive others reveals that our hearts do not understand the level of forgiveness we have received.

To forgive does not mean we necessarily forget; we may remember, but we choose not to allow the memory to keep us bitter. We don't replay the offense over and over in our mind. To forgive does not mean to say that what happened to hurt us doesn't matter; it *does* matter or it wouldn't need forgiveness. But we must remember that forgiving someone doesn't make that person right; it makes *you* free. When you forgive, you are set free from the bondage of carrying around the hurt, the pain, the grudge. You can let it go and move on with your life.

When we choose not to forgive, we end up stuck in the past and walking in the dark (1 John 2:9-11). Because we can't see clearly, we stumble around in confusion. This throws our judgment off and we make mistakes. We become weak, sick, and bitter. Other people notice all this because unforgiveness shows in the face, words, and actions of those who have it. People see it, even if they can't specifically identify what it is, and they don't feel comfortable around it.

The good news is that when we choose to forgive, not only do we benefit, but so do the people around us.

28"By what authority are you doing these things?" they asked. "And who gave you authority to do this?"

29Jesus replied, "I will ask you one question. Answer me, and I will tell you by what authority I am doing these things. 30John's baptism—was it from heaven, or from men? Tell me!"

31They discussed it among themselves and said, "If we say, 'From heaven,' he will ask, 'Then why didn't you believe him?' 32But if we say, 'From men'…" (They feared the people, for everyone held that John really was a prophet.)

33So they answered Jesus, "We don't know."

Jesus said, "Neither will I tell you by what authority I am doing these things."

The Parable of the Tenants

12 He then began to speak to them in parables: "A man planted a vineyard. He put a wall around it, dug a pit for the winepress and built a watchtower. Then he rented the vineyard to some farmers and went away on a journey. 2At harvest time he sent a servant to the tenants to collect from them some of the

fruit of the vineyard. [3]But they seized him, beat him and sent him away empty-handed. [4]Then he sent another servant to them; they struck this man on the head and treated him shamefully. [5]He sent still another, and that one they killed. He sent many others; some of them they beat, others they killed.

[6]"He had one left to send, a son, whom he loved. He sent him last of all, saying, 'They will respect my son.'

[7]"But the tenants said to one another, 'This is the heir. Come, let's kill him, and the inheritance will be ours.' [8]So they took him and killed him, and threw him out of the vineyard.

[9]"What then will the owner of the vineyard do? He will come and kill those tenants and give the vineyard to others. [10]Haven't you read this scripture:

"'The stone the builders rejected
  has become the capstone[a];
[11]the Lord has done this,
  and it is marvelous in our eyes'[b]?"

[12]Then they looked for a way to arrest him because they knew he had spoken the parable against them. But they were afraid of the crowd; so they left him and went away.

Paying Taxes to Caesar

[13]Later they sent some of the Pharisees and Herodians to Jesus to catch him in his words. [14]They came to him and said, "Teacher, we know you are a man of integrity. You aren't swayed by men, because you pay no attention to who they are; but you teach the way of God in accordance with the truth. Is it right to pay taxes to Caesar or not? [15]Should we pay or shouldn't we?"

But Jesus knew their hypocrisy. "Why are you trying to trap me?" he asked. "Bring me a denarius and let me look at it." [16]They brought the coin, and he asked them, "Whose portrait is this? And whose inscription?"

"Caesar's," they replied.

[17]Then Jesus said to them, "Give to Caesar what is Caesar's and to God what is God's."

And they were amazed at him.

Marriage at the Resurrection

[18]Then the Sadducees, who say there is no resurrection, came to him with a question. [19]"Teacher," they said, "Moses wrote for us that if a man's brother dies and leaves a wife but no children, the man must marry the widow and have children for his brother. [20]Now there were seven brothers. The first one married and died without leaving any children. [21]The second one married the widow, but he also died, leaving no child. It was the same with the third. [22]In fact, none of the seven left any children. Last of all, the woman died too. [23]At the resurrection[c] whose wife will she be, since the seven were married to her?"

[24]Jesus replied, "Are you not in error because you do not know the Scriptures or the power of God? [25]When the dead rise, they will neither marry nor be given in marriage; they will be like the angels in heaven. [26]Now about the dead rising—have you not read in the book of Moses, in the account of the bush, how God said to him, 'I am the God of Abraham, the God of Isaac, and the God of Jacob'[d]? [27]He is not the God of the dead, but of the living. You are badly mistaken!"

The Greatest Commandment

[28]One of the teachers of the law came and heard them debating. Noticing that Jesus had given them a good answer, he asked him, "Of all the commandments, which is the most important?"

[29]"The most important one," answered Jesus, "is this: 'Hear, O Israel, the Lord our God, the Lord is one.[e] [30]Love the Lord your God with all your heart and with all your soul and with all your mind

---

[a] 10 Or cornerstone   [b] 11 Psalm 118:22,23   [c] 23 Some manuscripts resurrection, when men rise from the dead,
[d] 26 Exodus 3:6   [e] 29 Or the Lord our God is one Lord

and with all your strength.'ª ³¹The second is this: 'Love your neighbor as yourself.'ᵇ There is no commandment greater than these."

Praying Mark 12:30

Lord, remove anything that keeps me from loving You with all my heart, soul, mind, and strength.

³²"Well said, teacher," the man replied. "You are right in saying that God is one and there is no other but him. ³³To love him with all your heart, with all your understanding and with all your strength, and to love your neighbor as yourself is more important than all burnt offerings and sacrifices."

³⁴When Jesus saw that he had answered wisely, he said to him, "You are not far from the kingdom of God." And from then on no one dared ask him any more questions.

Whose Son Is the Christ?

³⁵While Jesus was teaching in the temple courts, he asked, "How is it that the teachers of the law say that the Christ ͨ is the son of David? ³⁶David himself, speaking by the Holy Spirit, declared:

" 'The Lord said to my Lord:
  "Sit at my right hand
until I put your enemies
  under your feet." 'ᵈ

³⁷David himself calls him 'Lord.' How then can he be his son?"

The large crowd listened to him with delight.

³⁸As he taught, Jesus said, "Watch out for the teachers of the law. They like to walk around in flowing robes and be greeted in the marketplaces, ³⁹and have the most important seats in the synagogues and the places of honor at banquets. ⁴⁰They devour widows' houses and for a show make lengthy prayers. Such men will be punished most severely."

The Widow's Offering

⁴¹Jesus sat down opposite the place where the offerings were put and watched the crowd putting their money into the temple treasury. Many rich people threw in large amounts. ⁴²But a poor widow came and put in two very small copper coins,ᵉ worth only a fraction of a penny.ᶠ

⁴³Calling his disciples to him, Jesus said, "I tell you the truth, this poor widow has put more into the treasury than all the others. ⁴⁴They all gave out of their wealth; but she, out of her poverty, put in everything—all she had to live on."

Signs of the End of the Age

13 As he was leaving the temple, one of his disciples said to him, "Look, Teacher! What massive stones! What magnificent buildings!"

²"Do you see all these great buildings?" replied Jesus. "Not one stone here will be left on another; every one will be thrown down."

³As Jesus was sitting on the Mount of Olives opposite the temple, Peter, James, John and Andrew asked him privately, ⁴"Tell us, when will these things happen? And what will be the sign that they are all about to be fulfilled?"

⁵Jesus said to them: "Watch out that no one deceives you. ⁶Many will come in my name, claiming, 'I am he,' and will deceive many. ⁷When you hear of wars and rumors of wars, do not be alarmed. Such things must happen, but the end is still to come. ⁸Nation will rise against nation, and kingdom against kingdom. There will be earthquakes in various places, and famines. These are the beginning of birth pains.

⁹"You must be on your guard. You will be handed over to the local councils and flogged in the synagogues. On account of me you will stand before governors and kings as witnesses to them. ¹⁰And the gospel must first be preached to all nations. ¹¹Whenever you are arrested and brought

---

ª *30* Deut. 6:4,5   ᵇ *31* Lev. 19:18   ͨ *35* Or *Messiah*   ᵈ *36* Psalm 110:1   ᵉ *42* Greek *two lepta*   ᶠ *42* Greek *kodrantes* to trial, do not worry beforehand about what to say. Just say whatever is given you at the time, for it is not you speaking, but the Holy Spirit.

12"Brother will betray brother to death, and a father his child. Children will rebel against their parents and have them put to death. 13All men will hate you because of me, but he who stands firm to the end will be saved.

14"When you see 'the abomination that causes desolation'[a] standing where it[b] does not belong—let the reader understand—then let those who are in Judea flee to the mountains. 15Let no one on the roof of his house go down or enter the house to take anything out. 16Let no one in the field go back to get his cloak. 17How dreadful it will be in those days for pregnant women and nursing mothers! 18Pray that this will not take place in winter, 19because those will be days of distress unequaled from the beginning, when God created the world, until now—and never to be equaled again. 20If the Lord had not cut short those days, no one would survive. But for the sake of the elect, whom he has chosen, he has shortened them. 21At that time if anyone says to you, 'Look, here is the Christ[c]!' or, 'Look, there he is!' do not believe it. 22For false Christs and false prophets will appear and perform signs and miracles to deceive the elect—if that were possible. 23So be on your guard; I have told you everything ahead of time.

Praying Mark 13:21-22

Dear Jesus, keep me undeceived so that I will not listen to any false teaching or believe any lies of the enemy.

24"But in those days, following that distress,

"'the sun will be darkened,
    and the moon will not give its
        light;

25the stars will fall from the sky,
    and the heavenly bodies will be
        shaken.'[d]

26"At that time men will see the Son of Man coming in clouds with great power and glory. 27And he will send his angels and gather his elect from the four winds, from the ends of the earth to the ends of the heavens.

28"Now learn this lesson from the fig tree: As soon as its twigs get tender and its leaves come out, you know that summer is near. 29Even so, when you see these things happening, you know that it is near, right at the door. 30I tell you the truth, this generation[e] will certainly not pass away until all these things have happened. 31Heaven and earth will pass away, but my words will never pass away.

The Day and Hour Unknown

32"No one knows about that day or hour, not even the angels in heaven, nor the Son, but only the Father. 33Be on guard! Be alert[f]! You do not know when that time will come. 34It's like a man going away: He leaves his house and puts his servants in charge, each with his assigned task, and tells the one at the door to keep watch.

35"Therefore keep watch because you do not know when the owner of the house will come back—whether in the evening, or at midnight, or when the rooster crows, or at dawn. 36If he comes suddenly, do not let him find you sleeping. 37What I say to you, I say to everyone: 'Watch!'"

Jesus Anointed at Bethany

14 Now the Passover and the Feast of Unleavened Bread were only two days away, and the chief priests and the teachers of the law were looking for some sly way to arrest Jesus and kill him. 2"But not during the Feast," they said, "or the people may riot."

3While he was in Bethany, reclining at the table in the home of a man known as

---

a *14* Daniel 9:27; 11:31; 12:11   b *14* Or *he;* also in verse 29   c *21* Or *Messiah*   d *25* Isaiah 13:10; 34:4   e *30* Or *race*
f *33* Some manuscripts *alert and pray*

Simon the Leper, a woman came with an alabaster jar of very expensive perfume, made of pure nard. She broke the jar and poured the perfume on his head.

⁴Some of those present were saying indignantly to one another, "Why this waste of perfume? ⁵It could have been sold for more than a year's wages[a] and the money given to the poor." And they rebuked her harshly.

⁶"Leave her alone," said Jesus. "Why are you bothering her? She has done a beautiful thing to me. ⁷The poor you will always have with you, and you can help them any time you want. But you will not always have me. ⁸She did what she could. She poured perfume on my body beforehand to prepare for my burial. ⁹I tell you the truth, wherever the gospel is preached throughout the world, what she has done will also be told, in memory of her."

¹⁰Then Judas Iscariot, one of the Twelve, went to the chief priests to betray Jesus to them. ¹¹They were delighted to hear this and promised to give him money. So he watched for an opportunity to hand him over.

The Lord's Supper

¹²On the first day of the Feast of Unleavened Bread, when it was customary to sacrifice the Passover lamb, Jesus' disciples asked him, "Where do you want us to go and make preparations for you to eat the Passover?"

¹³So he sent two of his disciples, telling them, "Go into the city, and a man carrying a jar of water will meet you. Follow him. ¹⁴Say to the owner of the house he enters, 'The Teacher asks: Where is my guest room, where I may eat the Passover with my disciples?' ¹⁵He will show you a large upper room, furnished and ready. Make preparations for us there."

¹⁶The disciples left, went into the city and found things just as Jesus had told them. So they prepared the Passover.

¹⁷When evening came, Jesus arrived with the Twelve. ¹⁸While they were reclining at the table eating, he said, "I tell you the truth, one of you will betray me—one who is eating with me."

¹⁹They were saddened, and one by one they said to him, "Surely not I?"

²⁰"It is one of the Twelve," he replied, "one who dips bread into the bowl with me. ²¹The Son of Man will go just as it is written about him. But woe to that man who betrays the Son of Man! It would be better for him if he had not been born."

²²While they were eating, Jesus took bread, gave thanks and broke it, and gave it to his disciples, saying, "Take it; this is my body."

²³Then he took the cup, gave thanks and offered it to them, and they all drank from it.

²⁴"This is my blood of the[b] covenant, which is poured out for many," he said to them. ²⁵"I tell you the truth, I will not drink again of the fruit of the vine until that day when I drink it anew in the kingdom of God."

²⁶When they had sung a hymn, they went out to the Mount of Olives.

Jesus Predicts Peter's Denial

²⁷"You will all fall away," Jesus told them, "for it is written:

" 'I will strike the shepherd,
   and the sheep will be scattered.'[c]

²⁸But after I have risen, I will go ahead of you into Galilee."

²⁹Peter declared, "Even if all fall away, I will not."

³⁰"I tell you the truth," Jesus answered, "today—yes, tonight—before the rooster crows twice[d] you yourself will disown me three times."

³¹But Peter insisted emphatically, "Even if I have to die with you, I will never disown you." And all the others said the same.

---

[a] 5 Greek *than three hundred denarii*   [b] 24 Some manuscripts *the new*   [c] 27 Zech. 13:7   [d] 30 Some early manuscripts do not have *twice*.

Gethsemane

32 They went to a place called Gethsem-ane, and Jesus said to his disciples, "Sit here while I pray." 33 He took Peter, James and John along with him, and he began to be deeply distressed and troubled. 34 "My soul is overwhelmed with sorrow to the point of death," he said to them. "Stay here and keep watch."

> ## Prayer is . . .
> *telling God that it is His will you want and not your own.*

35 Going a little farther, he fell to the ground and prayed that if possible the hour might pass from him. 36 "*Abba*,[a] Father," he said, "everything is possible for you. Take this cup from me. Yet not what I will, but what you will."

37 Then he returned to his disciples and found them sleeping. "Simon," he said to Peter, "are you asleep? Could you not keep watch for one hour? 38 Watch and pray so that you will not fall into temptation. The spirit is willing, but the body is weak."

> ## Praying Mark 14:38
> *Father, keep me watchful and prayerful so that I do not enter into any kind of temptation.*

39 Once more he went away and prayed the same thing. 40 When he came back, he again found them sleeping, because their eyes were heavy. They did not know what to say to him.

41 Returning the third time, he said to them, "Are you still sleeping and resting? Enough! The hour has come. Look, the Son of Man is betrayed into the hands of sinners. 42 Rise! Let us go! Here comes my betrayer!"

Jesus Arrested

43 Just as he was speaking, Judas, one of the Twelve, appeared. With him was a crowd armed with swords and clubs, sent from the chief priests, the teachers of the law, and the elders.

44 Now the betrayer had arranged a signal with them: "The one I kiss is the man; arrest him and lead him away under guard." 45 Going at once to Jesus, Judas said, "Rabbi!" and kissed him. 46 The men seized Jesus and arrested him. 47 Then one of those standing near drew his sword and struck the servant of the high priest, cutting off his ear.

48 "Am I leading a rebellion," said Jesus, "that you have come out with swords and clubs to capture me? 49 Every day I was with you, teaching in the temple courts, and you did not arrest me. But the Scriptures must be fulfilled." 50 Then everyone deserted him and fled.

51 A young man, wearing nothing but a linen garment, was following Jesus. When they seized him, 52 he fled naked, leaving his garment behind.

Before the Sanhedrin

53 They took Jesus to the high priest, and all the chief priests, elders and teachers of the law came together. 54 Peter followed him at a distance, right into the courtyard of the high priest. There he sat with the guards and warmed himself at the fire.

55 The chief priests and the whole Sanhedrin were looking for evidence against Jesus so that they could put him to death, but they did not find any. 56 Many testified falsely against him, but their statements did not agree.

57 Then some stood up and gave this false testimony against him: 58 "We heard him say, 'I will destroy this man-made temple and in three days will build another, not made by man.'" 59 Yet even then their testimony did not agree.

60 Then the high priest stood up before them and asked Jesus, "Are you not

---

a 36 Aramaic for *Father*

going to answer? What is this testimony that these men are bringing against you?" 61But Jesus remained silent and gave no answer.

Again the high priest asked him, "Are you the Christ,a the Son of the Blessed One?"

62"I am," said Jesus. "And you will see the Son of Man sitting at the right hand of the Mighty One and coming on the clouds of heaven."

63The high priest tore his clothes. "Why do we need any more witnesses?" he asked. 64"You have heard the blasphemy. What do you think?"

They all condemned him as worthy of death. 65Then some began to spit at him; they blindfolded him, struck him with their fists, and said, "Prophesy!" And the guards took him and beat him.

Peter Disowns Jesus

66While Peter was below in the courtyard, one of the servant girls of the high priest came by. 67When she saw Peter warming himself, she looked closely at him.

"You also were with that Nazarene, Jesus," she said.

68But he denied it. "I don't know or understand what you're talking about," he said, and went out into the entryway.b

69When the servant girl saw him there, she said again to those standing around, "This fellow is one of them." 70Again he denied it.

After a little while, those standing near said to Peter, "Surely you are one of them, for you are a Galilean."

71He began to call down curses on himself, and he swore to them, "I don't know this man you're talking about."

72Immediately the rooster crowed the second time.c Then Peter remembered the word Jesus had spoken to him: "Before the rooster crows twiced you will disown me three times." And he broke down and wept.

Jesus Before Pilate

15 Very early in the morning, the chief priests, with the elders, the teachers of the law and the whole Sanhedrin, reached a decision. They bound Jesus, led him away and handed him over to Pilate.

2"Are you the king of the Jews?" asked Pilate.

"Yes, it is as you say," Jesus replied.

3The chief priests accused him of many things. 4So again Pilate asked him, "Aren't you going to answer? See how many things they are accusing you of."

5But Jesus still made no reply, and Pilate was amazed.

6Now it was the custom at the Feast to release a prisoner whom the people requested. 7A man called Barabbas was in prison with the insurrectionists who had committed murder in the uprising. 8The crowd came up and asked Pilate to do for them what he usually did.

9"Do you want me to release to you the king of the Jews?" asked Pilate, 10knowing it was out of envy that the chief priests had handed Jesus over to him. 11But the chief priests stirred up the crowd to have Pilate release Barabbas instead.

12"What shall I do, then, with the one you call the king of the Jews?" Pilate asked them.

13"Crucify him!" they shouted.

14"Why? What crime has he committed?" asked Pilate.

But they shouted all the louder, "Crucify him!"

15Wanting to satisfy the crowd, Pilate released Barabbas to them. He had Jesus flogged, and handed him over to be crucified.

The Soldiers Mock Jesus

16The soldiers led Jesus away into the palace (that is, the Praetorium) and called together the whole company of soldiers. 17They put a purple robe on him, then twisted together a crown of thorns and

---

a 61 Or Messiah   b 68 Some early manuscripts entryway and the rooster crowed   c 72 Some early manuscripts do not have the second time.   d 72 Some early manuscripts do not have twice.

set it on him. ¹⁸And they began to call out to him, "Hail, king of the Jews!" ¹⁹Again and again they struck him on the head with a staff and spit on him. Falling on their knees, they paid homage to him. ²⁰And when they had mocked him, they took off the purple robe and put his own clothes on him. Then they led him out to crucify him.

The Crucifixion

²¹A certain man from Cyrene, Simon, the father of Alexander and Rufus, was passing by on his way in from the country, and they forced him to carry the cross. ²²They brought Jesus to the place called Golgotha (which means The Place of the Skull). ²³Then they offered him wine mixed with myrrh, but he did not take it. ²⁴And they crucified him. Dividing up his clothes, they cast lots to see what each would get.

²⁵It was the third hour when they crucified him. ²⁶The written notice of the charge against him read: THE KING OF THE JEWS. ²⁷They crucified two robbers with him, one on his right and one on his left.ᵃ ²⁹Those who passed by hurled insults at him, shaking their heads and saying, "So! You who are going to destroy the temple and build it in three days, ³⁰come down from the cross and save yourself!"

³¹In the same way the chief priests and the teachers of the law mocked him among themselves. "He saved others," they said, "but he can't save himself! ³²Let this Christ,ᵇ this King of Israel, come down now from the cross, that we may see and believe." Those crucified with him also heaped insults on him.

The Death of Jesus

³³At the sixth hour darkness came over the whole land until the ninth hour. ³⁴And at the ninth hour Jesus cried out in a loud voice, *"Eloi, Eloi, lama sabachthani?"*—which means, "My God, my God, why have you forsaken me?"ᶜ

³⁵When some of those standing near heard this, they said, "Listen, he's calling Elijah."

³⁶One man ran, filled a sponge with wine vinegar, put it on a stick, and offered it to Jesus to drink. "Now leave him alone. Let's see if Elijah comes to take him down," he said.

³⁷With a loud cry, Jesus breathed his last.

³⁸The curtain of the temple was torn in two from top to bottom. ³⁹And when the centurion, who stood there in front of Jesus, heard his cry andᵈ saw how he died, he said, "Surely this man was the Sonᵉ of God!"

⁴⁰Some women were watching from a distance. Among them were Mary Magdalene, Mary the mother of James the younger and of Joses, and Salome. ⁴¹In Galilee these women had followed him and cared for his needs. Many other women who had come up with him to Jerusalem were also there.

The Burial of Jesus

⁴²It was Preparation Day (that is, the day before the Sabbath). So as evening approached, ⁴³Joseph of Arimathea, a prominent member of the Council, who was himself waiting for the kingdom of God, went boldly to Pilate and asked for Jesus' body. ⁴⁴Pilate was surprised to hear that he was already dead. Summoning the centurion, he asked him if Jesus had already died. ⁴⁵When he learned from the centurion that it was so, he gave the body to Joseph. ⁴⁶So Joseph bought some linen cloth, took down the body, wrapped it in the linen, and placed it in a tomb cut out of rock. Then he rolled a stone against the entrance of the tomb. ⁴⁷Mary Magdalene and Mary the mother of Joses saw where he was laid.

The Resurrection

16 When the Sabbath was over, Mary Magdalene, Mary the mother of James, and Salome bought spices so that

---

ᵃ 27 Some manuscripts *left,* ²⁸*and the scripture was fulfilled which says, "He was counted with the lawless ones"* (Isaiah 53:12)   ᵇ 32 Or *Messiah*   ᶜ 34 Psalm 22:1   ᵈ 39 Some manuscripts do not have *heard his cry and*   ᵉ 39 Or *a son* they might go to anoint Jesus' body. [2]Very early on the first day of the week, just after sunrise, they were on their way to the tomb [3]and they asked each other, "Who will roll the stone away from the entrance of the tomb?"

[4]But when they looked up, they saw that the stone, which was very large, had been rolled away. [5]As they entered the tomb, they saw a young man dressed in a white robe sitting on the right side, and they were alarmed.

[6]"Don't be alarmed," he said. "You are looking for Jesus the Nazarene, who was crucified. He has risen! He is not here. See the place where they laid him. [7]But go, tell his disciples and Peter, 'He is going ahead of you into Galilee. There you will see him, just as he told you.'"

[8]Trembling and bewildered, the women went out and fled from the tomb. They said nothing to anyone, because they were afraid.

[The earliest manuscripts and some other ancient witnesses do not have Mark 16:9–20.]

[9]When Jesus rose early on the first day of the week, he appeared first to Mary Magdalene, out of whom he had driven seven demons. [10]She went and told those who had been with him and who were mourning and weeping. [11]When they heard that Jesus was alive and that she had seen him, they did not believe it.

[12]Afterward Jesus appeared in a different form to two of them while they were walking in the country. [13]These returned and reported it to the rest; but they did not believe them either.

[14]Later Jesus appeared to the Eleven as they were eating; he rebuked them for their lack of faith and their stubborn refusal to believe those who had seen him after he had risen.

[15]He said to them, "Go into all the world and preach the good news to all creation. [16]Whoever believes and is baptized will be saved, but whoever does not believe will be condemned. [17]And these signs will accompany those who believe: In my name they will drive out demons; they will speak in new tongues; [18]they will pick up snakes with their hands; and when they drink deadly poison, it will not hurt them at all; they will place their hands on sick people, and they will get well."

Praying Mark 16:18

Jesus, I ask that You would give me the power to lay hands on the sick and pray in Your name for them to be healed and see them recover as You answer that prayer.

[19]After the Lord Jesus had spoken to them, he was taken up into heaven and he sat at the right hand of God. [20]Then the disciples went out and preached everywhere, and the Lord worked with them and confirmed his word by the signs that accompanied it.

Author: Luke

Date: AD 59-63 or 70-80

Audience: A man named Theophilus ("lover of God") and those to whom he would circulate this book

Luke's purpose in writing this very detailed, vivid, accurate, and orderly account of Jesus' life, priorities, activities, and teachings is to portray Him not only as the Savior of the world but also as the perfect human being.

Luke stresses Jesus' heroic mission: "The Son of Man came to seek and to save what was lost" (19:10). His compassion for hurting and suffering people inspires us to be the same way toward them. His emphasis on the importance of prayer, not only in His life but also in the lives of all who would be His followers, inspires us to think, act, and pray like Jesus did.

Prayer Themes:

• *Ask God to make Jesus' mission your own passion and priority: to declare the good news of God's salvation and grace, and to help those who are captive to sin find true freedom (4:16-19).*

• *Pray that you would understand more and more what it means to follow Jesus, and that you would not only be able to count the cost but also be willing to pay the price (14:25-33).*

• *Thank God for the gifts, abilities, and opportunities He has given you. Ask Him to make you a wise steward of all those things (19:11-27).*

Luke

Introduction

1 Many have undertaken to draw up an account of the things that have been fulfilled[a] among us, ²just as they were handed down to us by those who from the first were eyewitnesses and servants of the word. ³Therefore, since I myself have carefully investigated everything from the beginning, it seemed good also to me to write an orderly account for you, most excellent Theophilus, ⁴so that you may know the certainty of the things you have been taught.

The Birth of John the Baptist Foretold

⁵In the time of Herod king of Judea there was a priest named Zechariah, who belonged to the priestly division of Abijah; his wife Elizabeth was also a descendant of Aaron. ⁶Both of them were upright in the sight of God, observing all the Lord's commandments and regulations blamelessly. ⁷But they had no children, because Elizabeth was barren; and they were both well along in years.

⁸Once when Zechariah's division was on duty and he was serving as priest before God, ⁹he was chosen by lot, according to the custom of the priesthood, to go into the temple of the Lord and burn incense. ¹⁰And when the time for the burning of incense came, all the assembled worshipers were praying outside.

¹¹Then an angel of the Lord appeared to him, standing at the right side of the altar of incense. ¹²When Zechariah saw him, he was startled and was gripped with fear. ¹³But the angel said to him: "Do not be afraid, Zechariah; your prayer has been heard. Your wife Elizabeth will bear you a son, and you are to give him the name John. ¹⁴He will be a joy and

---

ª *1* Or *been surely believed*

delight to you, and many will rejoice because of his birth, [15]for he will be great in the sight of the Lord. He is never to take wine or other fermented drink, and he will be filled with the Holy Spirit even from birth.[a] [16]Many of the people of Israel will he bring back to the Lord their God. [17]And he will go on before the Lord, in the spirit and power of Elijah, to turn the hearts of the fathers to their children and the disobedient to the wisdom of the righteous—to make ready a people prepared for the Lord."

[18]Zechariah asked the angel, "How can I be sure of this? I am an old man and my wife is well along in years."

[19]The angel answered, "I am Gabriel. I stand in the presence of God, and I have been sent to speak to you and to tell you this good news. [20]And now you will be silent and not able to speak until the day this happens, because you did not believe my words, which will come true at their proper time."

[21]Meanwhile, the people were waiting for Zechariah and wondering why he stayed so long in the temple. [22]When he came out, he could not speak to them. They realized he had seen a vision in the temple, for he kept making signs to them but remained unable to speak.

[23]When his time of service was completed, he returned home. [24]After this his wife Elizabeth became pregnant and for five months remained in seclusion. [25]"The Lord has done this for me," she said. "In these days he has shown his favor and taken away my disgrace among the people."

The Birth of Jesus Foretold

[26]In the sixth month, God sent the angel Gabriel to Nazareth, a town in Galilee, [27]to a virgin pledged to be married to a man named Joseph, a descendant of David. The virgin's name was Mary. [28]The angel went to her and said, "Greetings, you who are highly favored! The Lord is with you."

[29]Mary was greatly troubled at his words and wondered what kind of greeting this might be. [30]But the angel said to her, "Do not be afraid, Mary, you have found favor with God. [31]You will be with child and give birth to a son, and you are to give him the name Jesus. [32]He will be great and will be called the Son of the Most High. The Lord God will give him the throne of his father David, [33]and he will reign over the house of Jacob forever; his kingdom will never end."

[34]"How will this be," Mary asked the angel, "since I am a virgin?"

[35]The angel answered, "The Holy Spirit will come upon you, and the power of the Most High will overshadow you. So the holy one to be born will be called[b] the Son of God. [36]Even Elizabeth your relative is going to have a child in her old age, and she who was said to be barren is in her sixth month. [37]For nothing is impossible with God."

[38]"I am the Lord's servant," Mary answered. "May it be to me as you have said." Then the angel left her.

Mary Visits Elizabeth

[39]At that time Mary got ready and hurried to a town in the hill country of Judea, [40]where she entered Zechariah's home and greeted Elizabeth. [41]When Elizabeth heard Mary's greeting, the baby leaped in her womb, and Elizabeth was filled with the Holy Spirit. [42]In a loud voice she exclaimed: "Blessed are you among women, and blessed is the child you will bear! [43]But why am I so favored, that the mother of my Lord should come to me? [44]As soon as the sound of your greeting reached my ears, the baby in my womb leaped for joy. [45]Blessed is she who has believed that what the Lord has said to her will be accomplished!"

Mary's Song

[46]And Mary said:

"My soul glorifies the Lord
[47]   and my spirit rejoices in God my
       Savior,

---

[a] 15 Or *from his mother's womb*   [b] 35 Or *So the child to be born will be called holy,*

48for he has been mindful
  of the humble state of his servant.
From now on all generations will call
  me blessed,
49 for the Mighty One has done great
    things for me—
  holy is his name.
50His mercy extends to those who fear
    him,
  from generation to generation.
51He has performed mighty deeds with
    his arm;
  he has scattered those who are
    proud in their inmost thoughts.
52He has brought down rulers from
    their thrones
  but has lifted up the humble.
53He has filled the hungry with good
    things
  but has sent the rich away empty.
54He has helped his servant Israel,
  remembering to be merciful
55to Abraham and his descendants
    forever,
  even as he said to our fathers."

56Mary stayed with Elizabeth for about
three months and then returned home.

The Birth of John the Baptist

57When it was time for Elizabeth to
have her baby, she gave birth to a son.
58Her neighbors and relatives heard that
the Lord had shown her great mercy, and
they shared her joy.

59On the eighth day they came to circumcise the child, and they were going
to name him after his father Zechariah,
60but his mother spoke up and said, "No!
He is to be called John."

61They said to her, "There is no one
among your relatives who has that
name."

62Then they made signs to his father,
to find out what he would like to name
the child. 63He asked for a writing tablet,
and to everyone's astonishment he wrote,
"His name is John." 64Immediately his
mouth was opened and his tongue was

loosed, and he began to speak, praising
God. 65The neighbors were all filled with
awe, and throughout the hill country of
Judea people were talking about all these
things. 66Everyone who heard this wondered about it, asking, "What then is this
child going to be?" For the Lord's hand
was with him.

Zechariah's Song

67His father Zechariah was filled with
the Holy Spirit and prophesied:

68"Praise be to the Lord, the God of
    Israel,
  because he has come and has
    redeemed his people.
69He has raised up a horn[a] of salvation
    for us
  in the house of his servant David
70(as he said through his holy prophets
    of long ago),
71salvation from our enemies
  and from the hand of all who hate
    us—
72to show mercy to our fathers
  and to remember his holy covenant,
73 the oath he swore to our father
    Abraham:
74to rescue us from the hand of our
    enemies,
  and to enable us to serve him
    without fear
75 in holiness and righteousness before
    him all our days.

76And you, my child, will be called a
    prophet of the Most High;
  for you will go on before the Lord
    to prepare the way for him,
77to give his people the knowledge of
    salvation
  through the forgiveness of their sins,
78because of the tender mercy of our
    God,
  by which the rising sun will come
    to us from heaven
79to shine on those living in darkness
  and in the shadow of death,

to guide our feet into the path of peace."

[80]And the child grew and became strong in spirit; and he lived in the desert until he appeared publicly to Israel.

The Birth of Jesus

2 In those days Caesar Augustus issued a decree that a census should be taken of the entire Roman world. [2](This was the first census that took place while Quirinius was governor of Syria.) [3]And everyone went to his own town to register.

[4]So Joseph also went up from the town of Nazareth in Galilee to Judea, to Bethlehem the town of David, because he belonged to the house and line of David. [5]He went there to register with Mary, who was pledged to be married to him and was expecting a child. [6]While they were there, the time came for the baby to be born, [7]and she gave birth to her firstborn, a son. She wrapped him in cloths and placed him in a manger, because there was no room for them in the inn.

The Shepherds and the Angels

[8]And there were shepherds living out in the fields nearby, keeping watch over their flocks at night. [9]An angel of the Lord appeared to them, and the glory of the Lord shone around them, and they were terrified. [10]But the angel said to them, "Do not be afraid. I bring you good news of great joy that will be for all the people. [11]Today in the town of David a Savior has been born to you; he is Christ[a] the Lord. [12]This will be a sign to you: You will find a baby wrapped in cloths and lying in a manger."

[13]Suddenly a great company of the heavenly host appeared with the angel, praising God and saying,

[14]"Glory to God in the highest,
    and on earth peace to men on
        whom his favor rests."

[15]When the angels had left them and gone into heaven, the shepherds said to one another, "Let's go to Bethlehem and see this thing that has happened, which the Lord has told us about."

[16]So they hurried off and found Mary and Joseph, and the baby, who was lying in the manger. [17]When they had seen him, they spread the word concerning what had been told them about this child, [18]and all who heard it were amazed at what the shepherds said to them. [19]But Mary treasured up all these things and pondered them in her heart. [20]The shepherds returned, glorifying and praising God for all the things they had heard and seen, which were just as they had been told.

Jesus Presented in the Temple

[21]On the eighth day, when it was time to circumcise him, he was named Jesus, the name the angel had given him before he had been conceived.

[22]When the time of their purification according to the Law of Moses had been completed, Joseph and Mary took him to Jerusalem to present him to the Lord [23](as it is written in the Law of the Lord, "Every firstborn male is to be consecrated to the Lord"[b]), [24]and to offer a sacrifice in keeping with what is said in the Law of the Lord: "a pair of doves or two young pigeons."[c]

[25]Now there was a man in Jerusalem called Simeon, who was righteous and devout. He was waiting for the consolation of Israel, and the Holy Spirit was upon him. [26]It had been revealed to him by the Holy Spirit that he would not die before he had seen the Lord's Christ. [27]Moved by the Spirit, he went into the temple courts. When the parents brought in the child Jesus to do for him what the custom of the Law required, [28]Simeon took him in his arms and praised God, saying:

[29]"Sovereign Lord, as you have
        promised,

---

[a] 11 Or Messiah. "The Christ" (Greek) and "the Messiah" (Hebrew) both mean "the Anointed One"; also in verse 26.
[b] 23 Exodus 13:2,12   [c] 24 Lev. 12:8

you now dismiss[a] your servant in
   peace.
30 For my eyes have seen your salvation,
31   which you have prepared in the
    sight of all people,
32 a light for revelation to the Gentiles
   and for glory to your people Israel."

33 The child's father and mother marveled at what was said about him. 34 Then Simeon blessed them and said to Mary, his mother: "This child is destined to cause the falling and rising of many in Israel, and to be a sign that will be spoken against, 35 so that the thoughts of many hearts will be revealed. And a sword will pierce your own soul too."

36 There was also a prophetess, Anna, the daughter of Phanuel, of the tribe of Asher. She was very old; she had lived with her husband seven years after her marriage, 37 and then was a widow until she was eighty-four.[b] She never left the temple but worshiped night and day, fasting and praying. 38 Coming up to them at that very moment, she gave thanks to God and spoke about the child to all who were looking forward to the redemption of Jerusalem.

39 When Joseph and Mary had done everything required by the Law of the Lord, they returned to Galilee to their own town of Nazareth. 40 And the child grew and became strong; he was filled with wisdom, and the grace of God was upon him.

The Boy Jesus at the Temple

41 Every year his parents went to Jerusalem for the Feast of the Passover. 42 When he was twelve years old, they went up to the Feast, according to the custom. 43 After the Feast was over, while his parents were returning home, the boy Jesus stayed behind in Jerusalem, but they were unaware of it. 44 Thinking he was in their company, they traveled on for a day. Then they began looking for him among their relatives and friends. 45 When they did not find him, they went back to Jerusalem to look for him. 46 After three days they found him in the temple courts, sitting among the teachers, listening to them and asking them questions. 47 Everyone who heard him was amazed at his understanding and his answers. 48 When his parents saw him, they were astonished. His mother said to him, "Son, why have you

---

[a] 29 Or promised, / now dismiss   [b] 37 Or widow for eighty-four years

---

God's people at prayer
SIMEON AND ANNA'S LONG-AWAITED ANSWER TO PRAYER

LUKE 2:29-38 How wonderful would it be to see the thing you'd prayed for all your life come true? Especially if your family had been praying for this same thing for countless years before you.

That's what happened to Simeon and Anna. Generations of Israelites had read the prophecies, knew the promises, and had been watching for the Messiah's arrival. For centuries people had been praying.

God always answers prayer, but in His way and in His time. And with the Lord, a thousand years is like a day (Psalm 90:4). This gives us perspective on waiting for answers. The answers to some prayers take a lot longer than others.

Many who prayed and waited for the Messiah never saw Him. But one day, the Lord allowed these two faithful elderly people to see the Christ child and joyously praise God for that long-awaited answer to prayer! When we pray, we must never give up hope that one day our prayers will be answered—no matter how long it takes.

treated us like this? Your father and I have been anxiously searching for you."

⁴⁹"Why were you searching for me?" he asked. "Didn't you know I had to be in my Father's house?" ⁵⁰But they did not understand what he was saying to them.

> ### Praying Luke 2:49
> *Jesus, help me to be like You—always aware that I need to be about my Father's business.*

⁵¹Then he went down to Nazareth with them and was obedient to them. But his mother treasured all these things in her heart. ⁵²And Jesus grew in wisdom and stature, and in favor with God and men.

John the Baptist Prepares the Way

3 In the fifteenth year of the reign of Tiberius Caesar—when Pontius Pilate was governor of Judea, Herod tetrarch of Galilee, his brother Philip tetrarch of Iturea and Traconitis, and Lysanias tetrarch of Abilene— ²during the high priesthood of Annas and Caiaphas, the word of God came to John son of Zechariah in the desert. ³He went into all the country around the Jordan, preaching a baptism of repentance for the forgiveness of sins. ⁴As is written in the book of the words of Isaiah the prophet:

> "A voice of one calling in the desert,
> 'Prepare the way for the Lord,
>   make straight paths for him.
> ⁵Every valley shall be filled in,
>   every mountain and hill made low.
> The crooked roads shall become
>   straight,
>   the rough ways smooth.
> ⁶And all mankind will see God's
>   salvation.' "ᵃ

⁷John said to the crowds coming out to be baptized by him, "You brood of vipers! Who warned you to flee from the coming wrath? ⁸Produce fruit in keeping with repentance. And do not begin to say to yourselves, 'We have Abraham as our father.' For I tell you that out of these stones God can raise up children for Abraham. ⁹The ax is already at the root of the trees, and every tree that does not produce good fruit will be cut down and thrown into the fire."

¹⁰"What should we do then?" the crowd asked.

¹¹John answered, "The man with two tunics should share with him who has none, and the one who has food should do the same."

¹²Tax collectors also came to be baptized. "Teacher," they asked, "what should we do?"

¹³"Don't collect any more than you are required to," he told them.

¹⁴Then some soldiers asked him, "And what should we do?"

He replied, "Don't extort money and don't accuse people falsely—be content with your pay."

¹⁵The people were waiting expectantly and were all wondering in their hearts if John might possibly be the Christ.ᵇ ¹⁶John answered them all, "I baptize you withᶜ water. But one more powerful than I will come, the thongs of whose sandals I am not worthy to untie. He will baptize you with the Holy Spirit and with fire. ¹⁷His winnowing fork is in his hand to clear his threshing floor and to gather the wheat into his barn, but he will burn up the chaff with unquenchable fire." ¹⁸And with many other words John exhorted the people and preached the good news to them.

¹⁹But when John rebuked Herod the tetrarch because of Herodias, his brother's wife, and all the other evil things he had done, ²⁰Herod added this to them all: He locked John up in prison.

The Baptism and Genealogy of Jesus

²¹When all the people were being baptized, Jesus was baptized too. And as he was praying, heaven was opened ²²and the Holy Spirit descended on him in bodily

---

ᵃ *6* Isaiah 40:3-5   ᵇ *15* Or *Messiah*   ᶜ *16* Or *in*

form like a dove. And a voice came from heaven: "You are my Son, whom I love; with you I am well pleased."

²³Now Jesus himself was about thirty years old when he began his ministry. He was the son, so it was thought, of Joseph,

the son of Heli, ²⁴the son of Matthat,
the son of Levi, the son of Melki,
the son of Jannai, the son of Joseph,
²⁵the son of Mattathias, the son of Amos,
the son of Nahum, the son of Esli,
the son of Naggai, ²⁶the son of Maath,
the son of Mattathias, the son of Semein,
the son of Josech, the son of Joda,
²⁷the son of Joanan, the son of Rhesa,
the son of Zerubbabel, the son of Shealtiel,
the son of Neri, ²⁸the son of Melki,
the son of Addi, the son of Cosam,
the son of Elmadam, the son of Er,
²⁹the son of Joshua, the son of Eliezer,
the son of Jorim, the son of Matthat,
the son of Levi, ³⁰the son of Simeon,
the son of Judah, the son of Joseph,
the son of Jonam, the son of Eliakim,
³¹the son of Melea, the son of Menna,
the son of Mattatha, the son of Nathan,
the son of David, ³²the son of Jesse,
the son of Obed, the son of Boaz,
the son of Salmon,ᵃ the son of Nahshon,
³³the son of Amminadab, the son of Ram,ᵇ
the son of Hezron, the son of Perez,
the son of Judah, ³⁴the son of Jacob,
the son of Isaac, the son of Abraham,
the son of Terah, the son of Nahor,
³⁵the son of Serug, the son of Reu,
the son of Peleg, the son of Eber,
the son of Shelah, ³⁶the son of Cainan,
the son of Arphaxad, the son of Shem,
the son of Noah, the son of Lamech,
³⁷the son of Methuselah, the son of Enoch,
the son of Jared, the son of Mahalalel,
the son of Kenan, ³⁸the son of Enosh,
the son of Seth, the son of Adam,
the son of God.

The Temptation of Jesus

4 Jesus, full of the Holy Spirit, returned from the Jordan and was led by the Spirit in the desert, ²where for forty days he was tempted by the devil. He ate nothing during those days, and at the end of them he was hungry.

³The devil said to him, "If you are the Son of God, tell this stone to become bread."

⁴Jesus answered, "It is written: 'Man does not live on bread alone.'ᶜ"

Praying Luke 4:3-4
Lord, help me to continually resist the lies and temptations of the enemy with the knowledge and power of Your Word.

⁵The devil led him up to a high place and showed him in an instant all the kingdoms of the world. ⁶And he said to him, "I will give you all their authority and splendor, for it has been given to me, and I can give it to anyone I want to. ⁷So if you worship me, it will all be yours."

⁸Jesus answered, "It is written: 'Worship the Lord your God and serve him only.'ᵈ"

⁹The devil led him to Jerusalem and had him stand on the highest point of the temple. "If you are the Son of God," he said, "throw yourself down from here.

ᵃ *32* Some early manuscripts *Sala*   ᵇ *33* Some manuscripts *Amminadab, the son of Admin, the son of Arni*; other manuscripts vary widely.   ᶜ *4* Deut. 8:3   ᵈ *8* Deut. 6:13

¹⁰For it is written:

> " 'He will command his angels
>   concerning you
>   to guard you carefully;
> ¹¹they will lift you up in their hands,
>   so that you will not strike your foot
>   against a stone.'ᵃ"

¹²Jesus answered, "It says: 'Do not put the Lord your God to the test.'ᵇ"

¹³When the devil had finished all this tempting, he left him until an opportune time.

Jesus Rejected at Nazareth

¹⁴Jesus returned to Galilee in the power of the Spirit, and news about him spread through the whole countryside. ¹⁵He taught in their synagogues, and everyone praised him.

¹⁶He went to Nazareth, where he had been brought up, and on the Sabbath day he went into the synagogue, as was his custom. And he stood up to read. ¹⁷The scroll of the prophet Isaiah was handed to him. Unrolling it, he found the place where it is written:

> ¹⁸"The Spirit of the Lord is on me,
>   because he has anointed me
>   to preach good news to the poor.
> He has sent me to proclaim freedom
>   for the prisoners
>   and recovery of sight for the blind,
> to release the oppressed,
> ¹⁹   to proclaim the year of the Lord's
>   favor."ᶜ

²⁰Then he rolled up the scroll, gave it back to the attendant and sat down. The eyes of everyone in the synagogue were fastened on him, ²¹and he began by saying to them, "Today this scripture is fulfilled in your hearing."

²²All spoke well of him and were amazed at the gracious words that came from his lips. "Isn't this Joseph's son?" they asked.

²³Jesus said to them, "Surely you will quote this proverb to me: 'Physician, heal yourself! Do here in your hometown what we have heard that you did in Capernaum.' "

²⁴"I tell you the truth," he continued, "no prophet is accepted in his hometown. ²⁵I assure you that there were many widows in Israel in Elijah's time, when the sky was shut for three and a half years and there was a severe famine throughout the land. ²⁶Yet Elijah was not sent to any of them, but to a widow in Zarephath in the region of Sidon. ²⁷And there were many in Israel with leprosyᵈ in the time of Elisha the prophet, yet not one of them was cleansed—only Naaman the Syrian."

²⁸All the people in the synagogue were furious when they heard this. ²⁹They got up, drove him out of the town, and took him to the brow of the hill on which the town was built, in order to throw him down the cliff. ³⁰But he walked right through the crowd and went on his way.

Jesus Drives Out an Evil Spirit

³¹Then he went down to Capernaum, a town in Galilee, and on the Sabbath began to teach the people. ³²They were amazed at his teaching, because his message had authority.

³³In the synagogue there was a man possessed by a demon, an evilᵉ spirit. He cried out at the top of his voice, ³⁴"Ha! What do you want with us, Jesus of Nazareth? Have you come to destroy us? I know who you are—the Holy One of God!"

³⁵"Be quiet!" Jesus said sternly. "Come out of him!" Then the demon threw the man down before them all and came out without injuring him.

³⁶All the people were amazed and said to each other, "What is this teaching? With authority and power he gives orders to evil spirits and they come out!" ³⁷And the news about him spread throughout the surrounding area.

ᵃ 11 Psalm 91:11,12   ᵇ 12 Deut. 6:16   ᶜ 19 Isaiah 61:1,2   ᵈ 27 The Greek word was used for various diseases affecting the skin—not necessarily leprosy.   ᵉ 33 Greek unclean; also in verse 36

Jesus Heals Many

38Jesus left the synagogue and went to the home of Simon. Now Simon's mother-in-law was suffering from a high fever, and they asked Jesus to help her. 39So he bent over her and rebuked the fever, and it left her. She got up at once and began to wait on them.

40When the sun was setting, the people brought to Jesus all who had various kinds of sickness, and laying his hands on each one, he healed them. 41Moreover, demons came out of many people, shouting, "You are the Son of God!" But he rebuked them and would not allow them to speak, because they knew he was the Christ.ª

42At daybreak Jesus went out to a solitary place. The people were looking for him and when they came to where he was, they tried to keep him from leaving them. 43But he said, "I must preach the good news of the kingdom of God to the other towns also, because that is why I was sent." 44And he kept on preaching in the synagogues of Judea.ᵇ

The Calling of the First Disciples

5 One day as Jesus was standing by the Lake of Gennesaret,ᶜ with the people crowding around him and listening to the word of God, 2he saw at the water's edge two boats, left there by the fishermen, who were washing their nets. 3He got into one of the boats, the one belonging to Simon, and asked him to put out a little from shore. Then he sat down and taught the people from the boat.

4When he had finished speaking, he said to Simon, "Put out into deep water, and let downᵈ the nets for a catch."

5Simon answered, "Master, we've worked hard all night and haven't caught anything. But because you say so, I will let down the nets."

6When they had done so, they caught such a large number of fish that their nets began to break. 7So they signaled their partners in the other boat to come and help them, and they came and filled both boats so full that they began to sink.

8When Simon Peter saw this, he fell at Jesus' knees and said, "Go away from me, Lord; I am a sinful man!" 9For he and all his companions were astonished at the catch of fish they had taken, 10and so were James and John, the sons of Zebedee, Simon's partners.

Then Jesus said to Simon, "Don't be afraid; from now on you will catch men." 11So they pulled their boats up on shore, left everything and followed him.

The Man With Leprosy

12While Jesus was in one of the towns, a man came along who was covered with leprosy.ᵉ When he saw Jesus, he fell with his face to the ground and begged him, "Lord, if you are willing, you can make me clean."

13Jesus reached out his hand and touched the man. "I am willing," he said. "Be clean!" And immediately the leprosy left him.

14Then Jesus ordered him, "Don't tell anyone, but go, show yourself to the priest and offer the sacrifices that Moses commanded for your cleansing, as a testimony to them."

15Yet the news about him spread all the more, so that crowds of people came to hear him and to be healed of their sicknesses. 16But Jesus often withdrew to lonely places and prayed.

Jesus Heals a Paralytic

17One day as he was teaching, Pharisees and teachers of the law, who had come from every village of Galilee and from Judea and Jerusalem, were sitting there. And the power of the Lord was present for him to heal the sick. 18Some men came carrying a paralytic on a mat and tried to take him into the house to lay him before Jesus. 19When they could not find a way to do this because of the crowd, they

---

ª 41 Or *Messiah*   ᵇ 44 Or *the land of the Jews*; some manuscripts *Galilee*   ᶜ 1 That is, Sea of Galilee   ᵈ 4 The Greek verb is plural.   ᵉ 12 The Greek word was used for various diseases affecting the skin—not necessarily leprosy.

went up on the roof and lowered him on his mat through the tiles into the middle of the crowd, right in front of Jesus.

20When Jesus saw their faith, he said, "Friend, your sins are forgiven."

21The Pharisees and the teachers of the law began thinking to themselves, "Who is this fellow who speaks blasphemy? Who can forgive sins but God alone?"

22Jesus knew what they were thinking and asked, "Why are you thinking these things in your hearts? 23Which is easier: to say, 'Your sins are forgiven,' or to say, 'Get up and walk'? 24But that you may know that the Son of Man has authority on earth to forgive sins..." He said to the paralyzed man, "I tell you, get up, take your mat and go home." 25Immediately he stood up in front of them, took what he had been lying on and went home praising God. 26Everyone was amazed and gave praise to God. They were filled with awe and said, "We have seen remarkable things today."

Praying Luke 5:27-28
Dear Jesus, help me to leave
all other things behind so that
I may follow You faithfully.

The Calling of Levi

27After this, Jesus went out and saw a tax collector by the name of Levi sitting at his tax booth. "Follow me," Jesus said to him, 28and Levi got up, left everything and followed him.

29Then Levi held a great banquet for Jesus at his house, and a large crowd of tax collectors and others were eating with them. 30But the Pharisees and the teachers of the law who belonged to their sect complained to his disciples, "Why do you eat and drink with tax collectors and 'sinners'?"

31Jesus answered them, "It is not the healthy who need a doctor, but the sick. 32I have not come to call the righteous, but sinners to repentance."

Jesus Questioned About Fasting

33They said to him, "John's disciples often fast and pray, and so do the disciples of the Pharisees, but yours go on eating and drinking."

34Jesus answered, "Can you make the guests of the bridegroom fast while he is with them? 35But the time will come when the bridegroom will be taken from them; in those days they will fast."

36He told them this parable: "No one tears a patch from a new garment and sews it on an old one. If he does, he will have torn the new garment, and the patch from the new will not match the old. 37And no one pours new wine into old wineskins. If he does, the new wine will burst the skins, the wine will run out and the wineskins will be ruined. 38No, new wine must be poured into new wineskins. 39And no one after drinking old wine wants the new, for he says, 'The old is better.'"

Lord of the Sabbath

6 One Sabbath Jesus was going through the grainfields, and his disciples began to pick some heads of grain, rub them in their hands and eat the kernels. 2Some of the Pharisees asked, "Why are you doing what is unlawful on the Sabbath?"

3Jesus answered them, "Have you never read what David did when he and his companions were hungry? 4He entered the house of God, and taking the consecrated bread, he ate what is lawful only for priests to eat. And he also gave some to his companions." 5Then Jesus said to them, "The Son of Man is Lord of the Sabbath."

6On another Sabbath he went into the synagogue and was teaching, and a man was there whose right hand was shriveled. 7The Pharisees and the teachers of the law were looking for a reason to accuse Jesus, so they watched him closely to see if he would heal on the Sabbath. 8But Jesus knew what they were thinking and said to the man with the shriveled hand, "Get up and stand in front of everyone." So he got up and stood there.

God's Word Makes Life Work

God gave us His Word so that we would know the right way to live. That's why we love it so much. It spells everything out. It tells us this is right and that is wrong. When you live *this* way, life works. When you live that way, life *doesn't* work. God's Word builds you up; it feeds your soul and gives you strength, direction, guidance, hope, encouragement, and faith.

God's laws are for *our* benefit. He doesn't come up with rules so that He will have a reason to strike us with lightning when we don't obey all of them perfectly. He wants to show us how to avoid the things that will hurt us or ruin our lives. That's why He has provided this wonderfully reliable tool. So we can always know the truth. And in it we will always find comfort and strength. Wisdom and knowledge. Love and faith. Peace and joy. Deliverance and liberty. Clarity and direction. Wholeness and restoration. Fruitfulness and purpose.

There are consequences for continued and willful disobedience to God's ways. And those of us who have tested those waters and paid the consequences know the pain of that testing. Those of us who have tried God's ways and have seen that they are good, understand how wonderful it is to have God's Word guiding us every day. When we refuse to look to the world for our counsel and instead find all we need in God's Word, then we become planted solidly where the river of God's life constantly flows into ours (Psalm 1:1-3). And that kind of life will bear fruit that lasts.

Believing in the promises of God enables us to escape the corruption that the lust of our eyes and flesh brings into our lives. God's Word has "given us his very great and precious promises," that through them we "may participate in the divine nature and escape the corruption in the world caused by evil desires" (2 Peter 1:4). His Word lifts us above ourselves and helps us to attain a holy nature like His.

God's Word is a weapon of spiritual warfare we can use to protect ourselves. "Take the helmet of salvation and the sword of the Spirit, which is the word of God" (Ephesians 6:17). But in order to use it as a weapon, we must *read* His Word, *think* about His Word, *speak* His Word, and *praise* God for His Word every day.

God's Word tells us how much He loves us and shows us to what extent He has gone to prove His love to us. That's why it touches a place deep in our hearts. Nothing penetrates our souls or changes our lives more profoundly than true love. And His is the truest of all. When we read God's love letter—the Bible— we can better understand His heart of love for us.

For the next "From Stormie's Heart" article, go to page 1268.

[9]Then Jesus said to them, "I ask you, which is lawful on the Sabbath: to do good or to do evil, to save life or to destroy it?"

[10]He looked around at them all, and then said to the man, "Stretch out your hand." He did so, and his hand was completely restored. [11]But they were furious and began to discuss with one another what they might do to Jesus.

The Twelve Apostles

[12]One of those days Jesus went out to a mountainside to pray, and spent the night praying to God. [13]When morning came, he called his disciples to him and chose twelve of them, whom he also designated apostles: [14]Simon (whom he named Peter), his brother Andrew, James, John, Philip, Bartholomew, [15]Matthew, Thomas, James son of Alphaeus, Simon who was called the Zealot, [16]Judas son of James, and Judas Iscariot, who became a traitor.

Blessings and Woes

[17]He went down with them and stood on a level place. A large crowd of his disciples was there and a great number of people from all over Judea, from Jerusalem, and from the coast of Tyre and Sidon, [18]who had come to hear him and to be healed of their diseases. Those troubled by evil[a] spirits were cured, [19]and the people all tried to touch him, because power was coming from him and healing them all.

[20]Looking at his disciples, he said:

"Blessed are you who are poor,
   for yours is the kingdom of God.
[21]Blessed are you who hunger now,
   for you will be satisfied.
Blessed are you who weep now,
   for you will laugh.
[22]Blessed are you when men hate
      you,
   when they exclude you and insult
      you
   and reject your name as evil,
      because of the Son of Man.

[23]"Rejoice in that day and leap for joy, because great is your reward in heaven. For that is how their fathers treated the prophets.

[24]"But woe to you who are rich,
   for you have already received your
      comfort.
[25]Woe to you who are well fed now,
   for you will go hungry.
Woe to you who laugh now,
   for you will mourn and weep.
[26]Woe to you when all men speak well
      of you,
   for that is how their fathers treated
      the false prophets.

Love for Enemies

[27]"But I tell you who hear me: Love your enemies, do good to those who hate you, [28]bless those who curse you, pray for those who mistreat you. [29]If someone strikes you on one cheek, turn to him the other also. If someone takes your cloak, do not stop him from taking your tunic. [30]Give to everyone who asks you, and if anyone takes what belongs to you, do not demand it back. [31]Do to others as you would have them do to you.

[32]"If you love those who love you, what credit is that to you? Even 'sinners' love those who love them. [33]And if you do good to those who are good to you, what credit is that to you? Even 'sinners' do that. [34]And if you lend to those from whom you expect repayment, what credit is that to you? Even 'sinners' lend to 'sinners,' expecting to be repaid in full. [35]But love your enemies, do good to them, and lend to them without expecting to get anything back. Then your reward will be great, and you will be sons of the Most High, because he is kind to the ungrateful and wicked. [36]Be merciful, just as your Father is merciful.

Judging Others

[37]"Do not judge, and you will not be judged. Do not condemn, and you will not be condemned. Forgive, and you will

---

[a] 18 Greek *unclean*

be forgiven. ³⁸Give, and it will be given to you. A good measure, pressed down, shaken together and running over, will be poured into your lap. For with the measure you use, it will be measured to you."

³⁹He also told them this parable: "Can a blind man lead a blind man? Will they not both fall into a pit? ⁴⁰A student is not above his teacher, but everyone who is fully trained will be like his teacher.

⁴¹"Why do you look at the speck of sawdust in your brother's eye and pay no attention to the plank in your own eye? ⁴²How can you say to your brother, 'Brother, let me take the speck out of your eye,' when you yourself fail to see the plank in your own eye? You hypocrite, first take the plank out of your eye, and then you will see clearly to remove the speck from your brother's eye.

A Tree and Its Fruit

⁴³"No good tree bears bad fruit, nor does a bad tree bear good fruit. ⁴⁴Each tree is recognized by its own fruit. People do not pick figs from thornbushes, or grapes from briers. ⁴⁵The good man brings good things out of the good stored up in his heart, and the evil man brings evil things out of the evil stored up in his heart. For out of the overflow of his heart his mouth speaks.

Praying Luke 6:45
Heavenly Father, fill my heart with the knowledge and remembrance of Your Word so that I only speak out of the abundance of a heart saturated with Your truth.

The Wise and Foolish Builders

⁴⁶"Why do you call me, 'Lord, Lord,' and do not do what I say? ⁴⁷I will show you what he is like who comes to me and hears my words and puts them into practice. ⁴⁸He is like a man building a house, who dug down deep and laid the foundation on rock. When a flood came, the torrent struck that house but could not

shake it, because it was well built. ⁴⁹But the one who hears my words and does not put them into practice is like a man who built a house on the ground without a foundation. The moment the torrent struck that house, it collapsed and its destruction was complete."

The Faith of the Centurion

7 When Jesus had finished saying all this in the hearing of the people, he entered Capernaum. ²There a centurion's servant, whom his master valued highly, was sick and about to die. ³The centurion heard of Jesus and sent some elders of the Jews to him, asking him to come and heal his servant. ⁴When they came to Jesus, they pleaded earnestly with him, "This man deserves to have you do this, ⁵because he loves our nation and has built our synagogue." ⁶So Jesus went with them.

He was not far from the house when the centurion sent friends to say to him: "Lord, don't trouble yourself, for I do not deserve to have you come under my roof. ⁷That is why I did not even consider myself worthy to come to you. But say the word, and my servant will be healed. ⁸For I myself am a man under authority, with soldiers under me. I tell this one, 'Go,' and he goes; and that one, 'Come,' and he comes. I say to my servant, 'Do this,' and he does it."

⁹When Jesus heard this, he was amazed at him, and turning to the crowd following him, he said, "I tell you, I have not found such great faith even in Israel." ¹⁰Then the men who had been sent returned to the house and found the servant well.

Jesus Raises a Widow's Son

¹¹Soon afterward, Jesus went to a town called Nain, and his disciples and a large crowd went along with him. ¹²As he approached the town gate, a dead person was being carried out—the only son of his mother, and she was a widow. And a large crowd from the town was with her. ¹³When the Lord saw her, his heart went out to her and he said, "Don't cry."

[14]Then he went up and touched the coffin, and those carrying it stood still. He said, "Young man, I say to you, get up!" [15]The dead man sat up and began to talk, and Jesus gave him back to his mother.

[16]They were all filled with awe and praised God. "A great prophet has appeared among us," they said. "God has come to help his people." [17]This news about Jesus spread throughout Judea[a] and the surrounding country.

Jesus and John the Baptist

[18]John's disciples told him about all these things. Calling two of them, [19]he sent them to the Lord to ask, "Are you the one who was to come, or should we expect someone else?"

[20]When the men came to Jesus, they said, "John the Baptist sent us to you to ask, 'Are you the one who was to come, or should we expect someone else?'"

[21]At that very time Jesus cured many who had diseases, sicknesses and evil spirits, and gave sight to many who were blind. [22]So he replied to the messengers, "Go back and report to John what you have seen and heard: The blind receive sight, the lame walk, those who have leprosy[b] are cured, the deaf hear, the dead are raised, and the good news is preached to the poor. [23]Blessed is the man who does not fall away on account of me."

[24]After John's messengers left, Jesus began to speak to the crowd about John: "What did you go out into the desert to see? A reed swayed by the wind? [25]If not, what did you go out to see? A man dressed in fine clothes? No, those who wear expensive clothes and indulge in luxury are in palaces. [26]But what did you go out to see? A prophet? Yes, I tell you, and more than a prophet. [27]This is the one about whom it is written:

"'I will send my messenger ahead of
    you,

who will prepare your way before
    you.'[c]

[28]I tell you, among those born of women there is no one greater than John; yet the one who is least in the kingdom of God is greater than he."

[29](All the people, even the tax collectors, when they heard Jesus' words, acknowledged that God's way was right, because they had been baptized by John. [30]But the Pharisees and experts in the law rejected God's purpose for themselves, because they had not been baptized by John.)

[31]"To what, then, can I compare the people of this generation? What are they like? [32]They are like children sitting in the marketplace and calling out to each other:

"'We played the flute for you,
    and you did not dance;
we sang a dirge,
    and you did not cry.'

[33]For John the Baptist came neither eating bread nor drinking wine, and you say, 'He has a demon.' [34]The Son of Man came eating and drinking, and you say, 'Here is a glutton and a drunkard, a friend of tax collectors and "sinners."' [35]But wisdom is proved right by all her children."

Jesus Anointed by a Sinful Woman

[36]Now one of the Pharisees invited Jesus to have dinner with him, so he went to the Pharisee's house and reclined at the table. [37]When a woman who had lived a sinful life in that town learned that Jesus was eating at the Pharisee's house, she brought an alabaster jar of perfume, [38]and as she stood behind him at his feet weeping, she began to wet his feet with her tears. Then she wiped them with her hair, kissed them and poured perfume on them.

[39]When the Pharisee who had invited him saw this, he said to himself, "If this

---

[a] 17 Or the land of the Jews   [b] 22 The Greek word was used for various diseases affecting the skin—not necessarily leprosy.
[c] 27 Mal. 3:1

man were a prophet, he would know who is touching him and what kind of woman she is—that she is a sinner."

⁴⁰Jesus answered him, "Simon, I have something to tell you."

"Tell me, teacher," he said.

⁴¹"Two men owed money to a certain moneylender. One owed him five hundred denarii,ᵃ and the other fifty. ⁴²Neither of them had the money to pay him back, so he canceled the debts of both. Now which of them will love him more?"

⁴³Simon replied, "I suppose the one who had the bigger debt canceled."

"You have judged correctly," Jesus said.

⁴⁴Then he turned toward the woman and said to Simon, "Do you see this woman? I came into your house. You did not give me any water for my feet, but she wet my feet with her tears and wiped them with her hair. ⁴⁵You did not give me a kiss, but this woman, from the time I entered, has not stopped kissing my feet. ⁴⁶You did not put oil on my head, but she has poured perfume on my feet. ⁴⁷Therefore, I tell you, her many sins have been forgiven—for she loved much. But he who has been forgiven little loves little."

⁴⁸Then Jesus said to her, "Your sins are forgiven."

⁴⁹The other guests began to say among themselves, "Who is this who even forgives sins?"

⁵⁰Jesus said to the woman, "Your faith has saved you; go in peace."

The Parable of the Sower

8 After this, Jesus traveled about from one town and village to another, proclaiming the good news of the kingdom of God. The Twelve were with him, ²and also some women who had been cured of evil spirits and diseases: Mary (called Magdalene) from whom seven demons had come out; ³Joanna the wife of Cuza, the manager of Herod's household; Susanna; and many others. These women

were helping to support them out of their own means.

⁴While a large crowd was gathering and people were coming to Jesus from town after town, he told this parable: ⁵"A farmer went out to sow his seed. As he was scattering the seed, some fell along the path; it was trampled on, and the birds of the air ate it up. ⁶Some fell on rock, and when it came up, the plants withered because they had no moisture. ⁷Other seed fell among thorns, which grew up with it and choked the plants. ⁸Still other seed fell on good soil. It came up and yielded a crop, a hundred times more than was sown."

When he said this, he called out, "He who has ears to hear, let him hear."

⁹His disciples asked him what this parable meant. ¹⁰He said, "The knowledge of the secrets of the kingdom of God has been given to you, but to others I speak in parables, so that,

" 'though seeing, they may not see;
though hearing, they may not
understand.'ᵇ

¹¹"This is the meaning of the parable: The seed is the word of God. ¹²Those along the path are the ones who hear, and then the devil comes and takes away the word from their hearts, so that they may not believe and be saved. ¹³Those on the rock are the ones who receive the word with joy when they hear it, but they have no root. They believe for a while, but in the time of testing they fall away. ¹⁴The seed that fell among thorns stands for those who hear, but as they go on their way they are choked by life's worries, riches and pleasures, and they do not mature. ¹⁵But the seed on good soil stands for those with a noble and good heart, who hear the word, retain it, and by persevering produce a crop.

A Lamp on a Stand

¹⁶"No one lights a lamp and hides it in a jar or puts it under a bed. Instead,

---

ᵃ *41* A denarius was a coin worth about a day's wages.   ᵇ *10* Isaiah 6:9

he puts it on a stand, so that those who come in can see the light. 17For there is nothing hidden that will not be disclosed, and nothing concealed that will not be known or brought out into the open. 18Therefore consider carefully how you listen. Whoever has will be given more; whoever does not have, even what he thinks he has will be taken from him."

Jesus' Mother and Brothers

19Now Jesus' mother and brothers came to see him, but they were not able to get near him because of the crowd. 20Someone told him, "Your mother and brothers are standing outside, wanting to see you."

21He replied, "My mother and brothers are those who hear God's word and put it into practice."

Jesus Calms the Storm

22One day Jesus said to his disciples, "Let's go over to the other side of the lake." So they got into a boat and set out. 23As they sailed, he fell asleep. A squall came down on the lake, so that the boat was being swamped, and they were in great danger.

24The disciples went and woke him, saying, "Master, Master, we're going to drown!"

He got up and rebuked the wind and the raging waters; the storm subsided, and all was calm. 25"Where is your faith?" he asked his disciples.

Praying Luke 8:23-25

Lord, I pray that when the storms of life come, no one will have to wonder where my faith is because I will fully trust that Your power is greater than anything I face.

In fear and amazement they asked one another, "Who is this? He commands even the winds and the water, and they obey him."

The Healing of a Demon-possessed Man

26They sailed to the region of the Gerasenes,ᵃ which is across the lake from Galilee. 27When Jesus stepped ashore, he was met by a demon-possessed man from the town. For a long time this man had not worn clothes or lived in a house, but had lived in the tombs. 28When he saw Jesus, he cried out and fell at his feet, shouting at the top of his voice, "What do you want with me, Jesus, Son of the Most High God? I beg you, don't torture me!" 29For Jesus had commanded the evilᵇ spirit to come out of the man. Many times it had seized him, and though he was chained hand and foot and kept under guard, he had broken his chains and had been driven by the demon into solitary places.

30Jesus asked him, "What is your name?"

"Legion," he replied, because many demons had gone into him. 31And they begged him repeatedly not to order them to go into the Abyss.

32A large herd of pigs was feeding there on the hillside. The demons begged Jesus to let them go into them, and he gave them permission. 33When the demons came out of the man, they went into the pigs, and the herd rushed down the steep bank into the lake and was drowned.

34When those tending the pigs saw what had happened, they ran off and reported this in the town and countryside, 35and the people went out to see what had happened. When they came to Jesus, they found the man from whom the demons had gone out, sitting at Jesus' feet, dressed and in his right mind; and they were afraid. 36Those who had seen it told the people how the demon-possessed man had been cured. 37Then all the people of the region of the Gerasenes asked Jesus to leave them, because they were overcome with fear. So he got into the boat and left.

ᵃ26 Some manuscripts *Gadarenes*; other manuscripts *Gergesenes*; also in verse 37   ᵇ29 Greek *unclean*

38 The man from whom the demons had gone out begged to go with him, but Jesus sent him away, saying, 39 "Return home and tell how much God has done for you." So the man went away and told all over town how much Jesus had done for him.

A Dead Girl and a Sick Woman

40 Now when Jesus returned, a crowd welcomed him, for they were all expecting him. 41 Then a man named Jairus, a ruler of the synagogue, came and fell at Jesus' feet, pleading with him to come to his house 42 because his only daughter, a girl of about twelve, was dying.

As Jesus was on his way, the crowds almost crushed him. 43 And a woman was there who had been subject to bleeding for twelve years,[a] but no one could heal her. 44 She came up behind him and touched the edge of his cloak, and immediately her bleeding stopped.

45 "Who touched me?" Jesus asked.

When they all denied it, Peter said, "Master, the people are crowding and pressing against you."

46 But Jesus said, "Someone touched me; I know that power has gone out from me."

47 Then the woman, seeing that she could not go unnoticed, came trembling and fell at his feet. In the presence of all the people, she told why she had touched him and how she had been instantly healed. 48 Then he said to her, "Daughter, your faith has healed you. Go in peace."

49 While Jesus was still speaking, someone came from the house of Jairus, the synagogue ruler. "Your daughter is dead," he said. "Don't bother the teacher any more."

50 Hearing this, Jesus said to Jairus, "Don't be afraid; just believe, and she will be healed."

51 When he arrived at the house of Jairus, he did not let anyone go in with him except Peter, John and James, and the child's father and mother. 52 Meanwhile, all the people were wailing and mourning for her. "Stop wailing," Jesus said. "She is not dead but asleep."

53 They laughed at him, knowing that she was dead. 54 But he took her by the hand and said, "My child, get up!" 55 Her spirit returned, and at once she stood up. Then Jesus told them to give her something to eat. 56 Her parents were astonished, but he ordered them not to tell anyone what had happened.

Jesus Sends Out the Twelve

9 When Jesus had called the Twelve together, he gave them power and authority to drive out all demons and to cure diseases, 2 and he sent them out to preach the kingdom of God and to heal the sick. 3 He told them: "Take nothing for the journey—no staff, no bag, no bread, no money, no extra tunic. 4 Whatever house you enter, stay there until you leave that town. 5 If people do not welcome you, shake the dust off your feet when you leave their town, as a testimony against them." 6 So they set out and went from village to village, preaching the gospel and healing people everywhere.

7 Now Herod the tetrarch heard about all that was going on. And he was perplexed, because some were saying that John had been raised from the dead, 8 others that Elijah had appeared, and still others that one of the prophets of long ago had come back to life. 9 But Herod said, "I beheaded John. Who, then, is this I hear such things about?" And he tried to see him.

Jesus Feeds the Five Thousand

10 When the apostles returned, they reported to Jesus what they had done. Then he took them with him and they withdrew by themselves to a town called Bethsaida, 11 but the crowds learned about it and followed him. He welcomed them and spoke to them about the kingdom of God, and healed those who needed healing.

---

[a] 43 Many manuscripts years, and she had spent all she had on doctors

¹²Late in the afternoon the Twelve came to him and said, "Send the crowd away so they can go to the surrounding villages and countryside and find food and lodging, because we are in a remote place here."

¹³He replied, "You give them something to eat."

They answered, "We have only five loaves of bread and two fish—unless we go and buy food for all this crowd." ¹⁴(About five thousand men were there.)

But he said to his disciples, "Have them sit down in groups of about fifty each." ¹⁵The disciples did so, and everybody sat down. ¹⁶Taking the five loaves and the two fish and looking up to heaven, he gave thanks and broke them. Then he gave them to the disciples to set before the people. ¹⁷They all ate and were satisfied, and the disciples picked up twelve basketfuls of broken pieces that were left over.

Peter's Confession of Christ

¹⁸Once when Jesus was praying in private and his disciples were with him, he asked them, "Who do the crowds say I am?"

¹⁹They replied, "Some say John the Baptist; others say Elijah; and still others, that one of the prophets of long ago has come back to life."

²⁰"But what about you?" he asked. "Who do you say I am?"

Peter answered, "The Christ[a] of God."

²¹Jesus strictly warned them not to tell this to anyone. ²²And he said, "The Son of Man must suffer many things and be rejected by the elders, chief priests and teachers of the law, and he must be killed and on the third day be raised to life."

²³Then he said to them all: "If anyone would come after me, he must deny himself and take up his cross daily and follow me. ²⁴For whoever wants to save his life will lose it, but whoever loses his life for me will save it. ²⁵What good is it for a man to gain the whole world, and yet

lose or forfeit his very self? ²⁶If anyone is ashamed of me and my words, the Son of Man will be ashamed of him when he comes in his glory and in the glory of the Father and of the holy angels. ²⁷I tell you the truth, some who are standing here will not taste death before they see the kingdom of God."

The Transfiguration

²⁸About eight days after Jesus said this, he took Peter, John and James with him and went up onto a mountain to pray. ²⁹As he was praying, the appearance of his face changed, and his clothes became as bright as a flash of lightning. ³⁰Two men, Moses and Elijah, ³¹appeared in glorious splendor, talking with Jesus. They spoke about his departure, which he was about to bring to fulfillment at Jerusalem. ³²Peter and his companions were very sleepy, but when they became fully awake, they saw his glory and the two men standing with him. ³³As the men were leaving Jesus, Peter said to him, "Master, it is good for us to be here. Let us put up three shelters—one for you, one for Moses and one for Elijah." (He did not know what he was saying.)

³⁴While he was speaking, a cloud appeared and enveloped them, and they were afraid as they entered the cloud. ³⁵A voice came from the cloud, saying, "This is my Son, whom I have chosen; listen to him." ³⁶When the voice had spoken, they found that Jesus was alone. The disciples kept this to themselves, and told no one at that time what they had seen.

The Healing of a Boy With an Evil Spirit

³⁷The next day, when they came down from the mountain, a large crowd met him. ³⁸A man in the crowd called out, "Teacher, I beg you to look at my son, for he is my only child. ³⁹A spirit seizes him and he suddenly screams; it throws him into convulsions so that he foams at the mouth. It scarcely ever leaves him and is

ᵃ 20 Or Messiah

destroying him. 40I begged your disciples to drive it out, but they could not."

41"O unbelieving and perverse generation," Jesus replied, "how long shall I stay with you and put up with you? Bring your son here."

42Even while the boy was coming, the demon threw him to the ground in a convulsion. But Jesus rebuked the evil[a] spirit, healed the boy and gave him back to his father. 43And they were all amazed at the greatness of God.

While everyone was marveling at all that Jesus did, he said to his disciples, 44"Listen carefully to what I am about to tell you: The Son of Man is going to be betrayed into the hands of men." 45But they did not understand what this meant. It was hidden from them, so that they did not grasp it, and they were afraid to ask him about it.

Who Will Be the Greatest?

46An argument started among the disciples as to which of them would be the greatest. 47Jesus, knowing their thoughts, took a little child and had him stand beside him. 48Then he said to them, "Whoever welcomes this little child in my name welcomes me; and whoever welcomes me welcomes the one who sent me. For he who is least among you all—he is the greatest."

49"Master," said John, "we saw a man driving out demons in your name and we tried to stop him, because he is not one of us."

50"Do not stop him," Jesus said, "for whoever is not against you is for you."

Samaritan Opposition

51As the time approached for him to be taken up to heaven, Jesus resolutely set out for Jerusalem. 52And he sent messengers on ahead, who went into a Samaritan village to get things ready for him; 53but the people there did not welcome him, because he was heading for Jerusa-

lem. 54When the disciples James and John saw this, they asked, "Lord, do you want us to call fire down from heaven to destroy them[b]?" 55But Jesus turned and rebuked them, 56and[c] they went to another village.

The Cost of Following Jesus

57As they were walking along the road, a man said to him, "I will follow you wherever you go."

58Jesus replied, "Foxes have holes and birds of the air have nests, but the Son of Man has no place to lay his head."

59He said to another man, "Follow me."

But the man replied, "Lord, first let me go and bury my father."

60Jesus said to him, "Let the dead bury their own dead, but you go and proclaim the kingdom of God."

61Still another said, "I will follow you, Lord; but first let me go back and say good-by to my family."

62Jesus replied, "No one who puts his hand to the plow and looks back is fit for service in the kingdom of God."

Jesus Sends Out the Seventy-two

10 After this the Lord appointed seventy-two[d] others and sent them two by two ahead of him to every town and place where he was about to go. 2He told them, "The harvest is plentiful, but the workers are few. Ask the Lord of the harvest, therefore, to send out workers into his harvest field. 3Go! I am sending you out like lambs among wolves. 4Do not take a purse or bag or sandals; and do not greet anyone on the road.

5"When you enter a house, first say, 'Peace to this house.' 6If a man of peace is there, your peace will rest on him; if not, it will return to you. 7Stay in that house, eating and drinking whatever they give you, for the worker deserves his wages. Do not move around from house to house.

---

[a] 42 Greek unclean   [b] 54 Some manuscripts them, even as Elijah did   [c] 55,56 Some manuscripts them. And he said, "You do not know what kind of spirit you are of, for the Son of Man did not come to destroy men's lives, but to save them." 56And
[d] 1 Some manuscripts seventy; also in verse 17

8"When you enter a town and are welcomed, eat what is set before you. 9Heal the sick who are there and tell them, 'The kingdom of God is near you.' 10But when you enter a town and are not welcomed, go into its streets and say, 11'Even the dust of your town that sticks to our feet we wipe off against you. Yet be sure of this: The kingdom of God is near.' 12I tell you, it will be more bearable on that day for Sodom than for that town.

13"Woe to you, Korazin! Woe to you, Bethsaida! For if the miracles that were performed in you had been performed in Tyre and Sidon, they would have repented long ago, sitting in sackcloth and ashes. 14But it will be more bearable for Tyre and Sidon at the judgment than for you. 15And you, Capernaum, will you be lifted up to the skies? No, you will go down to the depths.ª

16"He who listens to you listens to me; he who rejects you rejects me; but he who rejects me rejects him who sent me."

ª 15 Greek *Hades*

GOING *deeper*

Our God-Given Authority

READ AND CONSIDER: LUKE 10:17-22

"I have given you authority to trample on snakes and scorpions and to overcome all the power of the enemy; nothing will harm you" (Luke 10:19).

What does it mean that we have authority to overcome all the power of the enemy? Why did Jesus think it was so important to tell us this? Because our enemy is powerful and he is working every day to hurt us, destroy us, and make us ineffective for God.

If we don't take our enemy seriously, it is much easier for Satan to manipulate and deceive us. We are all involved in a spiritual battle with an enemy who won't let up. Even though it is people who do evil things to us, we have to keep in mind that it is our ultimate enemy, the devil, who is behind it. "For our struggle is not against flesh and blood, but against the rulers, against the authorities, against the powers of this dark world and against the spiritual forces of evil in the heavenly realms" (Ephesians 6:12). Even when we are being attacked by a person, recognizing who our real enemy is will be the first step in standing strong.

The second step has to do with acknowledging the authority that has been given to us by Christ Himself. Our enemy is not as powerful as he wants us to believe. Satan is not even close to being as powerful as God is, but he wants us to think he is. And he will overpower anyone who doesn't understand that. Because of what Jesus accomplished on the cross, the devil is a defeated foe. He can't take our life and do what he wants with it unless we allow him to. He can't have our soul unless we give it to him. He can only accomplish what he does through lies and deception. It's our responsibility to recognize his lies and expose them for what they are. We do that by standing on the ultimate truth, which is the Word of God. The Word of God says that we have been given authority "to overcome all the power of the enemy." But so often we let the enemy get away with too much because we don't exercise our God-given authority to control his access to our lives.

When we face difficulty or oppression, we never need to live under the assumption that it's "just our bad luck." Instead, we can go before God in prayer, asking Him for discernment, wisdom, and strength to exercise the authority He has given us. Then we can get up and walk through our day as children of the King with all the honors, privileges, and authority of rightful heirs.

17The seventy-two returned with joy and said, "Lord, even the demons submit to us in your name."

18He replied, "I saw Satan fall like lightning from heaven. 19I have given you authority to trample on snakes and scorpions and to overcome all the power of the enemy; nothing will harm you. 20However, do not rejoice that the spirits submit to you, but rejoice that your names are written in heaven."

21At that time Jesus, full of joy through the Holy Spirit, said, "I praise you, Father, Lord of heaven and earth, because you have hidden these things from the wise and learned, and revealed them to little children. Yes, Father, for this was your good pleasure.

22"All things have been committed to me by my Father. No one knows who the Son is except the Father, and no one knows who the Father is except the Son and those to whom the Son chooses to reveal him."

23Then he turned to his disciples and said privately, "Blessed are the eyes that see what you see. 24For I tell you that many prophets and kings wanted to see what you see but did not see it, and to hear what you hear but did not hear it."

The Parable of the Good Samaritan

25On one occasion an expert in the law stood up to test Jesus. "Teacher," he asked, "what must I do to inherit eternal life?"

26"What is written in the Law?" he replied. "How do you read it?"

27He answered: "'Love the Lord your God with all your heart and with all your soul and with all your strength and with all your mind'ᵃ; and, 'Love your neighbor as yourself.'ᵇ"

28"You have answered correctly," Jesus replied. "Do this and you will live."

29But he wanted to justify himself, so he asked Jesus, "And who is my neighbor?"

30In reply Jesus said: "A man was going down from Jerusalem to Jericho, when he fell into the hands of robbers. They stripped him of his clothes, beat him and went away, leaving him half dead. 31A priest happened to be going down the same road, and when he saw the man, he passed by on the other side. 32So too, a Levite, when he came to the place and saw him, passed by on the other side. 33But a Samaritan, as he traveled, came where the man was; and when he saw him, he took pity on him. 34He went to him and bandaged his wounds, pouring on oil and wine. Then he put the man on his own donkey, took him to an inn and took care of him. 35The next day he took out two silver coinsᶜ and gave them to the innkeeper. 'Look after him,' he said, 'and when I return, I will reimburse you for any extra expense you may have.'

36"Which of these three do you think was a neighbor to the man who fell into the hands of robbers?"

37The expert in the law replied, "The one who had mercy on him."

Jesus told him, "Go and do likewise."

At the Home of Martha and Mary

38As Jesus and his disciples were on their way, he came to a village where a woman named Martha opened her home to him. 39She had a sister called Mary, who sat at the Lord's feet listening to what he said. 40But Martha was distracted by all the preparations that had to be made. She came to him and asked, "Lord, don't you care that my sister has left me to do the work by myself? Tell her to help me!"

Prayer is . . .

simply sitting quietly in God's presence in thankful appreciation.

41"Martha, Martha," the Lord answered, "you are worried and upset about many things, 42but only one thing is needed.ᵈ

ᵃ27 Deut. 6:5 ᵇ27 Lev. 19:18 ᶜ35 Greek *two denarii* ᵈ42 Some manuscripts *but few things are needed—or only one*

Mary has chosen what is better, and it will not be taken away from her."

Jesus' Teaching on Prayer

11 One day Jesus was praying in a certain place. When he finished, one of his disciples said to him, "Lord, teach us to pray, just as John taught his disciples."

²He said to them, "When you pray, say:

" 'Father,[a]
hallowed be your name,
your kingdom come.[b]
³Give us each day our daily bread.
⁴Forgive us our sins,
    for we also forgive everyone who
        sins against us.[c]
And lead us not into temptation.[d]' "

⁵Then he said to them, "Suppose one of you has a friend, and he goes to him at midnight and says, 'Friend, lend me three loaves of bread, ⁶because a friend of mine on a journey has come to me, and I have nothing to set before him.'

⁷"Then the one inside answers, 'Don't bother me. The door is already locked, and my children are with me in bed. I can't get up and give you anything.' ⁸I tell you, though he will not get up and give him the bread because he is his friend, yet because of the man's boldness[e] he will get up and give him as much as he needs.

⁹"So I say to you: Ask and it will be given to you; seek and you will find; knock and the door will be opened to you. ¹⁰For everyone who asks receives; he who seeks finds; and to him who knocks, the door will be opened.

¹¹"Which of you fathers, if your son asks for[f] a fish, will give him a snake instead? ¹²Or if he asks for an egg, will give him a scorpion? ¹³If you then, though you are evil, know how to give good gifts to your children, how much more will your Father in heaven give the Holy Spirit to those who ask him!"

Jesus and Beelzebub

¹⁴Jesus was driving out a demon that was mute. When the demon left, the man who had been mute spoke, and the crowd was amazed. ¹⁵But some of them said, "By Beelzebub,[g] the prince of demons, he is driving out demons." ¹⁶Others tested him by asking for a sign from heaven.

¹⁷Jesus knew their thoughts and said to them: "Any kingdom divided against itself will be ruined, and a house divided against itself will fall. ¹⁸If Satan is divided against himself, how can his kingdom stand? I say this because you claim that I drive out demons by Beelzebub. ¹⁹Now if I drive out demons by Beelzebub, by whom do your followers drive them out? So then, they will be your judges. ²⁰But if I drive out demons by the finger of God, then the kingdom of God has come to you.

²¹"When a strong man, fully armed, guards his own house, his possessions are safe. ²²But when someone stronger attacks and overpowers him, he takes away the armor in which the man trusted and divides up the spoils.

²³"He who is not with me is against me, and he who does not gather with me, scatters.

²⁴"When an evil[h] spirit comes out of a man, it goes through arid places seeking rest and does not find it. Then it says, 'I will return to the house I left.' ²⁵When it arrives, it finds the house swept clean and put in order. ²⁶Then it goes and takes seven other spirits more wicked than itself, and they go in and live there. And the final condition of that man is worse than the first."

²⁷As Jesus was saying these things, a woman in the crowd called out, "Blessed is the mother who gave you birth and nursed you."

²⁸He replied, "Blessed rather are those who hear the word of God and obey it."

---

[a] 2 Some manuscripts *Our Father in heaven*   [b] 2 Some manuscripts *come. May your will be done on earth as it is in heaven.*
[c] 4 Greek *everyone who is indebted to us*   [d] 4 Some manuscripts *temptation but deliver us from the evil one*   [e] 8 Or *persistence*
[f] 11 Some manuscripts *for bread, will give him a stone; or if he asks for*   [g] 15 Greek *Beezeboul* or *Beelzeboul*; also in verses 18 and 19   [h] 24 Greek *unclean*

Why Prayer Works

READ AND CONSIDER: LUKE 11:5-13

"I tell you, though he will not get up and give him the bread because he is his friend, yet because of the man's boldness he will get up and give him as much as he needs" (Luke 11:8).

This parable about prayer gives us some insight into how Jesus expects us to pray—Boldly! Understandling why prayer works can help us to pray boldly. Here are a few reasons we can pray with confidence:

Prayer works because of what Jesus did. When we pray we are applying Jesus' victory through the cross, taking the rule away from Satan and establishing the rule of God. In that way we stop the devil's work and establish the Lord's will. We take things that are wrong and make them right. When we become believers, God doesn't take us to heaven right away—and for a good reason. There are things He has for us to do on earth. He wants us to expose the enemy's lies and proclaim God's truth. He wants us to bring down the enemy's strongholds and set the captives free. He wants us to bring health where there is sickness, love where there is fear, forgiveness where there is condemnation, revelation where there is spiritual blindness, and wholeness where there is a fracture in our lives. God's Word reveals that this can be accomplished when we pray. When we understand this, it's easier to pray boldly.

Prayer works because we live God's way. In order to get our prayers answered, we need to walk in obedience to God's laws. "We have confidence before God and receive from him anything we ask, because we obey his commands and do what pleases him" (1 John 3:21-22). You may be thinking that this is enough to disqualify you right there. How can you always do what pleases God? But God is merciful in this too, because we can pray about these issues as well. He will even help us to obey if we ask Him. Remember, the answers to our prayers are not earned by our obedience. But our privilege to pray boldly is rooted in our relationship with Father God. And He has called us to walk as obedient children.

Prayer works because we don't hesitate to ask. God wants us to be bold in our asking. Being bold isn't stomping into the throne room of God and demanding what we think we deserve, but it is recognizing that God wants to do above and beyond what we think possible (Ephesians 3:20). This knowledge makes us courageous to ask God to do great things in us, through us, and around us. Jesus' story about the man who persisted in asking for bread from his neighbor suggests that we not only ask persistently but boldly as well.

I once had someone tell me they prayed only about the "big stuff" because they didn't want to waste any of their prayers on small things, as if God only allows us a certain number of prayer requests per lifetime, so we had better make our prayers count. God says we are to ask continually—to pray without ceasing. Not like a chant or saying the same thing over and over, but praying *all* the time about *everything,* knowing that God has no limits and is never too busy or preoccupied. He is always ready to hear from us. He wants us to ask because He wants to answer. Such knowledge inspires bold praying.

Prayer works because God has set it up that way. The way God works His purposes in this world is through people who believe in Jesus. God says that if we pray, He will move on our behalf. And He will not only move, He will do what is impossible for us. He wants us to influence our part of this world by being in the prayer closet with Him, praying boldly.

The Sign of Jonah

29As the crowds increased, Jesus said, "This is a wicked generation. It asks for a miraculous sign, but none will be given it except the sign of Jonah. 30For as Jonah was a sign to the Ninevites, so also will the Son of Man be to this generation. 31The Queen of the South will rise at the judgment with the men of this generation and condemn them; for she came from the ends of the earth to listen to Solomon's wisdom, and now onea greater than Solomon is here. 32The men of Nineveh will stand up at the judgment with this generation and condemn it; for they repented at the preaching of Jonah, and now one greater than Jonah is here.

The Lamp of the Body

33"No one lights a lamp and puts it in a place where it will be hidden, or under a bowl. Instead he puts it on its stand, so that those who come in may see the light. 34Your eye is the lamp of your body. When your eyes are good, your whole body also is full of light. But when they are bad, your body also is full of darkness. 35See to it, then, that the light within you is not darkness. 36Therefore, if your whole body is full of light, and no part of it dark, it will be completely lighted, as when the light of a lamp shines on you."

Six Woes

37When Jesus had finished speaking, a Pharisee invited him to eat with him; so he went in and reclined at the table. 38But the Pharisee, noticing that Jesus did not first wash before the meal, was surprised.

39Then the Lord said to him, "Now then, you Pharisees clean the outside of the cup and dish, but inside you are full of greed and wickedness. 40You foolish people! Did not the one who made the outside make the inside also? 41But give what is inside ⌊the dish⌋b to the poor, and everything will be clean for you.

42"Woe to you Pharisees, because you give God a tenth of your mint, rue and all other kinds of garden herbs, but you neglect justice and the love of God. You should have practiced the latter without leaving the former undone.

43"Woe to you Pharisees, because you love the most important seats in the synagogues and greetings in the marketplaces.

44"Woe to you, because you are like unmarked graves, which men walk over without knowing it."

45One of the experts in the law answered him, "Teacher, when you say these things, you insult us also."

46Jesus replied, "And you experts in the law, woe to you, because you load people down with burdens they can hardly carry, and you yourselves will not lift one finger to help them.

47"Woe to you, because you build tombs for the prophets, and it was your forefathers who killed them. 48So you testify that you approve of what your forefathers did; they killed the prophets, and you build their tombs. 49Because of this, God in his wisdom said, 'I will send them prophets and apostles, some of whom they will kill and others they will persecute.' 50Therefore this generation will be held responsible for the blood of all the prophets that has been shed since the beginning of the world, 51from the blood of Abel to the blood of Zechariah, who was killed between the altar and the sanctuary. Yes, I tell you, this generation will be held responsible for it all.

52"Woe to you experts in the law, because you have taken away the key to knowledge. You yourselves have not entered, and you have hindered those who were entering."

53When Jesus left there, the Pharisees and the teachers of the law began to oppose him fiercely and to besiege him with questions, 54waiting to catch him in something he might say.

---

a 31 Or something; also in verse 32   b 41 Or what you have

Driving Under His Influence

If you want to move into new territory in your life, it is imperative that you decide exactly who is in the driver's seat. Is it going to be you, or is it going to be God? Are you going to head out on your own, or are you willing to let Him lead you? Will you be moving in the flesh, or will you be empowered by the Holy Spirit? It's important to make that crucial decision, because it will determine how effectively you pray.

Jesus *always* moved under the Holy Spirit's influence. His disciples observed that. They personally witnessed Him healing people, casting out demons, and performing many other miracles, and they wanted to know how these things happened. They recognized that Jesus had a source of power they didn't have. They also saw Him frequently go to a private place and pray, and whenever He did, the life and power of God would be infused in Him. They obviously knew there was a connection between power and prayer, because they didn't ask Him to teach them how to get power. They asked Him to teach them how to pray. And what He taught them is now known as the Lord's Prayer (Matthew 6:9-13; Luke 11:2-4).

Even though Jesus was the Son of God, He still went to His Father in prayer in order to receive power for all He needed to do. And He teaches us how to do the same. God wants us to draw on His resources by coming to Him in prayer and seeking a fresh infusion of power the way Jesus did. Many people think praying "Your kingdom come" is a prayer about sometime in the future.

But it is not a someday prayer. Just like the phrases "give us each day our daily bread" and "forgive us our sins," we are not talking about some day in the future. We are talking about *now*. When we pray "Your kingdom come," we are asking God's kingdom to invade our circumstances right now.

Moving forward with Jesus always calls us upward in prayer. Our constancy and consistency in prayer increases as we grow in our understanding of why prayer is so important. Essentially, it has to do with the power God invests in us—the power to touch His throne in heaven from our place on earth.

Just like Jesus, we need to be empowered by the Holy Spirit in all that we do. He is our Teacher, Helper, and Guide, and we must ask Him to teach us how to pray with fervency and passion so that our prayers have power. We must request that He help us have love and compassion for others, even those who are hard to love, so that our prayers are rightly motivated. We must invite Him to be in the driver's seat of our lives so that He can guide us where we need to go. When we move through each day under His influence, we will accomplish things we would otherwise never be able to do.

For the next "From Stormie's Heart" article, go to page 1293.

Warnings and Encouragements

12 Meanwhile, when a crowd of many thousands had gathered, so that they were trampling on one another, Jesus began to speak first to his disciples, saying: "Be on your guard against the yeast of the Pharisees, which is hypocrisy. ²There is nothing concealed that will not be disclosed, or hidden that will not be made known. ³What you have said in the dark will be heard in the daylight, and what you have whispered in the ear in the inner rooms will be proclaimed from the roofs.

⁴"I tell you, my friends, do not be afraid of those who kill the body and after that can do no more. ⁵But I will show you whom you should fear: Fear him who, after the killing of the body, has power to throw you into hell. Yes, I tell you, fear him. ⁶Are not five sparrows sold for two pennies^a? Yet not one of them is forgotten by God. ⁷Indeed, the very hairs of your head are all numbered. Don't be afraid; you are worth more than many sparrows.

⁸"I tell you, whoever acknowledges me before men, the Son of Man will also acknowledge him before the angels of God. ⁹But he who disowns me before men will be disowned before the angels of God. ¹⁰And everyone who speaks a word against the Son of Man will be forgiven, but anyone who blasphemes against the Holy Spirit will not be forgiven.

¹¹"When you are brought before synagogues, rulers and authorities, do not worry about how you will defend yourselves or what you will say, ¹²for the Holy Spirit will teach you at that time what you should say."

The Parable of the Rich Fool

¹³Someone in the crowd said to him, "Teacher, tell my brother to divide the inheritance with me."

¹⁴Jesus replied, "Man, who appointed me a judge or an arbiter between you?" ¹⁵Then he said to them, "Watch out! Be on your guard against all kinds of greed; a man's life does not consist in the abundance of his possessions."

¹⁶And he told them this parable: "The ground of a certain rich man produced a good crop. ¹⁷He thought to himself, 'What shall I do? I have no place to store my crops.'

¹⁸"Then he said, 'This is what I'll do. I will tear down my barns and build bigger ones, and there I will store all my grain and my goods. ¹⁹And I'll say to myself, "You have plenty of good things laid up for many years. Take life easy; eat, drink and be merry."'

²⁰"But God said to him, 'You fool! This very night your life will be demanded from you. Then who will get what you have prepared for yourself?'

²¹"This is how it will be with anyone who stores up things for himself but is not rich toward God."

Do Not Worry

²²Then Jesus said to his disciples: "Therefore I tell you, do not worry about your life, what you will eat; or about your body, what you will wear. ²³Life is more than food, and the body more than clothes. ²⁴Consider the ravens: They do not sow or reap, they have no storeroom or barn; yet God feeds them. And how much more valuable you are than birds! ²⁵Who of you by worrying can add a single hour to his life^b? ²⁶Since you cannot do this very little thing, why do you worry about the rest?

²⁷"Consider how the lilies grow. They do not labor or spin. Yet I tell you, not even Solomon in all his splendor was dressed like one of these. ²⁸If that is how God clothes the grass of the field, which is here today, and tomorrow is thrown into the fire, how much more will he clothe you, O you of little faith! ²⁹And do not set your heart on what you will eat or drink; do not worry about it. ³⁰For the pagan world runs after all such things, and your Father knows that you need

---

^{a} 6 Greek *two assaria* ^{b} 25 Or *single cubit to his height*

GOING *deeper*

Let Time With God Take the Place of Worrying

READ AND CONSIDER: LUKE 12:22-34

"Who of you by worrying can add a single hour to his life?" (Luke 12:25).

None of us can add a single moment to our lives by worrying. In fact, the opposite is probably more true; we actually *lose* life when we worry. We are wasting the time we spend worrying, and we may be causing health problems that could ultimately shorten our lives.

Jesus tells us to refuse to worry because no matter what problems we have, He has already overcome them. "In this world you will have trouble. But take heart! I have overcome the world" (John 16:33). We can find freedom from anxiety just by spending time with Him. "When anxiety was great within me, your consolation brought joy to my soul" (Psalm 94:19).

When you are anxious, it means you aren't trusting God to take care of you. But He will prove His faithfulness if you run to Him. "Do not set your heart on what you will eat or drink; do not worry about it. For the pagan world runs after all such things, and your Father knows that you need them. But seek his kingdom, and these things will be given to you as well" (Luke 12:29-31).

God says we don't need to be anxious about *anything*; we just need to pray about *everything*. So instead of worrying, actively bring your cares to Him. Prayer is not empty, powerless, wishful thinking. It is a powerful connection with the One who is the source of our comfort, strength, and hope. So take your worries about the future to the One who holds your future in his hands.

them. ³¹But seek his kingdom, and these things will be given to you as well.

³²"Do not be afraid, little flock, for your Father has been pleased to give you the kingdom. ³³Sell your possessions and give to the poor. Provide purses for yourselves that will not wear out, a treasure in heaven that will not be exhausted, where no thief comes near and no moth destroys. ³⁴For where your treasure is, there your heart will be also.

Watchfulness

³⁵"Be dressed ready for service and keep your lamps burning, ³⁶like men waiting for their master to return from a wedding banquet, so that when he comes and knocks they can immediately open the door for him. ³⁷It will be good for those servants whose master finds them watching when he comes. I tell you the truth, he will dress himself to serve, will have them recline at the table and will come and wait on them. ³⁸It will be good for those servants whose master finds them ready, even if he comes in the second or third watch of the night. ³⁹But understand this: If the owner of the house had known at what hour the thief was coming, he would not have let his house be broken into. ⁴⁰You also must be ready, because the Son of Man will come at an hour when you do not expect him."

⁴¹Peter asked, "Lord, are you telling this parable to us, or to everyone?"

⁴²The Lord answered, "Who then is the faithful and wise manager, whom the master puts in charge of his servants to give them their food allowance at the proper time? ⁴³It will be good for that servant whom the master finds doing so

when he returns. 44I tell you the truth, he will put him in charge of all his possessions. 45But suppose the servant says to himself, 'My master is taking a long time in coming,' and he then begins to beat the menservants and maidservants and to eat and drink and get drunk. 46The master of that servant will come on a day when he does not expect him and at an hour he is not aware of. He will cut him to pieces and assign him a place with the unbelievers.

47"That servant who knows his master's will and does not get ready or does not do what his master wants will be beaten with many blows. 48But the one who does not know and does things deserving punishment will be beaten with few blows. From everyone who has been given much, much will be demanded; and from the one who has been entrusted with much, much more will be asked.

Not Peace but Division

49"I have come to bring fire on the earth, and how I wish it were already kindled! 50But I have a baptism to undergo, and how distressed I am until it is completed! 51Do you think I came to bring peace on earth? No, I tell you, but division. 52From now on there will be five in one family divided against each other, three against two and two against three. 53They will be divided, father against son and son against father, mother against daughter and daughter against mother, mother-in-law against daughter-in-law and daughter-in-law against mother-in-law."

Interpreting the Times

54He said to the crowd: "When you see a cloud rising in the west, immediately you say, 'It's going to rain,' and it does. 55And when the south wind blows, you say, 'It's going to be hot,' and it is. 56Hypocrites! You know how to interpret the appearance of the earth and the sky. How is it that you don't know how to interpret this present time?

57"Why don't you judge for yourselves what is right? 58As you are going with your adversary to the magistrate, try hard to be reconciled to him on the way, or he may drag you off to the judge, and the judge turn you over to the officer, and the officer throw you into prison. 59I tell you, you will not get out until you have paid the last penny.ª"

Repent or Perish

13 Now there were some present at that time who told Jesus about the Galileans whose blood Pilate had mixed with their sacrifices. 2Jesus answered, "Do you think that these Galileans were worse sinners than all the other Galileans because they suffered this way? 3I tell you, no! But unless you repent, you too will all perish. 4Or those eighteen who died when the tower in Siloam fell on them— do you think they were more guilty than all the others living in Jerusalem? 5I tell you, no! But unless you repent, you too will all perish."

6Then he told this parable: "A man had a fig tree, planted in his vineyard, and he went to look for fruit on it, but did not find any. 7So he said to the man who took care of the vineyard, 'For three years now I've been coming to look for fruit on this fig tree and haven't found any. Cut it down! Why should it use up the soil?'

8"'Sir,' the man replied, 'leave it alone for one more year, and I'll dig around it and fertilize it. 9If it bears fruit next year, fine! If not, then cut it down.'"

A Crippled Woman Healed on the Sabbath

10On a Sabbath Jesus was teaching in one of the synagogues, 11and a woman was there who had been crippled by a spirit for eighteen years. She was bent over and could not straighten up at all. 12When Jesus saw her, he called her forward and said to her, "Woman, you are set free from your infirmity." 13Then he

ª 59 Greek lepton

put his hands on her, and immediately she straightened up and praised God.

¹⁴Indignant because Jesus had healed on the Sabbath, the synagogue ruler said to the people, "There are six days for work. So come and be healed on those days, not on the Sabbath."

¹⁵The Lord answered him, "You hypocrites! Doesn't each of you on the Sabbath untie his ox or donkey from the stall and lead it out to give it water? ¹⁶Then should not this woman, a daughter of Abraham, whom Satan has kept bound for eighteen long years, be set free on the Sabbath day from what bound her?"

¹⁷When he said this, all his opponents were humiliated, but the people were delighted with all the wonderful things he was doing.

The Parables of the Mustard Seed and the Yeast

¹⁸Then Jesus asked, "What is the kingdom of God like? What shall I compare it to? ¹⁹It is like a mustard seed, which a man took and planted in his garden. It grew and became a tree, and the birds of the air perched in its branches."

²⁰Again he asked, "What shall I compare the kingdom of God to? ²¹It is like yeast that a woman took and mixed into a large amount[a] of flour until it worked all through the dough."

The Narrow Door

²²Then Jesus went through the towns and villages, teaching as he made his way to Jerusalem. ²³Someone asked him, "Lord, are only a few people going to be saved?"

Praying Luke 13:24-25
Father, help me to always stay on the narrow path of life You have for me so that I don't end up outside of all You have prepared for my future.

He said to them, ²⁴"Make every effort to enter through the narrow door, be-

cause many, I tell you, will try to enter and will not be able to. ²⁵Once the owner of the house gets up and closes the door, you will stand outside knocking and pleading, 'Sir, open the door for us.'

"But he will answer, 'I don't know you or where you come from.'

²⁶"Then you will say, 'We ate and drank with you, and you taught in our streets.'

²⁷"But he will reply, 'I don't know you or where you come from. Away from me, all you evildoers!'

²⁸"There will be weeping there, and gnashing of teeth, when you see Abraham, Isaac and Jacob and all the prophets in the kingdom of God, but you yourselves thrown out. ²⁹People will come from east and west and north and south, and will take their places at the feast in the kingdom of God. ³⁰Indeed there are those who are last who will be first, and first who will be last."

Jesus' Sorrow for Jerusalem

³¹At that time some Pharisees came to Jesus and said to him, "Leave this place and go somewhere else. Herod wants to kill you."

³²He replied, "Go tell that fox, 'I will drive out demons and heal people today and tomorrow, and on the third day I will reach my goal.' ³³In any case, I must keep going today and tomorrow and the next day—for surely no prophet can die outside Jerusalem!

³⁴"O Jerusalem, Jerusalem, you who kill the prophets and stone those sent to you, how often I have longed to gather your children together, as a hen gathers her chicks under her wings, but you were not willing! ³⁵Look, your house is left to you desolate. I tell you, you will not see me again until you say, 'Blessed is he who comes in the name of the Lord.'[b]"

Jesus at a Pharisee's House

14 One Sabbath, when Jesus went to eat in the house of a prominent Pharisee, he was being carefully watched.

---

^a*21* Greek *three satas* (probably about 1/2 bushel or 22 liters)   ^b*35* Psalm 118:26

[2]There in front of him was a man suffering from dropsy. [3]Jesus asked the Pharisees and experts in the law, "Is it lawful to heal on the Sabbath or not?" [4]But they remained silent. So taking hold of the man, he healed him and sent him away.

[5]Then he asked them, "If one of you has a son[a] or an ox that falls into a well on the Sabbath day, will you not immediately pull him out?" [6]And they had nothing to say.

[7]When he noticed how the guests picked the places of honor at the table, he told them this parable: [8]"When someone invites you to a wedding feast, do not take the place of honor, for a person more distinguished than you may have been invited. [9]If so, the host who invited both of you will come and say to you, 'Give this man your seat.' Then, humiliated, you will have to take the least important place. [10]But when you are invited, take the lowest place, so that when your host comes, he will say to you, 'Friend, move up to a better place.' Then you will be honored in the presence of all your fellow guests. [11]For everyone who exalts himself will be humbled, and he who humbles himself will be exalted."

Praying Luke 14:11
Lord, pierce my conscience whenever I am drawn toward anything less than a humble attitude.

[12]Then Jesus said to his host, "When you give a luncheon or dinner, do not invite your friends, your brothers or relatives, or your rich neighbors; if you do, they may invite you back and so you will be repaid. [13]But when you give a banquet, invite the poor, the crippled, the lame, the blind, [14]and you will be blessed. Although they cannot repay you, you will be repaid at the resurrection of the righteous."

The Parable of the Great Banquet

[15]When one of those at the table with him heard this, he said to Jesus, "Blessed is the man who will eat at the feast in the kingdom of God."

[16]Jesus replied: "A certain man was preparing a great banquet and invited many guests. [17]At the time of the banquet he sent his servant to tell those who had been invited, 'Come, for everything is now ready.'

[18]"But they all alike began to make excuses. The first said, 'I have just bought a field, and I must go and see it. Please excuse me.'

[19]"Another said, 'I have just bought five yoke of oxen, and I'm on my way to try them out. Please excuse me.'

[20]"Still another said, 'I just got married, so I can't come.'

[21]"The servant came back and reported this to his master. Then the owner of the house became angry and ordered his servant, 'Go out quickly into the streets and alleys of the town and bring in the poor, the crippled, the blind and the lame.'

[22]"'Sir,' the servant said, 'what you ordered has been done, but there is still room.'

[23]"Then the master told his servant, 'Go out to the roads and country lanes and make them come in, so that my house will be full. [24]I tell you, not one of those men who were invited will get a taste of my banquet.'"

The Cost of Being a Disciple

[25]Large crowds were traveling with Jesus, and turning to them he said: [26]"If anyone comes to me and does not hate his father and mother, his wife and children, his brothers and sisters—yes, even his own life—he cannot be my disciple. [27]And anyone who does not carry his cross and follow me cannot be my disciple.

[28]"Suppose one of you wants to build a tower. Will he not first sit down and estimate the cost to see if he has enough money to complete it? [29]For if he lays the foundation and is not able to finish it, everyone who sees it will ridicule him,

[a] 5 Some manuscripts *donkey*

[30]saying, 'This fellow began to build and was not able to finish.'

[31]"Or suppose a king is about to go to war against another king. Will he not first sit down and consider whether he is able with ten thousand men to oppose the one coming against him with twenty thousand? [32]If he is not able, he will send a delegation while the other is still a long way off and will ask for terms of peace. [33]In the same way, any of you who does not give up everything he has cannot be my disciple.

[34]"Salt is good, but if it loses its saltiness, how can it be made salty again? [35]It is fit neither for the soil nor for the manure pile; it is thrown out.

"He who has ears to hear, let him hear."

The Parable of the Lost Sheep

15 Now the tax collectors and "sinners" were all gathering around to hear him. [2]But the Pharisees and the teachers of the law muttered, "This man welcomes sinners and eats with them."

[3]Then Jesus told them this parable: [4]"Suppose one of you has a hundred sheep and loses one of them. Does he not leave the ninety-nine in the open country and go after the lost sheep until he finds it? [5]And when he finds it, he joyfully puts it on his shoulders [6]and goes home. Then he calls his friends and neighbors together and says, 'Rejoice with me; I have found my lost sheep.' [7]I tell you that in the same way there will be more rejoicing in heaven over one sinner who repents than over ninety-nine righteous persons who do not need to repent.

The Parable of the Lost Coin

[8]"Or suppose a woman has ten silver coins[a] and loses one. Does she not light a lamp, sweep the house and search carefully until she finds it? [9]And when she finds it, she calls her friends and neighbors together and says, 'Rejoice with me; I have found my lost coin.' [10]In the same

way, I tell you, there is rejoicing in the presence of the angels of God over one sinner who repents."

The Parable of the Lost Son

[11]Jesus continued: "There was a man who had two sons. [12]The younger one said to his father, 'Father, give me my share of the estate.' So he divided his property between them.

[13]"Not long after that, the younger son got together all he had, set off for a distant country and there squandered his wealth in wild living. [14]After he had spent everything, there was a severe famine in that whole country, and he began to be in need. [15]So he went and hired himself out to a citizen of that country, who sent him to his fields to feed pigs. [16]He longed to fill his stomach with the pods that the pigs were eating, but no one gave him anything.

[17]"When he came to his senses, he said, 'How many of my father's hired men have food to spare, and here I am starving to death! [18]I will set out and go back to my father and say to him: Father, I have sinned against heaven and against you. [19]I am no longer worthy to be called your son; make me like one of your hired men.' [20]So he got up and went to his father.

"But while he was still a long way off, his father saw him and was filled with compassion for him; he ran to his son, threw his arms around him and kissed him.

[21]"The son said to him, 'Father, I have sinned against heaven and against you. I am no longer worthy to be called your son.[b]'

[22]"But the father said to his servants, 'Quick! Bring the best robe and put it on him. Put a ring on his finger and sandals on his feet. [23]Bring the fattened calf and kill it. Let's have a feast and celebrate. [24]For this son of mine was dead and is alive again; he was lost and is found.' So they began to celebrate.

[25]"Meanwhile, the older son was in the

---

[a] 8 Greek ten drachmas, each worth about a day's wages   [b] 21 Some early manuscripts son. Make me like one of your hired men.

field. When he came near the house, he heard music and dancing. 26So he called one of the servants and asked him what was going on. 27'Your brother has come,' he replied, 'and your father has killed the fattened calf because he has him back safe and sound.'

28"The older brother became angry and refused to go in. So his father went out and pleaded with him. 29But he answered his father, 'Look! All these years I've been slaving for you and never disobeyed your orders. Yet you never gave me even a young goat so I could celebrate with my friends. 30But when this son of yours who has squandered your property with prostitutes comes home, you kill the fattened calf for him!'

31" 'My son,' the father said, 'you are always with me, and everything I have is yours. 32But we had to celebrate and be glad, because this brother of yours was dead and is alive again; he was lost and is found.' "

The Parable of the Shrewd Manager

16 Jesus told his disciples: "There was a rich man whose manager was accused of wasting his possessions. 2So he called him in and asked him, 'What is this I hear about you? Give an account of your management, because you cannot be manager any longer.'

3"The manager said to himself, 'What shall I do now? My master is taking away my job. I'm not strong enough to dig, and I'm ashamed to beg— 4I know what I'll do so that, when I lose my job here, people will welcome me into their houses.'

5"So he called in each one of his master's debtors. He asked the first, 'How much do you owe my master?'

6" 'Eight hundred gallons[a] of olive oil,' he replied.

"The manager told him, 'Take your bill, sit down quickly, and make it four hundred.'

7"Then he asked the second, 'And how much do you owe?'

" 'A thousand bushels[b] of wheat,' he replied.

"He told him, 'Take your bill and make it eight hundred.'

8"The master commended the dishonest manager because he had acted shrewdly. For the people of this world are more shrewd in dealing with their own kind than are the people of the light. 9I tell you, use worldly wealth to gain friends for yourselves, so that when it is gone, you will be welcomed into eternal dwellings.

Praying Luke 16:10-13
God, I pray that I will always be faithful with the material possessions You have given me, and that with them I will serve and glorify only You.

10"Whoever can be trusted with very little can also be trusted with much, and whoever is dishonest with very little will also be dishonest with much. 11So if you have not been trustworthy in handling worldly wealth, who will trust you with true riches? 12And if you have not been trustworthy with someone else's property, who will give you property of your own?

13"No servant can serve two masters. Either he will hate the one and love the other, or he will be devoted to the one and despise the other. You cannot serve both God and Money."

14The Pharisees, who loved money, heard all this and were sneering at Jesus. 15He said to them, "You are the ones who justify yourselves in the eyes of men, but God knows your hearts. What is highly valued among men is detestable in God's sight.

Additional Teachings

16"The Law and the Prophets were proclaimed until John. Since that time, the good news of the kingdom of God is being preached, and everyone is forcing his way into it. 17It is easier for heaven

---

a 6 Greek *one hundred batous* (probably about 3 kiloliters)   b 7 Greek *one hundred korous* (probably about 35 kiloliters) and earth to disappear than for the least stroke of a pen to drop out of the Law.

18"Anyone who divorces his wife and marries another woman commits adultery, and the man who marries a divorced woman commits adultery.

The Rich Man and Lazarus

19"There was a rich man who was dressed in purple and fine linen and lived in luxury every day. 20At his gate was laid a beggar named Lazarus, covered with sores 21and longing to eat what fell from the rich man's table. Even the dogs came and licked his sores.

22"The time came when the beggar died and the angels carried him to Abraham's side. The rich man also died and was buried. 23In hell,ᵃ where he was in torment, he looked up and saw Abraham far away, with Lazarus by his side. 24So he called to him, 'Father Abraham, have pity on me and send Lazarus to dip the tip of his finger in water and cool my tongue, because I am in agony in this fire.'

25"But Abraham replied, 'Son, remember that in your lifetime you received your good things, while Lazarus received bad things, but now he is comforted here and you are in agony. 26And besides all this, between us and you a great chasm has been fixed, so that those who want to go from here to you cannot, nor can anyone cross over from there to us.'

27"He answered, 'Then I beg you, father, send Lazarus to my father's house, 28for I have five brothers. Let him warn them, so that they will not also come to this place of torment.'

29"Abraham replied, 'They have Moses and the Prophets; let them listen to them.'

30"'No, father Abraham,' he said, 'but if someone from the dead goes to them, they will repent.'

31"He said to him, 'If they do not listen to Moses and the Prophets, they will not be convinced even if someone rises from the dead.'"

Sin, Faith, Duty

17 Jesus said to his disciples: "Things that cause people to sin are bound to come, but woe to that person through whom they come. 2It would be better for him to be thrown into the sea with a millstone tied around his neck than for him to cause one of these little ones to sin. 3So watch yourselves.

"If your brother sins, rebuke him, and if he repents, forgive him. 4If he sins against you seven times in a day, and seven times comes back to you and says, 'I repent,' forgive him."

5The apostles said to the Lord, "Increase our faith!"

6He replied, "If you have faith as small as a mustard seed, you can say to this mulberry tree, 'Be uprooted and planted in the sea,' and it will obey you.

7"Suppose one of you had a servant plowing or looking after the sheep. Would he say to the servant when he comes in from the field, 'Come along now and sit down to eat'? 8Would he not rather say, 'Prepare my supper, get yourself ready and wait on me while I eat and drink; after that you may eat and drink'? 9Would he thank the servant because he did what he was told to do? 10So you also, when you have done everything you were told to do, should say, 'We are unworthy servants; we have only done our duty.'"

Ten Healed of Leprosy

11Now on his way to Jerusalem, Jesus traveled along the border between Samaria and Galilee. 12As he was going into a village, ten men who had leprosyᵇ met him. They stood at a distance 13and called out in a loud voice, "Jesus, Master, have pity on us!"

14When he saw them, he said, "Go, show yourselves to the priests." And as they went, they were cleansed.

15One of them, when he saw he was healed, came back, praising God in a loud voice. 16He threw himself at Jesus' feet and thanked him—and he was a Samaritan.

The Hidden Power of Praise

GOING **deeper**

READ AND CONSIDER: LUKE 17:11-19

"One of them, when he saw he was healed, came back, praising God in a loud voice" (Luke 17:15).

Ten lepers cried out to Jesus to heal them, and He did. But only one of the ten returned and glorified God. How often are we like the other nine? God does something great for us, and we just take it in stride and don't fall down on our face at His feet and thank Him for it. We often do that with healing, even when it is an answer to a specific prayer we prayed. Many people think, *Well, this would have happened anyway.* We often take the blessings of our health for granted, instead of praising Him every day and giving thanks that He is our Healer.

We need to praise Jesus that He is our healer whether we are healed at that moment or not. We have to remember that God heals in His way and in His time. Though Jesus came to earth as our Healer, not all sickness or injury gets healed in this lifetime—at least not the way *we* always want it to be. If He doesn't heal us the way we ask Him to, it's because He has a greater plan and His glory will be seen in it.

Some sickness comes from the enemy. God allowed Job to be made sick by Satan. God allowed it for a reason. And even though we don't understand the reason that God doesn't always heal us, we can trust that He will bring good out of our suffering. If nothing else, suffering forces us to draw closer to Him. And the closer we are to Him, the more we will praise Him.

Praying passionately and fervently for our own healing is not a problem because we are never apathetic about that, in fact we feel quite strongly about it. And the sicker, the more miserable, pained, and incapacitated we are, the more fervently we pray. The Bible says that if we are suffering, we are to pray, and we are to pray with passion. That means burning, devout, sincere, wholehearted, and enthusiastic prayer. That means with our whole heart. When we pray for healing, we pray passionately, knowing that the answer is all up to God. He is our Healer, but not all of us find the healing we want when we want it. Sometimes the healing is delayed and we can grow weary in the waiting. Time passes very slowly when we are in pain or are suffering.

In God's presence there is healing. When we praise God, it invites His presence into our lives in a powerful way. Praising God for His presence and healing power in the midst of our sickness, pain, weakness, or misery, opens up a channel through which His healing presence can penetrate our lives to heal us or to sustain us as He sees fit. That is the hidden power of praising God.

¹⁷Jesus asked, "Were not all ten cleansed? Where are the other nine? ¹⁸Was no one found to return and give praise to God except this foreigner?" ¹⁹Then he said to him, "Rise and go; your faith has made you well."

The Coming of the Kingdom of God

²⁰Once, having been asked by the Pharisees when the kingdom of God would come, Jesus replied, "The kingdom of God does not come with your careful observation, ²¹nor will people say, 'Here it is,' or 'There it is,' because the kingdom of God is within[a] you."

²²Then he said to his disciples, "The time is coming when you will long to see one of the days of the Son of Man, but you will not see it. ²³Men will tell you,

a 21 Or *among*

'There he is!' or 'Here he is!' Do not go running off after them. 24For the Son of Man in his day[a] will be like the lightning, which flashes and lights up the sky from one end to the other. 25But first he must suffer many things and be rejected by this generation.

26"Just as it was in the days of Noah, so also will it be in the days of the Son of Man. 27People were eating, drinking, marrying and being given in marriage up to the day Noah entered the ark. Then the flood came and destroyed them all.

28"It was the same in the days of Lot. People were eating and drinking, buying and selling, planting and building. 29But the day Lot left Sodom, fire and sulfur rained down from heaven and destroyed them all.

30"It will be just like this on the day the Son of Man is revealed. 31On that day no one who is on the roof of his house, with his goods inside, should go down to get them. Likewise, no one in the field should go back for anything. 32Remember Lot's wife! 33Whoever tries to keep his life will lose it, and whoever loses his life will preserve it. 34I tell you, on that night two people will be in one bed; one will be taken and the other left. 35Two women will be grinding grain together; one will be taken and the other left.[b]"

37"Where, Lord?" they asked.

He replied, "Where there is a dead body, there the vultures will gather."

The Parable of the Persistent Widow

18 Then Jesus told his disciples a parable to show them that they should always pray and not give up. 2He said: "In a certain town there was a judge who neither feared God nor cared about men. 3And there was a widow in that town who kept coming to him with the plea, 'Grant me justice against my adversary.'

4"For some time he refused. But finally he said to himself, 'Even though I don't fear God or care about men, 5yet because this widow keeps bothering me, I will see that she gets justice, so that she won't eventually wear me out with her coming!'"

6And the Lord said, "Listen to what the unjust judge says. 7And will not God bring about justice for his chosen ones, who cry out to him day and night? Will he keep putting them off? 8I tell you, he will see that they get justice, and quickly. However, when the Son of Man comes, will he find faith on the earth?"

Praying Luke 18:1-8
Heavenly Father, thank You that You are a God who is moved by persistent prayer and You hear me when I cry out to You day and night. Because of that I will always pray and not give up.

The Parable of the Pharisee and the Tax Collector

9To some who were confident of their own righteousness and looked down on everybody else, Jesus told this parable: 10"Two men went up to the temple to pray, one a Pharisee and the other a tax collector. 11The Pharisee stood up and prayed about[c] himself: 'God, I thank you that I am not like other men—robbers, evildoers, adulterers—or even like this tax collector. 12I fast twice a week and give a tenth of all I get.'

13"But the tax collector stood at a distance. He would not even look up to heaven, but beat his breast and said, 'God, have mercy on me, a sinner.'

14"I tell you that this man, rather than the other, went home justified before God. For everyone who exalts himself will be humbled, and he who humbles himself will be exalted."

The Little Children and Jesus

15People were also bringing babies to Jesus to have him touch them. When the disciples saw this, they rebuked them. 16But Jesus called the children to him

a 24 Some manuscripts do not have *in his day.* b 35 Some manuscripts *left.* 36 *Two men will be in the field; one will be taken and the other left.* c 11 Or *to* and said, "Let the little children come to me, and do not hinder them, for the kingdom of God belongs to such as these. [17]I tell you the truth, anyone who will not receive the kingdom of God like a little child will never enter it."

The Rich Ruler

[18]A certain ruler asked him, "Good teacher, what must I do to inherit eternal life?"

[19]"Why do you call me good?" Jesus answered. "No one is good—except God alone. [20]You know the commandments: 'Do not commit adultery, do not murder, do not steal, do not give false testimony, honor your father and mother.'[a]"

[21]"All these I have kept since I was a boy," he said.

[22]When Jesus heard this, he said to him, "You still lack one thing. Sell everything you have and give to the poor, and you will have treasure in heaven. Then come, follow me."

[23]When he heard this, he became very sad, because he was a man of great wealth. [24]Jesus looked at him and said, "How hard it is for the rich to enter the kingdom of God! [25]Indeed, it is easier for a camel to go through the eye of a needle than for a rich man to enter the kingdom of God."

[26]Those who heard this asked, "Who then can be saved?"

[27]Jesus replied, "What is impossible with men is possible with God."

[28]Peter said to him, "We have left all we had to follow you!"

[29]"I tell you the truth," Jesus said to them, "no one who has left home or wife or brothers or parents or children for the sake of the kingdom of God [30]will fail to receive many times as much in this age and, in the age to come, eternal life."

Jesus Again Predicts His Death

[31]Jesus took the Twelve aside and told them, "We are going up to Jerusalem, and everything that is written by the proph-

ets about the Son of Man will be fulfilled. [32]He will be handed over to the Gentiles. They will mock him, insult him, spit on him, flog him and kill him. [33]On the third day he will rise again."

[34]The disciples did not understand any of this. Its meaning was hidden from them, and they did not know what he was talking about.

A Blind Beggar Receives His Sight

[35]As Jesus approached Jericho, a blind man was sitting by the roadside begging. [36]When he heard the crowd going by, he asked what was happening. [37]They told him, "Jesus of Nazareth is passing by."

[38]He called out, "Jesus, Son of David, have mercy on me!"

[39]Those who led the way rebuked him and told him to be quiet, but he shouted all the more, "Son of David, have mercy on me!"

[40]Jesus stopped and ordered the man to be brought to him. When he came near, Jesus asked him, [41]"What do you want me to do for you?"

"Lord, I want to see," he replied.

[42]Jesus said to him, "Receive your sight; your faith has healed you." [43]Immediately he received his sight and followed Jesus, praising God. When all the people saw it, they also praised God.

Zacchaeus the Tax Collector

19 Jesus entered Jericho and was passing through. [2]A man was there by the name of Zacchaeus; he was a chief tax collector and was wealthy. [3]He wanted to see who Jesus was, but being a short man he could not, because of the crowd. [4]So he ran ahead and climbed a sycamore-fig tree to see him, since Jesus was coming that way.

[5]When Jesus reached the spot, he looked up and said to him, "Zacchaeus, come down immediately. I must stay at your house today." [6]So he came down at once and welcomed him gladly.

[7]All the people saw this and began to

---

a [20] Exodus 20:12-16; Deut. 5:16-20

mutter, "He has gone to be the guest of a 'sinner.'"

8But Zacchaeus stood up and said to the Lord, "Look, Lord! Here and now I give half of my possessions to the poor, and if I have cheated anybody out of anything, I will pay back four times the amount."

9Jesus said to him, "Today salvation has come to this house, because this man, too, is a son of Abraham. 10For the Son of Man came to seek and to save what was lost."

The Parable of the Ten Minas

11While they were listening to this, he went on to tell them a parable, because he was near Jerusalem and the people thought that the kingdom of God was going to appear at once. 12He said: "A man of noble birth went to a distant country to have himself appointed king and then to return. 13So he called ten of his servants and gave them ten minas.a 'Put this money to work,' he said, 'until I come back.'

14"But his subjects hated him and sent a delegation after him to say, 'We don't want this man to be our king.'

15"He was made king, however, and returned home. Then he sent for the servants to whom he had given the money, in order to find out what they had gained with it.

16"The first one came and said, 'Sir, your mina has earned ten more.'

17"'Well done, my good servant!' his master replied. 'Because you have been trustworthy in a very small matter, take charge of ten cities.'

18"The second came and said, 'Sir, your mina has earned five more.'

19"His master answered, 'You take charge of five cities.'

20"Then another servant came and said, 'Sir, here is your mina; I have kept it laid away in a piece of cloth. 21I was afraid of you, because you are a hard man. You take out what you did not put in and reap what you did not sow.'

22"His master replied, 'I will judge you by your own words, you wicked servant! You knew, did you, that I am a hard man, taking out what I did not put in, and reaping what I did not sow? 23Why then didn't you put my money on deposit, so that when I came back, I could have collected it with interest?'

24"Then he said to those standing by, 'Take his mina away from him and give it to the one who has ten minas.'

25"'Sir,' they said, 'he already has ten!'

26"He replied, 'I tell you that to everyone who has, more will be given, but as for the one who has nothing, even what he has will be taken away. 27But those enemies of mine who did not want me to be king over them—bring them here and kill them in front of me.'"

The Triumphal Entry

28After Jesus had said this, he went on ahead, going up to Jerusalem. 29As he approached Bethphage and Bethany at the hill called the Mount of Olives, he sent two of his disciples, saying to them, 30"Go to the village ahead of you, and as you enter it, you will find a colt tied there, which no one has ever ridden. Untie it and bring it here. 31If anyone asks you, 'Why are you untying it?' tell him, 'The Lord needs it.'"

32Those who were sent ahead went and found it just as he had told them. 33As they were untying the colt, its owners asked them, "Why are you untying the colt?"

34They replied, "The Lord needs it."

35They brought it to Jesus, threw their cloaks on the colt and put Jesus on it. 36As he went along, people spread their cloaks on the road.

37When he came near the place where the road goes down the Mount of Olives, the whole crowd of disciples began joyfully to praise God in loud voices for all the miracles they had seen:

38"Blessed is the king who comes in
    the name of the Lord!"b

---

a 13 A mina was about three months' wages.   b 38 Psalm 118:26

"Peace in heaven and glory in the highest!"

[39]Some of the Pharisees in the crowd said to Jesus, "Teacher, rebuke your disciples!"

[40]"I tell you," he replied, "if they keep quiet, the stones will cry out."

[41]As he approached Jerusalem and saw the city, he wept over it [42]and said, "If you, even you, had only known on this day what would bring you peace—but now it is hidden from your eyes. [43]The days will come upon you when your enemies will build an embankment against you and encircle you and hem you in on every side. [44]They will dash you to the ground, you and the children within your walls. They will not leave one stone on another, because you did not recognize the time of God's coming to you."

Jesus at the Temple

[45]Then he entered the temple area and began driving out those who were selling. [46]"It is written," he said to them, " 'My house will be a house of prayer'[a]; but you have made it 'a den of robbers.'[b]"

[47]Every day he was teaching at the temple. But the chief priests, the teachers of the law and the leaders among the people were trying to kill him. [48]Yet they could not find any way to do it, because all the people hung on his words.

The Authority of Jesus Questioned

20 One day as he was teaching the people in the temple courts and preaching the gospel, the chief priests and the teachers of the law, together with the elders, came up to him. [2]"Tell us by what authority you are doing these things," they said. "Who gave you this authority?"

[3]He replied, "I will also ask you a question. Tell me, [4]John's baptism—was it from heaven, or from men?"

[5]They discussed it among themselves and said, "If we say, 'From heaven,' he will ask, 'Why didn't you believe him?' [6]But

if we say, 'From men,' all the people will stone us, because they are persuaded that John was a prophet."

[7]So they answered, "We don't know where it was from."

[8]Jesus said, "Neither will I tell you by what authority I am doing these things."

Prayer is . . .

communicating with God.

The Parable of the Tenants

[9]He went on to tell the people this parable: "A man planted a vineyard, rented it to some farmers and went away for a long time. [10]At harvest time he sent a servant to the tenants so they would give him some of the fruit of the vineyard. But the tenants beat him and sent him away empty-handed. [11]He sent another servant, but that one also they beat and treated shamefully and sent away empty-handed. [12]He sent still a third, and they wounded him and threw him out.

[13]"Then the owner of the vineyard said, 'What shall I do? I will send my son, whom I love; perhaps they will respect him.'

[14]"But when the tenants saw him, they talked the matter over. 'This is the heir,' they said. 'Let's kill him, and the inheritance will be ours.' [15]So they threw him out of the vineyard and killed him.

"What then will the owner of the vineyard do to them? [16]He will come and kill those tenants and give the vineyard to others."

When the people heard this, they said, "May this never be!"

[17]Jesus looked directly at them and asked, "Then what is the meaning of that which is written:

" 'The stone the builders rejected
    has become the capstone'[c][d]?

---

[a] 46 Isaiah 56:7   [b] 46 Jer. 7:11   [c] 17 Or cornerstone   [d] 17 Psalm 118:22

18Everyone who falls on that stone will be broken to pieces, but he on whom it falls will be crushed."

19The teachers of the law and the chief priests looked for a way to arrest him immediately, because they knew he had spoken this parable against them. But they were afraid of the people.

Paying Taxes to Caesar

20Keeping a close watch on him, they sent spies, who pretended to be honest. They hoped to catch Jesus in something he said so that they might hand him over to the power and authority of the governor. 21So the spies questioned him: "Teacher, we know that you speak and teach what is right, and that you do not show partiality but teach the way of God in accordance with the truth. 22Is it right for us to pay taxes to Caesar or not?"

23He saw through their duplicity and said to them, 24"Show me a denarius. Whose portrait and inscription are on it?"

25"Caesar's," they replied.

He said to them, "Then give to Caesar what is Caesar's, and to God what is God's."

26They were unable to trap him in what he had said there in public. And astonished by his answer, they became silent.

The Resurrection and Marriage

27Some of the Sadducees, who say there is no resurrection, came to Jesus with a question. 28"Teacher," they said, "Moses wrote for us that if a man's brother dies and leaves a wife but no children, the man must marry the widow and have children for his brother. 29Now there were seven brothers. The first one married a woman and died childless. 30The second 31and then the third married her, and in the same way the seven died, leaving no children. 32Finally, the woman died too. 33Now then, at the resurrection whose wife will she be, since the seven were married to her?"

34Jesus replied, "The people of this age marry and are given in marriage. 35But those who are considered worthy of taking part in that age and in the resurrection from the dead will neither marry nor be given in marriage, 36and they can no longer die; for they are like the angels. They are God's children, since they are children of the resurrection. 37But in the account of the bush, even Moses showed that the dead rise, for he calls the Lord 'the God of Abraham, and the God of Isaac, and the God of Jacob.'a 38He is not the God of the dead, but of the living, for to him all are alive."

39Some of the teachers of the law responded, "Well said, teacher!" 40And no one dared to ask him any more questions.

Whose Son Is the Christ?

41Then Jesus said to them, "How is it that they say the Christb is the Son of David? 42David himself declares in the Book of Psalms:

" 'The Lord said to my Lord:
    "Sit at my right hand
43until I make your enemies
    a footstool for your feet." 'c

44David calls him 'Lord.' How then can he be his son?"

45While all the people were listening, Jesus said to his disciples, 46"Beware of the teachers of the law. They like to walk around in flowing robes and love to be greeted in the marketplaces and have the most important seats in the synagogues and the places of honor at banquets. 47They devour widows' houses and for a show make lengthy prayers. Such men will be punished most severely."

The Widow's Offering

21 As he looked up, Jesus saw the rich putting their gifts into the temple treasury. 2He also saw a poor widow put in two very small copper coins.d 3"I tell you the truth," he said, "this poor widow

---

a 37 Exodus 3:6   b 41 Or Messiah   c 43 Psalm 110:1   d 2 Greek two lepta has put in more than all the others. [4]All these people gave their gifts out of their wealth; but she out of her poverty put in all she had to live on."

Signs of the End of the Age

[5]Some of his disciples were remarking about how the temple was adorned with beautiful stones and with gifts dedicated to God. But Jesus said, [6]"As for what you see here, the time will come when not one stone will be left on another; every one of them will be thrown down."

[7]"Teacher," they asked, "when will these things happen? And what will be the sign that they are about to take place?"

[8]He replied: "Watch out that you are not deceived. For many will come in my name, claiming, 'I am he,' and, 'The time is near.' Do not follow them. [9]When you hear of wars and revolutions, do not be frightened. These things must happen first, but the end will not come right away."

[10]Then he said to them: "Nation will rise against nation, and kingdom against kingdom. [11]There will be great earthquakes, famines and pestilences in various places, and fearful events and great signs from heaven.

Praying Luke 21:12-15

Lord, I pray that every act of persecution or bias against me because I believe in You will be an opportunity for me to fearlessly testify as to who You are and what You have done.

[12]"But before all this, they will lay hands on you and persecute you. They will deliver you to synagogues and prisons, and you will be brought before kings and governors, and all on account of my name. [13]This will result in your being witnesses to them. [14]But make up your mind not to worry beforehand how you will defend yourselves. [15]For I will give you words and wisdom that none of your adversaries will be able to resist or contradict. [16]You will be betrayed even by par-

ents, brothers, relatives and friends, and they will put some of you to death. [17]All men will hate you because of me. [18]But not a hair of your head will perish. [19]By standing firm you will gain life.

[20]"When you see Jerusalem being surrounded by armies, you will know that its desolation is near. [21]Then let those who are in Judea flee to the mountains, let those in the city get out, and let those in the country not enter the city. [22]For this is the time of punishment in fulfillment of all that has been written. [23]How dreadful it will be in those days for pregnant women and nursing mothers! There will be great distress in the land and wrath against this people. [24]They will fall by the sword and will be taken as prisoners to all the nations. Jerusalem will be trampled on by the Gentiles until the times of the Gentiles are fulfilled.

[25]"There will be signs in the sun, moon and stars. On the earth, nations will be in anguish and perplexity at the roaring and tossing of the sea. [26]Men will faint from terror, apprehensive of what is coming on the world, for the heavenly bodies will be shaken. [27]At that time they will see the Son of Man coming in a cloud with power and great glory. [28]When these things begin to take place, stand up and lift up your heads, because your redemption is drawing near."

[29]He told them this parable: "Look at the fig tree and all the trees. [30]When they sprout leaves, you can see for yourselves and know that summer is near. [31]Even so, when you see these things happening, you know that the kingdom of God is near.

[32]"I tell you the truth, this generation[a] will certainly not pass away until all these things have happened. [33]Heaven and earth will pass away, but my words will never pass away.

[34]"Be careful, or your hearts will be weighed down with dissipation, drunkenness and the anxieties of life, and that

---

[a] 32 Or *race*

day will close on you unexpectedly like a trap. 35For it will come upon all those who live on the face of the whole earth. 36Be always on the watch, and pray that you may be able to escape all that is about to happen, and that you may be able to stand before the Son of Man."

37Each day Jesus was teaching at the temple, and each evening he went out to spend the night on the hill called the Mount of Olives, 38and all the people came early in the morning to hear him at the temple.

Judas Agrees to Betray Jesus

22 Now the Feast of Unleavened Bread, called the Passover, was approaching, 2and the chief priests and the teachers of the law were looking for some way to get rid of Jesus, for they were afraid of the people. 3Then Satan entered Judas, called Iscariot, one of the Twelve. 4And Judas went to the chief priests and the officers of the temple guard and discussed with them how he might betray Jesus. 5They were delighted and agreed to give him money. 6He consented, and watched for an opportunity to hand Jesus over to them when no crowd was present.

The Last Supper

7Then came the day of Unleavened Bread on which the Passover lamb had to be sacrificed. 8Jesus sent Peter and John, saying, "Go and make preparations for us to eat the Passover."

9"Where do you want us to prepare for it?" they asked.

10He replied, "As you enter the city, a man carrying a jar of water will meet you. Follow him to the house that he enters, 11and say to the owner of the house, 'The Teacher asks: Where is the guest room, where I may eat the Passover with my disciples?' 12He will show you a large upper room, all furnished. Make preparations there."

13They left and found things just as Jesus had told them. So they prepared the Passover.

14When the hour came, Jesus and his apostles reclined at the table. 15And he said to them, "I have eagerly desired to eat this Passover with you before I suffer. 16For I tell you, I will not eat it again until it finds fulfillment in the kingdom of God."

17After taking the cup, he gave thanks and said, "Take this and divide it among you. 18For I tell you I will not drink again of the fruit of the vine until the kingdom of God comes."

19And he took bread, gave thanks and broke it, and gave it to them, saying, "This is my body given for you; do this in remembrance of me."

20In the same way, after the supper he took the cup, saying, "This cup is the new covenant in my blood, which is poured out for you. 21But the hand of him who is going to betray me is with mine on the table. 22The Son of Man will go as it has been decreed, but woe to that man who betrays him." 23They began to question among themselves which of them it might be who would do this.

24Also a dispute arose among them as to which of them was considered to be greatest. 25Jesus said to them, "The kings of the Gentiles lord it over them; and those who exercise authority over them call themselves Benefactors. 26But you are not to be like that. Instead, the greatest among you should be like the youngest, and the one who rules like the one who serves. 27For who is greater, the one who is at the table or the one who serves? Is it not the one who is at the table? But I am among you as one who serves. 28You are those who have stood by me in my trials. 29And I confer on you a kingdom, just as my Father conferred one on me, 30so that you may eat and drink at my table in my kingdom and sit on thrones, judging the twelve tribes of Israel.

31"Simon, Simon, Satan has asked to sift you[a] as wheat. 32But I have prayed

---

a *31* The Greek is plural.

Pray That Your Faith Will Not Fail GOING *deeper*

READ AND CONSIDER: LUKE 22:24–34

"But I have prayed for you, Simon, that your faith may not fail. And when you have turned back, strengthen your brothers" (Luke 22:32).

Jesus prayed that Peter's faith wouldn't fail. And He told Peter this in the middle of their last Passover meal together—the Last Supper—just before revealing that Peter would deny Him. Peter did fail an important test when he denied Jesus, but ultimately his faith did not fail. He could have given up and hid himself in fear and refused to follow God's call. He had denied the very Son of God, after all. But his faith wasn't in works, or perfection, or in himself; it was in Jesus. Peter went on to lead the first-century church even after his failure on the night of Christ's trial. Jesus' prayer was answered. Peter's faith didn't fail.

Jesus' prayer shows us that if our faith doesn't fail, we can endure hardship, face temptation, and even act faithlessly at times, but ultimately we can be God's instruments to do great things. Faith is like the foundation of a house. If the foundation gives way, the house will crumble. Pray that your faith will not fail so your foundation will stay solid.

Pray the same for others as well. When you don't know what to pray for someone—when that person's needs are so great or when you just can't put your finger on the problem—one of the things you can pray for is that his or her faith will not fail. In fact, that's a good prayer to pray for people any time you pray. Who among us doesn't need to have stronger faith?

for you, Simon, that your faith may not fail. And when you have turned back, strengthen your brothers."

³³But he replied, "Lord, I am ready to go with you to prison and to death."

³⁴Jesus answered, "I tell you, Peter, before the rooster crows today, you will deny three times that you know me."

³⁵Then Jesus asked them, "When I sent you without purse, bag or sandals, did you lack anything?"

"Nothing," they answered.

³⁶He said to them, "But now if you have a purse, take it, and also a bag; and if you don't have a sword, sell your cloak and buy one. ³⁷It is written: 'And he was numbered with the transgressors'^a; and I tell you that this must be fulfilled in me. Yes, what is written about me is reaching its fulfillment."

³⁸The disciples said, "See, Lord, here are two swords."

"That is enough," he replied.

Jesus Prays on the Mount of Olives

³⁹Jesus went out as usual to the Mount of Olives, and his disciples followed him. ⁴⁰On reaching the place, he said to them, "Pray that you will not fall into temptation." ⁴¹He withdrew about a stone's throw beyond them, knelt down and prayed, ⁴²"Father, if you are willing, take this cup from me; yet not my will, but yours be done." ⁴³An angel from heaven appeared to him and strengthened him. ⁴⁴And being in anguish, he prayed more earnestly, and his sweat was like drops of blood falling to the ground.^b

⁴⁵When he rose from prayer and went back to the disciples, he found them asleep, exhausted from sorrow. ⁴⁶"Why are you sleeping?" he asked them. "Get up and pray so that you will not fall into temptation."

Jesus Arrested

⁴⁷While he was still speaking a crowd came up, and the man who was called

---

^a *37* Isaiah 53:12   ^b *44* Some early manuscripts do not have verses 43 and 44.

Judas, one of the Twelve, was leading them. He approached Jesus to kiss him, [48]but Jesus asked him, "Judas, are you betraying the Son of Man with a kiss?"

[49]When Jesus' followers saw what was going to happen, they said, "Lord, should we strike with our swords?" [50]And one of them struck the servant of the high priest, cutting off his right ear.

[51]But Jesus answered, "No more of this!" And he touched the man's ear and healed him.

[52]Then Jesus said to the chief priests, the officers of the temple guard, and the elders, who had come for him, "Am I leading a rebellion, that you have come with swords and clubs? [53]Every day I was with you in the temple courts, and you did not lay a hand on me. But this is your hour—when darkness reigns."

Peter Disowns Jesus

[54]Then seizing him, they led him away and took him into the house of the high priest. Peter followed at a distance. [55]But when they had kindled a fire in the middle of the courtyard and had sat down together, Peter sat down with them. [56]A servant girl saw him seated there in the firelight. She looked closely at him and said, "This man was with him."

[57]But he denied it. "Woman, I don't know him," he said.

[58]A little later someone else saw him and said, "You also are one of them."

"Man, I am not!" Peter replied.

[59]About an hour later another asserted, "Certainly this fellow was with him, for he is a Galilean."

[60]Peter replied, "Man, I don't know what you're talking about!" Just as he was speaking, the rooster crowed. [61]The Lord turned and looked straight at Peter. Then Peter remembered the word the Lord had spoken to him: "Before the rooster crows today, you will disown me three times." [62]And he went outside and wept bitterly.

The Guards Mock Jesus

[63]The men who were guarding Jesus began mocking and beating him. [64]They blindfolded him and demanded, "Prophesy! Who hit you?" [65]And they said many other insulting things to him.

Jesus Before Pilate and Herod

[66]At daybreak the council of the elders of the people, both the chief priests and teachers of the law, met together, and Jesus was led before them. [67]"If you are the Christ,[a]" they said, "tell us."

Jesus answered, "If I tell you, you will not believe me, [68]and if I asked you, you would not answer. [69]But from now on, the Son of Man will be seated at the right hand of the mighty God."

[70]They all asked, "Are you then the Son of God?"

He replied, "You are right in saying I am."

[71]Then they said, "Why do we need any more testimony? We have heard it from his own lips."

23 Then the whole assembly rose and led him off to Pilate. [2]And they began to accuse him, saying, "We have found this man subverting our nation. He opposes payment of taxes to Caesar and claims to be Christ,[b] a king."

[3]So Pilate asked Jesus, "Are you the king of the Jews?"

"Yes, it is as you say," Jesus replied.

[4]Then Pilate announced to the chief priests and the crowd, "I find no basis for a charge against this man."

[5]But they insisted, "He stirs up the people all over Judea[c] by his teaching. He started in Galilee and has come all the way here."

[6]On hearing this, Pilate asked if the man was a Galilean. [7]When he learned that Jesus was under Herod's jurisdiction, he sent him to Herod, who was also in Jerusalem at that time.

[8]When Herod saw Jesus, he was greatly pleased, because for a long time he had been wanting to see him. From what he

---

a 67 Or *Messiah*   b 2 Or *Messiah*; also in verses 35 and 39   c 5 Or *over the land of the Jews* had heard about him, he hoped to see him perform some miracle. [9]He plied him with many questions, but Jesus gave him no answer. [10]The chief priests and the teachers of the law were standing there, vehemently accusing him. [11]Then Herod and his soldiers ridiculed and mocked him. Dressing him in an elegant robe, they sent him back to Pilate. [12]That day Herod and Pilate became friends—before this they had been enemies.

[13]Pilate called together the chief priests, the rulers and the people, [14]and said to them, "You brought me this man as one who was inciting the people to rebellion. I have examined him in your presence and have found no basis for your charges against him. [15]Neither has Herod, for he sent him back to us; as you can see, he has done nothing to deserve death. [16]Therefore, I will punish him and then release him.[a]"

[18]With one voice they cried out, "Away with this man! Release Barabbas to us!" [19](Barabbas had been thrown into prison for an insurrection in the city, and for murder.)

[20]Wanting to release Jesus, Pilate appealed to them again. [21]But they kept shouting, "Crucify him! Crucify him!"

[22]For the third time he spoke to them: "Why? What crime has this man committed? I have found in him no grounds for the death penalty. Therefore I will have him punished and then release him."

[23]But with loud shouts they insistently demanded that he be crucified, and their shouts prevailed. [24]So Pilate decided to grant their demand. [25]He released the man who had been thrown into prison for insurrection and murder, the one they asked for, and surrendered Jesus to their will.

The Crucifixion

[26]As they led him away, they seized Simon from Cyrene, who was on his way in from the country, and put the cross on him and made him carry it behind Jesus. [27]A large number of people followed him, including women who mourned and wailed for him. [28]Jesus turned and said to them, "Daughters of Jerusalem, do not weep for me; weep for yourselves and for your children. [29]For the time will come when you will say, 'Blessed are the barren women, the wombs that never bore and the breasts that never nursed!' [30]Then

> " 'they will say to the mountains,
>   "Fall on us!"
> and to the hills, "Cover us!" ' [b]

[31]For if men do these things when the tree is green, what will happen when it is dry?"

[32]Two other men, both criminals, were also led out with him to be executed. [33]When they came to the place called the Skull, there they crucified him, along with the criminals—one on his right, the other on his left. [34]Jesus said, "Father, forgive them, for they do not know what they are doing."[c] And they divided up his clothes by casting lots.

[35]The people stood watching, and the rulers even sneered at him. They said, "He saved others; let him save himself if he is the Christ of God, the Chosen One."

[36]The soldiers also came up and mocked him. They offered him wine vinegar [37]and said, "If you are the king of the Jews, save yourself."

[38]There was a written notice above him, which read: THIS IS THE KING OF THE JEWS.

[39]One of the criminals who hung there hurled insults at him: "Aren't you the Christ? Save yourself and us!"

[40]But the other criminal rebuked him. "Don't you fear God," he said, "since you are under the same sentence? [41]We are punished justly, for we are getting what our deeds deserve. But this man has done nothing wrong."

[42]Then he said, "Jesus, remember me when you come into your kingdom.[d]"

---

[a] 16 Some manuscripts him." [17]Now he was obliged to release one man to them at the Feast.   [b] 30 Hosea 10:8   [c] 34 Some early manuscripts do not have this sentence.   [d] 42 Some manuscripts come with your kingly power

Father, I Forgive Them

READ AND CONSIDER: LUKE 23:32-34

"Jesus said, 'Father, forgive them, for they do not know what they are doing.' And they divided up his clothes by casting lots" (Luke 23:34).

I don't know about you, but when I've just been hurt by someone, the last thing I think about doing is praying for that person. Most of us are more interested in focusing on some kind of justice so that the offending person will have to pay for the hurt or damage he or she has inflicted. But not Jesus.

Jesus, who had done nothing wrong, was brutally beaten within an inch of His life. His head was pierced with a crown of long, thick thorns. His skin was slashed. His hands and feet had spikes driven through them. His cross was dropped into a hole in the ground. He hung there, naked and humiliated, for all the world to laugh at and scorn. Some said, "He saved others; let him save himself if he is the Christ of God, the Chosen One" (23:35). The way they crucified him is horrifying beyond what we can imagine. Yet as Jesus was hanging on the cross and dying in agony, He prayed for the men who were killing Him. "Father, forgive them, for they do not know what they are doing." Such amazing forgiveness and love is hard to fathom.

As we look at the injustices in our lives, how do they compare with what Jesus endured? If He could forgive His torturers, surely we can choose to forgive too. Some of us have very deep wounds that may require time before total forgiveness is worked in us. But in most injustices that we've experienced, we can decide to let go of them quickly and completely and choose to forgive the offenders.

The good news is we can ask God to help us forgive. We can ask Him to show us His perspective in the matter. We can pray for Him to help us remember what Jesus endured and be able to say, "Father, I forgive them whether they knew what they were doing or not. I forgive them, not because they deserve it, but because I want to be like You."

43Jesus answered him, "I tell you the truth, today you will be with me in paradise."

Jesus' Death

44It was now about the sixth hour, and darkness came over the whole land until the ninth hour, 45for the sun stopped shining. And the curtain of the temple was torn in two. 46Jesus called out with a loud voice, "Father, into your hands I commit my spirit." When he had said this, he breathed his last.

47The centurion, seeing what had happened, praised God and said, "Surely this was a righteous man." 48When all the people who had gathered to witness this sight saw what took place, they beat their breasts and went away. 49But all those who knew him, including the women who had followed him from Galilee, stood at a distance, watching these things.

Jesus' Burial

50Now there was a man named Joseph, a member of the Council, a good and upright man, 51who had not consented to their decision and action. He came from the Judean town of Arimathea and he was waiting for the kingdom of God. 52Going to Pilate, he asked for Jesus' body. 53Then he took it down, wrapped it in linen cloth and placed it in a tomb cut in the rock, one in which no one had yet been laid. 54It was Preparation Day, and the Sabbath was about to begin.

⁵⁵The women who had come with Jesus from Galilee followed Joseph and saw the tomb and how his body was laid in it. ⁵⁶Then they went home and prepared spices and perfumes. But they rested on the Sabbath in obedience to the commandment.

The Resurrection

24 On the first day of the week, very early in the morning, the women took the spices they had prepared and went to the tomb. ²They found the stone rolled away from the tomb, ³but when they entered, they did not find the body of the Lord Jesus. ⁴While they were wondering about this, suddenly two men in clothes that gleamed like lightning stood beside them. ⁵In their fright the women bowed down with their faces to the ground, but the men said to them, "Why do you look for the living among the dead? ⁶He is not here; he has risen! Remember how he told you, while he was still with you in Galilee: ⁷'The Son of Man must be delivered into the hands of sinful men, be crucified and on the third day be raised again.' " ⁸Then they remembered his words.

⁹When they came back from the tomb, they told all these things to the Eleven and to all the others. ¹⁰It was Mary Magdalene, Joanna, Mary the mother of James, and the others with them who told this to the apostles. ¹¹But they did not believe the women, because their words seemed to them like nonsense. ¹²Peter, however, got up and ran to the tomb. Bending over, he saw the strips of linen lying by themselves, and he went away, wondering to himself what had happened.

On the Road to Emmaus

¹³Now that same day two of them were going to a village called Emmaus, about seven miles[a] from Jerusalem. ¹⁴They were talking with each other about everything that had happened. ¹⁵As they talked and discussed these things with each other,

Jesus himself came up and walked along with them; ¹⁶but they were kept from recognizing him.

¹⁷He asked them, "What are you discussing together as you walk along?"

They stood still, their faces downcast. ¹⁸One of them, named Cleopas, asked him, "Are you only a visitor to Jerusalem and do not know the things that have happened there in these days?"

¹⁹"What things?" he asked.

"About Jesus of Nazareth," they replied. "He was a prophet, powerful in word and deed before God and all the people. ²⁰The chief priests and our rulers handed him over to be sentenced to death, and they crucified him; ²¹but we had hoped that he was the one who was going to redeem Israel. And what is more, it is the third day since all this took place. ²²In addition, some of our women amazed us. They went to the tomb early this morning ²³but didn't find his body. They came and told us that they had seen a vision of angels, who said he was alive. ²⁴Then some of our companions went to the tomb and found it just as the women had said, but him they did not see."

²⁵He said to them, "How foolish you are, and how slow of heart to believe all that the prophets have spoken! ²⁶Did not the Christ[b] have to suffer these things and then enter his glory?" ²⁷And beginning with Moses and all the Prophets, he explained to them what was said in all the Scriptures concerning himself.

²⁸As they approached the village to which they were going, Jesus acted as if he were going farther. ²⁹But they urged him strongly, "Stay with us, for it is nearly evening; the day is almost over." So he went in to stay with them.

³⁰When he was at the table with them, he took bread, gave thanks, broke it and began to give it to them. ³¹Then their eyes were opened and they recognized him, and he disappeared from their sight. ³²They asked each other, "Were not our

---

hearts burning within us while he talked with us on the road and opened the Scriptures to us?"

33 They got up and returned at once to Jerusalem. There they found the Eleven and those with them, assembled together 34 and saying, "It is true! The Lord has risen and has appeared to Simon." 35 Then the two told what had happened on the way, and how Jesus was recognized by them when he broke the bread.

Jesus Appears to the Disciples

36 While they were still talking about this, Jesus himself stood among them and said to them, "Peace be with you."

37 They were startled and frightened, thinking they saw a ghost. 38 He said to them, "Why are you troubled, and why do doubts rise in your minds? 39 Look at my hands and my feet. It is I myself! Touch me and see; a ghost does not have flesh and bones, as you see I have."

40 When he had said this, he showed them his hands and feet. 41 And while they still did not believe it because of joy and amazement, he asked them, "Do you have anything here to eat?" 42 They gave him a piece of broiled fish, 43 and he took it and ate it in their presence.

44 He said to them, "This is what I told you while I was still with you: Everything must be fulfilled that is written about me in the Law of Moses, the Prophets and the Psalms."

45 Then he opened their minds so they could understand the Scriptures. 46 He told them, "This is what is written: The Christ will suffer and rise from the dead on the third day, 47 and repentance and forgiveness of sins will be preached in his name to all nations, beginning at Jerusalem. 48 You are witnesses of these things. 49 I am going to send you what my Father has promised; but stay in the city until you have been clothed with power from on high."

The Ascension

50 When he had led them out to the vicinity of Bethany, he lifted up his hands and blessed them. 51 While he was blessing them, he left them and was taken up into heaven. 52 Then they worshiped him and returned to Jerusalem with great joy. 53 And they stayed continually at the temple, praising God.

Author: John

Date: AD 50-70, or possibly as late as 85-90

Audience: Unbelievers, skeptics, seekers, so that they might "believe that Jesus is the Christ, the Son of God, and that by believing . . . have life in his name" (20:31)

Prayer Themes:

- *Thank God for those who make it their life's ambition to point others to Jesus. Pray that they will have the strength to continue their ministry and resist all temptation to fall into sin (1:36).*

- *Pray that God will sensitize your heart to the hunger and thirst of people who need the freedom and life available to them only in Christ (4:1-42).*

- *Ask Jesus to draw you closer to Him in a deeper and richer way (15:1-5).*

John teaches us that the gospel of Jesus is not only about getting free of our *past* (all the sins we've committed that are now forgiven) and our *future* (going to heaven when we die), but it's also about living righteously and in a manner pleasing to God in the *present*. The explicit promise from Jesus is this: "I have come that they may have life, and have it to the full" (10:10).

That suggests that we can have a "maximum" existence, not a minimal one—it's the offer of a life that is abundant, rich, and overflowing!

Jesus also said that whatever we ask in His name He will do (14:13-14). That means this extraordinary life that is available to us right *now* in Christ comes about as we recognize the power of Jesus' name and pray as He instructs us to pray.

John

The Word Became Flesh

1 In the beginning was the Word, and the Word was with God, and the Word was God. ²He was with God in the beginning.

³Through him all things were made; without him nothing was made that has been made. ⁴In him was life, and that life was the light of men. ⁵The light shines in the darkness, but the darkness has not understood[a] it.

⁶There came a man who was sent from God; his name was John. ⁷He came as a witness to testify concerning that light, so that through him all men might believe. ⁸He himself was not the light; he came only as a witness to the light. ⁹The true light that gives light to every man was coming into the world.[b]

¹⁰He was in the world, and though the world was made through him, the world did not recognize him. ¹¹He came to that which was his own, but his own did not receive him. ¹²Yet to all who received him, to those who believed in his name, he gave the right to become children of God— ¹³children born not of natural descent,[c] nor of human decision or a husband's will, but born of God.

¹⁴The Word became flesh and made his dwelling among us. We have seen his glory, the glory of the One and Only,[d] who came from the Father, full of grace and truth.

¹⁵John testifies concerning him. He cries out, saying, "This was he of whom I said, 'He who comes after me has surpassed me because he was before me.'" ¹⁶From the fullness of his grace we have all received one blessing after another.

---

[a] 5 Or *darkness, and the darkness has not overcome*   [b] 9 Or *This was the true light that gives light to every man who comes into the world*   [c] 13 Greek *of bloods*   [d] 14 Or *the Only Begotten*

17For the law was given through Moses; grace and truth came through Jesus Christ. 18No one has ever seen God, but God the One and Only,[a,b] who is at the Father's side, has made him known.

John the Baptist Denies Being the Christ

19Now this was John's testimony when the Jews of Jerusalem sent priests and Levites to ask him who he was. 20He did not fail to confess, but confessed freely, "I am not the Christ.[c]"

21They asked him, "Then who are you? Are you Elijah?"

He said, "I am not."

"Are you the Prophet?"

He answered, "No."

22Finally they said, "Who are you? Give us an answer to take back to those who sent us. What do you say about yourself?"

23John replied in the words of Isaiah the prophet, "I am the voice of one calling in the desert, 'Make straight the way for the Lord.'"[d]

24Now some Pharisees who had been sent 25questioned him, "Why then do you baptize if you are not the Christ, nor Elijah, nor the Prophet?"

26"I baptize with[e] water," John replied, "but among you stands one you do not know. 27He is the one who comes after me, the thongs of whose sandals I am not worthy to untie."

28This all happened at Bethany on the other side of the Jordan, where John was baptizing.

Jesus the Lamb of God

29The next day John saw Jesus coming toward him and said, "Look, the Lamb of God, who takes away the sin of the world! 30This is the one I meant when I said, 'A man who comes after me has surpassed me because he was before me.' 31I myself did not know him, but the reason I came baptizing with water was that he might be revealed to Israel."

32Then John gave this testimony: "I saw the Spirit come down from heaven as a dove and remain on him. 33I would not have known him, except that the one who sent me to baptize with water told me, 'The man on whom you see the Spirit come down and remain is he who will baptize with the Holy Spirit.' 34I have seen and I testify that this is the Son of God."

Jesus' First Disciples

35The next day John was there again with two of his disciples. 36When he saw Jesus passing by, he said, "Look, the Lamb of God!"

37When the two disciples heard him say this, they followed Jesus. 38Turning around, Jesus saw them following and asked, "What do you want?"

They said, "Rabbi" (which means Teacher), "where are you staying?"

39"Come," he replied, "and you will see."

So they went and saw where he was staying, and spent that day with him. It was about the tenth hour.

40Andrew, Simon Peter's brother, was one of the two who heard what John had said and who had followed Jesus. 41The first thing Andrew did was to find his brother Simon and tell him, "We have found the Messiah" (that is, the Christ). 42And he brought him to Jesus.

Jesus looked at him and said, "You are Simon son of John. You will be called Cephas" (which, when translated, is Peter[f]).

Jesus Calls Philip and Nathanael

43The next day Jesus decided to leave for Galilee. Finding Philip, he said to him, "Follow me."

44Philip, like Andrew and Peter, was from the town of Bethsaida. 45Philip found Nathanael and told him, "We have found the one Moses wrote about in the Law, and about whom the prophets also

---

[a] 18 Or the Only Begotten [b] 18 Some manuscripts but the only (or only begotten) Son [c] 20 Or Messiah. "The Christ" (Greek) and "the Messiah" (Hebrew) both mean "the Anointed One"; also in verse 25. [d] 23 Isaiah 40:3 [e] 26 Or in; also in verses 31 and 33 [f] 42 Both Cephas (Aramaic) and Peter (Greek) mean rock.

Know to Whom You Belong

You will never really understand your true identity unless you can forever settle in your heart that you are a son or daughter of God. The Bible says of Jesus that "to all who received him, to those who believed in his name, he gave the right to become children of God" (1:12). Once you settle this issue and come to know God as your heavenly Father, your life will change. You'll begin to take on a family resemblance. You will have your Father's eyes, heart, and mind.

Have you ever heard someone talk about God in a way that made Him so stern and demanding that He seemed untouchable? He became someone to avoid because to be around Him meant being reminded of what a failure you are. If so, this is another good reason for you to learn to see God as your heavenly Father. He is only frightening when you don't know Him, don't love Him, and don't reverence Him as one who loves you. He wants to have a close relationship with you.

When Jesus taught us how to pray, He told us to first establish our relationship with God as our heavenly Father, and then praise and exalt His name. He said to pray, "Father, hallowed be your name, your kingdom come" (Luke 11:2). And He said, "When you pray, go into your room, close the door and pray to your Father, who is unseen. Then your Father, who sees what is done in secret, will reward you" (Matthew 6:6).

As a child of God, we have privileges that other people don't have. We have become part of a large family. We have a special place to live for eternity. We are provided for. We receive many wonderful blessings and gifts. We have security. We have an important position in the "family business." And we have an amazing inheritance. God says that the thoughts He thinks toward us are "plans to prosper you and not to harm you, plans to give you hope and a future" (Jeremiah 29:11).

One of the ways a parent loves a child is by having rules for their protection and benefit. God's rules are a sign of His love for us. Because we are His son or daughter, there are things that are expected of us. One of the ways we love and acknowledge Him as our Father is living by His rules. One of His rules is that we honor Him with worship and praise. That is also the way we come to know Him better.

The unconditional love of an earthly father is something you may have missed. But the unconditional love of your heavenly Father is something you need *never* live without. Your heavenly Father is waiting to hear from you, so call home.

For the next "From Stormie's Heart" article, go to page 1305.

wrote—Jesus of Nazareth, the son of Joseph."

⁴⁶"Nazareth! Can anything good come from there?" Nathanael asked.

"Come and see," said Philip.

⁴⁷When Jesus saw Nathanael approaching, he said of him, "Here is a true Israelite, in whom there is nothing false."

⁴⁸"How do you know me?" Nathanael asked.

Jesus answered, "I saw you while you were still under the fig tree before Philip called you."

⁴⁹Then Nathanael declared, "Rabbi, you are the Son of God; you are the King of Israel."

⁵⁰Jesus said, "You believeª because I told you I saw you under the fig tree. You shall see greater things than that." ⁵¹He then added, "I tell youᵇ the truth, youᵇ shall see heaven open, and the angels of God ascending and descending on the Son of Man."

Jesus Changes Water to Wine

2 On the third day a wedding took place at Cana in Galilee. Jesus' mother was there, ²and Jesus and his disciples had also been invited to the wedding. ³When the wine was gone, Jesus' mother said to him, "They have no more wine."

⁴"Dear woman, why do you involve me?" Jesus replied. "My time has not yet come."

⁵His mother said to the servants, "Do whatever he tells you."

⁶Nearby stood six stone water jars, the kind used by the Jews for ceremonial washing, each holding from twenty to thirty gallons.ᶜ

⁷Jesus said to the servants, "Fill the jars with water"; so they filled them to the brim.

⁸Then he told them, "Now draw some out and take it to the master of the banquet."

They did so, ⁹and the master of the banquet tasted the water that had been turned into wine. He did not realize where it had come from, though the servants who had drawn the water knew. Then he called the bridegroom aside ¹⁰and said, "Everyone brings out the choice wine first and then the cheaper wine after the guests have had too much to drink; but you have saved the best till now."

¹¹This, the first of his miraculous signs, Jesus performed at Cana in Galilee. He thus revealed his glory, and his disciples put their faith in him.

Jesus Clears the Temple

¹²After this he went down to Capernaum with his mother and brothers and his disciples. There they stayed for a few days.

¹³When it was almost time for the Jewish Passover, Jesus went up to Jerusalem. ¹⁴In the temple courts he found men selling cattle, sheep and doves, and others sitting at tables exchanging money. ¹⁵So he made a whip out of cords, and drove all from the temple area, both sheep and cattle; he scattered the coins of the money changers and overturned their tables. ¹⁶To those who sold doves he said, "Get these out of here! How dare you turn my Father's house into a market!"

¹⁷His disciples remembered that it is written: "Zeal for your house will consume me."ᵈ

¹⁸Then the Jews demanded of him, "What miraculous sign can you show us to prove your authority to do all this?"

¹⁹Jesus answered them, "Destroy this temple, and I will raise it again in three days."

²⁰The Jews replied, "It has taken forty-six years to build this temple, and you are going to raise it in three days?" ²¹But the temple he had spoken of was his body. ²²After he was raised from the dead, his disciples recalled what he had said. Then they believed the Scripture and the words that Jesus had spoken.

²³Now while he was in Jerusalem at

ª 50 Or Do you believe...? ᵇ 51 The Greek is plural. ᶜ 6 Greek two to three metretes (probably about 75 to 115 liters)
ᵈ 17 Psalm 69:9

the Passover Feast, many people saw the miraculous signs he was doing and believed in his name.[a] 24But Jesus would not entrust himself to them, for he knew all men. 25He did not need man's testimony about man, for he knew what was in a man.

Jesus Teaches Nicodemus

3 Now there was a man of the Pharisees named Nicodemus, a member of the Jewish ruling council. 2He came to Jesus at night and said, "Rabbi, we know you are a teacher who has come from God. For no one could perform the miraculous signs you are doing if God were not with him."

3In reply Jesus declared, "I tell you the truth, no one can see the kingdom of God unless he is born again.[b]"

4"How can a man be born when he is old?" Nicodemus asked. "Surely he cannot enter a second time into his mother's womb to be born!"

5Jesus answered, "I tell you the truth, no one can enter the kingdom of God unless he is born of water and the Spirit. 6Flesh gives birth to flesh, but the Spirit[c] gives birth to spirit. 7You should not be surprised at my saying, 'You[d] must be born again.' 8The wind blows wherever it pleases. You hear its sound, but you cannot tell where it comes from or where it

---

[a] 23 Or and believed in him   [b] 3 Or born from above; also in verse 7   [c] 6 Or but spirit   [d] 7 The Greek is plural.

GOING deeper

Responding to God's Love

READ AND CONSIDER: JOHN 3:1-21

"For God so loved the world that he gave his one and only Son, that whoever believes in him shall not perish but have eternal life" (John 3:16).

God loved us so much that He gave us His Son. Jesus loved us so much that He gave us His life. He did that so we could always be close to God and live with Him for eternity. He did that so we don't ever have to be separated from God. He did it so we could find healing and wholeness for our body, soul, and spirit. That's true love.

Jesus told Nicodemus the Old Testament story about the ancient Israelites wandering in the desert constantly complaining. As a punishment for their complaining, God sent snakes into the camp. But He also made a provision for those who would trust in Him. "The LORD said to Moses, 'Make a snake and put it up on a pole; anyone who is bitten can look at it and live" (Numbers 21:8). Jesus was making an analogy referring to His imminent death on the cross. "The Son of Man must be lifted up, that everyone who believes in him may have eternal life" (John 3:14-15).

Jesus died to save us not because we earned it, or we were good enough, or deserved it because of how tough our lives are, but because He loves us. Jesus did so much for us, yet all He asks in return is that we look to Him and lift Him up in our hearts and with our words.

God loves the whole world. He loves you and me. That kind of love requires a response. That kind of love is an amazing invitation that we must accept or in some way reject. Rejecting God's love can take many forms; accepting His love takes only one—believing in His Son, Jesus.

All we have to do to respond to God's great love for us is say, "Jesus, I believe You died on the cross for me in order to give me forgiveness for my sins and eternal life with You. I receive that gift of salvation and redemption today and every day. I will respond to Your great love by lifting You up in praise continually, and loving You with all my heart forever."

is going. So it is with everyone born of the Spirit."

9"How can this be?" Nicodemus asked.

10"You are Israel's teacher," said Jesus, "and do you not understand these things? 11I tell you the truth, we speak of what we know, and we testify to what we have seen, but still you people do not accept our testimony. 12I have spoken to you of earthly things and you do not believe; how then will you believe if I speak of heavenly things? 13No one has ever gone into heaven except the one who came from heaven—the Son of Man.[a] 14Just as Moses lifted up the snake in the desert, so the Son of Man must be lifted up, 15that everyone who believes in him may have eternal life.[b]

16"For God so loved the world that he gave his one and only Son,[c] that whoever believes in him shall not perish but have eternal life. 17For God did not send his Son into the world to condemn the world, but to save the world through him. 18Whoever believes in him is not condemned, but whoever does not believe stands condemned already because he has not believed in the name of God's one and only Son.[d] 19This is the verdict: Light has come into the world, but men loved darkness instead of light because their deeds were evil. 20Everyone who does evil hates the light, and will not come into the light for fear that his deeds will be exposed. 21But whoever lives by the truth comes into the light, so that it may be seen plainly that what he has done has been done through God."[e]

John the Baptist's Testimony About Jesus

22After this, Jesus and his disciples went out into the Judean countryside, where he spent some time with them, and baptized. 23Now John also was baptizing at Aenon near Salim, because there was plenty of water, and people were constantly coming to be baptized. 24(This was before John was put in prison.) 25An argument developed between some of John's disciples and a certain Jew[f] over the matter of ceremonial washing. 26They came to John and said to him, "Rabbi, that man who was with you on the other side of the Jordan—the one you testified about—well, he is baptizing, and everyone is going to him."

27To this John replied, "A man can receive only what is given him from heaven. 28You yourselves can testify that I said, 'I am not the Christ[g] but am sent ahead of him.' 29The bride belongs to the bridegroom. The friend who attends the bridegroom waits and listens for him, and is full of joy when he hears the bridegroom's voice. That joy is mine, and it is now complete. 30He must become greater; I must become less.

31"The one who comes from above is above all; the one who is from the earth belongs to the earth, and speaks as one from the earth. The one who comes from heaven is above all. 32He testifies to what he has seen and heard, but no one accepts his testimony. 33The man who has accepted it has certified that God is truthful. 34For the one whom God has sent speaks the words of God, for God[h] gives the Spirit without limit. 35The Father loves the Son and has placed everything in his hands. 36Whoever believes in the Son has eternal life, but whoever rejects the Son will not see life, for God's wrath remains on him."[i]

Jesus Talks With a Samaritan Woman

4 The Pharisees heard that Jesus was gaining and baptizing more disciples than John, 2although in fact it was not Jesus who baptized, but his disciples. 3When the Lord learned of this, he left Judea and went back once more to Galilee. 4Now he had to go through Samaria.

⁵So he came to a town in Samaria called Sychar, near the plot of ground Jacob had given to his son Joseph. ⁶Jacob's well was there, and Jesus, tired as he was from the journey, sat down by the well. It was about the sixth hour.

⁷When a Samaritan woman came to draw water, Jesus said to her, "Will you give me a drink?" ⁸(His disciples had gone into the town to buy food.)

⁹The Samaritan woman said to him, "You are a Jew and I am a Samaritan woman. How can you ask me for a drink?" (For Jews do not associate with Samaritans.ᵃ)

Prayer is . . .

filling the emptiness in your soul.

¹⁰Jesus answered her, "If you knew the gift of God and who it is that asks you for a drink, you would have asked him and he would have given you living water."

¹¹"Sir," the woman said, "you have nothing to draw with and the well is deep. Where can you get this living water? ¹²Are you greater than our father Jacob, who gave us the well and drank from it himself, as did also his sons and his flocks and herds?"

¹³Jesus answered, "Everyone who drinks this water will be thirsty again, ¹⁴but whoever drinks the water I give him will never thirst. Indeed, the water I give him will become in him a spring of water welling up to eternal life."

¹⁵The woman said to him, "Sir, give me this water so that I won't get thirsty and have to keep coming here to draw water."

¹⁶He told her, "Go, call your husband and come back."

¹⁷"I have no husband," she replied.

Jesus said to her, "You are right when you say you have no husband. ¹⁸The fact is, you have had five husbands, and the man you now have is not your husband. What you have just said is quite true."

¹⁹"Sir," the woman said, "I can see that you are a prophet. ²⁰Our fathers worshiped on this mountain, but you Jews claim that the place where we must worship is in Jerusalem."

²¹Jesus declared, "Believe me, woman, a time is coming when you will worship the Father neither on this mountain nor in Jerusalem. ²²You Samaritans worship what you do not know; we worship what we do know, for salvation is from the Jews. ²³Yet a time is coming and has now come when the true worshipers will worship the Father in spirit and truth, for they are the kind of worshipers the Father seeks. ²⁴God is spirit, and his worshipers must worship in spirit and in truth."

²⁵The woman said, "I know that Messiah" (called Christ) "is coming. When he comes, he will explain everything to us."

²⁶Then Jesus declared, "I who speak to you am he."

The Disciples Rejoin Jesus

²⁷Just then his disciples returned and were surprised to find him talking with a woman. But no one asked, "What do you want?" or "Why are you talking with her?"

²⁸Then, leaving her water jar, the woman went back to the town and said to the people, ²⁹"Come, see a man who told me everything I ever did. Could this be the Christᵇ?" ³⁰They came out of the town and made their way toward him.

³¹Meanwhile his disciples urged him, "Rabbi, eat something."

³²But he said to them, "I have food to eat that you know nothing about."

³³Then his disciples said to each other, "Could someone have brought him food?"

³⁴"My food," said Jesus, "is to do the will of him who sent me and to finish

his work. ³⁵Do you not say, 'Four months more and then the harvest'? I tell you, open your eyes and look at the fields! They are ripe for harvest. ³⁶Even now the reaper draws his wages, even now he harvests the crop for eternal life, so that the sower and the reaper may be glad together. ³⁷Thus the saying 'One sows and another reaps' is true. ³⁸I sent you to reap what you have not worked for. Others have done the hard work, and you have reaped the benefits of their labor."

Many Samaritans Believe

³⁹Many of the Samaritans from that town believed in him because of the woman's testimony, "He told me everything I ever did." ⁴⁰So when the Samaritans came to him, they urged him to stay with them, and he stayed two days. ⁴¹And because of his words many more became believers.

⁴²They said to the woman, "We no longer believe just because of what you said; now we have heard for ourselves, and we know that this man really is the Savior of the world."

Jesus Heals the Official's Son

⁴³After the two days he left for Galilee. ⁴⁴(Now Jesus himself had pointed out that a prophet has no honor in his own country.) ⁴⁵When he arrived in Galilee, the Galileans welcomed him. They had seen all that he had done in Jerusalem at the Passover Feast, for they also had been there.

⁴⁶Once more he visited Cana in Galilee, where he had turned the water into wine. And there was a certain royal official whose son lay sick at Capernaum. ⁴⁷When this man heard that Jesus had arrived in Galilee from Judea, he went to him and begged him to come and heal his son, who was close to death.

⁴⁸"Unless you people see miraculous signs and wonders," Jesus told him, "you will never believe."

⁴⁹The royal official said, "Sir, come down before my child dies."

⁵⁰Jesus replied, "You may go. Your son will live."

The man took Jesus at his word and departed. ⁵¹While he was still on the way, his servants met him with the news that his boy was living. ⁵²When he inquired as to the time when his son got better, they said to him, "The fever left him yesterday at the seventh hour."

⁵³Then the father realized that this was the exact time at which Jesus had said to him, "Your son will live." So he and all his household believed.

⁵⁴This was the second miraculous sign that Jesus performed, having come from Judea to Galilee.

The Healing at the Pool

5 Some time later, Jesus went up to Jerusalem for a feast of the Jews. ²Now there is in Jerusalem near the Sheep Gate a pool, which in Aramaic is called Bethesda[a] and which is surrounded by five covered colonnades. ³Here a great number of disabled people used to lie— the blind, the lame, the paralyzed.[b] ⁵One who was there had been an invalid for thirty-eight years. ⁶When Jesus saw him lying there and learned that he had been in this condition for a long time, he asked him, "Do you want to get well?"

⁷"Sir," the invalid replied, "I have no one to help me into the pool when the water is stirred. While I am trying to get in, someone else goes down ahead of me."

⁸Then Jesus said to him, "Get up! Pick up your mat and walk." ⁹At once the man was cured; he picked up his mat and walked.

The day on which this took place was a Sabbath, ¹⁰and so the Jews said to the man who had been healed, "It is the Sabbath; the law forbids you to carry your mat."

¹¹But he replied, "The man who made me well said to me, 'Pick up your mat and walk.'"

---

a 2 Some manuscripts Bethzatha; other manuscripts Bethsaida   b 3 Some less important manuscripts paralyzed—and they waited for the moving of the waters. ⁴From time to time an angel of the Lord would come down and stir up the waters. The first one into the pool after each such disturbance would be cured of whatever disease he had.

12So they asked him, "Who is this fellow who told you to pick it up and walk?"

13The man who was healed had no idea who it was, for Jesus had slipped away into the crowd that was there.

14Later Jesus found him at the temple and said to him, "See, you are well again. Stop sinning or something worse may happen to you." 15The man went away and told the Jews that it was Jesus who had made him well.

Life Through the Son

16So, because Jesus was doing these things on the Sabbath, the Jews persecuted him. 17Jesus said to them, "My Father is always at his work to this very day, and I, too, am working." 18For this reason the Jews tried all the harder to kill him; not only was he breaking the Sabbath, but he was even calling God his own Father, making himself equal with God.

19Jesus gave them this answer: "I tell you the truth, the Son can do nothing by himself; he can do only what he sees his Father doing, because whatever the Father does the Son also does. 20For the Father loves the Son and shows him all he does. Yes, to your amazement he will show him even greater things than these. 21For just as the Father raises the dead and gives them life, even so the Son gives life to whom he is pleased to give it. 22Moreover, the Father judges no one, but has entrusted all judgment to the Son, 23that all may honor the Son just as they honor the Father. He who does not honor the Son does not honor the Father, who sent him.

24"I tell you the truth, whoever hears my word and believes him who sent me has eternal life and will not be con-demned; he has crossed over from death to life. 25I tell you the truth, a time is coming and has now come when the dead will hear the voice of the Son of God and those who hear will live. 26For as the Father has life in himself, so he has granted the Son to have life in himself. 27And he has given him authority to judge because he is the Son of Man.

28"Do not be amazed at this, for a time is coming when all who are in their graves will hear his voice 29and come out—those who have done good will rise to live, and those who have done evil will rise to be condemned. 30By myself I can do nothing; I judge only as I hear, and my judgment is just, for I seek not to please myself but him who sent me.

Testimonies About Jesus

31"If I testify about myself, my testimony is not valid. 32There is another who testifies in my favor, and I know that his testimony about me is valid.

33"You have sent to John and he has testified to the truth. 34Not that I accept human testimony; but I mention it that you may be saved. 35John was a lamp that burned and gave light, and you chose for a time to enjoy his light.

36"I have testimony weightier than that of John. For the very work that the Father has given me to finish, and which I am doing, testifies that the Father has sent me. 37And the Father who sent me has himself testified concerning me. You have never heard his voice nor seen his form, 38nor does his word dwell in you, for you do not believe the one he sent. 39You diligently studya the Scriptures because you think that by them you possess eternal life. These are the Scriptures that testify about me, 40yet you refuse to come to me to have life.

41"I do not accept praise from men, 42but I know you. I know that you do not have the love of God in your hearts. 43I have come in my Father's name, and you do not accept me; but if someone

---

Praying John 5:24

Lord, I thank You that because I have received You and believe Your Word, I will have everlasting life and death is only a passage into life with You forever.

---

a 39 Or *Study diligently* (the imperative)

else comes in his own name, you will accept him. 44How can you believe if you accept praise from one another, yet make no effort to obtain the praise that comes from the only God[a]?

45"But do not think I will accuse you before the Father. Your accuser is Moses, on whom your hopes are set. 46If you believed Moses, you would believe me, for he wrote about me. 47But since you do not believe what he wrote, how are you going to believe what I say?"

Jesus Feeds the Five Thousand

6 Some time after this, Jesus crossed to the far shore of the Sea of Galilee (that is, the Sea of Tiberias), 2and a great crowd of people followed him because they saw the miraculous signs he had performed on the sick. 3Then Jesus went up on a mountainside and sat down with his disciples. 4The Jewish Passover Feast was near.

5When Jesus looked up and saw a great crowd coming toward him, he said to Philip, "Where shall we buy bread for these people to eat?" 6He asked this only to test him, for he already had in mind what he was going to do.

7Philip answered him, "Eight months' wages[b] would not buy enough bread for each one to have a bite!"

8Another of his disciples, Andrew, Simon Peter's brother, spoke up, 9"Here is a boy with five small barley loaves and two small fish, but how far will they go among so many?"

10Jesus said, "Have the people sit down." There was plenty of grass in that place, and the men sat down, about five thousand of them. 11Jesus then took the loaves, gave thanks, and distributed to those who were seated as much as they wanted. He did the same with the fish.

12When they had all had enough to eat, he said to his disciples, "Gather the pieces that are left over. Let nothing be wasted." 13So they gathered them and filled twelve baskets with the pieces of the five barley loaves left over by those who had eaten.

14After the people saw the miraculous sign that Jesus did, they began to say, "Surely this is the Prophet who is to come into the world." 15Jesus, knowing that they intended to come and make him king by force, withdrew again to a mountain by himself.

Jesus Walks on the Water

16When evening came, his disciples went down to the lake, 17where they got into a boat and set off across the lake for Capernaum. By now it was dark, and Jesus had not yet joined them. 18A strong wind was blowing and the waters grew rough. 19When they had rowed three or three and a half miles,[c] they saw Jesus approaching the boat, walking on the water; and they were terrified. 20But he said to them, "It is I; don't be afraid." 21Then they were willing to take him into the boat, and immediately the boat reached the shore where they were heading.

22The next day the crowd that had stayed on the opposite shore of the lake realized that only one boat had been there, and that Jesus had not entered it with his disciples, but that they had gone away alone. 23Then some boats from Tiberias landed near the place where the people had eaten the bread after the Lord had given thanks. 24Once the crowd realized that neither Jesus nor his disciples were there, they got into the boats and went to Capernaum in search of Jesus.

Jesus the Bread of Life

25When they found him on the other side of the lake, they asked him, "Rabbi, when did you get here?"

26Jesus answered, "I tell you the truth, you are looking for me, not because you saw miraculous signs but because you ate the loaves and had your fill. 27Do not work for food that spoils, but for food that endures to eternal life, which the Son of

---

[a] 44 Some early manuscripts the Only One   [b] 7 Greek two hundred denarii   [c] 19 Greek rowed twenty-five or thirty stadia (about 5 or 6 kilometers)

Man will give you. On him God the Father has placed his seal of approval."

28Then they asked him, "What must we do to do the works God requires?"

29Jesus answered, "The work of God is this: to believe in the one he has sent."

30So they asked him, "What miraculous sign then will you give that we may see it and believe you? What will you do? 31Our forefathers ate the manna in the desert; as it is written: 'He gave them bread from heaven to eat.'ᵃ"

Praying John 6:32-35

Jesus, You are the bread of heaven, and You give life to the world. I thank You that because I have come to You and received You, I will never hunger or thirst.

32Jesus said to them, "I tell you the truth, it is not Moses who has given you the bread from heaven, but it is my Father who gives you the true bread from heaven. 33For the bread of God is he who comes down from heaven and gives life to the world."

34"Sir," they said, "from now on give us this bread."

35Then Jesus declared, "I am the bread of life. He who comes to me will never go hungry, and he who believes in me will never be thirsty. 36But as I told you, you have seen me and still you do not believe. 37All that the Father gives me will come to me, and whoever comes to me I will never drive away. 38For I have come down from heaven not to do my will but to do the will of him who sent me. 39And this is the will of him who sent me, that I shall lose none of all that he has given me, but raise them up at the last day. 40For my Father's will is that everyone who looks to the Son and believes in him shall have eternal life, and I will raise him up at the last day."

41At this the Jews began to grumble about him because he said, "I am the bread that came down from heaven."

42They said, "Is this not Jesus, the son of Joseph, whose father and mother we know? How can he now say, 'I came down from heaven'?"

43"Stop grumbling among yourselves," Jesus answered. 44"No one can come to me unless the Father who sent me draws him, and I will raise him up at the last day. 45It is written in the Prophets: 'They will all be taught by God.'ᵇ Everyone who listens to the Father and learns from him comes to me. 46No one has seen the Father except the one who is from God; only he has seen the Father. 47I tell you the truth, he who believes has everlasting life. 48I am the bread of life. 49Your forefathers ate the manna in the desert, yet they died. 50But here is the bread that comes down from heaven, which a man may eat and not die. 51I am the living bread that came down from heaven. If anyone eats of this bread, he will live forever. This bread is my flesh, which I will give for the life of the world."

52Then the Jews began to argue sharply among themselves, "How can this man give us his flesh to eat?"

53Jesus said to them, "I tell you the truth, unless you eat the flesh of the Son of Man and drink his blood, you have no life in you. 54Whoever eats my flesh and drinks my blood has eternal life, and I will raise him up at the last day. 55For my flesh is real food and my blood is real drink. 56Whoever eats my flesh and drinks my blood remains in me, and I in him. 57Just as the living Father sent me and I live because of the Father, so the one who feeds on me will live because of me. 58This is the bread that came down from heaven. Your forefathers ate manna and died, but he who feeds on this bread will live forever." 59He said this while teaching in the synagogue in Capernaum.

Many Disciples Desert Jesus

60On hearing it, many of his disciples said, "This is a hard teaching. Who can accept it?"

ᵃ *31* Exodus 16:4; Neh. 9:15; Psalm 78:24,25   ᵇ *45* Isaiah 54:13

61Aware that his disciples were grumbling about this, Jesus said to them, "Does this offend you? 62What if you see the Son of Man ascend to where he was before! 63The Spirit gives life; the flesh counts for nothing. The words I have spoken to you are spirit[a] and they are life. 64Yet there are some of you who do not believe." For Jesus had known from the beginning which of them did not believe and who would betray him. 65He went on to say, "This is why I told you that no one can come to me unless the Father has enabled him."

66From this time many of his disciples turned back and no longer followed him.

67"You do not want to leave too, do you?" Jesus asked the Twelve.

68Simon Peter answered him, "Lord, to whom shall we go? You have the words of eternal life. 69We believe and know that you are the Holy One of God."

70Then Jesus replied, "Have I not chosen you, the Twelve? Yet one of you is a devil!" 71(He meant Judas, the son of Simon Iscariot, who, though one of the Twelve, was later to betray him.)

Jesus Goes to the Feast of Tabernacles

7 After this, Jesus went around in Galilee, purposely staying away from Judea because the Jews there were waiting to take his life. 2But when the Jewish Feast of Tabernacles was near, 3Jesus' brothers said to him, "You ought to leave here and go to Judea, so that your disciples may see the miracles you do. 4No one who wants to become a public figure acts in secret. Since you are doing these things, show yourself to the world." 5For even his own brothers did not believe in him.

6Therefore Jesus told them, "The right time for me has not yet come; for you any time is right. 7The world cannot hate you, but it hates me because I testify that what it does is evil. 8You go to the Feast. I am not yet[b] going up to this Feast, because for me the right time has not yet come." 9Having said this, he stayed in Galilee.

10However, after his brothers had left for the Feast, he went also, not publicly, but in secret. 11Now at the Feast the Jews were watching for him and asking, "Where is that man?"

12Among the crowds there was widespread whispering about him. Some said, "He is a good man."

Others replied, "No, he deceives the people." 13But no one would say anything publicly about him for fear of the Jews.

Jesus Teaches at the Feast

14Not until halfway through the Feast did Jesus go up to the temple courts and begin to teach. 15The Jews were amazed and asked, "How did this man get such learning without having studied?"

Praying John 7:18

God, help me never to speak for my own glory but for Your glory only.

16Jesus answered, "My teaching is not my own. It comes from him who sent me. 17If anyone chooses to do God's will, he will find out whether my teaching comes from God or whether I speak on my own. 18He who speaks on his own does so to gain honor for himself, but he who works for the honor of the one who sent him is a man of truth; there is nothing false about him. 19Has not Moses given you the law? Yet not one of you keeps the law. Why are you trying to kill me?"

20"You are demon-possessed," the crowd answered. "Who is trying to kill you?"

21Jesus said to them, "I did one miracle, and you are all astonished. 22Yet, because Moses gave you circumcision (though actually it did not come from Moses, but from the patriarchs), you circumcise a child on the Sabbath. 23Now if a child can be circumcised on the Sabbath so that the law of Moses may not be broken,

---

[a] 63 Or *Spirit*   [b] 8 Some early manuscripts do not have *yet*.

why are you angry with me for healing the whole man on the Sabbath? [24]Stop judging by mere appearances, and make a right judgment."

Is Jesus the Christ?

[25]At that point some of the people of Jerusalem began to ask, "Isn't this the man they are trying to kill? [26]Here he is, speaking publicly, and they are not saying a word to him. Have the authorities really concluded that he is the Christ[a]? [27]But we know where this man is from; when the Christ comes, no one will know where he is from."

[28]Then Jesus, still teaching in the temple courts, cried out, "Yes, you know me, and you know where I am from. I am not here on my own, but he who sent me is true. You do not know him, [29]but I know him because I am from him and he sent me."

[30]At this they tried to seize him, but no one laid a hand on him, because his time had not yet come. [31]Still, many in the crowd put their faith in him. They said, "When the Christ comes, will he do more miraculous signs than this man?"

[32]The Pharisees heard the crowd whispering such things about him. Then the chief priests and the Pharisees sent temple guards to arrest him.

[33]Jesus said, "I am with you for only a short time, and then I go to the one who sent me. [34]You will look for me, but you will not find me; and where I am, you cannot come."

[35]The Jews said to one another, "Where does this man intend to go that we cannot find him? Will he go where our people live scattered among the Greeks, and teach the Greeks? [36]What did he mean when he said, 'You will look for me, but you will not find me,' and 'Where I am, you cannot come'?"

[37]On the last and greatest day of the Feast, Jesus stood and said in a loud voice, "If anyone is thirsty, let him come to me and drink. [38]Whoever believes in me, as[b] the Scripture has said, streams of living water will flow from within him." [39]By this he meant the Spirit, whom those who believed in him were later to receive. Up to that time the Spirit had not been given, since Jesus had not yet been glorified.

[40]On hearing his words, some of the people said, "Surely this man is the Prophet."

[41]Others said, "He is the Christ."

Still others asked, "How can the Christ come from Galilee? [42]Does not the Scripture say that the Christ will come from David's family[c] and from Bethlehem, the town where David lived?" [43]Thus the people were divided because of Jesus. [44]Some wanted to seize him, but no one laid a hand on him.

Unbelief of the Jewish Leaders

[45]Finally the temple guards went back to the chief priests and Pharisees, who asked them, "Why didn't you bring him in?"

[46]"No one ever spoke the way this man does," the guards declared.

[47]"You mean he has deceived you also?" the Pharisees retorted. [48]"Has any of the rulers or of the Pharisees believed in him? [49]No! But this mob that knows nothing of the law—there is a curse on them."

[50]Nicodemus, who had gone to Jesus earlier and who was one of their own number, asked, [51]"Does our law condemn anyone without first hearing him to find out what he is doing?"

[52]They replied, "Are you from Galilee, too? Look into it, and you will find that a prophet[d] does not come out of Galilee."

[The earliest manuscripts and many other ancient witnesses do not have John 7:53–8:11.]

---

[a] 26 Or Messiah; also in verses 27, 31, 41 and 42   [b] 37,38 Or / If anyone is thirsty, let him come to me. / And let him drink, [38]who believes in me. / As   [c] 42 Greek seed   [d] 52 Two early manuscripts the Prophet

53 Then each went to his own home.

8 But Jesus went to the Mount of Olives. 2At dawn he appeared again in the temple courts, where all the people gathered around him, and he sat down to teach them. 3The teachers of the law and the Pharisees brought in a woman caught in adultery. They made her stand before the group 4and said to Jesus, "Teacher, this woman was caught in the act of adultery. 5In the Law Moses commanded us to stone such women. Now what do you say?" 6They were using this question as a trap, in order to have a basis for accusing him.

But Jesus bent down and started to write on the ground with his finger. 7When they kept on questioning him, he straightened up and said to them, "If any one of you is without sin, let him be the first to throw a stone at her." 8Again he stooped down and wrote on the ground.

9At this, those who heard began to go away one at a time, the older ones first, until only Jesus was left, with the woman still standing there. 10Jesus straightened up and asked her, "Woman, where are they? Has no one condemned you?"

11"No one, sir," she said.

"Then neither do I condemn you," Jesus declared. "Go now and leave your life of sin."

The Validity of Jesus' Testimony

12When Jesus spoke again to the people, he said, "I am the light of the world. Whoever follows me will never walk in darkness, but will have the light of life."

13The Pharisees challenged him, "Here you are, appearing as your own witness; your testimony is not valid."

14Jesus answered, "Even if I testify on my own behalf, my testimony is valid, for I know where I came from and where I am going. But you have no idea where I come from or where I am going. 15You judge by human standards; I pass judgment on no one. 16But if I do judge, my decisions are right, because I am not alone. I stand with the Father, who sent me. 17In your own Law it is written that the testimony of two men is valid. 18I am one who testifies for myself; my other witness is the Father, who sent me."

19Then they asked him, "Where is your father?"

"You do not know me or my Father," Jesus replied. "If you knew me, you would know my Father also." 20He spoke these words while teaching in the temple area near the place where the offerings were put. Yet no one seized him, because his time had not yet come.

21Once more Jesus said to them, "I am going away, and you will look for me, and you will die in your sin. Where I go, you cannot come."

22This made the Jews ask, "Will he kill himself? Is that why he says, 'Where I go, you cannot come'?"

23But he continued, "You are from below; I am from above. You are of this world; I am not of this world. 24I told you that you would die in your sins; if you do not believe that I am the one I claim to be,a you will indeed die in your sins."

25"Who are you?" they asked.

"Just what I have been claiming all along," Jesus replied. 26"I have much to say in judgment of you. But he who sent me is reliable, and what I have heard from him I tell the world."

27They did not understand that he was telling them about his Father. 28So Jesus said, "When you have lifted up the Son of Man, then you will know that I am the one I claim to be and that I do nothing on my own but speak just what the Father has taught me. 29The one who sent me is with me; he has not left me alone, for I always do what pleases him." 30Even as he spoke, many put their faith in him.

The Children of Abraham

31To the Jews who had believed him, Jesus said, "If you hold to my teaching,

---

a 24 Or I am he; also in verse 28

Finding the Light in the Midst of Dark Times

God allows us to go through dark times so that we will reach out for Him and find His light in them. He wants us so sure of His light in us that we never doubt it.

God says there are treasures hidden in darkness (Isaiah 45:3). Let me tell you that the treasure I've found hidden in darkness is *Him*. I know this because every time I'm in a dark situation and I reach out for God, I find Him waiting for me. And His light, which is a reflection of His glory, is who He is. His light is already there. We have to open our eyes and hearts to see it.

Whenever *you* reach out to God in the dark times of *your* life, you are always going to find His hand waiting for *you*. When you praise Him in the midst of whatever is happening, it turns on the switch that allows His light to flow freely through you and shine a light on your path.

But so often we don't reach out.

So often we don't praise Him.

We look for other sources of light instead, or we try to make light happen on our own. But the light we make on our own doesn't last.

You know how it is when a person is around someone they love? Their face lights up. They have a sparkle in their eyes and a radiant glow to their smile. And if that love is returned, their entire soul is illuminated. Love always lights up our lives. God's love does that for us too. Only in greater measure. He loved us enough to not let us sit in darkness. Jesus gave His all so we

could have His light forever, for He is the light of the world (8:12). There is no greater love than that. The light He brings into each of our lives is a reflection of His love for us, and it gives *us* a sparkle and glow.

Once you begin to see God's light in your darkest times, darkness will never be the same to you. It will never have the same foreboding. It will never bring with it the same fear. You will perceive things differently. When bad things happen in your life, you won't react with the same despair. You will be able to say, "Praise You, Lord. I worship You in the midst of this situation. I know that You are the Light of the World who lives in me, and Your light can never be put out. I know that You are with me now, and You will shine Your light on this situation. Your glory is over heaven and earth, and it is over my life today."

In the darkest times of your life, your praise to God should be the loudest. It will not only turn on the floodlights, but it will strengthen your faith and let the enemy know you're not afraid of the dark.

For the next "From Stormie's Heart" article, go to page 1357.

you are really my disciples. 32Then you will know the truth, and the truth will set you free."

33They answered him, "We are Abraham's descendants[a] and have never been slaves of anyone. How can you say that we shall be set free?"

34Jesus replied, "I tell you the truth, everyone who sins is a slave to sin. 35Now a slave has no permanent place in the family, but a son belongs to it forever. 36So if the Son sets you free, you will be free indeed. 37I know you are Abraham's descendants. Yet you are ready to kill me, because you have no room for my word. 38I am telling you what I have seen in the Father's presence, and you do what you have heard from your father.[b]"

39"Abraham is our father," they answered.

"If you were Abraham's children," said Jesus, "then you would[c] do the things Abraham did. 40As it is, you are determined to kill me, a man who has told you the truth that I heard from God. Abraham did not do such things. 41You are doing the things your own father does."

"We are not illegitimate children," they protested. "The only Father we have is God himself."

The Children of the Devil

42Jesus said to them, "If God were your Father, you would love me, for I came from God and now am here. I have not come on my own; but he sent me. 43Why is my language not clear to you? Because you are unable to hear what I say. 44You belong to your father, the devil, and you want to carry out your father's desire. He was a murderer from the beginning, not holding to the truth, for there is no truth in him. When he lies, he speaks his native language, for he is a liar and the father of lies. 45Yet because I tell the truth, you do not believe me! 46Can any of you prove me guilty of sin? If I am telling the truth, why don't you believe me? 47He who be-

longs to God hears what God says. The reason you do not hear is that you do not belong to God."

The Claims of Jesus About Himself

48The Jews answered him, "Aren't we right in saying that you are a Samaritan and demon-possessed?"

49"I am not possessed by a demon," said Jesus, "but I honor my Father and you dishonor me. 50I am not seeking glory for myself; but there is one who seeks it, and he is the judge. 51I tell you the truth, if anyone keeps my word, he will never see death."

52At this the Jews exclaimed, "Now we know that you are demon-possessed! Abraham died and so did the prophets, yet you say that if anyone keeps your word, he will never taste death. 53Are you greater than our father Abraham? He died, and so did the prophets. Who do you think you are?"

54Jesus replied, "If I glorify myself, my glory means nothing. My Father, whom you claim as your God, is the one who glorifies me. 55Though you do not know him, I know him. If I said I did not, I would be a liar like you, but I do know him and keep his word. 56Your father Abraham rejoiced at the thought of seeing my day; he saw it and was glad."

57"You are not yet fifty years old," the Jews said to him, "and you have seen Abraham!"

58"I tell you the truth," Jesus answered, "before Abraham was born, I am!" 59At this, they picked up stones to stone him, but Jesus hid himself, slipping away from the temple grounds.

Jesus Heals a Man Born Blind

9 As he went along, he saw a man blind from birth. 2His disciples asked him, "Rabbi, who sinned, this man or his parents, that he was born blind?"

3"Neither this man nor his parents sinned," said Jesus, "but this happened

a 33 Greek seed; also in verse 37   b 38 Or presence. Therefore do what you have heard from the Father.   c 39 Some early manuscripts "If you are Abraham's children," said Jesus, "then so that the work of God might be displayed in his life. ⁴As long as it is day, we must do the work of him who sent me. Night is coming, when no one can work. ⁵While I am in the world, I am the light of the world."

⁶Having said this, he spit on the ground, made some mud with the saliva, and put it on the man's eyes. ⁷"Go," he told him, "wash in the Pool of Siloam" (this word means Sent). So the man went and washed, and came home seeing.

⁸His neighbors and those who had formerly seen him begging asked, "Isn't this the same man who used to sit and beg?" ⁹Some claimed that he was.

Others said, "No, he only looks like him."

But he himself insisted, "I am the man."

¹⁰"How then were your eyes opened?" they demanded.

¹¹He replied, "The man they call Jesus made some mud and put it on my eyes. He told me to go to Siloam and wash. So I went and washed, and then I could see."

¹²"Where is this man?" they asked him.

"I don't know," he said.

The Pharisees Investigate the Healing

¹³They brought to the Pharisees the man who had been blind. ¹⁴Now the day on which Jesus had made the mud and opened the man's eyes was a Sabbath. ¹⁵Therefore the Pharisees also asked him how he had received his sight. "He put mud on my eyes," the man replied, "and I washed, and now I see."

¹⁶Some of the Pharisees said, "This man is not from God, for he does not keep the Sabbath."

But others asked, "How can a sinner do such miraculous signs?" So they were divided.

¹⁷Finally they turned again to the blind man, "What have you to say about him? It was your eyes he opened."

The man replied, "He is a prophet."

¹⁸The Jews still did not believe that he had been blind and had received his sight until they sent for the man's parents. ¹⁹"Is this your son?" they asked. "Is this the one you say was born blind? How is it that now he can see?"

²⁰"We know he is our son," the parents answered, "and we know he was born blind. ²¹But how he can see now, or who opened his eyes, we don't know. Ask him. He is of age; he will speak for himself." ²²His parents said this because they were afraid of the Jews, for already the Jews had decided that anyone who acknowledged that Jesus was the Christ[a] would be put out of the synagogue. ²³That was why his parents said, "He is of age; ask him."

²⁴A second time they summoned the man who had been blind. "Give glory to God,[b]" they said. "We know this man is a sinner."

²⁵He replied, "Whether he is a sinner or not, I don't know. One thing I do know. I was blind but now I see!"

²⁶Then they asked him, "What did he do to you? How did he open your eyes?"

²⁷He answered, "I have told you already and you did not listen. Why do you want to hear it again? Do you want to become his disciples, too?"

²⁸Then they hurled insults at him and said, "You are this fellow's disciple! We are disciples of Moses! ²⁹We know that God spoke to Moses, but as for this fellow, we don't even know where he comes from."

³⁰The man answered, "Now that is remarkable! You don't know where he comes from, yet he opened my eyes. ³¹We know that God does not listen to sinners. He listens to the godly man who does his will. ³²Nobody has ever heard of opening the eyes of a man born blind. ³³If this man were not from God, he could do nothing."

³⁴To this they replied, "You were steeped in sin at birth; how dare you lecture us!" And they threw him out.

ᵃ22 Or Messiah   ᵇ24 A solemn charge to tell the truth (see Joshua 7:19)

Spiritual Blindness

³⁵Jesus heard that they had thrown him out, and when he found him, he said, "Do you believe in the Son of Man?"

³⁶"Who is he, sir?" the man asked. "Tell me so that I may believe in him."

³⁷Jesus said, "You have now seen him; in fact, he is the one speaking with you."

³⁸Then the man said, "Lord, I believe," and he worshiped him.

³⁹Jesus said, "For judgment I have come into this world, so that the blind will see and those who see will become blind."

⁴⁰Some Pharisees who were with him heard him say this and asked, "What? Are we blind too?"

⁴¹Jesus said, "If you were blind, you would not be guilty of sin; but now that you claim you can see, your guilt remains.

The Shepherd and His Flock

10 "I tell you the truth, the man who does not enter the sheep pen by the gate, but climbs in by some other way, is a thief and a robber. ²The man who enters by the gate is the shepherd of his sheep. ³The watchman opens the gate for him, and the sheep listen to his voice. He calls his own sheep by name and leads them out. ⁴When he has brought out all his own, he goes on ahead of them, and his sheep follow him because they know his voice. ⁵But they will never follow a stranger; in fact, they will run away from him because they do not recognize a stranger's voice." ⁶Jesus used this figure of speech, but they did not understand what he was telling them.

Praying John 10:9-10

Dear Jesus, I thank You that You are the door through which I can enter and find salvation, security, provision, and abundance of life.

⁷Therefore Jesus said again, "I tell you the truth, I am the gate for the sheep. ⁸All who ever came before me were thieves and robbers, but the sheep did not listen to them. ⁹I am the gate; whoever enters through me will be saved.ᵃ He will come in and go out, and find pasture. ¹⁰The thief comes only to steal and kill and destroy; I have come that they may have life, and have it to the full.

¹¹"I am the good shepherd. The good shepherd lays down his life for the sheep. ¹²The hired hand is not the shepherd who owns the sheep. So when he sees the wolf coming, he abandons the sheep and runs away. Then the wolf attacks the flock and scatters it. ¹³The man runs away because he is a hired hand and cares nothing for the sheep.

¹⁴"I am the good shepherd; I know my sheep and my sheep know me— ¹⁵just as the Father knows me and I know the Father—and I lay down my life for the sheep. ¹⁶I have other sheep that are not of this sheep pen. I must bring them also. They too will listen to my voice, and there shall be one flock and one shepherd. ¹⁷The reason my Father loves me is that I lay down my life—only to take it up again. ¹⁸No one takes it from me, but I lay it down of my own accord. I have authority to lay it down and authority to take it up again. This command I received from my Father."

¹⁹At these words the Jews were again divided. ²⁰Many of them said, "He is demon-possessed and raving mad. Why listen to him?"

²¹But others said, "These are not the sayings of a man possessed by a demon. Can a demon open the eyes of the blind?"

The Unbelief of the Jews

²²Then came the Feast of Dedicationᵇ at Jerusalem. It was winter, ²³and Jesus was in the temple area walking in Solomon's Colonnade. ²⁴The Jews gathered around him, saying, "How long will you keep us in suspense? If you are the Christ,ᶜ tell us plainly."

²⁵Jesus answered, "I did tell you, but

ᵃ9 Or kept safe   ᵇ22 That is, Hanukkah   ᶜ24 Or Messiah

you do not believe. The miracles I do in my Father's name speak for me, [26]but you do not believe because you are not my sheep. [27]My sheep listen to my voice; I know them, and they follow me. [28]I give them eternal life, and they shall never perish; no one can snatch them out of my hand. [29]My Father, who has given them to me, is greater than all[a]; no one can snatch them out of my Father's hand. [30]I and the Father are one."

[31]Again the Jews picked up stones to stone him, [32]but Jesus said to them, "I have shown you many great miracles from the Father. For which of these do you stone me?"

[33]"We are not stoning you for any of these," replied the Jews, "but for blasphemy, because you, a mere man, claim to be God."

[34]Jesus answered them, "Is it not written in your Law, 'I have said you are gods'[b]? [35]If he called them 'gods,' to whom the word of God came—and the Scripture cannot be broken— [36]what about the one whom the Father set apart as his very own and sent into the world? Why then do you accuse me of blasphemy because I said, 'I am God's Son'? [37]Do not believe me unless I do what my Father does. [38]But if I do it, even though you do not believe me, believe the miracles, that you may know and understand that the Father is in me, and I in the Father." [39]Again they tried to seize him, but he escaped their grasp.

[40]Then Jesus went back across the Jordan to the place where John had been baptizing in the early days. Here he stayed [41]and many people came to him. They said, "Though John never performed a miraculous sign, all that John said about this man was true." [42]And in that place many believed in Jesus.

The Death of Lazarus

11 Now a man named Lazarus was sick. He was from Bethany, the village of Mary and her sister Martha. [2]This Mary, whose brother Lazarus now lay sick, was the same one who poured perfume on the Lord and wiped his feet with her hair. [3]So the sisters sent word to Jesus, "Lord, the one you love is sick."

[4]When he heard this, Jesus said, "This sickness will not end in death. No, it is for God's glory so that God's Son may be glorified through it." [5]Jesus loved Martha and her sister and Lazarus. [6]Yet when he heard that Lazarus was sick, he stayed where he was two more days.

[7]Then he said to his disciples, "Let us go back to Judea."

[8]"But Rabbi," they said, "a short while ago the Jews tried to stone you, and yet you are going back there?"

[9]Jesus answered, "Are there not twelve hours of daylight? A man who walks by day will not stumble, for he sees by this world's light. [10]It is when he walks by night that he stumbles, for he has no light."

[11]After he had said this, he went on to tell them, "Our friend Lazarus has fallen asleep; but I am going there to wake him up."

[12]His disciples replied, "Lord, if he sleeps, he will get better." [13]Jesus had been speaking of his death, but his disciples thought he meant natural sleep.

[14]So then he told them plainly, "Lazarus is dead, [15]and for your sake I am glad I was not there, so that you may believe. But let us go to him."

[16]Then Thomas (called Didymus) said to the rest of the disciples, "Let us also go, that we may die with him."

Jesus Comforts the Sisters

[17]On his arrival, Jesus found that Lazarus had already been in the tomb for four days. [18]Bethany was less than two miles[c] from Jerusalem, [19]and many Jews had come to Martha and Mary to comfort them in the loss of their brother. [20]When Martha heard that Jesus was coming, she went out to meet him, but Mary stayed at home.

---

[a] *29* Many early manuscripts *What my Father has given me is greater than all*   [b] *34* Psalm 82:6   [c] *18* Greek *fifteen stadia* (about 3 kilometers)

21"Lord," Martha said to Jesus, "if you had been here, my brother would not have died. 22But I know that even now God will give you whatever you ask."

23Jesus said to her, "Your brother will rise again."

24Martha answered, "I know he will rise again in the resurrection at the last day."

25Jesus said to her, "I am the resurrection and the life. He who believes in me will live, even though he dies; 26and whoever lives and believes in me will never die. Do you believe this?"

27"Yes, Lord," she told him, "I believe that you are the Christ,ᵃ the Son of God, who was to come into the world."

28And after she had said this, she went back and called her sister Mary aside. "The Teacher is here," she said, "and is asking for you." 29When Mary heard this, she got up quickly and went to him. 30Now Jesus had not yet entered the village, but was still at the place where Martha had met him. 31When the Jews who had been with Mary in the house, comforting her, noticed how quickly she got up and went out, they followed her, supposing she was going to the tomb to mourn there.

32When Mary reached the place where Jesus was and saw him, she fell at his feet and said, "Lord, if you had been here, my brother would not have died."

33When Jesus saw her weeping, and the Jews who had come along with her also weeping, he was deeply moved in spirit and troubled. 34"Where have you laid him?" he asked.

"Come and see, Lord," they replied.

35Jesus wept.

36Then the Jews said, "See how he loved him!"

37But some of them said, "Could not he who opened the eyes of the blind man have kept this man from dying?"

Jesus Raises Lazarus From the Dead

38Jesus, once more deeply moved, came to the tomb. It was a cave with a stone laid across the entrance. 39"Take away the stone," he said.

"But, Lord," said Martha, the sister of the dead man, "by this time there is a bad odor, for he has been there four days."

40Then Jesus said, "Did I not tell you that if you believed, you would see the glory of God?"

41So they took away the stone. Then Jesus looked up and said, "Father, I thank you that you have heard me. 42I knew that you always hear me, but I said this for the benefit of the people standing here, that they may believe that you sent me."

43When he had said this, Jesus called in a loud voice, "Lazarus, come out!" 44The dead man came out, his hands and feet wrapped with strips of linen, and a cloth around his face.

Jesus said to them, "Take off the grave clothes and let him go."

The Plot to Kill Jesus

45Therefore many of the Jews who had come to visit Mary, and had seen what Jesus did, put their faith in him. 46But some of them went to the Pharisees and told them what Jesus had done. 47Then the chief priests and the Pharisees called a meeting of the Sanhedrin.

"What are we accomplishing?" they asked. "Here is this man performing many miraculous signs. 48If we let him go on like this, everyone will believe in him, and then the Romans will come and take away both our placeᵇ and our nation."

49Then one of them, named Caiaphas, who was high priest that year, spoke up, "You know nothing at all! 50You do not realize that it is better for you that one man die for the people than that the whole nation perish."

51He did not say this on his own, but as high priest that year he prophesied that Jesus would die for the Jewish nation, 52and not only for that nation but also for the scattered children of God, to bring

ᵃ 27 Or Messiah ᵇ 48 Or temple

God Always Hears You When You Pray

READ AND CONSIDER JOHN 11:1-44

"Jesus looked up and said, 'Father, I thank you that you have heard me. I knew that you always hear me, but I said this for the benefit of the people standing here, that they may believe that you sent me'" (John 11:41-42).

Jesus showed up for a close friend's funeral—after he had already been buried. He deliberately missed it all. When Lazarus became sick, his sisters sent word to Jesus. But Jesus stayed where He was for two more days, saying to His disciples, "This sickness will not end in death" (11:4), and then, "Our friend Lazarus has fallen asleep; but I am going there to wake him up" (11:11). They didn't understand what He meant, so He finally told them, "Lazarus is dead" (11:14).

By the time Jesus arrived, Lazarus had been in the tomb for four days. Mary and Martha found it hard not to express their disappointment with Him. They knew He could have healed their brother, but now they would have to wait until the resurrection to see him again. In response Jesus said, "I am the resurrection and the life. He who believes in me will live, even though he dies" (11:25).

When He arrived at the burial site, Jesus asked that the tomb be opened. When the stone was rolled away, Jesus prayed, "Father, I thank you that you have heard me." But this sounded like the *end* of a prayer, not the beginning. Obviously, Jesus had been praying all along. He had been talking to His Father for days as He always did, but with full knowledge of this upcoming event.

It surely was difficult for Jesus to *not* be with His friends during this tragic time. But He talked with God and waited for the right moment so that God would be glorified in all that happened. He thanked His Father out loud for the benefit of all who were listening, and then He called Lazarus out of the tomb, grave clothes and all.

Jesus knew that His Father always heard Him. He knew days before that Lazarus would be resurrected. What a wonderful thing it is to be so certain that God always hears us when we pray. To trust completely that we are God's very own children and co-heirs with Christ (Romans 8:17).

God wants us to believe that He always listens to our prayers and will answer. He wants us to have an ongoing conversation with Him that keeps us in tune with His will and His purpose. He wants us to remember that Jesus brings life no matter how dead and helpless things seem. We just need to keep praying and believe in His ability and desire to answer.

them together and make them one. ⁵³So from that day on they plotted to take his life.

⁵⁴Therefore Jesus no longer moved about publicly among the Jews. Instead he withdrew to a region near the desert, to a village called Ephraim, where he stayed with his disciples.

⁵⁵When it was almost time for the Jewish Passover, many went up from the country to Jerusalem for their ceremonial cleansing before the Passover. ⁵⁶They kept looking for Jesus, and as they stood in the temple area they asked one another, "What do you think? Isn't he coming to the Feast at all?" ⁵⁷But the chief priests and Pharisees had given orders that if anyone found out where

Jesus was, he should report it so that they might arrest him.

Jesus Anointed at Bethany

12 Six days before the Passover, Jesus arrived at Bethany, where Lazarus lived, whom Jesus had raised from the dead. ²Here a dinner was given in Jesus' honor. Martha served, while Lazarus was among those reclining at the table with him. ³Then Mary took about a pint[a] of pure nard, an expensive perfume; she poured it on Jesus' feet and wiped his feet with her hair. And the house was filled with the fragrance of the perfume.

⁴But one of his disciples, Judas Iscariot, who was later to betray him, objected, ⁵"Why wasn't this perfume sold and the money given to the poor? It was worth a year's wages.[b]" ⁶He did not say this because he cared about the poor but because he was a thief; as keeper of the money bag, he used to help himself to what was put into it.

⁷"Leave her alone," Jesus replied. "It was intended that she should save this perfume for the day of my burial. ⁸You will always have the poor among you, but you will not always have me."

⁹Meanwhile a large crowd of Jews found out that Jesus was there and came, not only because of him but also to see Lazarus, whom he had raised from the dead. ¹⁰So the chief priests made plans to kill Lazarus as well, ¹¹for on account of him many of the Jews were going over to Jesus and putting their faith in him.

The Triumphal Entry

¹²The next day the great crowd that had come for the Feast heard that Jesus was on his way to Jerusalem. ¹³They took palm branches and went out to meet him, shouting,

"Hosanna![c]"

"Blessed is he who comes in the name of the Lord![d]"

"Blessed is the King of Israel!"

¹⁴Jesus found a young donkey and sat upon it, as it is written,

¹⁵"Do not be afraid, O Daughter of Zion;
    see, your king is coming,
    seated on a donkey's colt."[e]

¹⁶At first his disciples did not understand all this. Only after Jesus was glorified did they realize that these things had been written about him and that they had done these things to him.

¹⁷Now the crowd that was with him when he called Lazarus from the tomb and raised him from the dead continued to spread the word. ¹⁸Many people, because they had heard that he had given this miraculous sign, went out to meet him. ¹⁹So the Pharisees said to one another, "See, this is getting us nowhere. Look how the whole world has gone after him!"

Jesus Predicts His Death

²⁰Now there were some Greeks among those who went up to worship at the Feast. ²¹They came to Philip, who was from Bethsaida in Galilee, with a request. "Sir," they said, "we would like to see Jesus." ²²Philip went to tell Andrew; Andrew and Philip in turn told Jesus.

²³Jesus replied, "The hour has come for the Son of Man to be glorified. ²⁴I tell you the truth, unless a kernel of wheat falls to the ground and dies, it remains only a single seed. But if it dies, it produces many seeds. ²⁵The man who loves his life will lose it, while the man who hates his life in this world will keep it for eternal life. ²⁶Whoever serves me must follow me; and where I am, my servant also will be. My Father will honor the one who serves me.

²⁷"Now my heart is troubled, and what shall I say? 'Father, save me from this hour'? No, it was for this very rea-

---

a *3* Greek *a litra* (probably about 0.5 liter)   b *5* Greek *three hundred denarii*   c *13* A Hebrew expression meaning "Save!" which became an exclamation of praise   d *13* Psalm 118:25,26   e *15* Zech. 9:9

son I came to this hour. ²⁸Father, glorify your name!"

Then a voice came from heaven, "I have glorified it, and will glorify it again." ²⁹The crowd that was there and heard it said it had thundered; others said an angel had spoken to him.

³⁰Jesus said, "This voice was for your benefit, not mine. ³¹Now is the time for judgment on this world; now the prince of this world will be driven out. ³²But I, when I am lifted up from the earth, will draw all men to myself." ³³He said this to show the kind of death he was going to die.

³⁴The crowd spoke up, "We have heard from the Law that the Christ[a] will remain forever, so how can you say, 'The Son of Man must be lifted up'? Who is this 'Son of Man'?"

³⁵Then Jesus told them, "You are going to have the light just a little while longer. Walk while you have the light, before darkness overtakes you. The man who walks in the dark does not know where he is going. ³⁶Put your trust in the light while you have it, so that you may become sons of light." When he had finished speaking, Jesus left and hid himself from them.

The Jews Continue in Their Unbelief

³⁷Even after Jesus had done all these miraculous signs in their presence, they still would not believe in him. ³⁸This was to fulfill the word of Isaiah the prophet:

"Lord, who has believed our message
    and to whom has the arm of the
        Lord been revealed?"[b]

³⁹For this reason they could not believe, because, as Isaiah says elsewhere:

⁴⁰"He has blinded their eyes
    and deadened their hearts,
so they can neither see with their
        eyes,
    nor understand with their hearts,
    nor turn—and I would heal them."[c]

⁴¹Isaiah said this because he saw Jesus' glory and spoke about him.

⁴²Yet at the same time many even among the leaders believed in him. But because of the Pharisees they would not confess their faith for fear they would be put out of the synagogue; ⁴³for they loved praise from men more than praise from God.

⁴⁴Then Jesus cried out, "When a man believes in me, he does not believe in me only, but in the one who sent me. ⁴⁵When he looks at me, he sees the one who sent me. ⁴⁶I have come into the world as a light, so that no one who believes in me should stay in darkness.

> ### Praying John 12:46
> *Jesus, thank You that You are the light of the world. Because I walk with You, I will never have to live in darkness.*

⁴⁷"As for the person who hears my words but does not keep them, I do not judge him. For I did not come to judge the world, but to save it. ⁴⁸There is a judge for the one who rejects me and does not accept my words; that very word which I spoke will condemn him at the last day. ⁴⁹For I did not speak of my own accord, but the Father who sent me commanded me what to say and how to say it. ⁵⁰I know that his command leads to eternal life. So whatever I say is just what the Father has told me to say."

Jesus Washes His Disciples' Feet

13 It was just before the Passover Feast. Jesus knew that the time had come for him to leave this world and go to the Father. Having loved his own who were in the world, he now showed them the full extent of his love.[d]

²The evening meal was being served, and the devil had already prompted Judas Iscariot, son of Simon, to betray Jesus. ³Jesus knew that the Father had put all things under his power, and that he had come from God and was returning to

---

[a] *34* Or *Messiah*   [b] *38* Isaiah 53:1   [c] *40* Isaiah 6:10   [d] *1* Or *he loved them to the last*

God; [4]so he got up from the meal, took off his outer clothing, and wrapped a towel around his waist. [5]After that, he poured water into a basin and began to wash his disciples' feet, drying them with the towel that was wrapped around him.

[6]He came to Simon Peter, who said to him, "Lord, are you going to wash my feet?"

[7]Jesus replied, "You do not realize now what I am doing, but later you will understand."

[8]"No," said Peter, "you shall never wash my feet."

Jesus answered, "Unless I wash you, you have no part with me."

[9]"Then, Lord," Simon Peter replied, "not just my feet but my hands and my head as well!"

[10]Jesus answered, "A person who has had a bath needs only to wash his feet; his whole body is clean. And you are clean, though not every one of you." [11]For he knew who was going to betray him, and that was why he said not every one was clean.

[12]When he had finished washing their feet, he put on his clothes and returned to his place. "Do you understand what I have done for you?" he asked them. [13]"You call me 'Teacher' and 'Lord,' and rightly so, for that is what I am. [14]Now that I, your Lord and Teacher, have washed your feet, you also should wash one another's feet. [15]I have set you an example that you should do as I have done for you. [16]I tell you the truth, no servant is greater than his master, nor is a messenger greater than the one who sent him. [17]Now that you know these things, you will be blessed if you do them.

Jesus Predicts His Betrayal

[18]"I am not referring to all of you; I know those I have chosen. But this is to fulfill the scripture: 'He who shares my bread has lifted up his heel against me.'[a]

[19]"I am telling you now before it happens, so that when it does happen you will believe that I am He. [20]I tell you the truth, whoever accepts anyone I send accepts me; and whoever accepts me accepts the one who sent me."

[21]After he had said this, Jesus was troubled in spirit and testified, "I tell you the truth, one of you is going to betray me."

[22]His disciples stared at one another, at a loss to know which of them he meant. [23]One of them, the disciple whom Jesus loved, was reclining next to him. [24]Simon Peter motioned to this disciple and said, "Ask him which one he means."

[25]Leaning back against Jesus, he asked him, "Lord, who is it?"

[26]Jesus answered, "It is the one to whom I will give this piece of bread when I have dipped it in the dish." Then, dipping the piece of bread, he gave it to Judas Iscariot, son of Simon. [27]As soon as Judas took the bread, Satan entered into him.

"What you are about to do, do quickly," Jesus told him, [28]but no one at the meal understood why Jesus said this to him. [29]Since Judas had charge of the money, some thought Jesus was telling him to buy what was needed for the Feast, or to give something to the poor. [30]As soon as Judas had taken the bread, he went out. And it was night.

Jesus Predicts Peter's Denial

[31]When he was gone, Jesus said, "Now is the Son of Man glorified and God is glorified in him. [32]If God is glorified in him,[b] God will glorify the Son in himself, and will glorify him at once.

[33]"My children, I will be with you only a little longer. You will look for me, and just as I told the Jews, so I tell you now: Where I am going, you cannot come.

[34]"A new command I give you: Love one another. As I have loved you, so you must love one another. [35]By this all men

Praying John 13:34
Lord, help me to love others the way You have loved me and will always love me.

---

[a] 18 Psalm 41:9   [b] 32 Many early manuscripts do not have If God is glorified in him.

will know that you are my disciples, if you love one another."

³⁶Simon Peter asked him, "Lord, where are you going?"

Jesus replied, "Where I am going, you cannot follow now, but you will follow later."

³⁷Peter asked, "Lord, why can't I follow you now? I will lay down my life for you."

³⁸Then Jesus answered, "Will you really lay down your life for me? I tell you the truth, before the rooster crows, you will disown me three times!

Jesus Comforts His Disciples

14 "Do not let your hearts be troubled. Trust in God[a]; trust also in me. ²In my Father's house are many rooms; if it were not so, I would have told you. I am going there to prepare a place for you. ³And if I go and prepare a place for you, I will come back and take you to be with me that you also may be where I am. ⁴You know the way to the place where I am going."

Jesus the Way to the Father

⁵Thomas said to him, "Lord, we don't know where you are going, so how can we know the way?"

⁶Jesus answered, "I am the way and the truth and the life. No one comes to the Father except through me. ⁷If you really knew me, you would know[b] my Father as well. From now on, you do know him and have seen him."

⁸Philip said, "Lord, show us the Father and that will be enough for us."

⁹Jesus answered: "Don't you know me, Philip, even after I have been among you such a long time? Anyone who has seen me has seen the Father. How can you say, 'Show us the Father'? ¹⁰Don't you believe that I am in the Father, and that the Father is in me? The words I say to you are not just my own. Rather, it is the Father, living in me, who is doing

> ## Prayer is . . .
>
> *asking for whatever it is you desire in Jesus' name.*

his work. ¹¹Believe me when I say that I am in the Father and the Father is in me; or at least believe on the evidence of the miracles themselves. ¹²I tell you the truth, anyone who has faith in me will do what I have been doing. He will do even greater things than these, because I am going to the Father. ¹³And I will do whatever you ask in my name, so that the Son may bring glory to the Father. ¹⁴You may ask me for anything in my name, and I will do it.

Praying John 14:12-14

Dear Lord, give me the faith and power to pray for others in Your name and according to Your leading, and to see miraculous things happen in their lives because of Your answers to those prayers.

Jesus Promises the Holy Spirit

¹⁵"If you love me, you will obey what I command. ¹⁶And I will ask the Father, and he will give you another Counselor to be with you forever— ¹⁷the Spirit of truth. The world cannot accept him, because it neither sees him nor knows him. But you know him, for he lives with you and will be[c] in you. ¹⁸I will not leave you as orphans; I will come to you. ¹⁹Before long, the world will not see me anymore, but you will see me. Because I live, you also will live. ²⁰On that day you will realize that I am in my Father, and you are in me, and I am in you. ²¹Whoever has my commands and obeys them, he is the one who loves me. He who loves me will be loved by my Father, and I too will love him and show myself to him."

---

[a] *1 Or* You trust in God   [b] *7 Some early manuscripts* If you really have known me, you will know   [c] *17 Some early manuscripts* and is

22 Then Judas (not Judas Iscariot) said, "But, Lord, why do you intend to show yourself to us and not to the world?"

23 Jesus replied, "If anyone loves me, he will obey my teaching. My Father will love him, and we will come to him and make our home with him. 24 He who does not love me will not obey my teaching. These words you hear are not my own; they belong to the Father who sent me.

25 "All this I have spoken while still with you. 26 But the Counselor, the Holy Spirit, whom the Father will send in my name, will teach you all things and will remind you of everything I have said to you. 27 Peace I leave with you; my peace I give you. I do not give to you as the world gives. Do not let your hearts be troubled and do not be afraid.

28 "You heard me say, 'I am going away and I am coming back to you.' If you loved me, you would be glad that I am going to the Father, for the Father is greater than I. 29 I have told you now before it happens, so that when it does happen you will believe. 30 I will not speak with you much longer, for the prince of this world is coming. He has no hold on me, 31 but the world must learn that I love the Father and that I do exactly what my Father has commanded me.

"Come now; let us leave.

The Vine and the Branches

15 "I am the true vine, and my Father is the gardener. 2 He cuts off every branch in me that bears no fruit, while every branch that does bear fruit he prunes[a] so that it will be even more fruitful. 3 You are already clean because of the word I have spoken to you. 4 Remain in me, and I will remain in you. No branch can bear fruit by itself; it must remain in the vine. Neither can you bear fruit unless you remain in me.

5 "I am the vine; you are the branches. If a man remains in me and I in him, he will bear much fruit; apart from me you can do nothing. 6 If anyone does not re-

main in me, he is like a branch that is thrown away and withers; such branches are picked up, thrown into the fire and burned. 7 If you remain in me and my words remain in you, ask whatever you wish, and it will be given you. 8 This is to my Father's glory, that you bear much fruit, showing yourselves to be my disciples.

9 "As the Father has loved me, so have I loved you. Now remain in my love. 10 If you obey my commands, you will remain in my love, just as I have obeyed my Father's commands and remain in his love. 11 I have told you this so that my joy may be in you and that your joy may be complete. 12 My command is this: Love each other as I have loved you. 13 Greater love has no one than this, that he lay down his life for his friends. 14 You are my friends if you do what I command. 15 I no longer call you servants, because a servant does not know his master's business. Instead, I have called you friends, for everything that I learned from my Father I have made known to you. 16 You did not choose me, but I chose you and appointed you to go and bear fruit—fruit that will last. Then the Father will give you whatever you ask in my name. 17 This is my command: Love each other.

The World Hates the Disciples

18 "If the world hates you, keep in mind that it hated me first. 19 If you belonged to the world, it would love you as its own. As it is, you do not belong to the world, but I have chosen you out of the world. That is why the world hates you. 20 Remember the words I spoke to you: 'No servant is greater than his master.'[b] If they persecuted me, they will persecute you also. If they obeyed my teaching, they will obey yours also. 21 They will treat you this way because of my name, for they do not know the One who sent me. 22 If I had not come and spoken to them, they would not be guilty of sin. Now, however, they have no excuse for their sin. 23 He

---

a 2 The Greek for prunes also means cleans.   b 20 John 13:16

GOING *deeper*

Remaining in Him

"If you remain in me and my words remain in you, ask whatever you wish, and it will be given you" (John 15:7).

Eleven times the word *remain* is used in this short section. Eleven times Jesus chose this term to express the kind of relationship He wants us to have with Him. We are to remain in Christ. We are to remain in His love. If we do that, He will remain in us, His words will remain in us, and our lives will be fruitful.

So what does it mean to remain in Jesus? It means walking with Him and staying close and constantly plugged into Him, just like a branch remains with the vine. When a branch is part of the vine, it bears fruit. Conversely, when a branch is removed from the vine, it dies. Jesus says that if we remain in Him—spend time with Him, learn more about Him, get to know Him, be honest with Him, acknowledge our sins to Him—then we'll bear much fruit.

Jesus wants us to know His Word and allow it to become part of us. That means we need to be reading the Bible so that His words will be woven into the fabric of our being. We must know it so well that it becomes our guide, a source of renewal and knowledge of God's will. We must let it increase our understanding of who God is and who we are in Him.

God says if we remain in Him and let His words remain in us, we can ask of Him whatever we want and He will answer. That doesn't mean we will always get whatever we want. It means that because we are so closely entwined with Christ, we will have His mind and will learn how to pray for what He wants for our lives. When we do that, we end up doing His will and seeing answers to our prayers.

---

who hates me hates my Father as well. [24]If I had not done among them what no one else did, they would not be guilty of sin. But now they have seen these miracles, and yet they have hated both me and my Father. [25]But this is to fulfill what is written in their Law: 'They hated me without reason.'[a]

[26]"When the Counselor comes, whom I will send to you from the Father, the Spirit of truth who goes out from the Father, he will testify about me. [27]And you also must testify, for you have been with me from the beginning.

16 "All this I have told you so that you will not go astray. [2]They will put you out of the synagogue; in fact, a time is coming when anyone who kills you will think he is offering a service to God. [3]They will do such things because they have not known the Father or me. [4]I have told you this, so that when the time comes you will remember that I warned you. I did not tell you this at first because I was with you.

The Work of the Holy Spirit

[5]"Now I am going to him who sent me, yet none of you asks me, 'Where are you going?' [6]Because I have said these things, you are filled with grief. [7]But I tell you the truth: It is for your good that I am going away. Unless I go away, the Counselor will not come to you; but if I go, I will send him to you. [8]When he comes, he will convict the world of guilt[b] in regard to sin and righteousness and judgment: [9]in regard to sin, because men do not

---

[a] *25* Psalms 35:19; 69:4   [b] *8* Or *will expose the guilt of the world*

believe in me; 10in regard to righteousness, because I am going to the Father, where you can see me no longer; 11and in regard to judgment, because the prince of this world now stands condemned.

12"I have much more to say to you, more than you can now bear. 13But when he, the Spirit of truth, comes, he will guide you into all truth. He will not speak on his own; he will speak only what he hears, and he will tell you what is yet to come. 14He will bring glory to me by taking from what is mine and making it known to you. 15All that belongs to the Father is mine. That is why I said the Spirit will take from what is mine and make it known to you.

Praying John 16:13

Holy Spirit of God, in Jesus' name
I pray that You would teach me
all I need to know and guide me
in all things and into all truth.

16"In a little while you will see me no more, and then after a little while you will see me."

The Disciples' Grief Will Turn to Joy

17Some of his disciples said to one another, "What does he mean by saying, 'In a little while you will see me no more, and then after a little while you will see me,' and 'Because I am going to the Father'?" 18They kept asking, "What does he mean by 'a little while'? We don't understand what he is saying."

19Jesus saw that they wanted to ask him about this, so he said to them, "Are you asking one another what I meant when I said, 'In a little while you will see me no more, and then after a little while you will see me'? 20I tell you the truth, you will weep and mourn while the world rejoices. You will grieve, but your grief will turn to joy. 21A woman giving birth to a child has pain because her time has come; but when her baby is born she forgets the anguish because of her joy that

a child is born into the world. 22So with you: Now is your time of grief, but I will see you again and you will rejoice, and no one will take away your joy. 23In that day you will no longer ask me anything. I tell you the truth, my Father will give you whatever you ask in my name. 24Until now you have not asked for anything in my name. Ask and you will receive, and your joy will be complete.

25"Though I have been speaking figuratively, a time is coming when I will no longer use this kind of language but will tell you plainly about my Father. 26In that day you will ask in my name. I am not saying that I will ask the Father on your behalf. 27No, the Father himself loves you because you have loved me and have believed that I came from God. 28I came from the Father and entered the world; now I am leaving the world and going back to the Father."

29Then Jesus' disciples said, "Now you are speaking clearly and without figures of speech. 30Now we can see that you know all things and that you do not even need to have anyone ask you questions. This makes us believe that you came from God."

31"You believe at last!"[a] Jesus answered. 32"But a time is coming, and has come, when you will be scattered, each to his own home. You will leave me all alone. Yet I am not alone, for my Father is with me.

33"I have told you these things, so that in me you may have peace. In this world you will have trouble. But take heart! I have overcome the world."

Jesus Prays for Himself

17 After Jesus said this, he looked toward heaven and prayed:

"Father, the time has come. Glorify your Son, that your Son may glorify you. 2For you granted him authority over all people that he might give eternal life to all those you have

---

a 31 Or "Do you now believe?"

given him. ³Now this is eternal life: that they may know you, the only true God, and Jesus Christ, whom you have sent. ⁴I have brought you glory on earth by completing the work you gave me to do. ⁵And now, Father, glorify me in your presence with the glory I had with you before the world began.

Jesus Prays for His Disciples

⁶"I have revealed you[a] to those whom you gave me out of the world. They were yours; you gave them to me and they have obeyed your word. ⁷Now they know that everything you have given me comes from you. ⁸For I gave them the words you gave me and they accepted them. They knew with certainty that I came from you,

and they believed that you sent me. ⁹I pray for them. I am not praying for the world, but for those you have given me, for they are yours. ¹⁰All I have is yours, and all you have is mine. And glory has come to me through them. ¹¹I will remain in the world no longer, but they are still in the world, and I am coming to you. Holy Father, protect them by the power of your name—the name you gave me—so that they may be one as we are one. ¹²While I was with them, I protected them and kept them safe by that name you gave me. None has been lost except the one doomed to destruction so that Scripture would be fulfilled.

¹³"I am coming to you now, but I say these things while I am still in

---

[a] 6 Greek *your name*; also in verse 26

GOING *deeper*

Jesus' Prayer for You

READ AND CONSIDER JOHN 17:20-26

"My prayer is not for them alone. I pray also for those who will believe in me through their message, that all of them may be one, Father, just as you are in me and I am in you" (John 17:20-21).

Did you know that Jesus prayed for you and me? In this passage Jesus was interceding for His followers, but He was also speaking ultimately to every believer down through the ages.

We who have come to faith in Jesus can listen back in time to this moment when the Lord prayed for *us*. We were on His mind as He prepared to lay down His life in order to provide forgiveness for our sins, abundant life now, and life with Him for eternity.

Jesus prayed for us to have unity with other believers—across the nations, across cultures, across time, across the street, across the room, across the sanctuary. He also prayed for us to have unity with Him and the Father and the Holy Spirit so that our lives would convince others of who He is. He declared His love for us and promised to share His glory with us. He prayed for our salvation so that we could be with Him forever, and He promised to continue to make Himself known to us so we could experience more and more of His love.

Jesus was thinking of you centuries ago when He was praying. He lives today and every day to "intercede" for you (Hebrews 7:25). His desire is that you become one with Him and one with other believers, so that those who see you will believe in Him. Pray that you will always be one with Him and one with others. Thank Jesus that even way back then, He was already praying for you.

the world, so that they may have the full measure of my joy within them. [14]I have given them your word and the world has hated them, for they are not of the world any more than I am of the world. [15]My prayer is not that you take them out of the world but that you protect them from the evil one. [16]They are not of the world, even as I am not of it. [17]Sanctify[a] them by the truth; your word is truth. [18]As you sent me into the world, I have sent them into the world. [19]For them I sanctify myself, that they too may be truly sanctified.

Jesus Prays for All Believers

[20]"My prayer is not for them alone. I pray also for those who will believe in me through their message, [21]that all of them may be one, Father, just as you are in me and I am in you. May they also be in us so that the world may believe that you have sent me. [22]I have given them the glory that you gave me, that they may be one as we are one: [23]I in them and you in me. May they be brought to complete unity to let the world know that you sent me and have loved them even as you have loved me.

[24]"Father, I want those you have given me to be with me where I am, and to see my glory, the glory you have given me because you loved me before the creation of the world. [25]"Righteous Father, though the world does not know you, I know you, and they know that you have sent me. [26]I have made you known to them, and will continue to make you known in order that the love you have for me may be in them and that I myself may be in them."

Jesus Arrested

18 When he had finished praying, Jesus left with his disciples and crossed the Kidron Valley. On the other side there was an olive grove, and he and his disciples went into it.

[2]Now Judas, who betrayed him, knew the place, because Jesus had often met there with his disciples. [3]So Judas came to the grove, guiding a detachment of soldiers and some officials from the chief priests and Pharisees. They were carrying torches, lanterns and weapons.

[4]Jesus, knowing all that was going to happen to him, went out and asked them, "Who is it you want?"

[5]"Jesus of Nazareth," they replied.

"I am he," Jesus said. (And Judas the traitor was standing there with them.) [6]When Jesus said, "I am he," they drew back and fell to the ground.

[7]Again he asked them, "Who is it you want?"

And they said, "Jesus of Nazareth."

[8]"I told you that I am he," Jesus answered. "If you are looking for me, then let these men go." [9]This happened so that the words he had spoken would be fulfilled: "I have not lost one of those you gave me."[b]

[10]Then Simon Peter, who had a sword, drew it and struck the high priest's servant, cutting off his right ear. (The servant's name was Malchus.)

[11]Jesus commanded Peter, "Put your sword away! Shall I not drink the cup the Father has given me?"

Jesus Taken to Annas

[12]Then the detachment of soldiers with its commander and the Jewish officials arrested Jesus. They bound him [13]and brought him first to Annas, who was the father-in-law of Caiaphas, the high priest that year. [14]Caiaphas was the one who had advised the Jews that it would be good if one man died for the people.

Peter's First Denial

[15]Simon Peter and another disciple were following Jesus. Because this disciple was known to the high priest, he went with Jesus into the high priest's

---

[a] 17 Greek hagiazo (set apart for sacred use or make holy); also in verse 19 [b] 9 John 6:39

courtyard, [16]but Peter had to wait outside at the door. The other disciple, who was known to the high priest, came back, spoke to the girl on duty there and brought Peter in.

[17]"You are not one of his disciples, are you?" the girl at the door asked Peter.

He replied, "I am not."

[18]It was cold, and the servants and officials stood around a fire they had made to keep warm. Peter also was standing with them, warming himself.

The High Priest Questions Jesus

[19]Meanwhile, the high priest questioned Jesus about his disciples and his teaching.

[20]"I have spoken openly to the world," Jesus replied. "I always taught in synagogues or at the temple, where all the Jews come together. I said nothing in secret. [21]Why question me? Ask those who heard me. Surely they know what I said."

[22]When Jesus said this, one of the officials nearby struck him in the face. "Is this the way you answer the high priest?" he demanded.

[23]"If I said something wrong," Jesus replied, "testify as to what is wrong. But if I spoke the truth, why did you strike me?" [24]Then Annas sent him, still bound, to Caiaphas the high priest.[a]

Peter's Second and Third Denials

[25]As Simon Peter stood warming himself, he was asked, "You are not one of his disciples, are you?"

He denied it, saying, "I am not."

[26]One of the high priest's servants, a relative of the man whose ear Peter had cut off, challenged him, "Didn't I see you with him in the olive grove?" [27]Again Peter denied it, and at that moment a rooster began to crow.

Jesus Before Pilate

[28]Then the Jews led Jesus from Caiaphas to the palace of the Roman governor. By now it was early morning, and to avoid ceremonial uncleanness the Jews did not enter the palace; they wanted to be able to eat the Passover. [29]So Pilate came out to them and asked, "What charges are you bringing against this man?"

[30]"If he were not a criminal," they replied, "we would not have handed him over to you."

[31]Pilate said, "Take him yourselves and judge him by your own law."

"But we have no right to execute anyone," the Jews objected. [32]This happened so that the words Jesus had spoken indicating the kind of death he was going to die would be fulfilled.

[33]Pilate then went back inside the palace, summoned Jesus and asked him, "Are you the king of the Jews?"

[34]"Is that your own idea," Jesus asked, "or did others talk to you about me?"

[35]"Am I a Jew?" Pilate replied. "It was your people and your chief priests who handed you over to me. What is it you have done?"

[36]Jesus said, "My kingdom is not of this world. If it were, my servants would fight to prevent my arrest by the Jews. But now my kingdom is from another place."

[37]"You are a king, then!" said Pilate.

Jesus answered, "You are right in saying I am a king. In fact, for this reason I was born, and for this I came into the world, to testify to the truth. Everyone on the side of truth listens to me."

[38]"What is truth?" Pilate asked. With this he went out again to the Jews and said, "I find no basis for a charge against him. [39]But it is your custom for me to release to you one prisoner at the time of the Passover. Do you want me to release 'the king of the Jews'?"

[40]They shouted back, "No, not him! Give us Barabbas!" Now Barabbas had taken part in a rebellion.

Jesus Sentenced to Be Crucified

19 Then Pilate took Jesus and had him flogged. [2]The soldiers twisted together a crown of thorns and put it on his head. They clothed him in a

---

[a] 24 Or (Now Annas had sent him, still bound, to Caiaphas the high priest.)

purple robe ³and went up to him again and again, saying, "Hail, king of the Jews!" And they struck him in the face.

⁴Once more Pilate came out and said to the Jews, "Look, I am bringing him out to you to let you know that I find no basis for a charge against him." ⁵When Jesus came out wearing the crown of thorns and the purple robe, Pilate said to them, "Here is the man!"

⁶As soon as the chief priests and their officials saw him, they shouted, "Crucify! Crucify!"

But Pilate answered, "You take him and crucify him. As for me, I find no basis for a charge against him."

⁷The Jews insisted, "We have a law, and according to that law he must die, because he claimed to be the Son of God."

⁸When Pilate heard this, he was even more afraid, ⁹and he went back inside the palace. "Where do you come from?" he asked Jesus, but Jesus gave him no answer. ¹⁰"Do you refuse to speak to me?" Pilate said. "Don't you realize I have power either to free you or to crucify you?"

¹¹Jesus answered, "You would have no power over me if it were not given to you from above. Therefore the one who handed me over to you is guilty of a greater sin."

¹²From then on, Pilate tried to set Jesus free, but the Jews kept shouting, "If you let this man go, you are no friend of Caesar. Anyone who claims to be a king opposes Caesar."

¹³When Pilate heard this, he brought Jesus out and sat down on the judge's seat at a place known as the Stone Pavement (which in Aramaic is Gabbatha). ¹⁴It was the day of Preparation of Passover Week, about the sixth hour.

"Here is your king," Pilate said to the Jews.

¹⁵But they shouted, "Take him away! Take him away! Crucify him!"

"Shall I crucify your king?" Pilate asked.

"We have no king but Caesar," the chief priests answered.

¹⁶Finally Pilate handed him over to them to be crucified.

The Crucifixion

So the soldiers took charge of Jesus. ¹⁷Carrying his own cross, he went out to the place of the Skull (which in Aramaic is called Golgotha). ¹⁸Here they crucified him, and with him two others—one on each side and Jesus in the middle.

¹⁹Pilate had a notice prepared and fastened to the cross. It read: JESUS OF NAZARETH, THE KING OF THE JEWS. ²⁰Many of the Jews read this sign, for the place where Jesus was crucified was near the city, and the sign was written in Aramaic, Latin and Greek. ²¹The chief priests of the Jews protested to Pilate, "Do not write 'The King of the Jews,' but that this man claimed to be king of the Jews."

²²Pilate answered, "What I have written, I have written."

²³When the soldiers crucified Jesus, they took his clothes, dividing them into four shares, one for each of them, with the undergarment remaining. This garment was seamless, woven in one piece from top to bottom.

²⁴"Let's not tear it," they said to one another. "Let's decide by lot who will get it."

This happened that the scripture might be fulfilled which said,

"They divided my garments among them
    and cast lots for my clothing."ᵃ

So this is what the soldiers did.

²⁵Near the cross of Jesus stood his mother, his mother's sister, Mary the wife of Clopas, and Mary Magdalene. ²⁶When Jesus saw his mother there, and the disciple whom he loved standing nearby, he said to his mother, "Dear woman, here is your son," ²⁷and to the disciple, "Here is your mother." From that time on, this disciple took her into his home.

ᵃ 24 Psalm 22:18

The Death of Jesus

²⁸Later, knowing that all was now completed, and so that the Scripture would be fulfilled, Jesus said, "I am thirsty." ²⁹A jar of wine vinegar was there, so they soaked a sponge in it, put the sponge on a stalk of the hyssop plant, and lifted it to Jesus' lips. ³⁰When he had received the drink, Jesus said, "It is finished." With that, he bowed his head and gave up his spirit.

³¹Now it was the day of Preparation, and the next day was to be a special Sabbath. Because the Jews did not want the bodies left on the crosses during the Sabbath, they asked Pilate to have the legs broken and the bodies taken down. ³²The soldiers therefore came and broke the legs of the first man who had been crucified with Jesus, and then those of the other. ³³But when they came to Jesus and found that he was already dead, they did not break his legs. ³⁴Instead, one of the soldiers pierced Jesus' side with a spear, bringing a sudden flow of blood and water. ³⁵The man who saw it has given testimony, and his testimony is true. He knows that he tells the truth, and he testifies so that you also may believe. ³⁶These things happened so that the scripture would be fulfilled: "Not one of his bones will be broken,"ᵃ ³⁷and, as another scripture says, "They will look on the one they have pierced."ᵇ

The Burial of Jesus

³⁸Later, Joseph of Arimathea asked Pilate for the body of Jesus. Now Joseph was a disciple of Jesus, but secretly because he feared the Jews. With Pilate's permission, he came and took the body away. ³⁹He was accompanied by Nicodemus, the man who earlier had visited Jesus at night. Nicodemus brought a mixture of myrrh and aloes, about seventy-five pounds.ᶜ ⁴⁰Taking Jesus' body, the two of them wrapped it, with the spices, in strips of linen. This was in accordance with Jewish burial customs. ⁴¹At the place where Jesus was crucified, there was a garden, and in the garden a new tomb, in which no one had ever been laid. ⁴²Because it was the Jewish day of Preparation and since the tomb was nearby, they laid Jesus there.

The Empty Tomb

20 Early on the first day of the week, while it was still dark, Mary Magdalene went to the tomb and saw that the stone had been removed from the entrance. ²So she came running to Simon Peter and the other disciple, the one Jesus loved, and said, "They have taken the Lord out of the tomb, and we don't know where they have put him!"

³So Peter and the other disciple started for the tomb. ⁴Both were running, but the other disciple outran Peter and reached the tomb first. ⁵He bent over and looked in at the strips of linen lying there but did not go in. ⁶Then Simon Peter, who was behind him, arrived and went into the tomb. He saw the strips of linen lying there, ⁷as well as the burial cloth that had been around Jesus' head. The cloth was folded up by itself, separate from the linen. ⁸Finally the other disciple, who had reached the tomb first, also went inside. He saw and believed. ⁹(They still did not understand from Scripture that Jesus had to rise from the dead.)

Jesus Appears to Mary Magdalene

¹⁰Then the disciples went back to their homes, ¹¹but Mary stood outside the tomb crying. As she wept, she bent over to look into the tomb ¹²and saw two angels in white, seated where Jesus' body had been, one at the head and the other at the foot.

¹³They asked her, "Woman, why are you crying?"

"They have taken my Lord away," she said, "and I don't know where they have put him." ¹⁴At this, she turned around and saw Jesus standing there, but she did not realize that it was Jesus.

ᵃ 36 Exodus 12:46; Num. 9:12; Psalm 34:20   ᵇ 37 Zech. 12:10   ᶜ 39 Greek *a hundred litrai* (about 34 kilograms)

15"Woman," he said, "why are you crying? Who is it you are looking for?"

Thinking he was the gardener, she said, "Sir, if you have carried him away, tell me where you have put him, and I will get him."

16Jesus said to her, "Mary."

She turned toward him and cried out in Aramaic, "Rabboni!" (which means Teacher).

17Jesus said, "Do not hold on to me, for I have not yet returned to the Father. Go instead to my brothers and tell them, 'I am returning to my Father and your Father, to my God and your God.'"

18Mary Magdalene went to the disciples with the news: "I have seen the Lord!" And she told them that he had said these things to her.

Jesus Appears to His Disciples

19On the evening of that first day of the week, when the disciples were together, with the doors locked for fear of the Jews, Jesus came and stood among them and said, "Peace be with you!" 20After he said this, he showed them his hands and side. The disciples were overjoyed when they saw the Lord.

21Again Jesus said, "Peace be with you! As the Father has sent me, I am sending you." 22And with that he breathed on them and said, "Receive the Holy Spirit. 23If you forgive anyone his sins, they are forgiven; if you do not forgive them, they are not forgiven."

Jesus Appears to Thomas

24Now Thomas (called Didymus), one of the Twelve, was not with the disciples

GOING deeper

Believing Without Seeing

READ AND CONSIDER JOHN 20:19-29

"Then Jesus told him, 'Because you have seen me, you have believed; blessed are those who have not seen and yet have believed'" (John 20:29).

We've all known people like Thomas. People who are hard to convince, who frequently have doubt, and who are often negative. People who don't believe in what they can't see. Probably all of us have been that way ourselves at one time or another.

Even after all the other disciples believed in the resurrection because they had seen Jesus in person, Thomas still wouldn't believe *them*. He didn't believe it until Jesus appeared in the room where all of them were gathered behind a locked door. One might think that alone would be enough evidence. But Thomas still had to put his fingers on Jesus' hands where the nails had been driven though them and on His side where the spear had pierced it. Jesus told Thomas that he was only believing because he had seen it, but those who believed *without* seeing would be blessed.

Those of us who believe that Jesus died for us and was resurrected from the dead are among the blessed. But God wants to bless us in many ways that require faith. Faith in His Word. Faith in His promises. Faith in His love, power, and goodness. He wants us to believe for things we can't yet see. Thomas needed help to believe. Often we do too. And like the father who brought his son to Jesus for healing, we can cry out to God, "I do believe; help me overcome my unbelief!" (Mark 9:24).

In times of doubt, we must be honest with God. We don't want to be people who won't believe until we see it. Because when it comes to prayer, the truth is we won't see it until we believe.

when Jesus came. 25So the other disciples told him, "We have seen the Lord!"

But he said to them, "Unless I see the nail marks in his hands and put my finger where the nails were, and put my hand into his side, I will not believe it."

26A week later his disciples were in the house again, and Thomas was with them. Though the doors were locked, Jesus came and stood among them and said, "Peace be with you!" 27Then he said to Thomas, "Put your finger here; see my hands. Reach out your hand and put it into my side. Stop doubting and believe."

28Thomas said to him, "My Lord and my God!"

29Then Jesus told him, "Because you have seen me, you have believed; blessed are those who have not seen and yet have believed."

30Jesus did many other miraculous signs in the presence of his disciples, which are not recorded in this book. 31But these are written that you may[a] believe that Jesus is the Christ, the Son of God, and that by believing you may have life in his name.

Jesus and the Miraculous Catch of Fish

21 Afterward Jesus appeared again to his disciples, by the Sea of Tiberias.[b] It happened this way: 2Simon Peter, Thomas (called Didymus), Nathanael from Cana in Galilee, the sons of Zebedee, and two other disciples were together. 3"I'm going out to fish," Simon Peter told them, and they said, "We'll go with you." So they went out and got into the boat, but that night they caught nothing.

4Early in the morning, Jesus stood on the shore, but the disciples did not realize that it was Jesus.

5He called out to them, "Friends, haven't you any fish?"

"No," they answered.

6He said, "Throw your net on the right side of the boat and you will find some." When they did, they were unable to haul the net in because of the large number of fish.

7Then the disciple whom Jesus loved said to Peter, "It is the Lord!" As soon as Simon Peter heard him say, "It is the Lord," he wrapped his outer garment around him (for he had taken it off) and jumped into the water. 8The other disciples followed in the boat, towing the net full of fish, for they were not far from shore, about a hundred yards.[c] 9When they landed, they saw a fire of burning coals there with fish on it, and some bread.

10Jesus said to them, "Bring some of the fish you have just caught."

11Simon Peter climbed aboard and dragged the net ashore. It was full of large fish, 153, but even with so many the net was not torn. 12Jesus said to them, "Come and have breakfast." None of the disciples dared ask him, "Who are you?" They knew it was the Lord. 13Jesus came, took the bread and gave it to them, and did the same with the fish. 14This was now the third time Jesus appeared to his disciples after he was raised from the dead.

Jesus Reinstates Peter

15When they had finished eating, Jesus said to Simon Peter, "Simon son of John, do you truly love me more than these?"

"Yes, Lord," he said, "you know that I love you."

Jesus said, "Feed my lambs."

16Again Jesus said, "Simon son of John, do you truly love me?"

He answered, "Yes, Lord, you know that I love you."

Jesus said, "Take care of my sheep."

17The third time he said to him, "Simon son of John, do you love me?"

Peter was hurt because Jesus asked him the third time, "Do you love me?" He said, "Lord, you know all things; you know that I love you."

Jesus said, "Feed my sheep. 18I tell you the truth, when you were younger you dressed yourself and went where you wanted; but when you are old you will

---

a 31 Some manuscripts *may continue to*   b 1 That is, Sea of Galilee   c 8 Greek *about two hundred cubits* (about 90 meters) stretch out your hands, and someone else will dress you and lead you where you do not want to go." [19]Jesus said this to indicate the kind of death by which Peter would glorify God. Then he said to him, "Follow me!"

[20]Peter turned and saw that the disciple whom Jesus loved was following them. (This was the one who had leaned back against Jesus at the supper and had said, "Lord, who is going to betray you?") [21]When Peter saw him, he asked, "Lord, what about him?"

[22]Jesus answered, "If I want him to remain alive until I return, what is that to you? You must follow me." [23]Because of this, the rumor spread among the brothers that this disciple would not die. But Jesus did not say that he would not die; he only said, "If I want him to remain alive until I return, what is that to you?"

[24]This is the disciple who testifies to these things and who wrote them down. We know that his testimony is true.

[25]Jesus did many other things as well. If every one of them were written down, I suppose that even the whole world would not have room for the books that would be written.

Author: Luke

Date: AD 62

Audience: A man named Theophilus ("lover of God") and those to whom he would circulate the letter, to give a comprehensive, orderly account of the birth and growth of the Christian faith and the communities of believers across the world

Prayer Themes:

- Ask God's Spirit to fill you and empower you to do what He has called you to do (1:8).

- Pray for the strength and perseverance to live out your calling, even when life is difficult (14:19-20).

- Ask God to give you courage and opportunities to share your story—how you met Jesus, how He changed your life, and how He blesses you every day (26:1-32).

It is a mistake to think that the Christians of the first-century were a problem-free community of faith. The truth is that none of the churches and not a single believer in the New Testament "had it all together." From the beginning the followers of Christ have always struggled to trust and obey.

In spite of that, however, we must never *minimize* the impact of these imperfect saints. The book of Acts documents the supernatural way the message of Jesus Christ spread throughout Jerusalem, and then across diverse cultures, national borders, and vast seas (1:8).

Throughout Acts there is a noticeably consistent theme: Our first generation spiritual ancestors knew how to pray. They anticipated great things from God, and they expected to do great things for Him. But they knew to connect with God in prayer first and wait to be empowered by Him.

Acts

Jesus Taken Up Into Heaven

1 In my former book, Theophilus, I wrote about all that Jesus began to do and to teach ²until the day he was taken up to heaven, after giving instructions through the Holy Spirit to the apostles he had chosen. ³After his suffering, he showed himself to these men and gave many convincing proofs that he was alive. He appeared to them over a period of forty days and spoke about the kingdom of God. ⁴On one occasion, while he was eating with them, he gave them this command: "Do not leave Jerusalem, but wait for the gift my Father promised, which you have heard me speak about. ⁵For John baptized with[a] water, but in a few days you will be baptized with the Holy Spirit."

⁶So when they met together, they asked him, "Lord, are you at this time going to restore the kingdom to Israel?"

⁷He said to them: "It is not for you to know the times or dates the Father has set by his own authority. ⁸But you will receive power when the Holy Spirit comes on you; and you will be my witnesses in Jerusalem, and in all Judea and Samaria, and to the ends of the earth."

⁹After he said this, he was taken up before their very eyes, and a cloud hid him from their sight.

¹⁰They were looking intently up into the sky as he was going, when suddenly two men dressed in white stood beside them. ¹¹"Men of Galilee," they said, "why do you stand here looking into the sky? This same Jesus, who has been taken from you into heaven, will come back in the same way you have seen him go into heaven."

---

a 5 Or *in*

God's people at prayer
THE DISCIPLES WAITED—AND PRAYED

ACTS 1:12-14 After the emotional whirlwind of the previous weeks, the disciples needed to regroup. They had experienced the trauma of Jesus' trial, the shock of His crucifixion, the joy of His resurrection, the surprising encounters with Him as the risen Lord, and finally His ascension. One of Jesus' last commands was, "Wait for the gift my Father promised" (1:4). They went back to Jerusalem and waited. While they waited, they prayed.

What do we do while we wait for something God has promised—such as an answer to prayer, the guidance we need, or the provision He will give? The disciples' example reminds us that prayer is always the right thing to do in times of waiting. In fact, God sometimes seems to make us wait for the very purpose of teaching us to keep praying. Our tendency is to get worried when we can do nothing. His solution? See helplessness, anxiousness, impatience, and worry as a call to pray. Turn all your waiting times into prayer times.

Matthias Chosen to Replace Judas

¹²Then they returned to Jerusalem from the hill called the Mount of Olives, a Sabbath day's walk[a] from the city. ¹³When they arrived, they went upstairs to the room where they were staying. Those present were Peter, John, James and Andrew; Philip and Thomas, Bartholomew and Matthew; James son of Alphaeus and Simon the Zealot, and Judas son of James. ¹⁴They all joined together constantly in prayer, along with the women and Mary the mother of Jesus, and with his brothers.

¹⁵In those days Peter stood up among the believers[b] (a group numbering about a hundred and twenty) ¹⁶and said, "Brothers, the Scripture had to be fulfilled which the Holy Spirit spoke long ago through the mouth of David concerning Judas, who served as guide for those who arrested Jesus— ¹⁷he was one of our number and shared in this ministry."

¹⁸(With the reward he got for his wickedness, Judas bought a field; there he fell headlong, his body burst open and all his intestines spilled out. ¹⁹Everyone in Jerusalem heard about this, so they called that field in their language Akeldama, that is, Field of Blood.)

²⁰"For," said Peter, "it is written in the book of Psalms,

" 'May his place be deserted;
  let there be no one to dwell in it,'[c]

and,

" 'May another take his place of
    leadership.'[d]

²¹Therefore it is necessary to choose one of the men who have been with us the whole time the Lord Jesus went in and out among us, ²²beginning from John's baptism to the time when Jesus was taken up from us. For one of these must become a witness with us of his resurrection."

²³So they proposed two men: Joseph called Barsabbas (also known as Justus) and Matthias. ²⁴Then they prayed, "Lord, you know everyone's heart. Show us which of these two you have chosen ²⁵to take over this apostolic ministry, which Judas left to go where he belongs." ²⁶Then they cast lots, and the lot fell to Matthias; so he was added to the eleven apostles.

The Holy Spirit Comes at Pentecost

2 When the day of Pentecost came, they were all together in one place. ²Suddenly a sound like the blowing of a violent wind came from heaven and filled the whole house where they were sitting. ³They saw what seemed to be tongues of fire that separated and came to

---

[a] 12 That is, about 3/4 mile (about 1,100 meters)   [b] 15 Greek *brothers*   [c] 20 Psalm 69:25   [d] 20 Psalm 109:8

rest on each of them. [4]All of them were filled with the Holy Spirit and began to speak in other tongues[a] as the Spirit enabled them.

[5]Now there were staying in Jerusalem God-fearing Jews from every nation under heaven. [6]When they heard this sound, a crowd came together in bewilderment, because each one heard them speaking in his own language. [7]Utterly amazed, they asked: "Are not all these men who are speaking Galileans? [8]Then how is it that each of us hears them in his own native language? [9]Parthians, Medes and Elamites; residents of Mesopotamia, Judea and Cappadocia, Pontus and Asia, [10]Phrygia and Pamphylia, Egypt and the parts of Libya near Cyrene; visitors from Rome [11](both Jews and converts to Judaism); Cretans and Arabs—we hear them declaring the wonders of God in our own tongues!" [12]Amazed and perplexed, they asked one another, "What does this mean?"

[13]Some, however, made fun of them and said, "They have had too much wine.[b]"

Peter Addresses the Crowd

[14]Then Peter stood up with the Eleven, raised his voice and addressed the crowd: "Fellow Jews and all of you who live in Jerusalem, let me explain this to you; listen carefully to what I say. [15]These men are not drunk, as you suppose. It's only nine in the morning! [16]No, this is what was spoken by the prophet Joel:

[17]" 'In the last days, God says,
    I will pour out my Spirit on all
        people.
Your sons and daughters will
        prophesy,
    your young men will see visions,
    your old men will dream dreams.
[18]Even on my servants, both men and
        women,
    I will pour out my Spirit in those
        days,
    and they will prophesy.

[19]I will show wonders in the heaven
        above
    and signs on the earth below,
    blood and fire and billows of
        smoke.
[20]The sun will be turned to darkness
    and the moon to blood
    before the coming of the great and
        glorious day of the Lord.
[21]And everyone who calls
    on the name of the Lord will be
        saved.'[c]

[22]"Men of Israel, listen to this: Jesus of Nazareth was a man accredited by God to you by miracles, wonders and signs, which God did among you through him, as you yourselves know. [23]This man was handed over to you by God's set purpose and foreknowledge; and you, with the help of wicked men,[d] put him to death by nailing him to the cross. [24]But God raised him from the dead, freeing him from the agony of death, because it was impossible for death to keep its hold on him. [25]David said about him:

" 'I saw the Lord always before me.
    Because he is at my right hand,
    I will not be shaken.
[26]Therefore my heart is glad and my
        tongue rejoices;
    my body also will live in hope,
[27]because you will not abandon me to
        the grave,
    nor will you let your Holy One
        see decay.
[28]You have made known to me the
        paths of life;
    you will fill me with joy in your
        presence.'[e]

[29]"Brothers, I can tell you confidently that the patriarch David died and was buried, and his tomb is here to this day. [30]But he was a prophet and knew that God had promised him on oath that he would place one of his descendants on his throne. [31]Seeing what was ahead, he spoke of the

---

[a]4 Or languages; also in verse 11   [b]13 Or sweet wine   [c]21 Joel 2:28-32   [d]23 Or of those not having the law (that is, Gentiles)   [e]28 Psalm 16:8-11

resurrection of the Christ,[a] that he was not abandoned to the grave, nor did his body see decay. 32God has raised this Jesus to life, and we are all witnesses of the fact. 33Exalted to the right hand of God, he has received from the Father the promised Holy Spirit and has poured out what you now see and hear. 34For David did not ascend to heaven, and yet he said,

"'The Lord said to my Lord:
"Sit at my right hand
35until I make your enemies
a footstool for your feet."'[b]

36"Therefore let all Israel be assured of this: God has made this Jesus, whom you crucified, both Lord and Christ."

37When the people heard this, they were cut to the heart and said to Peter and the other apostles, "Brothers, what shall we do?"

38Peter replied, "Repent and be baptized, every one of you, in the name of Jesus Christ for the forgiveness of your sins. And you will receive the gift of the Holy Spirit. 39The promise is for you and your children and for all who are far off—for all whom the Lord our God will call."

40With many other words he warned

---

a 31 Or Messiah. "The Christ" (Greek) and "the Messiah" (Hebrew) both mean "the Anointed One"; also in verse 36.
b 35 Psalm 110:1

GOING *deeper*

Staying Devoted to Prayer

READ AND CONSIDER: ACTS 2:42-47

"They devoted themselves to the apostles' teaching and to the fellowship, to the breaking of bread and to prayer" (Acts 2:42).

When Peter preached the gospel to the crowds, they wanted to know what to do. After they had repented of their sins and been baptized, they devoted themselves to the apostles' teaching, to fellowship with one another, to communion, and to prayer. What was important to the new believers in the first century AD is just as important to believers today. Those four things mentioned above are essential for Christians to learn so they can mature and stay close to God. Studying the Bible, spending time with other believers, and partaking of communion are things that often occur in church but can happen anywhere. And they must be made a priority. Prayer, too, is something we deliberately need to set aside time for because it often gets set aside for other things.

So how can we be devoted to prayer like those early believers? They surely didn't quit their jobs or leave their family responsibilities in order to pray full-time. They went on with their lives in Christ but with a new focus—they were devoted to communication with God! What an awesome thought! They knew God was listening when they had a need or prayed for the needs of others.

We can be devoted to prayer in that same way as well. From the time we get up in the morning to when we go to bed at night, we always have a direct and open line to God. At any time we want, we can talk to God and He will hear and respond.

Devotion to prayer means that we are ready and willing to talk to God in Jesus' name whenever and wherever we feel the need to approach His throne. If we wake up in the middle of the night, we can ask God if there is someone who needs prayer right then. Wherever we are, at any time of day or night, for whatever needs God brings to mind, we can pray knowing God will hear and answer. That's devotion to prayer. That's how to make talking to God a priority.

them; and he pleaded with them, "Save yourselves from this corrupt generation." [41] Those who accepted his message were baptized, and about three thousand were added to their number that day.

The Fellowship of the Believers

[42] They devoted themselves to the apostles' teaching and to the fellowship, to the breaking of bread and to prayer. [43] Everyone was filled with awe, and many wonders and miraculous signs were done by the apostles. [44] All the believers were together and had everything in common. [45] Selling their possessions and goods, they gave to anyone as he had need. [46] Every day they continued to meet together in the temple courts. They broke bread in their homes and ate together with glad and sincere hearts, [47] praising God and enjoying the favor of all the people. And the Lord added to their number daily those who were being saved.

Peter Heals the Crippled Beggar

3 One day Peter and John were going up to the temple at the time of prayer—at three in the afternoon. [2] Now a man crippled from birth was being carried to the temple gate called Beautiful, where he was put every day to beg from those going into the temple courts. [3] When he saw Peter and John about to enter, he asked them for money. [4] Peter looked straight at him, as did John. Then Peter said, "Look at us!" [5] So the man gave them his attention, expecting to get something from them.

Praying Acts 3:6

Lord, my treasure is in You, and I ask You to help me generously share that treasure with others.

[6] Then Peter said, "Silver or gold I do not have, but what I have I give you. In the name of Jesus Christ of Nazareth, walk." [7] Taking him by the right hand, he helped him up, and instantly the man's feet

and ankles became strong. [8] He jumped to his feet and began to walk. Then he went with them into the temple courts, walking and jumping, and praising God. [9] When all the people saw him walking and praising God, [10] they recognized him as the same man who used to sit begging at the temple gate called Beautiful, and they were filled with wonder and amazement at what had happened to him.

Peter Speaks to the Onlookers

[11] While the beggar held on to Peter and John, all the people were astonished and came running to them in the place called Solomon's Colonnade. [12] When Peter saw this, he said to them: "Men of Israel, why does this surprise you? Why do you stare at us as if by our own power or godliness we had made this man walk? [13] The God of Abraham, Isaac and Jacob, the God of our fathers, has glorified his servant Jesus. You handed him over to be killed, and you disowned him before Pilate, though he had decided to let him go. [14] You disowned the Holy and Righteous One and asked that a murderer be released to you. [15] You killed the author of life, but God raised him from the dead. We are witnesses of this. [16] By faith in the name of Jesus, this man whom you see and know was made strong. It is Jesus' name and the faith that comes through him that has given this complete healing to him, as you can all see.

[17] "Now, brothers, I know that you acted in ignorance, as did your leaders. [18] But this is how God fulfilled what he had foretold through all the prophets, saying that his Christ[a] would suffer. [19] Repent, then, and turn to God, so that your sins may be wiped out, that times of refreshing may come from the Lord, [20] and that he may send the Christ, who has been appointed for you—even Jesus. [21] He must remain in heaven until the time comes for God to restore everything, as he promised long ago through his holy prophets. [22] For Moses said, 'The Lord your God will raise up

---

[a] 18 Or *Messiah*; also in verse 20

for you a prophet like me from among your own people; you must listen to everything he tells you. 23Anyone who does not listen to him will be completely cut off from among his people.'ᵃ

24"Indeed, all the prophets from Samuel on, as many as have spoken, have foretold these days. 25And you are heirs of the prophets and of the covenant God made with your fathers. He said to Abraham,'Through your offspring all peoples on earth will be blessed.'ᵇ 26When God raised up his servant, he sent him first to you to bless you by turning each of you from your wicked ways."

Peter and John Before the Sanhedrin

4 The priests and the captain of the temple guard and the Sadducees came up to Peter and John while they were speaking to the people. 2They were greatly disturbed because the apostles were teaching the people and proclaiming in Jesus the resurrection of the dead. 3They seized Peter and John, and because it was evening, they put them in jail until the next day. 4But many who heard the message believed, and the number of men grew to about five thousand.

5The next day the rulers, elders and teachers of the law met in Jerusalem. 6Annas the high priest was there, and so were Caiaphas, John, Alexander and the other men of the high priest's family. 7They had Peter and John brought before them and began to question them: "By what power or what name did you do this?"

8Then Peter, filled with the Holy Spirit, said to them: "Rulers and elders of the people! 9If we are being called to account today for an act of kindness shown to a cripple and are asked how he was healed, 10then know this, you and all the people of Israel: It is by the name of Jesus Christ of Nazareth, whom you crucified but whom God raised from the dead, that this man stands before you healed. 11He is

"'the stone you builders rejected, which has become the capstone.'ᶜ'ᵈ

12Salvation is found in no one else, for there is no other name under heaven given to men by which we must be saved."

13When they saw the courage of Peter and John and realized that they were unschooled, ordinary men, they were astonished and they took note that these men had been with Jesus. 14But since they could see the man who had been healed standing there with them, there was nothing they could say. 15So they ordered them to withdraw from the Sanhedrin and then conferred together. 16"What are we going to do with these men?" they asked. "Everybody living in Jerusalem knows they have done an outstanding miracle, and we cannot deny it. 17But to stop this thing from spreading any further among the people, we must warn these men to speak no longer to anyone in this name."

18Then they called them in again and commanded them not to speak or teach at all in the name of Jesus. 19But Peter and John replied, "Judge for yourselves whether it is right in God's sight to obey you rather than God. 20For we cannot help speaking about what we have seen and heard."

21After further threats they let them go. They could not decide how to punish them, because all the people were praising God for what had happened. 22For the man who was miraculously healed was over forty years old.

The Believers' Prayer

23On their release, Peter and John went back to their own people and reported all that the chief priests and elders had said to them. 24When they heard this, they raised their voices together in prayer to God. "Sovereign Lord," they said, "you made the heaven and the earth and the sea, and everything in them. 25You spoke by the Holy Spirit through the mouth of your servant, our father David:

ᵃ 23 Deut. 18:15,18,19 ᵇ 25 Gen. 22:18; 26:4 ᶜ 11 Or cornerstone ᵈ 11 Psalm 118:22

" 'Why do the nations rage
and the peoples plot in vain?
26 The kings of the earth take their
stand
and the rulers gather together
against the Lord
and against his Anointed One.'a'b

27 Indeed Herod and Pontius Pilate met together with the Gentiles and the people[c] of Israel in this city to conspire against your holy servant Jesus, whom you anointed. 28 They did what your power and will had decided beforehand should happen. 29 Now, Lord, consider their threats and enable your servants to speak your word with great boldness. 30 Stretch out your hand to heal and perform miraculous signs and wonders through the name of your holy servant Jesus."

31 After they prayed, the place where they were meeting was shaken. And they were all filled with the Holy Spirit and spoke the word of God boldly.

The Believers Share Their Possessions
32 All the believers were one in heart and mind. No one claimed that any of his possessions was his own, but they shared everything they had. 33 With great power the apostles continued to testify to the resurrection of the Lord Jesus, and much

grace was upon them all. 34 There were no needy persons among them. For from time to time those who owned lands or houses sold them, brought the money from the sales 35 and put it at the apostles' feet, and it was distributed to anyone as he had need.

36 Joseph, a Levite from Cyprus, whom the apostles called Barnabas (which means Son of Encouragement), 37 sold a field he owned and brought the money and put it at the apostles' feet.

Ananias and Sapphira
5 Now a man named Ananias, together with his wife Sapphira, also sold a piece of property. 2 With his wife's full knowledge he kept back part of the money for himself, but brought the rest and put it at the apostles' feet.

3 Then Peter said, "Ananias, how is it that Satan has so filled your heart that you have lied to the Holy Spirit and have kept for yourself some of the money you received for the land? 4 Didn't it belong to you before it was sold? And after it was

Praying Acts 5:4
Father God, keep me from ever being confused or influenced by the enemy so that I will never lie to You or anyone else.

a 26 That is, Christ or Messiah   b 26 Psalm 2:1,2   c 27 The Greek is plural.

sold, wasn't the money at your disposal? What made you think of doing such a thing? You have not lied to men but to God."

5When Ananias heard this, he fell down and died. And great fear seized all who heard what had happened. 6Then the young men came forward, wrapped up his body, and carried him out and buried him.

7About three hours later his wife came in, not knowing what had happened. 8Peter asked her, "Tell me, is this the price you and Ananias got for the land?"

"Yes," she said, "that is the price."

9Peter said to her, "How could you agree to test the Spirit of the Lord? Look! The feet of the men who buried your husband are at the door, and they will carry you out also."

10At that moment she fell down at his feet and died. Then the young men came in and, finding her dead, carried her out and buried her beside her husband. 11Great fear seized the whole church and all who heard about these events.

The Apostles Heal Many

12The apostles performed many miraculous signs and wonders among the people. And all the believers used to meet together in Solomon's Colonnade. 13No one else dared join them, even though they were highly regarded by the people. 14Nevertheless, more and more men and women believed in the Lord and were added to their number. 15As a result, people brought the sick into the streets and laid them on beds and mats so that at least Peter's shadow might fall on some of them as he passed by. 16Crowds gathered also from the towns around Jerusalem, bringing their sick and those tormented by evil[a] spirits, and all of them were healed.

The Apostles Persecuted

17Then the high priest and all his associates, who were members of the party of the Sadducees, were filled with jealousy. 18They arrested the apostles and put them in the public jail. 19But during the night an angel of the Lord opened the doors of the jail and brought them out. 20"Go, stand in the temple courts," he said, "and tell the people the full message of this new life."

21At daybreak they entered the temple courts, as they had been told, and began to teach the people.

When the high priest and his associates arrived, they called together the Sanhedrin—the full assembly of the elders of Israel—and sent to the jail for the apostles. 22But on arriving at the jail, the officers did not find them there. So they went back and reported, 23"We found the jail securely locked, with the guards standing at the doors; but when we opened them, we found no one inside." 24On hearing this report, the captain of the temple guard and the chief priests were puzzled, wondering what would come of this.

25Then someone came and said, "Look! The men you put in jail are standing in the temple courts teaching the people." 26At that, the captain went with his officers and brought the apostles. They did not use force, because they feared that the people would stone them.

27Having brought the apostles, they made them appear before the Sanhedrin to be questioned by the high priest. 28"We gave you strict orders not to teach in this name," he said. "Yet you have filled Jerusalem with your teaching and are determined to make us guilty of this man's blood."

29Peter and the other apostles replied: "We must obey God rather than men! 30The God of our fathers raised Jesus from the dead—whom you had killed by hanging him on a tree. 31God exalted him to his own right hand as Prince and Savior that he might give repentance and forgiveness of sins to Israel. 32We are

a 16 Greek unclean

witnesses of these things, and so is the Holy Spirit, whom God has given to those who obey him."

33When they heard this, they were furious and wanted to put them to death. 34But a Pharisee named Gamaliel, a teacher of the law, who was honored by all the people, stood up in the Sanhedrin and ordered that the men be put outside for a little while. 35Then he addressed them: "Men of Israel, consider carefully what you intend to do to these men. 36Some time ago Theudas appeared, claiming to be somebody, and about four hundred men rallied to him. He was killed, all his followers were dispersed, and it all came to nothing. 37After him, Judas the Galilean appeared in the days of the census and led a band of people in revolt. He too was killed, and all his followers were scattered. 38Therefore, in the present case I advise you: Leave these men alone! Let them go! For if their purpose or activity is of human origin, it will fail. 39But if it is from God, you will not be able to stop these men; you will only find yourselves fighting against God."

40His speech persuaded them. They called the apostles in and had them flogged. Then they ordered them not to speak in the name of Jesus, and let them go.

41The apostles left the Sanhedrin, rejoicing because they had been counted worthy of suffering disgrace for the Name. 42Day after day, in the temple courts and from house to house, they never stopped teaching and proclaiming the good news that Jesus is the Christ.[a]

The Choosing of the Seven

6 In those days when the number of disciples was increasing, the Grecian Jews among them complained against the Hebraic Jews because their widows were being overlooked in the daily distribution of food. 2So the Twelve gathered all the disciples together and said, "It would not be right for us to neglect the ministry of the word of God in order to wait on tables. 3Brothers, choose seven men from among you who are known to be full of the Spirit and wisdom. We will turn this responsibility over to them 4and will give our attention to prayer and the ministry of the word."

5This proposal pleased the whole group. They chose Stephen, a man full of faith and of the Holy Spirit; also Philip, Procorus, Nicanor, Timon, Parmenas, and Nicolas from Antioch, a convert to Judaism. 6They presented these men to the apostles, who prayed and laid their hands on them.

7So the word of God spread. The number of disciples in Jerusalem increased rapidly, and a large number of priests became obedient to the faith.

Stephen Seized

8Now Stephen, a man full of God's grace and power, did great wonders and miraculous signs among the people. 9Opposition arose, however, from members of the Synagogue of the Freedmen (as it was called)—Jews of Cyrene and Alexandria as well as the provinces of Cilicia and Asia. These men began to argue with Stephen, 10but they could not stand up against his wisdom or the Spirit by whom he spoke.

11Then they secretly persuaded some men to say, "We have heard Stephen speak words of blasphemy against Moses and against God."

12So they stirred up the people and the elders and the teachers of the law. They seized Stephen and brought him before the Sanhedrin. 13They produced false witnesses, who testified, "This fellow never stops speaking against this holy place and against the law. 14For we have heard him say that this Jesus of Nazareth will destroy this place and change the customs Moses handed down to us."

15All who were sitting in the Sanhedrin looked intently at Stephen, and they saw that his face was like the face of an angel.

---

a 42 Or Messiah

Praying for Spiritual Leaders and Servants

READ AND CONSIDER: ACTS 6:1-7

"They presented these men to the apostles, who prayed and laid their hands on them" (Acts 6:6).

People in full-time ministry need our prayer support. In the case of these men who were chosen to handle the food ministry, they were spiritually wise men who would be taking on a huge responsibility. Their job would allow the apostles to focus on preaching and teaching.

Every job within the body of Christ—the church—is important, as signified by the care in which the food-program workers were chosen in the early church. The men chosen to deal with the daily distribution of food had to be men who were "known to be full of the Spirit and wisdom" (6:3). When the apostles prayed for them and laid their hands on them, it signified that they were set apart for special service to God (Numbers 27:22-23; Deuteronomy 34:9).

Carefully choosing and praying for church workers is important because Satan's attacks go first to those who are making a difference for the cause of Christ. Have you ever noticed that when a church is winning souls, attacks seem to come from all sides? Little problems creep in, disagreements arise, temptations sprout like weeds. How do we fight this? By praying for those who minister and serve.

Pray for the Sunday school teacher who has a class full of children. Pray for the pastoral staff who must make decisions that affect the entire congregation. Pray for the administrative staff who carry a heavy load of paperwork each week. Pray for the people who volunteer their time with the youth group. Pray that each of them will be able to stand against every temptation and that none will fall into the traps of the enemy.

Spiritual leadership at all levels is serious business. Be sure to hold these servants up in prayer.

Stephen's Speech to the Sanhedrin

7 Then the high priest asked him, "Are these charges true?"

2 To this he replied: "Brothers and fathers, listen to me! The God of glory appeared to our father Abraham while he was still in Mesopotamia, before he lived in Haran. 3 'Leave your country and your people,' God said, 'and go to the land I will show you.'[a]

4 "So he left the land of the Chaldeans and settled in Haran. After the death of his father, God sent him to this land where you are now living. 5 He gave him no inheritance here, not even a foot of ground. But God promised him that he and his descendants after him would possess the land, even though at that time Abraham had no child. 6 God spoke to him in this way: 'Your descendants will be strangers in a country not their own, and they will be enslaved and mistreated four hundred years. 7 But I will punish the nation they serve as slaves,' God said, 'and afterward they will come out of that country and worship me in this place.'[b] 8 Then he gave Abraham the covenant of circumcision. And Abraham became the father of Isaac

---

[a] 3 Gen. 12:1   [b] 7 Gen. 15:13,14

and circumcised him eight days after his birth. Later Isaac became the father of Jacob, and Jacob became the father of the twelve patriarchs.

9"Because the patriarchs were jealous of Joseph, they sold him as a slave into Egypt. But God was with him 10and rescued him from all his troubles. He gave Joseph wisdom and enabled him to gain the goodwill of Pharaoh king of Egypt; so he made him ruler over Egypt and all his palace.

11"Then a famine struck all Egypt and Canaan, bringing great suffering, and our fathers could not find food. 12When Jacob heard that there was grain in Egypt, he sent our fathers on their first visit. 13On their second visit, Joseph told his brothers who he was, and Pharaoh learned about Joseph's family. 14After this, Joseph sent for his father Jacob and his whole family, seventy-five in all. 15Then Jacob went down to Egypt, where he and our fathers died. 16Their bodies were brought back to Shechem and placed in the tomb that Abraham had bought from the sons of Hamor at Shechem for a certain sum of money.

17"As the time drew near for God to fulfill his promise to Abraham, the number of our people in Egypt greatly increased. 18Then another king, who knew nothing about Joseph, became ruler of Egypt. 19He dealt treacherously with our people and oppressed our forefathers by forcing them to throw out their newborn babies so that they would die.

20"At that time Moses was born, and he was no ordinary child.ᵃ For three months he was cared for in his father's house. 21When he was placed outside, Pharaoh's daughter took him and brought him up as her own son. 22Moses was educated in all the wisdom of the Egyptians and was powerful in speech and action.

23"When Moses was forty years old, he decided to visit his fellow Israelites.

24He saw one of them being mistreated by an Egyptian, so he went to his defense and avenged him by killing the Egyptian. 25Moses thought that his own people would realize that God was using him to rescue them, but they did not. 26The next day Moses came upon two Israelites who were fighting. He tried to reconcile them by saying, 'Men, you are brothers; why do you want to hurt each other?'

27"But the man who was mistreating the other pushed Moses aside and said, 'Who made you ruler and judge over us? 28Do you want to kill me as you killed the Egyptian yesterday?'ᵇ 29When Moses heard this, he fled to Midian, where he settled as a foreigner and had two sons.

30"After forty years had passed, an angel appeared to Moses in the flames of a burning bush in the desert near Mount Sinai. 31When he saw this, he was amazed at the sight. As he went over to look more closely, he heard the Lord's voice: 32'I am the God of your fathers, the God of Abraham, Isaac and Jacob.'ᶜ Moses trembled with fear and did not dare to look.

33"Then the Lord said to him, 'Take off your sandals; the place where you are standing is holy ground. 34I have indeed seen the oppression of my people in Egypt. I have heard their groaning and have come down to set them free. Now come, I will send you back to Egypt.'ᵈ

35"This is the same Moses whom they had rejected with the words, 'Who made you ruler and judge?' He was sent to be their ruler and deliverer by God himself, through the angel who appeared to him in the bush. 36He led them out of Egypt and did wonders and miraculous signs in Egypt, at the Red Seaᵉ and for forty years in the desert.

37"This is that Moses who told the Israelites, 'God will send you a prophet like me from your own people.'ᶠ 38He was in the assembly in the desert, with the angel who spoke to him on Mount Sinai, and

---

ᵃ20 Or *was fair in the sight of God*   ᵇ28 Exodus 2:14   ᶜ32 Exodus 3:6   ᵈ34 Exodus 3:5,7,8,10   ᵉ36 That is, Sea of Reeds
ᶠ37 Deut. 18:15

with our fathers; and he received living words to pass on to us.

39"But our fathers refused to obey him. Instead, they rejected him and in their hearts turned back to Egypt. 40They told Aaron, 'Make us gods who will go before us. As for this fellow Moses who led us out of Egypt—we don't know what has happened to him!'[a] 41That was the time they made an idol in the form of a calf. They brought sacrifices to it and held a celebration in honor of what their hands had made. 42But God turned away and gave them over to the worship of the heavenly bodies. This agrees with what is written in the book of the prophets:

> " 'Did you bring me sacrifices and
>   offerings
>   forty years in the desert, O house
>   of Israel?
> 43You have lifted up the shrine of
>   Molech
>   and the star of your god Rephan,
>   the idols you made to worship.
> Therefore I will send you into exile'[b]
>   beyond Babylon.

44"Our forefathers had the tabernacle of the Testimony with them in the desert. It had been made as God directed Moses, according to the pattern he had seen. 45Having received the tabernacle, our fathers under Joshua brought it with them when they took the land from the nations God drove out before them. It remained in the land until the time of David, 46who enjoyed God's favor and asked that he might provide a dwelling place for the God of Jacob.[c] 47But it was Solomon who built the house for him.

48"However, the Most High does not live in houses made by men. As the prophet says:

> 49" 'Heaven is my throne,
>   and the earth is my footstool.
> What kind of house will you build
>   for me?
>   says the Lord.

Or where will my resting place be?
50Has not my hand made all these
    things?'[d]

51"You stiff-necked people, with uncircumcised hearts and ears! You are just like your fathers: You always resist the Holy Spirit! 52Was there ever a prophet your fathers did not persecute? They even killed those who predicted the coming of the Righteous One. And now you have betrayed and murdered him— 53you who have received the law that was put into effect through angels but have not obeyed it."

The Stoning of Stephen

54When they heard this, they were furious and gnashed their teeth at him. 55But Stephen, full of the Holy Spirit, looked up to heaven and saw the glory of God, and Jesus standing at the right hand of God. 56"Look," he said, "I see heaven open and the Son of Man standing at the right hand of God."

57At this they covered their ears and, yelling at the top of their voices, they all rushed at him, 58dragged him out of the city and began to stone him. Meanwhile, the witnesses laid their clothes at the feet of a young man named Saul.

59While they were stoning him, Stephen prayed, "Lord Jesus, receive my spirit." 60Then he fell on his knees and cried out, "Lord, do not hold this sin against them." When he had said this, he fell asleep.

8 And Saul was there, giving approval to his death.

The Church Persecuted and Scattered

On that day a great persecution broke out against the church at Jerusalem, and all except the apostles were scattered throughout Judea and Samaria. 2Godly men buried Stephen and mourned deeply for him. 3But Saul began to destroy the church. Going from house to house, he dragged off men and women and put them in prison.

---

[a] 40 Exodus 32:1   [b] 43 Amos 5:25-27   [c] 46 Some early manuscripts *the house of Jacob*   [d] 50 Isaiah 66:1,2

God's people at prayer
STEPHEN'S FINAL WORDS

ACTS 7:51-60 With his final breaths, Stephen spoke to heaven about the things of earth. He asked Jesus to receive his spirit and then requested forgiveness for those who at that moment were killing him. He spent his last moments on this side of eternity in God's presence through prayer.

Stephen's dying words were an imitation of Jesus' spirit, extending forgiveness to those who had murder in their hearts. As Jesus hung on the cross, among His last few statements were prayers to God on behalf of His tormentors, "Father, forgive them, for they do not know what they are doing" (Luke 23:34).

Forgiveness isn't easy; forgiveness doesn't mean the person deserves forgiveness. Forgiveness means letting go of the people and the situation and letting God do His work. With Stephen's death, the church in Jerusalem scattered, sending believers across the known world and igniting a missionary movement the likes of which had never been seen! Forgiveness releases powerfully.

Philip in Samaria

⁴Those who had been scattered preached the word wherever they went. ⁵Philip went down to a city in Samaria and proclaimed the Christ[a] there. ⁶When the crowds heard Philip and saw the miraculous signs he did, they all paid close attention to what he said. ⁷With shrieks, evil[b] spirits came out of many, and many paralytics and cripples were healed. ⁸So there was great joy in that city.

Simon the Sorcerer

⁹Now for some time a man named Simon had practiced sorcery in the city and amazed all the people of Samaria. He boasted that he was someone great, ¹⁰and all the people, both high and low, gave him their attention and exclaimed, "This man is the divine power known as the Great Power." ¹¹They followed him because he had amazed them for a long time with his magic. ¹²But when they believed Philip as he preached the good news of the kingdom of God and the name of Jesus Christ, they were baptized, both men and women. ¹³Simon himself believed and was baptized. And he followed Philip everywhere, astonished by the great signs and miracles he saw.

¹⁴When the apostles in Jerusalem heard that Samaria had accepted the word of God, they sent Peter and John to them. ¹⁵When they arrived, they prayed for them that they might receive the Holy Spirit, ¹⁶because the Holy Spirit had not yet come upon any of them; they had simply been baptized into[c] the name of the Lord Jesus. ¹⁷Then Peter and John placed their hands on them, and they received the Holy Spirit.

¹⁸When Simon saw that the Spirit was given at the laying on of the apostles' hands, he offered them money ¹⁹and said, "Give me also this ability so that everyone on whom I lay my hands may receive the Holy Spirit."

²⁰Peter answered: "May your money perish with you, because you thought you could buy the gift of God with money! ²¹You have no part or share in this ministry, because your heart is not right before God. ²²Repent of this wickedness and pray to the Lord. Perhaps he will forgive you for having such a thought in your heart. ²³For I see that you are full of bitterness and captive to sin."

²⁴Then Simon answered, "Pray to the Lord for me so that nothing you have said may happen to me."

²⁵When they had testified and proclaimed

ᵃ 5 Or *Messiah*   ᵇ 7 Greek *unclean*   ᶜ 16 Or *in*

the word of the Lord, Peter and John returned to Jerusalem, preaching the gospel in many Samaritan villages.

Philip and the Ethiopian

26 Now an angel of the Lord said to Philip, "Go south to the road—the desert road—that goes down from Jerusalem to Gaza." 27 So he started out, and on his way he met an Ethiopian[a] eunuch, an important official in charge of all the treasury of Candace, queen of the Ethiopians. This man had gone to Jerusalem to worship, 28 and on his way home was sitting in his chariot reading the book of Isaiah the prophet. 29 The Spirit told Philip, "Go to that chariot and stay near it."

Praying Acts 8:29

Help me to always respond to the prompting of Your Holy Spirit, Lord, so that I can be Your instrument to influence others for Your kingdom.

---

30 Then Philip ran up to the chariot and heard the man reading Isaiah the prophet. "Do you understand what you are reading?" Philip asked.

31 "How can I," he said, "unless someone explains it to me?" So he invited Philip to come up and sit with him.

32 The eunuch was reading this passage of Scripture:

"He was led like a sheep to the slaughter,
     and as a lamb before the shearer is
          silent,
     so he did not open his mouth.
33 In his humiliation he was deprived of
          justice.
     Who can speak of his descendants?
     For his life was taken from the
          earth."[b]

34 The eunuch asked Philip, "Tell me, please, who is the prophet talking about, himself or someone else?" 35 Then Philip began with that very passage of Scripture and told him the good news about Jesus.

36 As they traveled along the road, they came to some water and the eunuch said, "Look, here is water. Why shouldn't I be baptized?"[c] 38 And he gave orders to stop the chariot. Then both Philip and the eunuch went down into the water and Philip baptized him. 39 When they came up out of the water, the Spirit of the Lord suddenly took Philip away, and the eunuch did not see him again, but went on his way rejoicing. 40 Philip, however, appeared at Azotus and traveled about, preaching the gospel in all the towns until he reached Caesarea.

Saul's Conversion

9 Meanwhile, Saul was still breathing out murderous threats against the Lord's disciples. He went to the high priest 2 and asked him for letters to the synagogues in Damascus, so that if he found any there who belonged to the Way, whether men or women, he might take them as prisoners to Jerusalem. 3 As he neared Damascus on his journey, suddenly a light from heaven flashed around him. 4 He fell to the ground and heard a voice say to him, "Saul, Saul, why do you persecute me?"

5 "Who are you, Lord?" Saul asked.

"I am Jesus, whom you are persecuting," he replied. 6 "Now get up and go into the city, and you will be told what you must do."

7 The men traveling with Saul stood there speechless; they heard the sound but did not see anyone. 8 Saul got up from the ground, but when he opened his eyes he could see nothing. So they led him by the hand into Damascus. 9 For three days he was blind, and did not eat or drink anything.

10 In Damascus there was a disciple named Ananias. The Lord called to him in a vision, "Ananias!"

"Yes, Lord," he answered.

11 The Lord told him, "Go to the house of Judas on Straight Street and ask for a

---

a 27 That is, from the upper Nile region   b 33 Isaiah 53:7,8   c 36 Some late manuscripts *baptized?"* 37 *Philip said, "If you believe with all your heart, you may." The eunuch answered, "I believe that Jesus Christ is the Son of God."*

Seeing in the Dark

READ AND CONSIDER: ACTS 9:1-19

"The Lord told him, 'Go to the house of Judas on Straight Street and ask for a man from Tarsus named Saul, for he is praying'" (Acts 9:11).

Saul had probably grown up doing a lot of praying. He was, after all, a Pharisee. He was a well-educated Jew who felt that the Christian movement was heretical and so decided to persecute the Christians ruthlessly. But on that road to Damascus, a brilliant light caused him to stop in his tracks. Jesus spoke directly to Saul and blinded him. As a result, Saul was led into the city of Damascus where he fasted and prayed as he had never done before.

Why was Saul blinded? It's difficult to do much when you are suddenly without sight. Saul didn't know if this was a permanent condition—at least until God spoke to him in a vision that Ananias would come and restore his sight.

In a terrifying instant, Jesus had made Himself and His holiness evident to Saul. During those three days that Saul fasted and prayed, he surely turned his sight inward and examined his life. He believed he had been doing the right thing by persecuting and arresting Christians, but now he knew he had been persecuting Jesus. Even as Paul prayed, God spoke to Ananias to go to him and pray for him to receive his sight and be filled with the Holy Spirit.

Often God will allow us to get to a dark place in our lives where we can't see without His help. And He often does that just before the greatest revelation to us of our purpose and calling.

man from Tarsus named Saul, for he is praying. ¹²In a vision he has seen a man named Ananias come and place his hands on him to restore his sight."

¹³"Lord," Ananias answered, "I have heard many reports about this man and all the harm he has done to your saints in Jerusalem. ¹⁴And he has come here with authority from the chief priests to arrest all who call on your name."

¹⁵But the Lord said to Ananias, "Go! This man is my chosen instrument to carry my name before the Gentiles and their kings and before the people of Israel. ¹⁶I will show him how much he must suffer for my name."

¹⁷Then Ananias went to the house and entered it. Placing his hands on Saul, he said, "Brother Saul, the Lord—Jesus, who appeared to you on the road as you were coming here—has sent me so that you may see again and be filled with the Holy Spirit." ¹⁸Immediately, something like scales fell from Saul's eyes, and he could see again. He got up and was baptized, ¹⁹and after taking some food, he regained his strength.

Saul in Damascus and Jerusalem

Saul spent several days with the disciples in Damascus. ²⁰At once he began to preach in the synagogues that Jesus is the Son of God. ²¹All those who heard him were astonished and asked, "Isn't he the man who raised havoc in Jerusalem among those who call on this name? And hasn't he come here to take them as prisoners to the chief priests?" ²²Yet Saul grew more and more powerful and baffled the Jews living in Damascus by proving that Jesus is the Christ.ᵃ

²³After many days had gone by, the Jews conspired to kill him, ²⁴but Saul learned of their plan. Day and night they

---

ᵃ 22 Or *Messiah*

kept close watch on the city gates in order to kill him. 25But his followers took him by night and lowered him in a basket through an opening in the wall.

26When he came to Jerusalem, he tried to join the disciples, but they were all afraid of him, not believing that he really was a disciple. 27But Barnabas took him and brought him to the apostles. He told them how Saul on his journey had seen the Lord and that the Lord had spoken to him, and how in Damascus he had preached fearlessly in the name of Jesus. 28So Saul stayed with them and moved about freely in Jerusalem, speaking boldly in the name of the Lord. 29He talked and debated with the Grecian Jews, but they tried to kill him. 30When the brothers learned of this, they took him down to Caesarea and sent him off to Tarsus.

31Then the church throughout Judea, Galilee and Samaria enjoyed a time of peace. It was strengthened; and encouraged by the Holy Spirit, it grew in numbers, living in the fear of the Lord.

Aeneas and Dorcas

32As Peter traveled about the country, he went to visit the saints in Lydda. 33There he found a man named Aeneas, a paralytic who had been bedridden for eight years. 34"Aeneas," Peter said to him, "Jesus Christ heals you. Get up and take care of your mat." Immediately Aeneas got up. 35All those who lived in Lydda and Sharon saw him and turned to the Lord.

36In Joppa there was a disciple named Tabitha (which, when translated, is Dorcasª), who was always doing good and helping the poor. 37About that time she became sick and died, and her body was washed and placed in an upstairs room. 38Lydda was near Joppa; so when the disciples heard that Peter was in Lydda, they sent two men to him and urged him, "Please come at once!"

39Peter went with them, and when he arrived he was taken upstairs to the room. All the widows stood around him, crying and showing him the robes and other clothing that Dorcas had made while she was still with them.

40Peter sent them all out of the room; then he got down on his knees and prayed. Turning toward the dead woman, he said, "Tabitha, get up." She opened her eyes, and seeing Peter she sat up. 41He took her by the hand and helped her to her feet. Then he called the believers and the widows and presented her to them alive. 42This became known all over Joppa, and

---

ª 36 Both *Tabitha* (Aramaic) and *Dorcas* (Greek) mean *gazelle*.

God's people at prayer
PETER'S UNEXPECTED PRAYER

ACTS 9:36-43 We know very little about Tabitha (her Greek name was Dorcas). She probably began to follow Jesus during the time of Jesus' itinerant ministry. This was a woman with a "reputation"—she was always "doing good." Her kind and generous spirit had left a loving impression on people, so her death was deeply felt by many in her town.

When the local believers invited Peter to come for Tabitha's funeral, they probably only intended for him to honor her as one of God's special servants. Instead of presiding at her memorial, Peter prayed over her body and she came back to life. Peter was certainly led by the Lord to pray that way, and Tabitha certainly had unfinished work to do. The result of this miracle was that "many people believed in the Lord" (9:42).

Whenever God's Spirit moves us to pray for great things, we must not hesitate to do so. We must trust God to do the impossible, knowing that with Him, all things *are* possible.

God's people at prayer
CORNELIUS'S REWARD FOR FAITHFUL PRAYER

ACTS 10:1-8 Cornelius had quite a reputation in the community of Caesarea as a Roman centurion with a good heart. He feared God, helped those in need, and always prayed to God. Cornelius sought God, and God made sure Cornelius had the opportunity to find Him. At the same time, God prepared Peter to bring the message of salvation to Cornelius's household! Peter at first resisted, but God got through to him in a dream.

When we pray to God often and live to please Him, He brings situations and people into our lives that will be to our greatest blessing. He will work things out for our greatest good. God always rewards those who faithfully seek Him.

many people believed in the Lord. ⁴³Peter stayed in Joppa for some time with a tanner named Simon.

Cornelius Calls for Peter

10 At Caesarea there was a man named Cornelius, a centurion in what was known as the Italian Regiment. ²He and all his family were devout and God-fearing; he gave generously to those in need and prayed to God regularly. ³One day at about three in the afternoon he had a vision. He distinctly saw an angel of God, who came to him and said, "Cornelius!"

⁴Cornelius stared at him in fear. "What is it, Lord?" he asked.

The angel answered, "Your prayers and gifts to the poor have come up as a memorial offering before God. ⁵Now send men to Joppa to bring back a man named Simon who is called Peter. ⁶He is staying with Simon the tanner, whose house is by the sea."

⁷When the angel who spoke to him had gone, Cornelius called two of his servants and a devout soldier who was one of his attendants. ⁸He told them everything that had happened and sent them to Joppa.

Peter's Vision

⁹About noon the following day as they were on their journey and approaching the city, Peter went up on the roof to pray. ¹⁰He became hungry and wanted something to eat, and while the meal was being prepared, he fell into a trance. ¹¹He saw heaven opened and something like a large sheet being let down to earth by its four corners. ¹²It contained all kinds of four-footed animals, as well as reptiles of the earth and birds of the air. ¹³Then a voice told him, "Get up, Peter. Kill and eat."

¹⁴"Surely not, Lord!" Peter replied. "I have never eaten anything impure or unclean."

¹⁵The voice spoke to him a second time, "Do not call anything impure that God has made clean."

¹⁶This happened three times, and immediately the sheet was taken back to heaven.

¹⁷While Peter was wondering about the meaning of the vision, the men sent by Cornelius found out where Simon's house was and stopped at the gate. ¹⁸They called out, asking if Simon who was known as Peter was staying there.

¹⁹While Peter was still thinking about the vision, the Spirit said to him, "Simon, three[a] men are looking for you. ²⁰So get up and go downstairs. Do not hesitate to go with them, for I have sent them."

²¹Peter went down and said to the men, "I'm the one you're looking for. Why have you come?"

²²The men replied, "We have come from Cornelius the centurion. He is a

---

a 19 One early manuscript *two*; other manuscripts do not have the number.

righteous and God-fearing man, who is respected by all the Jewish people. A holy angel told him to have you come to his house so that he could hear what you have to say." 23 Then Peter invited the men into the house to be his guests.

Peter at Cornelius's House

The next day Peter started out with them, and some of the brothers from Joppa went along. 24 The following day he arrived in Caesarea. Cornelius was expecting them and had called together his relatives and close friends. 25 As Peter entered the house, Cornelius met him and fell at his feet in reverence. 26 But Peter made him get up. "Stand up," he said, "I am only a man myself."

27 Talking with him, Peter went inside and found a large gathering of people. 28 He said to them: "You are well aware that it is against our law for a Jew to associate with a Gentile or visit him. But God has shown me that I should not call any man impure or unclean. 29 So when I was sent for, I came without raising any objection. May I ask why you sent for me?"

30 Cornelius answered: "Four days ago I was in my house praying at this hour, at three in the afternoon. Suddenly a man in shining clothes stood before me 31 and said, 'Cornelius, God has heard your prayer and remembered your gifts to the poor. 32 Send to Joppa for Simon who is called Peter. He is a guest in the home of Simon the tanner, who lives by the sea.' 33 So I sent for you immediately, and it was good of you to come. Now we are all here in the presence of God to listen to everything the Lord has commanded you to tell us."

34 Then Peter began to speak: "I now realize how true it is that God does not show favoritism 35 but accepts men from every nation who fear him and do what is right. 36 You know the message God sent to the people of Israel, telling the good news of peace through Jesus Christ, who is Lord of all. 37 You know what has happened throughout Judea, beginning in Galilee after the baptism that John preached— 38 how God anointed Jesus of Nazareth with the Holy Spirit and power, and how he went around doing good and healing all who were under the power of the devil, because God was with him.

39 "We are witnesses of everything he did in the country of the Jews and in Jerusalem. They killed him by hanging him on a tree, 40 but God raised him from the dead on the third day and caused him to be seen. 41 He was not seen by all the people, but by witnesses whom God had already chosen—by us who ate and drank with him after he rose from the dead. 42 He commanded us to preach to the people and to testify that he is the one whom God appointed as judge of the living and the dead. 43 All the prophets testify about him that everyone who believes in him receives forgiveness of sins through his name."

44 While Peter was still speaking these words, the Holy Spirit came on all who heard the message. 45 The circumcised believers who had come with Peter were astonished that the gift of the Holy Spirit had been poured out even on the Gentiles. 46 For they heard them speaking in tongues[a] and praising God.

Then Peter said, 47 "Can anyone keep these people from being baptized with water? They have received the Holy Spirit just as we have." 48 So he ordered that they be baptized in the name of Jesus Christ. Then they asked Peter to stay with them for a few days.

Peter Explains His Actions

11 The apostles and the brothers throughout Judea heard that the Gentiles also had received the word of God. 2 So when Peter went up to Jerusalem, the circumcised believers criticized him 3 and said, "You went into the house of uncircumcised men and ate with them."

4 Peter began and explained everything

---

a 46 Or other languages

to them precisely as it had happened: 5"I was in the city of Joppa praying, and in a trance I saw a vision. I saw something like a large sheet being let down from heaven by its four corners, and it came down to where I was. 6I looked into it and saw four-footed animals of the earth, wild beasts, reptiles, and birds of the air. 7Then I heard a voice telling me, 'Get up, Peter. Kill and eat.'

8"I replied, 'Surely not, Lord! Nothing impure or unclean has ever entered my mouth.'

9"The voice spoke from heaven a second time, 'Do not call anything impure that God has made clean.' 10This happened three times, and then it was all pulled up to heaven again.

11"Right then three men who had been sent to me from Caesarea stopped at the house where I was staying. 12The Spirit told me to have no hesitation about going with them. These six brothers also went with me, and we entered the man's house. 13He told us how he had seen an angel appear in his house and say, 'Send to Joppa for Simon who is called Peter. 14He will bring you a message through which you and all your household will be saved.'

15"As I began to speak, the Holy Spirit came on them as he had come on us at the beginning. 16Then I remembered what the Lord had said: 'John baptized with[a] water, but you will be baptized with the Holy Spirit.' 17So if God gave them the same gift as he gave us, who believed in the Lord Jesus Christ, who was I to think that I could oppose God?"

18When they heard this, they had no further objections and praised God, saying, "So then, God has granted even the Gentiles repentance unto life."

The Church in Antioch

19Now those who had been scattered by the persecution in connection with Stephen traveled as far as Phoenicia, Cyprus and Antioch, telling the message only to Jews. 20Some of them, however, men from Cyprus and Cyrene, went to Antioch and began to speak to Greeks also, telling them the good news about the Lord Jesus. 21The Lord's hand was with them, and a great number of people believed and turned to the Lord.

22News of this reached the ears of the church at Jerusalem, and they sent Barnabas to Antioch. 23When he arrived and saw the evidence of the grace of God, he was glad and encouraged them all to remain true to the Lord with all their hearts. 24He was a good man, full of the Holy Spirit and faith, and a great number of people were brought to the Lord.

25Then Barnabas went to Tarsus to look for Saul, 26and when he found him, he brought him to Antioch. So for a whole year Barnabas and Saul met with the church and taught great numbers of people. The disciples were called Christians first at Antioch.

27During this time some prophets came down from Jerusalem to Antioch. 28One of them, named Agabus, stood up and through the Spirit predicted that a severe famine would spread over the entire Roman world. (This happened during the reign of Claudius.) 29The disciples, each according to his ability, decided to provide help for the brothers living in Judea. 30This they did, sending their gift to the elders by Barnabas and Saul.

Peter's Miraculous Escape From Prison

12 It was about this time that King Herod arrested some who belonged to the church, intending to persecute them. 2He had James, the brother of John, put to death with the sword. 3When he saw that this pleased the Jews, he proceeded to seize Peter also. This happened during the Feast of Unleavened Bread. 4After arresting him, he put him in prison, handing him over to be guarded by four squads of four soldiers each. Herod intended to bring him out for public trial after the Passover.

---

a 16 Or in

⁵So Peter was kept in prison, but the church was earnestly praying to God for him.

⁶The night before Herod was to bring him to trial, Peter was sleeping between two soldiers, bound with two chains, and sentries stood guard at the entrance. ⁷Suddenly an angel of the Lord appeared and a light shone in the cell. He struck Peter on the side and woke him up. "Quick, get up!" he said, and the chains fell off Peter's wrists.

⁸Then the angel said to him, "Put on your clothes and sandals." And Peter did so. "Wrap your cloak around you and follow me," the angel told him. ⁹Peter followed him out of the prison, but he had no idea that what the angel was doing was really happening; he thought he was seeing a vision. ¹⁰They passed the first and second guards and came to the iron gate leading to the city. It opened for them by itself, and they went through it. When they had walked the length of one street, suddenly the angel left him.

¹¹Then Peter came to himself and said, "Now I know without a doubt that the Lord sent his angel and rescued me from Herod's clutches and from everything the Jewish people were anticipating."

¹²When this had dawned on him, he went to the house of Mary the mother of John, also called Mark, where many people had gathered and were praying. ¹³Peter knocked at the outer entrance, and a servant girl named Rhoda came to answer the door. ¹⁴When she recognized Peter's voice, she was so overjoyed she ran back without opening it and exclaimed, "Peter is at the door!"

¹⁵"You're out of your mind," they told her. When she kept insisting that it was so, they said, "It must be his angel."

¹⁶But Peter kept on knocking, and when they opened the door and saw him, they were astonished. ¹⁷Peter motioned with his hand for them to be quiet and described how the Lord had brought him out of prison. "Tell James and the brothers about this," he said, and then he left for another place.

¹⁸In the morning, there was no small commotion among the soldiers as to what had become of Peter. ¹⁹After Herod had a thorough search made for him and did not find him, he cross-examined the guards and ordered that they be executed.

Herod's Death

Then Herod went from Judea to Caesarea and stayed there a while. ²⁰He had been quarreling with the people of Tyre

---

God's people at prayer
THE CHURCH'S SPEEDY ANSWER TO PRAYER

ACTS 12:1-17 After King Herod killed the apostle James, he then imprisoned Peter. Immediately, prayers for Peter were constantly being lifted to God by the church. As a result, the angel-led jailbreak seemed like an incredible dream to Peter. He didn't even believe it was happening until he was out in the street. When he arrived at the house where the people had gathered to pray, Rhoda came to answer the door but was so excited when she recognized his voice that she forgot to open the gate for him. Instead she ran to interrupt the prayer meeting, but her report was met with doubt. No one believed that God had already answered their prayer until they went to check for themselves and saw Peter standing there.

We must always leave the manner and timing of answers to our prayers in God's hands, including the possibility of God's swift action. If we always assume God will delay, then we've lost perspective. God is not on our timetable, and sometimes He decides to act even before we expect it! Isn't that good news?

and Sidon; they now joined together and sought an audience with him. Having secured the support of Blastus, a trusted personal servant of the king, they asked for peace, because they depended on the king's country for their food supply.

²¹On the appointed day Herod, wearing his royal robes, sat on his throne and delivered a public address to the people. ²²They shouted, "This is the voice of a god, not of a man." ²³Immediately, because Herod did not give praise to God, an angel of the Lord struck him down, and he was eaten by worms and died.

²⁴But the word of God continued to increase and spread.

²⁵When Barnabas and Saul had finished their mission, they returned from[a] Jerusalem, taking with them John, also called Mark.

Barnabas and Saul Sent Off

13 In the church at Antioch there were prophets and teachers: Barnabas, Simeon called Niger, Lucius of Cyrene, Manaen (who had been brought up with Herod the tetrarch) and Saul. ²While they were worshiping the Lord and

---

a 25 Some manuscripts to

GOING *deeper*

Changing the World With Our Prayers

READ AND CONSIDER: ACTS 13:1-3

"While they were worshiping the Lord and fasting, the Holy Spirit said, 'Set apart for me Barnabas and Saul for the work to which I have called them' " (Acts 13:2).

At a prayer meeting in the early church at Antioch, the Lord set forth a plan that changed the world (Acts 13:1-3). Members of that congregation recognized that change would involve two things: their response to the Holy Spirit that brought them to prayer and fasting, and their sending forth Barnabus and Saul in ministry.

And the world *was* changed. It is an observable fact that history turned on the basis of that prayer meeting in Antioch, Syria, nearly two thousand years ago. Any historical analysis shows that the flow of events that has shaped the world as we know it today—notably Western civilization—can be directly traced to that prayer meeting.

People who pray and understand who they have been made to be in Christ set the direction of history in their world—be it local, regional, national, or international. Most of the believing church today thinks of faith in Jesus Christ as an escape. But God says He wants us to be instruments of redemption through intercessory prayer, and ministry will flow out of that.

That's why it is so important to have prayer times with other believers. In fact, *it is impossible to grow and develop to your fullest potential independently of other believers.* It can't be "just me and God all the way." We have a mutual dependence upon one another because we are defined and refined within the context of a local body of believers. *Building a people to do God's work happens in the local church when we are connected to and grow with the rest of the body of Christ. It is within that context that we find who we are created to be and what we are created to do.*

One of the most important things about being in a spiritual family is finding power in prayer through unity. When believers are in unity, there is a dynamic that adds power to our prayers and the confidence that God will answer in power. Believers praying together can change the world.

fasting, the Holy Spirit said, "Set apart for me Barnabas and Saul for the work to which I have called them." [3]So after they had fasted and prayed, they placed their hands on them and sent them off.

On Cyprus

[4]The two of them, sent on their way by the Holy Spirit, went down to Seleucia and sailed from there to Cyprus. [5]When they arrived at Salamis, they proclaimed the word of God in the Jewish synagogues. John was with them as their helper.

[6]They traveled through the whole island until they came to Paphos. There they met a Jewish sorcerer and false prophet named Bar-Jesus, [7]who was an attendant of the proconsul, Sergius Paulus. The proconsul, an intelligent man, sent for Barnabas and Saul because he wanted to hear the word of God. [8]But Elymas the sorcerer (for that is what his name means) opposed them and tried to turn the proconsul from the faith. [9]Then Saul, who was also called Paul, filled with the Holy Spirit, looked straight at Elymas and said, [10]"You are a child of the devil and an enemy of everything that is right! You are full of all kinds of deceit and trickery. Will you never stop perverting the right ways of the Lord? [11]Now the hand of the Lord is against you. You are going to be blind, and for a time you will be unable to see the light of the sun."

Immediately mist and darkness came over him, and he groped about, seeking someone to lead him by the hand. [12]When the proconsul saw what had happened, he believed, for he was amazed at the teaching about the Lord.

In Pisidian Antioch

[13]From Paphos, Paul and his companions sailed to Perga in Pamphylia, where John left them to return to Jerusalem. [14]From Perga they went on to Pisidian Antioch. On the Sabbath they entered the synagogue and sat down. [15]After the reading from the Law and the Prophets, the synagogue rulers sent word to them, saying, "Brothers, if you have a message of encouragement for the people, please speak."

[16]Standing up, Paul motioned with his hand and said: "Men of Israel and you Gentiles who worship God, listen to me! [17]The God of the people of Israel chose our fathers; he made the people prosper during their stay in Egypt, with mighty power he led them out of that country, [18]he endured their conduct[a] for about forty years in the desert, [19]he overthrew seven nations in Canaan and gave their land to his people as their inheritance. [20]All this took about 450 years.

"After this, God gave them judges until the time of Samuel the prophet. [21]Then the people asked for a king, and he gave them Saul son of Kish, of the tribe of Benjamin, who ruled forty years. [22]After removing Saul, he made David their king. He testified concerning him: 'I have found David son of Jesse a man after my own heart; he will do everything I want him to do.'

[23]"From this man's descendants God has brought to Israel the Savior Jesus, as he promised. [24]Before the coming of Jesus, John preached repentance and baptism to all the people of Israel. [25]As John was completing his work, he said: 'Who do you think I am? I am not that one. No, but he is coming after me, whose sandals I am not worthy to untie.'

[26]"Brothers, children of Abraham, and you God-fearing Gentiles, it is to us that this message of salvation has been sent. [27]The people of Jerusalem and their rulers did not recognize Jesus, yet in condemning him they fulfilled the words of the prophets that are read every Sabbath. [28]Though they found no proper ground for a death sentence, they asked Pilate to have him executed. [29]When they had carried out all that was written about him, they took him down from the tree and

---

[a] 18 Some manuscripts *and cared for them*

laid him in a tomb. [30]But God raised him from the dead, [31]and for many days he was seen by those who had traveled with him from Galilee to Jerusalem. They are now his witnesses to our people.

[32]"We tell you the good news: What God promised our fathers [33]he has fulfilled for us, their children, by raising up Jesus. As it is written in the second Psalm:

> "'You are my Son;
>   today I have become your Father.'[a],[b]

[34]The fact that God raised him from the dead, never to decay, is stated in these words:

> "'I will give you the holy and sure
>   blessings promised to David.'[c]

[35]So it is stated elsewhere:

> "'You will not let your Holy One see
>   decay.'[d]

[36]"For when David had served God's purpose in his own generation, he fell asleep; he was buried with his fathers and his body decayed. [37]But the one whom God raised from the dead did not see decay.

[38]"Therefore, my brothers, I want you to know that through Jesus the forgiveness of sins is proclaimed to you. [39]Through him everyone who believes is justified from everything you could not be justified from by the law of Moses. [40]Take care that what the prophets have said does not happen to you:

> [41]"'Look, you scoffers,
>   wonder and perish,
> for I am going to do something in
>   your days
> that you would never believe,
>   even if someone told you.'[e]"

[42]As Paul and Barnabas were leaving the synagogue, the people invited them to speak further about these things on the next Sabbath. [43]When the congrega-

tion was dismissed, many of the Jews and devout converts to Judaism followed Paul and Barnabas, who talked with them and urged them to continue in the grace of God.

[44]On the next Sabbath almost the whole city gathered to hear the word of the Lord. [45]When the Jews saw the crowds, they were filled with jealousy and talked abusively against what Paul was saying.

[46]Then Paul and Barnabas answered them boldly: "We had to speak the word of God to you first. Since you reject it and do not consider yourselves worthy of eternal life, we now turn to the Gentiles. [47]For this is what the Lord has commanded us:

> "'I have made you[f] a light for the
>   Gentiles,
> that you[f] may bring salvation to the
>   ends of the earth.'[g]"

[48]When the Gentiles heard this, they were glad and honored the word of the Lord; and all who were appointed for eternal life believed.

[49]The word of the Lord spread through the whole region. [50]But the Jews incited the God-fearing women of high standing and the leading men of the city. They stirred up persecution against Paul and Barnabas, and expelled them from their region. [51]So they shook the dust from their feet in protest against them and went to Iconium. [52]And the disciples were filled with joy and with the Holy Spirit.

In Iconium

14 At Iconium Paul and Barnabas went as usual into the Jewish synagogue. There they spoke so effectively that a great number of Jews and Gentiles believed. [2]But the Jews who refused to believe stirred up the Gentiles and poisoned their minds against the brothers. [3]So Paul and Barnabas spent considerable time there, speaking boldly for the Lord, who confirmed the message of his grace by

---

[a] 33 Or have begotten you   [b] 33 Psalm 2:7   [c] 34 Isaiah 55:3   [d] 35 Psalm 16:10   [e] 41 Hab. 1:5   [f] 47 The Greek is singular.
[g] 47 Isaiah 49:6

enabling them to do miraculous signs and wonders. [4]The people of the city were divided; some sided with the Jews, others with the apostles. [5]There was a plot afoot among the Gentiles and Jews, together with their leaders, to mistreat them and stone them. [6]But they found out about it and fled to the Lycaonian cities of Lystra and Derbe and to the surrounding country, [7]where they continued to preach the good news.

In Lystra and Derbe

[8]In Lystra there sat a man crippled in his feet, who was lame from birth and had never walked. [9]He listened to Paul as he was speaking. Paul looked directly at him, saw that he had faith to be healed [10]and called out, "Stand up on your feet!" At that, the man jumped up and began to walk.

[11]When the crowd saw what Paul had done, they shouted in the Lycaonian language, "The gods have come down to us in human form!" [12]Barnabas they called Zeus, and Paul they called Hermes because he was the chief speaker. [13]The priest of Zeus, whose temple was just outside the city, brought bulls and wreaths to the city gates because he and the crowd wanted to offer sacrifices to them.

[14]But when the apostles Barnabas and Paul heard of this, they tore their clothes and rushed out into the crowd, shouting: [15]"Men, why are you doing this? We too are only men, human like you. We are bringing you good news, telling you to turn from these worthless things to the living God, who made heaven and earth and sea and everything in them. [16]In the past, he let all nations go their own way. [17]Yet he has not left himself without testimony: He has shown kindness by giving you rain from heaven and crops in their seasons; he provides you with plenty of food and fills your hearts with joy." [18]Even with these words, they had difficulty keeping the crowd from sacrificing to them.

[19]Then some Jews came from Antioch and Iconium and won the crowd over. They stoned Paul and dragged him outside the city, thinking he was dead. [20]But after the disciples had gathered around him, he got up and went back into the city. The next day he and Barnabas left for Derbe.

The Return to Antioch in Syria

[21]They preached the good news in that city and won a large number of disciples. Then they returned to Lystra, Iconium and Antioch, [22]strengthening the disciples and encouraging them to remain true to the faith. "We must go through many hardships to enter the kingdom of God," they said. [23]Paul and Barnabas appointed elders[a] for them in each church and, with prayer and fasting, committed them to the Lord, in whom they had put their trust. [24]After going through Pisidia, they came into Pamphylia, [25]and when they had preached the word in Perga, they went down to Attalia.

[26]From Attalia they sailed back to Antioch, where they had been committed to the grace of God for the work they had now completed. [27]On arriving there, they gathered the church together and reported all that God had done through them and how he had opened the door of faith to the Gentiles. [28]And they stayed there a long time with the disciples.

The Council at Jerusalem

15 Some men came down from Judea to Antioch and were teaching the brothers: "Unless you are circumcised, according to the custom taught by Moses, you cannot be saved." [2]This brought Paul and Barnabas into sharp dispute and debate with them. So Paul and Barnabas were appointed, along with some other believers, to go up to Jerusalem to see the apostles and elders about this question. [3]The church sent them on their way, and as they traveled through Phoenicia and Samaria, they told how the Gentiles

---

[a] 23 Or Barnabas ordained elders; or Barnabas had elders elected

When We Face Decisions and Difficulties

READ AND CONSIDER: ACTS 14:21-28

"Paul and Barnabas appointed elders for them in each church and, with prayer and fasting, committed them to the Lord, in whom they had put their trust" (Acts 14:23).

Whenever God said something important to His people, or whenever an important decision had to be made, prayer, often accompanied by fasting, preceded it.

When the apostles had to choose a replacement for Judas, they gathered all the believers and "joined together constantly in prayer" (1:14).

When the believers in the church in Jerusalem began to face severe persecution, they prayed for boldness, raising "their voices together in prayer" (4:24).

When it became apparent to the Christians who had converted from Judaism that even Samaritans could be saved, they sent Peter and John to pray for these new followers of Jesus (8:15).

When Saul (Paul) had been struck blind, he fasted and prayed for three days, waiting to see what God would do (9:9).

When God wanted to send His message beyond the borders of Jerusalem, Judea, and Samaria and to "the ends of the earth" (1:8), He sent His message to Peter as he was praying (10:9) and to Cornelius as he was praying (10:30).

When Peter was imprisoned, the church gathered to pray for him (12:12).

God set apart Saul (Paul) and Barnabas while the church at Antioch was worshiping and fasting (13:2).

It comes as no surprise then, that when Paul and Barnabas had to help organize the leadership in the churches they planted, they did so only after prayer and fasting (14:23). They couldn't stay in each church; they had to move on. For a church to continue to thrive, solid Spirit-filled leaders were needed. So Paul and Barnabas sought the Lord and waited for His guidance. As a result the churches grew even after Paul and Barnabas left.

When we face big decisions, difficult circumstances, or hard questions, we should always turn to God first and pray. When we combine prayer with fasting, our prayers gain new power. We are trusting God and only God to be our nourishment and fill our hunger with His Spirit. It is especially powerful when we do that in unity with other believers. So when seeking the Lord's guidance, whether for issues regarding your personal needs, or for the needs of others, in your family, community, nation, or world, don't take a step without seeking God in prayer first.

---

had been converted. This news made all the brothers very glad. 4When they came to Jerusalem, they were welcomed by the church and the apostles and elders, to whom they reported everything God had done through them.

5Then some of the believers who belonged to the party of the Pharisees stood up and said, "The Gentiles must be circumcised and required to obey the law of Moses."

6The apostles and elders met to consider

this question. [7]After much discussion, Peter got up and addressed them: "Brothers, you know that some time ago God made a choice among you that the Gentiles might hear from my lips the message of the gospel and believe. [8]God, who knows the heart, showed that he accepted them by giving the Holy Spirit to them, just as he did to us. [9]He made no distinction between us and them, for he purified their hearts by faith. [10]Now then, why do you try to test God by putting on the necks of the disciples a yoke that neither we nor our fathers have been able to bear? [11]No! We believe it is through the grace of our Lord Jesus that we are saved, just as they are."

[12]The whole assembly became silent as they listened to Barnabas and Paul telling about the miraculous signs and wonders God had done among the Gentiles through them. [13]When they finished, James spoke up: "Brothers, listen to me. [14]Simon[a] has described to us how God at first showed his concern by taking from the Gentiles a people for himself. [15]The words of the prophets are in agreement with this, as it is written:

[16]" 'After this I will return
    and rebuild David's fallen tent.
  Its ruins I will rebuild,
    and I will restore it,
[17]that the remnant of men may seek the
    Lord,
    and all the Gentiles who bear my
      name,
  says the Lord, who does these things'[b]
[18]   that have been known for ages.[c]

[19]"It is my judgment, therefore, that we should not make it difficult for the Gentiles who are turning to God. [20]Instead we should write to them, telling them to abstain from food polluted by idols, from sexual immorality, from the meat of strangled animals and from blood. [21]For Moses has been preached in every city

from the earliest times and is read in the synagogues on every Sabbath."

The Council's Letter to Gentile Believers

[22]Then the apostles and elders, with the whole church, decided to choose some of their own men and send them to Antioch with Paul and Barnabas. They chose Judas (called Barsabbas) and Silas, two men who were leaders among the brothers. [23]With them they sent the following letter:

The apostles and elders, your brothers,

To the Gentile believers in Antioch, Syria and Cilicia:

Greetings.

[24]We have heard that some went out from us without our authorization and disturbed you, troubling your minds by what they said. [25]So we all agreed to choose some men and send them to you with our dear friends Barnabas and Paul— [26]men who have risked their lives for the name of our Lord Jesus Christ. [27]Therefore we are sending Judas and Silas to confirm by word of mouth what we are writing. [28]It seemed good to the Holy Spirit and to us not to burden you with anything beyond the following requirements: [29]You are to abstain from food sacrificed to idols, from blood, from the meat of strangled animals and from sexual immorality. You will do well to avoid these things.

Farewell.

[30]The men were sent off and went down to Antioch, where they gathered the church together and delivered the letter. [31]The people read it and were glad for its encouraging message. [32]Judas and Silas,

---

[a] *14* Greek *Simeon*, a variant of *Simon*; that is, Peter   [b] *17* Amos 9:11,12   [c] *17,18* Some manuscripts *things'— / [18]known to the Lord for ages is his work*

who themselves were prophets, said much to encourage and strengthen the brothers. [33]After spending some time there, they were sent off by the brothers with the blessing of peace to return to those who had sent them.[a] [35]But Paul and Barnabas remained in Antioch, where they and many others taught and preached the word of the Lord.

Disagreement Between Paul and Barnabas

[36]Some time later Paul said to Barnabas, "Let us go back and visit the brothers in all the towns where we preached the word of the Lord and see how they are doing." [37]Barnabas wanted to take John, also called Mark, with them, [38]but Paul did not think it wise to take him, because he had deserted them in Pamphylia and had not continued with them in the work. [39]They had such a sharp disagreement that they parted company. Barnabas took Mark and sailed for Cyprus, [40]but Paul chose Silas and left, commended by the brothers to the grace of the Lord. [41]He went through Syria and Cilicia, strengthening the churches.

Timothy Joins Paul and Silas

16 He came to Derbe and then to Lystra, where a disciple named Timothy lived, whose mother was a Jewess and a believer, but whose father was a Greek. [2]The brothers at Lystra and Iconium spoke well of him. [3]Paul wanted to take him along on the journey, so he circumcised him because of the Jews who lived in that area, for they all knew that his father was a Greek. [4]As they traveled from town to town, they delivered the decisions reached by the apostles and elders in Jerusalem for the people to obey. [5]So the churches were strengthened in the faith and grew daily in numbers.

Paul's Vision of the Man of Macedonia

[6]Paul and his companions traveled throughout the region of Phrygia and Ga-

latia, having been kept by the Holy Spirit from preaching the word in the province of Asia. [7]When they came to the border of Mysia, they tried to enter Bithynia, but the Spirit of Jesus would not allow them to. [8]So they passed by Mysia and went down to Troas. [9]During the night Paul had a vision of a man of Macedonia standing and begging him, "Come over to Macedonia and help us." [10]After Paul had seen the vision, we got ready at once to leave for Macedonia, concluding that God had called us to preach the gospel to them.

Lydia's Conversion in Philippi

[11]From Troas we put out to sea and sailed straight for Samothrace, and the next day on to Neapolis. [12]From there we traveled to Philippi, a Roman colony and the leading city of that district of Macedonia. And we stayed there several days.

[13]On the Sabbath we went outside the city gate to the river, where we expected to find a place of prayer. We sat down and began to speak to the women who had gathered there. [14]One of those listening was a woman named Lydia, a dealer in purple cloth from the city of Thyatira, who was a worshiper of God. The Lord opened her heart to respond to Paul's message. [15]When she and the members of her household were baptized, she invited us to her home. "If you consider me a believer in the Lord," she said, "come and stay at my house." And she persuaded us.

Paul and Silas in Prison

[16]Once when we were going to the place of prayer, we were met by a slave girl who had a spirit by which she predicted the future. She earned a great deal of money for her owners by fortune-telling. [17]This girl followed Paul and the rest of us, shouting, "These men are servants of the Most High God, who are telling you the way to be saved." [18]She kept this up for many days. Finally Paul became so troubled that he turned around and said to the spirit, "In the name of Jesus Christ

I command you to come out of her!" At that moment the spirit left her.

¹⁹When the owners of the slave girl realized that their hope of making money was gone, they seized Paul and Silas and dragged them into the marketplace to face the authorities. ²⁰They brought them before the magistrates and said, "These men are Jews, and are throwing our city into an uproar ²¹by advocating customs unlawful for us Romans to accept or practice."

²²The crowd joined in the attack against Paul and Silas, and the magistrates ordered them to be stripped and beaten. ²³After they had been severely flogged, they were thrown into prison, and the jailer was commanded to guard them carefully. ²⁴Upon receiving such orders, he put them in the inner cell and fastened their feet in the stocks.

²⁵About midnight Paul and Silas were praying and singing hymns to God, and the other prisoners were listening to them. ²⁶Suddenly there was such a violent earthquake that the foundations of the prison were shaken. At once all the prison doors flew open, and everybody's chains came loose. ²⁷The jailer woke up, and when he saw the prison doors open, he drew his sword and was about to kill himself because he thought the prisoners had escaped. ²⁸But Paul shouted, "Don't harm yourself! We are all here!"

²⁹The jailer called for lights, rushed in and fell trembling before Paul and Silas. ³⁰He then brought them out and asked, "Sirs, what must I do to be saved?"

³¹They replied, "Believe in the Lord Jesus, and you will be saved—you and your household." ³²Then they spoke the word of the Lord to him and to all the others in his house. ³³At that hour of the night the jailer took them and washed their wounds; then immediately he and all his family were baptized. ³⁴The jailer brought them into his house and set a meal before them; he was filled with joy because he had come to believe in God—he and his whole family.

³⁵When it was daylight, the magistrates sent their officers to the jailer with the order: "Release those men." ³⁶The jailer told Paul, "The magistrates have ordered that you and Silas be released. Now you can leave. Go in peace."

³⁷But Paul said to the officers: "They beat us publicly without a trial, even though we are Roman citizens, and threw us into prison. And now do they want to

God's people at prayer
PAUL AND SILAS PRAY AND PRAISE IN PRISON

ACTS 16:16-34 In spite of the terrible beatings and being bound and imprisoned, Paul and Silas were "praying and singing hymns to God" at midnight in the jail (16:25). Their movements may have been limited, but they were exercising the greatest freedom of all—to worship. And they had a captive audience of fellow prisoners.

When an earthquake interrupted their prayer and praise service, it miraculously opened the prison doors. The prisoners, however, were more interested in Paul's message than in escaping, and that got the jailer's attention! Whatever Paul and Silas had, he wanted. That night he and his family received Jesus as Lord.

We can never underestimate the power of praising God—especially when we are going through tough times. It shakes up things in us and around us. If prayer is communicating with God, praise and worship are the purist forms of communication because they focus our attention entirely upon God. Every time we do that, we draw closer to God, and when we do, things change.

get rid of us quietly? No! Let them come themselves and escort us out."

38 The officers reported this to the magistrates, and when they heard that Paul and Silas were Roman citizens, they were alarmed. 39 They came to appease them and escorted them from the prison, requesting them to leave the city. 40 After Paul and Silas came out of the prison, they went to Lydia's house, where they met with the brothers and encouraged them. Then they left.

In Thessalonica

17 When they had passed through Amphipolis and Apollonia, they came to Thessalonica, where there was a Jewish synagogue. 2 As his custom was, Paul went into the synagogue, and on three Sabbath days he reasoned with them from the Scriptures, 3 explaining and proving that the Christ[a] had to suffer and rise from the dead. "This Jesus I am proclaiming to you is the Christ,[a]" he said. 4 Some of the Jews were persuaded and joined Paul and Silas, as did a large number of God-fearing Greeks and not a few prominent women.

5 But the Jews were jealous; so they rounded up some bad characters from the marketplace, formed a mob and started a riot in the city. They rushed to Jason's house in search of Paul and Silas in order to bring them out to the crowd.[b] 6 But when they did not find them, they dragged Jason and some other brothers before the city officials, shouting: "These men who have caused trouble all over the world have now come here, 7 and Jason has welcomed them into his house. They are all defying Caesar's decrees, saying that there is another king, one called Jesus." 8 When they heard this, the crowd and the city officials were thrown into turmoil. 9 Then they made Jason and the others post bond and let them go.

In Berea

10 As soon as it was night, the brothers sent Paul and Silas away to Berea. On arriving there, they went to the Jewish synagogue. 11 Now the Bereans were of more noble character than the Thessalonians, for they received the message with great eagerness and examined the Scriptures every day to see if what Paul said was true. 12 Many of the Jews believed, as did also a number of prominent Greek women and many Greek men.

13 When the Jews in Thessalonica learned that Paul was preaching the word of God at Berea, they went there too, agitating the crowds and stirring them up. 14 The brothers immediately sent Paul to the coast, but Silas and Timothy stayed at Berea. 15 The men who escorted Paul brought him to Athens and then left with instructions for Silas and Timothy to join him as soon as possible.

In Athens

16 While Paul was waiting for them in Athens, he was greatly distressed to see that the city was full of idols. 17 So he reasoned in the synagogue with the Jews and the God-fearing Greeks, as well as in the marketplace day by day with those who happened to be there. 18 A group of Epicurean and Stoic philosophers began to dispute with him. Some of them asked, "What is this babbler trying to say?" Others remarked, "He seems to be advocating foreign gods." They said this because Paul was preaching the good news about Jesus and the resurrection. 19 Then they took him and brought him to a meeting of the Areopagus, where they said to him, "May we know what this new teaching is that you are presenting? 20 You are bringing some strange ideas to our ears, and we want to know what they mean." 21 (All the Athenians and the foreigners who lived there spent their time doing nothing but talking about and listening to the latest ideas.)

22 Paul then stood up in the meeting of the Areopagus and said: "Men of Athens! I see that in every way you are very religious. 23 For as I walked around and looked

---

a 3 Or Messiah   b 5 Or the assembly of the people

carefully at your objects of worship, I even found an altar with this inscription: TO AN UNKNOWN GOD. Now what you worship as something unknown I am going to proclaim to you.

24 "The God who made the world and everything in it is the Lord of heaven and earth and does not live in temples built by hands. 25 And he is not served by human hands, as if he needed anything, because he himself gives all men life and breath and everything else. 26 From one man he made every nation of men, that they should inhabit the whole earth; and he determined the times set for them and the exact places where they should live. 27 God did this so that men would seek him and perhaps reach out for him and find him, though he is not far from each one of us. 28 'For in him we live and move and have our being.' As some of your own poets have said, 'We are his offspring.'

Praying Acts 17:26

Thank You, Lord, for making us to be brothers and sisters in Christ with all believers, regardless of race, culture, or nationality.

---

29 "Therefore since we are God's offspring, we should not think that the divine being is like gold or silver or stone—an image made by man's design and skill. 30 In the past God overlooked such ignorance, but now he commands all people everywhere to repent. 31 For he has set a day when he will judge the world with justice by the man he has appointed. He has given proof of this to all men by raising him from the dead."

32 When they heard about the resurrection of the dead, some of them sneered, but others said, "We want to hear you again on this subject." 33 At that, Paul left the Council. 34 A few men became followers of Paul and believed. Among them was Dionysius, a member of the Areopa-

gus, also a woman named Damaris, and a number of others.

In Corinth

18 After this, Paul left Athens and went to Corinth. 2 There he met a Jew named Aquila, a native of Pontus, who had recently come from Italy with his wife Priscilla, because Claudius had ordered all the Jews to leave Rome. Paul went to see them, 3 and because he was a tentmaker as they were, he stayed and worked with them. 4 Every Sabbath he reasoned in the synagogue, trying to persuade Jews and Greeks.

5 When Silas and Timothy came from Macedonia, Paul devoted himself exclusively to preaching, testifying to the Jews that Jesus was the Christ.[a] 6 But when the Jews opposed Paul and became abusive, he shook out his clothes in protest and said to them, "Your blood be on your own heads! I am clear of my responsibility. From now on I will go to the Gentiles."

7 Then Paul left the synagogue and went next door to the house of Titius Justus, a worshiper of God. 8 Crispus, the synagogue ruler, and his entire household believed in the Lord; and many of the Corinthians who heard him believed and were baptized.

9 One night the Lord spoke to Paul in a vision: "Do not be afraid; keep on speaking, do not be silent. 10 For I am with you, and no one is going to attack and harm you, because I have many people in this city." 11 So Paul stayed for a year and a half, teaching them the word of God.

Praying Acts 18:9-10

Lord, enable me to speak boldly about You and not be silenced by the fear of man.

---

12 While Gallio was proconsul of Achaia, the Jews made a united attack on Paul and brought him into court. 13 "This man," they charged, "is persuading the people to worship God in ways contrary to the law."

The Tests God Gives Us

God puts us through different kinds of tests, but He gives us three major tests that we will all have to take at one time or another. Can you think of times in your life when you have been tested in any of these three ways?

Test One: God Tests Our Heart

"I know, my God, that you test the heart and are pleased with integrity" (1 Chronicles 29:17). The famous "fall" that pride always goes before is something God allows in order to purify us from our inclination to be full of ourselves. Just when we have enough arrogance to think we can live one moment without Him, God searches our heart for humility. If found wanting, He allows us to hit rock bottom and gain a new perspective. Looking up! And this is exactly what we need if we've been looking down for too long. God doesn't give this kind of test to torture us. He does it so our hearts can be purified and we can see *Him*. "Blessed are the pure in heart, for they will see God" (Matthew 5:8).

Test Two: God Tests Our Faith

"Consider it pure joy, my brothers, whenever you face trials of many kinds, because you know that the testing of your faith develops perseverance" (James 1:2-3). One of the most profound times our faith is tested is when we are struggling with our finances. Few things are more upsetting than the prospect of losing our home, not having enough food, or not being able to pay our bills. This is especially frightening when it involves a family with dependent children. But learning to walk in the provision God gives us for the day in which we find ourselves opens our eyes to see how we must depend on Him for everything. It forces us to live in God's presence in a deeper way as we look to Him to work daily miracles on our behalf.

When our faith is tested during these times, our response to it is revealing. Do we trust Him to provide, or do we get angry and take it out on others? Do we view this as a time that God wants us to draw closer to Him, or do we see it as the termination of our future? Do we understand that God is testing us in order to prepare us for what He is going to do in our lives, or do we believe He is forsaking us? Will we lose patience in this time, or will we grow in faith? The answers we give to these questions are the keys to passing the test.

Test Three: God Tests Our Obedience

" 'In this way I will test them and see whether they will follow my instructions' " (Exodus 16:4). My own children have always determined the amount of privileges they enjoyed by how obedient they were to the rules we laid down in our home. If they didn't obey the rules, we didn't extend the rewards. Of course, we were committed to feed, clothe, educate, shelter, and love them no matter what they did. But the extra blessings they enjoyed over and above those things depended on their obedience. God does the same with us. He loves us no matter what, but there are certain blessings we forfeit if we don't obey Him.

A time of testing is God's way of preparing you for the great things He has ahead. Ask Him to help you learn each lesson well.

For the next "From Stormie's Heart" article, go to page 1369.

14Just as Paul was about to speak, Gallio said to the Jews, "If you Jews were making a complaint about some misdemeanor or serious crime, it would be reasonable for me to listen to you. 15But since it involves questions about words and names and your own law—settle the matter yourselves. I will not be a judge of such things." 16So he had them ejected from the court. 17Then they all turned on Sosthenes the synagogue ruler and beat him in front of the court. But Gallio showed no concern whatever.

Priscilla, Aquila and Apollos

18Paul stayed on in Corinth for some time. Then he left the brothers and sailed for Syria, accompanied by Priscilla and Aquila. Before he sailed, he had his hair cut off at Cenchrea because of a vow he had taken. 19They arrived at Ephesus, where Paul left Priscilla and Aquila. He himself went into the synagogue and reasoned with the Jews. 20When they asked him to spend more time with them, he declined. 21But as he left, he promised, "I will come back if it is God's will." Then he set sail from Ephesus. 22When he landed at Caesarea, he went up and greeted the church and then went down to Antioch.

23After spending some time in Antioch, Paul set out from there and traveled from place to place throughout the region of Galatia and Phrygia, strengthening all the disciples.

24Meanwhile a Jew named Apollos, a native of Alexandria, came to Ephesus. He was a learned man, with a thorough knowledge of the Scriptures. 25He had been instructed in the way of the Lord, and he spoke with great fervor[a] and taught about Jesus accurately, though he knew only the baptism of John. 26He began to speak boldly in the synagogue. When Priscilla and Aquila heard him, they invited him to their home and explained to him the way of God more adequately.

27When Apollos wanted to go to Achaia, the brothers encouraged him and wrote to the disciples there to welcome him. On arriving, he was a great help to those who by grace had believed. 28For he vigorously refuted the Jews in public debate, proving from the Scriptures that Jesus was the Christ.

Paul in Ephesus

19 While Apollos was at Corinth, Paul took the road through the interior and arrived at Ephesus. There he found some disciples 2and asked them, "Did you receive the Holy Spirit when[b] you believed?"

They answered, "No, we have not even heard that there is a Holy Spirit."

3So Paul asked, "Then what baptism did you receive?"

"John's baptism," they replied.

4Paul said, "John's baptism was a baptism of repentance. He told the people to believe in the one coming after him, that is, in Jesus." 5On hearing this, they were baptized into[c] the name of the Lord Jesus. 6When Paul placed his hands on them, the Holy Spirit came on them, and they spoke in tongues[d] and prophesied. 7There were about twelve men in all.

8Paul entered the synagogue and spoke boldly there for three months, arguing persuasively about the kingdom of God. 9But some of them became obstinate; they refused to believe and publicly maligned the Way. So Paul left them. He took the disciples with him and had discussions daily in the lecture hall of Tyrannus. 10This went on for two years, so that all the Jews and Greeks who lived in the province of Asia heard the word of the Lord.

11God did extraordinary miracles through Paul, 12so that even handkerchiefs and aprons that had touched him were taken to the sick, and their illnesses were cured and the evil spirits left them.

13Some Jews who went around driving out evil spirits tried to invoke the name

---

a 25 Or with fervor in the Spirit   b 2 Or after   c 5 Or in   d 6 Or other languages of the Lord Jesus over those who were demon-possessed. They would say, "In the name of Jesus, whom Paul preaches, I command you to come out." [14]Seven sons of Sceva, a Jewish chief priest, were doing this. [15]⌊One day⌋ the evil spirit answered them, "Jesus I know, and I know about Paul, but who are you?" [16]Then the man who had the evil spirit jumped on them and overpowered them all. He gave them such a beating that they ran out of the house naked and bleeding.

[17]When this became known to the Jews and Greeks living in Ephesus, they were all seized with fear, and the name of the Lord Jesus was held in high honor. [18]Many of those who believed now came and openly confessed their evil deeds. [19]A number who had practiced sorcery brought their scrolls together and burned them publicly. When they calculated the value of the scrolls, the total came to fifty thousand drachmas.[a] [20]In this way the word of the Lord spread widely and grew in power.

Praying Acts 19:19

Heavenly Father, help me to destroy anything in my life that is not of You.

[21]After all this had happened, Paul decided to go to Jerusalem, passing through Macedonia and Achaia. "After I have been there," he said, "I must visit Rome also." [22]He sent two of his helpers, Timothy and Erastus, to Macedonia, while he stayed in the province of Asia a little longer.

The Riot in Ephesus

[23]About that time there arose a great disturbance about the Way. [24]A silversmith named Demetrius, who made silver shrines of Artemis, brought in no little business for the craftsmen. [25]He called them together, along with the workmen in related trades, and said: "Men, you know we receive a good income from this business. [26]And you see and hear how this fellow Paul has convinced and led astray large numbers of people here in Ephesus and in practically the whole province of Asia. He says that man-made gods are no gods at all. [27]There is danger not only that our trade will lose its good name, but also that the temple of the great goddess Artemis will be discredited, and the goddess herself, who is worshiped throughout the province of Asia and the world, will be robbed of her divine majesty."

[28]When they heard this, they were furious and began shouting: "Great is Artemis of the Ephesians!" [29]Soon the whole city was in an uproar. The people seized Gaius and Aristarchus, Paul's traveling companions from Macedonia, and rushed as one man into the theater. [30]Paul wanted to appear before the crowd, but the disciples would not let him. [31]Even some of the officials of the province, friends of Paul, sent him a message begging him not to venture into the theater.

[32]The assembly was in confusion: Some were shouting one thing, some another. Most of the people did not even know why they were there. [33]The Jews pushed Alexander to the front, and some of the crowd shouted instructions to him. He motioned for silence in order to make a defense before the people. [34]But when they realized he was a Jew, they all shouted in unison for about two hours: "Great is Artemis of the Ephesians!"

[35]The city clerk quieted the crowd and said: "Men of Ephesus, doesn't all the world know that the city of Ephesus is the guardian of the temple of the great Artemis and of her image, which fell from heaven? [36]Therefore, since these facts are undeniable, you ought to be quiet and not do anything rash. [37]You have brought these men here, though they have neither robbed temples nor blasphemed our goddess. [38]If, then, Demetrius and his fellow craftsmen have a grievance against anybody, the courts are open and there are proconsuls. They can press charges.

---

[a] *19* A drachma was a silver coin worth about a day's wages.

39If there is anything further you want to bring up, it must be settled in a legal assembly. 40As it is, we are in danger of being charged with rioting because of today's events. In that case we would not be able to account for this commotion, since there is no reason for it." 41After he had said this, he dismissed the assembly.

Through Macedonia and Greece

20 When the uproar had ended, Paul sent for the disciples and, after encouraging them, said good-by and set out for Macedonia. 2He traveled through that area, speaking many words of encouragement to the people, and finally arrived in Greece, 3where he stayed three months. Because the Jews made a plot against him just as he was about to sail for Syria, he decided to go back through Macedonia. 4He was accompanied by Sopater son of Pyrrhus from Berea, Aristarchus and Secundus from Thessalonica, Gaius from Derbe, Timothy also, and Tychicus and Trophimus from the province of Asia. 5These men went on ahead and waited for us at Troas. 6But we sailed from Philippi after the Feast of Unleavened Bread, and five days later joined the others at Troas, where we stayed seven days.

Eutychus Raised From the Dead at Troas

7On the first day of the week we came together to break bread. Paul spoke to the people and, because he intended to leave the next day, kept on talking until midnight. 8There were many lamps in the upstairs room where we were meeting. 9Seated in a window was a young man named Eutychus, who was sinking into a deep sleep as Paul talked on and on. When he was sound asleep, he fell to the ground from the third story and was picked up dead. 10Paul went down, threw himself on the young man and put his arms around him. "Don't be alarmed," he said. "He's alive!" 11Then he went upstairs again and broke bread and ate. After talking until daylight, he left. 12The peo-

ple took the young man home alive and were greatly comforted.

Paul's Farewell to the Ephesian Elders

13We went on ahead to the ship and sailed for Assos, where we were going to take Paul aboard. He had made this arrangement because he was going there on foot. 14When he met us at Assos, we took him aboard and went on to Mitylene. 15The next day we set sail from there and arrived off Kios. The day after that we crossed over to Samos, and on the following day arrived at Miletus. 16Paul had decided to sail past Ephesus to avoid spending time in the province of Asia, for he was in a hurry to reach Jerusalem, if possible, by the day of Pentecost.

17From Miletus, Paul sent to Ephesus for the elders of the church. 18When they arrived, he said to them: "You know how I lived the whole time I was with you, from the first day I came into the province of Asia. 19I served the Lord with great humility and with tears, although I was severely tested by the plots of the Jews. 20You know that I have not hesitated to preach anything that would be helpful to you but have taught you publicly and from house to house. 21I have declared to both Jews and Greeks that they must turn to God in repentance and have faith in our Lord Jesus.

22"And now, compelled by the Spirit, I am going to Jerusalem, not knowing what will happen to me there. 23I only know that in every city the Holy Spirit warns me that prison and hardships are facing me. 24However, I consider my life worth nothing to me, if only I may finish the race and complete the task the Lord Jesus has given me—the task of testifying to the gospel of God's grace.

25"Now I know that none of you among whom I have gone about preaching the kingdom will ever see me again. 26Therefore, I declare to you today that I am innocent of the blood of all men. 27For I have not hesitated to proclaim to you the whole will of God. 28Keep watch over yourselves and all the flock of which the Holy Spirit has made you overseers.[a] Be shepherds of the church of God,[b] which he bought with his own blood. 29I know that after I leave, savage wolves will come in among you and will not spare the flock. 30Even from your own number men will arise and distort the truth in order to draw away disciples after them. 31So be on your guard! Remember that for three years I never stopped warning each of you night and day with tears.

On to Jerusalem

21 After we had torn ourselves away from them, we put out to sea and sailed straight to Cos. The next day we went to Rhodes and from there to Patara. 2We found a ship crossing over to Phoenicia, went on board and set sail. 3After sighting Cyprus and passing to the south of it, we sailed on to Syria. We landed at Tyre, where our ship was to unload its cargo. 4Finding the disciples there, we stayed with them seven days. Through

---

God's people at prayer
PAUL'S PRAYER-FILLED GOODBYE

ACTS 20:32-36 Paul was in a hurry to get to Jerusalem, but he also wanted to have a last encounter with the leaders and elders of Ephesus who would continue to watch over the church. He had instructions for them, but he also desired to pray with them. That intimate time of prayer as the group knelt together in God's presence was not simply the last item on the agenda but a moment of deep unity, love, and encouragement for God's servants. Everyone needed strength for the days that were before them.

We should never pass up the opportunity to pray with people we are with before we leave them or they leave us. We never know what protection our prayers might afford each other, or how they will empower us for what is ahead.

32"Now I commit you to God and to the word of his grace, which can build you up and give you an inheritance among all those who are sanctified. 33I have not coveted anyone's silver or gold or clothing. 34You yourselves know that these hands of mine have supplied my own needs and the needs of my companions. 35In everything I did, I showed you that by this kind of hard work we must help the weak, remembering the words the Lord Jesus himself said: 'It is more blessed to give than to receive.'"

36When he had said this, he knelt down with all of them and prayed. 37They all wept as they embraced him and kissed him. 38What grieved them most was his statement that they would never see his face again. Then they accompanied him to the ship.

the Spirit they urged Paul not to go on to Jerusalem. 5But when our time was up, we left and continued on our way. All the disciples and their wives and children accompanied us out of the city, and there on the beach we knelt to pray. 6After saying good-by to each other, we went aboard the ship, and they returned home.

7We continued our voyage from Tyre and landed at Ptolemais, where we greeted the brothers and stayed with them for a day. 8Leaving the next day, we reached Caesarea and stayed at the house of Philip the evangelist, one of the Seven. 9He had four unmarried daughters who prophesied.

10After we had been there a number of days, a prophet named Agabus came down from Judea. 11Coming over to us, he took Paul's belt, tied his own hands

---

a 28 Traditionally bishops   b 28 Many manuscripts of the Lord

A Parting Prayer

GOING deeper

READ AND CONSIDER: ACTS 21:1-16

"But when our time was up, we left and continued on our way. All the disciples and their wives and children accompanied us out of the city, and there on the beach we knelt to pray" **(Acts 21:5).**

Paul and some believers in Tyre had a chance to meet up as Paul was passing through and have fellowship for a week. The Holy Spirit allowed these Christians to foresee the persecution Paul would endure in Jerusalem (his destination), and they urged him not to go there. They were worried about his safety and rightly wanted to keep him from harm. But Paul knew where the Lord wanted him to go, and he would not be swayed from his purpose. As he departed, all of the disciples and their families accompanied him to the ship, where they knelt on the beach to pray before saying goodbye.

What better way to part from someone than to kneel in prayer? These friends knew the dangers that lay ahead for Paul—and perhaps eventually for them as persecution clouds began to build. Perhaps they prayed for safety, but they surely also prayed for guidance and boldness as they continued to work for the Lord, spreading His message throughout the land. Perhaps they prayed that God would bring them back together in fellowship again. And we know that they prayed for each other when they were apart—Paul says so in his letters.

We should remember to pray for people whenever we part from them or they part from us. We can pray for our spouse as he or she heads off to work. We can pray for our children as they go to school. We can pray for our friends as they go about their daily business. We can pray for our guests as they leave our home. Prayer is the most powerful tool we have as believers—our direct link with God. Let's not neglect it as we part from others.

and feet with it and said, "The Holy Spirit says, 'In this way the Jews of Jerusalem will bind the owner of this belt and will hand him over to the Gentiles.'"

¹²When we heard this, we and the people there pleaded with Paul not to go up to Jerusalem. ¹³Then Paul answered, "Why are you weeping and breaking my heart? I am ready not only to be bound, but also to die in Jerusalem for the name of the Lord Jesus." ¹⁴When he would not be dissuaded, we gave up and said, "The Lord's will be done."

¹⁵After this, we got ready and went up to Jerusalem. ¹⁶Some of the disciples from Caesarea accompanied us and brought us to the home of Mnason, where we were to stay. He was a man from Cyprus and one of the early disciples.

Paul's Arrival at Jerusalem

¹⁷When we arrived at Jerusalem, the brothers received us warmly. ¹⁸The next day Paul and the rest of us went to see James, and all the elders were present. ¹⁹Paul greeted them and reported in detail what God had done among the Gentiles through his ministry.

²⁰When they heard this, they praised God. Then they said to Paul: "You see, brother, how many thousands of Jews have believed, and all of them are zealous for the law. ²¹They have been informed that you teach all the Jews who live among the Gentiles to turn away from Moses, telling them not to circumcise their children or live according to our customs. ²²What shall we do? They will certainly hear that you have come, ²³so

do what we tell you. There are four men with us who have made a vow. 24Take these men, join in their purification rites and pay their expenses, so that they can have their heads shaved. Then everybody will know there is no truth in these reports about you, but that you yourself are living in obedience to the law. 25As for the Gentile believers, we have written to them our decision that they should abstain from food sacrificed to idols, from blood, from the meat of strangled animals and from sexual immorality."

26The next day Paul took the men and purified himself along with them. Then he went to the temple to give notice of the date when the days of purification would end and the offering would be made for each of them.

Paul Arrested

27When the seven days were nearly over, some Jews from the province of Asia saw Paul at the temple. They stirred up the whole crowd and seized him, 28shouting, "Men of Israel, help us! This is the man who teaches all men everywhere against our people and our law and this place. And besides, he has brought Greeks into the temple area and defiled this holy place." 29(They had previously seen Trophimus the Ephesian in the city with Paul and assumed that Paul had brought him into the temple area.)

30The whole city was aroused, and the people came running from all directions. Seizing Paul, they dragged him from the temple, and immediately the gates were shut. 31While they were trying to kill him, news reached the commander of the Roman troops that the whole city of Jerusalem was in an uproar. 32He at once took some officers and soldiers and ran down to the crowd. When the rioters saw the commander and his soldiers, they stopped beating Paul.

33The commander came up and arrested him and ordered him to be bound with two chains. Then he asked who he was

and what he had done. 34Some in the crowd shouted one thing and some another, and since the commander could not get at the truth because of the uproar, he ordered that Paul be taken into the barracks. 35When Paul reached the steps, the violence of the mob was so great he had to be carried by the soldiers. 36The crowd that followed kept shouting, "Away with him!"

Paul Speaks to the Crowd

37As the soldiers were about to take Paul into the barracks, he asked the commander, "May I say something to you?"

"Do you speak Greek?" he replied. 38"Aren't you the Egyptian who started a revolt and led four thousand terrorists out into the desert some time ago?"

39Paul answered, "I am a Jew, from Tarsus in Cilicia, a citizen of no ordinary city. Please let me speak to the people."

40Having received the commander's permission, Paul stood on the steps and motioned to the crowd. When they were all silent, he said to them in Aramaic[a]:

22 1"Brothers and fathers, listen now to my defense."

2When they heard him speak to them in Aramaic, they became very quiet.

Then Paul said: 3"I am a Jew, born in Tarsus of Cilicia, but brought up in this city. Under Gamaliel I was thoroughly trained in the law of our fathers and was just as zealous for God as any of you are today. 4I persecuted the followers of this Way to their death, arresting both men and women and throwing them into prison, 5as also the high priest and all the Council can testify. I even obtained letters from them to their brothers in Damascus, and went there to bring these people as prisoners to Jerusalem to be punished.

6"About noon as I came near Damascus, suddenly a bright light from heaven flashed around me. 7I fell to the ground and heard a voice say to me, 'Saul! Saul! Why do you persecute me?'

a 40 Or possibly Hebrew; also in 22:2

8 "'Who are you, Lord?' I asked.

"'I am Jesus of Nazareth, whom you are persecuting,' he replied. 9 My companions saw the light, but they did not understand the voice of him who was speaking to me.

10 "'What shall I do, Lord?' I asked.

"'Get up,' the Lord said, 'and go into Damascus. There you will be told all that you have been assigned to do.' 11 My companions led me by the hand into Damascus, because the brilliance of the light had blinded me.

12 "A man named Ananias came to see me. He was a devout observer of the law and highly respected by all the Jews living there. 13 He stood beside me and said, 'Brother Saul, receive your sight!' And at that very moment I was able to see him.

14 "Then he said: 'The God of our fathers has chosen you to know his will and to see the Righteous One and to hear words from his mouth. 15 You will be his witness to all men of what you have seen and heard. 16 And now what are you waiting for? Get up, be baptized and wash your sins away, calling on his name.'

17 "When I returned to Jerusalem and was praying at the temple, I fell into a trance 18 and saw the Lord speaking. 'Quick!' he said to me. 'Leave Jerusalem immediately, because they will not accept your testimony about me.'

19 "'Lord,' I replied, 'these men know that I went from one synagogue to another to imprison and beat those who believe in you. 20 And when the blood of your martyr[a] Stephen was shed, I stood there giving my approval and guarding the clothes of those who were killing him.'

21 "Then the Lord said to me, 'Go; I will send you far away to the Gentiles.'"

Paul the Roman Citizen

22 The crowd listened to Paul until he said this. Then they raised their voices and shouted, "Rid the earth of him! He's not fit to live!"

23 As they were shouting and throwing off their cloaks and flinging dust into the air, 24 the commander ordered Paul to be taken into the barracks. He directed that he be flogged and questioned in order to find out why the people were shouting at him like this. 25 As they stretched him out to flog him, Paul said to the centurion standing there, "Is it legal for you to flog a Roman citizen who hasn't even been found guilty?"

26 When the centurion heard this, he went to the commander and reported it. "What are you going to do?" he asked. "This man is a Roman citizen."

27 The commander went to Paul and asked, "Tell me, are you a Roman citizen?"

"Yes, I am," he answered.

28 Then the commander said, "I had to pay a big price for my citizenship."

"But I was born a citizen," Paul replied.

29 Those who were about to question him withdrew immediately. The commander himself was alarmed when he realized that he had put Paul, a Roman citizen, in chains.

Before the Sanhedrin

30 The next day, since the commander wanted to find out exactly why Paul was being accused by the Jews, he released him and ordered the chief priests and all the Sanhedrin to assemble. Then he brought Paul and had him stand before them.

23 Paul looked straight at the Sanhedrin and said, "My brothers, I have fulfilled my duty to God in all good conscience to this day." 2 At this the high priest Ananias ordered those standing near Paul to strike him on the mouth. 3 Then Paul said to him, "God will strike you, you whitewashed wall! You sit there to judge me according to the law, yet you yourself violate the law by commanding that I be struck!"

4 Those who were standing near Paul

said, "You dare to insult God's high priest?"

⁵Paul replied, "Brothers, I did not realize that he was the high priest; for it is written: 'Do not speak evil about the ruler of your people.'ᵃ"

⁶Then Paul, knowing that some of them were Sadducees and the others Pharisees, called out in the Sanhedrin, "My brothers, I am a Pharisee, the son of a Pharisee. I stand on trial because of my hope in the resurrection of the dead." ⁷When he said this, a dispute broke out between the Pharisees and the Sadducees, and the assembly was divided. ⁸(The Sadducees say that there is no resurrection, and that there are neither angels nor spirits, but the Pharisees acknowledge them all.)

> ## Prayer is . . .
> *daily communication with God, not something done only in an emergency.*

⁹There was a great uproar, and some of the teachers of the law who were Pharisees stood up and argued vigorously. "We find nothing wrong with this man," they said. "What if a spirit or an angel has spoken to him?" ¹⁰The dispute became so violent that the commander was afraid Paul would be torn to pieces by them. He ordered the troops to go down and take him away from them by force and bring him into the barracks.

¹¹The following night the Lord stood near Paul and said, "Take courage! As you have testified about me in Jerusalem, so you must also testify in Rome."

The Plot to Kill Paul

¹²The next morning the Jews formed a conspiracy and bound themselves with an oath not to eat or drink until they had killed Paul. ¹³More than forty men were involved in this plot. ¹⁴They went to the chief priests and elders and said, "We have taken a solemn oath not to eat anything until we have killed Paul. ¹⁵Now then, you and the Sanhedrin petition the commander to bring him before you on the pretext of wanting more accurate information about his case. We are ready to kill him before he gets here."

¹⁶But when the son of Paul's sister heard of this plot, he went into the barracks and told Paul.

¹⁷Then Paul called one of the centurions and said, "Take this young man to the commander; he has something to tell him." ¹⁸So he took him to the commander.

The centurion said, "Paul, the prisoner, sent for me and asked me to bring this young man to you because he has something to tell you."

¹⁹The commander took the young man by the hand, drew him aside and asked, "What is it you want to tell me?"

²⁰He said: "The Jews have agreed to ask you to bring Paul before the Sanhedrin tomorrow on the pretext of wanting more accurate information about him. ²¹Don't give in to them, because more than forty of them are waiting in ambush for him. They have taken an oath not to eat or drink until they have killed him. They are ready now, waiting for your consent to their request."

²²The commander dismissed the young man and cautioned him, "Don't tell anyone that you have reported this to me."

Paul Transferred to Caesarea

²³Then he called two of his centurions and ordered them, "Get ready a detachment of two hundred soldiers, seventy horsemen and two hundred spearmenᵇ to go to Caesarea at nine tonight. ²⁴Provide mounts for Paul so that he may be taken safely to Governor Felix."

²⁵He wrote a letter as follows:

²⁶Claudius Lysias,

To His Excellency, Governor Felix:

ᵃ 5 Exodus 22:28   ᵇ 23 The meaning of the Greek for this word is uncertain.

Greetings.

27This man was seized by the Jews and they were about to kill him, but I came with my troops and rescued him, for I had learned that he is a Roman citizen. 28I wanted to know why they were accusing him, so I brought him to their Sanhedrin. 29I found that the accusation had to do with questions about their law, but there was no charge against him that deserved death or imprisonment. 30When I was informed of a plot to be carried out against the man, I sent him to you at once. I also ordered his accusers to present to you their case against him.

31So the soldiers, carrying out their orders, took Paul with them during the night and brought him as far as Antipatris. 32The next day they let the cavalry go on with him, while they returned to the barracks. 33When the cavalry arrived in Caesarea, they delivered the letter to the governor and handed Paul over to him. 34The governor read the letter and asked what province he was from. Learning that he was from Cilicia, 35he said, "I will hear your case when your accusers get here." Then he ordered that Paul be kept under guard in Herod's palace.

The Trial Before Felix

24 Five days later the high priest Ananias went down to Caesarea with some of the elders and a lawyer named Tertullus, and they brought their charges against Paul before the governor. 2When Paul was called in, Tertullus presented his case before Felix: "We have enjoyed a long period of peace under you, and your foresight has brought about reforms in this nation. 3Everywhere and in every way, most excellent Felix, we acknowledge this with profound gratitude. 4But in order not to weary you further, I would request that you be kind enough to hear us briefly.

5"We have found this man to be a troublemaker, stirring up riots among the Jews all over the world. He is a ringleader of the Nazarene sect 6and even tried to desecrate the temple; so we seized him. 8Bya examining him yourself you will be able to learn the truth about all these charges we are bringing against him."

9The Jews joined in the accusation, asserting that these things were true.

10When the governor motioned for him to speak, Paul replied: "I know that for a number of years you have been a judge over this nation; so I gladly make my defense. 11You can easily verify that no more than twelve days ago I went up to Jerusalem to worship. 12My accusers did not find me arguing with anyone at the temple, or stirring up a crowd in the synagogues or anywhere else in the city. 13And they cannot prove to you the charges they are now making against me. 14However, I admit that I worship the God of our fathers as a follower of the Way, which they call a sect. I believe everything that agrees with the Law and that is written in the Prophets, 15and I have the same hope in God as these men, that there will be a resurrection of both the righteous and the wicked. 16So I strive always to keep my conscience clear before God and man.

17"After an absence of several years, I came to Jerusalem to bring my people gifts for the poor and to present offerings. 18I was ceremonially clean when they found me in the temple courts doing this. There was no crowd with me, nor was I involved in any disturbance. 19But there are some Jews from the province of Asia, who ought to be here before you and bring charges if they have anything against me. 20Or these who are here should state what crime they found in me when I stood before the Sanhe-

---

a 6-8 Some manuscripts him and wanted to judge him according to our law. 7But the commander, Lysias, came and with the use of much force snatched him from our hands 8and ordered his accusers to come before you. By drin— 21unless it was this one thing I shouted as I stood in their presence: 'It is concerning the resurrection of the dead that I am on trial before you today.' "

22Then Felix, who was well acquainted with the Way, adjourned the proceedings. "When Lysias the commander comes," he said, "I will decide your case." 23He ordered the centurion to keep Paul under guard but to give him some freedom and permit his friends to take care of his needs.

24Several days later Felix came with his wife Drusilla, who was a Jewess. He sent for Paul and listened to him as he spoke about faith in Christ Jesus. 25As Paul discoursed on righteousness, self-control and the judgment to come, Felix was afraid and said, "That's enough for now! You may leave. When I find it convenient, I will send for you." 26At the same time he was hoping that Paul would offer him a bribe, so he sent for him frequently and talked with him.

27When two years had passed, Felix was succeeded by Porcius Festus, but because Felix wanted to grant a favor to the Jews, he left Paul in prison.

The Trial Before Festus

25 Three days after arriving in the province, Festus went up from Caesarea to Jerusalem, 2where the chief priests and Jewish leaders appeared before him and presented the charges against Paul. 3They urgently requested Festus, as a favor to them, to have Paul transferred to Jerusalem, for they were preparing an ambush to kill him along the way. 4Festus answered, "Paul is being held at Caesarea, and I myself am going there soon. 5Let some of your leaders come with me and press charges against the man there, if he has done anything wrong."

6After spending eight or ten days with them, he went down to Caesarea, and the next day he convened the court and ordered that Paul be brought before him. 7When Paul appeared, the Jews who had come down from Jerusalem stood around

him, bringing many serious charges against him, which they could not prove.

8Then Paul made his defense: "I have done nothing wrong against the law of the Jews or against the temple or against Caesar."

9Festus, wishing to do the Jews a favor, said to Paul, "Are you willing to go up to Jerusalem and stand trial before me there on these charges?"

10Paul answered: "I am now standing before Caesar's court, where I ought to be tried. I have not done any wrong to the Jews, as you yourself know very well. 11If, however, I am guilty of doing anything deserving death, I do not refuse to die. But if the charges brought against me by these Jews are not true, no one has the right to hand me over to them. I appeal to Caesar!"

12After Festus had conferred with his council, he declared: "You have appealed to Caesar. To Caesar you will go!"

Festus Consults King Agrippa

13A few days later King Agrippa and Bernice arrived at Caesarea to pay their respects to Festus. 14Since they were spending many days there, Festus discussed Paul's case with the king. He said: "There is a man here whom Felix left as a prisoner. 15When I went to Jerusalem, the chief priests and elders of the Jews brought charges against him and asked that he be condemned.

16"I told them that it is not the Roman custom to hand over any man before he has faced his accusers and has had an opportunity to defend himself against their charges. 17When they came here with me, I did not delay the case, but convened the court the next day and ordered the man to be brought in. 18When his accusers got up to speak, they did not charge him with any of the crimes I had expected. 19Instead, they had some points of dispute with him about their own religion and about a dead man named Jesus who Paul claimed was alive. 20I was at a loss how to investigate such matters; so

I asked if he would be willing to go to Jerusalem and stand trial there on these charges. 21When Paul made his appeal to be held over for the Emperor's decision, I ordered him held until I could send him to Caesar."

22Then Agrippa said to Festus, "I would like to hear this man myself."

He replied, "Tomorrow you will hear him."

Paul Before Agrippa

23The next day Agrippa and Bernice came with great pomp and entered the audience room with the high ranking officers and the leading men of the city. At the command of Festus, Paul was brought in. 24Festus said: "King Agrippa, and all who are present with us, you see this man! The whole Jewish community has petitioned me about him in Jerusalem and here in Caesarea, shouting that he ought not to live any longer. 25I found he had done nothing deserving of death, but because he made his appeal to the Emperor I decided to send him to Rome. 26But I have nothing definite to write to His Majesty about him. Therefore I have brought him before all of you, and especially before you, King Agrippa, so that as a result of this investigation I may have something to write. 27For I think it is unreasonable to send on a prisoner without specifying the charges against him."

26 Then Agrippa said to Paul, "You have permission to speak for yourself."

So Paul motioned with his hand and began his defense: 2"King Agrippa, I consider myself fortunate to stand before you today as I make my defense against all the accusations of the Jews, 3and especially so because you are well acquainted with all the Jewish customs and controversies. Therefore, I beg you to listen to me patiently.

4"The Jews all know the way I have lived ever since I was a child, from the beginning of my life in my own country, and also in Jerusalem. 5They have known me for a long time and can testify, if they are willing, that according to the strictest sect of our religion, I lived as a Pharisee. 6And now it is because of my hope in what God has promised our fathers that I am on trial today. 7This is the promise our twelve tribes are hoping to see fulfilled as they earnestly serve God day and night. O king, it is because of this hope that the Jews are accusing me. 8Why should any of you consider it incredible that God raises the dead?

9"I too was convinced that I ought to do all that was possible to oppose the name of Jesus of Nazareth. 10And that is just what I did in Jerusalem. On the authority of the chief priests I put many of the saints in prison, and when they were put to death, I cast my vote against them. 11Many a time I went from one synagogue to another to have them punished, and I tried to force them to blaspheme. In my obsession against them, I even went to foreign cities to persecute them.

12"On one of these journeys I was going to Damascus with the authority and commission of the chief priests. 13About noon, O king, as I was on the road, I saw a light from heaven, brighter than the sun, blazing around me and my companions. 14We all fell to the ground, and I heard a voice saying to me in Aramaic,[a] 'Saul, Saul, why do you persecute me? It is hard for you to kick against the goads.'

15"Then I asked, 'Who are you, Lord?'

"'I am Jesus, whom you are persecuting,' the Lord replied. 16'Now get up and stand on your feet. I have appeared to you to appoint you as a servant and as a witness of what you have seen of me and what I will show you. 17I will rescue you from your own people and from the Gentiles. I am sending you to them 18to open their eyes and turn them from darkness to light, and from the power of Satan to

---

a 14 Or Hebrew

How to Maintain a Passion for His Presence

When you love God and want to be with Him simply because He *is*, one of the things that happens is that the joy of the Lord rises in you like a spring of pure water. It happens every time you praise Him. It is instantly felt in His presence. This joy comes from a source that never runs dry. It becomes your strength (John 4:14). No matter what else is happening, it's that underlying feeling that everything is going to ultimately be good.

Just being with God fills us with joy. We can experience the joy of the Lord in the midst of any situation because it's found in His presence. Does that mean people will never die, everyone will always be healed, and we will have our prayers answered every time just the way we prayed them? Of course not. It means that in the midst of whatever happens, He will never leave us or forsake us. He will always be everything He is. And we will have the joy of His presence, even when passing from earth to be with Him in heaven forever.

The way to maintain a passion for His presence is to be in His presence often. His presence is addictive. The more we experience Him, the more we want of Him.

Moses asked God what he should tell the children of Israel when they asked who sent him, and He said, "This is what you are to say to the Israelites: 'I am has sent me to you' " (Exodus 3:13-14).

That is about as basic and bottom line as it can get. He *is*. We can worship Him because He *is*. Because He *is*, I can live today. Because He *is*, I can get through tomorrow. Because He *is*, I can have joy.

We can read in the Bible about the many times God had to bring destruction into people's lives so they would know that He is God. He had to take away everything. He wants us to recognize that too. He says, "I am God, and there is none like me" (Isaiah 46:9). We don't need to lose everything or have a disaster happen in order to realize this. We just need to praise Him, and it will become clear.

"Be still, and know that I am God" (Psalm 46:10). It's not that He is necessarily trying to get us to shut up. Or perhaps He *is*. But God's ultimate goal is to get us to know *Him*. And we can't know Him fully unless we spend time with Him quietly. Just "being" in His presence. Just letting Him "be" in yours.

Have you ever talked with someone who was asking for advice but wouldn't stop talking long enough to hear what advice you had to give them? That's often the way we are when we come before God. It's not that we have to be still *all* the time, but perhaps *some* of the time. We need times when we simply come before Him quietly in worship. To be still before Him. To simply rest in His presence.

When you let all else go and just "be" with God, when you simply worship Him because He *is*, He will elevate you to His perspective and give you His joy and His rest.

For the next "From Stormie's Heart" article, go to page 1385.

God, so that they may receive forgiveness of sins and a place among those who are sanctified by faith in me.'

19"So then, King Agrippa, I was not disobedient to the vision from heaven. 20First to those in Damascus, then to those in Jerusalem and in all Judea, and to the Gentiles also, I preached that they should repent and turn to God and prove their repentance by their deeds. 21That is why the Jews seized me in the temple courts and tried to kill me. 22But I have had God's help to this very day, and so I stand here and testify to small and great alike. I am saying nothing beyond what the prophets and Moses said would happen— 23that the Christ[a] would suffer and, as the first to rise from the dead, would proclaim light to his own people and to the Gentiles."

24At this point Festus interrupted Paul's defense. "You are out of your mind, Paul!" he shouted. "Your great learning is driving you insane."

25"I am not insane, most excellent Festus," Paul replied. "What I am saying is true and reasonable. 26The king is familiar with these things, and I can speak freely to him. I am convinced that none of this has escaped his notice, because it was not done in a corner. 27King Agrippa, do you believe the prophets? I know you do."

28Then Agrippa said to Paul, "Do you think that in such a short time you can persuade me to be a Christian?"

29Paul replied, "Short time or long—I pray God that not only you but all who are listening to me today may become what I am, except for these chains."

30The king rose, and with him the governor and Bernice and those sitting with them. 31They left the room, and while talking with one another, they said, "This man is not doing anything that deserves death or imprisonment."

32Agrippa said to Festus, "This man could have been set free if he had not appealed to Caesar."

Paul Sails for Rome

27 When it was decided that we would sail for Italy, Paul and some other prisoners were handed over to a centurion named Julius, who belonged to the Imperial Regiment. 2We boarded a ship from Adramyttium about to sail for ports along the coast of the province of Asia, and we put out to sea. Aristarchus, a Macedonian from Thessalonica, was with us.

3The next day we landed at Sidon; and Julius, in kindness to Paul, allowed him to go to his friends so they might provide for his needs. 4From there we put out to sea again and passed to the lee of Cyprus because the winds were against us. 5When we had sailed across the open sea off the coast of Cilicia and Pamphylia, we landed at Myra in Lycia. 6There the centurion found an Alexandrian ship sailing for Italy and put us on board. 7We made slow headway for many days and had difficulty arriving off Cnidus. When the wind did not allow us to hold our course, we sailed to the lee of Crete, opposite Salmone. 8We moved along the coast with difficulty and came to a place called Fair Havens, near the town of Lasea.

9Much time had been lost, and sailing had already become dangerous because by now it was after the Fast.[b] So Paul warned them, 10"Men, I can see that our voyage is going to be disastrous and bring great loss to ship and cargo, and to our own lives also." 11But the centurion, instead of listening to what Paul said, followed the advice of the pilot and of the owner of the ship. 12Since the harbor was unsuitable to winter in, the majority decided that we should sail on, hoping to reach Phoenix and winter there. This was a harbor in Crete, facing both southwest and northwest.

The Storm

13When a gentle south wind began to blow, they thought they had obtained what they wanted; so they weighed an-

---

a 23 Or Messiah   b 9 That is, the Day of Atonement (Yom Kippur) chor and sailed along the shore of Crete. [14]Before very long, a wind of hurricane force, called the "northeaster," swept down from the island. [15]The ship was caught by the storm and could not head into the wind; so we gave way to it and were driven along. [16]As we passed to the lee of a small island called Cauda, we were hardly able to make the lifeboat secure. [17]When the men had hoisted it aboard, they passed ropes under the ship itself to hold it together. Fearing that they would run aground on the sandbars of Syrtis, they lowered the sea anchor and let the ship be driven along. [18]We took such a violent battering from the storm that the next day they began to throw the cargo overboard. [19]On the third day, they threw the ship's tackle overboard with their own hands. [20]When neither sun nor stars appeared for many days and the storm continued raging, we finally gave up all hope of being saved.

[21]After the men had gone a long time without food, Paul stood up before them and said: "Men, you should have taken my advice not to sail from Crete; then you would have spared yourselves this damage and loss. [22]But now I urge you to keep up your courage, because not one of you will be lost; only the ship will be destroyed. [23]Last night an angel of the God whose I am and whom I serve stood beside me [24]and said, 'Do not be afraid, Paul. You must stand trial before Caesar; and God has graciously given you the lives of all who sail with you.' [25]So keep up your courage, men, for I have faith in God that it will happen just as he told me. [26]Nevertheless, we must run aground on some island."

The Shipwreck

[27]On the fourteenth night we were still being driven across the Adriatic[a] Sea, when about midnight the sailors sensed they were approaching land. [28]They took soundings and found that the water was a hundred and twenty feet[b] deep. A short time later they took soundings again and found it was ninety feet[c] deep. [29]Fearing that we would be dashed against the rocks, they dropped four anchors from the stern and prayed for daylight. [30]In an attempt to escape from the ship, the sailors let the lifeboat down into the sea, pretending they were going to lower some anchors from the bow. [31]Then Paul said to the centurion and the soldiers, "Unless these men stay with the ship, you cannot be saved." [32]So the soldiers cut the ropes that held the lifeboat and let it fall away.

[33]Just before dawn Paul urged them all to eat. "For the last fourteen days," he said, "you have been in constant suspense and have gone without food—you haven't eaten anything. [34]Now I urge you to take some food. You need it to survive. Not one of you will lose a single hair from his head." [35]After he said this, he took some bread and gave thanks to God in front of them all. Then he broke it and began to eat. [36]They were all encouraged and ate some food themselves. [37]Altogether there were 276 of us on board. [38]When they had eaten as much as they wanted, they lightened the ship by throwing the grain into the sea.

[39]When daylight came, they did not recognize the land, but they saw a bay with a sandy beach, where they decided to run the ship aground if they could. [40]Cutting loose the anchors, they left them in the sea and at the same time untied the ropes that held the rudders. Then they hoisted the foresail to the wind and made for the beach. [41]But the ship struck a sandbar and ran aground. The bow stuck fast and would not move, and the stern was broken to pieces by the pounding of the surf.

[42]The soldiers planned to kill the prisoners to prevent any of them from swimming away and escaping. [43]But the centurion wanted to spare Paul's life

---

a 27 In ancient times the name referred to an area extending well south of Italy.   b 28 Greek *twenty orguias* (about 37 meters)
c 28 Greek *fifteen orguias* (about 27 meters)

and kept them from carrying out their plan. He ordered those who could swim to jump overboard first and get to land. ⁴⁴The rest were to get there on planks or on pieces of the ship. In this way everyone reached land in safety.

Ashore on Malta

28 Once safely on shore, we found out that the island was called Malta. ²The islanders showed us unusual kindness. They built a fire and welcomed us all because it was raining and cold. ³Paul gathered a pile of brushwood and, as he put it on the fire, a viper, driven out by the heat, fastened itself on his hand. ⁴When the islanders saw the snake hanging from his hand, they said to each other, "This man must be a murderer; for though he escaped from the sea, Justice has not allowed him to live." ⁵But Paul shook the snake off into the fire and suffered no ill effects. ⁶The people expected him to swell up or suddenly fall dead, but after waiting a long time and seeing nothing unusual happen to him, they changed their minds and said he was a god.

⁷There was an estate nearby that belonged to Publius, the chief official of the island. He welcomed us to his home and for three days entertained us hospitably. ⁸His father was sick in bed, suffering from fever and dysentery. Paul went in to see him and, after prayer, placed his hands on him and healed him. ⁹When this had happened, the rest of the sick on the island came and were cured. ¹⁰They honored us in many ways and when we were ready to sail, they furnished us with the supplies we needed.

Arrival at Rome

¹¹After three months we put out to sea in a ship that had wintered in the island. It was an Alexandrian ship with the figurehead of the twin gods Castor and Pollux. ¹²We put in at Syracuse and stayed there three days. ¹³From there we set sail and arrived at Rhegium. The next day

the south wind came up, and on the following day we reached Puteoli. ¹⁴There we found some brothers who invited us to spend a week with them. And so we came to Rome. ¹⁵The brothers there had heard that we were coming, and they traveled as far as the Forum of Appius and the Three Taverns to meet us. At the sight of these men Paul thanked God and was encouraged. ¹⁶When we got to Rome, Paul was allowed to live by himself, with a soldier to guard him.

Paul Preaches at Rome Under Guard

¹⁷Three days later he called together the leaders of the Jews. When they had assembled, Paul said to them: "My brothers, although I have done nothing against our people or against the customs of our ancestors, I was arrested in Jerusalem and handed over to the Romans. ¹⁸They examined me and wanted to release me, because I was not guilty of any crime deserving death. ¹⁹But when the Jews objected, I was compelled to appeal to Caesar—not that I had any charge to bring against my own people. ²⁰For this reason I have asked to see you and talk with you. It is because of the hope of Israel that I am bound with this chain."

²¹They replied, "We have not received any letters from Judea concerning you, and none of the brothers who have come from there has reported or said anything bad about you. ²²But we want to hear what your views are, for we know that people everywhere are talking against this sect."

²³They arranged to meet Paul on a certain day, and came in even larger numbers to the place where he was staying. From morning till evening he explained and declared to them the kingdom of God and tried to convince them about Jesus from the Law of Moses and from the Prophets. ²⁴Some were convinced by what he said, but others would not believe. ²⁵They disagreed among themselves and began to leave after Paul had made this final statement: "The Holy Spirit spoke the truth

to your forefathers when he said through Isaiah the prophet:

26 " 'Go to this people and say,
  "You will be ever hearing but never
      understanding;
    you will be ever seeing but never
      perceiving."
27 For this people's heart has become
      calloused;
    they hardly hear with their ears,
    and they have closed their eyes.
  Otherwise they might see with their
      eyes,

hear with their ears,
    understand with their hearts
  and turn, and I would heal
      them.'a

28 "Therefore I want you to know that God's salvation has been sent to the Gentiles, and they will listen!"b

30 For two whole years Paul stayed there in his own rented house and welcomed all who came to see him. 31 Boldly and without hindrance he preached the kingdom of God and taught about the Lord Jesus Christ.

---

a 27 Isaiah 6:9,10   b 28 Some manuscripts listen!" 29After he said this, the Jews left, arguing vigorously among themselves.

Author: Paul (formerly Saul of Tarsus)

Date: AD 56

Audience: The predominantly Gentile church at Rome

The book of Romans is all about understanding and living out the Christian faith. If you want to know what to believe, what truth to hang on to, and how to walk as a believer in this world, this book gives the answers.

Paul had traveled across much of Asia Minor bringing the gospel message to people who had never heard it. He had never been to Rome, but a thriving church already existed there, planted by believers who had heard the Good News while visiting Jerusalem at Pentecost (Acts 2:10). Remember, no one had Bibles at this time; believers relied on the teachings provided by the apostles to help them grow in their faith. Paul wrote this letter to help the believers understand that salvation is by God's grace alone, through faith in Christ.

Because of that salvation, we can come to God in prayer as we could go to a loving father. We can even address Him as "Abba," which is like calling Him "Daddy," suggesting a close, personal father and child relationship, because "the Spirit himself testifies with our spirit that we are God's children" (8:16).

Prayer Themes:

- *Ask God for the ability to see difficulties and suffering from His perspective—and to understand His purposes in them (5:3-5).*

- *Praise God that when your spirit is so troubled that the words won't come, or you don't even know what you ought to pray for, He has promised that His Spirit will intercede for you according to His will (8:26-27).*

- *Thank God that as you surrender your life to Him and refuse to let the world squeeze you into its mold, you will be transformed (12:1-2).*

Romans

1

Paul, a servant of Christ Jesus, called to be an apostle and set apart for the gospel of God— ²the gospel he promised beforehand through his prophets in the Holy Scriptures ³regarding his Son, who as to his human nature was a descendant of David, ⁴and who through the Spirit[a] of holiness was declared with power to be the Son of God[b] by his resurrection from the dead: Jesus Christ our Lord. ⁵Through him and for his name's sake, we received grace and apostleship to call people from among all the Gentiles to the obedience that comes from faith. ⁶And you also are among those who are called to belong to Jesus Christ.

⁷To all in Rome who are loved by God and called to be saints:

Grace and peace to you from God our Father and from the Lord Jesus Christ.

Paul's Longing to Visit Rome

⁸First, I thank my God through Jesus Christ for all of you, because your faith is being reported all over the world. ⁹God, whom I serve with my whole heart in preaching the gospel of his Son, is my witness how constantly I remember you ¹⁰in my prayers at all times; and I pray that now at last by God's will the way may be opened for me to come to you.

¹¹I long to see you so that I may impart to you some spiritual gift to make you strong— ¹²that is, that you and I may be mutually encouraged by each other's faith. ¹³I do not want you to be unaware, brothers, that I planned many times to come to you (but have been prevented from doing so until now) in order that I might have a harvest among you, just as I have had among the other Gentiles.

¹⁴I am obligated both to Greeks and

non-Greeks, both to the wise and the foolish. ¹⁵That is why I am so eager to preach the gospel also to you who are at Rome.

¹⁶I am not ashamed of the gospel, because it is the power of God for the salvation of everyone who believes: first for the Jew, then for the Gentile. ¹⁷For in the gospel a righteousness from God is revealed, a righteousness that is by faith from first to last,ᵃ just as it is written: "The righteous will live by faith."ᵇ

God's Wrath Against Mankind

¹⁸The wrath of God is being revealed from heaven against all the godlessness and wickedness of men who suppress the truth by their wickedness, ¹⁹since what may be known about God is plain to them, because God has made it plain to them. ²⁰For since the creation of the world God's invisible qualities—his eternal power and divine nature—have been clearly seen, being understood from what has been made, so that men are without excuse.

²¹For although they knew God, they neither glorified him as God nor gave thanks to him, but their thinking became futile and their foolish hearts were darkened. ²²Although they claimed to be wise, they became fools ²³and exchanged the glory of the immortal God for images made to look like mortal man and birds and animals and reptiles.

²⁴Therefore God gave them over in the sinful desires of their hearts to sexual impurity for the degrading of their bodies with one another. ²⁵They exchanged the truth of God for a lie, and worshiped and served created things rather than the Creator—who is forever praised. Amen.

²⁶Because of this, God gave them over to shameful lusts. Even their women exchanged natural relations for unnatural ones. ²⁷In the same way the men also abandoned natural relations with women and were inflamed with lust for one another. Men committed indecent acts with other men, and received in themselves the due penalty for their perversion.

²⁸Furthermore, since they did not think it worthwhile to retain the knowledge of God, he gave them over to a depraved mind, to do what ought not to be done. ²⁹They have become filled with every kind of wickedness, evil, greed and depravity. They are full of envy, murder,

---

ᵃ *17* Or *is from faith to faith*   ᵇ *17* Hab. 2:4

God's people at prayer
PAUL GIVES THANKS FOR THE BELIEVERS IN ROME

ROMANS 1:8-10 Paul lived at a time when the phrase "all roads lead to Rome" was an actual fact rather than just an expression. Rome was the capital of the world. In that swirling and decadent capital there was a thriving Christian church, probably started by people who had been in Jerusalem at Pentecost (where "visitors from Rome" had witnessed the manifestation of the Holy Spirit, Acts 2:10). Paul had never been to Rome, but the New Testament book of Romans is Paul's letter to that church.

Paul thanked God for these people because their faith was literally being reported all over the world. Travelers passed through Rome and caught a glimpse of people with a new kind of faith, a new way of living, a new approach to a personal God. It caught people's attention and made them listen! That's what the Holy Spirit in us can do. His presence in our lives can draw people to want to know what it is that makes us more loving, more hopeful, more peaceful, more fruitful. We need to ask God daily for a fresh flow of His Spirit in our lives that can be a refreshment for those around us, causing them to want to know Him!

strife, deceit and malice. They are gossips, [30]slanderers, God-haters, insolent, arrogant and boastful; they invent ways of doing evil; they disobey their parents; [31]they are senseless, faithless, heartless, ruthless. [32]Although they know God's righteous decree that those who do such things deserve death, they not only continue to do these very things but also approve of those who practice them.

God's Righteous Judgment

2 You, therefore, have no excuse, you who pass judgment on someone else, for at whatever point you judge the other, you are condemning yourself, because you who pass judgment do the same things. [2]Now we know that God's judgment against those who do such things is based on truth. [3]So when you, a mere man, pass judgment on them and yet do the same things, do you think you will escape God's judgment? [4]Or do you show contempt for the riches of his kindness, tolerance and patience, not realizing that God's kindness leads you toward repentance?

[5]But because of your stubbornness and your unrepentant heart, you are storing up wrath against yourself for the day of God's wrath, when his righteous judgment will be revealed. [6]God "will give to each person according to what he has done."[a] [7]To those who by persistence in doing good seek glory, honor and immortality, he will give eternal life. [8]But for those who are self-seeking and who reject the truth and follow evil, there will be wrath and anger. [9]There will be trouble and distress for every human being who does evil: first for the Jew, then for the Gentile; [10]but glory, honor and peace for everyone who does good: first for the Jew, then for the Gentile. [11]For God does not show favoritism.

[12]All who sin apart from the law will also perish apart from the law, and all who sin under the law will be judged by the law. [13]For it is not those who hear the law who are righteous in God's sight, but it is those who obey the law who will be declared righteous. [14](Indeed, when Gentiles, who do not have the law, do by nature things required by the law, they are a law for themselves, even though they do not have the law, [15]since they show that the requirements of the law are written on their hearts, their consciences also bearing witness, and their thoughts now accusing, now even defending them.) [16]This will take place on the day when God will judge men's secrets through Jesus Christ, as my gospel declares.

The Jews and the Law

[17]Now you, if you call yourself a Jew; if you rely on the law and brag about your relationship to God; [18]if you know his will and approve of what is superior because you are instructed by the law; [19]if you are convinced that you are a guide for the blind, a light for those who are in the dark, [20]an instructor of the foolish, a teacher of infants, because you have in the law the embodiment of knowledge and truth— [21]you, then, who teach others, do you not teach yourself? You who preach against stealing, do you steal? [22]You who say that people should not commit adultery, do you commit adultery? You who abhor idols, do you rob temples? [23]You who brag about the law, do you dishonor God by breaking the law? [24]As it is written: "God's name is blasphemed among the Gentiles because of you."[b]

[25]Circumcision has value if you observe the law, but if you break the law, you have become as though you had not been circumcised. [26]If those who are not circumcised keep the law's requirements, will they not be regarded as though they were circumcised? [27]The one who is not circumcised physically and yet obeys the law will condemn you who, even though you have the[c] written code and circumcision, are a lawbreaker.

[28]A man is not a Jew if he is only one outwardly, nor is circumcision merely out-

---

[a]6 Psalm 62:12; Prov. 24:12   [b]24 Isaiah 52:5; Ezek. 36:22   [c]27 Or who, by means of a

ward and physical. [29]No, a man is a Jew if he is one inwardly; and circumcision is circumcision of the heart, by the Spirit, not by the written code. Such a man's praise is not from men, but from God.

God's Faithfulness

3 What advantage, then, is there in being a Jew, or what value is there in circumcision? [2]Much in every way! First of all, they have been entrusted with the very words of God.

[3]What if some did not have faith? Will their lack of faith nullify God's faithfulness? [4]Not at all! Let God be true, and every man a liar. As it is written:

"So that you may be proved right
    when you speak
  and prevail when you judge."[a]

[5]But if our unrighteousness brings out God's righteousness more clearly, what shall we say? That God is unjust in bringing his wrath on us? (I am using a human argument.) [6]Certainly not! If that were so, how could God judge the world? [7]Someone might argue, "If my falsehood enhances God's truthfulness and so increases his glory, why am I still condemned as a sinner?" [8]Why not say—as we are being slanderously reported as saying and as some claim that we say—"Let us do evil that good may result"? Their condemnation is deserved.

No One Is Righteous

[9]What shall we conclude then? Are we any better[b]? Not at all! We have already made the charge that Jews and Gentiles alike are all under sin. [10]As it is written:

"There is no one righteous, not even
    one;
[11] there is no one who understands,
    no one who seeks God.
[12]All have turned away,
    they have together become
      worthless;
  there is no one who does good,

  not even one."[c]
[13]"Their throats are open graves;
    their tongues practice deceit."[d]
  "The poison of vipers is on their
      lips."[e]
[14] "Their mouths are full of cursing
      and bitterness."[f]
[15]"Their feet are swift to shed blood;
[16] ruin and misery mark their ways,
[17]and the way of peace they do not
      know."[g]
[18] "There is no fear of God before
      their eyes."[h]

[19]Now we know that whatever the law says, it says to those who are under the law, so that every mouth may be silenced and the whole world held accountable to God. [20]Therefore no one will be declared righteous in his sight by observing the law; rather, through the law we become conscious of sin.

Praying Romans 3:23

Thank You, Lord, that even though I have sinned and fallen short of all You have for me, You still love me and lead me on the path You want me to walk.

Righteousness Through Faith

[21]But now a righteousness from God, apart from law, has been made known, to which the Law and the Prophets testify. [22]This righteousness from God comes through faith in Jesus Christ to all who believe. There is no difference, [23]for all have sinned and fall short of the glory of God, [24]and are justified freely by his grace through the redemption that came by Christ Jesus. [25]God presented him as a sacrifice of atonement,[i] through faith in his blood. He did this to demonstrate his justice, because in his forbearance he had left the sins committed beforehand unpunished— [26]he did it to demonstrate his justice at the present time, so as to be just and the one who justifies those who have faith in Jesus.

---

[a] *4* Psalm 51:4   [b] *9* Or *worse*   [c] *12* Psalms 14:1-3; 53:1-3; Eccles. 7:20   [d] *13* Psalm 5:9   [e] *13* Psalm 140:3   [f] *14* Psalm 10:7
[g] *17* Isaiah 59:7,8   [h] *18* Psalm 36:1   [i] *25* Or *as the one who would turn aside his wrath, taking away sin*

27Where, then, is boasting? It is excluded. On what principle? On that of observing the law? No, but on that of faith. 28For we maintain that a man is justified by faith apart from observing the law. 29Is God the God of Jews only? Is he not the God of Gentiles too? Yes, of Gentiles too, 30since there is only one God, who will justify the circumcised by faith and the uncircumcised through that same faith. 31Do we, then, nullify the law by this faith? Not at all! Rather, we uphold the law.

Abraham Justified by Faith

4 What then shall we say that Abraham, our forefather, discovered in this matter? 2If, in fact, Abraham was justified by works, he had something to boast about—but not before God. 3What does the Scripture say? "Abraham believed God, and it was credited to him as righteousness."a

4Now when a man works, his wages are not credited to him as a gift, but as an obligation. 5However, to the man who does not work but trusts God who justifies the wicked, his faith is credited as righteousness. 6David says the same thing when he speaks of the blessedness of the man to whom God credits righteousness apart from works:

7"Blessed are they
    whose transgressions are forgiven,
    whose sins are covered.
8Blessed is the man
    whose sin the Lord will never
        count against him."b

9Is this blessedness only for the circumcised, or also for the uncircumcised? We have been saying that Abraham's faith was credited to him as righteousness. 10Under what circumstances was it credited? Was it after he was circumcised, or before? It was not after, but before! 11And he received the sign of circumcision, a seal of the righteousness that he had by faith while he was still uncircumcised. So then,

he is the father of all who believe but have not been circumcised, in order that righteousness might be credited to them. 12And he is also the father of the circumcised who not only are circumcised but who also walk in the footsteps of the faith that our father Abraham had before he was circumcised.

13It was not through law that Abraham and his offspring received the promise that he would be heir of the world, but through the righteousness that comes by faith. 14For if those who live by law are heirs, faith has no value and the promise is worthless, 15because law brings wrath. And where there is no law there is no transgression.

16Therefore, the promise comes by faith, so that it may be by grace and may be guaranteed to all Abraham's offspring—not only to those who are of the law but also to those who are of the faith of Abraham. He is the father of us all. 17As it is written: "I have made you a father of many nations."c He is our father in the sight of God, in whom he believed—the God who gives life to the dead and calls things that are not as though they were.

18Against all hope, Abraham in hope believed and so became the father of many nations, just as it had been said to him, "So shall your offspring be."d 19Without weakening in his faith, he faced the fact that his body was as good as dead—since he was about a hundred years old—and that Sarah's womb was also dead. 20Yet he did not waver through unbelief regarding the promise of God, but was strengthened in his faith and gave glory to God, 21being fully persuaded that God had power to do what he had promised. 22This is why "it was credited to him as righteousness." 23The words "it was credited to him" were written not for him alone, 24but also for us, to whom God will credit righteousness—for us who believe in him who raised Jesus our Lord from the dead. 25He was delivered over to death for our

---

a 3 Gen. 15:6; also in verse 22   b 8 Psalm 32:1,2   c 17 Gen. 17:5   d 18 Gen. 15:5

sins and was raised to life for our justification.

Peace and Joy

5 Therefore, since we have been justified through faith, we[a] have peace with God through our Lord Jesus Christ, [2]through whom we have gained access by faith into this grace in which we now stand. And we[a] rejoice in the hope of the glory of God. [3]Not only so, but we[a] also rejoice in our sufferings, because we know that suffering produces perseverance; [4]perseverance, character; and character, hope. [5]And hope does not disappoint us, because God has poured out his love into our hearts by the Holy Spirit, whom he has given us.

Praying Romans 5:3-5
Heavenly Father, I am grateful that
even in hard times I can feel Your love,
and You are always working in me
a greater sense of hope.

[6]You see, at just the right time, when we were still powerless, Christ died for the ungodly. [7]Very rarely will anyone die for a righteous man, though for a good man someone might possibly dare to die. [8]But God demonstrates his own love for us in this: While we were still sinners, Christ died for us.

[9]Since we have now been justified by his blood, how much more shall we be saved from God's wrath through him! [10]For if, when we were God's enemies, we were reconciled to him through the death of his Son, how much more, having been reconciled, shall we be saved through his life! [11]Not only is this so, but we also rejoice in God through our Lord Jesus Christ, through whom we have now received reconciliation.

Death Through Adam, Life Through Christ

[12]Therefore, just as sin entered the world through one man, and death through

sin, and in this way death came to all men, because all sinned— [13]for before the law was given, sin was in the world. But sin is not taken into account when there is no law. [14]Nevertheless, death reigned from the time of Adam to the time of Moses, even over those who did not sin by breaking a command, as did Adam, who was a pattern of the one to come.

[15]But the gift is not like the trespass. For if the many died by the trespass of the one man, how much more did God's grace and the gift that came by the grace of the one man, Jesus Christ, overflow to the many! [16]Again, the gift of God is not like the result of the one man's sin: The judgment followed one sin and brought condemnation, but the gift followed many trespasses and brought justification. [17]For if, by the trespass of the one man, death reigned through that one man, how much more will those who receive God's abundant provision of grace and of the gift of righteousness reign in life through the one man, Jesus Christ.

[18]Consequently, just as the result of one trespass was condemnation for all men, so also the result of one act of righteousness was justification that brings life for all men. [19]For just as through the disobedience of the one man the many were made sinners, so also through the obedience of the one man the many will be made righteous.

[20]The law was added so that the trespass might increase. But where sin increased, grace increased all the more, [21]so that, just as sin reigned in death, so also grace might reign through righteousness to bring eternal life through Jesus Christ our Lord.

Dead to Sin, Alive in Christ

6 What shall we say, then? Shall we go on sinning so that grace may increase? [2]By no means! We died to sin; how can we live in it any longer? [3]Or don't you know that all of us who were baptized into Christ Jesus were baptized into his

---

death? [4]We were therefore buried with him through baptism into death in order that, just as Christ was raised from the dead through the glory of the Father, we too may live a new life.

[5]If we have been united with him like this in his death, we will certainly also be united with him in his resurrection. [6]For we know that our old self was crucified with him so that the body of sin might be done away with,[a] that we should no longer be slaves to sin— [7]because anyone who has died has been freed from sin.

[8]Now if we died with Christ, we believe that we will also live with him. [9]For we know that since Christ was raised from the dead, he cannot die again; death no longer has mastery over him. [10]The death he died, he died to sin once for all; but the life he lives, he lives to God.

[11]In the same way, count yourselves dead to sin but alive to God in Christ Jesus. [12]Therefore do not let sin reign in your mortal body so that you obey its evil desires. [13]Do not offer the parts of your body to sin, as instruments of wickedness, but rather offer yourselves to God, as those who have been brought from death to life; and offer the parts of your body to him as instruments of righteousness. [14]For sin shall not be your master, because you are not under law, but under grace.

Slaves to Righteousness

[15]What then? Shall we sin because we are not under law but under grace? By no means! [16]Don't you know that when you offer yourselves to someone to obey him as slaves, you are slaves to the one whom you obey—whether you are slaves to sin, which leads to death, or to obedience, which leads to righteousness? [17]But thanks be to God that, though you used to be slaves to sin, you wholeheartedly obeyed the form of teaching to which you were entrusted. [18]You have been set free from sin and have become slaves to righteousness.

[19]I put this in human terms because you are weak in your natural selves. Just as you used to offer the parts of your body in slavery to impurity and to ever-increasing wickedness, so now offer them in slavery to righteousness leading to holiness. [20]When you were slaves to sin, you were free from the control of righteousness. [21]What benefit did you reap at that time from the things you are now ashamed of? Those things result in death! [22]But now that you have been set free from sin and have become slaves to God, the benefit you reap leads to holiness, and the result is eternal life. [23]For the wages of sin is death, but the gift of God is eternal life in[b] Christ Jesus our Lord.

An Illustration From Marriage

Do you not know, brothers—for I am speaking to men who know the law—that the law has authority over a man only as long as he lives? [2]For example, by law a married woman is bound to her husband as long as he is alive, but if her husband dies, she is released from the law of marriage. [3]So then, if she marries another man while her husband is still alive, she is called an adulteress. But if her husband dies, she is released from that law and is not an adulteress, even though she marries another man.

[4]So, my brothers, you also died to the law through the body of Christ, that you might belong to another, to him who was raised from the dead, in order that we might bear fruit to God. [5]For when we were controlled by the sinful nature,[c] the sinful passions aroused by the law were at work in our bodies, so that we bore fruit for death. [6]But now, by dying to what once bound us, we have been released from the law so that we serve in the new way of the Spirit, and not in the old way of the written code.

Struggling With Sin

[7]What shall we say, then? Is the law sin? Certainly not! Indeed I would not have

---

[a] 6 Or be rendered powerless   [b] 23 Or through   [c] 5 Or the flesh; also in verse 25

known what sin was except through the law. For I would not have known what coveting really was if the law had not said, "Do not covet."[a] 8But sin, seizing the opportunity afforded by the commandment, produced in me every kind of covetous desire. For apart from law, sin is dead. 9Once I was alive apart from law; but when the commandment came, sin sprang to life and I died. 10I found that the very commandment that was intended to bring life actually brought death. 11For sin, seizing the opportunity afforded by the commandment, deceived me, and through the commandment put me to death. 12So then, the law is holy, and the commandment is holy, righteous and good.

13Did that which is good, then, become death to me? By no means! But in order that sin might be recognized as sin, it produced death in me through what was good, so that through the commandment sin might become utterly sinful. 14We know that the law is spiritual; but I am unspiritual, sold as a slave to sin. 15I do not understand what I do. For what I want to do I do not do, but what I hate I do. 16And if I do what I do not want to do, I agree that the law is good. 17As it is, it is no longer I myself who do it, but it is sin living in me. 18I know that nothing good lives in me, that is, in my sinful nature.[b] For I have the desire to do what is good, but I cannot carry it out. 19For what I do is not the good I want to do; no, the evil I do not want to do—this I keep on doing. 20Now if I do what I do not want to do, it is no longer I who do it, but it is sin living in me that does it.

21So I find this law at work: When I want to do good, evil is right there with me. 22For in my inner being I delight in God's law; 23but I see another law at work in the members of my body, waging war against the law of my mind and making me a prisoner of the law of sin at work within my members. 24What a wretched man I am! Who will rescue me from this body of death? 25Thanks be to God— through Jesus Christ our Lord!

So then, I myself in my mind am a slave to God's law, but in the sinful nature a slave to the law of sin.

Life Through the Spirit

8 Therefore, there is now no condemnation for those who are in Christ Jesus,[c] 2because through Christ Jesus the law of the Spirit of life set me free from the law of sin and death. 3For what the law was powerless to do in that it was weakened by the sinful nature,[d] God did by sending his own Son in the likeness of sinful man to be a sin offering.[e] And so he condemned sin in sinful man,[f] 4in order that the righteous requirements of the law might be fully met in us, who do not live according to the sinful nature but according to the Spirit.

5Those who live according to the sinful nature have their minds set on what that nature desires; but those who live in accordance with the Spirit have their minds set on what the Spirit desires. 6The mind of sinful man[g] is death, but the mind controlled by the Spirit is life and peace; 7the sinful mind[h] is hostile to God. It does not submit to God's law, nor can it do so. 8Those controlled by the sinful nature cannot please God.

9You, however, are controlled not by the sinful nature but by the Spirit, if the Spirit of God lives in you. And if anyone does not have the Spirit of Christ, he does not belong to Christ. 10But if Christ is in you, your body is dead because of sin, yet your spirit is alive because of righteousness. 11And if the Spirit of him who raised Jesus from the dead is living in you, he who raised Christ from the dead will also give life to your mortal bodies through his Spirit, who lives in you.

12Therefore, brothers, we have an

---

a 7 Exodus 20:17; Deut. 5:21   b 18 Or my flesh   c 1 Some later manuscripts Jesus, who do not live according to the sinful nature but according to the Spirit,   d 3 Or the flesh; also in verses 4, 5, 8, 9, 12 and 13   e 3 Or man, for sin   f 3 Or in the flesh   g 6 Or mind set on the flesh   h 7 Or the mind set on the flesh obligation—but it is not to the sinful nature, to live according to it. [13]For if you live according to the sinful nature, you will die; but if by the Spirit you put to death the misdeeds of the body, you will live, [14]because those who are led by the Spirit of God are sons of God. [15]For you did not receive a spirit that makes you a slave again to fear, but you received the Spirit of sonship.[a] And by him we cry, "Abba,[b] Father." [16]The Spirit himself testifies with our spirit that we are God's children. [17]Now if we are children, then we are heirs—heirs of God and co-heirs with Christ, if indeed we share in his sufferings in order that we may also share in his glory.

Future Glory

[18]I consider that our present sufferings are not worth comparing with the glory that will be revealed in us. [19]The creation waits in eager expectation for the sons of God to be revealed. [20]For the creation was subjected to frustration, not by its own choice, but by the will of the one who subjected it, in hope [21]that[c] the creation itself will be liberated from its bondage to decay and brought into the glorious freedom of the children of God.

[22]We know that the whole creation has been groaning as in the pains of childbirth right up to the present time. [23]Not only so, but we ourselves, who have the firstfruits of the Spirit, groan inwardly as we wait eagerly for our adoption as sons, the redemption of our bodies. [24]For in this hope we were saved. But hope that is seen is no hope at all. Who hopes for what he already has? [25]But if we hope for what we do not yet have, we wait for it patiently.

[26]In the same way, the Spirit helps us in our weakness. We do not know what we ought to pray for, but the Spirit himself intercedes for us with groans that words cannot express. [27]And he who searches our hearts knows the mind of the Spirit, because the Spirit intercedes for the saints in accordance with God's will.

More Than Conquerors

[28]And we know that in all things God works for the good of those who love him,[d] who[e] have been called according to his purpose. [29]For those God foreknew he also predestined to be conformed to the likeness of his Son, that he might be the firstborn among many brothers. [30]And those he predestined, he also called; those he called, he also justified; those he justified, he also glorified.

[31]What, then, shall we say in response to this? If God is for us, who can be against us? [32]He who did not spare his own Son, but gave him up for us all—how will he not also, along with him, graciously give us all things? [33]Who will bring any charge against those whom God has chosen? It is God who justifies. [34]Who is he that condemns? Christ Jesus, who died—more than that, who was raised to life—is at the right hand of God and is also interceding for us. [35]Who shall separate us from the love of Christ? Shall trouble or hardship or persecution or famine or nakedness or danger or sword? [36]As it is written:

"For your sake we face death all day long;
we are considered as sheep to be slaughtered."[f]

[37]No, in all these things we are more than conquerors through him who loved us. [38]For I am convinced that neither death nor life, neither angels nor demons,[g] neither the present nor the future, nor any powers, [39]neither height nor depth, nor anything else in all creation, will be able to separate us from the love of God that is in Christ Jesus our Lord.

God's Sovereign Choice

9 I speak the truth in Christ—I am not lying, my conscience confirms it in the Holy Spirit— [2]I have great sorrow

---

[a] 15 Or adoption   [b] 15 Aramaic for Father   [c] 20,21 Or subjected it in hope. [21]For   [d] 28 Some manuscripts And we know that all things work together for good to those who love God   [e] 28 Or works together with those who love him to bring about what is good—with those who   [f] 36 Psalm 44:22   [g] 38 Or nor heavenly rulers

When Words Don't Come

GOING deeper

READ AND CONSIDER: ROMANS 8:18-30

"In the same way, the Spirit helps us in our weakness. We do not know what we ought to pray for, but the Spirit himself intercedes for us with groans that words cannot express. And he who searches our hearts knows the mind of the Spirit, because the Spirit intercedes for the saints in accordance with God's will" (Romans 8:26-27).

When we pray, we are talking to God—maybe out loud, or in a whisper, or silently. Probably most of us try to carefully choose the words we say. We want to get it just right, to be specific, to talk to God in a way that is pleasing to Him and that really expresses our hearts. But sometimes the words won't come. Sometimes the pain is too deep, the questions too difficult, the situation too confusing or complex, the fear too acute. We want to talk to God, but we don't know how to express what we feel. What then?

God promises that when we don't have the words, the Holy Spirit prays *for* us! He searches our hearts and knows what's going on, and intercedes. He pleads with God on our behalf.

In times of grief or suffering—when we can barely see past the pain to communicate with anyone . . . the Holy Spirit helps us to pray.

In times of uncertainty—when we are so unsure of the path ahead that we don't even know what kind of guidance to ask for . . . the Holy Spirit helps us to pray.

In times of fear—when we are so frightened that we don't know where to turn or who to trust . . . the Holy Spirit helps us to pray.

In times of feeling overwhelmed—when the crushing weight on our shoulders pushes us to our knees . . . the Holy Spirit helps us to pray.

When you can't find the words, simply sit with God and invite the Holy Spirit to enable you to communicate to God your deepest thoughts, feelings, fears, and doubts. He will help you pray.

and unceasing anguish in my heart. [3]For I could wish that I myself were cursed and cut off from Christ for the sake of my brothers, those of my own race, [4]the people of Israel. Theirs is the adoption as sons; theirs the divine glory, the covenants, the receiving of the law, the temple worship and the promises. [5]Theirs are the patriarchs, and from them is traced the human ancestry of Christ, who is God over all, forever praised![a] Amen.

[6]It is not as though God's word had failed. For not all who are descended from Israel are Israel. [7]Nor because they are his descendants are they all Abraham's children. On the contrary, "It is through Isaac that your offspring will be reckoned."[b] [8]In other words, it is not the natural children who are God's children, but it is the children of the promise who are regarded as Abraham's offspring. [9]For this was how the promise was stated: "At the appointed time I will return, and Sarah will have a son."[c]

[10]Not only that, but Rebekah's children had one and the same father, our father Isaac. [11]Yet, before the twins were born or had done anything good or bad—in order that God's purpose in election might stand: [12]not by works but by him who

---

[a] *5 Or Christ, who is over all. God be forever praised! Or Christ. God who is over all be forever praised!*   [b] *7 Gen. 21:12*
[c] *9 Gen. 18:10,14*

calls—she was told, "The older will serve the younger."ᵃ ¹³Just as it is written: "Jacob I loved, but Esau I hated."ᵇ

¹⁴What then shall we say? Is God unjust? Not at all! ¹⁵For he says to Moses,

"I will have mercy on whom I have mercy,
and I will have compassion on whom I have compassion."ᶜ

¹⁶It does not, therefore, depend on man's desire or effort, but on God's mercy. ¹⁷For the Scripture says to Pharaoh: "I raised you up for this very purpose, that I might display my power in you and that my name might be proclaimed in all the earth."ᵈ ¹⁸Therefore God has mercy on whom he wants to have mercy, and he hardens whom he wants to harden.

¹⁹One of you will say to me: "Then why does God still blame us? For who resists his will?" ²⁰But who are you, O man, to talk back to God? "Shall what is formed say to him who formed it, 'Why did you make me like this?'"ᵉ ²¹Does not the potter have the right to make out of the same lump of clay some pottery for noble purposes and some for common use?

²²What if God, choosing to show his wrath and make his power known, bore with great patience the objects of his wrath—prepared for destruction? ²³What if he did this to make the riches of his glory known to the objects of his mercy, whom he prepared in advance for glory— ²⁴even us, whom he also called, not only from the Jews but also from the Gentiles? ²⁵As he says in Hosea:

"I will call them 'my people' who are not my people;
and I will call her 'my loved one' who is not my loved one,"ᶠ

²⁶and,

"It will happen that in the very place where it was said to them,
'You are not my people,'

they will be called 'sons of the living God.'"ᵍ

²⁷Isaiah cries out concerning Israel:

"Though the number of the Israelites be like the sand by the sea,
only the remnant will be saved.
²⁸For the Lord will carry out his sentence on earth with speed and finality."ʰ

²⁹It is just as Isaiah said previously:

"Unless the Lord Almighty had left us descendants,
we would have become like Sodom,
we would have been like Gomorrah."ⁱ

Israel's Unbelief

³⁰What then shall we say? That the Gentiles, who did not pursue righteousness, have obtained it, a righteousness that is by faith; ³¹but Israel, who pursued a law of righteousness, has not attained it. ³²Why not? Because they pursued it not by faith but as if it were by works. They stumbled over the "stumbling stone." ³³As it is written:

"See, I lay in Zion a stone that causes men to stumble
and a rock that makes them fall,
and the one who trusts in him will never be put to shame."ʲ

10 Brothers, my heart's desire and prayer to God for the Israelites is that they may be saved. ²For I can testify about them that they are zealous for God, but their zeal is not based on knowledge. ³Since they did not know the righteousness that comes from God and sought to establish their own, they did not submit to God's righteousness. ⁴Christ is the end of the law so that there may be righteousness for everyone who believes.

⁵Moses describes in this way the righteousness that is by the law: "The man who does these things will live by them."ᵏ

ᵃ 12 Gen. 25:23   ᵇ 13 Mal. 1:2,3   ᶜ 15 Exodus 33:19   ᵈ 17 Exodus 9:16   ᵉ 20 Isaiah 29:16; 45:9   ᶠ 25 Hosea 2:23
ᵍ 26 Hosea 1:10   ʰ 28 Isaiah 10:22,23   ⁱ 29 Isaiah 1:9   ʲ 33 Isaiah 8:14; 28:16   ᵏ 5 Lev. 18:5

What Do I Do Now That I'm on My Knees?

Step 1: Tell God you are glad He is your heavenly Father.
Say, "Lord, I come before You today and thank You that You are my heavenly Father." This establishes your relationship with God in the clearest of terms, because this is who God ultimately is to you.

Step 2: Give God worship and praise.
Say, "Lord, I worship You for who You are and all that You have done." Then praise Him for everything that comes to your mind.

Step 3: Choose something that you are especially thankful for about God, and tell Him how grateful you are.
Say, "Lord, I thank You that You are more powerful than anything I face or any enemy that opposes me." Choose another attribute of God you are especially thankful for that day.

Step 4: Give your day to the Lord.
Say, "Lord, I give my day to You and ask You to bless it in every way." When you lift up your day before the Lord and put Him in charge of it, He will help you walk through it with great success.

Step 5: Present yourself to the Lord.
Say, "Lord, I present myself to You this day as a 'living sacrifice' and ask You to help me be a good steward of this temple of Your Spirit." When you present your body as "living sacrifices, holy and pleasing to God" (Romans 12:1), you are acknowledging your dependence upon Him physically as well as spiritually and emotionally.

Step 6: Confess your sins before God and ask Him to help you live His way.
Say, " 'Search me, O God, and know my heart; test me and know my anxious thoughts. See if there is any offensive way in me, and lead me in the way everlasting' (Psalm 139:23-24). Help me to live in obedience to your ways." The Bible says, "If we confess our sins, he is faithful and just and will forgive us our sins and purify us from all unrighteousness" (1 John 1:9).

Step 7: Ask God to help you speak only words that bring life.
Say, "Lord, may the words of my mouth and the meditation of my heart always be acceptable in Your sight (Psalm 19:14). May they bring life and truth to everyone who hears them." Prepare your heart by filling it with God's Word. And ask Him to put a monitor on your mouth so that every word proceeding from your lips is loving, truthful, kind, comforting, edifying, wise, encouraging, and God-glorifying.

Step 8: Ask God for what you need.
Say, "Lord, I ask You to meet all of my needs today. Specifically I ask for the following things..." Then tell the Lord whatever it is you need.

Step 9: Pray for God's will in your life.
Say, "Lord, may Your will be done in my life this day and every day." The more we ask God to keep us in His perfect will, the less chance we will end up *outside* of it.

Step 10: Pray for other people and situations.
Say, "Lord, I pray for the following people..." Then list all who come to your mind. Pray for any situation that you know needs your prayers.

End your prayer saying, "In Jesus' name I pray all these things."

For the next "From Stormie's Heart" article, go to page 1397.

6But the righteousness that is by faith says: "Do not say in your heart, 'Who will ascend into heaven?'ᵃ" (that is, to bring Christ down) 7"or 'Who will descend into the deep?'ᵇ" (that is, to bring Christ up from the dead). 8But what does it say? "The word is near you; it is in your mouth and in your heart,"ᶜ that is, the word of faith we are proclaiming: 9That if you confess with your mouth, "Jesus is Lord," and believe in your heart that God raised him from the dead, you will be saved. 10For it is with your heart that you believe and are justified, and it is with your mouth that you confess and are saved. 11As the Scripture says, "Anyone who trusts in him will never be put to shame."ᵈ 12For there is no difference between Jew and Gentile—the same Lord is Lord of all and richly blesses all who call on him, 13for, "Everyone who calls on the name of the Lord will be saved."ᵉ

14How, then, can they call on the one they have not believed in? And how can they believe in the one of whom they have not heard? And how can they hear without someone preaching to them? 15And how can they preach unless they are sent? As it is written, "How beautiful are the feet of those who bring good news!"ᶠ

Praying Romans 10:17

God, help me to be in Your Word and to understand it so that I will grow in faith every day.

16But not all the Israelites accepted the good news. For Isaiah says, "Lord, who has believed our message?"ᵍ 17Consequently, faith comes from hearing the message, and the message is heard through the word of Christ. 18But I ask: Did they not hear? Of course they did:

"Their voice has gone out into all the
    earth,
their words to the ends of the
    world."ʰ

19Again I ask: Did Israel not understand? First, Moses says,

"I will make you envious by those
    who are not a nation;
I will make you angry by a nation
    that has no understanding."ⁱ

20And Isaiah boldly says,

"I was found by those who did not
    seek me;
I revealed myself to those who did
    not ask for me."ʲ

21But concerning Israel he says,

"All day long I have held out my
    hands
to a disobedient and obstinate
    people."ᵏ

The Remnant of Israel

11 I ask then: Did God reject his people? By no means! I am an Israelite myself, a descendant of Abraham, from the tribe of Benjamin. 2God did not reject his people, whom he foreknew. Don't you know what the Scripture says in the passage about Elijah—how he appealed to God against Israel: 3"Lord, they have killed your prophets and torn down your altars; I am the only one left, and they are trying to kill me"ˡ? 4And what was God's answer to him? "I have reserved for myself seven thousand who have not bowed the knee to Baal."ᵐ 5So too, at the present time there is a remnant chosen by grace. 6And if by grace, then it is no longer by works; if it were, grace would no longer be grace.ⁿ

7What then? What Israel sought so earnestly it did not obtain, but the elect did. The others were hardened, 8as it is written:

"God gave them a spirit of stupor,
    eyes so that they could not see

ᵃ 6 Deut. 30:12   ᵇ 7 Deut. 30:13   ᶜ 8 Deut. 30:14   ᵈ 11 Isaiah 28:16   ᵉ 13 Joel 2:32   ᶠ 15 Isaiah 52:7   ᵍ 16 Isaiah 53:1   ʰ 18 Psalm 19:4   ⁱ 19 Deut. 32:21   ʲ 20 Isaiah 65:1   ᵏ 21 Isaiah 65:2   ˡ 3 1 Kings 19:10,14   ᵐ 4 1 Kings 19:18   ⁿ 6 Some manuscripts *be grace. But if by works, then it is no longer grace; if it were, work would no longer be work.*

and ears so that they could not hear, to this very day."[a]

[9]And David says:

"May their table become a snare and a trap,
a stumbling block and a retribution for them.
[10]May their eyes be darkened so they cannot see,
and their backs be bent forever."[b]

Ingrafted Branches

[11]Again I ask: Did they stumble so as to fall beyond recovery? Not at all! Rather, because of their transgression, salvation has come to the Gentiles to make Israel envious. [12]But if their transgression means riches for the world, and their loss means riches for the Gentiles, how much greater riches will their fullness bring!

[13]I am talking to you Gentiles. Inasmuch as I am the apostle to the Gentiles, I make much of my ministry [14]in the hope that I may somehow arouse my own people to envy and save some of them. [15]For if their rejection is the reconciliation of the world, what will their acceptance be but life from the dead? [16]If the part of the dough offered as firstfruits is holy, then the whole batch is holy; if the root is holy, so are the branches.

[17]If some of the branches have been broken off, and you, though a wild olive shoot, have been grafted in among the others and now share in the nourishing sap from the olive root, [18]do not boast over those branches. If you do, consider this: You do not support the root, but the root supports you. [19]You will say then, "Branches were broken off so that I could be grafted in." [20]Granted. But they were broken off because of unbelief, and you stand by faith. Do not be arrogant, but be afraid. [21]For if God did not spare the natural branches, he will not spare you either.

[22]Consider therefore the kindness and sternness of God: sternness to those who fell, but kindness to you, provided that you continue in his kindness. Otherwise, you also will be cut off. [23]And if they do not persist in unbelief, they will be grafted in, for God is able to graft them in again. [24]After all, if you were cut out of an olive tree that is wild by nature, and contrary to nature were grafted into a cultivated olive tree, how much more readily will these, the natural branches, be grafted into their own olive tree!

All Israel Will Be Saved

[25]I do not want you to be ignorant of this mystery, brothers, so that you may not be conceited: Israel has experienced a hardening in part until the full number of the Gentiles has come in. [26]And so all Israel will be saved, as it is written:

"The deliverer will come from Zion;
he will turn godlessness away from Jacob.
[27]And this is[c] my covenant with them when I take away their sins."[d]

[28]As far as the gospel is concerned, they are enemies on your account; but as far as election is concerned, they are loved on account of the patriarchs, [29]for God's gifts and his call are irrevocable. [30]Just as you who were at one time disobedient to God have now received mercy as a result of their disobedience, [31]so they too have now become disobedient in order that they too may now[e] receive mercy as a result of God's mercy to you. [32]For God has bound all men over to disobedience so that he may have mercy on them all.

Doxology

[33]Oh, the depth of the riches of the wisdom and[f] knowledge of God!
How unsearchable his judgments, and his paths beyond tracing out!
[34]"Who has known the mind of the Lord?

---

[a]8 Deut. 29:4; Isaiah 29:10   [b]10 Psalm 69:22,23   [c]27 Or will be   [d]27 Isaiah 59:20,21; 27:9; Jer. 31:33,34   [e]31 Some manuscripts do not have now.   [f]33 Or riches and the wisdom and the

Or who has been his counselor?"[a]
35"Who has ever given to God,
      that God should repay him?"[b]
36For from him and through him and
            to him are all things.

To him be the glory forever! Amen.

Living Sacrifices

12 Therefore, I urge you, brothers, in view of God's mercy, to offer your bodies as living sacrifices, holy and pleasing to God—this is your spiritual[c] act of worship. 2Do not conform any longer to the pattern of this world, but be transformed by the renewing of your mind. Then you will be able to test and approve what God's will is—his good, pleasing and perfect will.

3For by the grace given me I say to every one of you: Do not think of yourself more highly than you ought, but rather think of yourself with sober judgment, in accordance with the measure of faith God has given you. 4Just as each of us has one body with many members, and these members do not all have the same function, 5so in Christ we who are many form one body, and each member belongs to all the others. 6We have different gifts, according to the grace given us. If a man's gift is prophesying, let him use it in proportion to his[d] faith. 7If it is serving, let him serve; if it is teaching, let him teach; 8if it is encouraging, let him encourage; if it is contributing to the needs of others, let him give generously; if it is leadership, let him govern diligently; if it is showing mercy, let him do it cheerfully.

Love

9Love must be sincere. Hate what is evil; cling to what is good. 10Be devoted to one another in brotherly love. Honor one another above yourselves. 11Never be lacking in zeal, but keep your spiritual fervor, serving the Lord. 12Be joyful in hope,

---

[a] 34 Isaiah 40:13   [b] 35 Job 41:11   [c] 1 Or reasonable   [d] 6 Or in agreement with the

GOING deeper

Being Faithful in Prayer

READ AND CONSIDER: ROMANS 12:9-21

"Be joyful in hope, patient in affliction, faithful in prayer" (Romans 12:12).

A consistent prayer life requires faithfulness. We have to take the time, maintain focus, and commit to not allowing too much time to go in between each prayer. And we need to not grow weary when our prayers seem to go unanswered.

The words Paul wrote to the Romans offer us some insight into the expectations that God places on our prayer lives. God doesn't require eloquence. He doesn't ask that our prayers be a certain length or that we pray a certain number of times every day. God asks that we be "faithful in prayer."

So what does faithfulness in prayer mean? It means making prayer an ongoing, consistent part of our lives. It's being diligent to set aside time for prayer. It's developing a sense of awe and stillness before God. It's praying for someone when we promised we would. It's taking time to sit before God and ask for His direction rather than rushing through each decision. It's seeking out God's purpose in our lives rather than merely reacting to our circumstances. It's continuing to come to Him even when we don't feel that we're getting any answers. When we are faithful to pray—to talk to our heavenly Father—we establish intimacy with Him. That alone is reason enough to be faithful in prayer.

patient in affliction, faithful in prayer. [13]Share with God's people who are in need. Practice hospitality.

[14]Bless those who persecute you; bless and do not curse. [15]Rejoice with those who rejoice; mourn with those who mourn. [16]Live in harmony with one another. Do not be proud, but be willing to associate with people of low position.[a] Do not be conceited.

[17]Do not repay anyone evil for evil. Be careful to do what is right in the eyes of everybody. [18]If it is possible, as far as it depends on you, live at peace with everyone. [19]Do not take revenge, my friends, but leave room for God's wrath, for it is written: "It is mine to avenge; I will repay,"[b] says the Lord. [20]On the contrary:

"If your enemy is hungry, feed him;
    if he is thirsty, give him something
        to drink.
In doing this, you will heap burning
        coals on his head."[c]

[21]Do not be overcome by evil, but overcome evil with good.

Submission to the Authorities

13 Everyone must submit himself to the governing authorities, for there is no authority except that which God has established. The authorities that exist have been established by God. [2]Consequently, he who rebels against the authority is rebelling against what God has instituted, and those who do so will bring judgment on themselves. [3]For rulers hold no terror for those who do right, but for those who do wrong. Do you want to be free from fear of the one in authority? Then do what is right and he will commend you. [4]For he is God's servant to do you good. But if you do wrong, be afraid, for he does not bear the sword for nothing. He is God's servant, an agent of wrath to bring punishment on the wrongdoer. [5]Therefore, it is necessary to submit to the authorities, not only

because of possible punishment but also because of conscience.

[6]This is also why you pay taxes, for the authorities are God's servants, who give their full time to governing. [7]Give everyone what you owe him: If you owe taxes, pay taxes; if revenue, then revenue; if respect, then respect; if honor, then honor.

Love, for the Day Is Near

[8]Let no debt remain outstanding, except the continuing debt to love one another, for he who loves his fellowman has fulfilled the law. [9]The commandments, "Do not commit adultery," "Do not murder," "Do not steal," "Do not covet,"[d] and whatever other commandment there may be, are summed up in this one rule: "Love your neighbor as yourself."[e] [10]Love does no harm to its neighbor. Therefore love is the fulfillment of the law.

[11]And do this, understanding the present time. The hour has come for you to wake up from your slumber, because our salvation is nearer now than when we first believed. [12]The night is nearly over; the day is almost here. So let us put aside the deeds of darkness and put on the armor of light. [13]Let us behave decently, as in the daytime, not in orgies and drunkenness, not in sexual immorality and debauchery, not in dissension and jealousy. [14]Rather, clothe yourselves with the Lord Jesus Christ, and do not think about how to gratify the desires of the sinful nature.[f]

The Weak and the Strong

14 Accept him whose faith is weak, without passing judgment on disputable matters. [2]One man's faith allows him to eat everything, but another man, whose faith is weak, eats only vegetables. [3]The man who eats everything must not look down on him who does not, and the man who does not eat everything must not condemn the man who does, for God has accepted him. [4]Who are you to judge someone else's servant? To his

---

[a] *16* Or *willing to do menial work*   [b] *19* Deut. 32:35   [c] *20* Prov. 25:21,22   [d] *9* Exodus 20:13-15,17; Deut. 5:17-19,21
[e] *9* Lev. 19:18   [f] *14* Or *the flesh*

own master he stands or falls. And he will stand, for the Lord is able to make him stand.

5One man considers one day more sacred than another; another man considers every day alike. Each one should be fully convinced in his own mind. 6He who regards one day as special, does so to the Lord. He who eats meat, eats to the Lord, for he gives thanks to God; and he who abstains, does so to the Lord and gives thanks to God. 7For none of us lives to himself alone and none of us dies to himself alone. 8If we live, we live to the Lord; and if we die, we die to the Lord. So, whether we live or die, we belong to the Lord.

9For this very reason, Christ died and returned to life so that he might be the Lord of both the dead and the living. 10You, then, why do you judge your brother? Or why do you look down on your brother? For we will all stand before God's judgment seat. 11It is written:

"'As surely as I live,' says the Lord,
'every knee will bow before me;
    every tongue will confess to God.'"a

12So then, each of us will give an account of himself to God.

13Therefore let us stop passing judgment on one another. Instead, make up your mind not to put any stumbling block or obstacle in your brother's way. 14As one who is in the Lord Jesus, I am fully convinced that no foodb is unclean in itself. But if anyone regards something as unclean, then for him it is unclean. 15If your brother is distressed because of what you eat, you are no longer acting in love. Do not by your eating destroy your brother for whom Christ died. 16Do not allow what you consider good to be spoken of as evil. 17For the kingdom of God is not a matter of eating and drinking, but of righteousness, peace and joy in the Holy Spirit, 18because anyone who serves Christ in this way is pleasing to God and approved by men.

19Let us therefore make every effort to do what leads to peace and to mutual edification. 20Do not destroy the work of God for the sake of food. All food is clean, but it is wrong for a man to eat anything that causes someone else to stumble. 21It is better not to eat meat or drink wine or to do anything else that will cause your brother to fall.

22So whatever you believe about these things keep between yourself and God. Blessed is the man who does not condemn himself by what he approves. 23But the man who has doubts is condemned if he eats, because his eating is not from faith; and everything that does not come from faith is sin.

15 We who are strong ought to bear with the failings of the weak and not to please ourselves. 2Each of us should please his neighbor for his good, to build him up. 3For even Christ did not please himself but, as it is written: "The insults of those who insult you have fallen on me."c 4For everything that was written in the past was written to teach us, so that through endurance and the encouragement of the Scriptures we might have hope.

5May the God who gives endurance and encouragement give you a spirit of unity among yourselves as you follow Christ Jesus, 6so that with one heart and mouth you may glorify the God and Father of our Lord Jesus Christ.

7Accept one another, then, just as Christ accepted you, in order to bring praise to God. 8For I tell you that Christ has become a servant of the Jewsd on behalf of God's truth, to confirm the promises made to the patriarchs 9so that the Gentiles may glorify God for his mercy, as it is written:

"Therefore I will praise you among
    the Gentiles;
    I will sing hymns to your name."e

10Again, it says,

---

a 11 Isaiah 45:23   b 14 Or that nothing   c 3 Psalm 69:9   d 8 Greek circumcision   e 9 2 Samuel 22:50; Psalm 18:49

"Rejoice, O Gentiles, with his people."[a]

[11]And again,

"Praise the Lord, all you Gentiles,
    and sing praises to him, all you
        peoples."[b]

[12]And again, Isaiah says,

"The Root of Jesse will spring up,
    one who will arise to rule over the
        nations;
the Gentiles will hope in him."[c]

[13]May the God of hope fill you with all joy and peace as you trust in him, so that you may overflow with hope by the power of the Holy Spirit.

Paul the Minister to the Gentiles

[14]I myself am convinced, my brothers, that you yourselves are full of goodness, complete in knowledge and competent to instruct one another. [15]I have written you quite boldly on some points, as if to remind you of them again, because of the grace God gave me [16]to be a minister of Christ Jesus to the Gentiles with the priestly duty of proclaiming the gospel of God, so that the Gentiles might become an offering acceptable to God, sanctified by the Holy Spirit.

[17]Therefore I glory in Christ Jesus in my service to God. [18]I will not venture to speak of anything except what Christ has accomplished through me in leading the Gentiles to obey God by what I have said and done— [19]by the power of signs and miracles, through the power of the Spirit. So from Jerusalem all the way around to Illyricum, I have fully proclaimed the gospel of Christ. [20]It has always been my ambition to preach the gospel where Christ was not known, so that I would not be building on someone else's foundation. [21]Rather, as it is written:

"Those who were not told about him
    will see,
    and those who have not heard will
        understand."[d]

---

[a] *10* Deut. 32:43   [b] *11* Psalm 117:1   [c] *12* Isaiah 11:10   [d] *21* Isaiah 52:15

GOING deeper

Overflowing With Joy, Peace, and Hope

READ AND CONSIDER: ROMANS 15:7-13

"May the God of hope fill you with all joy and peace as you trust in him, so that you may overflow with hope by the power of the Holy Spirit" (Romans 15:13).

We live in a culture that is busy with activities and offers more options than we could ever have time for. We sometimes run on empty more than full, much less overflowing. Yet Paul's prayer for the believers in Rome was that their souls would be so full of joy, peace, and trust that they would overflow with hope. This was to happen not by their own strength or the sheer force of their wills, but "by the power of the Holy Spirit."

Would you like to overflow with hope? Would you like to be a person whose joy seems to light up every room, whose peace can be felt in even the tensest situations? Then by the power of the Holy Spirit, praise God! It's no accident that in this passage Paul quotes from Old Testament passages about praising God, singing hymns to His name, and rejoicing! That's how we find hope in God. Through praise and worship. When we connect to God and honor His presence in our lives, and when we praise Him for His character and the evidences of His works in us, we have so much of Him in us that He spills over. God's gifts in us become our gifts to those around us. That's when we overflow with the joy, peace, and hope that comes only from God.

22 This is why I have often been hindered from coming to you.

Paul's Plan to Visit Rome

23 But now that there is no more place for me to work in these regions, and since I have been longing for many years to see you, 24 I plan to do so when I go to Spain. I hope to visit you while passing through and to have you assist me on my journey there, after I have enjoyed your company for a while. 25 Now, however, I am on my way to Jerusalem in the service of the saints there. 26 For Macedonia and Achaia were pleased to make a contribution for the poor among the saints in Jerusalem. 27 They were pleased to do it, and indeed they owe it to them. For if the Gentiles have shared in the Jews' spiritual blessings, they owe it to the Jews to share with them their material blessings. 28 So after I have completed this task and have made sure that they have received this fruit, I will go to Spain and visit you on the way. 29 I know that when I come to you, I will come in the full measure of the blessing of Christ.

30 I urge you, brothers, by our Lord Jesus Christ and by the love of the Spirit, to join me in my struggle by praying to God for me. 31 Pray that I may be rescued from the unbelievers in Judea and that my service in Jerusalem may be acceptable to the saints there, 32 so that by God's will I may come to you with joy and together with you be refreshed. 33 The God of peace be with you all. Amen.

Personal Greetings

16 I commend to you our sister Phoebe, a servant[a] of the church in Cenchrea. 2 I ask you to receive her in the Lord in a way worthy of the saints and to give her any help she may need from you, for she has been a great help to many people, including me.

3 Greet Priscilla[b] and Aquila, my fellow workers in Christ Jesus. 4 They risked their lives for me. Not only I but all the churches of the Gentiles are grateful to them.

5 Greet also the church that meets at their house.

Greet my dear friend Epenetus, who was the first convert to Christ in the province of Asia.

6 Greet Mary, who worked very hard for you.

7 Greet Andronicus and Junias, my relatives who have been in prison with me. They are outstanding among the apostles, and they were in Christ before I was.

8 Greet Ampliatus, whom I love in the Lord.

9 Greet Urbanus, our fellow worker in Christ, and my dear friend Stachys.

10 Greet Apelles, tested and approved in Christ.

Greet those who belong to the household of Aristobulus.

11 Greet Herodion, my relative.

Greet those in the household of Narcissus who are in the Lord.

12 Greet Tryphena and Tryphosa, those women who work hard in the Lord.

Greet my dear friend Persis, another woman who has worked very hard in the Lord.

13 Greet Rufus, chosen in the Lord, and his mother, who has been a mother to me, too.

14 Greet Asyncritus, Phlegon, Hermes, Patrobas, Hermas and the brothers with them.

15 Greet Philologus, Julia, Nereus and his sister, and Olympas and all the saints with them.

16 Greet one another with a holy kiss.

All the churches of Christ send greetings.

17 I urge you, brothers, to watch out for those who cause divisions and put obstacles in your way that are contrary to the teaching you have learned. Keep away from them. 18 For such people are not

---

a 1 Or deaconess   b 3 Greek Prisca, a variant of Priscilla serving our Lord Christ, but their own appetites. By smooth talk and flattery they deceive the minds of naive people. [19]Everyone has heard about your obedience, so I am full of joy over you; but I want you to be wise about what is good, and innocent about what is evil.

[20]The God of peace will soon crush Satan under your feet.

The grace of our Lord Jesus be with you.

[21]Timothy, my fellow worker, sends his greetings to you, as do Lucius, Jason and Sosipater, my relatives.

[22]I, Tertius, who wrote down this letter, greet you in the Lord.

[23]Gaius, whose hospitality I and the whole church here enjoy, sends you his greetings.

Erastus, who is the city's director of public works, and our brother Quartus send you their greetings.[a]

[25]Now to him who is able to establish you by my gospel and the proclamation of Jesus Christ, according to the revelation of the mystery hidden for long ages past, [26]but now revealed and made known through the prophetic writings by the command of the eternal God, so that all nations might believe and obey him— [27]to the only wise God be glory forever through Jesus Christ! Amen.

---

[a] 23 Some manuscripts *their greetings.* [24]*May the grace of our Lord Jesus Christ be with all of you. Amen.*

Author: Paul

Date: AD 56

Audience: The church at Corinth, to answer specific questions posed to Paul and to encourage them to grow in grace and holiness

Being a Christian in the city of Corinth was not easy. The city was extremely decadent; even places like Rome looked down on Corinth! But believers who received Jesus and believed the gospel message were saved from sin and set on a different path and a new way of living.

After Paul moved on from Corinth, he received reports of problems in the church. People were not taking some sins seriously, others were *creating* rules for everyone to follow, and many were not being sensitive to the needs of their fellow believers. So Paul wrote this letter to explain how they should behave as Christians and as a church in order to be a good influence on the culture around them.

Prayer Themes:

- *Ask God to help you to be hungry for His truth and lose your appetite for the things of this world (3:1-3).*

- *Pray that God will help you remember that "you are not your own; you were bought at a price" (6:19-20).*

- *Seek God for the ability to see things from His perspective so that your priorities are established with eternity in mind (9:24-27).*

- *Pray for others so that you will develop God's heart of love for them (13:1-13).*

1 Corinthians

1 Paul, called to be an apostle of Christ Jesus by the will of God, and our brother Sosthenes,

²To the church of God in Corinth, to those sanctified in Christ Jesus and called to be holy, together with all those everywhere who call on the name of our Lord Jesus Christ—their Lord and ours:

³Grace and peace to you from God our Father and the Lord Jesus Christ.

Thanksgiving

⁴I always thank God for you because of his grace given you in Christ Jesus. ⁵For in him you have been enriched in every way—in all your speaking and in all your knowledge— ⁶because our testimony about Christ was confirmed in you. ⁷Therefore you do not lack any spiritual gift as you eagerly wait for our Lord Jesus Christ to be revealed. ⁸He will keep you strong to the end, so that you will be blameless on the day of our Lord Jesus Christ. ⁹God, who has called you into fellowship with his Son Jesus Christ our Lord, is faithful.

Divisions in the Church

¹⁰I appeal to you, brothers, in the name of our Lord Jesus Christ, that all of you agree with one another so that there may be no divisions among you and that you may be perfectly united in mind and thought. ¹¹My brothers, some from Chloe's household have informed me that there are quarrels among you. ¹²What I mean is this: One of you says, "I follow Paul"; another, "I follow Apollos"; another, "I follow Cephas[a]"; still another, "I follow Christ."

¹³Is Christ divided? Was Paul crucified for you? Were you baptized into[b] the name of Paul? ¹⁴I am thankful that

---

a *12* That is, Peter   b *13* Or *in*; also in verse 15

I did not baptize any of you except Crispus and Gaius, 15so no one can say that you were baptized into my name. 16(Yes, I also baptized the household of Stephanas; beyond that, I don't remember if I baptized anyone else.) 17For Christ did not send me to baptize, but to preach the gospel—not with words of human wisdom, lest the cross of Christ be emptied of its power.

Christ the Wisdom and Power of God

18For the message of the cross is foolishness to those who are perishing, but to us who are being saved it is the power of God. 19For it is written:

"I will destroy the wisdom of the
    wise;
  the intelligence of the intelligent I
    will frustrate."[a]

20Where is the wise man? Where is the scholar? Where is the philosopher of this age? Has not God made foolish the wisdom of the world? 21For since in the wisdom of God the world through its wisdom did not know him, God was pleased through the foolishness of what was preached to save those who believe. 22Jews demand miraculous signs and Greeks look for wisdom, 23but we preach Christ crucified: a stumbling block to Jews and foolishness to Gentiles, 24but to those whom God has called, both Jews and Greeks, Christ the power of God and the wisdom of God. 25For the foolishness of God is wiser than man's wisdom, and the weakness of God is stronger than man's strength.

26Brothers, think of what you were when you were called. Not many of you were wise by human standards; not many were influential; not many were of noble birth. 27But God chose the foolish things of the world to shame the wise; God chose the weak things of the world to shame the strong. 28He chose the lowly things of this world and the despised things—and the things that are not—to nullify the things that are, 29so that no one may boast before him. 30It is because of him that you are in Christ Jesus, who has become for us wisdom from God—that is, our righteousness, holiness and redemption. 31Therefore, as it is written: "Let him who boasts boast in the Lord."[b]

2 When I came to you, brothers, I did not come with eloquence or superior wisdom as I proclaimed to you the testimony about God.[c] 2For I resolved to know nothing while I was with you except Jesus Christ and him crucified. 3I came to you in weakness and fear, and with much trembling. 4My message and my preaching were not with wise and persuasive words, but with a demonstration of the Spirit's power, 5so that your faith might not rest on men's wisdom, but on God's power.

Wisdom From the Spirit

6We do, however, speak a message of wisdom among the mature, but not the wisdom of this age or of the rulers of this age, who are coming to nothing. 7No, we speak of God's secret wisdom, a wisdom that has been hidden and that God destined for our glory before time began. 8None of the rulers of this age understood it, for if they had, they would not have crucified the Lord of glory. 9However, as it is written:

"No eye has seen,
  no ear has heard,
  no mind has conceived
    what God has prepared for those
      who love him"[d]—

10but God has revealed it to us by his Spirit.

The Spirit searches all things, even the deep things of God. 11For who among men knows the thoughts of a man except the man's spirit within him? In the same way no one knows the thoughts of God except the Spirit of God. 12We have not received the spirit of the world but the Spirit who is from God, that we may understand what God has freely given us. 13This is what we speak, not in words taught us by human wisdom but in words taught by the Spirit, expressing spiritual truths in spiritual words.ª 14The man without the Spirit does not accept the things that come from the Spirit of God, for they are foolishness to him, and he cannot understand them, because they are spiritually discerned. 15The spiritual man makes judgments about all things, but he himself is not subject to any man's judgment:

16"For who has known the mind of the
  Lord
    that he may instruct him?"ᵇ

But we have the mind of Christ.

On Divisions in the Church

3 Brothers, I could not address you as spiritual but as worldly—mere infants in Christ. 2I gave you milk, not solid food, for you were not yet ready for it. Indeed, you are still not ready. 3You are still worldly. For since there is jealousy and quarreling among you, are you not worldly? Are you not acting like mere men? 4For when one says, "I follow Paul," and another, "I follow Apollos," are you not mere men?

5What, after all, is Apollos? And what is Paul? Only servants, through whom you came to believe—as the Lord has assigned to each his task. 6I planted the seed, Apollos watered it, but God made it grow. 7So neither he who plants nor he who waters is anything, but only God, who makes things grow. 8The man who plants and the man who waters have one purpose, and each will be rewarded according to his own labor. 9For we are God's fellow workers; you are God's field, God's building.

10By the grace God has given me, I laid a foundation as an expert builder, and someone else is building on it. But each one should be careful how he builds. 11For no one can lay any foundation other than the one already laid, which is Jesus Christ. 12If any man builds on this foundation using gold, silver, costly stones, wood, hay or straw, 13his work will be shown for what it is, because the Day will bring it to light. It will be revealed with fire, and the fire will test the quality of each man's work. 14If what he has built survives, he will receive his reward. 15If it is burned up, he will suffer loss; he himself will be saved, but only as one escaping through the flames.

16Don't you know that you yourselves are God's temple and that God's Spirit lives in you? 17If anyone destroys God's temple, God will destroy him; for God's temple is sacred, and you are that temple.

Praying 1 Corinthians 3:16-17

Lord, help me to always remember that I am the temple of Your Holy Spirit so that I never treat my body carelessly.

18Do not deceive yourselves. If any one of you thinks he is wise by the standards of this age, he should become a "fool" so that he may become wise. 19For the wisdom of this world is foolishness in God's sight. As it is written: "He catches the wise in their craftiness"ᶜ; 20and again, "The Lord knows that the thoughts of the wise are futile."ᵈ 21So then, no more boasting about men! All things are yours, 22whether Paul or Apollos or Cephasᵉ or the world or life or death or the present or the future—all are yours, 23and you are of Christ, and Christ is of God.

Apostles of Christ

4 So then, men ought to regard us as servants of Christ and as those entrusted with the secret things of God. 2Now it is required that those who have been given a trust must prove faithful. 3I care

---

ª 13 Or Spirit, interpreting spiritual truths to spiritual men   ᵇ 16 Isaiah 40:13   ᶜ 19 Job 5:13   ᵈ 20 Psalm 94:11   ᵉ 22 That
is, Peter

Walking in the Light of God's Word

In the theater, lights at the front of the stage that are level with the performer's feet are called "footlights." They act as a guide to help the actors know where to go and keep them from falling into the orchestra pit. God has provided footlights for us too—to guide us as we walk and to keep us from falling into the pit. When we read God's Word, it lights our path and keeps us surefooted. "Your word is a lamp to my feet and a light for my path" (Psalm 119:105). Walking step-by-step with God can only be done successfully if we have God's footlights showing us the way.

Those of us who have read the Bible many times from cover to cover have to be careful not to fall into the trap of thinking that the light we had last year, last month, last week, or even yesterday is enough to keep us safely on the path today. I have done enough writing to know that most of my preparation has to be done in prayer and in the Word of God. On my own, I am not able to write words that will transform anyone's life. Only the anointing power of God attending those words can bring them alive in the hearts of the people reading them. But I can't think that my time spent doing research in the Word of God is enough, even if I spend many hours doing it. If I do only that, I will find my message lacking in the very thing people want to experience—the Lord's touch. That means I don't just read the Bible to prepare for the message. I also must feed on God's Word to prepare my soul and spirit.

A miner will never go down into a dark mine without checking to make sure the light on his cap has sufficient power to last the entire time he's down there. We need to be that diligent about God's Word. We can't just read it once from cover to cover and then be finished like we can with any other book. The light we receive from God's Word must be renewed, revitalized, and solidly reestablished daily. When God's truth is renewed in us each day, it becomes like *our* miner's light. As we look in the direction God is leading us, we are better able to see where we are going. "The law of his God is in his heart; his feet do not slip" (Psalm 37:31). In order to take it in so deeply that it becomes a part of us, we have to open the Bible and say, "Lord, speak to me today and show me what I need to know." Then we must read until our light is recharged.

For the next "From Stormie's Heart" article, go to page 1421.

very little if I am judged by you or by any human court; indeed, I do not even judge myself. 4My conscience is clear, but that does not make me innocent. It is the Lord who judges me. 5Therefore judge nothing before the appointed time; wait till the Lord comes. He will bring to light what is hidden in darkness and will expose the motives of men's hearts. At that time each will receive his praise from God.

6Now, brothers, I have applied these things to myself and Apollos for your benefit, so that you may learn from us the meaning of the saying, "Do not go beyond what is written." Then you will not take pride in one man over against another. 7For who makes you different from anyone else? What do you have that you did not receive? And if you did receive it, why do you boast as though you did not?

8Already you have all you want! Already you have become rich! You have become kings—and that without us! How I wish that you really had become kings so that we might be kings with you! 9For it seems to me that God has put us apostles on display at the end of the procession, like men condemned to die in the arena. We have been made a spectacle to the whole universe, to angels as well as to men. 10We are fools for Christ, but you are so wise in Christ! We are weak, but you are strong! You are honored, we are dishonored! 11To this very hour we go hungry and thirsty, we are in rags, we are brutally treated, we are homeless. 12We work hard with our own hands. When we are cursed, we bless; when we are persecuted, we endure it; 13when we are slandered, we answer kindly. Up to this moment we have become the scum of the earth, the refuse of the world.

14I am not writing this to shame you, but to warn you, as my dear children. 15Even though you have ten thousand guardians in Christ, you do not have many fathers, for in Christ Jesus I became your father through the gospel. 16Therefore I urge you to imitate me. 17For this reason I am sending to you Timothy, my son whom I love, who is faithful in the Lord. He will remind you of my way of life in Christ Jesus, which agrees with what I teach everywhere in every church.

18Some of you have become arrogant, as if I were not coming to you. 19But I will come to you very soon, if the Lord is willing, and then I will find out not only how these arrogant people are talking, but what power they have. 20For the kingdom of God is not a matter of talk but of power. 21What do you prefer? Shall I come to you with a whip, or in love and with a gentle spirit?

Expel the Immoral Brother!

5 It is actually reported that there is sexual immorality among you, and of a kind that does not occur even among pagans: A man has his father's wife. 2And you are proud! Shouldn't you rather have been filled with grief and have put out of your fellowship the man who did this? 3Even though I am not physically present, I am with you in spirit. And I have already passed judgment on the one who did this, just as if I were present. 4When you are assembled in the name of our Lord Jesus and I am with you in spirit, and the power of our Lord Jesus is present, 5hand this man over to Satan, so that the sinful nature[a] may be destroyed and his spirit saved on the day of the Lord.

6Your boasting is not good. Don't you know that a little yeast works through the whole batch of dough? 7Get rid of the old yeast that you may be a new batch without yeast—as you really are. For Christ, our Passover lamb, has been sacrificed. 8Therefore let us keep the Festival, not with the old yeast, the yeast of malice and wickedness, but with bread without yeast, the bread of sincerity and truth.

9I have written you in my letter not to associate with sexually immoral peo-

---

a 5 Or that his body; or that the flesh

ple— [10]not at all meaning the people of this world who are immoral, or the greedy and swindlers, or idolaters. In that case you would have to leave this world. [11]But now I am writing you that you must not associate with anyone who calls himself a brother but is sexually immoral or greedy, an idolater or a slanderer, a drunkard or a swindler. With such a man do not even eat.

[12]What business is it of mine to judge those outside the church? Are you not to judge those inside? [13]God will judge those outside. "Expel the wicked man from among you."[a]

Lawsuits Among Believers

6 If any of you has a dispute with another, dare he take it before the ungodly for judgment instead of before the saints? [2]Do you not know that the saints will judge the world? And if you are to judge the world, are you not competent to judge trivial cases? [3]Do you not know that we will judge angels? How much more the things of this life! [4]Therefore, if you have disputes about such matters, appoint as judges even men of little account in the church![b] [5]I say this to shame you. Is it possible that there is nobody among you wise enough to judge a dispute between believers? [6]But instead, one brother goes to law against another—and this in front of unbelievers!

[7]The very fact that you have lawsuits among you means you have been completely defeated already. Why not rather be wronged? Why not rather be cheated? [8]Instead, you yourselves cheat and do wrong, and you do this to your brothers.

[9]Do you not know that the wicked will not inherit the kingdom of God? Do not be deceived: Neither the sexually immoral nor idolaters nor adulterers nor male prostitutes nor homosexual offenders [10]nor thieves nor the greedy nor drunkards nor slanderers nor swindlers will inherit the kingdom of God. [11]And that is what some of you were. But you were washed, you were sanctified, you were justified in the name of the Lord Jesus Christ and by the Spirit of our God.

Sexual Immorality

[12]"Everything is permissible for me"— but not everything is beneficial. "Everything is permissible for me"—but I will not be mastered by anything. [13]"Food for the stomach and the stomach for food"— but God will destroy them both. The body is not meant for sexual immorality, but for the Lord, and the Lord for the body. [14]By his power God raised the Lord from the dead, and he will raise us also. [15]Do you not know that your bodies are members of Christ himself? Shall I then take the members of Christ and unite them with a prostitute? Never! [16]Do you not know that he who unites himself with a prostitute is one with her in body? For it is said, "The two will become one flesh."[c] [17]But he who unites himself with the Lord is one with him in spirit.

Praying 1 Corinthians 6:18

Enable me to always glorify You in my body and spirit, Lord, and to stay completely free of any kind of inappropriate thoughts or actions.

[18]Flee from sexual immorality. All other sins a man commits are outside his body, but he who sins sexually sins against his own body. [19]Do you not know that your body is a temple of the Holy Spirit, who is in you, whom you have received from God? You are not your own; [20]you were bought at a price. Therefore honor God with your body.

Marriage

7 Now for the matters you wrote about: It is good for a man not to marry.[d] [2]But since there is so much immorality,

---

[a] *13* Deut. 17:7; 19:19; 21:21; 22:21,24; 24:7   [b] *4* Or *matters, do you appoint as judges men of little account in the church?*
[c] *16* Gen. 2:24   [d] *1* Or *"It is good for a man not to have sexual relations with a woman."*

each man should have his own wife, and each woman her own husband. ³The husband should fulfill his marital duty to his wife, and likewise the wife to her husband. ⁴The wife's body does not belong to her alone but also to her husband. In the same way, the husband's body does not belong to him alone but also to his wife. ⁵Do not deprive each other except by mutual consent and for a time, so that you may devote yourselves to prayer. Then come together again so that Satan will not tempt you because of your lack of self-control. ⁶I say this as a concession, not as a command. ⁷I wish that all men were as I am. But each man has his own gift from God; one has this gift, another has that.

⁸Now to the unmarried and the widows I say: It is good for them to stay unmarried, as I am. ⁹But if they cannot control themselves, they should marry, for it is better to marry than to burn with passion.

¹⁰To the married I give this command (not I, but the Lord): A wife must not separate from her husband. ¹¹But if she does, she must remain unmarried or else be reconciled to her husband. And a husband must not divorce his wife.

¹²To the rest I say this (I, not the Lord): If any brother has a wife who is not a believer and she is willing to live with him, he must not divorce her. ¹³And if a woman has a husband who is not a believer and he is willing to live with her, she must not divorce him. ¹⁴For the unbelieving husband has been sanctified through his wife, and the unbelieving wife has been sanctified through her believing husband. Otherwise your children would be unclean, but as it is, they are holy.

¹⁵But if the unbeliever leaves, let him do so. A believing man or woman is not bound in such circumstances; God has called us to live in peace. ¹⁶How do you know, wife, whether you will save your husband? Or, how do you know, husband, whether you will save your wife?

¹⁷Nevertheless, each one should retain the place in life that the Lord assigned to him and to which God has called him. This is the rule I lay down in all the churches. ¹⁸Was a man already circumcised when he was called? He should not become uncircumcised. Was a man uncircumcised when he was called? He should not be circumcised. ¹⁹Circumcision is nothing and uncircumcision is nothing. Keeping God's commands is what counts. ²⁰Each one should remain in the situation which he was in when God called him. ²¹Were you a slave when you were called? Don't let it trouble you—although if you can gain your freedom, do so. ²²For he who was a slave when he was called by the Lord is the Lord's freedman; similarly, he who was a free man when he was called is Christ's slave. ²³You were bought at a price; do not become slaves of men. ²⁴Brothers, each man, as responsible to God, should remain in the situation God called him to.

²⁵Now about virgins: I have no command from the Lord, but I give a judgment as one who by the Lord's mercy is trustworthy. ²⁶Because of the present crisis, I think that it is good for you to remain as you are. ²⁷Are you married? Do not seek a divorce. Are you unmarried? Do not look for a wife. ²⁸But if you do marry, you have not sinned; and if a virgin marries, she has not sinned. But those who marry will face many troubles in this life, and I want to spare you this.

²⁹What I mean, brothers, is that the time is short. From now on those who have wives should live as if they had none; ³⁰those who mourn, as if they did not; those who are happy, as if they were not; those who buy something, as if it were not theirs to keep; ³¹those who use the things of the world, as if not engrossed in them. For this world in its present form is passing away.

³²I would like you to be free from concern. An unmarried man is concerned about the Lord's affairs—how he can

please the Lord. 33But a married man is concerned about the affairs of this world—how he can please his wife— 34and his interests are divided. An unmarried woman or virgin is concerned about the Lord's affairs: Her aim is to be devoted to the Lord in both body and spirit. But a married woman is concerned about the affairs of this world—how she can please her husband. 35I am saying this for your own good, not to restrict you, but that you may live in a right way in undivided devotion to the Lord.

36If anyone thinks he is acting improperly toward the virgin he is engaged to, and if she is getting along in years and he feels he ought to marry, he should do as he wants. He is not sinning. They should get married. 37But the man who has settled the matter in his own mind, who is under no compulsion but has control over his own will, and who has made up his mind not to marry the virgin—this man also does the right thing. 38So then, he who marries the virgin does right, but he who does not marry her does even better.a

39A woman is bound to her husband as long as he lives. But if her husband dies, she is free to marry anyone she wishes, but he must belong to the Lord. 40In my judgment, she is happier if she stays as she is—and I think that I too have the Spirit of God.

Food Sacrificed to Idols

8 Now about food sacrificed to idols: We know that we all possess knowledge.b Knowledge puffs up, but love builds up. 2The man who thinks he knows something does not yet know as he ought to know. 3But the man who loves God is known by God.

4So then, about eating food sacrificed to idols: We know that an idol is nothing at all in the world and that there is no God but one. 5For even if there are so-called gods, whether in heaven or on earth (as indeed there are many "gods" and many "lords"), 6yet for us there is but one God, the Father, from whom all things came and for whom we live; and there is but one Lord, Jesus Christ, through whom all things came and through whom we live.

7But not everyone knows this. Some people are still so accustomed to idols that when they eat such food they think of it as having been sacrificed to an idol, and since their conscience is weak, it is defiled. 8But food does not bring us near to God; we are no worse if we do not eat, and no better if we do.

Prayer is . . .

allowing the Holy Spirit to be
in control of your life.

9Be careful, however, that the exercise of your freedom does not become a stumbling block to the weak. 10For if anyone with a weak conscience sees you who have this knowledge eating in an idol's temple, won't he be emboldened to eat what has been sacrificed to idols? 11So this weak brother, for whom Christ died, is destroyed by your knowledge. 12When you sin against your brothers in this way and wound their weak conscience, you sin against Christ. 13Therefore, if what I eat causes my brother to fall into sin, I will never eat meat again, so that I will not cause him to fall.

The Rights of an Apostle

9 Am I not free? Am I not an apostle? Have I not seen Jesus our Lord? Are you not the result of my work in the Lord? 2Even though I may not be

a 36-38 Or 36If anyone thinks he is not treating his daughter properly, and if she is getting along in years, and he feels she ought to marry, he should do as he wants. He is not sinning. He should let her get married. 37But the man who has settled the matter in his own mind, who is under no compulsion but has control over his own will, and who has made up his mind to keep the virgin unmarried—this man also does the right thing. 38So then, he who gives his virgin in marriage does right, but he who does not give her in marriage does even better.   b 1 Or "We all possess knowledge," as you say an apostle to others, surely I am to you! For you are the seal of my apostleship in the Lord.

3This is my defense to those who sit in judgment on me. 4Don't we have the right to food and drink? 5Don't we have the right to take a believing wife along with us, as do the other apostles and the Lord's brothers and Cephas[a]? 6Or is it only I and Barnabas who must work for a living?

7Who serves as a soldier at his own expense? Who plants a vineyard and does not eat of its grapes? Who tends a flock and does not drink of the milk? 8Do I say this merely from a human point of view? Doesn't the Law say the same thing? 9For it is written in the Law of Moses: "Do not muzzle an ox while it is treading out the grain."[b] Is it about oxen that God is concerned? 10Surely he says this for us, doesn't he? Yes, this was written for us, because when the plowman plows and the thresher threshes, they ought to do so in the hope of sharing in the harvest. 11If we have sown spiritual seed among you, is it too much if we reap a material harvest from you? 12If others have this right of support from you, shouldn't we have it all the more?

But we did not use this right. On the contrary, we put up with anything rather than hinder the gospel of Christ. 13Don't you know that those who work in the temple get their food from the temple, and those who serve at the altar share in what is offered on the altar? 14In the same way, the Lord has commanded that those who preach the gospel should receive their living from the gospel.

15But I have not used any of these rights. And I am not writing this in the hope that you will do such things for me. I would rather die than have anyone deprive me of this boast. 16Yet when I preach the gospel, I cannot boast, for I am compelled to preach. Woe to me if I do not preach the gospel! 17If I preach voluntarily, I have a reward; if not voluntarily, I am simply discharging the trust committed to me. 18What then is my reward? Just this: that in preaching the gospel I may offer it free of charge, and so not make use of my rights in preaching it.

19Though I am free and belong to no man, I make myself a slave to everyone, to win as many as possible. 20To the Jews I became like a Jew, to win the Jews. To those under the law I became like one under the law (though I myself am not under the law), so as to win those under the law. 21To those not having the law I became like one not having the law (though I am not free from God's law but am under Christ's law), so as to win those not having the law. 22To the weak I became weak, to win the weak. I have become all things to all men so that by all possible means I might save some. 23I do all this for the sake of the gospel, that I may share in its blessings.

24Do you not know that in a race all the runners run, but only one gets the prize? Run in such a way as to get the prize. 25Everyone who competes in the games goes into strict training. They do it to get a crown that will not last; but we do it to get a crown that will last forever. 26Therefore I do not run like a man running aimlessly; I do not fight like a man beating the air. 27No, I beat my body and make it my slave so that after I have preached to others, I myself will not be disqualified for the prize.

Warnings From Israel's History

10 For I do not want you to be ignorant of the fact, brothers, that our forefathers were all under the cloud and that they all passed through the sea. 2They were all baptized into Moses in the cloud and in the sea. 3They all ate the same spiritual food 4and drank the same spiritual drink; for they drank from the spiritual rock that accompanied them, and that rock was Christ. 5Nevertheless, God was not pleased with most of them;

---

[a] 5 That is, Peter   [b] 9 Deut. 25:4

their bodies were scattered over the desert.

[6]Now these things occurred as examples[a] to keep us from setting our hearts on evil things as they did. [7]Do not be idolaters, as some of them were; as it is written:"The people sat down to eat and drink and got up to indulge in pagan revelry."[b] [8]We should not commit sexual immorality, as some of them did—and in one day twenty-three thousand of them died. [9]We should not test the Lord, as some of them did—and were killed by snakes. [10]And do not grumble, as some of them did—and were killed by the destroying angel.

[11]These things happened to them as examples and were written down as warnings for us, on whom the fulfillment of the ages has come. [12]So, if you think you are standing firm, be careful that you don't fall! [13]No temptation has seized you except what is common to man. And God is faithful; he will not let you be tempted beyond what you can bear. But when you are tempted, he will also provide a way out so that you can stand up under it.

Praying 1 Corinthians 10:12-13
Thank You, Jesus, that because of the power of Your Spirit in me, I can never be tempted beyond my ability to resist.

Idol Feasts and the Lord's Supper
[14]Therefore, my dear friends, flee from idolatry. [15]I speak to sensible people; judge for yourselves what I say. [16]Is not the cup of thanksgiving for which we give thanks a participation in the blood of Christ? And is not the bread that we break a participation in the body of Christ? [17]Because there is one loaf, we, who are many, are one body, for we all partake of the one loaf.

[18]Consider the people of Israel: Do not those who eat the sacrifices participate in the altar? [19]Do I mean then that a sacrifice

offered to an idol is anything, or that an idol is anything? [20]No, but the sacrifices of pagans are offered to demons, not to God, and I do not want you to be participants with demons. [21]You cannot drink the cup of the Lord and the cup of demons too; you cannot have a part in both the Lord's table and the table of demons. [22]Are we trying to arouse the Lord's jealousy? Are we stronger than he?

The Believer's Freedom
[23]"Everything is permissible"—but not everything is beneficial. "Everything is permissible"—but not everything is constructive. [24]Nobody should seek his own good, but the good of others.

[25]Eat anything sold in the meat market without raising questions of conscience, [26]for, "The earth is the Lord's, and everything in it."[c]

[27]If some unbeliever invites you to a meal and you want to go, eat whatever is put before you without raising questions of conscience. [28]But if anyone says to you, "This has been offered in sacrifice," then do not eat it, both for the sake of the man who told you and for conscience' sake[d]— [29]the other man's conscience, I mean, not yours. For why should my freedom be judged by another's conscience? [30]If I take part in the meal with thankfulness, why am I denounced because of something I thank God for?

[31]So whether you eat or drink or whatever you do, do it all for the glory of God. [32]Do not cause anyone to stumble, whether Jews, Greeks or the church of God— [33]even as I try to please everybody in every way. For I am not seeking my own good but the good of many, so that they may be saved. **11** [1]Follow my example, as I follow the example of Christ.

Propriety in Worship
[2]I praise you for remembering me in everything and for holding to the

---

[a] *6* Or *types*; also in verse 11   [b] *7* Exodus 32:6   [c] *26* Psalm 24:1   [d] *28* Some manuscripts *conscience' sake, for "the earth is the Lord's and everything in it"*

teachings,[a] just as I passed them on to you.

[3]Now I want you to realize that the head of every man is Christ, and the head of the woman is man, and the head of Christ is God. [4]Every man who prays or prophesies with his head covered dishonors his head. [5]And every woman who prays or prophesies with her head uncovered dishonors her head—it is just as though her head were shaved. [6]If a woman does not cover her head, she should have her hair cut off; and if it is a disgrace for a woman to have her hair cut or shaved off, she should cover her head. [7]A man ought not to cover his head,[b] since he is the image and glory of God; but the woman is the glory of man. [8]For man did not come from woman, but woman from man; [9]neither was man created for woman, but woman for man. [10]For this reason, and because of the angels, the woman ought to have a sign of authority on her head.

[11]In the Lord, however, woman is not independent of man, nor is man independent of woman. [12]For as woman came from man, so also man is born of woman. But everything comes from God. [13]Judge for yourselves: Is it proper for a woman to pray to God with her head uncovered? [14]Does not the very nature of things

[a] 2 Or traditions   [b] 4-7 Or [4]Every man who prays or prophesies with long hair dishonors his head. [5]And every woman who prays or prophesies with no covering of hair, on her head dishonors her head—she is just like one of the "shorn women." [6]If a woman has no covering, let her be for now with short hair, but since it is a disgrace for a woman to have her hair shorn or shaved, she should grow it again. [7]A man ought not to have long hair

GOING *deeper*

The Importance of Spiritual Authority

READ AND CONSIDER: 1 CORINTHIANS 11:2-10

"For this reason, and because of the angels, the woman ought to have a sign of authority on her head" (1 Corinthians 11:10).

Paul wrote that women should have a sign of authority on their heads. This refers to spiritual authority, and it is still very important today. While we need not actually put a covering over our heads, we must submit to divinely appointed authority. It's part of God's order. God won't pour into our lives all He has for us until we are in a right relationship with the proper authority figures He has placed in our lives. They are there for our protection and benefit. God's power is too precious and too powerful to be let loose in an unsubmitted soul.

Women need this spiritual covering. It protects them from the enemy of their soul. When spiritual covering is done right—with strength, humility, kindness, and respect, and not with abuse, arrogance, harshness, or lovelessness—it becomes a place of safety for a woman. It brings a right order to her life.

More and more believing women are being given an open door to become all they were created to be. They are moving out in different areas of expertise and ministry and making important differences in their realms of influence. They are realizing that they are not just an afterthought in the order of God's creation, but were created for a special purpose. More and more they are enabled to fulfill their destiny because more men are rising up to their place of spiritual authority and leadership. This is an answer to the prayers of countless women and something for which everyone must praise God. If a woman will trust God's power to flow through the authorities He has placed over her, she can bloom and grow and change her world by the power of God's Spirit. Pray to be in right order with the spiritual authority in your life.

teach you that if a man has long hair, it is a disgrace to him, 15but that if a woman has long hair, it is her glory? For long hair is given to her as a covering. 16If anyone wants to be contentious about this, we have no other practice—nor do the churches of God.

The Lord's Supper

17In the following directives I have no praise for you, for your meetings do more harm than good. 18In the first place, I hear that when you come together as a church, there are divisions among you, and to some extent I believe it. 19No doubt there have to be differences among you to show which of you have God's approval. 20When you come together, it is not the Lord's Supper you eat, 21for as you eat, each of you goes ahead without waiting for anybody else. One remains hungry, another gets drunk. 22Don't you have homes to eat and drink in? Or do you despise the church of God and humiliate those who have nothing? What shall I say to you? Shall I praise you for this? Certainly not!

23For I received from the Lord what I also passed on to you: The Lord Jesus, on the night he was betrayed, took bread, 24and when he had given thanks, he broke it and said, "This is my body, which is for you; do this in remembrance of me." 25In the same way, after supper he took the cup, saying, "This cup is the new covenant in my blood; do this, whenever you drink it, in remembrance of me." 26For whenever you eat this bread and drink this cup, you proclaim the Lord's death until he comes.

27Therefore, whoever eats the bread or drinks the cup of the Lord in an unworthy manner will be guilty of sinning against the body and blood of the Lord. 28A man ought to examine himself before he eats of the bread and drinks of the cup. 29For anyone who eats and drinks without recognizing the body of the Lord eats and drinks judgment on himself. 30That is

why many among you are weak and sick, and a number of you have fallen asleep. 31But if we judged ourselves, we would not come under judgment. 32When we are judged by the Lord, we are being disciplined so that we will not be condemned with the world.

33So then, my brothers, when you come together to eat, wait for each other. 34If anyone is hungry, he should eat at home, so that when you meet together it may not result in judgment.

And when I come I will give further directions.

Spiritual Gifts

12 Now about spiritual gifts, brothers, I do not want you to be ignorant. 2You know that when you were pagans, somehow or other you were influenced and led astray to mute idols. 3Therefore I tell you that no one who is speaking by the Spirit of God says, "Jesus be cursed," and no one can say, "Jesus is Lord," except by the Holy Spirit.

4There are different kinds of gifts, but the same Spirit. 5There are different kinds of service, but the same Lord. 6There are different kinds of working, but the same God works all of them in all men.

7Now to each one the manifestation of the Spirit is given for the common good. 8To one there is given through the Spirit the message of wisdom, to another the message of knowledge by means of the same Spirit, 9to another faith by the same Spirit, to another gifts of healing by that one Spirit, 10to another miraculous powers, to another prophecy, to another distinguishing between spirits, to another speaking in different kinds of tongues,a and to still another the interpretation of tongues.a 11All these are the work of one and the same Spirit, and he gives them to each one, just as he determines.

One Body, Many Parts

12The body is a unit, though it is made up of many parts; and though all its parts

a 10 Or languages; also in verse 28

are many, they form one body. So it is with Christ. 13For we were all baptized by[a] one Spirit into one body—whether Jews or Greeks, slave or free—and we were all given the one Spirit to drink.

14Now the body is not made up of one part but of many. 15If the foot should say, "Because I am not a hand, I do not belong to the body," it would not for that reason cease to be part of the body. 16And if the ear should say, "Because I am not an eye, I do not belong to the body," it would not for that reason cease to be part of the body. 17If the whole body were an eye, where would the sense of hearing be? If the whole body were an ear, where would the sense of smell be? 18But in fact God has arranged the parts in the body, every one of them, just as he wanted them to be. 19If they were all one part, where would the body be? 20As it is, there are many parts, but one body.

21The eye cannot say to the hand, "I don't need you!" And the head cannot say to the feet, "I don't need you!" 22On the contrary, those parts of the body that seem to be weaker are indispensable, 23and the parts that we think are less honorable we treat with special honor. And the parts that are unpresentable are treated with special modesty, 24while our presentable parts need no special treatment. But God has combined the members of the body and has given greater honor to the parts that lacked it, 25so that there should be no division in the body, but that its parts should have equal concern for each other. 26If one part suffers, every part suffers with it; if one part is honored, every part rejoices with it.

27Now you are the body of Christ, and each one of you is a part of it. 28And in the church God has appointed first of all apostles, second prophets, third teachers, then workers of miracles, also those having gifts of healing, those able to help others, those with gifts of administration, and those speaking in different kinds of tongues. 29Are all apostles? Are all prophets? Are all teachers? Do all work miracles? 30Do all have gifts of healing? Do all speak in tongues[b]? Do all interpret? 31But eagerly desire[c] the greater gifts.

Love

And now I will show you the most excellent way.

13 If I speak in the tongues[d] of men and of angels, but have not love, I am only a resounding gong or a clanging cymbal. 2If I have the gift of prophecy and can fathom all mysteries and all knowledge, and if I have a faith that can move mountains, but have not love, I am nothing. 3If I give all I possess to the poor and surrender my body to the flames,[e] but have not love, I gain nothing.

4Love is patient, love is kind. It does not envy, it does not boast, it is not proud. 5It is not rude, it is not self-seeking, it is not easily angered, it keeps no record of wrongs. 6Love does not delight in evil but rejoices with the truth. 7It always protects, always trusts, always hopes, always perseveres.

8Love never fails. But where there are prophecies, they will cease; where there are tongues, they will be stilled; where there is knowledge, it will pass away. 9For we know in part and we prophesy in part, 10but when perfection comes, the imperfect disappears. 11When I was a child, I talked like a child, I thought like a child, I reasoned like a child. When I became a man, I put childish ways behind me. 12Now we see but a poor reflection as in a mirror; then we shall see face to face. Now I know in part; then I shall know fully, even as I am fully known.

13And now these three remain: faith, hope and love. But the greatest of these is love.

Gifts of Prophecy and Tongues

14 Follow the way of love and eagerly desire spiritual gifts, especially the gift of prophecy. 2For anyone who speaks

a 13 Or with; or in   b 30 Or other languages   c 31 Or But you are eagerly desiring   d 1 Or languages   e 3 Some early manuscripts body that I may boast in a tongue[a] does not speak to men but to God. Indeed, no one understands him; he utters mysteries with his spirit.[b] ³But everyone who prophesies speaks to men for their strengthening, encouragement and comfort. ⁴He who speaks in a tongue edifies himself, but he who prophesies edifies the church. ⁵I would like every one of you to speak in tongues,[c] but I would rather have you prophesy. He who prophesies is greater than one who speaks in tongues,[c] unless he interprets, so that the church may be edified.

⁶Now, brothers, if I come to you and speak in tongues, what good will I be to you, unless I bring you some revelation or knowledge or prophecy or word of instruction? ⁷Even in the case of lifeless things that make sounds, such as the flute or harp, how will anyone know what tune is being played unless there is a distinction in the notes? ⁸Again, if the trumpet does not sound a clear call, who will get ready for battle? ⁹So it is with you. Unless you speak intelligible words with your tongue, how will anyone know what you are saying? You will just be speaking into the air. ¹⁰Undoubtedly there are all sorts of languages in the world, yet none of them is without meaning. ¹¹If then I do not grasp the meaning of what someone is saying, I am a foreigner to the speaker, and he is a foreigner to me. ¹²So it is with you. Since you are eager to have spiritual gifts, try to excel in gifts that build up the church.

¹³For this reason anyone who speaks in a tongue should pray that he may interpret what he says. ¹⁴For if I pray in a tongue, my spirit prays, but my mind is unfruitful. ¹⁵So what shall I do? I will pray with my spirit, but I will also pray with my mind; I will sing with my spirit, but I will also sing with my mind. ¹⁶If you are praising God with your spirit, how can one who finds himself among those who do not understand[d] say "Amen" to your thanksgiving, since he does not know what you are saying? ¹⁷You may be giving thanks well enough, but the other man is not edified.

¹⁸I thank God that I speak in tongues more than all of you. ¹⁹But in the church I would rather speak five intelligible words to instruct others than ten thousand words in a tongue.

²⁰Brothers, stop thinking like children. In regard to evil be infants, but in your thinking be adults. ²¹In the Law it is written:

"Through men of strange tongues
   and through the lips of foreigners
I will speak to this people,
   but even then they will not listen
      to me,"[e]

says the Lord.

²²Tongues, then, are a sign, not for believers but for unbelievers; prophecy, however, is for believers, not for unbelievers. ²³So if the whole church comes together and everyone speaks in tongues, and some who do not understand[f] or some unbelievers come in, will they not say that you are out of your mind? ²⁴But if an unbeliever or someone who does not understand[g] comes in while everybody is prophesying, he will be convinced by all that he is a sinner and will be judged by all, ²⁵and the secrets of his heart will be laid bare. So he will fall down and worship God, exclaiming, "God is really among you!"

Orderly Worship

²⁶What then shall we say, brothers? When you come together, everyone has a hymn, or a word of instruction, a revelation, a tongue or an interpretation. All of these must be done for the strengthening of the church. ²⁷If anyone speaks in a tongue, two—or at the most three—should speak, one at a time, and someone must interpret. ²⁸If there is no interpreter, the speaker should keep quiet in the church and speak to himself and God.

---

[a] 2 Or *another language*; also in verses 4, 13, 14, 19, 26 and 27   [b] 2 Or *by the Spirit*   [c] 5 Or *other languages*; also in verses 6, 18, 22, 23 and 39   [d] 16 Or *among the inquirers*   [e] 21 Isaiah 28:11,12   [f] 23 Or *some inquirers*   [g] 24 Or *or some inquirer*

29Two or three prophets should speak, and the others should weigh carefully what is said. 30And if a revelation comes to someone who is sitting down, the first speaker should stop. 31For you can all prophesy in turn so that everyone may be instructed and encouraged. 32The spirits of prophets are subject to the control of prophets. 33For God is not a God of disorder but of peace.

As in all the congregations of the saints, 34women should remain silent in the churches. They are not allowed to speak, but must be in submission, as the Law says. 35If they want to inquire about something, they should ask their own husbands at home; for it is disgraceful for a woman to speak in the church.

36Did the word of God originate with you? Or are you the only people it has reached? 37If anybody thinks he is a prophet or spiritually gifted, let him acknowledge that what I am writing to you is the Lord's command. 38If he ignores this, he himself will be ignored.a

39Therefore, my brothers, be eager to prophesy, and do not forbid speaking in tongues. 40But everything should be done in a fitting and orderly way.

The Resurrection of Christ

15 Now, brothers, I want to remind you of the gospel I preached to you, which you received and on which you have taken your stand. 2By this gospel you are saved, if you hold firmly to the word I preached to you. Otherwise, you have believed in vain.

3For what I received I passed on to you as of first importanceb: that Christ died

---

a 38 Some manuscripts If he is ignorant of this, let him be ignorant   b 3 Or you at the first

---

GOING deeper

Finding Order and Peace

READ AND CONSIDER: 1 CORINTHIANS 14:26-40

"For God is not a God of disorder but of peace" (1 Corinthians 14:33).

God is not a God of disorder, He is a God of peace. Just as our households function better when there is some kind of order—you can find what you are looking for and things just make sense—our minds and hearts function better when there is a peaceful order to what we allow to influence us. We have to be careful what TV shows, magazines, and books we look at and what music, radio programs, or CDs we listen to. Those things should fill our minds with godly thoughts and feed our spirits so we are enriched, clear-minded, and peaceful. If, instead, they deplete us and leave us feeling empty, confused, anxious, and fearful, then we must turn them off and get them out of our lives.

It's important to remember that you have a choice about what you will accept into your mind and what you won't. You can choose to take every thought captive and let Christ's mind be in you (Philippians 2:5), or you can allow the devil to feed you lies and manipulate your life. Every sin begins as a thought in the mind (Mark 7:21-22), so if you don't take control of your mind, the devil will. That's why you must be diligent to monitor what you allow into your mind.

It's up to us to fill our minds with God's Word and the words of people in whom God's Spirit resides. It's up to us to fill our hearts and thoughts with praise so that we leave no room for the enemy's propaganda. It's up to us to find order by asking the God of peace to rule our lives. Only then will we know the peace that passes all understanding.

for our sins according to the Scriptures, [4]that he was buried, that he was raised on the third day according to the Scriptures, [5]and that he appeared to Peter,[a] and then to the Twelve. [6]After that, he appeared to more than five hundred of the brothers at the same time, most of whom are still living, though some have fallen asleep. [7]Then he appeared to James, then to all the apostles, [8]and last of all he appeared to me also, as to one abnormally born.

[9]For I am the least of the apostles and do not even deserve to be called an apostle, because I persecuted the church of God. [10]But by the grace of God I am what I am, and his grace to me was not without effect. No, I worked harder than all of them—yet not I, but the grace of God that was with me. [11]Whether, then, it was I or they, this is what we preach, and this is what you believed.

The Resurrection of the Dead

[12]But if it is preached that Christ has been raised from the dead, how can some of you say that there is no resurrection of the dead? [13]If there is no resurrection of the dead, then not even Christ has been raised. [14]And if Christ has not been raised, our preaching is useless and so is your faith. [15]More than that, we are then found to be false witnesses about God, for we have testified about God that he raised Christ from the dead. But he did not raise him if in fact the dead are not raised. [16]For if the dead are not raised, then Christ has not been raised either. [17]And if Christ has not been raised, your faith is futile; you are still in your sins. [18]Then those also who have fallen asleep in Christ are lost. [19]If only for this life we have hope in Christ, we are to be pitied more than all men.

[20]But Christ has indeed been raised from the dead, the firstfruits of those who have fallen asleep. [21]For since death came through a man, the resurrection of the dead comes also through a man. [22]For as in Adam all die, so in Christ all will be made alive. [23]But each in his own turn: Christ, the firstfruits; then, when he comes, those who belong to him. [24]Then the end will come, when he hands over the kingdom to God the Father after he has destroyed all dominion, authority and power. [25]For he must reign until he has put all his enemies under his feet. [26]The last enemy to be destroyed is death. [27]For he "has put everything under his feet."[b] Now when it says that "everything" has been put under him, it is clear that this does not include God himself, who put everything under Christ. [28]When he has done this, then the Son himself will be made subject to him who put everything under him, so that God may be all in all.

[29]Now if there is no resurrection, what will those do who are baptized for the dead? If the dead are not raised at all, why are people baptized for them? [30]And as for us, why do we endanger ourselves every hour? [31]I die every day—I mean that, brothers—just as surely as I glory over you in Christ Jesus our Lord. [32]If I fought wild beasts in Ephesus for merely human reasons, what have I gained? If the dead are not raised,

"Let us eat and drink,
    for tomorrow we die."[c]

[33]Do not be misled: "Bad company corrupts good character." [34]Come back to your senses as you ought, and stop sinning; for there are some who are ignorant of God—I say this to your shame.

The Resurrection Body

[35]But someone may ask, "How are the dead raised? With what kind of body will they come?" [36]How foolish! What you sow does not come to life unless it dies. [37]When you sow, you do not plant the body that will be, but just a seed, perhaps of wheat or of something else. [38]But God gives it a body as he has determined, and to each kind of seed he gives its own body. [39]All flesh is not the same: Men have one kind of flesh, animals have another, birds

---

[a] 5 Greek Cephas   [b] 27 Psalm 8:6   [c] 32 Isaiah 22:13

another and fish another. 40There are also heavenly bodies and there are earthly bodies; but the splendor of the heavenly bodies is one kind, and the splendor of the earthly bodies is another. 41The sun has one kind of splendor, the moon another and the stars another; and star differs from star in splendor.

42So will it be with the resurrection of the dead. The body that is sown is perishable, it is raised imperishable; 43it is sown in dishonor, it is raised in glory; it is sown in weakness, it is raised in power; 44it is sown a natural body, it is raised a spiritual body.

If there is a natural body, there is also a spiritual body. 45So it is written:"The first man Adam became a living being"a; the last Adam, a life-giving spirit. 46The spiritual did not come first, but the natural, and after that the spiritual. 47The first man was of the dust of the earth, the second man from heaven. 48As was the earthly man, so are those who are of the earth; and as is the man from heaven, so also are those who are of heaven. 49And just as we have borne the likeness of the earthly man, so shall web bear the likeness of the man from heaven.

50I declare to you, brothers, that flesh and blood cannot inherit the kingdom of God, nor does the perishable inherit the imperishable. 51Listen, I tell you a mystery: We will not all sleep, but we will all be changed— 52in a flash, in the twinkling of an eye, at the last trumpet. For the trumpet will sound, the dead will be raised imperishable, and we will be changed. 53For the perishable must clothe itself with the imperishable, and the mortal with immortality. 54When the perishable has been clothed with the imperishable, and the mortal with immortality, then the saying that is written will come true:"Death has been swallowed up in victory."c

55"Where, O death, is your victory?
    Where, O death, is your sting?"d

56The sting of death is sin, and the power of sin is the law. 57But thanks be to God! He gives us the victory through our Lord Jesus Christ.

58Therefore, my dear brothers, stand firm. Let nothing move you. Always give yourselves fully to the work of the Lord, because you know that your labor in the Lord is not in vain.

The Collection for God's People

16 Now about the collection for God's people: Do what I told the Galatian churches to do. 2On the first day of every week, each one of you should set aside a sum of money in keeping with his income, saving it up, so that when I come no collections will have to be made. 3Then, when I arrive, I will give letters of introduction to the men you approve and send them with your gift to Jerusalem. 4If it seems advisable for me to go also, they will accompany me.

Personal Requests

5After I go through Macedonia, I will come to you—for I will be going through Macedonia. 6Perhaps I will stay with you awhile, or even spend the winter, so that you can help me on my journey, wherever I go. 7I do not want to see you now and make only a passing visit; I hope to spend some time with you, if the Lord permits. 8But I will stay on at Ephesus until Pentecost, 9because a great door for effective work has opened to me, and there are many who oppose me.

10If Timothy comes, see to it that he has nothing to fear while he is with you, for he is carrying on the work of the Lord, just as I am. 11No one, then, should refuse to accept him. Send him on his way in peace so that he may return to me. I am expecting him along with the brothers.

12Now about our brother Apollos: I strongly urged him to go to you with the brothers. He was quite unwilling to go now, but he will go when he has the opportunity.

---

a 45 Gen. 2:7   b 49 Some early manuscripts *so let us*   c 54 Isaiah 25:8   d 55 Hosea 13:14

[13]Be on your guard; stand firm in the faith; be men of courage; be strong. [14]Do everything in love.

[15]You know that the household of Stephanas were the first converts in Achaia, and they have devoted themselves to the service of the saints. I urge you, brothers, [16]to submit to such as these and to everyone who joins in the work, and labors at it. [17]I was glad when Stephanas, Fortunatus and Achaicus arrived, because they have supplied what was lacking from you. [18]For they refreshed my spirit and yours also. Such men deserve recognition.

Final Greetings

[19]The churches in the province of Asia send you greetings. Aquila and Priscilla[a] greet you warmly in the Lord, and so does the church that meets at their house. [20]All the brothers here send you greetings. Greet one another with a holy kiss.

[21]I, Paul, write this greeting in my own hand.

[22]If anyone does not love the Lord—a curse be on him. Come, O Lord[b]!

[23]The grace of the Lord Jesus be with you.

[24]My love to all of you in Christ Jesus. Amen.[c]

---

[a] 19 Greek Prisca, a variant of Priscilla   [b] 22 In Aramaic the expression Come, O Lord is Marana tha.   [c] 24 Some manuscripts do not have Amen.

Author: Paul

Date: AD 55

Audience: The church at Corinth and the Christians throughout Greece south of Macedonia, who were hearing from a group of false teachers that Paul was not a true or a trustworthy apostle

Second Corinthians addresses the same audience as 1 Corinthians—the church in the city of Corinth.

While many of the issues mentioned in the first letter seem to have now been resolved, this letter addresses another problem common in many of the early churches. There were traveling preachers who arrived in Corinth and undermined Paul's teachings. In this letter, Paul set out to reestablish his credentials as an apostle and the truth of his message. For the sake of the gospel—not for his own reputation—Paul wrote to set the record straight. In this most soul-bearing of all his letters, we get to see the heart of a man who, because he clung to God in faith and prayer, was able to endure everything the world and the devil could throw at him.

Paul prayed that the believers would learn discernment—that they would not just be swayed by every changing wind of ideas that came their way, but would be rooted in the truth.

Prayer Themes:

• *Pray for others who are facing difficulty and danger, knowing that God will hear your prayers and help them (1:11).*

• *Thank God for all the ways He has blessed you, and ask Him to show you the many ways you can use what you have been given to bless others and thereby glorify Him (9:11).*

• *Praise God even when you receive a "no" answer from Him in response to your prayers, and ask Him to help you accept His perfect will with thanksgiving (12:1-10).*

2 Corinthians

1 Paul, an apostle of Christ Jesus by the will of God, and Timothy our brother,

To the church of God in Corinth, together with all the saints throughout Achaia:

²Grace and peace to you from God our Father and the Lord Jesus Christ.

The God of All Comfort

³Praise be to the God and Father of our Lord Jesus Christ, the Father of compassion and the God of all comfort, ⁴who comforts us in all our troubles, so that we can comfort those in any trouble with the comfort we ourselves have received from God. ⁵For just as the sufferings of Christ flow over into our lives, so also through Christ our comfort overflows. ⁶If we are distressed, it is for your comfort and salvation; if we are comforted, it is for your comfort, which produces in you patient endurance of the same sufferings we suffer. ⁷And our hope for you is firm, because we know that just as you share in our sufferings, so also you share in our comfort.

⁸We do not want you to be uninformed, brothers, about the hardships we suffered in the province of Asia. We were under great pressure, far beyond our ability to endure, so that we despaired even of life. ⁹Indeed, in our hearts we felt the sentence of death. But this happened that we might not rely on ourselves but on God, who raises the dead. ¹⁰He has delivered us from such a deadly peril, and

he will deliver us. On him we have set our hope that he will continue to deliver us, 11as you help us by your prayers. Then many will give thanks on our[a] behalf for the gracious favor granted us in answer to the prayers of many.

Paul's Change of Plans

12Now this is our boast: Our conscience testifies that we have conducted ourselves in the world, and especially in our relations with you, in the holiness and sincerity that are from God. We have done so not according to worldly wisdom but according to God's grace. 13For we do not write you anything you cannot read or understand. And I hope that, 14as you have understood us in part, you will come to understand fully that you can boast of us just as we will boast of you in the day of the Lord Jesus.

15Because I was confident of this, I planned to visit you first so that you might benefit twice. 16I planned to visit you on my way to Macedonia and to come back to you from Macedonia, and then to have you send me on my way to Judea. 17When I planned this, did I do it lightly? Or do I make my plans in a worldly manner so that in the same breath I say, "Yes, yes" and "No, no"?

18But as surely as God is faithful, our message to you is not "Yes" and "No." 19For the Son of God, Jesus Christ, who was preached among you by me and Silas[b] and Timothy, was not "Yes" and "No," but in him it has always been "Yes." 20For no matter how many promises God has made, they are "Yes" in Christ. And so through him the "Amen" is spoken by us to the glory of God. 21Now it is God who makes both us and you stand firm in Christ. He anointed us, 22set his seal of ownership on us, and put his Spirit in our hearts as a deposit, guaranteeing what is to come.

23I call God as my witness that it was in order to spare you that I did not return to Corinth. 24Not that we lord it over your

faith, but we work with you for your joy, because it is by faith you stand firm. 2 1So I made up my mind that I would not make another painful visit to you. 2For if I grieve you, who is left to make me glad but you whom I have grieved? 3I wrote as I did so that when I came I should not be distressed by those who ought to make me rejoice. I had confidence in all of you, that you would all share my joy. 4For I wrote you out of great distress and anguish of heart and with many tears, not to grieve you but to let you know the depth of my love for you.

Forgiveness for the Sinner

5If anyone has caused grief, he has not so much grieved me as he has grieved all of you, to some extent—not to put it too severely. 6The punishment inflicted on him by the majority is sufficient for him. 7Now instead, you ought to forgive and comfort him, so that he will not be overwhelmed by excessive sorrow. 8I urge you, therefore, to reaffirm your love for him. 9The reason I wrote you was to see if you would stand the test and be obedient in everything. 10If you forgive anyone, I also forgive him. And what I have forgiven—if there was anything to forgive—I have forgiven in the sight of Christ for your sake, 11in order that Satan might not outwit us. For we are not unaware of his schemes.

Ministers of the New Covenant

12Now when I went to Troas to preach the gospel of Christ and found that the Lord had opened a door for me, 13I still had no peace of mind, because I did not find my brother Titus there. So I said good-by to them and went on to Macedonia.

14But thanks be to God, who always leads us in triumphal procession in Christ and through us spreads everywhere the fragrance of the knowledge of him. 15For we are to God the aroma of Christ

a 11 Many manuscripts your   b 19 Greek Silvanus, a variant of Silas among those who are being saved and those who are perishing. ¹⁶To the one we are the smell of death; to the other, the fragrance of life. And who is equal to such a task? ¹⁷Unlike so many, we do not peddle the word of God for profit. On the contrary, in Christ we speak before God with sincerity, like men sent from God.

3 Are we beginning to commend ourselves again? Or do we need, like some people, letters of recommendation to you or from you? ²You yourselves are our letter, written on our hearts, known and read by everybody. ³You show that you are a letter from Christ, the result of our ministry, written not with ink but with the Spirit of the living God, not on tablets of stone but on tablets of human hearts.

⁴Such confidence as this is ours through Christ before God. ⁵Not that we are competent in ourselves to claim anything for ourselves, but our competence comes from God. ⁶He has made us competent as ministers of a new covenant—not of the letter but of the Spirit; for the letter kills, but the Spirit gives life.

The Glory of the New Covenant

⁷Now if the ministry that brought death, which was engraved in letters on stone, came with glory, so that the Israelites could not look steadily at the face of Moses because of its glory, fading though it was, ⁸will not the ministry of the Spirit be even more glorious? ⁹If the ministry that condemns men is glorious, how much more glorious is the ministry that brings righteousness! ¹⁰For what was glorious has no glory now in comparison with the surpassing glory. ¹¹And if what was fading away came with glory, how much greater is the glory of that which lasts!

¹²Therefore, since we have such a hope, we are very bold. ¹³We are not like Moses, who would put a veil over his face to keep the Israelites from gazing at it while the radiance was fading away. ¹⁴But their minds were made dull, for to this day the same veil remains when the old covenant is read. It has not been removed, because only in Christ is it taken away. ¹⁵Even to this day when Moses is read, a veil covers their hearts. ¹⁶But whenever anyone turns to the Lord, the veil is taken away. ¹⁷Now the Lord is the Spirit, and where the Spirit of the Lord is, there is freedom. ¹⁸And we, who with unveiled faces all reflect[a] the Lord's glory, are being transformed into his likeness with ever-increasing glory, which comes from the Lord, who is the Spirit.

Praying 2 Corinthians 3:16-18

Thank You, Jesus, that when I received
You I also received spiritual sight,
and that when I look to You
I am being transformed from glory to
glory by the power of Your Spirit.

Treasures in Jars of Clay

4 Therefore, since through God's mercy we have this ministry, we do not lose heart. ²Rather, we have renounced secret and shameful ways; we do not use deception, nor do we distort the word of God. On the contrary, by setting forth the truth plainly we commend ourselves to every man's conscience in the sight of God. ³And even if our gospel is veiled, it is veiled to those who are perishing. ⁴The god of this age has blinded the minds of unbelievers, so that they cannot see the light of the gospel of the glory of Christ, who is the image of God. ⁵For we do not preach ourselves, but Jesus Christ as Lord, and ourselves as your servants for Jesus' sake. ⁶For God, who said, "Let light shine out of darkness,"[b] made his light shine in our hearts to give us the light of the knowledge of the glory of God in the face of Christ.

⁷But we have this treasure in jars of clay to show that this all-surpassing power is from God and not from us. ⁸We are hard pressed on every side, but not crushed;

---

[a] *18* Or *contemplate*   [b] *6* Gen. 1:3

perplexed, but not in despair; [9]persecuted, but not abandoned; struck down, but not destroyed. [10]We always carry around in our body the death of Jesus, so that the life of Jesus may also be revealed in our body. [11]For we who are alive are always being given over to death for Jesus' sake, so that his life may be revealed in our mortal body. [12]So then, death is at work in us, but life is at work in you.

[13]It is written: "I believed; therefore I have spoken."[a] With that same spirit of faith we also believe and therefore speak, [14]because we know that the one who raised the Lord Jesus from the dead will also raise us with Jesus and present us with you in his presence. [15]All this is for your benefit, so that the grace that is reaching more and more people may cause thanksgiving to overflow to the glory of God.

[16]Therefore we do not lose heart. Though outwardly we are wasting away, yet inwardly we are being renewed day by day. [17]For our light and momentary troubles are achieving for us an eternal glory that far outweighs them all. [18]So we fix our eyes not on what is seen, but on what is unseen. For what is seen is temporary, but what is unseen is eternal.

Our Heavenly Dwelling

5 Now we know that if the earthly tent we live in is destroyed, we have a building from God, an eternal house in heaven, not built by human hands. [2]Meanwhile we groan, longing to be clothed with our heavenly dwelling, [3]because when we are clothed, we will not be found naked. [4]For while we are in this tent, we groan and are burdened, because we do not wish to be unclothed but to be clothed with our heavenly dwelling, so that what is mortal may be swallowed up by life. [5]Now it is God who has made us for this very purpose and has given us the Spirit as a deposit, guaranteeing what is to come.

[6]Therefore we are always confident and know that as long as we are at home in the body we are away from the Lord. [7]We live by faith, not by sight. [8]We are confident, I say, and would prefer to be away from the body and at home with the Lord. [9]So we make it our goal to please him, whether we are at home in the body or away from it. [10]For we must all appear before the judgment seat of Christ, that each one may receive what is due him for the things done while in the body, whether good or bad.

Prayer is . . .

talking to God, which means if you can talk, you can pray.

The Ministry of Reconciliation

[11]Since, then, we know what it is to fear the Lord, we try to persuade men. What we are is plain to God, and I hope it is also plain to your conscience. [12]We are not trying to commend ourselves to you again, but are giving you an opportunity to take pride in us, so that you can answer those who take pride in what is seen rather than in what is in the heart. [13]If we are out of our mind, it is for the sake of God; if we are in our right mind, it is for you. [14]For Christ's love compels us, because we are convinced that one died for all, and therefore all died. [15]And he died for all, that those who live should no longer live for themselves but for him who died for them and was raised again.

[16]So from now on we regard no one from a worldly point of view. Though we once regarded Christ in this way, we do so no longer. [17]Therefore, if anyone is in Christ, he is a new creation; the old has gone, the new has come! [18]All this is from God, who reconciled us to himself through Christ and gave us the ministry of reconciliation: [19]that God was

---

a *13* Psalm 116:10

reconciling the world to himself in Christ, not counting men's sins against them. And he has committed to us the message of reconciliation. 20We are therefore Christ's ambassadors, as though God were making his appeal through us. We implore you on Christ's behalf: Be reconciled to God. 21God made him who had no sin to be sin[a] for us, so that in him we might become the righteousness of God.

6 As God's fellow workers we urge you not to receive God's grace in vain. 2For he says,

"In the time of my favor I heard you,
   and in the day of salvation I helped
   you."[b]

I tell you, now is the time of God's favor, now is the day of salvation.

Paul's Hardships

3We put no stumbling block in anyone's path, so that our ministry will not be discredited. 4Rather, as servants of God we commend ourselves in every way: in great endurance; in troubles, hardships and distresses; 5in beatings, imprisonments and riots; in hard work, sleepless nights and hunger; 6in purity, understanding, patience and kindness; in the Holy Spirit and in sincere love; 7in truthful speech and in the power of God; with weapons of righteousness in the right hand and in the left; 8through glory and dishonor, bad report and good report; genuine, yet regarded as impostors; 9known, yet regarded as unknown; dying, and yet we live on; beaten, and yet not killed; 10sorrowful, yet always rejoicing; poor, yet making many rich; having nothing, and yet possessing everything.

11We have spoken freely to you, Corinthians, and opened wide our hearts to you. 12We are not withholding our affection from you, but you are withholding yours from us. 13As a fair exchange—I speak as to my children—open wide your hearts also.

Do Not Be Yoked With Unbelievers

14Do not be yoked together with unbelievers. For what do righteousness and wickedness have in common? Or what fellowship can light have with darkness? 15What harmony is there between Christ and Belial[c]? What does a believer have in common with an unbeliever? 16What agreement is there between the temple of God and idols? For we are the temple of the living God. As God has said: "I will live with them and walk among them, and I will be their God, and they will be my people."[d]

17"Therefore come out from them
   and be separate,
                           says the Lord.
Touch no unclean thing,
   and I will receive you."[e]
18"I will be a Father to you,
   and you will be my sons and
   daughters,
                  says the Lord Almighty."[f]

7 Since we have these promises, dear friends, let us purify ourselves from everything that contaminates body and spirit, perfecting holiness out of reverence for God.

Paul's Joy

2Make room for us in your hearts. We have wronged no one, we have corrupted no one, we have exploited no one. 3I do not say this to condemn you; I have said before that you have such a place in our hearts that we would live or die with you. 4I have great confidence in you; I take great pride in you. I am greatly encouraged; in all our troubles my joy knows no bounds.

5For when we came into Macedonia, this body of ours had no rest, but we were harassed at every turn—conflicts on the outside, fears within. 6But God, who comforts the downcast, comforted us by the coming of Titus, 7and not only by his coming but also by the comfort

---

you had given him. He told us about your longing for me, your deep sorrow, your ardent concern for me, so that my joy was greater than ever.

⁸Even if I caused you sorrow by my letter, I do not regret it. Though I did regret it—I see that my letter hurt you, but only for a little while— ⁹yet now I am happy, not because you were made sorry, but because your sorrow led you to repentance. For you became sorrowful as God intended and so were not harmed in any way by us. ¹⁰Godly sorrow brings repentance that leads to salvation and leaves no regret, but worldly sorrow brings death. ¹¹See what this godly sorrow has produced in you: what earnestness, what eagerness to clear yourselves, what indignation, what alarm, what longing, what concern, what readiness to see justice done. At every point you have proved yourselves to be innocent in this matter. ¹²So even though I wrote to you, it was not on account of the one who did the wrong or of the injured party, but rather that before God you could see for yourselves how devoted to us you are. ¹³By all this we are encouraged.

In addition to our own encouragement, we were especially delighted to see how happy Titus was, because his spirit has been refreshed by all of you. ¹⁴I had boasted to him about you, and you have not embarrassed me. But just as everything we said to you was true, so our boasting about you to Titus has proved to be true as well. ¹⁵And his affection for you is all the greater when he remembers that you were all obedient, receiving him with fear and trembling. ¹⁶I am glad I can have complete confidence in you.

Generosity Encouraged

8 And now, brothers, we want you to know about the grace that God has given the Macedonian churches. ²Out of the most severe trial, their overflowing joy and their extreme poverty welled up in rich generosity. ³For I testify that they gave as much as they were able, and even beyond their ability. Entirely on their own, ⁴they urgently pleaded with us for the privilege of sharing in this service to the saints. ⁵And they did not do as we expected, but they gave themselves first to the Lord and then to us in keeping with God's will. ⁶So we urged Titus, since he had earlier made a beginning, to bring also to completion this act of grace on your part. ⁷But just as you excel in everything—in faith, in speech, in knowledge, in complete earnestness and in your love for usª—see that you also excel in this grace of giving.

⁸I am not commanding you, but I want to test the sincerity of your love by comparing it with the earnestness of others. ⁹For you know the grace of our Lord Jesus Christ, that though he was rich, yet for your sakes he became poor, so that you through his poverty might become rich.

¹⁰And here is my advice about what is best for you in this matter: Last year you were the first not only to give but also to have the desire to do so. ¹¹Now finish the work, so that your eager willingness to do it may be matched by your completion of it, according to your means. ¹²For if the willingness is there, the gift is acceptable according to what one has, not according to what he does not have.

¹³Our desire is not that others might be relieved while you are hard pressed, but that there might be equality. ¹⁴At the present time your plenty will supply what they need, so that in turn their plenty will supply what you need. Then there will be equality, ¹⁵as it is written: "He who gathered much did not have too much, and he who gathered little did not have too little."ᵇ

Titus Sent to Corinth

¹⁶I thank God, who put into the heart of Titus the same concern I have for you. ¹⁷For Titus not only welcomed our appeal, but he is coming to you with much

ª 7 Some manuscripts in our love for you   ᵇ 15 Exodus 16:18

enthusiasm and on his own initiative. [18]And we are sending along with him the brother who is praised by all the churches for his service to the gospel. [19]What is more, he was chosen by the churches to accompany us as we carry the offering, which we administer in order to honor the Lord himself and to show our eagerness to help. [20]We want to avoid any criticism of the way we administer this liberal gift. [21]For we are taking pains to do what is right, not only in the eyes of the Lord but also in the eyes of men.

[22]In addition, we are sending with them our brother who has often proved to us in many ways that he is zealous, and now even more so because of his great confidence in you. [23]As for Titus, he is my partner and fellow worker among you; as for our brothers, they are representatives of the churches and an honor to Christ. [24]Therefore show these men the proof of your love and the reason for our pride in you, so that the churches can see it.

9 There is no need for me to write to you about this service to the saints. [2]For I know your eagerness to help, and I have been boasting about it to the Macedonians, telling them that since last year you in Achaia were ready to give; and your enthusiasm has stirred most of them to action. [3]But I am sending the brothers in order that our boasting about you in this matter should not prove hollow, but that you may be ready, as I said you would be. [4]For if any Macedonians come with me and find you unprepared, we—not to say anything about you— would be ashamed of having been so confident. [5]So I thought it necessary to urge the brothers to visit you in advance and finish the arrangements for the generous gift you had promised. Then it will be ready as a generous gift, not as one grudgingly given.

Sowing Generously

[6]Remember this: Whoever sows sparingly will also reap sparingly, and whoever sows generously will also reap generously. [7]Each man should give what he has decided in his heart to give, not reluctantly or under compulsion, for God loves a cheerful giver. [8]And God is

---

GOING *deeper*

Prayer Grows Love in Your Heart

READ AND CONSIDER: 2 CORINTHIANS 9:6-15

"And in their prayers for you their hearts will go out to you, because of the surpassing grace God has given you" (2 Corinthians 9:14).

It is a powerful thing when we pray for one another. Every time we pray for someone, we feel more connected to them. It is exactly as Paul said—your heart goes out to the person you are praying for. That's because God gives us His heart for them.

That's why praying for our enemies is a good thing. It not only softens our heart, but it opens a door for them to hear God and for their heart to be changed. When there are people we are angry with and don't feel like praying for at all, if we will make ourselves pray for them, even though we don't feel they deserve it, walls will come down and forgiveness will happen.

Intercessory prayer is powerful on many levels. It not only influences situations and people, it changes *us* in the very process. Is there a difficult person for whom you need to pray? Has someone hurt you? Ask God to help you pray for them. When you do, He will work love in your heart for them, which will ultimately be to your greatest blessing.

able to make all grace abound to you, so that in all things at all times, having all that you need, you will abound in every good work. [9]As it is written:

"He has scattered abroad his gifts to
    the poor;
  his righteousness endures forever."[a]

[10]Now he who supplies seed to the sower and bread for food will also supply and increase your store of seed and will enlarge the harvest of your righteousness. [11]You will be made rich in every way so that you can be generous on every occasion, and through us your generosity will result in thanksgiving to God.

[12]This service that you perform is not only supplying the needs of God's people but is also overflowing in many expressions of thanks to God. [13]Because of the service by which you have proved yourselves, men will praise God for the obedience that accompanies your confession of the gospel of Christ, and for your generosity in sharing with them and with everyone else. [14]And in their prayers for you their hearts will go out to you, because of the surpassing grace God has given you. [15]Thanks be to God for his indescribable gift!

Paul's Defense of His Ministry

10 By the meekness and gentleness of Christ, I appeal to you—I, Paul, who am "timid" when face to face with you, but "bold" when away! [2]I beg you that when I come I may not have to be as bold as I expect to be toward some people who think that we live by the standards of this world. [3]For though we live in the world, we do not wage war as the world does. [4]The weapons we fight with are not the weapons of the world. On the contrary, they have divine power to demolish strongholds. [5]We demolish arguments and every pretension that sets

itself up against the knowledge of God, and we take captive every thought to make it obedient to Christ. [6]And we will be ready to punish every act of disobedience, once your obedience is complete.

Praying 2 Corinthians 10:3-5

Help me, Lord, to bring every thought under godly control and to be entirely submitted to obeying You.

[7]You are looking only on the surface of things.[b] If anyone is confident that he belongs to Christ, he should consider again that we belong to Christ just as much as he. [8]For even if I boast somewhat freely about the authority the Lord gave us for building you up rather than pulling you down, I will not be ashamed of it. [9]I do not want to seem to be trying to frighten you with my letters. [10]For some say, "His letters are weighty and forceful, but in person he is unimpressive and his speaking amounts to nothing." [11]Such people should realize that what we are in our letters when we are absent, we will be in our actions when we are present.

[12]We do not dare to classify or compare ourselves with some who commend themselves. When they measure themselves by themselves and compare themselves with themselves, they are not wise. [13]We, however, will not boast beyond proper limits, but will confine our boasting to the field God has assigned to us, a field that reaches even to you. [14]We are not going too far in our boasting, as would be the case if we had not come to you, for we did get as far as you with the gospel of Christ. [15]Neither do we go beyond our limits by boasting of work done by others.[c] Our hope is that, as your faith continues to grow, our area of activity among you will greatly expand, [16]so that we can preach the gospel in the regions beyond you. For we do not want

---

[a] 9 Psalm 112:9   [b] 7 Or *Look at the obvious facts*   [c] 13-15 Or [13]*We, however, will not boast about things that cannot be measured, but we will boast according to the standard of measurement that the God of measure has assigned us—a measurement that relates even to you.* [14] ... [15]*Neither do we boast about things that cannot be measured in regard to the work done by others.*

to boast about work already done in another man's territory. 17But, "Let him who boasts boast in the Lord."a 18For it is not the one who commends himself who is approved, but the one whom the Lord commends.

Paul and the False Apostles

11 I hope you will put up with a little of my foolishness; but you are already doing that. 2I am jealous for you with a godly jealousy. I promised you to one husband, to Christ, so that I might present you as a pure virgin to him. 3But I am afraid that just as Eve was deceived by the serpent's cunning, your minds may somehow be led astray from your sincere and pure devotion to Christ. 4For if someone comes to you and preaches a Jesus other than the Jesus we preached, or if you receive a different spirit from the one you received, or a different gospel from the one you accepted, you put up with it easily enough. 5But I do not think I am in the least inferior to those "super-apostles." 6I may not be a trained speaker, but I do have knowledge. We have made this perfectly clear to you in every way.

7Was it a sin for me to lower myself in order to elevate you by preaching the gospel of God to you free of charge? 8I robbed other churches by receiving support from them so as to serve you. 9And when I was with you and needed something, I was not a burden to anyone, for the brothers who came from Macedonia supplied what I needed. I have kept myself from being a burden to you in any way, and will continue to do so. 10As surely as the truth of Christ is in me, nobody in the regions of Achaia will stop this boasting of mine. 11Why? Because I do not love you? God knows I do! 12And I will keep on doing what I am doing in order to cut the ground from under those who want an opportunity to be considered equal with us in the things they boast about.

13For such men are false apostles, deceitful workmen, masquerading as apostles of Christ. 14And no wonder, for Satan himself masquerades as an angel of light. 15It is not surprising, then, if his servants masquerade as servants of righteousness. Their end will be what their actions deserve.

Paul Boasts About His Sufferings

16I repeat: Let no one take me for a fool. But if you do, then receive me just as you would a fool, so that I may do a little boasting. 17In this self-confident boasting I am not talking as the Lord would, but as a fool. 18Since many are boasting in the way the world does, I too will boast. 19You gladly put up with fools since you are so wise! 20In fact, you even put up with anyone who enslaves you or exploits you or takes advantage of you or pushes himself forward or slaps you in the face. 21To my shame I admit that we were too weak for that!

What anyone else dares to boast about—I am speaking as a fool—I also dare to boast about. 22Are they Hebrews? So am I. Are they Israelites? So am I. Are they Abraham's descendants? So am I. 23Are they servants of Christ? (I am out of my mind to talk like this.) I am more. I have worked much harder, been in prison more frequently, been flogged more severely, and been exposed to death again and again. 24Five times I received from the Jews the forty lashes minus one. 25Three times I was beaten with rods, once I was stoned, three times I was shipwrecked, I spent a night and a day in the open sea, 26I have been constantly on the move. I have been in danger from rivers, in danger from bandits, in danger from my own countrymen, in danger from Gentiles; in danger in the city, in danger in the country, in danger at sea; and in danger from false brothers. 27I have labored and toiled and have often gone without sleep; I have known hunger and thirst and have often gone without food; I have been cold and naked. 28Besides everything else, I face

a 17 Jer. 9:24

Beginning to See the Light

Our lives are touched by many different kinds of light.

Sunlight and moonlight. Stoplights and spotlights. Firelight, city lights, candlelight, and lamplight. Headlights, night-lights, neon lights, and streetlights. Glittering and blinding lights. Confusing and deceiving lights.

All of these lights have one thing in common. They eventually go out. They're not reliable. They can never be the light we need to illuminate the path of our life. There is only one light that never goes out. It comes from God.

It *is* God.

God's light is the true light. His light makes clear. All other light confuses. His light *reveals* the truth. All other light obscures it. His light brings us out of our blindness and helps us see in a way we've never been able to see before. He says, "I will lead the blind by ways they have not known, along unfamiliar paths I will guide them; I will turn the darkness into light before them and make the rough places smooth. These are the things I will do; I will not forsake them" (Isaiah 42:16). God's light penetrates darkness, and darkness cannot put it out.

Unless we follow the true light, we are being led into darkness.

I have heard people talk about near-death experiences where they saw a bright light. I don't doubt that they saw it. But I know that when we who believe in the Lord die, we won't see a light. We will see *the* light. We will see Jesus, who is the Light of the World. The best way to make

sure we see His light after we die is to follow His light as long as we're alive.

We begin to see the light when we begin to see the Lord.

The way to keep from following the wrong light is to not follow any light except for the light of Jesus. The world wants us to follow *its* light. The devil wants us to follow *his* light. "For Satan himself masquerades as an angel of light" (2 Corinthians 11:14). We will encounter people who fancy themselves to be our savior and will want us to follow *their* light. But God does not have us follow a light. He has us follow *Him*. And He becomes our light. The more faithfully we follow Him, the more of His light we will have shining on our path. "In him was life, and that life was the light of men" (John 1:4).

God's light is constant because *He* is constant. He is without change. His light doesn't grow dim or go out. If it appears to, it's because we have stepped out of the light of His presence. Although God is omnipresent, we must remember that there are degrees of the fullness of His presence we can enjoy and experience. He gives us as much of His presence as we are able to receive. Although His light never goes out, we sometimes do things that separate us from the fullness of His life and cause His light to appear dim in our lives. But His light is always available to us. No matter how badly we think we've blown it in our lives, we are never truly in darkness when we look to Him.

For the next "From Stormie's Heart" article, go to page 1428.

daily the pressure of my concern for all the churches. ²⁹Who is weak, and I do not feel weak? Who is led into sin, and I do not inwardly burn?

³⁰If I must boast, I will boast of the things that show my weakness. ³¹The God and Father of the Lord Jesus, who is to be praised forever, knows that I am not lying. ³²In Damascus the governor under King Aretas had the city of the Damascenes guarded in order to arrest me. ³³But I was lowered in a basket from a window in the wall and slipped through his hands.

Paul's Vision and His Thorn

12 I must go on boasting. Although there is nothing to be gained, I will go on to visions and revelations from the Lord. ²I know a man in Christ who fourteen years ago was caught up to the third heaven. Whether it was in the body or out of the body I do not know—God knows. ³And I know that this man—whether in the body or apart from the body I do not know, but God knows— ⁴was caught up to paradise. He heard inexpressible things, things that man is not permitted to tell. ⁵I will boast about a man like that, but I will not boast about myself, except about my weaknesses. ⁶Even if I should choose to boast, I would not be a fool, because I would be speaking the truth. But I refrain, so no one will think more of me than is warranted by what I do or say.

⁷To keep me from becoming conceited because of these surpassingly great revelations, there was given me a thorn in my flesh, a messenger of Satan, to torment me. ⁸Three times I pleaded with the Lord to take it away from me. ⁹But he said to me, "My grace is sufficient for you, for my power is made perfect in weakness." Therefore I will boast all the more gladly about my weaknesses, so that Christ's power may rest on me. ¹⁰That is why, for Christ's sake, I delight in weaknesses, in insults, in hardships, in persecutions, in difficulties. For when I am weak, then I am strong.

Paul's Concern for the Corinthians

¹¹I have made a fool of myself, but you drove me to it. I ought to have been commended by you, for I am not in the least inferior to the "super-apostles," even though I am nothing. ¹²The things that mark an apostle—signs, wonders and miracles—were done among you with great perseverance. ¹³How were you inferior to the other churches, except that I was never a burden to you? Forgive me this wrong!

¹⁴Now I am ready to visit you for the third time, and I will not be a burden to you, because what I want is not your possessions but you. After all, children should not have to save up for their parents, but

---

God's people at prayer
PAUL HEARS GOD SAY NO

2 CORINTHIANS 12:7-10 Paul asked God to remove a hardship, a "thorn" in his flesh that was making his life difficult. Surely it made sense to pray for God to remove it. After all, it would make Paul that much more effective, wouldn't it? But God answered—and He said no. Paul knew what it was to want something from God, to ask in faith with pure motives, and yet to not receive the answer he was looking for. God only said, "My grace is sufficient . . . my power is made perfect in weakness" (12:9).

In essence, Paul said, "God, please take this hard thing away," and God said, "No, let the hard thing draw you closer to Me. I will give you grace to bear it and unexpected power through it. Trust Me." Our prayer lives are not about getting something out of God; instead, they are about finding our way to God. It's about a deeper relationship with Him. Prayer means accepting God's answer even if it is not what we prayed it would be.

parents for their children. ¹⁵So I will very gladly spend for you everything I have and expend myself as well. If I love you more, will you love me less? ¹⁶Be that as it may, I have not been a burden to you. Yet, crafty fellow that I am, I caught you by trickery! ¹⁷Did I exploit you through any of the men I sent you? ¹⁸I urged Titus to go to you and I sent our brother with him. Titus did not exploit you, did he? Did we not act in the same spirit and follow the same course?

¹⁹Have you been thinking all along that we have been defending ourselves to you? We have been speaking in the sight of God as those in Christ; and everything we do, dear friends, is for your strengthen-ing. ²⁰For I am afraid that when I come I may not find you as I want you to be, and you may not find me as you want me to be. I fear that there may be quarreling, jealousy, outbursts of anger, factions, slander, gossip, arrogance and disorder. ²¹I am afraid that when I come again my God will humble me before you, and I will be grieved over many who have sinned earlier and have not repented of the impurity, sexual sin and debauchery in which they have indulged.

Final Warnings

13 This will be my third visit to you. "Every matter must be established by the testimony of two or three

---

When the Failure of Others Tests Our Faith

READ AND CONSIDER: 2 CORINTHIANS 13:1-10

"Now we pray to God that you will not do anything wrong. Not that people will see that we have stood the test but that you will do what is right even though we may seem to have failed. For we cannot do anything against the truth, but only for the truth. We are glad whenever we are weak but you are strong; and our prayer is for your perfection" (2 Corinthians 13:7-9).

Paul addressed some criticism that had been spoken against him that had called into question his own faith. This led him to a discussion about passing the test of true faith. He prayed that even if his own faith seemed to fail the test, the faith of the Corinthians would not waver but instead remain strong.

Paul's prayer encouraging the Corinthians to do what was right was not the prayer of a perfectionistic leader who felt that the behavior of those he trained reflected on him. His prayer had to do with urging them on to authentic faith and not being dependent on him. Too often we become so connected to the people who mentor or teach us spiritually that when they fail in our eyes, our faith may fail too. But Paul's prayer was that the faith of these people would be so connected to *God* and to *His* faithfulness that nothing, not even disappointments in their mentors, could shake it.

We all need that kind of faith. People will let us down from time to time—even the best mentors, even our favorite preachers, even the people we need the most will disappoint us. But that won't shake us if the foundation of our faith is in God alone.

To have that kind of faith, we must invest in our relationship with Him. He will never change. We can always depend on Him. He won't fail us. If we ask Him to, He will strengthen *our* faith so we can lift up others who are struggling with *theirs*.

witnesses."[a] [2]I already gave you a warning when I was with you the second time. I now repeat it while absent: On my return I will not spare those who sinned earlier or any of the others, [3]since you are demanding proof that Christ is speaking through me. He is not weak in dealing with you, but is powerful among you. [4]For to be sure, he was crucified in weakness, yet he lives by God's power. Likewise, we are weak in him, yet by God's power we will live with him to serve you.

[5]Examine yourselves to see whether you are in the faith; test yourselves. Do you not realize that Christ Jesus is in you—unless, of course, you fail the test? [6]And I trust that you will discover that we have not failed the test. [7]Now we pray to God that you will not do anything wrong. Not that people will see that we have stood the test but that you will do what is right even though we may seem to have failed. [8]For we cannot do anything against the truth, but only for the truth. [9]We are glad whenever we are weak but you are strong; and our prayer is for your perfection. [10]This is why I write these things when I am absent, that when I come I may not have to be harsh in my use of authority—the authority the Lord gave me for building you up, not for tearing you down.

Final Greetings

[11]Finally, brothers, good-by. Aim for perfection, listen to my appeal, be of one mind, live in peace. And the God of love and peace will be with you.

[12]Greet one another with a holy kiss. [13]All the saints send their greetings.

[14]May the grace of the Lord Jesus Christ, and the love of God, and the fellowship of the Holy Spirit be with you all.

---

[a] [1] Deut. 19:15

Author: Paul

Date: Most likely written after Paul's first missionary journey in about AD 48–49, but before the Jerusalem council meeting recorded in Acts 15 in about AD 55–56, which formally addressed the issues Paul discusses in this letter.

Audience: The Christians in a number of towns and churches in Asia Minor who were being told that salvation required submitting to circumcision and keeping all the other requirements of the Old Testament law.

Prayer Themes:

- *Tell God you want to be set free from the enslaving idea that your efforts or works add anything to your salvation (3:1-5).*

- *Ask God to give you the ability to sense the prompting of His Spirit and follow His leading (5:25).*

- *Pray for God to give you a "second wind"—a renewed strength and fresh hope so that you might continue to powerfully serve and bless others (6:9).*

Galatia was a Roman province with several towns. Paul traveled through this region on his first missionary journey (Acts 13–14). He faced severe persecution and in one instance was stoned and left for dead (Acts 14:19-20). Nevertheless, on his second journey, Paul went back to those churches to "see how they are doing" (Acts 15:36). Paul deeply cared for the spiritual growth of the churches he planted.

Therefore, when he heard that false teachers had come into the churches after him, confusing the people by saying that they had to follow all of the Old Testament laws in order to be saved, Paul responded with this letter. He expressed astonishment that the people would so quickly desert the grace of Christ and the free salvation He offers and believe something that would make them work for their salvation.

No wonder Paul carried daily "concern for all the churches" (2 Corinthians 11:28). He wrote of his concerns, he sent trusted workers to guide the churches back to the truth, and he prayed that the believers would not be led astray.

Galatians

1 Paul, an apostle—sent not from men nor by man, but by Jesus Christ and God the Father, who raised him from the dead— ²and all the brothers with me,

To the churches in Galatia:

³Grace and peace to you from God our Father and the Lord Jesus Christ, ⁴who gave himself for our sins to rescue us from the present evil age, according to the will of our God and Father,

⁵to whom be glory for ever and ever. Amen.

No Other Gospel

⁶I am astonished that you are so quickly deserting the one who called you by the grace of Christ and are turning to a different gospel— ⁷which is really no gospel at all. Evidently some people are throwing you into confusion and are trying to pervert the gospel of Christ. ⁸But even if we

or an angel from heaven should preach a gospel other than the one we preached to you, let him be eternally condemned! ⁹As we have already said, so now I say again: If anybody is preaching to you a gospel other than what you accepted, let him be eternally condemned!

¹⁰Am I now trying to win the approval of men, or of God? Or am I trying to please men? If I were still trying to please men, I would not be a servant of Christ.

> *Prayer is . . .*
>
> *listening to God speak to your heart.*

Paul Called by God

¹¹I want you to know, brothers, that the gospel I preached is not something that man made up. ¹²I did not receive it from any man, nor was I taught it; rather, I received it by revelation from Jesus Christ.

¹³For you have heard of my previous way of life in Judaism, how intensely I persecuted the church of God and tried to destroy it. ¹⁴I was advancing in Judaism beyond many Jews of my own age and was extremely zealous for the traditions of my fathers. ¹⁵But when God, who set me apart from birthᵃ and called me by his grace, was pleased ¹⁶to reveal his Son in me so that I might preach him among the Gentiles, I did not consult any man, ¹⁷nor did I go up to Jerusalem to see those who were apostles before I was, but I went immediately into Arabia and later returned to Damascus.

¹⁸Then after three years, I went up to Jerusalem to get acquainted with Peterᵇ and stayed with him fifteen days. ¹⁹I saw none of the other apostles—only James, the Lord's brother. ²⁰I assure you before God that what I am writing you is no lie. ²¹Later I went to Syria and Cilicia. ²²I

was personally unknown to the churches of Judea that are in Christ. ²³They only heard the report: "The man who formerly persecuted us is now preaching the faith he once tried to destroy." ²⁴And they praised God because of me.

Paul Accepted by the Apostles

2 Fourteen years later I went up again to Jerusalem, this time with Barnabas. I took Titus along also. ²I went in response to a revelation and set before them the gospel that I preach among the Gentiles. But I did this privately to those who seemed to be leaders, for fear that I was running or had run my race in vain. ³Yet not even Titus, who was with me, was compelled to be circumcised, even though he was a Greek. ⁴This matter arose₎ because some false brothers had infiltrated our ranks to spy on the freedom we have in Christ Jesus and to make us slaves. ⁵We did not give in to them for a moment, so that the truth of the gospel might remain with you.

⁶As for those who seemed to be important—whatever they were makes no difference to me; God does not judge by external appearance—those men added nothing to my message. ⁷On the contrary, they saw that I had been entrusted with the task of preaching the gospel to the Gentiles,ᶜ just as Peter had been to the Jews.ᵈ ⁸For God, who was at work in the ministry of Peter as an apostle to the Jews, was also at work in my ministry as an apostle to the Gentiles. ⁹James, Peterᵉ and John, those reputed to be pillars, gave me and Barnabas the right hand of fellowship when they recognized the grace given to me. They agreed that we should go to the Gentiles, and they to the Jews. ¹⁰All they asked was that we should continue to remember the poor, the very thing I was eager to do.

Paul Opposes Peter

¹¹When Peter came to Antioch, I opposed him to his face, because he was

ᵃ *15* Or *from my mother's womb*   ᵇ *18* Greek *Cephas*   ᶜ *7* Greek *uncircumcised*   ᵈ *7* Greek *circumcised*; also in verses 8 and 9
ᵉ *9* Greek *Cephas*; also in verses 11 and 14

clearly in the wrong. [12]Before certain men came from James, he used to eat with the Gentiles. But when they arrived, he began to draw back and separate himself from the Gentiles because he was afraid of those who belonged to the circumcision group. [13]The other Jews joined him in his hypocrisy, so that by their hypocrisy even Barnabas was led astray.

[14]When I saw that they were not acting in line with the truth of the gospel, I said to Peter in front of them all, "You are a Jew, yet you live like a Gentile and not like a Jew. How is it, then, that you force Gentiles to follow Jewish customs?

[15]"We who are Jews by birth and not 'Gentile sinners' [16]know that a man is not justified by observing the law, but by faith in Jesus Christ. So we, too, have put our faith in Christ Jesus that we may be justified by faith in Christ and not by observing the law, because by observing the law no one will be justified.

[17]"If, while we seek to be justified in Christ, it becomes evident that we ourselves are sinners, does that mean that Christ promotes sin? Absolutely not! [18]If I rebuild what I destroyed, I prove that I am a lawbreaker. [19]For through the law I died to the law so that I might live for God. [20]I have been crucified with Christ and I no longer live, but Christ lives in me. The life I live in the body, I live by faith in the Son of God, who loved me and gave himself for me. [21]I do not set aside the grace of God, for if righteousness could be gained through the law, Christ died for nothing!"[a]

Faith or Observance of the Law

3 You foolish Galatians! Who has bewitched you? Before your very eyes Jesus Christ was clearly portrayed as crucified. [2]I would like to learn just one thing from you: Did you receive the Spirit by observing the law, or by believing what you heard? [3]Are you so foolish? After beginning with the Spirit, are you now trying to attain your goal by human effort? [4]Have you suffered so much for nothing—if it really was for nothing? [5]Does God give you his Spirit and work miracles among you because you observe the law, or because you believe what you heard?

[6]Consider Abraham: "He believed God, and it was credited to him as righteousness."[b] [7]Understand, then, that those who believe are children of Abraham. [8]The Scripture foresaw that God would justify the Gentiles by faith, and announced the gospel in advance to Abraham: "All nations will be blessed through you."[c] [9]So those who have faith are blessed along with Abraham, the man of faith.

[10]All who rely on observing the law are under a curse, for it is written: "Cursed is everyone who does not continue to do everything written in the Book of the Law."[d] [11]Clearly no one is justified before God by the law, because, "The righteous will live by faith."[e] [12]The law is not based on faith; on the contrary, "The man who does these things will live by them."[f] [13]Christ redeemed us from the curse of the law by becoming a curse for us, for it is written: "Cursed is everyone who is hung on a tree."[g] [14]He redeemed us in order that the blessing given to Abraham might come to the Gentiles through Christ Jesus, so that by faith we might receive the promise of the Spirit.

The Law and the Promise

[15]Brothers, let me take an example from everyday life. Just as no one can set aside or add to a human covenant that has been duly established, so it is in this case. [16]The promises were spoken to Abraham and to his seed. The Scripture does not say "and to seeds," meaning many people, but "and to your seed,"[h] meaning one person, who is Christ. [17]What I mean is this: The law, introduced 430 years later, does not set aside the covenant previously established by God and thus do away with the

---

[a] *21* Some interpreters end the quotation after verse 14.　　[b] *6* Gen. 15:6　　[c] *8* Gen. 12:3; 18:18; 22:18　　[d] *10* Deut. 27:26
[e] *11* Hab. 2:4　　[f] *12* Lev. 18:5　　[g] *13* Deut. 21:23　　[h] *16* Gen. 12:7; 13:15; 24:7

Nine Ways to Grow Spiritual Fruit

If we want to be fruitful for the Lord, this is what we need to plant:

1. *Plant seeds of love.* Ask God to plant His love in you in such a profound and powerful way that you are able to fully experience it. Ask also that His love will flow through you to others. Jesus said, "If you obey my commands, you will remain in my love, just as I have obeyed my Father's commands and remain in his love" (John 15:10).

2. *Plant seeds of joy.* Joy has nothing to do with your circumstances. You can have joy in spite of difficult and painful problems, because joy comes through a close, intimate relationship with the Lord. Jesus said, "I have told you this so that my joy may be in you and that your joy may be complete" (John 15:11).

3. *Plant seeds of peace.* Pray that the presence of the Lord planted in your life will provide peace that is beyond comprehension. "The peace of God, which transcends all understanding, will guard your hearts and your minds in Christ Jesus" (Philippians 4:7).

4. *Plant seeds of patience.* God's timing is not our timing. He is always doing more than we see or know, so we have to trust Him on how long He takes to bring things to pass. "Perseverance must finish its work so that you may be mature and complete, not lacking anything" (James 1:4).

5. *Plant seeds of kindness.* Kindness is something you choose to put on, like a garment. "Therefore, as God's chosen people, holy and dearly loved, clothe yourselves with compassion, kindness, humility, gentleness and patience" (Colossians 3:12). The ultimate act of kindness was when Jesus gave His life for us. Pray that His brand of kindness will grow in you so that you can sacrifice your life for others with acts of kindness too.

6. *Plant seeds of goodness.* When the goodness of God is sown in your soul, it leads you to produce good deeds. "The good man brings good things out of the good stored up in him, and the evil man brings evil things out of the evil stored up in him" (Matthew 12:35).

7. *Plant seeds of faithfulness.* When we are solid, steadfast, dependable, reliable, loyal, and trustworthy and do what is right no matter what, we exhibit faithfulness. "Whoever can be trusted with very little can also be trusted with much, and whoever is dishonest with very little will also be dishonest with much" (Luke 16:10).

8. *Plant seeds of gentleness.* Being considerate of the feelings and needs of others by exhibiting gentleness shows you are responding to the Spirit of God. Pray that you can be as gentle and meek as Jesus was (2 Corinthians 10:1).

9. *Plant seeds of self-control.* Self-control is not fragile like a strawberry plant; it's big and solid like an apple tree. Only God can plant something of that magnitude in you and make it bear fruit. "Make every effort to add to your faith goodness; and to goodness, knowledge; and to knowledge, self-control; and to self-control, perseverance; and to perseverance, godliness" (2 Peter 1:5-6).

If you've not been bearing the fruit of the Spirit in your life the way you'd like, ask God to help you plant good seeds and pull up any weeds that may have grown up around your soul. Feed the soil of your heart with the food of God's Word and ask the Holy Spirit to water it afresh every day. As long as you abide faithfully in the true vine, I guarantee you'll produce a crop of spiritual fruit that will make your heavenly Father proud.

For the next "From Stormie's Heart" article, go to page 1436.

promise. [18]For if the inheritance depends on the law, then it no longer depends on a promise; but God in his grace gave it to Abraham through a promise.

[19]What, then, was the purpose of the law? It was added because of transgressions until the Seed to whom the promise referred had come. The law was put into effect through angels by a mediator. [20]A mediator, however, does not represent just one party; but God is one.

[21]Is the law, therefore, opposed to the promises of God? Absolutely not! For if a law had been given that could impart life, then righteousness would certainly have come by the law. [22]But the Scripture declares that the whole world is a prisoner of sin, so that what was promised, being given through faith in Jesus Christ, might be given to those who believe.

[23]Before this faith came, we were held prisoners by the law, locked up until faith should be revealed. [24]So the law was put in charge to lead us to Christ[a] that we might be justified by faith. [25]Now that faith has come, we are no longer under the supervision of the law.

Sons of God

[26]You are all sons of God through faith in Christ Jesus, [27]for all of you who were baptized into Christ have clothed yourselves with Christ. [28]There is neither Jew nor Greek, slave nor free, male nor female, for you are all one in Christ Jesus. [29]If you belong to Christ, then you are Abraham's seed, and heirs according to the promise.

4 What I am saying is that as long as the heir is a child, he is no different from a slave, although he owns the whole estate. [2]He is subject to guardians and trustees until the time set by his father. [3]So also, when we were children, we were in slavery under the basic principles of the world. [4]But when the time had fully come, God sent his Son, born of a woman, born under law, [5]to redeem those under law, that we might receive the full rights

of sons. [6]Because you are sons, God sent the Spirit of his Son into our hearts, the Spirit who calls out, "Abba,[b] Father." [7]So you are no longer a slave, but a son; and since you are a son, God has made you also an heir.

Paul's Concern for the Galatians

[8]Formerly, when you did not know God, you were slaves to those who by nature are not gods. [9]But now that you know God—or rather are known by God—how is it that you are turning back to those weak and miserable principles? Do you wish to be enslaved by them all over again? [10]You are observing special days and months and seasons and years! [11]I fear for you, that somehow I have wasted my efforts on you.

[12]I plead with you, brothers, become like me, for I became like you. You have done me no wrong. [13]As you know, it was because of an illness that I first preached the gospel to you. [14]Even though my illness was a trial to you, you did not treat me with contempt or scorn. Instead, you welcomed me as if I were an angel of God, as if I were Christ Jesus himself. [15]What has happened to all your joy? I can testify that, if you could have done so, you would have torn out your eyes and given them to me. [16]Have I now become your enemy by telling you the truth?

[17]Those people are zealous to win you over, but for no good. What they want is to alienate you ⌊from us⌋, so that you may be zealous for them. [18]It is fine to be zealous, provided the purpose is good, and to be so always and not just when I am with you. [19]My dear children, for whom I am again in the pains of childbirth until Christ is formed in you, [20]how I wish I could be with you now and change my tone, because I am perplexed about you!

Hagar and Sarah

[21]Tell me, you who want to be under the law, are you not aware of what the law says? [22]For it is written that Abraham had

---

[a] 24 Or charge until Christ came   [b] 6 Aramaic for Father

two sons, one by the slave woman and the other by the free woman. ²³His son by the slave woman was born in the ordinary way; but his son by the free woman was born as the result of a promise.

²⁴These things may be taken figuratively, for the women represent two covenants. One covenant is from Mount Sinai and bears children who are to be slaves: This is Hagar. ²⁵Now Hagar stands for Mount Sinai in Arabia and corresponds to the present city of Jerusalem, because she is in slavery with her children. ²⁶But the Jerusalem that is above is free, and she is our mother. ²⁷For it is written:

"Be glad, O barren woman,
　who bears no children;
break forth and cry aloud,
　you who have no labor pains;
because more are the children of the
　　desolate woman
　than of her who has a husband."ᵃ

²⁸Now you, brothers, like Isaac, are children of promise. ²⁹At that time the son born in the ordinary way persecuted the son born by the power of the Spirit. It is the same now. ³⁰But what does the Scripture say? "Get rid of the slave woman and her son, for the slave woman's son will never share in the inheritance with the free woman's son."ᵇ ³¹Therefore, brothers, we are not children of the slave woman, but of the free woman.

Freedom in Christ

5 It is for freedom that Christ has set us free. Stand firm, then, and do not let yourselves be burdened again by a yoke of slavery.

²Mark my words! I, Paul, tell you that if you let yourselves be circumcised, Christ will be of no value to you at all. ³Again I declare to every man who lets himself be circumcised that he is obligated to obey the whole law. ⁴You who are trying to be justified by law have been alienated from Christ; you have fallen away from grace. ⁵But by faith we eagerly await through the Spirit the righteousness for which we hope. ⁶For in Christ Jesus neither circumcision nor uncircumcision has any value. The only thing that counts is faith expressing itself through love.

⁷You were running a good race. Who cut in on you and kept you from obeying the truth? ⁸That kind of persuasion does not come from the one who calls you. ⁹"A little yeast works through the whole batch of dough." ¹⁰I am confident in the Lord that you will take no other view. The one who is throwing you into confusion will pay the penalty, whoever he may be. ¹¹Brothers, if I am still preaching circumcision, why am I still being persecuted? In that case the offense of the cross has been abolished. ¹²As for those agitators, I wish they would go the whole way and emasculate themselves!

¹³You, my brothers, were called to be free. But do not use your freedom to indulge the sinful natureᶜ; rather, serve one another in love. ¹⁴The entire law is summed up in a single command: "Love your neighbor as yourself."ᵈ ¹⁵If you keep on biting and devouring each other, watch out or you will be destroyed by each other.

Life by the Spirit

¹⁶So I say, live by the Spirit, and you will not gratify the desires of the sinful nature. ¹⁷For the sinful nature desires what is contrary to the Spirit, and the Spirit what is contrary to the sinful nature. They are in conflict with each other, so that you do not do what you want. ¹⁸But if you are led by the Spirit, you are not under law.

¹⁹The acts of the sinful nature are obvious: sexual immorality, impurity and debauchery; ²⁰idolatry and witchcraft; hatred, discord, jealousy, fits of rage, selfish ambition, dissensions, factions ²¹and envy; drunkenness, orgies, and the like. I warn you, as I did before, that those who live like this will not inherit the kingdom of God.

ᵃ 27 Isaiah 54:1　ᵇ 30 Gen. 21:10　ᶜ 13 Or the flesh; also in verses 16, 17, 19 and 24　ᵈ 14 Lev. 19:18

Moving Into the Freedom God Has for Us

READ AND CONSIDER: GALATIANS 5:1-15

"It is for freedom that Christ has set us free. Stand firm, then, and do not let yourselves be burdened again by a yoke of slavery" (Galatians 5:1).

Did you inherit your mother's eyes or your father's nose? How about your grandmother's talent for art or your grandfather's gift of music?

There are many physical characteristics, gifts, abilities, and talents that we can inherit from our parents and grandparents. Unfortunately, though, we can also inherit character qualities that aren't so enviable—things like a bad temper, a propensity for lying, negativity, unforgiveness, perfectionism, or pride. These and other entrenched characteristics that have a spiritual base can also be passed along from our parents to us, and from us to our children. In a particular family there may be a tendency toward such things as addiction, suicide, depression, rejection, or being accident-prone—all mistakenly accepted as "fate" or "the way I am."

Some of what we accept about ourselves and our lives are actually family bondages, for children can inherit the consequences of their ancestors' sins. "I, the LORD your God, am a jealous God, punishing the children for the sin of the fathers to the third and fourth generation of those who hate me" (Exodus 20:5). This Scripture is referring to people who don't walk in a loving relationship with God, but how many of our ancestors didn't walk with God and how many times have we been less than lovingly obedient to Him?

Galatians warns us not to be burdened again by a yoke of slavery, or bondage. If it is not possible as a believer to become entangled again with a yoke of bondage, why does the Bible warn us about it? The answer is, even though Jesus set us free from sin, we can still make choices that put us back into bondage to it. Sometimes we accept certain tendencies toward sin in ourselves, without realizing that we don't have to. We can say no to them in our lives.

Sometimes we carry on a family tradition that we shouldn't and it affects our children. Unlike physical traits, tendencies toward sin are something we don't have to receive as an inheritance from our parents. That's because these tendencies are nothing more than the unquestioned acceptance of a firmly entrenched lie of the enemy. He wants us to believe that we are not a new creation in Christ and that we have not been set free from our old nature. He wants us to think that because Dad (or Grandpa) drank too much, or was a complainer, or cheated on his wife, or abused his family with his anger, or got divorced, or was dishonest in his business dealings, that this is just the way things are done in our family. But we can choose to break away from these old familial habits through prayer and the power of the Holy Spirit. And when we see things we don't like about ourselves reflected in our children, we can pray for them to be set free of that tendency as well. In Jesus' name we can be set free from any family bondage, and by the power of the Holy Spirit we can refuse to allow it any place in our own lives and in the lives of our children.

22But the fruit of the Spirit is love, joy, peace, patience, kindness, goodness, faithfulness, 23gentleness and self-control. Against such things there is no law. 24Those who belong to Christ Jesus have crucified the sinful nature with its passions and desires. 25Since we live by the Spirit, let us keep in step with the

Spirit. 26Let us not become conceited, provoking and envying each other.

Doing Good to All

6 Brothers, if someone is caught in a sin, you who are spiritual should restore him gently. But watch yourself, or you also may be tempted. 2Carry each other's burdens, and in this way you will fulfill the law of Christ. 3If anyone thinks he is something when he is nothing, he deceives himself. 4Each one should test his own actions. Then he can take pride in himself, without comparing himself to somebody else, 5for each one should carry his own load.

6Anyone who receives instruction in the word must share all good things with his instructor.

Praying Galatians 6:8-9

Lord, help me to not become weary of planting good spiritual seeds so that I can enjoy an everlasting harvest of spiritual fruit.

7Do not be deceived: God cannot be mocked. A man reaps what he sows. 8The one who sows to please his sinful nature, from that nature[a] will reap destruction; the one who sows to please the Spirit, from the Spirit will reap eternal life. 9Let us not become weary in doing good, for at the proper time we will reap a harvest if we do not give up. 10Therefore, as we have opportunity, let us do good to all people, especially to those who belong to the family of believers.

Not Circumcision but a New Creation

11See what large letters I use as I write to you with my own hand!

12Those who want to make a good impression outwardly are trying to compel you to be circumcised. The only reason they do this is to avoid being persecuted for the cross of Christ. 13Not even those who are circumcised obey the law, yet they want you to be circumcised that they may boast about your flesh. 14May I never boast except in the cross of our Lord Jesus Christ, through which[b] the world has been crucified to me, and I to the world. 15Neither circumcision nor uncircumcision means anything; what counts is a new creation. 16Peace and mercy to all who follow this rule, even to the Israel of God.

17Finally, let no one cause me trouble, for I bear on my body the marks of Jesus.

18The grace of our Lord Jesus Christ be with your spirit, brothers. Amen.

---

a 8 Or his flesh, from the flesh   b 14 Or whom

Author: Paul

Date: AD 60

Audience: Believers in Ephesus (ancient Asia Minor, modern-day Turkey) to remind them of their spiritual wealth and their high calling to live powerfully and purely

Prayer Themes:

• Pray for yourself as Paul prayed for the Ephesians—that you would have wisdom and revelation and know God better and that the eyes of your heart would be enlightened (1:15-23).

• Thank God for His grace and salvation and ask for deepening insight into His calling on your life (2:1-10).

• Follow Paul's directive to "pray in the Spirit on all occasions with all kinds of prayers and requests" and to "keep on praying for all the saints" (6:18).

• Be willing to ask for prayer when you need it, just as Paul did (6:19-20).

Ephesus was the capital of the Roman province of Asia. The record of Paul's visit to the cosmopolitan city of Ephesus is recorded in Acts 18:19-21. During his third missionary journey, Paul returned to Ephesus and stayed for almost three years (Acts 19). Clearly he had built such strong relationships with the believers there that when he was on his way to Jerusalem, he sent for the elders of the church so he could talk and pray with them (Acts 20:17). He was concerned that false teachers would come in like "savage wolves" (Acts 20:29) and hurt the flock of believers. He gave them a clear warning and then knelt and prayed with them.

Later, from his prison cell in Rome, Paul wrote the following letter to this beloved church. He told how he had "not stopped giving thanks" for them, remembering them in his prayers (1:16). He told them what he prayed for them—that they would have wisdom and revelation and know God better, that the eyes of their hearts would be enlightened in order to see the riches, the inheritance, and the power they have in Christ.

Ephesians

1 Paul, an apostle of Christ Jesus by the will of God,

To the saints in Ephesus,[a] the faithful[b] in Christ Jesus:

[2] Grace and peace to you from God our Father and the Lord Jesus Christ.

Spiritual Blessings in Christ

[3] Praise be to the God and Father of our Lord Jesus Christ, who has blessed us in the heavenly realms with every spiritual blessing in Christ. [4] For he chose us in him before the creation of the world to be holy and blameless in his sight. In love [5] he[c] predestined us to be adopted as his sons through Jesus Christ, in accordance with his pleasure and will— [6] to the praise of his glorious grace, which he has freely given us in the One he loves. [7] In him we have redemption through his blood, the forgiveness of sins, in accordance with the riches of God's grace [8] that he lavished on us with all wisdom and understanding. [9] And he[d] made known to us the mystery of his will according to his good pleasure, which he purposed in Christ, [10] to be put into effect when the times will have reached their fulfillment—to bring all things in heaven and on earth together under one head, even Christ.

[11] In him we were also chosen,[e] having been predestined according to the plan of him who works out everything in

---

[a] 1 Some early manuscripts do not have *in Ephesus.*   [b] 1 Or *believers who are*   [c] 4,5 Or *sight in love.* [5] He   [d] 8,9 Or *us. With all wisdom and understanding,* [9] he   [e] 11 Or *were made heirs*

conformity with the purpose of his will, 12in order that we, who were the first to hope in Christ, might be for the praise of his glory. 13And you also were included in Christ when you heard the word of truth, the gospel of your salvation. Having believed, you were marked in him with a seal, the promised Holy Spirit, 14who is a deposit guaranteeing our inheritance until the redemption of those who are God's possession—to the praise of his glory.

Thanksgiving and Prayer

15For this reason, ever since I heard about your faith in the Lord Jesus and your love for all the saints, 16I have not stopped giving thanks for you, remembering you in my prayers. 17I keep asking that the God of our Lord Jesus Christ, the glo-

Seeing the Power of God at Work   *GOING deeper*

READ AND CONSIDER: EPHESIANS 1:15-23

"I pray also that the eyes of your heart may be enlightened in order that you may know the hope to which he has called you, the riches of his glorious inheritance in the saints, and his incomparably great power for us who believe" (Ephesians 1:18-19).

The power of God is at work in our lives and in the world around us wherever He is invited. So if you ever find yourself thinking that you are not seeing His power manifesting in your life as much as you would like, then perhaps you have not invited Him into your situation with as much fervency as *He* would like. The Holy Spirit never forces Himself upon us. He waits for our invitation.

You can only move in the power of God's Spirit if you have first received Jesus as Savior. You need to "know this love that surpasses knowledge—that you may be filled to the measure of all the fullness of God" (3:19). When you have Jesus as ruler of your life, you will come to know Him as the one "who is able to do immeasurably more than all we ask or imagine, according to his power that is at work within us" (3:20). Because of His Holy Spirit in us—His power in us—He can do more in our lives than we can even think to ask for.

Once you receive Jesus and have the Holy Spirit in you, He will begin to work in your life as you pray. The more you pray—or seek God's presence—the more the Holy Spirit will guide and teach you. Jesus said, "The Counselor, the Holy Spirit, whom the Father will send in my name, will teach you all things and will remind you of everything I have said to you" (John 14:26). When you acknowledge the Holy Spirit and then invite Him to move in you freely, He will. You will see His power manifest.

God *wants* us to witness His power at work in the world. He wants us to understand "his incomparably great power for us who believe" (1:19). He desires that we know this power that raised Jesus "from the dead and seated him at his right hand in the heavenly realms, far above all rule and authority, power and dominion, and every title that can be given" (1:20-21). He wants us to understand that Jesus is not weak toward us, but powerful among us (2 Corinthians 13:3). He wants us to understand that though "he was crucified in weakness, yet he lives by God's power," and even though we are also weak, we live by the power of God too (2 Corinthians 13:4). God wants us to see that "we have not received the spirit of the world but the Spirit who is from God, that we may understand what God has freely given us" (1 Corinthians 2:12).

Invite God to open the eyes of your heart and understanding, so that you will be able to see Him and His power at work in you, in your life, and in the world around you.

rious Father, may give you the Spirit[a] of wisdom and revelation, so that you may know him better. [18]I pray also that the eyes of your heart may be enlightened in order that you may know the hope to which he has called you, the riches of his glorious inheritance in the saints, [19]and his incomparably great power for us who believe. That power is like the working of his mighty strength, [20]which he exerted in Christ when he raised him from the dead and seated him at his right hand in the heavenly realms, [21]far above all rule and authority, power and dominion, and every title that can be given, not only in the present age but also in the one to come. [22]And God placed all things under his feet and appointed him to be head over everything for the church, [23]which is his body, the fullness of him who fills everything in every way.

Made Alive in Christ

2 As for you, you were dead in your transgressions and sins, [2]in which you used to live when you followed the ways of this world and of the ruler of the kingdom of the air, the spirit who is now at work in those who are disobedient. [3]All of us also lived among them at one time, gratifying the cravings of our sinful nature[b] and following its desires and thoughts. Like the rest, we were by nature objects of wrath. [4]But because of his great love for us, God, who is rich in mercy, [5]made us alive with Christ even when we were dead in transgressions—it is by grace you have been saved. [6]And God raised us up with Christ and seated us with him in the heavenly realms in Christ Jesus, [7]in order that in the coming ages he might show the incomparable riches of his grace, expressed in his kindness to us in Christ Jesus. [8]For it is by grace you have been saved, through faith—and this not from yourselves, it is the gift of God— [9]not by works, so that no one can boast. [10]For we are God's workmanship, created in Christ Jesus to do good works, which God prepared in advance for us to do.

One in Christ

[11]Therefore, remember that formerly you who are Gentiles by birth and called "uncircumcised" by those who call themselves "the circumcision" (that done in the body by the hands of men)— [12]remember that at that time you were separate from Christ, excluded from citizenship in Israel and foreigners to the covenants of the promise, without hope and without God in the world. [13]But now in Christ Jesus you who once were far away have been brought near through the blood of Christ.

[14]For he himself is our peace, who has made the two one and has destroyed the barrier, the dividing wall of hostility, [15]by abolishing in his flesh the law with its commandments and regulations. His purpose was to create in himself one new man out of the two, thus making peace, [16]and in this one body to reconcile both of them to God through the cross, by which he put to death their hostility. [17]He came and preached peace to you who were far away and peace to those who were near. [18]For through him we both have access to the Father by one Spirit.

[19]Consequently, you are no longer foreigners and aliens, but fellow citizens with God's people and members of God's household, [20]built on the foundation of the apostles and prophets, with Christ Jesus himself as the chief cornerstone. [21]In him the whole building is joined together and rises to become a holy temple in the Lord. [22]And in him you too are being built together to become a dwelling in which God lives by his Spirit.

Paul the Preacher to the Gentiles

3 For this reason I, Paul, the prisoner of Christ Jesus for the sake of you Gentiles—

---

[a] 17 Or a spirit   [b] 3 Or our flesh

What to Do When You Feel Powerless

One of the most wonderful things about God is that He shares Himself with us. He gives us a portion of all that He is. He even shares His power, and He gives us a way to do and be what we couldn't do and be on our own. Who else would do that but Him? And He does that because He loves us.

God loves us enough to be strong on our behalf. To be strong where we are the weakest. "He gives strength to the weary and increases the power of the weak…those who hope in the LORD will renew their strength…they will run and not grow weary" (Isaiah 40:29-31). Because of God, you never have to feel powerless, no matter what is happening in your life.

The thing about God's power is that we have to wait on Him for it. We don't just throw it on like a light switch. *We* don't control it. *He* does. It's *His* power, and He dispenses it at will. He wants us to wait on Him. But the problem is, we don't like waiting. We want what we want when we want it. And what does it mean to wait, anyway? How exactly are we supposed to do that?

Waiting doesn't mean doing nothing. It's not like waiting for a bus or a cab. We aren't tapping our fingers and looking at the clock. While there can be desperation in prayer when we are seeking God for what we need, when we are waiting on the Lord our soul finds rest in Him. We find peace in the midst of strife.

The way we wait on the Lord is to spend time with Him in praise and worship. It means focusing and meditating on the greatness of God and praising Him for who He is and all that He has done. It's drawing close to God and telling Him how much we reverence Him. It's praising Him for being

our all-powerful Lord. That's how we can run the course and not grow weary. And as we continue to do that, He will lift us up.

God's power is not cheap. Just like the electric power that comes into our homes, there is a price to pay for it. Only the price is not monetary. The price is spending time filling ourselves with God's Word so we can *understand* the power. It's praying so we can *access* the power. It's living in obedience so we can *maximize* the power. It's praising and worshiping God so we *open up the lines* through which God's power flows into our lives.

Ask God to show you "his incomparably great power for us who believe. That power is like the working of his mighty strength, which he exerted in Christ when he raised him from the dead and seated him at his right hand in the heavenly realms, far above all rule and authority, power and dominion, and every title that can be given, not only in the present age but also in the one to come" (Ephesians 1:19-21).

Doesn't that sound like the kind of power we can't live without?

Jesus wasn't resurrected from the dead just so we could have a nice, happy life. He was raised up to save us from death and hell so we could live a life of *power* and purpose. That same power, which parted the Red Sea, opened blind eyes, broke the curse of death, and created heaven and earth, can transform your life and the lives of others around you. None of us wants to live a life without power. God doesn't want us to live that way either. He wants to empower us to live the life He has for us.

For the next "From Stormie's Heart" article, go to page 1446.

²Surely you have heard about the administration of God's grace that was given to me for you, ³that is, the mystery made known to me by revelation, as I have already written briefly. ⁴In reading this, then, you will be able to understand my insight into the mystery of Christ, ⁵which was not made known to men in other generations as it has now been revealed by the Spirit to God's holy apostles and prophets. ⁶This mystery is that through the gospel the Gentiles are heirs together with Israel, members together of one body, and sharers together in the promise in Christ Jesus.

⁷I became a servant of this gospel by the gift of God's grace given me through the working of his power. ⁸Although I am less than the least of all God's people, this grace was given me: to preach to the Gentiles the unsearchable riches of Christ, ⁹and to make plain to everyone the administration of this mystery, which for ages past was kept hidden in God, who created all things. ¹⁰His intent was that now, through the church, the manifold wisdom of God should be made known to the rulers and authorities in the heavenly realms, ¹¹according to his eternal purpose which he accomplished in Christ Jesus our Lord. ¹²In him and through faith in him we may approach God with freedom and confidence. ¹³I ask you, therefore, not to be discouraged because of my sufferings for you, which are your glory.

A Prayer for the Ephesians

¹⁴For this reason I kneel before the Father, ¹⁵from whom his whole family[a] in heaven and on earth derives its name. ¹⁶I pray that out of his glorious riches he may strengthen you with power through his Spirit in your inner being, ¹⁷so that Christ may dwell in your hearts through faith. And I pray that you, being rooted and established in love, ¹⁸may have power, together with all the saints, to grasp how wide and long and high and deep is the love of Christ, ¹⁹and to know this love that surpasses knowledge—that you may be filled to the measure of all the fullness of God.

²⁰Now to him who is able to do immeasurably more than all we ask or imagine, according to his power that is at work within us, ²¹to him be glory in the church and in Christ Jesus

---

a 15 Or whom all fatherhood

God's people at prayer
PAUL PRAYS FOR BELIEVERS TO KNOW GOD'S LOVE

EPHESIANS 3:14-21 Have you ever needed great strength—an extraordinary measure of ability to handle an extremely heavy problem? Sometimes we look at our situations and wonder how we can possibly make it through. The death of a loved one, a divorce, a rebellious child, a ravaging illness. It is beyond our ability to cope. But we can reach out to the only One who is able to provide everything we need to rise above it.

Paul prayed that God would give the Ephesians great inner strength out of God's own unlimited resources. His most impassioned plea was that the believers would begin to comprehend the vastness of God's love—its width, length, height, and depth. Corrie ten Boom, a Dutch woman who survived a Nazi death camp, once said that there is no pit so deep that God's love is not deeper still. She knew this firsthand from one of the darkest pits ever devised by humanity and the devil. No matter how great the storm in our lives, God will wrap His love around us, covering and protecting us as we walk through it. Thank God daily that His love is so powerful it can give you the strength and ability to transcend any situation.

throughout all generations, for ever and ever! Amen.

Unity in the Body of Christ

4 As a prisoner for the Lord, then, I urge you to live a life worthy of the calling you have received. ²Be completely humble and gentle; be patient, bearing with one another in love. ³Make every effort to keep the unity of the Spirit through the bond of peace. ⁴There is one body and one Spirit—just as you were called to one hope when you were called—⁵one Lord, one faith, one baptism; ⁶one God and Father of all, who is over all and through all and in all.

⁷But to each one of us grace has been given as Christ apportioned it. ⁸This is why it[a] says:

"When he ascended on high,
he led captives in his train
and gave gifts to men."[b]

⁹(What does "he ascended" mean except that he also descended to the lower, earthly regions[c]? ¹⁰He who descended is the very one who ascended higher than all the heavens, in order to fill the whole universe.) ¹¹It was he who gave some to be apostles, some to be prophets, some to be evangelists, and some to be pastors and teachers, ¹²to prepare God's people for works of service, so that the body of Christ may be built up ¹³until we all reach unity in the faith and in the knowledge of the Son of God and become mature, attaining to the whole measure of the fullness of Christ.

¹⁴Then we will no longer be infants, tossed back and forth by the waves, and blown here and there by every wind of teaching and by the cunning and craftiness of men in their deceitful scheming. ¹⁵Instead, speaking the truth in love, we will in all things grow up into him who is the Head, that is, Christ. ¹⁶From him the whole body, joined and held together by every supporting ligament, grows and builds itself up in love, as each part does its work.

Living as Children of Light

¹⁷So I tell you this, and insist on it in the Lord, that you must no longer live as the Gentiles do, in the futility of their thinking. ¹⁸They are darkened in their understanding and separated from the life of God because of the ignorance that is in them due to the hardening of their hearts. ¹⁹Having lost all sensitivity, they have given themselves over to sensuality so as to indulge in every kind of impurity, with a continual lust for more.

²⁰You, however, did not come to know Christ that way. ²¹Surely you heard of him and were taught in him in accordance with the truth that is in Jesus. ²²You were taught, with regard to your former way of life, to put off your old self, which is being corrupted by its deceitful desires; ²³to be made new in the attitude of your minds; ²⁴and to put on the new self, created to be like God in true righteousness and holiness.

Praying Ephesians 4:22-24
Dear Lord, enable me to resist
futile thoughts and blindness of heart
so that I can be renewed in my mind
and live the righteous and holy life
You have called me to live.

²⁵Therefore each of you must put off falsehood and speak truthfully to his neighbor, for we are all members of one body. ²⁶"In your anger do not sin"[d]: Do not let the sun go down while you are still angry, ²⁷and do not give the devil a foothold. ²⁸He who has been stealing must steal no longer, but must work, doing something useful with his own hands, that he may have something to share with those in need.

²⁹Do not let any unwholesome talk come out of your mouths, but only what is helpful for building others up according to their needs, that it may benefit those who listen. ³⁰And do not grieve the Holy Spirit of God, with whom you were

---

[a] *8 Or God*   [b] *8 Psalm 68:18*   [c] *9 Or the depths of the earth*   [d] *26 Psalm 4:4*

sealed for the day of redemption. ³¹Get rid of all bitterness, rage and anger, brawling and slander, along with every form of malice. ³²Be kind and compassionate to one another, forgiving each other, just as in Christ God forgave you.

5 Be imitators of God, therefore, as dearly loved children ²and live a life of love, just as Christ loved us and gave himself up for us as a fragrant offering and sacrifice to God.

³But among you there must not be even a hint of sexual immorality, or of any kind of impurity, or of greed, because these are improper for God's holy people. ⁴Nor should there be obscenity, foolish talk or coarse joking, which are out of place, but rather thanksgiving. ⁵For of this you can be sure: No immoral, impure or greedy person—such a man is an idolater—has any inheritance in the kingdom of Christ and of God.ᵃ ⁶Let no one deceive you with empty words, for because of such things God's wrath comes on those who are disobedient. ⁷Therefore do not be partners with them.

⁸For you were once darkness, but now you are light in the Lord. Live as children of light ⁹(for the fruit of the light consists in all goodness, righteousness and truth) ¹⁰and find out what pleases the Lord. ¹¹Have nothing to do with the fruitless deeds of darkness, but rather expose them. ¹²For it is shameful even to mention what the disobedient do in secret. ¹³But everything exposed by the light becomes visible, ¹⁴for it is light that makes everything visible. This is why it is said:

"Wake up, O sleeper,
    rise from the dead,
and Christ will shine on you."

¹⁵Be very careful, then, how you live— not as unwise but as wise, ¹⁶making the most of every opportunity, because the days are evil. ¹⁷Therefore do not be foolish, but understand what the Lord's will is. ¹⁸Do not get drunk on wine, which leads to debauchery. Instead, be filled with the Spirit. ¹⁹Speak to one another with psalms, hymns and spiritual songs. Sing and make music in your heart to the Lord, ²⁰always giving thanks to God the Father for everything, in the name of our Lord Jesus Christ.

²¹Submit to one another out of reverence for Christ.

Wives and Husbands

²²Wives, submit to your husbands as to the Lord. ²³For the husband is the head of the wife as Christ is the head of the church, his body, of which he is the Savior. ²⁴Now as the church submits to Christ, so also wives should submit to their husbands in everything.

²⁵Husbands, love your wives, just as Christ loved the church and gave himself up for her ²⁶to make her holy, cleansingᵇ her by the washing with water through the word, ²⁷and to present her to himself as a radiant church, without stain or wrinkle or any other blemish, but holy and blameless. ²⁸In this same way, husbands ought to love their wives as their own bodies. He who loves his wife loves himself. ²⁹After all, no one ever hated his own body, but he feeds and cares for it, just as Christ does the church— ³⁰for we are members of his body. ³¹"For this reason a man will leave his father and mother and be united to his wife, and the two will become one flesh."ᶜ ³²This is a profound mystery—but I am talking about Christ and the church. ³³However, each one of you also must love his wife as he loves himself, and the wife must respect her husband.

Children and Parents

6 Children, obey your parents in the Lord, for this is right. ²"Honor your father and mother"—which is the first commandment with a promise— ³"that it may go well with you and that you may enjoy long life on the earth."ᵈ

ᵃ5 Or kingdom of the Christ and God   ᵇ26 Or having cleansed   ᶜ31 Gen. 2:24   ᵈ3 Deut. 5:16

4Fathers, do not exasperate your children; instead, bring them up in the training and instruction of the Lord.

Slaves and Masters

5Slaves, obey your earthly masters with respect and fear, and with sincerity of heart, just as you would obey Christ. 6Obey them not only to win their favor when their eye is on you, but like slaves of Christ, doing the will of God from your heart. 7Serve wholeheartedly, as if you were serving the Lord, not men, 8because you know that the Lord will reward everyone for whatever good he does, whether he is slave or free.

9And masters, treat your slaves in the same way. Do not threaten them, since you know that he who is both their Master and yours is in heaven, and there is no favoritism with him.

The Armor of God

10Finally, be strong in the Lord and in his mighty power. 11Put on the full armor of God so that you can take your stand against the devil's schemes. 12For our struggle is not against flesh and blood, but

GOING *deeper*

Getting Armed for the Battle

READ AND CONSIDER: EPHESIANS 6:10-20

"Put on the full armor of God so that you can take your stand against the devil's schemes . . . Pray in the Spirit on all occasions with all kinds of prayers and requests. With this in mind, be alert and always keep on praying for all the saints" (Ephesians 6:11,18).

Scripture tells us that we are in a spiritual battle, and we need to be fully covered in the armor of God. From the moment we become believers and align ourselves with God and His purposes, the enemy of our soul wages war against us. Evil may be perpetrated against us by human beings, but we must never forget that it is our ultimate enemy, the devil, who is behind it. "For our struggle is not against flesh and blood, but against the rulers, against the authorities, against the powers of this dark world and against the spiritual forces of evil in the heavenly realms" (6:12).

God's Word, however, tells us how to protect ourselves. First, we are commanded to be strong in the Lord and in His power. Our own human strength is totally inadequate to do battle with our ultimate adversary, but God's power is invincible and His protection is complete.

The way we access that power and protection in this war that the enemy is waging against us is to put on God's armor. Paul tells us of the specific pieces of armor that each believer needs to consciously put on every day: the belt of truth (to fight Satan's lies), the breastplate of righteousness (to protect our hearts), shoes (for firm footing in our walk with Christ), the shield of faith (to repel Satan's accusations), the helmet of salvation (to protect our minds), and the sword of the Spirit—the Word of God (to give us knowledge, instruction, and ever-increasing faith).

Most of all, we must pray! Prayer strengthens us to stand against the enemy. Pray God's covering over yourself and your loved ones daily. Pray that He will reveal to you any place in your protective armor through which the evil one can secure a hook. Pray that any stronghold Satan is trying to erect in your life will be destroyed.

The enemy of our souls will always try to keep us from moving into all God has for us. But we can thwart his plans with prayer, praise, and the sword of the Spirit—which is the Word of God. These are our greatest weapons and the devil cannot stand against them.

against the rulers, against the authorities, against the powers of this dark world and against the spiritual forces of evil in the heavenly realms. 13Therefore put on the full armor of God, so that when the day of evil comes, you may be able to stand your ground, and after you have done everything, to stand. 14Stand firm then, with the belt of truth buckled around your waist, with the breastplate of righteousness in place, 15and with your feet fitted with the readiness that comes from the gospel of peace. 16In addition to all this, take up the shield of faith, with which you can extinguish all the flaming arrows of the evil one. 17Take the helmet of salvation and the sword of the Spirit, which is the word of God. 18And pray in the Spirit on all occasions with all kinds of prayers and requests. With this in mind,

be alert and always keep on praying for all the saints.

19Pray also for me, that whenever I open my mouth, words may be given me so that I will fearlessly make known the mystery of the gospel, 20for which I am an ambassador in chains. Pray that I may declare it fearlessly, as I should.

Final Greetings

21Tychicus, the dear brother and faithful servant in the Lord, will tell you everything, so that you also may know how I am and what I am doing. 22I am sending him to you for this very purpose, that you may know how we are, and that he may encourage you.

23Peace to the brothers, and love with faith from God the Father and the Lord Jesus Christ. 24Grace to all who love our Lord Jesus Christ with an undying love.

Author: Paul

Date: AD 61

Audience: The church at Philippi, to thank them for their financial gift, to encourage them to persevere, remain unified, and watch out for false teachers

Every day we have a choice. Will we be positive or negative? Optimistic or pessimistic? Will we choose to focus on God's blessings and the wonderful possibilities of a life lived for His glory? Or will we focus on life's troubles and resign ourselves to an existence that is far less than what God has for us?

Philippians shows us the better way of joy. It is essentially a thank-you note from the apostle Paul who had founded this church at Philippi on his second missionary journey (Acts 16:12-40). The church was a constant encouragement to him in many ways.

Though he was physically imprisoned, he was spiritually free. He consistently chose gratitude over grumbling. He chose joy over despondency. He chose trust in God over doubt. He would have preferred to be out traveling and preaching, and surely he wondered why God would keep him behind bars when there was so much work to be done. But Paul did what he could; he prayed and he wrote letters. And perhaps right there is the reason God kept him in prison—to provide us with the letters we read in our Bibles today. These letters give us lessons, encouragement, and warnings from the great apostle; letters we might not have had if God had not taken Paul through that experience during those years.

Prayer Themes:

- *Pray often for your family and friends, and tell them that you thank God for them every time you remember them in your prayers (1:3-6).*

- *Pray for an overwhelming hunger and thirst to know Christ and that He would become the greatest passion of your life (3:7-11).*

- *Take to heart Paul's suggestion to not worry about anything but "in everything, by prayer and petition, with thanksgiving, present your requests to God" (4:6).*

Philippians

1 Paul and Timothy, servants of Christ Jesus,

To all the saints in Christ Jesus at Philippi, together with the overseers[a] and deacons:

2 Grace and peace to you from God our Father and the Lord Jesus Christ.

Thanksgiving and Prayer

3 I thank my God every time I remember you. 4 In all my prayers for all of you, I always pray with joy 5 because of your partnership in the gospel from the first day until now, 6 being confident of this, that he who began a good work in you will carry it on to completion until the day of Christ Jesus.

7 It is right for me to feel this way about all of you, since I have you in my heart; for whether I am in chains or defending and confirming the gospel, all of you share in God's grace with me. 8 God can testify how I long for all of you with the affection of Christ Jesus.

9 And this is my prayer: that your love may abound more and more in knowledge and depth of insight, 10 so that you may be able to discern what is best and may be pure and blameless until the day of Christ, 11 filled with the fruit of righteousness that comes through

---

[a] 1 Traditionally *bishops*

God's people at prayer
PAUL'S PRAYER FOR HIS PARTNERS IN THE GOSPEL

PHILIPPIANS 1:3-11 The apostle Paul longed to see the Christians to whom he was writing in Philippi, and his prayer reflects both his confidence in them and their deep place in his affections. He affirms to all believers everywhere the wonderful reassurance that God's Spirit will continue the work begun in us when we accept Christ as Savior, reminding us that when Christ returns, that work will be stamped "Finished!" Paul also prayed that we will overflow with love for others—a true characteristic of the follower of Christ.

How would it make you feel to know that someone thanks God each and every time he or she thinks of you? What an honor to be the cause of so much gratitude and joy! When we support others who are serving Christ, whether they are pastors, missionaries, or fellow laborers in the body of Christ, we have the privilege of coming alongside them in ministry and being a great source of their joy.

Jesus Christ—to the glory and praise of God.

Paul's Chains Advance the Gospel

¹²Now I want you to know, brothers, that what has happened to me has really served to advance the gospel. ¹³As a result, it has become clear throughout the whole palace guard[a] and to everyone else that I am in chains for Christ. ¹⁴Because of my chains, most of the brothers in the Lord have been encouraged to speak the word of God more courageously and fearlessly.

¹⁵It is true that some preach Christ out of envy and rivalry, but others out of goodwill. ¹⁶The latter do so in love, knowing that I am put here for the defense of the gospel. ¹⁷The former preach Christ out of selfish ambition, not sincerely, supposing that they can stir up trouble for me while I am in chains.[b] ¹⁸But what does it matter? The important thing is that in every way, whether from false motives or true, Christ is preached. And because of this I rejoice.

Yes, and I will continue to rejoice, ¹⁹for I know that through your prayers and the help given by the Spirit of Jesus Christ, what has happened to me will turn out for my deliverance.[c] ²⁰I eagerly expect and hope that I will in no way be ashamed, but will have sufficient courage so that now as always Christ will be exalted in my body, whether by life or by death. ²¹For to me, to live is Christ and to die is gain. ²²If I am to go on living in the body, this will mean fruitful labor for me. Yet what shall I choose? I do not know! ²³I am torn between the two: I desire to depart and be with Christ, which is better by far; ²⁴but it is more necessary for you that I remain in the body. ²⁵Convinced of this, I know that I will remain, and I will continue with all of you for your progress and joy in the faith, ²⁶so that through my being with you again your joy in Christ Jesus will overflow on account of me.

²⁷Whatever happens, conduct yourselves in a manner worthy of the gospel of Christ. Then, whether I come and see you or only hear about you in my absence, I will know that you stand firm in one spirit, contending as one man for the faith of the gospel ²⁸without being frightened in any way by those who oppose you. This is a sign to them that they will be destroyed, but that you will be saved—and that by God. ²⁹For it has been granted to you on behalf of Christ not only to believe on him, but also to suffer for him, ³⁰since you are going through

the same struggle you saw I had, and now hear that I still have.

Imitating Christ's Humility

2 If you have any encouragement from being united with Christ, if any comfort from his love, if any fellowship with the Spirit, if any tenderness and compassion, 2then make my joy complete by being like-minded, having the same love, being one in spirit and purpose. 3Do nothing out of selfish ambition or vain conceit, but in humility consider others better than yourselves. 4Each of you should look not only to your own interests, but also to the interests of others.

> ### Praying Philippians 2:3-4
> *Jesus, teach me to love others the way You do so that I don't say or do anything out of selfishness or pride.*

5Your attitude should be the same as that of Christ Jesus:

6Who, being in very nature[a] God,
  did not consider equality with God
    something to be grasped,
7but made himself nothing,
  taking the very nature[b] of a
    servant,
  being made in human
    likeness.
8And being found in appearance as a
    man,
  he humbled himself
  and became obedient to death—
    even death on a cross!
9Therefore God exalted him to the
    highest place
  and gave him the name that is
    above every name,
10that at the name of Jesus every knee
    should bow,
  in heaven and on earth and under
    the earth,
11and every tongue confess that Jesus
    Christ is Lord,
  to the glory of God the Father.

Shining as Stars

12Therefore, my dear friends, as you have always obeyed—not only in my presence, but now much more in my absence—continue to work out your salvation with fear and trembling, 13for it is God who works in you to will and to act according to his good purpose.

14Do everything without complaining or arguing, 15so that you may become blameless and pure, children of God without fault in a crooked and depraved generation, in which you shine like stars in the universe 16as you hold out[c] the word of life—in order that I may boast on the day of Christ that I did not run or labor for nothing. 17But even if I am being poured out like a drink offering on the sacrifice and service coming from your faith, I am glad and rejoice with all of you. 18So you too should be glad and rejoice with me.

Timothy and Epaphroditus

19I hope in the Lord Jesus to send Timothy to you soon, that I also may be cheered when I receive news about you. 20I have no one else like him, who takes a genuine interest in your welfare. 21For everyone looks out for his own interests, not those of Jesus Christ. 22But you know that Timothy has proved himself, because as a son with his father he has served with me in the work of the gospel. 23I hope, therefore, to send him as soon as I see how things go with me. 24And I am confident in the Lord that I myself will come soon.

25But I think it is necessary to send back to you Epaphroditus, my brother, fellow worker and fellow soldier, who is also your messenger, whom you sent to take care of my needs. 26For he longs for all of you and is distressed because you heard he was ill. 27Indeed he was ill, and almost died. But God had mercy on him, and not on him only but also on me, to spare me sorrow upon sorrow. 28Therefore I am all the more eager to send him, so that when you see him again you may

---

a 6 Or *in the form of*   b 7 Or *the form*   c 16 Or *hold on to* be glad and I may have less anxiety. ²⁹Welcome him in the Lord with great joy, and honor men like him, ³⁰because he almost died for the work of Christ, risking his life to make up for the help you could not give me.

No Confidence in the Flesh

3 Finally, my brothers, rejoice in the Lord! It is no trouble for me to write the same things to you again, and it is a safeguard for you.

²Watch out for those dogs, those men who do evil, those mutilators of the flesh. ³For it is we who are the circumcision, we who worship by the Spirit of God, who glory in Christ Jesus, and who put no confidence in the flesh— ⁴though I myself have reasons for such confidence.

If anyone else thinks he has reasons to put confidence in the flesh, I have more: ⁵circumcised on the eighth day, of the people of Israel, of the tribe of Benjamin, a Hebrew of Hebrews; in regard to the law, a Pharisee; ⁶as for zeal, persecuting the church; as for legalistic righteousness, faultless.

⁷But whatever was to my profit I now consider loss for the sake of Christ. ⁸What is more, I consider everything a loss compared to the surpassing greatness of knowing Christ Jesus my Lord, for whose sake I have lost all things. I consider them rubbish, that I may gain Christ ⁹and be found in him, not having a righteousness of my own that comes from the law, but that which is through faith in Christ— the righteousness that comes from God and is by faith. ¹⁰I want to know Christ and the power of his resurrection and the fellowship of sharing in his sufferings, becoming like him in his death, ¹¹and so, somehow, to attain to the resurrection from the dead.

Pressing on Toward the Goal

¹²Not that I have already obtained all this, or have already been made perfect, but I press on to take hold of that for which Christ Jesus took hold of me. ¹³Brothers, I do not consider myself yet to have taken hold of it. But one thing I do: Forgetting what is behind and straining toward what is ahead, ¹⁴I press on toward the goal to win the prize for which God has called me heavenward in Christ Jesus.

¹⁵All of us who are mature should take such a view of things. And if on some point you think differently, that too God will make clear to you. ¹⁶Only let us live up to what we have already attained.

¹⁷Join with others in following my example, brothers, and take note of those who live according to the pattern we gave you. ¹⁸For, as I have often told you before and now say again even with tears, many live as enemies of the cross of Christ. ¹⁹Their destiny is destruction, their god is their stomach, and their glory is in their shame. Their mind is on earthly things. ²⁰But our citizenship is in heaven. And we eagerly await a Savior from there, the Lord Jesus Christ, ²¹who, by the power that enables him to bring everything under his control, will transform our lowly bodies so that they will be like his glorious body.

4 Therefore, my brothers, you whom I love and long for, my joy and crown, that is how you should stand firm in the Lord, dear friends!

Exhortations

²I plead with Euodia and I plead with Syntyche to agree with each other in the Lord. ³Yes, and I ask you, loyal yokefellow,ᵃ help these women who have contended at my side in the cause of the gospel, along with Clement and the rest of my fellow workers, whose names are in the book of life.

⁴Rejoice in the Lord always. I will say it again: Rejoice! ⁵Let your gentleness be evident to all. The Lord is near. ⁶Do not be anxious about anything, but in everything, by prayer and petition, with thanksgiving, present your requests to God. ⁷And the peace of God, which transcends

---

ᵃ 3 Or loyal Syzygus

Finding Freedom From Anxiety

Much of our anxiety comes from "what if" thoughts. What if I lose my job? What if I can't pay my bills? What if I never marry? What if I fail at what I am doing? What if I can't pass the test? What if my relationship falls apart? What if things never get better? What if I get seriously ill or injured?

On top of our own thoughts, we have television, newspapers, and magazines telling us all the reasons we should feel anxious. They remind us of the dangers around us and all too frequently bombard us with images of how we should look, talk, feel, and be. We sense great pressure to live a certain lifestyle, look a certain way, accomplish certain things, go along with certain attitudes and behavior, and mold to a certain image in order to fit in and avoid rejection. We are constantly being reminded of how we are falling short. We are losing the freedom to just be who we are and not have to look daily in the mirror to see if what is reflected there matches someone else's standard. All this makes us anxious. And that's one of the reasons why anxiety is epidemic in today's world.

God says in His Word, however, that we are not to be anxious about anything (Philippians 4:6). That's not the same as when something bad happens to you and someone says to you, "Don't worry. Just get over it." God is not saying, "Just forget about it." He is giving us the solution. He says the solution is to pray about everything and give all praise and thanks to Him. When we do that, He promises us peace beyond all comprehension. That means we will have peace even when it doesn't make sense. That kind of peace will protect our hearts and minds (Philippians 4:6-8).

So many times we think our fear and anxiety are actually connected to God. We believe we feel anxious because of something God didn't do or may not do for us. We think, *What if He doesn't provide for me? What if He doesn't protect us? Why hasn't He healed me? What if He doesn't give us what we want or need?* When we anticipate the worst and entertain a constant sense of foreboding, we create anxiety and mental stress that eventually can interfere with our ability to function. This lack of peace makes us miserable and can even make us sick because it is a burden we were not meant to carry. We will break down under it—whether in our minds, our emotions, or our bodies.

Anxiety can come into our souls at any time. And when it does we may look for any number of different ways to mask it. But anxiety can only be quieted by the peace of God. The moment we receive Jesus, we have access to His peace, which is beyond all understanding (Philippians 4:7). When you turn to Him, He can give you peace about who you are, what you are doing, and where you are going in your life. He can give you peace about your past, present, and future. He can give you peace about your circumstances regardless of what they are.

Even though life is unpredictable and too often filled with fearful things, God says that we don't have to live in fear. At the first sign of anxiety we can seek the peace of God—in His Word, in prayer, and in praise and worship—and we are assured we will find it.

For the next "From Stormie's Heart" article, go to page 1453.

GOING *deeper*
Prayer and Thanksgiving Bring Peace

READ AND CONSIDER: PHILIPPIANS 4:2-9

"Do not be anxious about anything, but in everything, by prayer and petition, with thanksgiving, present your requests to God. And the peace of God, which transcends all understanding, will guard your hearts and your minds in Christ Jesus" (Philippians 4:6-7).

This old familiar verse reminds us to pray and bring all our requests to God so that we can have His peace ruling our hearts. But what we often forget are the two words, "with thanksgiving." We neglect to thank God in the midst of whatever is happening (or *not* happening) to us at the time. We don't remember to praise Him first as the source of all that we will ever need. We don't always remember to worship Him for who He is. And we must do that, because all the things that are true of God are true of Him no matter what is going on inside of us or in our lives.

Just before this verse, Paul tells all of us to rejoice in God. He even says it twice for emphasis. We are instructed to "rejoice in the Lord always" (4:4), to find our joy in Him. So many times we think our fear and anxiety are connected to God. We think we feel that way because of something He didn't do or may not do for us. *What if He doesn't provide for us? What if He doesn't protect us? What if He doesn't give us what we want or need?* But what if we, instead, were to say in the face of these feared problems, "Thank You, Lord, that You will always provide for us." Or, "Thank You, Lord, that You are my protector and you will continue to protect me." Or, "Thank You, Lord, that You have promised to give us everything we need and give us the desires of our hearts."

Anxiety can come into our souls at any time. It often happens in the middle of the night when the house is quiet but the mind is not. There are pills that promise temporary relief, but when they wear off, the anxiety is still there. The problem has simply been masked. Such anxiety can only be quieted by the peace of God. And the moment we receive Jesus, we have access to peace that "transcends all understanding." When we are fearful, apprehensive, worried, or terrified, that peace of God can restore us to calm, assured confidence.

We have access to that peace every time we praise God and give Him thanks. It's best to do it the moment we sense anxiety over *anything*. And then *continue* to praise and thank Him until all anxiety leaves. Try it and you'll experience greater peace than you have ever known.

---

all understanding, will guard your hearts and your minds in Christ Jesus.

⁸Finally, brothers, whatever is true, whatever is noble, whatever is right, whatever is pure, whatever is lovely, whatever is admirable—if anything is excellent or praiseworthy—think about such things. ⁹Whatever you have learned or received or heard from me, or seen in me—put it into practice. And the God of peace will be with you.

Thanks for Their Gifts

¹⁰I rejoice greatly in the Lord that at last you have renewed your concern for me. Indeed, you have been concerned, but you had no opportunity to show it. ¹¹I am not saying this because I am in need, for I have learned to be content whatever the circumstances. ¹²I know what it is to be in need, and I know what it is to have plenty. I have learned the secret of being content in any and every

situation, whether well fed or hungry, whether living in plenty or in want. [13]I can do everything through him who gives me strength.

[14]Yet it was good of you to share in my troubles. [15]Moreover, as you Philippians know, in the early days of your acquaintance with the gospel, when I set out from Macedonia, not one church shared with me in the matter of giving and receiving, except you only; [16]for even when I was in Thessalonica, you sent me aid again and again when I was in need. [17]Not that I am looking for a gift, but I am looking for what may be credited to your account. [18]I have received full payment and even more; I am amply supplied, now that I have received from Epaphroditus the gifts you sent. They are a fragrant offering, an acceptable sacrifice, pleasing to God. [19]And my God will meet all your needs according to his glorious riches in Christ Jesus.

[20]To our God and Father be glory for ever and ever. Amen.

Final Greetings

[21]Greet all the saints in Christ Jesus. The brothers who are with me send greetings. [22]All the saints send you greetings, especially those who belong to Caesar's household.

[23]The grace of the Lord Jesus Christ be with your spirit. Amen.[a]

---

[a] 23 Some manuscripts do not have Amen.

Author: Paul

Date: About AD 60–61

Audience: The church at Colosse (ancient Asia Minor, present-day Turkey), to refute some heretical ideas that were gaining acceptance

Prayer Themes:

- Pray that God will enable you to live a powerful and fruitful life that reflects His love, His mercy, His truth, and His purity and is always pleasing to Him (1:9-12).

- Ask God to use you to help others become strong in their faith (1:28-29).

- Pray that you will have the discipline to set your mind on heavenly things—to have an eternal focus and not be depleted or scattered by worldly concerns (3:2-3).

The church in the city of Colosse was not founded by Paul but by one of Paul's disciples named Epaphras (1:7). Epaphras may have been converted during the years that Paul was in Ephesus; then Epaphras took the message back to his hometown. Later, when their paths crossed again, Epaphras told Paul about the problem with heretical teaching that was infecting the believers in Colosse. Paul wrote this letter to combat the heresy with the doctrine of truth.

At the beginning of this letter, Paul spoke of prayer—how he gave thanks for them and prayed always for them, asking God to fill them with the knowledge of His will, with spiritual wisdom and understanding so that they could bear fruit in every good work.

He prayed for them, then he talked to them about the difficult issues at hand. When we have to do a hard task or talk about tough issues, we would do well to first bring it all to God in prayer—especially to pray for the people to whom we need to give a difficult but important word.

Colossians

1 Paul, an apostle of Christ Jesus by the will of God, and Timothy our brother,

²To the holy and faithful[a] brothers in Christ at Colosse:

Grace and peace to you from God our Father.[b]

Thanksgiving and Prayer

³We always thank God, the Father of our Lord Jesus Christ, when we pray for you, ⁴because we have heard of your faith in Christ Jesus and of the love you have for all the saints— ⁵the faith and love that spring from the hope that is stored up for you in heaven and that you have already heard about in the word of truth, the gospel ⁶that has come to you. All over the world this gospel is bearing fruit and growing, just as it has been doing among you since the day you heard it and understood God's grace in all its truth. ⁷You learned it from Epaphras, our dear fellow servant, who is a faithful minister of Christ on our[c] behalf, ⁸and who also told us of your love in the Spirit.

⁹For this reason, since the day we heard about you, we have not stopped praying for you and asking God to fill you with the knowledge of his will through all spiritual wisdom and understanding. ¹⁰And we pray this in order that you may live a life worthy of the Lord and may please him in every way: bearing fruit in every good work, growing in the knowledge of God, ¹¹being strengthened with all power according to his glorious might so that you may have great endurance

---

a 2 Or *believing*   b 2 Some manuscripts *Father and the Lord Jesus Christ*   c 7 Some manuscripts *your*

GOING deeper

The Power of Praying for Others

READ AND CONSIDER: COLOSSIANS 1:9-14

"For this reason, since the day we heard about you, we have not stopped praying for you and asking God to fill you with the knowledge of his will through all spiritual wisdom and understanding" (Colossians 1:9).

For all the people we care about—parents, children, a spouse, friends, family, neighbors, co-workers, or people in need around the world—one of the best things we can do for them is pray. We may not be able to provide them with good health, financial security, or protection from all harm. But we can pray that *God* will heal them, provide for them, and keep them safe.

The promise to pray for others is one of the finest gifts we can give. Every time we seek the presence of God and the release of His power on behalf of someone else, great things happen. It is the most effective way we can touch others and make a difference in their lives.

The most important thing we can pray about for others is that they will know God better and that He will help them understand His will, grow in spiritual wisdom, and live lives that honor Him. We can pray that they will become more like Him and bear the fruit of His Spirit.

When we pray for others, we are asking God to make His presence known in their lives. We are asking Him to open their heart so they can hear from Him. That doesn't mean there will always be an immediate response. Sometimes it can take days, weeks, months, or even years. But our prayers are never lost or meaningless. If we are praying, something is happening in the lives of those for whom we pray, whether we see it or not. Everything that needs to happen in our lives and in the lives of our loved ones cannot happen without the presence and power of God. Prayer invites and ignites both.

and patience, and joyfully [12]giving thanks to the Father, who has qualified you[a] to share in the inheritance of the saints in the kingdom of light. [13]For he has rescued us from the dominion of darkness and brought us into the kingdom of the Son he loves, [14]in whom we have redemption,[b] the forgiveness of sins.

The Supremacy of Christ

[15]He is the image of the invisible God, the firstborn over all creation. [16]For by him all things were created: things in heaven and on earth, visible and invisible, whether thrones or powers or rulers or authorities; all things were created by him and for him. [17]He is before all things, and in him all things hold together. [18]And he is the head of the body, the church; he is the beginning and the firstborn from among the dead, so that in everything he might have the supremacy. [19]For God was pleased to have all his fullness dwell in him, [20]and through him to reconcile to himself all things, whether things on earth or things in heaven, by making peace through his blood, shed on the cross.

[21]Once you were alienated from God and were enemies in your minds because of[c] your evil behavior. [22]But now he has reconciled you by Christ's physical body through death to present you holy in his sight, without blemish and free from accusation— [23]if you continue in your faith, established and firm, not moved from

---

[a] *12* Some manuscripts *us*   [b] *14* A few late manuscripts *redemption through his blood*   [c] *21* Or *minds, as shown by*

the hope held out in the gospel. This is the gospel that you heard and that has been proclaimed to every creature under heaven, and of which I, Paul, have become a servant.

Paul's Labor for the Church

²⁴Now I rejoice in what was suffered for you, and I fill up in my flesh what is still lacking in regard to Christ's afflictions, for the sake of his body, which is the church. ²⁵I have become its servant by the commission God gave me to present to you the word of God in its fullness— ²⁶the mystery that has been kept hidden for ages and generations, but is now disclosed to the saints. ²⁷To them God has chosen to make known among the Gentiles the glorious riches of this mystery, which is Christ in you, the hope of glory.

²⁸We proclaim him, admonishing and teaching everyone with all wisdom, so that we may present everyone perfect in Christ. ²⁹To this end I labor, struggling with all his energy, which so powerfully works in me.

2 I want you to know how much I am struggling for you and for those at Laodicea, and for all who have not met me personally. ²My purpose is that they may be encouraged in heart and united in love, so that they may have the full riches of complete understanding, in order that they may know the mystery of God, namely, Christ, ³in whom are hidden all the treasures of wisdom and knowledge. ⁴I tell you this so that no one may deceive you by fine-sounding arguments. ⁵For though I am absent from you in body, I am present with you in spirit and delight to see how orderly you are and how firm your faith in Christ is.

Freedom From Human Regulations Through Life With Christ

⁶So then, just as you received Christ Jesus as Lord, continue to live in him, ⁷rooted and built up in him, strengthened in the faith as you were taught, and overflowing with thankfulness.

⁸See to it that no one takes you captive through hollow and deceptive philosophy, which depends on human tradition and the basic principles of this world rather than on Christ.

⁹For in Christ all the fullness of the Deity lives in bodily form, ¹⁰and you have been given fullness in Christ, who is the head over every power and authority. ¹¹In him you were also circumcised, in the putting off of the sinful nature,ᵃ not with a circumcision done by the hands of men but with the circumcision done by Christ, ¹²having been buried with him in baptism and raised with him through your faith in the power of God, who raised him from the dead.

> *Prayer is . . .*
>
> *tuning out the world and listening to God.*

¹³When you were dead in your sins and in the uncircumcision of your sinful nature,ᵇ God made youᶜ alive with Christ. He forgave us all our sins, ¹⁴having canceled the written code, with its regulations, that was against us and that stood opposed to us; he took it away, nailing it to the cross. ¹⁵And having disarmed the powers and authorities, he made a public spectacle of them, triumphing over them by the cross.ᵈ

¹⁶Therefore do not let anyone judge you by what you eat or drink, or with regard to a religious festival, a New Moon celebration or a Sabbath day. ¹⁷These are a shadow of the things that were to come; the reality, however, is found in Christ. ¹⁸Do not let anyone who delights in false humility and the worship of angels disqualify you for the prize. Such a person

ᵃ 11 Or the flesh   ᵇ 13 Or your flesh   ᶜ 13 Some manuscripts us   ᵈ 15 Or them in him goes into great detail about what he has seen, and his unspiritual mind puffs him up with idle notions. ¹⁹He has lost connection with the Head, from whom the whole body, supported and held together by its ligaments and sinews, grows as God causes it to grow.

²⁰Since you died with Christ to the basic principles of this world, why, as though you still belonged to it, do you submit to its rules: ²¹"Do not handle! Do not taste! Do not touch!"? ²²These are all destined to perish with use, because they are based on human commands and teachings. ²³Such regulations indeed have an appearance of wisdom, with their self-imposed worship, their false humility and their harsh treatment of the body, but they lack any value in restraining sensual indulgence.

Rules for Holy Living

3 Since, then, you have been raised with Christ, set your hearts on things above, where Christ is seated at the right hand of God. ²Set your minds on things above, not on earthly things. ³For you died, and your life is now hidden with Christ in God. ⁴When Christ, who is your[a] life, appears, then you also will appear with him in glory.

⁵Put to death, therefore, whatever belongs to your earthly nature: sexual immorality, impurity, lust, evil desires and greed, which is idolatry. ⁶Because of these, the wrath of God is coming.[b] ⁷You used to walk in these ways, in the life you once lived. ⁸But now you must rid yourselves of all such things as these: anger, rage, malice, slander, and filthy language from your lips. ⁹Do not lie to each other, since you have taken off your old self with its practices ¹⁰and have put on the new self, which is being renewed in knowledge in the image of its Creator. ¹¹Here there is no Greek or Jew, circumcised or uncircumcised, barbarian, Scythian, slave or free, but Christ is all, and is in all.

¹²Therefore, as God's chosen people, holy and dearly loved, clothe yourselves with compassion, kindness, humility, gentleness and patience. ¹³Bear with each other and forgive whatever grievances you may have against one another. Forgive as the Lord forgave you. ¹⁴And over all these virtues put on love, which binds them all together in perfect unity.

¹⁵Let the peace of Christ rule in your hearts, since as members of one body you were called to peace. And be thankful. ¹⁶Let the word of Christ dwell in you richly as you teach and admonish one another with all wisdom, and as you sing psalms, hymns and spiritual songs with gratitude in your hearts to God. ¹⁷And whatever you do, whether in word or deed, do it all in the name of the Lord Jesus, giving thanks to God the Father through him.

Rules for Christian Households

¹⁸Wives, submit to your husbands, as is fitting in the Lord.

¹⁹Husbands, love your wives and do not be harsh with them.

²⁰Children, obey your parents in everything, for this pleases the Lord.

²¹Fathers, do not embitter your children, or they will become discouraged.

²²Slaves, obey your earthly masters in everything; and do it, not only when their eye is on you and to win their favor, but with sincerity of heart and reverence for the Lord. ²³Whatever you do, work at it with all your heart, as working for the Lord, not for men, ²⁴since you know that you will receive an inheritance from the Lord as a reward. It is the Lord Christ you are serving. ²⁵Anyone who does wrong will be repaid for his wrong, and there is no favoritism.

4 Masters, provide your slaves with what is right and fair, because you know that you also have a Master in heaven.

Further Instructions

²Devote yourselves to prayer, being watchful and thankful. ³And pray for us,

---

[a] 4 Some manuscripts *our*   [b] 6 Some early manuscripts *coming on those who are disobedient*

Why Is It So Hard to Pray for Myself?

Do you find it is easier to pray for other people than it is to pray for yourself? I know I do. I can pray for my husband, my children, other family members, acquaintances, friends, and people I've never even met whom I hear about in the news far easier than I can pray for my own needs. For one thing, their needs are easy for me to identify. Mine are numerous, sometimes complicated, often difficult to determine, and certainly not easy to label. We women know what we *think* we need most of the time. We are able to recognize the obvious. But we are often too emotionally involved in the people around us and the day-to-day existence of our lives to be able to figure out how we should be praying for ourselves beyond the immediate and urgent.

Do you ever have times when your life seems out of control? Do you ever feel pressured, as if your days are so busy that you fear you're missing out on a certain quality of life because of it? Do you worry that you are neglecting one or more areas of your life because you are trying to fill numerous roles and meet many expectations?

Do you hunger for a greater sense of the Lord's presence in your life? Do you desire to know God in a deeper way? Do you want to serve Him better and more completely but don't feel you have the time, energy, or opportunity to do so? Do you need to spend more time with Him in prayer? Do you want your prayers to be accompanied by greater faith so that you can see greater answers to them? Do you need a more complete knowledge and understanding of God's Word? Do you ever just long to throw your arms wide open and embrace Jesus, white robes and all, and feel His embrace of you?

The good news is that this is the way God *wants* you to feel.

God wants you to long for *His* presence. He wants you to find your fulfillment in *Him* and nothing else. He wants you to walk closely with *Him*. He wants you to increase in faith and knowledge of *His* Word. He wants you to put all your hopes and dreams in *His* hands and look to *Him* to meet all of your needs. When you do, *He* will open the storehouse of blessing upon your life. That's because these things are *His* will for you.

But none of this happens without prayer. So that's why I think it's good to ask God to *help* you become a person of heartfelt and faith-filled prayer. Ask the Holy Spirit to *teach* you how to pray for every aspect of your life. He will answer those prayers.

For the next "From Stormie's Heart" article, go to page 1458.

too, that God may open a door for our message, so that we may proclaim the mystery of Christ, for which I am in chains. [4]Pray that I may proclaim it clearly, as I should. [5]Be wise in the way you act toward outsiders; make the most of every opportunity. [6]Let your conversation be always full of grace, seasoned with salt, so that you may know how to answer everyone.

Praying Colossians 4:2-5

Heavenly Father, I pray that You would open doors for me to speak of Your greatness to others and give me the perfect words to say at all times.

Final Greetings

[7]Tychicus will tell you all the news about me. He is a dear brother, a faithful minister and fellow servant in the Lord. [8]I am sending him to you for the express purpose that you may know about our[a] circumstances and that he may encourage your hearts. [9]He is coming with Onesimus, our faithful and dear brother, who is one of you. They will tell you everything that is happening here.

[10]My fellow prisoner Aristarchus sends you his greetings, as does Mark, the cousin of Barnabas. (You have received instructions about him; if he comes to you, welcome him.) [11]Jesus, who is called Justus, also sends greetings. These are the only Jews among my fellow workers for the kingdom of God, and they have proved a comfort to me. [12]Epaphras, who is one of you and a servant of Christ Jesus, sends greetings. He is always wrestling in prayer for you, that you may stand firm in all the will of God, mature and fully assured. [13]I vouch for him that he is working hard for you and for those at Laodicea and Hierapolis. [14]Our dear friend Luke, the doctor, and Demas send greetings. [15]Give my greetings to the brothers at Laodicea, and to Nympha and the church in her house.

[16]After this letter has been read to you, see that it is also read in the church of the Laodiceans and that you in turn read the letter from Laodicea.

[17]Tell Archippus: "See to it that you complete the work you have received in the Lord."

[18]I, Paul, write this greeting in my own hand. Remember my chains. Grace be with you.

---

[a] *8* Some manuscripts *that he may know about your*

Author: Paul

Date: AD 50–51

Audience: The largely Gentile church at Thessalonica (modern-day Greece), to encourage them to continue trusting and obeying God during a time of persecution

The apostle Paul had visited the city of Thessalonica during his second missionary journey (see Acts 17:1-10). He and his companions planted a church there, but then had to leave quickly because their lives were threatened. When it seemed safe to do so, Paul sent Timothy back to Thessalonica to check up on the believers. Timothy brought a good report back to Paul, but they also had a few questions about their new faith. Paul wrote this letter to help answer those questions.

The believers in Thessalonica were being persecuted externally by unbelievers and plagued internally by uncertainty and doubt. Paul wanted to encourage them that the Lord *is* coming back. So they should stay the course, keep living in a way that honors Him, and keep trusting and waiting. And while they worshiped and worked and waited, they should be joyful, pray continually, and give thanks in all circumstances.

We too face difficulties—whether from without or within—and Paul's advice to live in joy, thankfulness, and ongoing prayer should characterize our lives as well.

Prayer Themes:

- *Pray faithfully for the people God has put in your life—family, friends, neighbors, co-workers, etc. (1:2-3).*

- *Ask God to cause your love for others to grow (4:9-10).*

- *Thank God in every situation you face. Ask Him to help you develop a trusting perspective that sees His hand in all things (5:18).*

1 Thessalonians

1 Paul, Silas[a] and Timothy,

To the church of the Thessalonians in God the Father and the Lord Jesus Christ:

Grace and peace to you.[b]

Thanksgiving for the Thessalonians' Faith

²We always thank God for all of you, mentioning you in our prayers. ³We continually remember before our God and Father your work produced by faith, your labor prompted by love, and your endurance inspired by hope in our Lord Jesus Christ.

⁴For we know, brothers loved by God, that he has chosen you, ⁵because our gos-pel came to you not simply with words, but also with power, with the Holy Spirit and with deep conviction. You know how we lived among you for your sake. ⁶You became imitators of us and of the Lord; in spite of severe suffering, you welcomed the message with the joy given by the Holy Spirit. ⁷And so you became a model to all the believers in Macedonia and Achaia. ⁸The Lord's message rang out from you not only in Macedonia and Achaia—your faith in God has become known everywhere. Therefore we do not need to say anything about it, ⁹for they themselves report what kind of reception you gave us. They tell how you turned to God from idols to serve the living and true God, ¹⁰and to wait for his

---

a *1* Greek *Silvanus*, a variant of *Silas*   b *1* Some early manuscripts *you from God our Father and the Lord Jesus Christ*

Son from heaven, whom he raised from the dead—Jesus, who rescues us from the coming wrath.

Paul's Ministry in Thessalonica

2 You know, brothers, that our visit to you was not a failure. ²We had previously suffered and been insulted in Philippi, as you know, but with the help of our God we dared to tell you his gospel in spite of strong opposition. ³For the appeal we make does not spring from error or impure motives, nor are we trying to trick you. ⁴On the contrary, we speak as men approved by God to be entrusted with the gospel. We are not trying to please men but God, who tests our hearts. ⁵You know we never used flattery, nor did we put on a mask to cover up greed—God is our witness. ⁶We were not looking for praise from men, not from you or anyone else.

As apostles of Christ we could have been a burden to you, ⁷but we were gentle among you, like a mother caring for her little children. ⁸We loved you so much that we were delighted to share with you not only the gospel of God but our lives as well, because you had become so dear to us. ⁹Surely you remember, brothers, our toil and hardship; we worked night and day in order not to be a burden to anyone while we preached the gospel of God to you.

¹⁰You are witnesses, and so is God, of how holy, righteous and blameless we were among you who believed. ¹¹For you know that we dealt with each of you as a father deals with his own children, ¹²encouraging, comforting and urging you to live lives worthy of God, who calls you into his kingdom and glory.

¹³And we also thank God continually because, when you received the word of God, which you heard from us, you accepted it not as the word of men, but as it actually is, the word of God, which is at work in you who believe. ¹⁴For you, brothers, became imitators of God's churches in Judea, which are in Christ Jesus: You suffered from your own countrymen the same things those churches suffered from the Jews, ¹⁵who killed the Lord Jesus and the prophets and also drove us out. They displease God and are hostile to all men ¹⁶in their effort to keep us from speaking to the Gentiles so that they may be saved. In this way they always heap up their sins to the limit. The wrath of God has come upon them at last.ᵃ

Paul's Longing to See the Thessalonians

¹⁷But, brothers, when we were torn away from you for a short time (in person,

---

ᵃ *16 Or them fully*

not in thought), out of our intense longing we made every effort to see you. 18For we wanted to come to you—certainly I, Paul, did, again and again—but Satan stopped us. 19For what is our hope, our joy, or the crown in which we will glory in the presence of our Lord Jesus when he comes? Is it not you? 20Indeed, you are our glory and joy.

3 So when we could stand it no longer, we thought it best to be left by ourselves in Athens. 2We sent Timothy, who is our brother and God's fellow worker[a] in spreading the gospel of Christ, to strengthen and encourage you in your faith, 3so that no one would be unsettled by these trials. You know quite well that we were destined for them. 4In fact, when we were with you, we kept telling you that we would be persecuted. And it turned out that way, as you well know. 5For this reason, when I could stand it no longer, I sent to find out about your faith. I was afraid that in some way the tempter might have tempted you and our efforts might have been useless.

Timothy's Encouraging Report

6But Timothy has just now come to us from you and has brought good news about your faith and love. He has told us that you always have pleasant memories of us and that you long to see us, just as we also long to see you. 7Therefore, brothers, in all our distress and persecution we were encouraged about you because of your faith. 8For now we really live, since you are standing firm in the Lord. 9How can we thank God enough for you in return for all the joy we have in the presence of our God because of you? 10Night and day we pray most earnestly that we may see you again and supply what is lacking in your faith.

11Now may our God and Father himself and our Lord Jesus clear the way for us to come to you. 12May the Lord make your love increase and overflow for each other and for everyone else, just as ours does for you. 13May he strengthen your hearts so that you will be blameless and holy in the presence of our God and Father when our Lord Jesus comes with all his holy ones.

Living to Please God

4 Finally, brothers, we instructed you how to live in order to please God, as in fact you are living. Now we ask you and urge you in the Lord Jesus to do this more and more. 2For you know what instructions we gave you by the authority of the Lord Jesus.

Praying 1 Thessalonians 4:3-4

Lord, keep my heart, mind, and
body from any kind of immorality
so that I can live in the holiness to
which You have called me.

3It is God's will that you should be sanctified: that you should avoid sexual immorality; 4that each of you should learn to control his own body[b] in a way that is holy and honorable, 5not in passionate lust like the heathen, who do not know God; 6and that in this matter no one should wrong his brother or take advantage of him. The Lord will punish men for all such sins, as we have already told you and warned you. 7For God did not call us to be impure, but to live a holy life. 8Therefore, he who rejects this instruction does not reject man but God, who gives you his Holy Spirit.

9Now about brotherly love we do not need to write to you, for you yourselves have been taught by God to love each other. 10And in fact, you do love all the brothers throughout Macedonia. Yet we urge you, brothers, to do so more and more.

11Make it your ambition to lead a quiet life, to mind your own business and to work with your hands, just as we told you, 12so that your daily life may win the

---

a 2 Some manuscripts *brother and fellow worker*; other manuscripts *brother and God's servant*   b 4 Or *learn to live with his own wife*; or *learn to acquire a wife*

Embracing the Moment

Walking step-by-step with God requires embracing the moment you are in. For example, when you are tempted to become fearful, frustrated, uncertain, or panicked about what is happening in your life, stop and see that God is in it. And with Him, you have everything you need for the moment. Here and now.

It's amazing that when we open our eyes to the whole picture, we have a different perspective. When we embrace Him, we see the blessings that are right in front of us. We can be content right where we are no matter what state we are in—literally or figuratively—because *He* is there (see Philippians 4:11).

Regardless of what your situation is at this moment, God has an abundance of blessings for you. Right where you are, God is working powerfully in your life. He wants you to close your eyes, call out His name, and say, "Lord, show me Your hand in my life right now." He wants you to sense His presence. He wants you to trust that when you are afraid, you can turn to Him and find His peace. When you are weary, you will find His strength. When you are empty, you will find His fullness. When you are sad, you will find His joy.

When we have a deep and personal relationship with the Lord, our difficult times are not the same as they are for people who don't have Him. For unbelievers, their dark and troubled times are without hope. Even for believers who don't understand all that God has for them, their difficult experiences are filled with fear and doubt instead of a sense of God's sustaining presence.

When you embrace the heart of God in the nitty-gritty details of your life, you will find a oneness with Him you never dreamed possible. And you'll sense that He is in control and will not let you get off course. Whenever you feel angry, sad, depressed, or fearful, say, "God, reveal Yourself to me in this moment. What are You doing in my life that I am not seeing? If all things work together for good, then show me the good."

When you're determined to see the good, you will find it. If God knows your thoughts (Psalm 94:11), your heart (1 Samuel 16:7), when you stand up and sit down (Psalm 139:2), and how many hairs you have on your head (Matthew 10:30), then He knows where you are at any given moment. He sees your circumstances. Just because *you* can't see anything ahead doesn't mean *He* can't. He *can* and *does*. He knows where you've been. He knows where you're headed. He knows where you are supposed to be going. And He knows how to get you there. You have Him, and He is all you need.

For the next "From Stormie's Heart" article, go to page 1470.

respect of outsiders and so that you will not be dependent on anybody.

The Coming of the Lord

13Brothers, we do not want you to be ignorant about those who fall asleep, or to grieve like the rest of men, who have no hope. 14We believe that Jesus died and rose again and so we believe that God will bring with Jesus those who have fallen asleep in him. 15According to the Lord's own word, we tell you that we who are still alive, who are left till the coming of the Lord, will certainly not precede those who have fallen asleep. 16For the Lord himself will come down from heaven, with a loud command, with the voice of the archangel and with the trumpet call of God, and the dead in Christ will rise first. 17After that, we who are still alive

---

GOING *deeper*

How to Always Do God's Will

READ AND CONSIDER: 1 THESSALONIANS 5:12-28

"Be joyful always; pray continually; give thanks in all circumstances, for this is God's will for you in Christ Jesus" (1 Thessalonians 5:16-18).

What do you do when you pray and pray about something, and God doesn't seem to answer? For example, what if you've been praying about an important decision, and now time is running out? You have to know what to do right away, but still God seems silent. What do you do then? When that happens, always do what you *know* is God's will. And it is always God's will to be joyful, to *continue* praying, and to give Him thanks regardless of your circumstances (5:16-18). Praise, prayer, and a joyful heart are vital when you need to know God's will for your life.

To "be joyful always" means we have to make a choice. We can't always choose how we feel, but we *can* choose how we respond to our feelings. We can make a decision to be joyful *in spite* of how we feel. The way we do that is to never allow our feelings or our circumstances to interfere with our worship. Whatever the situation is, when we continually acknowledge God's greatness in the midst of whatever is happening, we experience the joy of the Lord.

To "pray continually" means to pray about everything right when you think about it, allowing prayer to become a natural first response to whatever is happening. Imagine how complicated our lives would be if we had to remember to tell our heart to beat and our lungs to breathe. How much time would we spend if we had to schedule all the body repairs that go on around the clock without our conscious attention? The challenge to pray continually is an invitation to develop a prayer life that simply goes on constantly in the background, like our lungs breathing and our heart beating, no matter what is happening in our life.

To "give thanks" is the main reason to pray. It's expressing gratitude for who God is and all He has done. It's deciding to be grateful even in the tough times—times of darkness, sadness, or despair. It's saying "thank you" to God in moments when we can't see the whole picture, knowing He will shed His light on the situation. We need to give thanks "in all circumstances" because something good always happens when we thank God. We become more receptive to God's will. We gain the mind of Christ and the leading of the Holy Spirit. We invite God to work in our situation. That means if we were leaning toward doing something that wasn't actually the will of God, our heart would open up to what He wants for us, and our mind would change.

So when you are waiting to know God's will for your future, do what you know is always God's will right now: Continue praying and praising and letting the joy of the Lord rise in your heart.

and are left will be caught up together with them in the clouds to meet the Lord in the air. And so we will be with the Lord forever. ¹⁸Therefore encourage each other with these words.

5 Now, brothers, about times and dates we do not need to write to you, ²for you know very well that the day of the Lord will come like a thief in the night. ³While people are saying, "Peace and safety," destruction will come on them suddenly, as labor pains on a pregnant woman, and they will not escape.

⁴But you, brothers, are not in darkness so that this day should surprise you like a thief. ⁵You are all sons of the light and sons of the day. We do not belong to the night or to the darkness. ⁶So then, let us not be like others, who are asleep, but let us be alert and self-controlled. ⁷For those who sleep, sleep at night, and those who get drunk, get drunk at night. ⁸But since we belong to the day, let us be self-controlled, putting on faith and love as a breastplate, and the hope of salvation as a helmet. ⁹For God did not appoint us to suffer wrath but to receive salvation through our Lord Jesus Christ. ¹⁰He died for us so that, whether we are awake or asleep, we may live together with him. ¹¹Therefore encourage one another and build each other up, just as in fact you are doing.

Final Instructions

¹²Now we ask you, brothers, to respect those who work hard among you, who are over you in the Lord and who admonish you. ¹³Hold them in the highest regard in love because of their work. Live in peace with each other. ¹⁴And we urge you, brothers, warn those who are idle, encourage the timid, help the weak, be patient with everyone. ¹⁵Make sure that nobody pays back wrong for wrong, but always try to be kind to each other and to everyone else.

¹⁶Be joyful always; ¹⁷pray continually; ¹⁸give thanks in all circumstances, for this is God's will for you in Christ Jesus.

¹⁹Do not put out the Spirit's fire; ²⁰do not treat prophecies with contempt. ²¹Test everything. Hold on to the good. ²²Avoid every kind of evil.

²³May God himself, the God of peace, sanctify you through and through. May your whole spirit, soul and body be kept blameless at the coming of our Lord Jesus Christ. ²⁴The one who calls you is faithful and he will do it.

²⁵Brothers, pray for us. ²⁶Greet all the brothers with a holy kiss. ²⁷I charge you before the Lord to have this letter read to all the brothers.

²⁸The grace of our Lord Jesus Christ be with you.

Author: Paul

Date: AD 50–52

Audience: The largely Gentile church at Thessalonica (modern-day Greece), to encourage them to continue trusting and obeying God during a time of persecution and to correct some misconceptions about the return of Christ

Prayer Themes:

- Praise God for His justice, that He will one day right every wrong (1:6).

- Ask the Lord for a deep hunger and thirst for His Word so that you desire His divine truth just as you desire food and water (2:15).

- Pray that you will never grow tired of doing the right thing (3:13).

Have you ever heard a Christian say: "I wish I could do more to help . . . Oh well, if nothing else, at least I can pray"? Paul never viewed prayer as a last resort. For him prayer wasn't some kind of last-ditch effort or a spiritual kind of wishful thinking. On the contrary, prayer was his initial response to any situation.

This is why, at the outset of his second letter to the beleaguered Christians in Thessalonica, Paul wrote, "We constantly pray for you" (1:11). This is why, at the end of the same letter, he pleaded, "Brothers, pray for us that the message of the Lord may spread rapidly and be honored . . . And pray that we may be delivered from wicked and evil men" (3:1-2).

In reading Paul's letters, it's clear that prayer isn't the "least we can do"; it's the *most powerful* thing we do and should be our first reaction.

2 Thessalonians

1 Paul, Silas[a] and Timothy,

To the church of the Thessalonians in God our Father and the Lord Jesus Christ:

²Grace and peace to you from God the Father and the Lord Jesus Christ.

Thanksgiving and Prayer

³We ought always to thank God for you, brothers, and rightly so, because your faith is growing more and more, and the love every one of you has for each other is increasing. ⁴Therefore, among God's churches we boast about your perseverance and faith in all the persecutions and trials you are enduring.

⁵All this is evidence that God's judgment is right, and as a result you will be counted worthy of the kingdom of God, for which you are suffering. ⁶God is just: He will pay back trouble to those who trouble you ⁷and give relief to you who are troubled, and to us as well. This will happen when the Lord Jesus is revealed from heaven in blazing fire with his powerful angels. ⁸He will punish those who do not know God and do not obey the gospel of our Lord Jesus. ⁹They will be punished with everlasting destruction and shut out from the presence of the Lord and from the majesty of his power ¹⁰on the day he comes to be glorified in his holy people and to be marveled at among all those who have believed. This includes you, because you believed our testimony to you.

¹¹With this in mind, we constantly

pray for you, that our God may count you worthy of his calling, and that by his power he may fulfill every good purpose of yours and every act prompted by your faith. [12]We pray this so that the name of our Lord Jesus may be glorified in you, and you in him, according to the grace of our God and the Lord Jesus Christ.[a]

The Man of Lawlessness

2 Concerning the coming of our Lord Jesus Christ and our being gathered to him, we ask you, brothers, [2]not to become easily unsettled or alarmed by some prophecy, report or letter supposed to have come from us, saying that the day of the Lord has already come. [3]Don't let anyone deceive you in any way, for ⌐that day will not come⌐ until the rebellion occurs and the man of lawlessness[b] is revealed, the man doomed to destruction. [4]He will oppose and will exalt himself over everything that is called God or is worshiped, so that he sets himself up in God's temple, proclaiming himself to be God.

[5]Don't you remember that when I was with you I used to tell you these things? [6]And now you know what is holding him back, so that he may be revealed at the proper time. [7]For the secret power of lawlessness is already at work; but the one who now holds it back will continue to do so till he is taken out of the way. [8]And then the lawless one will be revealed, whom the Lord Jesus will overthrow with the breath of his mouth and destroy by the splendor of his coming. [9]The coming of the lawless one will be in accordance with the work of Satan displayed in all kinds of counterfeit miracles, signs and wonders, [10]and in every sort of evil

that deceives those who are perishing. They perish because they refused to love the truth and so be saved. [11]For this reason God sends them a powerful delusion so that they will believe the lie [12]and so that all will be condemned who have not believed the truth but have delighted in wickedness.

Stand Firm

[13]But we ought always to thank God for you, brothers loved by the Lord, because from the beginning God chose you[c] to be saved through the sanctifying work of the Spirit and through belief in the truth. [14]He called you to this through our gospel, that you might share in the glory of our Lord Jesus Christ. [15]So then, brothers, stand firm and hold to the teachings[d] we passed on to you, whether by word of mouth or by letter.

[16]May our Lord Jesus Christ himself and God our Father, who loved us and by his grace gave us eternal encouragement and good hope, [17]encourage your hearts and strengthen you in every good deed and word.

Request for Prayer

3 Finally, brothers, pray for us that the message of the Lord may spread rapidly and be honored, just as it was with you. [2]And pray that we may be delivered from wicked and evil men, for not everyone has faith. [3]But the Lord is faithful, and he will strengthen and protect you from the evil one. [4]We have confidence in the Lord that you are doing and will continue to do the things we command. [5]May the Lord direct your hearts into God's love and Christ's perseverance.

Praying 2 Thessalonians 2:9-10

*Dear God, put in my heart an
unfailing love for your truth so that
I will never be deceived.*

Warning Against Idleness

[6]In the name of the Lord Jesus Christ, we command you, brothers, to keep away from every brother who is idle and does not live according to the teaching[e] you re-

---

[a] 12 Or *God and Lord, Jesus Christ*   [b] 3 Some manuscripts *sin*   [c] 13 Some manuscripts *because God chose you as his firstfruits*   [d] 15 Or *traditions*   [e] 6 Or *tradition*

Praying for People Who Need Good News

READ AND CONSIDER: 2 THESSALONIANS 3:1-5

"Finally, brothers, pray for us that the message of the Lord may spread rapidly and be honored, just as it was with you" (2 Thessalonians 3:1).

Do you remember the first time you heard about Jesus and His message of salvation, when the Good News really penetrated your soul? Do you recall that pivotal moment when your life changed for all eternity? Who brought Jesus' message to you? How did God use that person to reach out and touch your heart?

God is always intensely personal and masterfully creative in the ways He reaches out to us. Each one of us has a unique and wonderful story of our salvation. And all of our stories have one thing in common: Somewhere, somehow, *someone* responded to God's call to spread His love and bring His message. Whether we heard a pastor who preached a message that affected us, or listened to a friend who talked to us about Jesus, or someone gave us a Bible or a Christian book, or a person was praying for us . . . someone reached out because of a desire to help us discover the truth about God's love.

In this passage, the apostle Paul asked fellow Christians to pray for those who were spreading the message of the Lord, that it would be far-reaching and effective, "just as it was with you." This is a strong reminder to remember how Jesus saved us and all that He has done for us so that we will deeply desire that others experience His love too.

Praying is the most important thing you can do when trying to reach people for the Lord. Whether you feel confident or self-conscious about your own efforts to spread the good news, your prayers will pave the way for hearts to open up and receive what God wants to speak to them. Whether you are in the frontlines of evangelism or behind the scenes, as long as you are praying, you are a vital part of God's work here on earth. Along with everything else you are doing for the Lord, don't forget to share your own story about how you came to know Jesus. Tell it often. And let it remind you to pray for those who are searching for truth and need to hear about all the good news Jesus has for them.

ceived from us. 7For you yourselves know how you ought to follow our example. We were not idle when we were with you, 8nor did we eat anyone's food without paying for it. On the contrary, we worked night and day, laboring and toiling so that we would not be a burden to any of you. 9We did this, not because we do not have the right to such help, but in order to make ourselves a model for you to follow. 10For even when we were with you, we gave you this rule: "If a man will not work, he shall not eat."

11We hear that some among you are idle. They are not busy; they are busybodies. 12Such people we command and urge in the Lord Jesus Christ to settle down and earn the bread they eat. 13And as for you, brothers, never tire of doing what is right.

14If anyone does not obey our instruction in this letter, take special note of him. Do not associate with him, in order that he may feel ashamed. 15Yet do not regard him as an enemy, but warn him as a brother.

Final Greetings

16Now may the Lord of peace himself give you peace at all times and in every way. The Lord be with all of you.

17I, Paul, write this greeting in my own hand, which is the distinguishing mark in all my letters. This is how I write.

18The grace of our Lord Jesus Christ be with you all.

Author: Paul

Date: AD 63–65

Audience: Timothy, Paul's young protégé and leader of the church at Ephesus, to help him with the various pastoral issues (selecting leaders, refuting false doctrine, etc.)

Prayer Themes:

- Ask God to help you remember that the goal of your faith isn't knowledge or religious activity but to share the love of God that comes from a pure heart and a good conscience (1:5).

- Pray that the Holy Spirit will continually help you to be more concerned with your "internal" condition rather than your "external" appearance (2:9-10).

- Ask God to help you resist greed and learn to be content (6:7-10).

Timothy became one of Paul's right-hand men, traveling with Paul and many times on behalf of Paul to various churches. Paul often wanted to check back in on a congregation to see how they were doing and how they were growing in their faith after he had left, so he sent emissaries to go in his place. Timothy went to help those newly planted churches deal with issues of church leadership. In this letter to Timothy, Paul gave instructions about worship and qualifications for church leadership, and he issued warnings about watching out for false teachers.

Paul also demonstrated the priority of prayer. "I urge, then, first of all, that requests, prayers, intercession and thanksgiving be made for everyone" (2:1). It's clear that we are to be praying for others daily and giving thanks to God for them.

The book of 1 Timothy is a wise, concise summary of the issues that face every Christian leader. But clearly, Paul believes that our success in being world-changers hinges on how seriously we answer God's call to be people of prayer.

1 Timothy

1 Paul, an apostle of Christ Jesus by the command of God our Savior and of Christ Jesus our hope,

2 To Timothy my true son in the faith:

Grace, mercy and peace from God the Father and Christ Jesus our Lord.

Warning Against False Teachers of the Law

3 As I urged you when I went into Macedonia, stay there in Ephesus so that you may command certain men not to teach false doctrines any longer 4 nor to devote themselves to myths and endless genealogies. These promote controversies rather than God's work—which is by faith.

5 The goal of this command is love, which comes from a pure heart and a good conscience and a sincere faith. 6 Some have wandered away from these and turned to meaningless talk. 7 They want to be teachers of the law, but they do not know what they are talking about or what they so confidently affirm.

8 We know that the law is good if one uses it properly. 9 We also know that law[a] is made not for the righteous but for lawbreakers and rebels, the ungodly and sinful, the unholy and irreligious; for those who kill their fathers or mothers, for murderers, 10 for adulterers and perverts, for slave traders and liars and perjurers—and for whatever else is contrary to the sound

---

[a] 9 Or *that the law*

doctrine ¹¹that conforms to the glorious gospel of the blessed God, which he entrusted to me.

The Lord's Grace to Paul

¹²I thank Christ Jesus our Lord, who has given me strength, that he considered me faithful, appointing me to his service. ¹³Even though I was once a blasphemer and a persecutor and a violent man, I was shown mercy because I acted in ignorance and unbelief. ¹⁴The grace of our Lord was poured out on me abundantly, along with the faith and love that are in Christ Jesus.

¹⁵Here is a trustworthy saying that deserves full acceptance: Christ Jesus came into the world to save sinners—of whom I am the worst. ¹⁶But for that very reason I was shown mercy so that in me, the worst of sinners, Christ Jesus might display his unlimited patience as an ex-ample for those who would believe on him and receive eternal life. ¹⁷Now to the King eternal, immortal, invisible, the only God, be honor and glory for ever and ever. Amen.

¹⁸Timothy, my son, I give you this instruction in keeping with the prophecies once made about you, so that by following them you may fight the good fight, ¹⁹holding on to faith and a good conscience. Some have rejected these and so have shipwrecked their faith. ²⁰Among them are Hymenaeus and Alexander, whom I have handed over to Satan to be taught not to blaspheme.

Instructions on Worship

2 I urge, then, first of all, that requests, prayers, intercession and thanksgiving be made for everyone— ²for kings and all those in authority, that we may live peaceful and quiet lives in all godliness

GOING deeper

Praying Together in Unity

READ AND CONSIDER: 1 TIMOTHY 2:1-8

"I want men everywhere to lift up holy hands in prayer, without anger or disputing" (1 Timothy 2:8).

God wants all of us who believe in Him to be in unity. When we are unified, we stand together to glorify Him. Because Jesus "gave himself as a ransom for *all men*" (2:6), we are unified as recipients of His salvation and messengers of His love. That means regardless of how different we are from one another, we are all brought together by His sacrifice. But we have to make a decision to stay in unity. In fact, unity is such an important part of our spiritual foundation that our spiritual growth and the effectiveness of our prayer life depend on us being in unity with one another. God wants us to be unified in our beliefs, unified in our work for Him, and unified in our prayers. That means no arguing or fighting with our brothers and sisters.

Paul urges that "requests, prayers, intercession and thanksgiving be made for everyone," meaning both those who are already followers of Jesus and those who haven't yet met Him (2:1). But sometimes we Christians quarrel among ourselves. We get caught up in unimportant debates and useless arguments. Paul encourages all Christians to pray for others "without anger or disputing" for the common goal of winning people to the Lord (2:8).

When we are selfless in our prayers, increasingly grateful for our salvation, humbled by God's amazing love for us, staunch in our belief in Christ as Savior over all, and unified in prayer with other believers, then our prayers are powerful and will bear fruit beyond measure.

and holiness. ³This is good, and pleases God our Savior, ⁴who wants all men to be saved and to come to a knowledge of the truth. ⁵For there is one God and one mediator between God and men, the man Christ Jesus, ⁶who gave himself as a ransom for all men—the testimony given in its proper time. ⁷And for this purpose I was appointed a herald and an apostle—I am telling the truth, I am not lying—and a teacher of the true faith to the Gentiles.

⁸I want men everywhere to lift up holy hands in prayer, without anger or disputing.

⁹I also want women to dress modestly, with decency and propriety, not with braided hair or gold or pearls or expensive clothes, ¹⁰but with good deeds, appropriate for women who profess to worship God.

¹¹A woman should learn in quietness and full submission. ¹²I do not permit a woman to teach or to have authority over a man; she must be silent. ¹³For Adam was formed first, then Eve. ¹⁴And Adam was not the one deceived; it was the woman who was deceived and became a sinner. ¹⁵But women[a] will be saved[b] through childbearing—if they continue in faith, love and holiness with propriety.

Overseers and Deacons

3 Here is a trustworthy saying: If anyone sets his heart on being an overseer,[c] he desires a noble task. ²Now the overseer must be above reproach, the husband of but one wife, temperate, self-controlled, respectable, hospitable, able to teach, ³not given to drunkenness, not violent but gentle, not quarrelsome, not a lover of money. ⁴He must manage his own family well and see that his children obey him with proper respect. ⁵(If anyone does not know how to manage his own family, how can he take care of God's church?) ⁶He must not be a recent convert, or he may become conceited and fall under

the same judgment as the devil. ⁷He must also have a good reputation with outsiders, so that he will not fall into disgrace and into the devil's trap.

⁸Deacons, likewise, are to be men worthy of respect, sincere, not indulging in much wine, and not pursuing dishonest gain. ⁹They must keep hold of the deep truths of the faith with a clear conscience. ¹⁰They must first be tested; and then if there is nothing against them, let them serve as deacons.

¹¹In the same way, their wives[d] are to be women worthy of respect, not malicious talkers but temperate and trustworthy in everything.

¹²A deacon must be the husband of but one wife and must manage his children and his household well. ¹³Those who have served well gain an excellent standing and great assurance in their faith in Christ Jesus.

¹⁴Although I hope to come to you soon, I am writing you these instructions so that, ¹⁵if I am delayed, you will know how people ought to conduct themselves in God's household, which is the church of the living God, the pillar and foundation of the truth. ¹⁶Beyond all question, the mystery of godliness is great:

He[e] appeared in a body,[f]
 was vindicated by the Spirit,
was seen by angels,
 was preached among the nations,
was believed on in the world,
 was taken up in glory.

Instructions to Timothy

4 The Spirit clearly says that in later times some will abandon the faith and follow deceiving spirits and things taught by demons. ²Such teachings come through hypocritical liars, whose consciences have been seared as with a hot iron. ³They forbid people to marry and order them to abstain from certain

foods, which God created to be received with thanksgiving by those who believe and who know the truth. ⁴For everything God created is good, and nothing is to be rejected if it is received with thanksgiving, ⁵because it is consecrated by the word of God and prayer.

⁶If you point these things out to the brothers, you will be a good minister of Christ Jesus, brought up in the truths of the faith and of the good teaching that you have followed. ⁷Have nothing to do with godless myths and old wives' tales; rather, train yourself to be godly. ⁸For physical training is of some value, but godliness has value for all things, holding promise for both the present life and the life to come.

Praying 1 Timothy 4:8

God, help me to be disciplined in my mind, body, and soul for Your glory, and to always seek godliness as a priority over anything else in life.

---

⁹This is a trustworthy saying that deserves full acceptance ¹⁰(and for this we labor and strive), that we have put our hope in the living God, who is the Savior of all men, and especially of those who believe.

¹¹Command and teach these things. ¹²Don't let anyone look down on you because you are young, but set an example for the believers in speech, in life, in love, in faith and in purity. ¹³Until I come, devote yourself to the public reading of Scripture, to preaching and to teaching. ¹⁴Do not neglect your gift, which was given you through a prophetic message when the body of elders laid their hands on you.

¹⁵Be diligent in these matters; give yourself wholly to them, so that everyone may see your progress. ¹⁶Watch your life and doctrine closely. Persevere in them, because if you do, you will save both yourself and your hearers.

Advice About Widows, Elders and Slaves

5 Do not rebuke an older man harshly, but exhort him as if he were your father. Treat younger men as brothers, ²older women as mothers, and younger women as sisters, with absolute purity.

³Give proper recognition to those widows who are really in need. ⁴But if a widow has children or grandchildren, these should learn first of all to put their religion into practice by caring for their own family and so repaying their parents and grandparents, for this is pleasing to God. ⁵The widow who is really in need and left all alone puts her hope in God and continues night and day to pray and to ask God for help. ⁶But the widow who lives for pleasure is dead even while she lives. ⁷Give the people these instructions, too, so that no one may be open to blame. ⁸If anyone does not provide for his relatives, and especially for his immediate family, he has denied the faith and is worse than an unbeliever.

⁹No widow may be put on the list of widows unless she is over sixty, has been faithful to her husband,ᵃ ¹⁰and is well known for her good deeds, such as bringing up children, showing hospitality, washing the feet of the saints, helping those in trouble and devoting herself to all kinds of good deeds.

¹¹As for younger widows, do not put them on such a list. For when their sensual desires overcome their dedication to Christ, they want to marry. ¹²Thus they bring judgment on themselves, because they have broken their first pledge. ¹³Besides, they get into the habit of being idle and going about from house to house. And not only do they become idlers, but also gossips and busybodies, saying things they ought not to. ¹⁴So I counsel younger widows to marry, to have children, to manage their homes and to give the enemy no opportunity for slander. ¹⁵Some have in fact already turned away to follow Satan.

ᵃ 9 Or *has had but one husband*

[16]If any woman who is a believer has widows in her family, she should help them and not let the church be burdened with them, so that the church can help those widows who are really in need.

[17]The elders who direct the affairs of the church well are worthy of double honor, especially those whose work is preaching and teaching. [18]For the Scripture says, "Do not muzzle the ox while it is treading out the grain,"[a] and "The worker deserves his wages."[b] [19]Do not entertain an accusation against an elder unless it is brought by two or three witnesses. [20]Those who sin are to be rebuked publicly, so that the others may take warning.

[21]I charge you, in the sight of God and Christ Jesus and the elect angels, to keep these instructions without partiality, and to do nothing out of favoritism.

[22]Do not be hasty in the laying on of hands, and do not share in the sins of others. Keep yourself pure.

[23]Stop drinking only water, and use a little wine because of your stomach and your frequent illnesses.

[24]The sins of some men are obvious, reaching the place of judgment ahead of them; the sins of others trail behind them. [25]In the same way, good deeds are obvious, and even those that are not cannot be hidden.

6 All who are under the yoke of slavery should consider their masters worthy of full respect, so that God's name and our teaching may not be slandered. [2]Those who have believing masters are not to show less respect for them because they are brothers. Instead, they are to serve them even better, because those who benefit from their service are believers, and dear to them. These are the things you are to teach and urge on them.

Love of Money
[3]If anyone teaches false doctrines and does not agree to the sound instruction of our Lord Jesus Christ and to godly teaching, [4]he is conceited and understands nothing. He has an unhealthy interest in controversies and quarrels about words that result in envy, strife, malicious talk, evil suspicions [5]and constant friction between men of corrupt mind, who have been robbed of the truth and who think that godliness is a means to financial gain.

[6]But godliness with contentment is great gain. [7]For we brought nothing into the world, and we can take nothing out of it. [8]But if we have food and clothing, we will be content with that. [9]People who want to get rich fall into temptation and a trap and into many foolish and harmful desires that plunge men into ruin and destruction. [10]For the love of money is a root of all kinds of evil. Some people, eager for money, have wandered from the faith and pierced themselves with many griefs.

Paul's Charge to Timothy
[11]But you, man of God, flee from all this, and pursue righteousness, godliness, faith, love, endurance and gentleness. [12]Fight the good fight of the faith. Take hold of the eternal life to which you were called when you made your good confession in the presence of many witnesses. [13]In the sight of God, who gives life to everything, and of Christ Jesus, who while testifying before Pontius Pilate made the good confession, I charge you [14]to keep this command without spot or blame until the appearing of our Lord Jesus Christ, [15]which God will bring about in his own time—God, the blessed and only Ruler, the King of kings and Lord of lords, [16]who alone is immortal and who lives in unapproachable light, whom no one has seen or can see. To him be honor and might forever. Amen.

[17]Command those who are rich in this present world not to be arrogant nor to put their hope in wealth, which is so uncertain, but to put their hope in God, who richly provides us with everything

a 18 Deut. 25:4　b 18 Luke 10:7

Finding Freedom From Fear

Not all fear is bad. For example, fear of what *might* happen will keep you from allowing a child to run across a busy highway where cars are speeding by. It will stop you from playing with a loaded gun. It will cause you to seriously consider the consequences of disobeying God. It will inspire a deep reverence for who God is. That is *good* fear.

A good, healthy fear will cause us to do positive and productive things.

Being afraid of something is not wrong. But when we harbor fear, entertain it, and let it grow in us, it becomes a problem. The kind of fear that overtakes us, controls us, and paralyzes us is not of God. It is a spirit of fear. "For God did not give us a spirit of timidity, but a spirit of power, of love and of self-discipline" (2 Timothy 1:7). When you have that kind of destructive fear, take it to the Lord in prayer, and He will set you free from it by the *power* of His Spirit. He will rescue you from the torment of it by surrounding you with His *love*. He will keep your mind *sound* and give you peace.

God wants us to trust Him enough to take steps of faith in the face of all that we fear. When Pharaoh chased the Israelites to the Red Sea, they were terrified because they were facing an enormous body of water in front of them and Pharaoh's army fast approaching from behind. They saw no way out. But Moses said to the people, "Do not be afraid. Stand firm and you will see the deliverance the LORD will bring you today. The Egyptians you see today you will never see again. The LORD will fight for you; you need only to be still" (Exodus 14:13-14). And the Lord delivered them from a frightening and impossible situation.

The most important thing we can do when we feel afraid is to call upon God and ask Him to protect us and set us free from whatever it is we fear. In order to be free of fear, you need to have faith. Too often we don't "fight the good fight" in prayer (1 Timothy 6:12). We don't take the steps of faith God is asking us to take because of our unbelief. We doubt that God will really protect us or that He even hears our prayers. One of the greatest steps you can take is to read the Bible every day because faith comes by hearing and studying the Word of God.

Another step you can take is to lift up praise to God. Praise Him for His perfect love, which casts out all fear. Praise Him that He is more powerful than anything you face. Praise Him for His presence, for when you are in His presence, you have nothing to fear.

For the next "From Stormie's Heart" article, go to page 1489.

for our enjoyment. ¹⁸Command them to do good, to be rich in good deeds, and to be generous and willing to share. ¹⁹In this way they will lay up treasure for themselves as a firm foundation for the coming age, so that they may take hold of the life that is truly life.

²⁰Timothy, guard what has been entrusted to your care. Turn away from godless chatter and the opposing ideas of what is falsely called knowledge, ²¹which some have professed and in so doing have wandered from the faith.

Grace be with you.

Author: Paul

Date: AD 66–67

Audience: Timothy and the Ephesian church who need some final words from Paul before his martyrdom

At the end of his extraordinary life, the apostle Paul found himself "chained like a criminal" (2:9), awaiting Nero's executioners. But even though his body was imprisoned, his spirit remained free. With unwavering hope, Paul reveled in the fact that the gospel was spreading across the earth, transforming lives. He grasped the great truth that this world, this brief life, is merely the prelude to eternity. And so he spent his final days on earth entertaining visitors whenever possible and writing letters of encouragement. He exhorted others to press on, be strong, work hard, and teach the truth.

This letter has the sound of a man who knows his life is nearing its end. These are the final words he wants Timothy to hear. "Remember Timothy, to stand strong, to pass along the faith to others, who in turn will pass it on, that Scripture is infallible, that false teachers will come and make their mark. Timothy, know that I am ready to go because I have finished my course and kept the faith. You, however, have a job to do."

Paul had such strong faith and assurance because he walked closely with God. He could go to be with the Lord forever knowing that others would carry on the work he had begun.

Prayer Themes:

- Ask God to "fan into flame" your spiritual gifts. If you aren't sure what they are, ask Him to show you the gifts He has put within you (1:6).

- Pray that the Lord will give you a "Timothy," a younger person into whom you can invest some time helping them to grow in the ways of God (2:2).

- Ask God to show you any unclean attitudes or actions in your life that are keeping you from being used by Him for "noble purposes" (2:20-21).

2 Timothy

1 Paul, an apostle of Christ Jesus by the will of God, according to the promise of life that is in Christ Jesus,

2 To Timothy, my dear son:

Grace, mercy and peace from God the Father and Christ Jesus our Lord.

Encouragement to Be Faithful

3 I thank God, whom I serve, as my forefathers did, with a clear conscience, as night and day I constantly remember you in my prayers. 4 Recalling your tears, I long to see you, so that I may be filled with joy. 5 I have been reminded of your sincere faith, which first lived in your grandmother Lois and in your mother Eunice and, I am persuaded, now lives in you also. 6 For this reason I remind you to fan into flame the gift of God, which is in you through the laying on of my hands. 7 For God did not give us a spirit of timidity, but a spirit of power, of love and of self-discipline.

8 So do not be ashamed to testify about our Lord, or ashamed of me his prisoner. But join with me in suffering for the gospel, by the power of God, 9 who has saved us and called us to a holy life—not because of anything we have done but because of his own purpose and grace. This grace was given us in Christ Jesus before the beginning of time, 10 but it has now been revealed through the appearing of our Savior, Christ Jesus, who has destroyed death and has brought life and

Being Remembered in Prayer

READ AND CONSIDER: 2 TIMOTHY 1:3-7

"I thank God, whom I serve, as my forefathers did, with a clear conscience, as night and day I constantly remember you in my prayers" (2 Timothy 1:3).

We all want to be remembered. We all desire to make a positive and lasting impression on someone's life. None of us wants to be forgotten by the people who are near and dear to us—especially family and friends. And who doesn't want to make a profound impact on the world in some way? But most importantly, we all want to be remembered by others in prayer.

Imagine being remembered day and night in prayer. Think of how loved and cared for you would feel. When we are prayed for, we *feel* those prayers—even if we don't know people are praying, even if we don't fully understand what it is we are feeling. When we lift up each other in prayer, we are not only bound *together* in the love of God, but we also deepen and strengthen our *personal* bond with the Lord. We form a prayer circle with God at the center, and it grows stronger every time we pray. We experience great blessings whether we are the giver or the receiver of prayer.

If you need to be reminded to pray for others, keep a prayer journal with a list of the people who need your prayers and how you want to pray for them. Then pray as the Spirit leads. It's inspiring to think how Paul constantly remembered to pray for Timothy. We can do the same with people in our own lives.

---

immortality to light through the gospel. ¹¹And of this gospel I was appointed a herald and an apostle and a teacher. ¹²That is why I am suffering as I am. Yet I am not ashamed, because I know whom I have believed, and am convinced that he is able to guard what I have entrusted to him for that day.

¹³What you heard from me, keep as the pattern of sound teaching, with faith and love in Christ Jesus. ¹⁴Guard the good deposit that was entrusted to you—guard it with the help of the Holy Spirit who lives in us.

¹⁵You know that everyone in the province of Asia has deserted me, including Phygelus and Hermogenes.

¹⁶May the Lord show mercy to the household of Onesiphorus, because he often refreshed me and was not ashamed of my chains. ¹⁷On the contrary, when he was in Rome, he searched hard for me until he found me. ¹⁸May the Lord grant

that he will find mercy from the Lord on that day! You know very well in how many ways he helped me in Ephesus.

2 You then, my son, be strong in the grace that is in Christ Jesus. ²And the things you have heard me say in the presence of many witnesses entrust to reliable men who will also be qualified to teach others. ³Endure hardship with us like a good soldier of Christ Jesus. ⁴No one serving as a soldier gets involved in civilian affairs—he wants to please his commanding officer. ⁵Similarly, if anyone competes as an athlete, he does not receive the victor's crown unless he competes according to the rules. ⁶The hardworking farmer should be the first to receive a share of the crops. ⁷Reflect on what I am saying, for the Lord will give you insight into all this.

⁸Remember Jesus Christ, raised from the dead, descended from David. This is my gospel, ⁹for which I am suffering even to the point of being chained like a

criminal. But God's word is not chained. [10]Therefore I endure everything for the sake of the elect, that they too may obtain the salvation that is in Christ Jesus, with eternal glory.

[11]Here is a trustworthy saying:

If we died with him,
    we will also live with him;
[12]if we endure,
    we will also reign with him.
If we disown him,
    he will also disown us;
[13]if we are faithless,
    he will remain faithful,
    for he cannot disown himself.

A Workman Approved by God

[14]Keep reminding them of these things. Warn them before God against quarreling about words; it is of no value, and only ruins those who listen. [15]Do your best to present yourself to God as one approved, a workman who does not need to be ashamed and who correctly handles the word of truth. [16]Avoid godless chatter, because those who indulge in it will become more and more ungodly. [17]Their teaching will spread like gangrene. Among them are Hymenaeus and Philetus, [18]who have wandered away from the truth. They say that the resurrection has already taken place, and they destroy the faith of some. [19]Nevertheless, God's solid foundation stands firm, sealed with this inscription: "The Lord knows those who are his,"[a] and, "Everyone who confesses the name of the Lord must turn away from wickedness."

Praying 2 Timothy 2:20-21

Heavenly Father, I pray that You will help me to be separated and cleansed from all that is dishonorable so that I may be used as a vessel of honor that glorifies You.

[20]In a large house there are articles not only of gold and silver, but also of wood and clay; some are for noble purposes

and some for ignoble. [21]If a man cleanses himself from the latter, he will be an instrument for noble purposes, made holy, useful to the Master and prepared to do any good work.

[22]Flee the evil desires of youth, and pursue righteousness, faith, love and peace, along with those who call on the Lord out of a pure heart. [23]Don't have anything to do with foolish and stupid arguments, because you know they produce quarrels. [24]And the Lord's servant must not quarrel; instead, he must be kind to everyone, able to teach, not resentful. [25]Those who oppose him he must gently instruct, in the hope that God will grant them repentance leading them to a knowledge of the truth, [26]and that they will come to their senses and escape from the trap of the devil, who has taken them captive to do his will.

Godlessness in the Last Days

3 But mark this: There will be terrible times in the last days. [2]People will be lovers of themselves, lovers of money, boastful, proud, abusive, disobedient to their parents, ungrateful, unholy, [3]without love, unforgiving, slanderous, without self-control, brutal, not lovers of the good, [4]treacherous, rash, conceited, lovers of pleasure rather than lovers of God— [5]having a form of godliness but denying its power. Have nothing to do with them.

[6]They are the kind who worm their way into homes and gain control over weak-willed women, who are loaded down with sins and are swayed by all kinds of evil desires, [7]always learning but never able to acknowledge the truth. [8]Just as Jannes and Jambres opposed Moses, so also these men oppose the truth—men of depraved minds, who, as far as the faith is concerned, are rejected. [9]But they will not get very far because, as in the case of those men, their folly will be clear to everyone.

Paul's Charge to Timothy

[10]You, however, know all about my teaching, my way of life, my purpose,

---

[a] [19]Num. 16:5 (see Septuagint)

faith, patience, love, endurance, [11]persecutions, sufferings—what kinds of things happened to me in Antioch, Iconium and Lystra, the persecutions I endured. Yet the Lord rescued me from all of them. [12]In fact, everyone who wants to live a godly life in Christ Jesus will be persecuted, [13]while evil men and impostors will go from bad to worse, deceiving and being deceived. [14]But as for you, continue in what you have learned and have become convinced of, because you know those from whom you learned it, [15]and how from infancy you have known the holy Scriptures, which are able to make you wise for salvation through faith in Christ Jesus. [16]All Scripture is God-breathed and is useful for teaching, rebuking, correcting and training in righteousness, [17]so that the man of God may be thoroughly equipped for every good work.

Prayer is . . .

often begun by first thinking about a passage from God's Word.

4 In the presence of God and of Christ Jesus, who will judge the living and the dead, and in view of his appearing and his kingdom, I give you this charge: [2]Preach the Word; be prepared in season and out of season; correct, rebuke and encourage—with great patience and careful instruction. [3]For the time will come when men will not put up with sound doctrine. Instead, to suit their own desires, they will gather around them a great number of teachers to say what their itching ears want to hear. [4]They will turn their ears away from the truth and turn aside to myths. [5]But you, keep your head in all situations, endure hardship, do the work of an evangelist, discharge all the duties of your ministry.

[6]For I am already being poured out like a drink offering, and the time has come for my departure. [7]I have fought the good fight, I have finished the race, I have kept the faith. [8]Now there is in store for me the crown of righteousness, which the Lord, the righteous Judge, will award to me on that day—and not only to me, but also to all who have longed for his appearing.

Personal Remarks

[9]Do your best to come to me quickly, [10]for Demas, because he loved this world, has deserted me and has gone to Thessalonica. Crescens has gone to Galatia, and Titus to Dalmatia. [11]Only Luke is with me. Get Mark and bring him with you, because he is helpful to me in my ministry. [12]I sent Tychicus to Ephesus. [13]When you come, bring the cloak that I left with Carpus at Troas, and my scrolls, especially the parchments.

[14]Alexander the metalworker did me a great deal of harm. The Lord will repay him for what he has done. [15]You too should be on your guard against him, because he strongly opposed our message.

[16]At my first defense, no one came to my support, but everyone deserted me. May it not be held against them. [17]But the Lord stood at my side and gave me strength, so that through me the message might be fully proclaimed and all the Gentiles might hear it. And I was delivered from the lion's mouth. [18]The Lord will rescue me from every evil attack and will bring me safely to his heavenly kingdom. To him be glory for ever and ever. Amen.

Final Greetings

[19]Greet Priscilla[a] and Aquila and the household of Onesiphorus. [20]Erastus stayed in Corinth, and I left Trophimus sick in Miletus. [21]Do your best to get here before winter. Eubulus greets you, and so do Pudens, Linus, Claudia and all the brothers.

[22]The Lord be with your spirit. Grace be with you.

---

[a] *19* Greek *Prisca,* a variant of *Priscilla*

Author: Paul

Date: AD 63–65

Audience: Titus, a convert of Paul, who was ministering on the island of Crete, to advise him how to choose leaders for the church and how to deal with opposition and false teachers

Like Timothy, Titus was a fellow traveler with Paul who often was sent in Paul's place to minister. In the context of this letter, we find that Titus had been left on the island of Crete so that he might "straighten out what was left unfinished and appoint elders in every town" (1:5). And like Paul's first letter to Timothy, this letter instructs Titus in how to choose leaders and deal with false doctrine. It also offers advice in how Titus can help the believers live differently than their surrounding culture.

Consoling, urging, and guiding, Paul continually pointed Titus toward eternal truths. By warning, teaching, and reminding him, the apostle cast a vision for a community of faith—exceptionally pure and devout—committed to ministry.

If you want wise counsel on how to deal with problematic people, or if you need help on how to handle the "worldly passions" (2:12), this letter gives sound advice.

As you read this short book, pray that God will help you to depend more and more on Him as you live and serve in this godless age.

Prayer Themes:

- *Praise God for the promise that He is a God of truth and His Word can always be trusted (1:2).*

- *Ask the Holy Spirit to show you what specifically you need to do (or stop doing) in order to live in way that honors God (2:3-5).*

- *Ask God to give you a pure heart that is "eager to do what is good" (2:14).*

Titus

Paul, a servant of God and an apostle of Jesus Christ for the faith of God's elect and the knowledge of the truth that leads to godliness— ²a faith and knowledge resting on the hope of eternal life, which God, who does not lie, promised before the beginning of time, ³and at his appointed season he brought his word to light through the preaching entrusted to me by the command of God our Savior,

⁴To Titus, my true son in our common faith:

Grace and peace from God the Father and Christ Jesus our Savior.

Titus's Task on Crete

⁵The reason I left you in Crete was that you might straighten out what was left unfinished and appointª elders in every town, as I directed you. ⁶An elder must be blameless, the husband of but one wife, a man whose children believe and are not open to the charge of being wild and disobedient. ⁷Since an overseerᵇ is entrusted with God's work, he must be blameless—not overbearing, not quick-tempered, not given to drunkenness, not violent, not pursuing dishonest gain. ⁸Rather he must be hospitable, one who loves what is good, who is self-controlled, upright, holy and disciplined. ⁹He must hold firmly to the trustworthy message as it has been taught, so that he can encourage others by sound doctrine and refute those who oppose it.

¹⁰For there are many rebellious people, mere talkers and deceivers, especially those of the circumcision group. ¹¹They

must be silenced, because they are ruining whole households by teaching things they ought not to teach—and that for the sake of dishonest gain. [12]Even one of their own prophets has said, "Cretans are always liars, evil brutes, lazy gluttons." [13]This testimony is true. Therefore, rebuke them sharply, so that they will be sound in the faith [14]and will pay no attention to Jewish myths or to the commands of those who reject the truth. [15]To the pure, all things are pure, but to those who are corrupted and do not believe, nothing is pure. In fact, both their minds and consciences are corrupted. [16]They claim to know God, but by their actions they deny him. They are detestable, disobedient and unfit for doing anything good.

What Must Be Taught to Various Groups

2 You must teach what is in accord with sound doctrine. [2]Teach the older men to be temperate, worthy of respect, self-controlled, and sound in faith, in love and in endurance.

[3]Likewise, teach the older women to be reverent in the way they live, not to be slanderers or addicted to much wine, but to teach what is good. [4]Then they can train the younger women to love their husbands and children, [5]to be self-controlled and pure, to be busy at home, to be kind, and to be subject to their husbands, so that no one will malign the word of God.

[6]Similarly, encourage the young men to be self-controlled. [7]In everything set them an example by doing what is good. In your teaching show integrity, seriousness [8]and soundness of speech that cannot be condemned, so that those who oppose you may be ashamed because they have nothing bad to say about us.

[9]Teach slaves to be subject to their masters in everything, to try to please them, not to talk back to them, [10]and not to steal from them, but to show that they can be fully trusted, so that in every way they will make the teaching about God our Savior attractive.

[11]For the grace of God that brings salvation has appeared to all men. [12]It teaches us to say "No" to ungodliness and worldly passions, and to live self-controlled, upright and godly lives in this present age, [13]while we wait for the blessed hope—the glorious appearing of our great God and Savior, Jesus Christ, [14]who gave himself for us to redeem us from all wickedness and to purify for himself a people that are his very own, eager to do what is good.

Praying Titus 2:11-14
Jesus, enable me to rise above the lusts of the flesh and the temptations of the world so that I might be purified and made ready for the work You have for me to do.

[15]These, then, are the things you should teach. Encourage and rebuke with all authority. Do not let anyone despise you.

Doing What Is Good

3 Remind the people to be subject to rulers and authorities, to be obedient, to be ready to do whatever is good, [2]to slander no one, to be peaceable and considerate, and to show true humility toward all men.

[3]At one time we too were foolish, disobedient, deceived and enslaved by all kinds of passions and pleasures. We lived in malice and envy, being hated and hating one another. [4]But when the kindness and love of God our Savior appeared, [5]he saved us, not because of righteous things we had done, but because of his mercy. He saved us through the washing of rebirth and renewal by the Holy Spirit, [6]whom he poured out on us generously through Jesus Christ our Savior, [7]so that, having been justified by his grace, we might become heirs having the hope of eternal life. [8]This is a trustworthy saying. And I want you to stress these things, so that those who have trusted in God may be careful to devote themselves to doing what is good. These things are excellent and profitable for everyone.

⁹But avoid foolish controversies and genealogies and arguments and quarrels about the law, because these are unprofitable and useless. ¹⁰Warn a divisive person once, and then warn him a second time. After that, have nothing to do with him. ¹¹You may be sure that such a man is warped and sinful; he is self-condemned.

Final Remarks

¹²As soon as I send Artemas or Tychicus to you, do your best to come to me at Nicopolis, because I have decided to winter there. ¹³Do everything you can to help Zenas the lawyer and Apollos on their way and see that they have everything they need. ¹⁴Our people must learn to devote themselves to doing what is good, in order that they may provide for daily necessities and not live unproductive lives.

¹⁵Everyone with me sends you greetings. Greet those who love us in the faith.

Grace be with you all.

Author: Paul

Date: AD 60

Audience: Philemon, a Colossian Christian, urging him to welcome back and forgive Onesimus, his runaway servant whom Paul had introduced to Christ

Prayer Themes:

- Pray that you will mature spiritually and have the desire and the courage to share your faith openly (1:6).

- Pray that all relationships in your life will be marked by openness, respect, and clear communication (1:17-22).

- Pray that you can be a minister of reconciliation like Paul was and be able to help people love one another as brothers and sisters in Christ (1:15-16).

Reconciliation is the essence of the gospel: God pursuing us, offering us forgiveness, and inviting us to live in fellowship with Him. But as recipients of God's amazing grace, we are called to extend the same grace and forgiveness to others. God wants us to extend ourselves to our enemies, forgive all wrongs, and work to rebuild love and trust whenever possible.

Paul writes this short letter to Philemon who had become a Christian through Paul's ministry. He was a wealthy man who lived in Colosse and was a member of the church there. Onesimus was a slave who belonged to Philemon (and in the ancient Roman Empire, that meant Philemon had complete control of him). Onesimus stole some money and ran away. When he came to Rome, he ran into Paul and also became a Christian. The right thing for Onesimus to do was to return to his master, but Onesimus was understandably afraid to do that. So Paul sent this letter to Philemon, introducing the newly converted Onesimus and asking that Philemon treat this slave as a fellow member of God's family.

Paul told Philemon in the beginning of his letter that he always remembered him in his prayers. He made it clear that he expected Philemon to do the right thing. Surely he did.

Philemon

¹Paul, a prisoner of Christ Jesus, and Timothy our brother,

To Philemon our dear friend and fellow worker, ²to Apphia our sister, to Archippus our fellow soldier and to the church that meets in your home:

³Grace to you and peace from God our Father and the Lord Jesus Christ.

Thanksgiving and Prayer

⁴I always thank my God as I remember you in my prayers, ⁵because I hear about your faith in the Lord Jesus and your love for all the saints. ⁶I pray that you may be active in sharing your faith, so that you will have a full understanding of every good thing we have in Christ.

⁷Your love has given me great joy and encouragement, because you, brother, have refreshed the hearts of the saints.

Praying Philemon 1:6
Dear Jesus, give me the words to tell people of the good things in me because of You, and help me share my faith with others in a powerful and effective way.

Paul's Plea for Onesimus

⁸Therefore, although in Christ I could be bold and order you to do what you ought to do, ⁹yet I appeal to you on the basis of love. I then, as Paul—an old man and now also a prisoner of Christ Jesus— ¹⁰I appeal to you for my son

GOING *deeper*

Ask for Boldness to Share Your Faith

READ AND CONSIDER: PHILEMON 1:4-7

"I pray that you may be active in sharing your faith, so that you will have a full understanding of every good thing we have in Christ" (Philemon 1:6).

The moment we meet Jesus for the first time, our lives are changed forever. It's a moment we never forget. Why, then, is it so hard to introduce others to Him? After all, we understand the incredible effect knowing Jesus will have on their lives for all eternity. Jesus saves us and transforms our lives, and then He gives us the wonderful privilege of being a part of someone else's salvation and transformation. But when we have an opportunity to speak to others about Him, we can be filled with trepidation. For some of us, the pressure of wanting to be sure we say the right thing causes us to hesitate. We are afraid we might say something wrong, or say it insensitively, or turn someone off entirely. We fear we might be rejected and not be a good representative of Christ. That's why prayer in advance of that is crucial!

The apostle Paul's prayer is a model for us as believers and members of the family of God. Sharing our faith is a divine calling and is instrumental in furthering the work of God, but we can't do it without God's power. That's why we need to pray for God's enablement before we share our faith. We need to ask God to open up opportunities to talk about Jesus and to give us the ability to communicate His love in such a way that people can understand it and are attracted to it.

Pray often that you will be able to share your faith whenever the opportunity presents itself and that you will have the perfect words to say. Pray for God to soften the hearts of those you speak to and open their ears and eyes so that their hearts can receive the truth.

Onesimus,[a] who became my son while I was in chains. [11]Formerly he was useless to you, but now he has become useful both to you and to me.

[12]I am sending him—who is my very heart—back to you. [13]I would have liked to keep him with me so that he could take your place in helping me while I am in chains for the gospel. [14]But I did not want to do anything without your consent, so that any favor you do will be spontaneous and not forced. [15]Perhaps the reason he was separated from you for a little while was that you might have him back for good— [16]no longer as a slave, but better than a slave, as a dear brother. He is very dear to me but even dearer to you, both as a man and as a brother in the Lord.

[17]So if you consider me a partner, welcome him as you would welcome me. [18]If he has done you any wrong or owes you anything, charge it to me. [19]I, Paul, am writing this with my own hand. I will pay it back—not to mention that you owe me your very self. [20]I do wish, brother, that I may have some benefit from you in the Lord; refresh my heart in Christ. [21]Confident of your obedience, I write to you, knowing that you will do even more than I ask.

[22]And one thing more: Prepare a guest room for me, because I hope to be restored to you in answer to your prayers.

[23]Epaphras, my fellow prisoner in Christ Jesus, sends you greetings. [24]And so do Mark, Aristarchus, Demas and Luke, my fellow workers.

[25]The grace of the Lord Jesus Christ be with your spirit.

---

[a] 10 Onesimus means *useful*.

Author: Unknown (possibly Barnabas, Apollos, or Priscilla and Aquila)

Date: Before AD 70

Audience: Jewish believers in Christ, who—because of persecution—were contemplating reverting to Judaism

Prayer Themes:

- *Thank God that He is the Builder of all things in your life and that He is building great things in you today (3:1-6).*

- *Tell God that you submit your will to Him, and pray that He will help you become the kind of person who perseveres under any kind of pressure (12:1-4).*

- *Praise the Lord that He never changes—that He is the same yesterday and today and forever (13:8).*

This letter to the Hebrews was written to first-century converts from Judaism who were facing persecution by their fellow Jews. Many Jews were angry about the growth of the Christian movement and that some of their countrymen had accepted Jesus as the Messiah. As a result, Jewish Christians were severely persecuted. Many of them were tempted to abandon their newfound devotion to Jesus and return to their former, "safer" Jewish beliefs and practices. The unknown author of Hebrews pleaded with them to persevere.

This fascinating book takes us into the teachings and events of the Old Testament and explains how everything pointed to Jesus. The author wanted fellow Jewish Christians to hang on because of the faith they had. He explained that "faith is being sure of what we hope for and certain of what we do not see" (11:1).

This is true of our faith as well. We must be sure of what we hope for and certain of what we do not see. Jesus said, "Blessed are those who have not seen and yet have believed" (John 20:29). Faith means praying to a God you have never seen because you believe His promise to hear and answer. It means putting your hope in Him.

Hebrews

The Son Superior to Angels

1 In the past God spoke to our forefathers through the prophets at many times and in various ways, 2but in these last days he has spoken to us by his Son, whom he appointed heir of all things, and through whom he made the universe. 3The Son is the radiance of God's glory and the exact representation of his being, sustaining all things by his powerful word. After he had provided purification for sins, he sat down at the right hand of the Majesty in heaven. 4So he became as much superior to the angels as the name he has inherited is superior to theirs.

5For to which of the angels did God ever say,

"You are my Son;
today I have become your
Father[a]"[b]?

Or again,

"I will be his Father,
and he will be my Son"[c]?

6And again, when God brings his firstborn into the world, he says,

"Let all God's angels worship him."[d]

7In speaking of the angels he says,

"He makes his angels winds,
his servants flames of fire."[e]

8But about the Son he says,

---

[a] 5 Or *have begotten you* [b] 5 Psalm 2:7 [c] 5 2 Samuel 7:14; 1 Chron. 17:13 [d] 6 Deut. 32:43 (see Dead Sea Scrolls and Septuagint) [e] 7 Psalm 104:4

"Your throne, O God, will last for
ever and ever,
and righteousness will be the
scepter of your kingdom.
⁹You have loved righteousness and
hated wickedness;
therefore God, your God, has set
you above your companions
by anointing you with the oil of
joy."ᵃ

¹⁰He also says,

"In the beginning, O Lord, you laid
the foundations of the earth,
and the heavens are the work of
your hands.
¹¹They will perish, but you remain;
they will all wear out like a
garment.
¹²You will roll them up like a robe;
like a garment they will be
changed.
But you remain the same,
and your years will never end."ᵇ

¹³To which of the angels did God ever say,

"Sit at my right hand
until I make your enemies
a footstool for your feet"ᶜ?

¹⁴Are not all angels ministering spirits
sent to serve those who will inherit salvation?

Warning to Pay Attention

2 We must pay more careful attention,
therefore, to what we have heard, so
that we do not drift away. ²For if the message spoken by angels was binding, and every violation and disobedience received
its just punishment, ³how shall we escape

Praying Hebrews 2:1
*Lord, help me to stand strong in all I
know of You so that I will not drift away
from the path You have for me.*

if we ignore such a great salvation? This
salvation, which was first announced by
the Lord, was confirmed to us by those
who heard him. ⁴God also testified to it
by signs, wonders and various miracles,
and gifts of the Holy Spirit distributed
according to his will.

Jesus Made Like His Brothers

⁵It is not to angels that he has subjected
the world to come, about which we are
speaking. ⁶But there is a place where
someone has testified:

"What is man that you are mindful
of him,
the son of man that you care for
him?
⁷You made him a littleᵈ lower than the
angels;
you crowned him with glory and
honor
⁸ and put everything under his feet."ᵉ

In putting everything under him, God
left nothing that is not subject to him. Yet
at present we do not see everything subject to him. ⁹But we see Jesus, who was
made a little lower than the angels, now
crowned with glory and honor because
he suffered death, so that by the grace of
God he might taste death for everyone.

¹⁰In bringing many sons to glory, it was
fitting that God, for whom and through
whom everything exists, should make the
author of their salvation perfect through
suffering. ¹¹Both the one who makes men
holy and those who are made holy are of
the same family. So Jesus is not ashamed
to call them brothers. ¹²He says,

"I will declare your name to my
brothers;
in the presence of the congregation
I will sing your praises."ᶠ

¹³And again,

"I will put my trust in him."ᵍ

And again he says,

ᵃ 9 Psalm 45:6,7   ᵇ 12 Psalm 102:25-27   ᶜ 13 Psalm 110:1   ᵈ 7 Or *him for a little while*; also in verse 9   ᵉ 8 Psalm 8:4-6
ᶠ 12 Psalm 22:22   ᵍ 13 Isaiah 8:17

"Here am I, and the children God has given me."[a]

[14]Since the children have flesh and blood, he too shared in their humanity so that by his death he might destroy him who holds the power of death—that is, the devil— [15]and free those who all their lives were held in slavery by their fear of death. [16]For surely it is not angels he helps, but Abraham's descendants. [17]For this reason he had to be made like his brothers in every way, in order that he might become a merciful and faithful high priest in service to God, and that he might make atonement for[b] the sins of the people. [18]Because he himself suffered when he was tempted, he is able to help those who are being tempted.

Jesus Greater Than Moses

3 Therefore, holy brothers, who share in the heavenly calling, fix your thoughts on Jesus, the apostle and high priest whom we confess. [2]He was faithful to the one who appointed him, just as Moses was faithful in all God's house. [3]Jesus has been found worthy of greater honor than Moses, just as the builder of a house has greater honor than the house itself. [4]For every house is built by someone, but God is the builder of everything. [5]Moses was faithful as a servant in all God's house, testifying to what would be said in the future. [6]But Christ is faithful as a son over God's house. And we are his house, if we hold on to our courage and the hope of which we boast.

Warning Against Unbelief

[7]So, as the Holy Spirit says:

"Today, if you hear his voice,
[8] do not harden your hearts
 as you did in the rebellion,
    during the time of testing in the desert,
[9] where your fathers tested and
    tried me

and for forty years saw what I did.
[10]That is why I was angry with that generation,
    and I said, 'Their hearts are always going astray,
    and they have not known my ways.'
[11]So I declared on oath in my anger,
    'They shall never enter my rest.'"[c]

[12]See to it, brothers, that none of you has a sinful, unbelieving heart that turns away from the living God. [13]But encourage one another daily, as long as it is called Today, so that none of you may be hardened by sin's deceitfulness. [14]We have come to share in Christ if we hold firmly till the end the confidence we had at first. [15]As has just been said:

"Today, if you hear his voice,
    do not harden your hearts
 as you did in the rebellion."[d]

[16]Who were they who heard and rebelled? Were they not all those Moses led out of Egypt? [17]And with whom was he angry for forty years? Was it not with those who sinned, whose bodies fell in the desert? [18]And to whom did God swear that they would never enter his rest if not to those who disobeyed[e]? [19]So we see that they were not able to enter, because of their unbelief.

A Sabbath-Rest for the People of God

4 Therefore, since the promise of entering his rest still stands, let us be careful that none of you be found to have fallen short of it. [2]For we also have had the gospel preached to us, just as they did; but the message they heard was of no value to them, because those who heard did not combine it with faith.[f] [3]Now we who have believed enter that rest, just as God has said,

"So I declared on oath in my anger,
    'They shall never enter my rest.'"[g]

---

[a] 13 Isaiah 8:18   [b] 17 Or and that he might turn aside God's wrath, taking away   [c] 11 Psalm 95:7-11   [d] 15 Psalm 95:7,8
[e] 18 Or disbelieved   [f] 2 Many manuscripts because they did not share in the faith of those who obeyed   [g] 3 Psalm 95:11; also in verse 5

And yet his work has been finished since the creation of the world. ⁴For somewhere he has spoken about the seventh day in these words: "And on the seventh day God rested from all his work."ª ⁵And again in the passage above he says, "They shall never enter my rest."

⁶It still remains that some will enter that rest, and those who formerly had the gospel preached to them did not go in, because of their disobedience. ⁷Therefore God again set a certain day, calling it Today, when a long time later he spoke through David, as was said before:

"Today, if you hear his voice,
    do not harden your hearts."ᵇ

⁸For if Joshua had given them rest, God would not have spoken later about another day. ⁹There remains, then, a Sabbath-rest for the people of God; ¹⁰for anyone who enters God's rest also rests from his own work, just as God did from his. ¹¹Let us, therefore, make every effort to enter that rest, so that no one will fall by following their example of disobedience.

¹²For the word of God is living and active. Sharper than any double-edged sword, it penetrates even to dividing soul and spirit, joints and marrow; it judges the thoughts and attitudes of the heart. ¹³Nothing in all creation is hidden from God's sight. Everything is uncovered and laid bare before the eyes of him to whom we must give account.

Jesus the Great High Priest

¹⁴Therefore, since we have a great high priest who has gone through the heavens,ᶜ Jesus the Son of God, let us hold firmly to the faith we profess. ¹⁵For we do not have a high priest who is unable to sympathize with our weaknesses, but we have one who has been tempted in every way, just as we are—yet was with-

---

ª 4 Gen. 2:2   ᵇ 7 Psalm 95:7,8   ᶜ 14 Or gone into heaven

GOING deeper
Approach God's Throne With Confidence

READ AND CONSIDER: HEBREWS 4:14-16

"For we do not have a high priest who is unable to sympathize with our weaknesses, but we have one who has been tempted in every way, just as we are—yet was without sin. Let us then approach the throne of grace with confidence, so that we may receive mercy and find grace to help us in our time of need" (Hebrews 4:15-16).

Jesus understands us completely. That's because He left heaven and came to earth as a human being. He was "in very nature God, [but] did not consider equality with God something to be grasped, but made himself nothing, taking the very nature of a servant, being made in human likeness" (Philippians 2:6-7). He was fully God, yet a human being like us. He suffered heartache, persecution, pain, and suffering, so He is able to sympathize with *our* heartache, persecution, pain, and suffering. He was tempted in every way, so He understands *our* struggle with temptation. Though He never gave in to temptation, He understands that *we* often do.

That's why when we pray—especially in times of weakness, temptation, confusion, or shame—we must pray boldly and with confidence, knowing that Jesus understands us. Knowing that He is right there in the middle of whatever is troubling us, intervening on our behalf. Knowing that because we have aligned ourselves with Him—God's beloved Son who died to save us—God listens to our prayers as His beloved children. We can have confidence before God because of Jesus.

out sin. [16]Let us then approach the throne of grace with confidence, so that we may receive mercy and find grace to help us in our time of need.

[5]Every high priest is selected from among men and is appointed to represent them in matters related to God, to offer gifts and sacrifices for sins. [2]He is able to deal gently with those who are ignorant and are going astray, since he himself is subject to weakness. [3]This is why he has to offer sacrifices for his own sins, as well as for the sins of the people.

[4]No one takes this honor upon himself; he must be called by God, just as Aaron was. [5]So Christ also did not take upon himself the glory of becoming a high priest. But God said to him,

"You are my Son;
    today I have become your
        Father.[a]"[b]

[6]And he says in another place,

"You are a priest forever,
    in the order of Melchizedek."[c]

[7]During the days of Jesus' life on earth, he offered up prayers and petitions with loud cries and tears to the one who could save him from death, and he was heard because of his reverent submission. [8]Although he was a son, he learned obedience from what he suffered [9]and, once made perfect, he became the source of eternal salvation for all who obey him [10]and was designated by God to be high priest in the order of Melchizedek.

Warning Against Falling Away

[11]We have much to say about this, but it is hard to explain because you are slow to learn. [12]In fact, though by this time you ought to be teachers, you need someone to teach you the elementary truths of God's word all over again. You need milk, not solid food! [13]Anyone who lives on milk, being still an infant, is not acquainted with the teaching about righteousness. [14]But solid food is for the mature, who by constant use have trained themselves to distinguish good from evil.

[6]Therefore let us leave the elementary teachings about Christ and go on to maturity, not laying again the foundation of repentance from acts that lead to death,[d] and of faith in God, [2]instruction about baptisms, the laying on of hands, the resurrection of the dead, and eternal judgment. [3]And God permitting, we will do so.

[4]It is impossible for those who have once been enlightened, who have tasted the heavenly gift, who have shared in the Holy Spirit, [5]who have tasted the goodness of the word of God and the powers of the coming age, [6]if they fall away, to be brought back to repentance, because[e] to their loss they are crucifying the Son of God all over again and subjecting him to public disgrace.

Prayer is . . .

expressing your devotion to God.

[7]Land that drinks in the rain often falling on it and that produces a crop useful to those for whom it is farmed receives the blessing of God. [8]But land that produces thorns and thistles is worthless and is in danger of being cursed. In the end it will be burned.

[9]Even though we speak like this, dear friends, we are confident of better things in your case—things that accompany salvation. [10]God is not unjust; he will not forget your work and the love you have shown him as you have helped his people and continue to help them. [11]We want each of you to show this same diligence to the very end, in order to make your hope sure. [12]We do not want you to become lazy, but to imitate those who through faith and patience inherit what has been promised.

---

[a] 5 Or *have begotten you*   [b] 5 Psalm 2:7   [c] 6 Psalm 110:4   [d] 1 Or *from useless rituals*   [e] 6 Or *repentance while*

The Certainty of God's Promise

13When God made his promise to Abraham, since there was no one greater for him to swear by, he swore by himself, 14saying, "I will surely bless you and give you many descendants."a 15And so after waiting patiently, Abraham received what was promised.

16Men swear by someone greater than themselves, and the oath confirms what is said and puts an end to all argument. 17Because God wanted to make the unchanging nature of his purpose very clear to the heirs of what was promised, he confirmed it with an oath. 18God did this so that, by two unchangeable things in which it is impossible for God to lie, we who have fled to take hold of the hope offered to us may be greatly encouraged. 19We have this hope as an anchor for the soul, firm and secure. It enters the inner sanctuary behind the curtain, 20where Jesus, who went before us, has entered on our behalf. He has become a high priest forever, in the order of Melchizedek.

Melchizedek the Priest

7 This Melchizedek was king of Salem and priest of God Most High. He met Abraham returning from the defeat of the kings and blessed him, 2and Abraham gave him a tenth of everything. First, his name means "king of righteousness"; then also, "king of Salem" means "king of peace." 3Without father or mother, without genealogy, without beginning of days or end of life, like the Son of God he remains a priest forever.

4Just think how great he was: Even the patriarch Abraham gave him a tenth of the plunder! 5Now the law requires the descendants of Levi who become priests to collect a tenth from the people—that is, their brothers—even though their brothers are descended from Abraham. 6This man, however, did not trace his descent from Levi, yet he collected a tenth from Abraham and blessed him who had the promises. 7And without doubt the lesser person is blessed by the greater. 8In the one case, the tenth is collected by men who die; but in the other case, by him who is declared to be living. 9One might even say that Levi, who collects the tenth, paid the tenth through Abraham, 10because when Melchizedek met Abraham, Levi was still in the body of his ancestor.

Jesus Like Melchizedek

11If perfection could have been attained through the Levitical priesthood (for on the basis of it the law was given to the people), why was there still need for another priest to come—one in the order of Melchizedek, not in the order of Aaron? 12For when there is a change of the priesthood, there must also be a change of the law. 13He of whom these things are said belonged to a different tribe, and no one from that tribe has ever served at the altar. 14For it is clear that our Lord descended from Judah, and in regard to that tribe Moses said nothing about priests. 15And what we have said is even more clear if another priest like Melchizedek appears, 16one who has become a priest not on the basis of a regulation as to his ancestry but on the basis of the power of an indestructible life. 17For it is declared:

"You are a priest forever,
  in the order of Melchizedek."b

18The former regulation is set aside because it was weak and useless 19(for the law made nothing perfect), and a better hope is introduced, by which we draw near to God.

20And it was not without an oath! Others became priests without any oath, 21but he became a priest with an oath when God said to him:

"The Lord has sworn
  and will not change his mind:
'You are a priest forever.' "b

22Because of this oath, Jesus has become the guarantee of a better covenant.

---

a 14 Gen. 22:17   b 17,21 Psalm 110:4

²³Now there have been many of those priests, since death prevented them from continuing in office; ²⁴but because Jesus lives forever, he has a permanent priesthood. ²⁵Therefore he is able to save completely^a those who come to God through him, because he always lives to intercede for them.

²⁶Such a high priest meets our need— one who is holy, blameless, pure, set apart from sinners, exalted above the heavens. ²⁷Unlike the other high priests, he does not need to offer sacrifices day after day, first for his own sins, and then for the sins of the people. He sacrificed for their sins once for all when he offered himself. ²⁸For the law appoints as high priests men who are weak; but the oath, which came after the law, appointed the Son, who has been made perfect forever.

The High Priest of a New Covenant

8 The point of what we are saying is this: We do have such a high priest, who sat down at the right hand of the throne of the Majesty in heaven, ²and who serves in the sanctuary, the true tabernacle set up by the Lord, not by man.

³Every high priest is appointed to offer both gifts and sacrifices, and so it was necessary for this one also to have something to offer. ⁴If he were on earth, he would not be a priest, for there are already men who offer the gifts prescribed by the law. ⁵They serve at a sanctuary that is a copy and shadow of what is in heaven. This is why Moses was warned when he was about to build the tabernacle: "See to it that you make everything according to the pattern shown you on the mountain."^b ⁶But the ministry Jesus has received is as superior to theirs as the covenant of which he is mediator is superior to the old one, and it is founded on better promises.

⁷For if there had been nothing wrong with that first covenant, no place would have been sought for another. ⁸But God found fault with the people and said^c:

"The time is coming, declares the Lord,
  when I will make a new covenant
with the house of Israel
  and with the house of Judah.
⁹It will not be like the covenant
  I made with their forefathers
when I took them by the hand
  to lead them out of Egypt,
because they did not remain faithful
  to my covenant,
  and I turned away from them,
    declares the Lord.
¹⁰This is the covenant I will make with
  the house of Israel
after that time, declares the Lord.
I will put my laws in their minds
  and write them on their hearts.
I will be their God,
  and they will be my people.
¹¹No longer will a man teach his
  neighbor,
or a man his brother, saying, 'Know
  the Lord,'
because they will all know me,
  from the least of them to the
    greatest.
¹²For I will forgive their wickedness
  and will remember their sins no
    more."^d

¹³By calling this covenant "new," he has made the first one obsolete; and what is obsolete and aging will soon disappear.

Worship in the Earthly Tabernacle

9 Now the first covenant had regulations for worship and also an earthly sanctuary. ²A tabernacle was set up. In its first room were the lampstand, the table and the consecrated bread; this was called the Holy Place. ³Behind the second curtain was a room called the Most Holy Place, ⁴which had the golden altar of incense and the gold-covered ark of the covenant. This ark contained the gold jar of manna, Aaron's staff that had budded, and the stone tablets of the covenant. ⁵Above the ark were the cherubim of the Glory,

^a 25 Or forever   ^b 5 Exodus 25:40   ^c 8 Some manuscripts may be translated fault and said to the people.   ^d 12 Jer. 31:31-34

overshadowing the atonement cover.ª But we cannot discuss these things in detail now.

6When everything had been arranged like this, the priests entered regularly into the outer room to carry on their ministry. 7But only the high priest entered the inner room, and that only once a year, and never without blood, which he offered for himself and for the sins the people had committed in ignorance. 8The Holy Spirit was showing by this that the way into the Most Holy Place had not yet been disclosed as long as the first tabernacle was still standing. 9This is an illustration for the present time, indicating that the gifts and sacrifices being offered were not able to clear the conscience of the worshiper. 10They are only a matter of food and drink and various ceremonial washings—external regulations applying until the time of the new order.

The Blood of Christ

11When Christ came as high priest of the good things that are already here,ᵇ he went through the greater and more perfect tabernacle that is not man-made, that is to say, not a part of this creation. 12He did not enter by means of the blood of goats and calves; but he entered the Most Holy Place once for all by his own blood, having obtained eternal redemption. 13The blood of goats and bulls and the ashes of a heifer sprinkled on those who are ceremonially unclean sanctify them so that they are outwardly clean. 14How much more, then, will the blood of Christ, who through the eternal Spirit offered himself unblemished to God, cleanse our consciences from acts that lead to death,ᶜ so that we may serve the living God!

15For this reason Christ is the mediator of a new covenant, that those who are called may receive the promised eternal inheritance—now that he has died as a ransom to set them free from the sins committed under the first covenant.

16In the case of a will,ᵈ it is necessary to prove the death of the one who made it, 17because a will is in force only when somebody has died; it never takes effect while the one who made it is living. 18This is why even the first covenant was not put into effect without blood. 19When Moses had proclaimed every commandment of the law to all the people, he took the blood of calves, together with water, scarlet wool and branches of hyssop, and sprinkled the scroll and all the people. 20He said, "This is the blood of the covenant, which God has commanded you to keep."ᵉ 21In the same way, he sprinkled with the blood both the tabernacle and everything used in its ceremonies. 22In fact, the law requires that nearly everything be cleansed with blood, and without the shedding of blood there is no forgiveness.

23It was necessary, then, for the copies of the heavenly things to be purified with these sacrifices, but the heavenly things themselves with better sacrifices than these. 24For Christ did not enter a man-made sanctuary that was only a copy of the true one; he entered heaven itself, now to appear for us in God's presence. 25Nor did he enter heaven to offer himself again and again, the way the high priest enters the Most Holy Place every year with blood that is not his own. 26Then Christ would have had to suffer many times since the creation of the world. But now he has appeared once for all at the end of the ages to do away with sin by the sacrifice of himself. 27Just as man is destined to die once, and after that to face judgment, 28so Christ was sacrificed once to take away the sins of many people; and he will appear a second time, not to bear sin, but to bring salvation to those who are waiting for him.

Christ's Sacrifice Once for All

10 The law is only a shadow of the good things that are coming—not the realities themselves. For this reason it

---

ª5 Traditionally the mercy seat   ᵇ11 Some early manuscripts are to come   ᶜ14 Or from useless rituals   ᵈ16 Same Greek word as covenant; also in verse 17   ᵉ20 Exodus 24:8

Praying for My Enemies

God asks us to forgive and love our enemies and even to pray for them. And that's hard to do. But the reason He asks us to do that is not so we can help them feel good about what they've done. It's that God hates all sin, and our unforgiveness is a sin too. You may be thinking, *How bad is my unforgiveness compared to what that person did to me, or what those people did to my people?* But God says that *all* sin is bad. Jesus tells us to "love your enemies and pray for those who persecute you" (Matthew 5:44). If we don't love, forgive, and pray for our enemies, the evil won't stop—it will just continue to perpetuate itself. Unforgiveness fuels the constant fighting year after year in certain parts of the world where people or groups vent their hatred and take revenge on each other. Without forgiveness, the cycle of hatred never ends.

One of the best reasons to be free of unforgiveness is so our prayers will not be hindered. When we harbor evil in our hearts, we put up a wall between us and God. And the wall must be thick because it keeps Him from hearing our prayers. "The LORD is far from the wicked but he hears the prayer of the righteous" (Proverbs 15:29). Even prayers for our enemies must be prayed from a right heart. "And when you stand praying, if you hold anything against anyone, forgive him, so that your Father in heaven may forgive you your sins" (Mark 11:25). If we don't forgive our enemies, God doesn't forgive us for our sins or answer our prayers as we would like Him to.

God says, "There is a time for everything, and a season for every activity under heaven . . . a time for war and a time for peace" (Ecclesiastes 3:1,8). God is a God of justice, and He promises that the wicked will pay for their crimes. "The wicked will not go unpunished" (Proverbs 11:21). "I, the LORD, love justice" (Isaiah 61:8). When we forgive people who have done evil against us, they will still have to account for what they have done. If they need to be corrected, we can pray for them and commit them to the Lord so He can do that. If they remain unrepentant and steadfastly devoted to sin, if they continue to be set against living God's way, then their future is not bright. The Bible says, "It is a dreadful thing to fall into the hands of the living God" (Hebrews 10:31).

Let's commit those who hurt us into the Lord's hands and pray that they will have an encounter with the living God so they can be transformed by the power of His Holy Spirit. How much better than the sweet taste of revenge that turns bitter in our souls, or the reaping of consequences for our own sin of unforgiveness, would be our enemies' transformation into a devoted follower of Christ. Only God, through prayer, can accomplish all that.

For the next "From Stormie's Heart" article, go to page 1500.

can never, by the same sacrifices repeated endlessly year after year, make perfect those who draw near to worship. ²If it could, would they not have stopped being offered? For the worshipers would have been cleansed once for all, and would no longer have felt guilty for their sins. ³But those sacrifices are an annual reminder of sins, ⁴because it is impossible for the blood of bulls and goats to take away sins.

⁵Therefore, when Christ came into the world, he said:

"Sacrifice and offering you did not
    desire,
  but a body you prepared for me;
⁶with burnt offerings and sin offerings
  you were not pleased.
⁷Then I said, 'Here I am—it is written
    about me in the scroll—
  I have come to do your will,
    O God.' "ᵃ

⁸First he said, "Sacrifices and offerings, burnt offerings and sin offerings you did not desire, nor were you pleased with them" (although the law required them to be made). ⁹Then he said, "Here I am, I have come to do your will." He sets aside the first to establish the second. ¹⁰And by that will, we have been made holy through the sacrifice of the body of Jesus Christ once for all.

¹¹Day after day every priest stands and performs his religious duties; again and again he offers the same sacrifices, which can never take away sins. ¹²But when this priest had offered for all time one sacrifice for sins, he sat down at the right hand of God. ¹³Since that time he waits for his enemies to be made his footstool, ¹⁴because by one sacrifice he has made perfect forever those who are being made holy.

¹⁵The Holy Spirit also testifies to us about this. First he says:

¹⁶"This is the covenant I will make
  with them

after that time, says the Lord.
I will put my laws in their hearts,
  and I will write them on their
    minds."ᵇ

¹⁷Then he adds:

"Their sins and lawless acts
  I will remember no more."ᶜ

¹⁸And where these have been forgiven, there is no longer any sacrifice for sin.

A Call to Persevere

¹⁹Therefore, brothers, since we have confidence to enter the Most Holy Place by the blood of Jesus, ²⁰by a new and living way opened for us through the curtain, that is, his body, ²¹and since we have a great priest over the house of God, ²²let us draw near to God with a sincere heart in full assurance of faith, having our hearts sprinkled to cleanse us from a guilty conscience and having our bodies washed with pure water. ²³Let us hold unswervingly to the hope we profess, for he who promised is faithful. ²⁴And let us consider how we may spur one another on toward love and good deeds. ²⁵Let us not give up meeting together, as some are in the habit of doing, but let us encourage one another—and all the more as you see the Day approaching.

Praying Hebrews 10:23-25

*Jesus, help me to be in church when
I need to be and to always have words
of hope, love, and encouragement for
others when I see them.*

²⁶If we deliberately keep on sinning after we have received the knowledge of the truth, no sacrifice for sins is left, ²⁷but only a fearful expectation of judgment and of raging fire that will consume the enemies of God. ²⁸Anyone who rejected the law of Moses died without mercy on the testimony of two or three witnesses. ²⁹How much more severely do you think a man deserves to be punished who has

---

ᵃ 7 Psalm 40:6-8 (see Septuagint) ᵇ 16 Jer. 31:33 ᶜ 17 Jer. 31:34

trampled the Son of God under foot, who has treated as an unholy thing the blood of the covenant that sanctified him, and who has insulted the Spirit of grace? 30For we know him who said, "It is mine to avenge; I will repay,"a and again, "The Lord will judge his people."b 31It is a dreadful thing to fall into the hands of the living God.

32Remember those earlier days after you had received the light, when you stood your ground in a great contest in the face of suffering. 33Sometimes you were publicly exposed to insult and persecution; at other times you stood side by side with those who were so treated. 34You sympathized with those in prison and joyfully accepted the confiscation of your property, because you knew that you yourselves had better and lasting possessions.

35So do not throw away your confidence; it will be richly rewarded. 36You need to persevere so that when you have done the will of God, you will receive what he has promised. 37For in just a very little while,

"He who is coming will come and
    will not delay.
38   But my righteous onec will live by
    faith.
And if he shrinks back,
    I will not be pleased with him."d

39But we are not of those who shrink back and are destroyed, but of those who believe and are saved.

By Faith

11 Now faith is being sure of what we hope for and certain of what we do not see. 2This is what the ancients were commended for.

3By faith we understand that the universe was formed at God's command, so that what is seen was not made out of what was visible.

4By faith Abel offered God a better sacrifice than Cain did. By faith he was commended as a righteous man, when God spoke well of his offerings. And by faith he still speaks, even though he is dead.

5By faith Enoch was taken from this life, so that he did not experience death; he could not be found, because God had taken him away. For before he was taken, he was commended as one who pleased God. 6And without faith it is impossible to please God, because anyone who comes to him must believe that he exists and that he rewards those who earnestly seek him.

7By faith Noah, when warned about things not yet seen, in holy fear built an ark to save his family. By his faith he condemned the world and became heir of the righteousness that comes by faith.

8By faith Abraham, when called to go to a place he would later receive as his inheritance, obeyed and went, even though he did not know where he was going. 9By faith he made his home in the promised land like a stranger in a foreign country; he lived in tents, as did Isaac and Jacob, who were heirs with him of the same promise. 10For he was looking forward to the city with foundations, whose architect and builder is God.

11By faith Abraham, even though he was past age—and Sarah herself was barren—was enabled to become a father because hee considered him faithful who had made the promise. 12And so from this one man, and he as good as dead, came descendants as numerous as the stars in the sky and as countless as the sand on the seashore.

13All these people were still living by faith when they died. They did not receive the things promised; they only saw them and welcomed them from a distance. And they admitted that they were aliens and strangers on earth. 14People who say such things show that they are looking for a

a 30 Deut. 32:35   b 30 Deut. 32:36; Psalm 135:14   c 38 One early manuscript But the righteous   d 38 Hab. 2:3,4   e 11 Or By faith even Sarah, who was past age, was enabled to bear children because she country of their own. 15If they had been thinking of the country they had left, they would have had opportunity to return. 16Instead, they were longing for a better country—a heavenly one. Therefore God is not ashamed to be called their God, for he has prepared a city for them.

17By faith Abraham, when God tested him, offered Isaac as a sacrifice. He who had received the promises was about to sacrifice his one and only son, 18even though God had said to him, "It is through Isaac that your offspring[a] will be reckoned."[b] 19Abraham reasoned that God could raise the dead, and figuratively speaking, he did receive Isaac back from death.

20By faith Isaac blessed Jacob and Esau in regard to their future.

21By faith Jacob, when he was dying, blessed each of Joseph's sons, and worshiped as he leaned on the top of his staff.

22By faith Joseph, when his end was near, spoke about the exodus of the Israelites from Egypt and gave instructions about his bones.

23By faith Moses' parents hid him for three months after he was born, because they saw he was no ordinary child, and they were not afraid of the king's edict.

24By faith Moses, when he had grown up, refused to be known as the son of Pharaoh's daughter. 25He chose to be mistreated along with the people of God rather than to enjoy the pleasures of sin for a short time. 26He regarded disgrace for the sake of Christ as of greater value than the treasures of Egypt, because he was looking ahead to his reward. 27By faith he left Egypt, not fearing the king's anger; he persevered because he saw him who is invisible. 28By faith he kept the Passover and the sprinkling of blood, so that the destroyer of the firstborn would not touch the firstborn of Israel.

29By faith the people passed through the Red Sea[c] as on dry land; but when the Egyptians tried to do so, they were drowned.

30By faith the walls of Jericho fell, after the people had marched around them for seven days.

31By faith the prostitute Rahab, because she welcomed the spies, was not killed with those who were disobedient.[d]

32And what more shall I say? I do not have time to tell about Gideon, Barak, Samson, Jephthah, David, Samuel and the prophets, 33who through faith conquered kingdoms, administered justice, and gained what was promised; who shut the mouths of lions, 34quenched the fury of the flames, and escaped the edge of the sword; whose weakness was turned to strength; and who became powerful in battle and routed foreign armies. 35Women received back their dead, raised to life again. Others were tortured and refused to be released, so that they might gain a better resurrection. 36Some faced jeers and flogging, while still others were chained and put in prison. 37They were stoned[e]; they were sawed in two; they were put to death by the sword. They went about in sheepskins and goatskins, destitute, persecuted and mistreated— 38the world was not worthy of them. They wandered in deserts and mountains, and in caves and holes in the ground.

39These were all commended for their faith, yet none of them received what had been promised. 40God had planned something better for us so that only together with us would they be made perfect.

God Disciplines His Sons

12 Therefore, since we are surrounded by such a great cloud of witnesses, let us throw off everything that hinders and the sin that so easily entangles, and let us run with perseverance the race marked out for us. 2Let us fix our eyes on Jesus, the author and perfecter of our faith, who for the joy set before him endured the cross, scorning its shame, and

sat down at the right hand of the throne of God. ³Consider him who endured such opposition from sinful men, so that you will not grow weary and lose heart.

⁴In your struggle against sin, you have not yet resisted to the point of shedding your blood. ⁵And you have forgotten that word of encouragement that addresses you as sons:

"My son, do not make light of the
    Lord's discipline,
and do not lose heart when he
    rebukes you,
⁶because the Lord disciplines those he
    loves,
and he punishes everyone he
    accepts as a son."ᵃ

⁷Endure hardship as discipline; God is treating you as sons. For what son is not disciplined by his father? ⁸If you are not disciplined (and everyone undergoes discipline), then you are illegitimate children and not true sons. ⁹Moreover, we have all had human fathers who disciplined us and we respected them for it. How much more should we submit to the Father of our spirits and live! ¹⁰Our fathers disciplined us for a little while as they thought best; but God disciplines us for our good, that we may share in his holiness. ¹¹No discipline seems pleasant at the time, but painful. Later on, however, it produces a harvest of righteousness and peace for those who have been trained by it.

¹²Therefore, strengthen your feeble arms and weak knees. ¹³"Make level paths for your feet,"ᵇ so that the lame may not be disabled, but rather healed.

Warning Against Refusing God

¹⁴Make every effort to live in peace with all men and to be holy; without holiness no one will see the Lord. ¹⁵See to it that no one misses the grace of God and that no bitter root grows up to cause trouble and defile many. ¹⁶See that no one is sexually immoral, or is godless like Esau, who for a single meal sold his inheritance rights as the oldest son. ¹⁷Afterward, as you know, when he wanted to inherit this blessing, he was rejected. He could bring about no change of mind, though he sought the blessing with tears.

¹⁸You have not come to a mountain that can be touched and that is burning with fire; to darkness, gloom and storm; ¹⁹to a trumpet blast or to such a voice speaking words that those who heard it begged that no further word be spoken to them, ²⁰because they could not bear what was commanded: "If even an animal touches the mountain, it must be stoned."ᶜ ²¹The sight was so terrifying that Moses said, "I am trembling with fear."ᵈ

²²But you have come to Mount Zion, to the heavenly Jerusalem, the city of the living God. You have come to thousands upon thousands of angels in joyful assembly, ²³to the church of the firstborn, whose names are written in heaven. You have come to God, the judge of all men, to the spirits of righteous men made perfect, ²⁴to Jesus the mediator of a new covenant, and to the sprinkled blood that speaks a better word than the blood of Abel.

²⁵See to it that you do not refuse him who speaks. If they did not escape when they refused him who warned them on earth, how much less will we, if we turn away from him who warns us from heaven? ²⁶At that time his voice shook the earth, but now he has promised, "Once more I will shake not only the earth but also the heavens."ᵉ ²⁷The words "once more" indicate the removing of what can be shaken—that is, created things—so that what cannot be shaken may remain.

²⁸Therefore, since we are receiving a kingdom that cannot be shaken, let us be thankful, and so worship God acceptably with reverence and awe, ²⁹for our "God is a consuming fire."ᶠ

ᵃ 6 Prov. 3:11,12   ᵇ 13 Prov. 4:26   ᶜ 20 Exodus 19:12,13   ᵈ 21 Deut. 9:19   ᵉ 26 Haggai 2:6   ᶠ 29 Deut. 4:24

Concluding Exhortations

13 Keep on loving each other as brothers. [2] Do not forget to entertain strangers, for by so doing some people have entertained angels without knowing it. [3] Remember those in prison as if you were their fellow prisoners, and those who are mistreated as if you yourselves were suffering.

[4] Marriage should be honored by all, and the marriage bed kept pure, for God will judge the adulterer and all the sexually immoral. [5] Keep your lives free from the love of money and be content with what you have, because God has said,

"Never will I leave you;
never will I forsake you."[a]

[6] So we say with confidence,

"The Lord is my helper; I will not be
afraid.
What can man do to me?"[b]

[7] Remember your leaders, who spoke the word of God to you. Consider the outcome of their way of life and imitate their faith. [8] Jesus Christ is the same yesterday and today and forever.

[9] Do not be carried away by all kinds of strange teachings. It is good for our hearts to be strengthened by grace, not by ceremonial foods, which are of no value to those who eat them. [10] We have an altar from which those who minister at the tabernacle have no right to eat.

[11] The high priest carries the blood of animals into the Most Holy Place as a sin offering, but the bodies are burned outside the camp. [12] And so Jesus also suffered outside the city gate to make the people holy through his own blood. [13] Let us, then, go to him outside the camp, bearing the disgrace he bore. [14] For here we do not have an enduring city, but we are looking for the city that is to come.

[15] Through Jesus, therefore, let us continually offer to God a sacrifice of praise—the fruit of lips that confess his name. [16] And do not forget to do good and to share with others, for with such sacrifices God is pleased.

[17] Obey your leaders and submit to their authority. They keep watch over you as men who must give an account. Obey them so that their work will be a joy, not a burden, for that would be of no advantage to you.

[18] Pray for us. We are sure that we have a clear conscience and desire to live honorably in every way. [19] I particularly urge

---

[a] 5 Deut. 31:6   [b] 6 Psalm 118:6,7

God's people at prayer

WHAT TO PRAY WHEN YOU DON'T KNOW WHAT TO PRAY

HEBREWS 13:18-21 Have you ever wondered what to pray for someone? You believe that person has a need, but you don't know the specifics. Or maybe you want to ask someone to pray for *you*, but you don't want to divulge all the details of why you need prayer.

The author of the book of Hebrews—unknown to us but obviously known to the readers—said clearly, "Pray for us." He (or she) apparently wanted to maintain a clear conscience and live honorably. The writer also wanted to return home and so asked for prayer to be "restored to you soon."

Then the writer broke out into a beautiful prayer for the readers. You can make those words your prayer too. When you don't know what to pray for someone, pray for them to have a clear conscience, to be able to live honorably, to be equipped with everything good for doing God's will, and that God would work in their life what is pleasing to Him. Who wouldn't welcome that kind of prayer on their behalf?

you to pray so that I may be restored to you soon.

20 May the God of peace, who through the blood of the eternal covenant brought back from the dead our Lord Jesus, that great Shepherd of the sheep, 21 equip you with everything good for doing his will, and may he work in us what is pleasing to him, through Jesus Christ, to whom be glory for ever and ever. Amen.

22 Brothers, I urge you to bear with my word of exhortation, for I have written you only a short letter.

23 I want you to know that our brother Timothy has been released. If he arrives soon, I will come with him to see you.

24 Greet all your leaders and all God's people. Those from Italy send you their greetings.

25 Grace be with you all.

Author: James (the half-brother of Jesus, not the apostle)

Date: AD 50–61

Audience: Jewish Christians who had fled Jerusalem after the martyrdom of Stephen

The author of this book described himself as "a servant of God and of the Lord Jesus Christ." He could have given himself a more notable title: half-brother of Jesus. James knew Jesus before Jesus went into ministry. In fact, James had been one of those brothers who did not believe in Him (John 7:5). But eventually James *did* believe, perhaps through a personal appearance by Jesus after His resurrection (1 Corinthians 15:7), and he became one of the leaders in the church at Jerusalem.

James deals head-on with issues such as hypocrisy and unethical practices. He makes the point that true faith should inevitably produce good works. And prayer is one of his more prominent topics. About prayer, James wrote:

—Prayer is the way we find God's wisdom (1:5).

—Our prayers must be rooted and offered in faith (1:6; 5:13-18).

—God won't give us what we ask for if we ask with wrong or selfish motives (4:2-3).

—Whenever we move toward God, He comes near to us (4:8).

—If you're suffering, pray. If you need healing, pray. If you're sick, pray. If you're dealing with others' faults and sins, pray (5:13-16).

—The prayers of the righteous are powerful and effective (5:16).

Prayer Themes:

• *Pray for the ability to see trials as God's wise and good work in your life, designed to make you more like Christ (1:2-4).*

• *Ask the Holy Spirit to control your tongue, since it is untamable by human effort (3:8).*

• *Ask God to show you any pride that is in you, and whenever He does, confess it to Him as sin and acknowledge Him as Lord over every area of your life (4:10).*

James

1 James, a servant of God and of the Lord Jesus Christ,

To the twelve tribes scattered among the nations:

Greetings.

Trials and Temptations

2 Consider it pure joy, my brothers, whenever you face trials of many kinds, 3 because you know that the testing of your faith develops perseverance. 4 Perseverance must finish its work so that you may be mature and complete, not lacking anything. 5 If any of you lacks wisdom, he should ask God, who gives generously to all without finding fault, and it will be given to him. 6 But when he asks, he must believe and not doubt, because he who doubts is like a wave of the sea, blown and tossed by the wind. 7 That man should not think he will receive anything from the Lord; 8 he is a double-minded man, unstable in all he does.

9 The brother in humble circumstances ought to take pride in his high position. 10 But the one who is rich should take pride in his low position, because he will pass away like a wild flower. 11 For the sun rises with scorching heat and withers the plant; its blossom falls and its beauty is destroyed. In the same way, the rich man

Asking God for Wisdom

GOING *deeper*

READ AND CONSIDER: JAMES 1:2-18

"If any of you lacks wisdom, he should ask God, who gives generously to all without finding fault, and it will be given to him" (James 1:5).

If every time we pray for wisdom God will generously give it to us, then we should be praying for wisdom every day and not just when the need is urgent.

The most urgent time that we pray for wisdom is when we are in a difficult and pressing situation and we don't know what to do. We need help. We need to know which way to go. And we usually need to know immediately. In those times it's comforting to know that God is not only available to us and willing to help, but He has *promised* to do so.

However, we don't have to wait until we are in an emergency situation in order to pray for wisdom. We can pray now. How many times have we faced a quick decision or an immediate situation in which our response would have been a lot stronger, or better, or more effective if we'd had more of God's wisdom beforehand? King Solomon, when invited to make any request he wanted to God, asked for wisdom early in his reign. And God gladly granted his request (1 Kings 3:5-10). We need to do that too. In other words, we should ask *before* the need arises.

If you don't have God's wisdom, you will try to get through life on your own strength and understanding, and you may end up making bad decisions or doing stupid things. But when you ask God to give you wisdom every day, you will find yourself doing things so wise even *you* may be surprised. You will make a decision that turns out to be so completely right that you will be amazed. You will have insight you never had before. You will be able to give sound advice to someone who asks for it. You will sense danger when it is lurking. You will know when to speak and when not to, and what to say and how to say it. You will have a sense of what to do and what not to do in any situation.

Ask God for wisdom right now. You can trust that He will give it to you because He has promised it in His Word.

will fade away even while he goes about his business.

[12]Blessed is the man who perseveres under trial, because when he has stood the test, he will receive the crown of life that God has promised to those who love him. [13]When tempted, no one should say, "God is tempting me." For God cannot be tempted by evil, nor does he tempt anyone; [14]but each one is tempted when, by his own evil desire, he is dragged away and enticed. [15]Then, after desire has conceived, it gives birth to sin; and sin, when it is full-grown, gives birth to death. [16]Don't be deceived, my dear broth-

ers. [17]Every good and perfect gift is from above, coming down from the Father of the heavenly lights, who does not change like shifting shadows. [18]He chose to give us birth through the word of truth, that we might be a kind of firstfruits of all he created.

Listening and Doing

[19]My dear brothers, take note of this: Everyone should be quick to listen, slow to speak and slow to become angry, [20]for man's anger does not bring about the righteous life that God desires. [21]Therefore, get rid of all moral filth and the evil that is so prevalent and humbly

accept the word planted in you, which can save you.

22Do not merely listen to the word, and so deceive yourselves. Do what it says. 23Anyone who listens to the word but does not do what it says is like a man who looks at his face in a mirror 24and, after looking at himself, goes away and immediately forgets what he looks like. 25But the man who looks intently into the perfect law that gives freedom, and continues to do this, not forgetting what he has heard, but doing it—he will be blessed in what he does.

26If anyone considers himself religious and yet does not keep a tight rein on his tongue, he deceives himself and his religion is worthless. 27Religion that God our Father accepts as pure and faultless is this: to look after orphans and widows in their distress and to keep oneself from being polluted by the world.

Favoritism Forbidden

2 My brothers, as believers in our glorious Lord Jesus Christ, don't show favoritism. 2Suppose a man comes into your meeting wearing a gold ring and fine clothes, and a poor man in shabby clothes also comes in. 3If you show special attention to the man wearing fine clothes and say, "Here's a good seat for you," but say to the poor man, "You stand there" or "Sit on the floor by my feet," 4have you not discriminated among yourselves and become judges with evil thoughts?

5Listen, my dear brothers: Has not God chosen those who are poor in the eyes of the world to be rich in faith and to inherit the kingdom he promised those who love him? 6But you have insulted the poor. Is it not the rich who are exploiting you? Are they not the ones who are dragging you into court? 7Are they not the ones who are slandering the noble name of him to whom you belong?

8If you really keep the royal law found in Scripture, "Love your neighbor as yourself,"a you are doing right. 9But if you show favoritism, you sin and are convicted by the law as lawbreakers. 10For whoever keeps the whole law and yet stumbles at just one point is guilty of breaking all of it. 11For he who said, "Do not commit adultery,"b also said, "Do not murder."c If you do not commit adultery but do commit murder, you have become a lawbreaker.

12Speak and act as those who are going to be judged by the law that gives freedom, 13because judgment without mercy will be shown to anyone who has not been merciful. Mercy triumphs over judgment!

Faith and Deeds

14What good is it, my brothers, if a man claims to have faith but has no deeds? Can such faith save him? 15Suppose a brother or sister is without clothes and daily food. 16If one of you says to him, "Go, I wish you well; keep warm and well fed," but does nothing about his physical needs, what good is it? 17In the same way, faith by itself, if it is not accompanied by action, is dead.

18But someone will say, "You have faith; I have deeds."

Show me your faith without deeds, and I will show you my faith by what I do. 19You believe that there is one God. Good! Even the demons believe that—and shudder.

20You foolish man, do you want evidence that faith without deeds is useless[d]? 21Was not our ancestor Abraham considered righteous for what he did when he offered his son Isaac on the altar? 22You see that his faith and his actions were working together, and his faith was made complete by what he did. 23And the scripture was fulfilled that says, "Abraham believed God, and it was credited to him as righteousness,"e and he was called God's friend. 24You see that a person is justified by what he does and not by faith alone.

25In the same way, was not even Rahab the prostitute considered righteous

---

a 8 Lev. 19:18   b 11 Exodus 20:14; Deut. 5:18   c 11 Exodus 20:13; Deut. 5:17   d 20 Some early manuscripts dead   e 23 Gen. 15:6

for what she did when she gave lodging to the spies and sent them off in a different direction? 26As the body without the spirit is dead, so faith without deeds is dead.

Taming the Tongue

3 Not many of you should presume to be teachers, my brothers, because you know that we who teach will be judged more strictly. 2We all stumble in many ways. If anyone is never at fault in what he says, he is a perfect man, able to keep his whole body in check.

3When we put bits into the mouths of horses to make them obey us, we can turn the whole animal. 4Or take ships as an example. Although they are so large and are driven by strong winds, they are steered by a very small rudder wherever the pilot wants to go. 5Likewise the tongue is a small part of the body, but it makes great boasts. Consider what a great forest is set on fire by a small spark. 6The tongue also is a fire, a world of evil among the parts of the body. It corrupts the whole person, sets the whole course of his life on fire, and is itself set on fire by hell.

Praying James 3:8-10

Lord, I submit myself to Your control and pray that every word coming out of my mouth will glorify You and bring blessing and life to others.

7All kinds of animals, birds, reptiles and creatures of the sea are being tamed and have been tamed by man, 8but no man can tame the tongue. It is a restless evil, full of deadly poison.

9With the tongue we praise our Lord and Father, and with it we curse men, who have been made in God's likeness. 10Out of the same mouth come praise and cursing. My brothers, this should not be. 11Can both fresh water and salt[a] water flow from the same spring? 12My brothers, can a fig tree bear olives, or a grape-

vine bear figs? Neither can a salt spring produce fresh water.

Two Kinds of Wisdom

13Who is wise and understanding among you? Let him show it by his good life, by deeds done in the humility that comes from wisdom. 14But if you harbor bitter envy and selfish ambition in your hearts, do not boast about it or deny the truth. 15Such "wisdom" does not come down from heaven but is earthly, unspiritual, of the devil. 16For where you have envy and selfish ambition, there you find disorder and every evil practice.

17But the wisdom that comes from heaven is first of all pure; then peace-loving, considerate, submissive, full of mercy and good fruit, impartial and sincere. 18Peacemakers who sow in peace raise a harvest of righteousness.

Submit Yourselves to God

4 What causes fights and quarrels among you? Don't they come from your desires that battle within you? 2You want something but don't get it. You kill and covet, but you cannot have what you want. You quarrel and fight. You do not have, because you do not ask God. 3When you ask, you do not receive, because you ask with wrong motives, that you may spend what you get on your pleasures.

4You adulterous people, don't you know that friendship with the world is hatred toward God? Anyone who chooses to be a friend of the world becomes an enemy of God. 5Or do you think Scripture says without reason that the spirit he caused to live in us envies intensely?[b] 6But he gives us more grace. That is why Scripture says:

"God opposes the proud
    but gives grace to the humble."[c]

7Submit yourselves, then, to God. Resist the devil, and he will flee from you. 8Come near to God and he will come

---

Spending Time Alone With God

Our God is a God who can be found. A God who can be known. A God who wants to be close to us. That's why He is called Immanuel, which means "God *with* us." But He draws close to *us* as we draw close to *Him* (James 4:8).

If I could sit down and talk with you in person about your life, I would tell you that if you have received the Lord, the answer to what you need is within you. That's because the Holy Spirit of God is within you, and He will lead you in all things and teach you everything you need to know. He will transform you and your circumstances beyond your wildest dreams if you will give up trying to do it on your own and let *Him* do it *His* way and in *His* time.

This is not about striving to be good enough to get to God, for there is no way any of us can be. This is about letting all of the goodness of God be *in* you. It's about drawing closer to God and sensing Him drawing closer to you. This is about an intimate walk with God and the wholeness that will be worked in you because of it.

God wants us to want Him. And when we realize that it's Him that we want, we become free. We are free to identify the longings, loneliness, and emptiness inside of us as our signal that we need to draw near to God with open arms and ask Him to fill us with more of Himself. But this deep and intimate relationship with God that we all desire and can't live without doesn't just happen. It must be sought after, prayed for, nurtured, and treasured. And we must *continually* seek after, pray for, nurture, and treasure it.

We can never draw close to God and get to know Him well, or develop the kind of intimate relationship we want, unless we spend time alone with Him. It's in those private times that we are refreshed, strengthened, and rejuvenated. It's then we can see our lives from God's perspective and discover what is really important. That's where we understand who it is we belong to and believe in.

Here's something to keep in mind: If you haven't been praying much, you can't expect things to change overnight. It takes a while to get the enormous ocean liner of your life turned around and headed in a different direction. It doesn't immediately reposition itself the moment you begin steering. In fact, you may hardly see any changes at first. It's the same way with prayer. Prayer can turn your life around, but it doesn't always happen the moment you utter your first words. It may take a time of continued prayer before you actually see the scenery change. This is normal, so don't give up. You will soon be heading full speed in a new direction. Far too often people give up just before their breakthrough into the realm of answered prayer. Remember, this trip is not a mini-vacation tour around the harbor; it's a lifelong voyage to meet your destiny.

For the next "From Stormie's Heart" article, go to page 1508.

near to you. Wash your hands, you sinners, and purify your hearts, you double-minded. ⁹Grieve, mourn and wail. Change your laughter to mourning and your joy to gloom. ¹⁰Humble yourselves before the Lord, and he will lift you up.

¹¹Brothers, do not slander one another. Anyone who speaks against his brother or judges him speaks against the law and judges it. When you judge the law, you are not keeping it, but sitting in judgment on it. ¹²There is only one Lawgiver and Judge, the one who is able to save and destroy. But you—who are you to judge your neighbor?

Boasting About Tomorrow

¹³Now listen, you who say, "Today or tomorrow we will go to this or that city,

spend a year there, carry on business and make money." ¹⁴Why, you do not even know what will happen tomorrow. What is your life? You are a mist that appears for a little while and then vanishes. ¹⁵Instead, you ought to say, "If it is the Lord's will, we will live and do this or that." ¹⁶As it is, you boast and brag. All such boasting is evil. ¹⁷Anyone, then, who knows the good he ought to do and doesn't do it, sins.

Warning to Rich Oppressors

5 Now listen, you rich people, weep and wail because of the misery that is coming upon you. ²Your wealth has rotted, and moths have eaten your clothes. ³Your gold and silver are corroded. Their corrosion will testify against you and eat

GOING *deeper*

Powerful and Effective Praying

READ AND CONSIDER: JAMES 5:13-18

"Therefore confess your sins to each other and pray for each other so that you may be healed. The prayer of a righteous man is powerful and effective" (James 5:16).

Have you ever wondered, *Are my prayers powerful and effective? If they aren't, is it because I'm not righteous?* After all, James says the prayers of righteous people are powerful and effective. If you ever have doubts about the effectiveness of your prayers because you haven't seen very many answers to them, then you might be thinking that you are not good enough to deserve answers. But you would be mistaken.

Too often when we think about being a righteous person, we think in terms of our own behavior. The Bible does say that our faith should work itself out in what we do and the way we live our lives, but it also teaches that our righteousness comes not because of our good behavior but because of Christ's sacrifice. The work of Jesus on the cross and in His resurrection is what gives us righteousness before God. We are righteous in God's eyes because He sees Jesus' righteousness in us. We then behave in a righteous manner because we want to show our love for Jesus by living His way and doing what He asks us to do.

Too often we think that if our prayers aren't causing sicknesses to be healed, paralytics to walk, or mountains to be moved, then they aren't powerful. Too often we think that we have to see such astounding answers to our prayers in order to prove they are effective. But the truth is, we often don't get to see the results of our prayers at all. We don't know the ways in which God is working through our prayers to touch people or the circumstances of their lives. We don't know how much we have effected or prevented in our own lives through prayer.

Prayer is an act of faith. Our prayers are powerful because we pray them to a powerful God in whom we trust. We just have to pray and trust God to answer in His way and time.

your flesh like fire. You have hoarded wealth in the last days. [4]Look! The wages you failed to pay the workmen who mowed your fields are crying out against you. The cries of the harvesters have reached the ears of the Lord Almighty. [5]You have lived on earth in luxury and self-indulgence. You have fattened yourselves in the day of slaughter.[a] [6]You have condemned and murdered innocent men, who were not opposing you.

Patience in Suffering

[7]Be patient, then, brothers, until the Lord's coming. See how the farmer waits for the land to yield its valuable crop and how patient he is for the autumn and spring rains. [8]You too, be patient and stand firm, because the Lord's coming is near. [9]Don't grumble against each other, brothers, or you will be judged. The Judge is standing at the door!

[10]Brothers, as an example of patience in the face of suffering, take the prophets who spoke in the name of the Lord. [11]As you know, we consider blessed those who have persevered. You have heard of Job's perseverance and have seen what the Lord finally brought about. The Lord is full of compassion and mercy.

[12]Above all, my brothers, do not swear—not by heaven or by earth or by anything else. Let your "Yes" be yes, and your "No," no, or you will be condemned.

The Prayer of Faith

[13]Is any one of you in trouble? He should pray. Is anyone happy? Let him sing songs of praise. [14]Is any one of you sick? He should call the elders of the church to pray over him and anoint him with oil in the name of the Lord. [15]And the prayer offered in faith will make the sick person well; the Lord will raise him up. If he has sinned, he will be forgiven. [16]Therefore confess your sins to each other and pray for each other so that you may be healed. The prayer of a righteous man is powerful and effective.

[17]Elijah was a man just like us. He prayed earnestly that it would not rain, and it did not rain on the land for three and a half years. [18]Again he prayed, and the heavens gave rain, and the earth produced its crops.

[19]My brothers, if one of you should wander from the truth and someone should bring him back, [20]remember this: Whoever turns a sinner from the error of his way will save him from death and cover over a multitude of sins.

---

[a] 5 Or yourselves as in a day of feasting

Author: Peter

Date: Between AD 60 and 67

Audience: Jewish and Gentile Christians scattered throughout Asia Minor (modern-day Turkey)

Prayer Themes:

- Ask the Lord to show you the proper balance between working on your outer appearance and developing your inner beauty (3:1-6).

- Ask God for a servant mentality—that you will willingly use your God-given abilities to bless others (4:10).

- Pray for a discerning spirit so that you will always be aware of Satan's schemes and have the ability to resist him by standing firm in faith (5:8-9).

In the darkest hour of Christ's life as He struggled in Gethsemane about His coming task, Peter fell asleep. At one point, Jesus came upon His dozing disciples and asked, "Why are you sleeping? . . . Get up and pray so that you will not fall into temptation" (Luke 22:46). The consequences of Peter's prayerlessness were both immediate and tragic. In the ensuing hours, as all the forces of hell were unleashed, the disciple ironically nicknamed "the Rock" discovered that good intentions are not enough to withstand great temptation.

Reading Peter's first letter, it's clear that his failure to pray in Gethsemane changed him forever. Because of that regrettable experience, Peter became a devoted practitioner and advocate of prevailing prayer.

He reminded his scattered flock of believers, "The eyes of the Lord are on the righteous and his ears are attentive to their prayer" (3:12). A few verses later, he exhorted them: "The end of all things is near. Therefore be clear minded and self-controlled so that you can pray" (4:7).

Peter knew what he was talking about. He knew the problem of prayerlessness. We need to learn that lesson from him and pray that we don't make the same mistake ourselves.

1 Peter

1 Peter, an apostle of Jesus Christ,

To God's elect, strangers in the world, scattered throughout Pontus, Galatia, Cappadocia, Asia and Bithynia, ²who have been chosen according to the foreknowledge of God the Father, through the sanctifying work of the Spirit, for obedience to Jesus Christ and sprinkling by his blood:

Grace and peace be yours in abundance.

Praise to God for a Living Hope

³Praise be to the God and Father of our Lord Jesus Christ! In his great mercy he has given us new birth into a living hope through the resurrection of Jesus Christ from the dead, ⁴and into an inheritance that can never perish, spoil or fade—kept in heaven for you, ⁵who through faith are shielded by God's power until the coming of the salvation that is ready to be revealed in the last time. ⁶In this you greatly rejoice, though now for a little while you may have had to suffer grief in all kinds of trials. ⁷These have come so that your faith—of greater worth than gold, which perishes even though refined by fire—may be proved genuine and may result in praise, glory and honor when Jesus Christ is revealed. ⁸Though you have not seen him, you love him; and even though you do not see him now, you believe in him and are filled with an inexpressible and glorious joy, ⁹for you are receiving the goal of your faith, the salvation of your souls.

10Concerning this salvation, the prophets, who spoke of the grace that was to come to you, searched intently and with the greatest care, 11trying to find out the time and circumstances to which the Spirit of Christ in them was pointing when he predicted the sufferings of Christ and the glories that would follow. 12It was revealed to them that they were not serving themselves but you, when they spoke of the things that have now been told you by those who have preached the gospel to you by the Holy Spirit sent from heaven. Even angels long to look into these things.

Prayer is . . .

*telling God what you want,
not telling God what to do.*

Be Holy

13Therefore, prepare your minds for action; be self-controlled; set your hope fully on the grace to be given you when Jesus Christ is revealed. 14As obedient children, do not conform to the evil desires you had when you lived in ignorance. 15But just as he who called you is holy, so be holy in all you do; 16for it is written: "Be holy, because I am holy."a

17Since you call on a Father who judges each man's work impartially, live your lives as strangers here in reverent fear. 18For you know that it was not with perishable things such as silver or gold that you were redeemed from the empty way of life handed down to you from your forefathers, 19but with the precious blood of Christ, a lamb without blemish or defect. 20He was chosen before the creation of the world, but was revealed in these last times for your sake. 21Through him you believe in God, who raised him from

the dead and glorified him, and so your faith and hope are in God.

22Now that you have purified yourselves by obeying the truth so that you have sincere love for your brothers, love one another deeply, from the heart.b 23For you have been born again, not of perishable seed, but of imperishable, through the living and enduring word of God. 24For,

"All men are like grass,
    and all their glory is like the flowers
        of the field;
the grass withers and the flowers fall,
25   but the word of the Lord stands
        forever."c

And this is the word that was preached to you.

2 Therefore, rid yourselves of all malice and all deceit, hypocrisy, envy, and slander of every kind. 2Like newborn babies, crave pure spiritual milk, so that by it you may grow up in your salvation, 3now that you have tasted that the Lord is good.

The Living Stone and a Chosen People

4As you come to him, the living Stone—rejected by men but chosen by God and precious to him— 5you also, like living stones, are being built into a spiritual house to be a holy priesthood, offering spiritual sacrifices acceptable to God through Jesus Christ. 6For in Scripture it says:

"See, I lay a stone in Zion,
    a chosen and precious cornerstone,
and the one who trusts in him
    will never be put to shame."d

7Now to you who believe, this stone is precious. But to those who do not believe,

"The stone the builders rejected
    has become the capstone,e"f

---

a 16 Lev. 11:44,45; 19:2   b 22 Some early manuscripts *from a pure heart*   c 25 Isaiah 40:6-8   d 6 Isaiah 28:16
e 7 Or *cornerstone*   f 7 Psalm 118:22

8and,

"A stone that causes men to stumble
and a rock that makes them fall."[a]

They stumble because they disobey the message—which is also what they were destined for.

9But you are a chosen people, a royal priesthood, a holy nation, a people belonging to God, that you may declare the praises of him who called you out of darkness into his wonderful light. 10Once you were not a people, but now you are the people of God; once you had not received mercy, but now you have received mercy.

11Dear friends, I urge you, as aliens and strangers in the world, to abstain from sinful desires, which war against your soul. 12Live such good lives among the pagans that, though they accuse you of doing wrong, they may see your good deeds and glorify God on the day he visits us.

Submission to Rulers and Masters

13Submit yourselves for the Lord's sake to every authority instituted among men: whether to the king, as the supreme authority, 14or to governors, who are sent by him to punish those who do wrong and to commend those who do right. 15For it is God's will that by doing good you should silence the ignorant talk of foolish men. 16Live as free men, but do not use your freedom as a cover-up for evil; live as servants of God. 17Show proper respect to everyone: Love the brotherhood of believers, fear God, honor the king.

18Slaves, submit yourselves to your masters with all respect, not only to those who are good and considerate, but also to those who are harsh. 19For it is commendable if a man bears up under the pain of unjust suffering because he is conscious of God. 20But how is it to your credit if you receive a beating for doing wrong and endure it? But if you suffer for doing good and you endure it, this is commendable before God. 21To this you were called, because Christ suffered for you, leaving you an example, that you should follow in his steps.

22"He committed no sin,
and no deceit was found in his mouth."[b]

23When they hurled their insults at him, he did not retaliate; when he suffered, he made no threats. Instead, he entrusted himself to him who judges justly. 24He himself bore our sins in his body on the tree, so that we might die to sins and live for righteousness; by his wounds you have been healed. 25For you were like sheep going astray, but now you have returned to the Shepherd and Overseer of your souls.

Wives and Husbands

3 Wives, in the same way be submissive to your husbands so that, if any of them do not believe the word, they may be won over without words by the behavior of their wives, 2when they see the purity and reverence of your lives. 3Your beauty should not come from outward adornment, such as braided hair and the wearing of gold jewelry and fine clothes. 4Instead, it should be that of your inner self, the unfading beauty of a gentle and quiet spirit, which is of great worth in God's sight. 5For this is the way the holy women of the past who put their hope in God used to make themselves beautiful. They were submissive to their own husbands, 6like Sarah, who obeyed Abraham and called him her master. You are her daughters if you do what is right and do not give way to fear.

7Husbands, in the same way be considerate as you live with your wives, and treat them with respect as the weaker partner and as heirs with you of the gracious gift of life, so that nothing will hinder your prayers.

Suffering for Doing Good

8Finally, all of you, live in harmony with one another; be sympathetic, love

---

GOING *deeper*

God Hears Our Prayers and Sees Our Heart

READ AND CONSIDER: 1 PETER 3:8-12

"For the eyes of the Lord are on the righteous and his ears are attentive to their prayer, but the face of the Lord is against those who do evil" (1 Peter 3:12).

Have you ever wondered if God is really listening when you pray? If so, you're not alone. All of us have had that same question in our minds at one time or another. We pray about a specific thing and if nothing happens we wonder why we are praying at all.

When Peter wrote about God's attentive ears, he was quoting Psalm 34, a psalm written by David after he escaped with his life from the clutches of King Saul. David then traveled to a foreign land to seek asylum, but once he was in the court of the foreign king, he realized he had a reputation as someone who could threaten the king's authority. If this foreign king felt threatened (as Saul had), David would once again be running for his life. To free himself from this situation, David pretended to be crazy until the king literally threw him out of the city (1 Samuel 21). After such a shrewd escape, David wrote the psalm Peter quoted in this New Testament letter. David celebrated the fact that when he cried out to the Lord, God heard him. "I sought the LORD, and he answered me; he delivered me from all my fears . . . This poor man called, and the LORD heard him; he saved him out of all his troubles . . . The eyes of the LORD are on the righteous and his ears are attentive to their cry; . . . The righteous cry out, and the LORD hears them; he delivers them from all their troubles. The LORD is close to the brokenhearted and saves those who are crushed in spirit" (Psalm 34:4,6,15,17-18).

David's life was not easy. He went through horrible heartbreak, devastating loss, and extremely troubling situations. But through it all, he knew he was not alone. He knew that in every situation, God was there listening and answering.

We can know that too. We can have the same certainty that God not only hears our requests, He hears our heart. We may say something like, "Lord, help me get this job," but He will hear, "I'm desperate for a change. I feel so unimportant here." We may say, "God, please keep me safe," but He hears, "I am afraid of how dangerous, precarious, and out of control life seems right now." God not only hears what we want, He also knows what we need.

as brothers, be compassionate and humble. ⁹Do not repay evil with evil or insult with insult, but with blessing, because to this you were called so that you may inherit a blessing. ¹⁰For,

"Whoever would love life
    and see good days
must keep his tongue from evil
    and his lips from deceitful speech.
¹¹He must turn from evil and do good;
    he must seek peace and pursue it.

¹²For the eyes of the Lord are on the
    righteous
    and his ears are attentive to their
        prayer,
but the face of the Lord is against
    those who do evil."ᵃ

¹³Who is going to harm you if you are eager to do good? ¹⁴But even if you should suffer for what is right, you are blessed. "Do not fear what they fearᵇ; do not be frightened."ᶜ ¹⁵But in your

---

ᵃ *12* Psalm 34:12-16   ᵇ *14* Or *not fear their threats*   ᶜ *14* Isaiah 8:12

hearts set apart Christ as Lord. Always be prepared to give an answer to everyone who asks you to give the reason for the hope that you have. But do this with gentleness and respect, 16keeping a clear conscience, so that those who speak maliciously against your good behavior in Christ may be ashamed of their slander. 17It is better, if it is God's will, to suffer for doing good than for doing evil. 18For Christ died for sins once for all, the righteous for the unrighteous, to bring you to God. He was put to death in the body but made alive by the Spirit, 19through whom[a] also he went and preached to the spirits in prison 20who disobeyed long ago when God waited patiently in the days of Noah while the ark was being built. In it only a few people, eight in all, were saved through water, 21and this water symbolizes baptism that now saves you also—not the removal of dirt from the body but the pledge[b] of a good conscience toward God. It saves you by the resurrection of Jesus Christ, 22who has gone into heaven and is at God's right hand—with angels, authorities and powers in submission to him.

Living for God

4 Therefore, since Christ suffered in his body, arm yourselves also with the same attitude, because he who has suffered in his body is done with sin. 2As a result, he does not live the rest of his earthly life for evil human desires, but rather for the will of God. 3For you have spent enough time in the past doing what pagans choose to do—living in debauchery, lust, drunkenness, orgies, carousing and detestable idolatry. 4They think it strange that you do not plunge with them into the same flood of dissipation, and they heap abuse on you. 5But they will have to give account to him who is ready to judge the living and the dead. 6For this is the reason the gospel was preached even to those who are now dead, so that they

might be judged according to men in regard to the body, but live according to God in regard to the spirit.

7The end of all things is near. Therefore be clear minded and self-controlled so that you can pray. 8Above all, love each other deeply, because love covers over a multitude of sins. 9Offer hospitality to one another without grumbling. 10Each one should use whatever gift he has received to serve others, faithfully administering God's grace in its various forms. 11If anyone speaks, he should do it as one speaking the very words of God. If anyone serves, he should do it with the strength God provides, so that in all things God may be praised through Jesus Christ. To him be the glory and the power for ever and ever. Amen.

Suffering for Being a Christian

12Dear friends, do not be surprised at the painful trial you are suffering, as though something strange were happening to you. 13But rejoice that you participate in the sufferings of Christ, so that you may be overjoyed when his glory is revealed. 14If you are insulted because of the name of Christ, you are blessed, for the Spirit of glory and of God rests on you. 15If you suffer, it should not be as a murderer or thief or any other kind of criminal, or even as a meddler. 16However, if you suffer as a Christian, do not be ashamed, but praise God that you bear that name. 17For it is time for judgment to begin with the family of God; and if it begins with us, what will the outcome be for those who do not obey the gospel of God? 18And,

"If it is hard for the righteous to be
        saved,
    what will become of the ungodly
        and the sinner?"[c]

19So then, those who suffer according to God's will should commit themselves to their faithful Creator and continue to do good.

---

a 18,19 Or *alive in the spirit,* 19*through which*   b 21 Or *response*   c 18 Prov. 11:31

Finding Freedom From Discouragement

All of us go through times of discouragement in our lives. We all can get knocked down, set back, hurt, injured, or rejected. And most of the time we can pull ourselves together and get back up and on the path again. But sometimes tough things happen too often, too severely, and with too much devastation. At such times, the enemy of our souls will come in and stir things up with his lies. He'll try to poison your mind with thoughts like these: "You don't have what it takes." "You can't do anything right." "What made you think that you could ever succeed?" "No one really cares about you." "Things will never be any different." "God doesn't listen to your prayers." "You'll never be blessed like other people are." And he'll go on and on with whatever lie he can get you to listen to and believe.

The thing about discouragement is that it happens a little at a time and is therefore very subtle. The enemy likes to chip away at your courage when you are facing challenges and problems. Bit by bit, lie by lie, he attempts to wear you out, trying to convince you to give up. That's because he knows that if you give up in your situation, you also give up on God. And every time you do that, the enemy wins. He can't win the war, of course, even though he will try to convince you that he can. He just wins one of many battles. But it is a battle he doesn't have to win at all.

The good news is that God is a God of encouragement. And He wants us to come to Him at the first sign of discouragement so we can find our encouragement in *Him*. Or better yet, He wants us to trust His unfailing love for us so much that we don't fall for the devil's discouraging lies in the first place. But even the strongest of us can become discouraged at times. If that happens to you, turn immediately to God. Reach out to Him in prayer, and He will encourage you in your spirit. Spend time reading His Word, and you will find His encouragement there. Each time you worship and praise Him you will be encouraged by a wonderful sense of His presence. You will be encouraged whenever you think of the great things that are true about God. That He is a good God. That He loves you. That He makes all things new. That He is your Healer, Provider, Protector, Deliverer, and Savior. That He is all-powerful and therefore greater than anything you face. That with Him all things are possible.

When times are at their worst, seek God the most. Tell your mind to stop worrying about everything and put your hope in the Lord (Psalm 130:7). Say, "Lord, I am going to praise You regardless of what is happening." Take charge of your emotions and tell yourself, "Praise the Lord, O my soul; . . . and forget not all his benefits" (Psalm 103:1-2). Every time you turn to God in prayer, in His Word, and in praise and worship, you will open up the channels through which God's peace, love, and encouragement flow into your soul. Discouragement can't survive in that atmosphere.

For the next "From Stormie's Heart" article, go to page 1517.

To Elders and Young Men

5 To the elders among you, I appeal as a fellow elder, a witness of Christ's sufferings and one who also will share in the glory to be revealed: ²Be shepherds of God's flock that is under your care, serving as overseers—not because you must, but because you are willing, as God wants you to be; not greedy for money, but eager to serve; ³not lording it over those entrusted to you, but being examples to the flock. ⁴And when the Chief Shepherd appears, you will receive the crown of glory that will never fade away.

⁵Young men, in the same way be submissive to those who are older. All of you, clothe yourselves with humility toward one another, because,

"God opposes the proud
but gives grace to the humble."[a]

⁶Humble yourselves, therefore, under God's mighty hand, that he may lift you up in due time. ⁷Cast all your anxiety on him because he cares for you.

⁸Be self-controlled and alert. Your enemy the devil prowls around like a roaring lion looking for someone to devour. ⁹Resist him, standing firm in the faith, because you know that your brothers throughout the world are undergoing the same kind of sufferings.

¹⁰And the God of all grace, who called you to his eternal glory in Christ, after you have suffered a little while, will himself restore you and make you strong, firm and steadfast. ¹¹To him be the power for ever and ever. Amen.

Final Greetings

¹²With the help of Silas,[b] whom I regard as a faithful brother, I have written to you briefly, encouraging you and testifying that this is the true grace of God. Stand fast in it.

¹³She who is in Babylon, chosen together with you, sends you her greetings, and so does my son Mark. ¹⁴Greet one another with a kiss of love.

Peace to all of you who are in Christ.

Praying 1 Peter 5:8-9
Dear God, help me to be vigilant in intercession so that I can stand strong in resisting the enemy and all of his plans.

---

[a] 5 Prov. 3:34 [b] 12 Greek *Silvanus*, a variant of *Silas*

Author: Peter

Date: Between AD 65 and 68

Audience: The Christians under Peter's oversight, to equip them to deal with false teachers and to encourage them to grow spiritually

This is a letter of warning. Written to all believers, the apostle Peter knew that his time on earth was limited and there were certain things that needed to be put down on paper and learned by all followers of Christ. He sensed danger on the horizon. Just as there had been false prophets in the Old Testament, saying whatever people wanted to hear, there would come many false teachers trying to make the Christian faith become whatever they wanted it to be. They would mock Christianity and have disdain for all who believed in it.

Peter's warnings are especially timely today. Many people scoff at Christians. They think they've found a greater knowledge and arrogantly look down on those who believe in God's Word. The world is a spiritual battleground. All around us the forces of good and evil are at war. As events move steadily toward a climactic conflict, Peter urges us to cling to God's Word (1:20-21), be on high alert for false teachers (2:1-22), and commit to holy living (3:11). And we can do none of that without prayer.

Prayer Themes:

- Pray that you will embrace God's purpose of making you more like Christ, and that you will cooperate fully with His character-building plans for your life (1:3-9).

- Thank God for His Word—His inspired and trustworthy truth upon which you can build your life (1:19-21).

- Ask God to help you remember the fleeting and transitory nature of this world and the certainty of life with Him in eternity (3:10-12).

2 Peter

1

Simon Peter, a servant and apostle of Jesus Christ,

To those who through the righteousness of our God and Savior Jesus Christ have received a faith as precious as ours:

²Grace and peace be yours in abundance through the knowledge of God and of Jesus our Lord.

Making One's Calling and Election Sure

³His divine power has given us everything we need for life and godliness through our knowledge of him who called us by his own glory and goodness. ⁴Through these he has given us his very great and precious promises, so that through them you may participate in the divine nature and escape the corruption in the world caused by evil desires.

⁵For this very reason, make every effort to add to your faith goodness; and to goodness, knowledge; ⁶and to knowledge, self-control; and to self-control, perseverance; and to perseverance, godliness; ⁷and to godliness, brotherly kindness; and to brotherly kindness, love. ⁸For if you possess these qualities in increasing measure, they will keep you from being ineffective and unproductive in your knowledge of our Lord Jesus Christ. ⁹But if anyone does not have them, he is nearsighted and blind, and has forgotten that he has been cleansed from his past sins.

¹⁰Therefore, my brothers, be all the more eager to make your calling and election sure. For if you do these things, you will never fall, ¹¹and you will receive a rich welcome into the eternal kingdom of our Lord and Savior Jesus Christ.

Prophecy of Scripture

12So I will always remind you of these things, even though you know them and are firmly established in the truth you now have. 13I think it is right to refresh your memory as long as I live in the tent of this body, 14because I know that I will soon put it aside, as our Lord Jesus Christ has made clear to me. 15And I will make every effort to see that after my departure you will always be able to remember these things.

16We did not follow cleverly invented stories when we told you about the power and coming of our Lord Jesus Christ, but we were eyewitnesses of his majesty. 17For he received honor and glory from God the Father when the voice came to him from the Majestic Glory, saying, "This is my Son, whom I love; with him I am well pleased."a 18We ourselves heard this voice that came from heaven when we were with him on the sacred mountain.

19And we have the word of the prophets made more certain, and you will do well to pay attention to it, as to a light shining in a dark place, until the day dawns and the morning star rises in your hearts. 20Above all, you must understand that no prophecy of Scripture came about by the prophet's own interpretation. 21For prophecy never had its origin in the will of man, but men spoke from God as they were carried along by the Holy Spirit.

False Teachers and Their Destruction

2 But there were also false prophets among the people, just as there will be false teachers among you. They will secretly introduce destructive heresies, even denying the sovereign Lord who bought them—bringing swift destruction on themselves. 2Many will follow their shameful ways and will bring the way of truth into disrepute. 3In their greed these teachers will exploit you with stories they have made up. Their condemnation has long been hanging over them, and their destruction has not been sleeping.

4For if God did not spare angels when they sinned, but sent them to hell,b putting them into gloomy dungeonsc to be held for judgment; 5if he did not spare the ancient world when he brought the flood on its ungodly people, but protected Noah, a preacher of righteousness, and seven others; 6if he condemned the cities of Sodom and Gomorrah by burning them to ashes, and made them an example of what is going to happen to the ungodly; 7and if he rescued Lot, a righteous man, who was distressed by the filthy lives of lawless men 8(for that righteous man, living among them day after day, was tormented in his righteous soul by the lawless deeds he saw and heard)— 9if this is so, then the Lord knows how to rescue godly men from trials and to hold the unrighteous for the day of judgment, while continuing their punishment.d 10This is especially true of those who follow the corrupt desiree of the sinful nature and despise authority.

Bold and arrogant, these men are not afraid to slander celestial beings; 11yet even angels, although they are stronger and more powerful, do not bring slanderous accusations against such beings in the presence of the Lord. 12But these men blaspheme in matters they do not understand. They are like brute beasts, creatures of instinct, born only to be caught and destroyed, and like beasts they too will perish.

13They will be paid back with harm for the harm they have done. Their idea of pleasure is to carouse in broad daylight. They are blots and blemishes, reveling in their pleasures while they feast with you.f 14With eyes full of adultery, they never stop sinning; they seduce the unstable; they are experts in greed—an accursed brood! 15They have left the straight way and wandered off to follow the way of Balaam son of Beor, who loved the wages of

---

a 17 Matt. 17:5; Mark 9:7; Luke 9:35   b 4 Greek *Tartarus*   c 4 Some manuscripts *into chains of darkness*   d 9 Or *unrighteous for punishment until the day of judgment*   e 10 Or *the flesh*   f 13 Some manuscripts *in their love feasts* wickedness. 16But he was rebuked for his wrongdoing by a donkey—a beast without speech—who spoke with a man's voice and restrained the prophet's madness.

17These men are springs without water and mists driven by a storm. Blackest darkness is reserved for them. 18For they mouth empty, boastful words and, by appealing to the lustful desires of sinful human nature, they entice people who are just escaping from those who live in error. 19They promise them freedom, while they themselves are slaves of depravity—for a man is a slave to whatever has mastered him. 20If they have escaped the corruption of the world by knowing our Lord and Savior Jesus Christ and are again entangled in it and overcome, they are worse off at the end than they were at the beginning. 21It would have been better for them not to have known the way of righteousness, than to have known it and then to turn their backs on the sacred command that was passed on to them. 22Of them the proverbs are true: "A dog returns to its vomit,"a and, "A sow that is washed goes back to her wallowing in the mud."

Praying 2 Peter 2:20-21
Lord, help me to never return for even a moment to the things from which You have delivered me.

The Day of the Lord

3 Dear friends, this is now my second letter to you. I have written both of them as reminders to stimulate you to wholesome thinking. 2I want you to recall the words spoken in the past by the holy prophets and the command given by our Lord and Savior through your apostles.

3First of all, you must understand that in the last days scoffers will come, scoffing and following their own evil desires. 4They will say, "Where is this 'coming' he

promised? Ever since our fathers died, everything goes on as it has since the beginning of creation." 5But they deliberately forget that long ago by God's word the heavens existed and the earth was formed out of water and by water. 6By these waters also the world of that time was deluged and destroyed. 7By the same word the present heavens and earth are reserved for fire, being kept for the day of judgment and destruction of ungodly men.

Prayer is . . .
giving your day to God.

8But do not forget this one thing, dear friends: With the Lord a day is like a thousand years, and a thousand years are like a day. 9The Lord is not slow in keeping his promise, as some understand slowness. He is patient with you, not wanting anyone to perish, but everyone to come to repentance.

10But the day of the Lord will come like a thief. The heavens will disappear with a roar; the elements will be destroyed by fire, and the earth and everything in it will be laid bare.b

11Since everything will be destroyed in this way, what kind of people ought you to be? You ought to live holy and godly lives 12as you look forward to the day of God and speed its coming.c That day will bring about the destruction of the heavens by fire, and the elements will melt in the heat. 13But in keeping with his promise we are looking forward to a new heaven and a new earth, the home of righteousness.

14So then, dear friends, since you are looking forward to this, make every effort to be found spotless, blameless and at peace with him. 15Bear in mind that our Lord's patience means salvation, just as our dear brother Paul also wrote you with the wisdom that God gave him. 16He writes the same way in all his letters, speaking in them of these matters. His letters contain some things that are hard to understand, which ignorant and unstable people distort, as they do the other Scriptures, to their own destruction.

17Therefore, dear friends, since you already know this, be on your guard so that you may not be carried away by the error of lawless men and fall from your secure position. 18But grow in the grace and knowledge of our Lord and Savior Jesus Christ. To him be glory both now and forever! Amen.

1 John

Author: The apostle John
Date: Between AD 85 to 95
Audience: The churches of the province of Asia

Prayer Themes:

• Praise God that your faith is not rooted in wishful thinking or religious imagination, but in historical fact—that Jesus is the Son of God who lived among us, died for us, and rose again so that we who believe in Him can be with Him forever (1:1-3).

• Thank the Lord for His mercy that promises if we will confess our sins, He will not only forgive us, but He will also cleanse us from all that is not right in His sight (1:9).

• Pray that the certainty of eternity would grow in your heart, giving you an ever-increasing desire to live purely for Christ (3:1-3).

This letter was written by the apostle John (the same man who wrote the Gospel of John, the other two letters with his name, and the book of Revelation). John was getting old and may have been the last surviving apostle at this time, although he had not yet been banished to the island of Patmos where he would live the rest of his life in exile.

As an older man who had watched the initial growth of the church and as an eyewitness of Jesus' life, John wrote with a special kind of authority. He clearly saw the false teachers, the suspicions, the problems, the errors. So he wrote this letter to dispel doubts people might have begun having about who Jesus really was and to encourage all believers that because of God's great love, they are truly His children. In order to have that continued close relationship with our loving heavenly Father, we need to be in constant communication with Him through prayer.

1 John

The Word of Life

1 That which was from the beginning, which we have heard, which we have seen with our eyes, which we have looked at and our hands have touched—this we proclaim concerning the Word of life. ²The life appeared; we have seen it and testify to it, and we proclaim to you the eternal life, which was with the Father and has appeared to us. ³We proclaim to you what we have seen and heard, so that you also may have fellowship with us. And our fellowship is with the Father and with his Son, Jesus Christ. ⁴We write this to make our[a] joy complete.

Walking in the Light

⁵This is the message we have heard from him and declare to you: God is light; in him there is no darkness at all. ⁶If we claim to have fellowship with him yet walk in the darkness, we lie and do not live by the truth. ⁷But if we walk in the light, as he is in the light, we have fellowship with one another, and the blood of Jesus, his Son, purifies us from all[b] sin.

⁸If we claim to be without sin, we deceive ourselves and the truth is not in us. ⁹If we confess our sins, he is faithful and just and will forgive us our sins and purify us from all unrighteousness. ¹⁰If we claim we have not sinned, we make him out to be a liar and his word has no place in our lives.

2 My dear children, I write this to you so that you will not sin. But if anybody does sin, we have one who speaks to the Father in our defense—Jesus Christ, the Righteous One. ²He is the atoning sacrifice for our sins, and not only for ours but also for[c] the sins of the whole world.

---

[a] 4 Some manuscripts *your*   [b] 7 Or *every*   [c] 2 Or *He is the one who turns aside God's wrath, taking away our sins, and not only ours but also*

GOING *deeper*

Finding Forgiveness Through Confession

READ AND CONSIDER: 1 JOHN 1:5-10

"If we confess our sins, he is faithful and just and will forgive us our sins and purify us from all unrighteousness" (1 John 1:9).

God offers us three steps for changing our behavior.

The first step is *confession*, which is *admitting* what we did. Everyone makes mistakes. But there is an epidemic in the world today of people who can't admit they did something wrong. God says that all we have to do is confess our sins, and He will forgive us and purify us. Confession means admitting the truth to ourselves first, then to God, and then perhaps to someone else who might have been hurt because of our sin. Sometimes we need to confess to God in front of another person who can pray for us and help us truly get our mistakes off our chest. And confession is not just admitting the truth of what we did, but it is also taking responsibility for it. To own up to wrongdoing can seem like a monumental task, but it is well worth the effort. Confession is one of the best things you can do for yourself. It cleanses your heart by releasing the burden of guilt, and it makes way for God's total forgiveness.

The second step is *repentance*, which means *being sorry* about what we did and wanting to never do it again. We don't confess sin with the intention of clearing the slate and then continuing on with the same sinful behavior, knowing we can just confess it all over again. True repentance means being so sorry before God that we don't ever want to disappoint Him by doing the same thing again.

The third step is *asking for forgiveness* so we can be *cleansed and released* from the consequences of what we did. John didn't say, "If we beg and plead with all of our hearts, then God will forgive us." He said in essence that God's forgiveness flows freely the moment we simply ask for it. God is always waiting and ready to forgive. He doesn't have to be coerced or cajoled. He *wants* us to live free of guilt and shame. He wants us to live in complete forgiveness because only then can we ever find total restoration in our lives.

³We know that we have come to know him if we obey his commands. ⁴The man who says, "I know him," but does not do what he commands is a liar, and the truth is not in him. ⁵But if anyone obeys his word, God's love[a] is truly made complete in him. This is how we know we are in him: ⁶Whoever claims to live in him must walk as Jesus did.

⁷Dear friends, I am not writing you a new command but an old one, which you have had since the beginning. This old command is the message you have heard. ⁸Yet I am writing you a new command; its truth is seen in him and you, because the darkness is passing and the true light is already shining.

⁹Anyone who claims to be in the light but hates his brother is still in the darkness. ¹⁰Whoever loves his brother lives in the light, and there is nothing in him[b] to make him stumble. ¹¹But whoever hates his brother is in the darkness and walks around in the darkness; he does not know where he is going, because the darkness has blinded him.

[a] 5 Or *word, love for God*   [b] 10 Or *it*

12I write to you, dear children,
    because your sins have been
        forgiven on account of his
        name.
13I write to you, fathers,
    because you have known him who
        is from the beginning.
I write to you, young men,
    because you have overcome the evil
        one.
I write to you, dear children,
    because you have known the Father.
14I write to you, fathers,
    because you have known him who
        is from the beginning.
I write to you, young men,
    because you are strong,
    and the word of God lives in you,
    and you have overcome the evil
        one.

Prayer is . . .

telling God you love Him and letting Him assure you of His love for you.

Do Not Love the World

15Do not love the world or anything in the world. If anyone loves the world, the love of the Father is not in him. 16For everything in the world—the cravings of sinful man, the lust of his eyes and the boasting of what he has and does—comes not from the Father but from the world. 17The world and its desires pass away, but the man who does the will of God lives forever.

Warning Against Antichrists

18Dear children, this is the last hour; and as you have heard that the antichrist is coming, even now many antichrists have come. This is how we know it is the last hour. 19They went out from us, but they did not really belong to us. For if they had belonged to us, they would have remained with us; but their going showed that none of them belonged to us.

20But you have an anointing from the Holy One, and all of you know the truth.[a] 21I do not write to you because you do not know the truth, but because you do know it and because no lie comes from the truth. 22Who is the liar? It is the man who denies that Jesus is the Christ. Such a man is the antichrist—he denies the Father and the Son. 23No one who denies the Son has the Father; whoever acknowledges the Son has the Father also.

24See that what you have heard from the beginning remains in you. If it does, you also will remain in the Son and in the Father. 25And this is what he promised us—even eternal life.

26I am writing these things to you about those who are trying to lead you astray. 27As for you, the anointing you received from him remains in you, and you do not need anyone to teach you. But as his anointing teaches you about all things and as that anointing is real, not counterfeit—just as it has taught you, remain in him.

Children of God

28And now, dear children, continue in him, so that when he appears we may be confident and unashamed before him at his coming.

29If you know that he is righteous, you know that everyone who does what is right has been born of him.

3 How great is the love the Father has lavished on us, that we should be called children of God! And that is what we are! The reason the world does not know us is that it did not know him. 2Dear friends, now we are children of God, and what we will be has not yet been made known. But we know that when he appears,[b] we shall be like him, for we shall see him as he is. 3Everyone who has this hope in him purifies himself, just as he is pure.

4Everyone who sins breaks the law;

Loving God Through the Tough Times

When we experience tragedy or loss, we don't understand how anything good could possibly come out of it. We may have a hard time imagining ever feeling true happiness again. And even though God *promises* that "in all things God works for the good of those who love him, who have been called according to his purpose" (Romans 8:28), in a disastrous situation we may wonder how in the world God could ever bring anything good out of it. The truth is that He can, regardless of how bad our situation is. *How* He does it, only *He* knows. But it doesn't happen automatically. We must meet certain conditions.

First of all, we must *love God*. If we don't love God, or if we're mad at Him and have an angry, resentful, bitter, unforgiving, or hateful attitude, this promise will not be fulfilled. The Bible does *not* say that all things work together for the good of those who deny God's existence until disaster strikes and then run to Him and demand that He fix everything that's wrong. God knows what is in our hearts—we can't hide anything from Him. He works all things together for the good of those who *love* Him, and He knows whether we really love Him or not.

Loving God doesn't mean we just pray when we want something, as if God were a spiritual Santa Claus, a Sugar Daddy, or our fairy Godfather. He *wants* us to ask for things in accordance with His will. In fact, He says we don't have certain blessings because we don't ask for them (James 4:2). But He wants us to love Him enough to ask Him what *He* wants instead of just telling Him what *we* want. In other words, we can't just ignore His laws or reject His ways and then run to Him demanding that He give us everything we long to have. That is not loving God.

Loving God is a way of life that does not depend on circumstances. It depends on our knowledge of who God is. When we really know Him, we can't help but love Him. Loving God means trusting Him with all our heart and walking with Him through each day regardless of how difficult it may be. It means always knowing that God is on our side even if we don't sense His presence at the moment. It means praying with the leading of the Holy Spirit and refusing to give in to fear and doubt.

Secondly, loving God means loving others. It means praying for them. It means asking God to show you what you can do to help them through the tough situations they are experiencing. It's giving words of hope, comfort, and assurance that God loves them and hasn't forsaken them. Nothing helps us get through the tough times successfully more than showing God's love to others.

Remember that regardless of how much your world shakes, God is unshakeable. So don't doubt God when you are in the midst of a tough time. Continue to show your love for Him by praising Him for who He is and all that He has done. And thank Him ahead of time for the good He will soon bring out of your situation.

For the next "From Stormie's Heart" article, go to page 1531.

in fact, sin is lawlessness. [5]But you know that he appeared so that he might take away our sins. And in him is no sin. [6]No one who lives in him keeps on sinning. No one who continues to sin has either seen him or known him.

[7]Dear children, do not let anyone lead you astray. He who does what is right is righteous, just as he is righteous. [8]He who does what is sinful is of the devil, because the devil has been sinning from the beginning. The reason the Son of God appeared was to destroy the devil's work. [9]No one who is born of God will continue to sin, because God's seed remains in him; he cannot go on sinning, because he has been born of God. [10]This is how we know who the children of God are and who the children of the devil are: Anyone who does not do what is right is not a child of God; nor is anyone who does not love his brother.

Love One Another

[11]This is the message you heard from the beginning: We should love one another. [12]Do not be like Cain, who belonged to the evil one and murdered his brother. And why did he murder him? Because his own actions were evil and his brother's were righteous. [13]Do not be surprised, my brothers, if the world hates you. [14]We know that we have passed from death to life, because we love our brothers. Anyone who does not love remains in death. [15]Anyone who hates his brother is a murderer, and you know that no murderer has eternal life in him.

[16]This is how we know what love is: Jesus Christ laid down his life for us. And we ought to lay down our lives for our brothers. [17]If anyone has material possessions and sees his brother in need but has no pity on him, how can the love of God be in him? [18]Dear children, let us not love with words or tongue but with actions and in truth. [19]This then is how we know that we belong to the truth, and how we set our hearts at rest in his presence

[20]whenever our hearts condemn us. For God is greater than our hearts, and he knows everything.

[21]Dear friends, if our hearts do not condemn us, we have confidence before God [22]and receive from him anything we ask, because we obey his commands and do what pleases him. [23]And this is his command: to believe in the name of his Son, Jesus Christ, and to love one another as he commanded us. [24]Those who obey his commands live in him, and he in them. And this is how we know that he lives in us: We know it by the Spirit he gave us.

Test the Spirits

4 Dear friends, do not believe every spirit, but test the spirits to see whether they are from God, because many false prophets have gone out into the world. [2]This is how you can recognize the Spirit of God: Every spirit that acknowledges that Jesus Christ has come in the flesh is from God, [3]but every spirit that does not acknowledge Jesus is not from God. This is the spirit of the antichrist, which you have heard is coming and even now is already in the world.

> ### Praying 1 John 4:4
> *Help me to always remember, Lord, that Your Spirit in me is greater than anything I face.*

[4]You, dear children, are from God and have overcome them, because the one who is in you is greater than the one who is in the world. [5]They are from the world and therefore speak from the viewpoint of the world, and the world listens to them. [6]We are from God, and whoever knows God listens to us; but whoever is not from God does not listen to us. This is how we recognize the Spirit[a] of truth and the spirit of falsehood.

God's Love and Ours

[7]Dear friends, let us love one another, for love comes from God. Everyone who

---

loves has been born of God and knows God. [8]Whoever does not love does not know God, because God is love. [9]This is how God showed his love among us: He sent his one and only Son[a] into the world that we might live through him. [10]This is love: not that we loved God, but that he loved us and sent his Son as an atoning sacrifice for[b] our sins. [11]Dear friends, since God so loved us, we also ought to love one another. [12]No one has ever seen God; but if we love one another, God lives in us and his love is made complete in us.

[13]We know that we live in him and he in us, because he has given us of his Spirit. [14]And we have seen and testify that the Father has sent his Son to be the Savior of the world. [15]If anyone acknowledges that Jesus is the Son of God, God lives in him and he in God. [16]And so we know and rely on the love God has for us.

God is love. Whoever lives in love lives in God, and God in him. [17]In this way, love is made complete among us so that we will have confidence on the day of judgment, because in this world we are like him. [18]There is no fear in love. But perfect love drives out fear, because fear has to do with punishment. The one who fears is not made perfect in love.

[19]We love because he first loved us. [20]If anyone says, "I love God," yet hates his brother, he is a liar. For anyone who does not love his brother, whom he has seen, cannot love God, whom he has not seen. [21]And he has given us this command: Whoever loves God must also love his brother.

Faith in the Son of God

5 Everyone who believes that Jesus is the Christ is born of God, and everyone who loves the father loves his child as well. [2]This is how we know that we love the children of God: by loving God and carrying out his commands. [3]This is love for God: to obey his commands. And his commands are not burdensome, [4]for everyone born of God overcomes the world. This is the victory that has overcome the world, even our faith. [5]Who is it that overcomes the world? Only he who believes that Jesus is the Son of God.

[6]This is the one who came by water and blood—Jesus Christ. He did not come by water only, but by water and blood. And it is the Spirit who testifies, because the Spirit is the truth. [7]For there are three that testify: [8]the[c] Spirit, the water and the blood; and the three are in agreement. [9]We accept man's testimony, but God's testimony is greater because it is the testimony of God, which he has given about his Son. [10]Anyone who believes in the Son of God has this testimony in his heart. Anyone who does not believe God has made him out to be a liar, because he has not believed the testimony God has given about his Son. [11]And this is the testimony: God has given us eternal life, and this life is in his Son. [12]He who has the Son has life; he who does not have the Son of God does not have life.

Concluding Remarks

[13]I write these things to you who believe in the name of the Son of God so that you may know that you have eternal life. [14]This is the confidence we have in approaching God: that if we ask anything according to his will, he hears us. [15]And if we know that he hears us—whatever we ask—we know that we have what we asked of him.

[16]If anyone sees his brother commit a sin that does not lead to death, he should pray and God will give him life. I refer to those whose sin does not lead to death. There is a sin that leads to death. I am not saying that he should pray about that. [17]All wrongdoing is sin, and there is sin that does not lead to death.

[18]We know that anyone born of God does not continue to sin; the one who

---

[a] 9 Or *his only begotten Son*   [b] 10 Or *as the one who would turn aside his wrath, taking away*   [c] 7,8 Late manuscripts of the Vulgate *testify in heaven: the Father, the Word and the Holy Spirit, and these three are one.* [8]*And there are three that testify on earth: the* (not found in any Greek manuscript before the fourteenth century)

GOING *deeper*

Coming to Father God in Confidence

READ AND CONSIDER: 1 JOHN 5:13-21

"This is the confidence we have in approaching God: that if we ask anything according to his will, he hears us. And if we know that he hears us—whatever we ask—we know that we have what we asked of him" (1 John 5:14-15).

The Bible says our relationship to God is like a child's relationship with an adoring father. John spoke of God lavishing His love on us, calling us His own. What a powerful picture of the way we should always approach our heavenly Father. Imagine a small child coming to ask his or her father for something, knowing that it will be given. Would there be any hesitation before the child leaped into the father's arms, relaxed in the safety and security found there? Wouldn't the child be expectant and hopeful as every need is communicated and met?

How does that compare with the way we approach God? Too often we don't bound into His presence as joyfully as a small child. Perhaps we are worried that we're bothering Him with the same old request we've been praying about for years. Or maybe we fear that He is going to deny our request, and we don't want to set ourselves up for disappointment. Or perhaps we feel less than fit to be in His presence because of an area where we feel we are failing.

Whatever the reason we hesitate to come before God with confidence, we know from these verses that He is a good God who hears our requests and cares about our needs. If what we are asking for is wrong for us, He'll let us know. If it's right, He'll make it happen in His way and in His time. We can trust Him enough to run into His presence like a child who is loved and accepted, who can't imagine receiving anything but goodness from Father God.

was born of God keeps him safe, and the evil one cannot harm him. ¹⁹We know that we are children of God, and that the whole world is under the control of the evil one. ²⁰We know also that the Son of God has come and has given us understanding, so that we may know him who is true. And we are in him who is true—even in his Son Jesus Christ. He is the true God and eternal life.

²¹Dear children, keep yourselves from idols.

Author: The apostle John

Date: AD 85–95

Audience: To Christians engaged in the practice of housing and feeding traveling evangelists and teachers, urging them to be discerning in their hospitality

Prayer Themes:

- Thank God that although you live in a world that tolerates anything and everything, He has clearly drawn a line between what is true and what is not (1:1-2).

- Pray that you will show your love for God by obeying Him in all that He asks you to do (1:5-6).

- Pray for the boldness and courage to speak out against unbiblical and ungodly ideas in a loving but firm way (1:7-11).

The New Testament is full of "warning passages." Warnings about the world system in which we live, about fleshly desires lurking in our own souls, about the evil one who prowls the earth like a lion, looking for victims to devour. Warnings about our human tendency to forget what matters most. And warnings, like we find in 2 John, about the danger of following false teachers. Written by the apostle John, the purpose of this letter is to encourage believers to follow the truth, obey God, watch out for false teachers, and love the Lord and each other.

We are exposed to much teaching through radio, television, videos, books, lectures, and religious meetings. Most of it is good and helpful. But we have to always ask God to enable us to discern His truth from what is false so that we are never led astray. We need divine protection and a heavenly infusion of wisdom. And we need courage to take a stand against all who propagate ungodly ideas and promote sinful behavior. John reminds us in all of his warnings of our desperate need to cling to God.

2 John

¹The elder,

To the chosen lady and her children, whom I love in the truth—and not I only, but also all who know the truth—²because of the truth, which lives in us and will be with us forever:

³Grace, mercy and peace from God the Father and from Jesus Christ, the Father's Son, will be with us in truth and love.

⁴It has given me great joy to find some of your children walking in the truth, just as the Father commanded us. ⁵And now, dear lady, I am not writing you a new command but one we have had from the beginning. I ask that we love one another. ⁶And this is love: that we walk in obedience to his commands. As you have heard

Praying 2 John 1:6

Help me, Lord, to show my love for You by always living according to Your commands.

from the beginning, his command is that you walk in love.

⁷Many deceivers, who do not acknowledge Jesus Christ as coming in the flesh, have gone out into the world. Any such person is the deceiver and the antichrist. ⁸Watch out that you do not lose what you have worked for, but that you may be rewarded fully. ⁹Anyone who runs ahead and does not continue in the teaching of Christ does not have God; whoever continues in the teaching has both the Father and the Son. ¹⁰If anyone comes to you and does not bring this teaching, do not

take him into your house or welcome him. 11 Anyone who welcomes him shares in his wicked work.

12 I have much to write to you, but I do not want to use paper and ink. Instead, I hope to visit you and talk with you face to face, so that our joy may be complete.

13 The children of your chosen sister send their greetings.

Author: The apostle John

Date: AD 85–95

Audience: A Christian named Gaius in one of the churches of Asia Minor where a powerful church leader named Diotrephes was causing problems

Prayer Themes:

- Pray for the physical and spiritual health of your friends, family, and those whom the Lord puts on your heart (1:2).

- Ask the Lord to give you a strong desire to extend hospitality and to show you how to do it (1:5-8).

- Pray that God will give you the capacity to imitate the good behavior of strong believers you have observed (1:11).

The apostle John wrote this letter to Gaius, a leading Christian in one of the churches, who apparently had a very hospitable household. He often took in fellow believers even though they were strangers. Traveling missionaries depended on such hospitality in order to continue their ministries. John commended Gaius for his hospitality and kindness.

However, a man had risen to power in Gaius's church who apparently had a pride problem. Diotrephes loved "to be first," gossiped maliciously, and refused to give the kind of hospitality to traveling missionaries that Gaius showed. And those who *did* show hospitality were being put out of the church. Perhaps that had happened to Gaius, and perhaps Gaius had sent his concerns to John asking what to do.

The right thing to do, then *and* now, is to do good. It is always right to welcome those who come with Jesus' message. They need our friendship, support, encouragement, love, and hospitality. And they always need our ongoing prayer support.

3 John

¹The elder,

To my dear friend Gaius, whom I love in the truth.

²Dear friend, I pray that you may enjoy good health and that all may go well with you, even as your soul is getting along well. ³It gave me great joy to have some brothers come and tell about your faithfulness to the truth and how you continue to walk in the truth. ⁴I have no greater joy than to hear that my children are walking in the truth.

⁵Dear friend, you are faithful in what you are doing for the brothers, even though they are strangers to you. ⁶They have told the church about your love. You will do well to send them on their way in a manner worthy of God. ⁷It was for the sake of the Name that they went out, receiving no help from the pagans. ⁸We ought therefore to show hospitality to such men so that we may work together for the truth.

⁹I wrote to the church, but Diotrephes, who loves to be first, will have nothing to do with us. ¹⁰So if I come, I will call attention to what he is doing, gossiping maliciously about us. Not satisfied with that, he refuses to welcome the brothers. He also stops those who want to do so and puts them out of the church.

¹¹Dear friend, do not imitate what is evil but what is good. Anyone who does what is good is from God. Anyone who does what is evil has not seen God.

Praying 3 John 1:2

Heavenly Father, help me to prosper in all things and enjoy good health in my body, mind, and soul.

12Demetrius is well spoken of by everyone—and even by the truth itself. We also speak well of him, and you know that our testimony is true.

13I have much to write you, but I do not want to do so with pen and ink. 14I hope to see you soon, and we will talk face to face.

Peace to you. The friends here send their greetings. Greet the friends there by name.

Prayer Themes:

- Pray for an increasing hunger for God's truth and the discernment needed to think and live right in a world filled with deception (1:3-4).

- Pray for God to give you the courage, ability, and willingness to speak the truth in the face of theological error, and thereby help to rescue others from its consequences (1:22-23).

- Praise God for the reassuring promise that He is able to keep you from falling (1:24).

Author: Jude

Date: Approximately AD 65

Audience: Unclear; either Jewish Christians or Gentile believers, or both in a region not specified

Because life is dangerous, we do things to protect ourselves and our children. We put locks on our doors; we know what numbers to dial in an emergency; we teach our children to never go anywhere with a stranger.

But are we as vigilant about *moral* dangers? What do we do when faced with that questionable teaching by the new teacher who *seems* to be saying all the right things, yet not every word rings true?

Jude, the half brother of our Lord, wrote to address this timeless situation. His brief letter reminds us that, until the return of Christ, we will regularly be confronted with slick-tongued "experts" who claim to be enlightened. And Jude advises us: "Build yourselves up in your most holy faith and pray in the Holy Spirit. Keep yourselves in God's love as you wait for the mercy of our Lord Jesus Christ to bring you to eternal life" (1:20-21). Only when we do this can we be protected from the moral dangers and spiritual compromises that surround us.

Jude

¹Jude, a servant of Jesus Christ and a brother of James,

To those who have been called, who are loved by God the Father and kept by[a] Jesus Christ:

²Mercy, peace and love be yours in abundance.

The Sin and Doom of Godless Men

³Dear friends, although I was very eager to write to you about the salvation we share, I felt I had to write and urge you to contend for the faith that was once for all entrusted to the saints. ⁴For certain men whose condemnation was written about[b] long ago have secretly slipped in among you. They are godless men, who change the grace of our God into a license for immorality and deny Jesus Christ our only Sovereign and Lord.

⁵Though you already know all this, I want to remind you that the Lord[c] delivered his people out of Egypt, but later destroyed those who did not believe. ⁶And the angels who did not keep their positions of authority but abandoned their own home—these he has kept in darkness, bound with everlasting chains for judgment on the great Day. ⁷In a similar way, Sodom and Gomorrah and the surrounding towns gave themselves up to sexual immorality and perversion. They serve as an example of those who suffer the punishment of eternal fire.

⁸In the very same way, these dreamers pollute their own bodies, reject authority and slander celestial beings. ⁹But even the archangel Michael, when he was disputing with the devil about the body of Moses, did not dare to bring a slanderous

---

ᵃ *1 Or for; or in*   ᵇ *4 Or men who were marked out for condemnation*   ᶜ *5 Some early manuscripts Jesus* accusation against him, but said, "The Lord rebuke you!" [10]Yet these men speak abusively against whatever they do not understand; and what things they do understand by instinct, like unreasoning animals—these are the very things that destroy them.

[11]Woe to them! They have taken the way of Cain; they have rushed for profit into Balaam's error; they have been destroyed in Korah's rebellion.

[12]These men are blemishes at your love feasts, eating with you without the slightest qualm—shepherds who feed only themselves. They are clouds without rain, blown along by the wind; autumn trees, without fruit and uprooted—twice dead. [13]They are wild waves of the sea, foaming up their shame; wandering stars, for whom blackest darkness has been reserved forever.

[14]Enoch, the seventh from Adam, prophesied about these men: "See, the Lord is coming with thousands upon thousands of his holy ones [15]to judge everyone, and to convict all the ungodly of all the ungodly acts they have done in the ungodly way, and of all the harsh words ungodly sinners have spoken against him." [16]These men are grumblers and faultfinders; they follow their own evil desires; they boast about themselves and flatter others for their own advantage.

A Call to Persevere

[17]But, dear friends, remember what the apostles of our Lord Jesus Christ foretold. [18]They said to you, "In the last times there will be scoffers who will follow their own ungodly desires." [19]These are the men who divide you, who follow mere natural instincts and do not have the Spirit.

[20]But you, dear friends, build yourselves up in your most holy faith and pray in the Holy Spirit. [21]Keep yourselves in God's love as you wait for the mercy of our Lord Jesus Christ to bring you to eternal life.

[22]Be merciful to those who doubt; [23]snatch others from the fire and save them; to others show mercy, mixed with fear—hating even the clothing stained by corrupted flesh.

Praying Jude 1:24

Thank You, Jesus, that You are able to keep me from stumbling and falling and to present me before God without any fault.

Doxology

[24]To him who is able to keep you from falling and to present you before his glorious presence without fault and with great joy— [25]to the only God our Savior be glory, majesty, power and authority, through Jesus Christ our Lord, before all ages, now and forevermore! Amen.

Author: The apostle John

Date: Approximately AD 95

Audience: Christians in the seven churches of Asia Minor (modern-day Turkey), to remind them of the preeminence of Christ and to provide a glimpse of future events.

Prayer Themes:

- In light of the messages to the seven churches, ask God to show you the strengths and weaknesses in your own life (2:1–3:21).

- Praise God often that He is holy, almighty, eternal, and worthy to receive glory and honor (4:8-11).

- Thank God for the promise of an eternity of peace and joy in heaven where the curse of Eden has been forever erased (21:1-22:5).

John was given just a glimpse into heaven and of the future of our world. The apostle had been exiled to the island of Patmos because he wouldn't stop preaching the gospel message. One Sunday as he was worshiping the Lord, he received a vision and was told to "write on a scroll what you see and send it to the seven churches" (1:11). Even though John was in exile, that didn't stop God from using him to get out His message.

John obeyed God and the result is this final book of the Bible that lifts our eyes beyond the mundane world and gives us our clearest glimpse of ultimate reality. Even though it is just a peek, and even though there is much in these cryptic pages that we will never fully grasp this side of heaven, one thing is for sure: Jesus wins. The end of the story is already written. The future is secure. And we who await our place in eternity with God must continually praise Him on earth until we join that magnificent choir of angels singing around His throne.

Praise Him that your name is recorded in His Book of Life and that His presence is always with you.

Revelation

Prologue

1 The revelation of Jesus Christ, which God gave him to show his servants what must soon take place. He made it known by sending his angel to his servant John, ²who testifies to everything he saw—that is, the word of God and the testimony of Jesus Christ. ³Blessed is the one who reads the words of this prophecy, and blessed are those who hear it and take to heart what is written in it, because the time is near.

Greetings and Doxology

⁴John,

To the seven churches in the province of Asia:

Grace and peace to you from him who is, and who was, and who is to come, and from the seven spirits[a] before his throne, ⁵and from Jesus Christ, who is the faithful witness, the firstborn from the dead, and the ruler of the kings of the earth.

To him who loves us and has freed us from our sins by his blood, ⁶and has made us to be a kingdom and priests to serve his God and Father—to him be glory and power for ever and ever! Amen.

⁷Look, he is coming with the clouds,
  and every eye will see him,
  even those who pierced him;

---

and all the peoples of the earth will mourn because of him.

So shall it be! Amen.

8"I am the Alpha and the Omega," says the Lord God, "who is, and who was, and who is to come, the Almighty."

One Like a Son of Man

9I, John, your brother and companion in the suffering and kingdom and patient endurance that are ours in Jesus, was on the island of Patmos because of the word of God and the testimony of Jesus. 10On the Lord's Day I was in the Spirit, and I heard behind me a loud voice like a trumpet, 11which said: "Write on a scroll what you see and send it to the seven churches: to Ephesus, Smyrna, Pergamum, Thyatira, Sardis, Philadelphia and Laodicea."

12I turned around to see the voice that was speaking to me. And when I turned I saw seven golden lampstands, 13and among the lampstands was someone "like a son of man,"[a] dressed in a robe reaching down to his feet and with a golden sash around his chest. 14His head and hair were white like wool, as white as snow, and his eyes were like blazing fire. 15His feet were like bronze glowing in a furnace, and his voice was like the sound of rushing waters. 16In his right hand he held seven stars, and out of his mouth came a sharp double-edged sword. His face was like the sun shining in all its brilliance.

17When I saw him, I fell at his feet as though dead. Then he placed his right hand on me and said: "Do not be afraid. I am the First and the Last. 18I am the Living One; I was dead, and behold I am alive for ever and ever! And I hold the keys of death and Hades.

19"Write, therefore, what you have seen, what is now and what will take place later. 20The mystery of the seven stars that you saw in my right hand and of the seven golden lampstands is this: The seven stars are the angels[b] of the seven churches, and the seven lampstands are the seven churches.

To the Church in Ephesus

2 "To the angel[c] of the church in Ephesus write:

These are the words of him who holds the seven stars in his right hand and walks among the seven golden lampstands: 2I know your deeds, your hard work and your perseverance. I know that you cannot tolerate wicked men, that you have tested those who claim to be apostles but are not, and have found them false. 3You have persevered and have endured hardships for my name, and have not grown weary.

> *Praying Revelation 2:4-5*
> *Jesus, I pray that I will never lose the fervency of love for You that I should have and that You deserve.*

4Yet I hold this against you: You have forsaken your first love. 5Remember the height from which you have fallen! Repent and do the things you did at first. If you do not repent, I will come to you and remove your lampstand from its place. 6But you have this in your favor: You hate the practices of the Nicolaitans, which I also hate.

7He who has an ear, let him hear what the Spirit says to the churches. To him who overcomes, I will give the right to eat from the tree of life, which is in the paradise of God.

To the Church in Smyrna

8"To the angel of the church in Smyrna write:

These are the words of him who is the First and the Last, who died and came to life again. 9I know your afflictions and your poverty—yet you are rich! I know the slander of

---

[a] 13 Daniel 7:13   [b] 20 Or messengers   [c] 1 Or messenger; also in verses 8, 12 and 18

those who say they are Jews and are not, but are a synagogue of Satan. [10]Do not be afraid of what you are about to suffer. I tell you, the devil will put some of you in prison to test you, and you will suffer persecution for ten days. Be faithful, even to the point of death, and I will give you the crown of life.

[11]He who has an ear, let him hear what the Spirit says to the churches. He who overcomes will not be hurt at all by the second death.

To the Church in Pergamum

[12]"To the angel of the church in Pergamum write:

These are the words of him who has the sharp, double-edged sword. [13]I know where you live—where Satan has his throne. Yet you remain true to my name. You did not renounce your faith in me, even in the days of Antipas, my faithful witness, who was put to death in your city— where Satan lives.

[14]Nevertheless, I have a few things against you: You have people there who hold to the teaching of Balaam, who taught Balak to entice the Israelites to sin by eating food sacrificed to idols and by committing sexual immorality. [15]Likewise you also have those who hold to the teaching of the Nicolaitans. [16]Repent therefore! Otherwise, I will soon come to you and will fight against them with the sword of my mouth.

[17]He who has an ear, let him hear what the Spirit says to the churches. To him who overcomes, I will give some of the hidden manna. I will also give him a white stone with a new name written on it, known only to him who receives it.

To the Church in Thyatira

[18]"To the angel of the church in Thyatira write:

These are the words of the Son of God, whose eyes are like blazing fire and whose feet are like burnished bronze. [19]I know your deeds, your love and faith, your service and perseverance, and that you are now doing more than you did at first.

[20]Nevertheless, I have this against you: You tolerate that woman Jezebel, who calls herself a prophetess. By her teaching she misleads my servants into sexual immorality and the eating of food sacrificed to idols. [21]I have given her time to repent of her immorality, but she is unwilling. [22]So I will cast her on a bed of suffering, and I will make those who commit adultery with her suffer intensely, unless they repent of her ways. [23]I will strike her children dead. Then all the churches will know that I am he who searches hearts and minds, and I will repay each of you according to your deeds. [24]Now I say to the rest of you in Thyatira, to you who do not hold to her teaching and have not learned Satan's so-called deep secrets (I will not impose any other burden on you): [25]Only hold on to what you have until I come.

[26]To him who overcomes and does my will to the end, I will give authority over the nations—

[27]'He will rule them with an iron scepter;
   he will dash them to pieces like pottery'[a]—

just as I have received authority from my Father. [28]I will also give him the morning star. [29]He who has an ear, let him hear what the Spirit says to the churches.

To the Church in Sardis

3 "To the angel[b] of the church in Sardis write:

These are the words of him who

---

[a] 27 Psalm 2:9   [b] 1 Or messenger; also in verses 7 and 14

holds the seven spirits[a] of God and the seven stars. I know your deeds; you have a reputation of being alive, but you are dead. 2Wake up! Strengthen what remains and is about to die, for I have not found your deeds complete in the sight of my God. 3Remember, therefore, what you have received and heard; obey it, and repent. But if you do not wake up, I will come like a thief, and you will not know at what time I will come to you.

4Yet you have a few people in Sardis who have not soiled their clothes. They will walk with me, dressed in white, for they are worthy. 5He who overcomes will, like them, be dressed in white. I will never blot out his name from the book of life, but will acknowledge his name before my Father and his angels. 6He who has an ear, let him hear what the Spirit says to the churches.

To the Church in Philadelphia
7"To the angel of the church in Philadelphia write:

These are the words of him who is holy and true, who holds the key of David. What he opens no one can shut, and what he shuts no one can open. 8I know your deeds. See, I have placed before you an open door that no one can shut. I know that you have little strength, yet you have kept my word and have not denied my name. 9I will make those who are of the synagogue of Satan, who claim to be Jews though they are not, but are liars—I will make them come and fall down at your feet and acknowledge that I have loved you. 10Since you have kept my command to endure patiently, I will also keep you from the hour of trial that is going to come upon the whole world to test those who live on the earth.

11I am coming soon. Hold on to what you have, so that no one will take your crown. 12Him who overcomes I will make a pillar in the temple of my God. Never again will he leave it. I will write on him the name of my God and the name of the city of my God, the new Jerusalem, which is coming down out of heaven from my God; and I will also write on him my new name. 13He who has an ear, let him hear what the Spirit says to the churches.

To the Church in Laodicea
14"To the angel of the church in Laodicea write:

These are the words of the Amen, the faithful and true witness, the ruler of God's creation. 15I know your deeds, that you are neither cold nor hot. I wish you were either one or the other! 16So, because you are lukewarm—neither hot nor cold—I am about to spit you out of my mouth. 17You say, 'I am rich; I have acquired wealth and do not need a thing.' But you do not realize that you are wretched, pitiful, poor, blind and naked. 18I counsel you to buy from me gold refined in the fire, so you can become rich; and white clothes to wear, so you can cover your shameful nakedness; and salve to put on your eyes, so you can see.

19Those whom I love I rebuke and discipline. So be earnest, and repent. 20Here I am! I stand at the door and knock. If anyone hears my voice and opens the door, I will come in and eat with him, and he with me.

21To him who overcomes, I will give the right to sit with me on my throne, just as I overcame and sat down with my Father on his throne. 22He who has an ear, let him hear what the Spirit says to the churches."

a 1 Or the sevenfold Spirit

Remember What Jesus Did for You on the Cross

Jesus showed us who God is and what God's rule means. He demonstrated His authority over death, sickness, hopelessness, brokenness, poverty, and the enemy of our souls. He bore in His body the penalty of our sin so that we don't have to bear it ourselves. When He said, "It is finished" on the cross (John 19:30), it not only meant His life on earth was finished, but the things He accomplished on the cross were finished too. Done. Nothing can change that. The power of death and hell was conquered on the cross and defeated for all time. When we let our hearts fully grasp that reality, praise and worship can't be contained. It becomes like a sunrise in the heart that will shine out of us in one way or another. When that happens, we will shed our idea of worship as only a formal prescribed liturgy or a predictable order, and we will then know the newness of the living Christ in us.

Jesus does not want us to ever forget what He did. He wants us to remember it daily. He instructed His disciples in the way the sacrifice of His body and blood should be remembered in the drinking of wine and eating of bread. And we must do that often as well. But each time we worship and praise Him for His suffering, death, and resurrection, we give Him the reverence and worth He deserves. We remind ourselves of all that He sacrificed and accomplished.

There is an intimacy in sharing a meal with someone. There is a deepening or a connecting that happens in the relationship. Jesus waits for us to invite Him into our lives so we can do the same with Him. He says, "Here I am! I stand at the door and knock. If anyone hears my voice and opens the door, I will come in and eat with him, and he with me" (Revelation 3:20). That He will come and dine with us is a precious promise of intimacy. Every time we praise Him, we are opening that door and further deepening our relationship with Him.

I've often heard people say, "Isn't heaven going to be boring—wearing the same white robes and singing worship songs all day?" Actually, that sounds good to me. No pain, no sickness, no fear, no one hurting you, no more worry about where your next meal is coming from or how you're going to pay the bills or what you're going to wear. And, besides, I love white! As far as praise being boring—there's no way. We are going to be so impressed with the awesome wonder of God that we are not going to be able to contain it. Worship will pour out of us and be a continual thrill.

We owe Jesus so much. Our payment is to love Him and praise Him forever. Let's start now, shall we?

The Throne in Heaven

4 After this I looked, and there before me was a door standing open in heaven. And the voice I had first heard speaking to me like a trumpet said, "Come up here, and I will show you what must take place after this." [2]At once I was in the Spirit, and there before me was a throne in heaven with someone sitting on it. [3]And the one who sat there had the appearance of jasper and carnelian. A rainbow, resembling an emerald, encircled the throne. [4]Surrounding the throne were twenty-four other thrones, and seated on them were twenty-four elders. They were dressed in white and had crowns of gold on their heads. [5]From the throne came flashes of lightning, rumblings and peals of thunder. Before the throne, seven lamps were blazing. These are the seven spirits[a] of God. [6]Also before the throne there was what looked like a sea of glass, clear as crystal.

In the center, around the throne, were four living creatures, and they were covered with eyes, in front and in back. [7]The first living creature was like a lion, the second was like an ox, the third had a face like a man, the fourth was like a flying eagle. [8]Each of the four living creatures had six wings and was covered with eyes all around, even under his wings. Day and night they never stop saying:

> "Holy, holy, holy
> is the Lord God Almighty,
> who was, and is, and is to come."

[9]Whenever the living creatures give glory, honor and thanks to him who sits on the throne and who lives for ever and ever, [10]the twenty-four elders fall down before him who sits on the throne, and worship him who lives for ever and ever. They lay their crowns before the throne and say:

[11]"You are worthy, our Lord and God,
> to receive glory and honor and
> power,

> for you created all things,
> and by your will they were created
> and have their being."

The Scroll and the Lamb

5 Then I saw in the right hand of him who sat on the throne a scroll with writing on both sides and sealed with seven seals. [2]And I saw a mighty angel proclaiming in a loud voice, "Who is worthy to break the seals and open the scroll?" [3]But no one in heaven or on earth or under the earth could open the scroll or even look inside it. [4]I wept and wept because no one was found who was worthy to open the scroll or look inside. [5]Then one of the elders said to me, "Do not weep! See, the Lion of the tribe of Judah, the Root of David, has triumphed. He is able to open the scroll and its seven seals."

Prayer is . . .

*a means by which you
can find healing.*

---

[6]Then I saw a Lamb, looking as if it had been slain, standing in the center of the throne, encircled by the four living creatures and the elders. He had seven horns and seven eyes, which are the seven spirits[a] of God sent out into all the earth. [7]He came and took the scroll from the right hand of him who sat on the throne. [8]And when he had taken it, the four living creatures and the twenty-four elders fell down before the Lamb. Each one had a harp and they were holding golden bowls full of incense, which are the prayers of the saints. [9]And they sang a new song:

> "You are worthy to take the scroll
> and to open its seals,
> because you were slain,

---

[a] 5,6 Or *the sevenfold Spirit*

and with your blood you purchased
men for God
from every tribe and language and
people and nation.
10 You have made them to be a
kingdom and priests to serve
our God,
and they will reign on the earth."

11 Then I looked and heard the voice of many angels, numbering thousands upon thousands, and ten thousand times ten thousand. They encircled the throne and the living creatures and the elders. 12 In a loud voice they sang:

"Worthy is the Lamb, who was slain,
to receive power and wealth and
wisdom and strength
and honor and glory and praise!"

13 Then I heard every creature in heaven and on earth and under the earth and on the sea, and all that is in them, singing:

"To him who sits on the throne and
to the Lamb
be praise and honor and glory and
power,
for ever and ever!"

14 The four living creatures said, "Amen," and the elders fell down and worshiped.

The Seals

6 I watched as the Lamb opened the first of the seven seals. Then I heard one of the four living creatures say in a voice like thunder, "Come!" 2 I looked, and there before me was a white horse! Its rider held a bow, and he was given a crown, and he rode out as a conqueror bent on conquest.

3 When the Lamb opened the second seal, I heard the second living creature say, "Come!" 4 Then another horse came out, a fiery red one. Its rider was given power to take peace from the earth and to make men slay each other. To him was given a large sword.

5 When the Lamb opened the third seal, I heard the third living creature say, "Come!" I looked, and there before me was a black horse! Its rider was holding a pair of scales in his hand. 6 Then I heard what sounded like a voice among the four living creatures, saying, "A quart[a] of wheat for a day's wages,[b] and three quarts of barley for a day's wages,[b] and do not damage the oil and the wine!"

7 When the Lamb opened the fourth seal, I heard the voice of the fourth living creature say, "Come!" 8 I looked, and there before me was a pale horse! Its rider was named Death, and Hades was following close behind him. They were given power over a fourth of the earth to kill by sword, famine and plague, and by the wild beasts of the earth.

9 When he opened the fifth seal, I saw under the altar the souls of those who had been slain because of the word of God and the testimony they had maintained. 10 They called out in a loud voice, "How long, Sovereign Lord, holy and true, until you judge the inhabitants of the earth and avenge our blood?" 11 Then each of them was given a white robe, and they were told to wait a little longer, until the number of their fellow servants and brothers who were to be killed as they had been was completed.

12 I watched as he opened the sixth seal. There was a great earthquake. The sun turned black like sackcloth made of goat hair, the whole moon turned blood red, 13 and the stars in the sky fell to earth, as late figs drop from a fig tree when shaken by a strong wind. 14 The sky receded like a scroll, rolling up, and every mountain and island was removed from its place.

15 Then the kings of the earth, the princes, the generals, the rich, the mighty, and every slave and every free man hid in caves and among the rocks of the mountains. 16 They called to the mountains and the rocks, "Fall on us and hide us from the face of him who sits on the throne and from the wrath of the Lamb! 17 For

---

a 6 Greek *a choinix* (probably about a liter) b 6 Greek *a denarius* the great day of their wrath has come, and who can stand?"

144,000 Sealed

7 After this I saw four angels standing at the four corners of the earth, holding back the four winds of the earth to prevent any wind from blowing on the land or on the sea or on any tree. ²Then I saw another angel coming up from the east, having the seal of the living God. He called out in a loud voice to the four angels who had been given power to harm the land and the sea: ³"Do not harm the land or the sea or the trees until we put a seal on the foreheads of the servants of our God." ⁴Then I heard the number of those who were sealed: 144,000 from all the tribes of Israel.

⁵From the tribe of Judah 12,000 were sealed,
from the tribe of Reuben 12,000,
from the tribe of Gad 12,000,
⁶from the tribe of Asher 12,000,
from the tribe of Naphtali 12,000,
from the tribe of Manasseh 12,000,
⁷from the tribe of Simeon 12,000,
from the tribe of Levi 12,000,
from the tribe of Issachar 12,000,
⁸from the tribe of Zebulun 12,000,
from the tribe of Joseph 12,000,
from the tribe of Benjamin 12,000.

The Great Multitude in White Robes

⁹After this I looked and there before me was a great multitude that no one could count, from every nation, tribe, people and language, standing before the throne and in front of the Lamb. They were wearing white robes and were holding palm branches in their hands. ¹⁰And they cried out in a loud voice:

"Salvation belongs to our God,
who sits on the throne,
and to the Lamb."

¹¹All the angels were standing around the throne and around the elders and the four living creatures. They fell down on their faces before the throne and worshiped God, ¹²saying:

"Amen!
Praise and glory
and wisdom and thanks and honor
and power and strength
be to our God for ever and ever.
Amen!"

¹³Then one of the elders asked me, "These in white robes—who are they, and where did they come from?"

¹⁴I answered, "Sir, you know."

And he said, "These are they who have come out of the great tribulation; they have washed their robes and made them

God's people at prayer
PRACTICING FOR HEAVEN

REVELATION 7:9-17 This passage describes the one worship service we definitely don't want to miss. John saw a vision of the future; we can only imagine the actual event! What will it be like to join our voices with countless others, standing before God's throne, praising Him for His salvation? Whether we all instantly learn a new language for heaven or use our own, we'll all be saying the same thing—expressing our love, awe, and reverence to God.

That moment may be beyond our imaginations now, but we experience a touch of it whenever we worship God together with other believers. As we stand and sing together (no matter how many or how few), it's as if we're practicing for that day in heaven when we all will stand before God singing from the depths of our hearts with tears in our eyes for the joy we have in being with God for eternity. Then God will come and wipe away *all* our tears and welcome us to be with Him forever.

white in the blood of the Lamb. [15]Therefore,

> "they are before the throne of God
>   and serve him day and night in his
>   temple;
> and he who sits on the throne will
>   spread his tent over them.
> [16]Never again will they hunger;
>   never again will they thirst.
> The sun will not beat upon them,
>   nor any scorching heat.
> [17]For the Lamb at the center of the
>   throne will be their shepherd;
> he will lead them to springs of
>   living water.
> And God will wipe away every tear
>   from their eyes."

The Seventh Seal and the Golden Censer

8 When he opened the seventh seal, there was silence in heaven for about half an hour.

[2]And I saw the seven angels who stand before God, and to them were given seven trumpets.

[3]Another angel, who had a golden censer, came and stood at the altar. He was given much incense to offer, with the prayers of all the saints, on the golden altar before the throne. [4]The smoke of the incense, together with the prayers of the saints, went up before God from the angel's hand. [5]Then the angel took the censer, filled it with fire from the altar,

GOING *deeper*

Prayer Rises

READ AND CONSIDER: REVELATION 8:1-5

"The smoke of the incense, together with the prayers of the saints, went up before God from the angel's hand" (Revelation 8:4).

You've watched smoke rise from a lighted candle or from the chimney of a fireplace. It naturally goes up and disappears beyond sight. In his wonderful vision of heaven, John saw an angel carrying incense and the prayers of the saints. The aroma and smoke rising up from the angel's hand were offerings to God.

In the Old Testament, the incense that burned on the altar was also symbolic of prayers offered to God by the high priest: God directed the Israelites to place the altar for burning incense "in front of the curtain that is before the ark of the Testimony . . . where I will meet with you. Aaron must burn fragrant incense on the altar every morning when he tends the lamps. He must burn incense again when he lights the lamps at twilight so incense will burn regularly before the LORD for the generations to come" (Exodus 30:6-8).

This continued into the New Testament worship at the temple. Luke 1 describes the priest Zechariah (the father of John the Baptist) being chosen by lot to "go into the temple of the Lord and burn incense." Incense continued to be burned twice daily at the temple. And when the people saw the smoke rising, they prayed. Both the smoke and their prayers ascended to God's throne.

This is a particularly encouraging picture for us on those days when we feel as if our prayers don't have power enough to make it past the ceiling. As if they just hang there in space or evaporate into thin air. Or worse yet, as if they never even make it off the ground. At those times, it's wonderful to know that the distance our prayers travel does not depend on the fervency of our prayers or how loud or well we say them. Just as smoke rises, so do our prayers rise to heaven and to the ears of God, because that's what prayers born of faith do.

and hurled it on the earth; and there came peals of thunder, rumblings, flashes of lightning and an earthquake.

The Trumpets

⁶Then the seven angels who had the seven trumpets prepared to sound them.

⁷The first angel sounded his trumpet, and there came hail and fire mixed with blood, and it was hurled down upon the earth. A third of the earth was burned up, a third of the trees were burned up, and all the green grass was burned up.

⁸The second angel sounded his trumpet, and something like a huge mountain, all ablaze, was thrown into the sea. A third of the sea turned into blood, ⁹a third of the living creatures in the sea died, and a third of the ships were destroyed.

¹⁰The third angel sounded his trumpet, and a great star, blazing like a torch, fell from the sky on a third of the rivers and on the springs of water— ¹¹the name of the star is Wormwood.ᵃ A third of the waters turned bitter, and many people died from the waters that had become bitter.

¹²The fourth angel sounded his trumpet, and a third of the sun was struck, a third of the moon, and a third of the stars, so that a third of them turned dark. A third of the day was without light, and also a third of the night.

¹³As I watched, I heard an eagle that was flying in midair call out in a loud voice: "Woe! Woe! Woe to the inhabitants of the earth, because of the trumpet blasts about to be sounded by the other three angels!"

9 The fifth angel sounded his trumpet, and I saw a star that had fallen from the sky to the earth. The star was given the key to the shaft of the Abyss. ²When he opened the Abyss, smoke rose from it like the smoke from a gigantic furnace. The sun and sky were darkened by the smoke from the Abyss. ³And out of the smoke locusts came down upon the earth and were given power like that of scorpions of the earth. ⁴They were told not to harm the grass of the earth or any plant or tree, but only those people who did not have the seal of God on their foreheads. ⁵They were not given power to kill them, but only to torture them for five months. And the agony they suffered was like that of the sting of a scorpion when it strikes a man. ⁶During those days men will seek death, but will not find it; they will long to die, but death will elude them.

⁷The locusts looked like horses prepared for battle. On their heads they wore something like crowns of gold, and their faces resembled human faces. ⁸Their hair was like women's hair, and their teeth were like lions' teeth. ⁹They had breastplates like breastplates of iron, and the sound of their wings was like the thundering of many horses and chariots rushing into battle. ¹⁰They had tails and stings like scorpions, and in their tails they had power to torment people for five months. ¹¹They had as king over them the angel of the Abyss, whose name in Hebrew is Abaddon, and in Greek, Apollyon.ᵇ

¹²The first woe is past; two other woes are yet to come.

¹³The sixth angel sounded his trumpet, and I heard a voice coming from the hornsᶜ of the golden altar that is before God. ¹⁴It said to the sixth angel who had the trumpet, "Release the four angels who are bound at the great river Euphrates." ¹⁵And the four angels who had been kept ready for this very hour and day and month and year were released to kill a third of mankind. ¹⁶The number of the mounted troops was two hundred million. I heard their number.

¹⁷The horses and riders I saw in my vision looked like this: Their breastplates were fiery red, dark blue, and yellow as sulfur. The heads of the horses resembled the heads of lions, and out of their mouths came fire, smoke and sulfur. ¹⁸A third of mankind was killed by the three plagues of fire, smoke and sulfur that came out of their mouths. ¹⁹The power of the horses

---

ᵃ *11* That is, Bitterness   ᵇ *11* Abaddon and Apollyon mean *Destroyer.*   ᶜ *13* That is, projections was in their mouths and in their tails; for their tails were like snakes, having heads with which they inflict injury.

²⁰The rest of mankind that were not killed by these plagues still did not repent of the work of their hands; they did not stop worshiping demons, and idols of gold, silver, bronze, stone and wood— idols that cannot see or hear or walk. ²¹Nor did they repent of their murders, their magic arts, their sexual immorality or their thefts.

The Angel and the Little Scroll

10 Then I saw another mighty angel coming down from heaven. He was robed in a cloud, with a rainbow above his head; his face was like the sun, and his legs were like fiery pillars. ²He was holding a little scroll, which lay open in his hand. He planted his right foot on the sea and his left foot on the land, ³and he gave a loud shout like the roar of a lion. When he shouted, the voices of the seven thunders spoke. ⁴And when the seven thunders spoke, I was about to write; but I heard a voice from heaven say, "Seal up what the seven thunders have said and do not write it down."

⁵Then the angel I had seen standing on the sea and on the land raised his right hand to heaven. ⁶And he swore by him who lives for ever and ever, who created the heavens and all that is in them, the earth and all that is in it, and the sea and all that is in it, and said, "There will be no more delay! ⁷But in the days when the seventh angel is about to sound his trumpet, the mystery of God will be accomplished, just as he announced to his servants the prophets."

⁸Then the voice that I had heard from heaven spoke to me once more: "Go, take the scroll that lies open in the hand of the angel who is standing on the sea and on the land."

⁹So I went to the angel and asked him to give me the little scroll. He said to me, "Take it and eat it. It will turn your stomach sour, but in your mouth it will

be as sweet as honey." ¹⁰I took the little scroll from the angel's hand and ate it. It tasted as sweet as honey in my mouth, but when I had eaten it, my stomach turned sour. ¹¹Then I was told, "You must prophesy again about many peoples, nations, languages and kings."

The Two Witnesses

11 I was given a reed like a measuring rod and was told, "Go and measure the temple of God and the altar, and count the worshipers there. ²But exclude the outer court; do not measure it, because it has been given to the Gentiles. They will trample on the holy city for 42 months. ³And I will give power to my two witnesses, and they will prophesy for 1,260 days, clothed in sackcloth." ⁴These are the two olive trees and the two lampstands that stand before the Lord of the earth. ⁵If anyone tries to harm them, fire comes from their mouths and devours their enemies. This is how anyone who wants to harm them must die. ⁶These men have power to shut up the sky so that it will not rain during the time they are prophesying; and they have power to turn the waters into blood and to strike the earth with every kind of plague as often as they want.

⁷Now when they have finished their testimony, the beast that comes up from the Abyss will attack them, and overpower and kill them. ⁸Their bodies will lie in the street of the great city, which is figuratively called Sodom and Egypt, where also their Lord was crucified. ⁹For three and a half days men from every people, tribe, language and nation will gaze on their bodies and refuse them burial. ¹⁰The inhabitants of the earth will gloat over them and will celebrate by sending each other gifts, because these two prophets had tormented those who live on the earth.

¹¹But after the three and a half days a breath of life from God entered them, and they stood on their feet, and terror struck those who saw them. ¹²Then they

heard a loud voice from heaven saying to them, "Come up here." And they went up to heaven in a cloud, while their enemies looked on.

13 At that very hour there was a severe earthquake and a tenth of the city collapsed. Seven thousand people were killed in the earthquake, and the survivors were terrified and gave glory to the God of heaven.

14 The second woe has passed; the third woe is coming soon.

The Seventh Trumpet

15 The seventh angel sounded his trumpet, and there were loud voices in heaven, which said:

> "The kingdom of the world has
> become the kingdom of our
> Lord and of his Christ,
> and he will reign for ever and ever."

16 And the twenty-four elders, who were seated on their thrones before God, fell on their faces and worshiped God, 17 saying:

> "We give thanks to you, Lord God
> Almighty,
> the One who is and who was,
> because you have taken your great
> power
> and have begun to reign.
> 18 The nations were angry;
> and your wrath has come.
> The time has come for judging the
> dead,
> and for rewarding your servants the
> prophets
> and your saints and those who
> reverence your name,
> both small and great—
> and for destroying those who destroy
> the earth."

19 Then God's temple in heaven was opened, and within his temple was seen the ark of his covenant. And there came flashes of lightning, rumblings, peals of thunder, an earthquake and a great hailstorm.

The Woman and the Dragon

12 A great and wondrous sign appeared in heaven: a woman clothed with the sun, with the moon under her feet and a crown of twelve stars on her head. 2 She was pregnant and cried out in pain as she was about to give birth. 3 Then another sign appeared in heaven: an enormous red dragon with seven heads and ten horns and seven crowns on his heads. 4 His tail swept a third of the stars out of the sky and flung them to the earth. The dragon stood in front of the woman who was about to give birth, so that he might devour her child the moment it was born. 5 She gave birth to a son, a male child, who will rule all the nations with an iron scepter. And her child was snatched up to God and to his throne. 6 The woman fled into the desert to a place prepared for her by God, where she might be taken care of for 1,260 days.

7 And there was war in heaven. Michael and his angels fought against the dragon, and the dragon and his angels fought back. 8 But he was not strong enough, and they lost their place in heaven. 9 The great dragon was hurled down—that ancient serpent called the devil, or Satan, who leads the whole world astray. He was hurled to the earth, and his angels with him.

10 Then I heard a loud voice in heaven say:

> "Now have come the salvation and
> the power and the kingdom of
> our God,
> and the authority of his Christ.
> For the accuser of our brothers,
> who accuses them before our God
> day and night,
> has been hurled down.
> 11 They overcame him
> by the blood of the Lamb
> and by the word of their testimony;
> they did not love their lives so much
> as to shrink from death.
> 12 Therefore rejoice, you heavens
> and you who dwell in them!

But woe to the earth and the sea,
  because the devil has gone down
    to you!
He is filled with fury,
  because he knows that his time is
    short."

[13]When the dragon saw that he had been hurled to the earth, he pursued the woman who had given birth to the male child. [14]The woman was given the two wings of a great eagle, so that she might fly to the place prepared for her in the desert, where she would be taken care of for a time, times and half a time, out of the serpent's reach. [15]Then from his mouth the serpent spewed water like a river, to overtake the woman and sweep her away with the torrent. [16]But the earth helped the woman by opening its mouth and swallowing the river that the dragon had spewed out of his mouth. [17]Then the dragon was enraged at the woman and went off to make war against the rest of her offspring—those who obey God's commandments and hold to the testimony of Jesus. [1]And the dragon[a] stood on the shore of the sea.

The Beast out of the Sea

And I saw a beast coming out of the sea. He had ten horns and seven heads, with ten crowns on his horns, and on each head a blasphemous name. [2]The beast I saw resembled a leopard, but had feet like those of a bear and a mouth like that of a lion. The dragon gave the beast his power and his throne and great authority. [3]One of the heads of the beast seemed to have had a fatal wound, but the fatal wound had been healed. The whole world was astonished and followed the beast. [4]Men worshiped the dragon be-cause he had given authority to the beast, and they also worshiped the beast and asked, "Who is like the beast? Who can make war against him?"

[5]The beast was given a mouth to ut-ter proud words and blasphemies and to exercise his authority for forty-two months. [6]He opened his mouth to blas-pheme God, and to slander his name and his dwelling place and those who live in heaven. [7]He was given power to make war against the saints and to conquer them. And he was given authority over every tribe, people, language and nation. [8]All inhabitants of the earth will worship the beast—all whose names have not been written in the book of life belong-ing to the Lamb that was slain from the creation of the world.[b]

[9]He who has an ear, let him hear.

[10]If anyone is to go into captivity,
  into captivity he will go.
If anyone is to be killed[c] with the
    sword,
  with the sword he will be killed.

This calls for patient endurance and faith-fulness on the part of the saints.

The Beast out of the Earth

[11]Then I saw another beast, coming out of the earth. He had two horns like a lamb, but he spoke like a dragon. [12]He ex-ercised all the authority of the first beast on his behalf, and made the earth and its inhabitants worship the first beast, whose fatal wound had been healed. [13]And he performed great and miraculous signs, even causing fire to come down from heaven to earth in full view of men. [14]Be-cause of the signs he was given power to do on behalf of the first beast, he deceived the inhabitants of the earth. He ordered them to set up an image in honor of the beast who was wounded by the sword and yet lived. [15]He was given power to give breath to the image of the first beast, so that it could speak and cause all

---

[a] 1 Some late manuscripts *And I*   [b] 8 Or *written from the creation of the world in the book of life belonging to the Lamb that was slain*   [c] 10 Some manuscripts *anyone kills*

who refused to worship the image to be killed. 16He also forced everyone, small and great, rich and poor, free and slave, to receive a mark on his right hand or on his forehead, 17so that no one could buy or sell unless he had the mark, which is the name of the beast or the number of his name.

18This calls for wisdom. If anyone has insight, let him calculate the number of the beast, for it is man's number. His number is 666.

The Lamb and the 144,000

14 Then I looked, and there before me was the Lamb, standing on Mount Zion, and with him 144,000 who had his name and his Father's name written on their foreheads. 2And I heard a sound from heaven like the roar of rushing waters and like a loud peal of thunder. The sound I heard was like that of harpists playing their harps. 3And they sang a new song before the throne and before the four living creatures and the elders. No one could learn the song except the 144,000 who had been redeemed from the earth. 4These are those who did not defile themselves with women, for they kept themselves pure. They follow the Lamb wherever he goes. They were purchased from among men and offered as firstfruits to God and the Lamb. 5No lie was found in their mouths; they are blameless.

The Three Angels

6Then I saw another angel flying in mid-air, and he had the eternal gospel to proclaim to those who live on the earth—to every nation, tribe, language and people. 7He said in a loud voice, "Fear God and give him glory, because the hour of his judgment has come. Worship him who made the heavens, the earth, the sea and the springs of water."

8A second angel followed and said, "Fallen! Fallen is Babylon the Great, which made all the nations drink the maddening wine of her adulteries."

9A third angel followed them and said in a loud voice: "If anyone worships the beast and his image and receives his mark on the forehead or on the hand, 10he, too, will drink of the wine of God's fury, which has been poured full strength into the cup of his wrath. He will be tormented with burning sulfur in the presence of the holy angels and of the Lamb. 11And the smoke of their torment rises for ever and ever. There is no rest day or night for those who worship the beast and his image, or for anyone who receives the mark of his name." 12This calls for patient endurance on the part of the saints who obey God's commandments and remain faithful to Jesus.

> ## Prayer is . . .
> *something you can do in your mind, and God will hear your spirit talking to Him.*

13Then I heard a voice from heaven say, "Write: Blessed are the dead who die in the Lord from now on."

"Yes," says the Spirit, "they will rest from their labor, for their deeds will follow them."

The Harvest of the Earth

14I looked, and there before me was a white cloud, and seated on the cloud was one "like a son of man"ª with a crown of gold on his head and a sharp sickle in his hand. 15Then another angel came out of the temple and called in a loud voice to him who was sitting on the cloud, "Take your sickle and reap, because the time to reap has come, for the harvest of the earth is ripe." 16So he who was seated on the cloud swung his sickle over the earth, and the earth was harvested.

17Another angel came out of the temple

ª *14* Daniel 7:13

in heaven, and he too had a sharp sickle. [18]Still another angel, who had charge of the fire, came from the altar and called in a loud voice to him who had the sharp sickle, "Take your sharp sickle and gather the clusters of grapes from the earth's vine, because its grapes are ripe." [19]The angel swung his sickle on the earth, gathered its grapes and threw them into the great winepress of God's wrath. [20]They were trampled in the winepress outside the city, and blood flowed out of the press, rising as high as the horses' bridles for a distance of 1,600 stadia.[a]

Seven Angels With Seven Plagues

15 I saw in heaven another great and marvelous sign: seven angels with the seven last plagues—last, because with them God's wrath is completed. [2]And I saw what looked like a sea of glass mixed with fire and, standing beside the sea, those who had been victorious over the beast and his image and over the number of his name. They held harps given them by God [3]and sang the song of Moses the servant of God and the song of the Lamb:

"Great and marvelous are your deeds,
    Lord God Almighty.
Just and true are your ways,
    King of the ages.
[4]Who will not fear you, O Lord,
    and bring glory to your name?
For you alone are holy.
All nations will come
    and worship before you,
for your righteous acts have been
    revealed."

[5]After this I looked and in heaven the temple, that is, the tabernacle of the Testimony, was opened. [6]Out of the temple came the seven angels with the seven plagues. They were dressed in clean, shining linen and wore golden sashes around their chests. [7]Then one of the four living creatures gave to the seven angels seven golden bowls filled with the wrath of God, who lives for ever and ever. [8]And the temple was filled with smoke from the glory of God and from his power, and no one could enter the temple until the seven plagues of the seven angels were completed.

The Seven Bowls of God's Wrath

16 Then I heard a loud voice from the temple saying to the seven angels, "Go, pour out the seven bowls of God's wrath on the earth."

[2]The first angel went and poured out his bowl on the land, and ugly and painful sores broke out on the people who had the mark of the beast and worshiped his image.

[3]The second angel poured out his bowl on the sea, and it turned into blood like that of a dead man, and every living thing in the sea died.

[4]The third angel poured out his bowl on the rivers and springs of water, and they became blood. [5]Then I heard the angel in charge of the waters say:

"You are just in these judgments,
    you who are and who were, the
        Holy One,
    because you have so judged;
[6]for they have shed the blood of your
        saints and prophets,
    and you have given them blood to
        drink as they deserve."

[7]And I heard the altar respond:

"Yes, Lord God Almighty,
    true and just are your judgments."

[8]The fourth angel poured out his bowl on the sun, and the sun was given power to scorch people with fire. [9]They were seared by the intense heat and they cursed the name of God, who had control over these plagues, but they refused to repent and glorify him.

[10]The fifth angel poured out his bowl on the throne of the beast, and his kingdom was plunged into darkness. Men gnawed their tongues in agony [11]and

[a]20 That is, about 180 miles (about 300 kilometers)

cursed the God of heaven because of their pains and their sores, but they refused to repent of what they had done.

12 The sixth angel poured out his bowl on the great river Euphrates, and its water was dried up to prepare the way for the kings from the East. 13 Then I saw three evil[a] spirits that looked like frogs; they came out of the mouth of the dragon, out of the mouth of the beast and out of the mouth of the false prophet. 14 They are spirits of demons performing miraculous signs, and they go out to the kings of the whole world, to gather them for the battle on the great day of God Almighty.

15 "Behold, I come like a thief! Blessed is he who stays awake and keeps his clothes with him, so that he may not go naked and be shamefully exposed."

16 Then they gathered the kings together to the place that in Hebrew is called Armageddon.

17 The seventh angel poured out his bowl into the air, and out of the temple came a loud voice from the throne, saying, "It is done!" 18 Then there came flashes of lightning, rumblings, peals of thunder and a severe earthquake. No earthquake like it has ever occurred since man has been on earth, so tremendous was the quake. 19 The great city split into three parts, and the cities of the nations collapsed. God remembered Babylon the Great and gave her the cup filled with the wine of the fury of his wrath. 20 Every island fled away and the mountains could not be found. 21 From the sky huge hailstones of about a hundred pounds each fell upon men. And they cursed God on account of the plague of hail, because the plague was so terrible.

The Woman on the Beast

17 One of the seven angels who had the seven bowls came and said to me, "Come, I will show you the punishment of the great prostitute, who sits on many waters. 2 With her the kings of the earth committed adultery and the inhabitants of the earth were intoxicated with the wine of her adulteries."

3 Then the angel carried me away in the Spirit into a desert. There I saw a woman sitting on a scarlet beast that was covered with blasphemous names and had seven heads and ten horns. 4 The woman was dressed in purple and scarlet, and was glittering with gold, precious stones and pearls. She held a golden cup in her hand, filled with abominable things and the filth of her adulteries. 5 This title was written on her forehead:

MYSTERY
BABYLON THE GREAT
THE MOTHER OF PROSTITUTES
AND OF THE ABOMINATIONS OF THE EARTH.

6 I saw that the woman was drunk with the blood of the saints, the blood of those who bore testimony to Jesus.

When I saw her, I was greatly astonished. 7 Then the angel said to me: "Why are you astonished? I will explain to you the mystery of the woman and of the beast she rides, which has the seven heads and ten horns. 8 The beast, which you saw, once was, now is not, and will come up out of the Abyss and go to his destruction. The inhabitants of the earth whose names have not been written in the book of life from the creation of the world will be astonished when they see the beast, because he once was, now is not, and yet will come.

9 "This calls for a mind with wisdom. The seven heads are seven hills on which the woman sits. 10 They are also seven kings. Five have fallen, one is, the other has not yet come; but when he does come, he must remain for a little while. 11 The beast who once was, and now is not, is an eighth king. He belongs to the seven and is going to his destruction.

12 "The ten horns you saw are ten kings who have not yet received a kingdom, but who for one hour will receive authority as kings along with the beast.

---

a 13 Greek unclean

[13] They have one purpose and will give their power and authority to the beast. [14] They will make war against the Lamb, but the Lamb will overcome them because he is Lord of lords and King of kings—and with him will be his called, chosen and faithful followers."

[15] Then the angel said to me, "The waters you saw, where the prostitute sits, are peoples, multitudes, nations and languages. [16] The beast and the ten horns you saw will hate the prostitute. They will bring her to ruin and leave her naked; they will eat her flesh and burn her with fire. [17] For God has put it into their hearts to accomplish his purpose by agreeing to give the beast their power to rule, until God's words are fulfilled. [18] The woman you saw is the great city that rules over the kings of the earth."

The Fall of Babylon

18 After this I saw another angel coming down from heaven. He had great authority, and the earth was illuminated by his splendor. [2] With a mighty voice he shouted:

"Fallen! Fallen is Babylon the Great!
  She has become a home for demons
and a haunt for every evil[a] spirit,
  a haunt for every unclean and
    detestable bird.
[3] For all the nations have drunk
  the maddening wine of her
    adulteries.
The kings of the earth committed
    adultery with her,
  and the merchants of the earth
    grew rich from her excessive
    luxuries."

[4] Then I heard another voice from heaven say:

"Come out of her, my people,
  so that you will not share in her
    sins,
  so that you will not receive any of
    her plagues;

[5] for her sins are piled up to heaven,
  and God has remembered her
    crimes.
[6] Give back to her as she has given;
  pay her back double for what she
    has done.
  Mix her a double portion from her
    own cup.
[7] Give her as much torture and grief
  as the glory and luxury she gave
    herself.
In her heart she boasts,
  'I sit as queen; I am not a widow,
  and I will never mourn.'
[8] Therefore in one day her plagues will
    overtake her:
  death, mourning and famine.
She will be consumed by fire,
  for mighty is the Lord God who
    judges her.

[9] "When the kings of the earth who committed adultery with her and shared her luxury see the smoke of her burning, they will weep and mourn over her. [10] Terrified at her torment, they will stand far off and cry:

"'Woe! Woe, O great city,
  O Babylon, city of power!
In one hour your doom has come!'

[11] "The merchants of the earth will weep and mourn over her because no one buys their cargoes any more— [12] cargoes of gold, silver, precious stones and pearls; fine linen, purple, silk and scarlet cloth; every sort of citron wood, and articles of every kind made of ivory, costly wood, bronze, iron and marble; [13] cargoes of cinnamon and spice, of incense, myrrh and frankincense, of wine and olive oil, of fine flour and wheat; cattle and sheep; horses and carriages; and bodies and souls of men.

[14] "They will say, 'The fruit you longed for is gone from you. All your riches and splendor have vanished, never to be recovered.' [15] The merchants who sold these things and gained their wealth from

---

a 2 Greek unclean

her will stand far off, terrified at her torment. They will weep and mourn ¹⁶and cry out:

"'Woe! Woe, O great city,
   dressed in fine linen, purple and scarlet,
   and glittering with gold, precious stones and pearls!
¹⁷In one hour such great wealth has been brought to ruin!'

"Every sea captain, and all who travel by ship, the sailors, and all who earn their living from the sea, will stand far off. ¹⁸When they see the smoke of her burning, they will exclaim, 'Was there ever a city like this great city?' ¹⁹They will throw dust on their heads, and with weeping and mourning cry out:

"'Woe! Woe, O great city,
   where all who had ships on the sea
   became rich through her wealth!
In one hour she has been brought to ruin!
²⁰Rejoice over her, O heaven!
   Rejoice, saints and apostles and prophets!
God has judged her for the way she treated you.'"

²¹Then a mighty angel picked up a boulder the size of a large millstone and threw it into the sea, and said:

"With such violence
   the great city of Babylon will be thrown down,
   never to be found again.
²²The music of harpists and musicians,
   flute players and trumpeters,
   will never be heard in you again.
No workman of any trade
   will ever be found in you again.
The sound of a millstone
   will never be heard in you again.
²³The light of a lamp
   will never shine in you again.
The voice of bridegroom and bride
   will never be heard in you again.

Your merchants were the world's great men.
By your magic spell all the nations were led astray.
²⁴In her was found the blood of prophets and of the saints,
   and of all who have been killed on the earth."

Hallelujah!

19 After this I heard what sounded like the roar of a great multitude in heaven shouting:

"Hallelujah!
Salvation and glory and power belong to our God,
²   for true and just are his judgments.
He has condemned the great prostitute
   who corrupted the earth by her adulteries.
He has avenged on her the blood of his servants."

³And again they shouted:

"Hallelujah!
The smoke from her goes up for ever and ever."

⁴The twenty-four elders and the four living creatures fell down and worshiped God, who was seated on the throne. And they cried:

"Amen, Hallelujah!"

⁵Then a voice came from the throne, saying:

"Praise our God,
   all you his servants,
you who fear him,
   both small and great!"

⁶Then I heard what sounded like a great multitude, like the roar of rushing waters and like loud peals of thunder, shouting:

"Hallelujah!
   For our Lord God Almighty reigns.
⁷Let us rejoice and be glad

GOING *deeper*

Praising God for the Future

READ AND CONSIDER: REVELATION 19:1-10

"Let us rejoice and be glad and give him glory! For the wedding of the Lamb has come, and his bride has made herself ready" (Revelation 19:7).

We need to praise God for who He *is*. We must praise God for what He has *done*. We should also praise God for what He's *going* to do. The book of Revelation paints a picture of a future world. A world put right side up. It describes a wedding feast to which we are invited, a feast that inaugurates a new world where sadness and fear have no place.

Praising God for what we know is coming doesn't mean that we don't live fully in this day and in this moment. Instead, it means that part of the sweetness of this moment is the anticipation of the moments to come. In fact, knowing what is ahead allows us to better savor what we have, to endure the difficulties, and to continue on with courage.

Most often we praise God for the good things in our lives and the ways He has provided for us. This is right to do. But along with that, let's not forget to praise God that He will one day redeem this world in every possible way. Let's thank Him ahead of time for the feast that He will lay out before us—His beloved children—on the day when He brings all of history to a close and eternity with Him begins.

Let us rejoice in prayer right now that the wedding of the Lamb is coming, and we, as His bride, are being made ready to be with Him. Let us praise Him that our future is secure and good. Let's worship Him now and thank Him that we are going to have the privilege of worshiping Him in heaven forever.

and give him glory!
For the wedding of the Lamb has
come,
and his bride has made herself ready.
[8]Fine linen, bright and clean,
was given her to wear."
(Fine linen stands for the righteous acts of the saints.)

[9]Then the angel said to me, "Write: 'Blessed are those who are invited to the wedding supper of the Lamb!'" And he added, "These are the true words of God."

[10]At this I fell at his feet to worship him. But he said to me, "Do not do it! I am a fellow servant with you and with your brothers who hold to the testimony of Jesus. Worship God! For the testimony of Jesus is the spirit of prophecy."

The Rider on the White Horse

[11]I saw heaven standing open and there before me was a white horse, whose rider is called Faithful and True. With justice he judges and makes war. [12]His eyes are like blazing fire, and on his head are many crowns. He has a name written on him that no one knows but he himself. [13]He is dressed in a robe dipped in blood, and his name is the Word of God. [14]The armies of heaven were following him, riding on white horses and dressed in fine linen, white and clean. [15]Out of his mouth comes a sharp sword with which to strike down the nations. "He will rule them with an iron scepter."[a] He treads the winepress of the fury of the wrath of God Almighty. [16]On his robe and on his thigh he has this name written:

---

a *15* Psalm 2:9

KING OF KINGS AND LORD OF LORDS.

17And I saw an angel standing in the sun, who cried in a loud voice to all the birds flying in midair, "Come, gather together for the great supper of God, 18so that you may eat the flesh of kings, generals, and mighty men, of horses and their riders, and the flesh of all people, free and slave, small and great."

19Then I saw the beast and the kings of the earth and their armies gathered together to make war against the rider on the horse and his army. 20But the beast was captured, and with him the false prophet who had performed the miraculous signs on his behalf. With these signs he had deluded those who had received the mark of the beast and worshiped his image. The two of them were thrown alive into the fiery lake of burning sulfur. 21The rest of them were killed with the sword that came out of the mouth of the rider on the horse, and all the birds gorged themselves on their flesh.

The Thousand Years

20 And I saw an angel coming down out of heaven, having the key to the Abyss and holding in his hand a great chain. 2He seized the dragon, that ancient serpent, who is the devil, or Satan, and bound him for a thousand years. 3He threw him into the Abyss, and locked and sealed it over him, to keep him from deceiving the nations anymore until the thousand years were ended. After that, he must be set free for a short time.

4I saw thrones on which were seated those who had been given authority to judge. And I saw the souls of those who had been beheaded because of their testimony for Jesus and because of the word of God. They had not worshiped the beast or his image and had not received his mark on their foreheads or their hands. They came to life and reigned with Christ a thousand years. 5(The rest of the dead did not come to life until the thousand years were ended.) This is the first resurrection.

6Blessed and holy are those who have part in the first resurrection. The second death has no power over them, but they will be priests of God and of Christ and will reign with him for a thousand years.

Satan's Doom

7When the thousand years are over, Satan will be released from his prison 8and will go out to deceive the nations in the four corners of the earth—Gog and Magog—to gather them for battle. In number they are like the sand on the seashore. 9They marched across the breadth of the earth and surrounded the camp of God's people, the city he loves. But fire came down from heaven and devoured them. 10And the devil, who deceived them, was thrown into the lake of burning sulfur, where the beast and the false prophet had been thrown. They will be tormented day and night for ever and ever.

The Dead Are Judged

11Then I saw a great white throne and him who was seated on it. Earth and sky fled from his presence, and there was no place for them. 12And I saw the dead, great and small, standing before the throne, and books were opened. Another book was opened, which is the book of life. The dead were judged according to what they had done as recorded in the books. 13The sea gave up the dead that were in it, and death and Hades gave up the dead that were in them, and each person was judged according to what he had done. 14Then death and Hades were thrown into the lake of fire. The lake of fire is the second death. 15If anyone's name was not found written in the book of life, he was thrown into the lake of fire.

The New Jerusalem

21 Then I saw a new heaven and a new earth, for the first heaven and the first earth had passed away, and there was no longer any sea. 2I saw the Holy City, the new Jerusalem, coming down out of heaven from God, prepared as a bride beautifully dressed for her hus-

band. ³And I heard a loud voice from the throne saying, "Now the dwelling of God is with men, and he will live with them. They will be his people, and God himself will be with them and be their God. ⁴He will wipe every tear from their eyes. There will be no more death or mourning or crying or pain, for the old order of things has passed away."

Praying Revelation 21:4-5

Lord, thank You that You make all things new, and one day I will be with You and there will be no more death or sorrow or pain or tears.

⁵He who was seated on the throne said, "I am making everything new!" Then he said, "Write this down, for these words are trustworthy and true."

⁶He said to me: "It is done. I am the Alpha and the Omega, the Beginning and the End. To him who is thirsty I will give to drink without cost from the spring of the water of life. ⁷He who overcomes will inherit all this, and I will be his God and he will be my son. ⁸But the cowardly, the unbelieving, the vile, the murderers, the sexually immoral, those who practice magic arts, the idolaters and all liars— their place will be in the fiery lake of burning sulfur. This is the second death."

⁹One of the seven angels who had the seven bowls full of the seven last plagues came and said to me, "Come, I will show you the bride, the wife of the Lamb." ¹⁰And he carried me away in the Spirit to a mountain great and high, and showed me the Holy City, Jerusalem, coming down out of heaven from God. ¹¹It shone with the glory of God, and its brilliance was like that of a very precious jewel, like a jasper, clear as crystal. ¹²It had a great, high wall with twelve gates, and with twelve angels at the gates. On the gates were written the names of the twelve tribes of Israel. ¹³There were three gates on the east, three on the north, three on the south and three on the west. ¹⁴The wall of the city had twelve foundations, and on them were the names of the twelve apostles of the Lamb.

¹⁵The angel who talked with me had a measuring rod of gold to measure the city, its gates and its walls. ¹⁶The city was laid out like a square, as long as it was wide. He measured the city with the rod and found it to be 12,000 stadia[a] in length, and as wide and high as it is long. ¹⁷He measured its wall and it was 144 cubits[b] thick,[c] by man's measurement, which the angel was using. ¹⁸The wall was made of jasper, and the city of pure gold, as pure as glass. ¹⁹The foundations of the city walls were decorated with every kind of precious stone. The first foundation was jasper, the second sapphire, the third chalcedony, the fourth emerald, ²⁰the fifth sardonyx, the sixth carnelian, the seventh chrysolite, the eighth beryl, the ninth topaz, the tenth chrysoprase, the eleventh jacinth, and the twelfth amethyst.[d] ²¹The twelve gates were twelve pearls, each gate made of a single pearl. The great street of the city was of pure gold, like transparent glass.

²²I did not see a temple in the city, because the Lord God Almighty and the Lamb are its temple. ²³The city does not need the sun or the moon to shine on it, for the glory of God gives it light, and the Lamb is its lamp. ²⁴The nations will walk by its light, and the kings of the earth will bring their splendor into it. ²⁵On no day will its gates ever be shut, for there will be no night there. ²⁶The glory and honor of the nations will be brought into it. ²⁷Nothing impure will ever enter it, nor will anyone who does what is shameful or deceitful, but only those whose names are written in the Lamb's book of life.

The River of Life

22 Then the angel showed me the river of the water of life, as clear as crystal, flowing from the throne of God

---

[a] *16* That is, about 1,400 miles (about 2,200 kilometers)   [b] *17* That is, about 200 feet (about 65 meters)   [c] *17* Or *high*
[d] *20* The precise identification of some of these precious stones is uncertain.

and of the Lamb ²down the middle of the great street of the city. On each side of the river stood the tree of life, bearing twelve crops of fruit, yielding its fruit every month. And the leaves of the tree are for the healing of the nations. ³No longer will there be any curse. The throne of God and of the Lamb will be in the city, and his servants will serve him. ⁴They will see his face, and his name will be on their foreheads. ⁵There will be no more night. They will not need the light of a lamp or the light of the sun, for the Lord God will give them light. And they will reign for ever and ever.

⁶The angel said to me, "These words are trustworthy and true. The Lord, the God of the spirits of the prophets, sent his angel to show his servants the things that must soon take place."

Prayer is . . .
something God has called you to do.

Jesus Is Coming

⁷"Behold, I am coming soon! Blessed is he who keeps the words of the prophecy in this book."

⁸I, John, am the one who heard and saw these things. And when I had heard and seen them, I fell down to worship at the feet of the angel who had been showing them to me. ⁹But he said to me, "Do not do it! I am a fellow servant with you and with your brothers the prophets and of all who keep the words of this book. Worship God!"

¹⁰Then he told me, "Do not seal up the words of the prophecy of this book,

because the time is near. ¹¹Let him who does wrong continue to do wrong; let him who is vile continue to be vile; let him who does right continue to do right; and let him who is holy continue to be holy."

¹²"Behold, I am coming soon! My reward is with me, and I will give to everyone according to what he has done. ¹³I am the Alpha and the Omega, the First and the Last, the Beginning and the End.

¹⁴"Blessed are those who wash their robes, that they may have the right to the tree of life and may go through the gates into the city. ¹⁵Outside are the dogs, those who practice magic arts, the sexually immoral, the murderers, the idolaters and everyone who loves and practices falsehood.

¹⁶"I, Jesus, have sent my angel to give youᵃ this testimony for the churches. I am the Root and the Offspring of David, and the bright Morning Star."

¹⁷The Spirit and the bride say, "Come!" And let him who hears say, "Come!" Whoever is thirsty, let him come; and whoever wishes, let him take the free gift of the water of life.

¹⁸I warn everyone who hears the words of the prophecy of this book: If anyone adds anything to them, God will add to him the plagues described in this book. ¹⁹And if anyone takes words away from this book of prophecy, God will take away from him his share in the tree of life and in the holy city, which are described in this book.

²⁰He who testifies to these things says, "Yes, I am coming soon."

Amen. Come, Lord Jesus.

²¹The grace of the Lord Jesus be with God's people. Amen.

ᵃ *16* The Greek is plural.

TABLE OF *Weights and Measures*

BIBLICAL UNIT	APPROXIMATE AMERICAN EQUIVALENT	APPROXIMATE METRIC EQUIVALENT
WEIGHTS		
talent (60 minas)	75 pounds	34 kilograms
mina (50 shekels)	1¼ pounds	0.6 kilogram
shekel (2 bekas)	²/₅ ounce	11.5 grams
pim (²/₃ shekel)	¹/₃ ounce	7.6 grams
beka (10 gerahs)	¹/₅ ounce	5.5 grams
gerah	¹/₅₀ ounce	0.6 gram
LENGTH		
cubit	18 inches	0.5 meter
span	9 inches	23 centimeters
handbreadth	3 inches	8 centimeters
CAPACITY		
Dry Measure		
cor [homer] (10 ephahs)	6 bushels	220 liters
lethek (5 ephahs)	3 bushels	110 liters
ephah (10 omers)	³/₅ bushels	22 liters
seah (¹/₃ ephah)	7 quarts	7.3 liters
omer (¹/₁₀ ephah)	2 quarts	2 liters
cab (¹/₁₈ ephah)	1 quart	1 liter
Liquid Measure bath (1 ephah)	6 gallons	22 liters
hin (¹/₆ bath)	4 quarts	4 liters
log (¹/₇₂ bath)	¹/₃ quart	0.3 liter

The figures of the table are calculated on the basis of a shekel equaling 11.5 grams, a cubit equaling 18 inches and an ephah equaling 22 liters. The quart referred to is either a dry quart (slightly larger than a liter) or a liquid quart (slightly smaller than a liter), whichever is applicable. The ton referred to in the footnotes is the American ton of 2,000 pounds. Since most readers are more familiar with dry measures being given in weight rather than capacity (bushel, quart), dry measures have been converted in the footnotes to approximate weights.

This table is based upon the best available information, but it is not intended to be mathematically precise; like the measurement equivalents in the footnotes, it merely gives approximate amounts and distances. Weights and measures differed somewhat at various times and places in the ancient world. There is uncertainty particularly about the ephah and the bath; further discoveries may shed more light on these units of capacity.

INDEX TO THE *Going Deeper Notes*

INDEX TO THE *God's People at Prayer Notes*

INDEX TO THE *From Stormie's Heart Articles*

God's Promises About Prayer

God sees our tears and hears our prayers (2 Kings 20:5, page 477).

We can pray for our land and God will hear us (2 Chronicles 7:14, page 535).

The Lord will hear when we call to Him (Psalm 4:3, page 660).

We can call on the Lord, who is worthy of praise, and He saves us (Psalm 18:2-3, page 669).

When we acknowledge our sin, He forgives us (Psalm 32:5, page 680).

When we seek the Lord, He will deliver us from our fears (Psalm 34:4, page 682).

The Lord is attentive to our cries (Psalm 34:15-19, page 683).

God hears our cry and comes to our rescue (Psalm 40:1-3, page 688).

We can call on God in the day of trouble, and He will deliver us (Psalm 50:14-15, page 695).

At evening, morning, and noon—call and He will hear (Psalm 55:16-18, page 698).

God loves it when we praise Him (Psalm 100:4, page 731).

When we cry out to God, He will bring us out of the darkness (Psalm 107:13-14, page 741).

In the day when we cry out, He will answer (Psalm 138:1-3, page 761).

When we call out for wisdom, God gives it (Proverbs 2:3-6, page 771).

When we confess and renounce sin, we find mercy (Proverbs 28:13, page 803).

When we hope in the Lord, He renews our strength (Isaiah 40:31, page 878).

When we call and pray, He will listen (Jeremiah 29:12-13, page 959).

When we call to God, He will answer and show us great things (Jeremiah 33:3, page 966).

We can bring our children before the Lord (Lamentations 2:19, page 1000).

The Father knows our needs even before we ask (Matthew 6:5-8, page 1178).

Ask and it will be given; seek and we will find; knock and the door will be opened (Matthew 7:7, page 1180).

We need not be afraid of God's answers; He promises to give good gifts (Matthew 7:9-11, page 1180).

We must not only pray, but we must also act on what God tells us to do (Matthew 7:21, page 1181).

There is great power when even two or three gather in His name (Matthew 18:19-20, page 1198).

If we believe, we will receive what we ask for (Matthew 21:22, page 1201; Mark 11:23-24, page 1234).

We must forgive others so that our heavenly Father will forgive us (Mark 11:25, page 1234).

If we ask anything in His name, He will do it (John 14:13-14, page 1315).

If we remain in Him, He will answer our prayers (John 15:7, page 1316).

Ask and receive, and our joy will be complete (John 16:24, page 1318).

When we don't know what we ought to pray for, the Holy Spirit intercedes for us (Romans 8:26-28, page 1382).

God will give us peace when we give our requests to Him (Philippians 4:6-7, page 1445).

We should pray continually (1 Thessalonians 5:17, page 1460).

We can pray for others, that God will fulfill His purposes in them (2 Thessalonians 1:11, page 1461).

God will strengthen and protect us from the evil one (2 Thessalonians 3:2-3, page 1462).

We can approach the throne of grace with confidence (Hebrews 4:14-16, page 1484).

We should ask in faith, without doubting (James 1:6-8, page 1496).

Come near to God and He will come near to you (James 4:8, page 1499).

The prayer of a righteous person is powerful and effective (James 5:16, page 1502).

We can cast all of our anxiety on Him because He cares for us (1 Peter 5:7, page 1509).

If we confess our sins, God will forgive and purify us (1 John 1:8-9, page 1514).

We will receive His answers to our prayers because we obey and please Him (1 John 3:22, page 1518).

When we ask, God hears and promises to answer (1 John 5:14-15, page 1519).

The NIV Concordance, created by Edward W. Goodrick and John R. Kohlenberger III, has been developed specifically for use with the New International Version. Like all concordances, it is a special index which contains an alphabetical listing of words used in the Bible text. By looking up key words, readers can find verses and passages for which they remember a word or two but not their location.

This concordance contains 2,000 word entries, with some 13,000 Scripture references. Each word entry is followed by the Scripture references in which that particular word is found, as well as by a brief excerpt from the surrounding context. The first letter of the entry word is italicized to conserve space and to allow for a longer context excerpt. Variant spellings due to number and tense and compound forms follow the entry in parentheses, and direct the reader to check other forms of that word in locating a passage.

This concordance contains a number of "block entries," which highlight some of the key events and characteristics in the lives of certain Bible figures. The descriptive phrases replace the brief context surrounding each occurrence of the name. In those instances where more than one Bible character has the same name, that name is placed under one block entry, and each person is given a number (1), (2), etc. Insignificant names are not included.

Word or block entries marked with an asterisk (*) list every verse in the Bible in which the word appears.

Two entries are marked with a dagger (†) and two with a double-dagger (‡). LORD† and LORD'S† list occurrences of the title "Lord," spelled "Lord" and "lord," "Lord's" and "lord's" in the NIV. LORD‡ and LORD'S‡ list occurrences of the proper name of God, *Yahweh*, spelled "LORD" and "LORD'S" in the NIV. See the Preface to the New International Version on page iii.

This concordance is a valuable tool for Bible study. While one of its key purposes is to help the reader find forgotten references to verses, it can also be used to do word studies and to locate and trace biblical themes. Be sure to use this concordance as more than just a verse finder. Whenever you look up a verse, aim to discover the intended meaning of the verse in context. Give special attention to the flow of thought from the beginning of the passage to the end.

AARON
Priesthood of (Ex 28:1; Nu 17; Heb 5:1-4; 7), garments (Ex 28; 39), consecration (Ex 29), ordination (Lev 8).

Spokesman for Moses (Ex 4:14-16, 27-31; 7:1-2). Supported Moses' hands in battle (Ex 17:8-13). Built golden calf (Ex 32; Dt 9:20). Talked against Moses (Nu 12). Priesthood opposed (Nu 16); staff budded (Nu 17). Forbidden to enter land (Nu 20:1-12). Death (Nu 20:22-29; 33:38-39).

ABANDON
Dt   4:31 he will not-*a* or destroy you
1Ti   4: 1 in later times some will-*a* the faith

ABBA
Ro   8:15 And by him we cry,—"*A*, Father."
Gal   4: 6 the Spirit who calls out,—"*A*, Father

ABEL
Second son of Adam (Ge 4:2). Offered sacrifice (Ge 4:4; Heb 11:4). Murdered by Cain (Ge 4:8; Mt 23:35; Lk 11:51; 1Jn 3:12).

ABHORS
Pr 11: 1 The LORD-*a* dishonest scales,

ABIGAIL
Wife of Nabal (1Sa 25:30); pled for his life with David (1Sa 25:14-35). Became David's wife (1Sa 25:36-42).

ABIJAH
Son of Rehoboam; king of Judah (1Ki 14:31-15:8; 2Ch 12:16-14:1).

ABILITY (ABLE)
Ezr   2:69 According to their-*a* they gave
2Co   1: 8 far beyond our-*a* to endure,
        8: 3 were able, and even beyond their-*a*.

ABIMELECH
1. King of Gerar who took Abraham's wife Sarah, believing her to be his sister (Ge 20). Later made a covenant with Abraham (Ge 21:22-33).

2. King of Gerar who took Isaac's wife Rebekah, believing her to be his sister (Ge 26:1-11). Later made a covenant with Isaac (Ge 26:12-31).

ABLE (ABILITY ENABLE ENABLED ENABLES)
Eze   7:19 and gold will not be-*a* to save them
Da   3:17 The God we serve is-*a* to save us
Ro   8:39 will be-*a* to separate us
       14: 4 for the Lord is-*a* to make him stand
       16:25 to him who is-*a* to establish you
2Co   9: 8 God is-*a* to make all grace abound
Eph   3:20 him who is-*a* to do immeasurably
2Ti   1:12 and am convinced that he is-*a*
        3:15 which are-*a* to make you wise
Heb   7:25 he is-*a* to save completely
Jude :24 To him who is-*a* to keep you
Rev   5: 5 He is-*a* to open the scroll

ABOLISH
Mt   5:17 that I have come to-*a* the Law

ABOMINATION
Da 11:31 set up the-*a* that causes desolation.

ABOUND (ABOUNDING)
2Co   9: 8 able to make all grace-*a* to you,
Php   1: 9 that your love may-*a* more

ABOUNDING (ABOUND)
Ex   34: 6 slow to anger,-*a* in love
Ps   86: 5 in love to all who call to you.

ABRAHAM
Covenant relation with the LORD (Ge 12:1-3; 13:14-17; 15; 17; 22:15-18; Ex 2:24; Ne 9:8; Ps 105; Mic 7:20; Lk 1:68-75; Ro 4; Heb 6:13-15).
Called from Ur, via Haran, to Canaan (Ge 12:1; Ac 7:2-4; Heb 11:8-10). Moved to Egypt, nearly lost Sarah to Pharaoh (Ge 12:10-20). Divided the land with Lot (Ge 13). Saved Lot from four kings (Ge 14:1-16); blessed by Melchizedek (Ge 14:17-20; Heb 7:1-20). Declared righteous by faith (Ge 15:6; Ro 4:3; Gal 3:6-9). Fathered Ishmael by Hagar (Ge 16).
Name changed from Abram (Ge 17:5; Ne 9:7).

Circumcised (Ge 17; Ro 4:9-12). Entertained three visitors (Ge 18); promised a son by Sarah (Ge 18:9-15; 17:16). Moved to Gerar; nearly lost Sarah to Abimelech (Ge 20). Fathered Isaac by Sarah (Ge 21:1-7; Ac 7:8; Heb 11:11-12); sent away Hagar and Ishmael (Ge 21:8-21; Gal 4:22-30). Tested by offering Isaac (Ge 22; Heb 11:17-19; Jas 2:21-24). Sarah died; bought field of Ephron for burial (Ge 23). Secured wife for Isaac (Ge 24). Death (Ge 25:7-11).

ABSALOM
Son of David by Maacah (2Sa 3:3; 1Ch 3:2). Killed Amnon for rape of his sister Tamar; banished by David (2Sa 13). Returned to Jerusalem; received by David (2Sa 14). Rebelled against David; seized kingdom (2Sa 15-17). Killed (2Sa 18).

ABSTAIN (ABSTAINS)
1Pe   2:11 to-*a* from sinful desires,

ABSTAINS* (ABSTAIN)
Ro 14: 6 thanks to God; and he who-*a*,

ABUNDANCE (ABUNDANT)
Lk 12:15 consist in the-*a* of his possessions."
Jude : 2 peace and love be yours in-*a*.

ABUNDANT (ABUNDANCE)
Dt 28:11 will grant you-*a* prosperity—
Ps 145: 7 will celebrate your-*a* goodness
Pr 28:19 works his land will have-*a* food,
Ro   5:17 who receive God's-*a* provision

ACCEPT (ACCEPTED ACCEPTS)
Ex 23: 8 "Do not-*a* a bribe,
Pr 10: 8 The wise in heart-*a* commands,
       19:20 Listen to advice and-*a* instruction,
Ro 15: 7 *A* one another, then, just
Jas   1:21 humbly-*a* the word planted in you,

ACCEPTED (ACCEPT)
Lk   4:24 "no prophet is-*a* in his hometown.

ACCEPTS (ACCEPT)
Ps   6: 9 the LORD-*a* my prayer.

Jn 13:20 whoever-*a* anyone I send-*a* me;

ACCOMPANY
Mk 16:17 these signs will-*a* those who believe
Heb 6: 9 your case—things that-*a* salvation.

ACCOMPLISH
Isa 55:11 but will-*a* what I desire

ACCORD
Nu 24:13 not do anything of my own-*a*,
Jn 10:18 but I lay it down of my own-*a*.
       12:49 For I did not speak of my own-*a*,

ACCOUNT (ACCOUNTABLE)
Mt 12:36 to give-*a* on the day of judgment
Ro 14:12 each of us will give an-*a* of himself
Heb 4:13 of him to whom we must give-*a*.

ACCOUNTABLE (ACCOUNT)
Eze 33: 6 but I will hold the watchman-*a*
Ro   3:19 and the whole world held-*a* to God.

ACCUSATION (ACCUSE)
1Ti 5:19 Do not entertain an-*a*

ACCUSATIONS (ACCUSE)
2Pe 2:11 do not bring slanderous-*a*

ACCUSE (ACCUSATION ACCUSATIONS)
Pr   3:30 Do not-*a* a man for no reason—
Lk   3:14 and don't-*a* people falsely—

ACHAN*
Sin at Jericho caused defeat at Ai; stoned (Jos 7; 22:20; 1Ch 2:7).

ACHE*
Pr 14:13 Even in laughter the heart may-*a*,

ACKNOWLEDGE
Mt 10:32 *a* him before my Father in heaven.
1Jn 4: 3 spirit that does not-*a* Jesus is not

ACQUIT
Ex 23: 7 to death, for I will not-*a* the guilty.

ACTION (ACTIONS ACTIVE ACTS)
Jas 2:17 if it is not accompanied by-*a*,
1Pe 1:13 minds for-*a*; be self-controlled;

ACTIONS (ACTION)
Mt 11:19 wisdom is proved right by her-*a.*"
Gal 6:4 Each one should test his own-*a.*
Tit 1:16 but by their-*a* they deny him.

ACTIVE (ACTION)
Heb 4:12 For the word of God is living and-*a*

ACTS (ACTION)
Ps 145:12 all men may know of your mighty-*a* of power;
150:2 Praise him for his-*a* of power;
Isa 64:6 all our righteous-*a* are like filthy
Mt 6:1 not to do your-'*a* of righteousness'

ADAM
First man (Ge 1:26-2:25; Ro 5:14; 1Ti 2:13). Sin of (Ge 3; Hos 6:7; Ro 5:12-21). Children of (Ge 4:1-5:5). Death of (Ge 5:5; Ro 5:12-21; 1Co 15:22).

ADD
Dt 12:32 do not-*a* to it or take away from it.
Pr 30:6 Do not-*a* to his words,
Lk 12:25 by worrying can-*a* a single hour
Rev 22:18 God will-*a* to him the plagues

ADMIRABLE*
Php 4:8 whatever is lovely, whatever is-*a*—

ADMONISH
Col 3:16 and-*a* one another with all wisdom,

ADOPTED (ADOPTION)
Eph 1:5 In love he predestined us to be-*a*

ADOPTION (ADOPTED)
Ro 8:23 as we wait eagerly for our-*a* as sons,

ADORE*
SS 1:4 How right they are to-*a* you!

ADORNMENT* (ADORNS)
1Pe 3:3 should not come from outward-*a,*

ADORNS (ADORNMENT)
Ps 93:5 holiness-*a* your house

ADULTERY
Ex 20:14 "You shall not commit-*a.*
Mt 5:27 that it was said, 'Do not commit-*a.*'
5:28 lustfully has already committed-*a*
5:32 the divorced woman commits-*a.*
15:19 murder,-*a,* sexual immorality, theft

ADULTS*
1Co 14:20 but in your thinking be-*a.*

ADVANCED
Job 32:7 *a* years should teach wisdom.'

ADVANTAGE
Ex 22:22 "Do not take-*a* of a widow
Dt 24:14 Do not take-*a* of a hired man who is
1Th 4:6 should wrong his brother or take-*a*

ADVERSITY
Pr 17:17 and a brother is born for-*a.*

ADVICE
1Ki 12:8 rejected the-*a* the elders
12:14 he followed the-*a* of the young men
Pr 12:5 but the-*a* of the wicked is deceitful.
12:15 but a wise man listens to-*a.*
19:20 Listen to-*a* and accept instruction,
20:18 Make plans by seeking-*a;*

AFFLICTION
Ro 12:12 patient in-*a,* faithful in prayer.

AFRAID (FEAR)
Ge 26:24 Do not be-*a,* for I am with you;
Ex 3:6 because he was-*a* to look at God.
Ps 27:1 of whom shall I be-*a?*
56:3 When I am-*a,* / I will trust in you.
Pr 3:24 lie down, you will not be-*a;*
Jer 1:8 Do not be-*a* of them, for I am
Mt 8:26 You of little faith, why are you so-*a*
10:28 be-*a* of the One who can destroy

10:31 So don't be-*a;* you are worth more
Mk 5:36 "Don't be-*a;* just believe."
Jn 14:27 hearts be troubled and do not be-*a.*
Heb 13:6 Lord is my helper; I will not be-*a.*

AGED
Job 12:12 Is not wisdom found among the-*a?*
Pr 17:6 children are a crown to the-*a,*

AGREE
Mt 18:19 on earth-*a* about anything you ask
Ro 7:16 want to do, I-*a* that the law is good.
Php 4:2 with Syntyche to-*a* with each other

AHAB
Son of Omri; king of Israel (1Ki 16:28-22:40), husband of Jezebel (1Ki 16:31). Promoted Baal worship (1Ki 16:31-33); opposed by Elijah (1Ki 17:1; 18; 21), a prophet (1Ki 20:35-43), Micaiah (1Ki 22:1-28). Defeated Ben-Hadad (1Ki 20). Killed for failing to kill Ben-Hadad and for murder of Naboth (1Ki 20:35-21:40).

AHAZ
Son of Jotham; king of Judah, (2Ki 16; 2Ch 28; Isa 7).

AHAZIAH
1. Son of Ahab; king of Israel (1Ki 22:51-2Ki 1:18; 2Ch 20:35-37).
2. Son of Jehoram; king of Judah (2Ki 8:25-29; 9:14-29), also called Jehoahaz (2Ch 21:17-22:9; 25:23).

AIM
1Co 7:34 Her-*a* is to be devoted to the Lord
2Co 13:11 *A* for perfection, listen

AIR
Mt 8:20 and birds of the-*a* have nests,
1Co 9:26 not fight like a man beating the-*a.*
Eph 2:2 of the ruler of the kingdom of the-*a,*
1Th 4:17 clouds to meet the Lord in the-*a.*

ALABASTER
Mt 26:7 came to him with an-*a* jar

ALERT
Jos 8:4 All of you be on the-*a.*
Mk 13:33 Be-*a!* You do not know
Eph 6:18 be-*a* and always keep on praying
1Th 5:6 but let us be-*a* and self-controlled.

ALIEN (ALIENATED)
Ex 22:21 "Do not mistreat an-*a*

ALIENATED (ALIEN)
Gal 5:4 by law have been-*a* from Christ;

ALIVE (LIVE)
Ac 1:3 convincing proofs that he was-*a.*
Ro 6:11 but-*a* to God in Christ Jesus.
1Co 15:22 so in Christ all will be made-*a.*

ALMIGHTY (MIGHT)
Ge 17:1 "I am God-*A;* walk before me
Job 11:7 Can you probe the limits of the-*A?*
33:4 the breath of the-*A* gives me life.
Ps 91:1 will rest in the shadow of the-*A.*
Isa 6:3 "Holy, holy, holy is the Lord-*A;*

ALTAR
Ge 22:9 his son Isaac and laid him on the-*a,*
Ex 27:1 "Build an-*a* of acacia wood,
1Ki 18:30 and he repaired the-*a* of the Lord
2Ch 4:1 made a bronze-*a* twenty cubits
4:19 the golden-*a;* the tables

ALWAYS
Ps 16:8 I have set the Lord-*a* before me.
51:3 and my sin is-*a* before me.
Mt 26:11 The poor you will-*a* have with you,
28:20 And surely I will be with you-*a,*
1Co 13:7 *a* protects,-*a* trusts,-*a* hopes, *a*
Php 4:4 Rejoice in the Lord-*a.*

1Pe 3:15 *A* be prepared to give an answer

AMAZIAH
Son of Joash; king of Judah (2Ki 14; 2Ch 25).

AMBASSADORS
2Co 5:20 We are therefore Christ's-*a,*

AMBITION
Ro 15:20 It has always been my-*a*
1Th 4:11 Make it your-*a* to lead a quiet life,

AMON
Son of Manasseh; king of Judah (2Ki 21:18-26; 1Ch 3:14; 2Ch 33:21-25).

ANANIAS
1. Husband of Sapphira; died for lying to God (Ac 5:1-11).
2. Disciple who baptized Saul (Ac 9:10-19).
3. High priest at Paul's arrest (Ac 22:30-24:1).

ANCHOR
Heb 6:19 We have this hope as an-*a*

ANCIENT
Da 7:9 and the-*A* of Days took his seat.

ANDREW*
Apostle; brother of Simon Peter (Mt 4:18; 10:2; Mk 1:16-18, 29; 3:18; 13:3; Lk 6:14; Jn 1:35-44; 6:8-9; 12:22; Ac 1:13).

ANGEL (ANGELS ARCHANGEL)
Ps 34:7 The-*a* of the Lord encamps
Ac 6:15 his face was like the face of an-*a.*
2Co 11:14 Satan himself masquerades as an-*a*
Gal 1:8 or an-*a* from heaven should preach

ANGELS (ANGEL)
Ps 91:11 command his-*a* concerning you
Mt 18:10 For I tell you that their-*a*
25:41 prepared for the devil and his-*a.*
Lk 20:36 for they are like the-*a.*
1Co 6:3 you not know that we will judge-*a?*
Heb 1:4 as much superior to the-*a*
1:14 Are not all-*a* ministering spirits
2:7 made him a little lower than the-*a,*
13:2 some people have entertained-*a*
1Pe 1:12 Even-*a* long to look
2Pe 2:4 for if God did not spare-*a*

ANGER (ANGERED ANGRY)
Ex 32:10 alone so that my-*a* may burn
34:6 slow to-*a,* abounding in love
Dt 29:28 In furious-*a* and in great wrath
2Ki 22:13 Great is the Lord's-*a* that burns
Ps 30:5 For his-*a* lasts only a moment,
Pr 15:1 but a harsh word stirs up-*a.*
29:11 A fool gives full vent to his-*a,*

ANGERED (ANGER)
Pr 22:24 do not associate with one easily-*a,*
1Co 13:5 it is not easily-*a,* it keeps no record

ANGRY (ANGER)
Ps 2:12 Kiss the Son, lest he be-*a*
Pr 29:22 An-*a* man stirs up dissension,
Jas 1:19 slow to speak and slow to become-*a*

ANGUISH
Ps 118:5 In my-*a* I cried to the Lord,

ANOINT
Ps 23:5 You-*a* my head with oil;
Jas 5:14 and-*a* him with oil in the name

ANT*
Pr 6:6 Go to the-*a,* you sluggard;

ANTICHRIST
1Jn 2:18 have heard that the-*a* is coming,
2Jn :7 person is the deceiver and the-*a.*

ANTIOCH
Ac 11:26 were called Christians first at-*A.*

ANXIETY (ANXIOUS)
1Pe 5:7 Cast all your-*a* on him

ANXIOUS (ANXIETY)
Pr 12:25 An-*a* heart weighs a man down,
Php 4:6 Do not be-*a* about anything,

APOLLOS*
Christian from Alexandria, learned in the Scriptures; instructed by Aquila and Priscilla (Ac 18:24-28). Ministered at Corinth (Ac 19:1; 1Co 1:12; 3; Tit 3:13).

APOSTLES
See also Andrew, Bartholomew, James, John, Judas, Matthew, Nathanael, Paul, Peter, Philip, Simon, Thaddaeus, Thomas.
Mk 3:14 twelve—designating them-*a*—
Ac 1:26 so he was added to the eleven-*a.*
2:43 signs were done by the-*a.*
1Co 12:28 God has appointed first of all-*a,*
15:9 For I am the least of the-*a*
2Co 11:13 masquerading as-*a* of Christ.
Eph 2:20 built on the foundation of the-*a*

APPEAR (APPEARANCE APPEARING)
Mk 13:22 false prophets will-*a* and perform
2Co 5:10 we must all-*a* before the judgment
Col 3:4 also will-*a* with him in glory.
Heb 9:24 now to-*a* for us in God's presence.
9:28 and he will-*a* a second time,

APPEARANCE (APPEAR)
1Sa 16:7 Man looks at the outward-*a,*
Gal 2:6 God does not judge by external-*a*—

APPEARING (APPEAR)
2Ti 4:8 to all who have longed for his-*a.*
Tit 2:13 the glorious-*a* of our great God

APPLY
Pr 22:17 *a* your heart to what I teach,
23:12 *A* your heart to instruction

APPROACH
Eph 3:12 in him we may-*a* God with freedom
Heb 4:16 Let us then-*a* the throne of grace

APPROVED
2Ti 2:15 to present yourself to God as one-*a,*

AQUILA*
Husband of Priscilla; co-worker with Paul, instructor of Apollos (Ac 18; Ro 16:3; 1Co 16:19; 2Ti 4:19).

ARARAT
Ge 8:4 came to rest on the mountains of-*A.*

ARCHANGEL* (ANGEL)
1Th 4:16 with the voice of the-*a*
Jude :9 *a* Michael, when he was disputing

ARCHITECT*
Heb 11:10 whose-*a* and builder is God.

ARK
Ge 6:14 So make yourself an-*a*
Dt 10:5 put the tablets in the-*a* I had made,
2Ch 35:3 "Put the sacred-*a* in the temple that
Heb 9:4 This-*a* contained the gold jar

ARM (ARMY)
Nu 11:23 "Is the Lord's-*a* too short?
1Pe 4:1 *a* yourselves also with the same

ARMAGEDDON*
Rev 16:16 that in Hebrew is called-*A.*

ARMOR (ARMY)
1Ki 20:11 on his-*a* should not boast like one
Eph 6:11 Put on the full-*a* of God
6:13 Therefore put on the full-*a* of God,

ARMS (ARMY)
Dt 33:27 underneath are the everlasting-*a.*
Ps 18:32 It is God who-*a* me with strength

Pr 31:20 She opens her-*a* to the poor
Isa 40:11 he gathers the lambs in his-*a*
Mk 10:16 And he took the children in his-*a*,

ARMY (ARM ARMOR ARMS)
Ps 33:16 No king is saved by the size of his-*a*
Rev 19:19 the rider on the horse and his-*a*

AROMA
2Co 2:15 For we are to God the-*a* of Christ

ARRAYED*
Ps 110:3 *A* in holy majesty,
Isa 61:10 and-*a* me in a robe of righteousness

ARROGANT
Ro 11:20 Do not be-*a*, but be afraid.

ARROWS
Eph 6:16 you can extinguish all the flaming-*a*

ASA
King of Judah (1Ki 15:8-24; 1Ch 3:10; 2Ch 14-16).

ASCENDED
Eph 4: 8 "When he-*a* on high,

ASCRIBE
1Ch 16:28 *a* to the Lord glory and strength,
Job 36: 3 I will-*a* justice to my Maker.
Ps 29: 2 *A* to the Lord the glory due his

ASHAMED (SHAME)
Lk 9:26 If anyone is-*a* of me and my words,
Ro 1:16 I am not-*a* of the gospel,
2Ti 1: 8 So do not be-*a* to testify about our
2:15 who does not need to be-*a*

ASSIGNED
Mk 13:34 with his-*a* task, and tells the one
1Co 3: 5 as the Lord has-*a* to each his task.
7:17 place in life that the Lord-*a* to him

ASSOCIATE
Pr 22:24 do not-*a* with one easily angered,
Ro 12:16 but be willing to-*a* with people
1Co 5:11 am writing you that you must not-*a*
2Th 3:14 Do not-*a* with him,

ASSURANCE
Heb 10:22 with a sincere heart in full-*a* of faith

ASTRAY
Pr 10:17 ignores correction leads others-*a*.
Isa 53: 6 We all, like sheep, have gone-*a*,
Jer 50: 6 their shepherds have led them-*a*
Jn 16: 1 you so that you will not go-*a*.
1Pe 2:25 For you were like sheep going-*a*,
1Jn 3: 7 do not let anyone lead you-*a*.

ATHALIAH
Evil queen of Judah (2Ki 11; 2Ch 23).

ATHLETE*
2Ti 2: 5 if anyone competes as an-*a*,

ATONEMENT
Ex 25:17 "Make an-*a* cover of pure gold—
30:10 Once a year Aaron shall make-*a*
Lev 17:11 it is the blood that makes-*a*
23:27 this seventh month is the Day of *A*.
Nu 25:13 and made-*a* for the Israelites.
Ro 3:25 presented him as a sacrifice of-*a*,
Heb 2:17 that he might make-*a* for the sins

ATTENTION
Pr 4: 1 pay-*a* and gain understanding.
5: 1 My son, pay-*a* to my wisdom,
22:17 Pay-*a* and listen to the sayings
Tit 1:14 and will pay no-*a* to Jewish myths

ATTITUDE (ATTITUDES)
Eph 4:23 new in the-*a* of your minds,
Php 2: 5 Your-*a* should be the same
1Pe 4: 1 yourselves also with the same-*a*,

ATTITUDES (ATTITUDE)
Heb 4:12 it judges the thoughts and-*a*

ATTRACTIVE
Tit 2:10 teaching about God our Savior-*a*.

AUTHORITIES (AUTHORITY)
Ro 13: 5 it is necessary to submit to the-*a*,
13: 6 for the-*a* are God's servants,
Tit 3: 1 people to be subject to rulers and-*a*,
1Pe 3:22 *a* and powers in submission to him.

AUTHORITY (AUTHORITIES)
Mt 7:29 because he taught as one who had-*a*
9: 6 the Son of Man has-*a* on earth
28:18 "All-*a* in heaven and on earth has
Ro 13: 1 for there is no-*a* except that which
13: 2 rebels against the-*a* is rebelling
1Co 11:10 to have a sign of-*a* on her head.
1Ti 2: 2 for kings and all those in-*a*,
2:12 to teach or to have-*a* over a man;
Heb 13:17 your leaders and submit to their-*a*.

AVENGE (VENGEANCE)
Dt 32:35 It is mine to-*a*; I will repay.

AVOID
Pr 20: 3 It is to a man's honor to-*a* strife,
20:19 so-*a* a man who talks too much.
1Th 4: 3 you should-*a* sexual immorality;
5:22 *A* every kind of evil.
2Ti 2:16 *A* godless chatter, because those
Tit 3: 9 But-*a* foolish controversies

AWAKE
Ps 17:15 when I-*a*, I will be satisfied

AWE (AWESOME)
Job 25: 2 "Dominion and-*a* belong to God;
Ps 119:120 I stand in-*a* of your laws.
Ecc 5: 7 Therefore stand in-*a* of God.
Isa 29:23 will stand in-*a* of the God of Israel.
Jer 33: 9 they will be in-*a* and will tremble
Hab 3: 2 I stand in-*a* of your deeds,
Mal 2: 5 and stood in-*a* of my name.
Mt 9: 8 they were filled with-*a*;
Lk 7:16 They were all filled with-*a*
Ac 2:43 Everyone was filled with-*a*,
Heb 12:28 acceptably with reverence and-*a*,

AWESOME (AWE)
Ge 28:17 and said, "How-*a* is this place!
Ex 15:11 *a* in glory,
Dt 7:21 is among you, is a great and-*a* God.
10:17 the great God, mighty and-*a*,
28:58 revere this glorious and-*a* name—
Jdg 13: 6 like an angel of God, very-*a*.
Ne 1: 5 of heaven, the great and-*a* God,
9:32 the great, mighty and-*a* God,
Job 10:16 again display your-*a* power
37:22 God comes in-*a* majesty.
Ps 45: 4 let your right hand display-*a* deeds.
47: 2 How-*a* is the Lord Most High,
66: 5 how-*a* his works in man's behalf!
68:35 You are-*a*, O God,
89: 7 he is more-*a* than all who surround
99: 3 praise your great and-*a* name—
111: 9 holy and-*a* is his name.
145: 6 of the power of your-*a* works,
Da 9: 4 "O Lord, the great and-*a* God,

BAAL
1Ki 18:25 Elijah said to the prophets of-*B*,

BAASHA
King of Israel (1Ki 15:16-16:7; 2Ch 16:1-6).

BABIES (BABY)
Lk 18:15 also bringing-*b* to Jesus
1Pe 2: 2 Like newborn-*b*, crave pure

BABY (BABIES)
Isa 49:15 "Can a mother forget the-*b*

Lk 1:44 the-*b* in my womb leaped for joy.
2:12 You will find a-*b* wrapped in strips
Jn 16:21 but when her-*b* is born she forgets

BABYLON
Ps 137: 1 By the rivers of-*B* we sat and wept

BACKSLIDING
Jer 3:22 I will cure you of-*b*."
14: 7 For our-*b* is great;
Eze 37:23 them from all their sinful-*b*,

BALAAM
Prophet who attempted to curse Israel (Nu 22-24; Dt 23:4-5; 2Pe 2:15; Jude 11). Killed (Nu 31:8; Jos 13:22).

BALM
Jer 8:22 Is there no-*b* in Gilead?

BANISH
Jer 25:10 I will-*b* from them the sounds of joy

BANQUET
SS 2: 4 He has taken me to the-*b* hall,
Lk 14:13 when you give a-*b*, invite the poor,

BAPTIZE (BAPTIZED)
Mt 3:11 He will-*b* you with the Holy Spirit
Mk 1: 8 he will-*b* you with the Holy Spirit."
1Co 1:17 For Christ did not send me to-*b*,

BAPTIZED (BAPTIZE)
Mt 3: 6 they were-*b* by him in the Jordan
Mk 1: 9 and was-*b* by John in the Jordan.
10:38 or be-*b* with the baptism I am
16:16 believes and is-*b* will be saved,
Jn 4: 2 in fact it was not Jesus who-*b*,
Ac 1: 5 but in a few days you will be-*b*

BARABBAS
Mt 27:26 Then he released-*B* to them.

BARBS*
Nu 33:55 allow to remain will become-*b*

BARE
Heb 4:13 and laid-*b* before the eyes of him

BARNABAS*
Disciple, originally Joseph (Ac 4:36), prophet (Ac 13:1), apostle (Ac 14:14). Brought Paul to apostles (Ac 9:27), Antioch (Ac 11:22-29; Gal 2:1-13), on the first missionary journey (Ac 13-14). Together at Jerusalem Council, they separated over John Mark (Ac 15). Later co-workers (1Co 9:6; Col 4:10).

BARREN
Ps 113: 9 He settles the-*b* woman

BARTHOLOMEW*
Apostle (Mt 10:3; Mk 3:18; Lk 6:14; Ac 1:13). Possibly also known as Nathanael (Jn 1:45-49; 21:2).

BATH
Jn 13:10 person who has had a-*b* needs only

BATHSHEBA
Wife of Uriah who committed adultery with and became wife of David (2Sa 11), mother of Solomon (2Sa 12:24; 1Ki 1-2; 1Ch 3:5).

BATTLE
2Ch 20:15 For the-*b* is not yours, but God's.
Ps 24: 8 the Lord mighty in-*b*.
Ecc 9:11 or the-*b* to the strong,

BEAR (BEARING BIRTH BIRTHRIGHT BORN FIRSTBORN NEWBORN)
Ge 4:13 punishment is more than I can-*b*.
Ps 38: 4 like a burden too heavy to-*b*
Isa 53:11 and he will-*b* their iniquities.
Da 7: 5 beast, which looked like a-*b*.
Mt 7:18 A good tree cannot-*b* bad fruit,
Jn 15: 2 branch that does-*b* fruit he prunes

15:16 and appointed you to go and-*b* fruit—
Ro 15: 1 ought to-*b* with the failings
1Co 10:13 tempted beyond what you can-*b*.
Col 3:13 *B* with each other and forgive

BEARING (BEAR)
Eph 4: 2 *b* with one another in love.
Col 1:10 *b* fruit in every good work,

BEAST
Rev 13:18 him calculate the number of the-*b*,

BEAT (BEATING)
Isa 2: 4 They will-*b* their swords
Joel 3:10 *B* your plowshares into swords
1Co 9:27 I-*b* my body and make it my slave

BEATING (BEAT)
1Co 9:26 I do not fight like a man-*b* the air.
1Pe 2:20 if you receive a-*b* for doing wrong

BEAUTIFUL (BEAUTY)
Ge 6: 2 that the daughters of men were-*b*,
12:11 "I know what a-*b* woman you are.
12:14 saw that she was a very-*b* woman.
24:16 The girl was very-*b*, a virgin;
26: 7 of Rebekah, because she is-*b*."
29:17 Rachel was lovely in form, and-*b*.
Job 38:31 "Can you bind the-*b* Pleiades?
Pr 11:22 is a-*b* woman who shows no
Ecc 3:11 He has made everything-*b*
Isa 4: 2 of the Lord will be-*b*
52: 7 How-*b* on the mountains
Eze 20: 6 and honey, the most-*b* of all lands.
Zec 9:17 How attractive and-*b* they will be!
Mt 23:27 which look-*b* on the outside
26:10 She has done a-*b* thing to me.
Ro 10:15 "How-*b* are the feet
1Pe 3: 5 in God used to make themselves-*b*.

BEAUTY (BEAUTIFUL)
Ps 27: 4 to gaze upon the-*b* of the Lord
45:11 The king is enthralled by your-*b*;
Pr 31:30 is deceptive, and-*b* is fleeting;
Isa 33:17 Your eyes will see the king in his-*b*
53: 2 he had no-*b* or majesty
61: 3 to bestow on them a crown of-*b*
Eze 28:12 full of wisdom and perfect in-*b*.
1Pe 3: 4 the unfading-*b* of a gentle

BED
Heb 13: 4 and the marriage-*b* kept pure,

BEELZEBUB
Lk 11:15 "By-*B*, the prince of demons,

BEER
Pr 20: 1 Wine is a mocker and-*b* a brawler;

BEERSHEBA
Jdg 20: 1 all the Israelites from Dan to-*B*

BEGINNING
Ge 1: 1 In the-*b* God created the heavens
Ps 102:25 In the-*b* you laid the foundations
111:10 of the Lord is the-*b* of wisdom;
Pr 1: 7 of the Lord is the-*b* of knowledge
Jn 1: 1 In the-*b* was the Word,
1Jn 1: 1 That which was from the-*b*,
Rev 21: 6 and the Omega, the-*B* and the End.

BEHAVE
Ro 13:13 Let us-*b* decently, as in the daytime

BELIEVE (BELIEVED BELIEVER BELIEVERS BELIEVING)
Mt 18: 6 one of these little ones who-*b* in me
21:22 If you-*b*, you will receive whatever
Mk 1:15 Repent and-*b* the good news!"
9:24 "I do-*b*; help me overcome my
16:17 signs will accompany those who-*b*.
Lk 8:50 just-*b*, and she will be healed."
24:25 to-*b* all that the prophets have
Jn 1: 7 that through him all men might-*b*.

3:18 does not-*b* stands condemned
6:29 to-*b* in the one he has sent."
10:38 you do not-*b* me,-*b* the miracles,
11:27 "I-*b* that you are the Christ,
14:11 *B* me when I say that I am
16:30 This makes us-*b* that you came
16:31 "You-*b* at last!" Jesus answered.
17:21 that the world may-*b* that you have
20:27 Stop doubting and-*b*."
20:31 written that you may-*b* that Jesus is
Ac 16:31 They replied,-"*B* in the Lord Jesus,
24:14 I-*b* everything that agrees
Ro 3:22 faith in Jesus Christ to all who-*b*.
4:11 he is the father of all who-*b*
10:9 *b* in your heart that God raised him
10:14 And how can they-*b* in the one
16:26 so that all nations might-*b*
1Th 4:14 We-*b* that Jesus died and rose again
2Th 2:11 delusion so that they will-*b* the lie
1Ti 4:10 and especially of those who-*b*
Tit 1:6 a man whose children-*b*
Heb 11:6 comes to him must-*b* that he exists
Jas 2:19 Even the demons-*b* that—
1Jn 4:1 Dear friends, do not-*b* every spirit,

BELIEVED (BELIEVE)
Ge 15:6 Abram-*b* the Lord, and he
Jnh 3:5 The Ninevites-*b* God.
Jn 1:12 to those who-*b* in his name,
2:22 Then they-*b* the Scripture
3:18 because he has not-*b* in the name
20:8 He saw and-*b*.
20:29 who have not seen and yet have-*b*."
Ac 13:48 were appointed for eternal life-*b*.
Ro 4:3 Scripture say? "Abraham-*b* God,
10:14 call on the one they have not-*b* in?
1Co 15:2 Otherwise, you have-*b* in vain.
Gal 3:6 Consider Abraham: "He-*b* God,
2Ti 1:12 because I know whom I have-*b*,
Jas 2:23 that says, "Abraham-*b* God,

BELIEVER (BELIEVE)
1Co 7:12 brother has a wife who is not a-*b*
2Co 6:15 What does a-*b* have in common

BELIEVERS (BELIEVE)
Ac 4:32 All the-*b* were one in heart
5:12 And all the-*b* used to meet together
1Co 6:5 to judge a dispute between-*b*?
1Ti 4:12 set an example for the-*b* in speech,
1Pe 2:17 Love the brotherhood of-*b*,

BELIEVES (BELIEVE)
Pr 14:15 A simple man-*b* anything,
Mk 9:23 is possible for him who-*b*."
11:23 *b* that what he says will happen,
16:16 Whoever-*b* and is baptized will be
Jn 3:16 that whoever-*b* in him shall not
3:36 Whoever-*b* in the Son has eternal
5:24 *b* him who sent me has eternal life
6:35 and he who-*b* in me will never be
6:40 and-*b* in him shall have eternal life,
6:47 he who-*b* has everlasting life.
7:38 Whoever-*b* in me, as the Scripture
11:26 and-*b* in me will never die.
Ro 1:16 for the salvation of everyone who-*b*
10:4 righteousness for everyone who-*b*.
1Jn 5:1 Everyone who-*b* that Jesus is
5:5 Only he who-*b* that Jesus is the Son

BELIEVING (BELIEVE)
Jn 20:31 and that by-*b* you may have life

BELONG (BELONGS)
Dt 29:29 The secret things-*b*
Job 25:2 "Dominion and awe-*b* to God;
Ps 47:9 for the kings of the earth-*b* to God;
95:4 and the mountain peaks-*b* to him.
Jn 8:44 You-*b* to your father, the devil,
15:19 As it is, you do not-*b* to the world,

Ro 1:6 called to-*b* to Jesus Christ.
7:4 that you might-*b* to another,
14:8 we live or die, we-*b* to the Lord.
Gal 5:24 Those who-*b* to Christ Jesus have
1Th 5:8 But since we-*b* to the day, let us be

BELONGS (BELONG)
Job 41:11 Everything under heaven-*b* to me.
Ps 111:10 To him-*b* eternal praise.
Eze 18:4 For every living soul-*b* to me,
Jn 8:47 He who-*b* to God hears what God
Ro 12:5 each member-*b* to all the others.

BELOVED (LOVE)
Dt 33:12 "Let the-*b* of the Lord rest secure

BELT
Isa 11:5 Righteousness will be his-*b*
Eph 6:14 with the-*b* of truth buckled

BENEFIT (BENEFITS)
Ro 6:22 the-*b* you reap leads to holiness,
2Co 4:15 All this is for your-*b*,

BENEFITS (BENEFIT)
Ps 103:2 and forget not all his-*b*.
Jn 4:38 you have reaped the-*b* of their labor

BENJAMIN
Twelfth son of Jacob by Rachel (Ge 35:16-24; 46:19-21; 1Ch 2:2). Jacob refused to send him to Egypt, but relented (Ge 42-45).

BEREANS*
Ac 17:11 the-*B* were of more noble character

BESTOWS
Ps 84:11 the Lord-*b* favor and honor;

BETHLEHEM
Mt 2:1 After Jesus was born in-*B* in Judea,

BETRAY
Pr 25:9 do not-*b* another man's confidence,

BIND (BINDS)
Dt 6:8 and-*b* them on your foreheads.
Pr 6:21 *B* them upon your heart forever;
Isa 61:1 me to-*b* up the brokenhearted,
Mt 16:19 whatever you-*b* on earth will be

BINDS (BIND)
Ps 147:3 and-*b* up their wounds.
Isa 30:26 when the Lord-*b* up the bruises

BIRDS
Mt 8:20 and-*b* of the air have nests,

BIRTH (BEAR)
Ps 58:3 Even from-*b* the wicked go astray,
Mt 1:18 This is how the-*b* of Jesus Christ
1Pe 1:3 great mercy he has given us new-*b*

BIRTHRIGHT (BEAR)
Ge 25:34 So Esau despised his-*b*.

BLAMELESS
Ge 17:1 walk before me and be-*b*.
Job 1:1 This man was-*b* and upright;
Ps 84:11 from those whose walk is-*b*.
119:1 Blessed are they whose ways are-*b*,
Pr 19:1 Better a poor man whose walk is-*b*
1Co 1:8 so that you will be-*b* on the day
Eph 5:27 any other blemish, but holy and-*b*.
Php 2:15 so that you may become-*b* and pure
1Th 3:13 hearts so that you will be-*b*
5:23 and body be kept-*b* at the coming
Tit 1:6 An elder must be-*b*, the husband of
Heb 7:26 *b*, pure, set apart from sinners,
2Pe 3:14 effort to be found spotless,-*b*

BLASPHEMES
Mk 3:29 whoever-*b* against the Holy Spirit

BLEMISH
1Pe 1:19 a lamb without-*b* or defect.

BLESS (BLESSED BLESSING BLESSINGS)
Ge 12:3 I will-*b* those who-*b* you,
Ro 12:14 Bless those who persecute you;-*b*

BLESSED (BLESS)
Ge 1:22 God-*b* them and said, "Be fruitful
2:3 And God-*b* the seventh day
22:18 nations on earth will be-*b*,
Ps 1:1 *B* is the man
2:12 *B* are all who take refuge in him.
33:12 *B* is the nation whose God is
41:1 *B* is he who has regard for the weak
84:5 *B* are those whose strength is
106:3 *B* are they who maintain justice,
112:1 *B* is the man who fears the Lord,
118:26 *B* is he who comes in the name
Pr 29:18 but-*b* is he who keeps the law.
31:28 Her children arise and call her-*b*;
Mt 5:3 saying:-"*B* are the poor in spirit,
5:4 *B* are those who mourn,
5:5 *B* are the meek,
5:6 *B* are those who hunger
5:7 *B* are the merciful,
5:8 *B* are the pure in heart,
5:9 *B* are the peacemakers,
5:10 *B* are those who are persecuted
5:11 "*B* are you when people insult you,
Lk 1:48 on all generations will call me-*b*,
Jn 12:13 "*B* is he who comes in the name
Ac 20:35 'It is more-*b* to give than to receive
Tit 2:13 while we wait for the-*b* hope—
Jas 1:12 *B* is the man who perseveres
Rev 1:3 *B* is the one who reads the words
22:14 "*B* are those who wash their robes,

BLESSING (BLESS)
Eze 34:26 there will be showers of-*b*.

BLESSINGS (BLESS)
Pr 10:6 *B* crown the head of the righteous,

BLIND
Mt 15:14 a-*b* man leads a-*b* man, both will fall
23:16 "Woe to you,-*b* guides! You say,
Jn 9:25 I was-*b* but now I see!"

BLOOD
Ge 9:6 "Whoever sheds the-*b* of man,
Ex 12:13 and when I see the-*b*, I will pass
24:8 "This is the-*b* of the covenant that
Lev 17:11 For the life of a creature is in the-*b*,
Ps 72:14 for precious is their-*b* in his sight.
Pr 6:17 hands that shed innocent-*b*,
Mt 26:28 This is my-*b* of the covenant,
Ro 3:25 of atonement, through faith in his-*b*
5:9 have now been justified by his-*b*,
1Co 11:25 cup is the new covenant in my-*b*;
Eph 1:7 we have redemption through his-*b*,
2:13 near through the-*b* of Christ.
Col 1:20 by making peace through his-*b*,
Heb 9:12 once for all by his own-*b*,
9:22 of-*b* there is no forgiveness.
1Pe 1:19 but with the precious-*b* of Christ,
1Jn 1:7 and the-*b* of Jesus, his Son,
Rev 1:5 has freed us from our sins by his-*b*,
5:9 with your-*b* you purchased men
7:14 white in the-*b* of the Lamb.
12:11 him by the-*b* of the Lamb

BLOT (BLOTS)
Ex 32:32 then-*b* me out of the book you have
Ps 51:1 *b* out my transgressions.
Rev 3:5 I will never-*b* out his name

BLOTS (BLOT)
Isa 43:25 "I, even I, am he who-*b* out

BLOWN
Eph 4:14 and-*b* here and there by every wind
Jas 1:6 doubts is like a wave of the sea,-*b*

BOAST
1Ki 20:11 armor should not-*b* like one who
Ps 34:2 My soul will-*b* in the Lord;
44:8 In God we make our-*b* all day long,
Pr 27:1 Do not-*b* about tomorrow,
1Co 1:31 Let him who boasts-*b* in the Lord."
Gal 6:14 May I never-*b* except in the cross
Eph 2:9 not by works, so that no one can-*b*.

BOAZ
Wealthy Bethlehemite who showed favor to Ruth (Ru 2), married her (Ru 4). Ancestor of David (Ru 4:18-22; 1Ch 2:12-15), Jesus (Mt 1:5-16; Lk 3:23-32).

BODIES (BODY)
Ro 12:1 to offer your-*b* as living sacrifices,
1Co 6:15 not know that your-*b* are members
Eph 5:28 to love their wives as their own-*b*.

BODY (BODIES)
Zec 13:6 What are these wounds on your-*b*?'
Mt 10:28 afraid of those who kill the-*b*
26:26 saying, "Take and eat; this is my-*b*,
26:41 spirit is willing, but the-*b* is weak."
Jn 13:10 wash his feet; his whole-*b* is clean.
Ro 6:13 Do not offer the parts of your-*b*
12:4 us has one-*b* with many members,
1Co 6:19 not know that your-*b* is a temple
11:24 "This is my-*b*, which is for you;
12:12 The-*b* is a unit, though it is made up
Eph 5:30 for we are members of his-*b*.

BOLD (BOLDNESS)
Ps 138:3 you made me-*b* and stouthearted.
Pr 21:29 A wicked man puts up a-*b* front,
28:1 but the righteous are as-*b* as a lion.

BOLDNESS* (BOLD)
Ac 4:29 to speak your word with great-*b*.

BONDAGE
Ezr 9:9 God has not deserted us in our-*b*.

BOOK (BOOKS)
Jos 1:8 Do not let this-*B* of the Law depart
Ne 8:8 They read from the-*B* of the Law
Jn 20:30 which are not recorded in this-*b*.
Php 4:3 whose names are in the-*b* of life.
Rev 21:27 written in the Lamb's-*b* of life.

BOOKS (BOOK)
Ecc 12:12 Of making many-*b* there is no end,

BORN (BEAR)
Isa 9:6 For to us a child is-*b*,
Jn 3:7 at my saying, 'You must be-*b* again
1Pe 1:23 For you have been-*b* again,
1Jn 4:7 Everyone who loves has been-*b*
5:1 believes that Jesus is the Christ is-*b*

BORROWER
Pr 22:7 and the-*b* is servant to the lender.

BOUGHT
Ac 20:28 which he-*b* with his own blood.
1Co 6:20 You are not your own; you were-*b*
7:23 You were-*b* at a price; do not
2Pe 2:1 the sovereign Lord who-*b* them—

BOW
Ps 95:6 Come, let us-*b* down in worship,
Isa 45:23 Before me every knee will-*b*,
Ro 14:11 'every knee will-*b* before me;
Php 2:10 name of Jesus every knee should-*b*,

BRANCH (BRANCHES)
Isa 4:2 In that day the-*B* of the Lord will
Jer 33:15 I will make a righteous-*B* sprout

BRANCHES (BRANCH)
Jn 15:5 "I am the vine; you are the-*b*.

BRAVE
2Sa 2:7 Now then, be strong and-*b*,

BREAD

Dt 8:3 that man does not live on-*b* alone,
Pr 30:8 but give me only my daily-*b*.
Ecc 11:1 Cast your-*b* upon the waters,
Isa 55:2 Why spend money on what is not-*b*
Mt 4:4 'Man does not live on-*b* alone,
     6:11 Give us today our daily-*b*.
Jn 6:35 Jesus declared, "I am the-*b* of life.
  21:13 took the-*b* and gave it to them,
1Co 11:23 took-*b*, and when he had given

BREAK (BREAKING BROKEN)

Nu 30:2 he must not-*b* his word
Jdg 2:1 'I will never-*b* my covenant
Isa 42:3 A bruised reed he will not-*b*
Mt 12:20 A bruised reed he will not-*b*,

BREAKING (BREAK)

Jas 2:10 at just one point is guilty of-*b* all

BREASTPIECE (BREASTPLATE)

Ex 28:15 Fashion a-*b* for making decisions—

BREASTPLATE★ (BREASTPIECE)

Isa 59:17 He put on righteousness as his-*b*,
Eph 6:14 with the-*b* of righteousness in place
1Th 5:8 putting on faith and love as a-*b*,

BREATHED (GOD-BREATHED)

Ge 2:7 *b* into his nostrils the breath of life,
Jn 20:22 And with that he-*b* on them

BREEDS★

Pr 13:10 Pride only-*b* quarrels,

BRIBE

Ex 23:8 "Do not accept a-*b*,
Pr 6:35 will refuse the-*b*, however great it

BRIDE

Rev 19:7 and his-*b* has made herself ready,

BRIGHTER (BRIGHTNESS)

Pr 4:18 shining ever-*b* till the full light

BRIGHTNESS (BRIGHTER)

2Sa 22:13 Out of the-*b* of his presence
Da 12:3 who are wise will shine like the-*b*

BROAD

Mt 7:13 and-*b* is the road that leads

BROKEN (BREAK)

Ps 51:17 The sacrifices of God are a-*b* spirit;
Ecc 4:12 of three strands is not quickly-*b*.
Jn 10:35 and the Scripture cannot be-*b*—

BROKENHEARTED★ (HEART)

Ps 34:18 The Lord is close to the-*b*
  109:16 and the needy and the-*b*.
  147:3 He heals the-*b*
Isa 61:1 He has sent me to bind up the-*b*,

BROTHER (BROTHER'S BROTHERS)

Pr 17:17 and a-*b* is born for adversity.
  18:24 a friend who sticks closer than a-*b*.
  27:10 neighbor nearby than a-*b* far away.
Mt 5:24 and be reconciled to your-*b*;
  18:15 "If your-*b* sins against you,
Mk 3:35 Whoever does God's will is my-*b*
Lk 17:3 "If your-*b* sins, rebuke him,
1Co 8:13 if what I eat causes my-*b* to fall
1Jn 2:10 Whoever loves his-*b* lives
  4:21 loves God must also love his-*b*.

BROTHER'S (BROTHER)

Ge 4:9 "Am I my-*b* keeper?" The Lord

BROTHERS (BROTHER)

Ps 133:1 is when-*b* live together in unity!
Pr 6:19 who stirs up dissension among-*b*.
Mt 25:40 one of the least of these-*b* of mine,
Mk 10:29 or-*b* or sisters or mother or father
Heb 13:1 Keep on loving each other as-*b*.
1Pe 3:8 be sympathetic, love as-*b*,
1Jn 3:14 death to life, because we love our-*b*.

BUILD (BUILDING BUILDS BUILT)

Mt 16:18 and on this rock I will-*b* my church,
Ac 20:32 which can-*b* you up and give you
1Co 14:12 excel in gifts that-*b* up the church.
1Th 5:11 one another and-*b* each other up,

BUILDING (BUILD)

1Co 3:9 you are God's field, God's-*b*.
2Co 10:8 us for-*b* you up rather
Eph 4:29 helpful for-*b* others up according

BUILDS (BUILD)

Ps 127:1 Unless the Lord-*b* the house,
1Co 3:10 one should be careful how he-*b*.
  8:1 Knowledge puffs up, but love-*b* up.

BUILT (BUILD)

Mt 7:24 is like a wise man who-*b* his house
Eph 2:20 on the foundation of the apostles
  4:12 the body of Christ may be-*b* up

BURDEN (BURDENED BURDENS)

Ps 38:4 like a-*b* too heavy to bear.
Mt 11:30 my yoke is easy and my-*b* is light."

BURDENED (BURDEN)

Gal 5:1 do not let yourselves be-*b* again

BURDENS (BURDEN)

Ps 68:19 who daily bears our-*b*.
Gal 6:2 Carry each other's-*b*,

BURIED

Ro 6:4 *b* with him through baptism
1Co 15:4 that he was-*b*, that he was raised

BURNING

Lev 6:9 the fire must be kept-*b* on the altar.
Ro 12:20 you will heap-*b* coals on his head."

BUSINESS

Da 8:27 and went about the king's-*b*.
1Th 4:11 to mind your own-*b* and to work

BUSY

1Ki 20:40 While your servant was-*b* here
2Th 3:11 They are not-*b*; they are
Tit 2:5 to be-*b* at home, to be kind,

CAESAR

Mt 22:21 "Give to-*C* what is Caesar's,

CAIN

Firstborn of Adam (Ge 4:1), murdered brother
Abel (Ge 4:1-16; 1Jn 3:12).

CALEB

Judahite who spied out Canaan (Nu 13:6);
allowed to enter land because of faith (Nu
13:30-14:38; Dt 1:36). Possessed Hebron (Jos
14:6-15:19).

CALF

Ex 32:4 into an idol cast in the shape of a-*c*,
Lk 15:23 Bring the fattened-*c* and kill it.

CALL (CALLED CALLING CALLS)

Ps 105:1 to the Lord,-*c* on his name;
  145:18 near to all who-*c* on him,
Pr 31:28 children arise and-*c* her blessed;
Isa 5:20 Woe to those who-*c* evil good
  55:6 *c* on him while he is near.
  65:24 Before they-*c* I will answer;
Jer 33:3 'C to me and I will answer you
Mt 9:13 come to-*c* the righteous,
Ro 10:12 and richly blesses all who-*c* on him,
  11:29 gifts and his-*c* are irrevocable.
1Th 4:7 For God did not-*c* us to be impure,

CALLED (CALL)

1Sa 3:5 and said, "Here I am; you-*c* me."
2Ch 7:14 if my people, who are-*c*
Ps 34:6 This poor man-*c*, and the Lord
Mt 21:13 " 'My house will be-*c* a house
Ro 8:30 And those he predestined, he also-*c*
1Co 7:15 God has-*c* us to live in peace.

CALL

Gal 5:13 You, my brothers, were-*c* to be free
1Pe 2:9 of him who-*c* you out of darkness

CALLING (CALL)

Jn 1:23 I am the voice of one-*c* in the desert
Ac 22:16 wash your sins away,-*c* on his name
Eph 4:1 worthy of the-*c* you have received.
2Pe 1:10 all the more eager to make your-*c*

CALLS (CALL)

Joel 2:32 And everyone who-*c*
Jn 10:3 He-*c* his own sheep by name
Ro 10:13 "Everyone who-*c* on the name

CAMEL

Mt 19:24 it is easier for a-*c* to go
  23:24 strain out a gnat but swallow a-*c*.

CANAAN

1Ch 16:18 "To you I will give the land of-*C*

CANCELED

Lk 7:42 so he-*c* the debts of both.
Col 2:14 having-*c* the written code,

CAPITAL

Dt 21:22 guilty of a-*c* offense is put to death

CAPSTONE (STONE)

Ps 118:22 has become the-*c*;
1Pe 2:7 has become the-*c*,"

CARE (CAREFUL CARES CARING)

Ps 8:4 the son of man that you-*c* for him?
Pr 29:7 The righteous-*c* about justice
Lk 10:34 him to an inn and took-*c* of him.
Jn 21:16 Jesus said, "Take-*c* of my sheep."
Heb 2:6 the son of man that you-*c* for him?
1Pe 5:2 of God's flock that is under your-*c*,

CAREFUL (CARE)

Ex 23:13 "Be-*c* to do everything I have said
Dt 6:3 be-*c* to obey so that it may go well
Jos 23:6 be-*c* to obey all that is written
  23:11 be very-*c* to love the Lord your
Pr 13:24 he who loves him is-*c*
Mt 6:1 "Be-*c* not to do your 'acts
Ro 12:17 Be-*c* to do what is right in the eyes
1Co 3:10 each one should be-*c* how he builds
  8:9 Be-*c*, however, that the exercise
Eph 5:15 Be very-*c*, then, how you live—

CARELESS

Mt 12:36 for every-*c* word they have spoken.

CARES (CARE)

Ps 55:22 Cast your-*c* on the Lord
Na 1:7 He-*c* for those who trust in him,
Eph 5:29 but he feeds and-*c* for it, just
1Pe 5:7 on him because he-*c* for you.

CARING★ (CARE)

1Th 2:7 like a mother-*c* for her little
1Ti 5:4 practice by-*c* for their own family

CARRIED (CARRY)

Ex 19:4 and how I-*c* you on eagles' wings
Isa 53:4 and-*c* our sorrows,
Heb 13:9 Do not be-*c* away by all kinds
2Pe 1:21 as they were-*c* along by the Holy

CARRIES (CARRY)

Dt 32:11 and-*c* them on its pinions.
Isa 40:11 and-*c* them close to his heart;

CARRY (CARRIED CARRIES)

Lk 14:27 anyone who does not-*c* his cross
Gal 6:2 C each other's burdens,
  6:5 for each one should-*c* his own load.

CAST

Ps 22:18 and-*c* lots for my clothing.
  55:22 C your cares on the Lord
Ecc 11:1 C your bread upon the waters,
Jn 19:24 and-*c* lots for my clothing."
1Pe 5:7 C all your anxiety on him

CATCH (CAUGHT)

Lk 5:10 from now on you will-*c* men."

CATTLE

Ps 50:10 and the-*c* on a thousand hills.

CAUGHT (CATCH)

1Th 4:17 and are left will be-*c* up together

CAUSE (CAUSES)

Pr 24:28 against your neighbor without-*c*,
Ecc 8:3 Do not stand up for a bad-*c*,
Mt 18:7 of the things that-*c* people to sin!
Ro 14:21 else that will-*c* your brother
1Co 10:32 Do not-*c* anyone to stumble,

CAUSES (CAUSE)

Isa 8:14 a stone that-*c* men to stumble
Mt 18:6 if anyone-*c* one of these little ones

CAUTIOUS★

Pr 12:26 A righteous man is-*c* in friendship,

CEASE

Ps 46:9 He makes wars-*c* to the ends

CENSER

Lev 16:12 is to take a-*c* full of burning coals

CENTURION

Mt 8:5 had entered Capernaum, a-*c* came

CERTAIN (CERTAINTY)

2Pe 1:19 word of the prophets made more-*c*,

CERTAINTY★ (CERTAIN)

Lk 1:4 so that you may know the-*c*
Jn 17:8 They knew with-*c* that I came

CHAFF

Ps 1:4 They are like-*c*

CHAINED

2Ti 2:9 But God's word is not-*c*.

CHAMPION

Ps 19:5 like a-*c* rejoicing to run his course.

CHANGE (CHANGED)

1Sa 15:29 of Israel does not lie or-*c* his mind;
Ps 110:4 and will not-*c* his mind:
Jer 7:5 If you really-*c* your ways
Mal 3:6 "I the Lord do not-*c*.
Mt 18:3 unless you-*c* and become like little
Heb 7:21 and will not-*c* his mind:
Jas 1:17 who does not-*c* like shifting

CHANGED (CHANGE)

1Co 15:51 but we will all be-*c*— in a flash,

CHARACTER

Ru 3:11 that you are a woman of noble-*c*.
Pr 31:10 A wife of noble-*c* who can find?
Ro 5:4 perseverance,-*c*; and-*c*, hope.
1Co 15:33 "Bad company corrupts good-*c*."

CHARGE

Ro 8:33 Who will bring any-*c*
2Co 11:7 the gospel of God to you free of-*c*?
2Ti 4:1 I give you this-*c*: Preach the Word;

CHARIOTS

2Ki 6:17 and-*c* of fire all around Elisha.
Ps 20:7 Some trust in-*c* and some in horses,

CHARM

Pr 31:30 C is deceptive, and beauty is

CHASES

Pr 12:11 he who-*c* fantasies lacks judgment.

CHATTER★ (CHATTERING)

1Ti 6:20 Turn away from godless-*c*
2Ti 2:16 Avoid godless-*c*, because those

CHATTERING★ (CHATTER)

Pr 10:8 but a-*c* fool comes to ruin.
  10:10 and a-*c* fool comes to ruin.

CHEAT (CHEATED)

Mal 1:14 "Cursed is the-*c* who has

1Co 6: 8 you yourselves-c and do wrong,

CHEATED (CHEAT)
Lk 19: 8 if I have-c anybody out of anything,
1Co 6: 7 Why not rather be-c? Instead,

CHEEK
Mt 5:39 someone strikes you on the right-c,

CHEERFUL* (CHEERS)
Pr 15:13 A happy heart makes the face-c,
15:15 but the-c heart has a continual feast
15:30 A-c look brings joy to the heart,
17:22 A-c heart is good medicine,
2Co 9: 7 for God loves a-c giver.

CHEERS (CHEERFUL)
Pr 12:25 but a kind word-c him up.

CHILD (CHILDISH CHILDREN)
Pr 20:11 Even a-c is known by his actions,
22: 6 Train a-c in the way he should go,
22:15 Folly is bound up in the heart of a-c
23:13 not withhold discipline from a-c;
29:15 c left to himself disgraces his
mother.
Isa 7:14 The virgin will be with-c
9: 6 For to us a-c is born,
11: 6 and a little-c will lead them.
66:13 As a mother comforts her-c,
Mt 1:23 "The virgin will be with-c
18: 2 He called a little-c and had him
Lk 1:42 and blessed is the-c you will bear!
1:80 And the-c grew and became strong
1Co 13:11 When I was a-c, I talked like a-c,
1Jn 5: 1 who loves the father loves his-c

CHILDISH* (CHILD)
1Co 13:11 When I became a man, I put-c ways

CHILDREN (CHILD)
Dt 4: 9 Teach them to your-c
11:19 them to your-c, talking about them
Ps 8: 2 From the lips of-c and infants
Pr 17: 6 Children's-c are a crown
31:28 Her-c arise and call her blessed;
Mt 7:11 how to give good gifts to your-c,
11:25 and revealed them to little-c.
18: 3 you change and become like little-c
19:14 "Let the little-c come to me,
21:16 " 'From the lips of-c and infants
Mk 9:37 one of these little-c in my name
10:14 "Let the little-c come to me,
10:16 And he took the-c in his arms,
13:12 C will rebel against their parents
Lk 10:21 and revealed them to little-c.
18:16 "Let the little-c come to me,
Ro 8:16 with our spirit that we are God's-c.
2Co 12:14 parents, but parents for their-c.
Eph 6: 1 C, obey your parents in the Lord,
6: 4 do not exasperate your-c; instead,
Col 3:20 C, obey your parents in everything,
3:21 Fathers, do not embitter your-c,
1Ti 3: 4 and see that his-c obey him
3:12 and must manage his-c and his
5:10 bringing up-c, showing hospitality,
1Jn 3: 1 that we should be called-c of God!

CHOOSE (CHOOSES CHOSE CHOSEN)
Dt 30:19 Now-c life, so that you
Jos 24:15 then-c for yourselves this day
Pr 8:10 C my instruction instead of silver,
16:16 to-c understanding rather
Jn 15:16 You did not-c me, but I chose you

CHOOSES (CHOOSE)
Jn 7:17 If anyone-c to do God's will,

CHOSE (CHOOSE)
Ge 13:11 So Lot-c for himself the whole plain
Ps 33:12 the people he-c for his inheritance.
Jn 15:16 but I-c you and appointed you to go
1Co 1:27 But God-c the foolish things

Eph 1: 4 he-c us in him before the creation
2Th 2:13 from the beginning God-c you

CHOSEN (CHOOSE)
Isa 41: 8 Jacob, whom I have-c,
Mt 22:14 For many are invited, but few are-c
Lk 10:42 Mary has-c what is better,
23:35 the Christ of God, the-C One."
Jn 15:19 but I have-c you out of the world.
1Pe 1:20 He was-c before the creation
2: 9 But you are a-c people, a royal

CHRIST (CHRIST'S CHRISTIAN CHRISTS)
Mt 1:16 was born Jesus, who is called-C.
16:16 Peter answered, "You are the-C,
22:42 "What do you think about the-C?
Jn 1:41 found the Messiah" (that is, the-C).
20:31 you may believe that Jesus is the-C,
Ac 2:36 you crucified, both Lord and-C."
5:42 the good news that Jesus is the-C.
9:22 by proving that Jesus is the-C.
17: 3 proving that the-C had to suffer
18:28 the Scriptures that Jesus was the-C.
26:23 that the-C would suffer and,
Ro 3:22 comes through faith in Jesus-C
5: 6 we were still powerless,-C died
5: 8 While we were still sinners,-C died
5:17 life through the one man, Jesus-C.
6: 4 as-C was raised from the dead
8: 1 for those who are in-C Jesus,
8: 9 Spirit of-C, he does not belong to-C.
8:35 us from the love of-C?
10: 4 C is the end of the law
14: 9 C died and returned to life
15: 3 For even-C did not please himself
1Co 1:23 but we preach-C crucified:
2: 2 except Jesus-C and him crucified.
3:11 one already laid, which is Jesus-C.
5: 7 For-C, our Passover lamb,
8: 6 and there is but one Lord, Jesus-C,
10: 4 them, and that rock was-C.
11: 1 as I follow the example of-C.
11: 3 the head of every man is-C,
12:27 Now you are the body of-C,
15: 3 that-C died for our sins according
15:14 And if-C has not been raised,
15:22 so in-C all will be made alive.
15:57 victory through our Lord Jesus-C.
2Co 3: 3 show that you are a letter from-C,
4: 5 not preach ourselves, but Jesus-C
5:10 before the judgment seat of-C,
5:17 Therefore, if anyone is in-C,
11: 2 you to one husband, to-C,
Gal 2:20 I have been crucified with-C
3:13 C redeemed us from the curse
6:14 in the cross of our Lord Jesus-C,
Eph 1: 3 with every spiritual blessing in-C.
3: 8 the unsearchable riches of-C.
4:13 measure of the fullness of-C.
5: 2 as-C loved us and gave himself up
5:23 as-C is the head of the church,
5:25 just as-C loved the church
Php 1:21 to live is-C and to die is gain.
1:27 worthy of the gospel of-C.
4:19 to his glorious riches in-C Jesus.
Col 1:27 which is-C in you, the hope of glory
1:28 may present everyone perfect in-C.
2: 6 as you received-C Jesus as Lord,
2:17 the reality, however, is found in-C.
3:15 Let the peace of-C rule
2Th 2: 1 the coming of our Lord Jesus-C
1Ti 1:15 C Jesus came into the world
2: 5 the man-C Jesus, who gave himself
2Ti 2: 3 us like a good soldier of-C Jesus.
3:15 salvation through faith in-C Jesus.
Tit 2:13 our great God and Savior, Jesus-C,
Heb 3:14 to share in-C if we hold firmly

9:14 more, then, will the blood of-C,
9:15 For this reason-C is the mediator
9:28 so-C was sacrificed once
10:10 of the body of Jesus-C once for all.
13: 8 Jesus-C is the same yesterday
1Pe 1:19 but with the precious blood of-C,
2:21 because-C suffered for you,
3:18 For-C died for sins once for all,
4:14 insulted because of the name of-C,
1Jn 2:22 man who denies that Jesus is-C.
3:16 Jesus-C laid down his life for us.
5: 1 believes that Jesus is the-C is born
Rev 20: 4 reigned with-C a thousand years.

CHRIST'S (CHRIST)
2Co 5:14 For-C love compels us,
5:20 We are therefore-C ambassadors,
12: 9 so that-C power may rest on me.

CHRISTIAN (CHRIST)
1Pe 4:16 as a-C, do not be ashamed,

CHRISTS (CHRIST)
Mt 24:24 For false-C and false prophets will

CHURCH
Mt 16:18 and on this rock I will build my-c,
18:17 if he refuses to listen even to the-c,
Ac 20:28 Be shepherds of the-c of God,
1Co 5:12 of mine to judge those outside the-c
14: 4 but he who prophesies edifies the-c.
14:12 to excel in gifts that build up the-c.
14:26 done for the strengthening of the-c.
Eph 5:23 as Christ is the head of the-c,
Col 1:24 the sake of his body, which is the-c.

CIRCUMCISED
Ge 17:10 Every male among you shall be-c.

CIRCUMSTANCES
Php 4:11 to be content whatever the-c.
1Th 5:18 continually; give thanks in all-c,

CITIZENS (CITIZENSHIP)
Eph 2:19 but fellow-c with God's people

CITIZENSHIP (CITIZENS)
Php 3:20 But our-c is in heaven.

CITY
Mt 5:14 A-c on a hill cannot be hidden.
Heb 13:14 here we do not have an enduring-c,

CIVILIAN*
2Ti 2: 4 a soldier gets involved in-c affairs—

CLAIM (CLAIMS)
Pr 25: 6 do not-c a place among great men;
1Jn 1: 6 If we-c to have fellowship
1: 8 If we-c to be without sin, we
1:10 If we-c we have not sinned,

CLAIMS (CLAIM)
Jas 2:14 if a man-c to have faith
1Jn 2: 6 Whoever-c to live in him must walk
2: 9 Anyone who-c to be in the light

CLAP
Ps 47: 1 C your hands, all you nations;
Isa 55:12 will-c their hands.

CLAY
Isa 45: 9 Does the-c say to the potter,
64: 8 We are the-c, you are the potter;
Jer 18: 6 "Like-c in the hand of the potter,
La 4: 2 are now considered as pots of-c,
Da 2:33 partly of iron and partly of baked-c.
Ro 9:21 of the same lump of-c some pottery
2Co 4: 7 we have this treasure in jars of-c
2Ti 2:20 and-c; some are for noble purposes

CLEAN
Lev 16:30 you will be-c from all your sins.
Ps 24: 4 He who has-c hands and a pure
Mt 12:44 the house unoccupied, swept-c
23:25 You-c the outside of the cup

Mk 7:19 Jesus declared all foods- "c."
Jn 13:10 to wash his feet; his whole body is-c
15: 3 are already-c because of the word
Ac 10:15 impure that God has made-c."
Ro 14:20 All food is-c, but it is wrong

CLING (CLINGS)
Ro 12: 9 Hate what is evil;-c to what is good.

CLINGS (CLING)
Ps 63: 8 My soul-c to you;

CLOAK
2Ki 4:29 "Tuck your-c into your belt,

CLOSE (CLOSER)
Ps 34:18 LORD is-c to the brokenhearted
Isa 40:11 and carries them-c to his heart;
Jer 30:21 himself to be-c to me?'

CLOSER (CLOSE)
Ex 3: 5 "Do not come any-c," God said.
Pr 18:24 there is a friend who sticks-c

CLOTHE (CLOTHED CLOTHES CLOTHING)
Ps 45: 3 c yourself with splendor
Isa 52: 1 c yourself with strength.
Ro 13:14 c yourselves with the Lord Jesus
Col 3:12 c yourselves with compassion,
1Pe 5: 5 c yourselves with humility

CLOTHED (CLOTHE)
Ps 30:11 removed my sackcloth and-c me
Pr 31:25 She is-c with strength and dignity;
Lk 24:49 until you have been-c with power

CLOTHES (CLOTHE)
Mt 6:25 the body more important than-c?
6:28 "And why do you worry about-c?
Jn 11:44 Take off the grave-c and let him go

CLOTHING (CLOTHE)
Dt 22: 5 A woman must not wear men's-c,
Mt 7:15 They come to you in sheep's-c,

CLOUD (CLOUDS)
Ex 13:21 them in a pillar of-c to guide them
Isa 19: 1 See, the LORD rides on a swift-c
Lk 21:27 of Man coming in a-c with power
Heb 12: 1 by such a great-c of witnesses,

CLOUDS (CLOUD)
Ps 104: 3 He makes the-c his chariot
Da 7:13 coming with the-c of heaven.
Mk 13:26 coming in-c with great power
1Th 4:17 with them in the-c to meet the Lord

CO-HEIRS* (INHERIT)
Ro 8:17 heirs of God and-c with Christ,

COALS
Pr 25:22 you will heap burning-c on his head
Ro 12:20 you will heap burning-c on his head

COLD
Pr 25:25 Like-c water to a weary soul
Mt 10:42 if anyone gives even a cup of-c
water
24:12 the love of most will grow-c,

COMFORT (COMFORTED COMFORTS)
Ps 23: 4 rod and your staff, they-c me.
119:52 and I find-c in them.
119:76 May your unfailing love be my-c,
Zec 1:17 and the LORD will again-c Zion
1Co 14: 3 encouragement and-c.
2Co 1: 4 so that we can-c those
2: 7 you ought to forgive and-c him,

COMFORTED (COMFORT)
Mt 5: 4 for they will be-c.

COMFORTS* (COMFORT)
Job 29:25 I was like one who-c mourners.
Isa 49:13 For the LORD-c his people
51:12 "I, even I, am he who-c you.

66:13 As a mother-*c* her child,
2Co 1: 4 who-*c* us in all our troubles,
7: 6 But God, who-*c* the downcast,

COMMAND (COMMANDED
COMMANDING COMMANDMENT
COMMANDMENTS COMMANDS)
Ex 7: 2 You are to say everything I-*c* you,
Nu 24:13 to go beyond the-*c* of the LORD—
Dt 4: 2 Do not add to what I-*c* you
30:16 For I-*c* you today to love
32:46 so that you may-*c* your children
Ps 91:11 For he will-*c* his angels concerning
Pr 13:13 but he who respects a-*c* is rewarded
Ecc 8: 2 Obey the king's-*c*, I say,
Joel 2:11 mighty are those who obey his-*c*.
Jn 14:15 love me, you will obey what I-*c*,
15:12 My-*c* is this: Love each other
1Co 14:37 writing to you is the Lord's-*c*.
Gal 5:14 law is summed up in a single-*c*:
1Ti 1: 5 goal of this-*c* is love, which comes
Heb 11: 3 universe was formed at God's-*c*,
1Jn 3:23 this is his-*c*: to believe in the name
2Jn : 6 his-*c* is that you walk in love.

COMMANDED (COMMAND)
Ps 33: 9 he-*c*, and it stood firm.
148: 5 for he-*c* and they were created.
Mt 28:20 to obey everything I have-*c* you.
1Co 9:14 Lord has-*c* that those who preach
1Jn 3:23 and to love one another as he-*c* us.

COMMANDING (COMMAND)
2Ti 2: 4 he wants to please his-*c* officer.

COMMANDMENT (COMMAND)
Jos 22: 5 But be very careful to keep the-*c*
Mt 22:38 This is the first and greatest-*c*.
Jn 13:34 "A new-*c* I give you: Love one
Ro 7:12 and the-*c* is holy, righteous
Eph 6: 2 which is the first-*c* with a promise

COMMANDMENTS (COMMAND)
Ex 20: 6 who love me and keep my-*c*,
34:28 of the covenant—the Ten-*c*.
Ecc 12:13 Fear God and keep his-*c*,
Mt 5:19 one of the least of these-*c*
22:40 the Prophets hang on these two-*c*."

COMMANDS (COMMAND)
Dt 7: 9 those who love him and keep his-*c*.
11:27 the blessing if you obey the-*c*
Ps 112: 1 who finds great delight in his-*c*.
119:47 for I delight in your-*c*
119:86 All your-*c* are trustworthy;
119:98 Your-*c* make me wiser
119:127 Because I love your-*c*
119:143 but your-*c* are my delight.
119:172 for all your-*c* are righteous.
Pr 3: 1 but keep my-*c* in your heart,
6:23 For these-*c* are a lamp,
10: 8 The wise in heart accept-*c*,
Da 9: 4 all who love him and obey his-*c*,
Mt 5:19 teaches these-*c* will be called great
Jn 14:21 Whoever has my-*c* and obeys them,
Ac 17:30 but now he-*c* all people everywhere
1Co 7:19 Keeping God's-*c* is what counts.
1Jn 5: 3 And his-*c* are not burdensome,
5: 3 This is love for God: to obey his-*c*.

COMMEND (COMMENDED
COMMENDS)
Ecc 8:15 So I-*c* the enjoyment of life,
Ro 13: 3 do what is right and he will-*c* you.
1Pe 2:14 and to-*c* those who do right.

COMMENDED (COMMEND)
Heb 11:39 These were all-*c* for their faith,

COMMENDS (COMMEND)
2Co 10:18 not the one who-*c* himself who is

COMMIT (COMMITS COMMITTED)
Ex 20:14 "You shall not-*c* adultery.
Ps 37: 5 *C* your way to the LORD;
Mt 5:27 that it was said, 'Do not-*c* adultery.'
Lk 23:46 into your hands I-*c* my spirit."
Ac 20:32 I-*c* you to God and to the word
1Co 10: 8 We should not-*c* sexual immorality,
1Pe 4:19 to God's will should-*c* themselves

COMMITS (COMMIT)
Pr 6:32 man who-*c* adultery lacks
29:22 a hot-tempered one-*c* many sins.
Mt 19: 9 marries another woman-*c* adultery

COMMITTED (COMMIT)
Nu 5: 7 and must confess the sin he has-*c*.
1Ki 8:61 But your hearts must be fully-*c*
2Ch 16: 9 those whose hearts are fully-*c*
Mt 5:28 lustfully has already-*c* adultery
2Co 5:19 And he has-*c* to us the message
1Pe 2:22 "He-*c* no sin,

COMMON
Pr 22: 2 Rich and poor have this in-*c*:
1Co 10:13 has seized you except what is-*c*
2Co 6:14 and wickedness have in-*c*?

COMPANION (COMPANIONS)
Pr 13:20 but a-*c* of fools suffers harm.
28: 7 a-*c* of gluttons disgraces his father.
29: 3 *c* of prostitutes squanders his

COMPANIONS (COMPANION)
Pr 18:24 A man of many-*c* may come to ruin

COMPANY
Pr 24: 1 do not desire their-*c*;
Jer 15:17 I never sat in the-*c* of revelers,
1Co 15:33 "Bad-*c* corrupts good character."

COMPARED (COMPARING)
Eze 31: 2 Who can be-*c* with you in majesty?
Php 3: 8 I consider everything a loss-*c*

COMPARING* (COMPARED)
Ro 8:18 present sufferings are not worth-*c*
2Co 8: 8 the sincerity of your love by-*c* it
Gal 6: 4 without-*c* himself to somebody else

COMPASSION (COMPASSIONATE
COMPASSIONS)
Ex 33:19 I will have-*c* on whom I will have-*c*.
Ne 9:19 of your great-*c* you did not
9:28 in your-*c* you delivered them time
Ps 51: 1 according to your great-*c*,
103: 4 and crowns you with love and-*c*.
103:13 As a father has-*c* on his children,
145: 9 he has-*c* on all he has made.
Isa 49:13 and will have-*c* on his afflicted ones
49:15 and have no-*c* on the child she has
Hos 2:19 in love and-*c*,
11: 8 all my-*c* is aroused.
Jnh 3: 9 with-*c* turn from his fierce anger
Mt 9:36 When he saw the crowds, he had-*c*
Mk 8: 2 "I have-*c* for these people,
Ro 9:15 and I will have-*c* on whom I have-*c*
Col 3:12 clothe yourselves with-*c*, kindness,
Jas 5:11 The Lord is full of-*c* and mercy.

COMPASSIONATE (COMPASSION)
Ne 9:17 gracious and-*c*, slow to anger
Ps 103: 8 The LORD is-*c* and gracious,
112: 4 the gracious and-*c* and righteous
Eph 4:32 Be kind and-*c* to one another,
1Pe 3: 8 love as brothers, be-*c* and humble.

COMPASSIONS* (COMPASSION)
La 3:22 for his-*c* never fail.

COMPELLED (COMPEL)
Ac 20:22 "And now,-*c* by the Spirit,
1Co 9:16 I cannot boast, for I am-*c* to preach.

COMPELS (COMPELLED)
2Co 5:14 For Christ's love-*c* us, because we

COMPETENCE* (COMPETENT)
2Co 3: 5 but our-*c* comes from God.

COMPETENT* (COMPETENCE)
Lk 15:14 and-*c* to instruct one another.
1Co 6: 2 are you not-*c* to judge trivial cases?
2Co 3: 5 Not that we are-*c* in ourselves
3: 6 He has made us-*c* as ministers

COMPETES*
1Co 9:25 Everyone who-*c* in the games goes
2Ti 2: 5 Similarly, if anyone-*c* as an athlete,
2: 5 unless he-*c* according to the rules.

COMPLACENT
Am 6: 1 Woe to you who are-*c* in Zion,

COMPLAINING*
Php 2:14 Do everything without-*c* or arguing

COMPLETE
Jn 15:11 and that your joy may be-*c*.
16:24 will receive, and your joy will be-*c*.
17:23 May they be brought to-*c* unity
Ac 20:24 *c* the task the Lord Jesus has given
Php 2: 2 then make my joy-*c*
Col 4:17 to it that you-*c* the work you have
Jas 1: 4 so that you may be mature and-*c*,
2:22 his faith was made-*c* by what he did

CONCEAL (CONCEALED CONCEALS)
Ps 40:10 I do not-*c* your love and your truth
Pr 25: 2 It is the glory of God to-*c* a matter;

CONCEALED (CONCEAL)
Jer 16:17 nor is their sin-*c* from my eyes.
Mt 10:26 There is nothing-*c* that will not be
Mk 4:22 and whatever is-*c* is meant

CONCEALS (CONCEAL)
Pr 28:13 He who-*c* his sins does not prosper,

CONCEITED
Ro 12:16 Do not be-*c*.
Gal 5:26 Let us not become-*c*, provoking
1Ti 6: 4 he is-*c* and understands nothing.

CONCEIVED
Mt 1:20 what is-*c* in her is from the Holy
1Co 2: 9 no mind has-*c*

CONCERN (CONCERNED)
Eze 36:21 I had-*c* for my holy name, which
1Co 7:32 I would like you to be free from-*c*.
12:25 that its parts should have equal-*c*
2Co 11:28 of my-*c* for all the churches.

CONCERNED (CONCERN)
Jnh 4:10 "You have been-*c* about this vine,
1Co 7:32 An unmarried man is-*c* about

CONDEMN (CONDEMNATION
CONDEMNED CONDEMNING
CONDEMNS)
Job 40: 8 Would you-*c* me to justify yourself?
Isa 50: 9 Who is he that will-*c* me?
Lk 6:37 Do not-*c*, and you will not be
Jn 3:17 Son into the world to-*c* the world,
12:48 very word which I spoke will-*c* him
Ro 2:27 yet obeys the law will-*c* you who,
1Jn 3:20 presence whenever our hearts-*c* us.

CONDEMNATION (CONDEMN)
Ro 5:18 of one trespass was-*c* for all men,
8: 1 there is now no-*c* for those who are

CONDEMNED (CONDEMN)
Ps 34:22 no one will be-*c* who takes refuge
Mt 12:37 and by your words you will be-*c*."
23:33 How will you escape being-*c* to hell
Jn 3:18 Whoever believes in him is not-*c*,
5:24 has eternal life and will not be-*c*;
16:11 prince of this world now stands-*c*.
Ro 14:23 But the man who has doubts is-*c*
1Co 11:32 disciplined so that we will not be-*c*
Heb 11: 7 By his faith he-*c* the world

CONDEMNING (CONDEMN)
Pr 17:15 the guilty and-*c* the innocent—
Ro 2: 1 judge the other, you are-*c* yourself,

CONDEMNS (CONDEMN)
Ro 8:34 Who is he that-*c*? Christ Jesus,
2Co 3: 9 the ministry that-*c* men is glorious,

CONDUCT
Pr 10:23 A fool finds pleasure in evil-*c*,
20:11 by whether his-*c* is pure and right.
21: 8 but the-*c* of the innocent is upright.
Ecc 6: 8 how to-*c* himself before others?
Jer 4:18 "Your own-*c* and actions
17:10 to reward a man according to his-*c*,
Eze 7: 3 I will judge you according to your-*c*
Php 1:27 *c* yourselves in a manner worthy
1Ti 3:15 to-*c* themselves in God's household

CONFESS (CONFESSION)
Lev 16:21 and-*c* over it all the wickedness
26:40 " 'But if they will-*c* their sins
Nu 5: 7 must-*c* the sin he has committed.
Ro 10: 9 That if you-*c* with your mouth,
Php 2:11 every tongue-*c* that Jesus Christ is
Jas 5:16 Therefore-*c* your sins to each other
1Jn 1: 9 If we-*c* our sins, he is faithful

CONFESSION (CONFESS)
Ezr 10:11 Now make-*c* to the LORD,
2Co 9:13 obedience that accompanies your-*c*

CONFIDENCE
Ps 71: 5 my-*c* since my youth.
Pr 3:26 for the LORD will be your-*c*
11:13 A gossip betrays a-*c*,
25: 9 do not betray another man's-*c*,
31:11 Her husband has full-*c* in her
Isa 32:17 will be quietness and-*c* forever.
Jer 17: 7 whose-*c* is in him.
Php 3: 3 and who put no-*c* in the flesh—
Heb 3:14 till the end the-*c* we had at first.
4:16 the throne of grace with-*c*,
10:19 since we have-*c* to enter the Most
10:35 So do not throw away your-*c*;
1Jn 5:14 This is the-*c* we have

CONFORM* (CONFORMED)
Ro 12: 2 Do not-*c* any longer to the pattern
1Pe 1:14 do not-*c* to the evil desires you had

CONFORMED (CONFORM)
Ro 8:29 predestined to be-*c* to the likeness

CONQUERORS
Ro 8:37 than-*c* through him who loved us.

CONSCIENCE (CONSCIENCES)
Ro 13: 5 punishment but also because of-*c*.
1Co 8: 7 since their-*c* is weak, it is defiled.
8:12 in this way and wound their weak-*c*
10:25 without raising questions of-*c*,
10:29 freedom be judged by another's-*c*?
Heb 10:22 to cleanse us from a guilty-*c*
1Pe 3:16 and respect, keeping a clear-*c*,

CONSCIENCES* (CONSCIENCE)
Ro 2:15 their-*c* also bearing witness,
1Ti 4: 2 whose-*c* have been seared
Tit 1:15 their minds and-*c* are corrupted.
Heb 9:14 cleanse our-*c* from acts that lead

CONSCIOUS*
Ro 3:20 through the law we become-*c* of sin
1Pe 2:19 of unjust suffering because he is-*c*

CONSECRATE (CONSECRATED)
Ex 13: 2 "*C* to me every firstborn male.
Lev 20: 7 " '*C* yourselves and be holy,

CONSECRATED (CONSECRATE)
Ex 29:43 and the place will be-*c* by my glory.
1Ti 4: 5 because it is-*c* by the word of God

CONSIDER (CONSIDERATE CONSIDERED CONSIDERS)
1Sa 12:24 *c* what great things he has done
Job 37:14 stop and-*c* God's wonders.
Ps 8: 3 When I-*c* your heavens,
107:43 and-*c* the great love of the LORD.
143: 5 and-*c* what your hands have done.
Lk 12:24 *C* the ravens: They do not sow
12:27 about the rest?-"*C* how the lilies
Php 2: 3 but in humility-*c* others better
3: 8 I-*c* everything a loss compared
Heb 10:24 And let us-*c* how we may spur one
Jas 1: 2 *C* it pure joy, my brothers,

CONSIDERATE* (CONSIDER)
Tit 3: 2 to be peaceable and-*c*,
Jas 3:17 then peace-loving,-*c*, submissive,
1Pe 2:18 only to those who are good and-*c*,
3: 7 in the same way be-*c* as you live

CONSIDERED (CONSIDER)
Job 1: 8 "Have you-*c* my servant Job?
2: 3 "Have you-*c* my servant Job?
Ps 44:22 we are-*c* as sheep to be slaughtered.
Isa 53: 4 yet we-*c* him stricken by God,
Ro 8:36 we are-*c* as sheep to be slaughtered

CONSIDERS (CONSIDER)
Pr 31:16 She-*c* a field and buys it;
Ro 14: 5 One man-*c* one day more sacred
Jas 1:26 If anyone-*c* himself religious

CONSIST
Lk 12:15 a man's life does not-*c*

CONSOLATION
Ps 94:19 your-*c* brought joy to my soul.

CONSTRUCTIVE*
1Co 10:23 but not everything is-*c*.

CONSUME (CONSUMING)
Jn 2:17 "Zeal for your house will-*c* me."

CONSUMING (CONSUME)
Dt 4:24 For the LORD your God is a-*c* fire,
Heb 12:29 and awe, for our "God is a-*c* fire."

CONTAIN
1Ki 8:27 the highest heaven, cannot-*c* you.
2Pe 3:16 His letters-*c* some things that are

CONTAMINATES*
2Co 7: 1 from everything that-*c* body

CONTEMPT
Pr 14:31 He who oppresses the poor shows-*c*
17: 5 He who mocks the poor shows-*c*
18: 3 When wickedness comes, so does-*c*
Da 12: 2 others to shame and everlasting-*c*.
Ro 2: 4 Or do you show-*c* for the riches
Gal 4:14 you did not treat me with-*c*
1Th 5:20 do not treat prophecies with-*c*.

CONTEND (CONTENDING)
Jude : 3 you to-*c* for the faith that was once

CONTENDING* (CONTEND)
Php 1:27 *c* as one man for the faith

CONTENT (CONTENTMENT)
Pr 13:25 The righteous eat to their hearts'-*c*,
Php 4:11 to be-*c* whatever the circumstances
4:12 I have learned the secret of being-*c*
1Ti 6: 8 and clothing, we will be-*c* with that.
Heb 13: 5 and be-*c* with what you have,

CONTENTMENT (CONTENT)
1Ti 6: 6 But godliness with-*c* is great gain.

CONTINUAL (CONTINUE)
Pr 15:15 but the cheerful heart has a-*c* feast.

CONTINUE (CONTINUAL)
Php 2:12 *c* to work out your salvation
2Ti 3:14 *c* in what you have learned
1Jn 5:18 born of God does not-*c* to sin;

Rev 22:11 and let him who is holy-*c* to be holy
22:11 let him who does right-*c* to do right;

CONTRITE*
Ps 51:17 a broken and-*c* heart,
Isa 57:15 also with him who is-*c* and lowly
57:15 and to revive the heart of the-*c*.
66: 2 he who is humble and-*c* in spirit,

CONTROL (CONTROLLED SELF-CONTROL SELF-CONTROLLED)
Pr 29:11 a wise man keeps himself under-*c*.
1Co 7: 9 But if they cannot-*c* themselves,
7:37 but has-*c* over his own will,
1Th 4: 4 you should learn to-*c* his own body

CONTROLLED (CONTROL)
Ps 32: 9 but must be-*c* by bit and bridle
Ro 8: 6 but the mind-*c* by the Spirit is life
8: 8 Those-*c* by the sinful nature cannot

CONTROVERSIES
Tit 3: 9 But avoid foolish-*c* and genealogies

CONVERSATION
Col 4: 6 Let your-*c* be always full of grace,

CONVERT
1Ti 3: 6 He must not be a recent-*c*,

CONVICT
Jn 16: 8 he will-*c* the world of guilt in regard

CONVINCED (CONVINCING)
Ro 8:38 For I am-*c* that neither death
2Ti 1:12 and am-*c* that he is able
3:14 have learned and have become-*c*

CONVINCING* (CONVINCED)
Ac 1: 3 and gave many-*c* proofs that he was

CORNELIUS*
Roman to whom Peter preached; first Gentile Christian (Ac 10).

CORNERSTONE (STONE)
Isa 28:16 a precious-*c* for a sure foundation;
Eph 2:20 Christ Jesus himself as the chief-*c*.
1Pe 2: 6 a chosen and precious-*c*,

CORRECT (CORRECTING CORRECTION CORRECTS)
2Ti 4: 2 *c*, rebuke and encourage—

CORRECTING* (CORRECT)
2Ti 3:16 *c* and training in righteousness,

CORRECTION (CORRECT)
Pr 10:17 whoever ignores-*c* leads others
12: 1 but he who hates-*c* is stupid.
15: 5 whoever heeds-*c* shows prudence.
15:10 he who hates-*c* will die.
29:15 The rod of-*c* imparts wisdom,

CORRECTS* (CORRECT)
Job 5:17 "Blessed is the man whom God-*c*;
Pr 9: 7 Whoever-*c* a mocker invites insult;

CORRUPT (CORRUPTS)
Ge 6:11 Now the earth was-*c* in God's sight

CORRUPTS* (CORRUPT)
Ecc 7: 7 and a bribe-*c* the heart.
1Co 15:33 "Bad company-*c* good character."
Jas 3: 6 It-*c* the whole person, sets

COST
Pr 4: 7 Though it-*c* all you have, get
Isa 55: 1 milk without money and without-*c*.
Rev 21: 6 to drink without-*c* from the spring

COUNSEL (COUNSELOR)
1Ki 22: 5 "First seek the-*c* of the LORD."
Pr 15:22 Plans fail for lack of-*c*,
Rev 3:18 I-*c* you to buy from me gold refined

COUNSELOR (COUNSEL)
Isa 9: 6 Wonderful-*C*, Mighty God,
Jn 14:16 he will give you another-*C* to be

14:26 But the-*C*, the Holy Spirit,

COUNT (COUNTING COUNTS)
Ro 4: 8 whose sin the Lord will never-*c*
6:11 *c* yourselves dead to sin

COUNTING (COUNT)
2Co 5:19 not-*c* men's sins against them.

COUNTRY
Jn 4:44 prophet has no honor in his own-*c*.)

COUNTS (COUNT)
Jn 6:63 The Spirit gives life; the flesh-*c*
1Co 7:19 God's commands is what-*c*.
Gal 5: 6 only thing that-*c* is faith expressing

COURAGE (COURAGEOUS)
Ac 23:11 "Take-*c*! As you have testified
1Co 16:13 stand firm in the faith; be men of-*c*;

COURAGEOUS (COURAGE)
Dt 31: 6 Be strong and-*c*.
Jos 1: 6 and-*c*, because you will lead these

COURSE
Ps 19: 5 a champion rejoicing to run his-*c*.
Pr 15:21 of understanding keeps a straight-*c*.

COURTS
Ps 84:10 Better is one day in your-*c*
100: 4 and his-*c* with praise;

COVENANT (COVENANTS)
Ge 9: 9 "I now establish my-*c* with you
Ex 19: 5 if you obey me fully and keep my-*c*,
1Ch 16:15 He remembers his-*c* forever,
Job 31: 1 "I made a-*c* with my eyes
Jer 31:31 "when I will make a new-*c*
1Co 11:25 "This cup is the new-*c* in my blood;
Gal 4:24 One-*c* is from Mount Sinai
Heb 9:15 Christ is the mediator of a new-*c*,

COVENANTS (COVENANT)
Ro 9: 4 theirs the divine glory, the-*c*,
Gal 4:24 for the women represent two-*c*.

COVER (COVER-UP COVERED COVERS)
Ps 91: 4 he will-*c* you with his feathers,
Jas 5:20 and-*c* over a multitude of sins.

COVER-UP (COVER)
1Pe 2:16 but do not use your freedom as a-*c*

COVERED (COVER)
Ps 32: 1 whose sins are-*c*.
Isa 6: 2 With two wings they-*c* their faces,
Ro 4: 7 whose sins are-*c*.
1Co 11: 4 with his head-*c* dishonors his head.

COVERS (COVER)
Pr 10:12 but love-*c* over all wrongs.
1Pe 4: 8 love-*c* over a multitude of sins.

COVET
Ex 20:17 You shall not-*c* your neighbor's
Ro 13: 9 "Do not steal," "Do not-*c*,"

COWARDLY*
Rev 21: 8 But the-*c*, the unbelieving, the vile,

CRAFTINESS (CRAFTY)
1Co 3:19 "He catches the wise in their-*c*";

CRAFTY (CRAFTINESS)
Ge 3: 1 the serpent was more-*c* than any
2Co 12:16 *c* fellow that I am, I caught you

CRAVE
Pr 23: 3 Do not-*c* his delicacies,
1Pe 2: 2 newborn babies,-*c* pure spiritual

CREATE (CREATED CREATION CREATOR)
Ps 51:10 *C* in me a pure heart, O God,
Isa 45:18 he did not-*c* it to be empty,

CREATED (CREATE)
Ge 1: 1 In the beginning God-*c* the heavens
1:21 God-*c* the great creatures of the sea

1:27 So God-*c* man in his own image,
Ps 148: 5 for he commanded and they were-*c*
Isa 42: 5 he who-*c* the heavens and stretched
Ro 1:25 and served-*c* things rather
1Co 11: 9 neither was man-*c* for woman,
Col 1:16 For by him all things were-*c*:
1Ti 4: 4 For everything God-*c* is good,
Rev 10: 6 who-*c* the heavens and all that is

CREATION (CREATE)
Mk 16:15 and preach the good news to all-*c*.
Jn 17:24 me before the-*c* of the world.
Ro 8:19 The-*c* waits in eager expectation
8:39 depth, nor anything else in all-*c*,
2Co 5:17 he is a new-*c*; the old has gone,
Col 1:15 God, the firstborn over all-*c*.
1Pe 1:20 chosen before the-*c* of the world,
Rev 13: 8 slain from the-*c* of the world.

CREATOR (CREATE)
Ge 14:22 God Most High,-*C* of heaven
Ro 1:25 created things rather than the-*C*—

CREATURE (CREATURES)
Lev 17:11 For the life of a-*c* is in the blood,

CREATURES (CREATURE)
Ge 6:19 bring into the ark two of all living-*c*,
Ps 104:24 the earth is full of your-*c*.

CREDIT (CREDITED)
Ro 4:24 to whom God will-*c* righteousness
1Pe 2:20 it to your-*c* if you receive a beating

CREDITED (CREDIT)
Ge 15: 6 and he-*c* it to him as righteousness.
Ro 4: 5 his faith is-*c* as righteousness.
Gal 3: 6 and it was-*c* to him as righteousness
Jas 2:23 and it was-*c* to him as righteousness

CRIED (CRY)
Ps 18: 6 I-*c* to my God for help.

CRIMSON
Isa 1:18 though they are red as-*c*,

CRIPPLED
Mk 9:45 better for you to enter life-*c*

CRITICISM
2Co 8:20 We want to avoid any-*c*

CROOKED
Pr 10: 9 he who takes-*c* paths will be found
Php 2:15 children of God without fault in a-*c*

CROSS
Mt 10:38 and anyone who does not take his-*c*
Lk 9:23 take up his-*c* daily and follow me.
Ac 2:23 to death by nailing him to the-*c*.
1Co 1:17 lest the-*c* of Christ be emptied
Gal 6:14 in the-*c* of our Lord Jesus Christ,
Php 2: 8 even death on a-*c*!
Col 1:20 through his blood, shed on the-*c*.
2:14 he took it away, nailing it to the-*c*.
2:15 triumphing over them by the-*c*.
Heb 12: 2 set before him endured the-*c*,

CROWD
Ex 23: 2 Do not follow the-*c* in doing wrong.

CROWN (CROWNED CROWNS)
Pr 4: 9 present you with a-*c* of splendor.
10: 6 Blessings-*c* the head
12: 4 noble character is her husband's-*c*,
17: 6 Children's children are a-*c*
Isa 61: 3 to bestow on them a-*c* of beauty
Zec 9:16 like jewels in a-*c*.
Mt 27:29 then twisted together a-*c* of thorns
1Co 9:25 to get a-*c* that will last forever.
2Ti 4: 8 store for me the-*c* of righteousness,
Rev 2:10 and I will give you the-*c* of life.

CROWNED (CROWN)
Ps   8:5 and-*c* him with glory and honor.
Pr 14:18 the prudent are-*c* with knowledge.
Heb 2:7 you-*c* him with glory and honor

CROWNS (CROWN)
Rev 4:10 They lay their-*c* before the throne
      19:12 and on his head are many-*c*.

CRUCIFIED (CRUCIFY)
Mt 20:19 to be mocked and flogged and-*c*.
      27:38 Two robbers were-*c* with him,
Lk 24:7 be-*c* and on the third day be raised
Jn 19:18 Here they-*c* him, and with him two
Ac   2:36 whom you-*c*, both Lord and Christ
Ro   6:6 For we know that our old self was-*c*
1Co 1:23 but we preach Christ-*c*: a stumbling
       2:2 except Jesus Christ and him-*c*.
Gal 2:20 I have been-*c* with Christ
       5:24 Christ Jesus have-*c* the sinful

CRUCIFY (CRUCIFIED CRUCIFYING)
Mt 27:22 They all answered,-"*C* him!" "Why
      27:31 Then they led him away to-*c* him.

CRUCIFYING* (CRUCIFY)
Heb 6:6 to their loss they are-*c* the Son

CRUSH (CRUSHED)
Ge   3:15 he will-*c* your head,
Isa 53:10 it was the Lord's will to-*c* him
Ro 16:20 The God of peace will soon-*c* Satan

CRUSHED (CRUSH)
Ps 34:18 and saves those who are-*c* in spirit.
Isa 53:5 he was-*c* for our iniquities;
2Co 4:8 not-*c*; perplexed, but not in despair;

CRY (CRIED)
Ps 34:15 and his ears are attentive to their-*c*;
      40:1 he turned to me and heard my-*c*.
     130:1 Out of the depths I-*c* to you,

CUP
Ps 23:5 my-*c* overflows.
Mt 10:42 if anyone gives even a-*c* of cold
                water
      23:25 You clean the outside of the-*c*
      26:39 may this-*c* be taken from me.
1Co 11:25 after supper he took the-*c*, saying,

CURSE (CURSED)
Dt 11:26 before you today a blessing and a-*c*
      21:23 hung on a tree is under God's-*c*.
Lk   6:28 bless those who-*c* you, pray
Gal 3:13 of the law by becoming a-*c* for us,
Rev 22:3 No longer will there be any-*c*.

CURSED (CURSE)
Ge   3:17 "*C* is the ground because of you;
Dt 27:15 "*C* is the man who carves an image
      27:16 "*C* is the man who dishonors his
      27:17 "*C* is the man who moves his
      27:18 "*C* is the man who leads the blind
      27:19 *C* is the man who withholds justice
      27:20 "*C* is the man who sleeps
      27:21 "*C* is the man who has sexual
      27:22 "*C* is the man who sleeps
      27:23 "*C* is the man who sleeps
      27:24 "*C* is the man who kills his
      27:25 "*C* is the man who accepts a bribe
      27:26 "*C* is the man who does not uphold
Ro   9:3 I could wish that I myself were-*c*.
Gal 3:10 "*C* is everyone who does not

CURTAIN
Ex 26:33 The-*c* will separate the Holy Place
Lk 23:45 the-*c* of the temple was torn in two.
Heb 10:20 opened for us through the-*c*,

CYMBAL*
1Co 13:1 a resounding gong or a clanging-*c*.

DANCE (DANCING)
Ecc 3:4 a time to mourn and a time to-*d*,

Mt 11:17 and you did not-*d*;

DANCING (DANCE)
Ps 30:11 You turned my wailing into-*d*;
       149:3 Let them praise his name with-*d*

DANGER
Pr 27:12 The prudent see-*d* and take refuge,
Ro   8:35 famine or nakedness or-*d* or sword?

DANIEL
Hebrew exile to Babylon, name changed to Belteshazzar (Da 1:6-7). Refused to eat unclean food (Da 1:8-21). Interpreted Nebuchadnezzar's dreams (Da 2; 4), writing on the wall (Da 5). Thrown into lion's den (Da 6). Visions of (Da 7-12).

DARK (DARKNESS)
Job 34:22 There is no-*d* place, no deep
Pr 31:15 She gets up while it is still-*d*;
Ro   2:19 a light for those who are in the-*d*,
2Pe 1:19 as to a light shining in a-*d* place,

DARKNESS (DARK)
Ge   1:4 he separated the light from the-*d*.
2Sa 22:29 the Lord turns my-*d* into light.
Jn   3:19 but men loved-*d* instead of light
2Co 6:14 fellowship can light have with-*d*?
Eph 5:8 For you were once-*d*, but now you
1Pe 2:9 out of-*d* into his wonderful light.
1Jn 1:5 in him there is no-*d* at all.
       2:9 but hates his brother is still in the-*d*.

DAUGHTERS
Joel 2:28 sons and-*d* will prophesy,

DAVID
Son of Jesse (Ru 4:17-22; 1Ch 2:13-15), ancestor of Jesus (Mt 1:1-17; Lk 3:31).
Anointed king by Samuel (1Sa 16:1-13). Musician to Saul (1Sa 16:14-23; 18:10). Killed Goliath (1Sa 17). Relation with Jonathan (1Sa 18:1-4; 19-20; 23:16-18; 2Sa 1). Disfavor of Saul (1Sa 18:6-23:29). Spared Saul's life (1Sa 24; 26). Among Philistines (1Sa 21:10-14; 27-30). Lament for Saul and Jonathan (2Sa 1).
Anointed king of Judah (2Sa 2:1-11); of Israel (2Sa 5:1-4; 1Ch 11:1-3). Promised eternal dynasty (2Sa 7; 1Ch 17; Ps 132). Adultery with Bathsheba (2Sa 11-12). Absalom's revolt (2Sa 14-18). Last words (2Sa 23:1-7). Death (1Ki 2:10-12; 1Ch 29:28).

DAWN
Ps 37:6 your righteousness shine like the-*d*,
Pr   4:18 is like the first gleam of-*d*,

DAY (DAYS)
Ge   1:5 God called the light-"*d*,"
Ex 20:8 "Remember the Sabbath-*d*
Lev 23:28 because it is the-*D* of Atonement,
Nu 14:14 before them in a pillar of cloud by-*d*,
Jos 1:8 meditate on it-*d* and night,
Ps 84:10 Better is one-*d* in your courts
      96:2 proclaim his salvation-*d* after-*d*.
     118:24 This is the-*d* the Lord has made.
Pr 27:1 not know what a-*d* may bring forth.
Joel 2:31 and dreadful-*d* of the Lord.
Ob   :15 The-*d* of the Lord is near for
Lk 11:3 Give us each-*d* our daily bread.
Ac 17:11 examined the Scriptures every-*d*
2Co 4:16 we are being renewed-*d* by-*d*.
1Th 5:2 for you know very well that the-*d*
2Pe 3:8 With the Lord a-*d* is like

DAYS (DAY)
Dt 17:19 he is to read it all the-*d*, of his life
Ps 23:6 all the-*d* of my life,
      90:10 The length of our-*d* is seventy years
Ecc 12:1 Creator in the-*d* of your youth,
Joel 2:29 I will pour out my Spirit in those-*d*.

Mic   4:1 In the last-*d*
Heb 1:2 in these last-*d* he has spoken to us
2Pe 3:3 that in the last-*d* scoffers will come,

DEACONS
1Ti 3:8 *D*, likewise, are to be men worthy

DEAD (DIE)
Dt 18:11 or spiritist or who consults the-*d*.
Mt 28:7 'He has risen from the-*d*
Ro   6:11 count yourselves-*d* to sin
Eph 2:1 you were-*d* in your transgressions
1Th 4:16 and the-*d* in Christ will rise first.
Jas 2:17 is not accompanied by action, is-*d*.
       2:26 so faith without deeds is-*d*.

DEATH (DIE)
Nu 35:16 the murderer shall be put to-*d*.
Ps 23:4 the valley of the shadow of-*d*,
       116:15 is the death of-*d* his saints.
Pr   8:36 all who hate me love-*d*."
      14:12 but in the end it leads to-*d*.
Ecc 7:2 for-*d* is the destiny of every man;
Isa 25:8 he will swallow up-*d* forever.
      53:12 he poured out his life unto-*d*,
Jn   5:24 he has crossed over from-*d* to life.
Ro   5:12 and in this way-*d* came to all men,
       6:23 For the wages of sin is-*d*,
       8:13 put to-*d* the misdeeds of the body,
1Co 15:21 For since-*d* came through a man,
       15:55 Where, O-*d*, is your sting?"
Rev 1:18 And I hold the keys of-*d* and Hades
       20:6 The second-*d* has no power
       20:14 The lake of fire is the second-*d*.
       21:4 There will be no more-*d*

DEBAUCHERY
Ro 13:13 not in sexual immorality and-*d*,
Eph 5:18 drunk on wine, which leads to-*d*.

DEBORAH
Prophetess who led Israel to victory over Canaanites (Jdg 4-5).

DEBT (DEBTORS DEBTS)
Ro 13:8 Let no-*d* remain outstanding,
      13:8 continuing-*d* to love one another,

DEBTORS (DEBT)
Mt   6:12 as we also have forgiven our-*d*.

DEBTS (DEBT)
Dt 15:1 seven years you must cancel-*d*.
Mt   6:12 Forgive us our-*d*,

DECAY
Ps 16:10 will you let your Holy One see-*d*.
Ac   2:27 will you let your Holy One see-*d*.

DECEIT (DECEIVE)
Mk 7:22 greed, malice,-*d*, lewdness, envy,
1Pe 2:1 yourselves of all malice and all-*d*,
       2:22 and no-*d* was found in his mouth."

DECEITFUL (DECEIVE)
Jer 17:9 The heart is-*d* above all things
2Co 11:13 men are false apostles,-*d* workmen,

DECEITFULNESS (DECEIVE)
Mk 4:19 the-*d* of wealth and the desires
Heb 3:13 of you may be hardened by sin's-*d*.

DECEIVE (DECEIT DECEITFUL DECEITFULNESS DECEIVED DECEIVES DECEPTIVE)
Lev 19:11 "'Do not-*d* one another.
Pr 14:5 A truthful witness does not-*d*,
Mt 24:5 'I am the Christ,' and will-*d* many.
Ro 16:18 and flattery they-*d* the minds
1Co 3:18 Do not-*d* yourselves.
Eph 5:6 Let no one-*d* you with empty words
Jas 1:22 to the word, and so-*d* yourselves.
1Jn 1:8 we-*d* ourselves and the truth is not

DECEIVED (DECEIVE)
Ge   3:13 "The serpent-*d* me, and I ate."
Gal 6:7 Do not be-*d*: God cannot be
1Ti 2:14 And Adam was not the one-*d*;
2Ti 3:13 to worse, deceiving and being-*d*.
Jas 1:16 Don't be-*d*, my dear brothers.

DECEIVES (DECEIVE)
Gal 6:3 he is nothing, he-*d* himself.
Jas 1:26 he-*d* himself and his religion is

DECENCY*
1Ti 2:9 women to dress modestly, with-*d*

DECEPTIVE (DECEIVE)
Pr 31:30 Charm is-*d*, and beauty is fleeting;
Col 2:8 through hollow and-*d* philosophy,

DECLARE (DECLARED DECLARING)
1Ch 16:24 *D* his glory among the nations,
Ps 19:1 The heavens-*d* the glory of God;
      96:3 *D* his glory among the nations,
Isa 42:9 and new things I-*d*;

DECLARED (DECLARE)
Mk 7:19 Jesus-*d* all foods "clean.")
Ro   2:13 the law who will be-*d* righteous.
       3:20 no one will be-*d* righteous

DECLARING (DECLARE)
Ps 71:8 *d* your splendor all day long.
Ac   2:11 we hear them-*d* the wonders

DECREED (DECREES)
La   3:37 happen if the Lord has not-*d* it?
Lk 22:22 Son of Man will go as it has been-*d*,

DECREES (DECREED)
Lev 10:11 Israelites all the-*d* the Lord has
Ps 119:112 My heart is set on keeping your-*d*

DEDICATE (DEDICATION)
Nu   6:12 He must-*d* himself to the Lord
Pr 20:25 for a man to-*d* something rashly

DEDICATION (DEDICATE)
1Ti 5:11 sensual desires overcome their-*d*

DEED (DEEDS)
Col 3:17 you do, whether in word or-*d*,

DEEDS (DEED)
1Sa 2:3 and by him-*d* are weighed.
Ps 65:5 with awesome-*d* of righteousness,
      66:3 "How awesome are your-*d*!
      78:4 the praiseworthy-*d* of the Lord,
      86:10 you are great and do marvelous-*d*;
      92:4 For you make me glad by your-*d*,
       111:3 Glorious and majestic are his-*d*,
Hab 3:2 I stand in awe of your-*d*, O Lord.
Mt   5:16 that they may see your good-*d*
Ac 26:20 prove their repentance by their-*d*.
Jas 2:14 claims to have faith but has no-*d*?
       2:20 faith without-*d* is useless?
1Pe 2:12 they may see your good-*d*

DEEP (DEPTH)
1Co 2:10 all things, even the-*d* things
1Ti 3:9 hold of the-*d* truths of the faith

DEER
Ps 42:1 As the-*d* pants for streams of water,

DEFEND (DEFENSE)
Ps 74:22 Rise up, O God, and-*d* your cause;
Pr 31:9 *d* the rights of the poor and needy
Jer 50:34 He will vigorously-*d* their cause

DEFENSE (DEFEND)
Ps 35:23 Awake, and rise to my-*d*!
Php 1:16 here for the-*d* of the gospel.
1Jn 2:1 speaks to the Father in our-*d*—

DEFERRED*
Pr 13:12 Hope-*d* makes the heart sick,

DEFILE (DEFILED)
Da   1:8 Daniel resolved not to-*d* himself

DEFILED (DEFILE)
Isa 24: 5 The earth is-*d* by its people;

DEFRAUD
Lev 19:13 Do not-*d* your neighbor or rob him.

DEITY*
Col 2: 9 of the-*D* lives in bodily form,

DELIGHT (DELIGHTS)
1Sa 15:22 "Does the Lord-*d*
Ps 1: 2 But his-*d* is in the law of the Lord
16: 3 in whom is all my-*d*.
35: 9 and-*d* in his salvation.
37: 4 *D* yourself in the Lord
43: 4 to God, my joy and my-*d*.
51:16 You do not-*d* in sacrifice,
119:77 for your law is my-*d*.
Pr 29:17 he will bring-*d* to your soul.
Isa 42: 1 my chosen one in whom I-*d*
55: 2 and your soul will-*d* in the richest
61:10 I-*d* greatly in the Lord;
Jer 9:24 for in these I-*d*,
15:16 they were my joy and my heart's-*d*,
Mic 7:18 but-*d* to show mercy.
Zep 3:17 He will take great-*d* in you,
Mt 12:18 the one I love, in whom I-*d*;
1Co 13: 6 Love does not-*d* in evil
2Co 12:10 for Christ's sake, I-*d* in weaknesses,

DELIGHTS (DELIGHT)
Ps 22: 8 since he-*d* in him."
35:27 who-*d* in the well-being
36: 8 from your river of-*d*.
37:23 if the Lord-*d* in a man's way,
Pr 3:12 as a father the son he-*d* in.
12:22 but he-*d* in men who are truthful.
23:24 he who has a wise son-*d* in him.

DELILAH*
Woman who betrayed Samson (Jdg 16:4-22).

DELIVER (DELIVERANCE DELIVERED
DELIVERER DELIVERS)
Ps 72:12 For he will-*d* the needy who cry out
79: 9 *d* us and forgive our sins
Mt 6:13 but-*d* us from the evil one.'
2Co 1:10 hope that he will continue to-*d* us,

DELIVERANCE (DELIVER)
Ps 3: 8 From the Lord comes-*d*.
32: 7 and surround me with songs of-*d*.
33:17 A horse is a vain hope for-*d*;

DELIVERED (DELIVER)
Ps 34: 4 he-*d* me from all my fears.
Ro 4:25 He was-*d* over to death for our sins

DELIVERER (DELIVER)
Ps 18: 2 is my rock, my fortress and my-*d*;
40:17 You are my help and my-*d*;
140: 7 O Sovereign Lord, my strong-*d*,
144: 2 my stronghold and my-*d*,

DELIVERS (DELIVER)
Ps 34:17 he-*d* them from all their troubles.
34:19 but the Lord-*d* him from them all
37:40 The Lord helps them and-*d* them
37:40 *d* them from the wicked

DEMANDED
Lk 12:20 This very night your life will be-*d*
12:48 been given much, much will be-*d*;

DEMONS
Mt 12:27 And if I drive out-*d* by Beelzebub,
Mk 5:15 possessed by the legion of-*d*,
Ro 8:38 neither angels nor-*d*, neither
Jas 2:19 Good! Even the-*d* believe that—

DEMONSTRATE (DEMONSTRATES)
Ro 3:26 he did it to-*d* his justice

DEMONSTRATES* (DEMONSTRATE)
Ro 5: 8 God-*d* his own love for us in this:

DEN
Da 6:16 and threw him into the lions'-*d*.
Mt 21:13 you are making it a-*'d* of robbers.' "

DENARIUS
Mk 12:15 Bring me a-*d* and let me look at it."

DENIED (DENY)
1Ti 5: 8 he has-*d* the faith and is worse

DENIES (DENY)
1Jn 2:23 No one who-*d* the Son has

DENY (DENIED DENIES DENYING)
Ex 23: 6 "Do not-*d* justice to your poor
Job 27: 5 till I die, I will not-*d* my integrity.
La 3:35 to-*d* a man his rights
Lk 9:23 he must-*d* himself and take up his
Tit 1:16 but by their actions they-*d* him.

DENYING* (DENY)
Eze 22:29 mistreat the alien,-*d* them justice.
2Ti 3: 5 a form of godliness but-*d* its power.
2Pe 2: 1 *d* the sovereign Lord who bought

DEPART (DEPARTED)
Ge 49:10 The scepter will not-*d* from Judah,
Job 1:21 and naked I will-*d*.
Mt 25:41 '*D* from me, you who are cursed,
Php 1:23 I desire to-*d* and be with Christ,

DEPARTED (DEPART)
1Sa 4:21 "The glory has-*d* from Israel"—
Ps 119:102 I have not-*d* from your laws,

DEPOSIT
2Co 1:22 put his Spirit in our hearts as a-*d*,
5: 5 and has given us the Spirit as a-*d*,
Eph 1:14 who is a-*d* guaranteeing our
2Ti 1:14 Guard the good-*d* that was

DEPRAVED (DEPRAVITY)
Ro 1:28 he gave them over to a-*d* mind,
Php 2:15 fault in a crooked and-*d* generation,

DEPRAVITY (DEPRAVED)
Ro 1:29 of wickedness, evil, greed and-*d*.

DEPRIVE
Dt 24:17 Do not-*d* the alien or the fatherless
Pr 18: 5 or to-*d* the innocent of justice.
Isa 10: 2 to-*d* the poor of their rights
29:21 with false testimony-*d* the innocent
1Co 7: 5 Do not-*d* each other

DEPTH (DEEP)
Ro 8:39 any powers, neither height nor-*d*,
11:33 the-*d* of the riches of the wisdom

DESERT
Nu 32:13 wander in the-*d* forty years,
Ne 9:19 you did not abandon them in the-*d*.
Ps 78:19 "Can God spread a table in the-*d*?
78:52 led them like sheep through the-*d*.
Mk 1:13 and he was in the-*d* forty days,

DESERTED (DESERTS)
Ezr 9: 9 our God has not-*d* us
Mt 26:56 all the disciples-*d* him and fled.
2Ti 1:15 in the province of Asia has-*d* me,

DESERTING (DESERTS)
Gal 1: 6 are so quickly-*d* the one who called

DESERTS (DESERTED DESERTING)
Zec 11:17 who-*d* the flock!

DESERVE (DESERVES)
Ps 103:10 he does not treat us as our sins-*d*
Jer 21:14 I will punish you as your deeds-*d*,
Mt 22: 8 those I invited did not-*d* to come.
Ro 1:32 those who do such things-*d* death,

DESERVES (DESERVE)
2Sa 12: 5 the man who did this-*d* to die!
Lk 10: 7 for the worker-*d* his wages.
1Ti 5:18 and 'The worker-*d* his wages."

DESIRABLE (DESIRE)
Pr 22: 1 A good name is more-*d*

DESIRE (DESIRABLE DESIRES)
Ge 3:16 Your-*d* will be for your husband,
Dt 5:21 You shall not set your-*d*
1Ch 29:18 keep this-*d* in the hearts
Ps 40: 6 Sacrifice and offering you did not-*d*
40: 8 I-*d* to do your will, O my God;
73:25 earth has nothing I-*d* besides you
Pr 3:15 nothing you-*d* can compare
10:24 what the righteous-*d* will be
11:23 The-*d* of the righteous ends only
Isa 26: 8 are the-*d* of our hearts.
53: 2 appearance that we should-*d* him.
55:11 but will accomplish what I-*d*
Hos 6: 6 For I-*d* mercy, not sacrifice,
Mt 9:13 learn what this means: 'I-*d* mercy,
Ro 7:18 For I have the-*d* to do what is good,
1Co 12:31 But eagerly-*d* the greater gifts.
14: 1 and eagerly-*d* spiritual gifts,
Php 1:23 I-*d* to depart and be with Christ,
Heb 13:18 *d* to live honorably in every way.
Jas 1:15 Then, after-*d* has conceived,

DESIRES (DESIRE)
Ge 4: 7 at your door; it-*d* to have you,
Ps 34:12 and-*d* to see many good days,
37: 4 he will give you the-*d* of your heart.
103: 5 satisfies your-*d* with good things,
145:19 He fulfills the-*d* of those who fear
Pr 11: 6 the unfaithful are trapped by evil-*d*,
19:22 What a man-*d* is unfailing love;
Mk 4:19 and the-*d* for other things come in
Ro 8: 5 set on what that nature-*d*;
13:14 to gratify the-*d* of the sinful nature.
Gal 5:16 and you will not gratify the-*d*
5:17 The sinful nature-*d* what is contrary
1Ti 3: 1 an overseer, he-*d* a noble task.
6: 9 and harmful-*d* that plunge men
2Ti 2:22 Flee the evil-*d* of youth,
Jas 1:20 about the righteous life that God-*d*.
4: 1 from your-*d* that battle within you?
1Pe 2:11 to abstain from sinful-*d*, which war
1Jn 2:17 The world and its-*d* pass away,

DESOLATE
Isa 54: 1 are the children of the-*d* woman

DESPAIR
Isa 61: 3 instead of a spirit of-*d*.
2Co 4: 8 perplexed, but not in-*d*; persecuted,

DESPISE (DESPISED DESPISES)
Job 42: 6 Therefore I-*d* myself
Pr 1: 7 but fools-*d* wisdom and discipline.
3:11 do not-*d* the Lord's discipline
23:22 do not-*d* your mother
Lk 16:13 devoted to the one and-*d* the other.
Tit 2:15 Do not let anyone-*d* you.

DESPISED (DESPISE)
Ge 25:34 So Esau-*d* his birthright.
Isa 53: 3 He was-*d* and rejected by men,
1Co 1:28 of this world and the-*d* things—

DESPISES (DESPISE)
Pr 14:21 He who-*d* his neighbor sins,
15:20 but a foolish man-*d* his mother.
15:32 who ignores discipline-*d* himself,
Zec 4:10 "Who-*d* the day of small things?

DESTINED (DESTINY)
Lk 2:34 "This child is-*d* to cause the falling

DESTINY (DESTINED PREDESTINED)
Ps 73:17 then I understood their final-*d*.
Ecc 7: 2 for death is the-*d* of every man;

DESTITUTE
Pr 31: 8 for the rights of all who are-*d*.
Heb 11:37 *d*, persecuted and mistreated—

DESTROY (DESTROYED DESTROYS
DESTRUCTION)
Pr 1:32 complacency of fools will-*d* them;
Mt 10:28 of the One who can-*d* both soul

DESTROYED (DESTROY)
Job 19:26 And after my skin has been-*d*,
Isa 55:13 which will not be-*d*."
1Co 8:11 for whom Christ died, is-*d*
15:26 The last enemy to be-*d* is death.
2Co 5: 1 if the earthly tent we live in is-*d*
Heb 10:39 of those who shrink back and are-*d*,
2Pe 3:10 the elements will be-*d* by fire,

DESTROYS (DESTROY)
Pr 6:32 whoever does so-*d* himself.
11: 9 mouth the godless-*d* his neighbor,
18: 9 is brother to one who-*d*.
28:24 he is partner to him who-*d*.
Ecc 9:18 but one sinner-*d* much good.
1Co 3:17 If anyone-*d* God's temple,

DESTRUCTION (DESTROY)
Pr 16:18 Pride goes before-*d*,
Hos 13:14 Where, O grave, is your-*d*?
Mt 7:13 broad is the road that leads to-*d*,
Gal 6: 8 from that nature will reap-*d*;
2Th 1: 9 punished with everlasting-*d*
1Ti 6: 9 that plunge men into ruin and-*d*.
2Pe 2: 1 bringing swift-*d* on themselves.
3:16 other Scriptures, to their own-*d*.

DETERMINED (DETERMINES)
Job 14: 5 Man's days are-*d*;
Isa 14:26 This is the plan-*d* for the whole
Da 11:36 for what has been-*d* must take place
Ac 17:26 and he-*d* the times set for them

DETERMINES* (DETERMINED)
Ps 147: 4 He-*d* the number of the stars
Pr 16: 9 but the Lord-*d* his steps.
1Co 12:11 them to each one, just as he-*d*.

DETESTABLE (DETESTS)
Pr 21:27 The sacrifice of the wicked is-*d*—
28: 9 even his prayers are-*d*.
Isa 1:13 Your incense is-*d* to me.
Lk 16:15 among men is-*d* in God's sight.
Tit 1:16 They are-*d*, disobedient

DETESTS (DETESTABLE)
Dt 22: 5 Lord your God-*d* anyone who
23:18 the Lord your God-*d* them both.
25:16 Lord your God-*d* anyone who
Pr 12:22 The Lord-*d* lying lips,
15: 8 The Lord-*d* the sacrifice
15: 9 The Lord-*d* the way
15:26 The Lord-*d* the thoughts
16: 5 The Lord-*d* all the proud of heart
17:15 the Lord-*d* them both.
20:23 The Lord-*d* differing weights,

DEVIL (DEVIL'S)
Mt 13:39 the enemy who sows them is the-*d*.
25:41 the eternal fire prepared for the-*d*
Lk 4: 2 forty days he was tempted by the-*d*.
8:12 then the-*d* comes and takes away
Eph 4:27 and do not give the-*d* a foothold.
2Ti 2:26 and escape from the trap of the-*d*,
Jas 4: 7 Resist the-*d*, and he will flee
1Pe 5: 8 Your enemy the-*d* prowls
1Jn 3: 8 who does what is sinful is of the-*d*,
Rev 12: 9 that ancient serpent called the-*d*.

DEVIL'S (DEVIL)
Eph 6:11 stand against the-*d* schemes.
1Ti 3: 7 into disgrace and into the-*d* trap.
1Jn 3: 8 was to destroy the-*d* work.

DEVOTE (DEVOTED DEVOTING
DEVOTION DEVOUT)
Job 11:13 "Yet if you-*d* your heart to him
Jer 30:21 for who is he who will-*d* himself

Col 4:2 *D* yourselves to prayer, being
1Ti 4:13 *d* yourself to the public reading
Tit 3:8 may be careful to-*d* themselves

DEVOTED (DEVOTE)
Ezr 7:10 For Ezra had-*d* himself to the study
Ac 2:42 They-*d* themselves
Ro 12:10 Be-*d* to one another
1Co 7:34 Her aim is to be-*d* to the Lord

DEVOTING (DEVOTE)
1Ti 5:10 *d* herself to all kinds of good deeds.

DEVOTION (DEVOTE)
1Ch 28:9 and serve him with wholehearted-*d*
Eze 33:31 With their mouths they express-*d*,
1Co 7:35 way in undivided-*d* to the Lord.
2Co 11:3 from your sincere and pure-*d*

DEVOUR
2Sa 2:26 "Must the sword-*d* forever?
Mk 12:40 They-*d* widows' houses
1Pe 5:8 lion looking for someone to-*d*.

DEVOUT (DEVOTE)
Lk 2:25 Simeon, who was righteous and-*d*.

DIE (DEAD DEATH DIED DIES)
Ge 2:17 when you eat of it you will surely-*d*
Ex 11:5 Every firstborn son in Egypt will-*d*,
Ru 1:17 Where you-*d* I will-*d*, and there I
2Ki 14:6 each is to-*d* for his own sins."
Pr 5:23 He will-*d* for lack of discipline,
10:21 but fools-*d* for lack of judgment.
15:10 he who hates correction will-*d*.
23:13 with the rod, he will not-*d*.
Ecc 3:2 a time to be born and a time to-*d*,
Isa 66:24 their worm will not-*d*, nor will their
Eze 3:18 that wicked man will-*d* for his sin,
18:4 soul who sins is the one who will-*d*.
33:8 'O wicked man, you will surely-*d*,'
Mt 26:52 "for all who draw the sword will-*d*
Jn 11:26 and believes in me will never-*d*.
Ro 5:7 Very rarely will anyone-*d*
14:8 and if we-*d*, we-*d* to the Lord.
1Co 15:22 in Adam all-*d*, so in Christ all will
15:31 I-*d* every day—I mean that,
Php 1:21 to live is Christ and to-*d* is gain.
Heb 9:27 Just as man is destined to-*d* once,
Rev 14:13 Blessed are the dead who-*d*

DIED (DIE)
Ro 5:6 we were still powerless, Christ-*d*
6:2 By no means! We-*d* to sin;
6:8 if we-*d* with Christ, we believe that
14:15 brother for whom Christ-*d*
1Co 8:11 for whom Christ-*d*, is destroyed
15:3 that Christ-*d* for our sins according
2Co 5:14 for all, and therefore all-*d*.
Col 3:3 For you-*d*, and your life is now
1Th 5:10 for us so that, whether we are
2Ti 2:11 If we-*d* with him,
Heb 9:15 now that he has-*d* as a ransom
1Pe 3:18 For Christ-*d* for sins once for all,
Rev 2:8 who-*d* and came to life again.

DIES (DIE)
Job 14:14 If a man-*d*, will he live again?
Pr 11:7 a wicked man-*d*, his hope perishes;
Jn 11:25 in me will live, even though he-*d*;
1Co 15:36 does not come to life unless it-*d*.

DIFFERENCE (DIFFERENT)
Ro 10:12 For there is no-*d* between Jew

DIFFERENT (DIFFERENCE)
1Co 12:4 There are-*d* kinds of gifts,
2Co 11:4 or a-*d* gospel from the one you

DIGNITY
Pr 31:25 She is clothed with strength and-*d*;

DIGS
Pr 26:27 If a man-*d* a pit, he will fall into it;

DILIGENCE (DILIGENT)
Heb 6:11 to show this same-*d* to the very end

DILIGENT (DILIGENCE)
Pr 21:5 The plans of the-*d* lead to profit
1Ti 4:15 Be-*d* in these matters; give yourself

DIRECT (DIRECTS)
Ps 119:35 *D* me in the path of your
119:133 *D* my footsteps according
Jer 10:23 it is not for man to-*d* his steps.
2Th 3:5 May the Lord-*d* your hearts

DIRECTS (DIRECT)
Ps 42:8 By day the Lord-*d* his love,
Isa 48:17 who-*d* you in the way you should

DIRGE
Mt 11:17 we sang a-*d*,

DISAPPEAR
Mt 5:18 will by any means-*d* from the Law
Lk 16:17 earth to-*d* than for the least stroke

DISAPPOINT* (DISAPPOINTED)
Ro 5:5 And hope does not-*d* us,

DISAPPOINTED (DISAPPOINT)
Ps 22:5 in you they trusted and were not-*d*.

DISASTER
Ps 57:1 wings until the-*d* has passed.
Pr 3:25 Have no fear of sudden-*d*
17:5 over-*d* will not go unpunished.
Isa 45:7 I bring prosperity and create-*d*;
Eze 7:5 An unheard-of-*d* is coming.

DISCERN (DISCERNING DISCERNMENT)
Ps 19:12 Who can-*d* his errors?
139:3 You-*d* my going out and my lying
Php 1:10 you may be able to-*d* what is best

DISCERNING (DISCERN)
Pr 14:6 knowledge comes easily to the-*d*.
15:14 The-*d* heart seeks knowledge,
17:24 A-*d* man keeps wisdom in view,
17:28 and-*d* if he holds his tongue.
19:25 rebuke a-*d* man, and he will gain

DISCERNMENT (DISCERN)
Pr 17:10 A rebuke impresses a man of-*d*
28:11 a poor man who has-*d* sees

DISCIPLE (DISCIPLES)
Mt 10:42 these little ones because he is my-*d*,
Lk 14:27 and follow me cannot be my-*d*.

DISCIPLES (DISCIPLE)
Mt 28:19 Therefore go and make-*d*
Jn 8:31 to my teaching, you are really my-*d*
13:35 men will know that you are my-*d*
Ac 11:26 The-*d* were called Christians first

DISCIPLINE (DISCIPLINED DISCIPLINES)
Ps 38:1 or-*d* me in your wrath.
39:11 You rebuke and-*d* men for their sin;
94:12 Blessed is the man you-*d*, O Lord
Pr 1:7 but fools despise wisdom and-*d*.
3:11 do not despise the Lord's-*d*
5:12 You will say, "How I hated-*d*!
5:23 He will die for lack of-*d*,
6:23 and the corrections of-*d*
10:17 He who heeds-*d* shows the way
12:1 Whoever loves-*d* loves knowledge,
13:18 He who ignores-*d* comes to poverty
13:24 who loves him is careful to-*d* him.
15:5 A fool spurns his father's-*d*,
15:32 he who ignores-*d* despises himself,
19:18 *D* your son, for in that there is hope
22:15 the rod of-*d* will drive it far
23:13 Do not withhold-*d* from a child;
29:17 *D* your son, and he will give you
Heb 12:5 do not make light of the Lord's-*d*,
12:7 as-*d*; God is treating you

12:11 No-*d* seems pleasant at the time,
Rev 3:19 Those whom I love I rebuke and-*d*.

DISCIPLINED (DISCIPLINE)
Pr 1:3 for acquiring a-*d* and prudent life,
Jer 31:18 'You-*d* me like an unruly calf,
1Co 11:32 we are being-*d* so that we will not
Tit 1:8 upright, holy and-*d*.
Heb 12:7 For what son is not-*d* by his father?

DISCIPLINES (DISCIPLINE)
Dt 8:5 your heart that as a man-*d* his son,
Pr 3:12 the Lord-*d* those he loves,
Heb 12:6 because the Lord-*d* those he loves,
12:10 but God-*d* us for our good,

DISCLOSED
Lk 8:17 is nothing hidden that will not be-*d*.

DISCOURAGED
Jos 1:9 Do not be terrified; do not be-*d*,
10:25 "Do not be afraid; do not be-*d*.
1Ch 28:20 or-*d*, for the Lord God,
Isa 42:4 he will not falter or be-*d*
Col 3:21 children, or they will become-*d*.

DISCREDITED
2Co 6:3 so that our ministry will not be-*d*.

DISCRETION*
1Ch 22:12 May the Lord give you-*d*
Pr 1:4 knowledge and-*d* to the young—
2:11 *D* will protect you,
5:2 that you may maintain-*d*
8:12 I possess knowledge and-*d*
11:22 a beautiful woman who shows no-*d*.

DISCRIMINATED*
Jas 2:4 have you not-*d* among yourselves

DISFIGURED
Isa 52:14 his appearance was so-*d*

DISGRACE (DISGRACEFUL DISGRACES)
Pr 11:2 When pride comes, then comes-*d*,
14:34 but sin is a-*d* to any people.
19:26 is a son who brings shame and-*d*.
Ac 5:41 of suffering-*d* for the Name.
Heb 13:13 the camp, bearing the-*d* he bore.

DISGRACEFUL (DISGRACE)
Pr 10:5 during harvest is a-*d* son.
17:2 wise servant will rule over a-*d* son,

DISGRACES (DISGRACE)
Pr 28:7 of gluttons-*d* his father.
29:15 but a child left to itself-*d* his mother

DISHONEST
Pr 11:1 The Lord abhors-*d* scales,
29:27 The righteous detest the-*d*.
Lk 16:10 whoever is-*d* with very little will
1Ti 3:8 wine, and not pursuing-*d* gain.

DISHONOR (DISHONORS)
Lev 18:7 " 'Do not-*d* your father
Pr 30:9 and so-*d* the name of my God.
1Co 15:43 it is sown in-*d*, it is raised in glory;

DISHONORS (DISHONOR)
Dt 27:16 Cursed is the man who-*d* his father

DISMAYED
Isa 28:16 the one who trusts will never be-*d*.
41:10 do not be-*d*, for I am your God.

DISOBEDIENCE (DISOBEY)
Ro 5:19 as through the-*d* of the one man
11:32 to-*d* so that he may have mercy
Heb 2:2 and-*d* received its just punishment,
4:6 go in, because of their-*d*.
4:11 fall by following their example of-*d*.

DISOBEDIENT (DISOBEY)
2Ti 3:2 proud, abusive,-*d* to their parents,
Tit 1:6 to the charge of being wild and-*d*.
1:16 *d* and unfit for doing anything

DISOBEY (DISOBEDIENCE DISOBEDIENT)
Dt 11:28 the curse if you-*d* the commands
2Ch 24:20 'Why do you-*d* the Lord's
Ro 1:30 they-*d* their parents; they are

DISORDER
1Co 14:33 For God is not a God of-*d*
2Co 12:20 slander, gossip, arrogance and-*d*.
Jas 3:16 there you find-*d* and every evil

DISOWN
Pr 30:9 I may have too much and-*d* you
Mt 10:33 I will-*d* him before my Father
26:35 to die with you, I will never-*d* you."
2Ti 2:12 If we-*d* him,

DISPLAY (DISPLAYS)
Eze 39:21 I will-*d* my glory among the nations
1Ti 1:16 Christ Jesus might-*d* his unlimited

DISPLAYS (DISPLAY)
Isa 44:23 he-*d* his glory in Israel.

DISPUTE (DISPUTES)
Pr 17:14 before a-*d* breaks out.
1Co 6:1 If any of you has a-*d* with another,

DISPUTES (DISPUTE)
Pr 18:18 Casting the lot settles-*d*

DISQUALIFIED
1Co 9:27 I myself will not be-*d* for the prize.

DISREPUTE*
2Pe 2:2 will bring the way of truth into-*d*.

DISSENSION*
Pr 6:14 he always stirs up-*d*.
6:19 and a man who stirs up-*d*
10:12 Hatred stirs up-*d*,
15:18 A hot-tempered man stirs up-*d*,
16:28 A perverse man stirs up-*d*,
28:25 A greedy man stirs up-*d*,
29:22 An angry man stirs up-*d*,
Ro 13:13 debauchery, not in-*d* and jealousy.

DISSIPATION*
Lk 21:34 will be weighed down with-*d*,
1Pe 4:4 with them into the same flood of-*d*,

DISTINGUISH
1Ki 3:9 to-*d* between right and wrong.
Heb 5:14 themselves to-*d* good from evil.

DISTORT
2Co 4:2 nor do we-*d* the word of God.
2Pe 3:16 ignorant and unstable people-*d*,

DISTRESS (DISTRESSED)
Ps 18:6 In my-*d* I called to the Lord;
Jnh 2:2 "In my-*d* I called to the Lord,
Jas 1:27 after orphans and widows in their-*d*

DISTRESSED (DISTRESS)
Ro 14:15 If your brother is-*d*

DIVIDED (DIVISION)
Mt 12:25 household-*d* against itself will not
Lk 23:34 they-*d* up his clothes by casting lots
1Co 1:13 Is Christ-*d*? Was Paul crucified

DIVINATION
Lev 19:26 " 'Do not practice-*d* or sorcery.

DIVINE
Ro 1:20 his eternal power and-*d* nature—
2Co 10:4 they have-*d* power
2Pe 1:4 you may participate in the-*d* nature

DIVISION (DIVIDED DIVISIONS DIVISIVE)
Lk 12:51 on earth? No, I tell you, but-*d*
1Co 12:25 so that there should be no-*d*

DIVISIONS (DIVISION)
Ro 16:17 to watch out for those who cause-*d*
1Co 1:10 another so that there may be no-*d*
11:18 there are-*d* among you,

DIVISIVE* (DIVISION)
Tit 3:10 Warn a-*d* person once,

DIVORCE
Mal 2:16 "I hate-*d*," says the LORD God
Mt 19: 3 for a man to-*d* his wife for any
1Co 7:11 And a husband must not-*d* his wife.
7:27 Are you married? Do not seek a-*d*.

DOCTOR
Mt 9:12 "It is not the healthy who need a-*d*,

DOCTRINE
1Ti 4:16 Watch your life and-*d* closely.
Tit 2: 1 is in accord with sound-*d*.

DOMINION
Ps 22:28 for-*d* belongs to the LORD

DOOR
Ps 141: 3 keep watch over the-*d* of my lips.
Mt 6: 6 close the-*d* and pray to your Father
7: 7 and the-*d* will be opened to you.
Rev 3:20 I stand at the-*d* and knock.

DOORKEEPER
Ps 84:10 I would rather be a-*d* in the house

DOUBLE-EDGED
Heb 4:12 Sharper than any-*d* sword,
Rev 1:16 of his mouth came a sharp-*d* sword.
2:12 of him who has the sharp,-*d* sword.

DOUBLE-MINDED (MIND)
Ps 119:113 I hate-*d* men,
Jas 1: 8 he is a-*d* man, unstable

DOUBT
Mt 14:31 he said, "why did you-*d*?"
21:21 if you have faith and do not-*d*,
Mk 11:23 and does not-*d* in his heart
Jas 1: 6 he must believe and not-*d*,
Jude :22 Be merciful to those who-*d*;

DOWNCAST
Ps 42: 5 Why are you-*d*, O my soul?
2Co 7: 6 But God, who comforts the-*d*,

DRAW (DRAWING DRAWS)
Mt 26:52 "for all who-*d* the sword will die
Jn 12:32 up from the earth, will-*d* all men
Heb 10:22 let us-*d* near to God

DRAWING (DRAW)
Lk 21:28 because your redemption is-*d* near

DRAWS (DRAW)
Jn 6:44 the Father who sent me-*d* him,

DREADFUL
Heb 10:31 It is a-*d* thing to fall into the hands

DRESS
1Ti 2: 9 I also want women to-*d* modestly,

DRINK (DRUNK DRUNKARDS DRUNKENNESS)
Pr 5:15 *D* water from your own cistern,
Lk 12:19 Take life easy; eat,-*d* and be merry
Jn 7:37 let him come to me and-*d*.
1Co 12:13 were all given the one Spirit to-*d*,
Rev 21: 6 to-*d* without cost from the spring

DRIVES
1Jn 4:18 But perfect love-*d* out fear,

DROP
Pr 17:14 so-*d* the matter before a dispute
Isa 40:15 Surely the nations are like a-*d*

DRUNK (DRINK)
Eph 5:18 Do not get-*d* on wine, which leads

DRUNKARDS (DRINK)
Pr 23:21 for-*d* and gluttons become poor,
1Co 6:10 nor the greedy nor-*d* nor slanderers

DRUNKENNESS (DRINK)
Lk 21:34 weighed down with dissipation,-*d*
Ro 13:13 and-*d*, not in sexual immorality

DRY
Isa 53: 2 and like a root out of-*d* ground.
Eze 37: 4 *D* bones, hear the word

DUST
Ge 2: 7 man from the-*d* of the ground
Ps 103:14 he remembers that we are-*d*.
Ecc 3:20 all come from-*d*, and to-*d* all return.

DUTY
Ecc 12:13 for this is the whole-*d* of man.
Ac 23: 1 I have fulfilled my-*d* to God
1Co 7: 3 husband should fulfill his marital-*d*.

DWELL (DWELLING)
1Ki 8:27 "But will God really-*d* on earth?
Ps 23: 6 I will-*d* in the house of the LORD
Isa 43:18 do not-*d* on the past.
Eph 3:17 so that Christ may-*d* in your hearts
Col 1:19 to have all his fullness-*d* in him,
3:16 the word of Christ-*d* in you richly

DWELLING (DWELL)
Eph 2:22 to become a-*d* in which God lives

EAGER
Pr 31:13 and works with-*e* hands.
1Pe 5: 2 greedy for money, but-*e* to serve;

EAGLE'S (EAGLES)
Ps 103: 5 your youth is renewed like the-*e*.

EAGLES (EAGLE'S)
Isa 40:31 They will soar on wings like-*e*;

EAR (EARS)
1Co 2: 9 no-*e* has heard,
12:16 if the-*e* should say, "Because I am

EARNED
Pr 31:31 Give her the reward she has-*e*,

EARS (EAR)
Job 42: 5 My-*e* had heard of you
Ps 34:15 and his-*e* are attentive to their cry;
Pr 21:13 If a man shuts his-*e* to the cry
2Ti 4: 3 to say what their itching-*e* want

EARTH (EARTHLY)
Ge 1: 1 God created the heavens and the-*e*.
Ps 24: 1 *e* is the LORD's, and everything
108: 5 and let your glory be over all the-*e*.
Isa 6: 3 the whole-*e* is full of his glory."
51: 6 the-*e* will wear out like a garment
55: 9 the heavens are higher than the-*e*,
66: 1 and the-*e* is my footstool.
Jer 23:24 "Do not I fill heaven and-*e*?"
Hab 2:20 let all the-*e* be silent before him."
Mt 6:10 done on-*e* as it is in heaven.
16:19 bind on-*e* will be bound
24:35 Heaven and-*e* will pass away,
28:18 on-*e* has been given to me.
Lk 2:14 on-*e* peace to men
1Co 10:26 The-*e* is the Lord's, and everything
Php 2:10 in heaven and on-*e* and under the-*e*,
2Pe 3:13 to a new heaven and a new-*e*,

EARTHLY (EARTH)
Php 3:19 Their mind is on-*e* things.
Col 3: 2 on things above, not on-*e* things.

EAST
Ps 103:12 as far as the-*e* is from the west,

EASY
Mt 11:30 For my yoke is-*e* and my burden is

EAT (EATING)
Ge 2:17 but you must not-*e* from the tree
Isa 55: 1 come, buy and-*e*!
65:25 and the lion will-*e* straw like the ox,
Mt 26:26 "Take and-*e*; this is my body."
Ro 14: 2 faith allows him to-*e* everything,

1Co 8:13 if what I-*e* causes my brother to fall
10:31 So whether you-*e* or drink
2Th 3:10 man will not work, he shall not-*e*."

EATING (EAT)
Ro 14:17 kingdom of God is not a matter of-*e*

EDICT
Heb 11:23 they were not afraid of the king's-*e*.

EDIFIES
1Co 14: 4 but he who prophesies-*e* the church

EFFECT
Isa 32:17 *e* of righteousness will be quietness
Heb 9:18 put into-*e* without blood.

EFFORT
Lk 13:24 "Make every-*e* to enter
Ro 9:16 depend on man's desire or-*e*,
14:19 make every-*e* to do what leads
Eph 4: 3 Make every-*e* to keep the unity
Heb 4:11 make every-*e* to enter that rest,
12:14 Make every-*e* to live in peace
2Pe 1: 5 make every-*e* to add
3:14 make every-*e* to be found spotless,

ELAH
Son of Baasha; king of Israel (1Ki 16:6-14).

ELDERLY* (ELDERS)
Lev 19:32 show respect for the-*e*

ELDERS (ELDERLY)
1Ti 5:17 The-*e* who direct the affairs

ELECTION
Ro 9:11 God's purpose in-*e* might stand:
2Pe 1:10 to make your calling and-*e* sure.

ELI
High priest in youth of Samuel (1Sa 1-4).
Blessed Hannah (1Sa 1:12-18); raised Samuel
(1Sa 2:11-26).

ELIJAH
Prophet; predicted famine in Israel (1Ki 17:1;
Jas 5:17). Fed by ravens (1Ki 17:2-6). Raised
Sidonian widow's son (1Ki 17:7-24). Defeated
prophets of Baal at Carmel (1Ki 18:16-46). Ran
from Jezebel (1Ki 19:1-9). Prophesied death
of Azariah (2Ki 1). Succeeded by Elisha (1Ki
19:19-21; 2Ki 2:1-18). Taken to heaven in whirlwind (2Ki 2:11-12).
Return prophesied (Mal 4:5-6); equated with
John the Baptist (Mt 17:9-13; Mk 9:9-13; Lk
1:17). Appeared with Moses in transfiguration of
Jesus (Mt 17:1-8; Mk 9:1-8).

ELISHA
Prophet; successor of Elijah (1Ki 19:16-21);
inherited his cloak (2Ki 2:1-18). Miracles of
(2Ki 2-6).

ELIZABETH*
Mother of John the Baptist, relative of Mary
(Lk 1:5-58).

EMBITTER*
Col 3:21 Fathers, do not-*e* your children,

EMPTY
Eph 5: 6 no one deceive you with-*e* words,
1Pe 1:18 from the-*e* way of life handed

ENABLE (ABLE)
Lk 1:74 to-*e* us to serve him without fear
Ac 4:29 *e* your servants to speak your word

ENABLED (ABLE)
Lev 26:13 *e* you to walk with heads held high.
Jn 6:65 unless the Father has-*e* him."

ENABLES (ABLE)
Php 3:21 by the power that-*e* him

ENCAMPS*
Ps 34: 7 The angel of the LORD-*e*

ENCOURAGE (ENCOURAGEMENT)
Ps 10:17 you-*e* them, and you listen
Isa 1:17 *e* the oppressed.
Ac 15:32 to-*e* and strengthen the brothers.
Ro 12: 8 if it is encouraging, let him-*e*;
1Th 5:11 Therefore-*e* each other
2Ti 4: 2 rebuke and-*e*—with great patience
Tit 2: 6 *e* the young men to be
Heb 3:13 But-*e* one another daily, as long
10:25 but let us-*e* one another—

ENCOURAGEMENT (ENCOURAGE)
Ac 4:36 Barnabas (which means Son of-*E*),
Ro 15: 4 *e* of the Scriptures we might have
15: 5 and-*e* give you a spirit of unity
1Co 14: 3 to men for their strengthening,-*e*
Heb 12: 5 word of-*e* that addresses you

END
Ps 119:33 then I will keep them to the-*e*.
Pr 14:12 but in the-*e* it leads to death.
19:20 and in the-*e* you will be wise.
23:32 In the-*e* it bites like a snake
Ecc 12:12 making many books there is no-*e*,
Mt 10:22 firm to the-*e* will be saved.
Lk 21: 9 but the-*e* will not come right away
Ro 10: 4 Christ is the-*e* of the law
1Co 15:24 the-*e* will come, when he hands

ENDURANCE (ENDURE)
Ro 15: 4 through-*e* and the encouragement
15: 5 May the God who gives-*e*
2Co 1: 6 which produces in you patient-*e*
Col 1:11 might so that you may have great-*e*
1Ti 6:11 faith, love,-*e* and gentleness.
Tit 2: 2 and sound in faith, in love and in-*e*.

ENDURE (ENDURANCE ENDURES)
Ps 72:17 May his name-*e* forever;
Pr 12:19 Truthful lips-*e* forever,
27:24 for riches do not-*e* forever,
Ecc 3:14 everything God does will-*e* forever;
Mal 3: 2 who can-*e* the day of his coming?
2Ti 2: 3 *E* hardship with us like a good
2:12 if we-*e*, / we will also reign
Heb 12: 7 *E* hardship as discipline; God is
Rev 3:10 kept my command to-*e* patiently,

ENDURES (ENDURE)
Ps 112: 9 his righteousness-*e* forever;
136: 1 *His love is forever.*
Da 9:15 made for yourself a name that-*e*

ENEMIES (ENEMY)
Ps 23: 5 in the presence of my-*e*.
Mic 7: 6 a man's-*e* are the members
Mt 5:44 Love your-*e* and pray
Lk 20:43 hand until I make your-*e*

ENEMY (ENEMIES ENMITY)
Pr 24:17 Do not gloat when your-*e* falls;
25:21 If your-*e* is hungry, give him food
27: 6 but an-*e* multiplies kisses.
1Co 15:26 The last-*e* to be destroyed is death.
1Ti 5:14 and to give the-*e* no opportunity

ENJOY (JOY)
Dt 6: 2 and so that you may-*e* long life.
Eph 6: 3 and that you may-*e* long life
Heb 11:25 rather than to-*e* the pleasures of sin

ENJOYMENT (JOY)
Ecc 4: 8 and why am I depriving myself of-*e*?
1Ti 6:17 us with everything for our-*e*.

ENLIGHTENED* (LIGHT)
Eph 1:18 that the eyes of your heart may be-*e*
Heb 6: 4 for those who have once been-*e*,

ENMITY* (ENEMY)
Ge 3:15 And I will put-*e*

ENOCH
Walked with God and taken by him (Ge 5:18-24; Heb 11:5). Prophet (Jude 14).

ENTANGLED (ENTANGLES)
2Pe 2:20 and are again-*e* in it and overcome,

ENTANGLES* (ENTANGLED)
Heb 12: 1 and the sin that so easily-*e*,

ENTER (ENTERED ENTERS ENTRANCE)
Ps 100: 4 *E* his gates with thanksgiving
Mt 5:20 will certainly not-*e* the kingdom
7:13 "*E* through the narrow gate.
18: 8 It is better for you to-*e* life maimed
Mk 10:15 like a little child will never-*e* it."
10:23 is for the rich to-*e* the kingdom

ENTERED (ENTER)
Ro 5:12 as sin-*e* the world through one man,
Heb 9:12 but he-*e* the Most Holy Place once

ENTERS (ENTER)
Mk 7:18 you see that nothing that-*e* a man
Jn 10: 2 The man who-*e* by the gate is

ENTERTAIN
1Ti 5:19 Do not-*e* an accusation
Heb 13: 2 Do not forget to-*e* strangers,

ENTHRALLED*
Ps 45:11 The king is-*e* by your beauty;

ENTHRONED (THRONE)
1Sa 4: 4 who is-*e* between the cherubim.
Ps 2: 4 The One-*e* in heaven laughs;
102:12 But you, O LORD, sit-*e* forever;
Isa 40:22 He sits-*e* above the circle

ENTICE
Pr 1:10 My son, if sinners-*e* you,
2Pe 2:18 they-*e* people who are just escaping

ENTIRE
Gal 5:14 The-*e* law is summed up

ENTRUSTED (TRUST)
1Ti 6:20 guard what has been-*e* to your care.
2Ti 1:12 able to guard what I have-*e* to him
1:14 Guard the good deposit that was-*e*
Jude : 3 once for all-*e* to the saints.

ENVY
Pr 3:31 Do not-*e* a violent man
14:30 but-*e* rots the bones.
1Co 13: 4 It does not-*e*, it does not boast,

EPHRAIM
1. Second son of Joseph (Ge 41:52; 46:20). Blessed as firstborn by Jacob (Ge 48).
2. Synonymous with Northern Kingdom (Isa 7:17; Hos 5).

EQUAL
Isa 40:25 who is my-*e*?" says the Holy One.
Jn 5:18 making himself-*e* with God.
1Co 12:25 that its parts should have-*e* concern

EQUIP* (EQUIPPED)
Heb 13:21 *e* you with everything good

EQUIPPED (EQUIP)
2Ti 3:17 man of God may be thoroughly-*e*

ERROR
Jas 5:20 Whoever turns a sinner from the-*e*

ESAU
Firstborn of Isaac, twin of Jacob (Ge 25:21-26). Also called Edom (Ge 25:30). Sold Jacob his birthright (Ge 25:29-34); lost blessing (Ge 27). Reconciled to Jacob (Gen 33).

ESCAPE (ESCAPING)
Ro 2: 3 think you will-*e* God's judgment?
Heb 2: 3 how shall we-*e* if we ignore such

ESCAPING (ESCAPE)
1Co 3:15 only as one-*e* through the flames.

ESTABLISH
Ge 6:18 But I will-*e* my covenant with you,
1Ch 28: 7 I will-*e* his kingdom forever
Ro 10: 3 God and sought to-*e* their own,

ESTEEMED
Pr 22: 1 to be-*e* is better than silver or gold.
Isa 53: 3 he was despised, and we-*e* him not.

ESTHER
Jewess who lived in Persia; cousin of Mordecai (Est 2:7). Chosen queen of Xerxes (Est 2:8-18). Foiled Haman's plan to exterminate the Jews (Est 3-4; 7-9).

ETERNAL (ETERNALLY ETERNITY)
Ps 16:11 with-*e* pleasures at your right hand.
111:10 To him belongs-*e* praise.
119:89 Your word, O LORD, is-*e*;
Isa 26: 4 LORD, the LORD, is the Rock-*e*.
Mt 19:16 good thing must I do to get-*e* life?"
25:41 into the-*e* fire prepared for the devil
25:46 they will go away to-*e* punishment,
Jn 3:15 believes in him may have-*e* life.
3:16 him shall not perish but have-*e* life.
3:36 believes in the Son has-*e* life,
4:14 spring of water welling up to-*e* life."
5:24 believes him who sent me has-*e* life
6:68 You have the words of-*e* life.
10:28 I give them-*e* life, and they shall
17: 3 this is-*e* life: that they may know
Ro 1:20 his-*e* power and divine nature—
6:23 but the gift of God is-*e* life
2Co 4:17 for us an-*e* glory that far outweighs
4:18 temporary, but what is unseen is-*e*.
1Ti 1:16 believe on him and receive-*e* life.
1:17 Now to the King-*e*, immortal,
Heb 9:12 having obtained-*e* redemption.
1Jn 5:11 God has given us-*e* life,
5:13 you may know that you have-*e* life.

ETERNALLY (ETERNAL)
Gal 1: 8 let him be-*e* condemned! As we

ETERNITY (ETERNAL)
Ps 93: 2 you are from all-*e*.
Ecc 3:11 also set-*e* in the hearts of men;

ETHIOPIAN
Jer 13:23 Can the-*E* change his skin

EUNUCHS
Mt 19:12 For some are-*e* because they were

EVANGELIST (EVANGELISTS)
2Ti 4: 5 hardship, do the work of an-*e*,

EVANGELISTS* (EVANGELIST)
Eph 4:11 some to be prophets, some to be-*e*,

EVE
2Co 11: 3 as-*E* was deceived by the serpent's
1Ti 2:13 For Adam was formed first, then-*E*

EVEN-TEMPERED*
Pr 17:27 and a man of understanding is-*e*.

EVER (EVERLASTING FOREVER)
Ex 15:18 LORD will reign for-*e* and-*e*."
Dt 8:19 If you-*e* forget the LORD your
Ps 5:11 let them sing for joy.
10:16 The LORD is King for-*e* and-*e*;
25: 3 will-*e* be put to shame,
26: 3 for your love is-*e* before me,
45: 6 O God, will last for-*e* and-*e*;
52: 8 God's unfailing love for-*e* and-*e*.
89:33 nor will I-*e* betray my faithfulness.
145: 1 I will praise your name for-*e* and-*e*.
Pr 4:18 shining-*e* brighter till the full light
5:19 may you-*e* be captivated
Isa 66: 8 Who has-*e* heard of such a thing?

Jer 31:36 the descendants of Israel-*e* cease
Da 7:18 it forever—yes, for-*e* and-*e*.'
12: 3 like the stars for-*e* and *e*
Mk 4:12 *e* hearing but never understanding,
Jn 1:18 No one has-*e* seen God,
Rev 1:18 and behold I am alive for-*e* and-*e!*
22: 5 And they will reign for-*e* and-*e*.

EVER-INCREASING* (INCREASE)
Ro 6:19 to impurity and to-*e* wickedness,
2Co 3:18 into his likeness with-*e* glory,

EVERLASTING (EVER)
Dt 33:27 and underneath are the-*e* arms.
Ne 9: 5 your God, who is from-*e* to *e*."
Ps 90: 2 from-*e* to-*e* you are God.
139:24 and lead me in the way-*e*.
Isa 9: 6 *E* Father, Prince of Peace.
33:14 Who of us can dwell with-*e* burning
35:10 *e* joy will crown their heads.
45:17 the LORD with an-*e* salvation;
54: 8 but with-*e* kindness
55: 3 I will make an-*e* covenant with you,
63:12 to gain for himself-*e* renown,
Jer 31: 3 "I have loved you with an-*e* love;
Da 9:24 to bring in-*e* righteousness,
12: 2 some to-*e* life, others to shame
Jn 6:47 the truth, he who believes has-*e* life.
2Th 1: 9 punished with-*e* destruction
Jude : 6 bound with-*e* chains for judgment

EVER-PRESENT*
Ps 46: 1 an-*e* help in trouble

EVIDENCE (EVIDENT)
Jn 14:11 on the-*e* of the miracles themselves.

EVIDENT (EVIDENCE)
Php 4: 5 Let your gentleness be-*e* to all.

EVIL
Ge 2: 9 of the knowledge of good and-*e*.
Job 1: 1 he feared God and shunned-*e*.
1: 8 a man who fears God and shuns-*e*."
34:10 Far be it from God to do-*e*,
Ps 23: 4 I will fear no-*e*,
34:14 Turn from-*e* and do good;
51: 4 and done what is-*e* in your sight,
97:10 those who love the LORD hate-*e*,
101: 4 I will have nothing to do with-*e*.
Pr 8:13 To fear the LORD is to hate-*e*;
10:23 A fool finds pleasure in-*e* conduct,
11:27 *e* comes to him who searches for it.
24:19 Do not fret because of-*e* men
24:20 for the-*e* man has no future hope.
Isa 5:20 Woe to those who call-*e* good
13:11 I will punish the world for its-*e*,
55: 7 and the-*e* man his thoughts.
Hab 1:13 Your eyes are too pure to look on-*e*;
Mt 5:45 He causes his sun to rise on the-*e*
6:13 but deliver us from the-*e* one.'
7:11 If you, then, though you are-*e*,
12:35 and the-*e* man brings-*e* things out
Jn 17:15 you protect them from the-*e* one.
Ro 2: 9 for every human being who does-*e*:
12: 9 Hate what is-*e*; cling
12:17 Do not repay anyone-*e* for-*e*.
16:19 and innocent about what is-*e*.
1Co 13: 6 Love does not delight in-*e*
14:20 In regard to-*e* be infants,
Eph 6:16 all the flaming arrows of the-*e* one.
1Th 5:22 Avoid every kind of-*e*.
1Ti 6:10 of money is a root of all kinds of-*e*.
2Ti 2:22 Flee the-*e* desires of youth,
Jas 1:13 For God cannot be tempted by-*e*,
1Pe 2:16 your freedom as a cover-up for-*e*;
3: 9 Do not repay-*e* with-*e* or insult

EXACT
Heb 1: 3 the-*e* representation of his being,

EXALT (EXALTED EXALTS)
Ps 30: 1 I will-*e* you, O LORD,
34: 3 let us-*e* his name together.
118:28 you are my God, and I will-*e* you.
Isa 24:15 *e* the name of the LORD, the God

EXALTED (EXALT)
2Sa 22:47 *E* be God, the Rock, my Savior!
1Ch 29:11 you are-*e* as head over all.
Ne 9: 5 and may it be-*e* above all blessing
Ps 21:13 Be-*e*, O LORD, in your strength;
46:10 I will be-*e* among the nations,
57: 5 Be-*e*, O God, above the heavens;
97: 9 you are-*e* far above all gods.
99: 2 he is-*e* over all the nations.
108: 5 Be-*e*, O God, above the heavens,
148:13 for his name alone is-*e*;
Isa 6: 1 *e*, and the train of his robe filled
12: 4 and proclaim that his name is-*e*.
33: 5 The LORD is-*e*, for he dwells
Eze 21:26 The lowly will be-*e* and the-*e* will be
Mt 23:12 whoever humbles himself will be-*e*.
Php 1:20 always Christ will be-*e* in my body,
2: 9 Therefore God-*e* him

EXALTS (EXALT)
Ps 75: 7 He brings one down, he-*e* another.
Pr 14:34 Righteousness-*e* a nation,
Mt 23:12 For whoever-*e* himself will be

EXAMINE (EXAMINED)
Ps 26: 2 *e* my heart and my mind;
Jer 17:10 and-*e* the mind,
La 3:40 Let us-*e* our ways and test them,
1Co 11:28 A man ought to-*e* himself
2Co 13: 5 *E* yourselves to see whether you

EXAMINED (EXAMINE)
Ac 17:11 *e* the Scriptures every day to see

EXAMPLE (EXAMPLES)
Jn 13:15 have set you an-*e* that you should
1Co 11: 1 Follow my-*e*, as I follow
Tit 4:12 set an-*e* for the believers in speech,
Tit 2: 7 In everything set them an-*e*
1Pe 2:21 leaving you an-*e*, that you should

EXAMPLES* (EXAMPLE)
1Co 10: 6 Now these things occurred as-*e*
10:11 as-*e* and were written down
1Pe 5: 3 to you, but being-*e* to the flock.

EXASPERATE*
Eph 6: 4 Fathers, do not-*e* your children;

EXCEL (EXCELLENT)
1Co 14:12 to-*e* in gifts that build up the church
2Co 8: 7 But just as you-*e* in everything—

EXCELLENT (EXCEL)
1Co 12:31 now I will show you the most-*e* way
Php 4: 8 if anything is-*e* or praiseworthy—
1Ti 3:13 have served well gain an-*e* standing
Tit 3: 8 These things are-*e* and profitable

EXCHANGED
Ro 1:23 *e* the glory of the immortal God
1:25 They-*e* the truth of God for a lie,

EXCUSE (EXCUSES)
Jn 15:22 they have no-*e* for their sin.
Ro 1:20 so that men are without-*e*.

EXCUSES* (EXCUSE)
Lk 14:18 "But they all alike began to make-*e*.

EXISTS
Heb 2:10 and through whom everything-*e*,
11: 6 to him must believe that he-*e*

EXPECT (EXPECTATION)
Mt 24:44 at an hour when you do not-*e* him.

EXPECTATION (EXPECT)
Ro 8:19 waits in eager-*e* for the sons
Heb 10:27 but only a fearful-*e* of judgment

EXPEL★
1Co 5:13 *E* the wicked man from among you

EXPENSIVE
1Ti 2:9 or gold or pearls or-*e* clothes,

EXPLOIT
Pr 22:22 Do not-*e* the poor because they are
2Co 12:17 Did I-*e* you through any

EXPOSE
1Co 4:5 will-*e* the motives of men's hearts.
Eph 5:11 of darkness, but rather-*e* them.

EXTENDS
Pr 31:20 and-*e* her hands to the needy.
Lk 1:50 His mercy-*e* to those who fear him,

EXTINGUISHED
2Sa 21:17 the lamp of Israel will not be-*e*."

EXTOL★
Job 36:24 Remember to-*e* his work,
Ps 34:1 I will-*e* the LORD at all times;
68:4 *e* him who rides on the clouds—
95:2 and-*e* him with music and song.
109:30 mouth I will greatly-*e* the LORD;
111:1 I will-*e* the LORD with all my heart
115:18 it is we who-*e* the LORD,
117:1 *e* him, all you peoples.
145:2 and-*e* your name for ever and ever.
145:10 your saints will-*e* you.
147:12 *E* the LORD, O Jerusalem;

EXTORT★
Lk 3:14 "Don't-*e* money and don't accuse

EYE (EYES)
Ex 21:24 you are to take life for life,-*e* for-*e*,
Ps 94:9 Does he who formed the-*e* not see?
Mt 5:29 If your right-*e* causes you to sin,
5:38 '*E* for-*e*, and tooth for tooth.'
7:3 of sawdust in your brother's-*e*
1Co 2:9 "No-*e* has seen,
Col 3:22 not only when their-*e* is on you
Rev 1:7 and every-*e* will see him,

EYES (EYE)
Nu 33:55 remain will become barbs in your-*e*
Jos 23:13 on your backs and thorns in your-*e*,
2Ch 16:9 For the-*e* of the LORD range
Job 31:1 "I made a covenant with my-*e*
36:7 He does not take his-*e*
Ps 119:18 Open my-*e* that I may see
121:1 I lift up my-*e* to the hills—
141:8 But my-*e* are fixed on you,
Pr 3:7 Do not be wise in your own-*e*;
4:25 Let your-*e* look straight ahead,
15:3 The-*e* of the LORD are everywhere
Isa 6:5 and my-*e* have seen the King,
Hab 1:13 Your-*e* are too pure to look on evil;
Jn 4:35 open your-*e* and look at the fields!
2Co 4:18 So we fix our-*e* not on what is seen,
Heb 12:2 Let us fix our-*e* on Jesus, the author
Jas 2:5 poor in the-*e* of the world to be rich
1Pe 3:12 For the-*e* of the Lord are
Rev 7:17 wipe away every tear from their-*e*."
21:4 He will wipe every tear from their-*e*.

EZEKIEL
Priest called to be prophet to the exiles (Eze 1-3).

EZRA
Priest and teacher of the Law who led a return of exiles to Israel to reestablish temple and worship (Ezr 7-8). Corrected intermarriage of priests (Ezr 9-10). Read Law at celebration of Feast of Tabernacles (Neh 8).

FACE (FACES)
Ge 32:30 "It is because I saw God-*f* to-*f*,
Ex 34:29 was not aware that his-*f* was radiant

Nu 6:25 the LORD make his-*f* shine
1Ch 16:11 seek his-*f* always.
2Ch 7:14 and seek my-*f* and turn
Ps 4:6 Let the light of your-*f* shine upon us
27:8 Your-*f*, LORD, I will seek.
31:16 Let your-*f* shine on your servant;
105:4 seek his-*f* always.
119:135 Make your-*f* shine
Isa 50:7 Therefore have I set my-*f* like flint,
Mt 17:2 His-*f* shone like the sun,
1Co 13:12 mirror; then we shall see-*f* to-*f*.
2Co 4:6 the glory of God in the-*f* of Christ.
1Pe 3:12 but the-*f* of the Lord is
Rev 1:16 His-*f* was like the sun shining

FACES (FACE)
2Co 3:18 who with unveiled-*f* all reflect

FACTIONS
Gal 5:20 selfish ambition, dissensions,-*f*

FADE
1Pe 5:4 of glory that will never-*f* away.

FAIL (FAILING FAILINGS FAILS)
1Ch 28:20 He will not-*f* you or forsake you
2Ch 34:33 they did not-*f* to follow the LORD,
Ps 89:28 my covenant with him will never-*f*.
Pr 15:22 Plans-*f* for lack of counsel,
Isa 51:6 my righteousness will never-*f*.
La 3:22 for his compassions never-*f*.
2Co 13:5 unless, of course, you-*f* the test?

FAILING (FAIL)
1Sa 12:23 sin against the LORD by-*f* to pray

FAILINGS (FAIL)
Ro 15:1 ought to bear with the-*f* of the weak

FAILS (FAIL)
1Co 13:8 Love never-*f*.

FAINT
Isa 40:31 they will walk and not be-*f*.

FAIR
Pr 1:3 doing what is right and just and-*f*;
Col 4:1 slaves with what is right and-*f*,

FAITH (FAITHFUL FAITHFULLY FAITHFULNESS FAITHLESS)
2Ch 20:20 Have-*f* in the LORD your God
Hab 2:4 but the righteous will live by his-*f*—
Mt 9:29 According to your-*f* will it be done
17:20 if you have-*f* as small as a mustard
24:10 many will turn away from the-*f*
Mk 11:22 "Have-*f* in God," Jesus answered.
Lk 7:9 I have not found such great-*f*
12:28 will he clothe you, O you of little-*f*!
17:5 "Increase our-*f*!" He replied,
18:8 will he find-*f* on the earth?"
Ac 14:9 saw that he had-*f* to be healed
14:27 the door of-*f* to the Gentiles.
Ro 1:12 encouraged by each other's-*f*.
1:17 is by-*f* from first to last,
1:17 "The righteous will live by-*f*."
3:3 What if some did not have-*f*?
3:22 comes through-*f* in Jesus Christ
3:25 a sacrifice of atonement, through-*f*
4:5 his-*f* is credited as righteousness.
5:1 we have been justified through-*f*,
10:17 *f* comes from hearing the message,
14:1 Accept him whose-*f* is weak,
14:23 that does not come from-*f* is sin.
1Co 13:13 And now these three remain:-*f*,
13:13 stand firm in the-*f*; be men
16:13 in the-*f*; be men
2Co 5:7 We live by-*f*, not by sight.
13:5 to see whether you are in the-*f*;
Gal 2:16 Jesus that we may be justified by-*f*
2:20 I live by-*f* in the Son of God,
3:11 "The righteous will live by-*f*."
3:24 that we might be justified by-*f*.

Eph 2:8 through-*f*—and this not
4:5 one Lord, one-*f*, one baptism;
6:16 to all this, take up the shield of-*f*,
Col 1:23 continue in your-*f*, established
1Th 5:8 on-*f* and love as a breastplate,
1Ti 2:15 if they continue in-*f*, love
4:1 later times some will abandon the-*f*
5:8 he has denied the-*f* and is worse
6:12 Fight the good fight of the-*f*.
2Ti 3:15 wise for salvation through-*f*
4:7 finished the race, I have kept the-*f*.
Phm :6 may be active in sharing your-*f*
Heb 10:38 But my righteous one will live by-*f*.
11:1 *f* is being sure of what we hope for
11:3 By-*f* we understand that
11:5 By-*f* Enoch was taken from this life
11:6 And without-*f* it is impossible
11:7 By-*f* Noah, when warned about
11:8 By-*f* Abraham, when called to go
11:17 By-*f* Abraham, when God tested
11:20 By-*f* Isaac blessed Jacob
11:21 By-*f* Jacob, when he was dying,
11:22 By-*f* Joseph, when his end was near
11:24 By-*f* Moses, when he had grown up
11:31 By-*f* the prostitute Rahab,
12:2 the author and perfecter of our-*f*,
Jas 2:14 if a man claims to have-*f*
2:17 In the same way,-*f* by itself,
2:26 so-*f* without deeds is dead.
2Pe 1:5 effort to add to your-*f* goodness;
1Jn 5:4 overcome the world, even our-*f*.
Jude :3 to contend for the-*f* that was once

FAITHFUL (FAITH)
Nu 12:7 he is-*f* in all my house.
Dt 7:9 your God is God; he is the-*f* God,
32:4 A-*f* God who does no wrong,
2Sa 22:26 "To the-*f* you show yourself-*f*,
Ps 25:10 of the LORD are loving and-*f*
31:23 The LORD preserves the-*f*,
33:4 he is-*f* in all he does.
37:28 and will not forsake his-*f* ones.
97:10 for he guards the lives of his-*f* ones
145:13 The LORD is-*f* to all his promises
146:6 the LORD, who remains-*f* forever.
Pr 31:26 and-*f* instruction is on her tongue.
Mt 25:21 'Well done, good and-*f* servant!
Ro 12:12 patient in affliction,-*f* in prayer.
1Co 4:2 been given a trust must prove-*f*.
10:13 And God is-*f*; he will not let you be
1Th 5:24 The one who calls you is-*f*
2Ti 2:13 he will remain-*f*,
Heb 3:6 But Christ is-*f* as a son
10:23 for he who promised is-*f*.
1Pe 4:19 themselves to their-*f* Creator
1Jn 1:9 he is-*f* and just and will forgive us
Rev 1:5 who is the-*f* witness, the firstborn
2:10 Be-*f*, even to the point of death,
19:11 whose rider is called-*F* and True.

FAITHFULLY (FAITH)
Dt 11:13 if you-*f* obey the commands I am
1Sa 12:24 and serve him-*f* with all your heart;
1Ki 2:4 and if they walk-*f* before me
1Pe 4:10 *f* administering God's grace

FAITHFULNESS (FAITH)
Ps 57:10 your-*f* reaches to the skies.
85:10 Love and-*f* meet together;
86:15 to anger, abounding in love and-*f*
89:1 mouth I will make your-*f* known
89:14 love and-*f* go before you.
91:4 his-*f* will be your shield
117:2 the-*f* of the LORD endures forever.
119:75 and in-*f* you have afflicted me.
Pr 3:3 Let love and-*f* never leave you;
Isa 11:5 and-*f* the sash around his waist.
La 3:23 great is your-*f*.

Ro 3:3 lack of faith nullify God's-*f*?
Gal 5:22 patience, kindness, goodness,-*f*,

FAITHLESS (FAITH)
Ps 119:158 I look on the-*f* with loathing,
Jer 3:22 "Return,-*f* people;
Ro 1:31 they are senseless,-*f*, heartless,
2Ti 2:13 if we are-*f*,

FALL (FALLEN FALLING FALLS)
Ps 37:24 though he stumble, he will not-*f*,
55:22 he will never let the righteous-*f*.
69:9 of those who insult you-*f* on me.
Pr 11:28 Whoever trusts in his riches will-*f*,
Lk 11:17 a house divided against itself will-*f*.
Ro 3:23 and-*f* short of the glory of God,
Heb 6:6 if they-*f* away, to be brought back

FALLEN (FALL)
2Sa 1:19 How the mighty have-*f*!
Isa 14:12 How you have-*f* from heaven,
1Co 15:20 of those who have-*f* asleep.
Gal 5:4 you have-*f* away from grace.
1Th 4:15 precede those who have-*f* asleep.

FALLING (FALL)
Jude :24 able to keep you from-*f*

FALLS (FALL)
Pr 24:17 Do not gloat when your enemy-*f*;
Jn 12:24 a kernel of wheat-*f* to the ground
Ro 14:4 To his own master he stands or-*f*.

FALSE (FALSEHOOD FALSELY)
Ex 20:16 "You shall not give-*f* testimony
23:1 "Do not spread-*f* reports.
Pr 13:5 The righteous hate what is-*f*,
19:5 A-*f* witness will not go unpunished,
Mt 7:15 "Watch out for-*f* prophets.
19:18 not steal, do not give-*f* testimony,
24:11 and many-*f* prophets will appear
Php 1:18 whether from-*f* motives or true,
1Ti 1:3 not to teach-*f* doctrines any longer
2Pe 2:1 there will be-*f* teachers among you.

FALSEHOOD (FALSE)
Ps 119:163 I hate and abhor-*f*
Pr 30:8 Keep-*f* and lies far from me;
Eph 4:25 each of you must put off-*f*

FALSELY (FALSE)
Lev 19:12 "'Do not swear-*f* by my name
Lk 3:14 and don't accuse people-*f*—
1Ti 6:20 ideas of what is-*f* called knowledge,

FALTER★
Pr 24:10 If you-*f* in times of trouble,
Isa 42:4 he will not-*f* or be discouraged

FAMILIES (FAMILY)
Ps 68:6 God sets the lonely in-*f*,

FAMILY (FAMILIES)
Pr 15:27 greedy man brings trouble to his-*f*,
31:15 she provides food for her-*f*
Lk 9:61 go back and say good-by to my-*f*,"
12:52 in one-*f* divided against each other,
1Ti 3:4 He must manage his own-*f* well
3:5 how to manage his own-*f*,
5:4 practice by caring for their own-*f*
5:8 and especially for his immediate-*f*,

FAMINE
Ge 41:30 seven years of-*f* will follow them.
Am 8:11 but a-*f* of hearing the words
Ro 8:35 or persecution or-*f* or nakedness

FAN★
2Ti 1:6 you to-*f* into flame the gift of God,

FAST
Dt 13:4 serve him and hold-*f* to him.
Jos 22:5 to hold-*f* to him and to serve him
23:8 to hold-*f* to the LORD your God,
Ps 119:31 I hold-*f* to your statutes, O LORD;

139:10 your right hand will hold me-*f.*
Mt 6:16 "When you-*f,* do not look somber
1Pe 5:12 Stand-*f* in it.

FATHER (FATHER'S FATHERLESS
FATHERS FOREFATHERS)
Ge 2:24 this reason a man will leave his-*f*
17:4 You will be the-*f* of many nations.
Ex 20:12 "Honor your-*f* and your mother,
21:15 "Anyone who attacks his-*f*
21:17 "Anyone who curses his-*f*
Lev 18:7 " 'Do not dishonor your-*f*
19:3 you must respect his mother and-*f,*
Dt 5:16 "Honor your-*f* and your mother,
21:18 son who does not obey the-*f*
Ps 27:10 Though my-*f* and mother forsake
68:5 A-*f* to the fatherless, a defender
Pr 10:1 A wise son brings joy to his-*f*
17:21 there is no joy for the-*f* of a fool.
23:22 Listen to your-*f,* who gave you life,
23:24 *f* of a righteous man has great joy;
28:7 of gluttons disgraces his-*f.*
29:3 loves wisdom brings joy to his-*f,*
Isa 9:6 Everlasting-*f,* Prince of Peace.
Mt 6:9 " 'Our-*F* in heaven,
10:37 "Anyone who loves his-*f*
15:4 'Honor your-*f* and mother'
19:5 this reason a man will leave his-*f*
Lk 12:53 *f* against son and son against-*f,*
23:34 Jesus said,-*"f,* forgive them,
Jn 6:44 the-*F* who sent me draws him,
6:46 No one has seen the-*F*
8:44 You belong to your-*f,* the devil,
10:30 I and the-*f* are one."
14:6 No one comes to the-*F*
14:9 who has seen me has seen the-*F.*
Ro 4:11 he is the-*f* of all who believe
2Co 6:18 "I will be a-*f* to you,
Eph 6:2 "Honor your-*f* and mother"—
Heb 12:7 what son is not disciplined by his-*f?*

FATHER'S (FATHER)
Pr 13:1 A wise son heeds his-*f* instruction,
15:5 A fool spurns his-*f* discipline,
19:13 A foolish son is his-*f* ruin,
Lk 2:49 had to be in my-*f* house?"
Jn 2:16 How dare you turn my-*F* house
10:29 can snatch them out of my-*f* hand.
14:2 In my-*F* house are many rooms;

FATHERLESS (FATHER)
Dt 10:18 He defends the cause of the-*f*
24:17 Do not deprive the alien or the-*f*
24:19 Leave it for the alien, the-*f*
Ps 68:5 A father to the-*f,* a defender
Pr 23:10 or encroach on the fields of the-*f,*

FATHERS (FATHER)
Ex 20:5 for the sin of the-*f* to the third
Lk 11:11 "Which of you-*f,* if your son asks
Eph 6:4 *f,* do not exasperate your children;
Col 3:21 *f,* do not embitter your children,

FATHOM*
Job 11:7 "Can you-*f* the mysteries of God?
Ps 145:3 his greatness no one can-*f.*
Ecc 3:11 yet they cannot-*f* what God has
Isa 40:28 and his understanding no one can-*f*
1Co 13:2 and can-*f* all mysteries and all

FAULT (FAULTS)
Mt 18:15 and show him his-*f,* just
Php 2:15 of God without-*f* in a crooked
Jas 1:5 generously to all without finding-*f,*
Jude :24 his glorious presence without-*f*

FAULTFINDERS*
Jude :16 These men are grumblers and-*f;*

FAULTS (FAULT)
Ps 19:12 Forgive my hidden-*f.*

FAVORITISM*
Ex 23:3 and do not show-*f* to a poor man
Lev 19:15 to the poor or-*f* to the great,
Ac 10:34 true it is that God does not show-*f*
Ro 2:11 For God does not show-*f.*
Eph 6:9 and there is no-*f* with him.
Col 3:25 for his wrong, and there is no-*f.*
1Ti 5:21 and to do nothing out of-*f.*
Jas 2:1 Lord Jesus Christ, don't show-*f.*
2:9 But if you show-*f,* you sin

FEAR (AFRAID FEARS)
Dt 6:13 *F* the LORD your God, serve him
10:12 but to-*f* the LORD your God,
31:12 and learn to-*f* the LORD your God
Ps 19:9 The-*f* of the LORD is pure,
23:4 I will-*f* no evil,
27:1 whom shall I-*f?*
91:5 You will not-*f* the terror of night,
111:10 *f* of the LORD is the beginning
Pr 8:13 To-*f* the LORD is to hate evil;
9:10 *f* of the LORD is the beginning
10:27 The-*f* of the LORD adds length
14:27 The-*f* of the LORD is a fountain
15:33 *f* of the LORD teaches a man
16:6 through the-*f* of the LORD a man
19:23 The-*f* of the LORD leads to life:
29:25 *F* of man will prove to be a snare,
Isa 11:3 delight in the-*f* of the LORD.
41:10 So do not-*f,* for I am with you;
Lk 12:5 I will show you whom you should-*f:*
Php 2:12 to work out your salvation with-*f*
1Jn 4:18 But perfect love drives out-*f,*

FEARS (FEAR)
Job 1:8 a man who-*f* God and shuns evil."
Ps 34:4 he delivered me from all my-*f.*
Pr 31:30 a woman who-*f* the LORD is
1Jn 4:18 The one who-*f* is not made perfect

FEED
Jn 21:15 Jesus said,-"*f* my lambs."
21:17 Jesus said,-"*f* my sheep.
Ro 12:20 "If your enemy is hungry,-*f* him;
Jude :12 shepherds who-*f* only themselves.

FEET (FOOT)
Ps 8:6 you put everything under his-*f:*
22:16 have pierced my hands and my-*f.*
40:2 he set my-*f* on a rock
110:1 a footstool for your-*f."*
119:105 Your word is a lamp to my-*f*
Ro 10:15 "How beautiful are the-*f*
1Co 12:21 And the head cannot say to the-*f,*
15:25 has put all his enemies under his-*f.*
Heb 12:13 "Make level paths for your-*f,"*

FELLOWSHIP
2Co 6:14 what-*f* can light have with darkness
13:14 and the-*f* of the Holy Spirit be
Php 3:10 the-*f* of sharing in his sufferings,
1Jn 1:6 claim to have-*f* with him yet walk
1:7 we have-*f* with one another,

FEMALE
Ge 1:27 male and-*f* he created them.
Gal 3:28 *f,* for you are all one in Christ Jesus

FERVOR
Ro 12:11 but keep your spiritual-*f,* serving

FIELD (FIELDS)
Mt 6:28 See how the lilies of the-*f* grow.
13:38 *f* is the world, and the good seed
1Co 3:9 you are God's-*f,* God's building.

FIELDS (FIELD)
Lk 2:8 were shepherds living out in the-*f*
Jn 4:35 open your eyes and look at the-*f!*

FIG (FIGS)
Ge 3:7 so they sewed-*f* leaves together

FIGHT (FOUGHT)
Ex 14:14 The LORD will-*f* for you; you need
Dt 1:30 going before you, will-*f* for you,
3:22 the LORD your God himself will-*f*
Ne 4:20 Our God will-*f* for us!"
Ps 35:1 *f* against those who-*f* against me.
Jn 18:36 my servants would-*f*
1Co 9:26 I do not-*f* like a man beating the air.
2Co 10:4 The weapons we-*f*
1Ti 1:18 them you may-*f* the good-*f,*
6:12 Fight the good-*f* of the faith.
2Ti 4:7 fought the good-*f,* I have finished

FIGS (FIG)
Lk 6:44 People do not pick-*f*

FILL (FILLED FILLS FULL FULLNESS
FULLY)
Ge 1:28 and increase in number;-*f* the earth
Ps 16:11 you will-*f* me with joy
81:10 wide your mouth and I will-*f* it.
Pr 28:19 who chases fantasies will have his-*f*
Hag 2:7 and I will-*f* this house with glory,'
Jn 6:26 you ate the loaves and had your-*f.*
Ac 2:28 you will-*f* me with joy
Ro 15:13 The God of hope-*f* you with all joy

FILLED (FILL)
Ps 72:19 may the whole earth be-*f*
119:64 The earth is-*f* with your love,
Eze 43:5 the glory of the LORD-*f* the temple
Hab 2:14 For the earth will be-*f*
Lk 1:15 and he will be-*f* with the Holy Spirit
1:41 and Elizabeth was-*f* with the Holy
Jn 12:3 the house was-*f* with the fragrance
Ac 2:4 All of them were-*f*
4:8 Then Peter,-*f* with the Holy Spirit,
9:17 and be-*f* with the Holy Spirit."
13:9 called Paul,-*f* with the Holy Spirit,
Eph 5:18 Instead, be-*f* with the Spirit.
Php 1:11 *f* with the fruit of righteousness

FILLS (FILL)
Nu 14:21 of the LORD-*f* the whole earth,
Ps 107:9 and-*f* the hungry with good things.
Eph 1:23 fullness of him who-*f* everything

FILTHY
Isa 64:6 all our righteous acts are like-*f* rags;
Col 3:8 and-*f* language from your lips.
2Pe 2:7 by the-*f* lives of lawless men

FIND (FINDS FOUND)
Nu 32:23 be sure that your sin will-*f* you out.
Dt 4:29 you will-*f* him if you look for him
1Sa 23:16 and helped him-*f* strength in God.
Ps 36:7 *f* refuge in the shadow
91:4 under his wings you will-*f* refuge;
Pr 14:22 those who plan what is good-*f* love
31:10 A wife of noble character who can-*f*
Jer 6:16 and you will-*f* rest for your souls.
Mt 7:7 seek and you will-*f;* knock
11:29 and you will-*f* rest for your souls.
16:25 loses his life for me will-*f* it.
Lk 18:8 will he-*f* faith on the earth?"
Jn 10:9 come in and go out, and-*f* pasture.

FINDS (FIND)
Ps 62:1 My soul-*f* rest in God alone;
112:1 who-*f* great delight
119:162 like one who-*f* great spoil.
Pr 18:22 He who-*f* a wife *f* what is good
Mt 7:8 he who seeks-*f;* and to him who
10:39 Whoever-*f* his life will lose it,
Lk 12:37 whose master-*f* them watching
15:4 go after the lost sheep until he-*f?*

FINISH (FINISHED)
Jn 4:34 him who sent me and to-*f* his work.
5:36 that the Father has given me to-*f,*
Ac 20:24 if only I may-*f* the race
2Co 8:11 Now-*f* the work, so that your eager

Jas 1:4 Perseverance must-*f* its work

FINISHED (FINISH)
Ge 2:2 seventh day God had-*f* the work he
Jn 19:30 the drink, Jesus said, "It is-*f."*
2Ti 4:7 I have-*f* the race, I have kept

FIRE
Ex 13:21 in a pillar of-*f* to give them light,
Lev 6:12 *f* on the altar must be kept burning;
Isa 30:27 and his tongue is a consuming-*f.*
Jer 23:29 my word like-*f,"* declares
Mt 3:11 you with the Holy Spirit and with-*f.*
5:22 will be in danger of the-*f* of hell.
25:41 into the eternal-*f* prepared
Mk 9:43 where the-*f* never goes out.
Ac 2:3 to be tongues of-*f* that separated
1Co 3:13 It will be revealed with-*f,*
1Th 5:19 Do not put out the Spirit's-*f;*
Heb 12:29 for our "God is a consuming-*f."*
Jas 3:5 set on-*f* by a small spark.
2Pe 3:10 the elements will be destroyed by-*f,*
Jude :23 snatch others from the-*f*
Rev 20:14 The lake of-*f* is the second death.

FIRM
Ex 14:13 Stand-*f* and you will see
2Ch 20:17 stand-*f* and see the deliverance
Ps 33:11 of the LORD stand-*f* forever,
37:23 he makes his steps-*f;*
40:2 and gave me a-*f* place to stand.
89:2 that your love stands-*f* forever,
119:89 it stands-*f* in the heavens.
Pr 4:26 and take only ways that are-*f.*
Zec 8:23 nations will take-*f* hold of one Jew
Mk 13:13 he who stands-*f* to the end will be
1Co 16:13 on your guard; stand-*f* in the faith;
2Co 1:24 because it is by faith you stand-*f.*
Eph 6:14 Stand-*f* then, with the belt
Col 4:12 that you may stand-*f* in all the will
2Th 2:15 stand-*f* and hold to the teachings
2Ti 2:19 God's solid foundation stands-*f,*
Heb 6:19 an anchor for the soul,-*f* and secure
1Pe 5:9 Resist him, standing-*f* in the faith,

FIRST
Isa 44:6 I am the-*f* and I am the last;
48:12 I am the-*f* and I am the last.
Mt 5:24 *F* go and be reconciled
6:33 But seek-*f* his kingdom
7:5 *f* take the plank out
20:27 wants to be-*f* must be your slave—
22:38 This is the-*f* and greatest
23:26 *F* clean the inside of the cup
Mk 13:10 And the gospel must-*f* be preached
Ac 11:26 disciples were called Christians-*f*
Ro 1:16 for the Jew, then for the Gentile.
1Co 12:28 in the church God has appointed-*f*
2Co 8:5 they gave themselves-*f* to the Lord
1Ti 2:13 For Adam was formed-*f,* then Eve.
Jas 3:17 comes from heaven is-*f* of all pure;
1Jn 4:19 We love because he-*f* loved us.
3Jn :9 but Diotrephes, who loves to be-*f,*
Rev 1:17 I am the-*F* and the Last.
2:4 You have forsaken your-*f* love.

FIRSTBORN (BEAR)
Ex 11:5 Every-*f* son in Egypt will die,

FIRSTFRUITS
Ex 23:19 "Bring the best of the-*f* of your soil

FISHERS
Mk 1:17 "and I will make you-*f* of men."

FITTING*
Ps 33:1 it is-*f* for the upright to praise him.
147:1 how pleasant and-*f* to praise him!
Pr 10:32 of the righteous know what is-*f,*
19:10 It is not-*f* for a fool to live in luxury
26:1 honor is not-*f* for a fool.

1Co 14:40 everything should be done in a-*f*
Col 3:18 to your husbands, as is-*f* in the Lord
Heb 2:10 sons to glory, it was-*f* that God,

FIX
Dt 11:18 *F* these words of mine
Pr 4:25 *f* your gaze directly before you.
2Co 4:18 we-*f* our eyes not on what is seen,
Heb 3:1 heavenly calling,-*f* your thoughts
12:2 Let us-*f* our eyes on Jesus,

FLAME (FLAMES FLAMING)
2Ti 1:6 you to fan into-*f* the gift of God,

FLAMES (FLAME)
1Co 3:15 only as one escaping through the-*f*,
13:3 and surrender my body to the-*f*,

FLAMING (FLAME)
Eph 6:16 you can extinguish all the-*f* arrows

FLASH
1Co 15:52 in a-*f*, in the twinkling of an eye,

FLATTER (FLATTERING FLATTERY)
Job 32:21 nor will I-*f* any man;
Jude :16 *f* others for their own advantage.

FLATTERING (FLATTER)
Ps 12:2 their-*f* lips speak with deception.
12:3 May the Lord cut off all-*f* lips
Pr 26:28 and a-*f* mouth works ruin.

FLATTERY (FLATTER)
Ro 16:18 and-*f* they deceive the minds
1Th 2:5 You know we never used-*f*,

FLAWLESS*
2Sa 22:31 the word of the Lord is-*f*.
Job 11:4 You say to God, 'My beliefs are-*f*
Ps 12:6 And the words of the Lord are-*f*,
18:30 the word of the Lord is-*f*.
Pr 30:5 "Every word of God is-*f*;
SS 5:2 my dove, my-*f* one.

FLEE
Ps 139:7 Where can I-*f* from your presence?
1Co 6:18 *f* from sexual immorality.
10:14 my dear friends,-*f* from idolatry.
1Ti 6:11 But you, man of God,-*f* from all this
2Ti 2:22 *F* the evil desires of youth,
Jas 4:7 Resist the devil, and he will-*f*

FLEETING
Ps 89:47 Remember how-*f* is my life.
Pr 31:30 Charm is deceptive, and beauty is-*f*

FLESH
Ge 2:23 and-*f* of my-*f*;
2:24 and they will become one-*f*.
Job 19:26 yet in my-*f* I will see God;
Eze 11:19 of stone and give them a heart of-*f*.
36:26 of stone and give you a heart of-*f*.
Mk 10:8 and the two will become one-*f*.'
Jn 1:14 The Word became-*f* and made his
6:51 This bread is my-*f*, which I will give
1Co 6:16 "The two will become one-*f*."
Eph 5:31 and the two will become one-*f*."
6:12 For our struggle is not against-*f*

FLOCK (FLOCKS)
Isa 40:11 He tends his-*f* like a shepherd:
Eze 34:2 not shepherds take care of the-*f*?
Zec 11:17 who deserts the-*f*!
Mt 26:31 the sheep of the-*f* will be scattered.'
Ac 20:28 all the-*f* of which the Holy Spirit
1Pe 5:2 Be shepherds of God's-*f* that is

FLOCKS (FLOCK)
Lk 2:8 keeping watch over their-*f* at night.

FLOG
Ac 22:25 to-*f* a Roman citizen who hasn't

FLOODGATES
Mal 3:10 see if I will not throw open the-*f*

FLOURISHING
Ps 52:8 *f* in the house of God;

FLOW (FLOWING)
Nu 13:27 and it does-*f* with milk and honey!
Jn 7:38 streams of living water will-*f*

FLOWERS
Isa 40:7 The grass withers and the-*f* fall,

FLOWING (FLOW)
Ex 3:8 a land-*f* with milk and honey—

FOLDING
Pr 6:10 a little-*f* of the hands to rest—

FOLLOW (FOLLOWING FOLLOWS)
Ex 23:2 Do not-*f* the crowd in doing wrong.
Lev 18:4 and be careful to-*f* my decrees.
Dt 5:1 Learn them and be sure to-*f* them.
Ps 23:6 Surely goodness and love will-*f* me
Mt 16:24 and take up his cross and-*f* me.
Jn 10:4 his sheep-*f* him because they know
1Co 14:1 *F* the way of love and eagerly
Rev 14:4 They-*f* the Lamb wherever he goes.

FOLLOWING (FOLLOW)
1Ti 1:18 by-*f* them you may fight the good

FOLLOWS (FOLLOW)
Jn 8:12 Whoever-*f* me will never walk

FOOD (FOODS)
Pr 20:13 you will have-*f* to spare.
22:9 for he shares his-*f* with the poor.
25:21 If your enemy is hungry, give him-*f*
31:15 she provides-*f* for her family
Da 1:8 to defile himself with the royal-*f*
Jn 6:27 Do not work for-*f* that spoils,
Ro 14:14 fully convinced that no-*f* is unclean
1Co 8:8 But-*f* does not bring us near to God
1Ti 6:8 But if we have-*f* and clothing,
Jas 2:15 sister is without clothes and daily-*f*.

FOODS (FOOD)
Mk 7:19 Jesus declared all-*f* "clean.")

FOOL (FOOLISH FOOLISHNESS FOOLS)
Ps 14:1 The-*f* says in his heart,
Pr 15:5 A-*f* spurns his father's discipline,
17:28 Even a-*f* is thought wise
18:2 A-*f* finds no pleasure
26:5 Answer a-*f* according to his folly,
28:26 He who trusts in himself is a-*f*,
Mt 5:22 But anyone who says, 'You-*f*!'

FOOLISH (FOOL)
Pr 10:1 but a-*f* son grief to his mother.
17:25 A-*f* son brings grief to his father
Mt 7:26 practice is like a-*f* man who built
25:2 of them were-*f* and five were wise.
1Co 1:27 God chose the-*f* things of the world

FOOLISHNESS (FOOL)
1Co 1:18 of the cross is-*f* to those who are
1:25 For the-*f* of God is wiser
2:14 for they are-*f* to him, and he cannot
3:19 of this world is-*f* in God's sight.

FOOLS (FOOL)
Pr 14:9 *F* mock at making amends for sin,
1Co 4:10 We are-*f* for Christ, but you are

FOOT (FEET FOOTHOLD)
Jos 1:3 every place where you set your-*f*,
Isa 1:6 From the sole of your-*f* to the top
1Co 12:15 If the-*f* should say, "Because I am

FOOTHOLD (FOOT)
Eph 4:27 and do not give the devil a-*f*.

FORBEARANCE*
Ro 3:25 because in his-*f* he had left the sins

FORBID
1Co 14:39 and do not-*f* speaking in tongues.

FOREFATHERS (FATHER)
Heb 1:1 spoke to our-*f* through the prophets

FOREKNEW* (KNOW)
Ro 8:29 For those God-*f* he
11:2 not reject his people, whom he-*f*.

FOREVER (EVER)
1Ch 16:15 He remembers his covenant-*f*,
16:34 his love endures-*f*.
Ps 9:7 The Lord reigns-*f*;
23:6 dwell in the house of the Lord-*f*.
33:11 the plans of the Lord stand firm-*f*
86:12 I will glorify your name-*f*.
92:8 But you, O Lord, are exalted-*f*.
110:4 "You are a priest-*f*,
119:111 Your statutes are my heritage-*f*;
Jn 6:51 eats of this bread, he will live-*f*
14:16 Counselor to be with you-*f*—
1Co 9:25 it to get a crown that will last-*f*.
1Th 4:17 And so we will be with the Lord-*f*.
Heb 13:8 same yesterday and today and-*f*.
1Pe 1:25 but the word of the Lord stands-*f*."
1Jn 2:17 who does the will of God lives-*f*.

FORFEIT
Lk 9:25 and yet lose or-*f* his very self?

FORGAVE (FORGIVE)
Ps 32:5 and you-*f*
Eph 4:32 just as in Christ God-*f* you.
Col 2:13 He-*f* us all our sins, having
3:13 Forgive as the Lord-*f* you.

FORGET (FORGETS FORGETTING)
Dt 6:12 that you do not-*f* the Lord,
Ps 103:2 and-*f* not all his benefits.
137:5 may my right hand-*f* its skill.
Isa 49:15 "Can a mother-*f* the baby
Heb 6:10 he will not-*f* your work

FORGETS (FORGET)
Jn 16:21 her baby is born she-*f* the anguish
Jas 1:24 immediately-*f* what he looks like.

FORGETTING (FORGET)
Php 3:13 *F* what is behind and straining

FORGIVE (FORGAVE FORGIVENESS FORGIVING)
2Ch 7:14 will-*f* their sin and will heal their
Ps 19:12 *F* my hidden faults.
Mt 6:12 Forgive us our debts,
6:14 For if you-*f* men when they sin
18:21 many times shall I-*f* my brother
Mk 11:25 in heaven may-*f* you your sins."
Lk 11:4 For us our sins,
23:34 Jesus said, "Father,-*f* them,
Col 3:13 *F* as the Lord forgave you.
1Jn 1:9 and just and will-*f* us our sins

FORGIVENESS (FORGIVE)
Ps 130:4 But with you there is-*f*;
Ac 10:43 believes in him receives-*f* of sins
Eph 1:7 through his blood, the-*f* of sins,
Col 1:14 in whom we have redemption, the-*f*
Heb 9:22 the shedding of blood there is no-*f*.

FORGIVING (FORGIVE)
Ne 9:17 But you are a-*f* God, gracious
Eph 4:32 to one another,-*f* each other,

FORMED
Ge 2:7 And the Lord God-*f* man
Ps 103:14 for he knows how we are-*f*,
Isa 45:18 but-*f* it to be inhabited—
Ro 9:20 "Shall what is-*f* say to him who-*f* it,
1Ti 2:13 For Adam was-*f* first, then Eve.
Heb 11:3 understand that the universe was-*f*

FORSAKE (FORSAKEN)
Jos 1:5 I will never leave you nor-*f* you.
24:16 "Far be it from us to-*f* the Lord
2Ch 15:2 but if you-*f* him, he will-*f* you.

Ps 27:10 Though my father and mother-*f* me
Isa 55:7 Let the wicked-*f* his way
Heb 13:5 never will I-*f* you."

FORSAKEN (FORSAKE)
Ps 22:1 my God, why have you-*f* me?
37:25 I have never seen the righteous-*f*
Mt 27:46 my God, why have you-*f* me?"
Rev 2:4 You have-*f* your first love.

FORTRESS
Ps 18:2 The Lord is my rock, my-*f*
71:3 for you are my rock and my-*f*.

FOUGHT (FIGHT)
2Ti 4:7 I have-*f* the good fight, I have

FOUND (FIND)
1Ch 28:9 If you seek him, he will be-*f* by you;
Isa 55:6 Seek the Lord while he may be-*f*
Da 5:27 on the scales and-*f* wanting.
Lk 15:6 with me; I have-*f* my lost sheep.
15:9 with me; I have-*f* my lost coin."
Ac 4:12 Salvation is-*f* in no one else,

FOUNDATION
Isa 28:16 a precious cornerstone for a sure-*f*;
1Co 3:11 For no one can lay any-*f* other
Eph 2:20 built on the-*f* of the apostles
2Ti 2:19 God's solid-*f* stands firm,

FOXES
Mt 8:20 "*F* have holes and birds

FRAGRANCE
2Co 2:16 of death; to the other, the-*f* of life.

FREE (FREED FREEDOM FREELY)
Ps 146:7 The Lord sets prisoners-*f*,
Jn 8:32 and the truth will set you-*f*."
Ro 6:18 You have been set-*f* from sin
Gal 3:28 slave nor-*f*, male nor female,
1Pe 2:16 *f* men, but do not use your freedom

FREED (FREE)
Rev 1:5 has-*f* us from our sins by his blood,

FREEDOM (FREE)
Ro 8:21 into the glorious-*f* of the children
2Co 3:17 the Spirit of the Lord is, there is-*f*.
Gal 5:13 But do not use your-*f* to indulge
1Pe 2:16 but do not use your-*f* as a cover-up

FREELY (FREE)
Isa 55:7 and to our God, for he will-*f* pardon
Mt 10:8 Freely you have received,-*f* give.
Ro 3:24 and are justified-*f* by his grace
Eph 1:6 which he has-*f* given us

FRIEND (FRIENDS)
Ex 33:11 as a man speaks with his-*f*.
Pr 17:17 A-*f* loves at all times,
18:24 there is a-*f* who sticks closer
27:6 Wounds from a-*f* can be trusted,
27:10 Do not forsake your-*f* and the-*f*
Jas 4:4 Anyone who chooses to be a-*f*

FRIENDS (FRIEND)
Pr 16:28 and a gossip separates close-*f*.
Zec 13:6 given at the house of my-*f*.'
Jn 15:13 that he lay down his life for his-*f*.

FRUIT (FRUITFUL)
Ps 1:3 which yields its-*f* in season
Pr 11:30 The-*f* of the righteous is a tree
Mt 7:16 By their-*f* you will recognize them.
Jn 15:2 branch in me that bears no-*f*,
Gal 5:22 But the-*f* of the Spirit is love, joy,
Rev 22:2 of-*f*, yielding its-*f* every month.

FRUITFUL (FRUIT)
Ge 1:22 "Be-*f* and increase in number
Ps 128:3 Your wife will be like a-*f* vine
Jn 15:2 prunes so that it will be even more-*f*.

FULFILL (FULFILLED FULFILLMENT)
Ps 116:14 I will-*f* my vows to the Lord
Mt 5:17 come to abolish them but to-*f* them.
1Co 7: 3 husband should-*f* his marital duty

FULFILLED (FULFILL)
Pr 13:19 A longing-*f* is sweet to the soul,
Mk 14:49 But the Scriptures must be-*f.*"
Ro 13: 8 loves his fellowman has-*f* the law.

FULFILLMENT (FULFILL)
Ro 13:10 Therefore love is the-*f* of the law.

FULL (FILL)
Ps 127: 5 whose quiver is-*f* of them.
Pr 31:11 Her husband has-*f* confidence
Isa 6: 3 the whole earth is-*f* of his glory."
11: 9 for the earth will be-*f*
Jn 10:10 may have life, and have it to the-*f.*
Ac 6: 3 known to be-*f* of the Spirit

FULLNESS (FILL)
Col 1:19 to have all his-*f* dwell in him,
2: 9 in Christ all the-*f* of the Deity lives

FULLY (FILL)
1Ki 8:61 your hearts must be-*f* committed
2Ch 16: 9 whose hearts are-*f* committed
Ps 119: 4 that are to be-*f* obeyed.
119:138 they are-*f* trustworthy.
1Co 15:58 Always give yourselves-*f*

FUTURE
Ps 37:37 there is a-*f* for the man of peace.
Pr 23:18 There is surely a-*f* hope for you,
Ro 8:38 neither the present nor the-*f,*

GABRIEL*
Angel who interpreted Daniel's visions (Da 8:16-26; 9:20-27); announced births of John (Lk 1:11-20), Jesus (Lk 1:26-38).

GAIN (GAINED)
Ps 60:12 With God we will-*g* the victory,
Mk 8:36 it for a man to-*g* the whole world,
1Co 13: 3 but have not love, I-*g* nothing.
Php 1:21 to live is Christ and to die is-*g.*
3: 8 that I may-*g* Christ and be found
1Ti 6: 6 with contentment is great-*g.*

GAINED (GAIN)
Ro 5: 2 through whom we have-*g* access

GALILEE
Isa 9: 1 but in the future he will honor-*G*

GALL
Mt 27:34 mixed with-*g*; but after tasting it,

GAP
Eze 22:30 stand before me in the-*g* on behalf

GARDENER
Jn 15: 1 true vine, and my Father is the-*g.*

GARMENT (GARMENTS)
Ps 102:26 they will all wear out like a-*g.*
Mt 9:16 of unshrunk cloth on an old-*g.*
Jn 19:23 This-*g* was seamless, woven

GARMENTS (GARMENT)
Ge 3:21 The Lord God made-*g* of skin
Isa 61:10 me with-*g* of salvation
63: 1 with his-*g* stained crimson?
Jn 19:24 "They divided my-*g* among them

GATE (GATES)
Mt 7:13 For wide is the-*g* and broad is
Jn 10: 9 I am the-*g*; whoever enters

GATES (GATE)
Ps 100: 4 Enter his-*g* with thanksgiving
Mt 16:18 the-*g* of Hades will not overcome it

GATHER (GATHERS)
Zec 14: 2 I will-*g* all the nations to Jerusalem
Mt 12:30 he who does not-*g* with me scatters
23:37 longed to-*g* your children together,

GATHERS (GATHER)
Isa 40:11 He-*g* the lambs in his arms
Mt 23:37 a hen-*g* her chicks under her wings,

GAVE (GIVE)
Ezr 2:69 According to their ability they-*g*
Job 1:21 Lord-*g* and the Lord has taken
Jn 3:16 so loved the world that he-*g* his one
2Co 8: 5 they-*g* themselves first to the Lord
Gal 2:20 who loved me and-*g* himself for me
1Ti 2: 6 who-*g* himself as a ransom

GAZE
Ps 27: 4 to-*g* upon the beauty of the Lord
Pr 4:25 fix your-*g* directly before you.

GENEALOGIES
1Ti 1: 4 themselves to myths and endless-*g.*

GENERATIONS
Ps 22:30 future-*g* will be told about the Lord
102:12 your renown endures through all-*g.*
145:13 dominion endures through all-*g.*
Lk 1:48 now on all-*g* will call me blessed,
Eph 3: 5 not made known to men in other-*g*

GENEROUS
Ps 112: 5 Good will come to him who is-*g*
Pr 22: 9 A-*g* man will himself be blessed,
2Co 9: 5 Then it will be ready as a-*g* gift,
1Ti 6:18 and to be-*g* and willing to share.

GENTILE (GENTILES)
Ro 1:16 first for the Jew, then for the-*G.*
10:12 difference between Jew and-*G*—

GENTILES (GENTILE)
Isa 42: 6 and a light for the-*G,*
Ro 3: 9 and-*G* alike are all under sin.
11:13 as I am the apostle to the-*G,*
1Co 1:23 block to Jews and foolishness to-*G,*

GENTLE (GENTLENESS)
Pr 15: 1 A-*g* answer turns away wrath,
Zec 9: 9 *g* and riding on a donkey,
Mt 11:29 for I am-*g* and humble in heart,
21: 5 *g* and riding on a donkey,
1Co 4:21 or in love and with a-*g* spirit?
1Pe 3: 4 the unfading beauty of a-*g*

GENTLENESS* (GENTLE)
2Co 10: 1 By the meekness and-*g* of Christ,
Gal 5:23 faithfulness,-*g* and self-control.
Php 4: 5 Let your-*g* be evident to all.
Col 3:12 kindness, humility,-*g* and patience.
1Ti 6:11 faith, love, endurance and-*g.*
1Pe 3:15 But do this with-*g* and respect,

GETHSEMANE
Mt 26:36 disciples to a place called-*G,*

GIDEON*
Judge, also called Jerub-Baal; freed Israel from Midianites (Jdg 6-8; Heb 11:32). Given sign of fleece (Jdg 8:36-40).

GIFT (GIFTS)
Pr 21:14 A-*g* given in secret soothes anger,
Mt 5:23 if you are offering your-*g*
Ac 2:38 And you will receive the-*g*
Ro 6:23 but the-*g* of God is eternal life
1Co 7: 7 each man has his own-*g* from God,
2Co 8:12 the-*g* is acceptable according
9:15 be to God for his indescribable-*g!*
Eph 2: 8 it is the-*g* of God—not by works,
1Ti 4:14 not neglect your-*g*, which was
2Ti 1: 6 you to fan into flame the-*g* of God,
Jas 1:17 and perfect-*g* is from above,
1Pe 4:10 should use whatever-*g* he has

GIFTS (GIFT)
Ro 11:29 for God's-*g* and his call are
12: 6 We have different-*g*, according
1Co 12: 4 There are different kinds of-*g,*
12:31 But eagerly desire the greater-*g.*

14: 1 and eagerly desire spiritual-*g,*
14:12 excel in-*g* that build up the church.

GILEAD
Jer 8:22 Is there no balm in-*G?*

GIVE (GAVE GIVEN GIVER GIVES GIVING)
Nu 6:26 and-*g* you peace." '
1Sa 1:11 then I will-*g* him to the Lord
2Ch 15: 7 be strong and do not-*g* up,
Pr 21:26 but the righteous-*g* without sparing
23:26 My son,-*g* me your heart
30: 8 but-*g* me only my daily bread.
31:31 *G* her the reward she has earned,
Isa 42: 8 I will not-*g* my glory to another
Eze 36:26 I will-*g* you a new heart
Mt 6:11 *G* us today our daily bread.
10: 8 Freely you have received, freely-*g.*
22:21 "*G* to Caesar what is Caesar's,
Mk 8:37 Or what can a man-*g* in exchange
Lk 6:38 *G*, and it will be given to you.
11:13 Father in heaven-*g* the Holy Spirit
Jn 10:28 I-*g* them eternal life, and they shall
13:34 "A new commandment I-*g* you:
Ac 20:35 blessed to-*g* than to receive.' "
Ro 12: 8 let him-*g* generously;
13: 7 *G* everyone what you owe him:
14:12 each of us will-*g* an account
2Co 9: 7 Each man should-*g* what he has
Rev 14: 7 "Fear God and-*g* him glory,

GIVEN (GIVE)
Nu 8:16 are to be-*g* wholly to me.
Ps 115:16 but the earth he has-*g* to man.
Isa 9: 6 to us a son is-*g,*
Mt 6:33 and all these things will be-*g* to you
7: 7 "Ask and it will be-*g* to you;
Lk 22:19 saying, "This is my body-*g* for you;
Jn 3:27 man can receive only what is-*g* him
Ro 5: 5 the Holy Spirit, whom he has-*g* us.
1Co 4: 2 those who have been-*g* a trust must
12:13 we were all-*g* the one Spirit to drink
Eph 4: 7 to each one of us grace has been-*g*

GIVER* (GIVE)
Pr 18:16 A gift opens the way for the-*g*
2Co 9: 7 for God loves a cheerful-*g.*

GIVES (GIVE)
Ps 119:130 The unfolding of your words-*g* light;
Pr 14:30 A heart at peace-*g* life to the body,
15:30 good news-*g* health to the bones.
28:27 He who-*g* to the poor will lack
Isa 40:29 He-*g* strength to the weary
Mt 10:42 if anyone-*g* even a cup of cold water
Jn 6:63 The Spirit-*g* life; the flesh counts
1Co 15:57 he-*g* us the victory
2Co 3: 6 the letter kills, but the Spirit-*g* life.

GIVING (GIVE)
Ne 8: 8 *g* the meaning so that the people
Ps 19: 8 *g* joy to the heart.
Mt 6: 4 so that your-*g* may be in secret.
2Co 8: 7 also excel in this grace of-*g.*

GLAD (GLADNESS)
Ps 31: 7 I will be-*g* and rejoice in your love,
46: 4 whose streams make-*g* the city
97: 1 Lord reigns, let the earth be-*g;*
118:24 let us rejoice and be-*g* in it.
Pr 23:25 May your father and mother be-*g;*
Zec 2:10 and be-*g*, O Daughter of Zion.
Mt 5:12 be-*g*, because great is your reward

GLADNESS (GLAD)
Ps 45:15 They are led in with joy and-*g;*
51: 8 Let me hear joy and-*g;*
100: 2 Serve the Lord with-*g;*
Jer 31:13 I will turn their mourning into-*g;*

GLORIFIED (GLORY)
Jn 13:31 Son of Man-*g* and God is-*g* in him.
Ro 8:30 those he justified, he also-*g.*
2Th 1:10 comes to be-*g* in his holy people

GLORIFY (GLORY)
Ps 34: 3 *G* the Lord with me;
86:12 I will-*g* your name forever.
Jn 13:32 God will-*g* the Son in himself,
17: 1 *G* your Son, that your Son may

GLORIOUS (GLORY)
Ps 45:13 All-*g* is the princess
111: 3 *G* and majestic are his deeds,
145: 5 of the-*g* splendor of your majesty,
Isa 4: 2 the Lord will be beautiful and-*g.*
12: 5 for he has done-*g* things;
42:21 to make his law great and-*g.*
63:15 from your lofty throne, holy and-*g.*
Mt 19:28 the Son of Man sits on his-*g* throne,
Lk 9:31 appeared in-*g* splendor, talking
Ac 2:20 of the great and-*g* day of the Lord.
2Co 3: 8 of the Spirit be even more-*g?*
Php 3:21 so that they will be like his-*g* body.
4:19 to his-*g* riches in Christ Jesus.
Tit 2:13 the-*g* appearing of our great God
Jude :24 before his-*g* presence without fault

GLORY (GLORIFIED GLORIFY GLORIOUS)
Ex 15:11 awesome in-*g,*
33:18 Moses said, "Now show me your-*g*
1Sa 4:21 "The-*g* has departed from Israel"—
1Ch 16:24 Declare his-*g* among the nations,
16:28 ascribe to the Lord-*g*
29:11 and the-*g* and the majesty
Ps 8: 5 and crowned him with-*g* and honor
19: 1 The heavens declare the-*g* of God;
24: 7 that the King of-*g* may come in.
29: 1 ascribe to the Lord-*g*
72:19 the whole earth be filled with his-*g.*
96: 3 Declare his-*g* among the nations,
Pr 19:11 it is to his-*g* to overlook an offense.
25: 2 It is the-*g* of God to conceal
Isa 6: 3 the whole earth is full of his-*g.*"
48:11 I will not yield my-*g* to another
Eze 43: 2 and the land was radiant with his-*g.*
Mt 24:30 of the sky, with power and great-*g.*
25:31 the Son of Man comes in his-*g,*
Mk 8:38 in his Father's-*g* with the holy
13:26 in clouds with great power and-*g.*
Lk 2: 9 and the-*g* of the Lord shone
2:14 saying,-"*G* to God in the highest,
Jn 1:14 We have seen his-*g*, the-*g* of the One
17: 5 presence with the-*g* I had with you
17:24 to see my-*g*, the-*g* you have given
Ac 7: 2 The God of-*g* appeared
Ro 1:23 exchanged the-*g* of the immortal
3:23 and fall short of the-*g* of God,
8:18 with the-*g* that will be revealed
9: 4 theirs the divine-*g*, the covenants,
1Co 10:31 whatever you do, do it all for the-*g*
11: 7 but the woman is the-*g* of man.
15:43 it is raised in-*g*; it is sown
2Co 3:10 comparison with the surpassing-*g.*
3:18 faces all reflect the Lord's-*g,*
4:17 us an eternal-*g* that far outweighs
Col 1:27 Christ in you, the hope of-*g.*
3: 4 also will appear with him in-*g.*
1Ti 3:16 was taken up in-*g.*
Heb 1: 3 The Son is the radiance of God's-*g*
2: 7 you crowned him with-*g* and honor
1Pe 1:24 and all their-*g* is like the flowers
Rev 4:11 to receive-*g* and honor and power,
21:23 for the-*g* of God gives it light,

GLUTTONS
Tit 1:12 always liars, evil brutes, lazy-*g.*"

GNASHING
Mt 8:12 where there will be weeping and-*g*

GNAT*
Mt 23:24 You strain out a-*g* but swallow

GOAL
2Co 5: 9 So we make it our-*g* to please him,
Gal 3: 3 to attain your-*g* by human effort?
Php 3:14 on toward the-*g* to win the prize

GOAT (GOATS SCAPEGOAT)
Isa 11: 6 the leopard will lie down with the-*g*

GOATS (GOAT)
Nu 7:17 five male-*g* and five male lambs

GOD (GOD'S GODLINESS GODLY GODS)
Ge 1: 1 In the beginning-*G* created
1: 2 and the Spirit of-*G* was hovering
1:26 Then-*G* said, "Let us make man
1:27 So-*G* created man in his own image
1:31 *G* saw all that he had made,
2: 3 And-*G* blessed the seventh day
2:22 Then the Lord-*G* made a woman
3:21 The Lord-*G* made garments
3:23 So the Lord-*G* banished him
5:22 Enoch walked with-*G* 300 years
6: 2 sons of-*G* saw that the daughters
9:16 everlasting covenant between-*G*
17: 1 "I am-*G* Almighty; walk before me
21:33 name of the Lord, the Eternal-*G*.
22: 8 "*G* himself will provide the lamb
28:12 and the angels of-*G* were ascending
32:28 because you have struggled with-*G*
32:30 "It is because I saw-*G* face to face,
35:10 *G* said to him, "Your name is Jacob
41:51 *G* has made me forget all my
50:20 but-*G* intended it for good
Ex 2:24 *G* heard their groaning
3: 6 because he was afraid to look at-*G*.
6: 7 own people, and I will be your-*G*.
8:10 is no one like the Lord our-*G*.
13:18 So-*G* led the people
15: 2 He is my-*G*, and I will praise him,
17: 9 with the staff of-*G* in my hands."
19: 3 Then Moses went up to-*G*.
20: 2 the Lord your-*G*, who brought
20: 5 the Lord your-*G*, am a jealous-*G*,
20:19 But do not have-*G* speak to us
22:28 "Do not blaspheme-*G*
31:18 inscribed by the finger of-*G*.
34: 6 the compassionate and gracious-*G*,
34:14 name is Jealous, is a jealous-*G*.
Lev 18:21 not profane the name of your-*G*.
19: 2 the Lord your-*G*, am holy.
26:12 walk among you and be your-*G*,
Nu 22:38 I must speak only what-*G* puts
23:19 *G* is not a man, that he should lie,
Dt 1:17 for judgment belongs to-*G*.
3:22 Lord your-*G* himself will fight
3:24 For what-*g* is there in heaven
4:24 is a consuming fire, a jealous-*G*.
4:31 the Lord your-*G* is a merciful-*G*;
4:39 heart this day that the Lord is-*G*
5:11 the name of the Lord your-*G*,
5:14 a Sabbath to the Lord your-*G*.
5:26 of the living-*G* speaking out of fire,
6: 4 Lord our-*G*, the Lord is one.
6: 5 Love the Lord your-*G*
6:13 the Lord your-*G*, serve him only
6:16 Do not test the Lord your-*G*
7: 9 your-*G* is-*G*; he is the faithful-*G*,
7:12 the Lord your-*G* will keep his
7:21 is a great and awesome-*G*.
8: 5 the Lord your-*G* disciplines you.
10:12 but to fear the Lord your-*G*,
10:14 the Lord your-*G* belong
10:17 For the Lord your-*G* is *G* of gods
11:13 to love the Lord your-*G*

13: 3 the Lord your-*G* is testing you
13: 4 the Lord your-*G* you must
15: 6 the Lord your-*G* will bless you
19: 9 to love the Lord your-*G*
25:16 the Lord your-*G* detests anyone
29:29 belong to the Lord our-*G*,
30: 2 return to the Lord your-*G*
30:16 today to love the Lord your-*G*
30:20 you may love the Lord your-*G*
31: 6 for the Lord your-*G* goes
32: 3 Oh, praise the greatness of our-*G*!
32: 4 A faithful-*G* who does no wrong,
33:27 The eternal-*G* is your refuge,
Jos 1: 9 for the Lord your-*G* will be
14: 8 the Lord my-*G* wholeheartedly.
22: 5 to love the Lord your-*G*,
22:34 Between Us that the Lord is-*G*.
23:11 careful to love the Lord your-*G*
23:14 the Lord your-*G* gave you has
Jdg 16:28 O-*G*, please strengthen me just
Ru 1:16 be my people and your-*G* my-*G*.
1Sa 2: 2 there is no Rock like our-*G*.
2: 3 for the Lord is a-*G* who knows,
2:25 another man,-*G* may mediate
10:26 men whose hearts-*G* had touched.
12:12 the Lord your-*G* was your king.
17:26 defy the armies of the living-*G*?"
17:46 world will know that there is a-*G*
30: 6 strength in the Lord his-*G*.
2Sa 14:14 But-*G* does not take away life;
22: 3 my-*G* is my rock, in whom I take
22:31 "As for-*G*, his way is perfect;
1Ki 4:29 *G* gave Solomon wisdom
8:23 there is no-*G* like you in heaven
8:27 "But will-*G* really dwell on earth?
8:61 committed to the Lord our-*G*,
18:21 If the Lord is-*G*, follow him;
18:37 are-*G*, and that you are turning
20:28 a-*g* of the hills and not a-*g*
2Ki 19:15 *G* of Israel, enthroned
1Ch 16:35 Cry out, "Save us, O-*G* our Savior,
28: 2 for the footstool of our-*G*,
28: 9 acknowledge the-*G* of your father,
29:10 *G* of our father Israel,
29:17 my-*G*, that you test the heart
2Ch 2: 4 for the Name of the Lord my-*G*
5:14 of the Lord filled the temple of-*G*
6:18 "But will-*G* really dwell on earth
18:13 I can tell him only what my-*G* says
20: 6 are you not the-*G* who is in heaven?
25: 8 for-*G* has the power to help
30: 9 for the Lord your-*G* is gracious
33:12 the favor of the Lord his-*G*
Ezr 8:22 The good hand of our-*G* is
9: 6 "O my-*G*, I am too ashamed
9:13 our-*G*, you have punished us less
Ne 1: 5 the great and awesome-*G*,
8: 8 from the Book of the Law of-*G*,
9:17 But you are a forgiving-*G*,
9:32 the great, mighty and awesome-*G*,
Job 1: 1 he feared-*G* and shunned evil.
2:10 Shall we accept good from-*G*,
4:17 a mortal more righteous than-*G*?
5:17 is the man whom-*G* corrects;
11: 7 Can you fathom the mysteries of-*G*
19:26 yet in my flesh I will see-*G*;
22:13 Yet you say, 'What does-*G* know?
25: 4 can a man be righteous before-*G*?
33:14 For-*G* does speak—now one way,
34:12 is unthinkable that-*G* would do
36:26 is-*G*— beyond our understanding!
37:22 *G* comes in awesome majesty.
Ps 18: 2 my-*G* is my rock, in whom I take
18:28 my-*G* turns my darkness into light.
19: 1 The heavens declare the glory of-*G*;
22: 1 *G*, my-*G*, why have you forsaken

29: 3 the-*G* of glory thunders,
31:14 I say, "You are my-*G*."
40: 3 a hymn of praise to our-*G*.
40: 8 I desire to do your will, O my-*G*;
42: 2 thirsts for-*G*, for the living-*G*.
42:11 Put your hope in-*G*,
45: 6 O-*G*, will last for ever and ever;
46: 1 *G* is our refuge and strength,
46:10 "Be still, and know that I am-*G*;
47: 7 For-*G* is the King of all the earth;
50: 3 Our-*G* comes and will not be silent;
51: 1 Have mercy on me, O-*G*,
51:10 Create in me a pure heart, O-*G*,
51:17 O-*G*, you will not despise.
62: 7 my honor depend on-*G*;
65: 5 O-*G* our Savior,
66: 1 Shout with joy to-*G*, all the earth!
66:16 listen, all you who fear-*G*;
68: 6 *G* sets the lonely in families,
71:17 my youth, O-*G*, you have taught
71:19 reaches to the skies, O-*G*,
71:22 harp for your faithfulness, O my-*G*;
73:26 but-*G* is the strength of my heart
77:13 What-*g* is so great as our God?
78:19 Can-*G* spread a table in the desert?
81: 1 Sing for joy to-*G* our strength;
84: 2 out for the living-*G*.
84:10 a doorkeeper in the house of my-*G*
86:12 O Lord my-*G*, with all my heart;
89: 7 of the holy ones-*G* is greatly feared;
90: 2 to everlasting you are-*G*.
91: 2 my-*G*, in whom I trust."
95: 7 for he is our-*G*
100: 3 Know that the Lord is-*G*.
108: 1 My heart is steadfast, O-*G*;
113: 5 Who is like the Lord our-*G*,
139:23 Search me, O-*G*, and know my
Pr 3: 4 in the sight of-*G* and man.
25: 2 to conceal a matter;
30: 5 "Every word of-*G* is flawless;
Ecc 3:11 cannot fathom what-*G* has done
11: 5 cannot understand the work of-*G*,
12:13 Fear-*G* and keep his
Isa 9: 6 Wonderful Counselor, Mighty-*G*,
37:16 you alone are-*G* over all
40: 3 a highway for our-*G*.
40: 8 the word of our-*G* stands forever."
40:28 The Lord is the everlasting-*G*,
41:10 not be dismayed, for I am your-*G*.
44: 6 apart from me there is no-*G*.
52: 7 "Your-*G* reigns!"
55: 7 to our-*G*, for he will freely pardon.
59: 2 you from your-*G*;
61:10 my soul rejoices in my-*G*.
62: 5 so will your-*G* rejoice over you.
Jer 23:23 "Am I only a-*G* nearby,"
31:33 I will be their-*G*,
32:27 "I am the Lord, the-*G*
Eze 28:13 the garden of-*G*;
Da 3:17 the-*G* we serve is able to save us
9: 4 O Lord, the great and awesome-*G*,
Hos 12: 6 and wait for your-*G* always.
Joel 2:13 Return to the Lord your-*G*,
Am 4:12 prepare to meet your-*G*, O Israel."
Mic 6: 8 and to walk humbly with your-*G*.
Na 1: 2 Lord is a jealous and avenging-*G*;
Zec 14: 5 Then the Lord my-*G* will come,
Mal 3: 8 Will a man rob-*G*? Yet you rob me.
Mt 1:23 which means,-"*G* with us."
5: 8 for they will see-*G*.
6:24 You cannot serve both-*G*
19: 6 Therefore what-*G* has joined
19:26 but with-*G* all things are possible."
22:21 and to-*G* what is God's."
22:37 " 'Love the Lord your-*G*

27:46 which means, "My-*G*, my-*G*,
Mk 12:29 the Lord our-*G*, the Lord is one.
16:19 and he sat at the right hand of-*G*.
Lk 1:37 For nothing is impossible with-*G*."
1:47 my spirit rejoices in-*G* my Savior,
10: 9 'The kingdom of-*G* is near you.'
10:27 " 'Love the Lord your-*G*
18:19 "No one is good—except-*G* alone.
Jn 1: 1 was with-*G*, and the Word was-*G*.
1:18 seen-*G*, but-*G* the One and Only,
3:16 "For-*G* so loved the world that he
4:24 *G* is spirit, and his worshipers must
14: 1 Trust in-*G*; trust also in me.
20:28 "My Lord and my-*G*!"
Ac 2:24 But-*G* raised him from the dead,
5: 4 You have not lied to men but to-*G*."
5:29 "We must obey-*G* rather than men!
7:55 to heaven and saw the glory of-*G*,
17:23 TO AN UNKNOWN-*G*.
20:27 to you the whole will of-*G*.
20:32 "Now I commit you to-*G*
Ro 1:17 a righteousness from-*G* is revealed,
2:11 For-*G* does not show favoritism.
3: 4 Let-*G* be true, and every man a liar.
3:23 and fall short of the glory of-*G*,
4:24 to whom-*G* will credit
5: 8 *G* demonstrates his own love for us
6:23 but the gift of-*G* is eternal life
8:28 in all things-*G* works for the good
11:22 the kindness and sternness of-*G*:
14:12 give an account of himself to-*G*.
1Co 1:20 Has not-*G* made foolish
2: 9 what-*G* has prepared
3: 6 watered it, but-*G* made it grow.
6:20 Therefore honor-*G* with your body.
7:24 each man, as responsible to-*G*.
8: 8 food does not bring us near to-*G*;
10:13 *G* is faithful; he will not let you be
10:31 do it all for the glory of-*G*.
14:33 For-*G* is not a-*G* of disorder
15:28 so that-*G* may be all in all.
2Co 1: 9 rely on ourselves but on-*G*,
2:14 be to-*G*, who always leads us
3: 5 but our competence comes from-*G*.
4: 7 this all-surpassing power is from-*G*
5:19 that-*G* was reconciling the world
5:21 *G* made him who had no sin
6:16 we are the temple of the living-*G*.
9: 7 for-*G* loves a cheerful giver.
9: 8 *G* is able to make all grace abound
Gal 2: 6 *G* does not judge by external
6: 7 not be deceived:-*G* cannot be
Eph 2:10 which-*G* prepared in advance for us
4: 6 one baptism; one-*G* and Father
5: 1 Be imitators of-*G*, therefore,
Php 2:13 Who, being in very nature-*G*,
4:19 And my-*G* will meet all your needs
1Th 2: 4 trying to please men but-*G*,
4: 7 For-*G* did not call us to be impure,
4: 9 taught by-*G* to love each other.
5: 9 For-*G* did not appoint us
1Ti 2: 5 one mediator between-*G* and men,
4: 4 For everything-*G* created is good,
5: 4 for this is pleasing to-*G*.
Tit 2:13 glorious appearing of our great-*G*
Heb 1: 1 In the past-*G* spoke
4:12 For the word of-*G* is living
6:10 *G* is not unjust; he will not forget
10:31 to fall into the hands of the living-*G*
11: 6 faith it is impossible to please-*G*,
12:10 but-*G* disciplines us for our good,
12:29 for our "*G* is a consuming fire."
13:15 offer to-*G* a sacrifice of praise—
Jas 1:13 For-*G* cannot be tempted by evil,
2:19 You believe that there is one-*G*.
2:23 "Abraham believed-*G*,

4:4 the world becomes an enemy of-*G.*
4:8 Come near to-*G* and he will come
1Pe 4:11 it with the strength-*G* provides,
2Pe 1:21 but men spoke from-*G*
1Jn 1:5 *G* is light; in him there is no
3:20 For-*G* is greater than our hearts,
4:7 for love comes from-*G.*
4:9 This is how-*G* showed his love
4:11 Dear friends, since-*G* so loved us,
4:12 No one has ever seen-*G;*
4:16 *G* is love.
Rev 4:8 holy is the Lord-*G* Almighty,
7:17 *G* will wipe away every tear
19:6 For our Lord-*G* Almighty reigns.

GOD-BREATHED* (BREATHED)
2Ti 3:16 All Scripture is-*G* and is useful

GOD'S (GOD)
2Ch 20:15 For the battle is not yours, but-*G.*
Job 37:14 stop and consider-*G* wonders.
Ps 52:8 I trust in-*G* unfailing love
69:30 I will praise-*G* name in song
Mk 3:35 Whoever does-*G* will is my brother
Jn 7:17 If anyone chooses to do-*G* will,
10:36 'I am-*G* Son?' Do not believe me
Ro 2:3 think you will escape-*G* judgment?
2:4 not realizing that-*G* kindness leads
3:3 lack of faith nullify-*G* faithfulness?
7:22 in my inner being I delight in-*G* law
9:16 or effort, but on-*G* mercy.
11:29 for-*G* gifts and his call are
12:2 and approve what-*G* will is—
12:13 Share with-*G* people who are
13:6 for the authorities are-*G* servants,
1Co 7:19 Keeping-*G* commands is what
2Co 6:2 now is the time of-*G* favor,
Eph 1:7 riches of-*G* grace that he lavished
1Th 4:3 It is-*G* will that you should be
5:18 for this is-*G* will for you
1Ti 6:1 so that-*G* name and our teaching
2Ti 2:19 *G* solid foundation stands firm,
Tit 1:7 overseer is entrusted with-*G* work,
Heb 1:3 The Son is the radiance of-*G* glory
9:24 now to appear for us in-*G* presence.
11:3 was formed at-*G* command,
1Pe 2:15 For it is-*G* will that
3:4 which is of great worth in-*G* sight.
1Jn 2:5 *G* love is truly made complete

GODLINESS (GOD)
1Ti 2:2 and quiet lives in all-*g* and holiness.
4:8 but-*g* has value for all things,
6:6 *g* with contentment is great gain.
6:11 and pursue righteousness,-*g,* faith,

GODLY (GOD)
Ps 4:3 that the LORD has set apart the-*g*
2Co 7:10 *G* sorrow brings repentance that
11:2 jealousy for you with a-*g* jealousy.
2Ti 3:12 everyone who wants to live a-*g* life
2Pe 3:11 You ought to live holy and-*g* lives

GODS (GOD)
Ex 20:3 "You shall have no other-*g*
Ac 19:26 He says that man-made-*g* are no *g*

GOLD
Job 23:10 tested me, I will come forth as-*g.*
Ps 19:10 They are more precious than-*g,*
119:127 more than-*g,* more than pure-*g,*
Pr 22:1 esteemed is better than silver or-*g.*

GOLGOTHA
Jn 19:17 (which in Aramaic is called-*G*).

GOLIATH
Philistine giant killed by David (1Sa 17; 21:9).

GOOD
Ge 1:4 God saw that the light was-*g,*
1:31 he had made, and it was very-*g.*

2:18 "It is not-*g* for the man to be alone.
50:20 but God intended it for-*g.*
Job 2:10 Shall we accept-*g* from God,
Ps 14:1 there is no one who does-*g.*
34:8 Taste and see that the LORD is-*g;*
37:3 Trust in the LORD and do-*g;*
84:11 no-*g* thing does he withhold
86:5 You are forgiving and-*g,* O Lord
103:5 satisfies your desires with-*g* things,
119:68 You are-*g,* and what you do is-*g;*
133:1 How-*g* and pleasant it is
147:1 How-*g* it is to sing praises
Pr 3:4 you will win favor and a-*g* name
11:27 He who seeks-*g* finds-*g* will,
17:22 A cheerful heart is-*g* medicine,
18:22 He who finds a wife finds what is-*g*
22:1 A-*g* name is more desirable
31:12 She brings him-*g,* not harm,
Isa 5:20 Woe to those who call evil-*g*
52:7 the feet of those who bring-*g* news,
Jer 6:16 ask where the-*g* way is,
32:39 the-*g* of their children after them.
Mic 6:8 has showed you, O man, what is-*g*
Mt 5:45 sun to rise on the evil and the-*g,*
7:17 Likewise every-*g* tree bears-*g* fruit,
12:35 The-*g* man brings-*g* things out
19:17 "There is only One who is-*g.*
25:21 'Well done,-*g* and faithful servant!'
Mk 3:4 lawful on the Sabbath: to do-*g*
8:36 What-*g* is it for a man
Lk 6:27 do-*g* to those who hate you,
10:11 "I am the-*g* shepherd.
Ro 8:28 for the-*g* of those who love him,
10:15 feet of those who bring-*g* news!"
12:9 Hate what is evil; cling to what is-*g.*
1Co 10:24 should seek his own-*g,* but the-*g*
15:33 Bad company corrupts-*g* character
2Co 9:8 you will abound in every-*g* work.
Gal 6:9 us not become weary in doing-*g,*
6:10 as we have opportunity, let us do-*g*
Eph 2:10 in Christ Jesus to do-*g* works,
Php 1:6 that he who began a-*g* work
1Th 5:21 Hold on to the-*g.*
1Ti 3:7 have a-*g* reputation with outsiders,
4:4 For everything God created is-*g,*
6:12 Fight the-*g* fight of the faith.
6:18 them to do-*g,* to be rich in-*g* deeds,
2Ti 3:17 equipped for every-*g* work.
4:7 I have fought the-*g* fight, I have
Heb 12:10 but God disciplines us for our-*g,*
1Pe 2:3 you have tasted that the Lord is-*g.*
2:12 Live such-*g* lives among the pagans

GOSPEL
Ro 1:16 I am not ashamed of the-*g.*
15:16 duty of proclaiming the-*g* of God,
1Co 1:17 to preach the-*g*—not with words
9:16 Woe to me if I do not preach the-*g!*
15:1 you of the-*g* I preached to you,
Gal 1:7 a different-*g*—which is really no-*g*
Php 1:27 in a manner worthy of the-*g*

GOSSIP
Pr 11:13 A-*g* betrays a confidence,
16:28 and a-*g* separates close friends.
18:8 of a-*g* are like choice morsels;
26:20 without-*g* a quarrel dies down.
2Co 12:20 slander,-*g,* arrogance and disorder.

GRACE (GRACIOUS)
Ps 45:2 lips have been anointed with-*g,*
Jn 1:17 *g* and truth came through Jesus
Ac 20:32 to God and to the word of his-*g,*
Ro 3:24 and are justified freely by his-*g*
5:15 came by the-*g* of the one man,
5:17 God's abundant provision of-*g*
5:20 where sin increased,-*g* increased all
6:14 you are not under law, but under-*g.*

11:6 if by-*g,* then it is no longer by works
2Co 6:1 not to receive God's-*g* in vain.
8:9 For you know the-*g*
9:8 able to make all-*g* abound to you,
12:9 "My-*g* is sufficient for you,
Gal 2:21 I do not set aside the-*g* of God,
5:4 you have fallen away from-*g.*
Eph 1:7 riches of God's-*g* that he lavished
2:5 it is by-*g* you have been saved.
2:7 the incomparable riches of his-*g,*
2:8 For it is by-*g* you have been saved,
Php 1:7 all of you share in God's-*g* with me.
Col 4:6 conversation be always full of-*g,*
2Th 2:16 and by his-*g* gave us eternal
2Ti 2:1 be strong in the-*g* that is
Tit 2:11 For the-*g* of God that brings
3:7 having been justified by his-*g,*
Heb 2:9 that by the-*g* of God he might taste
4:16 find-*g* to help us in our time of need
4:16 the throne of-*g* with confidence,
Jas 4:6 but gives-*g* to the humble."
2Pe 3:18 But grow in the-*g* and knowledge

GRACIOUS (GRACE)
Nu 6:25 and be-*g* to you;
Pr 22:11 a pure heart and whose speech is-*g*
Isa 30:18 Yet the LORD longs to be-*g* to you

GRAIN
1Co 9:9 ox while it is treading out the-*g.*"

GRANTED
Php 1:29 For it has been-*g* to you on behalf

GRASS
Ps 103:15 As for man, his days are like-*g,*
1Pe 1:24 "All men are like-*g,*

GRAVE (GRAVES)
Pr 7:27 Her house is a highway to the-*g,*
Hos 13:14 Where, O-*g,* is your destruction?

GRAVES (GRAVE)
Jn 5:28 are in their-*g* will hear his voice
Ro 3:13 "Their throats are open-*g;*

GREAT (GREATER GREATEST GREATNESS)
Ge 12:2 "I will make you into a-*g* nation
Dt 10:17 the-*g* God, mighty and awesome,
2Sa 22:36 you stoop down to make me-*g.*
Ps 19:11 in keeping them there is-*g* reward.
89:1 of the LORD's-*g* love forever;
103:11 so-*g* is his love for those who fear
107:43 consider the-*g* love of the LORD.
108:4 For-*g* is your love, higher
119:165 *G* peace have they who love your
145:3 *G* is the LORD and most worthy
Pr 23:24 of a righteous man has-*g* joy;
Isa 42:21 to make his law-*g* and glorious.
La 3:23 *g* is your faithfulness.
Mk 10:43 whoever wants to become-*g*
Lk 21:27 in a cloud with power and-*g* glory.
1Ti 6:6 with contentment is-*g* gain.
Tit 2:13 glorious appearing of our-*g* God
Heb 2:3 if we ignore such a-*g* salvation?
1Jn 3:1 How-*g* is the love the Father has

GREATER (GREAT)
Mk 12:31 There is no commandment-*g*
Jn 1:50 You shall see-*g* things than that."
15:13 *G* love has no one than this,
1Co 12:31 But eagerly desire the-*g* gifts.
Heb 11:26 as of-*g* value than the treasures
1Jn 3:20 For God is-*g* than our hearts,
4:4 is in you is-*g* than the one who is

GREATEST (GREAT)
Mt 22:38 is the first and-*g* commandment.
Lk 9:48 least among you all—he is the-*g.*"
1Co 13:13 But the-*g* of these is love.

GREATNESS (GREAT)
Ps 145:3 his-*g* no one can fathom.
150:2 praise him for his surpassing-*g.*
Isa 63:1 forward in the-*g* of his strength?
Php 3:8 compared to the surpassing-*g*

GREED (GREEDY)
Lk 12:15 on your guard against all kinds of-*g*
Ro 1:29 kind of wickedness, evil,-*g*
Eph 5:3 or of any kind of impurity, or of-*g,*
Col 3:5 evil desires and-*g,* which is idolatry
2Pe 2:14 experts in-*g*— an accursed brood!

GREEDY (GREED)
Pr 15:27 A-*g* man brings trouble
1Co 6:10 nor thieves nor the-*g* nor drunkards
Eph 5:5 No immoral, impure or-*g* person—
1Pe 5:2 not-*g* for money, but eager to serve;

GREEN
Ps 23:2 makes me lie down in-*g* pastures,

GREW (GROW)
Lk 2:52 And Jesus-*g* in wisdom and stature,
Ac 16:5 in the faith and-*g* daily in numbers.

GRIEF (GRIEVE)
Ps 10:14 O God, do see trouble and-*g;*
Pr 14:13 and joy may end in-*g.*
La 3:32 Though he brings-*g,* he will show
Jn 16:20 but your-*g* will turn to joy.
1Pe 1:6 had to suffer-*g* in all kinds of trials.

GRIEVE (GRIEF)
Eph 4:30 do not-*g* the Holy Spirit of God,
1Th 4:13 or to-*g* like the rest of men,

GROUND
Ge 3:17 "Cursed is the-*g* because of you;
Ex 3:5 where you are standing is holy-*g.*"
Eph 6:13 you may be able to stand your-*g,*

GROW (GREW)
Pr 13:11 by little makes it-*g.*
1Co 3:6 watered it, but God made it-*g.*
2Pe 3:18 But-*g* in the grace and knowledge

GRUMBLE (GRUMBLING)
1Co 10:10 And do not-*g,* as some of them did
Jas 5:9 Don't-*g* against each other,

GRUMBLING (GRUMBLE)
Jn 6:43 "Stop-*g* among yourselves,"
1Pe 4:9 to one another without-*g.*

GUARANTEE (GUARANTEEING)
Heb 7:22 Jesus has become the-*g*

GUARANTEEING (GUARANTEE)
2Co 1:22 as a deposit,-*g* what is to come.
Eph 1:14 who is a deposit-*g* our inheritance

GUARD (GUARDS)
Ps 141:3 Set a-*g* over my mouth, O LORD;
Pr 4:23 Above all else,-*g* your heart,
Isa 52:12 the God of Israel will be your rear-*g.*
Mk 13:33 Be on-*g!* Be alert! You do not know
1Co 16:13 Be on your-*g;* stand firm in the faith
Php 4:7 will-*g* your hearts and your minds
1Ti 6:20 *g* what has been entrusted

GUARDS (GUARD)
Pr 13:3 He who-*g* his lips-*g* his life,
19:16 who obeys instructions-*g* his life,
21:23 He who-*g* his mouth and his tongue
22:5 he who-*g* his soul stays far

GUIDE
Ex 13:21 of cloud to-*g* them on their way
15:13 In your strength you will-*g* them
Ne 9:19 cease to-*g* them on their path,
Ps 25:5 me in your truth and teach me,
43:3 let them-*g* me;
48:14 he will be our-*g* even to the end.
67:4 and-*g* the nations of the earth.
73:24 You-*g* me with your counsel,

139:10 even there your hand will-*g* me,
Pr   4:11 I-*g* you in the way of wisdom
      6:22 When you walk, they will-*g* you;
Isa 58:11 The Lord will-*g* you always;
Jn 16:13 comes, he will-*g* you into all truth.

GUILTY
Ex 34: 7 does not leave the-*g* unpunished;
Jn   8:46 Can any of you prove me-*g* of sin?
Heb 10:22 to cleanse us from a-*g* conscience
Jas 2:10 at just one point is-*g* of breaking all

HADES
Mt 16:18 the gates of-*H* will not overcome it.

HAGAR
    Servant of Sarah, wife of Abraham, mother
of Ishmael (Ge 16:1-6; 25:12). Driven away by
Sarah while pregnant (Ge 16:5-16); after birth
of Isaac (Ge 21:9-21; Gal 4:21-31).

HAGGAI*
    Post-exilic prophet who encouraged rebuilding
of the temple (Ezr 5:1; 6:14; Hag 1-2).

HAIR (HAIRS)
Lk 21:18 But not a-*h* of your head will perish
1Co 11: 6 for a woman to have her-*h* cut

HAIRS (HAIR)
Mt 10:30 even the very-*h* of your head are all

HALLELUJAH*
Rev 19:1, 3, 4, 6

HALLOWED (HOLY)
Mt   6: 9 *h* be your name,

HAND (HANDS)
Ps 16: 8 Because he is at my right-*h*,
     37:24 the Lord upholds him with his-*h*.
    139:10 even there your-*h* will guide me,
Ecc 9:10 Whatever your-*h* finds to do,
Mt   6: 3 know what your right-*h* is doing,
Jn 10:28 one can snatch them out of my-*h*.
1Co 12:15 I am not a-*h*, I do not belong

HANDS (HAND)
Ps 22:16 they have pierced my-*h*
     24: 4 He who has clean-*h* and a pure
     31: 5 Into your-*h* I commit my spirit;
     31:15 My times are in your-*h*;
Pr 10: 4 Lazy-*h* make a man poor,
     31:20 and extends her-*h* to the needy.
Isa 55:12 will clap their-*h*.
     65: 2 All day long I have held out my-*h*
Lk 23:46 into your-*h* I commit my spirit."
1Th 4:11 and to work with your-*h*,
1Ti 2: 8 to lift up holy-*h* in prayer,
      5:22 hasty in the laying on of-*h*,

HANNAH*
    Wife of Elkanah, mother of Samuel (1Sa 1).
Prayer at dedication of Samuel (1Sa 2:1-10).
Blessed (1Sa 2:18-21).

HAPPY
Ps 68: 3 may they be-*h* and joyful.
Pr 15:13 A-*h* heart makes the face cheerful,
Ecc 5:12 better for men than to be-*h*
Jas 5:13 Is anyone-*h*? Let him sing songs

HARD (HARDEN HARDSHIP)
Ge 18:14 Is anything too-*h* for the Lord?
Mt 19:23 it is-*h* for a rich man
1Co 4:12 We work-*h* with our own hands.
1Th 5:12 to respect those who work-*h*

HARDEN (HARD)
Ro   9:18 he hardens whom he wants to-*h*.
Heb 3: 8 do not-*h* your hearts

HARDHEARTED* (HEART)
Dt 15: 7 do not be-*h* or tightfisted

HARDSHIP (HARD)
Ro   8:35 Shall trouble or-*h* or persecution
2Ti 2: 3 Endure-*h* with us like a good
      4: 5 endure-*h*, do the work
Heb 12: 7 Endure-*h* as discipline; God is

HARM
Ps 121: 6 the sun will not-*h* you by day,
Pr   3:29 not plot-*h* against your neighbor,
     31:12 She brings him good, not-*h*,
Ro 13:10 Love does no-*h* to its neighbor.
1Jn 5:18 and the evil one cannot-*h* him.

HARMONY
Ro 12:16 Live in-*h* with one another.
2Co 6:15 What-*h* is there between Christ
1Pe 3: 8 live in-*h* with one another;

HARVEST
Mt   9:37 *h* is plentiful but the workers are
Jn   4:35 at the fields! They are ripe for-*h*.
Gal 6: 9 at the proper time we will reap a-*h*
Heb 12:11 it produces a-*h* of righteousness

HASTE (HASTY)
Pr 21: 5 as surely as-*h* leads to poverty.
     29:20 Do you see a man who speaks in-*h*?

HASTY* (HASTE)
Pr 19: 2 nor to be-*h* and miss the way.
Ecc 5: 2 do not be-*h* in your heart
1Ti 5:22 Do not be-*h* in the laying

HATE (HATED HATES HATRED)
Lev 19:17 " 'Do not-*h* your brother
Ps   5: 5 you-*h* all who do wrong.
     45: 7 righteousness and-*h* wickedness;
     97:10 those who love the Lord-*h* evil,
    139:21 Do I not-*h* those who-*h* you,
Pr   8:13 To fear the Lord is to-*h* evil;
Am   5:15 *H* evil, love good;
Mal 2:16 "I-*h* divorce," says the Lord God
Mt   5:43 your neighbor and-*h* your enemy.'
     10:22 All men will-*h* you because of me,
Lk   6:27 do good to those who-*h* you,
Ro 12: 9 *H* what is evil; cling to what is good

HATED (HATE)
Ro   9:13 "Jacob I loved, but Esau I-*h*."
Eph 5:29 no one ever-*h* his own body,
Heb 1: 9 righteousness and-*h* wickedness;

HATES (HATE)
Pr   6:16 There are six things the Lord-*h*,
     13:24 He who spares the rod-*h* his son,
Jn   3:20 Everyone who does evil-*h* the light,
1Jn 2: 9 *h* his brother is still in the darkness.

HATRED (HATE)
Pr 10:12 *h* stirs up dissension,
Jas 4: 4 with the world is-*h* toward God?

HAUGHTY
Pr 16:18 a-*h* spirit before a fall.

HAY
1Co 3:12 costly stones, wood,-*h* or straw,

HEAD (HEADS HOTHEADED)
Ge   3:15 he will crush your-*h*,
Ps 23: 5 You anoint my-*h* with oil;
Pr 25:22 will heap burning coals on his-*h*,
Isa 59:17 and the helmet of salvation on his-*h*
Mt   8:20 of Man has no place to lay his-*h*."
Ro 12:20 will heap burning coals on his-*h*."
1Co 11: 3 and the-*h* of Christ is God.
     12:21 And the-*h* cannot say to the feet,
Eph 5:23 For the husband is the-*h* of the wife
2Ti 4: 5 keep your-*h* in all situations,
Rev 19:12 and on his-*h* are many crowns.

HEADS (HEAD)
Lev 26:13 you to walk with-*h* held high.
Isa 35:10 everlasting joy will crown their-*h*.

HEAL (HEALED HEALING HEALS)
2Ch 7:14 their sin and will-*h* their land.
Ps 41: 4 *h* me, for I have sinned against you
Mt 10: 8 *H* the sick, raise the dead,
Lk   4:23 to me: 'Physician,-*h* yourself!'
      5:17 present for him to-*h* the sick.

HEALED (HEAL)
Isa 53: 5 and by his wounds we are-*h*.
Mt   9:22 he said, "your faith has-*h* you."
     14:36 and all who touched him were-*h*.
Ac   4:10 this man stands before you-*h*.
     14: 9 saw that he had faith to be-*h*
Jas 5:16 for each other so that you may be-*h*
1Pe 2:24 by his wounds you have been-*h*.

HEALING (HEAL)
Eze 47:12 for food and their leaves for-*h*."
Mal 4: 2 rise with-*h* in its wings.
1Co 12: 9 to another gifts of-*h*
     12:30 Do all have gifts of-*h*? Do all speak
Rev 22: 2 are for the-*h* of the nations.

HEALS (HEAL)
Ex 15:26 for I am the Lord, who-*h* you."
Ps 103: 3 and-*h* all your diseases;
    147: 3 He-*h* the brokenhearted

HEALTH (HEALTHY)
Pr   3: 8 This will bring-*h* to your body
     15:30 and good news gives-*h* to the bones

HEALTHY (HEALTH)
Mk   2:17 "It is not the-*h* who need a doctor,

HEAR (HEARD HEARING HEARS)
Dt   6: 4 *H*, O Israel: The Lord our God,
     31:13 must-*h* it and learn
2Ch 7:14 then will I-*h* from heaven
Ps 94: 9 he who implanted the ear not-*h*?
Isa 29:18 that day the deaf will-*h* the words
     65:24 while they are still speaking I will-*h*
Mt 11:15 He who has ears, let him-*h*.
Jn   8:47 reason you do not-*h* is that you do
2Ti 4: 3 what their itching ears want to-*h*

HEARD (HEAR)
Job 42: 5 My ears had-*h* of you
Isa 66: 8 Who has ever-*h* of such a thing?
Mt   5:21 "You have-*h* that it was said
      5:27 "You have-*h* that it was said,
      5:33 you have-*h* that it was said
      5:38 "You have-*h* that it was said,
      5:43 "You have-*h* that it was said,
1Co 2: 9 no ear has-*h*,
1Th 2:13 word of God, which you-*h* from us,
2Ti 1:13 What you-*h* from me, keep
Jas 1:25 not forgetting what he has-*h*,

HEARING (HEAR)
Ro 10:17 faith comes from-*h* the message,

HEARS (HEAR)
Jn   5:24 whoever-*h* my word and believes
1Jn 5:14 according to his will, he-*h* us.
Rev 3:20 If anyone-*h* my voice and opens

HEART (BROKENHEARTED
HARDHEARTED HEARTS
WHOLEHEARTEDLY)
Ex 25: 2 each man whose-*h* prompts him
Lev 19:17 Do not hate your brother in your-*h*.
Dt   4:29 if you look for him with all your-*h*
      6: 5 Lord your God with all your-*h*
     10:12 Lord your God with all your-*h*
     15:10 and do so without a grudging-*h*;
     30: 6 you may love him with all your-*h*
     30:10 Lord your God with all your-*h*
Jos 22: 5 and to serve him with all your-*h*
1Sa 13:14 sought out a man after his own-*h*
     16: 7 but the Lord looks at the-*h*."
2Ki 23: 3 with all his-*h* and all his soul,
1Ch 28: 9 for the Lord searches every-*h*

2Ch 7:16 and my-*h* will always be there.
Job 22:22 and lay up his words in your-*h*.
     37: 1 "At this my-*h* pounds
Ps 14: 1 The fool says in his-*h*,
     19:14 and the meditation of my-*h*
     37: 4 will give you the desires of your-*h*.
     45: 1 My-*h* is stirred by a noble theme
     51:10 Create in me a pure-*h*, O God,
     51:17 a broken and contrite-*h*,
     66:18 If I had cherished sin in my-*h*,
     86:11 give me an undivided-*h*,
    119:11 I have hidden your word in my-*h*
    119:32 for you have set my-*h* free.
    139:23 Search me, O God, and know my-*h*
Pr   3: 5 Trust in the Lord with all your-*h*
      4:21 keep them within your-*h*;
      4:23 Above all else, guard your-*h*,
      7: 3 write them on the tablet of your-*h*.
     13:12 Hope deferred makes the-*h* sick,
     14:13 Even in laughter the-*h* may ache,
     15:30 A cheerful look brings joy to the-*h*,
     17:22 A cheerful-*h* is good medicine,
     24:17 stumbles, do not let your-*h* rejoice,
     27:19 so a man's-*h* reflects the man.
Ecc 8: 5 wise-*h* will know the proper time
SS   4: 9 You have stolen my-*h*, my sister,
Isa 40:11 and carries them close to his-*h*;
     57:15 and to revive the-*h* of the contrite.
Jer 17: 9 The-*h* is deceitful above all things
     29:13 when you seek me with all your-*h*.
Eze 36:26 I will give you a new-*h*
Mt   5: 8 Blessed are the pure in-*h*,
      6:21 treasure is, there your-*h* will be
     12:34 of the-*h* the mouth speaks.
     22:37 the Lord your God with all your-*h*
Lk   6:45 overflow of his-*h* his mouth speaks.
Ro   2:29 is circumcision of the-*h*,
     10:10 is with your-*h* that you believe
1Co 14:25 the secrets of his-*h* will be laid bare.
Eph 5:19 make music in your-*h* to the Lord,
      6: 6 doing the will of God from your-*h*.
Col 3:23 work at it with all your-*h*,
1Pe 1:22 one another deeply, from the-*h*.

HEARTS (HEART)
Dt 11:18 Fix these words of mine in your-*h*
1Ki 8:39 for you alone know the-*h* of all men
      8:61 your-*h* must be fully committed
Ps 62: 8 pour out your-*h* to him,
Ecc 3:11 also set eternity in the-*h* of men;
Jer 31:33 and write it on their-*h*.
Lk 16:15 of men, but God knows your-*h*.
     24:32 "Were not our-*h* burning within us
Jn 14: 1 "Do not let your-*h* be troubled.
Ac 15: 9 for he purified their-*h* by faith.
Ro   2:15 of the law are written on their-*h*,
2Co 3: 2 written on our-*h*, known
      3: 3 but on tablets of human-*h*.
      4: 6 shine in our-*h* to give us the light
Eph 3:17 dwell in your-*h* through faith.
Col 3: 1 set your-*h* on things above,
Heb 3: 8 do not harden your-*h*
     10:16 I will put my laws in their-*h*,
1Jn 3:20 For God is greater than our-*h*,

HEAT
2Pe 3:12 and the elements will melt in the-*h*.

HEAVEN (HEAVENLY HEAVENS)
Ge 14:19 Creator of-*h* and earth.
1Ki 8:27 the highest-*h*, cannot contain you.
2Ki 2: 1 up to-*h* in a whirlwind,
2Ch 7:14 then will I hear from-*h*
Isa 14:12 How you have fallen from-*h*,
     66: 1 "*H* is my throne,
Da   7:13 coming with the clouds of-*h*.
Mt   6: 9 " 'Our Father in-*h*,
      6:20 up for yourselves treasures in-*h*,

16:19 bind on earth will be bound in-*h*,
19:23 man to enter the kingdom of-*h*.
24:35 *H* and earth will pass away,
26:64 and coming on the clouds of-*h*."
28:18 "All authority in-*h*

Mk 16:19 he was taken up into-*h*
Lk 15:7 in-*h* over one sinner who repents
18:22 and you will have treasure in-*h*.
Ro 10:6 'Who will ascend into-*h*?' " (that is,
2Co 5:1 an eternal house in-*h*, not built
12:2 ago was caught up to the third-*h*.
Php 2:10 *h* and on earth and under the earth,
3:20 But our citizenship is in-*h*.
1Th 1:10 and to wait for his Son from-*h*,
Heb 8:5 and shadow of what is in-*h*.
9:24 he entered-*h* itself, now to appear
2Pe 3:13 we are looking forward to a new-*h*
Rev 21:1 Then I saw a new-*h* and a new earth

HEAVENLY (HEAVEN)
Ps 8:5 him a little lower than the-*h* beings
2Co 5:2 to be clothed with our-*h* dwelling,
Eph 1:3 in the-*h* realms with every spiritual
1:20 at his right hand in the-*h* realms,
2Ti 4:18 bring me safely to his-*h* kingdom.
Heb 12:22 to the-*h* Jerusalem, the city

HEAVENS (HEAVEN)
Ge 1:1 In the beginning God created the-*h*
1Ki 8:27 The-*h*, even the highest heaven,
2Ch 2:6 since the-*h*, even the highest
Ps 8:3 When I consider your-*h*,
19:1 The-*h* declare the glory of God;
102:25 the-*h* are the work of your hands.
108:4 is your love, higher than the-*h*;
119:89 it stands firm in the-*h*.
139:8 If I go up to the-*h*, you are there;
Isa 51:6 Lift up your eyes to the-*h*,
55:9 "As the-*h* are higher than the earth,
65:17 new-*h* and a new earth.
Joel 2:30 I will show wonders in the-*h*
Eph 4:10 who ascended higher than all the-*h*,
2Pe 3:10 The-*h* will disappear with a roar,

HEBREW
Ge 14:13 and reported this to Abram the-*H*.

HEEDS
Pr 13:1 wise son-*h* his father's instruction,
13:18 whoever correction is honored.
15:5 whoever-*h* correction shows
15:32 whoever-*h* correction gains

HEEL
Ge 3:15 and you will strike his-*h*."

HEIRS (INHERIT)
Ro 8:17 then we are-*h*—of God
Gal 3:29 and-*h* according to the promise.
Eph 3:6 gospel the Gentiles are-*h* together
1Pe 3:7 as-*h* with you of the gracious gift

HELL
Mt 5:22 will be in danger of the fire of-*h*.
Lk 16:23 In-*h*, where he was in torment,
2Pe 2:4 but sent them to-*h*, putting them

HELMET
Isa 59:17 and the-*h* of salvation on his head;
Eph 6:17 Take the-*h* of salvation
1Th 5:8 and the hope of salvation as a-*h*.

HELP (HELPED HELPER HELPING HELPS)
Ps 18:6 I cried to my God for-*h*.
30:2 my God, I called to you for-*h*
46:1 an ever-present-*h* in trouble.
79:9 *H* us, O God our Savior,
121:1 where does my-*h* come from?
Isa 41:10 I will strengthen you and-*h* you;
Jnh 2:2 depths of the grave I called for-*h*,
Mk 9:24 *h* me overcome my unbelief!"

Ac 16:9 Come over to Macedonia and-*h* us
1Co 12:28 those able to-*h* others, those

HELPED (HELP)
1Sa 7:12 "Thus far has the LORD-*h* us."

HELPER (HELP)
Ge 2:18 I will make a-*h* suitable for him."
Ps 10:14 you are the-*h* of the fatherless.
Heb 13:6 Lord is my-*h*; I will not be afraid.

HELPING (HELP)
Ac 9:36 always doing good and-*h* the poor.
1Ti 5:10 *h* those in trouble and devoting

HELPS (HELP)
Ro 8:26 the Spirit-*h* us in our weakness.

HEN
Mt 23:37 as a-*h* gathers her chicks

HERITAGE (INHERIT)
Ps 127:3 Sons are a-*h* from the LORD,

HEROD
1. King of Judea who tried to kill Jesus (Mt 2; Lk 1:5).
2. Son of 1. Tetrarch of Galilee who arrested and beheaded John the Baptist (Mt 14:1-12; Mk 6:14-29; Lk 3:1, 19-20; 9:7-9); tried Jesus (Lk 23:6-15).
3. Grandson of 1. King of Judea who killed James (Ac 12:2); arrested Peter (Ac 12:3-19). Death (Ac 12:19-23).

HERODIAS
Wife of Herod the Tetrarch who persuaded her daughter to ask for John the Baptist's head (Mt 14:1-12; Mk 6:14-29).

HEZEKIAH
King of Judah. Restored the temple and worship (2Ch 29-31). Sought the LORD for help against Assyria (2Ki 18-19; 2Ch 32:1-23; Isa 36-37). Illness healed (2Ki 20:1-11; 2Ch 32:24-26; Isa 38). Judged for showing Babylonians his treasures (2Ki 20:12-21; 2Ch 32:31; Isa 39).

HID (HIDE)
Ge 3:8 and they-*h* from the LORD God
Ex 2:2 she-*h* him for three months.
Jos 6:17 because she-*h* the spies we sent.
Heb 11:23 By faith Moses' parents-*h* him

HIDDEN (HIDE)
Ps 19:12 Forgive my-*h* faults.
119:11 I have-*h* your word in my heart
Pr 2:4 and search for it as for-*h* treasure,
Isa 59:2 your sins have-*h* his face from you,
Mt 5:14 A city on a hill cannot be-*h*.
13:44 of heaven is like treasure-*h*
Lk 1:26 the mystery that has been kept-*h*
2:3 in whom are-*h* all the treasures
3:3 and your life is now-*h* with Christ

HIDE (HID HIDDEN)
Ps 17:8 *h* me in the shadow of your wings
143:9 for I-*h* myself in you.

HILL (HILLS)
Mt 5:14 A city on a-*h* cannot be hidden.

HILLS (HILL)
Ps 50:10 and the cattle on a thousand-*h*.
121:1 I lift up my eyes to the-*h*—

HINDER (HINDERS)
1Sa 14:6 Nothing can-*h* the LORD
Mt 19:14 come to me, and do not-*h* them,
1Co 9:12 anything rather than-*h* the gospel
1Pe 3:7 so that nothing will-*h* your prayers.

HINDERS (HINDER)
Heb 12:1 let us throw off everything that-*h*

HINT*
Eph 5:3 even a-*h* of sexual immorality,

HOLD
Ex 20:7 LORD will not-*h* anyone guiltless
Lev 19:13 " 'Do not-*h* back the wages
Jos 22:5 to-*h* fast to him and to serve him
Ps 73:23 you-*h* me by my right hand.
Pr 4:4 "Lay-*h* of my words
Isa 54:2 do not-*h* back;
Mk 11:25 if you-*h* anything against anyone,
Php 2:16 as you-*h* out the word of life—
3:12 but I press on to take-*h* of that
Col 1:17 and in him all things-*h* together.
1Th 5:21 *H* on to the good.
1Ti 6:12 Take-*h* of the eternal life
Heb 10:23 Let us-*h* unswervingly

HOLINESS (HOLY)
Ex 15:11 majestic in-*h*,
Ps 29:2 in the splendor of his-*h*.
96:9 in the splendor of his-*h*;
Ro 6:19 to righteousness leading to-*h*.
2Co 7:1 perfecting-*h* out of reverence
Eph 4:24 God in true righteousness and-*h*.
Heb 12:10 that we may share in his-*h*.
12:14 without-*h* no one will see the Lord.

HOLY (HALLOWED HOLINESS)
Ex 19:6 kingdom of priests and a-*h* nation.'
20:8 the Sabbath day by keeping it-*h*.
Lev 11:44 and be-*h*, because I am-*h*.
20:7 " 'Consecrate yourselves and be-*h*,
20:26 You are to be-*h* to me because I,
21:8 Consider them-*h*, because I
22:32 Do not profane my-*h* name.
Ps 16:10 will you let your-*H* One see decay.
24:3 Who may stand in his-*h* place?
77:13 Your ways, O God, are-*h*.
99:3 he is-*h*.
99:5 he is-*h*.
99:9 for the LORD our God is-*h*.
111:9 *h* and awesome is his name.
Isa 5:16 the-*h* God will show himself-*h*
6:3 *H*, *h*,-*h* is the LORD Almighty;
40:25 who is my equal?" says the-*H* One.
57:15 who lives forever, whose name is-*h*:
Eze 28:25 I will show myself-*h* among them
Da 9:24 prophecy and to anoint the most-*h*.
Hab 2:20 But the LORD is in his-*h* temple;
Ac 2:27 will you let your-*H* One see decay.
Ro 7:12 and the commandment is-*h*,
12:1 as living sacrifices,-*h* and pleasing
Eph 5:3 improper for God's-*h* people.
2Th 1:10 to be glorified in his-*h* people
2Ti 1:9 saved us and called us to a-*h* life—
3:15 you have known the-*h* Scriptures,
Tit 1:8 upright,-*h* and disciplined.
1Pe 1:15 But just as he who called you is-*h*,
1:16 is written: "Be-*h*, because I am-*h*."
2:9 a royal priesthood, a-*h* nation,
2Pe 3:11 You ought to live-*h* and godly lives
Rev 4:8 "*H*,-*h*,-*h* is the Lord God

HOME (HOMES)
Dt 6:7 Talk about them when you sit at-*h*
Ps 84:3 Even the sparrow has found a-*h*,
Pr 3:33 but he blesses the-*h* of the righteous
Mk 10:29 "no one who has left-*h* or brothers
Jn 14:23 to him and make our-*h* with him.
Tit 2:5 to be busy at-*h*, to be kind,

HOMES (HOME)
Ne 4:14 daughters, your wives and your-*h*.
1Ti 5:14 to manage their-*h* and to give

HOMOSEXUAL*
1Co 6:9 male prostitutes nor-*h* offenders

HONEST
Lev 19:36 Use-*h* scales and-*h* weights,

Dt 25:15 and-*h* weights and measures,
Job 31:6 let God weigh me in-*h* scales
Pr 12:17 truthful witness gives-*h* testimony,

HONEY
Ex 3:8 a land flowing with milk and-*h*—
Ps 19:10 than-*h* from the comb.
119:103 sweeter than-*h* to my mouth!

HONOR (HONORABLE HONORABLY HONORED HONORS)
Ex 20:12 "*H* your father and your mother,
Nu 25:13 he was zealous for the-*h* of his God
Dt 5:16 "*H* your father and your mother,
1Sa 2:30 Those who-*h* me I will-*h*,
Ps 8:5 and crowned him with glory and-*h*.
Pr 3:9 *H* the LORD with your wealth,
15:33 and humility comes before-*h*.
20:3 It is to a man's-*h* to avoid strife,
Mt 15:4 '*H* your father and mother'
Ro 12:10 *H* one another above yourselves.
1Co 6:20 Therefore-*h* God with your body.
Eph 6:2 "*H* your father and mother"—
1Ti 5:17 well are worthy of double-*h*,
Heb 2:7 you crowned him with glory and-*h*
Rev 4:9 *h* and thanks to him who sits

HONORABLE (HONOR)
1Th 4:4 body in a way that is holy and-*h*,

HONORABLY (HONOR)
Heb 13:18 and desire to live-*h* in every way.

HONORED (HONOR)
Ps 12:8 when what is vile is-*h* among men.
Pr 13:18 but whoever heeds correction is-*h*.
1Co 12:26 if one part is-*h*, every part rejoices
Heb 13:4 Marriage should be-*h* by all,

HONORS (HONOR)
Ps 15:4 but-*h* those who fear the LORD,
Pr 14:31 to the needy-*h* God.

HOOKS
Isa 2:4 and their spears into pruning-*h*.
Joel 3:10 and your pruning-*h* into spears.

HOPE (HOPES)
Job 13:15 Though he slay me, yet will I-*h*
Ps 42:5 Put your-*h* in God,
62:5 my-*h* comes from him.
119:74 for I have put my-*h* in your word.
130:7 O Israel, put your-*h* in the LORD,
147:11 who put their-*h* in his unfailing love
Pr 13:12 *H* deferred makes the heart sick,
Isa 40:31 but those who-*h* in the LORD
Ro 5:4 character; and character,-*h*.
8:24 But-*h* that is seen is no-*h* at all.
12:12 Be joyful in-*h*, patient in affliction,
15:4 of the Scriptures we might have-*h*.
1Co 13:13 now these three remain: faith,-*h*
15:19 for this life we have-*h* in Christ,
Col 1:27 Christ in you, the-*h* of glory.
1Th 5:8 and the-*h* of salvation as a helmet.
1Ti 6:17 but to put their-*h* in God,
Tit 2:13 while we wait for the blessed-*h*—
Heb 6:19 We have this-*h* as an anchor
11:1 faith is being sure of what we-*h* for
1Jn 3:3 Everyone who has this-*h*

HOPES (HOPE)
1Co 13:7 always-*h*, always perseveres.

HORSE
Ps 147:10 not in the strength of the-*h*,
Pr 26:3 A whip for the-*h*, a halter
Zec 1:8 before me was a man riding a red-*h*
Rev 6:2 and there before me was a white-*h*!
6:4 Come!" Then another-*h* came out,
6:5 and there before me was a black-*h*!
6:8 and there before me was a pale-*h*!
19:11 and there before me was a white-*h*,

HOSANNA
Mt 21:9 *"H* in the highest!"

HOSHEA
Last king of Israel (2Ki 15:30; 17:1-6).

HOSPITABLE* (HOSPITALITY)
1Ti 3:2 self-controlled, respectable,-*h*,
Tit 1:8 Rather he must be-*h*, one who loves

HOSPITALITY (HOSPITABLE)
Ro 12:13 Practice-*h*.
1Ti 5:10 as bringing up children, showing-*h*,
1Pe 4:9 Offer-*h* to one another

HOSTILE
Ro 8:7 the sinful mind is-*h* to God.

HOT
1Ti 4:2 have been seared as with a-*h* iron.
Rev 3:15 that you are neither cold nor-*h*.

HOT-TEMPERED
Pr 15:18 A-*h* man stirs up dissension,
19:19 A-*h* man must pay the penalty;
22:24 Do not make friends with a-*h* man,
29:22 and a-*h* one commits many sins.

HOTHEADED (HEAD)
Pr 14:16 but a fool is-*h* and reckless.

HOUR
Ecc 9:12 knows when his-*h* will come:
Mt 6:27 you by worrying can add a single-*h*
Lk 12:40 the Son of Man will come at an-*h*
Jn 12:23 The-*h* has come for the Son of Man
12:27 for this very reason I came to this-*h*

HOUSE (HOUSEHOLD STOREHOUSE)
Ex 20:17 shall not covet your neighbor's-*h*.
Ps 23:6 I will dwell in the-*h* of the Lord
84:10 a doorkeeper in the-*h* of my God
122:1 "Let us go to the-*h* of the Lord."
127:1 Unless the Lord builds the-*h*,
Pr 7:27 Her-*h* is a highway to the grave,
21:9 than share a-*h* with a quarrelsome
Isa 56:7 a-*h* of prayer for all nations."
Zec 13:6 given at the-*h* of my friends.'
Mt 7:24 is like a wise man who built his-*h*
12:29 can anyone enter a strong man's-*h*
21:13 My-*h* will be called a-*h* of prayer,'
Mk 3:25 If a-*h* is divided against itself,
Lk 11:17 a-*h* divided against itself will fall.
Jn 2:16 How dare you turn my Father's-*h*
12:3 the-*h* was filled with the fragrance
14:2 In my Father's-*h* are many rooms;
Heb 3:3 the builder of a-*h* has greater honor

HOUSEHOLD (HOUSE)
Jos 24:15 my-*h*, we will serve the Lord."
Mic 7:6 are the members of his own-*h*.
Mt 10:36 will be the members of his own-*h*.'
12:25 or-*h* divided against itself will not
1Ti 3:12 manage his children and his-*h* well.
3:15 to conduct themselves in God's-*h*,

HUMAN (HUMANITY)
Gal 3:3 to attain your goal by-*h* effort?

HUMANITY (HUMAN)
Heb 2:14 he too shared in their-*h* so that

HUMBLE (HUMBLED HUMBLES HUMILIATE HUMILITY)
2Ch 7:14 will-*h* themselves and pray
Ps 25:9 He guides the-*h* in what is right
Pr 3:34 but gives grace to the-*h*.
Isa 66:2 he who is-*h* and contrite in spirit,
Mt 11:29 for I am gentle and-*h* in heart,
Eph 4:2 Be completely-*h* and gentle;
Jas 4:10 *H* yourselves before the Lord,
1Pe 5:6 *H* yourselves,

HUMBLED (HUMBLE)
Mt 23:12 whoever exalts himself will be-*h*,

Php 2:8 he-*h* himself

HUMBLES (HUMBLE)
Mt 18:4 whoever-*h* himself like this child is
23:12 whoever-*h* himself will be exalted.

HUMILIATE* (HUMBLE)
Pr 3:2 than for him to-*h* you
1Co 11:22 and-*h* those who have nothing?

HUMILITY (HUMBLE)
Pr 11:2 but with-*h* comes wisdom.
15:33 and-*h* comes before honor.
Php 2:3 but in-*h* consider others better
Tit 3:2 and to show true-*h* toward all men.
1Pe 5:5 clothe yourselves with-*h*

HUNGRY
Ps 107:9 and fills the-*h* with good things.
146:7 and gives food to the-*h*.
Pr 25:21 If your enemy is-*h*, give him food
Eze 18:7 but gives his food to the-*h*
Mt 25:35 For I was-*h* and you gave me
Lk 1:53 He has filled the-*h* with good things
Jn 6:35 comes to me will never go-*h*,
Ro 12:20 "If your enemy is-*h*, feed him;

HURT (HURTS)
Ecc 8:9 it over others to his own-*h*.
Mk 16:18 deadly poison, it will not-*h* them
Rev 2:11 He who overcomes will not be-*h*

HURTS* (HURT)
Ps 15:4 even when it-*h*,
Pr 26:28 A lying tongue hates those it-*h*,

HUSBAND (HUSBAND'S HUSBANDS)
1Co 7:3 The-*h* should fulfill his marital duty
7:10 wife must not separate from her-*h*.
7:11 And a-*h* must not divorce his wife.
7:13 And if a woman has a-*h* who is not
7:39 A woman is bound to her-*h* as long
2Co 11:2 I promised you to one-*h*, to Christ,
Eph 5:23 For the-*h* is the head of the wife
5:33 and the wife must respect her-*h*.
1Ti 3:2 the-*h* of but one wife, temperate,

HUSBAND'S (HUSBAND)
Pr 12:4 of noble character is her-*h* crown,
1Co 7:4 the-*h* body does not belong

HUSBANDS (HUSBAND)
Eph 5:22 submit to your-*h* as to the Lord.
5:25 *H*, love your wives, just
Tit 2:4 the younger women to love their-*h*
1Pe 3:1 same way be submissive to your-*h*
3:7 *H*, in the same way be considerate

HYMN
1Co 14:26 everyone has a-*h*, or a word

HYPOCRISY (HYPOCRITE HYPOCRITES)
Mt 23:28 but on the inside you are full of-*h*
1Pe 2:1 *h*, envy, and slander of every kind.

HYPOCRITE (HYPOCRISY)
Mt 7:5 You-*h*, first take the plank out

HYPOCRITES (HYPOCRISY)
Ps 26:4 nor do I consort with-*h*;
Mt 6:5 when you pray, do not be like the-*h*

HYSSOP
Ps 51:7 with-*h*, and I will be clean;

IDLE (IDLENESS)
1Th 5:14 those who are-*i*, encourage
2Th 3:6 away from every brother who is-*i*
1Ti 5:13 they get into the habit of being-*i*

IDLENESS* (IDLE)
Pr 31:27 and does not eat the bread of-*i*.

IDOL (IDOLATRY IDOLS)
Isa 44:17 From the rest he makes a god, his-*i*;
1Co 8:4 We know that an-*i* is nothing at all

IDOLATRY (IDOL)
Col 3:5 evil desires and greed, which is-*i*.

IDOLS (IDOL)
1Co 8:1 Now about food sacrificed to-*i*:

IGNORANT (IGNORE)
1Co 15:34 for there are some who are-*i* of God
Heb 5:2 to deal gently with those who are-*i*
1Pe 2:15 good you should silence the-*i* talk
2Pe 3:16 which-*i* and unstable people distort

IGNORE (IGNORANT IGNORES)
Dt 22:1 do not-*i* it but be sure
Ps 9:12 he does not-*i* the cry of the afflicted
Heb 2:3 if we-*i* such a great salvation?

IGNORES (IGNORE)
Pr 10:17 whoever-*i* correction leads others
15:32 He who-*i* discipline despises

ILLUMINATED*
Rev 18:1 and the earth was-*i* by his splendor.

IMAGE
Ge 1:26 "Let us make man in our-*i*,
1:27 So God created man in his own-*i*,
1Co 11:7 since he is the-*i* and glory of God;
Col 1:15 He is the-*i* of the invisible God,
3:10 in knowledge in the-*i* of its Creator.

IMAGINE
Eph 3:20 more than all we ask or-*i*,

IMITATE (IMITATORS)
1Co 4:16 Therefore I urge you to-*i* me.
Heb 6:12 but to-*i* those who through faith
13:7 the way of life and-*i* their faith.
3Jn :11 do not-*i* what is evil but what is

IMITATORS* (IMITATE)
Eph 5:1 Be-*i* of God, therefore,
1Th 1:6 You became-*i* of us and of the Lord
2:14 became-*i* of God's churches

IMMANUEL
Isa 7:14 birth to a son, and will call him-*I*.
Mt 1:23 and they will call him-*I*"—

IMMORAL* (IMMORALITY)
Pr 6:24 keeping you from the-*i* woman,
1Co 5:9 to associate with sexually-*i* people
5:10 the people of this world who are-*i*,
5:11 but is sexually-*i* or greedy,
6:9 Neither the sexually-*i* nor idolaters
Eph 5:5 No-*i*, impure or greedy person—
Heb 12:16 See that no one is sexually-*i*,
13:4 the adulterer and all the sexually-*i*.
Rev 21:8 the murderers, the sexually-*i*,
22:15 the sexually-*i*, the murderers,

IMMORALITY (IMMORAL)
1Co 6:13 The body is not meant for sexual-*i*,
6:18 Flee from sexual-*i*.
10:8 We should not commit sexual-*i*,
Gal 5:19 sexual-*i*, impurity and debauchery;
Eph 5:3 must not be even a hint of sexual-*i*,
1Th 4:3 that you should avoid sexual-*i*;
Jude :4 grace of our God into a license for-*i*

IMMORTAL* (IMMORTALITY)
Ro 1:23 glory of the-*i* God for images made
1Ti 1:17 Now to the King eternal,-*i*,
6:16 who alone is-*i* and who lives

IMMORTALITY (IMMORTAL)
Ro 2:7 honor and-*i*, he will give eternal life
1Co 15:53 and the mortal with-*i*.
2Ti 1:10 and-*i* to light through the gospel.

IMPERISHABLE*
1Pe 1:23 not of perishable seed, but of-*i*,

IMPORTANCE* (IMPORTANT)
1Co 15:3 passed on to you as of first-*i*:

IMPORTANT (IMPORTANCE)
Mt 6:25 Is not life more-*i* than food,
23:23 have neglected the more-*i* matters
Mk 12:29 "The most-*i* one," answered Jesus,
12:33 as yourself is more-*i* than all burnt
Php 1:18 The-*i* thing is that in every way,

IMPOSSIBLE
Mt 17:20 Nothing will be-*i* for you."
Lk 1:37 For nothing is-*i* with God."
18:27 "What is-*i* with men is possible
Heb 6:18 things in which it is-*i* for God to lie,
11:6 without faith it is-*i* to please God,

IMPROPER*
Eph 5:3 these are-*i* for God's holy people.

IMPURE (IMPURITY)
Ac 10:15 not call anything-*i* that God has
Eph 5:5 No immoral,-*i* or greedy person—
1Th 4:7 For God did not call us to be-*i*,
Rev 21:27 Nothing-*i* will ever enter it,

IMPURITY (IMPURE)
Ro 1:24 hearts to sexual-*i* for the degrading
Eph 5:3 or of any kind of-*i*, or of greed,

INCENSE
Ex 40:5 Place the gold altar of-*i* in front
Ps 141:2 my prayer be set before you like-*i*;
Mt 2:11 him with gifts of gold and of-*i*

INCOME
Ecc 5:10 wealth is never satisfied with his-*i*.
1Co 16:2 sum of money in keeping with his-*i*,

INCOMPARABLE*
Eph 2:7 ages he might show the-*i* riches

INCREASE (EVER-INCREASING INCREASED INCREASES INCREASING)
Ge 1:22 "Be fruitful and-*i* in number
Ps 62:10 though your riches-*i*,
Isa 9:7 Of the-*i* of his government
Lk 17:5 said to the Lord,-"*i* our faith!"
1Th 3:12 May the Lord make your love-*i*

INCREASED (INCREASE)
Ac 6:7 of disciples in Jerusalem-*i* rapidly,
Ro 5:20 But where sin-*i*, grace-*i* all the more

INCREASES (INCREASE)
Pr 24:5 and a man of knowledge-*i* strength;

INCREASING (INCREASE)
Ac 6:1 when the number of disciples was-*i*,
2Th 1:3 one of you has for each other is-*i*.
2Pe 1:8 these qualities in-*i* measure,

INDEPENDENT*
1Co 11:11 however, woman is not-*i* of man,
11:11 of man, nor is man-*i* of woman.

INDESCRIBABLE*
2Co 9:15 Thanks be to God for his-*i* gift!

INDISPENSABLE*
1Co 12:22 seem to be weaker are-*i*,

INEFFECTIVE*
2Pe 1:8 they will keep you from being-*i*

INEXPRESSIBLE*
2Co 12:4 He heard-*i* things, things that man
1Pe 1:8 are filled with an-*i* and glorious joy,

INFANTS
Mt 21:16 " 'From the lips of children and-*i*
1Co 14:20 In regard to evil be-*i*,

INFIRMITIES
Isa 53:4 Surely he took up our-*i*

INHERIT (CO-HEIRS HEIRS HERITAGE INHERITANCE)
Ps 37:11 But the meek will-*i* the land
37:29 the righteous will-*i* the land
Mt 5:5 for they will-*i* the earth.
Mk 10:17 "what must I do to-*i* eternal life?"

1Co 15:50 blood cannot-*i* the kingdom of God

INHERITANCE (INHERIT)
Dt 4:20 to be the people of his-*i*,
Pr 13:22 A good man leaves an-*i*
Eph 1:14 who is a deposit guaranteeing our-*i*
    5: 5 has any-*i* in the kingdom of Christ
Heb 9:15 receive the promised eternal-*i*—
1Pe 1: 4 and into an-*i* that can never perish,

INIQUITIES (INIQUITY)
Ps 78:38 he forgave their-*i*
    103:10 or repay us according to our-*i.*
Isa 59: 2 But your-*i* have separated
Mic 7:19 and hurl all our-*i* into the depths

INIQUITY (INIQUITIES)
Ps 51: 2 Wash away all my-*i*
Isa 53: 6 the-*i* of us all.

INJUSTICE
2Ch 19: 7 the Lord our God there is no-*i*

INNOCENT
Pr 17:26 It is not good to punish an-*i* man,
Mt 10:16 shrewd as snakes and as-*i* as doves.
    27: 4 "for I have betrayed-*i* blood."
1Co 4: 4 but that does not make me-*i.*

INSCRIPTION
Mt 22:20 And whose-*i?*" "Caesar's,"

INSOLENT
Ro 1:30 God-haters,-*i*, arrogant

INSTITUTED
Ro 13: 2 rebelling against what God has-*i*
1Pe 2:13 to every authority-*i* among men:

INSTRUCT (INSTRUCTION)
Ps 32: 8 I will-*i* you and teach you
Pr 9: 9 *I* a wise man and he will be wiser
Ro 15:14 and competent to-*i* one another.
2Ti 2:25 who oppose him he must gently-*i,*

INSTRUCTION (INSTRUCT)
Pr 1: 8 Listen, my son, to your father's-*i*
    4: 1 Listen, my sons, to a father's-*i;*
    4:13 Hold on to-*i*, do not let it go;
    8:10 Choose my-*i* instead of silver,
    8:33 Listen to my-*i* and be wise;
    13: 1 A wise son heeds his father's-*i,*
    13:13 He who scorns-*i* will pay for it,
    16:20 Whoever gives heed to-*i* prospers,
    16:21 and pleasant words promote-*i.*
    19:20 Listen to advice and accept-*i*,
    23:12 Apply your heart to-*i*
1Co 14: 6 or prophecy or word of-*i?*
    14:26 or a word of-*i*, a revelation,
Eph 6: 4 up in the training and-*i* of the Lord.
1Th 4: 8 he who rejects this-*i* does not reject
2Th 3:14 If anyone does not obey our-*i*
1Ti 1: 8 I give you this-*i* in keeping
    6: 3 to the sound-*i* of our Lord Jesus
2Ti 4: 2 with great patience and careful-*i.*

INSULT
Pr 9: 7 corrects a mocker invites-*i*,
    12:16 but a prudent man overlooks an-*i.*
Mt 5:11 Blessed are you when people-*i* you,
Lk 6:22 when they exclude you and-*i* you
1Pe 3: 9 evil with evil or-*i* with-*i*,

INTEGRITY
1Ki 9: 4 if you walk before me in-*i* of heart
Job 2: 3 And he still maintains his-*i*,
    27: 5 till I die, I will not deny my-*i.*
Pr 10: 9 The man of-*i* walks securely,
    11: 3 The-*i* of the upright guides them,
    29:10 Bloodthirsty men hate a man of-*i*
Tit 2: 7 your teaching show-*i*, seriousness

INTELLIGENCE
Isa 29:14 the-*i* of the intelligent will vanish."
1Co 1:19 *i* of the intelligent I will frustrate."

INTELLIGIBLE
1Co 14:19 I would rather speak five-*i* words

INTERCEDE (INTERCEDES INTERCESSION)
Heb 7:25 he always lives to-*i* for them.

INTERCEDES (INTERCEDE)
Ro 8:26 but the Spirit himself-*i* for us

INTERCESSION* (INTERCEDE)
Isa 53:12 and made-*i* for the transgressors.
1Ti 2: 1 *i* and thanksgiving be made

INTERESTS
1Co 7:34 his wife—and his-*i* are divided.
Php 2: 4 only to your own-*i*, but also to the-*i*
    2:21 everyone looks out for his own-*i*,

INTERMARRY (MARRY)
Dt 7: 3 Do not-*i* with them.

INVENTED*
2Pe 1:16 We did not follow cleverly-*i* stories

INVESTIGATED
Lk 1: 3 I myself have carefully-*i* everything

INVISIBLE
Ro 1:20 of the world God's-*i* qualities—
Col 1:15 He is the image of the-*i* God,
1Ti 1:17 immortal,-*i*, the only God,

INVITE (INVITED INVITES)
Lk 14:13 you give a banquet,-*i* the poor,

INVITED (INVITE)
Mt 22:14 For many are-*i*, but few are chosen
    25:35 I was a stranger and you-*i* me in,

INVITES (INVITE)
1Co 10:27 If some unbeliever-*i* you to a meal

INVOLVED
2Ti 2: 4 a soldier gets-*i* in civilian affairs—

IRON
1Ti 4: 2 have been seared as with a hot-*i.*
Rev 2:27 He will rule them with an-*i* scepter;

IRREVOCABLE*
Ro 11:29 for God's gifts and his call are-*i.*

ISAAC
Son of Abraham by Sarah (Ge 17:19; 21:1-7; 1Ch 1:28). Offered up by Abraham (Ge 22; Heb 11:17-19). Rebekah taken as wife (Ge 24). Fathered Esau and Jacob (Ge 25:19-26; 1Ch 1:34). Tricked into blessing Jacob (Ge 27). Father of Israel (Ex 3:6; Dt 29:13; Ro 9:10).

ISAIAH
Prophet to Judah (Isa 1:1). Called by the Lord (Isa 6).

ISHMAEL
Son of Abraham by Hagar (Ge 16; 1Ch 1:28). Blessed, but not son of covenant (Ge 17:18-21; Gal 4:21-31). Sent away by Sarah (Ge 21:8-21).

ISRAEL (ISRAELITES)
1. Name given to Jacob (see JACOB).
2. Corporate name of Jacob's descendants; often specifically Northern Kingdom.
Dt 6: 4 Hear, O-*I:* The Lord our God,
1Sa 4:21 "The glory has departed from-*I*"—
Isa 27: 6 *I* will bud and blossom
Jer 31:10 'He who scattered-*I* will gather
Eze 39:23 of-*I* went into exile for their sin,
Mk 12:29 'Hear, O-*I*, the Lord our God,
Lk 22:30 judging the twelve tribes of-*I.*
Ro 9: 6 all who are descended from-*I* are-*I.*
    11:26 And so all-*I* will be saved,
Eph 3: 6 Gentiles are heirs together with-*I*,

ISRAELITES (ISRAEL)
Ex 14:22 and the-*I* went through the sea
    16:35 The-*I* ate manna forty years,

Hos 1:10 "Yet the-*I* will be like the sand
Ro 9:27 the number of the-*I* be like the sand

ITCHING*
2Ti 4: 3 to say what their-*i* ears want to hear

JACOB
Second son of Isaac, twin of Esau (Ge 25:21-26; 1Ch 1:34). Bought Esau's birthright (Ge 25:29-34); tricked Isaac into blessing him (Ge 27:1-37). Abrahamic covenant perpetuated through (Ge 28:13-15; Mal 1:2). Vision at Bethel (Ge 28:10-22). Wives and children (Ge 29:1-30:24; 35:16-26; 1Ch 2-9). Wrestled with God; name changed to Israel (Ge 32:22-32). Sent sons to Egypt during famine (Ge 42-43). Settled in Egypt (Ge 46). Blessed Ephraim and Manasseh (Ge 48). Blessed sons (Ge 49:1-28; Heb 11:21). Death (Ge 49:29-33). Burial (Ge 50:1-14).

JAMES
1. Apostle; brother of John (Mt 4:21-22; 10:2; Mk 3:17; Lk 5:1-10). At transfiguration (Mt 17:1-13; Mk 9:1-13; Lk 9:28-36). Killed by Herod (Ac 12:2).
2. Apostle; son of Alphaeus (Mt 10:3; Mk 3:18; Lk 6:15).
3. Brother of Jesus (Mt 13:55; Mk 6:3; Lk 24:10; Gal 1:19) and Judas (Jude 1). With believers before Pentecost (Ac 1:13). Leader of church at Jerusalem (Ac 12:17; 15; 21:18; Gal 2:9, 12). Author of epistle (Jas 1:1).

JAPHETH
Son of Noah (Ge 5:32; 1Ch 1:4-5). Blessed (Ge 9:18-28).

JARS
2Co 4: 7 we have this treasure in-*j* of clay

JEALOUS (JEALOUSY)
Ex 20: 5 the Lord your God, am a-*j* God,
    34:14 whose name is Jealous, is a-*j* God.
Dt 4:24 God is a consuming fire, a-*j* God.
Joel 2:18 the Lord will be-*j* for his land
Zec 1:14 I am very-*j* for Jerusalem and Zion,
2Co 11: 2 I am-*j* for you with a godly jealousy

JEALOUSY (JEALOUS)
1Co 3: 3 For since there is-*j* and quarreling
2Co 11: 2 I am jealous for you with a godly-*j.*
Gal 5:20 hatred, discord,-*j*, fits of rage,

JEHOAHAZ
1. Son of Jehu; king of Israel (2Ki 13:1-9).
2. Son of Josiah; king of Judah (2Ki 23:31-34; 2Ch 36:1-4).

JEHOASH
Son of Jehoahaz; king of Israel (2Ki 13-14; 2Ch 25).

JEHOIACHIN
Son of Jehoiakim; king of Judah exiled by Nebuchadnezzar (2Ki 24:8-17; 2Ch 36:8-10; Jer 22:24-30; 24:1). Raised from prisoner status (2Ki 25:27-30; Jer 52:31-34).

JEHOIAKIM
Son of Josiah; king of Judah (2Ki 23:34-24:6; 2Ch 36:4-8; Jer 22:18-23; 36).

JEHORAM
Son of Jehoshaphat; king of Judah (2Ki 8:16-24).

JEHOSHAPHAT
Son of Asa; king of Judah (1Ki 22:41-50; 2Ki 3; 2Ch 17-20).

JEHU
King of Israel (1Ki 19:16-19; 2Ki 9-10).

JEPHTHAH
Judge from Gilead who delivered Israel from Ammon (Jdg 10:6-12:7). Made rash vow concerning his daughter (Jdg 11:30-40).

JEREMIAH
Prophet to Judah (Jer 1:1-3). Called by the Lord (Jer 1). Put in stocks (Jer 20:1-3). Threatened for prophesying (Jer 11:18-23; 26). Opposed by Hananiah (Jer 28). Scroll burned (Jer 36). Imprisoned (Jer 37). Thrown into cistern (Jer 38). Forced to Egypt with those fleeing Babylonians (Jer 43).

JEROBOAM
1. Official of Solomon; rebelled to become first king of Israel (1Ki 11:26-40; 12:1-20; 2Ch 10). Idolatry (1Ki 12:25-33); judgment for (1Ki 13-14; 2Ch 13).
2. Son of Jehoash; king of Israel (1Ki 14:23-29).

JERUSALEM
2Ki 23:27 and I will reject-*J*, the city I chose,
2Ch 6: 6 now I have chosen-*J* for my Name
Ne 2:17 Come, let us rebuild the wall of-*J*,
Ps 122: 6 Pray for the peace of-*J:*
    125: 2 As the mountains surround-*J*,
    137: 5 If I forget you, O-*J*,
Isa 40: 9 You who bring good tidings to-*J*,
    65:18 for I will create-*J* to be a delight
Joel 3:17 *J* will be holy;
Zep 3:16 On that day they will say to-*J*,
Zec 2: 4 '*J* will be a city without walls
    8: 8 I will bring them back to live in-*J;*
    14: 8 living water will flow out from-*J*,
Mt 23:37 "O-*J*, *J*, you who kill the prophets
Lk 13:34 die outside-*J!* "O-*J*, *J*,
    21:24 *J* will be trampled
Jn 4:20 where we must worship is in-*J.*"
Ac 1: 8 and you will be my witnesses in-*J*,
Gal 4:25 corresponds to the present city of-*J*
Rev 21: 2 I saw the Holy City, the new-*J*,

JESUS
LIFE: Genealogy (Mt 1:1-17; Lk 3:21-37). Birth announced (Mt 1:18-25; Lk 1:26-45). Birth (Mt 2:1-12; Lk 2:1-40). Escape to Egypt (Mt 2:13-23). As a boy in the temple (Lk 2:41-52). Baptism (Mt 3:13-17; Mk 1:9-11; Lk 3:21-22; Jn 1:32-34). Temptation (Mt 4:1-11; Mk 1:12-13; Lk 4:1-13). Ministry in Galilee (Mt 4:12-18:35; Mk 1:14-9:50; Lk 4:14-13:9; Jn 1:35-2:11; 4; 6), Transfiguration (Mt 17:1-8; Mk 9:2-8; Lk 9:28-36), on the way to Jerusalem (Mt 19-20; Mk 10; Lk 13:10-19:27), in Jerusalem (Mt 21-25; Mk 11-13; Lk 19:28-21:38; Jn 2:12-3:36; 5; 7-12). Last supper (Mt 26:17-35; Mk 14:12-31; Lk 22:1-38; Jn 13-17). Arrest and trial (Mt 26:36-27:31; Mk 14:43-15:20; Lk 22:39-23:25; Jn 18:1-19:16). Crucifixion (Mt 27:32-66; Mk 15:21-47; Lk 23:26-55; Jn 19:28-42). Resurrection and appearances (Mt 28; Mk 16; Lk 24; Jn 20-21; Ac 1:1-11; 7:56; 9:3-6; 1Co 15:1-8; Rev 1:1-20).
MIRACLES. Healings: official's son (Jn 4:43-54), demoniac in Capernaum (Mk 1:23-26; Lk 4:33-35), Peter's mother-in-law (Mt 8:14-17; Mk 1:29-31; Lk 4:38-39), leper (Mt 8:2-4; Mk 1:40-45; Lk 5:12-16), paralytic (Mt 9:1-8; Mk 2:1-12; Lk 5:17-26), cripple (Jn 5:1-9), shriveled hand (Mt 12:10-13; Mk 3:1-5; Lk 6:6-11), centurion's servant (Mt 8:5-13; Lk 7:1-10), widow's son raised (Lk 7:11-17), demoniac (Mt 12:22-23; Lk 11:14), Gadarene demoniacs (Mt 8:28-34; Mk 5:1-20; Lk 8:26-39), woman's bleeding and Jairus' daughter (Mt 9:18-26; Mk 5:21-43; Lk

8:40-56), blind man (Mt 9:27-31), mute man (Mt 9:32-33), Canaanite woman's daughter (Mt 15:21-28; Mk 7:24-30), deaf man (Mk 7:31-37), blind man (Mk 8:22-26), demoniac boy (Mt 17:14-18; Mk 9:14-29; Lk 9:37-43), ten lepers (Lk 17:11-19), man born blind (Jn 9:1-7), Lazarus raised (Jn 11), crippled woman (Lk 13:11-17), man with dropsy (Lk 14:1-6), two blind men (Mt 20:29-34; Mk 10:46-52; Lk 18:35-43), Malchus' ear (Lk 22:50-51). Other Miracles: water to wine (Jn 2:1-11), catch of fish (Lk 5:1-11), storm stilled (Mt 8:23-27; Mk 4:37-41; Lk 8:22-25), 5,000 fed (Mt 14:15-21; Mk 6:35-44; Lk 9:10-17; Jn 6:1-14), walking on water (Mt 14:25-33; Mk 6:48-52; Jn 6:15-21), 4,000 fed (Mt 15:32-39; Mk 8:1-9), money from fish (Mt 17:24-27), fig tree cursed (Mt 21:18-22; Mk 11:12-14), catch of fish (Jn 21:1-14).

MAJOR TEACHING: Sermon on the Mount (Mt 5-7; Lk 6:17-49), to Nicodemus (Jn 3), to Samaritan woman (Jn 4), Bread of Life (Jn 6:22-59), at Feast of Tabernacles (Jn 7-8), woes to Pharisees (Mt 23; Lk 11:37-54), Good Shepherd (Jn 10:1-18), Olivet Discourse (Mt 24-25; Mk 13; Lk 21:5-36), Upper Room Discourse (Jn 13-16).

PARABLES: Sower (Mt 13:3-23; Mk 4:3-25; Lk 8:5-18), seed's growth (Mk 4:26-29), wheat and weeds (Mt 13:24-30, 36-43), mustard seed (Mt 13:31-32; Mk 4:30-32), yeast (Mt 13:33; Lk 13:20-21), hidden treasure (Mt 13:44), valuable pearl (Mt 13:45-46), net (Mt 13:47-51), house owner (Mt 13:52), good Samaritan (Lk 10:25-37), unmerciful servant (Mt 18:15-35), lost sheep (Mt 18:10-14; Lk 15:4-7), lost coin (Lk 15:8-10), prodigal son (Lk 15:11-32), dishonest manager (Lk 16:1-13), rich man and Lazarus (Lk 16:19-31), persistent widow (Lk 18:1-8), Pharisee and tax collector (Lk 18:9-14), payment of workers (Mt 20:1-16), tenants and the vineyard (Mt 21:28-46; Mk 12:1-12; Lk 20:9-19), wedding banquet (Mt 22:1-14), faithful servant (Mt 24:45-51), ten virgins (Mt 25:1-13), talents (Mt 25:14-30; Lk 19:12-27).

DISCIPLES see APOSTLES. Call of (Jn 1:35-51; Mt 4:18-22; 9:9; Mk 1:16-20; 2:13-14; Lk 5:1-11, 27-28). Named Apostles (Mk 3:13-19; Lk 6:12-16). Twelve sent out (Mt 10; Mk 6:7-11; Lk 9:1-5). Seventy sent out (Lk 10:1-24). Defection of (Jn 6:60-71; Mt 26:56; Mk 14:50-52). Final commission (Mt 28:16-20; Jn 21:15-23; Ac 1:3-8).

Ac 2:32 God has raised this-J to life,
     9:5 "I am-J, whom you are persecuting
    15:11 of our Lord-J that we are saved,
    16:31 "Believe in the Lord-J
Ro 3:24 redemption that came by Christ-J.
     5:17 life through the one man,-J Christ.
     8:1 for those who are in Christ-J,
1Co 2:2 except-J Christ and him crucified.
     8:6 and there is but one Lord,-J Christ,
    12:3 and no one can say,-"J is Lord,"
2Co 4:5 not preach ourselves, but-J Christ
Gal 3:1 was clearly portrayed as crucified.
     3:28 for you are all one in Christ-J.
     5:6 in Christ-J neither circumcision
Eph 2:10 created in Christ-J
     2:20 with Christ-J himself as the chief
Php 1:6 until the day of Christ-J.
     2:5 be the same as that of Christ-J:
     2:10 name of-J every knee should bow,
Col 3:17 do it all in the name of the Lord-J,
2Th 2:1 the coming of our Lord-J Christ
1Ti 1:15 Christ-J came into the world
2Ti 3:12 life in Christ-J will be persecuted,

Tit 2:13 our great God and Savior,-J Christ,
Heb 2:9 But we see-J, who was made a little
      3:1 fix your thoughts on-J, the apostle
      4:14 through the heavens,-J the Son
      7:22 J has become the guarantee
      7:24 but because-J lives forever,
     12:2 Let us fix our eyes on-J, the author
2Pe 1:16 and coming of our Lord-J Christ,
1Jn 1:7 and the blood of-J, his Son,
      2:1 J Christ, the Righteous One.
      2:6 to live in him must walk as-J did.
      4:15 anyone acknowledges that-J is
Rev 22:20 Come, Lord-J.

JEW (JEWS JUDAISM)
Zec 8:23 of one-J by the edge of his robe
Ro   1:16 first for the-J, then for the Gentile.
     10:12 there is no difference between-J
1Co 9:20 To the Jews I became like a-J,
Gal 3:28 There is neither-J nor Greek,

JEWELRY (JEWELS)
1Pe 3:3 wearing of gold-J and fine clothes.

JEWELS (JEWELRY)
Isa 61:10 as a bride adorns herself with her-J.
Zec 9:16 like-J in a crown.

JEWS (JEW)
Mt 2:2 who has been born king of the-J?
    27:11 "Are you the king of the-J?" "Yes,
Jn   4:22 for salvation is from the-J.
Ro   3:29 Is God the God of-J only?
1Co 1:22 J demand miraculous signs
     9:20 To the-J I became like a Jew,
    12:13 whether-J or Greeks, slave or free
Gal 2:8 of Peter as an apostle to the-J,
Rev 3:9 claim to be-J though they are not,

JEZEBEL
Sidonian wife of Ahab (1Ki 16:31). Promoted Baal worship (1Ki 16:32-33). Killed prophets of the Lord (1Ki 18:4, 13). Opposed Elijah (1Ki 19:1-2). Had Naboth killed (1Ki 21). Death prophesied (1Ki 21:17-24). Killed by Jehu (2Ki 9:30-37).

JOASH
Son of Ahaziah; king of Judah. Sheltered from Athaliah by Jehoiada (2Ki 11; 2Ch 22:10-23:21). Repaired temple (2Ki 12; 2Ch 24).

JOB
Wealthy man from Uz; feared God (Job 1:1-5). Righteousness tested by disaster (Job 1:6-22), personal affliction (Job 2). Maintained innocence in debate with three friends (Job 3-31), Elihu (Job 32-37). Rebuked by the Lord (Job 38-41). Vindicated and restored to greater stature by the Lord (Job 42). Example of righteousness (Eze 14:14, 20).

JOHN
1. Son of Zechariah and Elizabeth (Lk 1). Called the Baptist (Mt 3:1-12; Mk 1:2-8). Witness to Jesus (Mt 3:11-12; Mk 1:7-8; Lk 3:15-18; Jn 1:6-35; 3:27-30; 5:33-36). Doubts about Jesus (Mt 11:2-6; Lk 7:18-23). Arrest (Mt 4:12; Mk 1:14). Execution (Mt 14:1-12; Mk 6:14-29; Lk 9:7-9). Ministry compared to Elijah (Mt 11:7-19; Mk 9:11-13; Lk 7:24-35).

2. Apostle; brother of James (Mt 4:21-22; 10:2; Mk 3:17; Lk 5:1-10). At transfiguration (Mt 17:1-13; Mk 9:1-13; Lk 9:28-36). Desire to be greatest (Mk 10:35-45). Leader of church at Jerusalem (Ac 4:1-3; Gal 2:9). Elder who wrote epistles (2Jn 1; 3Jn 1). Prophet who wrote Revelation (Rev 1:1; 22:8).

3. Cousin of Barnabas, co-worker with Paul, (Ac 12:12-13:13; 15:37), see MARK.

JOIN (JOINED)
Pr 23:20 Do not-J those who drink too much
           24:21 and do not-J with the rebellious,
Ro 15:30 to-J me in my struggle by praying
2Ti 1:8 J with me in suffering for the gospel

JOINED (JOIN)
Mt 19:6 Therefore what God has-J together,
Mk 10:9 Therefore what God has-J together,
Eph 2:21 him the whole building is-J together
      4:16 J and held together

JOINTS
Heb 4:12 even to dividing soul and spirit,-J

JOKING
Eph 5:4 or coarse-J, which are out of place,

JONAH
Prophet in days of Jeroboam II (2Ki 14:25). Called to Nineveh; fled to Tarshish (Jnh 1:1-3). Cause of storm; thrown into sea (Jnh 1:4-16). Swallowed by fish (Jnh 1:17). Prayer (Jnh 2). Preached to Nineveh (Jnh 3). Attitude reproved by the Lord (Jnh 4). Sign of (Mt 12:39-41; Lk 11:29-32).

JONATHAN
Son of Saul (1Sa 13:16; 1Ch 8:33). Valiant warrior (1Sa 13-14). Relation to David (1Sa 18:1-4; 19-20; 23:16-18). Killed at Gilboa (1Sa 31). Mourned by David (2Sa 1).

JORAM
1. Son of Ahab; king of Israel (2Ki 3; 8-9; 2Ch 22).

JORDAN
Nu 34:12 boundary will go down along the-J
Jos 4:22 Israel crossed the-J on dry ground.'
Mt   3:6 baptized by him in the-J River.

JOSEPH
1. Son of Jacob by Rachel (Ge 30:24; 1Ch 2:2). Favored by Jacob, hated by brothers (Ge 37:3-4). Dreams (Ge 37:5-11). Sold by brothers (Ge 37:12-36). Served Potiphar; imprisoned by false accusation (Ge 39). Interpreted dreams of Pharaoh's servants (Ge 40), of Pharaoh (Ge 41:4-40). Made greatest in Egypt (Ge 41:41-57). Sold grain to brothers (Ge 42-45). Brought Jacob and sons to Egypt (Ge 46-47). Sons Ephraim and Manasseh blessed (Ge 48). Blessed (Ge 49:22-26; Dt 33:13-17). Death (Ge 50:22-26; Ex 13:19; Heb 11:22). 12,000 from (Rev 7:8).

2. Husband of Mary, mother of Jesus (Mt 1:16-24; 2:13-19; Lk 1:27; 2; Jn 1:45).

3. Disciple from Arimathea, who gave his tomb for Jesus' burial (Mt 27:57-61; Mk 15:43-47; Lk 24:50-52).

4. Original name of Barnabas (Ac 4:36).

JOSHUA
1. Son of Nun; name changed from Hoshea (Nu 13:8, 16; 1Ch 7:27). Fought Amalekites under Moses (Ex 17:9-14). Servant of Moses on Sinai (Ex 24:13; 32:17). Spied Canaan (Nu 13). With Caleb, allowed to enter land (Nu 14:6, 30). Succeeded Moses (Dt 1:38; 31:1-8; 34:9).

Charged Israel to conquer Canaan (Jos 1). Crossed Jordan (Jos 3-4). Circumcised sons of wilderness wanderings (Jos 5). Conquered Jericho (Jos 6), Ai (Jos 7-8), five kings at Gibeon (Jos 10:1-28), southern Canaan (Jos 10:29-43), northern Canaan (Jos 11-12). Defeated at Ai (Jos 7). Deceived by Gibeonites (Jos 9). Renewed covenant (Jos 8:30-35; 24:1-27). Divided land among tribes (Jos 13-22). Last words (Jos 23). Death (Jos 24:28-31).

2. High priest during rebuilding of temple (Hag 1-2; Zec 3:1-9; 6:11).

JOSIAH
Son of Amon; king of Judah (2Ki 22-23; 2Ch 34-35).

JOTHAM
Son of Azariah (Uzziah); king of Judah (2Ki 15:32-38; 2Ch 26:21-27:9).

JOY (ENJOY ENJOYMENT JOYFUL OVERJOYED REJOICE REJOICES REJOICING)
Dt 16:15 and your-J will be complete.
1Ch 16:27 strength and-J in his dwelling place.
Ne   8:10 for the-J of the Lord is your
Est 9:22 their sorrow was turned into-J
Job 38:7 and all the angels shouted for-J?
Ps   4:7 have filled my heart with greater-J
     21:6 with the-J of your presence.
     30:11 sackcloth and clothed me with-J,
     43:4 to God, my-J and my delight.
     51:12 to me the-J of your salvation
     66:1 Shout with-J to God, all the earth!
     96:12 the trees of the forest will sing for-J;
     107:22 and tell of his works with songs of-J
     119:111 they are the-J of my heart.
Pr 10:1 A wise son brings-J to his father,
    10:28 The prospect of the righteous is-J,
    12:20 but-J for those who promote peace.
Isa 35:10 everlasting-J will crown their heads
    51:11 Gladness and-J will overtake them,
    55:12 You will go out in-J
Lk   1:44 the baby in my womb leaped for-J.
      2:10 news of great-J that will be
Jn 15:11 and that your-J may be complete.
    16:20 but your grief will turn to-J.
2Co 8:2 their overflowing-J and their
Php 2:2 then make my-J complete
      4:1 and long for, my-J and crown,
1Th 2:19 For what is our hope, our-J,
Phm :7 Your love has given me great-J
Heb 12:2 for the-J set before him endured
Jas 1:2 Consider it pure-J, my brothers,
1Pe 1:8 with an inexpressible and glorious-J
3Jn :4 It has given me great-J to find some
3Jn :4 I have no greater-J

JOYFUL (JOY)
Ps 100:2 come before him with-J songs.
Hab 3:18 I will be-J in God my Savior.
1Th 5:16 Be-J always; pray continually;

JUDAH
1. Son of Jacob by Leah (Ge 29:35; 35:23; 1Ch 2:1). Tribe of blessed as ruling tribe (Ge 49:8-12; Dt 33:7).

2. Name used for people and land of Southern Kingdom.
Jer 13:19 All-J will be carried into exile,
Zec 10:4 From-J will come the cornerstone,
Heb 7:14 that our Lord descended from-J,

JUDAISM (JEW)
Gal 1:13 of my previous way of life in-J,

JUDAS
1. Apostle (Lk 6:16; Jn 14:22; Ac 1:13). Probably also called Thaddaeus (Mt 10:3; Mk 3:18).

2. Brother of James and Jesus (Mt 13:55; Mk 6:3), also called Jude (Jude 1).

3. Apostle, also called Iscariot, who betrayed Jesus (Mt 10:4; 26:14-56; Mk 3:19; 14:10-50; Lk 6:16; 22:3-53; Jn 6:71; 12:4; 13:2-30; 18:2-11). Suicide of (Mt 27:3-5; Ac 1:16-25).

JUDGE (JUDGED JUDGES JUDGING JUDGMENT)
Ge 18:25 Will not the-J of all the earth do
1Ch 16:33 for he comes to-J the earth.

Ps 9:8 He will-*j* the world in righteousness
Joel 3:12 sit to-*j* all the nations on every side.
Mt 7:1 Do not-*j*, or you too will be judged.
Jn 12:47 For I did not come to-*j* the world,
Ac 17:31 a day when he will-*j* the world
Ro 2:16 day when God will-*j* men's secrets
1Co 4:3 indeed, I do not even-*j* myself.
6:2 that the saints will-*j* the world?
Gal 2:6 not-*j* by external appearance—
2Ti 4:1 who will-*j* the living and the dead,
4:8 which the Lord, the righteous-*J*,
Jas 4:12 There is only one Lawgiver and-*J*,
4:12 who are you to-*j* your neighbor?
Rev 20:4 who had been given authority to-*j*

JUDGED (JUDGE)
Mt 7:1 "Do not judge, or you too will be-*j*.
1Co 11:31 But if we-*j* ourselves, we would not
Jas 3:1 who teach will be-*j* more strictly.
Rev 20:12 The dead were-*j* according

JUDGES (JUDGE)
Jdg 2:16 Then the Lord raised up-*j*,
Ps 58:11 there is a God who-*j* the earth."
Heb 4:12 it-*j* the thoughts and attitudes
Rev 19:11 With justice he-*j* and makes war.

JUDGING (JUDGE)
Mt 19:28 *j* the twelve tribes of Israel.
Jn 7:24 Stop-*j* by mere appearances,

JUDGMENT (JUDGE)
Dt 1:17 of any man, for-*j* belongs to God.
Ps 1:5 the wicked will not stand in the-*j*,
119:66 Teach me knowledge and good-*j*,
Pr 6:32 man who commits adultery lacks-*j*;
12:11 but he who chases fantasies lacks-*j*.
Ecc 12:14 God will bring every deed into-*j*,
Isa 66:16 the Lord will execute-*j*
Mt 5:21 who murders will be subject to-*j*.'
10:15 on the day of-*j* than for that town.
12:36 have to give account on the day of-*j*
Jn 5:22 but has entrusted all-*j* to the Son,
7:24 appearances, and make a right-*j*."
16:8 to sin and righteousness and-*j*:
Ro 14:10 stand before God's-*j* seat.
14:13 Therefore let us stop passing-*j*
1Co 11:29 body of the Lord eats and drinks-*j*
2Co 5:10 appear before the-*j* seat of Christ,
Heb 9:27 to die once, and after that to face-*j*,
10:27 but only a fearful expectation of-*j*
1Pe 4:17 For it is time for-*j* to begin
Jude :6 bound with everlasting chains for-*j*

JUST (JUSTICE JUSTIFICATION
JUSTIFIED JUSTIFY JUSTLY)
Dt 32:4 and all his ways are-*j*.
Ps 37:28 For the Lord loves the-*j*
111:7 of his hands are faithful and-*j*;
Pr 1:3 doing what is right and-*j* and fair;
2:8 for he guards the course of the-*j*
Da 4:37 does is right and all his ways are-*j*.
Ro 3:26 as to be-*j* and the one who justifies
Heb 2:2 received its-*j* punishment,
1Jn 1:9 and-*j* and will forgive us our sins
Rev 16:7 true and-*j* are your judgments."

JUSTICE (JUST)
Ex 23:2 do not pervert-*j* by siding
23:6 "Do not deny-*j* to your poor people
Job 37:23 in his-*j* and great righteousness,
Ps 9:8 he will govern the peoples with-*j*;
9:16 The Lord is known by his-*j*;
11:7 he loves-*j*;
45:6 a scepter of-*j* will be the scepter
101:1 I will sing of your love and-*j*;
106:3 Blessed are they who maintain-*j*,
Pr 21:15 When-*j* is done, it brings joy
28:5 Evil men do not understand-*j*,
29:4 By-*j* a king gives a country stability

29:26 from the Lord that man gets-*j*.
Isa 9:7 it with-*j* and righteousness
28:17 I will make-*j* the measuring line
30:18 For the Lord is a God of-*j*.
42:1 and he will bring-*j* to the nations.
42:4 till he establishes-*j* on earth.
56:1 "Maintain-*j*
61:8 "For I, the Lord, love-*j*;
Jer 30:11 I will discipline you but only with-*j*;
Eze 34:16 I will shepherd the flock with-*j*.
Am 5:15 maintain-*j* in the courts.
5:24 But let-*j* roll on like a river,
Zec 7:9 'Administer true-*j*; show mercy
Lk 11:42 you neglect-*j* and the love of God.
Ro 3:25 He did this to demonstrate his-*j*,

JUSTIFICATION (JUST)
Ro 4:25 and was raised to life for our-*j*.
5:18 of righteousness was-*j* that brings

JUSTIFIED (JUST)
Ac 13:39 him everyone who believes is-*j*
Ro 3:24 and are-*j* freely by his grace
3:28 For we maintain that a man is-*j*
5:1 since we have been-*j* through faith,
5:9 Since we have now been-*j*
8:30 those he called, he also-*j*; those he-*j*,
1Co 6:11 you were-*j* in the name
Gal 2:16 observing the law no one will be-*j*,
3:11 Clearly no one is-*j* before God
3:24 to Christ that we might be-*j* by faith
Jas 2:24 You see that a person is-*j*

JUSTIFY (JUST)
Gal 3:8 that God would-*j* the Gentiles

JUSTLY (JUST)
Mic 6:8 To act-*j* and to love mercy

KEEP (KEEPER KEEPING KEEPS KEPT)
Ge 31:49 "May the Lord-*k* watch
Ex 20:6 and-*k* my commandments.
Nu 6:24 and-*k* you;
Ps 18:28 You, O Lord,-*k* my lamp burning
19:13 *K* your servant also from willful
119:9 can a young man-*k* his way pure?
121:7 The Lord will-*k* you
141:3 *k* watch over the door of my lips.
Pr 4:24 *k* corrupt talk far from your lips.
Isa 26:3 You will-*k* in perfect peace
Mt 10:10 for the worker is worth his-*k*.
Lk 12:35 and-*k* your lamps burning,
Gal 5:25 let us-*k* in step with the Spirit.
Eph 4:3 Make every effort to-*k* the unity
1Ti 5:22 *k* yourself pure.
2Ti 4:5 *k* your head in all situations,
Heb 13:5 *K* your lives free from the love
Jas 1:26 and yet does not-*k* a tight rein
2:8 If you really-*k* the royal law found
Jude :24 able to-*k* you from falling

KEEPER (KEEP)
Ge 4:9 I my brother's-*k*?" The Lord

KEEPING (KEEP)
Ex 20:8 the Sabbath day by-*k* it holy.
Ps 19:11 in-*k* them there is great reward.
Mt 3:8 Produce fruit in-*k* with repentance.
Lk 2:8 *k* watch over their flocks at night.
1Co 7:19 *K* God's commands is what counts.
2Pe 3:9 Lord is not slow in-*k* his promise,

KEEPS (KEEP)
Pr 17:28 a fool is thought wise if he-*k* silent,
Am 5:13 Therefore the prudent man-*k* quiet
1Co 13:5 is not easily angered, it-*k* no record
Jas 2:10 For whoever-*k* the whole law

KEPT (KEEP)
Ps 130:3 If you, O Lord,-*k* a record of sins,
2Ti 4:7 finished the race, I have-*k* the faith.
1Pe 1:4 spoil or fade—*k* in heaven for you,

KEYS
Mt 16:19 I will give you the-*k* of the kingdom

KILL (KILLS)
Mt 17:23 They will-*k* him, and on the third

KILLS (KILL)
Lev 24:21 but whoever-*k* a man must be put
2Co 3:6 for the letter-*k*, but the Spirit gives

KIND (KINDNESS KINDS)
Ge 1:24 animals, each according to its-*k*."
2Ch 10:7 "If you will be-*k* to these people
Pr 11:17 A-*k* man benefits himself,
12:25 but a-*k* word cheers him up.
14:21 blessed is he who is-*k* to the needy.
14:31 whoever is-*k* to the needy honors
19:17 He who is-*k* to the poor lends
Da 4:27 by being-*k* to the oppressed.
Lk 6:35 because he is-*k* to the ungrateful
1Co 13:4 Love is patient, love is-*k*.
15:35 With what-*k* of body will they
Eph 4:32 Be-*k* and compassionate
1Th 5:15 but always try to be-*k* to each other
2Ti 2:24 instead, he must be-*k* to everyone,
Tit 2:5 to be busy at home, to be-*k*,

KINDNESS (KIND)
Ac 14:17 He has shown-*k* by giving you rain
Ro 11:22 Consider therefore the-*k*
Gal 5:22 peace, patience,-*k*, goodness,
Eph 2:7 expressed in his-*k* to us
2Pe 1:7 brotherly-*k*; and to brotherly-*k*,

KINDS (KIND)
1Co 12:4 There are different-*k* of gifts,
1Ti 6:10 of money is a root of all-*k* of evil.

KING (KINGDOM KINGS)
1. Kings of Judah and Israel: see Saul, David, Solomon.
2. Kings of Judah: see Rehoboam, Abijah, Asa, Jehoshaphat, Jehoram, Ahaziah, Athaliah (Queen), Joash, Amaziah, Uzziah, Jotham, Ahaz, Hezekiah, Manasseh, Amon, Josiah, Jehoahaz, Jehoiakim, Jehoiachin, Zedekiah.
3. Kings of Israel: see Jeroboam I, Nadab, Baasha, Elah, Zimri, Tibni, Omri, Ahab, Ahaziah, Joram, Jehu, Jehoahaz, Jehoash, Jeroboam II, Zechariah, Shallum, Menahem, Pekah, Pekahiah, Hoshea.
Jdg 17:6 In those days Israel had no-*k*;
1Sa 12:12 the Lord your God was your-*k*.
Ps 24:7 that the-*K* of glory may come in.
Isa 32:1 See, a-*k* will reign in righteousness
Zec 9:9 See, your-*k* comes to you,
1Ti 6:15 the-*K* of kings and Lord of lords,
1Pe 2:17 of believers, fear God, honor the-*k*.
Rev 19:16 *K* OF KINGS AND LORD

KINGDOM (KING)
Ex 19:6 you will be for me a-*k* of priests
1Ch 29:11 Yours, O Lord, is the-*k*;
Ps 45:6 justice will be the scepter of your-*k*.
Da 4:3 His-*k* is an eternal-*k*;
Mt 3:2 Repent, for the-*k* of heaven is near
5:3 for theirs is the-*k* of heaven.
6:10 your-*k* come,
6:33 But seek first his-*k* and his
7:21 Lord,' will enter the-*k* of heaven,
11:11 least in the-*k* of heaven is greater
13:24 "The-*k* of heaven is like a man who
13:31 the-*k* of heaven is like a mustard seed,
13:33 "The-*k* of heaven is like yeast that
13:44 *k* of heaven is like treasure hidden
13:45 the-*k* of heaven is like a merchant
13:47 *k* of heaven is like a net that was let
16:19 the keys of the-*k* of heaven;
18:23 the-*k* of heaven is like a king who
19:24 for a rich man to enter the-*k* of God

24:7 rise against nation, and-*k* against-*k*.
24:14 gospel of the-*k* will be preached
25:34 the-*k* prepared for you
Mk 9:47 better for you to enter the-*k* of God
10:14 for the-*k* of God belongs to such
10:23 for the rich to enter the-*k* of God!"
Lk 10:9 'The-*k* of God is near you.'
12:31 seek his-*k*, and these things will be
17:21 because the-*k* of God is within you
Jn 3:5 no one can enter the-*k* of God
18:36 "My-*k* is not of this world.
1Co 6:9 the wicked will not inherit the-*k*
15:24 hands over the-*k* to God the Father
Rev 1:6 has made us to be a-*k* and priests
11:15 of the world has become the-*k*

KINGS (KING)
Ps 2:2 The-*k* of the earth take their stand
72:11 All-*k* will bow down to him
Da 7:24 ten horns are ten-*k* who will come
1Ti 2:2 for-*k* and all those in authority,
Rev 1:5 and the ruler of the-*k* of the earth.

KINSMAN-REDEEMER (REDEEM)
Ru 3:9 over me, since you are a-*k*."

KISS
Ps 2:12 *K* the Son, lest he be angry
Pr 24:26 is like a-*k* on the lips.
Lk 22:48 the Son of Man with a-*k*?"

KNEE (KNEES)
Isa 45:23 Before me every-*k* will bow;
Ro 14:11 'every-*k* will bow before me;
Php 2:10 name of Jesus every-*k* should bow,

KNEES (KNEE)
Isa 35:3 steady the-*k* that give way;
Heb 12:12 your feeble arms and weak-*k*.

KNEW (KNOW)
Job 23:3 If only I-*k* where to find him;
Jnh 4:2 I-*k* that you are a gracious
Mt 7:23 tell them plainly, 'I never-*k* you.

KNOCK
Mt 7:7 *k* and the door will be opened
Rev 3:20 I am! I stand at the door and-*k*.

KNOW (FOREKNEW KNEW KNOWING KNOWLEDGE KNOWN KNOWS)
Dt 18:21 "How can we-*k* when a message
Job 19:25 I-*k* that my Redeemer lives,
42:3 things too wonderful for me to-*k*.
Ps 46:10 "Be still, and-*k* that I am God;
139:1 and you-*k* me.
139:23 Search me, O God, and-*k* my heart;
Pr 27:1 for you do not-*k* what a day may
Jer 24:7 I will give them a heart to-*k* me,
31:34 his brother, saying,-'*K* the Lord,'
Mt 6:3 let your left hand-*k* what your right
24:42 you do not-*k* on what day your
Lk 1:4 so that you may-*k* the certainty
Jn 3:11 we speak of what we-*k*,
4:22 we worship what we-*k*,
9:25 One thing I do-*k*.
10:14 I-*k* my sheep and my sheep-*k* me—
17:3 that they may-*k* you, the only true
21:24 We-*k* that his testimony is true.
Ac 1:7 "It is not for you to-*k* the times
Ro 6:6 For we-*k* that our old self was
7:18 I-*k* that nothing good lives in me,
8:28 we-*k* that in all things God works
1Co 2:2 For I resolved to-*k* nothing
6:15 Do you not-*k* that your bodies are
6:19 Do you not-*k* that your body is
13:12 Now I-*k* in part; then I shall-*k* fully,
15:58 because you-*k* that your labor
Php 3:10 I want to-*k* Christ and the power
2Ti 1:12 because I-*k* whom I have believed,
Jas 4:14 *k* what will happen tomorrow.

1Jn 2:4 The man who says, "I-*k* him,"
3:14 We-*k* that we have passed
3:16 This is how we-*k* what love is:
5:2 This is how we-*k* that we love
5:13 so that you may-*k* that you have

KNOWING (KNOW)
Ge 3:5 and you will be like God,-*k* good
Php 3:8 of-*k* Christ Jesus my Lord,

KNOWLEDGE (KNOW)
Ge 2:9 the tree of the-*k* of good and evil.
Job 42:3 obscures my counsel without-*k*?"
Ps 19:2 night after night they display-*k*.
73:11 Does the Most High have-*k*?"
139:6 Such-*k* is too wonderful for me,
Pr 1:7 of the Lord is the beginning of-*k*,
10:14 Wise men store up-*k*,
12:1 Whoever loves discipline loves-*k*,
13:16 Every prudent man acts out of-*k*,
19:2 to have zeal without-*k*,
Isa 11:9 full of the-*k* of the Lord
Hab 2:14 filled with the-*k* of the glory
Ro 11:33 riches of the wisdom and-*k* of God!
1Co 8:1 *K* puffs up, but love builds up.
8:11 Christ died, is destroyed by your-*k*.
13:2 can fathom all mysteries and all-*k*,
2Co 2:14 everywhere the fragrance of the-*k*
4:6 light of the-*k* of the glory of God
Eph 3:19 to know this love that surpasses-*k*
Col 2:3 all the treasures of wisdom and-*k*
1Ti 6:20 ideas of what is falsely called-*k*,
2Pe 3:18 grow in the grace and-*k* of our Lord

KNOWN (KNOW)
Ps 16:11 You have made-*k* to me the path
105:1 make-*k* among the nations what he
Isa 46:10 *k* the end from the beginning,
Mt 10:26 or hidden that will not be made-*k*.
Ro 1:19 since what may be-*k* about God is
11:34 "Who has-*k* the mind of the Lord?
15:20 the gospel where Christ was not-*k*,
2Co 3:2 written on our hearts,-*k*
2Pe 2:21 than to have-*k* it and then

KNOWS (KNOW)
1Sa 2:3 for the Lord is a God who-*k*,
Job 23:10 But he-*k* the way that I take;
Ps 44:21 since he-*k* the secrets of the heart?
94:11 The Lord-*k* the thoughts of man;
Ecc 8:7 Since no man-*k* the future,
Mt 6:8 for your Father-*k* what you need
24:36 "No one-*k* about that day or hour,
Ro 8:27 who searches our hearts-*k* the mind
1Co 8:2 who thinks he-*k* something does
2Ti 2:19 The Lord-*k* those who are his," and

LABAN
Brother of Rebekah (Ge 24:29-51), father of Rachel and Leah (Ge 29-31).

LABOR
Ex 20:9 Six days you shall-*l* and do all your
Isa 55:2 and your-*l* on what does not satisfy
Mt 6:28 They do not-*l* or spin.
1Co 3:8 rewarded according to his own-*l*,
15:58 because you know that your-*l*

LACK (LACKING LACKS)
Pr 15:22 Plans fail for-*l* of counsel,
Ro 3:3 Will their-*l* of faith nullify God's
Col 2:23 *l* any value in restraining sensual

LACKING (LACK)
Ro 12:11 Never be-*l* in zeal, but keep your
Jas 1:4 and complete, not-*l* anything.

LACKS (LACK)
Pr 6:32 who commits adultery-*l* judgment;
12:11 he who chases fantasies-*l* judgment
Jas 1:5 any of you-*l* wisdom, he should ask

LAID (LAY)
Isa 53:6 and the Lord has-*l* on him
1Co 3:11 other than the one already-*l*,
1Jn 3:16 Jesus Christ-*l* down his life for us.

LAKE
Rev 19:20 into the fiery-*l* of burning sulfur.
20:14 The-*l* of fire is the second death.

LAMB (LAMB'S LAMBS)
Ge 22:8 "God himself will provide the-*l*
Ex 12:21 and slaughter the Passover-*l*.
Isa 11:6 The wolf will live with the-*l*,
53:7 he was led like a-*l* to the slaughter,
Jn 1:29 *L* of God, who takes away the sin
1Co 5:7 our Passover-*l*, has been sacrificed.
1Pe 1:19 a-*l* without blemish or defect.
Rev 5:6 Then I saw a-*L*, looking
5:12 "Worthy is the-*L*, who was slain,
14:4 They follow the-*L* wherever he

LAMB'S (LAMB)
Rev 21:27 written in the-*L* book of life.

LAMBS (LAMB)
Lk 10:3 I am sending you out like-*l*
Jn 21:15 Jesus said, "Feed my-*l*."

LAMENT
2Sa 1:17 took up this-*l* concerning Saul

LAMP (LAMPS)
2Sa 22:29 You are my-*l*, O Lord;
Ps 18:28 You, O Lord, keep my-*l* burning;
119:105 Your word is a-*l* to my feet
Pr 31:18 and her-*l* does not go out at night.
Lk 8:16 "No one lights a-*l* and hides it
Rev 21:23 gives it light, and the Lamb is its-*l*.

LAMPS (LAMP)
Mt 25:1 be like ten virgins who took their-*l*
Lk 12:35 for service and keep your-*l* burning,

LAND
Ge 1:10 God called the dry ground-"*l*,"
1:11 "Let the-*l* produce vegetation:
12:7 To your offspring I will give this-*l*."
Ex 3:8 a-*l* flowing with milk and honey—
Nu 35:33 Do not pollute the-*l* where you are.
Dt 34:1 Lord showed him the whole-*l*—
Jos 13:2 "This is the-*l* that remains:
14:4 Levites received no share of the-*l*
2Ch 7:14 their sin and will heal their-*l*.
7:20 then I will uproot Israel from my-*l*,
Eze 36:24 and bring you back into your own-*l*.

LANGUAGE
Ge 11:1 Now the whole world had one-*l*
Ps 19:3 There is no speech or-*l*
Jn 8:44 When he lies, he speaks his native-*l*
Ac 2:6 heard them speaking in his own-*l*,
Col 3:8 slander, and filthy-*l* from your lips.
Rev 5:9 from every tribe and-*l* and people

LAST (LASTING LASTS LATTER)
2Sa 23:1 These are the-*l* words of David:
Isa 44:6 I am the first and I am the-*l*;
Mt 19:30 But many who are first will be-*l*,
Mk 10:31 are first will be-*l*, and the-*l* first."
Jn 15:16 and bear fruit—fruit that will-*l*
Ro 1:17 is by faith from first to-*l*,
2Ti 3:1 will be terrible times in the-*l* days.
2Pe 3:3 in the-*l* days scoffers will come,
Rev 1:17 I am the First and the-*L*.
22:13 the First and the-*L*, the Beginning

LASTING (LAST)
Ex 12:14 to the Lord—a-*l* ordinance.
Lev 24:8 of the Israelites, as a-*l* covenant.
Nu 25:13 have a covenant of a-*l* priesthood.
Heb 10:34 had better and-*l* possessions.

LASTS (LAST)
Ps 30:5 For his anger-*l* only a moment,
2Co 3:11 greater is the glory of that which-*l*!

LATTER (LAST)
Job 42:12 The Lord blessed the-*l* part

LAUGH (LAUGHS)
Ecc 3:4 a time to weep and a time to-*l*,

LAUGHS (LAUGH)
Ps 2:4 The One enthroned in heaven-*l*;
37:13 but the Lord-*l* at the wicked,

LAVISHED
Eph 1:8 of God's grace that he-*l* on us
1Jn 3:1 great is the love the Father has-*l*

LAW (LAWS)
Dt 31:11 you shall read this-*l* before them
31:26 "Take this Book of the-*L*
Jos 1:8 of the-*L* depart from your mouth;
Ne 8:8 from the Book of the-*L* of God,
Ps 1:2 and on his-*l* he meditates day
19:7 The-*l* of the Lord is perfect,
119:18 wonderful things in your-*l*.
119:72 *l* from your mouth is more precious
119:97 Oh, how I love your-*l*!
119:165 peace have they who love your-*l*,
Isa 8:20 To the-*l* and to the testimony!
Jer 31:33 "I will put my-*l* in their minds
Mt 5:17 that I have come to abolish the-*L*
7:12 sums up the-*L* and the Prophets.
22:40 All the-*L* and the Prophets hang
Lk 16:17 stroke of a pen to drop out of the-*L*
Jn 1:17 For the-*l* was given through Moses;
Ro 2:12 All who sin apart from the-*l* will
2:15 of the-*l* are written on their hearts,
5:13 for before the-*l* was given,
5:20 *l* was added so that the trespass
6:14 because you are not under-*l*,
7:6 released from the-*l* so that we serve
7:12 is holy, and the commandment is-*l*
8:3 For what the-*l* was powerless to do
10:4 Christ is the end of the-*l*
13:10 love is the fulfillment of the-*l*.
Gal 3:13 curse of the-*l* by becoming a curse
3:24 So the-*l* was put in charge to lead us
5:3 obligated to obey the whole-*l*.
5:4 justified by-*l* have been alienated
5:14 The entire-*l* is summed up
Heb 7:19 (for the-*l* made nothing perfect),
10:1 The-*l* is only a shadow
Jas 1:25 intently into the perfect-*l* that gives
2:10 For whoever keeps the whole-*l*

LAWLESSNESS*
2Th 2:3 and the man of-*l* is revealed,
2:7 power of-*l* is already at work;
1Jn 3:4 sins breaks the law; in fact, sin is-*l*.

LAWS (LAW)
Lev 25:18 and be careful to obey my-*l*,
Ps 119:30 I have set my heart on your-*l*.
119:120 I stand in awe of your-*l*.
Heb 8:10 I will put my-*l* in their minds
10:16 I will put my-*l* in their hearts,

LAY (LAID LAYING)
Job 22:22 and-*l* up his words in your heart.
Isa 28:16 "See, I-*l* a stone in Zion,
Mt 8:20 of Man has no place to-*l* his head."
Jn 10:15 and I-*l* down my life for the sheep.
15:13 that he-*l* down his life
1Co 3:11 no one can-*l* any foundation other
1Jn 3:16 And we ought to-*l* down our lives
Rev 4:10 They-*l* their crowns

LAYING (LAY)
1Ti 5:22 Do not be hasty in the-*l* on of hands
Heb 6:1 not-*l* again the foundation

LAZARUS
1. Poor man in Jesus' parable (Lk 16:19-31).
2. Brother of Mary and Martha whom Jesus raised from the dead (Jn 11:1-12:19).

LAZY
Pr 10:4 *L* hands make a man poor,
Heb 6:12 We do not want you to become-*l*,

LEAD (LEADERS LEADERSHIP LEADS LED)
Ex 15:13 "In your unfailing love you will-*l*
Ps 27:11 *l* me in a straight path
61:2 *l* me to the rock that is higher
139:24 and-*l* me in the way everlasting.
143:10 *l* me on level ground.
Ecc 5:6 Do not let your mouth-*l* you
Isa 11:6 and a little child will-*l* them.
Da 12:3 those who-*l* many to righteousness,
Mt 6:13 And-*l* us not into temptation,
1Jn 3:7 do not let anyone-*l* you astray.

LEADERS (LEAD)
Heb 13:7 Remember your-*l*, who spoke
13:17 Obey your-*l* and submit

LEADERSHIP (LEAD)
Ro 12:8 if it is-*l*, let him govern diligently.

LEADS (LEAD)
Ps 23:2 he-*l* me beside quiet waters,
Pr 19:23 The fear of the Lord-*l* to life:
Isa 40:11 he gently-*l* those that have young.
Mt 7:13 and broad is the road that-*l*
15:14 If a blind man-*l* a blind man,
Jn 10:3 sheep by name and-*l* them out.
Ro 14:19 effort to do what-*l* to peace
2Co 2:14 always-*l* us in triumphal procession

LEAH
Wife of Jacob (Ge 29:16-30); bore six sons and one daughter (Ge 29:31-30:21; 34:1; 35:23).

LEAN
Pr 3:5 *l* not on your own understanding;

LEARN (LEARNED LEARNING)
Isa 1:17 *l* to do right!
Mt 11:29 yoke upon you and-*l* from me,

LEARNED (LEARN)
Php 4:11 for I have-*l* to be content whatever
2Ti 3:14 continue in what you have-*l*

LEARNING (LEARN)
Pr 1:5 let the wise listen and add to their-*l*,
2Ti 3:7 always-*l* but never able

LED (LEAD)
Ps 68:18 you-*l* captives in your train;
Isa 53:7 he was-*l* like a lamb to the slaughter
Am 2:10 and I-*l* you forty years in the desert
Ro 8:14 those who are-*l* by the Spirit
Eph 4:8 he-*l* captives in his train

LEFT
Jos 1:7 turn from it to the right or to the-*l*,
Pr 4:27 Do not swerve to the right or to the-*l*;
Mt 6:3 do not let your-*l* hand know what
25:33 on his right and the goats on his-*l*.

LEGION
Mk 5:9 "My name is-*L*," he replied,

LEND (LENDS)
Dt 15:8 freely-*l* him whatever he needs.
Ps 37:26 are always generous and-*l* freely;
Lk 6:34 if you-*l* to those from whom you

LENDS (LEND)
Pr 19:17 to the poor-*l* to the Lord,

LENGTH (LONG)
Ps 90:10 The-*l* of our days is seventy years—
Pr 10:27 The fear of the Lord adds-*l* to life

LEPROSY
2Ki 7:3 men with-/ at the entrance

LETTER (LETTERS)
Mt 5:18 not the smallest-/, not the least
2Co 3:2 You yourselves are our-/, written
3:6 for the-/ kills, but the Spirit gives
2Th 3:14 not obey our instruction in this-/,

LETTERS (LETTER)
2Co 3:7 which was engraved in-/ on stone,
10:10 "His-/ are weighty and forceful,
2Pe 3:16 His-/ contain some things that are

LEVEL
Ps 143:10 lead me on-/ ground.
Pr 4:26 Make-/ paths for your feet
Isa 26:7 The path of the righteous is-/;
Heb 12:13 "Make-/ paths for your feet,"

LEVI (LEVITES)
1. Son of Jacob by Leah (Ge 29:34; 46:11; 1Ch 2:1). Tribe of blessed (Ge 49:5-7; Dt 33:8-11), chosen as priests (Nu 3-4), numbered (Nu 3:39; 26:62), allotted cities, but not land (Nu 18; 35; Dt 10:9; Jos 13:14; 21), land (Eze 48:8-22), 12,000 from (Rev 7:7).
2. See MATTHEW.

LEVITES (LEVI)
Nu 1:53 The-/ are to be responsible
8:6 "Take the /. from among the other
18:21 I give to the-/ all the tithes in Israel

LEWDNESS
Mk 7:22 malice, deceit,-/, envy, slander,

LIAR (LIE)
Pr 19:22 better to be poor than a-/.
Jn 8:44 for he is a-/ and the father of lies.
Ro 3:4 Let God be true, and every man a-/.

LIBERATED*
Ro 8:21 that the creation itself will be-/

LIE (LIAR LIED LIES LYING)
Lev 19:11 " 'Do not-/.
Nu 23:19 God is not a man, that he should-/,
Dt 6:7 when you-/ down and when you get
Ps 23:2 me-/ down in green pastures,
Isa 11:6 leopard will-/ down with the goat,
Eze 34:14 they will-/ down in good grazing
Ro 1:25 exchanged the truth of God for a-/,
Col 3:9 Do not-/ to each other,
Heb 6:18 which it is impossible for God to-/,

LIED (LIE)
Ac 5:4 You have not-/ to men but to God."

LIES (LIE)
Ps 34:13 and your lips from speaking-/.
Jn 8:44 for he is a liar and the father of-/.

LIFE (LIVE)
Ge 2:7 into his nostrils the breath of-/,
2:9 of the garden were the tree of-/
9:11 Never again will all-/ be cut
Ex 21:23 you are to take-/ for-/, eye for eye,
Lev 17:14 the-/ of every creature is its blood.
24:18 must make restitution—/ for-/.
Dt 30:19 Now choose-/, so that you
Ps 16:11 known to me the path of-/;
23:6 all the days of my-/,
34:12 Whoever of you loves-/
39:4 let me know how fleeting is my-/.
49:7 No man can redeem the-/
104:33 I will sing to the LORD all my-/;
Pr 1:3 a disciplined and prudent-/,
6:23 are the way to-/,
7:23 little knowing it will cost him his-/.
8:35 For whoever finds me finds-/
11:30 of the righteous is a tree of-/,
21:21 finds-/, prosperity and honor.
Jer 10:23 that a man's-/ is not his own;

Eze 37:5 enter you, and you will come to-/.
Da 12:2 some to everlasting-/, others
Mt 6:25 Is not-/ more important than food,
7:14 and narrow the road that leads to-/,
10:39 Whoever finds his-/ will lose it,
16:25 wants to save his-/ will lose it,
20:28 to give his-/ as a ransom for many."
Mk 10:45 to give his-/ as a ransom for many."
Lk 12:15 a man's-/ does not consist
12:22 do not worry about your-/,
14:26 even his own-/— he cannot be my
Jn 1:4 In him was-/, and that-/ was
3:15 believes in him may have eternal-/.
3:36 believes in the Son has eternal-/,
4:14 of water welling up to eternal-/."
5:24 him who sent me has eternal-/
6:35 Jesus declared, "I am the bread of-/.
6:47 he who believes has everlasting-/.
6:68 You have the words of eternal-/.
10:10 I have come that they may have-/,
10:15 and I lay down my-/ for the sheep.
10:28 I give them eternal-/, and they shall
11:25 "I am the resurrection and the-/.
14:6 am the way and the truth and the-/.
15:13 lay down his-/ for his friends.
20:31 that by believing you may have-/
Ac 13:48 appointed for eternal-/ believed.
Ro 4:25 was raised to-/ for our justification.
6:13 have been brought from death to-/;
6:23 but the gift of God is eternal-/
8:38 convinced that neither death nor-/,
1Co 15:19 If only for this-/ we have hope
2Co 3:6 letter kills, but the Spirit gives-/
Gal 2:20 The-/ I live in the body, I live
Eph 4:1 I urge you to live a-/ worthy
Php 2:16 as you hold out the word of-/—
Col 1:10 order that you may live a-/ worthy
1Th 4:12 so that your daily-/ may win
1Ti 4:8 for both the present-/ and the-/.
4:16 Watch your-/ and doctrine closely.
6:19 hold of the-/ that is truly-/.
2Ti 3:12 to live a godly-/ in Christ Jesus will
Jas 1:12 crown of-/ that God has promised
3:13 Let him show it by his good-/,
1Pe 3:10 "Whoever would love-/
2Pe 1:3 given us everything we need for-/
1Jn 3:14 we have passed from death to-/,
5:11 has given us eternal-/, and this-/ is
Rev 13:8 written in the book of-/ belonging
20:12 was opened, which is the book of-/.
21:27 written in the Lamb's book of-/.
22:2 side of the river stood the tree of-/.

LIFT (LIFTED)
Ps 121:1 I-/ up my eyes to the hills—
134:2 /. up your hands in the sanctuary
La 3:41 Let us-/ up our hearts and our
1Ti 2:8 everywhere to-/ up holy hands

LIFTED (LIFT)
Ps 40:2 He-/ me out of the slimy pit,
Jn 3:14 Moses-/ up the snake in the desert,
12:32 when I am-/ up from the earth,

LIGHT (ENLIGHTENED)
Ge 1:3 "Let there be-/," and there was-/.
2Sa 22:29 LORD turns my darkness into-/.
Job 38:19 "What is the way to the abode of-/?
Ps 4:6 the-/ of your face shine upon us
19:8 giving-/ to the eyes.
27:1 LORD is my-/ and my salvation—
56:13 God in the-/ of life.
76:4 You are resplendent with-/,
104:2 He wraps himself in-/
119:105 and a-/ for my path.
119:130 The unfolding of your words gives-/;
Isa 2:5 let us walk in the-/ of the LORD.
9:2 have seen a great-/;

49:6 also make you a-/ for the Gentiles,
Mt 4:16 have seen a great-/;
5:16 let your-/ shine before men,
11:30 yoke is easy and my burden is-/."
Jn 3:19 but men loved darkness instead of-/
8:12 he said, "I am the-/ of the world.
2Co 4:6 made his-/ shine in our hearts
6:14 Or what fellowship can-/ have
11:14 masquerades as an angel of-/.
1Ti 6:16 and who lives in unapproachable-/,
1Pe 2:9 of darkness into his wonderful-/.
1Jn 1:5 God is-/; in him there is no
1:7 But if we walk in the-/,
Rev 21:23 for the glory of God gives it-/,

LIGHTNING
Da 10:6 his face like-/, his eyes like flaming
Mt 24:27 For as the-/ that comes from the east
28:3 His appearance was like-/,

LIKENESS
Ge 1:26 man in our image, in our-/,
Ps 17:15 I will be satisfied with seeing your-/
Isa 52:14 his form marred beyond human-/—
Ro 8:3 Son in the-/ of sinful man
8:29 to be conformed to the-/ of his Son,
2Co 3:18 his-/ with ever-increasing glory,
Php 2:7 being made in human-/,
Jas 3:9 who have been made in God's-/.

LILIES
Lk 12:27 "Consider how the-/ grow.

LION
Isa 11:7 and the-/ will eat straw like the ox.
1Pe 5:8 around like a roaring-/ looking
Rev 5:5 See, the-/ of the tribe of Judah,

LIPS
Ps 8:2 From the-/ of children and infants
34:1 his praise will always be on my-/.
119:171 May my-/ overflow with praise,
Pr 13:3 He who guards his-/ guards his life,
27:2 someone else, and not your own-/.
Isa 6:5 For I am a man of unclean-/,
Mt 21:16 " 'From the-/ of children
Col 3:8 and filthy language from your-/.

LISTEN (LISTENING LISTENS)
Dt 30:20 his voice, and hold fast to him.
Pr 1:5 let the wise-/ and add
Jn 10:27 My sheep-/ to my voice; I know
Jas 1:19 Everyone should be quick to-/,
1:22 Do not merely-/ to the word,

LISTENING (LISTEN)
1Sa 3:9 Speak, LORD, for your servant is-/
Pr 18:13 He who answers before-/—

LISTENS (LISTEN)
Pr 12:15 but a wise man-/ to advice.

LIVE (ALIVE LIFE LIVES LIVING)
Ex 20:12 so that you may-/ long
33:20 for no one may see me and-/."
Dt 8:3 to teach you that man does not-/
Job 14:14 If a man dies, will he-/ again?
Ps 119:175 Let me-/ that I may praise you,
Isa 55:3 hear me, that your soul may-/.
Eze 37:3 can these bones-/?" I said,
Hab 2:4 but the righteous will-/ by his faith
Mt 4:4 'Man does not-/ on bread alone,
Ac 17:24 does not-/ in temples built by hands
17:28 'For in him we-/ and move
Ro 1:17 "The righteous will-/ by faith."
2Co 5:7 We-/ by faith, not by sight.
Gal 2:20 The life I-/ in the body, I-/ by faith
5:25 Since we-/ by the Spirit, let us keep
Php 1:21 to-/ is Christ and to die is gain.
1Th 5:13 L in peace with each other.
2Ti 3:12 who wants to-/ a godly life

Heb 12:14 Make every effort to-/ in peace
1Pe 1:17 /your lives as strangers here

LIVES (LIVE)
Job 19:25 I know that my Redeemer-/,
Isa 57:15 he who-/ forever, whose name is
Da 3:28 to give up their-/ rather than serve
Jn 14:17 for he-/ with you and will be in you.
Ro 7:18 I know that nothing good-/ in me,
14:7 for none of us-/ to himself alone
1Co 3:16 and that God's Spirit-/ in you?
Gal 2:20 I no longer live, but Christ-/ in me.
Heb 13:5 Keep your-/ free from the love
2Pe 3:11 You ought to live holy and godly-/
1Jn 3:16 to lay down our-/ for our brothers.
4:16 Whoever-/ in love-/ in God,

LIVING (LIVE)
Ge 2:7 and man became a-/ being.
Jer 2:13 the spring of-/ water,
Mt 22:32 the God of the dead but of the-/."
Jn 7:38 streams of-/ water will flow
Ro 12:1 to offer your bodies as-/ sacrifices,
Heb 4:12 For the word of God is-/ and active.
10:31 to fall into the hands of the-/ God.
Rev 1:18 I am the-L One; I was dead,

LOAD
Gal 6:5 for each one should carry his own-/.

LOCUSTS
Mt 3:4 His food was-/ and wild honey.

LOFTY
Ps 139:6 too-/ for me to attain.
Isa 57:15 is what the high and-/ One says—

LONELY
Ps 68:6 God sets the-/ in families,

LONG (LENGTH LONGED LONGING LONGS)
1Ki 18:21 "How-/ will you waver
Jn 9:4 As-/ as it is day, we must do
Eph 3:18 to grasp how wide and-/ and high
1Pe 1:12 Even angels-/ to look

LONGED (LONG)
Mt 13:17 righteous men-/ to see what you see
23:37 how often I have-/
2Ti 4:8 to all who have-/ for his appearing.

LONGING (LONG)
Pr 13:19 A-/ fulfilled is sweet to the soul,
2Co 5:2 /to be clothed with our heavenly

LONGS (LONG)
Isa 30:18 Yet the LORD-/ to be gracious

LOOK (LOOKING LOOKS)
Dt 4:29 you will find him if you-/ for him
Job 31:1 not to-/ lustfully at a girl.
Ps 34:5 Those who-/ to him are radiant;
Pr 4:25 Let your eyes-/ straight ahead,
Isa 60:5 Then you will-/ and be radiant,
Hab 1:13 Your eyes are too pure to-/ on evil;
Zec 12:10 They will-/ on me, the one they
Mk 13:21 'L, here is the Christ!' or,-'L,
Lk 24:39 L at my hands and my feet.
Jn 1:36 he said,-"L, the Lamb of God!"
4:35 open your eyes and-/ at the fields!
19:37 "They will-/ on the one they have
Jas 1:27 to-/ after orphans and widows
1Pe 1:12 long to-/ into these things.

LOOKING (LOOK)
2Co 10:7 You are-/ only on the surface
Rev 5:6 I saw a Lamb,-/ as if it had been

LOOKS (LOOK)
1Sa 16:7 Man-/ at the outward appearance,
Lk 9:62 and-/ back is fit for service
Php 2:21 For everyone-/ out

LORD† (LORD'S† LORDING)

Ne 4:14 Remember the-L, who is great
Job 28:28 'The fear of the-L—that is wisdom,
Ps 54:4 the-L is the one who sustains me.
62:12 and that you, O-L, are loving.
86:5 You are forgiving and good, O-L,
110:1 The LORD says to my-L:
147:5 Great is our-L and mighty in power
Isa 6:1 I saw the-L seated on a throne,
Da 9:4 "O-L, the great and awesome God,
Mt 3:3 'Prepare the way for the-L,
4:7 'Do not put the-L your God
7:21 "Not everyone who says to me,-'L,
22:37 " 'Love the-L your God
22:44 For he says, " 'The L said to my-L:
Mk 12:11 has done this,
12:29 the-L our God, the-L is one.
Lk 2:9 glory of the-L shone around them,
6:46 "Why do you call me,-'L,-'L,'
10:27 " 'Love the-L your God
Ac 2:21 on the name of the-L will be saved.'
16:31 replied, "Believe in the-L Jesus,
Ro 10:9 with your mouth, "Jesus is-L,"
10:13 on the name of the-L will be saved
12:11 your spiritual fervor, serving the-L.
14:8 we live to the-L; and if we die,
1Co 1:31 Let him who boasts boast in the-L."
3:5 the-L has assigned to each his task.
7:34 to be devoted to the-L in both body
10:9 We should not test the-L,
11:23 For I received from the-L what I
12:3 "Jesus is-L," except by the Holy
15:57 victory through our-L Jesus Christ.
16:22 If anyone does not love the-L—
2Co 3:17 Now the-L is the Spirit,
8:5 they gave themselves first to the-L
10:17 Let him who boasts boast in the-L."
Gal 6:14 in the cross of our-L Jesus Christ,
Eph 4:5 one-L, one faith, one baptism;
5:10 and find out what pleases the-L.
5:19 make music in your heart to the-L,
Php 2:11 confess that Jesus Christ is-L,
3:1 my brothers, rejoice in the-L!
4:4 Rejoice in the-L always.
Col 2:6 as you received Christ Jesus as-L,
3:17 do it all in the name of the-L Jesus,
3:23 as working for the-L, not for men,
4:17 work you have received in the-L."
1Th 3:12 May the-L make your love increase
5:2 day of the-L will come like a thief
5:23 at the coming of our-L Jesus Christ.
2Th 2:1 the coming of our-L Jesus Christ
2Ti 2:19 "The-L knows those who are his,"
Heb 12:14 holiness no one will see the-L.
13:6 L is my helper; I will not be afraid.
Jas 4:15 you ought to say, "If it is the-L will,
1Pe 1:25 the word of the-L stands forever."
2:3 you have tasted that the-L is good.
3:15 in your hearts set apart Christ as-L.
2Pe 1:16 and coming of our-L Jesus Christ,
2:1 the sovereign-L who bought
3:9 The-L is not slow in keeping his
Jude :14 The-L is coming with thousands
Rev 4:8 holy, holy is the-L God Almighty,
4:11 "You are worthy, our-L and God,
17:14 he is-L of lords and King of kings—
22:20 Come,-L Jesus.

LORD'S† (LORD†)

Ac 21:14 and said, "The-L will be done."
1Co 10:26 "The earth is the-L, and everything
11:26 you proclaim the-L death
2Co 3:18 faces all reflect the-L glory,
2Ti 2:24 And the-L servant must not quarrel
Jas 4:15 you ought to say, "If it is the-L will,

LORDING* (LORD†)

1Pe 5:3 not-/it over those entrusted to you,

LORD‡ (LORD'S‡)

Ge 2:4 When the-L God made the earth
2:7 the-L God formed the man
3:21 The-L God made garments of skin
7:16 Then the-L shut him in.
15:6 Abram believed the-L,
18:14 Is anything too hard for the-L?
31:49 "May the-L keep watch
Ex 3:2 the angel of the-L appeared to him
9:12 the-L hardened Pharaoh's heart
14:30 That day the-L saved Israel
20:2 "I am the-L your God, who
33:11 The-L would speak to Moses face
40:34 glory of the-L filled the tabernacle.
Lev 2:4 'Be holy because I, the-L your God,
Nu 8:5 L said to Moses: "Take the Levites
14:21 glory of the-L fills the whole earth,
Dt 2:7 forty years the-L your God has
5:9 the-L your God, am a jealous God,
6:4 The-L our God, the-L is one.
6:5 Love the-L your God
6:16 Do not test the-L your God
10:14 To the-L your God belong
10:17 For the-L your God is God of gods
11:1 Love the-L your God and keep his
28:1 If you fully obey the-L your God
30:16 today to love the-L your God,
30:20 For the-L is your life, and he will
31:6 for the-L your God goes with you;
Jos 22:5 to love the-L your God, to walk
24:15 my household, we will serve the-L
1Sa 1:28 So now I give him to the-L
2:2 "There is no one holy like the-L;
7:12 "Thus far has the-L helped us."
12:22 his great name the-L will not reject
15:22 "Does the-L delight
2Sa 22:2 "The-L is my rock, my fortress
1Ki 2:3 and observe what the-L your God
8:11 the glory of the-L filled his temple.
8:61 fully committed to the-L our God,
18:21 If the-L is God, follow him;
2Ki 13:23 But the-L was gracious to them
1Ch 16:8 Give thanks to the-L, call
16:23 Sing to the-L, all the earth;
28:9 for the-L searches every heart
29:11 O-L, is the greatness and the power
2Ch 5:14 the glory of the-L filled the temple
16:9 of the-L range throughout the earth
19:6 judging for man but for the-L,
30:9 for the-L your God is gracious
Ne 1:5 Then I said: "O-L, God of heaven,
Job 1:21 L gave and the-L has taken away;
38:1 the-L answered Job out
42:9 and the-L accepted Job's prayer.
Ps 1:2 But his delight is in the law of the-L,
9:9 The-L is a refuge for the oppressed,
12:6 And the words of the-L are flawless
16:8 I have set the-L always before me.
18:30 the word of the-L is flawless
19:7 The law of the-L is perfect,
19:14 O-L, my Rock and my Redeemer.
23:1 The-L is my shepherd, I shall not be
23:6 I will dwell in the house of the-L
27:1 The-L is my light and my salvation
27:4 to gaze upon the beauty of the-L
29:1 Ascribe to the-L, O mighty ones,
32:2 whose sin the-L does not count
33:12 is the nation whose God is the-L,
33:18 But the eyes of the-L are
34:3 Glorify the-L with me;
34:7 The angel of the-L encamps
34:8 Taste and see that the-L is good;
34:18 The-L is close to the brokenhearted
37:4 Delight yourself in the-L
40:1 I waited patiently for the-L;
47:2 How awesome is the-L Most High,

48:1 Great is the-L, and most worthy
55:22 Cast your cares on the-L
75:8 In the hand of the-L is a cup
84:11 For the-L God is a sun and shield;
86:11 Teach me your way, O-L,
89:5 heavens praise your wonders, O-L,
91:2 I will say of the-L, "He is my refuge
95:1 Come, let us sing for joy to the-L;
96:1 Sing to the-L a new song;
98:4 Shout for joy to the-L, all the earth,
100:1 Shout for joy to the-L, all the earth.
103:1 Praise the-L, O my soul;
103:8 The-L is compassionate
104:1 O-L my God, you are very great;
107:8 to the-L for his unfailing love
110:1 The-L says to my Lord:
113:4 L is exalted over all the nations,
115:1 Not to us, O-L, not to us
116:15 Precious in the sight of the-L
118:1 Give thanks to the-L, for he is good
118:24 This is the day the-L has made;
121:2 My help comes from the-L,
121:5 The-L watches over you—
125:2 so the-L surrounds his people
127:1 Unless the-L builds the house,
127:3 Sons are a heritage from the-L,
130:3 If you, O-L, kept a record of sins,
135:6 The-L does whatever pleases him,
136:1 Give thanks to the-L, for he is good
139:1 O-L, you have searched me
144:3 O-L, what is man that you care
145:3 Great is the-L and most worthy
145:18 The-L is near to all who call on him
Pr 1:7 The fear of the-L is the beginning
3:5 Trust in the-L with all your heart
3:9 Honor the-L with your wealth,
3:12 the-L disciplines those he loves,
3:19 By wisdom the-L laid the earth's
5:21 are in full view of the-L,
6:16 There are six things the-L hates,
10:27 The fear of the-L adds length to life
11:1 The-L abhors dishonest scales,
12:22 The-L detests lying lips,
14:26 He who fears the-L has a secure
15:3 The eyes of the-L are everywhere,
16:2 but motives are weighed by the-L.
16:4 The-L works out everything
16:9 but the-L determines his steps.
16:33 but its every decision is from the-L.
18:10 The name of the-L is a strong tower
18:22 and receives favor from the-L.
19:14 but a prudent wife is from the-L.
19:17 to the poor lends to the-L,
21:3 to the-L than sacrifice.
21:30 that can succeed against the-L.
21:31 but victory rests with the-L.
22:2 The-L is the Maker of them all.
24:18 or the-L will see and disapprove
31:30 a woman who fears the-L is
Isa 6:3 holy, holy is the-L Almighty;
11:2 The Spirit of the-L will rest on him
11:9 full of the knowledge of the-L
12:2 The-L, the-L, is my strength
24:1 the-L is going to lay waste the earth
25:8 The Sovereign-L will wipe away
29:15 to hide their plans from the-L,
33:6 the fear of the-L is the key
35:10 the ransomed of the-L will return.
40:5 the glory of the-L will be revealed,
40:7 the breath of the-L blows on them.
40:10 the Sovereign-L comes with power,
40:28 The-L is the everlasting God,
40:31 but those who hope in the-L
42:8 "I am the-L; that is my name!
43:11 I, even I, am the-L,
44:24 I am the-L,

45:5 I am the-L, and there is no other;
45:21 Was it not I, the-L?
51:11 The ransomed of the-L will return.
53:6 and the-L has laid on him
53:10 and the will of the-L will prosper
55:6 Seek the-L while he may be found;
58:8 of the-L will be your rear guard.
58:11 The-L will guide you always;
59:1 the arm of the-L is not too short
61:3 a planting of the-L
61:10 I delight greatly in the-L;
Jer 1:9 Then the-L reached out his hand
9:24 I am the-L, who exercises kindness,
16:19 O-L, my strength and my fortress,
17:7 is the man who trusts in the-L,
La 3:40 and let us return to the-L.
Eze 1:28 of the likeness of the glory of the-L
Hos 1:7 horsemen, but by the-L their God."
3:5 They will come trembling to the-L.
6:1 "Come, let us return to the-L.
Joel 2:1 for the day of the-L is coming.
2:11 The day of the-L is great;
3:14 For the day of the-L is near
Am 5:18 long for the day of the-L?
Jnh 1:3 But Jonah ran away from the-L
Mic 4:2 up to the mountain of the-L,
6:8 And what does the-L require of you
Na 1:2 The-L takes vengeance on his foes
1:3 The-L is slow to anger
Hab 2:14 knowledge of the glory of the-L,
2:20 But the-L is in his holy temple;
Zep 3:17 The-L your God is with you,
Zec 1:17 and the-L will again comfort Zion
9:16 The-L their God will save them
14:5 Then the-L my God will come,
14:9 The-L will be king
Mal 4:5 and dreadful day of the-L comes.

LORD'S‡ (LORD‡)

Ex 34:34 he entered the-L presence
Nu 14:41 you disobeying the-L command?
Dt 6:18 is right and good in the-L sight,
32:9 For the-L portion is his people,
Jos 21:45 Not one of all the-L good promises
Ps 24:1 The earth is the-L, and everything
32:10 but the-L unfailing love
89:1 of the-L great love forever;
103:17 L love is with those who fear him,
Pr 3:11 do not despise the-L discipline
Isa 24:14 west they acclaim the-L majesty.
62:3 of splendor in the-L hand,
Jer 48:10 lax in doing the-L work!
La 3:22 of the-L great love we are not
Mic 4:1 of the-L temple will be established

LOSE (LOSES LOSS LOST)

1Sa 17:32 "Let no one-/heart on account
Mt 10:39 Whoever finds his life will-/it,
Lk 9:25 and yet-/or forfeit his very self?
Jn 6:39 that I shall-/none of all that he has
Heb 12:3 will not grow weary and-/heart.
12:5 do not-/heart when he rebukes you

LOSES (LOSE)

Mt 5:13 But if the salt-/its saltiness,
Lk 15:4 you has a hundred sheep and-/one
15:8 has ten silver coins and-/one.

LOSS (LOSE)

Ro 11:12 and their-/means riches
1Co 3:15 he will suffer-/; he himself will be
Php 3:8 I consider everything a-/compared

LOST (LOSE)

Ps 73:2 I had nearly-/my foothold.
Jer 50:6 "My people have been-/sheep;
Eze 34:4 the strays or searched for the-/.
34:16 for the-/and bring back the strays.
Mt 18:14 any of these little ones should be-/.
Lk 15:4 go after the-/sheep until he finds it?

15: 6 with me; I have found my-/ sheep.'
15: 9 with me; I have found my-/ coin.'
15:24 is alive again; he was-/ and is found
19:10 to seek and to save what was-/.''
Php 3: 8 for whose sake I have-/ all things.

LOT (LOTS)
Nephew of Abraham (Ge 11:27; 12:5). Chose to
live in Sodom (Ge 13). Rescued from four kings
(Ge 14). Rescued from Sodom (Ge 19:1-29;
2Pe 2:7). Fathered Moab and Ammon by his
daughters (Ge 19:30-38).
Est 3: 7 the-/l in the presence of Haman
       9:24 the-/l for their ruin and destruction.
Pr   16:33 The-/ is cast into the lap,
       18:18 Casting the-/ settles disputes
Ecc 3:22 his work, because that is his-/.
Ac   1:26 Then they drew lots, and the-/ fell

LOTS (LOT)
Ps 22:18 and cast-/ for my clothing.
Mt 27:35 divided up his clothes by casting-/.

LOVE (BELOVED LOVED LOVELY LOVER
LOVERS LOVES LOVING)
Ge 22: 2 your only son, Isaac, whom you-/,
Ex 15:13 "In your unfailing-/ you will lead
      20: 6 showing-/ to a thousand generations
      20: 6 of those who-/ me
      34: 6 abounding in-/ and faithfulness,
Lev 19:18 but-/ your neighbor as yourself.
      19:34 L him as yourself,
Nu 14:18 abounding in-/ and forgiving sin
Dt   5:10 showing-/ to a thousand generations
       5:10 of those who-/ me
       6: 5 L the LORD your God
       7:13 He will-/ you and bless you
      10:12 to walk in all his ways, to-/ him,
      11:13 to-/ the LORD your God
      13: 6 wife you-/, or your closest friend
      30: 6 so that you may-/ him
Jos 22: 5 to-/ the LORD your God, to walk
1Ki   3: 3 Solomon showed his-/
       8:23 you who keep your covenant of-/
2Ch   5:13 his-/ endures forever.''
Ne   1: 5 covenant of-/ with those who / him
Ps   18: 1 I-/ you, O LORD, my strength.
      23: 6 Surely goodness and-/ will follow
      25: 6 O LORD, your great mercy and-/,
      31:16 save me in your unfailing-/.
      32:10 but the LORD's unfailing-/
      33: 5 the earth is full of his unfailing-/,
      33:18 whose hope is in his unfailing-/,
      36: 5 Your-/, O LORD, reaches
      36: 7 How priceless is your unfailing-/!
      45: 7 You-/ righteousness and hate
      51: 1 according to your unfailing-/;
      57:10 For great is your-/, reaching
      63: 3 Because your-/ is better than life,
      66:20 or withheld his-/ from me!
      70: 4 may those who-/ your salvation
      77: 8 Has his unfailing-/ vanished forever
      85: 7 Show us your unfailing-/, O LORD
      85:10 L and faithfulness meet together;
      86:13 For great is your-/ toward me;
      89: 1 of the LORD's great-/ forever;
      89:33 but I will not take my-/ from him,
      92: 2 to proclaim your-/ in the morning
      94:18 your-/, O LORD, supported me.
     100: 5 is good and his-/ endures forever;
     101: 1 I will sing of your-/ and justice;
     103: 4 crowns you with-/ and compassion.
     103: 8 slow to anger, abounding in-/.
     103:11 so great is his-/ for those who fear
     107: 8 to the LORD for his unfailing-/
     108: 4 For great is your-/, higher
     116: 1 I-/ the LORD, for he heard my
     118: 1 his-/ endures forever.

119:47 because I-/ them.
119:64 The earth is filled with your-/,
119:76 May your unfailing-/ be my
119:97 Oh, how I-/ your law!
119:119 therefore I-/ your statutes.
119:124 your servant according to your-/
119:132 to those who-/ your name.
119:159 O LORD, according to your-/
119:163 but I-/ your law.
119:165 peace have they who-/ your law,
122: 6 "May those who-/ you be secure.
130: 7 for with the LORD is unfailing-/
136: 1 His l endures forever.
143: 8 of your unfailing-/,
145: 8 slow to anger and rich in-/.
145:20 over all who-/ him,
147:11 who put their hope in his unfailing-/
Pr   3: 3 Let-/ and faithfulness never leave
      4: 6 / her, and she will watch over you.
      5:19 you ever be captivated by her-/.
      8:17 I-/ those who-/ me,
      9: 8 rebuke a wise man and he will-/ you
     10:12 but-/ covers over all wrongs.
     14:22 those who plan what is good find-/
     15:17 of vegetables where there is-/
     17: 9 over an offense promotes-/,
     19:22 What a man desires is unfailing-/;
     20: 6 claims to have unfailing-/,
     20:13 Do not-/ sleep or you will grow
     20:28 through-/ his throne is made secure
     21:21 who pursues righteousness and-/
     27: 5 rebuke than hidden-/.
Ecc 9: 6 Their-/, their hate
      9: 9 life with your wife, whom you-/,
SS   2: 4 and his banner over me is-/.
      8: 6 for-/ is as strong as death,
      8: 7 Many waters cannot quench-/;
      8: 7 all the wealth of his house for-/,
Isa 5: 1 I will sing for the one I-/
     16: 5 In-/ a throne will be established;
     38:17 In your-/ you kept me
     54:10 yet my unfailing-/ for you will not
     55: 3 my faithful-/ promised to David.
     61: 8 "For I, the LORD,-/ justice;
     63: 9 In his-/ and mercy he redeemed
Jer   5:31 and my people-/ it this way.
     31: 3 you with an everlasting-/;
     32:18 You show-/ to thousands
     33:11 his-/ endures forever."
La   3:22 of the LORD's great-/ we are not
      3:32 so great is his unfailing-/.
Eze 33:32 more than one who sings-/ songs
Da   9: 4 covenant of-/ with all who-/ him
Hos 2:19 in-/ and compassion.
      3: 1 Go, show your-/ to your wife again,
     11: 4 with ties of-/.
     12: 6 maintain-/ and justice,
Joel 2:13 slow to anger and abounding in-/,
Am   5:15 Hate evil,-/ good;
Mic   3: 2 you who hate good and-/ evil;
      6: 8 To act justly and to-/ mercy
Zep   3:17 he will quiet you with his-/,
Zec   8:19 Therefore-/ truth and peace."
Mt   3:17 "This is my Son, whom I-/;
      5:44 L your enemies and pray
      6:24 he will hate the one and-/ the other,
     17: 5 "This is my Son, whom I-/,
     19:19 and- 'your neighbor as yourself.' ''
     22:37 " 'L the Lord your God
Lk   6:32 Even 'sinners'-/ those who-/ them.
      7:42 which of them will-/ him more?''
     20:13 whom I-/; perhaps they will respect
Jn   13:34 I give you:-L one another."
     13:35 disciples, if you-/ one another.''
     14:15 "If you-/ me, you will obey what I
     15:13 Greater-/ has no one than this,

15:17 This is my command:-L each other.
21:15 do you truly-/ me more than these
Ro   5: 5 because God has poured out his-/
     5: 8 God demonstrates his own-/ for us
     8:28 for the good of those who-/ him,
     8:35 us from the-/ of Christ?
     8:39 us from the-/ of God that is
    12: 9 L must be sincere.
    12:10 to one another in brotherly-/.
    13: 8 continuing debt to-/ one another,
    13: 9 "L your neighbor as yourself."
    13:10 Therefore-/ is the fulfillment
    13:10 L does no harm to its neighbor.
1Co 8: 1 prepared for those who-/ him"—
      8: 1 Knowledge puffs up, but-/ builds up
     13: 1 I have not-/, I am only a resounding
     13: 2 but have not-/, I am nothing.
     13: 3 but have not-/, I gain nothing.
     13: 4 Love is patient,-/ is kind.
     13: 4 L is patient, love is kind.
     13: 6 L does not delight in evil
     13: 8 L never fails.
     13:13 But the greatest of these is-/.
     13:13 three remain: faith, hope and-/.
     14: 1 way of-/ and eagerly desire spiritual
     16:14 Do everything in-/.
2Co 5:14 For Christ's-/ compels us,
      8: 8 sincerity of your-/ by comparing it
      8:24 show these men the proof of your-/
Gal   5: 6 is faith expressing itself through-/.
      5:13 rather, serve one another in-/.
      5:22 But the fruit of the Spirit is-/, joy,
Eph   1: 4 In-/ he predestined us
      2: 4 But because of his great-/ for us,
      3:17 being rooted and established in-/,
      3:18 and high and deep is the-/ of Christ,
      3:19 and to know this-/ that surpasses
      4: 2 bearing with one another in-/.
      4:15 Instead, speaking the truth in-/,
      5: 2 loved children and live a life of-/,
      5:25 / your wives, just as Christ loved
      5:28 husbands ought to-/ their wives
      5:33 each one of you also must-/ his wife
Php   1: 9 that your-/ may abound more
      2: 2 having the same-/, being one
Col   1: 5 that spring from the hope that is
      2: 2 in heart and united in-/,
      3:14 And over all these virtues put on-/,
      3:19 your wives and do not be harsh
1Th   1: 3 your labor prompted by-/,
      4: 9 taught by God to-/ each other.
      5: 8 on faith and-/ as a breastplate,
2Th   3: 5 direct your hearts into God's-/
1Ti   1: 5 The goal of this command is-/
      2:15 / and holiness with propriety.
      4:12 in life, in-/, in faith and in purity.
      6:10 For the-/ of money is a root
      6:11 faith,-/, endurance and gentleness.
2Ti   1: 7 of power, of-/ and of self-discipline.
      2:22 and pursue righteousness, faith,-/
      3:10 faith, patience,-/, endurance,
Tit   2: 4 women to-/ their husbands
Phm   9 yet I appeal to you on the basis of-/.
Heb   6:10 and the-/ you have shown him
     10:24 may spur one another on toward-/
     13: 5 free from the-/ of money
Jas   1:12 promised to those who-/ him.
      2: 5 he promised those who-/ him?
      2: 8 "L your neighbor as yourself,"
1Pe   1:22 the truth so that you have sincere-/
      1:22 / one another deeply,
      2:17 L the brotherhood of believers,
      3: 8 be sympathetic,-/ as brothers,
      3:10 "Whoever would-/ life
      4: 8 Above all,-/ each other deeply,
      4: 8 / covers over a multitude of sins.

5:14 Greet one another with a kiss of-/.
2Pe 1: 7 and to brotherly kindness,-/
      1:17 "This is my Son, whom I-/;
1Jn 2: 5 God's-/ is truly made complete
      2:15 Do not-/ the world or anything
      3: 1 How great is the-/ the Father has
      3:10 anyone who does not-/ his brother.
      3:11 We should-/ one another.
      3:14 Anyone who does not-/ remains
      3:16 This is how we know what-/ is:
      3:18 let us not-/ with words or tongue
      3:23 to-/ one another as he commanded
      4: 7 Dear friends, let us-/ one another,
      4: 7 for-/ comes from God.
      4: 8 Whoever does not-/ does not know
      4: 9 This is how God showed his-/
      4:10 This is-/: not that we loved God,
      4:11 we also ought to-/ one another.
      4:12 and his-/ is made complete in us.
      4:16 God is-/.
      4:16 Whoever lives in-/ lives in God,
      4:17 / is made complete among us
      4:18 But perfect-/ drives out fear,
      4:19 We-/ because he first loved us.
      4:20 If anyone says, "I-/ God,"
      4:21 loves God must also-/ his brother.
      5: 2 we know that we-/ the children
      5: 3 This is-/ for God: to obey his
2Jn   :5 I ask that we-/ one another.
       :6 his command is that you walk in-/.
       :6 this is-/: that we walk in obedience
Jude :12 men are blemishes at your-/ feasts,
       :21 Keep yourselves in God's-/
Rev 2: 4 You have forsaken your first-/.
      3:19 Those whom I-/ I rebuke
     12:11 they did not-/ their lives so much

LOVED (LOVE)
Ge 24:67 she became his wife, and he-/ her;
     29:30 and he-/ Rachel more than Leah.
     37: 3 Now Israel-/ Joseph more than any
Dt   7: 8 But it was because the LORD-/ you
1Sa   1: 5 a double portion because he-/ her,
     20:17 because he-/ him as he-/ himself.
Ps   44: 3 light of your face, for you-/ them.
Jer   2: 2 how as a bride you-/ me
     31: 3 "I have-/ you with an everlasting
Hos   2:23 to the one I called 'Not my-/ one.'
      3: 1 though she is-/ by another
      9:10 became as vile as the thing they-/.
     11: 1 "When Israel was a child, I-/ him,
Mal   1: 2 "But you ask, 'How have you-/ us?'
Mk   12: 6 left to send, a son, whom he-/.
Jn   3:16 so-/ the world that he gave his one
      3:19 but men-/ darkness instead of light
     11: 5 Jesus-/ Martha and her sister
     12:43 for they-/ praise from men more
     13: 1 Having-/ his own who were
     13:23 the disciple whom Jesus-/
     13:34 As I have-/ you, so you must love
     14:21 He who loves me will be-/
     15: 9 the Father has-/ me, so have I-/ you.
     15:12 Love each other as I have-/ you.
     19:26 the disciple whom he-/ standing
Ro   8:37 conquerors through him who-/ us.
      9:13 "Jacob I-/, but Esau I hated."
      9:25 her 'my-/ one' who is not my-/ one,"
     11:28 they are-/ on account
Gal   2:20 who-/ me and gave himself for me.
Eph   5: 2 as Christ-/ us and gave himself up
      5:25 just as Christ-/ the church
2Th   2:16 by his grace gave us
2Ti   4:10 for Demas, because he-/ this world,
Heb   1: 9 You have-/ righteousness
1Jn   4:10 This is love: not that we-/ God,
      4:11 Dear friends, since God so-/ us,
      4:19 We love because he first-/ us.

LOVELY (LOVE)
Ps 84: 1 How-/ is your dwelling place,
SS 2:14 and your face is-/.
   5:16 he is altogether-/.
Php 4: 8 whatever is-/, whatever is

LOVER (LOVE)
SS 2:16 *Beloved* My-/ is mine and I am his;
   7:10 I belong to my-/,
1Ti 3: 3 not quarrelsome, not a-/ of money.

LOVERS (LOVE)
2Ti 3: 2 People will be-/ of themselves,
   3: 3 without self-control, brutal, not-/
   3: 4 / of pleasure rather than-/ of God—

LOVES (LOVE)
Ps 11: 7 he-/ justice;
   33: 5 The Lord-/ righteousness
   34:12 Whoever of you-/ life
   91:14 Because he-/ me," says the Lord,
   127: 2 for he grants sleep to those he-/.
Pr 3:12 the Lord disciplines those he-/,
   12: 1 Whoever-/ discipline / knowledge,
   13:24 he who-/ him is careful
   17:17 A friend-/ at all times,
   17:19 He who-/ a quarrel-/ sin;
   22:11 He who-/ a pure heart and whose
Ecc 5:10 whoever-/ wealth is never satisfied
Mt 10:37 anyone who-/ his son or daughter
Lk 7:47 has been forgiven little-/ little."
Jn 3:35 Father-/ the Son and has placed
   10:17 reason my Father-/ me is that I lay
   12:25 The man who-/ his life will lose it,
   14:21 obeys them, he is the one who-/ me.
   14:23 Jesus replied, "If anyone-/ me,
Ro 13: 8 for he who-/ his fellowman has
2Co 9: 7 for God-/ a cheerful giver.
Eph 5:28 He who-/ his wife / himself.
   5:33 must love his wife as he-/ himself,
Heb 12: 6 the Lord disciplines those he-/,
1Jn 2:10 Whoever-/ his brother lives
   2:15 If anyone-/ the world, the love
   4: 7 Everyone who-/ has been born
   4:21 Whoever-/ God must also love his
   5: 1 who-/ the father-/ his child
3Jn : 9 but Diotrephes, who-/ to be first,
Rev 1: 5 To him who-/ us and has freed us

LOVING (LOVE)
Ps 25:10 All the ways of the Lord are-/.
   62:12 and that you, O Lord, are-/.
   145:17 and-/ toward all he has made.
Heb 13: 1 Keep on-/ each other as brothers.
1Jn 5: 2 by-/ God and carrying out his

LOWLY
Job 5:11 The-/ he sets on high,
Pr 29:23 but a man of-/ spirit gains honor.
Isa 57:15 also with him who is contrite and-/
Eze 21:26 / will be exalted and the exalted
1Co 1:28 He chose the-/ things of this world

LUKE*
   Co-worker with Paul (Col 4:14; 2Ti 4:11; Phm 24).

LUKEWARM*
Rev 3:16 So, because you are-/— neither hot

LUST
Pr 6:25 Do not-/ in your heart
Col 3: 5 sexual immorality, impurity,-/,
1Th 4: 5 not in passionate-/ like the heathen,
1Jn 2:16 the-/ of his eyes and the boasting

LYING (LIE)
Pr 6:17 a-/ tongue,
   26:28 A-/ tongue hates those it hurts,

MACEDONIA
Ac 16: 9 "Come over to-M and help us."

MADE (MAKE)
Ge 1:16 He also-*m* the stars.
   1:25 God-*m* the wild animals according
   2:22 Then the Lord God-*m* a woman
2Ki 19:15 You have-*m* heaven and earth.
Ps 95: 5 The sea is his, for he-*m* it,
   100: 3 It is he who-*m* us, and we are his;
   118:24 This is the day the Lord has-*m*;
   139:14 I am fearfully and wonderfully-*m*;
Ecc 3:11 He has-*m* everything beautiful
Mk 2:27 "The Sabbath was-*m* for man,
Jn 1: 3 Through him all things were-*m*;
Ac 17:24 "The God who-*m* the world
Heb 1: 2 through whom he-*m* the universe.
Rev 14: 7 Worship him who-*m* the heavens,

MAGI
Mt 2: 1 *M* from the east came to Jerusalem

MAGOG
Eze 38: 2 of the land of-*M*, the chief prince
   39: 6 I will send fire on-*M*
Rev 20: 8 and-*M*— to gather them for battle.

MAIDEN
Pr 30:19 and the way of a man with a-*m*.
Isa 62: 5 As a young man marries a-*m*,
Jer 2:32 Does a-*m* forget her jewelry,

MAIMED
Mt 18: 8 It is better for you to enter life-*m*

MAJESTIC (MAJESTY)
Ex 15: 6 was-*m* in power.
   15:11 *m* in holiness,
Ps 8: 1 how-*m* is your name in all the earth
   29: 4 the voice of the Lord is-*m*.
   111: 3 Glorious and-*m* are his deeds,
SS 6:10 *m* as the stars in procession?
2Pe 1:17 came to him from the-*M* Glory,

MAJESTY (MAJESTIC)
Ex 15: 7 In the greatness of your-*m*
Dt 33:26 and on the clouds in his-*m*.
1Ch 16:27 Splendor and-*m* are before him;
Est 1: 4 the splendor and glory of his-*m*.
Job 37:22 God comes in awesome-*m*.
   40:10 and clothe yourself in honor and-*m*
Ps 45: 4 In your-*m* ride forth victoriously
   93: 1 The Lord reigns, he is robed in-*m*
   110: 3 Arrayed in holy-*m*,
   145: 5 of the glorious splendor of your-*m*,
Isa 52: 2 or-*m* to attract us to him,
Eze 31: 2 can be compared with you in-*m*?
2Pe 1:16 but we were eyewitnesses of his-*m*.
Jude :25 only God our Savior be glory,-*m*,

MAKE (MADE MAKER MAKES MAKING)
Ge 1:26 "Let us-*m* man in our image,
   2:18 I will-*m* a helper suitable for him."
   12: 2 "I will-*m* you into a great nation
Ex 22: 3 thief must certainly-*m* restitution,
Nu 6:25 the Lord-*m* his face shine
Ps 108: 1 in music with all my soul.
Isa 14:14 I will-*m* myself like the Most High
   29:16 "He did not-*m* me"?
Jer 31:31 "when I will-*m* a new covenant
Mt 3: 3 *m* straight paths for him.' "
   28:19 and-*m* disciples of all nations,
Mk 1:17 "and I will-*m* you fishers of men."
Lk 13:24 *M* every effort to enter
   14:23 country lanes and-*m* them come in,
Ro 14:19 *m* every effort to do what leads
2Co 5: 9 So we-*m* it our goal to please him,
Eph 4: 3 *M* every effort to keep the unity
Col 4: 5 *m* the most of every opportunity.
1Th 4:11 *M* it your ambition
Heb 4:11 *m* every effort to enter that rest,
   12:14 *M* every effort to live in peace
2Pe 1: 5 *m* every effort to add
   3:14 *m* every effort to be found spotless,

MAKER (MAKE)
Job 4:17 Can a man be more pure than his-*M*
   36: 3 I will ascribe justice to my-*M*.
Ps 95: 6 kneel before the Lord our-*M*;
Pr 22: 2 The Lord is the-*M* of them all.
Isa 45: 9 to him who quarrels with his-*M*,
   54: 5 For your-*M* is your husband—
Jer 10:16 for he is the-*M* of all things,

MAKES (MAKE)
1Co 3: 7 but only God, who-*m* things grow.

MAKING (MAKE)
Ps 19: 7 *m* wise the simple.
Ecc 12:12 Of-*m* many books there is no end,
Jn 5:18 *m* himself equal with God.
Eph 5:16 *m* the most of every opportunity,

MALE
Ge 1:27 *m* and female he created them.
Gal 3:28 slave nor free,-*m* nor female,

MALICE (MALICIOUS)
Ro 1:29 murder, strife, deceit and-*m*.
Col 3: 8 *m*, slander, and filthy language
1Pe 2: 1 rid yourselves of all-*m*

MALICIOUS (MALICE)
Pr 26:24 A-*m* man disguises himself
1Ti 3:11 not-*m* talkers but temperate
   6: 4 *m* talk, evil suspicions

MAN (MEN WOMAN WOMEN)
Ge 1:26 "Let us make-*m* in our image,
   2: 7 God formed the-*m* from the dust
   2:18 for the-*m* to be alone
   2:23 she was taken out of-*m*.
   9: 6 Whoever sheds the blood of-*m*,
Dt 8: 3 *m* does not live on bread
1Sa 13:14 a-*m* after his own heart
   15:29 he is not a-*m* that he
Job 14: 1 *M* born of woman is of few
   14:14 If a-*m* dies, will he live
Ps 1: 1 Blessed is the-*m* who does
   8: 4 what is-*m* that you are
   119: 9 can a young-*m* keep his
   127: 5 Blessed is the-*m* whose quiver
Pr 14:12 that seems right to a-*m*,
   30:19 way of a-*m* with a maiden.
Isa 53: 3 a-*m* of sorrows,
Mt 19: 5 a-*m* will leave his father
Mk 8:36 What good is it for a-*m*
Lk 4: 4 '*M* does not live on bread
Ro 5:12 entered the world through one-*m*
1Co 7: 2 each-*m* should have his own
   11: 3 head of every-*m* is Christ,
   11: 3 head of woman is-*m*
   13:11 When I became a-*m*,
Php 2: 8 found in appearance as a-*m*,
1Ti 2: 5 the-*m* Christ Jesus,
   2:12 have authority over a-*m*;
Heb 9:27 as-*m* is destined to die

MANAGE
Jer 12: 5 how will you-*m* in the thickets
1Ti 3: 4 He must-*m* his own family well
   3:12 one wife and must-*m* his children
   5:14 to-*m* their homes and to give

MANASSEH
1. Firstborn of Joseph (Ge 41:51; 46:20). Blessed (Ge 48).
2. Son of Hezekiah; king of Judah (2Ki 21:1-18; 2Ch 33:1-20).

MANGER
Lk 2:12 in strips of cloth and lying in a-*m*."

MANNA
Ex 16:31 people of Israel called the bread-*m*.
Dt 8:16 He gave you-*m* to eat in the desert,
Jn 6:49 Your forefathers ate the-*m*
Rev 2:17 I will give some of the hidden-*m*.

MANNER
1Co 11:27 in an unworthy-*m* will be guilty
Php 1:27 conduct yourselves in a-*m* worthy

MARITAL (MARRY)
Ex 21:10 of her food, clothing and-*m* rights.
Mt 5:32 except for-*m* unfaithfulness,
   19: 9 except for-*m* unfaithfulness,
1Co 7: 3 husband should fulfill his-*m* duty

MARK (MARKS)
   Cousin of Barnabas (Col 4:10; 2Ti 4:11; Phm 24; 1Pe 5:13), see JOHN.
Ge 4:15 Then the Lord put a-*m* on Cain
Rev 13:16 to receive a-*m* on his right hand

MARKS (MARK)
Jn 20:25 Unless I see the nail-*m* in his hands
Gal 6:17 bear on my body the-*m* of Jesus.

MARRED
Isa 52:14 his form-*m* beyond human likeness

MARRIAGE (MARRY)
Mt 22:30 neither marry nor be given in-*m*;
   24:38 marrying and giving in-*m*,
Ro 7: 2 she is released from the law of-*m*.
Heb 13: 4 by all, and the-*m* bed kept pure,

MARRIED (MARRY)
Ro 7: 2 by law a-*m* woman is bound
1Co 7:27 Are you-*m*? Do not seek a divorce.
   7:33 But a-*m* man is concerned about
   7:36 They should get-*m*.

MARRIES (MARRY)
Mt 5:32 and anyone who-*m* the divorced
   19: 9 and-*m* another woman commits
Lk 16:18 the man who-*m* a divorced woman

MARRY (INTERMARRY MARITAL MARRIAGE MARRIED MARRIES)
Mt 22:30 resurrection people will neither-*m*
1Co 7: 1 It is good for a man not to-*m*.
   7: 9 control themselves, they should-*m*,
1Ti 5:14 So I counsel younger widows to-*m*,

MARTHA*
   Sister of Mary and Lazarus (Lk 10:38-42; Jn 11; 12:2).

MARVELED
Lk 2:33 mother-*m* at what was said about

MARY
1. Mother of Jesus (Mt 1:16-25; Lk 1:27-56; 2:1-40). With Jesus at temple (Lk 2:41-52), at the wedding in Cana (Jn 2:1-5), questioning his sanity (Mk 3:21), at the cross (Jn 19:25-27). Among disciples after Ascension (Ac 1:14).
2. Magdalene; former demoniac (Lk 8:2). Helped support Jesus' ministry (Lk 8:1-3). At the cross (Mt 27:56; Mk 15:40; Jn 19:25), burial (Mt 27:61; Mk 15:47). Saw angel after resurrection (Mt 28:1-10; Mk 16:1-9; Lk 24:1-12); also Jesus (Jn 20:1-18).
3. Sister of Martha and Lazarus (Jn 11). Washed Jesus' feet (Jn 12:1-8).

MASQUERADES*
2Co 11:14 for Satan himself-*m* as an angel

MASTER (MASTERED MASTERS)
Mt 10:24 nor a servant above his-*m*.
   23: 8 for you have only one-*M*
   24:46 that servant whose-*m* finds him
   25:21 "His-*m* replied, 'Well done,
Ro 6:14 For sin shall not be your-*m*,
   14: 4 To his own-*m* he stands or falls.
2Ti 2:21 useful to the-*M* and prepared

MASTERED* (MASTER)
1Co 6:12 but I will not be-*m* by anything.
2Pe 2:19 a slave to whatever has-*m* him.

MASTERS (MASTER)
Mt 6:24 "No one can serve two-*m*.
Eph 6:5 obey your earthly-*m* with respect
6:9 And-*m*, treat your slaves
Tit 2:9 subject to their-*m* in everything,

MATTHEW*
Apostle; former tax collector (Mt 9:9-13; 10:3;
Mk 3:18; Lk 6:15; Ac 1:13). Also called Levi (Mk
2:14-17; Lk 5:27-32).

MATURE (MATURITY)
Eph 4:13 of the Son of God and become-*m*,
Php 3:15 of us who are-*m* should take such
Heb 5:14 But solid food is for the-*m*,
Jas 1:4 work so that you may be-*m*

MATURITY* (MATURE)
Heb 6:1 about Christ and go on to-*m*,

MEAL
Pr 15:17 Better a-*m* of vegetables where
1Co 10:27 some unbeliever invites you to a-*m*
Heb 12:16 for a single-*m* sold his inheritance

MEANING
Ne 8:8 and giving the-*m* so that the people

MEANS
1Co 9:22 by all possible-*m* I might save some

MEAT
Ro 14:6 He who eats-*m*, eats to the Lord,
14:21 It is better not to eat-*m*

MEDIATOR
1Ti 2:5 and one-*m* between God and men,
Heb 8:6 of which he is-*m* is superior
9:15 For this reason Christ is the-*m*
12:24 to Jesus the-*m* of a new covenant,

MEDICINE*
Pr 17:22 A cheerful heart is good-*m*,

MEDITATE (MEDITATES MEDITATION)
Jos 1:8 from your mouth;-*m* on it day
Ps 119:15 I-*m* on your precepts
119:78 but I will-*m* on your precepts.
119:97 I-*m* on it all day long.
145:5 I will-*m* on your wonderful works.

MEDITATES* (MEDITATE)
Ps 1:2 and on his law he-*m* day and night.

MEDITATION* (MEDITATE)
Ps 19:14 of my mouth and the-*m* of my heart
104:34 May my-*m* be pleasing to him,

MEDIUM
Lev 20:27 " 'A man or woman who is a-*m*

MEEK (MEEKNESS)
Ps 37:11 But the-*m* will inherit the land
Mt 5:5 Blessed are the-*m*,

MEEKNESS* (MEEK)
2Co 10:1 By the-*m* and gentleness of Christ,

MEET (MEETING)
Ps 85:10 Love and faithfulness-*m* together;
Am 4:12 prepare to-*m* your God, O Israel."
1Th 4:17 them in the clouds to-*m* the Lord

MEETING (MEET)
Heb 10:25 Let us not give up-*m* together,

MELCHIZEDEK
Ge 14:18 *M* king of Salem brought out bread
Ps 110:4 in the order of-*M*."
Heb 7:11 in the order of-*M*, not in the order

MELT
2Pe 3:12 and the elements will-*m* in the heat.

MEMBERS
Mic 7:6 a man's enemies are the-*m*
Ro 7:23 law at work in the-*m* of my body,
12:4 of us has one body with many-*m*,
1Co 6:15 not know that your bodies are-*m*

12:24 But God has combined the-*m*
Eph 4:25 for we are all-*m* of one body,
Col 3:15 as-*m* of one body you were called

MEN (MAN)
Mt 4:19 will make you fishers of-*m*
5:16 your light shine before-*m*
12:36 *m* will have to give account
Jn 12:32 will draw all-*m* to myself
Ac 5:29 obey God rather than-*m*!
Ro 1:27 indecent acts with other-*m*,
5:12 death came to all-*m*,
1Co 9:22 all things to all-*m*
2Co 5:11 we try to persuade-*m*.
1Ti 2:4 wants all-*m* to be saved
2Ti 2:2 entrust to reliable-*m*
2Pe 1:21 but-*m* spoke from God

MENAHEM
King of Israel (2Ki 15:17-22).

MERCIFUL (MERCY)
Dt 4:31 the Lord your God is a-*m* God;
Ne 9:31 for you are a gracious and-*m* God.
Mt 5:7 Blessed are the-*m*,
Lk 6:36 Be-*m*, just as your Father is-*m*,
Heb 2:17 in order that he might become a-*m*
Jude :22 Be-*m* to those who doubt; snatch

MERCY (MERCIFUL)
Ex 33:19 *m* on whom I will have-*m*,
Ps 25:6 O Lord, your great-*m* and love,
Isa 63:9 and-*m* he redeemed them;
Hos 6:6 For I desire-*m*, not sacrifice,
Mic 6:8 To act justly and to love-*m*
Hab 3:2 in wrath remember-*m*.
Mt 12:7 'I desire-*m*, not sacrifice,' you
23:23 justice,-*m* and faithfulness.
Ro 9:15 "I will have-*m* on whom I have-*m*,
Eph 2:4 who is rich in-*m*, made us alive
Jas 2:13 *M* triumphs over judgment!
1Pe 1:3 In his great-*m* he has given us new

MESSAGE
Isa 53:1 Who has believed our-*m*
Jn 12:38 "Lord, who has believed our-*m*
Ro 10:17 faith comes from hearing the-*m*,
1Co 1:18 For the-*m* of the cross is
2Co 5:19 to us the-*m* of reconciliation.

MESSIAH*
Jn 1:41 "We have found the-*M*" (that is,
4:25 "I know that-*M*" (called Christ) "is

METHUSELAH
Ge 5:27 Altogether,-*M* lived 969 years,

MICHAEL
Archangel (Jude 9); warrior in angelic realm,
protector of Israel (Da 10:13, 21; 12:1; Rev
12:7).

MIDWIVES
Ex 1:17 The-*m*, however, feared God

MIGHT (ALMIGHTY MIGHTY)
Jdg 16:30 Then he pushed with all his-*m*
2Sa 6:14 before the Lord with all his-*m*,
Ps 21:13 we will sing and praise your-*m*.
Zec 4:6 'Not by-*m* nor by power,
1Ti 6:16 To him be honor and-*m* forever.

MIGHTY (MIGHT)
Ex 6:1 of my-*m* hand he will drive them
Dt 7:8 he brought you out with a-*m* hand
2Sa 1:19 How the-*m* have fallen!
23:8 the names of David's-*m* men:
Ps 24:8 The Lord strong and-*m*,
50:1 The-*M* One, God, the Lord,
89:8 You are-*m*, O Lord,
136:12 with a-*m* hand and outstretched
147:5 Great is our Lord and-*m* in power;
Isa 9:6 Wonderful Counselor,-*M* God,

Zep 3:17 he is-*m* to save.
Eph 6:10 in the Lord and in his-*m* power.

MILE*
Mt 5:41 If someone forces you to go one-*m*,

MILK
Ex 3:8 a land flowing with-*m* and honey—
Isa 55:1 Come, buy wine and-*m*
1Co 3:2 I gave you-*m*, not solid food,
Heb 5:12 You need-*m*, not solid food!
1Pe 2:2 babies, crave pure spiritual-*m*,

MILLSTONE (STONE)
Lk 17:2 sea with a-*m* tied around his neck

MIND (DOUBLE-MINDED MINDFUL MINDS)
1Sa 15:29 Israel does not lie or change his-*m*;
1Ch 28:9 devotion and with a willing-*m*,
Ps 26:2 examine my heart and my-*m*;
Isa 26:3 him whose-*m* is steadfast,
Mt 22:37 all your soul and with all your-*m*.'
Ac 4:32 believers were one in heart and-*m*.
Ro 7:25 I myself in my-*m* am a slave
8:7 the sinful-*m* is hostile to God,
12:2 by the renewing of your-*m*.
1Co 2:9 no-*m* has conceived
14:14 spirit prays, but my-*m* is unfruitful.
2Co 13:11 be of one-*m*, live in peace.
Php 3:19 Their-*m* is on earthly things.
1Th 4:11 to-*m* your own business
Heb 7:21 and will not change his-*m*:

MINDFUL* (MIND)
Ps 8:4 what is man that you are-*m* of him,
Lk 1:48 God my Savior, for he has been-*m*
Heb 2:6 What is man that you are-*m* of him,

MINDS (MIND)
Ps 7:9 who searches-*m* and hearts,
Jer 31:33 "I will put my law in their-*m*
Eph 4:23 new in the attitude of your-*m*;
Col 3:2 Set your-*m* on things above,
Heb 8:10 I will put my laws in their-*m*
Rev 2:23 I am he who searches hearts and-*m*,

MINISTERING (MINISTRY)
Heb 1:14 Are not all angels-*m* spirits sent

MINISTRY (MINISTERING)
Ac 6:4 to prayer and the-*m* of the word."
2Co 5:18 gave us the-*m* of reconciliation.
2Ti 4:5 discharge all the duties of your-*m*.

MIRACLES (MIRACULOUS)
1Ch 16:12 his-*m*, and the judgments he
Ps 77:14 You are the God who performs-*m*;
Mt 11:20 most of his-*m* had been performed,
11:21 If the-*m* that were performed
24:24 and perform great signs and-*m*
Mk 6:2 does-*m*! Isn't this the carpenter?
Jn 10:32 "I have shown you many great-*m*
14:11 the evidence of the-*m* themselves.
Ac 2:22 accredited by God to you by-*m*,
19:11 God did extraordinary-*m*
1Co 12:28 third teachers, then workers of-*m*,
Heb 2:4 it by signs, wonders and various-*m*,

MIRACULOUS (MIRACLES)
Jn 3:2 could perform the-*m* signs you are
9:16 "How can a sinner do such-*m* signs
20:30 Jesus did many other-*m* signs
1Co 1:22 Jews demand-*m* signs and Greeks

MIRE
Ps 40:2 out of the mud and-*m*;
Isa 57:20 whose waves cast up-*m* and mud.

MIRIAM
Sister of Moses and Aaron (Nu 26:59). Led
dancing at Red Sea (Ex 15:20-21). Struck with
leprosy for criticizing Moses (Nu 12). Death
(Nu 20:1).

MIRROR
Jas 1:23 a man who looks at his face in a-*m*

MISERY
Ex 3:7 "I have indeed seen the-*m*
Jdg 10:16 he could bear Israel's-*m* no longer.
Hos 5:15 in their-*m* they will earnestly seek
Ro 3:16 ruin and-*m* mark their ways,
Jas 5:1 of the-*m* that is coming upon you.

MISLED
1Co 15:33 Do not be-*m*: "Bad company

MISS
Pr 19:2 nor to be hasty and-*m* the way.

MIST
Hos 6:4 Your love is like the morning-*m*,
Jas 4:14 You are a-*m* that appears for a little

MISUSE*
Ex 20:7 "You shall not-*m* the name
Dt 5:11 "You shall not-*m* the name
Ps 139:20 your adversaries-*m* your name.

MOCK (MOCKED MOCKER MOCKERS MOCKING)
Ps 22:7 All who see me-*m* me;
Pr 14:9 Fools-*m* at making amends for sin,
Mk 10:34 who will-*m* him and spit on him,

MOCKED (MOCK)
Mt 27:29 knelt in front of him and-*m* him.
27:41 of the law and the elders-*m* him.
Gal 6:7 not be deceived: God cannot be-*m*.

MOCKER (MOCK)
Pr 9:7 corrects a-*m* invites insult;
9:12 if you are a-*m*, you alone will suffer
20:1 Wine is a-*m* and beer a brawler;
22:10 Drive out the-*m*, and out goes strife

MOCKERS (MOCK)
Ps 1:1 or sit in the seat of-*m*.

MOCKING (MOCK)
Isa 50:6 face from-*m* and spitting.

MODEL*
Eze 28:12 " 'You were the-*m* of perfection,
1Th 1:7 And so you became a-*m*
2Th 3:9 to make ourselves a-*m* for you

MOMENT
Job 20:5 the joy of the godless lasts but a-*m*.
Ps 30:5 For his anger lasts only a-*m*,
Isa 66:8 or a nation be brought forth in a-*m*?
Gal 2:5 We did not give in to them for a-*m*,

MONEY
Ecc 5:10 Whoever loves-*m* never has-*m*
Isa 55:1 and you who have no-*m*,
Mt 6:24 You cannot serve both God and-*M*.
Lk 9:3 no bread, no-*m*, no extra tunic.
1Co 16:2 set aside a sum of-*m* in keeping
1Ti 3:3 not quarrelsome, not a lover of-*m*,
6:10 For the love of-*m* is a root
2Ti 3:2 lovers of-*m*, boastful, proud,
Heb 13:5 free from the love of-*m*
1Pe 5:2 not greedy for-*m*, but eager to serve

MOON
Ps 121:6 nor the-*m* by night.
Joel 2:31 and the-*m* to blood
1Co 15:41 *m* another and the stars another;

MORNING
Ge 1:5 and there was-*m*— the first day.
Dt 28:67 In the-*m* you will say, "If only it
Ps 5:3 In the-*m*, O Lord,
2Pe 1:19 and the-*m* star rises in your hearts.
Rev 22:16 of David, and the bright-*M* Star."

MORTAL
1Co 15:53 and the-*m* with immortality.

MOSES

Levite; brother of Aaron (Ex 6:20; 1Ch 6:3). Put in basket into Nile; discovered and raised by Pharaoh's daughter (Ex 2:1-10). Fled to Midian after killing Egyptian (Ex 2:11-15). Married to Zipporah, fathered Gershom (Ex 2:16-22).

Called by the Lord to deliver Israel (Ex 3-4). Pharaoh's resistance (Ex 5). Ten plagues (Ex 7-11). Passover and Exodus (Ex 12-13). Led Israel through Red Sea (Ex 14). Song of deliverance (Ex 15:1-21). Brought water from rock (Ex 17:1-7). Raised hands to defeat Amalekites (Ex 17:8-16). Delegated judges (Ex 18; Dt 1:9-18).

Received Law at Sinai (Ex 19-23; 25-31; Jn 1:17). Announced Law to Israel (Ex 19:7-8; 24; 35). Broke tablets because of golden calf (Ex 32; Dt 9). Saw glory of the Lord (Ex 33-34). Supervised building of tabernacle (Ex 36-40). Set apart Aaron and priests (Lev 8-9). Numbered tribes (Nu 1-4; 26). Opposed by Aaron and Miriam (Nu 12). Sent spies into Canaan (Nu 13). Announced forty years of wandering for failure to enter land (Nu 14). Opposed by Korah (Nu 16). Forbidden to enter land for striking rock (Nu 20:1-13; Dt 1:37). Lifted bronze snake for healing (Nu 21:4-9; Jn 3:14). Final address to Israel (Dt 1-33). Succeeded by Joshua (Nu 27:12-23; Dt 34). Death (Dt 34:5-12).

"Law of Moses" (1Ki 2:3; Ezr 3:2; Mk 12:26; Lk 24:44). "Book of Moses" (2Ch 25:12; Ne 13:1). "Song of Moses" (Ex 15:1-21; Rev 15:3). "Prayer of Moses" (Ps 90).

MOTH
Mt 6:19 where-*m* and rust destroy,

MOTHER (MOTHER'S)
Ge 2:24 and-*m* and be united to his wife,
    3:20 because she would become the-*m*
Ex 20:12 "Honor your father and your-*m*,
Lev 20:9 " 'If anyone curses his father or-*m*,
Dt 5:16 "Honor your father and your-*m*,
    21:18 who does not obey his father and-*m*
    27:16 who dishonors his father or his-*m*."
1Sa 2:19 Each year his-*m* made him a little
Ps 113:9 as a happy-*m* of children.
Pr 23:25 May your father and-*m* be glad;
    29:15 child left to himself disgraces his-*m*.
    31:1 an oracle his-*m* taught him:
Isa 49:15 "Can a-*m* forget the baby
    66:13 As a-*m* comforts her child,
Mt 10:37 or-*m* more than me is not worthy
    15:4 'Honor your father and-*m*'
    19:5 and-*m* and be united to his wife,
Mk 7:10 'Honor your father and your-*m*,'
    10:19 honor your father and-*m*.' "
Jn 19:27 to the disciple, "Here is your-*m*."

MOTHER'S (MOTHER)
Job 1:21 "Naked I came from my-*m* womb,
Pr 1:8 and do not forsake your-*m* teaching

MOTIVES*
Pr 16:2 but-*m* are weighed by the Lord.
1Co 4:5 will expose the-*m* of men's hearts.
Php 1:18 whether from false-*m* or true,
1Th 2:3 spring from error or impure-*m*,
Jas 4:3 because you ask with wrong-*m*,

MOUNTAIN (MOUNTAINS)
Mic 4:2 let us go up to the-*m* of the Lord,
Mt 17:20 say to this-*m*, 'Move from here

MOUNTAINS (MOUNTAIN)
Isa 52:7 How beautiful on the-*m*
    55:12 the-*m* and hills
1Co 13:2 if I have a faith that can move-*m*,

MOURN (MOURNING)
Ecc 3:4 a time to-*m* and a time to dance,
Isa 61:2 to comfort all who-*m*,
    57:4 Blessed are those who-*m*,
Ro 12:15 *m* with those who-*m*.

MOURNING (MOURN)
Jer 31:13 I will turn their-*m* into gladness;
Rev 21:4 There will be no more death or-*m*

MOUTH
Jos 1:8 of the Law depart from your-*m*;
Ps 19:14 May the words of my-*m*
    40:3 He put a new song in my-*m*,
    119:103 sweeter than honey to my-*m*!
Pr 16:23 A wise man's heart guides his-*m*,
    27:2 praise you, and not your own-*m*;
Isa 51:16 I have put my words in your-*m*
Mt 12:34 overflow of the heart the-*m* speaks.
    15:11 into a man's-*m* does not make him
Ro 10:9 That if you confess with your-*m*,

MUD
Ps 40:2 out of the-*m* and mire;
Isa 57:20 whose waves cast up mire and-*m*.
2Pe 2:22 back to her wallowing in the-*m*."

MULTITUDE (MULTITUDES)
Isa 31:1 who trust in the-*m* of their chariots
1Pe 4:8 love covers over a-*m* of sins.
Rev 7:9 me was a great-*m* that no one could

MULTITUDES (MULTITUDE)
Joel 3:14 *M*,-*m* in the valley of decision!

MURDER (MURDERER MURDERERS)
Ex 20:13 "You shall not-*m*.
Mt 15:19 *m*, adultery, sexual immorality,
Ro 13:9 "Do not-*m*," "Do not steal,"
Jas 2:11 adultery," also said, "Do not-*m*."

MURDERER (MURDER)
Nu 35:16 he is a-*m*; the-*m* shall be put
Jn 8:44 He was a-*m* from the beginning,
1Jn 3:15 who hates his brother is a-*m*,

MURDERERS (MURDER)
1Ti 1:9 for-*m*, for adulterers and perverts,
Rev 21:8 the-*m*, the sexually immoral,

MUSIC
Jdg 5:3 I will make-*m* to the Lord,
Ps 27:6 and make-*m* to the Lord.
    95:2 and extol him with-*m* and song.
    98:4 burst into jubilant song with-*m*;
    108:1 make-*m* with all my soul.
Eph 5:19 make-*m* in your heart to the Lord,

MUSTARD
Mt 13:31 kingdom of heaven is like a-*m* seed,
    17:20 you have faith as small as a-*m* seed,

MUZZLE
Dt 25:4 Do not-*m* an ox while it is treading
Ps 39:1 I will put a-*m* on my mouth
1Co 9:9 "Do not-*m* an ox while it is

MYRRH
Mt 2:11 of gold and of incense and of-*m*.
Mk 15:23 offered him wine mixed with-*m*,

MYSTERY
Ro 16:25 to the revelation of the-*m* hidden
1Co 15:51 I tell you a-*m*: We will not all sleep,
Eph 5:32 This is a profound-*m*—
Col 1:26 the-*m* that has been kept hidden
1Ti 3:16 the-*m* of godliness is great:

MYTHS
1Ti 4:7 Have nothing to do with godless-*m*

NADAB
Son of Jeroboam I; king of Israel (1Ki 15:25-32).

NAIL* (NAILING)
Jn 20:25 "Unless I see the-*n* marks

NAILING* (NAIL)
Ac 2:23 him to death by-*n* him to the cross.
Col 2:14 he took it away,-*n* it to the cross.

NAKED
Ge 2:25 The man and his wife were both-*n*,
Job 1:21 *N*I came from my mother's womb,
Isa 58:7 when you see the-*n*, to clothe him,
2Co 5:3 are clothed, we will not be found-*n*.

NAME
Ex 3:15 This is my-*n* forever, the-*n*
    20:7 "You shall not misuse the-*n*
Dt 5:11 "You shall not misuse the-*n*
    28:58 this glorious and awesome-*n*—
1Ki 5:5 will build the temple for my-*N*.'
2Ch 7:14 my people, who are called by my-*n*,
Ps 34:3 let us exalt his-*n* together.
    103:1 my inmost being, praise his holy-*n*,
    147:4 and calls them each by-*n*.
Pr 22:1 A good-*n* is more desirable
    30:4 What is his-*n*, and the-*n* of his son?
Isa 40:26 and calls them each by-*n*.
    57:15 who lives forever, whose-*n* is holy:
Jer 14:7 do something for the sake of your-*n*,
Da 12:1 everyone whose-*n* is found written
Joel 2:32 on the-*n* of the Lord will be saved
Zec 14:9 one Lord, and his-*n* the only-*n*.
Mt 1:21 and you are to give him the-*n* Jesus,
    6:9 hallowed be your-*n*,
    18:20 or three come together in my-*n*,
Jn 10:3 he calls his own sheep by-*n*
    16:24 asked for anything in my-*n*.
Ac 4:12 for there is no other-*n*
Ro 10:13 "Everyone who calls on the-*n*
Php 2:9 him the-*n* that is above every-*n*,
Col 3:17 do it all in the-*n* of the Lord Jesus,
Heb 1:4 as the-*n* he has inherited is superior
Rev 20:15 If anyone's-*n* was not found written

NAOMI
Mother-in-law of Ruth (Ru 1). Advised Ruth to seek marriage with Boaz (Ru 2-4).

NARROW
Mt 7:13 "Enter through the-*n* gate.

NATHANAEL
Apostle (Jn 1:45-49; 21:2). Probably also called Bartholomew (Mt 10:3).

NATION (NATIONS)
Ge 12:2 "I will make you into a great-*n*
Ps 33:12 Blessed is the-*n* whose God is
Pr 14:34 Righteousness exalts a-*n*,
Isa 65:1 To a-*n* that did not call on my name
1Pe 2:9 a royal priesthood, a holy-*n*,
Rev 7:9 from every-*n*, tribe, people

NATIONS (NATION)
Ge 17:4 You will be the father of many-*n*.
    18:18 and all-*n* on earth will be blessed
Ex 19:5 of all-*n* you will be my treasured
Ne 1:8 I will scatter you among the-*n*,
Ps 96:3 Declare his glory among the-*n*,
Isa 40:15 Surely the-*n* are like a drop
Eze 36:23 *n* will know that I am the Lord,
Hag 2:7 and the desired of all-*n* will come,
Zec 8:23 *n* will take firm hold of one Jew
    14:2 I will gather all the-*n* to Jerusalem
Mt 28:19 and make disciples of all-*n*,
Rev 21:24 The-*n* will walk by its light,

NATURAL (NATURE)
Ro 6:19 you are weak in your-*n* selves.
1Co 15:44 If there is a-*n* body, there is

NATURE (NATURAL)
Ro 8:4 do not live according to the sinful-*n*
    8:8 by the sinful-*n* cannot please God.

NATURE (continued)
Gal 5:19 The acts of the sinful-*n* are obvious:
    5:24 Jesus have crucified the sinful-*n*
Php 2:6 Who, being in very-*n* God,

NAZARENE
Mt 2:23 prophets: "He will be called a-*N*."

NAZIRITE
Jdg 13:7 because the boy will be a-*N* of God

NECESSARY
Ro 13:5 it is-*n* to submit to the authorities,

NEED (NEEDS NEEDY)
Ps 116:6 when I was in great-*n*, he saved me.
Mt 6:8 for your Father knows what you-*n*
Ro 12:13 with God's people who are in-*n*.
1Co 12:21 say to the hand, "I don't-*n* you!"
1Jn 3:17 sees his brother in-*n* but has no pity

NEEDLE
Mt 19:24 go through the eye of a-*n*

NEEDS (NEED)
Isa 58:11 he will satisfy your-*n*
Php 4:19 God will meet all your-*n* according

NEEDY (NEED)
Pr 14:21 blessed is he who is kind to the-*n*.
    14:31 to the-*n* honors God.
    31:20 and extends her hands to the-*n*.
Mt 6:2 "So when you give to the-*n*,

NEGLECT (NEGLECTED)
Ne 10:39 We will not-*n* the house of our God
Ps 119:16 I will not-*n* your word.
Ac 6:2 for us to-*n* the ministry of the word
1Ti 4:14 Do not-*n* your gift, which was

NEGLECTED (NEGLECT)
Mt 23:23 But you have-*n* the more important

NEHEMIAH
Cupbearer of Artaxerxes (Ne 2:1); governor of Israel (Ne 8:9). Returned to Jerusalem to rebuild walls (Ne 2-6). With Ezra, reestablished worship (Ne 8). Prayer confessing nation's sin (Ne 9). Dedicated wall (Ne 12).

NEIGHBOR (NEIGHBOR'S)
Ex 20:16 give false testimony against your-*n*.
Lev 19:13 Do not defraud your-*n* or rob him.
    19:18 but love your-*n* as yourself.
Pr 27:10 better a-*n* nearby than a brother far
Mt 19:19 and 'love your-*n* as yourself.' "
Lk 10:29 who is my-*n*?" In reply Jesus said:
Ro 13:10 Love does no harm to its-*n*.

NEIGHBOR'S (NEIGHBOR)
Ex 20:17 You shall not covet your-*n* wife,
Dt 5:21 not set your desire on your-*n* house
    19:14 not move your-*n* boundary stone
Pr 25:17 Seldom set foot in your-*n* house—

NEW
Ps 40:3 He put a-*n* song in my mouth,
Ecc 1:9 there is nothing-*n* under the sun.
Isa 65:17 *n* heavens and a-*n* earth.
Jer 31:31 "when I will make a-*n* covenant
Eze 36:26 give you a-*n* heart and put a-*n* spirit
Mt 9:17 Neither do men pour-*n* wine
Lk 22:20 "This cup is the-*n* covenant
2Co 5:17 he is a-*n* creation; the old has gone,
Eph 4:24 and to put on the-*n* self, created
2Pe 3:13 to a-*n* heaven and a-*n* earth,
1Jn 2:8 Yet I am writing you a-*n* command;

NEWBORN (BEAR)
1Pe 2:2 Like-*n* babies, crave pure spiritual

NEWS
Isa 52:7 the feet of those who bring good-*n*,
Mk 1:15 Repent and believe the good-*n*!"
    16:15 preach the good-*n* to all creation.
Lk 2:10 I bring you good-*n*
Ac 5:42 proclaiming the good-*n* that Jesus

17:18 preaching the good-*n* about Jesus
Ro 10:15 feet of those who bring good-*n*!"

NICODEMUS*
Pharisee who visited Jesus at night (Jn 3).
Argued fair treatment of Jesus (Jn 7:50-52). With
Joseph, prepared Jesus for burial (Jn 19:38-42).

NIGHT
Job 35:10 who gives songs in the-*n*,
Ps 1:2 on his law he meditates day and-*n*,
91:5 You will not fear the terror of-*n*,
Jn 3:2 He came to Jesus at-*n* and said,
1Th 5:2 Lord will come like a thief in the-*n*.
5:5 We do not belong to the-*n*.
Rev 21:25 for there will be no-*n* there.

NOAH
Righteous man (Eze 14:14, 20) called to
build ark (Ge 6-8; Heb 11:7; 1Pe 3:20; 2Pe 2:5).
God's covenant with (Ge 9:1-17). Drunkenness
of (Ge 9:18-23). Blessed sons, cursed Canaan
(Ge 9:24-27).

NOBLE
Ru 3:11 you are a woman of-*n* character.
Ps 45:1 My heart is stirred by a-*n* theme
Pr 12:4 of-*n* character is her husband's
31:10 A wife of-*n* character who can find?
31:29 "Many women do-*n* things,
Isa 32:8 But the-*n* man makes-*n* plans,
Lk 8:15 good soil stands for those with a-*n*
Ro 9:21 of clay some pottery for-*n* purposes
Php 4:8 whatever is-*n*, whatever is right,
2Ti 2:20 some are for-*n* purposes

NOTHING
Ne 9:21 in the desert; they lacked-*n*,
Jer 32:17 *N* is too hard for you
Jn 15:5 apart from me you can do-*n*.

NULLIFY
Ro 3:31 Do we, then,-*n* the law by this faith

OATH
Dt 7:8 and kept the-*o* he swore

OBEDIENCE (OBEY)
2Ch 31:21 in-*o* to the law and the commands,
Pr 30:17 that scorns-*o* to a mother,
Ro 1:5 to the-*o* that comes from faith.
6:16 to-*o*, which leads to righteousness?
2Jn :6 that we walk in-*o* to his commands.

OBEDIENT (OBEY)
Lk 2:51 with them and was-*o* to them.
Php 2:8 and became-*o* to death—
1Pe 1:14 As-*o* children, do not conform

OBEY (OBEDIENCE OBEDIENT OBEYED)
Ex 12:24 "*O* these instructions as a lasting
Dt 6:3 careful to-*o* so that it may go well
13:4 Keep his commands and-*o* him;
21:18 son who does not-*o* his father
30:2 and-*o* him with all your heart
32:46 children to-*o* carefully all the words
1Sa 15:22 To-*o* is better than sacrifice,
Ps 119:34 and-*o* it with all my heart.
Mt 28:20 to-*o* everything I have commanded
Jn 14:23 loves me, he will-*o* my teaching.
Ac 5:29 "We must-*o* God rather than men!
Ro 6:16 slaves to the one whom you-*o*—
Gal 5:3 obligated to-*o* the whole law.
Eph 6:1 *o* your parents in the Lord,
6:5 *o* your earthly masters with respect
Col 3:20 *o* your parents in everything,
1Ti 3:4 and see that his children-*o* him
Heb 13:17 *O* your leaders and submit
1Jn 5:3 love for God: to-*o* his commands.

OBEYED (OBEY)
Ps 119:4 that are to be fully-*o*.

Jnh 3:3 Jonah-*o* the word of the Lord
Jn 17:6 and they have-*o* your word.
Ro 6:17 you wholeheartedly-*o* the form
Heb 11:8 *o* and went, even though he did not
1Pe 3:6 who-*o* Abraham and called her

OBLIGATED
Ro 1:14 I am-*o* both to Greeks
Gal 5:3 himself be circumcised that he is-*o*

OBSCENITY
Eph 5:4 Nor should there be-*o*, foolish talk

OBSOLETE
Heb 8:13 he has made the first one-*o*;

OBTAINED
Ro 9:30 not pursue righteousness, have-*o* it,
Php 3:12 Not that I have already-*o* all this,
Heb 9:12 having-*o* eternal redemption.

OFFENDED (OFFENSE)
Pr 18:19 An-*o* brother is more unyielding

OFFENSE (OFFENDED OFFENSIVE)
Pr 17:9 over an-*o* promotes love,
19:11 it is to his glory to overlook an-*o*.

OFFENSIVE (OFFENSE)
Ps 139:24 See if there is any-*o* way in me,

OFFER (OFFERED OFFERING OFFERINGS)
Ro 12:1 to-*o* your bodies as living sacrifices,
Heb 13:15 therefore, let us continually-*o*

OFFERED (OFFER)
Heb 7:27 once for all when he-*o* himself.
11:4 By faith Abel-*o* God a better

OFFERING (OFFER)
Ge 22:8 provide the lamb for the burnt-*o*,
Ps 40:6 Sacrifice and-*o* you did not desire,
Isa 53:10 the Lord makes his life a guilt-*o*,
Mt 5:23 if you are-*o* your gift at the altar
Eph 5:2 as a fragrant-*o* and sacrifice to God.
Heb 10:5 "Sacrifice and-*o* you did not desire,

OFFERINGS (OFFER)
Mal 3:8 do we rob you?' "In tithes and-*o*.
Mk 12:33 is more important than all burnt-*o*

OFFICER
2Ti 2:4 wants to please his commanding-*o*.

OFFSPRING
Ge 3:15 and between your-*o* and hers;
17:8 "To your-*o* I will give this land."

OIL
Ps 23:5 You anoint my head with-*o*;
Isa 61:3 the-*o* of gladness
Heb 1:9 by anointing you with the-*o* of joy."

OLIVE (OLIVES)
Zec 4:3 Also there are two-*o* trees by it,
Ro 11:17 and you, though a wild-*o* shoot,
Rev 11:4 These are the two-*o* trees

OLIVES (OLIVE)
Jas 3:12 a fig tree bear-*o*, or a grapevine bear

OMEGA
Rev 1:8 "I am the Alpha and the-*O*,"

OMRI
King of Israel (1Ki 16:21-26).

OPINIONS*
1Ki 18:21 will you waver between two-*o*?
Pr 18:2 but delights in airing his own-*o*.

OPPORTUNITY
Ro 7:11 seizing the-*o* afforded
Gal 6:10 as we have-*o*, let us do good
Eph 5:16 making the most of every-*o*,
Col 4:5 make the most of every-*o*,
1Ti 5:14 to give the enemy no-*o* for slander.

OPPOSES
Jas 4:6 "God-*o* the proud
1Pe 5:5 because, "God-*o* the proud

OPPRESS (OPPRESSED)
Ex 22:21 "Do not mistreat an alien or-*o* him,
Zec 7:10 Do not-*o* the widow

OPPRESSED (OPPRESS)
Ps 9:9 The Lord is a refuge for the-*o*,
Isa 53:7 He was-*o* and afflicted,
Zec 10:2 *o* for lack of a shepherd.

ORDAINED
Ps 8:2 you have-*o* praise

ORDERLY
1Co 14:40 done in a fitting and-*o* way.
Col 2:5 and delight to see how-*o* you are

ORGIES*
Ro 13:13 not in-*o* and drunkenness,
Gal 5:21 drunkenness,-*o*, and the like.
1Pe 4:3 *o*, carousing and detestable

ORIGIN
2Pe 1:21 For prophecy never had its-*o*

ORPHANS
Jn 14:18 will not leave you as-*o*; I will come
Jas 1:27 to look after-*o* and widows

OUTCOME
Heb 13:7 Consider the-*o* of their way of life
1Pe 4:17 what will the-*o* be for those who do

OUTSIDERS*
Col 4:5 wise in the way you act toward-*o*,
1Th 4:12 daily life may win the respect of-*o*
1Ti 3:7 also have a good reputation with-*o*,

OUTSTANDING
SS 5:10 *o* among ten thousand.
Ro 13:8 no debt remain-*o*,

OUTSTRETCHED
Ex 6:6 and will redeem you with an-*o* arm
Jer 27:5 and-*o* arm I made the earth
Eze 20:33 an-*o* arm and with outpoured wrath

OUTWEIGHS
2Co 4:17 an eternal glory that far-*o* them all.

OVERCOME (OVERCOMES)
Mt 16:18 and the gates of Hades will not-*o* it.
Mk 9:24 I do believe; help me-*o* my unbelief
Jn 16:33 But take heart! I have-*o* the world."
Ro 12:21 Do not be-*o* by evil, but-*o* evil
1Jn 5:4 is the victory that has-*o* the world,
Rev 17:14 but the Lamb will-*o* them

OVERCOMES (OVERCOME)
1Jn 5:4 born of God-*o* the world.
5:5 Who is it that-*o* the world?
Rev 2:7 To him who-*o*, I will give the right
2:11 He who-*o* will not be hurt at all
2:17 To him who-*o*, I will give some
2:26 To him who-*o* and does my will
3:5 He who-*o*, like them, be
3:12 Him who-*o* I will make a pillar
3:21 To him who-*o*, I will give the right
21:7 He who-*o* will inherit all this,

OVERFLOW (OVERFLOWS)
Ps 119:171 May my lips-*o* with praise,
Lk 6:45 out of the-*o* of his heart his mouth
Ro 15:13 so that you may-*o* with hope
2Co 4:15 to-*o* to the glory of God.
1Th 3:12 *o* for each other and for everyone

OVERFLOWS* (OVERFLOW)
Ps 23:5 my cup-*o*.
2Co 1:5 also through Christ our comfort-*o*.

OVERJOYED* (JOY)
Da 6:23 The king was-*o* and gave orders
Mt 2:10 they saw the star, they were-*o*.

Jn 20:20 The disciples were-*o*
Ac 12:14 she was so-*o* she ran back
1Pe 4:13 so that you may be-*o*

OVERSEER (OVERSEERS)
1Ti 3:1 anyone sets his heart on being an-*o*,
3:2 Now the-*o* must be above reproach,
Tit 1:7 Since an-*o* is entrusted

OVERSEERS* (OVERSEER)
Ac 20:28 the Holy Spirit has made you-*o*.
Php 1:1 together with the-*o* and deacons:
1Pe 5:2 as-*o*—not because you must,

OVERWHELMED
Ps 38:4 My guilt has-*o* me
65:3 When we were-*o* by sins,
Mt 26:38 "My soul is-*o* with sorrow
Mk 7:37 People were-*o* with amazement.

OWE
Ro 13:7 If you-*o* taxes, pay taxes; if revenue
Phm :19 to mention that you-*o* me your very

OX
Dt 25:4 Do not muzzle an-*o*
Isa 11:7 and the lion will eat straw like the-*o*
1Co 9:9 "Do not muzzle an-*o*

PAGANS
Mt 5:47 Do not even-*p* do that? Be perfect,
1Pe 2:12 such good lives among the-*p* that,

PAIN (PAINFUL)
Ge 3:16 with-*p* you will give birth
Job 33:19 may be chastened on a bed of-*p*
Jn 16:21 woman giving birth to a child has-*p*

PAINFUL (PAIN)
Ge 3:17 through-*p* toil you will eat of it
Heb 12:11 seems pleasant at the time, but-*p*.
1Pe 4:12 at the-*p* trial you are suffering,

PALMS
Isa 49:16 you on the-*p* of my hands;

PANTS
Ps 42:1 As the deer-*p* for streams of water,

PARADISE*
Lk 23:43 today you will be with me in-*p*."
2Co 12:4 God knows—was caught up to-*p*.
Rev 2:7 of life, which is in the-*p* of God.

PARALYTIC
Mk 2:3 bringing to him a-*p*, carried by four

PARDON (PARDONS)
Isa 55:7 and to our God, for he will freely-*p*.

PARDONS* (PARDON)
Mic 7:18 who-*p* sin and forgives

PARENTS
Pr 17:6 and-*p* are the pride of their children
Lk 18:29 left home or wife or brothers or-*p*
21:16 You will be betrayed even by-*p*,
Ro 1:30 they disobey their-*p*; they are
2Co 12:14 for their-*p*, but-*p* for their children.
Eph 6:1 Children, obey your-*p* in the Lord,
Col 3:20 obey your-*p* in everything,
2Ti 3:2 disobedient to their-*p*, ungrateful,

PARTIALITY
Dt 10:17 who shows no-*p* and accepts no
2Ch 19:7 our God there is no injustice or-*p*
Lk 20:21 and that you do not show-*p*

PARTICIPATION
1Co 10:16 is not the bread that we break a-*p*

PASS
Ex 12:13 and when I see the blood, I will-*p*
La 1:12 to you, all you who-*p* by?
Lk 21:33 Heaven and earth will-*p* away,
1Co 13:8 there is knowledge, it will-*p* away.

PASSION (PASSIONS)
1Co 7: 9 better to marry than to burn with-*p*.

PASSIONS (PASSION)
Gal 5:24 crucified the sinful nature with its-*p*,
Tit 2:12 to ungodliness and worldly-*p*,

PASSOVER
Ex 12:11 Eat it in haste; it is the LORD's-*P*.
Dt 16: 1 celebrate the-*P* of the LORD your
1Co 5: 7 our-*P* lamb, has been sacrificed.

PAST
Isa 43:18 do not dwell on the-*p*.
Ro 15: 4 in the-*p* was written to teach us,
Heb 1: 1 In the-*p* God spoke

PASTORS*
Eph 4:11 and some to be-*p* and teachers,

PASTURE (PASTURES)
Ps 37: 3 dwell in the land and enjoy safe-*p*.
100: 3 we are his people, the sheep of his-*p*
Jer 50: 7 against the LORD, their true-*p*,
Eze 34:13 I will-*p* them on the mountains
Jn 10: 9 come in and go out, and find-*p*.

PASTURES (PASTURE)
Ps 23: 2 He makes me lie down in green-*p*,

PATCH
Mt 9:16 No one sews a-*p* of unshrunk cloth

PATH (PATHS)
Ps 27:11 lead me in a straight-*p*,
119:105 and a light for my-*p*.
Pr 15:19 the-*p* of the upright is a highway.
15:24 The-*p* of life leads upward
Isa 26: 7 The-*p* of the righteous is level;
Lk 1:79 to guide our feet into the-*p* of peace
2Co 6: 3 no stumbling block in anyone's-*p*,

PATHS (PATH)
Ps 23: 3 He guides me in-*p* of righteousness
25: 4 teach me your-*p*,
Pr 3: 6 and he will make your-*p* straight.
Ro 11:33 and his-*p* beyond tracing out!
Heb 12:13 "Make level-*p* for your feet,"

PATIENCE (PATIENT)
Pr 19:11 A man's wisdom gives him-*p*;
2Co 6: 6 understanding,-*p* and kindness;
Gal 5:22 joy, peace,-*p*, kindness, goodness,
Col 1:11 may have great endurance and-*p*,
3:12 humility, gentleness and-*p*.

PATIENT (PATIENCE PATIENTLY)
Pr 15:18 but a-*p* man calms a quarrel.
Ro 12:12 Be joyful in hope,-*p* in affliction,
1Co 13: 4 Love is-*p*, love is kind.
Eph 4: 2 humble and gentle; be-*p*,
1Th 5:14 help the weak, be-*p* with everyone.

PATIENTLY (PATIENT)
Ps 40: 1 I waited-*p* for the LORD;
Ro 8:25 we do not yet have, we wait for it-*p*.

PATTERN
Ro 5:14 who was a-*p* of the one to come.
12: 2 longer to the-*p* of this world,
2Ti 1:13 keep as the-*p* of sound teaching,

PAUL
Also called Saul (Ac 13:9). Pharisee from Tarsus (Ac 9:11; Php 3:5). Apostle (Gal 1). At stoning of Stephen (Ac 8:1). Persecuted Church (Ac 9:1-2; Gal 1:13). Vision of Jesus on road to Damascus (Ac 9:4-9; 26:12-18). In Arabia (Gal 1:17). Preached in Damascus; escaped death through the wall in a basket (Ac 9:19-25). In Jerusalem; sent back to Tarsus (Ac 9:26-30).
Brought to Antioch by Barnabas (Ac 11:22-26). First missionary journey to Cyprus and Galatia (Ac 13-14). Stoned at Lystra (Ac 14:19-20). At Jerusalem council (Ac 15). Split with Barnabas over Mark (Ac 15:36-41).
Second missionary journey with Silas (Ac 16-20). Called to Macedonia (Ac 16:6-10). Freed from prison in Philippi (Ac 16:16-40). In Thessalonica (Ac 17:1-9). Speech in Athens (Ac 17:16-33). In Corinth (Ac 18). In Ephesus (Ac 19). Return to Jerusalem (Ac 20). Farewell to Ephesian elders (Ac 20:13-38). Arrival in Jerusalem (Ac 21:1-26). Arrested (Ac 21:27-36). Addressed crowds (Ac 22), Sanhedrin (Ac 23:1-11). Transferred to Caesarea (Ac 23:12-35). Trial before Felix (Ac 24), Festus (Ac 25:1-12). Before Agrippa (Ac 25:13-26:32). Voyage to Rome; shipwreck (Ac 27). Arrival in Rome (Ac 28).

PAY (REPAID REPAY)
Lev 26:43 They will-*p* for their sins
Pr 22:17 *P* attention and listen
Mt 22:17 Is it right to-*p* taxes to Caesar
Ro 13: 6 This is also why you-*p* taxes,
2Pe 1:19 you will do well to-*p* attention to it,

PEACE (PEACEMAKERS)
Nu 6:26 and give you-*p*." '
Ps 34:14 seek-*p* and pursue it.
85:10 righteousness and-*p* kiss each other
119:165 Great-*p* have they who love your
122: 6 Pray for the-*p* of Jerusalem:
Pr 14:30 A heart at-*p* gives life to the body,
17: 1 Better a dry crust with-*p* and quiet
Isa 9: 6 Everlasting Father, Prince of-*P*.
26: 3 You will keep in perfect-*p*
48:22 "There is no-*p*," says the LORD,
Zec 9:10 He will proclaim-*p* to the nations.
Mt 10:34 I did not come to bring-*p*,
Lk 2:14 on earth-*p* to men on whom his
Jn 14:27 *P* I leave with you; my-*p*
16:33 so that in me you may have-*p*.
Ro 5: 1 we have-*p* with God
1Co 7:15 God has called us to live in-*p*.
14:33 a God of disorder but of-*p*,
Gal 5:22 joy,-*p*, patience, kindness,
Eph 2:14 he himself is our-*p*, who has made
Php 4: 7 the-*p* of God, which transcends all
Col 1:20 by making-*p* through his blood,
3:15 Let the-*p* of Christ rule
1Th 5: 3 While people are saying,- "*P*
2Th 3:16 the Lord of-*p* himself give you-*p*
2Ti 2:22 righteousness, faith, love and-*p*,
1Pe 3:11 he must seek-*p* and pursue it.
Rev 6: 4 power to take-*p* from the earth

PEACEMAKERS* (PEACE)
Mt 5: 9 Blessed are the-*p*,
Jas 3:18 *P* who sow in peace raise a harvest

PEARL* (PEARLS)
Rev 21:21 each gate made of a single-*p*.

PEARLS (PEARL)
Mt 7: 6 do not throw your-*p* to pigs.
13:45 like a merchant looking for fine-*p*.
1Ti 2: 9 or gold or-*p* or expensive clothes,
Rev 21:21 The twelve gates were twelve-*p*,

PEKAH
King of Israel (2Ki 15:25-31; Isa 7:1).

PEKAHIAH*
Son of Menahem; king of Israel (2Ki 15:22-26).

PEN
Mt 5:18 letter, not the least stroke of a-*p*,

PENTECOST
Ac 2: 1 of-*P* came, they were all together

PEOPLE (PEOPLES)
Dt 32: 9 the LORD's portion is his-*p*,
Ru 1:16 Your-*p* will be my-*p*

2Ch 7:14 if my-*p*, who are called
Jer 24: 7 They will be my-*p*,
Zec 2:11 and will become my-*p*.
Lk 2:10 joy that will be for all the-*p*.
Ac 15:14 from the Gentiles a-*p*.
2Co 6:16 and they will be my-*p*."
1Pe 2: 9 you are a chosen-*p*,
Rev 21: 3 They will be his-*p*,

PEOPLES (PEOPLE)
Da 7:14 all-*p*, nations and men
Mic 4: 1 and-*p* will stream to it.

PERCEIVING
Isa 6: 9 be ever seeing, but never-*p*.'

PERFECT (PERFECTER PERFECTION)
SS 6: 9 but my dove, my-*p* one, is unique,
Isa 26: 3 You will keep in-*p* peace
Mt 5:48 as your heavenly Father is-*p*.
Ro 12: 2 his good, pleasing and-*p* will.
2Co 12: 9 for my power is made-*p*
Col 1:28 so that we may present everyone-*p*
3:14 binds them all together in-*p* unity.
Heb 9:11 and more-*p* tabernacle that is not
10:14 he has made-*p* forever those who
Jas 1:17 Every good and-*p* gift is from above
1:25 into the-*p* law that gives freedom,
3: 2 he is a-*p* man, able
1Jn 4:18 But-*p* love drives out fear,

PERFECTER* (PERFECT)
Heb 12: 2 the author and-*p* of our faith,

PERFECTION (PERFECT)
Ps 119:96 To all-*p* I see a limit;
2Co 13:11 Aim for-*p*, listen to my appeal,
Heb 7:11 If-*p* could have been attained

PERFORMS
Ps 77:14 You are the God who-*p* miracles;

PERISH (PERISHABLE)
Ps 1: 6 but the way of the wicked will-*p*.
102:26 They will-*p*, but you remain;
Lk 13: 3 unless you repent, you too will all-*p*
Jn 10:28 eternal life, and they shall never-*p*;
Col 2:22 These are all destined to-*p* with use,
Heb 1:11 They will-*p*, but you remain;
2Pe 3: 9 not wanting anyone to-*p*,

PERISHABLE (PERISH)
1Co 15:42 The body that is sown is-*p*,

PERJURERS
1Ti 1:10 for slave traders and liars and-*p*—

PERMISSIBLE (PERMIT)
1Co 10:23 "Everything is-*p*"—but not

PERMIT (PERMISSIBLE)
1Ti 2:12 I do not-*p* a woman to teach

PERSECUTE (PERSECUTED PERSECUTION)
Mt 5:11 *p* you and falsely say all kinds
Jn 15:20 they persecuted me, they will-*p* you
Ac 9: 4 why do you-*p* me?" "Who are you,
Ro 12:14 Bless those who-*p* you; bless

PERSECUTED (PERSECUTE)
1Co 4:12 when we are-*p*, we endure it;
2Ti 3:12 life in Christ Jesus will be-*p*,

PERSECUTION (PERSECUTE)
Ro 8:35 or hardship or-*p* or famine

PERSEVERANCE (PERSEVERE)
Ro 5: 3 we know that suffering produces-*p*;
5: 4 *p*, character; and character, hope.
Heb 12: 1 run with-*p* the race marked out
Jas 1: 3 the testing of your faith develops-*p*.
2Pe 1: 6 *p*; and to-*p*, godliness;

PERSEVERE* (PERSEVERANCE PERSEVERED PERSEVERES)
1Ti 4:16 *P* in them, because if you do,
Heb 10:36 You need to-*p* so that

PERSEVERED* (PERSEVERE)
Heb 11:27 he-*p* because he saw him who is
Jas 5:11 consider blessed those who have-*p*.
Rev 2: 3 You have-*p* and have endured

PERSEVERES* (PERSEVERE)
1Co 13: 7 trusts, always hopes, always-*p*.
Jas 1:12 Blessed is the man who-*p*

PERSUADE
2Co 5:11 is to fear the Lord, we try to-*p* men.

PERVERSION (PERVERT)
Lev 18:23 sexual relations with it; that is a-*p*.
Jude : 7 up to sexual immorality and-*p*.

PERVERT (PERVERSION PERVERTS)
Gal 1: 7 are trying to-*p* the gospel of Christ.

PERVERTS* (PERVERT)
1Ti 1:10 for murderers, for adulterers and-*p*,

PESTILENCE
Ps 91: 6 nor the-*p* that stalks in the darkness

PETER
Apostle, brother of Andrew, also called Simon (Mt 10:2; Mk 3:16; Lk 6:14; Ac 1:13), and Cephas (Jn 1:42). Confession of Christ (Mt 16:13-20; Mk 8:27-30; Lk 9:18-27). At transfiguration (Mt 17:1-8; Mk 9:2-8; Lk 9:28-36; 2Pe 1:16-18). Caught fish with coin (Mt 17:24-27). Denial of Jesus predicted (Mt 26:31-35; Mk 14:27-31; Lk 22:31-34; Jn 13:31-38). Denied Jesus (Mt 26:69-75; Mk 14:66-72; Lk 22:54-62; Jn 18:15-27). Commissioned by Jesus to shepherd his flock (Jn 21:15-23).
Speech at Pentecost (Ac 2). Healed beggar (Ac 3:1-10). Speech at temple (Ac 3:11-26), before Sanhedrin (Ac 4:1-22). In Samaria (Ac 8:14-25). Sent by vision to Cornelius (Ac 10). Announced salvation of Gentiles in Jerusalem (Ac 11; 15). Freed from prison (Ac 12). Inconsistency at Antioch (Gal 2:11-21). At Jerusalem Council (Ac 15).

PHARISEES
Mt 5:20 surpasses that of the-*P*

PHILIP
1. Apostle (Mt 10:3; Mk 3:18; Lk 6:14; Jn 1:43-48; 14:8; Ac 1:13).
2. Deacon (Ac 6:1-7); evangelist in Samaria (Ac 8:4-25), to Ethiopian (Ac 8:26-40).

PHILOSOPHY*
Col 2: 8 through hollow and deceptive-*p*,

PHYLACTERIES*
Mt 23: 5 They make their-*p* wide

PHYSICAL
1Ti 4: 8 For-*p* training is of some value,
Jas 2:16 but does nothing about his-*p* needs,

PIECES
Ge 15:17 and passed between the-*p*.
Jer 34:18 and then walked between its-*p*.

PIERCED
Ps 22:16 they have-*p* my hands and my feet.
Isa 53: 5 But he was-*p* for our transgressions,
Zec 12:10 look on me, the one they have-*p*,
Jn 19:37 look on the one they have-*p*."

PIGS
Mt 7: 6 do not throw your pearls to-*p*.

PILATE
Governor of Judea. Questioned Jesus (Mt 27:1-26; Mk 15:15; Lk 22:66-23:25; Jn 18:28-19:16); sent him to Herod (Lk 23:6-12); consented to

his crucifixion when crowds chose Barabbas
(Mt 27:15-26; Mk 15:6-15; Lk 23:13-25; Jn
19:1-10).

PILLAR
Ge 19:26 and she became a-*p* of salt.
Ex 13:21 ahead of them in a-*p* of cloud
1Ti 3:15 the-*p* and foundation of the truth.

PIT
Ps 40:2 He lifted me out of the slimy-*p*,
103:4 who redeems your life from the-*p*
Mt 15:14 a blind man, both will fall into a-*p*."

PITIED
1Co 15:19 we are to be-*p* more than all men.

PLAGUE
2Ch 6:28 "When famine or-*p* comes

PLAIN
Ro 1:19 what may be known about God is-*p*

PLAN (PLANNED PLANS)
Job 42:2 no-*p* of yours can be thwarted.
Pr 14:22 those who-*p* what is good find love
Eph 1:11 predestined according to the-*p*

PLANK
Mt 7:3 attention to the-*p* in your own eye?
Lk 6:41 attention to the-*p* in your own eye?

PLANNED (PLAN)
Ps 40:5 The things you-*p* for us
Isa 46:11 what I have-*p*, that will I do.
Heb 11:40 God had-*p* something better for us

PLANS (PLAN)
Ps 20:4 and make all your-*p* succeed.
33:11 *p* of the LORD stand firm forever,
Pr 20:18 Make-*p* by seeking advice;
Isa 32:8 But the noble man makes noble-*p*,

PLANTED (PLANTS)
Ps 1:3 He is like a tree-*p* by streams
Mt 15:13 Father has not-*p* will be pulled
1Co 3:6 I-*p* the seed, Apollos watered it,

PLANTS (PLANTED)
1Co 3:7 So neither he who-*p* nor he who
9:7 Who-*p* a vineyard and does not eat

PLATTER
Mk 6:25 head of John the Baptist on a-*p*."

PLAYED
Lk 7:32 " 'We-*p* the flute for you,
1Co 14:7 anyone know what tune is being-*p*

PLEADED
2Co 12:8 Three times I-*p* with the Lord

PLEASANT (PLEASE)
Ps 16:6 for me in-*p* places;
133:1 How good and-*p* it is
147:1 how-*p* and fitting to praise him!
Heb 12:11 No discipline seems-*p* at the time,

PLEASE (PLEASANT PLEASED PLEASES PLEASING PLEASURE PLEASURES)
Pr 20:23 and dishonest scales do not-*p* him.
Jer 6:20 your sacrifices do not-*p* me."
Jn 5:30 for I seek not to-*p* myself
Ro 8:8 by the sinful nature cannot-*p* God.
15:2 Each of us should-*p* his neighbor
1Co 7:32 affairs—how he can-*p* the Lord.
10:33 I try to-*p* everybody in every way.
2Co 5:9 So we make it our goal to-*p* him,
Gal 1:10 or of God? Or am I trying to-*p* men
1Th 4:1 how to live in order to-*p* God,
2Ti 2:4 wants to-*p* his commanding officer.
Heb 11:6 faith it is impossible to-*p* God,

PLEASED (PLEASE)
Mt 3:17 whom I love; with him I am well-*p*
1Co 1:21 God was-*p* through the foolishness
Col 1:19 For God was-*p* to have all his

PLEASES (PLEASE)
Ps 135:6 The LORD does whatever-*p* him,
Pr 15:8 but the prayer of the upright-*p* him.
Jn 3:8 The wind blows wherever it-*p*.
8:29 for I always do what-*p* him."
Col 3:20 in everything, for this-*p* the Lord.
1Ti 2:3 This is good, and-*p* God our Savior,
1Jn 3:22 his commands and do what-*p* him.

PLEASING (PLEASE)
Ps 104:34 May my meditation be-*p* to him,
Ro 12:1 *p* to God—which is your spiritual
Php 4:18 an acceptable sacrifice,-*p* to God.
Heb 13:21 may he work in us what is-*p* to him,

PLEASURE (PLEASE)
Ps 5:4 You are not a God who takes-*p*
147:10 His-*p* is not in the strength
Pr 21:17 He who loves-*p* will become poor;
Eze 18:32 For I take no-*p* in the death
Eph 1:5 in accordance with his-*p* and will—
1:9 of his will according to his good-*p*,
2Ti 3:4 lovers of-*p* rather than lovers

PLEASURES (PLEASE)
Ps 16:11 with eternal-*p* at your right hand.
Heb 11:25 rather than to enjoy the-*p* of sin
2Pe 2:13 reveling in their-*p* while they feast

PLENTIFUL
Mt 9:37 harvest is-*p* but the workers are

PLOW (PLOWSHARES)
Lk 9:62 "No one who puts his hand to the-*p*

PLOWSHARES (PLOW)
Isa 2:4 They will beat their swords into-*p*
Joel 3:10 Beat your-*p* into swords

PLUNDER
Ex 3:22 And so you will-*p* the Egyptians."

POINT
Jas 2:10 yet stumbles at just one-*p* is guilty

POISON
Mk 16:18 and when they drink deadly-*p*,
Jas 3:8 It is a restless evil, full of deadly-*p*.

POLLUTE* (POLLUTED)
Nu 35:33 " 'Do not-*p* the land where you are.
Jude :8 these dreamers-*p* their own bodies,

POLLUTED* (POLLUTE)
Ezr 9:11 entering to possess is a land-*p*
Pr 25:26 Like a muddied spring or a-*p* well
Ac 15:20 to abstain from food-*p* by idols,
Jas 1:27 oneself from being-*p* by the world.

PONDER
Ps 64:9 and-*p* what he has done.
119:95 but I will-*p* your statutes.

POOR (POVERTY)
Dt 15:4 there should be no-*p* among you,
15:11 There will always be-*p* people
Ps 34:6 This-*p* man called, and the LORD
82:3 maintain the rights of the-*p*
112:9 scattered abroad his gifts to the-*p*,
Pr 10:4 Lazy hands make a man-*p*,
13:7 to be-*p*, yet has great wealth.
14:31 oppresses the-*p* shows contempt
19:1 Better a-*p* man whose walk is
19:17 to the-*p* lends to the LORD,
22:2 Rich and-*p* have this in common:
22:9 for he shares his food with the-*p*.
28:6 Better a-*p* man whose walk is
31:20 She opens her arms to the-*p*
Isa 61:1 me to preach good news to the-*p*.
Mt 5:3 saying: "Blessed are the-*p* in spirit,
11:5 the good news is preached to the-*p*.
19:21 your possessions and give to the-*p*,

26:11 The-*p* you will always have
Mk 12:42 But a-*p* widow came and put
Ac 10:4 and gifts to the-*p* have come up
1Co 13:3 If I give all I possess to the-*p*
2Co 8:9 yet for your sakes he became-*p*,
Jas 2:2 and a-*p* man in shabby clothes

PORTION
Dt 32:9 For the LORD's-*p* is his people,
2Ki 2:9 "Let me inherit a double-*p*
La 3:24 to myself, "The LORD is my-*p*;

POSSESS (POSSESSING POSSESSION POSSESSIONS)
Nu 33:53 for I have given you the land to-*p*.
Jn 5:39 that by them you-*p* eternal life.

POSSESSING* (POSSESS)
2Co 6:10 nothing, and yet-*p* everything.

POSSESSION (POSSESS)
Ge 15:7 to give you this land to take-*p* of it
Nu 13:30 "We should go up and take-*p*
Eph 1:14 of those who are God's-*p*—

POSSESSIONS (POSSESS)
Lk 12:15 consist in the abundance of his-*p*."
2Co 12:14 what I want is not your-*p* but you.
1Jn 3:17 If anyone has material-*p*

POSSIBLE
Mt 19:26 but with God all things are-*p*."
Mk 9:23 "Everything is-*p* for him who
10:27 all things are-*p* with God."
Ro 12:18 If it is-*p*, as far as it depends on you,
1Co 9:22 by all-*p* means I might save some.

POT (POTSHERD POTTER POTTERY)
2Ki 4:40 there is death in the-*p*!"
Jer 18:4 But the-*p* he was shaping

POTSHERD (POT)
Isa 45:9 a-*p* among the potsherds

POTTER (POT)
Isa 29:16 Can the pot say of the-*p*,
45:9 Does the clay say to the-*p*,
64:8 We are the clay, you are the-*p*;
Jer 18:6 "Like clay in the hand of the-*p*,
Ro 9:21 Does not the-*p* have the right

POTTERY (POT)
Ro 9:21 of clay some-*p* for noble purposes

POUR (POURED)
Ps 62:8 *p* out your hearts to him,
Joel 2:28 I will-*p* out my Spirit on all people.
Mal 3:10 *p* out so much blessing that you
Ac 2:17 I will-*p* out my Spirit on all people.

POURED (POUR)
Ac 10:45 of the Holy Spirit had been-*p* out
Ro 5:5 because God has-*p* out his love

POVERTY (POOR)
Pr 14:23 but mere talk leads only to-*p*.
21:5 as surely as haste leads to-*p*.
30:8 give me neither-*p* nor riches,
Mk 12:44 out of her-*p*, put in everything—
2Co 8:2 and their extreme-*p* welled up
8:9 through his-*p* might become rich.

POWER (POWERFUL POWERS)
1Ch 29:11 LORD, is the greatness and the-*p*
2Ch 32:7 for there is a greater-*p* with us
Job 36:22 "God is exalted in his-*p*.
Ps 63:2 and beheld your-*p* and your glory.
68:34 Proclaim the-*p* of God,
147:5 Great is our Lord and mighty in-*p*;
Pr 24:5 A wise man has great-*p*,
Isa 40:10 the Sovereign LORD comes with-*p*,
Zec 4:6 nor by-*p*, but by my Spirit,'
Mt 22:29 do not know the Scriptures or the-*p*
24:30 on the clouds of the sky, with-*p*
Ac 1:8 you will receive-*p* when the Holy

4:33 With great-*p* the apostles
10:38 with the Holy Spirit and-*p*,
Ro 1:16 it is the-*p* of God for the salvation
1Co 1:18 to us who are being saved it is the-*p*
15:56 of death is sin, and the-*p*
2Co 12:9 for my-*p* is made perfect
Eph 1:19 and his incomparably great-*p*
Php 3:10 and the-*p* of his resurrection
Col 1:11 strengthened with all-*p* according
2Ti 1:7 but a spirit of-*p*, of love
Heb 7:16 of the-*p* of an indestructible life.
Rev 4:11 to receive glory and honor and-*p*,
19:1 and glory and-*p* belong to our God,
20:6 The second death has no-*p*

POWERFUL (POWER)
Ps 29:4 The voice of the LORD is-*p*;
Lk 24:19 *p* in word and deed before God
2Th 1:7 in blazing fire with his-*p* angels.
Heb 1:3 sustaining all things by his-*p* word.
Jas 5:16 The prayer of a righteous man is-*p*

POWERLESS
Ro 5:6 when we were still-*p*, Christ died
8:3 For what the law was-*p* to do

POWERS (POWER)
Ro 8:38 nor any-*p*, neither height nor depth
1Co 12:10 to another miraculous-*p*,
Col 1:16 whether thrones or-*p* or rulers
2:15 And having disarmed the-*p*

PRACTICE
Lev 19:26 " 'Do not-*p* divination or sorcery.
Mt 23:3 for they do not-*p* what they preach.
Lk 8:21 hear God's word and put it into-*p*."
Ro 12:13 *P* hospitality.
1Ti 5:4 to put their religion into-*p* by caring

PRAISE (PRAISED PRAISES PRAISING)
Ex 15:2 He is my God, and I will-*p* him,
Dt 32:3 Oh,-*p* the greatness of our God!
Ru 4:14 said to Naomi:- "*P* be to the LORD,
2Sa 22:47 The LORD lives!-*P* be to my Rock
1Ch 16:25 is the LORD and most worthy of-*p*;
2Ch 20:21 and to-*p* him for the splendor
Ps 8:2 you have ordained-*p*
33:1 it is fitting for the upright to-*p* him.
34:1 his-*p* will always be on my lips.
40:3 a hymn of-*p* to our God.
48:1 the LORD, and most worthy of-*p*,
68:19 *P* be to the Lord, to God our Savior
89:5 The heavens-*p* your wonders,
100:4 and his courts with-*p*;
105:2 Sing to him, sing-*p* to him;
106:1 *P* the LORD.
119:175 Let me live that I may-*p* you,
139:14 I-*p* you because I am fearfully
145:21 Let every creature-*p* his holy name
146:1 *P* the LORD, O my soul.
150:2 *p* him for his surpassing greatness.
150:6 that has breath-*p* the LORD.
Pr 27:2 Let another-*p* you, and not your
27:21 man is tested by the-*p* he receives.
31:31 let her works bring her-*p*.
Mt 15:8 and-*p* your Father in heaven.
21:16 you have ordained-*p*'?"
Jn 12:43 for they loved-*p* from men more
Eph 1:6 to the-*p* of his glorious grace,
1:12 might be for the-*p* of his glory.
1:14 to the-*p* of his glory.
Heb 13:15 offer to God a sacrifice of-*p*—
Jas 5:13 happy? Let him sing songs of-*p*.

PRAISED (PRAISE)
1Ch 29:10 David-*p* the LORD in the presence
Ne 8:6 Ezra-*p* the LORD, the great God;
Da 2:19 Then Daniel-*p* the God of heaven
Ro 9:5 who is God over all, forever-*p*!
1Pe 4:11 that in all things God may be-*p*

PRAISES (PRAISE)
2Sa 22:50 I will sing-p to your name.
Ps 47:6 Sing-p to God, sing-p;
147:1 How good it is to sing-p to our God,
Pr 31:28 her husband also, and he-p her:

PRAISING (PRAISE)
Ac 10:46 speaking in tongues and-p God.
1Co 14:16 If you are-p God with your spirit,

PRAY (PRAYED PRAYER PRAYERS
PRAYING)
Dt 4:7 is near us whenever we-p to him?
1Sa 12:23 the Lord by failing to-p for you.
2Ch 7:14 will humble themselves and-p
Job 42:8 My servant Job will-p for you,
Ps 122:6 P for the peace of Jerusalem:
Mt 5:44 and-p for those who persecute you,
6:5 "And when you-p, do not be like
6:9 "This, then, is how you should-p:
26:36 Sit here while I go over there and-p
Lk 6:28 p for those who mistreat you.
18:1 them that they should always-p
22:40 "P that you will not fall
Ro 8:26 do not know what we ought to-p,
1Co 14:13 in a tongue should-p that he may
1Th 5:17 Be joyful always;-p continually;
Jas 5:13 one of you in trouble? He should-p.
5:16 p for each other so that you may be

PRAYED (PRAY)
1Sa 1:27 I-p for this child, and the Lord
Jnh 2:1 From inside the fish Jonah-p
Mk 14:35 p that if possible the hour might

PRAYER (PRAY)
2Ch 30:27 for their-p reached heaven,
Ezr 8:23 about this, and he answered our-p.
Ps 6:9 the Lord accepts my-p.
86:6 Hear my-p, O Lord;
Pr 15:8 but the-p of the upright pleases him
Isa 56:7 a house of-p for all nations."
Mt 21:13 house will be called a house of-p,'
Mk 11:24 whatever you ask for in-p,
Jn 17:15 My-p is not that you take them out
Ac 6:4 and will give our attention to-p
Php 4:6 but in everything, by-p and petition
Jas 5:15 p offered in faith will make the sick
1Pe 3:12 and his ears are attentive to their-p,

PRAYERS (PRAY)
1Ch 5:20 He answered their-p, because they
Mk 12:40 and for a show make lengthy-p.
1Pe 3:7 so that nothing will hinder your-p.
Rev 5:8 which are the-p of the saints.

PRAYING (PRAY)
Mk 11:25 And when you stand-p,
Jn 17:9 I am not-p for the world,
Ac 16:25 and Silas were-p and singing hymns
Eph 6:18 always keep on-p for all the saints.

PREACH (PREACHED PREACHING)
Mt 23:3 they do not practice what they-p.
Mk 16:15 and-p the good news to all creation.
Ac 9:20 At once he began to-p
Ro 10:15 how can they-p unless they are sent
15:20 to-p the gospel where Christ was
1Co 1:17 to-p the gospel—not with words
1:23 wisdom, but we-p Christ crucified:
9:14 that those who-p the gospel should
9:16 Woe to me if I do not-p the gospel!
2Co 10:16 so that we can-p the gospel
Gal 1:8 from heaven should-p a gospel
2Ti 4:2 I give you this charge:-P the Word;

PREACHED (PREACH)
Mk 13:10 And the gospel must first be-p
Ac 8:4 had been scattered-p the word
1Co 9:27 so that after I have-p to others,
15:1 you of the gospel I-p to you,
2Co 11:4 other than the Jesus we-p,

Gal 1:8 other than the one we-p to you,
Php 1:18 false motives or true, Christ is-p.
1Ti 3:16 was-p among the nations,

PREACHING (PREACH)
Ro 10:14 hear without someone-p to them?
1Co 9:18 in-p the gospel I may offer it free
1Ti 4:13 the public reading of Scripture, to-p
5:17 especially those whose work is-p

PRECEPTS
Ps 19:8 The-p of the Lord are right,
111:7 all his-p are trustworthy.
111:10 who follow his-p have good
119:40 How I long for your-p!
119:69 I keep your-p with all my heart.
119:104 I gain understanding from your-p;
119:159 See how I love your-p;

PRECIOUS
Ps 19:10 They are more-p than gold,
116:15 P in the sight of the Lord
Pr 8:11 for wisdom is more-p than rubies,
Isa 28:16 a-p cornerstone for a sure
1Pe 1:19 but with the-p blood of Christ,
2:6 a chosen and-p cornerstone,
2Pe 1:4 us his very great and-p promises,

PREDESTINED* (DESTINY)
Ro 8:29 p to be conformed to the likeness
8:30 And those he-p, he also called;
Eph 1:5 In love he-p us to be adopted
1:11 having been-p according

PREDICTION*
Jer 28:9 only if his-p comes true."

PREPARE (PREPARED)
Ps 23:5 You-p a table before me
Am 4:12 p to meet your God, O Israel."
Jn 14:2 there to-p a place for you.
Eph 4:12 to-p God's people for works

PREPARED (PREPARE)
Mt 25:34 the kingdom-p for you
1Co 2:9 what God has-p for those who love
Eph 2:10 which God-p in advance for us
2Ti 4:2 be-p in season and out of season;
1Pe 3:15 Always be-p to give an answer

PRESENCE (PRESENT)
Ex 25:30 Put the bread of the-P on this table
Ezr 9:15 one of us can stand in your-p."
Ps 31:20 the shelter of your-p you hide them
89:15 who walk in the light of your-p,
90:8 our secret sins in the light of your-p
139:7 Where can I flee from your-p?
Jer 5:22 "Should you not tremble in my-p?
Heb 9:24 now to appear for us in God's-p.
Jude :24 before his glorious-p without fault

PRESENT (PRESENCE)
2Co 11:2 so that I might-p you as a pure
Eph 5:27 and to-p her to himself
2Ti 2:15 Do your best to-p yourself to God

PRESERVES
Ps 119:50 Your promise-p my life.

PRESS (PRESSED PRESSURE)
Php 3:14 I-p on toward the goal

PRESSED (PRESS)
Lk 6:38 p down, shaken together

PRESSURE (PRESS)
2Co 1:8 We were under great-p, far
11:28 I face daily the-p of my concern

PREVAILS
1Sa 2:9 "It is not by strength that one-p;

PRICE
Job 28:18 the-p of wisdom is beyond rubies.
1Co 6:20 your own; you were bought at a-p.
7:23 bought at a-p; do not become slaves

PRIDE (PROUD)
Pr 8:13 I hate-p and arrogance,
16:18 P goes before destruction,
Da 4:37 And those who walk in-p he is able
Gal 6:4 Then he can take-p in himself,
Jas 1:9 ought to take-p in his high position.

PRIEST (PRIESTHOOD PRIESTS)
Heb 4:14 have a great high-p who has gone
4:15 do not have a high-p who is unable
7:26 Such a high-p meets our need—
8:1 We do have such a high-p,

PRIESTHOOD (PRIEST)
Heb 7:24 lives forever, he has a permanent-p.
1Pe 2:5 into a spiritual house to be a holy-p,
2:9 you are a chosen people, a royal-p,

PRIESTS (PRIEST)
Ex 19:6 you will be for me a kingdom of-p
Rev 5:10 to be a kingdom and-p

PRINCE
Isa 9:6 Everlasting Father,-P of Peace.
Jn 12:31 now the-p of this world will be
Ac 5:31 as-P and Savior that he might give

PRISON (PRISONER)
Isa 42:7 to free captives from-p
Mt 25:36 I was in-p and you came to visit me
1Pe 3:19 spirits in-p who disobeyed long ago
Rev 20:7 Satan will be released from his-p

PRISONER (PRISON)
Ro 7:23 and making me a-p of the law of sin
Gal 3:22 declares that the whole world is a-p
Eph 3:1 the-p of Christ Jesus for the sake

PRIVILEGE*
2Co 8:4 pleaded with us for the-p of sharing

PRIZE
1Co 9:24 Run in such a way as to get the-p.
Php 3:14 on toward the goal to win the-p

PROCLAIM (PROCLAIMED
PROCLAIMING)
1Ch 16:23 p his salvation day after day.
Ps 19:1 the skies-p the work of his hands.
50:6 the heavens-p his righteousness,
68:34 P the power of God,
118:17 will-p what the Lord has done.
Zec 9:10 He will-p peace to the nations.
Ac 20:27 hesitated to-p to you the whole will
1Co 11:26 you-p the Lord's death

PROCLAIMED (PROCLAIM)
Ro 15:19 I have fully-p the gospel of Christ.
Col 1:23 that has been-p to every creature

PROCLAIMING (PROCLAIM)
Ro 10:8 the word of faith we are-p:

PRODUCE (PRODUCES)
Mt 3:8 P fruit in keeping with repentance.
3:10 tree that does not-p good fruit will

PRODUCES (PRODUCE)
Pr 30:33 so stirring up anger-p strife."
Ro 5:3 that suffering-p perseverance;
Heb 12:11 it-p a harvest of righteousness

PROFANE
Lev 22:32 Do not-p my holy name.

PROFESS*
1Ti 2:10 for women who-p to worship God.
Heb 4:14 let us hold firmly to the faith we-p.
10:23 unswervingly to the hope we-p,

PROMISE (PROMISED PROMISES)
1Ki 8:20 The Lord has kept the-p he made
Ac 2:39 The-p is for you and your children
Gal 3:14 that by faith we might receive the-p
1Ti 4:8 holding-p for both the present life
2Pe 3:9 Lord is not slow in keeping his-p,

PROMISED (PROMISE)
Ex 3:17 And I have-p to bring you up out
Dt 26:18 his treasured possession as he-p,
Ps 119:57 I have-p to obey your words.
Ro 4:21 power to do what he had-p.
Heb 10:23 for he who-p is faithful.
2Pe 3:4 "Where is this 'coming' he-p?

PROMISES (PROMISE)
Jos 21:45 one of all the Lord's good-p
Ro 9:4 the temple worship and the-p.
2Pe 1:4 us his very great and precious-p,

PROMPTED
1Th 1:3 your labor-p by love, and your
2Th 1:11 and every act-p by your faith.

PROPHECIES (PROPHESY)
1Co 13:8 where there are-p, they will cease;
1Th 5:20 do not treat-p with contempt.

PROPHECY (PROPHESY)
1Co 14:1 gifts, especially the gift of-p.
2Pe 1:20 you must understand that no-p

PROPHESY (PROPHECIES PROPHECY
PROPHESYING PROPHET PROPHETS)
Joel 2:28 Your sons and daughters will-p,
Mt 7:22 Lord, did we not-p in your name,
1Co 14:39 my brothers, be eager to-p,

PROPHESYING (PROPHESY)
Ro 12:6 If a man's gift is-p, let him use it

PROPHET (PROPHESY)
Dt 18:18 up for them a-p like you
Am 7:14 "I was neither a-p nor a prophet's
Mt 10:41 Anyone who receives a-p
Lk 4:24 "no-p is accepted in his hometown.

PROPHETS (PROPHESY)
Ps 105:15 do my-p no harm."
Mt 5:17 come to abolish the Law or the-p;
7:12 for this sums up the Law and the-p.
24:24 false Christs and false-p will appear
Lk 24:25 believe all that the-p have spoken!
Ac 10:43 All the-p testify about him that
1Co 12:28 second-p, third teachers, then
14:32 The spirits of-p are subject
Eph 2:20 foundation of the apostles and-p,
Heb 1:1 through the-p at many times
1Pe 1:10 Concerning this salvation, the-p,
2Pe 1:19 word of the-p made more certain,

PROSPER (PROSPERITY PROSPERS)
Pr 28:25 he who trusts in the Lord will-p.

PROSPERITY (PROSPER)
Ps 73:3 when I saw the-p of the wicked.
Pr 13:21 but-p is the reward of the righteous.

PROSPERS (PROSPER)
Ps 1:3 Whatever he does-p.

PROSTITUTE (PROSTITUTES)
1Co 6:15 of Christ and unite them with a-p?

PROSTITUTES (PROSTITUTE)
Lk 15:30 property with-p comes home,
1Co 6:9 male-p nor homosexual offenders

PROSTRATE
Dt 9:18 again I fell-p before the Lord

PROTECT (PROTECTS)
Ps 32:7 you will-p me from trouble
Pr 2:11 Discretion will-p you,
Jn 17:11 p them by the power of your name

PROTECTS (PROTECT)
1Co 13:7 It always-p, always trusts,

PROUD
Pr 16:5 The Lord detests all the-p
Ro 12:16 Do not be-p, but be willing
1Co 13:4 it does not boast, it is not-p.

PROVE
Ac 26:20 *p* their repentance by their deeds.
1Co 4:2 been given a trust must-*p* faithful.

PROVIDE (PROVIDED PROVIDES)
Ge 22:8 "God himself will-*p* the lamb
Isa 43:20 because I-*p* water in the desert
1Ti 5:8 If anyone does not-*p*

PROVIDED (PROVIDE)
Jnh 1:17 But the Lord-*p* a great fish
4:6 Then the Lord God-*p* a vine
4:7 dawn the next day God-*p* a worm,
4:8 God-*p* a scorching east wind,

PROVIDES (PROVIDE)
1Ti 6:17 who richly-*p* us with everything
1Pe 4:11 it with the strength God-*p*,

PROVOKED
Ecc 7:9 Do not be quickly-*p* in your spirit,

PRUDENT
Pr 14:15 a-*p* man gives thought to his steps.
19:14 but a-*p* wife is from the Lord.
Am 5:13 Therefore the-*p* man keeps quiet

PRUNING
Isa 2:4 and their spears into-*p* hooks.
Joel 3:10 and your-*p* hooks into spears.

PSALMS
Eph 5:19 Speak to one another with-*p*,
Col 3:16 and as you sing-*p*, hymns

PUBLICLY
Ac 20:20 have taught you-*p* and from house
1Ti 5:20 Those who sin are to be rebuked-*p*,

PUFFS
1Co 8:1 Knowledge-*p* up, but love builds up

PULLING
2Co 10:8 building you up rather than-*p* you

PUNISH (PUNISHED PUNISHES)
Ex 32:34 I will-*p* them for their sin."
Pr 23:13 if you-*p* him with the rod, he will
Isa 13:11 I will-*p* the world for its evil,
1Pe 2:14 by him to-*p* those who do wrong

PUNISHED (PUNISH)
La 3:39 complain when-*p* for his sins?
2Th 1:9 be-*p* with everlasting destruction
Heb 10:29 to be-*p* who has trampled the Son

PUNISHES (PUNISH)
Heb 12:6 and he-*p* everyone he accepts

PURE (PURIFIES PURIFY PURITY)
2Sa 22:27 to the-*p* you show yourself-*p*,
Ps 24:4 who has clean hands and a-*p* heart,
51:10 Create in me a-*p* heart, O God,
119:9 can a young man keep his way-*p*?
Pr 20:9 can say, "I have kept my heart-*p*;
Isa 52:11 Come out from it and be-*p*,
Hab 1:13 Your eyes are too-*p* to look on evil;
Mt 5:8 Blessed are the-*p* in heart,
2Co 11:2 I might present you as a-*p* virgin
Php 4:8 whatever is-*p*, whatever is lovely,
1Ti 5:22 Keep yourself-*p*.
Tit 1:15 To the-*p*, all things are-*p*,
2:5 to be self-controlled and-*p*,
Heb 13:4 and the marriage bed kept-*p*,
1Jn 3:3 him purifies himself, just as he is-*p*.

PURGE
Pr 20:30 and beatings-*p* the inmost being.

PURIFIES* (PURE)
1Jn 1:7 of Jesus, his Son,-*p* us from all sin.
3:3 who has this hope in him-*p* himself,

PURIFY (PURE)
Tit 2:14 to-*p* for himself a people that are
1Jn 1:9 and-*p* us from all unrighteousness.

PURITY (PURE)
2Co 6:6 in-*p*, understanding, patience
1Ti 4:12 in life, in love, in faith and in-*p*.

PURPOSE
Pr 19:21 but it is the Lord's-*p* that prevails
Isa 55:11 and achieve the-*p* for which I sent it
Ro 8:28 have been called according to his-*p*.
Php 2:2 love, being one in spirit and-*p*.

PURSES
Lk 12:33 Provide-*p* for yourselves that will

PURSUE
Ps 34:14 seek peace and-*p* it.
2Ti 2:22 and-*p* righteousness, faith,
1Pe 3:11 he must seek peace and-*p* it.

QUALITIES (QUALITY)
2Pe 1:8 For if you possess these-*q*

QUALITY (QUALITIES)
1Co 3:13 and the fire will test the-*q*

QUARREL (QUARRELSOME)
Pr 15:18 but a patient man calms a-*q*.
17:14 Starting a-*q* is like breaching a dam;
17:19 He who loves a-*q* loves sin;
2Ti 2:24 And the Lord's servant must not-*q*;

QUARRELSOME (QUARREL)
Pr 19:13 a-*q* wife is like a constant dripping.
1Ti 3:3 not violent but gentle, not-*q*,

QUICK-TEMPERED
Tit 1:7 not-*q*, not given to drunkenness,

QUIET (QUIETNESS)
Ps 23:2 he leads me beside-*q* waters,
Zep 3:17 he will-*q* you with his love,
Lk 19:40 he replied, "if they keep-*q*,
1Ti 2:2 we may live peaceful and-*q* lives
1Pe 3:4 beauty of a gentle and-*q* spirit,

QUIETNESS (QUIET)
Isa 30:15 in-*q* and trust is your strength,
32:17 the effect of righteousness will be-*q*
1Ti 2:11 A woman should learn in-*q*

QUIVER
Ps 127:5 whose-*q* is full of them.

RACE
Ecc 9:11 The-*r* is not to the swift
1Co 9:24 that in a-*r* all the runners run,
2Ti 4:7 I have finished the-*r*, I have kept
Heb 12:1 perseverance the-*r* marked out

RACHEL
Daughter of Laban (Ge 29:16); wife of Jacob (Ge 29:28); bore two sons (Ge 30:22-24; 35:16-24; 46:19).

RADIANCE (RADIANT)
Heb 1:3 The Son is the-*r* of God's glory

RADIANT (RADIANCE)
Ex 34:29 he was not aware that his face was-*r*
Ps 34:5 Those who look to him are-*r*;
SS 5:10 *Beloved* My lover is-*r* and ruddy,
Isa 60:5 Then you will look and be-*r*,
Eph 5:27 her to himself as a-*r* church,

RAIN (RAINBOW)
Mt 5:45 and sends-*r* on the righteous

RAINBOW (RAIN)
Ge 9:13 I have set my-*r* in the clouds,

RAISED (RISE)
Ro 4:25 was-*r* to life for our justification.
10:9 in your heart that God-*r* him
1Co 15:4 that he was-*r* on the third day

RAN (RUN)
Jnh 1:3 But Jonah-*r* away from the Lord

RANSOM
Mt 20:28 and to give his life as a-*r* for many."
Heb 9:15 as a-*r* to set them free

RAVENS
1Ki 17:6 The-*r* brought him bread
Lk 12:24 Consider the-*r*: They do not sow

READ (READS)
Jos 8:34 Joshua-*r* all the words of the law—
Ne 8:8 They-*r* from the Book of the Law
2Co 3:2 known and-*r* by everybody.

READS (READ)
Rev 1:3 Blessed is the one who-*r* the words

REAL (REALITY)
Jn 6:55 is-*r* food and my blood is-*r* drink.

REALITY* (REAL)
Col 2:17 the-*r*, however, is found in Christ.

REAP (REAPS)
Job 4:8 and those who sow trouble-*r* it.
2Co 9:6 generously will also-*r* generously.

REAPS (REAP)
Gal 6:7 A man-*r* what he sows.

REASON
Isa 1:18 "Come now, let us-*r* together,"
1Pe 3:15 to give the-*r* for the hope that you

REBEKAH
Sister of Laban, secured as bride for Isaac (Ge 24). Mother of Esau and Jacob (Ge 25:19-26). Taken by Abimelech as sister of Isaac; returned (Ge 26:1-11). Encouraged Jacob to trick Isaac out of blessing (Ge 27:1-17).

REBEL
Mt 10:21 children will-*r* against their parents

REBUKE (REBUKED REBUKING)
Pr 9:8 *r* a wise man and he will love you.
27:5 Better is open-*r*
Lk 17:3 "If your brother sins,-*r* him,
2Ti 4:2 correct,-*r* and encourage—
Rev 3:19 Those whom I love I-*r*

REBUKED (REBUKE)
1Ti 5:20 Those who sin are to be-*r* publicly,

REBUKING (REBUKE)
2Ti 3:16 *r*, correcting and training

RECEIVE (RECEIVED RECEIVES)
Ac 1:8 you will-*r* power when the Holy
20:35 'It is more blessed to give than to-*r*
2Co 6:17 and I will-*r* you."
Rev 4:11 to-*r* glory and honor and power,

RECEIVED (RECEIVE)
Mt 6:2 they have-*r* their reward in full.
10:8 Freely you have-*r*, freely give.
1Co 11:23 For I-*r* from the Lord what I
Col 2:6 just as you-*r* Christ Jesus as Lord,
1Pe 4:10 should use whatever gift he has-*r*

RECEIVES (RECEIVE)
Mt 7:8 everyone who asks-*r*; he who seeks
10:40 he who-*r* me-*r* the one who sent me.
Ac 10:43 believes in him-*r* forgiveness of sins

RECKONING
Isa 10:3 What will you do on the day of-*r*,

RECOGNIZE (RECOGNIZED)
Mt 7:16 By their fruit you will-*r* them.

RECOGNIZED (RECOGNIZE)
Mt 12:33 for a tree is-*r* by its fruit.
Ro 7:13 in order that sin might be-*r* as sin,

RECOMPENSE
Isa 40:10 and his-*r* accompanies him.

RECONCILE (RECONCILED RECONCILIATION)
Eph 2:16 in this one body to-*r* both of them

RECONCILED (RECONCILE)
Mt 5:24 First go and be-*r* to your brother;
Ro 5:10 we were-*r* to him through the death
2Co 5:18 who-*r* us to himself through Christ

RECONCILIATION* (RECONCILE)
Ro 5:11 whom we have now received-*r*.
11:15 For if their rejection is the-*r*
2Co 5:18 and gave us the ministry of-*r*:
5:19 committed to us the message of-*r*.

RECORD
Ps 130:3 If you, O Lord, kept a-*r* of sins,

RED
Isa 1:18 though they are-*r* as crimson,

REDEEM (KINSMAN-REDEEMER REDEEMED REDEEMER REDEMPTION)
2Sa 7:23 on earth that God went out to-*r*
Ps 49:7 No man can-*r* the life of another
Gal 4:5 under law, to-*r* those under law,

REDEEMED (REDEEM)
Gal 3:13 Christ-*r* us from the curse
1Pe 1:18 or gold that you were-*r*

REDEEMER (REDEEM)
Job 19:25 I know that my-*R* lives,

REDEMPTION (REDEEM)
Ps 130:7 and with him is full-*r*.
Lk 21:28 because your-*r* is drawing near."
Ro 8:23 as sons, the-*r* of our bodies.
Eph 1:7 In him we have-*r* through his blood
Col 1:14 in whom we have-*r*, the forgiveness
Heb 9:12 having obtained eternal-*r*.

REFLECT
2Co 3:18 unveiled faces all-*r* the Lord's

REFUGE
Nu 35:11 towns to be your cities of-*r*,
Dt 33:27 The eternal God is your-*r*,
Ru 2:12 wings you have come to take-*r*."
Ps 46:1 God is our-*r* and strength,
91:2 "He is my-*r* and my fortress,

REHOBOAM
Son of Solomon (1Ki 11:43; 1Ch 3:10). Harsh treatment of subjects caused divided kingdom (1Ki 12:1-24; 14:21-31; 2Ch 10-12).

REIGN
Ex 15:18 The Lord will-*r*
Ro 6:12 Therefore do not let sin-*r*
1Co 15:25 For he must-*r* until he has put all
2Ti 2:12 we will also-*r* with him.
Rev 20:6 will-*r* with him for a thousand years

REJECTED (REJECTS)
Ps 118:22 The stone the builders-*r*
Isa 53:3 He was despised and-*r* by men,
1Ti 4:4 nothing is to be-*r* if it is received
1Pe 2:4 *r* by men but chosen by God
2:7 "The stone the builders-*r*

REJECTS (REJECTED)
Lk 10:16 but he who-*r* me-*r* him who sent me
Jn 3:36 whoever-*r* the Son will not see life,

REJOICE (JOY)
Ps 2:11 and-*r* with trembling.
66:6 come, let us-*r* in him.
118:24 let us-*r* and be glad in it.
Pr 5:18 may you-*r* in the wife of your youth
Lk 10:20 but-*r* that your names are written
15:6 '*R* with me; I have found my lost
Ro 12:15 Rejoice with those who-*r*; mourn
Php 4:4 *R* in the Lord always.

REJOICES (JOY)
Isa 61:10 my soul-*r* in my God.
Lk 1:47 and my spirit-*r* in God my Savior,
1Co 12:26 if one part is honored, every part-*r*
13:6 delight in evil but-*r* with the truth.

REJOICING (JOY)
Ps 30:5 but-*r* comes in the morning.
Lk 15:7 in the same way there will be more-*r*
Ac 5:41 *r* because they had been counted

RELIABLE
2Ti 2:2 witnesses entrust to-*r* men who will

RELIGION
1Ti 5:4 all to put their-*r* into practice
Jas 1:27 *R* that God our Father accepts

REMAIN (REMAINS)
Nu 33:55 allow to-*r* will become barbs
Jn 15:7 If you-*r* in me and my words
Ro 13:8 Let no debt-*r* outstanding,
1Co 13:13 And now these three-*r*: faith,
2Ti 2:13 he will-*r* faithful,

REMAINS (REMAIN)
Ps 146:6 the Lord, who-*r* faithful forever.
Heb 7:3 Son of God he-*r* a priest forever.

REMEMBER (REMEMBERS REMEMBRANCE)
Ex 20:8 "*R* the Sabbath day
1Ch 16:12 *R* the wonders he has done,
Ecc 12:1 *R* your Creator
Jer 31:34 and will-*r* their sins no more."
Gal 2:10 we should continue to-*r* the poor,
Php 1:3 I thank my God every time I-*r* you.
Heb 8:12 and will-*r* their sins no more."

REMEMBERS (REMEMBER)
Ps 103:14 he-*r* that we are dust.
111:5 he-*r* his covenant forever.
Isa 43:25 and-*r* your sins no more.

REMEMBRANCE (REMEMBER)
1Co 11:24 which is for you; do this in-*r* of me

REMIND
Jn 14:26 will-*r* you of everything I have said

REMOVED
Ps 30:11 you-*r* my sackcloth and clothed me
103:12 so far has he-*r* our transgressions
Jn 20:1 and saw that the stone had been-*r*

RENEW (RENEWED RENEWING)
Ps 51:10 and-*r* a steadfast spirit within me.
Isa 40:31 will-*r* their strength.

RENEWED (RENEW)
Ps 103:5 that your youth is-*r* like the eagle's.
2Co 4:16 yet inwardly we are being-*r* day

RENEWING (RENEW)
Ro 12:2 transformed by the-*r* of your mind.

RENOUNCE (RENOUNCES)
Da 4:27 *R* your sins by doing what is right,

RENOUNCES (RENOUNCE)
Pr 28:13 confesses and-*r* them finds

RENOWN
Isa 63:12 to gain for himself everlasting-*r*,
Jer 32:20 have gained the-*r* that is still yours.

REPAID (PAY)
Lk 14:14 you will be-*r* at the resurrection
Col 3:25 Anyone who does wrong will be-*r*

REPAY (PAY)
Dt 32:35 It is mine to avenge; I will-*r*.
Ru 2:12 May the Lord-*r* you
Ps 116:12 How can I-*r* the Lord
Ro 12:19 "It is mine to avenge; I will-*r*,"
1Pe 3:9 Do not-*r* evil with evil

REPENT (REPENTANCE REPENTS)
Job 42:6 and-*r* in dust and ashes."
Jer 15:19 "If you-*r*, I will restore you
Mt 4:17 "*R*, for the kingdom of heaven is
Lk 13:3 unless you-*r*, you too will all perish.
Ac 2:38 Peter replied, "*R* and be baptized,
17:30 all people everywhere to-*r*.

REPENTANCE (REPENT)
Lk 3:8 Produce fruit in keeping with-*r*.
5:32 call the righteous, but sinners to-*r*."
Ac 26:20 and prove their-*r* by their deeds.
2Co 7:10 Godly sorrow brings-*r* that leads

REPENTS (REPENT)
Lk 15:10 of God over one sinner who-*r*."
17:3 rebuke him, and if he-*r*, forgive him

REPROACH
1Ti 3:2 Now the overseer must be above-*r*,

REPUTATION
1Ti 3:7 also have a good-*r* with outsiders,

REQUESTS
Ps 20:5 May the Lord grant all your-*r*.
Php 4:6 with thanksgiving, present your-*r*

REQUIRE
Mic 6:8 And what does the Lord-*r* of you

RESCUE (RESCUES)
Da 6:20 been able to-*r* you from the lions?"
2Pe 2:9 how to-*r* godly men from trials

RESCUES (RESCUE)
1Th 1:10 who-*r* us from the coming wrath.

RESIST
Jas 4:7 *R* the devil, and he will flee
1Pe 5:9 *R* him, standing firm in the faith,

RESOLVED
Ps 17:3 I have-*r* that my mouth will not sin.
Da 1:8 But Daniel-*r* not to defile himself
1Co 2:2 For I-*r* to know nothing while I was

RESPECT (RESPECTABLE)
Lev 19:3 " 'Each of you must-*r* his mother
19:32 show-*r* for the elderly and revere
Pr 11:16 A kindhearted woman gains-*r*,
Mal 1:6 where is the-*r* due me?" says
1Th 4:12 so that your daily life may win the-*r*
5:12 to-*r* those who work hard
1Ti 3:4 children obey him with proper-*r*,
1Pe 2:17 Show proper-*r* to everyone:
3:7 them with-*r* as the weaker partner

RESPECTABLE* (RESPECT)
1Ti 3:2 self-controlled,-*r*, hospitable,

REST
Ex 31:15 the seventh day is a Sabbath of-*r*,
Ps 91:1 will-*r* in the shadow
Jer 6:16 and you will find-*r* for your souls.
Mt 11:28 and burdened, and I will give you-*r*.

RESTITUTION
Ex 22:3 "A thief must certainly make-*r*,
Lev 6:5 He must make-*r* in full, add a fifth

RESTORE (RESTORES)
Ps 51:12 *R* to me the joy of your salvation
Gal 6:1 are spiritual should-*r* him gently.

RESTORES (RESTORE)
Ps 23:3 he-*r* my soul.

RESURRECTION
Mt 22:30 At the-*r* people will neither marry
Lk 14:14 repaid at the-*r* of the righteous."
Jn 11:25 Jesus said to her, "I am the-*r*
Ro 1:4 Son of God by his-*r* from the dead:
1Co 15:12 some of you say that there is no-*r*
Php 3:10 power of his-*r* and the fellowship
Rev 20:5 This is the first-*r*.

RETRIBUTION
Jer 51:56 For the Lord is a God of-*r*;

RETURN
2Ch 30:9 If you-*r* to the Lord, then your
Ne 1:9 but if you-*r* to me and obey my
Isa 55:11 It will not-*r* to me empty,
Hos 6:1 "Come, let us-*r* to the Lord.
Joel 2:12 "*r* to me with all your heart,

REVEALED (REVELATION)
Dt 29:29 but the things-*r* belong to us
Isa 40:5 the glory of the Lord will be-*r*,
Mt 11:25 and-*r* them to little children.
Ro 1:17 a righteousness from God is-*r*,
8:18 with the glory that will be-*r* in us.

REVELATION (REVEALED)
Gal 1:12 I received it by-*r* from Jesus Christ.
Rev 1:1 *r* of Jesus Christ, which God gave

REVENGE (VENGEANCE)
Lev 19:18 " 'Do not seek-*r* or bear a grudge
Ro 12:19 Do not take-*r*, my friends,

REVERE (REVERENCE)
Ps 33:8 let all the people of the world-*r* him

REVERENCE (REVERE)
Lev 19:30 and have-*r* for my sanctuary.
Ps 5:7 in-*r* will I bow down
Col 3:22 of heart and-*r* for the Lord.
1Pe 3:2 when they see the purity and-*r*

REVIVE (REVIVING)
Ps 85:6 Will you not-*r* us again,
Isa 57:15 to-*r* the spirit of the lowly

REVIVING (REVIVE)
Ps 19:7 *r* the soul.

REWARD (REWARDED)
Ps 19:11 in keeping them there is great-*r*.
127:3 children a-*r* from him.
Pr 19:17 he will-*r* him for what he has done.
25:22 and the Lord will-*r* you.
31:31 Give her the-*r* she has earned,
Jer 17:10 to-*r* a man according to his conduct
Mt 5:12 because great is your-*r* in heaven,
6:5 they have received their-*r* in full.
16:27 and then he will-*r* each person
1Co 3:14 built survives, he will receive his-*r*.
Rev 22:12 I am coming soon! My-*r* is with me

REWARDED (REWARD)
Ru 2:12 May you be richly-*r* by the Lord,
Ps 18:24 The Lord has-*r* me according
Pr 14:14 and the good man-*r* for his.
1Co 3:8 and each will be-*r* according

RICH (RICHES)
Pr 23:4 Do not wear yourself out to get-*r*;
Jer 9:23 or the-*r* man boast of his riches,
Mt 19:23 it is hard for a-*r* man
2Co 6:10 yet making many-*r*; having nothing
8:9 he was-*r*, yet for your sakes he
1Ti 6:17 Command those who are-*r*

RICHES (RICH)
Ps 119:14 as one rejoices in great-*r*.
Pr 30:8 give me neither poverty nor-*r*,
Isa 10:3 Where will you leave your-*r*?
Ro 9:23 to make the-*r* of his glory known
11:33 the depth of the-*r* of the wisdom
Eph 2:7 he might show the incomparable-*r*
3:8 to the Gentiles the unsearchable-*r*
Col 1:27 among the Gentiles the glorious-*r*

RID
Ge 21:10 "Get-*r* of that slave woman
1Co 5:7 Get-*r* of the old yeast that you may
Gal 4:30 "Get-*r* of the slave woman

RIGHT (RIGHTS)
Ge 18:25 the Judge of all the earth do-*r*?"
Ex 15:26 and do what is-*r* in his eyes,
Dt 5:32 do not turn aside to the-*r*
Ps 16:8 Because he is at my-*r* hand,
19:8 The precepts of the Lord are-*r*,
63:8 your-*r* hand upholds me.
110:1 "Sit at my-*r* hand
Pr 4:27 Do not swerve to the-*r* or the left;
14:12 There is a way that seems-*r*
Isa 1:17 learn to do-*r*!

ROBBERS
Jer 7:11 become a den of-*r* to you?

Jer 23:5 and do what is just and-*r* in the land
Hos 14:9 The ways of the Lord are-*r*;
Mt 6:3 know what your-*r* hand is doing,
Jn 1:12 he gave them the-*r* to become children
Ro 9:21 Does not the potter have the-*r*
12:17 careful to do what is-*r* in the eyes
Eph 1:20 and seated him at his-*r* hand
Php 4:8 whatever is-*r*, whatever is pure,
2Th 3:13 never tire of doing what is-*r*.

RIGHTEOUS (RIGHTEOUSNESS)
Ps 34:15 The eyes of the Lord are on the-*r*
37:25 yet I have never seen the-*r* forsaken
119:137 *R* are you, O Lord,
143:2 for no one living is-*r* before you.
Pr 3:33 but he blesses the home of the-*r*
11:30 The fruit of the-*r* is a tree of life,
18:10 the-*r* run to it and are safe.
Isa 64:6 and all our-*r* acts are like filthy rags
Hab 2:4 but the-*r* will live by his faith—
Mt 5:45 rain on the-*r* and the unrighteous.
9:13 For I have not come to call the-*r*,
13:49 and separate the wicked from the-*r*
25:46 to eternal punishment, but the-*r*
Ro 1:17 as it is written: "The-*r* will live
3:10 "There is no one-*r*, not even one;
1Ti 1:9 that law is made not for the-*r*
1Pe 3:18 the-*r* for the unrighteous,
1Jn 3:7 does what is right is-*r*, just as he is-*r*
Rev 19:8 stands for the-*r* acts of the saints.)

RIGHTEOUSNESS (RIGHTEOUS)
Ge 15:6 and he credited it to him as-*r*.
1Sa 26:23 Lord rewards every man for his-*r*
Ps 9:8 He will judge the world in-*r*,
23:3 He guides me in paths of-*r*
45:7 You love-*r* and hate wickedness;
85:10 *r* and peace kiss each other.
89:14 *R* and justice are the foundation
111:3 and his-*r* endures forever.
Pr 14:34 *R* exalts a nation,
21:21 He who pursues-*r* and love
Isa 5:16 will show himself holy by his-*r*.
59:17 He put on-*r* as his breastplate,
Eze 18:20 The-*r* of the righteous man will be
Da 9:24 to bring in everlasting-*r*,
12:3 and those who lead many to-*r*,
Mal 4:2 the sun of-*r* will rise with healing
Mt 5:6 those who hunger and thirst for-*r*,
5:20 unless your-*r* surpasses that
6:33 But seek first his kingdom and his-*r*
Ro 4:3 and it was credited to him as-*r*."
4:9 faith was credited to him as-*r*
6:13 body to him as instruments of-*r*.
2Co 5:21 that in him we might become the-*r*
Gal 2:21 for if-*r* could be gained
3:6 and it was credited to him as-*r*."
Eph 6:14 with the breastplate of-*r* in place,
Php 3:9 not having a-*r* of my own that
2Ti 3:16 correcting and training in-*r*,
4:8 is in store for me the crown of-*r*,
Heb 11:7 became heir of the-*r* that comes
2Pe 2:21 not to have known the way of-*r*,

RIGHTS (RIGHT)
La 3:35 to deny a man his-*r*
Gal 4:5 that we might receive the full-*r*

RISE (RAISED)
Isa 26:19 their bodies will-*r*.
Mt 27:63 'After three days I will-*r* again.'
Jn 5:29 those who have done good will-*r*
1Th 4:16 and the dead in Christ will-*r* first.

ROAD
Mt 7:13 and broad is the-*r* that leads

Mk 15:27 They crucified two-*r* with him,
Lk 19:46 but you have made it 'a den of-*r.*' "
Jn 10: 8 came before me were thieves and-*r,*

ROCK

Ps 18: 2 The Lord is my-*r,* my fortress
40: 2 he set my feet on a-*r*
Mt 7:24 man who built his house on the-*r.*
16:18 and on this-*r* I will build my church
Ro 9:33 and a-*r* that makes them fall,
1Co 10: 4 the spiritual-*r* that accompanied

ROD

Ps 23: 4 your-*r* and your staff,
Pr 13:24 He who spares the-*r* hates his son,
23:13 if you punish him with the-*r,*

ROOM (ROOMS)

Mt 6: 6 But when you pray, go into your-*r,*
Lk 2: 7 there was no-*r* for them in the inn.
Jn 21:25 the whole world would not have-*r*

ROOMS (ROOM)

Jn 14: 2 In my Father's house are many-*r;*

ROOT

Isa 53: 2 and like a-*r* out of dry ground.
1Ti 6:10 of money is a-*r* of all kinds of evil.

ROYAL

Jas 2: 8 If you really keep the-*r* law found
1Pe 2: 9 a-*r* priesthood, a holy nation,

RUBBISH*

Php 3: 8 I consider them-*r,* that I may gain

RUDE*

1Co 13: 5 It is not-*r,* it is not self-seeking,

RUIN (RUINS)

Pr 18:24 many companions may come to-*r,*
1Ti 6: 9 desires that plunge men into-*r*

RUINS (RUIN)

Pr 19: 3 A man's own folly-*r* his life,
2Ti 2:14 and only-*r* those who listen.

RULE (RULER RULERS RULES)

1Sa 12:12 'No, we want a king to-*r* over us'—
Ps 2: 9 You will-*r* them with an iron
119:133 let no sin-*r* over me.
Zec 9:10 His-*r* will extend from sea to sea
Col 3:15 the peace of Christ-*r* in your hearts,
Rev 2:27 He will-*r* them with an iron scepter;

RULER (RULE)

Ps 8: 6 You made him-*r* over the works
Eph 2: 2 of the-*r* of the kingdom of the air,
1Ti 6:15 God, the blessed and only-*R,*

RULERS (RULE)

Ps 2: 2 and the-*r* gather together
Col 1:16 or powers or-*r* or authorities;

RULES (RULE)

Ps 103:19 and his kingdom-*r* over all.
Lk 22:26 one who-*r* like the one who serves.
2Ti 2: 5 he competes according to the-*r.*

RUMORS

Mt 24: 6 You will hear of wars and-*r* of wars,

RUN (RAN)

Isa 40:31 they will-*r* and not grow weary,
1Co 9:24 *R* in such a way as to get the prize.
Heb 12: 1 let us-*r* with perseverance the race

RUST

Mt 6:19 where moth and-*r* destroy,

RUTH*

Moabitess; widow who went to Bethlehem with mother-in-law Naomi (Ru 1). Gleaned in field of Boaz; shown favor (Ru 2). Proposed marriage to Boaz (Ru 3). Married (Ru 4:1-12); bore Obed, ancestor of David (Ru 4:13-22), Jesus (Mt 1:5).

SABBATH

Ex 20: 8 "Remember the-*S* day
Dt 5:12 "Observe the-*S* day
Col 2:16 a New Moon celebration or a-*S* day

SACKCLOTH

Mt 11:21 would have repented long ago in-*s*

SACRED

Mt 7: 6 "Do not give dogs what is-*s;*
1Co 3:17 for God's temple is-*s,* and you are

SACRIFICE (SACRIFICED SACRIFICES)

Ge 22: 2 *S* him there as a burnt offering
Ex 12:27 'It is the Passover-*s* to the Lord,
1Sa 15:22 To obey is better than-*s,*
Hos 6: 6 For I desire mercy, not-*s,*
Mt 9:13 this means: 'I desire mercy, not-*s.*'
Heb 9:26 away with sin by the-*s* of himself.
13:15 offer to God a-*s* of praise—
1Jn 2: 2 He is the atoning-*s* for our sins,

SACRIFICED (SACRIFICE)

1Co 5: 7 our Passover lamb, has been-*s.*
8: 1 Now about food-*s* to idols:
Heb 9:28 so Christ was-*s* once

SACRIFICES (SACRIFICE)

Ps 51:17 The-*s* of God are a broken spirit;
Ro 12: 1 to offer your bodies as living-*s,*

SADDUCEES

Mk 12:18 *S,* who say there is no resurrection.

SAFE (SAVE)

Ps 37: 3 in the land and enjoy-*s* pasture.
Pr 18:10 the righteous run to it and are-*s.*

SAFETY (SAVE)

Ps 4: 8 make me dwell in-*s.*
1Th 5: 3 people are saying, "Peace and-*s,*"

SAINTS

Ps 116:15 is the death of his-*s.*
Ro 8:27 intercedes for the-*s* in accordance
Eph 1:18 of his glorious inheritance in the-*s,*
6:18 always keep on praying for all the-*s.*
Rev 5: 8 which are the prayers of the-*s.*
19: 8 for the righteous acts of the-*s.*)

SAKE

Ps 44:22 Yet for your-*s* we face death all day
Php 3: 7 loss for the-*s* of Christ.
Heb 11:26 He regarded disgrace for the-*s*

SALT

Ge 19:26 and she became a pillar of-*s.*
Mt 5:13 "You are the-*s* of the earth.

SALVATION (SAVE)

Ex 15: 2 he has become my-*s.*
1Ch 16:23 proclaim his-*s* day after day.
Ps 27: 1 The Lord is my light and my-*s*—
51:12 Restore to me the joy of your-*s*
62: 2 He alone is my rock and my-*s;*
85: 9 Surely his-*s* is near those who fear
96: 2 proclaim his-*s* day after day.
Isa 25: 9 let us rejoice and be glad in his-*s.*"
45:17 the Lord with an everlasting-*s;*
51: 6 But my-*s* will last forever,
59:17 and the helmet of-*s* on his head;
61:10 me with garments of-*s*
Jnh 2: 9 *S* comes from the Lord."
Zec 9: 9 righteous and having-*s,*
Lk 2:30 For my eyes have seen your-*s,*
Jn 4:22 for-*s* is from the Jews.
Ac 4:12 *S* is found in no one else,
13:47 that you may bring-*s* to the ends
Ro 11:11 *s* has come to the Gentiles
2Co 7:10 brings repentance that leads to-*s*
Eph 6:17 Take the helmet of-*s* and the sword
Php 2:12 to work out your-*s* with fear
1Th 5: 8 and the hope of-*s* as a helmet.
2Ti 3:15 wise for-*s* through faith

SAMARITAN

Lk 10:33 But a-*S,* as he traveled, came where

SAMSON

Danite judge. Birth promised (Jdg 13). Married to Philistine (Jdg 14). Vengeance on Philistines (Jdg 15). Betrayed by Delilah (Jdg 16:1-22). Death (Jdg 16:23-31). Feats of strength: killed lion (Jdg 14:6), 30 Philistines (Jdg 14:19), 1,000 Philistines with jawbone (Jdg 15:13-17), carried off gates of Gaza (Jdg 16:3), pushed down temple of Dagon (Jdg 16:25-30).

SAMUEL

Ephraimite judge and prophet (Heb 11:32). Birth prayed for (1Sa 1:10-18). Dedicated to temple by Hannah (1Sa 1:21-28). Raised by Eli (1Sa 2:11, 18-26). Called as prophet (1Sa 3). Led Israel to victory over Philistines (1Sa 7). Asked by Israel for a king (1Sa 8). Anointed Saul as king (1Sa 9-10). Farewell speech (1Sa 12). Rebuked Saul for sacrifice (1Sa 13). Announced rejection of Saul (1Sa 15). Anointed David as king (1Sa 16). Protected David from Saul (1Sa 19:18-24). Death (1Sa 25:1). Returned from dead to condemn Saul (1Sa 28).

SANCTIFIED (SANCTIFY)

Ac 20:32 among all those who are-*s.*
Ro 15:16 to God,-*s* by the Holy Spirit.
1Co 6:11 But you were washed, you were-*s,*
7:14 and the unbelieving wife has been-*s*
Heb 10:29 blood of the covenant that-*s* him,

SANCTIFY (SANCTIFIED SANCTIFYING)

1Th 5:23 *s* you through and through.

SANCTIFYING (SANCTIFY)

2Th 2:13 through the-*s* work of the Spirit

SANCTUARY

Ex 25: 8 "Then have them make a-*s* for me,

SAND

Ge 22:17 and as the-*s* on the seashore.
Mt 7:26 man who built his house on-*s.*

SANDALS

Ex 3: 5 off your-*s,* for the place where you
Jos 5:15 off your-*s,* for the place where you

SANG (SING)

Job 38: 7 while the morning stars-*s* together
Rev 5: 9 And they-*s* a new song:

SARAH

Wife of Abraham, originally named Sarai; barren (Ge 11:29-31; 1Pe 3:6). Taken by Pharaoh as Abraham's sister; returned (Ge 12:10-20). Gave Hagar to Abraham; sent her away in pregnancy (Ge 16). Name changed; Isaac promised (Ge 17:15-21; 18:10-15; Heb 11:1). Taken by Abimelech as Abraham's sister; returned (Ge 20). Isaac born; Hagar and Ishmael sent away (Ge 21:1-21; Gal 4:21-31). Death (Ge 23).

SATAN

Job 1: 6 and-*S* also came with them.
Zec 3: 2 said to-*S,* "The Lord rebuke you,
Mk 4:15 *S* comes and takes away the word
2Co 11:14 for-*S* himself masquerades
12: 7 a messenger of-*S,* to torment me.
Rev 12: 9 serpent called the devil, or-*S,*
20: 2 or-*S,* and bound him for a thousand
20: 7 *S* will be released from his prison

SATISFIED (SATISFY)

Isa 53:11 he will see the light of life ,and be-*s*

SATISFIES (SATISFY)

Ps 103: 5 who-*s* your desires with good things,

SATISFY (SATISFIED SATISFIES)

Isa 55: 2 and your labor on what does not-*s?*

SAUL

1. Benjamite; anointed by Samuel as first king of Israel (1Sa 9-10). Defeated Ammonites (1Sa 11). Rebuked for offering sacrifice (1Sa 13:1-15). Defeated Philistines (1Sa 14). Rejected as king for failing to annihilate Amalekites (1Sa 15). Soothed from evil spirit by David (1Sa 16:14-23). Sent David against Goliath (1Sa 17). Jealousy and attempted murder of David (1Sa 18:1-11). Gave David Michal as wife (1Sa 18:12-30). Second attempt to kill David (1Sa 19). Anger at Jonathan (1Sa 20:26-34). Pursued David: killed priests at Nob (1Sa 22), went to Keilah and Ziph (1Sa 23), life spared by David at En Gedi (1Sa 24) and in his tent (1Sa 26). Rebuked by Samuel's spirit for consulting witch at Endor (1Sa 28). Wounded by Philistines; took his own life (1Sa 31; 1Ch 10).

2. See PAUL

SAVE (SAFE SAFETY SALVATION SAVED SAVIOR)

Isa 63: 1 mighty to-*s.*"
Da 3:17 the God we serve is able to-*s* us
Zep 3:17 he is mighty to-*s.*
Mt 1:21 he will-*s* his people from their sins
16:25 wants to-*s* his life will lose it,
Lk 19:10 to seek and to-*s* what was lost."
Jn 3:17 but to-*s* the world through him.
1Ti 1:15 came into the world to-*s* sinners:
Jas 5:20 of his way will-*s* him from death

SAVED (SAVE)

Ps 34: 6 he-*s* him out of all his troubles.
Isa 45:22 "Turn to me and be-*s,*
Joel 2:32 on the name of the Lord will be-*s;*
Mk 13:13 firm to the end will be-*s.*
16:16 believes and is baptized will be-*s.*
Jn 10: 9 enters through me will be-*s.*
Ac 4:12 to men by which we must be-*s.*"
16:30 do to be-*s?*" They replied,
Ro 9:27 only the remnant will be-*s.*
10: 9 him from the dead, you will be-*s.*
1Co 3:15 will suffer loss; he himself will be-*s,*
15: 2 By this gospel you are-*s.*
Eph 2: 5 it is by grace you have been-*s.*
2: 8 For it is by grace you have been-*s,*
1Ti 2: 4 who wants all men to be-*s*

SAVIOR

Ps 89:26 my God, the Rock my-*S.*'
Isa 43:11 and apart from me there is no-*s.*
Hos 13: 4 no-*S* except me.
Lk 1:47 and my spirit rejoices in God my-*S,*
2:11 of David a-*S* has been born to you;
Jn 4:42 know that this man really is the-*S*
Eph 5:23 his body, of which he is the-*S.*
Tit 1: 4 who is the-*S* of all men,
2:10 about God our-*S* attractive.
2:13 appearing of our great God and-*S,*
3: 4 and love of God our-*S* appeared,
1Jn 4:14 Son to be the-*S* of the world.
Jude :25 to the only God our-*S* be glory,

SCALES

Lev 19:36 Use honest-*s* and honest weights,
Da 5:27 You have been weighed on the-*s*

SCAPEGOAT (GOAT)

Lev 16:10 by sending it into the desert as a-*s.*

SCARLET

Isa 1:18 "Though your sins are like-*s,*

SCATTERED
Jer 31:10 'He who-s Israel will gather them
Ac   8:4 who had been-s preached the word

SCEPTER
Rev 19:15 "He will rule them with an iron-s."

SCHEMES
2Co 2:11 For we are not unaware of his-s.
Eph 6:11 stand against the devil's-s.

SCOFFERS
2Pe 3:3 that in the last days-s will come,

SCORPION
Rev 9:5 sting of a-s when it strikes a man.

SCRIPTURE (SCRIPTURES)
Jn 10:35 and the-S cannot be broken—
1Ti   4:13 yourself to the public reading of-S,
2Ti   3:16 All-S is God-breathed
2Pe 1:20 that no prophecy of-S came about

SCRIPTURES (SCRIPTURE)
Lk 24:27 said in all the-S concerning himself.
Jn   5:39 These are the-S that testify about
Ac 17:11 examined the-S every day to see

SCROLL
Eze 3:1 eat what is before you, eat this-s;

SEA
Ex 14:16 go through the-s on dry ground.
Isa 57:20 the wicked are like the tossing-s,
Mic 7:19 iniquities into the depths of the-s.
Jas 1:6 who doubts is like a wave of the-s,
Rev 13:1 I saw a beast coming out of the-s.

SEAL (SEALS)
Jn   6:27 God the Father has placed his-s
2Co 1:22 set his-s of ownership on us,
Eph 1:13 you were marked in him with a-s,

SEALS (SEAL)
Rev 5:2 "Who is worthy to break the-s
       6:1 opened the first of the seven-s.

SEARCH (SEARCHED SEARCHES SEARCHING)
Ps   4:4 s your hearts and be silent.
   139:23 S me, O God, and know my heart;
Pr   2:4 and-s for it as for hidden treasure,
Jer 17:10 "I the LORD-s the heart
Eze 34:16 I will-s for the lost and bring back
Lk 15:8 and-s carefully until she finds it?

SEARCHED (SEARCH)
Ps 139:1 O LORD, you have-s me

SEARCHES (SEARCH)
Ro 8:27 And he who-s our hearts knows
1Co 2:10 The Spirit-s all things,

SEARCHING (SEARCH)
Am 8:12 s for the word of the LORD,

SEARED
1Ti 4:2 whose consciences have been-s

SEASON
2Ti 4:2 be prepared in-s and out of-s;

SEAT (SEATED SEATS)
Ps   1:1 or sit in the-s of mockers.
Da   7:9 and the Ancient of Days took his-s.
2Co 5:10 before the judgment-s of Christ,

SEATED (SEAT)
Ps 47:8 God is-s on his holy throne.
Isa 6:1 I saw the Lord-s on a throne,
Col 3:1 where Christ is-s at the right hand

SEATS (SEAT)
Lk 11:43 you love the most important-s

SECRET (SECRETS)
Dt 29:29 The-s things belong
Jdg 16:6 Tell me the-s of your great strength
Ps 90:8 our-s sins in the light

Pr 11:13 but a trustworthy man keeps a-s.
Mt   6:4 so that your giving may be in-s.
2Co 4:2 we have renounced-s and shameful
Php 4:12 I have learned the-s

SECRETS (SECRET)
Ps 44:21 since he knows the-s of the heart?
1Co 14:25 the-s of his heart will be laid bare.

SECURE (SECURITY)
Ps 112:8 His heart is-s, he will have no fear;
Heb 6:19 an anchor for the soul, firm and-s.

SECURITY (SECURE)
Job 31:24 or said to pure gold, 'You are my-s,'

SEED (SEEDS)
Lk   8:11 of the parable: The-s is the word
1Co 3:6 I planted the-s, Apollos watered it,
2Co 9:10 he who supplies-s to the sower
Gal 3:29 then you are Abraham's-s,
1Pe 1:23 not of perishable-s,

SEEDS (SEED)
Jn 12:24 But if it dies, it produces many-s.
Gal 3:16 Scripture does not say "and to-s,"

SEEK (SEEKS SELF-SEEKING)
Dt   4:29 if from there you-s the LORD your
1Ch 28:9 If you-s him, he will be found
2Ch 7:14 themselves and pray and-s my face
Ps 119:10 I-s you with all my heart;
Isa 55:6 S the LORD while he may be
       65:1 found by those who did not-s me.
Mt   6:33 But-s first his kingdom
Lk 19:10 For the Son of Man came to-s
Ro 10:20 found by those who did not-s me;
1Co 7:27 you married? Do not-s a divorce.

SEEKS (SEEK)
Jn   4:23 the kind of worshipers the Father-s.

SEER
1Sa 9:9 of today used to be called a-s.)

SELF-CONTROL (CONTROL)
1Co 7:5 you because of your lack of-s.
Gal 5:23 faithfulness, gentleness and-s.
2Pe 1:6 and to knowledge,-s; and to-s,

SELF-CONTROLLED* (CONTROL)
1Th   5:6 are asleep, but let us be alert and-s.
       8 let us be-s, putting on faith and love
1Ti   3:2 s, respectable, hospitable,
Tit   1:8 who is-s, upright, holy
       2:2 worthy of respect,-s, and sound
       2:5 to be-s and pure, to be busy at home
       2:6 encourage the young men to be-s.
       2:12 to live-s, upright and godly lives
1Pe 1:13 prepare your minds for action; be-s;
       4:7 and-s so that you can pray.
       5:8 Be-s and alert.

SELF-INDULGENCE
Mt 23:25 inside they are full of greed and-s.

SELF-SEEKING (SEEK)
1Co 13:5 it is not-s, it is not easily angered,

SELFISH*
Ps 119:36 and not toward-s gain.
Pr 18:1 An unfriendly man pursues-s ends;
Gal 5:20 fits of rage,-s ambition, dissensions,
Php 1:17 preach Christ out of-s ambition,
       2:3 Do nothing out of-s ambition
Jas 3:14 and-s ambition in your hearts,
       3:16 you have envy and-s ambition,

SEND (SENDING SENT)
Isa 6:8 S me!" He said, "Go and tell this
Mt   9:38 to-s out workers into his harvest
Jn 16:7 but if I go, I will-s him to you.

SENDING (SEND)
Jn 20:21 Father has sent me, I am-s you."

SENSES*
Lk 15:17 "When he came to his-s, he said,
1Co 15:34 Come back to your-s as you ought,
2Ti   2:26 and that they will come to their-s

SENSUAL
Col 2:23 value in restraining-s indulgence.

SENT (SEND)
Isa 55:11 achieve the purpose for which I-s it.
Mt 10:40 me receives the one who-s me.
Jn   4:34 "is to do the will of him who-s me
Ro 10:15 can they preach unless they are-s?
1Jn   4:10 but that he loved us and-s his Son

SEPARATE (SEPARATED SEPARATES)
Mt 19:6 has joined together, let man not-s."
Ro   8:35 Who shall-s us from the love
1Co 7:10 wife must not-s from her husband.
2Co 6:17 and be-s, says the Lord.

SEPARATED (SEPARATE)
Isa 59:2 But your iniquities have-s

SEPARATES (SEPARATE)
Pr 16:28 and a gossip-s close friends.

SERPENT
Ge   3:1 the-s was more crafty than any
Rev 12:9 that ancient-s called the devil

SERVANT (SERVANTS)
1Sa 3:10 "Speak, for your-s is listening."
Mt 20:26 great among you must be your-s,
       25:21 'Well done, good and faithful-s!
Lk 16:13 "No-s can serve two masters.
Php 2:7 taking the very nature of a-s,
2Ti 2:24 And the Lord's-s must not quarrel;

SERVANTS (SERVANT)
Lk 17:10 should say, 'We are unworthy-s;
Jn 15:15 longer call you-s, because a servant

SERVE (SERVICE SERVING)
Dt 10:12 to-s the LORD your God
Jos 22:5 and to-s him with all your heart
       24:15 this day whom you will-s,
Mt   4:10 Lord your God, and-s him only.'"
       6:24 "No one can-s two masters.
       20:28 but to-s, and to give his life
Eph 6:7 S wholeheartedly,

SERVICE (SERVE)
1Co 12:5 There are different kinds of-s,
Eph 4:12 God's people for works of-s,

SERVING (SERVE)
Ro 12:11 your spiritual fervor,-s the Lord.
Eph 6:7 as if you were-s the Lord, not men,
Col 3:24 It is the Lord Christ you are-s.
2Ti   2:4 No one-s as a soldier gets involved

SEVEN (SEVENTH)
Ge   7:2 Take with you-s of every kind
Jos   6:4 march around the city-s times,
1Ki 19:18 Yet I reserve-s thousand in Israel—
Pr   6:16 s that are detestable to him:
       24:16 a righteous man falls-s times,
Isa   4:1 In that day-s women
Da   9:25 comes, there will be-s 'sevens,'
Mt 18:21 Up to-s times?" Jesus answered,
Lk 11:26 takes-s other spirits more wicked
Ro 11:4 for myself-s thousand who have not
Rev 1:4 To the-s churches in the province
       6:1 opened the first of the-s seals.
       8:2 and to them were given-s trumpets.
       10:4 And when the-s thunders spoke,
       15:7 to the-s angels' golden bowls filled

SEVENTH (SEVEN)
Ge   2:2 By the-s day God had finished
Ex 23:12 but on the-s day do not work,

SEXUAL (SEXUALLY)
1Co 6:13 body is not meant for-s immorality,

6:18 Flee from-s immorality.
10:8 should not commit-s immorality,
Eph 5:3 even a hint of-s immorality,
1Th   4:3 that you should avoid-s immorality

SEXUALLY (SEXUAL)
1Co 5:9 to associate with-s immoral people
       6:18 he who sins-s sins against his own

SHADOW
Ps 23:4 through the valley of the-s of death,
       36:7 find refuge in the-s of your wings.
Heb 10:1 The law is only a-s

SHALLUM
King of Israel (2Ki 15:10-16).

SHAME (ASHAMED)
Ps 34:5 their faces are never covered with-s
Pr 13:18 discipline comes to poverty and-s,
Heb 12:2 endured the cross, scorning its-s,

SHARE (SHARED)
Ge 21:10 that slave woman's son will never-s
Lk   3:11 "The man with two tunics should-s
Gal 4:30 the slave woman's son will never-s
       6:6 in the word must-s all good things
Eph 4:28 something to-s with those in need.
1Ti   6:18 and to be generous and willing to-s.
Heb 12:10 that we may-s in his holiness.
       13:16 to do good and to-s with others,

SHARED (SHARE)
Heb 2:14 he too-s in their humanity so that

SHARON
SS   2:1 I am a rose of-S,

SHARPER*
Heb 4:12 S than any double-edged sword,

SHED (SHEDDING)
Ge   9:6 by man shall his blood be-s;
Col 1:20 through his blood,-s on the cross.

SHEDDING (SHED)
Heb 9:22 without the-s of blood there is no

SHEEP
Ps 100:3 we are his people, the-s
       119:176 I have strayed like a lost-s.
Isa 53:6 We all, like-s, have gone astray,
Jer 50:6 "My people have been lost-s;
Eze 34:11 I myself will search for my-s
Mt   9:36 helpless, like-s without a shepherd.
Jn 10:3 He calls his own-s by name
       10:15 and I lay down my life for the-s.
       10:27 My-s listen to my voice; I know
       21:17 Jesus said, "Feed my-s.
1Pe 2:25 For you were like-s going astray,

SHELTER
Ps 61:4 take refuge in the-s of your wings.
       91:1 in the-s of the Most High

SHEM
Son of Noah (Ge 5:32; 6:10). Blessed (Ge 9:26).
Descendants (Ge 10:21-31; 11:10-32).

SHEPHERD (SHEPHERDS)
Ps 23:1 LORD is my-s, I shall not be in want.
Isa 40:11 He tends his flock like a-s:
Jer 31:10 will watch over his flock like a-s.'
Eze 34:12 As a-s looks after his scattered
Zec 11:17 "Woe to the worthless-s,
Mt   9:36 and helpless, like sheep without a-s.
Jn 10:11 The good-s lays down his life
       10:16 there shall be one flock and one-s.
1Pe 5:4 And when the Chief-S appears,

SHEPHERDS (SHEPHERD)
Jer 23:1 "Woe to the-s who are destroying
Lk   2:8 there were-s living out in the fields
Ac 20:28 Be-s of the church of God,
1Pe 5:2 Be-s of God's flock that is

SHIELD
Ps 28:7 Lord is my strength and my-*s*;
Eph 6:16 to all this, take up the-*s* of faith,

SHINE (SHONE)
Ps 4:6 Let the light of your face-*s* upon us,
80:1 between the cherubim,-*s* forth
Isa 60:1 "Arise,-*s*, for your light has come,
Da 12:3 are wise will-*s* like the brightness
Mt 5:16 let your light-*s* before men,
13:43 the righteous will-*s* like the sun
2Co 4:6 made his light-*s* in our hearts
Eph 5:14 and Christ will-*s* on you."

SHIPWRECKED*
2Co 11:25 I was stoned, three times I was-*s*,
1Ti 1:19 and so have-*s* their faith.

SHONE (SHINE)
Mt 17:2 His face-*s* like the sun,
Lk 2:9 glory of the Lord-*s* around them,
Rev 21:11 It-*s* with the glory of God,

SHORT
Isa 59:1 of the Lord is not too-*s* to save,
Ro 3:23 and fall-*s* of the glory of God,

SHOULDERS
Isa 9:6 and the government will be on his-*s*
Lk 15:5 he joyfully puts it on his-*s*

SHOWED
1Jn 4:9 This is how God-*s* his love

SHREWD
Mt 10:16 Therefore be as-*s* as snakes and

SHUN*
Job 28:28 and to-*s* evil is understanding.' "
Pr 3:7 fear the Lord and-*s* evil.

SICK
Pr 13:12 Hope deferred makes the heart-*s*,
Mt 9:12 who need a doctor, but the-*s*,
25:36 I was-*s* and you looked after me,
Jas 5:14 of you-*s*? He should call the elders

SICKLE
Joel 3:13 Swing the-*s*,

SIDE
Ps 91:7 A thousand may fall at your-*s*,
124:1 If the Lord had not been on our-*s*
2Ti 4:17 But the Lord stood at my-*s*

SIGHT
Ps 90:4 For a thousand years in your-*s*,
116:15 Precious in the-*s* of the Lord
2Co 5:7 We live by faith, not by-*s*.
1Pe 3:4 which is of great worth in God's-*s*.

SIGN (SIGNS)
Isa 7:14 the Lord himself will give you a-*s*:

SIGNS (SIGN)
Mk 16:17 these-*s* will accompany those who
Jn 20:30 Jesus did many other miraculous-*s*

SILENT
Pr 17:28 a fool is thought wise if he keeps-*s*,
Isa 53:7 as a sheep before her shearers is-*s*,
Hab 2:20 let all the earth be-*s* before him."
1Co 14:34 women should remain-*s*
1Ti 2:12 over a man; she must be-*s*.

SILVER
Pr 25:11 is like apples of gold in settings of-*s*.
Hag 2:8 'The-*s* is mine and the gold is mine,'
1Co 3:12 *s*, costly stones, wood, hay or straw

SIMON
1. See PETER.
2. Apostle, called the Zealot (Mt 10:4; Mk 3:18; Lk 6:15; Ac 1:13).
3. Samaritan sorcerer (Ac 8:9-24).

SIN (SINFUL SINNED SINNER SINNERS SINNING SINS)
Nu 5:7 and must confess the-*s* he has
32:23 be sure that your-*s* will find you
Dt 24:16 each is to die for his own-*s*.
1Ki 8:46 for there is no one who does not-*s*
2Ch 7:14 and will forgive their-*s* and will heal
Ps 4:4 In your anger do not-*s*;
32:2 whose-*s* the Lord does not count
32:5 Then I acknowledged my-*s* to you
51:2 and cleanse me from my-*s*.
66:18 If I had cherished-*s* in my heart,
119:11 that I might not-*s* against you.
119:133 let no-*s* rule over me.
Isa 6:7 is taken away and your-*s* atoned
Mic 7:18 who pardons-*s* and forgives
Mt 18:6 little ones who believe in me to-*s*,
Jn 1:29 who takes away the-*s* of the world!
8:34 everyone who sins is a slave to-*s*.
Ro 5:12 as-*s* entered the world
5:20 where-*s* increased, grace increased
6:11 count yourselves dead to-*s*
6:23 For the wages of-*s* is death,
14:23 that does not come from faith is-*s*.
2Co 5:21 God made him who had no-*s* to be-*s*
Gal 6:1 if someone is caught in a-*s*,
Heb 9:26 to do away with-*s* by the sacrifice
11:25 the pleasures of-*s* for a short time.
12:1 and the-*s* that so easily entangles,
1Pe 2:22 "He committed no-*s*,
1Jn 1:8 If we claim to be without-*s*,
3:4 in fact,-*s* is lawlessness.
3:5 And in him is no-*s*.
3:9 born of God will continue to-*s*,
5:18 born of God does not continue to-*s*;

SINCERE
Ro 12:9 Love must be-*s*.
Heb 10:22 near to God with a-*s* heart

SINFUL (SIN)
Ps 51:5 Surely I was-*s* at birth
51:5 *s* from the time my mother
Ro 7:5 we were controlled by the-*s* nature,
8:4 not live according to the-*s* nature
8:9 are controlled not by the-*s* nature
Gal 5:19 The acts of the-*s* nature are obvious
5:24 Jesus have crucified the-*s* nature
1Pe 2:11 abstain from-*s* desires, which war

SING (SANG SINGING SONG SONGS)
Ps 30:4 *S* to the Lord, you saints of his;
47:6 *S* praises to God,-*s* praises;
59:16 But I will-*s* of your strength,
89:1 I will-*s* of the Lord's great love
101:1 I will-*s* of your love and justice;
Eph 5:19 *S* and make music in your heart

SINGING (SING)
Ps 63:5 with-*s* lips my mouth will praise
Ac 16:25 Silas were praying and-*s* hymns

SINNED (SIN)
2Sa 12:13 "I have-*s* against the Lord."
Job 1:5 "Perhaps my children have-*s*
Ps 51:4 Against you, you only, have I-*s*
Da 9:5 we have-*s* and done wrong.
Mic 7:9 Because I have-*s* against him,
Lk 15:18 I have-*s* against heaven
Ro 3:23 for all have-*s* and fall short
1Jn 1:10 claim we have not-*s*, we make him

SINNER (SIN)
Ecc 9:18 but one-*s* destroys much good.
Lk 15:7 in heaven over one-*s* who repents
18:13 'God, have mercy on me, a-*s*.'
1Co 14:24 convinced by all that he is a-*s*
Jas 5:20 Whoever turns a-*s* from the error
1Pe 4:18 become of the ungodly and the-*s*?"

SINNERS (SIN)
Ps 1:1 or stand in the way of-*s*
Pr 23:17 Do not let your heart envy-*s*,
Mt 9:13 come to call the righteous, but-*s*."
Ro 5:8 While we were still-*s*, Christ died
1Ti 1:15 came into the world to save-*s*—

SINNING (SIN)
Ex 20:20 be with you to keep you from-*s*.
1Co 15:34 stop-*s*; for there are some who are
Heb 10:26 If we deliberately keep on-*s*
1Jn 3:6 No one who lives in him keeps on-*s*
3:9 go on-*s*, because he has been born

SINS (SIN)
2Ki 14:6 each is to die for his own-*s*."
Ezr 9:6 our-*s* are higher than our heads
Ps 19:13 your servant also from willful-*s*;
32:1 whose-*s* are covered.
103:3 who forgives all your-*s*
130:3 O Lord, kept a record of-*s*,
Pr 28:13 who conceals his-*s* does not
Isa 1:18 "Though your-*s* are like scarlet,
43:25 and remembers your-*s* no more.
59:2 your-*s* have hidden his face
Eze 18:4 soul who-*s* is the one who will die.
Mt 1:21 he will save his people from their-*s*
18:15 "If your brother-*s* against you,
Lk 11:4 Forgive us our-*s*,
17:3 "If your brother-*s*, rebuke him,
Ac 22:16 be baptized and wash your-*s* away,
1Co 15:3 died for our-*s* according
Eph 2:1 dead in your transgressions and-*s*,
Col 2:13 us all our-*s*, having canceled
Heb 1:3 he had provided purification for-*s*,
7:27 He sacrificed for their-*s* once for all
8:12 and will remember their-*s* no more
10:12 for all time one sacrifice for-*s*,
Jas 4:17 ought to do and doesn't do it,-*s*.
5:16 Therefore confess your-*s*
5:20 and cover over a multitude of-*s*.
1Pe 2:24 He himself bore our-*s* in his body
3:18 For Christ died for-*s* once for all,
1Jn 1:9 If we confess our-*s*, he is faithful
Rev 1:5 has freed us from our-*s* by his blood

SITS
Ps 99:1 *s* enthroned between the cherubim,
Isa 40:22 He-*s* enthroned above the circle
Mt 19:28 of Man-*s* on his glorious throne,
Rev 4:9 thanks to him who-*s* on the throne

SKIN
Job 19:20 with only the-*s* of my teeth.
19:26 And after my-*s* has been destroyed,
Jer 13:23 Can the Ethiopian change his-*s*

SLAIN (SLAY)
Rev 5:12 "Worthy is the Lamb, who was-*s*,

SLANDER (SLANDERED SLANDERERS)
Lev 19:16 " 'Do not go about spreading-*s*
1Ti 5:14 the enemy no opportunity for-*s*.
Tit 3:2 to-*s* no one, to be peaceable

SLANDERED (SLANDER)
1Co 4:13 when we are-*s*, we answer kindly.

SLANDERERS (SLANDER)
Ro 1:30 They are gossips,-*s*, God-haters,
1Co 6:10 nor the greedy nor drunkards nor-*s*
Tit 2:3 not to be-*s* or addicted

SLAUGHTER
Isa 53:7 he was led like a lamb to the-*s*,

SLAVE (SLAVERY SLAVES)
Ge 21:10 "Get rid of that-*s* woman
Mt 20:27 wants to be first must be your-*s*—
Jn 8:34 everyone who sins is a-*s* to sin.
1Co 12:13 whether Jews or Greeks,-*s* or free
Gal 3:28 *s* nor free, male nor female,

4:30 Get rid of the-*s* woman and her son
2Pe 2:19 a man is a-*s* to whatever has

SLAVERY (SLAVE)
Ro 6:19 parts of your body in-*s* to impurity
Gal 4:3 were in-*s* under the basic principles

SLAVES (SLAVE)
Ro 6:6 that we should no longer be-*s* to sin
6:22 and have become-*s* to God,

SLAY (SLAIN)
Job 13:15 Though he-*s* me, yet will I hope

SLEEP (SLEEPING)
Ps 121:4 will neither slumber nor-*s*.
1Co 15:51 We will not all-*s*, but we will all be

SLEEPING (SLEEP)
Mk 13:36 suddenly, do not let him find you-*s*.

SLOW
Ex 34:6 and gracious God,-*s* to anger,
Jas 1:19 *s* to speak and-*s* to become angry,
2Pe 3:9 The Lord is not-*s* in keeping his

SLUGGARD
Pr 6:6 Go to the ant, you-*s*;
20:4 A-*s* does not plow in season;

SLUMBER
Ps 121:3 he who watches over you will not-*s*;
Pr 6:10 A little sleep, a little-*s*,
Ro 13:11 for you to wake up from your-*s*,

SNAKE (SNAKES)
Nu 21:8 "Make a-*s* and put it up on a pole;
Pr 23:32 In the end it bites like a-*s*
Jn 3:14 Moses lifted up the-*s* in the desert,

SNAKES (SNAKE)
Mt 10:16 as shrewd as-*s* and as innocent
Mk 16:18 they will pick up-*s* with their hands;

SNATCH
Jn 10:28 no one can-*s* them out of my hand.
Jude :23 *s* others from the fire and save

SNOW
Ps 51:7 and I will be whiter than-*s*.

SOAR
Isa 40:31 They will-*s* on wings like eagles;

SODOM
Ge 19:24 rained down burning sulfur on-*S*
Ro 9:29 we would have become like-*S*,

SOIL
Ge 4:2 kept flocks, and Cain worked the-*s*.
Mt 13:23 on good-*s* is the man who hears

SOLDIER
1Co 9:7 as a-*s* at his own expense?
2Ti 2:3 with us like a good-*s* of Christ Jesus

SOLE
Dt 28:65 place for the-*s* of your foot.
Isa 1:6 From the-*s* of your foot to the top

SOLID
2Ti 2:19 God's-*s* foundation stands firm,
Heb 5:12 You need milk, not-*s* food!

SOLOMON
Son of David by Bathsheba; king of Judah (2Sa 12:24; 1Ch 3:5, 10). Appointed king by David (1Ki 1); adversaries Adonijah, Joab, Shimei killed by Benaiah (1Ki 2). Asked for wisdom (1Ki 3; 2Ch 1). Judged between two prostitutes (1Ki 3:16-28). Built temple (1Ki 5-7, 2Ch 2-5); prayer of dedication (1Ki 8; 2Ch 6). Visited by Queen of Sheba (1Ki 10; 2Ch 9). Wives turned his heart from God (1Ki 11:1-13). Jeroboam rebelled against (1Ki 11:26-40). Death (1Ki 11:41-43; 2Ch 9:29-31).

Proverbs of (1Ki 4:32; Pr 1:1; 10:1; 25:1); psalms of (Ps 72; 127); song of (SS 1:1).

SON (SONS)

Ge 22: 2 "Take your-s, your only-s, Isaac,
Ex 11: 5 Every firstborn-s in Egypt will die,
Dt 21:18 rebellious-s who does not obey his
Ps 2: 7 He said to me, "You are my-S;
  2:12 Kiss the-S, lest he be angry
Pr 10: 1 A wise-s brings joy to his father,
  13:24 he who spares the rod hates his-s,
  29:17 Discipline your-s, and he will give
Isa 7:14 with child and will give birth to a-s,
Hos 11: 1 and out of Egypt I called my-s."
Mt 2:15 "Out of Egypt I called my-s."
  3:17 "This is my-S, whom I love;
  11:27 one knows the-S except the Father,
  16:16 "You are the Christ, the-S
  17: 5 "This is my-S, whom I love;
  20:18 and the-S of Man will be betrayed
  24:30 They will see the-S of Man coming
  24:44 the-S of Man will come at an hour
  27:54 "Surely he was the-S of God!"
  28:19 and of the-S and of the Holy Spirit,
Mk 10:45 even the-S of Man did not come
  14:62 you will see the-S of Man sitting
Lk 9:58 but the-S of Man has no place
  18: 8 when the-S of Man comes,
  19:10 For the-S of Man came to seek
Jn 3:14 so the-S of Man must be lifted up,
  3:16 that he gave his one and only-S,
  17: 1 Glorify your-S, that your-S may
Ro 8:29 conformed to the likeness of his-S,
  8:32 He who did not spare his own-S,
1Co 15:28 then the-S himself will be made
Gal 4:30 rid of the slave woman and her-s,
1Th 1:10 and to wait for his-S from heaven,
Heb 1: 2 days he has spoken to us by his-S,
  10:29 punished who has trampled the-S
1Jn 1: 7 his-S, purifies us from all sin.
  4: 9 only-S into the world that we might
  5: 5 he who believes that Jesus is the-S
  5:11 eternal life, and this life is in his-S.

SONG (SING)

Ps 40: 3 He put a new-s in my mouth,
  96: 1 Sing to the Lord a new-s;
  149: 1 Sing to the Lord a new-s.
Isa 49:13 burst into-s, O mountains!
  55:12 will burst into-s before you,
Rev 5: 9 And they sang a new-s:
  15: 3 and sang the-s of Moses the servant

SONGS (SING)

Job 35:10 who gives-s in the night,
Ps 100: 2 come before him with joyful-s.
Eph 5:19 with psalms, hymns and spiritual-s.
Jas 5:13 Is anyone happy? Let him sing-s

SONS (SON)

Joel 2:28 Your-s and daughters will prophesy
Jn 12:36 so that you may become-s of light."
Ro 8:14 by the Spirit of God are-s of God.
2Co 6:18 and you will be my-s and daughters
Gal 4: 5 we might receive the full rights of-s.
Heb 12: 7 discipline; God is treating you as-s.

SORROW (SORROWS)

Jer 31:12 and they will-s no more.
Ro 9: 2 I have great-s and unceasing
2Co 7:10 Godly-s brings repentance that

SORROWS (SORROW)

Isa 53: 3 a man of-s, and familiar

SOUL (SOULS)

Dt 6: 5 with all your-s and with all your
  10:12 all your heart and with all your-s,
Jos 22: 5 with all your heart and all your-s."
Ps 23: 3 he restores my-s.
  42: 1 so my-s pants for you, O God.
  42:11 Why are you downcast, O my-s?
  103: 1 Praise the Lord, O my-s;

Pr 13:19 A longing fulfilled is sweet to the-s,
Isa 55: 2 your-s will delight in the richest
Mt 10:28 kill the body but cannot kill the-s.
  16:26 yet forfeits his-s? Or what can
  22:37 with all your-s and with all your
Heb 4:12 even to dividing-s and spirit,

SOULS (SOUL)

Pr 11:30 and he who wins-s is wise.
Jer 6:16 and you will find rest for your-s.
Mt 11:29 and you will find rest for your-s.

SOUND

1Co 14: 8 if the trumpet does not-s a clear call
  15:52 the trumpet will-s, the dead will
2Ti 4: 3 men will not put up with-s doctrine.

SOVEREIGN

Da 4:25 that the Most High is-s

SOW (SOWS)

Job 4: 8 and those who-s trouble reap it.
Mt 6:26 they do not-s or reap or store away
2Pe 2:22 and, "A-s that is washed goes back

SOWS (SOW)

Pr 11:18 he who-s righteousness reaps a sure
  22: 8 he who-s wickedness reaps trouble
2Co 9: 6 Whoever-s sparingly will
Gal 6: 7 A man reaps what he-s.

SPARE (SPARES)

Ro 8:32 He who did not-s his own Son,
  11:21 natural branches, he will not-s you

SPARES (SPARE)

Pr 13:24 He who-s the rod hates his son,

SPEARS

Isa 2: 4 and their-s into pruning hooks.
Joel 3:10 and your pruning hooks into-s.
Mic 4: 3 and their-s into pruning hooks.

SPECTACLE

1Co 4: 9 We have been made a-s
Col 2:15 he made a public-s of them,

SPIN

Mt 6:28 They do not labor or-s.

SPIRIT (SPIRIT'S SPIRITS SPIRITUAL SPIRITUALLY)

Ge 1: 2 and the-S of God was hovering
  6: 3 "My-S will not contend
2Ki 2: 9 inherit a double portion of your-s,"
Job 33: 4 The-S of God has made me;
Ps 31: 5 Into your hands I commit my-s;
  51:10 and renew a steadfast-s within me.
  51:11 or take your Holy-S from me.
  51:17 sacrifices of God are a broken-s,
  139: 7 Where can I go from your-S?
Isa 57:15 him who is contrite and lowly in-s,
  63:10 and grieved his Holy-S.
Eze 11:19 an undivided heart and put a new-s
  36:26 you a new heart and put a new-s
Joel 2:28 I will pour out my-S on all people.
Zec 4: 6 but by my-S,' says the Lord
Mt 1:18 to be with child through the Holy-S
  3:11 will baptize you with the Holy-S
  3:16 he saw the-S of God descending
  4: 1 led by the-S into the desert
  5: 3 saying: "Blessed are the poor in-s,
  26:41 s is willing, but the body is weak."
  28:19 and of the Son and of the Holy-S,
Lk 1:80 child grew and became strong in-s;
  11:13 Father in heaven give the Holy-S
Jn 4:24 God is-s, and his worshipers must
  7:39 Up to that time the-S had not been
  14:26 But the Counselor, the Holy-S,
  16:13 But when he, the-S of truth, comes,
  20:22 and said, "Receive the Holy-S.
Ac 1: 5 will be baptized with the Holy-S."
  2: 4 of them were filled with the Holy-S

2:38 will receive the gift of the Holy-S.
  6: 3 who are known to be full of the-S
  19: 2 "Did you receive the Holy-S
Ro 8: 9 And if anyone does not have the-S
  8:26 the-S helps us in our weakness.
1Co 2:10 God has revealed it to us by his-S.
  2:14 man without the-S does not accept
  6:19 body is a temple of the Holy-S,
  12:13 baptized by one-S into one body—
2Co 3: 6 the letter kills, but the-S gives life.
  5: 5 and has given us the-S as a deposit,
Gal 5:16 by the-S, and you will not gratify
  5:22 But the fruit of the-S is love, joy,
  5:25 let us keep in step with the-S.
Eph 1:13 with a seal, the promised Holy-S,
  4:30 do not grieve the Holy-S of God,
  5:18 Instead, be filled with the-S.
  6:17 of salvation and the sword of the-S,
2Th 2:13 the sanctifying work of the-S,
Heb 4:12 even to dividing soul and-s,
1Pe 3: 4 beauty of a gentle and quiet-s,
2Pe 1:21 carried along by the Holy-S.
1Jn 4: 1 Dear friends, do not believe every-s

SPIRIT'S (SPIRIT)

1Th 5:19 not put out the-S fire; do not treat

SPIRITS (SPIRIT)

1Co 12:10 to another distinguishing between-s,
  14:32 The-s of prophets are subject
1Jn 4: 1 test the-s to see whether they are

SPIRITUAL (SPIRIT)

Ro 12: 1 this is your-s act of worship.
  12:11 but keep your-s fervor, serving
1Co 2:13 expressing-s truths in-s words.
  3: 1 I could not address you as-s but
  12: 1 Now about-s gifts, brothers,
  14: 1 of love and eagerly desire-s gifts,
  15:44 a natural body, it is raised a-s body.
Gal 6: 1 you who are-s should restore him
Eph 1: 3 with every-s blessing in Christ.
  5:19 with psalms, hymns and-s songs.
  6:12 and against the-s forces of evil
1Pe 2: 2 newborn babies, crave pure-s milk,
  2: 5 are being built into a-s house

SPIRITUALLY (SPIRIT)

1Co 2:14 because they are-s discerned.

SPLENDOR

1Ch 16:29 the Lord in the-s of his holiness.
  29:11 the glory and the majesty and the-s,
Job 37:22 of the north he comes in golden-s;
Ps 29: 2 in the-s of his holiness.
  45: 3 clothe yourself with-s and majesty.
  96: 6 S and majesty are before him;
  96: 9 in the-s of his holiness;
  104: 1 you are clothed with-s and majesty.
  145: 5 of the glorious-s of your majesty,
Isa 61: 3 the Lord for the display of his-s.
  63: 1 Who is this, robed in-s,
Lk 9:31 appeared in glorious-s, talking
2Th 2: 8 and destroy by the-s of his coming.

SPOIL

Ps 119:162 like one who finds great-s.

SPOTLESS

2Pe 3:14 make every effort to be found-s,

SPREAD (SPREADING)

Ac 12:24 of God continued to increase and-s,
  19:20 the word of the Lord-s widely

SPREADING (SPREAD)

1Th 3: 2 God's fellow worker in-s the gospel

SPRING

Jer 2:13 the-s of living water,
Jn 4:14 in him a-s of water welling up
Jas 3:12 can a salt-s produce fresh water.

SPUR*

Heb 10:24 how we may-s one another

SPURNS*

Pr 15: 5 A fool-s his father's discipline,

STAFF

Ps 23: 4 your rod and your-s,

STAKES

Isa 54: 2 strengthen your-s.

STAND (STANDING STANDS)

Ex 14:13 S firm and you will see
2Ch 20:17 s firm and see the deliverance
Ps 1: 5 Therefore the wicked will not-s
  40: 2 and gave me a firm place to-s.
  119:120 I-s in awe of your laws.
Eze 22:30 s before me in the gap on behalf
Zec 14: 4 On that day his feet will-s
Mt 12:25 divided against itself will not-s.
Ro 14:10 we will all-s before God's
  judgment
1Co 10:13 out so that you can-s up under it.
  15:58 Therefore, my dear brothers,-s firm
Eph 6:14 S firm then, with the belt
2Th 2:15 s firm and hold to the teachings we
Jas 5: 8 You too, be patient and-s firm,
Rev 3:20 Here I am! I-s at the door

STANDING (STAND)

Ex 3: 5 where you are-s is holy ground."
Jos 5:15 the place where you are-s is holy."
1Pe 5: 9 Resist him,-s firm in the faith,

STANDS (STAND)

Ps 89: 2 that your love-s firm forever,
  119:89 it-s firm in the heavens.
Mt 10:22 but he who-s firm to the end will be
2Ti 2:19 God's solid foundation-s firm,
1Pe 1:25 but the word of the Lord-s forever

STAR (STARS)

Nu 24:17 A-s will come out of Jacob;
Rev 22:16 and the bright Morning-S."

STARS (STAR)

Da 12: 3 like the-s for ever and ever.
Php 2:15 in which you shine like-s

STATURE

Lk 2:52 And Jesus grew in wisdom and-s,

STEADFAST

Ps 51:10 and renew a-s spirit within me.
Isa 26: 3 him whose mind is-s,
1Pe 5:10 and make you strong, firm and-s.

STEAL

Ex 20:15 "You shall not-s.
Mt 19:18 do not-s, do not give false
Eph 4:28 has been stealing must-s no longer,

STEP (STEPS)

Gal 5:25 let us keep in-s with the Spirit.

STEPS (STEP)

Pr 16: 9 but the Lord determines his-s.
Jer 10:23 it is not for man to direct his-s.
1Pe 2:21 that you should follow in his-s.

STICKS

Pr 18:24 there is a friend who-s closer

STIFF-NECKED

Ex 34: 9 Although this is a-s people,

STILL

Ps 46:10 "Be-s, and know that I am God;
Zec 2:13 Be-s before the Lord, all mankind

STIRS

Pr 6:19 and a man who-s up dissension
  10:12 Hatred-s up dissension,
  15: 1 but a harsh word-s up anger.
  15:18 hot-tempered man-s up dissension,
  16:28 A perverse man-s up dissension,

28:25 A greedy man-*s* up dissension,
29:22 An angry man-*s* up dissension,

STONE (CAPSTONE CORNERSTONE MILLSTONE)
1Sa 17:50 the Philistine with a sling and a-*s*;
Isa 8:14 a-*s* that causes men to stumble
Eze 11:19 remove from them their heart of-*s*
Mk 16:3 "Who will roll the-*s* away
Lk 4:3 tell this-*s* to become bread."
Jn 8:7 the first to throw a-*s* at her.
2Co 3:3 not on tablets of-*s* but on tablets

STOOP
2Sa 22:36 you-*s* down to make me great.

STORE
Pr 10:14 Wise men-*s* up knowledge,
Mt 6:19 not-*s* up for yourselves treasures

STOREHOUSE (HOUSE)
Mal 3:10 Bring the whole tithe into the-*s*,

STRAIGHT
Pr 3:6 and he will make your paths-*s*.
4:25 Let your eyes look-*s* ahead,
15:21 of understanding keeps a-*s* course.
Jn 1:23 'Make-*s* the way for the Lord.' "

STRAIN
Mt 23:24 You-*s* out a gnat but swallow

STRANGER (STRANGERS)
Mt 25:35 I was a-*s* and you invited me in,
Jn 10:5 But they will never follow a-*s*;

STRANGERS (STRANGER)
1Pe 2:11 as aliens and-*s* in the world,

STREAMS
Ps 1:3 He is like a tree planted by-*s*
46:4 is a river whose-*s* make glad
Ecc 1:7 All-*s* flow into the sea,
Jn 7:38 *s* of living water will flow

STRENGTH (STRONG)
Ex 15:2 The Lord is my-*s* and my song;
Dt 6:5 all your soul and with all your-*s*.
2Sa 22:33 It is God who arms me with-*s*
Ne 8:10 for the joy of the Lord is your-*s*."
Ps 28:7 The Lord is my-*s* and my shield;
46:1 God is our refuge and-*s*,
96:7 ascribe to the Lord glory and-*s*.
118:14 The Lord is my-*s* and my song;
147:10 not in the-*s* of the horse,
Isa 40:31 will renew their-*s*.
Mk 12:30 all your mind and with all your-*s*.'
1Co 1:25 of God is stronger than man's-*s*.
Php 4:13 through him who gives me-*s*.
1Pe 4:11 it with the-*s* God provides,

STRENGTHEN (STRONG)
2Ch 16:9 to-*s* those whose hearts are fully
Ps 119:28 *s* me according to your word.
Isa 35:3 *S* the feeble hands,
41:10 I will-*s* you and help you;
Eph 3:16 of his glorious riches he may-*s* you
2Th 2:17 and-*s* you in every good deed
Heb 12:12 *s* your feeble arms and weak knees.

STRENGTHENING (STRONG)
1Co 14:26 done for the-*s* of the church.

STRIFE
Pr 20:3 It is to a man's honor to avoid-*s*,
22:10 out the mocker, and out goes-*s*;

STRIKE (STRIKES)
Ge 3:15 and you will-*s* his heel."
Zec 13:7 "*S* the shepherd,
Mt 26:31 " 'I will-*s* the shepherd,

STRIKES (STRIKE)
Mt 5:39 If someone-*s* you on the right

STRONG (STRENGTH STRENGTHEN STRENGTHENING)
Dt 31:6 Be-*s* and courageous,
1Ki 2:2 "So be-*s*, show yourself a man,
Pr 18:10 The name of the Lord is a-*s* tower
31:17 her arms are-*s* for her tasks.
SS 8:6 for love is as-*s* as death,
Lk 2:40 And the child grew and became-*s*;
Ro 5:1 We who are-*s* ought to bear
1Co 1:27 things of the world to shame the-*s*.
16:13 in the faith; be men of courage; be-*s*
2Co 12:10 For when I am weak, then I am-*s*.
Eph 6:10 be-*s* in the Lord and in his mighty

STRUGGLE
Ro 15:30 me in my-*s* by praying to God
Eph 6:12 For our-*s* is not against flesh
Heb 12:4 In your-*s* against sin, you have not

STUDY
Ezr 7:10 Ezra had devoted himself to the-*s*
Ecc 12:12 and much-*s* wearies the body.
Jn 5:39 You diligently-*s* the Scriptures

STUMBLE (STUMBLING)
Ps 37:24 though he-*s*, he will not fall,
119:165 and nothing can make them-*s*.
Isa 8:14 a stone that causes men to-*s*
Jer 31:9 a level path where they will not-*s*
Eze 7:19 for it has made them-*s* into sin.
1Co 10:32 Do not cause anyone to-*s*,
1Pe 2:8 and, "A stone that causes men to-*s*

STUMBLING (STUMBLE)
Ro 14:13 up your mind not to put any-*s* block
1Co 8:9 freedom does not become a-*s* block
2Co 6:3 We put no-*s* block in anyone's path,

SUBDUE
Ge 1:28 in number; fill the earth and-*s* it.

SUBJECT (SUBJECTED)
1Co 14:32 of prophets are-*s* to the control
15:28 then the Son himself will be made-*s*
Tit 2:5 and to be-*s* to their husbands,
2:9 slaves to be-*s* to their masters
3:1 Remind the people to be-*s* to rulers

SUBJECTED (SUBJECT)
Ro 8:20 For the creation was-*s*

SUBMISSION (SUBMIT)
1Co 14:34 but must be in-*s*, as the Law says.
1Ti 2:11 learn in quietness and full-*s*.

SUBMISSIVE (SUBMIT)
Jas 3:17 then peace-loving, considerate,-*s*,
1Pe 3:1 in the same way be-*s*
5:5 in the same way be-*s*

SUBMIT (SUBMISSION SUBMISSIVE SUBMITS)
Ro 13:1 Everyone must-*s* himself
13:5 necessary to-*s* to the authorities,
1Co 16:16 to-*s* to such as these
Eph 5:21 *S* to one another out of reverence
Col 3:18 Wives,-*s* to your husbands,
Heb 12:9 How much more should we-*s*
13:17 Obey your leaders and-*s*
Jas 4:7 *S* yourselves, then, to God.
1Pe 2:18 *s* yourselves to your masters

SUBMITS* (SUBMIT)
Eph 5:24 Now as the church-*s* to Christ,

SUCCESSFUL
Jos 1:7 that you may be-*s* wherever you go.
2Ki 18:7 he was-*s* in whatever he undertook.
2Ch 20:20 in his prophets and you will be-*s*."

SUFFER (SUFFERED SUFFERING SUFFERINGS SUFFERS)
Isa 53:10 to crush him and cause him to-*s*,
Mk 8:31 the Son of Man must-*s* many things
Lk 24:26 the Christ have to-*s* these things

24:46 The Christ will-*s* and rise
Php 1:29 to-*s* for him, since you are going
1Pe 4:16 However, if you-*s* as a Christian,

SUFFERED (SUFFER)
Heb 2:9 and honor because he-*s* death,
2:18 Because he himself-*s*
1Pe 2:21 Christ-*s* for you, leaving you

SUFFERING (SUFFER)
Isa 53:3 of sorrows, and familiar with-*s*.
Ac 5:41 worthy of-*s* disgrace for the Name.
2Ti 1:8 But join with me in-*s* for the gospel,
Heb 2:10 of their salvation perfect through-*s*.

SUFFERINGS (SUFFER)
Ro 8:17 share in his-*s* in order that we may
8:18 that our present-*s* are not worth
2Co 1:5 as the-*s* of Christ flow
Php 3:10 the fellowship of sharing in his-*s*,

SUFFERS (SUFFER)
Pr 13:20 but a companion of fools-*s* harm.
1Co 12:26 If one part-*s*, every part-*s* with it;

SUFFICIENT
2Co 12:9 said to me, "My grace is-*s* for you,

SUITABLE
Ge 2:18 I will make a helper-*s* for him."

SUN
Ecc 1:9 there is nothing new under the-*s*.
Mal 4:2 the-*s* of righteousness will rise
Mt 5:45 He causes his-*s* to rise on the evil
17:2 His face shone like the-*s*,
Rev 1:16 His face was like the-*s* shining
21:23 The city does not need the-*s*

SUPERIOR
Heb 1:4 he became as much-*s* to the angels
8:6 ministry Jesus has received is as-*s*

SUPERVISION
Gal 3:25 longer under the-*s* of the law.

SUPREMACY* (SUPREME)
Col 1:18 in everything he might have the-*s*.

SUPREME (SUPREMACY)
Pr 4:7 Wisdom is-*s*; therefore get wisdom.

SURE
Nu 32:23 you may be-*s* that your sin will find
Dt 6:17 Be-*s* to keep the commands
14:22 Be-*s* to set aside a tenth
Isa 28:16 cornerstone for a-*s* foundation;
Heb 11:1 faith is being-*s* of what we hope for
2Pe 1:10 to make your calling and election-*s*.

SURPASS* (SURPASSES SURPASSING)
Pr 31:29 but you-*s* them all."

SURPASSES (SURPASS)
Mt 5:20 unless your righteousness-*s* that
Eph 3:19 to know this love that-*s* knowledge

SURPASSING* (SURPASS)
Ps 150:2 praise him for his-*s* greatness.
2Co 3:10 in comparison with the-*s* glory.
9:14 of the-*s* grace God has given you.
Php 3:8 the-*s* greatness of knowing Christ

SURROUNDED
Heb 12:1 since we are-*s* by such a great cloud

SUSPENDS*
Job 26:7 he-*s* the earth over nothing.

SUSTAINING* (SUSTAINS)
Heb 1:3 *s* all things by his powerful word.

SUSTAINS (SUSTAINING)
Ps 18:35 and your right hand-*s* me;
146:9 and-*s* the fatherless and the widow,
147:6 The Lord-*s* the humble
Isa 50:4 to know the word that-*s* the weary.

SWALLOWED
1Co 15:54 "Death has been-*s* up in victory."
2Co 5:4 so that what is mortal may be-*s* up

SWEAR
Mt 5:34 Do not-*s* at all: either by heaven,

SWORD (SWORDS)
Ps 45:3 Gird your-*s* upon your side,
Pr 12:18 Reckless words pierce like a-*s*,
Mt 10:34 come to bring peace, but a-*s*.
26:52 all who draw the-*s* will die by the-*s*.
Lk 2:35 a-*s* will pierce your own soul too."
Ro 13:4 for he does not bear the-*s*
Eph 6:17 of salvation and the-*s* of the Spirit,
Heb 4:12 Sharper than any double-edged-*s*,
Rev 1:16 came a sharp double-edged-*s*.

SWORDS (SWORD)
Isa 2:4 They will beat their-*s*
Joel 3:10 Beat your plowshares into-*s*

SYMPATHETIC*
1Pe 3:8 in harmony with one another; be-*s*,

SYNAGOGUE
Lk 4:16 the Sabbath day he went into the-*s*,
Ac 17:2 custom was, Paul went into the-*s*,

TABERNACLE
Ex 40:34 the glory of the Lord filled the-*t*.

TABLE (TABLES)
Ps 23:5 You prepare a-*t* before me

TABLES (TABLE)
Ac 6:2 word of God in order to wait on-*t*.

TABLET (TABLETS)
Pr 3:3 write them on the-*t* of your heart.
7:3 write them on the-*t* of your heart.

TABLETS (TABLET)
Ex 31:18 he gave him the two-*t*
Dt 10:5 and put the-*t* in the ark I had made,
2Co 3:3 not on-*t* of stone, but on-*t*

TAKE (TAKEN TAKES TAKING TOOK)
Dt 12:32 do not add to it or-*t* away from it.
31:26 "*T* this Book of the Law
Job 23:10 But he knows the way that I-*t*;
Ps 49:17 for he will-*t* nothing with him
51:11 or-*t* your Holy Spirit from me.
Mt 10:38 anyone who does not-*t* his cross
11:29 *T* my yoke upon you and learn
16:24 deny himself and-*t* up his cross

TAKEN (TAKE)
Lev 6:4 must return what he has stolen or-*t*
Isa 6:7 your guilt is-*t* away and your sin
Mt 24:40 one will be-*t* and the other left.
Mk 16:19 he was-*t* up into heaven
1Ti 3:16 was-*t* up in glory.

TAKES (TAKE)
1Ki 20:11 should not boast like one who-*t* it
Ps 5:4 You are not a God who-*t* pleasure
Jn 1:29 who-*t* away the sin of the world!
Rev 22:19 And if anyone-*t* words away

TAKING (TAKE)
Ac 15:14 by-*t* from the Gentiles a people
Php 2:7 *t* the very nature of a servant,

TALENT
Mt 25:15 to another one-*t*, each according

TAME*
Jas 3:8 but no man can-*t* the tongue.

TASK
Mk 13:34 each with his assigned-*t*,
Ac 20:24 complete the-*t* the Lord Jesus has
1Co 3:5 the Lord has assigned to each his-*t*.
2Co 2:16 And who is equal to such a-*t*?

TASTE (TASTED)
Ps 34:8 *T* and see that the Lord is good;

Col 2:21 Do not-*t*! Do not touch!"?
Heb 2:9 the grace of God he might-*t* death

TASTED (TASTE)
1Pe 2:3 now that you have-*t* that the Lord

TAUGHT (TEACH)
Mt 7:29 he-*t* as one who had authority,
1Co 2:13 but in words-*t* by the Spirit,
Gal 1:12 nor was I-*t* it; rather, I received it

TAXES
Mt 22:17 Is it right to pay-*t* to Caesar or not
Ro 13:7 If you owe-*t*, pay-*t*; if revenue,

TEACH (TAUGHT TEACHER TEACHERS
TEACHES TEACHING)
Ex 33:13 *t* me your ways so I may know you
Dt 4:9 Them to your children
    8:3 to-*t* you that man does not live
    11:19 Them to your children, talking
1Sa 12:23 I will-*t* you the way that is good
Ps 32:8 *t* you in the way you should go;
    51:13 I will-*t* transgressors your ways,
    90:12 *T* us to number our days aright,
    143:10 *T* me to do your will,
Jer 31:34 No longer will a man-*t* his neighbor
Lk 11:1 said to him, "Lord,-*t* us to pray,
Jn 14:26 will-*t* you all things and will remind
1Ti 2:12 I do not permit a woman to-*t*
    3:2 respectable, hospitable, able to-*t*,
Tit 2:1 You must-*t* what is in accord
Heb 8:11 No longer will a man-*t* his neighbor
Jas 3:1 know that we who-*t* will be judged
1Jn 2:27 you do not need anyone to-*t* you.

TEACHER (TEACH)
Mt 10:24 "A student is not above his-*t*,
Jn 13:14 and-*T*, have washed your feet,

TEACHERS (TEACH)
1Co 12:28 third-*t*, then workers of miracles,
Eph 4:11 and some to be pastors and-*t*,
Heb 5:12 by this time you ought to be-*t*,

TEACHES (TEACH)
1Ti 6:3 If anyone-*t* false doctrines

TEACHING (TEACH)
Pr 1:8 and do not forsake your mother's-*t*.
Mt 28:20 *t* them to obey everything I have
Jn 7:17 whether my-*t* comes from God or
    14:23 loves me, he will obey my-*t*.
1Ti 4:13 of Scripture, to preaching and to-*t*.
2Ti 3:16 is God-breathed and is useful for-*t*,
Tit 2:7 In your-*t* show integrity,

TEAR (TEARS)
Rev 7:17 God will wipe away every-*t*

TEARS (TEAR)
Ps 126:5 Those who sow in-*t*
Php 3:18 and now say again even with-*t*,

TEETH (TOOTH)
Mt 8:12 will be weeping and gnashing of-*t*."

TEMPERATE*
1Ti 3:2 *t*, self-controlled, respectable,
    3:11 not malicious talkers but-*t*
Tit 2:2 Teach the older men to be-*t*,

TEMPEST
Ps 55:8 far from the-*t* and storm."

TEMPLE (TEMPLES)
1Ki 8:27 How much less this-*t* I have built!
Hab 2:20 But the LORD is in his holy-*t*;
1Co 3:16 that you yourselves are God's-*t*
    6:19 you know that your body is God's-*t*
2Co 6:16 For we are the-*t* of the living God.

TEMPLES (TEMPLE)
Ac 17:24 does not live in-*t* built by hands.

TEMPT (TEMPTATION TEMPTED)
1Co 7:5 again so that Satan will not-*t* you

TEMPTATION (TEMPT)
Mt 6:13 And lead us not into-*t*,
    26:41 pray so that you will not fall into-*t*.
1Co 10:13 No-*t* has seized you except what is

TEMPTED (TEMPT)
Mt 4:1 into the desert to be-*t* by the devil.
1Co 10:13 he will not let you be-*t*
Heb 2:18 he himself suffered when he was-*t*,
    4:15 but we have one who has been-*t*
Jas 1:13 For God cannot be-*t* by evil,

TEN (TENTH TITHE TITHES)
Ex 34:28 covenant—the-*T* Commandments.
Ps 91:7 *t* thousand at your right hand,
Mt 25:28 it to the one who has the-*t* talents.
Lk 15:8 suppose a woman has-*t* silver coins

TENTH (TEN)
Dt 14:22 Be sure to set aside a-*t*

TERRIBLE (TERROR)
2Ti 3:1 There will be-*t* times

TERROR (TERRIBLE)
Ps 91:5 You will not fear the-*t* of night,
Lk 21:26 Men will faint from-*t*, apprehensive
Ro 13:3 For rulers hold no-*t*

TEST (TESTED TESTS)
Dt 6:16 Do not-*t* the LORD your God
Ps 139:23 *t* me and know my anxious
Ro 12:2 Then you will be able to-*t*
1Co 3:13 and the fire will-*t* the quality
1Jn 4:1 *t* the spirits to see whether they are

TESTED (TEST)
Ge 22:1 Some time later God-*t* Abraham.
Job 23:10 when he has-*t* me, I will come forth
Pr 27:21 man is-*t* by the praise he receives.
1Ti 3:10 They must first be-*t*; and then

TESTIFY (TESTIMONY)
Jn 5:39 are the Scriptures that-*t* about me,
2Ti 1:8 ashamed to-*t* about our Lord,

TESTIMONY (TESTIFY)
Isa 8:20 and to the-*t*! If they do not speak
Lk 18:20 not give false-*t*, honor your father

TESTS (TEST)
Pr 17:3 but the LORD-*t* the heart.
1Th 2:4 but God, who-*t* our hearts.

THADDAEUS
Apostle (Mt 10:3; Mk 3:18); probably also
known as Judas son of James (Lk 6:16; Ac 1:13).

THANKFUL (THANKS)
Heb 12:28 let us be-*t*, and so worship God

THANKS (THANKFUL THANKSGIVING)
1Ch 16:8 Give-*t* to the LORD, call
Ne 12:31 assigned two large choirs to give-*t*.
Ps 100:4 give-*t* to him and praise his name.
1Co 15:57 *t* be to God! He gives us the victory
2Co 2:14 *t* be to God, who always leads us
    9:15 *T* be to God for his indescribable
1Th 5:18 give-*t* in all circumstances,

THANKSGIVING (THANKS)
Ps 95:2 Let us come before him with-*t*
    100:4 Enter his gates with-*t*
Php 4:6 by prayer and petition, with-*t*,
1Ti 4:3 created to be received with-*t*

THIEF (THIEVES)
Ex 22:3 A-*t* must certainly make restitution
1Th 5:2 day of the Lord will come like a-*t*
Rev 16:15 I come like a-*t*! Blessed is he who

THIEVES (THIEF)
1Co 6:10 nor homosexual offenders nor-*t*

THINK (THOUGHT THOUGHTS)
Ro 12:3 Do not-*t* of yourself more highly
Php 4:8 praiseworthy—*t* about such things

THIRST (THIRSTY)
Ps 69:21 and gave me vinegar for my-*t*.
Mt 5:6 Blessed are those who hunger and-*t*
Jn 4:14 the water I give him will never-*t*.

THIRSTY (THIRST)
Isa 55:1 "Come, all you who are-*t*,
Jn 7:37 "If anyone is-*t*, let him come to me
Rev 22:17 Whoever is-*t*, let him come;

THOMAS
Apostle (Mt 10:3; Mk 3:18; Lk 6:15; Jn 11:16;
14:5; 21:2; Ac 1:13). Doubted resurrection (Jn
20-24-28).

THONGS
Mk 1:7 *t* of whose sandals I am not worthy

THORN (THORNS)
2Co 12:7 there was given me a-*t* in my flesh,

THORNS (THORN)
Nu 33:55 in your eyes and-*t* in your sides.
Mt 27:29 then twisted together a crown of-*t*
Heb 6:8 But land that produces-*t*

THOUGHT (THINK)
Pr 14:15 a prudent man gives-*t* to his steps.
1Co 13:11 I talked like a child, I-*t* like a child,

THOUGHTS (THINK)
Ps 94:11 The LORD knows the-*t* of man;
    139:23 test me and know my anxious-*t*.
Isa 55:8 "For my-*t* are not your-*t*,
Heb 4:12 it judges the-*t* and attitudes

THREE
Ecc 4:12 of-*t* strands is not quickly broken.
Mt 12:40 *t* nights in the belly of a huge fish,
    18:20 or-*t* come together in my name,
    27:63 'After-*t* days I will rise again.'
1Co 13:13 And now these-*t* remain: faith,
    14:27 or at the most-*t*— should speak,
2Co 13:1 testimony of two or-*t* witnesses."

THRESHING
2Sa 24:18 an altar to the LORD on the-*t* floor

THRONE (ENTHRONED)
2Sa 7:16 your-*t* will be established forever
Ps 45:6 Your-*t*, O God, will last for ever
    47:8 God is seated on his holy-*t*.
Isa 6:1 I saw the Lord seated on a-*t*,
    66:1 "Heaven is my-*t*
Heb 4:16 Let us then approach the-*t* of grace
    12:2 at the right hand of the-*t* of God.
Rev 4:10 They lay their crowns before the-*t*
    20:11 Then I saw a great white-*t*
    22:3 *t* of God and of the Lamb will be

THROW
Jn 8:7 the first to-*t* a stone at her."
Heb 10:35 So do not-*t* away your confidence,
    12:1 let us-*t* off everything that hinders

THWART*
Isa 14:27 has purposed, and who can-*t* him?

TIBNI
King of Israel (1Ki 16:21-22).

TIME (TIMES)
Est 4:14 come to royal position for such a-*t*
Da 7:25 to him for a-*t*, times and half a-*t*.
Hos 10:12 for it is-*t* to seek the LORD,
Ro 9:9 "At the appointed-*t* I will return,
Heb 9:28 and he will appear a second-*t*,
    10:12 for all-*t* one sacrifice for sins,
1Pe 4:17 For it is-*t* for judgment to begin

TIMES (TIME)
Ps 9:9 a stronghold in-*t* of trouble.
    31:15 My-*t* are in your hands;
    62:8 Trust in him at all-*t*, O people;
Pr 17:17 A friend loves at all-*t*,
Am 5:13 for the-*t* are evil.

Mt 18:21 how many-*t* shall I forgive my
Ac 1:7 "It is not for you to know the-*t*
Rev 12:14 *t* and half a time, out

TIMIDITY*
2Ti 1:7 For God did not give us a spirit of-*t*

TIMOTHY
Believer from Lystra (Ac 16:1). Joined Paul on
second missionary journey (Ac 16-20). Sent to
settle problems at Corinth (1Co 4:17; 16:10).
Led church at Ephesus (1Ti 1:3). Co-writer with
Paul (1Th 1:1; 2Th 1:1; Phm 1).

TIRE (TIRED)
2Th 3:13 never-*t* of doing what is right.

TIRED (TIRE)
Ex 17:12 When Moses' hands grew-*t*,
Isa 40:28 He will not grow-*t* or weary,

TITHE (TEN)
Lev 27:30 "'A-*t* of everything from the land,
Dt 12:17 eat in your own towns the-*t*
Mal 3:10 the whole-*t* into the storehouse,

TITHES (TEN)
Mal 3:8 'How do we rob you?' "In-*t*

TITUS
Gentile co-worker of Paul (Gal 2:1-3; 2Ti 4:10);
sent to Corinth (2Co 2:13; 7-8; 12:18), Crete
(Tit 1:4-5).

TODAY
Mt 6:11 Give us-*t* our daily bread.
Lk 23:43 *t* you will be with me in paradise."
Heb 3:13 daily, as long as it is called-*T*,
    13:8 Christ is the same yesterday and-*t*

TOIL
Ge 3:17 through painful-*t* you will eat of it

TOLERATE
Hab 1:13 you cannot-*t* wrong.
Rev 2:2 that you cannot-*t* wicked men,

TOMB
Mt 27:65 make the-*t* as secure as you know
Lk 24:2 the stone rolled away from the-*t*,

TOMORROW
Pr 27:1 Do not boast about-*t*,
Isa 22:13 "for-*t* we die!"
Mt 6:34 Therefore do not worry about-*t*,
Jas 4:13 "Today or-*t* we will go to this

TONGUE (TONGUES)
Ps 39:1 and keep my-*t* from sin;
Pr 12:18 but the-*t* of the wise brings healing.
1Co 14:2 speaks in a-*t* does not speak to men
    14:4 He who speaks in a-*t* edifies himself
    14:13 in a-*t* should pray that he may
    14:19 than ten thousand words in a-*t*.
Php 2:11 every-*t* confess that Jesus Christ is
Jas 1:26 does not keep a tight rein on his-*t*,
    3:8 but no man can tame the-*t*.

TONGUES (TONGUE)
Isa 28:11 with foreign lips and strange-*t*
    66:18 and gather all nations and-*t*,
Mk 16:17 in new-*t*; they will pick up snakes
Ac 2:4 and began to speak in other-*t*
    10:46 For they heard them speaking in-*t*
    19:6 and they spoke in-*t* and prophesied
1Co 12:30 Do all speak in-*t*? Do all interpret?
    14:18 speak in-*t* more than all of you.
    14:39 and do not forbid speaking in-*t*.

TOOK (TAKE)
1Co 11:23 the night he was betrayed,-*t* bread,
Php 3:12 for which Christ Jesus-*t* hold of me.

TOOTH (TEETH)
Ex 21:24 eye for eye, *t* for-*t*, hand for hand,
Mt 5:38 'Eye for eye, and-*t* for *t*.'

TORMENTED
Rev 20:10 They will be-*t* day and night

TORN
Gal 4:15 you would have-*t* out your eyes
Php 1:23 I do not know! I am-*t*

TOUCH (TOUCHED)
Ps 105:15 "Do not-*t* my anointed ones;
Lk 24:39 It is I myself!-*T* me and see;
2Co 6:17 *T* no unclean thing,
Col 2:21 Do not taste! Do not-*t*!"?

TOUCHED (TOUCH)
1Sa 10:26 men whose hearts God had-*t*.
Mt 14:36 and all who-*t* him were healed.

TOWER
Ge 11: 4 with a-*t* that reaches to the heavens
Pr 18:10 of the LORD is a strong-*t*;

TOWNS
Nu 35: 2 to give the Levites-*t* to live
35:15 These six-*t* will be a place of refuge

TRACING*
Ro 11:33 and his paths beyond-*t* out!

TRADITION
Mt 15: 6 word of God for the sake of your-*t*.
Col 2: 8 which depends on human-*t*

TRAIN (TRAINING)
Pr 22: 6 *T* a child in the way he should go,
Eph 4: 8 he led captives in his-*t*

TRAINING (TRAIN)
1Co 9:25 in the games goes into strict-*t*.
2Ti 3:16 correcting and-*t* in righteousness,

TRAMPLED
Lk 21:24 Jerusalem will be-*t*
Heb 10:29 to be punished who has-*t* the Son

TRANCE
Ac 10:10 was being prepared, he fell into a-*t*.

TRANSCENDS*
Php 4: 7 which-*t* all understanding,

TRANSFIGURED
Mt 17: 2 There he was-*t* before them.

TRANSFORM* (TRANSFORMED)
Php 3:21 will-*t* our lowly bodies

TRANSFORMED (TRANSFORM)
Ro 12: 2 be-*t* by the renewing of your mind.
2Co 3:18 are being-*t* into his likeness

TRANSGRESSION (TRANSGRESSIONS TRANSGRESSORS)
Isa 53: 8 for the-*t* of my people he was
Ro 4:15 where there is no law there is no-*t*.

TRANSGRESSIONS (TRANSGRESSION)
Ps 32: 1 whose-*t* are forgiven,
51: 1 blot out my-*t*.
103:12 so far has he removed our-*t* from us
Isa 53: 5 But he was pierced for our-*t*,
Eph 2: 1 you were dead in your-*t* and sins,

TRANSGRESSORS (TRANSGRESSION)
Ps 51:13 Then I will teach-*t* your ways,
Isa 53:12 and made intercession for the-*t*.
53:12 and was numbered with the-*t*.

TREADING
Dt 25: 4 an ox while it is-*t* out the grain.
1Co 9: 9 an ox while it is-*t* out the grain."

TREASURE (TREASURED TREASURES)
Isa 33: 6 of the LORD is the key to this-*t*.
Mt 6:21 For where your-*t* is, there your
2Co 4: 7 But we have this-*t* in jars of clay

TREASURED (TREASURE)
Dt 7: 6 to be his people, his-*t* possession.
Lk 2:19 But Mary-*t* up all these things

TREASURES (TREASURE)
Mt 6:19 up for yourselves-*t* on earth,
Col 2: 3 in whom are hidden all the-*t*
Heb 11:26 of greater value than the-*t* of Egypt,

TREAT
Lev 22: 2 sons to-*t* with respect the sacred
1Ti 5: 1 *T* younger men as brothers,
1Pe 3: 7 and-*t* them with respect

TREATY
Dt 7: 2 Make no-*t* with them, and show

TREE
Ge 2: 9 and the-*t* of the knowledge of good
2: 9 of the garden were the-*t* of life
Dt 21:23 hung on a-*t* is under God's curse.
Ps 1: 3 He is like a-*t* planted by streams
Mt 3:10 every-*t* that does not produce good
12:33 for a-*t* is recognized by its fruit.
Gal 3:13 is everyone who is hung on a-*t*."
Rev 22:14 they may have the right to the-*t*

TREMBLE (TREMBLING)
1Ch 16:30 *T* before him, all the earth!
Ps 114: 7 *T*, O earth, at the presence

TREMBLING (TREMBLE)
Ps 2:11 and rejoice with-*t*.
Php 2:12 out your salvation with fear and-*t*,

TRESPASS
Ro 5:17 For if, by the-*t* of the one man,

TRIALS
1Th 3: 3 one would be unsettled by these-*t*.
Jas 1: 2 whenever you face-*t* of many kinds,
2Pe 2: 9 how to rescue godly men from-*t*

TRIBES
Ge 49:28 All these are the twelve-*t* of Israel,
Mt 19:28 judging the twelve-*t* of Israel.

TRIBULATION*
Rev 7:14 who have come out of the great-*t*;

TRIUMPHAL* (TRIUMPHING)
Isa 60:11 their kings led in-*t* procession.
2Co 2:14 us in-*t* procession in Christ

TRIUMPHING* (TRIUMPHAL)
Col 2:15 of them,-*t* over them by the cross.

TROUBLE (TROUBLED TROUBLES)
Job 14: 1 is of few days and full of-*t*.
Ps 46: 1 an ever-present help in-*t*.
107:13 they cried to the LORD in their-*t*,
Pr 11:29 He who brings-*t* on his family will
24:10 If you falter in times of-*t*,
Mt 6:34 Each day has enough-*t* of its own.
Jn 16:33 In this world you will have-*t*.
Ro 8:35 Shall-*t* or hardship or persecution

TROUBLED (TROUBLE)
Jn 14: 1 "Do not let your hearts be-*t*.
14:27 Do not let your hearts be-*t*

TROUBLES (TROUBLE)
1Co 7:28 those who marry will face many-*t*
2Co 1: 4 who comforts us in all our-*t*,
4:17 and momentary-*t* are achieving

TRUE (TRUTH)
Dt 18:22 does not take place or come-*t*,
1Sa 9: 6 and everything he says comes-*t*.
Ps 119:160 All your words are-*t*;
Jn 17: 3 the only-*t* God, and Jesus Christ,
Ro 3: 4 Let God be-*t*, and every man a liar.
Php 4: 8 whatever is-*t*, whatever is noble,
Rev 22: 6 These words are trustworthy and-*t*.

TRUMPET
1Co 14: 8 if the-*t* does not sound a clear call,
15:52 For the-*t* will sound, the dead will

TRUST (ENTRUSTED TRUSTED TRUSTS TRUSTWORTHY)
Ps 20: 7 we-*t* in the name of the LORD our
37: 3 *T* in the LORD and do good;
56: 4 in God I-*t*; I will not be afraid.
119:42 for I-*t* in your word.
Pr 3: 5 *T* in the LORD with all your heart
Isa 30:15 in quietness and-*t* is your strength,
Jn 14: 1 *T* in God;-*t* also in me.
1Co 4: 2 been given a-*t* must prove faithful.

TRUSTED (TRUST)
Ps 26: 1 I have-*t* in the LORD
Isa 25: 9 we-*t* in him, and he saved us.
Da 3:28 They-*t* in him and defied the king's
Lk 16:10 *t* with very little can also be-*t*

TRUSTS (TRUST)
Ps 32:10 surrounds the man who-*t* in him.
Pr 11:28 Whoever-*t* in his riches will fall,
28:26 He who-*t* in himself is a fool,
Ro 9:33 one who-*t* in him will never be put

TRUSTWORTHY (TRUST)
Ps 119:138 they are fully-*t*.
Pr 11:13 but a-*t* man keeps a secret.
Rev 22: 6 "These words are-*t* and true.

TRUTH (TRUE TRUTHFUL TRUTHS)
Ps 51: 6 Surely you desire-*t*;
Isa 45:19 I, the LORD, speak the-*t*;
Zec 8:16 are to do: Speak the-*t* to each other,
Jn 4:23 worship the Father in spirit and-*t*,
8:32 Then you will know the-*t*,
8:32 and the-*t* will set you free."
14: 6 I am the way and the-*t* and the life.
16:13 comes, he will guide you into all-*t*.
18:38 "What is-*t*?" Pilate asked.
Ro 1:25 They exchanged the-*t* of God
1Co 13: 6 in evil but rejoices with the-*t*.
2Co 13: 8 against the-*t*, but only for the-*t*
Eph 4:15 Instead, speaking the-*t* in love,
6:14 with the belt of-*t* buckled
2Th 2:10 because they refused to love the-*t*
1Ti 2: 4 to come to a knowledge of the-*t*.
3:15 the pillar and foundation of the-*t*.
2Ti 2:15 correctly handles the word of-*t*.
3: 7 never able to acknowledge the-*t*.
Heb 10:26 received the knowledge of the-*t*,
1Pe 1:22 by obeying the-*t* so that you have
2Pe 2: 2 the way of-*t* into disrepute.
1Jn 1: 6 we lie and do not live by the-*t*.
1: 8 deceive ourselves and the-*t* is not

TRUTHFUL (TRUTH)
Pr 12:22 but he delights in men who are-*t*.
Jn 3:33 it has certified that God is-*t*.

TRUTHS (TRUTH)
1Co 2:13 expressing spiritual-*t*
1Ti 3: 9 hold of the deep-*t* of the faith
Heb 5:12 to teach you the elementary-*t*

TRY (TRYING)
Ps 26: 2 Test me, O LORD, and-*t* me,
Isa 7:13 enough to-*t* the patience of men?
1Co 14:12 to excel in gifts that build up
2Co 5:11 is to fear the Lord, we-*t*
1Th 5:15 always-*t* to be kind to each other

TRYING (TRY)
2Co 5:12 We are not-*t* to commend ourselves
1Th 2: 4 We are not-*t* to please men but God

TUNIC
Lk 6:29 do not stop him from taking your-*t*.

TURN (TURNED TURNS)
Ex 32:12 *T* from your fierce anger; relent
Dt 5:32 do not-*t* aside to the right
28:14 Do not-*t* aside from any
Jos 1: 7 do not-*t* from it to the right
2Ch 7:14 and-*t* from their wicked ways,

30: 9 He will not-*t* his face from you
Ps 78: 6 they in-*t* would tell their children.
Pr 22: 6 when he is old he will not-*t* from it.
Isa 29:16 You-*t* things upside down,
30:21 Whether you-*t* to the right
45:22 "*T* to me and be saved,
55: 7 Let him-*t* to the LORD,
Eze 33:11 *T!-T* from your evil ways!
Mal 4: 6 He will-*t* the hearts of the fathers
Mt 5:39 you on the right cheek,-*t*
10:35 For I have come to-*t*
Jn 12:40 nor-*t*— and I would heal them."
Ac 3:19 Repent, then, and-*t* to God,
26:18 and-*t* them from darkness to light,
1Ti 6:20 *T* away from godless chatter
1Pe 3:11 He must-*t* from evil and do good;

TURNED (TURN)
Ps 30:11 You-*t* my wailing into dancing;
40: 1 he-*t* to me and heard my cry.
Isa 53: 6 each of us has-*t* to his own way;
Hos 7: 8 Ephraim is a flat cake not-*t* over.
Joel 2:31 The sun will be-*t* to darkness
Ro 3:12 All have-*t* away,

TURNS (TURN)
2Sa 22:29 the LORD-*t* my darkness into light
Pr 15: 1 A gentle answer-*t* away wrath,
Isa 44:25 and-*t* it into nonsense,
Jas 5:20 Whoever-*t* a sinner from the error

TWELVE
Ge 49:28 All these are the-*t* tribes of Israel,
Mt 10: 1 He called his-*t* disciples to him

TWINKLING*
1Co 15:52 in a flash, in the-*t* of an eye,

UNAPPROACHABLE*
1Ti 6:16 immortal and who lives in-*u* light,

UNBELIEF (UNBELIEVER UNBELIEVERS UNBELIEVING)
Mk 9:24 help me overcome my-*u*!"
Ro 11:20 they were broken off because of-*u*,
Heb 3:19 able to enter, because of their-*u*.

UNBELIEVER* (UNBELIEF)
1Co 7:15 But if the-*u* leaves, let him do so.
10:27 If some-*u* invites you to a meal
14:24 if an-*u* or someone who does not
2Co 6:15 have in common with an-*u*?
1Ti 5: 8 the faith and is worse than an-*u*.

UNBELIEVERS (UNBELIEF)
1Co 6: 6 another—and this in front of-*u*!
2Co 6:14 Do not be yoked together with-*u*.

UNBELIEVING (UNBELIEF)
1Co 7:14 For the-*u* husband has been
Rev 21: 8 But the cowardly, the-*u*, the vile,

UNCERTAIN*
1Ti 6:17 which is so-*u*, but to put their hope

UNCHANGEABLE*
Heb 6:18 by two-*u* things in which it is

UNCIRCUMCISED
1Sa 17:26 Who is this-*u* Philistine that he
Col 3:11 circumcised or-*u*, barbarian,

UNCIRCUMCISION
1Co 7:19 is nothing and-*u* is nothing.
Gal 5: 6 neither circumcision nor-*u* has any

UNCLEAN
Isa 6: 5 ruined! For I am a man of-*u* lips,
Ro 14:14 fully convinced that no food is-*u*
2Co 6:17 Touch no-*u* thing,

UNCONCERNED*
Eze 16:49 were arrogant, overfed and-*u*;

UNCOVERED
Heb 4:13 Everything is-*u* and laid bare

UNDERSTAND (UNDERSTANDING UNDERSTANDS)
Job 42: 3 Surely I spoke of things I did not-u,
Ps 73:16 When I tried to-u all this,
119:125 that I may-u your statutes.
Lk 24:45 so they could-u the Scriptures.
Ac 8:30 "Do you-u what you are reading?"
Ro 7:15 I do not-u what I do.
1Co 2:14 and he cannot-u them,
Eph 5:17 but-u what the Lord's will is.
2Pe 3:16 some things that are hard to-u,

UNDERSTANDING (UNDERSTAND)
Ps 119:104 I gain-u from your precepts;
147: 5 his-u has no limit.
Pr 3: 5 and lean not on your own-u;
4: 7 Though it cost all you have, get-u.
10:23 but a man of-u delights in wisdom.
11:12 but a man of-u holds his tongue.
15:21 a man of-u keeps a straight course.
15:32 whoever heeds correction gains-u.
23:23 get wisdom, discipline and-u.
Isa 40:28 and his-u no one can fathom.
Da 5:12 a keen mind and knowledge and-u,
Mk 4:12 and ever hearing but never-u;
12:33 with all your-u and with all your
Php 4: 7 of God, which transcends all-u,

UNDERSTANDS (UNDERSTAND)
1Ch 28: 9 and-u every motive
1Ti 6: 4 he is conceited and-u nothing.

UNDIVIDED*
1Ch 12:33 to help David with-u loyalty—
Ps 86:11 give me an-u heart
Eze 11:19 I will give them an-u heart
1Co 7:35 way in-u devotion to the Lord.

UNDOING
Pr 18: 7 A fool's mouth is his-u,

UNDYING*
Eph 6:24 Lord Jesus Christ with an-u love.

UNFADING*
1Pe 3: 4 the-u beauty of a gentle

UNFAILING
Ps 33: 5 the earth is full of his-u love.
119:76 May your-u love be my comfort,
143: 8 bring me word of your-u love,
Pr 19:22 What a man desires is-u love;
La 3:32 so great is his-u love.

UNFAITHFUL (UNFAITHFULNESS)
Lev 6: 2 is-u to the Lord by deceiving his
1Ch 10:13 because he was-u to the Lord;
Pr 13:15 but the way of the-u is hard.

UNFAITHFULNESS (UNFAITHFUL)
Mt 5:32 except for marital-u, causes her
19: 9 for marital-u, and marries another

UNFOLDING
Ps 119:130 the-u of your words gives light;

UNGODLINESS
Tit 2:12 It teaches us to say "No" to-u

UNIT
1Co 12:12 body is a-u, though it is made up

UNITED (UNITY)
Ro 6: 5 If we have been-u with him
Php 2: 1 from being-u with Christ,
Col 2: 2 encouraged in heart and-u in love,

UNITY (UNITED)
Ps 133: 1 is when brothers live together in-u!
Ro 15: 5 a spirit of-u among yourselves
Eph 4: 3 effort to keep the-u of the Spirit
4:13 up until we all reach-u in the faith
Col 3:14 them all together in perfect-u.

UNIVERSE
Php 2:15 which you shine like stars in the-u

Heb 1: 2 and through whom he made the-u.

UNKNOWN
Ac 17:23 TO AN-U GOD.

UNLEAVENED
Ex 12:17 "Celebrate the Feast of-U Bread,

UNPROFITABLE
Tit 3: 9 because these are-u and useless.

UNPUNISHED
Ex 34: 7 Yet he does not leave the guilty-u;
Pr 19: 5 A false witness will not go-u,

UNREPENTANT*
Ro 2: 5 stubbornness and your-u heart,

UNRIGHTEOUS*
Zep 3: 5 yet the-u know no shame.
Mt 5:45 rain on the righteous and the-u.
1Pe 3:18 the righteous for the-u, to bring you
2Pe 2: 9 and to hold the-u for the day

UNSEARCHABLE
Ro 11:33 How-u his judgments,
Eph 3: 8 preach to the Gentiles the-u riches

UNSEEN
2Co 4:18 on what is seen, but on what is-u.
4:18 temporary, but what is-u is eternal.

UNSTABLE*
Jas 1: 8 he is a double-minded man,-u
2Pe 2:14 they seduce the-u; they are experts
3:16 ignorant and-u people distort,

UNTHINKABLE*
Job 34:12 It is-u that God would do wrong,

UNVEILED*
2Co 3:18 with-u faces all reflect the Lord's

UNWORTHY
Job 40: 4 "I am-u— how can I reply to you?
Lk 17:10 should say, 'We are-u servants;

UPRIGHT
Job 1: 1 This man was blameless and-u;
Pr 2: 7 he holds victory in store for the-u,
15: 8 but the prayer of the-u pleases him.
Tit 1: 8 who is self-controlled,-u, holy
2:12 u and godly lives in this present

UPROOTED
Jude :12 without fruit and-u— twice dead.

USEFUL
2Ti 2:21 u to the Master and prepared
3:16 Scripture is God-breathed and is-u

USELESS
1Co 15:14 our preaching is-u
Jas 2:20 faith without deeds is-u?

USURY
Ne 5:10 But let the exacting of-u stop!

UTTER
Ps 78: 2 I will-u hidden things, things from of

UZZIAH
Son of Amaziah; king of Judah also known as Azariah (2Ki 15:1-7; 1Ch 6:24; 2Ch 26).

VAIN
Ps 33:17 A horse is a-v hope for deliverance;
Isa 65:23 They will not toil in-v
1Co 15: 2 Otherwise, you have believed in-v.
15:58 labor in the Lord is not in-v.
2Co 6: 1 not to receive God's grace in-v.

VALLEY
Ps 23: 4 walk through the-v of the shadow
Isa 40: 4 Every-v shall be raised up,
Joel 3:14 multitudes in the-v of decision!

VALUABLE (VALUE)
Lk 12:24 And how much more-v you are

VALUE (VALUABLE)
Mt 13:46 When he found one of great-v,
1Ti 4: 8 For physical training is of some-v,
Heb 11:26 as of greater-v than the treasures

VEIL
Ex 34:33 to them, he put a-v over his face.
2Co 3:14 for to this day the same-v remains

VENGEANCE (AVENGE REVENGE)
Isa 34: 8 For the Lord has a day of-v,

VICTORIES (VICTORY)
Ps 18:50 He gives his king great-v;
21: 1 great is his joy in the-v you give!

VICTORIOUSLY* (VICTORY)
Ps 45: 4 In your majesty ride forth-v

VICTORY (VICTORIES VICTORIOUSLY)
Ps 60:12 With God we will gain the-v,
1Co 15:54 "Death has been swallowed up in-v
15:57 He gives us the-v through our Lord
1Jn 5: 4 This is the-v that has overcome

VINDICATED
1Ti 3:16 was-v by the Spirit,

VINE
Jn 15: 1 "I am the true-v, and my Father is

VINEGAR
Mk 15:36 filled a sponge with wine-v,

VIOLATION
Heb 2: 2 every-v and disobedience received

VIOLENCE
Isa 60:18 No longer will-v be heard
Eze 45: 9 Give up your-v and oppression

VIPERS
Ro 3:13 "The poison of-v is on their lips."

VIRGIN
Isa 7:14 The-v will be with child
Mt 1:23 "The-v will be with child
2Co 11: 2 that I might present you as a pure-v

VIRTUES*
Col 3:14 And over all these-v put on love,

VISION
Ac 26:19 disobedient to the-v from heaven.

VOICE
Ps 95: 7 Today, if you hear his-v,
Isa 30:21 your ears will hear a-v behind you,
Jn 5:28 are in their graves will hear his-v
10: 3 and the sheep listen to his-v.
Heb 3: 7 "Today, if you hear his-v,
Rev 3:20 If anyone hears my-v and opens

VOMIT
Pr 26:11 As a dog returns to its-v,
2Pe 2:22 "A dog returns to its-v," and,

VOW
Nu 30: 2 When a man makes a-v

WAGES
Lk 10: 7 for the worker deserves his-w.
Ro 4: 4 his-w are not credited to him
6:23 For the-w of sin is death,

WAILING
Ps 30:11 You turned my-w into dancing;

WAIST
2Ki 1: 8 with a leather belt around his-w."
Mt 3: 4 he had a leather belt around his-w.

WAIT (WAITED WAITS)
Ps 27:14 W for the Lord;
130: 5 I-w for the Lord, my soul waits,
Isa 30:18 Blessed are all who-w for him!
Ac 1: 4 w for the gift my Father promised,
Ro 8:23 as we-w eagerly for our adoption
1Th 1:10 and to-w for his Son from heaven,
Tit 2:13 while we-w for the blessed hope—

WAITED (WAIT)
Ps 40: 1 I-w patiently for the Lord;

WAITS (WAIT)
Ro 8:19 creation-w in eager expectation

WALK (WALKED WALKS)
Dt 11:19 and when you-w along the road,
Ps 1: 1 who does not-w in the counsel
23: 4 Even though I-w
89:15 who-w in the light of your presence
Isa 2: 5 let us-w in the light of the Lord.
30:21 saying, "This is the way,-w in it."
40:31 they will-w and not be faint.
Jer 6:16 ask where the good way is, and-w
Da 4:37 And those who-w in pride he is able
Am 3: 3 Do two-w together
Mic 6: 8 and to-w humbly with your God.
Mk 2: 9 'Get up, take your mat and-w'?
Jn 8:12 Whoever follows me will never-w
1Jn 1: 7 But if we-w in the light,
2Jn : 6 his command is that you-w in love.

WALKED (WALK)
Ge 5:24 Enoch-w with God; then he was no
Jos 14: 9 which your feet have-w will be your
Mt 14:29 w on the water and came toward

WALKS (WALK)
Pr 13:20 He who-w with the wise grows wise

WALL
Jos 6:20 w collapsed; so every man charged
Ne 2:17 let us rebuild the-w of Jerusalem,
Rev 21:12 It had a great, high-w

WALLOWING
2Pe 2:22 back to her-w in the mud."

WANT (WANTED WANTING WANTS)
1Sa 8:19 "We-w a king over us.
Ps 23: 1 is my shepherd, I shall not be in-w.
Lk 19:14 'We don't-w this man to be our king
Ro 7:15 For what I-w to do I do not do,
Php 3:10 I-w to know Christ and the power

WANTED (WANT)
1Co 12:18 of them, just as he-w them to be.

WANTING (WANT)
Da 5:27 weighed on the scales and found-w.
2Pe 3: 9 with you, not-w anyone to perish,

WANTS (WANT)
Mt 20:26 whoever-w to become great
Mk 8:35 For whoever-w to save his life will
Ro 9:18 he hardens whom he-w to harden.
1Ti 2: 4 who-w all men to be saved

WAR (WARS)
Isa 2: 4 nor will they train for-w anymore.
Da 9:26 W will continue until the end,
2Co 10: 3 we do not wage-w as the world does
Rev 19:11 With justice he judges and makes-w

WARN (WARNED WARNINGS)
Eze 3:19 But if you do-w the wicked man
33: 9 if you do-w the wicked man to turn

WARNED (WARN)
Ps 19:11 By them is your servant-w;

WARNINGS (WARN)
1Co 10:11 and were written down as-w for us,

WARS (WAR)
Mt 46: 9 He makes-w cease to the ends
Mt 24: 6 You will hear of-w and rumors of-w,

WASH (WASHED WASHING)
Ps 51: 7 w me, and I will be whiter
Jn 13: 5 and began to-w his disciples' feet,
Ac 22:16 be baptized and-w your sins away,
Rev 22:14 Blessed are those who-w their robes

WASHED (WASH)
1Co 6:11 you were-*w*, you were sanctified,
Rev 7:14 they have-*w* their robes

WASHING (WASH)
Eph 5:26 cleansing her by the-*w* with water
Tit 3:5 us through the-*w* of rebirth

WATCH (WATCHES WATCHING WATCHMAN)
Ge 31:49 "May the LORD keep-*w*
Jer 31:10 will-*w* over his flock like a shepherd
Mt 24:42 "Therefore keep-*w*, because you do
26:41 *W* and pray so that you will not fall
Lk 2:8 keeping-*w* over their flocks at night
1Ti 4:16 *W* your life and doctrine closely.

WATCHES (WATCH)
Ps 1:6 For the LORD-*w* over the way
121:3 he who-*w* over you will not slumber

WATCHING (WATCH)
Lk 12:37 whose master finds them-*w*

WATCHMAN (WATCH)
Eze 3:17 I have made you a-*w* for the house

WATER (WATERED WATERS)
Ps 1:3 like a tree planted by streams of-*w*,
22:14 I am poured out like-*w*,
Pr 25:21 if he is thirsty, give him-*w* to drink.
Isa 49:10 and lead them beside springs of-*w*,
Jer 2:13 broken cisterns that cannot hold-*w*.
Zec 14:8 On that day living-*w* will flow out
Mk 9:41 anyone who gives you a cup of-*w*
Jn 4:10 he would have given you living-*w*."
7:38 streams of living-*w* will flow
Eph 5:26 washing with-*w* through the word,
1Pe 3:21 this-*w* symbolizes baptism that now
Rev 21:6 cost from the spring of the-*w* of life.

WATERED (WATER)
1Co 3:6 I planted the seed, Apollos-*w* it,

WATERS (WATER)
Ps 23:2 he leads me beside quiet-*w*,
Ecc 11:1 Cast your bread upon the-*w*,
Isa 58:11 like a spring whose-*w* never fail.
1Co 3:7 plants nor he who-*w* is anything,

WAVE (WAVES)
Jas 1:6 he who doubts is like a-*w* of the sea,

WAVES (WAVE)
Isa 57:20 whose-*w* cast up mire and mud.
Mt 8:27 Even the winds and the-*w* obey him
Eph 4:14 tossed back and forth by the-*w*,

WAY (WAYS)
Dt 1:33 to show you the-*w* you should go.
2Sa 22:31 "As for God, his-*w* is perfect;
Job 23:10 But he knows the-*w* that I take;
Ps 1:1 or stand in the-*w* of sinners
37:5 Commit your-*w* to the LORD;
119:9 can a young man keep his-*w* pure?
139:24 See if there is any offensive-*w* in me
Pr 14:12 There is a-*w* that seems right
16:17 he who guards his-*w* guards his life.
22:6 Train a child in the-*w* he should go,
Isa 30:21 saying, "This is the-*w*; walk in it."
53:6 each of us has turned to his own-*w*;
55:7 Let the wicked forsake his-*w*
Jn 3:3 'Prepare the-*w* for the Lord,
14:6 "I am the-*w* and the truth
1Co 10:13 also provide a-*w* out so that you can
12:31 will show you the most excellent-*w*.
Heb 4:15 who has been tempted in every-*w*,
9:8 was showing by this that the-*w*
10:20 and living-*w* opened for us

WAYS (WAY)
Ex 33:13 teach me your-*w* so I may know
Ps 25:10 All the-*w* of the LORD are loving
51:13 I will teach transgressors your-*w*,

WEAK (WEAKER WEAKNESS)
Mt 26:41 spirit is willing, but the body is-*w*."
Ro 14:1 Accept him whose faith is-*w*,
1Co 1:27 God chose the-*w* things
8:9 become a stumbling block to the-*w*
9:22 To the-*w* I became-*w*, to win the-*w*.
2Co 12:10 For when I am-*w*, then I am strong.
Heb 12:12 your feeble arms and-*w* knees.

WEAKER (WEAK)
1Co 12:22 seem to be-*w* are indispensable,
1Pe 3:7 them with respect as the-*w* partner

WEAKNESS (WEAK)
Ro 8:26 the Spirit helps us in our-*w*.
1Co 1:25 and the-*w* of God is stronger
2Co 12:9 for my power is made perfect in-*w*.
Heb 5:2 since he himself is subject to-*w*.

WEALTH
Pr 3:9 Honor the LORD with your-*w*,
Mk 10:22 away sad, because he had great-*w*.
Lk 15:13 and there squandered his-*w*

WEAPONS
2Co 10:4 The-*w* we fight with are not

WEARIES (WEARY)
Ecc 12:12 and much study-*w* the body.

WEARY (WEARIES)
Isa 40:31 they will run and not grow-*w*,
Mt 11:28 all you who are-*w* and burdened,
Gal 6:9 Let us not become-*w* in doing good,

WEDDING
Mt 22:11 who was not wearing-*w* clothes.
Rev 19:7 For the-*w* of the Lamb has come,

WEEP (WEEPING WEPT)
Ecc 3:4 a time to-*w* and a time to laugh,
Lk 6:21 Blessed are you who-*w* now,

WEEPING (WEEP)
Ps 30:5 *w* may remain for a night,
126:6 He who goes out-*w*,
Mt 8:12 where there will be-*w* and gnashing

WELCOMES
Mt 18:5 whoever-*w* a little child like this
2Jn :11 Anyone who-*w* him shares

WELL
Lk 17:19 your faith has made you-*w*."
Jas 5:15 in faith will make the sick person-*w*

WEPT (WEEP)
Ps 137:1 of Babylon we sat and-*w*
Jn 11:35 Jesus-*w*.

WEST
Ps 103:12 as far as the east is from the-*w*,

WHIRLWIND (WIND)
2Ki 2:1 to take Elijah up to heaven in a-*w*,
Hos 8:7 and reap the-*w*.
Na 1:3 His way is in the-*w* and the storm,

WHITE (WHITER)
Isa 1:18 they shall be as-*w* as snow;
Da 7:9 His clothing was as-*w* as snow;
Rev 1:14 hair were-*w* like wool, as-*w* as snow,
3:4 dressed in-*w*, for they are worthy.
20:11 Then I saw a great-*w* throne

WHITER (WHITE)
Ps 51:7 and I will be-*w* than snow.

WHOLE
Mt 16:26 for a man if he gains the-*w* world,
24:14 will be preached in the-*w* world
Jn 13:10 to wash his feet; his-*w* body is clean
21:25 the-*w* world would not have room
Ac 20:27 proclaim to you the-*w* will of God.

WITNESS
Ro 3:19 and the-*w* world held accountable
8:22 know that the-*w* creation has been
Gal 3:22 declares that the-*w* world is
5:3 obligated to obey the-*w* law.
Eph 4:13 attaining to the-*w* measure
Jas 2:10 For whoever keeps the-*w* law
1Jn 2:2 but also for the sins of the-*w* world.

WHOLEHEARTEDLY (HEART)
Dt 1:36 because he followed the LORD-*w*
Eph 6:7 Serve-*w*, as if you were serving

WICKED (WICKEDNESS)
Ps 1:1 walk in the counsel of the-*w*
1:5 Therefore the-*w* will not stand
73:3 when I saw the prosperity of the-*w*.
Pr 10:20 the heart of the-*w* is of little value.
11:21 The-*w* will not go unpunished,
Isa 53:9 He was assigned a grave with the-*w*
55:7 Let the-*w* forsake his way
57:20 But the-*w* are like the tossing sea,
Eze 3:18 that-*w* man will die for his sin,
18:23 pleasure in the death of the-*w*?
33:14 to the-*w* man, 'You will surely die,'

WICKEDNESS (WICKED)
Eze 28:15 created till-*w* was found in you.

WIDE
Isa 54:2 stretch your tent curtains-*w*,
Mt 7:13 For-*w* is the gate and broad is
Eph 3:18 to grasp how-*w* and long and high

WIDOW (WIDOWS)
Dt 10:18 cause of the fatherless and the-*w*,
Lk 21:2 saw a poor-*w* put in two very small

WIDOWS (WIDOW)
Jas 1:27 look after orphans and-*w*

WIFE (WIVES)
Ge 2:24 and mother and be united to his-*w*,
24:67 she became his-*w*, and he loved her;
Ex 20:17 shall not covet your neighbor's-*w*,
Dt 5:21 shall not covet your neighbor's-*w*.
Pr 5:18 in the-*w* of your youth.
12:4 *w* of noble character is her
18:22 He who finds a-*w* finds what is
19:13 quarrelsome-*w* is like a constant
31:10 *w* of noble character who can find?
Mt 19:3 for a man to divorce his-*w* for any
1Co 7:2 each man should have his own-*w*,
7:33 how he can please his-*w*—
Eph 5:23 the husband is the head of the-*w*
5:33 must love his-*w* as he loves himself,
1Ti 3:2 husband of but one-*w*, temperate,
Rev 21:9 I will show you the bride, the-*w*

WILD
Lk 15:13 squandered his wealth in-*w* living.
Ro 11:17 and you, though a-*w* olive shoot,

WILL (WILLING WILLINGNESS)
Ps 40:8 I desire to do your-*w*, O my God;
143:10 Teach me to do your-*w*,
Isa 53:10 Yet it was the LORD's-*w*
Mt 6:10 your-*w* be done
26:39 Yet not as I-*w*, but as you-*w*."
Jn 7:17 If anyone chooses to do God's-*w*,
Ac 20:27 to you the whole-*w* of God.
Ro 12:2 and approve what God's-*w* is—
1Co 7:37 but has control over his own-*w*,
Eph 5:17 understand what the Lord's-*w* is.
Php 2:13 for it is God who works in you to-*w*
1Th 4:3 God's-*w* that you should be
5:18 for this is God's-*w* for you
Heb 9:16 In the case of a-*w*, it is necessary
10:7 I have come to do your-*w*, O God
Jas 4:15 "If it is the Lord's-*w*,
1Jn 5:14 we ask anything according to his-*w*,
Rev 4:11 and by your-*w* they were created

WILLING (WILL)
Ps 51:12 grant me a-*w* spirit, to sustain me.
Da 3:28 were-*w* to give up their lives rather
Mt 18:14 Father in heaven is not-*w* that any
23:37 her wings, but you were not-*w*.
26:41 The spirit is-*w*, but the body is weak

WILLINGNESS (WILL)
2Co 8:12 For if the-*w* is there, the gift is

WIN (WINS)
Php 3:14 on toward the goal to-*w* the prize
1Th 4:12 your daily life may-*w* the respect

WIND (WHIRLWIND)
Jas 1:6 blown and tossed by the-*w*.

WINE
Pr 20:1 *W* is a mocker and beer a brawler;
Isa 55:1 Come, buy-*w* and milk
Mt 9:17 Neither do men pour new-*w*
Lk 23:36 They offered him-*w* vinegar
Ro 14:21 not to eat meat or drink-*w*
Eph 5:18 on-*w*, which leads to debauchery.

WINESKINS
Mt 9:17 do men pour new wine into old-*w*

WINGS
Ru 2:12 under whose-*w* you have come
Ps 17:8 hide me in the shadow of your-*w*
Isa 40:31 They will soar on-*w* like eagles;
Mal 4:2 rise with healing in its-*w*.
Lk 13:34 hen gathers her chicks under her-*w*,

WINS (WIN)
Pr 11:30 and he who-*w* souls is wise.

WIPE
Rev 7:17 God will-*w* away every tear

WISDOM (WISE)
1Ki 4:29 God gave Solomon-*w* and very
Ps 111:10 of the LORD is the beginning of-*w*;
Pr 31:26 She speaks with-*w*,
Jer 10:12 he founded the world by his-*w*
Mt 11:19 But-*w* is proved right by her actions
Lk 2:52 And Jesus grew in-*w* and stature,
Ro 11:33 the depth of the riches of the-*w*
Col 2:3 are hidden all the treasures of-*w*
Jas 1:5 of you lacks-*w*, he should ask God,

WISE (WISDOM WISER)
1Ki 3:12 give you a-*w* and discerning heart,
Job 5:13 He catches the-*w* in their craftiness
Ps 19:7 making-*w* the simple.
Pr 3:7 Do not be-*w* in your own eyes;
9:8 rebuke a-*w* man and he will love
10:1 A-*w* son brings joy to his father,
11:30 and he who wins souls is-*w*.
13:20 he who walks with the-*w* grows-*w*,
17:28 Even a fool is thought-*w*
Da 12:3 Those who are-*w* will shine like
Mt 11:25 hidden these things from the-*w*
1Co 1:27 things of the world to shame the-*w*;
2Ti 3:15 able to make you-*w* for salvation

WISER (WISE)
1Co 1:25 of God is-*w* than man's wisdom,

WITHER (WITHERS)
Ps 1:3 and whose leaf does not-*w*.

WITHERS (WITHER)
Isa 40:7 The grass-*w* and the flowers fall,
1Pe 1:24 the grass-*w* and the flowers fall,

WITHHOLD
Ps 84:11 no good thing does he-*w*
Pr 23:13 Do not-*w* discipline from a child;

WITNESS (WITNESSES)
Jn 1:8 he came only as a-*w* to the light.

WITNESSES (WITNESS)
Dt 19:15 by the testimony of two or three-*w*.
Ac 1:8 and you will be my-*w* in Jerusalem,

WIVES (WIFE)
Eph 5:22 *W*, submit to your husbands
       5:25 love your-*w*, just as Christ loved
1Pe 3: 1 words by the behavior of their-*w*,

WOE
Isa 6: 5 "*W* to me!" I cried.

WOLF
Isa 65:25 *w* and the lamb will feed together,

WOMAN (MAN)
Ge 2:22 God made a-*w* from
       3:15 between you and the-*w*,
Lev 20:13 as one lies with a-*w*,
Dt 22: 5 *w* must not wear men's
Ru 3:11 a-*w* of noble character
Pr 31:30 a-*w* who fears the LORD
Mt 5:28 looks at a-*w* lustfully
Jn 8: 3 a-*w* caught in adultery.
Ro 7: 2 a married-*w* is bound to
1Co 11: 3 the head of the-*w* is man,
      11:13 a-*w* to pray to God with
1Ti 2:11 A-*w* should learn in

WOMEN (MAN)
Lk 1:42 Blessed are you among-*w*,
1Co 14:34 *w* should remain silent in
1Ti 2: 9 want-*w* to dress modestly
Tit 2: 3 teach the older-*w* to be
1Pe 3: 5 the holy-*w* of the past

WOMB
Job 1:21 Naked I came from my mother's-*w*,
Jer 1: 5 you in the-*w* I knew you,
Lk 1:44 the baby in my-*w* leaped for joy.

WONDER (WONDERFUL WONDERS)
Ps 17: 7 Show the-*w* of your great love,

WONDERFUL (WONDER)
Job 42: 3 things too-*w* for me to know.
Ps 31:21 for he showed his-*w* love to me
      119:18 *w* things in your law.
      119:129 Your statutes are-*w*;
      139: 6 Such knowledge is too-*w* for me,
Isa 9: 6 *W* Counselor, Mighty God,
1Pe 2: 9 out of darkness into his-*w* light.

WONDERS (WONDER)
Job 37:14 stop and consider God's-*w*.
Ps 119:27 then I will meditate on your-*w*.
Joel 2:30 I will show-*w* in the heavens
Ac 2:19 I will show-*w* in the heaven above

WOOD
Isa 44:19 Shall I bow down to a block of-*w*?"
1Co 3:12 costly stones,-*w*, hay or straw,

WORD (WORDS)
Dt 8: 3 but on every-*w* that comes
2Sa 22:31 the-*w* of the LORD is flawless.
Ps 119: 9 By living according to your-*w*.
      119:11 I have hidden your-*w* in my heart
      119:105 Your-*w* is a lamp to my feet
Pr 12:25 but a kind-*w* cheers him up.
      25:11 A-*w* aptly spoken
      30: 5 "Every-*w* of God is flawless;
Isa 55:11 so is my-*w* that goes out
Jn 1: 1 was the-*W*, and the-*W* was
       1:14 The-*W* became flesh and made his
2Co 2:17 we do not peddle the-*w* of God.
       4: 2 nor do we distort the-*w* of God.
Eph 6:17 of the Spirit, which is the-*w* of God.
Php 2:16 as you hold out the-*w* of life—

WORDS (WORD)
Dt 11:18 Fix these-*w* of mine in your hearts
Ps 119:103 How sweet are your-*w* to my taste
      119:130 The unfolding of your-*w* gives light;
      119:160 All your-*w* are true;
Pr 30: 6 Do not add to his-*w*,
Jer 15:16 When your-*w* came, I ate them;
Mt 24:35 but my-*w* will never pass away.
Jn 6:68 You have the-*w* of eternal life.
       15: 7 in me and my-*w* remain in you,
1Co 14:19 rather speak five intelligible-*w*
Rev 22:19 And if anyone takes-*w* away

WORK (WORKER WORKERS WORKING WORKMAN WORKMANSHIP WORKS)
Ex 23:12 "Six days do your-*w*,
Nu 8:11 ready to do the-*w* of the LORD.
Dt 5:14 On it you shall not do any-*w*,
Ecc 5:19 his lot and be happy in his-*w*—
Jer 48:10 lax in doing the Lord's-*w*!
Jn 6:27 Do not-*w* for food that spoils,
       9: 4 we must do the-*w* of him who sent
1Co 3:13 test the quality of each man's-*w*.
Php 1: 6 that he who began a good-*w*
       2:12 continue to-*w* out your salvation
Col 3:23 Whatever you do,-*w* at it
1Th 5:12 to respect those who-*w* hard
2Th 3:10 If a man will not-*w*, he shall not eat
2Ti 3:17 equipped for every good-*w*.
Heb 6:10 he will not forget your-*w*

WORKER (WORK)
Lk 10: 7 for the-*w* deserves his wages.
1Ti 5:18 and "The-*w* deserves his wages."

WORKERS (WORK)
Mt 9:37 is plentiful but the-*w* are few.
1Co 3: 9 For we are God's fellow-*w*;

WORKING (WORK)
Col 3:23 as-*w* for the Lord, not for men,

WORKMAN (WORK)
2Ti 2:15 a-*w* who does not need

WORKMANSHIP* (WORK)
Eph 2:10 For we are God's-*w*, created

WORKS (WORK)
Pr 31:31 let her-*w* bring her praise
Ro 8:28 in all things God-*w* for the good
Eph 2: 9 not by-*w*, so that no one can boast.
       4:12 to prepare God's people for-*w*

WORLD (WORLDLY)
Ps 50:12 for the-*w* is mine, and all that is in it
Isa 13:11 I will punish the-*w* for its evil,
Mt 5:14 You are the light of the-*w*.
      16:26 for a man if he gains the whole-*w*,
Mk 16:15 into all the-*w* and preach the good
Jn 1:29 who takes away the sin of the-*w*!
       3:16 so loved the-*w* that he gave his one
       8:12 he said, "I am the light of the-*w*.
      15:19 As it is, you do not belong to the-*w*,
      16:33 In this-*w* you will have trouble.
      18:36 "My kingdom is not of this-*w*.
Ro 3:19 and the whole-*w* held accountable
1Co 3:19 the wisdom of this-*w* is foolishness

2Co 5:19 that God was reconciling the-*w*
       10: 3 For though we live in the-*w*,
1Ti 6: 7 For we brought nothing into the-*w*,
1Jn 2: 2 but also for the sins of the whole-*w*.
       2:15 not love the-*w* or anything in the-*w*.
Rev 13: 8 slain from the creation of the-*w*.

WORLDLY (WORLD)
Tit 2:12 to ungodliness and-*w* passions,

WORM
Mk 9:48 " their-*w* does not die,

WORRY (WORRYING)
Mt 6:25 I tell you, do not-*w* about your life,
      10:19 do not-*w* about what to say

WORRYING (WORRY)
Mt 6:27 of you by-*w* can add a single hour

WORSHIP
1Ch 16:29 *w* the LORD in the splendor
Ps 95: 6 Come, let us bow down in-*w*,
Mt 2: 2 and have come to-*w* him."
Jn 4:24 and his worshipers must-*w* in spirit
Ro 12: 1 this is your spiritual act of-*w*.

WORTH (WORTHY)
Job 28:13 Man does not comprehend its-*w*;
Pr 31:10 She is-*w* far more than rubies.
Mt 10:31 are-*w* more than many sparrows.
Ro 8:18 sufferings are not-*w* comparing
1Pe 1: 7 of greater-*w* than gold,
       3: 4 which is of great-*w* in God's sight.

WORTHLESS
Pr 11: 4 Wealth is-*w* in the day of wrath,
Jas 1:26 himself and his religion is-*w*.

WORTHY (WORTH)
1Ch 16:25 For great is the LORD and most-*w*
Eph 4: 1 to live a life-*w* of the calling you
Php 1:27 in a manner-*w* of the gospel
3Jn   : 6 on their way in a manner-*w* of God.
Rev 5: 2 "Who is-*w* to break the seals

WOUNDS
Pr 27: 6 *W* from a friend can be trusted,
Isa 53: 5 and by his-*w* we are healed.
Zec 13: 6 'What are these-*w* on your body?'
1Pe 2:24 by his-*w* you have been healed.

WRATH
2Ch 36:16 scoffed at his prophets until the-*w*
Ps 2: 5 and terrifies them in his-*w*, saying,
      76:10 Surely your-*w* against men brings
Pr 15: 1 A gentle answer turns away-*w*,
Jer 25:15 filled with the wine of my-*w*
Ro 1:18 The-*w* of God is being revealed
       5: 9 saved from God's-*w* through him!
1Th 5: 9 God did not appoint us to suffer-*w*
Rev 6:16 and from the-*w* of the Lamb!

WRESTLED
Ge 32:24 and a man-*w* with him till daybreak

WRITE (WRITING WRITTEN)
Dt 6: 9 *W* them on the doorframes
Pr 7: 3 *w* them on the tablet of your heart.
Heb 8:10 and-*w* them on their hearts.

WRITING (WRITE)
1Co 14:37 him acknowledge that what I am-*w*

WRITTEN (WRITE)
Jos 1: 8 careful to do everything-*w* in it.
Da 12: 1 everyone whose name is found-*w*

Lk 10:20 but rejoice that your names are-*w*
Jn 20:31 these are-*w* that you may believe
1Co 4: 6 "Do not go beyond what is-*w*."
2Co 3: 3 *w* not with ink but with the Spirit
Col 2:14 having canceled the-*w* code,
Heb 12:23 whose names are-*w* in heaven.

WRONG (WRONGDOING WRONGED WRONGS)
Ex 23: 2 Do not follow the crowd in doing-*w*
Nu 5: 7 must make full restitution for his-*w*,
Job 34:12 unthinkable that God would do-*w*,
1Th 5:15 that nobody pays back-*w* for-*w*,

WRONGDOING (WRONG)
Job 1:22 sin by charging God with-*w*.

WRONGED (WRONG)
1Co 6: 7 not rather be-*w*? Why not rather

WRONGS (WRONG)
Pr 10:12 but love covers over all-*w*.
1Co 13: 5 angered, it keeps no record of-*w*.

YEARS
Ps 90: 4 For a thousand-*y* in your sight
      90:10 The length of our days is seventy-*y*
2Pe 3: 8 the Lord a day is like a thousand-*y*,
Rev 20: 2 and bound him for a thousand-*y*.

YESTERDAY
Heb 13: 8 Jesus Christ is the same-*y*

YOKE (YOKED)
Mt 11:29 Take my-*y* upon you and learn

YOKED (YOKE)
2Co 6:14 Do not be-*y* together

YOUNG (YOUTH)
Ps 119: 9 How can a-*y* man keep his way
1Ti 4:12 down on you because you are-*y*,

YOUTH (YOUNG)
Ps 103: 5 so that your-*y* is renewed like
Ecc 12: 1 Creator in the days of your-*y*,
2Ti 2:22 Flee the evil desires of-*y*,

ZEAL
Pr 19: 2 to have-*z* without knowledge,
Ro 12:11 Never be lacking in-*z*,

ZECHARIAH
1. Son of Jeroboam II; king of Israel (2Ki 15:8-12).

2. Post-exilic prophet who encouraged rebuilding of temple (Ezr 5:1; 6:14; Zec 1:1).

3. Father of John the Baptist (Lk 1:13; 3:2).

ZEDEKIAH
Mattaniah, son of Josiah (1Ch 3:15), made king of Judah by Nebuchadnezzar (2Ki 24:17-25:7; 2Ch 36:10-14; Jer 37-39; 52:1-11).

ZERUBBABEL
Descendant of David (1Ch 3:19; Mt 1:3). Led return from exile (Ezr 2-3; Ne 7:7; Hag 1-2; Zec 4).

ZIMRI
King of Israel (1Ki 16:9-20).

ZION
Ps 137: 3 "Sing us one of the songs of-*Z*!"
Jer 50: 5 They will ask the way to-*Z*
Ro 9:33 I lay in-*Z* a stone that causes men
      11:26 "The deliverer will come from-*Z*;